EU

HANDBOOK

20 10
11

THE EUROPEAN FOOTBALL YEARBOOK 2010/2011

General Editor
Mike Hammond

The only authoritative annual on the European game

**Further copies of The European Football Yearbook 2010/11
are available from:**
www.carltonbooks.co.uk
hotline number +44 (0) 141 306 3100

The European Football Yearbook 2010/11

First published by Carlton Books Ltd, England in 2010
Printed by m press (sales) Ltd, England

ISBN 978-1-84732-617-1

UEFA – the Union of European Football Associations – is the governing body of football on the continent of Europe. UEFA's core mission is to promote, protect and develop European football at every level of the game, to promote the principles of unity and solidarity, and to deal with all questions relating to European football.

UEFA is an association of associations based on representative democracy, and is the governing body of European football.

UEFA
Route de Genève 46
Case postale
CH-1260 Nyon 2
Switzerland

Tel: +41 (0) 848 00 2727
Fax: +41 (0) 848 01 2727
Web: UEFA.com
Email: info@uefa.com

Media Desk
Tel: +41 (0) 848 04 2727

All views expressed in the European Football Yearbook do not necessarily reflect those of UEFA. Every effort has been made to ensure the accuracy of the data in the European Football Yearbook, official and unofficial.

**The European Football Yearbook 2007/08,
The European Football Yearbook 2008/09 and
The European Football Yearbook 2009/10
are available from:**
www.calmproductions.com
orders@calmproductions.com
UK hotline 0845 408 2606

THE EUROPEAN FOOTBALL YEARBOOK 2010/11

General Editor
MIKE HAMMOND

Assistant Editor
Jesper Krogshede Sørensen

Nation-by-nation
Correspondents and Researchers
Mert Aydin (Turkey), Nikolai Belov (Russia), José Del Olmo (Spain), Sean DeLoughry (Republic of Ireland), Tamás Dénes (Hungary), Arno Funck (Luxembourg), Stoyan Georgiev (Bulgaria), Marshall Gillespie (Northern Ireland), Clas Glenning (Sweden), Miron Goihman (Moldova), Marcel Haisma (Netherlands), Michael Hansen (Denmark), Romeo Ionescu (Romania), Michel Jambonet (France), Valery Karpushkin (Latvia), Mikael Kirakosyan (Armenia), Jesper Krogshede Sørensen (Faroe Islands, Italy), Fuad & Feđa Krvavac (Bosnia-Herzegovina), Zdeněk Kučera (Czech Republic), Ambrosius Kutschera (Austria), Tarmo Lehiste (Estonia), Dag Lindholm (Norway), Ewan Macdonald (Scotland), Erlan Manashev (Kazakhstan), Goran Mancevski (Former Yugoslav Republic of Macedonia), Gabriel Mantz (Top 100 Players), Rasim Mövsümov (Azerbaijan), Giovanni Nappi (Albania), Kazimerz Oleszek (Poland), Olexandr Pauk (Belarus, Ukraine), Humberto Pereira Silva (Portugal), Ivan & Zdravko Reić (Croatia), Mike Ritter & Silvia Schäfer (Germany), Revaz Shengelia (Georgia), Vídir Sigurdsson (Iceland), Dušan Stamenković (Montenegro, Serbia), Andrej Stare (Slovenia), Algimantas Staskevičius (Lithuania), Edouard Stutz (Switzerland), Matej Széher (Slovakia), Mel Thomas (Wales), Vesa Tikander (Finland), Serge Van Hoof (Belgium), Victor Vassallo (Malta), Georgios J. Vassalos (Greece), Jacob Zelazo (Cyprus, Israel).

UEFA
Project management
David Farrelly, Rob Faulkner, Guillaume Sabran, Christophe Burri, Grégory Lepesqueux, Dan O'Toole
Editorial
Sam Adams, Kevin Ashby, John Atkin, Borja Bilbao, Chris Burke, Paul Bryan, Massimo Gonnella, Wayne Harrison, Michael Harrold, Patrick Hart, Simon Hart, Andrew Haslam, Thomas Kell, Mark Pettit, Paul Saffer, Graham Turner, James Wirth
Data
Jim Agnew, Robert Esteva, Jo Juvet, Kadira Malkoč, Dominique Maurer

Production
Print
m press (sales) Ltd, England; Cliff Moulder
Distribution
Carlton Books Ltd; Martin Corteel, Jim Greenough
Design
The Works
Artwork/Layout
Keith Jackson
Graphics
Mikhail Sipovich
Data Extraction
Delta3 (Antonio Bellissimo, Paolo Calva, Davide Giulietti, Vincenzo Gianno)
Photography
Getty Images, Sportsfile, Getty Images/AFP, Getty Images/Bongarts
Foreword
José Mourinho

NATIONAL THREE-LETTER CODES

There are many instances throughout the European Football Yearbook where country names are abbreviated using three-letter codes. These codes are shown below, listed alphabetically by nation and divided into Europe and the Rest of the World.

Europe

ALB	Alb	Albania
AND	And	Andorra
ARM	Arm	Armenia
AUT	Aut	Austria
AZE	Aze	Azerbaijan
BLR	Blr	Belarus
BEL	Bel	Belgium
BIH	Bih	Bosnia-Herzegovina
BUL	Bul	Bulgaria
CRO	Cro	Croatia
CYP	Cyp	Cyprus
CZE	Cze	Czech Republic
DEN	Den	Denmark
ENG	Eng	England
EST	Est	Estonia
FRO	Fro	Faroe Islands
FIN	Fin	Finland
FRA	Fra	France
GEO	Geo	Georgia
GER	Ger	Germany
GRE	Gre	Greece
HUN	Hun	Hungary
ISL	Isl	Iceland
ISR	Isr	Israel
ITA	Ita	Italy
KAZ	Kaz	Kazakhstan
LVA	Lva	Latvia
LIE	Lie	Liechtenstein
LTU	Ltu	Lithuania
LUX	Lux	Luxembourg
MKD	Mkd	Former Yugoslav Republic of Macedonia (FYROM)
MLT	Mlt	Malta
MDA	Mda	Moldova
MNE	Mne	Montenegro
NED	Ned	Netherlands
NIR	Nir	Northern Ireland
NOR	Nor	Norway
POL	Pol	Poland
POR	Por	Portugal
IRL	Irl	Republic of Ireland
ROU	Rou	Romania
RUS	Rus	Russia
SMR	Smr	San Marino
SCO	Sco	Scotland
SRB	Srb	Serbia
SVK	Svk	Slovakia
SVN	Svn	Slovenia
ESP	Esp	Spain
SWE	Swe	Sweden
SUI	Sui	Switzerland
TUR	Tur	Turkey
UKR	Ukr	Ukraine
WAL	Wal	Wales

Rest of the World

ALG	Alg	Algeria
ANG	Ang	Angola
ARG	Arg	Argentina
AUS	Aus	Australia
BHR	Bhr	Bahrain
BAN	Ban	Bangladesh
BRB	Brb	Barbados
BEN	Ben	Benin
BER	Ber	Bermuda
BOL	Bol	Bolivia
BOT	Bot	Botswana
BRA	Bra	Brazil
BFA	Bfa	Burkina Faso
BDI	Bdi	Burundi
CMR	Cmr	Cameroon
CAN	Can	Canada
CPV	Cpv	Cape Verde Islands
CAY	Cay	Cayman Islands
CTA	Cta	Central African Republic
CHA	Cha	Chad
CHI	Chi	Chile
CHN	Chn	China
COL	Col	Colombia
CGO	Cgo	Congo
COD	Cod	Congo DR
CRC	Crc	Costa Rica
CUB	Cub	Cuba
DOM	Dom	Dominican Republic
ECU	Ecu	Ecuador
EGY	Egy	Egypt
SLV	Slv	El Salvador
EQG	Eqg	Equatorial Guinea
ETH	Eth	Ethiopia
FIJ	Fij	Fiji
GAB	Gab	Gabon
GAM	Gam	Gambia
GHA	Gha	Ghana
GRN	Grn	Grenada
GUA	Gua	Guatemala
GUI	Gui	Guinea
GNB	Gnb	Guinea-Bissau
HAI	Hai	Haiti
HON	Hon	Honduras
HKG	Hkg	Hong Kong
IND	Ind	India
IRN	Irn	Iran
IRQ	Irq	Iraq
CIV	Civ	Ivory Coast
JAM	Jam	Jamaica
JPN	Jpn	Japan
JOR	Jor	Jordan
KEN	Ken	Kenya
PRK	Prk	North Korea
KOR	Kor	South Korea

KUW	Kuw	Kuwait
KGZ	Kgz	Kyrgyzstan
LIB	Lib	Lebanon
LBR	Lbr	Liberia
LBY	Lby	Libya
MAD	Mad	Madagascar
MWI	Mwi	Malawi
MLI	Mli	Mali
MTN	Mtn	Mauritania
MEX	Mex	Mexico
MAR	Mar	Morocco
MOZ	Moz	Mozambique
NAM	Nam	Namibia
ANT	Ant	Netherlands Antilles
NZL	Nzl	New Zealand
NIG	Nig	Niger
NGA	Nga	Nigeria
OMA	Oma	Oman
PAK	Pak	Pakistan
PAN	Pan	Panama
PAR	Par	Paraguay
PER	Per	Peru
QAT	Qat	Qatar
RWA	Rwa	Rwanda
KSA	Ksa	Saudi Arabia
SEN	Sen	Senegal
SLE	Sle	Sierra Leone
SIN	Sin	Singapore
SOL	Sol	Solomon Islands
SOM	Som	Somalia
RSA	Rsa	South Africa
SKN	Skn	St Kitts & Nevis
VIN	Vin	St Vincent & Grenadines
SYR	Syr	Syria
TAH	Tah	Tahiti
TJK	Tjk	Tajikistan
TAN	Tan	Tanzania
THA	Tha	Thailand
TOG	Tog	Togo
TRI	Tri	Trinidad & Tobago
TUN	Tun	Tunisia
TKM	Tkm	Turkmenistan
UGA	Uga	Uganda
UAE	Uae	United Arab Emirates
USA	Usa	United States
URU	Uru	Uruguay
UZB	Uzb	Uzbekistan
VEN	Ven	Venezuela
VIE	Vie	Vietnam
ZAM	Zam	Zambia
ZIM	Zim	Zimbabwe

Contents

EURO EAN
FOOTBALL
YEAR OOK
2010 11

Welcome

Foreword

It's good to be asked to write this page because it means you're a winning coach. It meant a lot to me to win the UEFA Champions League again. But I remember that, when I walked out of the Santiago Bernabéu, my emotions were all about other people's happiness rather than my own. For everybody at FC Internazionale Milano, it was an enormous occasion. For people on the outside, it's difficult to imagine the frustrations that built up during the long, long period when one of the great names in European football had not been the best. To be champions after over 40 years of waiting meant so much. Such frustration can build up complexes and inhibitions – so I hope that the whole Inter family will not just focus on celebrating the title but will set about starting a new era of success for the club.

For me, it was certainly special to achieve the treble of Serie A, Coppa Italia and the UEFA Champions League. If you consider yourself to be a winner, you want to win absolutely everything. But a lot of people consider themselves winners. Just look at the size of this book. How many clubs are in it?

What did they want when they started last season? How many clubs managed to achieve those expectations in Europe and in their domestic competitions?

That's why I'd like to mention Louis van Gaal. He has been a friend and colleague and it was an emotional moment to shake his hand at the end of the final in Madrid. This book also tells the story of the great job he did at FC Bayern München last season and, if you look at the way we both got to the final, you'll see that both teams had to deal with very difficult moments. When you look back at success, there is a temptation to think that everything on the way to it was easy. But success is never easy – especially in the UEFA Champions League.

We certainly had difficult moments at Inter. We drew our first three matches and we were 1-0 down five minutes from the end in our fourth. If we hadn't scored two at the end of that game in Kyiv, we would probably have been out. We had to play FC Barcelona four times – and I don't need to tell anyone how tough that was. If we came through all the delicate moments to win the title, it was because we had an exceptional group of players, an exceptional group of human beings.

This book has two values – and I'm not talking about money. First of all, it is a fantastic record of what happened last season all over Europe. But the facts and the statistics also bring back to life all the stories and the emotions behind the results. So, as you turn the pages, it's not just about what you see. It's also about what you remember and what you feel. Not everybody can win. But everybody can dream. And everybody can love the game of football.

José Mourinho
Head coach
FC Internazionale Milano
UEFA Champions League winners 2009/10

From the General Editor

Welcome to the 2010/11 edition of The European Football Yearbook.

I am proud to say that this is the fourth decade in which the Yearbook has been published. It has assumed many different forms and guises since the first edition in 1988, but its raison d'être remains unaltered – to provide a unique and comprehensive review of the past season of European football that will serve as an invaluable work of reference for many years to come.

This is the fourth Yearbook on which I have worked in conjunction with UEFA. The assistance and co-operation of European football's governing body lends an extra authority to the publication and, as ever, I am extremely grateful for their generous and loyal support.

I would also like to take this opportunity to thank all of the people who have routinely bought the 'EFY' year after year. You know who you are, and the publication could not have survived without you. My hope is that the Yearbook meets with your approval and that you will continue to support it.

This year, as some regular readers might already have noticed, we are giving you extra value for money with the addition of 48 pages – all of them in colour – without an increase in the cover price.

This, essentially, is to provide the space for full coverage of the 2010 FIFA World Cup without removing or cutting back on any of the other regular features. The World Cup is not, of course, a UEFA tournament, but its importance does not need overstating, and the European Football Yearbook would not be complete without a comprehensive review of the summer's events in South Africa.

On that subject, congratulations to Spain, the new world champions, and also to the Netherlands and Germany for making it a European one-two-three.

While the World Cup undoubtedly had its moments, the overall fare on offer in South Africa did not, in my opinion, match the high standards now regularly seen in the UEFA Champions League. You will, of course, find in these pages a comprehensive review of Europe's premier club competition as well as a full account of the inaugural UEFA Europa League. There is coverage too of all the other UEFA competitions, with youth tournaments, women's football and futsal all included.

Our Top 100 Players of the Season chapter is always good for a lively debate. I take great pleasure in overseeing the selection process, and you can take it as read that every possible candidate for inclusion had his criteria studiously analysed and evaluated before the final list was whittled down to the appropriate number and rubber-stamped.

The core of the Yearbook is the Nation-by-nation section, which contains 53 chapters within the chapter, one for each of UEFA's member associations, and includes statistical details on countries, clubs and players that cannot be found in such concise, easy-reference format anywhere else. This year we have expanded our research and included players' dates of birth in the club-by-club league appearances lists.

The popular Graphic Guide section containing maps, kits and logos has also been tweaked, with indication now made also of clubs that have been relegated as well as those promoted and qualified for the two European club competitions.

The Yearbook closes by looking ahead to the 2010/11 season with a calendar of UEFA events and a list of all the qualifying fixtures for UEFA EURO 2012.

Within the 1120 pages I trust there is something for everybody – from the passionate European football aficionado to the casual fan. Should you feel, however, that we have overlooked something – or indeed just want to wish us well - please do not hesitate to contact us on efy@uefa.ch.

Finally, I would like to thank everyone who has contributed to the Yearbook. Meeting the publication deadline is a massive and sometimes thankless task, and everyone's efforts are very much appreciated.

As ever, I am particularly grateful to David Farrelly, Jesper Krogshede Sørensen and Keith Jackson for immersing themselves in the project and repeatedly going beyond the call of duty. If only the football teams I support showed such dedication and commitment!

My sincere thanks also go to Paul Rosen for fixing my eye and to Chris Nawrat for those long, intellectually stimulating talks on the telephone.

And, of course, I could not deliver this publication without the much treasured love and support of my nearest and dearest – Sue, Rebecca and Charlie.

MIKE HAMMOND
August, 2010

THE EUROPEAN FOOTBALL YEARBOOK

TOP 100 PLAYERS OF THE SEASON

Turn to pages 365-416, where you will find pictorial, narrative and statistical profiles of the European Football Yearbook's Top 100 Players of the Season.

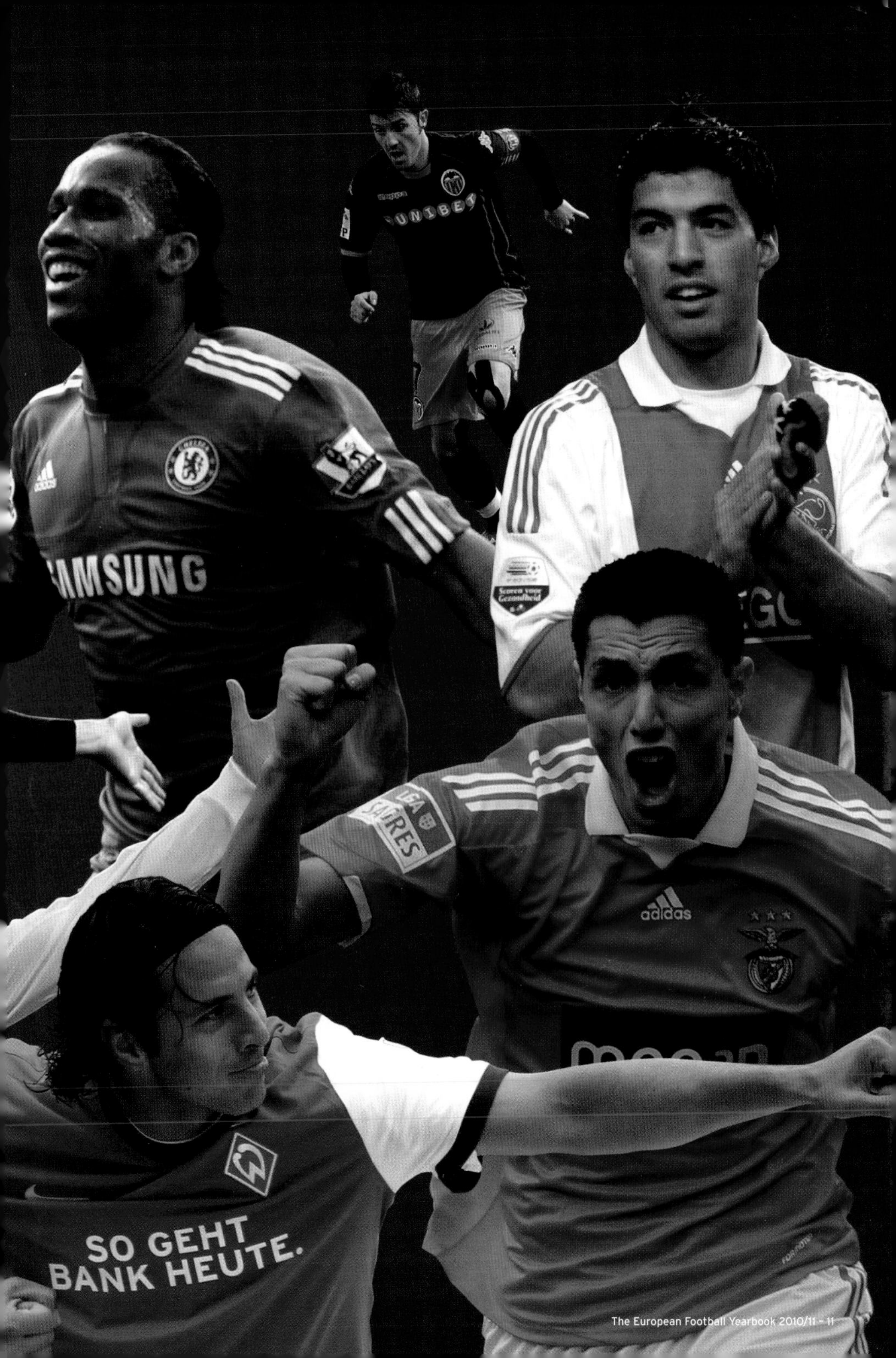
adidas
SO GEHT
BANK HEUTE.

INTRO

During the 2009/10 season, Spain ensured that Europe's domination of football was extended to the global stage, first with FC Barcelona's triumph at the FIFA Club World Cup and subsequently with the national team following their UEFA EURO 2008 success with victory in the 2010 FIFA World Cup in South Africa in an all-European final against the Netherlands.

Indeed, Spanish teams would come close to dominating the club scene as well, with Barcelona taking the UEFA Super Cup and Club Atlético de Madrid winning the inaugural UEFA Europa League. However, Barça were denied the clean sweep for Spain and a crack at defending their UEFA Champions League title when they lost out to eventual winners, FC Internazionale Milano, at the semi-final stage. For Inter, their defeat of FC Bayern München at Madrid's Santiago Bernabéu stadium ended a 45-year wait to claim European club football's premier title.

Elsewhere, in women's football, Germany continued their domination of the senior game, defeating England 6-2 in the UEFA Women's EURO 2009, an expanded 12-team final tournament which was held in Finland during August and September 2009. But the situation changed for Germany at under-age level where they failed to win a title for the first time in four seasons as honours went to France (WU19) and Spain (WU17).

Hungary played host to UEFA Futsal EURO 2010 (which also expanded to 12 teams), where Spain made it three in a row at Portugal's expense, but consolation for Portuguese futsal came at club level, where Lisbon hosted the UEFA Futsal Cup final four in April 2010 and SL Benfica came away as winners.

At youth level, there was a second 'host' success in two seasons as France followed the example of Ukraine in 2009 by capturing the UEFA European Under-19 Championship on home soil, with Spain denied in the final. Spain were also to end up on the losing side (and by the same 2-1 result) in Liechtenstein at Under-17 level where England triumphed at the international entry grade for the first time since the establishment of the UEFA European Under-16 Championship in 1980.

Looking ahead to the 2010/11 season, outside of all the annual finals, UEFA's major tournament will take place in June 2011 in Denmark when eight teams contest the UEFA European Under-21 Championship.

CHAPTER
01

UEFA CHAMPIONS LEAGUE

There were major changes to the UEFA Champions League format ahead of the 2009/10 campaign. Twenty-two, rather than 16, clubs qualified directly for the group stage, which still featured 32 teams but now contained 18 domestic champions.

While the qualifying tournament was revamped, with the introduction of two separate tributaries to the group phase - a Champions and Non-Champions Path - plus a play-off round, the format of the competition proper remained untouched. Instead, the novelties came on the field, with traditional heavyweights Liverpool FC and Juventus both failing to survive the group stage, and all four English clubs exiting before the semi-finals for the first time since 2002/03. FC Internazionale Milano, semi-final conquerors of holders FC Barcelona, and FC Bayern München made it through to the final at the Santiago Bernabéu – the latter for the first time since 2001, the former ending a 38-year wait – and it was the Italian side who prevailed, a clinical display in Madrid bringing a 2-0 victory that secured their third European crown - and their first since 1965.

2009/10

QUALIFYING PHASE

First/Second Qualifying Rounds

Barely a month after FC Barcelona had overcome Manchester United FC in the 2008/09 final, the 2009/10 edition of the UEFA Champions League kicked off with two contrasting first qualifying round ties.

Mogren in form

Montenegrin champions FK Mogren made light work of their Maltese counterparts Hibernians FC, winning 2-0 away in the first match of the new season - Marko Ćetković scoring the opening goal – before a 4-0 home victory in which Petar Grbić scored twice. The other tie, between San Marino's SP Tre Fiori and UE Sant Julià of Andorra, was considerably tighter, both legs finishing 1-1 before a penalty shoot-out win sent Sant Julià into the next stage.

The first-round victors found the going considerably tougher in the second qualifying round, Mogren going down 6-0 in each leg against FC København while Sant Julià lost 9-0 on aggregate to PFC Levski Sofia. FK Partizan were also 12-0 winners over the two legs, against Rhyl FC, with Cléo scoring a hat-trick in the 8-0 second-leg victory in Belgrade, while Maccabi Haifa FC put ten goals without reply past Glentoran FC.

Wisla shock

Wisla Kraków were the biggest name to fall in the second qualifying round, needing a last-gasp equaliser from substitute Piotr Ćwielong to salvage a 1-1 draw at home to FC Levadia Tallinn only for Vladislav Ivanov to score the solitary goal of the second leg in the 89th minute to take the Estonian champions through. FC Salzburg were close to becoming another high-profile casualty. Only four minutes of their tie against Bohemian FC remained when Patrik Ježek struck to seal a 2-1 aggregate success for the Austrian champions, while FK Ekranas and Bakı FK shared ten goals in an engrossing tie, the Azeri titleholders progressing 6-4 overall thanks to a 4-2 home win in the second leg.

Action from the opening tie of the 2009/10 UEFA Champions League between Hibernians FC (black and white stripes) and FK Mogren

UEFA Champions League

First Qualifying Round Results

30/6/09, Centenary, Ta' Qali
Hibernians FC 0-2 FK Mogren
Goal(s): 0-1 Ćetković 32, 0-2 Grbić 88
Referee: Wilmes (LUX)
8/7/09, Pod Goricom-Gradski, Podgorica
FK Mogren 4-0 Hibernians FC
Goal(s): 1-0 Milić 41, 2-0 Grbić 45, 3-0 Ćetković 51, 4-0 Grbić 79
Referee: Jones (WAL)
Aggregate: 6-0; FK Mogren qualify.

1/7/09, Montecchio, San Marino
SP Tre Fiori 1-1 UE Sant Julià
Goal(s): 0-1 Xinos 42 (p), 1-1 Andreini 75
Referee: Batinić (CRO)
7/7/09, Comunal, Andorra La Vella
UE Sant Julià 1-1 SP Tre Fiori (aet)
Goal(s): 1-0 Moreira 39, 1-1 Canarezza 82
Referee: Jareci (ALB)
Aggregate: 2-2; UE Sant Julià qualify 5-4 on penalties.

Second Qualifying Round Results

14/7/09, National Arena, Skopje
FK Makedonija GP Skopje 0-2 FC BATE Borisov
Goal(s): 0-1 Krivets 40, 0-2 Skavysh 50
Referee: Rasmussen (DEN)
21/7/09, Gorodskoi, Borisov
FC BATE Borisov 2-0 FK Makedonija GP Skopje
Goal(s): 1-0 Sosnovskiy 83, 2-0 Rodionov 90+3
Referee: Asumaa (FIN)
Aggregate: 4-0; FC BATE Borisov qualify.

14/7/09, Tórsvøllur, Torshavn
EB/Streymur 0-2 APOEL FC
Goal(s): 0-1 Mirosavljević 11, 0-2 Żewłakow 77
Referee: Oriekhov (UKR)
21/7/09, GSP, Nicosia
APOEL FC 3-0 EB/Streymur
Goal(s): 1-0 Żewłakow 42, 2-0 Alexandrou 63, 3-0 Mirosavljević 75
Referee: Zimmermann (SUI)
Aggregate: 5-0; APOEL FC qualify.

14/7/09, Belle Vue, Rhyl
Rhyl FC 0-4 FK Partizan
Goal(s): 0-1 Krstajić 17, 0-2 Cléo 18, 0-3 Diarra 45, 0-4 Đorđević 69
Referee: Muñiz Fernández (ESP)
21/7/09, FK Partizan, Belgrade
FK Partizan 8-0 Rhyl FC
Goal(s): 1-0 Diarra 4, 2-0 Cléo 17, 3-0 Đorđević 20, 4-0 B. Ilić 38, 5-0 Cléo 51, 6-0 B. Ilić 63, 7-0 Petrović 66, 8-0 Cléo 72 (p)
Referee: Strömbergsson (SWE)
Aggregate: 12-0; FK Partizan qualify.

14/7/09, Yerevan Republican, Yerevan
FC Pyunik 0-0 NK Dinamo Zagreb
Referee: Tagliavento (ITA)
21/7/09, Maksimir, Zagreb
NK Dinamo Zagreb 3-0 FC Pyunik
Goal(s): 1-0 Mandžukić 30, 2-0 Badelj 61, 3-0 Lovren 66
Referee: Pereira Gomes (POR)
Aggregate: 3-0; NK Dinamo Zagreb qualify.

14/7/09, Aukštaitija, Panevezys
FK Ekranas 2-2 Bakı FK
Goal(s): 1-0 Bička 52 (p), 1-1 Felipe 78, 1-2 William Batista 90+1, 2-2 Trakys 90+3
Referee: Kever (SUI)
21/7/09, Tofiq Bähramov, Baku
Bakı FK 4-2 FK Ekranas
Goal(s): 1-0 Felipe 59, 2-0 Mujiri 65, 3-0 Felipe 77, 3-1 Matović 81, 4-1 Šolić 90+1, 4-2 Gleveckas 90+2
Referee: Gumienny (BEL)
Aggregate: 6-4; Bakı FK qualify.

15/7/09, Ventspils Olimpiskais, Ventspils
FK Ventspils 3-0 F91 Dudelange
Goal(s): 1-0 Butriks 79, 2-0 Kačanovs 86, 3-0 Rimkus 87
Referee: Borski (POL)
22/7/09, Jos Nosbaum, Dudelange
F91 Dudelange 1-3 FK Ventspils
Goal(s): 1-0 Dan. Da Mota 15, 1-1 Astafjevs 27, 1-2 Butriks 57, 1-3 Mihadjuks 67
Referee: Ingvarsson (SWE)
Aggregate: 1-6; FK Ventspils qualify.

15/7/09, Turku, Turku
FC Inter Turku 0-1 FC Sheriff
Goal(s): 0-1 Suvorov 42 (p)
Referee: Szabó (HUN)
21/7/09, Sheriff, Tiraspol
FC Sheriff 1-0 FC Inter Turku
Goal(s): 1-0 Suvorov 69 (p)
Referee: Velasco Carballo (ESP)
Aggregate: 2-0; FC Sheriff qualify.

15/7/09, Kaplakrikavöllur, Hafnarfjördur
FH Hafnarfjördur 0-4 FC Aktobe
Goal(s): 0-1 Tleshev 48, 0-2 Golovskoy 57, 0-3 Khairullin 70, 0-4 Golovskoy 85
Referee: Malek (POL)
22/7/09, Centralny, Aktobe
FC Aktobe 2-0 FH Hafnarfjördur
Goal(s): 1-0 Smakov 20, 2-0 Tleshev 67
Referee: Kulbakov (BLR)
Aggregate: 6-0; FC Aktobe qualify.

15/7/09, Georgi Asparuhov, Sofia
PFC Levski Sofia 4-0 UE Sant Julià
Goal(s): 1-0 Tasevski 50, 2-0 Hristov 64, 3-0 Hristov 72, 4-0 Gadzhev 82
Referee: Paniashvili (GEO)
21/7/09, Comunal, Andorra La Vella
UE Sant Julià 0-5 PFC Levski Sofia
Goal(s): 0-1 Ognyanov 23, 0-2 Yovov 34, 0-3 Ognyanov 40, 0-4 Tsachev 83, 0-5 Kirov 87
Referee: Hyytiä (FIN)
Aggregate: 0-9; PFC Levski Sofia qualify.

15/7/09, Qemal Stafa, Tirana
KF Tirana 1-1 Stabæk Fotball
Goal(s): 0-1 Kobayashi 34, 1-1 Muka 50
Referee: Schörgenhofer (AUT)
21/7/09, Fornebu Arena, Oslo
Stabæk Fotball 4-0 KF Tirana
Goal(s): 1-0 Segerström 15, 2-0 Segerström 31, 3-0 Berglund 44, 4-0 Farnerud 55
Referee: Kinhöfer (GER)
Aggregate: 5-1; Stabæk Fotball qualify.

UEFA Champions League

15/7/09, Mikheil Meskhi, Tbilisi
FC WIT Georgia 0-0 NK Maribor
Referee: Kaasik (EST)
22/7/09, Ljudski vrt, Maribor
NK Maribor 3-1 FC WIT Georgia
Goal(s): 1-0 Bunderla 9, 2-0 Marcos Tavares 19, 2-1 Kvaratskhelia 45, 3-1 Mihelič 86
Referee: Tudor (ROU)
Aggregate: 3-1; NK Maribor qualify.

15/7/09, Debrecen, Debrecen
Debreceni VSC 2-0 Kalmar FF
Goal(s): 1-0 Varga 73, 2-0 Kiss 86
Referee: Fautrel (FRA)
22/7/09, Fredriksskans Idrottsplats, Kalmar
Kalmar FF 3-1 Debreceni VSC
Goal(s): 0-1 Varga 13, 1-1 R. Elm 19, 2-1 Daniel Mendes 32, 3-1 R. Elm 71 (p)
Referee: Sukhina (RUS)
Aggregate: 3-3; Debreceni VSC qualify on away goal.

15/7/09, Parken, Copenhagen
FC København 6-0 FK Mogren
Goal(s): 1-0 Kristensen 8, 2-0 M. Jørgensen 16, 3-0 Aílton 24, 4-0 N'Doye 69, 5-0 N'Doye 74, 6-0 Nordstrand 82
Referee: Dereli (TUR)
22/7/09, Pod Goricom-Gradski, Podgorica
FK Mogren 0-6 FC København
Goal(s): 0-1 N'Doye 10, 0-2 Nordstrand 16, 0-3 N'Doye 40, 0-4 Vingaard 43, 0-5 Delaney 47, 0-6 Aílton 87
Referee: Deaconu (ROU)
Aggregate: 0-12; FC København qualify.

15/7/09, Stadion Salzburg, Salzburg
FC Salzburg 1-1 Bohemian FC
Goal(s): 1-0 Dudić 25, 1-1 Ndo 60
Referee: Vollquartz (DEN)
22/7/09, Dalymount Park, Dublin
Bohemian FC 0-1 FC Salzburg
Goal(s): 0-1 Ježek 86
Referee: Stavrev (MKD)
Aggregate: 1-2; FC Salzburg qualify.

15/7/09, Gradski, Mostar
HŠK Zrinjski 1-0 ŠK Slovan Bratislava
Goal(s): 1-0 Kordić 48
Referee: McDonald (SCO)
21/7/09, Tehelné Pole, Bratislava
ŠK Slovan Bratislava 4-0 HŠK Zrinjski
Goal(s): 1-0 Halenár 13, 2-0 Gaúcho 19, 3-0 Halenár 60, 4-0 Sylvestr 90+2
Referee: Ennjimi (FRA)
Aggregate: 4-1; ŠK Slovan Bratislava qualify.

15/7/09, Pilkarski, Sosnowiec
Wisła Kraków 1-1 FC Levadia Tallinn
Goal(s): 0-1 Andreev 41, 1-1 Ćwielong 90+3
Referee: Skjerven (NOR)
22/7/09, Kadriorg, Tallinn
FC Levadia Tallinn 1-0 Wisła Kraków
Goal(s): 1-0 Ivanov 89
Referee: Çakır (TUR)
Aggregate: 2-1; FC Levadia Tallinn qualify.

Salzburg's Patrik Ježek scored the late goal that defeated Irish champions Bohemians in Dublin

15/7/09, Kiryat Eliazer, Haifa
Maccabi Haifa FC 6-0 Glentoran FC
Goal(s): 1-0 Refaelov 37, 2-0 Katan 53, 3-0 Dvalishvili 57, 4-0 Dvalishvili 81, 5-0 Arbeitman 83, 6-0 Ghdir 89
Referee: Nikolaev (RUS)
22/7/09, The Oval, Belfast
Glentoran FC 0-4 Maccabi Haifa FC
Goal(s): 0-1 Bello 9, 0-2 Bello 53, 0-3 Masilela 62, 0-4 Arbeitman 90+2
Referee: Berntsen (NOR)
Aggregate: 0-10; Maccabi Haifa FC qualify.

Third Qualifying Round

The third qualifying round highlighted the competition's increasingly even nature; of the 15 ties, four were settled on away goals and a further five by a one-goal margin.

Shakhtar slip up

Olympiacos FC were the exception, winning 2-0 twice against ŠK Slovan Bratislava, while a 5-0 first-leg victory ensured RSC Anderlecht's 3-1 defeat at Sivasspor was scant consolation for the Turkish team. Of the five sides who progressed on away goals, Sporting Clube de Portugal needed an own goal from Peter Wisgerhof five minutes into added time – Sporting goalkeeper Rui Patrício creating it – to draw 1-1 at FC Twente, and overall, to progress, while FC

UEFA Champions League

Timişoara unexpectedly ousted UEFA Cup holders FC Shakhtar Donetsk, drawing 2-2 in Ukraine and holding out for a goalless second leg.

SK Slavia Praha and FC BATE Borisov both had recent group-stage experience but neither was able to make it beyond qualifying this time around, losing out to FC Sheriff and FK Ventspils on away goals after respective 1-1 and 2-2 draws. Another big name to fall by the wayside was FK Partizan, unable to recover from a 2-0 defeat at APOEL FC despite their 1-0 home win, while Celtic FC looked like joining them after losing 1-0 at home to FC Dinamo Moskva, only for Scott McDonald to level the tie in the 45th minute of the second leg in Russia, paving the way for Georgios Samaras's added-time winner that completed Celtic's first away European win in 22 matches and six years.

Rousing fightbacks

The comeback of the round belonged to Panathinaikos FC, however, beaten 3-1 at AC Sparta Praha in the first leg but 3-0 winners in Athens. FC Zürich also recovered from a first-leg deficit having gone down 3-2 at home against NK Maribor, but winning 3-0 in Slovenia, while Robin Nelisse's 83rd-minute goal in Croatia earned FC Salzburg a 3-2 aggregate success against NK Dinamo Zagreb.

Celtic striker Georgios Samaras heads goalwards against Dinamo Moskva

Third Qualifying Round Results

28/7/09, Tofiq Bähramov, Baku
Bakı FK 0-0 PFC Levski Sofia
Referee: Moen (NOR)
5/8/09, Georgi Asparuhov, Sofia
PFC Levski Sofia 2-0 Bakı FK
Goal(s): 1-0 Yovov 64, 2-0 Hristov 80
Referee: Johannesson (SWE)
Aggregate: 2-0; PFC Levski Sofia qualify.

28/7/09, Generali Arena, Prague
AC Sparta Praha 3-1 Panathinaikos FC
Goal(s): 1-0 Holenda 26, 2-0 Vacek 32, 2-1 Salpingidis 67, 3-1 Kalouda 86
Referee: Bebek (CRO)
4/8/09, OACA Spyro Louis, Athens
Panathinaikos FC 3-0 AC Sparta Praha
Goal(s): 1-0 Sarriegi 45, 2-0 Katsouranis 54, 3-0 Salpingidis 89
Referee: Proença (POR)
Aggregate: 4-3; Panathinaikos FC qualify.

28/7/09, Constant Vanden Stock, Brussels
RSC Anderlecht 5-0 Sivasspor
Goal(s): 1-0 De Sutter 17, 2-0 Boussoufa 22, 3-0 Chatelle 32, 4-0 De Sutter 76, 5-0 Frutos 90+1
Referee: Thomson (SCO)
4/8/09, 4 Eylül, Sivas
Sivasspor 3-1 RSC Anderlecht
Goal(s): 1-0 Ersen Martin 12, 2-0 Kamanan 19 (p), 2-1 Van Damme 34, 3-1 Musa Aydin 58
Referee: Mejuto González (ESP)
Aggregate: 3-6; RSC Anderlecht qualify.

28/7/09, Centralny, Aktobe
FC Aktobe 0-0 Maccabi Haifa FC
Referee: Einwaller (AUT)
4/8/09, Kiryat Eliazer, Haifa
Maccabi Haifa FC 4-3 FC Aktobe
Goal(s): 0-1 Averchenko 8, 0-2 Chichulin 13, 0-3 Khairullin 15, 1-3 Katan 26, 2-3 Golasa 34, 3-3 Dvalishvili 59, 4-3 Dvalishvili 62
Referee: Gumienny (BEL)
Aggregate: 4-3; Maccabi Haifa FC qualify.

29/7/09, Ventspils Olimpiskais, Ventspils
FK Ventspils 1-0 FC BATE Borisov
Goal(s): 1-0 Chirkin 64
Referee: Čeferin (SVN)
5/8/09, Gorodskoi, Borisov
FC BATE Borisov 2-1 FK Ventspils
Goal(s): 0-1 Tigirlas 14, 1-1 Krivets 43, 2-1 Krivets 57
Referee: Tudor (ROU)
Aggregate: 2-2; FK Ventspils qualify on away goal.

29/7/09, Kadriorg, Tallinn
FC Levadia Tallinn 0-1 Debreceni VSC
Goal(s): 0-1 Leandro 70
Referee: Bruno Paixão (POR)
5/8/09, Debrecen, Debrecen
Debreceni VSC 1-0 FC Levadia Tallinn
Goal(s): 1-0 Coulibaly 70
Referee: Skomina (SVN)
Aggregate: 2-0; Debreceni VSC qualify.

Timişoara players celebrate one of their two crucial away goals against Shakhtar in Donetsk

29/7/09, Celtic Park, Glasgow
Celtic FC 0-1 FC Dinamo Moskva
Goal(s): 0-1 Kokorin 7
Referee: Rizzoli (ITA)
5/8/09, Arena Khimki, Moscow
FC Dinamo Moskva 0-2 Celtic FC
Goal(s): 0-1 McDonald 45, 0-2 Samaras 90+1
Referee: Eriksson (SWE)
Aggregate: 1-2; Celtic FC qualify.

29/7/09, Tehelné Pole, Bratislava
ŠK Slovan Bratislava 0-2 Olympiacos FC
Goal(s): 0-1 A. Papadopoulos 2, 0-2 Leonardo 21
Referee: Circhetta (SUI)
5/8/09, Georgios Karaiskakis, Piraeus
Olympiacos FC 2-0 ŠK Slovan Bratislava
Goal(s): 1-0 Maresca 35, 2-0 Diogo 56
Referee: Plautz (AUT)
Aggregate: 4-0; Olympiacos FC qualify.

29/7/09, GSP, Nicosia
APOEL FC 2-0 FK Partizan
Goal(s): 1-0 Mirosavljević 49, 2-0 Żewłakow 85
Referee: Kuipers (NED)
5/8/09, FK Partizan, Belgrade
FK Partizan 1-0 APOEL FC
Goal(s): 1-0 Moreira 3
Referee: Trefoloni (ITA)
Aggregate: 1-2; APOEL FC qualify.

29/7/09, Sheriff, Tiraspol
FC Sheriff 0-0 SK Slavia Praha
Referee: Kelly (IRL)
5/8/09, Eden, Prague
SK Slavia Praha 1-1 FC Sheriff
Goal(s): 1-0 Hloušek 15, 1-1 Nádson 90+3
Referee: Rocchi (ITA)
Aggregate: 1-1; FC Sheriff qualify on away goal.

29/7/09, RSC Olympiyskiy, Donetsk
FC Shakhtar Donetsk 2-2 FC Timişoara
Goal(s): 0-1 Bucur 20, 1-1 Hladkiy 60, 1-2 Bucur 80, 2-2 Fernandinho 86
Referee: Iturralde González (ESP)
5/8/09, Dan Păltinişanu, Timisoara
FC Timişoara 0-0 FC Shakhtar Donetsk
Referee: Hauge (NOR)
Aggregate: 2-2; FC Timişoara qualify on away goals.

29/7/09, Letzigrund, Zurich
FC Zürich 2-3 NK Maribor
Goal(s): 1-0 Vonlanthen 4, 1-1 Marcos Tavares 12, 1-2 Marcos Tavares 22, 2-2 Hassli 29, 2-3 Pavlovič 50
Referee: Braamhaar (NED)
5/8/09, Ljudski vrt, Maribor
NK Maribor 0-3 FC Zürich
Goal(s): 0-1 Djuric 21, 0-2 Margairaz 45, 0-3 Nikci 76
Referee: Duhamel (FRA)
Aggregate: 3-5; FC Zürich qualify.

UEFA Champions League

29/7/09, Parken, Copenhagen
FC København 3-1 Stabæk Fotball
Goal(s): 1-0 Grønkjær 11, 2-0 César Santin 41, 2-1 Pálmason 58,
3-1 César Santin 80 (p)
Referee: Baskakov (RUS)
5/8/09, Fornebu Arena, Oslo
Stabæk Fotball 0-0 FC København
Referee: Collum (SCO)
Aggregate: 1-3; FC København qualify.

29/7/09, Stadion Salzburg, Salzburg
FC Salzburg 1-1 NK Dinamo Zagreb
Goal(s): 1-0 Zickler 45, 1-1 Mandžukić 63
Referee: Kralovec (CZE)
4/8/09, Maksimir, Zagreb
NK Dinamo Zagreb 1-2 FC Salzburg
Goal(s): 0-1 Švento 33, 1-1 Papadopoulos 47, 1-2 Nelisse 83
Referee: Hamer (LUX)
Aggregate: 2-3; FC Salzburg qualify.

29/7/09, José Alvalade, Lisbon
Sporting Clube de Portugal 0-0 FC Twente
Referee: Brych (GER)
4/8/09, FC Twente, Enschede
FC Twente 1-1 Sporting Clube de Portugal
Goal(s): 1-0 Douglas 2, 1-1 Wisgerhof 90+5 (og)
Referee: Lannoy (FRA)
Aggregate: 1-1; Sporting Clube de Portugal qualify on away goal.

Play-Off Round

The qualifying competition for the group stage was revamped for the 2009/10 season following a decision by the UEFA Executive Committee in November 2007, with the addition of a play-off round in which the two new qualifying routes – the Champions Path and the Non-Champions Path – concluded with five ties in each section. The new format proved to be an immediate success, with the ten pairings producing relentless drama.

Lethal Lyon

Olympique Lyonnais were in the unusual position of having to qualify for the group stage having had their seven-year reign as French champions ended by FC Girondins de Bordeaux, yet Claude Puel's team produced the most ruthless display of the play-off round. RSC Anderlecht were defeated 5-1 at home and 3-1 away, with new signing Lisandro López offering an instant return on the club's investment with four goals in the tie, including a hat-trick in Brussels. Elsewhere in the Non-Champions Path Arsenal FC were also comfortable winners, a 2-0 triumph at Celtic Park preceding a 3-1 victory against the Glasgow club in north London as

Arsène Wenger's team emerged unscathed from the qualifying stages for the third season running.

FC Timişoara's interest in the competition was ended by VfB Stuttgart, the German side winning 2-0 in the first leg in Romania and holding out for a goalless draw in the return, while Club Atlético de Madrid gained the upper hand in their tie against Panathinaikos FC with a first-leg win in Athens. Although the home side twice fought back from a goal down, Sergio Agüero's 70th-minute strike gave Atlético a 3-2 away success, the subsequent 2-0 home victory assuring Abel Resino's team of a place in the group stage. ACF Fiorentina joined them there, edging through on away goals against Sporting Clube de Portugal, who had progressed in similar fashion in the previous stage. Alberto Gilardino's late equaliser gave the Viola a 2-2 first-leg draw in Lisbon, with young Montenegrin forward Stevan Jovetić striking in the second match to secure a 1-1 draw and progress.

APOEL advance

In the Champions Path, Olympiacos FC – beaten to a place in the group stage by Anorthosis Famagusta FC 12 months previously – made no such mistake against FC Sheriff, second-half goals from Dudu and substitute Kostas Mitroglou securing a 2-0 win in Moldova in the

New Lyon signing Lisandro López scored four goals against Anderlecht, including a hat-trick in Brussels

UEFA Champions League

opening leg and the latter grabbing the only goal of the second match in Greece to complete a 3-0 aggregate success. Anorthosis had become the first Cypriot club to reach the group stage in 2008/09 and APOEL FC repeated the feat by ousting FC København despite losing 1-0 in Denmark. Kamil Kosowski cancelled that out within two minutes of the return and Chrysis Michail put APOEL in front in the tie from the penalty spot in the 18th minute. Dame N'Doye quickly responded to put København back in the driving seat, but Michail's second in the 41st minute handed the overall lead back to APOEL, and Ivan Jovanović's team repelled further advances to squeeze through.

The three remaining ties were more straightforward affairs. Debreceni VSC's bid to become the first Hungarian side to compete in the group stage since Ferencvárosi TC in 1995/96 received a boost after they scored in either half to establish a 2-1 first-leg advantage away to PFC Levski Sofia. The Bulgarian side had reached the group stage in 2006/07 but had no answer to goals from József Varga and Gergely Rudolf in the first 35 minutes of the second leg as Debrecen qualified for the first time. Away first-leg wins also paved the way for Maccabi Haifa FC and FC

Zürich to progress, the Israeli champions winning 2-1 at Austria's FC Salzburg thanks to a goal six minutes from time from substitute Shlomi Arbeitman. Haifa duly booked their place in the last 32 for the first time since 2002/03 – when they became Israel's first group-stage participants – thanks to a 3-0 success in the return. Zürich beat FK Ventspils by a similar margin, taking a giant stride towards qualification in the first game in Riga thanks to a 3-0 victory. The Swiss champions ensured there would be a total of eight debutants in the group stage with a 2-1 home win against their Latvian counterparts.

Play-Off Round Results

18/8/09, Celtic Park, Glasgow
Celtic FC 0-2 Arsenal FC
Goal(s): 0-1 Gallas 43, 0-2 Caldwell 71 (og)
Referee: Busacca (SUI)
26/8/09, Arsenal Stadium, London
Arsenal FC 3-1 Celtic FC
Goal(s): 1-0 Eduardo 28 (p), 2-0 Eboué 53, 3-0 Arshavin 74, 3-1 Donati 90+2
Referee: Mejuto González (ESP)
Aggregate: 5-1; Arsenal FC qualify.

Kamil Kosowski of APOEL fires at goal in the Cypriot champions' 3-1 home win over FC København

UEFA Champions League

18/8/09, José Alvalade, Lisbon
Sporting Clube de Portugal 2-2 ACF Fiorentina
Goal(s): 0-1 Vargas 6, 1-1 Vukčević 58, 2-1 Miguel Veloso 66,
2-2 Gilardino 79
Referee: Kassai (HUN)
26/8/09, Artemio Franchi, Florence
ACF Fiorentina 1-1 Sporting Clube de Portugal
Goal(s): 0-1 João Moutinho 35, 1-1 Jovetić 54
Referee: Webb (ENG)
Aggregate: 3-3; ACF Fiorentina qualify on away goals.

18/8/09, Parken, Copenhagen
FC København 1-0 APOEL FC
Goal(s): 1-0 Pospěch 54
Referee: Hamer (LUX)
26/8/09, GSP, Nicosia
APOEL FC 3-1 FC København
Goal(s): 1-0 Kosowski 2, 2-0 Michail 18 (p), 2-1 N'Doye 22,
3-1 Michail 41
Referee: Plautz (AUT)
Aggregate: 3-2; APOEL FC qualify.

18/8/09, Sheriff, Tiraspol
FC Sheriff 0-2 Olympiacos FC
Goal(s): 0-1 Dudu Cearense 46, 0-2 Mitroglou 81
Referee: Atkinson (ENG)
26/8/09, Georgios Karaiskakis, Piraeus
Olympiacos FC 1-0 FC Sheriff
Goal(s): 1-0 Mitroglou 82
Referee: Undiano Mallenco (ESP)
Aggregate: 3-0; Olympiacos FC qualify.

18/8/09, Dan Păltinişanu, Timisoara
FC Timişoara 0-2 VfB Stuttgart
Goal(s): 0-1 Gebhart 28 (p), 0-2 Hleb 30
Referee: Olegário Benquerença (POR)
26/8/09, VfB Arena, Stuttgart
VfB Stuttgart 0-0 FC Timişoara
Referee: Rosetti (ITA)
Aggregate: 2-0; VfB Stuttgart qualify.

19/8/09, Stadion Salzburg, Salzburg
FC Salzburg 1-2 Maccabi Haifa FC
Goal(s): 0-1 Ghdir 22, 1-1 Zickler 57, 1-2 Arbeitman 84
Referee: Baskakov (RUS)
25/8/09, Ramat Gan, Ramat Gan
Maccabi Haifa FC 3-0 FC Salzburg
Goal(s): 1-0 Dvalishvili 31, 2-0 Golasa 57, 3-0 Ghdir 90
Referee: Layec (FRA)
Aggregate: 5-1; Maccabi Haifa FC qualify.

19/8/09, Gerland, Lyon
Olympique Lyonnais 5-1 RSC Anderlecht
Goal(s): 1-0 Pjanić 10, 2-0 Lisandro López 15 (p), 3-0 Michel Bastos 39,
4-0 Gomis 42, 4-1 Suárez 58, 5-1 Gomis 63
Referee: Stark (GER)
25/8/09, Constant Vanden Stock, Brussels
RSC Anderlecht 1-3 Olympique Lyonnais
Goal(s): 0-1 Lisandro López 26, 0-2 Lisandro López 32,
0-3 Lisandro López 41, 1-3 Suárez 51 (p)
Referee: Rizzoli (ITA)
Aggregate: 2-8; Olympique Lyonnais qualify.

Shlomi Arbeitman hit
Maccabi Haifa's winning
goal away to Salzburg

19/8/09, Skonto, Riga
FK Ventspils 0-3 FC Zürich
Goal(s): 0-1 Vonlanthen 12, 0-2 Aegerter 55, 0-3 Djuric 75
Referee: Øvrebø (NOR)
25/8/09, Arena St Gallen, St Gallen
FC Zürich 2-1 FK Ventspils
Goal(s): 1-0 Vonlanthen 6, 1-1 Tigirlas 8, 2-1 Abdi 90+2
Referee: Hauge (NOR)
Aggregate: 5-1; FC Zürich qualify.

19/8/09, Georgi Asparuhov, Sofia
PFC Levski Sofia 1-2 Debreceni VSC
Goal(s): 0-1 Bodnár 12, 1-1 Bardon 51, 1-2 Czvitkovics 76
Referee: Duhamel (FRA)
25/8/09, Ferenc Puskás, Budapest
Debreceni VSC 2-0 PFC Levski Sofia
Goal(s): 1-0 Varga 13, 2-0 Rudolf 35
Referee: Larsen (DEN)
Aggregate: 4-1; Debreceni VSC qualify.

19/8/09, OACA Spyro Louis, Athens
Panathinaikos FC 2-3 Club Atlético de Madrid
Goal(s): 0-1 Maxi Rodríguez 36, 1-1 Salpingidis 47, 1-2 Forlán 63,
1-3 Agüero 70, 2-3 Leto 74
Referee: Brych (GER)
25/8/09, Vicente Calderón, Madrid
Club Atlético de Madrid 2-0 Panathinaikos FC
Goal(s): 1-0 Vintra 4 (og), 2-0 Agüero 83
Referee: Vink (NED)
Aggregate: 5-2; Club Atlético de Madrid qualify.

GROUP STAGE

Group A

UEFA Champions League Group A brought together two of Europe's biggest clubs – FC Bayern München and Juventus – as well as the champions of France, FC Girondins de Bordeaux, while Maccabi Haifa FC returned to the group stage after seven seasons.

Tough at the top

The Israeli titleholders were quickly reminded of how harsh life at the top can be, Bayern inflicting only Haifa's second defeat in 29 competitive matches as they ran out 3-0 winners at the Ramat Gan Stadium on Matchday 1. Defender Daniel Van Buyten made the breakthrough before 20-year-old forward Thomas Müller's late brace wrapped up the points. In the other opening-night fixture, Juventus needed an inspired display from Gianluigi Buffon to hold Bordeaux at bay in Turin before taking a 63rd-minute lead through Vincenzo Iaquinta, but Jaroslav Plašil finally beat Buffon with 15 minutes left to ensure the points were shared.

Bordeaux playmaker Yoann Gourcuff opened the scoring in his team's 2-0 win at Bayern

The Italian giants were held again in the second round of games, extending their unbeaten run to 14 matches in all competitions with a goalless draw against Bayern in Munich. Bordeaux, meanwhile, built on their opening draw with a win against Haifa at the Stade Chaban-Delmas, although it took until the 83rd minute for Laurent Blanc's side to break through thanks to Michaël Ciani's header, the visitors ending with ten men following Baram Kayal's late red card.

Bayern beaten

Bordeaux's stock continued to rise on Matchday 3 as Bayern were beaten in south-west France despite taking a sixth-minute lead through Ciani's own goal. The Bordeaux defender found the net at the right end in the 27th minute, and Müller was dismissed before Marc Planus put Les Marine et Blanc ahead before half-time. Although Hans-Jörg Butt saved two second-half penalties from Yoann Gourcuff and Jussiê, the latter awarded after Van Buyten was also sent off, Bordeaux took the points. Haifa, however, were still looking for their first point and goal despite another disciplined defensive display in Italy, Juventus defender Giorgio Chiellini heading the only goal of the game two minutes into the second period with the Israeli outfit again finishing a man short as Tiago Dutra was sent off.

That 1-0 scoreline was repeated when the sides reconvened in Israel on Matchday 4, Mauro Camoranesi striking in first-half added time to keep Juve in contention. Bordeaux, however, left the Italian side to fight it out with Bayern for the runners-up berth with a 2-0 triumph in Germany, Gourcuff (37 minutes) and Marouane Chamakh (90) scoring late in each half to take Blanc's charges into the UEFA Champions League knockout stages for the first time.

Fourth straight win

There was no let-up on Matchday 5, however, Bordeaux recording a fourth successive win as goals from Fernando (54) and Chamakh (90+4) left Juve's hopes hanging in the balance. Bayern moved within a point of their final opponents with a vital home win against Haifa, Ivica Olić settling a tense game two minutes past the hour.

The German side still had to win in Turin to overtake Juventus, and the prospects for Louis van Gaal's side looked bleak when David Trezeguet volleyed the home team into a 19th-minute lead. Butt promptly levelled

UEFA Champions League

Juventus goalkeeper Gianluigi Buffon's efforts were not enough to keep the Bayern attack at bay on Matchday 6

from the penalty spot – curiously, the Bayern goalkeeper's third career goal against Juventus – and, despite another brilliant Buffon display, Olić gave Bayern the lead seven minutes into the second period. Late strikes from Mario Gómez and Anatoliy Tymoshchuk emphatically ended Juve's 16-match unbeaten home record in the competition and left Bayern celebrating a famous victory. In Israel, Jussiê's early strike gave Bordeaux a fifth straight win and ensured Haifa became only the second team in UEFA Champions League history, after RC Deportivo La Coruña in 2004/05, to finish the group stage without a goal and only the ninth to end it point-less.

Group A Results

15/9/09, Stadio Olimpico, Turin
Juventus 1-1 FC Girondins de Bordeaux
Attendance: 17513
Goal(s): 1-0 Iaquinta 63, 1-1 Plašil 75
Referee: Øvrebø (NOR)

15/9/09, Ramat Gan, Ramat Gan
Maccabi Haifa FC 0-3 FC Bayern München
Attendance: 38789
Goal(s): 0-1 Van Buyten 64, 0-2 Müller 85, 0-3 Müller 88
Referee: Skomina (SVN)

30/9/09, Fußball Arena München, Munich
FC Bayern München 0-0 Juventus
Attendance: 66000
Referee: Webb (ENG)

30/9/09, Chaban-Delmas, Bordeaux
FC Girondins de Bordeaux 1-0 Maccabi Haifa FC
Attendance: 28748
Goal(s): 1-0 Ciani 83
Referee: Braamhaar (NED)

21/10/09, Chaban-Delmas, Bordeaux
FC Girondins de Bordeaux 2-1 FC Bayern München
Attendance: 31321
Goal(s): 0-1 Ciani 6 (og), 1-1 Ciani 27, 2-1 Planus 40
Referee: Hauge (NOR)

21/10/09, Stadio Olimpico, Turin
Juventus 1-0 Maccabi Haifa FC
Attendance: 21303
Goal(s): 1-0 Chiellini 47
Referee: Olegário Benquerença (POR)

3/11/09, Fußball Arena München, Munich
FC Bayern München 0-2 FC Girondins de Bordeaux
Attendance: 66000
Goal(s): 0-1 Gourcuff 37, 0-2 Chamakh 90
Referee: Proença (POR)

3/11/09, Ramat Gan, Ramat Gan
Maccabi Haifa FC 0-1 Juventus
Attendance: 39120
Goal(s): 0-1 Camoranesi 45+2
Referee: Hauge (NOR)

25/11/09, Chaban-Delmas, Bordeaux
FC Girondins de Bordeaux 2-0 Juventus
Attendance: 32195
Goal(s): 1-0 Fernando 54, 2-0 Chamakh 90+4
Referee: Iturralde González (ESP)

25/11/09, Fußball Arena München, Munich
FC Bayern München 1-0 Maccabi Haifa FC
Attendance: 58000
Goal(s): 1-0 Olić 62
Referee: Thomson (SCO)

8/12/09, Stadio Olimpico, Turin
Juventus 1-4 FC Bayern München
Attendance: 27801
Goal(s): 1-0 Trezeguet 19, 1-1 Butt 30 (p), 1-2 Olić 52, 1-3 Gómez 83, 1-4 Tymoshchuk 90+2
Referee: Busacca (SUI)

8/12/09, Ramat Gan, Ramat Gan
Maccabi Haifa FC 0-1 FC Girondins de Bordeaux
Attendance: 25800
Goal(s): 0-1 Jussiê 13
Referee: Eriksson (SWE)

Group A Table

		Home				Away				Total				
	Pld	W	D	L	F A	W	D	L	F A	W	D	L	F A	Pts
1 FC Girondins de Bordeaux	6	3	0	0	5 1	2	1	0	4 1	5	1	0	9 2	16
2 FC Bayern München	6	1	1	1	1 2	2	0	1	8 3	3	1	2	9 5	10
3 Juventus	6	1	1	1	3 5	1	1	1	1 2	2	2	4	4 7	8
4 Maccabi Haifa FC	6	0	0	3	0 5	0	0	3	0 3	0	0	6	0 8	0

Group B

Having been in consecutive UEFA Champions League finals, Manchester United FC were clear favourites in Group B – although newly-crowned German champions VfL Wolfsburg, PFC CSKA Moskva and Beşiktaş JK represented a stiff test for Sir Alex Ferguson's men.

Typical United

United began in typical fashion in Istanbul, Paul Scholes heading the only goal against a spirited Beşiktaş with 13 minutes left at the Inönü stadium. Wolfsburg were more spectacular winners on Matchday 1, a hat-trick from Grafite ensuring Armin Veh's side enjoyed a competition debut to remember against CSKA. The Brazilian striker scored twice in six minutes shortly before half-time to put the home team in command. Although Alan Dzagoev halved the deficit with 14 minutes left, Grafite rounded off an evening to remember by completing his treble in the 87th minute.

The German champions carried that form into their trip to Old Trafford, their enterprise rewarded with Edin Džeko's towering 56th-minute header. Characteristically

United hit back, Ryan Giggs's deflected free-kick bringing them swiftly level before Michael Carrick struck a fine winner in the 78th minute. CSKA came out on top as the two opening-day losers met in Moscow, recording their first home UEFA Champions League win since October 2006. Dzagoev opened the scoring early on and Miloš Krasić added a second in the 61st minute. Ekrem Dağ pulled one back in added time, but already Beşiktaş hopes were hanging by a thread.

Gritty effort

The Turkish champions showed signs of life in their third outing with a gritty effort earning a goalless draw at Wolfsburg, for whom a frustrating night was completed with the 74th-minute dismissal of Grafite. United's bandwagon continued to gather pace in Moscow, Antonio Valencia opening his UEFA Champions League account in the 86th minute to secure a 1-0 victory for the English titleholders on their return to the Luzhniki stadium, scene of their 2008 final victory.

The return proved to be a different story, Dzagoev stunning Old Trafford with a spectacular 25th-minute opener. Michael Owen levelled within four minutes, but further goals from Krasić (31) and Vasiliy Berezutskiy (47) left United staring at a first home UEFA Champions League defeat in 22 matches. One of their famous

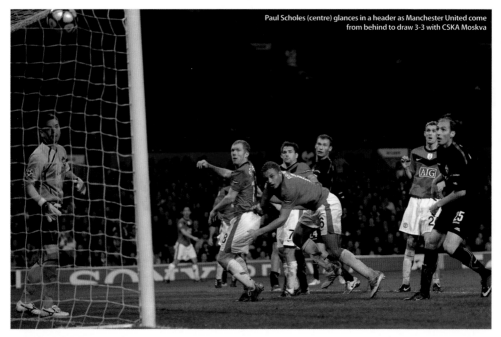
Paul Scholes (centre) glances in a header as Manchester United come from behind to draw 3-3 with CSKA Moskva

UEFA Champions League

fightbacks ensued, however, goals from Scholes (84) and Valencia (90+2) - the latter's effort taking a crucial deflection off CSKA full-back Georgi Schennikov - rescuing a point and securing progress. The visitors also lost Deividas Šemberas to a red card on a remarkable tournament debut for their new coach Leonid Slutskiy. Goals from Zvjezdan Misimović, Christian Gentner and Džeko ended injury-hit Beşiktaş's hopes of reaching the knockout phase on a freezing Istanbul night and strengthened Wolfsburg's hold on second place.

Krasić wondergoal

That grip looked to be further tightening when Džeko put Wolfsburg in front in Russia on Matchday 5, but Tomáš Necid levelled just before the hour and Krasić's wonderful long-range strike gave CSKA a deserved win. Meanwhile, in Manchester, already qualified United did fall to a home defeat, Rodrigo Tello ending an undefeated run stretching back to 2005 with the only goal of the game in the first half to finally give Beşiktaş something to cheer.

CSKA therefore needed to better Wolfsburg's result on Matchday 6 to reach the last 16 for the first time, and the Russian side looked to be heading for maximum points at Beşiktaş when Krasić put them in front after 41 minutes. Bobô equalised with four minutes left, but Yevgeniy Aldonin won the game deep in added time, and it was confirmed CSKA would qualify from the group stage at the fifth attempt as Wolfsburg went down 3-1 at home to United. Despite Džeko's 56th-minute header cancelling out Owen's first-half opener, the former England international struck twice late on to extend United's remarkable unbeaten run in the competition to 15 away games and leave Wolfsburg contemplating a consolation place in the UEFA Europa League.

Group B Results

15/9/09, VfL Wolfsburg Arena, Wolfsburg
VfL Wolfsburg 3-1 PFC CSKA Moskva
Attendance: 25017
Goal(s): 1-0 Grafite 36, 2-0 Grafite 41 (p), 2-1 Dzagoev 76, 3-1 Grafite 87
Referee: Lannoy (FRA)

15/9/09, Inönü, Istanbul
Beşiktaş JK 0-1 Manchester United FC
Attendance: 26448
Goal(s): 0-1 Scholes 77
Referee: Rizzoli (ITA)

30/9/09, Luzhniki, Moscow
PFC CSKA Moskva 2-1 Beşiktaş JK
Attendance: 19750
Goal(s): 1-0 Dzagoev 7, 2-0 Krasić 61, 2-1 Ekrem Dağ 90+2
Referee: Mejuto González (ESP)

30/9/09, Old Trafford, Manchester
Manchester United FC 2-1 VfL Wolfsburg
Attendance: 74037
Goal(s): 0-1 Džeko 56, 1-1 Giggs 59, 2-1 Carrick 78
Referee: Kassai (HUN)

21/10/09, Luzhniki, Moscow
PFC CSKA Moskva 0-1 Manchester United FC
Attendance: 51250
Goal(s): 0-1 Valencia 86
Referee: Larsen (DEN)

21/10/09, VfL Wolfsburg Arena, Wolfsburg
VfL Wolfsburg 0-0 Beşiktaş JK
Attendance: 25778
Referee: Rosetti (ITA)

3/11/09, Old Trafford, Manchester
Manchester United FC 3-3 PFC CSKA Moskva
Attendance: 73718
Goal(s): 0-1 Dzagoev 25, 1-1 Owen 29, 1-2 Krasić 31, 1-3 V. Berezutskiy 47, 2-3 Scholes 84, 3-3 Valencia 90+2
Referee: Olegário Benquerença (POR)

3/11/09, Inönü, Istanbul
Beşiktaş JK 0-3 VfL Wolfsburg
Attendance: 18116
Goal(s): 0-1 Misimović 14, 0-2 Gentner 80, 0-3 Džeko 87
Referee: Undiano Mallenco (ESP)

25/11/09, Old Trafford, Manchester
Manchester United FC 0-1 Beşiktaş JK
Attendance: 74242
Goal(s): 0-1 Tello 20
Referee: Lannoy (FRA)

25/11/09, Luzhniki, Moscow
PFC CSKA Moskva 2-1 VfL Wolfsburg
Attendance: 13478
Goal(s): 0-1 Džeko 19, 1-1 Necid 58, 2-1 Krasić 66
Referee: Rizzoli (ITA)

8/12/09, VfL Wolfsburg Arena, Wolfsburg
VfL Wolfsburg 1-3 Manchester United FC
Attendance: 26490
Goal(s): 0-1 Owen 44, 1-1 Džeko 56, 1-2 Owen 83, 1-3 Owen 90+1
Referee: Kuipers (NED)

8/12/09, Inönü, Istanbul
Beşiktaş JK 1-2 PFC CSKA Moskva
Attendance: 16129
Goal(s): 0-1 Krasić 41, 1-1 Bobô 86, 1-2 Aldonin 90+5
Referee: Hansson (SWE)

Group B Table

		Home					Away					Total					
	Pld	W	D	L	F	A	W	D	L	F	A	W	D	L	F	A	Pts
1 Manchester United FC	6	1	1	1	5	5	3	0	0	5	1	4	1	1	10	6	13
2 PFC CSKA Moskva	6	2	0	1	4	3	1	1	1	6	7	3	1	2	10	10	10
3 VfL Wolfsburg	6	1	1	1	4	4	1	0	2	5	4	2	1	3	9	8	7
4 Beşiktaş JK	6	0	0	3	1	6	1	1	1	2	2	1	1	4	3	8	4

Group C

Three winners of the UEFA Champions League were drawn together in Group C, with FC Zürich handed the unenviable task on their group-stage debut of overcoming Real Madrid CF, AC Milan and Olympique de Marseille.

Cruise control

The Swiss champions found the going tough from the outset, succumbing 5-2 to Madrid's new-look line-up at the Letzigrund stadium on Matchday 1. Goals from Cristiano Ronaldo (27), Raúl González (34) and Gonzalo Higuaín (45+1) had the Spanish side in cruise control by half-time and, although Xavier Margairaz scored from the penalty spot and Silvan Aegerter converted a 65th-minute header to reopen the contest, Ronaldo's 89th-minute set-piece sealed the points before Guti added a fifth. Two trademark Filippo Inzaghi strikes made the difference for Milan in Marseille, the 36-year-old showing that his predatory instincts remained as sharp as ever with goals either side of Gabriel Heinze's reply for Marseille.

The group was turned on its head in the next round of games as Zürich stunned San Siro with a 1-0 win in Milan thanks to Hannu Tihinen's impudent tenth-minute goal – a back-heel from Milan Gajić's corner. Madrid enjoyed a much more comfortable evening, brushing aside Marseille 3-0 at the Santiago Bernabéu although it took until the 58th minute for Ronaldo to open the scoring. Marseille's Souleymane Diawara collected a second yellow card in conceding the penalty from which Kaká made it 2-0 three minutes later, Ronaldo adding another in the 64th minute.

Pato double

The meeting of the two most successful teams in European Champion Clubs' Cup history ended in a morale-boosting Milan victory on Matchday 3 despite Raúl's opener. Andrea Pirlo levelled from long range in the 62nd minute before Pato struck four minutes later. It looked as if substitute Royston Drenthe had salvaged a point for Madrid in the 76th minute, only for Pato to pop up again with a decisive goal two minutes from time. Marseille, meanwhile, finally got their campaign up and running in Switzerland, Heinze getting the only goal midway through the second half against a Zürich team who had Laurent Bonnart sent off in added time.

Marseille again came out on top in the reverse meeting against Zürich, Fabrice Abriel producing a pair of free-kicks inside the opening eleven minutes, the first being turned in by Zürich midfielder Aegerter and the second flying straight into the net. Alexandre Alphonse replied for the visitors and it took an expertly taken Mamadou Niang goal on 51 minutes to settle the encounter before Hilton, Benoît Cheyrou and Brandão all registered late on. In the night's other game, Milan and Madrid shared a 1-1 draw, Ronaldinho cancelling out Karim Benzema's 29th-minute opener with a brilliantly executed penalty.

Held again

Leonardo's Milan team were again held 1-1 at home in their penultimate group game. Marco Borriello's first UEFA Champions League goal in the tenth minute was not enough to defeat a Marseille team for whom Lucho González levelled six minutes later. It was similarly tight in Madrid, only a 21st-minute Higuaín strike separating Manuel Pellegrini's charges from Zürich.

Marseille therefore needed to better Milan's Matchday 6 result to reach the last 16, and the signs were promising for the French side when Gajić gave Zürich a 29th-minute lead. Swiss hopes of a second famous win were dashed, however, as Ronaldinho replied from the penalty spot just past the hour after Alain Rochat had been dismissed. Ronaldo left Marseille with plenty of work to do as he gave the visitors a fifth-minute lead at the Stade Vélodrome and, although Lucho swiftly responded, second-half goals from Raúl Albiol and

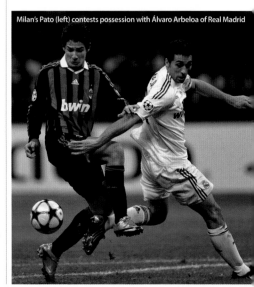

Milan's Pato (left) contests possession with Álvaro Arbeloa of Real Madrid

UEFA Champions League

Cristiano Ronaldo scores Real Madrid's third goal in their 3-1 win at Marseille

Ronaldo – the latter's strike his sixth in the group stage, making him the competition's leading scorer – took Madrid through as section winners and meant Marseille had to settle for third place.

Group C Results

15/9/09, Letzigrund, Zurich
FC Zürich 2-5 Real Madrid CF
Attendance: 24424
Goal(s): 0-1 Cristiano Ronaldo 27, 0-2 Raúl 34, 0-3 Higuaín 45+1, 1-3 Margairaz 64 (p), 2-3 Aegerter 65, 2-4 Cristiano Ronaldo 89, 2-5 Guti 90+4
Referee: Atkinson (ENG)

15/9/09, Vélodrome, Marseille
Olympique de Marseille 1-2 AC Milan
Attendance: 55434
Goal(s): 0-1 Inzaghi 28, 1-1 Heinze 49, 1-2 Inzaghi 74
Referee: Larsen (DEN)

30/9/09, Giuseppe Meazza, Milan
AC Milan 0-1 FC Zürich
Attendance: 32439
Goal(s): 0-1 Tihinen 10
Referee: Meyer (GER)

30/9/09, Santiago Bernabéu, Madrid
Real Madrid CF 3-0 Olympique de Marseille
Attendance: 67244
Goal(s): 1-0 Cristiano Ronaldo 58, 2-0 Kaká 61 (p), 3-0 Cristiano Ronaldo 64
Referee: Hansson (SWE)

21/10/09, Santiago Bernabéu, Madrid
Real Madrid CF 2-3 AC Milan
Attendance: 71569
Goal(s): 1-0 Raúl 19, 1-1 Pirlo 62, 1-2 Pato 66, 2-2 Drenthe 76, 2-3 Pato 88
Referee: De Bleeckere (BEL)

21/10/09, Letzigrund, Zurich
FC Zürich 0-1 Olympique de Marseille
Attendance: 22300
Goal(s): 0-1 Heinze 69
Referee: Skomina (SVN)

3/11/09, Giuseppe Meazza, Milan
AC Milan 1-1 Real Madrid CF
Attendance: 75092
Goal(s): 0-1 Benzema 29, 1-1 Ronaldinho 35 (p)
Referee: Brych (GER)

3/11/09, Vélodrome, Marseille
Olympique de Marseille 6-1 FC Zürich
Attendance: 56282
Goal(s): 1-0 Aegerter 3 (og), 2-0 Abriel 11, 2-1 Alphonse 31, 3-1 Niang 51, 4-1 Hilton 80, 5-1 Cheyrou 87, 6-1 Brandão 90
Referee: Thomson (SCO)

25/11/09, Santiago Bernabéu, Madrid
Real Madrid CF 1-0 FC Zürich
Attendance: 67867
Goal(s): 1-0 Higuaín 21
Referee: Hamer (LUX)

25/11/09, Giuseppe Meazza, Milan
AC Milan 1-1 Olympique de Marseille
Attendance: 49063
Goal(s): 1-0 Borriello 10, 1-1 Lucho González 16
Referee: Webb (ENG)

8/12/09, Letzigrund, Zurich
FC Zürich 1-1 AC Milan
Attendance: 24100
Goal(s): 1-0 Gajić 29, 1-1 Ronaldinho 64 (p)
Referee: Proença (POR)

8/12/09, Vélodrome, Marseille
Olympique de Marseille 1-3 Real Madrid CF
Attendance: 55722
Goal(s): 0-1 Cristiano Ronaldo 5, 1-1 Lucho González 11, 1-2 Albiol 60, 1-3 Cristiano Ronaldo 80
Referee: Stark (GER)

Group C Table

		Home					Away					Total					
	Pld	W	D	L	F	A	W	D	L	F	A	W	D	L	F	A	Pts
1 Real Madrid CF	6	2	0	1	6	3	2	1	0	9	4	4	1	1	15	7	13
2 AC Milan	6	0	2	1	2	3	2	1	0	6	4	2	3	1	8	7	9
3 Olympique de Marseille	6	1	0	2	8	6	1	1	1	2	4	2	1	3	10	10	7
4 FC Zürich	6	0	1	2	3	7	1	0	2	2	7	1	1	4	5	14	4

Group D

Seasoned UEFA Champions League campaigners Chelsea FC and FC Porto were the early favourites to progress from Group D, which also included Club Atlético de Madrid and APOEL FC, and so it proved as the pair duly made serene progress into the first knockout round again.

Anelka strikes

The eventual top two met at Stamford Bridge on the opening night of the group stage, Carlo Ancelotti's Chelsea continuing their impressive early-season form with a 1-0 home win. Nicolas Anelka – leading the attack in the absence of the suspended Didier Drogba – scored the only goal of the game three minutes after the interval, with Porto finishing a man short after Fernando collected a second yellow card in added time. APOEL – the second Cypriot team to reach the group stage in successive seasons following Anorthosis Famagusta FC's achievement in 2008/09 – served early notice of their intent by holding Atlético to a goalless draw at the Vicente Calderón.

APOEL produced another creditable display as they welcomed Chelsea to Cyprus on Matchday 2, but Anelka again proved to be the London club's match-winner with the only goal in the 18th minute. Porto, meanwhile, left it late to breathe life into their campaign as Radamel Falcao (75) and Rolando (82) struck in the closing stages to see off Atlético at the Estádio do Dragão.

Hulk weighs in

The Portuguese champions were once more victorious on home soil next time out, although again they had to survive a scare as defender Álvaro Pereira inadvertently put through his own goal to present APOEL with a 22nd-minute advantage. Hulk settled Porto nerves with an equaliser 11 minutes later and struck the decisive blow from the penalty spot three minutes after half-time, Jesualdo Ferreira's team holding on to give the coach his 100th victory in charge despite Mariano González's late red card. Chelsea, meanwhile, claimed a third successive win by dismissing Atlético 4-0 in London, Salomon Kalou scoring twice and Frank Lampard once with Luis Perea's added-time own goal completing the Spanish side's misery. Coach Abel Resino departed two days later.

Resino's replacement, Quique Sánchez Flores, made a more promising start to his reign on Matchday 4, Sergio Agüero opening the scoring at the Vicente Calderón only for Drogba to mark his first UEFA Champions League appearance of the season with two goals in the final eight minutes. A fine Agüero free-kick in added time at least spared Atlético a third successive defeat, although it was not enough to keep them in the competition – or deny Chelsea progress. Porto also reached the knockout stages, although again they were made to fight all the way by APOEL before Colombian international Falcao secured a 1-0 win with six minutes left.

Chelsea triumph

With qualification assured and two games to spare, first place was the only major issue at stake when Porto took on Chelsea in Portugal, and again it was the English side who emerged triumphant thanks to another Anelka strike. APOEL, meanwhile, were denied victory against Atlético after Nenad Mirosavljević's fifth-minute opener was cancelled out by Simão, keeping the Spanish side one point above their Cypriot rivals in the race for third place.

The Madrid club were left sweating when they slumped to a 3-0 home defeat against Porto on Matchday 6. Early goals from Bruno Alves and Falcao

Nicolas Anelka celebrates in familiar style after scoring Chelsea's winner at home to Porto

UEFA Champions League

effectively ended the contest before Hulk completed a fine away win late on. That meant APOEL would claim third with an unlikely win at Stamford Bridge. Polish international Marcin Żewłakow's early strike set them dreaming, but Michael Essien and Drogba had Chelsea breathing easier before half-time and, although substitute Mirosavljević made it 2-2 with three minutes to play, a famous draw was not enough to prolong APOEL's European season, Atlético clinging on to third position thanks to Simão's strike in Cyprus.

Hulk of Porto – a double goalscorer at home to APOEL

Group D Results

15/9/09, Stamford Bridge, London
Chelsea FC 1-0 FC Porto
Attendance: 39436
Goal(s): 1-0 Anelka 48
Referee: Plautz (AUT)

15/9/09, Vicente Calderón, Madrid
Club Atlético de Madrid 0-0 APOEL FC
Attendance: 30628
Referee: Thomson (SCO)

30/9/09, GSP, Nicosia
APOEL FC 0-1 Chelsea FC
Attendance: 21657
Goal(s): 0-1 Anelka 18
Referee: Layec (FRA)

30/9/09, Estádio do Dragão, Porto
FC Porto 2-0 Club Atlético de Madrid
Attendance: 37609
Goal(s): 1-0 Falcao 75, 2-0 Rolando 82
Referee: Rizzoli (ITA)

21/10/09, Estádio do Dragão, Porto
FC Porto 2-1 APOEL FC
Attendance: 31212
Goal(s): 0-1 Álvaro Pereira 22 (og), 1-1 Hulk 33, 2-1 Hulk 48 (p)
Referee: Brych (GER)

21/10/09, Stamford Bridge, London
Chelsea FC 4-0 Club Atlético de Madrid
Attendance: 39997
Goal(s): 1-0 Kalou 41, 2-0 Kalou 52, 3-0 Lampard 69, 4-0 Perea 90+1 (og)
Referee: Meyer (GER)

3/11/09, Vicente Calderón, Madrid
Club Atlético de Madrid 2-2 Chelsea FC
Attendance: 36284
Goal(s): 1-0 Agüero 66, 1-1 Drogba 82, 1-2 Drogba 88, 2-2 Agüero 90+1
Referee: Kuipers (NED)

3/11/09, GSP, Nicosia
APOEL FC 0-1 FC Porto
Attendance: 20825
Goal(s): 0-1 Falcao 84
Referee: Skomina (SVN)

25/11/09, Estádio do Dragão, Porto
FC Porto 0-1 Chelsea FC
Attendance: 38410
Goal(s): 0-1 Anelka 69
Referee: Eriksson (SWE)

25/11/09, GSP, Nicosia
APOEL FC 1-1 Club Atlético de Madrid
Attendance: 21178
Goal(s): 1-0 Mirosavljević 5, 1-1 Simão 62
Referee: De Bleeckere (BEL)

8/12/09, Stamford Bridge, London
Chelsea FC 2-2 APOEL FC
Attendance: 40917
Goal(s): 0-1 Żewłakow 6, 1-1 Essien 19, 2-1 Drogba 26, 2-2 Mirosavljević 87
Referee: Trefoloni (ITA)

8/12/09, Vicente Calderón, Madrid
Club Atlético de Madrid 0-3 FC Porto
Attendance: 24603
Goal(s): 0-1 Bruno Alves 2, 0-2 Falcao 14, 0-3 Hulk 76
Referee: Lannoy (FRA)

Group D Table

		Home					Away					Total					
	Pld	W	D	L	F	A	W	D	L	F	A	W	D	L	F	A	Pts
1 Chelsea FC	6	2	1	0	7	2	2	1	0	4	2	4	2	0	11	4	14
2 FC Porto	6	2	0	1	4	2	2	0	1	4	1	4	0	2	8	3	12
3 Club Atlético de Madrid	6	0	2	1	2	5	0	1	2	1	7	0	3	3	3	12	3
4 APOEL FC	6	0	1	2	1	3	0	2	1	3	4	0	3	3	4	7	3

Group E

Regular participants in the UEFA Champions League knockout stages, Liverpool FC and Olympique Lyonnais would nevertheless have been wary of the threat posed by ACF Fiorentina in Group E, while Debreceni VSC presented something of an unknown quantity.

Debutants denied

The Hungarian champions proved from the outset they would be no pushovers, Dirk Kuyt denying the debutants a point at Anfield with the only goal in first-half added time. The scoreline was the same in France, although it took the dismissal of Fiorentina striker Alberto Gilardino for violent conduct on the stroke of half-time to tip the balance Lyon's way, Miralem Pjanić finally beating the Viola's inspired French goalkeeper Sébastien Frey with 14 minutes left.

Lyon's bid to reach the knockout stages for the seventh successive season continued apace on Matchday 2 as Claude Puel's side ran out emphatic winners in Budapest, goals from Kim Källström (3), Pjanić (13), Sidney Govou (24) and Bafétimbi Gomis (51) securing the club's biggest away win in the competition. Fiorentina, meanwhile, took full advantage of a sluggish first-half Liverpool display at the Stadio

Artemio Franchi, Stevan Jovetić scoring twice in nine minutes before the interval to earn the points.

Liverpool crash

More trouble followed for Rafael Benítez's side on Matchday 3, although initially Yossi Benayoun's 41st-minute effort looked to have put the Reds' campaign back on track. Instead, 20-year-old substitute Maxime Gonalons headed Lyon level with 18 minutes remaining, and a minute into added time another replacement, César Delgado, pounced to send Liverpool to their fourth straight defeat in all competitions – their worst run since 1987. Once more Debrecen mustered a showing of considerable spirit, scoring their first group-stage goal as Péter Czvitkovics fired them in front early on against Fiorentina, only for two Adrian Mutu strikes and another from Gilardino to put the visitors 3-1 ahead. Gergely Rudolf and Fiorentina's Mario Santana then traded goals before Adamo Coulibaly headed in two minutes from time to set up a frantic finale.

The re-match in Italy was another high-scoring affair. Although Rudolf cancelled out Mutu's opener, Cesare Prandelli's men ran amok in the second half. Marco Marchionni, Riccardo Montolivo, Dario Dainelli and Gilardino all found the net to take the Serie A side second with a 4-2 win. In contrast, Lyon and Liverpool produced a tense encounter at the Stade de Gerland that Ryan Babel looked to have won for the visitors

Alberto Gilardino wins the group for Fiorentina with a late goal against Liverpool at Anfield

UEFA Champions League

CHAMPIONS
LEAGUE

with a fine strike seven minutes from time, only for Lisandro to level in the 90th minute, taking Lyon through and leaving Liverpool facing elimination.

TV torment

That was confirmed in the penultimate fixtures, although Liverpool at least kept their hopes alive initially with a 1-0 win in Hungary achieved through David N'Gog's early goal. Once the final whistle had sounded at the Ferenc Puskás stadium, Liverpool players crowded round TV screens to watch the final stages of Fiorentina-Lyon, yet they were left disappointed as the Viola held on to the advantage given to them by Juan Vargas' 28th-minute penalty.

Fiorentina then went on to steal first place in the standings by completing a double over Liverpool at Anfield. Trailing to Benayoun's first-half header, the Viola drew level through Martin Jørgensen before Gilardino snatched a dramatic victory in the final seconds to send the hosts to a second successive home defeat – an unwanted first in Europe for Liverpool – and earn Fiorentina's fifth consecutive victory. Lyon also ended their group campaign with a flourish, first-half goals from Gomis and Michel Bastos added to by Pjanić and Aly Cissokho in the second period. The latter's was the 19th goal Debrecen had conceded in their six matches, meaning they equalled the record held jointly by FC Dynamo Kyiv (2007/08) and compatriots Ferencvárosi TC (1995/96) for the competition's most porous defence.

Group E Results

16/9/09, Anfield, Liverpool
Liverpool FC 1-0 Debreceni VSC
Attendance: 41591
Goal(s): 1-0 Kuyt 45+1
Referee: Proença (POR)

16/9/09, Gerland, Lyon
Olympique Lyonnais 1-0 ACF Fiorentina
Attendance: 37169
Goal(s): 1-0 Pjanić 76
Referee: Vink (NED)

29/9/09, Artemio Franchi, Florence
ACF Fiorentina 2-0 Liverpool FC
Attendance: 33426
Goal(s): 1-0 Jovetić 28, 2-0 Jovetić 37
Referee: Brych (GER)

29/9/09, Ferenc Puskás, Budapest
Debreceni VSC 0-4 Olympique Lyonnais
Attendance: 41600
Goal(s): 0-1 Källström 3, 0-2 Pjanić 13, 0-3 Govou 24, 0-4 Gomis 51
Referee: Øvrebø (NOR)

20/10/09, Ferenc Puskás, Budapest
Debreceni VSC 3-4 ACF Fiorentina
Attendance: 41500
Goal(s): 1-0 Czvitkovics 2, 1-1 Mutu 6, 1-2 Gilardino 10, 1-3 Mutu 20, 2-3 Rudolf 28, 2-4 Santana 37, 3-4 Coulibaly 88
Referee: Thomson (SCO)

20/10/09, Anfield, Liverpool
Liverpool FC 1-2 Olympique Lyonnais
Attendance: 41562
Goal(s): 1-0 Benayoun 41, 1-1 Gonalons 72, 1-2 Delgado 90+1
Referee: Undiano Mallenco (ESP)

4/11/09, Artemio Franchi, Florence
ACF Fiorentina 5-2 Debreceni VSC
Attendance: 19676
Goal(s): 1-0 Mutu 14, 1-1 Rudolf 38, 2-1 Dainelli 52, 3-1 Montolivo 59, 4-1 Marchionni 61, 4-2 Coulibaly 70, 5-2 Gilardino 74
Referee: Mejuto González (ESP)

4/11/09, Gerland, Lyon
Olympique Lyonnais 1-1 Liverpool FC
Attendance: 39180
Goal(s): 0-1 Babel 83, 1-1 Lisandro López 90
Referee: De Bleeckere (BEL)

24/11/09, Ferenc Puskás, Budapest
Debreceni VSC 0-1 Liverpool FC
Attendance: 41500
Goal(s): 0-1 N'Gog 4
Referee: Kuipers (NED)

24/11/09, Artemio Franchi, Florence
ACF Fiorentina 1-0 Olympique Lyonnais
Attendance: 34301
Goal(s): 1-0 Vargas 28 (p)
Referee: Olegário Benquerença (POR)

9/12/09, Anfield, Liverpool
Liverpool FC 1-2 ACF Fiorentina
Attendance: 40863
Goal(s): 1-0 Benayoun 43, 1-1 Jørgensen 63, 1-2 Gilardino 90+2
Referee: Skomina (SVN)

9/12/09, Gerland, Lyon
Olympique Lyonnais 4-0 Debreceni VSC
Attendance: 36884
Goal(s): 1-0 Gomis 25, 2-0 Michel Bastos 45, 3-0 Pjanić 59, 4-0 Cissokho 76
Referee: Meyer (GER)

Group E Table

		Home				Away				Total				
	Pld	W	D	L	F A	W	D	L	F A	W	D	L	F A	Pts
1 ACF Fiorentina	6	3	0	0	8 2	2	0	1	6 5	5	0	1	14 7	15
2 Olympique Lyonnais	6	2	1	0	6 1	2	0	1	6 2	4	1	1	12 3	13
3 Liverpool FC	6	1	0	2	3 4	1	1	1	2 3	2	1	3	5 7	7
4 Debreceni VSC	6	0	0	3	3 9	0	0	3	2 10	0	0	6	5 19	0

Group F

Group F was the only one of the eight sections to contain four bona fide champions, with FC Barcelona and FC Internazionale Milano – title-holders in Spain and Italy respectively – facing long trips east to take on Russia's FC Rubin Kazan and FC Dynamo Kyiv of Ukraine.

San Siro stalemate

That prospect was put on hold for Matchday 1, with Inter welcoming holders Barça to San Siro – a fixture given extra frisson by the summer transfer swap involving Samuel Eto'o and Zlatan Ibrahimović. In the event, neither was able to find the net as the game finished goalless, and it was left to Dynamo and Rubin to provide the opening-night fireworks in Kyiv. Group-stage debutants Rubin – in only their second away game in UEFA competition – took a 25th-minute lead through Alejandro Domínguez's free-kick and, with Andriy Shevchenko spurning several chances on his first UEFA Champions League appearance for Dynamo since 1999, that looked to be enough for victory, only for Ayila Yussuf, Gérson Magrão and substitute Oleh Gusev all to find the net in the final 20 minutes and give Dynamo the points.

Rubin, however, showed their resilience again on Matchday 2, holding Inter to a 1-1 draw in Kazan, with Domínguez again on target in the 11th minute. Dejan Stanković replied 16 minutes later, but Inter's hopes of a win were effectively ended by Mario Balotelli's red card on the hour. The same night Barcelona ended Dynamo's 15-match unbeaten run, a goal in each half from Lionel Messi and substitute Pedro Rodríguez – who also scored the decisive goal against Dynamo's great rivals FC Shakhtar Donetsk in August's UEFA Super Cup – taking Josep Guardiola's team to the top of Group F.

Remarkable Rubin

If the defending champions thought the hard work was done, however, they were swiftly disabused of that notion in their second successive home game, Rubin earning a remarkable first European victory with a 2-1 win. Aleksandr Ryazantsev, with a stunning early long-range strike, and Gökdeniz Karadeniz did the damage despite Ibrahimović's 48th-minute response, leaving Guardiola to taste defeat against Russian opponents at the Camp Nou for the second time having been in the team beaten 3-2 by PFC CSKA

Moskva – and eliminated – in 1992/93. Dynamo also sprang a surprise, Taras Mykhalyk and a Lúcio own goal restricting Inter to a 2-2 draw in Milan despite equalisers from Stanković and Walter Samuel.

José Mourinho's team were up against it again when they trailed to a 21st-minute goal from old nemesis Shevchenko with just four minutes left at the Valeriy Lobanovskiy Stadium on Matchday 4, but Wesley Sneijder then set up Diego Milito for an equaliser and there was a sting in the tail for Dynamo as the Dutchman scored the 89th-minute winner himself to revive Inter's challenge. Rubin, however, had no such troubles, holding Barcelona to a goalless draw in Russia with a determined defensive effort.

All to play for

Having retained their Russian title the preceding weekend, Rubin earned a second successive goalless draw at home in the fifth round of games – although it took a spectacular save from Olexandr Shovkovskiy, on his 100th European appearance, to deny Domínguez and earn Dynamo a draw. Inter's revival ground to a swift halt, however, as Gerard Piqué and Pedro struck in the first 30 minutes at Camp Nou to give Barça a win that left all issues undecided going into Matchday 6.

Rubin players celebrate taking a shock early lead against Barcelona at Camp Nou

UEFA Champions League

CHAMPIONS LEAGUE

Inter's Samuel Eto'o lets fly against Dynamo Kyiv

29/9/09, Camp Nou, Barcelona
FC Barcelona 2-0 FC Dynamo Kyiv
Attendance: 68221
Goal(s): 1-0 Messi 26, 2-0 Pedro 76
Referee: Kuipers (NED)

20/10/09, Camp Nou, Barcelona
FC Barcelona 1-2 FC Rubin Kazan
Attendance: 55930
Goal(s): 0-1 Ryazantsev 2, 1-1 Ibrahimović 48, 1-2 Gökdeniz 73
Referee: Duhamel (FRA)

20/10/09, Giuseppe Meazza, Milan
FC Internazionale Milano 2-2 FC Dynamo Kyiv
Attendance: 34721
Goal(s): 0-1 Mykhalyk 5, 1-1 Stanković 35, 1-2 Lúcio 40 (og), 2-2 Samuel 47
Referee: Atkinson (ENG)

4/11/09, Centralniy, Kazan
FC Rubin Kazan 0-0 FC Barcelona
Attendance: 24600
Referee: Plautz (AUT)

4/11/09, Valeriy Lobanovskiy, Kyiv
FC Dynamo Kyiv 1-2 FC Internazionale Milano
Attendance: 15900
Goal(s): 1-0 Shevchenko 21, 1-1 Milito 86, 1-2 Sneijder 89
Referee: Layec (FRA)

24/11/09, Centralniy, Kazan
FC Rubin Kazan 0-0 FC Dynamo Kyiv
Attendance: 23185
Referee: Brych (GER)

24/11/09, Camp Nou, Barcelona
FC Barcelona 2-0 FC Internazionale Milano
Attendance: 93524
Goal(s): 1-0 Piqué 10, 2-0 Pedro 26
Referee: Busacca (SUI)

9/12/09, Giuseppe Meazza, Milan
FC Internazionale Milano 2-0 FC Rubin Kazan
Attendance: 49539
Goal(s): 1-0 Eto'o 31, 2-0 Balotelli 64
Referee: Vink (NED)

9/12/09, Valeriy Lobanovskiy, Kyiv
FC Dynamo Kyiv 1-2 FC Barcelona
Attendance: 16300
Goal(s): 1-0 Milevskiy 2, 1-1 Xavi 33, 1-2 Messi 86
Referee: Webb (ENG)

Barcelona were on the ropes at a chilly Valeriy Lobanovskiy Stadium when Artem Milevskiy headed Dynamo in front inside two minutes, but they fought back to level through Xavi Hernández just past the half-hour before Messi's imperious late winner confirmed top spot ahead of Inter – 2-0 home winners against Rubin, with Eto'o and Balotelli getting the goals – and denied Dynamo a place in the UEFA Europa League, with Rubin finishing third.

Group F Results

16/9/09, Giuseppe Meazza, Milan
FC Internazionale Milano 0-0 FC Barcelona
Attendance: 77321
Referee: Stark (GER)

16/9/09, Valeriy Lobanovskiy, Kyiv
FC Dynamo Kyiv 3-1 FC Rubin Kazan
Attendance: 15000
Goal(s): 0-1 Domínguez 25, 1-1 Yussuf 71, 2-1 Magrão 79, 3-1 Gusev 85
Referee: Hamer (LUX)

29/9/09, Centralniy, Kazan
FC Rubin Kazan 1-1 FC Internazionale Milano
Attendance: 23670
Goal(s): 1-0 Domínguez 11, 1-1 Stanković 27
Referee: Hauge (NOR)

Group F Table

	Pld	Home					Away					Total					Pts
		W	D	L	F	A	W	D	L	F	A	W	D	L	F	A	
1 FC Barcelona	6	2	0	1	5	2	1	2	0	2	1	3	2	1	7	3	11
2 FC Internazionale Milano	6	1	2	0	4	2	1	1	1	3	4	2	3	1	7	6	9
3 FC Rubin Kazan	6	0	3	0	1	1	1	0	2	3	6	1	3	2	4	7	6
4 FC Dynamo Kyiv	6	1	0	2	5	5	0	2	1	2	4	1	2	3	7	9	5

Group G

Group G promised to be one of the more closely-fought sections, but Sevilla FC went on to claim first position with two matches to spare, leaving VfB Stuttgart and Romanian debutants FC Unirea Urziceni to contest the runners-up berth as Rangers FC finished bottom after a disappointing campaign.

Perfect record

Sevilla made their mark almost from the first whistle, a 2-0 home win against Unirea on Matchday 1 achieved through a goal in each half from Luís Fabiano and Renato extending the Andalusian club's perfect UEFA Champions League record at the Ramón Sánchez-Pizjuán to six matches. Stuttgart had been paired with Rangers in each of their previous group-stage appearances, in 2003/04 and 2007/08, and familiarity bred caution for both teams, Madjid Bougherra cancelling out Pavel Pogrebnyak's first-half opener with a late equaliser to give Rangers a draw.

The Scottish champions' challenge started to unravel in the second round of matches, however, with Sevilla putting in a clinical display of counterattacking football to run out 4-1 winners in Glasgow. Four goals in 24 second-half minutes, from Abdoulay Konko, Adriano, Luís Fabiano and Frédéric Kanouté, did the damage, a late strike from Nacho Novo providing scant consolation for Rangers. Unirea, meanwhile, fought back from the shock of Serdar Taşçı's early goal for Stuttgart at Bucharest's Steaua stadium, with Dacian Varga levelling for the Romanian hosts three minutes after half-time.

Rangers self-destruct

Sevilla's serene progress to the knockout stages continued on Matchday 3 with another win, two set-piece headers from French international defender Sébastien Squillaci either side of a Jesús Navas strike doing the damage for the visitors at Stuttgart, whose sole response was Élson's 74th-minute consolation. Rangers, meanwhile, self-destructed against Unirea in Glasgow, suffering a second successive 4-1 home defeat and scoring two own goals into the bargain. Rangers in fact benefited from an early own goal themselves, Ricardo Vilana deflecting into his own net in the second minute, but Marius Bilaşco equalised midway through the first half, and after Daniel Tudor had saved Steven Davis's penalty, the second period

Sevilla's Frédéric Kanouté rises high against Rangers

began with both Rangers substitute Kyle Lafferty and team-mate Lee McCulloch scoring for Unirea, Pablo Brandán adding a clinching fourth.

McCulloch looked to have redeemed himself in Bucharest a fortnight later, giving Rangers a 79th-minute advantage, but Unirea hit back two minutes from time through Marius Onofraş's explosive equaliser. It was also 1-1 in Spain as Stuttgart halted the Sevilla bandwagon, Navas establishing a first-half lead for the Group G pacesetters, who were then hindered by injuries to Arouna Koné and substitute Aldo Duscher that left them a man short for the last 15 minutes. The result was Zdravko Kuzmanović's stunning effort that earned the visitors a point. It could not, however, prevent the hosts from reaching the last 16.

Bizarre own goal

Sevilla's wobble continued in their final away fixture, a bizarre Ivica Dragutinović own goal on the stroke of half-time giving Unirea a win that kept them clear in second place. Stuttgart, however, maintained the pressure by eliminating Rangers from European competition with a 2-0 victory in Glasgow, Sebastian Rudy and Kuzmanović scoring in either half to inflict a third straight home defeat on Walter Smith's team.

UEFA Champions League

Unirea still needed only a point at Stuttgart to pip their opponents to the runners-up berth but – with Christian Gross having replaced Markus Babbel as the German club's coach – the Romanian champions were blown away by goals in the first eleven minutes from Ciprian Marica, Christian Träsch and Pogrebnyak. That burst of scoring effectively wrapped up a last-16 place for the Bundesliga side, although António Semedo kept things interesting with a goal for Unirea early in the second period. Sevilla returned to winning ways with a 1-0 defeat of Rangers in Spain, Kanouté's eighth-minute penalty ensuring the Scottish side ended six points adrift at the foot of the table.

Group G Results

16/9/09, VfB Arena, Stuttgart
VfB Stuttgart 1-1 Rangers FC
Attendance: 38000
Goal(s): 1-0 Pogrebnyak 18, 1-1 Bougherra 77
Referee: Busacca (SUI)

16/9/09, Ramón Sánchez-Pizjuán, Seville
Sevilla FC 2-0 FC Unirea Urziceni
Attendance: 32691
Goal(s): 1-0 Luís Fabiano 45+1, 2-0 Renato 70
Referee: Trefoloni (ITA)

29/9/09, Steaua, Bucharest
FC Unirea Urziceni 1-1 VfB Stuttgart
Attendance: 13557
Goal(s): 0-1 Taşçi 5, 1-1 Varga 48
Referee: Duhamel (FRA)

29/9/09, Ibrox, Glasgow
Rangers FC 1-4 Sevilla FC
Attendance: 40572
Goal(s): 0-1 Konko 50, 0-2 Adriano 64, 0-3 Luís Fabiano 72, 0-4 Kanouté 74, 1-4 Nacho Novo 88
Referee: Eriksson (SWE)

20/10/09, Ibrox, Glasgow
Rangers FC 1-4 FC Unirea Urziceni
Attendance: 39476
Goal(s): 1-0 Ricardo Vilana 2 (og), 1-1 Bilaşco 32, 1-2 Lafferty 49 (og), 1-3 McCulloch 59 (og), 1-4 Brandán 65
Referee: Braamhaar (NED)

20/10/09, VfB Arena, Stuttgart
VfB Stuttgart 1-3 Sevilla FC
Attendance: 37000
Goal(s): 0-1 Squillaci 23, 0-2 Jesús Navas 55, 0-3 Squillaci 72, 1-3 Élson 74
Referee: Vink (NED)

4/11/09, Steaua, Bucharest
FC Unirea Urziceni 1-1 Rangers FC
Attendance: 9923
Goal(s): 0-1 McCulloch 79, 1-1 Onofraş 88
Referee: Larsen (DEN)

4/11/09, Ramón Sánchez-Pizjuán, Seville
Sevilla FC 1-1 VfB Stuttgart
Attendance: 32669
Goal(s): 1-0 Jesús Navas 14, 1-1 Kuzmanović 79
Referee: Atkinson (ENG)

24/11/09, Ibrox, Glasgow
Rangers FC 0-2 VfB Stuttgart
Attendance: 41468
Goal(s): 0-1 Rudy 16, 0-2 Kuzmanović 59
Referee: Rosetti (ITA)

24/11/09, Steaua, Bucharest
FC Unirea Urziceni 1-0 Sevilla FC
Attendance: 10007
Goal(s): 1-0 Dragutinović 45 (og)
Referee: Øvrebø (NOR)

9/12/09, VfB Arena, Stuttgart
VfB Stuttgart 3-1 FC Unirea Urziceni
Attendance: 37000
Goal(s): 1-0 Marica 5, 2-0 Träsch 8, 3-0 Pogrebnyak 11, 3-1 Semedo 46
Referee: Kassai (HUN)

9/12/09, Ramón Sánchez-Pizjuán, Seville
Sevilla FC 1-0 Rangers FC
Attendance: 31560
Goal(s): 1-0 Kanouté 8 (p)
Referee: Layec (FRA)

Pavel Pogrebnyak turns away after putting Stuttgart 3-0 up in their must-win final fixture against Unirea

Group G Table

		Home					Away					Total					
	Pld	W	D	L	F	A	W	D	L	F	A	W	D	L	F	A	Pts
1 Sevilla FC	6	2	1	0	4	1	2	0	1	7	3	4	1	1	11	4	13
2 VfB Stuttgart	6	1	1	1	5	5	1	2	0	4	2	2	3	1	9	7	9
3 FC Unirea Urziceni	6	1	2	0	3	2	1	0	2	5	6	2	2	2	8	8	8
4 Rangers FC	6	0	0	3	2	0	0	2	1	2	3	0	2	4	4	3	2

Group H

Group H contained the champions of the Netherlands (AZ Alkmaar), Belgium (R. Standard de Liège) and Greece (Olympiacos FC), yet the clear favourites to progress to the first knockout round were the team who had finished fourth in England in 2008/09, Arsenal FC.

Bad start

Arsène Wenger's side could hardly have made a worse start, however. The English side inflicted Standard's heaviest ever European defeat back in 1993, triumphing 7-0 at Stade Maurice Dufrasne, but it was the hosts who threatened to run up a big score this time around, centre-back Eliaquim Mangala finding the net with three minutes on the clock and Milan Jovanović following up with a spot-kick moments later. Arsenal failed to stir until Nicklas Bendtner's strike late in the first half, but they equalised through Thomas Vermaelen 13 minutes from time and claimed maximum points with a close-range Eduardo goal four minutes later. There was also defeat for the section's other group-stage debutants, AZ going down 1-0 at

Arsenal's Samir Nasri scored in successive home games against AZ and Standard

Olympiacos with Vasilios Torosidis scoring the only goal 11 minutes from time.

The Matchday 1 winners met in north London two weeks later and Arsenal again prevailed, although Wenger's side once more left it late before goals in the last 12 minutes from Robin van Persie and Andrei Arshavin finally ended the resolve of Olympiacos and goalkeeper Antonis Nikopolidis in particular. AZ and Standard each got off the mark thanks to a 1-1 draw in Alkmaar, although the visitors left the more satisfied with their point as Moussa Traoré cancelled out Mounir El Hamdaoui's 48th-minute opener a minute into added time.

Late goals

AZ then recorded a second successive 1-1 draw, although this time it was the home team who had more to celebrate, David Mendes da Silva volleying an equaliser deep into stoppage time after Cesc Fàbregas had swept Arsenal into a 36th-minute lead. Olympiacos also struck a crucial late goal, Ieroklis Stoltidis heading a 93rd-minute winner after Standard captain Igor De Camargo's composed finish in the 37th minute had been swiftly cancelled out by Kostas Mitroglou,

Standard bounced back in style on Matchday 4, recording a first UEFA Champions League win against Olympiacos in Liege with Dieumerci Mbokani's coolly taken strike after 31 minutes and Milan Jovanović's late header. Arsenal again conceded late against AZ, Jeremain Lens scoring with eight minutes left in north London, but by then it scarcely mattered as the hosts led 4-0 thanks to a Fàbregas double and further goals from Samir Nasri and Abou Diaby.

Convincing Gunners

The Gunners made sure of first place in the section with another routine home win next time out, first-half goals from Nasri and Denílson setting Arsenal on their way to a convincing success against Standard, who finished the match with ten men after an 86th-minute red card for Mehdi Carcela-González. AZ's first taste of the UEFA Champions League had proved to be brief, as a goalless home draw against Olympiacos ended the Dutch champions' interest in the competition and left their Greek counterparts in pole position to progress.

Needing just a draw against a youthful Arsenal team in Piraeus to secure qualification, Zico's side made no mistake. Leonardo scored the only goal two minutes

UEFA Champions League

Standard goalkeeper Sinan Bolat celebrates his incredible stoppage-time equaliser against AZ

after half-time to take Olympiacos through for the second time in three years. Instead the Matchday 6 drama was reserved for Liege. With the visitors leading from the 42nd minute thanks to Lens's close-range finish, it seemed Standard would be heading out of European competition altogether. However, in virtually the match's final action, home goalkeeper Sinan Bolat joined the attack for a free-kick and met Benjamin Nicaise's inswinging delivery with a powerful header to push AZ back down into fourth place and sensationally send the Belgian champions into the UEFA Europa League.

Group H Results

16/9/09, Maurice Dufrasne, Liege
R. Standard de Liège 2-3 Arsenal FC
Attendance: 23022
Goal(s): 1-0 Mangala 3, 2-0 Jovanović 5 (p), 2-1 Bendtner 45, 2-2 Vermaelen 77, 2-3 Eduardo 81
Referee: Iturralde González (ESP)

16/9/09, Georgios Karaiskakis, Piraeus
Olympiacos FC 1-0 AZ Alkmaar
Attendance: 29018
Goal(s): 1-0 Torosidis 79
Referee: Kassai (HUN)

29/9/09, Arsenal Stadium, London
Arsenal FC 2-0 Olympiacos FC
Attendance: 59884
Goal(s): 1-0 Van Persie 78, 2-0 Arshavin 86
Referee: Lannoy (FRA)

29/9/09, AZ, Alkmaar
AZ Alkmaar 1-1 R. Standard de Liège
Attendance: 16373
Goal(s): 1-0 El Hamdaoui 48, 1-1 Traoré 90+1
Referee: Stark (GER)

20/10/09, AZ, Alkmaar
AZ Alkmaar 1-1 Arsenal FC
Attendance: 16666
Goal(s): 0-1 Fàbregas 36, 1-1 Mendes da Silva 90+3
Referee: Hansson (SWE)

20/10/09, Georgios Karaiskakis, Piraeus
Olympiacos FC 2-1 R. Standard de Liège
Attendance: 29889
Goal(s): 0-1 De Camargo 37, 1-1 Mitroglou 43, 2-1 Stoltidis 90+3
Referee: Proença (POR)

4/11/09, Arsenal Stadium, London
Arsenal FC 4-1 AZ Alkmaar
Attendance: 59345
Goal(s): 1-0 Fàbregas 25, 2-0 Nasri 43, 3-0 Fàbregas 52, 4-0 Diaby 72, 4-1 Lens 82
Referee: Hamer (LUX)

4/11/09, Maurice Dufrasne, Liege
R. Standard de Liège 2-0 Olympiacos FC
Attendance: 24787
Goal(s): 1-0 Mbokani 31, 2-0 Jovanović 88
Referee: Rizzoli (ITA)

24/11/09, Arsenal Stadium, London
Arsenal FC 2-0 R. Standard de Liège
Attendance: 59941
Goal(s): 1-0 Nasri 35, 2-0 Denílson 45+2
Referee: Plautz (AUT)

24/11/09, AZ, Alkmaar
AZ Alkmaar 0-0 Olympiacos FC
Attendance: 16213
Referee: Undiano Mallenco (ESP)

9/12/09, Maurice Dufrasne, Liege
R. Standard de Liège 1-1 AZ Alkmaar
Attendance: 24359
Goal(s): 0-1 Lens 42, 1-1 Sinan 90+5
Referee: Atkinson (ENG)

9/12/09, Georgios Karaiskakis, Piraeus
Olympiacos FC 1-0 Arsenal FC
Attendance: 30277
Goal(s): 1-0 Leonardo 47
Referee: Cardoso Cortez Batista (POR)

Group H Table

		Home					Away					Total					
	Pld	W	D	L	F	A	W	D	L	F	A	W	D	L	F	A	Pts
1 Arsenal FC	6	3	0	0	8	1	1	1	1	4	4	4	1	1	12	5	13
2 Olympiacos FC	6	3	0	0	4	1	0	1	2	0	4	3	1	2	4	5	10
3 R. Standard de Liège	6	1	1	1	5	4	0	1	2	2	5	1	2	3	7	9	5
4 AZ Alkmaar	6	0	3	0	2	2	0	1	2	2	6	0	4	2	4	8	4

FIRST KNOCKOUT ROUND

When the draw for the UEFA Champions League first knockout round was made, the eye was immediately drawn by two high-profile reunions - David Beckham's AC Milan against his alma mater Manchester United FC, and José Mourinho's return to Chelsea FC with FC Internazionale Milano.

Rooney at the double

Beckham, on loan from LA Galaxy, was in the Milan starting line-up for the first leg at San Siro, with the Italian club in confident mood having won all four of the clubs' previous two-legged meetings. The Rossoneri made a perfect start as Ronaldinho's deflected shot gave them a third-minute lead and put United's 15-match unbeaten away run in the competition in jeopardy, yet Paul Scholes levelled in fortuitous circumstances with a miscued effort nine minutes before half-time – United's first goal against Milan in Italy. The second period belonged to the visitors, perfect crosses from Antonio Valencia and Darren Fletcher giving Wayne Rooney two headed opportunities that the striker clinically converted, although a fine flicked finish from Clarence Seedorf late on gave Milan a glimmer of hope to take to Manchester.

That was quickly snuffed out at Old Trafford, Rooney's 13th-minute strike setting United on their way to a sixth successive home win against Serie A visitors. The same player effectively sealed Milan's fate by supplying an assured finish to Nani's defence-splitting pass a minute after the interval and further goals from Park Ji-sung and Fletcher completed the rout, with Beckham restricted to a second-half cameo.

Tighter affair

Inter against Chelsea was an altogether tighter affair, Mourinho's current employers eking out a narrow first-leg advantage against his former team. Inter, who had lost in the first knockout round for three seasons running – the previous two defeats by English opposition – made the perfect start at San Siro when Diego Milito fired them in front in the third minute. Chelsea responded strongly, Didier Drogba striking the underside of the crossbar with a thunderous free-kick, and their improvement was rewarded six minutes into the second period when Salomon Kalou's shot

squirmed beyond Júlio César. Parity was short-lived, however, Esteban Cambiasso restoring Inter's lead at the second attempt to leave the tie delicately poised.

Chelsea went into the return at Stamford Bridge unbeaten in 21 home UEFA Champions League matches, yet they were unable to counter Mourinho's tactical switch, with Samuel Eto'o and Goran Pandev deployed in wide roles to stem the forays of the home full-backs. After a tense 78 minutes, Eto'o – who had also scored the decisive goal when FC Barcelona were the last side to win in west London in February 2006 (with Mourinho in the home dugout) – strode on to Wesley Sneijder's perfect pass to shoot Inter into the last eight for the first time since 2005/06. Drogba's late red card after a tangle with Thiago Motta encapsulated the Blues' frustrations.

Real lose

Karim Benzema recovered from a groin injury to take his place among the Real Madrid CF substitutes for their trip to his old club Olympique Lyonnais, but the striker failed to make it off the bench and had to watch as his new club fell to defeat at the Stade de

Inter midfielder Esteban Cambiasso is elated by his team's 1-0 win at Chelsea

UEFA Champions League

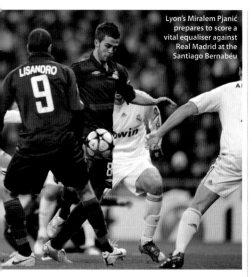

Lyon's Miralem Pjanić prepares to score a vital equaliser against Real Madrid at the Santiago Bernabéu

Stuttgart's fears were realised inside the first quarter of the match in Spain, where they had never won, as Barça marched serenely towards a ninth straight home win against German clubs. Lionel Messi's powerful strike broke the deadlock with 13 minutes gone and Barcelona never looked back, a dazzling interchange between Messi, Andrés Iniesta and Sergio Busquets ending with Pedro Rodríguez steering in Yaya Touré's pass. Second-half goals from Messi again and substitute Bojan Krkić rounded off another mesmeric attacking display from the Blaugrana.

Defensive lapses

Arsenal FC were another team left with work to do following a 2-1 first-leg defeat at FC Porto, who took an 11th-minute lead at the Estádio do Dragão when the visitors' stand-in goalkeeper Łukasz Fabiański pushed Silvestre Varela's cross into his own net. Sol Campbell marked his first UEFA Champions League appearance since the 2006 final by heading Arsenal level seven minutes later yet the Gunners were undone again by more defensive uncertainty shortly after half-time when Fabiański picked up Campbell's back-pass and Rúben Micael's quick free-kick gave Radamel Falcao a simple finish.

Gerland for the third time in five years. Jean II Makoun was allowed to advance unchecked two minutes into the second half and unleashed a thunderous shot for the only goal of the first leg.

Deprived of the suspended Marcelo and Xabi Alonso for the return, Madrid nevertheless started at breakneck speed and were level within six minutes, Cristiano Ronaldo scoring with a low left-foot shot. When Gonzalo Higuaín skipped past goalkeeper Hugo Lloris, Madrid looked set to take a commanding lead as they attempted to beat Lyon for the first time, only for the Argentinian to shoot against the inside of the post with the goal gaping. The home team were made to pay as the visitors improved substantially after half-time, Miralem Pjanić supplying a thumping finish to an incisive move 15 minutes from the end to condemn Madrid to a sixth successive last-16 exit and end their dreams of reaching the final at their Santiago Bernabéu home.

Taxing for Barça

Holders Barcelona also endured a taxing away first leg, VfB Stuttgart being rewarded for a sound tactical start midway through the first half when the in-form Cacau headed them in front against the team coach Christian Gross warned were "the best club side in the world". However, Zlatan Ibrahimović made the most of one of his few chances soon after the restart, getting the away goal – his long-awaited first in the knockout phase of the competition - to leave the German club facing a daunting trip to Camp Nou.

That left the Gunners needing to overturn a first-leg away defeat, something they had managed only once in nine previous attempts in UEFA competition, but any nerves were settled by Nicklas Bendtner's tenth-minute strike. Porto had their own unwanted record, having failed to win in 13 visits to England and lost six straight games in London, and that run was extended as Arsenal turned on the style, Bendtner adding two more goals – completing his hat-trick from the penalty spot in added time – with Samir Nasri's superb slalom effort and Emmanuel Eboué completing the scoring.

Gripping stuff

FC Bayern München and ACF Fiorentina shared eight goals in a gripping tie, the German side taking a 2-1 lead from the first leg in Munich. An Arjen Robben penalty in the closing seconds of the first half eased Bayern in front but Per Krøldrup, whose challenge had brought the spot-kick, deservedly equalised five minutes after the break. The Italian side looked set for a firm foothold in the tie despite Massimo Gobbi's 73rd-minute red card, yet Miroslav Klose's close-range header a minute from time – which television replays showed to be from an offside position - gave Bayern the edge.

That advantage was quickly overturned in Florence, however, as goals from Juan Vargas and Stevan Jovetić put the Serie A side on course for the last eight of Europe's elite competition for the first time since 1970. Yet Jovetić's 54th-minute effort was merely the start of a frenetic spell which brought four goals in 11 minutes, Mark van Bommel squaring the tie at 3-3 on the hour. Although Jovetić put Fiorentina back in front within four minutes, 60 seconds later Robben angled a stunning 25-metre strike into the top corner to take Bayern through on away goals.

Memorable equaliser

PFC CSKA Moskva welcomed Sevilla FC to the Russian capital for the first leg, and the home team, in the knockout stages for the first time, fell behind after 25 minutes when Álvaro Negredo struck for the visitors. Mark González fired a memorable long-range equaliser midway through the second half, but Sevilla's formidable home record left CSKA with it all to do in Andalusia.

The Spanish side had won seven of their eight UEFA Champions League matches at the Ramón Sánchez-Pizjuán and boasted a perfect record in three matches against Russian visitors, but they fell behind when Tomáš Necid struck in the 39th minute. Diego Perotti levelled before the break yet CSKA's only previous trip to Spain had ended in a 3-2 win at Barcelona in 1992/93 and another memorable victory was secured as home goalkeeper Andrés Palop fumbled Japanese midfielder Keisuke Honda's long-range free-kick into the Sevilla net.

Sixth straight win

FC Girondins de Bordeaux continued their impressive form with a sixth successive win in the competition at Olympiacos FC. Laurent Blanc's team, who collected the most points of the 32 teams in the group stage, soaked up long spells of home pressure and snatched victory with Michaël Ciani's third goal of the season two minutes into added time at the end of the first period, the centre-back muscling ahead of the home defence to head in Yoann Gourcuff's left-wing free-kick.

Bordeaux twice reached the last eight of the European Champion Clubs' Cup in the 1980s, and they looked set to qualify for the UEFA Champions League quarter-finals for the first time within five minutes of the second leg at the Stade Chaban-Delmas when another Gourcuff set piece produced a stunning shot from a tight angle over the hapless Antonis Nikopolidis and into the top corner. The goalscorer hit the crossbar with a similar free-kick before the break and Olympiacos's hopes seemed over when Matt Derbyshire collected a second yellow card on the hour.

Sevilla's Federico Fazio (left) challenges CSKA Moskva's Mark González

Yet five minutes later Kostas Mitroglou equalised – the first goal Bordeaux had conceded in the competition in 509 minutes – and the dismissal of home captain Alou Diarra shortly afterwards left the tie in the balance. Ludovic Sané's goal-line clearance denied Raúl Bravo as the visitors pressed for an all-important second, but Marouane Chamakh had the last say, heading in Benoît Trémoulinas's perfect cross two minutes from time to take the French champions through. Olympiacos ended with nine men after Olof Mellberg was sent off for dissent after the final whistle.

First Knockout Round Results

16/2/10, Gerland, Lyon
Olympique Lyonnais 1-0 Real Madrid CF
Attendance: 40327
Goal(s): 1-0 Makoun 47
Referee: Atkinson (ENG)
10/3/10, Santiago Bernabéu, Madrid
Real Madrid CF 1-1 Olympique Lyonnais
Attendance: 71569
Goal(s): 1-0 Cristiano Ronaldo 6, 1-1 Pjanić 75
Referee: Rizzoli (ITA)
Aggregate: 1-2; Olympique Lyonnais qualify.

16/2/10, Giuseppe Meazza, Milan
AC Milan 2-3 Manchester United FC
Attendance: 78587
Goal(s): 1-0 Ronaldinho 3, 1-1 Scholes 36, 1-2 Rooney 66, 1-3 Rooney 74, 2-3 Seedorf 85
Referee: Olegário Benquerença (POR)
10/3/10, Old Trafford, Manchester
Manchester United FC 4-0 AC Milan
Attendance: 74595
Goal(s): 1-0 Rooney 13, 2-0 Rooney 46, 3-0 Park 59, 4-0 Fletcher 88
Referee: Busacca (SUI)
Aggregate: 7-2; Manchester United FC qualify.

UEFA Champions League

17/2/10, Estádio do Dragão, Porto
FC Porto 2-1 Arsenal FC
Attendance: 40717
Goal(s): 1-0 Varela 11, 1-1 Campbell 18, 2-1 Falcao 51
Referee: Hansson (SWE)
9/3/10, Arsenal Stadium, London
Arsenal FC 5-0 FC Porto
Attendance: 59661
Goal(s): 1-0 Bendtner 10, 2-0 Bendtner 25, 3-0 Nasri 63,
4-0 Eboué 66, 5-0 Bendtner 90+1(p)
Referee: De Bleeckere (BEL)
Aggregate: 6-2; Arsenal FC qualify.

17/2/10, Fußball Arena München, Munich
FC Bayern München 2-1 ACF Fiorentina
Attendance: 66000
Goal(s): 1-0 Robben 45+3 (p), 1-1 Krøldrup 50, 2-1 Klose 89
Referee: Øvrebø (NOR)
9/3/10, Artemio Franchi, Florence
ACF Fiorentina 3-2 FC Bayern München
Attendance: 42762
Goal(s): 1-0 Vargas 28, 2-0 Jovetić 54, 2-1 Van Bommel 60,
3-1 Jovetić 64, 3-2 Robben 65
Referee: Undiano Mallenco (ESP)
Aggregate: 4-4; FC Bayern München qualify on away goals.

23/2/10, VfB Arena, Stuttgart
VfB Stuttgart 1-1 FC Barcelona
Attendance: 39430
Goal(s): 1-0 Cacau 25, 1-1 Ibrahimović 52
Referee: Kuipers (NED)
17/3/10, Camp Nou, Barcelona
FC Barcelona 4-0 VfB Stuttgart
Attendance: 88543
Goal(s): 1-0 Messi 13, 2-0 Pedro 22, 3-0 Messi 60, 4-0 Bojan 89
Referee: Hamer (LUX)
Aggregate: 5-1; FC Barcelona qualify.

23/2/10, Georgios Karaiskakis, Piraeus
Olympiacos FC 0-1 FC Girondins de Bordeaux
Attendance: 29773
Goal(s): 0-1 Ciani 45+2
Referee: Webb (ENG)
17/3/10, Chaban-Delmas, Bordeaux
FC Girondins de Bordeaux 2-1 Olympiacos FC
Attendance: 31004
Goal(s): 1-0 Gourcuff 5, 1-1 Mitroglou 65, 2-1 Chamakh 88
Referee: Olegário Benquerença (POR)
Aggregate: 3-1; FC Girondins de Bordeaux qualify.

24/2/10, Luzhniki, Moscow
PFC CSKA Moskva 1-1 Sevilla FC
Attendance: 28600
Goal(s): 1-0 Negredo 25, 1-1 Mark González 66
Referee: Brych (GER)
16/3/10, Ramón Sánchez-Pizjuán, Seville
Sevilla FC 1-2 PFC CSKA Moskva
Attendance: 29666
Goal(s): 0-1 Necid 39, 1-1 Perotti 41, 1-2 Honda 55
Referee: Kassai (HUN)
Aggregate: 2-3; PFC CSKA Moskva qualify.

24/2/10, Giuseppe Meazza, Milan
FC Internazionale Milano 2-1 Chelsea FC
Attendance: 78971
Goal(s): 1-0 Milito 3, 1-1 Kalou 51, 2-1 Cambiasso 55
Referee: Mejuto González (ESP)
16/3/10, Stamford Bridge, London
Chelsea FC 0-1 FC Internazionale Milano
Attendance: 38112
Goal(s): 0-1 Eto'o 78
Referee: Stark (GER)
Aggregate: 1-3; FC Internazionale Milano qualify.

Bordeaux players celebrate Michaël Ciani's winning goal away to Olympiacos

QUARTER-FINALS

The UEFA Champions League quarter-finals produced their usual mixture of high-quality football played by some of Europe's biggest clubs – but one man alone dominated the headlines.

Barcelona dazzle

FC Barcelona forward Lionel Messi had enjoyed a purple patch in early March, scoring ten goals in four appearances before going three matches without success – the last of which was the first leg of the holders' last-eight meeting against Arsenal FC. Barcelona were nevertheless firmly on top throughout the first half in north London. Manuel Almunia was forced to make fine stops from Sergio Busquets, Messi, Zlatan Ibrahimović and Xavi Hernández while Alex Song and Bacary Sagna blocked goalbound efforts from Messi and Pedro Rodríguez - all this inside the first 20 minutes.

Arsenal's woes deepened as Andrei Arshavin and William Gallas both went off injured before half-time, and less than 60 seconds after the restart they finally fell behind, Gerard Piqué playing a long ball for Ibrahimović, who caught out the advancing Almunia with a perfectly judged lob from the angle. Not long afterwards Ibrahimović was on target again, Xavi's

pass exposing the Arsenal defence and the Swedish striker thumping a powerful rising shot past the unprotected Almunia to make it 2-0.

Arsène Wenger responded by introducing Theo Walcott, and within three minutes the substitute had revived home hopes, sliding a shot under Víctor Valdés after good work from Samir Nasri and Nicklas Bendtner. Suddenly Barça found themselves under pressure and, although Arsenal fans broke off briefly to afford Barcelona replacement Thierry Henry a generous reception on his introduction with 13 minutes remaining, there was more to celebrate when Cesc Fàbregas was felled in the area by Carles Puyol, who was subsequently sent off. The Arsenal captain then smashed in the resulting penalty despite having cracked his right fibula in the challenge.

Messi magic

Fàbregas was therefore absent when the teams reconvened at Camp Nou, although the suspensions to Puyol and Piqué gave the visitors hope of extending Barça's winless home run against English clubs to six matches. Indeed it was Arsenal who struck first, Walcott racing away down the right in the 18th minute and crossing for Bendtner to prod in at the second attempt. The lead proved short-lived, however, Messi putting Barcelona back on course for a third successive semi-final within three minutes by crashing in a brilliant left-foot shot from the edge of the area.

With parity restored, the European champions began to find their passing rhythm. Eight minutes before the break Messi sent Eric Abidal through, and although Thomas Vermaelen got a foot to the left-back's low cross, Pedro tapped the loose ball to Messi. His first touch took him free of a challenge and his next dinked the ball over Almunia to put Barça in control. The young Argentine maestro's double soon became a treble when Arsenal were caught pushing up. Seydou Keita headed a loose ball into the path of Messi and the No10 bore down on Almunia before deftly scooping the ball up and over him to complete his hat-trick in style. Arsenal would not concede defeat and, although both were offside, Bendtner and Walcott hit the woodwork. Fittingly, though, the last word went to Messi with one final flourish in the 88th minute as he rounded Vermaelen and Gaël Clichy before clipping past Almunia at the second attempt. It was only the sixth time a player had scored four goals in a UEFA Champions League match.

Zlatan Ibrahimović scores his second goal against Arsenal

UEFA Champions League

Bayern Munich's Ivica Olić turns the tie against Manchester United with a goal just before half-time at Old Trafford

Final repeat

Elsewhere FC Bayern München met Manchester United FC in a repeat of the 1999 final and United – who had won all four of their previous away games in the competition – took the lead in Münich with barely 60 seconds on the clock, Wayne Rooney taking advantage of Martín Demichelis's slip to volley in Nani's right-wing free-kick. The United striker was only denied a second by the outstretched foot of Hans-Jörg Butt as a Bayern team deprived of the injured Arjen Robben struggled to get back into the game. However, 13 minutes from time fortune smiled on the German side, Franck Ribéry's free-kick taking a decisive deflection off Rooney to wrong-foot Edwin van der Sar. Although Nemanja Vidić headed powerfully against the crossbar, Van der Sar brilliantly parried Mario Gómez's point-blank effort in the final minute, but Bayern would not be denied and, when Patrice Evra hesitated, Ivica Olić stole in to make it 2-1 and tip the scales in their favour.

That balance was restored in the English team's favour, however, as United – buoyed by Rooney's unexpected recovery from an ankle problem sustained in the last minute in Munich – began the second leg at Old Trafford at breakneck speed. Darron Gibson's low shot

levelled the tie three minutes in, and four minutes later United were 2-0 up, Antonio Valencia teasing Holger Badstuber out on the right before driving in a low cross that Nani turned in with a magnificent flick of his heel. Michael Carrick and Rooney then went close as Bayern struggled to live with the pace of United's play, and the home team duly made it 3-0 in the 41st minute as Valencia again broke down the right and crossed for Nani to drive the ball high into the net.

Two minutes later United's celebrations were stifled as Olić muscled past Carrick to beat Van der Sar from an acute angle before the tide turned irrevocably in Bayern's favour when United were reduced to ten men five minutes into the second period, Rafael picking up a second yellow card for pulling back Ribéry. The visitors dominated the play thereafter but United defended valiantly and the decisive moment in the tie did not arrive until 16 minutes from time, the returning Robben finding space on the edge of the penalty area to volley Ribéry's left-wing corner like a guided missile into the far corner of the net. There was to be no way back for United and, just as in the previous round against Fiorentina, Bayern progressed on away goals thanks to a wonder goal from their flying Dutchman.

Inter through

FC Internazionale Milano, in contrast, made relatively light work of PFC CSKA Moskva to reach the semi-finals for the first time since 2003. The Russian club had never before featured in the last eight of the UEFA Champions League but acquitted themselves well in the first leg at San Siro, losing only to Diego Milito's 65th-minute strike. More costly were bookings picked up by Miloš Krasić and Yevgeniy Aldonin which ruled both out of the return fixture in Moscow - a game settled by Wesley Sneijder's free-kick in the sixth minute. Now needing to score three times, CSKA never looked capable of mounting an unlikely comeback, especially after substitute Chidi Odiah's 49th-minute red card.

The other quarter-final was an all-French affair. Olympique Lyonnais, aiming to reach the semi-finals for the first time having fallen at this stage three times previously, were up against FC Girondins de Bordeaux, who had not reached the last four of the European Champion Clubs' Cup since 1988. The former made full use of their first-leg home advantage, Lisandro López flicking in a tenth-minute opener from Mathieu Bodmer's driven cross after Michaël Ciani had failed to deal with Aly Cissokho's long ball. Four minutes later Yoann Gourcuff brilliantly turned past Jérémy Toulalan and crossed for Marouane Chamakh to head in an equaliser.

Powerful shot

More hesitant Bordeaux defending was punished again, however, on 32 minutes. Unmarked at the far post, Michel Bastos collected Benoît Trémoulinas's miscued header, jinked inside and curled a powerful shot into the top corner. Lyon goalkeeper Hugo Lloris made a remarkable stop to deny Chamakh just past the hour before Bordeaux's Wendel thundered an effort against the crossbar. More fortune favoured the home side 13 minutes from time as Matthieu Chalmé inadvertently blocked Cissokho's cross with his arm, giving Lyon a penalty which the outstanding Lisandro coolly converted, sending the goalkeeper the wrong way.

Lyon may have taken a two-goal cushion to the Stade Chaban-Delmas but suspensions for Lisandro and Sidney Govou restricted their attacking threat, and it took a resolute defensive display to hold the French champions at bay. Bordeaux had won all of their previous home games in the 2009/10 UEFA Champions League – the first-leg defeat had ended a seven-match winning run in the competition – and after a slow start they began to pose an increasing threat, finally breaking through in the 45th minute when Chamakh forced in his fifth goal of the season from close range seconds after home captain Alou

Diarra had struck the crossbar. Laurent Blanc's team continued to press in the second period, particularly from set pieces, but for once their favoured weapon failed to deliver. Ludovic Sané headed Gourcuff's corner wide with ten minutes remaining and Lloris pulled off a stunning save from Wendel's header on 87 minutes as time ran out for Bordeaux.

Quarter-Final Results

30/3/10, Gerland, Lyon
Olympique Lyonnais 3-1 FC Girondins de Bordeaux
Attendance: 37859
Goal(s): 1-0 Lisandro López 10, 1-1 Chamakh 14, 2-1 Michel Bastos 32, 3-1 Lisandro López 77 (p)
Referee: Brych (GER)
7/4/10, Chaban-Delmas, Bordeaux
FC Girondins de Bordeaux 1-0 Olympique Lyonnais
Attendance: 31962
Goal(s): 1-0 Chamakh 45
Referee: Undiano Mallenco (ESP)
Aggregate: 2-3; Olympique Lyonnais qualify.

30/3/10, Fußball Arena München, Munich
FC Bayern München 2-1 Manchester United FC
Attendance: 66000
Goal(s): 0-1 Rooney 1, 1-1 Ribéry 77, 2-1 Olić 90+2
Referee: De Bleeckere (BEL)
7/4/10, Old Trafford, Manchester
Manchester United FC 3-2 FC Bayern München
Attendance: 74482
Goal(s): 1-0 Gibson 3, 2-0 Nani 7, 3-0 Nani 41, 3-1 Olić 43, 3-2 Robben 74
Referee: Rizzoli (ITA)
Aggregate: 4-4; FC Bayern München qualify on away goals.

31/3/10, Arsenal Stadium, London
Arsenal FC 2-2 FC Barcelona
Attendance: 59572
Goal(s): 0-1 Ibrahimović 46, 0-2 Ibrahimović 59, 1-2 Walcott 69, 2-2 Fàbregas 85 (p)
Referee: Busacca (SUI)
6/4/10, Camp Nou, Barcelona
FC Barcelona 4-1 Arsenal FC
Attendance: 93330
Goal(s): 0-1 Bendtner 18, 1-1 Messi 21, 2-1 Messi 37, 3-1 Messi 42, 4-1 Messi 88
Referee: Stark (GER)
Aggregate: 6-3; FC Barcelona qualify.

31/3/10, Giuseppe Meazza, Milan
FC Internazionale Milano 1-0 PFC CSKA Moskva
Attendance: 69398
Goal(s): 1-0 Milito 65
Referee: Webb (ENG)
6/4/10, Luzhniki, Moscow
PFC CSKA Moskva 0-1 FC Internazionale Milano
Attendance: 54400
Goal(s): 0-1 Sneijder 6
Referee: Lannoy (FRA)
Aggregate: 0-2; FC Internazionale Milano qualify.

UEFA Champions League

SEMI-FINALS

There was a new name in the UEFA Champions League semi-finals, Olympique Lyonnais, but the French club were to come up short against FC Bayern München while FC Barcelona's bid to become the only team to successfully defend the trophy since its 1992 revamp – and the first to win successive European Champion Clubs' Cups since AC Milan in 1989 and 1990 – was thwarted by FC Internazionale Milano.

Pedro pounces

Flight disruption across Europe as a result of a volcanic ash cloud emanating from Iceland meant that Lyon and Barcelona faced lengthy coach journeys to get to Munich and Milan respectively for their first legs. Inter had never scored against Barça in four meetings, and their hopes of reaching the final for the first time since 1972 suffered a knock with 19 minutes on the clock at San Siro. Left-back Maxwell, one of Barcelona's two ex-Interistas (with Zlatan Ibrahimović), helped to hit his old club with a sucker-punch as, unchecked by Maicon, he broke into the box and delivered a perfect cutback for Pedro Rodríguez to slot the ball past Júlio César.

Inter had never lost at home in seven previous European Cup semi-finals, and 11 minutes after Pedro's opener they drew level. Diego Milito had already angled a shot fractionally wide after being sent through by Goran Pandev, but Barcelona failed to heed the warning. Milito made instant amends by cleverly diverting Samuel Eto'o's driven pass into the path of Wesley Sneijder, who, free of markers, drove in via the foot of Víctor Valdés.

Inter were faster out of the blocks for the second half and took the lead within three minutes. Pandev slipped in Milito who, though drawn wide of goal as he entered the area, still managed to tee up Maicon to finish adroitly from eight metres despite Seydou Keita's attentions. Barça looked shaken by the hosts' constant pressing yet stirred sufficiently for Lionel Messi to test Júlio César, who then produced a fine reflex save from Sergio Busquets' free header. The next aerial intervention brought a deserved goal for the hard-running Milito. Sneijder misdirected his header from Eto'o's firm right-wing cross, but the ball fortuitously fell for the Argentine striker, who, although perhaps fractionally offside, nodded the ball in from close range. It was the first time Barcelona had conceded three goals all season.

Wesley Sneijder equalises for Inter in the first leg of the semi-final against Barcelona

Frustrating evening

The holders therefore had it all to do in the Camp Nou return, although having overturned first-leg deficits on 11 previous occasions in UEFA competition, they had good cause for optimism. On the other hand, recent history was against Barça as they had failed to score in their previous four semi-final matches at the famous arena, and it was to prove another frustrating evening. José Mourinho made yet another high-profile return to his former employers, even surviving the late loss of Pandev, who broke down in the warm-up. Cristian Chivu was his replacement yet it had little effect on the modus operandi of the Italian side, whose blanket defence once again smothered their opponents and, crucially, largely negated the influence of Messi and Xavi.

Pedro and former Barcelona striker Eto'o swapped early chances, but Inter's task was made harder in the 28th minute when Thiago Motta put his hand into the face of Busquets and was shown a straight red card. Messi promptly brought the best out of Júlio César, whose athletic fingertip save to his right was as majestic as it was important, and as he continued to hold Barcelona in check, despite Josep Guardiola throwing Gérard Piqué forward as an extra attacker during the second period in a desperate quest for a Plan B. Substitute Bojan Krkić passed up a glorious chance to put Barcelona in front on the night, heading Messi's delicious cross wide when unmarked at the far post, but Piqué did finally break Inter's resistance with six minutes remaining, swivelling brilliantly on to Xavi's defence-splitting pass to take out goalkeeper and defender before shooting into the unguarded net. Deep into added time, Barcelona thought they were in a second successive final when Bojan shot into the top corner, but the goal was disallowed as the referee had already blown his whistle, penalising Yaya Touré for a handball on the edge of the penalty area in the build-up. Seconds later, the holders' defence was over.

Bayern in command

Bayern, in a first semi-final since lifting the trophy for the fourth time in 2001, were keen to capitalise on home advantage for the first leg against Lyon and assumed control from the first whistle. The opening chances duly went the home side's way, with the unmarked Daniel Van Buyten blazing a wayward volley into the Munich sky before Bastian Schweinsteiger headed Robben's corner wide after Hugo Lloris had missed his punch. Thomas Müller twice failed to find the target after impressive creative work from Franck Ribéry and Arjen Robben, but Bayern's momentum was checked eight minutes before half-time when

Lionel Messi takes on the Inter defence

Ribéry was shown a straight red card after catching Lisandro with his studs as the ball ran away from him.

The visitors promptly enjoyed their first spell of sustained possession and Kim Källström's powerful long-range effort drew a fine stop from Hans-Jörg Butt on the stroke of half-time. The interval gave the home team the chance to regroup, however, and they were again fastest out of the blocks after the restart. Danijel Pranjić forced Lloris into the half's first save with a dipping left-foot volley, Schweinsteiger sent a powerful header wide and Müller missed another glorious opportunity, failing to convert Philipp Lahm's low cross.

Bayern's prospects were further enhanced in the 54th minute when it became ten against ten, Jérémy Toulalan becoming the second French international to be dismissed as he let his team down by collecting a second yellow card in quick succession. With the teams again level numerically Bayern regained control, but it looked as if a frustrating night had been assured when unmarked substitute Mario Gómez nodded tamely into the arms of the grateful Lloris. Instead the moment the home fans had been longing for finally arrived in the 69th minute as Robben's thumping 25-metre strike wrong-footed Lloris after glancing off Müller's head. The goalkeeper may have been at fault on that occasion but he superbly denied Robben late on to keep Lyon in the hunt.

UEFA Champions League

CHAMPIONS LEAGUE

Lyon undone

The French side's hopes should have been crushed two minutes into the second leg as Bayern quickly picked up where they had left off, Ivica Olić dispossessing Cris and crossing for the unmarked Müller who somehow side-footed wide of the near post. The Bavarian club, thanks in no small part to captain Mark van Bommel – back after suspension – took charge, and Louis van Gaal's men were rewarded for their positive opening when Olić scored the all-important away goal on 26 minutes. The build-up was superb, Müller exchanging passes with Robben and surging into the box before cutting the ball back to the Croatia striker, whose fifth goal of the campaign left the hosts needing three. Lyon could ill-afford to squander clear openings yet Michel Bastos did just that on 31 minutes, steering his close-range volley wide having been picked out by Jean II Makoun's cross from the right.

Lyon continued to show spirit yet their chances of staging a dramatic fightback were dealt another heavy blow on 59 minutes as Cris was booked for a foul on Olić and then issued a second yellow card immediately afterwards for dissent. The sight of their inspirational captain trudging off effectively signalled the end of OL's chances. Olić made sure of Bayern's victory by adding two more excellent goals. Hamit

Altıntop's through ball laid on the first, with Olić hitting a crisp, low shot beyond Lloris before heading in Lahm's right-sided cross to confirm Bayern's eighth European Champion Clubs' Cup final appearance in considerable style.

Semi-Final Results

20/4/10, Giuseppe Meazza, Milan
FC Internazionale Milano 3-1 FC Barcelona
Attendance: 79000
Goal(s): 0-1 Pedro 19, 1-1 Sneijder 30, 2-1 Maicon 48, 3-1 Milito 61
Referee: Olegário Benquerença (POR)
28/4/10, Camp Nou, Barcelona
FC Barcelona 1-0 FC Internazionale Milano
Attendance: 96214
Goal(s): 1-0 Piqué 84
Referee: De Bleeckere (BEL)
Aggregate: 2-3; FC Internazionale Milano qualify.

21/4/10, Fußball Arena München, Munich
FC Bayern München 1-0 Olympique Lyonnais
Attendance: 66000
Goal(s): 1-0 Robben 69
Referee: Rosetti (ITA)
27/4/10, Gerland, Lyon
Olympique Lyonnais 0-3 FC Bayern München
Attendance: 39414
Goal(s): 0-1 Olić 26, 0-2 Olić 67, 0-3 Olić 78
Referee: Busacca (SUI)
Aggregate: 0-4; FC Bayern München qualify.

Arjen Robben strikes the winning goal for Bayern in the first leg of their semi-final against Lyon

FINAL

After a wait of 45 years, FC Internazionale Milano were crowned European champions for the third time as Diego Milito's brilliantly taken double put paid to FC Bayern München in Madrid.

Saturday night fever

Both sides came into the final at the Santiago Bernabéu – switched to a Saturday evening from the traditional Wednesday – after having won domestic doubles, and it was Bayern who initially looked the more likely to force a breakthrough. Inter had shown their ruthless, pragmatic side throughout the competition, however, and they demonstrated it again in the 35th minute as Milito rounded off a route-one attack with a sublime finish. Although the German side continued to dominate territory and possession, there was no way back when Milito again broke through with his second strike of the evening – another supremely composed effort - 20 minutes from time to secure Inter's first European Champion Clubs' Cup victory since their consecutive triumphs of 1964 and 1965 and, with it, a special treble – the Milan club becoming only the sixth team to be crowned domestic cup winners, league and European champions in the same season.

Although deprived of their suspended French international winger Franck Ribéry, it was the newly crowned German champions who made most of the early running against an Inter side representing Italy but featuring not one Italian. They were the quicker of the two teams to settle, and only Walter Samuel's timely intervention turned away Ivica Olić's dangerous cross before Bayern's Croatian international forward shot wide at the near post after Arjen Robben had skipped away from Cristian Chivu and Samuel down the right. Inter's Romanian international left-back had his hands full with the Dutchman, on whose shoulders much creative responsibility rested in the absence of Ribéry. Chivu collected a first-half caution as he struggled to contain Robben before Javier Zanetti – replacing the suspended Thiago Motta in a midfield holding role on his 700th Inter appearance – and compatriot Esteban Cambiasso were able to provide him with more regular support.

Milito quality

Although Wesley Sneijder's free-kick deflected off the head of Hamit Altıntop to bring the game's first save from Hans-Jörg Butt, Bayern had enjoyed 60% of the possession in the opening half-hour. Inter soon proved, however, that quality counts for more than quantity.

Wesley Sneijder launches a free-kick towards the Bayern goal

Diego Milito (No22) tucks away the first of his two goals

Júlio César's long kick was flicked to Sneijder by Milito, rising ahead of Martín Demichelis, and the Argentinian striker turned swiftly to race on to the Dutchman's perfectly weighted return and clip his shot over the advancing Butt, cleverly feinting a split-second before releasing the ball to wrong-foot the goalkeeper.

A variation of the same combination nearly put the match beyond Bayern before half-time, Sneijder finding Milito on the left wing with the German side's defence in retreat again. The striker's clever pass inside left Sneijder with just Butt to beat, but the Dutchman shot straight at the grateful goalkeeper, who blocked. Bayern should have capitalised on their reprieve less than 20 seconds into the second period, Altıntop drawing two defenders before slipping a pass to Thomas Müller, but with Inter exposed for what would prove the only time in the contest Júlio César preserved their slender advantage, saving adroitly with his legs.

Robben threat

Although Butt then had to tip a fine Goran Pandev effort over the crossbar after more good work from

Arjen Robben was Bayern's most dangerous attacker on his old Madrid stomping ground

Milito, Bayern continued to push Inter back into their own half, Altıntop picking up possession in the Inter area after a rare Lúcio error only to shoot into the side netting, and Robben running at the Nerazzurri defence with increasing regularity. It was the winger's free-kick that led to Müller delivering another goalbound shot that was unwittingly kept out by Cambiasso. Robben then took matters into his own hands, cutting in from the right again and working space for a trademark left-foot curler that Júlio César clawed away from the top corner.

Yet, like so many teams before them, Bayern were foundering on the rock of Inter's brilliantly organised defence, and their own rearguard was duly penetrated again on the counterattack in the 70th minute. Once more Milito proved their nemesis, the in-form striker

Diego Milito milks the applause after putting Inter 2-0 up

collecting another perfect pass from Samuel Eto'o – playing in his second successive UEFA Champions final following victory with FC Barcelona in 2008/09. Milito effectively ensured that Eto'o would become the 13th man to win the European Cup with two different clubs by making devastating use of the Cameroon striker's angled through-ball, leaving Daniel Van Buyten floundering in his wake before nervelessly beating Butt again with a composed right-footed shot inside the post. The Argentinian's second unerring finish – made possible by a prudent use of the advantage rule in the build-up by English referee Howard Webb – all but ended the contest, and although Bayern continued to seek a way back in the closing stages, Robben flashing another attempt across the face of goal, Inter's sharper cutting edge had already proved decisive.

Mourinho makes history

The result made José Mourinho, who had previously lifted the trophy with FC Porto in 2004, only the third coach to win the European Cup with two different

Inter coach José Mourinho passes on advice from the touchline

Inter captain Javier Zanetti lifts the trophy in Madrid

clubs - after Ernst Happel (Feyenoord 1970, Hamburger SV 1983) and Ottmar Hitzfeld (BV Borussia Dortmund 1997, Bayern 2001). "Everyone wants to win this competition but few have the privilege of winning, and it's an even bigger privilege to win it twice," said the Inter coach. "Some have asked if I feel different from how I felt after winning with Porto but I don't feel a major difference. I'm the same person with the same feelings - huge joy and happiness, with a tear here and there if I have to leave. I will always remember this season with Inter."

The Portuguese coach beat his old friend Louis van Gaal – under whom he had worked as assistant at FC Barcelona – to a second European title, the Dutchman having won with AFC Ajax 15 years previously. "It was no surprise to me how the match went; the surprise is we lost," said Van Gaal after becoming the seventh coach to lose two European Cup finals. "Mourinho told German television we won the championship and the cup and that that is a masterpiece," Van Gaal added. "Winning the Champions League is a bonus. You also need a bit of luck. The difference between the teams is not so big." For Inter, however, it was big enough.

Final Result

22/5/10, Santiago Bernabéu, Madrid
FC Bayern München 0-2 FC Internazionale Milano
Attendance: 75569
Bayern: Butt, Van Buyten, Demichelis, Hamit Altıntop (Klose 63), Robben, Olić (Gómez 74), Van Bommel, Lahm, Müller, Badstuber, Schweinsteiger. Coach: Louis van Gaal (NED)
Internazionale: Júlio César, Zanetti, Lúcio, Eto'o, Sneijder, Maicon, Cambiasso, Milito (Materazzi 90+2), Samuel, Chivu (Stanković 68), Pandev (Muntari 79). Coach: José Mourinho (POR)
Goal(s): 0-1 Milito 35, 0-2 Milito 70
Yellow Card(s): Demichelis 26 (Bayern), Chivu 30 (Internazionale), Van Bommel 78 (Bayern)
Referee: Webb (ENG)

TOP GOALSCORERS

8	Lionel Messi (Barcelona)
7	Cristiano Ronaldo (Real Madrid)
	Ivica Olić (Bayern)
6	Diego Milito (Inter)
5	Nicklas Bendtner (Arsenal)
	Wayne Rooney (Man. United)
	Marouane Chamakh (Bordeaux)
4	Michael Owen (Man. United)
	Stevan Jovetić (Fiorentina)
	Edin Džeko (Wolfsburg)
	Arjen Robben (Bayern)
	Cesc Fàbregas (Arsenal)
	Radamel Falcao (Porto)

UEFA EUROPA LEAGUE

UEFA
EUROPA
LEAGUE

CHAPTER
02

2009/10

The UEFA Europa League was given a cool reception when it replaced the UEFA Cup in the summer of 2009, but the first edition proved memorable – especially for the inaugural winners, Club Atlético de Madrid.

Without a continental title since lifting the 1961/62 UEFA Cup Winners' Cup, the Spanish side parachuted into the competition after edging Cypriot minnows APOEL FC to third place in their UEFA Champions League group by virtue of the number of goals scored in the two head-to-head encounters. It would prove a sign of things to come as, time and again, Atlético progressed by the skin of their teeth. In four ties leading up to the final in Hamburg they prevailed on away goals three times, the exception coming only courtesy of a last-minute Diego Forlán goal against Galatasaray AŞ in the round of 32. The final, against a Fulham FC side that had written a fairytale adventure by claiming the illustrious scalps of Juventus, Hamburger SV and UEFA Cup holders FC Shakhtar Donetsk, would be no different.

QUALIFYING PHASE

First Qualifying Round

Just 38 days after FC Shakhtar Donetsk marked the end of one era by becoming the 25th club to savour UEFA Cup glory, a new one dawned across the continent as the inaugural UEFA Europa League got under way.

Some 506 players lined up at 23 stadiums as the competition kicked off, but there was nothing anybody could do to push the most famous one, Henrik Larsson, out of the limelight. In his last season the 37-year-old Swedish striker struck twice to set Helsingborgs IF on course for a comfortable aggregate victory over FC Mika. It set up a second qualifying round meeting with FC Zestafoni, whose Jaba Dvali struck the UEFA Europa League's first hat-trick as the Georgian contenders overwhelmed Northern Ireland's Lisburn Distillery FC 11-1 over two legs – the biggest win of the round.

Into the unknown

Another Georgian player, FC Olimpi Rustavi's Giorgi Megreladze, had been responsible for the first goal of a competition that threw up some intrepid journeys. Kazakhstan pair FC Irtysh Pavlodar and FC Okzheptes Kokshetau each had 6,000km round trips as they took on Hungary's Szombathely Haladás and FC Zimbru Chisinau of Moldova, respectively. They were ultimately wasted journeys, too, as both bowed out.

First Qualifying Round Results

2/7/09, Gradski, Niksic
FK Sutjeska 1-1 FC MTZ-RIPO Minsk
Goal(s): 1-0 Međedović 48, 1-1 Bubnov 78
Referee: Amirkhanyan (ARM)
9/7/09, Traktor, Minsk
FC MTZ-RIPO Minsk 2-1 FK Sutjeska (aet)
Goal(s): 0-1 Todorović 63, 1-1 Ryndyuk 67, 2-1 Ryndyuk 111
Referee: Hagen (NOR)
Aggregate: 3-2; FC MTZ-RIPO Minsk qualify after extra time.

2/7/09, Poladi, Rustavi
FC Olimpi Rustavi 2-0 B36 Tórshavn
Goal(s): 1-0 Megreladze 10, 2-0 Megreladze 88
Referee: Kuchin (KAZ)
9/7/09, Gundadalur, Torshavn
B36 Tórshavn 0-2 FC Olimpi Rustavi
Goal(s): 0-1 Sirbiladze 5, 0-2 Khubua 28
Referee: Vlk (SVK)
Aggregate: 0-4; FC Olimpi Rustavi qualify.

2/7/09, Centenary, Ta' Qali
Valletta FC 3-0 Keflavík
Goal(s): 1-0 Falzon 25, 2-0 Priso 49, 3-0 Den Ouden 72
Referee: Radovanović (MNE)
9/7/09, Keflavíkurvöllur, Keflavik
Keflavík 2-2 Valletta FC
Goal(s): 0-1 Falzon 41, 1-1 Eysteinsson 55, 2-1 J. Gudmundsson 72, 2-2 Priso 82
Referee: Whitby (WAL)
Aggregate: 2-5; Valletta FC qualify.

2/7/09, Daugava, Daugavpils
FC Dinaburg 2-1 JK Nõmme Kalju
Goal(s): 1-0 Afanasjevs 63, 1-1 Haavistu 90+2, 2-1 Guchashvili 90+4
Referee: Gil (POL)
9/7/09, A Le Coq Arena, Tallinn
JK Nõmme Kalju 0-0 FC Dinaburg
Referee: Attwell (ENG)
Aggregate: 1-2; FC Dinaburg qualify.

2/7/09, Lahti, Lahti
FC Lahti 4-1 KS Dinamo Tirana
Goal(s): 1-0 Rafael 2, 1-1 Kuli 28, 2-1 Moilanen 43, 3-1 Haara 52, 4-1 Rafael 86
Referee: Reinert (FRO)
9/7/09, Qemal Stafa, Tirana
KS Dinamo Tirana 2-0 FC Lahti
Goal(s): 1-0 Diop 13, 2-0 Diop 70
Referee: Pamporidis (GRE)
Aggregate: 3-4; FC Lahti qualify.

2/7/09, Josy Barthel, Luxembourg
CS Grevenmacher 0-3 FK Vėtra
Goal(s): 0-1 Grigaitis 10, 0-2 Mašitšev 25, 0-3 Grigaitis 79
Referee: Ristoskov (BUL)
9/7/09, Vėtra, Vilnius
FK Vėtra 3-0 CS Grevenmacher
Goal(s): 1-0 Huss 18 (og), 2-0 Kijanskas 33, 3-0 Vėževičius 37
Referee: Spirkoski (MKD)
Aggregate: 6-0; FK Vėtra qualify.

2/7/09, Gundadalur, Torshavn
NSÍ Runavík 0-3 Rosenborg BK
Goal(s): 0-1 Zahora 21, 0-2 Zahora 59, 0-3 Lustig 89 (p)
Referee: Muir (SCO)
9/7/09, Lerkendal, Trondheim
Rosenborg BK 3-1 NSÍ Runavík
Goal(s): 0-1 Potemkin 6, 1-1 Iversen 39, 2-1 Konan Ya 90+2 (p), 3-1 Olsen 90+3
Referee: Direktorenko (LVA)
Aggregate: 6-1; Rosenborg BK qualify.

2/7/09, Rohonci Út, Szombathely
Szombathelyi Haladás 1-0 FC Irtysh Pavlodar
Goal(s): 1-0 Kenesei 79
Referee: Janku (ALB)
9/7/09, Shakhtyor, Karagandy
FC Irtysh Pavlodar 2-1 Szombathelyi Haladás
Goal(s): 1-0 Yurin 20, 1-1 Chernyshov 24 (og), 2-1 Rajos 36 (og)
Referee: Özkahya (TUR)
Aggregate: 2-2; Szombathelyi Haladás qualify on away goal.

2/7/09, The Showgrounds, Sligo
Sligo Rovers FC 1-2 KF Vllaznia
Goal(s): 0-1 Smajlaj 69, 0-2 Keane 75 (og), 1-2 Cretaro 89 (p)
Referee: Virant (BEL)
9/7/09, Loro Boriçi, Shkoder
KF Vllaznia 1-1 Sligo Rovers FC
Goal(s): 1-0 Shtupina 42, 1-1 Keane 84
Referee: Borg (MLT)
Aggregate: 3-2; KF Vllaznia qualify.

UEFA Europa League

2/7/09, Gradski, Koprivnica
NK Slaven Koprivnica 1-0 Birkirkara FC
Goal(s): 1-0 Csizmadia 3
Referee: Taborda Xistra (POR)
9/7/09, Centenary, Ta' Qali
Birkirkara FC 0-0 NK Slaven Koprivnica
Referee: Daloukas (GRE)
Aggregate: 0-1; NK Slaven Koprivnica qualify.

2/7/09, Zimbru, Chisinau
FC Zimbru Chisinau 1-2 FC Okzhetpes Kokshetau
Goal(s): 1-0 Demerji 48, 1-1 Karakulov 72, 1-2 Chonkayev 74
Referee: Grobelnik (AUT)
9/7/09, Okzhetpes, Kokshetau
FC Okzhetpes Kokshetau 0-2 FC Zimbru Chisinau
Goal(s): 0-1 O. Andronic 16, 0-2 G. Andronic 19
Referee: Shandor (UKR)
Aggregate: 2-3; FC Zimbru Chisinau qualify.

2/7/09, A Le Coq Arena, Tallinn
JK Trans Narva 0-3 NK Rudar Velenje
Goal(s): 0-1 Cipot 9 (p), 0-2 Omladič 61, 0-3 Trifkovič 89
Referee: Gestranius (FIN)
9/7/09, Ob Jezeru, Velenje
NK Rudar Velenje 3-1 JK Trans Narva
Goal(s): 1-0 Cipot 28, 2-0 Mahmutovič 69, 3-0 Cipot 73, 3-1 Starovoitov 74
Referee: Yusifov (AZE)
Aggregate: 6-1; NK Rudar Velenje qualify.

2/7/09, Antona Malatinského, Trnava
FC Spartak Trnava 2-1 İnter Bakı PİK
Goal(s): 1-0 Kožuch 20, 2-0 Kožuch 26, 2-1 Gutiérrez 80
Referee: Shvetsov (UKR)
9/7/09, Tofiq Bähramov, Baku
İnter Bakı PİK 1-3 FC Spartak Trnava
Goal(s): 1-0 Guglielmone 11, 1-1 Súkenník 34, 1-2 Kožuch 40, 1-3 Procházka 48
Referee: Vučemilović-Šimunović Jr. (CRO)
Aggregate: 2-5; FC Spartak Trnava qualify.

2/7/09, Dinamo, Minsk
FC Dinamo Minsk 2-1 FK Renova
Goal(s): 0-1 Ibraimi 41, 1-1 Kislyak 72 (p), 2-1 Strakhanovich 87
Referee: Thórisson (ISL)
9/7/09, National Arena, Skopje
FK Renova 1-1 FC Dinamo Minsk
Goal(s): 1-0 Ibraimi 12, 1-1 Kislyak 38 (p)
Referee: Silagava (GEO)
Aggregate: 2-3; FC Dinamo Minsk qualify.

2/7/09, Randers, Randers
Randers FC 4-0 Linfield FC
Goal(s): 1-0 Berg 36, 2-0 Sane 47, 3-0 Nygaard 79, 4-0 Lorentzen 80
Referee: Studer (SUI)
9/7/09, Mourneview Park, Lurgan
Linfield FC 0-3 Randers FC
Goal(s): 0-1 Olsen 21, 0-2 Lorentzen 51, 0-3 Berg 82
Referee: Masiah (ISR)
Aggregate: 0-7; Randers FC qualify.

2/7/09, Laugardalsvöllur, Reykjavik
Fram Reykjavík 2-1 The New Saints FC
Goal(s): 0-1 Evans 24, 1-1 S. Tillen 33 (p), 2-1 Júlíusson 48
Referee: Wouters (BEL)
9/7/09, The Venue, Shropshire
The New Saints FC 1-2 Fram Reykjavík
Goal(s): 1-0 Evans 11, 1-1 Ormarsson 16, 1-2 S. Tillen 66 (p)
Referee: Christoffersen (DEN)
Aggregate: 2-4; Fram Reykjavík qualify.

2/7/09, Mourneview Park, Lurgan
Lisburn Distillery FC 1-5 FC Zestafoni
Goal(s): 0-1 Gelashvili 11, 0-2 Grigalashvili 22, 0-3 Gelashvili 34, 0-4 Grigalashvili 38, 0-5 Aptsiauri 52, 1-5 Whelan 88
Referee: Bognár (HUN)
9/7/09, Tsentral, Zestaponi
FC Zestafoni 6-0 Lisburn Distillery FC
Goal(s): 1-0 Dvali 5, 2-0 Dvali 39, 3-0 Dvali 42, 4-0 Gelashvili 45, 5-0 Benashvili 87, 6-0 Benashvili 90
Referee: Constantin (ROU)
Aggregate: 11-1; FC Zestafoni qualify.

2/7/09, Antonis Papadopoulos, Larnaca
Anorthosis Famagusta FC 5-0 UN Käerjéng 97
Goal(s): 1-0 Da Costa 10 (og), 2-0 Katsavakis 25, 3-0 Frousos 62, 4-0 Cafú 67, 5-0 Frousos 90+1
Referee: Buttimer (IRL)
9/7/09, Josy Barthel, Luxembourg
UN Käerjéng 97 1-2 Anorthosis Famagusta FC
Goal(s): 0-1 Sosin 44, 0-2 Frousos 60, 1-2 Fiorani 90+3
Referee: Sevastsyanik (BLR)
Aggregate: 1-7; Anorthosis Famagusta FC qualify.

2/7/09, Yerevan Republican, Yerevan
FC Banants 0-2 NK Široki Brijeg
Goal(s): 0-1 Ivanković 40, 0-2 Tiago 65
Referee: Jílek (CZE)
9/7/09, Pecara, Široki Brijeg
NK Široki Brijeg 0-1 FC Banants
Goal(s): 0-1 Dashyan 87
Referee: Satchi (MDA)
Aggregate: 2-1; NK Široki Brijeg qualify.

2/7/09, Tofiq Bähramov, Baku
Simurq Zaqatala PFK 0-1 Bnei Yehuda Tel-Aviv FC
Goal(s): 0-1 Baldut 83
Referee: Trutz (SVK)
9/7/09, Bloomfield, Tel-Aviv
Bnei Yehuda Tel-Aviv FC 3-0 Simurq Zaqatala PFK
Goal(s): 1-0 Galván 27, 2-0 Galván 66, 3-0 Biton 86
Referee: Přhoda (CZE)
Aggregate: 4-0; Bnei Yehuda Tel-Aviv FC qualify.

2/7/09, Shyberry Excelsior, Airdrie
Motherwell FC 0-1 Llanelli AFC
Goal(s): 0-1 C. Jones 28
Referee: Nieminen (FIN)
9/7/09, Parc-Y-Scarlets, Llanelli
Llanelli AFC 0-3 Motherwell FC
Goal(s): 0-1 Sutton 8, 0-2 Sutton 25, 0-3 Murphy 72
Referee: Mažić (SRB)
Aggregate: 1-3; Motherwell FC qualify.

Giorgi Megreladze of Olimpi Rustavi - the first man to score a goal in the UEFA Europa League

2/7/09, Pod Goricom-Gradski, Podgorica
FK Budućnost Podgorica 0-2 KSP Polonia Warszawa
Goal(s): 0-1 Kozioł 54, 0-2 Jodłowiec 65
Referee: Stavridis (GRE)
9/7/09, W.O.S.I.R Polonia, Warsaw
KSP Polonia Warszawa 0-1 FK Budućnost Podgorica
Goal(s): 0-1 Vuković 51
Referee: Mažeika (LTU)
Aggregate: 2-1; KSP Polonia Warszawa qualify.

2/7/09, Olympia, Helsingborg
Helsingborgs IF 3-1 FC Mika
Goal(s): 1-0 Larsson 50, 1-1 Montenegro 66, 2-1 Larsson 86, 3-1 Sundin 90+2
Referee: Messner (AUT)
9/7/09, MIKA Sport Complex, Yerevan
FC Mika 1-1 Helsingborgs IF
Goal(s): 0-1 Makondele 68, 1-1 Ednei 83 (p)
Referee: Jovanetić (SRB)
Aggregate: 2-4; Helsingborgs IF qualify.

Second Qualifying Round

Former European Champion Clubs' Cup winners FK Crvena zvezda and FC Steaua Bucureşti were stirred into the pot for the second qualifying round as the UEFA Europa League stepped up a notch. They, 2000 UEFA Cup winners Galatasaray AŞ and twice UEFA Cup Winners' Cup finalists SK Rapid Wien all prevailed against less celebrated opposition.

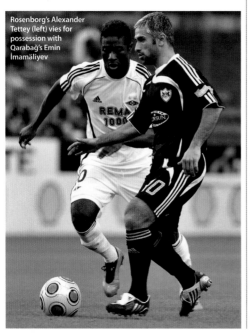
Rosenborg's Alexander Tettey (left) vies for possession with Qarabağ's Emin İmamäliyev

Some did it more convincingly than others. Rapid never looked back after brushing aside visitors KF Vllaznia 5-0 in the first leg of their tie, while Crvena zvezda and Steaua needed only to blow off the early-season cobwebs before sealing their own progress. Galatasaray were less impressive. Behind inside two minutes at Kazakhstan's FC Tobol Kostanay, Frank Rijkaard's side required a Milan Baroš equaliser to salvage a 1-1 first-leg stalemate.

Rijkaard managed to scrape away some of the rustiness over the coming week, and while hardly running at maximum capacity Galatasaray edged through in the return, Servet Çetin completing a 3-1 victory in the second minute of added time. There were no such problems for NAC Breda, who barely broke sweat in a 6-0 triumph at home to Armenian hopefuls FC Gandzasar Kapan. The Dutch side's aggregate scoreline of 8-0 was eclipsed by NK Slaven Koprivnica, 12-2 victors over FK Milano thanks in no small part to Aljoša Vojnović's five-minute hat-trick.

Qarabağ shock

Yet for every leisurely cruise there was a rough crossing. KAA Gent and FK Sevojno both progressed on the away-goals rule, while FC Vaduz, Helsingborgs IF and OFK Petrovac prevailed in extra time. Montenegro's Petrovac upset the odds as they overturned a 2-1 first-leg deficit against Anorthosis Famagusta FC, and FK Slavija Sarajevo accounted for another 2008/09 UEFA Champions League group stage participant, Aalborg BK. The shock of the round was Azerbaijani outfit Qarabağ FK, who heeded coach Qurban Qurbanov's call for "effort, discipline and a bit of luck" to see off seasoned European campaigners Rosenborg BK.

Second Qualifying Round Results

14/7/09, Centenary, Ta' Qali
Sliema Wanderers FC 0-0 Maccabi Netanya FC
Referee: Banari (MDA)
23/7/09, Bloomfield, Tel-Aviv
Maccabi Netanya FC 3-0 Sliema Wanderers FC
Goal(s): 1-0 Samya 58, 2-0 Ezra 84, 3-0 Saba'a 89
Referee: Nalbandyan (ARM)
Aggregate: 3-0; Maccabi Netanya FC qualify.

14/7/09, Mourneview Park, Lurgan
Crusaders FC 1-1 FK Rabotnicki
Goal(s): 0-1 B. Bozinovski 47, 1-1 Rainey 90
Referee: Kenan (ISR)
23/7/09, National Arena, Skopje
FK Rabotnicki 4-2 Crusaders FC
Goal(s): 1-0 B. Bozinovski 20, 2-0 Zé Carlos 35, 2-1 Owens 69, 3-1 Zé Carlos 79, 4-1 Petkovski 84, 4-2 Donnelly 90+3
Referee: Příhoda (CZE)
Aggregate: 5-3; FK Rabotnicki qualify.

UEFA Europa League

16/7/09, Gradski, Kumanovo
FK Milano 0-4 NK Slaven Koprivnica
Goal(s): 0-1 Csizmadia 26, 0-2 Vojnović 39, 0-3 Vojnović 41,
0-4 Vojnović 44
Referee: Teixeira Vitienes (ESP)
23/7/09, Gradski, Koprivnica
NK Slaven Koprivnica 8-2 FK Milano
Goal(s): 1-0 Poredski 24, 2-0 Vručina 45+3, 2-1 Stojanovic 59,
3-1 Tepurić 61, 4-1 Tepurić 74, 4-2 Alimi 75, 5-2 Vojnović 78, 6-2
Gregurina 80, 7-2 Jurić 81, 8-2 Vojnović 88
Referee: Svendsen (DEN)
Aggregate: 12-2; NK Slaven Koprivnica qualify.

16/7/09, Flamurtari, Vlora
KS Flamurtari 1-0 Motherwell FC
Goal(s): 1-0 Strati 66
Referee: Stuchlik (AUT)
23/7/09, Shyberry Excelsior, Airdrie
Motherwell FC 8-1 KS Flamurtari
Goal(s): 1-0 Murphy 16, 2-0 Murphy 19, 3-0 Slane 25, 4-0 Forbes 28 (p),
5-0 Murphy 34, 6-0 Hutchinson 38, 7-0 Forbes 50, 7-1 Roshi 64,
8-1 McHugh 72
Referee: Lerjeus (SWE)
Aggregate: 8-2; Motherwell FC qualify.

16/7/09, Pod Dubňon, Zilina
MŠK Žilina 2-0 FC Dacia Chisinau
Goal(s): 1-0 Oravec 57, 2-0 Lietava 77
Referee: Trifonos (CYP)
23/7/09, Zimbru, Chisinau
FC Dacia Chisinau 0-1 MŠK Žilina
Goal(s): 0-1 Oravec 47
Referee: McCourt (NIR)
Aggregate: 0-3; MŠK Žilina qualify.

16/7/09, Vitebsk Central sport complex, Vitebsk
FC Naftan Novopolotsk 2-1 KAA Gent
Goal(s): 1-0 Degterev 21, 2-0 Degterev 66, 2-1 Marić 90
Referee: Göçek (TUR)
23/7/09, Jules Otten, Gent
KAA Gent 1-0 FC Naftan Novopolotsk
Goal(s): 1-0 Elghanassy 54
Referee: Clos Gómez (ESP)
Aggregate: 2-2; KAA Gent qualify on away goal.

16/7/09, FK Partizan, Belgrade
FK Sevojno 0-0 FBK Kaunas
Referee: Buttimer (IRL)
23/7/09, S. Darius & S. Girenas, Kaunas
FBK Kaunas 1-1 FK Sevojno
Goal(s): 0-1 Vujović 48, 1-1 Fridrikas 76
Referee: Levi (ISR)
Aggregate: 1-1; FK Sevojno qualify on away goal.

16/7/09, Tsentral, Zestaponi
FC Zestafoni 1-2 Helsingborgs IF
Goal(s): 0-1 Jönsson 62, 1-1 Benashvili 70, 1-2 Larsson 89
Referee: Bertolini (SUI)
23/7/09, Olympia, Helsingborg
Helsingborgs IF 2-2 FC Zestafoni (aet)
Goal(s): 0-1 Dvali 29, 0-2 Gelashvili 32, 1-2 Ekstrand 90+3,
2-2 Sundin 100
Referee: Kaasik (EST)
Aggregate: 4-3; Helsingborgs IF qualify after extra time.

16/7/09, Lerkendal, Trondheim
Rosenborg BK 0-0 Qarabağ FK
Referee: Meckarovski (MKD)
23/7/09, Tofiq Bähramov, Baku
Qarabağ FK 1-0 Rosenborg BK
Goal(s): 1-0 R. F. Sadiqov 45+1
Referee: Fabian (HUN)
Aggregate: 1-0; Qarabağ FK qualify.

16/7/09, Daugava, Liepaja
SK Liepājas Metalurgs 2-1 FC Dinamo Tbilisi
Goal(s): 1-0 Karlsons 41, 2-0 Kirhners 54, 2-1 Khmaladze 68
Referee: Hermansen (DEN)
23/7/09, Boris Paichadze, Tbilisi
FC Dinamo Tbilisi 3-1 SK Liepājas Metalurgs
Goal(s): 1-0 Merebashvili 18, 1-1 Rafaļskis 49, 2-1 G. Kashia 53,
3-1 Merebashvili 63
Referee: Spasić (SRB)
Aggregate: 4-3; FC Dinamo Tbilisi qualify.

16/7/09, Andruv, Olomouc
SK Sigma Olomouc 1-1 Fram Reykjavík
Goal(s): 1-0 Fjóluson 21, 1-1 Daniel Rossi 89
Referee: Stalhammar (SWE)
23/7/09, Laugardalsvöllur, Reykjavik
Fram Reykjavík 0-2 SK Sigma Olomouc
Goal(s): 0-1 Hubník 47, 0-2 Otepka 57
Referee: Gomes Costa (POR)
Aggregate: 1-3; SK Sigma Olomouc qualify.

16/7/09, Tapiolan Urheilupuisto, Espoo
FC Honka Espoo 2-0 Bangor City FC
Goal(s): 1-0 Peruvuo 15, 2-0 Schüller 74
Referee: Jug (SVN)
23/7/09, The Racecourse, Wrexham
Bangor City FC 0-1 FC Honka Espoo
Goal(s): 0-1 Puustinen 39
Referee: Sippel (GER)
Aggregate: 0-3; FC Honka Espoo qualify.

16/7/09, Borås Arena, Boras
IF Elfsborg 3-0 Szombathelyi Haladás
Goal(s): 1-0 Svensson 60, 2-0 Ishizaki 82, 3-0 Avdic 89
Referee: Murray (SCO)
23/7/09, Rohonci Út, Szombathely
Szombathelyi Haladás 0-0 IF Elfsborg
Referee: João Ferreira (POR)
Aggregate: 0-3; IF Elfsborg qualify.

16/7/09, Dinamo, Minsk
FC Dinamo Minsk 0-0 Tromsø IL
Referee: Olsiak (SVK)
23/7/09, Alfheim, Tromso
Tromsø IL 4-1 FC Dinamo Minsk
Goal(s): 1-0 Knarvik 28, 2-0 Martynovich 76 (og), 2-1 Zita 83,
3-1 Moldskred 89, 4-1 Knarvik 90+1
Referee: Liesveld (NED)
Aggregate: 4-1; Tromsø IL qualify.

16/7/09, Graz Liebenau, Graz
SK Sturm Graz 2-1 NK Široki Brijeg
Goal(s): 1-0 Haas 12, 2-0 Hölzl 38, 2-1 Ljubić 67
Referee: Bergonzi (ITA)
23/7/09, Pecara, Siroki Brijeg
NK Široki Brijeg 1-1 SK Sturm Graz
Goal(s): 0-1 Jantscher 41, 1-1 Šilić 64
Referee: Szabó (HUN)
Aggregate: 2-3; SK Sturm Graz qualify.

16/7/09, Gerhard Hanappi, Vienna
SK Rapid Wien 5-0 KF Vllaznia
Goal(s): 1-0 Hofmann 33 (p), 2-0 Jelavić 69, 3-0 Jelavić 73,
4-0 Trimmel 83, 5-0 Hoffer 85
Referee: Bezborodov (RUS)
23/7/09, Loro Boriçi, Shkoder
KF Vllaznia 0-3 SK Rapid Wien
Goal(s): 0-1 Hofmann 66, 0-2 Maierhofer 76, 0-3 Hofmann 90+2
Referee: Yıldırım (TUR)
Aggregate: 0-8; SK Rapid Wien qualify.

16/7/09, KR-völlur, Reykjavik
KR Reykjavík 2-0 Larissa FC
Goal(s): 1-0 B. Sigurdsson 55, 2-0 Takefusa 90+3
Referee: Mikulski (POL)

23/7/09, Alkazar, Larissa
Larissa FC 1-1 KR Reykjavík
Goal(s): 1-0 Tsigas 28, 1-1 I. Sigurdsson 75
Referee: Strahonja (CRO)
Aggregate: 1-3; KR Reykjavík qualify.

16/7/09, Zimbru, Chisinau
FC Zimbru Chisinau 0-0 FC Paços de Ferreira
Referee: Kalt (FRA)
23/7/09, D. Afonso Henriques, Guimaraes
FC Paços de Ferreira 1-0 FC Zimbru Chişinău
Goal(s): 1-0 Cristiano 84
Referee: Aydınus (TUR)
Aggregate: 1-0; FC Paços de Ferreira qualify.

16/7/09, Aalborg, Aalborg
Aalborg BK 0-0 FK Slavija Sarajevo
Referee: Todorov (BUL)
23/7/09, Koševo, Sarajevo
FK Slavija Sarajevo 3-1 Aalborg BK
Goal(s): 1-0 Kutalia 35, 2-0 Ðermanovič 48, 2-1 Johansson 51, 3-1 Šćepanović 90+3
Referee: De Marco (ITA)
Aggregate: 3-1; FK Slavija Sarajevo qualify.

16/7/09, Metalurh, Donetsk
FC Metalurh Donetsk 3-0 FC MTZ-RIPO Minsk
Goal(s): 1-0 Mguni 34, 2-0 Mkhitaryan 42, 3-0 Godin 66
Referee: Rafati (GER)
23/7/09, Traktor, Minsk
FC MTZ-RIPO Minsk 1-2 FC Metalurh Donetsk
Goal(s): 1-0 Nicolas 15, 1-1 Mguni 35, 1-2 Mkhitaryan 85
Referee: Thual (FRA)
Aggregate: 1-5; FC Metalurh Donetsk qualify.

16/7/09, St. Jakob-Park, Basel
FC Basel 1893 3-0 FC Santa Coloma
Goal(s): 1-0 Sahin 23, 2-0 Streller 48, 3-0 Almerares 59
Referee: Richards (WAL)
23/7/09, Comunal, Andorra La Vella
FC Santa Coloma 1-4 FC Basel 1893
Goal(s): 0-1 Streller 12, 0-2 Gelabert 15, 0-3 Álvarez 40 (og), 1-3 Maicon 43 (p), 1-4 Almerares 88
Referee: Mrković (BIH)
Aggregate: 1-7; FC Basel 1893 qualify.

16/7/09, Falkirk Stadium, Falkirk
Falkirk FC 1-0 FC Vaduz
Goal(s): 1-0 Flynn 50
Referee: Ledentu (FRA)
23/7/09, Rheinpark, Vaduz
FC Vaduz 2-0 Falkirk FC (aet)
Goal(s): 1-0 Noll 24, 2-0 Burgmeier 105
Referee: Kovačić (CRO)
Aggregate: 2-1; FC Vaduz qualify after extra time.

16/7/09, Richmond Park, Dublin
Saint Patrick's Athletic FC 1-1 Valletta FC
Goal(s): 1-0 O'Brien 38, 1-1 G. Agius 65
Referee: Šipailo (LVA)
23/7/09, Centenary, Ta' Qali
Valletta FC 0-1 Saint Patrick's Athletic FC
Goal(s): 0-1 O'Brien 80
Referee: Jug (SVN)
Aggregate: 1-2; Saint Patrick's Athletic FC qualify.

16/7/09, Skonto, Riga
Skonto FC 1-1 Derry City FC
Goal(s): 1-0 Kozlovs 17, 1-1 McManus 44
Referee: Toussaint (LUX)
23/7/09, Brandywell, Derry
Derry City FC 1-0 Skonto FC
Goal(s): 1-0 Deery 57
Referee: Van Boekel (NED)
Aggregate: 2-1; Derry City FC qualify.

Daniel Wass of Brøndby (left) races for the ball with Flora Tallinn's Aivar Anniste

16/7/09, Športni Park, Nova Gorica
ND Gorica 1-0 FC Lahti
Goal(s): 1-0 Kršič 39
Referee: Malžinskas (LTU)
23/7/09, Lahti, Lahti
FC Lahti 2-0 ND Gorica
Goal(s): 1-0 Litmanen 66, 2-0 Rafael 79
Referee: Banti (ITA)
Aggregate: 2-1; FC Lahti qualify.

16/7/09, Josy Barthel, Luxembourg
FC Differdange 03 1-0 HNK Rijeka
Goal(s): 1-0 Piskor 61
Referee: Richmond (SCO)
23/7/09, Kantrida, Rijeka
HNK Rijeka 3-0 FC Differdange 03
Goal(s): 1-0 Cerić 20, 2-0 An. Sharbini 24, 3-0 Ah. Sharbini 64
Referee: Aliyev (AZE)
Aggregate: 3-1; HNK Rijeka qualify.

16/7/09, Marijampolė, Marijampole
FK Sūduva 0-1 Randers FC
Goal(s): 0-1 Beckmann 23
Referee: Stanković (SRB)
23/7/09, Randers, Randers
Randers FC 1-1 FK Sūduva
Goal(s): 1-0 Leimonas 17 (og), 1-1 Lukšys 58
Referee: Göçek (TUR)
Aggregate: 2-1; Randers FC qualify.

16/7/09, Wojska Polskiego, Warsaw
Legia Warszawa 3-0 FC Olimpi Rustavi
Goal(s): 1-0 Paluchowski 19, 2-0 Kiełbowicz 70, 3-0 Szałachowski 83
Referee: Kakos (GRE)
23/7/09, Poladi, Rustavi
FC Olimpi Rustavi 0-1 Legia Warszawa
Goal(s): 0-1 Szałachowski 8
Referee: Brugger (AUT)
Aggregate: 0-4; Legia Warszawa qualify.

UEFA Europa League

16/7/09, Vėtra, Vilnius
FK Vėtra 0-1 HJK Helsinki
Goal(s): 0-1 Bah 15
Referee: Vnuk (SVK)
23/7/09, Finnair, Helsinki
HJK Helsinki 1-3 FK Vėtra
Goal(s): 1-0 Kamara 3, 1-1 Grigalevičius 27, 1-2 Jankauskas 30, 1-3 Moroz 81
Referee: Borski (POL)
Aggregate: 2-3; FK Vėtra qualify.

16/7/09, Bloomfield, Tel-Aviv
Bnei Yehuda Tel-Aviv FC 4-0 FC Dinaburg
Goal(s): 1-0 Galván 25, 2-0 Mori 38, 3-0 Atar 67, 4-0 Zairi 90+3
Referee: Panić (BIH)
23/7/09, Daugava, Daugavpils
FC Dinaburg 0-1 Bnei Yehuda Tel-Aviv FC
Goal(s): 0-1 Atar 32
Referee: Sandmoen (NOR)
Aggregate: 0-5; Bnei Yehuda Tel-Aviv FC qualify.

16/7/09, Ob Jezeru, Velenje
NK Rudar Velenje 0-1 FK Crvena zvezda
Goal(s): 0-1 Perović 59
Referee: Laperriere (SUI)
23/7/09, FK Crvena zvezda, Belgrade
FK Crvena zvezda 4-0 NK Rudar Velenje
Goal(s): 1-0 Bogdanović 37, 2-0 Jevtić 74, 3-0 Cadú 85, 4-0 Jevtić 90+4
Referee: Layushkin (RUS)
Aggregate: 5-0; FK Crvena zvezda qualify.

16/7/09, Antonis Papadopoulos, Larnaca
Anorthosis Famagusta FC 2-1 OFK Petrovac
Goal(s): 1-0 Ricardo Fernandes 11, 2-0 Laban 14, 2-1 Lakić 84
Referee: Clattenburg (ENG)
23/7/09, Gradski, Niksic
OFK Petrovac 3-1 Anorthosis Famagusta FC (aet)
Goal(s): 1-0 Dragićević 15, 1-1 Katsavakis 45+2, 2-1 Rotković 76, 3-1 Rotković 102
Referee: Black (NIR)
Aggregate: 4-3; OFK Petrovac qualify after extra time.

16/7/09, Lazur, Burgas
PFC Cherno More Varna 1-0 FC Iskra-Stal
Goal(s): 1-0 Manolov 44
Referee: Tanner (ENG)
23/7/09, Sheriff, Tiraspol
FC Iskra-Stal 0-3 PFC Cherno More Varna
Goal(s): 0-1 Manolov 25, 0-2 Manolov 54, 0-3 Da. Georgiev 60
Referee: Hermansen (DEN)
Aggregate: 0-4; PFC Cherno More Varna qualify.

16/7/09, Brøndby, Brondby
Brøndby IF 0-1 FC Flora Tallinn
Goal(s): 0-1 Vanna 50
Referee: Valgeirsson (ISL)
23/7/09, A Le Coq Arena, Tallinn
FC Flora Tallinn 1-4 Brøndby IF
Goal(s): 0-1 Jallow 28, 0-2 Farnerud 35, 0-3 Holmén 45+1, 1-3 Kasimir 80, 1-4 Kristiansen 90+2
Referee: Verbist (BEL)
Aggregate: 2-4; Brøndby IF qualify.

16/7/09, Koševo, Sarajevo
FK Sarajevo 1-0 FC Spartak Trnava
Goal(s): 1-0 Muminović 14
Referee: Malcolm (NIR)
23/7/09, Antona Malatinského, Trnava
FC Spartak Trnava 1-1 FK Sarajevo
Goal(s): 1-0 Doležaj 19, 1-1 Jahovic 88
Referee: Trattou (CYP)
Aggregate: 1-2; FK Sarajevo qualify.

16/7/09, GSP, Nicosia
AC Omonia 4-0 HB Tórshavn
Goal(s): 1-0 Karipidis 3, 2-0 Patsatzoglou 11, 3-0 Żurawski 33, 4-0 Efrem 85
Referee: Rossi (SMR)
23/7/09, Gundadalur, Torshavn
HB Tórshavn 1-4 AC Omonia
Goal(s): 0-1 Konstantinou 27, 1-1 Jespersen 56, 1-2 Konstantinou 66, 1-3 Konstantinou 78, 1-4 Wenzel 90+1
Referee: Kaldma (EST)
Aggregate: 1-8; AC Omonia qualify.

16/7/09, Montecchio, San Marino
AC Juvenes-Dogana 0-1 KSP Polonia Warszawa
Goal(s): 0-1 Bah 15
Referee: Georgiev (BUL)
23/7/09, WOSIR Polonia, Warsaw
KSP Polonia Warszawa 4-0 AC Juvenes-Dogana
Goal(s): 1-0 Marcelo Sarvas 10, 2-0 Mierzejewski 45, 3-0 Chałbiński 54, 4-0 Marcelo Sarvas 65
Referee: Saliy (KAZ)
Aggregate: 5-0; KSP Polonia Warszawa qualify.

16/7/09, Steaua, Bucharest
FC Steaua Bucureşti 2-0 Újpest FC
Goal(s): 1-0 Surdu 46, 2-0 Stancu 72
Referee: Koukoulakis (GRE)
23/7/09, Szusza Ferenc, Budapest
Újpest FC 1-2 FC Steaua Bucureşti
Goal(s): 0-1 Székely 58, 0-2 Grzelak 66, 1-2 Vaskó 82
Referee: Marriner (ENG)
Aggregate: 1-4; FC Steaua Bucureşti qualify.

16/7/09, Rat Verlegh, Breda
NAC Breda 6-0 FC Gandzasar
Goal(s): 1-0 Kwakman 24, 2-0 De Graaf 55, 3-0 Amoah 57, 4-0 Amoah 61, 5-0 Lurling 68, 6-0 De Graaf 70
Referee: Kari (FIN)
23/7/09, Yerevan Republican, Yerevan
FC Gandzasar 0-2 NAC Breda
Goal(s): 0-1 Lurling 14, 0-2 De Graaf 34
Referee: Evans (WAL)
Aggregate: 0-8; NAC Breda qualify.

16/7/09, Centralny, Kostanay
FC Tobol Kostanay 1-1 Galatasaray AŞ
Goal(s): 1-0 Zhumaskaliyev 2, 1-1 Baroš 58
Referee: Kovařík (CZE)
23/7/09, Ali Sami Yen, Istanbul
Galatasaray AŞ 2-0 FC Tobol Kostanay
Goal(s): 1-0 Mustafa Sarp 64, 2-0 Servet Çetin 90+2
Referee: Rubinos Pérez (ESP)
Aggregate: 3-1; Galatasaray AŞ qualify.

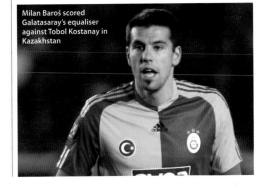

Milan Baroš scored Galatasaray's equaliser against Tobol Kostanay in Kazakhstan

Third Qualifying Round

Gone are the days when summer qualifying was reserved for second-string teams and far-flung clubs with unpronounceable names. Four former European champions lined up this time around, including a Hamburger SV side that reached the UEFA Cup semi-finals the previous season. Yet it was AS Roma who grabbed the headlines.

The Giallorossi were one of 30 clubs who entered the fray at this juncture, joining up with the 40 winners from the previous round. They did not disappoint. Not one to shy away from the limelight, it was captain Francesco Totti who caught the eye, contributing five goals in a 10-2 aggregate victory over Belgian contenders KAA Gent. Only Galatasaray AŞ mustered a bigger winning margin, coming from behind to overwhelm Israel's Maccabi Netanya FC 10-1.

Francesco Totti celebrates one of his five goals in Roma's romp against Gent

Lekić atonement

Former European champions FC Steaua Bucureşti, PSV Eindhoven and Hamburg also progressed at a canter, but for 1991 titleholders FK Crvena zvezda the ride was very uncomfortable. The writing was on the wall for the Serbian side when, having lost their first leg 2-0 at FC Dinamo Tbilisi, Dejan Lekić put through his own net early on in the return. The towering Lekić made amends in some style, completing a hat-trick with two minutes left to seal a 5-4 aggregate victory for Crvena zvezda. The hosts scored their last two goals despite being down to ten men.

FK Austria Wien trailed FK Vojvodina on away goals until two strikes in the last nine minutes took them through, and SK Rapid Wien needed Christopher Trimmel's extra-time goal to eliminate APOP/Kinyras Peyias FC. Club Brugge KV were also pushed hard by FC Lahti, while 16-year-old Iker Muniain's effort saw Athletic Club through against BSC Young Boys. Football romantics would not be completely ignored, however. Qarabağ FK continued their remarkable story by beating FC Honka Espoo, but even they were upstaged by Saint Patrick's Athletic FC, the Irish club overturning a first-leg deficit to beat Russia's PFC Krylya Sovetov Samara on away goals.

Third Qualifying Round Results

28/7/09, Bloomfield, Tel-Aviv
Bnei Yehuda Tel-Aviv FC 1-0 FC Paços de Ferreira
Goal(s): 1-0 Atar 55
Referee: Vollquartz (DEN)
6/8/09, D. Afonso Henriques, Guimaraes
FC Paços de Ferreira 0-1 Bnei Yehuda Tel-Aviv FC
Goal(s): 0-1 Atar 31
Referee: Stavrev (MKD)
Aggregate: 0-2; Bnei Yehuda Tel-Aviv FC qualify.

30/7/09, National Arena, Skopje
FK Rabotnicki 3-4 Odense BK
Goal(s): 0-1 Cacá 20, 1-1 Savic 21, 2-1 Wandeir 24, 2-2 Cacá 34, 2-3 Sørensen 62 (p), 2-4 Cacá 70, 3-4 Zé Carlos 74
Referee: Bezborodov (RUS)
6/8/09, Fionia Park, Odense
Odense BK 3-0 FK Rabotnicki
Goal(s): 1-0 Utaka 53, 2-0 Utaka 76, 3-0 Rodic 81 (og)
Referee: Kaasik (EST)
Aggregate: 7-3; Odense BK qualify.

30/7/09, Pod Goricom-Gradski, Podgorica
OFK Petrovac 1-2 SK Sturm Graz
Goal(s): 1-0 Divanović 13, 1-1 Haas 64 (p), 1-2 Lamotte 76
Referee: João Ferreira (POR)
6/8/09, Graz Liebenau, Graz
SK Sturm Graz 5-0 OFK Petrovac
Goal(s): 1-0 Muratović 30, 2-0 Hölzl 43, 3-0 Hölzl 49, 4-0 Hassler 56, 5-0 Weber 83
Referee: Borski (POL)
Aggregate: 7-1; SK Sturm Graz qualify.

30/7/09, Boris Paichadze, Tbilisi
FC Dinamo Tbilisi 2-0 FK Crvena zvezda
Goal(s): 1-0 Merebashvili 41, 2-0 Khmaladze 87
Referee: Van Boekel (NED)
6/8/09, FK Crvena zvezda, Belgrade
FK Crvena zvezda 5-2 FC Dinamo Tbilisi
Goal(s): 0-1 Lekić 3 (og), 1-1 Perović 18, 1-2 Vatsadze 24, 2-2 Lekić 26, 3-2 Lekić 45+2, 4-2 Cadú 76 (p), 5-2 Lekić 88
Referee: Ennjimi (FRA)
Aggregate: 5-4; FK Crvena zvezda qualify.

30/7/09, Finnair, Helsinki
FC Honka Espoo 0-1 Qarabağ FK
Goal(s): 0-1 E. Mämmädov 69
Referee: Toussaint (LUX)
6/8/09, Tofiq Bährnamov, Baku
Qarabağ FK 2-1 FC Honka Espoo
Goal(s): 1-0 E. Mämmädov 32, 1-1 Koskinen 34, 2-1 R. F. Sadiqov 80
Referee: Mikulski (POL)
Aggregate: 3-1; Qarabağ FK qualify.

UEFA Europa League

Lech Poznań go 6-1 up at Fredrikstad

30/7/09, Fredrikstad, Fredrikstad
Fredrikstad FK 1-6 Lech Poznań
Goal(s): 0-1 Wilk 10, 0-2 Arboleda 22, 0-3 Arboleda 25, 1-3 Borges 48,
1-4 Lewandowski 51, 1-5 Peszko 54, 1-6 Bandrowski 56
Referee: Clattenburg (ENG)
6/8/09, Amica, Wronki
Lech Poznań 1-2 Fredrikstad FK
Goal(s): 0-1 Gashi 31, 0-2 Piiroja 35, 1-2 Lewandowski 63
Referee: Zimmermann (SUI)
Aggregate: 7-3; Lech Poznań qualify.

30/7/09, Gamla Ullevi, Gothenburg
IFK Göteborg 1-3 Hapoel Tel-Aviv FC
Goal(s): 1-0 Hysén 21, 1-1 Shechter 73, 1-2 Yeboah 78, 1-3 Natcho 90+4
Referee: Schörgenhofer (AUT)
6/8/09, Bloomfield, Tel-Aviv
Hapoel Tel-Aviv FC 1-1 IFK Göteborg
Goal(s): 1-0 Zandberg 14, 1-1 Stiller 52
Referee: Hriňák (SVK)
Aggregate: 4-2; Hapoel Tel-Aviv FC qualify.

30/7/09, Ullevål, Oslo
Vålerenga Fotball 1-2 PAOK FC
Goal(s): 0-1 Lino 31, 0-2 Muslimović 37, 1-2 Storbæk 42
Referee: Deaconu (ROU)
6/8/09, Toumba, Thessalonika
PAOK FC 0-1 Vålerenga Fotball
Goal(s): 0-1 Berre 60
Referee: Banti (ITA)
Aggregate: 2-2; PAOK FC qualify on away goals.

30/7/09, Alfheim, Tromso
Tromsø IL 2-1 NK Slaven Koprivnica
Goal(s): 0-1 Šafarić 38 (p), 1-1 Moldskred 67, 2-1 Rushfeldt 69
Referee: Gil (POL)
6/8/09, Gradski, Koprivnica
NK Slaven Koprivnica 0-2 Tromsø IL
Goal(s): 0-1 Rushfeldt 14, 0-2 Rushfeldt 82
Referee: Jech (CZE)
Aggregate: 1-4; Tromsø IL qualify.

30/7/09, Brøndby, Brondby
Brøndby IF 1-1 Legia Warszawa
Goal(s): 0-1 Iwański 40 (p), 1-1 Farnerud 73 (p)
Referee: Velasco Carballo (ESP)
6/8/09, Wojska Polskiego, Warsaw
Legia Warszawa 2-2 Brøndby IF
Goal(s): 0-1 Von Schlebrügge 6, 1-1 Giza 16, 2-1 Iwański 55 (p), 2-2
Von Schlebrügge 59
Referee: Fautrel (FRA)
Aggregate: 3-3; Brøndby IF qualify on away goals.

30/7/09, Gerhard Hanappi, Vienna
SK Rapid Wien 2-1 APOP/Kinyras Peyias FC
Goal(s): 1-0 Maierhofer 25, 2-0 Jelavić 57, 2-1 Semedo 79
Referee: Paniashvili (GEO)
6/8/09, GSP, Nicosia
APOP/Kinyras Peyias FC 2-2 SK Rapid Wien (aet)
Goal(s): 0-1 Konrad 30, 1-1 Edgar Marcelino 43 (p), 2-1 González 80,
2-2 Trimmel 111
Referee: Berntsen (NOR)
Aggregate: 3-4; SK Rapid Wien qualify after extra time.

30/7/09, FK Crvena zvezda, Belgrade
FK Vojvodina 1-1 FK Austria Wien
Goal(s): 0-1 Jun 38, 1-1 Djurovski 45+2
Referee: Attwell (ENG)
6/8/09, Franz Horr, Vienna
FK Austria Wien 4-2 FK Vojvodina
Goal(s): 0-1 Mrđa 31, 1-1 Jun 45, 1-2 Tadić 58, 2-2 Sulimani 59,
3-2 Diabang 81, 4-2 Okotie 90+3
Referee: Oriekhov (UKR)
Aggregate: 5-3; FK Austria Wien qualify.

30/7/09, KR-völlur, Reykjavik
KR Reykjavík 2-2 FC Basel 1893
Goal(s): 1-0 Benediktsson 6, 2-0 I. Sigurdsson 9, 2-1 Chipperfield 58,
2-2 Almerares 83
Referee: Teixeira Vitienes (ESP)
6/8/09, St. Jakob-Park, Basel
FC Basel 1893 3-1 KR Reykjavík
Goal(s): 1-0 Frei 29, 1-1 Takefusa 45+1 (p), 2-1 Shaqiri 77, 3-1 Frei 80 (p)
Referee: Asumaa (FIN)
Aggregate: 5-3; FC Basel 1893 qualify.

30/7/09, Rheinpark, Vaduz
FC Vaduz 0-1 FC Slovan Liberec
Goal(s): 0-1 Blažek 43
Referee: Borg (MLT)
6/8/09, U Nisy, Liberec
FC Slovan Liberec 2-0 FC Vaduz
Goal(s): 1-0 Kerić 17, 2-0 Nezmar 22
Referee: Strömbergsson (SWE)
Aggregate: 3-0; FC Slovan Liberec qualify.

30/7/09, Pod Dubňon, Zilina
MŠK Žilina 1-1 HNK Hajduk Split
Goal(s): 0-1 Rafael Paraíba 52, 1-1 Kobylík 73 (p)
Referee: Kakos (GRE)
6/8/09, Poljud, Split
HNK Hajduk Split 0-1 MŠK Žilina
Goal(s): 0-1 Lietava 76
Referee: Nijhuis (NED)
Aggregate: 1-2; MŠK Žilina qualify.

30/7/09, Bloomfield, Tel-Aviv
Maccabi Netanya FC 1-4 Galatasaray AŞ
Goal(s): 1-0 Yampolski 25, 1-1 Hakan Balta 31, 1-2 Kewell 47,
1-3 Sabri Sarıoğlu 53, 1-4 Baroš 73
Referee: Ivanov (RUS)
6/8/09, Ali Sami Yen, Istanbul
Galatasaray AŞ 6-0 Maccabi Netanya FC
Goal(s): 1-0 Barış Özbek 2, 2-0 Keita 6, 3-0 Barış Özbek 51,
4-0 Nonda 56, 5-0 Nonda 60, 6-0 Nonda 90
Referee: Dean (ENG)
Aggregate: 10-1; Galatasaray AŞ qualify.

Elfsborg's English striker James Keene fires home one of his two goals as the Swedish team surprisingly knock out Portugal's Braga

30/7/09, Richmond Park, Dublin
Saint Patrick's Athletic FC 1-0 PFC Krylya Sovetov Samara
Goal(s): 1-0 O'Brien 71
Referee: Szabó (HUN)
6/8/09, Metallurg, Samara
PFC Krylya Sovetov Samara 3-2 Saint Patrick's Athletic FC
Goal(s): 1-0 Bober 41, 2-0 Savin 53, 3-0 Savin 57, 3-1 Bober 73 (og), 3-2 O'Brien 78
Referee: Skjerven (NOR)
Aggregate: 3-3; Saint Patrick's Athletic FC qualify on away goals.

30/7/09, Pittodrie, Aberdeen
Aberdeen FC 1-5 SK Sigma Olomouc
Goal(s): 0-1 Hubník 17, 1-1 Mulgrew 22, 1-2 Bajer 64, 1-3 Petr 69, 1-4 Ordoš 83, 1-5 Hořava 90
Referee: Laperrière (SUI)
6/8/09, Andruv, Olomouc
SK Sigma Olomouc 3-0 Aberdeen FC
Goal(s): 1-0 Janotka 5, 2-0 Kaščák 13 (p), 3-0 Hubník 45+1
Referee: Weiner (GER)
Aggregate: 8-1; SK Sigma Olomouc qualify.

30/7/09, Metalurh, Donetsk
FC Metalurh Donetsk 2-0 NK IB Ljubljana
Goal(s): 1-0 Godin 20, 2-0 Mário Sérgio 50 (p)
Referee: Malek (POL)

6/8/09, Športni Park, Domzale
NK IB Ljubljana 0-3 FC Metalurh Donetsk
Goal(s): 0-1 Mkhitaryan 67, 0-2 Mguni 73, 0-3 Dimitrov 85 (p)
Referee: Svendsen (DEN)
Aggregate: 0-5; FC Metalurh Donetsk qualify.

30/7/09, Vasil Levski National, Sofia
PFC CSKA Sofia 1-0 Derry City FC
Goal(s): 1-0 I. Stoyanov 73
Referee: Dereli (TUR)
6/8/09, Brandywell, Derry
Derry City FC 1-1 PFC CSKA Sofia
Goal(s): 0-1 Marquinhos 70, 1-1 Scullion 82
Referee: Efong Nzolo (BEL)
Aggregate: 1-2; PFC CSKA Sofia qualify.

30/7/09, WOSIR Polonia, Warsaw
KSP Polonia Warszawa 0-1 NAC Breda
Goal(s): 0-1 Kwakman 39
Referee: Kever (SUI)
6/8/09, Rat Verlegh, Breda
NAC Breda 3-1 KSP Polonia Warszawa
Goal(s): 1-0 Amoah 25, 2-0 Lurling 45, 2-1 Ivanovski 59, 3-1 Kwakman 81
Referee: Jakobsson (ISL)
Aggregate: 4-1; NAC Breda qualify.

UEFA Europa League

EUROPA LEAGUE

30/7/09, Vėtra, Vilnius
FK Vėtra 0-3 Fulham FC
Goal(s): 0-1 Zamora 45, 0-2 Murphy 57 (p), 0-3 Seol 85
Referee: Stuchlik (AUT)
6/8/09, Craven Cottage, London
Fulham FC 3-0 FK Vėtra
Goal(s): 1-0 Etuhu 57, 2-0 A. Johnson 80, 3-0 A. Johnson 84
Referee: Vad (HUN)
Aggregate: 6-0; Fulham FC qualify.

30/7/09, Koševo, Sarajevo
FK Slavija Sarajevo 0-2 MFK Košice
Goal(s): 0-1 Novák 11, 0-2 Škutka 60
Referee: Mažeika (LTU)
6/8/09, Lokomotiva Košice, Kosice
MFK Košice 3-1 FK Slavija Sarajevo
Goal(s): 1-0 Novák 2, 1-1 Đermanovič 17, 2-1 Bašista 55, 3-1 Cicman 90+1
Referee: Sukhina (RUS)
Aggregate: 5-1; MFK Košice qualify.

30/7/09, Jan Breydel, Bruges
Club Brugge KV 3-2 FC Lahti
Goal(s): 0-1 Moilanen 6, 1-1 Akpala 12, 2-1 Blondel 35, 2-2 Korte 50, 3-2 Blondel 90
Referee: Nikolaev (RUS)
6/8/09, Lahti, Lahti
FC Lahti 1-1 Club Brugge KV
Goal(s): 0-1 Akpala 76, 1-1 Vanninen 87
Referee: Pereira Gomes (POR)
Aggregate: 3-4; Club Brugge KV qualify.

30/7/09, Randers, Randers
Randers FC 0-4 Hamburger SV
Goal(s): 0-1 Guerrero 11, 0-2 Boateng 24, 0-3 Petrić 53, 0-4 Trochowski 80 (p)
Referee: Genov (BUL)
6/8/09, Hamburg Arena, Hamburg
Hamburger SV 0-1 Randers FC
Goal(s): 0-1 Berg 35
Referee: Blom (NED)
Aggregate: 4-1; Hamburger SV qualify.

30/7/09, Olympia, Helsingborg
Helsingborgs IF 2-1 FK Sarajevo
Goal(s): 1-0 C. Andersson 6 (p), 1-1 Hadžić 22, 2-1 Skúlason 58
Referee: Whitby (WAL)
6/8/09, Koševo, Sarajevo
FK Sarajevo 2-1 Helsingborgs IF (aet)
Goal(s): 0-1 Jönsson 2, 1-1 Hadžić 38, 2-1 Avdić 78
Referee: Kulbakov (BLR)
Aggregate: 3-3; FK Sarajevo qualify 5-4 on penalties.

30/7/09, Stadio Olimpico, Rome
AS Roma 3-1 KAA Gent
Goal(s): 0-1 Leye 22, 1-1 Totti 55, 2-1 Totti 73 (p), 3-1 Vučinić 85
Referee: Gomes Costa (POR)
6/8/09, Jules Otten, Gent
KAA Gent 1-7 AS Roma
Goal(s): 0-1 Totti 35, 0-2 Totti 56, 0-3 De Rossi 58, 0-4 Totti 64 (p), 0-5 De Rossi 74, 1-5 Smolders 78, 1-6 Ménez 79, 1-7 Okaka Chuka 86
Referee: Gräfe (GER)
Aggregate: 2-10; AS Roma qualify.

30/7/09, PSV Stadion, Eindhoven
PSV Eindhoven 1-0 PFC Cherno More Varna
Goal(s): 1-0 Marcellis 90+3
Referee: Cardoso Cortez Batista (POR)
6/8/09, Lazur, Burgas
PFC Cherno More Varna 0-1 PSV Eindhoven
Goal(s): 0-1 Coulibaly 30 (og)
Referee: Kinhöfer (GER)
Aggregate: 0-2; PSV Eindhoven qualify.

30/7/09, Steaua, Bucharest
FC Steaua Bucureşti 3-0 Motherwell FC
Goal(s): 1-0 Craigan 29 (og), 2-0 Nicoliță 45+1, 3-0 Stancu 61
Referee: Çakır (TUR)
6/8/09, Shyberry Excelsior, Airdrie
Motherwell FC 1-3 FC Steaua Bucureşti
Goal(s): 1-0 Forbes 17, 1-1 Marin 55 (p), 1-2 Stancu 67, 1-3 Stancu 84
Referee: Clos Gómez (ESP)
Aggregate: 1-6; FC Steaua Bucureşti qualify.

30/7/09, Municipal, Braga
SC Braga 1-2 IF Elfsborg
Goal(s): 0-1 Daníelsson 16, 1-1 Meyong 50 (p), 1-2 Bajrami 73
Referee: Muñiz Fernández (ESP)
6/8/09, Borås Arena, Boras
IF Elfsborg 2-0 SC Braga
Goal(s): 1-0 Keene 16, 2-0 Keene 32
Referee: Liesveld (NED)
Aggregate: 4-1; IF Elfsborg qualify.

30/7/09, FK Partizan, Belgrade
FK Sevojno 0-2 LOSC Lille Métropole
Goal(s): 0-1 Vittek 34, 0-2 Hazard 39
Referee: Ingvarsson (SWE)
6/8/09, Lille Métropole, Villeneuve d'Ascq
LOSC Lille Métropole 2-0 FK Sevojno
Goal(s): 1-0 Cabaye 72, 2-0 Túlio de Melo 85
Referee: Koukoulakis (GRE)
Aggregate: 4-0; LOSC Lille Métropole qualify.

30/7/09, Kantrida, Rijeka
HNK Rijeka 1-2 FC Metalist Kharkiv
Goal(s): 0-1 Eremenko Jr 43, 1-1 Ah. Sharbini 59, 1-2 Lysenko 85
Referee: Hyytiä (FIN)
6/8/09, Metalist, Kharkiv
FC Metalist Kharkiv 2-0 HNK Rijeka
Goal(s): 1-0 Gueye 12, 2-0 Oliynyk 60
Referee: Matějek (CZE)
Aggregate: 4-1; FC Metalist Kharkiv qualify.

30/7/09, Municipal, Vaslui
FC Vaslui 2-0 AC Omonia
Goal(s): 1-0 Temwanjera 20, 2-0 Temwanjera 55
Referee: McDonald (SCO)
4/8/09, GSP, Nicosia
AC Omonia 1-1 FC Vaslui
Goal(s): 0-1 Wesley 60, 1-1 Żurawski 84 (p)
Referee: Tagliavento (ITA)
Aggregate: 1-3; FC Vaslui qualify.

30/7/09, San Mamés, Bilbao
Athletic Club 0-1 BSC Young Boys
Goal(s): 0-1 Doumbia 23
Referee: Kapitanis (CYP)
6/8/09, Stade de Suisse, Berne
BSC Young Boys 1-2 Athletic Club
Goal(s): 0-1 Llorente 26, 0-2 Muniain 72, 1-2 Asamoah-Frimpong 90+2
Referee: Yefet (ISR)
Aggregate: 2-2; Athletic Club qualify on away goals.

30/7/09, Şükrü Saracoğlu, Istanbul
Fenerbahçe SK 5-1 Budapest Honvéd FC
Goal(s): 1-0 Roberto Carlos 13, 2-0 Güiza 30, 3-0 Güiza 40, 4-0 Güiza 61, 5-0 Alex 69, 5-1 Zsolnai 78
Referee: Kircher (GER)
6/8/09, József Bozsik, Budapest
Budapest Honvéd FC 1-1 Fenerbahçe SK
Goal(s): 0-1 André Santos 9, 1-1 Fritz 86
Referee: Allaerts (BEL)
Aggregate: 2-6; Fenerbahçe SK qualify.

Play-Off Round

The UEFA Europa League may have represented a new dawn, but the play-off round had a remarkably familiar feel about it. Three of the 2009 UEFA Cup semi-finalists were present, and Werder Bremen, Hamburger SV and eventual winners FC Shakhtar Donetsk made light work of unfancied opponents. Shocks were in short supply but CD Nacional ensured the big battalions did not have it all their own way.

Mladen Petrić – a hat-trick hero for Hamburg in France

Exactly three months after claiming the last UEFA Cup in Istanbul, Shakhtar returned to Turkey to begin their UEFA Europa League campaign at Sivasspor. Showing none of the rustiness that had led to their elimination from the UEFA Champions League third qualifying round by FC Timişoara, Mircea Lucescu's men cantered to a 5-0 aggregate victory, with UEFA Cup final goalscorers Jádson and Luiz Adriano both finding the net in the return.

Hanseatic goals

That second encounter was brought forward because of the UEFA Super Cup, so Shakhtar became the first side to book their place in the 48-strong group stage. In truth, a few had one foot already there following emphatic first-leg victories. SL Benfica, Valencia CF, Everton FC and Galatasaray AŞ all set up comfortable returns, though six goals were not enough to please Thomas Schaaf, who moaned "we should have scored more" after Bremen's 6-3 victory over FC Aktobe of Kazakhstan.

Hamburger SV were also on fire in sweltering temperatures at second-tier French Cup holders En Avant Guingamp, Mladen Petrić scoring a hat-trick in a 5-1 triumph. Impressive as that individual haul was, the Croatian was outgunned by Luis Suárez, responsible for four of AFC Ajax's five goals against ŠK Slovan Bratislava. Yet the prize for the round's top scorer went, again, to Francesco Totti. As he did in the third qualifying round, the AS Roma captain hit five as the Giallorossi racked up ten goals, but the Serie A giants did not have it all their own way against MFK Košice.

Nacional interests

Indeed, the Slovakian side travelled to the Italian capital with every hope of causing a shock after a 3-3 first-leg draw. Two Totti goals in the first ten minutes at the Stadio Olimpico put paid to those ambitions, however,

the forward completing his hat-trick and a 7-1 triumph as the final whistle approached. CD Nacional travelled to 2008 UEFA Cup winners FC Zenit St Petersburg fearing a similar backlash after a thrilling 4-3 first-leg victory. It failed to materialise, but the Russian side were heading through on the away-goals rule until a minute from time when Rúben Micael made it 1-1 on the night.

The biggest drama of all came in the Czech Republic. Awarded a 3-0 default win after the away leg of their tie against FC Dinamo Bucureşti was abandoned because of crowd trouble, FC Slovan Liberec looked poised for the group stage until Andrei Cristea's early goal put doubt in their minds. Dinamo substitute Marius Niculae struck twice after the break to send the game into extra time and then penalties, with the Romanian side eventually prevailing 9-8 from the spot.

Austrian attack

Club Brugge KV also needed spot-kicks to see off Lech Poznań, and while all three Austrian sides progressed, none did it the easy way. SK Rapid Wien surprisingly knocked out Aston Villa FC on the away goals rule, SK Sturm Graz held off a determined FC Metalist Kharkiv comeback while FK Austria Wien needed extra time to overcome another Ukrainian outfit, FC Metalurh Donetsk, 5-4 on aggregate. Villa were not the only former European champions to fall by the wayside, as a 3-0 first-leg defeat by SK Slavia Praha proved insurmountable for FK Crvena zvezda.

UEFA Europa League

Play-Off Round Results

20/8/09, Lokomotiva Košice, Kosice
MFK Košice 3-3 AS Roma
Goal(s): 1-0 Milinković 5, 1-1 Totti 38 (p), 1-2 Ménez 52, 1-3 Totti 67, 2-3 Novák 71 (p), 3-3 Novák 81
Referee: Rasmussen (DEN)
27/8/09, Stadio Olimpico, Rome
AS Roma 7-1 MFK Košice
Goal(s): 1-0 Totti 1, 2-0 Totti 6, 3-0 Guberti 8, 4-0 Cerci 17, 5-0 Ménez 18, 5-1 Novák 38, 6-1 Riise 70, 7-1 Totti 86
Referee: Dereli (TUR)
Aggregate: 10-4; AS Roma qualify.

20/8/09, Na Stínadlech, Teplice
FK Teplice 1-2 Hapoel Tel-Aviv FC
Goal(s): 0-1 Enyeama 74 (p), 1-1 Vondrášek 89, 1-2 Vermouth 90+4
Referee: Berntsen (NOR)
27/8/09, Bloomfield, Tel-Aviv
Hapoel Tel-Aviv FC 1-1 FK Teplice
Goal(s): 0-1 Klein 89, 1-1 Ben Dayan 90+1
Referee: Sukhina (RUS)
Aggregate: 3-2; Hapoel Tel-Aviv FC qualify.

20/8/09, Roudourou, Guingamp
En Avant Guingamp 1-5 Hamburger SV
Goal(s): 0-1 Guerrero 7, 0-2 Petrić 11, 0-3 Petrić 26, 0-4 Berg 51, 0-5 Petrić 86, 1-5 Hesl 88 (og)
Referee: Borski (POL)
27/8/09, Hamburg Arena, Hamburg
Hamburger SV 3-1 En Avant Guingamp
Goal(s): 1-0 Tesche 42, 2-0 Berg 47, 3-0 Tesche 51, 3-1 Mathis 90
Referee: Ingvarsson (SWE)
Aggregate: 8-2; Hamburger SV qualify.

20/8/09, Gorodskoi, Borisov
FC BATE Borisov 0-1 PFC Litex Lovech
Goal(s): 0-1 Sandrinho 81
Referee: Skjerven (NOR)
27/8/09, Gradski, Lovech
PFC Litex Lovech 0-4 FC BATE Borisov (aet)
Goal(s): 0-1 Sosnovskiy 86, 0-2 Rodionov 95, 0-3 Sosnovskiy 99, 0-4 Skavysh 118
Referee: Gräfe (GER)
Aggregate: 1-4; FC BATE Borisov qualify after extra time.

20/8/09, Rat Verlegh, Breda
NAC Breda 1-3 Villarreal CF
Goal(s): 0-1 Rossi 14, 1-1 Loran 17, 1-2 Ibagaza 49, 1-3 Llorente 90+2
Referee: Johannesson (SWE)
27/8/09, El Madrigal, Villarreal
Villarreal CF 6-1 NAC Breda
Goal(s): 1-0 Santi Cazorla 16, 2-0 Rossi 23 (p), 3-0 Rossi 37 (p), 4-0 Senna 46, 5-0 Jonathan Pereira 57, 6-0 Kiko 61, 6-1 De Graaf 80
Referee: Thomson (SCO)
Aggregate: 9-2; Villarreal CF qualify.

20/8/09, Gerhard Hanappi, Vienna
SK Rapid Wien 1-0 Aston Villa FC
Goal(s): 1-0 Jelavić 1
Referee: Tudor (ROU)
27/8/09, Villa Park, Birmingham
Aston Villa FC 2-1 SK Rapid Wien
Goal(s): 1-0 Milner 38 (p), 2-0 Carew 53, 2-1 Jelavić 76
Referee: Velasco Carballo (ESP)
Aggregate: 2-2; SK Rapid Wien qualify on away goal.

20/8/09, Graz Liebenau, Graz
SK Sturm Graz 1-1 FC Metalist Kharkiv
Goal(s): 1-0 Beichler 31, 1-1 Oliynyk 76
Referee: Braamhaar (NED)

27/8/09, Metalist, Kharkiv
FC Metalist Kharkiv 0-1 SK Sturm Graz
Goal(s): 0-1 Beichler 32
Referee: Moen (NOR)
Aggregate: 1-2; SK Sturm Graz qualify.

20/8/09, Bloomfield, Tel-Aviv
Bnei Yehuda Tel-Aviv FC 0-1 PSV Eindhoven
Goal(s): 0-1 Afellay 23
Referee: Eriksson (SWE)
27/8/09, PSV Stadion, Eindhoven
PSV Eindhoven 1-0 Bnei Yehuda Tel-Aviv FC
Goal(s): 1-0 Simons 25 (p)
Referee: Muñiz Fernández (ESP)
Aggregate: 2-0; PSV Eindhoven qualify.

20/8/09, Hüseyin Avni Aker, Trabzon
Trabzonspor 1-3 Toulouse FC
Goal(s): 0-1 Gignac 12, 1-1 Song 16, 1-2 Gignac 59, 1-3 Mansaré 90+1
Referee: Královec (CZE)
27/8/09, Stadium Municipal, Toulouse
Toulouse FC 0-1 Trabzonspor
Goal(s): 0-1 Ceyhun Gülselam 55
Referee: Gumienny (BEL)
Aggregate: 3-2; Toulouse FC qualify.

20/8/09, Estádio do Sport Lisboa e Benfica, Lisbon
SL Benfica 4-0 FC Vorskla Poltava
Goal(s): 1-0 Di María 31, 2-0 Cardozo 55 (p), 3-0 Saviola 57, 4-0 Weldon 77
Referee: Čeferin (SVN)
27/8/09, Vorskla, Poltava
FC Vorskla Poltava 2-1 SL Benfica
Goal(s): 1-0 Sachko 48, 1-1 Saviola 59, 2-1 Yesin 74
Referee: Circhetta (SUI)
Aggregate: 2-5; SL Benfica qualify.

20/8/09, Toumba, Thessalonika
PAOK FC 1-1 sc Heerenveen
Goal(s): 0-1 Paulo Henrique 45, 1-1 Ivić 54
Referee: Collum (SCO)
27/8/09, Abe Lenstra, Heerenveen
sc Heerenveen 0-0 PAOK FC
Referee: Iturralde González (ESP)
Aggregate: 1-1; sc Heerenveen qualify on away goal.

20/8/09, Goodison Park, Liverpool
Everton FC 4-0 SK Sigma Olomouc
Goal(s): 1-0 Saha 34, 2-0 Rodwell 40, 3-0 Rodwell 53, 4-0 Saha 72
Referee: Cardoso Cortez Batista (POR)
27/8/09, Andruv, Olomouc
SK Sigma Olomouc 1-1 Everton FC
Goal(s): 0-1 Pienaar 44, 1-1 Šultes 80
Referee: Fautrel (FRA)
Aggregate: 1-5; Everton FC qualify.

20/8/09, Craven Cottage, London
Fulham FC 3-1 FC Amkar Perm
Goal(s): 1-0 A. Johnson 4, 2-0 Dempsey 51, 3-0 Zamora 75, 3-1 Grishin 77
Referee: Proença (POR)
27/8/09, Zvezda, Perm
FC Amkar Perm 1-0 Fulham FC
Goal(s): 1-0 Kushev 90
Referee: Strömbergsson (SWE)
Aggregate: 2-3; Fulham FC qualify.

20/8/09, FC Twente, Enschede
FC Twente 3-1 Qarabağ FK
Goal(s): 0-1 Nadirov 8, 1-1 Ruiz 38, 2-1 Ruiz 66, 3-1 Douglas 81
Referee: Marriner (ENG)
27/8/09, Tofiq Bähramov, Baku
Qarabağ FK 0-0 FC Twente
Referee: Deaconu (ROU)
Aggregate: 1-3; FC Twente qualify.

UEFA Europa League

Play-Off Round

20/8/09, Vasil Levski National, Sofia
PFC CSKA Sofia 0-0 FC Dinamo Moskva
Referee: Schörgenhofer (AUT)
27/8/09, Arena Khimki, Moscow
FC Dinamo Moskva 1-2 PFC CSKA Sofia
Goal(s): 1-0 Kerzhakov 10, 1-1 Delev 14, 1-2 Ivanov 55
Referee: Weiner (GER)
Aggregate: 1-2; PFC CSKA Sofia qualify.

20/8/09, Tofiq Bähramov, Baku
Bakı FK 1-3 FC Basel 1893
Goal(s): 1-0 Pérez 49, 1-1 Streller 71, 1-2 Streller 74, 1-3 Huggel 77
Referee: Szabó (HUN)
27/8/09, St. Jakob-Park, Basel
FC Basel 1893 5-1 Bakı FK
Goal(s): 1-0 Almerares 32, 1-1 Felipe 33, 2-1 Gelabert 36, 3-1 Frei 63, 4-1 Shaqiri 74, 5-1 Mustafi 84
Referee: Kaasik (EST)
Aggregate: 8-2; FC Basel 1893 qualify.

0/8/09, Eden, Prague
SK Slavia Praha 3-0 FK Crvena zvezda
Goal(s): 1-0 Šenkeřík 34, 2-0 Šenkeřík 65, 3-0 Vlček 81
Referee: Allaerts (BEL)
27/8/09, FK Crvena zvezda, Belgrade
FK Crvena zvezda 2-1 SK Slavia Praha
Goal(s): 1-0 Bogdanović 23 (p), 2-0 Perović 45, 2-1 Vlček 63
Referee: Kinhöfer (GER)
Aggregate: 2-4; SK Slavia Praha qualify.

20/8/09, Metalurh, Donetsk
FC Metalurh Donetsk 2-2 FK Austria Wien
Goal(s): 0-1 Ačimovič 8, 1-1 Kingsley 17, 1-2 Diabang 48, 2-2 Dimitrov 90+2
Referee: Koukoulakis (GRE)
27/8/09, Franz Horr, Vienna
FK Austria Wien 3-2 FC Metalurh Donetsk (aet)
Goal(s): 0-1 Tănasă 20, 1-1 Okotie 36, 1-2 Mkhitaryan 54, 2-2 Ačimovič 70 (p), 3-2 Sulimani 115
Referee: Jakobsson (ISL)
Aggregate: 5-4; FK Austria Wien qualify after extra time.

20/8/09, FK Partizan, Belgrade
FK Partizan 1-1 MŠK Žilina
Goal(s): 1-0 Cléo 16 (p), 1-1 Adauto 34 (p)
Referee: Paniashvili (GEO)
27/8/09, Pod Dubňon, Zilina
MŠK Žilina 0-2 FK Partizan
Goal(s): 0-1 Diarra 59, 0-2 B. Ilić 65
Referee: Vollquartz (DEN)
Aggregate: 1-3; FK Partizan qualify.

20/8/09, Asim Ferhatović-Hase, Sarajevo
FK Sarajevo 1-1 CFR 1907 Cluj
Goal(s): 0-1 Dani 19, 1-1 Hadžić 77
Referee: Malek (POL)
27/8/09, Dr Constantin Rădulescu, Cluj-Napoca
CFR 1907 Cluj 2-1 FK Sarajevo
Goal(s): 1-0 Koné 40, 2-0 Mureşan 69, 2-1 Avdić 81
Referee: Pereira Gomes (POR)
Aggregate: 3-2; CFR 1907 Cluj qualify.

20/8/09, Amica, Wronki
Lech Poznań 1-0 Club Brugge KV
Goal(s): 1-0 Peszko 90+3
Referee: Neves Moreira de Sousa (POR)
27/8/09, Jan Breydel, Bruges
Club Brugge KV 1-0 Lech Poznań (aet)
Goal(s): 1-0 Sonck 79
Referee: Kelly (IRL)
Aggregate: 1-1; Club Brugge KV qualify 4-3 on penalties.

20/8/09, Brøndby, Brondby
Brøndby IF 2-1 Hertha BSC Berlin
Goal(s): 1-0 Bischoff 51, 1-1 Domovchiyski 53, 2-1 Pejčinović 70 (og)
Referee: Blom (NED)
27/8/09, Friedrich-Ludwig-Jahn Sportpark, Berlin
Hertha BSC Berlin 3-1 Brøndby IF
Goal(s): 0-1 M. Rasmussen 52, 1-1 Kačar 75, 2-1 Dárdai 80, 3-1 Kačar 86
Referee: Tagliavento (ITA)
Aggregate: 4-3; Hertha BSC Berlin qualify.

20/8/09, Steaua, Bucharest
FC Steaua Bucureşti 3-0 Saint Patrick's Athletic FC
Goal(s): 1-0 Niculiţă 56, 2-0 Stancu 65, 3-0 Stancu 80
Referee: Nikolaev (RUS)
27/8/09, Royal Dublin Society, Dublin
Saint Patrick's Athletic FC 1-2 FC Steaua Bucureşti
Goal(s): 1-0 O'Connor 49, 1-1 Niculiţă 80, 1-2 Ochiroşii 89
Referee: Jech (CZE)
Aggregate: 1-5; FC Steaua Bucureşti qualify.

20/8/09, Estádio da Madeira, Funchal
CD Nacional 4-3 FC Zenit St Petersburg
Goal(s): 1-0 Luís Alberto 30, 2-0 João Aurélio 37, 2-1 Semshov 43, 3-1 Rodrigo 53, 3-2 Semshov 55, 4-2 Rúben Micael 73, 4-3 Fatih Tekke 90+3
Referee: Çakır (TUR)
27/8/09, Petrovskiy, St Petersburg
FC Zenit St Petersburg 1-1 CD Nacional
Goal(s): 1-0 Fatih Tekke 34, 1-1 Rúben Micael 89
Referee: Bebek (CRO)
Aggregate: 4-5; CD Nacional qualify.

20/8/09, Dinamo, Bucharest
FC Dinamo Bucureşti 0-3 FC Slovan Liberec (w/o)
Referee: Einwaller (AUT)
27/8/09, U Nisy, Liberec
FC Slovan Liberec 0-3 FC Dinamo Bucureşti (aet)
Goal(s): 0-1 Andrei Cristea 2, 0-2 Niculae 57, 0-3 Niculae 81
Referee: Yefet (ISR)
Aggregate: 3-3; FC Dinamo Bucureşti qualify 9-8 on penalties.

20/8/09, Stade de Genève, Geneva
FC Sion 0-2 Fenerbahçe SK
Goal(s): 0-1 André Santos 45, 0-2 Kazım 85
Referee: Stalhammar (SWE)
27/8/09, Şükrü Saracoğlu, Istanbul
Fenerbahçe SK 2-2 FC Sion
Goal(s): 1-0 André Santos 2, 1-1 Vanczák 9, 1-2 Chihab 31 (p), 2-2 André Santos 41(p)
Referee: Bruno Paixão (POR)
Aggregate: 4-2; Fenerbahçe SK qualify.

20/8/09, Cristal Arena, Genk
KRC Genk 1-2 LOSC Lille Métropole
Goal(s): 0-1 Dumont 40, 0-2 Vittek 56, 1-2 Tőzsér 58
Referee: Genov (BUL)
27/8/09, Lille Métropole, Villeneuve d'Ascq
LOSC Lille Métropole 4-2 KRC Genk
Goal(s): 1-0 Túlio de Melo 10, 1-1 Barda 24 (p), 2-1 Dumont 59, 3-1 Hazard 70, 4-1 Túlio de Melo 73, 4-2 Tőzsér 86
Referee: Rocchi (ITA)
Aggregate: 6-3; LOSC Lille Métropole qualify.

20/8/09, Stadio Olimpico, Rome
S.S. Lazio 3-0 IF Elfsborg
Goal(s): 1-0 Kolarov 24, 2-0 Zárate 36, 3-0 Mauri 69
Referee: McDonald (SCO)
27/8/09, Borås Arena, Boras
IF Elfsborg 1-0 S.S. Lazio
Goal(s): 1-0 Avdic 70
Referee: Oriekhov (UKR)
Aggregate: 1-3; S.S. Lazio qualify.

UEFA Europa League

20/8/09, Amsterdam ArenA, Amsterdam
AFC Ajax 5-0 ŠK Slovan Bratislava
Goal(s): 1-0 Suárez 43, 2-0 Suárez 65, 3-0 Suárez 79, 4-0 Suárez 84, 5-0 Donald 90+2
Referee: Clattenburg (ENG)
27/8/09, Tehelné Pole, Bratislava
ŠK Slovan Bratislava 1-2 AFC Ajax
Goal(s): 0-1 De Jong 30, 1-1 Sylvestr 45+2, 1-2 Bakircioglü 84
Referee: Kapitanis (CYP)
Aggregate: 1-7; AFC Ajax qualify.

20/8/09, Ljudski vrt, Maribor
NK Maribor 0-2 AC Sparta Praha
Goal(s): 0-1 Wilfried 29, 0-2 Wilfried 86
Referee: Hyytiä (FIN)
27/8/09, Generali Arena, Prague
AC Sparta Praha 1-0 NK Maribor
Goal(s): 1-0 Wilfried 3
Referee: Kulbakov (BLR)
Aggregate: 3-0; AC Sparta Praha qualify.

20/8/09, Luigi Ferraris, Genoa
Genoa CFC 3-1 Odense BK
Goal(s): 1-0 Sørensen 9 (og), 2-0 Figueroa 48, 3-0 Figueroa 56, 3-1 Mesto 59 (og)
Referee: Lannoy (FRA)
27/8/09, Fionia Park, Odense
Odense BK 1-1 Genoa CFC
Goal(s): 1-0 Figueroa 45+2 (og), 1-1 Criscito 53
Referee: Kuipers (NED)
Aggregate: 2-4; Genoa CFC qualify.

20/8/09, Maksimir, Zagreb
NK Dinamo Zagreb 4-0 Heart of Midlothian FC
Goal(s): 1-0 Mandžukić 6, 2-0 Papadopoulos 36, 3-0 Vrdoljak 56, 4-0 Bišćan 60
Referee: Ivanov (RUS)
27/8/09, Tynecastle, Edinburgh
Heart of Midlothian FC 2-0 NK Dinamo Zagreb
Goal(s): 1-0 M. Stewart 18, 2-0 Žaliūkas 55
Referee: Kircher (GER)
Aggregate: 2-4; NK Dinamo Zagreb qualify.

20/8/09, Weserstadion, Bremen
Werder Bremen 6-3 FC Aktobe
Goal(s): 1-0 Boenisch 17, 1-1 Strukov 21, 2-1 Pizarro 28, 2-2 Strukov 32, 3-2 Naldo 36, 4-2 Hugo Almeida 60, 5-2 Naldo 65, 6-2 Özil 67 (p), 6-3 Smakov 87
Referee: Asumaa (FIN)
27/8/09, Centralny, Aktobe
FC Aktobe 0-2 Werder Bremen
Goal(s): 0-1 Pizarro 10, 0-2 Pizarro 45+1
Referee: Hriňák (SVK)
Aggregate: 3-8; Werder Bremen qualify.

20/8/09, 4 Eylül, Sivas
Sivasspor 0-3 FC Shakhtar Donetsk
Goal(s): 0-1 Hai 6, 0-2 Ilsinho 76, 0-3 Kobin 87
Referee: Dean (ENG)
25/8/09, RSC Olympiyskiy, Donetsk
FC Shakhtar Donetsk 2-0 Sivasspor
Goal(s): 1-0 Jádson 21 (p), 2-0 Luiz Adriano 59 (p)
Referee: Trefoloni (ITA)
Aggregate: 5-0; FC Shakhtar Donetsk qualify.

20/8/09, Municipal, Vaslui
FC Vaslui 2-1 AEK Athens FC
Goal(s): 1-0 Wesley 29, 1-1 Blanco 69 (p), 2-1 Wesley 83 (p)
Referee: Ennjimi (FRA)
27/8/09, OACA Spyro Louis, Athens
AEK Athens FC 3-0 FC Vaslui
Goal(s): 1-0 Manduca 59, 2-0 Scocco 74, 3-0 Scocco 79
Referee: Skomina (SVN)
Aggregate: 4-2; AEK Athens FC qualify.

20/8/09, Fornebu Arena, Oslo
Stabæk Fotball 0-3 Valencia CF
Goal(s): 0-1 Pablo Hernández 29, 0-2 David Villa 35, 0-3 Joaquín 80
Referee: Stavrev (MKD)
27/8/09, Mestalla, Valencia
Valencia CF 4-1 Stabæk Fotball
Goal(s): 1-0 Miku 28, 2-0 Miku 29, 2-1 Farnerud 36, 3-1 Žigić 77, 4-1 Miku 80
Referee: Nijhuis (NED)
Aggregate: 7-1; Valencia CF qualify.

20/8/09, Ali Sami Yen, Istanbul
Galatasaray AŞ 5-0 FC Levadia Tallinn
Goal(s): 1-0 Keita 21, 2-0 Keita 45, 3-0 Baroš 56 (p), 4-0 Kewell 78, 5-0 Leitan 88 (og)
Referee: Zimmermann (SUI)
27/8/09, A Le Coq Arena, Tallinn
FC Levadia Tallinn 1-1 Galatasaray AŞ
Goal(s): 1-0 E. Puri 50, 1-1 Nonda 64
Referee: Vad (HUN)
Aggregate: 1-6; Galatasaray AŞ qualify.

20/8/09, San Mamés, Bilbao
Athletic Club 3-2 Tromsø IL
Goal(s): 0-1 Moldskred 42, 1-1 Javi Martínez 62 (p), 1-2 Lindpere 78, 2-2 De Marcos 86, 3-2 Llorente 90
Referee: Kever (SUI)
27/8/09, Alfheim, Tromso
Tromsø IL 1-1 Athletic Club
Goal(s): 0-1 Javi Martínez 56 (p), 1-1 Rushfeldt 61
Referee: Chapron (FRA)
Aggregate: 3-4; Athletic Club qualify.

Gojko Kačar scored twice as Hertha Berlin came from behind to eliminate Brøndby.

GROUP STAGE

Group A

With nine major European titles between them, AFC Ajax and RSC Anderlecht were always expected to emerge from this section, but they did not have it all their own way.

Two games in and Dutch giants Ajax already had ground to make up. Draws against Anderlecht and a resilient FC Timişoara left them third in the section, but back-to-back victories over NK Dinamo Zagreb revived fortunes. It left Martin Jol's team needing a point in Timisoara to secure progress with a game to spare and although they came away with all three, Amsterdam's finest did it the hard way.

Penalty woe

Ajax would finish the group stage with more shots on goal than any other team, and 16 came in Romania as they wasted chance after chance following Dorin Goga's second-minute opener. A minute after half-time Marko Pantelić completed a turnaround when he made it 2-1 but hopes of coasting home were spoiled when Luis Suárez, who had earlier equalised, had two penalties saved – by different Timişoara goalkeepers.

On to Matchday 6 and Ajax had the chance to help end Anderlecht's ambitions; a home victory in Amsterdam and three points for Dinamo at home to Timişoara would be enough for the Croatian side to grab second place. For his part, Dinamo coach Krunoslav Jurčić "banned" his players from talking about the other game, but it proved in vain as Goga's late strike earned the visitors a surprise 2-1 win.

Mbark Boussoufa scored Anderlecht's winner at home to Timişoara – the Brussels club's 500th goal in Europe

Sweet 16

Anderlecht, of course, could not rely on events elsewhere. Put in their precarious predicament by a shock 1-0 defeat at home to Dinamo in the previous outing, Ariël Jacobs's side drove forward from the off. They forged ahead on 13 minutes when a cross from Mbark Boussoufa – scorer of Anderlecht's 500th goal in UEFA competition in the 3-1 Matchday 4 victory over FC Timişoara – was headed in by Romelu Lukaku.

At 16 years and 218 days, the competition's youngest player therefore became its youngest scorer. He added another soon after, and the Brussels side were on their way to a 3-1 win and, more importantly, a place in the round of 32.

Ajax hitman Luis Suárez scored and had two penalties saved in his team's 2-1 win over Timişoara

Group A Results

17/9/09, Amsterdam ArenA, Amsterdam
AFC Ajax 0-0 FC Timişoara
Attendance: 25391
Referee: Yefet (ISR)

17/9/09, Maksimir, Zagreb
NK Dinamo Zagreb 0-2 RSC Anderlecht
Attendance: 13844
Goal(s): 0-1 Bernárdez 74, 0-2 Legear 88
Referee: Szabó (HUN)

UEFA Europa League

1/10/09, Constant Vanden Stock, Brussels
RSC Anderlecht 1-1 AFC Ajax
Attendance: 17026
Goal(s): 0-1 Rommedahl 72, 1-1 Legear 85
Referee: Jakobsson (ISL)

1/10/09, Dan Păltinişanu, Timisoara
FC Timişoara 0-3 NK Dinamo Zagreb
Attendance: 5736
Goal(s): 0-1 Badelj 8, 0-2 Sammir 52, 0-3 Morales 59
Referee: Rasmussen (DEN)

22/10/09, Amsterdam ArenA, Amsterdam
AFC Ajax 2-1 NK Dinamo Zagreb
Attendance: 30700
Goal(s): 1-0 Suárez 3(p), 2-0 Rommedahl 81, 2-1 Tomečak 90+3
Referee: Einwaller (AUT)

22/10/09, Dan Păltinişanu, Timisoara
FC Timişoara 0-0 RSC Anderlecht
Attendance: 6893
Referee: Circhetta (SUI)

5/11/09, Constant Vanden Stock, Brussels
RSC Anderlecht 3-1 FC Timişoara
Attendance: 15991
Goal(s): 1-0 Suárez 30 (p), 1-1 Parks 51, 2-1 Boussoufa 69,
3-1 Legear 90+5
Referee: Chapron (FRA)

5/11/09, Maksimir, Zagreb
NK Dinamo Zagreb 0-2 AFC Ajax
Goal(s): 0-1 Pantelić 13, 0-2 De Zeeuw 45+1
Referee: Dean (ENG)

2/12/09, Constant Vanden Stock, Brussels
RSC Anderlecht 0-1 NK Dinamo Zagreb
Attendance: 15622
Goal(s): 0-1 Slepička 57
Referee: McDonald (SCO)

2/12/09, Dan Păltinişanu, Timisoara
FC Timişoara 1-2 AFC Ajax
Attendance: 8085
Goal(s): 1-0 Goga 2, 1-1 Suárez 8, 1-2 Pantelić 46
Referee: Tagliavento (ITA)

17/12/09, Amsterdam ArenA, Amsterdam
AFC Ajax 1-3 RSC Anderlecht
Attendance: 36156
Goal(s): 0-1 Lukaku 13, 0-2 Lukaku 22, 0-3 Legear 43,
1-3 Emanuelson 77
Referee: Çakır (TUR)

17/12/09, Maksimir, Zagreb
NK Dinamo Zagreb 1-2 FC Timişoara
Goal(s): 0-1 Bucur 67, 1-1 Scutaru 80 (og), 1-2 Goga 84
Referee: Velasco Carballo (ESP)

Group B

The normally prolific David Villa had scored just a solitary penalty in the group stage before he struck five minutes into added time on Matchday 6 to earn Valencia CF victory over Genoa CFC and a place in the last 32 as section winners.

Indeed, Unai Emery's charges went into the game in northern Italy still threatened with elimination. It was a peril they ultimately saw off with interest thanks to Villa, who shrugged off an earlier penalty miss to perform a typically decisive last act, sealing a 2-1 win five minutes into added time.

The Spain striker had not been so profligate from the spot earlier in the campaign, successfully converting on Matchday 2. Genoa were also the victims on that occasion and Villa's strike was again a telling one, sealing a 3-2 win in the midst of three draws at LOSC Lille Métropole (1-1) and SK Slavia Praha (2-2 and 1-1). Apparently stalling, Valencia moved up the gears to beat Lille 3-2 in their penultimate game of the round before Villa ensured they hit full throttle – better late than never.

David Villa gestures in celebration after scoring Valencia's stoppage-time winner at Genoa

Group A Table

	Pld	Home					Away					Total					Pts
		W	D	L	F	A	W	D	L	F	A	W	D	L	F	A	
1 RSC Anderlecht	6	1	1	1	4	3	2	1	0	5	1	3	2	1	9	4	11
2 AFC Ajax	6	1	1	1	3	4	2	1	0	5	2	3	2	1	8	6	11
3 NK Dinamo Zagreb	6	0	0	3	1	6	2	0	1	5	2	2	0	4	6	8	6
4 FC Timişoara	6	0	1	2	1	5	1	1	1	3	4	1	2	3	4	9	5

Lille steady

Rudi Garcia's Lille side rubber-stamped progress alongside the 2003/04 UEFA Cup winners with a more serene Matchday 6 victory; 3-1 at home to Slavia. As it transpired, Genoa's travails meant the Ligue 1 outfit were through regardless, though the manner of their triumph confirmed credentials worthy of advancement. They had, however, proved they were the real deal far earlier, following their opening-day draw against Valencia with a 5-1 defeat of Slavia in Prague.

The resounding nature of that result kick-started Lille's campaign while all but ending that of their opponents. Creditable draws against the eventual group winners came next, but Slavia rarely looked likely to be in the mix, eventually falling out of contention courtesy of a goalless draw at home to Genoa. Though a point was not sufficient for the Czech side, it did serve to prolong the hopes of their visitors until the last kick of the group. In the end, all the Serie A side had to show for it was Alberto Zapater's feat in scoring the first ever UEFA Europa League group-stage goal.

Group B Results

17/9/09, Lille Métropole, Villeneuve d'Ascq
LOSC Lille Métropole 1-1 Valencia CF
Attendance: 14676
Goal(s): 0-1 Mata 78, 1-1 Gervinho 86
Referee: Tudor (ROU)

17/9/09, Luigi Ferraris, Genoa
Genoa CFC 2-0 SK Slavia Praha
Attendance: 17356
Goal(s): 1-0 Zapater 4, 2-0 Sculli 39
Referee: Neves Moreira de Sousa (POR)

1/10/09, Eden, Prague
SK Slavia Praha 1-5 LOSC Lille Métropole
Attendance: 9158
Goal(s): 1-0 Belaid 6 (p), 1-1 Suchý 47 (og), 1-2 Frau 71, 1-3 Gervinho 85, 1-4 Souquet 88, 1-5 Gervinho 90+1
Referee: Schörgenhofer (AUT)

1/10/09, Mestalla, Valencia
Valencia CF 3-2 Genoa CFC
Attendance: 21333
Goal(s): 0-1 Floccari 43, 1-1 David Silva 52, 2-1 Žigić 56, 2-2 Kharja 64 (p), 3-2 David Villa 82 (p)
Referee: Çakır (TUR)

22/10/09, Mestalla, Valencia
Valencia CF 1-1 SK Slavia Praha
Attendance: 20632
Goal(s): 0-1 Naumov 28, 1-1 David Navarro 63
Referee: Gumienny (BEL)

22/10/09, Lille Métropole, Villeneuve d'Ascq
LOSC Lille Métropole 3-0 Genoa CFC
Attendance: 16518
Goal(s): 1-0 Obraniak 38, 2-0 Vittek 63, 3-0 Hazard 84
Referee: Čeferin (SVN)

5/11/09, Eden, Prague
SK Slavia Praha 2-2 Valencia CF
Attendance: 10624
Goal(s): 0-1 Joaquín 22 (p), 0-2 Maduro 47, 1-2 Janda 79, 2-2 Grajciar 82
Referee: Moen (NOR)

5/11/09, Luigi Ferraris, Genoa
Genoa CFC 3-2 LOSC Lille Métropole
Attendance: 18587
Goal(s): 1-0 Palacio 14, 2-0 Crespo 58, 2-1 Frau 76, 2-2 Gervinho 84, 3-2 Sculli 90+3
Referee: Nijhuis (NED)

Lille coach Rudi Garcia (right) congratulates Florent Balmont after the French side's Matchday 6 win at home to Slavia Praha

2/12/09, Mestalla, Valencia
Valencia CF 3-1 LOSC Lille Métropole
Attendance: 26193
Goal(s): 1-0 Joaquín 3, 2-0 Joaquín 32, 3-0 Mata 52, 3-1 Chedjou 90+1
Referee: Dean (ENG)

2/12/09, Eden, Prague
SK Slavia Praha 0-0 Genoa CFC
Attendance: 11799
Referee: Kircher (GER)

17/12/09, Lille Métropole, Villeneuve d'Ascq
LOSC Lille Métropole 3-1 SK Slavia Praha
Attendance: 15358
Goal(s): 1-0 Cabaye 25, 2-0 Gervinho 40, 2-1 Vlček 56, 3-1 Obraniak 80
Referee: Kaasik (EST)

17/12/09, Luigi Ferraris, Genoa
Genoa CFC 1-2 Valencia CF
Attendance: 23480
Goal(s): 0-1 Bruno 45+1, 1-1 Crespo 51, 1-2 David Villa 90+5
Referee: Kelly (IRL)

Group B Table

	Pld	Home W D L F A			Away W D L F A			Total W D L F A			Pts
1 Valencia CF	6	2 1 0 7 4			1 2 0 5 4			3 3 0 12 8			12
2 LOSC Lille Métropole	6	2 1 0 7 2			1 0 2 8 7			3 1 2 15 9			10
3 Genoa CFC	6	2 0 1 6 4			0 1 2 2 6			2 1 3 8 10			7
4 SK Slavia Praha	6	0 2 1 3 7			0 1 2 2 6			0 3 3 5 13			3

UEFA Europa League

Group C

When SK Rapid Wien defeated Hamburger SV 3-0 on the opening night it was a harbinger of what was to come in an unpredictable section. Indeed, in a group containing twice UEFA Cup Winners' Cup finalists Rapid and former European champions Hamburg and Celtic, it was Hapoel Tel-Aviv FC who came out on top.

Few would have predicted that outcome, less still that Rapid and Hapoel would be filling the top two places at the end of Matchday 1 after the Israeli underdogs struck twice in the last 15 minutes to beat Celtic 2-1. Eli Gutman's side lost to Hamburg next time out but back-to-back victories over previously unbeaten Rapid (5-1 at home, 3-0 away) put them on the brink of qualification for the last 32. On to Matchday 5 and Glasgow to face Celtic. The visitors lost 2-0 but still advanced as Hamburg's simultanoeus victory over Rapid gave the top two an unassailable lead.

Grand finale

It completed a miserable campaign for Celtic. Relegated to the competition after defeat to Arsenal FC in the UEFA Champions League play-offs, Tony Mowbray's side's were always up against it following their opening defeat at Hapoel. They managed just one goal and two points from their next three outings, and the damage was

done. Yet a club with such European pedigree refused to bow out without some cheer for their devoted fans, following up revenge against Hapoel with a dramatic fightback at Rapid in the tussle for third. Trailing 3-0 inside 19 minutes at the Ernst-Happel-Stadion, two goals from Marc-Antoine Fortuné dragged Mowbray's men back into the contest, paving the way for Paul McGowan's 91st-minute equaliser.

Celtic therefore took third, but the real intrigue lay in Tel-Aviv where Hapoel and Hamburg went head-to-head for first place. UEFA Cup semi-finalists the previous season, Hamburg were in pole position having picked up ten points in four games after their opening-day setback, Swedish youngster Marcus Berg scoring four goals. He threatened a fifth a few times on Matchday 6, but it was a 23-year-old in Hapoel's ranks who stole the headlines as Samuel Yeboah fired in the only goal midway through the first half to complete a memorable group campaign for his Israeli employers.

Group C Results

Marc-Antoine Fortuné starred in Celtic's 3-3 draw at Rapid Wien

UEFA Europa League

Tel Aviv players celebrate after scoring against Hamburg

Group D

A European campaign can represent a stretch on playing resources, but as coaches fell by the wayside amid domestic travails, it proved a welcome diversion for Sporting Clube de Portugal and Hertha BSC Berlin.

Sporting were struggling to hit their straps in the Portuguese Liga, but Liedson ensured they got off to a winning start at sc Heerenveen. The Brazilian-born striker completed what would prove the only hat-trick of the entire group stage two minutes before the final whistle to grab a 3-2 victory. It was the first of three successive narrow wins for Paulo Bento's team, who claimed their first success in 17 attempts against German opposition – Hertha – next time out before overcoming FK Ventspils 2-1 in Riga.

Coaching casualties

The Portuguese side would qualify with a game to spare, yet it was not enough to convince Bento, whose resignation heralded the arrival of Carlos Carvalhal before Matchday 5. The 40-year-old was not the only coaching casualty in Group D; Hertha had a different man in the dugout for each of their first three games. Lucien Favre was in charge for a 1-1 draw against Ventspils, his stand-in replacement Karsten Heine was on the bench for the 1-0 loss at Sporting before

5/11/09, Ernst Happel, Vienna
SK Rapid Wien 0-3 Hapoel Tel-Aviv FC
Attendance: 49000
Goal(s): 0-1 Yadin 13, 0-2 Vermouth 65, 0-3 Natcho 70
Referee: Skjerven (NOR)

2/12/09, Celtic Park, Glasgow
Celtic FC 2-0 Hapoel Tel-Aviv FC
Attendance: 35010
Goal(s): 1-0 Samaras 22, 2-0 Robson 68
Referee: Asumaa (FIN)

2/12/09, Hamburg Arena, Hamburg
Hamburger SV 2-0 SK Rapid Wien
Attendance: 45737
Goal(s): 1-0 Jansen 47, 2-0 Berg 53
Referee: Nijhuis (NED)

17/12/09, Ernst Happel, Vienna
SK Rapid Wien 3-3 Celtic FC
Attendance: 48300
Goal(s): 1-0 Jelavić 1, 2-0 Jelavić 8, 3-0 Salihi 19, 3-1 Fortuné 24, 3-2 Fortuné 67, 3-3 McGowan 90+1
Referee: Malek (POL)

17/12/09, Bloomfield, Tel-Aviv
Hapoel Tel-Aviv FC 1-0 Hamburger SV
Attendance: 13552
Goal(s): 1-0 Yeboah 23
Referee: Nikolaev (RUS)

Group C Table

	Pld	Home W D L F A	Away W D L F A	Total W D L F A	Pts
1 Hapoel Tel-Aviv FC	6	3 0 0 8 2	1 0 2 5 6	4 0 2 13 8	12
2 Hamburger SV	6	2 1 0 6 2	1 0 2 1 4	3 1 2 7 6	10
3 Celtic FC	6	1 1 1 3 2	0 2 1 4 5	1 3 2 7 7	6
4 SK Rapid Wien	6	1 1 1 6 6	0 1 2 2 8	1 2 3 8 14	5

Sporting striker Liedson (right) scored the only hat-trick of the group stage – against Heerenveen

UEFA Europa League

Friedhelm Funkel took the reins for a meeting with their main rivals for runners-up spot, Dutch Cup holders Heerenveen.

Hernán Losada's 36th-minute strike earned home side Heerenveen their first win in nine European outings, and the game looked up for the Bundesliga strugglers after 90 minutes of the rematch in Berlin a fortnight later. Despite twice coming from behind, a 2-2 draw better suited the visitors but Artur Wichniarek had other ideas, firing an injury-time winner. Hertha struck early next time out as they beat Ventspils, the first Latvian side to compete in the group stage of a major UEFA club competition.

Friedhelm Funkel – Hertha Berlin's third coach of the campaign

Final reckoning

Heerenveen again conceded a 91st-minute goal as they drew 1-1 at Sporting, leaving a team lying 14th in the 18-team Eredivisie needing to beat Ventspils on Matchday 6 and hope Hertha lost to Sporting to supplant the German side in second place. Jan de Jonge's side kept their side of the bargain, winning 5-0, but Gojko Kačar's 70th-minute goal in the Olympiastadion rendered that result academic.

Group D Results

17/9/09, Olympiastadion, Berlin
Hertha BSC Berlin 1-1 FK Ventspils
Attendance: 13454
Goal(s): 1-0 Piszczek 34, 1-1 Gauračs 48
Referee: Kelly (IRL)

17/9/09, Abe Lenstra, Heerenveen
sc Heerenveen 2-3 Sporting Clube de Portugal
Attendance: 13000
Goal(s): 1-0 Sibon 12, 1-1 Liedson 17, 1-2 Liedson 40, 2-2 Dingsdag 77, 2-3 Liedson 88
Referee: Nikolaev (RUS)

1/10/09, José Alvalade, Lisbon
Sporting Clube de Portugal 1-0 Hertha BSC Berlin
Attendance: 16197
Goal(s): 1-0 Adrien Silva 18
Referee: Gumienny (BEL)

1/10/09, Skonto, Riga
FK Ventspils 0-0 sc Heerenveen
Attendance: 3500
Referee: Oriekhov (UKR)

22/10/09, Olympiastadion, Berlin
Hertha BSC Berlin 0-1 sc Heerenveen
Attendance: 13134
Goal(s): 0-1 Losada 36
Referee: Kapitanis (CYP)

22/10/09, Skonto, Riga
FK Ventspils 1-2 Sporting Clube de Portugal
Attendance: 4500
Goal(s): 0-1 Miguel Veloso 6, 1-1 Laizāns 64 (p), 1-2 João Moutinho 85
Referee: Kever (SUI)

5/11/09, José Alvalade, Lisbon
Sporting Clube de Portugal 1-1 FK Ventspils
Attendance: 18103
Goal(s): 0-1 Zamperini 15, 1-1 Carlos Saleiro 22
Referee: Stavrev (MKD)

5/11/09, Abe Lenstra, Heerenveen
sc Heerenveen 2-3 Hertha BSC Berlin
Attendance: 20000
Goal(s): 1-0 Papadopulos 4, 1-1 Domovchiyski 21, 2-1 Papadopulos 36, 2-2 Domovchiyski 52, 2-3 Wichniarek 90+1
Referee: Balaj (ROU)

3/12/09, José Alvalade, Lisbon
Sporting Clube de Portugal 1-1 sc Heerenveen
Attendance: 12264
Goal(s): 0-1 Assaidi 47, 1-1 Grimi 90+1
Referee: Královec (CZE)

3/12/09, Skonto, Riga
FK Ventspils 0-1 Hertha BSC Berlin
Attendance: 7200
Goal(s): 0-1 Raffael 12
Referee: Vad (HUN)

16/12/09, Olympiastadion, Berlin
Hertha BSC Berlin 1-0 Sporting Clube de Portugal
Attendance: 14174
Goal(s): 1-0 Kačar 70
Referee: Kulbakov (BLR)

16/12/09, Abe Lenstra, Heerenveen
sc Heerenveen 5-0 FK Ventspils
Attendance: 16000
Goal(s): 1-0 Väyrynen 55, 2-0 Elm 58, 3-0 Sibon 77, 4-0 Sibon 78, 5-0 Janmaat 88
Referee: Schörgenhofer (AUT)

Group D Table

		Home					Away					Total					
	Pld	W	D	L	F	A	W	D	L	F	A	W	D	L	F	A	Pts
1 Sporting Clube de Portugal	6	1	2	0	3	2	2	0	1	5	4	3	2	1	8	6	11
2 Hertha BSC Berlin	6	1	1	1	2	2	2	0	1	4	3	3	1	2	6	5	10
3 sc Heerenveen	6	1	0	2	9	6	1	2	0	2	1	2	2	1	17	7	8
4 FK Ventspils	6	0	1	2	1	3	0	2	1	2	7	0	3	3	3	10	3

Group E

Fulham FC and PFC CSKA Sofia were considered outsiders in a section featuring two clubs who had participated in the UEFA Champions League group stage the previous season, AS Roma and FC Basel 1893.

The latter two met on Matchday 1 in Switzerland where, with CSKA and Fulham drawing 1-1 in Sofia, Basel took an early grip on Group E with a 2-0 victory. Fulham began the section unbeaten in nine home games since making their European debut in 2002, a record they extended as former Switzerland coach Roy Hodgson led his side to a 1-0 victory over Basel. That left the Londoners top of the pile, a point ahead of both Basel and a Roma team who registered their first win by defeating CSKA 2-0 at home.

Andreolli intervention

The leadership changed hands again on Matchday 3 when Marco Andreolli rescued a 1-1 draw for Roma at ten-man Fulham with a 93rd-minute equaliser, and Basel won 2-0 at CSKA. Thorsten Fink's team looked well placed to qualify after they overcame their Bulgarian opponents 3-1 in the return, while Roma once again left it late against Fulham, taking advantage of Erik Nevland's dismissal by scoring twice in the final 21 minutes to turn prospective defeat into a 2-1 win.

To remain in contention, Fulham knew victory was vital on Matchday 5 at home to CSKA, and the three points duly arrived thanks to Zoltán Gera's header. Meanwhile, Roma secured a place in the round of 32 with a 2-1 defeat of Basel, leaving the battle for second place intriguingly poised going into the final round of matches.

Judgment day

To join the Giallorossi, Basel needed to avoid defeat at home to Fulham while for the Londoners nothing less than victory would suffice on a ground where the Swiss club had won all five of their previous games during the campaign. Fulham, and Bobby Zamora in particular, ensured that run came to a halt. The striker's double before the break laid the foundations for a 3-2 win, sending Hodgson's charges through as runners-up, two points behind a Roma side that ended with a 3-0 triumph at CSKA.

Group E Results

Bobby Zamora took Fulham through to the round of 32 with two vital goals away to Basel

17/9/09, St. Jakob-Park, Basel
FC Basel 1893 2-0 AS Roma
Attendance: 16459
Goal(s): 1-0 Carlitos 11, 2-0 Almerares 87
Referee: Velasco Carballo (ESP)

17/9/09, Vasil Levski National, Sofia
PFC CSKA Sofia 1-1 Fulham FC
Attendance: 28000
Goal(s): 1-0 Michel 62, 1-1 Kamara 65
Referee: Čeferin (SVN)

1/10/09, Craven Cottage, London
Fulham FC 1-0 FC Basel 1893
Attendance: 16100
Goal(s): 1-0 Murphy 57
Referee: Weiner (GER)

1/10/09, Stadio Olimpico, Rome
AS Roma 2-0 PFC CSKA Sofia
Attendance: 16027
Goal(s): 1-0 Okaka Chuka 19, 2-0 Perrotta 23
Referee: Hriňák (SVK)

22/10/09, Craven Cottage, London
Fulham FC 1-1 AS Roma
Attendance: 23561
Goal(s): 1-0 Hangeland 24, 1-1 Andreolli 90+3
Referee: Allaerts (BEL)

22/10/09, Vasil Levski National, Sofia
PFC CSKA Sofia 0-2 FC Basel 1893
Attendance: 17664
Goal(s): 0-1 Frei 20, 0-2 Frei 63
Referee: Neves Moreira de Sousa (POR)

UEFA Europa League

Marco Andreolli strikes late to earn Roma a 1-1 draw against Fulham at Craven Cottage

Group F

Galatasaray AŞ and Panathinaikos FC rarely looked threatened as they confirmed their status as the Group F favourites, conceding just four goals apiece en route to a comfortable one-two finish. FC Dinamo Bucureşti and SK Sturm Graz played peripheral roles throughout.

UEFA Cup winners in 2000, it was Galatasaray who were quickest out of the blocks, beating Panathinaikos 3-1 on Matchday 1 in an ominous show of intent. Victory came courtesy of Elano, Milan Baroš and a Dimitrios Salpingidis own goal, the first of two the Greek side would concede during the group phase. It was not until Gilberto Silva turned into his own net to hand Galatasaray a 1-0 win on Matchday 5, however, that they were breached again.

5/11/09, St. Jakob-Park, Basel
FC Basel 1893 3-1 PFC CSKA Sofia
Attendance: 15255
Goal(s): 1-0 Gelabert 35, 2-0 Frei 41 (p), 2-1 Yanchev 61, 3-1 Frei 67
Referee: Oriekhov (UKR)

Nioplias introduction

By the time they were undone by Frank Rijkaard's charges a second time the Greek Super League runners-up were well on their way to the knockout phase, second-half goals earning three successive 1-0 wins, against Dinamo and Sturm (twice). It was a run that left them needing to avoid a two-goal reverse at home to the Romanian side to progress. They went into the game with a new coach, Nikolaos Nioplias

5/11/09, Stadio Olimpico, Rome
AS Roma 2-1 Fulham FC
Attendance: 14457
Goal(s): 0-1 Kamara 19 (p), 1-1 Riise 69, 2-1 Okaka Chuka 76
Referee: Blom (NED)

3/12/09, Craven Cottage, London
Fulham FC 1-0 PFC CSKA Sofia
Attendance: 23604
Goal(s): 1-0 Gera 15
Referee: Balaj (ROU)

3/12/09, Stadio Olimpico, Rome
AS Roma 2-1 FC Basel 1893
Attendance: 17332
Goal(s): 0-1 Huggel 18, 1-1 Totti 32 (p), 2-1 Vučinić 59
Referee: Chapron (FRA)

Galatasaray's Brazilian midfielder Elano in action against Dinamo Bucureşti

16/12/09, St. Jakob-Park, Basel
FC Basel 1893 2-3 Fulham FC
Attendance: 20063
Goal(s): 0-1 Zamora 42, 0-2 Zamora 45, 1-2 Frei 64 (p), 1-3 Gera 77, 2-3 Streller 87
Referee: Johannesson (SWE)

16/12/09, Vasil Levski National, Sofia
PFC CSKA Sofia 0-3 AS Roma
Attendance: 9700
Goal(s): 0-1 Cerci 45+1, 0-2 Cerci 52, 0-3 Scardina 89
Referee: Stavrev (MKD)

Group E Table

	Pld	Home					Away					Total					Pts
		W	D	L	F	A	W	D	L	F	A	W	D	L	F	A	
1 AS Roma	6	3	0	0	6	2	1	1	1	4	3	4	1	1	10	5	13
2 Fulham FC	6	2	1	0	3	1	1	1	1	5	5	3	2	1	8	6	11
3 FC Basel 1893	6	2	0	1	7	4	1	0	2	3	3	3	0	3	10	7	9
4 PFC CSKA Sofia	6	0	1	2	1	6	0	0	3	1	6	0	1	5	2	12	1

having replaced Henk ten Cate, and the former Greece midfielder enjoyed a charmed introduction to European football, Djibril Cissé scoring twice in a comfortable 3-0 win.

It was Galatasaray, however, that topped the pile. They followed their opening-day victory over Panathinaikos with a 1-1 draw at home to Sturm, but back-to-back triumphs (4-1 at home, 3-0 away) against a Dinamo side that went through three coaches over the course of the campaign – with Shabani Nonda scoring three times over those two games – brought a return to winning ways. The Cimbom roared into the round of 32 with their second triumph over Panathinaikos, making a last-day defeat at Sturm inconsequential – even if it did spoil a ten-match unbeaten run away from home in European competition.

It salvaged only pride for the Austrian side, who were already consigned to the foot of the section after picking up just that solitary point against Galatasaray over their first five games.

Group F Results

17/9/09, Graz Liebenau, Graz
SK Sturm Graz 0-1 FC Dinamo Bucureşti
Attendance: 15323
Goal(s): 0-1 Tamaş 80
Referee: Asumaa (FIN)

Panathinaikos striker Djibril Cissé gets in front of Sturm Graz's Mario Sonnleitner

17/9/09, OACA Spyro Louis, Athens
Panathinaikos FC 1-3 Galatasaray AŞ
Attendance: 46791
Goal(s): 0-1 Elano 5, 0-2 Baroš 48, 0-3 Sarriegi 58 (og), 1-3 Salpingidis 78
Referee: Tagliavento (ITA)

1/10/09, Dinamo, Bucharest
FC Dinamo Bucureşti 0-1 Panathinaikos FC
Attendance: 100
Goal(s): 0-1 Karagounis 79
Referee: Muñiz Fernández (ESP)

1/10/09, Ali Sami Yen, Istanbul
Galatasaray AŞ 1-1 SK Sturm Graz
Attendance: 18334
Goal(s): 0-1 Beichler 45+1, 1-1 Baroš 63
Referee: Nijhuis (NED)

22/10/09, Ali Sami Yen, Istanbul
Galatasaray AŞ 4-1 FC Dinamo Bucureşti
Attendance: 18902
Goal(s): 1-0 Kewell 32, 2-0 Nonda 42, 3-0 Nonda 46, 4-0 Elano 58 (p), 4-1 Boştină 61
Referee: Ingvarsson (SWE)

22/10/09, OACA Spyro Louis, Athens
Panathinaikos FC 1-0 SK Sturm Graz
Attendance: 31127
Goal(s): 1-0 Salpingidis 60 (p)
Referee: Rasmussen (DEN)

5/11/09, Graz Liebenau, Graz
SK Sturm Graz 0-1 Panathinaikos FC
Attendance: 15322
Goal(s): 0-1 Katsouranis 70
Referee: Královec (CZE)

5/11/09, Dinamo, Bucharest
FC Dinamo Bucureşti 0-3 Galatasaray AŞ
Goal(s): 0-1 Kewell 22, 0-2 Nonda 24, 0-3 Mehmet Topal 55
Referee: Weiner (GER)

3/12/09, Ali Sami Yen, Istanbul
Galatasaray AŞ 1-0 Panathinaikos FC
Attendance: 18566
Goal(s): 1-0 Gilberto Silva 50 (og)
Referee: Bebek (CRO)

3/12/09, Dinamo, Bucharest
FC Dinamo Bucureşti 2-1 SK Sturm Graz
Attendance: 1821
Goal(s): 0-1 Sonnleitner 5, 1-1 Niculae 41, 2-1 Niculae 57
Referee: Bruno Paixão (POR)

16/12/09, Graz Liebenau, Graz
SK Sturm Graz 1-0 Galatasaray AŞ
Attendance: 15232
Goal(s): 1-0 Beichler 21
Referee: Čeferin (SVN)

16/12/09, OACA Spyro Louis, Athens
Panathinaikos FC 3-0 FC Dinamo Bucureşti
Attendance: 19617
Goal(s): 1-0 Rukavina 54, 2-0 Cissé 80, 3-0 Cissé 85
Referee: Blom (NED)

Group F Table

		Pld	Home W D L F A	Away W D L F A	Total W D L F A	Pts
1	Galatasaray AŞ	6	2 1 0 6 2	2 0 1 6 2	4 1 1 12 4	13
2	Panathinaikos FC	6	2 0 1 5 3	2 0 1 2 1	4 0 2 7 4	12
3	FC Dinamo Bucureşti	6	1 0 2 2 5	1 0 2 2 7	2 0 4 4 12	6
4	SK Sturm Graz	6	1 0 2 1 2	0 1 2 2 4	1 1 4 3 6	4

UEFA Europa League

Admir Vladavić (left) congratulates Marc Janko after the latter's stoppage-time winner against Lazio in Rome

defeat, losing their opening two group games 1-0 to Villarreal and 4-0 to Lazio. Dostanić was consequently shown the door but his departure had little impact as Levski went on to record three more reverses before securing scant consolation with a 1-0 win at Lazio on Matchday 6, Hristo Yovov scoring their only goal of the group stage.

Cause for celebration was further restricted by the fact that their Italian hosts had already been eliminated after failing to build on their Matchday 2 drubbing of Levski and an ensuing 2-1 win against Villarreal. Beaten 4-1 by the Yellow Submarine in the rematch and 2-1 by Salzburg in their penultimate fixture, Davide Ballardini's side's wounds were salted by that closing loss to Levski. The path was thus paved for Ernesto Valverde's Liga charges to move forward into the last 32, even if they too had been left trailing in Salzburg's wake.

Group G

The group stage's only 100% record, the least prolific attack, and the meanest defence were the finer details of a section in which FC Salzburg ran riot and PFC Levski Sofia were simply run ragged.

Huub Stevens assumed the reins at Salzburg in summer 2009 and made a startling impact on the European stage, albeit on shaky foundations. The Austrian titleholders came into the competition following a deflating defeat by Maccabi Haifa FC in the UEFA Champions League play-offs and then looked set for further disappointment when S.S. Lazio's Pasquale Foggia put them behind on Matchday 1 in Rome.

Franz Schiemer levelled with eight minutes remaining, however, and Marc Janko completed the turnaround deep into added time. Salzburg never looked back. Three subsequent victories – 2-0 at home to Villarreal CF and 1-0 twice against Levski – were enough to all but secure their progression, although it was not until a 2-1 home win over Lazio on Matchday 5 that their round of 32 berth was rubber-stamped as section winners.

Levski flounder

It was a case of contrasting fortunes for the group's other three coaches, all of whom were also new to their respective posts. Ratko Dostanić's Levski side fared far worse than Salzburg in recovering from the disappointment of UEFA Champions League play-off

Group G Results

17/9/09, Stadio Olimpico, Rome
S.S. Lazio 1-2 FC Salzburg
Attendance: 12600
Goal(s): 1-0 Foggia 59, 1-1 Schiemer 82, 1-2 Janko 90+3
Referee: Ennjimi (FRA)

17/9/09, El Madrigal, Villarreal
Villarreal CF 1-0 PFC Levski Sofia
Attendance: 5244
Goal(s): 1-0 Nilmar 72
Referee: Dean (ENG)

Hristo Yovov scores Levski's only goal of the group stage - against Lazio

UEFA Europa League

EUROPA
LEAGUE

Group Stage

1/10/09, Stadion Salzburg, Salzburg
FC Salzburg 2-0 Villarreal CF
Attendance: 18800
Goal(s): 1-0 Janko 21, 2-0 Tchoyi 84
Referee: Kapitanis (CYP)

1/10/09, Georgi Asparuhov, Sofia
PFC Levski Sofia 0-4 S.S. Lazio
Attendance: 10000
Goal(s): 0-1 Matuzalém 22, 0-2 Zárate 45+1, 0-3 Meghni 67,
0-4 Rocchi 74
Referee: Ivanov (RUS)

22/10/09, Stadion Salzburg, Salzburg
FC Salzburg 1-0 PFC Levski Sofia
Attendance: 17800
Goal(s): 1-0 Švento 45+2
Referee: Kaasik (EST)

22/10/09, Stadio Olimpico, Rome
S.S. Lazio 2-1 Villarreal CF
Attendance: 14388
Goal(s): 1-0 Zárate 20, 1-1 Eguren 40, 2-1 Rocchi 90+2
Referee: Bebek (CRO)

5/11/09, El Madrigal, Villarreal
Villarreal CF 4-1 S.S. Lazio
Attendance: 14114
Goal(s): 1-0 Pirès 2, 2-0 Cani 13, 3-0 Pirès 15 (p), 3-1 Zárate 72,
4-1 Rossi 83 (p)
Referee: Kircher (GER)

5/11/09, Georgi Asparuhov, Sofia
PFC Levski Sofia 0-1 FC Salzburg
Attendance: 5000
Goal(s): 0-1 Schiemer 90+3
Referee: Çakır (TUR)

2/12/09, Stadion Salzburg, Salzburg
FC Salzburg 2-1 S.S. Lazio
Attendance: 26270
Goal(s): 1-0 Afolabi 52, 1-1 Foggia 57, 2-1 Tchoyi 78
Referee: Tudor (ROU)

2/12/09, Georgi Asparuhov, Sofia
PFC Levski Sofia 0-2 Villarreal CF
Attendance: 5600
Goal(s): 0-1 Rossi 37, 0-2 Senna 84
Referee: Allaerts (BEL)

17/12/09, Stadio Olimpico, Rome
S.S. Lazio 0-1 PFC Levski Sofia
Attendance: 8051
Goal(s): 0-1 Yovov 60
Referee: Collum (SCO)

17/12/09, El Madrigal, Villarreal
Villarreal CF 0-1 FC Salzburg
Attendance: 5860
Goal(s): 0-1 Švento 7
Referee: Hriňák (SVK)

Group H

FC Sheriff became the first Moldovan team to compete in the group stage of a UEFA club competition when they lined up in Group H alongside 1986 European champions FC Steaua Bucureşti, FC Twente and a Fenerbahçe SK side who would recover from an early setback in some style.

Hopes of a successful campaign for Sheriff were raised following a goalless draw away to Steaua on Matchday 1, although that achievement was upstaged by Twente's eye-catching 2-1 defeat of Fenerbahçe at the Şükrü Saracoğlu courtesy of two goals from veteran Swiss international striker Blaise Nkufo. Fenerbahçe were not to be denied next time out, winning 1-0 at Sheriff, while Steaua drew a blank once more, holding on for a goalless draw in Enschede.

Competitive results

Scoring was clearly Steaua's Achilles heel as the Romanian side came up short again on Matchday 3, losing 1-0 at home to a Fenerbahçe team now two points clear of Twente and Sheriff after the latter had ended Twente's 17-match unbeaten start to the season with a 2-0 victory. The Eredivisie club exacted

Blaise Nkufo of Twente contests an aerial challenge against Sheriff

Group G Table

	Pld	Home					Away					Total					Pts
		W	D	L	F	A	W	D	L	F	A	W	D	L	F	A	
1 FC Salzburg	6	3	0	0	5	1	3	0	0	4	1	6	0	0	9	2	18
2 Villarreal CF	6	2	0	1	5	2	1	0	2	3	4	3	0	3	8	6	9
3 S.S. Lazio	6	1	0	2	3	4	1	0	2	6	6	2	0	4	9	10	6
4 PFC Levski Sofia	6	0	0	3	0	7	1	0	2	1	2	1	0	5	1	9	3

UEFA Europa League

revenge two weeks later, when on-loan Chelsea FC winger Miroslav Stoch scored twice in a 2-1 win. Steaua's first goal of the section proved inconsequential at Fenerbahçe as the hosts emerged 3-1 winners.

Diego Lugano avenged Fenerbahçe's defeat at home to Twente by scoring the only goal when the teams met again on Matchday 5, a victory which confirmed the Istanbul outfit as group winners. Sheriff were well set to capitalise and move level with Twente until Juan Toja struck an 87th-minute equaliser for Steaua. The point was not enough, however, to prolong the Romanian club's interest in the competition.

Fenerbahçe celebrate Uğur Boral's winner against Sheriff in Istanbul

Steaua blunted

Needing victory on Matchday 6 to be sure of second spot, Twente's 1-1 draw at Steaua would not prove costly as Sheriff could find no answer to Uğur Boral's 15th-minute opener in Istabnbul, Fenerbahçe rounding off the section with a fifth successive win. Twente joined them in the last 32 and Sheriff earned plaudits for their efforts, yet for Steaua it was a different story. The Romanian side had won all six of their qualifying games but failed to claim a single three-point haul in the competition proper.

Group H Results

17/9/09, Steaua, Bucharest
FC Steaua Bucureşti 0-0 FC Sheriff
Referee: Královec (CZE)

17/9/09, Şükrü Saracoğlu, Istanbul
Fenerbahçe SK 1-2 FC Twente
Attendance: 27172
Goal(s): 1-0 Mehmet Topuz 71, 1-1 Nkufo 75, 1-2 Nkufo 80
Referee: Circhetta (SUI)

1/10/09, FC Twente, Enschede
FC Twente 0-0 FC Steaua Bucureşti
Attendance: 19200
Referee: Rocchi (ITA)

1/10/09, Sheriff, Tiraspol
FC Sheriff 0-1 Fenerbahçe SK
Attendance: 11634
Goal(s): 0-1 Alex 53
Referee: Stavrev (MKD)

22/10/09, Sheriff, Tiraspol
FC Sheriff 2-0 FC Twente
Attendance: 6350
Goal(s): 1-0 Balima 41, 2-0 Jymmy 90+4
Referee: Asumaa (FIN)

22/10/09, Steaua, Bucharest
FC Steaua Bucureşti 0-1 Fenerbahçe SK
Attendance: 10500
Goal(s): 0-1 Kazım Kazım 59
Referee: McDonald (SCO)

5/11/09, FC Twente, Enschede
FC Twente 2-1 FC Sheriff
Attendance: 20200
Goal(s): 1-0 Stoch 7, 1-1 Tioté 68 (og), 2-1 Stoch 89
Referee: Kulbakov (BLR)

5/11/09, Şükrü Saracoğlu, Istanbul
Fenerbahçe SK 3-1 FC Steaua Bucureşti
Attendance: 24080
Goal(s): 1-0 André Santos 15, 1-1 Kapetanos 38, 2-1 Fábio Bilica 51, 3-1 Alex 67
Referee: Einwaller (AUT)

2/12/09, FC Twente, Enschede
FC Twente 0-1 Fenerbahçe SK
Attendance: 23700
Goal(s): 0-1 Lugano 71
Referee: Muñiz Fernández (ESP)

2/12/09, Sheriff, Tiraspol
FC Sheriff 1-1 FC Steaua Bucureşti
Attendance: 10000
Goal(s): 1-0 Diedhiou 83, 1-1 Toja 87
Referee: Skjerven (NOR)

17/12/09, Steaua, Bucharest
FC Steaua Bucureşti 1-1 FC Twente
Attendance: 2400
Goal(s): 1-0 Kapetanos 18, 1-1 Stam 35
Referee: Neves Moreira de Sousa (POR)

17/12/09, Şükrü Saracoğlu, Istanbul
Fenerbahçe SK 1-0 FC Sheriff
Attendance: 15498
Goal(s): 1-0 Uğur Boral 15
Referee: Szabó (HUN)

Group H Table

		Pld	Home						Away						Total						Pts
			W	D	L	F	A		W	D	L	F	A		W	D	L	F	A		
1	Fenerbahçe SK	6	2	0	1	5	3		3	0	0	3	0		5	0	1	8	3		15
2	FC Twente	6	1	1	1	2	2		1	1	1	3	4		2	2	2	5	6		8
3	FC Sheriff	6	1	1	1	3	2		0	1	2	1	3		1	2	3	4	5		5
4	FC Steaua Bucureşti	6	0	2	1	1	2		0	2	1	2	4		0	4	2	3	6		4

Group I

SL Benfica's 5-0 defeat of Everton FC in Lisbon proved to be the group stage's most resounding victory, but both sides progressed from a section that provided more attempts on target (286) and more red cards (6) than any other.

Benfica striker Javier Saviola looks skywards after opening the scoring against Everton at Goodison Park

Alhough Everton would prove easy prey for the Eagles in the Portuguese capital, it was they who were first to catch the eye. AEK Athens FC were on the receiving end of a 4-0 Matchday 1 reverse that came courtesy of goals from Joseph Yobo, Sylvain Distin, Steven Pienaar and Jô. If such dominance from David Moyes's team was not indicative of things to come, the dismissal of a player apiece – Carlos Araujo and Louis Saha – would be symptomatic of the group as a whole.

Everton shocked

Benfica opened with a 2-0 triumph over FC BATE Borisov but ran into choppy waters on Matchday 2, losing 1-0 to ten-man AEK. The surprise nature of that result was confirmed as it turned out to be AEK's only victory and Benfica's sole defeat. Everton, meanwhile, came from behind to win 2-1 in Minsk and looked good value to take top spot. Then came the trip to Portugal.

Hugely depleted by injury, the visitors were lambs to the slaughter, two goals apiece from Javier Saviola and Óscar Cardozo and one from Luisão doing the damage. With Everton also losing 2-0 in the Goodison

Diniyar Bilyaletdinov lashes home Everton's winner against AEK in Athens

Park return, and BATE picking up four points from their AEK double-header – the first of which was a 2-1 win in which AEK ended with nine players – the group remained open with two rounds remaining.

Bilyaletdinov decider

Matchday 5 proved decisive, Diniyar Bilyaletdinov's goal giving Everton victory in rain-soaked Athens to assure them of qualification. They headed into the round of 32 as runners-up, though, Saviola again scoring for Benfica as they won 2-1 at BATE to guarantee top spot. That left only the wooden spoon to play for on Matchday 6, the dubious honour eventually going to AEK after they lost 2-1 at Benfica and BATE won 1-0 away to an experimental Everton side.

Group I Results

17/9/09, Estádio do Sport Lisboa e Benfica, Lisbon
SL Benfica 2-0 FC BATE Borisov
Attendance: 34953
Goal(s): 1-0 Nuno Gomes 36, 2-0 Cardozo 41
Referee: Kircher (GER)

17/9/09, Goodison Park, Liverpool
Everton FC 4-0 AEK Athens FC
Attendance: 26747
Goal(s): 1-0 Yobo 10, 2-0 Distin 17, 3-0 Pienaar 37, 4-0 Jô 82
Referee: Malek (POL)

UEFA Europa League

1/10/09, OACA Spyro Louis, Athens
AEK Athens FC 1-0 SL Benfica
Attendance: 12420
Goal(s): 1-0 Majstorović 43
Referee: Johannesson (SWE)

1/10/09, Dinamo, Minsk
FC BATE Borisov 1-2 Everton FC
Attendance: 21200
Goal(s): 1-0 Likhtarovich 16, 1-1 Fellaini 68, 1-2 Cahill 77
Referee: Balaj (ROU)

22/10/09, Estádio do Sport Lisboa e Benfica, Lisbon
SL Benfica 5-0 Everton FC
Attendance: 44534
Goal(s): 1-0 Saviola 14, 2-0 Cardozo 47, 3-0 Cardozo 48, 4-0 Luisão 52, 5-0 Saviola 83
Referee: Ivanov (RUS)

22/10/09, Dinamo, Minsk
FC BATE Borisov 2-1 AEK Athens FC
Attendance: 9200
Goal(s): 0-1 Blanco 31 (p), 1-1 Pavlov 51, 2-1 Alumona 85
Referee: Szabó (HUN)

5/11/09, Goodison Park, Liverpool
Everton FC 0-2 SL Benfica
Attendance: 30790
Goal(s): 0-1 Saviola 63, 0-2 Cardozo 76
Referee: Ennjimi (FRA)

5/11/09, OACA Spyro Louis, Athens
AEK Athens FC 2-2 FC BATE Borisov
Attendance: 9716
Goal(s): 1-0 Blanco 1, 1-1 Rodionov 17, 1-2 A. Volodko 26, 2-2 Manduca 38
Referee: Yefet (ISR)

2/12/09, Dinamo, Minsk
FC BATE Borisov 1-2 SL Benfica
Attendance: 11200
Goal(s): 0-1 Saviola 46, 0-2 Fábio Coentrão 63, 1-2 Miguel Vítor 68 (og)
Referee: Einwaller (AUT)

2/12/09, OACA Spyro Louis, Athens
AEK Athens FC 0-1 Everton FC
Attendance: 12141
Goal(s): 0-1 Bilyaletdinov 6
Referee: Circhetta (SUI)

17/12/09, Estádio do Sport Lisboa e Benfica, Lisbon
SL Benfica 2-1 AEK Athens FC
Attendance: 20155
Goal(s): 1-0 Di María 45, 2-0 Di María 73, 2-1 Blanco 84
Referee: Rocchi (ITA)

17/12/09, Goodison Park, Liverpool
Everton FC 0-1 FC BATE Borisov
Attendance: 18242
Goal(s): 0-1 Yurevich 75
Referee: Dereli (TUR)

Group I Table

	Pld	Home W D L F A	Away W D L F A	Total W D L F A	Pts
1 SL Benfica	6	3 0 0 9 1	2 0 1 4 2	5 0 1 13 3	15
2 Everton FC	6	1 0 2 4 3	2 0 1 3 6	3 0 3 7 9	9
3 FC BATE Borisov	6	1 0 2 4 5	1 1 1 3 4	2 1 3 7 9	7
4 AEK Athens FC	6	1 1 1 3 3	0 0 3 2 8	1 1 4 5 11	4

Group J

FC Shakhtar Donetsk blew away the opposition with their free-scoring displays, but it was the battle for second place between Club Brugge KV and Toulouse FC that provided the real intrigue in Group J.

Shakhtar showed no sign of any hangover after being surprisingly eliminated from UEFA Champions League qualifying, an opening-day 4-1 win at Club Brugge staking an early claim for supremacy. Toulouse, meanwhile, came from behind to defeat Partizan in Belgrade 3-2 thanks to two goals from Pantxi Sirieix.

Shakhtar irresistible

Partizan were the next to feel the force of Shakhtar's attacking armoury as they lost 4-1 in Ukraine, while the intervention of Ivan Perišić in added time salvaged Club Brugge a 2-2 draw with Toulouse that kept the French club in touching distance. Brugge moved level with Les Pitchounes on Matchday 3 thanks to a 2-0 victory – their 100th in UEFA competition – over bottom-placed Partizan, while Toulouse became the third side on the receiving end of four Shakhtar goals.

Shakhtar's Fernandinho shows his pleasure at scoring from the penalty spot against Toulouse

The UEFA Cup holders were restricted to two goals next time out, but the outcome remained the same as Shakhtar won again, 2-0 in Toulouse, to qualify for the last 32 with two matches to spare. Club Brugge took full advantage with a 4-2 triumph at Partizan, which ended the Serbian outfit's interest in the competition and lifted the visitors three points clear of Toulouse.

Showdown

Shakhtar's perfect record came to an end on Matchday 5 with a 0-0 draw against Club Brugge while Toulouse were busy edging past Partizan thanks to Daniel Braaten's second-half goal. It lifted Alain Casanova's team to within a point of their qualification rivals and set up a showdown to decide who would progress alongside Shakhtar, 1-0 losers to Partizan in snowy Belgrade on Matchday 6.

The French visitors had their chances in Bruges, with André-Pierre Gignac always a threat, and the game hung in the balance until the 93rd minute when, with Toulouse pushing for the goal they needed, Perišić slotted in at the other end.

Club Brugge's Croatian striker Ivan Perišić opened the scoring in both ties against Serbian champions Partizan

Group J Results

17/9/09, Jan Breydel, Bruges
Club Brugge KV 1-4 FC Shakhtar Donetsk
Attendance: 17770
Goal(s): 0-1 Hai 11, 0-2 Willian 19, 0-3 Srna 35, 1-3 Geraerts 62, 1-4 Kravchenko 75
Referee: Ingvarsson (SWE)

17/9/09, FK Partizan, Belgrade
FK Partizan 2-3 Toulouse FC
Attendance: 13860
Goal(s): 1-0 Krstajić 23, 1-1 Sirieix 30, 1-2 Sirieix 38, 1-3 Devaux 49, 2-3 Cléo 67
Referee: Dereli (TUR)

1/10/09, Stadium Municipal, Toulouse
Toulouse FC 2-2 Club Brugge KV
Attendance: 12275
Goal(s): 0-1 Akpala 52, 1-1 Sissoko 54, 2-1 Gignac 84, 2-2 Perišić 90+4
Referee: Kever (SUI)

1/10/09, Donbass Arena, Donetsk
FC Shakhtar Donetsk 4-1 FK Partizan
Attendance: 49480
Goal(s): 1-0 Lomić 24 (og), 2-0 Luiz Adriano 39, 3-0 Jádson 54, 4-0 Rakytskiy 67, 4-1 Ljajić 86
Referee: Collum (SCO)

22/10/09, Jan Breydel, Bruges
Club Brugge KV 2-0 FK Partizan
Attendance: 18903
Goal(s): 1-0 Perišić 4, 2-0 Brežančić 58 (og)
Referee: Dean (ENG)

22/10/09, Donbass Arena, Donetsk
FC Shakhtar Donetsk 4-0 Toulouse FC
Attendance: 50217
Goal(s): 1-0 Fernandinho 7 (p), 2-0 Luiz Adriano 24, 3-0 Hübschman 38, 4-0 Luiz Adriano 56
Referee: Bruno Paixão (POR)

5/11/09, Stadium Municipal, Toulouse
Toulouse FC 0-2 FC Shakhtar Donetsk
Attendance: 12046
Goal(s): 0-1 Luiz Adriano 49, 0-2 Hai 63
Referee: Muñiz Fernández (ESP)

5/11/09, FK Partizan, Belgrade
FK Partizan 2-4 Club Brugge KV
Attendance: 6290
Goal(s): 0-1 Perišić 28, 0-2 Kouemaha 36, 1-2 Ljajić 52, 1-3 Kouemaha 57, 2-3 Washington 66, 2-4 Odjidja-Ofoe 74
Referee: Schörgenhofer (AUT)

3/12/09, Stadium Municipal, Toulouse
Toulouse FC 1-0 FK Partizan
Attendance: 11123
Goal(s): 1-0 Braaten 54
Referee: Jakobsson (ISL)

3/12/09, Donbass Arena, Donetsk
FC Shakhtar Donetsk 0-0 Club Brugge KV
Attendance: 46089
Referee: Szabó (HUN)

16/12/09, Jan Breydel, Bruges
Club Brugge KV 1-0 Toulouse FC
Attendance: 23668
Goal(s): 1-0 Perišić 90+3
Referee: Moen (NOR)

16/12/09, FK Partizan, Belgrade
FK Partizan 1-0 FC Shakhtar Donetsk
Attendance: 2000
Goal(s): 1-0 Diarra 6
Referee: Weiner (GER)

Group J Table

		Pld	Home					Away					Total					Pts
			W	D	L	F	A	W	D	L	F	A	W	D	L	F	A	
1	FC Shakhtar Donetsk	6	2	1	0	8	1	2	0	1	6	2	4	1	1	14	3	13
2	Club Brugge KV	6	2	0	1	4	4	1	2	0	6	4	3	2	1	10	8	11
3	Toulouse FC	6	1	1	1	3	4	1	0	2	3	7	2	1	3	6	11	7
4	FK Partizan	6	1	0	2	5	7	0	0	3	1	7	1	0	5	6	14	3

UEFA Europa League

Group K

A resolute defence would prove the foundation for PSV Eindhoven's successful navigation through the waters of Group K as the Eredivisie outfit kept four clean sheets on their way to the round of 32.

Two of the three goals Fred Rutten's team conceded arrived on Matchday 1, when PSV were indebted to Brazilian import Jonathan Reis for securing a 2-2 draw at AC Sparta Praha. CFR 1907 Cluj had participated in the UEFA Champions League group stage the previous season and, as with their famous triumph over AS Roma at the Stadio Olimpico, the Transylvanian club kicked off with a win, defeating FC København 2-0.

All change

That would be as good as it got for CFR, however, as they narrowly lost to PSV on Matchday 2 while København defeated Sparta 1-0 in the Danish capital. A solitary goal from Reis, who had earlier had a penalty saved, proved the difference against FCK next time out as PSV consolidated their position at the summit, but perhaps the biggest story of the night was Sparta climbing off the bottom into second courtesy of a 2-0 defeat of CFR.

Jonathan Reis scored four goals in the group stage for PSV

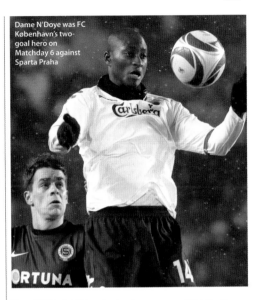

Dame N'Doye was FC København's two-goal hero on Matchday 6 against Sparta Praha

Bony Wilfried's 95th-minute winner ensured the Czech outfit completed the double over their Romanian opponents, which, coupled with PSV drawing 1-1 in Denmark, left Jozef Chovanec's team within a point of top spot and handily placed to progress with two matches remaining. The next of those ended in a narrow 1-0 loss to PSV – for whom Reis was again on target, on this occasion in added time – which resulted in Sparta relinquishing second spot to København, 2-0 winners against CFR, on head-to-head comparison.

Dual for second

That meant only a win would do for Sparta on Matchday 6 against their Danish visitors, who had not yet scored on the road. Dame N'Doye put that right with two goals in eight first-half minutes before Jesper Grønkjær added the third from the penalty spot. A thoroughly dispiriting night for the hosts was compounded with the dismissal of Manuel Pamić on the hour.

Group K Results

17/9/09, Generali Arena, Prague
AC Sparta Praha 2-2 PSV Eindhoven
Attendance: 16703
Goal(s): 1-0 Hubník 76, 1-1 Reis 80, 2-1 Zeman 87, 2-2 Reis 90+1 (p)
Referee: McDonald (SCO)

17/9/09, Dr Constantin Rădulescu, Cluj-Napoca
CFR 1907 Cluj 2-0 FC København
Attendance: 9000
Goal(s): 1-0 Culio 53, 2-0 Traoré 75
Referee: Kulbakov (BLR)

UEFA Europa League

1/10/09, Parken, Copenhagen
FC København 1-0 AC Sparta Praha
Attendance: 15043
Goal(s): 1-0 N'Doye 25
Referee: Kaasik (EST)

1/10/09, PSV Stadion, Eindhoven
PSV Eindhoven 1-0 CFR 1907 Cluj
Attendance: 13500
Goal(s): 1-0 Bakkal 9
Referee: Skjerven (NOR)

22/10/09, PSV Stadion, Eindhoven
PSV Eindhoven 1-0 FC København
Attendance: 17000
Goal(s): 1-0 Reis 72
Referee: Kelly (IRL)

22/10/09, Generali Arena, Prague
AC Sparta Praha 2-0 CFR 1907 Cluj
Attendance: 10134
Goal(s): 1-0 Kucka 15, 2-0 Hubník 32
Referee: Nikolaev (RUS)

5/11/09, Parken, Copenhagen
FC København 1-1 PSV Eindhoven
Attendance: 21605
Goal(s): 1-0 Grønkjær 40 (p), 1-1 Dzsudzsák 72
Referee: Hriňák (SVK)

5/11/09, Dr Constantin Rădulescu, Cluj-Napoca
CFR 1907 Cluj 2-3 AC Sparta Praha
Attendance: 7227
Goal(s): 0-1 Holenda 6, 0-2 Holenda 13, 1-2 Traoré 25, 2-2 Dubarbier 90+1, 2-3 Wilfried 90+5
Referee: Dereli (TUR)

3/12/09, PSV Stadion, Eindhoven
PSV Eindhoven 1-0 AC Sparta Praha
Attendance: 26400
Goal(s): 1-0 Reis 90+1
Referee: Ingvarsson (SWE)

3/12/09, Parken, Copenhagen
FC København 2-0 CFR 1907 Cluj
Attendance: 11567
Goal(s): 1-0 Vingaard 37, 2-0 N'Doye 43
Referee: Čeferin (SVN)

16/12/09, Generali Arena, Prague
AC Sparta Praha 0-3 FC København
Attendance: 17151
Goal(s): 0-1 N'Doye 22, 0-2 N'Doye 30, 0-3 Grønkjær 54 (p)
Referee: Kever (SUI)

16/12/09, Dr Constantin Rădulescu, Cluj-Napoca
CFR 1907 Cluj 0-2 PSV Eindhoven
Attendance: 3000
Goal(s): 0-1 Lazović 19 (p), 0-2 Amrabat 68
Referee: Ennjimi (FRA)

Group L

Beaten finalists in the last edition of the UEFA Cup, Werder Bremen showed no signs of any lingering disappointment as they contributed 17 of the 42 goals that made Group L the most prolific section in the inaugural UEFA Europa League.

Having eliminated FC Zenit St Petersburg in the play-offs, CD Nacional looked set for another eye-catching result on Matchday 1 when they recovered from two goals down at home to Bremen, only for Claudio Pizarro to strike the decisive blow with five minutes remaining. Athletic Club, meanwhile, were busy dispatching FK Austria Wien 3-0, striker Fernando Llorente beginning what would be a fruitful campaign by scoring two of the Basque club's goals.

Nacional woe

Llorente struck again on Matchday 2, although it would provide no more than consolation as Bremen ran out 3-1 winners in the Weserstadion, the German outfit now sitting pretty after two games with a three-point lead at the summit. Nacional and Austria each got off the mark with a 1-1 draw in Vienna but, as in their opening game, a late goal would prove the Madeiran club's undoing next time out.

Llorente scored it, his fourth in three games earning Athletic a 2-1 home win that left Joaquín Caparrós's charges comfortably in second place behind a Bremen team who dropped their first points by drawing 2-2 with Austria. Bremen made amends in the reverse fixture

Werder Bremen's Claudio Pizarro enjoys his winning goal against Nacional in Madeira

Group K Table

	Pld	Home					Away					Total					Pts
		W	D	L	F	A	W	D	L	F	A	W	D	L	F	A	
1 PSV Eindhoven	6	3	0	0	3	0	1	2	0	5	3	4	2	0	8	3	14
2 FC København	6	2	1	0	4	1	1	0	2	3	3	3	1	2	7	4	10
3 AC Sparta Praha	6	1	1	1	4	5	1	0	2	3	4	2	1	3	7	9	7
4 CFR 1907 Cluj	6	1	0	2	4	5	0	0	3	0	5	1	0	5	4	10	3

with a 2-0 victory that confirmed their qualification, while for the third time in four matches Nacional conceded in the final five minutes, Joseba Etxeberria's penalty salvaging a 1-1 draw for visitors Athletic.

European record

There was to be no let-up in Bremen's performance as Thomas Schaaf's team then defeated Nacional 4-1 at home. Athletic followed Bremen into the next round thanks to a 3-0 defeat of Austria, inspired by two more Llorente goals, the upshot being a meeting of the clubs on Matchday 6 to determine who would progress as group winners. Bremen duly completed the double over their Spanish hosts with a 3-0 win, while Nacional rounded off their first group-stage campaign in UEFA club competition by recording their biggest European win, 5-1 at home to Austria.

Fernando Llorente scored six times in Group L for Athletic

Group L Results

17/9/09, Estádio da Madeira, Funchal
CD Nacional 2-3 Werder Bremen
Attendance: 3082
Goal(s): 0-1 Frings 39 (p), 0-2 Pizarro 55, 1-2 Felipe Lopes 68, 2-2 Halliche 75, 2-3 Pizarro 85
Referee: Moen (NOR)

17/9/09, San Mamés, Bilbao
Athletic Club 3-0 FK Austria Wien
Attendance: 26000
Goal(s): 1-0 Llorente 8 (p), 2-0 Llorente 24, 3-0 Muniain 56
Referee: Blom (NED)

1/10/09, Weserstadion, Bremen
Werder Bremen 3-1 Athletic Club
Attendance: 24305
Goal(s): 1-0 Hunt 18, 2-0 Naldo 41, 2-1 Llorente 90+1, 3-1 Frings 90+4 (p)
Referee: Tudor (ROU)

1/10/09, Franz Horr, Vienna
FK Austria Wien 1-1 CD Nacional
Attendance: 11000
Goal(s): 0-1 Rúben Micael 35, 1-1 Schumacher 76
Referee: Chapron (FRA)

22/10/09, Franz Horr, Vienna
FK Austria Wien 2-2 Werder Bremen
Attendance: 11000
Goal(s): 0-1 Pizarro 19, 0-2 Pizarro 63, 1-2 Sulimani 73, 2-2 Schumacher 87
Referee: Tagliavento (ITA)

22/10/09, San Mamés, Bilbao
Athletic Club 2-1 CD Nacional
Attendance: 24569
Goal(s): 0-1 Rúben Micael 42, 1-1 Etxeberria 67, 2-1 Llorente 86
Referee: Vad (HUN)

5/11/09, Estádio da Madeira, Funchal
CD Nacional 1-1 Athletic Club
Attendance: 2945
Goal(s): 1-0 Edgar Silva 64 (p), 1-1 Etxeberria 85 (p)
Referee: Collum (SCO)

5/11/09, Weserstadion, Bremen
Werder Bremen 2-0 FK Austria Wien
Attendance: 25121
Goal(s): 1-0 Borowski 81, 2-0 Hugo Almeida 84
Referee: Johannesson (SWE)

3/12/09, Franz Horr, Vienna
FK Austria Wien 0-3 Athletic Club
Attendance: 11500
Goal(s): 0-1 Llorente 19, 0-2 San José 62, 0-3 Llorente 84
Referee: Moen (NOR)

3/12/09, Weserstadion, Bremen
Werder Bremen 4-1 CD Nacional
Attendance: 23784
Goal(s): 1-0 Rosenberg 31, 2-0 Rosenberg 34, 2-1 Rúben Micael 61, 3-1 Marcelo Moreno 84, 4-1 Marin 90+2
Referee: Yefet (ISR)

16/12/09, Estádio da Madeira, Funchal
CD Nacional 5-1 FK Austria Wien
Attendance: 1368
Goal(s): 0-1 Schumacher 21, 1-1 Rúben Micael 23, 2-1 Mateus 32, 3-1 Rúben Micael 57, 4-1 Tomašević 61, 5-1 Felipe Lopes 66
Referee: Kapitanis (CYP)

16/12/09, San Mamés, Bilbao
Athletic Club 0-3 Werder Bremen
Attendance: 27500
Goal(s): 0-1 Pizarro 13, 0-2 Naldo 20, 0-3 Rosenberg 36
Referee: Gumienny (BEL)

Group L Table

	Pld	Home W D L F A					Away W D L F A					Total W D L F A					Pts
1 Werder Bremen	6	3	0	0	9	2	2	1	0	8	4	5	1	0	17	6	16
2 Athletic Club	6	2	0	1	5	4	1	1	1	5	4	3	1	2	10	8	10
3 CD Nacional	6	1	1	1	8	5	0	1	2	3	7	1	2	3	11	12	5
4 FK Austria Wien	6	0	2	1	3	6	0	0	3	1	10	0	2	4	4	16	2

ROUND OF 32

AFC Ajax, AS Roma and 2008/09 UEFA Cup winners FC Shakhtar Donetsk were all high-prolife casualties in the round of 32 as the UEFA Europa League received an injection of talent in the form of clubs who finished third in the eight UEFA Champions League groups – Juventus, VfL Wolfsburg, Olympique de Marseille, Liverpool FC, FC Rubin Kazan, Club Atlético de Madrid, FC Unirea Urziceni and R. Standard de Liège.

Juve triumph

Of the eight sides parachuting down from Europe's top club competition, only Unirea did not make it to the next phase, losing 1-0 at home and 3-1 away against Liverpool. The Reds' Merseyside neighbours Everton FC were unable to join them in the round of 16, though, losing 3-0 at Sporting Clube de Portugal after winning the home leg 2-1.

Arguably the tie of the round brought together former European champions Juve and AFC Ajax. The pacy young Serbian, Miralem Sulejmani, broke the deadlock for the home side in Amsterdam but it was Juventus striker Amauri who stole the headlines as his two headers put the Bianconeri in charge. "Two or three chances and two beautiful goals – it was perfect for us," said Juve playmaker Diego, though Hasan Salihamidžić's added-time dismissal tempered the celebrations. A chanceless 0-0 draw in Turin saw them through.

Big guns silenced

Opportunities were rather easier to come by in AS Roma's double-header against Panathinaikos FC. The Giallorossi were Europe's in-form team as they went into the tie 20 matches unbeaten but, after the Greens had twice equalised, Djibril Cissé's last-minute winner ended that sequence in Athens. The French international was on target again in the return, scoring twice, but it was teenager Sotiris Ninis who caught the eye. In the space of six minutes before half-time he won a penalty, scored, and teed up Cissé for the third as the game again finished 3-2 in favour of the Greek side.

Shakhtar's early exit was no less surprising. Mircea Lucescu's side played beautifully to start with against Fulham FC at Craven Cottage but were never able to

fully recover from Bobby Zamora's thunderbolt that earned the Londoners a 2-1 advantage. Despite dominating again at home, it ended 1-1 in Donetsk. Lucescu's old side Galatasaray AŞ also bowed out, with Diego Forlán's 90th-minute goal in Istanbul earning Atlético a 2-1 win on the night and a 3-2 aggregate success. Fenerbahçe SK also came unstuck, Adil Rami's late goal earning LOSC Lille Métropole a 1-1 draw at the Şükrü Saraçoğlu Stadium and a 3-2 success overall.

Hamburg pushed

Beaten 2008/09 UEFA Cup finalists Werder Bremen, Wolfsburg, SL Benfica and RSC Anderlecht all scored four second-leg goals to eliminate FC Twente, Villarreal CF, Hertha BSC Berlin and Athletic Club, respectively. A 3-0 first-leg win in freezing Tatarstan set FC Rubin Kazan on their way against Hapoel Tel-Aviv FC, while a 3-2 home win (after going two goals down) proved enough to see Standard past the standout performers of the group stage, FC Salzburg.

Marseille won 3-1 away and at home against FC København, a 3-2 loss in the Netherlands earned Hamburger SV an away-goals win against PSV Eindhoven while, in the only tie to go to extra time, Valencia CF's Pablo Hernández struck twice to kill off Club Brugge KV.

Amauri of Juventus – his two headers accounted for Ajax in Amsterdam

UEFA Europa League

Round of 32 Results

16/2/10, Goodison Park, Liverpool
Everton FC 2-1 Sporting Clube de Portugal
Attendance: 28131
Goal(s): 1-0 Pienaar 35, 2-0 Distin 49,
2-1 Miguel Veloso 87 (p)
Referee: Čeferin (SVN)
25/2/10, José Alvalade, Lisbon
Sporting Clube de Portugal 3-0 Everton FC
Attendance: 17609
Goal(s): 1-0 Miguel Veloso 65, 2-0 Pedro
Mendes 76, 3-0 Matías Fernández 90+4
Referee: Yefet (ISR)
Aggregate: 4-2; Sporting Clube de Portugal qualify.

18/2/10, Centralniy, Kazan
FC Rubin Kazan 3-0 Hapoel Tel-Aviv FC
Attendance: 7152
Goal(s): 1-0 Bukharov 14, 2-0 Bukharov 23,
3-0 Semak 69
Referee: Collum (SCO)
25/2/10, Bloomfield, Tel-Aviv
Hapoel Tel-Aviv FC 0-0 FC Rubin Kazan
Attendance: 11330
Referee: Královec (CZE)
Aggregate: 0-3; FC Rubin Kazan qualify.

18/2/10, Amsterdam ArenA, Amsterdam
AFC Ajax 1-2 Juventus
Attendance: 51676
Goal(s): 1-0 Sulejmani 17, 1-1 Amauri 32,
1-2 Amauri 58
Referee: Bebek (CRO)
25/2/10, Stadio Olimpico, Turin
Juventus 0-0 AFC Ajax
Attendance: 16441
Referee: Duhamel (FRA)
Aggregate: 2-1; Juventus qualify.

18/2/10, Jan Breydel, Bruges
Club Brugge KV 1-0 Valencia CF
Attendance: 21657
Goal(s): 1-0 Kouemaha 56
Referee: Chapron (FRA)
25/2/10, Mestalla, Valencia
Valencia CF 3-0 Club Brugge KV (aet)
Attendance: 45297
Goal(s): 1-0 Mata 1, 2-0 Pablo Hernández 96,
3-0 Pablo Hernández 117
Referee: Larsen (DEN)
Aggregate: 3-1; Valencia CF qualify after extra time.

18/2/10, El Madrigal, Villarreal
Villarreal CF 2-2 VfL Wolfsburg
Attendance: 11384
Goal(s): 1-0 Senna 43, 1-1 Grafite 65, 1-2
Grafite 84 (p), 2-2 Marco Rubén 85
Referee: Blom (NED)
25/2/10, VfL Wolfsburg Arena, Wolfsburg
VfL Wolfsburg 4-1 Villarreal CF
Attendance: 16613
Goal(s): 1-0 Džeko 10, 2-0 Ángel 15 (og),
2-1 Capdevila 30, 3-1 Gentner 42, 4-1 Grafite 64
Referee: Tudor (ROU)
Aggregate: 6-3; VfL Wolfsburg qualify.

18/2/10, Maurice Dufrasne, Liege
R. Standard de Liège 3-2 FC Salzburg
Attendance: 20168
Goal(s): 0-1 Janko 4, 0-2 Janko 45, 1-2 Witsel 66 (p),
2-2 De Camargo 80, 3-2 Witsel 82
Referee: Balaj (ROU)

25/2/10, Stadion Salzburg, Salzburg
FC Salzburg 0-0 R. Standard de Liège
Attendance: 26500
Referee: Kelly (IRL)
Aggregate: 2-3; R. Standard de Liège qualify.

18/2/10, FC Twente, Enschede
FC Twente 1-0 Werder Bremen
Attendance: 22000
Goal(s): 1-0 Janssen 39
Referee: Cardoso Cortez Batista (POR)
25/2/10, Weserstadion, Bremen
Werder Bremen 4-1 FC Twente
Attendance: 20963
Goal(s): 1-0 Pizarro 15, 2-0 Pizarro 20,
3-0 Naldo 27, 3-1 De Jong 33, 4-1 Pizarro 58
Referee: Jakobsson (ISL)
Aggregate: 4-2; Werder Bremen qualify.

18/2/10, Lille Métropole, Villeneuve d'Ascq
LOSC Lille Métropole 2-1 Fenerbahçe SK
Attendance: 16783
Goal(s): 1-0 Balmont 3, 1-1 Wederson 5,
2-1 Frau 52
Referee: Iturralde González (ESP)
25/2/10, Şükrü Saracoğlu, Istanbul
Fenerbahçe SK 1-0 LOSC Lille Métropole
Attendance: 38740
Goal(s): 1-0 Emre Belözoğlu 35, 1-1 Rami 85
Referee: Meyer (GER)
Aggregate: 2-3; LOSC Lille Métropole qualify.

18/2/10, Craven Cottage, London
Fulham FC 2-1 FC Shakhtar Donetsk
Attendance: 21832
Goal(s): 1-0 Gera 3, 1-1 Luiz Adriano 32,
2-1 Zamora 63
Referee: Gumienny (BEL)
25/2/10, Donbass Arena, Donetsk
FC Shakhtar Donetsk 1-1 Fulham FC
Attendance: 47509
Goal(s): 0-1 Hangeland 33, 1-1 Jádson 69
Referee: Moen (NOR)
Aggregate: 2-3; Fulham FC qualify.

18/2/10, Anfield, Liverpool
Liverpool FC 1-0 FC Unirea Urziceni
Attendance: 40450
Goal(s): 1-0 N'Gog 81
Referee: Braamhaar (NED)
25/2/10, Steaua, Bucharest
FC Unirea Urziceni 1-3 Liverpool FC
Attendance: 17632
Goal(s): 1-0 Bruno Fernandes 19, 1-1
Mascherano 30, 1-2 Babel 41, 1-3 Gerrard 57
Referee: Johannesson (SWE)
Aggregate: 1-4; Liverpool FC qualify.

18/2/10, San Mamés, Bilbao
Athletic Club 1-1 RSC Anderlecht
Attendance: 38000
Goal(s): 0-1 Biglia 35, 1-1 San José 58
Referee: Trefoloni (ITA)
25/2/10, Constant Vanden Stock, Brussels
RSC Anderlecht 4-0 Athletic Club
Attendance: 19858
Goal(s): 1-0 Lukaku 4, 2-0 San José 27 (og),
3-0 Juhász 49, 4-0 Legear 68
Referee: Einwaller (AUT)
Aggregate: 5-1; RSC Anderlecht qualify.

18/2/10, Parken, Copenhagen
FC København 1-3 Olympique de Marseille
Attendance: 20334
Goal(s): 0-1 Niang 72, 1-1 Grønkjær 79 (p),
1-2 Ben Arfa 84, 1-3 Kaboré 90
Referee: Velasco Carballo (ESP)
25/2/10, Vélodrome, Marseille
Olympique de Marseille 3-1 FC København
Attendance: 27195
Goal(s): 1-0 Ben Arfa 84, 2-0 Koné 62, 3-0 Koné 78,
3-1 Aîlton 86
Referee: Çakır (TUR)
Aggregate: 6-2; Olympique de Marseille qualify.

18/2/10, Vicente Calderón, Madrid
Club Atlético de Madrid 1-1 Galatasaray AŞ
Attendance: 28056
Goal(s): 1-0 Reyes 23, 1-1 Keita 77
Referee: Nikolaev (RUS)
25/2/10, Ali Sami Yen, Istanbul
Galatasaray AŞ 1-2 Club Atlético de Madrid
Attendance: 22747
Goal(s): 0-1 Simão 63, 1-1 Keita 66, 1-2 Forlán 90
Referee: Rocchi (ITA)
Aggregate: 2-3; Club Atlético de Madrid qualify.

18/2/10, Hamburg Arena, Hamburg
Hamburger SV 1-0 PSV Eindhoven
Attendance: 35672
Goal(s): 1-0 Jansen 26 (p)
Referee: Circhetta (SUI)
25/2/10, PSV Stadion, Eindhoven
PSV Eindhoven 3-2 Hamburger SV
Attendance: 32000
Goal(s): 0-1 Toivonen 2, 2-0 Dzsudzsák 43,
2-1 Petrić 46, 2-2 Trochowski 79 (p), 3-2
Koevermans 90
Referee: Dean (ENG)
Aggregate: 3-3; Hamburger SV qualify on
away goals.

18/2/10, Olympiastadion, Berlin
Hertha BSC Berlin 1-1 SL Benfica
Attendance: 13684
Goal(s): 0-1 Di María 4, 1-1 Javi García 33 (og)
Referee: Hauge (NOR)
23/2/10, Estádio da Sport Lisboa e Benfica, Lisbon
SL Benfica 4-0 Hertha BSC Berlin
Attendance: 30402
Goal(s): 1-0 Aimar 25, 2-0 Cardozo 48,
3-0 Javi García 59, 4-0 Cardozo 62
Referee: Vink (NED)
Aggregate: 5-1; SL Benfica qualify.

18/2/10, OACA Spyro Louis, Athens
Panathinaikos FC 3-2 AS Roma
Attendance: 54274
Goal(s): 0-1 Vučinić 29, 1-1 Salpingidis 67,
1-2 Pizarro 81 (p), 2-2 Hristodoulopoulos 84,
3-2 Cissé 89
Referee: Skomina (SVN)
25/2/10, Stadio Olimpico, Rome
AS Roma 2-3 Panathinaikos FC
Attendance: 47825
Goal(s): 0-1 Riise 11, 1-1 Cissé 40 (p),
1-2 Ninis 43, 1-3 Cissé 45+1, 2-3 De Rossi 67
Referee: Bruno Paixão (POR)
Aggregate: 4-6; Panathinaikos FC qualify.

ROUND OF 16

The round of 16 enabled the UEFA Europa League to step temporarily out of the UEFA Champions League's shadow. Some tight, eventful first legs laid the foundations for some tense, gripping action a week later. And as the dust settled at the end of an exhausting evening of twists, turns and no fewer than 34 goals, eight clubs proceeded into the quarter-finals.

Juan Mata (right) celebrates with team-mate David Villa after putting Valencia 2-0 up in Bremen

Weser wonder

Eight of those goals came at the Weserstadion, where, having drawn the first leg 1-1, Werder Bremen and Valencia CF played out a memorable match. The depleted visitors were 2-0 up inside 15 minutes thanks to goals from David Villa and Juan Mata and, although Hugo Almeida pulled one back, Villa's second on the stroke of half-time looked decisive.

Yet dramatic European comebacks and Werder go hand in hand – the club's history is graced by countless 'Wunder von der Weser'. Torsten Frings converted a 57th-minute penalty and Marko Marin made it 3-3. Villa then raced away to fire Valencia's fourth, and put his team through, although not before Claudio Pizarro's 84th-minute equaliser had ensured a frenetic finale.

Juventus defender Jonathan Zebina is sent off against Fulham

Fulham shock Juve

Hat-trick hero Villa described it as "the craziest game I've ever played in"; an epithet that could have been applied to a few matches, not least the one at Craven Cottage. The writing appeared to be on the wall for Fulham FC when a second-minute goal from David Trezeguet put Italian giants Juventus 4-1 up on aggregate in their tie. But 88 minutes is a long time in football – long enough, in fact, for Juve to have two men sent off and for Fulham to score four goals – through Bobby Zamora, Zoltán Gera (two) and, with a memorable chip eight minutes from time, Clint Dempsey.

The Bianconeri were therefore left to rue squandering a 3-1 first-leg lead, and Hamburger SV were in a similar boat 15 minutes from time at RSC Anderlecht. The final hosts had been cruising after Jerome Boateng's 42nd-minute opener, only for Romelu Lukaku's header and a Matías Suárez penalty to put Anderlecht ahead before the break. Marcell Jansen's early second-half strike dampened home hopes, but efforts from Lucas Biglia and Mbark Boussoufa left Hamburg vulnerable until Mladen Petrić found the net 15 minutes before the end.

Last-gasp winners

SL Benfica and VfL Wolfsburg left it even later to claim 3-2 aggregate victories, with each indebted to the intervention of substitutes. Mid-season signing Alan Kardec silenced the Stade Vélodrome with an added-time decider for the Lisbon Eagles against Olympique de Marseille, while in Wolfsburg Obafemi Martins

UEFA Europa League

came off the bench to score one and set up Christian Gentner for a 119th-minute winner to ruin FC Rubin Kazan's dreams.

Sergio Agüero struck twice to take Club Atlético de Madrid through on away goals after a 2-2 draw with Sporting Clube de Portugal. Life was easier for R. Standard de Liège, 4-1 victors over Panathinaikos FC, and Liverpool FC, who overturned a 1-0 first-leg deficit with a 3-0 win at home to LOSC Lille Métropole.

Round of 16 Results

11/3/10, Hamburg Arena, Hamburg
Hamburger SV 3-1 RSC Anderlecht
Attendance: 34921
Goal(s): 1-0 Mathijsen 23, 2-0 Van Nistelrooy 40, 2-1 Legear 45, 3-1 Jarolím 76
Referee: Duhamel (FRA)
18/3/10, Constant Vanden Stock, Brussels
RSC Anderlecht 4-3 Hamburger SV
Attendance: 19669
Goal(s): 0-1 Boateng 42, 1-1 Lukaku 44, 2-1 Suárez 45+3 (p), 2-2 Jansen 54, 3-2 Biglia 59, 4-2 Boussoufa 66, 4-3 Petrić 75
Referee: Hauge (NOR)
Aggregate: 5-6; Hamburger SV qualify.

11/3/10, Vicente Calderón, Madrid
Club Atlético de Madrid 0-0 Sporting Clube de Portugal
Attendance: 34540
Referee: Vink (NED)
18/3/10, José Alvalade, Lisbon
Sporting Clube de Portugal 2-2 Club Atlético de Madrid
Attendance: 41919
Goal(s): 0-1 Agüero 3, 1-1 Liedson 19, 1-2 Agüero 33, 2-2 Anderson Polga 45+1
Referee: Kircher (GER)
Aggregate: 2-2; Club Atlético de Madrid qualify on away goals.

11/3/10, Lille Métropole, Villeneuve d'Ascq
LOSC Lille Métropole 1-0 Liverpool FC
Attendance: 17700
Goal(s): 1-0 Hazard 84
Referee: Larsen (DEN)
18/3/10, Anfield, Liverpool
Liverpool FC 3-0 LOSC Lille Métropole
Attendance: 38139
Goal(s): 1-0 Gerrard 9 (p), 2-0 Fernando Torres 49, 3-0 Fernando Torres 89
Referee: Rizzoli (ITA)
Aggregate: 3-1; Liverpool FC qualify.

11/3/10, Estádio do Sport Lisboa e Benfica, Lisbon
SL Benfica 1-1 Olympique de Marseille
Attendance: 46635
Goal(s): 1-0 Maxi Pereira 76, 1-1 Ben Arfa 90
Referee: Brych (GER)
18/3/10, Vélodrome, Marseille
Olympique de Marseille 1-2 SL Benfica
Attendance: 38386
Goal(s): 1-0 Niang 70, 1-1 Maxi Pereira 75, 1-2 Alan Kardec 90+1
Referee: Skomina (SVN)
Aggregate: 2-3; SL Benfica qualify.

11/3/10, Centralniy, Kazan
FC Rubin Kazan 1-1 VfL Wolfsburg
Attendance: 8432
Goal(s): 1-0 Noboa 29, 1-1 Misimović 67
Referee: Proença (POR)

18/3/10, VfL Wolfsburg Arena, Wolfsburg
VfL Wolfsburg 2-1 FC Rubin Kazan (aet)
Attendance: 15412
Goal(s): 0-1 Kasaev 21, 1-1 Martins 58, 2-1 Gentner 119
Referee: Eriksson (SWE)
Aggregate: 3-2; VfL Wolfsburg qualify after extra time.

11/3/10, Stadio Olimpico, Turin
Juventus 3-1 Fulham FC
Attendance: 11406
Goal(s): 1-0 Legrottaglie 9, 2-0 Zebina 25, 2-1 Etuhu 36, 3-1 Salihamidžić 45+3
Referee: Meyer (GER)
18/3/10, Craven Cottage, London
Fulham FC 4-1 Juventus
Attendance: 23458
Goal(s): 0-1 Trezeguet 2, 1-1 Zamora 9, 2-1 Gera 39, 3-1 Gera 48 (p), 4-1 Dempsey 82
Referee: Kuipers (NED)
Aggregate: 5-4; Fulham FC qualify.

Wolfsburg striker Obafemi Martins (left) tussles with Rubin defender César Navas

11/3/10, Mestalla, Valencia
Valencia CF 1-1 Werder Bremen
Attendance: 37223
Goal(s): 0-1 Frings 24 (p), 1-1 Mata 57
Referee: Atkinson (ENG)
18/3/10, Weserstadion, Bremen
Werder Bremen 4-4 Valencia CF
Attendance: 24200
Goal(s): 0-1 David Villa 3, 0-2 Mata 15, 1-2 Hugo Almeida 26, 1-3 David Villa 45, 2-3 Frings 57 (p), 3-3 Marin 62, 3-4 David Villa 66, 4-4 Pizarro 84
Referee: Blom (NED)
Aggregate: 5-5; Valencia CF qualify on away goals.

11/3/10, OACA Spyro Louis, Athens
Panathinaikos FC 1-3 R. Standard de Liège
Attendance: 50782
Goal(s): 0-1 Witsel 8, 0-2 Jovanović 16, 1-2 Vintra 48, 1-3 De Camargo 74
Referee: Thomson (SCO)
18/3/10, Maurice Dufrasne, Liege
R. Standard de Liège 1-0 Panathinaikos FC
Attendance: 26471
Goal(s): 1-0 Mbokani 45+2
Referee: Rocchi (ITA)
Aggregate: 4-1; R. Standard de Liège qualify.

QUARTER-FINALS

SL Benfica coach Jorge Jesus claimed the "two best teams in the UEFA Europa League will meet each other" when his team were drawn against Liverpool FC. It was a tie representative of the quarter-finals as a whole – a team in the UEFA Europa League from the start facing opposition that had crossed over mid-campaign from the UEFA Champions League.

'Perfect game'

Liverpool's exit from Europe's premier club competition did not look to have dampened their spirits in Lisbon, Daniel Agger giving them an early first-leg lead with a deft back-heel at a corner. Ryan Babel's dismissal later in the first half, though, presented the Merseysiders with an uphill struggle for an hour and Benfica duly capitalised – albeit thanks to two penalties, expertly converted, left-footed, by Óscar Cardozo.

The Portuguese side may have held sway going into the return but they were abruptly halted in their tracks at Anfield. Dirk Kuyt, who later praised his team-mates for producing "almost the perfect game", and Lucas turned the tie on its head with two goals inside 34 minutes before the irrepressible Fernando Torres, who had uncharacteristically missed a gilt-edged chance in Lisbon, allowed Liverpool breathing space with a tremendous third on the counterattack. Cardozo reignited the tie with a free-kick 20 minutes from time but Torres was on hand with a brilliant reply to seal the tie 5-3 on aggregate and book the Reds' place in their 15th major European semi-final.

Daniel Agger (centre) puts Liverpool ahead at Benfica with a deft flick

Fulham impress

Joining them for the first time would be either Fulham FC or VfL Wolfsburg, both of whom found themselves already in the uncharted territory of the last eight. As such, they took tentative first steps in the opening leg at Craven Cottage, but it was the home side who appeared to take charge thanks to a couple of well crafted goals from Bobby Zamora and Damien Duff.

Bobby Zamora (left) receives the congratulations of his Fulham team-mates after scoring with just 25 seconds on the clock in Wolfsburg

Roy Hodgson's side were on the verge of taking a two-goal advantage to the home of the Bundesliga champions, but they were denied at the death by Alexander Madlung's thunderous header following a short corner. It mattered not, however, because Zamora restored the Cottagers' cushion with a sharp turn and shot 25 seconds into the second leg. A stoic defensive display followed to see Fulham through 3-1 on aggregate.

Heaven and hell

It was therefore left to Hamburger SV to maintain German representation in the competition – though they already had motivation enough with the final set for their own stadium. They were in decent shape to progress after a 2-1 first-leg win at home to R. Standard de Liège, but after failing to convert any of a number of late chances, they could take nothing for granted as they headed to Belgium

UEFA Europa League

Early goals were traded in the second leg but HSV swiftly moved up a gear thanks to a breathtaking Mladen Petrić overhead kick that gave the Croatian striker his second goal of the night and put his team 4-2 ahead overall. The German side rubber-stamped their triumph with an additional goal from José Paolo Guerrero in stoppage time to set up a semi-final date with Fulham.

Mladen Petrić converts a penalty against Standard – the first of his three goals in the tie

Spanish rivals

The fourth quarter-final was an all-Spanish affair. Valencia CF and Club Atlético de Madrid had played 140 Spanish league fixtures prior to their first-leg encounter at the Mestalla, and there was little to choose between them historically, with Valencia amassing 53 victories to Atlético's 51.

A 37th draw transpired, with David Villa's equaliser eight minutes from time enabling Valencia to salvage a 2-2 draw prior to the return in Madrid. The second leg did not live up to its high-octane predecessor, a goalless stalemate ensuring the 2003/04 winners' demise after Atlético survived a late onslaught from the visitors in which Villa struck the underside of the crossbar and Nikola Žigić was denied a strong penalty claim.

Atlético players enjoy a celebratory huddle after eliminating Valencia

Quarter-Final Results

1/4/10, Craven Cottage, London
Fulham FC 2-1 VfL Wolfsburg
Attendance: 22307
Goal(s): 1-0 Zamora 59, 2-0 Duff 63, 2-1 Madlung 89
Referee: Skomina (SVN)
8/4/10, VfL Wolfsburg Arena, Wolfsburg
VfL Wolfsburg 0-1 Fulham FC
Attendance: 24843
Goal(s): 0-1 Zamora 1
Referee: Kassai (HUN)
Aggregate: 1-3; Fulham FC qualify.

1/4/10, Estádio do Sport Lisboa e Benfica, Lisbon
SL Benfica 2-1 Liverpool FC
Attendance: 62629
Goal(s): 0-1 Agger 9, 1-1 Cardozo 59 (p), 2-1 Cardozo 79 (p)
Referee: Eriksson (SWE)
8/4/10, Anfield, Liverpool
Liverpool FC 4-1 SL Benfica
Attendance: 42500
Goal(s): 1-0 Kuyt 27, 2-0 Lucas 34, 3-0 Fernando Torres 59, 3-1 Óscar Cardozo 70, 4-1 Fernando Torres 82
Referee: Kuipers (NED)
Aggregate: 5-3; Liverpool FC qualify.

1/4/10, Hamburg Arena, Hamburg
Hamburger SV 2-1 R. Standard de Liège
Attendance: 48437
Goal(s): 0-1 Mbokani 31, 1-1 Petrić 42 (p), 2-1 Van Nistelrooy 45
Referee: Atkinson (ENG)
8/4/10, Maurice Dufrasne, Liege
R. Standard de Liège 1-3 Hamburger SV
Attendance: 27129
Goal(s): 0-1 Petrić 20, 1-1 De Camargo 33, 1-2 Petrić 35, 1-3 Guerrero 90+4
Referee: Proença (POR)
Aggregate: 2-5; Hamburger SV qualify.

1/4/10, Mestalla, Valencia
Valencia CF 2-2 Club Atlético de Madrid
Attendance: 46310
Goal(s): 0-1 Forlán 59, 1-1 Manuel Fernandes 66, 1-2 Antonio López 72, 2-2 David Villa 82
Referee: Thomson (SCO)
8/4/10, Vicente Calderón, Madrid
Club Atlético de Madrid 0-0 Valencia CF
Attendance: 49907
Referee: Meyer (GER)
Aggregate: 2-2; Club Atlético de Madrid qualify on away goals.

SEMI-FINALS

The UEFA Europa League semi-finals featured a contest between two teams whose continental campaigns commenced nine months earlier in the third qualifying round and another involving a pair of sides who began the season in the UEFA Champions League.

Hamburger SV and Fulham FC had both already chalked up 16 matches during a European odyssey that started in late July. Club Atlético de Madrid and Liverpool FC – having finished third in their respective UEFA Champions League groups – were both attempting to salvage underwhelming seasons at home and abroad.

Hamburg falter

Hamburg, the 1983 continental champions, had the carrot of reaching the final at their own stadium dangling before them, yet they were unable to make home advantage count in the first leg against a Fulham team competing in a European semi-final for the first time and obliged to travel to northern Germany via land and sea because of a European flight ban caused by a giant cloud of ash from an Icelandic volcano. A match of few discernible chances for either side – the tenacious, well organised visitors failed to register a single shot on target – ended goalless, leaving the return in west London intriguingly poised.

If the upheaval caused by a 5-1 league defeat for HSV four days earlier and the resultant sacking of coach Bruno Labbadia was hardly ideal preparation, it did not initially appear to affect the Bundesliga outfit at Craven Cottage. A blistering free-kick from Mladen Petrić midway through the first half put temporary coach Ricardo Moniz's charges in firm control and left Fulham requiring two goals if they were to deny their opponents a dream date on home turf.

Fulham fantasy

A feature of Fulham's campaign had been their ability to repeatedly defy the odds, as FC Shakhtar Donetsk and Juventus, among others, bore witness, and once again Roy Hodgson's never-say-die warriors were to claim another memorable scalp. Two goals in the space of seven second-half minutes – from Simon Davies, who skilfully converted a deft Danny Murphy through-ball, and from Zoltán Gera, who twisted and scored from close range following a corner – sent the Cottagers through to their first major final since the 1975 FA Cup showdown at Wembley. As Hamburg's dream died, Bobby Zamora, whose eight goals were a cornerstone of Fulham's unexpected run to the final, summed up the feeling of euphoria among the home players and fans after the final whistle, saying "I'm lost for words."

Zoltán Gera scores Fulham's winning goal against Hamburg

UEFA Europa League

Atlético's Diego Forlán is surrounded by Liverpool players in the second leg at Anfield

Liverpool were also left dumbfounded for a very different reason after suffering extra-time agony at Anfield against Atlético. Having lost the first leg in Madrid – to which they, like Fulham, had been forced to make emergency travel plans because of the volcanic ash – as a result of a scrappy Diego Forlán goal, Alberto Aquilani's fine strike in the second meeting ensured the need for an additional 30 minutes on Merseyside. Yossi Benayoun then put the Reds into a winning position in the early stages of extra time with a sweet first-time strike before Forlán – a scorer of two goals on the same ground for Manchester United FC in 2002 – swept in the decisive goal from José Antonio Reyes's measured cross after 102 minutes.

Glorious ending

Also through to the Copa del Rey final and without a trophy since a domestic double in 1996, Atlético stood on the verge of a glorious ending to a campaign that reached its tipping point in the autumn when coach Quique Sánchez Flores replaced the sacked Abel Resino. "After so many years without reaching a final, to have two finals in front of us is incredible," said Forlán as his team celebrated success on the away-goals rule for the third round running.

Semi-Final Results

22/4/10, Vicente Calderón, Madrid
Club Atlético de Madrid 1-0 Liverpool FC
Attendance: 47042
Goal(s): 1-0 Forlán 9
Referee: Duhamel (FRA)
29/4/10, Anfield, Liverpool
Liverpool FC 2-1 Club Atlético de Madrid (aet)
Attendance: 42040
Goal(s): 1-0 Aquilani 44, 2-0 Benayoun 95, 2-1 Forlán 102
Referee: Hauge (NOR)
Aggregate: 2-2; Club Atlético de Madrid qualify after extra time on away goal.

22/4/10, Hamburg Arena, Hamburg
Hamburger SV 0-0 Fulham FC
Attendance: 49171
Referee: Larsen (DEN)
29/4/10, Craven Cottage, London
Fulham FC 2-1 Hamburger SV
Attendance: 23705
Goal(s): 0-1 Petrić 22, 1-1 Davies 69, 2-1 Gera 76
Referee: Çakır (TUR)
Aggregate: 2-1; Fulham FC qualify.

FINAL

After a competition full of drama, intrigue and no shortage of goals, the inaugural UEFA Europa League final, between Club Atlético de Madrid and giant-killing Fulham FC, had much to live up to. It did not disappoint, a tightly contested encounter from first whistle to the last being settled only late in extra time with a second goal of the game from Atlético's top scorer Diego Forlán.

Perennial underdogs throughout their European campaign, Atlético arrived in Germany as favourites to see off a club without a single major honour to its name – one, moreover, that had never finished higher than seventh in the English top flight. The Spanish club's coach Quique Sánchez Flores attempted to divert the spotlight but Fulham counterpart Roy Hodgson, the newly-crowned English manager of the year, switched it back on to the Spanish team. "Atlético's European pedigree speaks for itself," said the 62-year-old. Indeed, even if they had won only one of them, this was the Spanish side's fifth major European final. In contrast, it was only Fulham's second European campaign.

Atlético's Sergio Agüero attempts to squeeze his way through the Fulham defence

Agüero lively

On the night that Fulham introduced themselves to the big stage after 131 years in the shadows, there were few obvious signs of nerves as the match got under way in Hamburg. They started confidently, expansively, passing from the back. That almost proved their undoing on 12 minutes, however, as Sergio Agüero pounced on an uncharacteristically loose pass from Fulham skipper Danny Murphy. The young Argentine fed Forlán, but, with just goalkeeper Mark Schwarzer to beat, the in-form striker could only direct his low shot across goal against the far post.

Fulham heeded the warning, finding a more natural rhythm, and midway through the half a long-range shot from Simon Davies warmed David de Gea's hands. Agüero was knocking on the door in more subtle style at the other end, posing a consistent threat on the left flank. His contribution to the opening goal, though, was less refined. José Antonio Reyes outstripped Dickson Etuhu on the right, lofting a pass for Simão to direct into Agüero's path. The striker snatched at his shot but miscued it perfectly on to the right foot of the lurking Forlán, who this time tucked the ball into the corner of the net to give Atlético the lead.

Fulham manager Roy Hodgson savours his club's big night in Hamburg

UEFA Europa League

Fulham fightback

Fulham had staged countless comebacks during their journey to Hamburg and within five minutes they were at it again, levelling the scores with their first real goalscoring opportunity of the game. Bobby Zamora did well to turn inside Luis Perea on the left, but the opening it created had all but closed when the ball rolled to Zoltán Gera. The Hungarian international steadied himself and crossed towards the far post where Simon Davies lashed home a superb right-foot volley to make it 1-1.

After surviving more Atlético pressure as half-time approached, Fulham emerged for the restart a renewed force. The Spanish side were indebted to the reactions of De Gea, who first foiled Gera after a brilliant Murphy pass, then beat away another stinging Davies shot. In the meantime top scorer Zamora, an injury doubt before the game, had been withdrawn. Initially it failed to stem the Fulham tide, but as the game became more and more fractious Atlético re-established a measure of control.

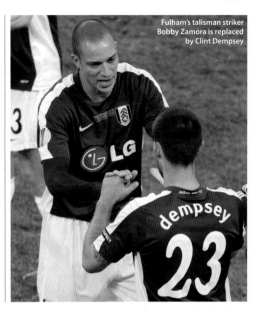

Fulham's talisman striker Bobby Zamora is replaced by Clint Dempsey

Simon Davies fires Fulham level with a spectacular volley

UEFA Europa League

Fina

Diego Forlán flicks in Atlético's winning goal

Forlán muscle

Extra time was increasingly inevitable. Thirty additional minutes of intense combat would have been a test for any side let alone two who had accumulated over 60 games during the season. Forlán had served in most of Atlético's but ominously for Fulham he looked as fresh as a daisy. The Uruguayan No7 made a surging run to the dead-ball line on 105 minutes, but neither Eduardo Salvio nor Agüero could turn in his clever cut-back. But four minutes from the end of the second extra period, with penalties looming, Forlán found himself in the right place at the right time, doing just enough to divert Agüero's cross from the left into the far corner via a slight deflection off his marker Brede Hangeland.

Atlético coach Quiqu
Sánchez Flores (left
celebrates his team'
victory at the final whistl

UEFA Europa League

As at Anfield in the semi-final, off came Forlán's shirt in celebration. Several Atlético fans in the stands copied him, for the club's long wait was over. Nearly half a century after the Madrid club had beaten ACF Fiorentina to claim their first major European trophy in the UEFA Cup Winners' Cup, they now, at last, had a second. Furthermore, the honour of being the inaugural winners of the UEFA Europa League would always be theirs.

Final Result

12/5/10, Hamburg Arena, Hamburg
Club Atlético de Madrid 2-1 Fulham FC (aet)
Attendance: 49000
Atlético: De Gea, Antonio López, Forlán, Raúl García, Agüero (Valera 119), Paulo Assunção, Ujfaluši, Álvaro Domínguez, Reyes (Salvio 78), Simão (Jurado 68), Perea. Coach: Quique Sánchez Flores (ESP)
Fulham: Schwarzer, Konchesky, Hangeland, Baird, Gera, Murphy (Greening 118), Duff (Nevland 84), Hughes, Etuhu, Zamora (Dempsey 55), Davies. Coach: Roy Hodgson (ENG)
Goal(s): 1-0 Forlán 32, 1-1 Davies 37, 2-1 Forlán 116
Yellow Card(s): Hangeland 63 (Fulham), Salvio 107 (Atlético), Raúl García 114 (Atlético), Forlán 117 (Atlético)
Referee: Rizzoli (ITA)

TOP GOALSCORERS

9	Claudio Pizarro (Werder)
	Óscar Cardozo (Benfica)
6	Jonathan Legear (Anderlecht)
	Fernando Llorente (Athletic)
	Diego Forlán (Atlético)
	David Villa (Valencia)
	Mladen Petrić (Hamburg)
	Bobby Zamora (Fulham)
	Zoltán Gera (Fulham)
5	Gervinho (Lille)
	Rúben Micael (Nacional)
	Alexander Frei (Basel)
	Luiz Adriano (Shakhtar)
	Djibril Cissé (Panathinaikos)
	Juan Mata (Valencia)
4	Jonathan Reis (PSV)
	Fernando Torres (Liverpool)
	Nikica Jelavić (Rapid Wien)
	Marc Janko (Salzburg)
	Marcus Berg (Hamburg)
	Javier Saviola (Benfica)
	Dame N'Doye (København)
	Romelu Lukaku (Anderlecht)
	Ivan Perišić (Club Brugge)
	Torsten Frings (Werder)
	Liedson (Sporting)

Claudio Pizarro

Óscar Cardozo

Atlético captain Antonio López raises the trophy for the inaugural UEFA Europa League winners

UEFA SUPER CUP

2009

FC Barcelona continued their trophy-laden year by collecting their fifth piece of silverware in 2009 thanks to a narrow victory in the UEFA Super Cup against FC Shakhtar Donetsk in Monaco, substitute Pedro Rodríguez scoring the only goal of the game five minutes from the end of extra time. Winners of the competition in 1992 and 1997 but beaten 3-0 by Sevilla FC on their last visit to Monaco in 2006, Josep Guardiola's charges had become the first Spanish side to win the treble in 2008/09 and had already added the domestic Super Cup to their collection by the time they met Shakhtar. The Ukrainian club proved a tough nut to crack, however, holding their opponents at bay until the 115th minute when the 22-year-old Pedro – a late substitute in the UEFA Champions League final win against Manchester United FC – finally struck the decisive blow to take the trophy to Spain for the seventh time.

A 115th-minute goal from substitute Pedro Rodríguez finally ended the resistance of FC Shakhtar Donetsk and gave FC Barcelona a third UEFA Super Cup triumph in Monaco.

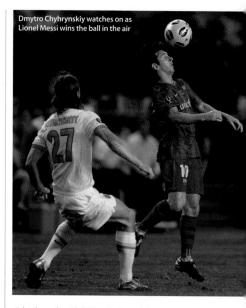

Dmytro Chyhrynskiy watches on as Lionel Messi wins the ball in the air

Dramatic victory

Spain's first 'treble' winners thanks to their triumphs in the Liga, Copa del Rey and UEFA Champions League, Barcelona had started the new campaign as they ended the old by collecting silverware the previous weekend with a 3-0 home win against Athletic Club that completed a 5-1 aggregate Spanish Super Cup victory, but Josep Guardiola's team struggled to unpick a well-drilled Shakhtar defence despite enjoying the vast majority of the possession. Shakhtar, bidding to become the 23rd side to lift the UEFA Super Cup and the first Ukrainian winners since FC Dynamo Kyiv's in 1975, held out to take the game into 30 additional minutes and looked to have earned a penalty shoot-out. Pedro had other ideas, however, exchanging passes with the tireless Lionel Messi to finally beat Shakhtar goalkeeper Andriy Pyatov with a low shot and add yet another trophy to Barça's ever-expanding collection.

Much attention pre-match focused on Barcelona's marquee summer signing Zlatan Ibrahimović, who joined from FC Internazionale Milano with the prolific Samuel Eto'o going in the other direction, while Messi

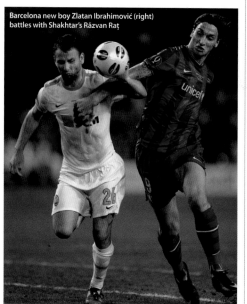

Barcelona new boy Zlatan Ibrahimović (right) battles with Shakhtar's Răzvan Raț

picked up the Club Footballer of the Year and Best Forward prizes at the UEFA Club Football Awards the day before the final, yet it was the third member of Josep Guardiola's attack who was first to threaten. Nine minutes in Thierry Henry expertly shook off Shakhtar captain Darijo Srna with a perfectly-executed turn before sending a fizzing shot fractionally too high from the edge of the area. That proved to be a misleading opening start, however, as a rearguard featuring Dmytro Chyhrynskiy in his final Shakhtar appearance before signing for Barça held the Spanish giants at bay.

Messi denied

Barcelona had won only three of their previous six meetings with Shakhtar, losing the sides' most recent encounter 3-2 at Camp Nou in December 2008, but although Víctor Valdés had to race from his line to whip the ball off the toes of Luiz Adriano, neither goalkeeper was called into serious action until the 33rd minute, when Messi played a swift one-two with Xavi Hernández and raced into the area, only for Pyatov to smother his shot. The Argentinian forward had another shooting opportunity as half-time approached but was unable to beat Shakhtar's defensive wall with his curling free-kick as the Spanish side stepped up their bid to add to their triumphs in this competition in 1992 and 1997. Xavi had also been a winner at the UEFA Club Football Awards, collecting the prize for Best Midfielder, and he put in a typically probing display in an attacking midfield role, yet despite their all-star lineup – Valdés, Gerard Piqué and Andrés Iniesta had also been nominated for prizes – Barcelona's frustrations were mounting.

Still without Iniesta due to a thigh injury that had kept the midfielder on the sidelines since the UEFA Champions League final, Barcelona nevertheless continued to control the tempo as the second half kicked off but struggled to carve out clear chances, Ibrahimović's sliced attempt encapsulating their difficulties. Henry failed to connect with an ambitious overhead kick before Pyatov produced two smart saves in quick succession to deny Messi and Henry.

Extra-time excitement

Messi was then unable to make the most of the time afforded to him by Dani Alves's cross, Pyatov easily gathering his tame right-foot effort, while Henry nearly turned in Carles Puyol's flick-on from a corner. With neither side able to find a breakthrough the match moved into extra time, where the introduction of Julius Aghahowa added verve to the Shakhtar attack, Valdés diving to his left to push away the striker's low shot. It was to be a Barcelona replacement who had the decisive word, however. Srna hacked away one Pedro effort, but the 22-year-old would not be denied and finally ended Shakhtar's resolve with a fine low shot after a typically intricate move to take the trophy to Spain again.

Guardiola, a winner in this competition in 1992 with Barcelona, was in characteristically modest mood after yet another triumph, saying: "It's a great evening. This is the second time I've won this trophy and I'm very lucky to have been chosen to coach these great players. I don't create players; I try to advise and support them. They've worked very hard and made sacrifices and it's all worked out. We haven't lost the essence of our side, it's been physically tough but it all came right in the end. In April or May you're on a roll. Right now we're still at an early stage of the season; suddenly it's August and you're contesting trophies. That's why it's hard to win this competition. We've managed to bring two Super Cups home already and that's not bad at all."

Result

28/8/09, Stade Louis II, Monaco
FC Barcelona 1-0 FC Shakhtar Donetsk (aet)
Attendance: 17738
Barcelona: Víctor Valdés, Dani Alves, Piqué, Puyol, Xavi, Ibrahimović (Pedro 81), Messi, Henry (Bojan 96), Keita, Abidal, Touré (Busquets 100). Coach: Josep Guardiola (ESP)
Shakhtar: Pyatov, Hübschman, Kucher, Fernandinho (Jádson 80), Ilsinho, Luiz Adriano, Gai (Kobin 80), Willian (Aghahowa 91), Raţ, Chyhrynskiy, Srna. Coach: Mircea Lucescu (ROU)
Goal(s): 1-0 Pedro 115
Yellow Card(s): Ilsinho 55 (Shakhtar), Srna 65 (Shakhtar), Messi 90+3 (Barcelona), Kucher 90+3 (Shakhtar), Pedro 107 (Barcelona), Kobin 119 (Shakhtar)
Referee: De Bleeckere (BEL)

Captain Carles Puyol lifts the UEFA Super Cup for Barcelona

04 UEFA Club Competitions 2009/10

ALBANIA

KF TIRANA

UEFA CHAMPIONS LEAGUE

Second Qualifying Round – Stabæk Fotball (NOR)
H 1-1 Muka (50)
Nallbani, Dabulla, Lila, Sefa, Muka, Devolli, Alechenwu, Muzaka (Mohellebi 59), Osmani, D. Xhafaj, Lilaj (Abilaliaj 85). Coach: Ilija Lončarević (CRO)
Yellow Card(s): Muka 33, Devolli 69, Lila 90
A 0-4
Nallbani, Dabulla, Pashaj, Lila, Sefa, Patushi (Abilaliaj 46), Devolli (Mohellebi 63), Alechenwu, Osmani, D. Xhafaj, Lilaj (Hajdari 71). Coach: Ilija Lončarević (CRO)
Red Card(s): Mohellebi 74
Yellow Card(s): Lila 15

KS FLAMURTARI

UEFA EUROPA LEAGUE

Second Qualifying Round – Motherwell FC (SCO)
H 1-0 Strati (66)
Moçka, Guga, Begaj, Alviž, Mema (Galica 78), Ngjela (Flávio Júnior 46), Veliu, Strati, Zeqiri, Shehaj (Roshi 37), Beqiri. Coach: Eqerem Memushi (ALB)
Yellow Card(s): Begaj 12, Guga 57, Strati 84
A 1-8 Roshi (64)
Moçka, Guga, Begaj, Alviž, Mema (Shehaj 46), Ngjele (Galica 78), Veliu, Strati, Zeqiri, Sakaj, Beqiri (Roshi 38). Coach: Eqerem Memushi (ALB)

KF VLLAZNIA

UEFA EUROPA LEAGUE

First Qualifying Round – Sligo Rovers FC (IRL)
A 2-1 Smajlaj (69), Keane (75og)
Grima, Smajlaj, Mrvaljević, Osja, Shtupina, Belisha, Sinani (Bala 85), Kasapi (Olsi 88), Hallaçi, E. Beqiri, Nallbani. Coach: Hasan Lika (ALB)
Red Card(s): Grima 86
Yellow Card(s): E. Beqiri 10, Sinani 25, Smajlaj 57, Shtupina 60
H 1-1 Shtupina (42)
Olsi, Smajlaj, Mrvaljević, Shtupina, Belisha, Sinani, Kasapi (Sykaj 90+3), Hallaçi, E. Beqiri (M. Bašić 61), Bala (Nika 64), Nallbani. Coach: Hasan Lika (ALB)
Red Card(s): Sinani 78
Yellow Card(s): Bala 45+2, Kasapi 73, Sinani 77

Second Qualifying Round – SK Rapid Wien (AUT)
A 0-5
Olsi, Smajlaj, Mrvaljević, Osja, Belisha, Kasapi (Vajushi 77), Nika, Hallaçi, E. Beqiri, Bala (M. Bašić 87), Nallbani. Coach: Hasan Lika (ALB)
H 0-3
Olsi, Smajlaj (Sykaj 68), Mrvaljević, Osja (Dibra 90), Belisha, Kasapi, Nika (Vajushi 62), Hallaçi, E. Beqiri, Bala, Nallbani. Coach: Hasan Lika (ALB)
Yellow Card(s): Smajlaj 63, Sykaj 75

KS DINAMO TIRANA

UEFA EUROPA LEAGUE

First Qualifying Round – FC Lahti (FIN)
A 1-4 Kuli (28)
Kotorri, Vrapi, Pisha, Kuli (Sosa 46), Poçi, Allmuça, Hadžibulić, Brkić (Plaku 46), Bakaj, Putinčanin (Sina 63), Diop. Coach: Shkëlqim Muça (ALB)
Yellow Card(s): Diop 61
H 2-0 Diop (13, 70)
Kotorri, Muça, Vrapi (Ferraj 78), Pisha, Kuli (Plaku 46), Allmuça, Hadžibulić, Bakaj, Putinčanin, Diop, Malacarne. Coach: Shkëlqim Muça (ALB)
Yellow Card(s): Kuli 17, Allmuça 52, Putinčanin 64

ANDORRA

UE SANT JULIÀ

UEFA CHAMPIONS LEAGUE

First Qualifying Round – SP Tre Fiori (SMR)
A 1-1 Xinos (42p)
Perianes, Wagner, Xinos, Moreira (Matamala 70), Romero, Peppe, Machado (Abdian 63), Muñoz, Nastri, Mejías (Gonçalves 87), Varela. Coach: Patricio González (ESP)
Red Card(s): Muñoz 60
Yellow Card(s): Varela 35, Nastri 72
H 1-1 Moreira (39) (aet; 5-4 on pens)
Perianes, Wagner, Abdian (Matamala 98), Xinos, Moreira (Gonçalves 79), Romero (Miraglia 77), Peppe, Machado, Nastri, Mejías, Varela. Coach: Patricio González (ESP)
Yellow Card(s): Abdian 55, Machado 69, Moreira 79

Second Qualifying Round – PFC Levski Sofia (BUL)
A 0-4
Burgos, Wagner, Abdian, Fontan (Miraglia 57), Xinos, Romero, Peppe, Machado (Vila 69), Nastri, Mejías (Bernales 77), Varela. Coach: Patricio González (ESP)
Red Card(s): Abdian 54, Romero 80
Yellow Card(s): Nastri 15, Fontan 19, Abdian 29, Romero 33, Abdian 54, Romero 80
H 0-5
Burgos, Wagner, Fontan, Xinos (Matamala 46), Moreira, Miraglia, Peppe, Machado (Vila 61) (Pérez 82), Gonçalves, Mejías, Varela. Coach: Patricio González (ESP)
Yellow Card(s): Peppe 65

FC SANTA COLOMA

UEFA EUROPA LEAGUE

Second Qualifying Round – FC Basel 1893 (SUI)
A 0-3
…ernández Lizarte, Ayala, Gil, Fernández, Albanell, Genís García (Medina
…3), Norberto Urbani (Juli Sánchez 51), Rodríguez Soria, Sánchez, Maciel
…ntunes (Maicon 64), Álvarez. Coach: Vicens Marques (AND)
Yellow Card(s): Albanell 40, Maicon 84, Juli Sánchez 90+2
H 1-4 Maicon (43p)
…errano, Maciel Antunes, Gil, Albanell, Fernández, Álvarez, Ayala, Rodríguez
…oria (Aguirre Santinelli 49), Genís García, Maicon (Da Cunha 76), Norberto
…rbani (Guida 72). Coach: Vicens Marques (AND)
Yellow Card(s): Ayala 35

ARMENIA

FC PYUNIK

UEFA CHAMPIONS LEAGUE

Second Qualifying Round – NK Dinamo Zagreb (CRO)
H 0-0
…. Hovhannisyan, Khachatryan, S. Hovsepyan, Mkrtchyan, Marcos (Aleksanyan
…8), Malakyan, Ghazaryan (Tadevosyan 78), Manoyan, Yusbashyan (Artur
…edigaryan 54), Minasyan, Mbola. Coach: Vardan Minasyan (ARM)
Yellow Card(s): Manoyan 25, Khachatryan 52
A 0-3
…. Hovhannisyan, Khachatryan, S. Hovsepyan, Artur Yedigaryan
…Yusbashyan 72), Mkrtchyan, Marcos, Malakyan, Ghazaryan, Minasyan,
…bola, Sahakyan (Artak Yedigaryan 66). Coach: Vardan Minasyan (ARM)

FC GANDZASAR KAPAN

UEFA EUROPA LEAGUE

Second Qualifying Round – NAC Breda (NED)
A 0-6
…ubuteishvili, K. Zakaryan, Antonyan, Aleksanyan, Marşavela (Davtyan 58),
…eandro, Simonyan (Hayrapetyan 71), Tatintsyan, Avetisyan (Sakhokia 64),
…hachatryan, D. Khanishvili. Coach: Slava Gabrielyan (ARM)
Yellow Card(s): Leandro 28, Antonyan 33
H 0-2
…ubuteishvili, K. Zakaryan, Antonyan, Aleksanyan, Marşavela (Sakhokia
…2), Simonyan (Hayrapetyan 55), Davtyan, Tatintsyan, Avetisyan (Avagyan
…'3), Khachatryan, D. Khanishvili. Coach: Slava Gabrielyan (ARM)
Red Card(s): Khachatryan 90+2
Yellow Card(s): Khachatryan 21, Khanishvili 63, Sakhokia 76

FC MIKA

UEFA EUROPA LEAGUE

First Qualifying Round – Helsingborgs IF (SWE)
A 1-3 Montenegro (66)
Harutyunyan, Petrosyan, Fursin, Pedro López, Mkrtchyan, Montenegro,
Demel (Beglaryan 88), Mikaelyan (A. Hakobyan 85), G. Poghosyan, Ednei,
Alex. Coach: Samvel Darbinyan (ARM)
Yellow Card(s): Fursin 42, Pedro López 59
H 1-1 Ednei (83p)
Harutyunyan, Petrosyan, Fursin, Pedro López (Morozov 83), Mkrtchyan,
Montenegro (Ednei 71), Demel, Mikaelyan (A. Hakobyan 80), M.
Poghosyan, Voskanyan, Alex. Coach: Samvel Darbinyan (ARM)

FC BANANTS

UEFA EUROPA LEAGUE

First Qualifying Round – NK Široki Brijeg (BIH)
H 0-2
Ghazaryan, Kavatsiv, Nazarenko, Voskanyan (Romanenko 74), Dashyan,
Kasule, Nasibyan (Gyozalyan 46), Kakosyan, Grigoryan, Melkonyan,
Mkhitaryan (Stepanyan 71). Coach: Armen Gyulbudaghyants (ARM)
A 1-0 Dashyan (87)
Ghazaryan, Nazarenko, Romanenko (Oseyan 83), Voskanyan, Dashyan,
Khachatryan, Kasule, Cherevko, Gyozalyan (Balabekyan 83), Melkonyan
(Nasibyan 85), Mkhitaryan. Coach: Armen Gyulbudaghyants (ARM)
Yellow Card(s): Melkonyan 71, Khachatryan 88, Kasule 90+3

AUSTRIA

FC SALZBURG

UEFA CHAMPIONS LEAGUE

Second Qualifying Round – Bohemian FC (IRL)
H 1-1 Dudić (25)
Gustafsson, Dudić, Schwegler, Opdam (Ježek 66), Švento, Cziommer (Ilić
63), Janko (Nelisse 73), Sekagya, Leitgeb, Aufhauser, Ngwat-Mahop.
Coach: Huub Stevens (NED)
Yellow Card(s): Sekagya 68
A 1-0 Ježek (86)
Gustafsson, Dudić, Schwegler, Augustinussen, Tchoyi, Schiemer, Ulmer
(Ježek 58), Švento, Janko, Ilić (Vladavić 62), Leitgeb (Nelisse 72). Coach:
Huub Stevens (NED)
Yellow Card(s): Janko 54, Schwegler 90+1, Gustafsson 90+3

CHAMPIONS LEAGUE EUROPA LEAGUE

Third Qualifying Round – NK Dinamo Zagreb (CRO)
H 1-1 Zickler (45)
Gustafsson, Dudić, Zickler (Janko 70), Augustinussen, Tchoyi, Schiemer, Ulmer, Švento (Ježek 73), Sekagya, Leitgeb, Vladavić (Ilić 85). Coach: Huub Stevens (NED)
Yellow Card(s): Vladavić 26, Augustinussen 53, Janko 77, Dudić 88, Schiemer 90+4
A 2-1 Švento (33), Nelisse (83)
Gustafsson, Dudić, Zickler (Cziommer 79), Nelisse, Tchoyi, Schiemer, Ulmer, Švento (Opdam 90+2), Sekagya, Leitgeb (Augustinussen 87), Aufhauser. Coach: Huub Stevens (NED)
Yellow Card(s): Sekagya 61

Play-Off Round – Maccabi Haifa FC (ISR)
H 1-2 Zickler (57)
Gustafsson, Dudić, Schwegler, Zickler (Janko 68), Augustinussen, Nelisse (Cziommer 60), Tchoyi, Schiemer, Ulmer, Švento (Ježek 80), Leitgeb. Coach: Huub Stevens (NED)
Yellow Card(s): Augustinussen 56, Schwegler 66
A 0-3
Gustafsson, Dudić (Vladavić 55), Tchoyi, Opdam, Schiemer, Ulmer, Švento, Cziommer (Zickler 55), Janko, Leitgeb, Ilsanker (Ilić 70). Coach: Huub Stevens (NED)
Yellow Card(s): Cziommer 21

UEFA EUROPA LEAGUE
Group G
Match 1 – S.S. Lazio (ITA)
A 2-1 Schiemer (82), Janko (90+3)
Gustafsson, Afolabi, Schwegler, Pokrivač (Cziommer 63), Tchoyi, Schiemer, Ulmer, Švento (Nelisse 80), Janko, Sekagya, Leitgeb (Vladavić 73). Coach: Huub Stevens (NED)
Yellow Card(s): Schiemer 56, Schwegler 90+1
Match 2 – Villarreal CF (ESP)
H 2-0 Janko (21), Tchoyi (84)
Gustafsson, Afolabi, Schwegler, Pokrivač, Tchoyi, Schiemer, Ulmer, Švento (Opdam 90), Janko (Zickler 79), Sekagya, Leitgeb (Cziommer 90+2). Coach: Huub Stevens (NED)
Match 3 – PFC Levski Sofia (BUL)
H 1-0 Švento (45+2)
Gustafsson, Afolabi, Schwegler, Zickler (Rakić 75), Pokrivač, Tchoyi, Schiemer, Ulmer, Švento (Vladavić 90), Sekagya, Leitgeb (Cziommer 80). Coach: Huub Stevens (NED)
Yellow Card(s): Pokrivač 64
Match 4 – PFC Levski Sofia (BUL)
A 1-0 Schiemer (90+3)
Gustafsson, Afolabi (Ježek 87), Schwegler, Pokrivač, Tchoyi, Schiemer, Ulmer, Švento (Zickler 73), Janko, Sekagya, Leitgeb. Coach: Huub Stevens (NED)
Yellow Card(s): Zickler 90, Schiemer 90+3
Match 5 – S.S. Lazio (ITA)
H 2-1 Afolabi (52), Tchoyi (78)
Gustafsson, Afolabi, Schwegler, Pokrivač (Cziommer 87), Tchoyi (Zickler 83), Opdam, Ulmer, Švento, Janko (Nelisse 90+2), Sekagya, Leitgeb. Coach: Huub Stevens (NED)
Yellow Card(s): Pokrivač 71
Match 6 – Villarreal CF (ESP)
A 1-0 Švento (7)
Gustafsson, Afolabi, Schwegler, Augustinussen, Nelisse (Rakić 64), Opdam, Ulmer, Švento, Cziommer (Vladavić 81), Sekagya, Leitgeb (Ježek 86). Coach: Huub Stevens (NED)
Yellow Card(s): Schwegler 34, Cziommer 76

Round of 32 – R. Standard de Liège (BEL)
A 2-3 Janko (4, 45)
Gustafsson, Afolabi, Schwegler, Tchoyi, Schiemer, Ulmer, Švento (Wallner 84), Cziommer (Pokrivač 74), Janko (Nelisse 88), Sekagya, Leitgeb. Coach: Huub Stevens (NED)
Yellow Card(s): Schwegler 60, Schiemer 65, Leitgeb 90+3
H 0-0
Gustafsson, Dudić (Zickler 74), Afolabi, Tchoyi, Opdam, Ulmer, Švento, Cziommer (Wallner 64), Janko, Sekagya, Leitgeb. Coach: Huub Stevens (NED)
Yellow Card(s): Cziommer 45, Sekagya 54

FK AUSTRIA WIEN

UEFA EUROPA LEAGUE
Third Qualifying Round – FK Vojvodina (SRB)
A 1-1 Jun (38)
Almer, Dragovic, Bąk, Jun, Ortlechner, Voříšek, Junuzovic (Klein 80), Okotie, Baumgartlinger, Ačimovič, Standfest. Coach: Karl Daxbacher (AUT)
Yellow Card(s): Okotie 61
H 4-2 Jun (45), Sulimani (63), Diabang (81), Okotie (90+3)
Almer, Dragovic, Bąk, Klein, Jun (Diabang 79), Ortlechner, Voříšek (Hattenberger 85), Junuzovic, Okotie, Baumgartlinger (Sulimani 60), Ačimovič. Coach: Karl Daxbacher (AUT)
Yellow Card(s): Diabang 82, Ortlechner 89

Play-Off Round – FC Metalurh Donetsk (UKR)
A 2-2 Ačimovič (8), Diabang (48)
Sáfár, Dragovic, Bąk, Diabang, Jun, Ortlechner, Voříšek, Junuzovic (Klein 46), Baumgartlinger, Ačimovič (Suttner 83), Standfest. Coach: Karl Daxbacher (AUT)
Red Card(s): Diabang 70
Yellow Card(s): Standfest 59, Klein 62, Diabang 69, Diabang 70, Jun 76, Baumgartlinger 83
H 3-2 Okotie (36), Ačimovič (70p), Sulimani (115)
Sáfár, Dragovic, Bąk, Klein, Jun (Sulimani 90+2), Ortlechner (Suttner 46), Voříšek, Okotie, Topić (64), Baumgartlinger, Ačimovič, Standfest. Coach: Karl Daxbacher (AUT)
Yellow Card(s): Baumgartlinger 82, Topić 105

Group L
Match 1 – Athletic Club (ESP)
A 0-3
Sáfár, Dragovic, Bąk, Klein, Diabang (Schumacher 59), Jun, Ortlechner, Voříšek (Madl 78), Sulimani (Liendl 31), Suttner, Standfest. Coach: Karl Daxbacher (AUT)
Red Card(s): Suttner 71
Yellow Card(s): Suttner 7
Match 2 – CD Nacional (POR)
H 1-1 Schumacher (76)
Sáfár, Dragovic, Bąk, Klein (Sulimani 70), Diabang (Schumacher 62), Jun, Ortlechner, Voříšek (Junuzovic 46), Baumgartlinger, Ačimovič, Standfest. Coach: Karl Daxbacher (AUT)
Yellow Card(s): Diabang 2, Standfest 50, Sulimani 84
Match 3 – Werder Bremen (GER)
H 2-2 Sulimani (73), Schumacher (87)
Almer, Dragovic, Bąk, Klein (Schumacher 64), Diabang, Ortlechner, Junuzovic, Sulimani, Baumgartlinger (Hattenberger 83), Ačimovič, Standfest. Coach: Karl Daxbacher (AUT)
Match 4 – Werder Bremen (GER)
A 0-2
Sáfár (Almer 46), Dragovic, Bąk, Klein, Hattenberger, Schumacher, Junuzovic, Liendl (Baumgartlinger 74), Leovac, Sulimani (Diabang 83), Ačimovič. Coach: Karl Daxbacher (AUT)
Yellow Card(s): Hattenberger 32
Match 5 – Athletic Club (ESP)
H 0-3
Sáfár, Dragovic, Bąk, Klein, Diabang (Topić 83), Junuzovic, Liendl (Schumacher 58), Sulimani (Krammer 49), Baumgartlinger, Suttner, Ačimovič. Coach: Karl Daxbacher (AUT)
Yellow Card(s): Sulimani 11, Dragovic 61
Match 6 – CD Nacional (POR)
A 1-5 Schumacher (21)
Almer, Bąk, Klein, Diabang (Topić 74), Schumacher (Hattenberger 68), Ortlechner, Voříšek, Junuzovic (Liendl 81), Baumgartlinger, Suttner, Ačimovič. Coach: Karl Daxbacher (AUT)
Yellow Card(s): Baumgartlinger 65, Bąk 77

SK RAPID WIEN

UEFA EUROPA LEAGUE

Second Qualifying Round – KF Vllaznia (ALB)
H 5-0 Hofmann (33p), Jelavić (68, 73), Trimmel (83), Hoffer (85)
Payer, Patocka, Heikkinen, Maierhofer (Jelavić 51), Hofmann, Katzer, Kavlak (Trimmel 74), Eder, Hoffer, Dober, Pehlivan (Drazan 29). Coach: Peter Pacult (AUT)
Yellow Card(s): Drazan 72
A 3-0 Hofmann (66, 90+2), Maierhofer (76)
Payer, Patocka, Heikkinen, Hofmann, Katzer, Eder, Drazan (Jelavić 60), Hoffer (Maierhofer 68), Dober, Trimmel (Konrad 78), Pehlivan. Coach: Peter Pacult (AUT)
Yellow Card(s): Heikkinen 62, Dober 77

Third Qualifying Round – APOP/Kinyras Peyias FC (CYP)
A 2-1 Maierhofer (25), Jelavić (57)
Payer, Jovanović, Heikkinen, Maierhofer, Hofmann, Katzer, Jelavić (Kulovits 77), Eder, Drazan, Dober (Thonhofer 66), Pehlivan (Trimmel 55). Coach: Peter Pacult (AUT)
Yellow Card(s): Katzer 45+1, Maierhofer 58, Eder 60, Dober 63
A 2-2 Konrad (30), Trimmel (111) (aet)
Payer, Jovanović, Thonhofer, Heikkinen, Hofmann, Katzer, Jelavić, Maierhofer 67), Eder, Trimmel, Konrad (Drazan 103), Pehlivan (Patocka 120). Coach: Peter Pacult (AUT)
Yellow Card(s): Pehlivan 9, Jovanović 43, Trimmel 66, Maierhofer 77, Hofmann 90+2

Play-Off Round – Aston Villa FC (ENG)
A 1-0 Jelavić (1)
Payer, Patocka, Jovanović, Heikkinen, Hofmann, Katzer, Jelavić, Drazan (Bošković 83), Dober, Konrad (Trimmel 62), Pehlivan. Coach: Peter Pacult (AUT)
Yellow Card(s): Dober 41
A 1-2 Jelavić (76)
Payer, Patocka, Heikkinen, Hofmann, Katzer, Jelavić (Bošković 87), Drazan, Soma, Dober, Trimmel (Maierhofer 56), Pehlivan. Coach: Peter Pacult (AUT)
Yellow Card(s): Dober 31, Payer 90

Group C
Match 1 – Hamburger SV (GER)
A 3-0 Hofmann (35), Jelavić (44), Drazan (76)
Payer, Kulovits, Heikkinen, Hofmann, Katzer, Jelavić (Salihi 86), Kavlak, Eder, Soma, Bošković (Drazan 60), Pehlivan. Coach: Peter Pacult (AUT)
Yellow Card(s): Bošković 42, Pehlivan 64
Match 2 – Celtic FC (SCO)
A 1-1 Jelavić (4)
Payer, Patocka, Heikkinen, Hofmann, Katzer, Jelavić, Kavlak, Soma, Dober, Bošković (Drazan 63), Pehlivan. Coach: Peter Pacult (AUT)
Yellow Card(s): Pehlivan 38, Kavlak 79
Match 3 – Hapoel Tel-Aviv FC (ISR)
A 1-5 Hofmann (31)
Payer, Patocka, Hofmann, Katzer, Jelavić, Kavlak, Soma, Dober (Salihi 66), Bošković (Jovanović 71), Trimmel (Kulovits 73), Pehlivan. Coach: Peter Pacult (AUT)
Match 4 – Hapoel Tel-Aviv FC (ISR)
A 0-0
Payer, Patocka, Heikkinen, Hofmann, Katzer, Jelavić (Salihi 80), Kavlak (Drazan 65), Soma, Dober, Bošković, Pehlivan (Gartler 57). Coach: Peter Pacult (AUT)
Match 5 – Hamburger SV (GER)
A 0-2
Payer, Jovanović, Kulovits, Heikkinen (Dober 66), Hofmann (Thonhofer 79), Katzer, Jelavić, Kavlak, Soma, Bošković, Pehlivan (Salihi 51). Coach: Peter Pacult (AUT)
Yellow Card(s): Pehlivan 24, Heikkinen 26, Katzer 35, Soma 40, Kulovits 73, Bošković 82, Thonhofer 90+2

Match 6 – Celtic FC (SCO)
H 3-3 Jelavić (1, 8), Salihi (19)
Hedl, Patocka, Kulovits, Salihi (Ildiz 78), Hofmann, Katzer, Jelavić, Kavlak (Drazan 59), Soma, Dober (Trimmel 30), Bošković. Coach: Peter Pacult (AUT)
Yellow Card(s): Patocka 15, Drazan 90

SK STURM GRAZ

UEFA EUROPA LEAGUE

Second Qualifying Round – NK Široki Brijeg (BIH)
H 2-1 Haas (12), Hölzl (38)
Gratzei, Lamotte, Sonnleitner, Feldhofer, Hlinka, Hölzl, Jantscher, Kienzl (Beichler 75), Kandelaki, Muratović (Weber 67), Haas. Coach: Franco Foda (GER)
Yellow Card(s): Beichler 85
A 1-1 Jantscher (41)
Gratzei, Lamotte, Sonnleitner, Feldhofer, Weber (Hassler 90+4), Hlinka, Hölzl, Haas (Beichler 63), Jantscher (Prettenthaler 83), Kandelaki, Kienzl. Coach: Franco Foda (GER)
Yellow Card(s): Kandelaki 39, Hlinka 78

Third Qualifying Round – OFK Petrovac (MNE)
A 2-1 Haas (64p), Lamotte (76)
Gratzei, Lamotte, Sonnleitner, Weber, Hlinka (Kienzl 66), Hölzl, Haas (Bukva 66), Kandelaki, Prettenthaler, Schildenfeld, Beichler (Hassler 89). Coach: Franco Foda (GER)
Yellow Card(s): Hölzl 55
H 5-0 Muratović (30), Hölzl (43, 49), Hassler (56), Weber (83)
Gratzei, Lamotte, Feldhofer, Weber, Hölzl (Bukva 70), Muratović (Foda 81), Hassler, Jantscher, Kandelaki (Prettenthaler 63), Kienzl, Schildenfeld. Coach: Franco Foda (GER)
Yellow Card(s): Feldhofer 58

Play-Off Round – FC Metalist Kharkiv (UKR)
H 1-1 Beichler (31)
Gratzei, Lamotte (Bukva 62), Sonnleitner, Weber, Hlinka, Hölzl, Muratović, Jantscher (Hassler 81), Kandelaki, Schildenfeld, Beichler (Weinberger 88). Coach: Franco Foda (GER)
Yellow Card(s): Weber 81, Bukva 90+2
A 1-0 Beichler (32)
Gratzei, Sonnleitner, Feldhofer, Weber, Hlinka, Hölzl, Muratović (Hassler 89), Jantscher, Kandelaki, Schildenfeld, Beichler. Coach: Franco Foda (GER)
Yellow Card(s): Hassler 90+4

Group F
Match 1 – FC Dinamo Bucureşti (ROU)
H 0-1
Gratzei, Sonnleitner, Feldhofer (Bukva 83), Weber (Hassler 83), Hlinka, Hölzl, Muratović, Jantscher, Kandelaki, Schildenfeld, Beichler (Lavrič 72). Coach: Franco Foda (GER)
Yellow Card(s): Beichler 71
Match 2 – Galatasaray AŞ (TUR)
A 1-1 Beichler (45+1)
Gratzei, Sonnleitner, Weber, Hlinka, Bukva (Prettenthaler 76), Muratović, Jantscher, Ehrenreich, Kandelaki, Schildenfeld, Beichler (Lavrič 89). Coach: Franco Foda (GER)
Match 3 – Panathinaikos FC (GRE)
A 0-1
Gratzei, Sonnleitner, Weber, Hlinka, Hölzl (Hassler 80), Bukva (Jantscher 63), Muratović, Ehrenreich, Prettenthaler (Feldhofer 46), Schildenfeld, Beichler. Coach: Franco Foda (GER)
Yellow Card(s): Bukva 45+1, Sonnleitner 59

Match 4 – Panathinaikos FC (GRE)
H 0-1
Gratzei, Sonnleitner, Weber, Hölzl, Muratović, Jantscher, Ehrenreich (Bukva 80), Kandelaki, Schildenfeld, Beichler (Lavrič 60), Foda (Weinberger 82). Coach: Franco Foda (GER)
Yellow Card(s): Hölzl 88
Match 5 – FC Dinamo Bucureşti (ROU)
A 1-2 *Sonnleitner (5)*
Gratzei, Sonnleitner (Jantscher 61), Feldhofer, Hlinka, Bukva, Muratović (Beichler 68), Ehrenreich, Prettenthaler, Schildenfeld, Weinberger (Hölzl 77), Lavrič. Coach: Franco Foda (GER)
Yellow Card(s): Schildenfeld 8, Feldhofer 33, Prettenthaler 56, Ehrenreich 84
Match 6 – Galatasaray AŞ (TUR)
H 1-0 *Beichler (21)*
Gratzei, Sonnleitner, Weber, Hlinka, Hölzl, Jantscher (Weinberger 90+2), Ehrenreich, Kandelaki, Schildenfeld, Beichler (Foda 90+3), Lavrič (Bukva 70). Coach: Franco Foda (GER)
Yellow Card(s): Hölzl 44, Lavrič 54, Schildenfeld 78, Bukva 90+4

AZERBAIJAN

BAKI FK

UEFA CHAMPIONS LEAGUE

Second Qualifying Round – FK Ekranas (LTU)
A 2-2 *Felipe (78), Batista (90+1)*
Sissokho, Rafael Barbosa, Boret, Bates, Skulić, Felipe, Fábio (Mujiri 69), Soltanov, Savinov, Adamia (Batista 81), Šolić. Coach: Gjokica Hadzievski (MKD)
Yellow Card(s): Boret 5, Adamia 17, Rafael Barbosa 51, Sissokho 52, Soltanov 86, Felipe 90+4
H 4-2 *Felipe (59, 77), Mujiri (65), Šolić (90+1)*
Sissokho, Rafael Barbosa, Boret, Bates, Skulić, Felipe (Batista 79), Mujiri (Qurbanov 69), Soltanov, Savinov, Adamia (Pérez 56), Šolić. Coach: Gjokica Hadzievski (MKD)
Yellow Card(s): Soltanov 49, Sissokho 81, Šolić 90+1

Third Qualifying Round – PFC Levski Sofia (BUL)
H 0-0
Šarlija, Rafael Barbosa, Boret, Bates, Qurbanov (Fábio 82), Skulić, Felipe (Batista 51), Mujiri (Adamia 68), Pérez, Savinov, Šolić. Coach: Gjokica Hadzievski (MKD)
Yellow Card(s): Mujiri 32, Bates 90+1
A 0-2
Sissokho, Rafael Barbosa, Boret, Bates, Skulić (Qurbanov 81), Felipe, Pérez (Mujiri 69), Fábio (Adamia 69), Soltanov, Savinov, Šolić. Coach: Gjokica Hadzievski (MKD)
Yellow Card(s): Felipe 2, Skulić 7

UEFA EUROPA LEAGUE

Play-Off Round – FC Basel 1893 (SUI)
H 1-3 *Pérez (49)*
Sissokho, Boret, Bates, Skulić, Mujiri, Pérez, Soltanov, Savinov, Yunisoğlu, Šolić (Adamia 74), Jabá (Qurbanov 64). Coach: Gjokica Hadzievski (MKD)
Yellow Card(s): Skulić 3
A 1-5 *Felipe (33)*
Sissokho, Ämirbäyov, Bates (Adamia 46), Felipe, Pérez (Mujiri 73), Mähärrämov, Tomash, Soltanov (Fábio 46), Yunisoğlu, Šolić, Jabá. Coach: Gjokica Hadzievski (MKD)
Yellow Card(s): Jabá 85, Fábio 85

QARABAĞ FK

UEFA EUROPA LEAGUE

Second Qualifying Round – Rosenborg BK (NOR)
Väliyev, Allahverdiyev, Medvedev (Äliyev 90), R.A. Sadiqov, A. Kärimov (Yusifov 72), E. Mämmädov, İmamäliyev (Häşimov 87), R.F. Sadiqov, Nadirov, Cavadov, Teli. Coach: Qurban Qurbanov (AZE)
Yellow Card(s): Allahverdiyev 36, İmamäliyev 47, Väliyev 89
H 1-0 *R.F. Sadiqov (45+1)*
Väliyev, Allahverdiyev, Medvedev, R.A. Sadiqov, A. Kärimov (Yusifov 68), E. Mämmädov (Häşimov 72), İmamäliyev (Äliyev 82), R.F. Sadiqov, Nadirov, Cavadov, Teli. Coach: Qurban Qurbanov (AZE)
Yellow Card(s): Mämmädov 47

Third Qualifying Round – FC Honka Espoo (FIN)
A 1-0 *E. Mämmädov (69)*
Väliyev, Allahverdiyev, Medvedev (Häşimov 66), R.A. Sadiqov, A. Kärimov (Yusifov 77), E. Mämmädov, İmamäliyev (Ismayılov 86), R.F. Sadiqov, Nadirov, Cavadov, Teli. Coach: Qurban Qurbanov (AZE)
H 2-1 *E. Mämmädov (32), R.F. Sadiqov (80)*
Väliyev, Allahverdiyev, Medvedev, R.A. Sadiqov, A. Kärimov (Yusifov 46), E. Mämmädov, R.F. Sadiqov, Nadirov (Äliyev 88), Cavadov, Ismayilov (Häşimov 79), Teli. Coach: Qurban Qurbanov (AZE)
Yellow Card(s): Teli 24, Allahverdiyev 73, Medvedev 76

Play-Off Round – FC Twente (NED)
A 1-3 *Nadirov (8)*
Väliyev, Häşimov, Medvedev, R.A. Sadiqov, A. Kärimov (Yusifov 64), E. Mämmädov (Hacıyev 81), Abbasov, Nadirov, Cavadov, Ismayilov (Äliyev 84), Teli. Coach: Qurban Qurbanov (AZE)
Yellow Card(s): Ismayilov 56, Abbasov 60
H 0-0
Väliyev, Allahverdiyev, Häşimov, Medvedev, R.A. Sadiqov, A. Kärimov (Yusifov 72), E. Mämmädov, Nadirov, Cavadov, Ismayilov (Äliyev 67), Teli. Coach: Qurban Qurbanov (AZE)
Yellow Card(s): Allahverdiyev 8, Häşimov 55, Mämmädov 90+2

İNTER BAKI PİK

UEFA EUROPA LEAGUE

First Qualifying Round – FC Spartak Trnava (SVK)
A 1-2 *Gutiérrez (80)*
Wilson Júnior, Accioly (Zagorac 85), Ismailov, Gutiérrez, Abbasov, Červenka, Zlatinov, Şükürov, Rubins (Mämmädov 63), Hüseynov (Xäya 57). Chertoganov. Coach: Kakhaber Tskhadadze (GEO)
Yellow Card(s): Şükürov 81
H 1-3 *Guglielmone (11)*
Wilson Júnior, Accioly, Ismailov (Rubins 64), Gutiérrez, Abbasov, Červenka, Zlatinov (Mämmädov 65), Şükürov, Guglielmone (Xäya 77), Hüseynov, Chertoganov. Coach: Kakhaber Tskhadadze (GEO)

SIMURQ ZAQATALA PFK

UEFA EUROPA LEAGUE

First Qualifying Round – Bnei Yehuda Tel-Aviv FC (ISR)
H 0-1
Mähdiyev, Malyhin, Sokolov, Soloņicins (Cälilov 64), Artyukh (E. Mämmädov 76), Chkhetiani, Bolkvadze, Bulychev, Makhviladze, Valev, Akhalkatsi (Dolidze 78). Coach: Roman Pokara (UKR)
Yellow Card(s): Soloņicins 52
A 0-3
Mähdiyev, Malyhin, Sokolov, Hunchak, E. Mämmädov (Soloņicins 66), Artyukh, Chkhetiani, Bolkvadze, Bulychev, Valev (Mazyar 46), Akhalkatsi (Popovici 77). Coach: Roman Pokara (UKR)
Yellow Card(s): Bolkvadze 35, Malyhin 59

BELARUS

FC BATE BORISOV

UEFA CHAMPIONS LEAGUE

Second Qualifying Round – FK Makedonija GP Skopje (MKD)
A 2-0 *Krivets (40), Skavysh (50)*
Veremko, Likhtarovich (Bordachev 69), Sosnovskiy, Shitov, Yurevich, A. Volodko, Krivets, Nekhaichik (Pavlov 85), Radkov, Skavysh (Alumona 75), Stasevich. Coach: Viktor Goncharenko (BLR)
H 2-0 *Sosnovskiy (83), Rodionov (90+3)*
Veremko, Likhtarovich (Bordachev 72), Sosnovskiy, Shitov, Yurevich, A. Volodko, Krivets, Nekhaichik (Rodionov 77), Radkov, Skavysh (Alumona 85), Stasevich. Coach: Viktor Goncharenko (BLR)
Yellow Card(s): Shitov 24, Sosnovskiy 48

Third Qualifying Round – FK Ventspils (LVA)
A 0-1
Veremko, Likhtarovich (A. Volodko 63), Sosnovskiy, Shitov, Yurevich, Krivets, Nekhaichik (Bordachev 74), Radkov, Skavysh, Rodionov (Alumona 88), Stasevich. Coach: Viktor Goncharenko (BLR)
Yellow Card(s): Rodionov 42, Bordachev 89, Radkov 90+2
H 2-1 *Krivets (43, 57)*
Veremko, Likhtarovich, Sosnovskiy, Shitov, Yurevich, A. Volodko (Pavlov 78), Krivets, Nekhaichik, Bordachev (Alumona 82), Rodionov (Skavysh 75), Stasevich. Coach: Viktor Goncharenko (BLR)
Yellow Card(s): Stasevich 82

UEFA EUROPA LEAGUE

Play-Off Round – PFC Litex Lovech (BUL)
H 0-1
Gutor, Sosnovskiy, Shitov, Yurevich, A. Volodko, Krivets (Rodionov 64), Nekhaichik, Skavysh (Goharyan 83), Pavlov, Bordachev, Stasevich (Alumona 84). Coach: Viktor Goncharenko (BLR)
Yellow Card(s): Nekhaichik 56, A. Volodko 76
A 4-0 *Sosnovskiy (86, 99), Rodionov (95), Skavysh (118) (aet)*
Gutor, Likhtarovich (Nekhaichik 58), Sosnovskiy, Shitov, Yurevich, Alumona (Krivets 46), Skavysh, Pavlov (Goharyan 77), Bordachev, Rodionov, Stasevich. Coach: Viktor Goncharenko (BLR)
Yellow Card(s): Shitov 37, Alumona 40, Stasevich 61, Krivets 65, Skavysh 95, Gutor 102, Goharyan 114

Group I
Match 1 – SL Benfica (POR)
A 0-2
Veremko, Likhtarovich (A. Volodko 64), Sosnovskiy, Yurevich, Krivets, Nekhaichik, Skavysh (Goharyan 56), Pavlov, Bordachev, Rodionov (Alumona 81), Rzhevskiy. Coach: Viktor Goncharenko (BLR)
Yellow Card(s): Yurevich 33, A. Volodko 90+1
Match 2 – Everton (ENG)
H 1-2 *Likhtarovich (16)*
Veremko, Likhtarovich (Goharyan 81), Sosnovskiy, Shitov, Yurevich, Krivets, Nekhaichik, Skavysh (Stasevich 28), Pavlov (A. Volodko 78), Bordachev, Rodionov. Coach: Viktor Goncharenko (BLR)
Yellow Card(s): Shitov 67, Krivets 73
Match 3 – AEK Athens FC (GRE)
H 2-1 *Pavlov (51), Alumona (85)*
Veremko, Likhtarovich (Goharyan 65), Sosnovskiy, Shitov, Yurevich, A. Volodko, Krivets, Nekhaichik, Pavlov (Skavysh 55), Bordachev (Alumona 85), Rodionov. Coach: Viktor Goncharenko (BLR)
Yellow Card(s): Sosnovskiy 30, A. Volodko 61, Goharyan 71
Match 4 – AEK Athens FC (GRE)
A 2-2 *Rodionov (17), A. Volodko (26)*
Veremko, Likhtarovich, Sosnovskiy, Shitov, Yurevich, A. Volodko, Krivets (Alumona 67), Nekhaichik (Pavlov 84), Skavysh (Radkov 76), Bordachev, Rodionov. Coach: Viktor Goncharenko (BLR)
Red Card(s): Shitov 75
Yellow Card(s): Yurevich 37, Nekhaichik 40, Shitov 52, Shitov 75, Radkov 81, Pavlov 90
Match 5 – SL Benfica (POR)
H 1-2 *Miguel Vitor (68og)*
Veremko, Likhtarovich (Skavysh 61), Sosnovskiy, Yurevich, A. Volodko, Krivets, Nekhaichik, Radkov, Pavlov (Alumona 56), Bordachev, Rodionov (Goharyan 79). Coach: Viktor Goncharenko (BLR)
Yellow Card(s): Bordachev 70, Nekhaichik 80
Match 6 – Everton (ENG)
A 1-0 *Yurevich (75)*
Veremko, Likhtarovich (Pavlov 56), Sosnovskiy, Shitov, Yurevich, A. Volodko, Krivets, Nekhaichik (Bulyga 82), Skavysh (Goharyan 74), Bordachev, Rodionov. Coach: Viktor Goncharenko (BLR)
Yellow Card(s): Sosnovskiy 14, Nekhaichik 34

FC NAFTAN NOVOPOLOTSK

UEFA EUROPA LEAGUE

Second Qualifying Round – KAA Gent (BEL)
H 2-1 *Degterev (21, 66)*
Kurskis, Gorbachev, Politevich, Rudik, Yatskevich, Komarovskiy, Degterev (Zuyev 72), Stripeikis (Zyulev 53), Belousov, Verkhovtsov, Trukhov (Bukatkin 83). Coach: Igor Kovalevich (BLR)
Yellow Card(s): Zyulev 69
A 0-1
Kurskis, Gorbachev, Politevich, Rudik, Yatskevich (Zyulev 58), Komarovskiy, Degterev (Volodenkov 74), Stripeikis (Zuyev 61), Belousov, Verkhovtsov, Trukhov. Coach: Igor Kovalevich (BLR)

CHAMPIONS LEAGUE   EUROPA LEAGUE

FC DINAMO MINSK

UEFA EUROPA LEAGUE

First Qualifying Round – FK Renova (MKD)
H 2-1 *Kislyak (72p), Strakhanovich (87)*
Gorbunov, Gigevich (Strakhanovich 58), Chukhlei (Dragun 71), Kislyak,
Pavlyukovich, Zita, Montaroup, Veretilo, Gavryushko (Lebedev 46),
Martynovich, Gurenko. Coach: Slavoljub Muslin (SRB)
Yellow Card(s): Pavlyukovich 90
A 1-1 *Kislyak (38p)*
Gorbunov, Lebedev, Chukhlei, Kislyak (Zita 51), Pavlyukovich, Putilo
(Strakhanovich 62), Montaroup, Veretilo, Shkabara (Gigevich 31), Šaraba,
Gurenko. Coach: Slavoljub Muslin (SRB)
Yellow Card(s): Montaroup 36, Šaraba 61

Second Qualifying Round – Tromsø IL (NOR)
H 0-0
Čanović, Dragun (Gigevich 53), Lebedev (Gavryushko 71), Chukhlei (Putilo
71), Kislyak, Zita, Montaroup, Veretilo, Martynovich, Šaraba, Gurenko.
Coach: Slavoljub Muslin (SRB)
A 1-4 *Zita (83)*
Čanović, Dragun (Gigevich 60), Lebedev, Chukhlei (Zaleskiy 72), Kislyak
(Strakhanovich 79), Pavlyukovich, Zita, Montaroup, Martynovich, Šaraba,
Gurenko. Coach: Slavoljub Muslin (SRB)
Red Card(s): Šaraba 66, Montaroup 85
Yellow Card(s): Montaroup 21, Šaraba 26, Šaraba 66, Montaroup 85

FC MTZ-RIPO MINSK

UEFA EUROPA LEAGUE

First Qualifying Round – FK Sutjeska (MNE)
A 1-1 *Bubnov (78)*
Sulima, Zrnanović, Camara (Makas 74), Kvaratskhelia (Bubnov 77),
Tolkanitsa, D. Shchegrikovich, Maltsev, Osipovich, Popel, Yeremchuk,
Ryndyuk (Ledenev 71). Coach: Yuriy Puntus (BLR)
H 2-1 *Ryndyuk (67, 111) (aet)*
Sulima, Skshynetskiy, Zrnanović, Camara (Sitko 113), Kvaratskhelia,
Tolkanitsa (Ryndyuk 60), D. Shchegrikovich (S. Shchegrikovich 70),
Maltsev, Osipovich, Popel, Yeremchuk. Coach: Yuriy Puntus (BLR)
Yellow Card(s): Camara 89, S. Shchegrikovich 105, Osipovich 122

Second Qualifying Round – FC Metalurh Donetsk (UKR)
A 0-3
Sulima, Zrnanović, Kvaratskhelia (Sitko 84), Tolkanitsa, D. Shchegrikovich,
Osipovich, Popel, Kharitonchik (Makas 60), Mayevskiy (Maltsev 69),
Yeremchuk, Nicolas. Coach: Yuriy Puntus (BLR)
Yellow Card(s): Kvaratskhelia 50, Zrnanović 54
H 1-2 *Nicolas (15)*
Sulima, Zrnanović (Maltsev 46), Camara (Kharitonchik 66), Kvaratskhelia,
Tolkanitsa, D. Shchegrikovich, Osipovich, Mayevskiy, Yeremchuk, Kendysh
(Makas 76), Nicolas. Coach: Yuriy Puntus (BLR)
Yellow Card(s): Zrnanović 22, Kvaratskhelia 56, Osipovich 87

BELGIUM

R. STANDARD DE LIÈGE

UEFA CHAMPIONS LEAGUE

Group H
Match 1 – Arsenal FC (ENG)
H 2-3 *Mangala (3), Jovanović (5p)*
Sinan, Ricardo Rocha, Dalmat (Goreux 80), Mbokani, De Camargo,
Marcos, Sarr, Mangala, Jovanović (Nicaise 59), Witsel (Traoré 84), Carcela-
González. Coach: László Bölöni (ROU)
Yellow Card(s): Sinan 44, Witsel 67, Nicaise 76
Match 2 – AZ Alkmaar (NED)
A 1-1 *Traoré (90+1)*
Sinan, Ricardo Rocha (Mulemo 53), Felipe, Dalmat (Traoré 77), Mbokani,
Marcos, Sarr (De Camargo 60), Mangala, Jovanović, Witsel, Carcela-
González. Coach: László Bölöni (ROU)
Yellow Card(s): Sarr 40, Jovanović 63
Match 3 – Olympiacos FC (GRE)
A 1-2 *De Camargo (37)*
Sinan, Ricardo Rocha, Felipe, Dalmat (Carcela-González 48), Mbokani, De
Camargo (Nicaise 89), Marcos, Sarr, Mangala, Jovanović, Witsel. Coach:
László Bölöni (ROU)
Yellow Card(s): Mangala 52, Ricardo Rocha 75
Match 4 – Olympiacos FC (GRE)
H 2-0 *Mbokani (31), Jovanović (88)*
Sinan, Ricardo Rocha, Felipe, Mbokani, De Camargo, Marcos, Sarr (Victor
Ramos 46), Mangala, Jovanović (Angeli 90+1), Witsel, Carcela-González
(Goreux 87). Coach: László Bölöni (ROU)
Yellow Card(s): Ricardo Rocha 27, Marcos 60, Mangala 64
Match 5 – Arsenal FC (ENG)
A 0-2
Sinan, Goreux, Felipe, Dalmat (Traoré 64), Mbokani (Cyriac 68), Mulemo,
Marcos, Sarr, Mangala, Witsel, Carcela-González. Coach: László Bölöni
(ROU)
Red Card(s): Carcela-González 86
Yellow Card(s): Mulemo 68, Mangala 70
Match 6 – AZ Alkmaar (NED)
H 1-1 *Sinan (90+5)*
Sinan, Felipe (Cyriac 85), Dalmat (Traoré 80), Mbokani, De Camargo,
Mulemo, Marcos, Sarr, Jovanović, Nicaise, Witsel. Coach: László Bölöni
(ROU)
Yellow Card(s): Traoré 90

No	Player	Nat	DoB	Aps	(s)	Gls
Goalkeeper						
38	Sinan Bolat	TUR	3/9/88	6		1
Defenders						
17	Marcos Camozzato	BRA	17/6/83	6		
5	Felipe	BRA	15/5/87	5		
2	Réginal Goreux		31/12/87	1	(2)	
22	Eliaquim Mangala	FRA	13/2/91	5		1
14	Landry Mulemo		17/9/86	2	(1)	
4	Ricardo Rocha	POR	3/10/78	4		
19	Mohamed Sarr	SEN	23/12/83	6		
3	Victor Ramos	BRA	5/5/89		(1)	
Midfielders						
27	Arnor Angeli		25/2/91		(1)	
33	Mehdi Carcela-González		1/7/89	4	(1)	
7	Wilfried Dalmat	FRA	17/7/82	5		
26	Benjamin Nicaise	FRA	28/9/80	1	(2)	
28	Axel Witsel		12/1/89	6		

Belgium

Forwards

29	Gohi Bi Cyriac	CIV	15/8/90		(2)	
10	Igor De Camargo		12/5/83	4	(1)	1
23	Milan Jovanović	SRB	18/4/81	5		2
9	Dieumerci Mbokani	COD	22/11/85	6		1
20	Moussa Traoré	CIV	19/4/90		(4)	1

UEFA EUROPA LEAGUE

Round of 32 – FC Salzburg (AUT)
H 3-2 *Witsel (66p, 82), De Camargo (80)*
Sinan, Goreux, Victor Ramos, Defour, Mbokani (Traoré 90+1), De Camargo, Mangala, Jovanović (Dalmat 90+3), Nicaise, Witsel, Pocognoli (Gershon 85). Coach: Dominique D'Onofrio (BEL)
Yellow Card(s): Goreux 52, De Camargo 75
A 0-0
Sinan, Victor Ramos, Defour, Mbokani (Traoré 90+4), De Camargo, Marcos, Sarr, Jovanović (Carcela-González 72), Nicaise (Mangala 82), Witsel, Pocognoli. Coach: Dominique D'Onofrio (BEL)
Yellow Card(s): Witsel 19, Pocognoli 69, Carcela-González 90+4

Round of 16 – Panathinaikos FC (GRE)
A 3-1 *Witsel (8), Jovanović (16), De Camargo (74)*
Sinan, Victor Ramos, Defour (Carcela-González 22), Mbokani, De Camargo, Marcos, Sarr, Jovanović (Dalmat 79), Gershon, Nicaise (Mangala 67), Witsel. Coach: Dominique D'Onofrio (BEL)
Yellow Card(s): Sarr 47, Gershon 58, Jovanović 61, Sinan 66
H 1-0 *Mbokani (45+2)*
Sinan, Victor Ramos, Dalmat (Goreux 72), Mbokani (Traoré 90), De Camargo, Marcos, Sarr, Jovanović (Mangala 82), Witsel, Carcela-González, Pocognoli. Coach: Dominique D'Onofrio (BEL)
Yellow Card(s): Pocognoli 24, Sarr 59

Quarter-Finals – Hamburger SV (GER)
A 1-2 *Mbokani (31)*
Sinan, Goreux (Grozav 76), Victor Ramos, Mbokani, De Camargo, Marcos, Mangala, Jovanović (Traoré 90+3), Witsel, Carcela-González, Pocognoli. Coach: Dominique D'Onofrio (BEL)
Yellow Card(s): Marcos 15, Mbokani 43, Mangala 79, Victor Ramos 81
H 1-3 *De Camargo (33)*
Sinan, Victor Ramos, Mbokani, De Camargo, Marcos, Sarr, Jovanović, Nicaise (Mangala 89), Witsel, Carcela-González (Dalmat 76), Pocognoli. Coach: Dominique D'Onofrio (BEL)
Yellow Card(s): Marcos 24, Victor Ramos 45+3, Mbokani 66, Pocognoli 85

RSC ANDERLECHT

UEFA CHAMPIONS LEAGUE

Third Qualifying Round – Sivasspor (TUR)
H 5-0 *De Sutter (17, 76), Boussoufa (22), Chatelle (32), Frutos (90+1)*
Proto, Deschacht, Biglia, Van Damme, Polák, Suárez (Frutos 74), Boussoufa, Chatelle (Legear 71), De Sutter (Gillet 78), Juhász, Wasilewski. Coach: Ariël Jacobs (BEL)
Yellow Card(s): Van Damme 64
A 1-3 *Van Damme (34)*
Proto, Deschacht, Van Damme, Polák, Boussoufa (Reynaldo 76), Chatelle, De Sutter (Frutos 57), Juhász, Wasilewski, Gillet, Saré. Coach: Ariël Jacobs (BEL)

Play-Off Round – Olympique Lyonnais (FRA)
A 1-5 *Suárez (58)*
Proto, Deschacht, Biglia, Van Damme, Polák, Suárez, Boussoufa, De Sutter (Lukaku 72), Juhász, Wasilewski, Gillet (Legear 46). Coach: Ariël Jacobs (BEL)
Yellow Card(s): Proto 14, Van Damme 15, Suárez 67, Polák 68

H 1-3 *Suárez (51p)*
Schollen, Mazuch, Deschacht, Polák (Biglia 46), Boussoufa, Chatelle (Reynaldo 66), De Sutter (Suárez 46), Juhász, Wasilewski, Gillet, Saré.
Coach: Ariël Jacobs (BEL)
Yellow Card(s): Boussoufa 69

UEFA EUROPA LEAGUE

Group A
Match 1 – NK Dinamo Zagreb (CRO)
A 2-0 *Bernárdez (74), Legear (88)*
Proto, Mazuch, Deschacht, Biglia, Suárez (Lukaku 85), Boussoufa (Chatelle 90), Kouyaté (Legear 71), Juhász, Bernárdez, Gillet, Saré. Coach: Ariël Jacobs (BEL)
Yellow Card(s): Saré 32
Match 2 – AFC Ajax (NED)
H 1-1 *Legear (85)*
Proto, Deschacht, Van Damme, Suárez (Legear 58), Kanu (De Sutter 79), Boussoufa, Juhász, Bernárdez, Gillet, Lukaku (Kruiswijk 87), Saré. Coach: Ariël Jacobs (BEL)
Red Card(s): Van Damme 82
Yellow Card(s): Bernárdez 69, Deschacht 77
Match 3 – FC Timişoara (ROU)
A 0-0
Proto, Mazuch, Deschacht, Biglia, Kanu (Rnić 46), Boussoufa, Juhász, Gillet, Diandy (Kouyaté 85), Lukaku (Suárez 64), Saré. Coach: Ariël Jacobs (BEL)
Yellow Card(s): Kanu 44
Match 4 – FC Timişoara (ROU)
H 3-1 *Suárez (30p), Boussoufa (69), Legear (90+5)*
Proto, Mazuch, Deschacht, Biglia, Suárez (Kouyaté 83), Kanu (Legear 62), Boussoufa, Juhász, Gillet, Lukaku (Frutos 77), Saré. Coach: Ariël Jacobs (BEL)
Match 5 – NK Dinamo Zagreb (CRO)
H 0-1
Proto, Mazuch, Deschacht (Kouyaté 85), Biglia, Van Damme, Boussoufa, Legear (Suárez 68), Juhász, Gillet, Lukaku, Saré (De Sutter 72). Coach: Ariël Jacobs (BEL)
Yellow Card(s): Deschacht 15, Mazuch 79, Van Damme 90+1
Match 6 – AFC Ajax (NED)
A 3-1 *Lukaku (13, 22), Legear (43)*
Proto, Mazuch, Deschacht, Biglia, Van Damme (Saré 90), Boussoufa, Legear (Suárez 79), Kouyaté, Juhász, Gillet, Lukaku (Frutos 64). Coach: Ariël Jacobs (BEL)
Yellow Card(s): Deschacht 75

Round of 32 – Athletic Club (ESP)
A 1-1 *Biglia (35)*
Proto, Mazuch, Biglia, Van Damme, Kanu, Boussoufa (Suárez 90+1), Legear, Kouyaté, Juhász, Gillet, Lukaku (De Sutter 80). Coach: Ariël Jacobs (BEL)
Yellow Card(s): Legear 20, Juhász 34, Kouyaté 60
H 4-0 *Lukaku (4), San José (27og), Juhász (49), Legear (68)*
Proto, Mazuch, Deschacht, Biglia, Van Damme, Boussoufa, Legear (Suárez 81), Kouyaté (Saré 73), Juhász, Gillet, Lukaku (De Sutter 66). Coach: Ariël Jacobs (BEL)
Yellow Card(s): Deschacht 8, Proto 43, Boussoufa 45+2, Lukaku 65

Round of 16 – Hamburger SV (GER)
A 1-3 *Legear (45)*
Proto, Mazuch, Deschacht, Biglia, Van Damme, Kanu (Suárez 77), Legear, Kouyaté, Juhász, Gillet, Lukaku. Coach: Ariël Jacobs (BEL)
H 4-3 *Lukaku (44), Suárez (45+3p), Biglia (59), Boussoufa (66)*
Proto, Mazuch, Deschacht (De Sutter 62), Biglia, Van Damme, Boussoufa, Kouyaté, Juhász, Gillet, Lukaku (Kanu 82). Coach: Ariël Jacobs (BEL)
Yellow Card(s): Van Damme 24, Suárez 72

Belgium

KRC GENK

Genk

UEFA EUROPA LEAGUE

Play-Off Round – LOSC Lille Métropole (FRA)
H 1-2 *Tőzsér (58)*
Verhulst, Daeseleire (De Bruyne 77), Hubert, Camus (Bakx 60), Tőzsér, Koïta, Barda, Ngcongca, Tóth (Matoukou 77), João Carlos, Pudil. Coach: Hein Van Haezebrouck (BEL)
Yellow Card(s): Hubert 22, Pudil 59, Tőzsér 63
A 2-4 *Barda (24p), Tőzsér (86)*
Verhulst, Daeseleire, Hubert (Cornelis 67), Joneleit, Camus (Ogunjimi 74), Tőzsér, Koïta, Barda (De Bruyne 46), Ngcongca, Tóth, Pudil. Coach: Hein Van Haezebrouck (BEL)
Red Card(s): Pudil 83
Yellow Card(s): Daeseleire 16, Koïta 61, Pudil 68, Pudil 83

CLUB BRUGGE KV

UEFA EUROPA LEAGUE

Third Qualifying Round – FC Lahti (FIN)
H 3-2 *Akpala (12), Blondel (35, 90)*
Stijnen, Daerden, Dirar, Sonck (Dahmane 79), Blondel, Simaeys, Akpala (Geraerts 89), Donk, Vermeulen, Alcaraz (Vargas 74), Odjidja-Ofoe. Coach: Adrie Koster (NED)
Yellow Card(s): Simaeys 22
A 1-1 *Akpala (76)*
Stijnen, Daerden, Dirar, Blondel, Simaeys, Akpala (Sonck 83), Donk, Vargas (Geraerts 75), Vermeulen, Alcaraz, Odjidja-Ofoe (Dahmane 88). Coach: Adrie Koster (NED)
Yellow Card(s): Vargas 13, Daerden 43

Play-Off Round – Lech Poznań (POL)
A 0-1
Stijnen, Klukowski, Dirar (Sonck 71), Blondel, Simaeys, Akpala, Vargas (Chávez 81), Vermeulen, Geraerts, Alcaraz, Odjidja-Ofoe. Coach: Adrie Koster (NED)
Yellow Card(s): Dirar 26
H 1-0 *Sonck (79) (aet; 4-3 on pens)*
Stijnen, Klukowski, Dirar, Sonck, Blondel (Geraerts 89), Simaeys, Akpala (Chávez 120+1), Vargas (Dahmane 94), Vermeulen, Alcaraz, Odjidja-Ofoe. Coach: Adrie Koster (NED)
Yellow Card(s): Vargas 23, Odjidja-Ofoe 37, Blondel 60, Vermeulen 72, Klukowski 90+2

Group J
Match 1 – FC Shakhtar Donetsk (UKR)
H 1-4 *Geraerts (62)*
De Vlieger, Klukowski, Dirar, Sonck, Simaeys, Akpala (Kouemaha 64), Vermeulen (Hoefkens 46), Geraerts, Alcaraz, Odjidja-Ofoe (Daerden 64), Perišić. Coach: Adrie Koster (NED)
Yellow Card(s): Alcaraz 38, Dirar 47, Akpala 61
Match 2 – Toulouse FC (FRA)
A 2-2 *Akpala (52), Perišić (90+4)*
Stijnen, Hoefkens, Klukowski, Daerden (Dahmane 87), Blondel (Dirar 63), Akpala (Kouemaha 60), Vargas, Geraerts, De Mets, Odjidja-Ofoe, Perišić. Coach: Adrie Koster (NED)
Yellow Card(s): Blondel 20, Odjidja-Ofoe 84, Perišić 90+4
Match 3 – FK Partizan (SRB)

H 2-0 *Perišić (4), Brežančić (58og)*
Stijnen, Hoefkens (Donk 72), Klukowski, Dirar, Blondel (Daerden 83), Akpala (Dahmane 68), Geraerts, De Mets, Alcaraz, Odjidja-Ofoe, Perišić. Coach: Adrie Koster (NED)
Yellow Card(s): Klukowski 60, Dahmane 83
Match 4 – FK Partizan (SRB)
A 4-2 *Perišić (28), Kouemaha (36, 57), Odjidja-Ofoe (74)*
Stijnen, Klukowski, Dirar (Akpala 58), Blondel, Donk, Geraerts, De Mets (Vermeulen 86), Alcaraz, Odjidja-Ofoe, Kouemaha, Perišić (Simaeys 81). Coach: Adrie Koster (NED)
Yellow Card(s): Dirar 55, Blondel 83
Match 5 – FC Shakhtar Donetsk (UKR)
A 0-0
Stijnen, Hoefkens, Klukowski, Sonck (Akpala 84), Blondel (Vargas 67), Simaeys, Donk, Geraerts, Alcaraz, Perišić (Odjidja-Ofoe 69), Dahmane. Coach: Adrie Koster (NED)
Yellow Card(s): Simaeys 37, Sonck 69, Klukowski 75, Stijnen 85
Match 6 – Toulouse FC (FRA)
H 1-0 *Perišić (90+3)*
Stijnen, Hoefkens, Dirar (Vargas 66), Blondel, Donk, Geraerts, Alcaraz, Odjidja-Ofoe, Kouemaha, Perišić. Coach: Adrie Koster (NED)
Yellow Card(s): Dirar 27

Round of 32 – Valencia CF (ESP)
H 1-0 *Kouemaha (56)*
Stijnen, Hoefkens, Klukowski, Blondel, Akpala (Lestienne 79), Donk, Geraerts, Alcaraz, Odjidja-Ofoe, Kouemaha, Perišić. Coach: Adrie Koster (NED)
Yellow Card(s): Blondel 19, Odjidja-Ofoe 86
A 0-3 *(aet)*
Stijnen, Hoefkens, Klukowski, Sonck (Akpala 91), Lestienne (Dahmane 81), Donk, Geraerts, Alcaraz, Odjidja-Ofoe (Chávez 102), Kouemaha, Perišić. Coach: Adrie Koster (NED)
Yellow Card(s): Kouemaha 7, Klukowski 60, Odjidja-Ofoe 90+2

KAA GENT

UEFA EUROPA LEAGUE

Second Qualifying Round – FC Naftan Novopolotsk (BLR)
A 1-2 *Marić (90)*
Jorgačević, Šuler, Hanstveit, Wils, Smolders, Leye (Elghanassy 63), Čustović, Lepoint, Marić, Ljubijankič, Grondin. Coach: Michel Preud'homme (BEL)
Yellow Card(s): Grondin 25
H 1-0 *Elghanassy (54)*
Jorgačević, Šuler, Hanstveit, Wils, Azofeifa (Adriano Duarte 85), Elghanassy (Leye 79), Lepoint, Marić (Čustović 90+3), Ljubijankič, Grondin. Coach: Michel Preud'homme (BEL)
Yellow Card(s): Adriano Duarte 76, Lepoint 81

Third Qualifying Round – AS Roma (ITA)
A 1-3 *Leye (22)*
Jorgačević, Šuler, Wils, Smolders, Leye (Hanstveit 77), Azofeifa (Lepoint 81), Thompson, Adriano Duarte, Marić, Ljubijankič (Čustović 58), Grondin. Coach: Michel Preud'homme (BEL)
Red Card(s): Thompson 75
Yellow Card(s): Azofeifa 29, Marić 51, Thompson 54, Jorgačević 58, Leye 71, Čustović 72, Thompson 75
H 1-7 *Smolders (78)*
Jorgačević, Šuler, Hanstveit, Wils, Azofeifa, Leye (Lepoint 63), Azofeifa, De Smet (Čustović 46), Marić, Ljubijankič (Adriano Duarte 46), Grondin. Coach: Michel Preud'homme (BEL)
Red Card(s): Šuler 45
Yellow Card(s): Marić 19, Šuler 45, Šuler 45, Smolders 47, Adriano Duarte 55

CHAMPIONS LEAGUE. EUROPA LEAGUE

BOSNIA-HERZEGOVINA

HŠK ZRINJSKI

UEFA CHAMPIONS LEAGUE

Second Qualifying Round – ŠK Slovan Bratislava (SVK)
H 1-0 *Kordić (48)*
Melher, Šunjić, Selimović, Žuržinov, P. Sušić (Afedzie 54), Ivanković, M. Sušić, Stojanović (Šarac 78), Kordić, Zadro (Rezdaušek 88), M. Aničić. Coach: Dragan Jović (BIH)
Yellow Card(s): Ivanković 30, Šunjić 37
A 0-4
Melher, Šunjić, Selimović, Žuržinov, P. Sušić (Musa 46), Ivanković, M. Sušić, Stojanović, Kordić, Zadro, M. Aničić. Coach: Dragan Jović (BIH)
Yellow Card(s): Zadro 26, Kordić 30

FK SLAVIJA SARAJEVO

UEFA EUROPA LEAGUE

Second Qualifying Round – Aalborg BK (DEN)
A 0-0
Lučić, Lackanović, Regoje, Simić (Nikolić 88), Radonja, Arsenijević, Šćepanović, Todorović (Radovanović 57), Đermanović (Šešlija 75), Kutalia, Stanković. Coach: Duško Petrović (BIH)
Yellow Card(s): Todorović 36, Lučić 73
H 3-1 *Kutalia (35), Đermanović (48), Šćepanović (90+3)*
Lučić, Lackanović, Regoje, Simić, Radonja, Arsenijević, Šćepanović, Todorović (Vuksanović 46) (Šešlija 90), Đermanović (Radovanović 80), Kutalia, Stanković. Coach: Duško Petrović (BIH)
Yellow Card(s): Kutalia 35, Regoje 84

Third Qualifying Round – MFK Košiće (SVK)
H 0-2
Lučić, Lackanović (Benović 68), Regoje, Simić, Radonja (Radovanović 46), Arsenijević, Šćepanović, Šešlija (Nikolić 67), Đermanović, Kutalia, Stanković. Coach: Duško Petrović (BIH)
Yellow Card(s): Nikolić 71, Šćepanović 90
A 1-3 *Đermanović (17)*
Lučić, Regoje, Benović, Simić (Nikolić 79), Arsenijević, Šćepanović (Todorović 85), Šešlija, Đermanović, Vuksanović (Radovanović 69), Kutalia, Stanković. Coach: Duško Petrović (BIH)
Yellow Card(s): Šešlija 4, Regoje 43

FK SARAJEVO

UEFA EUROPA LEAGUE

Second Qualifying Round – FC Spartak Trnava (SVK)
H 1-0 *Muminović (14)*
Alaim, Dudo, Torlak, Muminović (Hamzagić 85), Džakmić, Jahović (Avdić 75), Maksumić, Rizvanović, Belošević, Janjoš, Hadžić (Pliska 90+3). Coach: Mehmed Janjoš (BIH)
A 1-1 *Jahović (88)*
Alaim, Dudo (Pliska 46), Torlak, Džakmić, Hamzagić (Avdić 76), Jahović (Čomor 90+4), Maksumić, Rizvanović, Belošević, Janjoš, Hadžić. Coach: Mehmed Janjoš (BIH)
Yellow Card(s): Janjoš 8, Hadžić 80, Avdić 89

Third Qualifying Round – Helsingborgs IF (SWE)
A 1-2 *Hadžić (22)*
Alaim, Dudo, Torlak, Muminović (Pliska 86), Džakmić, Jahović (Avdić 69), Maksumić, Rizvanović, Belošević, Janjoš, Hadžić (Hamzagić 90+4). Coach: Mehmed Janjoš (BIH)
Red Card(s): Janjoš 50
Yellow Card(s): Torlak 5, Janjoš 45+3, Janjoš 50, Alaim 55, Maksumić 59
H 2-1 *Hadžić (38), Avdić (78)*
Alaim, Dudo (Ihtijarević 58), Torlak, Muminović, Avdić, Džakmić, Hamzagić, Maksumić, Rizvanović, Belošević (Jahović 70), Hadžić (Čomor 83). Coach: Mehmed Janjoš (BIH)
Yellow Card(s): Maksumić 49, Muminović 117

Play-Off Round – CFR 1907 Cluj (ROU)
H 1-1 *Hadžić (77)*
Alaim, Dudo, Torlak, Ihtijarević (Jahović 71), Muminović, Avdić (Pliska 82), Džakmić, Rizvanović, Belošević, Janjoš (Hamzagić 62), Hadžić. Coach: Mehmed Janjoš (BIH)
Yellow Card(s): Hamzagić 80
A 1-2 *Avdić (81)*
Alaim, Dudo, Torlak, Ihtijarević (Pliska 81), Muminović, Džakmić, Jahović (Avdić 71), Maksumić, Rizvanović, Belošević (Škoro 55), Hadžić. Coach: Mehmed Janjoš (BIH)
Yellow Card(s): Maksumić 39, Avdić 90+5

NK ŠIROKI BRIJEG

UEFA EUROPA LEAGUE

First Qualifying Round – FC Banants (ARM)
A 2-0 *Ivanković (40), Tiago (65)*
Marić, Renato, Barišić, Ljubić (Zovko 31), Topić (Brekalo 77), Šilić, Peraica (Tiago 62), Diogo, Wagner, Ivanković, Martinović. Coach: Ivica Barbarić (BIH)
Yellow Card(s): Martinović 77
H 0-1
Marić, Renato, Barišić, Topić, Šilić, Peraica (A. Pinjuh 89), Diogo (Brekalo 64), Wagner, Ivanković, Zovko (Ljubić 77), Martinović. Coach: Ivica Barbarić (BIH)
Yellow Card(s): Zovko 61

Second Qualifying Round – SK Sturm Graz (AUT)
A 1-2 *Ljubić (67)*
Marić, Diogo, Barišić, Martinović, Renato, Topić, Martínez (Ivanković 64), Wagner, Ljubić (Križanović 76), Šilić, Peraica (Varea 57). Coach: Ivica Barbarić (BIH)
Yellow Card(s): Šilić 4, Ljubić 18
H 1-1 *Šilić (64)*
Marić, Renato, Martínez (Peraica 57), Barišić, Ljubić (Ivanković 57), Topić, Šilić, Diogo (Križanović 85), Varea, Wagner, Martinović. Coach: Ivica Barbarić (BIH)
Yellow Card(s): Varea 27, Martinović 38, Renato 69, Šilić 90+2

CHAMPIONS LEAGUE EUROPA LEAGUE

Bulgaria

BULGARIA

PFC LEVSKI SOFIA

UEFA CHAMPIONS LEAGUE

Second Qualifying Round – UE Sant Julià (AND)
H 4-0 *Tasevski (50), Hristov (64, 72), Gadzhev (82)*
Petkov, Genev, Milanov, Rabeh, Yovov (Joãozinho 62), Minev, Tasevski, N. Dimitrov (Zé Soares 46), Bardon (Isa 78), Gadzhev, Hristov. Coach: Emil Velev (BUL)
Yellow Card(s): Bardon 41, Hristov 55
A 5-0 *Ognyanov (23, 40), Yovov (34), Tsachev (83), Kirov (87)*
Petkov, Milanov, Rabeh (Miliev 73), Sarmov, Yovov (Tsachev 57), Topuzakov, Minev, Ognyanov, Zé Soares (Kirov 46), Isa, Gadzhev. Coach: Emil Velev (BUL)
Red Card(s): Isa 44
Yellow Card(s): Ognyanov 11, Isa 27, Isa 44

Third Qualifying Round – Bakı FK (AZE)
A 0-0
Petkov, Milanov, Rabeh, Sarmov, Yovov (Hristov 72), Topuzakov, Minev, Deniran (N. Dimitrov 78), Zé Soares, Bardon (Genev 90+5), Gadzhev. Coach: Ratko Dostanić (SRB)
Yellow Card(s): Rabeh 23
H 2-0 *Yovov (64), Hristov (80)*
Petkov, Milanov, Rabeh, Sarmov, Yovov (Wagner 78), Topuzakov, Minev, Joãozinho (Tasevski 41), Zé Soares (Deniran 82), Bardon, Hristov. Coach: Ratko Dostanić (SRB)
Yellow Card(s): Sarmov 10, Rabeh 12, Zé Soares 51, Tasevski 75

Play-Off Round – Debreceni VSC (HUN)
H 1-2 *Bardon (51)*
Petkov, Genev, Sarmov, Yovov (Joãozinho 71), Topuzakov, Minev, Zé Soares (Deniran 60), Wagner, Bardon, Hristov (Krastovchev 85). Coach: Ratko Dostanić (SRB)
Yellow Card(s): Petkov 82
A 0-2
Petkov, Rabeh, Sarmov, Yovov (N. Dimitrov 71), Topuzakov, Minev, Benzoukane, Joãozinho (Tasevski 60), Zé Soares, Bardon, Hristov (Deniran 77). Coach: Ratko Dostanić (SRB)
Yellow Card(s): Sarmov 9, Zé Soares 52

UEFA EUROPA LEAGUE

Group G
Match 1 – Villarreal CF (ESP)
A 0-1
Petkov, Genev, Rabeh, Minev, Benzoukane, Joãozinho, Tasevski (Simonović 66), N. Dimitrov (Ognyanov 78), Bardon, Baltanov, Hristov (Yovov 62). Coach: Ratko Dostanić (SRB)
Yellow Card(s): Rabeh 86
Match 2 – S.S. Lazio (ITA)
H 0-4
T. Dimitrov, Rabeh, Sarmov, Topuzakov (Miliev 46), Minev, Benzoukane, Joãozinho, Zé Soares, Tasevski (Tabakov 46), Bardon, Hristov (Yovov 72). Coach: Ratko Dostanić (SRB)
Yellow Card(s): Benzoukane 33, Bardon 86
Match 3 – FC Salzburg (AUT)
A 0-1
Petkov, Genev, Milanov (Benzoukane 46), Sarmov, Yovov, Minev, Zé Soares, N. Dimitrov (Joãozinho 65), Bardon (Hristov 56), Baltanov, Miliev. Coach: Antoni Zdravkov (BUL)
Yellow Card(s): Baltanov 25, Yovov 45+1, Petkov 80

Match 4 – FC Salzburg (AUT)
H 0-1
Petkov, Milanov, Rabeh, Sarmov, Yovov (Baltanov 64), Minev, Zé Soares, Tasevski (Krastovchev 75), N. Dimitrov (Joãozinho 81), Bardon, Miliev. Coach: Antoni Zdravkov (BUL)
Red Card(s): Sarmov 62
Yellow Card(s): Bardon 33, Rabeh 90
Match 5 – Villarreal CF (ESP)
H 0-2
Mitrev, Milanov, Rabeh (Topuzakov 46; Benzoukane 65), Minev, Joãozinho, Zé Soares, Tasevski, Bardon, Miliev, Simonović, Hristov (Krastovchev 52). Coach: Antoni Zdravkov (BUL)
Yellow Card(s): Tasevski 52, Milanov 64
Match 6 – S.S. Lazio (ITA)
A 1-0 *Yovov (60)*
Mitrev, Milanov, Rabeh, Sarmov, Yovov (Simonović 88), Minev, Zé Soares, Tasevski (Hristov 76), N. Dimitrov (Joãozinho 58), Bardon, Miliev. Coach: Antoni Zdravkov (BUL)
Yellow Card(s): Rabeh 38, Milanov 86

PFC LITEX LOVECH

UEFA EUROPA LEAGUE

Play-Off Round – FC BATE Borisov (BLR)
A 1-0 *Sandrinho (81)*
Golubović, Barthe, Zanev, Petkov, Yanev (Todorov 57), Sandrinho, Doka Madureira (Venkov 90+1), Niflore, Nikolov, Jelenković, Kishishev. Coach: Stanimir Stoilov (BUL)
Yellow Card(s): Petkov 35, Barthe 73, Kishishev 87
H 0-4 *(aet)*
Golubović, Barthe, Zanev, Petkov (Yanev 98), Wellington (G. Milanov 104), Sandrinho, Doka Madureira, Niflore (Todorov 90+1), Nikolov, Jelenković, Kishishev. Coach: Stanimir Stoilov (BUL)
Yellow Card(s): Zanev 47, Petkov 58

PFC CSKA SOFIA

UEFA EUROPA LEAGUE

Third Qualifying Round – Derry City FC (IRL)
H 1-0 *I. Stoyanov (73)*
Chavdarov, Vidanov, Kotev, Timonov (Saidhodza 66), Rui Miguel (Todorov 80), S. Petrov (Orlinov 58), Ivanov, Yanev, Marquinhos, Minev, I. Stoyanov. Coach: Luboslav Penev (BUL)
Yellow Card(s): Ivanov 3, Marquinhos 48, I. Stoyanov 90+1
A 1-1 *Marquinhos (70)*
Chavdarov (Karadzhov 30), Vidanov, Kotev, Timonov (Rui Miguel 66), S. Petrov, Ivanov, Yanev, Marquinhos (Orlinov 83), Todorov, Minev, I. Stoyanov. Coach: Luboslav Penev (BUL)
Yellow Card(s): Marquinhos 15, I. Stoyanov 51, Vidanov 67, Karadzhov 76

Play-Off Round – FC Dinamo Moskva (RUS)
H 0-0
Karadzhov, Vidanov, Yanchev, Kotev, Timonov (Delev 58), Orlinov (Zehirov 62), Ivanov, Yanev(Paskov 70), Todorov, Morozs, Minev. Coach: Luboslav Penev (BUL)
Yellow Card(s): Orlinov 45, Yanchev 81

A 2-1 *Delev (14), Ivanov (55)*
Karadzhov, Vidanov, Yanchev, Kotev, Ivanov, Marquinhos (Timonov 21), Todorov (Yanev75), Morozs, Minev, I. Stoyanov, Delev (Paskov 85). Coach: Luboslav Penev (BUL)

Group E
Match 1 – Fulham FC (ENG)
H 1-1 *Michel (62)*
Karadzhov, K. Stoyanov, Yanchev, Kotev, Ivanov, Yanev(Manchev 78), Todorov, Morozs (Marquinhos 46), Minev, I. Stoyanov (Michel 54), Delev. Coach: Luboslav Penev (BUL)
Yellow Card(s): Minev 30, Michel 90, Marquinhos 90+3
Match 2 – AS Roma (ITA)
A 0-2
Karadzhov, K. Stoyanov, Yanchev (Delev 51), Kotev, Ivanov, Yanev, Marquinhos, Todorov (Manchev 65), Morozs (Michel 51), Minev, I. Stoyanov. Coach: Luboslav Penev (BUL)
Match 3 – FC Basel 1893 (SUI)
H 0-2
Karadzhov, Vidanov, Yanchev, Kotev (Branekov 46), Ivanov, Yanev, Michel, Marquinhos (Manchev 65), Todorov, Minev, I. Stoyanov (Rui Miguel 55). Coach: Luboslav Penev (BUL)
Yellow Card(s): Todorov 67, Branekov 70
Match 4 – FC Basel 1893 (SUI)
A 1-3 *Yanchev (61)*
Chavdarov, Vidanov, K. Stoyanov, Yanchev, Manchev (Rui Miguel 71), Branekov, Báez, Marquinhos, Morozs (Manchev 28), I. Stoyanov, Delev (Michel 56). Coach: Luboslav Penev (BUL)
Yellow Card(s): K. Stoyanov 15, Morozs 19
Match 5 – Fulham FC (ENG)
A 0-1
Chavdarov, Vidanov, K. Stoyanov, Yanchev, Timonov (Michel 54), Ivanov (Yanev64), Popov, Todorov (Rui Miguel 72), Morozs, Minev, Delev. Coach: Luboslav Penev (BUL)
Yellow Card(s): Morozs 36, Minev 62, K. Stoyanov 89
Match 6 – AS Roma (ITA)
H 0-2
Chavdarov, Vidanov, K. Stoyanov, Yanchev, Timonov (Manchev 60), S. Petrov, Popov (Rui Miguel 74), Yanev, Michel, Minev, Delev (Todorov 80). Coach: Luboslav Penev (BUL)
Yellow Card(s): S. Petrov 28, K. Stoyanov 55

PFC CHERNO MORE VARNA

UEFA EUROPA LEAGUE

Second Qualifying Round – FC Iskra-Stali (MDA)
H 1-0 *Manolov (44)*
Pirgov, Bachev (Petkov 85), Bornosuzov, A.D. Alexandrov, Z. Lazarov (Kakalov 65), A.Y. Alexandrov, Hristov, Rusev (Da. Georgiev 68), Manolov, Yurukov, Coulibaly. Coach: Nikola Spasov (BUL)
A 3-0 *Manolov (25, 54), Da. Georgiev (60)*
Pirgov, Bachev, A.D. Alexandrov, A.Y. Alexandrov, Hristov (Dyakov 60), Rusev, Da. Georgiev, Dimov (Petkov 66), Manolov, Yurukov (Stoyanov 57), Coulibaly. Coach: Nikola Spasov (BUL)

Third Qualifying Round – PSV Eindhoven (NED)
A 0-1
Pirgov, Bachev, A.Y. Alexandrov (Bornosuzov 90), Z. Lazarov (Da. Georgiev 46), A.D. Alexandrov, Hristov, Rusev (Petkov 80), Dimov, Manolov, Yurukov, Coulibaly. Coach: Nikola Spasov (BUL)
Yellow Card(s): Z. Lazarov 15, A.D. Alexandrov 17, Rusev 32, Coulibaly 87
H 0-1
Pirgov, Ademar Junior, Bornosuzov (Kakalov 65), A.D. Alexandrov (Stoyanov 81), Hristov, Rusev, Petkov, Da. Georgiev (Z. Lazarov 48), Manolov, Yurukov, Coulibaly. Coach: Nikola Spasov (BUL)
Yellow Card(s): Bornosuzov 39, Coulibaly 66, A.D. Alexandrov 79, Manolov 83

CROATIA

NK DINAMO ZAGREB

UEFA CHAMPIONS LEAGUE

Second Qualifying Round - FC Pyunik (ARM)
A 0-0
Butina, Lovren (Barbarić 46), Etto, Sammir, Carlos Santos, Badelj, Mandžukić, Vrdoljak, Bišćan, Sivonjić (Kramarić 78), Papadopoulos (Slepička 65). Coach: Krunoslav Jurčić (CRO)
Yellow Card(s): Lovren 45+1, Carlos Santos 50
H 3-0 *Mandžukić (30), Badelj (61), Lovren (66)*
Butina, Lovren, Etto, Sammir (Chago 75), Carlos Santos, Badelj, Mandžukić, Vrdoljak, Bišćan, Morales (Tomečak 79), Papadopoulos (Slepička 82). Coach: Krunoslav Jurčić (CRO)
Yellow Card(s): Sammir 36, Bišćan 83, Etto 86

Third Qualifying Round - FC Salzburg (AUT)
A 1-1 *Mandžukić (63)*
Butina, Lovren, Etto, Sammir (Barbarić 90+1), Glavina, Badelj, Mandžukić, Vrdoljak, Bišćan, Morales (Chago 86), Papadopoulos (Slepička 72). Coach: Krunoslav Jurčić (CRO)
Red Card(s): Mandžukić 90+4
Yellow Card(s): Mandžukić 30, Etto 60, Papadopoulos 70, Mandžukić 90+4
H 1-2 *Papadopoulos (47)*
Butina, Lovren, Sammir (Barbarić 89), Glavina, Chago (Slepička 46), Carlos Santos (Kramarić 84), Badelj, Vrdoljak, Bišćan, Morales, Papadopoulos. Coach: Krunoslav Jurčić (CRO)
Yellow Card(s): Lovren 69, Slepička 80

UEFA EUROPA LEAGUE

Play-Off Round - Heart of Midlothian FC (SCO)
H 4-0 *Mandžukić (6), Papadopoulos (36), Vrdoljak (56), Bišćan (60)*
Butina, Etto (Tomečak 20), Sammir (Kramarić 61), Carlos Santos, Badelj, Mandžukić, Barbarić, Vrdoljak, Bišćan, Morales (Calello 76), Papadopoulos. Coach: Krunoslav Jurčić (CRO)
A 0-2
Butina, Lovren, Sammir (Tomečak 68), Carlos Santos, Badelj, Mandžukić, Barbarić, Vrdoljak, Bišćan, Morales (Calello 87), Papadopoulos (Slepička 89). Coach: Krunoslav Jurčić (CRO)
Yellow Card(s): Barbarić 60, Lovren 78

Group A
Match 1 - RSC Anderlecht (BEL)
H 0-2
Butina, Kovač, Lovren, Etto (Tomečak 85), Sammir (Sivonjić 78), Badelj, Mandžukić, Vrdoljak, Cufré, Morales, Papadopoulos (Slepička 69). Coach: Krunoslav Jurčić (CRO)
Yellow Card(s): Badelj 69
Match 2 - FC Timişoara (ROU)
A 3-0 *Badelj (8), Sammir (52), Morales (59)*
Lončarić, Kovač, Lovren, Etto, Sammir, Badelj, Mandžukić, Vrdoljak, Sivonjić (Papadopoulos 74), Cufré (Barbarić 60), Morales (Calello 83). Coach: Krunoslav Jurčić (CRO)
Yellow Card(s): Badelj 47, Lovren 63
Match 3 - AFC Ajax (NED)
A 1-2 *Tomečak (90+3)*
Lončarić, Kovač, Lovren, Etto, Sammir, Badelj, Mandžukić (Kramarić 88), Vrdoljak, Lane, Morales (Sivonjić 62), Papadopoulos (Tomečak 68). Coach: Krunoslav Jurčić (CRO)
Yellow Card(s): Kovač 3, Badelj 55, Cufré 58

Match 4 - AFC Ajax (NED)
H 0-2
Butina, Tomečak, Kovač, Calello, Lovren, Etto, Sammir, Vrdoljak (Chago 46), Sivonjić (Ibáñez 77), Cufré, Morales (Barbarić 42). Coach: Krunoslav Jurčić (CRO)
Red Card(s): Cufré 35, Calello 73
Yellow Card(s): Calello 30, Calello 73, Lovren 73
Match 5 - RSC Anderlecht (BEL)
A 1-0 Slepička (57)
Butina, Tomečak (Chago 90+2), Ibáñez, Kovač, Lovren, Etto, Sammir (Barbarić 82), Badelj, Mandžukić, Slepička (Papadopoulos 66), Vrdoljak. Coach: Krunoslav Jurčić (CRO)
Yellow Card(s): Sammir 8, Ibáñez 41, Badelj 81, Mandžukić 89
Match 6 - FC Timişoara (ROU)
H 1-2 Scutaru (80og)
Butina, Ibáñez (Tomečak 72), Kovač, Lovren, Etto, Sammir, Badelj, Mandžukić, Slepička (Sivonjić 73), Vrdoljak, Morales (Kramarić 83). Coach: Krunoslav Jurčić (CRO)

HNK HAJDUK SPLIT

UEFA EUROPA LEAGUE
Third Qualifying Round - MŠK Žilina (SVK)
A 1-1 Rafael Paraíba (52)
Subašić, Šerić, Ibričić, Tomasov (Cernat 57), Gabrić, Skoko, Maloča, Rubil, Brkljača (Strinić 74), Pandža, Rafael Paraíba (Rodić 76). Coach: Ante Miše (CRO)
Yellow Card(s): Maloča 24, Šerić 30, Brkljača 45, Subašić 68, Rubil 72
H 0-1
Subašić, Šerić, Ibričić, Andrić, Tomasov (Rodić 80), Gabrić, Skoko, Maloča, Rubil (Cernat 85), Pandža, Rafael Paraíba (Brkljača 64). Coach: Ivica Kalinić (CRO)
Yellow Card(s): Rubil 3, Ibričić 64

HNK RIJEKA

UEFA EUROPA LEAGUE
Second Qualifying Round - FC Differdange 03 (LUX)
A 0-1
Radman, Čagalj, Čejvanović, Ah. Sharbini, An. Sharbini, Štrok (Smith 68), Križman (Kreilach 81), Budicin, Pamić, Fernández, Tadejević. Coach: Robert Rubčić (CRO)
Yellow Card(s): Čejvanović 18, Fernández 20, Pamić 76
H 3-0 Cerić (20), An. Sharbini (24), Ah. Sharbini (64)
Mance, Čagalj, Landeka, Ah. Sharbini, An. Sharbini, Štrok (Kreilach 69), Križman (Matko 77), Budicin, Pamić, Fernández (Smith 86), Cerić. Coach: Robert Rubčić (CRO)
Yellow Card(s): Ah. Sharbini 11

Third Qualifying Round - FC Metalist Kharkiv (UKR)
H 1-2 Ah. Sharbini (59)
Mance, Čagalj, Landeka, Ah. Sharbini, An. Sharbini (Smith 17), Matko (Turkalj 80), Štrok (Tadejević 75), Budicin, Pamić, Fernández, Cerić. Coach: Robert Rubčić (CRO)
Yellow Card(s): Matko 34, Fernández 71, Mance 85, Pamić 90+2

A 0-2
Mance, Smith (Datković 46), Čagalj, Landeka, Štrok (Čejvanović 65), Budicin, Kreilach, Gerc, Cerić (Stepčić 73), Turkalj, Tadejević. Coach: Robert Rubčić (CRO)
Yellow Card(s): Cerić 60, Turkalj 79

NK SLAVEN KOPRIVNICA

UEFA EUROPA LEAGUE
First Qualifying Round - Birkirkara FC (MLT)
H 1-0 Csizmadia (3)
Rodić, Kokalović, Rogulj, Poldrugač, Vojnović, Posavec (Delić 58), Vručina (Poredski 84), Lapić, Jurić, Nynkeu, Csizmadia. Coach: Milivoj Bračun (CRO)
Yellow Card(s): Lapić 50, Poldrugač 81, Csizmadia 85
A 0-0
Rodić, Rogulj, Poldrugač, Vojnović (Delić 60), Posavec (Bilen 74), Purić, Vručina, Jurić (Poredski 88), Nynkeu, Maras, Csizmadia. Coach: Milivoj Bračun (CRO)
Yellow Card(s): Vručina 87

Second Qualifying Round - FK Milano (MKD)
A 4-0 Csizmadia (26), Vojnović (39, 41, 44)
Rodić, Rogulj (Lapić 46), Poldrugač, Vojnović (Poredski 77), Posavec (Šafarić 56), Bilen, Purić, Vručina, Jurić, Maras, Csizmadia. Coach: Milivoj Bračun (CRO)
H 8-2 Poredski (24), Vručina (45+3), Tepurić (61, 74), Vojnović (78, 88), Gregurina (80), Jurić (81)
Rodić, Poredski (Tepurić 45+2), Rogulj, Šafarić, Vojnović, Delić (Gregurina 46), Purić, Vručina (Jurić 46), Nynkeu, Maras, Csizmadia. Coach: Milivoj Bračun (CRO)
Yellow Card(s): Purić 10

Third Qualifying Round - Tromsø IL (NOR)
A 1-2 Šafarić (38p)
Rodić, Kokalović, Rogulj, Poldrugač, Šafarić (Gregurina 90), Vojnović (Delić 70), Vručina (Tepurić 87), Jurić, Nynkeu, Maras, Csizmadia. Coach: Milivoj Bračun (CRO)
Yellow Card(s): Nynkeu 73
H 0-2
Rodić, Kokalović, Rogulj, Poldrugač, Šafarić, Vojnović (Poredski 69), Posavec (Vručina 46), Delić (Tepurić 55), Jurić, Maras, Csizmadia. Coach: Milivoj Bračun (CRO)
Yellow Card(s): Delić 29, Poldrugač 89

CYPRUS

APOEL FC

UEFA CHAMPIONS LEAGUE
Second Qualifying Round - EB/Streymur (FRO)
A 2-0 Mirosavljević (11), Žewłakow (77)
Chiotis, Poursaitidis, Charalambides (Žewłakow 65), Kosowski, Broerse, Hélio Pinto, Kontis, Nuno Morais (Grncarov 80), Mirosavljević, Haxhi, Michail (Satsias 84). Coach: Ivan Jovanović (SRB)
Yellow Card(s): Poursaitidis 90+3

H 3-0 Żewłakow (42), Alexandrou (63), Mirosavljević (75)
Chiotis, Paulo Jorge, Grncarov, Broerse, Satsias, Elia, Żewłakow
(Papathanasiou 71), Kontis, Alexandrou, Mirosavljević (Hélio Pinto 80),
Breška (Jean Paulista 69). Coach: Ivan Jovanović (SRB)

Third Qualifying Round - FK Partizan (SRB)
H 2-0 Mirosavljević (49), Żewłakow (85)
Chiotis, Poursaitidis, Charalambides, Kosowski (Alexandrou 82), Broerse,
Hélio Pinto (Żewłakow 73), Kontis, Nuno Morais, Mirosavljević, Haxhi,
Michail (Satsias 73). Coach: Ivan Jovanović (SRB)
Yellow Card(s): Alexandrou 87
A 0-1
Chiotis, Poursaitidis, Charalambides (Paulo Jorge 90+2), Kosowski
(Alexandrou 86), Broerse, Satsias, Żewłakow (Hélio Pinto 67), Kontis, Nuno
Morais, Mirosavljević, Haxhi. Coach: Ivan Jovanović (SRB)
Red Card(s): Broerse 89
Yellow Card(s): Poursaitidis 10, Żewłakow 26, Broerse 29, Satsias 70,
Broerse 89

Play-Off Round - FC København (DEN)
A 0-1
Chiotis, Paulo Jorge, Grncarov, Charalambides (Alexandrou 77), Kosowski
(Breška 86), Satsias (Żewłakow 69), Hélio Pinto, Kontis, Nuno Morais,
Mirosavljević, Haxhi. Coach: Ivan Jovanović (SRB)
Red Card(s): Haxhi 90+1
Yellow Card(s): Haxhi 50, Grncarov 61, Haxhi 90+1
H 3-1 Kosowski (2), Michail (18p,41)
Chiotis, Poursaitidis, Charalambides, Kosowski (Alexandrou 82), Broerse,
Elia, Żewłakow (Hélio Pinto 76), Kontis, Nuno Morais, Mirosavljević (Sikora
66), Michail. Coach: Ivan Jovanović (SRB)
Yellow Card(s): Alexandrou 86, Hélio Pinto 88, Poursaitidis 90+4

Group D
Match 1 - Club Atlético de Madrid (ESP)
A 0-0
Chiotis, Paulo Jorge (Grncarov 45+1), Poursaitidis, Charalambides (Satsias
67), Kosowski, Żewłakow (Jean Paulista 81), Hélio Pinto, Kontis, Nuno
Morais, Haxhi, Michail. Coach: Ivan Jovanović (SRB)
Yellow Card(s): Kontis 24, Satsias 88
Match 2 - Chelsea FC (ENG)
H 0-1
Chiotis, Grncarov, Poursaitidis, Charalambides (Jean Paulista 85), Hélio
Pinto, Kontis, Nuno Morais, Alexandrou (Kosowski 58), Mirosavljević,
Haxhi, Michail (Breška 80). Coach: Ivan Jovanović (SRB)
Match 3 - FC Porto (POR)
A 1-2 Álvaro Pereira (22og)
Chiotis, Grncarov, Charalambides, Kosowski (Breška 38), Broerse, Satsias
(Papathanasiou 78), Elia, Hélio Pinto, Nuno Morais, Mirosavljević, Michail
(Alexandrou 60). Coach: Ivan Jovanović (SRB)
Yellow Card(s): Satsias 23, Grncarov 37, Breška 57, Broerse 83
Match 4 - FC Porto (POR)
H 0-1
Chiotis, Poursaitidis, Charalambides, Broerse, Satsias, Elia (Grncarov 57),
Jean Paulista (Alexandrou 61), Hélio Pinto, Kontis (Papathanasiou 87),
Nuno Morais, Mirosavljević. Coach: Ivan Jovanović (SRB)
Yellow Card(s): Charalambides 51, Elia 52, Hélio Pinto 74
Match 5 - Club Atlético de Madrid (ESP)
H 1-1 Mirosavljević (5)
Chiotis, Paulo Jorge, Poursaitidis, Kosowski (Żewłakow 77), Elia (Breška
70), Hélio Pinto, Kontis, Nuno Morais, Alexandrou, Mirosavljević, Michail
(Broerse 71). Coach: Ivan Jovanović (SRB)
Yellow Card(s): Paulo Jorge 1, Breška 80
Match 6 - Chelsea FC (ENG)
A 2-2 Żewłakow (6), Mirosavljević (87)
Chiotis, Paulo Jorge, Poursaitidis, Charalambides, Kosowski (Mirosavljević
70), Broerse, Żewłakow (Breška 83), Hélio Pinto, Nuno Morais, Haxhi (Elia
34), Michail. Coach: Ivan Jovanović (SRB)
Yellow Card(s): Poursaitidis 85

No	Player	Nat	DoB	Aps	(s)	Gls
Goalkeeper						
22	Dionissis Chiotis	GRE	4/6/77	6		
Defenders						
14	Joost Broerse	NED	8/5/79	3	(1)	
19	Marios Elia		14/4/79	3	(1)	
5	Boban Grncarov	MKD	12/8/82	2	(2)	
24	Christos Kontis	GRE	13/5/75	4		
26	Nuno Morais	POR	29/1/84	6		
3	Paulo Jorge	POR	16/6/80	3		
Midfielders						
29	Nektarios Alexandrou		19/12/83	2	(2)	
10	Kostas Charalambides		25/7/81	5		
32	Altin Haxhi	ALB	17/6/75	3		
23	Hélio Pinto	POR	29/2/84	6		
11	Kamil Kosowski	POL	30/8/77	4	(1)	
33	Chrysis Michail		26/5/77	5		
7	Savvas Poursaitidis	GRE	23/6/76	5		
17	Marinos Satsias		24/5/78	2	(1)	
Forwards						
37	Mário Breška	SVK	27/12/79		(4)	
20	Jean Paulista	BRA	28/11/77	1	(2)	
21	Marcin Żewłakow	POL	22/4/76	2	(1)	1
30	Nenad Mirosavljević	SRB	4/9/77	4	(1)	2
9	Andreas Papathanasiou		3/10/83		(2)	

APOP/KINYRAS PEYIAS FC

UEFA EUROPA LEAGUE

Third Qualifying Round - SK Rapid Wien (AUT)
A 1-2 Semedo (79)
Fani, Buyse, Tall, Galanis, Edgar Marcelino (González 70), Semedo
(Bengelloun 88), Vitali, Željkovič, Grimaldi, Liri (Rodrigues da Silva 65),
Grabič. Coach: Giorgos Polyviou (CYP)
Yellow Card(s): Buyse 22, Tall 39, Semedo 88
H 2-2 Edgar Marcelino (43p), González (80)
Fani, Buyse, Tall, Galanis, Edgar Marcelino (Rodrigues da Silva 78),
Semedo, Vitali (González 69), Samaras (Liri 56), Željkovič, Grimaldi, Grabič.
Coach: Giorgos Polyviou (CYP)
Yellow Card(s): Buyse 22, Samaras 27, Vitali 37, Gonzalez Valdes 90,
Rodrigues Da Silva 104, Semedo 113

AC OMONIA

UEFA EUROPA LEAGUE

Second Qualifying Round - HB Tórshavn (FRO)
H 4-0 Karipidis (3), Patsatzoglou (11), Żurawski (33), Efrem (85)
Kotsolis, Alabi, Davidson, Karipidis, Żurawski (Efrem 83), Bruno Aguiar,
Cáceres, Patsatzoglou, Aloneftis, Christofi
(Konstantinou 69). Coach: Takis Lemonis (GRE)
A 4-1 Konstantinou (27, 66, 78), Wenzel (90+1)
Kotsolis, Wenzel, Karipidis, Efrem, Żlogar, Bruno Aguiar, Kaseke (Panagi
68), Konstantinou, Pantić, Charalambous, Christofi (Kyriakos 60). Coach:
Takis Lemonis (GRE)

Cyprus/Czech Republic

Third Qualifying Round - FC Vaslui (ROU)
A 0-2
Kotsolis, Alabi, Davidson, Žlogar, Žurawski, Bruno Aguiar, Kaseke (Konstantinou 77), Patsatzoglou, Charalambous, Aloneftis, Christofi (Efrem 66). Coach: Takis Lemonis (GRE)
Yellow Card(s): Kaseke 30, Alabi 90, Konstantinou 90+3
H 1-1 *Żurawski (84p)*
Kotsolis, Alabi, Davidson, Wenzel, Żurawski, Bruno Aguiar, Grammozis (Kyriakos 57), Konstantinou, Patsatzoglou (Žlogar 79), Charalambous, Aloneftis (Efrem 62). Coach: Takis Lemonis (GRE)
Red Card(s): Charalambous 90+4
Yellow Card(s): Grammozis 11, Konstantinou 90+4

ANORTHOSIS FAMAGUSTA FC

UEFA EUROPA LEAGUE
First Qualifying Round - UN Käerjéng 97 (LUX)
H 5-0 *Da Costa (10og), Katsavakis (25), Frousos (62, 90+1), Café (67)*
Supić, Katsavakis, Marangos (Frousos 57), Sosin, Ricardo Fernandes (Dellas 79), Leiwakabessy, Cristóvão (Garpozis 71), Café, Laban, Janício, Konstantinou. Coach: Ernst Middendorp (GER)
Yellow Card(s): Ricardo Fernandes 66
A 2-1 *Sosin (44), Frousos (60)*
Supić, Katsavakis, Sosin, Ricardo Fernandes (Garpozis 61), Leiwakabessy, Cristóvão (Frousos 46), Café, Laban, Janício, Konstantinou, Georgiou (Dellas 46). Coach: Ernst Middendorp (GER)

Second Qualifying Round - OFK Petrovac (MNE)
H 2-1 *Ricardo Fernandes (11), Laban (14)*
Supić, Katsavakis, Skopelitis, Ricardo Fernandes, Leiwakabessy, Cristóvão (Sosin 72), Café, Agali (Frousos 62), Laban, Janício, Konstantinou. Coach: Ernst Middendorp (GER)
A 1-3 *Katsavakis (45+2) (aet)*
Supić, Katsavakis, Dellas (Cristóvão 95), Skopelitis, Ricardo Fernandes (Marangos 71), Leiwakabessy, Café, Agali (Sosin 106), Laban, Janício, Konstantinou. Coach: Ernst Middendorp (GER)
Yellow Card(s): Katsavakis 68, Janício 100, Cristovão 109

CZECH REPUBLIC

SK SLAVIA PRAHA

UEFA CHAMPIONS LEAGUE
Third Qualifying Round - FC Sheriff (MDA)
A 0-0
Hanuš, Čelůstka, Ragued, Vlček (Belaid 86), Janda (Volešák 90+2), Hloušek, Jarolím (Šenkeřík 66), M. Černý, Suchý, Vomáčka, J. Černý. Coach: Pavel Řehák
H 1-1 *Hloušek (15)*
Hanuš, Hubáček, Čelůstka, Ragued, Vlček, Janda, Hloušek (M. Černý 74), Jarolím (Vasiljević 62), Suchý, Vomáčka, J. Černý (Tafat 89). Coach: Pavel Řehák
Yellow Card(s): Suchý 84, J. Černý 89

UEFA EUROPA LEAGUE
Play-Off Round - FK Crvena zvezda (SRB)
H 3-0 *Šenkeřík (34, 65), Vlček (81)*
Hanuš, Hubáček, Čelůstka (Krajčík 62), Ragued, Hloušek (Janda 89), Šenkeřík (Vlček 72), Suchý, Belaid, Vomáčka, Volešák, J. Černý. Coach: Karel Jarolím (CZE)
Yellow Card(s): Šenkeřík 18
A 1-2 *Vlček (63)*
Vaniak, Hubáček, Čelůstka, Janda (Trapp 46), Hloušek, Šenkeřík (Vlček 57), Suchý, Belaid (Krajčík 85), Vomáčka, Volešák, J. Černý. Coach: Karel Jarolím (CZE)
Yellow Card(s): Hubáček 45+1, Trapp 87

Group B
Match 1 - Genoa CFC (ITA)
A 0-2
Vaniak, Čelůstka, Ragued, Janda, Hloušek, Vasiljević (Grajciar 79), Šenkeřík (Naumov 46), Suchý, Krajčík, Belaid (Volešák 71), Vomáčka. Coach: Karel Jarolím (CZE)
Match 2 - LOSC Lille Métropole (FRA)
H 1-5 *Belaid (6p)*
Vaniak, Hubáček, Ragued (Grajciar 62), Janda, Hloušek, Šenkeřík (Vlček 76), Suchý, Krajčík, Belaid (Vasiljević 76), Vomáčka, Volešák. Coach: Karel Jarolím (CZE)
Yellow Card(s): Volešák 58
Match 3 - Valencia CF (ESP)
A 1-1 *Naumov (28)*
Vaniak, Trapp, Hubáček, Čelůstka, Ragued, Hloušek, Šenkeřík (Belaid 78), Suchý, Naumov (Krajčík 86), Vomáčka, Grajciar (Vlček 90). Coach: Karel Jarolím (CZE)
Red Card(s): Ragued 76
Yellow Card(s): Ragued 58, Hloušek 66, Ragued 76, Trapp 76, Vomáčka 86
Match 4 - Valencia CF (ESP)
H 2-2 *Janda (79), Grajciar (82)*
Romanovs (Vaniak 28), Trapp, Hubáček, Čelůstka, Hloušek, Šenkeřík, Suchý, Naumov (Janda 46), Krajčík, Vomáčka, Grajciar (Šmicer 86). Coach: Karel Jarolím (CZE)
Red Card(s): Šenkeřík 48
Yellow Card(s): Šenkeřík 45+2, Šenkeřík 48, Trapp 69, Grajciar 84, Šmicer 90+2
Match 5 - Genoa CFC (ITA)
H 0-0
Romanovs, Hubáček, Čelůstka, Ragued, Vlček (Naumov 88), Hloušek, Suchý, Belaid (Koreš 71), Trubila (Mareš 81), Grajciar. Coach: Karel Jarolím (CZE)
Match 6 - LOSC Lille Métropole (FRA)
A 1-3 *Vlček (56)*
Romanovs, Hubáček, Čelůstka, Ragued, Vlček (Naumov 87), Janda (Belaid 84), Hloušek, Krajčík, Trubila (Šenkeřík 73), Hošek, Grajciar. Coach: Karel Jarolím (CZE)
Yellow Card(s): Hubáček 45, Janda 51

AC SPARTA PRAHA

UEFA CHAMPIONS LEAGUE
Third Qualifying Round - Panathinaikos FC (GRE)
H 3-1 *Holenda (26), Vacek (32), Kalouda (86)*
Blažek, Řepka, Pamić, Hubník, Žofčák, Wilfried (Střeštík 90+2), Kušnír, Holenda (Prudnikov 59), Zeman (Kalouda 76), Vacek, Hušek. Coach: Jozef Chovanec (CZE)
Yellow Card(s): Řepka 23, Blažek 33, Kušnír 90+3, Hubník 90+4
A 0-3
Blažek, Pamić, Hoheneder, Hubník, Berger, Žofčák, Wilfried (Prudnikov 69), Kušnír, Zeman (Kadlec 58), Vacek, Hušek (Kalouda 78). Coach: Jozef Chovanec (CZE)
Yellow Card(s): Hoheneder 44, Blažek 89

CHAMPIONS LEAGUE EUROPA LEAGUE

UEFA EUROPA LEAGUE

Play-Off Round - NK Maribor (SVN)
A 2-0 *Wilfried (29, 86)*
Kozáčík, Řepka, Pamić, Hubník, Žofčák, Wilfried, Kušnír, Kadlec (Kalouda 77), Zeman, Vacek (Kovba 77), Hušek (Hoheneder 74). Coach: Jozef Chovanec (SVK)
Yellow Card(s): Vacek 26, Pamić 70
H 1-0 *Wilfried (3)*
Blažek, Řepka, Pamić, Hubník, Žofčák, Wilfried (Jirouš 75), Kušnír, Kadlec (Prudnikov 62), Zeman (Střeštík 81), Kovba, Vacek. Coach: Jozef Chovanec (SVK)
Yellow Card(s): Pamić 57

Group K
Match 1 - PSV Eindhoven (NED)
H 2-2 *Hubník (76), Zeman (87)*
Blažek, Řepka, Hoheneder, Hubník, Žofčák, Wilfried, Kušnír, Holenda (Kadlec 79), Zeman (Kalouda 90+4), Vacek (Kucka 85), Hušek. Coach: Jozef Chovanec (SVK)
Yellow Card(s): Řepka 63, Hoheneder 69, Wilfried 90+1, Blažek 90+4
Match 2 - FC København (DEN)
A 0-1
Blažek, Řepka, Pamić, Hubník, Prudnikov, Žofčák (Střeštík 46), Kušnír, Holenda (Wilfried 55), Kalouda, Vacek, Hušek (Kadlec 80). Coach: Jozef Chovanec (SVK)
Yellow Card(s): Kušnír 32
Match 3 - CFR 1907 Cluj (ROU)
H 2-0 *Kucka (15), Hubník (32)*
Blažek, Řepka, Pamić, Hubník, Wilfried, Kušnír, Kadlec (Prudnikov 74), Kalouda (Střeštík 90+1), Kucka, Kovba, Vacek (Hoheneder 89). Coach: Jozef Chovanec (SVK)
Yellow Card(s): Kušnír 58, Kalouda 68
Match 4 - CFR 1907 Cluj (ROU)
A 3-2 *Holenda (6, 13), Wilfried (90+5)*
Blažek, Řepka, Pamić, Hubník, Žofčák (Kalouda 90), Wilfried, Kušnír, Holenda (Kadlec 74), Kucka, Zeman (Hoheneder 90+2). Coach: Jozef Chovanec (SVK)
Yellow Card(s): Kucka 28, Řepka 52
Match 5 - PSV Eindhoven (NED)
A 0-1
Blažek, Řepka, Pamić, Hoheneder, Žofčák (Kadlec 68), Wilfried (Kalouda 90), Kušnír, Holenda, Kucka, Vacek (Prudnikov 90+4), Hušek. Coach: Jozef Chovanec (SVK)
Yellow Card(s): Řepka 15, Wilfried 73, Hušek 82
Match 6 - FC København (DEN)
H 0-3
Blažek, Pamić, Hoheneder, Žofčák, Wilfried (Jirouš 66), Kušnír, Holenda, Kucka (Kladrubský 78), Zeman, Vacek (Kadlec 52), Hušek. Coach: Jozef Chovanec (SVK)
Red Card(s): Pamić 60
Yellow Card(s): Kušnír 25, Pamić 42, Kucka 55, Pamić 60

FK TEPLICE

UEFA EUROPA LEAGUE

Play-Off Round - Hapoel Tel-Aviv FC (ISR)
H 1-2 *Vondrášek (89)*
Grigar, Klein, Ljevaković, Vidlička, Vachoušek, Stožický, Lukáš, Mareš (Vondrášek 59), Matula, Rosa (Merzić 46), Mahmutović (Verbíř 80). Coach: Jiří Plíšek (CZE)
Yellow Card(s): Vidlicka 30
A 1-1 *Klein (89)*
Grigar, Klein, Ljevaković (Doležal 73), Vidlicka, Vachoušek, Stožický, Hesek (Verbíř 46), Merzić, Lukáš, Vondrášek, Mareš (Mahmutović 82). Coach: Zdeněk Klucký (CZE)
Yellow Card(s): Ljevaković 70, Vachoušek 73, Lukáš 90+2

FC SLOVAN LIBEREC

UEFA EUROPA LEAGUE

Third Qualifying Round - FC Vaduz (LIE)
A 1-0 *Blažek (43)*
Zlámal, Liška, Gecov, Holeňák, Kerić, Dočkal (Vácha 76), Vulin (Kelić 69), Dejmek, Čorić, Blažek (Nezmar 81), Gebre Selassie. Coach: Ladislav Škorpil (CZE)
Yellow Card(s): Čorić 65, Kelić 70, Blažek 72
H 2-0 *Kerić (17), Nezmar (22)*
Hauzr, Nezmar (Diviš 69), Gecov, Holeňák, Kerić, Dočkal, Vulin, Dejmek, Čorić (Frejlach 84), Blažek (Vácha 15), Gebre Selassie. Coach: Ladislav Škorpil (CZE)
Yellow Card(s): Vácha 45

Play-Off Round - FC Dinamo Bucureşti (ROU)
A 3-0 *Liška (5), Blažek (84) (w/o)*
Hauzr, Liška, Gecov, Holeňák, Kerić, Dočkal, Vulin, Dejmek, Čorić (Blažek 73), Papoušek (Vácha 63), Gebre Selassie. Coach: Ladislav Škorpil (CZE)
Yellow Card(s): Gecov 30
H 0-3 *(aet; 8-9 on pens)*
Hauzr, Nezmar (Vácha 61), Liška, Gecov, Holeňák, Kerić (Blažek 73), Dočkal, Vulin, Dejmek, Čorić (Papoušek 88), Gebre Selassie. Coach: Ladislav Škorpil (CZE)
Yellow Card(s): Čorić 48, Vácha 70, Blažek 90+3, Vulin 105

SK SIGMA OLOMOUC

UEFA EUROPA LEAGUE

Second Qualifying Round - Fram Reykjavík (ISL)
H 1-1 *Daniel Rossi (89)*
Drobisz, Dreksa, Kaščák, Onofrej, Daniel Rossi, Otepka, Škerle, Hořava (Murín 87), Petr (Hubník 56), Janotka, Šultes (Caihame 75). Coach: Zdeněk Psotka (CZE)
Yellow Card(s): Petr 6, Dreksa 26, Daniel Rossi 55
A 2-0 *Hubník (47), Otepka (57)*
Drobisz, Dreksa, Kaščák (Bajer 80), Onofrej, Daniel Rossi, Otepka, Hubník (Caihame 74), Škerle, Hořava (Vepřek 88), Janotka, Šultes. Coach: Zdeněk Psotka (CZE)
Yellow Card(s): Onofrej 70, Caihame 79

Third Qualifying Round - Aberdeen FC (SCO)
A 5-1 *Hubník (17), Bajer (64), Petr (69), Ordoš (83), Hořava (90)*
Drobisz, Dreksa, Onofrej, Daniel Rossi, Otepka, Kaščák 57), Hubník (Heidenreich 85), Škerle, Bajer, Hořava, Petr (Ordoš 74), Janotka. Coach: Zdeněk Psotka (CZE)
Yellow Card(s): Janotka 48, Heidenreich 88
H 3-0 *Janotka (5), Kaščák (13p), Hubník (45+1)*
Drobisz, Dreksa, Kaščák, Onofrej, Daniel Rossi, Hubník (Otepka 66), Škerle, Bajer, Hořava (Ordoš 46), Petr (Šultes 58), Janotka. Coach: Zdeněk Psotka (CZE)

Play-Off Round – Everton FC (ENG)
A 0-4
Drobisz, Dreksa, Kaščák, Onofrej, Ordoš (Šultes 46), Daniel Rossi, Otepka (Bajer 61), Hubník, Škerle, Hořava, Petr (Janotka 74). Coach: Zdeněk Psotka (CZE)
Yellow Card(s): Hubník 8
H 1-1 *Šultes (80)*
Lovásik, Dreksa, Kaščák, Onofrej, Ordoš, Daniel Rossi, Škerle, Bajer (Otepka 73), Hořava, Petr (Štěpán 84), Janotka (Šultes 73). Coach: Zdeněk Psotka (CZE)
Yellow Card(s): Onofrej 23

Denmark

DENMARK

FC KØBENHAVN

UEFA CHAMPIONS LEAGUE

Second Qualifying Round - FK Mogren (MNE)
H 6-0 *Kristensen (8), M. Jørgensen (16), Aílton (24), N'Doye (69, 74), Nordstrand (82)*
Christiansen, Pospěch, Nørregaard, Aílton (Nordstrand 65), W.K. Jørgensen, César Santin (N'Doye 65), Antonsson, Kristensen (Grønkjær 60), Wendt, Vingaard, M. Jørgensen. Coach: Ståle Solbakken (NOR)
Yellow Card(s): Kristensen 17
A 6-0 *N'Doye (10, 40), Nordstrand (16), Vingaard (43), Delaney (47), Aílton (87)*
Wiland, Jensen, Laursen, W.K. Jørgensen (Larsson 66), Nordstrand (Aílton 66), N'Doye, Kristensen, Vingaard (Özdogan 46), Sionko, M. Jørgensen, Delaney. Coach: Ståle Solbakken (NOR)
Yellow Card(s): Özdogan 76

Third Qualifying Round - Stabæk IF (NOR)
H 3-1 *Grønkjær (11), César Santin (41, 80p)*
Christiansen, Pospěch, Nørregaard (Vingaard 71), Aílton (Nordstrand 64), W.K. Jørgensen, Grønkjær (Kristensen 82), César César Santin, Hutchinson, Antonsson, Wendt, M. Jørgensen. Coach: Ståle Solbakken (NOR)
Yellow Card(s): M. Jørgensen 87
A 0-0
Christiansen, Pospěch, Nørregaard, Aílton (Nordstrand 68), W.K. Jørgensen, Grønkjær (Kristensen 73), César Santin (N'Doye 86), Hutchinson, Antonsson, Wendt, M. Jørgensen. Coach: Ståle Solbakken (NOR)
Yellow Card(s): Antonsson 63

Play-Off Round - APOEL FC (CYP)
H 1-0 *Pospěch (54)*
Christiansen, Pospěch, Nørregaard, Aílton (Nordstrand 75), W.K. Jørgensen, Grønkjær, César Santin (N'Doye 22), Hutchinson, Antonsson, Wendt, M. Jørgensen. Coach: Ståle Solbakken (NOR)
A 1-3 *N'Doye (22)*
Christiansen, Pospěch, Nørregaard (Sionko 66), Aílton (Nordstrand 79), W.K. Jørgensen, Hutchinson, N'Doye, Antonsson, Wendt, Vingaard (Grønkjær 46), M. Jørgensen. Coach: Ståle Solbakken (NOR)
Yellow Card(s): Hutchinson 18, Nordstrand 82

UEFA EUROPA LEAGUE

Group K
Match 1 - CFR 1907 Cluj (ROU)
A 0-2
Wiland, Pospěch, Aílton (N'Doye 28), W.K. Jørgensen, César Santin, Larsson, Hutchinson, Antonsson, Kristensen (Delaney 77), Wendt, Vingaard (Sionko 63). Coach: Ståle Solbakken (NOR)
Yellow Card(s): W.K. Jørgensen 50, Kristensen 74
Match 2 - AC Sparta Praha (CZE)
H 1-0 *N'Doye (25)*
Wiland, Pospěch, W.K. Jørgensen, Grønkjær, César Santin (Aílton 67), Larsson, Hutchinson, N'Doye, Antonsson, Wendt, Vingaard (Nørregaard 86). Coach: Ståle Solbakken (NOR)
Match 3 - PSV Eindhoven (NED)
A 0-1
Wiland, Pospěch, Nørregaard (Vingaard 77), Laursen, W.K. Jørgensen, Grønkjær, Hutchinson, N'Doye (Aílton 76), Antonsson, Kristensen (César Santin 76), Wendt. Coach: Ståle Solbakken (NOR)
Yellow Card(s): Antonsson 32, Grønkjær 50, Pospěch 83

Match 4 - PSV Eindhoven (NED)
H 1-1 *Grønkjær (40p)*
Wiland, Pospěch, Nørregaard (Sionko 84), Laursen, W.K. Jørgensen, Grønkjær (César Santin 71), Hutchinson, N'Doye, Antonsson, Wendt, Vingaard. Coach: Ståle Solbakken (NOR)
Yellow Card(s): N'Doye 7
Match 5 - CFR 1907 Cluj (ROU)
H 2-0 *Vingaard (37), N'Doye (43)*
Wiland, Pospěch, Nørregaard (Kristensen 80), Laursen, W.K. Jørgensen, Grønkjær (Aílton 72), Hutchinson, N'Doye, Wendt, Vingaard (Jensen 90), M. Jørgensen. Coach: Ståle Solbakken (NOR)
Match 6 - AC Sparta Praha (CZE)
A 3-0 *N'Doye (22, 30), Grønkjær (54p)*
Wiland, Pospěch, Nørregaard (Delaney 82), Laursen, W.K. Jørgensen, Grønkjær (Aílton 87), Hutchinson, N'Doye, Antonsson, Wendt, Vingaard (Sionko 71). Coach: Ståle Solbakken (NOR)
Yellow Card(s): N'Doye 65

Round of 32 - Olympique de Marseille (FRA)
H 1-3 *Grønkjær (79p)*
Wiland, Pospěch, Nørregaard (César Santin 75), W.K. Jørgensen, Grønkjær, Hutchinson, N'Doye, Antonsson, Wendt, Vingaard, M. Jørgensen. Coach: Ståle Solbakken (NOR)
Yellow Card(s): Nørregaard 63
A 1-3 *Aílton (86)*
Wiland, Nørregaard, W.K. Jørgensen, Grønkjær (Aílton 61), César Santin (Kristensen 71), Hutchinson, N'Doye (Özdogan 80), Antonsson, Wendt, Vingaard, M. Jørgensen. Coach: Ståle Solbakken (NOR)

ODENSE BK

UEFA EUROPA LEAGUE

Third Qualifying Round - FK Rabotnicki (MKD)
A 4-3 *Cacá (20, 34, 70), Sørensen (62p)*
Lindegaard, Ruud, Håland, Christensen, H. Hansen (Andreasen 64), Absalonsen, Sørensen, Cacá (Utaka 71), Djemba-Djemba, Gíslason, Demba-Nyrén (E. Hansen 78). Coach: Lars Olsen (DEN)
Yellow Card(s): H. Hansen 44
H 3-0 *Utaka (53, 76), Rodic (81og)*
Lindegaard, Håland, Andreasen (Ruud 78), Christensen, Utaka, H. Hansen (Gíslason 56), Absalonsen, Sørensen, Troest, Djemba-Djemba, Demba-Nyrén (Cacá 46). Coach: Lars Olsen (DEN)
Yellow Card(s): Absalonsen 34, Utaka 39

Play-Off Round - Genoa CFC (ITA)
A 1-3 *Mesto (59og)*
Carroll, Ruud, Håland, Andreasen, Christensen, Helveg (Utaka 65), Absalonsen, Sørensen, Djemba-Djemba, Gíslason, Demba-Nyrén (Cacá 77). Coach: Lars Olsen (DEN)
Yellow Card(s): Helveg 12, Christensen 55, Sørensen 64, Utaka 85, Djemba-Djemba 90+2
H 1-1 *Figueroa (45+2og)*
Carroll, Ruud, Håland (H. Hansen 80), Andreasen, Christensen, Absalonsen, Sørensen, Cacá, Djemba-Djemba, Gíslason, Demba-Nyrén (Helveg 78). Coach: Lars Olsen (DEN)
Yellow Card(s): Djemba-Djemba 11, Cacá 39

BRØNDBY IF

UEFA EUROPA LEAGUE

Second Qualifying Round - FC Flora Tallinn (EST)
H 0-1
Andersen, Randrup (Jensen 26), Von Schlebrügge, Holmén, Nilsson, Farnerud, T. Rasmussen, Jallow (Madsen 84), Krohn-Dehli, Bischoff, Kristiansen (Agger 65). Coach: Kent Nielsen (DEN)
A 4-1 *Jallow (28), Farnerud (35), Holmén (45+1), Kristiansen (90+2)*
Andersen, Von Schlebrügge, Holmén (Kristiansen 73), Nilsson, Farnerud (Agger 62), Jönsson, T. Rasmussen (Frederiksen 54), Jallow, Krohn-Dehli, Bischoff, Jensen. Coach: Kent Nielsen (DEN)
Yellow Card(s): Holmén 17, Jönsson 33

Third Qualifying Round - Legia Warszawa (POL)
H 1-1 *Farnerud (73p)*
Andersen, Von Schlebrügge, Holmén, Nilsson, Farnerud, Jönsson (M. Rasmussen 60), T. Rasmussen, Jallow, Krohn-Dehli (Kristiansen 81), Bischoff (Randrup 33), Jensen. Coach: Kent Nielsen (DEN)
A 2-2 *Von Schlebrügge (6, 59)*
Andersen, Randrup, Von Schlebrügge, Frederiksen, Holmén, Nilsson, Farnerud (Gíslason 77), Madsen (Jallow 62), Jönsson, Krohn-Dehli Kristiansen 87), Jensen. Coach: Kent Nielsen (DEN)
Yellow Card(s): Frederiksen 52, Madsen 53, Krohn-Dehli 55

Play-Off Round - Hertha BSC Berlin (GER)
H 2-1 *Bischoff (51), Pejčinović (70og)*
Andersen, Randrup, Von Schlebrügge, Holmén, Nilsson (Jensen 90+2), M. Rasmussen (Farnerud 79), Madsen (Bernburg 64), Gíslason, T. Rasmussen, Krohn-Dehli, Bischoff. Coach: Kent Nielsen (DEN)
Yellow Card(s): Gíslason 72, Bernburg 89
A 1-3 *M. Rasmussen (52)*
Andersen, Randrup, Von Schlebrügge, Holmén, Nilsson, M. Rasmussen (Jensen 79), Madsen (Bernburg 61), Gíslason, T. Rasmussen (Farnerud 89), Krohn-Dehli, Bischoff. Coach: Kent Nielsen (DEN)
Yellow Card(s): Von Schlebrügge 68

RANDERS FC

UEFA EUROPA LEAGUE

First Qualifying Round - Linfield FC (NIR)
H 4-0 *Berg (36), Sane (47), Nygaard (79), Lorentzen (80)*
Ellegaard, Ahmed, Lorentzen, Addy, S. Pedersen, Grahn (Beckmann 73), Berg, K.M. Pedersen (Damborg 82), Nygaard, Sane (Olsen 73), Fenger. Coach: John Jensen (DEN)
A 3-0 *Olsen (21), Lorentzen (51), Berg (82)*
Ellegaard, Olesen (Fischer 73), Friberg da Cruz, Jepsen, Lorentzen, Berg, Beckmann (Byskov 77), Damborg, Olsen, Nygaard (König 63), Fenger. Coach: John Jensen (DEN)

Second Qualifying Round - FK Sūduva (LTU)
A 1-0 *Beckmann (23)*
Ellegaard, Ahmed, Jepsen, Lorentzen (Damborg 82), S. Pedersen, Grahn, Berg, Beckmann (König 76), K.M. Pedersen, Sane (Olsen 68), Fenger. Coach: John Jensen (DEN)
Yellow Card(s): Sane 36
H 1-1 *Leimonas (17og)*
Ellegaard, Friberg da Cruz, Jepsen, Lorentzen, S. Pedersen, Grahn (Damborg 82), Berg, K.M. Pedersen, Nygaard (Beckmann 58), Sane (Olsen 71), Fenger. Coach: John Jensen (DEN)
Yellow Card(s): Grahn 39, Olsen 82

Third Qualifying Round - Hamburger SV (GER)
H 0-4
Ellegaard, Friberg da Cruz, Lorentzen (Jepsen 60), Addy, S. Pedersen (Fischer 53), Berg, Beckmann (Damborg 76), K.M. Pedersen, Olsen, Sane, Fenger. Coach: John Jensen (DEN)
Yellow Card(s): Olsen 55, Ellegaard 80
A 1-0 *Berg (35)*
Ellegaard, Ahmed, Jepsen, Addy (König 62), S. Pedersen, Berg, Beckmann, Damborg, K.M. Pedersen (Fenger 79), Arzumanyan, Sane (Olesen 71). Coach: John Jensen (DEN)
Yellow Card(s): Beckmann 20

AALBORG BK

UEFA EUROPA LEAGUE

Second Qualifying Round - FK Slavija Sarajevo (BIH)
H 0-0
Zaza, Jakobsen, Chanko, Due, Johansson, Curth (Fredheim Holm 79), Tracy (Dalsgaard 67), Gaardsøe, Enevoldsen (Christensen 70), Kristensen, L. Nielsen. Coach: Magnus Pehrsson (SWE)
Yellow Card(s): Gaardsøe 90+4
A 1-3 *Johansson (51)*
Zaza, Jakobsen, Chanko, Due (Kristensen 68), Johansson, Curth, Fredheim Holm (Tracy 73), Bøgelund (Christensen 84), Gaardsøe, Enevoldsen, L. Nielsen. Coach: Magnus Pehrsson (SWE)
Yellow Card(s): Kristensen 77, Johansson 80, Chanko 90+3

ENGLAND

MANCHESTER UNITED FC

UEFA CHAMPIONS LEAGUE

Group B
Match 1 - Beşiktaş JK (TUR)
A 1-0 *Scholes (77)*
Foster, Neville, Evra, Anderson, Rooney (Owen 63), Vidić, Carrick (Berbatov 63), Nani, Scholes, Evans, Valencia (Park 83). Coach: Sir Alex Ferguson (SCO)
Yellow Card(s): Vidić 89
Match 2 - VfL Wolfsburg (GER)
H 2-1 *Giggs (59), Carrick (78)*
Kuszczak, Evra, Ferdinand, Owen (Berbatov 20), Anderson, Rooney, Giggs, Vidić, Carrick, O'Shea, Valencia (Fletcher 82). Coach: Sir Alex Ferguson (SCO)
Yellow Card(s): Vidić 39

CHAMPIONS LEAGUE **EUROPA LEAGUE**

Match 3 - PFC CSKA Moskva (RUS)
A 1-0 *Valencia (86)*
Van der Sar, Neville, Ferdinand (Brown 57), Anderson, Berbatov, Vidić,
Nani, Scholes (Owen 71), Fábio (Carrick 88), O'Shea, Valencia. Coach: Sir
Alex Ferguson (SCO)
Yellow Card(s): Berbatov 53
Match 4 - PFC CSKA Moskva (RUS)
H 3-3 *Owen (29), Scholes (84), Valencia (90+2)*
Van der Sar, Neville, Brown, Owen, Nani (Rooney 58), Scholes, Fábio (Evra
59), Evans, Fletcher, Valencia, Macheda (Obertan 82). Coach: Sir Alex
Ferguson (SCO)
Yellow Card(s): Fletcher 50, Macheda 75, Obertan 90+5
Match 5 - Beşiktaş JK (TUR)
H 0-1
Foster, Neville, Brown, Anderson, Park (Owen 69), Vidić, Welbeck,
Rafael (Evra 74), Obertan, Macheda, Gibson (Carrick 74). Coach: Sir Alex
Ferguson (SCO)
Match 6 - VfL Wolfsburg (GER)
A 3-1 *Owen (44, 83, 90+1)*
Kuszczak, Evra, Owen, Anderson, Park, Carrick, Nani (Valencia 74), Scholes,
Welbeck (Obertan 74), Fletcher, Gibson. Coach: Sir Alex Ferguson (SCO)

First Knockout Round - AC Milan (ITA)
A 3-2 *Scholes (36), Rooney (66, 74)*
Van der Sar, Evra, Ferdinand, Rooney, Park, Carrick, Nani (Valencia 65),
Scholes, Rafael (Brown 90+3), Evans, Fletcher. Coach: Sir Alex Ferguson (SCO)
Red Card(s): Carrick 90+3
Yellow Card(s): Rooney 44, Carrick 63, Carrick 90+3
H 4-0 *Rooney (13, 46), Park (59), Fletcher (88)*
Van der Sar, Neville (Rafael 66), Evra, Ferdinand, Rooney (Berbatov 66),
Park, Vidić, Nani, Scholes (Gibson 73), Fletcher, Valencia. Coach: Sir Alex
Ferguson (SCO)
Yellow Card(s): Scholes 68

Quarter-Finals - FC Bayern München (GER)
A 1-2 *Rooney (1)*
Van der Sar, Neville, Evra, Ferdinand, Rooney, Park (Berbatov 70), Vidić,
Carrick (Valencia 70), Nani (Giggs 82), Scholes, Fletcher. Coach: Sir Alex
Ferguson (SCO)
Yellow Card(s): Neville 76, Scholes 78, Rooney 88
H 3-2 *Gibson (3), Nani (7, 41)*
Van der Sar, Evra, Ferdinand, Rooney (O'Shea 55), Vidić, Carrick (Berbatov
80), Nani, Rafael, Fletcher, Valencia, Gibson (Giggs 81). Coach: Sir Alex
Ferguson (SCO)
Red Card(s): Rafael 50
Yellow Card(s): Rafael 18, Rafael 50

No	Player	Nat	DoB	Aps	(s)	Gls
Goalkeepers						
12	Ben Foster		3/4/83	2		
29	Tomasz Kuszczak	POL	20/3/82	2		
1	Edwin van der Sar	NED	29/10/70	6		
Defenders						
6	Wes Brown		13/10/79	2	(2)	
23	Jonny Evans	NIR	3/1/88	3		
3	Patrice Evra	FRA	15/5/81	7	(2)	
20	Fábio	BRA	9/7/90	2		
5	Rio Ferdinand		7/11/78	6		
2	Gary Neville		18/2/75	6		
22	John O'Shea	IRL	30/4/81	2	(1)	
21	Rafael	BRA	9/7/90	3	(1)	
15	Nemanja Vidić	SRB	21/10/81	7		
Midfielders						
8	Anderson	BRA	13/4/88	5		
16	Michael Carrick		28/7/81	6	(2)	1
24	Darren Fletcher	SCO	1/2/84	6	(1)	1
28	Darron Gibson	IRL	25/10/87	3	(1)	1
11	Ryan Giggs	WAL	29/11/73	1	(2)	
17	Nani	POR	17/11/86	8		2
13	Park Ji-sung	KOR	25/2/81	5	(1)	1
18	Paul Scholes		16/11/74	7		3
25	Luis Antonio Valencia	ECU	4/8/85	6	(3)	2
Forwards						

9	Dimitar Berbatov	BUL	30/1/81	1	(5)	
27	Federico Macheda	ITA	22/8/91	2		
26	Gabriel Obertan	FRA	26/2/89	1	(2)	
7	Michael Owen		14/12/79	3	(3)	4
10	Wayne Rooney		24/10/85	6	(1)	5
19	Daniel Welbeck		26/11/90	2		

LIVERPOOL FC

UEFA CHAMPIONS LEAGUE

Group E
Match 1 - Debreceni VSC (HUN)
H 1-0 *Kuyt (45+1)*
Reina, Johnson, Gerrard, Fernando Torres, Riera (Babel 80), Benayoun
(Mascherano 88), Kuyt (Fábio Aurélio 90+2), Lucas, Insúa, Carragher,
Škrtel. Coach: Rafael Benítez (ESP)
Yellow Card(s): Gerrard 26
Match 2 - ACF Fiorentina (ITA)
A 0-2
Reina, Johnson, Gerrard, Fernando Torres, Fábio Aurélio, Benayoun, Kuyt
(Voronin 80), Lucas, Insúa (Babel 72), Carragher, Škrtel. Coach: Rafael
Benítez (ESP)
Match 3 - Olympique Lyonnais (FRA)
H 1-2 *Benayoun (41)*
Reina, Agger, Gerrard (Fábio Aurélio 25), Benayoun (Voronin 85), Kuyt,
Mascherano, Lucas, Insúa, Carragher, N'Gog, Kelly (Škrtel 74). Coach:
Rafael Benítez (ESP)
Yellow Card(s): N'Gog 45+4
Match 4 - Olympique Lyonnais (FRA)
A 1-1 *Babel (83)*
Reina, Agger, Fernando Torres (N'Gog 87), Voronin (Babel 67), Benayoun,
Kyrgiakos, Kuyt, Mascherano, Lucas, Insúa, Carragher. Coach: Rafael
Benítez (ESP)
Yellow Card(s): Agger 33
Match 5 - Debreceni VSC (HUN)
A 1-0 *N'Gog (4)*
Reina, Johnson, Agger, Gerrard (Aquilani 90+2), Fábio Aurélio (Dossena
89), Kuyt, Mascherano, Lucas, Insúa, Carragher, N'Gog (Benayoun 77).
Coach: Rafael Benítez (ESP)
Match 6 - ACF Fiorentina (ITA)
H 1-2 *Benayoun (43)*
Cavalieri, Aquilani (Pacheco 76), Agger, Gerrard, Benayoun, Kuyt
(Fernando Torres 65), Mascherano (Fábio Aurélio 86), Insúa, Darby, Škrtel,
Dossena. Coach: Rafael Benítez (ESP)

No	Player	Nat	DoB	Aps	(s)	Gls
Goalkeepers						
1	Diego Cavalieri	BRA	1/12/82	1		
25	Pepe Reina	ESP	31/8/82	5		
Defenders						
5	Daniel Agger	DEN	12/12/84	4		
23	Jamie Carragher		28/1/78	5		
32	Stephen Darby		6/10/88	1		
38	Andrea Dossena	ITA	11/9/81	1	(1)	
12	Fábio Aurélio	BRA	24/9/79	2	(3)	
22	Emiliano Insúa	ARG	7/1/89	6		
2	Glen Johnson		23/8/84	3		
34	Martin Kelly		27/4/90	1		
16	Sotirios Kyrgiakos	GRE	23/7/79	1		
37	Martin Škrtel	SVK	15/12/84	3	(1)	
Midfielders						
4	Alberto Aquilani	ITA	7/7/84	1	(1)	
15	Yossi Benayoun	ISR	5/5/80	5	(1)	2
8	Steven Gerrard		30/5/80	5		

CHAMPIONS LEAGUE   EUROPA LEAGUE

1	Lucas	BRA	9/1/87	5		
0	Javier Mascherano	ARG	8/6/84	4	(1)	
7	Daniel Pacheco	ESP	5/1/91		(1)	
1	Albert Riera	ESP	15/4/82	1		
Forwards						
9	Ryan Babel	NED	19/12/86		(3)	1
8	Dirk Kuyt	NED	22/7/80	6		1
4	David N'Gog	FRA	1/4/89	2	(1)	1
	Fernando Torres	ESP	20/3/84	3	(1)	
0	Andriy Voronin	UKR	21/7/79	1	(2)	

UEFA EUROPA LEAGUE

Round of 32 - FC Unirea Urziceni (ROU)
1-0 *N'Gog (81)*
Reina, Aquilani (Pacheco 75), Agger, Gerrard, Riera (Babel 63), Fábio Aurélio, Kuyt, Mascherano, Carragher, N'Gog (Lucas 89), Škrtel. Coach: Rafael Benítez (ESP)
Yellow Card(s): Mascherano 68
3-1 *Mascherano (30), Babel (41), Gerrard (57)*
Reina, Agger, Gerrard, Benayoun (Fábio Aurélio 77), Babel, Mascherano, Lucas, Insúa, Carragher (Kelly 61), N'Gog, Škrtel (Kyrgiakos 66). Coach: Rafael Benítez (ESP)
Yellow Card(s): Babel 20, Mascherano 61

Round of 16 - LOSC Lille Métropole (FRA)
0-1
Reina, Johnson, Agger, Gerrard, Fernando Torres, Kuyt (El Zhar 88), Babel (Riera 73), Mascherano, Lucas, Insúa, Carragher. Coach: Rafael Benítez (ESP)
Yellow Card(s): Insúa 62, Fernando Torres 67
3-0 *Gerrard (9p), Fernando Torres (49, 89)*
Reina, Johnson, Aquilani (Kyrgiakos 90+1), Gerrard, Fernando Torres (N'Gog 90+2), Kuyt, Babel (Benayoun 80), Mascherano, Lucas, Insúa, Carragher. Coach: Rafael Benítez (ESP)
Yellow Card(s): Insúa 42, Fernando Torres 73

Quarter-Finals - SL Benfica (POR)
1-2 *Agger (9)*
Reina, Johnson, Agger, Gerrard (Benayoun 90+1), Fernando Torres (N'Gog 92), Kuyt, Babel, Mascherano, Lucas, Insúa, Carragher. Coach: Rafael Benítez (ESP)
Red Card(s): Babel 30
Yellow Card(s): Insúa 45+1, Reina 74, Carragher 78
4-1 *Kuyt (27), Lucas (34), Fernando Torres (59, 82)*
Reina, Johnson, Agger, Gerrard (Aquilani 88), Fernando Torres (N'Gog 86), Benayoun (El Zhar 90+1), Kyrgiakos, Kuyt, Mascherano, Lucas, Carragher. Coach: Rafael Benítez (ESP)
Yellow Card(s): Benayoun 75

Semi-Finals - Club Atlético de Madrid (ESP)
0-1
Reina, Johnson, Agger, Gerrard, Benayoun (El Zhar 83), Kyrgiakos, Kuyt, Mascherano, Lucas, Carragher, N'Gog (Babel 64). Coach: Rafael Benítez (ESP)
Yellow Card(s): Kyrgiakos 83
2-1 *Aquilani (44), Benayoun (95) (aet)*
Reina, Johnson, Aquilani (El Zhar 90), Agger, Gerrard, Benayoun (Pacheco 14), Kuyt, Babel, Mascherano (Degen 110), Lucas, Carragher. Coach: Rafael Benítez (ESP)
Yellow Card(s): Gerrard 43, Aquilani 51, Carragher 82

CHELSEA FC

UEFA CHAMPIONS LEAGUE

Group D
Match 1 - FC Porto (POR)
H 1-0 *Anelka (48)*
Čech, Ivanović, A. Cole, Essien, Ricardo Carvalho, Lampard, Ballack, Malouda, Kalou (Belletti 77), Terry, Anelka. Coach: Carlo Ancelotti (ITA)
Yellow Card(s): Essien 15, Malouda 18
Match 2 - APOEL FC (CYP)
A 1-0 *Anelka (18)*
Čech, Ivanović, A. Cole, Essien, Ricardo Carvalho, Lampard, Malouda, Kalou (J. Cole 80), Terry, Belletti (Deco 68), Anelka. Coach: Carlo Ancelotti (ITA)
Yellow Card(s): Kalou 44, Ivanović 79
Match 3 - Club Atlético de Madrid (ESP)
H 4-0 *Kalou (41, 52), Lampard (69), Perea (90+1og)*
Čech, Ivanović, A. Cole (Malouda 75), Essien, Lampard, Ballack, Deco, Kalou (Zhirkov 73), Terry, Belletti, Anelka (Sturridge 78). Coach: Carlo Ancelotti (ITA)
Yellow Card(s): Belletti 86
Match 4 - Club Atlético de Madrid (ESP)
A 2-2 *Drogba (82, 88)*
Čech, A. Cole, Essien (Ballack 59), Lampard, J. Cole (Deco 70), Drogba, Malouda, Kalou (Anelka 70), Terry, Alex, Belletti. Coach: Carlo Ancelotti (ITA)
Yellow Card(s): Essien 17, Terry 87
Match 5 - FC Porto (POR)
A 1-0 *Anelka (69)*
Čech, Ivanović, Ricardo Carvalho, Drogba, Mikel, Ballack (Essien 68), Malouda, Zhirkov, Deco (J. Cole 76), Terry, Anelka. Coach: Carlo Ancelotti (ITA)
Yellow Card(s): Ballack 58
Match 6 - APOEL FC (CYP)
H 2-2 *Essien (19), Drogba (26)*
Turnbull, Essien (Lampard 26), Ricardo Carvalho, J. Cole, Drogba, Mikel, Malouda, Zhirkov, Terry, Belletti, Kakuta (Borini 73). Coach: Carlo Ancelotti (ITA)
Yellow Card(s): Zhirkov 18

First Knockout Round - FC Internazionale Milano (ITA)
A 1-2 *Kalou (51)*
Čech (Hilário 61), Ivanović, Ricardo Carvalho, Lampard, Drogba, Mikel, Ballack, Malouda, Kalou (Sturridge 78), Terry, Anelka. Coach: Carlo Ancelotti (ITA)
Yellow Card(s): Kalou 23
H 0-1
Turnbull, Ivanović, Lampard, Drogba, Mikel, Ballack (J. Cole 62), Malouda, Zhirkov (Kalou 74), Terry, Alex, Anelka. Coach: Carlo Ancelotti (ITA)
Red Card(s): Drogba 87
Yellow Card(s): Malouda 55, Drogba 57, Alex 83, Terry 89

No	Player	Nat	DoB	Aps	(s)	Gls
Goalkeepers						
1	Petr Čech	CZE	20/5/82	6		
40	Henrique Hilário	POR	21/10/75		(1)	
22	Ross Turnbull		4/1/85	2		
Defenders						
3	Ashley Cole		20/12/80	4		
33	Alex	BRA	17/6/82	2		
35	Juliano Belletti	BRA	20/6/76	4	(1)	
6	Ricardo Carvalho	POR	18/5/78	5		
2	Branislav Ivanović	SRB	22/2/84	6		
26	John Terry		7/12/80	8		
Midfielders						
13	Michael Ballack	GER	26/9/76	5	(1)	
20	Deco	POR	27/8/77	2	(2)	
5	Michael Essien	GHA	3/12/82	5	(1)	1
10	Joe Cole		8/11/81	2	(3)	
8	Frank Lampard		20/6/78	6	(1)	1
15	Florent Malouda	FRA	13/6/80	7	(1)	
12	John Obi Mikel	NGA	22/4/87	4		
18	Yuriy Zhirkov	RUS	20/8/83	3	(1)	
Forwards						
39	Nicolas Anelka	FRA	14/3/79	6	(1)	4
45	Fabio Borini	ITA	23/3/91		(1)	
11	Didier Drogba	CIV	11/3/78	5		3
44	Gaël Kakuta	FRA	21/6/91	1		
21	Salomon Kalou	CIV	5/8/85	5	(1)	3
23	Daniel Sturridge		1/9/89		(2)	

ARSENAL FC

UEFA CHAMPIONS LEAGUE

Play-Off Round - Celtic FC (SCO)
A 2-0 *Gallas (43), Caldwell (71og)*
Almunia, Sagna, Fàbregas, Vermaelen, Gallas, Van Persie, Denílson, Song, Clichy, Arshavin (Diaby 70), Bendtner. Coach: Arsène Wenger (FRA)
Yellow Card(s): Clichy 84
H 3-1 *Eduardo (28p), Eboué (53), Arshavin (74)*
Almunia, Diaby (Ramsey 61), Sagna, Vermaelen, Eduardo (Arshavin 72), Gallas, Denílson, Song, Clichy, Eboué (Wilshere 72), Bendtner. Coach: Arsène Wenger (FRA)
Yellow Card(s): Eboué 54, Denílson 83

Group H
Match 1 - R. Standard de Liège (BEL)
A 3-2 *Bendtner (45), Vermaelen (77), Eduardo (81)*
Mannone, Diaby, Fàbregas, Vermaelen, Rosický (Ramsey 70), Eduardo (Wilshere 86), Gallas, Song, Clichy, Eboué (Sagna 78), Bendtner. Coach: Arsène Wenger (FRA)
Yellow Card(s): Clichy 34
Match 2 - Olympiacos FC (GRE)
H 2-0 *Van Persie (78), Arshavin (86)*
Mannone, Diaby (Vela 77), Fàbregas, Vermaelen, Rosický (Eduardo 66), Gallas, Van Persie (Ramsey 85), Song, Clichy, Arshavin, Eboué. Coach: Arsène Wenger (FRA)
Yellow Card(s): Van Persie 52, Fàbregas 90
Match 3 - AZ Alkmaar (NED)
A 1-1 *Fàbregas (36)*
Mannone, Diaby, Sagna, Fàbregas, Vermaelen, Gallas, Van Persie (Vela 74), Song, Clichy, Arshavin, Eboué (Ramsey 83). Coach: Arsène Wenger (FRA)
Yellow Card(s): Van Persie 48, Clichy 66, Vela 77
Match 4 - AZ Alkmaar (NED)
H 4-1 *Fàbregas (25, 52), Nasri (43), Diaby (72)*
Almunia, Diaby, Fàbregas (Ramsey 67), Vermaelen, Nasri, Gallas, Van Persie (Eduardo 67), Song, Arshavin (Rosický 75), Eboué, Gibbs. Coach: Arsène Wenger (FRA)
Match 5 - R. Standard de Liège (BEL)
H 2-0 *Nasri (35), Denílson (45+2)*
Almunia, Fàbregas, Vermaelen, Nasri (Walcott 60), Gallas (Silvestre 46), Vela, Denílson (Rosický 67), Song, Arshavin, Eboué, Gibbs. Coach: Arsène Wenger (FRA)
Yellow Card(s): Fàbregas 86
Match 6 - Olympiacos FC (GRE)
A 0-1
Fabiański, Vela, Walcott, Ramsey, Song, Silvestre, Wilshere (Sunu 76), Fran Mérida, Bartley, Cruise, Gilbert. Coach: Arsène Wenger (FRA)
Yellow Card(s): Mérida 40

First Knockout Round - FC Porto (POR)
A 1-2 *Campbell (18)*
Fabiański, Diaby, Sagna, Fàbregas, Vermaelen, Rosický (Walcott 68), Nasri (Eboué 88), Denílson, Clichy, Campbell, Bendtner (Vela 83). Coach: Arsène Wenger (FRA)
Yellow Card(s): Diaby 31
H 5-0 *Bendtner (10, 25, 90+1p), Nasri (63), Eboué (66)*
Almunia, Diaby, Sagna, Fàbregas, Vermaelen, Rosický (Eboué 57), Nasri (Denílson 73), Song, Clichy, Arshavin (Walcott 77), Campbell, Bendtner. Coach: Arsène Wenger (FRA)
Yellow Card(s): Vermaelen 38, Bendtner 44

Quarter-Finals - FC Barcelona (ESP)
H 2-2 *Walcott (69), Fàbregas (85p)*
Almunia, Diaby, Sagna (Walcott 66), Fàbregas, Vermaelen, Nasri, Gallas (Denílson 44), Song, Clichy, Arshavin (Eboué 27), Bendtner. Coach: Arsène Wenger (FRA)

Yellow Card(s): Arshavin 21, Song 40, Fàbregas 44, Eboué 74, Diaby 79
A 1-4 *Bendtner (18)*
Almunia, Diaby, Sagna, Vermaelen, Rosický (Eduardo 73), Nasri, Walcott, Denílson, Silvestre (Eboué 63), Clichy, Bendtner. Coach: Arsène Wenger (FRA)
Yellow Card(s): Denílson 31, Rosický 44, Eboué 67

No	Player	Nat	DoB	Aps	(s)	Gls
Goalkeepers						
1	Manuel Almunia	ESP	19/5/77	5		
21	Łukasz Fabiański	POL	18/4/85	2		
24	Vito Mannone	ITA	2/3/88	3		
Defenders						
34	Kyle Bartley		22/5/91	1		
31	Sol Campbell		18/9/74	2		1
22	Gaël Clichy	FRA	26/7/85	7		
36	Thomas Cruise		9/3/91	1		
27	Emmanuel Eboué	CIV	4/6/83	5	(4)	1
10	William Gallas	FRA	17/8/77	6		
42	Kerrea Gilbert		28/2/87	1		
3	Bacary Sagna	FRA	14/2/83	5	(1)	
18	Mikaël Silvestre	FRA	9/8/77	2	(1)	
5	Thomas Vermaelen	BEL	14/11/85	9		1
Midfielders						
15	Denílson	BRA	16/2/88	3	(2)	1
2	Abou Diaby	FRA	11/5/86	8		1
4	Cesc Fàbregas	ESP	4/5/87	7		4
28	Kieran Gibbs		26/9/89	2		
32	Fran Mérida	ESP	4/3/90	1		
8	Samir Nasri	FRA	26/6/87	6		3
16	Aaron Ramsey	WAL	26/12/90	1	(4)	
7	Tomáš Rosický	CZE	4/10/80	5	(2)	
17	Alex Song	CMR	9/9/87	8		
19	Jack Wilshere		1/1/92	1	(1)	
Forwards						
23	Andrei Arshavin	RUS	29/5/81	6		1
52	Nicklas Bendtner	DEN	16/1/88	5		5
9	Eduardo	CRO	25/2/83	1	(3)	1
51	Gilles Sunu	FRA	30/3/91		(1)	
11	Robin van Persie	NED	6/8/83	3		1
12	Carlos Vela	MEX	1/3/89	2	(3)	
14	Theo Walcott		16/3/89	2	(4)	1

EVERTON FC

UEFA EUROPA LEAGUE

Play-Off Round - SK Sigma Olomouc (CZE)
H 4-0 *Saha (34, 72), Rodwell (40, 53)*
Howard, Hibbert, Baines, Yobo, Saha (Jô 78), Cahill, Neville, Pienaar (Vaughan 82), Osman, Fellaini, Rodwell (Gosling 76). Coach: David Moyes (SCO)
Yellow Card(s): Neville 61
A 1-1 *Pienaar (44)*
Howard, Hibbert, Baines, Yobo, Jô (Yakubu 76), Neville, Gosling, Pienaar (Wallace 66), Osman (Baxter 66), Fellaini, Rodwell. Coach: David Moyes (SCO)
Red Card(s): Hibbert 7
Yellow Card(s): Gosling 24

Group I
Match 1 - AEK Athens FC (GRE)
H 4-0 *Yobo (10), Distin (17), Pienaar (37), Jô (82)*
Howard, Baines, Yobo, Distin, Bilyaletdinov (Yakubu 52), Jô, Distin, Cahill (Osman 46), Gosling, Pienaar, Saha (58), Fellaini, Rodwell. Coach: David Moyes (SCO)
Red Card(s): Saha 90+2
Yellow Card(s): Cahill 42

Match 2 - FC BATE Borisov (BLR)
A 2-1 *Fellaini (68), Cahill (77)*
Howard, Hibbert, Baines, Bilyaletdinov (Baxter 90+1), Jô, Distin, Cahill, Gosling, Osman, Yakubu (Agard 78), Fellaini. Coach: David Moyes (SCO)
Yellow Card(s): Osman 74, Agard 90+3
Match 3 - SL Benfica (POR)
A 0-5
Howard, Hibbert, Bilyaletdinov (Saha 60), Jô, Distin, Cahill, Gosling, Yakubu (Baxter 71), Fellaini, Rodwell, Coleman. Coach: David Moyes (SCO)
Yellow Card(s): Gosling 32, Saha 76
Match 4 - SL Benfica (POR)
H 0-2
Howard, Hibbert, Baines, Yobo, Bilyaletdinov, Distin, Cahill, Gosling (Jô 69), Yakubu (Agard 81), Fellaini, Rodwell. Coach: David Moyes (SCO)
Yellow Card(s): Yakubu 20, Rodwell 51, Hibbert 79
Match 5 - AEK Athens FC (GRE)
A 1-0 *Bilyaletdinov (6)*
Howard, Hibbert, Baines, Bilyaletdinov, Jô (Yakubu 73), Distin (Duffy 18), Cahill, Gosling (Baxter 10), Pienaar, Fellaini, Coleman. Coach: David Moyes (SCO)
Yellow Card(s): Hibbert 18, Cahill 50, Howard 56, Bilyaletdinov 67, Baxter 88
Match 6 - FC BATE Borisov (BLR)
H 0-1
Nash, Hibbert (Mustafi 75), Osman (Craig 82), Yakubu, Rodwell (Akpan 9), Forshaw, Coleman, Duffy, Agard, Bidwell, Baxter. Coach: David Moyes (SCO)
Yellow Card(s): Coleman 50, Duffy 51

Round of 32 - Sporting Clube de Portugal (POR)
H 2-1 *Pienaar (35), Distin (49)*
Howard, Baines, Yobo, Saha (Bilyaletdinov 83), Donovan, Arteta (Rodwell 78), Distin, Cahill (Yakubu 62), Neville, Pienaar, Osman. Coach: David Moyes (SCO)
Red Card(s): Distin 86
A 0-3
Howard, Baines, Yobo, Bilyaletdinov (Rodwell 62), Saha, Donovan (Yakubu 73), Arteta, Neville, Pienaar, Osman, Senderos (Jagielka 52). Coach: David Moyes (SCO)
Yellow Card(s): Pienaar 79

ASTON VILLA FC

UEFA EUROPA LEAGUE
Play-Off Round - SK Rapid Wien (AUT)
A 0-1
Guzan, Sidwell, Young, Milner, Davies (Lowry 81), Heskey, Reo-Coker, Shorey, Beye, Cuéllar, Gardner (Agbonlahor 55). Coach: Martin O'Neill (NIR)
Yellow Card(s): Sidwell 41
H 2-1 *Milner (38p), Carew (53)*
Guzan, Young, Milner, Carew, Davies (Lowry 83), Delph (Albrighton 86), Heskey (Agbonlahor 82), Petrov, Shorey, Beye, Cuéllar. Coach: Martin O'Neill (NIR)
Yellow Card(s): Cuéllar 20, Young 32, Carew 36

FULHAM FC

UEFA EUROPA LEAGUE
Third Qualifying Round - FK Vėtra (LTU)
A 3-0 *Zamora (45), Murphy (57p), Seol (85)*
Schwarzer, Konchesky, Pantsil, Hangeland, Baird, A. Johnson (Nevland 69), Gera, Murphy (Riise 87), Hughes, Dempsey (Seol 81), Zamora. Coach: Roy Hodgson (ENG)
H 3-0 *Etuhu (57), A. Johnson (80, 84)*
Schwarzer, Konchesky, Pantsil (Kelly 78), Hangeland, A. Johnson, Gera (Riise 78), Murphy, Hughes, Etuhu, Dempsey, Zamora (E. Johnson 82). Coach: Roy Hodgson (ENG)
Yellow Card(s): Kelly 90+2

Play-Off Round - FC Amkar Perm (RUS)
H 3-1 *A. Johnson (4), Dempsey (51), Zamora (75)*
Schwarzer, Konchesky, Pantsil, Hangeland, A. Johnson (Nevland 68), Gera (Duff 75), Murphy, Hughes, Etuhu (Baird 78), Dempsey, Zamora. Coach: Roy Hodgson (ENG)
Yellow Card(s): Dempsey 82
A 0-1
Schwarzer, Kelly, Pantsil, Hangeland, Baird, Nevland (Kamara 68), Gera, Duff, Riise (Seol 76), Hughes, Etuhu. Coach: Roy Hodgson (ENG)
Yellow Card(s): Pantsil 63, Baird 88

Group E
Match 1 - PFC CSKA Sofia (BUL)
A 1-1 *Kamara (65)*
Stockdale, Kelly, Pantsil, Baird, Nevland, Gera, Kamara, Riise, Smalling, Greening, Davies. Coach: Roy Hodgson (ENG)
Yellow Card(s): Greening 23, Smalling 47, Kamara 89
Match 2 - FC Basel 1893 (SUI)
H 1-0 *Murphy (57)*
Schwarzer, Kelly, Konchesky, Baird, A. Johnson, Murphy, Riise, Dempsey, Zamora, Smalling, Greening. Coach: Roy Hodgson (ENG)
Yellow Card(s): Greening 63, Baird 85
Match 3 - AS Roma (ITA)
H 1-1 *Hangeland (24)*
Schwarzer, Kelly, Konchesky (Pantsil 46), Hangeland, Baird, Gera, Kamara, Riise (Duff 75), Hughes, Zamora (Nevland 61), Greening. Coach: Roy Hodgson (ENG)
Red Card(s): Kelly 77
Match 4 - AS Roma (ITA)
A 1-2 *Kamara (19p)*
Schwarzer, Konchesky, Pantsil, Hangeland, Gera, Kamara (Nevland 46), Riise (Zamora 70), Hughes, Etuhu (Baird 77), Dempsey, Greening. Coach: Roy Hodgson (ENG)
Red Card(s): Nevland 49, Konchesky 90+1
Yellow Card(s): Greening 34, Hangeland 45, Baird 89
Match 5 - PFC CSKA Sofia (BUL)
H 1-0 *Gera (15)*
Schwarzer, Kelly, Pantsil, Hangeland (Hughes 46), Baird, Gera, Murphy (Duff 79), Riise, Zamora, Smalling, Davies (Dempsey 70). Coach: Roy Hodgson (ENG)
Yellow Card(s): Baird 41, Pantsil 81
Match 6 - FC Basel 1893 (SUI)
A 3-2 *Zamora (42, 45), Gera (77)*
Schwarzer, Kelly, Pantsil, Gera, Murphy, Riise, Hughes, Etuhu, Zamora (Duff 80), Smalling, Greening (Dempsey 70). Coach: Roy Hodgson (ENG)
Yellow Card(s): Zamora 30, Greening 51

Round of 32 - FC Shakhtar Donetsk (UKR)
H 2-1 *Gera (3), Zamora (63)*
Schwarzer, Kelly, Hangeland, Baird, Gera (Elm 89), Murphy, Duff, Hughes, Etuhu, Zamora, Davies. Coach: Roy Hodgson (ENG)
Yellow Card(s): Murphy 53

A 1-1 *Hangeland (33)*
Schwarzer, Kelly, Hangeland, Baird, Gera, Murphy, Duff, Hughes, Etuhu, Zamora (Elm 72), Davies (Riise 89). Coach: Roy Hodgson (ENG)
Red Card(s): Murphy 90+4
Yellow Card(s): Gera 77

Round of 16 - Juventus (ITA)
A 1-3 *Etuhu (36)*
Schwarzer, Konchesky, Hangeland, Baird, Gera, Duff, Hughes, Etuhu, Zamora, Greening, Davies (Dempsey 60). Coach: Roy Hodgson (ENG)
Yellow Card(s): Greening 84
H 4-1 *Zamora (9), Gera (39, 48p), Dempsey (82)*
Schwarzer, Kelly (Dempsey 71), Konchesky, Hangeland, Baird, Gera (Riise 85), Duff, Hughes, Etuhu, Zamora, Davies. Coach: Roy Hodgson (ENG)
Yellow Card(s): Konchesky 90

Quarter-Finals - VfL Wolfsburg (GER)
H 2-1 *Zamora (59), Duff (63)*
Schwarzer, Konchesky, Hangeland, Gera, Murphy (Baird 87), Duff, Hughes, Etuhu, Dempsey, Zamora, Davies. Coach: Roy Hodgson (ENG)
Yellow Card(s): Zamora 39
A 1-0 *Zamora (1)*
Schwarzer, Konchesky, Hangeland, Baird, Gera (Nevland 82), Murphy, Duff, Hughes, Etuhu, Zamora, Davies (Riise 86). Coach: Roy Hodgson (ENG)
Yellow Card(s): Baird 48, Konchesky 63

Semi-Finals - Hamburger SV (GER)
A 0-0
Schwarzer, Konchesky, Hangeland, Baird, Gera, Murphy, Duff, Hughes, Etuhu, Zamora, Davies. Coach: Roy Hodgson (ENG)
Yellow Card(s): Baird 55, Gera 68
H 2-1 *Davies (69), Gera (76)*
Schwarzer, Konchesky, Pantsil (Nevland 74), Hangeland, Gera, Murphy, Duff, Hughes, Etuhu, Zamora (Dempsey 57), Davies. Coach: Roy Hodgson (ENG)
Yellow Card(s): Hangeland 65, Dempsey 90+3

Final - Club Atlético de Madrid (ESP)
1-2 *Davies (37) (aet)*
Schwarzer, Konchesky, Hangeland, Baird, Gera, Murphy (Greening 118), Duff (Nevland 84), Hughes, Etuhu, Zamora (Dempsey 55), Davies. Coach: Roy Hodgson (ENG)
Yellow Card(s): Hangeland 63

ESTONIA

FC LEVADIA TALLINN

UEFA CHAMPIONS LEAGUE
Second Qualifying Round - Wisła Kraków (POL)
A 1-1 *Andreev (41)*
Kaalma, Kalimullin, Morozov, Nahk, Gussev, Ivanov (E. Puri 85), Marmor (Šišov 46), Malov, Andreev (Zelinski 83), S. Puri, Teniste. Coach: Igor Prins (EST)
Yellow Card(s): S. Puri 65, Nahk 90+1
H 1-0 *Ivanov (89)*
Kaalma, Kalimullin, Morozov, Šišov, Nahk, Gussev (Zelinski 90+3), Ivanov, Malov, Andreev (Leitan 86), S. Puri, Teniste. Coach: Igor Prins (EST)

Third Qualifying Round - Debreceni VSC (HUN)
H 0-1
Kaalma, Kalimullin, Morozov, Šišov, Nahk, Gussev (Zelinski 86), Ivanov, Malov (Leitan 74), Andreev, S. Puri (E. Puri 89), Teniste. Coach: Igor Prins (EST)
Yellow Card(s): Nahk 43, Malov 58, Andreev 80

A 0-1
Kaalma, Kalimullin, Morozov, Gussev, Ivanov, Marmor (Šišov 21), Malov, Saarelma, Andreev (Zelinski 46), S. Puri, Teniste. Coach: Igor Prins (EST)
Red Card(s): Malov 80
Yellow Card(s): Malov 24, Saarelma 31, Malov 80

UEFA EUROPA LEAGUE
Play-Off Round - Galatasaray AŞ (TUR)
A 0-5
Kaalma, Teniste (E. Puri 73), Morozov, Kalimullin, Šišov, Nahk, Leitan, Ivanov, Gussev, S. Puri (Saarelma 19), Zelinski. Coach: Igor Prins (EST)
H 1-1 *E. Puri (50)*
Kaalma, Kalimullin, Morozov, Leitan (Mones 89), Šišov, Nahk, Gussev, Saarelma, Neemelo (Zelinski 81), E. Puri, Teniste. Coach: Igor Prins (EST)
Yellow Card(s): Saarelma 68

FC FLORA TALLINN

UEFA EUROPA LEAGUE
Second Qualifying Round - Brøndby IF (DEN)
A 1-0 *Vanna (50)*
Aksalu, Rooba (Jürgenson 65), Kasimir, Vunk, Mošnikov (Kallaste 83), Konsa, Zahovaiko (Dupikov 58), Vanna, Kams, Palatu, Anniste. Coach: Tarmo Rüütli (EST)
H 1-4 *Kasimir (80)*
Aksalu, Rooba (Kallaste 46), Kasimir, Vunk, Konsa, He. Anier, Zahovaiko (Dupikov 70), Vanna, Jürgenson, Palatu, Anniste (Tamm 70). Coach: Tarmo Rüütli (EST)
Yellow Card(s): Jürgenson 81

JK TRANS NARVA

UEFA EUROPA LEAGUE
First Qualifying Round - NK Rudar Velenje (SVN)
H 0-3
Stonys, Rimas, Gorškov, Kazakov, Tarassenkov (Fjodorov 90+3), Lõsanov (Starovoitov 77), Lepik, Bazyukin, Kitto, E. Ratnikov, D. Ratnikov. Coach: Sergei Ratnikov (EST)
Yellow Card(s): Bazjukin 49
A 1-3 *Starovoitov (74)*
Stonys, E. Ratnikov, Kitto, Bazjukin (D. Ratnikov 67), Lepik, Lõsanov, Tarassenkov, Kazakov (Leontovitš 75), Gorškov, Starovoitov (Eder 76), Rimas. Coach: Sergei Ratnikov (EST)

CHAMPIONS EUROPA
LEAGUE, LEAGUE

JK NÕMME KALJU

UEFA EUROPA LEAGUE

First Qualifying Round - FC Dinaburg (LVA)
1-2 *Haavistu (90+2)*
...aas, Haavistu, Diego, Felipe, Marcio (Novikov 65), Arruda, Tükk, Terehhov ...aukvere 68), Rafael, Shuhanau (Smirnov 77), Hurt. Coach: Fredo Getúlio ...urélio (BRA)
Yellow Card(s): Tükk 66, Novikov 70
0-0
...aas, Haavistu, Diego, Felipe, Novikov, Arruda, Smirnov (Kaukvere 55), ...accari (Tükk 70), Terehhov, Rafael (Shuhanov 64), Hurt. Coach: Fredo ...etúlio Aurélio (BRA)
...ed Card(s): Haavistu 68
...ellow Card(s): Terehhov 38, Arruda 90

EB/STREYMUR

UEFA CHAMPIONS LEAGUE

...econd Qualifying Round - APOEL FC (CYP)
...0-2
...eig, Davidsen, L. Hanssen, Bø, Anghel (Jacobsen 89), Samuelsen, ...jurhuus (Br. Olsen 83), Bá. Olsen, A.T. Hansen (P.G. Hansen 82), Niclasen, ...ielsen . Coach: Sigfrídur Clementsen (FRO)
...ellow Card(s): Djurhuus 59, Anghel 73
0-3
...eig, Davidsen, L. Hanssen, Anghel, Samuelsen (Alex 76), Djurhuus, Bá. ...lsen, P.G. Hansen (Jacobsen 58), A.T. Hansen, Niclasen, Nielsen (Br. Olsen ...). Coach: Sigfrídur Clementsen (FRO)

HB TÓRSHAVN

UEFA EUROPA LEAGUE

...econd Qualifying Round - AC Omonia (CYP)
...0-4
...awid, Lag, Ólavsstovu (R. Nolsøe 77), Fløtum, B. Jørgensen (Joensen 74), ...uljić, Dam, Poulsen, Mortensen, P.T. Jørgensen, Jespersen. Coach: Sámal ...rik Hentze (FRO)
1-4 *Jespersen (56)*
...awid, R. Nolsøe, Benjaminsen, Fløtum, J. Mouritsen (K. Nielsen 70), Kuljić ...oulsen 83), Dam, Mortensen, P.T. Jørgensen, Jespersen, Joensen (B. ...ørgensen 67). Coach: Sámal Erik Hentze (FRO)
...ellow Card(s): Benjaminsen 54, Mortensen 68

B36 TÓRSHAVN

UEFA EUROPA LEAGUE

First Qualifying Round - FC Olimpi Rustavi (GEO)
A 0-2
Jakobsen, Færø, Midjord (Hermansen 82), R. Jacobsen, Ellingsgaard, Koroma (Eysturoy 75), Olsen, Matras, Malsom (Borg 46), Gunnarsson, H. Jacobsen. Coach: Mikkjal Thomasen (FRO)
Yellow Card(s): Koroma 45, Midjord 74, Matras 77, Hermansen 90+4
H 0-2
Jakobsen, Færø, Midjord (Holmberg 17), R. Jacobsen, Ellingsgaard, Koroma, Olsen (Hermansen 90), Matras, Malsom (Borg 65), Gunnarsson, H. Jacobsen. Coach: Danjal Jákup Joensen (FRO)
Yellow Card(s): Ellingsgaard 18

NSÍ RUNAVÍK

UEFA EUROPA LEAGUE

First Qualifying Round - Rosenborg BK (NOR)
H 0-3
M. Joensen, Ó. Hansen, J. Hansen, Davidsen, Potemkin (Madsen 79), Elttør (Olsen 76), Petersen, E. Hansen, Løkin, Frederiksberg (J. Joensen 56), C.H. Jacobsen. Coach: Pauli Poulsen (FRO)
Yellow Card(s): Madsen 83
A 1-3 *Potemkin (6)*
M. Joensen, Ó. Hansen, J. Hansen, Davidsen, Potemkin (Olsen 70), Elttør, Petersen, E. Hansen, Løkin (J. Joensen 89), Frederiksberg, C.H. Jacobsen (Mortensen 61). Coach: Pauli Poulsen (FRO)
Yellow Card(s): J. Davidsen 43, Frederiksberg 90+1

FINLAND

FC INTER TURKU

UEFA CHAMPIONS LEAGUE

Second Qualifying Round - FC Sheriff (MDA)
H 0-1
Bantamoi, Verino, Ramírez, Nyman, Furuholm, Aho, Paajanen, Ojala (Nwanganga 69), Purje (Grot 71), Kauko, Lehtonen. Coach: Job Dragtsma (NED)
Yellow Card(s): Purje 19, Bantamoi 41, Kauko 47, Furuholm 64, Paajanen 90+1
A 0-1
Bantamoi, Ramírez, Gustafsson (Verino 81), Nyman, Tumanto (Purje 58), Furuholm, Aho, Paajanen, Ojala (Nwanganga 64), Kauko, Lehtonen. Coach: Job Dragtsma (NED)
Yellow Card(s): Bantamoi 68, Ramírez Torres 74

CHAMPIONS LEAGUE EUROPA LEAGUE

Finland/France

HJK HELSINKI

UEFA EUROPA LEAGUE

Second Qualifying Round - FK Vėtra (LTU)
A 1-0 *Bah (15)*
Wallén, Hauhia, Kamara, Sauso, Fowler, Sorsa (Taulo 88), Kärkkäinen, Parikka (Popovich 74), Bah, Raitala, Pelvas (Mäkelä 61). Coach: Antti Muurinen (FIN)
H 1-3 *Kamara (3)*
Wallén, Hauhia (Popovich 79), Kamara, Sauso, Fowler, Sorsa, Kärkkäinen, Parikka (Oravainen 66), Bah, Raitala, Pelvas (Mäkelä 46). Coach: Antti Muurinen (FIN)
Yellow Card(s): Kamara 84

FC HONKA ESPOO

UEFA EUROPA LEAGUE

Second Qualifying Round - Bangor City FC (WAL)
H 2-0 *Perovuo (15), Schüller (74)*
Henriksson, Koskinen, Aalto, Vuorinen, Koskimaa, Kokko (Puustinen 77), Savage (Otaru 89), Hakanpää, Perovuo, Lepola (Vasara 46), Schüller. Coach: Mika Lehkosuo (FIN)
Yellow Card(s): Savage 45+1
A 1-0 *Puustinen (39)*
Henriksson, Koskinen (Haarala 69), Aalto, Vuorinen (Kokko 77), Puustinen, Koskimaa, Vasara, Savage (Otaru 61), Hakanpää, Perovuo, Schüller. Coach: Mika Lehkosuo (FIN)

Third Qualifying Round - Qarabağ FK (AZE)
H 0-1
Henriksson, Koskinen (Aalto 64), Vuorinen, Puustinen (Simpanen 78), Haarala, Koskimaa (Heilala 72), Vasara, Savage, Hakanpää, Perovuo, Lepola. Coach: Mika Lehkosuo (FIN)
A 1-2 *Koskinen (34)*
Henriksson, Koskinen, Heilala, Vuorinen, Puustinen, Haarala, Vasara (Savage 63), Hakanpää, Otaru, Perovuo, Schüller. Coach: Mika Lehkosuo (FIN)
Yellow Card(s): Vuorinen 24, Hakanpää 58, Schüller 84

FC LAHTI

UEFA EUROPA LEAGUE

First Qualifying Round - KS Dinamo Tirana (ALB)
H 4-1 *Rafael (2, 86), Moilanen (43), Haara (52)*
Szentpéteri, Haara, Toivomäki, Moilanen, Eerola, Fofana (Heini 61), Rafael (Länsitalo 87), Litmanen, Hietanen (Shala 46), Vanninen, Korte. Coach: Ilkka Mäkelä (FIN)

A 0-2
Szentpéteri, Haara (Huuhka 72), Toivomäki, Moilanen, Eerola, Fofana, Rafael (Kemppinen 26), Litmanen, Shala (Heini 46), Vanninen, Korte. Coach: Ilkka Mäkelä (FIN)
Yellow Card(s): Fofana 69, Szentpéteri 74

Second Qualifying Round - ND Gorica (SVN)
A 0-1
Szentpéteri, Toivomäki, Moilanen, Eerola, Fofana (Shala 88), Rafael (Kemppinen 68), Litmanen, Huuhka, Hietanen (Heini 46), Vanninen, Korte. Coach: Ilkka Mäkelä (FIN)
Yellow Card(s): Heini 77, Eerola 88
H 2-0 *Litmanen (66), Rafael (79)*
Szentpéteri, Toivomäki, Moilanen, Eerola, Fofana (Heini 74), Rafael (Kemppinen 68), Litmanen, Huuhka, Hietanen (Shala 64), Vanninen, Korte. Coach: Ilkka Mäkelä (FIN)
Yellow Card(s): Rafael 81

Third Qualifying Round - Club Brugge KV (BEL)
A 2-3 *Moilanen (6), Korte (50)*
Szentpéteri, Haara, Toivomäki, Moilanen, Eerola, Fofana (Heini 72), Rafael, Litmanen, Shala (Hietanen 46), Vanninen, Korte. Coach: Ilkka Mäkelä (FIN)
Yellow Card(s): Vanninen 41, Eerola 63
H 1-1 *Vanninen (87)*
Szentpéteri, Haara, Toivomäki, Moilanen, Fofana, Rafael, Litmanen, Hietanen, Vanninen, Korte, Heini (Shala 56). Coach: Ilkka Mäkelä (FIN)
Yellow Card(s): Hietanen 64, Toivomäki 70

FRANCE

FC GIRONDINS DE BORDEAUX

UEFA CHAMPIONS LEAGUE

Group A
Match 1 - Juventus (ITA)
A 1-1 *Plašil (75)*
Carrasso (Ramé 55), Ciani, Diarra, Fernando, Gourcuff, Wendel, Plašil (Gouffran 77), Chalmé, Planus, Trémoulinas, Chamakh. Coach: Laurent Blanc (FRA)
Yellow Card(s): Ciani 65
Match 2 - Maccabi Haifa FC (ISR)
H 1-0 *Ciani (90)*
Carrasso, Ciani, Diarra, Gourcuff (Fernando 46), Cavenaghi (Bellion 60), Wendel, Plašil (Sertic 71), Chalmé, Planus, Trémoulinas, Chamakh. Coach: Laurent Blanc (FRA)
Yellow Card(s): Planus 38
Match 3 - FC Bayern München (GER)
H 2-1 *Ciani (27), Planus (40)*
Carrasso, Ciani, Diarra, Fernando, Gourcuff, Wendel (Jussiê 85), Plašil (Gouffran 85), Chalmé, Planus, Trémoulinas, Chamakh. Coach: Laurent Blanc (FRA)
Yellow Card(s): Chamakh 52, Gourcuff 55
Match 4 - FC Bayern München (GER)
A 2-0 *Gourcuff (37), Chamakh (90)*
Carrasso, Ciani, Diarra, Fernando, Gourcuff, Wendel (Jussiê 68), Plašil (Sané 84), Chalmé, Planus, Trémoulinas, Chamakh. Coach: Laurent Blanc (FRA)
Yellow Card(s): Diarra 30, Planus 73
Match 5 - Juventus (ITA)
H 2-0 *Fernando (54), Chamakh (90+4)*
Carrasso, Ciani, Diarra, Fernando, Gouffran (Traoré 75), Wendel, Plašil, Chalmé, Planus, Trémoulinas, Chamakh. Coach: Laurent Blanc (FRA)
Yellow Card(s): Fernando 60, Traoré 90

CHAMPIONS LEAGUE

EUROPA LEAGUE

atch 6 - Maccabi Haifa FC (ISR)
1-0 *Jussiê (13)*
amé, Fernando, Jurietti, Cavenaghi, Jussiê, Bellion, Placente, Wendel,
aivet, Traoré (Sertic 78), Sané. Coach: Laurent Blanc (FRA)

rst Knockout Round - Olympiacos FC (GRE)
1-0 *Ciani (45+2)*
arrasso, Ciani, Fernando, Gourcuff, Wendel (Jussiê 83), Plašil (Gouffran 82),
halmé, Sané, Planus, Trémoulinas, Chamakh. Coach: Laurent Blanc (FRA)
ellow Card(s): Sané 29, Ciani 75
2-1 *Gourcuff (5), Chamakh (88)*
arrasso, Ciani, Diarra, Fernando, Gourcuff, Wendel (Jussiê 90), Plašil (Sertic
4), Chalmé, Sané, Trémoulinas, Chamakh. Coach: Laurent Blanc (FRA)
ed Card(s): Diarra 68
ellow Card(s): Diarra 65, Diarra 68

uarter-Finals - Olympique Lyonnais (FRA)
1-3 *Chamakh (14)*
arrasso, Ciani, Fernando, Gouffran (Bellion 84), Gourcuff, Wendel (Jussiê
1), Plašil, Chalmé (Henrique 82), Sané, Trémoulinas, Chamakh. Coach:
aurent Blanc (FRA)
1-0 *Chamakh (45)*
arrasso, Ciani, Diarra (Chalmé 70), Gourcuff, Jussiê (Gouffran 77), Wendel,
lašil, Sané, Planus (Cavenaghi 85), Trémoulinas, Chamakh. Coach: Laurent
lanc (FRA)

o	Player	Nat	DoB	Aps	(s)	Gls
oalkeepers						
	Cédric Carrasso		30/12/81	9		
6	Ulrich Ramé		19/9/72	1	(1)	
efenders						
1	Matthieu Chalmé		7/10/80	8	(1)	
	Michaël Ciani		6/4/84	9		3
	Henrique	BRA	2/5/83		(1)	
	Franck Jurietti		30/3/75	1		
3	Diego Placente	ARG	24/4/77	1		
7	Marc Planus		7/3/82	7		1
5	Ludovic Sané		22/3/87	5	(1)	
8	Benoît Trémoulinas		28/12/85	9		
idfielders						
	Alou Diarra		15/7/81	7		
	Fernando	BRA	3/5/81	8	(1)	1
	Yoann Gourcuff		11/7/86	8		2
8	Jaroslav Plašil	CZE	5/1/82	9		1
2	Grégory Sertic		5/8/89		(3)	
4	Abdou Traoré	MLI	17/1/88	1	(1)	
7	Wendel	BRA	8/4/82	10		
orwards						
1	David Bellion		27/11/82	1	(2)	
	Fernando Cavenaghi	ARG	21/9/83	2	(1)	
9	Marouane Chamakh	MAR	10/1/84	9		5
	Yoan Gouffran		25/5/86	2	(4)	
0	Jussiê	BRA	19/9/83	2	(5)	1
0	Henri Saivet		26/10/90	1		

OLYMPIQUE DE MARSEILLE

DROIT AU BUT

UEFA CHAMPIONS LEAGUE

Group C
Match 1 - AC Milan (ITA)
1-2 *Heinze (49)*
Mandanda, Taiwo, Cissé (Morientes 88), Cheyrou, Lucho González (Ben
Arfa 75), Brandão, Niang, Kaboré, Mbia, Heinze, Diawara. Coach: Didier
Deschamps (FRA)

Match 2 - Real Madrid CF (ESP)
A 0-3
Mandanda, Taiwo, Cheyrou, Lucho González, Niang (Ben Arfa 87), Mbia,
Abriel (Rodriguez 62), Heinze, Diawara, Morientes (Brandão 63), Bonnart.
Coach: Didier Deschamps (FRA)
Red Card(s): Diawara 60
Yellow Card(s): Diawara 47, Mbia 54, Diawara 60, Heinze 62, Rodriguez 67
Match 3 - FC Zürich (SUI)
A 1-0 *Heinze (69)*
Mandanda, Hilton, Cissé, Cheyrou (Abriel 64), Lucho González (Kaboré 82),
Brandão, Niang, Mbia, Heinze, Bonnart, Valbuena (Koné 65). Coach: Didier
Deschamps (FRA)
Red Card(s): Bonnart 90+2
Yellow Card(s): Bonnart 68, Brandão 78, Bonnart 90+2
Match 4 - FC Zürich (SUI)
H 6-1 *Aegerter (3og), Abriel (11), Niang (51), Hilton (80), Cheyrou (87),
Brandão (90)*
Mandanda, Bocaly, Hilton, Cheyrou, Brandão, Niang, Koné (Valbuena 61),
Mbia (Cissé 84), Abriel (Kaboré 68), Heinze, Diawara. Coach: Didier
Deschamps (FRA)
Yellow Card(s): Brandão 20, Mbia 66, Cheyrou 67
Match 5 - AC Milan (ITA)
A 1-1 *Lucho González (16)*
Mandanda, Taiwo, Cissé, Cheyrou (Morientes 85), Lucho González (Koné
66), Brandão, Niang (Ben Arfa 73), Abriel, Heinze, Diawara, Bonnart.
Coach: Didier Deschamps (FRA)
Yellow Card(s): Heinze 90+3
Match 6 - Real Madrid CF (ESP)
H 1-3 *Lucho González (11)*
Mandanda, Taiwo, Cissé (Koné 62), Cheyrou, Lucho González, Brandão
(Morientes 78), Niang (Valbuena 68), Abriel, Heinze, Diawara, Bonnart.
Coach: Didier Deschamps (FRA)
Yellow Card(s): Brandão 9, Heinze 63

No	Player	Nat	DoB	Aps	(s)	Gls
Goalkeeper						
30	Steve Mandanda		28/3/85	6		
Defenders						
2	Garry Bocaly		19/4/88	1		
24	Laurent Bonnart		25/12/79	4		
21	Souleymane Diawara	SEN	24/12/78	5		
19	Gabriel Heinze	ARG	19/4/78	6		2
5	Hilton	BRA	13/9/77	2		1
4	Julien Rodriguez		11/6/78		(1)	
3	Taye Taiwo	NGA	16/4/85	4		
Midfielders						
18	Fabrice Abriel		6/7/79	4	(1)	1
10	Hatem Ben Arfa		7/3/87		(3)	
7	Benoît Cheyrou		3/5/81	6		1
6	Edouard Cissé		30/3/78	4	(1)	
12	Charles Kaboré	BFA	9/2/88	1	(2)	
8	Lucho González	ARG	19/1/81	5		2
17	Stéphane Mbia	CMR	20/5/86	4		
28	Mathieu Valbuena		28/9/84	1	(2)	
Forwards						
9	Brandão	BRA	16/6/80	5	(1)	1
14	Bakari Koné	CIV	17/9/81	1	(3)	
23	Fernando Morientes	ESP	5/4/76	1	(3)	
11	Mamadou Niang	SEN	13/10/79	6		1

UEFA EUROPA LEAGUE

Round of 32 - FC København (DEN)
A 3-1 *Niang (72), Ben Arfa (84), Kaboré (90)*
Mandanda, Taiwo, Cissé, Cheyrou (Abriel 73), Lucho González, Niang,
Koné (Kaboré 81), Mbia, Diawara, Bonnart, Valbuena (Ben Arfa 63). Coach:
Didier Deschamps (FRA)
Yellow Card(s): Diawara 23, Niang 79, Mbia 81
H 3-1 *Ben Arfa (43), Koné (62,78)*
Mandanda, Taiwo, Hilton, Cheyrou (M'Bow 65), Ben Arfa (Valbuena 79),
Kaboré, Koné, Abriel, Diawara (Heinze 65), Morientes, Bonnart. Coach:
Didier Deschamps (FRA)

France

Round of 16 - SL Benfica (POR)
A 1-1 *Ben Arfa (90)*
Mandanda, Taiwo, Cissé, Cheyrou, Lucho González, Brandão, Niang (Ben Arfa 75), Mbia, Abriel (Valbuena 70), Diawara, Bonnart. Coach: Didier Deschamps (FRA)
Yellow Card(s): Lucho González 48, Brandão 72
H 1-2 *Niang (70)*
Mandanda, Taiwo, Cissé, Cheyrou, Kaboré 76), Lucho González, Brandão, Niang, Mbia, Abriel (Koné 44; Ben Arfa 90+2), Diawara, Bonnart. Coach: Didier Deschamps (FRA)
Red Card(s): Ben Arfa 90+3
Yellow Card(s): Koné 55, Taiwo 83, Kaboré 90+3

OLYMPIQUE LYONNAIS

UEFA CHAMPIONS LEAGUE
Play-Off Round - RSC Anderlecht (BEL)
H 5-1 *Pjanić (10), Lisandro López (15p), Michel Bastos (39), Gomis (42, 63)*
Lloris, Cris, Bodmer, Källström (Makoun 64), Michel Bastos, Pjanić, Lisandro López (Delgado 72), Réveillère, Gomis (Ederson 82), Cissokho, Toulalan. Coach: Claude Puel (FRA)
A 3-1 *Lisandro López (26, 32, 41)*
Lloris, Cris, Bodmer, Källström (Pjanić 80), Michel Bastos, Lisandro López (Belfodil 60), Réveillère, Makoun, Delgado, Cissokho, Toulalan (Gonalons 73). Coach: Claude Puel (FRA)
Yellow Card(s): Toulalan 66

Group E
Match 1 - ACF Fiorentina (ITA)
H 1-0 *Pjanić (76)*
Lloris, Cris, Källström, Michel Bastos (Govou 26), Pjanić (Ederson 82), Lisandro López, Réveillère, Makoun, Gomis (Delgado 70), Cissokho, Toulalan. Coach: Claude Puel (FRA)
Yellow Card(s): Lisandro López 34, Pjanić 38, Toulalan 54
Match 2 - Debreceni VSC (HUN)
A 4-0 *Källström (3), Pjanić (13), Govou (24), Gomis (51)*
Lloris, Clerc, Cris, Källström, Pjanić (Gonalons 57), Réveillère, Govou, Makoun, Gomis (Ederson 54), Cissokho (Kolodziejczak 78), Toulalan. Coach: Claude Puel (FRA)
Yellow Card(s): Gonalons 68
Match 3 - Liverpool FC (ENG)
A 2-1 *Gonalons (72), Delgado (90+1)*
Lloris, Cris (Gonalons 43), Källström, Pjanić, Lisandro López (Delgado 86), Ederson (Gomis 61), Réveillère, Govou, Makoun, Cissokho, Toulalan. Coach: Claude Puel (FRA)
Yellow Card(s): Cris 34, Govou 55, Réveillère 90
Match 4 - Liverpool FC (ENG)
H 1-1 *Lisandro López (90)*
Lloris, Cris, Källström, Michel Bastos, Pjanić (Ederson 40), Lisandro López, Réveillère (Gassama 18), Makoun, Gomis (Govou 73), Cissokho, Toulalan. Coach: Claude Puel (FRA)
Yellow Card(s): Lisandro López 34
Match 5 - ACF Fiorentina (ITA)
A 0-1
Lloris, Cris, Boumsong, Källström, Michel Bastos (Lisandro López 67), Pjanić, Govou (Delgado 74), Makoun, Gomis, Cissokho, Gassama. Coach: Claude Puel (FRA)
Yellow Card(s): Cissokho 21, Pjanić 88, Källström 90+1
Match 6 - Debreceni VSC (HUN)
H 4-0 *Gomis (25), Michel Bastos (45), Pjanić (59), Cissokho (76)*
Lloris, Cris, Boumsong, Michel Bastos, Réveillère, Govou (Pjanić 29), Makoun (Källström 73), Gomis (Lisandro López 67) Delgado, Cissokho, Gonalons. Coach: Claude Puel (FRA)

First Knockout Round - Real Madrid CF (ESP)
H 1-0 *Makoun (47)*
Lloris, Cris, Boumsong, Pjanić (Källström 78), Lisandro López (Gomis 81), Réveillère, Govou, Makoun, Delgado (Michel Bastos 89), Cissokho, Toulalan. Coach: Claude Puel (FRA)
Yellow Card(s): Govou 29
A 1-1 *Pjanić (75)*
Lloris, Cris, Boumsong (Källström 46), Pjanić (Ederson 84), Lisandro López, Réveillère, Govou, Makoun (Gonalons 46), Delgado, Cissokho, Toulalan. Coach: Claude Puel (FRA)
Yellow Card(s): Cris 26, Delgado 67

Quarter-Finals - FC Girondins de Bordeaux (FRA)
H 3-1 *Lisandro López (10, 77p), Michel Bastos (32)*
Lloris, Cris, Bodmer, Michel Bastos (Govou 65), Pjanić (Källström 65), Lisandro López, Réveillère, Makoun, Delgado (Gonalons 86), Cissokho, Toulalan. Coach: Claude Puel (FRA)
Yellow Card(s): Govou 74, Lisandro López 80
A 0-1
Lloris, Cris, Boumsong (Bodmer 77), Källström, Michel Bastos (Ederson 88), Réveillère, Gomis (Pjanić 66), Delgado, Cissokho, Toulalan, Gonalons. Coach: Claude Puel (FRA)
Yellow Card(s): Cissokho 34, Gonalons 67, Toulalan 69, Källström 78, Delgado 89

Semi-Finals - FC Bayern München (GER)
A 0-1
Lloris, Cris, Källström, Pjanić (Makoun 56), Lisandro López, Ederson (Michel Bastos 70), Réveillère, Delgado (Govou 79), Cissokho, Toulalan, Gonalons. Coach: Claude Puel (FRA)
Red Card(s): Toulalan 54
Yellow Card(s): Toulalan 51, Toulalan 54, Michel Bastos 79
H 0-3
Lloris, Cris, Boumsong, Michel Bastos, Lisandro López (Ederson 79), Réveillère, Govou, Makoun, Gonalons (Pjanić 67), Cissokho (Gomis 46), Gonalons. Coach: Claude Puel (FRA)
Red Card(s): Cris 59
Yellow Card(s): Gonalons 23, Cris 59, Cris 59

No	Player	Nat	DoB	Aps	(s)	Gls
Goalkeeper						
1	Hugo Lloris		26/12/86	12		
Defenders						
4	Jean-Alain Boumsong		14/12/79	6		
20	Aly Cissokho		15/9/87	12		1
2	François Clerc		18/4/83	1		
3	Cris	BRA	3/6/77	12		
32	Lamine Gassama		20/10/89	1	(1)	
12	Timothée Kolodziejczak		1/10/91		(1)	
13	Anthony Réveillère		10/11/79	11		
Midfielders						
7	Michel Bastos	BRA	2/8/83	7	(2)	2
5	Mathieu Bodmer		22/11/82	1	(1)	
19	César Delgado	ARG	18/8/81	7	(3)	1
10	Ederson	BRA	13/1/86	2	(7)	
41	Maxime Gonalons		10/3/89	4	(4)	1
6	Kim Källström	SWE	24/8/82	7	(4)	1
17	Jean II Makoun	CMR	29/5/83	10	(1)	1
8	Miralem Pjanić	BIH	2/4/90	9	(3)	4
28	Jérémy Toulalan		10/9/83	9		
Forwards						
18	Bafétimbi Gomis		6/8/85	6	(3)	2
14	Sidney Govou		27/7/79	7	(4)	1
9	Lisandro López	ARG	2/3/83	8	(2)	3

CHAMPIONS LEAGUE   EUROPA LEAGUE

EN AVANT GUINGAMP

UEFA EUROPA LEAGUE

ay-Off Round - Hamburger SV (GER)
1-5 *Hesl (88og)*
évisan, Deroff, Mathis, Diallo, Koné, Grax (Scarpelli 8), Bellugou, El
deyaoui (Giresse 57), Colleau, Ogunbiyi (Hamroun 68), Felipe Saad.
oach: Victor Zvunka (FRA)
llow Card(s): Colleau 53, Diallo 75
1-3 *Mathis (90)*
auclin, Deroff, Bellugou (Scarpelli 57), Bazile, Hamroun, Colleau,
oman (Diallo 62), Ogunbiyi, Giresse (Mathis 57), Felipe Saad, Delgado.
oach: Victor Zvunka (FRA)
llow Card(s): Deroff 29

TOULOUSE FC

UEFA EUROPA LEAGUE

ay-Off Round - Trabzonspor (TUR)
3-1 *Gignac (12, 59), Mansaré (90+1)*
ondel, Fofana (Congré 83), Cetto, Paulo Machado (Mansaré 82), Devaux
raaten 65), Didot, Gignac, M'Bengué, Sissoko, Ebondo, Capoue. Coach:
ain Casanova (FRA)
llow Card(s): Ebondo 85
0-1
ondel, Congré, Cetto, Devaux (Braaten 74), Mansaré (M'Bengué 82),
ounkeu, Sirieix, Pentecôte (Gignac 75), Sissoko, Ebondo, Capoue. Coach:
ain Casanova (FRA)
llow Card(s): Sirieix 60, Capoue 77, Gignac 78, Ebondo 90

roup J
atch 1 - FK Partizan (SRB)
3-2 *Sirieix (30, 38), Devaux (49)*
elé, Congré, Devaux (Braaten 65), M'Bengué (Paulo Machado 75),
ounkeu, Sirieix, Pentecôte (Gignac 61), Berson, Sissoko, Tabanou,
apoue. Coach: Alain Casanova (FRA)
llow Card(s): Pelé 57, Sissoko 76
atch 2 - Club Brugge KV (BEL)
2-2 *Sissoko (54), Gignac (84)*
elé, Congré, Paulo Machado (Soukouna 77), Devaux (Sissoko 34),
ansaré (Tabanou 46)) Gignac, M'Bengué, Nounkeu, Sirieix, Berson,
apoue. Coach: Alain Casanova (FRA)
llow Card(s): Capoue 26, Berson 50
atch 3 - FC Shakhtar Donetsk (UKR)
0-4
elé, Congré, Didot, Luan (Tabanou 46), M'Bengué, Nounkeu, Sirieix
issoko 46), Pentecôte (Soukouna 87), Ebondo, Braaten, Capoue. Coach:
ain Casanova (FRA)
llow Card(s): M'Bengué 57
atch 4 - FC Shakhtar Donetsk (UKR)
0-2
elé, Congré, Paulo Machado (Braaten 66), Didot, Luan, M'Bengué,
ounkeu, Sirieix, Pentecôte, Berson (Sissoko 83), Ebondo. Coach: Alain
asanova (FRA)
llow Card(s): Sirieix 45+3, M'Bengué 49, Berson 72

Match 5 - FK Partizan (SRB)
H 1-0 *Braaten (54)*
Blondel, Paulo Machado, Luan (Tabanou 72), M'Bengué, Nounkeu, Sirieix,
Berson, Ebondo, Braaten (N'Gadi Kakou 83), Soukouna, Capoue. Coach:
Alain Casanova (FRA)
Yellow Card(s): Berson 19
Match 6 - Club Brugge KV (BEL)
A 0-1
Valverde, Fofana, Paulo Machado (Regattin 82), Didot, Gignac, M'Bengué,
Nounkeu, Sissoko, Ebondo, Tabanou (Braaten 58), Capoue. Coach: Alain
Casanova (FRA)
Yellow Card(s): Ebondo 27

LOSC LILLE MÉTROPOLE

UEFA EUROPA LEAGUE

Third Qualifying Round - FK Sevojno (SRB)
A 2-0 *Vittek (34), Hazard (39)*
Butelle, Balmont (Debuchy 83), Cabaye, Obraniak, Vittek (Túlio de Melo
67), Emerson, Béria, Rami, Mavuba, Plestan, Hazard (Gervinho 74). Coach:
Rudi Garcia (FRA)
Red Card(s): Plestan 90
Yellow Card(s): Rami 25, Plestan 41, Obraniak 53, Plestan 90
H 2-0 *Cabaye (72), Túlio de Melo (85)*
Butelle, Debuchy, Balmont (Dumont 77), Túlio de Melo, Vittek (Balmont 46),
Emerson, Touré (Aubameyang 64), Chedjou, Rami, Mavuba, Gervinho.
Coach: Rudi Garcia (FRA)
Yellow Card(s): Balmont 49, Chedjou 69, Butelle 87

Play-Off Round - KRC Genk (BEL)
A 2-1 *Dumont (40), Vittek (56)*
Butelle, Debuchy, Balmont (Cabaye 86), Vittek (Touré 80), Béria, Chedjou,
Rami, Mavuba, Hazard (Obraniak 67), Gervinho, Dumont. Coach: Rudi
Garcia (FRA)
Yellow Card(s): Debuchy 13, Rami 60
H 4-2 *Túlio de Melo (10, 73), Dumont (59), Hazard (70)*
Butelle, Debuchy (Balmont 51), Cabaye, Túlio de Melo, Aubameyang,
Emerson, Béria, Chedjou, Mavuba (Vandam 79), Gervinho (Hazard 62),
Dumont. Coach: Rudi Garcia (FRA)
Yellow Card(s): Cabaye 15

Group B
Match 1 - Valencia CF (ESP)
H 1-1 *Gervinho (86)*
Butelle, Balmont (Mavuba 77), Obraniak, Aubameyang (Frau 64), Vittek
(Gervinho 69), Emerson, Béria, Chedjou, Rami, Hazard, Dumont. Coach:
Rudi Garcia (FRA)
Yellow Card(s): Balmont 46, Obraniak 73
Match 2 - SK Slavia Praha (CZE)
A 5-1 *Suchý (47og), Frau (71), Gervinho (85, 90+1), Souquet (88)*
Butelle, Vandam, Cabaye (Mavuba 83), Aubameyang (Gervinho 61), Vittek
(Frau 67), Emerson, Béria, Rami, Hazard, Dumont, Souquet. Coach: Rudi
Garcia (FRA)
Yellow Card(s): Butelle 5, Dumont 50
Match 3 - Genoa CFC (ITA)
H 3-0 *Obraniak (38), Vittek (63), Hazard (84)*
Butelle, Vandam, Balmont, Cabaye (Béria 81), Obraniak (Hazard 74),
Aubameyang (Gervinho 65), Vittek, Emerson, Chedjou, Rami, Mavuba.
Coach: Rudi Garcia (FRA)
Yellow Card(s): Cabaye 23, Obraniak 71, Hazard 85
Match 4 - Genoa CFC (ITA)
A 2-3 *Frau (70), Gervinho (84)*
Landreau, Vandam, Balmont (Cabaye 62), Obraniak, Aubameyang
(Gervinho 62), Vittek, Emerson, Béria, Touré (Frau 73), Rami, Dumont.
Coach: Rudi Garcia (FRA)
Yellow Card(s): Béria 56, Vandam 64, Landreau 90+3

Match 5 - Valencia CF (ESP)
A 1-3 *Chedjou (90+1)*
Landreau, Balmont, Cabaye (Obraniak 71), Emerson (Debuchy 46), Frau (Vittek 46), Béria, Chedjou, Rami, Mavuba, Hazard, Gervinho. Coach: Rudi Garcia (FRA)
Yellow Card(s): Gervinho 20, Cabaye 56, Chedjou 89, Debuchy 90+4
Match 6 - SK Slavia Praha (CZE)
H 3-1 *Cabaye (25), Gervinho (40), Obraniak (80)*
Landreau, Vandam, Balmont, Cabaye (Dumont 46), Obraniak, Frau (Túlio de Melo 81), Béria, Chedjou, Rami, Mavuba, Gervinho (Hazard 68). Coach: Rudi Garcia (FRA)
Yellow Card(s): Balmont 73

Round of 32 - Fenerbahçe SK (TUR)
H 2-1 *Balmont (3), Frau (52)*
Landreau, Balmont, Obraniak, Emerson, Frau (Gervinho 69), Béria, Chedjou, Rami, Mavuba, Hazard (Touré 84), Dumont (Cabaye 60). Coach: Rudi Garcia (FRA)
Yellow Card(s): Balmont 6, Cabaye 79
A 1-1 *Rami (85)*
Landreau, Obraniak, Aubameyang (Touré 68), Emerson, Frau, Béria, Chedjou, Rami, Mavuba, Hazard, Dumont (Vandam 79). Coach: Rudi Garcia (FRA)

Round of 16 - Liverpool FC (ENG)
H 1-0 *Hazard (84)*
Landreau, Balmont, Cabaye (Dumont 73), Obraniak (Touré 83), Emerson, Frau (Aubameyang 77), Béria, Chedjou, Rami, Mavuba, Hazard. Coach: Rudi Garcia (FRA)
Yellow Card(s): Touré 85, Aubameyang 88
A 0-3
Landreau, Balmont (Aubameyang 71), Cabaye, Obraniak, Emerson, Frau (Touré 59), Béria, Chedjou, Rami, Mavuba, Hazard (Vandam 86). Coach: Rudi Garcia (FRA)
Yellow Card(s): Cabaye 80, Obraniak 90

GEORGIA

FC WIT GEORGIA

UEFA CHAMPIONS LEAGUE

Second Qualifying Round - NK Maribor (SVN)
H 0-0
Bediashvili, Lomaia, Lipartia (Zakradze 63), Razmadze, Kakhelishvili (Kvelashvili 90+2), Japaridze, Kvaratskhelia (Beriashvili 68), Klimiashvili, Datunaishvili, Bechvaia, Kvakhadze. Coach: Nestor Mumladze (GEO)
Red Card(s): Klimiashvili 83
Yellow Card(s): Razmadze 37, Kvaratskhelia 60, Klimiashvili 64, Zakradze 75, Klimiashvili 83
A 1-3 *Kvaratskhelia (45)*
Bediashvili, Lomaia, Lipartia (Zakradze 81), Razmadze, Kakhelishvili, Japaridze, Kvaratskhelia, Datunaishvili, Bechvaia, Kvakhadze, Janelidze. Coach: Nestor Mumladze (GEO)
Yellow Card(s): Lomaia 47, Datunaishvili 59, Kakhelishvili 70, Kvaratskhelia 90+3

FC DINAMO TBILISI

UEFA EUROPA LEAGUE

Second Qualifying Round - SK Liepājas Metalurgs (LVA)
A 1-2 *Khmaladze (68)*
Loria, Tomashvili, Koshkadze, Khmaladze, S. Kashia, Merebashvili, Vatsadze, Djousse, Digmelashvili, Nergadze, G. Kashia. Coach: Kakha Kacharava (GEO)
Yellow Card(s): S. Kashia 49
H 3-1 *Merebashvili (18, 63), G. Kashia (53)*
Loria, Tomashvili, Koshkadze (Lomia 56), Khmaladze, S. Kashia, Merebashvili, Vatsadze (Kakubava 90+2), Djousse (Akieremy 71), Digmelashvili, Nergadze, G. Kashia. Coach: Kakha Kacharava (GEO)
Yellow Card(s): Vatsadze 5, Khmaladze 35, Tomashvili 42, Merebashvili 55, Loria 90+4

Third Qualifying Round - FK Crvena zvezda (SRB)
H 2-0 *Merebashvili (41), Khmaladze (87)*
Loria, Tomashvili, Koshkadze (Pirtskhalava 78), Khmaladze, S. Kashia, Merebashvili (Akieremy 86), Vatsadze, Digmelashvili, Nergadze, Kakubava (Lomia 63), G. Kashia. Coach: Kakha Kacharava (GEO)
Yellow Card(s): Merebashvili 44, Pirtskhalava 87
A 2-5 *Lekić (3og), Vatsadze (24)*
Loria, Tomashvili (Sikharulidze 90+5), Koshkadze (Lomia 55), Khmaladze, S. Kashia, Vatsadze, Digmelashvili, Nergadze, Kakubava (Pirtskhalava 67), Akieremy, G. Kashia. Coach: Kakha Kacharava (GEO)
Red Card(s): Akieremy 83
Yellow Card(s): Lomia 61, Kakubava 68

FC OLIMPI RUSTAVI

UEFA EUROPA LEAGUE

First Qualifying Round - B36 Tórshavn (FRO)
H 2-0 *Megreladze (10, 88)*
Alavidze, Gongadze, Gilauri, Machavariani, Rekhviashvili (Khubua 46), Babunashvili, Megreladze, Seturidze (G. Chelidze 72), Dobrovolski, Sirbiladze, Z. Chelidze (Pipia 60). Coach: Varlam Kilasonia (GEO)
Red Card(s): Babunashvili 90+4
Yellow Card(s): Sirbiladze 80
A 2-0 *Sirbiladze (5), Khubua (28)*
Alavidze, Gongadze, Gilauri, Machavariani, Chkhetiani (Megreladze 59), Dobrovolski, Seturidze, Khubua (G. Chelidze 57), Sirbiladze (Pipia 65), Z. Chelidze, Lomidze. Coach: Varlam Kilasonia (GEO)
Yellow Card(s): Lomidze 60

Second Qualifying Round - Legia Warszawa (POL)
A 0-3
Alavidze, Gongadze, Gilauri, Machavariani (Lomidze 84), Chkhetiani (G. Chelidze 61), Seturidze, Dobrovolski, Z. Chelidze, Jonatas (Sirbiladze 84), Anderson Aquino, Alex. Coach: Varlam Kilasonia (GEO)
Yellow Card(s): Jonatas 35, Gilauri 69, Dobrovolski 90+2
H 0-1
Alavidze, Gongadze (Gerônimo 46), Gilauri, Machavariani, Babunashvili, Seturidze, Dobrovolski, Jonatas, Choco (G. Chelidze 61), Anderson Aquino, Alex. Coach: Varlam Kilasonia (GEO)
Yellow Card(s): Gilauri 17, Gerônimo 87

FC ZESTAFONI

UEFA EUROPA LEAGUE

rst Qualifying Round - Lisburn Distillery FC (NIR)
5-1 *Gelashvili (11, 34), Grigalashvili (22, 38), Aptsiauri (52)*
amaladze, Oniani, Todua, Daushvili, Gelashvili, Dzaria (Benashvili 58),
vali (N. Kvaskhvadze 88), Khidesheli, Aptsiauri, Grigalashvili (Gorgiashvili
4), Eliava. Coach: Giorgi Geguchadze (GEO)
6-0 *Dvali (5, 39, 42), Gelashvili (45), Benashvili (87, 90)*
amaladze, Lobjanidze, Oniani, Daushvili (Benashvili 46), Gelashvili,
zaria (Gorgiashvili 60), Dvali, Khidesheli, Aptsiauri, Grigalashvili, Eliava
1akariani 46). Coach: Giorgi Geguchadze (GEO)
ellow Card(s): Benashvili 89

econd Qualifying Round - Helsingborgs IF (SWE)
1-2 *Benashvili (70)*
amaladze, Lobjanidze, Oniani, Daushvili, Gelashvili, Dzaria (Benashvili
3), Dvali (Ionanidze 80), Khidesheli, Aptsiauri (N. Kvaskhvadze 85),
rigalashvili, Eliava. Coach: Giorgi Geguchadze (GEO)
ellow Card(s): Daushvili 13, Dzaria 52, Ionanidze 87
2-2 *Dvali (29), Gelashvili (32)*
amaladze, Lobjanidze, Oniani, Daushvili (Tskhadaia 84), Gelashvili (N.
vaskhvadze 90+2), Dzaria (Benashvili 74), Dvali, Khidesheli, Aptsiauri,
rigalashvili, Eliava. Coach: Giorgi Geguchadze (GEO)
ellow Card(s): Daushvili 36, Aptsiauri 51, Grigalashvili 65, Lobjanidze 89

GERMANY

VFL WOLFSBURG

UEFA CHAMPIONS LEAGUE

iroup B
1atch 1 - PFC CSKA Moskva (RUS)
3-1 *Grafite (36, 41p, 87)*
enaglio, Schäfer, Josué, Dżeko, Misimović, Martins (Ziani 65), Madlung,
iether, Grafite (Santana 89), Gentner (Hasebe 90+2), Barzagli. Coach:
rmin Veh (GER)
1atch 2 - Manchester United FC (ENG)
1-2 *Dżeko (56)*
enaglio, Schäfer, Ricardo Costa, Josué, Dżeko, Misimović, Hasebe (Ziani 73),
1adlung, Riether, Grafite (Martins 82), Gentner. Coach: Armin Veh (GER)
ellow Card(s): Ricardo Costa 61
1atch 3 - Beşiktaş JK (TUR)
1 0-0
enaglio, Schäfer, Ricardo Costa, Josué, Dżeko, Misimović, Hasebe
)ejagah 67), Madlung, Riether, Grafite, Gentner. Coach: Armin Veh (GER)
ed Card(s): Grafite 74
1atch 4 - Beşiktaş JK (TUR)
3-0 *Misimović (14), Gentner (80), Dżeko (87)*
enaglio, Schäfer, Ricardo Costa, Josué, Dżeko, Misimović (Santana 89),
1artins (Dejagah 69), Hasebe (Pekarík 46), Madlung, Riether, Gentner.
oach: Armin Veh (GER)
ellow Card(s): Misimović 43

Match 5 - PFC CSKA Moskva (RUS)
A 1-2 *Dżeko (19)*
Benaglio, Schäfer, Ricardo Costa, Josué, Dżeko, Misimović, Martins (Ziani
68), Hasebe, Madlung, Riether, Gentner. Coach: Armin Veh (GER)
Yellow Card(s): Madlung 87
Match 6 - Manchester United FC (ENG)
H 1-3 *Dżeko (56)*
Benaglio, Schäfer, Ricardo Costa, Josué, Dżeko, Misimović, Hasebe (Ziani 72),
Riether, Grafite (Dejagah 72), Gentner, Barzagli. Coach: Armin Veh (GER)

No	Player	Nat	DoB	Aps	(s)	Gls
Goalkeeper						
1	Diego Benaglio	SUI	8/9/83	6		
Defenders						
43	Andrea Barzagli	ITA	8/5/81	2		
17	Alexander Madlung		11/7/82	5		
19	Peter Pekarík	SVK	30/10/86		(1)	
5	Ricardo Costa	POR	16/5/81	5		
20	Sascha Riether		23/3/83	6		
4	Marcel Schäfer		7/6/84	6		
Midfielders						
25	Christian Gentner		14/8/85	6		1
13	Makoto Hasebe	JPN	18/1/84	5	(1)	
7	Josué	BRA	19/7/79	6		
10	Zvjezdan Misimović	BIH	5/6/82	6		1
14	Jonathan Santana	PAR	19/10/81		(2)	
15	Karim Ziani	ALG	17/8/82		(4)	
Forwards						
24	Ashkan Dejagah		5/7/86		(3)	
9	Edin Dżeko	BIH	17/3/86	6		4
23	Grafite	BRA	2/4/79	4		3
11	Obafemi Martins	NGA	28/10/84	3	(1)	

UEFA EUROPA LEAGUE

Round of 32 - Villarreal CF (ESP)
A 2-2 *Grafite (65, 84p)*
Hitz, Schäfer, Šimůnek, Josué, Dżeko, Misimović, Madlung, Pekarík, Riether,
Grafite, Gentner (Dejagah 58). Coach: Lorenz-Günther Köstner (GER)
Yellow Card(s): Riether 42
H 4-1 *Dżeko (10), Ángel (15og), Gentner (42), Grafite (64)*
Hitz, Schäfer, Šimůnek (Barzagli 50), Josué, Dżeko, Misimović, Madlung,
Pekarík, Riether (Hasebe 79), Grafite, Gentner (Schindzielorz 90+1). Coach:
Lorenz-Günther Köstner (GER)
Yellow Card(s): Šimůnek 19, Barzagli 90+1

Round of 16 - FC Rubin Kazan (RUS)
A 1-1 *Misimović (67)*
Hitz, Schäfer, Josué, Dżeko, Misimović, Martins (Dejagah 83), Hasebe,
Madlung, Pekarík, Riether, Gentner. Coach: Lorenz-Günther Köstner (GER)
H 2-1 *Martins (58), Gentner (119) (aet)*
Hitz, Schäfer, Šimůnek (Johnson 75), Josué, Dżeko, Misimović, Madlung,
Pekarík (Martins 46), Riether, Dejagah, Gentner. Coach: Lorenz-Günther
Köstner (GER)
Yellow Card(s): Gentner 116

Quarter-Finals - Fulham FC (ENG)
A 1-2 *Madlung (89)*
Benaglio, Schäfer, Josué, Dżeko, Misimović, Madlung, Pekarík (Martins 74),
Riether, Grafite, Gentner (Dejagah 84), Barzagli. Coach: Lorenz-Günther
Köstner (GER)
Yellow Card(s): Madlung 72
H 0-1
Benaglio, Schäfer, Šimůnek (Réver 76), Josué, Dżeko, Misimović, Pekarík
(Dejagah 35), Riether, Grafite, Gentner (Martins 61), Barzagli. Coach:
Lorenz-Günther Köstner (GER)
Yellow Card(s): Dżeko 34, Dejagah 63, Josué 84

FC BAYERN MÜNCHEN

UEFA CHAMPIONS LEAGUE

Group A
Match 1 - Maccabi Haifa FC (ISR)
A 3-0 *Van Buyten (64), Müller (85, 88)*
Butt, Van Buyten, Ribéry (Gómez 64), Robben (Ottl 77), Olić (Sosa 86), Lahm, Pranjić, Müller, Badstuber, Schweinsteiger, Tymoshchuk. Coach: Louis van Gaal (NED)
Yellow Card(s): Ribéry 48, Lahm 84
Match 2 - Juventus (ITA)
H 0-0
Butt, Braafheid, Van Buyten, Ribéry, Robben (Olić 45), Ottl, Klose (Gómez 74), Lahm, Müller, Badstuber, Schweinsteiger. Coach: Louis van Gaal (NED)
Match 3 - FC Girondins de Bordeaux (FRA)
A 1-2 *Ciani (6og)*
Butt, Van Buyten, Hamit Altıntop, Toni (Gómez 78), Van Bommel (Ottl 78), Klose (Pranjić 74), Lahm, Müller, Badstuber, Schweinsteiger, Tymoshchuk. Coach: Louis van Gaal (NED)
Red Card(s): Müller 30, Van Buyten 88
Yellow Card(s): Müller 13, Badstuber 17, Müller 30, Tymoshchuk 63
Match 4 - FC Girondins de Bordeaux (FRA)
H 0-2
Butt, Braafheid (Gómez 59), Demichelis, Toni, Van Bommel, Klose (Robben 46), Lahm, Pranjić, Badstuber, Schweinsteiger, Tymoshchuk. Coach: Louis van Gaal (NED)
Yellow Card(s): Pranjić 45+1, Schweinsteiger 75
Match 5 - Maccabi Haifa FC (ISR)
H 1-0 *Olić (62)*
Butt, Van Buyten, Demichelis, Olić (Tymoshchuk 81), Van Bommel, Lahm, Pranjić (Ottl 70), Müller, Gómez. Coach: Louis van Gaal (NED)
Match 6 - Juventus (ITA)
A 4-1 *Butt (30p), Olić (52), Gómez (83), Tymoshchuk (90+2)*
Butt, Van Buyten, Demichelis, Olić (Tymoshchuk 79), Van Bommel, Lahm, Pranjić (Robben 73), Müller, Schweinsteiger, Gómez. Coach: Louis van Gaal (NED)
Yellow Card(s): Pranjić 7, Schweinsteiger 58, Demichelis 71

First Knockout Round - ACF Fiorentina (ITA)
H 2-1 *Robben (45+3p), Klose (89)*
Butt, Van Buyten (Contento 46), Demichelis, Ribéry, Robben, Van Bommel, Lahm, Müller (Olić 66), Badstuber, Schweinsteiger, Gómez (Klose 66). Coach: Louis van Gaal (NED)
Yellow Card(s): Van Bommel 28, Klose 78
A 2-3 *Van Bommel (60), Robben (65)*
Butt, Van Buyten, Ribéry (Pranjić 90+2), Robben, Van Bommel, Lahm, Müller, Alaba, Badstuber, Schweinsteiger, Gómez (Klose 30). Coach: Louis van Gaal (NED)
Yellow Card(s): Schweinsteiger 22, Van Bommel 85

Quarter-Finals - Manchester United FC (ENG)
H 2-1 *Ribéry (77), Olić (90+2)*
Butt, Van Buyten, Demichelis, Ribéry, Hamit Altıntop (Klose 86), Olić, Van Bommel, Lahm, Pranjić (Tymoshchuk 89), Müller (Gómez 73), Badstuber. Coach: Louis van Gaal (NED)
Yellow Card(s): Badstuber 57, Olić 90+3
A 2-3 *Olić (43), Robben (74)*
Butt, Van Buyten, Demichelis, Ribéry, Robben (Hamit Altıntop 76), Olić (Pranjić 85), Van Bommel, Lahm, Müller (Gómez 46), Badstuber, Schweinsteiger. Coach: Louis van Gaal (NED)
Yellow Card(s): Van Bommel 27, Badstuber 54

Semi-Finals - Olympique Lyonnais (FRA)
H 1-0 *Robben (69)*
Butt, Van Buyten, Demichelis, Ribéry, Robben (Hamit Altıntop 85), Olić (Tymoshchuk 46), Lahm, Pranjić (Gómez 63), Müller, Contento, Schweinsteiger. Coach: Louis van Gaal (NED)
Red Card(s): Ribéry 37
Yellow Card(s): Pranjić 27
A 3-0 *Olić (26, 67, 78)*
Butt, Van Buyten (Demichelis 46), Hamit Altıntop, Robben (Klose 76), Olić, Van Bommel, Lahm, Müller, Contento, Badstuber, Schweinsteiger (Alaba 78). Coach: Louis van Gaal (NED)
Yellow Card(s): Hamit Altıntop 24

Final - FC Internazionale Milano (ITA)
0-2
Butt, Van Buyten, Demichelis, Hamit Altıntop (Klose 63), Robben, Olić (Gómez 74), Van Bommel, Lahm, Müller, Badstuber, Schweinsteiger. Coach: Louis van Gaal (NED)
Yellow Card(s): Demichelis 26, Van Bommel 78

No	Player	Nat	DoB	Aps	(s)	Gls
Goalkeeper						
22	Hans-Jörg Butt		28/5/74	13		1
Defenders						
28	Holger Badstuber		13/3/89	12		
4	Edson Braafheid	NED	8/4/83	2		
26	Diego Contento		1/5/90	2	(1)	
6	Martín Demichelis	ARG	20/12/80	8	(1)	
21	Philipp Lahm		11/11/83	13		
5	Daniel Van Buyten	BEL	7/2/78	12		1
Midfielders						
27	David Alaba	AUT	24/6/92	1	(1)	
8	Hamit Altıntop	TUR	8/12/82	4	(2)	
16	Andreas Ottl		1/3/85	1	(3)	
23	Danijel Pranjić	CRO	2/12/81	6	(3)	
7	Franck Ribéry	FRA	7/4/83	7		1
10	Arjen Robben	NED	23/1/84	8	(2)	4
31	Bastian Schweinsteiger		1/8/84	12		
20	José Ernesto Sosa	ARG	19/6/85		(1)	
44	Anatoliy Tymoshchuk	UKR	30/3/79	3	(4)	1
17	Mark van Bommel	NED	22/4/77	10		1
Forwards						
33	Mario Gómez		10/7/85	4	(8)	1
18	Miroslav Klose		9/6/78	3	(5)	1
25	Thomas Müller		13/9/89	12		2
11	Ivica Olić	CRO	14/9/79	8	(2)	7
9	Luca Toni	ITA	26/5/77	2		

VFB STUTTGART

UEFA CHAMPIONS LEAGUE
Play-Off Round - FC Timişoara (ROU)
A 2-0 *Gebhart (28p), Hleb (30)*
Lehmann, Taşçı, Marica, Hitzlsperger, Gebhart (Rudy 86), Delpierre, Magnin, Hleb (Élson 61), Celozzi, Khedira, Pogrebnyak (Schieber 77). Coach: Markus Babbel (GER)
Yellow Card(s): Delpierre 49, Hleb 60
H 0-0
Lehmann, Taşçı, Marica (Schieber 79), Hitzlsperger, Gebhart (Élson 90), Rudy (Šimák 67), Delpierre, Magnin, Celozzi, Khedira, Pogrebnyak. Coach: Markus Babbel (GER)

CHAMPIONS LEAGUE,   EUROPA LEAGUE

Group G
Match 1 - Rangers FC (SCO)
1-1 *Pogrebnyak (18)*
ehmann, Taşçı, Hitzlsperger, Boka, Delpierre, Cacau (Schieber 88), Hilbert, leb (Gebhart 67), Khedira, Pogrebnyak, Träsch. Coach: Markus Babbel (GER)
Match 2 - FC Unirea Urziceni (ROU)
1-1 *Taşçı (5)*
ehmann, Taşçı, Marica (Schieber 64), Hitzlsperger, Gebhart, Boka, Delpierre, ilbert, Celozzi, Khedira, Pogrebnyak. Coach: Markus Babbel (GER)
ellow Card(s): Schieber 78, Gebhart 80
Match 3 - Sevilla FC (ESP)
1-3 *Élson (74)*
ehmann, Osorio, Boulahrouz, Taşçı, Boka, Cacau (Pogrebnyak 69), Hleb Élson 69), Khedira, Kuzmanović, Träsch (Hitzlsperger 69), Schieber. Coach: Markus Babbel (GER)
ellow Card(s): Taşçı 71
Match 4 - Sevilla FC (ESP)
1-1 *Kuzmanović (79)*
ehmann, Boulahrouz (Celozzi 46), Taşçı, Hitzlsperger (Schieber 65), Boka, elpierre, Hilbert (Rudy 46), Hleb, Élson, Pogrebnyak, Kuzmanović. Coach: Markus Babbel (GER)
ellow Card(s): Élson 12, Hilbert 45+1, Boka 49
Match 5 - Rangers FC (SCO)
2-0 *Rudy (16), Kuzmanović (59)*
ehmann, Osorio, Niedermeier, Boka, Rudy (Gebhart 90), Delpierre, Cacau Schieber 82), Hleb, Pogrebnyak, Kuzmanović (Hitzlsperger 75), Träsch. Coach: Markus Babbel (GER)
ellow Card(s): Träsch 25, Cacau 74
Match 6 - FC Unirea Urziceni (ROU)
3-1 *Marica (5), Träsch (8), Pogrebnyak (11)*
ehmann, Taşçı, Marica (Cacau 83), Gebhart, Boka, Hleb (Rudy 5), Celozzi, Khedira (Kuzmanović 60), Pogrebnyak, Träsch. Coach: Christian Gross (SUI)

First Knockout Round - FC Barcelona (ESP)
1-1 *Cacau (25)*
ehmann, Molinaro, Taşçı, Gebhart (Rudy 84), Delpierre, Cacau, Hleb, Celozzi, Khedira, Pogrebnyak (Marica 64), Träsch (Kuzmanović 58). Coach: Christian Gross (SUI)
ellow Card(s): Gebhart 51, Molinaro 84, Khedira 90+2
0-4
ehmann, Molinaro, Niedermeier, Delpierre, Cacau, Hleb, Celozzi (Gebhart 46), Khedira, Pogrebnyak (Marica 70), Kuzmanović, Träsch. Coach: Christian Gross (SUI)
ellow Card(s): Lehmann 43, Pogrebnyak 45, Kuzmanović 54

No	Player	Nat	DoB	Aps	(s)	Gls
Goalkeeper						
	Jens Lehmann		10/11/69	8		
Defenders						
5	Arthur Boka	CIV	2/4/83	6		
4	Khalid Boulahrouz	NED	28/12/81	2		
27	Stefano Celozzi		2/11/88	4	(1)	
17	Matthieu Delpierre	FRA	26/4/81	7		
2	Cristian Molinaro	ITA	30/7/83	2		
5	Georg Niedermeier		26/2/86	2		
3	Ricardo Osorio	MEX	30/3/80	2		
5	Serdar Taşçı		24/4/87	6		1
35	Christian Träsch		1/9/87	6		1
Midfielders						
25	Élson	BRA	16/11/81	1	(1)	1
13	Timo Gebhart		12/4/89	3	(3)	
19	Roberto Hilbert		16/10/84	3		
11	Thomas Hitzlsperger		5/4/82	3	(2)	
23	Aleksandr Hleb	BLR	1/5/81	7		
8	Sami Khedira		4/4/87	6		
32	Zdravko Kuzmanović	SRB	22/9/87	4	(2)	2
16	Sebastian Rudy		28/2/90	1	(3)	1
Forwards						
18	Cacau		27/3/81	5	(1)	1
9	Ciprian Marica	ROU	2/10/85	2	(2)	1
29	Pavel Pogrebnyak	RUS	8/11/83	7	(1)	2
9	Julian Schieber		13/2/89	1	(4)	

WERDER BREMEN

UEFA EUROPA LEAGUE

Play-Off Round - FC Aktobe (KAZ)
H 6-3 *Boenisch (17), Pizarro (28), Naldo (36, 65), Hugo Almeida (60), Özil (67p)*
Wiese, Boenisch, Naldo (Pasanen 76), Borowski, Fritz, Marin (Hugo Almeida 46), Özil, Hunt, Frings, Pizarro (Marcelo Moreno 82), Mertesacker. Coach: Thomas Schaaf (GER)
Yellow Card(s): Naldo 37, Frings 90
A 2-0 *Pizarro (10, 45+1)*
Wiese, Pasanen, Naldo, Borowski (Bargfrede 60), Fritz, Özil (Marin 73), Hunt, Frings, Pizarro (Marcelo Moreno 60), Niemeyer, Mertesacker. Coach: Thomas Schaaf (GER)
Yellow Card(s): Wiese 44

Group L
Match 1 - CD Nacional (POR)
A 3-2 *Frings (39p), Pizarro (55, 85)*
Wiese, Boenisch, Naldo, Borowski, Fritz, Marin (Niemeyer 74), Hunt, Frings, Pizarro (Marcelo Moreno 90+3), Mertesacker, Bargfrede. Coach: Thomas Schaaf (GER)
Yellow Card(s): Boenisch 8, Bargfrede 80
Match 2 - Athletic Club (ESP)
H 3-1 *Hunt (18), Naldo (41), Frings (90+4p)*
Wiese, Pasanen, Naldo, Fritz, Marin (Rosenberg 75), Özil, Hunt (Oehrl 89), Frings, Pizarro, Mertesacker, Bargfrede (Niemeyer 60). Coach: Thomas Schaaf (GER)
Red Card(s): Niemeyer 64
Yellow Card(s): Niemeyer 61, Niemeyer 64, Hunt 67
Match 3 - FK Austria Wien (AUT)
A 2-2 *Pizarro (19, 63)*
Wiese, Boenisch, Naldo, Fritz, Marin (Rosenberg 59), Özil, Hunt, Frings, Pizarro, Mertesacker, Bargfrede (Borowski 63). Coach: Thomas Schaaf (GER)
Yellow Card(s): Hunt 53, Boenisch 74, Mertesacker 85, Rosenberg 90+3
Match 4 - FK Austria Wien (AUT)
H 2-0 *Borowski (81), Hugo Almeida (84)*
Wiese, Pasanen, Naldo, Borowski, Fritz, Marin (Rosenberg 60), Özil, Hunt, Niemeyer (Jensen 75), Mertesacker, Bargfrede (Hugo Almeida 46). Coach: Thomas Schaaf (GER)
Yellow Card(s): Bargfrede 30
Match 5 - CD Nacional (POR)
H 4-1 *Rosenberg (31, 34), Marcelo Moreno (84), Marin (90+2)*
Mielitz, Pasanen, Fritz, Rosenberg, Hunt (Borowski 46), Prödl, Jensen, Frings, Niemeyer (Marin 79), Mertesacker, Marcelo Moreno. Coach: Thomas Schaaf (GER)
Yellow Card(s): Mielitz 60, Jensen 79
Match 6 - Athletic Club (ESP)
A 3-0 *Pizarro (13), Naldo (20), Rosenberg (36)*
Wiese, Pasanen, Naldo, Rosenberg, Özil (Marin 75), Prödl, Jensen, Frings (Niemeyer 69), Pizarro (Hugo Almeida 62), Mertesacker. Coach: Thomas Schaaf (GER)
Yellow Card(s): Rosenberg 11, Jensen 83

Round of 32 - FC Twente (NED)
A 0-1
Wiese, Pasanen (Abdennour 32), Naldo, Fritz, Marin, Özil (Hugo Almeida 67), Hunt, Frings, Pizarro, Niemeyer (Borowski 77), Mertesacker. Coach: Thomas Schaaf (GER)
Yellow Card(s): Marin 40, Hunt 60
H 4-1 *Pizarro (15, 20, 58), Naldo (27)*
Vander, Pasanen, Naldo, Marin (Ayık 74), Özil (Borowski 83), Abdennour, Frings, Hugo Almeida, Pizarro, Niemeyer (Bargfrede 58), Mertesacker. Coach: Thomas Schaaf (GER)
Yellow Card(s): Abdennour 68

Round of 16 - Valencia CF (ESP)
A 1-1 *Frings (24p)*
Wiese, Pasanen, Naldo, Borowski, Fritz, Marin (Bargfrede 61), Özil (Jensen 76), Hunt, Frings, Pizarro, Mertesacker. Coach: Thomas Schaaf (GER)
Yellow Card(s): Borowski 35, Frings 37, Pasanen 47, Bargfrede 72, Naldo 79, Wiese 87
H 4-4 *Hugo Almeida (26), Frings (57p), Marin (62), Pizarro (84)*
Wiese, Pasanen, Naldo, Borowski (Hugo Almeida 22), Fritz (Rosenberg 80), Marin, Özil, Hunt, Frings, Pizarro, Mertesacker. Coach: Thomas Schaaf (GER)
Yellow Card(s): Rosenberg 87

Round of 32 - SL Benfica (POR)
H 1-1 *Javi García (33og)*
Drobný, Friedrich, Von Bergen, Janker, Cícero, Ramos, Raffael (Gekas 88), Ebert, Kobiashvili, Nicu (Kringe 61), Piszczek. Coach: Friedhelm Funkel (GER)
A 0-4
Drobný, Friedrich, Von Bergen, Janker, Cícero, Ramos (Gekas 63), Raffael (Wichniarek 63), Kringe, Ebert, Nicu, Piszczek (Pejčinović 72). Coach: Friedhelm Funkel (GER)
Yellow Card(s): Friedrich 14, Von Bergen 75

HERTHA BSC BERLIN

UEFA EUROPA LEAGUE

Play-Off Round - Brøndby IF (DEN)
A 1-2 *Domovchiyski (53)*
Drobný, Von Bergen, Pejčinović, Cícero (Nicu 80), Dárdai, Raffael, Stein, Wichniarek (Domovchiyski 31), Ebert, Kačar (Piszczek 83). Coach: Lucien Favre (SUI)
Yellow Card(s): Ebert 60, Domovchiyski 86
H 3-1 *Kačar (75, 86), Dárdai (80)*
Drobný, Von Bergen, Pejčinović, Janker, Cícero, Dárdai, Wichniarek (Nicu 66), Ebert (Bengtsson 90+4), Domovchiyski (Piszczek 61), Kačar. Coach: Lucien Favre (SUI)
Yellow Card(s): Janker 19, Von Bergen 62, Drobný 90+2

Group D
Match 1 - FK Ventspils (LVA)
H 1-1 *Piszczek (34)*
Drobný (Burchert 21), Friedrich, Janker, Cícero, Ramos, Stein, Bengtsson, Domovchiyski, Nicu, Piszczek (César 67), Hartmann (Dárdai 77). Coach: Lucien Favre (SUI)
Yellow Card(s): R.Bengtsson 45+3, Stein 83
Match 2 - Sporting Clube de Portugal (POR)
A 0-1
Burchert, Kaká, Von Bergen, Pejčinović, Janker, Dárdai, Ramos (Piszczek 46), Raffael, Wichniarek (Domovchiyski 80), César, Kačar (Nicu 67). Coach: Carsten Heine (GER)
Yellow Card(s): Pejčinović 16, Wichniarek 30, Kaká 45+1, Janker 73, Raffael 85
Match 3 - sc Heerenveen (NED)
H 0-1
Burchert, Friedrich, Von Bergen, Pejčinović, Cícero (Kačar 62), Ramos, Stein, Wichniarek (Domovchiyski 46), Ebert, Lustenberger, Bigalke (Raffael 68). Coach: Friedhelm Funkel (GER)
Red Card(s): Ebert 90+4
Yellow Card(s): Friedrich 62, Lustenberger 71, Ebert 78, Ebert 90+4
Match 4 - sc Heerenveen (NED)
A 3-2 *Domovchiyski (21, 52), Wichniarek (90+1)*
Drobný, Friedrich, Von Bergen, Pejčinović, Cícero, Stein, Wichniarek, Domovchiyski (Janker 90+2), Nicu (Piszczek 72), Lustenberger, Bigalke (Raffael 60). Coach: Friedhelm Funkel (GER)
Yellow Card(s): Friedrich 45
Match 5 - FK Ventspils (LVA)
A 1-0 *Raffael (12)*
Drobný, Von Bergen, Janker, Cícero, Ramos (Kačar 68), Raffael, Wichniarek, Nicu, Piszczek, Lustenberger, Radjabali-Fardi. Coach: Friedhelm Funkel (GER)
Red Card(s): Raffael 87
Yellow Card(s): Raffael 73, Raffael 87
Match 6 - Sporting Clube de Portugal (POR)
H 1-0 *Kačar (70)*
Drobný, Von Bergen, Pejčinović, Janker, Cícero, Ramos, Wichniarek (Domovchiyski 69), Nicu (Kaká 90+2), Piszczek, Lustenberger, Kačar (Kringe 86). Coach: Friedhelm Funkel (GER)
Yellow Card(s): Kačar 71

HAMBURGER SV

UEFA EUROPA LEAGUE

Third Qualifying Round - Randers FC (DEN)
A 4-0 *Guerrero (11), Boateng (24), Petrić (53), Trochowski (80p)*
Rost, Mathijsen, Aogo, Zé Roberto, Guerrero (Choupo-Moting 66), Petrić, Jarolím (Tesche 66), Trochowski, Boateng, Demel (Benjamin 7), Pitroipa. Coach: Bruno Labbadia (GER)
H 0-1
Hesl, Rozehnal, Mathijsen, Jansen, Jarolím, Berg, Castelen, Tavares, Benjamin (Rincón 46), Ben-Hatira (Petrić 46), Torun (Pitroipa 62). Coach: Bruno Labbadia (GER)
Yellow Card(s): Tavares 21

Play-Off Round - EA Guingamp (FRA)
A 5-1 *Guerrero (7), Petrić (11, 26, 86), Berg (51)*
Hesl, Mathijsen, Aogo, Zé Roberto (Tesche 60), Guerrero (Berg 46), Petrić, Elia (Benjamin 70), Jarolím, Trochowski, Boateng, Demel. Coach: Bruno Labbadia (GER)
Yellow Card(s): Jarolím 45, Boateng 74, Tesche 80
H 3-1 *Tesche (42, 51), Berg (47)*
Hesl, Rozehnal, Guerrero (Torun 46), Tesche, Berg, Boateng (Aogo 46), Castelen (Elia 73), Pitroipa, Rincón, Tavares, Benjamin. Coach: Bruno Labbadia (GER)
Yellow Card(s): Castelen 40

Group C
Match 1 - SK Rapid Wien (AUT)
A 0-0
Rost, Rozehnal, Mathijsen, Aogo, Zé Roberto, Petrić, Elia, Jarolím, Trochowski (Pitroipa 46), Berg (Torun 73), Boateng (Demel 46). Coach: Bruno Labbadia (GER)
Yellow Card(s): Trochowski 42
Match 2 - Hapoel Tel-Aviv FC (ISR)
H 4-2 *Berg (5, 12), Elia (41), Zé Roberto (77)*
Rost, Mathijsen, Aogo, Zé Roberto (Tesche 84), Petrić (Pitroipa 84), Elia (Castelen 46), Jarolím, Berg, Boateng, Demel, Torun. Coach: Bruno Labbadia (GER)
Match 3 - Celtic FC (SCO)
A 1-0 *Berg (63)*
Rost, Rozehnal, Mathijsen, Aogo, Jansen (Trochowski 77), Zé Roberto, Elia, Jarolím, Berg, Demel, Pitroipa (Tesche 89). Coach: Bruno Labbadia (GER)
Yellow Card(s): Trochowski 82
Match 4 - Celtic FC (SCO)
H 0-0
Rost, Rozehnal, Mathijsen, Aogo, Jansen (Trochowski 82), Zé Roberto, Elia, Jarolím, Berg, Pitroipa (Torun 87), Rincón. Coach: Bruno Labbadia (GER)
Yellow Card(s): Jarolím 66
Match 5 - SK Rapid Wien (AUT)
H 2-0 *Jansen (47), Berg (53)*
Rost, Mathijsen, Aogo (Bertram 87), Jansen (Tavares 83), Tesche, Jarolím, Trochowski, Berg (Petrić 76), Boateng, Demel, Rincón. Coach: Bruno Labbadia (GER)
Yellow Card(s): Jarolím 38

CHAMPIONS LEAGUE,   EUROPA LEAGUE

Match 6 - Hapoel Tel-Aviv FC (ISR)
0-1
…esl, Rozehnal, Mathijsen, Jansen, Petrić, Tesche, Trochowski (Elia 46), …erg, Demel, Rincón, Tavares (Torun 46). Coach: Bruno Labbadia (GER)
…ellow Card(s): Rozehnal 62, Jansen 77, Torun 86, Rincón 90+1

…ound of 32 - PSV Eindhoven (NED)
…1-0 Jansen (26p)
…ost, Rozehnal, Mathijsen, Aogo (Zé Roberto 60), Jansen, Petrić, Tesche, …arolím, Berg (Van Nistelrooy 65), Demel (Boateng 81), Rincón. Coach: …runo Labbadia (GER)
…ellow Card(s): Petrić 14, Aogo 57, Jansen 76, Jarolím 82
…2-3 Petrić (46), Trochowski (79p)
…ost, Rozehnal, Mathijsen, Aogo, Zé Roberto, Petrić (Boateng 76), Elia, …esche (Pitroipa 46), Trochowski (Berg 89), Demel, Rincón. Coach: Bruno …abbadia (GER)
…ed Card(s): Demel 74
…ellow Card(s): Tesche 43, Rincón 61, Mathijsen 63, Demel 65, Demel 74

…ound of 16 - RSC Anderlecht (BEL)
…3-1 Mathijsen (23), Van Nistelrooy (40), Jarolím (76)
…ost, Rozehnal, Mathijsen, Aogo, Jansen, Zé Roberto, Petrić, Elia (Trochowski …8), Jarolím, Van Nistelrooy, Rincón. Coach: Bruno Labbadia (GER)
…3-4 Boateng (42), Jansen (54), Petrić (75)
…ost, Rozehnal, Mathijsen, Jansen (Tesche 79), Zé Roberto, Petrić, Jarolím, …oateng (Elia 63), Van Nistelrooy, Rincón, Torun (Trochowski 83). Coach: …runo Labbadia (GER)
…ellow Card(s): Boateng 33

…uarter-Finals - R. Standard de Liège (BEL)
…2-1 Petrić (42p), Van Nistelrooy (45)
…ost, Mathijsen, Aogo, Zé Roberto, Petrić (Berg 72), Jarolím, Boateng, …emel, Pitroipa, Van Nistelrooy, Torun (Trochowski 72). Coach: Bruno …abbadia (GER)
…ellow Card(s): Van Nistelrooy 56, Zé Roberto 90+1
…3-1 Petrić (20, 35), Guerrero (90+4)
…ost, Mathijsen, Aogo, Zé Roberto, Petrić (Guerrero 66), Tesche, Jarolím, …oateng, Demel, Pitroipa (Trochowski 76), Van Nistelrooy (Berg 89). Coach: …runo Labbadia (GER)
…ellow Card(s): Jarolím 28, Rost 45+3, Aogo 60, Tesche 80, Demel 85

…emi-Finals - Fulham FC (ENG)
…0-0
…ost, Mathijsen, Aogo, Zé Roberto, Guerrero (Petrić 72), Jarolím, …rochowski, Boateng, Demel (Rincón 82) Pitroipa, Van Nistelrooy. Coach: …runo Labbadia (GER)
…ellow Card(s): Mathijsen 32, Trochowski 90+1
…1-2 Petrić (22)
…ost, Mathijsen, Aogo, Zé Roberto, Petrić, Tesche (Rincón 55; Guerrero 79), …arolím (Rozehnal 90+1), Boateng, Demel, Pitroipa, Van Nistelrooy. Coach: …icardo Moniz (NED)
…ellow Card(s): Boateng 62, Rost 90+3

GREECE

OLYMPIACOS FC

UEFA CHAMPIONS LEAGUE

…hird Qualifying Round - ŠK Slovan Bratislava (SVK)
…2-0 A. Papadopoulos (2), Leonardo (21)
…ikopolidis, Mellberg, Zairi, Żewłakow, Raúl Bravo, Dudu Cearense, A. …apadopoulos, Mitroglou (Diogo 84), Leonardo (Galletti 60), Ledesma, I. …apadopoulos (Maresca 70). Coach: Temuri Ketsbaia (GEO)
…ellow Card(s): Maresca 90

H 2-0 Maresca (35), Diogo (56)
Nikopolidis, Mellberg, Galletti (Leonardo 69), Zairi, Żewłakow, Raúl Bravo, Dudu Cearense, A. Papadopoulos, Mitroglou (Diogo 46), Maresca (K. Papadopoulos 79), Ledesma. Coach: Temuri Ketsbaia (GEO)

Play-Off Round - FC Sheriff (MDA)
A 2-0 Dudu Cearense (46), Mitroglou (81)
Nikopolidis, Mellberg, Galletti (Leonardo 62), Diogo (Mitroglou 80), Zairi, Żewłakow, Raúl Bravo, Dudu Cearense, A. Papadopoulos, Maresca, Ledesma. Coach: Temuri Ketsbaia (GEO)
Yellow Card(s): Raúl Bravo 45+3, Domi 59
H 1-0 Mitroglou (82)
Nikopolidis, K. Papadopoulos (Ledesma 46), Mellberg, Galletti (Galitsios 65), Żewłakow, Raúl Bravo, Dudu Cearense (Diogo 62), A. Papadopoulos, Mitroglou, Leonardo, Maresca. Coach: Temuri Ketsbaia (GEO)

Group H
Match 1 - AZ Alkmaar (NED)
H 1-0 Torosidis (79)
Nikopolidis, Mellberg, Diogo (Mitroglou 74), Zairi, Żewłakow, Raúl Bravo, Dudu Cearense, A. Papadopoulos, Leonardo (Stoltidis 81), Ledesma, Torosidis (Óscar 85). Coach: Božidar Bandović (SRB)
Match 2 - Arsenal FC (ENG)
A 0-2
Nikopolidis, Mellberg, Diogo, Zairi (Stoltidis 46), Żewłakow, Raúl Bravo, Dudu Cearense, A. Papadopoulos, Leonardo (Óscar 83), Ledesma (Mitroglou 79), Torosidis. Coach: Zico (BRA)
Yellow Card(s): Żewłakow 52, Dudu Cearense 66, Torosidis 80, Raúl Bravo 89
Match 3 - R. Standard de Liège (BEL)
H 2-1 Mitroglou (43), Stoltidis (90+3)
Nikopolidis, Mellberg, Galletti, Óscar, Zairi (Stoltidis 72), Żewłakow, Raúl Bravo, Dudu Cearense, A. Papadopoulos, Mitroglou, Maresca. Coach: Zico (BRA)
Yellow Card(s): Mellberg 69
Match 4 - R. Standard de Liège (BEL)
A 0-2
Nikopolidis, Mellberg, Galitsios, Galletti (Fetfatzidis 42), Óscar (Stoltidis 78), Żewłakow, Raúl Bravo, Dudu Cearense, A. Papadopoulos (I. Papadopoulos 78), Mitroglou, Maresca. Coach: Zico (BRA)
Yellow Card(s): Dudu Cearense 20, Óscar 73
Match 5 - AZ Alkmaar (NED)
A 0-0
Nikopolidis, Mellberg, Galitsios, Óscar, Zairi (Pantos 90+3), Żewłakow, Raúl Bravo, Dudu Cearense, Mitroglou, Leonardo, Maresca. Coach: Zico (BRA)
Yellow Card(s): Mitroglou 73, Raúl Bravo 81
Match 6 - Arsenal FC (ENG)
H 1-0 Leonardo (47)
Nikopolidis, Mellberg, Galitsios, Galletti, Óscar (Pantos 90+3), Raúl Bravo, Dudu Cearense (Domi 86), A. Papadopoulos, Mitroglou, Leonardo, Maresca. Coach: Zico (BRA)
Yellow Card(s): Leonardo 24

First Knockout Round - FC Girondins de Bordeaux (FRA)
H 0-1
Nikopolidis, Mellberg, Stoltidis, Raúl Bravo, Dátolo, A. Papadopoulos, Mitroglou (Derbyshire 77), Maresca, Ledesma (Zairi 64), LuaLua, Torosidis. Coach: Božidar Bandović (SRB)
Yellow Card(s): A. Papadopoulos 55, Zairi 80
A 1-2 Mitroglou (65)
Nikopolidis, Mellberg, Stoltidis (Ledesma 80), Derbyshire, Zairi (Mitroglou 63), Raúl Bravo, Dátolo, A. Papadopoulos, Maresca, LuaLua, Torosidis. Coach: Božidar Bandović (SRB)
Red Card(s): Derbyshire 60, Mellberg 90+4
Yellow Card(s): Torosidis 4, Derbyshire 54, Derbyshire 60, Mellberg 74, A. Papadopoulos 79, Mellberg 90+4

Greece

No	Player	Nat	DoB	Aps	(s)	Gls
Goalkeeper						
71	Antonios Nikopolidis		14/1/71	8		
Defenders						
21	Avraam Papadopoulos		3/12/84	7		
3	Didier Domi	FRA	2/5/78		(1)	
5	Georgios Galitsios		6/7/86	3		
24	Leonardo	BRA	4/8/85	4		1
4	Olof Mellberg	SWE	3/9/77	8		
30	Anastasios Pantos		5/5/76		(2)	
15	Raúl Bravo	ESP	14/4/81	8		
35	Vasilios Torosidis		10/6/85	4		1
14	Michał Żewłakow	POL	22/4/76	5		
Midfielders						
19	Jesús Alberto Dátolo	ARG	19/5/84	2		
20	Dudu Cearense	BRA	15/4/83	6		
18	Ioannis Fetfatzidis		21/12/90		(1)	
33	Ioannis Papadopoulos		9/3/89		(1)	
7	Luciano Galletti	ARG	9/4/80	3		
28	Cristian Ledesma	ARG	29/12/78	3		(1)	
25	Enzo Maresca	ITA	10/2/80	6		
8	Óscar	ESP	12/11/82	4		(2)	
6	Ieroklis Stoltidis		2/2/75	2	(4)	1
11	Jaouad Zairi	MAR	14/4/82	5	(1)	
Forwards						
9	Matt Derbyshire	ENG	14/4/86	1	(1)	
10	Diogo	BRA	26/5/87	2		
32	Lomana LuaLua	COD	28/12/80	2		
22	Konstantinos Mitroglou		12/3/88	5	(3)	2

PANATHINAIKOS FC

UEFA CHAMPIONS LEAGUE

Third Qualifying Round - AC Sparta Praha (CZE)
A 1-3 *Salpingidis (67)*
Galinović, Kanté (Sarriegi 69), Cissé, Salpingidis, Gilberto Silva (Katsouranis 83), Bjärsmyr, Kanté (Leto 59), Simão, Vintra, Karagounis, Spiropoulos. Coach: Henk ten Cate (NED)
Yellow Card(s): Sarriegi 70, Cissé 88
H 3-0 *Sarriegi (45), Katsouranis (54), Salpingidis (89)*
Galinović, Moon, Sarriegi, Cissé, Leto (Simão 74), Salpingidis, Gilberto Silva, Vintra, Karagounis (Gabriel 77), Katsouranis, Spiropoulos. Coach: Henk ten Cate (NED)
Yellow Card(s): Sarriegi 30, Gabriel 79

Play-Off Round - Club Atlético de Madrid (ESP)
H 2-3 *Salpingidis (47), Leto (74)*
Galinović, Moon, Mattos (Leto 46), Cissé, Salpingidis, Gilberto Silva, Simão (Hristodoulopoulos 80), Vintra, Karagounis, Katsouranis, Spiropoulos. Coach: Henk ten Cate (NED)
Yellow Card(s): Spiropoulos 77, Moon 87
A 0-2
Galinović, Moon (Salpingidis 52), Sarriegi, Ninis (Hristodoulopoulos 63), Cissé, Leto, Gilberto Silva, Gabriel, Darlas, Vintra, Katsouranis (Simão 87). Coach: Henk ten Cate (NED)
Red Card(s): Cissé 71
Yellow Card(s): Katsouranis 54, Gilberto Silva 60, Salpingidis 68, Hristodoulopoulos 76, Sarriegi 85

UEFA EUROPA LEAGUE

Group F
Match 1 - Galatasaray AŞ (TUR)
H 1-3 *Salpingidis (78)*
Galinović, Sarriegi, Leto, Salpingidis, Gilberto Silva, Hristodoulopoulos (Petropoulos 50), Bjärsmyr, Marinos, Karagounis (Ninis 50), Spiropoulos. Coach: Henk ten Cate (NED)
Yellow Card(s): Sarriegi 19, Spiropoulos 56

Match 2 - FC Dinamo Bucureşti (ROU)
A 1-0 *Karagounis (79)*
Tzorvas, Sarriegi, Kanté, Leto (Ninis 45+1), Salpingidis (Rukavina 67), Gilberto Silva, Bjärsmyr, Simão, Vintra, Karagounis (Hristodoulopoulos 83), Katsouranis. Coach: Henk ten Cate (NED)
Yellow Card(s): Leto 4, Bjärsmyr 87
Match 3 - SK Sturm Graz (AUT)
H 1-0 *Salpingidis (60p)*
Tzorvas, Sarriegi, Cissé, Leto (Simão 75), Salpingidis, Gilberto Silva, Gabriel, Vintra, Karagounis (Rukavina 85), Katsouranis (Ninis 46), Spiropoulos. Coach: Henk ten Cate (NED)
Yellow Card(s): Karagounis 37, Gabriel 65
Match 4 - SK Sturm Graz (AUT)
A 1-0 *Katsouranis (70)*
Tzorvas, Sarriegi, Cissé (Rukavina 90+2), Salpingidis (Leto 66), Gilberto Silva, Gabriel, Simão, Vintra, Karagounis (Ninis 40), Katsouranis, Spiropoulos. Coach: Henk ten Cate (NED)
Yellow Card(s): Spiropoulos 59
Match 5 - Galatasaray AŞ (TUR)
A 0-1
Tzorvas, Sarriegi, Rukavina, Kanté, Cissé, Gilberto Silva, Darlas (Spiropoulos 46), Simão, Vintra, Karagounis (Ninis 74), Katsouranis (Hristodoulopoulos 63). Coach: Henk ten Cate (NED)
Yellow Card(s): Darlas 41, Cissé 53
Match 6 - FC Dinamo Bucureşti (ROU)
H 3-0 *Rukavina (54), Cissé (80, 85)*
Tzorvas, Rukavina (Salpingidis 82), Ninis (Leto 69), Kanté, Cissé, Gilberto Silva, Bjärsmyr, Simão, Vintra, Karagounis (Katsouranis 56), Spiropoulos. Coach: Nikolaos Nioplias (GRE)

Round of 32 - AS Roma (ITA)
H 3-2 *Salpingidis (67), Hristodoulopoulos (84), Cissé (89)*
Tzorvas, Sarriegi, Ninis (Hristodoulopoulos 84), Kanté, Cissé, Leto (Marinos 85), Simão, Vintra, Karagounis, Katsouranis (Salpingidis 64), Spiropoulos. Coach: Nikolaos Nioplias (GRE)
Yellow Card(s): Simão 60, Salpingidis 80, Tzorvas 90+1
A 3-2 *Cissé (40p, 45+1), Ninis (43)*
Tzorvas, Sarriegi, Ninis (Gilberto Silva 72), Kanté, Cissé (Hristodoulopoulos 90+2), Salpingidis (Leto 87), Marinos, Simão, Vintra, Katsouranis, Spiropoulos. Coach: Nikolaos Nioplias (GRE)
Red Card(s): Katsouranis 90
Yellow Card(s): Salpingidis 12, Katsouranis 27, Marinos 37, Vintra 77, Cissé 82, Katsouranis 90

First Knockout Round - R. Standard de Liège (BEL)
H 1-3 *Vintra (48)*
Galinović, Sarriegi, Rukavina (Hristodoulopoulos 71), Ninis (Karagounis 46), Kanté, Cissé, Leto (Salpingidis 46), Gilberto Silva, Darlas, Simão, Vintra. Coach: Nikolaos Nioplias (GRE)
Red Card(s): Simão 90+4
Yellow Card(s): Vintra 35, Karagounis 61, Sarriegi 61, Simão 61, Simão 90+4
A 0-1
Tzorvas, Sarriegi, Kanté, Cissé, Leto (Hristodoulopoulos 82), Salpingidis (Rukavina 69), Gilberto Silva, Bjärsmyr (Nisim 56), Vintra, Karagounis, Katsouranis. Coach: Nikolaos Nioplias (GRE)
Yellow Card(s): Leto 27, Gilberto Silva 65, Sarriegi 73, Hristodoulopoulos 88

AEK ATHENS FC

UEFA EUROPA LEAGUE

Play-Off Round - FC Vaslui (ROU)
A 1-2 *Blanco (69p)*
Saja, Geraldo, Majstorović, Nsaliwa, Leonardo (Gentsoglou 90+3), Djebbour, Manduca, Koutromanos, Makos, Blanco (Iordache 89), Georgeas. Coach: Dušan Bajević (SRB)
Yellow Card(s): Majstorović 49, Georgeas 65

3-0 *Manduca (59), Scocco (74, 79)*
aja, Kafes (Nsaliwa 72), Araujo, Geraldo, Majstorović, Juanfran, Leonardo
ahtsidis 67), Manduca, Makos, Blanco, Scocco (Karabelas 85). Coach:
ušan Bajević (SRB)
ellow Card(s): Araujo 41, Majstorović 62

roup I
latch 1 – Everton FC (ENG)
0-4
aja, Kafes, Araujo, Geraldo (Nsaliwa 13; Manduca 46), Juanfran, Leonardo
Yahaya 71), Jahić, Makos, Blanco, Scocco, Arce. Coach: Dušan Bajević (SRB)
ed Card(s): Araujo 55
ellow Card(s): Kafes 65
latch 2 - SL Benfica (POR)
1-0 *Majstorović (43)*
aja, Kafes (Gentsoglou 69), Hersi (Leonardo 78), Majstorović, Juanfran,
Manduca, Jahić, Blanco, Georgeas, Scocco (Karabelas 89), Arce. Coach:
ušan Bajević (SRB)
ed Card(s): Georgeas 86
ellow Card(s): Georgeas 9, Jahić 66, Georgeas 86, Gentsoglou 87
latch 3 - FC BATE Borisov (BLR)
1-2 *Blanco (31p)*
aja, Kafes, Majstorović, Juanfran (Karabelas 62), Nsaliwa, Manduca, Jahić,
lanco (Makos 58), Németh (Leonardo 83), Scocco, Arce. Coach: Dušan
ajević (SRB)
ted Card(s): Majstorović 52, Arce 90+1
ellow Card(s): Majstorović 38, Majstorović 52, Kafes 80, Manduca 86,
rce 87, Arce 90+1
latch 4 - FC BATE Borisov (BLR)
2-2 *Blanco (1), Manduca (38)*
aja, Kafes (Leonardo 81), Nsaliwa (Yahaya 66), Manduca (Hersi 68), Jahić,
arabelas, Blanco, Németh, Georgeas, Scocco, Gentsoglou. Coach:
yssandros Georgamlis (GRE)
ellow Card(s): Gentsoglou 49, Yahaya 74, Németh 90+1
latch 5 - Everton (ENG)
0-1
aja, Kafes, Hersi, Geraldo, Majstorović, Juanfran, Leonardo (Scocco 46),
lakos (Manduca 30), Pavlis (Blanco 62), Georgeas, Tahtsidis. Coach: Dušan
ajević (SRB)
ellow Card(s): Geraldo 75
Match 6 - SL Benfica (POR)
1-2 *Blanco (84)*
aja, Kafes, Araujo, Hersi, Geraldo, Majstorović (Jahić 46), Manduca
ordache 78), Makos (Nsaliwa 46), Blanco, Georgeas, Gentsoglou. Coach:
Dušan Bajević (SRB)
ellow Card(s): Araujo 14, Geraldo 90+3, Georgeas 90+4

PAOK FC

UEFA EUROPA LEAGUE
Third Qualifying Round - Vålerenga Fotball (NOR)
2-1 *Lino (31), Muslimović (37)*
Chalkias, Pablo García, Sérgio Conceição, Cirillo, Sorlin (Malezas 87),
Muslimović (Anastasakos 40), Lino, Fotakis, Ivić (Filomeno 64), Bizera,
sznaucner. Coach: Fernando Santos (POR)
Yellow Card(s): Cirillo 74
H 0-1
Chalkias, Pablo García, Sérgio Conceição (Papazoglou 76), Cirillo,
Anastasakos (Koutsianikoulis 72), Sorlin, Lino, Fotakis, Ivić (Filomeno 64),
Bizera, Sznaucner. Coach: Fernando Santos (POR)
Yellow Card(s): Fotakis 87, Papazoglou 90+2

Play-Off Round - sc Heerenveen (NED)
H 1-1 *Ivić (54)*
Chalkias, Pablo García, Vitolo, Conceição (Koutsianikoulis 66), Cirillo,
Muslimović (Filomeno 66), Malezas, Lino, Vieirinha (Anastasakos 86), Ivić,
Savini. Coach: Fernando Santos (POR)
Yellow Card(s): Vieirinha 52, Malezas 61, Vitolo 62
A 0-0
Chalkias, Pablo García (Koutsianikoulis 77), Vitolo, Cirillo, Muslimović, Lino,
Fotakis (Filomeno 63), Vieirinha, Ivić, Bizera, Savini (Anastasakos 84).
Coach: Fernando Santos (POR)
Yellow Card(s): Vitolo 69, Bizera 86, Cirillo 90+5

LARISSA FC

UEFA EUROPA LEAGUE
Second Qualifying Round - KR Reykjavík (ISL)
A 0-2
Seremet, Boukouvalas, Dabizas, Vlassopoulos (Lampropoulos 59), Toama,
Simić (Siatravanis 81), Aarab, Romeu, Tripotseris, Iglesias (Balis 66), Tsigas.
Coach: Marinos Ouzounidis (GRE)
Yellow Card(s): Vlassopoulos 49
H 1-1 *Tsigas (28)*
Malarz, Boukouvalas, Dabizas, Vlassopoulos (Siatravanis 76), Toama
(Müller 83), Tümer, Simić (Lampropoulos 70), Aarab, Romeu, Tripotseris,
Tsigas. Coach: Marinos Ouzounidis (GRE)
Yellow Card(s): Dabizas 83

HUNGARY

DEBRECENI VSC

UEFA CHAMPIONS LEAGUE
Second Qualifying Round - Kalmar FF (SWE)
H 2-0 *Varga (73), Kiss (86)*
Poleksić, Leandro, Rudolf (Katona 90+1), Mészáros, Máté, Bernáth, Kiss,
Varga, Szakály (Dombi 85), Czvitkovics, Dudu (Oláh 58). Coach: András
Herczeg (HUN)
Yellow Card(s): Bernáth 65, Varga 72
A 1-3 *Varga (13)*
Poleksić, Leandro, Rudolf (Komlósi 87), Mészáros, Máté, Bernáth, Kiss, Varga, Oláh
(Szilágyi 64), Szakály (Dombi 73), Czvitkovics. Coach: András Herczeg (HUN)
Red Card(s): Máté 86
Yellow Card(s): Kiss 45, Varga 60, Máté 71, Leandro 72, Dombi 79, Máté 86

Third Qualifying Round - FC Levadia Tallinn (EST)
A 1-0 *Leandro (70)*
Poleksić, Leandro, Rudolf, Komlósi, Mészáros, Bernáth, Szilágyi (Coulibaly
58), Kiss, Szakály (Szűcs 84), Czvitkovics, Katona (Dombi 67). Coach:
András Herczeg (HUN)
Yellow Card(s): Leandro 32, Coulibaly 72
H 1-0 *Coulibaly (70)*
Poleksić, Rudolf (Szűcs 89), Komlósi, Mészáros, Fodor, Bernáth (Dombi 64),
Kiss, Varga, Coulibaly (Oláh 71), Szakály, Czvitkovics. Coach: András
Herczeg (HUN)
Yellow Card(s): Varga 22, Rudolf 48, Fodor 87

CHAMPIONS EUROPA
LEAGUE LEAGUE

Hungary

Play-Off Round - PFC Levski Sofia (BUL)
A 2-1 *Bodnár (12), Czvitkovics (76)*
Poleksić, Leandro, Bodnár, Rudolf, Mészáros, Máté (Komlósi 15), Kiss,
Varga, Coulibaly, Szakály (Dombi 55), Czvitkovics (Ramos 79). Coach:
Zoran Spisljak (SRB)
Yellow Card(s): Kiss 82
H 2-0 *Varga (13), Rudolf (35)*
Poleksić, Leandro, Ramos, Bodnár, Rudolf (Oláh 88), Komlósi, Mészáros,
Varga, Coulibaly, Szakály (Dombi 58), Czvitkovics (Fodor 81). Coach:
András Herczeg (HUN)
Yellow Card(s): Leandro 21, Ramos 37, Varga 61, Dombi 76

Group E
Match 1 - Liverpool FC (ENG)
A 0-1
Poleksić, Leandro, Ramos (Laczkó 67), Bodnár, Komlósi, Mészáros, Fodor, Kiss,
Coulibaly, Szakály (Feczesin 79), Czvitkovics. Coach: András Herczeg (HUN)
Yellow Card(s): Fodor 21
Match 2 - Olympique Lyonnais (FRA)
H 0-4
Poleksić, Leandro, Bodnár, Komlósi, Fodor, Kiss, Varga, Coulibaly, Szakály
(Dombi 85), Czvitkovics, Laczkó (Rudolf 46). Coach: András Herczeg (HUN)
Yellow Card(s): Szakály 58
Match 3 - ACF Fiorentina (ITA)
H 3-4 *Czvitkovics (2), Rudolf (28), Coulibaly (88)*
Poleksić, Leandro, Bodnár, Rudolf, Komlósi, Mészáros (Szelesi 30), Kiss
(Laczkó 88), Varga, Coulibaly, Szakály (Dombi 57), Czvitkovics. Coach:
András Herczeg (HUN)
Yellow Card(s): Rudolf 28, Bodnár 81
Match 4 - ACF Fiorentina (ITA)
A 2-5 *Rudolf (38), Coulibaly (70)*
Pantić, Leandro, Ramos (Coulibaly 53), Bodnár, Rudolf, Komlósi (Kiss 10),
Fodor, Szelesi, Varga, Czvitkovics, Laczkó (Szakály 65). Coach: András
Herczeg (HUN)
Yellow Card(s): Ramos 27
Match 5 - Liverpool FC (ENG)
H 0-1
Poleksić, Bodnár, Rudolf, Mészáros, Fodor (Dombi 78), Mijadinoski, Szelesi,
Kiss, Szakály (Coulibaly 62), Czvitkovics, Laczkó. Coach: András Herczeg
(HUN)
Yellow Card(s): Szelesi 23
Match 6 - Olympique Lyonnais (FRA)
A 0-4
Pantić, Ramos (Kiss 57), Bodnár (Bernáth 52), Mészáros, Mijadinoski,
Szelesi, Varga, Coulibaly, Szakály (Feczesin 74), Czvitkovics, Laczkó. Coach:
András Herczeg (HUN)
Yellow Card(s): Ramos 39

No	Player	Nat	DoB	Aps	(s)	Gls
Goalkeepers						
12	Đorđe Pantić	SRB	27/1/80	2		
1	Vukašin Poleksić	MNE	30/8/82	4		
Defenders						
22	Csaba Bernáth		26/3/79		(1)	
10	László Bodnár		25/2/79	6		
21	Marcell Fodor		27/10/87	4		
16	Ádám Komlósi		6/12/77	4		
17	Norbert Mészáros		19/8/80	4		
24	Mirsad Mijadinoski	SUI	1/10/81	2		
Midfielders						
77	Péter Czvitkovics		10/2/83	6		1
7	Tibor Dombi		11/11/73		(3)	
30	Zoltán Kiss		18/8/80	4	(2)	
4	Leandro		19/3/82	4		
6	Luis Ramos	HON	11/4/85	3		
55	Péter Szakály		17/8/86	5	(1)	
25	Zoltán Szélesi		22/11/81	3	(1)	
33	József Varga		6/6/88	4		
86	Zsolt Laczkó		18/12/86	4	(2)	
Forwards						
39	Adamo Coulibaly	FRA	14/8/81	4	(2)	2
11	Róbert Feczesin		22/2/86		(2)	
14	Gergely Rudolf		9/3/85	3	(1)	2

BUDAPEST HONVÉD FC

UEFA EUROPA LEAGUE

Third Qualifying Round - Fenerbahçe SK (TUR)
A 1-5 *Zsolnai (78)*
Németh, Benjamin, Botiş, Hajdu (Guilherme 88), Macko, Hrepka (Zsolnai
53), Debreceni, Pastva, Abraham, Hidi (Horváth 63), Vukmir. Coach: Tibor
Sisa (HUN)
Yellow Card(s): Benjamin 16
H 1-1 *Fritz (86)*
Németh, Fazakas (Zsolnai 46), Benjamin, Botiş, Hajdu, Macko, Debreceni,
Pastva, Abraham, Horváth, Takács (Fritz 82). Coach: Tibor Sisa (HUN)
Yellow Card(s): Debreceni 15

ÚJPEST FC

UEFA EUROPA LEAGUE

Second Qualifying Round - FC Steaua Bucureşti (ROU)
A 0-2
Balajcza, Dudić, Sándor, Stokes, Rajczi (Tisza 81), Lambulić, Vermes, Vaskó,
Korcsmár, Kabát, Pollák. Coach: Willie McStay (SCO)
Red Card(s): Korcsmár 54
Yellow Card(s): Kabát 23, Korcsmár 34, Vaskó 43, Pollák 44, Korcsmár 54
H 1-2 *Vaskó (82)*
Balajcza, Dudić, Sándor, Stokes, Rajczi, Tisza, Lambulić, Vermes, Vaskó,
Kabát (Foxi 59), Pollák (Tóth 66). Coach: Willie McStay (SCO)
Yellow Card(s): Tisza 22, Dudić 30

SZOMBATHELYI HALADÁS

UEFA EUROPA LEAGUE

First Qualifying Round - FC Irtysh Pavlodar (KAZ)
H 1-0 *Kenesei (79)*
Rózsa, Rajos, Maikel (Skriba 62), Molnár, Oross, Vörös, Tóth, Kenesei,
Guzmics, Szabolcs, Kuttor. Coach: Aurél Csertői (HUN)
Yellow Card(s): Rajos 78
A 1-2 *Chernyshov (24og)*
Rózsa, Rajos, Maikel (Skriba 45), Molnár, Oross, Vörös (Irhás 88), Tóth,
Kenesei (At. Simon 55), Guzmics, Szabolcs, Kuttor. Coach: Aurél Csertői
(HUN)
Yellow Card(s): Vörös 35, Oross 85

Second Qualifying Round - IF Elfsborg (SWE)
A 0-3
Rózsa, Molnár, Nagy, Oross, Irhás (Lattenstein 67), Tóth, Skriba (Ugrai 66),
Guzmics, Szabolcs (Csontos 87), Kuttor, Iszlai. Coach: Aurél Csertői (HUN)
Yellow Card(s): Molnár 27, Iszlai 48

0-0
...ózsa, Molnár, Nagy, Oross (At. Simon 70), Irhás (Lattenstein 73), Tóth, ...kriba (Csontos 89), Guzmics, Szabolcs, Kuttor, Iszlai. Coach: Aurél ...sertői (HUN)
Yellow Card(s): Tóth 31

ICELAND

FH HAFNARFJÖRDUR

UEFA CHAMPIONS LEAGUE

Second Qualifying Round - FK Aktobe (KAZ)
A 0-4
...árusson, Søderlund (M. Gudmundsson 54), Nielsen, Ásgeirsson (T. Gudmundsson 54), P. Vidarsson, D. Vidarsson, Vilhjálmsson, Gudnason, ...Björnsson (Sverrisson 71), Gardarsson, V. Gudmundsson. Coach: Heimir Gudjónsson (ISL)
Red Card(s): V. Gudmundsson 54
Yellow Card(s): D. Vidarsson 40, V. Gudmundsson 43, V. Gudmundsson 64, Gudnason 80, P. Vidarsson 84
A 0-2
...árusson, Søderlund (Benediktsson 85), Nielsen, D. Vidarsson, T. Gudmundsson, Vilhjálmsson, Gudnason (Kuld 85), Kristjánsson, M. Gudmundsson, Gardarsson (Hallfredsson 83), Sverrisson. Coach: Heimir Gudjónsson (ISL)
Yellow Card(s): Søderlund 33, D. Vidarsson 79

KR REYKJAVÍK

UEFA EUROPA LEAGUE

Second Qualifying Round - Larissa FC (GRE)
H 2-0 *B. Sigurdsson (55), Takefusa (90+3)*
Magnússon, I. Sigurdsson, Gudjónsson, Sævarsson, Fridgeirsson, Hauksson (Kristjánsson 86), Benediktsson (Takefusa 72), B. Sigurdsson, Rutgers, Jónsson (Gunnarsson 77), Diogo. Coach: Logi Ólafsson (ISL)
Yellow Card(s): Fridgeirsson 86
A 1-1 *I. Sigurdsson (75)*
Magnússon, I. Sigurdsson, Gudjónsson, Sævarsson, Fridgeirsson, Hauksson, Benediktsson (Takefusa 46), B. Sigurdsson (Gunnarsson 86), Rutgers, Jónsson (Jóhannsson 86), Diogo. Coach: Logi Ólafsson (ISL)
Yellow Card(s): I. Sigurdsson 23, Gudjónsson 54

Third Qualifying Round - FC Basel 1893 (SUI)
H 2-2 *Benediktsson (6), I. Sigurdsson (9)*
Magnússon, I. Sigurdsson, Gudjónsson, Fridgeirsson, Jóhannsson, Hauksson, Benediktsson (Takefusa 61), B. Sigurdsson, Rutgers, Jónsson (Gunnarsson 61), Diogo. Coach: Logi Ólafsson (ISL)
A 1-3 *Takefusa (45+1p)*
Magnússon, I. Sigurdsson, Gudjónsson, Fridgeirsson, Jóhannsson (Benediktsson 71), Hauksson, Takefusa, B. Sigurdsson, Rutgers, Jónsson (Gunnarsson 75), Diogo. Coach: Logi Ólafsson (ISL)
Yellow Card(s): B. Sigurdsson 76, Magnússon 78, Rutgers 79

KEFLAVÍK

UEFA EUROPA LEAGUE

First Qualifying Round - Valletta FC (MLT)
A 0-3
L. Jørgensen, Sutej, Antoníusson, N. Jørgensen, Eysteinsson (Matthíasson 73), Sveinsson, Samuelsen, Thorsteinsson, Einarsson, Adalsteinsson, H. Gudmundsson (Arnarson 85). Coach: Kristján Gudmundsson (ISL)
Yellow Card(s): Thorsteinsson 47, Samuelsen 90+3
H 2-2 *Eysteinsson (55), J. Gudmundsson (72)*
L. Jørgensen, Sutej, Antoníusson, Gudnason (Arnarson 65), N. Jørgensen (H. Gudmundsson 46), Eysteinsson, Sveinsson, Samuelsen, Thorsteinsson (J. Gudmundsson 70), Einarsson, Adalsteinsson. Coach: Kristján Gudmundsson (ISL)

FRAM REYKJAVÍK

UEFA EUROPA LEAGUE

First Qualifying Round - The New Saints FC (WAL)
H 2-1 *S. Tillen (33p), Júlíusson (48)*
Halldórsson, McShane, Ólason (Hl. Magnússon 87), Hauksson, Jónsson, Gudmundsson, Júlíusson (J. Tillen 70), S. Tillen, H. Thórarinsson, Ormarsson (Björnsson 70), Fjóluson. Coach: Thorvaldur Örlygsson (ISL)
A 2-1 *Ormarsson (16), S. Tillen (66p)*
Halldórsson, McShane, Ólason, Hauksson, Jónsson (Ólafsson 90), Gudmundsson, Júlíusson (J. Tillen 87), S. Tillen, H. Thórarinsson, Ormarsson (Björnsson 82), Fjóluson. Coach: Thorvaldur Orlygsson (ISL)
Yellow Card(s): S. Tillen 76, Thórarinsson 81, Hauksson 85

Second Qualifying Round - SK Sigma Olomouc (CZE)
A 1-1 *Fjóluson (21)*
Halldórsson, McShane (J. Tillen 61), Ólason, Hauksson, Jónsson, Gudmundsson, Júlíusson, S. Tillen, H. Thórarinsson (Björnsson 75), Ormarsson (Hl. Magnússon 85), Fjóluson. Coach: Thorvaldur Örlygsson (ISL)
Yellow Card(s): McShane 34, Júlíusson 90+2
H 0-2
Halldórsson, McShane, Ólason (Gudmundsson 68), Hauksson, Helgason, Jónsson, Júlíusson, S. Tillen, H. H. Thórarinsson, Ormarsson, Fjóluson. Coach: Thorvaldur Örlygsson (ISL)
Yellow Card(s): S. Tillen 50, Ólason 57, Fjóluson 60

Israel

ISRAEL

MACCABI HAIFA FC

UEFA CHAMPIONS LEAGUE

Second Qualifying Round - Glentoran FC (NIR)
H 6-0 *Refaelov (37), Katan (53), Dvalishvili (57, 81), Arbeitman (83), Ghdir (89)*
Davidovich, Jorge Teixeira, Culma (Golasa 55), Dvalishvili, Ghdir, Masilela, Katan (Arbeitman 72), Keinan, Kayal, Refaelov (Boccoli 61), Meshumar. Coach: Elisha Levi (ISR)
A 4-0 *Bello (9, 53), Masilela (62), Arbeitman (90+2)*
Davidovich, Jorge Teixeira, Culma (Boccoli 46), Dvalishvili, Bello (Arbeitman 64), Golasa (Ghdir 57), Masilela, Keinan, Kayal, Refaelov, Meshumar. Coach: Elisha Levi (ISR)
Yellow Card(s): Culma 17, Golasa 24

Third Qualifying Round - FC Aktobe (KAZ)
A 0-0
Davidovich, Jorge Teixeira, Culma, Dvalishvili (Bello 64), Ghdir, Masilela, Katan (Golasa 86), Keinan, Kayal, Refaelov (Boccoli 64), Meshumar. Coach: Elisha Levi (ISR)
Yellow Card(s): Jorge Teixeira 52
H 4-3 *Katan (26), Golasa (34), Dvalishvili (59, 62)*
Davidovich, Jorge Teixeira, Culma, Dvalishvili, Ghdir (Boccoli 65), Masilela, Katan, Keinan, Kayal (Arbeitman 58), Refaelov (Golasa 31), Meshumar. Coach: Elisha Levi (ISR)
Yellow Card(s): Refaelov 24, Keinan 56, Davidovich 76, Jorge Teixeira 84

Play-Off Round - FC Salzburg (AUT)
A 2-1 *Ghdir (22), Arbeitman (84)*
Davidovich, Maymon, Culma, Dvalishvili (Arbeitman 76), Golasa, Ghdir (Boccoli 65) Masilela, Katan, Keinan, Kayal (Refaelov 69), Meshumar. Coach: Elisha Levi (ISR)
Yellow Card(s): Meshumar 17, Keinan 72, Masilela 88
H 3-0 *Dvalishvili (31), Golasa (57), Ghdir (90)*
Davidovich, Maymon, Jorge Teixeira, Culma, Dvalishvili (Refaelov 73), Golasa (Boccoli 62), Ghdir, Masilela, Katan, Kayal, Meshumar (Harazi 63). Coach: Elisha Levi (ISR)
Yellow Card(s): Culma 22, Kayal 25

Group A
Match 1 - FC Bayern München (GER)
H 0-3
Davidovich, Jorge Teixeira, Boccoli, Dvalishvili, Golasa, Ghdir (Osman 68), Masilela, Katan, Keinan, Kayal (Arbeitman 68), Meshumar (Refaelov 73). Coach: Elisha Levi (ISR)
Yellow Card(s): Boccoli 80
Match 2 - FC Girondins de Bordeaux (FRA)
A 0-1
Davidovich, Jorge Teixeira, Culma, Dvalishvili (Arbeitman 58), Golasa (Boccoli 84), Ghdir (Refaelov 66), Masilela, Katan, Keinan, Kayal, Meshumar. Coach: Elisha Levi (ISR)
Red Card(s): Kayal 88
Yellow Card(s): Meshumar 66
Match 3 - Juventus (ITA)
A 0-1
Davidovich, Jorge Teixeira, Boccoli, Culma, Dvalishvili, Masilela (Zaguri 46), Osman, Arbeitman (Ghdir 46), Keinan, Refaelov (Dutra 56), Meshumar. Coach: Elisha Levi (ISR)
Red Card(s): Dutra 68
Yellow Card(s): Culma 11, Jorge Teixeira 31, Osman 38, Zaguri 51, Boccoli 90

Match 4 - Juventus (ITA)
H 0-1
Davidovich, Jorge Teixeira, Boccoli (Zaguri 71), Culma (Ghdir 46), Dvalishvili (Refaelov 56), Masilela, Osman, Arbeitman, Katan, Keinan, Meshumar. Coach: Elisha Levi (ISR)
Yellow Card(s): Masilela 26, Culma 36, Osman 71
Match 5 - FC Bayern München (GER)
A 0-1
Davidovich, Maymon, Culma (Refaelov 69), Dvalishvili (Arbeitman 63), Ghdir, Masilela, Osman (Golasa 74), Katan, Keinan, Kayal, Meshumar. Coach: Elisha Levi (ISR)
Yellow Card(s): Masilela 57, Arbeitman 81
Match 6 - FC Girondins de Bordeaux (FRA)
H 0-1
Davidovich, Jorge Teixeira, Culma, Dvalishvili (Arbeitman 54), Golasa (Harazi 71), Ghdir, Masilela (Tawatha 62), Keinan, Kayal, Refaelov, Meshumar. Coach: Elisha Levi (ISR)
Yellow Card(s): Culma 39

No	Player	Nat	DoB	Aps	(s)	Gls
Goalkeeper						
1	Nir Davidovich		17/12/76	6		
Defenders						
3	Alon Harazi		13/2/71		(1)	
21	Dekel Keinan		15/9/84	6		
17	Tsepo Masilela	RSA	5/5/85	6		
4	Shai Maymon		18/3/86	1		
27	Eyal Meshumar		10/8/83	6		
18	Ali Osman		8/2/87	3	(1)	
13	Taleb Tawatha		21/6/92		(1)	
5	Jorge Teixeira	POR	27/8/86	5		
Midfielders						
7	Gustavo Boccoli	BRA	16/2/78	3	(1)	
8	John Jairo Culma	COL	17/3/81	5		
14	Tiago Dutra	BRA	17/9/90		(1)	
15	Eyal Golasa		7/10/91	3	(1)	
23	Biram Kayal		2/5/88	4		
26	Lior Refaelov		26/4/86	2	(4)	
24	Israel Zaguri		29/1/90		(2)	
Forwards						
19	Shlomi Arbeitman		14/5/85	2	(4)	
9	Vladimer Dvalishvili	GEO	20/4/86	6		
16	Mohammad Ghdir		21/1/91	4	(2)	
20	Yaniv Katan		27/1/81	4		

HAPOEL TEL-AVIV FC

UEFA EUROPA LEAGUE

Third Qualifying Round - IFK Göteborg (SWE)
A 3-1 *Shechter (73), Yeboah (78), Natcho (90+4)*
Enyeama, Douglas, Bondarv, Zandberg (Menteshashvili 78), Natcho, Badir, Yeboah (Lala 86), Vermouth, Zhavi (Shechter 46), Ben Dayan, Yadin. Coach: Eli Gutman (ISR)
Yellow Card(s): Badir 4, Ben Dayan 53, Menteshashvili 88, Douglas 90+4
H 1-1 *Zandberg (14)*
Enyeama, Douglas, Bondarv, Zandberg (Zhavi 67), Natcho (Menteshashvili 76), Shechter (Lala 82), Badir, Yeboah, Vermouth, Ben Dayan, Yadin. Coach: Eli Gutman (ISR)
Yellow Card(s): Shechter 46, Bondarv 88

Play-Off Round - FK Teplice (CZE)
A 2-1 *Enyeama (74p), Vermouth (90+4)*
Enyeama, Douglas, Bondarv, Zandberg (Zhavi 62), Natcho, Shechter (Lala 86), Badir, Yeboah (Menteshashvili 80), Vermouth, Ben Dayan, Yadin. Coach: Eli Gutman (ISR)
Yellow Card(s): Yadin 37, Zandberg 41, Enyeama 66

1-1 *Ben Dayan (90+1)*
[E]nyeama, Douglas, Bondarv, Zandberg (Zhavi 62), Natcho, Shechter (Menteshashvili 82), Badir, Yeboah (Lala 68), Vermouth, Ben Dayan, Yadin.
[C]oach: Eli Gutman (ISR)
Yellow Card(s): Bondarv 57, Shechter 67

Group C
Match 1 - Celtic FC (SCO)
H 2-1 *Vučićević (75), Lala (88)*
[E]nyeama, Douglas, Natcho (Zhavi 60), Vučićević (Maree 80), Badir, Yeboah, [V]ermouth, Menteshashvili (Lala 54), Ben Dayan, Kenda, Yadin. Coach: Eli [G]utman (ISR)
Yellow Card(s): Yadin 44, Natcho 51
Match 2 - Hamburger SV (GER)
A 2-4 *Shechter (36), Yeboah (61)*
[E]nyeama, Douglas, Bondarv (Zhavi 84), Natcho, Vučićević (Duani 68), [B]adir, Yeboah, Vermouth, Menteshashvili (Shechter 28), Ben Dayan, Yadin.
[C]oach: Eli Gutman (ISR)
Red Card(s): Badir 65
Yellow Card(s): Yeboah 72
Match 3 - SK Rapid Wien (AUT)
H 5-1 *Dober (30og), Menteshashvili (54), Shechter (59), Vermouth (69), Lala (90)*
[E]nyeama, Douglas, Bondarv, Natcho, Vučićević (Zhavi 82), Shechter [(Maree 87), Yeboah (Lala 77), Vermouth, Menteshashvili, Ben Dayan, Yadin.
[C]oach: Eli Gutman (ISR)
Yellow Card(s): Yeboah 41, Menteshashvili 52, Vermouth 81
Match 4 - SK Rapid Wien (AUT)
A 3-0 *Yadin (13), Vermouth (65), Natcho (70)*
[E]nyeama, Douglas, Bondarv, Natcho, Vučićević (Menteshashvili 59), [S]hechter, Badir, Yeboah (Lala 73), Vermouth, Ben Dayan, Yadin (Zandberg [87]). Coach: Eli Gutman (ISR)
Yellow Card(s): Yadin 36
Match 5 - Celtic FC (SCO)
A 0-2
Enyeama, Douglas, Bondarv, Natcho, Shechter, Badir, Yeboah (Vučićević 46), Vermouth, Menteshashvili (Lala 46), Ben Dayan, Yadin (Zhavi 79).
Coach: Eli Gutman (ISR)
Yellow Card(s): Yadin 71
Match 6 - Hamburger SV (GER)
H 1-0 *Yeboah (23)*
Enyeama, Douglas, Natcho, Shechter (Zandberg 90), Badir, Yeboah (Lala 68), Vermouth, Menteshashvili, Zhavi (Maree 81), Ben Dayan, Kenda.
Coach: Eli Gutman (ISR)
Yellow Card(s): Maree 82

Round of 32 - FC Rubin Kazan (RUS)
A 0-3
Enyeama, Douglas, Bondarv, Natcho, Shechter, Badir, Vermouth, Menteshashvili (Zhavi 46), Lala (Maree 46), Shish, Yadin (De Ridder 75).
Coach: Eli Gutman (ISR)
Yellow Card(s): Yadin 30, Bondarv 37, Shish 79, De Ridder 87
H 0-0
Enyeama, Douglas, Bondarv (Kenda 56), Natcho, Shechter, Badir, Vermouth, Zhavi, Lala (Maree 56), Shish, Yadin (Huta 81). Coach: Eli Gutman (ISR)
Yellow Card(s): Kenda 64, Shish 65

MACCABI NETANYA FC

UEFA EUROPA LEAGUE

Second Qualifying Round - Sliema Wanderers FC (MLT)
A 0-0
Lifshitz, Haimovich, Saban, Gazal, Saba'a, Cohen, Yampolski (Vaysberg 71), Dgani, Magharbeh (Goata 53), Samya, Menashe. Coach: Nati Azaria (ISR)
Yellow Card(s): Samya 68

H 3-0 *Samya (58), Ezra (84), Saba'a (89)*
Lifshitz, Haimovich, Saban, Gazal, Saba'a, Cohen, Goata (Magharbeh 46), Yampolski (Ezra 82), Dgani, Samya, Menashe (Messika 86). Coach: Nati Azaria (ISR)
Yellow Card(s): Menashe 72, Saban 77

Third Qualifying Round - Galatasaray AŞ (TUR)
H 1-4 *Yampolski (25)*
Lifshitz, Saban, Gazal, Saba'a (Awudu 46), Cohen, Yampolski (Ezra 81), Dgani, Magharbeh (Taga 57), Fransman, Ma'abi, Menashe. Coach: Nati Azaria (ISR)
Yellow Card(s): Cohen 27, Fransman 53, Ma'abi 61, Gazal 68
A 0-6
Lifshitz, Gazal, Saba'a (Vaysberg 76), Cohen, Yampolski (Ezra 85), Dgani (Shollkovsky 70), Taga, Fransman, Ma'abi, Samya, Menashe. Coach: Nati Azaria (ISR)
Red Card(s): Samya 90+1
Yellow Card(s): Vaysberg 89, Fransman 90, Samya 90+1, Samya 90+1

BNEI YEHUDA TEL-AVIV FC

UEFA EUROPA LEAGUE

First Qualifying Round - Simurq Zaqatala PFK (AZE)
A 1-0 *Baldut (83)*
Aiyenugba, Mori, Rali, Baldut, Radi, Zairi (Azoz 86), Atar (Biton 78), Galván (Garrido 90), Hadad, Edri, Abu Zeid. Coach: Guy Luzon (ISR)
H 3-0 *Galván (27, 66), Biton (86)*
Aiyenugba, Mori, Garrido, Rali, Baldut, Radi, Zairi (Amsis 83), Atar, Galván (Biton 70), Edri (Azoz 80), Abu Zeid. Coach: Guy Luzon (ISR)
Yellow Card(s): Zairi 38, Mori 53, Rali 63

Second Qualifying Round - FC Dinaburg (LVA)
H 4-0 *Galván (25), Mori (38), Atar (67), Zairi (90+3)*
Aiyenugba, Mori, Garrido, Rali, Baldut (Amsis 78), Radi (Biton 64), Zairi, Atar, Galván (Azoz 83), Edri, Abu Zeid. Coach: Guy Luzon (ISR)
Yellow Card(s): Radi 10, Mori 39, Abu Zeid 61
A 1-0 *Atar (32)*
Aiyenugba, Garrido, Baldut, Radi, Atar (Amsis 56), Biton, Azoz, Galván (Hatari 74), Hadad, Edri, Abu Zeid (Ha'aronovic 65). Coach: Guy Luzon (ISR)
Yellow Card(s): Ha'aronovic 72, Amsis 72, Garrido 75

Third Qualifying Round - FC Paços de Ferreira (POR)
H 1-0 *Atar (55)*
Aiyenugba, Mori, Garrido, Rali, Baldut (Afek 71), Radi, Zairi, Biton (Atar 52), Galván (Azoz 88), Edri, Abu Zeid. Coach: Guy Luzon (ISR)
Yellow Card(s): Biton 11, Rali 56, Atar 84
A 1-0 *Atar (31)*
Aiyenugba, Mori, Garrido, Baldut, Radi, Zairi (Linić 74), Atar, Azoz, Galván (Afek 66), Edri, Abu Zeid. Coach: Guy Luzon (ISR)
Yellow Card(s): Atar 27, Mori 64, Abu Zeid 80

Play-Off Round - PSV Eindhoven (NED)
H 0-1
Aiyenugba, Mori, Linić (Amsis 81), Garrido, Rali (Ha'aronovic 88), Baldut, Radi, Biton, Azoz, Galván, Edri. Coach: Guy Luzon (ISR)
Yellow Card(s): Garrido 14
A 0-1
Aiyenugba, Mori, Rali (Zairi 77), Baldut (Biton 71), Radi (Linić 65), Atar, Azoz, Galván, Hadad, Edri, Abu Zeid. Coach: Guy Luzon (ISR)
Yellow Card(s): Edri 34, Abu Zeid 42, Linić 63

ITALY

FC INTERNAZIONALE MILANO

UEFA CHAMPIONS LEAGUE

Group F
Match 1 - FC Barcelona (ESP)
H 0-0
Júlio César, Zanetti, Lúcio, Thiago Motta, Eto'o, Sneijder (Santon 80), Muntari (Stanković 62), Maicon, Milito (Balotelli 85), Samuel, Chivu. Coach: José Mourinho (POR)
Yellow Card(s): Chivu 90
Match 2 - FC Rubin Kazan (RUS)
A 1-1 Stanković (27)
Júlio César, Zanetti, Stanković, Lúcio, Eto'o, Maicon, Cambiasso (Vieira 80), Samuel, Chivu, Mancini (Ricardo Quaresma 64), Balotelli. Coach: José Mourinho (POR)
Red Card(s): Balotelli 60
Yellow Card(s): Samuel 14, Balotelli 20, Balotelli 60, Maicon 63
Match 3 - FC Dynamo Kyiv (UKR)
H 2-2 Stanković (35), Samuel (47)
Júlio César, Zanetti, Stanković (Vieira 85), Lúcio, Eto'o, Sneijder, Muntari (Suazo 46), Maicon, Cambiasso (Materazzi 86), Samuel, Chivu. Coach: José Mourinho (POR)
Yellow Card(s): Stanković 23, Maicon 29, Chivu 52, Zanetti 83
Match 4 - FC Dynamo Kyiv (UKR)
A 2-1 Milito (86), Sneijder (89)
Júlio César, Zanetti, Stanković, Lúcio, Eto'o, Sneijder, Maicon, Cambiasso (Thiago Motta 46), Milito, Samuel (Muntari 79), Chivu (Balotelli 46). Coach: José Mourinho (POR)
Yellow Card(s): Samuel 23, Lúcio 45
Match 5 - FC Barcelona (ESP)
A 0-2
Júlio César, Zanetti, Stanković (Balotelli 71), Lúcio, Thiago Motta, Eto'o, Maicon, Cambiasso (Muntari 46), Milito (Ricardo Quaresma 81), Samuel, Chivu. Coach: José Mourinho (POR)
Yellow Card(s): Thiago Motta 18, Chivu 80, Zanetti 89
Match 6 - FC Rubin Kazan (RUS)
H 2-0 Eto'o (31), Balotelli (64)
Júlio César, Zanetti, Stanković (Cambiasso 52), Lúcio, Thiago Motta, Eto'o, Sneijder, Maicon, Milito, Samuel (Córdoba 15), Balotelli (Muntari 77). Coach: José Mourinho (POR)
Yellow Card(s): Balotelli 46, Lúcio 69

First Knockout Round - Chelsea FC (ENG)
H 2-1 Milito (3), Cambiasso (55)
Júlio César, Zanetti, Stanković (Muntari 84), Lúcio, Thiago Motta (Balotelli 57), Eto'o (Pandev 68), Sneijder, Maicon, Cambiasso, Milito, Samuel. Coach: José Mourinho (POR)
Yellow Card(s): Thiago Motta 9, Milito 22
A 1-0 Eto'o (78)
Júlio César, Zanetti, Lúcio, Thiago Motta (Materazzi 90+2), Eto'o, Sneijder (Mariga 85), Maicon, Cambiasso, Milito, Samuel, Pandev (Stanković 75). Coach: José Mourinho (POR)
Yellow Card(s): Eto'o 17, Thiago Motta 48, Lúcio 54, Júlio César 82

Quarter-Finals - PFC CSKA Moskva (RUS)
H 1-0 Milito (65)
Júlio César, Zanetti, Eto'o, Sneijder, Maicon, Cambiasso, Milito, Materazzi, Samuel, Pandev (Mariga 90+4). Coach: José Mourinho (POR)
Yellow Card(s): Materazzi 12
A 1-0 Sneijder (6)
Júlio César, Zanetti, Stanković, Eto'o, Sneijder (Muntari 86), Maicon, Cambiasso, Milito (Balotelli 74), Samuel, Pandev (Chivu 63). Coach: José Mourinho (POR)
Yellow Card(s): Stanković 16

Semi-Finals - FC Barcelona (ESP)
H 3-1 Sneijder (30), Maicon (48), Milito (61)
Júlio César, Zanetti, Lúcio, Thiago Motta, Eto'o, Sneijder, Maicon (Chivu 73), Cambiasso, Milito (Balotelli 75), Samuel, Pandev (Stanković 56). Coach: José Mourinho (POR)
Yellow Card(s): Eto'o 12, Stanković 82
A 0-1
Júlio César, Zanetti, Lúcio, Thiago Motta, Eto'o (Mariga 86), Sneijder (Muntari 66), Maicon, Cambiasso, Milito (Córdoba 81), Samuel, Chivu.
Red Card(s): Thiago Motta 28
Yellow Card(s): Thiago Motta 10, Júlio César 34, Chivu 43, Muntari 82, Lúcio 82

Final - FC Bayern München (GER)
2-0 Milito (35, 70)
Júlio César, Zanetti, Lúcio, Eto'o, Sneijder, Maicon, Cambiasso, Milito (Materazzi 90+2), Samuel, Chivu (Stanković 68), Pandev (Muntari 79). Coach: José Mourinho (POR)
Yellow Card(s): Chivu 30

No	Player	Nat	DoB	Aps	(s)	Gls
Goalkeeper						
12	Júlio César	BRA	3/9/79	13		
Defenders						
26	Cristian Chivu	ROU	26/10/80	7	(2)	
2	Iván Córdoba	COL	11/8/76		(2)	
6	Lúcio	BRA	8/5/78	12		
13	Maicon	BRA	26/7/81	13		1
23	Marco Materazzi		19/8/73	1	(3)	
25	Walter Samuel	ARG	23/3/78	13		1
39	Davide Santon		2/1/91		(1)	
4	Javier Zanetti	ARG	10/8/73	13		
Midfielders						
19	Esteban Cambiasso	ARG	18/8/80	11	(1)	1
30	Mancini	BRA	1/8/80	1		
17	McDonald Mariga	KEN	4/4/87		(3)	
11	Sulley Muntari	GHA	27/8/84	2	(7)	
7	Ricardo Quaresma	POR	26/9/83		(2)	
10	Wesley Sneijder	NED	9/6/84	11		3
5	Dejan Stanković	SRB	11/9/78	8	(4)	2
8	Thiago Motta	BRA	28/8/82	7	(1)	
14	Patrick Vieira	FRA	23/6/76		(2)	
Forwards						
45	Mario Balotelli		12/8/90	2	(6)	1
9	Samuel Eto'o	CMR	10/3/81	13		2
22	Diego Milito	ARG	12/6/79	11		6
27	Goran Pandev	MKD	27/7/83	5	(1)	
18	David Suazo	HON	5/11/79		(1)	

JUVENTUS

UEFA CHAMPIONS LEAGUE

Group A
Match 1 - FC Girondins de Bordeaux (FRA)
H 1-1 Iaquinta (63)
Buffon, Cáceres, Felipe Melo, Cannavaro (Zebina 66), Grosso, Marchisio, Iaquinta, Amauri, Giovinco (Camoranesi 73), Tiago (Poulsen 81), Legrottaglie. Coach: Ciro Ferrara (ITA)
Yellow Card(s): Iaquinta 63, Giovinco 68
Match 2 - FC Bayern München (GER)
A 0-0
Buffon, Chiellini, Felipe Melo, Grosso, Marchisio, Iaquinta, Camoranesi (Tiago 90), Trezeguet (Amauri 74), Grygera, Diego (Poulsen 60), Legrottaglie. Coach: Ciro Ferrara (ITA)
Yellow Card(s): Trezeguet 8, Camoranesi 37, Marchisio 57

Italy

Match 3 - Maccabi Haifa FC (ISR)
H 1-0 *Chiellini (47)*
Buffon, Chiellini, Felipe Melo (Poulsen 62), Cannavaro, Grosso, Zebina (Cáceres 35), Camoranesi, Trezeguet (Amauri 81), Giovinco, Sissoko, Diego. Coach: Ciro Ferrara (ITA)
Match 4 - Maccabi Haifa FC (ISR)
A 1-0 *Camoranesi (45+2)*
Buffon, Cáceres, Chiellini, Felipe Melo, Grosso, Amauri (Trezeguet 84), Camoranesi, Poulsen, Diego, Tiago (De Ceglie 60), Legrottaglie. Coach: Ciro Ferrara (ITA)
Yellow Card(s): Felipe Melo 36
Match 5 - FC Girondins de Bordeaux (FRA)
A 0-2
Buffon, Cáceres, Chiellini, Felipe Melo, Grosso, Del Piero (Immobile 68), Amauri (Giovinco 77), Camoranesi, Sissoko (Marchisio 89), Diego, Legrottaglie. Coach: Ciro Ferrara (ITA)
Yellow Card(s): Camoranesi 33, Felipe Melo 45, Legrottaglie 51, Cáceres 58
Match 6 - FC Bayern München (GER)
H 1-4 *Trezeguet (19)*
Buffon, Cáceres, Felipe Melo (Giovinco 81), Cannavaro, Grosso, Marchisio, Del Piero (Poulsen 46), Camoranesi, Trezeguet, Diego (Amauri 65), Legrottaglie. Coach: Ciro Ferrara (ITA)

No	Player	Nat	DoB	Aps	(s)	Gls
Goalkeeper						
1	Gianluigi Buffon		28/1/78	6		
Defenders						
5	Fabio Cannavaro		13/9/73	3		
3	Giorgio Chiellini		14/8/84	4		1
6	Fabio Grosso		28/11/77	6		
21	Zdeněk Grygera	CZE	14/5/80	1		
33	Nicola Legrottaglie		20/10/76	5		
2	Martín Cáceres	URU	7/4/87	4	(1)	
15	Jonathan Zebina	FRA	19/7/78	1	(1)	
Midfielders						
16	Mauro Camoranesi		4/10/76	5	(1)	1
29	Paolo De Ceglie		17/9/86		(1)	
28	Diego	BRA	28/2/85	5		
4	Felipe Melo	BRA	26/6/83	6		
8	Claudio Marchisio		19/1/86	3	(1)	
18	Christian Poulsen	DEN	28/2/80	1	(4)	
22	Mohamed Sissoko	MLI	22/1/85	2		
30	Tiago	POR	2/5/81	2	(1)	
Forwards						
11	Amauri	BRA	3/6/80	3	(3)	
10	Alessandro Del Piero		9/11/74	2		
20	Sebastian Giovinco		26/1/87	2	(2)	
9	Vincenzo Iaquinta		21/11/79	2		1
40	Ciro Immobile		20/2/90		(1)	
17	David Trezeguet	FRA	15/10/77	3	(1)	1

UEFA EUROPA LEAGUE

Round of 32 - AFC Ajax (NED)
A 2-1 *Amauri (32, 58)*
Buffon, Chiellini, Felipe Melo, Marchisio, Del Piero, Amauri (Salihamidžić 71), Zebina (Grygera 46), Sissoko, Diego (Trezeguet 80), De Ceglie, Legrottaglie. Coach: Alberto Zaccheroni (ITA)
Red Card(s): Salihamidžić 90+2
Yellow Card(s): Legrottaglie 29, Marchisio 42, Diego 51
H 0-0
Manninger, Chiellini, Felipe Melo, Marchisio, Del Piero (Candreva 87), Amauri (Trezeguet 15), Grygera, Sissoko, Diego (Camoranesi 71), De Ceglie, Legrottaglie. Coach: Alberto Zaccheroni (ITA)
Yellow Card(s): Felipe Melo 62

Round of 16 - Fulham FC (ENG)
H 3-1 *Legrottaglie (9), Zebina (25), Salihamidžić (45+3)*
Manninger, Cannavaro, Grosso, Salihamidžić (Camoranesi 46), Marchisio, Zebina, Trezeguet (Iaquinta 62), Poulsen (Sissoko 76), Candreva, Diego, Legrottaglie. Coach: Alberto Zaccheroni (ITA)
Yellow Card(s): Legrottaglie 67

A 1-4 *Trezeguet (2)*
Chimenti, Felipe Melo, Cannavaro, Grosso (Del Piero 85), Salihamidžić, Zebina, Camoranesi (De Ceglie 51), Trezeguet, Sissoko, Candreva (Grygera 28), Diego. Coach: Alberto Zaccheroni (ITA)
Red Card(s): Cannavaro 26, Zebina 90+1
Yellow Card(s): Camoranesi 12, Diego 48, Felipe Melo 90+2

AC MILAN

UEFA CHAMPIONS LEAGUE

Group C
Match 1 - Olympique de Marseille (FRA)
A 2-1 *Inzaghi (28, 74)*
Storari, Pato, Inzaghi (Huntelaar 87), Seedorf (Abate 90+3), Nesta, Zambrotta, Flamini, Pirlo, Ambrosini (Gattuso 58), Thiago Silva, Oddo. Coach: Leonardo (BRA)
Yellow Card(s): Zambrotta 57, Flamini 61, Storari 81
Match 2 - FC Zürich (SUI)
H 0-1
Storari, Kaladze, Pato, Inzaghi, Seedorf (Ronaldinho 46), Nesta (Onyewu 60), Flamini (Zambrotta 46), Jankulovski, Abate, Pirlo, Ambrosini. Coach: Leonardo (BRA)
Yellow Card(s): Kaladze 35, Abate 51, Jankulovski 80
Match 3 - Real Madrid CF (ESP)
A 3-2 *Pirlo (62), Pato (66, 88)*
Dida, Pato, Inzaghi (Borriello 60), Seedorf, Nesta, Zambrotta, Pirlo, Ambrosini, Thiago Silva, Oddo, Ronaldinho (Flamini 90+1). Coach: Leonardo (BRA)
Yellow Card(s): Zambrotta 71, Nesta 86, Ronaldinho 86
Match 4 - Real Madrid CF (ESP)
H 1-1 *Ronaldinho (35p)*
Dida, Pato, Seedorf, Nesta, Zambrotta, Pirlo, Borriello (Inzaghi 79), Ambrosini, Thiago Silva, Oddo, Ronaldinho. Coach: Leonardo (BRA)
Yellow Card(s): Pato 55
Match 5 - Olympique de Marseille (FRA)
H 1-1 *Borriello (10)*
Dida, Pato, Seedorf, Nesta, Zambrotta, Pirlo, Borriello, Ambrosini, Thiago Silva, Oddo (Abate 28), Ronaldinho. Coach: Leonardo (BRA)
Yellow Card(s): Ambrosini 34, Zambrotta 59
Match 6 - FC Zürich (SUI)
A 1-1 *Ronaldinho (64p)*
Dida, Pato, Seedorf, Nesta, Abate, Pirlo, Borriello (Inzaghi 84), Ambrosini (Flamini 55), Thiago Silva (Kaladze 20), Antonini, Ronaldinho. Coach: Leonardo (BRA)
Yellow Card(s): Abate 77, Seedorf 86

First Knockout Round - Manchester United FC (ENG)
H 2-3 *Ronaldinho (3), Seedorf (85)*
Dida, Pato, Huntelaar (Inzaghi 77), Nesta, Pirlo, Ambrosini, Bonera, Beckham (Seedorf 72), Thiago Silva, Antonini (Favalli 38), Ronaldinho. Coach: Leonardo (BRA)
Yellow Card(s): Ronaldinho 90+3
A 0-4
Abbiati, Huntelaar, Flamini, Jankulovski, Abate (Beckham 64), Pirlo, Borriello (Inzaghi 69), Ambrosini, Bonera (Seedorf 46), Thiago Silva, Ronaldinho. Coach: Leonardo (BRA)
Yellow Card(s): Ronaldinho 71, Flamini 85

No	Player	Nat	DoB	Aps	(s)	Gls
Goalkeepers						
12	Christian Abbiati		8/7/77	1		
1	Dida	BRA	7/10/73	5		
30	Marco Storari		7/1/77	2		

CHAMPIONS LEAGUE EUROPA LEAGUE

Italy

Defenders						
77	Luca Antonini		4/8/82	2		
25	Daniele Bonera		31/5/81	2		
19	Giuseppe Favalli		8/1/72		(1)	
18	Marek Jankulovski	CZE	9/5/77	2		
4	Kakha Kaladze	GEO	27/2/78	1	(1)	
13	Alessandro Nesta		19/3/76	7		
44	Massimo Oddo		14/6/76	4		
5	Oguchi Onyewu	USA	13/5/82		(1)	
33	Thiago Silva	BRA	22/9/84	7		
15	Gianluca Zambrotta		19/2/77	4	(1)	
Midfielders						
20	Ignazio Abate		12/11/86	3	(2)	
23	Massimo Ambrosini		29/5/77	8		
32	David Beckham	ENG	2/5/75	1	(1)	
16	Mathieu Flamini	FRA	7/3/84	3	(2)	
8	Gennaro Gattuso		9/1/78		(1)	
21	Andrea Pirlo		19/5/79	8		1
10	Clarence Seedorf	NED	1/4/76	6	(2)	1
Forwards						
22	Marco Borriello		18/6/82	4	(1)	1
11	Klaas Jan Huntelaar	NED	12/8/83	2	(1)	
9	Filippo Inzaghi		9/8/73	3	(4)	2
7	Pato	BRA	2/9/89	7		2
80	Ronaldinho	BRA	21/3/80	6	(1)	3

ACF FIORENTINA

UEFA CHAMPIONS LEAGUE

Play-Off Round - Sporting Clube de Portugal (POR)
A 2-2 *Vargas (6), Gilardino (79)*
Frey, Dainelli, Gamberini, Vargas, Mutu (Jović 64), Gilardino, Zanetti, Montolivo (Donadel 80), Gobbi, Comotto, Marchionni. Coach: Cesare Prandelli (ITA)
Yellow Card(s): Gamberini 12, Zanetti 15, Dainelli 29
H 1-1 *Jović (54)*
Frey, Dainelli, Gamberini, Vargas, Mutu (Jørgensen 72), Gilardino, Zanetti (Donadel 81), Montolivo, Gobbi (Jović 46), Comotto, Marchionni. Coach: Cesare Prandelli (ITA)
Yellow Card(s): Comotto 33, Zanetti 60, Jović 68

Group E
Match 1 - Olympique Lyonnais (FRA)
A 0-1
Frey, Dainelli, Donadel, Gamberini, Vargas, Mutu (Jović 58), Gilardino, Montolivo, Gobbi, Santana (Marchionni 72). Coach: Cesare Prandelli (ITA)
Red Card(s): Gilardino 45+1
Yellow Card(s): Donadel 40, Dainelli 45+1, Gamberini 50
Match 2 - Liverpool FC (ENG)
H 2-0 *Jović (28, 37)*
Frey, Dainelli, Gamberini, Vargas (Jørgensen 75), Jović, Mutu (Donadel 83), Zanetti, Montolivo, Gobbi, Comotto, Marchionni (De Silvestri 90). Coach: Cesare Prandelli (ITA)
Match 3 - Debreceni VSC (HUN)
A 4-3 *Mutu (6, 20), Gilardino (10), Santana (37)*
Frey, Dainelli (Natali 55), Donadel, Gamberini, Vargas, Mutu, Gilardino, Zanetti (Montolivo 46), Pasqual, Santana (Jørgensen 68), Comotto. Coach: Cesare Prandelli (ITA)
Yellow Card(s): Donadel 16
Match 4 - Debreceni VSC (HUN)
H 5-2 *Mutu (14), Dainelli (52), Montolivo (59), Marchionni (61), Gilardino (74)*
Avramov, Dainelli, Donadel, Gamberini (Krøldrup 33), Vargas (Santana 77), Mutu, Gilardino, Zanetti (Montolivo 46), Pasqual, Comotto, Marchionni. Coach: Cesare Prandelli (ITA)
Yellow Card(s): Dainelli 28

Match 5 - Olympique Lyonnais (FRA)
H 1-0 *Vargas (28p)*
Frey, Krøldrup, Dainelli, Vargas, Gilardino, Zanetti (Jørgensen 80), Montolivo, Gobbi, Santana (Donadel 70), De Silvestri (Comotto 86), Marchionni. Coach: Cesare Prandelli (ITA)
Yellow Card(s): Gilardino 32, Dainelli 35, Gobbi 70
Match 6 - Liverpool FC (ENG)
A 2-1 *Jørgensen (63), Gilardino (90+2)*
Frey, Krøldrup, Donadel, Gilardino, Natali, Montolivo, Jørgensen (Vargas 72), Pasqual, Santana (Marchionni 72), Comotto, De Silvestri (Castillo 83). Coach: Cesare Prandelli (ITA)
Yellow Card(s): Montolivo 66, Gilardino 90+3

First Knockout Round - FC Bayern München (GER)
A 1-2 *Krøldrup (50)*
Frey, Krøldrup, Vargas, Jović (Felipe 75), Gilardino, Natali (Pasqual 85), Montolivo (Donadel 84), Gobbi, Bolatti, De Silvestri, Marchionni. Coach: Cesare Prandelli (ITA)
Red Card(s): Gobbi 73
Yellow Card(s): De Silvestri 52, Dainelli 77, Vargas 90
H 3-2 *Vargas (28), Jović (54, 64)*
Frey, Krøldrup, Vargas (Keirrison 82), Jović, Gilardino, Natali, Zanetti, Felipe (Pasqual 79), Montolivo, De Silvestri, Marchionni. Coach: Cesare Prandelli (ITA)
Yellow Card(s): Krøldrup 39, Felipe 78

No	Player	Nat	DoB	Aps	(s)	Gls
Goalkeepers						
35	Vlada Avramov	SRB	5/4/79	1		
1	Sébastien Frey	FRA	18/3/80	7		
Defenders						
25	Gianluca Comotto		16/10/78	5	(1)	
3	Dario Dainelli		9/6/79	5		1
29	Lorenzo De Silvestri		23/5/88	4	(1)	
16	Felipe	BRA	31/7/84	1	(1)	
5	Alessandro Gamberini		27/8/81	4		
2	Per Krøldrup	DEN	31/7/79	4	(1)	1
14	Cesare Natali		5/4/79	3	(1)	
23	Manuel Pasqual		13/3/82	3	(2)	
6	Juan Vargas	PER	5/10/83	7	(1)	2
Midfielders						
28	Mario Bolatti	ARG	17/2/85	1		
4	Marco Donadel		21/4/83	4	(3)	
19	Massimo Gobbi		31/10/80	4		
20	Martin Jørgensen	DEN	6/10/75	1	(3)	1
32	Marco Marchionni		22/7/80	6	(1)	1
18	Riccardo Montolivo		18/1/85	6	(2)	1
24	Mario Santana	ARG	23/12/81	3	(2)	1
15	Cristiano Zanetti		14/4/77	5		
Forwards						
9	José Ignacio Castillo	ARG	4/11/75		(1)	
11	Alberto Gilardino		5/7/82	7		3
8	Stevan Jović	MNE	2/11/89	3	(1)	4
39	Keirrison	BRA	3/12/88		(1)	
10	Adrian Mutu	ROU	8/1/79	4		3

S.S. LAZIO

UEFA EUROPA LEAGUE

Play-Off Round - IF Elfsborg (SWE)
H 3-0 *Kolarov (24), Zárate (36), Mauri (69)*
Muslera, Lichtsteiner, Mauri (Diakité 86), Matuzalém (Dabo 58), Zárate (Eliseu 75), Kolarov, Siviglia, Cribari, Brocchi, Baronio, Cruz. Coach: Davide Ballardini (ITA)
Yellow Card(s): Siviglia 63

A 0-1
Muslera, Lichtsteiner, Matuzalém, Rocchi, Siviglia (Kolarov 23), Meghni, Cribari, Radu, Brocchi (Eliseu 52), Baronio, Cruz (Zárate 66). Coach: Davide Ballardini (ITA)
Red Card(s): Kolarov 82
Yellow Card(s): Meghni 16, Lichtsteiner 73, Matuzalém 82, Muslera 88

Group G
Match 1 - FC Salzburg (AUT)
H 1-2 *Foggia (59)*
Bizzarri, Lichtsteiner, Dabo (Foggia 46), Matuzalém, Zárate, Meghni (Eliseu 71), Cribari, Radu, Baronio, Cruz (Mauri 62), Diakité. Coach: Davide Ballardini (ITA)
Yellow Card(s): Cruz 61, Mauri 72, Zárate 89
Match 2 - PFC Levski Sofia (BUL)
A 4-0 *Matuzalém (22), Zárate (45+1), Meghni (67), Rocchi (74)*
Bizzarri, Lichtsteiner, Eliseu, Matuzalém (Mauri 74), Rocchi, Zárate (Foggia 62), Meghni, Cribari, Radu, Baronio (Dabo 55), Perpetuini. Coach: Davide Ballardini (ITA)
Yellow Card(s): Lichtsteiner 9
Match 3 - Villarreal CF (ESP)
H 2-1 *Zárate (20), Rocchi (90+2)*
Bizzarri, Lichtsteiner, Dabo (Diakité 46), Matuzalém, Zárate, Kolarov, Foggia (Rocchi 76), Cribari, Radu, Baronio, Cruz (Mauri 72). Coach: Davide Ballardini (ITA)
Red Card(s): Matuzalém 68
Yellow Card(s): Kolarov 39, Matuzalém 42, Lichtsteiner 45, Foggia 63, Matuzalém 68
Match 4 - Villarreal CF (ESP)
A 1-4 *Zárate (72)*
Bizzarri, Lichtsteiner, Mauri, Eliseu, Rocchi (Makinwa 64), Siviglia (Zárate 53), Foggia, Radu, Baronio, Diakité, Perpetuini (Kolarov 53). Coach: Davide Ballardini (ITA)
Red Card(s): Baronio 3
Yellow Card(s): Radu 7, Diakité 14, Foggia 29, Rocchi 29, Eliseu 63, Zárate 90+3
Match 5 - FC Salzburg (AUT)
A 1-2 *Foggia (57)*
Muslera, Lichtsteiner, Mauri, Eliseu (Meghni 46), Zárate, Kolarov, Foggia, Cribari, Radu (Rocchi 55), Brocchi (Makinwa 81), Diakité. Coach: Davide Ballardini (ITA)
Yellow Card(s): Muslera 32, Eliseu 34, Diakité 38, Brocchi 51, Mauri 68, Foggia 79, Zárate 81
Match 6 - PFC Levski Sofia (BUL)
H 0-1
Muslera, Scaloni, Eliseu, Makinwa, Cribari, Baronio, Sevieri (Cinque 61), Cavanda, Luciani, Diakité, Perpetuini. Coach: Davide Ballardini (ITA)

GENOA CFC

UEFA EUROPA LEAGUE

Play-Off Round - Odense BK (DEN)
H 3-1 *Sørensen (9og), Figueroa (48, 56)*
Amelia, Criscito, Palacio, Sculli, Mesto, Moretti, Biava, Bocchetti (Papastathopoulos 74), Jurić, Figueroa (Kharja 84), Milanetto (Zapater 66). Coach: Gian Piero Gasperini (ITA)
Yellow Card(s): Biava 17, Bocchetti 45
A 1-1 *Criscito (53)*
Amelia, Criscito, Rossi, Sculli, Papastathopoulos, Mesto (Palacio 78), Zapater, Moretti, Biava, Jurić (Milanetto 13), Figueroa (Kharja 83). Coach: Gian Piero Gasperini (ITA)
Yellow Card(s): Biava 45+3, Papastathopoulos 77

Group B
Match 1 - SK Slavia Praha (CZE)
H 2-0 *Zapater (4), Sculli (39)*
Amelia, Criscito, Kharja (Milanetto 81), Rossi, Palacio, Crespo (Figueroa 81), Sculli, Zapater (Mesto 85), Moretti, Bocchetti, Tomović. Coach: Gian Piero Gasperini (ITA)
Match 2 - Valencia CF (ESP)
A 2-3 *Floccari (43), Kharja (64p)*
Amelia, Kharja, Palladino, Papastathopoulos (Milanetto 74), Mesto, Zapater, Modesto (Esposito 58), Moretti, Bocchetti, Floccari, Tomović (Sculli 74). Coach: Gian Piero Gasperini (ITA)
Yellow Card(s): Moretti 72, Mesto 74, Esposito 81
Match 3 - LOSC Lille Métropole (FRA)
A 0-3
Amelia, Criscito (Sculli 44), Rossi, Palacio, Esposito (Palladino 46), Mesto, Moretti, Bocchetti, Jurić, Floccari (Figueroa 63), Milanetto. Coach: Gian Piero Gasperini (ITA)
Yellow Card(s): Bocchetti 27, Mesto 35, Esposito 40, Palacio 71
Match 4 - LOSC Lille Métropole (FRA)
H 3-2 *Palacio (14), Crespo (58), Sculli (90+3)*
Scarpi, Rossi, Palacio (Figueroa 84), Crespo (Sculli 81), Palladino, Zapater, Modesto (Papastathopoulos 79), Moretti, Biava, Bocchetti, Tomović. Coach: Gian Piero Gasperini (ITA)
Yellow Card(s): Moretti 36, Zapater 43, Sculli 90+3
Match 5 - SK Slavia Praha (CZE)
A 0-0
Scarpi, Crespo (Sculli 52), Papastathopoulos, Mesto (Palladino 78), Zapater, Modesto, Biava, Bocchetti, Jurić (Criscito 52), Floccari, Tomović. Coach: Gian Piero Gasperini (ITA)
Yellow Card(s): Palladino 87
Match 6 - Valencia CF (ESP)
H 1-2 *Crespo (51)*
Scarpi, Criscito, Rossi, Palacio, Crespo, Palladino (Sculli 30), Zapater (Floccari 82), Moretti, Biava, Bocchetti, Jurić. Coach: Gian Piero Gasperini (ITA)
Yellow Card(s): Jurić 25, Sculli 42, Bocchetti 85

AS ROMA

UEFA EUROPA LEAGUE

Third Qualifying Round - KAA Gent (BEL)
H 3-1 *Totti (55, 73p), Vučinić (85)*
Artur, Mexès, Pizarro, Totti, Taddei (Cerci 66), Motta (Cassetti 87), De Rossi, Riise, Guberti, Tonetto, Okaka Chuka (Vučinić 78). Coach: Luciano Spalletti (ITA)
Yellow Card(s): Totti 43
A 7-1 *Totti (35, 56, 64p), De Rossi (58, 74), Ménez (79), Okaka Chuka (86)*
Artur, Andreolli, Mexès, Pizarro, Totti (Okaka Chuka 65), Taddei (Cerci 70), Motta (Cassetti 66), De Rossi, Riise, Brighi, Ménez. Coach: Luciano Spalletti (ITA)
Yellow Card(s): Taddei 67, Mexès 83

Play-Off Round - MFK Košice (SVK)
A 3-3 *Totti (38p, 67), Ménez (52)*
Artur, Andreolli, Mexès, Pizarro, Totti, Motta (Cassetti 84), De Rossi, Riise, Cerci (Taddei 51), Brighi, Ménez (Guberti 74). Coach: Luciano Spalletti (ITA)
Yellow Card(s): De Rossi 27
H 7-1 *Totti (1, 6, 86), Guberti (8), Cerci (17), Ménez (18), Riise (70)*
Artur, Mexès, Pizarro, Totti, Motta, De Rossi (Faty 46), Riise, Guberti, Cerci, Cassetti (Juan 56), Ménez (Vučinić 56). Coach: Luciano Spalletti (ITA)

Group E
Match 1 - FC Basel 1893 (SUI)
A 0-2
Júlio Sérgio, Mexès, Pizarro, Totti, Taddei, Motta, De Rossi, Riise (Tonetto 64), Júlio Baptista (Vučinić 64), Burdisso, Ménez (Guberti 46). Coach: Claudio Ranieri (ITA)
Yellow Card(s): Ménez 45+1, Pizarro 78

CHAMPIONS EUROPA
LEAGUE LEAGUE

Italy/Kazakhstan

Match 2 - PFC CSKA Sofia (BUL)
H 2-0 *Okaka Chuka (19), Perrotta (23)*
Júlio Sérgio, Juan (Andreolli 71), Pizarro, Vučinić (Ménez 46), Motta, De Rossi, Riise, Perrotta, Cerci (Tonetto 74), Burdisso, Okaka Chuka. Coach: Claudio Ranieri (ITA)
Yellow Card(s): Ménez 90+2
Match 3 - Fulham FC (ENG)
A 1-1 *Andreolli (90+3)*
Doni, Andreolli, Mexès, Taddei (Vučinić 63), De Rossi, Riise, Guberti, Burdisso, Brighi (Pizarro 46), Okaka Chuka (Perrotta 46), Ménez. Coach: Claudio Ranieri (ITA)
Yellow Card(s): Vučinić 84
Match 4 - Fulham FC (ENG)
H 2-1 *Riise (69), Okaka Chuka (76)*
Doni (Júlio Sérgio 46), Cicinho (Taddei 46), Andreolli, Mexès, Pizarro, De Rossi, Riise, Júlio Baptista, Guberti (Ménez 66), Cassetti, Okaka Chuka. Coach: Claudio Ranieri (ITA)
Yellow Card(s): Andreolli 18, Okaka Chuka 38, De Rossi 72
Match 5 - FC Basel 1893 (SUI)
H 2-1 *Totti (32p), Vučinić (59)*
Júlio Sérgio, Cicinho (Juan 73), Mexès, Pizarro, Vučinić (Júlio Baptista 60), Totti, De Rossi, Riise, Perrotta, Burdisso, Ménez (Taddei 60). Coach: Claudio Ranieri (ITA)
Yellow Card(s): De Rossi 32, Ménez 44, Juan 90+2
Match 6 - PFC CSKA Sofia (BUL)
A 3-0 *Cerci (45+1, 52), Scardina (89)*
Lobonţ, Andreolli, Pizarro (Brighi 46), Motta, De Rossi, Riise, Júlio Baptista, Perrotta, Cerci (Pettinari 74), Burdisso, Okaka Chuka (Scardina 81). Coach: Claudio Ranieri (ITA)
Yellow Card(s): Okaka Chuka 29, Cerci 30

Round of 32 - Panathinaikos FC (GRE)
A 2-3 *Vučinić (29), Pizarro (81p)*
Júlio Sérgio (Doni 40), Juan, Pizarro, Vučinić (Ménez 70), Taddei (Cerci 75), Motta, De Rossi, Riise, Júlio Baptista, Burdisso, Brighi. Coach: Claudio Ranieri (ITA)
Yellow Card(s): Pizarro 25, Taddei 30, Cerci 90
H 2-3 *Riise (11), De Rossi (67)*
Doni, Juan, Mexès, Taddei, De Rossi, Riise, Perrotta, Cerci (Ménez 68), Brighi (Júlio Baptista 46), Cassetti. Coach: Claudio Ranieri (ITA)
Yellow Card(s): De Rossi 39, Taddei 54, Cassetti 84, Mexès 90+2

KAZAKHSTAN

FC AKTOBE

UEFA CHAMPIONS LEAGUE
Second Qualifying Round - FH Hafnarfjördur (ISL)
A 4-0 *Tleshev (48), Golovskoy (57, 85), Khairullin (70)*
Sidelnikov, Chichulin, Smakov, Khairullin (Khokhlov 86), Golovskoy, Tleshev, Kenzhesariev, Asanbaev, Logvinenko, Averchenko (Strukov 68), Lavrik (Mitrofanov 82). Coach: Vladimir Mukhanov (RUS)
Yellow Card(s): Tleshev 25, Lavrik 40, Strukov 85
H 2-0 *Smakov (20), Tleshev (67)*
Sidelnikov, Chichulin, Smakov, Khairullin, Golovskoy, Tleshev (Strukov 71), Kenzhesariev, Asanbaev, Logvinenko, Averchenko (Mitrofanov 84), Lavrik (Badlo 75). Coach: Vladimir Mukhanov (RUS)

Third Qualifying Round - Maccabi Haifa FC (ISR)
H 0-0
Sidelnikov, Chichulin, Smakov, Khairullin, Golovskoy (Badlo 85), Tleshev, Kenzhesariev, Asanbaev (Strukov 66), Logvinenko, Averchenko

(Mitrofanov 75), Lavrik. Coach: Vladimir Mukhanov (RUS)
A 3-4 *Averchenko (8), Chichulin (13), Khairullin (15)*
Sidelnikov, Chichulin, Smakov, Mitrofanov (Tleshev 60), Khairullin, Golovskoy (Asanbaev 67), Kenzhesariev, Logvinenko, Strukov (Badlo 72), Averchenko, Lavrik. Coach: Vladimir Mukhanov (RUS)
Yellow Card(s): Golovskoy 38, Chichulin 89

UEFA EUROPA LEAGUE
Play-Off Round - Werder Bremen (GER)
A 3-6 *Strukov (21, 32), Smakov (87)*
Sidelnikov, Badlo, Smakov, Khairullin, Golovskoy (Chichulin 72), Kenzhesariev, Asanbaev (Mitrofanov 70), Logvinenko, Strukov (Tleshev 84), Averchenko, Lavrik. Coach: Vladimir Mukhanov (RUS)
Yellow Card(s): Lavrik 80
H 0-2
Sidelnikov, Badlo, Smakov, Khairullin, Golovskoy, Tleshev (Chichulin 46), Kenzhesariev, Asanbaev (Khokhlov 90+1), Logvinenko, Strukov, Averchenko (Mitrofanov 75). Coach: Vladimir Mukhanov (RUS)
Red Card(s): Kenzhesariev 36
Yellow Card(s): Kenzhesariev 18, Badlo 32, Kenzhesariev 36, Smakov 90

FC TOBOL KOSTANAY

UEFA EUROPA LEAGUE
Second Qualifying Round - Galatasaray AŞ (TUR)
H 1-1 *Zhumaskaliyev (2)*
Petukhov, Chelyadinskiy, Nurgaliev (Baltiyev 83), Zhumaskaliyev (Dimitrov 83), Skorykh, Kharabara, Irismetov, Yakovlev, Mukanov, Golban, Bayramov (Alekperzade 89). Coach: Dmitriy Ogai (KAZ)
Yellow Card(s): Mukanov 14, Nurgaliev 38, Irismetov 90+1
A 0-2
Petukhov, Chelyadinskiy, Nurgaliev, Zhumaskaliyev (Aubakirov 87), Skorykh, Kharabara, Irismetov, Yakovlev, Mukanov, Golban (Baltiyev 70), Bayramov (Alekperzade 84). Coach: Dmitriy Ogai (KAZ)

FC IRTYSH PAVLODAR

UEFA EUROPA LEAGUE
First Qualifying Round – Szombathelyi Haladás (HUN)
A 0-1
Rikhard, Chernyshov, Kolomyts, Maltsev (Malinin 64), Yurin (Sobolev 70), Ivanov, Shomko, Parkhamchuk (Noskov 82), Andreev, Rimavičius, Nakov. Coach: Leonid Nazarenko (RUS)
Yellow Card(s): Andreev 32, Shomko 48, Parkhamchuk 72, Sobolev 85
H 2-1 *Yurin (20), Rajos (36og)*
Rikhard, Chernyshov, Kolomyts, Maltsev (Bayzhanov 70), Noskov (Shabalin 59), Yurin, Ivanov (Zarechni 78), Shomko, Andreev, Rimavičius, Nakov. Coach: Leonid Nazarenko (RUS)

FC OKZHETPES KOKSHETAU

UEFA EUROPA LEAGUE

First Qualifying Round - FC Zimbru Chisinau (MDA)
A 2-1 *Karakulov (72), Chonkayev (74)*
Gatybaldin, Cuznetsov, Pischulin, Karakulov (Mokrousov 78),
Dosmanbetov, Keker, Nurgaliyev (Dyak 68), Aliyev, Chonkayev (Maymakov 86), Bekmukhayev, Krutskevich. Coach: Eduard Glazunov (KAZ)
Red Card(s): Krutskevich 90
Yellow Card(s): Krutskevich 51, Krutskevich 90
H 0-2
Gatybaldin, Cuznetsov, Pischulin, Karakulov (Dyak 60), Mokrousov (Maymakov 70), Dosmanbetov, Keker, Nurgaliyev, Aliyev (Ledenev 79), Chonkayev, Bekmukhayev. Coach: Eduard Glazunov (KAZ)

LATVIA

FK VENTSPILS

UEFA CHAMPIONS LEAGUE

Second Qualifying Round - F91 Dudelange (LUX)
H 3-0 *Butriks (79), Kačanovs (86), Rimkus (87)*
Pavlovs, Astafjevs, Žigajevs (Lazdiņš 90), Kosmačovs, Cilinšek, Kačanovs, Rimkus (João Martins 90+1), Chirkin, Mihadjuks, Dedov (Butriks 65), Tigirlas. Coach: Roman Grigorchuk (UKR)
Yellow Card(s): Tigirlas 17
A 3-1 *Astafjevs (27), Butriks (57), Mihadjuks (67)*
Pavlovs, Astafjevs (Lazdiņš 71), Žigajevs (João Martins 63), Kosmačovs, Cilinšek, Kačanovs, Rimkus, Chirkin, Mihadjuks, Dedov (Shpakov 46), Butriks. Coach: Roman Grigorchuk (UKR)
Yellow Card(s): Astafjevs 69, Mihadjuks 84

Third Qualifying Round - FC BATE Borisov (BLR)
H 1-0 *Chirkin (64)*
Pavlovs, Astafjevs, Žigajevs, Kosmačovs (Lazdiņš 72), Cilinšek, Kačanovs, Rimkus, Chirkin (A. Višņakovs 83), Mihadjuks, Tigirlas, Butriks (Shpakov 77). Coach: Roman Grigorchuk (UKR)
Yellow Card(s): Kačanovs 15, Kosmačovs 42
A 1-2 *Tigirlas (14)*
Pavlovs, Astafjevs, Žigajevs (Dedov 86), Cilinšek, Kačanovs, Rimkus, A. Višņakovs (Lazdiņš 46), Shpakov (Rugins 63), Chirkin, Mihadjuks, Tigirlas. Coach: Roman Grigorchuk (UKR)
Red Card(s): Chirkin 90+5
Yellow Card(s): Rimkus 30, Chirkin 35, Cilinšek 60, Rugins 68, Chirkin 90+5

Play-Off Round - FC Zürich (SUI)
H 0-3
Pavlovs, Astafjevs, Žigajevs (Cilinšek 69), Kosmačovs, Kačanovs, Rimkus, A. Višņakovs (João Martins 74), Ndeki, Mihadjuks, Dedov (Butriks 60), Tigirlas. Coach: Nunzio Zavettieri (ITA)
Yellow Card(s): Astafjevs 26, Cilinšek 90+2
A 1-2 *Tigirlas (8)*
Chesnovskiy, Kosmačovs, Kačanovs, Rimkus, A. Višņakovs (Rugins 55), Savčenkovs, Chirkin, Ndeki, Tigirlas, Baimatov (Shpakov 62), Butriks (Dedov 72). Coach: Nunzio Zavettieri (ITA)
Yellow Card(s): Baimatov 51

UEFA EUROPA LEAGUE

Group D
Match 1 - Hertha BSC Berlin (GER)
A 1-1 *Gauračs (48)*
Chesnovski, Žigajevs (Ndeki 86), Kosmačovs, Laizans, A. Višņakovs (Butriks 72), Chirkin, Mihadjuks, Zamperini, Tigirlas (Astafjevs 75), Gauračs, Solovjovs. Coach: Nunzio Zavettieri (ITA)
Yellow Card(s): Žigajevs 41
Match 2 - sc Heerenveen (NED)
H 0-0
Koļinko, Žigajevs (Butriks 63), Kosmačovs, Chirkin, Ndeki, Mihadjuks, Zamperini, Tigirlas, Gauračs (E. Višņakovs 88), Hodel, Solovjovs (Rugins 90+1). Coach: Nunzio Zavettieri (ITA)
Match 3 - Sporting Clube de Portugal (POR)
H 1-2 *Laizans (64p)*
Koļinko, Kosmačovs (Žigajevs 60), Laizans (Astafjevs 83), Chirkin, Ndeki, Mihadjuks, Zamperini, Tigirlas, Gauračs, Hodel, Butriks (A. Višņakovs 53). Coach: Nunzio Zavettieri (ITA)
Match 4 - Sporting Clube de Portugal (POR)
A 1-1 *Zamperini (15)*
Koļinko, Žigajevs (João Martins 50), Kosmačovs, Laizans, Chirkin, Ndeki, Mihadjuks, Zamperini, Tigirlas (Rugins 90), Gauračs (Butriks 71), Hodel. Coach: Nunzio Zavettieri (ITA)
Yellow Card(s): Žigajevs 45
Match 5 - Hertha BSC Berlin (GER)
H 0-1
Koļinko, Kosmačovs, Laizans (Butriks 83), Chirkin, Ndeki, Zamperini, Tigirlas, E. Višņakovs (A. Višņakovs 56), Hodel (Gauračs 46), João Martins, Solovjovs. Coach: Nunzio Zavettieri (ITA)
Yellow Card(s): Laizans 35, Tigirlas 72, Zamperini 81, Gauračs 83
Match 6 - sc Heerenveen (NED)
A 0-5
Chesnovskiy, Žigajevs (Gauračs 59), Kosmačovs, Chirkin (Dedov 68), Ndeki, Zamperini, Tigirlas, Rugins (A. Višņakovs 55), E. Višņakovs, Butriks, Solovjovs. Coach: Nunzio Zavettieri (ITA)
Yellow Card(s): Rugins 30, Chirkin 40

SK LIEPĀJAS METALURGS

UEFA EUROPA LEAGUE

Second Qualifying Round - FC Dinamo Tbilisi (GEO)
H 2-1 *Karlsons (41), Kirhners (54)*
Spole, Kļava, Zirnis, Ivanovs, Rafaļskis, Tamošauskas, Surņins, Kirhners, Karlsons, Grebis (Prohorenkovs 83), Jemeļins (Kastner 61). Coach: Rüdiger Abramczik (GER)
Yellow Card(s): Jemeļins 10, Surņins 64, Kļava 71, Ivanovs 88
A 1-3 *Rafaļskis (49)*
Spole, Kļava (Prohorenkovs 70), Zirnis (Rakeļs 87), Ivanovs, Rafaļskis, Tamošauskas, Surņins, Kirhners, Karlsons, Grebis, Jemeļins (Kastner 72). Coach: Rüdiger Abramczik (GER)
Yellow Card(s): Zirnis 45, Surņins 88, Kirhners 90+3

SKONTO FC

UEFA EUROPA LEAGUE
Second Qualifying Round - Derry City FC (IRL)
H 1-1 *Kozlovs (17)*
Māliņš, Golubevs, Hščanovičs, Gamezardashvili, Kozlovs, Fertovs, Laizāns (Agafonov 77), Júnior, Semjonovs (Cauņa 62), Smirnovs, Tarasovs. Coach: Paul Ashworth (ENG)
Yellow Card(s): Fertovs 90, Nathan Junior 90+3
A 0-1
Māliņš, Golubevs, Hščanovičs, Gamezardashvili, Kozlovs, Fertovs (Mingazov 66), Blanks, Júnior (Agafonov 84), Smirnovs, Tarasovs (Laizāns 69), Cauņa. Coach: Paul Ashworth (ENG)
Yellow Card(s): Smirnovs 18, Golubevs 45

FC DINABURG

UEFA EUROPA LEAGUE
First Qualifying Round - JK Nõmme Kalju (EST)
H 2-1 *Afanasjevs (63), Guchashvili (90+4)*
Davidovs, Danilin, Kuleshov, Sokolovs, Guchashvili, Afanasjevs, Simonovs (Zizilevs 60), Gabovs, Logins, Krjauklis, Hong (Koļcovs 78). Coach: Tamaz Pertia (GEO)
Red Card(s): Koļcovs 90
Yellow Card(s): Koļcovs 84, Koļcovs 90, Logins 90+1
A 0-0
Davidovs, Danilin, Zizilevs, Kuleshov, Sokolovs, Guchashvili (Ri 79; Denisevičs 93), Afanasjevs, Gabovs, Logins, Krjauklis, Hong (Kortua 59). Coach: Tamaz Pertia (GEO)
Yellow Card(s): Sokolovs 5, Krjauklis 30, Guchashvili 65, Afanasjevs 87

Second Qualifying Round - Bnei Yehuda Tel-Aviv FC (ISR)
A 0-4
Davidovs, Danilin, Kuleshov, Sokolovs, Guchashvili (Ri 56), Afanasjevs, Simonovs (Kortua 72), Gabovs, Logins, Krjauklis, Hong (Zizilevs 46). Coach: Tamaz Pertia (GEO)
Yellow Card(s): Danilin 54, Simonovs 58
H 0-1
Fjodorovs, Danilin, Kuleshov, Sokolovs, Kokins (Kovaljovs 46), Afanasjevs, Simonovs (Denisevičs 59), Gabovs, Logins (Kortua 63), Krjauklis, Hong. Coach: Tamaz Pertia (GEO)

LIECHTENSTEIN

FC VADUZ

UEFA EUROPA LEAGUE
Second Qualifying Round - Falkirk FC (SCO)
A 0-1
Jehle, Steil, Stuckmann (Sutter 84), Bellon, Colocci (Rebronja 67), Proschwitz, Koitka (Franjic 79), Burgmeier, Cerrone, Stegmayer, Noll. Coach: Pierre Littbarski (GER)
Yellow Card(s): Stuckmann 39, Noll 49
H 2-0 *Noll (24), Burgmeier (105) (aet)*
Jehle, Steil, Stuckmann, Bellon, Colocci (Bader 119), Proschwitz (Franjic 110), Koitka (Kempe 73), Burgmeier, Cerrone, Stegmayer, Noll. Coach: Pierre Littbarski (GER)
Yellow Card(s): Burgmeier 27, Stuckmann 41, Kempe 107, Franjic 114

Third Qualifying Round - FC Slovan Liberec (CZE)
H 0-1
Jehle, Steil, Bellon, Colocci (Petrick 58), Proschwitz, Koitka (Kempe 49), Burgmeier (Ritzberger 85), Franjic, Cerrone, Stegmayer, Noll. Coach: Pierre Littbarski (GER)
Yellow Card(s): Koitka 5, Burgmeier 28, Stegmayer 64, Noll 70, Ritzberger 90+3
A 0-2
Jehle, Bader, Steil, Stuckmann, Bellon, Proschwitz, Franjic, Rebronja (Löppert 86), Cerrone, Stegmayer (Rechsteiner 79), Kempe (Colocci 46). Coach: Pierre Littbarski (GER)
Red Card(s): Steil 74
Yellow Card(s): Stegmayer 53, Cerrone 54, Stuckmann 64

LITHUANIA

FK EKRANAS

UEFA CHAMPIONS LEAGUE
Second Qualifying Round - Bakı FK (AZE)
H 2-2 *Bička (52p), Trakys (90+3)*
Černiauskas, Gleveckas, Ademolu, Trakys, Šidlauskas, Arlauskas, Varnas (Pogreban 79), Bička, Matović, Tomkevičius, Galkevičius (Aranđelović 46). Coach: Valdas Urbonas (LTU)
Yellow Card(s): Gleveckas 65, Pogreban 82, Matović 89
A 2-4 *Matović (81), Gleveckas (90+2)*
Černiauskas, Gleveckas, Ademolu, Trakys, Šidlauskas, Sasnauskas, Arlauskas, Varnas (Pogreban 71), Bička (Aranđelović 82), Matović, Tomkevičius. Coach: Valdas Urbonas (LTU)
Yellow Card(s): Gleveckas 24, Sasnauskas 54, Ademolu 81

FK SŪDUVA

UEFA EUROPA LEAGUE
Second Qualifying Round - Randers FC (DEN)
H 0-1
S. Klevinskas, Skinderis, Radavičius, Skroblas, G. Slavickas (Zagurskas 88), Kozyuberda, Lukšys, Leimonas, Urbšys, V. Slavickas, Gardzijauskas (Brokas 46). Coach: Gedas Jarmalavičius (LTU)
Yellow Card(s): Radavičius 14

1-1 *Lukšys (58)*
Klevinskas, Skinderis, Radavičius, Skroblas, G. Slavickas (Brokas 71), Kozyuberda, Lukšys, Leimonas, Urbšys (Krasnovskis 81), V. Slavickas, Kardijauskas (Zagurskas 76). Coach: Gedas Jarmalavičius (LTU)
Yellow Card(s): Kozyuberda 33, V. Slavickas 89

FBK KAUNAS

UEFA EUROPA LEAGUE

Second Qualifying Round - FK Sevojno (SRB)
0-0
Vertelis, Vaikasas, Vičius, Vertelis, Kočanauskas (Smaryginas 27), Razulis, Andriuškevičius (Antonovas 55), Miklinevičius (Paulius 82), Fridrikas, Tinikas, Pehlić. Coach: Saulius Vertelis (LTU)
Yellow Card(s): Vaikasas 29, Vičius 49
1-1 *Fridrikas (76)*
Vertelis, Vaikasas, Vičius, Račkus (Smaryginas 71), Vertelis, Razulis, Macežinskas 66), Andriuškevičius (Juozaitis 82), Miklinevičius, Fridrikas, Tinikas, Pehlić. Coach: Saulius Vertelis (LTU)
Yellow Card(s): Vičius 77, Vaikasas 90+1, Juozaitis 90+2

FK VĖTRA

UEFA EUROPA LEAGUE

First Qualifying Round - CS Grevenmacher (LUX)
3-0 *Grigaitis (10, 79), Mašitšev (25)*
Kalinčius, Borovskij, Kijanskas, Jankauskas, Moroz, Grigaitis, Mašitšev, Vasiliauskas 79), Paulauskas, Eliošius (Věževičius 57), Stanaitis, Grigalevičius (Kulbis 81). Coach: Virginijus Liubšys (LTU)
Yellow Card(s): Eliošius 54, Kulbis 87
3-0 *Huss (180g), Kijanskas (33), Věževičius (37)*
Kalinčius, Borovskij, Kijanskas, Jankauskas, Moroz (Kulbis 61), Grigaitis, Vasiliauskas 82), Mašitšev, Paulauskas, Věževičius (Eliošius 65), Stanaitis, ažanauskas. Coach: Virginijus Liubšys (LTU)

Second Qualifying Round - HJK Helsinki (FIN)
0-1
Kalinčius, Borovskij, Kijanskas, Jankauskas, Grigaitis (Moroz 25; Vasiliauskas 76), Mašitšev, Paulauskas, Věževičius, Stanaitis (Ngapounou 56), ažanauskas, Grigalevičius. Coach: Virginijus Liubšys (LTU)
Yellow Card(s): Věževičius 42, Moroz 45
3-1 *Grigalevičius (27), Jankauskas (30), Moroz (81)*
Kalinčius, Borovskij, Kijanskas, Jankauskas, Ngapounou, Mašitšev, aulauskas, Vasiliauskas (Stanaitis 88), Věževičius (Eliošius 57), ažanauskas, Grigalevičius (Moroz 69). Coach: Virginijus Liubšys (LTU)
Yellow Card(s): Mašitšev 39, Paulauskas 87

Third Qualifying Round - Fulham FC (ENG)
0-3
Kalinčius, Borovskij, Kijanskas, Jankauskas, Ngapounou (Stanaitis 46), Grigaitis (Eliošius 76), Mašitšev, Paulauskas, Vasiliauskas (Moroz 58), Věževičius, Ražanauskas. Coach: Virginijus Liubšys (LTU)
Yellow Card(s): Ngapounou 26, Jankauskas 56
0-3
Kalinčius, Borovskij, Kijanskas, Jankauskas, Grigaitis, Paulauskas, Vasiliauskas (Žulpa 80), Věževičius (Eliošius 46), Stanaitis, Ražanauskas, Grigalevičius (Moroz 57). Coach: Virginijus Liubšys (LTU)

LUXEMBOURG

F91 DUDELANGE

UEFA CHAMPIONS LEAGUE

Second Qualifying Round - FK Ventspils (LVA)
A 0-3
Joubert, Franceschi, Bendaha (Payal 88), Walter, Dan. Da Mota, Hareau, Françoise, Guthleber, Zeghdane, Amado, Diakite. Coach: Marc Grosjean (BEL)
Yellow Card(s): Amado 30, Walter 82, Zeghdane 85
H 1-3 *Dan. Da Mota (15)*
Joubert, Walter (Payal 62), Dan. Da Mota (Remy 72), Hareau, Molnar, Hammami, Françoise, Guthleber, Zeghdane, Amado (Bendaha 76), Diakite. Coach: Marc Grosjean (BEL)
Red Card(s): Françoise 69
Yellow Card(s): Guthleber 26, Françoise 62, Françoise 69

FC DIFFERDANGE 03

UEFA EUROPA LEAGUE

Second Qualifying Round - HNK Rijeka (CRO)
H 1-0 *Piskor (61)*
Weber, Siebenaler, May, Soraire, Mendes (Diop 76), Jänisch, Lebresne, Piskor (Pace 79), Kintziger, Wagner, Joachim (Kettenmeyer 61). Coach: Dan Theis (LUX)
Yellow Card(s): Piskor 5
A 0-3
Weber, Siebenaler, May (Diop 54), Soraire, Mendes (Piskor 46), Kettenmeyer (Pace 66), Jänisch, Lebresne, Kintziger, Wagner, Joachim. Coach: Dan Theis (LUX)
Yellow Card(s): Kettenmeyer 15, Kintziger 50, Piskor 55, Diop 89

CS GREVENMACHER

UEFA EUROPA LEAGUE

First Qualifying Round - FK Větra (LTU)
H 0-3
Pleimling, Marić, Schmitt (Thimmesch 72), Federspiel, Habte, Omerović (Müller 46), Huss, Hoffmann, Boussi (Tejerina 46), Heinz, Lorig. Coach: Claude Osweiler (LUX)
Yellow Card(s): Lorig 32, Hoffmann 35, Habte 78
A 0-3
Diederich, Marić, Schmitt (Omerović 77), Habte, Huss, Meriem (Stojadinović 64), Hoffmann, Tejerina, Heinz, Lorig, Müller (Boussi 72). Coach: Claude Osweiler (LUX)
Yellow Card(s): Huss 55, Schmitt 75

UN KÄERJÉNG 97

UEFA EUROPA LEAGUE

First Qualifying Round - Anorthosis Famagusta FC (CYP)
A 0-5
Castellani, Shoffner, Abeid (Leite 79), Ramedović, Spinelli, Rolandi, Zewe (Sagramola 82), Mukenge (Polidori 71), Boulahfari, Da Costa, Marinelli. Coach: Claude Heinz (LUX)
Yellow Card(s): Zewe 45, Rolandi 75
H 1-2 *Fiorani (90+3)*
Castellani, Shoffner, Abeid, Ramedović, Spinelli (Betorangal 84), Rolandi, Zewe, Mukenge, Marinelli, Boulahfari (Fiorani 71), Carl (Cleyton 78). Coach: Claude Heinz (LUX)

FORMER YUGOSLAV REPUBLIC OF
MACEDONIA

FK MAKEDONIJA GP SKOPJE

UEFA CHAMPIONS LEAGUE

Second Qualifying Round - FC BATE Borisov (BLR)
H 0-2
Pustinjaković, Ambourouet, Milevski, Mojsov, Ilievski, Lena, Brnjarcevski, Ivanovski (Felipe 46), Carlos Augusto (Felipe Montanari 61), Gligorovski (Kleckarovski 52), Mitrev. Coach: Ilco Gjorgioski (MKD)
Yellow Card(s): Lena 59, Mitrev 90
A 0-2
Pustinjaković, Ambourouet, Mojsov, Felipe Montanari, Ilievski, Kleckarovski (Felipe 63), Ivanovski (Gjurgjevic 82), Carlos Augusto, Kiende (Gligorovski 72), Mitrev, Kralevski. Coach: Ilco Gjorgioski (MKD)
Yellow Card(s): Mitrev 44, Kleckarovski 57, Kralevski 64

FK RABOTNICKI

UEFA EUROPA LEAGUE

Second Qualifying Round - Crusaders FC (NIR)
A 1-1 *B. Bozinovski (47)*
Naumovski, Ristov, Sekulovski, Bojović, B. Bozinovski, Muarem (Carlos Roberto 70), Savic, Todorovski, Gligorov, V. Bozinovski, Wandeir. Coach: Zoran Stratev (MKD)
Red Card(s): Naumovski 87
Yellow Card(s): Gligorov 48, B. Bozinovski 54, Wandeir 60
H 4-2 *B. Bozinovski (20), Zé Carlos (35,79), Petkovski (84)*
Bogatinov, Ristov, Sekulovski, Bojović, B. Bozinovski, Savic (Petkovski 67), Zé Carlos (Muarem 79), Todorovski, Gligorov, V. Bozinovski, Wandeir (Carlos Roberto 84). Coach: Zoran Stratev (MKD)
Red Card(s): Petkovski 90+1
Yellow Card(s): Bojović 47, V. Bozinovski 54, Bogatinov 59, Petkovski 84, Petkovski 90+1

Third Qualifying Round - Odense BK (DEN)
H 3-4 *Savic (21), Wandeir (24), Zé Carlos (74)*
Naumovski, Ristov, Sekulovski, Bojović, B. Bozinovski (Carlos Roberto 69), Savic, Zé Carlos, Todorovski, Gligorov, V. Bozinovski (Dimovski 84), Wandeir (Márcio 51). Coach: Zoran Stratev (MKD)
Yellow Card(s): Sekulovski 41, Wandeir 48, Todorovski 61, Gligorov 75
A 0-3
Naumovski, Ristov (Rodic 69), Sekulovski, Bojović, Dimovski, B. Bozinovski, Muarem (Márcio 80), Savic (Fábio 88), Zé Carlos, Todorovski, V. Bozinovski. Coach: Zoran Stratev (MKD)
Yellow Card(s): Naumovski 5

FK MILANO

UEFA EUROPA LEAGUE

Second Qualifying Round - NK Slaven Koprivnica (CRO)
H 0-4
Markovski, Cecelia, Aliji (Arijeton 46), F. Shabani, Aziri, Lazarev (Beluli 66), Limani, F. Trajkovski, Erdogan (Stojanović 46), Bogatinov, Alimi. Coach: Erkan Jusuf (MKD)
A 2-8 *Stojanović (59), Alimi (75)*
Danić, Puzović, Cecelia, B. Shabani, Limani, Bajlozov, F. Trajkovski (F. Shabani 46), Erdogan, Arijeton (Stojanović 46; Beluli 75), Bogatinov, Alimi. Coach: Erkan Jusuf (MKD)
Yellow Card(s): F. Shabani 71

FK RENOVA

UEFA EUROPA LEAGUE

First Qualifying Round - FC Dinamo Minsk (BLR)
A 1-2 *Ibraimi (41)*
Kovačević, Memedi, Despotovski, Emini, Ibraimi (Ademi 88), Ali (Ignjatovski 90+3), Nuhiu, Ismaili (Gafuri 63), Statovci, Angelovski, Stojanov. Coach: Vlatko Kostov (MKD)
Yellow Card(s): Kovačević 71, Gafuri 76, Ali 79
H 1-1 *Ibraimi (12)*
Kovačević, Memedi, Despotovski, Emini, Ibraimi, Ali, Nuhiu, Ismaili (Gafuri 81), Statovci, Angelovski (Gasi 56; Ademi 87), Stojanov. Coach: Vlatko Kostov (MKD)
Yellow Card(s): Ali 23, Statovci 37, Stojanov 38, Despotovski 48

CHAMPIONS LEAGUE   EUROPA LEAGUE

MALTA

HIBERNIANS FC

UEFA CHAMPIONS LEAGUE

First Qualifying Round - FK Mogren (MNE)
A 0-2
Muscat, J. Caruana, Herrera, Pulis, Xuereb, Callejas (Pearson 62), Cohen, Cvetić, Mintoff (Grech 62), B. Camilleri, R. Camilleri. Coach: Mark Miller (ENG)
Yellow Card(s): Cohen 44, Mintoff 45+3, Callejas 56
H 0-4
Muscat, J. Caruana, Herrera, Pulis, Xuereb, Pearson (Galabov 34), Cohen, Cvetić, Mintoff, B. Camilleri (E. Cauchi 72), R. Camilleri (Grech 65). Coach: Mark Miller (ENG)
Yellow Card(s): R. Camilleri 49, Galabov 73

SLIEMA WANDERERS FC

UEFA EUROPA LEAGUE

Second Qualifying Round - Maccabi Netanya FC (ISR)
H 0-0
Agius, Muscat (Mintoff 58), Azzopardi, Mifsud, Fenech, Scerri, Mifsud Triganza (Gatt Baldacchino 74), Woods, Dronca, I. Ciantar, Failla (Bartolo 90). Coach: Stephen Azzopardi (MLT)
Red Card(s): Mifsud 59
A 0-3
Agius, Muscat (Bartolo 74), Azzopardi, Fenech, Scerri, Mifsud Triganza, Gatt Baldacchino, Woods, Dronca, I. Ciantar (Turner 85), Failla (Mintoff 79). Coach: Stephen Azzopardi (MLT)
Yellow Card(s): Azzopardi 38, Scerri 72, Agius 90+3

VALLETTA FC

UEFA EUROPA LEAGUE

First Qualifying Round - Keflavík (ISL)
H 3-0 Falzon (25), Priso (49), Den Ouden (72)
Hogg, G. Agius, Briffa, Bezzina, Scicluna, Pace (E. Agius 77), Falzon (Zammit 82), Den Ouden (Giglio 90+4), Priso, Dimech, Cruyff. Coach: Ton Caanen (NED)
A 2-2 Falzon (41), Priso (82)
Hogg, G. Agius, Briffa, Bezzina, Scicluna (Borg 90), Pace, Falzon (Grioli 77), Den Ouden, Priso (Grima 90), Dimech, Cruyff. Coach: Ton Caanen (NED)
Yellow Card(s): Dimech 33, Priso 80

Second Qualifying Round - Saint Patrick's Athletic FC (IRL)
A 1-1 G. Agius (65)
Hogg, G. Agius, Briffa, Bezzina, Scicluna, Pace, Falzon (Zammit 77), Den Ouden (E. Agius 90), Priso, Dimech, Cruyff. Coach: Ton Caanen (NED)
Yellow Card(s): G. Agius 28, Priso 41, Scicluna 78, Hogg 90+2
H 0-1
Hogg, Grioli (E. Agius 70), G. Agius, Briffa, Bezzina, Scicluna, Pace, Falzon (Zammit 81), Den Ouden, Dimech, Cruyff. Coach: Ton Caanen (NED)
Yellow Card(s): Zammit 89

BIRKIRKARA FC

UEFA EUROPA LEAGUE

First Qualifying Round - NK Slaven Koprivnica (CRO)
A 0-1
O. Borg, Paris, P. Borg, Fenech, Cilia (Muscat 86), Tabone, Comvalius, Bajada, Zerafa, Buhagiar (Sciberras 74), Scicluna. Coach: Paul Zammit (MLT)
Yellow Card(s): Scicluna 47, Cilia 50, P. Borg 69, O. Borg 70, Zerafa 76, Bajada 80, Paris 90+4
H 0-0
Borg, Paris (Zammit 89), Borg, Fenech (Muscat 85), Cilia, Tabone, Comvalius, Bajada, Zerafa, Buhagiar (Sciberras 76), Scicluna. Coach: Paul Zammit (MLT)
Yellow Card(s): Borg 87, Sciberras 90+1

MOLDOVA

FC SHERIFF

UEFA CHAMPIONS LEAGUE

Second Qualifying Round - FC Inter Turku (FIN)
A 1-0 Suvorov (42p)
Namasco, Tarkhnishvili, Corneencov, Suvorov (Da Costa 90+1), Balima, Karpovich, Rouamba, Diedhiou (Mandricenco 72), Rodríguez, Bulat (Verbetchi 74), Nádson. Coach: Leonid Kuchuk (BLR)
Yellow Card(s): Karpovich 68
H 1-0 Suvorov (69p)
Namasco, Tarkhnishvili, Corneencov, Suvorov, Balima, Karpovich, Rouamba, Diedhiou, Rodríguez, Bulat (Verbetchi 69), Nádson. Coach: Leonid Kuchuk (BLR)
Yellow Card(s): Bulat 52, Suvorov 74

Third Qualifying Round - SK Slavia Praha (CZE)
H 0-0
Namasco, Tarkhnishvili, Corneencov, Suvorov (Jymmy 66), Balima, Rouamba, Arbănaş, Diedhiou (Volkov 90+2), Rodríguez, Mamah, Nádson. Coach: Leonid Kuchuk (BLR)
Yellow Card(s): Jymmy 78
A 1-1 Nádson (90+3)
Namasco, Tarkhnishvili, Corneencov, Suvorov (Volkov 81), Balima, Rouamba, Arbănaş, Diedhiou (Jymmy 59), Rodríguez, Mamah (Bulat 72), Nádson. Coach: Leonid Kuchuk (BLR)
Yellow Card(s): Mamah 44, Balima 71

Play-Off Round - Olympiacos FC (GRE)
H 0-2
Namasco, Tarkhnishvili, Corneencov, Erokhin, Suvorov (Volkov 55), Balima, Karpovich, Rouamba, Arbănaş (Bulat 70), Diedhiou (Branković 81), Rodríguez. Coach: Leonid Kuchuk (BLR)
Yellow Card(s): Tarkhnishvili 87
A 0-1
Namasco, Da Costa, Tarkhnishvili, Corneencov, Erokhin (Kuchuk 65), Balima (Volkov 80), Rouamba, Arbănaş, Tsynya, Diedhiou (Suvorov 58), Rodríguez. Coach: Leonid Kuchuk (BLR)
Yellow Card(s): Rodríguez 83, Kuchuk 90

UEFA EUROPA LEAGUE

Group H
Match 1 - FC Steaua Bucureşti (ROU)
A 0-0
Namasco, Da Costa, Volkov (Diedhiou 64) (Suvorov 90), Verbetchi (Bulat 81), Tarkhnishvili, Erokhin, Balima, Rouamba, Tsynya, Rodríguez, Kuchuk. Coach: Leonid Kuchuk (BLR)
Yellow Card(s): Kuchuk 22, Rodríguez 32, Tsynya 81
Match 2 - Fenerbahçe SK (TUR)
H 0-1
Namasco, Tarkhnishvili, Erokhin, Suvorov (Volkov 78), Balima, Karpovich, Rouamba, Arbănaş (Corneencov 65), Tsynya (Diedhiou 70), Rodríguez, Kuchuk. Coach: Leonid Kuchuk (BLR)
Yellow Card(s): Erokhin 45, Karpovich 78
Match 3 - FC Twente (NED)
H 2-0 Balima (41), Jymmy (90+4)
Namasco, Tarkhnishvili, Corneencov, Erokhin (Arbănaş 90+3), Balima, Rouamba, Diedhiou (Volkov 66), Rodríguez, Mamah, Nádson, Kuchuk (Jymmy 78). Coach: Leonid Kuchuk (BLR)
Yellow Card(s): Jymmy 90+2, Erokhin 90+3
Match 4 - FC Twente (NED)
A 1-2 Tioté (68og)
Namasco, Tarkhnishvili, Corneencov, Erokhin, Suvorov (Volkov 72), Balima (Diedhiou 65) (Arbănaş 90), Rouamba, Rodríguez, Mamah, Nádson, Kuchuk. Coach: Leonid Kuchuk (BLR)
Yellow Card(s): Kuchuk 80
Match 5 - FC Steaua Bucureşti (ROU)
H 1-1 Diedhiou (83)
Namasco, Da Costa, Volkov (Diedhiou 77), Tarkhnishvili, Jymmy (Kuchuk 88), Erokhin, Balima, Rouamba, Arbănaş, Rodríguez, Mamah. Coach: Leonid Kuchuk (BLR)
Yellow Card(s): Rouamba 79, Rodríguez 80
Match 6 - Fenerbahçe SK (TUR)
A 0-1
Namasco, Da Costa, Volkov (Rodríguez 55), Tarkhnishvili, Corneencov (Erokhin 66), Jymmy (Kuchuk 68), Balima, Rouamba, Arbănaş, Mamah, Branković. Coach: Leonid Kuchuk (BLR)
Yellow Card(s): Jymmy 42, Tarkhnishvili 72, Rouamba 90+1

FC DACIA CHISINAU

UEFA EUROPA LEAGUE

Second Qualifying Round - MŠK Žilina (SVK)
A 0-2
Matiughin, Mekang, Orbu, Demchenko (Buza 85), Bulat, Negrescu, Zgura (Popovici 84), Grosev, Caraulan, Sackey, Trinitatskiy. Coach: Roman Pylypchuk (UKR)
Yellow Card(s): Grosev 23
H 0-1
Mosneaga, Mekang, Onica, Orbu, Demchenko (Zgura 61), Bulat, Negrescu (Buza 65), Grosev (Popovici 46), Caraulan, Sackey, Trinitatskiy. Coach: Roman Pylypchuk (UKR)
Red Card(s): Trinitatskiy 86
Yellow Card(s): Orbu 6, Sackey 64, Trinitatskiy 65, Bulat 76, Trinitatskiy 86

FC ISKRA-STAL

UEFA EUROPA LEAGUE

Second Qualifying Round - PFC Cherno More Varna (BUL)
A 0-1
Gaiduchevici, Stinga, Osipenco (Romaniuc 85), Hauşi, Rudac, Tofan, Manaliu (Kilikevych 62), Feshchenko (Ochinca 86), Jurca, Stahiv, Burcovsh
Coach: Vlad Goian (MDA)
Yellow Card(s): Stahiv 19, Burcovshi 49
H 0-3
Gaiduchevici, Stinga, Osipenco, Hauşi, Rudac (Romaniuc 62), Tofan, Kilikevych (Manaliu 57), Feshchenko (Ochinca 53), Jurca, Stahiv, Burcovsh
Coach: Vlad Goian (MDA)
Yellow Card(s): Stahiv 28, Osipenco 68

FC ZIMBRU CHISINAU

UEFA EUROPA LEAGUE

First Qualifying Round - FC Okzhetpes Kokshetau (KAZ)
H 1-2 Demerji (48)
Calancea, Ternavschi, I. Andronic, Demerji (Catan 80), A. Antoniuc, Erhan, Hvorosteanov, Sofroni, Clonin, Sidorenco (O. Andronic 46), Onila (G. Andronic 59). Coach: Ivan Tabanov (MDA)
Yellow Card(s): A. Antoniuc 83
A 2-0 O. Andronic (16), G. Andronic (19)
Chirinciuc, Ternavschi, I. Andronic, Demerji, A. Antoniuc (Sidorenco 67), O
Andronic, Erhan, Hvorosteanov, Sofroni, Clonin, G. Andronic (Onila 75).
Coach: Ivan Tabanov (MDA)
Yellow Card(s): Erhan 9, O. Andronic 73

Second Qualifying Round - FC Paços de Ferreira (POR)
H 0-0
Chirinciuc, Ternavschi, I. Andronic, Demerji (Catan 87), A. Antoniuc (Sidorenco 71), O. Andronic, Erhan, Hvorosteanov, Sofroni, Clonin, G. Andronic (Onila 76). Coach: Ivan Tabanov (MDA)
Yellow Card(s): Clonin 90
A 0-1
Chirinciuc, Ternavschi, I. Andronic, Demerji, A. Antoniuc, O. Andronic, Erhan, Hvorosteanov, Sofroni (Sidorenco 61), Clonin (Secrieru 90), G. Andronic (Onila 72). Coach: Ivan Tabanov (MDA)
Yellow Card(s): Erhan 30, O. Andronic 43

CHAMPIONS LEAGUE EUROPA LEAGUE

MONTENEGRO

FK MOGREN

UEFA CHAMPIONS LEAGUE

First Qualifying Round - Hibernians FC (MLT)
H 2-0 Ćetković (32), Grbić (88)
...anjušević, Pejović, Belada, Simović, Grbić, D. Božović, G. Jovanović, Rakič ...iodorović 70), Milić (B. Božović 63), Stojaković (Kalezić 85), Ćetković.
...oach: Dejan Vukićević (SRB)
...ellow Card(s): Belada 16, Simović 64
A 4-0 Milić (41), Grbić (45, 79), Ćetković (51)
...anjušević, Pejović, Belada, Simović, Grbić, D. Božović, G. Jovanović, Rakič ...alezić 46), Milić (Tiodorović 46), Stojaković (B. Božović 69), Ćetković.
...oach: Dejan Vukićević (SRB)

...econd Qualifying Round - FC København (DEN)
...0-6
...anjušević, Pejović, Simović (Novaković 36), Janičić, Grbić, D. Božović, ...iodorović (Rakić 78), G. Jovanović, Milić, B. Božović (Kalezić 61), Ćetković.
...oach: Dejan Vukićević (SRB)
...ellow Card(s): Grbić 19, D. Božović 54
...0-6
...anjušević, Pejović, Simović (Kapisoda 46), Janičić, Grbić, D. Božović, ...iodorović, G. Jovanović (B. Božović 66), Milić (Sekulić 56), Stojaković, ...etković. Coach: Dejan Vukićević (SRB)
...ellow Card(s): D. Božović 82

OFK PETROVAC

UEFA EUROPA LEAGUE

...econd Qualifying Round - Anorthosis Famagusta FC (CYP)
...1-2 Lakić (84)
...raić, Radulović, Graovac, Mikijelj, Lakić, Obradović, Lopičić, Radović ...aičević 46), Dragićević, Divanović (Boljević 89), Đurašković (Rotković 65).
...oach: Aleksandar Miljenović (MNE)
...ellow Card(s): Lopičić 26, Rotković 79, Graovac 89
...3-1 Dragićević (15), Rotković (76, 102) (aet)
...raić, Radulović (Raičević 73), Graovac, Mikijelj, Lakić, Obradović, Lopičić, ...adović, Dragićević (Boljević 113), Divanović , Djurašković (Rotković 62).
...oach: Aleksandar Miljenović (MNE)
...ellow Card(s): Mikijelj 21, Graovac 45+4, Obradović 64, Divanović 68, ...otković 121

...hird Qualifying Round - SK Sturm Graz (AUT)
...1-2 Divanović (13)
...raić, Radulović, Mikijelj (Skenderi 90+2), Lakić, Obradović, Lopičić, ...adović, Dragićević (Boljević 73), Divanović , Djurašković, Raičević. Coach: ...leksandar Miljenović (MNE)
...ellow Card(s): Radović 64
...0-5
...raić, Radulović (Rotković 59), Graovac, Mikijelj, Lakić, Obradović, Lopičić, ...adović (Raičević 55), Dragićević (Boljević 90+2), Divanović , Đurašković.
...oach: Aleksandar Miljenović (MNE)
...ellow Card(s): Obradović 68

FK BUDUĆNOST PODGORICA

UEFA EUROPA LEAGUE

First Qualifying Round - KSP Polonia Warszawa (POL)
H 0-2
Vujadinović, N. Vukčević (Nikolić 88), Perišić, Delić (Ajković 48), Brnović, P. Vukčević, Bošković (Vešović 62), Kudemor, Vuković, Bećiraj, Višnjić. Coach: Mihailo Ivanović (SRB)
Yellow Card(s): Višnjić 23, Vuković 59, N. Vukčević 61, Vesović 69
A 1-0 Vuković (51)
Vujadinović, N. Vukčević (Đurišić 87), Ajković, Brnović, P. Vukčević, Milan Radulović, Bošković (Delić 74), Kudemor, Vuković, Bećiraj (Vešović 81), Višnjić. Coach: Mihailo Ivanovic (SRB)
Red Card(s): Kudemor 66
Yellow Card(s): Brnović 29, P. Vukčević 40, Kudemor 59, Kudemor 66, Milan Radulović 82

FK SUTJESKA

UEFA EUROPA LEAGUE

First Qualifying Round - FC MTZ-RIPO Minsk (BLR)
H 1-1 Međedović (48)
Giljen, Delić, Bulatović, Đikanović, Adrović, Međedović, Bulajić (Marković 89), N. Dževerdanović (M. Dževerdanović 85), Todorović (Banda 83), Dubljević, Zvicer. Coach: Nikola Rakojević (SRB)
Yellow Card(s): Bulajić 56, Bulatović 63, Adrović 67
A 1-2 Todorović (63) (aet)
Giljen, Delić, Bulatović, Đikanović, Adrović, Međedović, Bulajić (M. Dževerdanović 117), N. Dževerdanović (Vuković 75), Todorović (Banda 111), Dubljević, Zvicer. Coach: Nikola Rakojević (SRB)
Yellow Card(s): Đikanović 43, Delić 122

NETHERLANDS

AZ ALKMAAR

UEFA CHAMPIONS LEAGUE

Group H
Match 1 - Olympiacos FC (GRE)
A 0-1
Romero, Jaliens, Moreno, Pocognoli, Mendes da Silva (Luijckx 71), Schaars, El Hamdaoui (Pellè 77), Martens (Lens 80), Dembélé, Moisander, Holman. Coach: Ronald Koeman (NED)
Yellow Card(s): Mendes da Silva 37, Schaars 84

Match 2 - R. Standard de Liège (BEL)
H 1-1 El Hamdaoui (48)
Romero, Jaliens, Moreno, Pocognoli (Klavan 82), Mendes da Silva, Schaars, El Hamdaoui, Martens (Poulsen 71), Dembélé, Holman, Swerts. Coach: Ronald Koeman (NED)
Yellow Card(s): El Hamdaoui 18
Match 3 - Arsenal FC (ENG)
H 1-1 Mendes da Silva (90+3)
Romero, Jaliens, Moreno, Mendes da Silva, Schaars, El Hamdaoui, Martens (Lens 69), Poulsen, Dembélé, Moisander (Wernbloom 84), Holman (Pellè 73). Coach: Ronald Koeman (NED)
Yellow Card(s): Lens 89
Match 4 - Arsenal FC (ENG)
A 1-4 Lens (82)
Romero, Jaliens, Moreno, Mendes da Silva (Wernbloom 70), Schaars, Martens, Poulsen (Pocognoli 64), Dembélé (Lens 58), Moisander, Holman, Pellè. Coach: Ronald Koeman (NED)
Yellow Card(s): Moisander 66
Match 5 - Olympiacos FC (GRE)
H 0-0
Romero, Moreno, Pocognoli, Mendes da Silva, Lens, Schaars (Martens 89), Wernbloom, Dembélé (Pellè 68), Moisander, Holman (Ari 78), Swerts. Coach: Ronald Koeman (NED)
Yellow Card(s): Pocognoli 65, Moreno 90+1
Match 6 - R. Standard de Liège (BEL)
A 1-1 Lens (42)
Romero, Jaliens, Moreno, Pocognoli, Mendes da Silva, Lens (Wernbloom 72), Schaars, El Hamdaoui (Pellè 90+1), Dembélé, Moisander, Holman (Martens 46). Coach: Martin Haar (NED)
Yellow Card(s): Pocognoli 43, Jaliens 87

No	Player	Nat	DoB	Aps	(s)	Gls
Goalkeeper						
22	Sergio Romero	ARG	22/2/87	6		
Defenders						
2	Kew Jaliens		15/9/78	5		
25	Niklas Moisander	FIN	29/9/85	5		
4	Héctor Moreno	MEX	17/1/88	6		
5	Sébastien Pocognoli	BEL	1/8/87	4	(1)	
Midfielders						
27	Brett Holman	AUS	27/3/84	6		
14	Ragnar Klavan	EST	30/10/85		(1)	
19	Kees Luijckx		11/2/86		(1)	
11	Maarten Martens	BEL	2/7/84	4	(2)	
6	David Mendes da Silva		4/8/82	6		1
15	Simon Poulsen	DEN	7/10/84	2	(1)	
8	Stijn Schaars		11/1/84	6		
28	Gill Swerts	BEL	23/9/82	2		
16	Pontus Wernbloom	SWE	25/6/86	1	(3)	
Forwards						
9	Ari	BRA	11/12/85		(1)	
18	Moussa Dembélé	BEL	16/7/87	6		
10	Mounir El Hamdaoui	MAR	14/7/84	4		1
7	Jeremain Lens		24/11/87	2	(3)	2
29	Graziano Pellè	ITA	15/7/85	1	(4)	

FC TWENTE

UEFA CHAMPIONS LEAGUE

Third Qualifying Round - Sporting Clube de Portugal (POR)
A 0-0
Boschker, Wisgerhof, Rajković, Brama, Stam, Nkufo, Perez (Mihaylov 27), Stoch (Tioté 74), Douglas, Ruiz (Rukavytsya 61), Janssen. Coach: Steve McClaren (ENG)
Red Card(s): Boschker 24
Yellow Card(s): Nkufo 87

H 1-1 Douglas (2)
Mihaylov, Wisgerhof, Rajković, Brama, Stam, Nkufo, Perez (Tioté 59), Stoch (Rukavytsya 79), Douglas, Ruiz (Vujičević 90+1), Janssen. Coach: Steve McClaren (ENG)

UEFA EUROPA LEAGUE

Play-Off Round - Qarabağ FK (AZE)
H 3-1 Ruiz (38, 66), Douglas (81)
Boschker, Wisgerhof, Brama, Stam, Nkufo, Perez (Vujičević 73), Heubach, Stoch (Tioté 87), Douglas, Ruiz, Janssen. Coach: Steve McClaren (ENG)
A 0-0
Boschker, Kuiper, Wisgerhof, Brama, Stam, Nkufo, Stoch (Vujičević 62), Tioté, Douglas, Ruiz (Akram 90+2), Janssen (Perez 46). Coach: Steve McClaren (ENG)
Yellow Card(s): Stam 35

Group H
Match 1 - Fenerbahçe SK (TUR)
A 2-1 Nkufo (75, 80)
Boschker, Kuiper, Wisgerhof, Brama, Stam, Nkufo, Perez (Akram 90+1), Stoch (Vujičević 70), Tioté (Janssen 40), Douglas, Ruiz. Coach: Steve McClaren (ENG)
Yellow Card(s): Tioté 29, Douglas 71, Kuiper 83
Match 2 - FC Steaua București (ROU)
H 0-0
Boschker, Kuiper, Wisgerhof, Brama, Stam, Nkufo, Perez (Parker 62), Stoch (Vujičević 85), Tioté (Janssen 62), Douglas, Ruiz. Coach: Steve McClaren (ENG)
Yellow Card(s): Stoch 54
Match 3 - FC Sheriff (MDA)
A 0-2
Boschker, Carney, Wisgerhof, Brama (Tioté 58), Stam, Nkufo, Perez (Parker 57), Stoch (De Jong 78), Douglas, Ruiz, Janssen. Coach: Steve McClaren (ENG)
Yellow Card(s): Douglas 89
Match 4 - FC Sheriff (MDA)
H 2-1 Stoch (7, 89)
Boschker, Carney, Wisgerhof, Brama (Akram 57), Stam, Nkufo, Perez (Tioté 46), Stoch, Douglas, Ruiz, Janssen (Parker 79). Coach: Steve McClaren (ENG)
Yellow Card(s): Nkufo 86, Stoch 90
Match 5 - Fenerbahçe SK (TUR)
H 0-1
Boschker, Carney, Wisgerhof, Brama (De Jong 82), Stam, Nkufo, Perez, Stoch, Tioté (Parker 82), Douglas, Ruiz. Coach: Steve McClaren (ENG)
Yellow Card(s): Douglas 69, Perez 88, Boschker 90+1
Match 6 - FC Steaua București (ROU)
A 1-1 Stam (35)
Boschker, Kuiper, Wisgerhof, Brama, Stam, Nkufo, Perez, Heubach (Rajković 74), Stoch, Tioté (Akram 76), Ruiz (Parker 62). Coach: Steve McClaren (ENG)

Round of 32 - Werder Bremen (GER)
H 1-0 Janssen (39)
Boschker, Wisgerhof, Brama, Stam, Nkufo, Perez (Tioté 70), Stoch (De Jong 86), Douglas, Ruiz, Janssen, Tiendalli. Coach: Steve McClaren (ENG)
Yellow Card(s): Janssen 89
A 1-4 De Jong (33)
Boschker, Wisgerhof, Brama, Stam (Kuiper 62), Perez (Tioté 62), Parker, Douglas, De Jong, Ruiz (Vujičević 74), Janssen, Tiendalli. Coach: Steve McClaren (ENG)
Yellow Card(s): Douglas 17, Stam 44, Brama 76

SC HEERENVEEN

UEFA EUROPA LEAGUE

Play-Off Round - PAOK FC (GRE)
H 1-1 *Paulo Henrique (45)*
Hejsal, Breuer, Dingsdag, Beerens (Paulo Henrique 20), Papadopulos (Sibon 82), Švec, Grindheim, Popov, Kalou, Losada (Janmaat 90+3), Koning. Coach: Trond Sollied (NOR)
Yellow Card(s): Paulo Henrique 50, Koning 56
A 0-0
Hejsal, Bak Nielsen, Breuer, Dingsdag, Papadopulos, Paulo Henrique (Angelsten 90+3), Grindheim, Popov, Losada, Sibon (Kalou 79), Koning.
Coach: Trond Sollied (NOR)
Yellow Card(s): Breuer 25, Dingsdag 56, Losada 61, Djurić 89, Bak Nielsen 90+5

Group D
Match 1 - Sporting Clube de Portugal (POR)
H 2-3 *Sibon (12), Dingsdag (77)*
Hejsal, Bak Nielsen, Breuer, Dingsdag, Beerens, Paulo Henrique, Švec, Grindheim (Assaidi 73), Popov (Elm 52), Losada, Sibon (Papadopulos 86). Coach: Jan de Jonge (NED)
Yellow Card(s): Assaidi 79
Match 2 - FK Ventspils (LVA)
A 0-0
Vandenbussche, Breuer, Dingsdag, Elm, Paulo Henrique (Assaidi 70), Švec, Beerens 54), Grindheim, Janmaat, Popov, Losada, Sibon (Papadopulos 83). Coach: Jan de Jonge (NED)
Yellow Card(s): Dingsdag 90+3
Match 3 - Hertha BSC Berlin (GER)
A 1-0 *Losada (36)*
Vandenbussche, Bak Nielsen, Breuer, Dingsdag, Elm, Papadopulos, Grindheim (Janmaat 73), Popov, Assaidi (Paulo Henrique 83), Losada, Sibon (Švec 66). Coach: Jan de Jonge (NED)
Red Card(s): Janmaat 76
Yellow Card(s): Bak Nielsen 55, Assaidi 65
Match 4 - Hertha BSC Berlin (GER)
H 2-3 *Papadopulos (4, 36)*
Vandenbussche, Bak Nielsen, Breuer, Elm, Beerens (Väyrynen 66), Papadopulos, Švec, Popov, Assaidi, Losada (Paulo Henrique 82), Koning. Coach: Jan de Jonge (NED)
Match 5 - Sporting Clube de Portugal (POR)
A 1-1 *Assaidi (47)*
Vandenbussche, Bak Nielsen, Breuer, Dingsdag, Elm, Beerens, Papadopulos (Paulo Henrique 80), Grindheim (Väyrynen 72), Popov, Assaidi (Elyounoussi 85), Losada. Coach: Jan de Jonge (NED)
Yellow Card(s): Popov 67, Elm 78
Match 6 - FK Ventspils (LVA)
H 5-0 *Väyrynen (55), Elm (58), Sibon (77, 78), Janmaat (88)*
Vandenbussche, Bak Nielsen, Breuer, Elm, Beerens, Väyrynen (Losada 81), Papadopulos (Sibon 66), Grindheim, Janmaat, Popov, Assaidi (Elyounoussi 83). Coach: Jan de Jonge (NED)
Yellow Card(s): Papadopulos 41

AFC AJAX

UEFA EUROPA LEAGUE

Play-Off Round - ŠK Slovan Bratislava (SVK)
H 5-0 *Suárez (43, 65, 79, 84), Donald (90+2)*
Stekelenburg, Van der Wiel, Vertonghen, Atouba (Emanuelson 72), Sulejmani (Zeegelaar 69), Suárez, Alderweireld, Enoh, De Jong (Donald 80), Rommedahl, De Zeeuw. Coach: Martin Jol (NED)
A 2-1 *De Jong (30), Bakircioglü (84)*
Stekelenburg, Van der Wiel, Vertonghen, Atouba (De Zeeuw 75), Emanuelson, Suárez (Sulejmani 46), Wielaert, Cvitanich, Enoh (Bakircioglü 89), De Jong, Donald. Coach: Martin Jol (NED)
Yellow Card(s): Enoh 58, Vertonghen 77

Group A
Match 1 - FC Timişoara (ROU)
H 0-0
Stekelenburg, Van der Wiel, Vertonghen, Emanuelson, Aissati (Rommedahl 83), Suárez, Alderweireld, Cvitanich (Pantelić 58), De Jong, Bakircioglü (Sulejmani 71), De Zeeuw. Coach: Martin Jol (NED)
Yellow Card(s): Vertonghen 27
Match 2 - RSC Anderlecht (BEL)
A 1-1 *Rommedahl (72)*
Stekelenburg, Van der Wiel, Vertonghen, Emanuelson, Pantelić, Aissati (Sulejmani 88), Suárez, Alderweireld, Enoh, Bakircioglü (Rommedahl 58), De Zeeuw. Coach: Martin Jol (NED)
Yellow Card(s): De Zeeuw 82, Vertonghen 90+2
Match 3 - NK Dinamo Zagreb (CRO)
H 2-1 *Suárez (3p), Rommedahl (81)*
Stekelenburg, Van der Wiel, Vertonghen, Emanuelson, Pantelić (Rommedahl 74), Suárez (Gabri 79), Alderweireld, Suárez (Cvitanich 90+1), Alderweireld, Enoh, Anita, De Zeeuw. Coach: Martin Jol (NED)
Yellow Card(s): Anita 9, Emanuelson 14, Sulejmani 69
Match 4 - NK Dinamo Zagreb (CRO)
A 2-0 *Pantelić (13), De Zeeuw (45+1)*
Stekelenburg, Van der Wiel, Vertonghen (Oleguer 80), Emanuelson (Sulejmani 77), Pantelić, Suárez, Alderweireld, Enoh (Donald 65), De Jong, Anita, De Zeeuw. Coach: Martin Jol (NED)
Yellow Card(s): De Jong 89
Match 5 - FC Timişoara (ROU)
A 2-1 *Suárez (8), Pantelić (46)*
Stekelenburg, Van der Wiel (Silva 64), Vertonghen, Emanuelson (Oleguer 46), Pantelić, Suárez, Alderweireld, Enoh, Anita (Sulejmani 59), Donald, De Zeeuw. Coach: Martin Jol (NED)
Yellow Card(s): Suárez 66
Match 6 - RSC Anderlecht (BEL)
H 1-3 *Emanuelson (77)*
Stekelenburg, Van der Wiel, Oleguer, Vertonghen, Emanuelson, Pantelić, Sulejmani, Enoh (Rommedahl 59), De Jong (De Zeeuw 83), Anita, Donald (Suárez 79). Coach: Martin Jol (NED)
Yellow Card(s): Suárez 90+3

Round of 32 - Juventus (ITA)
H 1-2 *Sulejmani (17)*
Stekelenburg, Van der Wiel, Oleguer, Vertonghen, Emanuelson (Eriksen 73), Sulejmani (Rommedahl 80), Suárez, Alderweireld, Enoh (Suk 86), De Jong, De Zeeuw. Coach: Martin Jol (NED)
Yellow Card(s): Sulejmani 30, Oleguer 45+1, Suárez 61
A 0-0
Stekelenburg, Van der Wiel, Oleguer, Vertonghen, Pantelić (Emanuelson 75), Sulejmani (Suk 64), Alderweireld, Enoh (Rommedahl 77), De Jong, De Zeeuw, Eriksen. Coach: Martin Jol (NED)
Yellow Card(s): Enoh 70, Eriksen 85, Vertonghen 86

PSV EINDHOVEN

UEFA EUROPA LEAGUE

Third Qualifying Round - PFC Cherno More Varna (BUL)
H 1-0 *Marcellis (90+3)*
Isaksson, Kromkamp, Salcido, Simons (Bakkal 79), Toivonen (Lazović 62), Amrabat (Koevermans 62), Engelaar, Afellay, Dzsudzsák, Ooijer, Marcellis. Coach: Fred Rutten (NED)
Yellow Card(s): Ooijer 34, Salcido 79
A 1-0 *Coulibaly (30og)*
Isaksson, Salcido (Pieters 89), Simons, Toivonen, Amrabat (Bakkal 46), Engelaar (Wuytens 46), Afellay, Dzsudzsák, Ooijer, Marcellis, Manolev. Coach: Fred Rutten (NED)
Red Card(s): Manolev 44
Yellow Card(s): Manolev 24, Isaksson 42, Manolev 44, Ooijer 45+1

Netherlands/Northern Ireland

Play-Off Round - Bnei Yehuda Tel-Aviv FC (ISR)
A 1-0 *Afellay (23)*
Isaksson, Kromkamp (Ojo 78), Salcido, Rodríguez, Simons, Toivonen (Koevermans 69), Lazović (Amrabat 61), Pieters, Afellay, Dzsudzsák, Bakkal. Coach: Fred Rutten (NED)
H 1-0 *Simons (25p)*
Isaksson, Rodríguez, Simons (Engelaar 46), Lazović, Koevermans (Reis 77; Toivonen 83), Pieters, Afellay, Dzsudzsák, Ooijer, Manolev, Bakkal. Coach: Fred Rutten (NED)

Group K
Match 1 - AC Sparta Praha (CZE)
A 2-2 *Reis (80, 90+1p)*
Isaksson, Simons, Toivonen, Lazović, Koevermans (Reis 64), Pieters, Engelaar, Dzsudzsák, Ooijer, Manolev, Bakkal. Coach: Fred Rutten (NED)
Yellow Card(s): Ooijer 42, Manolev 45+1
Match 2 - CFR 1907 Cluj (ROU)
H 1-0 *Bakkal (9)*
Isaksson, Rodríguez, Toivonen (Simons 80), Lazović, Pieters (Salcido 57), Engelaar, Afellay, Dzsudzsák, Ooijer, Manolev, Bakkal (Reis 69). Coach: Fred Rutten (NED)
Match 3 - FC København (DEN)
H 1-0 *Reis (72)*
Isaksson, Rodríguez, Simons (Salcido 61), Lazović, Pieters (Vuković 86), Engelaar, Afellay, Dzsudzsák, Manolev, Bakkal (Toivonen 61), Reis. Coach: Fred Rutten (NED)
Yellow Card(s): Simons 53, Manolev 80
Match 4 - FC København (DEN)
A 1-1 *Dzsudzsák (72)*
Isaksson, Salcido, Rodríguez, Lazović, Pieters (Vuković 80), Engelaar (Toivonen 71), Afellay, Dzsudzsák, Manolev, Bakkal, Reis (Simons 90+1). Coach: Fred Rutten (NED)
Yellow Card(s): Pieters 39, Engelaar 47
Match 5 - AC Sparta Praha (CZE)
H 1-0 *Reis (90+1)*
Isaksson, Salcido, Rodríguez (Ooijer 78), Lazović, Pieters, Engelaar, Afellay, Dzsudzsák, Manolev, Bakkal (Toivonen 62), Reis. Coach: Fred Rutten (NED)
Yellow Card(s): Manolev 72
Match 6 - CFR 1907 Cluj (ROU)
A 2-0 *Lazović (19p), Amrabat (68)*
Isaksson, Rodríguez, Simons, Toivonen, Lazović (Vuković 80), Pieters, Afellay (Koevermans 66), Dzsudzsák (Amrabat 46), Ooijer, Marcellis, Bakkal. Coach: Fred Rutten (NED)
Yellow Card(s): Afellay 30, Toivonen 43, Rodríguez 53

Round of 32 - Hamburger SV (GER)
A 0-1
Isaksson, Salcido, Rodríguez, Toivonen (Koevermans 78), Lazović, Pieters (Vuković 81), Engelaar, Afellay, Dzsudzsák, Manolev (Ooijer 46), Bakkal. Coach: Fred Rutten (NED)
Yellow Card(s): Manolev 25, Pieters 59, Afellay 89
H 3-2 *Toivonen (2), Dzsudzsák (43), Koevermans (90)*
Isaksson, Salcido, Rodríguez (Koevermans 79), Toivonen, Lazović, Pieters, Engelaar, Afellay, Dzsudzsák, Manolev (Ooijer 25), Bakkal (Labyad 71). Coach: Fred Rutten (NED)
Red Card(s): Dzsudzsák 57
Yellow Card(s): Toivonen 25, Engelaar 47, Dzsudzsák 57, Salcido 78, Ooijer 83, Koevermans 86

NAC BREDA

UEFA EUROPA LEAGUE

Second Qualifying Round - FC Gandzasar Kapan (ARM)
H 6-0 *Kwakman (24), De Graaf (55, 70), Amoah (57, 61), Lurling (68)*
Ten Rouwelaar, Kwakman, Gilissen (Van der Leegte 67), De Graaf (Cairo 71), Lurling, Kolkka, Fehér, Amoah, Gorter (Snoyl 83), Schilder, Loran. Coach: Robert Maaskant (NED)

A 2-0 *Lurling (14), De Graaf (34)*
Ten Rouwelaar, Zwaanswijk, Gilissen (Kwakman 53), De Graaf (Reuser 72), Lurling, Fehér, Amoah, Cairo, Schilder, Loran, Snoyl (Gorter 61). Coach: Robert Maaskant (NED)
Yellow Card(s): Kwakman 54, Reuser 86

Third Qualifying Round - KSP Polonia Warszawa (POL)
A 1-0 *Kwakman (39)*
Ten Rouwelaar, Zwaanswijk, Kwakman, Gilissen, De Graaf (Gorter 57), Lurling (Cairo 83), Kolkka, Fehér, Amoah, Schilder, Loran. Coach: Robert Maaskant (NED)
Yellow Card(s): Lurling 23, De Graaf 23, Gorter 67
H 3-1 *Amoah (25), Lurling (45), Kwakman (81)*
Ten Rouwelaar, Zwaanswijk, Kwakman (Snoyl 87), Gilissen, De Graaf (Gorter 61), Lurling, Kolkka, Fehér, Amoah, Schilder, Loran. Coach: Robert Maaskant (NED)

Play-Off Round - Villarreal CF (ESP)
H 1-3 *Loran (17)*
Ten Rouwelaar, Zwaanswijk, Kwakman, Gilissen (Penders 87), De Graaf (Idabdelhay 76), Lurling, Kolkka, Fehér, Reuser (Gorter 66), Schilder, Loran. Coach: Robert Maaskant (NED)
Yellow Card(s): Fehér 13, Gilissen 32, Lurling 45+1
A 1-6 *De Graaf (80)*
Ten Rouwelaar, Zwaanswijk, Kwakman, De Graaf (Benomar 84), Kolkka, Reuser, Gorter, Cairo (Amoah 66), Schilder, Snoyl, Hofstede (Penders 77). Coach: Robert Maaskant (NED)
Yellow Card(s): Gorter 36, Snoyl 89

NORTHERN IRELAND

GLENTORAN FC

UEFA CHAMPIONS LEAGUE

Second Qualifying Round - Maccabi Haifa FC (ISR)
A 0-6
Morris, Nixon, Neill, Clarke (Fitzgerald 68), Leeman, Ward, Fordyce (Hall 79), Hamilton, Waterworth (Halliday 68), Jo. Taylor, Black. Coach: Alan McDonald (NIR)
Yellow Card(s): Clarke 21, Black 62
H 0-6
Morris, Neill, Clarke, Leeman (Nixon 32), McCabe, Ward, Fordyce, Hamilton, Waterworth (Halliday 67), Jo. Taylor, Black (Gardiner 61). Coach: Alan McDonald (NIR)

CRUSADERS FC

UEFA EUROPA LEAGUE

Second Qualifying Round - FK Rabotnicki (MKD)
H 1-1 *Rainey (90)*
Keenan, McKeown, McBride, Magowan, Coates, McCann, Doherty (Black 74), Dickson, Rainey, Donnelly, Morrow (Owens 63). Coach: Stephen Baxter (NIR)
Red Card(s): Coates 68
Yellow Card(s): Keenan 63

2-4 *Owens (69), Donnelly (90+3)*
enan, McKeown, McBride, Black (Caddell 67), Magowan, McCann,
oherty, Dickson, Donnelly, Morrow (Rainey 46), Magee (Owens 46).
ach: Stephen Baxter (NIR)
llow Card(s): Caddell 76, Rainey 81, McCann 88

LINFIELD FC

UEFA EUROPA LEAGUE

rst Qualifying Round - Randers FC (DEN)
0-4
ayney, Douglas, Lowry (Allen 62), Carville, Bailie, B. Burns (Curran 69),
Kane, Garrett, Ervin, Mulgrew, McAllister (McHugh 74). Coach: David
ffrey (NIR)
llow Card(s): McHugh 78
0-3
ayney, Douglas, Lowry, Carville (Allen 59), Bailie, B. Burns, O'Kane,
arrett, Ervin, Mulgrew (Gault 67), McAllister (Miskimmon 78). Coach:
avid Jeffrey (NIR)
llow Card(s): O'Kane 65

LISBURN DISTILLERY FC

UEFA EUROPA LEAGUE

rst Qualifying Round - FC Zestafoni (GEO)
1-5 *Whelan (88)*
urphy, McShane, S. Thompson, Simpson, Melaugh, Kilmartin, Whelan,
mour (Kingsberry 69), G. Thompson (Corey 55), Shaw (Browne 56),
allaghan. Coach: Jimmy Brown (NIR)
llow Card(s): S. Thompson 66
0-6
urphy, McShane, S. Thompson, Simpson, Melaugh, Kilmartin, Whelan,
mour (G. Thompson 73), Kingsberry (Shaw 46), Browne (Corey 46),
allaghan. Coach: Jimmy Brown (NIR)
llow Card(s): S. Thompson 63, Simpson 78

NORWAY

STABÆK FOTBALL

UEFA CHAMPIONS LEAGUE

econd Qualifying Round - KF Tirana (ALB)
1-1 *Kobayashi (34)*
nudsen, Segerström, Hauger, Keller, Kobayashi (Hoff 87), Skjønsberg,
rnerud, Olsen, Diskerud (Pálmason 80), Hedenstad, Berglund (Nannskog
). Coach: Jan Jönsson (SWE)
llow Card(s): Keller 87

H 4-0 *Segerström (15, 17), Berglund (44), Farnerud (55)*
Knudsen, Segerström, Hauger, Keller (Andersen Aase 76), Kobayashi
(Skjelvik 80), Nannskog, Skjønsberg, Farnerud, Olsen, Hedenstad,
Berglund (Hoff 67). Coach: Jan Jönsson (SWE)
Yellow Card(s): Segerström 50, Keller 74

Third Qualifying Round - FC København (DEN)
A 1-3 *Pálmason (58)*
Knudsen, Segerström, Hauger, Kobayashi (Diskerud 90), Nannskog
(Andersson 77), Pálmason, Skjønsberg, Farnerud, Rogne, Hedenstad,
Berglund (Hoff 70). Coach: Jan Jönsson (SWE)
H 0-0
Knudsen, Segerström, Hauger, Kobayashi (Diskerud 86), Nannskog,
Pálmason (Hoff 52), Skjønsberg (Andersson 80), Farnerud, Rogne,
Hedenstad, Berglund. Coach: Jan Jönsson (SWE)
Yellow Card(s): Farnerud 68

UEFA EUROPA LEAGUE

Play-Off Round - Valencia CF (ESP)
H 0-3
Knudsen, Segerström, Hauger, Kobayashi (Diskerud 69), Nannskog (Hoff
63), Pálmason, Skjønsberg, Farnerud, Rogne, Hedenstad, Berglund
(Andersen Aase 63). Coach: Jan Jönsson (SWE)
A 1-4 *Farnerud (36)*
Austbø, Høiland (Skjønsberg 74), Segerström, Hauger, Hoff (Stenvoll 78),
Kobayashi, Farnerud, Rogne, Diskerud, Hedenstad, Andersen Aase
(Berglund 69). Coach: Jan Jönsson (SWE)

VÅLERENGA FOTBALL

UEFA EUROPA LEAGUE

Third Qualifying Round - PAOK FC (GRE)
H 1-2 *Storbæk (42)*
Perkins, Hagen (Singh 59), Andresen, Storbæk, Sæternes, Fuenmayor,
Leigh (Fellah 46), Hæstad, Moh. Abdellaoue (Berre 75), Zajić, Nouri. Coach:
Tor Ole Skullerud (NOR)
Yellow Card(s): Zajić 44
A 1-0 *Berre (60)*
Perkins, Hagen (Singh 88), Andresen, Berre, Sæternes, Leigh (Fellah 78),
Hæstad, Moh. Abdellaoue, Zajić, Brix, Nouri. Coach: Tor Ole Skullerud (NOR)
Yellow Card(s): Hagen 29

FREDRIKSTAD FK

UEFA EUROPA LEAGUE

Third Qualifying Round - Lech Poznań (POL)
H 1-6 *Borges (48)*
Staw, Wehrman (Elvestad 62), Piiroja, Éverton, Kvisvik (Tegström 46),
Thomassen, Askar, Gashi, Borges, Ophaug, Barsom (Martinsen 46). Coach:
Tom Freddy Aune (NOR)
A 2-1 *Gashi (31), Piiroja (35)*
Staw, Wehrman, Piiroja, Adiyah (Trulsen 83), Thomassen, Elvestad, Askar,
Tegström (Jóhannsson 73), Gashi, Ophaug, Barsom. Coach: Tom Freddy
Aune (NOR)
Yellow Card(s): Gashi 49, Piiroja 56, Wehrman 62, Askar 65, Barsom 72

TROMSØ IL

UEFA EUROPA LEAGUE

Second Qualifying Round - FC Dinamo Minsk (BLR)
A 0-0
Sahlman, T. Reginiussen, Moldskred, Larsen, Rushfeldt, Yttergård Yttergård Jensen, Strand (Knudsen 65), Knarvik (Haugen 30), Lindpere (M. Reginiussen 86), Høgli, Sequeira. Coach: Per-Mathias Høgmo (NOR)
Yellow Card(s): Haugen 57
H 4-1 Knarvik (28, 90+1), Martynovich (76og), Moldskred (89)
Ramović, T. Reginiussen, Moldskred, Larsen, Rushfeldt (Koppinen 77), Yttergård Jensen, Strand (Haugen 87), Knarvik, Lindpere (Knudsen 80), Høgli, Sequeira. Coach: Per-Mathias Høgmo (NOR)
Yellow Card(s): T. Reginiussen 74

Third Qualifying Round - NK Slaven Koprivnica (CRO)
H 2-1 Moldskred (67), Rushfeldt (69)
Sahlman, T. Reginiussen, Moldskred, Larsen, Koppinen, Rushfeldt (Sequeira 75), Yttergård Jensen, Strand (Knudsen 87), Knarvik, Lindpere (Yndestad 89), Høgli. Coach: Per-Mathias Høgmo (NOR)
A 2-0 Rushfeldt (14, 82)
Ramović, T. Reginiussen, Moldskred (Sequeira 81), Larsen (Yndestad 72), Koppinen, Rushfeldt, Yttergård Jensen, Knarvik (Haugen 62), Knudsen, Lindpere, Høgli. Coach: Per-Mathias Høgmo (NOR)
Yellow Card(s): Larsen 59

Play-Off Round - Athletic Club (ESP)
A 2-3 Moldskred (42), Lindpere (78)
Ramović, T. Reginiussen, Moldskred (M. Reginiussen 89), Larsen, Koppinen, Rushfeldt, Yttergård Jensen, Knarvik, Knudsen (Strand 81), Lindpere (Haugen 90+3), Høgli. Coach: Per-Mathias Høgmo (NOR)
Yellow Card(s): Moldskred 16, Larsen 61
H 1-1 Rushfeldt (61)
Ramović, T. Reginiussen, Moldskred, Koppinen, Rushfeldt, Yttergård Jensen, Yndestad (Taboga 90), Knarvik (Isaksen 90+4), Knudsen (Strand 82), Lindpere, Høgli. Coach: Per-Mathias Høgmo (NOR)
Red Card(s): Ramović 90+3
Yellow Card(s): Moldskred 77

ROSENBORG BK

UEFA EUROPA LEAGUE

First Qualifying Round - NSÍ Runavík (FRO)
A 3-0 Zahora (21, 59), Lustig (89p)
Jarstein, Lustig, Annan (Tettey 71), Konan Ya, Stadsgaard (Miller 46), Iversen (Olsen 65), Skjelbred, Lago, Nordvik, Sellin, Zahora. Coach: Erik Hamrén (SWE)
Yellow Card(s): Lago 65, Nordvik 73
H 3-1 Iversen (39), Konan Ya (90+2p), Olsen (90+3)
Jarstein, Annan (Tettey 65), Strand, Olsen, Konan Ya, Iversen (Sellin 65), Skjelbred (Traoré 76), Lago, Nordvik, Miller, Zahora. Coach: Erik Hamrén (SWE)

Second Qualifying Round - Qarabağ FK (AZE)
H 0-0
Jarstein, Lustig, Dorsin, Annan (Strand 68), Olsen (Konan Ya 68), Tettey, Stadsgaard, Iversen, Skjelbred (Traoré 83), Lago, Prica. Coach: Erik Hamrén (SWE)
Yellow Card(s): Konan Ya 90+2, Stadsgaard 90+4

A 0-1
Jarstein, Lustig, Dorsin, Annan, Konan Ya (Olsen 46), Tettey (Miller 85), Stadsgaard, Iversen, Skjelbred (Zahora 74), Lago, Prica. Coach: Erik Hamrén (SWE)
Yellow Card(s): Annan 37, Stadsgaard 44, Lustig 72, Zahora 77, Prica 90+2

POLAND

WISŁA KRAKÓW

UEFA CHAMPIONS LEAGUE

Second Qualifying Round - FC Levadia Tallinn (EST)
H 1-1 Ćwielong (90+3)
Pawełek, Marcelo, Sobolewski, Pi. Brożek, Díaz, Jirsák (Cantoro 73), Kirm, Małecki, Łobodziński (Ćwielong 46), Jop, Pa. Brożek. Coach: Maciej Skorża (POL)
A 0-1
Pawełek, Marcelo, Głowacki, Sobolewski, Pi. Brożek, Díaz, Jirsák, Kirm, Małecki, Pa. Brożek (Łobodziński 73). Coach: Maciej Skorża (POL)
Yellow Card(s): Díaz 81, Pawełek 88

LECH POZNAŃ

UEFA EUROPA LEAGUE

Third Qualifying Round - Fredrikstad FK (NOR)
A 6-1 Wilk (10), Arboleda (22, 25), Lewandowski (51), Peszko (54), Bandrowski (56)
Kasprzik, Đurđević, Arboleda, Bandrowski, Wilk (Handžić 79), Lewandowski (Mikołajczak 71), Rengifo, Štilić, Peszko (Chrapek 61), Bosacki, Injac. Coach: Jacek Zieliński (POL)
Yellow Card(s): Peszko 42
H 1-2 Lewandowski (63)
Kotorowski, Đurđević, Arboleda, Wilk, Lewandowski, Rengifo (Bandrowski 46), Štilić (Golik 81), Bosacki, Injac, Kikut, Chrapek (Mikołajczak 75). Coach: Jacek Zieliski (POL)

Play-Off Round - Club Brugge KV (BEL)
H 1-0 Peszko (90+3)
Kasprzik, Gancarczyk, Arboleda, Bandrowski, Wilk (Kikut 71), Lewandowski (Mikołajczak 89), Rengifo, Štilić (Golik 64), Peszko, Bosacki, Injac. Coach: Jacek Zieliński (POL)
Yellow Card(s): Bandrowski 33, Arboleda 63, Golik 69, Peszko 90+4
A 0-1 (aet; 3-4 on pens)
Kasprzik, Gancarczyk, Đurđević, Arboleda, Bandrowski, Lewandowski (Chrapek 116), Rengifo, Štilić (Wilk 66), Bosacki, Injac (Golik 120+1), Kikut. Coach: Jacek Zieliński (POL)
Yellow Card(s): Arboleda 6, Bandrowski 11, Đurđević 45, Kikut 107

LEGIA WARSZAWA

UEFA EUROPA LEAGUE

cond Qualifying Round - FC Olimpi Rustavi (GEO)
3-0 *Paluchowski (19), Kiełbowicz (70), Szałachowski (83)*
ucha, Szala, Choto, Giza, Iwański, Kiełbowicz, Paluchowski (Mięciel 71),
aki Astiz, Szałachowski (Borysiuk 83), Radović (Rybus 46), Ostrowski.
ach: Jan Urban (POL)
llow Card(s): Radović 35, Rybus 49, Mucha 66
-0 *Szałachowski (8)*
ucha, Szala, Choto (Rzeźniczak 83), Giza, Iwański, Kiełbowicz,
uchowski (Mięciel 59), Iñaki Astiz, Szałachowski (Borysiuk 66), Rybus,
trowski. Coach: Jan Urban (POL)
llow Card(s): Giza 46

ird Qualifying Round - Brøndby IF (DEN)
1-1 *Iwański (40p)*
ucha, Szala, Roger, Giza (Borysiuk 76), Iwański, Kiełbowicz, Iñaki Astiz
drzejczyk 83), Szałachowski, Mięciel, Rzeźniczak, Radović (Rybus 68).
ach: Jan Urban (POL)
llow Card(s): Rzeźniczak 72
2-2 *Giza (16), Iwański (55p)*
ucha, Szala, Roger (Paluchowski 83), Giza (Borysiuk 90), Iwański,
ełbowicz, Iñaki Astiz, Szałachowski (Radović 67), Mięciel, Rzeźniczak,
bus. Coach: Jan Urban (POL)
llow Card(s): Iwański 59, Iñaki Astiz 75

KSP POLONIA WARSZAWA

UEFA EUROPA LEAGUE

rst Qualifying Round - FK Budućnost Podgorica (MNE)
2-0 *Kozioł (54), Jodłowiec (65)*
zyrowski, Mynář, Jodłowiec, Ivanovski (Chałbiński 70), Sokołowski (Mąka
), Skrzyński, Zasada, Kozioł, Lato, Majewski, Marcelo Sarvas
ierzejewski 55). Coach: Jacek Grembocki (POL)
llow Card(s): Mynář 9, Zasada 50
0-1
zyrowski, Mynář, Jodłowiec, Ivanovski (Chałbiński 60), Sokołowski
ierzejewski 68), Skrzyński, Zasada, Kozioł, Lato, Majewski, Marcelo
rvas (Piątek 89). Coach: Jacek Grembocki (POL)
llow Card(s): Lato 50

cond Qualifying Round - AC Juvenes-Dogana (SMR)
1-0 *Kokosiński (2)*
zyrowski, Mynář, Jodłowiec, Mierzejewski (Piątek 85), Ivanovski (Mąka
'), Zasada, Kozioł, Lato, Majewski, Kokosiński, Marcelo Sarvas
ołębiewski 46). Coach: Jacek Grembocki (POL)
4-0 *Marcelo Sarvas (10, 65), Mierzejewski (45), Chałbiński (54)*
zyrowski, Mynář (Piątek 46), Jodłowiec, Mierzejewski, Chałbiński,
sada, Kozioł (Trałka 56), Lato (Gołębiewski 56), Mąka, Kokosiński,
arcelo Sarvas. Coach: Jacek Grembocki (POL)

ird Qualifying Round - NAC Breda (NED)
0-1
zyrowski, Mynář, Jodłowiec, Mierzejewski, Chałbiński (Kosmalski 58),
sada, Kozioł (Kulcsar 69), Trałka (Sokołowski 46), Lato, Kokosiński,
arcelo Sarvas. Coach: Jacek Grembocki (POL)
ed Card(s): Mynář 43
llow Card(s): Mynář 41, Mynář 42, Marcelo Sarvas 89

A 1-3 *Ivanovski (59)*
Przyrowski, Jodłowiec, Ivanovski, Sokołowski, Skrzyński, Zasada, Kozioł,
Trałka (Kosmalski 46), Lato, Ciach (Kulcsar 77), Marcelo Sarvas
(Mierzejewski 59). Coach: Jacek Grembocki (POL)
Yellow Card(s): Sokołowski 35, Ciach 41, Trałka 42

PORTUGAL

FC PORTO

UEFA CHAMPIONS LEAGUE

Group D
Match 1 - Chelsea FC (ENG)
A 0-1
Hélton, Bruno Alves, Raul Meireles, Guarín, Rodríguez (Varela 64), Mariano
González (Falcao 54), Hulk, Fucile, Rolando, Álvaro Pereira, Fernando.
Coach: Jesualdo Ferreira (POR)
Red Card(s): Fernando 90+2
Yellow Card(s): Fernando 78, Fernando 90+2
Match 2 - Club Atlético de Madrid (ESP)
H 2-0 *Falcao (75), Rolando (82)*
Hélton, Bruno Alves, Raul Meireles, Belluschi, Falcao (Farías 88), Mariano
González (Valeri 90+1), Hulk, Fucile, Rolando, Álvaro Pereira, Tomás Costa
(Guarín 67). Coach: Jesualdo Ferreira (POR)
Match 3 - APOEL FC (CYP)
H 2-1 *Hulk (33, 48p)*
Hélton, Bruno Alves, Raul Meireles (Săpunaru 90+3), Falcao (Farías 87),
Rodríguez (Guarín 69), Mariano González, Hulk, Fucile, Rolando, Álvaro
Pereira, Fernando. Coach: Jesualdo Ferreira (POR)
Red Card(s): Mariano González 74
Yellow Card(s): Hélton 90+2
Match 4 - APOEL FC (CYP)
A 1-0 *Falcao (84)*
Hélton, Bruno Alves, Raul Meireles, Guarín (Tomás Costa 83), Falcao
(Belluschi 90), Rodríguez (Farías 69), Hulk, Rolando, Álvaro Pereira,
Săpunaru, Fernando. Coach: Jesualdo Ferreira (POR)
Yellow Card(s): Álvaro Pereira 86
Match 5 - Chelsea FC (ENG)
H 0-1
Beto, Bruno Alves, Raul Meireles, Belluschi (Guarín 71), Falcao, Rodríguez,
Rolando, Álvaro Pereira, Varela (Hulk 60), Săpunaru (Farías 79), Fernando.
Coach: Jesualdo Ferreira (POR)
Yellow Card(s): Fernando 51, Raul Meireles 79
Match 6 - Club Atlético de Madrid (ESP)
A 3-0 *Bruno Alves (2), Falcao (14), Hulk (76)*
Hélton, Bruno Alves, Raul Meireles, Valeri (Guarín 62), Falcao (Varela 70),
Rodríguez, Hulk, Fucile, Álvaro Pereira, Maicon (Săpunaru 59), Fernando.
Coach: Jesualdo Ferreira (POR)
Yellow Card(s): Guarín 72

First Knockout Round - Arsenal FC (ENG)
H 2-1 *Varela (11), Falcao (51)*
Hélton, Bruno Alves, Raul Meireles (Tomás Costa 68), Falcao, Hulk
(Mariano González 81), Fucile, Rolando, Álvaro Pereira, Varela, Fernando,
Rúben Micael (Belluschi 85). Coach: Jesualdo Ferreira (POR)
Yellow Card(s): Bruno Alves 34, Fucile 64, Álvaro Pereira 78, Fernando 84
A 0-5
Hélton, Bruno Alves, Raul Meireles, Falcao, Hulk, Fucile, Rolando, Álvaro
Pereira, Varela (Mariano González 76), Nuno Coelho (Rodríguez 46), Rúben
Micael (Guarín 76). Coach: Jesualdo Ferreira (POR)
Yellow Card(s): Falcao 24, Álvaro Pereira 59, Fucile 90

No	Player	Nat	DoB	Aps	(s)	Gls
Goalkeepers						
24	Beto		1/5/82	1		
1	Hélton	BRA	18/5/78	7		
Defenders						
15	Álvaro Pereira	URU	28/11/85	8		
2	Bruno Alves		27/11/81	8		1
13	Jorge Fucile	URU	19/11/84	6		
16	Maicon	BRA	14/9/88	1		
18	Nuno Coelho		7/1/86	1		
14	Rolando		31/8/85	7		1
21	Cristian Săpunaru	ROU	5/4/84	2	(2)	
Midfielders						
7	Fernando Belluschi	ARG	10/9/83	2	(2)	
25	Fernando	BRA	25/7/87	6		
6	Freddy Guarín	COL	30/6/86	2	(5)	
11	Mariano González	ARG	5/5/81	3	(2)	
3	Raul Meireles		17/3/83	8		
10	Cristian Rodríguez	URU	30/9/85	5	(1)	
28	Rúben Micael		19/8/86	2		
20	Tomás Costa	ARG	30/1/85	1	(2)	
8	Diego Valeri	ARG	1/5/86	1	(1)	
Forwards						
9	Radamel Falcao	COL	10/2/86	7	(1)	4
19	Ernesto Farías	ARG	29/5/80		(4)	
12	Hulk	BRA	25/7/86	7	(1)	3
17	Silvestre Varela		2/2/85	3	(2)	1

SPORTING CLUBE DE PORTUGAL

UEFA CHAMPIONS LEAGUE

Third Qualifying Round - FC Twente (NED)
H 0-0
Rui Patrício, Daniel Carriço, Anderson Polga, Pedro Silva (Fábio Rochemback 77), Vukčević (Yannick Djaló 69), Marco Caneira (Pereirinha 57), Matías Matías Fernández, Hélder Postiga, Miguel Veloso, João Moutinho, Liedson. Coach: Paulo Bento (POR)
Yellow Card(s): Miguel Veloso 49
A 1-1 *Wisgerhof (90+5og)*
Rui Patrício, Daniel Carriço, Anderson Polga, Matías Fernández (Pereirinha 46), Yannick Djaló, Hélder Postiga (Caicedo 63), Miguel Veloso, João Moutinho, Liedson, André Marques (Vukčević 63), Abel. Coach: Paulo Bento (POR)
Yellow Card(s): Hélder Postiga 43

Play-Off Round - ACF Fiorentina (ITA)
H 2-2 *Vukčević (58), Miguel Veloso (66)*
Rui Patrício, Daniel Carriço, Anderson Polga, Pedro Silva (Pereirinha 57), Vukčević, Matías Fernández, Hélder Postiga (Yannick Djaló 81), Miguel Veloso, João Moutinho, Liedson, André Marques (Marco Caneira 67). Coach: Paulo Bento (POR)
Red Card(s): Vukčević 59
Yellow Card(s): Vukčević 12, Vukčević 59
A 1-1 *João Moutinho (35)*
Rui Patrício, Daniel Carriço, Anderson Polga, Pedro Silva (Tonel 81), Matías Fernández (Carlos Saleiro 62), Yannick Djaló, Miguel Veloso, Pereirinha, João Moutinho, Liedson, André Marques. Coach: Paulo Bento (POR)
Yellow Card(s): Pedro Silva 49, André Marques 70, Marco Caneira 90+2

UEFA EUROPA LEAGUE

Group D
Match 1 - sc Heerenveen (NED)
A 3-2 *Liedson (17, 40, 88)*
Rui Patrício, Daniel Carriço, Anderson Polga, Vukčević (Tonel 89), Marco

Caneira, Matías Fernández (Angulo 82), Yannick Djaló (Hélder Postiga 6), Miguel Veloso, João Moutinho, Liedson, Abel. Coach: Paulo Bento (POR)
Yellow Card(s): Miguel Veloso 66
Match 2 - Hertha BSC Berlin (GER)
H 1-0 *Adrien Silva (18)*
Rui Patrício, Daniel Carriço, Adrien Silva, Vukčević (Grimi 78), Caicedo (Yannick Djaló 68), Tonel, Matías Fernández (Pereirinha 46), Miguel Velo João Moutinho, Liedson, Abel. Coach: Paulo Bento (POR)
Red Card(s): Adrien Silva 90+3
Yellow Card(s): Matías Fernández 20, Adrien Silva 32, João Moutinho 3 Adrien Silva 90+3
Match 3 - FK Ventspils (LVA)
A 2-1 *Miguel Veloso (6), João Moutinho (85)*
Rui Patrício, Daniel Carriço, Vukčević (Pereirinha 63), Caicedo (Hélder Postiga 73), Tonel, Matías Fernández (Angulo 80), Grimi, Miguel Veloso, João Moutinho, Liedson, Abel. Coach: Paulo Bento (POR)
Yellow Card(s): Angulo 88, Liedson 90
Match 4 - FK Ventspils (LVA)
H 1-1 *Carlos Saleiro (22)*
Rui Patrício, Daniel Carriço (Grimi 53), Pedro Silva, Carlos Saleiro, Vukčevi (Hélder Postiga 74), Tonel, Matías Fernández, Miguel Veloso, João Moutinho, Liedson, André Marques (Angulo 46). Coach: Paulo Bento (PC
Yellow Card(s): André Marques 14, Matías Fernández 60, Pedro Silva 8
Match 5 - sc Heerenveen (NED)
H 1-1 *Grimi (90+1)*
Rui Patrício, Daniel Carriço, Anderson Polga, Pedro Silva, Adrien Silva, Marco Caneira (Grimi 46), Matías Fernández (Izmailov 46), Hélder Postig (Caicedo 79), Miguel Veloso, João Moutinho, Liedson. Coach: Carlos Carvalhal (POR)
Yellow Card(s): Liedson 52
Match 6 - Hertha BSC Berlin (GER)
A 0-0
Rui Patrício, Daniel Carriço, Pedro Silva (Abel 67), Adrien Silva, Izmailov (Vukčević 46), Carlos Saleiro, Tonel, Matías Fernández, Grimi, Pereirinha, João Moutinho (Miguel Veloso 73). Coach: Carlos Carvalhal (POR)
Yellow Card(s): Daniel Carriço 42, Carlos Saleiro 82

Round of 32 – Everton FC (ENG)
A 1-2 *Miguel Veloso (87p)*
Rui Patrício, Pedro Mendes, Daniel Carriço, Izmailov, Tonel, Matías Fernández (Carlos Saleiro 67), Grimi, Miguel Veloso, João Moutinho (Yannick Djaló 67), Liedson, Abel. Coach: Carlos Carvalhal (POR)
Yellow Card(s): João Moutinho 54, Daniel Carriço 74
H 3-0 *Miguel Veloso (65), Pedro Mendes (76), Matías Fernández (90+4)*
Rui Patrício, Pedro Mendes, Daniel Carriço, Izmailov (Matías Fernández 90+ Tonel, Grimi (Carlos Saleiro 62), Yannick Djaló, Miguel Veloso, João Moutinh Liedson (Anderson Polga 90+3), Abel. Coach: Carlos Carvalhal (POR)
Yellow Card(s): Abel 81

Round of 16 - Club Atlético de Madrid (ESP)
A 0-1
Rui Patrício, Pedro Mendes, Anderson Polga, Izmailov, Tonel, Grimi, Mig Veloso (Adrien Silva 85), Pereirinha (Pedro Silva 61), João Moutinho, Liedson (Carlos Saleiro 90+1), Abel. Coach: Carlos Carvalhal (POR)
Red Card(s): Grimi 31, Tonel 89
Yellow Card(s): Grimi 9, Grimi 31, Miguel Veloso 53, Pereirinha 60, Carl Saleiro 90+4
H 2-2 *Liedson (19), Anderson Polga (45+1)*
Rui Patrício, Pedro Mendes, Anderson Polga, Pedro Silva (Vukčević 54), Carlos Saleiro, Marco Caneira, Miguel Veloso, Pereirinha (Matías Fernánc 70), João Moutinho, Liedson, Abel. Coach: Carlos Carvalhal (POR)
Yellow Card(s): Pedro Silva 51, Abel 76, Anderson Polga 80

SL BENFICA

UEFA EUROPA LEAGUE

ay-Off Round - FC Vorskla Poltava (UKR)
4-0 Di María (31), Cardozo (55p), Saviola (57), Weldon (77)
Jim, Shaffer, Luisão, Rúben Amorim, Javi García, Cardozo (Weldon 75),
mar, Fábio Coentrão (Ramires 62), Di María, David Luiz, Saviola (César
eixoto 80). Coach: Jorge Jesus (POR)
ellow Card(s): Shaffer 30, Ramires 84
1-2 Saviola (59)
oreira, Luisão, Javi García, Ramires (Rúben Amorim 71), Keirrison, Fábio
entrão (Di María 63), Nuno Gomes (Saviola 46), Luís Filipe, David Luiz,
sar Peixoto, Sidnei. Coach: Jorge Jesus (POR)
ellow Card(s): Nuno Gomes 10, Saviola 68, Javi García 75

roup I
atch 1 - FC BATE Borisov (BLR)
2-0 Cardozo (36), Cardozo (41)
lio César, Luisão, Javi García, Cardozo, Ramires, Maxi Pereira, Di María
úben Amorim 77), Nuno Gomes (Saviola 66), David Luiz, Felipe Menezes
ábio Coentrão (59), César Peixoto. Coach: Jorge Jesus (POR)
atch 2 - AEK Athens FC (GRE)
0-1
lio César, Luisão, Javi García, Cardozo, Ramires, Aimar (Nuno Gomes 80),
axi Pereira (Fábio Coentrão 59), Di María, David Luiz, César Peixoto,
viola (Weldon 59). Coach: Jorge Jesus (POR)
ellow Card(s): Maxi Pereira 48, Ramires 74, Cardozo 87
atch 3 – Everton FC (ENG)
5-0 Saviola (14, 83), Cardozo (47, 48), Luisão (52)
lio César, Luisão, Rúben Amorim, Javi García, Cardozo (Fábio Coentrão
7), Ramires, Aimar (Carlos Martins 69), Di María, David Luiz, César
eixoto, Saviola (Weldon 84). Coach: Jorge Jesus (POR)
atch 4 – Everton FC (ENG)
2-0 Saviola (63), Cardozo (76)
lio César, Luisão, Rúben Amorim, Javi García, Cardozo, Ramires (Maxi
ereira 45+1), Fábio Coentrão (Aimar 61), Di María, David Luiz, Sidnei,
viola (Felipe Menezes 87). Coach: Jorge Jesus (POR)
ellow Card(s): Saviola 74, Júlio César 87
atch 5 - FC BATE Borisov (BLR)
2-1 Saviola (46), Fábio Coentrão (63)
lio César, Javi García, Cardozo, Maxi Pereira (Rúben Amorim
+2), Fábio Coentrão (Di María 79), David Luiz, Felipe Menezes, César
eixoto, Miguel Vítor, Saviola (Aimar 67). Coach: Jorge Jesus (POR)
ellow Card(s): David Luiz 31, Ramires 84
atch 6 - AEK Athens FC (GRE)
2-1 Di María (45, 73)
lio César, Shaffer, Roderick, Carlos Martins, Fábio Coentrão (César
eixoto 46), Weldon, Di María, Nuno Gomes (Cardozo 72), Luís Filipe,
elipe Menezes (Javi García 65), Miguel Vítor. Coach: Jorge Jesus (POR)
ellow Card(s): Felipe Menezes 42, Shaffer 75, Carlos Martins 90+2

ound of 32 - Hertha BSC Berlin (GER)
1-1 Di María (4)
lio César, Luisão, Rúben Amorim, Javi García, Cardozo, Ramires (Felipe
enezes 63), Carlos Martins (Aimar 63), Di María, David Luiz, César
eixoto, Saviola (Miguel Vítor 83). Coach: Jorge Jesus (POR)
ellow Card(s): César Peixoto 23, Ramires 43, Júlio César 74
4-0 Aimar (25), Cardozo (48, 62), Javi García (59)
lio César, Luisão, Rúben Amorim, Javi García, Cardozo, Aimar (Carlos
artins 66), Maxi Pereira, Fábio Coentrão, Di María (Nuno Gomes 74),
avid Luiz, Saviola (César Peixoto 69). Coach: Jorge Jesus (POR)

ound of 16 - Olympique de Marseille (FRA)
1-1 Maxi Pereira (76)
lio César, Luisão, Javi García, Cardozo, Ramires, Aimar (Carlos Martins
5), Maxi Pereira, Di María, David Luiz, César Peixoto (Fábio Coentrão 77),
viola (Éder Luís 88). Coach: Jorge Jesus (POR)
ellow Card(s): Maxi Pereira 66
2-1 Maxi Pereira (75), Alan Kardec (90+1)
lio César, Luisão, Javi García, Cardozo, Ramires, Maxi Pereira (Miguel
tor 90+5), Carlos Martins (Alan Kardec 86), Fábio Coentrão, Di María,
avid Luiz, Saviola (Aimar 77). Coach: Jorge Jesus (POR)
ellow Card(s): Cardozo 32, Di María 54, Luisão 81, Javi García 83, Alan
ardec 90+2, Aimar 90+5

Quarter-Finals - Liverpool FC (ENG)
H 2-1 Cardozo (59p, 79p)
Júlio César, Luisão, Javi García, Cardozo, Ramires, Aimar (Aírton 87), Maxi
Pereira (Nuno Gomes 66), Carlos Martins (Rúben Amorim 72), Fábio
Coentrão, Di María, David Luiz. Coach: Jorge Jesus (POR)
Yellow Card(s): Luisão 29, David Luiz 37
A 1-4 Cardozo (70)
Júlio César (Moreira 80), Luisão, Rúben Amorim, Javi García, Cardozo,
Ramires, Aimar (Fábio Coentrão 86), Carlos Martins (Alan Kardec 67), Di
María, David Luiz, Sidnei. Coach: Jorge Jesus (POR)
Yellow Card(s): Aimar 84

CD NACIONAL

UEFA EUROPA LEAGUE

Play-Off Round - FC Zenit St Petersburg (RUS)
H 4-3 Luís Alberto (30), João Aurélio (37), Rodrigo (53), Rúben Micael (73)
Rafael Bracali, Patacas, Felipe Lopes, Wellington (Tomašević 83), Cléber,
Luís Alberto, Pečnik (Nuno Pinto 55), Rúben Micael, João Aurélio, Rodrigo
(Guirassy 87), Leandro Salino. Coach: Manuel Machado (POR)
Yellow Card(s): João Aurélio 38, Cléber 35, Patacas 55, Luís Alberto 66
A 1-1 Rúben Micael (89)
Rafael Bracali, Patacas, Felipe Lopes, Halliche (Nuno Pinto 46), Wellington
(Tomašević 80), Cléber, Luís Alberto, Pečnik, Rúben Micael (Guirassy
90+4), João Aurélio, Leandro Salino. Coach: Manuel Machado (POR)
Yellow Card(s): Rúben Micael 14, Nuno Pinto 63, Felipe Lopes 66, Patacas 76

Group L
Match 1 - Werder Bremen (GER)
H 2-3 Felipe Lopes (68), Halliche (75)
Rafael Bracali, Felipe Lopes, Halliche, Wellington (Tomašević 46), Cléber,
Luís Alberto, Edgar Silva, Pečnik (Mateus 46), Rúben Micael, João Aurélio,
Leandro Salino (Amuneke 58). Coach: Manuel Machado (POR)
Match 2 - FK Austria Wien (AUT)
A 1-1 Rúben Micael (35)
Rafael Bracali, Patacas, Felipe Lopes, Halliche (Pečnik 66), Cléber, Luís
Alberto, Edgar Silva, Rúben Micael, Leandro Salino, Mateus (Amuneke 50),
Tomašević (João Aurélio 82). Coach: Manuel Machado (POR)
Yellow Card(s): Mateus 6, Edgar Silva 35, Halliche 45+1, Felipe Lopes 53,
Leandro Salino 87
Match 3 - Athletic Club (ESP)
A 1-2 Rúben Micael (42)
Rafael Bracali, Patacas, Felipe Lopes, Halliche, Cléber, Luís Alberto (João
Aurélio 74), Edgar Silva (Clebão 75), Pečnik (Mateus 66), Rúben Micael,
Leandro Salino, Nuno Pinto. Coach: Manuel Machado (POR)
Yellow Card(s): Patacas 38, Luís Alberto 62, Cléber 69
Match 4 - Athletic Club (ESP)
H 1-1 Edgar Silva (64p)
Rafael Bracali, Patacas, Felipe Lopes, Halliche, Luís Alberto (João Aurélio
69), Edgar Silva, Pečnik, Rúben Micael, Mateus (Leandro Salino 46),
Tomašević (Cléber 45), Nuno Pinto. Coach: Manuel Machado (POR)
Red Card(s): Nuno Pinto 79
Yellow Card(s): Pečnik 30, Nuno Pinto 39, Edgar Silva 45, Cléber 77, Nuno Pinto 79
Match 5 - Werder Bremen (GER)
A 1-4 Rúben Micael (61)
Rafael Bracali, Patacas, Felipe Lopes, Cléber, Luís Alberto, Pečnik, Rúben
Micael, João Aurélio (Amuneke 74), Leandro Salino (Anselmo 87), Mateus,
Tomašević. Coach: José Augusto Araujo (POR)
Yellow Card(s): Tomašević 28, Cléber 83
Match 6 - FK Austria Wien (AUT)
H 5-1 Rúben Micael (23, 57), Mateus (32), Tomašević (61), Felipe Lopes (66)
Rafael Bracali, Patacas, Felipe Lopes, Halliche, Edgar Silva (Amuneke 69),
Pečnik (João Aurélio 60), Rúben Micael (Pedro Melo 75), Leandro Salino,
Mateus, Tomašević, Nuno Pinto. Coach: Predrag Jokanović (SRB)

SC BRAGA

UEFA EUROPA LEAGUE

Third Qualifying Round - IF Elfsborg (SWE)
H 1-2 *Meyong (50p)*
Eduardo, Rodríguez, Paulão, Evaldo, Paulo César (Márcio Mossoró 61), Frechaut, Meyong, Alan, Fernando Alexandre (Yazalde 76), Vandinho, Matheus (Diogo Valente 55). Coach: Domingos Paciência (POR)
Yellow Card(s): Matheus 47, Frechaut 87
A 0-2
Eduardo, Rodríguez, Evaldo, Márcio Mossoró (Paulo César 76), Diogo Valente (Matheus 56), Frechaut, Meyong, Possebon (Kalaba 34), Alan, João Pereira, Vandinho. Coach: Domingos Paciência (POR)
Yellow Card(s): Vandinho 57, Evaldo 84

FC PAÇOS DE FERREIRA

UEFA EUROPA LEAGUE

Second Qualifying Round - FC Zimbru Chisinau (MDA)
A 0-0
Cássio, Ozéia, Pedrinha, William (Romeu 86), Leandrinho (Rondon 90+3), Jorginho, Leonel Olímpio, Kelly, Ricardo, Carlitos (Baiano 90+1), Filipe Anunciação. Coach: Paulo Sérgio (POR)
Yellow Card(s): Ricardo 54, William 64
H 1-0 *Cristiano (84)*
Cássio, Ozéia (Manuel José 77), Pedrinha, Leandrinho (Cristiano 64), Jorginho (Pedro Queirós 90), Leonel Olímpio, Kelly, Ricardo, Romeu, Carlitos, Filipe Anunciação. Coach: Paulo Sérgio (POR)
Yellow Card(s): Cristiano 84

Third Qualifying Round - Bnei Yehuda Tel-Aviv FC (ISR)
A 0-1
Cássio, Ozéia (Leal 86), Pedrinha, Leandrinho (Cristiano 62), Jorginho, Baiano, Leonel Olímpio, Kelly, Ricardo, Romeu (Rondon 82), Filipe Anunciação. Coach: Paulo Sérgio (POR)
Yellow Card(s): Jorginho 36, Ricardo 67
H 0-1
Cássio, Ozéia, Pedrinha, Cristiano, Leandrinho (William 46), Jorginho, Baiano, Leonel Olímpio, Kelly (Rondon 72), Romeu, Filipe Anunciação (Carlitos 63). Coach: Paulo Sérgio (POR)
Yellow Card(s): Filipe Anunciação 27, Ozéia 40, Kelly 50, Cristiano 54

REPUBLIC OF IRELAND

BOHEMIAN FC

UEFA CHAMPIONS LEAGUE

Second Qualifying Round - FC Salzburg (AUT)
A 1-1 *Ndo (60)*
B. Murphy, Powell, Rossiter (Madden 90+2), Oman, Crowe, J. Byrne (A. Murphy 73), Brennan, Shelley, Deegan, Keegan, Ndo. Coach: Pat Fenlon (IR
H 0-1
B. Murphy, Powell, Rossiter (McGuinness 87), Oman, Crowe, J. Byrne (Cronin 84), Brennan (A. Murphy 65), Shelley, Deegan, Keegan, Ndo. Coach: Pat Fenlon (IRL)
Yellow Card(s): A. Murphy 68

SAINT PATRICK'S ATHLETIC FC

UEFA EUROPA LEAGUE

Second Qualifying Round - Valletta FC (MLT)
H 1-1 *O'Brien (38)*
Rogers, Maher, Partridge, Harris, Byrne, Cawley, B. Ryan (Fitzpatrick 70), O'Connor, Guy, Stevens, O'Brien. Coach: Jeff Kenna (IRL)
A 1-0 *O'Brien (80)*
Rogers, Maher (Lynch 80), Partridge, Harris, Byrne (Cawley 58), B. Ryan (D Ryan 73), O'Connor, Gavin, Guy, Stevens, O'Brien. Coach: Jeff Kenna (IRL)
Red Card(s): Ryan 77
Yellow Card(s): Stevens 54, Gavin 56

Third Qualifying Round - PFC Krylya Sovetov Samara (RUS)
H 1-0 *O'Brien (71)*
Rogers, Partridge, Harris, Lynch, Byrne (Dempsey 72), Fitzpatrick (B. Ryan 46), O'Connor, Gavin, Guy, Stevens, O'Brien. Coach: Jeff Kenna (IRL)
A 2-3 *Bober (73og), O'Brien (78)*
Rogers, Partridge, Harris, Lynch, Byrne, B. Ryan (Cawley 63), O'Connor, Gavi (Maher 66), Guy, Stevens (D. Ryan 76), O'Brien. Coach: Jeff Kenna (IRL)
Yellow Card(s): O'Brien 27, Byrne 39

Play-Off Round - FC Steaua Bucureşti (ROU)
A 0-3
Rogers, Partridge, Harris, Lynch (Cawley 86), Byrne (Dempsey 70), Fitzpatrick (Quigley 61), O'Connor, Gavin, Guy, Stevens, O'Brien. Coach: Jeff Kenna (IRL)
Yellow Card(s): Fitzpatrick 27, Quigley 63
H 1-2 *O'Connor (49)*
Rogers, Partridge, Harris (Gavin 86), Lynch, Byrne (Dempsey 79), Cawley, Quigley (Scullion 89), O'Connor, Guy, Stevens (D. Ryan 46), O'Brien. Coach: Jeff Kenna (IRL

DERRY CITY FC

UEFA EUROPA LEAGUE

Second Qualifying Round - Skonto FC (LVA)
A 1-1 *McManus (44)*
Doherty, Delaney, Hutton, Gray (McCallion 81), Higgins, Martyn, O'Brien, McGlynn, Molloy, Farren (Stewart 87), McManus (Morrow 81). Coach: Stephen Kenny (IRL)
Yellow Card(s): O'Brien 57
H 1-0 *Deery (57)*
Doherty, McCallion, Delaney, Hutton, Morrow (Higgins 50), Stewart (Farren 75), O'Brien, McGlynn (Scullion 89), Deery, Molloy, McManus. Coach: Stephen Kenny (IRL)

hird Qualifying Round - PFC CSKA Sofia (BUL)
0-1
oherty, Delaney, Hutton, Gray, Higgins (Martyn 81), Stewart, O'Brien, cGlynn (McCallion 73), Deery, Molloy, McManus (Farren 71). Coach: :ephen Kenny (IRL)
ellow Card(s): Doherty 72, Gray 73
1-1 Scullion (82)
oherty, Delaney, Hutton, Gray, Higgins, Stewart, O'Brien, Deery, Molloy cullion (74), Farren (McGlynn 53), McManus (Nash 90). Coach: Stephen enny (IRL)
ed Card(s): McGlynn 87
ellow Card(s): Gray 27, Molloy 68

SLIGO ROVERS FC

UEFA EUROPA LEAGUE

irst Qualifying Round - KF Vllaznia (ALB)
1-2 Cretaro (89p)
rush, Keane, Holmes, Ventre, O'Grady, Cash (Doherty 73), Ryan, Boco, retaro, Morrison, Feeney (Noctor 64). Coach: Paul Cook (ENG)
ellow Card(s): O'Grady 67, Ryan 90+5
1-1 Keane (84)
:ush, Keane, Holmes, Ventre, O'Grady, Cash (Ch. Kelly 57), Ryan, Boco, retaro, Doherty (Morrison 66), Feeney. Coach: Paul Cook (ENG)
ed Card(s): O'Grady 90+4
ellow Card(s): Cretaro 44, Keane 53

ROMANIA

FC UNIREA URZICENI

UEFA CHAMPIONS LEAGUE

roup G
latch 1 - Sevilla FC (ESP)
0-2
rlauskis, Mehmedović, Galamaz, Bilaşco, Varga (Semedo 73), Ricardo ilana (Onofraş 81), Brandán, Bălan (Paraschiv 65), Maftei, Frunză, Apostol. oach: Dan Petrescu (ROU)
ellow Card(s): Mehmedović 10, Frunză 26, Maftei 31, Galamaz 54
latch 2 - VfB Stuttgart (GER)
1-1 Varga (48)
rlauskis, Galamaz, Bilaşco (Rusescu 64), Varga (Pădureţu 90), Nicu, icardo Vilana, Brandán, Bălan (Frunză 46), Bruno Fernandes, Maftei, postol. Coach: Dan Petrescu (ROU)
ellow Card(s): Maftei 85
latch 3 - Rangers FC (SCO)
4-1 Bilaşco (32), Lafferty (49og), McCulloch (59og), Brandán (65)
udor, Galamaz, Bilaşco, Varga (Pădureţu 89), Nicu (Onofraş 19), Ricardo ilana, Brandán, Bălan (Frunză 75), Bruno Fernandes, Maftei, Apostol. oach: Dan Petrescu (ROU)
ellow Card(s): Brandán 37, Ricardo Vilana 61

Match 4 - Rangers FC (SCO)
H 1-1 Onofraş (88)
Arlauskis, Galamaz, Bilaşco, Varga (Semedo 81), Ricardo Vilana (Pădureţu 81), Brandán, Bălan (Onofraş 28), Bordeanu, Maftei, Frunză, Apostol. Coach: Dan Petrescu (ROU)
Yellow Card(s): Bilaşco 69
Match 5 - Sevilla FC (ESP)
H 1-0 Dragutinović (45og)
Arlauskis, Mehmedović, Galamaz, Bilaşco, Varga (Semedo 89), Ricardo Vilana (Pădureţu 90+4), Brandán, Bordeanu, Maftei, Frunză (Bălan 64), Apostol. Coach: Dan Petrescu (ROU)
Yellow Card(s): Ricardo Vilana 23, Apostol 49, Galamaz 75, Maftei 83
Match 6 - VfB Stuttgart (GER)
A 1-3 Semedo (46)
Arlauskis, Mehmedović, Bilaşco, Pădureţu, Onofraş (Varga 46), Semedo, Brandán, Bordeanu, Bruno Fernandes, Bordeanu, Apostol (Todoran 86). Coach: Dan Petrescu (ROU)
Yellow Card(s): Bilaşco 43, Apostol 68, Brandán 75

No	Player	Nat	DoB	Aps	(s)	Gls
Goalkeepers						
1	Giedrius Arlauskis	LTU	1/12/87	5		
74	Daniel Tudor		1/6/74	1		
Defenders						
23	Valeriu Bordeanu		2/2/77	3		
19	Pablo Brandán	ARG	5/3/83	6		1
22	Bruno Fernandes	GNB	6/11/78	3		
6	George Galamaz		5/4/81	5		
24	Vasile Maftei		1/1/81	5		
16	Epaminonda Nicu		17/12/79	2		
Midfielders						
32	Iulian Apostol		3/12/80	6		
21	Tiberiu Bălan		17/2/81	5	(1)	
30	Sorin Frunză		29/3/78	3	(2)	
4	Ersin Mehmedović	SRB	10/5/81	3		
10	Răzvan Pădureţu		19/6/81	1	(4)	
8	Sorin Paraschiv		17/6/81		(1)	
18	Ricardo Vilana	BRA	18/7/81	5		
5	Dinu Todoran		8/9/78		(1)	
9	Şerban Varga		15/10/84	5	(1)	1
Forwards						
7	Marius Ioan Bilaşco		13/7/81	6		1
11	Marius Onofraş		17/8/80	1	(3)	1
14	Raul Rusescu		9/7/88		(2)	
17	António Semedo	POR	1/6/79	1	(3)	1

UEFA EUROPA LEAGUE

Round of 32 - Liverpool FC (ENG)
A 0-1
Arlauskis, Galamaz, Bilaşco, Paraschiv (Ricardo Vilana 86), Pădureţu (Rusescu 90+1), Onofraş (Marinescu 75), Brandán, Bruno Fernandes, Maftei, Frunză, Apostol. Coach: Roni Levi (ISR)
Yellow Card(s): Bruno Fernandes 41, Brandán 58
H 1-3 Bruno Fernandes (19)
Arlauskis, Galamaz (Mehmedović 27), Bilaşco, Paraschiv (Ricardo Vilana 56), Pădureţu, Bruno Fernandes, Bordeanu, Maftei, Onofraş (Semedo 62), Frunză, Apostol. Coach: Roni Levi (ISR)
Yellow Card(s): Onofraş 28, Bruno Fernandes 31, Arlauskis 54

FC TIMIŞOARA

UEFA CHAMPIONS LEAGUE

Third Qualifying Round - FC Shakhtar Donetsk (UKR)
A 2-2 Bucur (20, 80)
Pantilimon, Éder Bonfim, Alexa (Stancu 71), Nibombé, Parks (Magera 26), Art. Karamyan, Arm. Karamyan, Bucur (Ionescu 90+3), Čišovský, Bourceanu, Curtean. Coach: Ioan Ovidiu Sabău (ROU)
Yellow Card(s): Bourceanu 37, Art. Karamyan 39, Magera 74, Stancu 74

CHAMPIONS LEAGUE   EUROPA LEAGUE

Romania

H 0-0
Pantilimon, Éder Bonfim, Alexa (Scutaru 67), Nibombé, Stancu (Ionescu 82), Parks, Art. Karamyan, Arm. Karamyan, Bucur (Magera 89), Čišovský, Bourceanu. Coach: Ioan Ovidiu Sabău (ROU)
Yellow Card(s): Alexa 24, Arm. Karamyan 45+1, Bourceanu 87

Play-Off Round - VfB Stuttgart (GER)
H 0-2
Pantilimon, Éder Bonfim, Alexa, Nibombé, Stancu, Art. Karamyan (Latovlevici 77), Arm. Karamyan, Scutaru (Borbély 46), Bucur, Magera (Ionescu 69), Čišovský. Coach: Ioan Ovidiu Sabău (ROU)
Yellow Card(s): Alexa 4, Pantilimon 27, Art. Karamyan 68
A 0-0
Pantilimon, Éder Bonfim (Ionescu 60), Latovlevici, Nibombé, Parks, Arm. Karamyan, Borbély (Stancu 46), Bucur, Čišovský (Scutaru 73), Bourceanu, Curtean. Coach: Ioan Ovidiu Sabău (ROU)
Yellow Card(s): Arm. Karamyan 20, Éder Bonfim 35, Bourceanu 88

UEFA EUROPA LEAGUE
Group A
Match 1 - AFC Ajax (NED)
A 0-0
Pantilimon, Éder Bonfim, Alexa, Nibombé, Parks (Stancu 59), Art. Karamyan, Mera, Bucur, Goga (Poparadu 84), Bourceanu, Curtean (Ionescu 67). Coach: Ioan Ovidiu Sabău (ROU)
Yellow Card(s): Alexa 62, Bucur 87, Ionescu 90+1, Pantilimon 90+2
Match 2 - NK Dinamo Zagreb (CRO)
H 0-3
Pantilimon, Éder Bonfim, Alexa, Nibombé, Art. Karamyan, Arm. Karamyan (Parks 46), Mera, Bucur, Goga, Ionescu (Bourceanu 55), Curtean (Magera 69). Coach: Ioan Ovidiu Sabău (ROU)
Yellow Card(s): Magera 90+3
Match 3 - RSC Anderlecht (BEL)
H 0-0
Pantilimon, Éder Bonfim, Alexa (Magera 81), Nibombé, Art. Karamyan, Arm. Karamyan (Curtean 72), Scutaru, Mera, Bucur (Parks 74), Goga, Bourceanu. Coach: Ioan Ovidiu Sabău (ROU)
Yellow Card(s): Éder Bonfim 19, Mera 67, Parks 87
Match 4 - RSC Anderlecht (BEL)
A 1-3 *Parks (51)*
Pantilimon, Éder Bonfim, Alexa, Nibombé, Parks, Art. Karamyan (Curtean 80), Scutaru, Bucur (Goga 76), Maxim, Magera, Bourceanu (Stancu 67). Coach: Ioan Ovidiu Sabău (ROU)
Yellow Card(s): Maxim 29
Match 5 - AFC Ajax (NED)
H 1-2 *Goga (2)*
Pantilimon, Éder Bonfim, Alexa, Stancu, Art. Karamyan, Scutaru, Mera, Bucur (Taborda 62), Goga (Maxim 73), Magera (Parks 53), Bourceanu. Coach: Ioan Ovidiu Sabău (ROU)
Red Card(s): Éder Bonfim 50, Pantilimon 62
Yellow Card(s): Alexa 20, Scutaru 25, Goga 67
Match 6 - NK Dinamo Zagreb (CRO)
A 2-1 *Bucur (67), Goga (84)*
Taborda, Alexa, Nibombé, Stancu, Parks (Ionescu 90+2), Scutaru, Mera, Bucur (Matei 88), Maxim, Bourceanu, Curtean (Goga 75). Coach: Ioan Ovidiu Sabău (ROU)
Yellow Card(s): Mera 61, Nibombé 62, Taborda 90+3

CFR 1907 CLUJ

UEFA EUROPA LEAGUE
Play-Off Round - FK Sarajevo (BIH)
A 1-1 *Dani (19)*
Nuno Claro, Tony, Panin, Peralta (Leão 73), Alcântara, Koné, Culio, Cadú, Mara (Edimar 63), Dani, Nei (Traoré 77). Coach: Toni (POR)

H 2-1 *Koné (40), Mureşan (69)*
Nuno Claro, Tony, Panin, Mureşan, Dubarbier (Buş 90+4), Peralta (Traoré 88), Koné, Culio, Cadú, Dani, Nei (Mara 62). Coach: Toni (POR)
Yellow Card(s): Tony 32, Dubarbier 66

Group K
Match 1 - FC København (DEN)
H 2-0 *Culio (53), Traoré (75)*
Nuno Claro, Tony, Panin, Mureşan, Dubarbier (Mara 54), Peralta (Dani 77), Hugo Alcântara, Koné (Traoré 46), Culio, Cadú, Deac. Coach: Toni (POR)
Yellow Card(s): Mureşan 67
Match 2 - PSV Eindhoven (NED)
A 0-1
Nuno Claro, Tony, Panin, Mureşan (Dani 9), Dubarbier (Mara 70), Peralta, Traoré, Hugo Alcântara, Culio, Cadú, Deac (Nei 78). Coach: Toni (POR)
Yellow Card(s): Dani 34, Mara 88
Match 3 - AC Sparta Praha (CZE)
A 0-2
Nuno Claro, Cabrera, Panin, Peralta (Mara 46), Traoré (Buş 72), Culio, Cadú, Dani, Edimar, Deac (Dubarbier 46), Nei. Coach: Toni (POR)
Yellow Card(s): Deac 16, Traoré 38, Cadú 45+2, Nuno Claro 90+3
Match 4 - AC Sparta Praha (CZE)
H 2-3 *Traoré (25), Dubarbier (90+1)*
Nuno Claro, Tony, Panin, Mureşan, Peralta, Traoré, Hugo Alcântara, Culio (Dubarbier 58), Cadú, Deac (Mara 63), Nei (Buş 83). Coach: Toni (POR)
Red Card(s): Mureşan 64, Mara 88
Yellow Card(s): Mureşan 26, Cadú 43, Mureşan 64, Mara 86, Mara 88, Dani 8
Match 5 - FC København (DEN)
A 0-2
Nuno Claro, Tony, Cabrera, Panin, Dubarbier, Traoré (Deac 46), Koné (E. Dică 79), Culio, Cadú, Leão (Nei 67), Dani. Coach: Andrea Mandorlini (ITA)
Yellow Card(s): Cadú 42, Dani 52
Match 6 - PSV Eindhoven (NED)
H 0-2
Peškovič, Tony, Cabrera, Panin, Mureşan, Dubarbier (Buş 85), Koné (Mara 78), Culio, Leão (Traoré 75), E. Dică, Deac. Coach: Andrea Mandorlini (ITA)
Yellow Card(s): Peškovič 18, Panin 61, Tony 63, Leão 72

FC DINAMO BUCUREŞTI

UEFA EUROPA LEAGUE
Play-Off Round - FC Slovan Liberec (CZE)
H 0-3 (w/o)
Dolha, Pulhac, Rus (Zicu 55), Niculae (Niculescu 82), Dănciulescu (An. Cristea 46), Ad. Cristea, Grigore, Torje, Scarlatache, N'Doye, Tamaş. Coach: Dario Bonetti (ITA)
Yellow Card(s): Zicu 72
A 3-0 *An. Cristea (2), Niculae (57, 81) (aet; 9-8 on pens)*
Matache, Diabaté, Moţi, Koné, Zicu, Boştină, Dănciulescu (Niculae 46), Molinero, An. Cristea (Niculescu 75), Ad. Cristea (Torje 64), Grigore. Coach: Dario Bonetti (ITA)
Yellow Card(s): Moţi 51, Diabaté 74, Zicu 75, Niculae 78

Group F
Match 1 - SK Sturm Graz (AUT)
A 1-0 *Tamaş (80)*
Dolha, Diabaté, Koné (Boştină 90+2), An. Cristea, Goian, Ad. Cristea (Niculescu 76), Torje (Zé Kalanga 80), Scarlatache, N'Doye, Tamaş, Alexe. Coach: Dario Bonetti (ITA)
Yellow Card(s): N'Doye 71, Goian 83
Match 2 - Panathinaikos FC (GRE)
H 0-1
Dolha, Diabaté, Koné, Boştină (Rus 74), An. Cristea, Goian, Ad. Cristea (Niculescu 86), Torje, Scarlatache, Tamaş, Alexe (Zicu 52). Coach: Dario Bonetti (ITA)
Yellow Card(s): Diabaté 78, Goian 89

CHAMPIONS LEAGUE   EUROPA LEAGUE

atch 3 - Galatasaray AŞ (TUR)
1-4 *Boştină (61)*
ılha, Diabaté, Rus (Boştină 46), An. Cristea, Goian, Ad. Cristea, Torje
iculescu 75), Scarlatache, N'Doye, Tamaş, Alexe (Zicu 58). Coach: Marin
າ (ROU)
llow Card(s): N'Doye 64
atch 4 - Galatasaray AŞ (TUR)
0-3
ılha, Pulhac, Moţi, Koné (Boştină 60), Ad. Cristea (Rus 65), Torje,
arlatache, N'Doye, Tamaş, Alexe, Niculescu. Coach: Cornel Ţălnar (ROU)
d Card(s): N'Doye 68
llow Card(s): N'Doye 48, Pulhac 53, N'Doye 68
atch 5 - SK Sturm Graz (AUT)
2-1 *Niculae (41, 57)*
ılha, Diabaté, Moţi, Rus, Boştină, Niculae (Niculescu 90+2), Molinero, An. Cristea
ɔian 84), Ad. Cristea, Torje (Koné 58), Tamaş. Coach: Cornel Ţălnar (ROU)
d Card(s): Rus 43
llow Card(s): Rus 4, Rus 43, Moţi 67, Molinero 76, Ad. Cristea 89
atch 6 - Panathinaikos FC (GRE)
0-3
ılha, Diabaté, Moţi, Koné, Niculae, Molinero, An. Cristea (Niculescu 67), Torje
cu 60), N'Doye, Tamaş, Alexe (Ad. Cristea 46). Coach: Cornel Ţălnar (ROU)
llow Card(s): N'Doye 21, Tamaş 50, An. Cristea 56

FC VASLUI

UEFA EUROPA LEAGUE

hird Qualifying Round - AC Omonia (CYP)
2-0 *Temwanjera (20, 55)*
ıciak, Genchev, Burdujan, Gerlem (Gângioveanu 78), Buhuş, Zubar,
ălace, Temwanjera (Jovanović 74), Ljubinković (Pavlović 68), Cânu, Wesley.
ɔach: Cristian Dulca (ROU)
ellow Card(s): Buhuş 76, Bălace 86
1-1 *Wesley (60)*
ıciak, Genchev, Burdujan, Gerlem (Gângioveanu 66), Buhuş, Zubar,
ălace, Temwanjera (Jovanović 74), Pavlović, Cânu, Wesley (Zmeu 87).
ɔach: Cristian Dulca (ROU)
ed Card(s): Kuciak 88
ellow Card(s): Buhuş 2, Gerlem 33, Pavlović 82

ay-Off Round - AEK Athens FC (GRE)
2-1 *Wesley (29, 83p)*
äisan, Genchev, Gerlem (Zmeu 85), Akakpo, Zubar, Bălace, Temwanjera
ɔvanović 90), Ljubinković, Pavlović (Gângioveanu 75), Farkaš, Wesley.
ɔach: Cristian Dulca (ROU)
ellow Card(s): Akakpo 34, Zubar 50
0-3
ıciak, Zmeu (Costin 70), Gerlem, Buhuş, Zubar, Bălace, Temwanjera,
ubinković (Jovanović 78), Pavlović, Farkaš, Wesley. Coach: Cristian
ulca (ROU)
ellow Card(s): Pavlović 45, Ljubinković 77

FC STEAUA BUCUREŞTI

UEFA EUROPA LEAGUE

Second Qualifying Round - Újpest FC (HUN)
H 2-0 *Surdu (46), Stancu (72)*
Tătăruşanu, Goian, Székely, Kapetanos, Surdu (Grzelak 88), Toja (Ionescu
83), Marin, Ochiroşii (Stancu 46), Ghionea, Onicaş, Ninu. Coach: Cristiano
Bergodi (ITA)
Red Card(s): Kapetanos 42
Yellow Card(s): Ochiroşii 35, Goian 59, Toja 62, Marin 69
A 2-1 *Székely (58), Grzelak (66)*
Tătăruşanu, Goian, Golański, Székely, Surdu, Toja (Ionescu 83), Nicoliţă
(Grzelak 65), Baciu, Marin, Bicfalvi (Onicaş 46), Stancu. Coach: Cristiano
Bergodi (ITA)
Yellow Card(s): Marin 18, Toja 63, Székely 72

Third Qualifying Round - Motherwell FC (SCO)
H 3-0 *Craigan (29og), Nicoliţă (45+1), Stancu (61)*
Tătăruşanu, Goian, Golański, Székely (Grzelak 26), Surdu (Bibishkov 72),
Nicoliţă (Ochiroşii 87), Baciu, Ionescu, Onicaş, Stancu, Ninu. Coach:
Cristiano Bergodi (ITA)
Yellow Card(s): Goian 49, Ninu 73
A 3-1 *Marin (55p), Stancu (67, 84)*
Zapata, Grzelak, Nicoliţă, Baciu, Marin, Ghionea (Tudose 76),
Onicaş (Iacob 81), Stancu, Ninu, Bibishkov (Ochiroşii 62). Coach: Cristiano
Bergodi (ITA)
Yellow Card(s): Ionescu 63, Ninu 75

Play-Off Round - Saint Patrick's Athletic FC (IRL)
H 3-0 *Nicoliţă (56), Stancu (65, 80)*
Tătăruşanu, Golański (Tininho 86), Kapetanos (Grzelak 81), Surdu, Tudose,
Nicoliţă, Baciu, Marin, Ionescu, Ochiroşii (Stancu 53), Onicaş. Coach:
Cristiano Bergodi (ITA)
A 2-1 *Nicoliţă (80), Ochiroşii (89)*
Zapata, Golański, Székely (Ochiroşii 86), Grzelak (Nicoliţă 57), Tudose,
Ionescu, Ghionea, Onicaş, Stancu (Surdu 79), Ninu, Bibishkov. Coach:
Cristiano Bergodi (ITA)

Group H
Match 1 - FC Sheriff (MDA)
H 0-0
Zapata, Rada, Székely, Surdu (Tănase 79), Nicoliţă, Marin, Ionescu,
Ghionea, Onicaş (Toja 57), Stancu (Kapetanos 70), Ninu. Coach: Cristiano
Bergodi (ITA)
Yellow Card(s): Ninu 88
Match 2 - FC Twente (NED)
A 0-0
Zapata, Rada, Székely (Ninu 90+2), Kapetanos, Surdu (Onicaş 77), Toja,
Nicoliţă, Marin, Ghionea, Bicfalvi, Stancu (Ionescu 90+3). Coach: Mihai
Stoichiţă (ROU)
Yellow Card(s): Rada 26, Székely 87
Match 3 - Fenerbahçe SK (TUR)
H 0-1
Zapata, Golański, Rada, Székely (Dayro Moreno 67), Kapetanos, Surdu,
Toja, Nicoliţă, Baciu, Ghionea, Bicfalvi (Onicaş 42). Coach: Mihai Stoichiţă
(ROU)
Yellow Card(s): Bicfalvi 19, Golański 37, Toja 88
Match 4 - Fenerbahçe SK (TUR)
A 1-3 *Kapetanos (38)*
Zapata, Rada, Tănase (Dayro Moreno 63), Székely (Surdu 66), Kapetanos,
Toja, Nicoliţă, Baciu, Marin, Ghionea, Bicfalvi (Golański 72). Coach: Mihai
Stoichiţă (ROU)
Match 5 - FC Sheriff (MDA)
A 1-1 *Toja (87)*
Zapata, Rada, Tănase (Ionescu 66), Székely (Marin 20), Surdu, Toja, Nicoliţă,
Baciu, Ghionea, Bicfalvi, Stancu (Kapetanos 54). Coach: Mihai Stoichiţă (ROU)
Red Card(s): Marin 90+3
Yellow Card(s): Bicfalvi 27, Surdu 89
Match 6 - FC Twente (NED)
H 1-1 *Kapetanos (18)*
Zapata, Golański (Ninu 63), Rada, Tănase, Székely (Ochiroşii 78),
Kapetanos, Toja, Nicoliţă, Ghionea, Bicfalvi (Dayro Moreno 73), Emeghara.
Coach: Mihai Stoichiţă (ROU)
Yellow Card(s): Tănase 37, Rada 39, Golański 57, Ninu 79

RUSSIA

FC RUBIN KAZAN

UEFA CHAMPIONS LEAGUE

Group F
Match 1 - FC Dynamo Kyiv (UKR)
A 1-3 *Domínguez (25)*
Ryzhikov, Ansaldi, César Navas, Semak, Domínguez (Murawski 77), Bukharov, Ryazantsev (Kasaev 83), Noboa, Kaleshin, Gökdeniz Karadeniz, Sharonov. Coach: Kurban Berdyev (TKM)
Yellow Card(s): Sharonov 28, Ansaldi 68, Semak 81
Match 2 - FC Internazionale Milano (ITA)
H 1-1 *Domínguez (11)*
Ryzhikov, Ansaldi, César Navas, Semak, Salukvadze, Domínguez (Kasaev 86), Bukharov, Ryazantsev, Noboa, Gökdeniz Karadeniz, Sharonov. Coach: Kurban Berdyev (TKM)
Yellow Card(s): Gökdeniz Karadeniz 9
Match 3 - FC Barcelona (ESP)
A 2-1 *Ryazantsev (2), Gökdeniz Karadeniz (73)*
Ryzhikov, Ansaldi, César Navas, Semak (Murawski 43), Salukvadze, Domínguez, Ryazantsev (Kasaev 83), Noboa, Kaleshin, Gökdeniz Karadeniz (Popov 90+3), Sharonov. Coach: Kurban Berdyev (TKM)
Yellow Card(s): Murawski 78, Ansaldi 90
Match 4 - FC Barcelona (ESP)
H 0-0
Ryzhikov, Ansaldi, César Navas, Semak, Salukvadze, Domínguez, Ryazantsev, Noboa, Kaleshin, Gökdeniz Karadeniz (Bukharov 62), Sharonov. Coach: Kurban Berdyev (TKM)
Yellow Card(s): Semak 73, Ryzhikov 90+1
Match 5 - FC Dynamo Kyiv (UKR)
H 0-0
Ryzhikov, Ansaldi, César Navas, Semak, Salukvadze, Domínguez, Bukharov, Ryazantsev, Noboa, Gökdeniz Karadeniz (Bystrov 75), Sharonov (Kaleshin 53). Coach: Kurban Berdyev (TKM)
Yellow Card(s): Domínguez 56, Noboa 59
Match 6 - FC Internazionale Milano (ITA)
A 0-2
Ryzhikov, César Navas, Semak, Salukvadze, Domínguez, Ryazantsev (Balyaikin 84), Noboa (Bystrov 81), Kaleshin, Popov, Murawski, Gökdeniz Karadeniz (Kasaev 74). Coach: Kurban Berdyev (TKM)
Yellow Card(s): Murawski 28, César Navas 43

No	Player	Nat	DoB	Aps	(s)	Gls
Goalkeeper						
77	Sergei Ryzhikov		19/9/80	6		
Defenders						
3	Cristian Ansaldi	ARG	20/9/86	5		
4	César Navas	ESP	14/2/80	6		
19	Vitaliy Kaleshin		3/10/80	4	(1)	
24	Aleksei Popov		7/7/78	1	(1)	
9	Lasha Salukvadze	GEO	21/12/81	5		
76	Roman Sharonov		8/9/76	5		
Midfielders						
23	Yevgeniy Balyaikin		19/5/88		(1)	
5	Pyotr Bystrov		15/7/79		(2)	
61	Gökdeniz Karadeniz	TUR	11/1/80	6		1
88	Alan Kasaev		8/4/86		(4)	
42	Rafał Murawski	POL	9/10/81	1	(2)	
16	Christian Noboa	ECU	9/4/85	6		
15	Aleksandr Ryazantsev		5/9/86	6		1
7	Sergei Semak		27/2/76	6		

Forwards
| 11 | Aleksandr Bukharov | | 12/3/85 | 3 | (1) |
| 10 | Alejandro Domínguez | ARG | 10/6/81 | 6 | 2 |

UEFA EUROPA LEAGUE
Round of 32 - Hapoel Tel-Aviv FC (ISR)
H 3-0 *Bukharov (14, 23), Semak (69)*
Ryzhikov, Ansaldi, César Navas, Semak, Salukvadze, Bukharov, Ryazantsev (Kasaev 40), Noboa, Kaleshin, Murawski, Gökdeniz Karadeniz (Gorbanets 88). Coach: Kurban Berdyev (TKM)
A 0-0
Ryzhikov, Ansaldi, César Navas, Semak, Salukvadze, Bukharov (Hasan Kabze 82), Noboa, Kaleshin (Balyaikin 51), Murawski, Gökdeniz Karadeniz, Kasaev. Coach: Kurban Berdyev (TKM)
Yellow Card(s): Semak 48, Balyaikin 59, César Navas 64

Round of 16 - VfL Wolfsburg (GER)
H 1-1 *Noboa (29)*
Ryzhikov, Ansaldi, César Navas, Sibaya (Murawski 79), Salukvadze, Bukharov, Noboa, Orekhov, Gökdeniz Karadeniz (Balyaikin 81), Kasaev (Portnyagin 85), Hasan Kabze. Coach: Kurban Berdyev (TKM)
A 1-2 *Kasaev (21) (aet)*
Ryzhikov, Ansaldi (Salukvadze 97), César Navas, Bukharov, Noboa, Orekhov, Balyaikin, Murawski (Sibaya 97), Gökdeniz Karadeniz, Kasaev (Gorbanets 82), Hasan Kabze. Coach: Kurban Berdyev (TKM)
Red Card(s): César Navas 109
Yellow Card(s): César Navas 25, Orekhov 57, Kasaev 77, Gorbanets 90+1 César Navas 109

PFC CSKA MOSKVA

UEFA CHAMPIONS LEAGUE
Group B
Match 1 - VfL Wolfsburg (GER)
A 1-3 *Dzagoev (76)*
Akinfeev, Šembaras, Ignashevich, A. Berezutskiy, Dzagoev, Krasić, Guilherme, Aldonin (Mamayev 68), V. Berezutskiy (Necid 84), Rahimić, Schennikov (Piliev 57). Coach: Juande Ramos (ESP)
Yellow Card(s): Rahimić 34
Match 2 - Beşiktaş JK (TUR)
H 2-1 *Dzagoev (7), Krasić (61)*
Akinfeev, Šembaras, Ignashevich, A. Berezutskiy (Grigoryev 46), Dzagoev, Mamayev, Mark González (Schennikov 78), Odiah, Krasić, V. Berezutskiy, Necid (Rahimić 64). Coach: Juande Ramos (ESP)
Yellow Card(s): A. Berezutskiy 35, Odiah 37, Krasić 61, Ignashevich 82
Match 3 - Manchester United FC (ENG)
H 0-1
Akinfeev, Šembaras, Ignashevich, A. Berezutskiy, Dzagoev, Odiah, Krasić, V. Berezutskiy, Rahimić (Daniel Carvalho 90), Schennikov (Mamayev 62), Necid (Piliev 73). Coach: Juande Ramos (ESP)
Match 4 - Manchester United FC (ENG)
A 3-3 *Dzagoev (25), Krasić (31), V. Berezutskiy (47)*
Akinfeev, Šembaras, Ignashevich, A. Berezutskiy, Dzagoev (Daniel Carvalho 72), Mamayev (Rahimić 70), Krasić, Aldonin, V. Berezutskiy, Schennikov, Necid (Piliev 85). Coach: Leonid Slutskiy (RUS)
Red Card(s): Šembaras 90+5
Yellow Card(s): Necid 25, Aldonin 54, Šembaras 72, Daniel Carvalho 89, Šembaras 90+5
Match 5 - VfL Wolfsburg (GER)
H 2-1 *Necid (58), Krasić (66)*
Akinfeev, Ignashevich, A. Berezutskiy, Dzagoev, Mamayev, Krasić, Aldonin, V. Berezutskiy, Rahimić, Schennikov, Necid. Coach: Leonid Slutskiy (RUS)

atch 6 - Beşiktaş JK (TUR)
2-1 *Krasić (41), Aldonin (90+5)*
kinfeev, Šemberas, Dzagoev (Grigoryev 90+6), Mamayev, Odiah, Krasić
liseh 82), Aldonin, V. Berezutskiy, Rahimić, Schennikov, Necid. Coach:
eonid Slutskiy (RUS)
ellow Card(s): Odiah 27, Mamayev 37, Krasić 42

rst Knockout Round - Sevilla FC (ESP)
1-1 *Mark González (66)*
kinfeev, Šemberas, Ignashevich, A. Berezutskiy, Mark González, Krasić,
onda (Mamayev 83), Aldonin, V. Berezutskiy, Schennikov, Necid. Coach:
eonid Slutskiy (RUS)
ellow Card(s): Aldonin 78, Mark González 80, Honda 82
2-1 *Necid (39), Honda (55)*
kinfeev, Šemberas, Ignashevich, A. Berezutskiy, Mark González
Mamayev 88), Krasić (Odiah 72), Honda (Rahimić 82), Aldonin, V.
erezutskiy, Schennikov, Necid. Coach: Leonid Slutskiy (RUS)
ellow Card(s): A. Berezutskiy 20, Schennikov 61, Mark González 70,
emberas 71

uarter-Finals - FC Internazionale Milano (ITA)
0-1
kinfeev, Šemberas, Ignashevich, A. Berezutskiy, Mamayev (Mark
onzález 73), Krasić, Honda (Dzagoev 70), Aldonin (Rahimić 76), V.
erezutskiy, Schennikov, Necid. Coach: Leonid Slutskiy (RUS)
ellow Card(s): Krasić 32, Aldonin 37
0-1
kinfeev, Šemberas, Ignashevich, A. Berezutskiy, Dzagoev, Mamayev,
ark González, Honda (Rahimić 77), V. Berezutskiy (Odiah 14),
chennikov, Necid (Guilherme 71). Coach: Leonid Slutskiy (RUS)
ed Card(s): Odiah 49
ellow Card(s): Odiah 38, Odiah 49, Mamayev 63

o	Player	Nat	DoB	Aps	(s)	Gls
oalkeeper						
5	Igor Akinfeev		8/4/86	10		
efenders						
	Aleksei Berezutskiy		20/6/82	9		
0	Anton Grigoryev		13/12/85		(2)	
	Sergei Ignashevich		14/7/79	9		
5	Chidi Odiah	NGA	17/12/83	3	(2)	
2	Georgiy Schennikov		27/4/91	9	(1)	
	Deividas Šemberas	LTU	2/8/78	9		
4	Vasiliy Berezutskiy		20/6/82	10		1
idfielders						
2	Yevgeniy Aldonin		22/1/80	7		1
	Daniel Carvalho	BRA	1/3/83		(2)	
0	Alan Dzagoev		17/6/90	7	(1)	3
8	Keisuke Honda	JPN	13/6/86	4		1
7	Miloš Krasić	SRB	1/11/84	9		4
1	Pavel Mamayev		17/9/88	6	(4)	
3	Mark González	CHI	10/7/84	4	(1)	1
6	Sekou Oliseh	NGA	5/6/90		(1)	
3	Nika Piliev		21/3/91		(3)	
5	Elvir Rahimić	BIH	4/4/76	4	(5)	
orwards						
0	Guilherme	BRA	22/10/88	1	(1)	
9	Tomáš Necid	CZE	13/8/89	9	(1)	2

FC DINAMO MOSKVA

UEFA CHAMPIONS LEAGUE

hird Qualifying Round - Celtic FC (SCO)
1-0 *Kokorin (7)*
Gabulov, Kowalczyk, Fernández, K. Kombarov, D. Kombarov, Kerzhakov,
Granat, Wilkshire, Kolodin, Svezhov, Kokorin (Smolov 74). Coach: Andrei
Kobelev (RUS)
Yellow Card(s): Wilkshire 72, Svezhov 90

H 0-2
Gabulov, Kowalczyk, Fernández (Ropotan 90+6), K. Kombarov, Khokhlov,
D. Kombarov, Kerzhakov, Granat, Wilkshire, Kolodin, Svezhov (Kokorin 84).
Coach: Andrei Kobelev (RUS)
Yellow Card(s): Svezhov 68

UEFA EUROPA LEAGUE

Play-Off Round - PFC CSKA Sofia (BUL)
A 0-0
Gabulov, Kowalczyk, Fernández, K. Kombarov, Khokhlov (Ropotan 85), D.
Kombarov, Kerzhakov, Granat, Wilkshire, Kolodin, Kokorin (Aguiar 68).
Coach: Andrei Kobelev (RUS)
Yellow Card(s): Fernández 42, K. Kombarov 45, Ropotan 90+2
H 1-2 *Kerzhakov (10)*
Gabulov, Kowalczyk (Smolov 61), Fernández, K. Kombarov, Khokhlov, D.
Kombarov, Kerzhakov, Granat (Kokorin 56), Aguiar (Dimidko 46), Wilkshire,
Kolodin. Coach: Andrei Kobelev (RUS)
Yellow Card(s): K. Kombarov 86

FC AMKAR PERM

UEFA EUROPA LEAGUE

Play-Off Round - Fulham FC (ENG)
A 1-3 *Grishin (77)*
Zhilyaev (Grishin 60), Narubin, Peev, Novaković (Telkiyski 68), Sirakov,
Gaál, Jean Carlos (Junuzović 85), Drinčić, Belorukov, Cherenchikov,
Kushev. Coach: Dimitar Dimitrov (BUL)
Yellow Card(s): Belorukov 63, Cherenchikov 75
H 1-0 *Kushev (90)*
Narubin, Grishin (Junuzović 76), Telkiyski (Novaković 60), Peev, Sirakov,
Gaál, Jean Carlos (Zhilyaev 64), Drinčić, Belorukov, Cherenchikov, Kushev.
Coach: Dimitar Dimitrov (BUL)
Yellow Card(s): Belorukov 84

FC ZENIT ST PETERSBURG

UEFA EUROPA LEAGUE

Play-Off Round - CD Nacional (POR)
A 3-4 *Semshov (43, 55), Fatih Tekke (90+3)*
Malafeev, Anyukov, Fernando Meira, Lombaerts, Hubočan, Shirokov,
Zyryanov, Kornilenko (Fatih Tekke 68), Semshov, Huszti (Rosina 58),
Denisov (Ignatovich 76). Coach: Anatoliy Davydov (RUS)
Yellow Card(s): Anyukov 21, Shirokov 35, Fernando Meira 79
H 1-1 *Fatih Tekke (34)*
Čontofalský, Anyukov, Fernando Meira, Kim, Lombaerts, Fatih Tekke
(Rosina 71), Shirokov (Križanac 71), Zyryanov, Kornilenko, Semshov, Huszti
(Ignatovich 90+1). Coach: Anatoliy Davydov (RUS)
Yellow Card(s): Huszti 66, Zyryanov 77, Križanac 80, Kim 90+4

PFC KRYLYA SOVETOV SAMARA

UEFA EUROPA LEAGUE

Third Qualifying Round - Saint Patrick's Athletic FC (IRL)
A 0-1
Lobos, Kalachev, Leílton, Shishkin, Bober, Savin, Jarošík, Adjindjal, Ignatyev, Belozyorov, Ivanov (Kulik 78). Coach: Leonid Slutskiy (RUS)
Yellow Card(s): Kalachev 37
H 3-2 Bober (41), Savin (53, 57)
Lobos, Kalachev, Shishkin, Bober, Taranov, Savin, Adjindjal, Ignatyev (Kulik 39), Budylin (Leílton 68), Belozyorov, Ivanov. Coach: Leonid Slutskiy (RUS)
Yellow Card(s): Adjindjal 32, Kulik 72

SAN MARINO

SP TRE FIORI

UEFA CHAMPIONS LEAGUE

First Qualifying Round - UE Sant Julià (AND)
H 1-1 Andreini (75)
Micheletti, Nardone, Ballanti, Tombetti (Vendemini 85), Macerata, Benedettini, Andreini, Canarezza (Simoncini 62), Lisi, Rodríguez, Amici (Giunta 55). Coach: Floriano Sperindio (SMR)
Yellow Card(s): Rodríguez 24, Ballanti 33, Simoncini 70
A 1-1 Canarezza (82) (aet; 4-5 on pens)
Micheletti, Nardone (Vendemini 75), Ballanti, Tombetti (Giunta 65), Macerata, Benedettini, Andreini, Canarezza (Macina 114), Lisi, Simoncini, Rodríguez. Coach: Floriano Sperindio (SMR)
Red Card(s): Simoncini 60
Yellow Card(s): Canarezza 7, Rodríguez 14, Simoncini 26, Simoncini 60, Lisi 90

AC JUVENES-DOGANA

UEFA EUROPA LEAGUE

Second Qualifying Round - KSP Polonia Warszawa (POL)
H 0-1
Montanari, Renzi, Ceci, Marzocchi, Perrotta, Rossi, Tasso, Galli, Nanni (Gasperoni 85), Gamberini, Selva. Coach: Alberto Manca (ITA)
A 0-4
Montanari, Renzi, Ceci, Marzocchi, Perrotta, Rossi, Tasso, Galli, Gasperoni (Nanni 46), Gamberini (Fantini 50), Selva. Coach: Alberto Manca (ITA)

SCOTLAND

RANGERS FC

UEFA CHAMPIONS LEAGUE

Group G
Match 1 - VfB Stuttgart (GER)
A 1-1 Bougherra (77)
McGregor, Pedro Mendes, Papac, McCulloch, Davis, Thomson, Rothen, Naismith, Whittaker, Miller (Nacho Novo 90+3), Bougherra. Coach: Walter Smith (SCO)
Yellow Card(s): Papac 71
Match 2 - Sevilla FC (ESP)
H 1-4 Nacho Novo (88)
McGregor, Weir, Pedro Mendes, Papac, McCulloch (Boyd 73), Davis, Thomson, Rothen (Nacho Novo 73), Naismith, Whittaker, Bougherra. Coach: Walter Smith (SCO)
Yellow Card(s): Naismith 58
Match 3 - FC Unirea Urziceni (ROU)
H 1-4 Ricardo Vilana (2og)
McGregor, Weir, Pedro Mendes (Lafferty 46), Papac, McCulloch, Davis, Thomson, Rothen (Nacho Novo 66), Naismith, Whittaker, Miller. Coach: Walter Smith (SCO)
Yellow Card(s): Naismith 58
Match 4 - FC Unirea Urziceni (ROU)
A 1-1 McCulloch (79)
McGregor, Weir, Papac, McCulloch, Davis, Thomson (Fleck 85), Naismith, Whittaker, Miller, Nacho Novo 82), Lafferty, Wilson. Coach: Walter Smith (SCO)
Yellow Card(s): Lafferty 28, Wilson 76
Match 5 - VfB Stuttgart (GER)
H 0-2
McGregor, Weir, Papac, McCulloch, Davis, Thomson (Fleck 77), Boyd, Whittaker, Miller (Nacho Novo 69), Lafferty (Beasley 85), Wilson. Coach: Walter Smith (SCO)
Yellow Card(s): Boyd 19, Thomson 26, McCulloch 34
Match 6 - Sevilla FC (ESP)
A 0-1
McGregor, Weir, Papac, McCulloch, Davis, Thomson, Whittaker, Miller (Nacho Novo 46), Beasley (Lafferty 46), Bougherra, Smith (Fleck 85). Coach: Walter Smith (SCO)
Yellow Card(s): Papac 35, Lafferty 74, Bougherra 84

No	Player	Nat	DoB	Aps	(s)	Gls
Goalkeeper						
1	Allan McGregor		31/1/82	6		
Defenders						
24	Madjid Bougherra	ALG	7/10/82	3		1
5	Saša Papac	BIH	7/2/80	6		
26	Steven Smith		30/8/85	1		
3	David Weir		10/5/70	5		
16	Steven Whittaker		16/6/84	6		
66	Danny Wilson		27/12/91	2		
Midfielders						
20	DaMarcus Beasley	USA	24/5/82	1	(1)	
7	Steven Davis	NIR	1/1/85	6		
29	John Fleck		24/8/91		(3)	
6	Lee McCulloch		14/5/78	6		1
4	Pedro Mendes	POR	26/2/79	3		
11	Jérôme Rothen	FRA	31/3/78	3		
8	Kevin Thomson		14/10/84	6		
Forwards						
9	Kris Boyd		18/8/83	1	(1)	
27	Kyle Lafferty	NIR	16/9/87	2	(2)	
18	Kenny Miller		23/12/79	5		
14	Steven Naismith		14/9/86	4		
10	Nacho Novo	ESP	26/3/79		(6)	1

CELTIC FC

UEFA CHAMPIONS LEAGUE

Third Qualifying Round - FC Dinamo Moskva (RUS)
A 0-1
Boruc, Hinkel, Naylor, Caldwell, N'Guémo, McDonald (Killen 61), Fortuné (Samaras 60), Maloney, Donati (Fox 67), Loovens, McGeady. Coach: Tony Mowbray (ENG)
Yellow Card(s): Hinkel 67, Killen 87
H 2-0 McDonald (45), Samaras (90+1)
Boruc, Hinkel, Caldwell, N'Guémo, McDonald (Samaras 79), Fortuné (Brown 69), Fox, Maloney, Donati, Loovens, McGeady. Coach: Tony Mowbray (ENG)
Yellow Card(s): N'Guémo 78

Play-Off Round - Arsenal FC (ENG)
A 0-2
Boruc, Hinkel, Caldwell, N'Guémo (McCourt 76), Brown, Samaras (Fortuné 65), Fox, Maloney, Donati (McDonald 56), Loovens, McGeady. Coach: Tony Mowbray (ENG)
Yellow Card(s): Fox 52, N'Guémo 58, Loovens 86
H 1-3 Donati (90+2)
Boruc, Hinkel, Caldwell (O'Dea 46), McDonald, Brown, Fortuné, Fox, Maloney (Flood 61), Donati, Loovens, McGeady (Naylor 61). Coach: Tony Mowbray (ENG)
Yellow Card(s): Caldwell 33, McGeady 56, Brown 83

UEFA EUROPA LEAGUE

Group C
Match 1 - Hapoel Tel-Aviv FC (ISR)
A 1-2 Samaras (25)
Boruc, Hinkel, McManus, Caldwell (McDonald 89), N'Guémo (McGinn 66), Brown, Samaras (Killen 70), Fox, Maloney, Loovens, McGeady. Coach: Tony Mowbray (ENG)
Yellow Card(s): McGeady 44, McDonald 90+1
Match 2 - SK Rapid Wien (AUT)
H 1-1 McDonald (21)
Boruc, McManus, Caldwell, N'Guémo (Robson 81), McDonald, Brown, Samaras, Fox, Wilson, Maloney (Killen 81), McGeady (McGinn 81). Coach: Tony Mowbray (ENG)
Yellow Card(s): N'Guémo 59
Match 3 - Hamburger SV (GER)
A 0-1
Boruc, Naylor, McManus, Caldwell, N'Guémo, McDonald (Samaras 62), Brown (McCourt 76), Wilson, Maloney (McGinn 76), Robson, McGeady. Coach: Tony Mowbray (ENG)
Yellow Card(s): McManus 31, Naylor 52
Match 4 - Hamburger SV (GER)
H 0-0
Zaluska, Hinkel, Caldwell, N'Guémo, McDonald (Naylor 58), Samaras, Fox, Crosas, Robson (McGinn 75), Loovens, McGeady (Fortuné 58). Coach: Tony Mowbray (ENG)
Yellow Card(s): Caldwell 19, Samaras 65, Robson 66
Match 5 - Hapoel Tel-Aviv FC (ISR)
H 2-0 Samaras (22), Robson (68)
Zaluska, Hinkel, Caldwell, N'Guémo, McDonald, Samaras (Fortuné 63), Fox, Crosas, Robson, Loovens, McGeady (Naylor 74). Coach: Tony Mowbray (ENG)
Match 6 - SK Rapid Wien (AUT)
A 3-3 Fortuné (24, 67), McGowan (90+1)
Boruc, McManus, N'Guémo, Fortuné (Killen 90), Wilson, McGinn (Carey 78), Flood, Crosas, Loovens, Caddis, McGowan. Coach: Tony Mowbray (ENG)

HEART OF MIDLOTHIAN FC

UEFA EUROPA LEAGUE

Play-Off Round - NK Dinamo Zagreb (CRO)
A 0-4
Kello, Wallace, Jónnson, Gonçalves, Rubén Palazuelos, Suso Santana (Novikovas 81), Obua, Nadé (Glen 58), Bouzid (Black 46), M. Stewart, Žaliūkas. Coach: Csaba László (HUN)
Yellow Card(s): Nadé 45, Žaliūkas 66
H 2-0 M. Stewart (18), Žaliūkas (55)
Balogh, Gonçalves, Rubén Palazuelos (Black 82), Suso Santana, Obua, Nadé (Smith 55), Bouzid, M. Stewart, Žaliūkas, Glen (Driver 60), C. Thomson. Coach: Csaba László (HUN)
Yellow Card(s): M. Stewart 57, Black 90+3

ABERDEEN FC

UEFA EUROPA LEAGUE

Third Qualifying Round - SK Sigma Olomouc (CZE)
H 1-5 Mulgrew (22)
Langfield, Mulgrew, Foster, McDonald, Considine, Kerr, Miller, Mackie (Maguire 60), Aluko (Paton 72), Young, Duff. Coach: Mark McGhee (SCO)
Yellow Card(s): Foster 76
A 0-3
Langfield, Mulgrew, Foster, McDonald, Considine, Maguire (Megginson 85), Kerr, Miller, Mackie, Aluko, Duff. Coach: Mark McGhee (SCO)
Yellow Card(s): Langfield 48, Foster 78

FALKIRK FC

UEFA EUROPA LEAGUE

Second Qualifying Round - FC Vaduz (LIE)
H 1-0 Flynn (50)
Olejnik, Barr, Scobbie, Twaddle, McNamara, McLean, O'Brien, Finnigan (Robertson 77), Arfield, Flynn (Mitchell 75), Macdonald (Sludden 89). Coach: Eddie May (SCO)
Yellow Card(s): Arfield 45, Finnigan 62, McNamara 69, Robertson 90+2
A 0-2 (aet)
Olejnik, Barr, Scobbie, Twaddle, McNamara, McLean, O'Brien (Lynch 90+1), Finnigan, Arfield, Mitchell (Sludden 106), McDonald (Flynn 59). Coach: Eddie May (SCO)
Red Card(s): Finnigan 120+3
Yellow Card(s): Barr 27, Scobbie 30, O'Brien 35, Finnigan 39, Flynn 60

MOTHERWELL FC

UEFA EUROPA LEAGUE

First Qualifying Round - Llanelli AFC (WAL)
H 0-1
Fraser, Hammell, Reynolds, Craigan, Sutton, Lasley (Slane 46), Murphy, O'Brien (McHugh 74), McGarry, Forbes, Saunders. Coach: Jim Gannon (IRL)
A 3-0 Sutton (8,25), Murphy (72)
Fraser, Hammell, Reynolds, Craigan, Sutton (Archdeacon 76), Lasley, O'Brien, McGarry (Murphy 69), Forbes, Saunders (Page 78), Slane. Coach: Jim Gannon (IRL)

Second Qualifying Round - KS Flamurtari (ALB)
A 0-1
Fraser, Hammell, Reynolds, Craigan, Sutton, Lasley, O'Brien, McGarry (Fitzpatrick 65), Forbes (Murphy 75), Saunders (Page 40), Slane. Coach: Jim Gannon (IRL)
Yellow Card(s): Forbes 35, Hammell 58
H 8-1 Murphy (16, 19, 34), Slane (25), Forbes (28p, 50), Hutchinson (38), McHugh (72)
Fraser, Reynolds, Craigan, Humphrey (McHugh 67), Jennings (Lasley 68), Sutton, Murphy, O'Brien, Forbes, Hutchinson, Slane (Page 77). Coach: Jim Gannon (IRL)

Third Qualifying Round - FC Steaua Bucureşti (ROU)
A 0-3
Ruddy, Reynolds, Craigan, Coke, Humphrey (O'Brien 55), Jennings (Murphy 77), Sutton, Forbes (Hammell 37), Hutchinson, Saunders, Slane. Coach: Jim Gannon (IRL)
Yellow Card(s): Craigan 78
H 1-3 Forbes (17)
Ruddy, Hammell, Reynolds (McHugh 60), Craigan, Coke (Jennings 71), Sutton, Murphy (Humphrey 60), O'Brien, Forbes, Hutchinson, Slane. Coach: Jim Gannon (IRL)
Yellow Card(s): Forbes 58

SERBIA

FK PARTIZAN

UEFA CHAMPIONS LEAGUE

Second Qualifying Round - Rhyl FC (WAL)
A 4-0 Krstajić (17), Cléo (18), Diarra (45), Đorđević (69)
Božović, Stevanović (Knežević 72), Đorđević (Vujović 72), Petrović, Cléo (Bogunović 83), Moreira, B. Ilić, Krstajić, Diarra, Gavrančić. Coach: Slaviša Jokanović (SRB)
H 8-0 Diarra (4), Cléo (17, 51, 72p), Đorđević (20), B. Ilić (38, 63), Petrović (66)
Božović, Stevanović, Đorđević (Brežančić 60), Tomić (Bogunović 69), Petrović, Cléo, Moreira (B. Jovanović 60), B. Ilić, Krstajić, Diarra, Gavrančić. Coach: Slaviša Jokanović (SRB)

Third Qualifying Round - APOEL FC (CYP)
A 0-2
Božović, Stevanović (Knežević 84), Đorđević, Tomić (Fejsa 61), Petrović, Cléo, Moreira, B. Ilić (Bogunović 72), Diarra, Obradović, Gavrančić. Coach: Slaviša Jokanović (SRB)
Yellow Card(s): Stevanović 23, Diarra 29, Petrović 48, Gavrančić 83

H 1-0 Moreira (3)
Božović, Đorđević, Tomić (B. Jovanović 85), Petrović, Cléo (Bogunović 67), Moreira, Ljajić (Washington 57), Knežević, Diarra, Obradović, Gavrančić. Coach: Slaviša Jokanović (SRB)
Yellow Card(s): Ljajić 23, Petrović 57, Diarra 76

UEFA EUROPA LEAGUE

Play-Off Round - MŠK Žilina (SVK)
H 1-1 Cléo (16p)
Božović, Đorđević, Fejsa (M. Jovanović 46), Tomić (B. Ilić 63), Cléo, Moreir Bogunović, Krstajić, Ljajić, Obradović, Gavrančić (Knežević 69). Coach: Slaviša Jokanović (SRB)
Yellow Card(s): Božović 32, Cléo 41, Obradović 54, Đorđević 88, Moreira 90+
A 2-0 Diarra (59), B. Ilić (65)
Božović, Stevanović (Gavrančić 85), Đorđević, Tomić, Petrović, B. Ilić, Krstajić (Knežević 56), B. Jovanović (Fejsa 67), Ljajić, Diarra, Obradović. Coach: Slaviša Jokanović (SRB)
Yellow Card(s): Ljajić 78, Diarra 85

Group J
Match 1 - Toulouse FC (FRA)
H 2-3 Krstajić (23), Cléo (67)
Božović, Đorđević, Fejsa, Petrović, Moreira, Lomić, B. Ilić (Cléo 62), Krstajić Knežević (Stevanović 46), Diarra, Gavrančić (Tomić 52). Coach: Goran Stevanović (SRB)
Yellow Card(s): Lomić 41, Gavrančić 50
Match 2 - FC Shakhtar Donetsk (UKR)
A 1-4 Ljajić (86)
Radosavljević, Stevanović, Đorđević, Fejsa, Petrović (Ljajić 46), Moreira, Lomić (Tomić 69), B. Ilić (Cléo 57), Krstajić, Diarra, Gavrančić. Coach: Gorar Stevanović (SRB)
Match 3 - Club Brugge KV (BEL)
A 0-2
Radosavljević, Stevanović, Fejsa, Tomić, Moreira (Cléo 46), Krstajić, B. Jovanović (Petrović 88), Ljajić, Diarra, Brežančić, Gavrančić (Đorđević 14). Coach: Goran Stevanović (SRB)
Yellow Card(s): Đorđević 18, Krstajić 33, Fejsa 83, B. Jovanović 88, Petrović 89
Match 4 - Club Brugge KV (BEL)
H 2-4 Ljajić (52), Washington (66)
Radosavljević, Đorđević, Fejsa, Moreira, Lomić, B. Ilić (Bogunović 46), Krstajić, B. Jovanović (Tomić 75), Ljajić, Knežević, Diarra (Washington 50). Coach: Goran Stevanović (SRB)
Red Card(s): Krstajić 80
Yellow Card(s): B. Jovanović 56, Krstajić 57, Krstajić 80, Moreira 83, Đorđević 90+1
Match 5 - Toulouse FC (FRA)
A 0-1
Božović, Stevanović, Đorđević, Fejsa, Tomić, Petrović (B. Jovanović 85), Cléo (Washington 75), Moreira, M. Jovanović, Ljajić (Bogunović 52), Knežević. Coach: Goran Stevanović (SRB)
Yellow Card(s): Petrović 37
Match 6 - FC Shakhtar Donetsk (UKR)
H 1-0 Diarra (6)
Božović, Fejsa, Tomić, Petrović (B. Jovanović 69), Moreira (B. Ilić 60), Lomić M. Jovanović, Krstajić, Ljajić, Knežević, Diarra (Bogunović 79). Coach: Goran Stevanović (SRB)
Yellow Card(s): Petrović 16, Ljajić 29, Fejsa 70, Tomić 82

FK VOJVODINA

UEFA EUROPA LEAGUE

Third Qualifying Round - FK Austria Wien (AUT)
H 1-1 Djurovski (45+2)
Brkić, Peković, Ajuru, Stoića (Tumbasević 46), Djurovski (Grozdanovski 85) Stjepanović, Vulićević, Karan, Lovrić, Tadić (Maksimović 62), Mrđa. Coach: Dragoslav Stepanović (SRB)
Yellow Card(s): Stjepanović 27, Djurovski 45+3, Mrđa 70, Tumbasević 84

2-4 Mrđa (31), Tadić (58)
kić, Peković, Ajuru, Grozdanovski, Djurovski (Khutsishvili 84),
jepanović (Smiljanić 72), Tumbasević (Stoića 84), Vulićević, Karan, Tadić,
rđa. Coach: Dragoslav Stepanović (SRB)
llow Card(s): Vulićević 59

FK CRVENA ZVEZDA

UEFA EUROPA LEAGUE

econd Qualifying Round - NK Rudar Velenje (SVN)
1-0 Perović (59)
avlović, Sávio, Ignjatijević, Lekić, Tutorić, Lazetić (Cvetković 90+1),
orđević, Perović (Jevtić 90+3), Ninkov, Awal Issah, Bogdanović (Nikolić
3). Coach: Vladimir Petrović (SRB)
llow Card(s): Đorđević 39, Lazetić 55
4-0 Bogdanović (37), Jevtić (74, 90+4), Cadú (85)
avlović, Sávio, Ignjatijević, Lekić, Tutorić, Lazetić (Cadú 76), Đorđević,
erović (Jevtić 69), Ninkov, Awal Issah, Bogdanović (Nikolić 80). Coach:
ladimir Petrović (SRB)

hird Qualifying Round - FC Dinamo Tbilisi (GEO)
0-2
avlović, Sávio, Ignjatijević, Lekić, Tutorić, Lazetić (Nikolić 73), Đorđević,
vtić (Perović 63), Ninkov, Awal Issah, Bogdanović (Cadú 57). Coach:
adimir Petrović (SRB)
llow Card(s): Awal Issah 10, Bogdanović 30
5-2 Perović (18), Lekić (26, 45+2, 88), Cadú (76p)
avlović, Sávio (Cadú 58), Savić, Lekić, Lazetić, Đorđević, Cvetković
ogdanović 65), Perović, Ninkov, Blažić (Nikolić 73), Awal Issah. Coach:
adimir Petrović (SRB)
ed Card(s): Đorđević 70
llow Card(s): Perović 33, Sávio 37, Lekić 82

ay-Off Round - SK Slavia Praha (CZE)
0-3
avlović, Sávio, Lekić, Tutorić, Vilotić, Srečković (Perović 46), Lazetić,
inkov, Awal Issah (Ignjatijević 70), Savić, Bogdanović (Nikolić 90+2).
oach: Vladimir Petrović (SRB)
llow Card(s): Ninkov 61
2-1 Bogdanović (23p), Perović (45)
tamenković, Ignjatijević (Cadú 38), Lekić, Vilotić, Lazetić, Perović, Ninkov,
ažić, Awal Issah, Savić (Sávio 74), Bogdanović (Nikolić 46). Coach:
ladimir Petrović (SRB)
llow Card(s): Lekić 55, Savić 58, Cadú 87

FK SEVOJNO

UEFA EUROPA LEAGUE

econd Qualifying Round - FBK Kaunas (LTU)
0-0
ikolić, Kamberović, Virić, Bulatović, Raković, Sunjevarić (Timić 58),
avićević, Vujović (Pejović 83), Stanisavljević, Janković, Maksimović
ović 49). Coach: Ljubiša Stamenković (SRB)
llow Card(s): Raković 17

A 1-1 Vujović (48)
Nikolić, Kamberović, Virić (Sunjevarić 70), Bulatović, Raković, Jovičić,
Pavićević, Vujović, Stanisavljević, Janković, Timić (Maksimović 86). Coach:
Ljubiša Stamenković (SRB)
Yellow Card(s): Sunjevarić 74

Third Qualifying Round - LOSC Lille Métropole (FRA)
H 0-2
Nikolić, Kamberović, Virić (Maksimović 74), Bulatović, Sandulović, Raković,
Jovičić, Pavićević, Vujović (Timić 58), Stanisavljević, Janković. Coach:
Ljubiša Stamenković (SRB)
Yellow Card(s): Bulatović 16, Vujović 39, Raković 75, Timić 87
A 0-2
Nikolić, Kamberović (Ljubičić 86), Virić (Timić 77), Bulatović, Sandulović,
Pavićević, Vujović, Stanisavljević, Janković, Ćosić, Mudrinić (Sunjevarić 64).
Coach: Ljubiša Stamenković (SRB)
Yellow Card(s): Ćosić 59, Pavićević 70, Janković 78

SLOVAKIA

ŠK SLOVAN BRATISLAVA

UEFA CHAMPIONS LEAGUE

Second Qualifying Round - HŠK Zrinjski (BIH)
A 0-1
Bičík, Saláta, Dobrotka, Valachovič, Slovák, Božić (Čerňák 78), Obžera
(Sylvestr 83), M. Petráš, Masaryk, Kozák (Gaúcho 88), Dosoudil. Coach:
Dušan Uhrin (CZE)
Yellow Card(s): Dobrotka 52
H 4-0 Halenár (13, 60), Gaúcho (19), Sylvestr (90+2)
Bičík, Saláta, Dobrotka, Valachovič, Halenár (Čerňák 75), Slovák, M. Petráš,
Masaryk (Božić 89), Kozák, Gaúcho (Sylvestr 84), Dosoudil. Coach: Dušan
Uhrin (CZE)
Yellow Card(s): Saláta 37, M. Petráš 78

Third Qualifying Round - Olympiacos FC (GRE)
H 0-2
Bičík, Saláta (Čerňák 79), Dobrotka, Valachovič, Halenár, Slovák, M. Petráš,
Masaryk (Sylvestr 58), Kozák, Gaúcho (Ivana 74), Dosoudil. Coach: Dušan
Uhrin (CZE)
Yellow Card(s): Dobrotka 33, M. Petráš 49, Kozák 67
A 0-2
Bičík, Saláta, Valachovič, Halenár (Čerňák 85), Slovák, Božić, Masaryk
(Obžera 61), Kozák, Gaúcho (Sylvestr 53), Dosoudil, Simão. Coach: Dušan
Uhrin (CZE)
Yellow Card(s): Slovák 12, Dosoudil 16, Obžera 73, Halenár 82

UEFA EUROPA LEAGUE

Play-Off Round - AFC Ajax (NED)
A 0-5
Bičík, Saláta, Dobrotka, Valachovič, Halenár (Čerňák 71), Slovák, Božić,
Obžera (Gaúcho 18), M. Petráš, Masaryk (Sylvestr 57), Kozák. Coach: Dušan
Uhrin (CZE)
Yellow Card(s): Bičík 22, Kozák 61
H 1-2 Sylvestr (45+2)
Putnocký, Saláta, Dobrotka, Halenár, Slovák (Serrano 46), Božić, Sylvestr,
Bagayoko, M. Petráš (Simão 59), Gaúcho (Masaryk 75), Dosoudil. Coach:
Michal Hipp (SVK)
Yellow Card(s): Gaúcho 32, Božić 38, Bagayoko 81

MFK KOŠICE

UEFA EUROPA LEAGUE

Third Qualifying Round - FK Slavija Sarajevo (BIH)
A 2-0 *Novák (11), Škutka (60)*
Schreng, Kišš, Kaminský, Kuzma, Dobias, Milinković (Karaš 82), Cicman, Viazanko, Novák (Serečin 90+4), Bašista, Škutka (Janič 61). Coach: Ján Kozák (SVK)
Yellow Card(s): Škutka 37, Dobias 78
H 3-1 *Novák (2), Bašista (55), Cicman (90+1)*
Schreng, Kišš, Smrek, Dobias, Milinković (Serečin 84), Cicman, Viazanko (Karaš 81), Janič, Novák (Hovančík 76), Bašista, Škutka. Coach: Ján Kozák (SVK)
Yellow Card(s): Bašista 13

Play-Off Round - AS Roma (ITA)
H 3-3 *Milinković (5), Novák (71p, 81)*
Schreng, Kišš, Kaminský (Matić 58), Dobias, Milinković (Janič 69), Juhar, Cicman, Viazanko, Novák, Bašista, Škutka (Karaš 69). Coach: Ján Kozák (SVK)
A 1-7 *Novák (38)*
Schreng, Kišš (Matić 46), Kaminský (Škutka 46), Smrek, Dobias, Milinković, Juhar, Cicman, Viazanko (Serečin 60), Novák, Bašista. Coach: Ján Kozák (SVK)

MŠK ŽILINA

UEFA EUROPA LEAGUE

Second Qualifying Round - FC Dacia Chisinau (MDA)
H 2-0 *Oravec (57), Lietava (77)*
Perniš, Angelovič, Guldan, Mráz, Kobylík (Babatunde 89), Adauto (Lietava 56), Jež, Oravec, Piaček, Zlatkovič (Žilák 76), Šourek. Coach: Pavel Hapal (CZE)
Yellow Card(s): Zlatković 67
A 1-0 *Oravec (47)*
Perniš, Angelovič, Žilák, Guldan, Mráz, Leitner (Zlatkovič 69), Kobylík (Adauto 63), Jež, Oravec (Lietava 79), Piaček, Šourek. Coach: Pavel Hapal (CZE)
Yellow Card(s): Leitner 60, Jež 80

Third Qualifying Round - HNK Hajduk Split (CRO)
H 1-1 *Kobylík (73p)*
Perniš, Angelovič, Žilák (Babatunde 60), Guldan, Mráz, Kobylík (Zlatkovič 79), Adauto, Jež, Piaček, Šourek, Lietava. Coach: Pavel Hapal (CZE)
Yellow Card(s): Guldan 45, Mráz 54, Piaček 88
A 1-0 *Lietava (76)*
Perniš, Guldan (Pečalka 74), Mráz, Leitner, Kobylík (Chupáč 84), Adauto, Jež, Oravec, Piaček, Šourek, Babatunde (Lietava 54). Coach: Pavel Hapal (CZE)
Yellow Card(s): Kobylík 39, Oravec 57, Lietava 70, Pečalka 78

Play-Off Round - FK Partizan (SRB)
A 1-1 *Adauto (34p)*
Perniš, Pečalka (Guldan 59), Mráz, Leitner, Adauto (Babatunde 87), Vyskočil (Rilke 82), Jež, Oravec, Piaček, Šourek, Tsimakuridze. Coach: Pavel Hapal (CZE)
Yellow Card(s): Tsimakuridze 15, Šourek 20
H 0-2
Perniš, Pečalka, Mráz (Kobylík 72), Leitner, Adauto (Lietava 63), Vyskočil (Rilke 64), Jež, Oravec, Piaček, Šourek, Tsimakuridze. Coach: Pavel Hapal (CZE)
Yellow Card(s): Pečalka 46, Lietava 82, Kobylík 90

FC SPARTAK TRNAVA

UEFA EUROPA LEAGUE

First Qualifying Round - İnter Bakı PİK (AZE)
H 2-1 *Kožuch (20, 26)*
Kralj, Doležaj, Procházka, Ďuriš, Kožuch (Bernáth 68), Kopúnek, Hruška, Ľ. Hanzel, Kotula, Gueye, Súkenník (Guldan 86). Coach: Karol Pecze (SVK)
Yellow Card(s): Kožuch 51, Procházka 75, Bernáth 90+1
A 3-1 *Súkenník (34), Kožuch (40), Procházka (48)*
Kralj, Doležaj, Procházka, Ďuriš, Kožuch (Bernáth 79), Kopúnek, Hruška (Jakubička 68), Ľ. Hanzel, Kotula, Gueye, Súkenník (Železník 74). Coach: Karol Pecze (SVK)
Red Card(s): Ľ. Hanzel 59
Yellow Card(s): Ľ. Hanzel 42, Kopúnek 65

Second Qualifying Round - FK Sarajevo (BIH)
A 0-1
Kralj, Jakubička, Doležaj, Kotula, Procházka, Ďuriš (Železník 89), Kožuch (Bernáth 82), Kopúnek, Hruška (Danilo 69), Gueye, Súkenník. Coach: Karol Pecze (SVK)
H 1-1 *Doležaj (19)*
Hrdina, Jakubička, Doležaj, Kotula, Procházka, Ďuriš, Kožuch (Koné 75), Kopúnek, Bernáth, Hruška (Súkenník 67), Gueye. Coach: Karol Pecze (SVK)
Yellow Card(s): Procházka 14, Kotula 72

SLOVENIA

NK MARIBOR

UEFA CHAMPIONS LEAGUE

Second Qualifying Round - FC WIT Georgia (GEO)
A 0-0
Ranilovič, Džinič, Jurkič, Marcos Tavares, Mihelič, Jelič (Bunderla 70), Lunder, Bačinovič, Popović, Pavlovič, Mertelj (Školnik 69). Coach: Darko Milanič (SVN)
Yellow Card(s): Lunder 54, Školnik 83
H 3-1 *Bunderla (9), Marcos Tavares (19), Mihelič (86)*
Ranilovič, Džinič, Jurkič, Marcos Tavares, Mihelič, Lunder, Bačinovič, Pavlovič (Volaš 90), Bunderla (Jelič 70), Školnik (Mertelj 63). Coach: Darko Milanič (SVN)
Yellow Card(s): Školnik 33, Džinič 58, Jurkič 79

Third Qualifying Round - FC Zürich (SUI)
A 3-2 *Marcos Tavares (12, 22), Pavlovič (50)*
Ranilovič, Džinič (Kljajević 77), Mejač (Jurkič 78), Marcos Tavares, Mihelič, Lunder, Bačinovič, Popović, Volas (Jelič 70), Pavlovič, Mertelj. Coach: Darko Milanič (SVN)
Yellow Card(s): Mertelj 23, Mejač 67
H 0-3
Ranilovič, Džinič, Jurkič, Marcos Tavares, Mihelič, Samardžič, Bačinovič (Bunderla 78), Popović, Volaš (Jelič 46), Pavlovič, Mertelj (Mezga 65). Coach: Darko Milanič (SVN)
Yellow Card(s): Bačinovič 67

UEFA EUROPA LEAGUE

Play-Off Round - AC Sparta Praha (CZE)
A 0-2
Kanilović, Džinić, Jurkić (Aljančič 57), Marcos Tavares, Mihelič (Mertelj 80), Samardžić, Bačinović, Popović, Pavlović (Volaš 63), Bunderla, Školnik. Coach: Darko Milanič (SVN)
Yellow Card(s): Bunderla 57, Samardžić 72, Bačinović 90

Kanilović, Marcos Tavares, Mihelič, Jelić (Bunderla 63), Aljančič, Lunder, Samardžić, Popović, Pavlović, Školnik, Mertelj (Črnič 46). Coach: Darko Milanič (SVN)

NK IB LJUBLJANA

UEFA EUROPA LEAGUE

Third Qualifying Round - FC Metalurh Donetsk (UKR)
A 0-2
Rozman, Tabot, Brezič, E. Rakovič, Mišura (Gerič 50), Kokot, Gill, Jelečevič, Horvat (Zadnikar 78), Iličič (Fink 83), Grabus. Coach: Igor Benedejčič (SVN)
Yellow Card(s): Brezič 86
H 0-3
Rozman, Tabot, Brezič, E. Rakovič (Majcen 70), Mišura (Zadnikar 55), Kokot, Ntamé, Gill, Jelečevič, Iličič, Fink (Milenković 46). Coach: Igor Benedejčič (SVN)
Yellow Card(s): Jelečevič 55, Iličič 72

ND GORICA

UEFA EUROPA LEAGUE

Second Qualifying Round - FC Lahti (FIN)
H 1-0 *Kršič (39)*
Simčič, Gorinšek, Balažič, Kršič (Cvijanović 63), Velikonja (Žigon 90+2), Škarabot, Galešić, Demirović, Đukić, Rakušček, Osterc (Arčon 87). Coach: Miran Srebrnič (SVN)
Yellow Card(s): Balažič 83
A 0-2
Simčič, Gorinšek, Balažič, Kršič, Velikonja, Škarabot, Galešić, Demirović, Đukić, Rakušček, Osterc. Coach: Miran Srebrnič (SVN)
Yellow Card(s): Osterc 79

NK RUDAR VELENJE

UEFA EUROPA LEAGUE

First Qualifying Round - JK Trans Narva (EST)
A 3-0 *Cipot (9p), Omladič (61), Trifković (89)*
Savić, Kolsi, Sulejmanovič, Cipot, Trifković, Golob (Kreft 81), Prašnikar, Pokleka, Omladič (Mujakovič 61), Tolimir, Dedič (Jeseničnik 66). Coach: Marjan Pušnik (SVN)
Yellow Card(s): Jeseničnik 84
H 3-1 *Cipot (28, 73), Mahmutovič (69)*
Savić, Dedič, Tolimir (Mujakovič 46), Omladič (Grbič 46), Pokleka, Prašnikar (Mahmutovič 65), Golob, Trifković, Cipot, Sulejmanovič, Kolsi. Coach: Marjan Pušnik (SVN)
Yellow Card(s): Dedič 53

Second Qualifying Round - FK Crvena zvezda (SRB)
H 0-1
Savić, Kolsi (Đukič 61), Sulejmanovič, Cipot, Trifković (Grbič 57), Golob, Prašnikar (Mešič 70), Pokleka, Omladič, Tolimir, Dedič. Coach: Marjan Pušnik (SVN)
Yellow Card(s): Golob 22, Dedič 22, Omladič 63
A 0-4
Savić, Kolsi (Renato 46), Sulejmanovič, Cipot, Mešič, Stojnič (Jeseničnik 53), Golob, Prašnikar (Trifković 42), Pokleka, Omladič, Tolimir. Coach: Marjan Pušnik (SVN)
Yellow Card(s): Pokleka 36

SPAIN

FC BARCELONA

UEFA CHAMPIONS LEAGUE

Group F
Match 1 - FC Internazionale Milano (ITA)
A 0-0
Víctor Valdés, Dani Alves, Piqué, Puyol, Xavi, Ibrahimović, Messi, Henry (Iniesta 77), Keita, Abidal, Touré. Coach: Josep Guardiola (ESP)
Yellow Card(s): Henry 54, Touré 83
Match 2 - FC Dynamo Kyiv (UKR)
H 2-0 *Messi (26), Pedro (76)*
Víctor Valdés, Dani Alves, Piqué, Puyol, Xavi, Iniesta (Pedro 46), Ibrahimović (Jeffrén 85), Messi, Keita, Abidal, Touré (Busquets 68). Coach: Josep Guardiola (ESP)
Match 3 - FC Rubin Kazan (RUS)
H 1-2 *Ibrahimović (48)*
Víctor Valdés, Dani Alves (Busquets 90+3), Piqué, Márquez (Keita 80), Xavi, Iniesta, Ibrahimović, Messi, Pedro (Bojan 66), Abidal, Touré. Coach: Josep Guardiola (ESP)
Yellow Card(s): Iniesta 43, Dani Alves 88
Match 4 - FC Rubin Kazan (RUS)
A 0-0
Víctor Valdés, Dani Alves, Piqué, Puyol, Xavi, Iniesta, Ibrahimović, Messi, Keita (Henry 83), Abidal, Touré. Coach: Josep Guardiola (ESP)
Yellow Card(s): Puyol 75
Match 5 - FC Internazionale Milano (ITA)
H 2-0 *Piqué (10), Pedro (26)*
Víctor Valdés, Dani Alves, Piqué, Puyol, Xavi, Iniesta (Jonathan 90+4), Henry, Keita, Busquets, Pedro (Bojan 85), Abidal (Maxwell 89). Coach: Josep Guardiola (ESP)
Yellow Card(s): Puyol 34, Pedro 50
Match 6 - FC Dynamo Kyiv (UKR)
A 2-1 *Xavi (33), Messi (86)*
Víctor Valdés, Dani Alves, Piqué (Márquez 88), Puyol, Xavi, Iniesta (Pedro 82), Ibrahimović, Messi, Keita, Busquets, Abidal. Coach: Josep Guardiola (ESP)
Yellow Card(s): Piqué 45, Ibrahimović 77, Xavi 81

UEFA EUROPA LEAGUE

Play-Off Round - AC Sparta Praha (CZE)
H 0-2
Ranilović, Džinić, Jurkič (Aljančič 57), Marcos Tavares, Mihelič (Mertelj 80), Samardžič, Bačinovič, Popovič, Pavlovič (Volaš 63), Bunderla, Školnik. Coach: Darko Milanič (SVN)
Yellow Card(s): Bunderla 57, Samardžič 72, Bačinovič 90
A 0-1
Ranilović, Marcos Tavares, Mihelič, Jelič (Bunderla 63), Aljančič, Lunder, Samardžič, Popovič, Pavlovič, Školnik, Mertelj (Črnič 46). Coach: Darko Milanič (SVN)

NK IB LJUBLJANA

UEFA EUROPA LEAGUE

Third Qualifying Round - FC Metalurh Donetsk (UKR)
A 0-2
Rozman, Tabot, Brezič, E. Rakovič, Mišura (Gerič 50), Kokot, Gill, Jelečevič, Horvat (Zadnikar 78), Iličič (Fink 83), Grabus. Coach: Igor Benedejčič (SVN)
Yellow Card(s): Brezič 86
H 0-3
Rozman, Tabot, Brezič, E. Rakovič (Majcen 70), Mišura (Zadnikar 55), Kokot, Ntamé, Gill, Jelečevič, Iličič, Fink (Milenković 46). Coach: Igor Benedejčič (SVN)
Yellow Card(s): Jelečevič 55, Iličič 72

ND GORICA

UEFA EUROPA LEAGUE

Second Qualifying Round - FC Lahti (FIN)
H 1-0 Kršič (39)
Simčič, Gorinšek, Balažič, Kršič (Cvijanovič 63), Velikonja (Žigon 90+2), Škarabot, Galešić, Demirovic, Đukić, Rakuščck, Osterc (Arčon 87). Coach: Miran Srebrnič (SVN)
Yellow Card(s): Balažič 83
A 0-2
Simčič, Gorinšek, Balažič, Kršič, Velikonja, Škarabot, Galešić, Demirovic, Đukić, Rakuščck, Osterc. Coach: Miran Srebrnič (SVN)
Yellow Card(s): Osterc 79

NK RUDAR VELENJE

UEFA EUROPA LEAGUE

First Qualifying Round - JK Trans Narva (EST)
A 3-0 Cipot (9p), Omladič (61), Trifkovič (89)
Savić, Kolsi, Sulejmanovič, Cipot, Trifkovič, Golob (Kreft 81), Prašnikar, Pokleka, Omladič (Mujakovič 61), Tolimir, Dedič (Jeseničnik 66). Coach: Marjan Pušnik (SVN)
Yellow Card(s): Jeseničnik 84
H 3-1 Cipot (28, 73), Mahmutovič (69)
Savić, Dedič, Tolimir (Mujakovič 46), Omladič (Grbič 46), Pokleka, Prašnika (Mahmutovič 65), Golob, Trifkovič, Cipot, Sulejmanovič, Kolsi. Coach: Marjan Pušnik (SVN)
Yellow Card(s): Dedič 53

Second Qualifying Round - FK Crvena zvezda (SRB)
H 0-1
Savić, Kolsi (Đukič 61), Sulejmanovič, Cipot, Trifkovič (Grbič 57), Golob, Prašnikar (Mešič 70), Pokleka, Omladič, Tolimir, Dedič. Coach: Marjan Pušnik (SVN)
Yellow Card(s): Golob 22, Dedič 22, Omladič 63
A 0-4
Savić, Kolsi (Renato 46), Sulejmanovič, Cipot, Mešič, Stojnič (Jeseničnik 53), Golob, Prašnikar (Trifkovič 42), Pokleka, Omladič, Tolimir. Coach: Marjan Pušnik (SVN)
Yellow Card(s): Pokleka 36

SPAIN

FC BARCELONA

UEFA CHAMPIONS LEAGUE

Group F
Match 1 - FC Internazionale Milano (ITA)
A 0-0
Víctor Valdés, Dani Alves, Piqué, Puyol, Xavi, Ibrahimović, Messi, Henry (Iniesta 77), Keita, Abidal, Touré. Coach: Josep Guardiola (ESP)
Yellow Card(s): Henry 54, Touré 83
Match 2 - FC Dynamo Kyiv (UKR)
H 2-0 Messi (26), Pedro (76)
Víctor Valdés, Dani Alves, Piqué, Puyol, Xavi, Iniesta (Pedro 46), Ibrahimović (Jeffrén 85), Messi, Keita, Abidal, Touré (Busquets 68). Coach: Josep Guardiola (ESP)
Match 3 - FC Rubin Kazan (RUS)
H 1-2 Ibrahimović (48)
Víctor Valdés, Dani Alves (Busquets 90+3), Piqué, Márquez (Keita 80), Xavi, Iniesta, Ibrahimović, Messi, Pedro (Bojan 66), Abidal, Touré. Coach: Josep Guardiola (ESP)
Yellow Card(s): Iniesta 43, Dani Alves 88
Match 4 - FC Rubin Kazan (RUS)
A 0-0
Víctor Valdés, Dani Alves, Piqué, Puyol, Xavi, Iniesta, Ibrahimović, Messi, Keita (Henry 83), Abidal, Touré. Coach: Josep Guardiola (ESP)
Yellow Card(s): Puyol 75
Match 5 - FC Internazionale Milano (ITA)
H 2-0 Piqué (10), Pedro (26)
Víctor Valdés, Dani Alves, Piqué, Puyol, Xavi, Iniesta (Jonathan 90+4), Henry, Keita, Busquets, Pedro (Bojan 85), Abidal (Maxwell 89). Coach: Josep Guardiola (ESP)
Yellow Card(s): Puyol 34, Pedro 50
Match 6 - FC Dynamo Kyiv (UKR)
A 2-1 Xavi (33), Messi (86)
Víctor Valdés, Dani Alves, Piqué (Márquez 88), Puyol, Xavi, Iniesta (Pedro 82), Ibrahimović, Messi, Keita, Busquets, Abidal. Coach: Josep Guardiola (ESP)
Yellow Card(s): Piqué 45, Ibrahimović 77, Xavi 81

SEVILLA FC

UEFA CHAMPIONS LEAGUE

Group G
Match 1 - FC Unirea Urziceni (ROU)
H **2-0** Luís Fabiano (45+1), Renato (70)
Palop, Squillaci, Jesús Navas, Zokora (Lolo 76), Luís Fabiano, Renato,
Kanouté (Negredo 63), Escudé, Diego Capel (Perotti 56), Sergio Sánchez,
Fernando Navarro. Coach: Manuel Jiménez (ESP)
Yellow Card(s): Zokora 72
Match 2 - Rangers FC (SCO)
A **4-1** Konko (50), Adriano (64), Luís Fabiano (72), Kanouté (74)
Palop, Squillaci, Adriano (Diego Capel 66), Jesús Navas, Zokora, Luís
Fabiano (Romaric 79), Kanouté (Negredo 75), Escudé, Fernando Navarro,
Lolo, Konko. Coach: Manuel Jiménez (ESP)
Yellow Card(s): Diego Capel 77, Fernando Navarro 90+3
Match 3 - VfB Stuttgart (GER)
H **3-1** Squillaci (23, 72), Jesús Navas (55)
Javi Varas, Dragutinović, Squillaci, Adriano (Perotti 37), Jesús Navas,
Zokora, Luís Fabiano (Duscher 46), Kanouté (Koné 90+4), Sergio Sánchez,
Fernando Navarro, Lolo. Coach: Manuel Jiménez (ESP)
Yellow Card(s): Fernando Navarro 57, Dragutinović 73, Duscher 79
Match 4 - VfB Stuttgart (GER)
H **1-1** Jesús Navas (14)
Javi Varas, Squillaci, Jesús Navas, Zokora, Koné (Negredo 31), Luís Fabiano,
Escudé, Diego Capel (Perotti 58), Fernando Navarro, Romaric (Duscher 62),
Konko. Coach: Manuel Jiménez (ESP)
Yellow Card(s): Escudé 54
Match 5 - FC Unirea Urziceni (ROU)
A **0-1**
Javi Varas, Dragutinović, Jesús Navas, Zokora, Kanouté, Diego Capel (Luís
Fabiano 62), Sergio Sánchez, Fernando Navarro, Negredo (Perotti 70), Lolo
(Renato 62), Konko. Coach: Manuel Jiménez (ESP)
Yellow Card(s): Jesús Navas 52
Match 6 - Rangers FC (SCO)
H **1-0** Kanouté (8p)
Palop, Dragutinović, Jesús Navas (Koné 81), Zokora, Renato, Kanouté
(Negredo 60), Diego Capel, Fernando Navarro, Romaric (Duscher 74),
Konko, Cala. Coach: Manuel Jiménez (ESP)

First Knockout Round - PFC CSKA Moskva (RUS)
A **1-1** Negredo (25)
Palop, Fazio, Adriano (Perotti 59), Jesús Navas, Zokora, Renato (Acosta 89),
Escudé, Fernando Navarro, Negredo (Kanouté 76), Romaric, Stankevičius.
Coach: Manuel Jiménez (ESP)
H **1-2** Perotti (41)
Palop, Fazio, Dragutinović, Jesús Navas, Zokora, Luís Fabiano, Renato
(Negredo 71), Diego Capel (Kanouté 46), Fernando Navarro (Adriano 74),
Perotti, Stankevičius. Coach: Manuel Jiménez (ESP)
Yellow Card(s): Luís Fabiano 52

No	Player	Nat	DoB	Aps	(s)	Gls
Goalkeepers						
13	Javi Varas		10/9/82	3		
1	Andrés Palop		22/10/73	5		
Defenders						
28	Cala		26/11/89	1		
3	Ivica Dragutinović	SRB	13/11/75	4		
14	Julien Escudé	FRA	17/8/79	4		
2	Federico Fazio	ARG	17/3/87	2		
18	Fernando Navarro		25/6/82	8		
24	Abdoulay Konko	FRA	9/3/84	4		1
23	Lolo		22/8/84	3	(1)	
17	Sergio Sánchez		3/4/86	3		
4	Sébastien Squillaci	FRA	11/8/80	4		2
35	Marius Stankevičius	LTU	15/7/81	2		

Midfielders						
6	Adriano	BRA	26/10/84	3	(1)	1
5	Aldo Duscher	ARG	22/3/79		(3)	
25	Diego Perotti	ARG	26/7/88	1	(5)	1
11	Renato	BRA	15/5/79	4	(1)	1
22	Romaric	CIV	4/6/83	3	(1)	
8	Didier Zokora	CIV	14/12/80	8		
Forwards						
21	Lautaro Acosta	ARG	14/3/88		(1)	
16	Diego Capel		16/2/88	5	(1)	
7	Jesús Navas		21/11/85	8		2
12	Frédéric Kanouté	MLI	2/9/77	5	(2)	2
9	Arouna Koné	CIV	11/11/83	1	(2)	
10	Luís Fabiano	BRA	8/11/80	5	(1)	2
19	Álvaro Negredo		20/8/85	2	(5)	1

CLUB ATLÉTICO DE MADRID

UEFA CHAMPIONS LEAGUE

Play-Off Round - Panathinaikos FC (GRE)
A **3-2** Maxi Rodríguez (36), Forlán (63), Agüero (70)
Asenjo, Antonio López, Heitinga, Forlán, Raúl García (Cléber Santana 72),
Agüero (Jurado 75), Maxi Rodríguez (Sinama-Pongolle 86), Paulo
Assunção, Juanito, Ujfaluši, Simão. Coach: Abel Resino (ESP)
H **2-0** Vintra (4og), Agüero (90)
Asenjo, Antonio López, Heitinga, Forlán (Jurado 82), Raúl García (Cléber
Santana 62), Agüero, Maxi Rodríguez, Paulo Assunção, Juanito, Ujfaluši,
Simão (Reyes 86). Coach: Abel Resino (ESP)

Group D
Match 1 - APOEL FC (CYP)
H **0-0**
Asenjo, Forlán, Jurado, Agüero, Paulo Assunção, Ujfaluši, Álvaro
Domínguez, Simão, Perea (Sinama-Pongolle 67), Pablo, Cléber Santana
(Maxi Rodríguez 51). Coach: Abel Resino (ESP)
Yellow Card(s): Paulo Assunção 90+1
Match 2 - FC Porto (POR)
A **0-2**
Roberto (De Gea 26), Forlán, Jurado (Reyes 79), Agüero, Paulo Assunção,
Juanito, Ujfaluši, Simão (Maxi Rodríguez 70), Perea, Pablo, Cléber Santana.
Coach: Abel Resino (ESP)
Yellow Card(s): Paulo Assunção 36, Perea 48
Match 3 - Chelsea FC (ENG)
A **0-4**
Asenjo, Antonio López, Forlán, Raúl García, Agüero, Paulo Assunção
(Jurado 54), Ujfaluši, Álvaro Domínguez, Simão (Reyes 77), Perea, Cléber
Santana (Maxi Rodríguez 65). Coach: Abel Resino (ESP)
Yellow Card(s): Raúl García 74, Álvaro Domínguez 90
Match 4 - Chelsea FC (ENG)
H **2-2** Agüero (66, 90+1)
Asenjo, Antonio López, Forlán, Paulo Assunção, Sinama-Pongolle (Agüero
53), Juanito, Reyes (Maxi Rodríguez 73), Simão (Jurado 83), Perea, Pablo,
Cléber Santana. Coach: Quique Sánchez Flores (ESP)
Yellow Card(s): Reyes 26, Paulo Assunção 33
Match 5 - APOEL FC (CYP)
A **1-1** Simão (62)
Asenjo, Camacho, Forlán (Reyes 87), Jurado (Maxi Rodríguez 79), Agüero,
Juanito, Ujfaluši, Simão (Antonio López 90+2), Perea,
Cléber Santana. Coach: Quique Sánchez Flores (ESP)
Yellow Card(s): Forlán 3, Álvaro Domínguez 21
Match 6 - FC Porto (POR)
H **0-3**
Asenjo, Valera (Antonio López 46), Forlán, Agüero (Jurado 48), Maxi
Rodríguez (Reyes 68), Paulo Assunção, Juanito, Álvaro Domínguez, Simão,
Perea, Cléber Santana. Coach: Quique Sánchez Flores (ESP)
Yellow Card(s): Simão 43, Agüero 44, Juanito 88

Spain

No	Player	Nat	DoB	Aps	(s)	Gls
Goalkeepers						
43	David de Gea		7/11/90		(1)	
13	Roberto		10/2/86	1		
1	Asenjo		28/6/89	5		
Defenders						
18	Álvaro Domínguez		15/5/89	4		
3	Antonio López		13/9/81	2	(2)	
16	Juanito		23/7/76	4		
22	Pablo Ibáñez		3/8/81	3		
21	Luis Perea	COL	30/1/79	6		
17	Tomáš Ujfaluši	CZE	24/3/78	4		
2	Juan Valera		21/12/84	1		
Midfielders						
6	Ignacio Camacho		4/5/90	1		
23	Cléber Santana	BRA	27/6/81	6		
11	Maxi Rodríguez	ARG	2/1/81	1	(5)	
12	Paulo Assunção	BRA	25/1/80	5		
8	Raúl García		11/7/86	1		
19	José Antonio Reyes		1/9/83	1	(4)	
20	Simão	POR	31/10/79	6		1
Forwards						
10	Sergio Agüero	ARG	2/6/88	5	(1)	2
7	Diego Forlán	URU	19/5/79	6		
9	José Manuel Jurado		29/6/86	3	(3)	
14	Florent Sinama-Pongolle	FRA	20/10/84	1	(1)	

UEFA EUROPA LEAGUE

Round of 32 - Galatasaray AŞ (TUR)
H 1-1 *Reyes (23)*
De Gea (Asenjo 71), Valera, Forlán (Jurado 58), Raúl García, Agüero, Paulo Assunção, Ujfaluši, Álvaro Domínguez, Reyes (Salvio 86), Simão, Perea. Coach: Quique Sánchez Flores (ESP)
Yellow Card(s): Álvaro Domínguez 90+2
A 2-1 *Simão (63), Forlán (90)*
Asenjo, Valera, Antonio López, Raúl García, Jurado (Camacho 90+4), Agüero (Forlán 42), Paulo Assunção, Ujfaluši, Reyes (Salvio 90+2), Simão, Perea. Coach: Quique Sánchez Flores (ESP)

Round of 16 - Sporting Clube de Portugal (POR)
H 0-0
De Gea, Antonio López, Forlán, Raúl García (Jurado 72), Agüero, Paulo Assunção, Ujfaluši, Álvaro Domínguez, Reyes, Simão (Salvio 58), Perea (Valera 13). Coach: Quique Sánchez Flores (ESP)
Yellow Card(s): Ujfaluši 81
A 2-2 *Agüero (3, 33)*
De Gea, Antonio López, Raúl García, Jurado (Camacho 90), Agüero (Forlán 81), Paulo Assunção, Ujfaluši, Álvaro Domínguez, Reyes, Simão (Valera 68), Perea. Coach: Quique Sánchez Flores (ESP)

Quarter-Finals - Valencia CF (ESP)
A 2-2 *Forlán (59), Antonio López (72)*
De Gea, Antonio López, Forlán (Salvio 78), Raúl García, Jurado (Camacho 90+2), Agüero, Paulo Assunção, Ujfaluši, Álvaro Domínguez, Simão, Perea. Coach: Quique Sánchez Flores (ESP)
Yellow Card(s): Ujfaluši 66, Raúl García 69, Agüero 90+4
H 0-0
De Gea, Antonio López, Forlán (Camacho 84), Raúl García, Agüero (Salvio 90+5), Paulo Assunção, Juanito, Ujfaluši, Álvaro Domínguez, Reyes (Jurado 46), Simão. Coach: Quique Sánchez Flores (ESP)
Yellow Card(s): Reyes 24, Agüero 90+5

Semi-Finals - Liverpool FC (ENG)
H 1-0 *Forlán (9)*
De Gea, Antonio López, Forlán (Salvio 85), Raúl García, Jurado, Paulo Assunção, Ujfaluši, Álvaro Domínguez, Reyes (Camacho 90+2), Simão (Valera 78), Perea. Coach: Quique Sánchez Flores (ESP)
Yellow Card(s): Valera 85
A 1-2 *Forlán (102) (aet)*
De Gea, Valera, Antonio López, Forlán (Camacho 117), Raúl García, Agüero (Salvio 120+1), Paulo Assunção (Jurado 99), Álvaro Domínguez, Reyes, Simão, Perea. Coach: Quique Sánchez Flores (ESP)
Yellow Card(s): Paulo Assunção 52, Valera 67, Forlán 103, Álvaro Domínguez 104

Final - Fulham FC (ENG)
H 2-1 *Forlán (32, 116) (aet)*
De Gea, Antonio López, Forlán, Raúl García, Agüero (Valera 119), Paulo Assunção, Ujfaluši, Álvaro Domínguez, Reyes (Salvio 78), Simão (Jurado 68), Perea. Coach: Quique Sánchez Flores (ESP)
Yellow Card(s): Salvio 107, Raúl García 114, Forlán 117

VILLARREAL CF

UEFA EUROPA LEAGUE

Play-Off Round - NAC Breda (NED)
A 3-1 *Rossi (14), Ibagaza (49), Llorente (90+2)*
Diego López, Gonzalo Rodríguez Rodríguez, Godín, Capdevila, Santi Cazorla, Cani, Ibagaza (David Fuster 80), Nilmar (Pires 75), Ángel López, Senna, Rossi (Llorente 66). Coach: Ernesto Valverde (ESP)
Yellow Card(s): Senna 40, Ángel López 43, Gonzalo Rodríguez 45+1, Santi Cazorla 59
H 6-1 *Santi Cazorla (16), Rossi (23p, 37p), Senna (46), Jonathan Pereira (57), Kiko (61)*
Diego López, Godín (Kiko 52), Capdevila, Santi Cazorla, Llorente, Cani, Ibagaza, Fabricio Fuentes, Ángel López, Senna (David Fuster 58), Rossi (Jonathan Pereira 46). Coach: Ernesto Valverde (ESP)
Yellow Card(s): Ibagaza 90

Group G
Match 1 - PFC Levski Sofia (BUL)
H 1-0 *Nilmar (72)*
Diego López, Gonzalo Rodríguez, Capdevila, Eguren, Pires (Escudero 82), Cani, Nilmar, Javi Venta, Marcano, Bruno (Ibagaza 55), Jonathan Pereira (Rossi 66). Coach: Ernesto Valverde (ESP)
Match 2 - FC Salzburg (AUT)
A 0-2
Diego López, Gonzalo Rodríguez (Senna 57), Capdevila, Eguren, Santi Cazorla, Llorente (Nilmar 76), Cani (Escudero 64), Ángel, Marcano, Bruno, Rossi. Coach: Ernesto Valverde (ESP)
Yellow Card(s): Ángel 20, Gonzalo Rodríguez 49
Match 3 - S.S. Lazio (ITA)
A 1-2 *Eguren (40)*
Diego López, Gonzalo Rodríguez, Capdevila, Eguren, Pires, Cani (Santi Cazorla 74), Nilmar (Jonathan Pereira 81), Ángel, Senna, Marcano, Rossi (Llorente 78). Coach: Ernesto Valverde (ESP)
Yellow Card(s): Nilmar 16, Eguren 73, Marcano 84
Match 4 - S.S. Lazio (ITA)
H 4-1 *Pires (2, 15p), Cani (13), Rossi (83p)*
Diego López, Gonzalo Rodríguez, Godín, Capdevila, Eguren, Pires (Rossi 77), Llorente (Marcano 57), Cani, Nilmar, Ángel, Bruno. Coach: Ernesto Valverde (ESP)
Red Card(s): Gonzalo Rodríguez 32
Yellow Card(s): Llorente 52, Bruno 59
Match 5 - PFC Levski Sofia (BUL)
A 2-0 *Rossi (37), Senna (84)*
Diego López, Godín, Capdevila, Eguren, Pires (Cani 60), Ibagaza, David Fuster (Nilmar 69), Ángel, Marcano, Rossi (Senna 80), Escudero. Coach: Ernesto Valverde (ESP)
Yellow Card(s): Eguren 50, Ibagaza 77
Match 6 - FC Salzburg (AUT)
H 0-1
Oliva, Gonzalo Rodríguez (Capdevila 46), Eguren, Llorente, Nilmar, Ángel, Marcano, Bruno, Jonathan Pereira (Rossi 72), Escudero, Kiko (Matilla 61). Coach: Ernesto Valverde (ESP)
Yellow Card(s): Gonzalo Rodríguez 28, Jonathan Pereira 51

Round of 32 - VfL Wolfsburg (GER)
H 2-2 *Senna (43), Marco Rubén (85)*
Diego López, Godín, Capdevila, Pires (Marco Rubén 77), Llorente, Ibagaza
(Cani 64), Nilmar, Ángel, Senna, Marcano, Bruno (Matilla 77). Coach: Juan
Carlos Garrido (ESP)
Red Card(s): Marcano 83
A 1-4 *Capdevila (30)*
Diego López, Gonzalo Rodríguez, Godín (Musacchio 46), Capdevila, Pires
Jefferson Montero 70), Cani (Llorente 46), Nilmar, David Fuster, Ángel,
Senna, Bruno. Coach: Juan Carlos Garrido (ESP)
Yellow Card(s): David Fuster 45, Capdevila 73

VALENCIA CF

UEFA EUROPA LEAGUE

Play-Off Round - Stabæk IF (NOR)
A 3-0 *Pablo Hernández (29), David Villa (35), Joaquín (80)*
César Sánchez, Bruno, Marchena, David Villa (Žigić 76), Dealbert, Mata,
Pablo Hernández (Joaquín 71), Alexis, David Silva (Míchel 82), Miguel, Éver
Banega. Coach: Unai Emery (ESP)
Yellow Card(s): David Villa 73
H 4-1 *Miku (28, 29, 80), Žigić (77)*
Moyá, Maduro, David Navarro, Albelda (Éver Banega 69), Žigić, Mata
(Olcina 57), Joaquín, Mathieu, Miguel (Bruno 73), Miku, Míchel. Coach:
Unai Emery (ESP)

Group B
Match 1 - LOSC Lille Métropole (FRA)
A 1-1 *Mata (78)*
César Sánchez, Bruno, Maduro, David Navarro, Albelda, Žigić (David Villa
82), Miku (Éver Banega 67), Joaquín, Mathieu, Jordi Alba (Mata 77),
Míchel. Coach: Unai Emery (ESP)
Yellow Card(s): Bruno 25, Jordi Alba 63, Maduro 90+3
Match 2 - Genoa CFC (ITA)
H 3-2 *David Silva (52), Žigić (56), David Villa (82p)*
César Sánchez, David Navarro, Albelda (Maduro 79), Žigić (David Villa 65),
Mata, Dealbert, Pablo Hernández (Joaquín 79), David Silva, Mathieu,
Miguel, Éver Banega. Coach: Unai Emery (ESP)
Yellow Card(s): Mathieu 63, David Silva 86, Éver Banega 90
Match 3 - SK Slavia Praha (CZE)
H 1-1 *David Navarro (63)*
Moyá, Maduro (Éver Banega 78), David Navarro, Baraja, Žigić, Pablo
Hernández, Alexis, Mathieu, Miguel, Jordi Alba (David Villa 62), Míchel
(Mata 46). Coach: Unai Emery (ESP)
Red Card(s): David Villa 85
Yellow Card(s): Mathieu 34
Match 4 - SK Slavia Praha (CZE)
A 2-2 *Joaquín (22p), Maduro (47)*
Moyá, Bruno, Maduro, David Navarro, Marchena, Baraja, Žigić, Mata (Jordi
Alba 64), Joaquín, David Silva (Pablo Hernández 58), Mathieu (Del Horno
70). Coach: Unai Emery (ESP)
Red Card(s): Baraja 90+4
Yellow Card(s): Pablo Hernández 60, Mathieu 62, Del Horno 84, Baraja 88,
Baraja 90+4
Match 5 - LOSC Lille Métropole (FRA)
H 3-1 *Joaquín (3, 32), Mata (52)*
Moyá, Bruno, Maduro, David Navarro, Marchena (Manuel Fernandes 80),
Mata (Miku 72), Joaquín (Jordi Alba 77), Pablo Hernández, Alexis, Miguel,
Éver Banega. Coach: Unai Emery (ESP)
Yellow Card(s): Alexis 44, Éver Banega 67, Miku 89
Match 6 - Genoa CFC (ITA)
A 2-1 *Bruno (45+1), David Villa (90+5)*
Moyá, Bruno, David Navarro, Marchena (Maduro 31), Albelda, David Villa,
Mata (Pablo Hernández 76), Joaquín (Jordi Alba 90+1), Alexis, Miguel, Éver
Banega. Coach: Unai Emery (ESP)
Yellow Card(s): David Villa 20, Bruno 33, Éver Banega 70, Moyá 74, Albelda 86

Round of 32 - Club Brugge KV (BEL)
A 0-1
Moyá, Marchena, Albelda, David Villa, Baraja, Mata, Dealbert, Joaquín
(Pablo Hernández 63), David Silva, Mathieu (Maduro 25), Miguel. Coach:
Unai Emery (ESP)
Red Card(s): David Silva 51
Yellow Card(s): David Silva 31, David Silva 51, Albelda 54, Pablo
Hernández 90+4
H 3-0 *Mata (1), Pablo Hernández (96, 117) (aet)*
César Sánchez, Marchena, Albelda, David Villa, Baraja (Alexis 46), Žigić
(Joaquín 57), Mata (Maduro 118), Dealbert, Pablo Hernández, Miguel, Éver
Banega. Coach: Unai Emery (ESP)
Yellow Card(s): David Villa 34, Baraja 40

Round of 16 - Werder Bremen (GER)
H 1-1 *Mata (57)*
César Sánchez, David Navarro, Marchena, David Villa (Baraja 84), David
(Joaquín 76), Dealbert, Pablo Hernández, Alexis (Jordi Alba 46), David
Silva, Miguel, Éver Banega. Coach: Unai Emery (ESP)
Red Card(s): Éver Banega 55
Yellow Card(s): César Sánchez 55, Marchena 67, Pablo Hernández 76
A 4-4 *David Villa (3, 45, 66), Mata (15)*
César Sánchez, Bruno (Jordi Alba 46), Maduro, Marchena (Míchel 65),
David Villa, Baraja, Mata, Dealbert, Joaquín (Manuel Fernandes 55), David
Silva, Miguel. Coach: Unai Emery (ESP)
Yellow Card(s): Joaquín 55, Jordi Alba 57, Miguel 67, Mata 82, Baraja 90+2

Quarter-Finals - Club Atlético de Madrid (ESP)
H 2-2 *Manuel Fernandes (66), David Villa (82)*
César Sánchez, Bruno, Maduro, David Villa, Baraja, Mata (Vicente 76),
Dealbert, Manuel Fernandes (Žigić 81), Pablo Hernández (Joaquín 70),
David Silva, Jordi Alba. Coach: Unai Emery (ESP)
Yellow Card(s): Bruno 44, Mata 54, Pablo Hernández 63
A 0-0
César Sánchez, Maduro, David Villa, Baraja, Mata (Vicente 70), Joaquín
(Žigić 70), Manuel Fernandes, Pablo Hernández, Alexis (David Navarro 80),
David Silva, Jordi Alba. Coach: Unai Emery (ESP)
Yellow Card(s): Joaquín 34, Mata 40, David Silva 74

ATHLETIC CLUB

UEFA EUROPA LEAGUE

Third Qualifying Round - BSC Young Boys (SUI)
H 0-1
Iraizoz, Toquero (Muniain 59), Amorebieta, Llorente, Yeste (David López
46), Susaeta (Etxeberria 71), Iraola, Orbaiz, Aitor Ocio, Castillo, Javi
Martínez. Coach: Joaquín Caparrós (ESP)
Yellow Card(s): Yeste 40, Javi Martínez 77
A 2-1 *Llorente (26), Muniain (72)*
Iraizoz, Toquero, Amorebieta, Llorente, Yeste (Gurpegui 86), Susaeta
(Muniain 70), Iraola, Aitor Ocio, Castillo, Javi Martínez, De Marcos (Orbaiz
80). Coach: Joaquín Caparrós (ESP)
Yellow Card(s): Castillo 50

Play-Off Round - Tromsø IL (NOR)
H 3-2 *Javi Martínez (62p), De Marcos (86), Llorente (90)*
Iraizoz, Amorebieta, Llorente, Yeste (Iturraspe 80), Susaeta (David López
85), Iraola, Aitor Ocio, Castillo, Javi Martínez, Muniain (Toquero 74), De
Marcos. Coach: Joaquín Caparrós (ESP)
Yellow Card(s): Amorebieta 70, De Marcos 76
A 1-1 *Javi Martínez (56p)*
Iraizoz, Toquero, Amorebieta, Llorente, Yeste (Gurpegui 90+3), Susaeta
(Koikili 90), Iraola, Aitor Ocio, Castillo, Javi Martínez, De Marcos (Iturraspe
69). Coach: Joaquín Caparrós (ESP)
Yellow Card(s): De Marcos 38, Iraizoz 53, Javi Martínez 76

Group L
Match 1 - FK Austria Wien (AUT)
H 3-0 *Llorente (8p, 24), Muniain (56)*
Iraizoz, Amorebieta, Llorente (David López 59), Yeste, Susaeta, Iraola (Zubiaurre 76), Etxeberria, Gurpegui (San José 83), Aitor Ocio, Castillo, Muniain. Coach: Joaquín Caparrós (ESP)
Yellow Card(s): Susaeta 53
Match 2 - Werder Bremen (GER)
A 1-3 *Llorente (90+1)*
Iraizoz, Toquero (Muniain 46), Amorebieta, Llorente, Yeste, Gabilondo (David López 46), Iraola, Gurpegui, Aitor Ocio, Castillo, Javi Martínez (Etxeberria 75). Coach: Joaquín Caparrós (ESP)
Yellow Card(s): Iraola 40, Gurpegui 54, Castillo 69
Match 3 - CD Nacional (POR)
H 2-1 *Etxeberria (67), Llorente (86)*
Iraizoz, Ustaritz, Amorebieta, Llorente, Yeste (Javi Martínez 46), Gabilondo (De Marcos 46), Susaeta, Iraola, Orbaiz, Etxeberria (Toquero 72), Castillo. Coach: Joaquín Caparrós (ESP)
Yellow Card(s): Ustaritz 55
Match 4 - CD Nacional (POR)
A 1-1 *Etxeberria (85p)*
Iraizoz, Ustaritz, Amorebieta, David López (Díaz de Cerio 60), Llorente (De Marcos 40), Gabilondo, Iraola, Etxeberria, Gurpegui, Castillo, Javi Martínez (Orbaiz 71). Coach: Joaquín Caparrós (ESP)
Yellow Card(s): Javi Martínez 58, Iraizoz 62, Gurpegui 78, Etxeberria 90+2
Match 5 - FK Austria Wien (AUT)
A 3-0 *Llorente (19, 84), San José (62)*
Iraizoz, Amorebieta, Llorente (Díaz de Cerio 85), Yeste, San José, Iraola, Gurpegui (Etxeberria 72), Castillo, Javi Martínez, Iturraspe, Muniain (De Marcos 61). Coach: Joaquín Caparrós (ESP)
Yellow Card(s): San José 34
Match 6 - Werder Bremen (GER)
H 0-3
Iraizoz, Toquero (David López 55), Amorebieta, Etxeita, Yeste (Iñigo Pérez 70), San José, Susaeta, Díaz de Cerio (Etxeberria 55), Javi Martínez, Muniain, Aurtenetxe. Coach: Joaquín Caparrós (ESP)
Yellow Card(s): Iñigo Pérez 78

Round of 32 - RSC Anderlecht (BEL)
H 1-1 *San José (58)*
Iraizoz, Ustaritz, Llorente, Yeste (Muniain 46), San José, Iraola, Orbaiz, Gurpegui (Susaeta 55), Castillo, Javi Martínez, De Marcos (Toquero 66). Coach: Joaquín Caparrós (ESP)
A 0-4
Iraizoz, Toquero (De Marcos 54), Amorebieta, Llorente, Yeste, San José, Susaeta, Iraola, Orbaiz (Muniain 46; Gabilondo 59), Castillo, Javi Martínez. Coach: Joaquín Caparrós (ESP)
Yellow Card(s): San José 2, Yeste 64, Amorebieta 65, Javi Martínez 90+2

KALMAR FF

UEFA CHAMPIONS LEAGUE

Second Qualifying Round - Debreceni VSC (HUN)
A 0-2
Wastå, Lantz, Rydström, Larsson, Daniel Sobralense, D. Elm (Ricardo Santos 84), Ålander, Daniel Mendes (Dauda 84), R. Elm, Eriksson, Nouri. Coach: Nanne Bergstrand (SWE)
H 3-1 *R. Elm (19, 71p), Daniel Mendes (32)*
Wastå, Lantz, Carlsson (Johansson 56), Rydström, Larsson, Daniel Sobralense (Smylie 69), D. Elm (Ricardo Santos 56), Daniel Mendes, R. Elm, Eriksson, Nouri. Coach: Nanne Bergstrand (SWE)
Yellow Card(s): Rydström 46, R. Elm 89

IFK GÖTEBORG

UEFA EUROPA LEAGUE
Third Qualifying Round - Hapoel Tel-Aviv FC (ISR)
H 1-3 *Hysén (21)*
Christensen, Turunen, Hysén, Olsson (J. Johansson 70), Selakovic (K. Svensson 89), Sigurdsson, G. Svensson, Jónsson, Lund, Eriksson, Bjarnason (D. Alexandersson 72). Coach: Stefan Rehn (SWE)
Yellow Card(s): Eriksson 59, Olsson 60, Jónsson 90
A 1-1 *Stiller (52)*
Christensen, Hysén, Olsson (Bjarnason 56), Selakovic (K. Svensson 77), Sigurdsson, G. Svensson, Jónsson, Lund, Stiller, Bärkroth (Mustafa 69), Eriksson. Coach: Stefan Rehn (SWE)
Yellow Card(s): Lund 60, Sigurdsson 64, Jónsson 72

IF ELFSBORG

UEFA EUROPA LEAGUE
Second Qualifying Round – Szombathelyi Haladás (HUN)
H 3-0 *Svensson (60), Ishizaki (82), Avdic (89)*
Covic, M. Florén, Karlsson, Daníelsson, Svensson (Nordmark 88), Ericsson (Ishizaki 46), Mobaeck, Wikström, Lucic, Keene (Avdic 72), Bajrami. Coach: Magnus Haglund (SWE)
Yellow Card(s): Wikström 36, Keene 51
A 0-0
Covic, M. Florén, Karlsson, Daníelsson, Svensson (J. Florén 84), Avdic (Johansson 73), Mobaeck, Wikström, Lucic (Andersson 84), Nordmark, Ishizaki. Coach: Magnus Haglund (SWE)
Yellow Card(s): J. Florén 85, Daníelsson 88

Third Qualifying Round - SC Braga (POR)
A 2-1 *Daníelsson (16), Bajrami (73)*
Covic, Karlsson, Andersson, Daníelsson, Svensson (Avdic 59), Mobaeck, Lucic, Nordmark (Wikström 69), Keene, Bajrami, Ishizaki (Johansson 85). Coach: Magnus Haglund (SWE)
Yellow Card(s): Nordmark 19, Svensson 21, Wikström 90+3
H 2-0 *Keene (16,32)*
Covic, J. Florén, Karlsson, Andersson, Daníelsson, Svensson, Mobaeck, Lucic, Keene (Avdic 77), Bajrami (Nordmark 81), Ishizaki (Johansson 89). Coach: Magnus Haglund (SWE)
Yellow Card(s): Andersson 12, Keene 70, Nordmark 83

Play-Off Round - S.S. Lazio (ITA)
A 0-3
Covic, M. Florén, Karlsson, Andersson, Daníelsson, Svensson (J. Florén 74), Avdic, Mobaeck, Jawo (Johansson 74), Lucic, Ishizaki. Coach: Magnus Haglund (SWE)
H 1-0 *Avdic (70)*
Covic, J. Florén, Karlsson, Andersson, Daníelsson (Jawo 84), Svensson, Mobaeck, Lucic, Keene (Avdic 46), Bajrami, Ishizaki (Nordmark 77). Coach: Magnus Haglund (SWE)
Yellow Card(s): Keene 15, Mobaeck 21, Svensson 82

HELSINGBORGS IF

UEFA EUROPA LEAGUE

First Qualifying Round - FC Mika (ARM)
A 3-1 *Larsson (50, 86), Sundin (90+2)*
Jansson, Tamboura, Sundin, Lantz, Bergholtz (Landgren 74), Holgersson (Wahlstedt 46), Makondele, Larsson, C. Andersson (Jönsson 36), Nilsson, Ekstrand. Coach: Bo Nilsson (SWE)
Yellow Card(s): Sundin 88
H 1-1 *Makondele (68) (aet)*
Jansson, Tamboura, Landgren, Patronen, Svanbäck, Bergholtz (Ekstrand 98), Makondele, Jönsson (Unkuri 65), C. Andersson (Skúlason 74), Wahlstedt, Nilsson. Coach: Bo Nilsson (SWE)
Yellow Card(s): Tamboura 31, Wahlstedt 47, Skúlason 82

Second Qualifying Round - FC Zestafoni (GEO)
A 2-1 *Jönsson (62), Larsson (89)*
Jansson, Tamboura, Landgren, Lantz (Skúlason 83), Makondele, Holgersson 80), Larsson, Jönsson (Unkuri 83), C. Andersson, Wahlstedt, Nilsson, Ekstrand. Coach: Bo Nilsson (SWE)
Yellow Card(s): Tamboura 72
H 2-2 *Ekstrand (90+3), Sundin (100) (aet)*
Jansson, Landgren (Skúlason 46), Lantz (Bergholtz 86), Holgersson, Makondele (Sundin 64), Larsson, Jönsson, C. Andersson, Wahlstedt, Nilsson, Ekstrand. Coach: Bo Nilsson (SWE)
Yellow Card(s): Lantz 77

Third Qualifying Round - FK Sarajevo (BIH)
H 2-1 *C. Andersson (6p), Skúlason (58)*
Jansson, Tamboura, Landgren, Patronen, Skúlason, Makondele, Larsson, Svanbäck 23), Jönsson (Sundin 75), C. Andersson, Wahlstedt, Nilsson. Coach: Bo Nilsson (SWE)
Yellow Card(s): Skúlason 26
A 1-2 *Jönsson (2) (aet; 4-5 on pens)*
Jansson, Tamboura, Svanbäck, Sundin, Bergholtz (Unkuri 106), Holgersson, Makondele, Jönsson (Mahlangu 46), C. Andersson (Wahlstedt 105+1), Nilsson, Ekstrand. Coach: Bo Nilsson (SWE)
Yellow Card(s): Ekstrand 26, Tamboura 90

SWITZERLAND

FC ZÜRICH

UEFA CHAMPIONS LEAGUE

Third Qualifying Round - NK Maribor (SVN)
A 2-3 *Vonlanthen (4), Hassli (29)*
Guatelli, Lampi, Margairaz (Nikci 64), Aegerter, Vonlanthen, Tico, Djuric (Alphonse 76), Rochat, Gajić, Hassli, Tihinen. Coach: Bernard Challandes (SUI)
Yellow Card(s): Gajić 82, Aegerter 86
H 3-0 *Djuric (21), Margairaz (45), Nikci (76)*
Leoni, Lampi, Margairaz, Aegerter, Vonlanthen, Stahel (P. Koch 75), Djuric (Nikci 65), Rochat, Gajić, Hassli (Tico 82), Tihinen. Coach: Bernard Challandes (SUI)
Yellow Card(s): Gajić 86

Play-Off Round - FK Ventspils (LVA)
A 3-0 *Vonlanthen (12), Aegerter (55), Djuric (75)*
Leoni, Margairaz (Abdi 79), Aegerter, Vonlanthen (Nikci 84), Tico, Stahel, Djuric, P. Koch, Rochat, Hassli (Alphonse 73), Tihinen. Coach: Bernard Challandes (SUI)
H 2-1 *Vonlanthen (6), Abdi (90+2)*
Leoni, Lampi, Margairaz (Abdi 64), Aegerter, Vonlanthen, Tico, Alphonse (Hassli 84), Stahel, Djuric (Gajić 78) Rochat, Tihinen. Coach: Bernard Challandes (SUI)

Group C
Match 1 - Real Madrid CF (ESP)
H 2-5 *Margairaz (64p), Aegerter (65)*
Leoni, Margairaz, Aegerter, Vonlanthen, Tico (Abdi 66), Alphonse, Stahel (Gajić 88), P. Koch, Rochat, Hassli (Djuric 46), Tihinen. Coach: Bernard Challandes (SUI)
Yellow Card(s): Stahel 24, Tico 50
Match 2 - AC Milan (ITA)
A 1-0 *Tihinen (10)*
Leoni, Margairaz, Aegerter, Vonlanthen (Nikci 76), Tico, Djuric (Alphonse 86), P. Koch, Rochat (Stahel 80), Gajić, Barmettler, Tihinen. Coach: Bernard Challandes (SUI)
Yellow Card(s): Leoni 50, Tico 51, Margairaz 90+5
Match 3 - Olympique de Marseille (FRA)
H 0-1
Leoni, Margairaz (Abdi 84), Aegerter, Vonlanthen (Nikci 84), Tico, Alphonse, Stahel, P. Koch, Rochat, Gajić (Djuric 72), Tihinen. Coach: Bernard Challandes (SUI)
Yellow Card(s): Margairaz 61, Aegerter 63
Match 4 - Olympique de Marseille (FRA)
A 1-6 *Alphonse (31)*
Leoni, Margairaz, Aegerter (Gajić 46), Vonlanthen (Mehmedi 9), Tico, Alphonse (Nikci 76), Stahel, Djuric, P. Koch, Rochat, Tihinen. Coach: Bernard Challandes (SUI)
Yellow Card(s): Tico 48, Tihinen 66, Stahel 79
Match 5 - Real Madrid CF (ESP)
A 0-1
Leoni, Margairaz, Aegerter, Alphonse (Mehmedi 86), Stahel, Djuric (Schönbächler 88), P. Koch, Rochat, Gajić (Vonlanthen 76), Barmettler, Tihinen. Coach: Bernard Challandes (SUI)
Yellow Card(s): Barmettler 56, Djuric 63, Stahel 65
Match 6 - AC Milan (ITA)
H 1-1 *Gajić (29)*
Leoni, Aegerter, Tico, Nikci (Vonlanthen 74), Alphonse, Djuric (Lampi 66), P. Koch, Rochat, Gajić (Margairaz 82), Barmettler, Tihinen. Coach: Bernard Challandes (SUI)
Red Card(s): Rochat 63
Yellow Card(s): Barmettler 43

No	Player	Nat	DoB	Aps	(s)	Gls
Goalkeeper						
1	Johnny Leoni		30/6/84	6		
Defenders						
16	Philippe Koch		8/2/91	6		
2	Veli Lampi	FIN	18/7/84		(1)	
19	Alain Rochat		1/2/83	6		
13	Florian Stahel		10/3/85	4	(1)	
30	Hannu Tihinen	FIN	1/7/76	6		1
Midfielders						
23	Almen Abdi		21/10/86		(2)	
7	Silvan Aegerter		5/5/80	6		1
21	Heinz Barmettler		21/7/87	3		
14	Dusan Djuric	SWE	16/9/84	4	(2)	
20	Milan Gajić	SRB	17/11/86	4	(2)	1
5	Xavier Margairaz		7/1/84	5	(1)	1
25	Admir Mehmedi		16/3/91		(2)	
10	Onyekachi Okonkwo "Tico"	NGA	13/5/82	5		
Forwards						
12	Alexandre Alphonse	FRA	17/6/82	5	(1)	1
29	Éric Hassli	FRA	3/5/81	1		
11	Adrian Nikci		10/11/89	1	(3)	
27	Marco Schönbächler		11/1/90		(1)	
8	Johan Vonlanthen		1/2/86	4	(2)	

FC SION

UEFA EUROPA LEAGUE

Play-Off Round - Fenerbahçe SK (TUR)
H 0-2
Vaņins, Chihab, Marin (M'Futi 78), Alioui, Paíto, Serey Die, Fermino, Vanczák, Obradović (Yoda 60), Domínguez (Afonso 78), Mpenza. Coach: Didier Tholot (FRA)
Yellow Card(s): Paíto 81
A 2-2 Vanczák (9), Chihab (31p)
Vaņins, Mohamed, Nwaneri, Chihab, Alioui, Paíto (Mpenza 69), Serey Die, Vanczák (Marin 46), Obradović, Dabo (M'Futi 73), Bühler. Coach: Didier Tholot (FRA)
Yellow Card(s): Yusuf 14, Bühler 40

BSC YOUNG BOYS

UEFA EUROPA LEAGUE

Third Qualifying Round - Athletic Club (ESP)
A 1-0 Doumbia (23)
Wölfli, Ghezal, Dudar, Doumbia (Pasche 90+3), Sutter, Yapi Yapo, Degen, Hochstrasser, Regazzoni (Affolter 76), Schneuwly (Asamoah-Frimpong 84), Merdassi . Coach: Vladimir Petković (BIH)
Yellow Card(s): Degen 16, Regazzoni 46
H 1-2 Asamoah-Frimpong (90+2)
Wölfli, Ghezal, Dudar, Doumbia, Sutter (Pasche 78), Yapi Yapo, Degen, Hochstrasser (Traoré 80), Regazzoni (Asamoah-Frimpong 74), Schneuwly, Merdassi . Coach: Vladimir Petković (BIH)
Red Card(s): Yapi Yapo 90+6
Yellow Card(s): Merdassi 33, Degen 34, Yapi Yapo 45

FC BASEL 1893

UEFA EUROPA LEAGUE

Second Qualifying Round - FC Santa Coloma (AND)
H 3-0 Sahin (23), Streller (48), Almerares (59)
Costanzo, Çağdaş Atan, Huggel (Gelabert 80), Streller (Mustafi 72), Stocker, Almerares, Safari (Shaqiri 68), Inkoom, Antônio da Silva, Ferati, Sahin. Coach: Thorsten Fink (GER)
A 4-1 Streller (12), Gelabert (15), Álvarez (40og), Almerares (88)
Costanzo, Ritter, Gelabert (Antônio da Silva 51), Huggel, Streller (Almerares 46), Perović, Shaqiri, Safari, Cabral, Aratore, Sahin (Stocker 71). Coach: Thorsten Fink (GER)
Yellow Card(s): Huggel 37, Sahin 43, Gelabert 52, Safari 87

Third Qualifying Round - KR Reykjavík (ISL)
A 2-2 Chipperfield (58), Almerares (83)
Costanzo, Çağdaş Atan, Gelabert (Carlitos 85), Huggel, Chipperfield (Almerares 70), Frei, Shaqiri (Stocker 61), Safari, Cabral, Antônio da Silva, Sahin. Coach: Thorsten Fink (GER)
H 3-1 Frei (29, 80p), Shaqiri (77)
Costanzo, Gelabert, Streller, Chipperfield, Frei, Shaqiri (Ritter 84), Inkoom, Cabral, Antônio da Silva (Huggel 46), Ferati, Carlitos (Aratore 82). Coach: Thorsten Fink (GER)
Red Card(s): Gelabert 45
Yellow Card(s): Gelabert 28, Gelabert 45, Frei 62

Play-Off Round - Bakı FK (AZE)
A 3-1 Streller (71, 74), Huggel (77)
Costanzo, Çağdaş Atan, Huggel, Streller (Almerares 86), Chipperfield, Frei, Safari (Shaqiri 53), Inkoom (Carlitos 53), Cabral, Antônio da Silva, Sahin. Coach: Thorsten Fink (GER)
Yellow Card(s): Sahin 45, Inkoom 51
H 5-1 Almerares (32), Gelabert (36), Frei (63), Shaqiri (74), Mustafi (84)
Costanzo, Çağdaş Atan (Ritter 64), Gelabert, Chipperfield, Frei (Mustafi 71), Almerares, Shaqiri, Abraham (Huggel 46), Inkoom, Antônio da Silva, Aratore. Coach: Thorsten Fink (GER)
Yellow Card(s): Gelabert 7, Antônio da Silva 60, Huggel 69, Mustafi 85, Shaqiri 90+1

Group E
Match 1 - AS Roma (ITA)
H 2-0 Carlitos (11), Almerares (87)
Costanzo, Çağdaş Atan, Streller (Almerares 85), Chipperfield, Frei (Ferati 90+3), Stocker (Unal 90+1), Abraham, Safari, Inkoom, Cabral, Carlitos. Coach: Thorsten Fink (GER)
Yellow Card(s): Cabral 33, Costanzo 50, Abraham 65, Çağdaş Atan 73, Almerares 88
Match 2 - Fulham FC (ENG)
A 0-1
Costanzo, Çağdaş Atan, Gelabert (Chipperfield 86), Huggel, Streller, Frei, Stocker, Abraham (Antônio da Silva 69), Safari, Carlitos (Almerares 82), Sahin. Coach: Thorsten Fink (GER)
Yellow Card(s): Almerares 85
Match 3 - PFC CSKA Sofia (BUL)
A 2-0 Frei (20, 63)
Colomba, Çağdaş Atan, Huggel, Streller (Almerares 86), Frei (Cabral 81), Stocker, Abraham, Safari, Inkoom, Antônio da Silva, Carlitos (Shaqiri 88). Coach: Thorsten Fink (GER)
Yellow Card(s): Safari 34
Match 4 - PFC CSKA Sofia (BUL)
H 3-1 Gelabert (35), Frei (41p, 67)
Colomba, Çağdaş Atan, Gelabert (Aratore 64), Huggel, Chipperfield, Frei, Stocker (Perović 88), Almerares, Safari (Shaqiri 78), Inkoom, Cabral. Coach: Thorsten Fink (GER)
Match 5 - AS Roma (ITA)
A 1-2 Huggel (18)
Wessels, Çağdaş Atan, Gelabert, Huggel, Streller, Frei, Stocker, Abraham, Safari (Shaqiri 80), Inkoom, Carlitos. Coach: Thorsten Fink (GER)
Yellow Card(s): Gelabert 32, Carlitos 75
Match 6 - Fulham FC (ENG)
H 2-3 Frei (64p), Streller (87)
Colomba, Çağdaş Atan, Huggel, Streller, Frei, Stocker, Abraham, Safari (Shaqiri 46), Inkoom, Cabral (Almerares 46), Carlitos (Schürpf 79). Coach: Thorsten Fink (GER)
Yellow Card(s): Abraham 40, Frei 45

TURKEY

BEŞİKTAŞ JK

UEFA CHAMPIONS LEAGUE

Group B
Match 1 - Manchester United FC (ENG)
0-1
...akan Arıkan, İbrahim Kaş, Sivok, Nobre, Rodrigo Tabata (Tello 66), Ekrem
...ağ, İbrahim Üzülmez, Serdar Özkan (Yusuf Şimşek 58), Hološko (Nihat
...ahveci 83), Ferrari, Ernst. Coach: Mustafa Denizli (TUR)
Yellow Card(s): Sivok 5, Nobre 52
Match 2 - PFC CSKA Moskva (RUS)
1-2 Ekrem Dağ (90+2)
...üştü Reçber, İsmail Köybaşı, İbrahim Kaş, Sivok, Nihat Kahveci (Serdar
...zkan 73), Nobre, Tello (Bobô 75), Ekrem Dağ, Hološko (Yusuf Şimşek 34),
...errari, Ernst. Coach: Mustafa Denizli (TUR)
Yellow Card(s): İsmail Köybaşı 21, Sivok 79
Match 3 - VfL Wolfsburg (GER)
0-0
...üştü Reçber, İbrahim Kaş, Fink (Uğur İnceman 87), Sivok, Nihat Kahveci,
...obô (Nobre 88), Tello (Rodrigo Tabata 81), Ekrem Dağ, İbrahim Üzülmez,
...errari, Ernst. Coach: Mustafa Denizli (TUR)
Yellow Card(s): İbrahim Üzülmez 17
Match 4 - VfL Wolfsburg (GER)
0-3
...akan Arıkan, İbrahim Kaş, Fink, Sivok, Bobô, Rodrigo Tabata (Nobre 69),
...krem Dağ, İbrahim Üzülmez (İsmail Köybaşı 78), Serdar Özkan (Tello 46),
...ğur İnceman, Ferrari. Coach: Mustafa Denizli (TUR)
Yellow Card(s): Ekrem Dağ 36, Tello 49, Uğur İnceman 59, Sivok 90
Match 5 - Manchester United FC (ENG)
1-0 Tello (20)
...üştü Reçber, İsmail Köybaşı, İbrahim Kaş, Fink, Bobô (Batuhan Karadeniz
...4), Tello (Uğur İnceman 75), Ekrem Dağ, İbrahim Üzülmez, Ferrari, Ernst,
...rahim Toraman (Erhan Güven 67). Coach: Mustafa Denizli (TUR)
Yellow Card(s): Batuhan Karadeniz 85, Rüştü Reçber 90+5
Match 6 - PFC CSKA Moskva (RUS)
1-2 Bobô (86)
...üştü Reçber, İbrahim Kaş, Fink (Uğur İnceman 77), Sivok, Bobô, Tello
...obre 87), Ekrem Dağ (Nihat Kahveci 68), İbrahim Üzülmez, Ferrari, Ernst,
...rahim Toraman. Coach: Mustafa Denizli (TUR)
Yellow Card(s): Fink 66, İbrahim Toraman 85, Sivok 90+4

No	Player	Nat	DoB	Aps	(s)	Gls
Goalkeepers						
1	Hakan Arıkan		17/8/82	2		
	Rüştü Reçber		10/5/73	4		
Defenders						
4	Erhan Güven		15/5/82		(1)	
7	Matteo Ferrari	ITA	5/12/79	6		
	İbrahim Kaş		20/9/86	6		
3	İbrahim Toraman		20/11/81	2		
9	İbrahim Üzülmez		10/3/74	5		
	İsmail Köybaşı		10/7/89	2	(1)	
	Tomáš Sivok	CZE	15/9/83	5		
Midfielders						
7	Ekrem Dağ	AUT	5/12/80	6		1
8	Fabian Ernst	GER	30/5/79	5		
	Fink	GER	1/2/82	4		
5	Rodrigo Tabata	BRA	19/11/80	2	(1)	
	Serdar Özkan		1/1/87	2	(1)	
4	Rodrigo Tello	CHI	14/10/79	4	(2)	1
6	Uğur İnceman		25/5/81	1	(3)	
9	Yusuf Şimşek		20/7/75		(2)	

Forwards

9	Batuhan Karadeniz		24/4/91		(1)	
13	Bobô	BRA	9/1/85	4	(1)	1
23	Filip Hološko	SVK	17/1/84	2		
11	Mert Nobre	BRA	6/11/80	2	(3)	
8	Nihat Kahveci		23/11/79	2	(2)	

SIVASSPOR

UEFA CHAMPIONS LEAGUE

Third Qualifying Round - RSC Anderlecht (BEL)
A 0-5
Petković, Sedat Bayrak, Musa Aydın, İbrahim Dağaşan, Erman Kılıç, Yasin
Çakmak, Ersen Martin (Kamanan 46), Mbemba (Uğur Kavuk 46), Hayrettin
Yerlikaya, Abdurrahman Dereli, Onur Tuncer (Cihan Yılmaz 71). Coach:
Bülent Uygun (TUR)
Yellow Card(s): Abdurrahman Dereli 26, Sedat Bayrak 35, Onur Tuncer 64
H 3-1 Ersen Martin (12), Kamanan (19p), Musa Aydın (58)
Akın Vardar, Sedat Bayrak, Murat Sözgelmez, Musa Aydın (İbrahim
Dağaşan 60), Erman Kılıç (Agbetu 58), Kamanan, Cihan Yılmaz, Ersen
Martin (Murat Erdoğan 76), Hayrettin Yerlikaya, Uğur Kavuk, Onur Tuncer.
Coach: Bülent Uygun (TUR)
Yellow Card(s): Uğur Kavuk 5

UEFA EUROPA LEAGUE

Play-Off Round - FC Shakhtar Donetsk (UKR)
H 0-3
Petković, Sedat Bayrak, Musa Aydın (Ersen Martin 46), İbrahim Dağaşan,
Cihan Yılmaz (Onur Tuncer 79), Kadir Bekmezci, İbrahim Şahin, Bouazza
(Kamanan 61), Yasin Çakmak, Hayrettin Yerlikaya, Abdurrahman Dereli.
Coach: Bülent Uygun (TUR)
Red Card(s): Petković 90+1
Yellow Card(s): Yasin Çakmak 25, İbrahim Dağaşan 75, Sedat Bayrak 86
A 0-2
Akın Vardar, Murat Sözgelmez (Ferhat Bıkmaz 72), İbrahim Dağaşan,
Erman Kılıç, Kamanan, Cihan Yılmaz (Agbetu 62), Kadir Bekmezci, Yasin
Çakmak, Mbemba, Abdurrahman Dereli (Uğur Kavuk 55), Onur Tuncer.
Coach: Bülent Uygun (TUR)
Yellow Card(s): Murat Sözgelmez 34, Yasin Çakmak 67, Uğur Kavuk 89

TRABZONSPOR

UEFA EUROPA LEAGUE

Play-Off Round - Toulouse FC (FRA)
H 1-3 Song (16)
Sylva, Čale (Giray Kaçar 80), Song, Engin Baytar, Selçuk İnan, Umut Bulut,
Egemen Korkmaz, Tayfun Cora (Alanzinho 65), Colman, Tjikuzu (Gökhan
Ünal 70), Serkan Balci. Coach: Hugo Broos (BEL)
Red Card(s): Engin Baytar 86
Yellow Card(s): Egemen Korkmaz 68, Engin Baytar 76, Engin Baytar 86
A 1-0 Ceyhun Gülselam (55)
Sylva, Čale, Song, Gülselam, Selçuk İnan (Tjikuzu 85), Gökhan Ünal, Barış
Memiş, Tayfun Cora (Serkan Balci 73), Colman, Giray Kaçar, Alanzinho
(Umut Bulut 54). Coach: Hugo Broos (BEL)
Yellow Card(s): Tayfun Cora 41, Giray Kaçar 75, Colman 80

FENERBAHÇE SK

UEFA EUROPA LEAGUE

Third Qualifying Round - Budapest Honvéd FC (HUN)
H 5-1 *Roberto Carlos (13), Güiza (30, 40, 61), Alex (69)*
Volkan Demirel, Roberto Carlos (Deivid 17), Emre Belözoğlu (Deniz Barış 85), Kazım Kazım, Güiza (Mehmet Topuz 71), Alex, Cristian, Önder Turacı, André Santos, Fábio Bilica, Gökhan Gönül. Coach: Christoph Daum (GER)
A 1-1 *André Santos (9)*
Volkan Demirel, Wederson (Deniz Barış 69), Güiza, Alex, Cristian, Ali Bilgin, Önder Turacı, Selçuk Şahin, André Santos (Uğur Boral 80), Fábio Fábio Bilica, Deivid (Bekir İrtegün 75). Coach: Christoph Daum (GER)
Red Card(s): Fábio Bilica 31

Play-Off Round - FC Sion (SUI)
A 2-0 *André Santos (45), Kazım Kazım (85)*
Volkan Demirel, Lugano, Roberto Carlos, Emre Belözoğlu (Uğur Boral 76), Kazım Kazım, Güiza, Cristian, Deniz Barış (Önder Turacı 29), André Santos, Gökhan Gönül, Deivid (Semih Şentürk 63). Coach: Christoph Daum (GER)
Yellow Card(s): Cristian 52, Güiza 68, Gökhan Gönül 89
H 2-2 *André Santos (2, 41p)*
Volkan Demirel, Lugano, Wederson, Kazım Kazım (Özer Hurmacı 90+1), Cristian, Önder Turacı, Selçuk Şahin, Semih Şentürk (Güiza 77), Uğur Boral (Emre Belözoğlu 77), André Santos, Gökhan Gönül. Coach: Christoph Daum (GER)
Yellow Card(s): Volkan Demirel 30, Lugano 37

Group H
Match 1 - FC Twente (NED)
H 1-2 *Mehmet Topuz (71)*
Volkan Demirel, Lugano, Roberto Carlos (Mehmet Topuz 64), Emre Belözoğlu, Kazım Kazım (Deivid 79), Güiza (Semih Şentürk 79), Alex, Cristian, André Santos, Fábio Bilica, Gökhan Gönül. Coach: Christoph Daum (GER)
Yellow Card(s): André Santos 41
Match 2 - FC Sheriff (MDA)
A 1-0 *Alex (53)*
Volkan Demirel, Lugano, Roberto Carlos, Emre Belözoğlu, Kazım Kazım (Mehmet Topuz 70), Alex, Cristian, Önder Turacı, Semih Şentürk (Wederson 83), Uğur Boral (Deivid 70), Fábio Bilica. Coach: Christoph Daum (GER)
Match 3 - FC Steaua Bucureşti (ROU)
A 1-0 *Kazım Kazım (59)*
Volkan Demirel, Lugano, Roberto Carlos, Emre Belözoğlu, Kazım Kazım (Selçuk Şahin 85), Cristian, Özer Hurmacı (Wederson 71), André Santos (Ali Bilgin 89), Fábio Bilica, Mehmet Topuz, Gökhan Gönül. Coach: Christoph Daum (GER)
Yellow Card(s): Lugano 28, Kazım Kazım 45+3, Emre Belözoğlu 82, Gökhan Gönül 90+2
Match 4 - FC Steaua Bucureşti (ROU)
H 3-1 *André Santos (15), Fábio Bilica (51), Alex (67)*
Volkan Demirel, Lugano, Roberto Carlos, Emre Belözoğlu (Özer Hurmacı 70), Kazım Kazım (Güiza 70), Alex (Selçuk Şahin 85), Cristian, André Santos, Fábio Bilica, Mehmet Topuz, Gökhan Gönül. Coach: Christoph Daum (GER)
Yellow Card(s): André Santos 43, Mehmet Topuz 66, Kazım Kazım 70
Match 5 - FC Twente (NED)
A 1-0 *Lugano (71)*
Volkan Demirel, Lugano, Roberto Carlos (André Santos 75), Wederson, Güiza (Semih Şentürk 82), Alex, Cristian, Selçuk Şahin, Fábio Bilica, Mehmet Topuz (Deniz Barış 90), Gökhan Gönül. Coach: Christoph Daum (GER)
Yellow Card(s): Roberto Carlos 29, Volkan Demirel 39, Alex 63, Wederson 81, Lugano 87

Match 6 - FC Sheriff (MDA)
H 1-0 *Uğur Boral (15)*
Volkan Babacan, Lugano, Güiza, Bekir İrtegün, Özer Hurmacı (Mehmet Topuz 46), Selçuk Şahin, Semih Şentürk (Roberto Carlos 89), Deniz Barış, Uğur Boral (Ali Bilgin 86), André Santos, Fábio Bilica. Coach: Christoph Daum (GER)

Round of 32 - LOSC Lille Métropole (FRA)
A 1-2 *Wederson (5)*
Volkan Demirel, Lugano (Deniz Barış 10), Emre Belözoğlu, Wederson, Güiza, Alex (Selçuk Şahin 90+3), Cristian, Özer Hurmacı (Mehmet Topuz 73), André Santos, Fábio Bilica, Gökhan Gönül. Coach: Christoph Daum (GER)
Yellow Card(s): Emre Belözoğlu 39, André Santos 71
H 1-1 *Emre Belözoğlu (35)*
Volkan Demirel, Emre Belözoğlu, Wederson, Güiza (Cristian 74), Alex, Bekir İrtegün, Önder Turacı, Selçuk Şahin, Deniz Barış (Semih Şentürk 79), Fábio Bilica, Gökhan Gönül. Coach: Christoph Daum (GER)
Yellow Card(s): Wederson 60, Fábio Bilica 85

GALATASARAY AŞ

UEFA EUROPA LEAGUE

Second Qualifying Round - FC Tobol Kostanay (KAZ)
A 1-1 *Baroš (58)*
Orkun Uşak, Gökhan Zan, Aydın Yılmaz (Uğur Uçar 75), Barış Özbek (Arda Turan 46), Mustafa Sarp, Yaser Yıldız, Ayhan Akman, Erhan Şentürk (Baroš 46), Sabri Sarıoğlu, Alparslan Erdem, Servet Çetin. Coach: Frank Rijkaard (NED)
Red Card(s): Alparslan Erdem 72
Yellow Card(s): Mustafa Sarp 40, Gökhan Zan 53, Aydın Yılmaz 61, Alparslan Erdem 67, Alparslan Erdem 72
H 2-0 *Mustafa Sarp (64), Servet Çetin (90+2)*
Orkun Uşak, Gökhan Zan, Arda Turan, Baroš (Nonda 90+2), Mustafa Sarp, Yıldız (Kewell 46), Ayhan Akman, Hakan Balta, Serdar Eylik (Linderoth 57), Sabri Sarıoğlu, Servet Çetin. Coach: Frank Rijkaard (NED)

Third Qualifying Round - Maccabi Netanya FC (ISR)
A 4-1 *Hakan Balta (31), Kewell (47), Sabri Sarıoğlu (53), Baroš (73)*
Leo Franco, Gökhan Zan, Aydın Yılmaz (Barış Özbek 71), Arda Turan, Baroš (Nonda 78), Mustafa Sarp, Ayhan Akman, Kewell (Keita 66), Hakan Balta, Sabri Sarıoğlu, Servet Çetin. Coach: Frank Rijkaard (NED)
Yellow Card(s): Mustafa Sarp 65, Baroš 76
H 6-0 *Barış Özbek (2, 51), Keita (6), Nonda (56, 60, 90)*
Leo Franco, Emre Güngör, Uğur Uçar, Linderoth (Ayhan Akman 58), Aydın Yılmaz, Barış Özbek, Arda Turan (Serdar Eylik 74), Keita (Kewell 46), Nonda, Emre Aşık, Hakan Balta. Coach: Frank Rijkaard (NED)

Play-Off Round - FC Levadia Tallinn (EST)
H 5-0 *Keita (21, 45), Baroš (56p), Kewell (78), Leitan (88og)*
Leo Franco, Gökhan Zan, Aydın Yılmaz (Kewell 62), Arda Turan, Keita, Baroš (Elano 69), Mustafa Sarp (Mehmet Topal 74), Ayhan Akman, Hakan Balta, Sabri Sarıoğlu, Servet Çetin. Coach: Frank Rijkaard (NED)
A 1-1 *Nonda (64)*
Leo Franco, Emre Güngör, Aydın Yılmaz (Arda Turan 65), Barış Özbek, Elano, Mehmet Topal, Nonda (Mustafa Sarp 74), Emre Aşık, Serdar Eylik, Sabri Sarıoğlu, Alparslan Erdem (Serkan Kurtuluş 59). Coach: Frank Rijkaard (NED)
Yellow Card(s): Emre Güngör 22, Elano 90

Group F

Match 1 - Panathinaikos FC (GRE)
3-1 *Elano (5), Baroš (48), Sarriegi (58og)*
Leo Franco, Emre Güngör (Uğur Uçar 24), Elano (Arda Turan 62), Keita (Barış Özbek 72), Mehmet Topal, Baroš, Mustafa Sarp, Kewell, Emre Aşık, Hakan Balta, Sabri Sarıoğlu. Coach: Frank Rijkaard (NED)
Yellow Card(s): Leo Franco 44, Emre Aşık 70, Uğur Uçar 76

Match 2 - SK Sturm Graz (AUT)
1-1 *Baroš (63)*
Leo Franco, Elano, Arda Turan, Keita, Mehmet Topal (Mustafa Sarp 77), Baroš (Nonda 86), Ayhan Akman (Kewell 61), Emre Aşık, Hakan Balta, Sabri Sarıoğlu, Servet Çetin. Coach: Frank Rijkaard (NED)
Yellow Card(s): Emre Aşık 67, Sabri Sarıoğlu 73

Match 3 - FC Dinamo Bucureşti (ROU)
4-1 *Kewell (32), Nonda (42, 46), Elano (58p)*
Leo Franco, Elano, Keita (Aydın Yılmaz 57), Mehmet Topal, Mustafa Sarp, Ayhan Akman (Barış Özbek 74), Kewell, Nonda, Sabri Sarıoğlu (Uğur Uçar 45), Servet Çetin, Caner Erkin. Coach: Frank Rijkaard (NED)
Yellow Card(s): Ayhan Akman 50, Kewell 64

Match 4 - FC Dinamo Bucureşti (ROU)
3-0 *Kewell (22), Nonda (24), Mehmet Topal (55)*
Leo Franco, Gökhan Zan (Emre Güngör 86), Barış Özbek, Arda Turan, Mehmet Topal, Mustafa Sarp (Elano 79), Kewell, Nonda (Keita 72), Hakan Balta, Sabri Sarıoğlu, Servet Çetin. Coach: Frank Rijkaard (NED)

Match 5 - Panathinaikos FC (GRE)
1-0 *Gilberto Silva (50og)*
Leo Franco, Gökhan Zan (Barış Özbek 30), Elano (Ayhan Akman 73), Arda Turan, Mehmet Topal, Mustafa Sarp, Kewell (Keita 63), Nonda, Hakan Balta, Sabri Sarıoğlu, Servet Çetin. Coach: Frank Rijkaard (NED)
Yellow Card(s): Arda Turan 25, Kewell 44, Mustafa Sarp 90+1

Match 6 - SK Sturm Graz (AUT)
0-1
Aykut Erçetin, Linderoth (Mustafa Sarp 64), Aydın Yılmaz, Barış Özbek, Keita, Ayhan Akman, Emre Aşık, Serdar Eylik, Alparslan Erdem (Çetin Güngör 68), Servet Çetin (Hakan Balta 74), Caner Erkin. Coach: Frank Rijkaard (NED)

Round of 32 - Club Atlético de Madrid (ESP)
1-1 *Keita (77)*
Leo Franco, Uğur Uçar, Elano (Ayhan Akman 82), Arda Turan (Barış Özbek 90), Keita, Neill, Mehmet Topal, Mustafa Sarp, Hakan Balta, Servet Çetin, Caner Erkin (Giovani 36). Coach: Frank Rijkaard (NED)
Yellow Card(s): Servet Çetin 40

1-2 *Keita (66)*
Leo Franco, Uğur Uçar, Elano (Ayhan Akman 50), Arda Turan, Keita, Neill, Mehmet Topal, Mustafa Sarp (Giovani 90+3), Hakan Balta, Servet Çetin, Caner Erkin. Coach: Frank Rijkaard (NED)
Red Card(s): Caner Erkin 82
Yellow Card(s): Mehmet Topal 59, Arda Turan 61, Uğur Uçar 68, Caner Erkin 80, Caner Erkin 81

Match 2 - FC Barcelona (ESP)
A 0-2
Shovkovskiy, Vukojević, Shevchenko, Milevskiy, Eremenko, Gusev (Ninković 86), Magrão (Betão 73), Yussuf (Ghioane 46), Khacheridi, Leandro Almeida, Yarmolenko. Coach: Valeriy Gazzayev (RUS)
Yellow Card(s): Magrão 37, Leandro Almeida 55

Match 3 - FC Internazionale Milano (ITA)
A 2-2 *Mykhalyk (5), Lúcio (40og)*
Bohush, Vukojević, Shevchenko, Milevskiy (Kravets 90+3), Eremenko, Mykhalyk, Magrão (Betão 70), Khacheridi, Ninković (Gusev 69), Leandro Almeida, Yarmolenko. Coach: Valeriy Gazzayev (RUS)
Yellow Card(s): Leandro Almeida 31, Shevchenko 61, Milevskiy 68, Vukojević 82

Match 4 - FC Internazionale Milano (ITA)
H 1-2 *Shevchenko (21)*
Bohush, Vukojević, Shevchenko, Milevskiy (Gusev 70), Eremenko, Mykhalyk, Magrão, Khacheridi, Ninković, Leandro Almeida, Yarmolenko. Coach: Valeriy Gazzayev (RUS)
Yellow Card(s): Leandro Almeida 28, Mykhalyk 53

Match 5 - FC Rubin Kazan (RUS)
A 0-0
Shovkovskiy, Betão, Vukojević, Shevchenko, Milevskiy, Eremenko, Mykhalyk, Magrão, Yussuf, Ninković (Ghioane 86), Yarmolenko. Coach: Valeriy Gazzayev (RUS)
Yellow Card(s): Shevchenko 37

Match 6 - FC Barcelona (ESP)
H 1-2 *Milevskiy (2)*
Shovkovskiy, Betão, Vukojević, Shevchenko, Milevskiy, Eremenko, Mykhalyk, Magrão (Ninković 75), Yussuf, Leandro Almeida, Yarmolenko. Coach: Valeriy Gazzayev (RUS)
Yellow Card(s): Leandro Almeida 51, Vukojević 55, Mykhalyk 78, Shevchenko 88

No	Player	Nat	DoB	Aps	(s)	Gls
Goalkeepers						
31	Stanislav Bohush		25/10/83	2		
1	Olexandr Shovkovskiy		2/1/75	4		
Defenders						
3	Betão	BRA	11/11/83	2	(3)	
34	Yevhen Khacheridi		28/7/87	4		
44	Leandro Almeida	BRA	14/3/87	5		
17	Taras Mykhalyk		28/10/83	4		1
Midfielders						
11	Roman Eremenko	FIN	19/3/87	6		
4	Tiberiu Ghioane	ROU	18/6/81		(3)	
20	Oleh Gusev		25/4/83	1	(3)	1
21	Magrão	BRA	13/6/85	6		1
36	Miloš Ninković	SRB	25/12/84	4	(2)	
5	Ognjen Vukojević	CRO	20/12/83	6		
25	Ayila Yussuf	NGA	4/11/84	4		1
Forwards						
22	Artem Kravets		3/6/89		(1)	
10	Artem Milevskiy		12/1/85	6		1
7	Andriy Shevchenko		29/9/76	6		1
70	Andriy Yarmolenko		23/10/89	6		

UKRAINE

FC DYNAMO KYIV

UEFA CHAMPIONS LEAGUE

Group F
Match 1 - FC Rubin Kazan (RUS)
3-1 *Yussuf (71), Magrão (79), Gusev (85)*
Shovkovskiy, Vukojević, Shevchenko (Betão 90), Milevskiy, Eremenko, Magrão, Yussuf, Khacheridi, Ninković (Ghioane 57), Leandro Almeida, Yarmolenko (Gusev 65). Coach: Valeriy Gazzayev (RUS)
Yellow Card(s): Milevskiy 62, Magrão 80

FC SHAKHTAR DONETSK

UEFA CHAMPIONS LEAGUE

Third Qualifying Round - FC Timişoara (ROU)
H 2-2 *Hladkiy (60), Fernandinho (86)*
Pyatov, Hübschman, Kucher, Fernandinho, Jádson, Ilsinho, Shevchuk (Hladkiy 46), Luiz Adriano (Aghahowa 80), Willian, Ishchenko (Chyhrynskiy 46), Srna. Coach: Mircea Lucescu (ROU)
Yellow Card(s): Srna 75

A 0-0
Pyatov, Hübschman, Kucher, Fernandinho, Jádson (Hladkiy 69), Ilsinho, Luiz Adriano (Aghahowa 32), Hai (Willian 54), Raţ, Chyhrynskiy, Srna.
Coach: Mircea Lucescu (ROU)
Yellow Card(s): Hübschman 56, Kucher 82, Srna 86

UEFA EUROPA LEAGUE

Play-Off Round - Sivasspor (TUR)
A 3-0 *Hai (6), Ilsinho (76), Kobin (87)*
Pyatov, Hübschman, Kucher, Fernandinho, Jádson (Willian 67), Ilsinho, Kobin, Hai (Polyanskiy 77), Hladkiy (Aghahowa 71), Raţ, Chyhrynskiy.
Coach: Mircea Lucescu (ROU)
Yellow Card(s): Jádson 16, Hai 75
H 2-0 *Jádson (21p), Luiz Adriano (59p)*
Khudzhamov, Jádson, Ilsinho (Rakytskiy 60), Kobin, Hai (Fernandinho 60), Willian, Polyanskiy, Ishchenko, Srna, Chizhov, Aghahowa (Luiz Adriano 46).
Coach: Mircea Lucescu (ROU)
Yellow Card(s): Polyanskiy 51

Group J
Match 1 - Club Brugge KV (BEL)
A 4-1 *Hai (11), Willian (19), Srna (35), Kravchenko (75)*
Pyatov, Kucher, Fernandinho, Jádson (Polyanskiy 71), Luiz Adriano, Lewandowski, Hai (Kobin 46), Willian (Kravchenko 63), Raţ, Srna, Rakytskiy.
Coach: Mircea Lucescu (ROU)
Yellow Card(s): Luiz Adriano 67
Match 2 - FK Partizan (SRB)
H 4-1 *Lomić (24og), Luiz Adriano (39), Jádson (54), Rakytskiy (67)*
Pyatov, Hübschman (Duljaj 72), Kucher (Ishchenko 72), Fernandinho, Jádson, Ilsinho, Luiz Adriano, Willian, Raţ, Srna (Kobin 75), Rakytskiy.
Coach: Mircea Lucescu (ROU)
Match 3 - Toulouse FC (FRA)
H 4-0 *Fernandinho (7p), Luiz Adriano (24, 56), Hübschman (38)*
Pyatov, Hübschman (Lewandowski 46), Kucher, Fernandinho, Jádson (Hai 71), Ilsinho, Luiz Adriano, Willian (Aghahowa 71), Raţ, Srna, Rakytskiy.
Coach: Mircea Lucescu (ROU)
Match 4 - Toulouse FC (FRA)
A 2-0 *Luiz Adriano (49), Hai (63)*
Pyatov, Hübschman, Kucher, Fernandinho, Jádson (Lewandowski 77), Luiz Adriano (Hladkiy 83), Hai, Willian, Raţ, Srna (Kobin 73), Rakytskiy. Coach: Mircea Lucescu (ROU)
Yellow Card(s): Raţ 34
Match 5 - Club Brugge KV (BEL)
H 0-0
Pyatov, Hübschman (Lewandowski 80), Kucher, Fernandinho, Jádson (Kravchenko 71), Ilsinho, Luiz Adriano, Willian, Raţ, Srna, Rakytskiy. Coach: Mircea Lucescu (ROU)
Yellow Card(s): Srna 67
Match 6 - FK Partizan (SRB)
A 0-1
Pyatov, Hübschman, Duljaj (Hai 77), Fernandinho, Jádson (Vitsenets 77), Kobin, Luiz Adriano (Hladkiy 81), Willian, Raţ, Ishchenko, Rakytskiy. Coach: Mircea Lucescu (ROU)
Yellow Card(s): Raţ 74

Round of 32 - Fulham FC (ENG)
A 1-2 *Luiz Adriano (32)*
Pyatov, Hübschman (Kravchenko 78), Kucher, Fernandinho, Jádson (Douglas Costa 75), Ilsinho, Luiz Adriano, Willian, Raţ, Srna, Rakytskiy.
Coach: Mircea Lucescu (ROU)
Yellow Card(s): Luiz Adriano 21, Srna 45
H 1-1 *Jádson (69)*
Pyatov, Hübschman (Kravchenko 46), Kucher, Fernandinho, Jádson, Ilsinho, Luiz Adriano (Hladkiy 76), Willian (Douglas Costa 53), Raţ, Srna, Rakytskiy. Coach: Mircea Lucescu (ROU)
Yellow Card(s): Ilsinho 90+3

FC VORSKLA POLTAVA

UEFA EUROPA LEAGUE

Play-Off Round - SL Benfica (POR)
A 0-4
Dolhanskiy, Despotovski, Dallku, Krasnoperov, Markoski (Chichkov 87), Kulakov, Sachko (Yanuzi 46), Curri, Medvedev, Yarmash (Bezus 60), Yesin.
Coach: Mykola Pavlov (UKR)
Yellow Card(s): Yarmash 37, Kulakov 44, Dallku 51, Yanuzi 74
H 2-1 *Sachko (48), Yesin (74)*
Dolhanskiy, Despotovski, Dallku, Krasnoporov, Markoski (Chesnakov 88), Kulakov, Sachko (Chichikov 72), Curri, Medvedev, Yarmash (Bezus 46), Yesin. Coach: Mykola Pavlov (UKR)
Yellow Card(s): Yarmash 22, Curri 47, Bezus 86

FC METALIST KHARKIV

UEFA EUROPA LEAGUE

Third Qualifying Round - HNK Rijeka (CRO)
A 2-1 *Eremenko Jr (43), Lysenko (85)*
Goryainov, Shelayev, Valyayev, Edmar, Eremenko Jr (Oliynyk 65), Lysenko, Pshenychnykh (Berezovchuk 79), Obradović, Maidana, Gueye, Dević (Trišović 65). Coach: Myron Markevych (UKR)
Red Card(s): Valyayev 67
Yellow Card(s): Edmar 39, Maidana 45+1
H 2-0 *Gueye (12), Oliynyk (60)*
Goryainov, Shelayev, Edmar (Zézé 75), Eremenko Jr, Oliynyk (Barylko 87), Lysenko (Fredes 62), Pshenychnykh, Obradović, Maidana, Gueye, Dević.
Coach: Myron Markevych (UKR)
Yellow Card(s): Gueye 24, Dević 81

Play-Off Round - SK Sturm Graz (AUT)
A 1-1 *Oliynyk (76)*
Goryainov, Edmar, Eremenko Jr (Bordian 68), Oliynyk (Fredes 88), Lysenko (Shelayev 46), Pshenychnykh, Obradović, Maidana, Gueye, Dević, Jajá.
Coach: Myron Markevych (UKR)
Yellow Card(s): Obradović 58, Edmar 85
H 0-1
Goryainov, Shelayev (Eremenko Jr 46), Slyusar, Oliynyk, Burkhardt (Phantskhava 58), Pshenychnykh, Obradović, Maidana, Gueye, Dević (Zézé 75), Jajá. Coach: Myron Markevych (UKR)
Yellow Card(s): Shelayev 37, Jajá 90+3

FC METALURH DONETSK

UEFA EUROPA LEAGUE

cond Qualifying Round - FC MTZ-RIPO Minsk (BLR)
3-0 *Mguni (34), Mkhitaryan (42), Godin (66)*
šljenković, Korotetskiy, Checher, Mguni, Lazić, Makrides (Tănasă 87), khitaryan, Godin (Danylovskiy 83), China, Mário Mário Sérgio, Kingsley olovyk 68). Coach: Nikolai Nikolov (BUL)
llow Card(s): Checher 59
2-1 *Mguni (35), Mkhitaryan (85)*
robyov, Korotetskiy (Bilozor 70), Checher, Mguni (Tănasă 67), Lazić, olovyk, Makrides, Mkhitaryan, Godin, Mário Sérgio, Kingsley (Tkachenko). Coach: Nikolai Nikolov (BUL)

ird Qualifying Round - NK IB Ljubljana (SVN)
2-0 *Godin (20), Mário Sérgio (50p)*
šljenković, Korotetskiy, Checher, Mguni (Tănasă 89), Lazić, Volovyk, akrides, Mkhitaryan, Godin (Tkachenko 81), Mário Sérgio, Kingsley abinho 76). Coach: Nikolai Nikolov (BUL)
3-0 *Mkhitaryan (67), Mguni (73), Dimitrov (85p)*
šljenković, Korotetskiy (Bilozor 77), Checher, Mguni, Lazić, Volovyk, akrides, Mkhitaryan, Godin (Fabinho 72), Mário Sérgio, Kingsley imitrov 46). Coach: Nikolai Nikolov (BUL)

ay-Off Round - FK Austria Wien (AUT)
2-2 *Kingsley (17), Dimitrov (90+2)*
šljenković, Korotetskiy, Checher, Lazić, Volovyk (China 68), Dimitrov, akrides (Fabinho 73), Mkhitaryan, Godin (Tănasă 57), Mário Sérgio, ngsley. Coach: Nikolai Nikolov (BUL)
ellow Card(s): Kingsley 50, Lazić 80
2-3 *Tănasă (20), Mkhitaryan (54)*
šljenković, Korotetskiy, Checher, Lazić, Volovyk (China 3), Tănasă, Dimitrov, Makrides, Mkhitaryan, Mário Sérgio, Kingsley abinho 109). Coach: Nikolai Nikolov (BUL)
ed Card(s): Dimitrov 90
ellow Card(s): Dimitrov 61, Dimitrov 90, Mário Sérgio 112, Lazić 121

WALES

RHYL FC

UEFA CHAMPIONS LEAGUE

econd Qualifying Round - FK Partizan (SRB)
0-4
endall, Naylor, Strong, Horan, Leah, Owen, Holden , Roberts, M. Williams unt 55), Sherbon (Connolly 70), Stones. Coach: Alan Bickerstaff (WAL)
ellow Card(s): Sherbon 33, M. Williams 36, Connolly 86
0-8
endall (Pritchard 86), Connolly, Naylor, Strong, Horan, Leah, Owen, olden, Roberts, Sherbon (M. Williams 60), Stones. Coach: Alan ickerstaff (WAL)
ellow Card(s): Horan 72

BANGOR CITY FC

UEFA EUROPA LEAGUE

Second Qualifying Round - FC Honka Espoo (FIN)
A 0-2
Smith, Johnston, Brewerton, Morley, Limbert (Beattie 87), Stott, Sharp, Roberts, Hoy, Killackey, Smyth (Edwards 77). Coach: Nev Powell (ENG)
Yellow Card(s): Hoy 34, Brewerton 71, Smith 76
H 0-1
Smith, Johnston, Brewerton (Williams 78), Morley, Limbert (Edwards 59), Stott, Sharp, Roberts, Hoy, Killackey, Smyth. Coach: Nev Powell (ENG)
Yellow Card(s): Limbert 21, Brewerton 73, Edwards 90

LLANELLI AFC

UEFA EUROPA LEAGUE

First Qualifying Round - Motherwell FC (SCO)
A 1-0 *S. Jones (28)*
Morris, Mumford, S. Jones, Corbisiero, Griffiths, C. Jones (Follows 65), Venables, Jarman (Thomas 16), Legg (Warlow 51), Phillips, Howard. Coach: Andy Legg (WAL)
Yellow Card(s): S. Jones 4, Griffiths 30, Howard 45+2
H 0-3
Morris, Mumford, S. Jones (Jenkins 67), Thomas, Corbisiero, Griffiths, Venables, Follows, Legg (Warlow 76), Phillips (Moses 80), Howard. Coach: Andy Legg (WAL)

THE NEW SAINTS FC

UEFA EUROPA LEAGUE

First Qualifying Round - Fram Reykjavík (ISL)
A 1-2 *Evans (24)*
Harrison, Hogan, T. Holmes, Evans, Baker (McKenna 89), Ruscoe, Berkeley, Wood, Jones, Murtagh (Darlington 73), D. Holmes (C. Marriott 83). Coach: Andy Cale (ENG)
Yellow Card(s): Berkeley 20
H 1-2 *Evans (11)*
Harrison, Hogan, R. Marriott, T. Holmes, Evans, Baker, Ruscoe, Darlington (Seargeant 70), Williams (Berkeley 74), Jones (Wood 70), D. Holmes. Coach: Andy Cale (ENG)
Yellow Card(s): R. Marriott 17

2010 FIFA WORLD CUP

Spain became the eighth different nation to win the FIFA World Cup – and the fifth from Europe - after defeating the Netherlands with a late extra-time goal from Andrés Iniesta in the 2010 final at the Soccer City stadium in Johannesburg. In so doing they also became the first European team to lift the trophy on non-European soil. Vicente del Bosque's side recovered well from a shock opening defeat by Switzerland, winning each of their remaining six games, the last four all by a 1-0 margin. The victory enabled them to add the world title to the European crown they won at UEFA EURO 2008.

Although Europe took the first three places, with an adventurous young Germany side featuring Golden Boot winner Thomas Müller claiming the bronze medals, South America dominated the early stages of the tournament before three teams from that region, including record champions Brazil, dropped out at the quarter-final stage, leaving only Uruguay, inspired by Player of the Tournament Diego Forlán, to advance into the last four. The first World Cup in Africa proved to be a disappointing one for the African teams, with only one of the continent's six participants, Ghana, surviving the group stage and South Africa becoming the first host nation in the history of the tournament to be eliminated in the first round.

GROUP A

After months of feverish expectation, the 19th FIFA World Cup kicked off in Johannesburg's spectacular Soccer City stadium with the Opening Match between hosts South Africa and Mexico.

The game actually started five minutes later than scheduled, and it was the home side, featuring eight locally-based players and three from England's Premier League, who seemed the more adversely affected by the hold-up as they allowed Mexico to dominate the early stages. Set up by their coach Javier Aguirre in a fluid 4-3-3 formation, the Mexicans attacked with pace and purpose, with full-backs Paul Aguilar and Carlos Salcido repeatedly getting forward to support the attack, in which young Giovani dos Santos, with his darting bursts and skilful left-footed technique, was the liveliest and most effective contributor.

Chances squandered

Pressed into repeatedly conceding possession in dangerous areas, South Africa appeared as poor as their 83rd place in the FIFA world rankings suggested they might be – despite a run of 12 friendly games

unbeaten going into the tournament – and they were fortunate not to go behind when Guillermo Franco, the Mexico No9, squandered two decent chances, the first of them well saved by Itumeleng Khune, the second headed wastefully over the bar.

Bafana Bafana, finally aroused by the ear-splitting drone of the vuvuzelas, began to show something in attack just before the interval, and ten minutes into the second half they took the lead when a fabulous angled through-ball from midfielder Kagisho Dikgacoi found Siphiwe Tshabalala, who raced clear down the left before thumping a magnificent left-footed shot across Óscar Pérez into the top corner of the net. It was a stunning strike, totally out of keeping with what the hosts had offered up to that point, and it galvanised both the team and the crowd into a much-improved second-half display.

Mexico, though rocked by the goal, kept themselves in the game and brought a temporary halt to the din when, 11 minutes from time, Rafael Márquez coolly converted at the far post after being found unmarked from substitute Andrés Guardado's well flighted cross from the left. Over the game as a whole it was an

Siphiwe Tshabalala opens the scoring for South Africa against Mexico with a stunning strike

equaliser that the Central Americans deserved, but they almost lost the game in the last minute when Katlego Mphela, South Africa's centre-forward, raced on to a long ball over the top but could not control it sufficiently on the bounce to find the net, his effort tamely brushing the outside of the post instead.

Diego Forlán puts Uruguay 2-0 up against South Africa from the penalty spot

Exciting contest

That dramatic late incident concluded an exciting, superbly officiated contest, but the second game of the group, between Uruguay and France later that evening, was to rank considerably lower on the entertainment scale. Both previous meetings between the two nations had finished goalless, and this fixture in Cape Town was to complete the hat-trick.

It was a scrappy and uneventful encounter, with France having marginally the better of the play but creating very little. Sidney Govou failed to get a proper connection on to Franck Ribéry's low cross after seven minutes, glancing his effort wide, and that was as close as Raymond Domenech's side would get to piercing the defence of a Uruguayan side in which Diego Forlán was the sole attacking threat. The last ten minutes were a period of anxiety for the South Americans, however, after substitute Nicolás Lodeiro became the tournament's first red card victim – for a studs-up challenge on Bacary Sagna that brought him a second yellow – but France's siege came to nought, the ironic sight of Thierry Henry frantically appealing for a last-minute handball penalty – correctly turned down by the excellent Japanese referee – rather summing up his team's desperation on a disappointing night both for France and the competition.

Carlos Alberto Parreira, South Africa's Brazilian coach, went into his 22nd World Cup finals match, against Uruguay in Pretoria, by making just one change to the starting XI, with Tsepo Masilela, of Israeli club Maccabi Haifa FC, replacing Lucas Thwala at left-back. Uruguay boss Óscar Tabárez brought in a third forward, Edinson Cavani, which enabled Forlán to operate in a more withdrawn attacking role. The Club Atlético de Madrid striker would go on to be the star of the show, destroying South African dreams with a virtuoso performance.

Spectacular shot

It was Forlán's spectacular dipping long-range shot – deflected off the back of South Africa skipper Aaron Mokoena – that gave Uruguay a deserved 1-0 half-time lead, and the South Americans continued to dominate in the second period, with almost all of their

attacks being channelled through their dynamic No10. The hosts, in contrast, could not put together any moves of consequence, and on 76 minutes their hopes of getting back into the game were effectively dashed when goalkeeper Khune brought down Luis Suárez, earning himself a red card and Uruguay a penalty. Despite having to wait several minutes before he could take the spot-kick, Forlán held his nerve, lifting his right-foot shot high into the net just past the flailing hand of replacement 'keeper Moeneeb Josephs. South Africa's plight looked desperate now, and there was further agony for the home fans in the last minute of stoppage time when Álvaro Pereira bundled in a third goal for Uruguay following incisive build-up pay by Forlán and Suárez.

There was a gap of more than 24 hours before the next Group A fixture, between France and Mexico – the two teams that had contested the very first World Cup finals fixture, in Uruguay, 80 years previously. France won that game 4-1 and Mexico had never beaten them since, but that statistic was to change as the Central Americans battered the 2006 runners-up in Polokwane, claiming a comprehensive 2-0 victory that betrayed the lack of spirit and unity within the French camp.

Mexico were all over their ragged opponents for the first 45 minutes in Polokwane, doing everything but score. The lack of an end-product was a source of consternation, but the introduction of young Manchester United FC-bound striker Javier Hernández just after half-time resolved that problem. The 22-year-old had been on the pitch less than ten minutes when he sprang the French offside trap, collected Márquez's ball over the top and neatly evaded goalkeeper Hugo Lloris's challenge before tucking the ball into the empty net. At 1-0 down and with their tournament survival at stake, a response was demanded from France, but they simply had nothing to offer. Instead, they conceded a second goal. Again it was the work of Mexican substitutes, Pablo Barrera's excellent run being halted only by a foul in the area by Éric Abidal and veteran playmaker Cuauhtémoc Blanco sliding the ensuing penalty low into the corner past Lloris.

Strong incentive

A third goal would have put Mexico on top of the group but, as things stood, if they and Uruguay drew their final match, both were guaranteed to go through to the knockout phase, thereby sending both South Africa and France out. There was a strong incentive to finish first, however, as that would almost certainly mean avoiding Argentina. To do that, Mexico had to win, whereas a draw sufficed for Uruguay.

With qualification out of their hands, South Africa and France could only win and hope. Given that Rustenburg, the venue for Mexico v Uruguay, had hosted three draws already and that the two Latin American teams' only previous World Cup meeting, in 1966, had ended 0-0, the portents were not exactly encouraging. Furthermore, the French appeared to be in total disarray after mutiny had broken out in the camp following the sending-home of striker Nicolas Anelka, who had insulted coach Domenech at half-time during the Mexico game.

Domenech prepared for what seemed likely to be his last game in charge by making several changes in Bloemfontein, but by half-time his team were two goals and one man down, Yoann Gourcuff having been red-carded for reckless use of the elbow in between wildly celebrated, if rather scrappily executed, South African strikes from Bongani Khumalo and Mphela. Meanwhile, in Rustenburg, there appeared to be no hint of collusion as Mexico and Uruguay both attacked each other with gusto, Guardado crashing a stunning left-foot strike against the crossbar for Mexico before Uruguay rekindled South Africa's hopes by taking the lead just before

half-time, Suárez heading in a right-wing cross from Cavani at the end of a fluid counterattack.

Mphela misses

A two-goal swing, in either game or a combination of both, was still required to take South Africa above Mexico in the table. Mphela had two glorious opportunities to extend Bafana Bafana's lead but hit the outside of the post with the first of them and the side-netting with the second, while Mexico's diminutive 'keeper Pérez was forced to make a fine diving save to prevent Uruguay skipper Diego Lugano from doubling his team's advantage. Had one of those three efforts gone in, the excitement would have been intense. Instead, the next goal went to France – their first of the competition – as Florent Malouda tapped in Ribéry's square-ball, and that effectively was that. Mexico's urgency for an equaliser subsided, and South Africa seemed happy simply to settle for the win.

There were no further goals, so Uruguay, with seven points, went through as group winners, with Mexico, on four, accompanying them on goal difference ahead of South Africa, who thus became the first host nation in the history of the World Cup to be eliminated in the first round. As for bottom-of-the-heap France, their disastrous tournament ended with just one point, one goal and a major inquest to face when they arrived home.

Katlego Mphela (left) is in a hurry to get on with the game after putting South Africa 2-0 up against France

2010 FIFA WORLD CUP

Mexico goalkeeper
Óscar Pérez

Group A Results

11/6/10, Soccer City, Johannesburg
South Africa 1-1 Mexico
Attendance: 84490
South Africa: Khune; Gaxa, Mokoena, Khumalo, Thwala (Masilela 46); Modise, Letsholonyane, Dikgacoi, Tshabalala; Pienaar (Parker 83); Mphela. Coach: Carlos Alberto Parreira (BRA)
Mexico: Pérez; Aguilar (Guardado 55), Osorio, Rodríguez, Salcido; Torrado, Márquez, Juárez; Giovani, Franco (Hernández 73), Vela (Blanco 69). Coach: Javier Aguirre (MEX)
Goal(s): 1-0 Tshabalala 55, 1-1 Márquez 79
Yellow Card(s): Juárez 18 (Mexico), Dikgacoi 27 (South Africa), Torrado 57 (Mexico), Masilela 70 (South Africa)
Referee: Irmatov (UZB)

11/6/10, Green Point, Cape Town
Uruguay 0-0 France
Attendance: 64100
Uruguay: Muslera; Victorino, Lugano, Godín; Maxi Pereira, Diego Pérez (Eguren 87), Arévalo, Álvaro Pereira; González (Lodeiro 63); Suárez (Abreu 74), Forlán. Coach: Óscar Tabárez (URU)
France: Lloris; Sagna, Abidal, Gallas, Evra; Diaby, Toulalan; Govou (Gignac 85), Gourcuff (Malouda 75), Ribéry; Anelka (Henry 72). Coach: Raymond Domenech (FRA)
Red Card(s): Lodeiro 81 (Uruguay)
Yellow Card(s): Evra 12 (France), Ribéry 19 (France), Victorino 59 (Uruguay), Lodeiro 65 (Uruguay), Toulalan 68 (France), Lodeiro 81 (Uruguay), Lugano 90+3 (Uruguay)
Referee: Nishimura (JPN)

16/6/10, Loftus Versfeld, Pretoria
South Africa 0-3 Uruguay
Attendance: 42658
South Africa: Khune; Gaxa, Mokoena, Khumalo, Masilela; Modise, Dikgacoi, Letsholonyane (Moriri 57), Tshabalala; Pienaar (Josephs 79); Mphela. Coach: Carlos Alberto Parreira (BRA)
Uruguay: Muslera; Maxi Pereira, Lugano, Godín, Fucile (Á. Fernández 71); Diego Pérez (Gargano 90), Arévalo, Álvaro Pereira; Forlán; Suárez, Cavani (S. Fernández 89). Coach: Óscar Tabárez (URU)
Goal(s): 0-1 Forlán 24, 0-2 Forlán 80 (p), 0-3 Álvaro Pereira 90+5
Red Card(s): Khune 76 (South Africa)
Yellow Card(s): Pienaar 6 (South Africa), Dikgacoi 42 (South Africa)
Referee: Busacca (SUI)

17/6/10, Peter Mokaba, Polokwane
France 0-2 Mexico
Attendance: 45372
France: Lloris; Sagna, Abidal, Gallas, Evra; Toulalan, Diaby; Govou (Valbuena 69), Ribéry, Malouda; Anelka (Gignac 46). Coach: Raymond Domenech (FRA)
Mexico: Pérez; Osorio, Moreno, Rodríguez, Salcido; Márquez; Juárez (Hernández 55), Torrado; Giovani, Franco (Blanco 62), Vela (Barrera 31). Coach: Javier Aguirre (MEX)
Goal(s): 0-1 Hernández 64, 0-2 Blanco 79 (p)
Yellow Card(s): Franco 4 (Mexico), Toulalan 45+1 (France), Juárez 48 (Mexico), Moreno 49 (Mexico), Abidal 78 (France), Rodríguez 82 (Mexico)
Referee: Al Ghamdi (KSA)

22/6/10, Royal Bafokeng, Rustenburg
Mexico 0-1 Uruguay
Attendance: 33425
Mexico: Pérez; Osorio, Rodríguez, Moreno (Castro 57), Salcio; Márquez; Torrado, Guardado (Barrera 46); Blanco (Hernández 63); Giovani, Franco. Coach: Javier Aguirre (MEX)
Uruguay: Muslera; Maxi Pereira, Lugano, Victorino, Fucile; Diego Pérez, Arévalo, Álvaro Pereira (Scotti 77); Forlán; Cavani, Suárez (Á. Fernández 85). Coach: Óscar Tabárez (URU)
Goal(s): 0-1 Suárez 43
Yellow Card(s): Fucile 68 (Uruguay), Hernández 77 (Mexico), Castro 86 (Mexico)
Referee: Kassai (HUN)

22/6/10, Free State, Bloemfontein
France 1-2 South Africa
Attendance: 39415
France: Lloris; Sagna, Squillaci, Gallas, Clichy; Diarra (Govou 82), Diaby; Gignac (Malouda 46), Gourcuff, Ribéry; Cissé (Henry 55), Coach: Raymond Domenech (FRA)
South Africa: Josephs; Ngcongca (Gaxa 55), Mokoena, Khumalo, Masilela; Pienaar, Sibaya, Khuboni (Modise 78), Tshabalala; Parker (Nomvethe 68), Mphela. Coach: Carlos Alberto Parreira (BRA)
Goal(s): 0-1 Khumalo 20, 0-2 Mphela 37, 1-2 Malouda 70
Red Card(s): Gourcuff 25 (France)
Yellow Card(s): Diaby 71 (France)
Referee: Ruiz (COL)

Group A Table

	Pld	W	D	L	F	A	Pts
1 Uruguay	3	2	1	0	4	0	7
2 Mexico	3	1	1	1	3	2	4
3 South Africa	3	1	1	1	3	5	4
4 France	3	0	1	2	1	4	1

GROUP B

The Group B action kicked off in the early afternoon of the competition's second day as South Korea and Greece met in Port Elizabeth.

With Argentina taking on Nigeria later in the day, it was seen as an appetiser for the main event, but it hardly tickled the taste buds. Greece, seeking their first goal and point at the FIFA World Cup finals, appeared hampered by that burden throughout a drab encounter, which their Asian opponents, showing intermittent speed and thrust on the counterattack but little else, deservedly won 2-0 with a goal at the start of each half, claiming only their second World Cup finals victory on foreign soil in the process.

Seventh-minute lead

Lee Jung-soo, Korea's Japan-based centre-back, gave his team the lead with just seven minutes on the clock as he volleyed in Ki Sung-yong's well flighted free-kick from close range. Greece offered no response, and the Koreans should have made it 2-0 on 28 minutes when Park Chu-young wasted an opportunity brilliantly set up for him by his captain, Park Ji-sung. The Manchester

Lee Jung-soo is a happy man after scoring for South Korea against Greece

United FC midfielder was the liveliest player on view and he duly doubled his team's advantage seven minutes into the second period, dispossessing dallying Greece defender Loukas Vintra before clipping the ball left-footed over the goalkeeper with impressive composure.

Otto Rehhagel's team finally woke up following the introduction of attacking substitutes Dimitris Salpingidis and Pantelis Kapetanos, but their best chance fell to Theofanis Gekas – the top scorer in the European qualifying zone – whose fine shot on the turn forced a spectacular tip-over from Jung Sung-ryong. Generally, though, Greece were devoid of ideas and could have no complaints about their defeat.

A few hours later South Korea would find themselves still holding top spot in the group after Argentina could only beat Nigeria 1-0 in Johannesburg, a supreme performance from the African side's acrobatic goalkeeper, Vincent Enyeama, keeping the score down in a match that the South Americans, inspired by the supreme individual skills of the world's No1 player, Lionel Messi, largely bossed.

Messi magic

The FC Barcelona magician was up and at Nigeria right from the off, superbly setting up Gonzalo Higuaín for an easy chance that the Real Madrid CF striker lazily spurned, then letting fly with a shot that produced the first of Enyeama's many excellent saves. That was all before Argentina took a sixth-minute lead, defender Gabriel Heinze losing his marker at a corner and stooping to power in an excellent header. The atmosphere in Ellis Park was electric, the football from Argentina exciting, but Higuaín was guilty of another bad miss when Enyeama denied him on 21 minutes. The moment of the half came 16 minutes later when a lovely curled effort by Messi was kept out of the net with extraordinary agility by the Nigeria No1.

Argentina's efforts to seal the win with a second goal should have been rewarded with a four-against-two breakaway midway through the second half, but somehow they contrived to let Nigeria off the hook, and as the game entered its closing phase, with Enyeama continuing to thwart Argentina in general and Messi in particular, the Africans sniffed an opportunity to grab an unlikely point. Two half-chances for Obafemi Martins and Yakubu sandwiched a gilt-edged opportunity for substitute Kalu Uche, but he failed to finish off Nigeria's best move of the game, lifting his left-foot shot over the

Nigeria goalkeeper Vincent Enyeama makes one of his many saves from Argentina's Lionel Messi in Johannesburg

bar. So victory went to Argentina – their third out of three against Nigeria in the World Cup – with the final whistle being greeted by a spectacular show of emotion from coach Diego Maradona.

There would be even more celebratory poses from the great man five days later across town at Soccer City as Argentina recorded another win, this time by a resounding 4-1 margin, against South Korea. It was as one-sided a contest as the competition had witnessed to that point, and it featured the first – and, as it transpired, only – hat-trick of the tournament as Higuaín made amends for his first-match aberrations by scoring once in the first half and twice in the second.

Opening own goal

The first of Argentina's four goals, on 17 minutes, was scored by a South Korean, striker Park Chu-young inadvertently deflecting Messi's left-wing free-kick into his own net off his standing leg. With the South Americans completely on top, Higuaín made it 2-0 on 33 minutes, nodding in unmarked at the far post following a flick-on from a short corner. A joyous piece of skill from Messi just before half-time, when he jinked past three defenders before chipping fractionally wide, suggested that Argentina were in cruise mode, but

their confidence was jolted on the stroke of half-time when casual defending by Martín Demichelis allowed Lee Chung-yong to steal in and score.

Suddenly the game had become a contest again, and although Argentina continued to control it after the interval, the next big chance fell to South Korea, the ebullient Lee Chung-yong setting up Yeom Ki-hun, who was unable to seize the moment, shooting awkwardly and wide. The Asian side never threatened again, the final quarter of the contest being played almost entirely in and around the Korean penalty area. More Messi brilliance gifted Higuaín his second goal, the young striker tapping in after the No10's shot conveniently rebounded to him off the inside of the post, and his hat-trick was completed when he headed substitute Sergio Agüero's chip skilfully back across goal at the end of an incisive counterattack.

Argentina's 4-1 win would have been sufficient to guarantee their place in the knockout phase if, later that afternoon, Greece and Nigeria had drawn in Bloemfontein, but the match in the Free State stadium was to produce a winner, and it was the Europeans, against the odds, who came from behind to claim all three points and thus secure their first World Cup finals victory.

Self-inflicted wound

Nigeria had only themselves to blame for coming out of the game with nothing. Ahead after 16 minutes when a free-kick into a crowded penalty area from Uche evaded everyone before settling into the far corner of the embarrassed Alexandros Tzorvas's net, the Africans were in control until midfielder Sani Kaita completely lost his head, petulantly kicking out at Vassilis Torosidis and being punished for his stupidity with a red card. Greece had been a blunt attacking force until then, but to their credit they capitalised on their one-man advantage and twice came close to equalising before the goal they had been threatening – their first at the World Cup finals, after over 400 minutes without one – arrived just before the interval via a shot from Salpingidis that took a wicked deflection off the head of Lukman Haruna, giving no chance to Enyeama.

Two golden opportunities – one for each team – were squandered within the space of a minute on the hour mark when, firstly, Gekas, free in the area after a misplaced headed clearance, put his shot straight at Enyeama, then, immediately afterwards at the other end, Chinedu Obasi shot wastefully wide after a Yakubu shot, well saved by Tzorvas, had fallen to him in front of an open goal. Victory was there for the taking, but Nigeria's fatigue began to show and Greece made their numerical advantage count when they exploited an error from, of all people, Enyeama, who, outstanding hitherto, could only half-parry a low drive from Alexandros Tzilois into Torosidis's path.

Work to do

Greece's history-making win was greeted with appropriate glee, but, with Argentina up next, Rehhagel's side still had their work cut out to stay in the competition. As for Nigeria, they had played twice and lost twice but were still very much in the competition, knowing that they would qualify on goal difference if they defeated South Korea while Argentina maintained their 100 success rate against Greece.

Greece's chances of survival were boosted when Maradona decided to make seven changes to his starting XI, the Argentina coach's assumption being that only a miraculous combination of scorelines could send his team home. He did retain Messi, but Rehhagel already had plans for the little maestro, burdening him with a full-time man-marker in Sokratis Papastathopoulos. It worked a treat as Argentina's second string struggled to make an impression without their stifled superstar.

Dimitris Salpingidis turns away in jubilation after scoring Greece's first ever World Cup finals goal

Goalless at half-time in Polokwane, the other game in Durban was also evenly contested, with Uche putting Nigeria into the lead for the second game running only for Lee Jung-soo, also with his second goal of the competition, to equalise. The drama intensified in the second half as Park Chu-young made it 2-1 to South Korea – with the first direct free-kick goal of the tournament – before Yakubu contrived to miss an absolute sitter for Nigeria and then partly make amends five minutes later by stroking home a penalty.

Perfect record

With Argentina finally breaking the deadlock against Greece, through defender Demichelis, Nigeria knew that one more goal would take them through. They pressed hard but Martins missed a good chance and South Korea held on for the 2-2 draw that sent them into the last 16 for the first time on foreign soil. Argentina's perfect record, meanwhile, was cemented with a late second goal from substitute Martín Palermo as Greece disappointingly ended Rehhagel's long and successful reign with nothing more than a whimper.

2010 FIFA WORLD CUP

Group B Results

12/6/10, Nelson Mandela Bay, Port Elizabeth
South Korea 2-0 Greece
Attendance: 31513
South Korea: Jung Sung-ryong; Cha Du-ri, Cho Yong-hyung, Lee Jung-soo, Lee Young-pyo; Lee Chung-yong (Kim Jae-sung 90+1), Kim Jung-woo, Ki Sung-yong (Kim Nam-il 74), Park Ji-sung; Yeom Ki-hun; Park Chu-young (Lee Seung-yeoul 87). Coach: Huh Jung-moo (KOR)
Greece: Tzorvas; Seitaridis, Vintra, Papadopoulos, Torosidis; Tziolis, Katsouranis, Karagounis (Patsatzoglou 46); Charisteas (Kapetanos 61), Gekas, Samaras (Salpingidis 59). Coach: Otto Rehhagel (GER)
Goal(s): 1-0 Lee Jung-soo 7, 2-0 Park Ji-sung 52
Yellow Card(s): Torosidis 56 (Greece)
Referee: Hester (NZL)

12/6/10, Ellis Park, Johannesburg
Argentina 1-0 Nigeria
Attendance: 55686
Argentina: Romero; Gutiérrez, Demichelis, Samuel, Heinze; Verón (Maxi Rodríguez 74), Mascherano, Di María (Burdisso 85); Messi; Higuaín (Milito 79), Tévez. Coach: Diego Maradona (ARG)
Nigeria: Enyeama; Odiah, Yobo, Shittu, Taiwo (Uche 75); Kaita, Etuhu, Haruna; Obinna (Martins 52), Yakubu, Obasi (Odemwingie 60). Coach: Lars Lagerbäck (SWE)
Goal(s): 1-0 Heinze 6
Yellow Card(s): Gutiérrez 41 (Argentina), Haruna 77 (Nigeria)
Referee: Stark (GER)

17/6/10, Soccer City, Johannesburg
Argentina 4-1 South Korea
Attendance: 82174
Argentina: Romero; Gutiérrez, Demichelis, Samuel (Burdisso 23), Heinze; Mascherano; Maxi Rodríguez, Di María; Messi; Higuaín (Bolatti 82), Tévez (Milito 75). Coach: Diego Maradona (ARG)

Diego Maradona enjoys the moment as Argentina go 1-0 up against Greece

South Korea: Jung Sung-ryong; Oh Beom-seok, Cho Yong-hyung, Lee Jung-soo, Lee Young-pyo; Kim Jung-woo, Ki Sung-yong (Kim Nam-il 46); Lee Chung-yong, Park Ji-sung, Yeom Ki-hun; Park Chu-young (Lee Dong-gook 81). Coach: Huh Jung-moo (KOR)
Goal(s): 1-0 Park Chu-young 17 (og), 2-0 Higuaín 33, 2-1 Lee Chung-yong 45+1, 3-1 Higuaín 76, 4-1 Higuaín 80
Yellow Card(s): Yeom Ki-hun 10 (South Korea), Lee Chung-yong 34 (South Korea), Gutiérrez 54 (Argentina), Mascherano 55 (Argentina), Heinze 74 (Argentina)
Referee: De Bleeckere (BEL)

17/6/10, Free State, Bloemfontein
Greece 2-1 Nigeria
Attendance: 31593
Greece: Tzorvas; Papadopoulos, Papastathopoulos (Samaras 37), Kyrgiakos; Vintra, Katsouranis, Tziolis, Torosidis; Karagounis; Salpingidis, Gekas (Ninis 79). Coach: Otto Rehhagel (GER)
Nigeria: Enyeama; Odiah, Yobo, Shittu, Taiwo (Echiéjilé 55; Afolabi 77); Haruna, Etuhu, Kaita, Uche; Odemwingie (Obasi 46); Yakubu. Coach: Lars Lagerbäck (SWE)
Goal(s): 0-1 Uche 16, 1-1 Salpingidis 44, 2-1 Torosidis 71
Red Card(s): Kaita 33 (Nigeria)
Yellow Card(s): Papastathopoulos 15 (Greece), Tziolis 59 (Greece), Samaras 88 (Greece), Obasi 89 (Nigeria)
Referee: Ruiz (COL)

22/6/10, Moses Mabhida, Durban
Nigeria 2-2 South Korea
Attendance: 61874
Nigeria: Enyeama; Odiah, Yobo (Echiéjilé 46), Shittu, Afolabi, Obasi, Etuhu, Yussuf, Uche; Kanu (Martins 57); Yakubu (Obinna 70). Coach: Lars Lagerbäck (SWE)
South Korea: Jung Sung-ryong; Cha Du-ri, Cho Yong-hyung, Lee Jung-soo, Lee Young-pyo; Ki Sung-yong (Kim Jae-sung 87), Kim Jung-woo; Lee Chung-yong, Yeom Ki-hun (Kim Nam-il 64), Park Ji-sung; Park Chu-young (Kim Dong-jin 90+3). Coach: Huh Jung-moo (KOR)
Goal(s): 1-0 Uche 12, 1-1 Lee Jung-soo 38, 1-2 Park Chu-young 49, 2-2 Yakubu 69 (p)
Yellow Card(s): Enyeama 31 (Nigeria), Obasi 37 (Nigeria), Yussuf 42 (Nigeria), Kim Nam-il 68 (South Korea)
Referee: Olegário Benquerença (POR)

22/6/10, Peter Mokaba, Polokwane
Greece 0-2 Argentina
Attendance: 38891
Greece: Tzorvas; Papadopoulos, Moras, Kyrgiakos; Papastathopoulos; Vintra, Katsouranis (Ninis 54), Tziolis, Torosidis (Patsatzoglou 55); Karagounis (Spiropoulos 46); Samaras. Coach: Otto Rehhagel (GER)
Argentina: Romero; Otamendi, Demichelis, Burdisso, C. Rodríguez; Verón, Bolatti, Maxi Rodríguez (Di María 63); Messi; Milito (Palermo 80), Agüero (Pastore 77). Coach: Diego Maradona (ARG)
Goal(s): 0-1 Demichelis 77, 0-2 Palermo 89
Yellow Card(s): Katsouranis 30 (Greece), Bolatti 76 (Argentina)
Referee: Irmatov (UZB)

Group B Table

	Pld	W	D	L	F	A	Pts
1 Argentina	3	3	0	0	7	1	9
2 South Korea	3	1	1	1	5	6	4
3 Greece	3	1	0	2	2	5	3
4 Nigeria	3	0	1	2	3	5	1

GROUP C

England, the seeded team in Group C, suffered a major blow before the tournament got underway with the loss of their captain – and most consistent player of the previous two FIFA World Cups – Rio Ferdinand, who suffered serious knee ligament damage shortly after the team's arrival in South Africa.

Ferdinand's replacement as skipper, Steven Gerrard, could hardly have wished for a better start to the tournament, however, as he gave England a fourth-minute lead in their opening game against the United States in Rustenburg. Running on to a smart lay-off from Emile Heskey, the Liverpool FC midfielder calmly slid the ball past Tim Howard, of Merseyside rivals Everton FC, with the outside of his right foot. As one of the favourites coming into the tournament, England would have been expected to build on that early advantage, but they were unable to gain any control against diligently organised opponents, and after right-winger Aaron Lennon wasted an inviting

opening on 20 minutes, it was the US, set up well by coach Bob Bradley, who began to look the more comfortable team in possession.

Cardinal sin

Even so, there appeared to be no threat to England's goal when, on 40 minutes, Clint Dempsey escaped the attentions of Gerrard and fired in a tame low shot from just outside the area. Incredibly, though, goalkeeper Robert Green, who had been selected ahead of the more experienced David James, committed the cardinal sin of not getting his body behind the ball, allowing it to bounce off his palms across the line and into the net. It was the softest of goals for England to concede but they should have restored their advantage early in the second half when a measured pass from Lennon sent Heskey clean through, only for the big striker, not uncharacteristically, to spurn the chance by firing straight at Howard. The Americans, though seemingly content to soak up pressure and take the draw, also created a gilt-edged chance midway through the second period when Jozy

England captain Steven Gerrard celebrates after giving his team an early lead against the United States

Altidore, who had headed badly wide in the first half, outpaced Jamie Carragher down the left before firing in a shot that Green only just turned on to the inside of his near post. England also missed a late chance when Frank Lampard messed up a three-on-two break, but they did not do enough to win and 1-1 was a fair and fitting outcome.

The draw in Rustenburg provided an opportunity for either Algeria or Slovenia to go top of the group the following afternoon in Polokwane. Neither team, though, seemed capable of seizing it. A dreadful first half, low on both quality and incident, was brought to life only two minutes before the break by a superb left-foot strike from Slovenian midfielder Valter Birsa that Algeria goalkeeper Faouzi Chaouchi tipped over the bar. Nothing much of interest happened in the second half either until Algerian substitute Abdelkader Ghezzal was sent off on 73 minutes for a deliberate handball after he had already been yellow-carded within seconds of his arrival. That senseless act was further punished six minutes later when Slovenia skipper Robert Koren gave his team the lead with an accurate but seemingly unthreatening shot that Chaouchi completely misread, helping the ball into the corner of the net as he attempted to push it round the post. It was an error almost – but not quite – as bad as Green's the night before, and with his ten-man team unable to respond, just as costly. Slovenia, strong in defence but weak in attack, were fortunate winners, but there was no sign of that in their post-match jubilation as they celebrated their first ever victory at a major tournament with wild abandon.

Better was to come from Matjaž Kek's team five days later in Johannesburg, where they took on the United States. It was the tournament's smallest participating country against its largest, but size isn't everything in football and by half-time Slovenia, thanks to a wonder strike from Birsa – a left-foot snapshot from distance that fizzed into the top corner past a motionless Howard – and a second goal, totally against the run of play but neatly converted by Zlatan Ljubijankič, found themselves 2-0 up and scenting not just another victory but a guaranteed place in the last 16.

Stern stuff

The Americans, though, as they had shown against England, were made of stern stuff, and three minutes into the second half they got themselves back into the game when Landon Donovan skipped his marker, ambled into the area from the right and suddenly unleashed an unstoppable rising shot past Slovenia's impressive goalkeeper Samir Handanovič. From that

Robert Koren (left) is congratulated by Aleksandar Radosavljevič after scoring Slovenia's winner against Algeria

moment on the European side retreated into their shell and the US, led from the front by Donovan, pounded forward. Good, organised defending kept them at bay until eight minutes from time when Michael Bradley, son of the coach, burst forward on to Altidore's knockdown and poked his shot into the roof of the net. Now the Americans pressed for the winner and appeared to have scored it when substitute Maurice Edu volleyed in at the far post from a Donovan free-kick, but the referee from Mali disallowed the goal for an infringement that extensive TV replay scrutiny was unable to detect.

The group was now wide open, with England expected to take command as they travelled south from their Rustenburg base to Cape Town to face an Algeria team that had lost five of their previous six games, scoring just one goal – a penalty. It was England coach Fabio Capello's 64th birthday, and the Green Point stadium was packed with England supporters. James had returned in goal, with Gareth Barry also reintroduced to midfield after his recovery from injury. With the exception of Ferdinand, whose place was taken by Carragher, substituting the injured Ledley King, the Three Lions were at full strength. It was time for them to deliver.

What they produced over the next 90 minutes, however, was an affront to those thousands of white-and-red bedecked followers bellowing them on in the stands. They started the game badly and got progressively worse. Incapable of retaining the ball for any length of time, their play was riddled with unforced errors and they created virtually nothing up front, where the man wearing the No10 shirt looked like Wayne Rooney but certainly didn't play like him. The only positive thing they took from the game was a point, and that was only because Algeria were as unambitious as England were atrocious.

Win or bust

Third in the table going into their final game, against Slovenia in Port Elizabeth, it was a case of win or bust for Capello's team, three points providing their only sure means of progress. Changes were made to the team, with Matthew Upson replacing the suspended Carragher in central defence (thus giving John Terry his third different partner in as many games), the ineffectual, non-scoring Heskey making way for Jermain Defoe and Lennon ceding his place to James Milner. All three choices would be vindicated during the course of an eventful, highly-charged yet fraught encounter for

No way through for England's Wayne Rooney against Algeria

England, Milner's excellent 23rd-minute cross being volleyed in emphatically by Defoe – albeit off his shin and through the hands of Handanovič – and Upson making a crucial, goal-saving 90th-minute tackle to preserve that 1-0 lead through to the final whistle.

In between those two incidents there was much for England supporters to savour as the team improved a hundred-fold from the Algeria nightmare, with strong performances from James, Terry and Gerrard as well as the three newcomers. During the middle third of the game they created numerous opportunities to double their lead, but alarmingly none were taken, the best of them falling to Rooney, who, out of sorts again, scuffed his shot against the post via Handanovič's fingertips when the goalkeeper should not have stood a chance. The Manchester United FC striker was substituted, perhaps to spare him further embarrassment, but before he departed England survived an almighty scare when Slovenia broke forward on the counter and fired in three shots in quick succession that only desperate, last-ditch defending repelled.

Nervous at the finish, England were happy to count down the final minutes with the ball at the corner flag, but while 1-0 was enough to keep them in the competition, it was insufficient to take them through as group winners. At the final whistle they held first place, but while they were bouncing around in celebration, news came through from Pretoria that the United States, on the point of elimination, had scored a dramatic stoppage-time winner against Algeria. On top throughout the match and denied a good goal in the first half when Dempsey was incorrectly adjudged to have scored from an offside position, their winning goal, from the ever-reliable Donovan, might have come late, but it was thoroughly deserved.

Cruel elimination

So as the United States leapfrogged England to the top of the table on the number of goals scored, they also relegated Slovenia to third place, cruelly eliminating the eastern Europeans from the competition. While Algeria, unable to score in their three matches, could have no complaints about making an early exit, the Slovenians were entitled to feel they had done enough to survive. As for England, they had scraped through to the last 16, thus maintaining their proud World Cup record of never having finished outside the top two in a first-round group, but, as runners-up, the road ahead now looked far more daunting than it would have done had they scored that second goal against Slovenia and finished first.

2010 FIFA WORLD CUP

Group C Results

12/6/10, Royal Bafokeng, Rustenburg
England 1-1 United States
Attendance: 38646
England: Green; Johnson, King (Carragher 46), Terry, A. Cole;
Lennon, Gerrard, Lampard, Milner (Wright-Phillips 31); Rooney,
Heskey (Crouch 79). Coach: Fabio Capello (ITA)
United States: Howard; Cherundolo, DeMerit, Onyewu, Bocanegra;
Donovan, Bradley, Clark, Dempsey; Altidore (Holden 86), Findley
(Buddle 77). Coach: Bob Bradley (United States)
Goal(s): 1-0 Gerrard 4, 1-1 Dempsey 40
Yellow Card(s): Milner 26 (England), Cherundolo 39 (United States),
DeMerit 47 (United States), Carragher 60 (England), Gerrard 61
(England), Findley 74 (United States)
Referee: Simon (BRA)

Landon Donovan strikes in stoppage time for the United States against Algeria

13/6/10, Peter Mokaba, Polokwane
Algeria 0-1 Slovenia
Attendance: 30325
Algeria: Chaouchi; Bougherra, Halliche, Yahia; Kadir (Guedioura 82),
Lacen, Yebda, Belhadj; Matmour (Saïfi 81), Ziani; Djebbour (Ghezzal
58). Coach: Rabah Saâdane (ALG)
Slovenia: S. Handanovič; Brečko, Šuler, Cesar, Jokič; Kirm,
Radosavljevič (Komac 87), Koren, Birsa (Pečnik 84); Novakovič, Dedič
(Ljubijankič 53). Coach: Matjaž Kek (SVN)
Goal(s): 0-1 Koren 79
Red Card(s): Ghezzal 73 (Algeria)
Yellow Card(s): Radosavljevič 35 (Slovenia), Ghezzal 59 (Algeria),
Ghezzal 73 (Algeria), Komac 90+3 (Slovenia), Yebda 90+5 (Algeria)
Referee: Batres (GUA)

18/6/10, Ellis Park, Johannesburg
Slovenia 2-2 United States
Attendance: 45573
Slovenia: S. Handanovič; Brečko, Šuler, Cesar, Jokič; Birsa (Dedič 87),
Radosavljevič, Koren, Kirm; Ljubijankič (Pečnik 74) Komac 90+4),
Novakovič. Coach: Matjaž Kek (SVN)
United States: Howard; Cherundolo, DeMerit, Onyewu (Gomez 80),
Bocanegra; Donovan, Bradley, Torres (Edu 46), Dempsey; Altidore,
Findley (Feilhaber 46). Coach: Bob Bradley (United States)
Goal(s): 1-0 Birsa 13, 2-0 Ljubijankič 42, 2-1 Donovan 48, 2-2 Bradley 82
Yellow Card(s): Cesar 35 (Slovenia), Findley 40 (United States), Šuler
69 (Slovenia), Kirm 72 (Slovenia)
Referee: Coulibaly (MLI)

18/6/10, Green Point, Cape Town
England 0-0 Algeria
Attendance: 64100
England: James; Johnson, Carragher, Terry, A. Cole; Lennon (Wright-
Phillips 63), Lampard, Barry (Crouch 84), Gerrard; Rooney, Heskey
(Defoe 74). Coach: Fabio Capello (ITA)
Algeria: M'Bohli; Bougherra, Halliche, Yahia; Kadir, Yebda (Mesbah
89), Lacen, Belhadj; Boudebouz (Abdoun 74), Ziani (Guedioura 81);
Matmour. Coach: Rabah Saâdane (ALG)
Yellow Card(s): Carragher 58 (England), Lacen 85 (Algeria)
Referee: Irmatov (UZB)

23/6/10, Nelson Mandela Bay, Port Elizabeth
Slovenia 0-1 England
Attendance: 36893
Slovenia: S. Handanovič; Brečko, Šuler, Cesar, Jokič; Birsa, Koren,
Radosavljevič, Kirm (Matavž 79); Ljubijankič (Dedič 62); Novakovič.
Coach: Matjaž Kek (SVN)
England: James; Johnson, Terry, Upson, A. Cole; Milner, Lampard,
Barry, Gerrard; Defoe (Heskey 85), Rooney (J. Cole 72). Coach: Fabio
Capello (ITA)
Goal(s): 0-1 Defoe 23
Yellow Card(s): Jokič 40 (Slovenia), Johnson 48 (England), Birsa 79
(Slovenia), Dedič 81 (Slovenia)
Referee: Stark (GER)

23/6/10, Loftus Versfeld, Pretoria
United States 1-0 Algeria
Attendance: 35827
United States: Howard; Cherundolo, DeMerit, Bocanegra, Bornstein
(Beasley 81); Donovan, Bradley, Edu (Buddle 64); Dempsey; Altidore,
Gomez (Feilhaber 46). Coach: Bob Bradley (United States)
Algeria: M'Bohli; Bougherra, Halliche, Yahia; Kadir, Lacen, Yebda,
Belhadj; Matmour (Saïfi 86), Ziani (Guedioura 69); Djebbour (Ghezzal
65). Coach: Rabah Saâdane (ALG)
Goal(s): 1-0 Donovan 90+1
Red Card(s): Yahia 90+3 (Algeria)
Yellow Card(s): Yebda 12 (Algeria), Altidore 62 (United States), Yahia
76 (Algeria), Lacen 83 (Algeria), Beasley 90 (United States), Yahia
90+3 (Algeria)
Referee: De Bleeckere (BEL)

Group C Table

	Pld	W	D	L	F	A	Pts
1 United States	3	1	2	0	4	3	5
2 England	3	1	2	0	2	1	5
3 Slovenia	3	1	1	1	3	3	4
4 Algeria	3	0	1	2	0	2	1

GROUP D

Although generally perceived to be one of the most evenly balanced sections when the Final Draw was made in December 2009, Group D was headed by Germany, the European vice-champions and FIFA World Cup mainstays, who were widely expected to go through to the next round along with one of Australia, Ghana and Serbia.

The first match pitted Serbia against a Ghana team coached by a Serbian, Milovan Rajevac. Another curiosity was that both teams fielded goalkeepers who had ended the 2009/10 season at the same club – English Premier League outfit Wigan Athletic FC. Unfortunately, neither Vladimir Stojković of Serbia nor Richard Kingson of Ghana would be overworked in Pretoria as the defenders in front of them largely stood firm in a dull and lacklustre encounter. There was very little to choose between either the 'keepers or the teams until the 74th minute when Serbian defender Aleksandar Luković was handed a second yellow card for pulling back Asamoah Gyan, the game's most dangerous attacker.

Ghana's Serbian coach
Milovan Rajevac

Needless penalty

Strangely, though, it was the team reduced to ten men rather than the one with numerical advantage that began to seize the initiative, with Serbia twice coming close to opening the scoring soon afterwards through Miloš Krasić and Nemanja Vidić. But just as the game appeared to be petering out into the goalless stalemate that had been on the cards from the first whistle, Serbian substitute Zdravko Kuzmanović needlessly raised his arm in his own penalty area and handled a harmless cross. It was a moment of madness that would earn him a yellow card and cost his team the game as Gyan stepped up to take the ensuing penalty and confidently smashed it past Stojković to give Ghana a barely deserved 85th-minute lead. Kuzmanović had the chance to redeem himself a minute later when the ball landed invitingly at his feet at the edge of the other penalty area, but he lashed it wildly over the bar and that was that – 1-0 to Ghana, a first victory for Africa, but nothing for Serbia.

Germany, beset by injuries in the lead-up to the tournament, fielded only five survivors from the UEFA EURO 2008 final as they took on Australia on a warm evening in Durban. Support for the Socceroos was large and vocal at kick-off, but it was the German fans who would have all the fun as their team produced by far the best opening performance of any of the 32 teams. Fluent in possession and full of energy, Joachim Löw's young side were outstanding from start to finish, blowing away their Antipodean adversaries with a comprehensive 4-0 win.

It took only seven minutes for Germany to create their first chance – which Miroslav Klose mis-hit, allowing Mark Schwarzer to save – and eight for them to open the scoring, Lukas Podolski rifling in a left-foot shot that was too powerfully struck for Schwarzer to keep out. It was one-way traffic for the remainder of the half as Germany sought to hammer home their superiority. Klose missed a sitter but immediately made amends, meeting a perfect cross from Germany's new captain Philipp Lahm with a thunderous header as Schwarzer failed to collect. It was the striker's 11th World Cup finals goal and his 49th for Germany.

Total domination

Germany's domination was so total that they scarcely needed the help they received from the Mexican referee on 56 minutes when he sent off Australia's Tim

Thomas Müller blows a kiss after scoring Germany's third goal in the 4-0 victory over Australia

With the Spanish referee producing a yellow card for virtually every foul in the early stages, the first of them for an accidental trip by Klose on Branislav Ivanović, it was perhaps inevitable that someone would see red, but if Germany were aggrieved by their main goalscorer's dismissal, their response to having their numbers reduced was positive, Sami Khedira striking the underside of the bar just before half-time and several further chances coming their way in the third quarter. All of them, however, fell to Podolski, who had forgotten to put on his shooting boots. Having butchered two marvellous opportunities brilliantly created for him by Özil, it was surprising that he was the man who stepped forward shortly afterwards to take a penalty – awarded for a handball by Vidić that was as unnecessary as Kuzmanović's against Ghana – but not surprising that he missed it, shooting weakly and allowing Stojković to save. It was the first penalty missed by Germany at a World Cup – shoot-outs included – since 1982.

Chances squandered

Alerted by that close shave, Serbia began to make their own chances, but Jovanović and Žigić both struck the frame of the goal and several other openings were squandered by wasteful final balls. In the end the final whistle came as a relief, but although Serbia had claimed a famous World Cup scalp, their failure to score a second goal - and therefore give their overall goal difference a positive balance – slightly took the shine off their achievement. It might not have mattered so much had Australia defeated Ghana the following day, thus giving all four teams a win and three points after two matches, but the game in Rustenburg ended 1-1, which dropped Serbia to third place in the group – and put the African side on top.

It was another match shaped by a first-half sending-off. Australia were already 1-0 up, thanks to Brett Holman's alertness after Ghana 'keeper Kingson failed to hold a Marco Bresciano free-kick, when Harry Kewell, back in the team after missing the opening game through injury, was red-carded after a goalbound shot from Jonathan Mensah struck him on the right arm as he was standing on the goal-line. As an inconsolable Kewell trooped off pleading his innocence, Gyan did as he had done against Serbia and successfully converted the spot-kick, sending Schwarzer the wrong way with a low drive into the corner. Although Ghana had the advantage of an extra player, they showed little inclination to press it home. Indeed, it was the Socceroos who went for the kill in the second half, but having created two huge chances, they failed to

Cahill for an over-enthusiastic tackle on Bastian Schweinsteiger. Just before that incident they had conjured the best move of the tournament, with Lahm and the ubiquitous young playmaker Mesut Özil thrillingly setting up Thomas Müller, who clipped his finish over the bar. The young FC Bayern München starlet would not have too much longer to wait for his first international goal, however, swivelling superbly to wrong-foot the defence before driving an accurate right-foot shot in off the post. Two minutes later, Cacau, just on as a substitute for Klose, made it 4-0, sliding in to convert a perfect pass from the left by man of the match Özil.

Germany could not have made a more impressive start, yet five days later they were brought crashing down to earth by an unexpected defeat, going down 1-0 to Serbia in Port Elizabeth. The match was transformed by a red card brandished to Klose in the 37th minute, immediately after which Serbia took the lead as Milan Jovanović, their top scorer in qualifying, volleyed in smartly from close range from Nikola Žigić's headed pass.

Tim Cahill puts Australia ahead against Serbia in Nelspruit

convert either, substitute Scott Chipperfield putting an easy header over the bar a minute after coming on and Luke Wilkshire being denied by Kingson before Josh Kennedy messed up the follow-up.

Ghana were yet to score either from open play or against 11 men yet they went into their final match, against Germany at Soccer City stadium, knowing that even a defeat could send them through. Germany, on the other hand, had to win to be sure of making progress. It was a similar story for Serbia, while for bottom-of-the-table Australia it was simply a case of win and hope.

End-to-end action

Both matches proved eventful, with lots of end-to-end action. Ghana, now serving as Africa's standard-bearers after a wretchedly disappointing first round for the continent, had plenty of opportunities to go ahead, but so too did Germany as the two teams traded missed chances in an entertaining but goalless first half. There was no score over in Nelspruit, either,

but when Kwadwo Asamoah blew Ghana's biggest chance of all just after the interval, the sense of inevitability grew that Germany would not let their opponents get away with such largesse and, sure enough, they took the lead on the hour as Özil, given too much time and space to shoot on the edge of the area, finished off a patient build-up with a powerful left-foot strike that soared past Kingson.

From that moment on Germany had total control, and Ghana's fate looked set to be decided by events elsewhere. Their plight was helped as Australia went 2-0 up with goals from Cahill – a trademark header – and Holman – a brilliant long-range shot – but hindered when Serbia pulled one back six minutes from time through Marko Pantelić. One more goal for Serbia would put them through at Ghana's expense, but although there was drama at the death when the ball struck Cahill's arm in the penalty area, prompting vehement Serbian claims for a penalty, the game finished 2-1 to Australia, sending both teams out while Germany, as group winners, and Ghana, as relieved runners-up, advanced.

Group D Results

13/6/10, Loftus Versfeld, Pretoria
Serbia 0-1 Ghana
Attendance: 38833
Serbia: Stojković; Ivanović, Vidić, Luković, Kolarov; Krasić, Stanković, Milijaš (Kuzmanović 62), Jovanović (Subotić 76); Pantelić, Žigić (Lazović 69). Coach: Radomir Antić (SRB)
Ghana: Kingson; Pantsil, Vorsah, John Mensah, Sarpei; Annan; Tagoe, Asamoah (Appiah 73), K. Boateng (Addy 90+1), A. Ayew; Gyan (Owusu-Abeyie 90+3). Coach: Milovan Rajevac (SRB)
Goal(s): 0-1 Gyan 85 (p)
Red Card(s): Luković 74 (Serbia)
Yellow Card(s): Žigić 19 (Serbia), Vorsah 26 (Ghana) Luković 54 (Serbia), Luković 74 (Serbia), Kuzmanović 83 (Serbia), Tagoe 89 (Ghana)
Referee: Baldassi (ARG)

13/6/10, Moses Mabhida, Durban
Germany 4-0 Australia
Attendance: 62660
Germany: Neuer; Lahm, Mertesacker, Friedrich, Badstuber; Khedira, Schweinsteiger; Müller, Özil (Gómez 74), Podolski (Marin 81); Klose (Cacau 68). Coach: Joachim Löw (GER)
Australia: Schwarzer; Wilkshire, Neill, Moore, Chipperfield; Valeri, Grella (Holman 46); Emerton (Jedinak 74), Culina, Garcia (Rukavytsya 64); Cahill. Coach: Pim Verbeek (NED)
Goal(s): 1-0 Podolski 8, 2-0 Klose 26, 3-0 Müller 68, 4-0 Cacau 70
Red Card(s): Cahill 56 (Australia)
Yellow Card(s): Özil 12 (Germany), Moore 24 (Australia), Neill 46 (Australia), Valeri 58 (Australia), Cacau 90+2 (Germany)
Referee: Rodríguez (MEX)

18/6/10, Nelson Mandela Bay, Port Elizabeth
Germany 0-1 Serbia
Attendance: 38294
Germany: Neuer; Lahm, Mertesacker, Friedrich, Badstuber (Gómez 77); Khedira, Schweinsteiger; Müller (Cacau 70), Özil (Marin 70), Podolski; Klose. Coach: Joachim Löw (GER)
Serbia: Stojković; Ivanović, Vidić, Subotić, Kolarov; Stanković; Krasić, Kuzmanović (Petrović 75), Ninković (Kačar 70); Jovanović (Lazović 79); Žigić. Coach: Radomir Antić (SRB)
Goal(s): 0-1 Jovanović 38
Red Card(s): Klose 37 (Germany)
Yellow Card(s): Klose 12 (Germany), Ivanović 18 (Serbia), Kolarov 19 (Serbia), Khedira 22 (Germany), Lahm 32 (Germany), Klose 37 (Germany), Subotić 57 (Serbia), Vidić 59 (Serbia), Schweinsteiger 73 (Germany)
Referee: Undiano Mallenco (ESP)

19/6/10, Royal Bafokeng, Rustenburg
Ghana 1-1 Australia
Attendance: 34812
Ghana: Kingson; Pantsil, Jonathan Mensah, Addy, Sarpei; Annan; Tagoe (Owusu-Abeyie 56), Asamoah (Muntari 77), K. Boateng (Amoah 87), A. Ayew; Gyan. Coach: Milovan Rajevac (SRB)
Australia: Schwarzer; Wilkshire (Rukavytsya 84), Neill, Moore, Carney; Culina, Valeri; Emerton, Holman (Kennedy 68), Bresciano (Chipperfield 66); Kewell. Coach: Pim Verbeek (NED)
Goal(s): 0-1 Holman 11, 1-1 Gyan 25 (p)
Red Card(s): Kewell 24 (Australia)
Yellow Card(s): Addy 40 (Ghana), Jonathan Mensah 79 (Ghana), Annan 84 (Ghana), Moore 85 (Australia)
Referee: Rosetti (ITA)

23/6/10, Soccer City, Johannesburg
Ghana 0-1 Germany
Attendance: 86000
Ghana: Kingson; Pantsil, John Mensah, Jonathan Mensah, Sarpei; Annan; Tagoe (Muntari 64), Asamoah, K. Boateng, A. Ayew (Adiyiah 90+2); Gyan (Amoah 82). Coach: Milovan Rajevac (SRB)
Germany: Neuer; Lahm, Mertesacker, Friedrich, Boateng (Jansen 73); Khedira, Schweinsteiger (Kroos 81); Müller (Trochowski 67), Özil, Podolski; Cacau. Coach: Joachim Löw (GER)
Goal(s): 0-1 Özil 60
Yellow Card(s): A. Ayew 40 (Ghana), Müller 43 (Germany)
Referee: Simon (BRA)

23/6/10, Mbombela, Nelspruit
Australia 2-1 Serbia
Attendance: 38836
Australia: Schwarzer; Wilkshire (Garcia 82), Neill, Beauchamp, Carney; Culina, Valeri (Holman 66); Emerton, Cahill, Bresciano (Chipperfield 66); Kennedy. Coach: Pim Verbeek (NED)
Serbia: Stojković; Ivanović, Vidić, Luković, Obradović; Stanković; Krasić (Tošić 62), Kuzmanović (Lazović 77), Ninković, Jovanović, Žigić (Pantelić 67). Coach: Radomir Antić (SRB)
Goal(s): 1-0 Cahill 69, 2-0 Holman 73, 2-1 Pantelić 84
Yellow Card(s): Luković 18 (Serbia), Beauchamp 49 (Australia), Wilkshire 50 (Australia), Ninković 59 (Serbia), Emerton 67 (Australia)
Referee: Larrionda (URU)

André Ayew parades the Ghanaian flag at Soccer City in celebration of the Black Stars' qualification for the round of 16

Group D Table

	Pld	W	D	L	F	A	Pts
1 Germany	3	2	0	1	5	1	6
2 Ghana	3	1	1	1	2	2	4
3 Australia	3	1	1	1	3	6	4
4 Serbia	3	1	0	2	2	3	3

GROUP E

Group E began with the first all-European tie of the competition as the Netherlands met Denmark at Soccer City in Johannesburg. The stadium's orange seats helped the Dutch feel at home, and the group seeds went into the game full of confidence on the back of a 19-match unbeaten run. It was also a day of celebration for captain Giovanni van Bronckhorst, winning his 100th cap.

Time for a communal hug as Dirk Kuyt (centre) gives the Netherlands a 2-0 lead against Denmark

Bert van Marwijk's side showed little fluency in the early exchanges, however. Denied the services of their flying winger Arjen Robben, who was still nursing a hamstring injury sustained in the team's final warm-up game, the Oranje clearly missed his pace and flair, and Denmark gave as good as they got in a fairly soporific first half. Indeed, Morten Olsen's side came closest to breaking the deadlock when Nicklas Bendtner headed just wide from Dennis Rommedahl's cross following a superb diagonal crossfield pass from defender Daniel Agger.

Stroke of fortune

The Scandinavians would offer nothing in attack after the interval, though, after gifting the Netherlands the lead within seconds of the restart. Robin van Persie's cross from the left appeared to pose little danger but Simon Poulsen, who had been selected to fill Denmark's problem position at left-back, completely miscued his header, which hit Agger's back and deflected into the net. Spurred by that stroke of good fortune, the Dutch began to command the play, and for the final quarter, after the introduction of Eljero Elia for the disappointing Rafael van der Vaart, they even started to entertain. It was Elia, after receiving a lovely pass from Wesley Sneijder, who was chiefly responsible for his team's game-clinching second goal, weaving inside and clipping a shot against the post – via Thomas Sørensen's fingertips – before Dirk Kuyt took advantage of Simon Kjær's ball-watching to race in and tap home the rebound. Another lively substitute, Ibrahim Afellay, was denied a third goal a few minutes later with a magnificently athletic goal-line clearance from Simon Poulsen, but that would have flattered the Dutch, who were off and running with a victory but only with a very workmanlike performance.

The following afternoon Japan met Cameroon in Bloemfontein. Both teams had endured a very poor build-up to the tournament, and it showed as between them they struggled to put together any moves of substance or quality. There were no shots on target until Cameroon managed one in the 38th minute with a harmless daisy-cutting drive from Eyong Enoh. A minute later Japan had their first effort on goal…and it went in, Keisuke Honda smartly tucking the ball home at the far post from Daisuke Matsui's cross. The second half was just as dull as Cameroon struggled to find their rhythm, their efforts not helped by the deployment of dangerman Samuel Eto'o on the right wing. It was only in the last few minutes that Paul Le Guen's side put the Japanese defence under any real pressure, but the Asian side comfortably repelled the late onslaught – most of it from aimless long balls – and went on to celebrate their first FIFA World Cup finals victory on foreign soil.

With three points each, the Netherlands and Japan both followed the old maxim of never changing a winning team as they went into battle in Durban. Unfortunately, the drab standard of the group's opening two games was maintained. The first half passed almost without incident before the Dutch took the lead eight minutes into the second period, Sneijder connecting perfectly with a long-range snapshot that deceived Japan goalkeeper Eiji Kawashima as it swerved in flight, forcing him to go one way then the next before he palmed the ball into the net. Japan upped their game in response, but there were no further gilt-edged scoring opportunities until the closing minutes when, after Kawashima had twice denied vibrant Dutch substitute Afellay with fine saves, Shinji Okazaki lashed a glorious late chance to equalise wastefully over the bar.

Mini-classic

The group was in desperate need of a good game, and fortunately it got one that evening in Pretoria, where Cameroon and Denmark served up a World Cup mini-classic. Right from the start it was obvious that both teams had decided to shed the cloaks of caution that had brought them nothing in their opening games, and the result was a match of end-to-end endeavour that provided tremendous – albeit error-strewn – entertainment throughout its 90 minutes.

Cameroon took a tenth-minute lead when Eto'o, now back in the centre of the attack, drilled in an emphatic low shot from Pierre Webo's pass after Denmark midfielder Christian Poulsen was caught daydreaming.

It was the FC Internazionale Milano striker's 43rd international goal and potentially one of his most important. Denmark, with Jesper Grønkjær and Jon Dahl Tomasson recalled to their line-up, responded positively to the setback, and after each of those two veterans had been denied by brave defending, the equaliser duly arrived with one of the best goals of the tournament, Bendtner sliding in to convert a perfect square ball from Dennis Rommedahl, who had brilliantly controlled Kjær's wonderful long diagonal pass with his chest. Before the half was out, both teams squandered chances created by defensive mistakes, with Tomasson and Jørgensen missing for Denmark and Eto'o and Achille Emana failing to convert for Cameroon.

If anything, the action intensified after the interval. Cameroon appeared to be getting on top, but after Webo missed another chance and left-back Benoît Assou-Ekotto was caught upfield, Denmark exploited the space to perfection as Rommedahl cut in from the right past covering midfielder Jean II Makoun and curled a superb left-foot shot into the far corner. Although they were in the lead, Denmark could have done with another goal to make their qualifying task simpler. Tomasson had the chance to score it after more fine work from Rommedahl but he was denied by Souleymanou Hamidou. Thereafter the focus for

Keisuke Honda (top left) scores Japan's winning goal against Cameroon

Cameroon captain Samuel Eto'o scored two goals in South Africa but his team lost all three matches

Matsui was denied an opening goal by Sørensen's legs and Makoto Hasebe drove just wide before, in the 17th minute, Honda beat Sørensen with a superb swerving long-range free-kick. The PFC CSKA Moskva star had scored a similar goal to knock Sevilla FC out of the UEFA Champions League a few months earlier, and his set-piece skills were matched on 30 minutes by Asian Footballer of the Year Yasuhito Endo, who doubled Japan's lead with an equally stunning strike into the top corner. The same player almost performed the same trick with another free-kick early in the second half, causing Sørensen all sorts of problems, but the Denmark 'keeper was rescued by his post.

Now needing three goals to qualify, Denmark's efforts to get back into the game seemed half-hearted. Tomasson, who had not scored for his country in two and a half years and needed just one goal to equal Denmark's all-time record, missed a sitter on 70 minutes but he did finally get that goal, albeit in comical fashion, nine minutes from time. His weakly struck penalty – awarded for a clumsy foul on Agger by Hasebe – was easily saved by Kawashima, but it returned to his feet, and even then Tomasson struggled to squeeze in the rebound, slicing it off the outside of his right foot and injuring himself to such an extent that for the remainder of the game, with all three Danish substitutes used up, he was forced to hobble around as a virtual passenger. During that time Denmark looked a spent force and Japan punished them with a third goal, scored by Okazaki and beautifully created with an extravagant piece of skill from the outstanding Honda.

Denmark was to hold on to what they had as the African side came on strong in the last 15 minutes. Sørensen made a superb one-handed save to deny Emana, then Vincent Aboubakar's goalbound shot struck the head of a prostrate Christian Poulsen.

First team out

It was not to be Cameroon's night. Their second defeat meant that they were the first team to be eliminated and the Netherlands the first to qualify for the last 16. As for Denmark, they lived to fight another day but would have to defeat Japan to go through. A third goal against Cameron would have left them requiring just a draw.

Thus, while the Netherlands and Cameroon played out a dead rubber in Cape Town, everything was to play for between Denmark and Japan in Rustenburg. Japan coach Takeshi Okada chose to keep the same starting XI once again despite the defeat against the Dutch, while Denmark had to make do in defence without Kjær, who was suspended after picking up a late booking against Cameroon.

Although Japan required only a draw to advance, it was evident early on that they were going for the win.

Through in style

With two wins out of three, Japan were through to the last 16 in style. First place went to the Netherlands, who maintained their 100 per cent record by overcoming Cameroon 2-1. Van Persie put the Oranje ahead with a right-foot shot from a tight angle, and although Eto'o equalised from the penalty spot after a Geremi free-kick struck Van der Vaart's raised arm, the African side's third defeat was sealed by an exceptional winning goal from the Netherlands that featured a central contribution from the returning Robben. Just ten minutes after coming on as a substitute to make his first appearance in the tournament, he gathered a fantastic outside-of-the-foot pass from Sneijder, cut inside on to his left foot in familiar style and whipped in a superb shot that thudded against the inside of the far post. Fortunately fellow substitute Klaas Jan Huntelaar was on hand to slide in the rebound with a composed first-time finish and give the Netherlands their third successive victory.

Group E Results

14/6/10, Soccer City, Johannesburg
Netherlands 2-0 Denmark
Attendance: 83465
Netherlands: Stekelenburg; Van der Wiel, Heitinga, Mathijsen, Van Bronckhorst; Van Bommel, De Jong (De Zeeuw 88); Kuyt, Sneijder, Van der Vaart (Elia 67); Van Persie (Afellay 77). Coach: Bert van Marwijk (NED)
Denmark: Sørensen; Jacobsen, Kjær, Agger, S. Poulsen; Enevoldsen (Grønkjær 56); C. Poulsen, Kahlenberg (Eriksen 73); Rommedahl, Bentdner (Beckmann 62), Jørgensen. Coach: Morten Olsen (DEN)
Goal(s): 1-0 Agger 46 (og), 2-0 Kuyt 85
Yellow Card(s): De Jong 44 (Netherlands), Van Persie 49 (Netherlands), Kjær 63 (Denmark)
Referee: Lannoy (FRA)

14/6/10, Free State, Bloemfontein
Japan 1-0 Cameroon
Attendance: 30620
Japan: Kawashima; Komano, Nakazawa, Tulio Tanaka, Nagatomo; Hasebe (Inamoto 88), Abe, Endo, Matsui (Okazaki 69), Okubo (Yano 82); Honda. Coach: Takeshi Okada (JPN)
Cameroon: Hamidou; Mbia, N'Koulou, Bassong, Assou-Ekotto; Matip (Emana 63), Makoun (Geremi 75), Enoh; Eto'o, Webo, Choupo-Moting (Idrissou 75). Coach: Paul Le Guen (FRA)
Goal(s): 1-0 Honda 39
Yellow Card(s): N'Koulou 72 (Cameroon), Abe 90+1 (Japan)
Referee: Olegário Benquerença (POR)

Denmark's Jon Dahl Tomasson scores but injures himself against Japan

19/6/10, Moses Mabhida, Durban
Netherlands 1-0 Japan
Attendance: 62010
Netherlands: Stekelenburg; Van der Wiel, Heitinga, Mathijsen, Van Bronckhorst; Van Bommel, De Jong, Kuyt, Sneijder (Afellay 83), Van der Vaart (Elia 72); Van Persie (Huntelaar 88). Coach: Bert van Marwijk (NED)
Japan: Kawashima; Komano, Nakazawa, Tulio Tanaka, Nagatomo; Hasebe (Okazaki 77), Abe, Endo; Matsui (S. Nakamura 64), Okubo (Tamada 77); Honda. Coach: Takeshi Okada (JPN)
Goal(s): 1-0 Sneijder 53
Yellow Card(s): Van der Wiel 36 (Netherlands)
Referee: Baldassi (ARG)

19/6/10, Loftus Versfeld, Pretoria
Cameroon 1-2 Denmark
Attendance: 38704
Cameroon: Hamidou; Mbia, N'Koulou, Bassong (Idrissou 72), Assou-Ekotto; Geremi, A. Song, Enoh (Makoun 46); Emana, Eto'o, Webo (Aboubakar 78). Coach: Paul Le Guen (FRA)
Denmark: Sørensen; Jacobsen, Kjær, Agger, S. Poulsen; C. Poulsen, Jørgensen (Jensen 46); Tomasson (J. Poulsen 86); Rommedahl, Bentdner, Grønkjær (Kahlenberg 67). Coach: Morten Olsen (DEN)
Goal(s): 1-0 Eto'o 10, 1-1 Bentdner 33, 1-2 Rommedahl 61
Yellow Card(s): Bassong 49 (Cameroon), Mbia 75 (Cameroon), Sørensen 86 (Denmark), Kjær 87 (Denmark)
Referee: Larrionda (URU)

24/6/10, Royal Bafokeng, Rustenburg
Denmark 1-3 Japan
Attendance: 27967
Denmark: Sørensen; Jacobsen, Krøldrup (Larsen 56), Agger, S. Poulsen; C. Poulsen, Jørgensen (J. Poulsen 34); Tomasson; Rommedahl, Bentdner, Kahlenberg (Eriksen 63). Coach: Morten Olsen (DEN)
Japan: Kawashima; Komano, Nakazawa, Tulio Tanaka, Nagatomo; Hasebe, Abe, Endo (Inamoto 90+1); Matsui (Okazaki 74), Okubo (Konno 88); Honda. Coach: Takeshi Okada (JPN)
Goal(s): 0-1 Honda 17, 0-2 Endo 30, 1-2 Tomasson 81, 1-3 Okazaki 87
Yellow Card(s): Endo 12 (Japan), Nagatomo 26 (Japan), Krøldrup 29 (Denmark), C. Poulsen 48 (Denmark), Bentdner 66 (Denmark)
Referee: Damon (RSA)

24/6/10, Green Point, Cape Town
Cameroon 1-2 Netherlands
Attendance: 63093
Cameroon: Hamidou; Geremi, N'Koulou (R. Song 73), Mbia, Assou-Ekotto; N'Guémo, Makoun, Chedjou, Bong (Aboubakar 56); Choupo-Moting (Idrissou 72), Eto'o. Coach: Paul Le Guen (FRA)
Netherlands: Stekelenburg; Boularouz, Heitinga, Mathijsen, Van Bronckhorst; Van Bommel, De Jong; Kuyt (Elia 66), Sneijder, Van der Vaart (Robben 73); Van Persie (Huntelaar 59). Coach: Bert van Marwijk (NED)
Goal(s): 0-1 Van Persie 36, 1-1 Eto'o 65 (p), 1-2 Huntelaar 83
Yellow Card(s): Kuyt 17 (Netherlands), N'Koulou 25 (Cameroon), Van der Vaart 65 (Netherlands), Van Bronckhorst 70 (Netherlands), Mbia 81 (Cameroon)
Referee: Pozo (CHI)

Group E Table

	Pld	W	D	L	F	A	Pts
1 Netherlands	3	3	0	0	5	1	9
2 Japan	3	2	0	1	4	2	6
3 Denmark	3	1	0	2	3	6	3
4 Cameroon	3	0	0	3	2	5	0

GROUP F

There was a wild, wet and windy start to proceedings in Group F as Italy and Pargauay, the two teams favoured to progress from the section, opened their 2010 FIFA World Cup programme in Cape Town.

The world champions were without their injured playmaker Andrea Pirlo, and although his replacement, Riccardo Montolivo, did his best to fill the gap, the Azzurri offered very little invention in their attempts to break down a solid, well constructed Paraguay defence. Indeed, the South Americans looked anything but overawed and deserved the lead that came their way on 39 minutes when centre-back Antolín Alcaraz rose above Italy skipper Fabio Cannavaro to head in Aureliano Torres's teasing free-kick. The game certainly needed a goal to liven it up, and Italy were more active in attack in the second period, which they began with a new goalkeeper as the injured Gianluigi Buffon had to be replaced by Federico Marchetti. It was an error of judgment from Paraguay's No1, however, that led to the next goal, Daniele De Rossi sliding in at the far post to score after Justo Villar completely misread the flight of

Simone Pepe's inswinging corner from the left. Villar redeemed himself with a couple of late saves from Pepe and Montolivo to ensure that Paraguay emerged from the contest with a point. Italy, frankly, did not do enough to win and provided scant evidence that they could go on to defend their trophy.

Low-key contest

The group's second game, between New Zealand and Slovakia, took place in the early afternoon of the following day several hundred miles to the north in Rustenburg. Apart from a few impressive runs and touches from winger Vladimír Weiss, the namesake son of the Slovakia coach, the first-half entertainment level was low, but a goal from the European side five minutes after the interval raised it a couple of notches. Róbert Vittek was just offside when he met Stanislav Šesták's cross from the right with a well-placed header, but Slovakia deserved their lead and they continued to have the better of the play for the remainder of the game until, fatally, they switched off in the last minute of stoppage-time, allowing New Zealand to equalise. With perfect timing Winston Reid rose to head in at the far post after Shane Smeltz's quick and accurate cross

Daniele De Rossi (second right) equalises for Italy against Paraguay

caught the Slovakian defence flat-footed. The Kiwis thus claimed their first ever World Cup point, and although Slovakia did likewise, their overriding feeling was of two precious points needlessly thrown away.

Slovakia's dejection seemed to carry forward into their next game, in Bloemfontein, where they hardly came out to play against a Paraguay side that maintained South America's excellent start to the tournament with an easy 2-0 win. Weiss's ultra-conservative tactics did not change even after Paraguay took the lead on 27 minutes with a sweetly struck finish from midfielder Enrique Vera, who skilfully despatched Lucas Barrios's neat lay-off with the outside of his right foot. Slovakia's lack of ambition left the spectators in the Free State stadium crying out for some meaningful action in a desperately disappointing second half. They finally got some four minutes from time when Paraguay sealed a straightforward win with a second goal, Cristian Riveros smashing home a loose ball after a free-kick.

With the exception of the injured Buffon, Italy were unchanged against New Zealand in Nelspruit. Had this been a rugby union international, the Azzurri would have been the underdogs, but it was the All Whites that Italy were up against rather than the All Blacks and were therefore overwhelming favourites to rack up the three points that would put them level with Paraguay at the top of the table. Within seven minutes, though, they were behind. As against Paraguay, captain Cannavaro struggled to deal with a free-kick swung into the Italy box and Smeltz, the Kiwis' top scorer in qualifying, poked the ball home from close range. Replays showed that the goal should have been disallowed for offside but Marcello Lippi's side had plenty of time to recover from the shock. Indeed, they had almost all of the play for the remainder of the first half, but as New Zealand defended stoutly, their only reward was a penalty. Although it was a soft decision – De Rossi having flung himself to the ground after a slight shirt tug – the spot-kick was clinically despatched by Vincenzo Iaquinta.

Kiwis hold firm

With over an hour remaining, it seemed only a matter of time before Italy went ahead. But although the one-way traffic largely continued, the world champions' attacks lacked the necessary guile and subtlety to destabilise the Kiwi rearguard. One beautifully struck shot from Montolivo brought an equally fine save from Mark Paston, but although the pressure increased in the final ten minutes, keeping Paston and his defensive colleagues busy, that was about as close as Italy got to winning the game. They even had to survive a moment of alarm when New Zealand's 18-year-old substitute

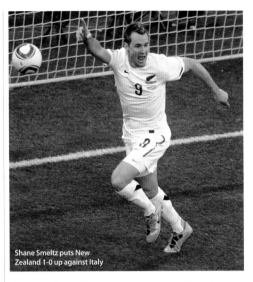

Shane Smeltz puts New Zealand 1-0 up against Italy

Chris Wood barged his way into the area and flashed a shot narrowly wide. When Kiwi skipper Ryan Nelsen capped a superb individual performance by blocking Gianluca Zambrotta's effort in the 90th minute, Italy's last chance went begging. It was a humiliating result for Marcello Lippi's team but a momentous one for their opponents, who now went into their final game still bidding for a place in the last 16.

The match between Ricki Herbert's rank outsiders and group leaders Paraguay in Polokwane would prove to be something of an anti-climax, finishing goalless and thus sending the South Americans through and the Kiwis out – albeit with an unbeaten record. But there would be drama aplenty at Ellis Park in Johannesburg as Slovakia and Italy took part in an epic encounter that will live long in the memory of the fans from both countries – if for entirely different reasons.

Aware at kick-off that only a win would guarantee their progress, both teams tried to establish an early foothold, but there was not much quality on offer in the opening exchanges and some awful Italian defending allowed Slovakia's Italy-based captain, SSC Napoli midfielder Marek Hamšík, an early sight of goal that he should probably have made better use of. It was a warning to Italy that their opponents would not be re-deploying the craven safety-first tactics that had cost them against Paraguay, but it was not heeded and on 25 minutes Slovakia took the lead. A sloppy pass out of defence by De Rossi was intercepted by Juraj Kucka, and the AC Sparta Praha midfielder, making his first start of the competition, fed Vittek, who skilfully steered his right-foot shot past Marchetti into the bottom corner. There was a further indication of Italian defensive insecurity when Cannavaro was yellow-carded for a deliberate block on the lively Kucka, who ended an excellent half for both himself and his team with a fantastic first-time volley from 30 metres that grazed the outside of Marchetti's post.

Vittek strikes again

Italy had to react, and 11 minutes into the second half Pirlo was finally introduced to the World Cup fray. With Fabio Quagliarella having also been brought on at half-time, the Azzurri began to look much more creative and dangerous. The Napoli striker thought he had equalised when his goalbound flick was blocked on the goal-line by Martin Škrteľ, but as Italy started committing more men forward, the game began to stretch, enabling Slovakia also to advance with more purpose. On 73 minutes Vittek struck his second goal of the game to send Slovakia into dreamland, getting in front of his marker to meet Hamšík's low cross from the right and turn it adroitly past Marchetti at the near post.

The last ten minutes were to provide the most pulsating passage of play in the entire tournament. Italy, increasing the pressure, pulled a goal back through Antonio Di Natale, who tapped in after Quagliarella's low shot was only half-saved by Ján Mucha. Then

Quagliarella's close-range flick found the net, only for the linesman to raise his flag and indicate – correctly – that the Italy striker had been fractionally offside. Slovakia were hanging on precariously to their lead, but then, with one minute left of normal time, they cleared the ball upfield and won a throw-in on the right. Italy, forgetting that they still had to defend, stood and watched as the ball was delivered infield for substitute Kamil Kopúnek, who ran unopposed into the area and, with his very first touch of the tournament, lifted it over Marchetti into the far corner.

It was a magnificent goal, but Italy were not finished yet. With two of the four minutes of stoppage time elapsed, Quagliarella got the goal he deserved with an audacious and superbly executed chip from the edge of the area. The Azzurri piled forward in the final seconds in search of the equalising goal that would keep them in the tournament. They won a throw-in on the right. It was launched into the crowded penalty area and somehow found its way at the back post to the unmarked figure of Pepe. With history beckoning, he took fractionally too long to get his shot away and as the defenders desperately tried to close him down he miscued his shot wide. With that last breathless piece of action it was all over. Italy, the defending champions, were out – succumbing to their first opening-round exit since 1974 - and Slovakia, the World Cup novices, were through – after the greatest win in their history.

Slovakia striker Róbert Vittek celebrates his second goal against Italy

2010 FIFA WORLD CUP

Cristian Riveros – a goalscorer for Paraguay against Slovakia

Group F Results

14/6/10, Green Point, Cape Town
Italy 1-1 Paraguay
Attendance: 65000
Italy: Buffon (Marchetti 46); Zambrotta, Cannavaro, Chiellini, Criscito; De Rossi, Montolivo; Pepe, Marchisio (Camoranesi 59), Iaquinta; Gilardino (Di Natale 72). Coach: Marcello Lippi (ITA)
Paraguay: Villar; Bonet, Da Silva, Alcaraz, Morel; Vera, V. Cáceres, Riveros, Torres (Santana 60); Barrios (Cardozo 76), Valdez (Santa Cruz 68). Coach: Gerardo Martino (ARG)
Goal(s): 0-1 Alcaraz 39, 1-1 De Rossi 63
Yellow Card(s): V. Cáceres 62 (Paraguay), Camoranesi 70 (Italy)
Referee: Archundia (MEX)

15/6/10, Royal Bafokeng, Rustenburg
New Zealand 1-1 Slovakia
Attendance: 33820
New Zealand: Paston; Reid, Nelsen, Smith; Bertos, Vicelich (Christie 78), Elliott, Lochhead; Fallon, Killen (Wood 72); Smeltz. Coach: Ricki Herbert (NZL)
Slovakia: Mucha; Zabavník, Škrteľ, Ďurica, Čech; Štrba; Weiss (Kucka 90+1), Hamšík, Jendrišek; Šesták (Hološko 81), Vittek (Stoch 84). Coach: Vladimír Weiss (SVK)
Goal(s): 0-1 Vittek 50, 1-1 Reid 90+3
Yellow Card(s): Lochhead 42 (New Zealand), Štrba 55 (Slovakia), Reid 90+3 (New Zealand)
Referee: Damon (RSA)

20/6/10, Free State, Bloemfontein
Slovakia 0-2 Paraguay
Attendance: 26643
Slovakia: Mucha; Pekarík, Škrteľ, Saláta (Stoch 83), Ďurica; Štrba; Šesták (Hološko 70), Hamšík, Kozák, Weiss; Vittek. Coach: Vladimír Weiss (SVK)
Paraguay: Villar; Bonet, Da Silva, Alcaraz, Morel; Vera (É. Barreto 88), V. Cáceres, Riveros; Barrios (Cardozo 82), Santa Cruz, Valdez (Torres 68). Coach: Gerardo Martino (ARG)
Goal(s): 0-1 Vera 27, 0-2 Riveros 86
Yellow Card(s): Ďurica 42 (Slovakia), Vera 45 (Paraguay), Šesták 47 (Slovakia), Weiss 84 (Slovakia)
Referee: Maillet (SEY)

20/6/10, Mbombela, Nelspruit
Italy 1-1 New Zealand
Attendance: 38229
Italy: Marchetti; Zambrotta, Cannavaro, Chiellini, Criscito; Pepe (Camoranesi 46), De Rossi, Montolivo, Marchisio (Pazzini 61); Iaquinta, Gilardino (Di Natale 46). Coach: Marcello Lippi (ITA)
New Zealand: Paston; Reid, Nelsen, Smith; Bertos, Vicelich (Christie 81), Elliott, Lochhead; Fallon (Wood 63), Killen (Barron 90+3); Smeltz. Coach: Ricki Herbert (NZL)
Goal(s): 0-1 Smeltz 7, 1-1 Iaquinta 29 (p)
Yellow Card(s): Fallon 14 (New Zealand), Smith 28 (New Zealand), Nelsen 87 (New Zealand)
Referee: Batres (GUA)

24/6/10, Ellis Park, Johannesburg
Slovakia 3-2 Italy
Attendance: 53412
Slovakia: Mucha; Pekarík, Škrteľ, Ďurica, Zabavník; Štrba (Kopúnek 87), Kucka; Stoch, Hamšík, Jendrišek (Petráš 90+4); Vittek (Šesták 90+2). Coach: Vladimír Weiss (SVK)
Italy: Marchetti; Zambrotta, Cannavaro, Chiellini, Criscito (Maggio 46); Gattuso (Quagliarella 46), De Rossi, Montolivo (Pirlo 56); Pepe, Iaquinta, Di Natale. Coach: Marcello Lippi (ITA)
Goal(s): 1-0 Vittek 25, 2-0 Vittek 73, 2-1 Di Natale 81, 3-1 Kopúnek 89, 3-2 Quagliarella 90+2
Yellow Card(s): Štrba 16 (Slovakia), Cannavaro 31 (Italy), Vittek 40 (Slovakia), Pekarík 50 (Slovakia), Chiellini 67 (Italy), Pepe 76 (Italy), Mucha 82 (Slovakia), Quagliarella 83 (Italy)
Referee: Webb (ENG)

24/6/10, Peter Mokaba, Polokwane
Paraguay 0-0 New Zealand
Attendance: 34850
Paraguay: Villar; Caniza, J. Cáceres, Da Silva, Morel; Vera, V. Cáceres, Riveros; Santa Cruz, Cardozo (Barrios 66), Valdez (Benítez 67). Coach: Gerardo Martino (ARG)
New Zealand: Paston; Reid, Nelsen, Smith; Bertos, Elliott Vicelich, Lochhead; Killen (Brockie 79), Fallon (Wood 69), Smeltz. Coach: Ricki Herbert (NZL)
Yellow Card(s): V. Cáceres 10 (Paraguay), Santa Cruz 41 (Paraguay), Nelsen 56 (New Zealand)
Referee: Nishimura (JPN)

Group F Table

	Pld	W	D	L	F	A	Pts
1 Paraguay	3	1	2	0	3	1	5
2 Slovakia	3	1	1	1	4	5	4
3 New Zealand	3	0	3	0	2	2	3
4 Italy	3	0	2	1	4	5	2

GROUP G

The so-called 'Group of Death' kicked off with an intriguing clash between Ivory Coast and Portugal. With Brazil expected to top the section and North Korea the firm favourites to finish bottom, this match in Port Elizabeth was potentially a face-off for second place.

Unfortunately, because it was the first match rather than the last, the overriding objective for both the Africans and the Europeans was not to win but to ensure that they avoided defeat. As a consequence the intrigue was replaced by inertia, leading to yet another dull, pedestrian group opener. Cristiano Ronaldo, Portugal's superstar captain, drew some gasps from the crowd early on when he turned and shot from 30 metres, his ferocious effort thudding spectacularly against the post, but that was about the only moment to savour in the first half as the two defences remained rigid, with neither side willing to make any kind of sacrifice to attack.

Broken arm

Didier Drogba, the Ivory Coast captain, had broken his arm in a pre-tournament friendly and was not declared fit to start by the Elephants' recently appointed coach, Sven-Göran Eriksson. He did make an appearance from the bench, to a huge roar, midway through the second half but was unable to make an impact, his only chance coming in stoppage time when he latched on to Abdul Kader Keita's pass but could not make the contact he needed as he stretched to shoot and pulled the ball harmlessly across goal.

The goalless draw kept the group interesting and also provided an open invitation for Brazil to make an early claim on group leadership as they took on North Korea in the evening game at Ellis Park – the same stadium in which they had won the FIFA Confederations Cup 12 months earlier. Dunga's team were at full strength but the expected avalanche of goals did not materialise as the Koreans defended with great diligence, and by half-time, to widespread astonishment, Group G was still awaiting its first goal.

Brazil upped the pace in the second half and duly opened the scoring on 55 minutes when Maicon drove in a shot from an acute angle that fooled goalkeeper Ri Myong-guk and swerved past him at his near post.

There was some debate as to whether the full-back meant to shoot or cross, but it looked so spectacular that it would have been a shame if it had not been authentic. Whether or not it was a stroke of genius or luck, it gave Brazil the lead, and from then on the game became even more one-sided. Although the South Americans struggled to find their traditional fluency, their second goal was a genuine thing of beauty, Elano slotting a first-time shot into the bottom corner from Robinho's geometrically perfect angled through-ball. At 2-0 it was game over, but North Korea, for whom shaven-headed striker Jong Tae-se was a bundle of energy throughout, had the last say as Ji Yun-nam latched on to Jong's back header and lifted the ball precisely over Júlio César to score arguably the most wildly celebrated consolation goal of all time. Although they had been on the back foot throughout the game, it was a goal the underdogs deserved for their determined efforts over the 90 minutes.

Didier Drogba enters the fray for Ivory Coast against Portugal

Brazil's Maicon drives in from a tight angle to open the scoring against North Korea

Goal out of the blue

Although it was not the opening scoreline Brazil had anticipated, the three points were nevertheless welcome. Dunga chose to field the same starting XI five days later in Soccer City against Ivory Coast, for whom Drogba was deemed fit to start. The Chelsea FC striker did a passable impression of the Invisible Man for most of the first half, however, as Brazil, though disappointing again with their lack of invention and ingenuity, took the lead with a terrific goal out of the blue from Luís Fabiano. The Seleção centre-forward moved on to Kaká's poked pass before lashing a ferocious angled shot past Boubacar Barry.

There would be a second goal for the Brazil No9 five minutes after the interval. It might have classified as even more spectacular than the first had video evidence not confirmed that in juggling the ball over a defender before driving home with his left foot he had twice used his arm to control it. Drogba came out of his shell to head an Aruna Dindane cross wide shortly afterwards but Brazil were beginning to buzz now, and almost immediately after a wonderful flowing move involving Maicon, Robinho and Kaká came frustratingly to nought, they went 3-0 up as Elano

applied a measured finish to Kaká's square-ball from the left. The goalscorer would not last much longer, however, as a nasty challenge left him with a badly damaged shinbone. In fact, the latter stages of the game turned quite ugly, with Kaká being shown a red card on the basis of a shameful piece of playacting from Keita, who reacted to a gentle hand-off by theatrically clutching his face. This came after Drogba had reduced the deficit to 3-1 with a fine header from a Yaya Touré cross, but although that goal promised to be useful if qualification came down to goal difference, the defeated Africans could not dispute that the better side had won.

Dark grey skies and driving rain greeted Portugal and North Korea the following afternoon in Cape Town. The Asian side knew that a second defeat would eliminate them and they gave as good as they got for the first quarter, surviving a Ricardo Carvalho header against the post to launch a number of pot-shots at Eduardo's goal. But once Portugal took the lead on 29 minutes, as Raul Meireles charged into the area to drive home Tiago's fine pass, the heart seemed to go out of Kim Jong-hun's team and they went to pieces in the second half as Portugal ploughed through their defence at will, plundering another six goals.

Second-half onslaught

Simão made it 2-0 on 53 minutes, slotting his shot under the 'keeper after neat link-up play between Raul Meireles and Hugo Almeida, who three minutes later scored himself, heading home unmarked from flying full-back Fábio Coentrão's left-wing cross. Tiago supplied an excellent low drive to make it 4-0 and there were countless chances created and missed over the next 20 minutes before substitute Liedson, with his first touch, added the fifth goal. Cristiano Ronaldo had not scored for his country in 16 months but, having come close with one majestic strike against the crossbar, he got in the act, making it 6-0 with a cool sidefoot finish after the ball had rolled down off his neck. The onslaught was concluded a couple of minutes later as Tiago, perhaps the pick of the Portuguese players, scored his second goal of the afternoon with a superb glancing header from another Fábio Coentrão cross.

Cristiano Ronaldo controls the ball with his neck before scoring against North Korea in Portugal's 7-0 win

With a plus-seven goal difference compared to Ivory Coast's minus-two, Portugal appeared to have done enough in that one game to secure their place, alongside Brazil, in the last 16. Only a miraculous turnaround could save the Africans from their second successive World Cup first-round exit. Their only means of progress was to emulate Portugal with a high-scoring win against now eliminated North Korea in Nelspruit while hoping that Brazil did them a favour by convincingly beating Carlos Queiroz's team in Durban.

What was a long shot at the start never became anything else. As they had done in Germany four years earlier, Ivory Coast would bow out with a victory, but again it would be futile. The three goals they scored – from Yaya Touré and Romaric in the first half and Salomon Kalou near the end – would have been insufficient even if Brazil had put five without reply past Portugal. Instead the match in the spectacular Moses Mabhida stadium failed to live up to either its surroundings or its pre-tournament hype and ended in a mutually convenient 0-0 draw.

Total commitment

Not that it started out as such. Although both teams were without key men - Brazil allowing Robinho to rest up on the sidelines with the injured Elano and the suspended Kaká, and Portugal making several changes, particularly in attack - the commitment in the first half was total. The two countries may have shared the same language and a cultural heritage, but there appeared to be no love lost between them as the tackles and challenges flew in from both sides during a fractious and niggly opening period that, alas, produced little goalmouth action. No fewer than seven yellow cards were dished out before half-time, with Pepe, the Brazilian-born Portugal holding midfielder playing his first game for seven months, lucky to stay on the field after a horrible rake on Felipe Melo.

By comparison the second half was placid and uneventful. Portugal, knowing that only a win would put them top of the group, tried the harder to break the deadlock, but after Raul Meireles wasted the best chance of the game, set up by an explosive charge down the right by Ronaldo, the European side showed no further inclination to adjust the scoreline. With Brazil also happy to take the goalless draw, the game petered out into a stand-off, the only interruption coming in stoppage time when a deflected shot by Brazilian substitute Ramires forced Eduardo into a superb scrambling save to protect his third clean sheet in as many matches.

2010 FIFA WORLD CUP

Ji Yun-nam scores North Korea's consolation goal against Brazil

Group G Results

15/6/10, Nelson Mandela Bay, Port Elizabeth
Ivory Coast 0-0 Portugal
Attendance: 37034
Ivory Coast: Barry; Demel, K. Touré, Zokora, Tiéné; Eboué (Romaric 89), Y. Touré, Tioté; Dindane, Kalou (Drogba 66); Gervinho (Keita 82). Coach: Sven-Göran Eriksson (SWE)
Portugal: Eduardo; Paulo Ferreira, Ricardo Carvalho, Bruno Alves, Fábio Coentrão; Deco (Tiago 62), Pedro Mendes, Raul Meireles (Rúben Amorim 85); Cristiano Ronaldo, Liedson, Danny (Simão 55). Coach: Carlos Queiroz (POR)
Yellow Card(s): Zokora 7 (Ivory Coast), Demel 21 (Ivory Coast), Cristiano Ronaldo 21 (Portugal)
Referee: Larrionda (URU)

15/6/10, Ellis Park, Johannesburg
Brazil 2-1 North Korea
Attendance: 54331
Brazil: Júlio César; Maicon, Lúcio, Juan, Michel Bastos; Gilberto Silva, Felipe Melo (Ramires 84); Elano (Dani Alves 73), Kaká (Nilmar 78), Robinho; Luís Fabiano. Coach: Dunga (BRA)
North Korea: Ri Myong-guk; Cha Jong-hyok, Pak Chol-jin, Ri Jun-il, Pak Nam-chol (I), Ri Kwang-chon; Mun In-guk (Kim Kum-il 80), An Yong-hak, Ji Yun-nam; Hong Yong-jo; Jong Tae-se. Coach: Kim Jong-hun (PRK)
Goal(s): 1-0 Maicon 55, 2-0 Elano 72, 2-1 Ji Yun-nam 89
Yellow Card(s): Ramires 88 (Brazil)
Referee: Kassai (HUN)

20/6/10, Soccer City, Johannesburg
Brazil 3-1 Ivory Coast
Attendance: 84455
Brazil: Júlio César; Maicon, Lúcio, Juan, Michel Bastos; Gilberto Silva, Felipe Melo; Elano (Dani Alves 67), Kaká, Robinho (Ramires 90+3); Luís Fabiano. Coach: Dunga (BRA)

Ivory Coast: Barry; Demel, K. Touré, Zokora, Tiéné; Eboué (Romaric 72), Y. Touré, Tioté; Dindane (Gervinho 54), Kalou (Keita 68); Drogba. Coach: Sven-Göran Eriksson (SWE)
Goal(s): 1-0 Luís Fabiano 25, 2-0 Luís Fabiano 50, 3-0 Elano 62, 3-1 Drogba 79
Red Card(s): Kaká 88 (Brazil)
Yellow Card(s): Tiéné 31 (Ivory Coast), Keita 75 (Ivory Coast), Kaká 85 (Brazil), Tioté 86 (Ivory Coast), Kaká 88 (Brazil)
Referee: Lannoy (FRA)

21/6/10, Green Point, Cape Town
Portugal 7-0 North Korea
Attendance: 63644
Portugal: Eduardo; Miguel, Ricardo Carvalho, Bruno Alves, Fábio Coentrão; Tiago, Pedro Mendes, Raul Meireles (Miguel Veloso 70); Simão (Duda 74), Hugo Almeida (Liedson 77), Cristiano Ronaldo. Coach: Carlos Queiroz (POR)
North Korea: Ri Myong-guk; Cha Jong-hyok (Nam Song-chol 75), Pak Chol-jin, Ri Jun-il, , Ji Yun-nam, Ri Kwang-chon; Mun In-guk (Kim Yong-jun 58), An Yong-hak, Pak Nam-chol (I) (Kim Kum-il 58); Hong Yong-jo; Jong Tae-se. Coach: Kim Jong-hun (PRK)
Goal(s): 1-0 Raul Meireles 29, 2-0 Simão 53, 3-0 Hugo Almeida 56, 4-0 Tiago 60, 5-0 Liedson 81, 6-0 Cristiano Ronaldo 87, 7-0 Tiago 89
Yellow Card(s): Pak Chol-jin 32 (North Korea), Pedro Mendes 39 (Portugal), Hong Yong-jo 47 (North Korea), Hugo Almeida 70 (Portugal)
Referee: Pozo (CHI)

25/6/10, Moses Mabhida, Durban
Portugal 0-0 Brazil
Attendance: 62712
Portugal: Eduardo; Ricardo Costa, Ricardo Carvalho, Bruno Alves, Fábio Coentrão; Pepe (Pedro Mendes 64); Danny, Tiago, Raul Meireles (Miguel Veloso 84); Duda (Simão 54); Cristiano Ronaldo. Coach: Carlos Queiroz (POR)
Brazil: Júlio César; Maicon, Lúcio, Juan, Michel Bastos; Felipe Melo (Josué 44); Dani Alves, Júlio Baptista (Ramires 82), Nilmar; Luís Fabiano (Grafite 85). Coach: Dunga (BRA)
Yellow Card(s): Luís Fabiano 15 (Brazil), Duda 25 (Portugal), Juan 25 (Brazil), Tiago 31 (Portugal), Pepe 40 (Portugal), Felipe Melo 43 (Brazil), Fábio Coentrão 45 (Portugal)
Referee: Archundia (MEX)

25/6/10, Mbombela, Nelspruit
North Korea 0-3 Ivory Coast
Attendance: 34634
North Korea: Ri Myong-guk; Cha Jong-hyok, Pak Chol-jin, Ri Jun-il, Ji Yun-nam, Ri Kwang-chon; Mun In-guk (Choe Kum-chol 67), An Yong-hak, Pak Nam-chol (I); Hong Yong-jo; Jong Tae-se. Coach: Kim Jong-hun (PRK)
Ivory Coast: Barry; Eboué, K. Touré, Zokora, Boka; Y. Touré; Romaric (Doumbia 79), Tioté; Keita (Kalou 64), Gervinho (Dindane 64); Drogba. Coach: Sven-Göran Eriksson (SWE)
Goal(s): 0-1 Y. Touré 14, 0-2 Romaric 20, 0-3 Kalou 82
Referee: Undiano Mallenco (ESP)

Group G Table

	Pld	W	D	L	F	A	Pts
1 Brazil	3	2	1	0	5	2	7
2 Portugal	3	1	2	0	7	0	5
3 Ivory Coast	3	1	1	1	4	3	4
4 North Korea	3	0	0	3	1	12	0

GROUP H

The four teams in Group H had to wait until the sixth day of competition before they got their campaigns underway. The first two in action were Honduras and Chile, who met in an all-Latin American affair in Nelspruit.

Jean Beausejour (No15) smiles after scoring for Chile against Honduras

Chile, under their Argentinian coach Marcelo Bielsa, arrived in South Africa with a reputation for lively, adventurous football and they did not disappoint, putting the squeeze on the Hondurans, whose Colombian coach Reinaldo Rueda was suspended, for most of the 90 minutes with their incessant commitment to attack. That they managed just a single goal for all their efforts – and a rather fortuitous one at that - was something of a letdown, but their priority was to get off to a winning start, and despite the scoreline they achieved that in comfort.

Poor finishing

The Chileans' early pressure eventually paid off on 34 minutes when their left-winger with the French name, Jean Beausejour, finished off an incisive move as a defender's attempt to clear a low cross from wing-back Mauricio Isla struck him on the thigh and went in. It was a lucky goal but one that Chile deserved. With Alexis Sánchez, Beausejour's counterpoint on the right flank, showing impressive craft and skill, further goals should have followed, but the team's excellent build-up play was repeatedly spoilt by imprecise finishing, the worst culprit being centre-back Waldo Ponce who somehow failed to head in from almost on the goal-line. As for Honduras, they defended well but never looked likely to score, their only gripe being a penalty appeal that fell on deaf ears just after half-time when Édgar Álvarez appeared to be taken out by Gary Medel.

Spain, the European champions, began their World Cup assault in Durban against Switzerland, a team that had never beaten them in 18 attempts. With two key players in Valon Behrami and captain Alexander Frei both injured, Ottmar Hitzfeld's team had a huge mountain to climb against a side entering its 50th World Cup finals match with 33 wins in their last 34 internationals.

Spain had seven starters from the UEFA EURO 2008 final, with injured English Premier League duo Fernando Torres and Cesc Fàbregas only making it on to the bench. It was obvious straight away that Switzerland's sole strategy was to sit back in their defensive banks and absorb pressure. Vicente del Bosque's side seemed happy initially to join in with this we-attack-you-defend contest but as time wore on and they struggled to make any inroads, a certain anxiety began to creep in. Although David Villa looked lively, the only clear-cut chance Spain created in a goalless first half – the ninth in the competition's first 16 matches – fell to defender Gerard Piqué, who, having received Andrés Iniesta's smart pass and evaded his marker with a sharp turn, saw his shot saved by the leg of goalkeeper Diego Benaglio.

Shock goal

Switzerland's defending was more than admirable, but they barely crossed the halfway line, so it was an enormous shock when, on 52 minutes, they took the lead with their first meaningful attack. It was a shambolic goal from Spain's perspective, with bodies all over the place as Gelson Fernandes bundled the ball home from close range at the end of a move started from a hopeful long punt from the back. Now

2010 FIFA WORLD CUP

Spain were in big trouble. Their attacks intensified, but Benaglio was in brilliant form and they appeared to be out of luck, too, as Iniesta shot narrowly wide and Xabi Alonso crashed a superb shot against the the crossbar. Incredibly, Switzerland almost made it 2-0 on 74 minutes when Eren Derdiyok struck the inside of the post after some bewitching footwork. Spain kept probing patiently in their familiar style, but they lacked penetration and variation. By the last few minutes they had run out of ideas and Switzerland, with one of the biggest shocks in World Cup history, had not only beaten Spain for the first time but had done it with a record-equalling fifth successive clean sheet at the World Cup finals.

Next up for Hitfeld's side was Chile in Port Elizabeth. Another attack-against-defence encounter loomed, and when Behrami, back from injury, was red-carded on 31 minutes by an over-zealous Saudi Arabian referee who had already brandished four yellows, that was exactly what it became. It was no less intriguing for it, though, as Chile, with Sánchez again prominent, attempted to use their pace and energy to deconstruct the Swiss rearguard. The Udinese Calcio forward thought he had scored early in the second half before discovering – about 30 seconds later - that a team-mate had been flagged for offside. Sánchez also drew a majestic save from Benaglio, who in so doing helped to take his team past the 67-minute

mark without conceding, which enabled Switzerland to break Italy's World Cup record of 549 minutes without conceding a goal.

Eight minutes later, however, just as Chile appeared to have given up hope of a breakthrough, they scored. A tight offside call went their way, enabling Esteban Paredes to cross to the far post where his fellow substitute Mark González headed the ball down and in to give the South Americans the lead. The goal sparked a frantic flurry of activity in the final 15 minutes, with Paredes fluffing two golden opportunities to make it 2-0 and Derdiyok, with almost the last kick of the game, sliding a shot wide with the goal at his mercy.

Villa on target

Chile's second win was not the result Spain wanted as they took the field later that evening at Ellis Park. It effectively left them having to win their last two games to remain in the competition. Fortunately their next opponents were Honduras, and sure enough Del Bosque's side would tear into the Central Americans in the same manner as Chile. Spain took the lead on 17 minutes when David Villa, who had earlier struck the crossbar, cut in from his left-wing station and picked out the top corner with a sweeping right-foot shot. Fernando Torres, who had taken Villa's central berth

Switzerland midfielder Gelson Fernandes falls over goalkeeper Iker Casillas as he stabs in the winning goal against Spain

after returning from injury, was uncharacteristically off target with two simple chances within the space of a few seconds, but the European champions sealed the game with a deflected second from Villa just after the interval. The FC Barcelona-bound striker should have completed his hat-trick when Jesús Navas was upended in the area but slid his penalty wide of the post. Many more chances were created and spurned as the mismatch drew to its conclusion. The final score of 2-0 was very flattering to Honduras. Had Spain's finishing been more clinical, they could have reached double figures.

A much sterner test awaited Spain in Pretoria four nights later. Chile, with six points already in the bag, needed one more to secure top place in the group, whereas Spain could only be certain of progress with a victory. Furthermore, if Switzerland simultaneously

David Villa (right) celebrates with team-mate Xavi after putting Spain ahead against Chile

overcame already eliminated Honduras by two goals, then one of Chile and Spain would be out.

With no South American side having yet suffered a defeat in the competition – after 14 matches – and Chile starting the game with a fierce determination to make sure that they would not become the first, Spain were up against it. Unfortunately for Bielsa's team, their lively start could not be sustained, and after David Villa had punished a terrible error from Chile's goalkeeper-captain Claudio Bravo with a brilliant first-time lob from the left touchline, their response to conceding their first goal of the tournament was to lose their discipline. Enthusiasm turned to recklessness and they were lucky to have 11 men on the pitch before Marco Estrada was expelled for clipping Fernando Torres in the build-up to a second goal for Spain, clinically despatched by Iniesta from Villa's pull-back. Estrada might have been given the benefit of doubt that his collision with the Liverpool FC striker was accidental had he not already tested the referee's patience with two lunging fouls. Ponce, already booked and out of the next game, should have joined him in the changing-room after a malicious stamp on Xabi Alonso just before half-time.

Good news

As Spain went in at the interval to lick their wounds, they could reflect gleefully on being two goals up without really playing. The good news for Chile was that Switzerland had failed to score against Honduras, and their plight was eased further when, two minutes after the interval, they scored themselves, half-time substitute Rodrigo Millar taking just two minutes to make his mark as his shot, with a big deflection off Piqué's knee, soared past Iker Casillas. And that, pretty much, was that. For the rest of the match both teams seemed happy with their lot and just passed the ball around among themselves with one ear on what was happening in Bloemfontein. The answer was not a lot. Though outstanding in defence, the Swiss were ineffective in attack. Indeed, it was Honduras who had the better second-half chances, David Suazo glancing a simple header wide before Álvarez was denied by a magnificent one-handed save from the consistently excellent Benaglio.

And so, with the scores unchanged, Switzerland – despite their fine defence and that historic win against Spain – were on their way home, while Chile and Spain progressed, the latter as group winners thanks to their superior goal difference. Although they played only half a game in Pretoria, it was fair to say that the two most attractive teams in Group H were going through.

2010 FIFA WORLD CUP

Group H Results

16/6/10, Mbombela, Nelspruit
Honduras 0-1 Chile
Attendance: 32664
Honduras: Valladares; Mendoza, Chávez, Figueroa, Izaguirre; W. Palacios, Guevara (Thomas 66); Álvarez, Núñez (Martínez 78), Espinoza; Pavón (Welcome 60). Coach: Alexis Mendoza (COL)
Chile: Bravo; Isla, Medel, Ponce, Vidal (Contreras 81); Carmona, Millar (Jara 52); Fernández; Sánchez, Valdivia (González 87), Beausejour. Coach: Marcelo Bielsa (ARG)
Goal(s): 0-1 Beausejour 34
Yellow Card(s): Carmona 4 (Chile), Fernández 19 (Chile), W. Palacios 33 (Honduras)
Referee: Maillet (SEY)

16/6/10, Moses Mabhida, Durban
Spain 0-1 Switzerland
Attendance: 62453
Spain: Casillas; Sergio Ramos, Piqué, Puyol, Capdevila; Xabi Alonso, Busquets (Fernando Torres 61); David Silva (Jesús Navas 62); Xavi, Iniesta (Pedro 77); David Villa. Coach: Vicente del Bosque (ESP)
Switzerland: Benaglio; Lichtsteiner, Senderos (Von Bergen 36), Grichting, Ziegler; Barnetta (Eggimann 90+2), Huggel, Inler, Fernandes; Derdiyok (Yakin 79); Nkufo. Coach: Ottmar Hitzfeld (GER)
Goal(s): 0-1 Fernandes 52
Yellow Card(s): Grichting 30 (Switzerland), Ziegler 73 (Switzerland), Benaglio 90+1 (Switzerland), Yakin 90+4 (Switzerland)
Referee: Webb (ENG)

21/6/10, Nelson Mandela Bay, Port Elizabeth
Chile 1-0 Switzerland
Attendance: 34872
Chile: Bravo; Medel, Ponce, Jara; Isla, Carmona, Vidal (González 46); Fernández (Paredes 65); Sánchez, Suazo (Valdivia 46), Beausejour. Coach: Marcelo Bielsa (ARG)
Switzerland: Benaglio; Lichtsteiner, Von Bergen, Grichting, Ziegler; Behrami, Inler, Huggel, Fernandes (Bunjaku 77); Frei (Barnetta 42); Nkufo (Derdiyok 68). Coach: Ottmar Hitzfeld (GER)
Goal(s): 1-0 González 75
Red Card(s): Behrami 31 (Switzerland)
Yellow Card(s): Suazo 2 (Chile), Nkufo 18 (Switzerland), Carmona 22 (Chile), Ponce 25 (Chile), Barnetta 48 (Switzerland), Fernández 60 (Chile), Inler 60 (Switzerland), Medel 61 (Chile), Valdivia 90+2 (Chile)
Referee: Al Ghamdi (KSA)

21/6/10, Ellis Park, Johannesburg
Spain 2-0 Honduras
Attendance: 54386
Spain: Casillas; Sergio Ramos (Arbeloa 77), Piqué, Puyol, Capdevila; Xabi Alonso, Busquets; Jesús Navas, Xavi (Fàbregas 66), David Villa; Fernando Torres (Mata 70). Coach: Vicente del Bosque (ESP)
Honduras: Valladares; Mendoza, Chávez, Figueroa, Izaguirre; W. Palacios, Guevara; Martínez, Turcios (Núñez 63), Espinoza (Welcome 46); Suazo (Je. Palacios 84). Coach: Reinaldo Rueda (COL)
Goal(s): 1-0 David Villa 17, 2-0 David Villa 51
Yellow Card(s): Turcios 8 (Honduras), Izaguirre 38 (Honduras)
Referee: Nishimura (JPN)

25/6/10, Loftus Versfeld, Pretoria
Chile 1-2 Spain
Attendance: 41958
Chile: Bravo; Medel, Ponce, Jara; Isla, Estrada, Vidal; González (Millar 46); Sánchez (Orellana 65), Valdivia (Paredes 46), Beausejour. Coach: Marcelo Bielsa (ARG)

David Suazo of Honduras

Spain: Casillas; Sergio Ramos, Piqué, Puyol, Capdevila; Xabi Alonso (Javi Martínez 73), Busquets; Iniesta, Xavi, David Villa; Fernando Torres (Fàbregas 55). Coach: Vicente del Bosque (ESP)
Goal(s): 0-1 David Villa 24, 0-2 Iniesta 37, 1-2 Millar 47
Red Card(s): Estrada 38 (Chile)
Yellow Card(s): Medel 15 (Chile), Ponce 19 (Chile), Estrada 21 (Chile), Estrada 37 (Chile)
Referee: Rodríguez (MEX)

25/6/10, Free State, Bloemfontein
Switzerland 0-0 Honduras
Attendance: 28042
Switzerland: Benaglio; Lichtsteiner, Von Bergen, Grichting, Ziegler; Barnetta, Huggel (Shaqiri 78), Inler, Fernandes (Yakin 46); Derdiyok; Nkufo (Frei 69). Coach: Ottmar Hitzfeld (GER)
Honduras: Valladares; Sabillón, Chávez, Bernárdez, Figueroa; W. Palacios, Thomas; Álvarez, Núñez (Martínez 67); Je. Palacios (Welcome 78), Suazo (Turcios 87). Coach: Reinaldo Rueda (COL)
Yellow Card(s): Thomas 4 (Honduras), Fernandes 34 (Switzerland), Suazo 58 (Honduras), Chávez 64 (Honduras), W. Palacios 89 (Honduras)
Referee: Baldassi (ARG)

Group H Table

	Pld	W	D	L	F	A	Pts
1 Spain	3	2	0	1	4	2	6
2 Chile	3	2	0	1	3	2	6
3 Switzerland	3	1	1	1	1	1	4
4 Honduras	3	0	1	2	0	3	1

ROUND OF 16

The knockout phase of the 2010 FIFA World Cup was notable in featuring all five of the South American participants but, disappointingly for the host continent, just one of the original six from Africa. Europe took six of its 13 teams forward, but with all of them drawn together, only three could advance to the quarter-finals. Asia and CONCACAF completed the line-up with two teams apiece.

The first of the eight matches brought together Uruguay and South Korea in Port Elizabeth. The Group A winners had yet to concede a goal and had not lost in five previous meetings with their Asian adversaries. It was South Korea who supplied the game's first moment of excitement, when Park Chu-young smacked a free-kick against the post, but Uruguay, three minutes later, who opened the scoring, Luis Suárez tucking the ball home first time from a tight angle as the Korean defence was caught napping from Diego Forlán's teasing low cross from the left.

Pouring rain

Although the first half was even, Uruguay began to retreat into their defensive shell as the rain poured down in the second period, allowing South Korea to make most of the running. Park Chu-young blasted a good chance over and a Park Ji-sung header brought a decent save from Fernando Muslera before the South Americans' defence was finally breached, Lee Chung-yong nodding in on 68 minutes after Uruguay failed to clear their lines and Muslera found himself in no man's land.

Uruguay came alive again as an attacking force in the closing stages and were rewarded on 80 minutes when the ever-dangerous Suárez curled in a beautiful right-foot shot off the inside of the far post to restore his team's lead. Another big chance fell to South Korea before the end, but substitute Lee Dong-gook snatched at his shot and the danger was averted. As South Korea departed with their heads held high, Uruguay proceeded into their first World Cup quarter-final for 40 years.

Later that evening, in Rustenburg, the United States took on Ghana in a repeat of the 2006 group game that the Black Stars had won 2-1 in Nuremberg to become their continent's only representatives in the last 16. Now here they were again carrying Africa's

hopes alone. With their group-stage goal tally consisting of just two penalties, the 2010 Africa Cup of Nations runners-up clearly had more to give, and they proved that just five minutes in when Kevin-Prince Boateng, a new recruit since that tournament in Angola, put his team ahead with a sumptuous goal, stealing possession in the centre circle before racing forward and steering a measured left-foot shot past Tim Howard.

Chasing the game

For the third time in four matches the United States were behind early and having to chase the game. They had come back against England and Slovenia and managed to do so again, their efforts rewarded just past the hour when Clint Dempsey was fouled in the area by Jonathan Mensah and Landon Donovan, with his third goal in as many games, converted the penalty – albeit off the inside of the post. The excitement now intensified, with the Americans, spurred on by inspirational midfielder Michael Bradley, pressing particularly hard for a winner.

The goal did not come, though, so the tournament had its first period of extra time. That was a positive portent for Ghana as Africa's only two previous quarter-finalists – Cameroon in 1990 and Senegal in 2002 – had both won their last-16 games in extra time, and, sure enough, just three minutes of additional play

Match-winner Asamoah Gyan in action for Ghana against the United States

had elapsed before Milovan Rajevac's team regained the lead, Asamoah Gyan winning a footrace with American captain Carlos Bocanegra before smashing the ball left-footed past Howard. It would prove to be the decisive action of the game. The USA strove valiantly to find a reply, especially in the dying seconds, but, much to the delight of the locals, the Ghanaian defence held firm through to the finish.

The first of the three all-European ties took place the following afternoon in Bloemfontein as old rivals Germany and England came face to face for the first time at the World Cup finals since their epic 1990 semi-final. Both teams had needed 1-0 wins in their final group game to reach the knockout phase, and the respective coaches, Joachim Löw and Fabio Capello, both stuck with the same formations and personnel that had seen them through those matches, the only change to either side being the return to the German attack, after suspension, of Miroslav Klose.

Klose strikes

With 20 minutes gone, the World Cup veteran's value was clear for all to see as he exploited a large hole in the England defence – and hesitation from goalkeeper David James – to latch on to a long punt upfield from Manuel Neuer, outmuscle his marker and slide his shot inside the post. It was his 50th international goal and 12th at the World Cup finals, and, ominously for England, Germany had never lost a match in which he had scored. Capello's ragged team certainly didn't look like overturning this one as the fluid passing and movement of the German midfielders carved them apart, creating another chance for Klose, which James saved, and a second goal, driven in low by Lukas Podolski, despite a poor first touch that narrowed his angle, after he arrived unmarked into the area on the left.

Outplayed and overrun, England needed to gain a foothold fast. Frank Lampard forced a good save from Neuer as he ran in to meet a James Milner cross, and two minutes later poor German defending allowed Matthew Upson to reduce the deficit with a firm header from Steven Gerrard's free-kick. Now, suddenly, Germany were on the back foot, and with their massive support urging them on, England struck again, Lampard picking up a loose ball just outside the area and firing in a superb dipping shot that beat Neuer and struck the underside of the bar before bouncing over the line. To England's absolute horror, though, neither the Uruguayan referee nor his assistant saw fit to award the goal. It was an aberration that beggared belief, the ball having landed so far behind the line that the decision was not even contentious. Yet, as the two

Miroslav Klose (right) evades Thomas Müller's embrace after opening the scoring against England with his 50th goal for Germany

teams trooped off at half-time, the scoreboard indicated that Germany were still 2-1 ahead. England had 45 minutes in which to right the wrong.

Not surprisingly, it was England who started the second half on the attack. The unfortunate Lampard smashed another shot against the bar from a free-kick, but this time it skimmed over the top. Their frustration mounting, the Three Lions began to over-commit players forward, and Germany made them pay – not once but twice as Thomas Müller finished off two brilliant counterattacks, the first set up by Bastian Schweinsteiger, the second by Mesut Özil, to put his team 4-1 up and kill the contest stone dead with 20 minutes still to go. England's lack of tactical nous had been brutally exposed, and as one last hope of a late fightback was dashed with Neuer's brilliant one-handed save from Gerrard, Germany cantered home in cruise control. Had Lampard's goal counted, the outcome might have been different, but before and after that turning point Germany had been as ruthlessly efficient as ever and the better of the two teams by some margin. So, as England, one of the pre-tournament favourites, were left to digest elimination and a heaviest ever World Cup defeat, Germany marched confidently on into the quarter-finals.

Repeat encounter

There would be more controversy in the fourth quarter-final later that evening as Argentina took on Mexico at Soccer City in a repeat of their 2006 last-16 clash. The Mexicans were eager to avenge that 2-1 extra-time defeat and made a bold, bright start, but on 26 minutes they fell behind to a goal that should not have been given, Carlos Tévez receiving Lionel Messi's chip forward in a clear offside position – with not even one opposing player between him and the goal – before heading it in. Mexico were still cursing their luck when Argentina went 2-0 up seven minutes later, Gonzalo Higuaín exploiting an error by Ricardo Osorio before finishing with skill and composure to take his tournament tally to four goals and move to the top of the Golden Boot standings.

The game having swung on Tévez's first goal, it was settled by his second – a sensational right-foot strike from distance that was still gaining in speed as it soared past the helpless Óscar Pérez into the top corner. Thirty-eight minutes remained, but there was no way back for Mexico. To their credit they took the game to Argentina and created several openings before Javier Hernández scored a goal almost as

Carlos Tévez lets fly with a thunderous shot to put Argentina 3-0 up against Mexico

spectacular as Tévez's second, turning brilliantly and lifting a powerful left-foot shot high into the net, but there was too much ground to make up and so for the fifth World Cup in succession Mexico had to endure elimination at the last-16 stage, while Argentina, for whom Messi had a disturbingly quiet game, progressed with their fourth win out of four.

The Netherlands also had a 100 per cent record to maintain as they took on Slovakia in Durban. Firm favourites to do so despite Slovakia's heroics against Italy, the Oranje were boosted by the return to the starting line-up of Arjen Robben, and he was to make an early impact, putting his team 1-0 up after 18 minutes with a goal so familiar from his repertoire that the opposing defenders should really have seen it coming. Gathering a long pass on the right wing, he cut inside on to his favoured left foot and rifled a low shot past goalkeeper Ján Mucha.

Superb saves

The Slovakia 'keeper was forced to make two superb stops – from Robben and Joris Mathijsen – to deny the Dutch a second goal early in the second half, but his opposite number Maarten Stekelenburg was no less influential, pulling off two equally fine saves in quick succession – from Miroslav Stoch and Róbert Vittek – as Slovakia finally put together a decent attack. Although the eastern Europeans had their moments in an increasingly absorbing second half, the Netherlands deserved the second goal that came their way when Sneijder drove home Dirk Kuyt's square pass following a quickly taken free-kick. Vittek converted a penalty to make it 2-1, but as it was with the very last kick of the game, the striker's fourth goal of the competition was sure to be his last.

The Netherlands' quarter-final opponents would be South American, but they had to wait until later that day to discover whether it would be Brazil or Chile. The odds favoured the former, who had not only slayed their opponents 4-1 at France 98, but had also defeated them home and away in qualifying. Furthermore, Chile had three players suspended, including key defenders Waldo Ponce and Gary Medel.

Once again Marcelo Bielsa's side promised much with their quick, enterprising play but in Brazil they found an opponent that knew their style and knew how to defeat it, and by the end of the 90 minutes Dunga's side had delivered their most impressive performance of the tournament, both in attack and defence, providing rich entertainment for the Ellis Park crowd in a comprehensive 3-0 win.

2010 FIFA WORLD CUP

Brazil take control

Brazil assumed control with two goals in three first-half minutes. Defender Juan, exceptional all evening, powered in the first with a firm header from Maicon's corner. The second came from a more familiar source as Luís Fabiano rounded off a swashbuckling counterattack involving Robinho and Kaká with a classic goalpoacher's finish. The game was wrapped up with a fine first-time strike from Robinho after a forceful run from the halfway line by Ramires, who had been selected in place of the injured Felipe Melo. The SL Benfica midfielder had an impressive game but would spoil it with a yellow card for a foul on Alexis Sánchez that ruled him out of the quarter-final.

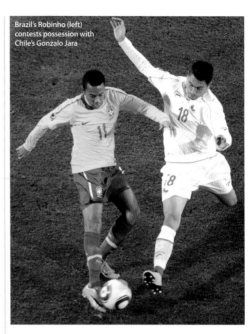

Brazil's Robinho (left) contests possession with Chile's Gonzalo Jara

The first six of the second-round ties had delivered drama and entertainment aplenty, but the seventh, between Paraguay and Japan, was even more lifeless than some of the tournament's early encounters. Neither of the two countries had reached the World Cup quarter-finals before, and the prospect of making history seemed to fill both sets of players with utter dread. The consequence was two turgid hours of emptiness, during which defences were totally on top and barely a goalscoring opportunity of note was created. The inevitable penalty shoot-out – the first of the competition – finally brought some meaningful action, and it was Paraguay who prevailed, scoring from all five of their spot-kicks – the last of them, coolly and decisively, from Óscar Cardozo – as Japan, fatally, missed one of theirs, full-back Yuichi Komano proving to be the fall-guy as he struck the third of his team's efforts against the crossbar. With that, Asia's interest in the competition ended as Paraguay became the fourth South American side to progress.

The round of 16 was concluded by its third all-European clash, between Iberian rivals Spain and Portugal. It was their first World Cup finals meeting, and although Portugal were the outsiders, they had yet to concede a goal at the tournament and were looking to make it 20 successive games without defeat. Spain marked the second anniversary of their UEFA EURO 2008 triumph by fielding the same XI that had started against Chile, with Xabi Alonso passed fit for a team that had gone through the entire group stage without picking up a yellow card.

Counterattack threat

Spain started the stronger, with Fernando Torres and David Villa (twice) forcing fine early saves from Eduardo, but although La Roja made the play in their customary style, pressing Portugal back into their own half, the ability of Carlos Queiroz's side to strike on the counterattack offered menace, with Tiago and Cristiano Ronaldo both forcing unconvincing saves from an edgy-looking Iker Casillas. At half-time Queiroz was definitely winning the tactical battle against the man he replaced as Real Madrid CF coach in 2003, Vicente del Bosque, but in the second half the tide turned.

Having failed to score when they had their chance, Portugal began to fade as an attacking force, with Ronaldo cutting an increasingly isolated and frustrated figure up front. Del Bosque took off Fernando Torres, and almost immediately his replacement, Fernando Llorente, brought another fabulous save from Eduardo. The Portugal goalkeeper seemed unbeatable, but three minutes later he finally conceded. Xavi's flick sent in David Villa on the left, and although Eduardo saved the prolific striker's first effort, he had no chance with his second as it scooped over him and into the net via the underside of the bar. A goal to the good, Spain ran the game from there on in. Although they were unable to bolster their lead – not least because of more brilliance from Eduardo – their monopoly of possession prevented Portugal from making any inroads at the other end. A late red card for Ricardo Costa added to Portugal's woes as Spain, with their third successive victory and Villa's fourth goal of the tournament, moved ominously forward into the quarter-finals.

First Knockout Round Results

26/6/10, Nelson Mandela Bay, Port Elizabeth
Uruguay 2-1 South Korea
Attendance: 30597
Uruguay: Muslera; Maxi Pereira, Lugano, Godín (Victorino 46); Fucile; Diego Pérez, Arévalo, Álvaro Pereira (Lodeiro 74); Forlán; Cavani, Suárez (Á. Fernández 84). Coach: Óscar Tabárez (URU)
South Korea: Jung Sung-ryong; Cha Du-ri, Cho Yong-hyung, Lee Jung-soo, Lee Young-pyo; Ki Sung-yong (Yeom Ki-hun 85), Kim Jung-woo; Kim Jae-sung (Lee Dong-gook 61), Park Ji-sung, Lee Chung-yong; Park Chu-young. Coach: Huh Jung-moo (KOR)
Goal(s): 1-0 Suárez 8, 1-1 Lee Chung-yong 68, 2-1 Suárez 80
Yellow Card(s): Kim Jung-woo 38 (South Korea), Cha Du-ri 69 (South Korea), Cho Yong-hyung 83 (South Korea)
Referee: Stark (GER)

26/6/10, Royal Bafokeng, Rustenburg
United States 1-2 Ghana (aet)
Attendance: 32976
United States: Howard; Cherundolo, DeMerit, Bocanegra, Bornstein; Donovan, Bradley, Clark (Edu 31), Dempsey; Altidore (Gomez 91), Findley (Feilhaber 46). Coach: Bob Bradley (United States)
Ghana: Kingson; Pantsil, Jonathan Mensah, John Mensah, Sarpei (Addy 73); Annan; Inkoom (Muntari 113), Asamoah, K. Boateng (Appiah 78), A. Ayew; Gyan. Coach: Milovan Rajevac (SRB)
Goal(s): 0-1 K. Boateng 5, 1-1 Donovan 62 (p), 1-2 Gyan 93
Yellow Card(s): Clark 7 (United States), Cherundolo 18 (United States), Jonathan Mensah 61 (Ghana), Bocanegra 68 (United States), A. Ayew 90+2 (Ghana)
Referee: Kassai (HUN)

27/6/10, Free State, Bloemfontein
Germany 4-1 England
Attendance: 40510
Germany: Neuer; Lahm, Mertesacker, Friedrich, Boateng; Khedira, Schweinsteiger; Müller (Trochowski 72), Özil (Kiessling 83), Podolski; Klose (Gómez 72). Coach: Joachim Löw (GER)
England: James; Johnson (Wright-Phillips 87), Terry, Upson, A. Cole; Milner (J. Cole 64), Lampard, Barry, Gerrard; Defoe (Heskey 71), Rooney. Coach: Fabio Capello (ITA)
Goal(s): 1-0 Klose 20, 2-0 Podolski 32, 2-1 Upson 37, 3-1 Müller 67, 4-1 Müller 70
Yellow Card(s): Friedrich 47 (Germany), Johnson 81 (England)
Referee: Larrionda (URU)

27/6/10, Soccer City, Johannesburg
Argentina 3-1 Mexico
Attendance: 84377
Argentina: Romero; Otamendi, Demichelis, Burdisso, Heinze; Mascherano; Maxi Rodríguez (Pastore 87), Di María (Gutiérrez 79); Messi (Agüero 69), Higuaín. Coach: Diego Maradona (ARG)
Mexico: Pérez; Juárez, Osorio, Rodríguez, Salcido; Márquez, Torrado; Giovani, Bautista (Barrera 46), Guardado (Franco 61); Hernández. Coach: Javier Aguirre (MEX)
Goal(s): 1-0 Tévez 26, 2-0 Higuaín 33, 3-0 Tévez 52, 3-1 Hernández 71
Yellow Card(s): Márquez 28 (Mexico)
Referee: Rosetti (ITA)

28/6/10, Moses Mabhida, Durban
Netherlands 2-1 Slovakia
Attendance: 61962
Netherlands: Stekelenburg; Van der Wiel, Heitinga, Mathijsen, Van Bronckhorst; Van Bommel, De Jong; Robben (Elia 71), Sneijder (Afellay 90+2), Kuyt; Van Persie (Huntelaar 80). Coach: Bert van Marwijk (NED)
Slovakia: Mucha; Pekarík, Škrteľ, Ďurica, Zabavník (Jakubko 88); Kucka, Stoch, Hamšík (Sapara 87), Weiss, Jendrišek (Kopúnek 71); Vittek. Coach: Vladimír Weiss (SVK)
Goal(s): 1-0 Robben 18, 2-0 Sneijder 84, 2-1 Vittek 90+4 (p)
Yellow Card(s): Robben 31 (Netherlands), Kucka 40 (Slovakia), Kopúnek 72 (Slovakia), Škrteľ 84 (Slovakia), Stekelenburg 90+3 (Netherlands)
Referee: Undiano Mallenco (ESP)

Óscar Cardozo is congratulated by goalkeeper Justo Villar after scoring the decisive spot-kick in Paraguay's penalty shoot-out victory over Japan

28/6/10, Ellis Park, Johannesburg
Brazil 3-0 Chile
Attendance: 54096
Brazil: Júlio César; Maicon, Lúcio, Juan, Michel Bastos; Gilberto Silva, Ramires; Dani Alves, Kaká (Kléberson 81), Robinho (Gilberto 85); Luís Fabiano (Nilmar 76). Coach: Dunga (BRA)
Chile: Bravo; Jara, Fuentes, Contreras (Tello 46), Isla (Millar 62); Carmona, Vidal; Beausejour; Sánchez, Suazo, González (Valdivia 46). Coach: Marcelo Bielsa (ARG)
Goal(s): 1-0 Juan 35, 2-0 Luís Fabiano 38, 3-0 Robinho 59
Yellow Card(s): Kaká 30 (Brazil), Vidal 47 (Chile), Fuentes 68 (Chile), Ramires 72 (Brazil), Millar 80 (Chile)
Referee: Webb (ENG)

29/6/10, Loftus Versfeld, Pretoria
Paraguay 0-0 Japan (aet; 5-3 on pens)
Attendance: 36742
Paraguay: Villar; Bonet, Da Silva, Alcaraz, Morel; Ortigoza (É. Barreto 75); Vera, Riveros, Santa Cruz (Cardozo 94); Barrios, Benítez (Valdez 60). Coach: Gerardo Martino (ARG)
Japan: Kawashima; Komano, Nakazawa, Tulio Tanaka, Nagatomo; Abe (K. Nakamura 81); Hasebe, Endo; Matsui (Okazaki 65), Okubo, Honda. Coach: Takeshi Okada (JPN)
Penalties: 1-0 É. Barreto; 1-1 Endo; 2-1 Barrios; 2-2 Hasebe; 3-2 Riveros; 4-2 Valdez; 4-3 Honda; 5-3 Cardozo
Yellow Card(s): Matsui 58 (Japan), Nagatomo 72 (Japan), Honda 90+3 (Japan), Endo 113 (Japan), Riveros 118 (Paraguay)
Referee: De Bleeckere (BEL)

29/6/10, Green Point, Cape Town
Spain 1-0 Portugal
Attendance: 62955
Spain: Casillas; Sergio Ramos, Piqué, Puyol, Capdevila; Xabi Alonso (Marchena 90+3), Busquets; Iniesta, Xavi, David Villa (Pedro 88); Fernando Torres (Llorente 58). Coach: Vicente del Bosque (ESP)
Portugal: Eduardo; Ricardo Costa, Ricardo Carvalho, Bruno Alves, Fábio Coentrão; Tiago, Pepe (Pedro Mendes 72), Raul Meireles; Cristiano Ronaldo, Hugo Almeida (Danny 58), Simão (Liedson 72). Coach: Carlos Queiroz (POR)
Goal(s): 1-0 David Villa 63
Red Card(s): Ricardo Costa 89 (Portugal)
Yellow Card(s): Xabi Alonso 74 (Spain), Tiago 80 (Portugal)
Referee: Baldassi (ARG)

QUARTER-FINALS

The quarter-final line-up was a case of South America against the world, with the prospect of all four semi-finalists coming from the region for the first time in FIFA World Cup history.

The continent's standard-bearers, five-time winners Brazil, were the first of the quartet into action as they took on the Netherlands in Port Elizabeth. With the Oranje having gone 23 games unbeaten and won all 12 of their World Cup fixtures under Bert van Marwijk, Dunga and his players knew they had a formidable obstacle to overcome. Another challenge was the uneven playing surface in the Nelson Mandela Bay stadium – far and away the poorest of all the World Cup pitches.

Defence carved open

The Oranje had yet to concede in open play during their four games in South Africa, but it took just ten minutes for Brazil to carve them open and take the lead as Robinho raced on to Felipe Melo's measured pass through a gaping hole in the centre of the Dutch defence before confidently clipping the ball past Maarten Stekelenburg. Although Kaká was a peripheral figure early on, he suddenly emerged at the end of a sumptuous move to force a wonderful flying save from Stekelenburg, and there was more work for the Dutch 'keeper just before half-time as he tipped Maicon's shot wide at the end of a sweeping move reminiscent of the one that produced Brazil's famous fourth goal in the 1970 World Cup final.

But if Brazil were dominant during the first half, they carelessly allowed their opponents back into the game early in the second period when a free-kick floated in from the right by Wesley Sneijder – awarded for a bad foul on Arjen Robben by Michel Bastos – was misjudged by the normally ultra-reliable Júlio César. As the goalkeeper came out to collect, he bumped into Felipe Melo, who inadvertently deflected the ball with his head into the net. It was a goal out of nothing for the Netherlands, who had hardly conjured up a worthwhile attack to that point. Dani Alves and Kaká put decent chances wide as Brazil attempted to restore order to the scoreline, but there was more defensive disaster to come soon afterwards as Sneijder, generously credited with the first goal, scored again, glancing in a header flicked on by Dirk Kuyt from a routine Robben corner.

At 2-1 down and with their World Cup hopes hanging by a thread, Brazil now had to show what they were made

Wesley Sneijder (No10) gives the Netherlands the lead against Brazil with a close-range header

of. But instead of calmly regrouping, they completely lost the plot. Felipe Melo kicked and stamped on Robben, giving the Japanese referee no option but to send him off, and with their reduced numbers they could find no way back. Indeed, the Dutch should have finished them off with a third goal, but errant finishing by Robin van Persie, Kuyt and, in the last seconds, Klaas Jan Huntelaar let them off the hook. Not that it mattered. With their fifth win in a row, the Netherlands were through to the semi-finals while Brazil, vanquished by their own defensive negligence and indiscipline, were out.

Adopted team

Most of the spectators in the Soccer City stadium were hoping for more South American suffering in the day's evening game between Uruguay and Ghana. The Black Stars had been adopted by the South Africans in an act of continental brotherhood, but as the only group runners-up to have reached the last eight, they went into the game as slight underdogs in their bid to become Africa's first World Cup semi-finalists.

Uruguay made much the brighter start, with star strikers Diego Forlán and Luis Suárez especially menacing, but after the Celeste lost skipper Diego Lugano to injury Ghana began to take charge. Kevin-Prince Boateng was especially prominent, superbly setting up Asamoah Gyan for the best chance of the first half, which the big striker wasted, before trying an acrobatic overhead kick that flashed just over. The half-time interval was imminent when Sulley Ali Muntari, making his first start of the tournament, tried his luck from 35 metres. It seemed an overly speculative strike but, with goalkeeper Fernando Muslera unsighted, found its target, giving Ghana an unlikely but spectacular lead.

Within ten minutes of the restart, however, Uruguay were level, Forlán curling in a superb free-kick from the left that deceived Ghana goalkeeper Richard Kingson with its deadly combination of power, accuracy and swerve. It was the striker's fourth World Cup finals goal, all of them against African opposition. Having taken the captain's armband from the departed Lugano, Forlán led his team by example and for the remainder of the 90 minutes Uruguay were the superior side, but despite Forlán's best efforts they could not find a winner and the contest continued into extra time.

Last-kick agony

Uruguay might have had a penalty when John Pantsil caught substitute Sebastián Abreu, but Ghana survived that scare and came on strong in the second extra

Luis Suárez uses his hands to keep out Dominic Adiyiah's header in the last minute of the Uruguay-Ghana quarter-final

period. Gyan and Boateng both went close before, in the very last minute, a goalmouth scramble led to young Dominic Adiyiah sending in a header that Suárez deliberately kept out on the line with his hands. It was an instinctive reaction - perhaps understandable in the circumstances – but it was also an illegal infringement that not only brought the striker a red card but also gave Ghana a penalty with what was the last kick of the game. Up stood Gyan, a man with two successful penalty kicks in the tournament already. The whole of Africa willed him to score, but the pressure was too much and he smashed his kick wildly against the bar.

It was not all over for Ghana. They still had the shoot-out, and courageously Gyan came up to take their first kick, which he converted superbly to level Forlán's opener. However, two of Gyan's team-mates – John Mensah and Adiyiah – could not emulate him, and with only Maxi Pereira missing for Uruguay, the decisive kick fell to Abreu, who, with an audacious chip, sent his country into the semi-finals, destroying the African dream in the process.

In a repeat of the Berlin quarter-final of 2006, Argentina re-encountered Germany in Cape Town. The two teams had met in the countdown to South Africa, with Diego Maradona's side overcoming Joachim Löw's men 1-0 in Munich. The tournament's two top-scoring teams were both at full strength and in form, and there appeared little to choose between them. However, with just two minutes and 40 seconds on the clock Germany drew first blood, Thomas Müller glancing in Bastian

Schweinsteiger's inswinging free-kick, and from that moment on the European side were in control.

Argentina struggle

Argentina's attempts to equalise were, as ever, largely dependent on Lionel Messi, but Germany were far too organised to allow the FC Barcelona maestro a free ride, and although they enjoyed plenty of possession, the South Americans threatened only intermittently, struggling to carve out clear chances. In fact, Miroslav Klose should have doubled Germany's lead when set up by Müller midway through the first half. Throughout the second period – as against England - Germany were happy to protect their lead with contain-and-counter tactics, and once again they bore fruit.

As Argentina, increasingly frustrated, despatched greater numbers forward, Germany pounced. On 68 minutes Klose had the simplest of tap-ins to make it 2-0 after Müller and Lukas Podolski set him up, and not long afterwards a wonderful jinking run to the byline by the outstanding Schweinsteiger allowed defender Arne Friedrich to finish off the contest with a third goal. The best was saved till last, though, as one minute from time Podolski sent Özil clear on the left with a superb through-ball, and the little playmaker's perfectly flighted cross was met with an equally exquisite volleyed finish

Argentina's Lionel Messi (No10) is crowded out by German opponents in Cape Town

from Klose. It was a goal that oozed quality. It put Klose just one shy of Brazilian striker Ronaldo's all-time World Cup record of 15 goals, it gave Germany their third four-goal win of the tournament, and it also took them into their record 11th World Cup semi-final. For Argentina, Messi and Maradona, though, the tournament was over.

Ellis Park staged the fourth of the quarter-finals, with Spain heavily tipped to complete a hat-trick of European wins over South America. Paraguay had been poor against Japan, and none of their strikers had yet scored, but in the first half against the European champions they were unquestionably the better team. Spain could not get their passing game going at all, surrendering possession with alarming and unusual frequency, and Paraguay should really have capitalised. But after a debatable offside decision had denied Nélson Haedo Valdez, it remained 0-0 at the interval.

Penalty drama

The removal of the completely out-of-form Fernando Torres had worked for Spain against Portugal, but no sooner had he been replaced by Cesc Fàbregas than Paraguay were awarded a penalty as Gerard Piqué hauled down Óscar Cardozo. The big striker, who had struck the winning spot-kick against Japan, looked much less composed this time and his weak effort was easily saved by Iker Casillas. If that was bad for Paraguay, things immediately got worse as Spain raced up to the other end and were awarded a penalty themselves as David Villa went down under a challenge from Antolín Alcaraz. Xabi Alonso converted it but was then asked to retake it because of encroachment. Amazingly, his second effort was saved, but as Justo Villar moved to his left to push the ball to safety, he connected only with the legs of Fàbregas. Luckily for Paraguay, the officials were unsighted, so there was no fourth spot-kick..

After that whirlwind activity Spain finally began to impose themselves, and after putting the Paraguayan defence under their first sustained spell of pressure, they scored. Once again it was David Villa, with his fifth goal in four games, who emerged as Spain's saviour. As against Portugal, though, he required the intervention of the woodwork – the inside of both posts, in fact – before his right-foot shot eventually settled in the net. Paraguay still had a chance to level but the curse on their strikers continued as Roque Santa Cruz's 89th-minute effort struck Casillas's outstretched leg. That was the end of the road for Gerardo Martino's side. Ironically they had produced their best performance of the tournament, and Spain their worst, but it was the Europeans not the South Americans who made it through to their first World Cup semi-final.

Iker Casillas saves Óscar Cardozo's penalty to help Spain defeat Paraguay

Quarter-Final Results

2/7/10, Nelson Mandela Bay, Port Elizabeth
Netherlands 2-1 Brazil
Attendance: 40186
Netherlands: Stekelenburg; Van der Wiel, Heitinga, Ooijer, Van Bronckhorst; Van Bommel, De Jong; Robben, Sneijder, Kuyt; Van Persie (Huntelaar 85). Coach: Bert van Marwijk (NED)
Brazil: Júlio César; Maicon, Lúcio, Juan, Michel Bastos (Gilberto 62); Felipe Melo, Gilberto Silva; Dani Alves, Kaká, Robinho; Luís Fabiano (Nilmar 77). Coach: Dunga (BRA)
Goal(s): 0-1 Robinho 10, 1-1 Sneijder 53, 2-1 Sneijder 68
Red Card(s): Felipe Melo 73 (Brazil)
Yellow Card(s): Heitinga 14 (Netherlands), Michel Bastos 37 (Brazil), Van der Wiel 47 (Netherlands), De Jong 64 (Netherlands), Ooijer 76 (Netherlands)
Referee: Nishimura (JPN)

2/7/10, Soccer City, Johannesburg
Uruguay 1-1 Ghana (aet; 4-2 on pens)
Attendance: 84017
Uruguay: Muslera; Maxi Pereira, Lugano (Scotti 38), Victorino, Fucile; Diego Pérez, Arévalo, Á. Fernández (Lodeiro 46); Forlán; Cavani (Abreu 76), Suárez. Coach: Óscar Tabárez (URU)
Ghana: Kingson; Pantsil, Vorsah, John Mensah, Sarpei; Annan; Inkoom (Appiah 74), Asamoah, K. Boateng, Muntari (Adiyiah 88); Gyan. Coach: Milovan Rajevac (SRB)
Goal(s): 0-1 Muntari 45+2, 1-1 Forlán 55
Penalties: 1-0 Forlán; 1-1 Gyan; 2-1 Victorino; 2-2 Appiah; 3-2 Scotti; 4-2 Abreu
Red Card(s): Suárez 120+1 (Uruguay)
Yellow Card(s): Fucile 20 (Uruguay), Arévalo 48 (Uruguay), Pantsil 54 (Ghana), Diego Pérez 59 (Uruguay), Sarpei 77 (Ghana), John Mensah 93 (Ghana)
Referee: Olegário Benquerença (POR)

3/7/10, Green Point, Cape Town
Argentina 0-4 Germany
Attendance: 64100
Argentina: Romero; Otamendi (Pastore 70), Demichelis, Burdisso, Heinze; Mascherano; Maxi Rodríguez, Di María (Agüero 75); Messi; Higuaín, Tévez. Coach: Diego Maradona (ARG)
Germany: Neuer; Lahm, Mertesacker, Friedrich, Boateng (Jansen 72); Khedira (Kroos 77), Schweinsteiger; Müller (Trochowski 84), Özil, Podolski; Klose. Coach: Joachim Löw (GER)
Goal(s): 0-1 Müller 3, 0-2 Klose 68, 0-3 Friedrich 74, 0-4 Klose 89
Yellow Card(s): Otamendi 11 (Argentina), Müller 35 (Germany), Mascherano 80 (Argentina)
Referee: Irmatov (UZB)

3/7/10, Ellis Park, Johannesburg
Paraguay 0-1 Spain
Attendance: 55359
Paraguay: Villar; Verón, Da Silva, Alcaraz, Morel; V. Cáceres (Barrios 84); É. Barreto (Vera 64), Santana, Riveros; Valdez (Santa Cruz 72), Cardozo. Coach: Gerardo Martino (ARG)
Spain: Casillas; Sergio Ramos, Piqué, Puyol (Marchena 84), Capdevila; Xabi Alonso (Pedro 75), Busquets; Iniesta, Xavi, David Villa; Fernando Torres (Fàbregas 56). Coach: Vicente del Bosque (ESP)
Goal(s): 0-1 David Villa 83
Yellow Card(s): Piqué 57 (Spain), Alcaraz 59 (Paraguay), V. Cáceres 59 (Paraguay), Busquets 63 (Spain), Morel 71 (Paraguay), Santana 88 (Paraguay)
Referee: Batres (GUA)

SEMI-FINALS

Uruguay's penalty shoot-out victory over Ghana had saved South America from a quarter-final wipeout, but now Óscar Tabárez's side were the only team that could prevent Europe from claiming its first FIFA World Cup victory on foreign soil.

Both Uruguay and their opponents in Cape Town, the Netherlands, came into the semi-final without key players. While the Celeste were missing injured captain Diego Lugano as well as suspended pair Jorge Fucile and Luis Suárez, the Oranje were forced to make changes at right-back and central midfield to cover the suspensions of, respectively, Gregory van der Wiel and Nigel de Jong.

Captains strike

There was a disappointingly dull and lifeless start to the game, but it perked up on 18 minutes when Oranje skipper Giovanni van Bronckhorst unleashed a stunning left-foot strike from all of 40 metres that flew past Fernando Muslera's outstretched hand into the top corner. It was an exceptional strike, but it was accompanied by little else of note from Bert van

Marwijk's side in the remainder of the half, and on 41 minutes their lack of ambition was punished when Uruguay drew level with another fabulous left-footed strike from their captain, Diego Forlán, his swerving snapshot deceiving Maarten Stekelenburg and bringing him a fourth goal of the competition.

Both sides had their chances to score in an even third quarter, but it was the Netherlands who eventually restored their lead on 70 minutes as Sneijder, with his fifth goal of the tournament, squeezed in a speculative low shot that narrowly missed the ankles of Robin van Persie, who was standing in an offside position. There was some substance to Uruguay's claim that the Arsenal FC striker was interfering with play, but the referee from Uzbekistan allowed the goal to stand. There was nothing controversial about the goal the Oranje scored three minutes later to make it 3-1, Arjen Robben planting a header into the bottom corner of Muslera's net from Dirk Kuyt's measured left-wing cross. Curiously, as with the Netherlands' two previous goals, the ball went in via the inside of the post.

Robben should have made it 4-1 when sent clean through by Van Persie with four minutes to go, but he got his attempt at a chip horribly wrong. It didn't seem

Giovanni van Bronckhorst is ecstatic after his long-range screamer puts the Netherlands in front against Uruguay

Arjen Robben (left) heads in to put the Netherlands 3-1 up

World Cup semi-final full of confidence. Villa nearly scored his sixth goal of the tournament as Pedro slid him in with an exquisite pass after six minutes, and Carles Puyol should have done better than head Andrés Iniesta's firmly driven cross over the bar. Germany, as expected, sat back and allowed Spain to dictate the tempo, but while that was intrinsically a negative tactic, the quality of football from both teams was exceptionally high. With the Hungarian referee allowing the game to flow and the two teams helping him out by not committing fouls, the game simmered nicely. The only element it lacked was pace, with Spain's build-up play, though attractive and ornate, rather too slow and over-elaborate at times to trouble the well organised German defence.

Germany were refused a penalty just before half-time when Mesut Özil appeared to have his legs clipped by Sergio Ramos, but it was Spain who became stronger after the interval, with Xavi and Iniesta increasingly asserting their midfield authority. More and more shots began to rain in on Manuel Neuer's goal, and after the Germany 'keeper had made an excellent save from Pedro, he was lucky to see Iniesta's follow-up flash across goal just fractionally ahead of David Villa's outstretched foot. When Spain finally did score a goal, on 73 minutes, it was laced with heavy irony – firstly

too important at the time, but when Maxi Pereira pulled a goal back for Uruguay in stoppage time with a low curling drive, the last few minutes became tense and anxious for the Dutch, and the final whistle was greeted more with relief than elation at reaching their first World Cup final in 32 years. Uruguay, committed to the last, had enjoyed an excellent tournament, with Forlán immense, but, for their impressive second-half performance and a sixth victory on the trot, the Netherlands deserved their place in the final.

EURO final re-match

The following evening, Germany faced Spain in an eagerly awaited encounter in Durban. It was a repeat of the UEFA EURO 2008 final in Vienna, which Spain had won 1-0, but the match-winner from that game, Fernando Torres, was predictably dropped by Vicente del Bosque after his poor displays against Portugal and Paraguay. Less predictable was his replacement, the inexperienced Pedro Rodríguez, who was preferred to both Fernando Llorente and Cesc Fàbregas and thus raised to six the number of FC Barcelona players in the team – seven including new summer signing David Villa. Germany, having put four goals past both England and Argentina, would have fielded an unchanged side but for the suspension that deprived them of four-goal Thomas Müller. Piotr Trochowski was introduced instead for his first start.

Although Spain had struggled past Paraguay and scored only six goals to Germany's 13, they began their first

Andrés Iniesta of Spain holds off Germany's Toni Kroos

2010 FIFA WORLD CUP

Spain defender Carles Puyol (No5) flings himself forward to head the winning goal against Germany

because it arrived just as Germany were starting to look dangerous themselves, substitute Toni Kroos wasting their first clear opening with a tame sidefoot finish that Iker Casillas easily saved, and secondly because it came from a routine set piece, Xavi's corner from the left being met with a well-timed leap and thumping header from Puyol.

Spain march on

As ever, Spain were at their best when in front. The replacement of Villa by Fernando Torres seemed a gamble at the time, but Germany were not given a sniff of a chance to equalise. In contrast, Spain should have made the game safe when Pedro, sent clear by Xavi's majestic pass, opted to go alone rather than square to Torres, standing all alone in the centre. Iniesta was guilty too of trying to walk the ball into the net, but it was all academic. Germany were down and out. Their contain-and-counter tactics had worked against England and Argentina, but Spain were too clever, too comfortable and confident in possession to fall into their trap. Thanks to their best performance of the tournament, the European champions were through to the final – an all-European final against the Netherlands.

Semi-Final Results

6/7/10, Green Point, Cape Town
Uruguay 2-3 Netherlands
Attendance: 62479
Uruguay: Muslera; Maxi Pereira, Victorino, Godín, Cáceres; Arévalo; Diego Pérez, Gargano, Álvaro Pereira (Abreu 78); Forlán (S. Fernández 84), Cavani. Coach: Óscar Tabárez (URU)
Netherlands: Stekelenburg; Boulahrouz, Heitinga, Mathijsen, Van Bronckhorst; Van Bommel, De Zeeuw (Van der Vaart 46); Robben (Elia 89), Sneijder, Kuyt; Van Persie, Coach: Bert van Marwijk (NED)
Goal(s): 0-1 Van Bronckhorst 18, 1-1 Forlán 41, 1-2 Sneijder 70, 1-3 Robben 73, 2-3 Maxi Pereira 90+2
Yellow Card(s): Maxi Pereira 21 (Uruguay), Cáceres 29 (Uruguay), Sneijder 29 (Netherlands), Boulahrouz 78 (Netherlands), Van Bommel 90+5 (Netherlands)
Referee: Irmatov (UZB)

7/7/10, Moses Mabhida, Durban
Germany 0-1 Spain
Attendance: 60960
Germany: Neuer; Lahm, Mertesacker, Friedrich, Boateng (Jansen 52); Khedira (Gómez 81), Schweinsteiger; Trochowski (Kroos 62), Özil, Podolski; Klose. Coach: Joachim Löw (GER)
Spain: Casillas; Sergio Ramos, Piqué, Puyol, Capdevila; Xabi Alonso (Marchena 90+3), Busquets; Pedro (David Silva 86), Xavi, Iniesta; David Villa (Fernando Torres 81). Coach: Vicente del Bosque (ESP)
Goal(s): 0-1 Puyol 73
Referee: Kassai (HUN)

THIRD PLACE PLAY-OFF

The third place play-off may not be to everyone's taste, but it is a FIFA World Cup tradition and, with the pressure off, can often produce an excellent game full of goals and entertainment. That was precisely what happened in Port Elizabeth as Germany came from behind to defeat Uruguay 3-2 and claim the bronze medals for the second tournament in succession.

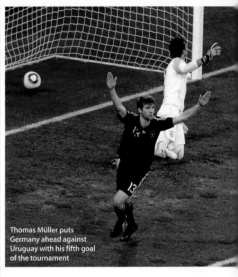

Thomas Müller puts Germany ahead against Uruguay with his fifth goal of the tournament

Both coaches took the fixture seriously, fielding strong teams, although there was disappointment for Miroslav Klose, just one goal short of Ronaldo's all-time World Cup finals scoring record but not considered fit enough to play. That also scuppered his chances of winning back-to-back World Cup Golden Boots, but the trophy did go to another German, his team-mate Thomas Müller, who returned from suspension to open the scoring with his fifth goal of the tournament, slotting in the rebound after Bastian Schweinsteiger's shot was only partially saved by Fernando Muslera.

Spectacular volley

Schweinsteiger was at fault for Uruguay's equaliser, ceding possession and enabling Luis Suárez to play in Edinson Cavani, but there was nothing Germany could do to prevent a majestic second goal for the South Americans, drilled in spectacularly on the volley by Diego

Forlán from Egidio Arévalo's right-wing cross. It was also Forlán's fifth goal of the competition, and although he lost the Golden Boot to Müller on the assists count, his strike was voted Goal of the Tournament and he would also leave South Africa in possession of the Golden Ball – the prize accorded to the World Cup's best player.

Forlán's last act of the World Cup was to strike Germany's crossbar with a free-kick. Had it gone in, he would probably have added the Golden Boot to his collection and certainly taken the game into extra time. But it missed and so Germany, who had came back to lead with headed goals from Marcell Jansen and Sami Khedira, the latter eight minutes from the end, ensured that for the second successive World Cup the top three places would be filled by teams from Europe.

Third Place Play-Off Result

10/7/10, Nelson Mandela Bay, Port Elizabeth
Uruguay 2-3 Germany
Attendance: 36007
Uruguay: Muslera; Fucile, Lugano, Godín, Cáceres; Maxi Pereira, Diego Pérez (Gargano 77), Arévalo, Cavani (Abreu 88); Suárez, Forlán. Coach: Óscar Tabárez (URU)
Germany: Butt; Boateng, Mertesacker, Friedrich, Aogo; Khedira, Schweinsteiger; Müller, Özil (Tasci 90+1), Jansen (Kroos 81); Cacau (Kiessling 73). Coach: Joachim Löw (GER)
Goal(s): 0-1 Müller 19, 1-1 Cavani 28, 2-1 Forlán 51, 2-2 Jansen 56, 2-3 Khedira 82
Yellow Card(s): Aogo 5 (Germany), Cacau 7 (Germany), Diego Pérez 61 (Uruguay), Friedrich 90+2 (Germany)
Referee: Archundia (MEX)

Diego Forlán celebrates his spectacular strike against Germany

FINAL

One outcome from the 19th FIFA World Cup final was guaranteed. There would be a new name on the trophy, the first since France in 1998 and the first from a non-host nation since 40 years before that when Brazil triumphed for the first time in Sweden.

Remarkably, in all their years of major tournament combat, including a combined total of 97 World Cup finals matches, the paths of Spain and the Netherlands had never crossed. Their only previous competitive encounters had been two qualifying ties for the 1984 UEFA European Championship, in which they registered one home win apiece. Now here they were contesting the biggest, most important football match of them all.

In-form teams

With Spain having won 50 of their previous 54 matches and the Netherlands unbeaten in their last 25, there could be no disputing that the world's two most in-form and consistent teams had reached the final. Furthermore, they were the only two of the participating teams in South Africa who had qualified with an unblemished record.

The results and the statistics were impressive, but it was fair to say that neither team had provided exceptional quality or entertainment en route to the Soccer City showpiece. Vicente del Bosque's team, though always seeking to make the play, had struggled to turn their fancy possession football into goals, while Bert van Marwijk's side, despite the odd moment of individual brilliance, had largely been functional and pragmatic. What the whole world wanted was for it all to come together in the final, for the two teams to raise their game and deliver performances worthy of the occasion, for the last and the most important game of the tournament to also be the best. Unfortunately, it was not to be.

The match started promisingly enough, particularly for Spain, with Sergio Ramos's bullet header from Xavi's free-kick bringing a fine save from Maarten Stekelenburg and David Villa volleying just wide, but before long the match had deteriorated into a fractious, low-quality spectacle in which referee Howard Webb's patience was severely and repeatedly tested by a succession of fouls - some just niggly and annoying, others dangerous and violent. The Dutch were the main offenders, with their defensive midfield pair Mark van Bommel and Nigel de Jong seemingly on a pre-planned mission to apply a wrecking ball to Spain's much-vaunted midfield. By half-time Webb had been forced to remove the yellow card from his pocket five times. It was perhaps only the magnitude of the occasion that had held him back from producing the red.

Spain's Sergio Ramos heads a good chance over the bar in the World Cup final against the Netherlands

Robben denied

Amidst all the aggression there was not much opportunity for quality football or indeed goalmouth action. Joris Mathijsen contrived to miss the ball completely when it fell invitingly to him in the area, and at the other end Pedro drove a decent effort wide, but the game was over an hour old before the first clear-cut chance arrived. It fell to the Netherlands, and it was created by a majestic defence-splitting pass from their player of the tournament, Wesley Sneijder. Its recipient was Arjen Robben, who raced clean through on goal but, with just Iker Casillas to beat, put his left-foot shot fractionally too close to the goalkeeper's body, allowing the Spanish captain to deflect the ball wide with his right foot.

Spurred into action by that almighty scare, Spain intensified their attacking efforts and finally began to put the Dutch goal under concerted pressure. David Villa looked certain to score as he was found at the far post, but a fantastic last-ditch block by John Heitinga catapulted the ball to safety. Then Sergio Ramos rose unmarked at a corner and, with World Cup glory at his mercy, sent a simple header over the bar. He nearly had double cause to regret his profligacy because soon afterwards Robben was back up the other end causing more panic in the Spanish defence, allowing Casillas to save at his feet when he might have gone down following a slight challenge from behind. The excitement was building, but frustratingly there was nobody on the field who could apply that final touch of quality to break the deadlock, and so at 0-0 the final carried on into extra time.

The game was crying out for a hero, but the fear was that he would not emerge until the penalty shoot-out. Spain, as in all of their previous games, got stronger the longer the game went on, and that continued into the first period of extra time, where they created four clear chances to the Netherlands' one, the best of them falling to substitute Cesc Fàbregas, who, like Robben before him, was unable to win his one-on-one duel with the goalkeeper, shooting timidly with his left foot after Iniesta had sent him through.

Moment of truth

The red card that had been threatened for so long was finally brandished four minutes into the second extra period when Heitinga, already cautioned, pulled back Iniesta on the edge of the area. Xavi sent the ensuing free-kick harmlessly over the bar, but the Dutch could ill afford a shortage of numbers and with 116 minutes on the clock, just after the Netherlands had been denied a clear corner from a deflected Sneijder free-kick, Spain broke upfield and worked the ball to Fàbregas, who, seeing Iniesta free of attention just inside the right-hand side of the area, served him with a finely measured pass. It was Spain's moment of truth and the little midfielder seized it with aplomb, crashing his right-foot shot firmly and decisively across Stekelenburg and into the net.

The goal of deliverance had finally arrived, and fittingly it went to Spain. There was no way back for the Dutch. Their long winning run was over. Their crude tactics had failed to pay off. The glory instead was Spain's. The European champions were now the world champions. They had been the better, more positive team in a poor

Arjen Robben (right) is denied by Iker Casillas as the Netherlands go close to taking the lead

2010 FIFA WORLD CUP

Andrés Iniesta shapes to shoot and score Spain's winning goal

Final Result

11/7/10, Soccer City, Johannesburg
Netherlands 0-1 Spain (aet)
Attendance: 84490
Netherlands: Stekelenburg; Van der Wiel, Heitinga, Mathijsen, Van Bronckhorst (Braafheid 105); Van Bommel, De Jong (Van der Vaart 99); Robben, Sneijder, Kuyt (Elia 71); Van Persie. Coach: Bert van Marwijk (NED)
Spain: Casillas; Sergio Ramos, Piqué, Puyol, Capdevila; Xabi Alonso (Fàbregas 87), Busquets; Pedro (Jesús Navas 60), Xavi, Iniesta; David Villa (Fernando Torres 106), Coach: Vicente del Bosque (ESP)
Goal(s): 0-1 Iniesta 116
Red Card(s): Heitinga 109 (Netherlands)
Yellow Card(s): Van Persie 15 (Netherlands), Puyol 16 (Spain), Van Bommel 22 (Netherlands), Sergio Ramos 23 (Spain), De Jong 28 (Netherlands), Van Bronckhorst 54 (Netherlands), Heitinga 57 (Netherlands), Capdevila 67 (Spain), Robben 84 (Netherlands), Heitinga 109 (Netherlands), Van der Wiel 111 (Netherlands), Mathijsen 117 (Netherlands), Iniesta 118 (Spain), Xavi 120+1 (Spain)
Referee: Webb (ENG)

TOP GOALSCORERS

5   Thomas MÜLLER (Germany)
    Wesley SNEIJDER (Netherlands)
    DAVID VILLA (Spain)
    Diego FORLÁN (Uruguay)

4   Gonzalo HIGUAÍN (Argentina)
    Miroslav KLOSE (Germany)
    Róbert VITTEK (Slovakia)

3   LUÍS FABIANO (Brazil)
    Asamoah GYAN (Ghana)
    Landon DONOVAN (United States)
    Luis SUÁREZ (Uruguay)

Thomas Müller

game, completely outplaying their opponents in extra time. In the tournament as a whole, they had scored only eight goals in seven matches, and had even lost the first of them, but they had been the most consistently creative side on show, the most cultured 'footballing' team by far. The FIFA World Cup was Spain's at last, and they lifted the most treasured trophy in the game as proud and worthy winners.

2010 FIFA World Cup winners Spain lift the trophy in Johannesburg

GROUP A

SOUTH AFRICA

SOUTH AFRICAN
FOOTBALL ASSOCIATION

		DoB	Aps (s)	Gls	Club
Goalkeepers					
1	Moeneeb JOSEPHS	19/5/80	1 (1)		Orlando Pirates
16	Itumeleng KHUNE	20/6/87	2		Kaizer Chiefs
22	Shu-Aib WALTERS	26/12/81			Maritzburg Utd.
Defenders					
2	Siboniso GAXA	6/4/84	2 (1)		Mamelodi Sundowns
3	Tsepo MASILELA	5/5/85	2 (1)		M. Haifa (ISR)
4	Aaron MOKOENA	25/11/80	3		Portsmouth (ENG)
5	Calvin Anele NGCONGCA	20/10/87	1		Genk (BEL)
14	Matthew BOOTH	14/3/77			Mamelodi Sundowns
15	Lucas THWALA	19/10/81	1		Orlando Pirates
20	Bongani KHUMALO	6/1/87	3	1	SuperSport Utd.
21	Siyabonga SANGWENI	29/9/81			Golden Arrows
Midfielders					
6	MacBeth SIBAYA	25/11/77	1		Rubin (RUS)
7	Lance DAVIDS	11/4/85			Ajax Cape Town
8	Siphiwe TSHABALALA	25/9/84	3	1	Kaizer Chiefs
10	Steven PIENAAR	17/3/82	3		Everton (ENG)
11	Teko MODISE	22/12/82	2 (1)		Orlando Pirates
12	Reneilwe LETSHOLONYANE	9/6/82	2		Kaizer Chiefs
13	Kagisho DIKGACOI	24/11/84	2		Fulham (ENG)
19	Surprise MORIRI	20/3/80	(1)		Mamelodi Sundowns
23	Thanduyise KHUBONI	23/5/86	1		Golden Arrows
Forwards					
9	Katlego MPHELA	29/11/84	3	1	Mamelodi Sundowns
17	Bernard PARKER	16/3/86	1 (1)		Twente (NED)
18	Siyabonga NOMVETHE	2/12/77	(1)		Moroka Swallows

MEXICO

		DoB	Aps (s)	Gls	Club
Goalkeepers					
1	Óscar PÉREZ	1/2/73	4		Jaguares
13	Guillermo OCHOA	13/7/85			América
23	Luis Ernesto MICHEL	21/7/79			Chivas
Defenders					
2	Francisco RODRÍGUEZ	20/10/81	4		PSV (NED)
3	Carlos SALCIDO	2/4/80	4		PSV (NED)
4	Rafael MÁRQUEZ	13/2/79	4	1	Barcelona (ESP)
5	Ricardo OSORIO	30/3/80	4		Stuttgart (GER)
15	Héctor MORENO	17/1/88	2		AZ (NED)
19	Jonny MAGALLÓN	21/11/81			Chivas
Midfielders					
6	Gerardo TORRADO	30/4/79	4		Cruz Azul
8	Israel CASTRO	20/12/80	(1)		Pumas UNAM
12	Paul AGUILAR	6/3/86	1		Pachuca
16	Efraín JUÁREZ	22/2/88	3		Pumas UNAM
18	Andrés GUARDADO	28/9/86	2 (1)		Deportivo (ESP)
20	Jorge TORRES	16/1/88			Atlas
21	Adolfo BAUTISTA	15/5/79	1		Chivas
Forwards					
7	Pablo BARRERA	21/6/87	(3)		Pumas UNAM
9	Guillermo FRANCO	3/11/76	3 (1)		West Ham (ENG)
10	Cuauhtémoc BLANCO	17/1/73	1 (2)	1	Veracruz
11	Carlos VELA	1/3/89	2		Arsenal (ENG)
14	Javier HERNÁNDEZ	1/6/88	1 (3)	2	Chivas
17	GIOVANI dos Santos	11/5/89	4		Galatasaray (TUR)
22	Alberto MEDINA	29/5/83			Chivas

URUGUAY

		DoB	Aps (s)	Gls	Club
Goalkeepers					
1	Fernando MUSLERA	16/6/86	7		Lazio (ITA)
12	Juan CASTILLO	17/4/78			Deportivo Cali (COL)
23	Martín SILVA	25/3/83			Defensor Sporting
Defenders					
2	Diego LUGANO	2/11/80	6		Fenerbahçe (TUR)
3	Diego GODÍN	16/2/86	5		Villarreal (ESP)
4	Jorge FUCILE	19/11/84	5		Porto (POR)
6	Mauricio VICTORINO	11/10/82	4 (1)		Univ. de Chile (CHI)
16	MAXI PEREIRA	8/6/84	7	1	Benfica (POR)
19	Andrés SCOTTI	14/12/75	(2)		Colo-Colo (CHI)
22	Martín CÁCERES	7/4/87	2		Juventus (ITA)
Midfielders					
5	Walter GARGANO	23/7/84	1 (2)		Napoli (ITA)
8	Sebastián EGUREN	8/1/81	(1)		AIK (SWE)
11	ÁLVARO PEREIRA	28/11/85	5		Porto (POR)
14	Nicolás LODEIRO	21/3/89	(3)		Ajax (NED)
15	DIEGO PÉREZ	18/5/80	7		Monaco (FRA)
17	Egidio ARÉVALO Ríos	1/1/82	7		Peñarol
18	Ignacio GONZÁLEZ	14/5/82	1		Levadiakos (GRE)
20	Álvaro FERNÁNDEZ	11/10/85	1 (3)		Univ. de Chile (CHI)
Forwards					
7	Edinson CAVANI	14/2/87	6	1	Palermo (ITA)
9	Luis SUÁREZ	24/1/87	6	3	Ajax (NED)
10	Diego FORLÁN	19/5/79	7	5	Atlético (ESP)
18	Sebastián ABREU	17/10/76	(4)		Botafogo (BRA)
21	Sebastián FERNÁNDEZ	23/5/85	(2)		Banfield (ARG)

FRANCE

		DoB	Aps (s)	Gls	Club
Goalkeepers					
1	Hugo LLORIS	26/12/86	3		Lyon
16	Steve MANDANDA	28/3/85			Marseille
23	Cédric CARRASSO	30/12/81			Bordeaux
Defenders					
2	Bacary SAGNA	14/2/83	3		Arsenal (ENG)
3	Éric ABIDAL	11/9/79	2		Barcelona (ESP)
4	Anthony RÉVEILLÈRE	10/11/79			Lyon
5	William GALLAS	17/8/77	3		Arsenal (ENG)
6	Marc PLANUS	7/3/82			Bordeaux
13	Patrice EVRA	15/5/81	2		Man. United (ENG)
17	Sébastien SQUILLACI	11/8/80	1		Sevilla (ESP)
22	Gaël CLICHY	26/7/85	1		Arsenal (ENG)
Midfielders					
7	Franck RIBÉRY	7/4/83	3		Bayern (GER)
8	Yoann GOURCUFF	11/7/86	2		Bordeaux
14	Jérémy TOULALAN	10/9/83	2		Lyon
18	Florent MALOUDA	13/6/80	1 (2)	1	Chelsea (ENG)
19	Alou DIARRA	15/7/81	1		Bordeaux
19	Abou DIABY	11/5/86	3		Arsenal (ENG)
20	Mathieu VALBUENA	28/9/84	(1)		Marseille
Forwards					
9	Djibril CISSÉ	12/8/81	1		Panathinaikos (GRE)
10	Sidney GOVOU	27/7/79	2 (1)		Lyon
11	André-Pierre GIGNAC	5/12/85	1 (2)		Toulouse
12	Thierry HENRY	17/8/77	(2)		Barcelona (ESP)
21	Nicolas ANELKA	14/3/79	2		Chelsea (ENG)

2010 FIFA WORLD CUP

GROUP B

ARGENTINA

NIGERIA

	DoB	Aps	(s)	Gls	Club
Goalkeepers					
Diego POZO	16/2/78				Atlético Colón
21 Mariano ANDÚJAR	30/7/83				Catania (ITA)
12 Sergio ROMERO	22/2/87	5			AZ (NED)
Defenders					
2 Martín DEMICHELIS	20/12/80	5		1	Bayern (GER)
4 Clemente RODRÍGUEZ	31/7/81	1			Estudiantes
8 Nicolás BURDISSO	12/4/81	3	(2)		Roma (ITA)
6 Gabriel HEINZE	19/4/78	4		1	Marseille (FRA)
12 Ariel GARCÉ	14/7/79				Atlético Colón
13 Walter SAMUEL	23/3/78	2			Inter (ITA)
15 Nicolás OTAMENDI	12/2/88	3			Vélez Sársfield
17 Jonás GUTIÉRREZ	5/7/83	2	(1)		Newcastle (ENG)
Midfielders					
5 Mario Ariel BOLATTI	17/2/85	1	(1)		Fiorentina (ITA)
7 Ángel DI MARÍA	14/2/88	4	(1)		Benfica (POR)
8 Juan Sebastián VERÓN	9/3/75	2	(1)		Estudiantes
10 Lionel MESSI	24/6/87	5			Barcelona (ESP)
14 Javier MASCHERANO	8/6/84	4			Liverpool (ENG)
20 MAXI RODRÍGUEZ	2/1/81	4			Liverpool (ENG)
23 Javier PASTORE	20/6/89		(3)		Palermo (ITA)
Forwards					
9 Gonzalo HIGUAÍN	10/12/87	4		4	Real Madrid (ESP)
11 Carlos TÉVEZ	5/2/84	4		2	Man. City (ENG)
16 Sergio AGÜERO	2/6/88	1	(2)		Atlético (ESP)
18 Martín PALERMO	7/11/73		(1)	1	Boca Juniors
19 Diego MILITO	12/6/79	1	(1)		Inter (ITA)

	DoB	Aps	(s)	Gls	Club
Goalkeepers					
1 Vincent ENYEAMA	29/8/82	3			H. Tel-Aviv (ISR)
16 Austin EJIDE	8/4/84				H. Petach-Tikva (ISR)
23 Bamidele AIYENUGBA	20/11/83				Bnei Yehuda (ISR)
Defenders					
2 Joseph YOBO	6/9/80	3			Everton (ENG)
3 Taye TAIWO	16/4/85	2			Marseille (FRA)
5 Rabiu AFOLABI	18/4/80	1	(1)		Salzburg (AUT)
6 Danny SHITTU	2/9/80	3			Bolton (ENG)
17 Chidi ODIAH	17/12/83	3			CSKA Moskva (RUS)
21 Uwa ECHIÉJILÉ	20/1/88		(2)		Rennes (FRA)
22 Ayodele ADELEYE	25/12/88				Sparta (NED)
Midfielders					
4 Nwankwo KANU	1/8/76	1			Portsmouth (ENG)
12 Kalu UCHE	15/11/82	2	(1)	2	Almería (ESP)
13 Ayila YUSSUF	4/11/84	1			Dynamo Kyiv (UKR)
14 Sani KAITA	2/5/86	2			Alania (RUS)
15 Lukman HARUNA	4/12/90	2			Monaco (FRA)
20 Dickson ETUHU	8/6/82	3			Fulham (ENG)
Forwards					
7 John UTAKA	8/1/82				Portsmouth (ENG)
8 YAKUBU Aiyegbeni	22/11/82	3		1	Everton (ENG)
9 Obafemi MARTINS	28/10/84		(2)		Wolfsburg (GER)
10 Ideye Aide BROWN	10/10/88				Sochaux (FRA)
11 Peter ODEMWINGIE	15/7/81	1	(1)		Lokomotiv Moskva (RUS)
18 Victor OBINNA	25/3/87	1	(1)		Málaga (ESP)
19 Chinedu OBASI	1/6/86	2	(1)		Hoffenheim (GER)

SOUTH KOREA

GREECE

	DoB	Aps	(s)	Gls	Club
Goalkeepers					
1 LEE Woon-jae	26/4/73				Suwon Bluewings
18 JUNG Sung-ryong	4/1/85	4			Seongnam Ilhwa Chunma
21 KIM Young-kwang	28/6/83				Ulsan Hyundai
Defenders					
2 OH Beom-seok	29/7/84	1			Ulsan Hyundai
3 KIM Hyung-il	27/4/84				Pohang Steelers
4 CHO Yong-hyung	3/11/83	4			Jeju Utd.
12 LEE Young-pyo	23/4/77	4			Al-Hilal (KSA)
14 LEE Jung-soo	8/1/80	4		2	Kashima Antlers (JPN)
15 KIM Dong-jin	29/1/82		(1)		Ulsan Hyundai
22 CHA Du-ri	25/7/80	3			Freiburg (GER)
23 KANG Min-soo	14/2/86				Suwon Bluewings
Midfielders					
5 KIM Nam-il	14/3/77		(3)		Tom (RUS)
6 KIM Bo-kyung	6/10/89				Oita Trinita (JPN)
7 PARK Ji-sung	25/2/81	4		1	Man. United (ENG)
8 KIM Jung-woo	9/5/82	4			Gwangju Sangmu
13 KIM Jae-sung	3/10/83	1	(2)		Pohang Steelers
16 KI Sung-yong	24/1/89	4			Celtic (SCO)
17 LEE Chung-yong	2/7/88	4		2	Bolton (ENG)
19 YEOM Ki-hun	30/3/83	3	(1)		Suwon Bluewings
Forwards					
9 AHN Jung-hwan	27/1/76				Dalian Shide (CHN)
10 PARK Chu-young	10/7/85	4		1	Monaco (FRA)
11 LEE Seung-yeoul	6/3/89		(1)		Seoul
20 LEE Dong-gook	29/4/79		(2)		Jeonbuk Motors

	DoB	Aps	(s)	Gls	Club
Goalkeepers					
1 Kostas CHALKIAS	30/5/74				PAOK
12 Alexandros TZORVAS	12/8/82	3			Panathinaikos
13 Mihail SIFAKIS	9/9/84				Aris
Defenders					
2 Giourkas SEITARIDIS	4/6/81	1			Panathinaikos
3 Christos PATSATZOGLOU	19/3/79		(2)		Omonia (CYP)
4 Nikolaos SPIROPOULOS	10/10/83		(1)		Panathinaikos
5 Vangelis MORAS	26/8/81	1			Bologna (ITA)
8 Avraam PAPADOPOULOS	3/12/84	3			Olympiacos
11 Loukas VINTRA	5/2/81	3			Panathinaikos
15 Vassilis TOROSIDIS	10/6/85	3		1	Olympiacos
16 Sotirios KYRGIAKOS	23/7/79	2			Liverpool (ENG)
19 Sokratis PAPASTATHOPOULOS	9/6/88	2			Genoa (ITA)
22 Stilianos MALEZAS	11/3/85				PAOK
Midfielders					
6 Alexandros TZIOLIS	13/2/85	3			Siena (ITA)
10 Georgios KARAGOUNIS	6/3/77	3			Panathinaikos
18 Sotirios NINIS	3/4/90		(2)		Panathinaikos
21 Kostas KATSOURANIS	21/6/79	3			Panathinaikos
23 Athanasios PRITTAS	9/1/79				Aris
Forwards					
7 Georgios SAMARAS	21/2/85	2	(1)		Celtic (SCO)
9 Angelos CHARISTEAS	9/2/80	1			Nürnberg (GER)
14 Dimitris SALPINGIDIS	18/8/81	1	(1)	1	Panathinaikos
17 Theofanis GEKAS	23/5/80	2			Hertha (GER)
20 Pantelis KAPETANOS	8/6/83		(1)		Steaua (ROU)

GROUP C

  ### ENGLAND

		DoB	Aps (s)	Gls	Club
Goalkeepers					
1	David JAMES	1/8/70	3		Portsmouth
12	Robert GREEN	18/1/80	1		West Ham
23	Joe HART	19/4/87			Birmingham
Defenders					
2	Glen JOHNSON	23/8/84	4		Liverpool
3	Ashley COLE	20/12/80	4		Chelsea
5	Michael DAWSON	18/11/83			Tottenham
6	John TERRY	7/12/80	4		Chelsea
13	Stephen WARNOCK	12/12/81			Aston Villa
15	Matthew UPSON	18/4/79	2	1	West Ham
18	Jamie CARRAGHER	28/1/78	1	(1)	Liverpool
20	Ledley KING	12/10/80	1		Tottenham
Midfielders					
4	Steven GERRARD	30/5/80	4	1	Liverpool
7	Aaron LENNON	16/4/87	2		Tottenham
8	Frank LAMPARD	20/6/78	4		Chelsea
11	Joe COLE	8/11/81	(2)		Chelsea
14	Gareth BARRY	23/2/81	3		Man. City
16	James MILNER	4/1/86	3		Aston Villa
17	Shaun WRIGHT-PHILLIPS	25/10/81	(3)		Man. City
22	Michael CARRICK	28/7/81			Man. United
Forwards					
9	Peter CROUCH	30/1/81	(2)		Tottenham
10	Wayne ROONEY	24/10/85	4		Man. United
19	Jermain DEFOE	7/10/82	2	(1) 1	Tottenham
21	Emile HESKEY	11/1/78	2	(2)	Aston Villa

  ### UNITED STATES

		DoB	Aps (s)	Gls	Club
Goalkeepers					
1	Tim HOWARD	6/3/79	4		Everton (ENG)
18	Brad GUZAN	9/9/84			Aston Villa (ENG)
23	Marcus HAHNEMANN	15/6/72			Wolves (ENG)
Defenders					
2	Jonathan SPECTOR	1/3/86			West Ham (ENG)
3	Carlos BOCANEGRA	25/5/79	4		Rennes (FRA)
5	Oguchi ONYEWU	13/5/82	2		Milan (ITA)
6	Steve CHERUNDOLO	19/2/79	4		Hannover (GER)
12	Jonathan BORNSTEIN	7/11/84	2		Chivas USA
15	Jay DeMERIT	4/12/79	4		Watford (ENG)
21	Clarence GOODSON	17/5/82			Start (NOR)
Midfielders					
4	Michael BRADLEY	31/7/87	4	1	Mönchengladbach (GER)
7	DaMarcus BEASLEY	24/5/82	(1)		Rangers (SCO)
8	Clint DEMPSEY	9/3/83	4	1	Fulham (ENG)
10	Landon DONOVAN	4/3/82	4	3	Los Angeles Galaxy
11	Stuart HOLDEN	1/8/85	(1)		Bolton (ENG)
13	Ricardo CLARK	10/2/83	2		Eintracht (GER)
16	José Francisco TORRES	29/10/87	1		Pachuca (MEX)
19	Maurice EDU	18/4/86	1	(2)	Rangers (SCO)
22	Benny FEILHABER	19/1/85	(3)		AGF (DEN)
Forwards					
9	Herculez GOMEZ	6/4/82	(2)		Puebla (MEX)
14	Edson BUDDLE	21/5/81	(2)		Los Angeles Galaxy
17	Jozy ALTIDORE	6/11/89	4		Hull (ENG)
20	Robbie FINDLEY	4/8/85	3		Real Salt Lake

  ### ALGERIA

		DoB	Aps (s)	Gls	Club
Goalkeepers					
1	Lounes GAOUAOUI	28/9/77			Chlef
16	Faouzi CHAOUCHI	5/12/84	1		Setif
23	Raïs M'BOLHI	25/4/86	2		Slavia Sofia (BUL)
Defenders					
2	Madjid BOUGHERRA	7/10/82	3		Rangers (SCO)
4	Anther YAHIA	21/3/82	3		Bochum (GER)
5	Rafik HALLICHE	2/9/86	3		Nacional (POR)
12	Habib BELLAID	28/3/86			Boulogne (FRA)
14	Abdelkader LAÏFAOUI	29/7/81			Setif
18	Carl MEDJANI	15/5/85			Ajaccio (FRA)
20	Djamel MESBAH	9/10/84	(1)		Lecce (ITA)
Midfielders					
3	Nadir BELHADJ	18/6/82	3		Portsmouth (ENG)
6	Yazid MANSOURI	25/2/78			Lorient (FRA)
7	Ryad BOUDEBOUZ	19/2/90	1		Sochaux (FRA)
15	Medhi LACEN	15/5/84	3		Racing (ESP)
17	Adlène GUEDIOURA	12/11/85	(3)		Wolves (ENG)
19	Hassan YEBDA	14/5/84	3		Portsmouth (ENG)
21	Foued KADIR	5/12/83	3		Valenciennes (FRA)
22	Djamal ABDOUN	14/2/86	(1)		Nantes (FRA)
Forwards					
9	Abdelkader GHEZZAL	5/12/84	(2)		Siena (ITA)
10	Rafik SAÏFI	7/2/75	(2)		Istres (FRA)
11	Rafik DJEBBOUR	8/3/84	2		AEK (GRE)
13	Karim MATMOUR	25/6/85	3		Mönchengladbach (GER)

  ### SLOVENIA

		DoB	Aps (s)	Gls	Club
Goalkeepers					
1	Samir HANDANOVIČ	14/7/84	3		Udinese (ITA)
12	Jasmin HANDANOVIČ	28/1/78			Mantova (ITA)
16	Aleksander ŠELIGA	1/2/80			Sparta (NED)
Defenders					
2	Mišo BREČKO	1/5/84	3		Köln (GER)
3	Elvedin DŽINIČ	25/8/85			Maribor
4	Boštjan CESAR	9/3/83	3		Gent (BEL)
5	Boštjan CESAR	9/7/82	3		Grenoble (FRA)
6	Branko ILIČ	6/2/83			Lokomotiv Moskva (RUS)
13	Bojan JOKIČ	17/5/86	3		Chievo (ITA)
19	Suad FILEKOVIČ	16/9/78			Maribor
22	Matej MAVRIČ	29/1/79			Koblenz (GER)
Midfielders					
8	Robert KOREN	20/9/80	3	1	West Brom (ENG)
10	Valter BIRSA	7/8/86	3	1	Auxerre (FRA)
15	René KRHIN	21/5/90			Inter (ITA)
17	Andraž KIRM	6/9/84	3		Wisła Kraków (POL)
18	Aleksandar RADOSAVLJEVIĆ	25/4/79	3		Larissa (GRE)
20	Andrej KOMAC	4/12/79	(2)		M. Tel-Aviv (ISR)
21	Dalibor STEVANOVIČ	27/9/84			Vitesse (NED)
Forwards					
7	Nejc PEČNIK	3/1/86	(2)		Nacional (POR)
9	Zlatan LJUBIJANKIČ	15/12/83	2	(1) 1	Gent (BEL)
11	Milivoje NOVAKOVIČ	18/5/79	3		Köln (GER)
14	Zlatko DEDIČ	5/10/84	1	(2)	Bochum (GER)
23	Tim MATAVŽ	13/1/89	(1)		Groningen (NED)

2010 FIFA WORLD CUP

GROUP D

GERMANY

	DoB	Aps (s)	Gls	Club
Goalkeepers				
Manuel NEUER	27/3/86	6		Schalke
Tim WIESE	17/12/81			Werder
Hans-Jörg BUTT	28/5/74	1		Bayern
Defenders				
Arne FRIEDRICH	29/5/79	7	1	Hertha
Dennis AOGO	14/1/87	1		Hamburg
Serdar TAŞCI	24/4/87	(1)		Stuttgart
Holger BADSTUBER	13/3/89	2		Bayern
Philipp LAHM	11/11/83	6		Bayern
Per MERTESACKER	29/9/84	7		Werder
Jérôme BOATENG	3/9/88	5		Hamburg
Midfielders				
Marcell JANSEN	4/11/85	1 (3)	1	Hamburg
Sami KHEDIRA	4/4/87	7	1	Stuttgart
Bastian SCHWEINSTEIGER	1/8/84	7		Bayern
Mesut ÖZIL	15/10/88	7	1	Werder
Thomas MÜLLER	13/9/89	6	5	Bayern
Piotr TROCHOWSKI	22/3/84	1 (3)		Hamburg
Toni KROOS	4/1/90	(4)		Leverkusen
Marko MARIN	13/3/89	(2)		Werder
Forwards				
Stefan KIESSLING	25/1/84	(2)		Leverkusen
Lukas PODOLSKI	4/6/85	6	2	Köln
Miroslav KLOSE	9/6/78	5	4	Bayern
CACAU	27/3/81	2 (2)	1	Stuttgart
Mario GÓMEZ	10/7/85	(4)		Bayern

AUSTRALIA

FOOTBALL FEDERATION AUSTRALIA

	DoB	Aps (s)	Gls	Club
Goalkeepers				
1 Mark SCHWARZER	6/10/72	3		Fulham (ENG)
12 Adam FEDERICI	31/1/85			Reading (ENG)
18 Eugene GALEKOVIC	12/6/81			Adelaide United
Defenders				
2 Lucas NEILL	9/3/78	3		Galatasaray (TUR)
3 Craig MOORE	12/12/75	2		unattached
6 Michael BEAUCHAMP	8/3/81	1		Al-Jazira (UAE)
8 Luke WILKSHIRE	2/10/81	3		Dinamo Moskva (RUS)
11 Scott CHIPPERFIELD	30/12/75	1 (2)		Basel (SUI)
20 Mark MILLIGAN	4/8/85			JEF United (JPN)
21 David CARNEY	30/11/83	2		Twente (NED)
Midfielders				
5 Jason CULINA	5/8/80	3		Gold Coast United
7 Brett EMERTON	22/2/79	3		Blackburn (ENG)
13 Vince GRELLA	5/10/79	1		Blackburn (ENG)
14 Brett HOLMAN	27/3/84	1 (2)	2	AZ (NED)
15 Mile JEDINAK	3/8/84	(1)		Antalyaspor (TUR)
16 Carl VALERI	14/8/84	3		Sassuolo (ITA)
22 Dario VIDOŠIC	8/4/87			Duisburg (GER)
23 Marco BRESCIANO	11/2/80	2		Palermo (ITA)
Forwards				
4 Tim CAHILL	6/12/79	2	1	Everton (ENG)
9 Joshua KENNEDY	20/8/82	1 (1)		Nagoya Grampus Eight (JPN)
10 Harry KEWELL	22/9/78	1		Galatasaray (TUR)
17 Nikita RUKAVYTSYA	22/6/87	(2)		Twente (NED)
19 Richard GARCIA	4/9/81	1 (1)		Hull (ENG)

SERBIA

	DoB	Aps (s)	Gls	Club
Goalkeepers				
Vladimir STOJKOVIC	28/7/83	3		Wigan (ENG)
2 Bojan ISAILOVIC	25/3/80			Zagłębie Lubin (POL)
3 Andelko DURICIC	21/11/80			Leiria (POR)
Defenders				
Antonio RUKAVINA	26/1/84			1860 München (GER)
Aleksandar KOLAROV	10/11/85	2		Lazio (ITA)
Nemanja VIDIC	21/10/81	3		Man. United (ENG)
Branislav IVANOVIC	22/2/84	3		Chelsea (ENG)
3 Aleksandar LUKOVIC	23/10/82	2		Udinese (ITA)
6 Ivan OBRADOVIC	25/7/88	1		Zaragoza (ESP)
0 Neven SUBOTIC	10/12/88	1 (1)		Dortmund (GER)
Midfielders				
Gojko KAČAR	26/1/87	(1)		Hertha (GER)
Zoran TOŠIC	28/4/87	(1)		Köln (GER)
0 Dejan STANKOVIC	11/9/78	3		Inter (ITA)
1 Nenad MILIJAŠ	30/4/83	1		Wolves (ENG)
2 Milan JOVANOVIC	18/4/81	3	1	Standard (BEL)
Miloš KRASIC	1/11/84	3		CSKA Moskva (RUS)
8 Miloš NINKOVIC	25/12/84	2		Dynamo Kyiv (UKR)
9 Radosav PETROVIC	8/3/89	1		Partizan
2 Zdravko KUZMANOVIC	22/9/87	2 (1)		Stuttgart (GER)
Forwards				
Danko LAZOVIC	17/5/83	(3)		Zenit (RUS)
Marko PANTELIC	15/9/78	1 (1)	1	Ajax (NED)
5 Nikola ŽIGIC	25/9/80	3		Valencia (ESP)
1 Dragan MRDA	23/1/84			Vojvodina

GHANA

GHANA FOOTBALL ASSOCIATION

	DoB	Aps (s)	Gls	Club
Goalkeepers				
1 Daniel AGYEI	10/11/89			Liberty
16 Stephen AHORLU	5/9/88			Heart of Lions
22 Richard KINGSON	13/6/78	5		Wigan (ENG)
Defenders				
2 Hans SARPEI	28/6/76	5		Leverkusen (GER)
4 John PANTSIL	15/6/81	5		Fulham (ENG)
5 John MENSAH	29/11/82	4		Sunderland (ENG)
8 Jonathan MENSAH	13/7/90	3		Free State Stars (RSA)
15 Isaac VORSAH	21/6/88	2		Hoffenheim (GER)
17 Ibrahim AYEW	16/4/88			Zamalek (EGY)
19 Lee ADDY	7/7/90	1 (2)		Bechem Chelsea
Midfielders				
6 Anthony ANNAN	21/7/86	5		Rosenborg (NOR)
7 Samuel INKOOM	22/8/89	2		Basel (SUI)
9 Derek BOATENG	2/5/83			Getafe (ESP)
10 Stephen APPIAH	24/12/80	(3)		Bologna (ITA)
11 Sulley Ali MUNTARI	27/8/84	1 (3)	1	Inter (ITA)
12 Prince TAGOE	9/11/86	3		Hoffenheim (GER)
13 André AYEW	17/12/89	4		Arles-Avignon (FRA)
21 Kwadwo ASAMOAH	9/12/88	5		Udinese (ITA)
23 Kevin-Prince BOATENG	6/3/87	5	1	Portsmouth (ENG)
Forwards				
3 Asamoah GYAN	22/11/85	5	3	Rennes (FRA)
14 Matthew AMOAH	24/10/80	(2)		NAC (NED)
18 Dominic ADIYIAH	29/11/89	(2)		Milan (ITA)
20 Quincy OWUSU-ABEYIE	15/4/86	(2)		Al-Sadd (QAT)

GROUP E

NETHERLANDS

KNVB

DENMARK

DBU 1889

		DoB	Aps	(s)	Gls	Club
Goalkeepers						
1	Maarten STEKELENBURG	22/9/82	7			Ajax
16	Michel VORM	20/10/83				Utrecht
22	Sander BOSCHKER	20/10/70				Twente
Defenders						
2	Gregory VAN DER WIEL	3/2/88	5			Ajax
3	John HEITINGA	15/11/83	7			Everton (ENG)
4	Joris MATHIJSEN	5/4/80	6			Hamburg (GER)
5	Giovanni VAN BRONCKHORST	5/2/75	7		1	Feyenoord
12	Khalid BOULAHROUZ	28/12/81	2			Stuttgart (GER)
13	André OOIJER	11/7/74	1			PSV
15	Edson BRAAFHEID	8/4/83		(1)		Celtic (SCO)
Midfielders						
6	Mark VAN BOMMEL	22/4/77	7			Bayern (GER)
8	Nigel DE JONG	30/11/84	6			Man. City (ENG)
10	Wesley SNEIJDER	9/6/84	7		5	Inter (ITA)
14	Demy DE ZEEUW	26/5/83	1	(1)		Ajax
18	Stijn SCHAARS	11/1/84				AZ
20	Ibrahim AFELLAY	2/4/86		(3)		PSV
23	Rafael VAN DER VAART	11/2/83	3	(2)		Real Madrid (ESP)
Forwards						
7	Dirk KUYT	22/7/80	7		1	Liverpool (ENG)
9	Robin VAN PERSIE	6/8/83	7		1	Arsenal (ENG)
11	Arjen ROBBEN	23/1/84	4	(1)	2	Bayern (GER)
17	Eljero ELIA	13/2/87		(6)		Hamburg (GER)
19	Ryan BABEL	19/12/86				Liverpool (ENG)
21	Klaas Jan HUNTELAAR	12/8/83		(4)	1	Milan (ITA)

		DoB	Aps	(s)	Gls	Club
Goalkeepers						
1	Thomas SØRENSEN	12/6/76	3			Stoke (ENG)
16	Stephan ANDERSEN	26/11/81				Brøndby
22	Jesper CHRISTIANSEN	24/4/78				København
Defenders						
3	Simon KJÆR	26/3/89	2			Palermo (ITA)
4	Daniel AGGER	12/12/84	3			Liverpool (ENG)
6	Lars JACOBSEN	20/9/79	3			Blackburn (ENG)
13	Per KRØLDRUP	31/7/79	1			Fiorentina (ITA)
15	Simon Busk POULSEN	7/4/84	3			AZ (NED)
23	Patrick MTILIGA	28/1/81				Málaga (ESP)
Midfielders						
2	Christian POULSEN	28/2/80	3			Juventus (ITA)
5	William Kvist JØRGENSEN	24/2/85				København
7	Daniel JENSEN	25/6/79		(1)		Werder (GER)
10	Martin JØRGENSEN	6/10/75	3			AGF
12	Thomas KAHLENBERG	20/3/83	2	(1)		Wolfsburg (GER)
14	Jakob POULSEN	7/7/83		(2)		AGF
20	Thomas ENEVOLDSEN	27/7/87	1			Groningen (NED)
21	Christian ERIKSEN	14/2/92		(2)		Ajax (NED)
Forwards						
8	Jesper GRØNKJÆR	12/8/77	1	(1)		København
9	Jon Dahl TOMASSON	29/8/76	2		1	Feyenoord (NED)
11	Nicklas BENDTNER	16/1/88	3		1	Arsenal (ENG)
17	Mikkel BECKMANN	24/10/83		(1)		Randers
18	Søren LARSEN	6/9/81		(1)		Duisburg (GER)
19	Dennis ROMMEDAHL	22/7/78	3		1	Ajax (NED)

JAPAN

CAMEROON

		DoB	Aps	(s)	Gls	Club
Goalkeepers						
1	Seigo NARAZAKI	15/4/76				Nagoya Grampus
21	Eiji KAWASHIMA	20/3/83	4			Kawasaki Frontale
23	Yoshikatsu KAWAGUCHI	15/8/75				Júbilo Iwata
Defenders						
3	Yuichi KOMANO	25/7/81	4			Júbilo Iwata
4	Marcus Tulio TANAKA	24/4/81	4			Nagoya Grampus
5	Yuto NAGATOMO	12/9/86	4			FC Tokyo
6	Atsuto UCHIDA	27/3/88				Kashima Antlers
13	Daiki IWAMASA	30/1/82				Kashima Antlers
15	Yasuyuki KONNO	25/1/83		(1)		FC Tokyo
22	Yuji NAKAZAWA	25/2/78	4			Yokohama F Marinos
Midfielders						
2	Yuki ABE	6/9/81	4			Urawa Reds
7	Yasuhito ENDO	28/1/80	4		1	Gamba Osaka
8	Daisuke MATSUI	11/5/81	4			Grenoble (FRA)
10	Shunsuke NAKAMURA	24/6/78		(1)		Yokohama F Marinos
14	Kengo NAKAMURA	31/10/80		(1)		Kawasaki Frontale
16	Yoshito OKUBO	9/6/82	4			Vissel Kobe
17	Makoto HASEBE	18/1/84	4			Wolfsburg (GER)
20	Junichi INAMOTO	18/9/79		(2)		Kawasaki Frontale
Forwards						
9	Shinji OKAZAKI	16/4/86		(4)	1	Shimizu S-Pulse
11	Keiji TAMADA	11/4/80		(2)		Nagoya Grampus
12	Kisho YANO	5/4/84		(1)		Albirex Niigata
18	Keisuke HONDA	13/6/86	4		2	CSKA Moskva (RUS)
19	Takayuki MORIMOTO	7/5/88				Catania (ITA)

		DoB	Aps	(s)	Gls	Club
Goalkeepers						
1	Idriss Carlos KAMENI	18/2/84				Espanyol (ESP)
16	Souleymanou HAMIDOU	22/11/73	3			Kayserispor (TUR)
22	Guy Roland N'DY ASSEMBÉ	28/2/86				Valenciennes (FRA)
Defenders						
2	Benoît ASSOU-EKOTTO	24/3/84	3			Tottenham (ENG)
3	Nicolas N'KOULOU	27/3/90	3			Monaco (FRA)
4	Rigobert SONG	1/7/76		(1)		Trabzonspor (TUR)
5	Sébastien BASSONG	9/7/86	2			Tottenham (ENG)
14	Aurélien CHEDJOU	20/6/85	1			Lille (FRA)
19	Stéphane MBIA	20/5/86	3			Marseille (FRA)
Midfielders						
6	Alex SONG	9/9/87	1			Arsenal (ENG)
7	Landry N'GUÉMO	28/11/85	1			Celtic (SCO)
8	GEREMI Njitap	20/12/78	2	(1)		Ankaragücü (TUR)
10	Achille EMANA	5/6/82	1	(1)		Betis (ESP)
11	Jean II MAKOUN	29/5/83	2	(1)		Lyon (FRA)
12	Gaëtan BONG	25/4/88	1			Valenciennes (FRA)
18	Eyong ENOH	23/3/86	2			Ajax (NED)
20	Georges MANDJECK	9/12/88				Kaiserslautern (GER)
21	Joël MATIP	8/8/91	1			Schalke (GER)
Forwards						
9	Samuel ETO'O	10/3/81	3		2	Inter (ITA)
14	Eric CHOUPO-MOTING	23/3/89	2			Nürnberg (GER)
15	Pierre WEBO	20/1/82	2			Mallorca (ESP)
17	Mohamadou IDRISSOU	8/3/80		(3)		Freiburg (GER)
23	Vincent ABOUBAKAR	22/1/92		(2)		Coton Sport

2010 FIFA WORLD CUP

GROUP F

ITALY

PARAGUAY

	DoB	Aps (s)	Gls	Club
Goalkeepers				
Gianluigi BUFFON	28/1/78	1		Juventus
Federico MARCHETTI	7/2/83	2 (1)		Cagliari
Morgan DE SANCTIS	26/3/77			Napoli
Defenders				
Christian MAGGIO	11/2/82	(1)		Napoli
Domenico CRISCITO	30/12/86	3		Genoa
Giorgio CHIELLINI	14/8/84	3		Juventus
Fabio CANNAVARO	13/9/73	3		Juventus
Salvatore BOCCHETTI	30/11/86			Genoa
Gianluca ZAMBROTTA	19/2/77	3		Milan
Leonardo BONUCCI	1/5/87			Bari
Midfielders				
Daniele DE ROSSI	24/7/83	3	1	Roma
Simone PEPE	30/8/83	3		Udinese
Gennaro GATTUSO	9/1/78	1		Milan
Claudio MARCHISIO	19/1/86	2		Juventus
Mauro CAMORANESI	4/10/76	(2)		Juventus
Angelo PALOMBO	25/9/81			Sampdoria
Andrea PIRLO	19/5/79	(1)		Milan
Riccardo MONTOLIVO	18/1/85	3		Fiorentina
Forwards				
Vincenzo IAQUINTA	21/11/79	3	1	Juventus
Antonio DI NATALE	13/10/77	1 (2)	1	Udinese
Alberto GILARDINO	5/7/82	2		Fiorentina
Fabio QUAGLIARELLA	31/1/83	(1)		Napoli
Giampaolo PAZZINI	2/8/84	(1)		Sampdoria

	DoB	Aps (s)	Gls	Club
Goalkeepers				
1 Justo VILLAR	30/6/77	5		Valladolid (ESP)
12 Diego BARRETO	16/7/81			Cerro Porteño
22 Aldo BOBADILLA	20/4/76			Independiente (COL)
Defenders				
2 Darío VERÓN	26/7/79	1		Pumas UNAM (MEX)
3 Claudio MOREL Rodríguez	2/2/78	5		Boca Juniors (ARG)
4 Denis CANIZA	29/8/74	1		León (MEX)
5 Julio César CÁCERES	5/10/79	1		Atlético Mineiro (BRA)
14 Paulo DA SILVA	1/2/80	5		Sunderland (ENG)
17 Aureliano TORRES	16/6/82	1 (1)		San Lorenzo (ARG)
21 Antolín ALCARAZ	30/7/82	4	1	Club Brugge (BEL)
Midfielders				
6 Carlos BONET	2/10/77	3		Olimpia Asunción
8 Édgar BARRETO	15/7/84	1 (2)		Atalanta (ITA)
10 Édgar BENÍTEZ	8/11/87	1 (1)		Pachuca (MEX)
11 Jonathan SANTANA	19/10/81	1 (1)		Wolfsburg (GER)
13 Enrique VERA	10/3/79	4 (1)	1	LDU Quito (ECU)
15 Víctor CÁCERES	25/3/85	4		Libertad
16 Cristian RIVEROS	16/10/82	5	1	Cruz Azul (MEX)
20 Néstor ORTIGOZA	7/10/84	1		Argentinos Juniors (ARG)
Forwards				
7 Óscar CARDOZO	20/5/83	2 (3)		Benfica (POR)
9 Roque SANTA CRUZ	16/8/81	3 (2)		Man. City (ENG)
18 Nelson Haedo VALDEZ	28/11/83	4 (1)		Dortmund (GER)
19 Lucas BARRIOS	13/11/84	3 (2)		Dortmund (GER)
23 Rodolfo GAMARRA	10/12/88			Libertad

NEW ZEALAND

SLOVAKIA

	DoB	Aps (s)	Gls	Club
Goalkeepers				
Mark PASTON	13/12/76	3		Wellington Phoenix
2 Glen MOSS	19/1/83			Melbourne Victory (AUS)
3 James BANNATYNE	30/6/75			Team Wellington
Defenders				
Ben SIGMUND	3/2/81			Wellington Phoenix
Winston REID	3/7/88	3	1	Midtjylland (DEN)
Ryan NELSEN	18/10/77	3		Blackburn (ENG)
8 Andy BOYENS	18/9/83			New York Red Bulls (USA)
9 Tommy SMITH	31/3/90	3		Ipswich (ENG)
Midfielders				
Tony LOCHHEAD	12/1/82	3		Wellington Phoenix
Ivan VICELICH	3/9/76	3		Auckland City
Simon ELLIOTT	10/6/74	3		unattached
Tim BROWN	6/3/81			Wellington Phoenix
Leo BERTOS	20/12/81	3		Wellington Phoenix
3 Andy BARRON	24/12/80	(1)		Team Wellington
5 Michael McGLINCHEY	7/1/87			Motherwell (SCO)
6 Aaron CLAPHAM	15/1/87			Canterbury United
7 Dave MULLIGAN	24/3/82			unattached
Jeremy CHRISTIE	22/5/83	(2)		Tampa Bay (USA)
Forwards				
Shane SMELTZ	29/9/81	3	1	Gold Coast United (AUS)
0 Chris KILLEN	8/10/81	3		Middlesbrough (ENG)
4 Rory FALLON	20/3/82	3		Plymouth (ENG)
0 Chris WOOD	7/12/91	(3)		West Brom (ENG)
2 Jeremy BROCKIE	7/10/87	(1)		North Queensland Fury (AUS)

	DoB	Aps (s)	Gls	Club
Goalkeepers				
1 Ján MUCHA	5/12/82	4		Legia (POL)
12 Dušan PERNIŠ	28/11/84			Dundee United (SCO)
23 Dušan KUCIAK	21/5/85			Vaslui (ROU)
Defenders				
2 Peter PEKARÍK	30/10/86	3		Wolfsburg (GER)
3 Martin ŠKRTEĽ	15/12/84	4		Liverpool (ENG)
4 Marek ČECH	26/1/83	1		West Brom (ENG)
5 Radoslav ZABAVNÍK	16/9/80	3		Mainz (GER)
16 Ján ĎURICA	10/12/81	4		Hannover (GER)
21 Kornel SALÁTA	24/1/85	1		Slovan Bratislava
22 Martin PETRÁŠ	2/11/79	(1)		Cesena (ITA)
Midfielders				
6 Zdeno ŠTRBA	9/6/76	3		Xanthi (GRE)
7 Vladimír WEISS	30/11/89	3		Bolton (ENG)
8 Ján KOZÁK	22/4/80	1		Timişoara (ROU)
10 Marek SAPARA	31/7/82	(1)		Ankaragücü (TUR)
15 Miroslav STOCH	19/10/89	2 (1)		Twente (NED)
17 Marek HAMŠÍK	27/7/87	4		Napoli (ITA)
19 Juraj KUCKA	26/2/87	2 (1)		Sparta Praha (CZE)
20 Kamil KOPÚNEK	18/5/84	(2)	1	Spartak Trnava
Forwards				
9 Stanislav ŠESTÁK	16/12/82	2 (1)		Bochum (GER)
11 Róbert VITTEK	1/4/82	4	4	Ankaragücü (TUR)
13 Filip HOLOŠKO	17/1/84	(2)		Beşiktaş (TUR)
14 Martin JAKUBKO	26/2/80	(1)		Saturn (RUS)
18 Erik JENDRIŠEK	26/10/86	3		Kaiserslautern (GER)

GROUP G

BRAZIL

		DoB	Aps (s)	Gls	Club
Goalkeepers					
1	JÚLIO CÉSAR	3/9/79	5		Inter (ITA)
12	GOMES	15/2/81			Tottenham (ENG)
22	DONI	22/10/79			Roma (ITA)
Defenders					
2	MAICON	26/7/81	5	1	Inter (ITA)
3	LÚCIO	8/5/78	5		Inter (ITA)
4	JUAN	1/2/79	5		Roma (ITA)
6	MICHEL BASTOS	2/8/83	5		Lyon (FRA)
13	DANI ALVES	6/5/83	3	(2)	Barcelona (ESP)
14	LUISÃO	13/2/81			Benfica (POR)
15	THIAGO SILVA	22/9/84			Milan (ITA)
16	GILBERTO MELO	25/4/76		(2)	Cruzeiro
Midfielders					
5	FELIPE MELO	26/6/83	4		Juventus (ITA)
7	ELANO	14/6/81	2	2	Galatasaray (TUR)
8	GILBERTO SILVA	7/10/76	5		Panathinaikos (GRE)
10	KAKÁ	22/4/82	4		Real Madrid (ESP)
17	JOSUÉ	19/7/79	(1)		Wolfsburg (GER)
18	RAMIRES	24/3/87	1	(3)	Benfica (POR)
19	JÚLIO BAPTISTA	1/10/81	1		Roma (ITA)
20	KLÉBERSON	19/6/79	(1)		Flamengo
Forwards					
9	LUÍS FABIANO	8/11/80	5	3	Sevilla (ESP)
11	ROBINHO	25/1/84	4	2	Santos
21	NILMAR	14/7/84	1	(3)	Villarreal (ESP)
23	GRAFITE	2/4/79	(1)		Wolfsburg (GER)

NORTH KOREA

		DoB	Aps (s)	Gls	Club
Goalkeepers					
1	RI Myong-guk	9/9/86	3		Pyongyang City
18	KIM Myong-gil	16/10/84			Amrokgang
20	KIM Myong-won	15/7/83			Amrokgang
Defenders					
3	RI Jun-il	24/8/87	3		Sobaeksu
5	RI Kwang-chon	4/9/85	3		April 25
13	PAK Chol-jin	5/9/85	3		Amrokgang
14	PAK Nam-chol (II)	3/10/88			Amrokgang
16	NAM Song-chol	7/5/82		(1)	April 25
21	RI Kwang-hyok	17/8/87			Kyonggongop
Midfielders					
2	CHA Jong-hyok	25/9/85	3		Amrokgang
4	PAK Nam-chol (I)	2/7/85	3		April 25
6	KIM Kum-il	10/10/87	2		April 25
8	JI Yun-nam	20/11/76	3	1	April 25
10	HONG Yong-jo	22/5/82	3		Rostov (RUS)
11	MUN In-guk	29/9/78	3		April 25
15	KIM Yong-jun	19/7/83	(1)		Pyongyang City
17	AN Yong-hak	25/10/78	3		Omiya Ardija (JPN)
19	RI Chol-myong	18/2/88			Pyongyang City
22	KIM Kyong-il	11/12/88			Rimyongsu
23	PAK Sung-hyok	30/5/90			Sobaeksu
Forwards					
7	AN Chol-hyok	27/6/87			Rimyongsu
9	JONG Tae-se	2/3/84	3		Kawasaki Frontale (JPN)
12	CHOE Kum-chol	9/2/87	(1)		April 25

IVORY COAST

		DoB	Aps (s)	Gls	Club
Goalkeepers					
1	Boubacar BARRY	30/12/79	3		Lokeren (BEL)
16	Aristide ZOGBO	30/12/81			M. Netanya (ISR)
23	Daniel YEBOAH	13/11/84			ASEC Mimosas
Defenders					
2	Benjamin ANGOUA	28/11/86			Valenciennes (FRA)
3	Arthur BOKA	2/4/83	1		Stuttgart (GER)
4	Kolo TOURÉ	19/3/81	3		Man. City (ENG)
5	Didier ZOKORA	14/12/80	3		Sevilla (ESP)
6	Steve GOHOURI	8/2/81			Wigan (ENG)
17	Siaka TIÉNÉ	22/2/82	2		Valenciennes (FRA)
20	Guy DEMEL	13/6/81	2		Hamburg (GER)
22	Souleymane BAMBA	13/1/85			Hibernian (SCO)
Midfielders					
9	Cheik TIOTÉ	21/6/86	3		Twente (NED)
12	Jean-Jacques GOSSO	15/3/83			Monaco (FRA)
13	ROMARIC	4/6/83	1	(2) 1	Sevilla (ESP)
14	Emmanuel KONÉ	31/12/86			International Curtea (ROU)
18	Abdul Kader KEITA	6/8/81	1	(2)	Galatasaray (TUR)
19	Yaya TOURÉ	13/5/83	3	1	Barcelona (ESP)
21	Emmanuel EBOUÉ	4/6/83	3		Arsenal (ENG)
Forwards					
7	Seydou DOUMBIA	31/12/87	(1)		Young Boys (SUI)
8	Salomon KALOU	5/8/85	2	(1) 1	Chelsea (ENG)
10	GERVINHO	27/5/87	2	(1)	Lille (FRA)
14	Didier DROGBA	11/3/78	2	(1) 1	Chelsea (ENG)
15	Aruna DINDANE	26/11/80	2	(1)	Portsmouth (ENG)

PORTUGAL

		DoB	Aps (s)	Gls	Club
Goalkeepers					
1	EDUARDO	19/9/82	4		Braga
12	BETO	1/5/82			Porto
22	DANIEL FERNANDES	25/9/83			Iraklis (GRE)
Defenders					
2	BRUNO ALVES	27/11/81	4		Porto
3	PAULO FERREIRA	18/1/79	1		Chelsea (ENG)
4	ROLANDO	31/8/85			Porto
5	DUDA	27/6/80	1	(1)	Málaga (ESP)
6	RICARDO CARVALHO	18/5/78	4		Chelsea (ENG)
13	MIGUEL	4/1/80	1		Valencia (ESP)
21	RICARDO COSTA	16/5/81	2		Lille (FRA)
23	FÁBIO COENTRÃO	11/3/88	4		Benfica
Midfielders					
8	PEDRO MENDES	26/2/79	2	(2)	Sporting
14	MIGUEL VELOSO	11/5/86	2	(2)	Sporting
15	PEPE	26/2/83	2		Real Madrid (ESP)
16	RAUL MEIRELES	17/3/83	4	1	Porto
17	RÚBEN AMORIM	27/1/85	(1)		Benfica
19	TIAGO	2/5/81	3	(1) 2	Atlético (ESP)
20	DECO	27/8/77	1		Chelsea (ENG)
Forwards					
7	CRISTIANO RONALDO	5/2/85	4	1	Real Madrid (ESP)
9	LIEDSON	17/12/77	1	(2) 1	Sporting
10	DANNY	7/8/83	2	(1)	Zenit (RUS)
11	SIMÃO	31/10/79	2	(2) 1	Atlético (ESP)
18	HUGO ALMEIDA	23/5/84	2		Werder (GER)

2010 FIFA WORLD CUP

GROUP H

 SPAIN

	DoB	Aps	(s)	Gls	Club
Goalkeepers					
Iker CASILLAS	20/5/81	7			Real Madrid
VÍCTOR VALDÉS	14/1/82				Barcelona
José Manuel REINA	31/8/82				Liverpool (ENG)
Defenders					
Raúl ALBIOL	4/9/85				Real Madrid
Gerard PIQUÉ	2/2/87	7			Barcelona
Carlos MARCHENA	31/7/79		(3)		Valencia
Carles PUYOL	13/4/78	7		1	Barcelona
Joan CAPDEVILA	3/2/78	7			Villarreal
SERGIO RAMOS	30/3/86	7			Real Madrid
Álvaro ARBELOA	17/1/83		(1)		Real Madrid
Midfielders					
Andrés INIESTA	11/5/84	6		2	Barcelona
XAVI Hernández	25/1/80	7			Barcelona
Cesc FÁBREGAS	4/5/87		(4)		Arsenal (ENG)
XABI ALONSO	25/11/81	7			Real Madrid
Sergio BUSQUETS	16/7/88	7			Barcelona
JAVI MARTÍNEZ	2/9/88		(1)		Athletic
DAVID SILVA	8/1/86	1	(1)		Valencia
Forwards					
DAVID VILLA	3/12/81	7		5	Valencia
FERNANDO TORRES	20/3/84	4	(3)		Liverpool (ENG)
Juan Manuel MATA	28/4/88		(1)		Valencia
PEDRO Rodríguez	28/7/87	2	(3)		Barcelona
Fernando LLORENTE	26/2/85		(1)		Athletic
JESÚS NAVAS	21/11/85	1	(2)		Sevilla

 SWITZERLAND

		DoB	Aps	(s)	Gls	Club
Goalkeepers						
1	Diego BENAGLIO	8/9/83	3			Wolfsburg (GER)
12	Marco WÖLFLI	22/8/82				Young Boys
21	Johnny LEONI	30/6/84				Zürich
Defenders						
2	Stephan LICHTSTEINER	16/1/84	3			Lazio (ITA)
3	Ludovic MAGNIN	20/4/79				Zürich
4	Philippe SENDEROS	14/2/85	1			Everton (ENG)
5	Steve VON BERGEN	10/6/83	2	(1)		Hertha (GER)
13	Stéphane GRICHTING	30/3/79	3			Auxerre (FRA)
17	Reto ZIEGLER	16/1/86	3			Sampdoria (ITA)
22	Mario EGGIMANN	24/1/81		(1)		Hannover (GER)
Midfielders						
6	Benjamin HUGGEL	7/7/77	3			Basel
7	Tranquillo BARNETTA	22/5/85	2	(1)		Leverkusen (GER)
8	Gökhan INLER	27/6/84	3			Udinese (ITA)
11	Valon BEHRAMI	19/4/85	1			West Ham (ENG)
14	Marco PADALINO	8/12/83				Sampdoria (ITA)
15	Hakan YAKIN	22/2/77		(2)		Luzern
16	Gelson FERNANDES	2/9/86	3		1	St-Étienne (FRA)
20	Pirmin SCHWEGLER	9/3/87				Eintracht (GER)
23	Xherdan SHAQIRI	10/10/91		(1)		Basel
Forwards						
9	Alexander FREI	15/7/79	1	(1)		Basel
10	Blaise NKUFO	25/5/75	3			Twente (NED)
18	Albert BUNJAKU	29/11/83		(1)		Nürnberg (GER)
19	Eren DERDIYOK	12/6/88	2	(1)		Leverkusen (GER)

 HONDURAS

		DoB	Aps	(s)	Gls	Club
Goalkeepers						
	Ricardo CANALES	30/5/82				Motagua
	Noel VALLADARES	3/5/77	3			Olimpia Tegucigalpa
	Donis ESCOBER	3/2/81				Olimpia Tegucigalpa
Defenders						
	Osman CHÁVEZ	29/7/84	3			Platense
	Maynor FIGUEROA	2/5/83	3			Wigan (ENG)
	Jhony PALACIOS	20/12/86				Olimpia Tegucigalpa
	Víctor BERNÁRDEZ	24/5/82	1			Anderlecht (BEL)
	Sergio MENDOZA	4/9/84				Olimpia Tegucigalpa
	Mauricio SABILLÓN	11/11/78	1			Hangzhou Greentown (CHN)
	Emilio IZAGUIRRE	10/5/86	2			Motagua
	Sergio MENDOZA	23/5/81	2			Motagua
Midfielders						
	Hendry THOMAS	23/2/85	1	(1)		Wigan (ENG)
	Ramón NÚÑEZ	14/11/85	2	(1)		Olimpia Tegucigalpa
	Wilson PALACIOS	29/7/84	3			Tottenham (ENG)
	Jerry PALACIOS	13/5/82	1	(1)		Hangzhou Greentown (CHN)
	Édgar ÁLVAREZ	18/1/80	2			Bari (ITA)
	Danilo TURCIOS	8/5/78	1	(1)		Olimpia Tegucigalpa
	Amado GUEVARA	2/5/76	2			Motagua
Forwards						
	Carlos PAVÓN	9/10/73	1			Real España
	David SUAZO	5/11/79	2			Genoa (ITA)
	Georgie WELCOME	9/3/85		(3)		Motagua
	Roger ESPINOZA	25/10/86	2			Kansas City Wizards (USA)
	Walter MARTÍNEZ	24/3/82	1	(2)		Marathón

 CHILE

		DoB	Aps	(s)	Gls	Club
Goalkeepers						
1	Claudio BRAVO	13/4/83	4			Real Sociedad (ESP)
12	Miguel PINTO	4/7/83				Univ. de Chile
23	Luis MARÍN	18/5/83				Unión Española
Defenders						
2	Ismael FUENTES	4/8/81	1			Univ. Católica
3	Waldo PONCE	4/12/82	3			Univ. Católica
4	Pablo CONTRERAS	11/9/78	1	(1)		PAOK (GRE)
17	Gary MEDEL	3/8/87	3			Boca Juniors (ARG)
18	Gonzalo JARA	29/8/85	3	(1)		West Brom (ENG)
Midfielders						
4	Mauricio ISLA	12/6/88	4			Udinese (ITA)
6	Carlos CARMONA	21/2/87	3			Reggina (ITA)
8	Arturo VIDAL	22/5/87	4			Leverkusen (GER)
10	Jorge VALDIVIA	19/10/83	2	(2)		Al-Ain (UAE)
13	Marco ESTRADA	28/5/83	1			Univ. de Chile
14	Matías FERNÁNDEZ	15/5/86	2			Sporting (POR)
20	Gonzalo FIERRO	21/3/83				Flamengo (BRA)
20	Rodrigo MILLAR	3/11/81	1	(2)	1	Colo-Colo
21	Rodrigo TELLO	14/10/79		(1)		Beşiktaş (TUR)
Forwards						
7	Alexis SÁNCHEZ	19/12/88	4			Udinese (ITA)
9	Humberto SUAZO	10/5/81	2			Zaragoza (ESP)
11	Mark GONZÁLEZ	10/7/84	2	(2)	1	CSKA Moskva (RUS)
15	Jean BEAUSEJOUR	1/6/84	4		1	América (MEX)
16	Fabián ORELLANA	27/1/86		(1)		Xerez (ESP)
22	Esteban PAREDES	1/8/80		(2)		Colo-Colo

EUROPEAN QUALIFYING ROUND

GROUP 1

Denmark secured their fourth appearance on world football's biggest stage by topping Qualifying Group 1 with 21 points from their ten matches, finishing with a two-point advantage over a Portugal side whose autumn revival earned them a play-off berth at the expense of Sweden and Hungary.

Bendtner strikes

Morten Olsen's side entered the new season on the back of a five-match winning run, but their progress stalled in September with two successive draws. Arsenal FC striker Nicklas Bendtner's spectacular half-volley, later voted Danish Goal of the Year for 2009, looked to have earned them three points at home against Portugal, but Liedson, the Brazilian-born

Nicklas Bendtner (left) is congratulated by team-mates after scoring for Denmark against Portugal

Sporting Clube de Portugal forward, came off the bench and levelled four minutes from time on his first appearance for his adopted country, earning the visitors a precious – and deserved - point.

Four days later the Danes, despite another strike from Bendtner, dropped further points in a rather more surprising 1-1 draw away to fifth-placed Albania. Yet Denmark, absent from both the 2006 FIFA World Cup and UEFA EURO 2008, made amends for that slip-up when they welcomed their old rivals Sweden to Copenhagen for their penultimate qualifier in October.

Jakob Poulsen's first goal for his country, after 78 minutes, earned a narrow 1-0 victory at the Parken stadium, the midfielder's drive from distance bouncing beyond the reach of Sweden goalkeeper Andreas Isaksson. It proved a thoroughly frustrating night for Lars Lagerbäck's visitors, who saw second-half goals from Henrik Larsson and Anders Svensson disallowed.

Costly for Swedes

Denmark had never recorded a competitive victory over their neighbours until winning in Solna the previous June; now they had two in the space of five months and, moreover, a ticket to their first World Cup since 2002. Defeat proved costly to the Swedes, leaving second place within Portugal's grasp.

It was actually Erwin Koeman's Hungary who had held second spot going into the autumn but their last-gasp loss to Sweden in Budapest in September was followed by home-and-away defeats against a Portugal side finally asserting their authority.

Semi-finalists at the 2006 World Cup, Portugal had looked in danger of missing out on the 2010 finals after winning only two of their six qualifying matches the previous season, but after gaining that vital point in Denmark, they then travelled to Budapest and came away with three more through Pepe's early headed goal.

At that stage Hungary were still level on points with Portugal but they suffered further punishment when the countries met again in the 10 October return, going down 3-0 in Lisbon. Club Atlético de Madrid winger Simão opened the scoring for Carlos Queiroz's side, and although Roland Juhász then rattled the crossbar for the visitors, Portugal made sure of victory in the last 20 minutes as Liedson and Simão again found the net.

2010 FIFA WORLD CUP

Portugal in the clear

Suddenly Portugal were a point clear of the Swedes with just a home game against bottom-placed Malta left to play. They made no mistake in Guimaraes, goals from Nani, Simão, Miguel Veloso and Edinho securing the 4-0 triumph that opened the door to the play-offs.

Thus, for Sweden, the closing 4-1 win over Malta counted for nothing. Condemned to watch the World Cup finals from home for the first time since 1998, the failure brought an end to Lagerbäck's ten–year reign as coach (the first four spent as joint-coach with Tommy Söderberg). He would later be handed the reins of World Cup-bound Nigeria while his old job went to Erik Hamrén. Hungary also gained little consolation from their concluding win – 1-0 against a demob-happy Denmark in Copenhagen – with their dream of a first World Cup finals appearance since 1986 long since shattered.

Pepe heads Portugal's winning goal against Hungary in Budapest

Group 1 Results

6/9/08
Hungary 0-0 Denmark
Malta 0-4 Portugal
Albania 0-0 Sweden
10/9/08
Sweden 2-1 Hungary
Portugal 2-3 Denmark
Albania 3-0 Malta
11/10/08
Hungary 2-0 Albania
Denmark 3-0 Malta
Sweden 0-0 Portugal
15/10/08
Malta 0-1 Hungary
Portugal 0-0 Albania

11/2/09
Malta 0-0 Albania
28/3/09
Malta 0-3 Denmark
Albania 0-1 Hungary
Portugal 0-0 Sweden
1/4/09
Hungary 3-0 Malta
Denmark 3-0 Albania
6/6/09
Sweden 0-1 Denmark
Albania 1-2 Portugal
10/6/09
Sweden 4-0 Malta

5/9/09, Ferenc Puskás, Budapest
Hungary 1-2 Sweden
Attendance: 40169
Hungary: Babos, Gyepes, Szélesi, Juhász (Tímár 64), Dárdai (Torghelle 46), Hajnal (Buzsáky 85), Halmosi, Gera, Huszti, Vadócz, Dzsudzsák. Coach: Erwin Koeman (NED)
Sweden: Isaksson, Mellberg, Nilsson, Majstorović, Safari, Svensson, Källström, Holmén (Hysén 85), R. Elm, Ibrahimović, Elmander (Berg 75). Coach: Lars Lagerbäck (SWE)
Goal(s): 0-1 Mellberg 9, 1-1 Huszti 79 (p), 1-2 Ibrahimović 90+3
Yellow Card(s): Svensson 22 (Sweden), Dárdai 31 (Hungary), Gera 81 (Hungary), Mellberg 81 (Sweden)
Referee: Rizzoli (ITA)

5/9/09, Parken, Copenhagen
Denmark 1-1 Portugal
Attendance: 37998
Denmark: Andersen, Jacobsen, Christensen, Kjær, C. Poulsen, Silberbauer (W.K. Jørgensen 66), Rommedahl, J. Poulsen (Grønkjær 88), M. Jørgensen (Nørregaard 61), Tomasson, Bendtner. Coach: Morten Olsen (DEN)
Portugal: Eduardo, Bosingwa, Ricardo Carvalho, Pepe, Bruno Alves, Tiago (Liedson 46), Deco, Duda, Raul Meireles (Nuno Gomes 80), Simão (Nani 70), Cristiano Ronaldo. Coach: Carlos Queiroz (POR)
Goal(s): 0-1 Mellberg 43, 1-1 Liedson 86
Yellow Card(s): Liedson 48 (Portugal), Kjær 60 (Denmark), Andersen 85 (Denmark)
Referee: Busacca (SUI)

9/9/09, Ta' Qali, Ta' Qali
Malta 0-1 Sweden
Attendance: 4705
Malta: Hogg, Said, Scicluna, Azzopardi, A. Muscat (Briffa 61), G. Agius, E. Muscat, Bajada (Failla 72), Cohen, Pace, Mifsud. Coach: John Buttigieg (MLT)
Sweden: Isaksson, Mellberg, Nilsson, Majstorović, Safari, Svensson (Berg 70), Källström, Holmén (Hysén 57), R. Elm, Ibrahimović, Elmander (S. Larsson 82). Coach: Lars Lagerbäck (SWE)
Goal(s): 0-1 Azzopardi 82 (og)
Yellow Card(s): Majstorović 45 (Sweden), Safari 45+1 (Sweden), Mifsud 85 (Malta)
Referee: McCourt (NIR)

9/9/09, Qemal Stafa, Tirana
Albania 1-1 Denmark
Attendance: 4500
Albania: Ujkani, Beqiri (Hyka 46), Agolli, Dallku, Curri, Skela (Vila 82), Duro, Cana, Bulku, Bogdani (Lika 78), Salihi. Coach: Josip Kuže (CRO)
Denmark: Sørensen, Jacobsen, Christensen, W.K. Jørgensen, Kjær, C. Poulsen, Rommedahl, J. Poulsen (Grønkjær 54), M. Jørgensen (Nørregaard 69), Tomasson (Larsen 73), Bendtner. Coach: Morten Olsen (DEN)
Goal(s): 0-1 Bendtner 40, 1-1 Bogdani 69
Yellow Card(s): Agolli 49 (Albania), Dallku 65 (Albania)
Referee: Çakır (TUR)

9/9/09, Ferenc Puskás, Budapest
Hungary 0-1 Portugal
Attendance: 42000
Hungary: Babos, Bodnár, Gyepes, Juhász, Tóth (Buzsáky 83), Dárdai (Hajnal 65), Halmosi, Huszti (Priskin 65), Vadócz, Dzsudzsák, Torghelle. Coach: Erwin Koeman (NED)
Portugal: Eduardo, Bosingwa, Ricardo Carvalho, Pepe, Bruno Alves, Tiago (Rolando 89), Deco (Simão 49), Duda, Raul Meireles, Cristiano Ronaldo, Liedson (Nani 81). Coach: Carlos Queiroz (POR)
Goal(s): 0-1 Pepe 10
Yellow Card(s): Tóth 51 (Hungary), Pepe 69 (Portugal), Duda 77 (Portugal), Halmosi 90 (Hungary)
Referee: Lannoy (FRA)

Sweden's Olof Mellberg (No3) rises highest in
Sweden's 1-0 win away to Malta

10/10/09, Parken, Copenhagen
Denmark 1-0 Sweden
Attendance: 37800
Denmark: Sørensen, Jacobsen, Jakobsen, Agger, Kjær, C. Poulsen,
Rommedahl, J. Poulsen, M. Jørgensen (Silberbauer 46), Tomasson,
Bendtner. Coach: Morten Olsen (DEN)
Sweden: Isaksson, Mellberg, Nilsson (Rosenberg 88), Majstorović,
Safari, Svensson, Källström, Holmén (S. Larsson 63), R. Elm (Berg 80),
H. Larsson, Ibrahimović. Coach: Lars Lagerbäck (SWE)
Goal(s): 1-0 J. Poulsen 78
Referee: Mejuto González (ESP)

10/10/09, Estádio do Sport Lisboa e Benfica, Lisbon
Portugal 3-0 Hungary
Attendance: 50115
Portugal: Eduardo, Bosingwa, Ricardo Carvalho, Bruno Alves, Deco,
Pedro Mendes, Duda, Raul Meireles, Simão (Miguel Veloso 81),
Cristiano Ronaldo (Nani 27), Liedson (Nuno Gomes 83). Coach:
Carlos Queiroz (POR)
Hungary: Babos, Bodnár, Gyepes, Juhász, Vanczák, Gera, Tóth, Huszti
(Buzsáky 67), Vadócz (Priskin 56), Dzsudzsák (Varga 84), Torghelle.
Coach: Erwin Koeman (NED)
Goal(s): 1-0 Simão 18, 2-0 Liedson 74, 3-0 Simão 79
Referee: Hamer (LUX)

14/10/09, D. Afonso Henriques, Guimaraes
Portugal 4-0 Malta
Attendance: 29350
Portugal: Eduardo, Bosingwa, Ricardo Carvalho, Pepe, Deco, Pedro
Mendes, Raul Meireles (Nuno Assis 62), Nani (João Moutinho 73),
Miguel Veloso, Simão, Liedson (Edinho 62). Coach: Carlos Queiroz (POR)
Malta: Hogg, Said, Scicluna, Azzopardi, Bajada (Fenech 73), Muscat,
Cohen (Failla 23), Briffa (Sammut 88), Pace, Hutchinson, Mifsud.
Coach: John Buttigieg (MLT)
Goal(s): 1-0 Nani 14, 2-0 Simão 45, 3-0 Miguel Veloso 52, 4-0 Edinho 90
Yellow Card(s): Scicluna 43 (Malta), Failla 76 (Malta), Bosingwa 78
(Portugal), Pepe 84 (Portugal)
Referee: Kelly (IRL)

14/10/09, Råsunda, Solna
Sweden 4-1 Albania
Attendance: 25342
Sweden: Isaksson, Mellberg, Nilsson, Majstorović, Safari, Svensson,
Källström (Andersson 21), S. Larsson, R. Elm, Ibrahimović (Rosenberg
77), Elmander (Berg 37). Coach: Lars Lagerbäck (SWE)
Albania: Ujkani, Beqiri, Dallku, Curri, Skela, Haxhi (Hyka 22), Duro,
Cana, Bulku, Bogdani (Berisha 87), Salihi (Kapllani 79). Coach: Josip
Kuže (CRO)
Goal(s): 1-0 Mellberg 6, 2-0 Berg 40, 3-0 Mellberg 42, 3-1 Salihi 57,
4-1 Svensson 86
Yellow Card(s): Dallku 22 (Albania), Svensson 28 (Sweden)
Referee: Ivanov (RUS)

14/10/09, Parken, Copenhagen
Denmark 0-1 Hungary
Attendance: 36956
Denmark: Sørensen, Jacobsen, Christensen, Jakobsen, Agger, C.
Poulsen, Rommedahl (Silberbauer 71), J. Poulsen, Enevoldsen (Larsen
46), Tomasson (Jensen 62), Bendtner. Coach: Morten Olsen (DEN)
Hungary: Babos, Bodnár, Juhász, Vanczák, Halmosi, Buzsáky (Huszti
76), Tóth, Dzsudzsák (Priskin 89), Varga, Torghelle, Rudolf (Vadócz
87). Coach: Erwin Koeman (NED)
Goal(s): 0-1 Buzsáky 35
Yellow Card(s): Christensen 19 (Denmark), Jensen 78 (Denmark)
Referee: Meyer (GER)

Group 1 Table

	Pld	Home					Away					Total					Pts
		W	D	L	F	A	W	D	L	F	A	W	D	L	F	A	
1 Denmark	10	3	1	1	8	2	3	2	0	8	3	6	3	1	16	5	21
2 Portugal	10	2	2	1	9	3	3	2	0	8	2	5	4	1	17	5	19
3 Sweden	10	3	1	1	10	3	2	2	1	3	2	5	3	2	13	5	18
4 Hungary	10	2	1	2	6	3	3	0	2	4	5	5	1	4	10	8	16
5 Albania	10	1	2	2	5	4	0	2	3	1	9	1	4	5	6	13	7
6 Malta	10	0	1	4	0	9	0	0	5	0	17	0	1	9	0	26	1

GROUP 2

Switzerland ensured a second consecutive FIFA World Cup finals berth for the first time since 1966 after topping Group 2 ahead of a Greece side who had to settle for second place and the play-offs.

Crucial victories

With just one point separating the countries at the close of the qualifying programme, Switzerland owed their success very much to the two victories they secured against their closest rivals.

Ottmar Hitzfeld's men had already defeated Greece 2-1 in Piraeus the previous October when the countries squared off in their second summit meeting in Basel on 5 September 2009. With the pair tied on 13 points at the top of the section going into the new season, the stakes were high – and not surprisingly a tightly fought contest unfolded.

Greece contained their hosts comfortably for much of the first half at St. Jakob-Park and even after the 41st-minute dismissal of Loukas Vintra for a second yellow card, they went close to opening the scoring in the second period when Nikos Spiropoulos had a shot tipped on to the crossbar by Switzerland goalkeeper Diego Benaglio. But instead it was Switzerland who broke through with a Stéphane Grichting header from Hakan Yakin's cross after 84 minutes. Soon afterwards Marco Padalino salted Greek wounds by nodding in a second goal, this time from an Alexander Frei cross.

Greece slip up

Although Switzerland were then held 2-2 by Latvia in Riga four days later, they retained their three-point advantage at the top because Otto Rehhagel's Greeks surprisingly dropped two points away to bottom-placed Moldova, conceding a 90th-minute equaliser to Valeriu Andronic in a 1-1 draw in Chisinau.

From pursuing top spot, Greece suddenly found themselves level on points with the third-placed Latvians. The Baltic team had enjoyed a successful September, winning 1-0 in Israel through a Kaspars Gorkšs goal (which effectively killed off their hosts' hopes), then holding the Swiss.

Latvia's hopes of a play-off place were demolished, however, when they crashed to a 5-2 defeat in Greece the following month. Aleksandrs Starkovs' visitors

actually took a 2-1 half-time lead before the Greeks reasserted their superiority. Four of their five goals came from Germany-based forward Theofanis Gekas, two of them from the penalty spot.

Gekas in the goals

It was fitting that Gekas then struck the final goal of Greece's Group 2 programme – in a nervy 2-1 defeat of Luxembourg on 14 October – for with that effort he secured his place at the top of the European Zone scoring chart with ten, one clear of both England's Wayne Rooney and Bosnia-Herzegovina's Edin Džeko.

Despite Gekas's exploits, it was Switzerland – whose leading marksmen Alexander Frei and Blaise Nkufo each managed exactly half the Greek striker's tally – who were celebrating that night. Having defeated Luxembourg 3-0 in their penultimate fixture, their goalless home draw against ten-man Israel was sufficient to see them across the finishing line with 21 points.

For the visiting Israel coach Dror Kashtan it was a last competitive match at the helm after a disappointing fourth-placed finish for a team who lost just twice but - not for the first time in a qualifying campaign - paid the price for too many draws.

Marco Padalino puts Switzerland 2-0 up against Greece in Basel

No such worries for his counterpart Hitzfield, who, having taken the Swiss post after the co-hosts' disappointing early exit at UEFA EURO 2008, could take satisfaction from a job well done. He had succeeded in righting their course after a rocky start that brought an embarrassing 2-1 home loss to Luxembourg. Indeed, that proved to be the team's only defeat as the former BV Borussia Dortund and FC Bayern München coach got the better of his compatriot Rehhagel to steer the Swiss to their ninth World Cup finals.

Group 2 Results

6/9/08
Moldova 1-2 Latvia
Luxembourg 0-3 Greece
Israel 2-2 Switzerland
10/9/08
Switzerland 1-2 Luxembourg
Moldova 1-2 Israel
Latvia 0-2 Greece
11/10/08
Switzerland 2-1 Latvia
Luxembourg 1-3 Israel
Greece 3-0 Moldova

15/10/08
Latvia 1-1 Israel
Luxembourg 0-0 Moldova
Greece 1-2 Switzerland
28/3/09
Luxembourg 0-4 Latvia
Moldova 0-2 Switzerland
Israel 1-1 Greece
1/4/09
Latvia 2-0 Luxembourg
Switzerland 2-0 Moldova
Greece 2-1 Israel

5/9/09, Zimbru, Chisinau
Moldova 0-0 Luxembourg
Attendance: 7820
Moldova: St. Namaşco, Lascencov, Catinsus, Golovatenco, Armas, Gatcan, Onica, Comleonoc (Andronic 81), Calincov, Bugaiov (Suvorov 77), Sofroni. Coach: Igor Dobrovolski (MDA)
Luxembourg: Joubert, Strasser, Hoffmann, Kintziger, Jänisch (Collette 57), Blaise, Peters, Lombardelli (Leweck 78), Bettmer, Payal, Pupovac (Da Mota 84). Coach: Guy Hellers (LUX)
Yellow Card(s): Lombardelli 9 (Luxembourg), Blaise 32 (Luxembourg), Onica 36 (Moldova), Joubert 81 (Luxembourg), Strasser 84 (Luxembourg), Gatcan 84 (Moldova), Golovatenco 85 (Moldova), Payal 86 (Luxembourg)
Referee: Mažeika (LTU)

Elyaniv Barda hurdles a challenge against Luxembourg – he scored a hat-trick in Israel's 7-0 win

5/9/09, St. Jakob-Park, Basel
Switzerland 2-0 Greece
Attendance: 38500
Switzerland: Benaglio, Nef (Derdiyok 61), Von Bergen, Grichting, Magnin, Padalino, Huggel, Fernandes (Yakin 68), Barnetta, Frei, Nkufo (Vonlanthen 81). Coach: Ottmar Hitzfeld (GER)
Greece: Chalkias, Papasthopoulos, Moras, Kyrgiakos, Vintra, Patsatzoglou, Katsouranis, Spiropoulos, Salpingidis (Samaras 46), Charisteas (Papadopoulos 73), Amanatidis (Gekas 81). Coach: Otto Rehhagel (GER)
Goal(s): 1-0 Grichting 83, 2-0 Padalino 88
Red Card(s): Vintra 42 (Greece)
Yellow Card(s): Vintra 7 (Greece), Vintra 42 (Greece), Kyrgiakos 65 (Greece), Spiropoulos 83 (Greece), Magnin 87 (Switzerland)
Referee: De Bleeckere (BEL)

5/9/09, Ramat Gan, Ramat Gan
Israel 0-1 Latvia
Attendance: 25625
Israel: Awat, Ben Dayan, Keinan, Strul, Shpungin, Benayoun (Baruchyan 67), Cohen (Alberman 46), Kayal, Katan, Golan (Sahar 63), Barda. Coach: Dror Kashtan (ISR)
Latvia: Vaņins, Ivanovs, Gorkšs, Kačanovs, Kļava, Rubins (Zirnis 82), Astafjevs, Koļesničenko, Cauņa (Žigajevs 82), Verpakovskis (Perepļotkins 90+2), Karlsons. Coach: Aleksandrs Starkovs (LVA)
Goal(s): 0-1 Gorkss 59
Yellow Card(s): Shpungin 66 (Israel), Keinan 71 (Israel), Verpakovskis 81 (Latvia), Zirnis 88 (Latvia)
Referee: Kircher (GER)

9/9/09, Ramat Gan, Ramat Gan
Israel 7-0 Luxembourg
Attendance: 7038
Israel: Awat (Davidovich 46), Ben Haim, Ben Dayan, Strul, Ziv, Benayoun, Cohen, Baruchyan, Kayal, Golan (Itzhaki 67), Barda (Sahar 59). Coach: Dror Kashtan (ISR)
Luxembourg: Oberweis, Hoffmann, Mutsch, Kintziger, Jänisch (Collette 50), Blaise, Peters, Lombardelli (Leweck 63), Bettmer, Payal (Pedro 46), Pupovac. Coach: Ronny Bonvini (LUX)
Goal(s): 1-0 Barda 9, 2-0 Baruchyan 15, 3-0 Barda 21, 4-0 Barda 43, 5-0 Golan 58, 6-0 Sahar 63, 7-0 Sahar 84
Yellow Card(s): Golan 62 (Israel)
Referee: Svendsen (DEN)

9/9/09, Skonto, Riga
Latvia 2-2 Switzerland
Attendance: 8600
Latvia: Vanins, Ivanovs, Gorkšs, Kačanovs, Kļava, Rubins, Astafjevs, Koļesničenko (Rafaļskis 86), Cauņa (Zirnis 89), Verpakovskis, Karlsons (Grebis 85). Coach: Aleksandrs Starkovs (LVA)
Switzerland: Benaglio, Spycher, Grichting, Lichtsteiner, Von Bergen, Padalino (Vonlanthen 76), Huggel, Fernandes (Derdiyok 76), Barnetta (Yakin 76), Frei, Nkufo. Coach: Ottmar Hitzfeld (GER)
Goal(s): 0-1 Frei 43, 1-1 Cauņa 62, 2-1 Astafjevs 75, 2-2 Derdiyok 80
Yellow Card(s): Ivanovs 16 (Latvia), Grichting 23 (Switzerland), Koļesničenko 72 (Latvia), Astafjevs 73 (Latvia)
Referee: Královec (CZE)

9/9/09, Zimbru, Chisinau
Moldova 1-1 Greece
Attendance: 9870
Moldova: St. Namaşco, Lascencov, Savinov (Andronic 79), Catinsus, Epureanu, Armas, Gatcan, Se. Namasco (Comleonoc 56), Bulat, Calincov, Bugaiov (Sofroni 46). Coach: Igor Dobrovolski (MDA)
Greece: Chalkias, Kyrgiakos, Moras (Papadopoulos 58), Spiropoulos, Patsatzoglou, Karagounis (Amanatidis 76), Katsouranis, Tziolis, Charisteas, Gekas, Samaras. Coach: Otto Rehhagel (GER)
Goal(s): 0-1 Gekas 33, 1-1 Andronic 90
Yellow Card(s): Gatcan 11 (Moldova), Tziolis 15 (Greece), Kyrgiakos 45 (Greece), Papadopoulos 81 (Greece), Charisteas 89 (Greece), Lascencov 90+2 (Moldova)
Referee: Stalhammar (SWE)

2010 FIFA WORLD CUP

10/10/09, Josy Barthel, Luxembourg
Luxembourg 0-3 Switzerland
Attendance: 8031
Luxembourg: Joubert, Strasser, Collette (Jänisch 73), Mutsch, Kintziger, Blaise, Peters, Bettmer, Payal, Laterza (Leweck 46), Kitenge (Pupovac 60). Coach: Guy Hellers (LUX)
Switzerland: Benaglio, Spycher, Senderos, Lichtsteiner, Von Bergen, Huggel, Barnetta (Ziegler 82), Inler, Vonlanthen (Yakin 65), Frei (Derdiyok 65), Nkufo. Coach: Ottmar Hitzfeld (GER)
Goal(s): 0-1 Senderos 6, 0-2 Senderos 8, 0-3 Huggel 22
Yellow Card(s): Von Bergen 40 (Switzerland), Bettmer 42 (Luxembourg), Barnetta 79 (Switzerland)
Referee: Iturralde González (ESP)

10/10/09, Ramat Gan, Ramat Gan
Israel 3-1 Moldova
Attendance: 8700
Israel: Awat, Ben Haim, Ben Dayan, Strul, Ziv (Saban 29), Benayoun, Cohen, Vermouth, Yadin, Barda (Colautti 72), Sahar (Shechter 61). Coach: Dror Kashtan (ISR)
Moldova: St. Namaşco, Lascencov, Savinov, Catinsus, Epureanu, Golovatenco, Bulat, Cebotari (Andronic 67), Calincov, Bugaiov (Suvorov 74), Sofroni (Ovseannicov 79). Coach: Igor Dobrovolski (MDA)
Goal(s): 1-0 Barda 21, 2-0 Ben Dayan 65, 3-0 Barda 70, 3-1 Calincov 90+2
Yellow Card(s): Cohen 20 (Israel), Bulat 20 (Moldova), Ben Dayan 41 (Israel), Sahar 53 (Israel), Bugaiov 60 (Moldova)
Referee: Blom (NED)

10/10/09, OACA Spyro Louis, Athens
Greece 5-2 Latvia
Attendance: 18981
Greece: Tzorvas, Seitaridis, Moras, Torosidis, Papastathopoulos, Karagounis (Pliatsikas 89), Katsouranis, Tziolis (Patsatzoglou 46), Gekas, Salpingidis (Amanatidis 46), Samaras. Coach: Otto Rehhagel (GER)
Latvia: Vanins, Ivanovs, Gorkšs, Kačanovs, Kļava, Rubins (Soloņicins 78), Koļesničenko, Laizāns, Cauņa, Verpakovskis (Pereplotkins 84), Karlsons (Grebis 71). Coach: Aleksandrs Starkovs (LVA)
Goal(s): 1-0 Gekas 4, 1-1 Verpakovskis 12, 1-2 Verpakovskis 40, 2-2 Gekas 47 (p), 3-2 Gekas 57, 4-2 Samaras 73, 5-2 Gekas 90+1
Yellow Card(s): Samaras 50 (Greece), Seitaridis 51 (Greece), Patsatzoglou 79 (Greece)
Referee: Øvrebø (NOR)

14/10/09, St. Jakob-Park, Basel
Switzerland 0-0 Israel
Attendance: 38500
Switzerland: Wölfli, Spycher, Senderos, Grichting, Lichtsteiner, Barnetta, Fernandes, Padalino, Inler, Derdiyok (Frei 70), Nkufo. Coach: Ottmar Hitzfeld (GER)
Israel: Awat, Saban, Ben Haim, Strul, Ziv, Benayoun, Cohen, Kayal, Yadin, Barda (Vermouth 85), Colautti (Shechter 68). Coach: Dror Kashtan (ISR)
Red Card(s): Yadin 60 (Israel)
Yellow Card(s): Ziv 14 (Israel), Padalino 25 (Switzerland), Yadin 33 (Israel), Inler 45+1 (Switzerland), Kayal 47 (Israel), Yadin 60 (Israel), Colautti 65 (Israel), Fernandes 65 (Switzerland), Lichtsteiner 71 (Switzerland)
Referee: Tudor (ROU)

14/10/09, OACA Spyro Louis, Athens
Greece 2-1 Luxembourg
Attendance: 13932
Greece: Sifakis, Kyrgiakos (Moras 43), Papadopoulos, Torosidis, Vintra (Ninis 83), Spiropoulos, Karagounis, Patsatzoglou, Fotakis (Pliatsikas 46), Gekas, Salpingidis. Coach: Otto Rehhagel (GER)
Luxembourg: Joubert, Strasser, Hoffmann, Mutsch, Kintziger (Martino 80), Jänisch (Leweck 46), Blaise, Peters, Bettmer, Payal, Kitenge (Pupovac 73). Coach: Guy Hellers (LUX)
Goal(s): 1-0 Torosidis 30, 2-0 Gekas 33, 2-1 Papadopoulos 90 (og)
Red Card(s): Payal 58 (Luxembourg)
Yellow Card(s): Payal 16 (Luxembourg), Payal 58 (Luxembourg), Pliatsikas 59 (Greece), Mutsch 90+2 (Luxembourg)
Referee: Čeferin (SVN)

Theofanis Gekas celebrates one of his four goals in Greece's 5-2 win over Latvia

14/10/09, Skonto, Riga
Latvia 3-2 Moldova
Attendance: 3800
Latvia: Vanins, Ivanovs, Gorkšs, Kačanovs, Kļava, Rubins (Soloņicins 63), Astafjevs, Koļesničenko (Laizāns 74), Cauņa, Verpakovskis, Karlsons (Grebis 69). Coach: Aleksandrs Starkovs (LVA)
Moldova: St. Namaşco, Lascencov, Savinov, Epureanu, Golovatenco, Armas (Andronic 81), Catinsus, Se. Namasco, Calincov, Ovseannicov (Sofroni 76), Bugaiov (Suvorov 70). Coach: Igor Dobrovolski (MDA)
Goal(s): 0-1 Ovseannicov 25, 1-1 Rubins 32, 2-1 Rubins 44, 3-1 Grebis 76, 3-2 Sofroni 90
Yellow Card(s): Karlsons 11 (Latvia), Golovatenco 40 (Moldova), Rubins 58 (Latvia)
Referee: Hyytiä (FIN)

Group 2 Table

		Pld	Home					Away					Total					Pts
			W	D	L	F	A	W	D	L	F	A	W	D	L	F	A	
1	Switzerland	10	3	1	1	7	3	3	2	0	11	5	6	3	1	18	8	21
2	Greece	10	4	0	1	13	6	2	2	1	7	4	6	2	2	20	10	20
3	Latvia	10	2	2	1	8	7	3	0	2	10	8	5	2	3	18	15	17
4	Israel	10	2	2	1	13	5	2	2	1	7	5	4	4	2	20	10	16
5	Luxembourg	10	0	1	4	1	13	1	1	3	3	12	1	2	7	4	25	5
6	Moldova	10	0	2	3	3	7	0	1	4	3	11	0	3	7	6	18	3

GROUP 3

Slovakia stepped out of the shadow of the Czech Republic, their neighbours and erstwhile compatriots, to qualify for their first FIFA World Cup finals as an independent state as winners of Group 3. They held off a late challenge from a Slovenia side who hit a rich vein of form in the final straight to earn a second chance in the play-offs.

Hopes high

Slovakia had ended the 2008/09 season on course for a place in South Africa after winning five of their first six qualifying games. Hopes were duly high when Vladimír Weiss's men resumed their campaign at home to the Czech Republic on 5 September. They had already prevailed when the countries met in Prague but this time had to settle for a point after twice losing the lead in a 2-2 draw.

After a scoreless first half, Stanislav Šesták put them in front before Daniel Pudil replied for the Czechs. Classy playmaker Marek Hamšík restored the hosts' advantage from the penalty spot only to be sent off two minutes later for a second bookable offence. The Czechs took advantage as Milan Baroš headed their second equaliser in the 83rd minute. Four days later Šesták – who managed six goals in six qualifying appearances – was on the mark again in a vital 2-0 victory away to Northern Ireland. Filip Hološko struck the second goal two minutes after taking the field as Slovakia cemented their place at the top with a stirring display at Windsor Park.

Slovenia on the up

Second in the group going into the autumn qualifiers, Nigel Worthington's Northern Ireland had now slipped to third on goal difference behind Slovenia and would eventually finish fourth. The Slovenians, by contrast, were on the up. They had gone into the autumn in fifth place, with eight points from six matches. Six further points were added to their total at the expense of San Marino and Poland, and Matjaž Kek's men made it three wins in a row with an impressive 2-0 defeat of Slovakia in Bratislava on 10 October.

AJ Auxerre midfielder Valter Birsa struck the visitors' first goal with a swerving long-range shot in the 56th minute before Nejc Pečnik sealed the win on a breakaway in added time. Slovakia had needed just a point against Slovenia to book their ticket to South Africa but now travelled to Poland for their final qualifier minus four suspended players and, with just a two-point advantage over the Slovenians, who faced the easier-looking task of a home fixture against San Marino, requiring a win to stay top.

Slovakia prevail in snow

It was no surprise when Slovenia beat the Sammarinese, the European Zone's second meanest defence keeping a fourth successive clean sheet in the 3-0 win, but they were denied first place as Slovakia scraped the win they needed on a snow-covered pitch in Chorzow. A third-minute own goal by Poland's Seweryn Gancarczyk gifted them a lead they defended with a combination of fine goalkeeping from Ján Mucha and good fortune, with the crossbar coming to the rescue when Mucha was beaten by a Mariusz Lewandowski shot.

Slovakia's Stanislav Šesták points the way forward after scoring in the 2-2 draw against the Czech Republic

Footballers from Slovakia had competed at previous World Cups under the flag of Czechoslovakia – indeed national coach Weiss was in the squad that reached the last eight at Italia 90. Now, for the first time since independence, a generation of Slovakian players had won through to compete in a major tournament.

It was a considerably less satisfying outcome for their Czech neighbours who, despite finishing with a four-match unbeaten run under Ivan Hašek, missed out on a major tournament for the first time since 2002. They responded by appointing Michal Bílek as their fourth coach in the space of a year. Poland did the same after a disheartening fifth-place finish. Leo Beenhakker had quit after the 3-0 loss in Slovenia that ended their hopes of a third successive World Cup participation, and after Stefan Majewski deputised for the final qualifiers, the mantle was passed to Franciszek Smuda with the remit of rebuilding for the UEFA EURO 2012 tournament that the Poles will co-host.

Slovenia's star midfielder Valter Birsa

Group 3 Results

6/9/08
Poland 1-1 Slovenia
Slovakia 2-1 Northern Ireland
Northern Ireland 0-0 Czech Republic
10/9/08
San Marino 0-2 Poland
Slovenia 2-1 Slovakia
San Marino 1-3 Slovakia
11/10/08
Poland 2-1 Czech Republic
Slovenia 2-0 Northern Ireland
Czech Republic 1-0 Slovenia
15/10/08
Northern Ireland 4-0 San Marino
Slovakia 2-1 Poland

19/11/08
San Marino 0-3 Czech Republic
11/2/09
San Marino 0-3 Northern Ireland
28/3/09
Northern Ireland 3-2 Poland
Slovenia 0-0 Czech Republic
1/4/09
Northern Ireland 1-0 Slovenia
Czech Republic 1-2 Slovakia
Poland 10-0 San Marino
6/6/09
Slovakia 7-0 San Marino

12/8/09, Ljudski vrt, Maribor
Slovenia 5-0 San Marino
Attendance: 4400
Slovenia: S. Handanovič, Brecko, Šuler, Cesar, Jokič, Pečnik (Kirm 46), Radosavljevič (Bačinovič 74), Koren, Birsa, Ljubijankič, Velikonja (Novakovič 72). Coach: Matjaž Kek (SVN)
San Marino: A. Simoncini, F. Vitaioli (M. Vitaioli 59), Andreini, Bacciocchi, Della Valle, D. Simoncini (Albani 66), Vannucci, Bugli, Berretti, Man. Marani (Bonini 80), Ciacci. Coach: Giampaolo Mazza (ITA)
Goal(s): 1-0 Koren 19, 2-0 Radosavljevič 39, 3-0 Kirm 54, 4-0 Koren 74 5-0 Ljubijankič 90+3
Yellow Card(s): D. Simoncini 41 (San Marino), A. Simoncini 55 (San Marino), Bugli 79 (San Marino)
Referee: Meckarovski (MKD)

5/9/09, Śląski, Chorzow
Poland 1-1 Northern Ireland
Attendance: 45000
Poland: Boruc, Żewłakow, Dudka, Golański, Krzynówek, M. Lewandowski, Obraniak (Smolarek 46), Błaszczykowski, Roger, Murawski (R. Lewandowski 61), Pa. Brożek. Coach: Leo Beenhakker (NED)
Northern Ireland: Taylor, Craigan, Hughes, McAuley, J. Evans, Johnson, McCann, Clingan, Davis, Healy, Lafferty (Paterson 54). Coach: Nigel Worthington (NIR)
Goal(s): 0-1 Lafferty 38, 1-1 M. Lewandowski 80
Yellow Card(s): Golański 62 (Poland)
Referee: Mejuto González (ESP)

5/9/09, Tehelné Pole, Bratislava
Slovakia 2-2 Czech Republic
Attendance: 23800
Slovakia: Mucha, Zabavník, Ďurica, Škrteľ, Pekarík, Štrba, Šesták (Čech 82), Weiss (Sapara 74), Hamšík, Vittek, Hološko (Jendrišek 87). Coach: Vladimír Weiss (SVK)
Czech Republic: Čech, Jankulovski, Grygera, Hübschman, Sivok, Kadlec, Štajner (Svěrkoš 83), Jarolím (Necid 65), Plašil, Pudil, Koller (Baroš 55). Coach: Ivan Hašek (CZE)
Goal(s): 1-0 Šesták 59, 1-1 Pudil 68, 2-1 Hamšík 73 (p), 2-2 Baroš 84
Red Card(s): Hamšík 75 (Slovakia)
Yellow Card(s): Grygera 11 (Czech Republic), Hamšík 74 (Slovakia), Hamšík 75 (Slovakia)
Referee: Øvrebø (NOR)

9/9/09, Stonký, Uherske Hradiste
Czech Republic 7-0 San Marino
Attendance: 8121
Czech Republic: Čech, Rozehnal, Grygera (Štajner 77), Hübschman, Hubník, Kadlec (Pudil 46), Rosický (Jarolím 56), Plašil, Baroš, Svěrkoš, Necid. Coach: Ivan Hašek (CZE)
San Marino: A. Simoncini, Mau. Marani (Bonini 65), Bacciocchi, Della Valle, Andreini, F. Vitaioli, Vannucci, Bugli (Cervellini 89), Berretti, Ciacci (M. Vitaioli 75), Selva. Coach: Giampaolo Mazza (ITA)
Goal(s): 1-0 Baroš 28, 2-0 Baroš 44, 3-0 Baroš 45+3 (p), 4-0 Svěrkoš 47, 5-0 Baroš 66, 6-0 Necid 86, 7-0 Svěrkoš 90+4
Red Card(s): Bacciocchi 82 (San Marino)
Yellow Card(s): Della Valle 4 (San Marino), Berretti 23 (San Marino), F. Vitaioli 45+2 (San Marino), Pudil 49 (Czech Republic), Bacciocchi 54 (San Marino), Mau. Marani 58 (San Marino), Bacciocchi 82 (San Marino), Vannucci 90+2 (San Marino)
Referee: Amirkhanyan (ARM)

2010 FIFA WORLD CUP

9/9/09, Windsor Park, Belfast
Northern Ireland 0-2 Slovakia
Attendance: 13019
Northern Ireland: Taylor, Craigan, Hughes, McAuley, J. Evans, Johnson, McCann (McGinn 70), Clingan (Baird 70), Davis, Healy, Paterson (Brunt 76). Coach: Nigel Worthington (NIR)
Slovakia: Mucha, Zabavník, Ďurica, Škrteľ, Pekarík, Štrba, Šesták (Hološko 65), Kopúnek, Weiss (Sapara 90+1), Stoch (Jendrišek 80), Vittek. Coach: Vladimír Weiss (SVK)
Goal(s): 0-1 Šesták 15, 0-2 Hološko 67
Yellow Card(s): Clingan 17 (Northern Ireland), Šesták 18 (Slovakia), Healy 83 (Northern Ireland)
Referee: Kuipers (NED)

9/9/09, Ljudski vrt, Maribor
Slovenia 3-0 Poland
Attendance: 10226
Slovenia: S. Handanovič, Mavrič, Brecko, Šuler, Jokič, Radosavljević (Pečnik 89), Koren, Kirm, Dedič (Ljubijankič 58), Birsa (Komac 71), Novakovič. Coach: Matjaž Kek (SVN)
Poland: Boruc, Żewłakow, Bosacki, Dudka, Gancarczyk (Smolarek 61), Krzynówek, M. Lewandowski, Obraniak (Łobodziński 46), Błaszczykowski, Roger, Pa.Brożek (R. Lewandowski 61). Coach: Leo Beenhakker (NED)
Goal(s): 1-0 Dedič 13, 2-0 Novakovič 44, 3-0 Birsa 62
Yellow Card(s): Dedič 9 (Slovenia), Brecko 39 (Slovenia), Błaszczykowski 39 (Poland), Obraniak 45+2 (Poland)
Referee: Collum (SCO)

10/10/09, Generali Arena, Prague
Czech Republic 2-0 Poland
Attendance: 14010
Czech Republic: Čech, Jankulovski, Hübschman, Sivok, Pospěch, Hubník, Rosický (Jarolím 78), Plašil, Pudil (Štajner 86), Baroš, Papadopulos (Necid 46). Coach: Ivan Hašek (CZE)
Poland: Kowalewski, Głowacki, Gancarczyk, Polczak, Rzeźniczak, M. Lewandowski, Obraniak, Błaszczykowski (Peszko 68), Iwanski, Jeleń (R. Lewandowski 63), Grosicki (Janczyk 81). Coach: Stefan Majewski (POL)
Goal(s): 1-0 Necid 51, 2-0 Plašil 72
Yellow Card(s): Jankulovski 7 (Czech Republic), Polczak 38 (Poland), Iwanski 49 (Poland), Głowacki 59 (Poland), Necid 88 (Czech Republic)
Referee: Larsen (DEN)

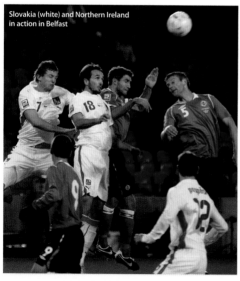

Slovakia (white) and Northern Ireland in action in Belfast

10/10/09, Tehelné Pole, Bratislava
Slovakia 0-2 Slovenia
Attendance: 23800
Slovakia: Mucha, Zabavník, Ďurica, Škrteľ, Pekarík, Štrba (Novák 84), Weiss, Hamšík, Stoch, Vittek (Jendrišek 80), Jakubko (Karhan 46). Coach: Vladimír Weiss (SVK)
Slovenia: S. Handanovič, Cesar, Brecko, Šuler, Jokič, Radosavljević, Koren, Kirm, Dedič (Pečnik 78), Birsa (Stevanovič 90+4), Novakovič. Coach: Matjaž Kek (SVN)
Goal(s): 0-1 Birsa 56, 0-2 Pečnik 90+3
Yellow Card(s): Stoch 28 (Slovakia), Ďurica 48 (Slovakia), Weiss 75 (Slovakia), Koren 76 (Slovenia), Zabavník 81 (Slovakia), Škrteľ 85 (Slovakia)
Referee: Stark (GER)

14/10/09, Eden, Prague
Czech Republic 0-0 Northern Ireland
Attendance: 8002
Czech Republic: Čech, Jankulovski, Sivok, Pospěch, Hubník, Rosický (Štajner 72), Jarolím (Papadopulos 83), Hübschman, Plašil, Baroš, Necid (Hloušek 59). Coach: Ivan Hašek (CZE)
Northern Ireland: Taylor, Craigan, Baird, Hughes, McAuley, McGivern, Johnson (Kirk 83), McCann (O'Connor 80), Davis, McGinn, Healy (Feeney 69). Coach: Nigel Worthington (NIR)
Yellow Card(s): Baroš 74 (Czech Republic), Feeney 75 (Northern Ireland)
Referee: Duhamel (FRA)

14/10/09, Śląski, Chorzow
Poland 0-1 Slovakia
Attendance: 5000
Poland: Dudek, Głowacki, Bieniuk, Gancarczyk, Rzeźniczak, M. Lewandowski, Obraniak, Błaszczykowski, Roger (Peszko 60), Pa.Brożek (Janczyk 86), Jeleń (R. Lewandowski 68). Coach: Stefan Majewski (POL)
Slovakia: Mucha, M. Petráš, Saláta, Pekarík, Štrba, Šesták (Švento 74), Kozák (Karhan 85), Kopúnek, Weiss (Novák 65), Hamšík, Jendrišek. Coach: Vladimír Weiss (SVK)
Goal(s): 0-1 Gancarczyk 3 (og)
Yellow Card(s): Weiss 57 (Slovakia)
Referee: Eriksson (SWE)

14/10/09, Olimpico, Serravalle
San Marino 0-3 Slovenia
Attendance: 1745
San Marino: A. Simoncini, Albani, Mau. Marani, Valentini (Cervellini 77), D. Simoncini, F. Vitaioli, Mic. Marani, Berretti (Bugli 46), Man. Marani, Selva (Rinaldi 62), M. Vitaioli. Coach: Giampaolo Mazza (ITA)
Slovenia: S. Handanovič, Cesar, Brecko (Krhin 85), Šuler, Jokič, Radosavljević, Stevanovič (Ilič 85), Kirm, Dedič (Ljubijankič 51), Birsa, Novakovič. Coach: Matjaž Kek (SVN)
Goal(s): 0-1 Novakovič 24, 0-2 Stevanovič 68, 0-3 Šuler 81
Yellow Card(s): Man. Marani 12 (San Marino), Berretti 24 (San Marino), Bugli 48 (San Marino), M. Vitaioli 74 (San Marino), Albani 80 (San Marino), Stevanovič 83 (Slovenia)
Referee: Szabó (HUN)

Group 3 Table

	Pld	Home W	D	L	F	A	Away W	D	L	F	A	Total W	D	L	F	A	Pts
1 Slovakia	10	3	1	1	13	6	4	0	1	9	4	7	1	2	22	10	22
2 Slovenia	10	4	1	0	12	1	2	1	2	6	3	6	2	2	18	4	20
3 Czech Republic	10	3	1	1	11	2	1	3	1	6	4	4	4	2	17	6	16
4 Northern Ireland	10	3	1	1	8	4	1	2	2	5	5	4	3	3	13	9	15
5 Poland	10	2	2	1	14	4	1	0	4	5	10	3	2	5	19	14	11
6 San Marino	10	0	0	5	1	14	0	0	5	0	33	0	0	10	1	47	0

GROUP 4

Germany demonstrated once more their time-honoured knack of winning when it matters as they booked their trip to South Africa with a hard-fought 1-0 victory away to Russia in October. While Joachim Löw's men turned their attentions to preparing for a 15th successive FIFA World Cup appearance, the defeated Russians were forced to settle for the play-offs.

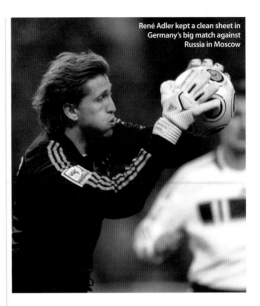

René Adler kept a clean sheet in Germany's big match against Russia in Moscow

Vogts reunion

Germany entered the 2009/10 campaign holding a one-point lead at the top of the standings and they consolidated their position with routine home-and-away wins over an Azerbaijan side coached by Berti Vogts, the former World Cup winner who led the Nationalmannschaft to the UEFA European Championship title in 1996.

Germany picked up six points – winning 2-0 in Baku in August and then 4-0 in Hanover the following month against opponents reduced to ten men by Samir Abbasov's 50th-minute sending-off. Miroslav Klose put three goals past the Azeris and eventually finished as Germany's top scorer in the qualifying competition.

In pursuit

Going into that penultimate group fixture on 10 October, Germany stood a point clear of the Russians, who had sustained their pursuit of the leaders with victories over Liechtenstein and Wales the previous month. Tottenham Hotspur FC forward Roman Pavlyuchenko was on target in both matches, converting two penalties in the 3-0 home success over Liechtenstein on 5 September before his added-time strike sealed a 3-1 win away to fourth-placed Wales.

Although Igor Semshov gave Russia a half-time lead in Cardiff, James Collins equalised soon after the restart and it took a 71st-minute free-kick from Sergei Ignashevich to restore the visitors' lead before Pavlyuchenko's late third.

Russians rue luck

If that scoreline flattered Russia, they were left ruing their misfortune after Germany's 1-0 triumph in Moscow. Miroslav Klose's first-half strike, his seventh and last of the campaign, settled a tight, tense contest at the Luzhniki stadium and in the process ensured yet another World Cup appearance for the Germans.

Löw's charges were well organised but they rode their luck, surviving early Russia pressure and then a late onslaught after the 69th-minute sending-off of debutant Jerome Boateng for a foul on Vladimir Bystrov. It was Bystrov who spurned the hosts' best first-half opening, foiled by René Adler when clean through, and ten minutes before the break Klose, the Golden Shoe winner at the 2006 finals, hit the all-important goal with a near-post finish from a clever cut-back by Mesut Özil. The Werder Bremen playmaker had made his full debut only the previous month after helping Germany win the UEFA European Under-21 Championship the previous June and already his influence was evident.

No way past Adler

Russia pinned Germany back as they sought a reply after the restart but Adler was equal to everything the home side threw at him – notably shots by Andrei Arshavin and Yuriy Zhirkov. Two substantial late penalty appeals by the home side were then rejected as Germany held out to win. Russia's second narrow defeat to the Germans – who had scraped a 2-1 victory in Dortmund 12 months earlier – dispatched them into the play-offs. Their only other dropped points were to come in their final game, away to Azerbaijan, with their fate already sealed. Their subsequent failure in the play-off against Slovenia would lead to coach Guus Hiddink's departure for a new challenge with Turkey.

With the pressure off, Germany almost slipped up in their final qualifier at home against Finland, needing a last-minute Lukas Podolski effort to cancel out Jonathan Johansson's goal – his fifth in qualifying – and preserve their unbeaten record in the group. For Stuart Baxter's Finns, it was the second time they had been denied a win by a late German equaliser but this was not the main reason why they had to settle for third place. Two 3-0 defeats against Russia the previous season had left them off the pace, and their hopes evaporated entirely with a 1-1 draw against Liechtenstein, the bottom team, in Vaduz in September.

Group 4 Results

6/9/08
Wales 1-0 Azerbaijan
Liechtenstein 0-6 Germany
10/9/08
Russia 2-1 Wales
Finland 3-3 Germany
Azerbaijan 0-0 Liechtenstein
11/10/08
Finland 1-0 Azerbaijan
Wales 2-0 Liechtenstein
Germany 2-1 Russia
15/10/08
Russia 3-0 Finland
Germany 1-0 Wales

28/3/09
Wales 0-2 Finland
Russia 2-0 Azerbaijan
Germany 4-0 Liechtenstein
1/4/09
Liechtenstein 0-1 Russia
Wales 0-2 Germany
6/6/09
Finland 2-1 Liechtenstein
Azerbaijan 0-1 Wales
10/6/09
Finland 0-3 Russia

Azerbaijan's Räşäd A. Sadiqov (grounded) attempts a tackle on Russia's Renat Yanbayev

12/8/09, Tofiq Bähramov, Baku
Azerbaijan 0-2 Germany
Attendance: 22500
Azerbaijan: Väliyev, Sükürov, Yunisoğlu, Mälikov, Abbasov, Allahverdiyev, Räşad F. Sadiqov, Mämmädov, Chertoganov, Nadirov (Axtyamov 74), Cavadov. Coach: Berti Vogts (GER)
Germany: Enke, Schäfer, Taşçi, Mertesacker, Lahm, Ballack, Trochowski (Jansen 76), Schweinsteiger, Hitzlsperger, Klose (Cacau 71), Gómez (Özil 83). Coach: Joachim Löw (GER)
Goal(s): 0-1 Schweinsteiger 11, 0-2 Klose 53
Yellow Card(s): Allahverdiyev 39 (Azerbaijan), Sükürov 42 (Azerbaijan), Mälikov 53 (Azerbaijan), Chertoganov 81 (Azerbaijan)
Referee: Kelly (IRL)

5/9/09, Petrovskiy, St Petersburg
Russia 3-0 Liechtenstein
Attendance: 21000
Russia: Akinfeev, Ignashevich, V. Berezutskiy (A. Berezutskiy 58), Anyukov, Zyryanov (Semshov 46), Semak, Bilyaletdinov, Bystrov, Denisov (Rebko 69), Kerzhakov, Pavlyuchenko. Coach: Guus Hiddink (NED)
Liechtenstein: Jehle, Mi. Stocklasa, Vogt (S. Büchel 82), Ritzberger, Oehri, Rechsteiner, Burgmeier, R. Büchel, Frick, T. Beck (Hasler 57), Christen (R. Beck 72). Coach: Hans-Peter Zaugg (SUI)
Goal(s): 1-0 V. Berezutskiy 17, 2-0 Pavlyuchenko 39 (p), 3-0 Pavlyuchenko 45 (p)
Yellow Card(s): Burgmeier 35 (Liechtenstein), Denisov 42 (Russia), Vogt 45 (Liechtenstein), Pavlyuchenko 48 (Russia)
Referee: Constantin (ROU)

5/9/09, City, Lankaran
Azerbaijan 1-2 Finland
Attendance: 12000
Azerbaijan: Ağayev, Abbasov, Sükürov, Räşad Ä. Sadiqov, Abişov (Hüseynov 46), Yunisoğlu, Levin, Allahverdiyev, Mämmädov (Ämirquliyev 84), Cavadov, Nadirov (Axtyamov 73). Coach: Berti Vogts (GER)
Finland: Jääskeläinen, Pasanen, Tihinen, Moisander, Lampi, Tainio (Litmanen 45), Heikkinen, R. Eremenko, Kuqi (Sjölund 72) (Kolkka 83), Johansson, A. Eremenko Jr. Coach: Stuart Baxter (ENG)
Goal(s): 1-0 Mämmädov 49, 1-1 Heikkinen 74, 1-2 Johansson 85
Yellow Card(s): Yunisoğlu 77 (Azerbaijan)
Referee: Trifonos (CYP)

9/9/09, Rheinpark, Vaduz
Liechtenstein 1-1 Finland
Attendance: 3132
Liechtenstein: Jehle, Mi. Stocklasa, Ritzberger, Oehri, Rechsteiner, Burgmeier, Rohrer (R. Beck 85), M. Büchel (Polverino 65), R. Büchel, Frick, Hasler (T. Beck 79). Coach: Hans-Peter Zaugg (SUI)
Finland: Jääskeläinen, Pasanen, Tihinen, Hyypiä, Moisander, Litmanen (Kuqi 82), Heikkinen, R. Eremenko, Johansson, A. Eremenko Jr, Sadik (Kolkka 59). Coach: Stuart Baxter (ENG)
Goal(s): 0-1 Litmanen 74 (p), 1-1 Polverino 75
Red Card(s): M. Büchel 75 (Liechtenstein)
Yellow Card(s): Jehle 33 (Liechtenstein), Hasler 55 (Liechtenstein), Polverino 66 (Liechtenstein), Heikkinen 72 (Finland), Frick 90+2 (Liechtenstein)
Referee: Panić (BIH)

9/9/09, Millennium, Cardiff
Wales 1-3 Russia
Attendance: 14505
Wales: Hennessey, Collins, Gabbidon (Vokes 74), Ricketts, Williams, Gunter, Stock, Edwards, Ledley, Ramsey, Bellamy. Coach: John Toshack (WAL)
Russia: Akinfeev, Ignashevich, V. Berezutskiy, Anyukov, Yanbayev, Zyryanov, Semshov (Pavlyuchenko 70), Semak, Arshavin, Bystrov, Kerzhakov (Rebko 84). Coach: Guus Hiddink (NED)
Goal(s): 0-1 Semshov 36, 1-1 Collins 53, 1-2 Ignashevich 71, 1-3 Pavlyuchenko 90+1
Yellow Card(s): Anyukov 55 (Russia), Ricketts 89 (Wales)
Referee: Neves Moreira de Sousa (POR)

2010 FIFA WORLD CUP

9/9/09, AWD-Arena, Hannover
Germany 4-0 Azerbaijan
Attendance: 35369
Germany: Adler, Lahm, Westermann, Mertesacker, Schäfer (Beck 46), Hitzlsperger, Ballack, Rolfes, Schweinsteiger (Trochowski 65), Podolski, Gómez (Klose 46). Coach: Joachim Löw (GER)
Azerbaijan: Ağayev, Allahverdiyev, Sükürov, Rǎşad Ä. Sadiqov, Yunisoğlu, Levin, Chertoganov, Abbasov, Mämmädov (Hüseynov 67), Cavadov, Nadirov (Ernani 56). Coach: Berti Vogts (GER)
Goal(s): 1-0 Ballack 15 (p), 2-0 Klose 55, 3-0 Klose 66, 4-0 Podolski 71
Red Card(s): Abbasov 50 (Azerbaijan)
Yellow Card(s): Abbasov 13 (Azerbaijan), Abbasov 50 (Azerbaijan), Ernani 81 (Azerbaijan)
Referee: Kakos (GRE)

10/10/09, Olympic, Helsinki
Finland 2-1 Wales
Attendance: 14000
Finland: Jääskeläinen, Pasanen, Tihinen, Hyypiä, Moisander, Litmanen (A. Eremenko Jr 90), Kolkka (Hämäläinen 68), Sparv, Eremenko, Johansson (Kuqi 88), Porokara. Coach: Stuart Baxter (ENG)
Wales: Hennessey, Collins, Williams, Nyatanga (Eardley 83), Bale, Gunter, Vaughan, Edwards, Ramsey, Bellamy, Church (Vokes 62). Coach: John Toshack (WAL)
Goal(s): 1-0 Porokara 5, 1-1 Bellamy 17, 2-1 Moisander 77
Yellow Card(s): Bellamy 47 (Wales), Tihinen 47 (Finland), Hennessey 72 (Wales), Pasanen 86 (Finland)
Referee: Mažić (SRB)

10/10/09, Luzhniki, Moscow
Russia 0-1 Germany
Attendance: 72100
Russia: Akinfeev, Ignashevich, V. Berezutskiy, Anyukov, Zhirkov, Zyryanov, Semshov (Pogrebnyak 77), Bystrov, Denisov (Torbinskiy 46), Arshavin, Kerzhakov (Pavlyuchenko 55). Coach: Guus Hiddink (NED)
Germany: Adler, Lahm, Westermann, Mertesacker, Boateng, Ballack, Rolfes, Schweinsteiger, Özil (A. Friedrich 72), Klose (Gómez 89), Podolski (Trochowski 85). Coach: Joachim Löw (GER)
Goal(s): 0-1 Klose 35
Red Card(s): Boateng 69 (Germany)
Yellow Card(s): Boateng 42 (Germany), Zhirkov 58 (Russia), Boateng 69 (Germany), Semshov 73 (Russia)
Referee: Busacca (SUI)

10/10/09, Rheinpark, Vaduz
Liechtenstein 0-2 Azerbaijan
Attendance: 1635
Liechtenstein: Jehle, Ritzberger (Christen 82), Rechsteiner, Oehri, D'Elia, Rohrer (R. Beck 60), Kieber, Burgmeier, S. Büchel (T. Beck 68), R. Büchel, Hasler. Coach: Hans-Peter Zaugg (SUI)
Azerbaijan: Ağayev, Allahverdiyev, Sükürov, Abişov, Chertoganov, Levin, Mämmädov, Medvedev (Mälikov 90+4), Cavadov (Hüseynov 90+1), Nadirov (Rǎşad Ä. Sadiqov 46), Axtyamov. Coach: Berti Vogts (GER)
Goal(s): 0-1 Cavadov 55, 0-2 Mämmädov 82
Yellow Card(s): Chertoganov 37 (Azerbaijan), Axtyamov 66 (Azerbaijan), T. Beck 69 (Liechtenstein), Kieber 73 (Liechtenstein), Cavadov 73 (Azerbaijan), Burgmeier 75 (Liechtenstein), R. Beck 79 (Liechtenstein), Allahverdiyev 88 (Azerbaijan), Rechsteiner 89 (Liech
Referee: Radovanović (MNE)

14/10/09, Hamburg Arena, Hamburg
Germany 1-1 Finland
Attendance: 51500
Germany: Adler, A. Friedrich, Lahm, Westermann, Beck, Hitzlsperger (Gentner 46), Ballack (Özil 46), Trochowski, Cacau, Podolski, Gómez (Klose 77). Coach: Joachim Löw (GER)
Finland: Jääskeläinen, Hyypiä, Moisander, Lampi, Litmanen (Nyman 87), Heikkinen, Sparv, Eremenko, Hämäläinen (Kolkka 66), Johansson, Porokara (Kuqi 72). Coach: Stuart Baxter (ENG)
Goal(s): 0-1 Johansson 11, 1-1 Podolski 90
Yellow Card(s): Sparv 74 (Finland)
Referee: Atkinson (ENG)

Finland players celebrate taking the lead against Germany in Hamburg

14/10/09, Rheinpark, Vaduz
Liechtenstein 0-2 Wales
Attendance: 1858
Liechtenstein: Jehle, D'Elia, Ritzberger, Oehri, Eberle, Rohrer (R. Beck 36), Kieber, R. Büchel (Polverino 70), Rechsteiner, Frick, Hasler (Christen 72). Coach: Hans-Peter Zaugg (SUI)
Wales: Myhill, Collins, Williams, Morgan, Bale (Nyatanga 84), Gunter (Eardley 88), Vaughan, Edwards (King 80), Ramsey, Easter, Church. Coach: John Toshack (WAL)
Goal(s): 0-1 Vaughan 16, 0-2 Ramsey 80
Yellow Card(s): Morgan 48 (Wales), R. Büchel 48 (Liechtenstein), D'Elia 83 (Liechtenstein), Eberle 86 (Liechtenstein)
Referee: Kaldma (EST)

14/10/09, Tofiq Bähramov, Baku
Azerbaijan 1-1 Russia
Attendance: 17000
Azerbaijan: Ağayev, Sükürov, Rǎşad Ä. Sadiqov (Nadirov 46), Mälikov, Abişov, Levin, Chertoganov, Mämmädov, Cavadov, Medvedev (Hüseynov 73). Coach: Berti Vogts (GER)
Russia: Akinfeev, Ignashevich, A. Berezutskiy, Yanbayev, Semak, Rebko (Denisov 64), Torbinskiy, Bystrov (Bukharov 64), Bilyaletdinov, Dzagoev, Arshavin. Coach: Guus Hiddink (NED)
Goal(s): 0-1 Arshavin 13, 1-1 Cavadov 53
Yellow Card(s): Sükürov 36 (Azerbaijan), Yanbayev 41 (Russia), Semak 86 (Russia), Torbinskiy 90+1 (Russia)
Referee: Webb (ENG)

Group 4 Table

	Pld	Home				Away				Total				Pts
		W	D	L	F A	W	D	L	F A	W	D	L	F A	
1 Germany	10	4	1	0	12 2	4	1	0	14 3	8	2	0	26 5	26
2 Russia	10	4	0	1	10 2	3	1	1	9 4	7	1	2	19 6	22
3 Finland	10	3	1	1	8 8	2	2	1	6 6	5	3	2	14 14	18
4 Wales	10	2	0	3	4 7	2	0	3	5 5	4	0	6	9 12	12
5 Azerbaijan	10	0	2	3	2 6	1	0	4	2 8	1	2	7	4 14	5
6 Liechtenstein	10	0	1	4	1 12	0	1	4	1 11	0	2	8	2 23	2

GROUP 5

Spain maintained the imperious standards that had earned them the 2008 UEFA European Championship title as they qualified for their ninth consecutive FIFA World Cup with a 100 per cent winning record. They were the only team in the European Zone to record ten straight victories, scoring 28 goals and conceding just five. Miroslav Blažević's Bosnia-Herzegovina held off the challenge of Turkey to secure the runners-up spot.

No twists

There were no late twists in a section that had already taken clear shape in spring 2009. Vicente del Bosque's Spain stood six points clear at the top after winning both matches of their double-header against Turkey – notably a last-gasp 2-1 triumph in Istanbul on 1 April – while Bosnia-Herzegovina held a four-point advantage in second place after their own six-point haul against Belgium.

When qualifying resumed on 5 September, Spain underlined their supremacy with a 5-0 rout of Belgium in La Coruna. Valencia CF duo David Silva and David Villa scored two goals apiece, with defender Gerard Piqué adding the other. The winning margin could have been even greater as Villa, Spain's seven-goal leading scorer in qualifying, had a penalty saved by Belgium goalkeeper Jean-François Gillet while a post denied Fernando Torres. Four days later, Del Bosque's men confirmed their place in South Africa with a 3-0 defeat of Estonia, Cesc Fàbregas, Santi Cazorla and Juan Manuel Mata supplying the goals.

Bosnian momentum

While Spain were cruising to qualification, Bosnia-Herzegovina maintained their momentum with a 2-0 win in Armenia on 5 September. Senijad Ibričić gave them a sixth-minute lead, and although Edin Džeko then missed a penalty, the striker made amends by crossing for his VfL Wolfsburg colleague Zlatan Misimović to seal the victory late on.

With Turkey beating Estonia 4-2 on the same night, that success ensured Bosnia-Herzegovina went into their showdown against the Turks four days later with their four-point lead intact. Crucially, it was still intact after they came from behind to hold Turkey 1-1 in Zenica thanks to a Sejad Salihović free-kick. Turkey made the

David Silva (facing) embrac Álvaro Arbeloa after scorir against Belgiu

perfect start as Emre Belözoğlu put them in front after four minutes but Salihović pegged the visitors back with a superbly curled strike into the top corner in the 25th minute. The Bosnians made sure of a play-off berth with a subsequent 2-0 win in Estonia on 10 October courtesy of goals from Džeko and Vedad Ibišević.

Coaches pay price

Later that evening there was a winning start for Dick Advocaat as Belgium coach. The Red Devils had turned to Advocaat after a 2-1 loss in Armenia concluded a run of five straight qualifying defeats under Frank Vercauteren. The Dutchman's first match brought a 2-0 win over Turkey yet there was no new dawn: Belgium lost their last qualifier in Estonia and by April 2010 Advocaat had quit. He was not alone, Fatih Terim making way for Guus Hiddink as Turkey coach after failing to build on his team's semi-final run at UEFA EURO 2008.

Spain may have assured qualification with two games to spare but Del Bosque's men did not take their foot off the gas. Indeed, having defeated Armenia 2-1 in their penultimate qualifier, they underlined their

2010 FIFA WORLD CUP

superiority by putting five past the Bosnians in Zenica. After Ibisević had missed an open goal for the home side after rounding Iker Casillas, the visitors took control through Piqué's 13th-minute header and a Silva strike 60 seconds later. Sevilla FC forward Álvaro Negredo opened his international account with a quickfire double shortly after the break and Mata made it five in the 81st minute.

Spanish supremacy

Džeko – with his ninth qualifying goal – and Mismović both struck in added time but Spain had made their point. Head and shoulders above their Group 5 rivals, they would be journeying to South Africa as one of the favourites to lift the trophy. Unfortunately for Bosnia-Herzegovina, their ensuing play-off loss meant they would not be following Spain to the finals, and by the close of 2009 Safet Sušić had replaced Blažević at the helm.

Group 5 Results

6/9/08
Belgium 3-2 Estonia
Armenia 0-2 Turkey
Spain 1-0 Bosnia-Herzegovina
10/9/08
Bosnia-Herzegovina 7-0 Estonia
Turkey 1-1 Belgium
Spain 4-0 Armenia
11/10/08
Belgium 2-0 Armenia
Turkey 7-1 Bosnia-Herzegovina
Estonia 0-3 Spain

15/10/08
Bosnia-Herzegovina 4-1 Armenia
Belgium 1-2 Spain
Estonia 0-0 Turkey
28/3/09
Armenia 2-2 Estonia
Belgium 2-4 Bosnia-Herzegovina
Spain 1-0 Turkey
1/4/09
Estonia 1-0 Armenia
Bosnia-Herzegovina 2-1 Belgium
Turkey 1-2 Spain

5/9/09, Yerevan Republican, Yerevan
Armenia 0-2 Bosnia-Herzegovina
Attendance: 1800
Armenia: Kasparov, Hovsepyan, A. Mkrtchyan, Arzumanyan, Tadevosyan, Artavazd Karamyan, Arakelyan (Minasyan 66), Artur Yedigaryan (Yagan 76), Arman Karamyan, Yavruyan (Goharyan 46), Coach: Vardan Minasyan (ARM)
Bosnia-Herzegovina: Supić, Jahić, Spahić, Nadarević, Muratović (Pjanić 65), Rahimić, Salihović, Ibričić (Bajramović 84), Džeko, Ibišević (Muslimović 69), Vladavić. Coach: Miroslav Blažević (CRO)
Goal(s): 0-1 Ibričić 6, 0-2 Muslimović 75
Yellow Card(s): Kasparov 32 (Armenia), Artavazd Karamyan 59 (Armenia), Bajramović 87 (Bosnia-Herzegovina), Mkhitaryan 90+2 (Armenia)
Referee: Braamhaar (NED)

5/9/09, Kadir Has, Kayseri
Turkey 4-2 Estonia
Attendance: 32000
Turkey: Volkan Demirel, Servet, Gökhan Zan (Önder 36), Hakan, Gökhan Gönül, Hamit, Arda, Emre Belözoğlu (Ceyhun Gülselam 78), Kazım (Halil 61), Tuncay, Sercan. Coach: Fatih Terim (TUR)
Estonia: Pareiko, Piiroja, Klavan, Jääger, Bärengrub, Kruglov, Lindpere, Dmitrijev (Vunk 73), Vassiljev, Oper (Kink 74), Voskoboinikov (Zenjov 54). Coach: Tarmo Rüütli (EST)
Goal(s): 0-1 Voskoboinikov 7, 1-1 Tuncay 28, 2-1 Sercan 37, 2-2 Vassiljev 52, 3-2 Arda 62, 4-2 Tuncay 72
Yellow Card(s): Voskoboinikov 8 (Estonia), Gökhan Gönül 75 (Turkey)
Referee: Skjerven (NOR)

5/9/09, Riazor, La Coruna
Spain 5-0 Belgium
Attendance: 30441
Spain: Casillas, Puyol, Capdevila, Arbeloa (Albiol 82), Piqué, Xavi (Fàbregas 70), Xabi Alonso, David Silva, Busquets, Fernando Torres (Riera 66), David Villa. Coach: Vicente del Bosque (ESP)
Belgium: Gillet, Van Buyten, Vermaelen, Vanden Borre, Vertonghen (Deschacht 29), Simons, Defour, Fellaini, Hazard (Mirallas 58), Sonck (De Camargo 70), Dembélé. Coach: Frank Vercauteren (BEL)
Goal(s): 1-0 David Silva 41, 2-0 David Villa 49, 3-0 Piqué 51, 4-0 David Silva 68, 5-0 David Villa 85
Yellow Card(s): Vermaelen 10 (Belgium), Busquets 24 (Spain), Fellaini 43 (Belgium), Puyol 79 (Spain)
Referee: Layec (FRA)

9/9/09, Bilino Polje, Zenica
Bosnia-Herzegovina 1-1 Turkey
Attendance: 14000
Bosnia-Herzegovina: Supić, Jahić, Spahić, Nadarević, Ibričić (Vladavić 79), Muratović (Pjanić 61), Rahimić, Salihović, Misimović, Džeko, Ibišević (Muslimović 68). Coach: Miroslav Blažević (CRO)
Turkey: Volkan Demirel, Önder (İsmail 46), Servet, Hakan, Gökhan Gönül, Emre Belözoğlu, Hamit (Sercan 46), Arda, Ceyhun Gülselam, Tuncay, Semih. Coach: Fatih Terim (TUR)
Goal(s): 0-1 Emre Belözoğlu 4, 1-1 Salihović 25
Yellow Card(s): Emre Belözoğlu 24 (Turkey), Rahimić 38 (Bosnia-Herzegovina), Arda 44 (Turkey), Ceyhun Gülselam 64 (Turkey), Pjanić 68 (Bosnia-Herzegovina), Semih 81 (Turkey), Supić 84 (Bosnia-Herzegovina), Misimović 90+2 (Bosnia-Herzegovina)
Referee: Olegário Benquerença (POR)

9/9/09, Yerevan Republican, Yerevan
Armenia 2-1 Belgium
Attendance: 4000
Armenia: Kasparov, Hovsepyan, A. Mkrtchyan, Arzumanyan, Mkoyan, Goharyan (Yavruyan 32), Artavazd Karamyan, Arakelyan (K. Mkrtchyan 14), Artur Yedigaryan (Kakosyan 89), Arman Karamyan, Mkhitaryan. Coach: Vardan Minasyan (ARM)
Belgium: Gillet, Van Buyten, Deschacht, Swerts, Simons, Martens (De Sutter 53), Defour, Sonck (Lamah 81), De Camargo, Mirallas (Hazard 72), Dembélé. Coach: Frank Vercauteren (BEL)
Goal(s): 1-0 Goharyan 22, 2-0 Hovsepyan 51, 2-1 Van Buyten 90+2
Yellow Card(s): Mkhitaryan 18 (Armenia), Sonck 54 (Belgium), Yavruyan 55 (Armenia), Simons 58 (Belgium)
Referee: Stavrev (MKD)

Sejad Salihović scored Bosnia-Herzegovina's crucial equaliser in the 1-1 draw away to Turkey

Belgium coach Dick Advocaat watches on as his team defeat Turkey 2-0 in Brussels

9/9/09, Romano, Merida
Spain 3-0 Estonia
Attendance: 14362
Spain: Casillas, Marchena, Capdevila, Albiol, Piqué, Xabi Alonso, Senna, Fàbregas, David Silva (Mata 77), Fernando Torres (Güiza 54), David Villa (Santi Cazorla 66). Coach: Vicente del Bosque (ESP)
Estonia: Pareiko, Piiroja, Klavan, Rähn, Šišov (Jääger 64), Kruglov, Vunk, Vassiljev, Oper, Kink (Lindpere 71), Zenjov (Voskoboinikov 46). Coach: Tarmo Rüütli (EST)
Goal(s): 1-0 Fàbregas 33, 2-0 Santi Cazorla 82, 3-0 Mata 90+2
Yellow Card(s): Piiroja 14 (Estonia), Vassiljev 50 (Estonia), Rähn 52 (Estonia)
Referee: Oriekhov (UKR)

10/10/09, A Le Coq Arena, Tallinn
Estonia 0-2 Bosnia-Herzegovina
Attendance: 6450
Estonia: Pareiko, Klavan, Rähn, Jääger, Bärengrub, Kruglov, Dmitrijev, Vassiljev, S. Puri, Kink (Purje 73), Voskoboinikov (Saag 60). Coach: Tarmo Rüütli (EST)
Bosnia-Herzegovina: Hasagić (Begović 90+2), Jahić, Spahić, Nadarević, Misimović, Muratović (Berberović 85), Rahimić, Salihović, Ibričić, Džeko, Ibišević. Coach: Miroslav Blažević (CRO)
Goal(s): 0-1 Džeko 30, 0-2 Ibišević 64
Yellow Card(s): Ibričić 45 (Bosnia-Herzegovina), Dmitrijev 88 (Estonia)
Referee: Rizzoli (ITA)

10/10/09, Roi Baudouin, Brussels
Belgium 2-0 Turkey
Attendance: 30131
Belgium: Bailly, Van Buyten, Swerts, Vermaelen, Lombaerts, Vertonghen, Fellaini, Mpenza (De Sutter 89), Mirallas (Hazard 74), Dembélé, Lamah (Mudingayi 78). Coach: Dick Advocaat (NED)
Turkey: Volkan Demirel, Önder, Servet, Hakan, Gökhan Gönül, Ceyhun Eriş (Semih 46), Ayhan (Kazım 61), Tuncay, Hamit, Nuri, Nihat (Yusuf 71). Coach: Fatih Terim (TUR)
Goal(s): 1-0 Mpenza 7, 2-0 Mpenza 84
Yellow Card(s): Van Buyten 25 (Belgium), Lombaerts 56 (Belgium), Mpenza 84 (Belgium), Semih 86 (Turkey)
Referee: Trefoloni (ITA)

10/10/09, Hrazdan, Yerevan
Armenia 1-2 Spain
Attendance: 10500
Armenia: Berezovski, Hovsepyan, A. Mkrtchyan, Arzumanyan, Mkoyan, Goharyan (Melkonyan 60), Artavazd Karamyan, Artur Yedigaryan (Arakelyan 74), K. Mkrtchyan, Arman Karamyan, Marcos (Dashyan 66). Coach: Vardan Minasyan (ARM)
Spain: Reina, Marchena (Piqué 46), Puyol, Sergio Ramos, Monreal, Xavi, Senna, Fàbregas, Santi Cazorla, Fernando Torres (Negredo 55), Mata (Iniesta 67). Coach: Vicente del Bosque (ESP)
Goal(s): 0-1 Fàbregas 33, 1-1 Arzumanyan 58, 1-2 Mata 64 (p)
Yellow Card(s): Marchena 18 (Spain), Berezovski 64 (Armenia), Puyol 66 (Spain), Hovsepyan 88 (Armenia)
Referee: Jech (CZE)

14/10/09, Bilino Polje, Zenica
Bosnia-Herzegovina 2-5 Spain
Attendance: 13500
Bosnia-Herzegovina: Supić, Jahić, Spahić, Nadarević, Misimović, Muratović (Vladavić 67), Rahimić (Bajramović 46), Salihović (Hrgović 73), Pjanić, Džeko, Ibišević. Coach: Miroslav Blažević (CRO)
Spain: Casillas, Capdevila, Iraola, Albiol, Piqué (Sergio Ramos 77), Riera, Xabi Alonso, Iniesta (Senna 67), Busquets, David Silva (Mata 82), Negredo. Coach: Vicente del Bosque (ESP)
Goal(s): 0-1 Piqué 13, 0-2 David Silva 14, 0-3 Negredo 50, 0-4 Negredo 55, 0-5 Mata 89, 1-5 Džeko 90, 2-5 Misimović 90+2
Yellow Card(s): Iniesta 63 (Spain)
Referee: Plautz (AUT)

14/10/09, Atatürk, Bursa
Turkey 2-0 Armenia
Attendance: 16200
Turkey: Volkan Demirel (Rüştü 90+1), Servet, Gökhan Gönül, İsmail, Ayhan, Tuncay (İbrahim 46), Hamit (Kazım 83), Emre Belözoğlu, Arda, Ceyhun Gülselam, Halil. Coach: Fatih Terim (TUR)
Armenia: Berezovski, Hovsepyan, A. Mkrtchyan, Arzumanyan, Mkoyan, Goharyan (Melkonyan 46), Artavazd Karamyan, Arakelyan (Marcos 58), K. Mkrtchyan, Arman Karamyan (Kakosyan 77), Mkhitaryan. Coach: Vardan Minasyan (ARM)
Goal(s): 1-0 Halil 16, 2-0 Servet 28
Red Card(s): Ceyhun Gülselam 33 (Turkey)
Yellow Card(s): Ceyhun Gülselam 3 (Turkey), Goharyan 25 (Armenia), Ceyhun Gülselam 33 (Turkey), Arman Karamyan 68 (Armenia), Mkoyan 68 (Armenia), Emre Belözoğlu 90 (Turkey)
Referee: Hansson (SWE)

14/10/09, A Le Coq Arena, Tallinn
Estonia 2-0 Belgium
Attendance: 4680
Estonia: Pareiko, Piiroja (Morozov 63), Rähn, Jääger, Kruglov, Lindpere, Dmitrijev, Vunk, Vassiljev, Kink (S. Puri 60), Saag (Voskoboinikov 72). Coach: Tarmo Rüütli (EST)
Belgium: Bailly, Van Buyten (Alderweireld 46), Swerts (De Sutter 76), Vermaelen, Lombaerts, Vertonghen, Mudingayi (Buffel 46), Mpenza, Mirallas, Dembélé, Lamah. Coach: Dick Advocaat (NED)
Goal(s): 1-0 Piiroja 30, 2-0 Vassiljev 67
Yellow Card(s): Swerts 52 (Belgium), Vunk 79 (Estonia)
Referee: Vollquartz (DEN)

Group 5 Table

	Pld	Home W	D	L	F	A	Away W	D	L	F	A	Total W	D	L	F	A	Pts
1 Spain	10	5	0	0	14	0	5	0	0	14	5	10	0	0	28	5	30
2 Bosnia-Herzegovina	10	3	1	1	16	8	3	0	2	9	5	6	1	3	25	13	19
3 Turkey	10	3	1	1	10	6	1	2	2	3	4	4	3	3	13	10	15
4 Belgium	10	3	0	2	10	8	0	1	4	3	12	3	1	6	13	20	10
5 Estonia	10	2	1	2	3	5	0	1	4	6	19	2	2	6	9	24	8
6 Armenia	10	1	1	3	5	9	0	0	5	1	13	1	1	8	6	22	4

GROUP 6

England may have missed out on UEFA EURO 2008 but they qualified in impressive fashion for the 2010 FIFA World Cup by topping their section with 27 points from a possible 30 and outscoring every other team in Europe. They won eight straight games to secure their ticket to South Africa with two matches to spare and leave Ukraine and Croatia scrapping it out for second place – a contest the Ukrainians eventually won.

Crushing win

Fabio Capello's charges were already well on course for qualification entering the 2009/10 campaign, with a ten-point lead at the group summit. Although they had scored ten goals in their two previous matches against Kazakhstan and Andorra, few would have predicted that they could maintain that scoring rate against Croatia on 9 September, but that is precisely what happened in a crushing 5-1 win at Wembley that secured their 13th World Cup finals appearance.

Wayne Rooney scores his ninth goal of the qualifying competition to seal England's 5-1 win against Croatia at Wembley

England started on the front foot and were two goals ahead by the 18th minute, Frank Lampard converting a penalty before Steven Gerrard struck with a header. Both midfielders nodded another goal each in the second half to cement victory, and although Eduardo pulled a goal back for Croatia in the 71st minute, Wayne Rooney struck England's fifth six minutes later, capitalising on a miskick by Croatia goalkeeper Vedran Runje. It was the young Manchester United FC striker's 25th goal for his country and the last of his nine in qualifying, leaving him joint-second in the European scoring chart.

Sweet symmetry

For England there was a sweet symmetry about their dismantling of a Croatia team that had proved their nemesis in UEFA EURO 2008 qualifying. It was Croatia's 3-2 win at Wembley in November 2007 that confirmed the absence of Steve McClaren's England from the following summer's European extravaganza. England had already gained some revenge for the home-and-away losses suffered against Croatia in that EURO campaign with a 4-1 win in September 2008. Now, 12 months on, with their ticket to the FIFA World Cup booked, they had proved that the earlier triumph in Zagreb was anything but a flash in the pan.

In their next match, on 10 October, England surrendered their unbeaten run in competitive matches under Capello with a 1-0 defeat in Ukraine. It was an unhappy evening for Rio Ferdinand who looked vulnerable on his return from injury – and even more so for Robert Green who became the first England goalkeeper sent off after bringing down Artem Milevskiy when the striker broke through in the 13th minute following Ferdinand's early mistake.

Ukraine earn crucial victory

Although Andriy Shevchenko missed the resulting spot-kick, Serhiy Nazarenko's 29th-minute goal – deflected in off Ashley Cole – earned Ukraine a crucial victory in their battle for second place with Croatia, taking them above Slaven Bilić's men for the first time in 12 months.

The two countries had drawn their two direct encounters and ended the previous season locked on 11 points apiece before Croatia moved three points ahead with a 3-1 win in Belarus in August. Although Ukraine put six past Andorra on 5 September, Croatia retained their advantage with a narrow victory in their return fixture against Belarus on the same day. With playmaker Luka Modrić missing with a broken leg, it took goalkeeper Runje to preserve their 1-0 lead after Vedran Ćorluka was sent off.

Pole position

Four days later came Croatia's Wembley nightmare and Ukraine profited by narrowing the gap to two points with a draw in Belarus – the only point Bernd Stange's team took against the three countries above them. When Ukraine then won their game in hand against England, they were suddenly in pole position.

Needing only to beat Andorra in their final qualifier, Ukraine made no mistake with a 6-0 rout, rendering Croatia's subsequent 2-1 win in Kazakhstan meaningless. Play-off disappointment would beckon for Ukraine boss Olexiy Mykhailychenko – costing him his job – but there were no such worries for Capello who saw his England team sign off with a 3-0 defeat of Belarus at Wembley, lifting their goal haul to 34, the highest in the European Zone by some distance.

Group 6 Results

20/8/08
Kazakhstan 3-0 Andorra
6/9/08
Ukraine 1-0 Belarus
Andorra 0-2 England
Croatia 3-0 Kazakhstan
10/9/08
Andorra 1-3 Belarus
Croatia 1-4 England
Kazakhstan 1-3 Ukraine
11/10/08
England 5-1 Kazakhstan
Ukraine 0-0 Croatia

15/10/08
Croatia 4-0 Andorra
Belarus 1-3 England
1/4/09
England 2-1 Ukraine
Andorra 0-2 Croatia
Kazakhstan 1-5 Belarus
6/6/09
Belarus 5-1 Andorra
Croatia 2-2 Ukraine
Kazakhstan 0-4 England
10/6/09
Ukraine 2-1 Kazakhstan
England 6-0 Andorra

12/8/09, Dinamo, Minsk
Belarus 1-3 Croatia
Attendance: 21651
Belarus: Zhevnov, Omelyanchuk, Yurevich, Verkhovtsov, Sosnovskiy, Kulchiy, A. Hleb, Kalachev, Kashevskiy (Kovel 54), Kutuzov (Bliznyuk 85), Kornilenko (Rodionov 69). Coach: Bernd Stange (GER)
Croatia: Runje, Šimunić, Križanac (Rakitić 46), Ćorluka, Srna, Kranjčar (Mandžukić 66), Pranjić, Modrić, Vukojević, Eduardo (Jurić 88), Olić. Coach: Slaven Bilić (CRO)
Goal(s): 0-1 Olić 22, 0-2 Eduardo 69, 1-2 Verkhovtsov 81, 1-3 Olić 85
Yellow Card(s): Sosnovskiy 57 (Belarus), Mandžukić 71 (Croatia), Kutuzov 75 (Belarus)
Referee: Brych (GER)

5/9/09, Valeriy Lobanovskiy, Kyiv
Ukraine 5-0 Andorra
Attendance: 14870
Ukraine: Pyatov, Chyhrynskiy, Kucher, Mandzyuk, Kobin, Tymoshchuk, Gusev (Hai 71), Yarmolenko, Shevchenko (Homenyuk 81), Voronin (Seleznev 66), Milevskiy. Coach: Olexiy Mykhailychenko (UKR)
Andorra: Gómes, Sonejee, Martínez, Jiménez, Ayala, Pujol, Vales, Silva, Moreno (G. García 82), Vieira (Escura 76), Toscano (Hugo 84). Coach: David Rodrigo (ESP)
Goal(s): 1-0 Yarmolenko 18, 2-0 Milevskiy 45+2, 3-0 Shevchenko 72 (p), 4-0 Milevskiy 90+2 (p), 5-0 Seleznev 90+4 (p)
Yellow Card(s): Voronin 24 (Ukraine), Pujol 34 (Andorra), Vales 90+1 (Andorra), Ayala 90+4 (Andorra)
Referee: Šipailo (LVA)

5/9/09, Maksimir, Zagreb
Croatia 1-0 Belarus
Attendance: 25628

Croatia: Runje, Križanac, Ćorluka, Šimunić, Vukojević, Kranjčar, Srna, Rakitić (Mandžukić 65), Pranjić, Olić (Petrić 73), Eduardo (Jurić 81). Coach: Slaven Bilić (CRO)
Belarus: Zhevnov, Yurevich, Sosnovskiy, Shitov, Verkhovtsov, Omelyanchuk, Bordachev (Stasevich 55), Kulchiy, Kalachev, V. Hleb (Krivets 63), Kornilenko (Kovel 77). Coach: Bernd Stange (GER)
Goal(s): 1-0 Rakitić 24
Red Card(s): Ćorluka 78 (Croatia)
Yellow Card(s): Bordachev 12 (Belarus), Kornilenko 25 (Belarus), Ćorluka 28 (Croatia), V. Hleb 57 (Belarus), Verkhovtsov 75 (Belarus), Ćorluka 78 (Croatia), Kovel 88 (Belarus), Kalachev 89 (Belarus), Križanac 89 (Croatia)
Referee: Plautz (AUT)

9/9/09, Comunal, Andorra La Vella
Andorra 1-3 Kazakhstan
Attendance: 510
Andorra: Gómes, Sonejee, Lima, Martínez, Vales (Escura 46), Ayala, Bernaus, Vieira (Riera 87), Moreno, Jiménez (Toscano 54), Silva. Coach: David Rodrigo (ESP)
Kazakhstan: Mokin, Kislitsin, Logvinenko, Kirov, Abdulin, Baltiyev, Karpovich, Kukeev (Nurgaliev 87), Finonchenko (Skorykh 78), Averchenko, Khizhnichenko (Erbes 90+2). Coach: Bernd Storck (GER)
Goal(s): 0-1 Khizhnichenko 13, 0-2 Baltiyev 28 (p), 0-3 Khizhnichenko 34, 1-3 Sonejee 70
Yellow Card(s): Vieira 16 (Andorra), Khizhnichenko 68 (Kazakhstan), Sonejee 77 (Andorra), Karpovich 78 (Kazakhstan), Moreno 89 (Andorra)
Referee: Toussaint (LUX)

9/9/09, Dinamo, Minsk
Belarus 0-0 Ukraine
Attendance: 21727
Belarus: Zhevnov, Omelyanchuk, Yurevich, Plaskonnyi (Lentsevich 57), Shitov, Sosnovskiy, A. Hleb, Kalachev, Kulchiy, Kutuzov (V. Hleb 88), Kornilenko (Kovel 76). Coach: Bernd Stange (GER)
Ukraine: Pyatov, Chyhrynskiy, Kucher, Mandzyuk, Kobin, Tymoshchuk, Hai, Gusev (Nazarenko 60), Yarmolenko, Shevchenko (Voronin 89), Milevskiy. Coach: Olexiy Mykhailychenko (UKR)
Yellow Card(s): Shitov 42 (Belarus), Omelyanchuk 68 (Belarus), Mandzyuk 82 (Ukraine), Shevchenko 88 (Ukraine)
Referee: Kassai (HUN)

Croatia's Niko Kranjčar (left) battles for possession with Kazakhstan's Sergei Skorykh

9/9/09, Wembley, London
England 5-1 Croatia
Attendance: 87319
England: Green, Upson, A. Cole, Terry, G. Johnson, Gerrard (Milner 81), Barry, Lampard, Lennon (Beckham 81), Heskey (Defoe 59), Rooney. Coach: Fabio Capello (ITA)
Croatia: Runje, Šimunić, Križanac, Srna, Kranjčar, Pranjić, Vukojević, Pokrivač (Rakitić 46), Mandžukić, Eduardo (Klasnić 73), Olić (Petrić 46). Coach: Slaven Bilić (CRO)
Goal(s): 1-0 Lampard 7 (p), 2-0 Gerrard 18, 3-0 Lampard 59, 4-0 Gerrard 67, 4-1 Eduardo 71, 5-1 Rooney 77
Yellow Card(s): Šimunić 44 (Croatia), Terry 85 (England)
Referee: Undiano Mallenco (ESP)

10/10/09, Brestskiy, Brest
Belarus 4-0 Kazakhstan
Attendance: 9530
Belarus: Zhevnov, Omelyanchuk, Yurevich, Shitov, Verkhovtsov, Sosnovskiy, Bordachev (Krivets 83), Kalachev, Kulchiy (Rodionov 90), Kutuzov (Kovel 73), Kornilenko. Coach: Bernd Stange (GER)
Kazakhstan: Mokin, Kislitsin, Logvinenko, Kirov, Abdulin, Baltiyev (Nuserbayev 61), Karpovich, Skorykh (Erbes 79), Kukeev, Averchenko, Khizhnichenko. Coach: Bernd Storck (GER)
Goal(s): 1-0 Bordachev 23, 2-0 Kalachev 69, 3-0 Kovel 86, 4-0 Kalachev 90+2
Yellow Card(s): Karpovich 57 (Kazakhstan)
Referee: Ennjimi (FRA)

10/10/09, Dnipro Arena, Dnipropetrovsk
Ukraine 1-0 England
Attendance: 31000
Ukraine: Pyatov, Kucher, Kobin, Khacheridi, Rakytskiy, Tymoshchuk, Rotan, Nazarenko (Yarmolenko 67), Hai, Shevchenko (Gusev 90+2), Milevskiy. Coach: Olexiy Mykhailychenko (UKR)
England: Green, Ferdinand, A. Cole, Terry, G. Johnson, Gerrard (Milner 46), Carrick, Lampard, Lennon (James 12), Heskey (C. Cole 72), Rooney. Coach: Fabio Capello (ITA)
Goal(s): 1-0 Nazarenko 29
Red Card(s): Green 12 (England)
Yellow Card(s): Kobin 45+2 (Ukraine), Khacheridi 68 (Ukraine), Tymoshchuk 69 (Ukraine), Rotan 79 (Ukraine), Pyatov 90 (Ukraine)
Referee: Skomina (SVN)

14/10/09, Comunal, Andorra La Vella
Andorra 0-6 Ukraine
Attendance: 820
Andorra: Gómes, Lima, Martínez, Maneiro, Vales, Andorrà (G. García 89), Ayala, Pujol, Jiménez (Moreno 74), Silva, Sánchez (Riera 79). Coach: David Rodrigo (ESP)
Ukraine: Pyatov, Kobin, Kucher, Rakytskiy, Khacheridi, Yarmolenko, Mykhalyk, Gusev, Nazarenko (Hai 74), Shevchenko (Aliyev 74), Milevskiy (Seleznev 76). Coach: Olexiy Mykhailychenko (UKR)
Goal(s): 0-1 Shevchenko 22, 0-2 Gusev 61, 0-3 Lima 69 (og), 0-4 Rakytskiy 80, 0-5 Seleznev 81, 0-6 Yarmolenko 83
Yellow Card(s): Sánchez 14 (Andorra), Jiménez 37 (Andorra), Pujol 72 (Andorra), Lima 81 (Andorra)
Referee: Thomson (SCO)

14/10/09, Wembley, London
England 3-0 Belarus
Attendance: 76897
England: Foster, Ferdinand, Bridge (Milner 78), Terry, G. Johnson, Wright-Phillips, Barry, Lampard, Lennon (Beckham 58), Crouch, Agbonlahor (C. Cole 66). Coach: Fabio Capello (ITA)
Belarus: Zhevnov, Omelyanchuk, Yurevich, Shitov, Verkhovtsov, Sosnovskiy, Bordachev (Kashevskiy 83), Kalachev, Kulchiy, Kutuzov (Rodionov 46), Kornilenko (Kovel 76). Coach: Bernd Stange (GER)
Goal(s): 1-0 Crouch 4, 2-0 Wright-Phillips 60, 3-0 Crouch 76
Yellow Card(s): Kornilenko 53 (Belarus)
Referee: Cardoso Cortez Batista (POR)

Ukraine's Andriy Yarmolenko (right) on the attack against Andorra

14/10/09, Astana Arena, Astana
Kazakhstan 1-2 Croatia
Attendance: 10250
Kazakhstan: Mokin, Kislitsin, Logvinenko, Kirov, Abdulin, Skorykh, Nurgaliev (Kukeev 54), Erbes (Baltiyev 90), Nuserbayev (Malinin 76), Averchenko, Khizhnichenko. Coach: Bernd Storck (GER)
Croatia: Runje, Kovač, Ćorluka, Lovren, Srna (Pokrivač 90+4), Kranjčar, Pranjić, Rakitić, Vukojević, Klasnić (Jelavić 76), Mandžukić (Bilic 63). Coach: Slaven Bilić (CRO)
Goal(s): 0-1 Vukojević 10, 1-1 Khizhnichenko 26, 1-2 Kranjčar 90+3
Yellow Card(s): Nurgaliev 1 (Kazakhstan), Kranjčar 44 (Croatia), Nuserbayev 70 (Kazakhstan), Vukojević 82 (Croatia), Srna 87 (Croatia), Baltiyev 90+3 (Kazakhstan), Jelavić 90+4 (Croatia)
Referee: Circhetta (SUI)

Group 6 Table

	Pld	Home W	D	L	F	A	Away W	D	L	F	A	Total W	D	L	F	A	Pts
1 England	10	5	0	0	21	3	4	0	1	13	3	9	0	1	34	6	27
2 Ukraine	10	4	1	0	9	1	2	2	1	12	5	6	3	1	21	6	21
3 Croatia	10	3	1	1	11	6	3	1	1	8	7	6	2	2	19	13	20
4 Belarus	10	2	1	2	11	7	2	0	3	8	7	4	1	5	19	14	13
5 Kazakhstan	10	1	0	4	6	14	1	0	4	5	15	2	0	8	11	29	6
6 Andorra	10	0	0	5	2	16	0	0	5	1	23	0	0	10	3	39	0

GROUP 7

Serbia qualified for their second consecutive FIFA World Cup having competed under the flag of Serbia and Montenegro in Germany four years earlier. Radomir Antić's side did so with a game to spare – and in style too with a 5-0 victory over Romania. The Serbs' success forced France, World Cup runners-up in 2006, to settle for second place.

French frustrated

Serbia had gone into the summer break with an eight-point lead over France at the head of the standings, albeit with Les Bleus benefiting from two games in hand. France began narrowing the deficit with a 1-0 August victory away to the Faroe Islands but they missed the chance to cut it to two points before the 9 September summit meeting in Belgrade when they could only draw 1-1 at home to Romania at the Stade de France four days earlier. Although Thierry Henry opened the scoring, Julien Escudé's own goal left the French frustrated.

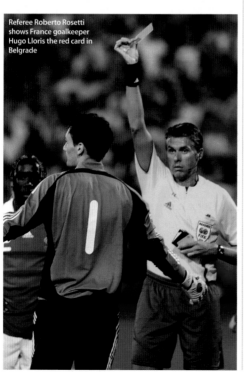

Referee Roberto Rosetti shows France goalkeeper Hugo Lloris the red card in Belgrade

So to the Serbian capital where France made the worst possible start, goalkeeper Hugo Lloris earning a red card for bringing down Milan Jovanović, and Nenad Milijaš duly tucking away the penalty with just 12 minutes on the clock. Henry, however, pounced to equalise before half-time after Vladimir Stojković could only parry a shot by Nicolas Anelka. The match finished 1-1 with the Serbs also ending the game a man short after Danko Lazović's late dismissal.

Despite the disappointment of drawing at home against ten men, the point was more useful to Serbia than France and Antić's men confirmed their qualification as group winners in emphatic fashion on 10 October by putting five goals past Romania in Belgrade. The struggling Romanians had shown signs of improvement after Răzvan Lucescu replaced Victor Pițurcă in the spring but the scale of this defeat underlined the fact that this was the country's worst World Cup campaign for 25 years.

Serbs turn on style

After Nikola Žigić had headed Serbia into a half-time lead, Marko Pantelić doubled that advantage five minutes after the restart. The home side then turned on the style in front of their celebrating fans. From Marko Pantelić's cutback, substitute Zdravko Kuzmanović volleyed into the roof of the net in the 77th minute. Then, in the closing moments, R. Standard de Liège forward Jovanović gilded the lily with two superbly struck efforts from outside the box – one into each corner of Dănuț Coman's net – enabling him to finish as his country's five-goal top scorer in qualifying.

On the same night France made sure of second place with their own five-goal victory, albeit against less illustrious opposition in the shape of the Faroe Islands. Raymond Domenech's men might have been struggling for form but they signed off on a high note four days later by beating Austria 3-1 at the Stade de France, thus avenging an identical defeat by the same opponents in their opening qualifying game. The highlight was a spectacular third goal by Toulouse FC striker André-Pierre Gignac – the fourth of the campaign for the 2008/09 Ligue 1 top scorer.

Win for Faroes

With that victory, France finished up a point shy of the Serbs, who could be forgiven for closing out their campaign with defeat in Lithuania. For José Couceiro's Lithuanians that 2-1 victory ended a run of five straight defeats, the most striking away to the Faroe

Islands a month earlier. Arnbjørn Hansen's winner for the Faroes that day secured for Brian Kerr's charges their first victory in a World Cup qualifying tie since 2001.

Lithuania – who later replaced Couceiro with ex-international Raimondas Žutautas – also lost in Vienna against an Austria side whose haul of ten points from six games after Dietmar Constantini had replaced Karel Brückner allowed them to leapfrog the Baltic state and take third place. Although they signed off with defeat in France, their supporters had a glimpse of the future that day with a first cap for FC Bayern München's David Alaba, who became, at 17, Austria's youngest ever senior international.

Group 7 Results

Bartal Eliasen (left) of the Faroe Islands gets past Lithuania's Tomas Danilevičius

6/9/08
Serbia 2-0 Faroe Islands
Austria 3-1 France
Romania 0-3 Lithuania
10/9/08
Faroe Islands 0-1 Romania
Lithuania 2-0 Austria
France 2-1 Serbia
11/10/08
Faroe Islands 1-1 Austria
Serbia 3-0 Lithuania
Romania 2-2 France

15/10/08
Lithuania 1-0 Faroe Islands
Austria 1-3 Serbia
28/3/09
Romania 2-3 Serbia
Lithuania 0-1 France
1/4/09
Austria 2-1 Romania
France 1-0 Lithuania
6/6/09
Serbia 1-0 Austria
Lithuania 0-1 Romania
10/6/09
Faroe Islands 0-2 Serbia

12/8/09, Tórsvøllur, Torshavn
Faroe Islands 0-1 France
Attendance: 2974
Faroe Islands: Mikkelsen, Gregersen, Næs, Davidsen, Danielsen (Petersen 42), Bø, Benjaminsen, S. Olsen (Borg 85), Løkin, Samuelsen, Holst (Edmundsson 28). Coach: Brian Kerr (IRL)
France: Lloris, Gallas, Evra, Escudé, Sagna, Malouda (Ribéry 65), Gourcuff, L. Diarra, Toulalan, Gignac, Anelka. Coach: Raymond Domenech (FRA)
Goal(s): 0-1 Gignac 41
Yellow Card(s): Gregersen 18 (Faroe Islands), Benjaminsen 45+2 (Faroe Islands), Næs 74 (Faroe Islands)
Referee: Koukoulakis (GRE)

5/9/09, Graz-Liebenau, Graz
Austria 3-1 Faroe Islands
Attendance: 12300
Austria: Payer, Schiemer, Fuchs, Patocka (Ortlechner 46), Dragović, Hölzl, Beichler (Wallner 78), Jantscher, Pehlivan, Janko, Maierhofer (Hoffer 60). Coach: Dietmar Constantini (AUT)
Faroe Islands: Mikkelsen, E. Hansen, Gregersen, Danielsen, Næs, Bø, S. Olsen (Hanssen 67), Benjaminsen (Petersen 80), Samuelsen, Holst (A. L. Olsen 71), Løkin. Coach: Brian Kerr (IRL)
Goal(s): 1-0 Maierhofer 1, 2-0 Janko 15, 3-0 Janko 58 (p), 3-1 A. L. Olsen 82
Yellow Card(s): Janko 51 (Austria), Danielsen 52 (Faroe Islands), Benjaminsen 55 (Faroe Islands), E. Hansen 60 (Faroe Islands), Løkin 68 (Faroe Islands), Wallner 88 (Austria)
Referee: Borg (MLT)

5/9/09, Stade de France, Paris
France 1-0 Romania
Attendance: 80000
France: Lloris, Gallas, Escudé, Evra, Sagna, Toulalan, Gourcuff (Benzema 73), L. Diarra, Henry, Anelka, Gignac (Ribéry 57). Coach: Raymond Domenech (FRA)

Romania: Coman, Chivu, Rădoi, Raţ, Maftei, Mara (Roman 61), Ghioane, Apostol, Nicu (Bucur 77), Marica, Surdu (Codrea 87). Coach: Răzvan Lucescu (ROU)
Goal(s): 1-0 Henry 48, 1-1 Escudé 55 (og)
Yellow Card(s): Apostol 75 (Romania), Sagna 79 (France)
Referee: Bebek (CRO)

9/9/09, Svangaskard, Toftir
Faroe Islands 2-1 Lithuania
Attendance: 1942
Faroe Islands: Mikkelsen, Davidsen, E. Hansen, Eliasen, Gregersen, Borg (B. Olsen 90), Petersen, S. Olsen, Holst, Samuelsen, A. Hansen (A. L. Olsen 68). Coach: Brian Kerr (IRL)
Lithuania: Karčemarskas, Skerla, Stankevičius, Dedura, Klimavičius (Mikoliūnas 60), Ivaškevičius (Kalonas 82), Šemberas, E. Česnauskis, Pilibaitis (Trakys 60), Danilevičius, Šernas. Coach: José Couceiro (POR)
Goal(s): 1-0 S. Olsen 15, 1-1 Danilevičius 23 (p), 2-1 A. Hansen 35
Yellow Card(s): Klimavičius 12 (Lithuania), Holst 35 (Faroe Islands), Borg 38 (Faroe Islands), E. Hansen 40 (Faroe Islands), Samuelsen 50 (Faroe Islands), Mikoliūnas 61 (Lithuania), Mikkelsen 62 (Faroe Islands), Ivaškevičius 78 (Lithuania)
Referee: Vad (HUN)

9/9/09, Steaua, Bucharest
Romania 1-1 Austria
Attendance: 7505
Romania: Coman, Chivu, Rădoi, Raţ, Săpunaru, Codrea (Lazăr 70), Ghioane, Ad. Cristea (Surdu 86), Roman, Marica (Mazilu 78), Bucur. Coach: Răzvan Lucescu (ROU)
Austria: Payer, Schiemer, Fuchs, Dragović, Pehlivan, Beichler (Wallner 72), Jantscher (Trimmel 62), Scharner, Hölzl, Hoffer (Maierhofer 46), Baumgartlinger. Coach: Dietmar Constantini (AUT)
Goal(s): 1-0 Bucur 54, 1-1 Schiemer 82
Yellow Card(s): Scharner 60 (Austria), Chivu 72 (Romania), Bucur 79 (Romania), Fuchs 84 (Austria), Pehlivan 87 (Austria)
Referee: Atkinson (ENG)

9/9/09, FK Crvena Zvezda, Belgrade
Serbia 1-1 France
Attendance: 49256
Serbia: Stojković, Vidić, Luković, Ivanović, Obradović, D. Stanković, Krasić, Milijaš (Kuzmanović 70), Jovanović (Lazović 73), Kačar (Ninković 46), Žigić. Coach: Radomir Antić (SRB)
France: Lloris, Gallas, Abidal, Evra, Sagna, Toulalan, Gourcuff (A. Diarra 85), L. Diarra, Henry (Ribéry 77), Anelka, Gignac (Mandanda 12). Coach: Raymond Domenech (FRA)
Goal(s): 1-0 Milijaš 13 (p), 1-1 Henry 35
Red Card(s): Lloris 12 (France)
Yellow Card(s): Stanković 48 (Serbia), Evra 52 (France), Abidal 61 (France), Jovanović 61 (Serbia), L. Diarra 79 (France), Kuzmanović 88 (Serbia)
Referee: Rosetti (ITA)

10/10/09, Tivoli, Innsbruck
Austria 2-1 Lithuania
Attendance: 14200
Austria: Payer, Scharner, Schiemer, Ulmer, Dragović, Prager (Baumgartlinger 57), Kavlak, Beichler (Drazan 57), Pehlivan, Wallner, Janko (Maierhofer 73). Coach: Dietmar Constantini (AUT)
Lithuania: Karčemarskas, Stankevičius, Dedura, Alunderis (Lukša 82), Kijanskas, Ražanauskas (Kalonas 46), Šemberas, E. Česnauskis, Panka (Trakys 89), Danilevičius, Šernas. Coach: José Couceiro (POR)
Goal(s): 1-0 Janko 16, 1-1 Stankevičius 66, 2-1 Wallner 80 (p)
Yellow Card(s): Danilevičius 24 (Lithuania), Dedura 36 (Lithuania), Schiemer 39 (Austria), Kavlak 54 (Austria), Alunderis 69 (Lithuania), Drazan 72 (Austria), Šemberas 78 (Lithuania)
Referee: Gumienny (BEL)

10/10/09, FK Crvena Zvezda, Belgrade
Serbia 5-0 Romania
Attendance: 39839
Serbia: Stojković, Vidić (Subotić 73), Luković (Dragutinović 46), Ivanović, Kolarov, D. Stanković, Krasić, Milijaš (Kuzmanović 64), Jovanović, Žigić, Pantelić. Coach: Radomir Antić (SRB)
Romania: Coman, Chivu, Rădoi, Raţ, Maftei, Ghioane (Bucur 60), Apostol, Ad. Cristea, Varga, Mutu (An. Cristea 75), Marica (Goian 60). Coach: Răzvan Lucescu (ROU)
Goal(s): 1-0 Žigić 36, 2-0 Pantelić 50, 3-0 Kuzmanović 77, 4-0 Jovanović 87, 5-0 Jovanović 90+3
Red Card(s): Chivu 85 (Romania)
Yellow Card(s): Ad. Cristea 27 (Romania), Raţ 30 (Romania), Varga 31 (Romania), Mutu 32 (Romania), Luković 33 (Serbia), Stanković 43 (Serbia), Kuzmanović 66 (Serbia)
Referee: Kapitanis (CYP)

10/10/09, Roudourou, Guingamp
France 5-0 Faroe Islands
Attendance: 16755
France: Mandanda, Gallas, Abidal, Evra, Sagna, Toulalan (Sissoko 62), L. Diarra, Henry, Anelka, Govou (Malouda 62), Gignac (Benzema 73). Coach: Raymond Domenech (FRA)
Faroe Islands: Mikkelsen, Benjaminsen, S. Olsen (B. Olsen 90), Danielsen, Bø, Gregersen, Petersen (Næs 64), Davidsen, Løkin, C. H. Jacobsen, R. Jacobsen (A. L. Olsen 79). Coach: Brian Kerr (IRL)
Goal(s): 1-0 Gignac 34, 2-0 Gignac 39, 3-0 Gallas 53, 4-0 Anelka 85, 5-0 Benzema 87
Yellow Card(s): L. Diarra 90+4 (France)
Referee: Malek (POL)

14/10/09, Stade de France, Paris
France 3-1 Austria
Attendance: 78099
France: Lloris, Fanni, Squillaci, Escudé, Clichy, Malouda, A. Diarra, Sissoko, Henry (Gignac 51), Govou, Benzema (Gomis 79). Coach: Raymond Domenech (FRA)
Austria: Payer (Gratzei 46), Scharner, Patocka, Pehlivan, Dragović, Fuchs (Alaba 80), Jantscher, Kavlak, Baumgartlinger, Janko, Maierhofer (Hoffer 46). Coach: Dietmar Constantini (AUT)
Goal(s): 1-0 Benzema 18, 2-0 Henry 26 (p), 2-1 Janko 49, 3-1 Gignac 66
Yellow Card(s): Fuchs 25 (Austria), Kavlak 45+1 (Austria)
Referee: Proença (POR)

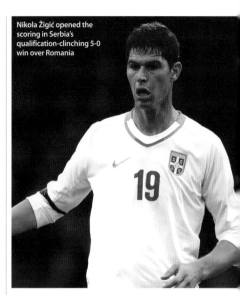

Nikola Žigić opened the scoring in Serbia's qualification-clinching 5-0 win over Romania

14/10/09, Ceahlăul, Piatra Neamt
Romania 3-1 Faroe Islands
Attendance: 13000
Romania: Pantilimon, Rădoi, Raţ , Goian (Galamaz 25), Panin, Mara, Grigore, Apostol, Varga, Marica (Mazilu 82), Bucur (An. Cristea 76). Coach: Răzvan Lucescu (ROU)
Faroe Islands: Mikkelsen, Benjaminsen (C. H. Jacobsen 81), S. Olsen, Danielsen, Bø, Næs, Gregersen, Borg, R. Jacobsen (A. Hansen 73), Holst (Løkin 70), Samuelsen. Coach: Brian Kerr (IRL)
Goal(s): 1-0 Apostol 16, 2-0 Bucur 65, 2-1 Bø 83, 3-1 Mazilu 87
Yellow Card(s): Bø 29 (Faroe Islands), Borg 43 (Faroe Islands), Panin 45 (Romania), Samuelsen 50 (Faroe Islands), Grigore 53 (Romania), Gregersen 82 (Faroe Islands)
Referee: Gvardis (RUS)

14/10/09, Sūduva, Marijampole
Lithuania 2-1 Serbia
Attendance: 2000
Lithuania: Karčemarskas, Stankevičius, Dedura, Klimavičius, Kijanskas, Ivaškevičius, Mikoliūnas (Lukša 67), Panka, Pilibaitis, Kalonas (Ražanauskas 82), Šernas (Trakys 89). Coach: José Couceiro (POR)
Serbia: Dišljenković, Dragutinović, Ivanović, Subotić, Obradović (Luković 61), Krasić (Tošić 46), Jovanović, Kačar, Petrović, Žigić, Pantelić (Ninković 73). Coach: Radomir Antić (SRB)
Goal(s): 1-0 Kalonas 20 (p), 1-1 Tošić 60, 2-1 Stankevičius 68 (p)
Yellow Card(s): Subotić 19 (Serbia), Obradović 30 (Serbia), Tošić 60 (Serbia), Dragutinović 67 (Serbia)
Referee: Genov (BUL)

Group 7 Table

	Pld	Home					Away					Total					Pts
		W	D	L	F	A	W	D	L	F	A	W	D	L	F	A	
1 Serbia	10	4	1	0	12	1	3	0	2	10	7	7	1	2	22	8	22
2 France	10	4	1	0	12	3	2	2	1	6	6	6	3	1	18	9	21
3 Austria	10	4	0	1	11	7	0	2	3	3	8	4	2	4	14	15	14
4 Lithuania	10	3	0	2	5	2	1	0	4	5	9	4	0	6	10	11	12
5 Romania	10	1	2	2	8	10	2	1	2	4	8	3	3	4	12	18	12
6 Faroe Islands	10	1	1	3	3	6	0	0	5	2	14	1	1	8	5	20	4

2010 FIFA WORLD CUP

GROUP 8

World champions Italy could look forward to their 17th FIFA World Cup finals after emerging victorious from a two-way tussle with a Republic of Ireland side coached by one of their own, Italian football legend Giovanni Trapattoni. Marcello Lippi's men qualified undefeated thanks to Alberto Gilardino's last-minute leveller in the Dublin showdown, and the Irish merited praise too for finishing unbeaten themselves – one of only five teams in the European Zone to achieve the feat.

Kaladze's helping hand

Italy went into the final straight holding a one-point advantage over the Irish as well as a game in hand. They profited from two own goals by long-serving AC Milan defender Kakha Kaladze in their 2-0 win in Georgia on 5 September before beating Bulgaria by the same margin in Turin four days later. Fittingly, both goals came from Juventus men, left-back Fabio Grosso volleying in the first after a one-two with Andrea Pirlo in the 11th minute and Vincenzo Iaquinta adding a second before the break.

Georgia's Kakha Kaladze scored two own goals in his team's 2-0 defeat by Italy

Those two wins allowed Italy to open up a four-point lead on the Irish, who played only once in September, beating Cyprus in Nicosia thanks to Robbie Keane's 40th international goal, headed in with just seven minutes left. For the Irish, therefore, only victory would do to keep alive their hopes of direct qualification when they welcomed the Azzurri to Dublin on 10 October. As in the countries' 1-1 draw in Bari the previous April, there would be late drama.

Before a 70,640 Croke Park crowd, Glenn Whelan gave the hosts an eighth-minute lead when he collected Stoke City FC colleague Liam Lawrence's sideways free-kick and drove a blistering shot beyond Gianluigi Buffon. Mauro Camoranesi nodded Italy level from a Pirlo corner after 26 minutes, however, and an offside flag then denied Iaquinta as he turned in another Pirlo dead-ball delivery.

Gilardino to the rescue

When Sean St Ledger headed in his first goal for his country with just three minutes remaining, it looked like the Irish had narrowed Italy's lead to a point. However, the home supporters were silenced by a 90th-minute equaliser from Gilardino, who deftly turned in Iaquinta's cross to secure the holders' ticket to South Africa. It was, as Lippi noted afterwards, the third time the Azzurri had booked their FIFA World Cup place with a game to spare. On the previous two occasions, in 1982 and 2006, they went on to lift the trophy.

ACF Fiorentina front man Gilardino was the Azzurri hero again four days later when he turned around almost singlehandedly a two-goal deficit with a hat-trick in a 3-2 victory over Cyprus in Parma. With Lippi having changed his entire starting XI from the Ireland game, Cyprus took advantage by scoring twice through Yiannis Okkas and Chrysis Michail. Cue Gilardino's rescue act. After heading a goal back with 12 minutes remaining, he equalised with a close-range volley before sliding in to poke Fabio Quagliarella's deflected effort over the line two minutes into added time. Italy's campaign had ended as it began – with an injury-time win over an improving Cyprus side.

Irish centurions

As for the Irish, they signed off with a drab goalless home draw against second-bottom Montenegro on the night that Shay Given and Kevin Kilbane both collected their 100th cap. It was perhaps a predictable outcome given that these were the two teams that had registered the highest number of draws in European qualifying – six apiece.

2010 FIFA WORLD CUP

Dimitar Berbatov scores for Bulgaria in their 6-2 win over Georgia

Third-placed Bulgaria, meanwhile, could only admire Ireland's unbeaten record as they resigned themselves to missing out on a third successive World Cup. The eastern Europeans had escaped defeat in their first six qualifiers, albeit winning only one of them despite the change of coach that brought in Stanimir Stoilov in place of Plamen Markov. Further mixed results followed in the autumn, however – notably a 4-1 loss in Cyprus and a 6-2 final-day win over Georgia that featured a hat-trick from captain Dimitar Berbatov, who would end the year as his country's record goalscorer.

Group 8 Results

6/9/08
Georgia 1-2 Republic of Ireland
Montenegro 2-2 Bulgaria
Cyprus 1-2 Italy
10/9/08
Montenegro 0-0 Republic of Ireland
Italy 2-0 Georgia
11/10/08
Georgia 1-1 Cyprus
Bulgaria 0-0 Italy
15/10/08
Republic of Ireland 1-0 Cyprus
Georgia 0-0 Bulgaria
Italy 2-1 Montenegro

11/2/09
Republic of Ireland 2-1 Georgia
28/3/09
Republic of Ireland 1-1 Bulgaria
Cyprus 1-2 Georgia
Montenegro 0-2 Italy
1/4/09
Bulgaria 2-0 Cyprus
Italy 1-1 Republic of Ireland
Georgia 0-0 Montenegro
6/6/09
Bulgaria 1-1 Republic of Ireland
Cyprus 2-2 Montenegro

5/9/09, Vasil Levski National, Sofia
Bulgaria 4-1 Montenegro
Attendance: 15000
Bulgaria: Ivankov, Il. Stoyanov, Kotev (Telkiyski 46), Manolev, S. Petrov, Kishishev, Angelov, Yankov, M. Petrov (Georgiev 76), Berbatov, Rangelov (Domovchiyski 82). Coach: Stanimir Stoilov (BUL)
Montenegro: Poleksić, Baša (Fatić 73), Pejović, Pavićević, Džudović, S. Vukčević, Peković (Vučinić 66), Drinčić, Božović (Bošković 58), Jovetić, Damjanović. Coach: Zoran Filipović (MNE)
Goal(s): 0-1 Jovetić 9, 1-1 Kishishev 45+1, 2-1 Telkiyski 49, 3-1 Berbatov 83 (p), 4-1 Domovchiyski 90+1

Yellow Card(s): Kotev 22 (Bulgaria), Božović 41 (Montenegro), Damjanović 45 (Montenegro), M. Petrov 51 (Bulgaria), Peković 62 (Montenegro), Džudović 73 (Montenegro), Rangelov 81 (Bulgaria), Fatić 83 (Montenegro)
Referee: Asumaa (FIN)

5/9/09, GSP, Nicosia
Cyprus 1-2 Republic of Ireland
Attendance: 5191
Cyprus: Avgousti, Nicolaou, Elia, Charalambous, Christou, Satsias (Marangos 89), Charalambides, Michail (Alexandrou 72), Aloneftis, Avraam, Okkas (Christofi 89). Coach: Angelos Anastasiadis (GRE)
Republic of Ireland: Given, O'Shea, Dunne, St Ledger, Whelan, Andrews, S. Hunt (McGeady 67), Duff, Kilbane, Keane, Doyle (Folan 75). Coach: Giovanni Trapattoni (ITA)
Goal(s): 0-1 Doyle 5, 1-1 Elia 30, 1-2 Keane 83
Yellow Card(s): Elia 42 (Cyprus), Avraam 59 (Cyprus), Folan 81 (Republic of Ireland)
Referee: Einwaller (AUT)

5/9/09, Boris Paichadze, Tbilisi
Georgia 0-2 Italy
Attendance: 50000
Georgia: Lomaia, Khizanishvili, Kaladze, Sanaia, Lobjanidze, Kobiashvili, Khmaladze, Kenia, Razmadze (Tskitishvili 73), Ananidze (Vatsadze 59), Dvalishvili. Coach: Héctor Cúper (ARG)
Italy: Buffon, Zambrotta, Cannavaro, Chiellini, Criscito, Camoranesi (Santon 71), Marchionni (D'Agostino 57), Pirlo, Palombo, Iaquinta, Rossi (Quagliarella 57). Coach: Marcello Lippi (ITA)
Goal(s): 0-1 Kaladze 56 (og), 0-2 Kaladze 66 (og)
Yellow Card(s): Criscito 26 (Italy), Khmaladze 80 (Georgia), Kobiashvili 90 (Georgia)
Referee: Borski (POL)

9/9/09, Pod Goricom-Gradski, Podgorica
Montenegro 1-1 Cyprus
Attendance: 4000
Montenegro: Poleksić, Baša, Pejović, Pavićević, Fatić, S. Vukčević, Peković (Damjanović 70), Bošković (Kašćelan 62), Drinčić, Jovetić, Vučinić. Coach: Zoran Filipović (MNE)
Cyprus: Avgousti, Nicolaou (Marangos 83), Charalambous, Christou, Satsias, Alexandrou (Aloneftis 46), Michail, Makridis, Avraam, Okkas (Efrem 90+1), Konstantinou. Coach: Angelos Anastasiadis (GRE)
Goal(s): 1-0 Vučinić 56 (p), 1-1 Okkas 63
Yellow Card(s): Peković 24 (Montenegro), Pavićević 51 (Montenegro), Jovetić 64 (Montenegro), Konstantinou 73 (Cyprus), Charalambous 80 (Cyprus), Okkas 87 (Cyprus)
Referee: Zimmermann (SUI)

9/9/09, Stadio Olimpico, Turin
Italy 2-0 Bulgaria
Attendance: 26122
Italy: Buffon, Zambrotta, Cannavaro, Chiellini, Grosso, Camoranesi, De Rossi, Pirlo, Marchisio (Pepe 73), Gilardino (Rossi 58), Iaquinta (D'Agostino 83). Coach: Marcello Lippi (ITA)
Bulgaria: Ivankov, Il. Stoyanov, Manolev, Angelov, Kishishev, S. Petrov, Sarmov, Yankov (Domovchiyski 72), M. Petrov (Bojinov 57), Berbatov, Rangelov (Georgiev 57). Coach: Stanimir Stoilov (BUL)
Goal(s): 1-0 Grosso 11, 2-0 Iaquinta 40
Yellow Card(s): Yankov 58 (Bulgaria), Cannavaro 74 (Italy)
Referee: Meyer (GER)

10/10/09, Pod Goricom-Gradski, Podgorica
Montenegro 2-1 Georgia
Attendance: 5420
Montenegro: Poleksić, Baša, Batak, Pejović (Jovanović 46), Zverotić, Novaković (Kašćelan 71), Bošković, S. Vukčević, Drinčić, Jovetić, Damjanović (Delibašić 61). Coach: Zoran Filipović (MNE)
Georgia: Lomaia, Khizanishvili, Kaladze, Sanaia (Popkhadze 79), Lobjanidze, Khmaladze, Razmadze, Iashvili, Dvalishvili, Merebashvili (Odikadze 76), Gelashvili (Lipartia 67). Coach: Héctor Cúper (ARG)
Goal(s): 1-0 Batak 14, 1-1 Dvalishvili 45, 2-1 Delibašić 78
Yellow Card(s): Jovetić 26 (Montenegro), Lobjanidze 26 (Georgia),

Novaković 45 (Montenegro), Merebashvili 47 (Georgia), Kaladze 53 (Georgia), Lomaia 65 (Georgia), Delibašić 78 (Montenegro), Drinčić 86 (Montenegro), Dvalishvili 86 (Georgia)
Referee: Dereli (TUR)

10/10/09, Antonis Papadopoulos, Larnaca
Cyprus 4-1 Bulgaria
Attendance: 3700
Cyprus: Avgousti, Elia (Nicolaou 75), Christou, Michail, Satsias, Avraam, Konstantinou (Papathanasiou 89), Makridis, Aloneftis (Efrem 86), Charalambides, Dobrašinović. Coach: Angelos Anastasiadis (GRE)
Bulgaria: Ivankov (Mihaylov 68), Ivan Ivanov, Minev, Nikolov, K. Stoyanov, S. Petrov (Yanev 68), Angelov, Georgiev, M. Petrov, Berbatov, Bojinov (Domovchiyski 62). Coach: Stanimir Stoilov (BUL)
Goal(s): 1-0 Charalambides 11, 2-0 Charalambides 20, 2-1 Berbatov 44, 3-1 Konstantinou 58, 4-1 Aloneftis 78
Yellow Card(s): Charalambides 53 (Cyprus), S. Petrov 63 (Bulgaria), Yanev 72 (Bulgaria)
Referee: Allaerts (BEL)

Sean St Ledger scored his first international goal to put the Republic of Ireland 2-1 up against Italy at Croke Park

10/10/09, Croke Park, Dublin
Republic of Ireland 2-2 Italy
Attendance: 70640
Republic of Ireland: Given, O'Shea, Dunne, St Ledger, Whelan (Rowlands 70), Andrews, Lawrence, Kilbane, McGeady (S. Hunt 78), Keane, Doyle (Best 67). Coach: Giovanni Trapattoni (ITA)
Italy: Buffon, Zambrotta, Legrottaglie, Chiellini, Grosso (Bocchetti 76), Camoranesi, Pirlo, De Rossi, Palombo (Pepe 89), Iaquinta, Di Natale (Gilardino 76). Coach: Marcello Lippi (ITA)
Goal(s): 1-0 Whelan 8, 1-1 Camoranesi 26, 2-1 St Ledger 87, 2-2 Gilardino 90
Yellow Card(s): Whelan 33 (Republic of Ireland), De Rossi 67 (Italy), Best 83 (Republic of Ireland)
Referee: Hauge (NOR)

14/10/09, Croke Park, Dublin
Republic of Ireland 0-0 Montenegro
Attendance: 50212
Republic of Ireland: Given, Dunne, St Ledger, McShane, Miller, Rowlands (O'Shea 40), S. Hunt (Keogh 88), Duff, Kilbane, Keane, N. Hunt (Best 69). Coach: Giovanni Trapattoni (ITA)
Montenegro: Poleksić, Baša, Batak (Džudović 31), Jovanović, Zverotić, Novaković, Bošković (Kaščelan 81), Peković, S. Vukčević, Drinčić, Delibašić (Damjanović 69). Coach: Zoran Filipović (MNE)
Yellow Card(s): Rowlands 35 (Republic of Ireland), Peković 47 (Montenegro), Jovanović 82 (Montenegro)
Referee: Hriňák (SVK)

14/10/09, Ennio Tardini, Parma
Italy 3-2 Cyprus
Attendance: 15009
Italy: Marchetti, Gamberini, Cannavaro, Bocchetti, Santon, Pepe (Camoranesi 46), Gattuso, D'Agostino (De Rossi 66), Quagliarella, Gilardino, Rossi (Di Natale 46). Coach: Marcello Lippi (ITA)
Cyprus: Avgousti, Michail, Charalambous, Christou (Satsias 30), Elia, Avraam, Aloneftis (Konstantinou 74), Makridis, Charalambides, Dobrašinović, Okkas (Alexandrou 85). Coach: Angelos Anastasiadis (GRE)
Goal(s): 0-1 Okkas 12, 0-2 Michail 48, 1-2 Gilardino 78, 2-2 Gilardino 81, 3-2 Gilardino 90+2
Yellow Card(s): Satsias 35 (Cyprus), Gattuso 44 (Italy), Elia 75 (Cyprus)
Referee: Yefet (ISR)

14/10/09, Vasil Levski National, Sofia
Bulgaria 6-2 Georgia
Attendance: 700
Bulgaria: Mihaylov, Ivan Ivanov, Minev, Nikolov, K. Stoyanov (Bandalovski 46), Angelov (Bojinov 78), Georgiev, Yanev, M. Petrov, Berbatov, Rangelov (Iv. Stoyanov 64). Coach: Stanimir Stoilov (BUL)
Georgia: Lomaia (Mamaladze 29), Khizanishvili, Kaladze, Sanaia (Merebashvili 78), Lobjanidze, Kobiashvili, Khmaladze, Kenia (Odikadze 88), Razmadze, Iashvili, Dvalishvili. Coach: Héctor Cúper (ARG)
Goal(s): 1-0 Berbatov 6, 2-0 M. Petrov 14, 3-0 Berbatov 23, 4-0 Angelov 31, 4-1 Dvalishvili 34, 5-1 Berbatov 35, 6-1 M. Petrov 44, 6-2 Kobiashvili 51 (p)
Red Card(s): Khmaladze 58 (Georgia)
Yellow Card(s): Kenia 18 (Georgia), Khmaladze 33 (Georgia), Khmaladze 58 (Georgia), Bandalovski 87 (Bulgaria)
Referee: Jakobsson (ISL)

Group 8 Table

	Pld	Home						Away						Total						Pts
		W	D	L	F	A		W	D	L	F	A		W	D	L	F	A		
1 Italy	10	4	1	0	10	4		3	2	0	8	3		7	3	0	18	7		24
2 Republic of Ireland	10	2	3	0	6	4		2	3	0	6	4		4	6	0	12	8		18
3 Bulgaria	10	3	2	0	13	4		0	3	2	4	9		3	5	2	17	13		14
4 Cyprus	10	2	1	2	10	8		0	2	3	4	8		2	3	5	14	16		9
5 Montenegro	10	1	3	1	5	6		0	3	2	4	8		1	6	3	9	14		9
6 Georgia	10	0	3	2	2	5		0	0	5	5	14		0	3	7	7	19		3

GROUP 9

Bert van Marwijk's Netherlands had longer than any other European team to prepare for the 2010 FIFA World Cup having secured their qualification the previous June. That just left the task of trying to maintain their 100 per cent record in their final qualifier against Scotland – which they duly did to shatter the Scots' hopes of a play-off place. Instead it was Norway who snatched the runners-up spot - only to discover that their relatively meagre points total meant they were the one second-placed team to miss out.

Race for second

With the Dutch already assured of a place in South Africa after beating Iceland in Reykjavik on 6 June, the Group 9 focus switched to the race for second place. Scotland looked favourites to claim it as they were the team in possession with seven points from five matches. Although the Former Yugoslav Republic of Macedonia (FYROM) had the same tally, they had played a game more. Norway, by contrast, were bottom of the group with three points from a possible 15.

The Norwegians had brought back Egil 'Drillo' Olsen, architect of their qualification for USA 94, in place of Åge Hareide in January 2009. Although he had overseen a friendly win in Germany, his first two qualifiers had brought a draw in FYROM and defeat against the Netherlands. It was third time lucky, however, when Scotland visited Oslo in mid-August and Olsen's men subjected them to a 4-0 hammering.

Caldwell sees red

Scotland manager George Burley had opted for a centre-back pairing of brothers Gary and Steven Caldwell but they did not last long on the field together. Just after the half-hour Gary received a yellow card for fouling Morten Gamst Pedersen and within 60 seconds he was sent off after referee Alain Hamer adjudged him to have pulled the shirt of John Carew. Norway full-back John Arne Riise added insult to injury by scoring from the resulting free-kick, with the help of a big deflection off Scott Brown.

Pedersen doubled Norway's lead on the stroke of half-time, and the Scots' evening deteriorated further in the second period. Erik Huseklepp turned in the third on the hour after a Carew shot had rebounded off

Netherlands coach Bert van Marwijk (left) led his country to eight wins out of eight in Group 9

both posts. Carew then hit the underside of the crossbar before Pedersen completed Norway's victory with a last-minute free-kick.

Jonuz tastes defeat

With that victory Norway climbed above Iceland into fourth place, while Scotland slipped to third behind FYROM on goal difference. Burley's charges then climbed back into second place by beating the Macedonians 2-0 at Hampden Park in their next outing on 5 September. Brown headed his first international goal before James McFadden produced a late solo strike to condemn the visitors to a first defeat since Mirsad Jonuz replaced Srečko Katanec as coach in the spring.

Norway's draw in Iceland on the same day left Scotland with a three-point lead going into their final qualifier against the Dutch at Hampden on 9 September.

Unfortunately for Burley, the Scots' luck was out. Roared on by the Hampden crowd, they created several good scoring chances, with Kenny Miller and Steven Naismith both denied by the woodwork, but paid the price for not taking any of them. With eight minutes left Netherlands substitute Eljero Elia latched on to a weak David Weir header and rounded goalkeeper David Marshall to score the only goal.

Norway miss the cut

For the Oranje it was time to celebrate qualification with a 100 per cent record; for Scotland the hope of a play-off place had vanished, with Norway, 2-1 winners against FYROM, supplanting them in second place. The Norwegians owed their victory to first-half efforts from Thorstein Helstad and Riise, with Boban Grncarov replying for the visitors with his first international goal. Still, when the dust settled on European qualifying the next month, Norway's efforts proved in vain – their haul of ten points from eight games constituted the weakest record of the nine group runners-up so they missed the cut for the play-offs.

Group 9 Results

6/9/08
FYROM 1-0 Scotland
Norway 2-2 Iceland
10/9/08
Iceland 1-2 Scotland
FYROM 1-2 Netherlands
11/10/08
Scotland 0-0 Norway
Netherlands 2-0 Iceland
15/10/08
Iceland 1-0 FYROM
Norway 0-1 Netherlands
28/3/09

Netherlands 3-0 Scotland
1/4/09
Netherlands 4-0 FYROM
Scotland 2-1 Iceland
6/6/09
FYROM 0-0 Norway
Iceland 1-2 Netherlands
10/6/09
FYROM 2-0 Iceland
Netherlands 2-0 Norway

12/8/09, Ullevål, Oslo
Norway 4-0 Scotland
Attendance: 24493
Norway: Knudsen, Høgli, Wæhler, Hangeland, J.A. Riise, B.H. Riise (Skjelbred 84), Grindheim, Hoseth, Gamst Pedersen, Carew (Helstad 84), Huseklepp (Iversen 76). Coach: Åge Hareide (NOR)
Scotland: Marshall, Hutton, G. Caldwell, S. Caldwell, Davidson (McFadden 48), Alexander, D. Fletcher, Commons, Brown, McCormack (Berra 37)(Whittaker 78), Miller. Coach: George Burley (SCO)
Goal(s): J.A. Riise 35, Gamst Pedersen 45+1, Huseklepp 60, Gamst Pedersen 90+2
Red Card(s): G. Caldwell 34 (Scotland)
Yellow Card(s): Carew 11 (Norway), Hoseth 19 (Norway), G. Caldwell 32 (Scotland), J.A. Riise 31 (Norway), G. Caldwell 34 (Scotland), S. Caldwell 44 (Scotland)
Referee: Hamer (LUX)

James McFadden scores for Scotland in their 2-0 home win against FYROM

Thorstein Helstad (left) is pursued by John Carew and Bjørn Helge Riise after giving Norway the lead against FYROM

5/9/09, Hampden Park, Glasgow
Scotland 2-0 FYROM
Attendance: 50214
Scotland: Gordon, Alexander, Weir, Davidson (Whittaker 14), Hutton, McManus, Fletcher, Brown (Hartley 73), McFadden, Miller, D. Fletcher (Maloney 68). Coach: George Burley (SCO)
FYROM: Nikoloski, Mitreski, Sedloski, Noveski, G. Popov, Sumulikoski, Georgievski (Grozdanovski 69), Despotovski, Naumoski (Tasevski 64), Stojkov (B. Ibraimi 79), Pandev. Coach: Mirsad Jonuz (MKD)
Goal(s): 1-0 Brown 56, 2-0 McFadden 80
Yellow Card(s): Mitreski 18 (FYROM), Despotovski 45 (FYROM), Brown 45 (Scotland), McFadden 45+2 (Scotland)
Referee: Stark (GER)

5/9/09, Laugardalsvöllur, Reykjavik
Iceland 1-1 Norway
Attendance: 6321
Iceland: Gunnleifsson, Steinsson, I. Sigurdsson, K. Sigurdsson, Ottesen (R. Sigurdsson 90), B. Gunnarsson, Hallfredsson (V. P. Gunnarsson 89), A. Gunnarsson (S. Gíslason 81), R. Gíslason, Helguson, Gudjohnsen. Coach: Ólafur Jóhannesson (ISL)
Norway: Knudsen, Hangeland, Wæhler, Høgli, J.A. Riise, Gamst Pedersen, Grindheim, Hoseth (Brenne 46), Carew, Moldskred (Helstad 87), Huseklepp (B.H. Riise 78). Coach: Egil Olsen (NOR)
Goal(s): 0-1 J.A. Riise 11, 1-1 Gudjohnsen 29
Yellow Card(s): Hallfredsson 75 (Iceland), I. Sigurdsson 78 (Iceland), Helguson 83 (Iceland), Wæhler 86 (Norway)
Referee: Tudor (ROU)

9/9/09, Hampden Park, Glasgow
Scotland 0-1 Netherlands
Attendance: 51230
Scotland: Marshall, Weir, Whittaker, Hutton, McManus, Maloney (O'Connor 83), Hartley (Commons 67), D. Fletcher, Brown, Miller, Naismith. Coach: George Burley (SCO)

Netherlands: Vorm, Van Bronckhorst, Mathijsen, Ooijer, Van der Wiel, Robben (Elia 73), De Jong, Sneijder (Van der Vaart 77), De Zeeuw, Kuyt, Van Persie (Huntelaar 84). Coach: Bert van Marwijk (NED)
Goal(s): 0-1 Elia 82
Yellow Card(s): Naismith 13 (Scotland), Van Persie 18 (Netherlands), Hartley 45 (Scotland), D. Fletcher 56 (Scotland), Kuyt 62 (Netherlands), Robben 65 (Netherlands)
Referee: Larsen (DEN)

9/9/09, Ullevål, Oslo
Norway 2-1 FYROM
Attendance: 147660
Norway: Knudsen, Hangeland, Wæhler, Høiland, J.A. Riise, Grindheim (Winsnes 71), Hauger, B.H. Riise, Gamst Pedersen, Helstad (Moldskred 77), Carew (Braaten 84). Coach: Egil Olsen (NOR)
FYROM: Pacovski, Mitreski, Sedloski, Grncarov, G. Popov, Sumulikoski, Georgievski, Tasevski (Alimi 65), Naumoski (Ivanovski 75), Stojkov (B. Ibraimi 60), Pandev. Coach: Mirsad Jonuz (MKD)
Goal(s): 1-0 Helstad 2, 2-0 J.A. Riise 25, 2-1 Grncarov 79
Yellow Card(s): Mitreski 23 (FYROM), G. Popov 40 (FYROM)
Referee: Bruno Paixão (POR)

Group 9 Table

		Home					Away					Total					
	Pld	W	D	L	F	A	W	D	L	F	A	W	D	L	F	A	Pts
1 Netherlands	8	4	0	0	11	0	4	0	0	6	2	8	0	0	17	2	24
2 Norway	8	2	1	1	8	4	0	3	1	3	6	2	4	2	11	10	10
3 Scotland	8	2	1	1	4	2	1	0	3	2	9	3	1	4	6	11	10
4 FYROM	8	2	1	1	4	2	0	0	4	1	9	2	1	5	5	11	7
5 Iceland	8	1	1	2	4	5	0	1	3	3	8	1	2	5	7	13	5

PLAY-OFFS

If the play-offs had generated controversy even before a ball was kicked through FIFA's decision to seed the draw, that was nothing beside the furore that followed when France beat the Republic of Ireland with the help of a Thierry Henry handball. Henry twice used his left arm before teeing up William Gallas to head the goal that sent France to South Africa alongside fellow play-off winners Greece, Portugal and a Slovenia side who provided the big surprise by defeating Russia.

Dramatic events

Not many would have foreseen the dramatic events at the Stade de France on 18 November when France deservedly won the first leg against the Irish four days earlier. Raymond Domenech's men looked to have done the hard bit after Nicolas Anelka beat Shay Given with a deflected shot in the 72nd minute. The Dublin crowd could hardly complain about the result, for while the visitors survived an early scare when Liam Lawrence shot against Patrice Evra with the goal at his

Damien Duff shows his dejection after the Republic of Ireland go out to France

mercy, France upped a gear in the second half and would have added to Anelka's goal had André-Pierre Gignac not shot wide of an open net.

Yet Irish players and supporters were left seething with injustice after the second leg. Giovanni Trapattoni's side levelled the aggregate score after 33 minutes when Robbie Keane converted Damien Duff's low cross, and they squandered several chances to score again as they outplayed their nervous hosts for long spells. John O'Shea shot over from close range, Duff broke clear but could not beat Hugo Lloris, then Keane overran the ball after taking it past the France goalkeeper. So to extra time and after Swedish referee Martin Hansson had ignored French appeals for a penalty after Shay Given saved at the feet of Nicolas Anelka, the match official and his touchline assistant failed to spot Henry's indiscretion leading up to the equaliser and decisive goal. As a result Henry's reputation was tarnished, but Domenech's stuttering France side were through to their fourth successive World Cup.

Slovenia shock

The other major talking point of the play-offs was Slovenia's shock victory over Guus Hiddink's Russia. The UEFA EURO 2008 semi-finalists were strong favourites but instead Slovenia – the small Balkan state with a population of around 2m – prevailed on the away-goals rule to qualify for their first major finals since Korea/Japan 2002. Russia were actually two goals up in the first leg in Moscow but instead were left to count the cost of the late goal they conceded in that 2-1 win after falling 1-0 in the return.

The Russians made the breakthrough at the Luzhniki stadium with a spectacular 40th-minute strike by Diniyar Bilyaletdinov. Collecting a pass from Roman Pavlyuchenko inside Slovenia's area, he left two defenders for dead with a superb turn before rifling home with his supposedly weaker right foot. The Everton midfielder struck again after 52 minutes with a close-range finish but Slovenia grabbed a lifeline two minutes from time when Nejc Pečnik nodded in the rebound after Igor Akinfeev had saved from Robert Koren. Zlatko Dedič then provided the solitary goal Slovenia required back in Maribor, volleying in from Valter Birsa's inswinging cross a minute before half-time. Russia were unable to break down a stout Slovenia defence breached only once at home in five group games and they ended with nine men after the second-half sendings-off of substitute Aleksandr Kerzhakov – harshly penalised for a challenge on the goalkeeper – and Vladimir Bystrov.

Denied by woodwork

There was no such slip-up by Germany 2006 semi-finalists Portugal despite the absence of the injured Cristiano Ronaldo as they overcame Bosnia-Herzegovina 2-0 on aggregate. The Bosnians' coach, Miroslav Blažević, may have steered Croatia to third in the world in 1998 but Lady Luck frowned on his men in the first leg in Lisbon where they were denied three times by the woodwork.

Bruno Alves scored the only goal after 31 minutes when he nodded home a Nani cross but before half-time the visitors were frustrated for the first time as Senijad Ibričić headed against the goalframe. Although Liedson missed a golden opportunity to double the lead, Portugal had a bigger let-off in the 90th minute as Edin Džeko headed against the crossbar and Zlatan Muslimović hit the rebound against the post. Almost as costly for Bosnia-Herzegovina were the bookings picked up by Emir Spahić, Elvir Rahimić, Samir Muratović and Zvjezdan Misimović that caused the quartet to miss the return. Portugal fashioned the clearer chances in Zenica, where goalkeeper Kenan Hasagić foiled Tiago in the first half but was helpless to stop Raul Meireles finding the corner of the net from a Nani pass in the 56th minute. Home

Raul Meireles (facing) congratulates team-mate Bruno Alves after the defender's winning goal against Bosnia-Herzegovina in Lisbon

hopes vanished altogether with Sejad Salihović's dismissal 15 minutes from time.

Ukraine unstuck

The fourth play-off winners were Greece, who advanced to their first World Cup since their finals debut at USA 94 with a 1-0 aggregate success against Ukraine. Olexiy Mykhailychenko's team appeared to have taken the upper hand after a stalemate in Athens only to come unstuck back in Donetsk.

Both sides had chances in the first leg. Ruslan Rotan and Taras Mykhalyk, with a free-kick beaten away by Alexandros Tzorvas, threatened for Ukraine while Greece's Theofanis Gekas and Georgios Samaras went close before Sotirios Kyrgiakos summed up the hosts' frustrations with a late header wide. Yet Otto Rehhagel's 2004 European champions resisted Ukraine's pressure in the return and found the decisive goal through Dimitris Salpingidis after 31 minutes, the Panathinaikos FC striker breaking on to Samaras's wonderful through-ball and beating Andriy Pyatov with a smart low finish. Ukraine created openings – Andriy Shevchenko shot wide of an empty net early on while Greece goalkeeper Tzorvas was increasingly busy in the second period – but their efforts proved in vain. Their focus now turned to preparing for UEFA EURO 2012 on home soil.

Play-Off Results

14/11/09, Luzhniki, Moscow
Russia 2-1 Slovenia
Attendance: 71600
Russia: Akinfeev, Ignashevich, V. Berezutskiy, Anyukov, Zhirkov, Zyryanov, Semak (Bystrov 61), Bilyaletdinov, Denisov, Arshavin, Pavlyuchenko (Sychev 80). Coach: Guus Hiddink (NED)
Slovenia: S. Handanovič, Cesar, Brecko, Šuler, Jokič, Radosavljevič, Koren, Kirm (Pečnik 82), Dedič (Ljubijankič 67), Birsa (Stevanovič 77), Novakovič. Coach: Matjaž Kek (SVN)
Goal(s): 1-0 Bilyaletdinov 40, 2-0 Bilyaletdinov 52, 2-1 Pečnik 88
Yellow Card(s): Arshavin 45+1 (Russia), Sychev 82 (Russia)
Referee: Larsen (DEN)
18/11/09, Ljudski vrt, Maribor
Slovenia 1-0 Russia
Attendance: 12510
Slovenia: S. Handanovič, Cesar, Brecko, Šuler, Jokič, Radosavljevič, Koren, Kirm, Dedič (Stevanovič 90+4), Birsa (Pečnik 78), Novakovič. Coach: Matjaž Kek (SVN)
Russia: Akinfeev, Ignashevich, V. Berezutskiy, Anyukov, Zhirkov, Zyryanov, Yanbayev (Semak 46), Bilyaletdinov (Pogrebnyak 77), Denisov, Arshavin, Pavlyuchenko (Kerzhakov 46). Coach: Guus Hiddink (NED)
Goal(s): 1-0 Dedič 44
Red Card(s): Kerzhakov 66 (Russia), Zhirkov 90+2 (Russia)
Yellow Card(s): Zhirkov 7 (Russia), Bilyaletdinov 22 (Russia), Birsa 55 (Slovenia), S. Handanovič 66 (Slovenia), Denisov 73 (Russia), Koren 76 (Slovenia), Zhirkov 90+2 (Russia)
Referee: Hauge (NOR)
Aggregate: 2-2; Slovenia qualify on away goal.

Slovenia's players erupt with joy after knocking out Russia

Ukraine: Pyatov, Mykhalyk, Kucher, Khacheridi, Kobin, Rakytskiy, Tymoshchuk, Rotan (Yarmolenko 46), Gusev (Aliyev 53), Milevskiy, Shevchenko. Coach: Olexiy Mykhailychenko (UKR)
Yellow Card(s): Papastathopoulos 60 (Greece)
Referee: Duhamel (FRA)
18/11/09, Donbass Arena, Donetsk
Ukraine 0-1 Greece
Attendance: 31648
Ukraine: Pyatov, Mykhalyk (Hai 66), Kucher, Khacheridi, Kobin, Rakytskiy, Tymoshchuk, Yarmolenko (Gusev 69), Aliyev (Seleznev 57), Milevskiy, Shevchenko. Coach: Olexiy Mykhailychenko (UKR)
Greece: Tzorvas, Vintra, Spiropoulos, Papastathopoulos (Pliatsikas 29), Moras, Kyrgiakos, Katsouranis, Karagounis, Samaras (Gekas 63), Charisteas (Tziolis 71), Salpingidis. Coach: Otto Rehhagel (GER)
Goal(s): 0-1 Salpingidis 31
Yellow Card(s): Katsouranis 17 (Greece), Yarmolenko 52 (Ukraine), Vintra 63 (Greece), Kyrgiakos 78 (Greece)
Referee: Olegário Benquerença (POR)
Aggregate: 0-1; Greece qualify.

14/11/09, Estádio do Sport Lisboa e Benfica, Lisbon
Portugal 1-0 Bosnia-Herzegovina
Attendance: 60588
Portugal: Eduardo, Paulo Ferreira, Bruno Alves, Ricardo Carvalho, Pepe, Deco (Tiago 84), Duda, Raul Meireles, Nani (Fábio Coentrão 69), Simão (Hugo Almeida 88), Liedson. Coach: Carlos Queiroz (POR)
Bosnia-Herzegovina: Hasagić, Jahić, Spahić, Nadarević, Misimović (Muslimović 81), Muratović (Pjanić 87), Rahimić, Salihović, Ibričić, Džeko, Ibišević. Coach: Miroslav Blažević (CRO)
Goal(s): 1-0 Bruno Alves 31
Yellow Card(s): Deco 14 (Portugal), Ibišević 15 (Bosnia-Herzegovina), Muratović 37 (Bosnia-Herzegovina), Rahimić 48 (Bosnia-Herzegovina), Spahić 71 (Bosnia-Herzegovina)
Referee: Atkinson (ENG)
18/11/09, Bilino Polje, Zenica
Bosnia-Herzegovina 0-1 Portugal
Attendance: 15000
Bosnia-Herzegovina: Hasagić, Pandža, Nadarević, Jahić, Salihović, Pjanić, Medunjanin (Muslimović 46), Ibričić, Bajramović (Berberović 83), Ibišević, Džeko. Coach: Miroslav Blažević (CRO)
Portugal: Eduardo, Paulo Ferreira, Bruno Alves, Ricardo Carvalho, Pepe, Tiago, Duda, Raul Meireles, Nani (Edinho 73), Simão (Deco 80), Liedson (Miguel Veloso 90+1). Coach: Carlos Queiroz (POR)
Goal(s): 0-1 Raul Meireles 56
Yellow Card(s): Simão 11 (Portugal), Jahić 25 (Bosnia-Herzegovina), Nadarević 37 (Bosnia-Herzegovina), Džeko 58 (Bosnia-Herzegovina), Salihović 77 (Bosnia-Herzegovina), Salihović 77 (Bosnia-Herzegovina), Berberović 90+2 (Bosnia-Herzegovina)
Referee: Rosetti (ITA)
Aggregate: 0-2; Portugal qualify.

14/11/09, Croke Park, Dublin
Republic of Ireland 0-1 France
Attendance: 74103
Republic of Ireland: Given, St Ledger, O'Shea, Dunne, Whelan, Lawrence (S. Hunt 80), Kilbane, Duff (McGeady 76), Andrews, Keane, Doyle (Best 71). Coach: Giovanni Trapattoni (ITA)
France: Lloris, Sagna, Gallas, Evra, Abidal, Gourcuff, L. Diarra, Diarra, Henry, Gignac (Malouda 90+1), Anelka. Coach: Raymond Domenech (FRA)
Goal(s): 0-1 Anelka 72
Referee: Brych (GER)
18/11/09, Stade de France, Paris
France 1-1 Republic of Ireland (aet)
Attendance: 79145
France: Lloris, Sagna, Gallas, Evra, Escudé (Squillaci 9), Gourcuff (Malouda 88), L. Diarra, Diarra, Henry, Gignac (Govou 57), Anelka. Coach: Raymond Domenech (FRA)
Republic of Ireland: Given, St Ledger, O'Shea (McShane 67), Dunne, Whelan (Gibson 63), Lawrence (McGeady 287), Kilbane, Duff, Andrews, Keane, Doyle. Coach: Giovanni Trapattoni (ITA)
Goal(s): 0-1 Keane 33, 1-1 Gallas 193
Yellow Card(s): Kilbane 59 (Republic of Ireland), McShane 75 (Republic of Ireland), Squillaci 79 (France), Malouda 90+2 (France), Duff 104 (Republic of Ireland), Govou 107 (France)
Referee: Hansson (SWE)
Aggregate: 2-1; France qualify after extra time.

14/11/09, OACA Spyro Louis, Athens
Greece 0-0 Ukraine
Attendance: 39045
Greece: Tzorvas, Papastathopoulos, Kyrgiakos, Moras, Vintra, Spiropoulos, Katsouranis, Karagounis, Samaras, Salpingidis (Mitroglou 71), Gekas (Charisteas 65). Coach: Otto Rehhagel (GER)

TOP GOALSCORERS
(including Play-Offs)

10	Theofanis GEKAS (Greece)
9	Edin DŽEKO (Bosnia-Herzegovina)
	Wayne ROONEY (England)
7	Miroslav KLOSE (Germany)
	DAVID VILLA (Spain)
6	Marc JANKO (Austria)
	Wesley SONCK (Belgium)
	Lukas PODOLSKI (Germany)
	Elyaniv BARDA (Israel)
	Euzebiusz SMOLAREK (Poland)
	Robbie KEANE (Republic of Ireland)
	Stanislav ŠESTÁK (Slovakia)
	Andriy SHEVCHENKO (Ukraine)

UEFA
UNDER21
CHAMPIONSHIP

2011 U21 CHAMPIONSHIP

A year after winning the UEFA European Under-21 Championship for the first time, Germany's hopes of retaining the trophy hung in the balance. That was just one of a number of surprises as qualifying for the 2011 finals in Denmark entered the 2010 summer break. Germany triumphed 4-0 against England in the 2009 final in Malmo, but Rainer Adrion's new-look side faltered early in their title defence. Defeat by the Czech Republic left them playing catch-up from the start of the group stage, and they were not the only traditional powerhouse that found the going tough. Five-times winners Italy won just three of their first six games as Wales took command of Group 3, while England saw Greece wrest control of Group 9. Less surprising was the return to strength of 2006 and 2007 champions the Netherlands, who won all six of their matches going into the break. They and the Czech Republic were the only two sides boasting perfect records at that point.

Qualifying for the 2011 UEFA European Under-21 Championship finals kicked off with a goalless draw between Luxembourg and Wales in Ettelbruck on 27 March 2009 and was already well under way by the time Germany lifted the trophy at the Malmo Arena to bring the 2009 edition of the competition to a close. With Denmark already qualified as hosts, the 52 other UEFA member associations took part in the qualifying group stage, with the winners of each section and the four best runners-up advancing to the play-offs, to be held between 9 and 13 October 2010 and which would determine the seven countries to join Denmark at the final tournament from 12 to 25 June 2011.

GROUP 1

Romania and Russia were among the first teams into action, both starting with victories against Andorra in Group 1. Russia's hopes of reaching the play-offs looked bleak, though, after losing 1-0 to the Faroe Islands in their second game.

It was only the second competitive victory at this level for the North Atlantic minnows and did not bode well for Russia, but they recovered to win their next five matches to go into the summer recess locked on 18 points with Romania, whose only loss came against Latvia, 5-1. Russia and Romania were scheduled to meet home and away on 4 and 7 September 2010 in their final two games to decide the section.

Group 1 Results

28/3/09, Francisc Neuman, Arad
Romania 2-0 Andorra
Goal(s): 1-0 Gângioveanu 63(p), 2-0 Ganea 72

1/4/09, Kuban, Krasnodar
Russia 4-0 Andorra
Goal(s): 1-0 A. Ionov 14, 2-0 Ryzhov 21, 3-0 Mamaev 33(p), 4-0 Koslov 88

6/6/09, Skonto, Riga
Latvia 4-0 Andorra
Goal(s): 1-0 Gauračs 41(p), 2-0 Rudņevs 70, 3-0 Rugins 74, 4-0 Žulevs 90

6/6/09, Gundadalur, Torshavn
Faroe Islands 0-4 Romania
Goal(s): 0-1 Rusescu 14, 0-2 Gângioveanu 36, 0-3 Rusescu 56, 0-4 Torje 67

9/6/09, Gundadalur, Torshavn
Faroe Islands 1-0 Russia
Goal(s): 1-0 Edmundson 1

12/8/09, Comunal, Andorra La Vella
Andorra 0-2 Romania
Goal(s): 0-1 Gâman 8(p), 0-2 Torje 64

12/8/09, Sheriff, Tiraspol
Moldova 1-0 Latvia
Goal(s): 1-0 Ionita 59

5/9/09, Gundadalur, Torshavn
Faroe Islands 1-1 Moldova
Goal(s): 0-1 Sidorenco 24, 1-1 K. Jacobsen 36

5/9/09, Daugava, Liepaja
Latvia 0-4 Russia
Goal(s): 0-1 Kazura 17(og), 0-2 Yakovlev 28, 0-3 Ryzhov 48, 0-4 Gorbatenko 54

8/9/09, Comunal, Andorra La Vella
Andorra 0-4 Russia
Goal(s): 0-1 Gorbatenko 17, 0-2 Ryzhov 26, 0-3 Smolov 47, 0-4 Gatagov 84

8/9/09, Ion Oblemenco, Craiova
Romania 3-0 Moldova
Goal(s): 1-0 Torje 12, 2-0 Ochiroşii 15, 3-0 Torje 48

9/9/09, Gundadalur, Torshavn
Faroe Islands 1-3 Latvia
Goal(s): 0-1 Gauračs 1, 0-2 Gauračs 20, 1-2 Poulsen 38, 1-3 Gauračs 44

9/10/09, Daugava, Riga
Latvia 5-1 Romania
Goal(s): 1-0 Rudņevs 30, 2-0 Gauračs 39, 3-0 Gauračs 63, 4-0 Gauračs 66, 5-0 Rudņevs 85, 5-1 Torje 90+4(p)

10/10/09, Arena Khimki, Moscow
Russia 2-0 Faroe Islands
Goal(s): 1-0 Ryzhov 21, 2-0 Salughin 90+2

10/10/09, Sheriff, Tiraspol
Moldova 1-0 Andorra
Goal(s): 1-0 Bogdan 41

13/10/09, Municipal, Botosani
Romania 3-0 Faroe Islands
Goal(s): 1-0 Bicfalvi 5, 2-0 Ganea 39, 3-0 Ionescu 58

14/10/09, Arena Khimki, Moscow
Russia 3-1 Moldova
Goal(s): 1-0 Kokorin 5, 2-0 Balyaykin 38, 3-0 Kokorin 41, 3-1 Vornisel 62

14/11/09, Gloria, Buzau
Romania 4-1 Latvia
Goal(s): 1-0 Sburlea 10, 2-0 Costea 28, 3-0 Papp 43, 4-0 Hora 82, 4-1 I. Tarasovs 90+1

14/11/09, Sheriff, Tiraspol
Moldova 0-3 Russia
Goal(s): 0-1 Balyaykin 17, 0-2 Mamaev 28, 0-3 Gatagov 89(p)

18/11/09, Daugava, Riga
Latvia 0-1 Faroe Islands
Goal(s): 0-1 Edmundson 55

21/11/09, Comunal, Andorra La Vella
Andorra 1-1 Faroe Islands
Goal(s): 0-1 Edmundson 32, 1-1 Madeira 51

3/3/10, Comunal, Andorra La Vella
Andorra 1-3 Moldova
Goal(s): 0-1 Patras 10, 0-2 Dedov 11, 0-3 Dedov 45, 1-3 Vieira 62

Group 1 Fixtures

11/8/10
Russia - Latvia
Faroe Islands - Andorra
Moldova - Romania
4/9/10
Moldova - Faroe Islands
Romania - Russia
Andorra - Latvia
7/9/10
Russia - Romania
Latvia - Moldova

Group 1 Table

	Pld	Home W D L F A	Away W D L F A	Total W D L F A	Pts
1 Russia	7	3 0 0 9 1	3 0 1 11 1	6 0 1 20 2	18
2 Romania	7	4 0 0 12 1	2 0 1 7 5	6 0 1 19 6	18
3 Moldova	7	2 0 1 2 3	1 1 2 5 8	3 1 3 7 11	10
4 Latvia	7	2 0 2 9 6	1 0 2 4 6	3 0 4 13 12	9
5 Faroe Islands	8	1 1 2 3 8	1 1 2 2 6	2 2 4 5 14	8
6 Andorra	8	0 1 3 2 10	0 0 4 0 11	0 1 7 2 21	1

GROUP 2

Switzerland had the opportunity to confirm top spot in Group 2 early. A draw against Turkey in St Gallen on 26 May would have been enough for them to do so, but they fell 2-0 to the second-placed side.

They had another chance four days later but again failed to grasp it as Georgia held Pierluigi Tami's team to a goalless draw. Nevertheless, as the competition closed for the summer the Swiss led Turkey, who had a game in hand, by four points and were set to host bottom side the Republic of Ireland in their final match on 10 August.

Group 2 Results

31/3/09, Turner's Cross, Cork
Republic of Ireland 0-3 Turkey
Goal(s): 0-1 Deniz Yılmaz 13, 0-2 Emre Özkan 40, 0-3 Ömer Şişmanoğlu 90+1

5/6/09, Bergholz, Wil
Switzerland 2-1 Armenia
Goal(s): 1-0 Derdiyok 16, 2-0 Gashi 20, 2-1 Manasyan 84

UEFA European Under-21 Championship

UNDER21.
CHAMPIONSHIP

6/09, Yerevan Republican, Yerevan
Armenia 2-5 Turkey
Goal(s): 0-1 Deniz Yılmaz 5,
2 Aydın Yılmaz 45+1, 0-3 Ferhat
kmaz 49(p), 0-4 Mustafa
ektemek 60, 1-4 Mkhitaryan 69,
5 Yiğit Gökoğlan 70, 2-5 Dashyan 81

2/8/09, Breite, Schaffhausen
witzerland 0-1 Estonia
Goal(s): 0-1 Saag 31

9/09, MIKA Sport Complex, Yerevan
Armenia 1-3 Switzerland
Goal(s): 0-1 Hochstrasser 4,
1 Yagan 10, 1-2 Rossini 35,
3 F. Feltscher 39

9/09, A Le Coq Arena, Tallinn
stonia 2-0 Georgia
Goal(s): 1-0 Mošnikov 42, 2-0 Anier 90

9/09, Tsentral, Zestaponi
eorgia 4-0 Turkey
Goal(s): 1-0 Ivanishvili 1,
0 Khidesheli 35, 3-0 Totadze 80,
0 Gugava 88

9/09, Rakvere, Rakvere
stonia 1-1 Republic of Ireland
Goal(s): 1-0 Saag 4, 1-1 Sheridan 7

10/09, Kadriorg, Tallinn
stonia 1-4 Switzerland
Goal(s): 1-0 Zenjov 7, 1-1 Ciarocchi 10,
2 Gavranovic 21, 1-3 F. Feltscher 23,
4 Koch 26

10/09, Tallaght Stadium, Dublin
epublic of Ireland 1-1 Georgia
Goal(s): 1-0 Judge 28,
1 Ivanishvili 89

3/10/09, Atatürk, Eskisehir
urkey 1-0 Armenia
oal(s): 1-0 Aydın Yılmaz 90+4

3/10/09, Regional Sports Centre,
Waterford
epublic of Ireland 1-1 Switzerland
oal(s): 0-1 Frei 58, 1-1 Garvan 90+3

4/11/09, Mikheil Meskhi, Tbilisi
eorgia 1-1 Republic of Ireland
oal(s): 0-1 Carey 48,
1 Kvaratskhelia 84

4/11/09, Yerevan Republican, Yerevan
rmenia 1-1 Estonia
oal(s): 1-0 Mkhitaryan 24,
1 Artjunin 90+2

14/11/09, Hüseyin Avni Aker, Trabzon
Turkey 1-3 Switzerland
Goal(s): 0-1 Stocker 7, 0-2 Stocker 43,
1-2 Caner Erkin 51, 1-3 Gashi 89

17/11/09, Yerevan Republican, Yerevan
Armenia 4-1 Republic of Ireland
Goal(s): 1-0 Mkhitaryan 30,
2-0 Mkhitaryan 61, 2-1 Sheridan 65,
3-1 Goharyan 75, 4-1 Mkhitaryan 82(p)

18/11/09, Rize Atatürk, Rize
Turkey 0-0 Estonia

18/11/09, Cornaredo, Lugano
Switzerland 1-0 Georgia
Goal(s): 1-0 Gavranovic 43

3/3/10, Mikheil Meskhi, Tbilisi
Georgia 2-0 Estonia
Goal(s): 1-0 Barabadze 44,
2-0 Ananidze 90+2

3/3/10, Tallaght Stadium, Dublin
Republic of Ireland 1-2 Armenia
Goal(s): 0-1 Hayrapetyan 34,
0-2 Ghazaryan 40, 1-2 Daly 80

20/5/10, Kadriorg, Tallinn
Estonia 2-3 Armenia
Goal(s): 0-1 Ghazaryan 18,
1-1 Saag 32, 1-2 Manoyan 55,
1-3 Ghazaryan 68, 2-3 Kallaste 81

23/5/10, Kadriorg, Tallinn
Estonia 1-0 Turkey
Goal(s): 1-0 Saag 13

26/5/10, Arena St. Gallen, St Gallen
Switzerland 0-2 Turkey
Goal(s): 0-1 Affolter 66(og),
0-2 Özgür Çek 89

30/5/10, Boris Paichadze National
Stadium, Tbilisi
Georgia 0-0 Switzerland

Group 2 Fixtures

10/8/10
Republic of Ireland - Estonia
11/8/10
Armenia - Georgia
3/9/10
Switzerland - Republic of Ireland
4/9/10
Turkey – Georgia
7/9/10
Georgia - Armenia
Turkey - Republic of Ireland

GROUP 3

Wales came close to beating England in the 2009 play-offs and Brian Flynn's side re-affirmed their pedigree at this level. Group 3 was set for an exciting finish as Wales led Italy, semi-finalists in 2009, by three points with two games to play.

Hungary were also just a point behind the Azzurrini with a game in hand. Italy kicked off their campaign against Wales in Swansea and Arsenal FC starlet Aaron Ramsey scored the decisive goal in a memorable 2-1 victory for the home team. Pierluigi Casiraghi's side surprisingly won just one of their opening four games, also dropping points against Bosnia-Herzegovina (1-1) and Hungary (0-2), and they were grateful still to be in with a chance after Wales fell to their first defeat in six matches, 2-1 against Bosnia-Herzegovina, in November 2009. Italy hoped to exact revenge when they met Wales again in their final game on 7 September.

Aaron Ramsey scored the winning goal for Wales against Italy in Swansea

Group 2 Table

		Home					Away					Total					
	Pld	W	D	L	F	A	W	D	L	F	A	W	D	L	F	A	Pts
Switzerland	9	2	0	2	3	4	3	2	0	11	4	5	2	2	14	8	17
Turkey	8	1	1	1	2	3	3	0	2	10	7	4	1	3	12	10	13
Estonia	9	2	1	2	7	8	1	2	1	2	3	3	3	3	9	11	12
Armenia	8	1	1	2	8	10	2	0	2	6	6	3	1	4	14	16	10
Georgia	7	2	2	0	7	1	0	1	2	1	4	2	3	2	8	5	9
Republic of Ireland	7	0	2	2	3	7	0	2	1	3	6	0	4	3	6	13	4

Group 3 Results

27/3/09, Deich, Ettelbruck
Luxembourg 0-0 Wales

31/3/09, Parc-Y-Scarlets, Llanelli
Wales 5-1 Luxembourg
Goal(s): 1-0 Eardley 11(p),
2-0 Brown 12, 3-0 King 34,
4-0 Church 41, 4-1 Polidori 57,
5-1 Wilson 79

6/6/09, Györi Eto, Gyor
Hungary 3-0 Luxembourg
Goal(s): 1-0 Présinger 14, 2-0
Koman 36, 3-0 Korcsmár 72

10/6/09, Jos Nosbaum, Dudelange
Luxembourg 0-1 Hungary
Goal(s): 0-1 Filkor 26

12/8/09, The Racecourse, Wrexham
Wales 4-1 Hungary
Goal(s): 1-0 MacDonald 16,
1-1 Korcsmár 18, 2-1 Evans 36,
3-1 Evans 41, 4-1 King 90+1

4/9/09, Koševo, Sarajevo
Bosnia-Herzegovina 0-1
Luxembourg
Goal(s): 0-1 Twimumu 75

4/9/09, Liberty Stadium, Swansea
Wales 2-1 Italy
Goal(s): 1-0 Ribeiro 8,
1-1 Paloschi 23, 2-1 Ramsey 68

8/9/09, Silvio Piola, Novara
Italy 2-0 Luxembourg
Goal(s): 1-0 Poli 45+1,
2-0 Balotelli 90+3

10/10/09, The Racecourse, Wrexham
Wales 2-0 Bosnia-Herzegovina
Goal(s): 1-0 Evans 56,
2-0 Evans 90+2

13/10/09, Danilo Martelli, Mantova
Italy 1-1 Bosnia-Herzegovina
Goal(s): 1-0 Marilungo 8,
1-1 Ćorić 30

13/11/09, Györi Eto, Gyor
Hungary 2-0 Italy
Goal(s): 1-0 Németh 15,
2-0 Koman 88

17/11/09, Josy Barthel, Luxembourg
Luxembourg 0-4 Italy
Goal(s): 0-1 Barillà 38, 0-2 Soriano 68,
0-3 Barillà 77, 0-4 Marilungo 83

18/11/09, Grbavica, Sarajevo
Bosnia-Herzegovina 2-1 Wales
Goal(s): 0-1 Allen 5,
1-1 Haurdić 29, 2-1 Haurdić 66

2/3/10, Alphonse Theis, Hesperange
Luxembourg 0-1 Bosnia-
Herzegovina
Goal(s): 0-1 Ćorić 73(p)

3/3/10, Centro d'Italia, Rieti
Italy 2-0 Hungary
Goal(s): 1-0 Okaka Chuka 25,
2-0 Marrone 81

Group 3 Fixtures

11/8/10
Bosnia-Herzegovina - Hungary
3/9/10
Bosnia-Herzegovina - Italy
4/9/10
Hungary - Wales
7/9/10
Italy - Wales
Hungary - Bosnia-Herzegovina

Group 3 Table

		Home				Away				Total				
	Pld	W	D	L	F A	W	D	L	F A	W	D	L	F A	Pt
1 Wales	6	4	0	0	13 3	0	1	1	1 2	4	1	1	14 5	1:
2 Italy	6	2	1	0	5 1	1	0	2	5 4	3	1	2	10 5	1(
3 Hungary	5	2	0	0	5 0	1	0	2	2 6	3	0	2	7 6	9
4 Bosnia-Herzegovina	5	1	0	1	2 2	1	1	1	2 3	2	1	2	4 5	7
5 Luxembourg	8	0	1	3	0 6	1	0	3	2 10	1	1	6	2 16	4

GROUP 4

As other fancied teams struggled, there were no such problems for the Netherlands, who, after missing out on the 2009 finals, returned to their best, demonstrating the sort of form that took them to the title in 2006 and 2007 under Foppe de Haan.

New coach Cor Pot's side is built along the traditional Dutch 4-3-3 lines, with Pot stressing team-building as the key to their success. Only goalkeeper Tim Krul and captain Erik Pieters have survived from the 2007 title-winning squad, but after failing to reach the finals in Sweden, the team's winning mentality returned, notably with a crucial 2-1 victory against second-placed Spain in November 2009 that hoisted them six points clear at the top. Spain had won their previous 14 group stage qualifiers stretching back to October 2005, and they had the opportunity to make amends when the pair faced off again with first place at stake on 3 September.

Group 4 Results

9/6/09, MZOS Znicz, Pruszkow
Poland 2-0 Liechtenstein
Goal(s): 1-0 Korzym 35, 2-0 Rybus 56

4/9/09, Nuevo Carlos Tartiere, Oviedo
Spain 2-0 Poland
Goal(s): 1-0 Joselú 7, 2-0 Parejo 58

4/9/09, FC Emmen, Emmen
Netherlands 2-0 Finland
Goal(s): 1-0 De Jong 16,
2-0 Biseswar 75

7/9/09, Rheinpark, Vaduz
Liechtenstein 0-4 Spain
Goal(s): 0-1 Parejo 15,
0-2 Javi Martínez 23, 0-3 Diego
Capel 82, 0-4 Aarón Ñíguez 86

8/9/09, Groclin Dyskobolia, Grodzisk Wielkopolski
Poland 2-1 Finland
Goal(s): 1-0 Glik 44, 1-1 Pukki 51,
2-1 Grosicki 56

9/10/09, Sportpark Eschen-Mauren, Eschen
Liechtenstein 0-5 Poland
Goal(s): 0-1 Kiełb 43, 0-2 Małecki 59,
0-3 Małecki 73, 0-4 Kiełb 80,
0-5 Sobiech 90+1

9/10/09, Finnair Stadium, Helsinki
Finland 0-1 Netherlands
Goal(s): 0-1 Pieters 24

13/10/09, Kielce, Kielce
Poland 0-4 Netherlands
Goal(s): 0-1 Van Wolfswinkel 41,
0-2 Kuiper 45, 0-3 Van Wolfswinkel 49
0-4 Van Wolfswinkel 66

13/10/09, Sportpark Eschen-Mauren, Eschen
Liechtenstein 0-4 Finland
Goal(s): 0-1 Pukki 48, 0-2 Hjelm 65
0-3 Hjelm 75, 0-4 Kangaskolkka 90+:

13/11/09, El Arcangel, Cordoba
Spain 1-0 Finland
Goal(s): 1-0 Míchel 79

13/11/09, De Vliert, 's-hertogenbosch
Netherlands 3-0 Liechtenstein
Goal(s): 1-0 De Jong 8,
2-0 Falkenburg 68, 3-0 John 90+3

17/11/09, Sparta, Rotterdam
Netherlands 2-1 Spain
Goal(s): 1-0 Falkenburg 14,
2-0 Wijnaldum 63, 2-1 Azpilicueta 8(

Italy's Luca Marrone celebrates his goal against Hungary

3/10, El Toralin, Ponferrada
ain 3-1 Liechtenstein
al(s): 1-0 Parejo 13,
1 Hanselmann 58, 2-1 Adrián 73,
1 Diego Capel 89(p)

3/10, Vijverberg, Doetinchem
etherlands 3-2 Poland
al(s): 0-1 Cetnarski 22,
1 Biseswar 57, 2-1 Biseswar 71,
1 De Jong 75, 3-2 Kielb 82

Group 4 Fixtures

11/8/10
Finland - Spain
Liechtenstein - Netherlands
3/9/10
Spain - Netherlands
Finland - Poland
7/9/10
Poland - Spain
Finland - Liechtenstein

roup 4 Table

	Pld	Home					Away					Total					Pts
		W	D	L	F	A	W	D	L	F	A	W	D	L	F	A	
Netherlands	6	4	0	0	10	3	2	0	0	5	0	6	0	0	15	3	18
Spain	5	3	0	0	6	1	1	0	1	5	2	4	0	1	11	3	12
Poland	6	2	0	1	4	5	1	0	2	7	5	3	0	3	11	10	9
Finland	5	0	0	1	0	1	1	0	3	5	5	1	0	4	5	6	3
Liechtenstein	6	0	0	3	0	13	0	0	3	1	8	0	0	6	1	21	0

Joshua John (centre) is surrounded by Spanish opponents in the Netherlands' 2-1 win in Rotterdam

GROUP 5

he Czech Republic went into the summer reak with a maximum yield of points and onfident of reaching their first finals since hey won the competition in 2002. Michael labušic scored twice as the team lay down n early marker with an impressive 2-1 ictory against title holders Germany in Viesbaden in September 2009.

line months later they headed the section on 15 points, wo clear of surprise package Iceland, the competition's eading scorers on 24 goals, and five ahead of Germany.

lorst Hrubesch was replaced by Rainer Adrion after eading Germany to victory in 2009, and the new coach as assembled a fresh side. Fourteen players from the 2009

squad were no longer eligible, and Adrion's task became more difficult with the promotion of Holger Badstuber, Thomas Müller, Toni Kroos and Jerome Boateng to the senior set-up. With the pressure on, it remained to be seen whether that talented quartet, all part of Germany's FIFA World Cup squad in South Africa, would return for the big match against the Czechs on 3 September.

Group 5 Results

9/6/09, Olimpico, Serravalle
San Marino 0-8 Czech Republic
Goal(s): 0-1 Pekhart 19, 0-2 Hořava
29, 0-3 Pekhart 31, 0-4 Pekhart 38,
0-5 Valenta 45, 0-6 Dockal 49(p),
0-7 Dockal 70, 0-8 Chramosta 86

12/8/09, KR-völlur, Reykjavik
Iceland 0-2 Czech Republic
Goal(s): 0-1 Rabušic 58,
0-2 Čelůstka 79

4/9/09, Tivoli, Aachen
Germany 6-0 San Marino
Goal(s): 1-0 Naki 4, 2-0 J. Boateng
19, 3-0 Hummels 31, 4-0 Schieber
33, 5-0 Höwedes 41, 6-0 Schieber 56

4/9/09, Chance Arena, Jablonec nad Nisou
Czech Republic 2-0 Northern Ireland
Goal(s): 1-0 Gecov 72, 2-0 Dockal 83

8/9/09, The Showgrounds, Coleraine
Northern Ireland 2-6 Iceland
Goal(s): 0-1 Vidarsson 15(p),
0-2 Gunnarsson 32, 0-3
Finnbogason 42, 0-4 Gíslason 44,
0-5 Gudmundsson 57,
1-5 Magennis 58, 1-6 Gíslason 64,
2-6 Magennis 76

8/9/09, BRITA-Arena, Wiesbaden
Germany 1-2 Czech Republic
Goal(s): 0-1 Rabušic 21,
0-2 Rabušic 70(p), 1-2 Hummels
90+2(p)

9/10/09, Laugardalsvöllur, Reykjavik
Iceland 8-0 San Marino
Goal(s): 1-0 Gudmundsson 4,
2-0 Eyjólfsson 24, 3-0 Gíslason 25,
4-0 Gudmundsson 40, 5-0 Gíslason
75(p), 6-0 Ormarsson 79,
7-0 Gudmundsson 86,
8-0 Steindorsson 89

13/10/09, Grindavíkurvöllur, Grindavik
Iceland 2-1 Northern Ireland
Goal(s): 1-0 Gudmundsson 56,
2-0 Jósefsson 70, 2-1 Lawrie 80

13/11/09, The Oval, Belfast
Northern Ireland 1-1 Germany
Goal(s): 0-1 Choupo-Moting 90,
1-1 Norwood 90+4

13/11/09, Olimpico, Serravalle
San Marino 0-6 Iceland
Goal(s): 0-1 Sigthórsson 8,
0-2 Sigurdsson 15, 0-3 Vidarsson
18(p), 0-4 Sigurdsson 31,
0-5 Finnbogason 60,
0-6 Finnbogason 82

17/11/09, The Showgrounds, Ballymena
Northern Ireland 1-2 Czech Republic
Goal(s): 0-1 Zeman 36, 0-2 Kozák
38, 1-2 Norwood 82

17/11/09, Olimpico, Serravalle
San Marino 0-11 Germany
Goal(s): 0-1 Hummels 4,
0-2 Choupo-Moting 11,
0-3 Schwaab 31(p), 0-4 Badstuber
33, 0-5 Schürrle 44, 0-6 Sam 49,
0-7 Hummels 56, 0-8 Müller 58,
0-9 Sukuta-Pasu 69, 0-10 Hummels
71(p), 0-11 Bargfrede 82

2/3/10, Magdeburg, Magdeburg
Germany 2-2 Iceland
Goal(s): 1-0 Gebhart 10,
1-1 Sigthórsson 13, 2-1 Schieber
50, 2-2 Vidarsson 77

2/3/10, Olimpico Serravalle, Serravalle
San Marino 0-3 Northern Ireland
Goal(s): 0-1 Norwood 24,
0-2 Lawrie 38, 0-3 Norwood 78

Group 5 Fixtures

11/8/10
Czech Republic - San Marino
Iceland - Germany
3/9/10
Northern Ireland - San Marino
Czech Republic - Germany
7/9/10
Germany - Northern Ireland
Czech Republic - Iceland

Group 5 Table

	Pld	Home					Away					Total					Pts
		W	D	L	F	A	W	D	L	F	A	W	D	L	F	A	
1 Czech Republic	5	1	0	0	2	0	4	0	0	14	2	5	0	0	16	2	15
2 Iceland	6	2	0	1	10	3	2	1	0	14	4	4	1	1	24	7	13
3 Germany	5	1	1	1	9	4	1	1	0	12	1	2	2	1	21	5	8
4 Northern Ireland	6	0	1	2	4	9	1	0	2	4	4	1	1	4	8	13	4
5 San Marino	6	0	0	4	0	28	0	0	2	0	14	0	0	6	0	42	0

GROUP 6

Tournament hosts Sweden were unfortunate to lose to England on penalties in the 2009 semi-finals and they continued to impress in the qualifying competition for 2011.

They led Group 6 by three points from Montenegro, whom they beat 2-0 home and away, and coaches Jörgen Lennartsson and Tommy Söderberg looked likely to ensure a second successive finals appearance for their side across the Oresund in Denmark. Striker Marcus Berg stole the show in the 2009 finals with his tournament-record haul of seven goals, and it was influential captain Emir Bajrami who particularly caught the eye on the road to Denmark. The 22-year-old's efforts earned him promotion to the senior Sweden side and his pace and wing play earned him a summer move from IF Elfsborg to Dutch champions FC Twente. Sweden, whose only dropped points came in a 1-1 draw in Kazakhstan, were poised to win the section with a draw at home to Israel on 3 September.

Emir Bajrami skippere
Sweden to the top o
Group

Group 6 Results

29/3/09, Kiryat Eliezer, Haifa
Israel 1-1 Kazakhstan
Goal(s): 1-0 Bar Buzaglo 44,
1-1 Kenetayev 62

2/4/09, Centralny, Almaty
Kazakhstan 2-0 Bulgaria
Goal(s): 1-0 Ibrayev 70,
2-0 Erbes 90+1

7/6/09, Centralny, Almaty
Kazakhstan 0-2 Montenegro
Goal(s): 0-1 Jovetić 17,
0-2 Lakicevič 48

10/6/09, Georgi Asparuhov, Sofia
Bulgaria 3-4 Israel
Goal(s): 1-0 Baltanov 2, 1-1 Zhairi 6,
1-2 Kayal 28, 1-3 Tamuz 53,
2-3 Tsvetanov 59, 3-3 I. Ivanov 76,
3-4 Sahar 89

4/9/09, Gradski, Lovech
Bulgaria 3-0 Kazakhstan
Goal(s): 1-0 Tonev 57, 2-0 Baltanov
64, 3-0 Baltanov 90+4

*4/9/09, Pod Goricom-Gradski,
Podgorica*
Montenegro 0-2 Sweden
Goal(s): 0-1 Ekdal 84, 0-2 Mehmeti 89

*9/9/09, Kazhimukan Munaytpasov,
Astana*
Kazakhstan 1-2 Israel
Goal(s): 1-0 Natcho 56, 1-1 Dautov
58, 1-2 Tamuz 90

9/9/09, Vångavallen, Trelleborg
Sweden 2-1 Bulgaria
Goal(s): 1-0 Olsson 31, 1-1 Genev
34, 2-1 Bajrami 89

10/10/09, Gradski, Lovech
Bulgaria 1-1 Montenegro
Goal(s): 1-0 Baltanov 68(p),
1-1 Đurović 77

*11/10/09, Kazhimukan
Munaytpasov, Astana*
Kazakhstan 1-1 Sweden
Goal(s): 1-0 Shabalin 51,1-1
Almebäck 88

14/10/09, Gradski, Niksic
Montenegro 3-1 Kazakhstan
Goal(s): 1-0 Adrović 10, 2-0 Đurović
42, 3-0 N. Nikolić 81, 3-1
Abdukarimov 83

*14/11/09, Pod Goricom-Gradski,
Podgorica*
Montenegro 1-0 Israel
Goal(s): 1-0 S. Nikolić 5

*15/11/09, Malmö New Stadium,
Malmo*
Sweden 5-1 Kazakhstan
Goal(s): 1-0 Fejzullahu 32,
2-0 Fejzullahu 50, 3-0 Fejzullahu 56,
4-0 Ekdal 60, 5-0 Fejzullahu 67,
5-1 Shomko 89

18/11/09, Ramat Gan, Ramat Gan
Israel 4-0 Bulgaria
Goal(s): 1-0 Sahar 7, 2-0 Sahar 24,
3-0 Vered 32, 4-0 Sahar 57

*3/3/10, Pod Goricom-Gradski,
Podgorica*
Montenegro 2-0 Bulgaria
Goal(s): 1-0 Đurović 24,
2-0 D. Božović 89

4/6/10, Nes-Ziona, Nes-Ziona
Israel 0-1 Sweden
Goal(s): 0-1 Avdic 58

8/6/10, Örjans vall, Halmstad
Sweden 2-0 Montenegro
Goal(s): 1-0 Avdic 33(p),
2-0 Jönsson 89

Group 6 Fixtures

3/9/10
Sweden - Israel

7/9/10
Israel - Montenegro
Bulgaria - Sweden

Group 6 Table

	Pld	Home W	D	L	F	A	Away W	D	L	F	A	Total W	D	L	F	A	P
1 Sweden	6	3	0	0	9	2	2	1	0	4	1	5	1	0	13	3	1
2 Montenegro	7	3	0	1	6	3	1	1	1	3	3	4	1	2	9	6	1
3 Israel	6	1	1	1	5	2	2	0	1	6	5	3	1	2	11	7	1
4 Kazakhstan	8	1	1	2	4	5	0	1	3	3	12	1	2	5	7	17	5
5 Bulgaria	7	1	1	1	7	5	0	0	4	1	10	1	1	5	8	15	4

GROUP 7

Group 7 was building towards an exciting early-autumn climax as a tight three-way tussle developed between Croatia, top on 13 points, Slovakia, two behind, and perennial challengers Serbia, who lay third on nine points with a game in hand.

Croatia began with a surprise 2-0 defeat at home to Cyprus, but subsequent victories against each of their rivals put them in command. Established senior internationals bolstered the ranks of many sides, and FIFA World Cup participants Vladimír Weiss Jr and Miroslav Stoch proved particularly prominent for Slovakia. Ivan Rakitić, a regular for the senior Croatia side, scored a stunning equaliser against Slovakia in May, while Serbia had their own full international to thank for remaining in contention as Miralem Sulejmani struck a hat-trick to help his side recover from 2-0 down to beat Norway in November. Serbia still had Croatia and Slovakia to face in the run-in, so everything was still very much to play for.

Group 7 Results

5/09, Gradski, Koprivnica
oatia 0-2 Cyprus
oal(s): 0-1 Kolokoudias 12,
2 Kolokoudias 39

/6/09, Viking, Stavanger
orway 2-2 Slovakia
oal(s): 0-1 Sylvestr 26,
1 Berget 52(p), 1-2 Juhar 75,
2 Orry Larsen 90+1

/8/09, Dasaki Achnas, Famagusta
prus 1-3 Norway
oal(s): 0-1 Singh 29, 0-2
younoussi 58, 0-3 Katsis 66(og),
3 Efrem 80(p)

9/09, Vojvodina, Novi Sad
rbia 1-2 Slovakia
oal(s): 0-1 Gergel 55, 1-1 Bosančić
, 1-2 Lačný 90

9/09, Fredrikstad, Fredrikstad
orway 1-3 Croatia
oal(s): 0-1 Jajalo 12, 1-1 Berget 19,
2 Jajalo 55, 1-3 Kramarić 82

9/09, FK Senica, Senica
ovakia 1-0 Cyprus
oal(s): 1-0 Sylvestr 68

9/09, Fredrikstad, Fredrikstad
orway 0-1 Serbia
oal(s): 0-1 Milanović 90+2

10/09, Vojvodina, Novi Sad
erbia 2-0 Cyprus
oal(s): 1-0 Milanović 18,
0 Aleksić 89

13/10/09, NK Varteks, Varazdin
Croatia 3-1 Serbia
Goal(s): 1-0 Oremuš 32,
2-0 Kramarić 52, 2-1 Tomić 69,
3-1 K. Ljubičić 83

14/10/09, Dasaki Achnas,
Famagusta
Cyprus 0-1 Slovakia
Goal(s): 0-1 Stoch 46

14/11/09, Peyia Municipal, Paphos
Cyprus 1-2 Croatia
Goal(s): 1-0 Christofi 25, 1-1 Vida 60,
1-2 Rakitić 65

15/11/09, Vojvodina, Novi Sad
Serbia 3-2 Norway
Goal(s): 0-1 Forren 2, 0-2 Elyounoussi
34, 1-2 Sulejmani 42, 2-2 Sulejmani
52, 3-2 Sulejmani 72

18/11/09, FC ViOn, Zlate Moravce
Slovakia 1-2 Croatia
Goal(s): 0-1 Kalinić 28, 1-1 Sylvestr
48, 1-2 Vida 86

19/5/10, NK Varteks, Varazdin
Croatia 1-1 Slovakia
Goal(s): 0-1 Duris 30, 1-1 Rakitić 32

Group 7 Fixtures

11/8/10
Croatia - Norway
Slovakia - Serbia
3/9/10
Norway - Cyprus
4/9/10
Serbia - Croatia
7/9/10
Slovakia - Norway
Cyprus - Serbia

Group 7 Table

	Pld	Home W D L F A					Away W D L F A					Total W D L F A					Pts
Croatia	6	1	1	1	4	4	3	0	0	7	3	4	1	1	11	7	13
Slovakia	6	1	0	1	2	2	2	2	0	6	4	3	2	1	8	6	11
Serbia	5	2	0	1	6	4	1	0	1	2	3	3	0	2	8	7	9
Norway	5	0	1	2	3	6	1	0	1	5	4	1	1	3	8	10	4
Cyprus	6	0	0	3	2	6	1	0	2	2	3	1	0	5	4	9	3

Miralem Sulejmani
scored a hat-trick for
Serbia in their 3-2 win
at home to Norway

France's Étienne Capoue (left)
is challenged by Belgium's
Romelu Lukaku in the Group 8
fixture in Mouscron

GROUP 8

While experience provided the thrust for some sides as they targeted a finals place in Denmark, youth came to the fore for several others, with some exciting new faces breaking through during the campaign.

Foremost among those was striker Romelu Lukaku, who, having played his part in strengthening Belgium's hand in Group 8, won his first senior cap still aged just 16 on 3 March 2010. The RSC Anderlecht teenager, blessed with pace and power, opened his Under-21 account with a goal in a 2-0 win against Slovenia, but despite that Belgium still had their work cut out to advance from the section. Ukraine led at the summer break on 14 points, three ahead of France, who had a game in hand, and Belgium. Much seemed likely to hinge on the next two matches in the group, with France hosting Belgium on 11 August then travelling to Ukraine the following month.

Group 8 Results

31/3/09, Hibernians Ground, Corradino
Malta 0-2 Slovenia
Goal(s): 0-1 Mihelič 33,
0-2 Mihelič 65(p)

9/6/09, Borex, Borodinka
Ukraine 1-0 Malta
Goal(s): 1-0 Konoplyanka 65

4/9/09, Ta' Qali, Ta' Qali
Malta 0-1 Belgium
Goal(s): 0-1 Kitoko 33

5/9/09, Ob Jezeru, Velenje
Slovenia 1-3 France
Goal(s): 0-1 Modeste 18,
0-2 Bakar 43, 1-2 Mihelič 69,
1-3 Škarabot 90+1(og)

8/9/09, 't Kuipje, Westerlo
Belgium 2-0 Slovenia
Goal(s): 1-0 Nainggolan 56,
2-0 Lukaku 77

8/9/09, Jean Laville, Gueugnon
France 2-2 Ukraine
Goal(s): 1-0 Modeste 3,
2-0 Sakho 26, 2-1 Chesnakov 44,
2-2 Chesnakov

9/9/09, Valeriy Lobanovskiy, Kyiv
Ukraine 1-1 Belgium
Goal(s): 0-1 Mujangi 67,
1-1 Zozulya 69

9/10/09, Ta' Qali, Ta' Qali
Malta 0-2 France
Goal(s): 0-1 Modeste 54,
0-2 Aït-Fana 77

13/10/09, Le Canonnier, Mouscron
Belgium 0-0 France

14/10/09, Arena Petrol, Celje
Slovenia 0-2 Ukraine
Goal(s): 0-1 Morozyuk 34,
0-2 Lugachev 44

13/11/09, Športni Park, Nova Gorica
Slovenia 1-0 Malta
Goal(s): 1-0 Črnčič 48

13/11/09, Staaien, Sint-Truiden
Belgium 0-2 Ukraine
Goal(s): 0-1 Golodiuk 36,
0-2 Golodiuk 73

17/11/09, Auguste-Delaune, Reims
France 1-0 Slovenia
Goal(s): 1-0 Sankhare 90+3

3/3/10, Daknam, Lokeren
Belgium 1-0 Malta
Goal(s): 1-0 Kums 74(p)

29/5/10, Ta' Qali, Ta' Qali
Malta 0-3 Ukraine
Goal(s): 0-1 Rakitskiy 87(p),
0-2 Yarmolenko 89,
0-3 Fedorchuk 90+4

Group 8 Fixtures

11/8/10
France - Belgium
3/9/10
Ukraine - France
Slovenia - Belgium
7/9/10
France - Malta
Ukraine - Slovenia

Group 8 Table

	Pld	Home					Away					Total					P
		W	D	L	F	A	W	D	L	F	A	W	D	L	F	A	
1 Ukraine	6	1	1	0	2	1	3	1	0	9	2	4	2	0	11	3	1
2 France	5	1	1	0	3	2	2	1	0	5	1	3	2	0	8	3	1
3 Belgium	6	2	1	1	3	2	1	1	0	2	1	3	2	1	5	3	1
4 Slovenia	6	1	0	2	2	5	1	0	2	2	3	2	0	4	4	8	(
5 Malta	7	0	0	4	0	8	0	0	3	0	3	0	0	7	0	11	(

GROUP 9

Greece opened up a five-point lead over 2009 runners-up England at the top of Group 9 thanks to a pair of good results against Stuar Pearce's side, whose only comfort was their game in hand.

Exciting prospect Sotirios Ninis cancelled out Daniel Sturridge's early strike in Tripoli Arkadia in September 2009 to earn Greece a 1-1 draw. Georgios Georgiadis's team went one better against the 2009 finalists in Doncaster in March, a shock 2-1 win leaving them in complete control of the section. Greece's only defeat came against Portugal, who, although nine points off the pace in third, still had two games in hand on the leaders and remained hopeful as they prepared to host England on 3 September. Pearce was able to call on no fewer than eight players from the side that featured in the 2009 final defeat by Germany and would have been banking on tha experience as his team looked to end a run of two games without victory in Portugal.

Danny Rose scores
England's winner against
Portugal at Wembley

UEFA European Under-21 Championship

roup 9 Results

/3/09, Asteras Tripolis, Tripoli
kadia
eece 3-1 FYROM
oal(s): 1-0 Mitroglou 7, 2-0
troglou 48, 2-1 Fazli 50, 3-1
annidis 61

6/09, Súduva, Marijampole
thuania 0-1 Greece
oal(s): 0-1 Papastathopoulos 76

9/09, Goce Delcev, Prilep
FROM 1-2 England
oal(s): 1-0 Ibraimi 34, 1-1 Sears
, 1-2 Cattermole 83(p)

9/09, Dr Jorge Sampaio, Vila Nova
Gaia
rtugal 4-1 Lithuania
oal(s): 1-0 Ukra 25,
1 Chvedukas 26, 2-1 Ukra 55,
1 Rui Pedro 63, 4-1 João Aurélio 85

9/09, Asteras Tripolis, Tripoli
kadia
eece 1-1 England
oal(s): 0-1 Sturridge 5, 1-1 Ninis 41

9/09, Goce Delcev, Prilep
FROM 1-1 Lithuania
oal(s): 1-0 Muarem 1,
1 Novikovas 58

10/09, Asteras Tripolis, Tripoli Arkadia
eece 2-1 Portugal
oal(s): 1-0 Koutsianikoulis 4,
1 Miguel Vítor 83, 2-1 K.
apadopoulos 90

10/09, Ricoh Arena, Coventry
ngland 6-3 FYROM
oal(s): 1-0 Gibbs 22, 2-0 Richards
), 2-1 Muarem 42, 2-2 Ibraimi 53,
2 Carroll 54, 3-3 Gibbs 58(og),
3 Hines 67, 5-3 Carroll 87,
3 Hines 90

13/10/09, Goce Delcev, Prilep
FYROM 1-1 Portugal
Goal(s): 1-0 Muarem 68,
1-1 Adrien Silva 90

13/10/09, Asteras Tripolis, Tripoli
Arkadia
Greece 1-0 Lithuania
Goal(s): 1-0 Koutsianikoulis 80

13/11/09, S. Darius & S. Girenas,
Kaunas
Lithuania 1-0 FYROM
Goal(s): 1-0 Zagurskas 5

14/11/09, Wembley, London
England 1-0 Portugal
Goal(s): 1-0 Rose 40

17/11/09, Vetra, Vilnius
Lithuania 0-0 England

17/11/09, José Arcanjo, Olhao
Portugal 2-1 Greece
Goal(s): 1-0 Rui Pedro 51, 2-0
Yazalde 74, 2-1 Dimoutsos 90+2

3/3/10, Keepmoat, Doncaster
England 1-2 Greece
Goal(s): 0-1 K. Papadopoulos 28,
0-2 G. Papadopoulos 49,
1-2 Delfouneso 80

Group 9 Fixtures

11/8/10
Lithuania - Portugal
3/9/10
Portugal - England
4/9/10
FYROM - Greece
7/9/10
England - Lithuania
Portugal - FYROM

roup 9 Table

	Pld	Home W D L F A	Away W D L F A	Total W D L F A	Pts
Greece	7	3 1 0 7 3	2 0 1 4 3	5 1 1 11 6	16
England	6	2 0 1 8 5	1 2 0 3 2	3 2 1 11 7	11
Portugal	5	2 0 0 6 2	0 1 2 2 4	2 1 2 8 6	7
Lithuania	6	1 1 1 1 1	0 1 2 2 6	1 2 3 3 7	5
FYROM	6	0 2 1 3 4	0 0 3 4 10	0 2 4 7 14	2

GROUP 10

A tight three-way race emerged in Group 10, with Austria ahead of Scotland on head-to-head records after six matches and Belarus, who reached the final tournament in 2009, a point behind with a game in hand.

ustria reached the play-offs in 2009 and mounted nother strong challenge. FC Bayern München midfielder David Alaba shot to prominence during the course of the

campaign and made his senior debut aged just 17 in October 2009, while Atdhe Nuhiu found the net five times, second only to Latvia's Edgars Gauračs, on seven, in the scoring charts. Belarus were set to play both front-runners in their next two matches before Scotland hosted Austria on 7 October. Debutant Andreas Weimann scored the only goal for Austria when the two sides met in September 2009 as Andreas Herzog's team made up for an opening-game defeat by Belarus, whose only dropped points came in a 1-0 defeat away to Scotland.

Group 10 Results

28/3/09, Ruzhdi Bizhuta, Elbasan
Albania 0-1 Scotland
Goal(s): 0-1 Maguire 85(p)

1/4/09, Falkirk Stadium, Falkirk
Scotland 5-2 Albania
Goal(s): 1-0 Goodwillie 36,
2-0 Maguire 51, 3-0 Shinnie 54,
3-1 Hyka 73, 4-1 Murphy 75,
4-2 Vila 89, 5-2 McGinn 90+1

12/8/09, Gorodskoi, Molodechno
Belarus 2-1 Austria
Goal(s): 1-0 Yurchenko 6,
1-1 Beichler 30, 2-1 Filipenko 60

5/9/09, Niko Dovana, Durres
Albania 1-0 Azerbaijan
Goal(s): 1-0 E. Guliyev 63(og)

5/9/09, Bundesstadion Südstadt,
Maria Enzersdorf
Austria 1-0 Scotland
Goal(s): 1-0 Murphy 57

9/9/09, Franz Fürst, Wiener Neudorf
Austria 3-1 Albania
Goal(s): 1-0 Nuhiu 3, 2-0 Weimann
5, 3-0 Nuhiu 13, 3-1 Roshi 41

9/9/09, Tofiq Bähramov, Baku
Azerbaijan 2-3 Belarus
Goal(s): 1-0 Abdullayev 26,
1-1 Sivakov 36, 1-2 Karpovich 43,
1-3 Rekish 56, 2-3 Narimanov 66

10/10/09, Saint Mirren Park, Paisley
Scotland 1-0 Belarus
Goal(s): 1-0 Murphy 90+2

10/10/09, Tofiq Bähramov, Baku
Azerbaijan 1-2 Austria
Goal(s): 1-0 Soltanov 34,
1-1 Margreitter 90(p), 1-2 Grünwald
90+3

14/10/09, Gorodskoi, Molodechno
Belarus 4-2 Albania
Goal(s): 1-0 Nekhaychik 25, 2-0
Voronkov 38, 3-0 Skavysh 41,
4-0 Voronkov 72, 4-1 Januzi 75,
4-2 Hysa 78

13/11/09, Qemal Stafa, Tirana
Albania 2-2 Austria
Goal(s): 1-0 Sykaj 20, 2-0 Roshi 50,
2-1 Samina 52(og), 2-2 Perstaller 79

14/11/09, Tofiq Bähramov, Baku
Azerbaijan 0-4 Scotland
Goal(s): 1-0 Murphy 26,
0-2 Arfield 36, 0-3 Murphy 54,
0-4 Loy 83

17/11/09, Niko Dovana, Durres
Albania 2-1 Belarus
Goal(s): 0-1 Skavysh 8,
0-2 Skavysh 38, 1-2 Roshi 76

18/11/09, Franz Fürst, Wiener
Neudorf
Austria 4-0 Azerbaijan
Goal(s): 1-0 Nuhiu 10,
2-0 Nuhiu 19, 3-0 Nuhiu 79,
4-0 Weimann 83

2/3/10, Falkirk Stadium, Falkirk
Scotland 2-2 Azerbaijan
Goal(s): 0-1 Hajiyev 13,
1-1 Maguire 32(p), 1-2 Abdullayev 65,
2-2 Griffiths 86

Group 10 Fixtures

11/8/10
Austria - Belarus
3/9/10
Belarus - Scotland
4/9/10
Azerbaijan - Albania
7/9/10
Scotland - Austria
Belarus - Azerbaijan

Group 10 Table

		Pld	Home W D L F A	Away W D L F A	Total W D L F A	Pts
1	Austria	6	3 0 0 8 1	1 1 1 5 5	4 1 1 13 6	13
2	Scotland	6	2 1 0 8 4	2 0 1 5 1	4 1 1 13 5	13
3	Belarus	5	2 0 0 6 3	2 0 1 5 4	4 0 1 11 7	12
4	Albania	7	1 1 2 4 5	0 0 3 5 12	1 1 5 9 17	4
5	Azerbaijan	6	0 0 3 3 9	0 1 2 2 7	0 1 5 5 16	1

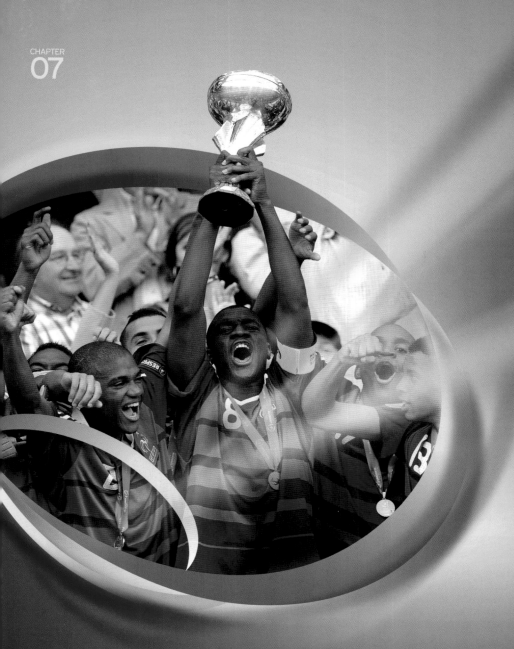

UEFA
UNDER19™
CHAMPIONSHIP

U19

UEFA

2009/10

Until Ukraine's triumph in 2009, no UEFA European Under-19 Championship had been won by the host nation. In 2010, France made it a second home victory in succession, claiming the crown with a surprise win in the final against what had previously been a highly impressive Spain side, turning round a half-time deficit in Caen with a vibrant second-half display. Having suffered two poor tournaments by their own high standards, falling at the group stage in both 2008 and 2009, Luis Milla's Spain team looked to be back in the groove as they advanced to the Stade Michel-d'Ornano with four successive wins, including a comprehensive semi-final victory over England. However, they were undone in the final by opponents who produced their best football when it mattered most, Francis Smerecki's side avenging their emphatic defeat at Spanish hands in the U17 final two years earlier to claim the U19 prize for the second time.

QUALIFYING ROUND

Group 1 Results

13/11/09, Olimpico, Serravalle
Italy 5-0 Albania
13/11/09, Montecchio, San Marino
Republic of Ireland 5-0 San Marino
15/11/09, Montecchio, San Marino
Republic of Ireland 2-0 Albania
15/11/09, Olimpico, Serravalle
San Marino 0-4 Italy
18/11/09, Olimpico, Serravalle
Italy 2-0 Republic of Ireland
18/11/09, Olimpico, Serravalle
Albania 4-1 San Marino

Group 1 Table

	Pld	W	D	L	F	A	Pts
1 Italy	3	3	0	0	11	0	9
2 Republic of Ireland	3	2	0	1	7	2	6
3 Albania	3	1	0	2	4	8	3
4 San Marino	3	0	0	3	1	13	0

Group 2 Results

9/10/09, Športni Park, Lendava
Slovakia 1-0 Slovenia
9/10/09, Fazanerija, Murska Sobota
England 3-1 Finland
11/10/09, Športni Park, Lendava
Slovakia 4-0 Finland
11/10/09, Fazanerija, Murska Sobota
Slovenia 1-3 England
14/10/09, Športni Park, Lendava
England 2-0 Slovakia
14/10/09, Fazanerija, Murska Sobota
Finland 2-0 Slovenia

Group 2 Table

	Pld	W	D	L	F	A	Pts
1 England	3	3	0	0	8	2	9
2 Slovakia	3	2	0	1	5	2	6
3 Finland	3	1	0	2	3	7	3
4 Slovenia	3	0	0	3	1	6	0

Group 3 Results

7/10/09, Rodange, Rodange
Turkey 1-0 Moldova
7/10/09, Alphonse Theis, Hesperange
Germany 3-0 Luxembourg
9/10/09, Alphonse Theis, Hesperange
Moldova 0-5 Germany
9/10/09, Rodange, Rodange
Turkey 1-1 Luxembourg
12/10/09, Josy Barthel, Luxembourg
Germany 1-2 Turkey
12/10/09, Op Biirk, Mensdorf
Luxembourg 1-2 Moldova

Group 3 Table

	Pld	W	D	L	F	A	Pts
1 Turkey	3	2	1	0	4	2	7
2 Germany	3	2	0	1	9	2	6
3 Moldova	3	1	0	2	2	7	3
4 Luxembourg	3	0	1	2	2	6	1

Group 4 Results

23/9/09, Marijampolė FC, Marijampole
Switzerland 5-0 Lithuania
23/9/09, Sūduva, Marijampole
Croatia 3-0 Estonia
25/9/09, Sūduva, Marijampole
Switzerland 5-0 Estonia
25/9/09, Marijampolė FC, Marijampole
Lithuania 1-2 Croatia
28/9/09, Sūduva, Marijampole
Croatia 1-0 Switzerland
28/9/09, Marijampolė FC, Marijampole
Estonia 1-2 Lithuania

Group 4 Table

	Pld	W	D	L	F	A	Pts
1 Croatia	3	3	0	0	6	1	9
2 Switzerland	3	2	0	1	10	1	6
3 Lithuania	3	1	0	2	3	8	3
4 Estonia	3	0	0	3	1	10	0

Group 5 Results

6/10/09, Gradski, Jagodina
Greece 2-0 Faroe Islands
6/10/09, Cika Daca, Kragujevac
Serbia 5-0 Belarus

Cenk Tosun of Germany

8/10/09, Cika Daca, Kragujevac
Greece 1-0 Belarus
8/10/09, Gradski, Jagodina
Faroe Islands 0-2 Serbia
11/10/09, Cika Daca, Kragujevac
Serbia 1-0 Greece
11/10/09, Gradski, Jagodina
Belarus 0-0 Faroe Islands

Group 5 Table

	Pld	W	D	L	F	A
1 Serbia	3	3	0	0	8	0
2 Greece	3	2	0	1	3	1
3 Faroe Islands	3	0	1	2	0	4
4 Belarus	3	0	1	2	0	6

Group 6 Results

10/10/09, Jacques Lemans Arena, St Veit an der Glc
Scotland 3-0 Romania
10/10/09, Wigo-Haus Arena, Feldkirchen
Austria 5-1 Armenia
12/10/09, Wigo-Haus Arena, Feldkirchen
Armenia 1-6 Scotland
12/10/09, Jacques Lemans Arena, St Veit an der Gla
Austria 0-4 Romania
15/10/09, Jacques Lemans Arena, St Veit an der Gla.
Scotland 0-1 Austria
15/10/09, Villach-Lind, Villach
Romania 1-0 Armenia

Group 6 Table

	Pld	W	D	L	F	A	
1 Scotland	3	2	0	1	9	2	
2 Romania	3	2	0	1	5	3	
3 Austria	3	2	0	1	6	5	
4 Armenia	3	0	0	3	2	12	

Group 7 Results

7/10/09, Grbavica, Sarajevo
Bulgaria 1-1 Northern Ireland
7/10/09, Asim Ferhatović-Hase, Sarajevo
Iceland 0-1 Bosnia-Herzegovina
9/10/09, Asim Ferhatović-Hase, Sarajevo
Bulgaria 1-2 Bosnia-Herzegovina
9/10/09, Grbavica, Sarajevo
Northern Ireland 0-0 Iceland
12/10/09, Grbavica, Sarajevo
Iceland 3-2 Bulgaria
12/10/09, Asim Ferhatović-Hase, Sarajevo
Bosnia-Herzegovina 0-4 Northern Ireland

Group 7 Table

	Pld	W	D	L	F	A	F
1 Bosnia-Herzegovina	3	2	0	1	3	5	
2 Northern Ireland	3	1	2	0	5	1	
3 Iceland	3	1	1	1	3	3	
4 Bulgaria	3	0	1	2	4	6	

UEFA European Under-19 Championship

Salvador Agra of Portugal

25/10/09, Városi, Nyiregyhaza
Hungary 5-1 Latvia
28/10/09, Városi, Nyiregyhaza
Russia 2-1 Hungary
28/10/09, Tiszaújváros, Tiszaujvaros
Latvia 4-0 Liechtenstein

Group 9 Table

	Pld	W	D	L	F	A	Pts
1 Russia	3	2	1	0	9	2	7
2 Hungary	3	2	0	1	10	3	6
3 Latvia	3	1	1	1	6	6	4
4 Liechtenstein	3	0	0	3	0	14	0

Group 10 Results

12/11/09, Centenary, Ta' Qali
Netherlands 1-0 Malta
12/11/09, Centenary, Ta' Qali
Czech Republic 3-1 Cyprus
14/11/09, Centenary, Ta' Qali
Netherlands 5-1 Cyprus
14/11/09, Centenary, Ta' Qali
Malta 0-4 Czech Republic
17/11/09, Hibernians Ground, Corradino
Czech Republic 0-1 Netherlands
17/11/09, Centenary, Ta' Qali
Cyprus 1-1 Malta

Group 10 Table

	Pld	W	D	L	F	A	Pts
1 Netherlands	3	3	0	0	7	1	9
2 Czech Republic	3	2	0	1	7	2	6
3 Malta	3	0	1	2	1	6	1
4 Cyprus	3	0	1	2	3	9	1

Mattia Destro of Italy

roup 8 Results

1/09, Luis Suner Pico, Alzira
'tugal 3-0 Wales
1/09, La Forana, Alginet
ain 5-1 FYR Macedonia
1/09, La Forana, Alginet
'tugal 3-0 FYR Macedonia
1/09, La Forana, Alginet
les 0-1 Spain
1/09, Luis Suner Pico, Alzira
ain 0-1 Portugal
1/09, La Forana, Alginet
R Macedonia 1-3 Wales

roup 8 Table

	Pld	W	D	L	F	A	Pts
'ortugal	3	3	0	0	7	0	9
pain	3	2	0	1	6	2	6
Vales	3	1	0	2	3	5	3
YR Macedonia	3	0	0	3	2	11	0

roup 9 Results

10/09, Tiszaújváros, Tiszaujvaros
ssia 1-1 Latvia
10/09, Városi, Nyiregyhaza
ngary 4-0 Liechtenstein
10/09, Tiszaújváros, Tiszaujvaros
chtenstein 0-6 Russia

Group 11 Results

13/11/09, RS Waasland, St Nicolas
Norway 2-0 Kazakhstan
13/11/09, FC VW Hamme, Hamme
Belgium 4-0 Andorra
15/11/09, FC VW Hamme, Hamme
Norway 5-0 Andorra
15/11/09, Freethiel, Beveren
Kazakhstan 0-4 Belgium
18/11/09, RS Waasland, St Nicolas
Belgium 2-4 Norway
18/11/09, Freethiel, Beveren
Andorra 1-2 Kazakhstan

Group 11 Table

	Pld	W	D	L	F	A	Pts
1 Norway	3	3	0	0	11	2	9
2 Belgium	3	2	0	1	10	4	6
3 Kazakhstan	3	1	0	2	2	7	3
4 Andorra	3	0	0	3	1	11	0

Group 12 Results

9/10/09, Starke Arvid, Ljungskile
Sweden 0-0 Montenegro
9/10/09, Edsborgs IP, Trollhattan
Ukraine 1-0 Georgia
11/10/09, Edsborgs IP, Trollhattan
Sweden 0-0 Georgia
11/10/09, Rimnersvallen, Udevalla
Montenegro 1-1 Ukraine
14/10/09, Rimnersvallen, Udevalla
Ukraine 1-0 Sweden
14/10/09, Starke Arvid, Ljungskile
Georgia 1-1 Montenegro

Group 12 Table

	Pld	W	D	L	F	A	Pts
1 Ukraine	3	2	1	0	3	1	7
2 Montenegro	3	0	3	0	2	2	3
3 Georgia	3	0	2	1	1	2	2
4 Sweden	3	0	2	1	0	1	2

Group 13 Results

9/10/09, Lavita, Kfar-Saba
Poland 2-1 Denmark
9/10/09, Nes-Ziona, Nes-Ziona
Israel 0-3 Azerbaijan
11/10/09, Lavita, Kfar-Saba
Poland 1-2 Azerbaijan
11/10/09, Nes-Ziona, Nes-Ziona
Denmark 1-0 Israel
14/10/09, Nes-Ziona, Nes-Ziona
Israel 1-1 Poland
14/10/09, Lavita, Kfar-Saba
Azerbaijan 0-3 Denmark

Group 13 Table

	Pld	W	D	L	F	A	Pts
1 Denmark	3	2	0	1	5	2	6
2 Azerbaijan	3	2	0	1	5	4	6
3 Poland	3	1	1	1	4	4	4
4 Israel	3	0	1	2	1	5	1

UEFA European Under-19 Championship

ELITE ROUND

Group 1 Results

19/5/10, Lučko, Zagreb
Croatia 2-1 Belgium
Goal(s): 1-0 Maglica 45+3, 1-1 Van Eenoo 50, 2-1 Ozobić 68

19/5/10, SRC Velika Gorika, Velika Gorica
Scotland 4-0 Montenegro
Goal(s): 1-0 McHugh 13, 1-0 Robinson 29, 1-0 Armstrong 74, 4-0 Armstrong 85

21/5/10, Gradski, Vrbovec
Belgium 2-1 Scotland
Goal(s): 1-0 Badibanga 69, 1-1 Inman 87, 2-1 Sterckx y Calle 90+2

21/5/10, Branko Čavlović-Čavlek, Karlovac
Croatia 3-0 Montenegro
Goal(s): 1-0 Ozobić 34, 2-0 Tičinović 84, 3-0 Maglica 90+2

24/5/10, NK Inter Zaprešić, Zapresic
Scotland 0-1 Croatia
Goal(s): 0-1 Adrijašević 19

24/5/10, SRC Velika Gorika, Velika Gorica
Montenegro 1-4 Belgium
Goal(s): 0-1 Van Damme 9, 0-2 Lestienne 16, 0-3 Badibanga 28, 1-3 Van Damme 32(og), 1-4 Bruno 73

Group 1 Table

	Pld	W	D	L	F	A	Pts
1 Croatia	3	3	0	0	6	1	9
2 Belgium	3	2	0	1	7	4	6
3 Scotland	3	1	0	2	5	3	3
4 Montenegro	3	0	0	3	1	11	0

Group 2 Results

3/5/10, Globall Football Park, Telki
Portugal 3-1 Romania
Goal(s): 1-0 Sérgio Oliveira 2, 2-0 Nélson Oliveira 9, 2-1 Matei 10, 3-1 Alex 68

3/5/10, Tatabánya Városi, Tatabany
Hungary 0-1 Greece
Goal(s): 0-1 Vellios 83

5/5/10, Globall Football Park, Telki
Portugal 1-1 Greece
Goal(s): 1-0 Baldé 83, 1-1 Potouridis 90+2

5/5/10, Tatabánya Városi, Tatabany
Romania 0-3 Hungary
Goal(s): 0-1 Simon 9, 0-2 Simon 83, 0-3 Skriba 90+2(p)

Anton Maglica scored two goals for Croatia in Elite Group 1

8/5/10, Tatabánya Városi, Tatabany
Hungary 2-3 Portugal
Goal(s): 0-1 Salvador Agra 21, 1-1 Kulcsár 27, 2-1 Skriba 32(p), 2-2 Alex 43, 2-3 Nélson Oliveira 59

8/5/10, Globall Football Park, Telki
Greece 2-0 Romania
Goal(s): 1-0 Mantalos 61, 2-0 Mantalos 86

Group 2 Table

	Pld	W	D	L	F	A	Pts
1 Portugal	3	2	1	0	7	4	7
2 Greece	3	2	1	0	4	1	7
3 Hungary	3	1	0	2	5	4	3
4 Romania	3	0	0	3	1	8	0

Group 3 Results

26/5/10, FFU Training complex, Kyiv
England 1-0 Republic of Ireland
Goal(s): 1-0 Parrett 37

26/5/10, Borex, Borodyanka
Ukraine 4-1 Bosnia-Herzegovina
Goal(s): 1-0 Chaykovskiy 10, 2-0 Chaykovskiy 43(p), 2-1 Pandža 45, 3-1 Zubko 56, 4-1 Sydorchuk 72

28/5/10, FFU Training complex, Kyiv
England 4-0 Bosnia-Herzegovina
Goal(s): 1-0 Noble 2, 2-0 Phillips 18, 3-0 Bostock 69, 4-0 Delfouneso 79

28/5/10, Borex, Borodyanka
Republic of Ireland 1-0 Ukraine
Goal(s): 1-0 Clifford 60(p)

31/5/10, Borex, Borodyanka
Ukraine 1-1 England
Goal(s): 1-0 Zubko 81, 1-1 Parrett 83

31/5/10, FFU Training complex, Kyiv
Bosnia-Herzegovina 0-1 Republic of Irela
Goal(s): 0-1 Clifford 68(p)

Group 3 Table

	Pld	W	D	L	F	A
1 England	3	2	1	0	6	1
2 Republic of Ireland	3	2	0	1	2	1
3 Ukraine	3	1	1	1	5	3
4 Bosnia-Herzegovina	3	0	0	3	1	9

Group 4 Results

14/4/10, Anadolu University, Eskisehir
Norway 1-1 Spain
Goal(s): 1-0 Lehne Olsen 44, 1-1 Rochina 62

14/4/10, Atatürk, Eskisehir
Turkey 2-0 Azerbaijan
Goal(s): 1-0 Emre Çolak 55(p), 2-0 Emre Çolak 58

16/4/10, Anadolu University, Eskisehir
Norway 1-1 Azerbaijan
Goal(s): 1-0 Lehne Olsen 37, 1-1 Hasanov 81

16/4/10, Atatürk, Eskisehir
Spain 3-2 Turkey
Goal(s): 1-0 Keko 8, 1-1 Necip Uysal 14, 2-1 Thiago 44, 2-2 Muhammet Demir 48, 3-2 Oriol 54

19/4/10, Atatürk, Eskisehir
Turkey 2-1 Norway
Goal(s): 1-0 Emre Çolak 16, 1-1 Ringstad 21, 2-1 Volkan Dikmen 64

19/4/10, Anadolu University, Eskisehir
Azerbaijan 0-4 Spain
Goal(s): 0-1 Rochina 29, 0-2 Rochina 31, 0-3 Thiago 36(p), 0-4 Rodri 70

Group 4 Table

	Pld	W	D	L	F	A
1 Spain	3	2	1	0	8	3
2 Turkey	3	2	0	1	6	4
3 Norway	3	0	2	1	3	4
4 Azerbaijan	3	0	1	2	1	7

UEFA European Under-19 Championship

roup 5 Results

'5/10, Spartak, Schelkovo
ly 2-0 Czech Republic
al(s): 1-0 Destro 27, 2-0 Borini 75

'5/10, Krylya Sovetov, Moscow
ssia 2-2 Northern Ireland
al(s): 1-0 Gatagov 17, 2-0 Kokorin 49, 2-1
rwood 82, 2-2 Norwood 90+3

'5/10, Spartak, Schelkovo
ly 3-2 Northern Ireland
al(s): 0-1 Norwood 32(p), 1-1 Destro 40,
Tremolada 42, 2-2 C. McLaughlin 58,
Destro 66

'5/10, Krylya Sovetov, Moscow
ech Republic 3-3 Russia
al(s): 0-1 Gatagov 12, 1-1 Krejčí 28,
Skalák 32, 2-2 Kokorin 45, 3-2 Kadlec 78,
Kanunnikov 82

'5/10, Krylya Sovetov, Moscow
ssia 3-1 Italy
al(s): 1-0 Logua 5, 2-0 Kanunnikov 47,
Borini 62, 3-1 Bashkirov 65

icky van Haaren scored twice for the
etherlands in their 3-0 victory over
ermany

26/5/10, Spartak, Schelkovo
Northern Ireland 1-3 Czech Republic
Goal(s): 0-1 Krejčí 42, 0-2 Fantiš 57, 1-2 Gray 74,
1-3 Kaderabek 90

Group 5 Table

	Pld	W	D	L	F	A	Pts
1 Italy	3	2	0	1	6	5	6
2 Russia	3	1	2	0	8	6	5
3 Czech Republic	3	1	1	1	6	6	4
4 Northern Ireland	3	0	1	2	5	8	1

Group 6 Results

18/5/10, Sportpark "In de Bandert", Echt
Netherlands 0-0 Slovakia

18/5/10, Bakenbos, Tegelen
Germany 4-1 Poland
Goal(s): 0-1 Kucharczyk 6, 1-1 Tosun 15,
2-1 Tosun 21, 3-1 Tosun 55, 4-1 Alvarez 68

20/5/10, Sportpark "In de Bandert", Echt
Slovakia 2-1 Germany
Goal(s): 0-1 Sauter 8, 1-1 Banović 45+1,
2-1 Mikuš 87

20/5/10, Bakenbos, Tegelen
Netherlands 2-0 Poland
Goal(s): 1-0 Castaignos 53, 2-0 Castaignos 64

23/5/10, De Koel, Venlo
Germany 0-3 Netherlands
Goal(s): 0-1 Cabral 7, 0-2 Van Haaren 37,
0-3 Van Haaren 52

23/5/10, Bakenbos, Tegelen
Poland 1-0 Slovakia
Goal(s): 1-0 Borysiuk 18

Group 6 Table

	Pld	W	D	L	F	A	Pts
1 Netherlands	3	2	1	0	5	0	7
2 Slovakia	3	1	1	1	2	2	4
3 Germany	3	1	0	2	5	6	3
4 Poland	3	1	0	2	2	6	3

Group 7 Results

25/5/10, Hall, Hall in Tirol
Serbia 3-2 Denmark
Goal(s): 0-1 N. Jørgensen 15, 1-1 Aleksić 23,
2-1 Đuričić 28, 2-2 Kadrii 45, 3-2 Šćepović 57

25/5/10, Sportzentrum Schwaz, Schwaz
Switzerland 3-2 Austria
Goal(s): 0-1 Weimann 6, 1-1 Sauthier 26,
2-1 Zuber 74, 3-1 Xhaka 90, 3-2 Djuricin 90+4

27/5/10, Hall, Hall in Tirol
Denmark 1-0 Switzerland
Goal(s): 1-0 N. Jørgensen 34

27/5/10, Sportzentrum Schwaz, Schwaz
Serbia 0-2 Austria
Goal(s): 0-1 Klem 70, 0-2 Knasmüllner 90

30/5/10, Sportzentrum Schwaz, Schwaz
Switzerland 2-4 Serbia
Goal(s): 0-1 Ljajić 19, 0-2 Đuričić 29,
1-2 Mehmedi 58, 2-2 Lang 67, 2-3 Aleksić 69(p),
2-4 Ljajić 77

30/5/10, Hall, Hall in Tirol
Austria 4-3 Denmark
Goal(s): 0-1 E. Larsen 11, 1-1 Holzhauser 16,
2-1 Knasmüllner 24, 2-2 N. Jørgensen 34,
2-3 N. Jørgensen 61, 3-3 Djuricin 73(p),
4-3 Knasmüllner 77

Group 13 Table

	Pld	W	D	L	F	A	Pts
1 Austria	3	2	0	1	8	6	6
2 Serbia	3	2	0	1	7	6	6
3 Denmark	3	1	0	2	6	7	3
4 Switzerland	3	1	0	2	5	7	3

FINAL TOURNAMENT

GROUP A

Group A brought together two of the teams that had contested the 2008/09 UEFA European Under-19 Championship semi-finals, England and France, while Austria featured in the tournament for the first time since hosting it in 2007 and the Netherlands made their finals debut – surprisingly the first time the Oranje had qualified since the competition's U18 forerunner in 2000.

Initially the new boys both found the going tough, Austria finding themselves two goals down inside 29 minutes against England at the Stade du Hazé in Flers as Frank Nouble supplied two assured left-foot finishes. David Alaba's free-kick restored Austrian hopes six minutes after half-time and, although Thomas Cruise restored England's two-goal cushion almost immediately, Noel Blake's side still had to endure a tense finale as Gernot Trauner reduced the deficit again with 17 minutes left.

France also started at breakneck speed at the Stade Michel-d'Ornano in Caen, solo goals from Gaël Kakuta and Cédric Bakambu giving Francis Smerecki's side a two-goal half-time cushion. Netherlands winger Jerson Cabral pulled one back with a deflected free-kick early in the second period, but France held firm and made the game safe in the last five minutes thanks to a Bruno Martins Indi own goal and Bakambu's second.

Exquisite strike

The hosts picked up where they had left off against Austria in the second round of matches, taking the lead thanks to an exquisite Antoine Griezmann strike in the 19th minute. Andreas Heraf's young Austria side refused to be cowed, however, only running out of steam once Alexandre Lacazette had doubled France's lead in the 66th minute. Griezmann and Lacazette both added further goals, with substitute Enzo Reale also joining the party as Les Bleus ran out 5-0 winners.

In Bayeux, meanwhile, the Netherlands bounced back to edge past England and revive their qualification hopes. Steven Berghuis headed the only goal of a tight contest in the sixth minute from a Cabral cross.

That meant France were in the semi-finals barring a remarkable reversal of fortune in the final game, a prospect that never looked likely even before Yannis Tafer headed Smerecki's team into a 56th-minute lead against England at the Stade Louis Villemer in Saint-Lo. Blake's England, knowing their hopes were hanging by a thread, pushed forward with time running out and snatched a dramatic draw in the last seconds, Matt Phillips heading the equaliser through the hands of goalkeeper Abdoulaye Diallo deep into added time.

A point at the Stade Michel Farré in Mondeville would still have been enough for Wim van Zwam's Netherlands to reach the last four. Initially it looked like they would take all three, Luc Castaignos striking the crossbar with a deflected shot early in the second period. Although the Oranje lost Leandro Bacuna to an 80th-minute red card following a tangle with Emir Dilaver they still looked the more likely scorers, Castaignos hitting the bar again and Lorenzo Ebicilio being denied by goalkeeper Philip Petermann from point-blank range. Three minutes from time, however, Ricky van Rhijn felled Georg Teigl and Marco Djuricin – who had passed up five gilt-edged opportunities – made amends from the spot, giving Austria third position and a place in the 2011 FIFA U-20 World Cup while leaving the Dutch empty-handed.

Frank Nouble opens the scoring for England against Austria

UEFA European Under-19 Championship

UNDER-19
CHAMPIONSHIP

Group A Results

18/7/10, Stade du Hazé, Flers
Austria 2-3 England
Austria: Petermann, Dilaver, Imamoglu, Schimpelsberger (Rath 59), Kainz (Gucher 82), Alaba, Weimann, Knasmüllner, Djuricin (Tiffner 71), Trauner, Klem. Coach: Andreas Heraf (AUT)
England: Rudd, Briggs (Clyne 54), James, Caulker (Thompson 86), Baker, Parrett, Delfouneso, Nouble, Bostock (Mellis 77), Cruise, Brown. Coach: Noel Blake (ENG)
Goal(s): 0-1 Nouble 13, 0-2 Nouble 29, 1-2 Alaba 51, 1-3 Cruise 53, 2-3 Trauner 73
Yellow Card(s): Schimpelsberger 41 (Austria), Kainz 70 (Austria), Brown 85 (England)
Referee: Strömbergsson (SWE)

18/7/10, Michel-d'Ornano, Caen
France 4-1 Netherlands
France: Diallo, Nego, Mavinga, Faure, Grenier (Reale 80), Kakuta, Fofana, Griezmann (Lacazette 73), Coquelin, Kolodziejczak, Bakambu. Coach: Francis Smerecki (FRA)
Netherlands: Zoet, Najah, Schouten (Sneijder 46), Martins Indi, Clasie (Ebicilio 77), Van la Parra, Bacuna (Pröpper 46), Castaignos, Van Haaren, Cabral, Eekman. Coach: Wim van Zwam (NED)
Goal(s): 1-0 Kakuta 20, 2-0 Bakambu 37, 2-1 Cabral 51, 3-1 Martins Indi 84(og), 4-1 Bakambu 90+3
Yellow Card(s): Najah 28 (Netherlands), Bakambu 41 (France), Kolodziejczak 42 (France), Fofana 83 (France), Castaignos 88 (Netherlands), Van la Parra 88 (Netherlands), Lacazette 89 (France)
Referee: Bezborodov (RUS)

21/7/10, Stade du Hazé, Flers
France 5-0 Austria
France: Diallo, Nego, Mavinga, Faure, Grenier (Reale 67), Kakuta, Fofana, Griezmann, Coquelin (Sunu 84), Kolodziejczak, Bakambu (Lacazette 58). Coach: Francis Smerecki (FRA)
Austria: Petermann, Dilaver, Imamoglu, Alaba, Gucher, Weimann (Djuricin 46), Trauner (Knasmüllner 67), Rath, Holzhauser, Teigl, Meilinger (Tiffner 67). Coach: Andreas Heraf (AUT)
Goal(s): 1-0 Griezmann 19, 2-0 Lacazette 66, 3-0 Griezmann 73, 4-0 Reale 80, 5-0 Lacazette 83
Yellow Card(s): Trauner 39 (Austria), Mavinga 42 (France), Teigl 55 (Austria)
Referee: Black (NIR)

21/7/10, Henry Jeanne, Bayeux
Netherlands 1-0 England
Netherlands: Zoet, Van Rhijn, Najah, Martins Indi, Clasie, Bacuna, Castaignos (Ebicilio 72), Van Haaren, Cabral (Jozefzoon 89), Sneijder, Berghuis (Van la Parra 75). Coach: Wim van Zwam (NED)
England: Rudd, Clyne, James, Caulker, Baker, Mellis (Donaldson 83), Parrett, Delfouneso, Nouble, Brown, Phillips (Noble 72). Coach: Noel Blake (ENG)
Goal(s): 1-0 Berghuis 6
Yellow Card(s): Parrett 48 (England), Najah 73 (Netherlands)
Referee: Mazeika (LTU)

24/7/10, Louis Villemer, Saint-Lo
England 1-1 France
England: Rudd, Clyne, James, Caulker, Mellis (Bostock 78), Parrett (Noble 74), Delfouneso, Nouble, Cruise, Thompson, Donaldson (Phillips 76). Coach: Noel Blake (ENG)

France: Diallo, Nego, Martial, Faure, Grenier, Kakuta (Lacazette 62), Tafer (Kolodziejczak 80), Sunu (Griezmann 73), Reale, Bakambu, Bussmann. Coach: Francis Smerecki (FRA)
Goal(s): 0-1 Tafer 56, 1-1 Phillips 90+3
Yellow Card(s): Parrett 73 (England)
Referee: Studer (SUI)

24/7/10, Michel Farré, Mondeville
Netherlands 0-1 Austria
Netherlands: Zoet, Van Rhijn, Martins Indi, Clasie (Pröpper 44), Bacuna, Castaignos, Van Haaren, Cabral (Van la Parra 85), Eekman, Sneijder, Berghuis (Ebicilio 63). Coach: Wim van Zwam (NED)
Austria: Petermann, Dilaver, Schimpelsberger, Kainz, Gucher, Weimann (Teigl 63), Djuricin, Trauner, Rath (Imamoglu 46), Holzhauser (Meilinger 68), Klem. Coach: Andreas Heraf (AUT)
Goal(s): 0-1 Djuricin 87(p)
Red Card(s): Bacuna 80 (Netherlands)
Yellow Card(s): Clasie 33 (Netherlands), Martins Indi 47 (Netherlands), Schimpelsberger 56 (Austria), Gucher 69 (Austria), Djuricin 78 (Austria), Van Rhijn 86 (Netherlands), Teigl 90+2 (Austria)
Referee: Jug (SVN)

Group A Table

	Pld	W	D	L	F	A	Pts
1 France	3	2	1	0	10	2	7
2 England	3	1	1	1	4	4	4
3 Austria	3	1	0	2	3	8	3
4 Netherlands	3	1	0	2	2	5	3

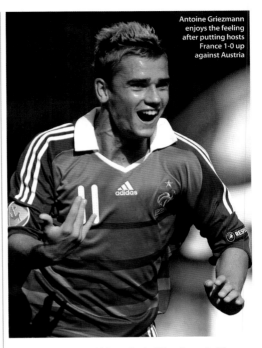

Antoine Griezmann enjoys the feeling after putting hosts France 1-0 up against Austria

GROUP B

Group B provided plenty of incident and excitement, with the section's eventual victors Spain taking a maximum nine points en route to the semi-finals. Entering the last round of matches Portugal, Croatia and Italy were all in contention to join La Roja in the last four, but it was Ivica Grnja's Croatian side that eventually won through.

Having failed to get beyond the group stage since 2007, Luis Milla led his Spain side into the finals with the intention of succeeding where he had failed the previous year in Ukraine. In the opening stages against Croatia it was evident that Spain's teenagers were intent on imitating the slick passing and quick movement of their senior FIFA World Cup-winning counterparts yet despite dominating possession it was Croatia who took the lead late in the first half thanks to Franko Andrijašević's long-range strike. It took just 11 second-half minutes for the four-time winners to finally make their dominance count, Thiago Alcántara and Rodrigo finding the net to turn the match around.

Out for revenge

Elsewhere on Matchday 1, Portugal were seeking a long-delayed revenge against Italy in a repeat of the 2003 final, won 2-0 by the Azzurrini in Liechtenstein. This time around Ilídio Vale's team gained an immediate advantage as they ran out 2-0 winners against opponents who finished with ten men following Marco D'Alessandro's late red card. Nélson Oliveira had opened the scoring in the 51st minute, and Sérgio Oliveira's powerful effort from distance 12 minutes later was enough to ensure that Portugal joined their Iberian neighbours and next opponents on three points.

Ezequiel Calvente (left) is congratulated by team-mate Iker Muniain after scoring a penalty against Italy

When the early leaders met in Saint-Lo three days later it was Spain who took the initiative, left-sided midfielder Daniel Pacheco opening the scoring from inside the area after 12 minutes. Milla's team tired after the break, however, and Rúben Pinto sent the ball in off the woodwork with 12 minutes remaining to level. There was still time for Spain to regain the advantage, Pacheco working his way into the Portugal area before firing in at the near post to wrap up the points. Croatia and Italy's goalless draw in the day's other game meant Spain were guaranteed first place, yet it might have worked out differently had Arijan Ademi's late effort not struck the upright for Croatia. Italy again ended a man short after left-back Michelangelo Albertazzi collected two yellow cards.

Knowing a draw in Bayeux would be enough to take them through to the semi-finals as runners-up, Portugal were stunned early on by Andrijašević's opener for a Croatia. That set the scene for an impressive attacking display from the tournament debutants, Zvonko Pamić registering a hat-trick and Filip Ozobić also putting his name on the scoresheet as the Croatians made light of a 54th-minute red card for captain Renato Kelić to complete a resounding 5-0 triumph. Despite making six changes Spain comfortably overcame Italy 3-0 in Flers, Rúben Rochina and Daniel Pacheco taking advantage of defensive lapses in the first half before Ezequiel Calvente's audacious penalty wrapped things up.

Group B Results

18/7/10, Henry Jeanne, Bayeux
Croatia 1-2 Spain
Croatia: Delač, Vrsaljko, Rugašević, Andrijašević, Kelić, Glumac, Ademi, Ozobić, Kramarić (Tičinović 65), Pamić (Punčec 81), Maglica (Vukušić 65). Coach: Ivan Grnja (CRO)
Spain: Álex, Montoya, Planas, Bartra, Pulido, Oriol Romeu, Keko (Muniain 45+1), Thiago Alcántara, Rodrigo (Rochina 71), Canales, Pacheco (Ezequiel Calvente 89). Coach: Luis Milla (ESP)
Goal(s): 1-0 Andrijašević 42, 1-1 Thiago Alcántara 53, 1-2 Rodrigo 64
Yellow Card(s): Vrsaljko 17 (Croatia), Montoya 39 (Spain), Kelić 63 (Croatia)
Referee: Black (NIR)

18/7/10, Michel Farré, Mondeville
Italy 0-2 Portugal
Italy: Colombi, Crescenzi, Albertazzi, Soriano, Caldirola, Sala (Galano 54), Bertolacci (Taddei 46), Destro, Borini (Nicolao Dumitru 80), Adamo, D'Alessandro. Coach: Massimo Piscedda (ITA)
Portugal: Tiago Maia, Aníbal Capela, Roderick, Agostinho Cá, Nélson Oliveira (Baldé 87), Cédric, Sana (Evandro 79), Alex (Rúben Pinto 90+2), Danilo, Mário Rui, Sérgio Oliveira. Coach: Ilídio Vale (POR)
Goal(s): 0-1 Nélson Oliveira 51, 0-2 Sérgio Oliveira 63
Red Card(s): D'Alessandro 90+2 (Italy)
Yellow Card(s): Sana 43 (Portugal)
Referee: Mazeika (LTU)

UEFA European Under-19 Championship

Croatia's Zvonko Pamić lets fly to score the second of his three goals against Portugal

24/7/10, Henry Jeanne, Bayeux

Portugal 0-5 Croatia

Portugal: João Amorim, Tiago Maia, Nuno Reis, Roderick, Nélson Oliveira, Sana, Evandro (Alex 46), Danilo (Salvador Agra 68), Mário Rui (Baldé 46), Sérgio Oliveira, Rúben Pinto. Coach: Ilídio Vale (POR)

Croatia: Delač, Vrsaljko, Rugašević, Andrijašević (Bičvić 86), Kelić, Glumac, Ademi, Ozobić, Tičinović (Jonjić 57), Pamić, Maglica (Kramarić 31). Coach: Ivan Grnja (CRO)

Goal(s): 0-1 Andrijašević 19(p), 0-2 Pamić 25, 0-3 Pamić 37, 0-4 Ozobić 67, 0-5 Pamić 69

Red Card(s): Kelić 54 (Croatia)

Yellow Card(s): Roderick 18 (Portugal), Kramarić 41 (Croatia), Baldé 58 (Portugal), Nuno Reis 78 (Portugal), Sérgio Oliveira 86 (Portugal)

Referee: Strömbergsson (SWE)

24/7/10, Stade du Hazé, Flers

Spain 3-0 Italy

Spain: Aitor, Planas, Bartra, Keko, Thiago Alcántara (Oriol Romeu 46), Pacheco (Ezequiel Calvente 46), Hugo Mallo, Muniain, Mayor, Koke (Pulido 66), Rochina. Coach: Luis Milla (ESP)

Italy: Colombi, Crescenzi, Soriano, Brosco, Caldirola, Sala (Nicolao Dumitru 46), Destro, Borini, Adamo (Malomo 26), Tremolada (Galano 46), Taddei. Coach: Massimo Piscedda (ITA)

Goal(s): 1-0 Rochina 17, 2-0 Pacheco 23, 3-0 Ezequiel Calvente 57(p)

Yellow Card(s): Adamo 19 (Italy), Destro 58 (Italy), Colombi 58 (Italy), Pulido 89 (Spain), Taddei 90+2 (Italy)

Referee: Bezborodov (RUS)

Group B Table

	Pld	W	D	L	F	A	Pts
1 Spain	3	3	0	0	7	2	9
2 Croatia	3	1	1	1	6	2	4
3 Portugal	3	1	0	2	3	7	3
4 Italy	3	0	1	2	0	5	1

21/7/10, Louis Villemer, Saint-Lo

Spain 2-1 Portugal

Spain: Álex, Montoya, Planas, Bartra, Pulido, Oriol Romeu, Keko (Koke 90+1), Thiago Alcántara, Rodrigo (Rochina 79), Canales (Muniain 73), Pacheco. Coach: Luis Milla (ESP)

Portugal: Tiago Maia, Nuno Reis, Roderick, Agostinho Cá (Rúben Pinto 46), Nélson Oliveira (Baldé 86), Cédric, Sana, Alex (Evandro 46), Danilo, Mário Rui, Sérgio Oliveira. Coach: Ilídio Vale (POR)

Goal(s): 1-0 Pacheco 12, 1-1 Rúben Pinto 78, 2-1 Pacheco 88

Yellow Card(s): Canales 44 (Spain), Sérgio Oliveira 47 (Portugal), Montoya 71 (Spain), Roderick 81 (Portugal), Cédric 82 (Portugal)

Referee: Jug (SVN)

21/7/10, Michel Farré, Mondeville

Croatia 0-0 Italy

Croatia: Delač, Vrsaljko, Rugašević, Andrijašević (Mlinar 83), Kelić, Glumac, Ademi, Ozobić, Tičinović (Kramarić 77), Vukušić, Punčec (Pamić 68). Coach: Ivan Grnja (CRO)

Italy: Colombi, Crescenzi, Albertazzi, Soriano, Caldirola, Bertolacci (Brosco 64), Destro, Borini, Adamo (Malomo 52), Tremolada (Sala 69), Taddei. Coach: Massimo Piscedda (ITA)

Red Card(s): Albertazzi 59 (Italy)

Yellow Card(s): Borini 12 (Italy), Albertazzi 58 (Italy), Albertazzi 59 (Italy), Ademi 61 (Croatia)

Referee: Studer (SUI)

Semi-Finals

As many had expected, Spain and France emerged victorious in the semi-finals, although the manner of their successes could scarcely have been more different.

Luis Milla's Spain side were in the last four for the first time since lifting the trophy in 2007, and they took on 2009 runners-up England in the first semi-final in Saint-Lo. Noel Blake's side started promisingly, Ryan Donaldson threatening with a header inside the first minute, but Spain quickly found their rhythm and went ahead with 12 minutes on the clock. Sergio Canales escaped down the right and picked out the fast-arriving Daniel Pacheco at the far post, where the Liverpool FC player slotted his fourth goal of the finals beyond Declan Rudd.

Spain continued to monopolise possession and doubled their advantage in the 34th minute with another well-worked goal. Thiago Alcántara and

Canales were both involved in the quick-fire one-touch passing move that ended with Keko wrong-footing Steven Caulker and rolling a shot past Rudd. Although England reduced the arrears three minutes later, substitute John Bostock finding the bottom corner of the net with a low volley from the edge of the area, the match was effectively settled in the 57th minute by another Spanish move straight from the training ground. With Oriol Romeu shaping to strike a free-kick, a clever flick from Thiago over the wall put Canales in on goal and his finish was predictably composed.

Shock start

With Spain through, attention switched to the Stade Michel-d'Ornano in Caen, where the majority of the 9,000-strong crowd suffered a shock in the fourth minute as Arijan Ademi got ahead of Gilles Sunu to flick Zvonko Pamić's free-kick beyond France goalkeeper Abdoulaye Diallo via the underside of the crossbar. Sunu nearly made amends just past the half-hour, sending two defenders the wrong way with a drag-back and digging out a lofted shot that struck the outside of Matej Delač's right-hand post with the goalkeeper beaten.

With French pressure steadily mounting, however, the Croatian defence cracked eight minutes before half-time as Mario Tičinović's misdirected header across his own penalty area found only Gaël Kakuta, who duly tucked the ball home past the exposed Delač. France continued to control the tempo as the second period progressed but struggled to penetrate the Croatia rearguard until the closing stages. When they did, it proved decisive, Francis Coquelin skipping past three challenges before sliding a pass through for substitute Cédric Bakambu, who curled his shot low into the net to send the hosts through to the final.

Semi-Final Results

27/7/10, Louis Villemer, Saint-Lo
Spain 3-1 England
Spain: Álex, Montoya, Planas, Bartra, Pulido, Oriol Romeu, Keko, Thiago Alcántara, Rodrigo (Rochina 58), Canales (Koke 69), Pacheco (Muniain 75). Coach: Luis Milla (ESP)
England: Rudd, Clyne, James, Caulker, Baker (Bostock 18), Mellis (Noble 59), Delfouneso, Nouble, Cruise, Thompson, Donaldson (Phillips 71). Coach: Noel Blake (ENG)
Goal(s): 1-0 Pacheco 12, 2-0 Keko 34, 2-1 Bostock 37, 3-1 Canales 57
Yellow Card(s): Planas 40 (Spain), Bostock 41 (England), Caulker 81 (England), Álex 81 (Spain)
Referee: Strömbergsson (SWE)

27/7/10, Michel-d'Ornano, Caen
France 2-1 Croatia
France: Diallo, Nego, Mavinga, Faure, Kakuta, Fofana, Tafer (Bakambu 74), Sunu (Lacazette 68), Griezmann, Coquelin, Kolodziejczak. Coach: Francis Smerecki (FRA)

Gaël Kakuta calls for silence after equalising for France against Croatia

Croatia: Delač, Vrsaljko, Rugašević, Andrijašević (Punčec 74), Glumac, Ademi, Ozobić, Tičinović (Kramarić 58), Vukušić, Jonjić, Pamić. Coach: Ivan Grnja (CRO)
Goal(s): 0-1 Ademi 4, 1-1 Kakuta 37, 2-1 Bakambu 83
Yellow Card(s): Rugašević 55 (Croatia), Vrsaljko 59 (Croatia), Punčec 79 (Croatia)
Referee: Bezborodov (RUS)

FINAL

France fought back from a goal down in Caen to defeat Spain in the 9th UEFA European Under-19 Championship final as Alexandre Lacazette came off the bench to delight the home fans with an 85th-minute winner.

Francis Smerecki's team, bidding to become the second successive host nation to win the U19 title following Ukraine's triumph in 2009, were on the back foot from the first whistle and fell behind to Rodrigo's first-half strike. The teams had also met two years previously in the European U17 Championship final, in which La Roja ran out 4-0 winners, and a repeat of that one-sided contest looked to be on the cards during a dominant first-half Spanish display, only for Gilles Sunu to bring the hosts level four minutes into the second period. Just as the match appeared to be heading for extra time, France's revival brought a dramatic winner as Lacazette headed in Gaël Kakuta's cross to give his country the trophy for the second time.

Spain in control

Eleven of the 22 starters in Caen also began that U17 final and, as in Antalya two years earlier, Spain swiftly took control. In the tenth minute clever interplay down the right from Martín Montoya and Keko worked an opening for Sergio Canales, who turned sharply inside the penalty area only to shoot against the legs of Abdoulaye Diallo. France were struggling to get a foothold in the match and paid the price eight minutes later.

Daniel Pacheco had scored four goals coming into the final, but he showed that his game was not just about finishing with his creative contribution to the opening goal. There seemed little danger when the midfielder received possession inside his own half but he spotted Rodrigo's clever run and, one perfectly-weighted pass and an impeccable first touch later, the striker was sliding a low left-footed shot across the goalkeeper and into the net.

Timely equaliser

Spain continued to dominate both territory and possession, but their failure to increase their lead allowed France hope of a second-half recovery. Smerecki introduced Yannis Tafer in an attempt to give his attack more punch, yet three minutes after half-time his side might have been two down, Diallo having to scramble to deny Canales. Seconds later, Sunu headed the goalkeeper's long clearance to Tafer and raced on to the return pass, lifting his shot over Álex to equalise.

With a reinvigorated crowd behind them, France strove to press home their advantage, and when Cédric Bakambu fed Tafer, Álex came to Spain's rescue, touching the shot to safety at his near post. The goalkeeper then denied Kakuta after the latter had burst through, but he was powerless when the France midfielder regained possession and lifted a perfect cross to the far post for Lacazette to head gleefully home and bring France the title.

France's match-winner in the final, Alexandre Lacazette, tries his luck from a free-kick

Final Result

30/7/10, Michel-d'Ornano, Caen
France 2-1 Spain
Attendance: 20188
France: Diallo, Nego, Mavinga, Faure, Kakuta, Fofana, Sunu (Lacazette 69), Griezmann (Tafer 46), Coquelin, Kolodziejczak, Bakambu. Coach: Francis Smerecki (FRA)
Spain: Álex, Montoya, Planas, Bartra, Pulido (Ezequiel Calvente 87), Oriol Romeu, Keko (Muniain 64), Thiago Alcántara, Rodrigo (Rochina 73), Canales, Pacheco. Coach: Luis Milla (ESP)
Goal(s): 0-1 Rodrigo 18, 1-1 Sunu 49, 2-1 Lacazette 85
Yellow Card(s): Pacheco 23 (Spain), Fofana 26 (France), Pulido 63 (Spain), Rochina 82 (Spain), Coquelin 84 (France), Faure 89 (France), Muniain 89 (Spain)
Referee: Studer (SUI)

TOP GOALSCORERS

4	Daniel Pacheco (Spain)
3	Alexandre Lacazette (France)
	Zvonko Pamić (Croatia)
	Cédric Bakambu (France)
2	Rodrigo (Spain)
	Antoine Griezmann (France)
	Franko Andrijašević (Croatia)
	Frank Nouble (England)
	Gaël Kakuta (France)

2010 European Under-19 champions France pose with the trophy

UEFA UNDER17 CHAMPIONSHIP

UEFA U17

2009/10

England etched their name on the UEFA European Under-17 Championship trophy for the first time, and there was no doubt that John Peacock's athletic and skilful side deserved their triumph. They won all six of their qualifying games and increased that number to 11 with five victories out of five at the final tournament in Liechtenstein. Peacock had led England to their only other final at this level in 2007 when they lost 1-0 to the tournament's historically dominant team, Spain, with Bojan Krkić scoring the winner. Three years on, the teams were matched again in the decider, Spain having also picked up four straight wins. Once again England fell behind, but this time they were able to recover and secured their first continental men's crown since the year most of the squad were born, the 1993 UEFA European Under-18 Championship, when Sol Campbell, Robbie Fowler, Nicky Butt and Paul Scholes, among others, triumphed on home soil.

UNDER17.
CHAMPIONSHIP

QUALIFYING ROUND

Group 1

26/10/09, Ismet Qaibov, Baku
England 6-2 Kazakhstan
26/10/09, Tofiq Bähramov, Baku
Serbia 0-0 Azerbaijan
28/10/09, Tofiq Ismayilov, Baku
Serbia 1-0 Kazakhstan
28/10/09, Tofiq Bähramov, Baku
Azerbaijan 0-4 England
31/10/09, Ismet Qaibov, Baku
England 1-0 Serbia
31/10/09, Tofiq Bähramov, Baku
Kazakhstan 1-3 Azerbaijan

Group 1 Table

	Pld	W	D	L	F	A	Pts
1 England	3	3	0	0	11	2	9
2 Serbia	3	1	1	1	1	1	4
3 Azerbaijan	3	1	1	1	3	5	4
4 Kazakhstan	3	0	0	3	3	10	0

Group 2

16/10/09, Town Stadium, Buftea
Romania 1-0 Lithuania
16/10/09, Concordia, Chiajna
Spain 6-0 Faroe Islands
18/10/09, Town Stadium, Buftea
Romania 4-0 Faroe Islands
18/10/09, Concordia, Chiajna
Lithuania 1-9 Spain
21/10/09, Concordia, Chiajna
Spain 4-1 Romania
21/10/09, Town Stadium, Buftea
Faroe Islands 2-3 Lithuania

Group 2 Table

	Pld	W	D	L	F	A	Pts
1 Spain	3	3	0	0	19	2	9
2 Romania	3	2	0	1	6	4	6
3 Lithuania	3	1	0	2	4	12	3
4 Faroe Islands	3	0	0	3	2	13	0

Group 3

23/9/09, Pod Goricom-Gradski, Podgorica
Croatia 1-1 Montenegro
23/9/09, Training Camp, Podgorica
Belgium 3-1 Denmark
25/9/09, Gradski, Niksic
Croatia 2-1 Denmark
25/9/09, Training Camp, Podgorica
Montenegro 1-1 Belgium
28/9/09, Training Camp, Podgorica
Belgium 0-1 Croatia
28/9/09, Gradski, Niksic
Denmark 8-1 Montenegro

Group 3 Table

	Pld	W	D	L	F	A	Pts
1 Croatia	3	2	1	0	4	2	7
2 Belgium	3	1	1	1	4	3	4
3 Denmark	3	1	0	2	10	6	3
4 Montenegro	3	0	2	1	3	10	2

Group 4

9/10/09, City Stadium GOS, Nadarzyn
Poland 2-4 Austria
9/10/09, MZOS Znicz, Pruszkow
Israel 6-1 Armenia
11/10/09, City Stadium OSIR, Grodzisk Mazowiecki
Armenia 1-4 Poland
11/10/09, MZOS Znicz, Pruszkow
Israel 0-2 Austria
14/10/09, MZOS Znicz, Pruszkow
Poland 7-0 Israel
14/10/09, City Stadium OSIR, Grodzisk Mazowiecki
Austria 1-1 Armenia

Group 4 Table

	Pld	W	D	L	F	A	Pts
1 Austria	3	2	1	0	7	2	7
2 Poland	3	2	0	1	13	5	6
3 Israel	3	1	0	2	6	10	3
4 Armenia	3	0	1	2	3	11	1

Group 5

23/10/09, FC Turnovo, Strumica
Turkey 2-0 Finland
23/10/09, Mladost, Strumica
Germany 2-0 FYROM
25/10/09, FC Turnovo, Strumica
Turkey 2-1 FYROM
25/10/09, Mladost, Strumica
Finland 1-0 Germany
28/10/09, FC Turnovo, Strumica
Germany 2-1 Turkey
28/10/09, Mladost, Strumica
FYROM 2-5 Finland

Group 5 Table

	Pld	W	D	L	F	A	Pts
1 Turkey	3	2	0	1	5	3	6
2 Germany	3	2	0	1	4	2	6
3 Finland	3	2	0	1	6	4	6
4 FYROM	3	0	0	3	3	9	0

Group 6

27/9/09, Albena 1, Albena
Sweden 2-0 Latvia
27/9/09, Druzhba, Dobrich
Republic of Ireland 2-1 Bulgaria
29/9/09, Albena 1, Albena
Republic of Ireland 1-0 Latvia
29/9/09, Druzhba, Dobrich
Bulgaria 0-0 Sweden
2/10/09, Albena 1, Albena
Sweden 0-0 Republic of Ireland
2/10/09, Druzhba, Dobrich
Latvia 0-4 Bulgaria

Group 6 Table

	Pld	W	D	L	F	A	Pts
1 Republic of Ireland	3	2	1	0	3	1	7
2 Sweden	3	1	2	0	2	0	5
3 Bulgaria	3	1	1	1	5	2	4
4 Latvia	3	0	0	3	0	7	0

Group 7

17/10/09, Rakvere, Rakvere
France 3-1 Slovenia
17/10/09, Kadriorg, Tallinn
Ukraine 0-0 Estonia
19/10/09, Rakvere, Rakvere
Slovenia 0-1 Ukraine
19/10/09, Kadriorg, Tallinn
France 3-1 Estonia
22/10/09, Rakvere, Rakvere
Ukraine 1-1 France
22/10/09, Kadriorg, Tallinn
Estonia 1-0 Slovenia

Group 7 Table

	Pld	W	D	L	F	A	Pts
1 France	3	2	1	0	7	3	7
2 Ukraine	3	1	2	0	2	1	5
3 Estonia	3	1	1	1	2	3	4
4 Slovenia	3	0	0	3	1	5	0

Group 8

22/10/09, Comunal, Andorra la Vella
Netherlands 4-0 Andorra
22/10/09, Comunal, Andorra la Vella
Northern Ireland 2-0 Malta
24/10/09, Comunal, Andorra la Vella
Andorra 0-2 Northern Ireland
24/10/09, Comunal, Andorra la Vella
Netherlands 1-2 Malta
27/10/09, Comunal, Andorra la Vella
Northern Ireland 0-1 Netherlands
27/10/09, Camp d'Esports del M.I. Consell General, Andorra la Vella
Malta 0-0 Andorra

Group 8 Table

	Pld	W	D	L	F	A	Pts
1 Netherlands	3	2	0	1	6	2	6
2 Northern Ireland	3	2	0	1	4	1	6
3 Malta	3	1	1	1	2	3	4
4 Andorra	3	0	1	2	0	6	1

UEFA European Under-17 Championship

UNDER17.
CHAMPIONSHIP

Group 9

24/10/09, Comunale, Teramo
Norway 0-1 Greece
24/10/09, Rubens Fadini, Giulianova
Italy 5-0 Moldova
26/10/09, Rubens Fadini, Giulianova
Moldova 0-0 Norway
26/10/09, Comunale, Teramo
Italy 0-0 Greece
29/10/09, Rubens Fadini, Giulianova
Norway 2-0 Italy
29/10/09, Comunale, Teramo
Greece 2-2 Moldova

Group 9 Table

	Pld	W	D	L	F	A	Pts
1 Greece	3	1	2	0	3	2	5
2 Norway	3	1	1	1	2	1	4
3 Italy	3	1	1	1	5	2	4
4 Moldova	3	0	2	1	2	7	2

Group 10

20/10/09, East End Park, Dunfermline
Scotland 1-2 Cyprus
20/10/09, Forthbank Stadium, Stirling
Portugal 2-0 Georgia
22/10/09, Stark's Park, Kirkcaldy
Scotland 1-2 Georgia
22/10/09, Bayview, Methil
Cyprus 1-2 Portugal
25/10/09, Stark's Park, Kirkcaldy
Portugal 2-2 Scotland
25/10/09, Forthbank Stadium, Stirling
Georgia 4-2 Cyprus

Group 10 Table

	Pld	W	D	L	F	A	Pts
1 Portugal	3	2	1	0	6	3	7
2 Georgia	3	2	0	1	6	5	6
3 Cyprus	3	1	0	2	5	7	3
4 Scotland	3	0	1	2	4	6	1

Group 11

25/9/09, Globall Football Park, Telki
Slovakia 2-0 Luxembourg
25/9/09, Globall Football Park, Telki
Hungary 5-0 Albania
27/9/09, Tatai Honvéd Atletikai Klub, Tata
Hungary 1-1 Luxembourg
27/9/09, Globall Football Park, Telki
Albania 0-3 Slovakia
30/9/09, Tatai Honvéd Atletikai Klub, Tata
Slovakia 0-1 Hungary
30/9/09, Globall Football Park, Telki
Luxembourg 3-2 Albania

Group 11 Table

	Pld	W	D	L	F	A	Pts
1 Hungary	3	2	1	0	7	1	7
2 Slovakia	3	2	0	1	5	1	6
3 Luxembourg	3	1	1	1	4	5	4
4 Albania	3	0	0	3	2	11	0

Group 12

28/9/09, Richmond Park, Carmarthen
Wales 3-2 Iceland
28/9/09, Stebonheath Park, Llanelli
Russia 0-0 Bosnia-Herzegovina
30/9/09, Stebonheath Park, Llanelli
Wales 2-2 Bosnia-Herzegovina
30/9/09, Bridge Meadow, Haverfordwest
Iceland 1-1 Russia
3/10/09, Bridge Meadow, Haverfordwest
Russia 1-2 Wales
3/10/09, Richmond Park, Carmarthen
Bosnia-Herzegovina 1-1 Iceland

Group 12 Table

	Pld	W	D	L	F	A	Pts
1 Wales	3	2	1	0	7	5	7
2 Bosnia-Herzegovina	3	0	3	0	3	3	3
3 Iceland	3	0	2	1	4	5	2
4 Russia	3	0	2	1	2	3	2

Group 13

5/9/09, Gorodskoi, Molodechno
Switzerland 10-0 San Marino
5/9/09, Dinamo-Juni, Minsk
Czech Republic 1-0 Belarus
7/9/09, Torpedo, Minsk
San Marino 0-4 Czech Republic
7/9/09, Dinamo-Juni, Minsk
Switzerland 2-0 Belarus
10/9/09, Gorodskoi, Molodechno
Czech Republic 4-0 Switzerland
10/9/09, Gorodskoi, Borisov
Belarus 4-0 San Marino

Group 13 Table

	Pld	W	D	L	F	A	Pts
1 Czech Republic	3	3	0	0	9	0	9
2 Switzerland	3	2	0	1	12	4	6
3 Belarus	3	1	0	2	4	3	3
4 San Marino	3	0	0	3	0	18	0

Youssouf Sabaly of Group 7 winners France

ELITE ROUND

Group 1

25/3/10, Na Slajsi, Lanzhot
Czech Republic 0-1 Georgia
Goal(s): 0-1 Kazaishvili 40+1

25/3/10, Banik Ratiskovice, Ratiskovice
Netherlands 2-0 Ukraine
Goal(s): 1-0 Locadia 7, 2-0 Klaassen 63

27/3/10, 1. FC Kyjov, Kyjov
Czech Republic 2-1 Ukraine
Goal(s): 1-0 Hurka 15, 1-1 Khamid 64,
2-1 P. Twardzik 80+1

27/3/10, Mestsky sportovni klub Breclav, Breclav
Georgia 1-2 Netherlands
Goal(s): 0-1 Maher 14, 1-1 Chanturia 16,
1-2 Locadia 69

30/3/10, Mestsky sportovni klub Breclav, Breclav
Netherlands 0-1 Czech Republic
Goal(s): 0-1 Hurka 16

30/3/10, Na Slajsi, Lanzhot
Ukraine 2-2 Georgia
Goal(s): 0-1 Kazaishvili 45, 1-1 Khamid 63,
2-1 Lukanyuk 71(p), 2-2 Kazaishvili 78(p)

Group 1 Table

		Pld	W	D	L	F	A	Pts
1	Czech Republic	3	2	0	1	3	2	6
2	Netherlands	3	2	0	1	4	2	6
3	Georgia	3	1	1	1	4	4	4
4	Ukraine	3	0	1	2	3	6	1

Group 2

19/3/10, Grbavica, Sarajevo
Portugal 4-1 Romania
Goal(s): 1-0 João Mário 24(p), 1-1 Vatajelu 26,
2-1 Tobias Figueiredo 31, 3-1 Betinho 43,
4-1 Tó Zé 80+2

19/3/10, Asim Ferhatović-Hase, Sarajevo
Croatia 2-1 Bosnia-Herzegovina
Goal(s): 1-0 Aleksić 33, 1-1 Ćemalović 51,
2-1 Kukavica 65(og)

21/3/10, Asim Ferhatović-Hase, Sarajevo
Portugal 1-1 Bosnia-Herzegovina
Goal(s): 0-1 Kukavica 13, 1-1 Bruma 19

21/3/10, Grbavica, Sarajevo
Romania 0-3 Croatia
Goal(s): 0-1 Livaja 9, 0-2 Ivančić 14,
0-3 Džoni 30

24/3/10, Asim Ferhatović-Hase, Sarajevo
Croatia 0-2 Portugal
Goal(s): 0-1 Ricardo Esgaio 53,
0-2 Ivan Cavaleiro 80+1

24/3/10, Grbavica, Sarajevo
Bosnia-Herzegovina 3-3 Romania
Goal(s): 1-0 Sivišić 1, 2-0 Ćemalović 12,
2-1 Baluta 39, 3-1 Ćemalović 45, 3-2 Baluta 66,
3-3 Gavra 80

Group 2 Table

		Pld	W	D	L	F	A	Pts
1	Portugal	3	2	1	0	7	2	7
2	Croatia	3	2	0	1	5	3	6
3	Bosnia-Herzegovina	3	0	2	1	5	6	2
4	Romania	3	0	1	2	4	10	1

Group 3

19/3/10, Municipal, Kato Achaia
Republic of Ireland 0-3 Greece
Goal(s): 0-1 Katidis 57, 0-2 Katidis 70,
0-3 Diamantakos 79

19/3/10, Pampeloponnisiako, Patras
Austria 3-3 Finland
Goal(s): 0-1 Väyrynen 8, 1-1 Burusic 17,
1-2 Paananen 27, 1-3 Väyrynen 42(p),
2-3 Holzhauser 68(p), 3-3 Traunmüller 80+1

21/3/10, Municipal, Kato Achaia
Austria 2-2 Greece
Goal(s): 0-1 Rougkalas 5, 1-1 Burusic 8,
2-1 Burusic 32(p), 2-2 Diamantakos 80+4(p)

21/3/10, Pampeloponnisiako, Patras
Finland 0-1 Republic of Ireland
Goal(s): 0-1 Knight 54

24/3/10, Pampeloponnisiako, Patras
Republic of Ireland 3-0 Austria
Goal(s): 1-0 O'Brien 20, 2-0 Knight 44,
3-0 O'Brien 72

24/3/10, Panahaiki, Patras
Greece 2-1 Finland
Goal(s): 0-1 Väyrynen 48, 1-1 Diamantakos 72,
2-1 Diamantakos 79

Group 3 Table

		Pld	W	D	L	F	A	Pts
1	Greece	3	2	1	0	7	3	7
2	Republic of Ireland	3	2	0	1	4	3	6
3	Austria	3	0	2	1	5	8	2
4	Finland	3	0	1	2	4	6	1

Robert Mariotti helped the Czech Republic to top spot in Group 1

UEFA European Under-17 Championship

Group 4

17/3/10, Shamrock Park, Portadown
Poland 0-2 Belgium
Goal(s): 0-1 Lallemand 17, 0-2 Arslanagic 66

17/3/10, The Showgrounds, Coleraine
Spain 4-0 Northern Ireland
Goal(s): 1-0 Jiménez 43, 2-0 Alcacer 69, 3-0
Jiménez 75, 4-0 Alcacer 77

19/3/10, Mourneview Park, Lurgan
Spain 0-1 Belgium
Goal(s): 0-1 Raman 63

19/3/10, The Oval, Belfast
Northern Ireland 1-0 Poland
Goal(s): 1-0 Ball 70

22/3/10, The Showgrounds, Coleraine
Poland 0-2 Spain
Goal(s): 0-1 Alcacer 3, 0-2 Alcacer 79(p)

22/3/10, Mourneview Park, Lurgan
Belgium 0-1 Northern Ireland
Goal(s): 0-1 McAlinden 43

Group 4 Table

		Pld	W	D	L	F	A	Pts
1	Spain	3	2	0	1	6	1	6
2	Belgium	3	2	0	1	3	1	6
3	Northern Ireland	3	2	0	1	2	4	6
4	Poland	3	0	0	3	0	5	0

Group 5

26/3/10, François Le Parco, La Rochelle
Wales 0-0 Norway

26/3/10, Complexe Sportif, Perigny
France 0-1 Turkey
Goal(s): 0-1 Derici 34

28/3/10, François Le Parco, La Rochelle
Turkey 1-1 Wales
Goal(s): 1-0 Derici 44, 1-1 March 57

28/3/10, Complexe Sportif, Perigny
France 1-0 Norway
Goal(s): 1-0 Dure 75(og)

31/3/10, François Le Parco, La Rochelle
Wales 0-4 France
Goal(s): 0-1 Koura 35, 0-2 Omrani 52, 0-3
Omrani 70, 0-4 Omrani 71

31/3/10, Complexe Sportif, Perigny
Norway 0-2 Turkey
Goal(s): 0-1 Yokuslu 11, 0-2 Azgar 44

Group 5 Table

		Pld	W	D	L	F	A	Pts
1	Turkey	3	2	1	0	4	1	7
2	France	3	2	0	1	5	1	6
3	Wales	3	0	2	1	1	5	2
4	Norway	3	0	1	2	0	3	1

Arlind Ajeti of Switzerland, who eliminated Germany in Group 6

Group 6

25/3/10, Esp, Baden
Hungary 0-1 Germany
Goal(s): 0-1 Pusch 17(p)

25/3/10, Trinermatten, Zofingen
Switzerland 1-2 Serbia
Goal(s): 1-0 Vuleta 10, 1-1 Nastasič 32,
1-2 Nastasič 60

27/3/10, Trinermatten, Zofingen
Hungary 0-0 Serbia

27/3/10, Brügglifeld, Aarau
Germany 0-1 Switzerland
Goal(s): 0-1 Savic 56

30/3/10, Esp, Baden
Switzerland 3-1 Hungary
Goal(s): 1-0 Vuleta 16, 2-0 Vuleta 23,
3-0 Savic 43, 3-1 Adorján 52

30/3/10, Brügglifeld, Aarau
Serbia 1-4 Germany
Goal(s): 0-1 Kittel 6, 0-2 Parker 18,
0-3 Bittencourt 30, 1-3 Georgijevič 35,
1-4 Younes 50

Group 6 Table

		Pld	W	D	L	F	A	Pts
1	Switzerland	3	2	0	1	5	3	6
2	Germany	3	2	0	1	5	2	6
3	Serbia	3	1	1	1	3	5	4
4	Hungary	3	0	1	2	1	4	1

Group 7

27/3/10, Pirelli Stadium, Burton-on-Trent
Slovakia 2-0 Malta
Goal(s): 1-0 Schranz 52, 2-0 Špilár 58

27/3/10, Sixfields, Northampton
England 4-0 Sweden
Goal(s): 1-0 Wickham 21, 2-0 Afobe 32,
3-0 Hall 73, 4-0 Keane 80+2

29/3/10, Sixfields, Northampton
Sweden 2-0 Slovakia
Goal(s): 1-0 Ohlander 13(p), 2-0 Söderqvist 55

29/3/10, Pirelli Stadium, Burton-on-Trent
England 5-0 Malta
Goal(s): 1-0 Aneke 20, 2-0 Keane 30,
3-0 Aneke 36, 4-0 Afobe 38, 5-0 Kane 72(p)

1/4/10, Sixfields, Northampton
Slovakia 0-2 England
Goal(s): 0-1 Wickham 60, 0-2 Kane 76

1/4/10, Pirelli Stadium, Burton-on-Trent
Malta 0-5 Sweden
Goal(s): 0-1 Azulay 24, 0-2 Sandberg
Magnusson 31, 0-3 Sandberg Magnusson 51,
0-4 Tönros 68, 0-5 Tönros 76

Group 7 Table

		Pld	W	D	L	F	A	Pts
1	England	3	3	0	0	11	0	9
2	Sweden	3	2	0	1	7	4	6
3	Slovakia	3	1	0	2	2	4	3
4	Malta	3	0	0	3	0	12	0

FINAL TOURNAMENT

GROUP A

Four former champions – France, Spain, Switzerland and Turkey – were drawn in this section, and it produced an enthralling contest.

France actually finished second in their elite round group, but Liechtenstein's decision to withdraw their team from the finals – on the grounds that they did not consider themselves sufficiently competitive - opened the door for the best runners-up to qualify for the first time. That gave France their chance, and for the fourth U17 finals running they found themselves in a group with Spain. Since they beat Spain in the 2004 final, France had not overcome their southern neighbours in this competition, and although Les Mini-Bleus had plenty of the play they went down 2-1. Juan Bernat's first-half header was cancelled out with a quarter of an hour to go by Anthony Koura, but

France's Wesley Yamnaine was then sent off and Spain striker Paco won it with six minutes left. It was more comfortable for Portugal against Switzerland as they streaked to a 3-0 win against a side who, since eliminating holders Germany in the elite round, had been beset by injuries and suspension. There was a Sporting Clube de Portugal theme to the goals, the first and third coming as Bruma set up Ricardo Esgaio and the second resulting from Betinho's assist for Mateus Fonseca; all four players hailed from the Lisbon club.

Swiss rolled

Switzerland, winners of the 2009 FIFA Under-17 World Cup in Nigeria, were effectively eliminated three days later after a 4-0 defeat by Spain. Valencia CF striker Paco, who had top-scored in qualifying with eight goals, took his finals tally to four with a hat-trick, striking twice before the break then again just after the interval. Not long afterwards he turned provider,

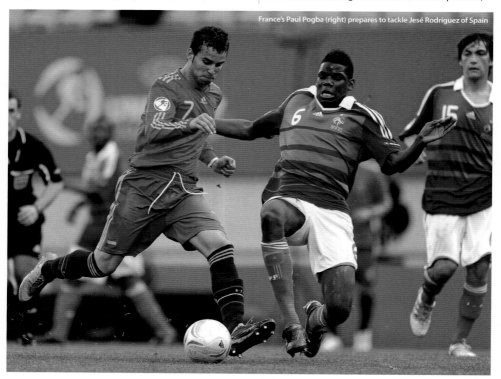

France's Paul Pogba (right) prepares to tackle Jesé Rodríguez of Spain

cleverly pulling back Jesé Rodríguez's scooped pass for Jorge Ortí to complete the scoring. That result gave Portugal the chance to clinch a last-four place with victory against France, but Rui Bento's side fell to third after losing 1-0. Manchester United FC midfielder Paul Pogba, only a substitute in the opening game, was given a start for France and he struck on 29 minutes. In the second half France had substitutes Billel Omrani and Vincent Leroux sent off but remained defiant and held out for victory.

Nothing was therefore decided before the final day, and during the first half of the simultaneous games Portugal moved up provisionally to second place as they held Spain 0-0 and France – without suspended Omrani, Leroux and Youssouf Sabaly – trailed Switzerland 1-0 to a deflected Aleksandar Zarkovic free-kick. However, within seven minutes of the restart France striker Yaya Sanogo, who had made his Ligue 1 debut for AJ Auxerre earlier in the month, scored two goals to put France in control and Koura clinched a 3-1 win just past the hour. A two-goal margin of victory could still have taken Portugal through, but despite their pressure it was Spain who scored twice in the last 11 minutes, winger Gerard producing a fine solo goal then scoring direct from a corner to ensure a 2-0 triumph and first place ahead of France.

Group A Results

18/5/10, Rheinpark, Vaduz
France 1-2 Spain
France: Aréola, Sabaly, Yamnaine, Doucouré, Le Pogam (Koura 53), Sanogo, Deligny (Arrondel 71), Digne, Obin, Rosenfelder (Pogba 41), Sorin. Coach: Guy Ferrier (FRA)
Spain: Ortolá, Edu, Ramalho, Víctor Álvarez (Galas 70), Sergi Darder, Jesé Rodríguez, Campaña, Paco, Bernat (Castro 56), Israel, Pablo (Gerard 58). Coach: Ginés Meléndez (ESP)
Goal(s): 0-1 Bernat 24, 1-1 Koura 65, 1-2 Paco 74
Red Card(s): Yamnaine 69 (France)
Yellow Card(s): Edu 21 (Spain), Sabaly 59 (France), Yamnaine 63 (France), Yamnaine 69 (France)
Referee: Norris (SCO)

18/5/10, Sportpark Eschen-Mauren, Eschen
Portugal 3-0 Switzerland
Portugal: André Pereira, Pedro Almeida, Tiago Ferreira, Tobias Figueiredo, Ricardo Esgaio, João Mário, Betinho (Sancidino Silva 54), Mateus Fonseca (Agostinho Cá 56), Daniel Martins, Bruma (Ivan Cavaleiro 61), João Carlos. Coach: Rui Bento (POR)
Switzerland: Brecher, Schmid, Desole, Zarkovic, Martinelli (Riva 62), Lavanchy, Zwimpfer, Kleiber (Karlen 72), Zangger, Miani (Adili 41), Geissmann. Coach: Heinz Moser (SUI)
Goal(s): 1-0 Ricardo Esgaio 25, 2-0 Mateus Fonseca 48, 3-0 Ricardo Esgaio 50
Yellow Card(s): Bruma 38 (Portugal), João Mário 45 (Portugal), Kleiber 64 (Switzerland), Zwimpfer 66 (Switzerland)
Referee: Kuchin (KAZ)

21/5/10, Rheinpark, Vaduz
Spain 4-0 Switzerland
Spain: Ortolá, Edu (Uxío 52), Ramalho, Víctor Álvarez, Jesé Rodríguez (Saúl Ñíguez 72), Campaña, Paco (Bernat 57), Israel, Castro, Gerard, Ortí. Coach: Ginés Meléndez (ESP)
Switzerland: Brecher, Schmid, Desole, Zarkovic, Ajeti, Martinelli, Lavanchy, Zwimpfer (Riva 50), Kleiber (Adili 54), Vuleta, Geissmann. Coach: Heinz Moser (SUI)
Goal(s): 1-0 Paco 12, 2-0 Paco 36, 3-0 Paco 43, 4-0 Ortí 48
Yellow Card(s): Zwimpfer 31 (Switzerland), Ajeti 70 (Switzerland), Desole 74 (Switzerland)
Referee: Munukka (FIN)

21/5/10, Sportpark Eschen-Mauren, Eschen
France 1-0 Portugal
France: Aréola, Sabaly, Arrondel, Pogba, Doucouré, Sanogo (Leroux 64), Deligny (Omrani 52), Digne, Obin, Sorin. Coach: Guy Ferrier (FRA)
Portugal: André Pereira, Pedro Almeida, Tiago Ferreira, Tobias Figueiredo, Ricardo Esgaio, João Mário, Betinho, Mateus Fonseca (Agostinho Cá 52), Daniel Martins (Sancidino Silva 61), Bruma, João Carlos (Rodolfo Simões 74). Coach: Rui Bento (POR)
Goal(s): 1-0 Pogba 29
Red Card(s): Omrani 56 (France), Leroux 80+4 (France)
Yellow Card(s): Tobias Figueiredo 15 (Portugal), Sabaly 32 (France), Deligny 45 (France), Tiago Ferreira 53 (Portugal), Digne 72 (France), Pedro Almeida 78 (Portugal)
Referee: Virant (BEL)

24/5/10, Sportpark Eschen-Mauren, Eschen
Switzerland 1-3 France
Switzerland: Brecher, Schmid (Riva 72), Desole, Zarkovic (Naili 51), Ajeti, Martinelli, Lavanchy (Adili 51), Kleiber, Vuleta, Zangger, Geissmann. Coach: Heinz Moser (SUI)
France: Dupé, Arrondel, Umtiti, Pogba, Doucouré (Rosenfelder 67), Sanogo (Le Pogam 76), Koura, Deligny, Digne, Obin (Yamnaine 72), Sorin. Coach: Guy Ferrier (FRA)
Goal(s): 1-0 Zarkovic 30, 1-1 Sanogo 43, 1-2 Sanogo 47, 1-3 Koura 64
Yellow Card(s): Desole 20 (Switzerland), Obin 22 (France), Pogba 62 (France), Schmid 70 (Switzerland)
Referee: Direktorenko (LVA)

24/5/10, Rheinpark, Vaduz
Spain 2-0 Portugal
Spain: Ortolá (Herrero 77), Edu, Ramalho, Víctor Álvarez, Jesé Rodríguez (Pablo 68), Campaña, Paco, Israel, Castro, Gerard, Ortí (Sergi Darder 59). Coach: Ginés Meléndez (ESP)
Portugal: André Pereira, Pedro Almeida (Ivan Cavaleiro 73), Tiago Ferreira, Tobias Figueiredo, Ricardo Esgaio, João Mário, Sancidino Silva (Betinho 62), Daniel Martins, Agostinho Cá, Bruma, João Carlos (Mateus Fonseca 59). Coach: Rui Bento (POR)
Goal(s): 1-0 Gerard 69, 2-0 Gerard 73
Yellow Card(s): Daniel Martins 38 (Portugal), Israel 58 (Spain), Jesé Rodríguez 67 (Spain)
Referee: Todorov (BUL)

Group A Table

	Pld	W	D	L	F	A	Pts
1 Spain	3	3	0	0	8	1	9
2 France	3	2	0	1	5	3	6
3 Portugal	3	1	0	2	3	3	3
4 Switzerland	3	0	0	3	1	10	0

GROUP B

A little bit of history was made on the opening day as for the first time in a UEFA final tournament Greece and Turkey came face to face.

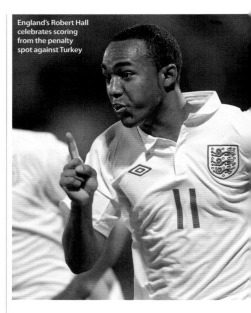

England's Robert Hall celebrates scoring from the penalty spot against Turkey

Turkey are regulars in the U17 finals, taking the 2005 title, but Greece were making their debut and they fell behind in rainy conditions on 16 minutes when Oğuzhan Azğar struck from distance to the delight of the noisy Turkish support. Turkey took this as their cue to dominate and on the hour mark Okan Derıcı strode down the left and sent in a low cross for captain Artun Akçakin to turn in. Two minutes later Dimitrios Diamantakos converted a penalty to get Greece back in the game but they lost defender Ioannis Polychronakis to a second bookable offence – a foul on substitute Recep Nıyaz, the youngest player ever to appear in a U17 finals at 15 years and 137 days. Turkey completed a 3-1 win with Artun's injury-time penalty. It was the same result in the other match as England overcame the Czech Republic. Although the Czechs scored first through Jakub Plšek on seven minutes, Ross Barkley equalised for England and the only side to win all six of their qualifiers ensured the points late on with further goals from Joshua McEachran and Benik Afobe.

England edge it

The Czech Republic now needed to respond against Turkey but could not make their first-half pressure tell and, just after the break, Artun pounced to give his side the lead. Turkey now retreated into defence and paid the price for their conservatism when, with ten minutes to go, Matěj Hybš's cross was headed in by Roman Haša for a 1-1 draw. England therefore had the opportunity to book their semi-final place – and eliminate Greece – with a victory in the evening game, and they duly edged a tight encounter 1-0 when Barkley produced a fine header after a 35th-minute cross from Everton colleague Luke Garbutt, who was celebrating his 17th birthday.

England took the opportunity to make the maximum possible seven changes to their starting line-up for their last group game against Turkey, who needed a point to make sure of progress and a win to pip John Peacock's side to first place. Turkey took a deserved lead just past the half-hour when Taşkın Çalış's deep corner found Servan Taştan, whose volley into the ground bounced high for Okan Derıcı to head in just ahead of stand-in England goalkeeper Jack Butland.

Within four minutes, though, England were level after some superb skill and a neat finish by Saido Berahino – only called up after the tournament had begun to replace injured Chuks Aneke. England were on top in the second half and secured victory through Robert Hall's 62nd-minute penalty following a foul by goalkeeper Alperen Uysal on Afobe. Had the Czech Republic beaten Greece by three goals, Turkey would have been in trouble, but instead the other concluding match finished 0-0. Tomáš Kalas's sending-off left the Czech Republic with ten men for the last 15 minutes and Greece almost clinched a valedictory victory.

Group B Results

18/5/10, Sportpark Eschen-Mauren, Eschen
Greece 1-3 Turkey
Greece: Kapino, Lykogiannis, Rougkalas, Polychronakis, Diamantakos, Arianoutsos, Kousidis (Provatidis 59), Marinakis, Mavrias (Gianniotas 73), Katidis, Stafylidis (Kaimakamoudis 41). Coach: Leonidas Vokolos (GRE)
Turkey: Alperen Uysal, Erhan Kartal, Onur Yavuz, Metin Aydin, Oğuzhan Azğar, Servan Taştan, Taşkın Çalış, Artun Akçakin, Çağrı Tekin (Bilal Gülden 80+1), Okan Derıcı (Rıdvan Armut 78), Okay Yokuşlu (Recep Nıyaz 67). Coach: Abdullah Ercan (TUR)
Goal(s): 0-1 Okay Yokuşlu 16, 0-2 Artun Akçakin 60, 1-2 Diamantakos 62(p), 1-3 Artun Akçakin 80+2(p)
Red Card(s): Polychronakis 79 (Greece)
Yellow Card(s): Taşkın Çalış 10 (Turkey), Arianoutsos 14 (Greece), Lykogiannis 40+1 (Greece), Polychronakis 46 (Greece), Polychronakis 79 (Greece)
Referee: Virant (BEL)

UEFA European Under-17 Championship

UNDER17.
CHAMPIONSHIP

18/5/10, Rheinpark, Vaduz
England 3-1 Czech Republic
England: Johnstone, Pilatos, Garbutt, Chalobah, Wisdom, Keane (Hall 58), Thorne (Thorpe 75), Afobe, McEachran (Williams 75), Barkley, Wickham. Coach: John Peacock (ENG)
Czech Republic: Veselý, Kalas, Mižič, Plšek, Krátký (Mariotti 65), Hurka, Mandula (Haša 77), Česlák, Hybš, F. Twardzik, P. Twardzik. Coach: Jiří Štol (CZE)
Goal(s): 0-1 Plšek 7, 1-1 Barkley 21, 2-1 McEachran 68, 3-1 Afobe 69
Yellow Card(s): Chalobah 7 (England), Mižič 31 (Czech Republic), Wickham 32 (England)
Referee: Todorov (BUL)

21/5/10, Sportpark Eschen-Mauren, Eschen
Turkey 1-1 Czech Republic
Turkey: Alperen Uysal, Erhan Kartal, Onur Yavuz, Metin Aydin, Oğuzhan Azğar, Servan Taştan, Taşkın Çalış, Artun Akçakin (Beykan Şimşek 75), Çağrı Tekin (Bilal Gülden 41), Okan Derıcı, Okay Yokuşlu (Recep Nıyaz 53). Coach: Abdullah Ercan (TUR)
Czech Republic: Veselý, Kalas, Plšek, Toms (Mandula 52), Krátký, Hurka, Česlák (P. Twardzik 64), Hybš, F. Twardzik, Haša, Mariotti (Kučera 73). Coach: Jiří Štol (CZE)
Goal(s): 1-0 Artun Akçakin 43, 1-1 Haša 70
Yellow Card(s): Artun Akçakin 63 (Turkey), Erhan Kartal 66 (Turkey), Recep Nıyaz 73 (Turkey), Servan Taştan 74 (Turkey)
Referee: Direktorenko (LVA)

21/5/10, Rheinpark, Vaduz
Greece 0-1 England
Greece: Kapino (Giannikoglou 40), Lykogiannis, Rougkalas, Bougaidis (Karagkounis 12), Fourlanos, Diamantakos, Arianoutsos (Stafylidis 52), Marinakis, Kaimakamoudis, Mavrias, Katidis. Coach: Leonidas Vokolos (GRE)
England: Johnstone, Pilatos, Garbutt, Coady, Chalobah, Wisdom, Keane (Williams 73), Afobe (Hall 51), McEachran (Thorne 80), Barkley, Wickham. Coach: John Peacock (ENG)
Goal(s): 0-1 Barkley 35
Yellow Card(s): Karagkounis 38 (Greece), Marinakis 74 (Greece)
Referee: Kuchin (KAZ)

24/5/10, Sportpark Eschen-Mauren, Eschen
Czech Republic 0-0 Greece
Czech Republic: Veselý (Adamuška 74), Kalas, Plšek, Krátký, Hurka, Kučera, Česlák (Mižič 67), Hybš, F. Twardzik, Haša (Štancl 50), Mariotti. Coach: Jiří Štol (CZE)
Greece: Giannikoglou, Karagkounis, Lykogiannis, Rougkalas, Polychronakis, Gianniotas (Mavrias 41), Fourlanos, Diamantakos, Kousidis (Kaimakamoudis 41), Marinakis, Katidis. Coach: Leonidas Vokolos (GRE)
Red Card(s): Kalas 65 (Czech Republic)
Yellow Card(s): Krátký 20 (Czech Republic), Hybš 47 (Czech Republic), Mariotti 50 (Czech Republic), Lykogiannis 57 (Greece), Rougkalas 78 (Greece), Kučera 80+1 (Czech Republic)
Referee: Norris (SCO)

24/5/10, Rheinpark, Vaduz
Turkey 1-2 England
Turkey: Alperen Uysal, Erhan Kartal, Onur Yavuz, Metin Aydin, Oğuzhan Azğar, Servan Taştan, Taşkın Çalış, Artun Akçakin (İlker Sayan 69), Çağrı Tekin (Recep Nıyaz 74), Okan Derıcı (Rıdvan Armut 77), Okay Yokuşlu. Coach: Abdullah Ercan (TUR)
England: Butland, Pilatos, Coady, Wisdom, Thorne, Afobe, Berahino (Garbutt 72), Hall, Gibson, Thorpe, Williams (Barkley 66). Coach: John Peacock (ENG)

Goal(s): 1-0 Okan Derıcı 31, 1-1 Berahino 35, 1-2 Hall 62(p)
Yellow Card(s): Coady 9 (England)
Referee: Munukka (FIN)

Group B Table

	Pld	W	D	L	F	A	Pts
1 England	3	3	0	0	6	2	9
2 Turkey	3	1	1	1	5	4	4
3 Czech Republic	3	0	2	1	2	4	2
4 Greece	3	0	1	2	1	4	1

SEMI-FINALS

England restored their six rested outfield players for the first semi-final against France, and, duly recharged, they dominated the early stages.

William Keane had an early header saved but he was to be withdrawn due to injury soon afterwards. No matter. Robert Hall came on and proved just as adept on the right as he had against Turkey. The deadlock was broken on 23 minutes, Benik Afobe picking up the ball near the France box and holding it up long enough for Connor Wickham to get into position. Afobe fed the Ipswich Town FC striker, whose angled shot found the net. Jack Butland, retaining his place in goal, made a superb save from Yaya Sanogo, and just before the break Wickham produced an identical finish to his first goal, set up this time by Conor Coady. France emerged for the second half in determined

Spain's Paco fires in the first of his two goals in the semi-final against Turkey

fashion, and with 24 minutes to go they were back in the game when Abdoulaye Doucouré's cross was headed in by Paul Pogba. England were now clinging on and they survived several scares, not least when Butland was fortunate to block a point-blank mis-kick from team-mate Nathaniel Chalobah. But a place in the final was England's as France's comeback heroics for once deserted them.

Spain on top

That evening, also at the Rheinpark stadium, Spain faced a Turkey team missing midfielder Çağrı Tekin due to a hamstring injury. Turkey almost took an early lead as Artun Akçakin broke clear and shot just wide, but Spain were not to be kept quiet for long and soon began to boss the game, Alperen Uysal having to deny both José Campaña and Jorge Ortí. However, the Turkey goalkeeper was beaten by Jesé Rodríguez on 14 minutes following a run from the left. Spain now looked to close the game by dominating possession and waiting for a Turkey error, but after half-time coach Abdullah Ercan introduced Recep Nıyaz and his side started to stage a fightback. Indeed, within seven minutes of the restart they drew level courtesy of Taşkın Çalış's powerful strike. Suddenly Spain were uneasy but within four minutes Turkey lost Erhan Kartal to a second booking for a foul on Jesé and the game swung back the other way. Just past the hour mark Jesé set up Paco to put Spain back ahead, and three minutes later Okay Yokuşlu brought down Gerard inside the box. Paco converted the penalty to

Connor Wickham (No17) scored England's winning goal in the final against Spain

send Spain into the final and, in so doing, become the first player to reach 14 goals, including qualifying, in the history of the U17 Championship.

Semi-Final Results

27/5/10, Rheinpark, Vaduz
England 2-1 France
England: Butland, Pilatos, Garbutt, Coady, Chalobah, Wisdom, Keane (Hall 16) (Gibson 81), Afobe, McEachran (Thorne 68), Barkley, Wickham. Coach: John Peacock (ENG)
France: Aréola, Sabaly, Arrondel, Umtiti, Pogba, Doucouré, Sanogo, Koura (Omrani 68), Obin, Rosenfelder (Deligny 46), Sorin. Coach: Guy Ferrier (FRA)
Goal(s): 1-0 Wickham 23, 2-0 Wickham 40, 2-1 Pogba 56
Yellow Card(s): Butland 80+2 (England)
Referee: Todorov (BUL)

27/5/10, Rheinpark, Vaduz
Spain 3-1 Turkey
Spain: Ortolá, Edu, Ramalho (Uxío 41), Víctor Álvarez, Sergi Darder (Castro 67), Jesé Rodríguez, Campaña, Paco, Israel, Gerard, Ortí (Pablo 55). Coach: Ginés Meléndez (ESP)
Turkey: Alperen Uysal, Erhan Kartal, Onur Yavuz, Oğuzhan Azğar, Servan Taştan, Taşkın Çalış, Artun Akçakin, Okan Derıcı (Metin Aydin 54), Okay Yokuşlu (Rıdvan Armut 72), Bilal Gülden (Recep Nıyaz 41), Kani Özdıl. Coach: Abdullah Ercan (TUR)
Goal(s): 1-0 Jesé Rodríguez 11, 1-1 Taşkın Çalış 47, 2-1 Paco 63, 3-1 Paco 66(p)
Red Card(s): Erhan Kartal 51 (Turkey)
Yellow Card(s): Erhan Kartal 28 (Turkey), Erhan Kartal 51 (Turkey), Artun Akçakin 51 (Turkey), Recep Nıyaz 73 (Turkey)
Referee: Norris (SCO)

FINAL

Heavy rain had fallen in the hours leading up to kick-off of the final – the tournament in that sense ending as it began - and in the early stages the surface water seemed to trouble England to a much greater degree than Spain.

Gerard gave left-back Luke Garbutt a tough time while on the other flank Jesé Rodríguez got around Bruno Pilatos and crossed for Jorge Ortí to turn the ball wide. England eventually settled, however, with Joshua McEachran finding Connor Wickham whose strike was deflected over.

Wisdom redemption

There was relief for England in the 21st minute as José Campaña's free-kick struck the head of Ross Barkley before hitting the outside of the post. However, the resulting corner was played short, and Gerard's cross from the left was inadvertently deflected in by Andre

UEFA European Under-17 Championship

England captain Conor Coady lifts the UEFA Under-17 Championship trophy

Wisdom to put Spain 1-0 up. Redemption, however, was not long in coming for the Liverpool FC defender. William Keane, who passed a late fitness test, helped win England a corner and Josh McEachran sent it in perfectly for Wisdom to head in the equaliser. The goal came against the run of play, but England found new zest from it and McEachran shot over from distance before Keane crossed for Wickham, who forced Adrián Ortolá into a save.

If Spain thought they could swiftly restore their superiority in the second half, Wickham soon set them straight. Entering the left of the box parallel to the goal he went past three defenders before giving Ortolá no chance with a superb finish to give England a 2-1 lead. Spain sent on Pablo, a useful introduction after they had lost the lead in the semi-final against Turkey, and Gerard was soon back in action, curling a shot just wide. Spain were not coming to terms with Wickham's combination of skill and size, though, and he got around the defence again only to see his effort on goal float off target. Gerard responded, outsmarting Bruno Pilatos and looping a shot above the angle of post and bar. Soon afterwards Gerard blazed off target when Butland could only palm a Pablo cross.

England hold on

Jesé was not having the same impact as his fellow winger but he showed fine skill to create a chance that was equally well saved by Butland, who had begun the finals as England's second-choice 'keeper. He watched on helplessly, though, as England survived a scare when Wisdom's clearance hit Garbutt and then the post. Spain were pushing hard to equalise, but Paco was frustrated in his attempt to add to his six goals in Liechtenstein and England stoutly held on to their lead through to the final whistle, claiming a first men's European title for the country in 17 years.

Final Result

30/5/10, Rheinpark, Vaduz
Spain 1-2 England
Attendance: 3990
Spain: Ortolá, Edu (Bernat 72), Ramalho, Víctor Álvarez, Sergi Darder, Jesé Rodríguez, Campaña, Paco, Israel, Gerard, Ortí (Pablo 45). Coach: Ginés Meléndez (ESP)
England: Butland, Pilatos, Garbutt, Coady, Chalobah, Wisdom, Keane (Thorne 66), Afobe (Hall 72), McEachran (Thorpe 79), Barkley, Wickham. Coach: John Peacock (ENG)
Goal(s): 1-0 Gerard 22, 1-1 Wisdom 30, 1-2 Wickham 42
Yellow Card(s): McEachran 62 (England), Garbutt 69 (England)
Referee: Munukka (FIN)

TOP GOALSCORERS

6 Paco (Spain)

3 Artun Akçakin (Turkey)
   Connor Wickham (England)
   Gerard (Spain)

UEFA WOMEN'S EURO

2009

Continuing a reign which began in 1995, Germany won the EURO crown for the fifth consecutive time with a 6-2 defeat of England in the final. That result in Helsinki may have been harsh on Hope Powell's side but there was no doubting the clinical nature of Germany's run, from their 34 goals in eight qualifying wins to ten more in three group victories and their gritty knockout eliminations of Italy and Norway. However, while Germany maintained their dominance, there were plenty of surprises in the first finals to feature 12 rather than eight contenders – England's nerve-shredding run to the final, the Netherlands reaching the last four on their debut, and Norway silencing their doubters to make up the semi-final quartet.

CHAPTER
09

GROUP STAGE

Group A

Two newcomers to this level opened the tournament, with the Netherlands making a superb start by overcoming Ukraine 2-0 thanks to goals in the first nine minutes from Kerstin van de Ven and Karin Stevens.

However, Ukraine did set two records on their debut: Olena Mazurenko became the oldest player in UEFA European Women's Championship finals history aged 39 years and 303 days (she was to add six days to that record), while Oksana Yakovishyn's appearance made her the youngest at 16 years and 156 days. Another milestone was set that day at Helsinki's Olympic Stadium, where the biggest crowd to watch a women's international in Finland, 16,324, saw the hosts beat Denmark courtesy of Maija Saari's 49th-minute free-kick that floated in from wide on the right.

Hosts progress

Denmark bounced back three days later, defeating Ukraine 2-1 with Maiken Pape's 87th-minute goal;

Daryna Apanaschenko having cancelled out Camilla Sand Andersen's opener. Finland thus knew a victory against the Netherlands would confirm their quarter-final place as group winners with a game to spare. They made the perfect start towards reaching that objective when, on seven minutes, Laura Österberg Kalmari headed in Petra Vaelma's cross. Finland pushed for a second but in the 25th minute their lead was wiped out with a superb solo run from Van de Ven that began in her own half and ended with a low shot into the left-hand corner. Vaelma then hit the crossbar but on 69 minutes Finland were back in front, Österberg Kalmari this time turning in Saari's cross. Netherlands coach Vera Pauw knew her side remained ahead of Denmark on goal difference and told her players not to push for an equaliser and thus run the risk of jeopardising second place ahead of their final match.

Finland met Ukraine with the hosts through and the newcomers out, but Lyudmyla Pekur's goal ensured her side at least departed with a first win. In contrast, the stakes were high in Lahti, where Denmark needed to beat the Netherlands. Although Pape hit the crossbar for a dominant Denmark team, Sylvia Smit half-volleyed the Netherlands in front before the hour,

Finland players crowd around Maija Saari (hidden) after her winning strike against Denmark

and eight minutes later Manon Melis doubled the lead. Johanna Rasmussen, so impressive on the wing in all of Denmark's games, pulled one back with 19 minutes left but the Netherlands clung on. Denmark now had two nervous days before discovering if they were to progress as one of the two best third-placed sides. The results, however, would not go their way.

Group A Results

23/8/09, Turku Stadium, Turku
Ukraine 0-2 Netherlands
Attendance: 2571
Ukraine: Baranova, Mazurenko, Chorna, Pekur, Khodyreva, Boychenko, Dyatel (Vasylyuk 83), Zinchenko, Lyshafay, Apanaschenko, Sukhorukova (Yakovishyn 46). Coach: Anatoliy Kutsev (UKR)
Netherlands: Geurts, Bito, Koster, Meulen, Hogewoning, Hoogendijk, Kiesel-Griffioen, Van de Ven (Pieëte 79), Melis, Stevens (De Ridder 86), Smit. Coach: Vera Pauw (NED)
Goal(s): 0-1 Van de Ven 4, 0-2 Stevens 9
Yellow Card(s): Hogewoning 35 (Netherlands), Boychenko 39 (Ukraine), Dyatel 54 (Ukraine), Pekur 80 (Ukraine)
Referee: Dorcioman (ROU)

23/8/09, Olympic Stadium, Helsinki
Finland 1-0 Denmark
Attendance: 16324
Finland: Korpela, Vaelma, Julin (Sjölund 84), Valkonen, Salmén, Mäkinen, Österberg Kalmari, Westerlund (Lehtinen 73), Sainio (Talonen 60), Saari. Coach: Michael Käls (FIN)
Denmark: Johansen, Brogaard, K. Pedersen, M. Jensen (Nadim 72), Røddik Hansen, Paaske-Sørensen, Rydahl Bukh (M. Pedersen 89), Pape, Sand Andersen, J. Rasmussen, T. Rasmussen (Veje 46). Coach: Kenneth Heiner-Møller (DEN)
Goal(s): 1-0 Saari 49
Yellow Card(s): Westerlund 87 (Finland)
Referee: Damkova (CZE)

26/8/09, Helsinki Football Stadium, Helsinki
Ukraine 1-2 Denmark
Attendance: 1372
Ukraine: Baranova, Mazurenko, Chorna, Yakovishyn (Boychenko 64), Pekur, Khodyreva, Dyatel, Zinchenko, Tytova, Lyshafay, Apanaschenko. Coach: Anatoliy Kutsev (UKR)
Denmark: Johansen, Brogaard, K. Pedersen, M. Jensen, Røddik Hansen, Paaske-Sørensen, Rydahl Bukh, Pape, Sand Andersen, Nadim (Veje 56), J. Rasmussen (L. Jensen 90+1). Coach: Kenneth Heiner-Møller (DEN)
Goal(s): 0-1 Sand Andersen 49, 1-1 Apanaschenko 62, 1-2 Pape 87
Yellow Card(s): Khodyreva 29 (Ukraine), Chorna 87 (Ukraine)
Referee: Gaál (HUN)

26/8/09, Olympic Stadium, Helsinki
Netherlands 1-2 Finland
Attendance: 16148
Netherlands: Geurts, Bito, Koster, Meulen, Hogewoning, Hoogendijk, Kiesel-Griffioen, Van de Ven, Melis, Stevens (De Ridder 68), Smit. Coach: Vera Pauw (NED)
Finland: Korpela, Vaelma, Julin (Rantanen 78), Valkonen, Salmén, Mäkinen, Österberg Kalmari, Westerlund (Sjölund 46), Sällström, Sainio, Saari. Coach: Michael Käls (FIN)
Goal(s): 0-1 Österberg Kalmari 7, 1-1 Van de Ven 25, 1-2 Österberg Kalmari 69
Referee: Palmqvist (SWE)

29/8/09, Olympic Stadium, Helsinki
Finland 0-1 Ukraine
Attendance: 15318
Finland: Meriluoto, Vaelma, Julin, Salmén (Niemi 58), Mäkinen (Sällström 46), Nokso-Koivisto (Talonen 54), Österberg Kalmari, Rantanen, Hyyrynen, Sjölund, Saari. Coach: Michael Käls (FIN)
Ukraine: Zvarych (Baranova 39), Mazurenko, Chorna, Yakovishyn (Boychenko 77), Pekur, Khodyreva, Dyatel, Zinchenko, Vaschenko (Vasylyuk 85), Lyshafay, Apanaschenko. Coach: Anatoliy Kutsev (UKR)
Goal(s): 0-1 Pekur 69
Yellow Card(s): Vaelma 76 (Finland)
Referee: Avdonchenko (RUS)

29/8/09, Lahti Stadium, Lahti
Denmark 1-2 Netherlands
Attendance: 1712
Denmark: Johansen, Brogaard, K. Pedersen, Røddik Hansen, Paaske-Sørensen, Rydahl Bukh, Pape, Sand Andersen, Nadim (Veje 46), J. Rasmussen, Troelsgaard Nielsen (M. Pedersen 72). Coach: Kenneth Heiner-Møller (DEN)
Netherlands: Geurts, Bito, Koster, Meulen, Hogewoning, Hoogendijk, Kiesel-Griffioen, Van de Ven (Van den Heiligenberg 76), Melis, Smit (Pieëte 90+1), De Ridder (Stevens 46). Coach: Vera Pauw (NED)
Goal(s): 0-1 Smit 58, 0-2 Melis 66, 1-2 J. Rasmussen 71
Yellow Card(s): Rydahl Bukh 73 (Denmark), Stevens 84 (Netherlands)
Referee: Palmqvist (SWE)

Group A Table

	Pld	W	D	L	F	A	Pts
1 Finland	3	2	0	1	3	2	6
2 Netherlands	3	2	0	1	5	3	6
3 Denmark	3	1	0	2	3	4	3
4 Ukraine	3	1	0	2	2	4	3

Group B

The two teams that met in the 2005 final, as well as in their opening match in England, were pitted against each other again.

Just as on those two occasions, Germany got the better of Norway, who came into the tournament in wretched form with several key players having bowed out of international football since qualification. Linda Bresonik broke the deadlock from the penalty spot after Birgit Prinz was fouled just past the half-hour, and the score remained that way until the last minute when Germany goalkeeper Nadine Angerer denied teenage substitute Cecilie Pedersen - a third-division player whose unexpected international debut had only come the previous week - and, on the break, Fatmire Bajramaj doubled the lead. In injury time Anja Mittag and fellow substitute Bajramaj both struck to make it 4-0. Finals debutants Iceland took the lead six minutes in against France through Hólmfríður Magnúsdóttir, but either side of the break Camille Abily and Sonia Bompastor converted penalties before Louisa Nécib made it 3-1. Iceland won a penalty of their own but Sarah Bouhaddi denied Margrét Lára Vidarsdóttir, the top scorer in qualifying, whose tally had been a winner against France.

Norway's 18-year-old starlet Cecilie Pedersen (centre) takes on the Iceland defence

No comeback

France found themselves behind early in their next game against Germany to Inka Grings but this time there was no comeback as Annike Krahn and Melanie Behringer made it 3-0 before half-time. Bresonik added a fourth from the spot, and after Gaëtane Thiney pulled one back, substitute Simone Laudehr completed a 5-1 win at the death. That proved enough for Germany to clinch first place as Iceland, despite a lively performance, were beaten 1-0 by Norway. Iceland did hit the post through a floated Dóra María Lárusdóttir cross on 12 minutes but fell to a fine turn and finish from 18-year-old Pedersen just before the break.

Iceland could not now avoid elimination in fourth place but, nonetheless, went down fighting against Germany to a 50th-minute Grings goal, the holders' coach Silvia Neid giving her fringe players an outing, with even matchwinner Grings starting on the bench. Qualification was at stake in the other match and Norway – needing a win for second place – led France after four minutes thanks to Lene Storløkken. Twelve minutes later Abily equalised with a shot while lying on the ground, sending France through as runners-up on goal difference. Norway, though, knew they would join them in the quarter-finals having finished third with a better record than Denmark.

Group B Results

24/8/09, Tampere Stadium, Tampere
Germany 4-0 Norway
Attendance: 6552
Germany: Angerer, Peter, Krahn, Behringer (Mittag 86), Grings (Da Mbabi 65), Prinz, Bresonik, Kulig, Hingst, Garefrekes (Bajramaj 66), Schmidt. Coach: Silvia Neid (GER)
Norway: Hjelmseth, Akerhaugen, Stensland, Huse, Rønning, Gulbrandsen, Herlovsen, Løvbræk (Pedersen 72), Thorsnes (Kaurin 58), Mjelde, Storløkken (Giske 80). Coach: Bjarne Berntsen (NOR)
Goal(s): 1-0 Bresonik 33(p), 2-0 Bajramaj 90, 3-0 Mittag 90+2, 4-0 Bajramaj 90+4
Yellow Card(s): Kulig 5 (Germany), Mjelde 33 (Norway), Bresonik 64 (Germany)
Referee: Ihringova (ENG)

24/8/09, Tampere Stadium, Tampere
Iceland 1-3 France
Attendance: 1460
Iceland: Helgadóttir, G.S. Gunnarsdóttir, Ó. Vidarsdóttir, Gardarsdóttir, Magnúsdóttir (Fridriksdóttir 89), K. Jónsdóttir, M. Vidarsdóttir, Lárusdóttir, S. Gunnarsdóttir (E. Arnardóttir 76), E. Sigurdardóttir, Ómarsdóttir (Hönnudóttir 71). Coach: Sigurdur Ragnar Eyjólfsson (ISL)
France: Bouhaddi, Meilleroux, Georges, Soubeyrand, Franco (Viguier 37), Bompastor, Herbert (Brétigny 40), Abily, Thomis (Le Sommer 86), Nécib, Bussaglia. Coach: Bruno Bini (FRA)
Goal(s): 1-0 Magnúsdóttir 6, 1-1 Abily 18(p), 1-2 Bompastor 53(p), 1-3 Nécib 67
Yellow Card(s): Ó. Vidarsdóttir 17 (Iceland), Thomis 17 (France)
Referee: Avdonchenko (RUS)

27/8/09, Tampere Stadium, Tampere
France 1-5 Germany
Attendance: 3331
France: Bouhaddi, Meilleroux, Georges, Viguier (Lepailleur 68), Soubeyrand, Bompastor, Abily, Thomis, Nécib (Le Sommer 68), Bussaglia (Brétigny 79), Thiney. Coach: Bruno Bini (FRA)
Germany: Angerer, Peter, Krahn, Behringer (Laudehr 46), Grings (Da Mbabi 77), Prinz, Bresonik, Kulig (Bartusiak 66), Hingst, Garefrekes, Schmidt. Coach: Silvia Neid (GER)
Goal(s): 0-1 Grings 9, 0-2 Krahn 17, 0-3 Behringer 45+1, 0-4 Bresonik 47(p), 1-4 Thiney 51, 1-5 Laudehr 90+1
Yellow Card(s): Bompastor 47 (France), Bartusiak 68 (Germany)
Referee: Monzul (UKR)

27/8/09, Lahti Stadium, Lahti
Iceland 0-1 Norway
Attendance: 1399
Iceland: Helgadóttir, G.S. Gunnarsdóttir, Ó. Vidarsdóttir, Gardarsdóttir, Magnúsdóttir, Stefánsdóttir (Logadóttir 60), K. Jónsdóttir, M. Vidarsdóttir, Lárusdóttir, S. Gunnarsdóttir, E. Sigurdardóttir (Hönnudóttir 82). Coach: Sigurdur Ragnar Eyjólfsson (ISL)
Norway: Hjelmseth, Akerhaugen, Stensland, Giske, Huse, Rønning, Gulbrandsen, Herlovsen (Isaksen 86), Mjelde, Storløkken, Pedersen (Lie 90+1). Coach: Bjarne Berntsen (NOR)
Goal(s): 0-1 Pedersen 45
Yellow Card(s): Rønning 80 (Norway)
Referee: Dorcioman (ROU)

30/8/09, Tampere Stadium, Tampere
Germany 1-0 Iceland
Attendance: 3101
Germany: Angerer, Bartusiak, Peter, Krahn, Laudehr, Prinz (Grings 46; Da Mbabi 59), Müller, Fuss (Stegemann 46), Mittag, Hingst, Bajramaj. Coach: Silvia Neid (GER)
Iceland: G. Gunnarsdóttir, G.S. Gunnarsdóttir, Ó. Vidarsdóttir, Gardarsdóttir, Magnúsdóttir (Hönnudóttir 71), K. Jónsdóttir, M. Vidarsdóttir, Lárusdóttir (E. Arnardóttir 71), S. Gunnarsdóttir, Ómarsdóttir (Fridriksdóttir 87), Atladóttir. Coach: Sigurdur Ragnar Eyjólfsson (ISL)
Goal(s): 1-0 Grings 50
Yellow Card(s): Atladóttir 49 (Iceland)
Referee: Heikkinen (FIN)

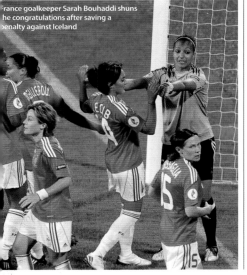
France goalkeeper Sarah Bouhaddi shuns the congratulations after saving a penalty against Iceland

30/8/09, Helsinki Football Stadium, Helsinki
Norway 1-1 France
Attendance: 1537
Norway: Hjelmseth, Akerhaugen, Stensland, Giske, Huse, Rønning, Gulbrandsen, Herlovsen (Løvbræk 89), Mjelde, Storløkken, Pedersen (Kaurin 46). Coach: Bjarne Berntsen (NOR)
France: Bouhaddi, Meilleroux, Georges, Soubeyrand, Bompastor, Abily, Thomis, Nécib, Bussaglia, Thiney (Le Sommer 83), Blanc. Coach: Bruno Bini (FRA)
Goal(s): 1-0 Storløkken 4, 1-1 Abily 16
Referee: Ihringova (ENG)

Group B Table

	Pld	W	D	L	F	A	Pts
1 Germany	3	3	0	0	10	1	9
2 France	3	1	1	1	5	7	4
3 Norway	3	1	1	1	2	5	4
4 Iceland	3	0	0	3	1	5	0

Group C

Italy had been eliminated without a point in 2005 but they opened their campaign this time with a surprise 2-1 win against one of the pre-tournament favourites, England, who had Casey Stoney sent off on 28 minutes for a foul on Melanie Gabbiadini.

Ten minutes later Fara Williams put England ahead from the spot but early in the second half Patrizia Panico's fine finish levelled matters and eight minutes remained when Alessia Tuttino's 25-metre shot won it for the Azzurre. Sweden avoided any upsets against Russia, defender Charlotte Rohlin and captain Victoria Sandell Svensson putting them two up within 15 minutes and Caroline Seger securing a 3-0 victory near the end.

Sensational goal

Sweden ensured a quarter-final berth three days later, again going 2-0 up before the midway point of the first half, Lotta Schelin and Kosovare Asllani scoring to decide the game against Italy. There were two other early goals in Helsinki, where Ksenia Tsybutovich's bullet header and Olesya Kurochkina's subtle strike put Russia in control against England, who knew defeat meant elimination. Maybe that spurred Powell's side into action because by half-time they led 3-2. Karen Carney pulled one back with an angled shot and then set up Eniola Aluko to equalise before Kelly Smith, an injury doubt before the tournament and only a substitute against Italy, scored a sensational goal from the centre circle, controlling Elena Kochneva's drop-kick in the air and half-volleying it straight back over the keeper's head. The second half was just as frantic but, to England's relief, goalless.

Unlike in the other two groups, the simultaneous matches to conclude this pool both had plenty at stake. Russia were hoping for a win against Italy in Helsinki - which would have needed to be by three goals if England did not lose to Sweden - and they began in a lively manner. Over in Turku, meanwhile, England captain Faye White put her side ahead on 28 minutes before Sandell Svensson equalised from the penalty spot late in the first half. A draw was enough to take England through at least in third place and the main interest now switched to the Finnish capital. Russia had to go for broke but could not produce a breakthrough and, with 12 minutes left, Italy took the lead, Gabbiadini pouncing on Elisabetta Tona's parried header. Substitute Tatiana Zorri's clever free-kick then sealed a 2-0 win for Italy and second place behind Sweden after their draw with England.

Group C Results

25/8/09, Lahti Stadium, Lahti
England 1-2 Italy
Attendance: 2950
England: Brown, A. Scott, Stoney, F. Williams, Asante (Unitt 73), Carney, Chapman, Aluko (K. Smith 46), S. Smith (Sanderson 85), J. Scott, White. Coach: Hope Powell (ENG)
Italy: Picarelli, Gama, D'Adda, Tuttino, Tona, Schiavi, Domenichetti (Parisi 53), Gabbiadini (Manieri 90+3), Panico, Zorri, Pini (Guagni 77). Coach: Pietro Ghedin (ITA)
Goal(s): 1-0 F. Williams 38(p), 1-1 Panico 56, 1-2 Tuttino 82
Red Card(s): Stoney 28 (England)
Yellow Card(s): F. Williams 65 (England), D'Adda 90 (Italy)
Referee: Steinhaus (GER)

25/8/09, Turku Stadium, Turku
Sweden 3-0 Russia
Attendance: 4697
Sweden: Lindahl, Rohlin, Paulson, Seger, Thunebro, S. Larsson, Schelin, Asllani (Nilsson 76), Sandell Svensson (Fischer 87), Sjögran, Dahlkvist (Liljegärd 69). Coach: Thomas Dennerby (SWE)
Russia: Kochneva, Skotnikova (Kharchenko 87), Shmachkova, Savchenkova, Fomina, Kurochkina (Danilova 46), Poryadina, Petrova (Terekhova 62), Pertseva, Tsybutovich, Morozova. Coach: Igor Shalimov (RUS)
Goal(s): 1-0 Rohlin 5, 2-0 Sandell Svensson 15, 3-0 Seger 82
Referee: Heikkinen (FIN)

28/8/09, Turku Stadium, Turku
Italy 0-2 Sweden
Attendance: 5947
Italy: Picarelli, Gama, D'Adda, Tuttino, Tona, Schiavi, Domenichetti, Gabbiadini (Fuselli 69), Panico, Zorri (Parisi 75), Pini. Coach: Pietro Ghedin (ITA)
Sweden: Lindahl, Rohlin, Segerström, Paulson, Seger, Thunebro, Schelin, Asllani (Liljegärd 79), Sandell Svensson, Sjögran (Fors 89), Dahlkvist (Fischer 66). Coach: Thomas Dennerby (SWE)
Goal(s): 0-1 Schelin 9, 0-2 Asllani 19
Yellow Card(s): Fischer 85 (Sweden)
Referee: Steinhaus (GER)

28/8/09, Helsinki Football Stadium, Helsinki
England 3-2 Russia
Attendance: 1462
England: Brown, A. Scott, F. Williams, Johnson, Carney, Chapman, Aluko, K. Smith, S. Smith (Clarke 66), White, Unitt. Coach: Hope Powell (ENG)

Sweden go 1-0 up against Russia in Turku

Russia: Kochneva, Skotnikova, Shmachkova, Savchenkova, Fomina (Barbashina 76), Kurochkina, Poryadina (Myskiv 90), Pertseva, Danilova (Petrova 43), Tsybutovich, Morozova. Coach: Igor Shalimov (RUS)
Goal(s): 0-1 Tsybutovich 2, 0-2 Kurochkina 22, 1-2 Carney 24, 2-2 Aluko 32, 3-2 K. Smith 42
Referee: Damkova (CZE)

31/8/09, Olympic Stadium, Helsinki
Russia 0-2 Italy
Attendance: 1112
Russia: Todua, Kozhnikova, Skotnikova (Sochneva 46), Savchenkova (Barbashina 68), Fomina, Kurochkina, Poryadina (Danilova 60), Petrova, Pertseva, Tsybutovich, Morozova. Coach: Igor Shalimov (RUS)
Italy: Picarelli, Gama, D'Adda, Tuttino (Zorri 74), Tona, Schiavi, Domenichetti, Gabbiadini, Panico, Pini (Guagni 64), Carissimi. Coach: Pietro Ghedin (ITA)
Goal(s): 0-1 Gabbiadini 77, 0-2 Zorri 90+3
Yellow Card(s): Carissimi 49 (Italy), Pertseva 77 (Russia), Tsybutovich 90+2 (Russia)
Referee: Gaál (HUN)

31/8/09, Turku Stadium, Turku
Sweden 1-1 England
Attendance: 6142
Sweden: Lindahl, Rohlin, Segerström, Paulson, Seger, Thunebro, Schelin (Lindén 90+3), Asllani (Nilsson 68), Sandell Svensson, Sjögran, Dahlkvist (Landström 60). Coach: Thomas Dennerby (SWE)
England: Brown, A. Scott, Stoney, F. Williams, Johnson, Carney, Chapman, Aluko (Westwood 65), K. Smith, S. Smith (Clarke 90+1), White. Coach: Hope Powell (ENG)
Goal(s): 0-1 White 28, 1-1 Sandell Svensson 40(p)
Yellow Card(s): Sjögran 27 (Sweden), Asllani 64 (Sweden)
Referee: Monzul (UKR)

Group C Table

	Pld	W	D	L	F	A	Pts
1 Sweden	3	2	1	0	6	1	7
2 Italy	3	2	0	1	4	3	6
3 England	3	1	1	1	5	5	4
4 Russia	3	0	0	3	2	8	0

QUARTER-FINALS

England knew they needed to silence the Turku crowd early against Finland, and a superb team move after 14 minutes was finished coolly by Eniola Aluko.

There was a blow to England when captain Faye White was forced off after taking a blow to her face in the 35th minute but they doubled their lead early in the second half, Fara Williams getting first to the rebound after Tinja-Riikka Korpela saved from Katie Chapman. Finland substitute Annica Sjölund bundled in a 66th-minute corner but virtually from the restart Aluko set off on a mazy run which ended with an accurate strike. The hosts rallied again with 11 minutes left when Linda Sällström headed in a corner, but Rachel Brown in the England goal stood firm thereafter to end Finland's campaign.

Penalty shoot-out

Goals were at more of a premium that evening in Tampere. Netherlands coach Vera Pauw had been staunch in the defence of her hitherto cautious tactics during nearly half an hour of questioning from Dutch journalists following the defeat of Denmark and stuck with that approach against France despite the absence of regular goalkeeper Sarah Bouhaddi through injury. It was the Dutch No1 Loes Guerts who was the busier, denying Camille Abily, while Gaëtane Thiney shot wide. Manon Melis embarked on a solo run that forced Bouhaddi's replacement, Céline Deville, into action but the Netherlands were defending staunchly, marshalled by captain Daphne

Koster. The game was goalless into extra time and despite Candie Herbert heading just past the post in the 119th minute, penalties were needed. Both teams converted their first four spot kicks, only to each miss their next two. Herbert then shot over and Anouk Hoogendijk converted, ensuring the Netherlands emulated Finland's feat of 2005, reaching the last four on their finals debut.

Germany, by contrast, had not missed a semi-final since 1987 and that run looked certain to be extended when Inka Grings put them ahead against Italy in Lahti four minutes in, receiving Melanie Behringer's pass and producing a low shot on the turn. The holders were unlikely to be satisfied with that and stretched Italy in their push for a second. That goal arrived two minutes after the interval and again Grings was the scorer. Half-time substitute Simone Laudher delivered a cross from the left that deflected off Marta Carissimi into the path of the grateful Grings, who was firmly on course to be top scorer for the second straight finals. In the 63rd minute Italy had a lifeline, however, when Melanie Gabbiadini found Patrizia Panico to reduce the arrears. The Azzurri captain would have equalised in added time with a diving header but for a superb stop by Nadine Angerer.

Scandinavian derby

The fourth quarter-final in Helsinki matched two old rivals, with Sweden favourites to reverse their 2005 last-four defeat by Norway. Sweden nearly broke the early deadlock when Kosovare Asllani struck the

nouk Hoogendijk of the Netherlands converts the decisive penalty past France's Céline Deville in the quarter-final shoot-out

crossbar midway through the first half but, out of nowhere, Norway took a 39th-minute lead when Elise Thorsnes's shot deflected in off Sweden defender Stina Segerström. By half-time it was 2-0. Trine Rønning, winning her 100th Norway cap, sent in a free-kick from the right which Sweden's Sara Thunebro could only direct into the path of Anneli Giske to score from close range. Sweden coach Thomas Dennerby sent on striker Jessica Landström, who swiftly hit the post, but Norway's Bjarne Berntsen responded with the introduction of Cecilie Pedersen and within three minutes the teenager had made it 3-0, running on to Isabell Herlovsen's flick. Victoria Sandell Svensson claimed her 68th goal for Sweden with ten minutes left on her 166th and final appearance, but it was only a consolation.

Quarter-Final Results

3/9/09, Turku Stadium, Turku
Finland 2-3 England
Attendance: 7247
Finland: Korpela, Vaelma, Julin (Westerlund 72), Salmén, Mäkinen, Österberg Kalmari, Hyyrynen, Sällström, Sainio (Sjölund 52), Talonen (Lehtinen 75), Saari. Coach: Michael Käls (FIN)
England: Brown, Stoney, F. Williams, Johnson (Bassett 68), Asante, Carney, Chapman, Aluko, K. Smith, S. Smith, White (J. Scott 41). Coach: Hope Powell (ENG)
Goal(s): 0-1 Aluko 14, 0-2 F. Williams 49, 1-2 Sjölund 66, 1-3 Aluko 67, 2-3 Sällström 79
Referee: Damkova (CZE)

3/9/09, Tampere Stadium, Tampere
Netherlands 0-0 France (aet; 5-4 on penalties)
Attendance: 2766
Netherlands: Geurts, Bito, Koster, Meulen, Hogewoning, Hoogendijk, Kiesel-Griffioen, Van de Ven (Van den Heiligenberg 77), Melis, Stevens, Smit. Coach: Vera Pauw (NED)
France: Deville, Meilleroux, Georges, Soubeyrand, Franco, Bompastor, Abily, Thomis, Nécib (Le Sommer 55), Thiney (Herbert 87), Henry. Coach: Bruno Bini (FRA)
Yellow Card(s): Koster 83 (Netherlands)
Referee: Heikkinen (FIN)

4/9/09, Lahti Stadium, Lahti
Germany 2-1 Italy
Attendance: 1866
Germany: Angerer, Peter, Krahn, Behringer, Grings, Prinz (Müller 83), Bresonik, Kulig, Hingst (Fuss 46), Garefrekes, Schmidt (Laudehr 46). Coach: Silvia Neid (GER)
Italy: Picarelli, Gama, D'Adda, Tuttino, Tona, Schiavi, Domenichetti, Gabbiadini, Panico, Pini (Fuselli 87), Carissimi (Zorri 82). Coach: Pietro Ghedin (ITA)
Goal(s): 1-0 Grings 4, 2-0 Grings 47, 2-1 Panico 63
Yellow Card(s): Gabbiadini 32 (Italy)
Referee: Palmqvist (SWE)

4/9/09, Helsinki Football Stadium, Helsinki
Sweden 1-3 Norway
Attendance: 1708
Sweden: Lindahl, Rohlin, Segerström (Fors 67), Paulson, Seger, Thunebro, Schelin, Asllani (Nilsson 46), Sandell Svensson, Sjögran, Fischer (Landström 46). Coach: Thomas Dennerby (SWE)
Norway: Hjelmseth, Akerhaugen, Stensland, Giske, Huse, Rønning, Gulbrandsen, Herlovsen (Isaksen 76), Thorsnes (Pedersen 57), Mjelde, Storløkken (Lund 90+2). Coach: Bjarne Berntsen (NOR)
Goal(s): 0-1 Segerström 39(og), 0-2 Giske 45, 0-3 Pedersen 60, 1-3 Sandell Svensson 80
Yellow Card(s): Sjögran 90 (Sweden)
Referee: Steinhaus (GER)

The hair flies as Scandinavian rivals Sweden (yellow) and Norway go head to head in Helsinki

UEFA Women's EURO 2009

SEMI-FINALS

Hope Powell sprung a surprise with her selection of Jessica Clarke on the right in place of Karen Carney for England's Tampere meeting with the Netherlands.

Making her first competitive start, the 20-year-old did her job of pinning down dangerous full-back Dyanne Bito and when Carney replaced Sue Smith at the break, England took control. They went ahead in the 61st minute when Eniola Aluko's cut-back was swept in by Kelly Smith, who celebrated the goal as if it were the winner. Three minutes later, though, Marlous Pieëte, also given a first competitive start, equalised from Manon Melis's cross.

Late winner

A breakthrough in extra time was thwarted when substitute Lianne Sanderson hit the underside of the bar from point-blank range but England kept attacking and substitute Jill Scott and Katie Chapman both went close. A penalty shoot-out loomed, but with only four minutes remaining Carney's corner was turned in by Scott and this time the Netherlands were unable to produce a response. There was a consolation, though, as their run earned the squad two-year professional contracts from the Dutch government, having attracted record viewing figures for Eurosport in the Netherlands.

The following night in Helsinki, Germany were behind for the first time in the finals when Isabell Herlovsen headed Norway in front from Ingvild Stensland's corner. Germany were clearly missing the injured Ariane Hingst in central defence, struggling especially from Stensland corners, while Lene Storløkken hit the post after Nadine Angerer could not gather.

Germany in control

Simone Laudehr had already taken over from Linda Bresonik for Germany just before half-time and at the break Silvia Neid revamped her side further, sending on Célia Okoyino da Mbabi for right-back Bianca Schmidt in a bold attacking move. The game was transformed and Germany took control, Birgit Prinz and Inka Grings both threatening. Just before the hour the scores were levelled when Laudher turned in Melanie Behringer's cross. Two minutes later Laudehr set up Da Mbabi to put the holders in front. Norway responded and nearly equalised when Stensland's delivery was fumbled by Angerer before the goalkeeper did well to stop Cecilie Pedersen's

Dyanne Bito of the Netherlands (left) holds off England's Jessica Clark

ambitious lob. A goal looked likely at either end, and just before the final whistle a clincher arrived for Germany, their third substitute Fatmire Bajramaj turning in a loose ball to end Bjarne Berntsen's impressive four-year reign as Norway coach.

Semi-Final Results

6/9/09, Tampere Stadium, Tampere
England 2-1 Netherlands (aet)
Attendance: 4621
England: Brown, A. Scott, Stoney, F. Williams, Johnson, Asante, Chapman, Aluko (Sanderson 70), K. Smith, S. Smith (Carney 46), Clarke (J. Scott 91). Coach: Hope Powell (ENG)
Netherlands: Geurts, Bito (De Boer 117), Koster, Meulen, Hogewoning, Hoogendijk, Kiesel-Griffioen, Melis, Stevens (Van de Sanden 120), Smit, Pieëte (Van de Ven 86). Coach: Vera Pauw (NED)
Goal(s): 1-0 K. Smith 61, 1-1 Pieëte 64, 2-1 J. Scott 116
Yellow Card(s): Stoney 86 (England)
Referee: Gaál (HUN)

7/9/09, Helsinki Football Stadium, Helsinki
Germany 3-1 Norway
Attendance: 2765
Germany: Angerer, Bartusiak, Peter, Krahn, Behringer (Bajramaj 59), Grings, Prinz, Bresonik (Laudehr 46), Kulig, Garefrekes, Schmidt (Da Mbabi 46). Coach: Silvia Neid (GER)
Norway: Hjelmseth, Akerhaugen, Lund, Stensland, Giske, Huse (Gardsjord 82), Gulbrandsen (Løvbræk 76), Herlovsen, Kaurin (Pedersen 62), Mjelde, Storløkken. Coach: Bjarne Berntsen (NOR)
Goal(s): 0-1 Herlovsen 10, 1-1 Laudehr 59, 2-1 Da Mbabi 61, 3-1 Bajramaj 90+3
Yellow Card(s): Mjelde 78 (Norway), Akerhaugen 81 (Norway)
Referee: Heikkinen (FIN)

FINAL

Germany won their fifth title in a row but only after a valiant fight from an England team showing every bit of the attacking spirit that had carried them to their first final in 25 years

England captain Faye White started in a mask having broken her cheekbone in the quarter-final against Finland, and within a few minutes produced a vital saving tackle on Birgit Prinz. It was a reshuffled England attack, with Kelly Smith pushed forward and Karen Carney restored on the right, while Jill Scott came into midfield to give Fara Williams, whose ninth-minute free-kick came very close, freedom to advance. The holders also made a tactical change with Simone Laudehr starting in midfield and Linda Bresonik moved to right-back. It was from down that flank that the opening goal came, as Inka Grings chased Laudehr's pass and squared for veteran campaigner Prinz to score in the fourth of the five European finals she has won. Two minutes later Melanie Behringer doubled the lead with a thunderous, long-range strike that caught out Rachel Brown – just as Smith had done to the Russia goalkeeper in the group stage. In that game England recovered from two down to lead at the break, and

Kelly Smith scores for England

they responded two minutes later when Smith muscled her way to the byline and cut back for Carney to turn the ball into an empty net. Already a physical tussle, the rest of the half passed in a torrent of attacks at both ends, with a Scott header cleared off the line by Behringer the best of the chances.

England goalkeeper Rachel Brown is unable to prevent Birgit Prinz (grounded) scoring Germany's opening goal

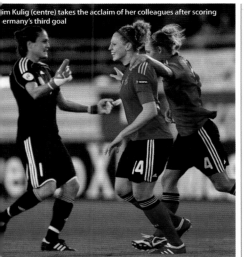

im Kulig (centre) takes the acclaim of her colleagues after scoring ermany's third goal

Title retained in style

Half-time did little to suppress the tempo. Six minutes into the second period Laudehr's effort from a corner struck the post and rolled across the line. It was cleared by Casey Stoney but only as far as Kim Kulig, who smashed in her first competitive senior international goal to make it 3-1. Again England responded immediately, Carney finding Smith, who twisted clear of her marker and gave Angerer no chance with her shot. Seven minutes later, though, Kerstin Garefrekes' cross from the left was headed in by Grings to restore Germany's two-goal lead. Alex Scott's deflection from substitute Célia Okoyino da Mbabi's cross then bounced off the England post, before Grings skipped past Anita Asante and White to produce her competition record sixth finals goal, sealing the Golden Boot award. Grings then set up Prinz for another, both now level with Heidi Mohr on ten finals goals, as Germany retained their title with a resounding, if slightly flattering, 6-2 win.

Germany celebrate their fifth successive European title

Final Result

10/9/09, Olympic Stadium, Helsinki
England 2-6 Germany
Attendance: 15877
England: Brown, A. Scott, Stoney, F. Williams, Asante, Carney, Chapman (Westwood 86), Aluko (Sanderson 81), K. Smith, J. Scott, White. Coach: Hope Powell (ENG)
Germany: Angerer, Bartusiak, Peter, Krahn, Laudehr, Behringer (Da Mbabi 60), Grings, Prinz, Bresonik, Kulig, Garefrekes (Bajramaj 83). Coach: Silvia Neid (GER)
Goal(s): 0-1 Prinz 20, 0-2 Behringer 22, 1-2 Carney 24, 1-3 Kulig 51, 2-3 K. Smith 55, 2-4 Grings 62, 2-5 Grings 73, 2-6 Prinz 76
Yellow Card(s): Stoney 44 (England)
Referee: Damkova (CZE)

TOP GOALSCORERS
6 Inka Grings (Germany)

3 Fatmire Bajramaj (Germany)
   Victoria Sandell Svensson (Sweden)
   Eniola Aluko (England)
   Kelly Smith (England)

UEFA WOMEN'S CHAMPIONS LEAGUE

2009/10

There was a fresh look to European female club competition in 2009/10. The UEFA Women's Champions League replaced the UEFA Women's Cup with the aim of raising the profile, standard and standing of women's club football – and the format was duly altered to enhance the new tournament. Eight nations were given two entrants, with Germany allowed three as the last UEFA Women's Cup winners, FCR 2001 Duisburg, had finished third in their domestic league. The final was to be a one-off game played in, or near, the same city as the UEFA Champions League final taking place two nights later. While some things change, others remain the same, however, and once again a team from Germany – the dominant force in the UEFA Women's Cup era – claimed the trophy, 1. FFC Turbine Potsdam beating Olympique Lyonnais on penalties in the final at the Coliseum Alfonso Pérez in Getafe on the outskirts of Madrid.

QUALIFYING ROUND

Group 1 Results

30/7/09, City Stadium, Siauliai
FC Bayern München 5-2 Glasgow City LFC
30/7/09, City Stadium, Siauliai
Gintra Universitetas FC 7-1 FC Norchi Dinamoeli Tbilisi
1/8/09, City Stadium, Siauliai
FC Bayern München 19-0 FC Norchi Dinamoeli Tbilisi
1/8/09, City Stadium, Siauliai
Glasgow City LFC 2-0 Gintra Universitetas FC
4/8/09, City Stadium, Siauliai
Gintra Universitetas FC 0-8 FC Bayern München
4/8/09, Aukštaitija, Panevezys
FC Norchi Dinamoeli Tbilisi 0-9 Glasgow City LFC

Group 1 Table

		Pld	W	D	L	F	A	Pts
1	FC Bayern München	3	3	0	0	32	2	9
2	Glasgow City LFC	3	2	0	1	13	5	6
3	Gintra Universitetas FC	3	1	0	2	7	11	3
4	FC Norchi Dinamoeli Tbilisi	3	0	0	3	1	35	0

Group 2 Results

30/7/09, Mladost, Strumica
Montpellier Hérault SC 2-0 KÍ Klaksvík
30/7/09, FC Turnovo, Strumica
FC NSA Sofia 5-0 ZFK Tikvesanka
1/8/09, Mladost, Strumica
Montpellier Hérault SC 7-1 ZFK Tikvesanka
1/8/09, FC Turnovo, Strumica
KÍ Klaksvík 1-2 FC NSA Sofia
4/8/09, Mladost, Strumica
FC NSA Sofia 0-3 Montpellier Hérault SC
4/8/09, FC Turnovo, Strumica
ZFK Tikvesanka 2-4 KÍ Klaksvík

Group 2 Table

		Pld	W	D	L	F	A	Pts
1	Montpellier Hérault SC	3	3	0	0	12	1	9
2	FC NSA Sofia	3	2	0	1	7	4	6
3	KÍ Klaksvík	3	1	0	2	5	6	3
4	ZFK Tikvesanka	3	0	0	3	3	16	0

Group 3 Results

30/7/09, Brøndby 2, Brondby
SU 1° Dezembro 10-0 Birkirkara FC
30/7/09, Brøndby 2, Brondby
Brøndby IF 5-0 Cardiff City LFC
1/8/09, Brøndby 2, Brondby
Cardiff City LFC 0-3 SU 1° Dezembro
1/8/09, Brøndby 2, Brondby
Brøndby IF 6-0 Birkirkara FC
4/8/09, Brøndby 2, Brondby
Birkirkara FC 1-10 Cardiff City LFC
4/8/09, Brøndby, Brondby
SU 1° Dezembro 0-1 Brøndby IF

Group 3 Table

		Pld	W	D	L	F	A	Pts
1	Brøndby IF	3	3	0	0	12	0	9
2	SU 1° Dezembro	3	2	0	1	13	1	6
3	Cardiff City LFC	3	1	0	2	10	9	3
4	Birkirkara FC	3	0	0	3	1	26	0

Group 4 Results

30/7/09, Matija Gubec, Krsko
ASD Torres Calcio 1-0 FK Slovan Duslo Šaľa
30/7/09, Matija Gubec, Krsko
ŽNK Krka 0-2 Trabzonspor
1/8/09, Matija Gubec, Krsko
ASD Torres Calcio 9-0 Trabzonspor
1/8/09, Matija Gubec, Krsko
FK Slovan Duslo Šaľa 2-2 ŽNK Krka
4/8/09, Matija Gubec, Krsko
ŽNK Krka 0-3 ASD Torres Calcio
4/8/09, NK Livar Ivančna Gorica
Trabzonspor 1-2 FK Slovan Duslo Šaľa

Group 4 Table

		Pld	W	D	L	F	A	Pts
1	ASD Torres Calcio	3	3	0	0	13	0	9
2	FK Slovan Duslo Šaľa	3	1	1	1	4	4	4
3	Trabzonspor	3	1	0	2	3	11	3
4	ŽNK Krka	3	0	1	2	2	7	1

Group 5 Results

30/7/09, Folkungavallen, Linkoping
CFF Clujana 1-0 Glentoran Belfast United WFC
30/7/09, Folkungavallen, Linkoping
Linköpings FC 11-0 FC Roma Calfa
1/8/09, Folkungavallen, Linkoping
FC Roma Calfa 0-9 CFF Clujana
1/8/09, Folkungavallen, Linkoping
Linköpings FC 3-0 Glentoran Belfast United WFC
4/8/09, Folkungavallen, Linkoping
Glentoran Belfast United WFC 2-0 FC Roma Calfa
4/8/09, Folkungavallen, Linkoping
CFF Clujana 0-6 Linköpings FC

Group 5 Table

		Pld	W	D	L	F	A
1	Linköpings FC	3	3	0	0	20	0
2	CFF Clujana	3	2	0	1	10	6
3	Glentoran Belfast United WFC	3	1	0	2	2	4
4	FC Roma Calfa	3	0	0	3	0	22

Group 6 Results

30/7/09, Tsirion, Limassol
WFC Rossiyanka 11-0 St Francis FC
30/7/09, Tsirion, Limassol
Maccabi Holon FC 0-4 Apollon Limassol L
1/8/09, Tsirion, Limassol
WFC Rossiyanka 1-0 Apollon Limassol LF
1/8/09, Tsirion, Limassol
St Francis FC 0-2 Maccabi Holon FC
4/8/09, Paphiakos, Paphos
Maccabi Holon FC 0-7 WFC Rossiyanka
4/8/09, Tsirion, Limassol
Apollon Limassol LFC 2-0 St Francis FC

Group 6 Table

		Pld	W	D	L	F	A
1	WFC Rossiyanka	3	3	0	0	19	0
2	Apollon Limassol LFC	3	2	0	1	6	1
3	Maccabi Holon FC	3	1	0	2	2	11
4	St Francis FC	3	0	0	3	0	15

Group 7 Results

30/7/09, Gradski vrt, Osijek
Everton LFC 3-1 WFC Osijek
30/7/09, Gradski vrt, Osijek
Lillestrøm FK Kvinner 5-0 Tallinna FC Levadia
1/8/09, Gradski vrt, Osijek
Everton LFC 7-0 Tallinna FC Levadia
1/8/09, Gradski vrt, Osijek
WFC Osijek 0-9 Lillestrøm FK Kvinner
4/8/09, Cibalia Vinkovci, Vinkovci
Lillestrøm FK Kvinner 0-1 Everton LFC
4/8/09, Gradski vrt, Osijek
Tallinna FC Levadia 4-1 WFC Osijek

Group 7 Table

		Pld	W	D	L	F	A
1	Everton LFC	3	3	0	0	11	1
2	Lillestrøm FK Kvinner	3	2	0	1	14	1
3	Tallinna FC Levadia	3	1	0	2	4	13
4	WFC Osijek	3	0	0	3	2	16

ROUND OF 32

9/09, OSiR, Racibórz
Unia Racibórz 1-3 SV Neulengbach
al(s): 0-1 Brandtner 12, 0-2 Ruiss 38,
Burger 51, 1-3 Sznyrowska 90+2
9/09, Wienerwaldstadion, Neulengbach
Neulengbach 0-1 RTP Unia Racibórz
al(s): 0-1 Winczo 69
gregate: 3-2; SV Neulengbach qualify.

9/09, Vanni Sanna, Sassari
Torres Calcio 4-1 Valur Reykjavík
al(s): 1-0 Panico 40, 2-0 Manieri 45,
Tona 68, 3-1 Gísladóttir 68, 4-1 Stracchi 80
9/09, Hlídarendi, Reykjavik
ur Reykjavík 1-2 ASD Torres Calcio
al(s): 0-1 Iannella 42, 1-1 K. Jónsdóttir 69,
Panico 81
gregate: 2-6; ASD Torres Calcio qualify.

9/09, Gelios-Arena, Kharkiv
lstroy-1 Kharkov 0-5 Umeå IK
al(s): 0-1 Jakobsson 10, 0-2 Dahlkvist 26,
Bachmann 44, 0-4 Yamaguchi 46,
Edlund 65
9/09, Gammliavallen, Umeå
eå IK 6-0 Zhilstroy-1 Kharkov
al(s): 1-0 Andrushchak 34(og),
Masalska 38(og), 3-0 Bachmann 45+2,
Bachmann 46, 5-0 Konradsson 56,
Åberg Zingmark 88
gregate: 11-0; Umeå IK qualify.

9/09, Okzhetpes, Kokshetau
na KTZH 1-0 AC Sparta Praha
al(s): 1-0 Zhanatayeva 49
9/09, TJ Lokomotiva Praha, Prague
Sparta Praha 2-0 Alma KTZH
al(s): 1-0 Ondrušová 16, 2-0 Ondrušová 37
gregate: 2-1; AC Sparta Praha qualify.

9/09, Grbavica, Sarajevo
K SFK 2000 Sarajevo 0-3 Zvezda-2005
al(s): 0-1 Apanaschenko 9,
Tsybutovich 37, 0-3 Zinchenko 49
9/09, Zvezda, Perm
zda-2005 5-0 ŽNK SFK 2000 Sarajevo
al(s): 1-0 Apanaschenko 8,
Kurochkina 15, 3-0 Barbashina 32,
Dyatel 41, 5-0 Zinchenko 76
gregate: 8-0; Zvezda-2005 qualify.

9/09, Delijski Vis, Nis
K Mašinac Niš 0-3 Olympique Lyonnais (w/o)
9/09, Stade de Gerland, Lyon
mpique Lyonnais 5-0 ŽFK Mašinac Niš
al(s): 1-0 Nécib 55, 2-0 Thomis 71, 3-0
elin 74, 4-0 Brétigny 80, 5-0 Nécib 89
gregate: 8-0; Olympique Lyonnais qualify.

30/9/09, Røabanen, Oslo
Røa IL 3-0 Everton LFC
Goal(s): 1-0 Thorsnes 15, 2-0 M. Knutsen 40,
3-0 Haavi 68
7/10/09, Marine AFC Rossett Park, Liverpool
Everton LFC 2-0 Røa IL
Goal(s): 1-0 Westwood 8, 2-0 Hinnigan 57
Aggregate: 2-3; Røa IL qualify.

30/9/09, Maurice Dufrasne, Liege
**Standard Femina de Liège 0-0 Montpellier
Hérault SC**
7/10/09, La Mosson, Montpellier
**Montpellier Hérault SC 3-1 Standard Femina
de Liège**
Goal(s): 0-1 Meunier 28, 1-1 Lattaf 63,
2-1 Ramos 64, 3-1 Delie 78
Aggregate: 3-1; Montpellier Hérault SC qualify.

30/9/09, Rohonci Út, Szombathely
**Viktória FC Szombathely 0-5 FC Bayern
München**
Goal(s): 0-1 Bürki 9, 0-2 Baunach 17,
0-3 Islacker 31, 0-4 Rech 45+1, 0-5 Mayr 90+1
7/10/09, Sportpark Aschheim, Aschheim
**FC Bayern München 4-2 Viktória FC
Szombathely**
Goal(s): 1-0 Mayr 9, 1-1 G. Tóth 12, 2-1 Mayr 60,
2-2 G. Tóth 76, 3-2 Mayr 80, 4-2 Banecki 84
Aggregate: 9-2; FC Bayern München qualify.

30/9/09, Schützenwiese, Winterthur
FC Zürich Frauen 0-2 Linköpings FC
Goal(s): 0-1 Seger 15, 0-2 Landström 30
7/10/09, Folkungavallen, Linkoping
Linköpings FC 3-0 FC Zürich Frauen
Goal(s): 1-0 Brännström 25, 2-0 Karlsson II 37,
3-0 J. Andersson 60
Aggregate: 5-0; Linköpings FC qualify.

30/9/09, Vitebsk Central sport complex, Vitebsk
**WFC Universitet Vitebsk 1-5 FCR 2001
Duisburg**
Goal(s): 0-1 Hegering 6, 0-2 Maes 33,0-3 Grings 37,
0-4 Grings 40, 0-5 Oliveira Leite 69, 1-5 Yalova 76
7/10/09, Niederrhein, Oberhausen
**FCR 2001 Duisburg 6-3 WFC Universitet
Vitebsk**
Goal(s): 1-0 Grings 5(p), 2-0 Grings 22, 3-0
Maes 26, 3-1 Yalova 27, 3-2 Aniskovtseva 35,
4-2 Grings 38, 5-2 Grings 45, 6-2 Grings 48, 6-3
Ryzhevich 52
Aggregate: 11-4; FCR 2001 Duisburg qualify.

30/9/09, Tapiolan Urheilupuisto, Espoo
FC Honka Espoo 1-8 1. FFC Turbine Potsdam
Goal(s): 0-1 Mittag 8, 0-2 Mittag 10, 0-3 Zietz
14(p), 0-4 Helenius 16(og), 0-5 Kessler 58,
0-6 Mittag 60, 0-7 Draws 71, 1-7 Jessi Hietanen 89,
1-8 Tervo 90+3(og)

7/10/09, Karl Liebknecht, Potsdam
1. FFC Turbine Potsdam 8-0 FC Honka Espoo
Goal(s): 1-0 Mittag 10, 2-0 Zietz 17,
3-0 Bagehorn 40, 4-0 Odebrecht 52,
5-0 Bajramaj 64, 6-0 Bajramaj 71, 7-0 Mittag 79,
8-0 Mittag 90+2
Aggregate: 16-1; 1. FFC Turbine Potsdam
qualify.

30/9/09, Toumba, Thessalonika
FC PAOK Thessaloniki 0-9 Arsenal LFC
Goal(s): 0-1 Yankey 8, 0-2 Little 13, 0-3 Little 32,
0-4 Little 35, 0-5 Lander 44, 0-6 Lander 62,
0-7 Yankey 72, 0-8 Ludlow 87, 0-9 Little 90+4
7/10/09, Meadow Park, Borehamwood
Arsenal LFC 9-0 FC PAOK Thessaloniki
Goal(s): 1-0 Little 11, 2-0 Little 13,
3-0 Chapman 17, 4-0 Beattie 21,
5-0 Kynossidou 44(og), 6-0 Little 47,
7-0 Davison 74, 8-0 Bruton 77, 9-0 Coombs 84
Aggregate: 18-0; Arsenal LFC qualify.

30/9/09, Hjørring, Hjorring
**Fortuna Hjørring 4-0 ASD CF Bardolino
Verona**
Goal(s): 1-0 Igbo 28, 2-0 Boni 50(og),
3-0 Munk 72, 4-0 Christensen 81
7/10/09, Marc'Antonio Bentegodi, Verona
**ASD CF Bardolino Verona 2-1 Fortuna
Hjørring**
Goal(s): 0-1 Christensen 27, 1-1 Paliotti 33,
2-1 Villar 77
Aggregate: 2-5; Fortuna Hjørring qualify.

30/9/09, TATA Steel, Velsen
AZ Alkmaar 1-2 Brøndby IF
Goal(s): 0-1 Christiansen 22, 0-2 Madsen 35, 1-
2 Demarteau 42
7/10/09, Brøndby, Brondby
Brøndby IF 1-1 AZ Alkmaar
Goal(s): 0-1 Røddik Hansen 9(og),
1-1 Christiansen 88
Aggregate: 3-2; Brøndby IF qualify.

30/9/09, Teresa Rivero, Madrid
**Rayo Vallecano de Madrid 1-3 WFC
Rossiyanka**
Goal(s): 0-1 Petrova 4, 0-2 Oghiabeva 15,
1-2 Adriana 86, 1-3 Shmachkova 90+2
7/10/09, Krasnoarmeysk, Krasnoarmeysk
**WFC Rossiyanka 2-1 Rayo Vallecano de
Madrid**
Goal(s): 1-0 Oghiabeva 5, 2-0 Danilova 55,
2-1 Natalia 73
Aggregate: 5-2; WFC Rossiyanka qualify.

ROUND OF 16

4/11/09, Røabanen, Oslo
Røa IL 0-0 Zvezda-2005
11/11/09, Zvezda, Perm
Zvezda-2005 1-1 Røa IL
Goal(s): 0-1 Knutsen Mienna 2, 1-1 Barbashina 61
Aggregate: 1-1; Røa IL qualify on away goal.

4/11/09, Saturn, Ramenskoye
WFC Rossiyanka 0-1 Umeå IK
Goal(s): 0-1 Jakobsson 51
11/11/09, Gammliavallen, Umeå
Umeå IK 1-1 WFC Rossiyanka
Goal(s): 1-0 Jakobsson 2, 1-1 Chorna 37
Aggregate: 2-1; Umeå IK qualify.

4/11/09, La Mosson, Montpellier
Montpellier Hérault SC 0-0 FC Bayern München
11/11/09, Sportpark Aschheim, Aschheim
FC Bayern München 0-1 Montpellier
Hérault SC (aet)
Goal(s): 0-1 Lattaf 107
Aggregate: 0-1; Montpellier Hérault SC qualify after extra time.

4/11/09, Generali Arena, Prague
AC Sparta Praha 0-3 Arsenal LFC
Goal(s): 0-1 Flaherty 11, 0-2 Grant 27,
0-3 Little 55(p)
11/11/09, Meadow Park, Borehamwood
Arsenal LFC 2-0 AC Sparta Praha
Goal(s): 1-0 Heroldová 31(og), 2-0 Little 56
Aggregate: 5-0; Arsenal LFC qualify.

4/11/09, Karl Liebknecht, Potsdam
1. FFC Turbine Potsdam 1-0 Brøndby IF
Goal(s): 1-0 Bajramaj 17
11/11/09, Brøndby, Brondby
Brøndby IF 0-4 1. FFC Turbine Potsdam
Goal(s): 0-1 Kessler 6, 0-2 Wich 65,
0-3 Mittag 66, 0-4 Kessler 88
Aggregate: 0-5; 1. FFC Turbine Potsdam qualify.

4/11/09, Wienerwaldstadion, Neulengbach
SV Neulengbach 1-4 ASD Torres Calcio
Goal(s): 0-1 Iannella 12, 0-2 Fuselli 15,
0-3 Iannella 27, 1-3 Novotny 43, 1-4 Iannella 44
11/11/09, Vanni Sanna, Sassari
ASD Torres Calcio 4-1 SV Neulengbach
Goal(s): 1-0 Manieri 46, 1-1 Burger 67,
2-1 Tona 74, 3-1 Stracchi 87, 4-1 Fuselli 90+2
Aggregate: 8-2; ASD Torres Calcio qualify.

4/11/09, Niederrhein, Oberhausen
FCR 2001 Duisburg 1-1 Linköpings FC
Goal(s): 0-1 Asllani 30, 1-1 Laudehr 86
11/11/09, NYA Parken, Norrkoping
Linköpings FC 0-2 FCR 2001 Duisburg
Goal(s): 0-1 Popp 59, 0-2 Grings 90+3
Aggregate: 1-3; FCR 2001 Duisburg qualify.

5/11/09, Hjørring, Hjorring
Fortuna Hjørring 0-1 Olympique Lyonnais
Goal(s): 0-1 Thomis 16
12/11/09, Stade de Gerland, Lyon
Olympique Lyonnais 5-0 Fortuna Hjørring
Goal(s): 1-0 Thomis 11, 2-0 Schelin 26, 3-0 Franco 36, 4-0 Schelin 81,
5-0 Katia 83
Aggregate: 6-0; Olympique Lyonnais qualify.

Arsenal's Kim Little (right) goes through on goal against Sparta Prah

UEFA Women's Champions League

QUARTER-FINALS

Under the new format of the UEFA Women's Champions League, the knockout stage began in the last 32 rather than the quarter-finals.

Two sides reached the last eight for the first time, in the company of four past UEFA Women's Cup winners. One of the debutant quarter-finalists, Røa IL, lost 5-0 away and at home against 2004/05 champions 1. FFC Turbine Potsdam, with seven different players from the German club finding the net. Reigning European champions FCR 2001 Duisburg knocked out 2006/07 winners Arsenal LFC to set up a semi-final with domestic rivals Potsdam. An Inka Grings own goal in Germany had given Arsenal hope in a 2-1 first-leg loss but Duisburg consolidated their lead in the return, winning 2-0.

Lyon hat-trick

The other club in their first quarter-final, ASD Torres Calcio, fell to Olympique Lyonnais, who advanced to the last four for the third year running. Lyon were in control after a 3-0 victory at Stade de Gerland and could afford a 1-0 second-leg defeat in Italy. Lyon would next face two-time continental champions Umeå IK - as they had in the 2007/08 semi-finals. The Swedish side had changed much of their squad and appointed a new coach, Joakim Blomqvist, since the previous round. Held 0-0 at home in their quarter-final first leg against Montpellier Hérault SC, Umeå looked doomed when Montpellier took a 2-0 lead late in the return, but the visitors showed their mettle by scoring twice in the last four minutes through substitute Emma Åberg Zingmark and Sofia Jakobsson to get through on away goals. The elimination of Montpellier and Torres meant that all the teams that had entered as league runners-up were now out.

Quarter-Final Results

10/3/10, Stade de Gerland, Lyon
Olympique Lyonnais 3-0 ASD Torres Calcio
Lyon: Nilsen, Renard, Schelin (Herlovsen 88), Katia (Thomis 88), Nécib (Stensland 83), Cruz Trana, Franco, Ducher, Dickenmann, Henry, Rybeck. Coach: Farid Benstiti (FRA)
Torres: Cupido, Manieri, Valenti (Fadda 58), Stracchi, Tona, Fuselli (Iacchelli 90+3), Domenichetti, Cortesi, Panico, Iannella, Sorvillo (Pintus 83). Coach: Salvatore Arca (ITA)
Goal(s): 1-0 Cruz Trana 19, 2-0 Schelin 30, 3-0 Schelin 62
Yellow Card(s): Manieri 69 (Torres), Renard 75 (Lyon)
Referee: Brohet (BEL)

Sofia Jakobsson scored in the last minute to give Umeå an away-goals victory over Montpellier

17/3/10, Vanni Sanna, Sassari
ASD Torres Calcio 1-0 Olympique Lyonnais
Torres: Cupido, Manieri, Stracchi, Tona, Fuselli, Domenichetti (Valenti 76), Cortesi, Panico, Iannella (Ruotsalainen 90), Fadda (Pintus 85), Sorvillo. Coach: Salvatore Arca (ITA)
Lyon: Nilsen, Renard, Stensland, Schelin, Katia (Herlovsen 55), Nécib, Cruz Trana, Franco, Dickenmann, Henry, Rybeck. Coach: Farid Benstiti (FRA)
Goal(s): 1-0 Cruz Trana 18(og)
Yellow Card(s): Iannella 26 (Torres), Cruz Trana 42 (Lyon), Cortesi 85 (Torres), Fuselli 90+1 (Torres)
Referee: Steinhaus (GER)
Aggregate: 1-3; Olympique Lyonnais qualify.

10/3/10, Gammliavallen, Umeå
Umeå IK 0-0 Montpellier Hérault SC
Umeå: Jönsson, Paulson, Berglund, Saari, Konradsson, Nordlund, Jakobsson, Molin, Chikwelu, Kapstad (Åberg Zingmark 61), Östberg. Coach: Joakim Blomqvist (SWE)
Montpellier: Deville, Torrent, Viguier, Rubio, Hamou Maamar, Diguelman, Plaza, Blanc, Lattaf (Asseyi 83), Roux, Delie. Coach: Sarah M'barek (FRA)
Referee: Albon (ROU)

17/3/10, La Mosson, Montpellier
Montpellier Hérault SC 2-2 Umeå IK
Montpellier: Deville, Torrent, Viguier, Rubio (Wenger 90+2), Hamou Maamar, Diguelman, Plaza, Blanc, Lattaf, Delie, Asseyi (Roux 83). Coach: Sarah M'barek (FRA)
Umeå: Jönsson, Paulson, Berglund, Saari, Konradsson, Nordlund (Molin 82), Jakobsson, Åberg Zingmark, Chikwelu, Kapstad (Åberg Zingmark 69), Östberg. Coach: Joakim Blomqvist (SWE)
Goal(s): 1-0 Diguelman 54, 2-0 Plaza 76, 2-1 Åberg Zingmark 86, 2-2 Jakobsson 90
Referee: Schett (AUT)
Aggregate: 2-2; Umeå IK qualify on away goals.

Turbine Potsdam goalkeeper Anna Felicitas Sarholz

10/3/10, Karl Liebknecht, Potsdam
1. FFC Turbine Potsdam 5-0 Røa IL
Potsdam: Schumann, Peter, Henning, Wich (Nagasato 46), Bajramaj, Zietz, Odebrecht, Schmidt, Draws, Kessler (Kerschowski 73), Mittag. Coach: Bernd Schröder (GER)
Røa: C. Knutsen, Vikre (Finskud 75), Johansen, Mykjaland, Thorsnes, Haavi (Kvalsvik 69), Gardsjord, Andreassen (Sondena 63), Christensen, Knutsen Mienna, Nordby. Coach: Geir Kristian Nordby (NOR)
Goal(s): 1-0 Kessler 20, 2-0 Odebrecht 43, 3-0 Peter 49, 4-0 Kessler 69, 5-0 Nagasato 80
Referee: Monzul (UKR)

17/3/10, Røabanen, Oslo
Røa IL 0-5 1. FFC Turbine Potsdam
Røa: C. Knutsen, Johansen, Mykjaland, Thorsnes, Finskud (Rolness 70), Gardsjord (Minge Olsen 84), Andreassen, Christensen, Knutsen Mienna, Nordby, Kvalsvik (Haavi 46). Coach: Geir Kristian Nordby (NOR)
Potsdam: Sarholz, Peter, Henning, Wich, Bajramaj (Bagehorn 64), Zietz, Odebrecht (Schröder 64), Nagasato, Schmidt, Draws, Mittag (Kemme 64). Coach: Bernd Schröder (GER)
Goal(s): 0-1 Mittag 30, 0-2 Bajramaj 56, 0-3 Mittag 63, 0-4 Nagasato 73, 0-5 Wich 82
Yellow Card(s): Thorsnes 45+2 (Røa), Draws 89 (Potsdam)
Referee: Ihringova (ENG)
Aggregate: 0-10; 1. FFC Turbine Potsdam qualify.

10/3/10, MSV Arena, Duisburg
FCR 2001 Duisburg 2-1 Arsenal LFC
Duisburg: Holl, Wensing, Oster (Himmighofen 88), Kiesel-Griffioen, Grings, Bresonik, Laudehr (Knaak 46), Krahn, Maes, Hegering, Popp. Coach: Martina Voss-Tecklenburg (GER)
Arsenal: Byrne, Yorston, Ludlow, Flaherty, White, Grant, Yankey, Davison (Bruton 90+1), Little, Fahey, Carter (Beattie 78). Coach: Laura Harvey (ENG)
Goal(s): 1-0 Grings 24(p), 2-0 Hegering 49, 2-1 Grings 66(og)
Yellow Card(s): Little 24 (Arsenal), Ludlow 71 (Arsenal)
Referee: Palmqvist (SWE)

14/3/10, Woodside Park, Bishop's Stortford
Arsenal LFC 0-2 FCR 2001 Duisburg
Arsenal: Byrne, Yorston, Ludlow, Flaherty, White (Tracy 90+1), Grant, Yankey (Bruton 70), Davison, Beattie, Fahey, Carter. Coach: Laura Harvey (ENG)
Duisburg: Holl, Wensing, Oster (Himmighofen 82), Kiesel-Griffioen, Grings, Bresonik, Laudehr (Knaak 72), Krahn, Maes (Kayikci 88), Hegering, Popp. Coach: Martina Voss-Tecklenburg (GER)
Goal(s): 0-1 Oster 49, 0-2 Himmighofen 88
Yellow Card(s): Flaherty 48 (Arsenal), Popp 79 (Duisburg)
Referee: Heikkinen (FIN)
Aggregate: 1-4; FCR 2001 Duisburg qualify.

UEFA Women's Champions League

SEMI-FINALS

In between booking their place in the semi-final and playing the first leg, 1. FFC Turbine Potsdam and FCR 2001 Duisburg actually met twice – Turbine prevailed 2-1 at home in a crucial league game before losing 1-0 away in the German Cup semis.

That proved a useful form guide as, eight days on from that second encounter, Duisburg again overcame Potsdam 1-0 at home in the first leg of their European tie, with Femke Maes scoring the goal. Unsurprisingly, the return match a week later was tight. Two minutes after her introduction as substitute on the hour, Tabea Kemme headed Potsdam level in the tie. With no further goals, the third penalty shoot-out in UEFA women's club competition history ensued. Potsdam's 17-year-old goalkeeper Anna Felicitas Sarholz was the hero, saving from Inka Grings, Linda Bresonik and – after Fatmire Bajramaj had missed a potentially decisive penalty against her former club – Irini Ioannidou to send Turbine through 3-1.

Second leg postponed

Goals were less hard to come by in the first leg of the other tie, which Olympique Lyonnais won 3-2 at home

Lyon's Louisa Nécib scored twice against Umeå to help her team into their first European final

to Umeå IK. Twice Louisa Nécib put Lyon in front, only for Hanna Pettersson to equalise on each occasion, before, with seven minutes left, Katia nodded the winner. The sequel was scheduled for the following weekend, but flight restrictions enforced by Icelandic volcanic ash postponed the game by ten days. On the night before the rescheduled match Lyon's men exited the UEFA Champions League, but the women ensured the club would still contest a first European final with a 0-0 draw that earned a showdown in Spain against Potsdam.

Semi-Final Results

10/4/10, Stade de Gerland, Lyon
Olympique Lyonnais 3-2 Umeå IK
Lyon: Nilsen, Renard, Stensland (Thomis 74), Georges, Schelin, Nécib, Cruz Trana, Franco, Dickenmann (Katia 82), Henry, Rybeck. Coach: Farid Benstiti (FRA)
Umeå: Jönsson, Paulson, Berglund, Saari, Pettersson (Åberg Zingmark 85), Konradsson, Jakobsson, Åberg Zingmark, Chikwelu, Kapstad (Molin 46), Östberg. Coach: Joakim Blomqvist (SWE)
Goal(s): 1-0 Nécib 3, 1-1 Pettersson 19, 2-1 Nécib 42, 2-2 Pettersson 71, 3-2 Katia 83
Referee: Beck (GER)

28/4/10, Gammliavallen, Umeå
Umeå IK 0-0 Olympique Lyonnais
Umeå: Jönsson, Paulson, Berglund, Saari, Pettersson (Molin 20), Konradsson, Jakobsson, Åberg Zingmark (Kapstad 45+3), Åberg Zingmark (Nordlund 45+2), Chikwelu, Östberg. Coach: Joakim Blomqvist (SWE)
Lyon: Bouhaddi, Renard, Stensland, Georges, Nécib, Cruz Trana, Thomis, Franco, Dickenmann, Henry, Rybeck. Coach: Farid Benstiti (FRA)
Yellow Card(s): Stensland 25 (Lyon), Nécib 66 (Lyon), Chikwelu 80 (Umeå), Molin 84 (Umeå)
Referee: Dorcioman (ROU)
Aggregate: 2-3; Olympique Lyonnais qualify.

11/4/10, PCC Stadion, Duisburg
FCR 2001 Duisburg 1-0 1. FFC Turbine Potsdam
Duisburg: Holl, Oster (Knaak 69), Kiesel-Griffioen, Grings, Bresonik, Laudehr, Krahn, Maes, Hegering (Ioannidou 79), Popp, Ando (Beckmann 89). Coach: Martina Voss-Tecklenburg (GER)
Potsdam: Schumann, Peter, Henning, Bajramaj, Zietz, Odebrecht, Schmidt, Kemme (Nagasato 67), Draws, Kessler, Mittag. Coach: Bernd Schröder (GER)
Goal(s): 1-0 Maes 28
Referee: Damkova (CZE)

18/4/10, Karl Liebknecht, Potsdam
1. FFC Turbine Potsdam 1-0 FCR 2001 Duisburg (aet)
Potsdam: Sarholz, Peter, Henning, Wich (Nagasato 46), Bajramaj, Zietz, Odebrecht, Schröder (Kemme 60), Schmidt, Kessler (Draws 119), Mittag. Coach: Bernd Schröder (GER)
Duisburg: Holl, Wensing, Kiesel-Griffioen, Grings, Bresonik, Laudehr (Ioannidou 109), Krahn, Maes, Hegering (Wermelt 91), Popp, Ando (Oster 57). Coach: Martina Voss-Tecklenburg (GER)
Goal(s): 1-0 Kemme 62
Yellow Card(s): Mittag 59 (Potsdam), Bresonik 85 (Duisburg)
Referee: Gaál (HUN)
Aggregate: 1-1; 1. FFC Turbine Potsdam qualify 3-1 on penalties.

FINAL

The first UEFA Women's Champions League final was held at Getafe CF's Coliseum Alfonso Pérez two days before the UEFA Champions League final in Madrid.

1. FFC Turbine Potsdam eventually emerged victorious against Olympique Lyonnais 7-6 on penalties following a goalless draw after extra time. As in the semi-final, Potsdam's teenaged goalkeeper Anna Felicitas Sarholz was the key figure, saving two spot kicks and scoring one herself after the German side had fallen two behind in the shoot-out.

Free-flowing spectacle

That the game finished goalless after 120 minutes was testament to Sarholz and her opposite number, Lyon's Sarah Bouhaddi. In front of a crowd of 10,372, both teams created numerous opportunities in a free-flowing spectacle, with Lyon threatening in the early stages, especially when Louisa Nécib's free-kick hit the crossbar on 15 minutes. Despite playing their first European final, Lyon showed few signs of nerves, and it was Potsdam who took time to settle. After the break, though, the Frauen-Bundesliga club began to take control. Fatmire Bajramaj had been their biggest threat to that point and she teed up Tabea Kemme shortly before the hour, only for Bouhaddi to pull off a brilliant reflex stop from the left-back's close-range shot.

Six minutes from time Anja Mittag went closer still as her curling effort rattled the base of the post. Bouhaddi produced more heroics for the French titleholders in extra time, first combining with Laura Georges to deny Viola Odebrecht and Mittag, then keeping out a stinging strike from substitute Isabell Kerschowski. And so it went to penalties.

Potsdam's Fatmire Bajmaraj (centre) takes on the Lyon defence

Potsdam's match-winning goalkeeper Anna Felicitas Sarholz smiles after converting a penalty past her opposite number Sarah Bouhaddi

Final Result

20/5/10, Coliseum Alfonso Pérez, Getafe

Olympique Lyonnais 0-0 1. FFC Turbine Potsdam (aet; 6-7 on pens)
Attendance: 10372
Lyon: Bouhaddi, Renard, Stensland (Kaci 70), Georges, Nécib (Herlovsen 90), Cruz Trana (Simone 105), Thomis, Franco, Dickenmann, Henry, Rybeck. Coach: Farid Benstiti (FRA)
Potsdam: Sarholz, Peter, Henning, Wich (Nagasato 66), Bajramaj, Zietz, Odebrecht, Schmidt, Kemme (Schröder 106), Kessler (I. Kerschowski 66), Mittag. Coach: Bernd Schröder (GER)
Yellow Card(s): Renard 8 (Lyon), Kemme 15 (Potsdam), Georges 68 (Lyon), Cruz Trana 89 (Lyon), Mittag 97 (Potsdam)
Referee: Heikkinen (FIN)

Vanessa Bürki

TOP GOALSCORERS

11	Vanessa Bürki (Bayern)
10	Ida Brännström (Linköping)
9	Kim Little (Arsenal)
	Inka Grings (Duisburg)
	Anja Mittag (Potsdam)
7	Katharina Würmseer (Bayern)
	Elena Danilova (Rossiyanka)
	Emueje Oghiabeva (Rossiyanka)
	Julia Simic (Bayern)

Bouhaddi looked to have put Lyon into a winning position after saving attempts from Jennifer Zietz and Mittag, but Sarholz had the last word, saving twice in succession with the title on the line before scoring one herself to swing the momentum Potsdam's way. The first UEFA Women's Champions League crown belonged to Potsdam when Lyon's Élodie Thomis fired the 18th penalty against the crossbar.

. FFC Turbine Potsdam, the inaugural UEFA Women's Champions League winners, celebrate with the trophy

WU19

CHAPTER
11

2009/10

In recent years one team has invariably emerged from the pack to dominate and claim the UEFA Women's European Under-19 Championship, but the 2010 edition was a more even affair – a triumph for calm endeavour. Such fine margins meant that both the Netherlands and Germany returned home early from the finals in the Former Yugoslav Republic of Macedonia (FYROM) despite being unbeaten, the Jong Oranje without even conceding a goal. Holders England were made to pay for a couple of major defensive errors in the final as France inscribed their name on the trophy for a second time. A third final in four years at least enabled England to console themselves with the fact that they are now firmly established among the elite at this level. The Netherlands have further to go, but having lost five of their six previous games at the final tournament, 2010 marked an encouraging watershed. So too Scotland, who bowed out with their first point, and while the host nation conceded 19 goals in their three outings, star player Natasa Andonova at least gave the locals something to cheer about.

UEFA European Women's Under-19 Championship

QUALIFYING ROUNDS

First Qualifying Round

Group 1 Results

19/9/09, Sports Centre, Samobor
Republic of Ireland 3-0 Croatia

19/9/09, Town stadium, Vrbovec
Finland 1-0 Faroe Islands

21/9/09, SRC Velika Gorika, Velika Gorica
Republic of Ireland 7-0 Faroe Islands

21/9/09, Town stadium, Vrbovec
Croatia 1-2 Finland

24/9/09, Sports Centre, Samobor
Finland 2-3 Republic of Ireland

24/9/09, SRC Velika Gorika, Velika Gorica
Faroe Islands 0-3 Croatia

Group 1 Table

	Pld	W	D	L	F	A	Pts
1 Republic of Ireland	3	3	0	0	13	2	9
2 Finland	3	2	0	1	5	4	6
3 Croatia	3	1	0	2	4	5	3
4 Faroe Islands	3	0	0	3	0	11	0

Group 2 Results

19/9/09, Kohila, Kohila
Sweden 2-2 Slovenia

19/9/09, Kuusalu, Kuusalu
Czech Republic 3-1 Estonia

21/9/09, Kohila, Kohila
Czech Republic 2-1 Slovenia

21/9/09, Kuusalu, Kuusalu
Estonia 0-8 Sweden

24/9/09, Kohila, Kohila
Sweden 1-0 Czech Republic

24/9/09, Kuusalu, Kuusalu
Slovenia 0-1 Estonia

Group 2 Table

	Pld	W	D	L	F	A	Pts
1 Sweden	3	2	1	0	11	2	7
2 Czech Republic	3	2	0	1	5	3	6
3 Estonia	3	1	0	2	2	11	3
4 Slovenia	3	0	1	2	3	5	1

Group 3 Results

19/9/09, Vanløse Idrætspark, Vanlose
Wales 2-6 Bosnia-Herzegovina

19/9/09, Vanløse Idrætspark, Vanlose
Denmark 5-0 Moldova

21/9/09, Lyngby, Lyngby
Wales 5-0 Moldova

21/9/09, Lyngby, Lyngby
Bosnia-Herzegovina 0-7 Denmark

24/9/09, Vanløse Idrætspark, Vanlose
Denmark 2-1 Wales

24/9/09, Lyngby, Lyngby
Moldova 0-3 Bosnia-Herzegovina

Group 3 Table

	Pld	W	D	L	F	A	Pts
1 Denmark	3	3	0	0	14	1	9
2 Bosnia-Herzegovina	3	2	0	1	9	9	6
3 Wales	3	1	0	2	8	8	3
4 Moldova	3	0	0	3	0	13	0

Group 4 Results

19/9/09, Albena 1, Albena
Scotland 2-0 Northern Ireland

19/9/09, Druzhba, Dobrich
Italy 6-0 Bulgaria

21/9/09, Albena 1, Albena
Northern Ireland 0-6 Italy

Isobel Christiansen of England

21/9/09, Druzhba, Dobrich
Scotland 5-1 Bulgaria

24/9/09, Albena 1, Albena
Italy 2-0 Scotland

24/9/09, Druzhba, Dobrich
Bulgaria 1-0 Northern Ireland

Group 4 Table

	Pld	W	D	L	F	A	P
1 Italy	3	3	0	0	14	0	
2 Scotland	3	2	0	1	7	3	
3 Bulgaria	3	1	0	2	2	11	
4 Northern Ireland	3	0	0	3	0	9	

Group 5 Results

19/9/09, Sportpark Oostenburg, Oosterwolde
Poland 3-0 Lithuania

19/9/09, Sportpark Skoatterwald, Heerenveen
Netherlands 9-1 Israel

21/9/09, Sportpark Skoatterwald, Heerenveen
Israel 0-6 Poland

21/9/09, Sportpark Oostenburg, Oosterwolde
Netherlands 7-0 Lithuania

24/9/09, Sportpark Skoatterwald, Heerenveen
Poland 1-1 Netherlands

24/9/09, Sportpark Oostenburg, Oosterwolde
Lithuania 1-3 Israel

Group 5 Table

	Pld	W	D	L	F	A	P
1 Netherlands	3	2	1	0	17	2	7
2 Poland	3	2	1	0	10	1	
3 Israel	3	1	0	2	4	16	
4 Lithuania	3	0	0	3	1	13	0

Group 6 Results

19/9/09, Tameside, Ashton-under-Lyne
Norway 5-1 Slovakia

19/9/09, Spotland Stadium, Rochdale
England 4-0 Belarus

21/9/09, Tameside, Ashton-under-Lyne
Belarus 0-12 Norway

21/9/09, Gigg Lane, Bury
England 3-1 Slovakia

24/9/09, Spotland Stadium, Rochdale
Norway 1-1 England

24/9/09, Tameside, Ashton-under-Lyne
Slovakia 5-1 Belarus

Group 6 Table

	Pld	W	D	L	F	A	Pts
Norway	3	2	1	0	18	2	7
England	3	2	1	0	8	2	7
Slovakia	3	1	0	2	7	9	3
Belarus	3	0	0	3	1	21	0

Group 7 Results

9/9/09, Yeni Buca, Izmir
Serbia 1-1 Turkey

9/9/09, Buca Sehir, Izmir
France 7-0 Georgia

1/9/09, Yeni Buca, Izmir
France 5-1 Turkey

1/9/09, Buca Sehir, Izmir
Georgia 0-3 Serbia

4/9/09, Buca Sehir, Izmir
Serbia 0-5 France

4/9/09, Yeni Buca, Izmir
Turkey 13-0 Georgia

Group 7 Table

	Pld	W	D	L	F	A	Pts
France	3	3	0	0	17	1	9
Turkey	3	1	1	1	15	6	4
Serbia	3	1	1	1	4	6	4
Georgia	3	0	0	3	0	23	0

Group 8 Results

9/9/09, Városi, Kozármisleny
Hungary 7-0 Latvia

9/9/09, Pécsi Mecsek, Pecs
Belgium 10-0 Armenia

1/9/09, Városi, Kozármisleny
Latvia 2-4 Belgium

1/9/09, Pécsi Mecsek, Pecs
Hungary 4-0 Armenia

4/9/09, Pécsi Mecsek, Pecs
Belgium 0-0 Hungary

4/9/09, Városi, Kozármisleny
Armenia 2-6 Latvia

Group 8 Table

	Pld	W	D	L	F	A	Pts
Belgium	3	2	1	0	14	2	7
Hungary	3	2	1	0	11	0	7
Latvia	3	1	0	2	8	13	3
Armenia	3	0	0	3	2	20	0

Group 9 Results

19/9/09, Lindabrunn, Lindabrunn
Russia 5-1 Greece

19/9/09, Lindabrunn, Lindabrunn
Austria 2-1 Kazakhstan

21/9/09, Lindabrunn, Lindabrunn
Kazakhstan 0-3 Russia

21/9/09, Sportzentrum, Trumau
Austria 2-0 Greece

24/9/09, Schwadorf, Schwadorf
Russia 1-0 Austria

24/9/09, Sportzentrum, Trumau
Greece 1-2 Kazakhstan

Group 9 Table

	Pld	W	D	L	F	A	Pts
1 Russia	3	3	0	0	9	1	9
2 Austria	3	2	0	1	4	2	6
3 Kazakhstan	3	1	0	2	3	6	3
4 Greece	3	0	0	3	2	9	0

Group 10 Results

19/9/09, Ismet Qaibov, Baku
Ukraine 2-0 Cyprus

19/9/09, Tofiq Ismayilov, Baku
Spain 3-0 Azerbaijan

21/9/09, Ismet Qaibov, Baku
Spain 4-1 Cyprus

21/9/09, Tofiq Bähramov, Baku
Azerbaijan 0-3 Ukraine

24/9/09, Ismet Qaibov, Baku
Ukraine 0-4 Spain

24/9/09, Tofiq Bähramov, Baku
Cyprus 3-0 Azerbaijan

Group 10 Table

	Pld	W	D	L	F	A	Pts
1 Spain	3	3	0	0	11	1	9
2 Ukraine	3	2	0	1	5	4	6
3 Cyprus	3	1	0	2	4	6	3
4 Azerbaijan	3	0	0	3	0	9	0

Group 11 Results

19/9/09, Municipal, Albufeira
Switzerland 5-0 Romania

19/9/09, Municipal, Albufeira
Portugal 0-2 Iceland

21/9/09, Fernando Cabrita, Lagos
Iceland 1-1 Switzerland

21/9/09, Fernando Cabrita, Lagos
Portugal 1-2 Romania

24/9/09, Municipal, Albufeira
Switzerland 4-1 Portugal

24/9/09, Fernando Cabrita, Lagos
Romania 0-5 Iceland

Group 11 Table

	Pld	W	D	L	F	A	Pts
1 Switzerland	3	2	1	0	10	2	7
2 Iceland	3	2	1	0	8	1	7
3 Romania	3	1	0	2	2	11	3
4 Portugal	3	0	0	3	2	8	0

Second Qualifying Round

Group 1 Results

27/3/10, Behrn, Orebro
Sweden 3-0 Turkey
Goal(s): 1-0 Schough 38, 2-0 Wegerman 48, 3-0 Schough 51

27/3/10, Behrn, Orebro
Republic of Ireland 0-3 England
Goal(s): 0-1 Duggan 40, 0-2 Stokes 53, 0-3 Flaherty 66

29/3/10, Tunavallen, Eskilstuna
Republic of Ireland 3-2 Turkey
Goal(s): 1-0 Shelby Murphy 32, 2-0 Ryan 40, 2-1 Fatma Kara 42, 3-1 Grant 75, 3-2 Ertürk 80

29/3/10, Swedbank Park, Vasteras
England 3-2 Sweden
Goal(s): 0-1 Wegerman 2, 1-1 Duggan 17, 2-1 Duggan 37, 2-2 Klinga 53, 3-2 Stokes 82

1/4/10, Tunavallen, Eskilstuna
Sweden 4-0 Republic of Ireland
Goal(s): 1-0 Schough 10, 2-0 Heimersson 44(p), 3-0 K. Carlsson 49, 4-0 Erlandsson 51

1/4/10, Swedbank Park, Vasteras
Turkey 0-3 England
Goal(s): 0-1 Nobbs 18, 0-2 Jane 23, 0-3 Nobbs 42

Group 1 Table

	Pld	W	D	L	F	A	Pts
1 England	3	3	0	0	9	2	9
2 Sweden	3	2	0	1	9	3	6
3 Republic of Ireland	3	1	0	2	3	9	3
4 Turkey	3	0	0	3	2	9	0

Group 2 Results

27/3/10, Tatabánya Városi, Tatabanya
Hungary 1-3 Austria
Goal(s): 1-0 Vágó 2, 1-1 Feiersinger 11, 1-2 Puntigam 68, 1-3 Makas 89

27/3/10, Globall Football Park, Telki
France 1-0 Switzerland
Goal(s): 1-0 Rubio 4

UEFA European Women's Under-19 Championship

29/3/10, Tatabánya Várósi, Tatabanya
Switzerland 5-1 Hungary
Goal(s): 1-0 Fimian 32, 2-0 Spahr 45+2,
3-0 Canetta 53, 4-0 Susuri 70, 5-0 Bouakaz 82,
5-1 Sipos 84

29/3/10, Globall Football Park, Telki
France 0-0 Austria

1/4/10, Tatabánya Várósi, Tatabanya
Hungary 0-4 France
Goal(s): 0-1 Barbance 2, 0-2 Barbance 29,
0-3 Crammer 42, 0-4 Thomas 89

1/4/10, Globall Football Park, Telki
Austria 1-1 Switzerland
Goal(s): 0-1 Spahr 74, 1-1 Wenninger 87

Group 2 Table

	Pld	W	D	L	F	A	Pts
1 France	3	2	1	0	5	0	7
2 Austria	3	1	2	0	4	2	5
3 Switzerland	3	1	1	1	6	3	4
4 Hungary	3	0	0	3	2	12	0

Group 3 Results

27/3/10, FK Tavankut, Tavankut
Germany 7-0 Poland
Goal(s): 1-0 Huth 34, 2-0 Huth 43, 3-0
Bagehorn 52, 4-0 Maier 61, 5-0 Malinowski 62,
6-0 Rolser 72, 7-0 Rolser 90+2

27/3/10, Backa, Subotica
Norway 4-0 Serbia
Goal(s): 1-0 Christensen 10, 2-0 Gausdal 69,
3-0 Wigdahl Hegland 86, 4-0 Bjanesoy 88

29/3/10, Backa, Subotica
Germany 8-0 Serbia
Goal(s): 1-0 Doppler 14, 2-0 Simon 28,
3-0 Bagehorn 35, 4-0 Malinowski 36,
5-0 Doppler 40, 6-0 Doppler 69, 7-0 Kayikci 84,
8-0 Malinowski 88

29/3/10, Gradski, Subotica
Poland 1-6 Norway
Goal(s): 0-1 Bjanesoy 13, 0-2 Haavi 45+2,
1-2 Zdunek 49, 1-3 Kleppa 72, 1-4 Bjanesoy 79,
1-5 Christensen 82, 1-6 Bjanesoy 90+4

1/4/10, Backa, Subotica
Norway 0-3 Germany
Goal(s): 0-1 Knaak 56, 0-2 Huth 58,
0-3 Marozsan 60

1/4/10, Gradski, Subotica
Serbia 1-1 Poland
Goal(s): 1-0 Marković 18, 1-1 Smiljković 78(og)

Group 3 Table

	Pld	W	D	L	F	A	Pts
1 Germany	3	3	0	0	18	0	9
2 Norway	3	2	0	1	10	4	6
3 Poland	3	0	1	2	2	14	1
4 Serbia	3	0	1	2	1	13	1

Anna Cholovyaga scored four goals for Russia against the Czech Republic

Group 4 Results

27/3/10, Sputnik-Sport, Sochi
Spain 2-3 Iceland
Goal(s): 1-0 Ana 9, 1-1 Thorvaldsdóttir 10,
2-1 María Losada 39, 2-2 Sigfúsdóttir 53, 2-3
Sigfúsdóttir 77

27/3/10, Sputnik-Sport, Sochi
Russia 6-0 Czech Republic
Goal(s): 1-0 Cholovyaga 18, 2-0 Ziyastinova 25,
3-0 Cholovyaga 36(p), 4-0 Cholovyaga 38,
5-0 Gasparyan 55, 6-0 Cholovyaga 83

29/3/10, Sputnik-Sport, Sochi
Spain 5-0 Czech Republic
Goal(s): 1-0 Amaia 19, 2-0 Diez 21, 3-0 Ana 63,
4-0 Esther 65, 5-0 Serrano 87

29/3/10, Sputnik-Sport, Sochi
Iceland 0-1 Russia
Goal(s): 0-1 Cholovyaga 21

1/4/10, "South-Sport", Sochi
Russia 0-1 Spain
Goal(s): 0-1 Ananyeva 78(og)

1/4/10, Sputnik-Sport, Sochi
Czech Republic 2-1 Iceland
Goal(s): 1-0 Kožárová 18, 2-0 Kožárová 45+1,
2-1 Ásbjörnsdóttir 48

Group 4 Table

	Pld	W	D	L	F	A	Pts
1 Spain	3	2	0	1	8	3	6
2 Russia	3	2	0	1	7	1	6
3 Czech Republic	3	1	0	2	2	12	3
4 Iceland	3	1	0	2	4	5	3

Group 5 Results

27/3/10, De Strokel, Harderwijk
Netherlands 4-0 Finland
Goal(s): 1-0 Van de Wetering 22, 2-0 Martens
45, 3-0 Van de Sanden 58, 4-0 Jansen 71

27/3/10, Oderbos, Apeldoorn
Denmark 1-2 Scotland
Goal(s): 1-0 Harder 22, 1-1 Dempster 73, 1-2
Borthwick 81

29/3/10, Oderbos, Apeldoorn
Denmark 2-1 Finland
Goal(s): 1-0 Junge Pedersen 53, 2-0 Boye
Sørensen 73, 2-1 Vatanen 75

29/3/10, De Strokel, Harderwijk
Scotland 0-0 Netherlands

1/4/10, Oderbos, Apeldoorn
Netherlands 2-1 Denmark
Goal(s): 0-1 Harder 17, 1-1 Jansen 59,
2-1 Grimberg 66

1/4/10, De Strokel, Harderwijk
Finland 1-3 Scotland
Goal(s): 0-1 Dempster 18, 0-2 Dempster 29,
1-2 Yli-Anttila 71, 1-3 Porali 80(og)

Group 5 Table

	Pld	W	D	L	F	A	P
1 Netherlands	3	2	1	0	6	1	
2 Scotland	3	2	1	0	5	2	
3 Denmark	3	1	0	2	4	5	
4 Finland	3	0	0	3	2	9	

Group 6 Results

27/3/10, Gemeentelijk Sportstadion,
Maasmechelen
Italy 3-0 Ukraine
Goal(s): 1-0 Marchese 7, 2-0 Bonetti 41,
3-0 Marchese 51(p)

27/3/10, Mijnstadion, Beringen
Belgium 2-0 Bosnia-Herzegovina
Goal(s): 1-0 Van Gils 45+1, 2-0 Hofman 86

29/3/10, Eburons Dome Op De Keiberg, Tongeren
Ukraine 1-2 Belgium
Goal(s): 1-0 Basanska 29, 1-1 Berrens 65,
1-2 Van Haevermaet 84

29/3/10, Mijnstadion, Beringen
Italy 3-1 Bosnia-Herzegovina
Goal(s): 1-0 Lotto 7, 2-0 Bonansea 21,
3-0 Bonetti 45+1, 3-1 Kuliš 80

1/4/10, Gemeentelijk Sportstadion,
Maasmechelen
Belgium 0-5 Italy
Goal(s): 0-1 Bonetti 4, 0-2 Rosucci 13, 0-3
Bonansea 27, 0-4 Bonansea 32, 0-5 Lotto 85

1/4/10, Eburons Dome Op De Keiberg, Tongeren
Bosnia-Herzegovina 0-6 Ukraine
Goal(s): 0-1 Stets 36, 0-2 Tyelna 59,
0-3 Yakovishyn 61(p), 0-4 Yakovishyn 68,
0-5 Sorokina 74, 0-6 Yakovishyn 89

Group 6 Table

	Pld	W	D	L	F	A	Pts
1 Italy	3	3	0	0	11	1	9
2 Belgium	3	2	0	1	4	6	6
3 Ukraine	3	1	0	2	7	5	3
4 Bosnia-Herzegovina	3	0	0	3	1	11	0

FINAL TOURNAMENT

GROUP A

The final standings suggested a cakewalk for Germany and England but they failed to tell the whole story of a section that remained up for grabs until fatigue shackled the ambitions of Italy and Scotland.

Three-time winners Germany and holders England arrived in Skopje as tournament favourites, and there was little in their opening games to detract from that assessment, England cruising to a 3-1 victory against Scotland while Germany put four past a stunned Italy inside the opening 47 minutes before easing off. The Azzurrine pulled one back through Marta Mason, whose calming piano concert that evening looked to have had the desired effect next time out against England.

Dramatic turnaround

Only in the side after a tournament-ending injury to Roberta Filippozzi, Francesca Vitale's sixth-minute header gave Italy a dream start against the holders, who laboured for an equaliser. Right up until three minutes from time, in fact, when the excellent Toni Duggan orchestrated a dramatic turnaround. She it was who scored an equaliser before her back-heel helped set up the winner, Lauren Bruton's first touch

of the game ending Italy's last-four ambitions as Germany beat Scotland 5-1. The scoreline flattered the Germans as it was 1-1 until 21 minutes from time when Turid Knaak's second goal of the evening suddenly opened the floodgates.

Knaak would claim a hat-trick as Scotland tired, and she was on target again three days later, along with Annika Doppler, as Germany and England vied for top spot. Bruton pulled one back, and although England were unable to prevent a first defeat in 20 games, Germany's 2-1 victory was overshadowed by tournament-ending injuries to substitutes Hasret Kayikci and Laura Vetterlein. Scotland's third finals appearance ended with a third last-place group finish but they ended on a high as two Rebecca Dempster goals helped them come from 3-1 down to earn their first ever point against an Italy side already with one eye on the 2011 finals in Rimini.

Group A Results

24/5/10, Zelezarnica, Skopje
Scotland 1-3 England
Scotland: Clark, Beattie, Robertson, McSorley, Small (Emslie 90+3), Ross, Thomson (Docherty 80), Mitchell, Dempster, Campbell, Borthwick (Ewens 59). Coach: Michelle Kerr (SCO)
England: Spencer, Cunningham, Flaherty, Prosser (Jane 77), Bronze, Bonner, Christiansen, Nobbs, Duggan, Holbrook (Coombs 62), Stokes (Bruton 90+2). Coach: Mo Marley (ENG)
Goal(s): 0-1 Duggan 20, 0-2 Christiansen 34, 1-2 Beattie 67, 1-3 Coombs 72
Yellow Card(s): Robertson 74 (Scotland)
Referee: Azzopardi (MLT)

Laura Coombes (No14) is congratulated by England team-mates after scoring against Scotland

24/5/10, Milano Arena, Kumanovo
Germany 4-1 Italy
Germany: Schult, Maier (Wesely 54), Simon, Elsig, Kleiner, Hendrich (Rolser 54), Knaak (Doppler 64), Bagehorn, Kayikci, Petzelberger, Malinowski. Coach: Maren Meinert (GER)
Italy: Schroffenegger, Ledri, Franco, Filippozzi, Sampietro, Bonetti (Pedretti 73), Ferrandi (Alborghetti 46), Marchese, Rosucci, Bonansea (Mason 46), De Angelis. Coach: Corrado Corradini (ITA)
Goal(s): 1-0 Malinowski 15, 2-0 Kayikci 25, 3-0 Bagehorn 34, 4-0 Simon 47, 4-1 Mason 59
Yellow Card(s): Filippozzi 46 (Italy), Elsig 90+4 (Germany)
Referee: Daly (IRL)

27/5/10, Boris Trajkovski, Skopje
Scotland 1-5 Germany
Scotland: Clark (Alexander 75), Beattie, Robertson, McSorley (McLean 66), Ross, Evans (Emslie 26), Thomson, Ewens, Mitchell, Dempster, Campbell. Coach: Michelle Kerr (SCO)
Germany: Schult, Maier, Kleiner, Knaak, Bagehorn, Kayikci (Doppler 59), Petzelberger, Ioannidou, Wesely, Beckmann (Rolser 70), Malinowski (Hendrich 80). Coach: Maren Meinert (GER)
Goal(s): 0-1 Knaak 45+2, 1-1 Dempster 66, 1-2 Knaak 69, 1-3 Kleiner 82(p), 1-4 Knaak 90+1, 1-5 Doppler 90+2
Yellow Card(s): Beattie 25 (Scotland), Mitchell 41 (Scotland), Campbell 82 (Scotland)
Referee: Karagiorgi (CYP)

27/5/10, Milano Arena, Kumanovo
England 2-1 Italy
England: Spencer, Cunningham (Bruton 90), Flaherty, Bronze, Bonner, Christiansen, Nobbs, Duggan, Holbrook, Stokes (Jane 63), Coombs. Coach: Mo Marley (ENG)
Italy: Schroffenegger, Bartoli (Ferrandi 64), Ledri, Franco, Sampietro, Bonetti, Marchese, Rosucci, Bonansea (Mason 78), Vitale, Alborghetti (Pedretti 59). Coach: Corrado Corradini (ITA)
Goal(s): 0-1 Vitale 6, 1-1 Duggan 87, 2-1 Bruton 90+1
Yellow Card(s): Bonner 12 (England), Bonetti 82 (Italy)
Referee: Chuda (SVK)

30/5/10, Boris Trajkovski, Skopje
Italy 3-3 Scotland
Italy: Valzolgher, Bartoli, Ledri, Franco, Marchese, Rosucci, Bonansea (Pedretti 54), Vitale, Linari, Mason, Pederzoli (Alborghetti 54). Coach: Corrado Corradini (ITA)
Scotland: Alexander, Beattie, Robertson, McSorley, Small, Ross, Thomson (Docherty 66), Ewens (Fitzpatrick 90), Mitchell (Emslie 58), Dempster, Campbell. Coach: Michelle Kerr (SCO)
Goal(s): 1-0 Bonansea 17, 1-1 Ewens 20, 2-1 Franco 22, 3-1 Vitale 29, 3-2 Dempster 64, 3-3 Dempster 73
Yellow Card(s): Bartoli 78 (Italy), Small 78 (Scotland), Franco 85 (Italy)
Referee: Azzopardi (MLT)

30/5/10, National Arena, Skopje
England 1-2 Germany
England: Spencer, Flaherty (Stokes 78), Prosser, Bronze, Christiansen, Nobbs, Holbrook (Spence 76), Hills, Chappell (Cunningham 51), Bruton, Jane. Coach: Mo Marley (ENG)
Germany: Benkarth, Simon, Elsig, Kleiner, Hendrich (Vetterlein 19), Knaak (Kayikci 60), Bagehorn (Petzelberger 46), Rolser, Wesely, Doppler, Beckmann (GER)
Goal(s): 0-1 Doppler 12, 0-2 Knaak 40, 1-2 Bruton 45+1
Yellow Card(s): Flaherty 66 (England), Rolser 85 (Germany)
Referee: Kulcsar (HUN)

Group A Table

	Pld	W	D	L	F	A	Pts
1 Germany	3	3	0	0	11	3	9
2 England	3	2	0	1	6	4	6
3 Italy	3	0	1	2	5	9	1
4 Scotland	3	0	1	2	5	11	1

GROUP B

Previous winners France and Spain both hoped to bend Group B to their will, but it was the Netherlands who impressed most.

The Jong Oranje opened up by defeating Les Bleuettes 2-0 thanks to a pair of first-half headers from corners, Lieke Martens scoring the second almost immediately after coming on as a substitute. Spain fared better against FYROM, and a competition record 8,000-strong crowd at Skopje's National Arena witnessed their 6-0 win against the hosts, with four goals coming in the final nine minutes as the home team's valiant efforts were ultimately undone by fatigue.

French revival

The Netherlands enjoyed an even more convincing outing against Dobrislav Dimovski's charges as they triumphed 7-0, Martens again making an instant impact - this time inside the first minute. She was one of three players to score twice in a match that contrasted wildly with the tight affair at the National Arena, where soaring temperatures made for a tense

Lieke Martens scores the first of the Netherlands' seven goals against FYROM

meeting between France and Spain. Needing a victory to relaunch their campaign, Jean-Michel Degrange's side clinched it thanks to Léa Le Garrec's 69th-minute header and some fine saves from Laetitia Philippe. France's tournament still hung in the balance, however, as a slender win for Spain over the Netherlands in the last round of matches would have brought about their elimination.

All France could do was maximise their chances by seeing off the hosts, and they did that in a 6-1 success that yielded the moment the whole of FYROM had been waiting for – a goal. And what a goal it was as local favourite Natasa Andonova hit the target from fully 40 metres out. It was Les Bleuettes who had more to celebrate, though, as they finished second behind Hesterine de Reus's Jong Oranje, who downed Spain 2-0 – a game in which Martens plundered her fourth goal of the competition – to finish with a perfect nine-point haul.

FYROM's star player
Natasa Andonova

Group B Results

24/5/10, Boris Trajkovski, Skopje
Netherlands 2-0 France
Netherlands: Van den Berg, Van Es, Heemskerk, Worm, Jansen, Van Dongen, Oudejans (Van de Sanden 58), Van de Wetering, Manduapessij, Lewerissa (Martens 34), Bakker (Van Lunteren 71). Coach: Hesterine de Reus (NED)
France: Chauvet, La Villa (Barbetta 46), Gadea, Rousseau, Rubio, Makanza, Catala (Lavaud 46), Crammer, Barbance (Butel 64), Jaurena, Torrent. Coach: Jean-Michel Degrange (FRA)
Goal(s): 1-0 Van Dongen 8, 2-0 Martens 35
Red Card(s): Rousseau 88 (France)
Yellow Card(s): Crammer 43 (France), Jansen 49 (Netherlands), Barbetta 62 (France), Van Dongen 90+4 (Netherlands)
Referee: Karagiorgi (CYP)

24/5/10, National Arena, Skopje
FYROM 0-6 Spain
FYROM: Petrova, Angelova (Dukova 56), Ginovska, Stojanova, Andonova, Miloseska, Andreevska, Petrova (Naceva 90), N. Andonova, Gjorgjieva (Angelovska 61), Rochi. Coach: Dobrislav Dimovski (MKD)
Spain: Paños, Galán, Yazmina, Serano, Corredera (Rodríguez 66), Buceta, Esther (Lareo 71), del Río (Ferez Mendez 60), Losada, Méndez, Beristain. Coach: Angel Vilda Serrano (ESP)
Goal(s): 0-1 Galán 38, 0-2 del Río 53, 0-3 Ferez Mendez 81, 0-4 Losada 85, 0-5 Buceta 87, 0-6 Beristain 90+2
Referee: Radzik-Johan (POL)

27/5/10, Zelezarnica, Skopje
FYROM 0-7 Netherlands
FYROM: Petrova, Ginovska (Dukova 83), Stojanova, Andonova, Kirovska (Angelova 78), Miloseska, Andreevska, Petrova, N. Andonova, Gjorgjieva, Rochi. Coach: Dobrislav Dimovski (MKD)
Netherlands: Van den Berg, Heemskerk, Worm, Van Lunteren, Reichardt (Oudejans 46), Martens, Van de Sanden (Van de Wetering 46), Van der Gragt (Van Es 58), Koopmans, Manduapessij, Lewerissa. Coach: Hesterine de Reus (NED)
Goal(s): 0-1 Martens 1, 0-2 Lewerissa 10, 0-3 Koopmans 23, 0-4 Lewerissa 45, 0-5 Koopmans 56, 0-6 Martens 66, 0-7 Van de Wetering 79
Yellow Card(s): Andonova 71 (FYROM), Oudejans 83 (Netherlands)
Referee: Daly (IRL)

27/5/10, National Arena, Skopje
Spain 0-1 France
Spain: Paños, Galán, Yazmina, Serano, Buceta, Ferez Mendez (Corredera 72), Lareo (Esther 67), Losada, Rodríguez, Ruiz, Beristain (del Río 64). Coach: Angel Vilda Serrano (ESP)
France: Philippe, Butel, La Villa, Gadea, Makanza, Crammer, Le Garrec, Godart (Barbetta 46), Jaurena (Rubio 46), Lavaud (Barbance 46), Torrent. Coach: Jean-Michel Degrange (FRA)
Goal(s): 0-1 Le Garrec 69
Yellow Card(s): Galán 43 (Spain), Serano 57 (Spain)
Referee: Kulcsar (HUN)

30/5/10, Milano Arena, Kumanovo
France 6-1 FYROM
France: Philippe, Butel, Gadea (Torrent 46), Rousseau, Makanza (Lavaud 46), Catala, Barbance (Le Garrec 46), Godart, Berthet, Jaurena, Barbetta. Coach: Jean-Michel Degrange (FRA)
FYROM: Petrova, Angelova , Stojanova (Dukova 86), Andonova, Kirovska (Rochi 46), Miloseska, Andreevska, Petrova, N. Andonova, Gjorgjieva (Ginovska 46), Naceva. Coach: Dobrislav Dimovski (MKD)
Goal(s): 1-0 Makanza 12, 2-0 Catala 14, 3-0 Barbetta 15, 4-0 Makanza 40, 4-1 N. Andonova 66, 5-1 Le Garrec 72, 6-1 Barbetta 88
Referee: Chuda (SVK)

30/5/10, Zelezarnica, Skopje
Spain 0-2 Netherlands
Spain: Paños, Merino, Luna, Galán, Serano, Corredera, Buceta, Esther (Lareo 72), del Río, Losada, Méndez (Ruiz 89). Coach: Angel Vilda Serrano (ESP)
Netherlands: Van den Berg, Van Es, Heemskerk, Worm, Jansen (Koopmans 73), Van Dongen (Lewerissa 66), Martens, Oudejans (Van de Sanden 53), Van de Wetering, Manduapessij, Bakker. Coach: Hesterine de Reus (NED)
Goal(s): 0-1 Van Dongen 37, 0-2 Martens 39
Referee: Radzik-Johan (POL)

Group B Table

	Pld	W	D	L	F	A	Pts
1 Netherlands	3	3	0	0	11	0	9
2 France	3	2	0	1	7	3	6
3 Spain	3	1	0	2	6	3	3
4 FYROM	3	0	0	3	1	19	0

SEMI-FINALS

Prior to the 2010 finals, only three games in the nine-year history of the tournament had gone to a penalty shoot-out. Both semi-finals would be decided in that fashion in FYROM.

Few gave France much hope against a Germany side that had coasted through the group stage with a 100% record. Defeated in their opening game and forced to endure an avalanche of late pressure before winning the second, Les Bleuettes had relied on the Netherlands beating Spain to scrape through. Yet they were a different proposition in Kumanovo. Solène Barbance opened the scoring for France, just as she had done when the two teams met in the group stage the previous year, and she must have been having flashbacks as Kyra Malinowski quickly levelled. Germany went on to win that 2009 encounter 2-1, but this time it took spot-kicks to separate the teams and while France converted all of their penalties, Germany captain Valeria Kleiner crucially shot wide for the three-time winners.

Worm turns

Dutch skipper Siri Worm also had the unwelcome distinction of being the only player to miss in the other semi-final shoot-out, allowing England's Gilly Flaherty

Solène Barbance opened the scoring for France in the semi-final against Germany

to convert the decisive kick. Netherlands coach Hesterine de Reus graciously acknowledged that it was little more than the holders deserved after they had had the better of the previous 120 minutes. A combination of goal-line blocks, English profligacy and Roxanne van den Berg saves had conspired to thwart England and keep the game goalless. Manager Mo Marley admitted that she had "begun to think maybe it's not our day" but she need not have worried. Van den Berg was given no chance in the shoot-out as the holders confidently sealed a return to the National Arena to face France in the final.

Semi-Final Results

2/6/10, Milano Arena, Kumanovo
Germany 1-1 France (aet; 3-5 on pens)
Germany: Schult, Maier, Simon (Ioannidou 97), Elsig, Kleiner, Hendrich (Beckmann 51), Knaak, Bagehorn, Petzelberger, Doppler (Rolser 84), Malinowski. Coach: Bettina Wiegmann (GER)
France: Philippe, Butel, La Villa, Gadea, Rousseau (Torrent 60), Rubio, Makanza (Catala 78), Crammer, Barbance (Le Garrec 69), Jaurena, Barbetta. Coach: Jean-Michel Degrange (FRA)
Goal(s): 0-1 Barbance 28, 1-1 Malinowski 37
Referee: Azzopardi (MLT)

2/6/10, National Arena, Skopje
Netherlands 0-0 England (aet; 4-5 on pens)
Netherlands: Van den Berg, Van Es, Heemskerk (Van der Gragt 118), Worm, Jansen, Van Dongen, Martens, Oudejans (Koopmans 79), Van de Wetering, Manduapessij (Van Lunteren 68), Bakker. Coach: Hesterine de Reus (NED)
England: Spencer, Cunningham, Flaherty, Prosser, Bronze, Bonner, Christiansen, Nobbs, Duggan, Holbrook, Stokes (Jane 117). Coach: Mo Marley (ENG)
Yellow Card(s): Van de Wetering 115 (Netherlands)
Referee: Kulcsar (HUN)

Gilly Flaherty puts England into the final with the winning penalty against the Netherlands

FINAL

England, bidding to retain the title won 12 months earlier in Belarus, initially lived up to their billing as favourites in Skopje but then it all unravelled as two defensive lapses gifted France their second title at this level.

It was all going to plan for Mo Marley's team when Jessica Holbrook gave them a deserved lead midway through the first half. Yet within four minutes a Lucia Bronze error allowed Rose Lavaud to equalise, and shortly after the interval goalkeeper Rebecca Spencer's poor clearance afforded Pauline Crammer the simplest of finishes. There was no way back for a tired-looking England as France merely grew stronger in preparation for the full-time celebrations.

Finals often start at a sedentary pace, a victory for caution over adventure, but there was never a hint of that in this contest. Much of the early endeavour came from Toni Duggan as England's lone striker ran at the France defence. With 25 minutes gone the 18-year-old cut in from the left and teed up Holbrook, who made a difficult finish in a crowded box look easy by shrugging off Adeline Rousseau and firing low into the bottom corner.

Clinical finishes

Twice beaten finalists since claiming their only title in 2003, France must have feared the worst, but having been handed a surprise starting berth, Lavaud repaid coach Jean-Michel Degrange with interest. With Bronze prevaricating, the winger blocked her eventual clearance and gratefully ran on to the favourable rebound before planting a crisp finish into the far corner.

If Bronze could point to some ill fortune, Spencer's culpability for France's second was less in doubt, the goalkeeper directing a pass straight at the only red shirt in England's half ten minutes after the break. Crammer duly slotted into the empty net, and although Spencer made partial amends when she denied the lively Lavaud and Léa Le Garrec, the damage had been done. The title belonged to France.

Final Result

5/6/10, National Arena, Skopje
France 2-1 England
Attendance: 4000
France: Philippe, La Villa, Gadea, Rousseau, Rubio, Makanza (Le Garrec 59), Crammer (Catala 80), Barbance (Butel 59), Jaurena, Barbetta, Lavaud. Coach: Jean-Michel Degrange (FRA)
England: Spencer, Cunningham, Flaherty (Jane 62), Prosser, Bronze, Bonner, Christiansen (Bruton 77), Nobbs, Duggan, Holbrook, Stokes. Coach: Mo Marley (ENG)
Goal(s): 0-1 Holbrook 25, 1-1 Lavaud 29, 2-1 Crammer 55
Referee: Radzik-Johan (POL)

TOP GOALSCORERS

4   Turid Knaak (Germany)
    Lieke Martens (Netherlands)

3   Rebecca Dempster (Scotland)

Turid Knaak   Lieke Martens

France celebrate with the trophy after becoming UEFA Women's Under-19 champions for the second time

WOMEN'S
UNDER17.
CHAMPIONSHIP

WU17

2009/10

Twelve months after the ignominy of losing the UEFA European Women's Under-17 Championship final 7-0 to Germany, Spain returned to Nyon and claimed the title. For the first time in the competition's three-year history Germany failed to become champions. They were eliminated 1-0 in the semi-finals by a Republic of Ireland team making their first appearance at this level. Spain were no less impressive as they swept aside the Netherlands 3-0, and in a year when their men's U17 team were pipped in the European final by England, the women went one better. Spain came close to winning the final in regulation time but in the end the first penalty shoot-out in the tournament's history was required. There, two Dolores Gallardo saves proved crucial for a side coached by Jorge Vilda, whose father Ángel had been in charge a year earlier. Germany beat the Netherlands 2-0 for the consolation of third place.

UEFA European Women's Under-17 Championship

QUALIFYING ROUNDS

First Qualifying Round

Group 1 Results

12/10/09, Mladost, Strumica
England 7-0 Belarus

12/10/09, FC Turnovo, Strumica
Wales 1-1 FYROM

14/10/09, Mladost, Strumica
England 7-0 FYROM

14/10/09, FC Turnovo, Strumica
Belarus 0-2 Wales

17/10/09, Mladost, Strumica
Wales 0-3 England

17/10/09, FC Turnovo, Strumica
FYROM 0-1 Belarus

Group 1 Table

	Pld	W	D	L	F	A	Pts
1 England	3	3	0	0	17	0	9
2 Wales	3	1	1	1	3	4	4
3 Belarus	3	1	0	2	1	9	3
4 FYROM	3	0	1	2	1	9	1

Group 2 Results

16/10/09, Margelacker, Muttenz
Switzerland 23-0 Georgia

16/10/09, In den Sandgruben, Pratteln
Italy 7-0 Faroe Islands

18/10/09, Gitterli, Liestal
Switzerland 7-0 Faroe Islands

18/10/09, Margelacker, Muttenz
Georgia 0-27 Italy

21/10/09, In den Sandgruben, Pratteln
Italy 1-2 Switzerland

21/10/09, Gitterli, Liestal
Faroe Islands 7-0 Georgia

Group 2 Table

	Pld	W	D	L	F	A	Pts
1 Switzerland	3	3	0	0	32	1	9
2 Italy	3	2	0	1	35	2	6
3 Faroe Islands	3	1	0	2	7	14	3
4 Georgia	3	0	0	3	0	57	0

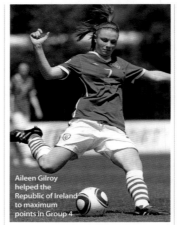

Aileen Gilroy helped the Republic of Ireland to maximum points in Group 4

Group 3 Results

12/10/09, Tatai Honvéd Atletikai Klub, Tata
Hungary 3-2 Croatia

12/10/09, Globall Football Park, Telki
Norway 5-0 Greece

14/10/09, Tatai Honvéd Atletikai Klub, Tata
Croatia 0-4 Norway

14/10/09, Globall Football Park, Telki
Hungary 3-0 Greece

17/10/09, Tatai Honvéd Atletikai Klub, Tata
Norway 5-1 Hungary

17/10/09, Globall Football Park, Telki
Greece 0-2 Croatia

Group 3 Table

	Pld	W	D	L	F	A	Pts
1 Norway	3	3	0	0	14	1	9
2 Hungary	3	2	0	1	7	7	6
3 Croatia	3	1	0	2	4	7	3
4 Greece	3	0	0	3	0	10	0

Group 4 Results

10/10/09, Šmartna, Smartno ob Paki
Republic of Ireland 5-0 Slovenia

10/10/09, Športni Center, Dravograd
Denmark 3-0 Turkey

12/10/09, Športni Center, Dravograd
Republic of Ireland 3-0 Turkey

12/10/09, Ob Jezeru, Velenje
Slovenia 0-2 Denmark

15/10/09, Šmartna, Smartno ob Paki
Denmark 0-1 Republic of Ireland

15/10/09, Športni Center, Dravograd
Turkey 1-0 Slovenia

Group 4 Table

	Pld	W	D	L	F	A	P
1 Republic of Ireland	3	3	0	0	9	0	
2 Denmark	3	2	0	1	5	1	
3 Turkey	3	1	0	2	1	6	
4 Slovenia	3	0	0	3	0	8	

Group 5 Results

22/10/09, CWKS Resowia, Rzeszow
Belgium 3-1 Romania

22/10/09, Stal ZKS, Rzeszow
Poland 2-0 Bulgaria

24/10/09, Stal ZKS, Rzeszow
Bulgaria 1-7 Belgium

24/10/09, CWKS Resowia, Rzeszow
Poland 3-0 Romania

27/10/09, Stal ZKS, Rzeszow
Belgium 1-1 Poland

27/10/09, CWKS Resowia, Rzeszow
Romania 1-0 Bulgaria

Group 5 Table

	Pld	W	D	L	F	A	P
1 Belgium	3	2	1	0	11	3	
2 Poland	3	2	1	0	6	1	
3 Romania	3	1	0	2	2	6	
4 Bulgaria	3	0	0	3	1	10	

Group 6 Results

21/10/09, District Sport Complex, Orhei
Ukraine 6-1 Kazakhstan

21/10/09, Zimbru, Chisinau
Netherlands 9-0 Moldova

23/10/09, Zimbru, Chisinau
Ukraine 5-0 Moldova

23/10/09, District Sport Complex, Orhei
Kazakhstan 0-2 Netherlands

26/10/09, Zimbru, Chisinau
Moldova 1-2 Kazakhstan

UEFA European Women's Under-17 Championship

/10/09, District Sport Complex, Orhei
etherlands 2-1 Ukraine

Group 6 Table

	Pld	W	D	L	F	A	Pts
Netherlands	3	3	0	0	13	1	9
Ukraine	3	2	0	1	12	3	6
Kazakhstan	3	1	0	2	3	9	3
Moldova	3	0	0	3	1	16	0

Group 7 Results

'9/09, KR-völlur, Reykjavik
'ance 8-0 Israel

'9/09, Hlídarendi, Valsvollur
ermany 0-0 Iceland

'9/09, Grindavíkurvöllur, Grindavik
'ance 2-1 Iceland

'9/09, Keflavíkurvöllur, Keflavik
rael 0-10 Germany

'9/09, Akranesvöllur, Akranes
ermany 1-0 France

'9/09, Kópavogsvöllur, Kopavogur
eland 7-0 Israel

Group 7 Table

	Pld	W	D	L	F	A	Pts
Germany	3	2	1	0	11	0	7
France	3	2	0	1	10	2	6
Iceland	3	1	1	1	8	2	4
Israel	3	0	0	3	0	25	0

Group 8 Results

5/9/09, Hallsta IP, Hallstavik
weden 8-0 Latvia

5/9/09, Midgårdsvallen, Marsta
nland 7-0 Estonia

'7/9/09, Studentarnas Idrottspark, Uppsala
nland 5-0 Latvia

'7/9/09, Midgårdsvallen, Marsta
stonia 0-14 Sweden

0/9/09, Studentarnas Idrottspark, Uppsala
weden 4-1 Finland

0/9/09, Hallsta IP, Hallstavik
atvia 3-0 Estonia

Group 8 Table

	Pld	W	D	L	F	A	Pts
Sweden	3	3	0	0	26	1	9
Finland	3	2	0	1	13	4	6
Latvia	3	1	0	2	3	13	3
Estonia	3	0	0	3	0	24	0

Group 9 Results

7/10/09, Sūduva, Marijampole
Czech Republic 1-5 Austria

7/10/09, Marijampolė FC, Marijampole
Scotland 13-0 Lithuania

9/10/09, Marijampolė FC, Marijampole
Czech Republic 18-0 Lithuania

9/10/09, Sūduva, Marijampole
Austria 3-1 Scotland

12/10/09, Sūduva, Marijampole
Scotland 0-5 Czech Republic

12/10/09, Marijampolė FC, Marijampole
Lithuania 1-13 Austria

Group 9 Table

	Pld	W	D	L	F	A	Pts
1 Austria	3	3	0	0	21	3	9
2 Czech Republic	3	2	0	1	24	5	6
3 Scotland	3	1	0	2	14	8	3
4 Lithuania	3	0	0	3	1	44	0

Group 10 Results

24/10/09, Mirko Vucurević, Banatski Dvor
Spain 2-2 Serbia

24/10/09, FK Zadrugar, Lazarevo
Russia 19-0 Armenia

26/10/09, FK Zadrugar, Lazarevo
Spain 21-0 Armenia

26/10/09, Mirko Vucurević, Banatski Dvor
Serbia 2-1 Russia

29/10/09, Mirko Vucurević, Banatski Dvor
Russia 0-3 Spain

29/10/09, FK Zadrugar, Lazarevo
Armenia 0-12 Serbia

Group 10 Table

	Pld	W	D	L	F	A	Pts
1 Spain	3	2	1	0	26	2	7
2 Serbia	3	2	1	0	16	3	7
3 Russia	3	1	0	2	20	5	3
4 Armenia	3	0	0	3	0	52	0

Tashira Renfurm of Group 6 winners the Netherlands

Second Qualifying Round

Group 1 Results

8/4/10, Comunale Fioroni, Ellera
England 3-1 Serbia
Goal(s): 1-0 Wilkinson 5, 2-0 Wilkinson 40+2, 2-1 Popov 61, 3-1 Ayisi 80+6

8/4/10, Comunale Ornari, Perugia
Netherlands 2-0 Italy
Goal(s): 1-0 Zeeman 4, 2-0 Renfurm 8

10/4/10, Comunale Migagheli, Santa Maria Degli Angeli
England 0-0 Italy

10/4/10, Comunale Morandi, Umbertide
Serbia 0-1 Netherlands
Goal(s): 0-1 Bakker 22

13/4/10, Comunale, Deruta
Netherlands 2-1 England
Goal(s): 0-1 Wilkinson 57, 1-1 Zeeman 59(p), 2-1 Schoenmakers 77

13/4/10, Comunale, Bastia Umbra
Italy 6-1 Serbia
Goal(s): 1-0 Pugnali 13, 2-0 Alborghetti 15(p), 3-0 Alborghetti 17, 4-0 Mason 24, 5-0 Moscia 53, 5-1 Savanović 69, 6-1 Piai 80+2

Group 1 Table

	Pld	W	D	L	F	A	Pts
1 Netherlands	3	3	0	0	5	1	9
2 Italy	3	1	1	1	6	3	4
3 England	3	1	1	1	4	3	4
4 Serbia	3	0	0	3	2	10	0

Germany goalkeeper Lena Nuding

Spain's Iraia Pérez de Heredia

Group 2 Results

10/4/10, Pabellón de la Ciudad del Fútbol 1, Madrid
Switzerland 0-0 Belgium

10/4/10, Pabellón de la Ciudad del Fútbol 1, Madrid
Spain 5-1 Denmark
Goal(s): 1-0 Pinel 2, 2-0 Mérida 23, 3-0 Putellas Segura 40+5, 4-0 Pinel 51, 4-1 Iversen 57, 5-1 Mérida 63

12/4/10, Pabellón de la Ciudad del Fútbol 1, Madrid
Switzerland 0-2 Denmark
Goal(s): 0-1 R. Jensen 28, 0-2 Neilsen 31

12/4/10, Pabellón de la Ciudad del Fútbol 1, Madrid
Belgium 0-2 Spain
Goal(s): 0-1 Tazo 80+1, 0-2 García 80+3

15/4/10, Pabellón de la Ciudad del Fútbol 1, Madrid
Spain 0-0 Switzerland

15/4/10, Pabellón de la Ciudad del Fútbol 2, Madrid
Denmark 1-0 Belgium
Goal(s): 1-0 Neilsen 66

Group 2 Table

	Pld	W	D	L	F	A	Pts
1 Spain	3	2	1	0	7	1	7
2 Denmark	3	2	0	1	4	5	6
3 Switzerland	3	0	2	1	0	2	2
4 Belgium	3	0	1	2	0	3	1

Group 3 Results

10/4/10, Fiolent, Simferopol
Republic of Ireland 3-1 Ukraine
Goal(s): 1-0 Gorman 14, 1-1 Vorontsova 38, 2-1 Donnelly 61, 3-1 O'Sullivan 74

10/4/10, Sport KT Arena, Simferopol
Sweden 4-1 Poland
Goal(s): 1-0 J. Andersson 21, 2-0 Rubensson 29, 3-0 J. Andersson 35, 3-1 Królikowska 47, 4-1 Stegius 80+2

13/4/10, Fiolent, Simferopol
Sweden 6-0 Ukraine
Goal(s): 1-0 P. Andersson 14, 2-0 Rolfö 23, 3-0 Rolfö 26, 4-0 J. Andersson 48, 5-0 Rubensson 65(p), 6-0 Holmgren 77

13/4/10, Sport KT Arena, Simferopol
Poland 1-1 Republic of Ireland
Goal(s): 0-1 McLaughlin 11(p), 1-1 Cichosz 24

15/4/10, Sport KT Arena, Simferopol
Republic of Ireland 2-1 Sweden
Goal(s): 0-1 Ericsson 2, 1-1 Jarrett 58(p), 2-1 Campbell 66

15/4/10, Fiolent, Simferopol
Ukraine 2-2 Poland
Goal(s): 1-0 Tyelna 10, 1-1 Gusciora 40, 1-2 Cichosz 45, 2-2 Tyelna 47

Group 3 Table

	Pld	W	D	L	F	A	P
1 Republic of Ireland	3	2	1	0	6	3	
2 Sweden	3	2	0	1	11	3	6
3 Poland	3	0	2	1	4	7	
4 Ukraine	3	0	1	2	3	11	

Group 4 Results

10/4/10, Lindabrunn, Lindabrunn
Norway 2-1 Finland
Goal(s): 0-1 Liljedahl 12, 1-1 Birkeland 31, 2-1 Halvorsen 40+1

10/4/10, Sportzentrum, Trumau
Austria 0-1 Germany
Goal(s): 0-1 Petermann 26

12/4/10, Lindabrunn, Lindabrunn
Germany 4-0 Norway
Goal(s): 1-0 Chojnowski 10, 2-0 Thorisdottir 32(og), 3-0 Petermann 34, 4-0 Petermann 56

12/4/10, Sportzentrum, Trumau
Austria 1-0 Finland
Goal(s): 1-0 Zadrazil 47

15/4/10, Lindabrunn, Lindabrunn
Finland 0-3 Germany
Goal(s): 0-1 Moik 15, 0-2 Petermann 33, 0-3 Romert 58

15/4/10, Lindabrunn, Lindabrunn
Norway 1-0 Austria
Goal(s): 1-0 Hegerberg 76

Group 4 Table

	Pld	W	D	L	F	A	Pt
1 Germany	3	3	0	0	8	0	9
2 Norway	3	2	0	1	3	5	6
3 Austria	3	1	0	2	1	2	3
4 Finland	3	0	0	3	1	6	0

FINAL TOURNAMENT

SEMI-FINALS

Germany arrived in Switzerland as overwhelming favourites to claim a hat-trick of titles at this level, but the semi-final fixtures proved to be anything but predictable.

Spain's Raquel Pirel celebrates scoring her team's second goal against the Netherlands

When the decorated holders were paired with the Republic of Ireland, a team making their bow in a women's final tournament, there were fears of a scoreline similar to Germany's 7-0 final victory over Spain a year earlier. But the underdogs had their day, Megan Campbell's free-kick late in the first half proving enough to give Ireland a 1-0 win and wholly dispelling notions that their 2-1 defeat of fancied Sweden in the qualifying round had been a fluke.

Disappointing end

For Germany it was a disappointing end to a campaign that had begun with their failure to win a match for the first time in the tournament's history, drawing 0-0 with Iceland in their opening qualifier, before they went on to win their next five games with 19 unanswered goals. How coach Ralf Peter must have longed for their five-goal star from the previous year's final, Kyra Malinowski, still eligible but promoted to the U19s.

The Netherlands had qualified impressively for the final-four showpiece event, collecting six wins from as many matches culminating in a 2-1 victory over England. Although they missed out on the first two final tournaments, the Jong Oranje arrived in Nyon having never actually lost a match in the competition. However, that record abruptly came to an end as Spain eased through to a second successive final with goals from Raquel Pinel, substitute Paloma Lazaro and skipper Amanda Sampedro – one of five survivors from the 2009 squad

Semi-Final Results

22/6/10, Colovray, Nyon
Netherlands 0-3 Spain
Netherlands: Huisman, Kelleners, Victoria, Zeeman, Van der Veen (Lardinois 41), Bakker, Scheepers, Renfurm, Moorrees (Bakker 41), Schoenmakers (Bruininberg 60), Tang. Coach: Maria van Kortenhof (NED)
Spain: Gallardo, Sáenz de Pipaon (Nicart 78), Catala, Ivana, Laura, Gema (García 70), Amanda Sampedro, Putellas Segura, Pérez de Heredia, Mérida, Pinel (Lazaro 54). Coach: Jorge Vilda (ESP)
Goal(s): 0-1 Amanda Sampedro 32, 0-2 Pinel 52, 0-3 Lazaro 80+3
Yellow Card(s): Laura 30 (Spain)
Referee: Pirie (SCO)

22/6/10, Colovray, Nyon
Republic of Ireland 1-0 Germany
Republic of Ireland: Moloney , Gleeson, O'Brien, Campbell, Byrne, Grant, Gilroy, Gorman, O'Sullivan, Killeen, Donnelly (Jarrett 63). Coach: Noel King (IRL)
Germany: Nuding, Wensing, Demann, Cramer, Schmid, Jäger, Magull (Pyko 69), Petermann (Leupolz 55), Chojnowski, Romert, Moik (Lotzen 59). Coach: Ralf Peter (GER)
Goal(s): 1-0 Campbell 38
Yellow Card(s): Moloney 73 (Republic of Ireland)
Referee: Pustovoitova (RUS)

Republic of Ireland players show their collective delight at defeating holders and favourites Germany

UEFA European Women's Under-17 Championship

FINAL

The 2009 final had been a one-sided affair, but the 2010 edition proved much tighter, with nothing to separate the Republic of Ireland and Spain after 100 minutes. It took the competition's first penalty shoot-out to decide the winner.

Spain goalkeeper Dolores Gallardo saves from Jessica Gleeson in the penalty shoot-out

With defences refusing to buckle in high temperatures at the Colovray stadium – situated across the road from UEFA headquarters - the final went to spot-kicks, handing the goalkeepers the opportunity to take centre stage. Dolores Gallardo needed no invitation as she denied Rianna Jarrett and Jessica Gleeson. Ciara O'Brien did beat the Spain No1 to prevent a whitewash, but Ana Maria Catala converted to put Spain out of reach. Twelve months after being overwhelmed 7-0 by Germany, La Roja became the second team to etch their name on to the three-year-old trophy.

Birthday honour

Fittingly, the honour of lifting it went to captain and inspiration Amanda Sampedro on her 17th birthday.

She converted Spain's third penalty with confidence and had come as close as anybody to breaking the deadlock in regulation time, actually having the ball in the net before her second-half effort was ruled out for offside. Another fierce strike was met by a save from Grace Moloney, the Irish 'keeper who impressed throughout. She was beaten when Laura Gutiérrez ghosted in at the far post to meet Sara Mérida's cross, but her effort came back off the post.

Laura Gutiérrez of Spain is tackled by Ireland's Niamh McLaughlin

Gutiérrez was indebted to Gallardo at the other end for saving her blushes following a weak back pass, and on an afternoon for redemption she then tucked away Spain's second penalty after Mérida had converted the opener. Defending champions Germany could only watch and wonder, although they did end the tournament on a happy note with a 3-0 win against the Netherlands in the third-place play-off. They therefore booked a place at the 2010 FIFA U-17 Women's World Cup in Trinidad and Tobago alongside Ireland and new European champions Spain.

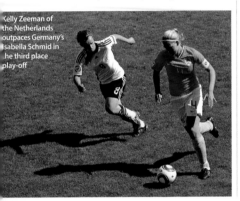

Kelly Zeeman of the Netherlands outpaces Germany's Isabella Schmid in the third place play-off

Third Place Play-Off Result

26/6/10, Colovray, Nyon

Netherlands 0-3 Germany

Netherlands: Van der Wiel, Kelleners, Victoria, Zeeman, Van der Veen (Lardinois 74), De Roest, Bakker (Veltrop 80), Scheepers, Renfurm, Schoenmakers (Moorrees 73), Bakker. Coach: Maria van Kortenhof (NED)

Germany: Nuding, Wensing, Demann, Cramer, Schmid (Leupolz 52), Jäger (Savin 75), Magull, Petermann (Rheinheimer 73), Chojnowski, Romert, Lotzen. Coach: Ralf Peter (GER)

Goal(s): 0-1 Petermann 23, 0-2 Leupolz 56, 0-3 Chojnowski 70

Yellow Card(s): Cramer 33 (Germany), Schoenmakers 61 (Netherlands)

Referee: Pirie (SCO)

Final Result

26/6/10, Colovray, Nyon

Spain 0-0 Republic of Ireland (aet; 4-1 on pens)

Spain: Gallardo, Sáenz de Pipaon, Catala, Ivana, Laura, García, Amanda Sampedro, Putellas Segura (Altonaga 88), Pérez de Heredia (Calderón 69), Mérida, Pinel (Lazaro 58). Coach: Jorge Vilda (ESP)

Republic of Ireland: Moloney, Gleeson, O'Brien, Campbell (Scott 49), Byrne, Grant, Gilroy (Jarrett 97), Gorman, O'Sullivan, Killeen (McLaughlin 69), Donnelly. Coach: Noel King (IRL)

Yellow Card(s): Amanda Sampedro 65 (Spain), Gilroy 107 (Republic of Ireland)

Referee: Pustovoitova (RUS)

Spain are the 2010 UEFA Women's Under-17 champions

UEFA FUTSAL

UEFA
FUTSAL
EURO

EURO
2010

The 2010 UEFA European Futsal Championship in Hungary provided several new features - the January date; the expansion to 12 finalists instead of the previous eight; and the competition being a nationwide affair in Budapest and Debrecen rather than based in a single city. But one thing did not change - the dominance of Spain. They began the finals with a competition record 9-1 defeat of Belarus, and by the time they had lifted the trophy for the third time in a row by beating Portugal 4-2 they had scored 27 goals in their five fixtures, with captain Javi Rodríguez, goalkeeper Luis Amado, defender Kike and winger Daniel all claiming fourth winner's medals. Still, there were plenty of surprises along the way, with Portugal recovering from a wretched start to reach their first final and both the Czech Republic and newcomers Azerbaijan impressing many by reaching the last four.

GROUP STAGE

GROUP A

Boasting a team loaded with Brazilian and Russian-born talent, Azerbaijan were to upstage all-comers in Group A.

Alésio's men took the lead within the first minute of their opener against Hungary through Biro Jade's powerful shot, and while the hosts levelled, further goals from Serjão and Alves ensured a 3-1 win. The oddball contenders then overcame the Czech Republic 6-1 to win the section and set up a decider between Hungary and the Czech Republic, with the hosts only needing a point. A crowd of over 7,000 in Budapest saw Hungary take a 4-0 lead only for the deployment of David Frič as flying goalkeeper to tear them apart. Five-four down in the final minute, the hosts then appeared to have a foot in the last eight thanks to Zsolt Gyurcsányi's effort, but with just 19 seconds to go Marek Kopecký stabbed home a loose ball to snatch a 6-5 win.

Group A Results

19/1/10, Papp László Aréna, Budapest
Hungary 1-3 Azerbaijan
Attendance: 6000
Hungary: Balázs, Reveland, Tóth, Lódi, Madarász, Gyurcsányi, G. Nagy, Trencsényi, Lovas, Sivák, Dróth, Angyalos. Coach: Mihály Kozma (HUN)
Azerbaijan: Tveryankin, Salyanski, Serjão, Felipe, Farzaliyev, Biro Jade, Chuykov, Alves, Thiago, Namig Mammadkarimov, Borisov. Coach: José Alésio da Silva (AZE)
Goal(s): 0-1 Biro Jade 0, 1-1 Lódi 2, 1-2 Serjão 12, 1-3 Alves 16

21/1/10, Papp László Aréna, Budapest
Azerbaijan 6-1 Czech Republic
Attendance: 2069
Azerbaijan: Tveryankin, Salyanski, Serjão, Felipe, Farzaliyev, Biro Jade, Chuykov, Alves, Farajzade, Thiago, Namig Mammadkarimov, Borisov. Coach: José Alésio da Silva (AZE)

Azerbaijan's Felipe and Alves embrace after beating hosts Hungary

Czech Republic: Gerčák, Meller, Polášek, Frič, Sláma, Janovský, Blažej, Kroulík, Havel, Kopecký, Rešetár, Belej. Coach: Tomáš Neumann (CZE)
Goal(s): 1-0 Biro Jade 2, 2-0 Borisov 7, 3-0 Serjão 10, 4-0 Thiago 23, 4-1 Rešetár 26, 5-1 Borisov 28, 6-1 Biro Jade 37 penalty second mark

23/1/10, Papp László Aréna, Budapest
Czech Republic 6-5 Hungary
Attendance: 7066
Czech Republic: Gerčák, Meller, Dlouhý, Kopecký, Frič, Rešetár, Blažej, Polášek, Havel, Belej, Sláma, Janovský. Coach: Tomáš Neumann (CZE)
Hungary: Balázs, Reveland, Trencsényi, Lovas, T. Nagy, Angyalos, G. Nagy, Lódi, Sivák, Madarász, Gyurcsányi, Dróth. Coach: Mihály Kozma (HUN)
Goal(s): 0-1 Dróth 5, 0-2 Lódi 9, 0-3 Lódi 24, 0-4 Dróth 24, 1-4 Rešetár 25, 2-4 Belej 32, 3-4 Dlouhý 34, 4-4 Frič 37, 5-4 Dlouhý 38, 5-5 Gyurcsányi 39, 6-5 Kopecký 39
Yellow Card(s): Blažej 9 (Czech Republic), Kopecký 31 (Czech Republic)

Group A Table

		Pld	W	D	L	F	A	Pts
1	Azerbaijan	2	2	0	0	9	2	6
2	Czech Republic	2	1	0	1	7	11	3
3	Hungary	2	0	0	2	6	9	0

GROUP B

Italy were aiming to improve on their runners-up finish in 2007 and their team, refreshed with young players under new coach Roberto Menichelli, opened with a 4-0 defeat of Belgium.

Saad Assis goals at the start of each half were complemented by a penalty from Luca Ippoliti – back in the team having dropped out not long after their 2003 triumph – and a Clayton Baptistella strike. Belgium's first final campaign since 2003 was then ended by a 4-2 loss to Ukraine, two Karim Bachar goals trumped by Valeriy Zamyatin, Denys Ovsyannikov, Valeriy Legchanov's double penalty and Maxym Pavlenko. That meant two-time runners-up Ukraine, who had gone out in the group stage in 2007, were through alongside Italy. First place went to the Azurrri thanks to a 4-2 win inspired by a Baptistella hat-trick, continuing the form that made him the top scorer in qualifying. Assis was also on target for Italy.

Group B Results

19/1/10, Fönix Arena, Debrecen
Italy 4-0 Belgium
Attendance: 2226
Italy: Feller, Mammarella, Forte, Baptistella, Ippoliti, Saad Assis, Ercolessi, Romano, Botta, Bácaro, Vinicius Duarte, Patrick Nora. Coach: Roberto Menichelli (ITA)

Italy's Vincenzo Botta fires in a shot against Ukraine

GROUP C

Slovenia always looked likely to struggle in a group featuring futsal superpower Russia and a capable Serbia team, and so it proved, with a 5-1 loss to Russia in their opener and a 2-0 defeat by Serbia thereafter ending their campaign in the space of three days.

That, however, set up a thrilling tie to decide who would win the section – and perhaps more importantly avoid Spain in the last eight. Things looked to be going with form as Konstantin Maevski slid the ball through goalkeeper Vladimir Ranisavljević's legs to make it 2-0 to Russia just after the break. However, goals from Bojan Pavićević, schemer-in-chief Marko Perić and Vladimir Lazić turned the tide in the space of two minutes. Mladen Kocić made it 4-2 on the break, and while Perić deflected past his own 'keeper late on, Serbia had caused an upset and Russia were off to Debrecen to meet Spain.

Group C Results

20/1/10, Papp László Aréna, Budapest
Russia 5-1 Slovenia
Attendance: 2287
Russia: Zuev, Garagulya, Fukin, Pula, Maevski, Cirilo, Shayakhmetov, Agapov, Abyshev, Sergeev, Khamadiyev, Chistopolov. Coach: Sergei Skorovich (RUS)
Slovenia: Mohorič, Pertovt, Osojnik, Drobnič, Goranović, Melink, Kragelj, Čujec, Osredkar, R. Uršič, Sovdat, Pertič. Coach: Andrej Dobovičnik (SVN)
Goal(s): 1-0 Chistopolov 3, 2-0 Chistopolov 18, 3-0 Pula 18, 4-0 Khamadiyev 23, 4-1 Čujec 36, 5-1 Shayakhmetov 39
Yellow Card(s): Maevski 15 (Russia)

Serbia's Predrag Rajić celebrates scoring against Russia

Belgium: Morant, Paggetta, Achahbar, Chaibai, Bachar, Sababti, Aabbassi, André, Lúcio, Ferrian, Zico, Fossé. Coach: Benjamin Meurs (BEL)
Goal(s): 1-0 Saad Assis 1, 2-0 Saad Assis 22, 3-0 Ippoliti 22(p), 4-0 Baptistella 37

21/1/10, Fönix Arena, Debrecen
Belgium 2-4 Ukraine
Attendance: 1583
Belgium: Morant, Paggetta, Aabbassi, Chaibai, Bachar, Sababti, Achahbar, André, Lúcio, Neukermans, Zico, Salhi. Coach: Benjamin Meurs (BEL)
Ukraine: Kardash, Lysenko, Pavlenko, Cheporniuk, Legchanov, Kondratyuk, Ivanov, Rogachov, Valyenko, Ovsyannikov, Zamyatin, Silchenko. Coach: Gennadiy Lisenchuk (UKR)
Goal(s): 0-1 Zamyatin 10, 0-2 Ovsyannikov 15, 1-2 Bachar 17, 1-3 Legchanov 19penalty second mark, 1-4 Pavlenko 34, 2-4 Bachar 39
Red Card(s): Aabbassi 27 (Belgium)
Yellow Card(s): Aabbassi 25 (Belgium), Aabbassi 27 (Belgium)

23/1/10, Fönix Arena, Debrecen
Ukraine 2-4 Italy
Attendance: 2339
Ukraine: Kardash, Lysenko, Pavlenko, Cheporniuk, Legchanov, Kondratyuk, Romanov, Ivanov, Rogachov, Ovsyannikov, Zamyatin, Silchenko. Coach: Gennadiy Lisenchuk (UKR)
Italy: Feller, Mammarella, Forte, Baptistella, Ippoliti, Saad Assis, Romano, Botta, Bácaro, Rizzo, Patrick Nora, Gabriel Lima. Coach: Roberto Menichelli (ITA)
Goal(s): 0-1 Baptistella 12, 1-1 Cheporniuk 22, 1-2 Baptistella 27, 1-3 Saad Assis 30, 1-4 Baptistella 30, 2-4 Pavlenko 38

Group B Table

		Pld	W	D	L	F	A	Pts
1	Italy	2	2	0	0	8	2	6
2	Ukraine	2	1	0	1	6	6	3
3	Belgium	2	0	0	2	2	8	0

22/1/10, Papp László Aréna, Budapest
Slovenia 0-2 Serbia
Attendance: 2236
Slovenia: Mohorič, Pertovt, Osojnik, Drobnič, Goranovič, Melink, Kragelj, Čujec, R. Uršič, Brkić, Sovdat, Pertič. Coach: Andrej Dobovičnik (SVN)
Serbia: Stojanović, V. Ranisavljević, Perić, Pavićević, Rakić, Borojević, Kocić, Janjić, Lazić, Tomin, Bojović, Rajčević. Coach: Aca Kovačević (SRB)
Goal(s): 0-1 Rakić 20, 0-2 Janjić 28
Yellow Card(s): Lazić 18 (Serbia)

24/1/10, Papp László Aréna, Budapest
Serbia 4-3 Russia
Attendance: 1977
Serbia: Stojanović, V. Ranisavljević, Perić, Kocić, Pavićević, Rakić, Janjić, Bogdanović, Lazić, Borojević, Bojović, Rajčević. Coach: Aca Kovačević (SRB)
Russia: Zuev, Garagulya, Fukin, Pula, Maevski, Cirilo, Shayakhmetov, Agapov, Timoschenkov, Sergeev, Khamadiyev, Chistopolov. Coach: Sergei Skorovich (RUS)
Goal(s): 0-1 Chistopolov 16, 0-2 Maevski 21, 1-2 Pavićević 29, 2-2 Perić 30, 3-2 Lazić 31, 4-2 Kocić 35, 4-3 Perić 37(og)
Yellow Card(s): Perić 14 (Serbia), Chistopolov 32 (Russia)

Group C Table

		Pld	W	D	L	F	A	Pts
1	Serbia	2	2	0	0	6	3	6
2	Russia	2	1	0	1	8	5	3
3	Slovenia	2	0	0	2	1	7	0

GROUP D

Belarus could not have asked for a tougher game on their debut finals appearance than Spain and although Juanra's early strike was cancelled out by Vladimir Levus, Kike made it 2-1 almost immediately.

Spain piled on the pressure and in the last 13 minutes it told with seven unanswered goals, including a Javi Rodríguez hat-trick, for a finals record 9-1 win. It all seemed to be going wrong again for Belarus when they fell two down to Portugal but by the 31st minute the underdogs held a 4-2 lead. Portugal responded to go 5-4 up and the drama was not over as with one second left Belarus won a double penalty and Aleksei Popov claimed his third of the game. A draw was now sufficient for Portugal provided they avoided losing to Spain by more than Belarus did. However, despite scoring first they only just avoided that fate, going down 6-1.

Group D Results

20/1/10, Fönix Arena, Debrecen
Spain 9-1 Belarus
Attendance: 1729
Spain: Luis Amado, Juanjo, Ortiz, Juanra, Borja, Lin, Javi Eseverri, Torras, Álvaro, Javi Rodríguez, Kike, Daniel. Coach: José Venancio López Hierro (ESP)

Aleksei Popov of Belarus (right) races past two Portuguese opponent

Belarus: Navoichik, Golovnyov, Chernik, Yeliseev, Savintsev, Levus, Gayduk, Miranovich, Komarov, Kuznetsov, Gorbenko, Popov. Coach: Valeriy Dosko (BLR)
Goal(s): 1-0 Juanra 2, 1-1 Levus 7, 2-1 Kike 8, 3-1 Torras 27, 4-1 Javi Rodríguez 29, 5-1 Javi Rodríguez 30, 6-1 Ortiz 31, 7-1 Juanra 34, 8-1 Lin 36, 9-1 Javi Rodríguez 39
Yellow Card(s): Levus 25 (Belarus), Chernik 33 (Belarus)

22/1/10, Fönix Arena, Debrecen
Belarus 5-5 Portugal
Attendance: 2087
Belarus: Navoichik, Golovnyov, Chernik, Savintsev, Levus, Popov, Gayduk, Yuraga, Yeliseev, Komarov, Kuznetsov, Gorbenko. Coach: Valeriy Dosko (BLR)
Portugal: João Benedito, Bébé, Leitão, Pedro Costa, Arnaldo, Gonçalo Alves, Evandro, Joel Queirós, Cardinal, Israel, Paulinho, Pedro Cary. Coach: Orlando Francisco Alves Duarte (POR)
Goal(s): 0-1 Cardinal 6, 0-2 Joel Queirós 13, 1-2 Chernik 16, 2-2 Popov 25, 3-2 Popov 29, 4-2 Gayduk 31, 4-3 Joel Queirós 31(p), 4-4 Cardinal 36, 4-5 Arnaldo 38, 5-5 Popov 39penalty second mark
Yellow Card(s): Komarov 13 (Belarus), Chernik 31 (Belarus)

24/1/10, Fönix Arena, Debrecen
Portugal 1-6 Spain
Attendance: 3740
Portugal: João Benedito, André Sousa, Pedro Costa, Arnaldo, Cardinal, Gonçalo Alves, Evandro, Leitão, Joel Queirós, Israel, Joaõ Matos, Pedro Cary. Coach: Orlando Francisco Alves Duarte (POR)
Spain: Luis Amado, Juanjo, Álvaro, Javi Rodríguez, Kike, Juanra, Ortiz, Javi Eseverri, Torras, Fernandao, Lin, Daniel. Coach: José Venancio López Hierro (ESP)
Goal(s): 1-0 Arnaldo 5, 1-1 Torras 14, 1-2 Torras 15, 1-3 Juanra 23, 1-4 Kike 29, 1-5 Fernandao 31, 1-6 Lin 38
Yellow Card(s): Ortiz 28 (Spain)

Group D Table

		Pld	W	D	L	F	A	Pts
1	Spain	2	2	0	0	15	2	6
2	Portugal	2	0	1	1	6	11	1
3	Belarus	2	0	1	1	6	14	1

QUARTER-FINALS

Relative unknowns at the start of the finals, Azerbaijan – and their burly pivot Serjão in particular - quickly gained a cult following in Budapest, but their 42-year-old goalkeeper Andrey Tveryankin was to be their quarter-final hero, saving two penalties in a 4-2 shoot-out success after Ukraine's diligent craftsmen had held Alésio's wearying fine artists to a 3-3 draw. Rizvan Farzaliyev – one of the handful of Azeri-born players in Alésio's squad – had the honour of hitting the winner.

Faint praise

Serbia captain Bojan Pavićević damned Portugal with faint praise before the other Budapest semi-final, saying: "It's just their pace that makes them stand out." It was to prove a grimly prophetic statement as a revived Portugal ran Serbia ragged. Joel Queirós scored before the break as relentless running and sharp interceptions cut Serbia's attacking lines, and further goals from Cardinal, Joel, Leitão and Arnaldo contributed to a well-deserved 5-1 victory.

Over in Debrecen, there was an upset as the Czech Republic knocked out 2007 runners-up Italy on penalties after a 3-3 draw. Italy led twice in the first half but in the end needed an Assis goal, his second of the match and fifth of the finals, to force spot kicks. Libor Gerčák, selected ahead of Tomáš Meller in the Czech goal, saved Italy's first three attempts and Frič converted for a decisive 3-1 lead.

David Frič takes the acclaim after scoring the winning penalty for the Czech Republic in their quarter-final shoot-out against Italy

Shoot-out success

Penalties were also needed to split Spain and Russia, a fixture many had expected in the final. Spain had the better of the 40 minutes but could find no way past Sergei Zuev in the first goalless knockout game in Futsal EURO history. The shoot-out score was 4-4 after five attempts each and both teams converted their next two kicks. Fernandao then made it 7-6 and Luis Amado's save from Konstantin Timoschenkov took Spain through.

Quarter-Final Results

25/1/10, Fönix Arena, Debrecen
Czech Republic 3-3 Italy (3-1 on penalties)
Attendance: 1860
Czech Republic: Gerčák, Meller, Dlouhý, Kopecký, Frič, Rešetár, Kroulík, Havel, J. Novotný, Belej, Sláma, Janovský. Coach: Tomáš Neumann (CZE)
Italy: Feller, Mammarella, Forte, Baptistella, Ippoliti, Saad Assis, Ercolessi, Romano, Botta, Bácaro, Vinicius Duarte, Patrick Nora. Coach: Roberto Menichelli (ITA)
Goal(s): 0-1 Vinicius Duarte 5, 1-1 Kopecký 7, 1-2 Saad Assis 17, 2-2 Sláma 23, 3-2 Vinicius Duarte 27(og), 3-3 Saad Assis 32
Yellow Card(s): Ippoliti 39 (Italy), Kopecký 39 (Czech Republic)

25/1/10, Papp László Aréna, Budapest
Azerbaijan 3-3 Ukraine (4-2 on penalties)
Attendance: 2207
Azerbaijan: Tveryankin, Salyanski, Serjão, Felipe, Farzaliyev, Biro Jade, Chuykov, Alves, Farajzade, Thiago, Namig Mammadkarimov, Borisov. Coach: José Alésio da Silva (AZE)
Ukraine: Kornyeyev, Lysenko, Romanov, Rogachov, Cheporniuk, Zamyatin, Pavlenko, Ivanov, Ovsyannikov, Legchanov, Kondratyuk, Silchenko. Coach: Gennadiy Lisenchuk (UKR)
Goal(s): 0-1 Romanov 0, 1-1 Farzaliyev 2, 1-2 Cheporniuk 10, 2-2 Thiago 17, 3-2 Biro Jade 24, 3-3 Kondratyuk 33
Yellow Card(s): Biro Jade 14 (Azerbaijan), Silchenko 26 (Ukraine), Thiago 34 (Azerbaijan), Tveryankin 35 (Azerbaijan), Farzaliyev 39 (Azerbaijan)

26/1/10, Fönix Arena, Debrecen
Russia 0-0 Spain (6-7 on penalties)
Attendance: 2045
Russia: Zuev, Garagulya, Shayakhmetov, Pula, Maevski, Cirilo, Fukin, Timoschenkov, Abyshev, Sergeev, Khamadiyev, Chistopolov. Coach: Sergei Skorovich (RUS)
Spain: Luis Amado, Juanjo, Fernandao, Álvaro, Javi Rodríguez, Kike, Ortiz, Torras, Juanra, Borja, Lin, Daniel. Coach: José Venancio López Hierro (ESP)
Yellow Card(s): Javi Rodríguez 40 (Spain), Fernandao 40 (Spain)

26/1/10, Papp László Aréna, Budapest
Serbia 1-5 Portugal
Attendance: 2843
Serbia: Stojanović, V. Ranisavljević, Perić, Kocić, Pavićević, Rakić, Janjić, Bogdanović, Lazić, Borojević, Bojović, Rajčević. Coach: Aca Kovačević (SRB)
Portugal: João Benedito, Bébé, Leitão, Pedro Costa, Arnaldo, Gonçalo Alves, Evandro, Joel Queirós, Cardinal, Israel, João Matos, Pedro Cary. Coach: Orlando Francisco Alves Duarte (POR)
Goal(s): 0-1 Joel Queirós 12, 0-2 Cardinal 22, 0-3 Joel Queirós 29, 0-4 Leitão 33, 1-4 Bojović 36, 1-5 Arnaldo 38
Yellow Card(s): Rajčević 12 (Serbia), Bojović 29 (Serbia), Kocić 30 (Serbia), Leitão 37 (Portugal)

SEMI-FINALS

Two of the quarter-finals had finished 3-3 and gone to penalties; likewise the first of the last-four encounters in Debrecen between Azerbaijan and Portugal, who had drawn by the same scoreline in qualifying.

Portugal's Gonçalo Alves steps up to convert the decisive penalty in the semi-final shoot-out against Azerbaijan

Azerbaijan coach Alésio, without the injured Alves, had an ace up his sleeve with the early use of Biro Jade as a flying goalkeeper – indeed the move would have been used from the kick-off had his side had the honour. In the eighth minute they went ahead in a fine passing move finished off by Thiago. With regular Azerbaijan No1 Andrey Tveryankin back in goal, Cardinal quickly equalised but Felipe then made it 2-1 to Azerbaijan. Then, in a thrilling 81-second period starting in the 28th minute, Joaõ Matos and Pedro Costa edged Portugal ahead before Biro Jade's immediate equaliser. Penalties were to go Portugal's way as Bébé blocked Azerbaijan's second strike from Thiago and eventually Gonçalo Alves converted for a 5-3 win to take his nation into a major futsal final for the first time, erasing the memories of their spot-kick elimination by Spain in the last four on home soil in 2007.

Super Spain

The game that followed was not quite as close, Spain defeating the Czech Republic 8-1, the most convincing margin of victory in any Futsal EURO knockout game. Captain Javi Rodríguez headed the opener and Ortiz made it 2-0 in the seventh minute. He added another

later in the half, also after a clever set-piece move, and with the Czechs committed to attack, Spain goalkeeper Luis Amado drop-kicked in just before the break for his first goal in 11 years of UEFA club and national-team competition. Spain continued to dominate throughout the second half and Borja and Fernandao both increased the lead before two quickfire goals from Daniel. Martin Dlouhý did manage a late consolation.

Spain's Daniel (left) and Lin celebrate Spain's eighth goal against the Czech Republic

Semi-Final Results

28/1/10, Fönix Arena, Debrecen
Azerbaijan 3-3 Portugal (3-5 on penalties)
Attendance: 2840
Azerbaijan: Tveryankin, Salyanski, Serjão, Felipe, Farzaliyev, Borisov, Chuykov, Farajzade, Thiago, Biro Jade, Namig Mammadkarimov. Coach: José Alésio da Silva (AZE)
Portugal: João Benedito, Bébé, Leitão, Arnaldo, Gonçalo Alves, Joaõ Matos, Evandro, Pedro Costa, Joel Queirós, Cardinal, Israel, Pedro Cary. Coach: Orlando Francisco Alves Duarte (POR)
Goal(s): 1-0 Thiago 7, 1-1 Cardinal 9, 2-1 Felipe 17, 2-2 Joaõ Matos 27, 2-3 Pedro Costa 28, 3-3 Biro Jade 28
Yellow Card(s): Biro Jade 18 (Azerbaijan)

28/1/10, Fönix Arena, Debrecen
Czech Republic 1-8 Spain
Attendance: 3269
Czech Republic: Gerčák, Meller, Blažej, Dlouhý, Frič, Rešetár, Polášek, Havel, J. Novotný, Belej, Sláma, Janovský. Coach: Tomáš Neumann (CZE)
Spain: Luis Amado, Juanjo, Álvaro, Javi Rodríguez, Kike, Juanra, Ortiz, Torras, Fernandao, Borja, Lin, Daniel. Coach: José Venancio López Hierro (ESP)
Goal(s): 0-1 Javi Rodríguez 4, 0-2 Ortiz 6, 0-3 Ortiz 16, 0-4 Luis Amado 19, 0-5 Borja 25, 0-6 Fernandao 32, 0-7 Daniel 36, 0-8 Daniel 38, 1-8 Dlouhý 38
Yellow Card(s): Frič 28 (Czech Republic)

THIRD PLACE PLAY-OFF

The third-place play-off proved an entertaining curtain-raiser for the final in Debrecen as the Czech Republic defeated Azerbaijan 5-3, having led on 27 seconds through Michal Belej. By half-time Azerbaijan led 2-1 but were 4-2 down with five minutes left.

Rajab Farajzadeh set up an exciting finish but Marek Kopecký rolled the ball into an empty net from defence with nine seconds left. Still, Azerbaijan's performance was the best by a Futsal EURO debutant since the inaugural tournament.

Third place Play-off Result

1/1/10, Fönix Arena, Debrecen
Azerbaijan 3-5 Czech Republic
Attendance: 3603
Azerbaijan: Tveryankin, Salyanski, Serjão, Felipe, Farzaliyev, Thiago, Zhuykov, Farajzade, Namig Mammadkarimov, Borisov. Coach: José Alésio da Silva (AZE)
Czech Republic: Gerčák, Meller, Dlouhý, Kopecký, Frič, Rešetár, Kroulík, Pavel, J. Novotný, Belej, Sláma, Janovský. Coach: Tomáš Neumann (CZE)
Goal(s): 0-1 Belej 0, 1-1 Borisov 7, 2-1 Serjão 18, 2-2 Sláma 23, 2-3 Farzaliyev 25(og), 2-4 J. Novotný 35, 3-4 Farajzade 37, 3-5 Kopecký 39
Yellow Card(s): Serjão 10 (Azerbaijan), Borisov 13 (Azerbaijan), Janovský 30 (Czech Republic)

Ortiz opens the scoring for Spain in the final against Portugal

FINAL

For 37 minutes and 49 seconds, the final was a procession for Spain, reviving memories of their 6-1 defeat of Portugal only six days earlier in the same venue. With nine minutes gone Ortiz intercepted a Pedro Costa pass and shot in to open the scoring. Four minutes later Javi Rodríguez received the ball on the edge of the box with Israel between him and the goal but his back-heel surprised both the defender and goalkeeper Bébé, making it 2-0.

Portugal were still playing a cautious game and Bébé was racking up the saves both before and after half-time, while Álvaro hit the post. At the other end Leitão's lob came off the woodwork but Spain seemed to have sealed it when Lin added a third in the 36th minute. However, Portugal now went for broke and earned immediate reward as Gonçalo pulled one back and Joel scrambled in with 92 seconds remaining. In the end, though, Spain sealed it thanks to Daniel claiming his 16th Futsal EURO finals goal to go outright second on the all-time list. It was a fitting end to his stellar international career while the other stalwart bowing out, Javi Rodríquez, had an extra reward as his fifth goal of the finals – and 99th international strike – ensured he shared the Golden Boot with Saad Assis and Joel Queirós.

Final Result

30/1/10, Fönix Arena, Debrecen
Portugal 2-4 Spain
Attendance: 4845
Portugal: João Benedito, Bébé, Pedro Costa, Arnaldo, Gonçalo Alves, Pedro Cary, Evandro, Leitão, Joel Queirós, Cardinal, Israel, João Matos. Coach: Orlando Francisco Alves Duarte (POR)
Spain: Luis Amado, Juanjo, Álvaro, Javi Rodríguez, Kike, Borja, Ortiz, Torras, Fernandao, Juanra, Lin, Daniel. Coach: José Venancio López Hierro (ESP)
Goal(s): 0-1 Ortiz 8, 0-2 Javi Rodríguez 12, 0-3 Lin 35, 1-3 Gonçalo Alves 37, 2-3 Joel Queirós 38, 2-4 Daniel 39
Yellow Card(s): Cardinal 28 (Portugal), Kike 38 (Spain)

TOP GOALSCORERS

5	Saad Assis (Italy), Javi Rodríguez (Spain), Joel Queirós (Portugal)
4	Cleyton Baptistella (Italy), Biro Jade (Azerbaijan), Cardinal (Portugal), Ortiz (Spain)

Saad Assis   Javi Rodriguez   Joel Queirós

2009/10

UEFA FUTSAL CUP

SL Benfica famously won two European Champion Clubs' Cups in the early 1960s and now they have a continental honour in the small-sided game to go alongside them after victory on home territory in the UEFA Futsal Cup. They had reached the old two-legged final in 2004 and lost to Interviú Madrid, but six years later they turned the tables on the three-time champions with a 3-2 extra-time victory in front of a competition-record crowd of 9,400 at Lisbon's Pavilhão Atlântico to become the first ever Portuguese winners. Benfica's historic triumph was not the only fresh thing about the 2010 finals. Whereas all previous final-four tournaments since the showpiece format was introduced in 2007 had featured the top four seeds, this time three established names fell in the elite round. Benfica ousted 2008 winners MFK Viz-Sinara Ekaterinburg, Azerbaijan's Araz Naxçivan defeated three-time semi-finalists Kairat Almaty, and Italy's Luparense C/5 pipped Spanish champions ElPozo Murcia FS.

WINNERS
Futsal Cup Finals 2009

PRELIMINARY ROUND

Group A Results

20/8/09, Vladislav, Varna
SC Tornado Chisinau 4-1 Gazi Üniversitesi
20/8/09, Vladislav, Varna
MFC Varna 8-3 Cork City FC
21/8/09, Vladislav, Varna
Cork City FC 0-10 SC Tornado Chisinau
21/8/09, Vladislav, Varna
MFC Varna 5-2 Gazi Üniversitesi
23/8/09, Vladislav, Varna
Gazi Üniversitesi 5-2 Cork City FC
23/8/09, Vladislav, Varna
SC Tornado Chisinau 4-3 MFC Varna

Group A Table

		Pld	W	D	L	F	A	Pts
1	SC Tornado Chisinau	3	3	0	0	18	4	9
2	MFC Varna	3	2	0	1	16	6	6
3	Gazi Üniversitesi	3	1	0	2	8	11	3
4	Cork City FC	3	0	0	3	5	23	0

Group B Results

17/8/09, Tassos Papadopoulos, Nicosia
RCS Košice 4-2 Nidaros Futsal Trondheim
17/8/09, Tassos Papadopoulos, Nicosia
AC Omonia 10-3 FC Seefeld Zürich
18/8/09, Tassos Papadopoulos, Nicosia
FC Seefeld Zürich 2-2 RCS Košice
18/8/09, Tassos Papadopoulos, Nicosia
AC Omonia 5-4 Nidaros Futsal Trondheim
20/8/09, Tassos Papadopoulos, Nicosia
RCS Košice 2-5 AC Omonia
20/8/09, Tassos Papadopoulos, Nicosia
Nidaros Futsal Trondheim 2-1 FC Seefeld Zürich

Group B Table

		Pld	W	D	L	F	A	Pts
1	AC Omonia	3	3	0	0	20	9	9
2	RCS Košice	3	1	1	1	8	9	4
3	Nidaros Futsal Trondheim	3	1	0	2	8	10	3
4	FC Seefeld Zürich	3	0	1	2	6	14	1

Group C Results

17/8/09, Bregovi, Trebinje
KMF Leotar Trebinje 6-0 Futsal Panthers Köln
17/8/09, Bregovi, Trebinje
FK Nikars Riga 6-4 JK Sillamäe Kalev
18/8/09, Bregovi, Trebinje
Futsal Panthers Köln 3-7 FK Nikars Riga
18/8/09, Bregovi, Trebinje
KMF Leotar Trebinje 11-0 JK Sillamäe Kalev
20/8/09, Bregovi, Trebinje
JK Sillamäe Kalev 2-6 Futsal Panthers Köln
20/8/09, Bregovi, Trebinje
FK Nikars Riga 9-5 KMF Leotar Trebinje

Group C Table

		Pld	W	D	L	F	A	Pts
1	FK Nikars Riga	3	3	0	0	22	12	9
2	KMF Leotar Trebinje	3	2	0	1	22	9	6
3	Futsal Panthers Köln	3	1	0	2	9	15	3
4	JK Sillamäe Kalev	3	0	0	3	6	23	0

Group D Results

20/8/09, Tapiola Urheiluhalli, Espoo
Golden Futsal Team 6-2 FC Santos
20/8/09, Tapiola Urheiluhalli, Espoo
Roubaix AFS 4-6 Helvécia Futsal London
22/8/09, Tapiola Urheiluhalli, Espoo
Golden Futsal Team 6-4 Helvécia Futsal London
22/8/09, Tapiola Urheiluhalli, Espoo
FC Santos 0-4 Roubaix AFS
23/8/09, Tapiola Urheiluhalli, Espoo
Helvécia Futsal London 11-2 FC Santos
23/8/09, Tapiola Urheiluhalli, Espoo
Roubaix AFS 1-7 Golden Futsal Team

Group D Table

		Pld	W	D	L	F	A	Pts
1	Golden Futsal Team	3	3	0	0	19	7	9
2	Helvécia Futsal London	3	2	0	1	21	12	6
3	Roubaix AFS	3	1	0	2	9	13	3
4	FC Santos	3	0	0	3	4	21	0

Group E Results

19/8/09, S.Darius & S.Girenas Sport Center, Kaunas
Tirana 4-3 White Eagles FC
19/8/09, S.Darius & S.Girenas Sport Center, Kaunas
FK Nautara Kaunas 4-1 FC Madriu
20/8/09, S.Darius & S.Girenas Sport Center, Kaunas
FC Madriu 2-4 Tirana
20/8/09, S.Darius & S.Girenas Sport Center, Kaunas
FK Nautara Kaunas 9-7 White Eagles FC
22/8/09, S.Darius & S.Girenas Sport Center, Kaunas
White Eagles FC 1-1 FC Madriu
22/8/09, S.Darius & S.Girenas Sport Center, Kaunas
Tirana 3-4 FK Nautara Kaunas

Group E Table

		Pld	W	D	L	F	A	Pts
1	FK Nautara Kaunas	3	3	0	0	17	11	9
2	Tirana	3	2	0	1	11	9	6
3	White Eagles FC	3	0	1	2	11	14	1
4	FC Madriu	3	0	1	2	4	9	1

Group F Results

19/8/09, SHS Wr. Neustadt Dr. Fred Sinowatz Schule, Wiener Neustadt
ASA Tel-Aviv 5-2 Hvöt Blonduosi
19/8/09, SHS Wr. Neustadt Dr. Fred Sinowatz Schule, Wiener Neustadt
1. FC Allstars Wiener Neustadt 2-3 Erebuni Yerevan
20/8/09, SHS Wr. Neustadt Dr. Fred Sinowatz Schule, Wiener Neustadt
Erebuni Yerevan 3-3 ASA Tel-Aviv
20/8/09, SHS Wr. Neustadt Dr. Fred Sinowatz Schule, Wiener Neustadt
1. FC Allstars Wiener Neustadt 5-4 Hvöt Blonduosi
22/8/09, SHS Wr. Neustadt Dr. Fred Sinowatz Schule, Wiener Neustadt
Hvöt Blonduosi 0-7 Erebuni Yerevan
22/8/09, SHS Wr. Neustadt Dr. Fred Sinowatz Schule, Wiener Neustadt
ASA Tel-Aviv 6-3 1. FC Allstars Wiener Neustadt

Group F Table

		Pld	W	D	L	F	A	Pts
1	Erebuni Yerevan	3	2	1	0	13	5	7
2	ASA Tel-Aviv	3	2	1	0	14	8	7
3	1. FC Allstars Wiener Neustadt	3	1	0	2	10	13	3
4	Hvöt Blonduosi	3	0	0	3	6	17	0

Group G Results

21/8/09, Sport Halle Kale, Skopje
KMF Zelezarec Skopje 3-5 Futsal BGA
22/8/09, Sport Halle Kale, Skopje
Futsal BGA 3-8 Montenegro Stars Budva
23/8/09, Sport Halle Kale, Skopje
Montenegro Stars Budva 2-3 KMF Zelezarec Skopje

Group G Table

		Pld	W	D	L	F	A	Pts
1	Montenegro Stars Budva	2	1	0	1	10	6	3
2	KMF Zelezarec Skopje	2	1	0	1	6	7	3
3	Futsal BGA	2	1	0	1	8	11	3

MAIN ROUND

Group 1 Results

1/10/09, Fönix Arena, Debrecen
Luparense C/5 10-0 SC Tornado Chisinau
1/10/09, Fönix Arena, Debrecen
MVFC Berettyóújfalu 0-6 Time Lviv
2/10/09, Fönix Arena, Debrecen
Time Lviv 3-3 Luparense C/5
2/10/09, Fönix Arena, Debrecen
MVFC Berettyóújfalu 4-2 SC Tornado Chisinau
4/10/09, Fönix Arena, Debrecen
SC Tornado Chisinau 1-11 Time Lviv
4/10/09, Fönix Arena, Debrecen
Luparense C/5 10-0 MVFC Berettyóújfalu

Group 1 Table

	Pld	W	D	L	F	A	Pts
1 Luparense C/5	3	2	1	0	23	3	7
2 Time Lviv	3	2	1	0	20	4	7
3 MVFC Berettyóújfalu	3	1	0	2	4	18	3
4 SC Tornado Chisinau	3	0	0	3	3	25	0

Group 2 Results

28/9/09, Zimní Stadión, Chrudim
Hurtap Łęczyca 9-1 FK Nautara Kaunas
28/9/09, Zimní Stadión, Chrudim
FK Era-Pack Chrudim 10-1 FK Nikars Riga
29/9/09, Zimní Stadión, Chrudim
FK Nikars Riga 4-3 Hurtap Łęczyca
29/9/09, Zimní Stadión, Chrudim
FK Era-Pack Chrudim 8-1 FK Nautara Kaunas
1/10/09, Zimní Stadión, Chrudim
FK Nautara Kaunas 2-3 FK Nikars Riga
1/10/09, Zimní Stadión, Chrudim
Hurtap Łęczyca 3-5 FK Era-Pack Chrudim

Group 2 Table

	Pld	W	D	L	F	A	Pts
1 FK Era-Pack Chrudim	3	3	0	0	23	5	9
2 FK Nikars Riga	3	2	0	1	8	15	6
3 Hurtap Łęczyca	3	1	0	2	15	10	3
4 FK Nautara Kaunas	3	0	0	3	4	20	0

Group 3 Results

30/9/09, La Garenne, Charleroi
Skövde AIK 3-9 Golden Futsal Team
30/9/09, La Garenne, Charleroi
Action 21 Charleroi 4-2 Athina '90 Athens
1/10/09, La Garenne, Charleroi
Athina '90 Athens 11-2 Skövde AIK
1/10/09, La Garenne, Charleroi
Action 21 Charleroi 3-0 Golden Futsal Team
3/10/09, La Garenne, Charleroi
Golden Futsal Team 3-3 Athina '90 Athens
3/10/09, La Garenne, Charleroi
Skövde AIK 1-10 Action 21 Charleroi

Group 3 Table

	Pld	W	D	L	F	A	Pts
1 Action 21 Charleroi	3	3	0	0	17	3	9
2 Athina '90 Athens	3	1	1	1	16	9	4
3 Golden Futsal Team	3	1	1	1	12	9	4
4 Skövde AIK	3	0	0	3	6	30	0

Group 4 Results

1/10/09, Solski Center, Tolmin
SL Benfica 15-1 Montenegro Stars Budva
1/10/09, Solski Center, Tolmin
KMN Puntar 3-0 Viten Orsha
2/10/09, Solski Center, Tolmin
Viten Orsha 1-7 SL Benfica
2/10/09, Solski Center, Tolmin
KMN Puntar 7-0 Montenegro Stars Budva
4/10/09, Solski Center, Tolmin
Montenegro Stars Budva 1-2 Viten Orsha
4/10/09, Solski Center, Tolmin
SL Benfica 4-2 KMN Puntar

Group 4 Table

	Pld	W	D	L	F	A	Pts
1 SL Benfica	3	3	0	0	26	4	9
2 KMN Puntar	3	2	0	1	12	4	6
3 Viten Orsha	3	1	0	2	3	11	3
4 Montenegro Stars Budva	3	0	0	3	2	24	0

Group 5 Results

1/10/09, Dom Sportova "Mate Parlov", Pula
Araz Naxçivan 4-1 AC Omonia
1/10/09, Dom Sportova "Mate Parlov", Pula
MNK Potpićan 98 4-3 KMF Kolubara Lazarevac
2/10/09, Dom Sportova "Mate Parlov", Pula
KMF Kolubara Lazarevac 0-4 Araz Naxçivan
2/10/09, Dom Sportova "Mate Parlov", Pula
MNK Potpićan 98 3-3 AC Omonia
4/10/09, Dom Sportova "Mate Parlov", Pula
AC Omonia 3-7 KMF Kolubara Lazarevac
4/10/09, Dom Sportova "Mate Parlov", Pula
Araz Naxçivan 4-4 MNK Potpićan 98

Group 5 Table

	Pld	W	D	L	F	A	Pts
1 Araz Naxçivan	3	2	1	0	12	5	7
2 MNK Potpićan 98	3	1	2	0	11	10	5
3 KMF Kolubara Lazarevac	3	1	0	2	10	11	3
4 AC Omonia	3	0	1	2	7	14	1

Group 6 Results

1/10/09, Sports Hall, Deva
Iberia Star Tbilisi 5-0 Erebuni Yerevan
1/10/09, Sports Hall, Deva
FC CIP Deva 0-3 FC Marlène
2/10/09, Sports Hall, Deva
FC Marlène 0-2 Iberia Star Tbilisi
2/10/09, Sports Hall, Deva
FC CIP Deva 9-1 Erebuni Yerevan
4/10/09, Sports Hall, Deva
Erebuni Yerevan 0-9 FC Marlène
4/10/09, Sports Hall, Deva
Iberia Star Tbilisi 3-5 FC CIP Deva

Group 6 Table

	Pld	W	D	L	F	A	Pts
1 FC Marlène	3	2	0	1	12	2	6
2 Iberia Star Tbilisi	3	2	0	1	10	5	6
3 FC CIP Deva	3	2	0	1	14	7	6
4 Erebuni Yerevan	3	0	0	3	1	23	0

UEFA Futsal Cup

ELITE ROUND

Group A Results

19/11/09, Zoppas Arena, Conegliano
Murcia FS 12-0 Iberia Star Tbilisi
19/11/09, Zoppas Arena, Conegliano
Luparense C/5 6-0 Action 21 Charleroi
20/11/09, Zoppas Arena, Conegliano
Action 21 Charleroi 2-9 Murcia FS
20/11/09, Zoppas Arena, Conegliano
Luparense C/5 4-1 Iberia Star Tbilisi
22/11/09, Zoppas Arena, Conegliano
Iberia Star Tbilisi 4-3 Action 21 Charleroi
22/11/09, Zoppas Arena, Conegliano
Murcia FS 4-5 Luparense C/5

Group A Table

	Pld	W	D	L	F	A	Pts
1 Luparense C/5	3	3	0	0	15	5	9
2 Murcia FS	3	2	0	1	25	7	6
3 Iberia Star Tbilisi	3	1	0	2	5	19	3
4 Action 21 Charleroi	3	0	0	3	5	19	0

Humberto Honorio (left) and Poncio Danieli celebrate a goal for Luparense

Group B Results

19/11/09, Indoor Pavilhão do SL Benfica, Lisbon
MFK Viz-Sinara Ekaterinburg 2-0 MNK Potpićan 98
19/11/09, Indoor Pavilhão do SL Benfica, Lisbon
SL Benfica 4-0 FC Marlène
20/11/09, Indoor Pavilhão do SL Benfica, Lisbon
FC Marlène 0-9 MFK Viz-Sinara Ekaterinburg
20/11/09, Indoor Pavilhão do SL Benfica, Lisbon
SL Benfica 8-1 MNK Potpićan 98
22/11/09, Indoor Pavilhão do SL Benfica, Lisbon
MNK Potpićan 98 2-1 FC Marlène
22/11/09, Indoor Pavilhão do SL Benfica, Lisbon
MFK Viz-Sinara Ekaterinburg 2-2 SL Benfica

Group B Table

	Pld	W	D	L	F	A	Pts
1 SL Benfica	3	2	1	0	14	3	7
2 MFK Viz-Sinara Ekaterinburg	3	2	1	0	13	2	7
3 MNK Potpićan 98	3	1	0	2	3	11	3
4 FC Marlène	3	0	0	3	1	15	0

Group C Results

19/11/09, CEZ Arena Pardubice, Pardubice
Interviú Madrid 3-0 KMN Puntar
19/11/09, CEZ Arena Pardubice, Pardubice
FK Era-Pack Chrudim 2-4 Time Lviv
20/11/09, CEZ Arena Pardubice, Pardubice
Time Lviv 1-3 Interviú Madrid
20/11/09, CEZ Arena Pardubice, Pardubice
FK Era-Pack Chrudim 4-3 KMN Puntar
22/1/09, CEZ Arena Pardubice, Pardubice
KMN Puntar 0-5 Time Lviv
22/11/09, CEZ Arena Pardubice, Pardubice
Interviú Madrid 5-1 FK Era-Pack Chrudim

Group C Table

	Pld	W	D	L	F	A	Pts
1 Interviú Madrid	3	3	0	0	11	2	9
2 Time Lviv	3	2	0	1	10	5	6
3 FK Era-Pack Chrudim	3	1	0	2	7	12	3
4 KMN Puntar	3	0	0	3	3	12	0

Group D Results

19/11/09, Palace of Sport, Baku
Kairat Almaty 3-2 Athina '90 Athens
19/11/09, Palace of Sport, Baku
Araz Naxçivan 7-1 FK Nikars Riga
20/11/09, Palace of Sport, Baku
FK Nikars Riga 2-3 Kairat Almaty
20/11/09, Palace of Sport, Baku
Araz Naxçivan 7-0 Athina '90 Athens
22/11/09, Palace of Sport, Baku
Athina '90 Athens 3-0 FK Nikars Riga
22/11/09, Palace of Sport, Baku
Kairat Almaty 3-4 Araz Naxçivan

Group D Table

	Pld	W	D	L	F	A	Pts
1 Araz Naxçivan	3	3	0	0	18	4	9
2 Kairat Almaty	3	2	0	1	9	8	6
3 Athina '90 Athens	3	1	0	2	5	10	3
4 FK Nikars Riga	3	0	0	3	3	13	0

Araz Naxçivan's Aleksei Petrov jumps for joy as team-mate Felipe looks on

FINAL FOUR

The choice of the Pavilhão Atlântico as the venue marked a return to the competition's roots as the first edition in 2001/02 concluded uniquely with an eight-team final tournament at the Lisbon waterfront venue, hosted on that occasion by Sporting Clube de Portugal and won by Spain's Playas de Castellón.

Interviú pushed hard

Interviú, who in 2009 moved clear of domestic rivals Castellón on the UEFA Futsal Cup all-time roll of honour with their record third victory, were tipped to give Spain their sixth triumph in nine editions, but they did not have things all their own way in their semi-final with Araz, who shared a coach – Alésio – and the core of the squad with the Azerbaijan side that had reached the UEFA Futsal EURO 2010 last four three months earlier in Hungary. Jordi Torras and Gabriel gave Interviú the lead in each half, only for Biro Jade and Serjão to equalise. With seven minutes left Betão swivelled to restore Interviú's advantage, and this time they held on as Luis Amado pulled off a fine save from Biro Jade before shortly afterwards punting into an empty net. Amado's fellow veteran of all three previous Interviú triumphs, Daniel, cemented a 5-2 win late on.

Interviú goalkeeper Luis Amada makes a flying save against Araz

Goals continued to flow that evening as Benfica defeated Luparense 8-4. In the first five minutes the Eagles were 2-1 up as Joel Queirós and Ricardinho struck either side of Humberto Honorio's equaliser. Joel scored again, and although Vampeta pulled one back before the break, Arnaldo scored 33 seconds after the interval and Davi made it 5-2. Cleyton Baptistella reduced arrears with five minutes left but Ricardinho, Arnaldo and César Paulo scored for Benfica before Zé Maria's late own goal.

Eagles swoop

Araz took third place 5-4 on penalties against Luparense after Thiago had equalised late on for the Azerbaijani side, and by the time of the final the arena was almost full. Marquinho struck on seven minutes for Interviú in their fifth final but Joel quickly equalised from Ricardinho's free-kick, his 12th goal of the competition making him the season's top scorer. Arnaldo, who, like Zé Maria, Pedro Costa, Ricardinho, substitute goalkeeper Zé Carlos and current coach André Lima, played in the Benfica side that lost the 2004 final, made it 2-1 to the hosts early in the second half with a back-heel before Betão responded in similar style three minutes later. Benfica kept pushing and in extra time had their reward when Amado's loose pass was turned in by Davi under the gaze of the club's famed eagle mascot, perched behind the Interviú goal. Coincidentally, Davi was also a winner in 2005 with Action 21 Charleroi of Belgium, the only other time a team from outside Spain or Russia has won the UEFA Futsal Cup.

Davi puts Benfica 5-2 up against Luparense

Semi-Final Results

23/4/10, Pavilhão Atlántico, Lisbon
Araz Naxçivan 2-5 Interviú Madrid
Araz: Tveryankin, Salyanski, Serjão, Farzaliyev, Biro Jade, Felipe,
Sultanov, Dushkevich, Farajzade, Thiago, Borisov, Petrov. Coach: José
Alésio da Silva (BRA)
Interviú Madrid: Luis Amado, Alberto, Neto, Gabriel, Schumacher,
Betão, Marquinho, Torras, Juanra, Borja, Ortiz, Daniel. Coach: Jesús
Candelas Rodrigo (ESP)
Goal(s): 0-1 Torras 9, 1-1 Biro Jade 17, 1-2 Gabriel 22, 2-2 Serjão 22,
2-3 Betão 33, 2-4 Luis Amado 37, 2-5 Daniel 38
Yellow Card(s): Serjão 39 (Araz)

23/4/10, Pavilhão Atlántico, Lisbon
SL Benfica 8-4 Luparense C/5
Benfica: Bébé, Zé Carlos, Pedro Costa, Arnaldo, Ricardinho, Joel
Queirós, Zé Maria, Gonçalo Alves, Davi, César Paulo, Marinho, Rúben
Simões. Coach: André Lima (POR)
Luparense: Weber, Putano, Danieli, Muñoz Calvo, Honorio, Chilavert
Gennaro, Vasconcelos, Barro, De Oliveira, Vampeta, Baptistella, Nuno.
Coach: Sito Rivera (ESP)
Goal(s): 1-0 Joel Queirós 3, 1-1 Honorio 3, 2-1 Ricardinho 4,
3-1 Joel Queirós 12, 3-2 Vampeta 13, 4-2 Arnaldo 20, 5-2 Davi 22,
5-3 Baptistella 35, 6-3 Ricardinho 35, 7-3 Arnaldo 36, 8-3 César Paulo 38,
8-4 Zé Maria 38(og)

Third Place Play-off Result

25/4/10, Pavilhão Atlántico, Lisbon
Araz Naxçivan 2-2 Luparense C/5 (aet; 5-4 on pens)
Araz: Tveryankin, Salyanski, Thiago, Biro Jade, Felipe, Borisov,
Sultanov, Dushkevich, Farajzade, Farzaliyev, Petrov. Coach: José
Alésio da Silva (BRA)
Luparense: Weber, Putano, Vasconcelos, De Oliveira, Vampeta,
Nuno, Danieli, Barro, Muñoz Calvo, Honorio, Baptistella, Chilavert
Gennaro. Coach: Sito Rivera (ESP)
Goal(s): 1-0 Borisov 3, 1-1 Muñoz Calvo 6, 1-2 Baptistella 17,
2-2 Thiago 36
Yellow Card(s): Dushkevich 15 (Araz), Muñoz Calvo 16 (Luparense)

Final Result

25/4/10, Pavilhão Atlántico, Lisbon
Interviú Madrid 2-3 SL Benfica (aet)
Interviú Madrid: Luis Amado, Alberto, Torras, Gabriel, Schumacher,
Betão, Marquinho, Neto, Juanra, Borja, Ortiz, Daniel. Coach: Jesús
Candelas Rodrigo (ESP)
Benfica: Zé Carlos, Bébé, Pedro Costa, Arnaldo, Ricardinho, Joel
Queirós, Zé Maria, Gonçalo Alves, Davi, César Paulo, Marinho, Rúben
Simões. Coach: André Lima (POR)
Goal(s): 1-0 Marquinho 7, 1-1 Joel Queirós 11, 1-2 Arnaldo 21,
2-2 Betão 24, 2-3 Davi 42
Yellow Card(s): Betão 14 (Interviú Madrid), Arnaldo 22 (Benfica),
César Paulo 26 (Benfica), Torras 32 (Interviú Madrid)

Futsal Cup winners Benfica start the party at the Pavilhão Atlántico
after their 3-2 win over Interviú

THE EUROPEAN FOOTBALL YEARBOOK

TOP 100 PLAYERS OF THE SEASON 2009/10

Welcome to the chapter of the European Football Yearbook that provokes the most debate – the Top 100 Players of the Season.

As ever, much careful thought and consideration has gone into the selection of the hundred players who, in the collective opinion of the Yearbook's editorial team and UEFA.com's network of continental correspondents, have done most to impress during the 2009/10 season.

The list of nominees was generated, monitored and revised as the season progressed, although naturally events in South Africa in June and July had a strong bearing on the eventual outcome. The final cut was made the day after the FIFA World Cup final.

Overleaf you will find the names of the players who have made it into this year's selection, followed on the subsequent 50 pages by narrative, pictorial and statistical profiles. The players are listed purely in alphabetical order, with no other classification or demarcation.

Please note that the information pertaining to international caps, goals and club careers is up to date as of 6 August, 2010.

Enjoy the read.

MIKE HAMMOND
General Editor

Igor AKINFEEV (PFC CSKA Moskva, Russia)
Darren BENT (Sunderland AFC, England)
Valter BIRSA (AJ Auxerre, Slovenia)
Mbark BOUSSOUFA (RSC Anderlecht, Morocco)
Aleksandr BUKHAROV (FC Rubin Kazan, Russia)
Sergio BUSQUETS (FC Barcelona, Spain)
Esteban CAMBIASSO (FC Internazionale Milano, Argentina)
Óscar CARDOZO (SL Benfica, Paraguay)
Iker CASILLAS (Real Madrid CF, Spain)
Antonio CASSANO (UC Sampdoria, Italy)
Marouane CHAMAKH (FC Girondins de Bordeaux, Morocco)
Djibril CISSÉ (Panathinaikos FC, France)
Ashley COLE (Chelsea FC, England)
CRISTIANO RONALDO (Real Madrid CF, Portugal)
DAVID VILLA (Valencia CF, Spain)
Michael DAWSON (Tottenham Hotspur FC, England)
Nigel DE JONG (Manchester City FC, Netherlands)
Eren DERDIYOK (Bayer 04 Leverkusen, Switzerland)
Ángel DI MARÍA (SL Benfica, Argentina)
Antonio DI NATALE (Udinese Calcio, Italy)
Alejandro DOMÍNGUEZ (FC Rubin Kazan/Valencia CF, Argentina)
DOUGLAS (FC Twente, Brazil)
Didier DROGBA (Chelsea FC, Ivory Coast)
Edin DŽEKO (VfL Wolfsburg, Bosnia-Herzegovina)
Balász DZSUDZSÁK (PSV Eindhoven, Hungary)
EDUARDO (SC Braga, Portugal)
FÁBIO COENTRÃO (SL Benfica, Portugal)
Cesc FÀBREGAS (Arsenal FC, Spain)
Radamel FALCAO (FC Porto, Colombia)
Diego FORLÁN (Club Atlético de Madrid, Uruguay)
GERVINHO (LOSC Lille Métropole, Ivory Coast)
GILBERTO SILVA (Panathinaikos FC, Brazil)
Shay GIVEN (Manchester City FC, Republic of Ireland)
Marek HAMŠÍK (SSC Napoli, Slovakia)
Brede HANGELAND (Fulham FC, Norway)
Joe HART (Birmingham City FC, England)
Eden HAZARD (LOSC Lille Métropole, Belgium)
Gonzalo HIGUAÍN (Real Madrid CF, Argentina)
Steffen HOFMANN (SK Rapid Wien, Germany)
Keisuke HONDA (VVV-Venlo/PFC CSKA Moskva, Japan)
Andrés INIESTA (FC Barcelona, Spain)
Branislav IVANOVIĆ (Chelsea FC, Serbia)
JESÚS NAVAS (Sevilla FC, Spain)
JÚLIO CÉSAR (FC Internazionale Milano, Brazil)
Sami KHEDIRA (VfB Stuttgart, Germany)
Stefan KIESSLING (Bayer 04 Leverkusen, Germany)
Simon KJÆR (US Città di Palermo, Denmark)
Miroslav KLOSE (FC Bayern München, Germany)
Miloš KRASIĆ (PFC CSKA Moskva, Serbia)
Sergei KRIVETS (FC BATE Borisov/Lech Poznań, Belarus)
Kevin KURÁNYI (FC Schalke 04, Germany)
Dirk KUYT (Liverpool FC, Netherlands)
Philipp LAHM (FC Bayern München, Germany)
Frank LAMPARD (Chelsea FC, England)
Robert LEWANDOWSKI (Lech Poznań, Poland)

LISANDRO LÓPEZ (Olympique Lyonnais, Argentina)
Hugo LLORIS (Olympique Lyonnais, France)
LUCHO GONZÁLEZ (Olympique de Marseille, Argentina)
LÚCIO (FC Internazionale Milano, Brazil)
Romelu LUKAKU (RSC Anderlecht, Belgium)
MAICON (FC Internazionale Milano, Brazil)
Florent MALOUDA (Chelsea FC, France)
Lionel MESSI (FC Barcelona, Argentina)
Fabrizio MICCOLI (US Città di Palermo, Italy)
Artem MILEVSKIY (FC Dynamo Kyiv, Ukraine)
Diego MILITO (FC Internazionale Milano, Argentina)
James MILNER (Aston Villa FC, England)
Thomas MÜLLER (FC Bayern München, Germany)
Manuel NEUER (FC Schalke 04, Germany)
Mamadou NIANG (Olympique de Marseille, Senegal)
Ivica OLIĆ (FC Bayern München, Croatia)
Mesut ÖZIL (Werder Bremen, Germany)
Giampaolo PAZZINI (UC Sampdoria, Italy)
PEDRO Rodríguez (FC Barcelona, Spain)
Mladen PETRIĆ (Hamburger SV, Croatia)
Gerard PIQUÉ (FC Barcelona, Spain)
Claudio PIZARRO (Werder Bremen, Peru)
Carles PUYOL (FC Barcelona, Spain)
John Arne RIISE (AS Roma, Norway)
Arjen ROBBEN (FC Bayern München, Netherlands)
Wayne ROONEY (Manchester United FC, England)
Bryan RUIZ (FC Twente, Costa Rica)
Walter SAMUEL (FC Internazionale Milano, Argentina)
Bastian SCHWEINSTEIGER (FC Bayern München, Germany)
Sergei SEMAK (FC Rubin Kazan, Russia)
SERGIO RAMOS (Real Madrid CF, Spain)
Wesley SNEIJDER (FC Internazionale Milano, Netherlands)
Luis SUÁREZ (AFC Ajax, Uruguay)
Carlos TÉVEZ (Manchester City FC, Argentina)
Mathieu VALBUENA (Olympique de Marseille, France)
Luis Antonio VALENCIA (Manchester United FC, Ecuador)
Mark VAN BOMMEL (FC Bayern München, Netherlands)
Giovanni VAN BRONCKHORST (Feyenoord, Netherlands)
Gregory VAN DER WIEL (AFC Ajax, Netherlands)
Thomas VERMAELEN (Arsenal FC, Belgium)
VÍCTOR VALDÉS (FC Barcelona, Spain)
Mirko VUČINIĆ (AS Roma, Montenegro)
XAVI Hernández (FC Barcelona, Spain)
Bobby ZAMORA (Fulham FC, England)
Javier ZANETTI (FC Internazionale Milano, Argentina)

NB Clubs indicated are those the players belonged to in the 2009/10 season.

Key to competitions: WCF = FIFA World Cup final tournament; WCQ = FIFA World Cup qualifying round; ECF = UEFA EURO final tournament; ECQ = UEFA EURO qualifying round; CC = FIFA Confederations Cup; CA = Copa América; ANF = Africa Cup of Nations final tournament; ANQ = Africa Cup of Nations qualifying round; CGC = Concacaf Gold Cup

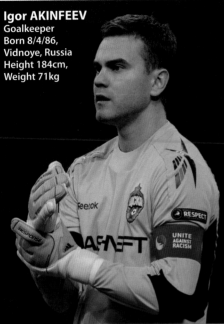

Igor AKINFEEV
Goalkeeper
Born 8/4/86,
Vidnoye, Russia
Height 184cm,
Weight 71kg

With 40 international caps accumulated before his 24th birthday, Igor Akinfeev has a growing reputation as one of the world's best young goalkeepers. Indeed, his continuing excellence in 2009 and 2010 for PFC CSKA Moskva added further weight to the argument that he is the finest practitioner of the art produced by Russia since the legendary Lev Yashin. For the second successive season he started all 30 of CSKA's Premier-Liga matches and was particularly prominent as the Army Men reached the quarter-finals of the UEFA Champions League, starting all ten matches and impressing foreign scouts with top-class displays at Old Trafford and San Siro. Akinfeev's extraordinary agility and reflex speed were also on view in the FIFA World Cup qualifying play-offs, but Russia's away-goals defeat to Slovenia denied him a debut on the game's greatest stage in South Africa. Fortunately, he is young enough to be able to look forward to appearing in two, maybe three, World Cups in the future.

International Career
RUSSIA
Debut – 28/4/04 v Norway (a, Oslo, friendly), lost 2-3
Caps 40; **Goals** 0
Major Tournaments – UEFA EURO 2004, UEFA EURO 2008

Club Career
Major Honours – UEFA Cup (2005); Russian Championship (2003, 2005, 2006); Russian Cup (2005, 2006, 2008, 2009)
Clubs: 2003- PFC CSKA Moskva

Darren BENT
Striker
Born 6/2/84,
London, England
Height 180cm,
Weight 73kg

Selected in England's preliminary 2010 FIFA World Cup squad, Darren Bent was unfortunate to be one of the seven players excluded from Fabio Capello's final party. Having also just missed out on a World Cup call-up four years earlier, it was a bitter blow for the 26-year-old striker, who had just completed an outstanding first season for Sunderland AFC in the Premier League, scoring 24 goals – exactly half the club's total – to take third place behind Didier Drogba and Wayne Rooney in the final Golden Boot standings. Two thirds of his goals were registered at the Stadium of Light, a ground where he scored twice on his top-flight debut for Charlton Athletic FC in 2005. One strike in particular entered Premier League folklore, his winning goal against Liverpool FC in October crossing the line after deflecting off a plastic beach ball that a Liverpool supporter had thrown on to the pitch. The following month Bent was selected to lead England's attack in a friendly against Brazil.

International Career
ENGLAND
Debut – 1/3/06 v Uruguay (h, Liverpool, friendly), won 2-1
Caps 6; **Goals** 0

Club Career
Major Honours – English League Cup (2008)
Clubs: 01-05 Ipswich Town FC; 05-07 Charlton Athletic FC; 07-09 Tottenham Hotspur FC; 09- Sunderland AFC

Valter BIRSA
Attacking Midfielder/
Winger
Born 7/8/86,
Sempeter pri Gorici,
Slovenia
Height 184cm,
Weight 79kg

After spending the second half of the 2008/09 season on loan at AJ Auxerre, Valter Birsa joined the Burgundy club on a permanent basis and went on to star in the team's unexpected challenge for the Ligue 1 title. The crafty left foot of the Slovenia international proved to be a potent weapon, especially at set-pieces, and his late winning penalty at home to defending champions FC Girondins de Bordeaux in mid-October turned out to be a season-defining moment for the club who eventually went on to finish third. Birsa also enjoyed his finest season yet for Slovenia, starting in every match and helping his country to an unexpected place at the finals of the 2010 FIFA World Cup. The 23-year-old further enhanced his reputation there with some classy displays on the right wing and one absolutely fabulous long-range goal that opened the scoring in the team's 2-2 draw against the United States.

International Career

SLOVENIA
Debut – 28/2/06 v Cyprus (a, Larnaca, friendly), won 1-0
First Goal – 9/9/09 v Poland (h, Maribor, WCQ), won 3-0
Caps 37; **Goals** 3
Major Tournaments – FIFA World Cup 2010

Club Career

Major Honours – Slovenian Championship (2004, 2005); French Cup (2007)
Clubs: 03-04 NK Primorje; 04-06 ND Gorica; 06-09 FC Sochaux-Montbéliard (FRA); 09 AJ Auxerre (FRA) (loan); 09- AJ Auxerre (FRA)

Moubarak 'Mbark' BOUSSOUFA
Attacking Midfielder
Born 15/8/84,
Amsterdam,
Netherlands
Height 167cm,
Weight 59kg

International football with Morocco has been a secondary sideshow so far in the burgeoning career of Mbark Boussoufa, who once again displayed his skills to an appreciative audience in Belgium during a 2009/10 season that brought him his second Pro League championship title with RSC Anderlecht and a second successive Belgian Professional Footballer of the Year award. The diminutive Dutch-born schemer became the first player to retain that individual honour since another Anderlecht midfield maestro, Swede Pär Zetterberg, 12 years earlier. Once again he was the man who pulled the strings for the Mauves, scoring 14 goals and supplying another 20 assists in their procession to a 30th domestic league title. He was also a key figure in Anderlecht's run to the last 16 of the UEFA Europa League, although ironically his most eye-catching display came in the 4-3 home win against Hamburger SV with which the Brussels club exited the competition.

International Career

MOROCCO
Debut – 23/5/06 v United States (a, Nashville, friendly), drew 1-1
First Goal – 3/9/06 v Malawi (h, Rabat, ANQ), won 2-0
Caps 15; **Goals** 1

Club Career

Major Honours – Belgian Championship (2007, 2010); Belgian Cup (2008)
Clubs: 04-06 KAA Gent (BEL); 06- RSC Anderlecht (BEL)

Aleksandr BUKHAROV

Striker
Born 12/3/85,
Naberezhnye
Chelny, Russia
Height 191cm,
Weight 83kg

A modest contributor to FC Rubin Kazan's 2008 Russian Premier-Liga title triumph, Aleksandr Bukharov developed into one of the team's most important and consistent players as they successfully defended the title in 2009. The tall, athletic striker upped his goal tally from six to 16 – the same number as his attacking partner Alejandro Domínguez – and particularly enjoyed his visits to the capital, scoring in away wins against FC Moskva, FC Spartak Moskva and PFC CSKA Moskva. He was unable to score in the UEFA Champions League, missing two big chances for glory in the home tie against holders FC Barcelona, but partly made amends with a brace on his UEFA Europa League debut against Hapoel Tel-Aviv FC. Called up for his Russian international debut in October 2009, he will expect to feature prominently under new head coach Dick Advocaat during the UEFA EURO 2012 campaign – particularly after leaving Rubin for Russia's wealthiest club, FC Zenit St Petersburg, in July 2010.

International Career

RUSSIA
Debut – 14/10/09 v Azerbaijan (a, Baku, WCQ), drew 1-1
Caps 1; **Goals** 0

Club Career

Major Honours – Russian Championship (2008, 2009)
Clubs: Clubs: 02 FC Krasnodar-2000; 03 FC Chernomorets Novorossiisk; 04-10 FC Rubin Kazan; 10- FC Zenit St Petersburg

Sergio BUSQUETS Burgos

Midfielder
Born 16/7/88,
Sabadell, Spain
Height 189cm,
Weight 73kg

Sergio Busquets' fledgling career continued its meteoric rise in 2009/10. Having come from nowhere to help FC Barcelona win a unique treble in 2008/09, the young midfielder was even more effective in his second season, holding down a near-permanent place in Josep Guardiola's team and not only capturing a second successive Spanish title but also adding winner's medals in the UEFA Super Cup and FIFA Club World Cup to his international collection. As if serial success for his club was not enough, he went on to win the FIFA World Cup with Spain. As the replacement for UEFA EURO 2008 hero Marcos Senna in the holding role, the 21-year-old started all seven matches in South Africa and was one of only three outfield players to remain on the field from start to finish in all of the team's six victories. Notwithstanding a shameful piece of playacting in the UEFA Champions League semi-final against FC Internazionale Milano, it was another glorious season for one of European football's brightest young stars.

International Career

SPAIN
Major Honours – FIFA World Cup (2010)
Debut – 1/4/09 v Turkey (a, Istanbul, WCQ), won 2-1
Caps 20; **Goals** 0
Major Tournaments – FIFA World Cup 2010

Club Career

Major Honours – UEFA Champions League (2009); UEFA Super Cup (2009); FIFA Club World Cup (2009); Spanish Championship (2009, 2010); Spanish Cup (2009)
Clubs: 07- FC Barcelona

Esteban Matías CAMBIASSO Deleau
Midfielder
Born 18/8/80,
Buenos Aires,
Argentina
Height 177cm,
Weight 78kg

Controversially, but not surprisingly, overlooked by Diego Maradona for Argentina's 2010 FIFA World Cup squad, Esteban Cambiasso had done more than enough to justify selection for his country in South Africa after a season of total fulfilment for his club FC Internazionale Milano. A fifth successive Serie A title and a third Coppa Italia triumph further expanded his collection of domestic silverware, but it was victory in the UEFA Champions League that the combative, shaven-headed left-footer desired the most, and he helped the Nerazzurri to attain that objective with a string of pitch-perfect midfield performances. Coach José Mourinho kept him on the field for every minute of the knockout phase, and it was in the first of those seven games that he scored his only goal of the competition, a timely winning strike at home to Chelsea FC. With a further four years to run on his contract, the 30-year-old can expect more days of glory for Inter and perhaps, with Maradona gone, a return to international football with Argentina.

International Career
ARGENTINA
Debut – 20/12/00 v Mexico (n, Los Angeles, friendly), won 2-0
First Goal – 21/6/05 v Germany (a, Nuremburg, CC), drew 2-2
Caps 46; Goals 4
Major Tournaments – FIFA Confederations Cup 2005; FIFA World Cup 2006; Copa América 2007

Club Career
Major Honours – UEFA Champions League (2010); World Club Cup (2002); Argentine Championship (2002 clausura); Spanish Championship (2003); Italian Championship (2006, 2007, 2008, 2009, 2010); Italian Cup (2005, 2006, 2010)
Clubs: 98-01 CA Independiente; 01-02 CA River Plate; 02-04 Real Madrid CF (ESP); 04- FC Internazionale Milano (ITA)

Óscar René CARDOZO
Striker
Born 20/5/83,
Juan Eulogio Estigarribia,
Paraguay
Height 194cm,
Weight 83kg

The 2010 FIFA World Cup was a bittersweet experience for Paraguay striker Óscar Cardozo. Injured then omitted, he came in to claim national hero status with his decisive winning penalty in the round-of-16 shoot-out against Japan, only to miss from the spot in regular play at a decisive moment of the quarter-final against Spain. The lanky left-footer had journeyed to South Africa as one of the world's most in-form strikers following a season of ceaseless productivity for SL Benfica. His third season at the Lisbon club lifted his stature to a new level as he finished top scorer in the Portuguese Liga – with 26 goals – and joint-leading marksman in the UEFA Europa League – with nine (two thirds of them against opposition from the city of Liverpool). His domestic league tally, which included four hat-tricks, proved decisive in bringing Benfica their first domestic championship title for five seasons, and he also scored twice in the Portuguese League Cup, including once in the final – a 3-0 victory over FC Porto.

International Career
PARAGUAY
Debut – 7/10/06 v Australia (a, Brisbane, friendly), drew 1-1
First Goal – 5/6/07 v Mexico (a, Mexico City, friendly), won 1-0
Caps 34; Goals 4
Major Tournaments – Copa América 2007; FIFA World Cup 2010

Club Career
Major Honours – Portuguese Championship (2010)
Clubs: 05 3 de Febrero; 05-06 Club Nacional; 06-07 Newell's Old Boys (ARG); 07- SL Benfica (POR)

Iker CASILLAS Fernández
Goalkeeper
Born 20/5/81,
Madrid, Spain
Height 185cm,
Weight 79kg

Iker Casillas fulfilled every footballer's fantasy as he lifted the FIFA World Cup in Johannesburg's Soccer City stadium on 11 July 2010. The captain of Spain, he was also one of the team's most decisive figures. Great players find their form in the big matches, and the Real Madrid CF goalkeeper made a number of key saves at crucial times to help Spain become the new champions of the world. His four clean sheets in the knockout phase supplemented the three he kept at UEFA EURO 2008, and the only goals he conceded in the group stage were a scrappy effort from Switzerland and a deflected shot against Chile. There were some concerns about his form going into the tournament after a less-than-vintage season with Real, but Casillas got better and better as it progressed and was deservedly honoured with the Golden Glove as the tournament's best goalkeeper. A Spanish sporting saint to rank with the very best, 'San Iker' won his 111th cap in the final – just 15 short of the national record – and is still only 29 years of age.

International Career

SPAIN
Major Honours – FIFA World Cup (2010); UEFA European Championship (2008)
Debut – 3/6/00 v Sweden (a, Gothenburg, friendly), drew 1-1
Caps 111; **Goals** 0
Major Tournaments – UEFA EURO 2000; FIFA World Cup 2002; UEFA EURO 2004; FIFA World Cup 2006; UEFA EURO 2008; FIFA Confederations Cup 2009; FIFA World Cup 2010

Club Career

Major Honours – UEFA Champions League (2000, 2002); UEFA Super Cup (2002); World Club Cup (2002); Spanish Championship (2001, 2003, 2007, 2008)
Clubs: 99- Real Madrid CF

Antonio CASSANO
Striker
Born 12/7/82,
Bari, Italy
Height 175cm,
Weight 75kg

There were incessant calls from the Italian public and media for Antonio Cassano to be restored to the national squad in 2009/10, but the louder the pleas, the less Marcello Lippi seemed to listen. The Azzurri coach had never been one to threaten the harmony of the group with a disruptive maverick, and so Italy went to the FIFA World Cup without Cassano…and played with such a lack of flair and variety in attack that the issue of the UC Sampdoria forward's omission became more heated than ever. It remains to be seen whether Lippi's successor, Cesare Prandelli, will have a different view on the multi-talented 28-year-old. In fact, Cassano almost left for Prandelli's ACF Fiorentina in January after a fall-out with Sampdoria coach Luigi Del Neri that left him idle for two months in mid-season, but he was at his very best before and after that enforced six-match break, finishing the campaign with nine goals to steer Samp to fourth place in Serie A.

International Career

ITALY
Debut – 12/11/03 v Poland (a, Warsaw, friendly), lost 1-3
First Goal – 12/11/03 v Poland (a, Warsaw, friendly), lost 1-3
Caps 15; **Goals** 3
Major Tournaments – UEFA EURO 2004; UEFA EURO 2008

Club Career

Major Honours – Spanish Championship (2007)
Clubs: 99-01 AS Bari; 01-06 AS Roma; 06-08 Real Madrid CF; 07/08 UC Sampdoria (loan); 08- UC Sampdoria

Marouane CHAMAKH
Striker
Born 10/1/84,
Tonneins, France
Height 185cm,
Weight 70kg

Marouane Chamakh ended an eight-year association with FC Girondins de Bordeaux at the conclusion of the 2009/10 season as he packed his bags for a new career in England with Arsenal FC. The French-born Moroccan international striker had long been coveted by Arsenal manager Arsène Wenger, and his physical presence and exceptional power in the air were put to good use by Bordeaux as they reached the quarter-finals of the UEFA Champions League. Chamakh scored five goals in the competition, all against quality opposition, including one in each leg of the quarter-final tie against Olympique Lyonnais, against whom he also scored at home and away in the domestic league. Voted Ligue 1's best foreign player at the end of 2009, he was unable to prevent the defending champions' dramatic spring slump, but he did end the campaign with ten league goals and was afforded a long and emotional standing ovation by the Bordeaux fans in his final game at the Stade Chaban-Delmas.

International Career

MOROCCO
Debut – 8/6/03 v Sierra Leone (h, Casablanca, ANQ), won 1-0
First Goal – 10/9/03 v Trinidad & Tobago (h, Marrakech, friendly), won 2-0
Caps 52; **Goals** 15
Major Tournaments – Africa Cup of Nations 2004; Africa Cup of Nations 2006; Africa Cup of Nations 2008

Club Career

Major Honours – French Championship (2009); French League Cup (2007, 2009)
Clubs: 02-10 FC Girondins de Bordeaux (FRA); 10- Arsenal FC (ENG)

Djibril CISSÉ
Striker
Born 12/8/81, Arles, France
Height 182cm, Weight 78kg

Although the four-year contract he signed for Panathinaikos FC in June 2009 was financially appealing, many critics in France claimed that Djibril Cissé's transfer from Olympique de Marseille to the Athens club constituted a backward career move. Twelve months later, however, the striker was travelling to the FIFA World Cup in South Africa, having been recalled to the French national squad for his first major tournament in seven years. His first season in Greek football could scarcely have gone better. Not only did he win the domestic double with Panathinaikos, he was the main reason for their return to power, scoring 23 league goals – more than twice as many as anyone else in the Super League and almost half of his club's total – to claim the first championship winner's medal of his career. He was also on target five times in the UEFA Europa League, three of those goals coming at the expense of AS Roma in an epic round of 32 tie.

International Career

FRANCE
Major Honours – FIFA Confederations Cup (2003)
Debut – 18/5/02 v Belgium (h, Saint-Denis, friendly), lost 1-2
First Goal – 7/9/02 v Cyprus (a, Nicosia, ECQ), won 2-1
Caps 40; **Goals** 9
Major Tournaments – FIFA World Cup 2002; FIFA Confederations Cup 2003; FIFA World Cup 2010

Club Career

Major Honours – UEFA Champions League (2005); UEFA Super Cup (2005); Greek Championship (2010); French Cup (2003); English FA Cup (2006); Greek Cup (2010)
Clubs: 98-04 AJ Auxerre; 04-06 Liverpool FC (ENG); 06-09 Olympique de Marseille; 08-09 Sunderland AFC (ENG) (loan); 09- Panathinaikos FC (GRE)

Ashley COLE
Left-Back
Born 20/12/80,
London, England
Height 172cm,
Weight 67kg

2009/10 was a season in which Ashley Cole fractured his left ankle and began divorce proceedings after a split from his glamorous celebrity wife Cheryl, but, on the positive side, it was also one in which he won the second English league and cup double of his career, became the first footballer to win the FA Cup six times and, having made a lightning recovery from his injury, also appeared in his third FIFA World Cup for England. He travelled to South Africa as the world's best left-back, that tag having been re-attributed to him as a result of his outstanding contributions to Chelsea FC's double triumph. Although he missed a large chunk of the campaign, it was the most impressive of the four he had spent at Stamford Bridge following his 2006 transfer from Arsenal FC. He even trebled his goal tally for the west London club with four Premier League goals, one of which, a brilliant strike in a 7-2 win against Sunderland AFC, was voted as the Chelsea goal of the year.

International Career

ENGLAND
Debut – 28/3/01 v Albania (a, Tirana, WCQ), won 3-1
Caps 82; **Goals** 0
Major Tournaments – FIFA World Cup 2002; UEFA EURO 2004; FIFA World Cup 2006; FIFA World Cup 2010

Club Career

Major Honours – English Premier League (2002, 2004, 2010); English FA Cup (2002, 2003, 2005, 2007, 2009, 2010); English League Cup (2007)
Clubs: 98-06 Arsenal FC; 99-00 Crystal Palace FC (loan); 06- Chelsea FC

CRISTIANO RONALDO
Santos Aveiro
Winger/Attacking
Midfielder
Born 5/2/85,
Funchal, Madeira,
Portugal
Height 184cm,
Weight 78kg

As the world's best paid footballer as well as its costliest, Cristiano Ronaldo was expected to spearhead Real Madrid CF to Spanish and European glory following his €92m transfer from Manchester United FC in June 2009. He may well go on to do that but it didn't happen in his first season at the Santiago Bernabéu. From a personal standpoint, however, the brilliant Portuguese winger enjoyed a superb debut campaign, scoring 26 goals in 29 Liga games for Real and another seven in just six UEFA Champions League appearances. There were occasional rumblings of discontent that he did not channel his energies to the benefit of the team, but those formidable goalscoring statistics overrode any accusations of over-elaborate Olé-style showmanship. The FIFA World Cup in South Africa brought only the odd moment of magic from the 25-year-old as Portugal exited in the round of 16 to Spain, but he did at least end a long goal drought for his country in the 7-0 annihilation of North Korea.

International Career

PORTUGAL
Debut – 20/8/03 v Kazakhstan (h, Chaves, friendly), won 1-0
First Goal – 12/6/04 v Greece (h, Porto, ECF), lost 1-2
Caps 76; **Goals** 23
Major Tournaments – UEFA EURO 2004; FIFA World Cup 2006; UEFA EURO 2008; FIFA World Cup 2010

Club Career

Major Honours – UEFA Champions League (2008); FIFA Club World Cup (2008); English Premiership (2007, 2008, 2009); English FA Cup (2004); English League Cup (2006, 2009)
Clubs: 02-03 Sporting Clube de Portugal; 03-09 Manchester United FC (ENG); 09- Real Madrid CF (ESP)

DAVID VILLA Sánchez
Striker
Born 3/12/81,
Langreo, Spain
Height 175cm,
Weight 69kg

David Villa's status as the best finisher in world football was confirmed at the 2010 FIFA World Cup, where he scored five goals, all of them of crucial importance, to help Spain become the champions of the world for the first time. His formidable efforts in South Africa left him just one short of Raúl González's all-time national record of 44 goals, but with an international goals-per-game ratio of better than two in three the 28-year-old surely qualifies already as his country's greatest ever marksman. Mobile and incisive as well as supremely composed in the danger zone, Villa went to the World Cup in a buoyant frame of mind having just signed a four-year contract with FC Barcelona. The transfer was worth €40m to Valencia CF, for whom he was as prolific as ever in his fifth and final season, registering 28 goals in all competitions including 21 in the league to take his all-time Liga tally for the club to 107 in 166 matches.

International Career

SPAIN
Major Honours – FIFA World Cup (2010); UEFA European Championship (2008)
Debut – 9/2/05 v San Marino (h, Almeria, WCQ), won 5-0
First Goal – 16/11/05 v Slovakia (a, Bratislava, WCQ) drew 1-1
Caps 65; **Goals** 43
Major Tournaments - FIFA World Cup 2006; UEFA EURO 2008; FIFA Confederations Cup 2009; FIFA World Cup 2010

Club Career

Major Honours – Spanish Cup (2004, 2008)
Clubs: 00-03 Sporting Gijón; 03-05 Real Zaragoza; 05-10 Valencia CF; 10- FC Barcelona

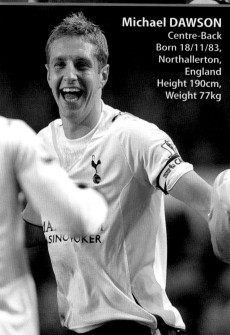

Michael DAWSON
Centre-Back
Born 18/11/83,
Northallerton,
England
Height 190cm,
Weight 77kg

At the end of a Premier League campaign in which Tottenham Hotspur FC achieved their pre-season target of UEFA Champions League qualification by finishing fourth, Michael Dawson was voted by supporters as the club's player of the year. The 26-year-old central defender was appointed temporarily as team captain halfway through the season, and the added responsibility appeared to bring out the best in him. Not even a first choice in Harry Redknapp's side during the early weeks of the season, he ended it as a member of England's FIFA World Cup squad. Although omitted from the original 30-man party, an injury to captain Rio Ferdinand enabled him to take the Manchester United FC centre-back's No5 shirt in the final 23. By the time England's tournament was over, Dawson was yet to win his first senior international cap, but it can safely be assumed that he will be part of Fabio Capello's plans as the team is remodelled for UEFA EURO 2012 and beyond.

International Career

ENGLAND
Uncapped
Major Tournaments – FIFA World Cup 2010

Club Career

Major Honours – English League Cup (2008)
Clubs: 01-05 Nottingham Forest FC; 05- Tottenham Hotspur FC

Nigel DE JONG
Midfielder
Born 30/11/84,
Amsterdam,
Netherlands
Height 174cm,
Weight 72kg

Having become a fixture for the Netherlands in Marco van Basten's team at UEFA EURO 2008, Nigel de Jong re-established his defensive midfield credentials under new Bondscoach Bert van Marwijk during the qualifying campaign for the 2010 FIFA World Cup and was firmly rooted as a fixture of the side at the finals in South Africa, where the Oranje finished as runners-up to Spain. Suspended for the semi-final against Uruguay, he might have been sent off in the final for a reckless studs-up challenge that caught Xabi Alonso in the ribs, but while the 25-year-old occasionally crossed the line with his eagerness to win the ball, his tenacity and tactical nous were central components in the smooth running of Van Marwijk's mean machine. De Jong's combative and competitive attributes were also much appreciated by fans of Manchester City FC – and managers Mark Hughes and Roberto Mancini - in his first full season of Premier League football.

International Career
NETHERLANDS
Debut – 31/3/04 v France (h, Rotterdam, friendly), drew 0-0
First Goal – 6/6/09 v Iceland (a, Reykjavik, WCQ), won 2-1
Caps 48; **Goals** 1
Major Tournaments - UEFA EURO 2008; FIFA World Cup 2010

Club Career
Major Honours – Dutch Championship (2004); Dutch Cup (2006)
Clubs: 02-06 AFC Ajax; 06-09 Hamburger SV (GER); 09- Manchester City FC (ENG)

Eren DERDIYOK
Striker
Born 12/6/88,
Basel, Switzerland
Height 191cm,
Weight 92kg

Eren Derdiyok's debut season in the German Bundesliga was a successful one. Bought by Bayer 04 Leverkusen from FC Basel 1893 on a four-year contract, the powerful young striker benefited from a long-term injury to Patrick Helmes, the club's leading goalscorer in 2008/09, and formed a complementary and productive strike partnership with Stefan Kiessling that took the club to the top of the table at the winter break and onwards to a record run of 24 games without defeat. Unfortunately, the goals dried up for the Swiss international during the run-in as Leverkusen's title hopes also faded, but he had already done enough, with 12 goals in total, to convince coach Jupp Heynckes to keep him in the team even after Helmes' recovery. There would be no goals for Derdiyok at the 2010 FIFA World Cup finals, but his strength and skill made him Switzerland's main attacking threat and he was unlucky to see a superb effort hit the post in the opening victory against eventual winners Spain.

International Career
SWITZERLAND
Debut – 6/2/08 v England (a, Wembley, friendly), lost 1-2
First Goal – 6/2/08 v England (a, Wembley, friendly), lost 1-2
Caps 24; **Goals** 2
Major Tournaments – UEFA EURO 2008; FIFA World Cup 2010

Club Career
Major Honours – Swiss Championship (2008); Swiss Cup (2008)
Clubs: 05-06 BSC Old Boys; 06-09 FC Basel 1893; 09- Bayer 04 Leverkusen (GER)

Ángel Fabián DI MARÍA
Midfielder/Winger
Born 14/2/88, Rosario, Argentina
Height 180cm, Weight 65kg

A winner of the FIFA U-20 World Cup in 2007 and the Olympic football tournament in 2008, Ángel Di María was unable to complete the international hat-trick with Argentina at the 2010 FIFA World Cup, but he earned a regular place in Diego Maradona's side in South Africa on the back of a wonderful season at club level with SL Benfica. Relatively discreet in his first two years at the Lisbon club, the willowy young left-winger exploded into life in 2009/10 under the tutelage of new coach Jorge Jesus. His combination of speed, elaborate technique and left-footed power shooting at times made him unplayable. A decisive figure in the Eagles' long-awaited Portuguese title triumph, he also raised his profile internationally with some exquisite displays in the UEFA Europa League. Despite the prospect of guaranteed UEFA Champions League football in 2010/11, Benfica were powerless to keep him and he left for Real Madrid CF in the summer on a highly lucrative six-year contract.

International Career

ARGENTINA
Debut – 6/9/08 v Paraguay (h, Buenos Aires, WCQ), drew 1-1
First Goal – 24/5/10 v Canada (h, Buenos Aires, friendly), won 5-0
Caps 13; **Goals** 1
Major Tournaments – FIFA World Cup 2010

Club Career

Major Honours – Portuguese Championship (2010)
Clubs: 05-07 Rosario Central; 07-10 SL Benfica (POR); 10- Real Madrid CF (ESP)

Antonio DI NATALE
Striker/Winger
Born 13/10/77,
Naples, Italy
Height 177cm,
Weight 70kg

Overlooked by Marcello Lippi when Italy won the FIFA World Cup in 2006, Antonio Di Natale was a shoo-in for South Africa. In fact, he even got to wear the celebrated No10 shirt. The Azzurri coach could hardly ignore the claims of a player who had just scored 29 goals to become the top scorer in Serie A – and for a club, moreover, in the wrong half of the table. The speedy, opportunistic 32-year-old striker was responsible for more than half of Udinese Calcio's goals, and his final tally, completed with eight in the last seven games, set a club record as he surpassed German striker Oliver Bierhoff's 27-goal haul in 1997/98. The highlight of his prolific season was the hat-trick he scored against his hometown club SSC Napoli in February, but the joy of his club campaign was counterbalanced by the pain of early World Cup elimination by Slovakia in a match that brought Di Natale his long-awaited tenth international goal but left him a tearful, inconsolable figure at the final whistle.

International Career

ITALY
Debut – 20/11/02 v Turkey (h, Pescara, friendly), drew 1-1
First Goal – 18/2/04 v Czech Republic (h, Palermo, friendly), drew 2-2
Caps 36; **Goals** 10
Major Tournaments – UEFA EURO 2008; FIFA World Cup 2010

Club Career

Clubs: 96-04 Empoli FC; 97-98 Iperzola Ponteroncariale (loan); 98 AS Varese 1910 (loan); 98-99 FCE Viareggio (loan); 04- Udinese Calcio

Alejandro Damián DOMÍNGUEZ

Attacking Midfielder/Striker
Born 10/6/81,
Lanus, Argentina
Height 175cm,
Weight 73kg

A Russian champion and UEFA Cup winner during a two-year spell at FC Zenit St Petersburg, Alejandro Domínguez returned to his first Russian club, FC Rubin Kazan, at the start of the 2009 season and played a leading role as the team from Tatarstan regained the Premier-Liga title. Free-kicks and penalties made up the bulk of the Argentine set-piece specialist's 16-goal haul, and his all-round creativity and effectiveness earned him the post-season honour of Premier-Liga Player of the Year. With the addition of goals in each of his first two UEFA Champions League games, including an absolute belter against FC Internazionale Milano – the first goal conceded in the competition by the eventual champions – Domínguez entered the radar of Europe's heavyweight clubs, and he was duly signed by Valencia CF in December 2009. Things did not go to plan for him in his first half-season at the Mestalla, but with three further years on his contract, there is plenty of time for him to make his mark in La Liga.

International Career

ARGENTINA
Uncapped

Club Career

Major Honours – UEFA Cup (2008); UEFA Super Cup (2008); Argentinian Championship (2002 clausura, 2003 clausura); Russian Championship (2007, 2009);
Clubs: 00-01 Quilmes AC; 01-04 CA River Plate; 04-06 FC Rubin Kazan (RUS); 07-08 FC Zenit St Petersburg (RUS); 09 FC Rubin Kazan (RUS); 10- Valencia CF (ESP)

DOUGLAS Franco Teixeira

Centre-Back
Born 12/1/88,
Florianopolis, Brazil
Height 192cm,
Weight 80kg

Brazilian footballers come to Europe in their droves to find employment. Many of them go home without making a mark, others arrive largely unannounced but go on to become major stars in their adopted land. Douglas is one of the latter. The tall centre-back was an obscure nobody from Brazil's third division when he was recruited by Dutch club FC Twente in 2007. Within three years, however, he had become arguably the most impressive defender in the Netherlands. He was certainly a major factor in the Enschede club's shock Eredivisie title win in 2009/10. Tough, powerful and rock solid from the start of the season to the end, the 22-year-old missed only three league games and was the defensive linchpin of Steve McClaren's title-winning side. He even scored two goals, the first in an early 1-1 draw at home to PSV Eindhoven, and increasingly attracted scouts from England, Italy and Spain. Should he maintain his rapid progress, he could yet be one to watch when Brazil host the FIFA World Cup in 2014.

International Career

BRAZIL
Uncapped

Club Career

Major Honours – Dutch Championship (2010)
Clubs: 06-07 Joinville EC; 07- FC Twente (NED)

Didier DROGBA
Striker
Born 11/3/78,
Abidjan, Ivory Coast
Height 189cm, Weight 80kg

Didier Drogba's sixth season at Chelsea FC, and first under Italian coach Carlo Ancelotti, brought spectacular results. Despite being away at the Africa Cup of Nations with Ivory Coast for the whole of January, the bustling centre-forward spearheaded the Blues to victory in the Premier League with magnificent Golden Boot-winning tally of 29 goals, which he concluded with a second-half hat-trick in the title-clinching final game, an 8-0 win over Wigan Athletic FC. He also scored record-breaking sixth goal in an English domestic cup final the following weekend to beat Portsmouth FC 1-0 at Wembley and secure Chelsea's first ever league and FA Cup double. Everything seemed on track for a successful FIFA World Cup for the Ivory Coast skipper until he broke his arm in a pre-tournament friendly against Japan. It was a cruel blow for the reigning African Footballer of the Year, and although he scored a fine goal against Brazil, it had no real value and, as in Germany four years earlier, Drogba and his team trudged disconsolately out of the tournament after just three matches.

International Career

IVORY COAST
Debut – 8/9/02 v South Africa (h, Abidjan, ANQ), drew 0-0
First Goal – 11/2/03 v Cameroon (n, Chateauroux, friendly), won 3-0
Caps 71; **Goals** 45
Major Tournaments – Africa Cup of Nations 2006; FIFA World Cup 2006; Africa Cup of Nations 2008; Africa Cup of Nations 2010; FIFA World Cup 2010

Club Career

Major Honours – English Premier League (2005, 2006, 2010); English FA Cup (2007, 2009, 2010); English League Cup (2005, 2007)
Clubs: 98-02 Le Mans UC 72 (FRA); 02-03 En Avant Guingamp (FRA); 03-04 Olympique de Marseille (FRA); 04- Chelsea FC (ENG)

Edin DŽEKO
Striker
Born 17/3/86,
Doboj,
Bosnia-Herzegovina
Height 193cm,
Weight 84kg

His nine goals were insufficient to take Bosnia-Herzegovina to the 2010 FIFA World Cup, but Edin Džeko further advanced his mushrooming reputation as one of European football's most complete strikers with four goals for VfL Wolfsburg in his debut UEFA Champions League campaign – including one in each of the team's two matches against Manchester United FC – and a top-scoring tally of 22 goals in the German Bundesliga. Although Wolfsburg came nowhere near to defending the title they had won so thrillingly in 2008/09, with Džeko scoring 26 goals and his Brazilian strike-partner Grafite grabbing 28, the 24-year-old Bosnian remained a painful thorn in the side of Bundesliga defenders, and a late burst of eight goals in the last seven matches of the season enabled him to overtake Bayer 04 Leverkusen's Stefan Kiessling and succeed Grafite as Germany's Torschützenkönig (goal king), courting ever more interest from wealthy would-be purchasers such as AC Milan, Juventus and Manchester City FC.

International Career

BOSNIA-HERZEGOVINA
Debut – 2/6/07 v Turkey (h, Sarajevo, ECQ), won 3-2
First Goal – 2/6/07 v Turkey (h, Sarajevo, ECQ), won 3-2
Caps 26; **Goals** 15

Club Career

Major Honours – German Championship (2009)
Clubs: 03-05 FK Željezničar; 05 FK Ústí nad Labem (CZE); 06-07 FK Teplice (CZE); 07- VfL Wolfsburg (GER)

Balázs DZSUDZSÁK
Left Midfielder/ Winger
Born 23/12/86, Nyirlugos, Hungary
Height 179cm, Weight 72kg

A season without silverware is never a good one for a team of PSV Eindhoven's lofty repute, but a shining light amidst the general gloom of the Dutch club's trophyless 2009/10 campaign was provided by the excellent form of their lively left-footed winger from Hungary, Balázs Dzsudzsák. He got off to a brilliant start with two fantastic free-kick goals in a 4-3 win at home to AFC Ajax in August and ended up as the club's top scorer in the Eredivisie with 14 goals, to which he added 16 assists. It was a long season for the 23-year-old, with 47 matches in all competitions for PSV plus another eight for the Hungarian national team. It ended in the Amsterdam ArenA on 2 June with Dzsudzsák opening the scoring for Hungary in a friendly against the Netherlands with his second international goal. Unfortunately for him, the Oranje came back to score six in reply, getting Hungary's Dutch coach Erwin Koeman the sack.

International Career
HUNGARY
Debut – 2/6/07 v Greece (a, Heraklion, ECQ), lost 0-2
First Goal – 24/5/08 v Greece (h, Budapest, friendly), won 3-2
Caps 26; Goals 2

Club Career
Major Honours – Hungarian Championship (2005, 2006, 2007); Dutch Championship (2008)
Clubs: 04-08 Debreceni VSC; 08- PSV Eindhoven (NED)

EDUARDO dos Reis Carvalho
Goalkeeper
Born 19/9/82, Mirandela, Portugal
Height 187cm, Weight 84kg

The Portuguese national team's goalkeeping gloves would appear to be on safe hands for the foreseeable future. Fresh from an outstanding domestic campaign, in which he conceded only 20 goals in 30 matches for SC Braga as the club infiltrated the country's traditional hierarchy by finishing above FC Porto and Sporting Clube de Portugal as Liga runners-up to SL Benfica, the 27-year-old enjoyed a splendid FIFA World Cup in South Africa. A more than convincing heir to the long-serving Ricardo, he marked his major tournament debut by keeping clean sheets in each of Portugal's three group games and was even more impressive in the round of 16 clash against Spain, repeatedly keeping the opposition attack at bay with a string of top-class saves. Agile, courageous and dependable, Eduardo left Braga shortly after his return from South Africa, joining Italian Serie A club Genoa CFC on a four-year contract as the replacement 'keeper for Marco Amelia, who departed on loan to AC Milan.

International Career
PORTUGAL
Debut – 11/2/09 v Finland (h, Faro, friendly), won 1-0
Caps 19; Goals 0
Major Tournaments – FIFA World Cup 2010

Club Career
Clubs: 01-05 SC Braga B; 05-10 SC Braga; 07 SC Beira-Mar (loan); 07-08 Vitória FC (loan); 10- Genoa CFC (ITA)

FÁBIO Alexandre da Silva COENTRÃO

Left-Back/Left-Winger
Born 11/3/88,
Vila do Conde, Portugal
Height 178cm,
Weight 66kg

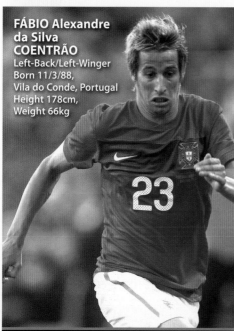

The potential that Fábio Coentrão hinted at as a Portuguese youth international was finally realised in 2009/10 as the stylish young left-footer made the big breakthrough both fo SL Benfica and the senior national side. Generally renowned a winger, he reinvented himself as a left-back and it was in that position that he caught the eye at the FIFA World Cup in South Africa. Defensively sound, he was dynamic going forward as he raced down the left flank and whipped in delicious crosses, playing a fulsome part in the destruction c North Korea and also standing out in the other three matche against Ivory Coast, Brazil and Spain. The youngster was promoted ahead of Duda for the role after an excellent seas with Benfica – his first at the club after several spells on loan that brought him a championship winner's medal and some valuable experience in the UEFA Europa League.

International Career

PORTUGAL
Debut – 14/11/09 v Bosnia-Herzegovina (h, Lisbon, WCQ), won 1-0
Caps 8; Goals 0
Major Tournaments – FIFA World Cup 2010

Club Career

Major Honours – Portuguese Championship (2010)
Clubs: 05-07 Rio Ave FC; 07- SL Benfica; 08 CD Nacional (loan 08 Real Zaragoza (ESP) (loan); 09 Rio Ave FC (loan)

Francesc "Cesc" FÀBREGAS i Soler

Midfielder
Born 4/5/87,
Vilassar de Mar,
Spain
Height177cm,
Weight 69kg

Perhaps the best indication of the strength of Spain's FIFA Word Cup-winning team was that Cesc Fàbregas couldn't ge into it. The sublimely gifted young midfielder would have been a guaranteed starter in every one of the other 31 teams in South Africa. In the event, the best he could manage for La Roja was four substitute appearances. He did get on in the final, though, and after missing one good chance to score himself in extra time he made amends by setting up Andrés Iniesta's winner. Until he cracked a bone in his right leg playing against FC Barcelona at the end of March, Fàbregas had been in supreme form for Arsenal FC. He was the Gunne top scorer in the Premier League with a personal best tally of 15 goals, to which he added the same number of assists. Frustratingly, however, his first trophy as club captain remained elusive as Arsène Wenger's team completed their fifth successive season without silverware, leading to persistent speculation throughout the summer about a prospective move 'home' to Barcelona.

International Career

SPAIN
Major Honours – FIFA World Cup (2010); UEFA European Championship (2008)
Debut – 1/3/06 v Ivory Coast (h, Valladolid, friendly), won 3-2
First Goal – 10/6/08 v Russia (n, Innsbruck, ECF), won 4-1
Caps 54; Goals 6
Major Tournaments – FIFA World Cup 2006; UEFA EURO 2008 FIFA Confederations Cup 2009; FIFA World Cup 2010

Club Career

Major Honours – English FA Cup (2005)
Clubs: 03- Arsenal FC (ENG)

Radamel FALCAO García Zárate
Striker
Born 10/2/86,
Magdalena,
Colombia
Height 175cm,
Weight 78kg

FC Porto were unable to retain the Portuguese Liga title in 2009/10, but they did find a top-class replacement up front for the departed Lisandro López. Colombian international striker Radamel Falcao – named after the famous Brazilian midfielder Falcão – arrived amidst much fanfare from CA River Plate – after Porto had gazumped SL Benfica for his signature – and immediately endeared himself to the local populace by scoring in each of his first four league games. It would be no false dawn, either. By the end of term the dynamic, pacy 24-year-old had struck another 21 times in the Liga to finish just behind Benfica's Óscar Cardozo in the goal charts. He also scored five goals in the Portuguese Cup, including the winner in the final against GD Chaves, and his consistent output on the domestic front was supplemented by four goals – and several lively performances – in the UEFA Champions League.

International Career
COLOMBIA
Debut – 7/2/07 v Uruguay (h, Cucuta, friendly), lost 1-3
First Goal – 3/6/07 v Montenegro (n, Matsumoto, Kirin Cup), won 1-0
Caps 22; **Goals** 5

Club Career
Major Honours – Argentine Championship (2008 clausura); Portuguese Cup (2010)
Clubs: 05-09 CA River Plate (ARG); 09- FC Porto (POR)

Diego Martín FORLÁN Corazo
Striker
Born 19/5/79,
Montevideo, Uruguay
Height 174cm,
Weight 74kg

The Golden Ball for the best player at the 2010 FIFA World Cup went to Diego Forlán, and rightly so. It was a tournament in which most of the game's superstars struggled to shine, but while the poster boys wilted under the pressure, Uruguay's classy No10 thrived on it. Despite a long, tiring season for Club Atlético de Madrid, the 31-year-old's form never dropped for a minute over the entire month. He was excellent in every match and decisive in most of them, scoring five goals and inspiring his country to their best World Cup performance for 40 years. Nobody at the tournament struck the controversial Jabulani football with greater power or precision, and Forlán provided several contenders for Goal of the Tournament, including the eventual winner – a wonderful snap-volley on the run in the third place play-off against Germany. His World Cup exploits came hot on the heels of another high-profile international success story, Atlético having won the inaugural UEFA Europa League thanks to his six goals, which included both in the final – a 2-1 extra-time win over Fulham FC in Hamburg.

International Career
URUGUAY
Debut – 27/3/02 v Saudi Arabia (a, Riyadh, friendly), lost 2-3
First Goal – 27/3/02 v Saudi Arabia (a, Riyadh, friendly), lost 2-3
Caps 68; **Goals** 29
Major Tournaments – FIFA World Cup 2002; Copa América 2004; Copa América 2007; FIFA World Cup 2010

Club Career
Major Honours – UEFA Europa League (2010); English Premier League (2003); English FA Cup (2004)
Clubs: 98-02 CA Independiente (ARG); 02-04 Manchester United FC (ENG); 04-07 Villarreal CF (ESP); 07- Club Atlético de Madrid (ESP)

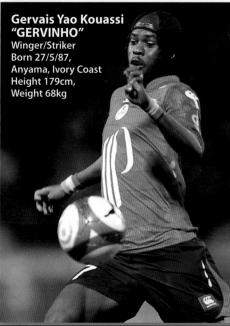

Gervais Yao Kouassi "GERVINHO"
Winger/Striker
Born 27/5/87,
Anyama, Ivory Coast
Height 179cm,
Weight 68kg

LOSC Lille Métropole were Ligue 1's top-scoring team in 2009/10, and Ivory Coast international Gervinho was largely responsible for that, especially during the first half of the campaign when he announced his arrival from Le Mans UC 72 with a flurry of goals and assists. From October through to December he found the net 11 times in the league and performed with a similar rate of efficiency in the UEFA Europa League, scoring five goals in the group stage, four of them after coming on as a substitute. His purple patch was brought to a halt by a visit to the Africa Cup of Nations in Angola in January but Gervinho offered his his team more than just goals. Fast, skilful and direct, he was deployed mostly on the right wing by Lille boss Rudi Garcia but can also operate through the centre as he did in Ivory Coast's opening game of the 2010 FIFA World Cup, where he stood in for injured captain Didier Drogba.

International Career
IVORY COAST
Debut – 1/11/07 v Qatar (a, Doha, friendly), won 6-1
First Goal – 14/11/09 v Guinea (h, Abidjan, WCQ), won 3-0
Caps 16; **Goals** 3
Major Tournaments – Africa Cup of Nations 2008; Africa Cup of Nations 2010; FIFA World Cup 2010

Club Career
Clubs: 05-07 KSK Beveren (BEL); 07-09 Le Mans UC 72 (FRA); 09- LOSC Lille Métropole (FRA)

GILBERTO Aparecido da SILVA
Midfielder
Born 7/10/76,
Lagoa da Prata, Brazil
Height 185cm,
Weight 78kg

Perceived by many to be over the hill, not least by Arsenal FC manager Arsène Wenger, who allowed him to leave the club in 2008, Gilberto Silva reminded everyone in South Africa – in his third FIFA World Cup – that his ability to perform effectively at the highest level was still very much intact. A starter in all of Brazil's five matches, he was one of the team's most consistent, if unspectacular, players, holding the midfield fort with strength and purpose and embodying the work ethic of coach Dunga. There would be no second World Cup winner's medal for the 33-year-old, but he did go into the tournament in celebratory mood having helped his club Panathinaikos FC dethrone arch-rivals Olympiacos FC as the kings of Greek football with a domestic double. The Brazilian veteran formed a productive midfield triumvirate with Greek internationals Georgios Karagounis and Kostas Katsouranis to claim his first club honours for five years.

International Career
BRAZIL
Major Honours – FIFA World Cup (2002); Copa América (2007); FIFA Confederations Cup (2005, 2009)
Debut – 7/11/01 v Bolivia (a, La Paz, WCQ), lost 1-3
First Goal – 31/1/02 v Bolivia (h, Goiania, friendly), won 6-0
Caps 92; **Goals** 3
Major Tournaments – FIFA World Cup 2002; FIFA Confederations Cup 2005; FIFA World Cup 2006; Copa América 2007; FIFA Confederations Cup 2009; FIFA World Cup 2010

Club Career
Major Honours – English Premier League (2004); English FA Cup (2003, 2005); Greek Championship (2010); Greek Cup (2010)
Clubs: 97-00 América MG; 00-02 Clube Atleico Mineiro; 02-08 Arsenal FC (ENG); 08- Panathinaikos FC (GRE)

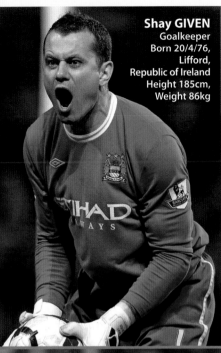

Shay GIVEN
Goalkeeper
Born 20/4/76,
Lifford,
Republic of Ireland
Height 185cm,
Weight 86kg

A Republic of Ireland international since he was 19, Shay Given collected his 100th senior cap in a 2010 FIFA World Cup qualifier against Montenegro in October 2009. It was his record-equalling 102nd appearance, against France in Paris a month later, however, that he would have greater cause to reflect upon as Ireland were held to a controversial 1-1 draw in the second leg of their qualifying play-off and therefore eliminated from the World Cup. A man of sound principles, Given appeared more traumatised than any other Ireland player by the so-called 'Hand of Henry' but he did not let it affect his domestic form in England with Manchester City FC. One of the team's most reliable and, on occasions, spectacular performers, he was an ever present during his first full season at the club until he dislocated a shoulder against Arsenal FC in late April, which kept him out of the big UEFA Champions League qualifying decider against Tottenham Hotspur FC – a game that, in his regrettable absence, City lost 1-0.

International Career

REPUBLIC OF IRELAND
Debut – 27/3/96 v Russia (h, Dublin, friendly), lost 0-2
Caps 103; **Goals** 0
Major Tournaments – FIFA World Cup 2002

Club Career

Clubs: 94-97 Blackburn Rovers FC (ENG); 95 Swindon Town FC (ENG) (loan); 96 Sunderland AFC (ENG) (loan); 97-09 Newcastle United FC (ENG); 09- Manchester City FC (ENG)

Marek HAMŠÍK
Midfielder
Born 27/7/87,
Banska Bystrica,
Slovakia
Height 180cm,
Weight 73kg

Slovakia's spiky-haired skipper will doubtless have enjoyed his team's momentous victory over Italy at the 2010 FIFA World Cup even more than his team-mates. For Marek Hamšík not only produced his best performance of the tournament against the Azzurri, he did so as a long-time Italian resident. The leading attraction at SSC Napoli since joining the club from Brescia Calcio in the summer of 2007, Hamšík maintained his annual progress by delivering his best season yet in 2009/10. Having scored nine Serie A goals in each of the previous two campaigns, he was relieved to make it third time lucky and break into double figures at last, the goal that carried him over that threshold coming in a rather special 3-1 home win over Juventus. The young playmaker ended the campaign as he had each of the previous two, as Napoli's top scorer, edging out Italian international striker Fabio Quagliarella – one of his Azzurri victims in Johannesburg – by one goal.

International Career

SLOVAKIA
Debut – 7/2/07 v Poland (n, Jerez, friendly), drew 2-2
First Goal – 13/10/07 v San Marino (h, Dubnica, ECQ), won 7-0
Caps 36; **Goals** 8
Major Tournaments – FIFA World Cup 2010

Club Career

Clubs: 04 ŠK Slovan Bratislava; 04-07 Brescia Calcio (ITA); 07- SSC Napoli (ITA)

**Brede Paulsen
HANGELAND**
Centre-Back
Born 20/6/81,
Houston, Texas,
USA
Height 195cm,
Weight 92kg

When Brede Hangeland left FC København for Fulham FC in January 2008, he probably assumed that he would be waving goodbye to European football for a while. But in 2009/10 he was right back in the heart of the action as the west London side made stunning progress to the UEFA Europa League final where they were narrowly defeated by Club Atlético de Madrid. Fulham's European adventure lasted 19 matches – half a Premier League season – and their towering Norwegian centre-back started 16 of them, including all of the knockout games in the spring. Solid and dependable in defence, he even scored vital goals against AS Roma and FC Shakhtar Donetsk. He also had an impressive international season, captaining his country to five wins in seven matches, the first of them a 4-0 thrashing of Scotland in a FIFA World Cup qualifier. Although eyed by bigger clubs, he signed a new contract with Fulham in November 2009 that should keep him at Craven Cottage until 2013.

International Career

NORWAY
Debut – 20/11/02 v Austria (a, Vienna, friendly), won 1-0
Caps 60; **Goals** 0

Club Career

*Major Honours – Danish Championship (2006, 2007);
Norwegian Cup (2001)*
Clubs: 00-05 Viking FK; 05-08 FC København (DEN);
08- Fulham FC (ENG)

Joe Hart went to the FIFA World Cup with just three international caps – all won as a half-time substitute – but there were still widespread calls for England's head coach Fabio Capello to make him the team's first-choice goalkeeper in South Africa ahead of Robert Green and David James. The reason for the recommendation was the 23-year-old's exceptional form for Birmingham City FC in the Premier League season just finished. Sent on a long-term loan to the newly promoted Midlands club from Manchester City FC, where he was second choice to Shay Given, Hart delivered one top-class display after another, helping Alex McLeish's side to a 12-match unbeaten run and a final position in the top half of the Premier League table. Recognised for his efforts with a place in the PFA Team of the Year, Hart will have looked on in envy at the World Cup as his opposite number in the 2009 UEFA European Under-21 Championship final, Manuel Neuer, kept goal for Germany while he remained unemployed on the sidelines.

International Career

ENGLAND
Debut – 1/6/08 v Trinidad & Tobago (a, Port of Spain, friendly), won 3-0
Caps 3; **Goals** 0
Major Tournaments – FIFA World Cup 2010

Club Career

Clubs: 03-06 Shrewsbury Town FC; 06- Manchester City FC;
07 Tranmere Rovers FC (loan); 07 Blackpool FC (loan);
09-10 Birmingham City FC (loan)

Joe HART
Goalkeeper
Born 19/4/87, Shrewsbury, England
Height 191cm, Weight 80kg

Very few modern-day footballers have the ability, or indeed the inclination or the licence from their coach, to run at defenders. Eden Hazard belongs to the alternative Lionel Messi school of thought, which holds that if you have a special ability, then you should use it. LOSC Lille Métropole coach Rudi Garcia was also of that belief during a 2009/10 season in which he allowed the diminutive 19-year-old from Belgium to express himself fully – and was amply rewarded as the teenager scooped France's Young Player of the Year award for the second successive season. Hazard's dribbling and creative skills helped Lille to rack up the goals in both Ligue 1 and the UEFA Europa League. A provider more than a finisher, he nevertheless supplied five goals in the domestic league and another four in Europe, including the winner at home to Liverpool FC. Many hopes have already been invested in the youngster by long-suffering supporters of the Belgian national team, who are banking on him making an impact in the UEFA EURO 2012 qualifiers and for a long time beyond.

International Career

BELGIUM
Debut – 19/11/08 v Luxembourg (a, Luxembourg, friendly), drew 1-1
Caps 12; **Goals** 0

Club Career

Clubs: 07- LOSC Lille Métropole (FRA)

Eden HAZARD
Attacking Midfielder
Born 7/1/91,
La Louviere, Belgium
Height 170cm, Weight 69kg

Gonzalo Gerardo HIGUAÍN
Striker
Born 10/12/87,
Brest, France
Height 184cm,
Weight 75kg

If the arrival at Real Madrid CF in summer 2009 of a new wave of galácticos, including Cristiano Ronaldo and Karim Benzema, was greeted by most Madridistas with uncontained enthusiasm, Gonzalo Higuaín was hardly likely to join in with the cheerleading. Although he had finished the 2008/09 season as Real's top scorer, the threat to the young Argentine striker's position was considerable. Sure enough, he started the season as a substitute, but by the onset of winter his consistent ability to make the most of the opportunities offered to him resulted in his restoration as the chief focal point of the Real attack. By the end of the season he would have 27 league goals to his name, one more than Ronaldo and second only in the entire division to Lionel Messi of FC Barcelona. Higuaín joined his compatriot in Argentina's FIFA World Cup team, scoring four goals – to Messi's none – in South Africa, but although they may be brothers in arms for their country, the new six-year contract signed for Real by Higuaín in June suggests that the pair will be arch-enemies at club level for some time to come.

International Career

ARGENTINA
Debut – 10/10/09 v Peru (h, Buenos Aires, WCQ), won 2-1
First Goal – 10/10/09 v Peru (h, Buenos Aires, WCQ), won 2-1
Caps 9; **Goals** 6
Major Tournaments – FIFA World Cup 2010

Club Career

Major Honours – Spanish Championship (2007, 2008)
Clubs: 04-06 CA River Plate; 07- Real Madrid CF (ESP)

Steffen HOFMANN
Attacking Midfielder
Born 9/9/80,
Wurzburg,
Germany
Height 170cm,
Weight 67kg

For most of his highly productive career with SK Rapid Wien, Steffen Hofmann had stood out for his ability to make goals for others. A phenomenally consistent supply of assists, many from set-pieces but a good number also from his defence-splitting through-balls, had defined him as the Austrian Bundesliga's playmaker par excellence. In 2009/10, however, he added another string to his bow by scoring as many goals as he created. With the assistance, admittedly, of six penalties, the 29-year-old German helped himself to 20 Bundesliga goals, which was not just more than Rapid's strikers, Nikica Jelavić and Hamdi Salihi, managed but the highest tally in the whole division, enabling Hofmann to make history as the first midfielder ever to top the Bundesliga score charts. Unfortunately, his efforts were not enough to bring the title back to Rapid, but further individual recognition did come his way when he was voted Austrian Footballer of the Year.

International Career

GERMANY
Uncapped

Club Career

Major Honours – Austrian Championship (2005, 2008)
Clubs: 00-02 FC Bayern München; 02-05 SK Rapid Wien (AUT); 06 TSV 1860 München; 06- SK Rapid Wien (AUT)

Keisuke HONDA
Attacking Midfielder/
Striker
Born 13/6/86,
Osaka, Japan
Height 182cm,
Weight 74kg

A new Japanese footballing icon was unearthed at the 2010 FIFA World Cup as Keisuke Honda assumed the mantle previously held by the likes of Hidetoshi Nakata and Shunsuke Nakamura. Such is the depth and variety of the 24-year-old's talent that it will be a surprise if he does not go on to bigger and better things. At the beginning of the 2009/10 season he was known outside his homeland only in the Netherlands, where he had been a roaring success in helping VVV-Venlo win promotion. The skilful left-footed schemer scored five goals in his first four Eredivisie games and made such a splash that he was recruited in January by PFC CSKA Moskva. His impact there was just as immediate as he helped the Russian club into the UEFA Champions League quarter-finals with two brilliant performances – capped by a wonderful winning goal from a trademark free-kick – against Sevilla FC. At the World Cup he was used as an out-and-out striker and looked comfortable in the role, finding the net in the victories over Cameroon and Denmark and also converting his penalty in the shoot-out defeat by Paraguay.

International Career

JAPAN
Debut – 22/6/08 v Bahrain (h, Saitama, WCQ), won 1-0
First Goal – 27/5/09 v Chile (h, Osaka, Kirin Cup), won 4-0
Caps 19; **Goals** 6
Major Tournaments – FIFA World Cup 2010

Club Career

Clubs: 05-08 Nagoya Grampus Eight; 08-09 VVV-Venlo (NED); 10- PFC CSKA Moskva (RUS)

Andrés INIESTA Luján
Attacking Midfielder
Born 11/5/84,
Fuentealbilla, Spain
Height 170cm,
Weight 65kg

Although Dutch fans may disagree, Andrés Iniesta did the world a huge favour when he scored the winning goal in the FIFA World Cup final. His dramatic strike in the Soccer City stadium, with just four minutes of extra time remaining, brought a proper and fitting conclusion to football's biggest occasion, saving it from the unsatisfactory anti-climax of penalties. The 26-year-old Spaniard's seventh international goal will be replayed from now to eternity, and whatever Iniesta goes on to achieve over the rest of his career – and he is such a huge talent that there will surely be much more for him to celebrate – nothing can ever come close to that magical dream-come-true moment in Johannesburg. Curiously, Iniesta did not have a great 2009/10 season for FC Barcelona. Often injured and out of sorts, his contribution to the Spanish title defence was no more than modest. He was evidently saving himself for the 'Mundial', because in South Africa his form and staying power were exceptional.

International Career
SPAIN
Major Honours – FIFA World Cup (2010); UEFA European Championship (2008)
Debut – 27/5/06 v Russia (h, Albacete, friendly), drew 0-0
First Goal – 7/2/07 v England (a, Manchester, friendly), won 1-0
Caps 49; **Goals** 7
Major Tournaments – FIFA World Cup 2006; UEFA EURO 2008; FIFA World Cup 2010

Club Career
Major Honours – UEFA Champions League (2006, 2009); UEFA Super Cup (2009); FIFA Club World Cup (2009); Spanish Championship (2005, 2006, 2009, 2010); Spanish Cup (2009)
Clubs: 00- FC Barcelona

Branislav IVANOVIĆ
Right-Back/Centre-Back
Born 22/2/84,
Sremska Mitrovica,
Serbia
Height 188cm,
Weight 83kg

When regular Chelsea FC right-back José Bosingwa picked up a serious knee injury in October 2009, it opened the door for the club's versatile Serbian defender Branislav Ivanović to shake off his 'understudy' tag and claim a permanent place in the Blues' first XI. It was a challenge he rose to with such fervour and distinction that by the end of the season he had claimed the right-back slot in the PFA's Team of the Year – a selection that included just one other player from the Premier League champions, striker Didier Drogba. The 26-year-old ended a memorable season by helping the Blues complete the domestic double with victory over Portsmouth FC at Wembley. His first appearance in the FA Cup final was followed a few weeks later by his major tournament debut at the FIFA World Cup. Although Serbia failed to get beyond the opening round in South Africa, Ivanović was one of their better players, starting all three matches in his now familiar right-back role.

International Career
SERBIA
Debut – 8/6/05 v Italy (n, Toronto, friendly), drew 1-1
First Goal – 12/9/07 v Portugal (a, Lisbon, ECQ), drew 1-1
Caps 34; **Goals** 4
Major Tournaments – FIFA World Cup 2010

Club Career
Major Honours – English Premier League (2010); Russian Cup (2007); English FA Cup (2009, 2010)
Clubs: 02-03 FK Srem; 03-05 OFK Beograd; 06-07 FC Lokomotiv Moskva (RUS); 08- Chelsea FC (ENG)

JESÚS NAVAS
González
Right-Winger
Born 21/11/85,
Seville, Spain
Height 170cm,
Weight 60kg

A genuine right-winger of traditional virtues, such as the ability to beat the full-back for pace and get to the byline, Jesús Navas was just a local hero in his native Andalusia until, in 2009/10, he finally conquered a psychological fear of homesickness and made himself available not only for Sevilla FC's away trips but also to the Spanish national team. Selected by Vicente del Bosque for the first time in November 2009, the lightweight flier won himself a place in Spain's FIFA World Cup squad with some fabulous performances for Sevilla, helping the club to win their UEFA Champions League group and then to re-qualify for the competition with a fourth-place finish in La Liga. Furthermore, he also won his second Copa del Rey with the club, scoring four goals including one in the final against Club Atlético de Madrid. In South Africa he was used sparingly by Del Bosque but he did come on as a substitute in the final and was at the source of the move that led to Andrés Iniesta's winning goal.

International Career

SPAIN
Major Honours – FIFA World Cup (2010)
Debut – 14/11/09 v Argentina (h, Madrid, friendly), won 2-1
First Goal – 3/6/10 v South Korea (n, Innsbruck, friendly), won 1-0
Caps 9; **Goals** 1
Major Tournaments – FIFA World Cup 2010

Club Career

Major Honours – UEFA Cup (2006, 2007); UEFA Super Cup (2006); Spanish Cup (2007, 2010)
Clubs: 03- Sevilla FC

JÚLIO CÉSAR
Soares
e Espíndola
Goalkeeper
Born 3/9/79,
Duque de Caxias,
Brazil
Height 186cm,
Weight 79kg

One mistake was all it took to transform Júlio César from the greatest Brazilian goalkeeper of all time into a FIFA World Cup flop. At least that was the way some of the enraged local media preferred to interpret his uncharacteristic error of judgment in the quarter-final against the Netherlands when, with Brazil leading 1-0, he failed to gather a seemingly harmless free-kick into the area by his FC Internazionale Milano club colleague Wesley Sneijder and allowed the ball to deflect off a team-mate and gift the Oranje an equaliser. That moment apart, Júlio César had a fabulous season, reinforcing his claims to be the world's No1 'keeper with a succession of top-grade displays for club and country. A treble-winner with Inter, he was a UEFA Champions League ever-present – even reporting for duty against Chelsea FC a few days after a car crash – and conceded only three goals in the seven knockout games. He also pulled off the save of the season with a staggering fingertip stop from Lionel Messi in the second leg of the semi-final against FC Barcelona.

International Career

BRAZIL
Major Honours – Copa América (2004); FIFA Confederations Cup (2009)
Debut – 8/7/04 v Chile (n, Arequipa, CA), won 1-0
Caps 54; **Goals** 0
Major Tournaments – FIFA Confederations Cup 2003; Copa América 2004; FIFA World Cup 2006; FIFA Confederations Cup 2009; FIFA World Cup 2010

Club Career

Major Honours – UEFA Champions League (2010); Italian Championship (2006, 2007, 2008, 2009, 2010); Italian Cup (2006, 2010)
Clubs: 98-04 CR Flamengo; 05- FC Internazionale Milano (ITA); 05 AC Chievo Verona (ITA) (loan)

Sami KHEDIRA
Midfielder
Born 4/4/87,
Stuttgart,
Germany
Height 189cm,
Weight 83kg

One footballer's misfortune can often be the making of another. If Michael Ballack had not sustained an injury in the FA Cup final that put him out of the 2010 FIFA World Cup, Sami Khedira would probably not have left his hometown club VfB Stuttgart later in the summer for Real Madrid CF. The captain of Germany's triumphant UEFA European Under-21 Championship team in June 2009, Khedira made his senior debut for the Nationalmannschaft three months later but had not even started a full international when skipper Ballack suffered that unfortunate brush with fate at Wembley. From that moment on Germany coach Joachim Löw did not hesitate to nominate the 23-year-old as his preferred central midfield partner to Bastian Schweinsteiger, and Khedira would go on to not only start all seven of Germany's matches in South Africa but star in most of them. He crowned a superb tournament by heading in the winning goal in the third place play-off against Uruguay, and no sooner was the World Cup party over than in came the offer of a five-year contract from Real that neither he nor Stuttgart could possibly refuse.

International Career

GERMANY
Debut – 5/9/09 v South Africa (h, Leverkusen, friendly), won 2-0
First Goal – 10/7/10 v Uruguay (n, Port Elizabeth, WCF), won 3-2
Caps 12; **Goals** 1
Major Tournaments – FIFA World Cup 2010

Club Career

Major Honours – German Championship (2007)
Clubs: 06-10 VfB Stuttgart; 10- Real Madrid CF (ESP)

Stefan KIESSLING
Striker
Born 25/1/84,
Lichtenfels,
Germany
Height 191cm,
Weight 78kg

Stefan Kiessling made it into Germany's 2010 FIFA World Cup squad despite having played no part in the qualifying campaign. Although some questioned his value at international level, the tall blond striker demanded inclusion for South Africa with his prolific goalscoring for Bayer 04 Leverkusen. Unluckily pipped at the last by VfL Wolfsburg's Edin Džeko for the Bundesliga top scorer prize, Kiessling's marksmanship was the key constant in the Rhineland club's concerted bid for a first ever Bundesliga title. It came to nought in the end – indeed, they finished a disappointing fourth – but Kiessling showed repeatedly that he could take on the goalscoring mantle of long-term injury victim Patrick Helmes, the player he had partnered in all 34 of the previous season's league games, scoring 12 goals to his team-mate's 21. A new liaison was forged in 2009/10 with Swiss striker Eren Derdiyok, and once again it yielded 33 Bundesliga goals – only this time Kiessling was the senior partner on 21.

International Career

GERMANY
Debut – 28/3/07 v Denmark (h, Duisburg, friendly), lost 0-1
Caps 6; **Goals** 0
Major Tournaments – FIFA World Cup 2010

Club Career

Clubs: 01-06 1. FC Nürnberg; 06- Bayer 04 Leverkusen

Simon KJÆR
Centre-Back
Born 26/3/89,
Horsens, Denmark
Height 189cm,
Weight 82kg

A year after making his debut for the Danish national team – in a famous FIFA World Cup qualifying win in Sweden – Simon Kjær travelled to South Africa as one of the key figures in Morten Olsen's side. The 21-year-old centre-back was in the form of his young life after a fabulous season in Serie A with US Città di Palermo during which he made 35 starts, scored two goals and established himself as one of the classiest and consistent defenders in Italy. The Sicilians only just missed out on a UEFA Champions League place, finishing fifth, and while that brought frustration, there was more disappointment for the Rosanero fans when Kjær was sold in early July to German club VfL Wolfsburg. Before then he fulfilled his date with Denmark in South Africa, where he earned mixed reviews, making one bad error (against the Netherlands), helping to create one glorious goal (against Cameroon), and picking up two yellow cards that excluded him from the decisive third game against Japan.

International Career

DENMARK
Debut – 6/6/09 v Sweden (a, Solna, WCQ), won 1-0
Caps 11; Goals 0
Major Tournaments – FIFA World Cup 2010

Club Career

Clubs: 07-08 FC Midtjylland; 08-10 US Città di Palermo (ITA); 10- VfL Wolfsburg (GER)

Miroslav Klose's 2009/10 season at club level was probably the most frustrating of his career. Although FC Bayern München won the German league and cup double and reached the UEFA Champions League final, he played only a bit-part role in the success, coach Louis van Gaal preferring to use Ivica Olić alone up front and for the most part leaving Klose to twiddle his thumbs on the bench. Despite that inactivity, Germany coach Joachim Löw was never going to leave his most prized attacking asset sitting idle at the FIFA World Cup. Germany's top scorer in qualifying with seven goals, including the all-important winner away to Russia in Moscow, Klose proved his evergreen class in South Africa, scoring four times to take his cumulative tally of World Cup finals goals to a staggering 14 – one behind Brazilian striker Ronaldo's all-time record. He celebrated his 100th cap with a brace of goals against Argentina, the second of which, to make it 4-0, was unquestionably the best collective 'team' goal of the tournament.

International Career

GERMANY
Debut – 24/3/01 v Albania (h, Leverkusen, WCQ), won 2-1
First Goal – 24/3/01 v Albania (h, Leverkusen, WCQ), won 2-1
Caps 101; Goals 52
Major Tournaments – FIFA World Cup 2002; UEFA EURO 2004; FIFA World Cup 2006; UEFA EURO 2008; FIFA World Cup 2010

Club Career

Major Honours – German Championship (2008, 2010); German Cup (2008, 2010)
Clubs: 98/99 FC Homburg; 99-04 1. FC Kaiserslautern; 04-07 Werder Bremen; 07- FC Bayern München

Miroslav KLOSE
Striker
Born 9/6/78,
Opole, Poland
Height 182cm,
Weight 81kg

PFC CSKA Moskva's unexpected run to the quarter-finals of the 2009/10 UEFA Champions League had much to do with the skilful and speedy contributions of their scurrying Serbian right-winger Miloš Krasić. The 25-year-old with the conspicuous blond mane scored four goals in the group stage, including one against Manchester United FC at Old Trafford and both winning strikes at home to Beşiktaş JK and VfL Wolfsburg, the latter a contender for European goal of the season. He was badly missed through suspension, however, when CSKA's dreams died at home to FC Internazionale Milano. A key member also of the Serbia team that qualified for the 2010 FIFA World Cup (he set up three of the goals in the qualification-clinching 5-0 win at home to Romania), more was expected of him than he delivered in South Africa, which was probably good news for CSKA given the number of top European clubs who were rumoured to be chasing his signature in the build-up to the tournament.

International Career

SERBIA

Debut – 15/11/06 v Norway (h, Belgrade, friendly), drew 1-1
First Goal – 11/10/08 v Lithuania (h, Belgrade, WCQ), won 3-0
Caps 34; **Goals** 3
Major Tournaments – FIFA World Cup 2010

Club Career

Major Honours – UEFA Cup (2005); Russian Championship (2005, 2006); Russian Cup (2005, 2006, 2008, 2009)
Clubs: 99-04 FK Vojvodina; 04- PFC CSKA Moskva (RUS)

Miloš KRASIĆ
Midfielder/Right-Winger
Born 1/11/84,
Kosovska Mitrovica, Serbia
Height 185cm, Weight 75kg

Sergei KRIVETS
Midfielder
Born 8/6/86,
Grodno, Belarus
Height 177cm,
Weight 77kg

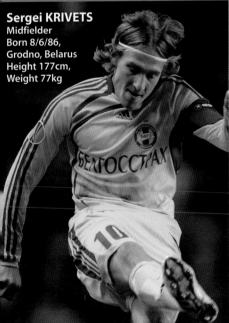

Sergei Krivets qualified for the 2010/11 UEFA Champions League twice over – firstly as a champion of Belarus with FC BATE Borisov, then, six months later, as a champion of Poland with Lech Poznań. The gifted young Belarusian international midfielder played in the group stage of Europe's flagship club competition with BATE in 2008/09 and he enjoyed another extended sojourn in the UEFA Europa League in 2009/10, his last game with the club bringing a memorable 1-0 victory away to Everton FC. Five days later he signed a three-and-a-half-year contract with Lech. Krivets contributed 14 goals to BATE's 2009 Belarusian Premier League triumph – his and the club's fourth in succession – and he was also on target twice in his first three games for Lech, but it was his third goal that proved the most crucial, his last-minute strike at KS Ruch Chorzów in the penultimate round enabling Lech to seize the initiative from Wisła Kraków in the clubs' two-horse race for the Ekstraklasa title.

International Career

BELARUS

Debut – 2/2/08 v Iceland (n, Ta' Qali, friendly), won 2-0
Caps 8; **Goals** 0

Club Career

Major Honours – Belarusian Championship (2006, 2007, 2008, 2009); Polish Championship (2010); Belarusian Cup (2006)
Clubs: 03-05 FC Lokomotiv Minsk; 06-09 FC BATE Borisov; 10- Lech Poznań (POL)

Kevin KURÁNYI
Striker
Born 2/3/82,
Rio de Janeiro,
Brazil
Height 190cm,
Weight 83kg

FC Schalke 04's concerted bid to win a first Bundesliga title in 2009/10 was founded on the consistent goalscoring of Kevin Kuranyi. The 28-year-old German international striker had fallen out with the Schalke fans for a spell the previous season, but he rekindled the love affair during a campaign in which his formidable finishing skills, and especially his strength in the air, turned the Gelsenkirchen club into genuine title challengers. There was huge disappointment for the player when he was informed by Germany head coach Joachim Löw that, despite his 18 Bundesliga goals, he would not be considered for the 2010 FIFA World Cup. With his Schalke contract at an end, Kuranyi decided to quit the Bundesliga and join Russian club FC Dinamo Moskva. He left behind a little legacy, however, having become only the third player in Bundesliga history to have scored ten goals or more in eight successive seasons. His Bundesliga tally stands at 111 in 261 matches.

International Career
GERMANY
Debut – 29/3/03 v Lithuania (h, Nuremberg, ECQ) drew 1-1
First Goal – 11/10/03 v Iceland (h, Hamburg, ECQ), won 3-0
Caps 52; **Goals** 19
Major Tournaments – UEFA EURO 2004; FIFA Confederations Cup 2005; UEFA EURO 2008

Club Career
Clubs: 00-05 VfB Stuttgart; 05-10 FC Schalke 04; 10- FC Dinamo Moskva (RUS)

Dirk KUYT
Striker/
Wide Midfielder
Born 22/7/80,
Katwijk aan Zee,
Netherlands
Height 184cm,
Weight 84kg

Dirk Kuyt played 70 matches in the 2009/10 season, 53 for Liverpool FC and 17 for the Netherlands, ending his marathon campaign with a starting appearance in the FIFA World Cup final in Johannesburg. His two coaches, Rafael Benítez and Bert van Marwijk, never thought to give a rest to a player who always showed willing and seldom, if ever, let them down. It was not the greatest of seasons for Liverpool but Kuyt was one of the team's most consistent and productive players. He scored in both derby wins over Everton FC and took his tally of goals for the club past the 50 mark, but it was his ceaseless endeavour and fearless commitment that were equally important in the eyes of the ever-demanding Kop. He displayed similar qualities in helping the Netherlands go all the way to the World Cup final. In addition to his goal in the first game against Denmark, he set up three for his team-mates in the knockout phase, making him the joint-leading provider of assists in the competition.

International Career
NETHERLANDS
Debut – 3/9/04 v Liechtenstein (h, Utrecht, friendly), won 3-0
First Goal – 9/10/04 v FYR Macedonia (a, Skopje, WCQ), drew 2-
Caps 70; **Goals** 16
Major Tournaments – FIFA World Cup 2006; UEFA EURO 2008; FIFA World Cup 2010

Club Career
Major Honours – Dutch Cup (2003)
Clubs: 98-03 FC Utrecht; 03-06 Feyenoord; 06- Liverpool FC (ENG)

Philipp LAHM
Full-Back
Born 11/11/83,
Munich, Germany
Height 170cm,
Weight 62kg

With Michael Ballack injured, Philipp Lahm was pressed into emergency service as Germany's captain for the FIFA World Cup finals. Although that made him, at 26, Germany's youngest ever World Cup skipper, the FC Bayern München full-back fulfilled the obligation like the consummate professional he is – without fuss or fanfare – and almost led the team to the final. Remarkably, the third place play-off against Uruguay was Germany's first World Cup game for eight years, qualifiers included, in which Lahm did not feature. Moreover, in each of the previous 23 he had played from start to finish. In South Africa, unlike in 2006, Lahm operated as a right-back rather than on the left. Although more than capable in both positions, it was a logical move given that he had spent the 2009/10 season playing there for Bayern, coach Louis van Gaal having preferred to pair him up with Arjen Robben on the right flank. It proved a smart move as Bayern won the Bundesliga/DFB-Pokal double and finished runners-up in the UEFA Champions League, with Lahm, assiduous as ever, barely missing a minute of the action.

International Career

GERMANY
Debut – 18/2/04 v Croatia (a, Split, friendly), won 2-1
First Goal – 28/4/04 v Romania (a, Bucharest, friendly), lost 1-5
Caps 71; **Goals** 4
Major Tournaments – UEFA EURO 2004; FIFA World Cup 2006; UEFA EURO 2008; FIFA World Cup 2010

Club Career

Major Honours – German Championship (2006, 2008, 2010); German Cup (2006, 2008, 2010)
Clubs: 03-05 VfB Stuttgart; 05- FC Bayern München

Frank LAMPARD
Midfielder
Born 20/6/78,
Romford, England
Height 183cm,
Weight 79kg

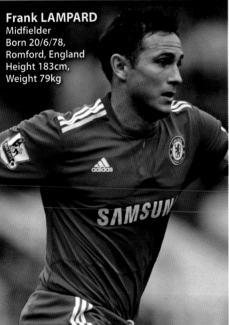

One of many England players who failed to do themselves justice at the 2010 FIFA World Cup, Frank Lampard did at least elicit widespread sympathy for the 'goal' he scored against Germany that was not ratified by the referee. That unfortunate incident in Bloemfontein meant that, officially at least, Lampard had failed to score in nine World Cup finals matches, having also endured a miserable time of it at the 2006 tournament. His lacklustre displays in South Africa were particularly surprising because he headed there fresh from the finest season of his club career – albeit one that ended with a missed penalty in the FA Cup final. A Premier League/FA Cup double-winner with Chelsea FC, he registered a total of 27 goals in all competitions, including 22 in the Premier League – six more than his previous best tally, in 2005/06. In so doing he surpassed 100 league goals for the club and 150 in all, becoming Chelsea's third highest scorer of all time – a prodigious achievement for a midfielder.

International Career

ENGLAND
Debut – 10/10/99 v Belgium (h, Sunderland, friendly), won 2-1
First Goal – 20/8/03 v Croatia (h, Ipswich, friendly), won 3-1
Caps 82; **Goals** 20
Major Tournaments – UEFA EURO 2004; FIFA World Cup 2006; FIFA World Cup 2010

Club Career

Major Honours – English Premier League (2005, 2006, 2010); English FA Cup (2007, 2009, 2010); English League Cup (2005, 2007)
Clubs: 95-01 West Ham United FC; 96 Swansea City FC (loan); 01- Chelsea FC

Robert LEWANDOWSKI
Striker
Born 21/8/88,
Warsaw,
Poland
Height 181cm,
Weight 71kg

Poland failed to qualify for the 2010 FIFA World Cup but, as hosts of UEFA EURO 2012, they are guaranteed to be present at the next major tournament, and the man most likely to lift the nation at those finals is Robert Lewandowski. The striker left his homeland in June 2010 for a new career in Germany with BV Borussia Dortmund. It took several weeks of negotiations before Dortmund sport director Michael Zorc got his man, but the 21-year-old was hot property after all, his reputation as one of the continent's most gifted young strikers having risen with his 18-goal contribution to Lech Poznań's 2009/10 Polish Ekstraklasa title triumph. Lewandowski was Lech's star turn – and the league's top scorer - as they won their first Polish championship for 17 years. His goalscoring was consistent – nine in the autumn, nine in the spring, with his last five coming just when his team needed them most, in the final four matches. His development in Germany will be of considerable interest both to Polish fans and, of course, to those enormous crowds that regularly fill Dortmund's cavernous Signal-Iduna-Park.

International Career

POLAND
Debut – 10/9/08 v San Marino (a, Serravalle, WCQ), won 2-0
First Goal – 10/9/08 v San Marino (a, Serravalle, WCQ), won 2-
Caps 23; **Goals** 6

Club Career

Major Honours – Polish Championship (2010); Polish Cup (2009)
Clubs: 06-08 Znicz Pruszków; 08-10 Lech Poznań; 10- BV Borussia Dortmund (GER)

Signed by Olympique Lyonnais as the replacement for Real Madrid CF-bound Karim Benzema in a €27m deal, Lisandro López went on to justify the outlay with an excellent debut season in French football, scoring just as freely for Lyon in both domestic and European competition as he had done over a number of campaigns for FC Porto and winning end-of-season acclaim with the prize of Ligue 1 Player of the Year. Unlike in Portugal, the 27-year-old striker did not win the domestic title, Lyon finishing runners-up to Olympique de Marseille despite his 15-goal contribution, but he did help to take his new club further than ever before in the UEFA Champions League, scoring four goals in their play-off round tie against RSC Anderlecht, a crucial last-minute equaliser at home to Liverpool FC in the group stage and another two in the first leg of the quarter-final tie against FC Girondins de Bordeaux that Lyon won 3-2 on aggregate to reach the semi-finals for the first time.

International Career

ARGENTINA
Debut – 9/3/05 v Mexico (n, Los Angeles, friendly), drew 1-1
First Goal – 12/8/09 v Russia (a, Moscow, friendly), won 3-2
Caps 7; **Goals** 1

Club Career

Major Honours – Portuguese Championship (2006, 2007, 2008, 2009); Portuguese Cup (2006, 2009)
Clubs: 02-05 Racing Club; 05-09 FC Porto (POR); 09- Olympique Lyonnais (FRA)

LISANDRO LÓPEZ
Striker
Born 2/3/83,
Buenos Aires, Argentina
Height 175cm, Weight 74kg

Hugo LLORIS
Goalkeeper
Born 26/12/86,
Nice, France
Height 188cm,
Weight 78kg

On reflection, given what transpired in South Africa, it might have been better for all concerned had France not been present at the 2010 FIFA World Cup finals, but they would not have got there without the brilliance of their goalkeeper in the qualifying play-off against the Republic of Ireland. As other French players froze, Hugo Lloris was majestic in both legs of the tie, his confident and decisive interventions not just saving Les Bleus from elimination but also confirming once and for all his position as the team's undisputed No1 'keeper after a protracted tussle for the jersey with Steve Mandanda. Lloris appeared to have lost ground in that contest with a red card in France's big group game against Serbia in Belgrade, but coach Raymond Domenech kept faith in him and was duly rewarded. Lloris also enjoyed an excellent season for Olympique Lyonnais, especially in Europe, where he was inspirational in helping his club knock out, among others, Liverpool FC and Real Madrid CF. His fine domestic form also earned him a second successive Ligue 1 Goalkeeper of the Year award.

International Career

FRANCE
Debut – 19/11/08 v Uruguay (h, Saint-Denis, friendly), drew 0-0
Caps 14; **Goals** 0
Major Tournaments – FIFA World Cup 2010

Club Career

Clubs: 05-08 OGC Nice; 08- Olympique Lyonnais

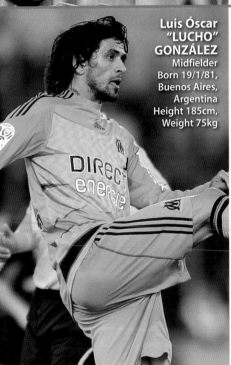

Luis Óscar "LUCHO" GONZÁLEZ
Midfielder
Born 19/1/81,
Buenos Aires,
Argentina
Height 185cm,
Weight 75kg

Having won four consecutive domestic league titles with FC Porto, Lucho González promptly made it five in a row as he helped his new club Olympique de Marseille to their first French championship title in 18 years. Signed for a club-record fee of €18m, the pressure was on the Argentine playmaker to perform, but his debut campaign in France turned out to be a season of two halves. Injured and out of kilter in the autumn, he burst into life after Christmas, providing the X factor that Marseille needed to turn championship-winning promise into fulfilment. His subtle skills, set-piece expertise and on-field leadership proved to be key assets for Didier Deschamps' team and he ended the Ligue 1 season with 11 assists – the highest figure in the division – and five goals. There was disappointment for him, particularly as an ex-Porto captain, as Marseille exited the UEFA Europa League at the hands of SL Benfica, and despite his excellent end to the season he was not recalled by Diego Maradona to serve his country at the 2010 FIFA World Cup.

International Career

ARGENTINA
Debut – 31/1/03 v Honduras (a, San Pedro Sula, friendly), won 3-1
First Goal - 31/1/03 v Honduras (a, San Pedro Sula, friendly), won 3-1
Caps 43; **Goals** 7
Major Tournaments – Copa América 2004; FIFA Confederations Cup 2005; FIFA World Cup 2006; Copa América 2007

Club Career

Major Honours – Argentine Championship (clausura 2004); Portuguese Championship (2006, 2007, 2008, 2009); French Championship (2010); Portuguese Cup (2006, 2009); French League Cup (2010)
Clubs: 98-02 CA Huracán; 02-05 CA River Plate; 05-09 FC Porto (POR); 09- Olympique de Marseille (FRA)

Lucimar Ferreira da Silva "LÚCIO"
Centre-Back
Born 8/5/78,
Brasilia, Brazil
Height 188cm,
Weight 80kg

Having lifted the FIFA Confederations Cup in Johannesburg in 2009 – after scoring the winning goal in the final – Brazil captain Lúcio returned to South Africa a year later looking for a FIFA World Cup encore. Sadly for him and his team, it was not to be as the Netherlands eliminated the Seleção in the quarter-finals, but from a personal perspective Lúcio was entitled to feel that he had given his best. For the third World Cup finals in a row the tall, tough-tackling centre-back started every one of Brazil's matches, stretching his aggregate tally to 17. Whether he will still be around on home soil in 2014 to prolong that run at the age of 36 is debatable, but there was nothing remotely wrong with his fitness and athleticism during a 2009/10 campaign in which he helped FC Internazionale Milano to an unprecedented clean sweep of trophies in his first season at the club. Doubly delicious for Lúcio was the fact that Inter won the UEFA Champions League final against the club that sold him, FC Bayern München. His form both in Madrid and throughout the run to the final was nothing short of majestic.

International Career

BRAZIL
Major Honours – FIFA World Cup (2002); FIFA Confederations Cup (2005, 2009)
Debut – 15/11/00 v Colombia (h, Sao Paulo, WCQ), won 1-0
First Goal – 9/2/05 v Hong Kong (a, Hong Kong, friendly), won 7-1
Caps 96; **Goals** 4
Major Tournaments – FIFA Confederations Cup 2001; FIFA World Cup 2002; FIFA Confederations Cup 2003; FIFA Confederations Cup 2005; FIFA World Cup 2006; FIFA Confederations Cup 2009; FIFA World Cup 2010

Club Career

Major Honours – UEFA Champions League (2010); German Championship (2005, 2006, 2008); Italian Championship (2010); German Cup (2005, 2006, 2008); Italian Cup (2010)
Clubs: 97-00 SC Internacional; 01-04 Bayer 04 Leverkusen (GER); 04-09 FC Bayern München (GER); 09- FC Internazionale Milano (ITA)

Romelu LUKAKU
Striker
Born 13/5/93,
Antwerp,
Belgium
Height 190cm,
Weight 94kg

Romelu Lukaku's goalscoring feats for RSC Anderlecht in 2009/10 constituted one of the most remarkable stories of the European season. The figures alone were not overly astonishing – 15 goals in Belgium's Pro League and another four in the UEFA Europa League – but they became so when accompanied by the fact that the player who scored them was only 16 years old. Big, fast and strong, Lukaku certainly looked older than the schoolboy he actually was, but there was nothing deceptive about his talent, which, if carefully harnessed, should go on to serve Belgian football royally for at least the next decade and a half. Lukaku's first season as a professional yielded both a championship winner's medal and the individual prize of the Golden Boot as the Pro League's top scorer (during the regular part of the two-phase campaign). He was also handed his first two international caps for Belgium. Not surprisingly, the youngster's exploits attracted widespread interest from abroad, but his immediate future lies with Anderlecht, who will hope to hold on to him until he at least exits his teens - which, astonishingly, would give them another three seasons of his services.

International Career

BELGIUM
Debut – 3/3/10 v Croatia (h, Brussels, friendly), lost 0-1
Caps 2; **Goals** 0

Club Career

Major Honours – Belgian Championship (2010)
Clubs: 09- RSC Anderlecht

MAICON Douglas Sisenando
Right-Back
Born 26/7/81,
Criciuma, Brazil
Height 184cm,
Weight 77kg

Universally recognised as the finest attacking right-back in the world, Maicon consolidated that status in helping FC Internazionale Milano to their historic treble of UEFA Champions League, Serie A and Coppa Italia in 2009/10. He was unable to make it the perfect season at the FIFA World Cup, where Brazil were prematurely eliminated by the Netherlands, but not even the best can have everything. Even so, Maicon made a mark on his first World Cup, scoring on his finals debut against North Korea. Futile debate raged afterwards as to whether his spectacular effort was a shot or a cross – only the perpetrator himself will ever know the truth – but the case for the former was strengthened by the full-back's excellent goalscoring record, not least in the season just passed, in which he registered memorable strikes against, among others, AC Milan, Juventus and FC Barcelona. Maicon's post-World Cup summer was dominated by speculation surrounding a long-proposed move for him to rejoin ex-Inter coach José Mourinho at Real Madrid CF.

International Career

BRAZIL
Major Honours – Copa América (2004, 2007); FIFA Confederations Cup (2005, 2009)
Debut – 13/7/03 v Mexico (a, Mexico City, CGC), lost 0-1
First Goal – 15/7/03 v Honduras (n, Mexico City, CGC), won 2-1
Caps 63; **Goals** 6
Major Tournaments – CONCACAF Gold Cup 2003; Copa América 2004; FIFA Confederations Cup 2005; Copa América 2007; FIFA Confederations Cup 2009; FIFA World Cup 2010

Club Career

Major Honours – UEFA Champions League (2010); Brazilian Championship (2003); Italian Championship (2007, 2008, 2009, 2010); Brazilian Cup (2003); Italian Cup (2010)
Clubs: 01-04 Cruzeiro EC; 04-06 AS Monaco FC (FRA); 06- FC Internazionale Milano (ITA)

The excellent form with which Florent Malouda ended the 2008/09 season under temporary Chelsea FC manager Guus Hiddink was carried forward with interest into the following campaign under permanent new boss Carlo Ancelotti. Comforted by a new four-year contract, the French international made positive contributions to the Chelsea cause throughout the season, displaying a consistency that had eluded him during his early days at Stamford Bridge. He also doubled his Premier League goal tally from the previous season to 12, scoring five times in March, which won him the league's player of the month vote. Frequently shifted by Ancelotti from his familiar left-wing berth into a more central midfield role, Malouda enjoyed the extra involvement and responsibility. Having played such a major role in Chelsea's double triumph, he was expected to be one of France's top players at the FIFA World Cup. In the event, he did score a goal, but it proved to be the only one the team managed in their three games, providing scant consolation in a disastrous campaign.

International Career

FRANCE
Debut – 17/11/04 v Poland (h, Saint-Denis, friendly), drew 0-0
First Goal – 31/5/05 v Hungary (h, Metz, friendly), won 2-1
Caps 57; **Goals** 4
Major Tournaments – FIFA World Cup 2006; UEFA EURO 2008; FIFA World Cup 2010

Florent MALOUDA
Left-Winger/Midfielder
Born 13/6/80, Cayenne, French Guiana
Height 176cm, Weight 75kg

Club Career

Major Honours – French Championship (2004, 2005, 2006, 2007); English Premier League (2010); English FA Cup (2009, 2010)
Clubs: 96-00 La Berrichonne de Châteauroux; 00-03 En Avant Guingamp; 03-07 Olympique Lyonnais ; 07- Chelsea FC (ENG)

Lionel Andrés MESSI
Attacking Midfielder/Striker
Born 24/6/87,
Rosario, Argentina
Height 170cm,
Weight 65kg

Admission to the pantheon of football's all-time greats was denied to Lionel Messi after a disappointing FIFA World Cup wit Argentina, but if he keeps knocking on the portal as he did repeatedly with FC Barcelona during a glorious 2009/10 season, one day he will surely be welcomed inside to join Pelé, Maradona and co. 'El Diego', alas, was unable, as feared, to bring the best out of the little genius in South Africa. Messi started brilliantly against Nigeria but faded gradually thereafter and wa practically powerless in the quarter-final against Germany. As the reigning Ballon d'Or and FIFA World Player of the Year, more was expected of Messi at the World Cup than any other player. He won those awards for his exploits in 2009, and his game ascended to an even loftier plane during the first few months of 2010. Boosted by his winning goal in the FIFA Club World Cup final against Estudiantes in December, he scored 25 goals in La Liga from January through to May, giving him 34 in total, which won him the Pichichi and Barça the title. He also topped the UEFA Champions League goal charts for the second successive season, half of his eight-goal tally coming in a magnificent virtuoso performance against Arsenal FC at Camp Nou that, even with his enormous talent and so many years still ahead of him, Messi may struggle to better.

International Career
ARGENTINA
Debut – 17/8/05 v Hungary (a, Budapest, friendly), won 2-1
First Goal – 1/3/06 v Croatia (n, Basel, friendly), lost 2-3
Caps 50; **Goals** 13
Major Tournaments – FIFA World Cup 2006; Copa América 2007; FIFA World Cup 2010

Club Career
Major Honours – UEFA Champions League (2006, 2009); UEFA Super Cup (2009); FIFA Club World Cup (2009); Spanish Championship (2005, 2006, 2009, 2010); Spanish Cup (2009)
Clubs: 04- FC Barcelona (ESP)

Fabrizio MICCOLI
Striker
Born 27/6/79,
Nardo, Italy
Height 165cm,
Weight 60kg

Fabrizio Miccoli's international career ended in 2004 so there was never a realistic chance that, despite a media lobby in his favour, he would be recalled for the 2010 FIFA World Cup – even before he injured himself in the penultimate game of a Serie A season that was unquestionably the finest of his career. The stocky striker scored a personal-best tally of 19 Serie A goals, helping unsung US Città di Palermo to finish fifth. Had the Rosanero won their round 37 game at home to UC Sampdoria, rather than drawing it 1-1, they would have taken fourth spot and a UEFA Champions League qualifying berth. Hailing from the south of Italy, Miccoli felt at home in Sicily, and the attacking trident he formed with Javier Pastore and Edinson Cavani concocted some of the tastiest football served up by any Serie A club. Unbeaten at home, Palermo even attacked on their travels, with two of Miccoli's more memorable goals coming in a thrill-a-minute 5-3 defeat at FC Internazionale Milano. His appetite for the big games also brought him goals against Juventus, Milan and Roma.

International Career
ITALY
Debut – 12/2/03 v Portugal (h, Genoa, friendly), won 1-0
First Goal – 31/3/04 v Portugal (a, Braga, friendly), won 2-1
Caps 10; **Goals** 2

Club Career
Clubs: 96-98 ASD Virtus Casarano; 98-02 Ternana Calcio; 02-04 Juventus; 02-03 Perugia Calcio (loan); 04-05 ACF Fiorentina; 05-07 Juventus; 05-07 SL Benfica (POR) (loan); 07- US Città di Palermo

Artem
MILEVSKIY
Striker
Born 12/1/85,
Mozyr, Belarus
Height 190cm,
Weight 78kg

Ukraine will be looking for a hero to spark their challenge on home soil at UEFA EURO 2012, and Belarus-born Artem Milevskiy, who made his international debut for Ukraine at the 2006 FIFA World Cup, offered himself up as a prime contender with some impressive displays for club and country in 2009/10. The tall, technically proficient striker was the top scorer in the Ukrainian Premier League with 17 goals for FC Dynamo Kyiv, pipping FC Metalist Kharkiv's Brazilian striker Jajá to the prize with a last-day double at home to FC Metalurh Zaporizhya. Although his efforts were not enough to keep the title in Kyiv as Dynamo allowed FC Shakhtar Donetsk to catch and overtake them, Milevskiy stole some of the thunder from national sporting icon Andriy Shevchenko on his return to Ukraine, outscoring the ex-AC Milan and Chelsea FC striker by ten goals. Milevskiy also opened the scoring in the UEFA Champions League at home to FC Barcelona before the holders came back to win 2-1.

International Career
UKRAINE
Debut – 19/6/06 v Saudi Arabia (n, Hamburg, WCF), won 4-0
First Goal – 6/2/08 v Cyprus (a, Nicosia, friendly), drew 1-1
Caps 29; **Goals** 4
Major Tournaments – FIFA World Cup 2006

Club Career
Major Honours – Ukrainian Championship (2003, 2004, 2007, 2009); Ukrainian Cup (2003, 2005, 2006, 2007)
Clubs: 01-02 FC Borysfen-2 Boryspil; 02- FC Dynamo Kyiv

Diego Alberto MILITO
Striker
Born 12/6/79, Bernal, Argentina
Height 179cm, Weight 78kg

As debut seasons go, Diego Milito's at FC Internazionale Milano was just about as good as it gets. The Argentinian international arrived at the San Siro aged 30 having never previously played for a big club. He had scored reams of goals for mid-ranking Real Zaragoza and Genoa CFC but there were doubts about whether he could hack it at Inter. One man who had every confidence in him, though, was José Mourinho, and Milito repaid the faith shown in him by the Inter coach with an avalanche of goals, scoring 30 in all competitions as the Nerazzurri won the treble of Serie A, Coppa Italia and UEFA Champions League. Moreover, Milito delivered when it really mattered, scoring the winner in the Coppa Italia final against AS Roma, the decisive scudetto-clinching goal in the last league game of the season at AC Siena and, to cap it all, both goals in the 2-0 win over FC Bayern München in Madrid that enabled Inter to become champions of Europe again for the first time in 45 years. Those two exquisite finishes in the Santiago Bernabéu were not enough, however, to convince Diego Maradona to make Milito a regular starter at the FIFA World Cup but, in fairness, with Lionel Messi, Carlos Tévez, Gonzalo Higuaín and Sergio Agüero also at his disposal, the Argentina coach was rather spoilt for choice in attack.

International Career
ARGENTINA
Debut – 31/1/03 v Honduras (a, San Pedro Sula, friendly), won 3-1
First Goal – 31/1/03 v Honduras (a, San Pedro Sula, friendly), won 3-1
Caps 23; **Goals** 4
Major Tournaments – Copa América 2007; FIFA World Cup 2010

Club Career
Major Honours – UEFA Champions League (2010); Argentine Championship (2001 apertura); Italian Championship (2010); Italian Cup (2010)
Clubs: 99-03 Racing Club Avellaneda; 04-05 Genoa CFC (ITA); 05-08 Real Zaragoza (ESP); 08-09 Genoa CFC (ITA); 09- FC Internazionale Milano (ITA)

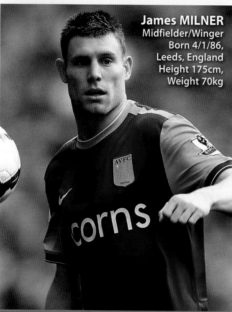

James MILNER
Midfielder/Winger
Born 4/1/86,
Leeds, England
Height 175cm,
Weight 70kg

A prolific collector of international caps for England at youth and Under-21 level, James Milner was handed his senior debut by Fabio Capello in the first international of the 2009/10 season, against the Netherlands in Amsterdam, and by the end of it he was appearing as a starter for his country at the FIFA World Cup in South Africa. Highly versatile, the Yorkshire-born youngster began his career as a striker then established himself as winger, but during the course of the 2009/10 campaign his Aston Villa FC manager Martin O'Neill decided to try him out in a central midfield role. It worked a treat as Milner suddenly tapped into the best form of his career. While other young World Cup hopefuls in the Villa side, such as Gabriel Agbonlahor, Ashley Young and Stewart Downing, floundered, Milner flourished. He ended the campaign with seven goals in his 36 Premier League appearances and was voted by the PFA as their Young Player of the Year.

International Career

ENGLAND
Debut – 12/8/09 v Netherlands (a, Amsterdam, friendly), drew 2-2
Caps 11; Goals 0
Major Tournaments – FIFA World Cup 2010

Club Career

Clubs: 02-04 Leeds United AFC; 03 Swindon Town FC (loan); 04-08 Newcastle United FC; 05-06 Aston Villa FC (loan); 08- Aston Villa FC

Thomas MÜLLER
Attacking Midfielder
Born 13/9/89,
Weilheim, Germany
Height 186cm,
Weight 74kg

Prior to the 2009/10 season Thomas Müller was a footballer known only to those in the inner circle at FC Bayern München. By the end of it the 20-year-old was a global superstar. With just a handful of substitute appearances to his name before the campaign began, there was not the remotest slither of evidence to suggest that the tall, tousle-haired academy graduate would go on and emulate his great Bavarian namesake Gerd by winning the Golden Boot at the FIFA World Cup. But thanks to the faith shown in him by coaches Louis van Gaal (at Bayern) and Joachim Löw (Germany), coupled with an abundance of natural talent and extraordinary self-belief, that is precisely what he did. He worked his way into the national team with a succession of top-notch displays for Bayern, two goals on his first European start, against Maccabi Haifa FC, giving an early indication of his special powers. A regular in the Bayern side that won the German double and finished runners-up in the UEFA Champions League, he lay claim to a starting berth on the right-hand side of Germany's attack at the World Cup and turned out to be the revelation of the finals, his five goals and three assists bringing him the Golden Boot and his overall excellence earning him the tournament's Best Young Player award.

International Career

GERMANY
Debut – 3/3/10 v Argentina (h, Munich, friendly), lost 0-1
First Goal – 13/6/10 v Australia (n, Durban, WCF), won 4-0
Caps 8; Goals 5
Major Tournaments – FIFA World Cup 2010

Club Career

Major Honours – German Championship (2010); German Cup (2010)
Clubs: 08- FC Bayern München

Manuel NEUER
Goalkeeper
Born 27/3/86, Gelsenkirchen, Germany
Height 193cm, Weight 90kg

A year after winning the UEFA European Under-21 Championship with Germany, Manuel Neuer represented his country at the FIFA World Cup, starting all six of the games that mattered before resting up for the third place play-off. He was not coach Joachim Löw's original choice to fill the role. Even before the tragic suicide of Robert Enke in November 2009 the No1 jersey appeared to have been promised to René Adler, who performed superbly in the all-important World Cup qualifier against Russia in Moscow. But the Bayer 04 Leverkusen 'keeper suffered a serious rib injury before the tournament and Neuer, who had enjoyed an excellent season between the posts for FC Schalke 04, starting all 34 Bundesliga matches and helping the Gelsenkirchen outfit to an unexpected runners-up spot, was promoted by Löw to first choice. Neuer did not let his coach or his country down, showing no sign of stage fright and conceding just three goals in his six matches as Germany took third place for the second successive World Cup.

International Career
GERMANY
Debut – 2/6/09 v United Arab Emirates (a, Dubai, friendly), won 7-2
Caps 11; **Goals** 0
Major Tournaments – FIFA World Cup 2010

Club Career
Clubs: 05- FC Schalke 04

Mamadou NIANG
Striker
Born 13/10/79, Matam, Senegal
Height 178cm, Weight 80kg

Mamadou Niang completed his fifth season at Olympique de Marseille by captaining the club to the Ligue 1 and League Cup double, bringing the Mediterranean port club their first major trophies in 17 years. On top of that the Senegalese striker achieved a triple goalscoring feat, his penalty against relegated Grenoble Foot 38 on the last day of the season not only enabling him to finish on top of the Ligue 1 scoring charts, with 18 for the season, but also bringing both his all-time total in France's top division and his cumulative tally in all competitions for Marseille to a nice round 100. Renowned for his power and direct running, the added responsibility of the captaincy, granted to him by new coach Didier Deschamps following the departure of Lorik Cana, seemed to inspire him to new heights, improving his all-round game and above all his composure in front of goal. Fielded predominantly by Deschamps at centre-forward, rather than in his alternative role on the left wing, Niang confirmed that it was his best position, not least when scoring the long-awaited first hat-trick of his club career in a 3-1 home win over AS Nancy-Lorraine in February.

International Career
SENEGAL
Debut – 27/3/02 v Bolivia (h, Dakar, friendly), won 2-1
First Goal – 27/3/02 v Bolivia (h, Dakar, friendly), won 2-1
Caps 43; **Goals** 15
Major Tournaments – Africa Cup of Nations 2004; Africa Cup of Nations 2006; Africa Cup of Nations 2008

Club Career
Major Honours – French Championship (2010); French League Cup (2005, 2010)
Clubs: 99-03 ES Troyes AC (FRA); 03 FC Metz (FRA) (loan); 03-05 RC Strasbourg (FRA); 05- Olympique de Marseille (FRA)

Ivica OLIĆ
Winger/Striker
Born 14/9/79,
Slavonski Brod,
Croatia
Height 182cm,
Weight 182kg

FC Bayern München bought Ivica Olić on a free transfer from Hamburger SV in the summer of 2009 while paying a club record €35m for another striker, Mario Gomez. It was the Croatian, however, who found favour with the German club's new coach Louis van Gaal as they hunted three trophies during the spring. Olić's non-stop running and chasing of seemingly lost causes contrasted with the German international's more laboured approach, and he also scored some very important goals, especially in Europe. Not content with his winning strikes in each of Bayern's last two UEFA Champions League group games – which might or might not have saved Van Gaal from the sack – and two highly opportune goals, one in each leg, in the quarter-final against Manchester United FC, Olić put his team into the final with the finest performance of his career, scoring the perfect hat-trick – with right foot, left foot and head – as Bayern trounced Olympique Lyonnais 3-0 in the Stade de Gerland.

International Career

CROATIA
Debut – 13/2/02 v Bulgaria (h, Rijeka, friendly), drew 0-0
First Goal – 17/4/02 v Bosnia-Herzegovina (h, Zagreb, friendly), won 2-0
Caps 69; **Goals** 13
Major Tournaments – FIFA World Cup 2002; UEFA EURO 2004; FIFA World Cup 2006; UEFA EURO 2008

Club Career
Major Honours – UEFA Cup (2005); Croatian Championship (2002, 2003); Russian Championship (2003, 2005, 2006); German Championship (2010); Russian Cup (2005, 2006); German Cup (2010)
Clubs: 96-98 NK Marsonia; 98-99 Hertha BSC Berlin (GER); 99-01 NK Marsonia; 01-02 NK Zagreb (loan); 02-03 NK Dinamo Zagreb; 03-07 PFC CSKA Moskva (RUS); 07-09 Hamburger SV (GER); 09- FC Bayern München (GER)

Mesut ÖZIL
Attacking
Midfielder
Born 15/10/88,
Gelsenkirchen,
Germany
Height 182cm,
Weight 73kg

A prominent member of the Germany team that won the 2009 UEFA European Under-21 Championship in Sweden, Mesut Özil's talent was always destined to flower in the senior Nationalmannschaft. That it reached full bloom so quickly, with a stunning performance at the 2010 FIFA World Cup, was nevertheless something of a surprise. The little left-footed schemer made his first major contribution to Germany's World Cup challenge by brilliantly setting up Miroslav Klose for the winning goal in the qualification-clinching 1-0 win in Russia. That secured him a place in Joachim Löw's team, and he consolidated his new status by helping Werder Bremen to third place in the Bundesliga with nine goals and a league-best tally of 15 assists. He carried that fine form to South Africa, where he was arguably the most eye-catching player of the group phase, starring in the opener against Australia and scoring a brilliant winner against Ghana. He continued to perform well in the latter stages and was one of the ten nominees for the Golden Ball.

International Career

GERMANY
Debut – 11/2/09 v Norway (h, Dusseldorf, friendly), lost 0-1
First Goal – 5/9/09 v South Africa (h, Leverkusen, friendly), won 2-0
Caps 17; **Goals** 2
Major Tournaments – FIFA World Cup 2010

Club Career
Major Honours – German Cup (2009)
Clubs: 06-08 FC Schalke 04; 08- Werder Bremen

Giampaolo PAZZINI
Striker
Born 2/8/84,
Pescia, Italy
Height 180cm,
Weight 74kg

UC Sampdoria surpassed expectations by finishing fourth in Serie A, and the man who did most to take them to the brink of the 2010/11 UEFA Champions League was Giampaolo Pazzini. The sharpshooting striker scored 19 goals in 37 appearances, including a brilliant brace in a late-season 2-1 win at AS Roma that effectively handed the scudetto to FC Internazionale Milano. That deadly double in the Stadio Olimpico aside, all of Pazzini's goals came in singles. Apart from a lean winter spell when he went six games without scoring, his consistency was remarkable. He also delivered when it mattered most, coolly converting a penalty away to US Città di Palermo in round 37 that put Samp in the driving seat for fourth spot and clinching that UEFA Champions League ticket with the winner against SSC Napoli seven days later. Pazzini's season didn't end there, though, as he was selected for Italy's FIFA World Cup squad. He might have shone in South Africa had the Azzurri lasted beyond the first round. As it was, he only managed half an hour against New Zealand.

International Career
ITALY
Debut – 28/3/09 v Montenegro (a, Podgorica, WCQ), won 2-1
First Goal – 28/3/09 v Montenegro (a, Podgorica, WCQ), won 2-1
Caps 9; **Goals** 1
Major Tournaments – FIFA World Cup 2010

Club Career
Clubs: 03-05 Atalanta BC; 05-09 ACF Fiorentina; 09- UC Sampdoria

PEDRO Rodríguez Ledesma
Winger/Striker
Born 28/7/87,
Santa Cruz,
Tenerife, Spain
Height 169cm,
Weight 64kg

Although he came on as a stoppage-time substitute for FC Barcelona in the 2009 UEFA Champions League final, Pedro Rodríguez could not really consider himself a bona fide contributor to the Catalan club's landmark treble triumph. By the end of the year, however, he had made history of his own by becoming the first player to score in six different competitions in the same season, finding the net successively in the Spanish Super Cup, the UEFA Super Cup, the UEFA Champions League, La Liga, the Copa del Rey and, to complete the set, the FIFA Club World Cup. It was an astounding feat, made even more special by the fact that he had never previously scored a senior goal for Barça in any of the competitions. The Canary Islander's rags-to-riches rise continued into the new year as he scored nine further league goals, including one at Real Madrid CF, to help the Catalans defend their Spanish title; then onwards into the FIFA World Cup, where, having made his international debut on the eve of the tournament, he started both the semi-final and the final as Spain went on to claim the trophy for the first time.

International Career
SPAIN
Major Honours – FIFA World Cup (2010)
Debut – 29/5/10 v Saudi Arabia (n, Innsbruck, friendly), won 3-2
First Goal – 8/6/10 v Poland (h, Murcia, friendly), won 6-0
Caps 8; **Goals** 1
Major Tournaments – FIFA World Cup 2010

Club Career
Major Honours – UEFA Champions League (2009); UEFA Super Cup (2009); FIFA Club World Cup (2009); Spanish Championship (2009, 2010); Spanish Cup (2009)
Clubs: 07- FC Barcelona

Mladen PETRIĆ
Striker
Born 1/1/81,
Dubrave,
Bosnia-Herzegovina
Height 185cm,
Weight 81kg

The arrival of the UEFA Europa League may have drawn a lukewarm response from some quarters but not in Hamburg. Having been granted hosting rights for the new competition's inaugural final, Hamburger SV made it a mission of theirs right from the outset, when they launched their campaign in the third qualifying round, to go all the way to the final. They eventually fell frustratingly one round short, going out to Fulham FC in the semi-final, the same round in which they had exited the previous season's UEFA Cup, but their valiant effort was a personal success story nonetheless for Croatian striker Mladen Petrić, who helped himself to ten goals during the long European run, including at least one in each away leg of the knockout phase. There were some spectacular strikes among his collection, too, including one sensational bicycle kick in Liege and a fantastic long-distance free-kick at Craven Cottage. Like his club, Petrić was not quite so impressive in the Bundesliga, although he did score the winning goal early in the season at home to FC Bayern München.

International Career

CROATIA
Debut – 10/11/01 v South Korea (a, Seoul, friendly), lost 0-2
First Goal – 21/8/02 v Wales (h, Varazdin, friendly), drew 1-1
Caps 37; **Goals** 11
Major Tournaments – UEFA EURO 2008

Club Career

Major Honours – Swiss Championship (2001, 2003, 2005); Swiss Cup (2007)
Clubs: 98-99 FC Baden (SUI); 99-04 Grasshopper-Club (SUI); 04-07 FC Basel 1893 (SUI); 07- BV Borussia Dortmund (GER); 08- Hamburger SV (GER)

Gerard PIQUÉ
Bernabéu
Central Defender
Born 2/2/87,
Barcelona,
Spain
Height 190cm,
Weight 84kg

If there were an official award for the world's best defender, Gerard Piqué would be a strong candidate to win it. Since he left Manchester United FC for FC Barcelona, the giant young centre-back has developed with lightning speed into a colossal figure both for Barça and the Spanish national team. If 2008/09 was his breakthrough season, 2009/10 brought confirmation of his world-class prowess. Peerless in the air and mobile on the ground, he is also useful up front, as he showed in scoring twice against FC Internazionale Milano in the UEFA Champions League, the second of those goals almost turning the semi-final. His presence in Spain's 2010 FIFA World Cup team was one of the major changes to the side since UEFA EURO 2008, and he was on the field for all 660 minutes of La Roja's triumph in South Africa. Twice a champion of Europe at club level and now on top of the world with his country, Piqué has already scaled the game's heights at the age of 23.

International Career

SPAIN
Major Honours – FIFA World Cup (2010)
Debut – 11/2/09 v England (h, Seville, friendly), won 2-0
First Goal – 28/3/09 v Turkey (h, Madrid, WCQ), won 1-0
Caps 23; **Goals** 4
Major Tournaments – FIFA Confederations Cup 2009; FIFA World Cup 2010

Club Career

Major Honours – UEFA Champions League (2008, 2009); UEFA Super Cup (2009); FIFA Club World Cup (2009); English Premier League (2008); Spanish Championship (2009, 2010); Spanish Cup (2009); English League Cup (2006)
Clubs: 04-08 Manchester United FC (ENG); 06-07 Real Zaragoza (loan); 08- FC Barcelona

Claudio Miguel PIZARRO Bosio
Striker
Born 3/10/78,
Callao, Peru
Height 186cm,
Weight 80kg

Claudio Pizarro drew level with Giovane Élber as the Bundesliga's all-time top-scoring foreigner when he found the net for Werder Bremen against Hamburger SV on the final day of the 2009/10 season. It was the 16th league goal of another prolific campaign for the 31-year-old Peruvian, lifting his all-time tally in Germany's top division to 133 in 282 matches and also, in the process, ensuring that his club finished in third place to secure a ticket for the play-off round of the 2010/11 UEFA Champions League. Pizarro's first season back at Bremen on a permanent basis – after a year-long loan spell from Chelsea FC – was packed with goals. If his domestic output was prolific, his yield in Europe was phenomenal – 12 goals in ten games as Bremen went from the play-off round of the UEFA Europa League to the round of 16. The highlight was a hat-trick in the Weserstadion that knocked out in-form Dutch side FC Twente, but the most notable aspect of his feat was that he scored at least one goal against every one of the six teams Bremen faced.

International Career
PERU
Debut – 10/2/99 v Ecuador (h, Lima, friendly), lost 1-2
First Goal – 17/2/99 v Ecuador (a, Guayaquil, friendly), won 2-1
Caps 55; **Goals** 13
Major Tournaments – Copa América 1999; Copa América 2004; Copa América 2007

Club Career
Major Honours – World Club Cup (2001); German Championship (2003, 2005, 2006); German Cup (2003, 2005, 2006, 2009)
Clubs: 96-97 Deportivo Pesquero; 97-99 Alianza Lima; 99-01 Werder Bremen (GER); 01-07 FC Bayern München (GER); 07-Chelsea FC (ENG); 08-09 Werder Bremen (GER) (loan); 09-Werder Bremen (GER)

Carles PUYOL i Saforcada
Centre-Back
Born 13/4/78,
Pobla de Segur,
Spain
Height 180cm,
Weight 79kg

FC Barcelona captain Carles Puyol raised another four trophies in 2009/10 – the Spanish Super Cup, the UEFA Super Cup, the FIFA Club World Cup and the Liga trophy – to go with the three he had lifted the previous season in the club's historic treble, but while, as a proud Catalan, every one of those triumphs meant a great deal, none can have compared with the elation he felt at helping Spain to win the 2010 FIFA World Cup. The indefatigable shaggy-haired stopper was arguably the most consistent performer in Vicente del Bosque's victorious team during their seven-match sojourn in South Africa. Resilient to the last, he even had his moment of glory when he headed in Spain's winning goal in the semi-final against Germany. It was only his third international goal but far and away the most important, the previous two having come in a friendly against Northern Ireland and a World Cup qualifier in Estonia. The 32-year-old won his 90th cap in the World Cup final and has already indicated that he will carry on playing for his country for at least another two years.

International Career
SPAIN
Major Honours – FIFA World Cup (2010); UEFA European Championship (2008)
Debut – 15/11/00 v Netherlands (h, Seville, friendly), lost 1-2
First Goal – 17/4/02 v Northern Ireland (a, Belfast, friendly), won 5-0
Caps 90; **Goals** 3
Major Tournaments – FIFA World Cup 2002; UEFA EURO 2004; FIFA World Cup 2006; UEFA EURO 2008; FIFA Confederations Cup 2009; FIFA World Cup 2010

Club Career
Major Honours – UEFA Champions League (2006, 2009); UEFA Super Cup (2009); FIFA Club World Cup (2009); Spanish Championship (1999, 2005, 2006, 2009, 2010); Spanish Cup (2009)
Clubs: 99- FC Barcelona

John Arne RIISE
Left-Back
Born 24/9/80, Aalesund, Norway
Height 185cm, Weight 78kg

AS Roma's challenge to FC Internazionale Milano for the 2009/1 Serie A title lasted all the way to the finish. It was a tremendous effort from Claudio Ranieri's team, and the man who made mor appearances for the Giallorossi than any other was their lung-busting, sharpshooting left-back, John Arne Riise. The majority of Roma's 68 Serie A goals came from set-pieces, and the Norwegian red-head was at the source of many of them. He scored five goals himself, including one memorable stoppage-time header against Juventus that brought three valuable point back to the capital from Turin. Riise also starred for Roma in Europe, one of his two goals curiously going in via a deflection off his younger brother, Bjørn Helge, in the UEFA Europa League group game at home to Fulham FC. The two siblings were on the same side, however, for Norway, as the Roma man scored in each of his country's last three 2010 FIFA World Cup qualifiers to take his international goal tally into double figures.

International Career
NORWAY
Debut – 31/1/00 v Iceland (n, La Manga, friendly), drew 0-0
First Goal – 23/2/00 v Turkey (a, Istanbul, friendly), won 2-0
Caps 87; **Goals** 12
Major Tournaments – UEFA EURO 2000

Club Career
Major Honours – UEFA Champions League (2005); UEFA Super Cup (2001, 2005); French Championship (2000); English FA Cup (2006); English League Cup (2003)
Clubs: 97-98 Aalesunds FK; 98-01 AS Monaco FC (FRA); 01-08 Liverpool FC (ENG); 08- AS Roma (ITA)

Arjen ROBBEN
Winger
Born 23/1/84,
Bedum, Netherlands
Height 180cm, Weight 75kg

The best season of Arjen Robben's career was also the most frustrating. A brilliant debut campaign in Germany with FC Bayern München, in which he handsomely paid off his €25m transfer fee from Real Madrid CF, was supplemented by an impressive FIFA World Cup for the Netherlands in South Africa. But while the 26-year-old with the lethal left foot won both domestic prizes with Bayern, thus adding a German championship title to those he had already won in the Netherlands, England and Spain, he was on the losing side in both the UEFA Champions League and World Cup finals. As tricky and elusive as any winger in the modern game, Robben reinvented himself as a serial goalscorer under the tutelage of his fellow Dutchman Louis van Gaal. He scored 23 goals in 37 games for Bayern, including spectacular, important strikes against ACF Fiorentina, Manchester United FC and Olympique Lyonnais in Europe, and he recovered from a hamstring injury to score against Slovakia and Uruguay in the latter stages of the World Cup, but the precious chance he missed in the final, when one-against-one with Iker Casillas with the game delicately poised at 0-0, will doubtless prey on his mind for a long time to come.

International Career
NETHERLANDS
Debut – 30/4/03 v Portugal (h, Eindhoven, friendly), drew 1-1
First Goal – 11/10/03 v Moldova (h, Eindhoven, ECQ), won 5-0
Caps 52; **Goals** 15
Major Tournaments – UEFA EURO 2004; FIFA World Cup 2006; UEFA EURO 2008; FIFA World Cup 2010

Club Career
Major Honours – Dutch Championship (2003); English Premier League (2005, 2006); Spanish Championship (2008); German Championship (2010); English FA Cup (2007); German Cup (2010); English League Cup (2005, 2007)
Clubs: 00-02 FC Groningen; 02-04 PSV Eindhoven; 04-07 Chelsea FC (ENG); 07-09 Real Madrid CF (ESP); 09- FC Bayern München (GER)

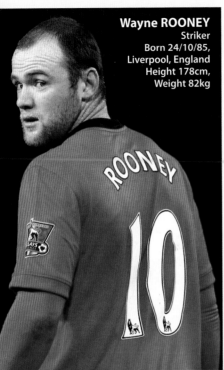

Wayne ROONEY
Striker
Born 24/10/85,
Liverpool, England
Height 178cm,
Weight 82kg

The Dr Jekyll and Mr Hyde nature of Wayne Rooney was encapsulated in 2009/10 as he followed a breathtakingly brilliant season for Manchester United FC with a woeful performance for England at the FIFA World Cup. With Cristiano Ronaldo departed for Real Madrid CF, Rooney became the main man at Old Trafford and revelled in the spotlight, scoring 26 goals in the Premier League and another five in the UEFA Champions League, four of them against AC Milan in the first knockout round. United did not win either of those two glittering prizes but Rooney's individual excellence won him the vote for both PFA Player of the Year and FWA Footballer of the Year. Shunted forward into a lone striker role by Sir Alex Ferguson, the 24-year-old was particularly prolific in the early spring, but then, on 30 March, disaster struck as he turned his ankle in the last minute of the European quarter-final first leg against FC Bayern München in Munich. He was never the same player again – either for United or, despite being passed fully fit for action, for England. So much was expected of him at the World Cup, but the man who scored nine goals in qualifying never looked like adding to that total in South Africa as his touch, technique and even his renowned competitive spirit completely deserted him in his country's greatest hour of need.

International Career
ENGLAND
Debut – 12/2/03 v Australia (h, London, friendly), lost 1-3
First Goal – 6/9/03 v FYR Macedonia (a, Skopje, ECQ), won 2-1
Caps 64; **Goals** 25
Major Tournaments – UEFA EURO 2004; FIFA World Cup 2006; FIFA World Cup 2010

Club Career
Major Honours – UEFA Champions League (2008); FIFA Club World Cup (2008); English Premier League (2007, 2008, 2009); English League Cup (2006, 2009, 2010)
Clubs: 02-04 Everton FC; 04- Manchester United FC

Perhaps if Costa Rica had defeated Uruguay in their 2010 FIFA World Cup play-off, Bryan Ruiz would have gone on to become the Golden Ball winner in South Africa rather than Diego Forlán. The tall, left-footed striker would certainly have travelled there in good heart after scoring 24 league goals in his first season for FC Twente to help the team from Enschede win the Dutch Eredivisie title. His total was second to that of another Uruguayan striker, AFC Ajax's Luis Suárez, in the league's top-scorer standings but, with Ajax pipped to the title by a point, the bigger prize certainly belonged to the Costa Rican. A starter for Twente in all 34 Eredivisie matches following his €5m cross-border move from KAA Gent, he found the net with phenomenal consistency. He scored in ten successive matches – one goal in each – from late September through to the winter break and, in March, poached a hat-trick in less than five minutes against Sparta Rotterdam. Fittingly he also opened the scoring in the last-day 2-0 win at NAC Breda that secured the title.

International Career
COSTA RICA
Debut – 19/6/05 v China (a, Changsha, friendly), drew 2-2
First Goal – 16/7/05 v Honduras (n, Foxboro, CGC), lost 2-3
Caps 34; **Goals** 9
Major Tournaments – CONCACAF Gold Cup 2005

Club Career
Major Honours – CONCACAF Champions' Cup (2004); Costa Rican Championship (2005); Dutch Championship (2010)
Clubs: 03-06 LD Alajuelense; 06-09 KAA Gent (BEL); 09- FC Twente (NED)

Bryan RUIZ
Gonzalez
Left-Winger/Striker
Born 18/8/85,
San Jose, Costa Rica
Height 188cm, Weight 78kg

Walter Adrián SAMUEL
Centre-Back
Born 23/3/78,
Firmat, Argentina
Height 183cm,
Weight 83kg

Walter Samuel's fifth successive Serie A title with FC Internazionale Milano meant much more than the previous four. Not only did it form part of a glorious treble (alongside victories in the UEFA Champions League and Coppa Italia); it was also the one to which he made his most significant contribution. Previously injured or simply ignored, Samuel was fit, healthy and very much in demand as José Mourinho's team conquered all before them. The tough, experienced Argentinian centre-back lived up to his nickname of Il Muro (The Wall) as he developed a rock-solid new partnership with Lúcio. He was ever present in the club's run to European glory, saving his best form for the big games against Chelsea FC and FC Barcelona. Although he played no part in Argentina's qualification for the 2010 FIFA World Cup, he was recalled for the finals, where he started the first two games before picking up a muscular injury. Although recovered for the quarter-final against Germany, he was not recalled by coach Diego Maradona – a controversial move at the time and a bad one in retrospect as, without him, Argentina conceded four goals and were eliminated.

International Career

ARGENTINA
Debut – 3/2/99 v Venezuela (a, Maracaibo, friendly), won 2-0
First Goal – 3/2/99 v Venezuela (a, Maracaibo, friendly), won 2-0
Caps 56; **Goals** 5
Major Tournaments – Copa América 1999; FIFA World Cup 2002; FIFA Confederations Cup 2005; FIFA World Cup 2010

Club Career

Major Honours – UEFA Champions League (2010); Copa Libertadores (2000); Argentina Championship (1998 apertura, 1999 clausura); Italian Championship (2001, 2006, 2007, 2008, 2009, 2010); Italian Cup (2006, 2010)
Clubs: 96-97 Newell's Old Boys; 97-00 CA Boca Juniors; 00-04 AS Roma (ITA); 04-05 Real Madrid CF (ESP); 05- FC Internazionale Milano (ITA)

Bastian SCHWEINSTEIGER
Midfielder
Born 1/8/84,
Kolbermoor,
Germany
Height 183cm,
Weight 79kg

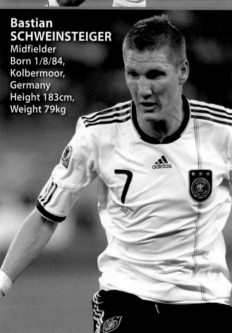

True to his 'my way or the highway' reputation, Louis van Gaal made many changes at FC Bayern München during his first season as coach. One of his most successful improvisations was to bring Bastian Schweinsteiger in from the flanks and convert him into a top-class central midfielder. One of Bayern's longest-serving and most experienced players – despite his relative youth – Schweinsteiger took to the new role with relish and was one of the chief contributors to the Bavarian club's highly successful season, winning his fifth Bundesliga/DFB-Pokal double and also reaching the final of the UEFA Champions League. There was even better to come from him at the FIFA World Cup, where, with Germany boss Joachim Löw following van Gaal's lead and depositing him in central midfield, he enjoyed his most impressive major tournament to date, improving even on his sterling efforts at the 2006 World Cup and UEFA EURO 2008 as he helped steer Germany to the semi-finals. His man-of-the-match display in the quarter-final against Argentina was possibly the finest all-round midfield performance of the tournament.

International Career

GERMANY
Debut – 6/6/04 v Hungary (h, Kaiserslautern, friendly), lost 0-2
First Goal – 8/6/05 v Russia (h, Monchengladbach, friendly), drew 2-2
Caps 81; **Goals** 21
Major Tournaments – UEFA EURO 2004; FIFA Confederations Cup 2005; FIFA World Cup 2006; UEFA EURO 2008; FIFA World Cup 2010

Club Career

Major Honours – German Championship (2003, 2005, 2006, 2008, 2010); German Cup (2003, 2005, 2006, 2008, 2010)
Clubs: 02- FC Bayern München

For the second successive year the Russian Premier-Liga was won by FC Rubin Kazan, and once again the most inspirational and influential figure in their triumph was captain Sergei Semak. Like the claret of the team's shirts, the veteran Russian international midfielder seems to improve with age. Some of the speed he once displayed as an attacking midfielder at PFC CSKA Moskva may have vanished, but that has been counterbalanced by the improvement in his organisational, tactical and playmaking skills. As well as setting up myriad chances for Alejandro Domínguez and Aleksandr Bukharov, Semak got in on the goalscoring act himself, registering six goals, the last of them to open the scoring in an emphatic and vital 3-0 win at closest title rivals FC Spartak Moskva. He also led Rubin in all six of their UEFA Champions League group games, although injury restricted him to just 43 minutes of the team's famous 2-1 win away to FC Barcelona. In August 2010 he left Rubin to join FC Zenit St Petersburg.

International Career

RUSSIA
Debut – 15/11/97 v Italy (a, Naples, WCQ), lost 0-1
First Goal –6/6/01 v Luxembourg (a, Luxembourg, WCQ), won 2-1
Caps 65; **Goals** 4
Major Tournaments – FIFA World Cup 2002; UEFA EURO 2008

Club Career

Major Honours – Russian Championship (2003, 2008, 2009); Russian Cup (2002)
Clubs: 92 FC Presnya Moskva; 92 FC Karelia Petrozadovsk; 93-94 FC Asmaral Moskva; 94-04 PFC CSKA Moskva; 05-06 Paris Saint-Germain FC (FRA); 06-07 FC Moskva; 08-10 FC Rubin Kazan; 10- FC Zenit St Petersburg

Sergei SEMAK
Midfielder
Born 27/2/76, Luhansk, Ukraine
Height 178cm, Weight 73kg

Amidst the joy of winning the FIFA World Cup with Spain there must have been a tinge of frustration for Sergio Ramos that he did not score the winning goal in the final against the Netherlands. Fortunately, though, the easy headed chance that he sent soaring over a gaping goal in the 77th minute of the Soccer City showdown will not haunt him for ever thanks to Andrés Iniesta's more measured finish in the same goalmouth some 45 minutes or so later. It would not have been inappropriate for the Real Madrid CF right-back to have taken the match-winning acclaim because he enjoyed an outstanding final and an outstanding tournament – both in defence and in his consistent support of the attack. Although he won no trophies for Real in the season leading up to the World Cup, he did reach two landmark figures for the club – 150 Liga appearances and 200 in all competitions. Both milestones were arrived at simultaneously in a 6-2 victory at home to Villarreal CF in February.

International Career

SPAIN
Major Honours – FIFA World Cup (2010); UEFA European Championship (2008)
Debut – 26/3/05 v China (h, Salamanca, friendly), won 3-0
First Goal – 13/10/05 v San Marino (a, Serravalle, WCQ), won 6-0
Caps 67; **Goals** 5
Major Tournaments – FIFA World Cup 2006; UEFA EURO 2008; FIFA World Cup 2010

Club Career

Major Honours – Spanish Championship (2007, 2008)
Clubs: 02-05 Sevilla FC; 05- Real Madrid CF

SERGIO RAMOS García
Right-Back/Centre-Back
Born 30/3/86, Seville, Spain
Height 183cm, Weight 73kg

Wesley SNEIJDER
Midfielder
Born 9/6/84,
Utrecht,
Netherlands
Height 170cm,
Weight72kg

Wesley Sneijder came within one match of becoming the first footballer in history to win a domestic double, the top European club trophy and the FIFA World Cup in the same season. The Netherlands' narrow defeat to Spain in Johannesburg denied him that unique pleasure, but there were many more positives than negatives for the 26-year-old Oranje playmaker to take home from South Africa. As at UEFA EURO 2008 he was his country's most impressive player. He scored five goals (all in the second half, all in coastal cities), provided a stream of beautiful passes, and scooped no fewer than four man-of-the-match awards plus the Silver Ball and the Bronze Boot. His World Cup exploits were no surprise because he had been playing at the same exalted level for most of the season with FC Internazionale Milano. Freshly landed from Real Madrid CF in a bargain €15m transfer, Sneijder helped Inter beat AC Milan 4-0 on his debut and went on to become the team's principal playmaker and set-piece specialist, making a massive contribution to their treble success, not least with some vintage displays in the UEFA Champions League against Chelsea FC, FC Barcelona and, in the final back at the Santiago Bernabéu, FC Bayern München.

International Career
NETHERLANDS
Debut – 30/4/03 v Portugal (h, Eindhoven, friendly), drew 1-1
First Goal – 11/10/03 v Moldova (h, Eindhoven, ECQ), won 5-0
Caps 68; **Goals** 19
Major Tournaments – UEFA EURO 2004; FIFA World Cup 2006; UEFA EURO 2008; FIFA World Cup 2010

Club Career
Major Honours – UEFA Champions League (2010); Dutch Championship (2004); Spanish Championship (2008); Italian Championship (2010; Dutch Cup (2006, 2007); Italian Cup (2010)
Clubs: 02-07 AFC Ajax; 07-09 Real Madrid CF (ESP); 09- FC Internazionale Milano (ITA)

Luis Alberto SUÁREZ Díaz
Striker
Born 24/1/87,
Salto, Uruguay
Height 181cm,
Weight 81kg

If Golden Ball winner Diego Forlán was the hero of the 2010 FIFA World Cup, then Luis Suárez was its villain, his instinctive handled goal-line clearance in the last minute of the quarter-final against Ghana bringing him a red card, suspension from the semi-final and a cacophony of jeers and whistles from the African public every time he touched the ball in the third place play-off against Germany. It was the fact that he got away with his indiscretion, with Asamoah Gyan missing the ensuing penalty and Ghana the ensuing shoot-out, that turned so many against him. There was no ill feeling towards the striker from his compatriots, though. Indeed, until that moment of controversy Suárez, with three goals, had been almost as impressive up front for his country as he had been throughout an extraordinarily prolific season in the Netherlands as captain of AFC Ajax that brought him 35 goals in the Eredivisie, eight in the KNVB Beker (which Ajax won), six in Europe and the title of Dutch Footballer of the Year.

International Career
URUGUAY
Debut – 7/2/07 v Colombia (a, Cucuta, friendly), won 3-1
First Goal – 13/10/07 v Bolivia (h, Montevideo, WCQ), won 5-0
Caps 36; **Goals** 13
Major Tournaments – FIFA World Cup 2010

Club Career
Major Honours – Uruguayan Championship (2006); Dutch Cup (2010)
Clubs: 05-06 Club Nacional; 06-07 FC Groningen (NED); 07- AFC Ajax (NED)

Carlos Alberto TÉVEZ

Striker
Born 5/2/84,
Buenos Aires,
Argentina
Height 173cm,
Weight 74kg

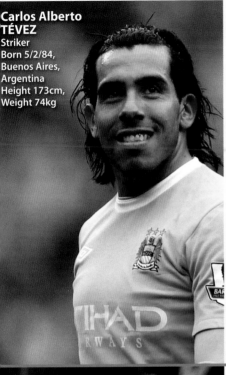

Carlos Tévez emulated his Argentina coach by scoring one highly controversial and one brilliant goal in a FIFA World Cup finals match, but whereas Diego Maradona's beauty-after-the-beast brace against England in 1986 contributed to his team's World Cup triumph, Tévez's double whammy in the 3-1 win against Mexico was followed by quarter-final elimination against Germany. Thus ended a season for Tévez that had begun 12 months earlier with the multi-talented striker's intriguing transfer from Manchester United FC to Manchester City FC. There was immense pressure on Tévez to deliver the goods for his new club, and he did not disappoint, winning over the hearts and minds of the City fans with his formidable commitment and a welter of spectacular goals. He started slowly but by December he was in irrepressible form and he carried that through to the end of term, finishing up with 23 Premier League goals and six in the League Cup, half of them in an epic two-legged semi-final against his former club from across the city.

International Career

ARGENTINA
Debut – 30/3/04 v Ecuador (h, Buenos Aires, WCQ), won 1-0
First Goal – 17/7/04 v Peru (a, Chiclayo, CA), won 1-0
Caps 56; **Goals** 11
Major Tournaments – Copa América 2004; FIFA Confederations Cup 2005; FIFA World Cup 2006; Copa América 2007; FIFA World Cup 2010

Club Career

Major Honours – UEFA Champions League (2008); Copa Libertadores (2003); World Club Cup (2003); Argentinian Championship (apertura 2003); Brazilian Championship (2005); English Premier League (2008)
Clubs: 01-04 CA Boca Juniors; 05-06 SC Corinthians (BRA); 06-07 West Ham United FC (ENG); 07-09 Manchester United FC (ENG); 09- Manchester City (ENG)

Mathieu VALBUENA

Attacking Midfielder
Born 28/9/84,
Bruges, France
Height 67cm,
Weight 57kg

Out of favour at Olympique de Marseille in the first half of the 2009/10 season, Mathieu Valbuena seemed certain to leave during the winter break after failing to impress the club's new coach Didier Deschamps, but the diminutive jack-in-the-box midfielder decided instead to knuckle down and win back his place in the team. He succeeded to such an extent that by the end of the season he had not only won over Deschamps but also seduced Raymond Domenech into selecting him for France's 2010 FIFA World Cup squad. A game-changing substitute appearance, and goal, in the League Cup final against FC Girondins de Bordeaux – which ended Marseille's 17-year trophy drought – marked the turning point in Valbuena's fortunes. He was a Ligue 1 regular thereafter, scoring three goals in the next four games to set the team up for their successful title assault. He scored the winning goal in a friendly against Costa Rica on his France debut but managed only 21 minutes of World Cup action as Les Bleus limped home after just three matches.

International Career

FRANCE
Debut – 26/5/10 v Costa Rica (h, Lens, friendly), won 2-1
First Goal – 26/5/10 v Costa Rica (h, Lens, friendly), won 2-1
Caps 3; **Goals** 1
Major Tournaments – FIFA World Cup 2010

Club Career

Major Honours – French Championship (2010); French League Cup (2010)
Clubs: 04-06 FC Libourne-Saint-Seurin; 06- Olympique de Marseille

Luis Antonio VALENCIA Mosquera
Right-Winger
Born 5/8/85, Lago Agrio, Ecuador
Height 178cm, Weight 78kg

Filling Cristiano Ronaldo's boots at Manchester United FC was always going to be an impossible job, but Luis Antonio Valencia the man Sir Alex Ferguson brought in to do it, made a more tha passable attempt. The Ecuador international had won acclaim during a three-year stint at Wigan Athletic FC for his purposeful running and pin-point crossing, and he continued to display the qualities at United while also making his mark as a goalscorer w five Premier League strikes before Christmas and one in each of United's UEFA Champions League group games against PFC CSK Moskva. His most memorable performance came in the League Cup final against Aston Villa FC at Wembley, where he provided the cross for Wayne Rooney's winning goal and won the Alan Hardaker Trophy attributed to the man of the match. At the end the season his efforts were further recognised with a place in the PFA Premier League Team of the Year.

International Career

ECUADOR
Debut – 28/4/04 v Honduras (n, Fort Lauderdale, friendly), drew 1-1
First Goal – 27/3/05 v Paraguay (h, Quito, WCQ), won 5-2
Caps 41; **Goals** 6
Major Tournaments – FIFA World Cup 2006; Copa América 20

Club Career

Major Honours – Ecuadorian Championship (2005 clausura); English League Cup (2010)
Clubs: 03-05 CD El Nacional; 05-08 Villarreal CF (ESP); 05-06 F Recreativo de Huelva (ESP) (loan); 06-08 Wigan Athletic FC (ENG) (loan); 08-09 Wigan Athletic FC (ENG); 09- Manchester United FC (ENG)

Mark VAN BOMMEL
Midfielder
Born 22/4/77, Maasbracht, Netherlands
Height 187cm, Weight 85kg

FC Bayern München are accustomed to winning trophies, but the two they claimed in 2009/10 – the Bundesliga shield and the German Cup – were unusual in that they were the first to lifted for the club by a non-German captain. The man afforded that mould-breaking privilege was Dutchman Mark van Bommel. The 33-year-old midfielder would have been even happier to have emulated such Bayern luminaries as Franz Beckenbauer and Stefan Effenberg and lifted the 'Cup with the big ears' as a UEFA Champions League winner, but that particular pleasure eluded him after the Bavarians' 2-0 defeat the final by FC Internazionale Milano. Van Bommel was to suff more big-match heartache a few weeks later at the 2010 FIFA World Cup as his Netherlands team lost to Spain in the final. Neither he nor his team-mates distinguished themselves in th game with their ill-disciplined display, but Van Bommel had been a key figure in the Oranje's progress to Soccer City, his presence at the heart of the midfield providing security, authority and experience – not to mention the odd tactical fou – as they won all six of their matches en route to the final.

International Career

NETHERLANDS
Debut – 7/10/00 v Cyprus (a, Nicosia, WCQ), won 4-0
First Goal – 24/3/01 v Andorra (a, Barcelona, WCQ), won 5-0
Caps 63; **Goals** 10
Major Tournaments – FIFA World Cup 2006; FIFA World Cup 201

Club Career

Major Honours – UEFA Champions League (2006); Dutch Championship (2000, 2001, 2003, 2005); Spanish Championship (2006); German Championship (2008, 2010); Dutch Cup (2005); German Cup (2008, 2010)
Clubs: 92-99 Fortuna Sittard; 99-05 PSV Eindhoven; 05-06 F Barcelona (ESP); 06- FC Bayern München (GER)

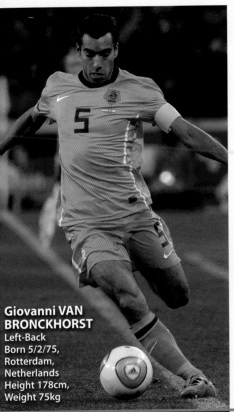

Like Zinédine Zidane four years earlier, Giovanni van Bronckhorst played his last football match as a professional in the FIFA World Cup final. Unlike the great French midfielder, he did not spoil the occasion by getting sent off, but he did share the disappointment of ending up as the losing captain. Having won his 100th international cap in the Oranje's opening game against Denmark, Van Bronckhorst returned to the Soccer City stadium against Spain desperate to bow out on the ultimate high. Although, sadly, he did not get to lift the trophy, the veteran left-back scored one of the tournament's best goals – a beautifully struck long-range thunderbolt against Uruguay in the semi-final – and, even with retirement imminent, showed the necessary fitness and stamina to remain on the field from first whistle to last in almost every game. The only exception was the last 15 minutes of the final when, without their inspirational skipper and best player on the night, the Netherlands went down to ten men and conceded the late winner to Andrés Iniesta - from a position where, irony of ironies, Van Bronckhorst would in all probability have been standing.

International Career

NETHERLANDS
Debut – 31/8/96 v Brazil (h, Amsterdam, friendly), drew 2-2
First Goal – 4/6/97 v South Africa (a, Johannesburg, friendly), won 2-0
Caps 106; **Goals** 6
Major Tournaments – FIFA World Cup 1998; UEFA EURO 2000; UEFA EURO 2004; FIFA World Cup 2006; UEFA EURO 2008; FIFA World Cup 2010

Club Career

Major Honours – UEFA Champions League (2006); Scottish Championship (1999, 2000); English Premier League (2002); Spanish Championship (2005, 2006); Dutch Cup (1995, 2008); Scottish Cup (1999, 2000); English FA Cup (2002, 2003); Scottish League Cup (1998)
Clubs: 93-94 RKC Waalwijk; 94-98 Feyenoord; 98-01 Rangers FC (SCO); 01-03 Arsenal FC (ENG); 03-07 FC Barcelona (ESP); 07- Feyenoord

Giovanni VAN BRONCKHORST
Left-Back
Born 5/2/75,
Rotterdam,
Netherlands
Height 178cm,
Weight 75kg

Gregory VAN DER WIEL
Right-Back
Born 3/2/88,
Amsterdam,
Netherlands
Height 182cm,
Weight 69kg

As the winner in 2010 of the esteemed Johan Cruyff Trophy awarded to the Netherlands' Young Talent of the Year – a prize claimed in previous years by the likes of Arjen Robben and Wesley Sneijder – there was a lot of expectation riding on 22-year-old Gregory van der Wiel as he headed to the FIFA World Cup finals in South Africa. Although he had embedded himself in Bert van Marwijk's team as the first-choice right-back with some top-class performances in the warm-up games, his lack of experience and rebellious reputation led some to identify him as a potential weakness in the Dutch defence. As it transpired, those fears proved unfounded, the youngster performing for his country with the same level of confidence and commitment that he had shown throughout the season at club level for AFC Ajax, for whom he was an Eredivisie ever-present and a victor in the Dutch Cup.

International Career

NETHERLANDS
Debut – 11/2/09 v Tunisia (a, Rades, friendly), drew 1-1
Caps 15; **Goals** 0
Major Tournaments – FIFA World Cup 2010

Club Career

Major Honours – Dutch Cup (2010)
Clubs: 06- AFC Ajax

Thomas VERMAELEN
Centre-Back
Born 14/11/85,
Kapellen, Belgium
Height 182cm,
Weight 82kg

Arsenal FC bought Thomas Vermaelen from AFC Ajax to plug the gap in the centre of a defence that had leaked too many goals during a disappointing 2008/09 season. With Kolo Touré offloaded to Manchester City FC, the brawny, left-footed Belgian international stepped straight into Arsène Wenger's team and stayed there for the rest of the season, racking up appearances in all competitions and also scoring eight goals. On target on his debut for the Gunners in both the Premier League – at Everton FC – and the UEFA Champions League – back in his homeland against R. Standard de Liège - he also scored his first international goal in a November 2009 friendly against Hungary, having been appointed as the new captain of Belgium the previous month. If his finishing was impressive, so too was his defending, and although once again Arsenal failed to win a trophy, Vermaelen's excellent first season in England was rewarded with a place in the PFA Premier League Team of the Year.

International Career

BELGIUM

Debut – 1/3/06 v Luxembourg (a, Luxembourg, friendly), won 2 (abandoned)
First Goal – 14/11/09 v Hungary (h, Ghent, friendly), won 3-0
Caps 28; **Goals** 1

Club Career

Major Honours – Dutch Championship (2004);
Dutch Cup (2006, 2007)
Clubs: 03-09 AFC Ajax (NED); 04-05 RKC Waalwijk (NED) (loan); 09- Arsenal FC (ENG)

VÍCTOR VALDÉS i Arribas
Goalkeeper
Born 14/1/82,
L'Hospitalet
de Llobregat,
Spain
Height 186cm,
Weight 76kg

Ignored for so long at international level despite his repeated exploits for FC Barcelona, Víctor Valdés was finally awarded his first cap for Spain on the eve of the 2010 FIFA World Cup finals, and although he did not play in South Africa – skipper Iker Casillas was never going to be shifted – his presence in the winning squad entitled him to a gold medal the same as every other member of Vicente del Bosque's 23-man party. The 28-year-old 'keeper was accustomed, of course, to winning things, and after Barça's ground-breaking treble triumph of 2008/09, he and his team were at it again in 2009/10, winning the UEFA Super Cup and FIFA Club World Cup as well as retaining the Spanish Liga title. Fresh from signing a new five-year contract, Valdés was the only ever-present in Barça's championship win, starting and finishing all 38 matches. His concession of only 24 goals made him a clear winner of the esteemed Trofeo Zamora, which he won for the third time and with the best winning average (0.63 goals per game) for 16 years.

International Career

SPAIN

Major Honours – FIFA World Cup (2010)
Debut – 3/6/10 v South Korea (n, Innsbruck, friendly), won 1-0
Caps 1; **Goals** 0
Major Tournaments – FIFA World Cup 2010

Club Career

Major Honours – UEFA Champions League (2006, 2009); UEFA Super Cup (2009); FIFA Club World Cup (2009); Spanish Championship (2005, 2006, 2009, 2010); Spanish Cup (2009)
Clubs: 02- FC Barcelona

Mirko VUČINIĆ
Striker
Born 1/10/83,
Niksic, Montenegro
Height 186cm,
Weight 76kg

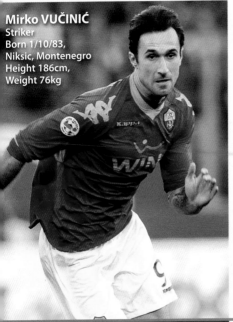

The captain of Montenegro, Mirko Vučinić maintained a 50 per cent strike rate for his country in 2009/10, and he was close to that level of consistency for AS Roma in Serie A, scoring 14 times in his 34 appearances. Above all it was the timing of his Giallorossi goals that made him such an invaluable contributor to the team's unlikely title challenge. It was November before he found the net for the first time, but once his duck was broken, he was off and running, repeatedly chipping in when Roma needed him most. Thirteen of Vučinić's goals came during a record 24-match unbeaten run, and with the exception of one of his goals in a hat-trick against Udinese Calcio, all were 'point-collectors', turning either a defeat into a draw or, more commonly, a draw into a victory. His double in the 2-1 win against S.S. Lazio in April brought a very different reaction from the same fans who had whistled him in the early part of the campaign, and for a while his opening goal on the last day at AC Chievo Verona looked like it would win the scudetto…until Diego Milito stole his thunder with Inter's winner in Siena.

International Career
SERBIA & MONTENEGRO
Debut – 4/6/05 v Belgium (h, Belgrade, WCQ), drew 0-0
Caps 3; **Goals** 0
MONTENEGRO
Debut – 24/3/07 v Hungary (h, Podgorica, friendly), won 2-1
First Goal – 24/3/07 v Hungary (h, Podgorica, friendly), won 2-1
Caps 18; **Goals** 9

Club Career
Major Honours – Italian Cup (2007, 2008)
Clubs: 99-00 FK Sutjeska; 00-06 US Lecce (ITA); 06- AS Roma (ITA)

XAVI Hernández Creus
Midfielder
Born 25/1/80,
Terrassa, Spain
Height 170cm,
Weight 68kg

Xavi Hernández re-affirmed his status as the world's most accomplished midfielder at the 2010 FIFA World Cup. His ability to control the tempo of every game he plays in is unmatched by any of his contemporaries. He played for Spain in South Africa just like he always plays for FC Barcelona – as the central constructor-in-chief, constantly prompting and probing, never losing possession. Unlike so many other players who went to the World Cup with bill-topping reputations, Xavi lived up to his. He wasn't at his very best in every game, but he was always Spain's focal point, and against Germany in the semi-final – as he had been against the same opponents in the final of UEFA EURO 2008 – he was the master of all he surveyed, producing the best individual performance of the tournament in its most absorbing match. A more than worthy World Cup winner with his country, Xavi had also become a world champion with his club seven months earlier as Barça captured the FIFA Club World Cup. He also claimed his fifth Spanish Liga title, with many locals insisting that, at 30 years of age, he had never played better.

International Career
SPAIN
Major Honours – FIFA World Cup (2010); UEFA European Championship (2008)
Debut – 15/11/00 v Netherlands (h, Seville, friendly), lost 1-2
First Goal – 26/3/05 v China (h, Salamanca, friendly), won 3-0
Caps 94; **Goals** 9
Major Tournaments – FIFA World Cup 2002; UEFA EURO 2004; FIFA World Cup 2006; UEFA EURO 2008; FIFA Confederations Cup 2009; FIFA World Cup 2010

Club Career
Major Honours – UEFA Champions League (2006, 2009); UEFA Super Cup (2009); FIFA Club World Cup (2009); Spanish Championship (1999, 2005, 2006, 2009, 2010); Spanish Cup (2009)
Clubs: 97- FC Barcelona

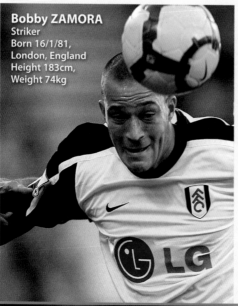

Bobby ZAMORA
Striker
Born 16/1/81,
London, England
Height 183cm,
Weight 74kg

If Fulham FC's fairytale run to the final of the UEFA Europa League was English football's most unlikely success story in 2009/10, the contribution of Bobby Zamora to the team's marathon 19-match campaign was not far behind. The journeyman striker from London with Caribbean roots was set to launch a belated international career with Trinidad & Tobago in August 2009 but an injury prevented him from playing in a FIFA World Cup qualifier. Nine months later he was in a similar situation for England, having to decline an invitation from Fabio Capello to form part of his provisional World Cup finals squad. The Italian, like every other football follower in England, had been seduced by Zamora's extraordinary explosion of form in Europe. He scored eight goals on Fulham's run to Hamburg, with the defenders of FC Basel 1893, FC Shakhtar Donetsk, Juventus and VfL Wolfsburg all struggling to cope with his lethal combination of physical power, deft technique and formidable left foot. Unfortunately, an Achilles injury severely reduced his effectiveness in the semi-final and final, but he had already left his calling-card on the competition and, at the age of 29, totally revitalised his career.

International Career
ENGLAND
Uncapped

Club Career
Clubs: 99-00 Bristol Rovers FC; 00 Bath City FC (loan); 00 Brighton & Hove Albion FC (loan); 00-03 Brighton & Hove Albion FC; 03-04 Tottenham Hotspur FC; 04-08 West Ham United FC; 08- Fulham FC

Javier Adelmar ZANETTI
Full-Back/Midfielder
Born 10/8/73,
Buenos Aires,
Argentina
Height 178 cm,
Weight 73kg

Javier Zanetti celebrated his 700th match for FC Internazionale Milano by captaining the club to victory in the UEFA Champions League final against FC Bayern München in Madrid and thus securing the last, and most important, part of a glorious and unprecedented trophy-winning treble. The 2009/10 European club season could hardly have come to a more fitting conclusion. An Inter player since 1995, and the team captain since 1999, Zanetti simply had to be the man in the spotlight as the Nerazzurri ended their long 45-year wait for club football's most treasured piece of silverware. The versatile veteran was not there for show, either. His contribution to the team's success, both in Europe and on the domestic front, was as fulsome as ever. Although his long unbroken run of Serie A appearances finally ended on 137 as he sat out the home game against Bologna FC in early April through suspension, he was on the field of play for every minute of Inter's UEFA Champions League triumph. Remarkably, there was no place for Zanetti in Argentina's FIFA World Cup squad - for the second successive tournament - as Diego Maradona chose not to take the country's record cap-holder to South Africa. To the football world at large and to Inter supporters in particular, it was a decision that defied all logic and reason.

International Career
ARGENTINA
Debut – 16/11/94 v Chile (a, Santiago, friendly), won 3-0
First Goal – 22/6/95 v Slovakia (h, Mendoza, friendly), won 6-0
Caps 136; **Goals** 5
Major Tournaments – Copa América 1995, FIFA World Cup 1998; Copa América 1999; FIFA World Cup 2002; Copa América 2004; FIFA Confederations Cup 2005; Copa América 2007

Club Career
Major Honours – UEFA Champions League (2010); UEFA Cup (1998); Italian Championship (2006, 2007, 2008, 2009, 2010); Italian Cup (2005, 2006, 2010);
Clubs: 92-93 CA Talleres; 93-95 CA Banfield; 95- FC Internazionale Milano (ITA)

Nation-by-nation

Welcome to the Nation-by-nation section of the European Football Yearbook.

Here you will find separate chapters, alphabetically arranged, on each of the 53 UEFA member associations.

Nation-by-nation explained

Included for each UEFA member association is a narrative and pictorial review of the season accompanied by the following statistics:

ASSOCIATION DIRECTORY

Address, contact details and senior officials followed by international honours, major international tournament appearances and the member association's top five international cap-holders and goalscorers.

NATIONAL TEAM RESULTS

Details on all international matches played between August 2009 and July 2010 with date, opponent, venue, result and scorer details.

Key: H = home, A = away, N = neutral, og = own-goal, (p) = penalty, (aet) = after extra time, (WCQ) = FIFA World Cup qualification round match, (WCF) = FIFA World Cup final tournament match.

NATIONAL TEAM APPEARANCES

Details on all participants in the aforementioned matches (coaches and players), including name, date of birth and, for each player, club, match-by-match appearances, minutes played and all-time international caps and goals scored.

Opponents are ranged across the top and abbreviated with the appropriate three-letter country codes – capital letters identify a FIFA World Cup qualification round or final tournament match.

Changes of national team coach are indicated with the appropriate date; temporary coaches are indicated in brackets.

Non-native clubs are indicated with the appropriate three-letter country code.

*Key: G = goalkeeper, D = defender, M = midfielder, A = attacker, s = substitute, * = sending-off.*

The number appearing after the letter indicates the time a substitution took place. The number preceding an asterisk indicates the time a sending-off took place.

DOMESTIC LEAGUE

FINAL TABLE

The final standings of the member association's top division including home, away and total records.

Key: Pld = matches played, W = matches won, D = matches drawn, L = matches lost, F = goals for (scored), A = goals against (conceded), Pts = points.

·············· = play-off line
– – – – – – – – = relegation line

Any peculiarities, such as the deduction of points or clubs withdrawn, are indicated as NB at the foot of the table.

TOP GOALSCORERS

A list of the top ten goalscorers (with clubs) in the member association's top division (league goals only).

CLUB-BY-CLUB

Information on each top-division club is provided in four parts:

1) Club name followed by the coach(es)/manager(s) used during the season and, in the case of new appointments, the dates on which they took place.
2) The year the club was founded and the club's home stadium (with capacity), followed by, where applicable, major honours, including European, international and domestic competitions. National 'super cups', secondary leagues and minor or age-restricted knockout competitions are not included.
3) League fixtures, including dates, opponents, results and scorers.

Key: h = home, a = away, og = own-goal, (p) = penalty, (w/o) = walkover/forfeit

4) A list of all players used in the league campaign, including name, nationality, date of birth, playing position, appearances and goals. Where applicable, and known, squad numbers are also included.

Key: No = squad (jersey) number, Name = full name (listed alphabetically with family name or football nickname in capitals), Nat = nationality (native unless listed with three-letter country code), DoB = date of birth, Pos = playing position, Aps = number of appearances in the starting line-up, (s) = number of appearances as a substitute, Gls = number of goals scored, G = goalkeeper, D = defender, M = midfielder; A = attacker.

INDEX

PROMOTED CLUB(S)

Information on each promoted club is provided in two parts:

1) Club name followed by the coach(es)/manager(s) used during the season and, in the case of new appointments, the dates on which they took place.

2) The year the club was founded and the club's home stadium (with capacity), followed, where applicable, by major honours, including European, international and domestic competitions. National 'super cups', secondary leagues and minor or age-restricted knockout competitions are not included.

SECOND LEVEL FINAL TABLE

The final classification of the member association's second level (i.e. feeder league to the top division) table(s). Play-off details, where applicable, are also indicated.

Key: Pld = matches played, W = matches won, D = matches drawn, L = matches lost, F = goals for (scored), A = goals against (conceded), Pts = points.

```
-------- = promotion line (at the top)
............. = play-off line
-------- = relegation line (at the bottom)
```

Any peculiarities, such as the deduction of points or clubs withdrawn, are indicated as NB at the foot of the final league table.

DOMESTIC CUP(S)

Results from the member association's main domestic knockout competition, beginning at the round in which the top-division clubs (or some of them) enter. Goalscorers and times of goals are indicated from the quarter-final stage with complete line-ups for the final.

Details of the latter stages of significant secondary knockout competitions are also included for some member associations.

Key: (aet) = after extra time

NB A complete key to all three-letter country codes can be found on page 6.

Domestic roll

Country	Champions	Top league goalscorer(s)	Cup winners
ALB	KS Dinamo Tirana	Daniel Xhafa (Besa) 18	KS Besa
AND	FC Santa Coloma	Gabriel Riera (Sant Julià) 19	UE Sant Julià
ARM**	FC Pyunik	Artur Kocharyan (Ulisses) 15	FC Pyunik
AUT	FC Salzburg	Steffen Hofmann (Rapid) 20	SK Sturm Graz
AZE	İnter Bakı PİK	Färid Quliyev (Standard) 16	Bakı FK
BLR**	FC BATE Borisov	Maicon (Gomel) 15	FC BATE Borisov
BEL	RSC Anderlecht	Romelu Lukaku (Anderlecht) 15	KAA Gent
BIH	FK Željezničar	Feđa Dudić (Travnik) 16	FK Borac Banja Luka
BUL	PFC Litex Lovech	Wilfried Niflore (Litex) 19	PFC Beroe Stara Zagora
CRO	NK Dinamo Zagreb	Davor Vugrinec (Zagreb) 18	HNK Hajduk Split
CYP	AC Omonia	Semedo (APOP), Joeano (Ermis) 22	Apollon Limassol FC
CZE	AC Sparta Praha	Michal Ordoš (Sigma) 12	FC Viktoria Plzeň
DEN	FC København	Peter Utaka (OB) 18	FC Nordsjælland
ENG	Chelsea FC	Didier Drogba (Chelsea) 29	Chelsea FC
EST**	FC Levadia Tallinn	Vitali Gussev (Levadia) 26	FC Levadia Tallinn
FRO*	HB Tórshavn	Finnur Justinussen (Víkingur) 19	Víkingur
FIN*	HJK Helsinki	Hermanni Vuorinen (Honka) 16	FC Inter Turku
FRA	Olympique de Marseille	Mamadou Niang (Marseille) 18	Paris Saint-Germain FC
GEO	FC Olimpi Rustavi	Anderson Aquino (Olimpi) 26	FC Dinamo Tbilisi
GER	FC Bayern München	Edin Džeko (Wolfsburg) 22	FC Bayern München
GRE	Panathinaikos FC	Djibril Cissé (Panathinaikos) 23	Panathinaikos FC
HUN	Debreceni VSC	Nemanja Nikolić (Kaposvár/Videoton) 18	Debreceni VSC
ISL*	FH Hafnarfjördur	Björgólfur Takefusa (KR) 16	Breidablik
ISR	Hapoel Tel-Aviv FC	Shlomi Arbeitman (M. Haifa) 28	Hapoel Tel-Aviv FC
ITA	FC Internazionale Milano	Antonio Di Natale (Udinese) 29	FC Internazionale Milano
KAZ*	FC Aktobe	Murat Tleshev (Aktobe), Vladimir Bayramov (Tobol) 20	FC Atyrau
LVA**	SK Liepājas Metalurgs	Kristaps Grebis (Liepājas Metalurgs) 30	FK Jelgava

untry	Champions	Top league goalscorer(s)	Cup winners
	-	-	FC Vaduz
J**	FK Ekranas	Valdas Trakys (Ekranas) 20	FK Ekranas
X	AS Jeunesse Esch	Daniel Huss (Grevenmacher) 22	FC Differdange 03
KD	FK Renova	Bobi Bozinovski (Rabotnicki) 14	FK Teteks
T	Birkirkara FC	Camilo (Qormi) 24	Valletta FC
DA	FC Sheriff	Jymmy (Sheriff), Alexandru Maximov (Viitorul) 13	FC Sheriff
NE	FK Rudar Pljevlja	Ivan Bošković (Grbalj) 28	FK Rudar Pljevlja
D	FC Twente	Luis Suárez (Ajax) 35	AFC Ajax
R	Linfield FC	Rory Patterson (Coleraine) 30	Linfield FC
OR*	Rosenborg BK	Rade Prica (Rosenborg) 17	Aalesunds FK
L	Lech Poznań	Robert Lewandowski (Lech) 18	Jagiellonia Białystok
R	SL Benfica	Óscar Cardozo (Benfica) 26	FC Porto
.*	Bohemian FC	Gary Twigg (Shamrock Rovers) 24	Sporting Fingal FC
U	CFR 1907 Cluj	Andrei Cristea (Dinamo) 16	CFR 1907 Cluj
S**	FC Rubin Kazan	Welliton (Spartak Moskva) 21	FC Zenit St Petersburg
IR	SP Tre Fiori	Simon Parma (La Fiorita) 13	SP Tre Fiori
O	Rangers FC	Kris Boyd (Rangers) 23	Dundee United FC
B	FK Partizan	Dragan Mrđa (Vojvodina) 22	FK Crvena zvezda
K	MŠK Žilina	Róbert Rák (Nitra) 18	ŠK Slovan Bratislava
N	FC Koper	Milan Osterc (Gorica) 23	NK Maribor
P	FC Barcelona	Lionel Messi (Barcelona) 34	Sevilla FC
VE*	AIK Solna	Wanderson (GAIS), Tobias Hysén (Göteborg) 18	AIK Solna
I	FC Basel 1893	Seydou Doumbia (Young Boys) 30	FC Basel 1893
R	Bursaspor	Ariza Makukula (Kayserispor) 21	Trabzonspor
KR	FC Shakhtar Donetsk	Artem Milevskiy (Dynamo) 17	SC Tavriya Simferopol
AL	The New Saints FC	Rhys Griffiths (Llanelli) 30	Bangor City FC

*eague and Cup in 2009   ** League in 2009; Cup in 2010*

Relegated/pr

Country	Relegated clubs	Promoted clubs
ALB	(2) KS Gramozi, KF Apolonia	(2) KS Bylis, KF Elbasani
AND	(1) UE Engordany	(1) FC Casa del Benfica
ARM	(1) FC Ararat Yerevan	(1) FC Impuls
AUT	(1) SK Austria Kärnten	(1) FC Wacker Innsbruck
AZE	(2) Karvan İK, Standard Sumqayıt FK	(2) Gäncä PFK, MOİK Bakı PFK
BLR	(3) FC Smorgon, FC Granit Mikashevichi, FC Gomel	(1) FC Belshina Bobruisk
BEL	(2) R. Excelsior Mouscron*, KSV Roeselare	(2) K. Lierse SK, K. AS Eupen
BIH	(2) FK Modriča, FK Laktaši	(2) FK Budućnost Banovici, FK Drina Zvornik
BUL	(3) PFC Botev Plovdiv, PFC Sportist Svoge, PFC Lokomotiv Mezdra	(3) PFC Kaliakra Kavarna, PFC Vidima-Rakovski Sevlievo, PFC Akademik Sofia
CRO	(2) NK Croatia Sesvete, NK Međimurje,	(2) RNK Split, NK Hrvatski dragovoljac Zagreb
CYP	(3) APEP Kyperounda FC, Nea Salamis FC, Aris Limassol FC	(3) Alki Larnaca FC, AEK Larnaca FC, Olympiakos Nicosia FC
CZE	(2) FC Bohemians Praha, SK Kladno	(2) FC Hradec Králové, FK Ústí nad Labem
DEN	(2) HB Køge, AGF Århus	(2) AC Horsens, Lyngby BK
ENG	(3) Portsmouth FC, Burnley FC, Hull City AFC	(3) Newcastle United FC, West Bromwich Albion F Blackpool FC
EST	(1) JK Tallinna Kalev	(1) FC Lootus Kohtla-Järve
FRO	(2) 07 Vestur, KÍ Klaksvik	(2) VB/Sumba Vágur, B71 Sandoy
FIN	(1) RoPS Rovaniemi	(1) AC Oulu
FRA	(3) Grenoble Foot 38, US Boulogne CO, Le Mans UC 72	(3) SM Caen, Stade Brestois 29, AC Arles-Avignon
GEO	(2) FC Gagra, FC Lokomotivi Tbilisi	(2) FC Torpedo-2008 Kutaisi, FC Kolkheti-1913 Poti
GER	(2) Hertha BSC Berlin, VfL Bochum 1848	(2) 1. FC Kaiserslautern, FC St Pauli
GRE	(3) Panthrakakos FC, PAS Giannina FC, Levadiakos FC	(3) Olympiacos Volou FC, Kerkyra FC, Panserraikos FC
HUN	(2) Diósgyőri VTK, Nyíregyháza Spartacus FC	(2) Szolnoki MÁV FC, BFC Siófok
ISL	(2) Fjölnir, Thróttur Reykjavík	(2) Selfoss, Haukar
ISR	(2) Maccabi Ahi Nazareth FC, Hapoel Ra'anana FC	(2) Hapoel Kiryat Shmona FC, Hapoel Ashkelon FC
ITA	(3) AS Livorno Calcio, AC Siena, Atalanta BC	(3) US Lecce, AC Cesena, Brescia Calcio
KAZ	(4) FC Kyzylzhar Petropavlovsk, FC Kaisar Kyzylorda, FC Kazakhmys, FC Vostok*	(2) FC Kairat Almaty, FC Akzhaiyk Uralsk

09/10

noted/clubs

untry	Relegated clubs	Promoted clubs
A	(2) FC Dinaburg, FK Daugava Rīga	(3) FK Jelgava, FK Jaunība Rīga, FC Daugava Daugavpils
U	(0)	(3) FK Mažeikiai, FK Klaipėda, VMFD Žalgiris
JX	(2) FC Mondercange, US Rumelange	(2) FC Wiltz 71, FC Jeunesse Canach
KD	(4) FK Sloga Jugomagnat*, FK Makedonija GP Skopje*, FK Pobeda, FK Milano	(4) FK Skendija 79, FK Skopje, FK Napredok, FK Bregalnica Stip
LT	(2) Msida St Jospeh FC, Dingli Swallows FC	(2) Marsaxlokk FC, Vittoriosa Stars FC
DA	(0)	(2) FC Costuleni, CF Gagauziya Comrat
NE	(2) FK Kom, FK Berane	(2) FK Mladost Podgorica, OFK Bar
ED	(2) RKC Waalwijk, Sparta Rotterdam	(2) De Graafschap, SBV Excelsior
R	(1) Institute FC	(1) Donegal Celtic FC
OR	(3) FC Lyn Oslo, FK Bodø/Glimt, Fredrikstad FK	(3) FK Haugesund, Hønefoss BK, Kongsvinger IL
OL	(2) GKS Piast Gliwice, MKS Odra Wodzisław Śląski	(2) RTS Widzew Łódź, Górnik Zabrze
OR	(2) Leixões SC, CF Os Belenenses	(2) SC Beira-Mar, Portimonense SC
L	(2) Derry City FC*, Cork City FC*	(2) University College Dublin AFC, Sporting Fingal FC
OU	(4) FC Unirea Alba Iulia, FC Ceahlăul Piatra Neamț, FC Politehnica Iași, FC Internațional Curtea de Argeș*	(4) FC Victoria Brănești, FCM Târgu Mureș FC Sportul Studențesc București, FC Universitatea Cluj
US	(3) FC Khimki, FC Kuban Krasnodar, FC Moskva*	(3) FC Anzhi Makhachkala, FC Sibir Novosibirsk, FC Alania Vladikavkaz
CO	(1) Falkirk FC	(1) Inverness Caledonian Thistle FC
RB	(2) FK Mladi radnik, FK Napredak	(2) FK Inđija, FK Sloboda Sevojno
VK	(1) MFK Petržalka	(1) FC ViOn Zlaté Moravce
VN	(2) NK Drava, NK IB Ljubljana	(2) FK Primorje, ND Triglav
SP	(3) Xerez CD, CD Tenerife, Real Valladolid CF	(3) Real Sociedad de Fútbol, Hércules CF, Levante UD
WE	(2) Hammarby Fotboll, Örgryte IS	(2) Mjällby AIF, Åtvidabergs FF
UI	(1) FC Aarau	(1) FC Thun
UR	(3) Ankaraspor*, Denizlispor, Diyarbakırspor	(3) Karademir Karabükspor, Bucaspor, Konyaspor
KR	(2) FC Zakarpattya Uzhhorod, FC Chernomorets Odesa	(2) PFC Sevastopol, FC Volyn Lutsk
VAL	(6) Cefn Druids AFC, Caersws FC, Welshpool Town FC, CPD Porthmadog, Connah's Quay FC, Rhyl FC*	(0)

excluded/withdrawn club

Dinamo withstand spring collapse

t is not often that a club wins a national championship by a handsome margin despite losing seven matches in a row during the run-in. That, however, was the remarkable story of KS Dinamo Tirana's 2009/10 Superliga title triumph.

Dinamo, coached by one of Albania's finest footballers of the 1980s, Shkëlqim Muça, were so dominant during the first two thirds of the campaign, winning 17 and drawing three of their first 22 matches, that they were able to coast home in carefree fashion towards their 18th title.

Nobody quite foresaw how spectacularly the wheels would come off, however, as their exuberant championship-winning form totally deserted them in the spring. Rocked by a couple of defeats to KS Shkumbini in the quarter-finals of the Albanian Cup, Dinamo completely lost the plot in the league. The comfort of a huge, virtually insurmountable lead led to a slackening of application that resulted in all six of their April fixtures, plus the next one in May, ending in

defeat. Fortunately, they had so many points stored away that they were able to secure the title after the fourth defeat of that sequence, 1-2 at home to KS Teuta, when the only team that could conceivably catch them, defending champions KF Tirana, also lost at home by the same scoreline to KF Laçi.

Muted celebrations

Although, given the circumstances, the championship celebrations were understandably muted, the bare facts and figures did not lie. By the end of the season, four weeks later, after three further defeats and a welcome last-day 4-3 win at home to runners-up KS Besa, Dinamo still had an eight-point lead. Whether a team that lost ten of their 33 games and conceded 42 goals – more than every other club in the division bar the two automatically relegated (who each conceded 43) – could be considered worthy champions was a matter for debate, but with 56 goals scored Dinamo did boast by far the most potent attack. And, of course, for the first six months of the season they had been majestic.

Elis Bakaj of Dinamo Tirana was voted Albania's Player of the Year

Powered up front by the potent all-Albanian strikeforce of Elis Bakaj and Fatjon Sefa, who between them scored exactly half of the team's goals, Dinamo were also indebted to foreign assistance, notably from Argentina in the shape of talented trio Lucas Malacarne, Alfredo Sosa and Nicolás Delmonte. Defenders Marko Putinčanin, from Serbia, and Albaye Papa Diop, from Senegal, were also important contributors, the latter even scoring both goals in the club's 2-0 UEFA Europa League qualifying win over FC Lahti – a result which, alas, was insufficient to take Dinamo through after a first-leg 4-1 defeat in Finland.

Albania's three other European participants – Tirana, KS Flamurtari and KF Vllaznia – fared little better, with only the latter winning a tie, and the trio would all go on to endure disappointing domestic campaigns, finishing third, fifth and sixth, respectively in the league. Title-holders Tirana were torn apart by internal disruption and went through five different coaches, while Flamurtari and Vllaznia, despite their mid-table finishes, were never free from relegation worries.

Thrilling Cup final

Flamurtari lost their hold on the Albanian Cup at an early juncture but 2008 winners Vllaznia did make amends for their poor league form by reaching the final. Their opponents at the Qemal Stafa were 2007 winners Besa, and Shpetim Duro's all-Albanian outfit were to stage a memorable comeback to see off Vllaznia in a thrilling final, equalising five minutes from the end of normal time and snatching an extra-time winner through 30-year-old midfielder Paulin Dhëmbi, who had joined Besa from Vllaznia the previous summer.

The Cup final triumph brought a happy end to a traumatic week for Besa boss Duro, who only a few days earlier had been controversially sacked, only to be reinstated after a revolt by the players. To outsiders as well as insiders his reprieve was certainly warranted. With Besa also taking runners-up spot in the league and providing the Superliga's leading marksman in 18-goal Daniel Xhafa (a champion the previous season with Tirana), 2009/10 was undoubtedly the best season in the club's history.

Another all-Albanian team with plenty to celebrate were Laç, who, fresh from winning promotion, defied pre-season predictions by finishing fourth and qualifying for Europe for the first time. Coach Stavri Nica skilfully oversaw the development of an enthusiastic group of youngsters, and with the strongest defence in the league allied to a regular goalgetter in striker Arlind Nora, not to mention warm and loyal support, Laç fully deserved that European passport.

Laç had been one of four teams promoted in 2009, but that number was halved in 2010 as KS Kastrioti and KS Skëndebeu, ninth and tenth respectively in the top division, both won their play-off ties, leaving only the champions and runners-up from the second tier, KS

Bylis and KF Elbasani, to make the move up. KF Apolonia and KS Gramozi were relegated, the latter finding life at the higher level too hot to handle, with their fans repeatedly getting the club into trouble as a result of their unruly behaviour.

Kuže continues

Josip Kuže, the new head coach of the Albanian national team, was confirmed in his position for the UEFA EURO 2012 campaign despite two defeats and a draw in the three 2010 FIFA World Cup qualifiers for which he was in charge. Within that sequence he led Albania to an emphatic 6-1 win over Cyprus in a Tirana friendly, and there was more good news in the spring of 2010 as the Croatian masterminded a trio of 1-0 victories over Northern Ireland, Montenegro and Andorra.

Kuže's way forward appears to be by injecting a more youthful element into the team. Key senior players, however, include Lorik Cana - who enjoyed a creditable season in England with Sunderland AFC - and Debatik Curri - who, uniquely among Albanian footballers, appeared for every minute of the World Cup qualifying campaign – while 26-year-old Austrian Bundesliga star Hamdi Salihi, who scored the winning goals against both Montenegro and Andorra, looks to possess both the talent and strength of character to lead Albania's forward line for many years to come.

Federata Shqiptarë e Futbollit (FShF)

Rruga e Elbasanit
AL-TIRANË
tel - +355 42 346 605
fax - +355 42 346 609
website – fshf.org
email – fshf@fshf.org.al
Year of Formation - 1930

President - Armand Duka
General Secretary - Eduard Prodani
Media Officer – Tritan Kokona
National Stadium – Qemal Stafa, Tirana (16,230)

TOP FIVE ALL-TIME CAPS
Foto Strakosha (73); Altin Lala (70); Igli Tare (68); Alban Bushi,
Altin Haxhi & Ervin Skela (67)
TOP FIVE ALL-TIME GOALS
Alban Bushi (14); Ervin Skela (13); Erjon Bogdani (12);
Altin Rraklli (11); Sokol Kushta & Igli Tare (10)

NATIONAL TEAM RESULTS 2009/10

Date	Opponent		Venue	Score	Scorers
12/8/09	Cyprus	H	Tirana	6-1	Skela (25p, 44p), Bogdani (65), Duro (67), Agolli (71), Vila (75)
9/9/09	Denmark (WCQ)	H	Tirana	1-1	Bogdani (50)
14/10/09	Sweden (WCQ)	A	Solna	1-4	Salihi (57)
14/11/09	Estonia	A	Tallinn	0-0	
3/3/10	Northern Ireland	H	Tirana	1-0	Skela (25)
25/5/10	Montenegro	A	Podgorica	1-0	Salihi (79)
2/6/10	Andorra	H	Tirana	1-0	Salihi (44)

NATIONAL TEAM APPEARANCES 2009/10

Coach – Josip KUŽE (CRO) 13/11/52

Player	DOB	Club	Cyp	DEN	SWE	Est	Nir	Mne	And	Caps	Goals
Samir UJKANI	5/7/88	Novara (ITA)	G	G	G					4	-
Kristi VANGJELI	5/9/85	Aris (GRE)	D60				D		D78	21	-
Armend DALLKU	16/6/83	Vorskla (UKR)	D	D	D	D89	D	D		38	1
Debatik CURRI	28/12/83	Vorskla (UKR)	D	D	D	D	D	D		31	1
Lorik CANA	27/7/83	Sunderland (ENG)	D72	D	D	D	s61	D		43	1
Ansi AGOLLI	11/10/82	Kryvbas (UKR)	M	M		D	M61	M	D	17	2
Ervin BULKU	3/3/81	Kryvbas (UKR)	M	M	M		M84	M84	M57	26	-
Ervin SKELA	17/11/76	unattached /Koblenz (GER)	M66	M82	M	M	M81	M18	M	67	13
Klodian DURO	21/12/77	Apollon (CYP)	M76	M	M	M	M72	M64	M88	64	4
Erjon BOGDANI	14/4/77	Chievo (ITA)	A67	A78	A87		A46	A64		55	12
Hamdi SALIHI	19/1/84	Ried (AUT) /Rapid Wien (AUT)	A73	A	A79	A75	s46	A81	A	21	4
Jahmir HYKA	8/3/88	Mainz (GER)	s60	s46	s22	M	s61	s18	M57	17	1
Gilman LIKA	31/1/87	Boluspor (TUR)	s66	s78		M75		s84	s57	10	-
Emiljano VILA	12/3/88	Lokomotiva Zagreb (CRO) /Dinamo Tirana	s67	s82	s71	s89	s81			6	1
Elvin BEQIRI	27/9/80	Vllaznia	s72	D46	D					47	-
Elis BAKAJ	25/6/87	Dinamo Tirana	s73			M71	s72	s81	s58	8	-
Jetmir SEFA	30/1/87	Tirana	s76							1	-
Altin HAXHI	17/6/75	APOEL (CYP)		M22						67	3
Edmond KAPLLANI	31/7/82	Augsburg (GER) /Koblenz (GER)		s79	s75		s84	s64	A58	29	6
Besart BERISHA	29/7/85	Arminia (GER)			s87					17	1
Isli HIDI	15/10/80	Kryvbas (UKR)				G	G	G	G89	14	-
Gjergji MUZAKA	26/9/84	Tirana					s75	s64	s78	5	-
Andi LILA	12/2/86	Tirana				s89	D	D89	D	10	-
Altin LALA	18/11/75	Hannover (GER)					M61			70	3
Endrit VRAPI	23/5/82	Besa						D88		8	-
Parid XHIHANI	18/7/83	Zorya (UKR)							s57	1	-
Ditmar BICI	26/2/89	Tirana							s88	1	-
Emiljano VELIAJ	9/2/85	Laç							s88	1	-
Ervin LLANI	24/4/83	Laç							s89	1	-

DOMESTIC LEAGUE 2009/10

SUPERLIGA FINAL TABLE

		Pld	Home					Away					Total					Pts
			W	D	L	F	A	W	D	L	F	A	W	D	L	F	A	
1	KS Dinamo Tirana	33	12	2	3	34	19	7	2	7	22	23	19	4	10	56	42	61
2	KS Besa	33	10	4	3	24	12	5	4	7	18	21	15	8	10	42	33	53
3	KF Tirana	33	8	3	6	22	17	7	4	5	16	15	15	7	11	38	32	52
4	KF Laçi	33	10	5	2	20	9	4	4	8	15	19	14	9	10	35	28	51
5	KS Flamurtari	33	10	3	3	25	14	3	5	9	17	25	13	8	12	42	39	47
6	KF Vllaznia	33	8	3	5	19	16	5	4	8	15	23	13	7	13	34	39	46
7	KS Shkumbini	33	13	2	2	27	8	0	4	12	6	25	13	6	14	33	33	45
8	KS Teuta	33	9	4	4	20	15	4	2	10	13	25	13	6	14	33	40	45
9	KS Kastrioti	33	9	3	4	23	14	4	3	10	10	21	13	6	14	33	35	42
10	KS Skënderbeu	33	7	5	4	28	21	4	4	9	13	20	11	9	13	41	41	42
11	KF Apolonia	33	8	4	4	23	13	2	4	11	13	30	10	8	15	36	43	38
12	KS Gramozi	33	5	5	6	14	11	1	3	13	11	32	6	8	19	25	43	26

TOP GOALSCORERS

18 Daniel XHAFA (Besa)

15 Mladen BRKIĆ (Apolonia)
Elis BAKAJ (Dinamo)
Migen MEMELLI (Tirana/Flamurtari)

14 Arlind NORA (Laç)

13 Fatjon SEFA (Dinamo)

11 Milaim GUERRIB (Skënderbeu)

10 Vangjëll MILE (Teuta)
Gjergji MUZAKA (Tirana)

9 Orjand ABAZAJ (Kastrioti)
Bekim BALA (Vllaznia)

CLUB-BY-CLUB

KF APOLONIA

Coach – Esad Karišik (SRB); (13/11/09) Hasan Lika
Founded – 1925
Stadium – Loni Papuçiu (7,000)
MAJOR HONOURS:
Albanian Cup – (1) 1998.

2009

23/8	Teuta	h	2-0	*Hoti 2*
29/8	Vllaznia	a	0-1	
13/9	Shkumbini	h	1-0	*Ribaj*
19/9	Laç	a	2-3	*Hadžibulić Sea. (p), Brkić*
26/9	Tirana	h	2-0	*Meto, Brkić*
3/10	Skënderbeu	a	3-2	*Hadžibulić Sea., Hadžibulić Sem., Brkić*
17/10	Gramozi	h	3-0	*Ferizović, Hadzibulić Sea., Meto*
26/10	Besa	a	0-0	
31/10	Flamurtari	h	1-1	*Ofoyen*
7/11	Kastrioti	h	2-3	*Hadžibulić Sea., Kaçi*
21/11	Dinamo	a	2-3	*Capo, Hadžibulić Sem.*
29/11	Teuta	a	2-0	*Brkić, Kaçi*
5/12	Vllaznia	h	1-1	*Meto*
12/12	Shkumbini	a	0-3	
16/12	Laç	h	2-0	*Brkić 2*
20/12	Tirana	a	1-4	*Dhrami*
23/12	Skënderbeu	h	1-1	*Hadžibulić Sea.*

2010

24/1	Gramozi	a	0-1	
30/1	Besa	h	0-2	
8/2	Flamurtari	a	0-2	
13/2	Kastrioti	a	1-1	*Brkić*
21/2	Dinamo	h	3-0	*Brkić 2, Mone*
7/3	Teuta	a	1-1	*Brkić (p)*
20/3	Shkumbini	h	0-0	
28/3	Laç	a	0-2	
2/4	Tirana	h	1-2	*Brkić (p)*
11/4	Besa	a	0-2	
17/4	Dinamo	h	2-1	*Brkić 2*
21/4	Skënderbeu	a	1-1	*Ragipović*
25/4	Kastrioti	h	2-1	*Brkić 2*
30/4	Flamurtari	a	0-1	
14/5	Vllaznia	h	0-1	
19/5	Gramozi	a	0-3	

No	Name	Nat	DoB	Pos	Aps	(s)	Gls
9	Mladen BRKIĆ	SRB	3/10/75	A	30		15
14	Arbër CAPO		30/7/87	M	9	(4)	1
17	Sokol ÇELA		17/6/88	M	7	(2)	
15	Gazmend CIMILI		17/4/87	M	15	(11)	
23	Xhynejt ÇUTRA		23/11/88	M	8	(3)	
19	Arbër DHRAMI		23/6/88	A	2	(6)	1
3	Erald ELMAZI		18/5/88	D	4	(6)	
5	Edin FERIZOVIĆ	SRB	12/10/77	D	12	(3)	1
	Elton GRAMI		6/6/84	D	9		
10	Sead HADŽIBULIĆ	SRB	30/1/83	A	17		5
16	Semir HADŽIBULIĆ	SRB	16/8/86	A	11	(2)	2
1	Egland HAXHO		10/11/88	G	13		
	Erjon HOTI		8/5/83	M	8		2
12	Sulejman HOXHA		13/2/90	G	20		
17	Miloš JEVĐEVIĆ	SRB	11/1/81	M	14	(1)	
21	Albert KAÇI		11/6/81	A	15	(1)	2
24	Shkëlzen KELMENDI		16/2/86	D	15	(3)	
	Elis KOKALARI		18/1/91	M	1	(1)	
4	Hekuran KORRESHI		30/5/87	D	6	(1)	
	Ilirjan MËRTIRI		1/4/79	D	1	(1)	
7	Agim METO		2/2/86	M	25	(4)	3
22	Goran MIROVIĆ	SRB	18/5/82	M	12	(1)	
16	Arbën MONE		8/6/88	A	3	(4)	1
5	Petar MUDRESA	SRB	1/1/85	M	14		
	Eraldo MUSABELLIU		2/3/90	M		(1)	
2	Charles OFOYEN	NGA	26/7/85	D	14	(5)	1
	Ibezito OGBONNA	NGA	27/3/83	A	2	(4)	
8	Kenan RAGIPOVIĆ	SRB	16/9/82	M	27		1
	Besmir RAMAJ			M		(1)	
20	Andi RIBAJ		21/11/89	A	6	(14)	1
	Marsel RUSHANI		8/10/86	M	1	(4)	
6	Marenglen SHOSHI		29/1/85	D	31		
15	Norjon SPAHO		11/6/86	D	11		
	Leons TAFA			D		(1)	

ALBANIA

KS BESA

Coach – Shpetim Duro
Founded – 1922
Stadium – Besa (7,000)
MAJOR HONOURS:
Albanian Cup – (2) 2007, 2010.

2009

23/8	Vllaznia	h	2-0	Xhafa 2
29/8	Shkumbini	a	2-1	Çikalleshi, Mihani
13/9	Laç	h	1-0	Mançaku
19/9	Tirana	a	0-0	
26/9	Skënderbeu	h	1-0	Xhafa
3/10	Gramozi	a	0-0	
18/10	Flamurtari	h	1-0	Mançaku (p)
26/10	Apolonia	h	0-0	
1/11	Kastrioti	a	0-1	
9/11	Dinamo	h	0-1	
22/11	Teuta	a	1-1	Dragusha
29/11	Vllaznia	a	3-2	Xhafa, Çikalleshi, Leçi
5/12	Shkumbini	h	2-0	Mançaku (p), Xhafa
12/12	Laç	a	0-0	
17/12	Tirana	h	1-1	Babamusta
24/12	Gramozi	h	1-0	Dhëmbi

2010

24/1	Flamurtari	a	0-1	(result annulled; replayed 3/2)
27/1	Skënderbeu	a	2-0	Babamusta, Xhafa
30/1	Apolonia	a	2-0	Sinani, Xhafa
3/2	Flamurtari	a	0-3	
8/2	Kastrioti	h	1-0	Xhafa
15/2	Dinamo	a	0-1	
20/2	Teuta	h	1-1	Xhafa
7/3	Skënderbeu	h	1-2	Xhafa
19/3	Kastrioti	a	2-3	Sinani, Xhafa
28/3	Flamurtari	h	1-2	Xhafa
2/4	Vllaznia	a	0-2	
11/4	Apolonia	h	2-0	Shkëmbi, Sinani
17/4	Teuta	a	2-3	Shtini, Xhafa
21/4	Shkumbini	h	2-0	Shkëmbi, Sinani
25/4	Laç	a	1-0	Dragusha
30/4	Tirana	h	1-1	Xhafa (p)
14/5	Gramozi	h	6-4	Sinani, Xhafa 3, Shtini, Mançaku
19/5	Dinamo	a	3-4	Xhafa, Poçi (p), Mançaku

No	Name	Nat	DoB	Pos	Aps	(s)	Gls
6	Renato ARAPI		28/8/86	D	31		
14	Dritan BABAMUSTA		6/9/81	M	14	(1)	2
12	Edvan BAKAJ		9/10/87	G	2	(1)	
17	Sajmir ÇELHAKA		21/11/90	M	1	(3)	
7	Sokol ÇIKALLESHI		27/7/90	M	19	(8)	2
	Rigers ÇOBANI		14/6/90	D		(1)	
	Eglajd DEDEJ		2/3/90	D		(1)	
20	Paulin DHËMBI		9/8/79	M	16	(4)	1
5	Alban DRAGUSHA		11/12/81	D	24	(1)	2
	Aldo DURO		23/2/91	M	1		
8	Erbim FAGU		15/4/87	M	31		
25	Blerim HASALLA		16/8/73	D	7	(13)	
15	Erand HOXHA		27/12/81	M	5	(6)	
2	Liridon LEÇI		11/2/85	M	6	(8)	1
21	Bledar MANÇAKU		5/1/82	A	26	(5)	5
23	Meglid MIHANI		1/9/83	M	22	(1)	1
11	Bruno OKSHTUNI		16/3/87	A		(3)	
13	Artion POÇI		23/7/77	M	27		1
	Mario RROKAJ		6/9/91	M	1		
	Elidon SELAÇI		3/5/90	A		(2)	
1	Orges SHEHI		20/9/77	G	31		
10	Bledi SHKËMBI		13/8/79	M	14		2
30	Arjel SHTINI		7/2/92	A	2	(8)	2
9	Vioresin SINANI		4/11/77	A	16		5

16	Bazjon TROGAJ		16/8/88	D	6	(12)	
4	Endrit VRAPI		23/5/82	D	29		
	Ledio VRAPI		10/4/90	D	2	(4)	
22	Daniel XHAFA		1/5/77	A	30	(1)	18

KS DINAMO TIRANA

Coach – Shkëlqim Muça
Founded – 1950
Stadium – Selman Stermasi (8,000)
MAJOR HONOURS:
Albanian League – (18) 1950, 1951, 1952, 1953, 1955, 1956, 1960, 1967,
1973, 1975, 1976, 1977, 1980, 1986, 1990, 2002, 2008, 2010;
Albanian Cup – (13) 1950, 1951, 1952, 1953, 1954, 1960, 1971, 1974, 1978,
1982, 1989, 1990, 2003.

2009

23/8	Kastrioti	a	3-1	Bakaj, Muça, Kuli (p)
29/8	Flamurtari	a	3-0	Bakaj, Sefa, Plaku
13/9	Teuta	h	1-0	Malacarne
19/9	Vllaznia	a	0-0	
26/9	Shkumbini	h	2-1	Bakaj 2
3/10	Laç	a	1-0	Malacarne
18/10	Tirana	h	2-1	Bakaj, Sefa
25/10	Skënderbeu	a	1-1	Sosa
31/10	Gramozi	h	4-0	Sefa 2, Muça, Bakaj
9/11	Besa	a	1-0	Sosa
21/11	Apolonia	h	3-2	Sefa 2, Diop
28/11	Kastrioti	h	2-0	Bakaj 2
5/12	Flamurtari	h	1-0	Sosa
12/12	Teuta	a	3-1	Kuli, Sosa, Bakaj
16/12	Vllaznia	h	4-2	Sefa 3, Bakaj
19/12	Shkumbini	a	0-4	
24/12	Laç	h	1-1	Plaku (p)

2010

25/1	Tirana	a	2-1	Malacarne, Bakaj
30/1	Skënderbeu	h	3-0	Muça, Malacarne, Vila
6/2	Gramozi	a	1-0	Timpanaro
15/2	Besa	h	1-0	Sosa
21/2	Apolonia	a	0-3	
7/3	Gramozi	h	1-0	Delmonte
20/3	Skënderbeu	a	3-4	Bakaj 2 (1p), Putinčanin
27/3	Kastrioti	h	1-1	Timpanaro
2/4	Flamurtari	a	1-2	Sosa
11/4	Vllaznia	h	1-2	Vila
17/4	Apolonia	a	1-2	Sefa
21/4	Teuta	h	1-2	Diop
25/4	Shkumbini	a	0-1	
30/4	Laç	h	2-4	Sefa, Mallota
14/5	Tirana	a	2-3	Mallota, Bakaj
19/5	Besa	h	4-3	Kuli, Sefa 2, Bakaj

No	Name	Nat	DoB	Pos	Aps	(s)	Gls
14	Igli ALLMUÇA		25/10/80	M	30		
19	Elis BAKAJ		25/6/87	A	29		15
26	Odeon BERDUFI		20/10/90	D		(6)	
4	Asjon DAJA		14/3/90	M		(2)	
8	Nicolás DELMONTE	ARG	5/10/89	M	19	(3)	1
23	Albaye Papa DIOP	SEN	12/12/84	D	29	(2)	2
7	Nertil FERRAJ		11/9/87	M	11	(8)	
12	Alban HOXHA		23/5/87	G	5	(1)	
20	Eni IMAMI		19/12/92	D		(4)	
1	Elvis KOTORRI		30/4/79	G	28	(1)	
10	Bekim KULI		19/2/82	A	12	(12)	3
18	Lucas Damián MALACARNE	ARG	25/11/89	M	21		4
13	Renato MALLOTA		26/1/85	M	17	(2)	2
3	Gentian MUÇA		13/5/87	D	13	(6)	3
	Roland PEQINI		25/11/90	M	6	(9)	
5	Arjan PISHA		18/1/77	D	29		
11	Sebino PLAKU		20/5/85	A	5	(10)	2

21	Gerard PROGRI		6/11/86	M		(4)	
	Marko PUTINČANIN	SRB	16/12/87	D	23		1
26	Fatjon SEFA		23/7/84	A	26	(4)	13
17	Alfredo Rafael SOSA	ARG	7/5/88	A	25	(2)	6
9	Maximiliano TIMPANARO	ARG	26/3/88	A	3	(8)	2
11	Emiljano VILA		12/3/88	A	15		2
6	Erjon XHAFA		31/5/82	D	17	(7)	

KS FLAMURTARI

Coach – Eqerem Memushi; (30/9/09) Gugash Magani
Founded – 1923
Stadium – Flamurtari (9,000)
MAJOR HONOURS:
Albanian League – (1) 1991;
Albanian Cup – (3) 1985, 1988, 2009.

2009

23/8	Tirana	a	3-1	*Alviž, Roshi, Mema (p)*
29/8	Dinamo	h	0-3	
13/9	Skënderbeu	a	0-1	
19/9	Teuta	h	0-3	
26/9	Gramozi	a	0-2	
3/10	Vllaznia	h	2-0	*Roshi 2*
18/10	Besa	a	0-1	
25/10	Shkumbini	h	1-1	*Mema (p)*
31/10	Apolonia	a	1-1	*Sakaj*
8/11	Laç	h	0-0	
21/11	Kastrioti	a	1-1	*Alviž*
30/11	Tirana	h	0-2	
5/12	Dinamo	a	0-1	
12/12	Skënderbeu	h	1-1	*Mema (p)*
16/12	Teuta	a	0-1	
19/12	Gramozi	h	2-0	*Flávio Júnior (p), Đukič*
23/12	Vllaznia	a	2-2	*Zeqiri 2*

2010

24/1	Besa	h	1-0	*Shehaj (result annulled; replayed 3/2)*
30/1	Shkumbini	a	1-2	*Veliu*
3/2	Besa	h	3-0	*Sakaj (p), Memelli, Lena*
8/2	Apolonia	h	2-0	*Grami, Memelli*
12/2	Laç	a	2-3	*Memelli, Grami*
21/2	Kastrioti	h	2-0	*(w/o; match abandoned at 1-1 Sakaj (p))*
7/3	Laç	a	1-3	*Zeqiri*
21/3	Tirana	h	3-1	*Veliu, Shehaj, Memelli*
28/3	Besa	a	2-1	*Memelli 2*
2/4	Dinamo	h	2-1	*Lena, Memelli*
11/4	Skënderbeu	a	1-0	*Veliu*
17/4	Kastrioti	h	3-0	*Liçaj, Memelli 2*
21/4	Gramozi	a	1-1	*Memelli*
25/4	Vllaznia	a	1-1	*Memelli*
30/4	Apolonia	h	1-0	*Memelli (p)*
14/5	Teuta	a	1-3	*Memelli (p)*
19/5	Shkumbini	h	3-2	*Shehaj, Lena, Memelli*

No	Name	Nat	DoB	Pos	Aps	(s)	Gls
8	Roberto ALVIŽ	CRO	6/9/84	D	12	(3)	2
17	Besmir ARIFAJ		6/5/86	D	9		
5	Marko BAŠIĆ	CRO	13/9/84	D	3		
6	Halim BEGAJ		29/11/85	D	15	(7)	
13	Amarildo BELISHA		11/7/81	M	15		
33	Orjand BEQIRI		21/2/85	D	5	(1)	
	Mario BILAN	CRO	23/1/85	D	7		
21	Alvaro BISHAJ		2/10/91	M		(2)	
16	Albano ÇAUSHI		26/3/90	A	2	(7)	
15	Darko ĐUKIĆ	SVN	13/8/80	A	7	(7)	1
7	FLÁVIO Beck JÚNIOR	BRA	14/3/87	M	12	(3)	1
	Herbert GJONDEDA		21/5/90	D		(1)	
5	Elton GRAMI		6/6/84	A	14		2

4	Bledion GUGA		20/2/86	D	11	(1)	
1	Argjent HALILI		16/11/82	G	7	(2)	
20	Taulant KUQI		11/11/85	M	25	(1)	
17	Njasi LENA	MKD	25/6/86	A	7	(6)	3
18	Ledio LIÇAJ		19/5/87	M	7		1
9	Devis MEMA		13/2/85	A	11	(8)	3
25	Migen MEMELLI		25/4/80	A	15		14
12	Shpëtim MOÇKA		20/10/89	G	26		
	Armando MYRTAJ		1/3/90	M	4	(1)	
23	Marius NGJELA		22/1/83	A	3	(3)	
7	Gerard PROGRI		6/11/86	M	14		
15	Jurica PULJIZ	CRO	13/12/79	D	14		
22	Odhise ROSHI		22/5/91	A	24	(5)	3
28	Artan SAKAJ		8/12/80	M	29	(2)	3
	Andi SHABANI		30/1/91	D	1	(2)	
10	Ardit SHEHAJ		23/9/90	A	9	(9)	2
	Sinan SINAJ		8/7/91	M		(1)	
14	Ermir STRATI		11/11/85	M	5	(12)	
11	Franc VELIU		11/11/89	M	30	(1)	3
	Klodian XHELILI		23/11/88	G		(1)	
19	Hajr ZEQIRI		11/10/88	M	20	(5)	3

KS GRAMOZI

Coach – Ilir Qirjako; (27/9/09) Agim Canaj
Founded – 1925
Stadium – Gramozi (5,000)

2009

23/8	Shkumbini	h	0-0	
29/8	Laç	a	1-1	*Hyseni*
13/9	Tirana	h	0-1	
19/9	Skënderbeu	a	1-4	*Sadiku*
26/9	Flamurtari	h	2-0	*Hyseni, Sadiku*
3/10	Besa	a	0-0	
17/10	Apolonia	a	0-3	
24/10	Kastrioti	h	0-0	
31/10	Dinamo	a	0-4	
7/11	Teuta	h	2-0	*Sadiku 2*
21/11	Vllaznia	a	0-1	
28/11	Shkumbini	a	1-1	*Sadiku*
5/12	Laç	h	1-2	*Hyseni*
12/12	Tirana	a	1-1	*Marcos (p)*
16/12	Skënderbeu	h	2-0	*Oliveira, Rustemi*
19/12	Flamurtari	a	0-2	
24/12	Besa	h	0-1	

2010

24/1	Apolonia	h	1-0	*Semina*
30/1	Kastrioti	a	0-1	
6/2	Dinamo	h	0-1	
14/2	Teuta	a	0-2	
21/2	Vllaznia	h	1-1	*Sadiku*
7/3	Dinamo	a	0-1	
20/3	Teuta	a	2-0	*Marcos, Hadžibulić*
27/3	Skënderbeu	h	0-2	*(w/o; match abandoned at 0-1)*
2/4	Shkumbini	a	1-2	*Hoti*
11/4	Kastrioti	h	0-1	
17/4	Laç	a	0-1	
21/4	Flamurtari	h	1-1	*Sadiku*
25/4	Tirana	a	0-1	
30/4	Vllaznia	h	1-2	*Sadiku*
14/5	Besa	a	4-6	*Oliveira (p), Lena, Caka, Ngjela*
19/5	Apolonia	h	3-0	*Marcos 2, Metani*

No	Name	Nat	DoB	Pos	Aps	(s)	Gls
12	Olgert AMETLI		30/9/82	G	21		
20	Shpëtim BABAJ		9/12/81	D	23		
10	Olsi BEJOLLARI		17/4/85	M	3	(11)	
	Armand CAKA		22/12/82	M		(1)	1
	Aleksandar GROSEVSKI	MKD	24/12/86	M	20	(1)	

		Nat	DoB	Pos	Aps	(s)	Gls
	Semir HADŽIBULIĆ	SRB	16/8/86	A	11	(1)	1
	Erjon HOTI		8/5/83	M	13	(1)	1
	Genc HYSENI		28/3/83	A	7	(5)	3
	Erjon ISLAMI		28/8/81	M	1	(2)	
14	Elvis ISMOLLI		9/2/85	D	1	(2)	
8	Liridon KUKAJ		22/6/83	D	28	(1)	
7	Bledar LENA		16/6/85	M	18	(12)	1
	LEONARDO Martins	BRA	29/3/78	M	3	(4)	
17	MARCOS Paulo dos Santos	BRA	18/5/81	A	28	(1)	4
	Ermal MATA		24/1/86	D	4		
	Migen METANI		29/6/86	M	12	(8)	1
	Marius NGJELA		22/1/83	A	11	(3)	1
9	OLIVEIRA Juriander da Silva	BRA	28/2/82	M	19	(8)	2
	Elvis PEÇI		13/1/82	M	14		
	Klaudio REXHEPI		29/5/89	M	21		
	Arlindo RUSTEMI		7/2/86	M	17	(2)	1
13	Armando SADIKU		27/5/87	A	18	(11)	8
	Klodian SEMINA		19/1/89	D	24	(1)	1
16	Ardit SHAQIRI	MKD	14/11/85	M	19	(8)	
	Hyserion SHUPE		30/10/83	D	1	(4)	
	Ergys TARE		25/9/88	D		(1)	
1	Irakli TOÇI		30/6/82	G	12		
	Klement XHYRA		5/5/84	M	14		

KS KASTRIOTI
Coach – Ramazan Ndreu
Founded – 1926
Stadium – Kastrioti (5,500)

2009

23/8	Dinamo	h	1-3	Abazaj
29/8	Teuta	a	1-2	Abazaj
13/9	Vllaznia	h	1-0	Grizha
19/9	Shkumbini	a	0-1	
26/9	Laç	h	0-0	
3/10	Tirana	a	1-1	Roshi
18/10	Skënderbeu	h	2-1	Braho, Roshi (p)
24/10	Gramozi	a	0-0	
1/11	Besa	h	1-0	Abazaj
7/11	Apolonia	a	3-2	Abazaj, Turdiu, Grizha
21/11	Flamurtari	h	1-1	Teqja
28/11	Dinamo	a	0-2	
4/12	Teuta	h	1-2	Pema
12/12	Vllaznia	a	0-1	
16/12	Shkumbini	h	4-1	Kalari, Abazaj 2, Pema
19/12	Laç	a	0-1	
23/12	Tirana	h	0-1	

2010

24/1	Skënderbeu	a	1-0	Abazaj
30/1	Gramozi	h	1-0	Shameti
8/2	Besa	a	0-1	
13/2	Apolonia	h	1-1	Abazaj
21/2	Flamurtari	a	0-2	(w/o; match abandoned at 1-1 Pema)
6/3	Tirana	a	1-0	Djarmati
19/3	Besa	h	3-2	Abazaj, Babić 2
27/3	Dinamo	a	1-1	Pema
2/4	Skënderbeu	h	1-2	Babić
11/4	Gramozi	a	1-0	Babić
17/4	Flamurtari	a	0-3	
21/4	Vllaznia	h	2-0	Babić 2
25/4	Apolonia	a	1-2	Pema
30/4	Teuta	h	3-0	Hoxha, Kalari, Goçaj
14/5	Shkumbini	a	0-2	
19/5	Laç	h	1-0	Kalari

No	Name	Nat	DoB	Pos	Aps	(s)	Gls
8	Orjand ABAZAJ		17/1/85	A	33		9
17	Besmir ARIFAJ		5/6/86	D	8	(5)	
7	Ivan BABIĆ	CRO	29/4/84	A	11	(4)	6
17	Florjan BRAHO		25/5/85	M	7	(4)	1
6	Vinko BUDEN	CRO	18/1/86	M	16		
2	Fatmir CACA		28/5/85	D	8	(6)	
	Matko DJARMATI	CRO	24/2/82	M	13		1
2	Genti GJONDEDA		23/6/80	A	7	(1)	
21	Olsi GOÇAJ		30/9/89	M	29	(1)	1
6	Robert GRIZHA		10/3/82	D	13	(1)	2
5	Rigels HOXHA		3/9/85	M	8	(7)	1
7	Pëllumb JUSUFI	CRO	10/2/88	M	27	(2)	
9	Renaldo KALARI		25/6/84	D	23	(6)	3
1	Ilion LIKA		17/5/80	G	15		
15	Vilson LILA		6/10/89	M		(3)	
	Arbër MALAJ		11/4/89	D	1		
1	Arjon MUSTAFA		29/1/80	G	17		
19	Eleandro PEMA		9/2/85	A	23	(8)	5
10	Klevis ROSHI		11/7/84	A	15		2
8	Antonio RUKAVINA	CRO	6/5/85	D	5	(4)	
3	Raimond SHALA		15/4/83	M	15	(1)	
13	Ylli SHAMETI		7/6/84	D	29		1
	Fejzo SHENAJ		24/11/84	M	6	(5)	
	Roland SHULLAZI		18/10/87	M		(1)	
32	Gledis TAFAJ		29/6/85	G	1	(1)	
14	Sokol TALI		12/8/88	D		(2)	
4	Olsi TEQJA		27/7/88	D	10	(7)	1
11	Erald TURDIU		15/7/84	A	23		1

KF LAÇI
Coach – Stavri Nica
Founded – 1965
Stadium – Laçi (3,500)

2009

23/8	Skënderbeu	a	3-4	Nimani, Kaja, Malo
29/8	Gramozi	h	1-1	Nora (p)
13/9	Besa	a	0-1	
19/9	Apolonia	h	3-2	Brahja 2, Malo
26/9	Kastrioti	a	0-0	
3/10	Dinamo	h	0-1	
18/10	Teuta	a	1-2	Nora (p)
24/10	Vllaznia	h	3-1	Nora, Veliaj, Nimani
31/10	Shkumbini	a	0-1	
8/11	Flamurtari	a	0-0	
22/11	Tirana	h	1-0	og (Osmani)
28/11	Skënderbeu	h	0-0	
5/12	Gramozi	a	2-1	Nora, Jushi
12/12	Besa	h	0-0	
16/12	Apolonia	a	0-2	
19/12	Kastrioti	h	1-0	Brahja
24/12	Dinamo	a	1-1	Nora

2010

24/1	Teuta	h	0-0	
30/1	Vllaznia	a	2-1	Nora 2
7/2	Shkumbini	h	1-0	Nora (p)
12/2	Flamurtari	h	3-2	Kaja, Veliaj, Tanushaj
20/2	Tirana	a	0-1	
7/3	Flamurtari	h	3-1	Nora 2, Veliaj
21/3	Vllaznia	a	0-1	
28/3	Apolonia	h	2-0	Brahja, Kastrati
2/4	Teuta	a	0-0	
11/4	Shkumbini	h	0-0	
17/4	Gramozi	h	1-0	Kaja
21/4	Tirana	a	2-1	Nimani, Nora
25/4	Besa	h	0-1	
30/4	Dinamo	a	4-2	Vuçaj, Nora 2 (1p), Jushi
14/5	Skënderbeu	h	1-0	Nora
19/5	Kastrioti	a	0-1	

ALBANIA

No	Name	Nat	DoB	Pos	Aps	(s)	Gls
	Fisnik BLLACA		13/2/86	D		(3)	
9	Julian BRAHJA		6/12/80	D	30		4
	Besnik BURAKU		13/1/88	D		(1)	
3	Emiljano ÇELA		21/7/85	D	28	(2)	
	Kelvin JUSHI		18/4/89	M	7	(9)	2
29	Ervis KAJA		29/7/87	M	31	(1)	3
6	Saimir KASTRATI		7/3/87	M	20	(10)	1
1	Ervin LLANI		24/4/83	G	33		
	Rezart MAHO		8/2/84	A	1	(5)	
	Julian MALO		2/2/85	A	6	(3)	2
9	Bledar MARASHI		3/10/90	A	4	(7)	
17	Denis MUSTAFARAJ		2/4/85	D	29	(2)	
19	Valdano NIMANI		5/3/87	A	29		3
22	Jetmir NINA		21/5/86	D	29	(1)	
18	Arlind NORA		4/7/80	A	29	(1)	14
	Armand PASHA		17/1/91	D	1		
11	Taulant SEFGJINI		21/7/86	M	9	(13)	
23	Elio SHAZIVARI		14/4/85	M	21	(8)	
	Renato SULA		6/7/86	A	2	(5)	
	Alsid TAFILI		2/6/87	A	1	(2)	
13	Eduart TANUSHAJ		20/6/83	A	7	(4)	1
28	Emiljano VELIAJ		9/2/85	M	32		3
14	Erjon VUÇAJ		25/12/90	A	14	(6)	1
7	Sajmir XHETANI		28/6/74	M		(3)	

No	Name	Nat	DoB	Pos	Aps	(s)	Gls
19	Endri BAKIU		6/11/87	A	24	(8)	3
	Denald BALLIU		21/2/90	D	6	(11)	
1	Ibrahim BEJTJE		15/9/89	G	31		
	Kadri BIRJA		30/9/89	G	2	(1)	
	Klejdis BRANICA		10/5/92	A		(3)	2
21	Hetlen ÇAPJA		3/2/83	M	12	(3)	
17	Ilirjan ÇAUSHAJ		18/3/87	A	27	(1)	8
	Asjon DAJA		14/3/90	M	2	(6)	
18	Roland DERVISHI		16/2/82	A	10	(3)	5
	Edin FERIZOVIĆ	SRB	12/10/77	D	14		
22	Arvis GJATA		23/6/87	D		(2)	
3	Saso GJOREVSKI	MKD	18/9/82	D	13	(12)	1
11	Viktor GJYLA		11/5/83	M	30	(2)	2
	Altin GRBOVIĆ	SRB	13/3/86	A	3	(3)	2
	Albano ISAJ		19/4/91	M	1	(3)	
4	Hekuran KORRESHI		30/5/87	M	11	(2)	
	Driton KRASNIQI		15/8/84	D	13		
14	Emiljan LLUCA		27/9/88	M	2	(10)	
	Amarildo LUNDRAXHIU		27/12/92	D		(1)	
5	Ahmed MUJDRAGIĆ	SRB	13/6/86	D	31		
10	Erjon MUSTAFAJ		29/1/89	M	27	(1)	6
7	Lorenc PASHA		24/1/78	M	28		1
2	Ardian SEKSERI		9/8/81	A	12	(1)	
20	Isidor SEKSERI		16/11/86	D	24	(2)	2
	Fejzo SHENAJ		24/11/84	M	11		1
16	Erjon XHAFA		29/4/86	D	23	(2)	
15	Klement XHYRA		5/5/84	M	6	(4)	

KS SHKUMBINI

Coach – Gugash Magani; (30/9/09) Kristaq Mile; (19/12/09) Përparim Daiu
Founded – 1924
Stadium – Fusha Sportive (6,000)

2009
23/8 Gramozi a 0-0
29/8 Besa h 1-2 Mustafaj
13/9 Apolonia a 0-1
19/9 Kastrioti h 1-0 Mustafaj
26/9 Dinamo a 1-2 Bakiu
3/10 Teuta h 4-1 Dervishi 2 (1p), Çaushaj, Mustafaj
18/10 Vllaznia a 0-2
25/10 Flamurtari a 1-1 Dervishi
31/10 Laç h 1-0 Dervishi
7/11 Tirana a 0-2
21/11 Skënderbeu h 1-0 Mustafaj
28/11 Gramozi h 1-1 Mustafaj
6/12 Besa a 0-2
12/12 Apolonia h 3-0 Çaushaj 2 (1p), Dervishi
16/12 Kastrioti a 1-4 Pasha
19/12 Dinamo h 4-0 Sekseri I., Çaushaj (p), Bakiu, Gjorevski
24/12 Teuta a 0-1

2010
23/1 Vllaznia h 2-1 Shenaj, Grbović
30/1 Flamurtari h 2-1 Çaushaj 2 (2p)
7/2 Laç a 0-1
14/2 Tirana h 1-0 Sekseri I.
21/2 Skënderbeu a 0-1
10/3 Vllaznia h 0-0
20/3 Apolonia a 0-0
28/3 Teuta h 1-0 Bakiu (p)
2/4 Gramozi h 2-0 Gjyla, Çaushaj
11/4 Laç a 0-0
17/4 Tirana h 0-1
21/4 Besa a 0-2
25/4 Dinamo h 1-0 Mustafaj
30/4 Skënderbeu a 1-3 Branica
14/5 Kastrioti h 2-0 Çaushaj (p), Grbović
19/5 Flamurtari a 2-3 Branica, Gjyla

KS SKËNDERBEU

Coach – Gjert Haxhiu; (1/1/10) Andrea Marko; (7/2/10) Mirel Josa
Founded – 1923
Stadium – Skënderbeu (7,000)
MAJOR HONOURS:
Albanian League – (1) 1933.

2009
23/8 Laç h 4-3 Guerrib 2, Rukavina, Çipi
29/8 Tirana a 0-1
13/9 Flamurtari h 1-0 Rukavina
19/9 Gramozi h 4-1 Çajku 3, Shkëmbi
26/9 Besa a 0-1
3/10 Apolonia h 2-3 Çajku, Guerrib
18/10 Kastrioti a 1-2 Guerrib
25/10 Dinamo h 1-1 Frashëri
1/11 Teuta a 0-2
8/11 Vllaznia h 1-1 Lako
21/11 Shkumbini a 0-1
28/11 Laç a 0-0
6/12 Tirana h 1-1 Guerrib
12/12 Flamurtari a 1-1 Guerrib
16/12 Gramozi a 0-2
23/12 Apolonia a 1-1 Shkëmbi (p)

2010
24/1 Kastrioti h 0-1
27/1 Besa h 0-2
30/1 Dinamo a 0-3
13/2 Tirana a 2-3 Malindi, Roshi
25/2 Teuta h 3-0 Roshi 2, Guerrib
28/2 Shkumbini h 1-0 Grizha
7/3 Besa a 2-1 Lika, Guerrib
20/3 Dinamo h 4-3 Guerrib 2, Frashëri, Nestorović
27/3 Gramozi a 2-0 (w/o; match abandoned at 1-0 Guerrib)
2/4 Kastrioti a 2-1 Roshi, Marković
11/4 Flamurtari h 0-1
17/4 Vllaznia a 2-0 (w/o; original result 2-3 Malindi, Asllani)
21/4 Apolonia h 1-1 Asllani

ALBANIA

25/4	Teuta	a	0-0	
30/4	Shkumbini	h	3-1	Guerrib, Lika, Malindi
14/5	Laç	a	0-1	
19/5	Tirana	h	2-2	Nestorović, Çajku

No	Name	Nat	DoB	Pos	Aps	(s)	Gls
	Arbër ALIU		13/1/88	D		(3)	
	Klodian ASLLANI		2/8/77	A	10	(2)	2
	Elvis BALLA		14/5/82	M		(1)	
	Vasian BALLÇO		6/2/82	M	6	(3)	
17	Edi ÇAJKU		25/2/82	A	24	(4)	5
	Rigers ÇEKA		2/5/84	D	2	(1)	
	Besian ÇELIKU		18/7/87	D	1		
23	Jorgo ÇIPI		5/1/87	D	12	(14)	1
25	Matko DJARMATI	CRO	24/2/82	M	14	(1)	
2	Elton DOKU		1/10/86	D	24	(5)	
8	Erlis FRASHËRI		13/5/88	M	17	(12)	2
	Arvis GJATA		23/6/87	M	1	(1)	
5	Genti GJONDEDA		23/6/80	M	13		
	Robert GRIZHA		10/3/82	D	13		1
9	Milaim GUERRIB	CRO	5/11/85	A	25	(4)	12
	Erjon ISLAMI		28/8/81	M	1	(2)	
	Igli KOKONA		10/6/90	D		(1)	
	Dejan KOSTURANOV	MKD	7/8/86	G	5	(1)	
23	Ervis KRAJA		20/6/83	D	10	(1)	
	Fidel KREKA		7/4/88	M		(1)	
28	Staviron LAKO		24/3/80	D	29		1
12	Erjon LAPANJI		10/5/85	G	16	(1)	
	Dejan LESKAROVSKI	MKD	17/10/85	D	11		
14	Ledio LIÇAJ		19/5/87	M	3	(11)	
24	Elton LIKA		9/10/80	M	23	(1)	2
	Enco MALINDI		15/1/88	A	14		3
	Vlado MARKOVIĆ	SRB	26/8/85	M	12		1
	Emiljano MEMELLI		18/7/88	M	1		
	Aldo MITRAJ		12/1/87	D	1	(2)	
	Lorenc MUÇA		30/10/84	M	3		
	Marko NESTOROVIĆ	SRB	15/7/84	M	12		2
	Klevis ROSHI		11/7/84	A	13		4
29	Antonio RUKAVINA	CRO	6/5/85	D	15		2
10	Bledi SHKËMBI		13/8/79	M	15		2
1	Marijan TOMAŠIĆ	CRO	6/12/86	G	12		
	Erstel VIEROS		2/7/84	D		(3)	
22	Arlind XAKA		18/7/88	A	5	(11)	

KS TEUTA
Coach – Mirel Josa; (31/1/10) Ylli Shehu
Founded – 1925
Stadium – Niko Dovana (8,000)
MAJOR HONOURS:
Albanian League – (1) 1994;
Albanian Cup – (3) 1995, 2000, 2005.

2009

23/8	Apolonia	a	0-2	
29/8	Kastrioti	h	2-1	Mile 2 (1p)
13/9	Dinamo	a	0-1	
19/9	Flamurtari	a	3-0	Hodo, og (Moçka), Mile
26/9	Vllaznia	h	1-0	Hysa
3/10	Shkumbini	a	1-4	Hysa
18/10	Laç	h	2-1	Hysa, Mersini
24/10	Tirana	a	0-2	
1/11	Skënderbeu	h	2-0	Hodo, Hysa
7/11	Gramozi	a	0-2	
22/11	Besa	h	1-1	Mile
29/11	Apolonia	h	0-2	
4/12	Kastrioti	a	2-1	Hysa, Mile
12/12	Dinamo	h	1-3	Mile (p)
16/12	Flamurtari	h	1-0	Dushku
20/12	Vllaznia	a	1-2	Muçollari
24/12	Shkumbini	h	1-0	Hyseni

2010

24/1	Laç	a	0-0	
30/1	Tirana	h	0-1	
14/2	Gramozi	h	2-0	Hodo, Dushku
20/2	Besa	a	1-1	Dosti
25/2	Skënderbeu	a	0-3	
7/3	Apolonia	h	1-1	Imeraj
20/3	Gramozi	h	0-2	
28/3	Shkumbini	a	0-1	
2/4	Laç	h	0-0	
11/4	Tirana	a	1-2	og (Devolli)
17/4	Besa	h	3-2	Hodo 2, Dosti
21/4	Dinamo	a	2-1	Muçollari, Mile
25/4	Skënderbeu	h	0-0	
30/4	Kastrioti	a	0-3	
14/5	Flamurtari	h	3-1	Mile 2, Hodo
19/5	Vllaznia	a	2-0	Mile 2

No	Name	Nat	DoB	Pos	Aps	(s)	Gls
3	Fatmir CACA		28/5/85	D	4	(4)	
26	Mirel ÇOTA		14/5/88	A	9	(4)	
19	Erald DELIALLISI		12/3/82	M	30	(1)	
	Albi DOSTI		13/9/91	A	3	(9)	2
16	Erjon DUSHKU		25/2/85	D	27		2
3	Endrit FERRAJ		13/1/89	M		(5)	
	Eraldo GUNA		18/2/85	M		(1)	
13	Bledar HODO		21/6/85	M	32		6
14	Altin HOXHA		21/10/90	D	23	(9)	
	Rrustem HOXHA		4/7/91	D		(1)	
10	Vilfor HYSA		9/9/89	A	18	(3)	5
8	Berat HYSENI		26/10/86	A	12	(4)	1
21	Shpëtim IMERAJ		4/4/78	M	24	(2)	1
20	Akil JAKUPI		1/8/82	D	31		
	Albert KAÇI		11/6/81	A	1	(1)	
5	Arbën LIKMETA		3/3/87	D	8	(6)	
11	Ergys MERSINI		30/9/89	M	2	(10)	1
9	Vangjëll MILE		1/7/86	A	28		11
23	Elton MUÇOLLARI		14/9/80	D	24	(2)	2
4	Henri NDREKA		27/3/83	D	15		
18	Ergys RAKIPI		9/1/90	D	1	(7)	
12	Bledian RIZVANI		2/7/85	G	15	(1)	
	Dardan Rexhep ROGOVA		8/9/89	A		(1)	
28	Sokol SELACI		8/12/88	M	2	(4)	
22	Shaqir STAFA		23/4/87	M	23	(3)	
	Jozef THANA		14/12/88	M		(1)	
	Sajmir VAROSHI		1/3/87	A		(2)	
1	Bledi VASHAKU		8/1/80	G	18		
17	Orjon XHEMALAJ		7/6/89	D	13	(7)	

KF TIRANA
Coach – Ilija Lončarević (CRO); (4/10/09) Alban Tafaj;
(26/1/10) Nevil Dede; (14/2/10) Luan Sengla;
(29/3/10) Sulejman Starova
Founded – 1920
Stadium – Selman Stermasi (8,000)
MAJOR HONOURS:
Albanian League – (25) 1930, 1931, 1932, 1933, 1934, 1936, 1937, 1965,
1966, 1968, 1970, 1982, 1985, 1988, 1989, 1995, 1996, 1997, 1999, 2000,
2003, 2004, 2005, 2007, 2009;
Albanian Cup – (13) 1939, 1963, 1976, 1977, 1983, 1984, 1986, 1994, 1996,
1999, 2001, 2002, 2006.

2009

23/8	Flamurtari	h	1-3	Abilaliaj
29/8	Skënderbeu	h	1-0	Nallbani (p)
13/9	Gramozi	a	1-0	Abilaliaj
19/9	Besa	h	0-0	
26/9	Apolonia	a	0-2	
3/10	Kastrioti	h	1-1	Muzaka

18/10	Dinamo	a	1-2	*Abilaliaj*
24/10	Teuta	h	2-0	*Muzaka, Devolli*
30/10	Vllaznia	a	1-0	*Muzaka*
7/11	Shkumbini	h	2-0	*Sefa 2*
22/11	Laç	a	0-1	
30/11	Flamurtari	a	2-0	*Sefa, Ahmataj*
6/12	Skënderbeu	a	1-1	*Lila*
12/12	Gramozi	h	1-1	*Muka (p)*
17/12	Besa	a	1-1	*Ahmataj*
20/12	Apolonia	h	4-1	*Abilaliaj, Muzaka, Hajdari, Memelli*
23/12	Kastrioti	a	1-0	*Hajdari*
2010				
25/1	Dinamo	h	1-2	*Muzaka (p)*
30/1	Teuta	a	1-0	*Plaku*
7/2	Vllaznia	h	0-1	
14/2	Shkumbini	a	0-1	
20/2	Laç	h	1-0	*Abilaliaj*
6/3	Kastrioti	h	0-1	
21/3	Flamurtari	a	1-3	*Plaku*
28/3	Vllaznia	h	1-2	*Muzaka (p)*
2/4	Apolonia	a	2-1	*Muka, Muzaka*
11/4	Teuta	h	2-1	*Devolli, Muzaka*
17/4	Shkumbini	a	1-0	*Muka*
21/4	Laç	h	1-2	*Ahmataj*
25/4	Gramozi	a	1-0	*Hajdari*
30/4	Besa	a	1-1	*Plaku*
14/5	Dinamo	h	3-2	*Muzaka 2 (1p), Plaku*
19/5	Skënderbeu	a	2-2	*Abilaliaj, Sorra*

No	Name	Nat	DoB	Pos	Aps	(s)	Gls
	Arbër ABILALIAJ		6/6/86	A	21	(4)	6
7	Julian AHMATAJ		24/5/79	M	24	(6)	3
16	Abraham ALECHENWU	NGA	16/3/86	D	24	(3)	
15	Ditmar BICI		26/2/89	D	11	(3)	
	Rezart DABULLA		24/10/79	D	3	(3)	
14	Bledar DEVOLLI		15/1/78	M	29	(1)	2
	Endrit FERRAJ		15/10/90	M		(1)	
	Blerti HAJDARI		1/9/90	M	8	(8)	3
13	Erando KARABECI		6/9/88	M	6	(12)	
12	Pece KORUNOVSKI	MKD	5/10/82	G	5	(2)	
6	Andi LILA		12/2/86	D	22	(1)	1
	Sabien LILAJ		10/2/89	M	10	(15)	
25	Enco MALINDI		15/1/88	A	2	(4)	
11	Migen MEMELLI		25/4/80	A	8	(1)	1
	Laurent MOHELLEBI	FRA	5/1/84	M	2		
10	Devis MUKA		21/12/76	M	18	(1)	3
17	Gjergji MUZAKA		26/9/84	M	28	(2)	10
1	Blendi NALLBANI		30/5/71	G	28		1
	Tefik OSMANI		8/6/85	D	24	(1)	
5	Entonio PASHAJ		10/11/84	D	25	(3)	
	Sajmir PATUSHI		28/9/76	M	1	(1)	
	Sebino PLAKU		20/5/85	A	15		4
	Jetmir SEFA		30/1/87	A	30	(1)	3
2	Elvis SINA		14/11/78	D	19	(8)	
	Ergys SORRA		23/7/89	M		(7)	1
13	Gerard TUSHA		2/5/91	M		(3)	

KF VLLAZNIA

Coach – Hasan Lika; (4/10/09) Roland Luçi;
(22/12/09) Edi Martini
Founded – 1919
Stadium – Loro Boriçi (16,000)
MAJOR HONOURS:
Albanian League – (9) 1945, 1946, 1972, 1974, 1978, 1983, 1992, 1998, 2001;
Albanian Cup – (6) 1965, 1972, 1979, 1981, 1987, 2008.

2009				
23/8	Besa	a	0-2	
29/8	Apolonia	h	1-0	*Nallbani*
13/9	Kastrioti	a	0-1	
19/9	Dinamo	h	0-0	
26/9	Teuta	a	0-1	
3/10	Flamurtari	a	0-2	
18/10	Shkumbini	h	2-0	*Bala 2*
24/10	Laç	a	1-3	*Kasapi*
30/10	Tirana	h	0-1	
8/11	Skënderbeu	a	1-1	*Bala*
21/11	Gramozi	h	1-0	*Osja*
29/11	Besa	h	2-3	*Sinani, Bala*
5/12	Apolonia	a	1-1	*Beqiri E.*
12/12	Kastrioti	h	1-0	*Alikaj*
16/12	Dinamo	a	2-4	*Rajović, Beqiri E.*
20/12	Teuta	h	2-1	*Bala, Alikaj*
23/12	Flamurtari	h	2-2	*Nallbani, Bala*
2010				
23/1	Shkumbini	a	1-2	*Shtupina*
30/1	Laç	h	1-2	*Bala*
7/2	Tirana	a	1-0	*Bala*
13/2	Skënderbeu	h	3-2	*Belisha, Hadžibulić (p), Shtupina*
20/2	Gramozi	a	1-1	*Rajović*
10/3	Shkumbini	a	0-0	
21/3	Laç	h	1-0	*Kraja*
28/3	Tirana	a	2-1	*Rajović (p), og (Alechenwu)*
2/4	Besa	h	2-0	*Kraja, Shtupina*
11/4	Dinamo	a	2-1	*Nika, Rajović (p)*
17/4	Skënderbeu	h	0-2	*(w/o; original result 3-2 Alikaj, Rajović 2 (2p)*
21/4	Kastrioti	a	0-2	
25/4	Flamurtari	h	1-1	*Shtupina*
30/4	Gramozi	a	2-1	*Mrvaljević, Shtupina*
14/5	Apolonia	a	1-0	*Bala*
19/5	Teuta	h	0-2	

No	Name	Nat	DoB	Pos	Aps	(s)	Gls
	Enkeleid ALIKAJ		27/12/81	M	16	(4)	3
19	Bekim BALA		11/1/91	A	23	(7)	9
	Amarildo BELISHA		11/7/81	M	15		1
4	Ardit BEQIRI		13/2/79	D	9	(1)	
18	Elvin BEQIRI		27/9/80	D	16		2
31	Olti BISHANI		11/1/88	G	6	(1)	
	Ari DJEPAXHIJA		4/10/92	D	2	(4)	
22	Edmond DOÇI		1/3/81	A	15	(8)	
	Elham GALICA		30/1/89	A	3	(2)	
1	Armir GRIMA		16/6/74	G	26		
9	Sead HADŽIBULIĆ	SRB	30/1/83	A	10	(3)	1
13	Rahman HALLAÇI		12/11/83	D	10	(3)	
28	Edom HASANI		9/1/92	M		(2)	
25	Fetim KASAPI		9/5/83	M	5	(2)	1
4	Ervis KRAJA		20/6/83	D	13		2
8	LEANDRO Teófilo Santos Pinto	BRA	3/5/81	M	5	(4)	
11	Liridon LEÇI		11/2/85	M	11	(1)	
	Ilion LIKA		17/5/80	G	1		
3	Željko MRVALJEVIĆ	MNE	8/4/81	D	21	(1)	1
20	Ilir NALLBANI		11/7/82	M	32		2
15	Ansi NIKA		11/5/90	A	1	(10)	1
5	Safet OSJA		17/10/75	D	12	(7)	1
6	Jamie PHOENIX	ENG	15/1/84	A	5	(1)	
18	Blažo RAJOVIĆ	BIH	26/3/86	A	21	(1)	6
15	Erjon RIZVANOLLI		14/8/81	A		(6)	
6	Blerim RUSTEMI		4/2/83	D	7	(3)	
7	Ndriçim SHTUPINA		18/3/87	M	32		5
9	Vioresin SINANI		4/11/77	A	13		1
2	Dritan SMAJLAJ		12/2/85	D	28		
17	Arsen SYKAJ		11/4/90	M	5	(10)	
14	Armando VAJUSHI		3/12/91	M		(11)	

ALBANIA

PROMOTED CLUBS

KS BYLIS
Coach – Ilir Spahiu
Founded – 1972
Stadium – Adush Muça (5,000)

KF ELBASANI
Coach – Muharrem Dosti; (19/12/09) Krenar Alimehmeti
Founded – 1923
Stadium – Ruzhdi Bizhuta (9,000)
MAJOR HONOURS:
Albanian League - 1984, 2006;
Albanian Cup – 1975, 1992.

SECOND LEVEL FINAL TABLE 2009/10

		Pld	W	D	L	F	A	Pts
1	KS Bylis	30	22	3	5	57	26	69
2	KF Elbasani	30	19	5	6	56	25	62
3	KS Dajti Kamëz	30	19	5	6	50	21	62
4	KS Lushnja	30	17	9	4	59	10	60
5	FK Partizani	30	17	6	7	49	35	57
6	KS Pogradeci	30	14	6	10	40	38	48
7	KS Ada Velipojë	30	13	3	14	45	33	42
8	KS Luftëtari Gjirokastër	30	10	6	14	39	46	36
9	KS Besëlidhja Lezhë	30	9	8	13	32	40	35
10	KF Gramshi	30	8	8	14	23	34	32
11	KF Bilisht Sport	30	9	5	16	30	50	32
12	KS Burreli	30	7	10	13	27	42	31
13	KF Skrapari	30	9	4	17	29	56	31
14	KF Memaliaj	30	7	8	15	23	37	29
15	KS Turbina Cërrik	30	7	7	16	35	53	28
16	KS Sopoti Librazhd	30	5	3	22	14	62	18

PROMOTION/RELEGATION PLAY-OFFS

(26/5/10)
Skënderbeu 1, Lushnja 0

(27/5/10)
Kastrioti 1, Dajti 0

DOMESTIC CUP 2009/10

KUPA E SHQIPËRISË

FIRST ROUND

(21/10/09 & 4/11/09)
Adriatiku v Dinamo 2-3; 0-2 *(2-5)*
Bilisht v Apolonia 3-1; 0-7 *(3-8)*
Burreli v Lushnja 0-0; 1-3 *(1-3)*
Dajti v Elbasan 2-1; 0-0 *(2-1)*
Gramshi v Flamurtari 0-3; 0-0 *(0-3)*
Luftëtari v Gramozi 1-3; 1-4 *(2-7)*
Luzi v Tirana 3-1; 0-3 *(3-4)*
Memaliaj v Shkumbini 1-2; 0-2 *(1-4)*
Pogradeci v Besa 1-2; 0-1 *(1-3)*
Skrapari v Skënderbeu 5-3; 5-9 *(10-12)*
Sopoti v Kastrioti 0-3; 1-3 *(1-6)*

Tomori v Vllaznia 0-4; 1-5 *(1-9)*
Turbina v Bylis 1-0; 0-3 *(1-3)*
Vlora v Teuta 0-3 *(w/o)*; 0-1 *(0-4)*

(21/10/09 & 11/11/09)
Ada v Partizani 0-0; 1-2 *(1-2)*
Besëlidhja v Laç 1-2; 1-4 *(2-6)*

SECOND ROUND

(25/11/09 & 9/12/09)
Bylis v Dinamo 1-0; 1-3 *(2-3)*
Dajti v Vllaznia 1-3; 2-2 *(3-5)*
Gramozi v Flamurtari 1-0; 1-1 *(2-1)*
Kastrioti v Shkumbini 1-1; 0-1 *(1-2)*
Laç v Besa 0-1; 1-1 *(1-2)*
Lushnja v Tirana 2-2; 1-2 *(3-4)*
Partizani v Teuta 1-1; 0-2 *(1-3)*
Skënderbeu v Apolonia 1-0; 1-2 *(2-2 Skënderbeu on away goal)*

QUARTER-FINALS

(10/2/10 & 24/2/10)
Besa 2 *(Mançaku 11p, Xhafa 78)*, Tirana 0
Tirana 4 *(Ahmataj 47, 68, Plaku 49, Lila 51p)*, Besa 2 *(Mançaku 72p, Xhafa 80)*
(4-4; Besa on away goals)

(10/2/10 & 16/3/10)
Skënderbeu 0, Vllaznia 0
Vllaznia 4 *(Bala 23, 63, Kraja 29, Shtupina 59)*, Skënderbeu 0
(Vllaznia 4-0)

(24/2/10 & 16/3/10)
Shkumbini 2 *(Bakiu 65p, 76p)*, Dinamo 1 *(Kuli 55)*
Dinamo 0, Shkumbini 1 *(Bakiu 90)*
(Shkumbini 3-1)

(2/3/10 & 17/3/10)
Gramozi 1 *(Hoti 46)*, Teuta 1 *(Hodo 62p)*
Teuta 0, Gramozi 0
(1-1; Teuta on away goal)

SEMI-FINALS

(24/3/10 & 7/4/10)
Besa 1 *(Xhafa 26)*, Shkumbini 1 *(Bakiu 5)*
Shkumbini 0, Besa 1 *(Çikalleshi 70)*
(Besa 2-1)

Teuta 1 *(Mile 45)*, Vllaznia 0
Vllaznia 2 *(Hadžibulić 72, Smajlaj 77)*, Teuta 0
(Vllaznia 2-1)

FINAL

(9/5/10)
Qemal Stafa, Tirana
KS BESA 2 *(Arapi 85, Dhëmbi 97)*
KF VLLAZNIA 1 *(Bala 63)*
(aet)
Referee – Ceferin (SVN)
BESA – Shehi, Dragusha, Vrapi E., Fagu, Mihani, Poçi (Babamusta 120), Sinani (Hasalla 79), Xhafa, Mançaku (Dhëmbi 67), Arapi, Shkëmbi.
VLLAZNIA – Grima, Smajlaj, Kraja, Osja (Hadžibulić 90), Phoenix (Djepaxhija 95), Shtupina, Belisha, Rajović, Bala, Nallbani, Doçi (Alikaj 100).

Unbeaten champions challenged to the end

FC Santa Coloma regained the Andorran Primera Divisió crown from their regular sparring partners UE Sant Julià in 2009/10, taking the title for the fifth time in the decade. They did so with an unbeaten record, but despite that their victory was still uncertain as they went into their final fixture.

It was only with a 1-1 draw against closest challengers UE Santa Coloma in the last game of the play-off round at the end of March that FC Santa Coloma wrapped up the title. Their opponents had gone into the match needing a four-goal victory to unseat them from first place. It was always a remote possibility, but for UE Santa Coloma to have taken their village rivals to the wire was nevertheless a victory in itself as the club had only been promoted to the top flight two years earlier. Second place, two points ahead of defending champions Sant Julià, was a considerable over-achievement, although there would be a major disappointment for the new kids on the block when, in mid-May, they lost 1-0 to Sant Julià in the final of the Copa Constitució, enabling their opponents to win the trophy for the second time in three seasons.

Rare success

Sant Julià had scored a rare international success for Andorra the previous summer when they defeated San Marino's SP Tre Fiori in a penalty shoot-out after two hard-fought 1-1 draws in their UEFA Champions League first qualifying round tie. There would be further good news for Andorran football with the doubling of the country's European representation from two clubs to four, enabling FC Lusitans, who finished fourth in the league, to join Sant Julià and the two Santa Coloma clubs in continental combat in 2010/11.

The other big story of the season was the appointment of Koldo, Andorra's long-serving goalkeeper, as the new head coach of the national team. The popular 39-year-old was handed the job in February 2010, thus ending the 11-year reign of David Rodrigo, under whom Koldo had won the vast majority of his 78 caps.

Former Andorra goalkeeper Koldo – the country's new head coach

Federació Andorrana de Fútbol (FAF)

Avinguda Carlemany 67 3° pis
Apartado postal 65
AD-Escaldes-Engordany
tel - +376 805 830
fax - +376 862 006
website – fedandfut.com
email – info@fedandfut.com
Year of Formation – 1994

President – Antoni Giribet Fiter
General Secretary – Tomás Gea
Media Officer – Andrea Vidal
National Stadium – Comunal, Andorra la Vella (1,249)

TOP FIVE ALL-TIME CAPS
Óscar Sonojee (83); Jesús Álvarez "Koldo" (78); José Manuel García "Txema" (72); Manolo Jiménez (69); Justo Ruíz (67)
TOP FIVE ALL-TIME GOALS
Ildefons Lima (7); Jesús Julián Lucendo (3); Emiliano González, Marc Pujol, Justo Ruiz, Juli Sánchez, Óscar Sonojee & Fernando Silva (2)

ANDORRA

NATIONAL TEAM RESULTS 2009/10

Date	Opponent	H/A	Venue	Score	Scorers
5/9/09	Ukraine (WCQ)	A	Kyiv	0-5	
9/9/09	Kazakhstan (WCQ)	H	Andorra la Vella	1-3	*Sonejee (70)*
14/10/09	Ukraine (WCQ)	H	Andorra la Vella	0-6	
29/5/10	Iceland	A	Reyjkavik	0-4	
2/6/10	Albania	A	Tirana	0-1	

NATIONAL TEAM APPEARANCES 2009/10

Coach – David RODRIGO (ESP) 8/5/68
/(2/2/10) Jesús Álvarez "KOLDO" 4/9/70

Player	DOB	Club	UKR	KAZ	UKR	Isl	Alb	Caps	Goals
José Antonio GÓMES	3/12/86	unattached /Ciadad Vícar (ESP)	G	G	G	G	G85	11	-
José Manuel AYALA	8/4/80	FC Santa Coloma	D	M	M	M	M	48	-
Cristian MARTÍNEZ	16/10/89	FC Andorra (ESP)	D	D	D			3	-
Óscar SONEJEE	26/3/76	FC Santa Coloma	D	D			s70	83	2
Fernando SILVA	16/5/77	Badajoz (ESP)	D	A	D	D70	D70	33	2
Marc VALES	4/4/90	Atlético Monzon (ESP)	D	D46	M			13	-
Marc PUJOL	21/8/82	Balaguer (ESP)	M		M	M82	M80	45	2
Marcio VIEIRA	10/10/84	Atlético Monzon (ESP)	M76	M87		M	M	28	-
Manolo JIMÉNEZ	12/8/76	FC Santa Coloma	M	M54	M74	M	M73	69	1
Sergi MORENO	25/11/87	Gimnástico Alcázar (ESP)	M82	A	s74	M51	M	27	-
Juan Carlos TOSCANO	14/8/84	FC Andorra (ESP)	A84	s54				18	-
Jordi ESCURA	19/4/80	Balaguer (ESP) /Alcarràs (ESP)	s76	s46		D77	D85	61	-
Genís GARCÍA	18/5/78	FC Santa Coloma	s82	s89			s73	37	-
Víctor HUGO Moreira	5/10/82	Sant Julià	s84					5	-
Ildefons LIMA	10/12/79	Bellinzona (SUI)				D	D	61	7
Marc BERNAUS	2/2/77	Girona (ESP)				M		18	1
Gabriel RIERA	5/6/85	Sant Julià				s87	s79	15	1
David MANEIRO	16/2/89	FC Andorra (ESP)				D		1	-
Xavier ANDORRÀ	7/6/85	FC Andorra (ESP)				M89	s70	19	-
Juli SÁNCHEZ	20/6/78	FC Santa Coloma		A79				61	2
Jordi RUBIO	1/11/87	UE Santa Coloma				D51	D55	7	-
Emili GARCÍA	11/1/89	FC Andorra (ESP)				D	D	3	-
Sebastià GOMEZ	1/11/83	Sant Julià				A71	A76	2	-
Marc GARCÍA	21/3/88	Fraga (ESP)				s51 /77		1	-
Daniel MEJÍAS	26/7/82	FC Andorra (ESP)				s51		1	-
Àlex SOMOZA	7/7/86	FC Andorra (ESP)				s77		8	-
Àlexandre MARTÍNEZ	4/3/87	UE Santa Coloma				s77		1	-
Samir BOUSENINE	7/2/91	FC Andorra (ESP)				s82	s76	2	-
Xavier GIL Sánchez	24/5/82	FC Santa Coloma					s55	3	-
Ferran POL	28/2/83	Sants (ESP)					s85	1	-
David RIBOLLEDA	13/2/85	FC Santa Coloma					s85	3	-

DOMESTIC LEAGUE 2009/10

PRIMERA DIVISIÓ FINAL TABLES

PLAY-OFFS

Championship Group	Pld	W	D	L	F	A	Pts
1 FC Santa Coloma	20	13	7	0	46	14	46
2 UE Santa Coloma	20	13	4	3	50	26	43
3 UE Sant Julià	20	12	5	3	69	18	41
4 FC Lusitans	20	7	3	10	34	32	24

Relegation Group	Pld	W	D	L	F	A	Pts
5 CE Principat	20	8	2	10	42	50	26
6 Inter Club d'Escaldes	20	6	1	13	25	49	19
7 FC Encamp	20	4	3	13	31	67	15
8 UE Engordany	20	4	1	15	22	63	13

FIRST PHASE

	Pld	W	D	L	F	A	Pts
1 FC Santa Coloma	14	11	3	0	38	10	36
2 UE Sant Julià	14	10	2	2	59	12	32
3 UE Santa Coloma	14	10	2	2	41	20	32
4 FC Lusitans	14	7	2	5	30	17	23
5 CE Principat	14	7	0	7	27	33	21
6 FC Encamp	14	3	1	10	19	50	10
7 Inter Club d'Escaldes	14	1	1	12	10	41	4
8 UE Engordany	14	1	1	12	11	52	4

NB League split into two groups of four after 14 matches.

TOP GOALSCORERS

19 Gabriel RIERA (Sant Julià)

16 LUIS MIGUEL do Nascimiento (UE Santa Coloma)

12 Alejandro ROMERO (Sant Julià)
Norberto URBANI (FC Santa Coloma)

11 PEDRO Reis (Lusitans)
Victor HUGO Moreira (Sant Julià)

10 LUIS dos Reis (Lusitans)

9 Carles SIRVAN Jimenez (UE Santa Coloma)

SECOND LEVEL FINAL TABLE

PLAY-OFFS

Promotion Pool	Pld	W	D	L	F	A	Pts
1 SE Casa del Benfica	20	13	3	4	47	25	42
2 UE Extremenya	20	13	2	5	47	23	41
3 FC Lusitans B	20	13	1	6	49	19	40
4 CE Jenlai	20	10	5	5	51	30	32

NB CE Jenlai - 3 pts deducted.

FIRST PHASE

	Pld	W	D	L	F	A	Pts
1 SE Casa del Benfica	14	10	2	2	37	15	32
2 CE Jenlai	14	9	4	1	44	15	31
3 UE Extremenya	14	10	1	3	36	16	31
4 FC Lusitans B	14	10	0	4	37	11	30
5 FC Rànger's	14	5	3	6	28	22	18
6 Atlètic Club d'Escaldes	14	2	3	9	13	37	6
7 Penya Encarnada	14	1	0	13	13	57	3
8 CE Principat B	14	1	3	10	17	52	0

NB CE Principat B - 6 pts deducted; Atlètic Club d'Escaldes - 3 pts deducted.

PROMOTION/RELEGATION PLAY-OFFS

(25/4/10)
FC Encamp 2, UE Extremenya 1

(15/5/10)
UE Extremenya 1, FC Encamp 3
(FC Encamp 5-2)

DOMESTIC CUP 2009/10

COPA CONSTITUCIÓ

SECOND ROUND

(4/1/10)
Casa del Benfica 0, Inter Escaldes 2
Extremenya 2, Encamp 1
Jenlai 1, Engordany 2
Lusitans B 0, Lusitans 4

Byes – FC Santa Coloma, UE Santa Coloma, Sant Julià, Principat

QUARTER-FINALS

(11/4/10 & 18/4/10)
Engordany v Sant Julià 0-5; 0-8 *(0-13)*
Extremenya v Principat 0-2; 0-3 *(0-5)*
Inter Escaldes v UE Santa Coloma 3-0; 0-4 *(3-4)*
Lusitans v FC Santa Coloma 6-0; 1-1 *(7-1)*

SEMI-FINALS

(25/4/10 & 9/5/10)
Sant Julià 1 *(Sebas Gómez 25)*, Lusitans 0
Lusitans 0, Sant Julià 2 *(Romero 33, 76)*
(Sant Julià 3-0)

UE Santa Coloma 3 *(Sirvan 45+1, Bernat 72, Rodríguez V. 90)*, Principat 1 *(Nuevo 62)*
Principat 3 *(Àlex Montoto 12, Àlex Godoy 29, 52p)*, UE Santa Coloma 2 *(Àlex Martínez 25, Gerard Aloy 61)*
(UE Santa Coloma 5-4)

FINAL

(16/5/10)
Aixovall Stadium, Andorra la Vella
UE SANT JULIÀ 1 *(Sebas Gómez 82)*
UE SANTA COLOMA 0
Referee – Sanchez
SANT JULIÀ – Burgos, Wagner, Fontan, Matamala, Xinos, Vítor Pinto (Bernales 90+2), Romero, Peppe, Sebas Gómez, Nastri, Varela.
UE SANTA COLOMA – Rivas, Nieto, Àlex Martínez, Sirvan, Gerard Aloy, Rodríguez V., Lafoz, Rodríguez X., Bernat, Luis Miguel, Rubio.

ARMENIA

Pyunik complete decade of dominance

F C Pyunik's domination of Armenian domestic football during the first decade of the 21st century was sustained through to the end as they captured their ninth successive Armenian championship title.

Unlike in 2008, when they had been taken to extra time in a title play-off by city rivals FC Ararat Yerevan (who slumped alarmingly in 2009 and were relegated), Pyunik retained their crown in comparative tranquility, finishing the 28-match campaign seven points clear of FC Mika after overcoming their closest pursuers 4-0 at home on the final day. The title had been secured six days earlier with a 3-1 win at FC Shirak in which teenaged striker Albert Tadevosyan, the double-goalscoring hero of the Golden Match against Ararat 12 months earlier, bagged a hat-trick.

Scoring burst

It was Tadevosyan's burst of scoring in the closing weeks – he registered ten goals in as many games – that helped to ensure a repeat triumph for Pyunik in coach Vardan Minasyan's first full season in charge. Minasyan had taken over as coach in July 2008, replacing Armen Gyulbudaghyants, and although he led the team to victory in the 2009 Armenian Independence Cup final, a narrow 1-0 win over FC Banants, a stuttering run of form during the middle section of the Premier League campaign, coupled with an early exit from the UEFA Champions League qualifying competition against NK Dinamo Zagreb (0-3 on aggregate), led to some uncertainty about his position – not least because he was also doubling up at the time as the interim head coach of the Armenian national team.

Back-to-back away defeats against Mika and Banants in September left both Minasyan and Pyunik in a position of vulnerability, but they regrouped and responded to the crisis in championship-winning style with victories in each of their last six matches. By the close of the campaign their superiority was once again borne out by the statistics – 20 wins in 28 matches,

Pyunik defender Sargis Hovsepyan – a valuable veteran for club and country

only three defeats (none at home) and the best attack (64 goals) and defence (13) in the division.

The champions' top scorer was 20-year-old Armenian international striker Henrikh Mkhitaryan, who plundered 11 goals in the early weeks of the season, including two hat-tricks, before moving to Ukrainian club FC Metalurh Donetsk. His departure hit Pyunik hard, but the recruitment of naturalised Brazilian striker Marcos Pizelli from Ararat (after a loan spell in France) eventually filled the void as he, in tandem with Tadevosyan, struck a rich vein of form in the run-in. Pyunik's top performer over the whole campaign, however, was captain Sargis Hovsepyan, who turned 37 a day after the title win – a veteran in a team stocked chiefly with up-and-coming talents in the embryonic phase of their careers.

Cup retained

Pyunik gave a firm indication to their rivals that the onset of a new decade would not diminish their powers when Minasyan's young, vibrant team retained the domestic cup in 2010, again overcoming Banants in the final, this time by a resounding 4-0 margin with goals from David Manoyan, Marcos and Gevorg Ghazaryan (two).

It was Banants' fourth Cup final appearance in as many years and their third successive defeat in the fixture. Their presence in the final once again ensured their European qualification, putting them into the 2010/11 UEFA Europa League alongside Premier League runners-up Mika and the team that had surprisingly beaten them to third place, Ulisses FC.

Led by coach Sevada Arzumanyan, Ulisses increased their points tally from 29 in 2008 to 53 in 2009, rising three places in the process and thereby reaching the highest position in their history. Although they won none of their eight games against the two teams that finished above them, the club formerly known as Dinamo-Zenit FC had the distinction of being the only team in the division to score away to Pyunik (a feat they achieved three times). They also possessed the Premier League's top scorer in 15-goal veteran striker Artur Kocharyan and the player of the year in towering 23-year-old centre-back Hrayr Mkoyan.

Only victory

There was a first call-up for Mkoyan to the Armenian national team in September 2009, and the Ulisses youngster enjoyed a memorable debut alongside old-timer Hovsepyan in central defence as Armenia recorded their only win of the 2010 FIFA World Cup qualifying campaign, defeating Belgium 2-1 in Yerevan. Team captain Hovsepyan, on his record 107th international appearance, scored the winning goal – only his second for Armenia – and would go on to become his country's only ever present during the 2009/10 season, appearing from start to finish in all seven matches and extending his all-time cap record to 111.

Despite the disappointment of seeing his team finish bottom of their World Cup qualifying group, Minasyan, who had overseen the final five fixtures, was confirmed as Armenia's coach for the UEFA EURO 2012 qualifiers. Grouped alongside Russia, Slovakia, the Republic of Ireland, FYR Macedonia and Andorra, Armenia were scheduled to begin their campaign at home to the Irish on 3 September 2010.

Buoyed by that World Cup win over Belgium, a subsequent 2-1 home defeat by European champions Spain and a May 2010 friendly success against Uzbekistan (3-1), in which the great hope of Armenian football, striker Edgar Manucharyan, re-emerged with a couple of goals, Minasyan and his team will hope to claim another prized scalp or two on the road to Poland/Ukraine.

Hayastani Futboli Federacia (HFF)

Khanjyan Street 27
AM-0010 Yerevan
tel – +374 10 568883
fax – +374 10 547173
website – ffa.am
email – media@ffa.am
Year of Formation – 1992

President – Ruben Hayrapetyan
General Secretary – Armen Minasyan
Media Officer – Tigran Israelyan
National Stadium – Hanrapetakan, Yerevan (14,403)

TOP FIVE ALL-TIME CAPS
Sargis Hovsepyan (111); Artur Petrosyan (69); Harutyun Vardanyan (63); Roman Berezovski (59); Hamlet Mkhitaryan (56)
TOP FIVE ALL-TIME GOALS
Artur Petrosyan (11); Ara Hakobyan (7); Armen Shahgeldyan (6); Arman Karamyan (5); Robert Arzumanyan, Edgar Manucharyan & Tigran Yessayan (4)

NATIONAL TEAM RESULTS 2009/10

12/8/09	Moldova	H	Yerevan	1-4	Arakelyan (75)
5/9/09	Bosnia-Herzegovina (WCQ)	H	Yerevan	0-2	
9/9/09	Belgium (WCQ)	H	Yerevan	2-1	Goharyan (22), Hovsepyan (51)
10/10/09	Spain (WCQ)	H	Yerevan	1-2	Arzumanyan (58)
14/10/09	Turkey (WCQ)	A	Bursa	0-2	
3/3/10	Belarus	N	Antalya (TUR)	1-3	Pachajyan (59)
25/5/10	Uzbekistan	H	Yerevan	3-1	Mkhitaryan (7), Manucharyan (18p, 28)

NATIONAL TEAM APPEARANCES 2009/10

Coach – Vardan MINASYAN	5/1/74		Mda	BIH	BEL	ESP	TUR	Blr	Uzb	Caps	Goals
Gevorg KASPAROV	25/7/80	Ulisses	G	G	G					17	-
Vahagn MINASYAN	25/4/85	Pyunik	D	s66					D 76*	12	1
Sargis HOVSEPYAN	2/11/72	Pyunik	D	D	D	D	D	D	D	111	2
Alexander TADEVOSYAN	9/8/80	Mika	D	D				D		41	-
Aghvan MKRTCHYAN	27/2/81	Mika	D	D	D	D	D	D		44	-
Edgar MALAKYAN	22/9/90	Pyunik	M46						s88	2	-
David Zh. GRIGORYAN	28/12/82	Ulisses	M84							9	-
Ararat ARAKELYAN	1/2/84	Metalurh Donetsk (UKR) /Banants	M90	M66	M14	s74	M58	M46		28	2
Henrikh MKHITARYAN	21/1/89	Metalurh Donetsk (UKR)	M	M	M		M		M79	15	2
Yeghia YAVRUYAN	18/10/81	M. Tel-Aviv (ISR)	A58	A46	s32			s78		4	-
MARCOS Pizelli Pinheiro	3/10/84	Pyunik	A54			A66	s58	A71	s51	7	1
David MANOYAN	5/7/90	Pyunik	s46						s56	3	-
Hovhannes GOHARYAN	18/3/88	BATE (BLR)	s54	s46	A32	A60	A46			5	1
Hiraç YAGAN	3/1/89	Standard (BEL)	s58	s76						2	-
Artur YEDIGARYAN	26/6/87	Pyunik /PAS Hamedan (IRN)	s84	M76	M89	M74		s46	M56	11	-
Edvard KAKOSYAN	4/6/86	Banants	s90		s89		s77			3	-
Robert ARZUMANYAN	24/7/85	Randers (DEN)		D	D	D	D	D		42	4
Arman KARAMYAN	14/11/79	Timişoara (ROU) /Steaua (ROU)		M	M	M	M77	s88		48	5
Artavazd KARAMYAN	14/11/79	Timişoara (ROU) /Steaua (ROU)		M	M	M	M	M46		50	2
Hrayr MKOYAN	2/9/86	Ulisses / Mika			D	D	D	D		4	-
Karlen MKRTCHYAN	25/11/88	Pyunik			s14	M	M	M46	M	9	-
Roman BEREZOVSKI	5/8/74	Khimki (RUS)				G	G	G		59	-
Samvel MELKONYAN	15/3/84	Banants				s60	s46	s46	s60	28	-
Artak DASHYAN	20/11/89	Banants				s66				2	-
Levon PACHAJYAN	20/9/83	Sanat Naft (IRN)						M88	M60	33	2
Edgar MANUCHARYAN	19/1/87	AGOVV (NED)						A78	A51	22	4
Artak ALEKSANYAN	10/3/91	Ural (RUS)						s46		1	-
Artur VOSKANYAN	13/8/76	Banants						s71		52	1
Stepan GHAZARYAN	11/1/85	Banants							G	1	-
Artak YEDIGARYAN	18/3/90	Pyunik							D	1	-
Gevorg GHAZARYAN	5/4/88	Pyunik							A88	12	1
Artur YUSBASHYAN	7/9/89	Pyunik							s79	1	-

DOMESTIC LEAGUE 2009

PREMIER LEAGUE FINAL TABLE

		Pld	Home					Away					Total					Pts
			W	D	L	F	A	W	D	L	F	A	W	D	L	F	A	
1	FC Pyunik	28	12	2	0	37	3	8	3	3	27	10	20	5	3	64	13	65
2	FC Mika	28	11	2	1	37	12	7	2	5	22	22	18	4	6	59	34	58
3	Ulisses FC	28	8	2	4	26	13	8	3	3	21	12	16	5	7	47	25	53
4	FC Banants	28	7	2	5	23	15	6	3	5	17	14	13	5	10	40	29	44
5	FC Gandzasar Kapan	28	7	0	7	21	23	5	2	7	11	24	12	2	14	32	47	38
6	FC Shirak	28	3	6	5	11	16	2	2	10	13	39	5	8	15	24	55	23
7	FC Kilikia	28	4	3	7	14	22	1	2	11	8	29	5	5	18	22	51	20
8	FC Ararat Yerevan	28	1	4	9	10	25	1	4	9	10	29	2	8	18	20	54	14

TOP GOALSCORERS

15 Artur KOCHARYAN (Ulisses)
14 Arsen AVETISYAN (Gandzasar)
   Boti DEMEL (Mika)
12 Samvel MELKONYAN (Banants)
11 Artyom ADAMYAN (Ulisses)
   Henrikh MKHITARYAN (Pyunik)
10 Aram VOSKANYAN (Mika)
   Albert TADEVOSYAN (Pyunik)
9 MARCOS (Pyunik)
8 Andranik BARIKYAN (Shirak)

CLUB-BY-CLUB

FC ARARAT YEREVAN

Coach – Ashot Kirakosyan; (12/4/09) Albert Safaryan
Founded – 1935
Stadium – City, Abovyan (5,500)
MAJOR HONOURS:
USSR League - (1) 1973; Armenian League - (1) 1993; USSR Cup - (2) 1973, 1975 ; Armenian Cup - (5) 1993, 1994, 1995, 1997, 2008.

2009

22/3	Shirak	a	0-1	
4/4	Kilikia	h	0-2	
11/4	Mika	a	0-2	
18/4	Pyunik	h	0-2	
26/4	Banants	a	0-1	
3/5	Gandzasar	h	0-2	
10/5	Ulisses	h	0-1	
17/5	Shirak	h	1-3	*Erzrumyan S.*
24/5	Kilikia	a	2-3	*Petrosyan G. 2*
31/5	Mika	h	0-1	
14/6	Banants	h	0-3	*(w/o; original result 0-2)*
20/6	Gandzasar	a	0-1	
27/6	Ulisses	a	0-3	
7/7	Pyunik	a	0-0	
25/7	Shirak	a	2-2	*Grigoryan A., Tsiganenko*
1/8	Kilikia	h	1-1	*Nranyan (p)*
7/8	Mika	a	1-5	*Petrosyan A.*
16/8	Pyunik	h	1-0	*Nranyan*
23/8	Banants	a	0-0	
30/8	Gandzasar	h	1-2	*Grigoryan A.*
12/9	Ulisses	h	1-1	*Avoyan*
19/9	Shirak	h	2-4	*Rajab, Safaryan R.*
28/9	Kilikia	a	0-0	
4/10	Mika	h	2-2	*Avoyan, Minasyan (p)*
20/10	Pyunik	a	0-6	
25/10	Banants	h	1-1	*Harkusha*
1/11	Gandzasar	a	3-2	*Harkusha, Hovhannisyan Ara 2*
7/11	Ulisses	a	2-3	*Avoyan 2*

No	Name	Nat	DoB	Pos	Aps	(s)	Gls
21	Karen AVOYAN		22/8/86	M	9	(2)	4
4	Arkadi CHILINGARYAN		9/5/79	D	9		
10	Nshan ERZRUMYAN		17/12/79	A	3		
9	Sergei ERZRUMYAN		22/11/80	M	12	(1)	1
14	Artak G. GRIGORYAN		19/10/87	D	21	(3)	2
8	David G. GRIGORYAN		17/7/89	M	13	(8)	
21	Roman HARKUSHA	BLR	2/6/84	M	10		2
11	Ara HOVHANNISYAN		13/9/86	A	5	(7)	2
14	Artak HOVHANNISYAN		8/9/88	M		(1)	
22	Gevorg KARAPETYAN		10/6/90	A	5	(7)	
13	Vachagan KARAPETYAN		12/3/83	D	7	(2)	
2	Giorgi KRASOVSKI	GEO	20/12/79	M	23	(2)	
3	Narek MACHKALYAN		31/5/91	M		(6)	
19	Gor MARTIROSYAN		18/2/91	D		(4)	
20	Vahe MEHRABYAN		25/8/86	D	6	(2)	
12	David MELIKSETYAN		1/2/89	M	1	(5)	
18	Virab MEYTIKHANYAN		25/9/81	D	16	(1)	
1	Jeofak MILLER	GHA	12/8/85	G	1	(1)	
17	Artur H. MINASYAN		4/6/77	M	21	(4)	1
5	Sargis MOVSISYAN		10/7/84	A	4	(2)	
19	Jugoslav MUNISEVIĆ	SRB	11/9/89	M	1	(4)	
14	Semyon MURADYAN		21/3/88	A		(2)	
6	Karen NAVOYAN		10/8/79	M	4	(5)	
17	Gevorg NRANYAN		9/3/86	A	18	(4)	2
22	Goran OBRADOVIĆ	SRB	25/12/86	M	11		
18	Artur PETROSYAN		15/6/83	D	20	(1)	1
10	Galust PETROSYAN		5/9/81	A	9	(3)	2
21	Vardan PETROSYAN		27/2/82	M	9		
12	Sergei POLTOVETS	RUS	11/4/81	M	3	(1)	
33	Gevorg PRAZYAN		24/7/89	G	22		
15	Khaled RAJAB	IRN	1/1/87	A	4		1
20	Edgar SAFARYAN		26/5/78	A	2	(2)	
6	Rafayel SAFARYAN		30/1/86	M	10	(2)	1
3	Dejan SAINOVIĆ	SRB	15/3/90	D	6	(2)	
16	Nikolai SARGSYAN		9/5/81	G	5		
12	Andranik TADEVOSYAN		2/3/85	D		(1)	
8	Valeri TSIGANENKO	BLR	21/7/81	A	10	(1)	1
4	Bidzina TSINTSADZE	GEO	4/6/89	D	7	(1)	
22	Ara VOSKANYAN		1/1/78	M	1	(1)	

ARMENIA

FC BANANTS

Coach – Armen Gyulbudaghyants
Founded - 1992
Stadium – Nairi (2,000)
MAJOR HONOURS:
Armenian Cup - (2) 1992, 2007.

2009

22/3	Pyunik	a	0-1
4/4	Gandzasar	h	1-0 *Melkonyan*
11/4	Shirak	a	2-1 *Melkonyan, Kakosyan*
19/4	Mika	a	3-2 *Kavatsiv, Balabekyan, Melkonyan*
26/4	Ararat	h	1-0 *Dashyan (p)*
3/5	Ulisses	a	1-0 *Oseyan*
13/5	Kilikia	h	3-0 *Gyozalyan, Nasibyan, Stepanyan*
17/5	Pyunik	h	1-4 *Dashyan*
24/5	Gandzasar	a	1-2 *Dashyan*
30/5	Shirak	h	5-1 *Dashyan, Oseyan, Kavatsiv, Stepanyan, Ohanyan G.K.*
14/6	Ararat	a	3-0 *(w/o; original result 2-0 Gevorgyan, Melkonyan)*
17/6	Mika	h	1-2 *Oseyan*
21/6	Ulisses	h	1-3 *Nasibyan*
27/6	Kilikia	a	2-0 *Gyozalyan, Melkonyan*
2/8	Gandzasar	h	0-1
7/8	Shirak	a	0-0
15/8	Mika	h	2-1 *Gyozalyan, Melkonyan*
19/8	Pyunik	a	0-1
23/8	Ararat	h	0-0
29/8	Ulisses	a	0-1
12/9	Kilikia	h	5-0 *Melkonyan, Balabekyan, Gevorgyan, Oseyan 2*
20/9	Pyunik	h	1-0 *Melkonyan*
26/9	Gandzasar	a	2-1 *Melkonyan 2*
3/10	Shirak	h	0-0
20/10	Mika	a	1-3 *Melkonyan*
25/10	Ararat	a	1-1 *Balabekyan*
1/11	Ulisses	h	2-3 *Gyozalyan, Melkonyan (p)*
7/11	Kilikia	a	1-1 *Hambartsumyan*

No	Name	Nat	DoB	Pos	Aps	(s)	Gls
11	Arsen BALABEKYAN		24/11/86	A	18	(2)	3
7	Aram BAREGHAMYAN		1/6/88	M	12	(3)	
3	Gagik DAGHBASHYAN		19/10/90	D	10	(2)	
9	Artak DASHYAN		20/11/89	M	16	(3)	4
8	Hrant GEVORGYAN		20/7/88	A	12	(5)	2
22	Stepan GHAZARYAN		11/1/85	G	23		
20	Hovhannes GRIGORYAN		9/3/85	D	8		
18	Norayr GYOZALYAN		15/3/90	A	11	(8)	4
19	Hovhannes HAMBARTSUMYAN		4/10/90	D	10	(5)	1
4	Aghvan HAYRAPETYAN		19/1/87	M	2	(4)	
15	Edvard KAKOSYAN		4/6/86	D	23		1
17	Sargis KARAPETYAN		24/4/90	M	9	(1)	
13	Noah Babadi KASULE	UGA	5/5/85	M	22		
2	Yarema KAVATSIV	UKR	10/2/86	D	12		2
12	Grisha KHACHATRYAN		1/3/92	D	12	(4)	
23	Oleg KHROMTSOV	RUS	8/7/86	M	1	(1)	
21	Samvel MELKONYAN		15/3/84	A	25		12
9	Hamlet MKHITARYAN		24/11/73	M	9	(1)	
14	Sargis NASIBYAN		7/7/90	D	9	(6)	2
4	Dmytro NAZARENKO	UKR	14/9/87	D	14		
22	Gevorg H. OHANYAN		31/3/92	A		(4)	
16	Gevorg K. OHANYAN		29/1/92	M		(11)	1
10	Artak OSEYAN		16/5/87	M	11	(12)	5
1	Oleh OSTAPENKO	UKR	27/10/77	G	4		
17	Argishti PETROSYAN		16/10/92	M		(1)	
16	Valter PETROSYAN		16/5/92	M		(5)	
6	Volodymyr ROMANENKO	UKR	8/6/85	M	10	(2)	
16	Nikolai SARGSYAN		9/5/81	G	1		
5	ZhoraSTEPANYAN		31/1/91	M	2	(23)	2
8	Artur VOSKANYAN		13/8/76	D	22		

FC GANDZASAR KAPAN

Coach – Samvel Petrosyan; (12/4/09) Avetik Sargsyan;
(20/5/09) Slava Gabrielyan
Founded - 2004
Stadium – Kapan City (5,500)

2009

22/3	Mika	h	0-2
4/4	Banants	a	0-1
11/4	Ulisses	h	1-2 *Avetisyan*
18/4	Kilikia	a	1-2 *Avetisyan*
26/4	Pyunik	h	0-4
3/5	Ararat	a	2-0 *Tatintsyan (p), Davtyan*
10/5	Shirak	h	0-0
16/5	Mika	a	0-2
24/5	Banants	h	2-1 *Davtyan, Avagyan*
31/5	Ulisses	a	0-5
7/6	Kilikia	h	1-0 *Marşavela*
13/6	Pyunik	a	0-0
20/6	Ararat	h	1-0 *Avetisyan*
27/6	Shirak	h	2-1 *Avetisyan 2*
27/7	Mika	h	3-1 *og (Poghosyan G.), Simonyan, Sakhokia*
2/8	Banants	a	1-0 *Avetisyan*
7/8	Ulisses	h	0-3
15/8	Kilikia	a	1-0 *Davtyan*
23/8	Pyunik	h	0-2
30/8	Ararat	a	2-1 *Khachatryan A., Sakhokia*
12/9	Shirak	a	1-2 *Erzrumyan*
19/9	Mika	a	1-3 *Marşavela*
27/9	Banants	h	1-2 *Davtyan*
4/10	Ulisses	a	2-1 *Avetisyan, Marşavela*
20/10	Kilikia	h	4-1 *Avetisyan 2, Davtyan 2*
25/10	Pyunik	a	0-7
1/11	Ararat	h	2-3 *Avetisyan 2*
7/11	Shirak	h	4-1 *Avetisyan 3, Badoyan*

No	Name	Nat	DoB	Pos	Aps	(s)	Gls
6	Valeri ALEKSANYAN		4/9/84	D	24		
5	Artashes ANTONYAN		15/1/80	M	15	(1)	
18	Hayrapet AVAGYAN		8/5/89	D	4	(11)	1
20	Arsen AVETISYAN		8/10/73	A	23	(1)	14
22	Zaven BADOYAN		22/12/89	M	7	(8)	1
1	Levan BUBUTEISHVILI	GEO	14/7/83	G	24		
11	Vahe DAVTYAN		17/8/83	M	21	(4)	6
18	Sergei ERZRUMYAN		22/11/80	M	14		1
22	Dragan GALIĆ	SRB	20/9/82	A	1	(3)	
7	Hakob GHAZARYAN		27/4/90	D		(2)	
5	Arman GRIGORYAN		20/10/92	D		(2)	
16	Alen HAMBARTSUMYAN		1/3/92	M		(5)	
14	Aghvan HAYRAPETYAN		19/1/87	M	1	(6)	
23	Ara KHACHATRYAN		21/10/81	D	24	(1)	1
14	Romik KHACHATRYAN		23/8/78	M	1	(1)	
24	David KHANISHVILI	GEO	27/4/82	M	22	(1)	
7	Koba KHANISHVILI	GEO	4/2/85	M	3	(3)	
11	Milan KRIVOKAPICH	MKD	1/7/81	M		(1)	
8	LEANDRO Santos Pinto	BRA	3/5/81	M	12	(1)	
33	Vladimir LUKIĆ	SRB	12/6/86	G	3		
9	Beniamin MANUCHARYAN		2/1/81	A	8	(8)	
2	Virgil MARŞAVELA	ROU	10/3/74	M	14	(6)	3
10	Alexander PETROSYAN		28/5/86	A	3		
15	Vladan RADOVANOVIĆ	SRB	20/1/85	M	2		
30	Zaza SAKHOKIA	GEO	12/2/84	A	4	(7)	2
8	Andranik SARGSYAN		7/3/85	M	10	(3)	
4	Mikhel SIMONYAN		29/7/87	D	26	(1)	1
32	Gor TADEVOSYAN		30/4/87	G	1		
13	Armen TATINTSYAN		4/10/81	D	18	(1)	1
15	Suren VOSKANYAN		26/8/90	D		(2)	
2	Artashes ZAKARYAN		29/11/87	D		(3)	
25	Karen ZAKARYAN		28/1/78	D	23		

ARMENIA

FC KILIKIA

Coach – Abraham Khashmanyan
Founded - 1992
Stadium - Hrazdan (55,000)

2009

21/3	Ulisses	h	0-1	
4/4	Ararat	a	2-0	Sargsyan A. (p), Mkrtchyan R.
11/4	Pyunik	a	0-1	
18/4	Gandzasar	h	2-1	Khachatryan K. (p), Gharabaghtsyan
25/4	Shirak	a	1-3	Movsisyan G.
2/5	Mika	h	1-2	Gharabaghtsyan
13/5	Banants	a	0-3	
17/5	Ulisses	a	0-1	
24/5	Ararat	h	3-2	Gharabaghtsyan, Mkrtchyan R. 2 (2p)
30/5	Pyunik	h	1-3	Gharabaghtsyan
7/6	Gandzasar	a	0-1	
14/6	Shirak	h	1-1	Mkrtchyan R.
20/6	Mika	a	1-2	Mkrtchyan R. (p)
27/6	Banants	h	0-2	
26/7	Ulisses	h	0-3	
1/8	Ararat	a	1-1	Khachatryan K.
7/8	Pyunik	a	0-1	
15/8	Gandzasar	h	0-1	
22/8	Shirak	a	1-1	Mkrtchyan H.
30/8	Mika	h	3-2	Movsisyan S., Khachatryan K. 2
12/9	Banants	a	0-5	
20/9	Ulisses	a	0-4	
28/9	Ararat	h	0-0	
3/10	Pyunik	h	0-3	
20/10	Gandzasar	a	1-4	Khachatryan K.
25/10	Shirak	h	2-0	Movsisyan S., Khachatryan K.
1/11	Mika	a	1-2	Minasyan
7/11	Banants	h	1-1	Movsisyan S.

No	Name	Nat	DoB	Pos	Aps	(s)	Gls
22	Artashes ARAKELYAN		11/2/85	D	26		
20	Artyom ARAKELYAN		11/2/85	M	17	(2)	
9	Artur AVAGYAN		4/7/87	M	20	(1)	
2	Vahagn GEVORGYAN		4/8/88	D	15	(6)	
24	Tigran GHARABAGHTSYAN		6/6/84	A	18	(7)	4
3	Avetis GHAZARYAN		2/8/90	D	18	(2)	
12	Ashot GRIGORYAN		5/10/79	D	12		
8	Grigor GRIGORYAN		28/10/80	M	24		
13	Mkhitar GRIGORYAN		20/2/86	M	10	(3)	
19	Tigran GRIGORYAN		22/3/91	M	3		
25	Roman HOVHANNISYAN		28/8/91	M	7	(10)	
77	Armen KHACHATRYAN		25/4/84	G	22		
17	Karen N. KHACHATRYAN		10/6/85	A	21	(5)	6
26	Gegham KOCHARYAN		27/3/85	D	8	(5)	
18	Artur S. MINASYAN		9/8/78	M	5	(5)	1
10	Hayk MKRTCHYAN		5/11/89	A	9	(10)	1
11	Rafayel MKRTCHYAN		4/1/85	A	18	(7)	5
1	Martik MKRTUMYAN		4/3/85	G	6		
14	Grigor MOVSISYAN		27/7/89	A	3	(7)	1
7	Sargis MOVSISYAN		10/7/84	A	9	(1)	3
4	Andranik SARGSYAN		7/3/85	M	10		1
23	Suren SARGSYAN		15/3/84	A	4	(5)	
16	Vladimir STEPANYAN		7/8/84	D	22	(1)	
6	Hrach YEGHIAZARYAN		8/11/92	M	1	(1)	

FC MIKA

Coach – Ivo Šušak (CRO); (27/4/09) Samvel Darbinyan;
(1/9/09) Babken Melikyan
Founded - 1997
Stadium - Mika (8,000)
MAJOR HONOURS:
Armenian Cup - (5) 2000, 2001, 2003, 2005, 2006.

2009

22/3	Gandzasar	a	2-0	Demel 2
5/4	Shirak	h	3-2	Hakobyan A. 2, Alex
11/4	Ararat	h	2-0	Demel 2
19/4	Banants	h	2-3	Voskanyan 2
26/4	Ulisses	h	0-0	
2/5	Kilikia	a	2-1	Ednei, Voskanyan
13/5	Pyunik	h	2-2	Ednei, Demel
16/5	Gandzasar	h	2-0	Voskanyan, Hakobyan S.
24/5	Shirak	a	4-0	Voskanyan, Demel 2, Petrosyan
31/5	Ararat	a	1-0	Demel
13/6	Ulisses	h	2-1	Voskanyan 2
17/6	Banants	a	2-1	Demel, Montenegro
20/6	Kilikia	h	2-1	Alex, Hakobyan A.
28/6	Pyunik	a	0-3	
27/7	Gandzasar	a	1-3	Hakobyan A.
2/8	Shirak	h	7-0	Voskanyan 2, Hakobyan A. 2, Fursin, Beglaryan 2 (1p)
7/8	Ararat	h	5-1	Montenegro 2, Voskanyan, Hakobyan A., Beglaryan
15/8	Banants	a	1-2	Demel
22/8	Ulisses	h	2-0	Demel, Ednei
30/8	Kilikia	a	2-3	Alex, Tadevosyan
14/9	Pyunik	h	2-0	Alex, Tadevosyan (p)
19/9	Gandzasar	h	3-1	Ednei, Montenegro 2
26/9	Shirak	h	1-0	Montenegro (p)
4/10	Ararat	a	2-2	Montenegro, Demel
20/10	Banants	h	3-1	Ednei, Demel, Beglaryan
24/10	Ulisses	a	2-2	Beglaryan, Alex
1/11	Kilikia	h	2-1	Demel, Ednei
7/11	Pyunik	a	0-4	

No	Name	Nat	DoB	Pos	Aps	(s)	Gls
22	ALEX Henrique da Silva	BRA	6/1/82	D	24		5
25	Armen AVAGYAN		5/2/90	M		(2)	
10	Narek BEGLARYAN		1/9/85	A	4	(18)	5
9	Boti DEMEL	CIV	3/3/89	A	24		14
15	EDNEI Fereira de Oliveira	BRA	30/11/85	M	23	(2)	6
4	Nikita FURSIN	RUS	9/3/83	D	17		1
1	Soso GRISHIKASHVILI	GEO	25/12/73	G	19		
17	Ara HAKOBYAN		4/11/80	A	15	(5)	7
81	Felix HAKOBYAN		11/3/81	G	2		
3	Stepan HAKOBYAN		21/1/85	D	11	(6)	1
14	Vigen HAMBARTSUMYAN		14/1/87	M		(8)	
12	Artur HARUTYUNYAN		8/12/85	G	7	(2)	
24	Hayk ISHKHANYAN		24/6/89	M		(1)	
11	Hrachya MIKAYELYAN		9/1/75	D	18	(5)	
7	Aghvan MKRTCHYAN		27/2/81	D	17	(1)	
8	Ulisses Kano MONTENEGRO	ESP	5/5/83	M	23	(3)	7
19	Maksim MOROZOV	RUS	28/9/78	M	2	(13)	
6	PEDRO Jesús LÓPEZ Pérez de Tudela	ESP	25/8/83	M	24		
2	Armen PETROSYAN		26/9/85	M	19	(3)	1
13	Gevorg POGHOSYAN		26/8/86	D	24	(3)	
21	Mikael POGHOSYAN		25/1/91	M		(2)	
18	Alexander TADEVOSYAN		9/8/80	D	11		2
16	Manoel de Souza "THIAGO"	BRA	20/10/84	M		(1)	
23	Irakli TSANAVA	GEO	28/10/85	M	6	(4)	
20	Aram VOSKANYAN		28/8/75	A	18	(4)	10

ARMENIA

FC PYUNIK
Coach – Vardan Minasyan
Founded - 1992
Stadium – Hanrapetakan (14,403) & Nairi (2,000)
MAJOR HONOURS:
Armenian League - (12) 1992 (shared), 1996, 1997, 2001, 2002, 2003, 2004,
2005, 2006, 2007, 2008, 2009;
Armenian Cup – (5) 1996 , 2002, 2004, 2009, 2010.

2009

22/3	Banants	h	1-0	Mkhitaryan
4/4	Ulisses	a	3-0	og (Grigoryan D.), Mkhitaryan, Malakyan
11/4	Kilikia	h	1-0	Ghazaryan
18/4	Ararat	a	2-0	Yedigaryan Artur, Manasyan
26/4	Gandzasar	a	4-0	Mkhitaryan 3, Ghazaryan
2/5	Shirak	h	4-0	Hovsepyan S. (p), Ghazaryan, Manasyan 2
13/5	Mika	a	2-2	Yedigaryan Artur, Mkhitaryan
17/5	Banants	a	4-1	Malakyan, Mkhitaryan 3
23/5	Ulisses	h	3-2	Ghazaryan, Mkhitaryan 2
30/5	Kilikia	a	3-1	Yedigaryan Artak, Aleksanyan, Manasyan
13/6	Gandzasar	h	0-0	
21/6	Shirak	a	0-0	
28/6	Mika	h	3-0	Ghazaryan 2, Mkrtchyan
7/7	Ararat	h	0-0	
1/8	Ulisses	a	1-1	Marcos
7/8	Kilikia	h	1-0	Hovsepyan S. (p)
16/8	Ararat	a	0-1	
19/8	Banants	h	1-0	Mkrtchyan
23/8	Gandzasar	a	2-0	Tadevosyan, Hovakimyan
29/8	Shirak	h	4-0	Tadevosyan, Hovsepyan S. (p), Manoyan, Sahakyan
14/9	Mika	a	0-2	
20/9	Banants	a	0-1	
27/9	Ulisses	h	2-1	Tadevosyan, Marcos
3/10	Kilikia	a	3-0	Malakyan, Marcos 2
20/10	Ararat	h	6-0	Yedigaryan Artur 2, Yedigaryan Artak 2, Manoyan, Tadevosyan
25/10	Gandzasar	h	7-0	Marcos 2, Tadevosyan 2, Hovsepyan S. 2 (2p), Ghazaryan
1/11	Shirak	a	3-1	Tadevosyan 3
7/11	Mika	h	4-0	Marcos 3, Tadevosyan

No	Name	Nat	DoB	Pos	Aps	(s)	Gls
91	Artak ALEKSANYAN		10/3/91	M	12	(12)	1
24	Artak ANDRIKYAN		24/1/88	D	7	(1)	
25	Vahe GHASABOGHLYAN		7/2/91	A		(1)	
8	Gevorg GHAZARYAN		5/4/88	M	14	(6)	7
20	Varazdat HAROYAN		24/8/92	D		(5)	
22	Albert HOVAKIMYAN		16/9/91	M		(6)	1
99	Edvard HOVHANNISYAN		28/2/90	G	10		
29	Kamo HOVHANNISYAN		5/10/92	M		(4)	
81	Aram HOVSEPYAN		6/6/91	A		(1)	
4	Sargis HOVSEPYAN		2/11/72	D	26		5
3	Karen V. KHACHATRYAN		22/4/88	D	17		
9	Edgar MALAKYAN		22/9/90	A	24		3
14	Mihran MANASYAN		13/1/89	A	2	(5)	4
11	David MANOYAN		5/7/90	A	19	(5)	2
10	MARCOS Pizelli Pinheiro		3/10/84	A	10	(2)	9
23	Emmanuel MBOLA	ZAM	10/5/93	D	22	(1)	
1	Grigor MELIKSETYAN		18/8/86	G	18		
16	Vahagn MINASYAN		25/4/85	D	26		
22	Henrikh MKHITARYAN		21/1/89	A	8	(2)	11
6	Karlen MKRTCHYAN		25/11/88	M	17	(1)	2
	Gagik POGHOSYAN		4/5/93	M		(1)	
77	Norayr SAHAKYAN		7/10/87	M	15	(9)	1
19	Albert TADEVOSYAN		13/9/90	D	9	(12)	10
20	Marcos Gabriel TORRES	ARG	8/2/86	D	1		

17	Artak YEDIGARYAN		18/3/90	D	6	(14)	3
5	Artur YEDIGARYAN		26/6/87	M	22	(2)	4
15	Artur YUSBASHYAN		7/9/79	M	23	(2)	

FC SHIRAK
Coach – Zhora Barseghyan; (27/5/09) Vardan Bichakhchyan
Founded - 1958
Stadium - Gyumri City (8,500)
MAJOR HONOURS:
Armenian League - (3) 1992 (shared), 1994, 1999.

2009

22/3	Ararat	h	1-0	Barikyan
5/4	Mika	a	2-3	Barikyan, Davtyan
11/4	Banants	h	1-2	Khachatryan
18/4	Ulisses	a	0-3	
25/4	Kilikia	h	3-1	Hovhannisyan G., Sargsyan, Nalbandyan
2/5	Pyunik	a	0-4	
10/5	Gandzasar	h	0-0	
17/5	Ararat	a	3-1	Barikyan 3 (1p)
23/5	Mika	h	0-4	
30/5	Banants	a	1-5	Barikyan
6/6	Ulisses	h	0-0	
14/6	Kilikia	a	1-1	Mkrtchyan
21/6	Pyunik	h	0-0	
27/6	Gandzasar	a	1-2	Barikyan
25/7	Ararat	h	2-2	Davtyan, Khachatryan
2/8	Mika	a	0-7	
7/8	Banants	h	0-0	
16/8	Ulisses	a	0-1	
22/8	Kilikia	h	1-1	Khachatryan
29/8	Pyunik	a	0-4	
12/9	Gandzasar	h	2-1	Davtyan 2
19/9	Ararat	a	4-2	Barikyan, Harutyunyan, Mkrtchyan 2
26/9	Mika	h	0-1	
3/10	Banants	a	0-0	
10/10	Ulisses	h	0-1	
25/10	Kilikia	a	0-2	
1/11	Pyunik	h	1-3	og (Minasyan)
7/11	Gandzasar	a	1-4	Davtyan

No	Name	Nat	DoB	Pos	Aps	(s)	Gls
22	Norayr ABRAHAMYAN		30/10/85	G	21		
19	Henrik BADIKYAN		12/2/77	M	12	(7)	
12	Andranik BARIKYAN		11/9/80	M	22		8
5	Tigran DAVTYAN		10/6/78	A	22	(3)	5
4	Hovhannes DEMIRCHYAN		18/5/75	D	20	(1)	
8	Vladimir GASPARYAN		31/8/80	A	2	(14)	
6	Armen GHAZARYAN		30/1/88	D	21	(3)	
3	Artak V. GRIGORYAN		24/4/79	D	1	(3)	
15	Ararat HARUTYUNYAN		24/8/75	M	22	(2)	1
21	Gevorg HOVHANNISYAN		16/6/83	D	22	(2)	1
3	Tigran HOVHANNISYAN		26/11/80	D	7	(1)	
1	Yervand HUNANYAN		10/10/82	G	7		
11	Hayk ISHKHANYAN		24/6/89	M		(4)	
26	Artashes KAGHZVANTSYAN		3/11/87	M		(1)	
14	Karen KARAPETYAN		4/6/87	M		(3)	
7	Karen G. KHACHATRYAN		8/5/81	M	23		3
2	Felix KHOJOYAN		22/12/74	D	26		
18	Ara MKRTCHYAN		3/11/84	A	25	(2)	3
10	Hrachya MNATSAKANYAN		16/12/85	M	13	(4)	
16	Mkrtich NALBANDYAN		5/2/89	A	1	(11)	1
20	Rafayel PALTAJYAN		2/2/84	M	1	(5)	
13	Edvard PANOSYAN		4/2/86	M		(8)	
17	Garnik SARGSYAN		11/3/83	A	18	(5)	1
23	Hovhannes TAHMAZYAN		11/1/70	D	19	(1)	
11	Edvard VARDANYAN		20/6/82	M	3	(6)	

ULISSES FC

Coach – Sevada Arzumanyan
Founded - 2006
Stadium - Hanrapetakan (14,403) & Mika (8,000)

2009

Date	Opponent		Score	Scorers
21/3	Kilikia	a	1-0	Kocharyan
4/4	Pyunik	h	0-3	
11/4	Gandzasar	a	2-1	Kocharyan, Muradyan S.
18/4	Shirak	h	3-0	Kocharyan 2, Muradyan S.
26/4	Mika	a	0-0	
3/5	Banants	h	0-1	
10/5	Ararat	a	1-0	Adamyan
17/5	Kilikia	h	1-0	Mkoyan
23/5	Pyunik	a	2-3	Tbilashvili (p), Mkoyan
31/5	Gandzasar	h	5-0	Adamyan, Tbilashvili, Grigoryan D., og (Khanishvili D.), Hovhannisyan
6/6	Shirak	a	0-0	
13/6	Mika	h	1-2	Tbilashvili
21/6	Banants	a	3-1	Grigoryan D., Kocharyan 2
27/6	Ararat	h	3-0	Adamyan 2, Kocharyan
26/7	Kilikia	a	3-0	Kocharyan, Adamyan 2 (1p)
1/8	Pyunik	h	1-1	Adamyan
7/8	Gandzasar	a	3-0	Kocharyan (p), Adamyan, Petrosyan A.
16/8	Shirak	h	1-0	Kocharyan
22/8	Mika	a	0-2	
29/8	Banants	h	1-0	Tbilashvili
12/9	Ararat	a	1-1	Tbilashvili
20/9	Kilikia	h	4-0	Kocharyan, Adamyan, Muradyan K., Davtyan
27/9	Pyunik	a	1-2	Kocharyan (p)
4/10	Gandzasar	h	1-2	Kocharyan (p)
20/10	Shirak	a	1-0	Petrosyan A.
25/10	Mika	h	2-2	Mkoyan, Kocharyan
1/11	Banants	a	3-2	Adamyan, Tigranyan, Petrosyan A.
7/11	Ararat	h	3-2	og (Safaryan R.), Adamyan, Kocharyan

No	Name	Nat	DoB	Pos	Aps	(s)	Gls
18	Artyom ADAMYAN		2/9/80	M	22	(5)	11
1	Manvel AFRIKYAN		8/8/85	G	11		
23	Levan AKOBIA	GEO	11/2/80	M	25	(1)	
3	Karen ALEKSANYAN		17/6/80	M	12	(2)	
12	Mayis AZIZYAN		1/5/78	G	5		
7	Artur BARSEGHYAN		16/11/86	A	5	(10)	
14	Narek DAVTYAN		24/8/88	M	2	(9)	1
8	David Zh. GRIGORYAN		28/12/82	M	21	(3)	2
5	Norayr GRIGORYAN		7/1/83	D	21	(1)	
15	Tigran HAKHNAZARYAN		18/4/87	D	4	(3)	
9	Martun HAKOBYAN		26/11/90	D		(2)	
18	Henrik HARUTYUNYAN		16/12/91	M		(12)	
11	Ara HOVHANNISYAN		13/9/86	M	8	(3)	1
1	Gevorg KASPAROV		25/7/80	G	12		
19	Gorik KHACHATRYAN		16/6/88	A		(1)	
13	Avetik KIRAKOSYAN		21/6/83	M	2	(3)	
10	Artur KOCHARYAN		14/9/81	A	23	(2)	15
9	Vahe MARTIROSYAN		19/1/88	M	1	(2)	
21	Yeghishe MELIKYAN		13/8/79	M	5	(2)	
15	Hayk MINASYAN		16/10/88	M		(2)	
25	Hrayr MKOYAN		2/9/86	D	27		3
4	Karen MURADYAN		11/8/81	A	16	(4)	1
14	Semyon MURADYAN		21/3/88	A	5	(7)	2
11	Karen NAVOYAN		10/8/79	M	5	(6)	
9	Alexander PETROSYAN		28/5/86	A	2	(8)	3
20	Galust PETROSYAN		5/9/81	A		(1)	
16	Karen STEPANYAN		1/12/85	D	4	(1)	
22	Gaga TBILASHVILI	GEO	1/10/84	A	25	(1)	5
6	Armen TIGRANYAN		16/8/85	M	19		1
17	Tengiz UGREKELIDZE	GEO	29/7/81	D	24		
2	Arkadi YEPREMYAN		10/9/80	D	2	(2)	

PROMOTED CLUB

FC IMPULS

Coach – Varuzhan Sukiasyan
Founded – 2008
Stadium – Dilijan City (2,300)

SECOND LEVEL FINAL TABLE 2009

		Pld	W	D	L	F	A	Pts
1	FC Impuls	24	18	4	2	57	22	58
2	FC Shengavit	24	16	4	4	59	32	52
3	FC Pyunik–2	24	12	4	8	58	30	40
4	FC Banants-2	24	11	3	10	40	26	36
5	FC Gandzasar-2 Kapan	24	11	2	11	42	42	35
6	FC Mika-2	24	10	5	9	36	33	35
7	FC Pyunik–3	24	8	2	14	37	57	26
8	FC Shirak-2	24	4	3	17	21	60	15
9	FC Banants-3	24	3	3	18	22	70	12

DOMESTIC CUP 2010

ARMENIAN INDEPENDENCE CUP

QUARTER-FINALS

(23/3/10 & 6/4/10)
Gandzasar 1 *(Avetisyan 47)*, Ulisses 1 *(Adamyan 78p)*
Ulisses 2 *(Tbilashvili 15, Grigoryan D. 73)*, Gandzasar 0
(Ulisses 3-1)

Pyunik 1 *(Marcos 59)*, Impuls 0
Impuls 0, Pyunik 1 *(Tadevosyan 65)*
(Pyunik 2-0)

(24/3/10 & 7/4/10)
Mika 3 *(Montenegro 20p, Edilson 30, Hambartsumyan 87)*, Kilikia 0
Kilikia 0, Mika 1 *(Demel 69)*
(Mika 4-0)

Shirak 0, Banants 1 *(Lovrić 61)*
Banants 3 *(Melkonyan 5, 27, Ortega 63)*, Shirak 0
(Banants 4-0)

SEMI-FINALS

(13/4/10 & 20/4/10)
Ulisses 0, Pyunik 2 *(Marcos 19, Tadevosyan 54)*
Pyunik 1 *(Mkrtchyan 75)*, Ulisses 0
(Pyunik 3-0)

(14/4/10 & 21/4/10)
Banants 1 *(Beto 15)*, Mika 1 *(Beglaryan 12)*
Mika 0, Banants 2 *(Santos Du Bala 22, Ortega 45)*
(Banants 3-1)

FINAL

(10/5/10)
Hanrapetakan stadium, Yerevan
FC PYUNIK 4 *(Manoyan 13, Marcos 41, Ghazaryan 45, 70)*
FC BANANTS 0
Referee – Chagharyan
PYUNIK – Lesko, Yedigaryan Artak, Minasyan (Haroyan 85), Hovsepyan S., Yusbashyan, Ghazaryan, Mkrtchyan , Tadevosyan, Malakyan (Hovhannisyan K. 80), Marcos, Manoyan.
BANANTS – Ghazaryan, Nikolov, Hambartsumyan, Daghbashyan, Lovrić, Beto (Kasule 80), Karapetyan, Voskanyan (Gyozalyan 69), Santos Du Bala, Ortega (Arakelyan 52), Melkonyan.

Salzburg hang on to retain Bundesliga title

FC Salzburg's third Austrian Bundesliga triumph in four seasons looked all but assured throughout the 2009/10 campaign. There seemed no threat to their position at the top of the table until suddenly, in the final month of combat, their confidence deserted them and, with just five points taken from a possible 15, they found themselves having to win their final game, away to SK Sturm Graz, to hold off a belated two-pronged challenge from FK Austria Wien and SK Rapid Wien.

Had Salzburg managed a draw at home to Austria Wien in the penultimate round, the title would have been theirs. They were just seconds away from doing so when visiting midfielder Zlatko Junuzovic scored a dramatic winner to reopen the title race. Now Salzburg's lead was down to just one over the Violetten and three over Rapid, who had the superior goal difference.

Test of nerve

Having led for so long, it seemed inconceivable that Salzburg could throw away the title. The situation now demanded that they take all three points in Graz or suffer the consequences. It was a massive test of nerve for both the team and their coach, Huub Stevens, who had succeeded his fellow Dutchman Co Adriaanse the previous summer. In the event, they passed it with flying colours, two quickfire goals from Simon Cziommer and mid-season signing Roman Wallner easing the pressure and enabling them to cruise to a 2-0 victory that rendered results elsewhere redundant.

Austria and Rapid both won, but the title was Salzburg's – the sixth in their history and third since the rebranding of the club by energy-drink tycoon Didi Mateschitz. Despite the late-season dip, Salzburg registered two points more than in the previous season's title-winning campaign. Their goal tally was significantly reduced, however, with top scorer Marc Janko's final total of 18 barely comparable with his incredible 39-goal haul of 2008/09. Conversely,

Salzburg's defensive figures were much improved, with just 27 goals conceded under Stevens compared to 50 under Adriaanse. While Janko and his fellow Austrians Wallner and Christoph Leitgeb did their bit, there were strong contributions from the African branch of the team's sizeable foreign legion, with Cameroonian attacking midfielder Somen Tchoyi and Nigerian defender Rabiu Afolabi the pick of the imports.

Six out of six

Much to the pleasure of Mateschitz, Salzburg also finally made some waves in Europe – not, alas, in the UEFA Champions League, from which they made an ignominious exit against Maccabi Haifa FC, but in the UEFA Europa League, in which they were the only team to win all six group-stage matches. S.S. Lazio, Villarreal CF and PFC Levski Sofia were all defeated twice in an impressive show of strength from Stevens' men, but joy in the autumn turned to despair in the spring when Salzburg allowed a two-goal lead against R. Standard de Liège to become a 3-2 aggregate defeat.

Somen Tchoyi had a fine season for Austrian champions Salzburg

Salzburg were the only Austrian club to extend their European involvement beyond Christmas, but remarkably all four representatives made it through to the group stage of the UEFA Europa League. Sturm and Austria Wien both unexpectedly accounted for Ukrainian opposition in the play-off round while Rapid eclipsed them by knocking out Aston Villa FC, one goal in each leg from Croatian striker Nikica Jelavić doing the trick.

Jelavić scored nine goals in all during Rapid's European run, and the 25-year-old doubled that tally in the Bundesliga, leaving him just two shy of his Rapid captain Steffen Hofmann, who, outstanding all season long, became the first midfielder in history to head the Austrian top flight's score charts. Albanian striker Hamdi Salihi also added 15 goals as Peter Pacult's adventurous side once again boasted the Bundesliga's best attack – an impressive effort given that both of their high-scoring strikers from the previous season, Stefan Maierhofer and Erwin Hoffer, had been sold

Sturm success

Austria Wien, led diligently by Karl Daxbacher, could not match Rapid's firepower – especially after losing young gun Robin Okotie to serious injury in August – but they closed the season brilliantly, with ten wins and two draws in their last 12 matches, and were delighted to finish above their city rivals. For once, however, the Violetten were found wanting in the Austrian Cup, ending a lengthy run of success by losing to LASK Linz in the third round. The final was won by Sturm, who defeated Bundesliga newcomers SC Wiener Neustadt 1-0 in Klagenfurt, with Slovenian striker Klemen Lavrič heading in the late winner. Sturm's first major trophy for 11 years enabled Austria to go into the 2010/11 European competitions with the same quartet that had hit the headlines in 2009/10.

Österreichischer Fussball-Bund (ÖFB)

Ernst-Happel-Stadion
Sektor A/F
Meiereistrasse 7
AT-1020 Wien
tel – +43 1 727 180
fax – +43 1 728 1632
website – oefb.at
email – office@oefb.at
Year of Formation – 1904

President – Leo Windtner
General Secretary – Alfred Ludwig
Media Officer – Peter Klinglmüller
National Stadium - Ernst-Happel-Stadion, Vienna (50,000)

INTERNATIONAL TOURNAMENT APPEARANCES
FIFA World Cup Finals - (7) 1934 (4th), 1954 (3rd), 1958, 1978 (2nd phase), 1982 (2nd phase), 1990, 1998.
UEFA European Championship – (1) 2008.
TOP FIVE ALL-TIME CAPS
Andreas Herzog (103); Anton Polster (95); Gerhard Hanappi (93); Karl Koller (86); Friedl Koncilia & Bruno Pezzey (84)
TOP FIVE ALL-TIME GOALS
Anton Polster (44); Hans Krankl (34); Johann Horvath (29); Erich Hof (28); Anton Schall (27)

It was a season of conflicting fortunes for Dietmar Constantini's young national team. Already consigned to 2010 FIFA World Cup qualifying failure, they ended the campaign with spirits reasonably high before Spain returned to the Ernst-Happel-Stadion, scene of their UEFA EURO 2008 triumph, and humbled them 5-1. Constantini was clearly on a mission to rejuvenate the squad almost from scratch, refusing to recall in-form ex-skipper Andreas Ivanschitz while promoting several players from the youth ranks. The most promising of these was 19-year-old Austria Wien centre-back Aleksandar Dragovic, a player already widely tipped for the very top.

NATIONAL TEAM RESULTS 2009/10

Date	Opponent	H/A	Venue	Score	Scorers
12/8/09	Cameroon	H	Klagenfurt	0-2	
5/9/09	Faroe Islands (WCQ)	H	Graz	3-1	Maierhofer (1), Janko (15, 58p)
9/9/09	Romania (WCQ)	A	Bucharest	1-1	Schiemer (82)
10/10/09	Lithuania (WCQ)	H	Innsbruck	2-1	Janko (16), Wallner (80p)
14/10/09	France (WCQ)	A	Saint-Denis	1-3	Janko (49)
18/11/09	Spain	H	Vienna	1-5	Jantscher (8)
3/3/10	Denmark	H	Vienna	2-1	Schiemer (12), Wallner (37)
19/5/10	Croatia	H	Klagenfurt	0-1	

AUSTRIA

NATIONAL TEAM APPEARANCES 2009/10

Coach – Dietmar CONSTANTINI	30/5/55		Cmr	FRO	ROU	LTU	FRA	Esp	Den	Cro	Caps	Goals
Jürgen MACHO	24/8/77	unattached /LASK	G46							G	19	-
Manuel ORTLECHNER	4/3/80	Austria Wien	D	s46						D	6	-
Franz SCHIEMER	21/3/86	Salzburg	D46	D	D	D			M	M	13	2
Aleksandar DRAGOVIC	6/3/91	Austria Wien	D	D	D	D	D	D	D64	D	9	
György GARICS	8/3/84	Atalanta (ITA)	D46						D		23	1
Jakob JANTSCHER	8/1/89	Sturm	M	M	M62		M	M60			6	1
Yasin PEHLIVAN	5/1/89	Rapid Wien	M	M	M	M	M	M27*			8	-
Paul SCHARNER	11/3/80	Wigan (ENG)	M40		D	D	D	D	D		30	-
Andreas HÖLZL	16/3/85	Sturm	M67	M	M			M46			9	2
Marc JANKO	25/6/83	Salzburg	A	A		A73	A	A62	A	A	16	7
Erwin HOFFER	14/4/87	Napoli (ITA)	A61	s60	A46		s46	s62			16	2
Christoph LEITGEB	14/4/85	Salzburg	s40						M37	s63	27	-
Helge PAYER	9/8/79	Rapid Wien	s46	G	G	G	G46				20	-
Sebastian PRÖDL	21/6/87	Werder (GER)	s46						s64	D	23	2
Christian FUCHS	7/4/86	Bochum (GER)	s46	D	D		D80	D	D	D	31	-
Stefan MAIERHOFER	16/8/82	Rapid Wien /Wolves (ENG)	s61	A60	s46	s73	A46				10	1
Christopher TRIMMEL	24/2/87	Rapid Wien	s67		s62					s89	3	-
Jürgen PATOCKA	30/7/77	Rapid Wien		D46			D	s46			5	-
Daniel BEICHLER	13/10/88	Sturm			M78	M72	M57		M89		5	-
Roman WALLNER	4/2/82	LASK /Salzburg		s78	s72	A	A68		A63	A63	29	7
Julian BAUMGARTLINGER	2/1/88	Austria Wien			M	s57	M	s37	M		5	-
Andreas ULMER	30/10/85	Salzburg				D					2	-
Veli KAVLAK	3/11/88	Rapid Wien					M	M	s60	M73	8	-
Thomas PRAGER	13/9/85	LASK					M57				14	1
Christopher DRAZAN	2/10/90	Rapid Wien					s57			s73	2	-
Christian GRATZEI	19/9/81	Sturm					s46	G	G		3	-
David ALABA	24/6/92	Bayern (GER)						s80	s68	s73	3	-
Ekrem DAĞ	5/12/80	Beşiktaş (TUR)							D		1	-
Patrick WOLF	4/5/81	Wiener Neustadt							s63		1	-
Martin HARNIK	10/6/87	Düsseldorf (GER)								M39	16	2
Zlatko JUNUZOVIC	26/9/87	Austria Wien								M	5	-
Ümit KORKMAZ	17/9/85	Eintracht (GER)								M73	7	-
Florian KLEIN	17/11/86	Austria Wien								s39	1	-

DOMESTIC LEAGUE 2009/10

BUNDESLIGA FINAL TABLE

		Pld	|	Home				|	Away				|	Total					Pts
			W	D	L	F	A	W	D	L	F	A	W	D	L	F	A		
1	FC Salzburg	36	13	4	1	41	12	9	6	3	27	15	22	10	4	68	27	76
2	FK Austria Wien	36	14	3	1	33	10	9	3	6	27	24	23	6	7	60	34	75
3	SK Rapid Wien	36	15	2	1	48	14	6	8	4	32	24	21	10	5	80	38	73
4	SK Sturm Graz	36	8	6	4	26	15	8	4	6	24	21	16	10	10	50	36	58
5	SC Wiener Neustadt	36	10	4	4	36	23	3	4	11	18	35	13	8	15	54	58	47
6	SV Mattersburg	36	9	3	6	33	30	3	2	13	12	41	12	5	19	45	71	41
7	LASK Linz	36	7	8	3	38	22	2	5	11	21	48	9	13	14	59	70	40
8	SV Ried	36	8	3	7	28	20	2	5	11	11	27	10	8	18	39	47	38
9	Kapfenberger SV	36	6	5	7	26	23	2	4	12	18	44	8	9	19	44	67	33
10	SK Austria Kärnten	36	2	6	10	16	34	0	3	15	13	46	2	9	25	29	80	15

TOP GOALSCORERS

20 Steffen HOFMANN (Rapid)
19 Roman WALLNER (LASK/Salzburg)
18 Nikica JELAVIĆ (Rapid)
   Marc JANKO (Salzburg)
17 Hamdi SALIHI (Ried/Rapid)
14 Róbert WALTNER (Mattersburg)
11 Daniel BEICHLER (Sturm)
10 Milenko AČIMOVIČ (Austria Wien)
   Christian MAYRLEB (LASK)
   Hannes AIGNER (Wiener Neustadt)

CLUB-BY-CLUB

SK AUSTRIA KÄRNTEN

Coach – Frenkie Schinkels; (26/11/09) Joze Prelogar
Founded – 2007
Stadium – Hypo Group Arena (32,000)

2009

17/7	Wiener Neustadt	a	1-3	*Hinum*
26/7	Kapfenberg	a	2-3	*Schembri, Sandro*
2/8	Rapid	a	1-5	*Gramann*
9/8	Sturm	h	1-3	*Pusztai*
21/8	Ried	h	0-0	
28/8	Mattersburg	a	1-4	*Sand*
12/9	Austria Wien	h	2-1	*Hinum, Mair*
23/9	LASK	a	1-3	*Hinum*
26/9	Salzburg	h	1-2	*Hiden*
4/10	Salzburg	a	1-7	*Blanchard*
17/10	Wiener Neustadt	h	0-0	
24/10	Kapfenberg	h	1-1	*Sandro*
28/10	Rapid	h	1-3	*Kaufmann*
31/10	Sturm	a	0-4	
8/11	Ried	a	0-1	
21/11	Mattersburg	h	0-3	
28/11	Austria Wien	a	0-1	
6/12	LASK	h	1-1	*Hierländer*
11/12	Salzburg	a	0-1	
2010				
14/2	Sturm	h	0-3	
20/2	Austria Wien	a	1-4	*Troyanski*
27/2	Kapfenberg	h	0-1	
6/3	Mattersburg	h	2-4	*Sandro 2 (1p)*
12/3	LASK	a	0-0	
20/3	Ried	h	1-0	*Hierländer*
24/3	Wiener Neustadt	a	1-2	*Kaufmann*
27/3	Rapid	h	2-4	*Kaufmann, Gramann*
3/4	Rapid	a	0-1	
10/4	Salzburg	h	0-2	
14/4	Sturm	a	2-3	*Hinum, Hierländer*
17/4	Austria Wien	h	0-2	
24/4	Kapfenberg	a	0-0	
1/5	Mattersburg	a	1-1	*Pink*
5/5	LASK	h	2-2	*Kaufmann 2*
9/5	Ried	a	1-3	*Dollinger (p)*
13/5	Wiener Neustadt	h	2-2	*Hierländer, Pusztai*

No	Name	Nat	DoB	Pos	Aps	(s)	Gls
20	Goran ALEKSIĆ	CRO	5/4/85	A	3	(4)	
21	Jocelyn BLANCHARD	FRA	28/5/72	M	21		1
22	Georg BLATNIK		6/7/92	G	1		
19	Matthias DOLLINGER		12/9/79	M	22	(2)	1
7	Luka ELSNER	SVN	2/8/82	D	15		
23	Daniel GRAMANN		6/1/87	D	16	(2)	2
8	Martin HIDEN		11/3/73	D	11		1
25	Stefan HIERLÄNDER		3/2/91	M	26	(4)	4
18	Thomas HINUM		24/7/87	M	28	(2)	4
7	Modou JAGNE	GAM	14/2/83	A	3	(1)	
17	Leonhard KAUFMANN		12/1/89	M	27	(7)	5
32	Mario KRÖPFL		21/12/89	A	7	(7)	
9	Wolfgang MAIR		17/2/80	A	13	(1)	1
8	Admir MEDJEDOVIC		25/9/85	A		(4)	
9	Atdhe NUHIU		29/7/89	A		(3)	
31	Markus PINK		24/2/91	M	12	(13)	1
15	Christian PRAWDA		6/8/82	D	16	(1)	
29	Peter PUCKER		8/2/88	M	11	(3)	
4	Oliver PUSZTAI	HUN	14/10/81	D	12	(2)	2
34	Roland PUTSCHE		22/3/91	D		(1)	
6	Thomas RIEDL	GER	18/6/76	M	19	(3)	
35	Marcel RITZMAIER		22/4/93	M		(1)	
2	Marco SALVATORE		2/2/86	D	20	(3)	
39	Marc SAND		23/1/88	A	5	(7)	1
11	SANDRO José Ferreira da Silva	BRA	19/3/86	D	17	(7)	4
10	André SCHEMBRI	MLT	27/5/86	A	8	(5)	1
30	Christian SCHIMMEL		19/9/92	M		(1)	
1	Andreas SCHRANZ		2/5/79	G	25		
26	Michael SOLLBAUER		15/5/90	D	17	(1)	
3	Fernando TROYANSKI	ARG	24/11/77	D	14	(1)	1
24	Heinz WEBER		5/12/76	G	10	(2)	
39	Matthias WRIENZ		19/2/92	A	1	(5)	
33	Martin ŽIVNÝ	CZE	20/3/81	D	16	(1)	

 **AUSTRIA**

FK AUSTRIA WIEN

Coach – Karl Daxbacher
Founded – 1911
Stadium – Franz Horr Stadion (13,400)
MAJOR HONOURS:
Austrian League – (23) 1924, 1926, 1949, 1950, 1953, 1961, 1962, 1963,
1969, 1970, 1976, 1978, 1979, 1980, 1981, 1984, 1985, 1986, 1991, 1992,
1993, 2003, 2006;
Austrian Cup – (27) 1921, 1924, 1925, 1926, 1933, 1935, 1936, 1948, 1949,
1960, 1962, 1963, 1967, 1971, 1974, 1977, 1980, 1982, 1986, 1990, 1992,
1994, 2003, 2005, 2006, 2007, 2009.

2009
19/7	Salzburg	a	1-2	Junuzovic
24/7	LASK	a	5-4	Klein, Bąk, Okotie 2, Ortlechner
2/8	Kapfenberg	h	3-0	Junuzovic, Okotie 2 (1p)
9/8	Wiener Neustadt	h	2-1	Ortlechner, Ačimovič (p)
23/8	Sturm	a	1-0	Ačimovič
30/8	Rapid	h	1-1	Jun
12/9	Austria Kärnten	a	1-2	Ačimovič (p)
23/9	Ried	h	1-1	Diabang
26/9	Mattersburg	a	3-1	Jun 2, Standfest
4/10	Mattersburg	h	1-0	Jun
17/10	Salzburg	h	1-0	Junuzovic
25/10	LASK	h	3-0	Ortlechner, Diabang, Liendl
28/10	Kapfenberg	a	0-1	
31/10	Wiener Neustadt	a	3-4	Schumacher, Ačimovič, Diabang
8/11	Sturm	h	1-0	Bąk
22/11	Rapid	a	1-4	Hattenberger
28/11	Austria Kärnten	h	1-0	Sulimani
6/12	Ried	a	2-0	Ačimovič 2
13/12	Sturm	a	2-2	Ačimovič, Klein

2010
13/2	Kapfenberg	h	4-3	Linz 2, Klein, Ačimovič (p)
20/2	Austria Kärnten	h	4-1	Schumacher 2, Standfest, Ačimovič
26/2	Mattersburg	a	1-1	Ačimovič (p)
6/3	LASK	h	0-1	
14/3	Rapid	a	0-2	
21/3	Salzburg	h	1-1	Linz
24/3	Ried	a	1-0	Sulimani
27/3	Wiener Neustadt	h	1-0	Klein (p)
4/4	Wiener Neustadt	a	1-0	Junuzovic
11/4	Sturm	h	1-0	Linz
14/4	Kapfenberg	a	1-1	Liendl
17/4	Austria Kärnten	a	2-0	Liendl, Voříšek
25/4	Mattersburg	h	5-1	Jun, Ortlechner, Linz 2, Junuzovic
2/5	LASK	a	1-0	Jun
5/5	Rapid	h	1-0	Jun
9/5	Salzburg	a	1-0	Junuzovic
13/5	Ried	h	2-0	Jun 2

No	Name	Nat	DoB	Pos	Aps	(s)	Gls
30	Milenko AČIMOVIČ	SVN	15/2/77	M	26		10
21	Robert ALMER		20/3/84	G	5	(1)	
6	Jacek BĄK	POL	24/3/73	D	20	(3)	2
26	Julian BAUMGARTLINGER		2/1/88	M	24	(6)	
9	Mamadou DIABANG	SEN	21/1/79	A	13	(13)	3
4	Aleksandar DRAGOVIC		6/3/91	D	30	(2)	
8	Matthias HATTENBERGER		30/11/78	M	11	(8)	1
11	Tomáš JUN	CZE	17/1/83	A	17	(4)	9
16	Zlatko JUNUZOVIC		26/9/87	M	29	(1)	6
7	Florian KLEIN		17/11/86	M	31	(4)	4
27	Thomas KRAMMER		18/2/83	M	1	(2)	
22	Marin LEOVAC	CRO	7/1/88	D	4	(4)	
18	Michael LIENDL		25/10/85	M	12	(8)	3
13	Heinz LINDNER		17/7/90	G	15	(1)	
32	Roland LINZ		9/8/81	A	15		6
25	Michael MADL		21/3/88	D		(1)	
19	Rubin OKOTIE		6/6/87	A	4		4
14	Manuel ORTLECHNER		4/3/80	D	28	(1)	4
1	Szabolcs SÁFÁR	HUN	20/8/74	G	16		
10	Thiago Maier dos Santos "SCHUMACHER"	BRA	31/8/86	A	14	(14)	3
31	Joachim STANDFEST		30/5/80	D	32		2
23	Emin SULIMANI		4/8/86	M	14	(10)	2
29	Markus SUTTNER		16/4/87	D	26	(1)	
20	Eldar TOPIĆ	BIH	29/5/83	A		(5)	
15	Petr VOŘÍŠEK	CZE	19/3/79	M	9	(12)	1

KAPFENBERGER SV

**Coach – Werner Gregoritsch; (29/8/09) (Manfred Unger);
(12/9/09) Werner Gregoritsch**
Founded – 1919
Stadium – Franz Fekete Stadion (10,000)

2009
18/7	Ried	h	0-1	
26/7	Austria Kärnten	h	3-2	Pitter, Hüttenbrenner, Sencar
2/8	Austria Wien	a	0-3	
7/8	LASK	a	0-4	
23/8	Mattersburg	h	0-1	
29/8	Salzburg	a	0-4	
12/9	Wiener Neustadt	a	3-2	Scharrer (p), Sencar, Fukal
23/9	Rapid	h	0-1	
26/9	Sturm	h	0-1	
4/10	Sturm	a	0-0	
17/10	Ried	a	0-3	
24/10	Austria Kärnten	a	1-1	Alar
28/10	Austria Wien	h	1-0	Felfernig
1/11	LASK	h	7-2	Schmid 2, Alar 2, Heinz 2 (1p), Sencar
7/11	Mattersburg	a	1-4	Scharrer
21/11	Salzburg	h	0-2	
28/11	Wiener Neustadt	h	3-1	Fukal, Pavlov, Schellander
5/12	Rapid	a	1-3	Heinz
12/12	Mattersburg	h	2-2	Hüttenbrenner, Schönberger

2010
13/2	Austria Wien	a	3-4	Pavlov 2, Heinz
20/2	Ried	h	1-1	Pavlov
27/2	Austria Kärnten	a	1-0	Rauscher
7/3	Rapid	h	2-2	Heinz, Felfernig
13/3	Salzburg	a	0-1	
19/3	Wiener Neustadt	h	2-3	Siegl 2 (1p)
24/3	LASK	a	1-1	Pavlov
27/3	Sturm	h	0-3	
3/4	Sturm	a	1-1	Pavlov
10/4	Mattersburg	a	1-3	Sencar
14/4	Austria Wien	h	1-1	Gregoritsch
17/4	Ried	a	1-2	Pavlov
24/4	Austria Kärnten	h	0-0	
30/4	Rapid	a	3-5	Felfernig, Alar 2
4/5	Salzburg	h	2-0	Sencar, Alar
9/5	Wiener Neustadt	a	1-3	Pavlov
13/5	LASK	h	2-0	Pavlov, Tieber

No	Name	Nat	DoB	Pos	Aps	(s)	Gls
19	Deni ALAR		18/1/90	A	16	(12)	6
9	Antonio DI SALVO	ITA	5/6/79	A	1	(6)	
1	Martin EISL		14/11/82	G	1		
13	Stefan ERKINGER		1/9/81	M		(1)	
14	Markus FELFERNIG		18/6/83	M	22	(6)	3
5	Milan FUKAL	CZE	16/5/75	D	33		
4	Gerald GANSTERER		29/10/82	D	21	(1)	
37	Manfred GOLLNER		22/12/90	D	1	(1)	
34	Michael GREGORITSCH		14/4/94	M		(4)	1
38	Mario GRGIC		10/9/91	M	2		
30	Marek HEINZ	CZE	4/8/77	M	23	(4)	4
33	Daniel HOFER		18/12/83	M	1	(1)	

20	Boris HÜTTENBRENNER		23/9/85	M	21	(10)	2
11	Arno KOZELSKY		1/11/81	A	5	(12)	
35	Georg KRENN		4/10/90	M		(2)	
8	Mario MAJSTOROVIC		1/3/77	D	18	(2)	
31	Patrick OSOINIK		29/1/85	D	24	(1)	
28	Srđan PAVLOV	SRB	28/1/84	A	19	(6)	9
9	Pero PEJIĆ	CRO	28/11/82	A	1		
2	René PITTER		8/7/89	M	4	(2)	1
22	Andreas RAUSCHER		25/1/78	D	22		1
18	Markus SCHARRER		3/7/74	M	6	(4)	2
16	Robert SCHELLANDER		31/1/83	M	26		1
23	Manuel SCHMID		23/8/81	M	13	(8)	2
6	Thomas SCHÖNBERGER		14/10/86	D	21	(1)	1
10	David SENCAR		29/1/84	M	26	(4)	5
15	Patrik SIEGL	CZE	26/2/76	M	26	(7)	2
21	Pa Ousman SONKO	GAM	26/12/84	D	1		
17	Lukas STADLER		28/10/90	A	1	(1)	
4	Dominique TABOGA		6/11/82	D	1		
21	Michael TIEBER		4/9/88	A	4	(7)	1
29	Philipp WENDLER		2/6/91	A		(1)	
7	Herbert WIEGER		7/2/72	A	1	(3)	
36	Raphael WOLF	GER	6/6/88	G	35		

LASK LINZ
Coach – Matthias Hamann (GER); (5/2/10) Helmut Kraft
Founded – 1908
Stadium – Stadion der Stadt Linz Gugl (18,400)
MAJOR HONOURS:
Austrian League – (1) 1965;
Austrian Cup – (1) 1965.

2009

Date	Opponent		Score	Scorers
18/7	Mattersburg	h	4-0	Saurer, Wallner, Metz, Mayrleb
24/7	Austria Wien	h	4-5	Prager, Mayrleb 2, Metz
1/8	Salzburg	a	2-3	Prager, Mayrleb
7/8	Kapfenberg	h	4-0	Mayrleb, Prager 2, Wallner
23/8	Rapid	a	1-4	Prager
30/8	Wiener Neustadt	h	4-2	Mayrleb, Majavbi, Wallner 2
12/9	Sturm	a	3-3	Prager, Saurer, Margreitter
23/9	Austria Kärnten	h	3-1	Wallner 3
27/9	Ried	a	2-5	Saurer, Wallner
3/10	Ried	h	2-2	Wallner (p), Prager
17/10	Mattersburg	a	2-3	Wallner, Margreitter
25/10	Austria Wien	a	0-3	
28/10	Salzburg	h	0-0	
1/11	Kapfenberg	a	2-7	Wallner 2 (1p)
8/11	Rapid	h	3-3	Mayrleb 2, Prager
25/11	Wiener Neustadt	a	1-4	Kobleder
28/11	Sturm	h	2-2	Mayrleb, Wallner
6/12	Austria Kärnten	a	1-1	Wallner
12/12	Wiener Neustadt	a	0-4	

2010

Date	Opponent		Score	Scorers
12/2	Rapid	h	4-2	Metz, Panis 2, Saurer
21/2	Salzburg	a	0-3	
27/2	Sturm	h	1-2	Škuletić
6/3	Austria Wien	a	1-0	Aufhauser
12/3	Austria Kärnten	h	0-0	
20/3	Mattersburg	a	1-2	og (Malić)
24/3	Kapfenberg	h	1-1	Chinchilla
28/3	Ried	h	3-0	Hart, Mayrleb, Alunderis
3/4	Ried	a	2-2	og (Burgstaller), Aufhauser
10/4	Wiener Neustadt	h	1-1	Kragl
13/4	Rapid	a	0-0	
18/4	Salzburg	h	0-0	
24/4	Sturm	a	1-0	Prager
2/5	Austria Wien	h	0-1	
5/5	Austria Kärnten	a	2-2	Kragl, Saurer
9/5	Mattersburg	h	2-0	Chinchilla, Gunnlaugsson
13/5	Kapfenberg	a	0-2	

No	Name	Nat	DoB	Pos	Aps	(s)	Gls
2	Vidas ALUNDERIS	LTU	27/3/79	D	19	(6)	1
6	René AUFHAUSER		21/6/76	M	13		2
22	Paul BICHELHUBER		22/2/87	M	6	(6)	
21	Wolfgang BUBENIK		31/3/81	M	29	(3)	
1	Silvije ČAVLINA	CRO	22/4/77	G	15		
31	Pablo CHINCHILLA Vega	CRC	21/12/78	D	31		2
33	Gardar GUNNLAUGSSON	ISL	7/9/83	A	4	(1)	1
27	Ali HAMDEMIR		1/5/89	M		(2)	
3	Florian HART		11/5/90	D	2	(10)	1
15	Christoph KOBLEDER		3/3/90	D	8	(3)	1
17	Lukas KRAGL		12/1/90	A	8	(1)	2
32	Jürgen MACHO		24/8/77	G	13		
28	Justice MAJABVI	ZIM	26/3/84	M	33	(1)	1
4	Georg MARGREITTER		7/11/88	D	20		2
9	Christian MAYRLEB		8/6/72	A	30	(2)	10
5	Florian METZ		18/9/85	D	29		3
8	Jürgen PANIS		21/4/75	M	13	(9)	2
30	Sascha PICHLER		31/1/86	A		(1)	
24	Thomas PIERMAYR		2/8/89	D	17	(12)	
14	Thomas PRAGER		13/9/85	M	29	(4)	9
26	Mark PRETTENTHALER		11/4/83	D	12		
23	Siegfried RASSWALDER		13/5/87	M	7	(7)	
10	Klaus SALMUTTER		3/1/84	A	1	(3)	
20	Christoph SAURER		22/1/86	M	29	(3)	5
18	Petar ŠKULETIĆ	SRB	29/6/90	A	3	(12)	1
25	Marco VUJIC		21/2/84	A		(4)	
7	Roman WALLNER		4/2/82	A	17		14
11	Markus WEISSENBERGER		8/3/75	M		(3)	
12	Michael ZAGLMAIR		7/12/87	G	8	(3)	
29	Sandro ZAKANY		23/9/87	A		(8)	

SV MATTERSBURG
Coach – Franz Lederer
Founded – 1922
Stadium – Pappelstadion (15,700)

2009

Date	Opponent		Score	Scorers
18/7	LASK	a	0-4	
26/7	Rapid	h	2-1	Mörz (p), Waltner
2/8	Sturm	a	0-2	
8/8	Salzburg	h	2-3	Sedloski, Spuller
23/8	Kapfenberg	a	1-0	Atan
28/8	Austria Kärnten	h	4-1	Naumoski 2, Schmidt, Atan
12/9	Ried	h	3-0	og (Burgstaller), Waltner, Spuller
22/9	Wiener Neustadt	a	0-3	
26/9	Austria Wien	h	1-3	Naumoski
4/10	Austria Wien	a	0-1	
17/10	LASK	h	3-2	Naumoski 3 (1p)
25/10	Rapid	a	0-4	
28/10	Sturm	h	0-2	
31/10	Salzburg	a	0-2	
7/11	Kapfenberg	h	4-1	Naumoski 2, Spuller 2
21/11	Austria Kärnten	a	3-0	Waltner 3
27/11	Ried	a	0-0	
4/12	Wiener Neustadt	h	1-3	Malić
12/12	Kapfenberg	a	2-2	Naumoski, Mörz

2010

Date	Opponent		Score	Scorers
13/2	Wiener Neustadt	h	1-0	Waltner
20/2	Sturm	a	0-4	
26/2	Austria Wien	h	1-1	Waltner
6/3	Austria Kärnten	a	4-2	Waltner, Spuller 2 (1p), Doleschal
13/3	Ried	a	0-3	
20/3	LASK	h	2-1	Spuller, Waltner
23/3	Rapid	a	0-3	
27/3	Salzburg	h	1-6	Waltner
2/4	Salzburg	a	0-2	
10/4	Kapfenberg	h	3-1	Doleschal, Spuller, Lindner
14/4	Wiener Neustadt	a	1-2	Waltner
17/4	Sturm	h	0-0	

25/4	Austria Wien	a	1-5	Waltner
1/5	Austria Kärnten	h	1-1	Lindner
5/5	Ried	h	3-1	Lindner, Waltner 2
9/5	LASK	a	0-2	
13/5	Rapid	h	1-3	Doleschal

No	Name	Nat	DoB	Pos	Aps	(s)	Gls
27	Cem ATAN		30/6/85	M	17	(7)	2
21	Stefan BLIEM		5/5/83	G	25		
1	Thomas BORENITSCH		19/12/80	G	11		
26	Peter CHRAPPAN		21/12/84	D	16		
14	Dominik DOLESCHAL		9/5/89	A	12	(4)	3
17	Patrick FARKAS		9/9/92	M	15	(1)	
25	Christian GARTNER		3/4/94	M		(1)	
7	Josef HAMOUZ	CZE	8/4/80	M	13	(4)	
31	Alois HÖLLER		15/3/89	M	3	(1)	
11	Matthias LINDNER		7/9/88	A	4	(3)	3
4	Nedeljko MALIĆ	BIH	15/5/88	D	34		1
15	Jürgen MANSBERGER		13/1/88	M		(1)	
5	Michael MÖRZ		2/4/80	M	34		2
24	Ilco NAUMOSKI	MKD	29/7/83	A	23	(1)	9
6	Anton PAUSCHENWEIN		24/1/81	D	20	(5)	
2	Alexander PÖLLHUBER		30/4/85	D	14	(4)	
18	Lukas RATH		18/1/92	D	17	(4)	
20	Thomas SALAMON		18/1/89	M	4	(8)	
19	Markus SCHMIDT		12/10/77	M	21	(4)	1
8	Tomáš SEDLÁK	SVK	3/2/83	M	3	(2)	
3	Goce SEDLOSKI	MKD	10/4/74	D	21	(8)	1
12	Manuel SEIDL		26/10/88	D	28	(4)	
28	Ronald SPULLER		22/6/81	M	25	(10)	8
23	Ostoja STJEPANOVIC	MKD	17/1/85	A	3	(11)	
9	Thomas WAGNER		9/10/76	A	5	(10)	
29	Róbert WALTNER	HUN	20/9/77	A	28	(7)	14

SK RAPID WIEN
Coach – Peter Pacult
Founded – 1899
Stadium – Gerhard Hanappi Stadion (17,500)
MAJOR HONOURS:
Austrian League – (32) 1912, 1913, 1916, 1917, 1919, 1920, 1921, 1923, 1929, 1930, 1935, 1938, 1940, 1941, 1946, 1948, 1951, 1952, 1954, 1956, 1957, 1960, 1964, 1967, 1968, 1982, 1983, 1987, 1988, 1996, 2005, 2008;
German League – (1) 1941;
Austrian Cup – (14) 1919, 1920, 1927, 1946, 1961, 1968, 1969, 1972, 1976, 1983, 1984, 1985, 1987, 1995;
German Cup – (1) 1938.

2009

26/7	Mattersburg	a	1-2	Heikkinen
2/8	Austria Kärnten	h	5-1	Hofmann, Konrad, Trimmel 3
9/8	Ried	a	1-1	Hofmann
23/8	LASK	h	4-1	og (Alunderis), Jelavić 2, Hofmann
30/8	Austria Wien	a	1-1	Maierhofer
13/9	Salzburg	h	2-2	Hofmann, Salihi
23/9	Kapfenberg	a	1-0	Dober
26/9	Wiener Neustadt	h	3-1	Salihi 2, Soma
4/10	Wiener Neustadt	a	4-0	Jelavić 2, Kavlak, Salihi
18/10	Sturm	a	0-1	
25/10	Mattersburg	h	4-0	Katzer, Gartler, Salihi, Hofmann
28/10	Austria Kärnten	a	3-1	Drazan 2, Gartler
31/10	Ried	h	1-0	Katzer
8/11	LASK	a	3-3	Jelavić, Hofmann (p), Salihi
22/11	Austria Wien	h	4-1	Hofmann 2, Jelavić, Salihi
25/11	Sturm	h	2-1	Jelavić, Salihi (p)
29/11	Salzburg	a	0-0	
5/12	Kapfenberg	h	3-1	Hofmann (p), Jelavić, Salihi
12/12	Ried	h	2-1	Katzer, Salihi

2010

| 12/2 | LASK | a | 2-4 | Hofmann 2 (1p) |

19/2	Wiener Neustadt	a	2-2	Gartler, Trimmel
28/2	Salzburg	h	0-1	
7/3	Kapfenberg	a	2-2	Katzer, Konrad
14/3	Austria Wien	h	2-0	Hofmann (p), Jelavić
20/3	Sturm	a	1-1	Jelavić
23/3	Mattersburg	h	3-0	Patocka, Jelavić, Salihi
27/3	Austria Kärnten	a	4-2	Kavlak, Hofmann (p), Trimmel, Jelavić
3/4	Austria Kärnten	h	1-0	Hofmann
9/4	Ried	a	3-1	Bošković, Jelavić, Hofmann (p)
13/4	LASK	h	0-0	
17/4	Wiener Neustadt	h	3-0	Jelavić 2, Hofmann
23/4	Salzburg	a	1-1	Hofmann
30/4	Kapfenberg	h	5-3	Jelavić 2, Bošković 2, Hofmann
5/5	Austria Wien	a	0-1	
9/5	Sturm	h	4-1	Salihi, Hofmann 2, Jelavić
13/5	Mattersburg	a	3-1	Salihi 3

No	Name	Nat	DoB	Pos	Aps	(s)	Gls
27	Branko BOŠKOVIĆ	MNE	21/6/80	M	21	(8)	3
23	Andreas DOBER		31/3/86	D	23	(5)	1
19	Christopher DRAZAN		2/10/90	M	13	(17)	2
18	Hannes EDER		5/9/83	D	18	(1)	
20	Rene GARTLER		21/10/85	A	9	(10)	3
1	Raimund HEDL		31/8/74	G	14		
8	Markus HEIKKINEN	FIN	13/10/78	M	28		1
21	Erwin HOFFER		14/4/87	A	1		
11	Steffen HOFMANN	GER	9/9/80	M	36		20
16	Nikica JELAVIĆ	CRO	27/8/85	A	31	(2)	18
4	Milan JOVANOVIĆ	MNE	21/7/83	D	4	(5)	
31	Markus KATZER		11/12/79	D	26		4
17	Veli KAVLAK		3/11/88	M	21	(3)	2
33	Mario KONRAD		22/1/83	A	5	(10)	2
7	Stefan KULOVITS		19/4/83	M	16	(3)	
9	Stefan MAIERHOFER		16/8/82	A	2	(1)	1
3	Jürgen PATOCKA		30/7/77	D	18	(4)	1
24	Helge PAYER		9/8/79	G	22		
35	Yasin PEHLIVAN		5/1/89	M	24	(4)	
9	Hamdi SALIHI	ALB	19/1/84	A	13	(10)	15
22	Ragnvald SOMA	NOR	10/11/79	D	33		1
6	Christian THONHOFER		26/5/85	M	12	(1)	
28	Christopher TRIMMEL		24/2/87	A	6	(18)	5

SV RIED
Coach – Paul Gludovatz
Founded – 1912
Stadium – Keine Sorgen Arena (7,680)
MAJOR HONOURS:
Austrian Cup – (1) 1998.

2009

18/7	Kapfenberg	a	1-0	Glasner
25/7	Salzburg	h	1-0	Salihi
31/7	Wiener Neustadt	h	1-2	Lexa
9/8	Rapid	h	1-1	Salihi
21/8	Austria Kärnten	a	0-0	
30/8	Sturm	h	1-2	Drechsel
12/9	Mattersburg	a	0-3	
23/9	Austria Wien	a	1-1	Nuhiu
27/9	LASK	h	5-2	Lexa, Nacho 2, Nuhiu, Brenner
3/10	LASK	a	2-2	Nuhiu, Glasner
17/10	Kapfenberg	h	3-0	Mader, Nacho 2
25/10	Salzburg	a	1-1	Hadžić
28/10	Wiener Neustadt	h	3-0	Nuhiu 2, Huspek
31/10	Rapid	a	0-1	
8/11	Austria Kärnten	h	1-0	Brenner
21/11	Sturm	a	2-0	Lexa, Nacho
27/11	Mattersburg	h	0-0	
6/12	Austria Wien	h	0-2	
12/12	Rapid	a	1-2	Burgstaller

2010

13/2	Salzburg	h	1-2	Nuhiu
20/2	Kapfenberg	a	1-1	Mader
27/2	Wiener Neustadt	h	0-1	
6/3	Sturm	a	0-1	
13/3	Mattersburg	h	3-0	Jonathan Carrill, Hammerer, Sturm
20/3	Austria Kärnten	a	0-1	
24/3	Austria Wien	h	0-1	
28/3	LASK	a	0-3	
3/4	LASK	h	2-2	Hammerer, Lexa
9/4	Rapid	h	1-3	Hammerer
14/4	Salzburg	a	0-2	
17/4	Kapfenberg	h	2-1	Drechsel 2 (2p)
24/4	Wiener Neustadt	a	0-2	
1/5	Sturm	h	1-2	Lexa
5/5	Mattersburg	a	1-3	og (Seidl)
9/5	Austria Kärnten	h	3-1	Stocklasa, Sturm 2
13/5	Austria Wien	a	0-2	

No	Name	Nat	DoB	Pos	Aps	(s)	Gls
33	Hubert AUER		19/12/81	G	1		
18	Ewald BRENNER		26/6/75	M	31	(1)	2
23	Thomas BURGSTALLER		9/1/80	D	34		1
16	Herwig DRECHSEL		4/9/73	M	24	(4)	3
24	Thomas GEBAUER	GER	30/6/82	G	35		
5	Oliver GLASNER		28/8/74	D	17		2
4	Martin GRASEGGER		10/1/89	D	12	(11)	
19	Peter HACKMAIR		26/6/87	M	19	(2)	
20	Anel HADŽIĆ	BIH	16/8/89	M	29	(2)	1
21	Markus HAMMERER		31/8/89	A	7	(6)	3
25	Philipp HUSPEK		5/2/91	M	5	(15)	1
9	JONATHAN CARRILL Regueiro	ESP	28/2/84	A	1	(13)	1
8	Stefan LEXA		1/11/76	M	34		5
10	Florian MADER		14/9/82	A	29	(4)	2
11	Ignacio "NACHO" Rodriguez Ortiz	ESP	6/11/82	A	24	(4)	5
34	Atdhe NUHIU		29/7/89	A	19	(8)	6
15	Mihael RAJIĆ	CRO	8/10/84	M	1	(2)	
28	Thomas REIFELTSHAMMER		13/7/87	D	3	(2)	
14	Hamdi SALIHI	ALB	19/1/84	A	5	(1)	2
3	Thomas SCHRAMMEL		5/9/87	M	29	(1)	
2	Martin STOCKLASA	LIE	29/5/79	D	26	(1)	1
7	Florian STURM		6/5/82	M	6	(12)	3
29	Marcel ZIEGL		20/12/92	D	5	(16)	

FC SALZBURG
Coach – Huub Stevens (NED)
Founded – 1933
Stadium – Bullen Arena Wals-Siezenheim (30,900)
MAJOR HONOURS:
Austrian League – (6) 1994, 1995, 1997, 2007, 2009, 2010.

2009

19/7	Austria Wien	h	2-1	Zickler, Tchoyi
25/7	Ried	a	0-1	
1/8	LASK	h	3-2	Tchoyi, Janko, Zickler
8/8	Mattersburg	a	3-2	Nelisse, Švento, Cziommer
22/8	Wiener Neustadt	a	1-1	Janko
29/8	Kapfenberg	h	4-0	Zickler, Tchoyi, Cziommer, Pokrivač
13/9	Rapid	a	2-2	Tchoyi, Švento
23/9	Sturm	h	4-2	Afolabi, Tchoyi, Janko 2
26/9	Austria Kärnten	a	2-1	Pokrivač, Tchoyi
4/10	Austria Kärnten	a	7-1	Leitgeb, Pokrivač, Janko 4, Vladavić (p)
17/10	Austria Wien	a	0-1	
25/10	Ried	h	1-1	Leitgeb
28/10	LASK	a	0-0	
31/10	Mattersburg	h	2-0	Janko, Schiemer
8/11	Wiener Neustadt	a	3-2	Janko, Pokrivač, Leitgeb

21/11	Kapfenberg	a	2-0	Leitgeb, Opdam
29/11	Rapid	h	0-0	
6/12	Sturm	a	0-0	
11/12	Austria Kärnten	h	1-0	og (Sollbauer)

2010

13/2	Ried	a	2-1	Janko 2
21/2	LASK	h	3-0	Wallner, Švento 2
28/2	Rapid	a	1-0	Afolabi
6/3	Wiener Neustadt	h	1-1	Wallner
13/3	Kapfenberg	a	1-0	Janko
21/3	Austria Wien	a	1-1	Zickler
24/3	Sturm	h	3-0	Švento, Wallner, Leitgeb
27/3	Mattersburg	a	6-1	Cziommer, Wallner (p), Schiemer, Tchoyi, Schwegler, Janko
2/4	Mattersburg	h	2-0	Janko 2
10/4	Austria Kärnten	a	2-0	Cziommer, Tchoyi
14/4	Ried	h	2-0	Cziommer, og (Hadžić)
18/4	LASK	a	0-0	
23/4	Rapid	h	1-1	Afolabi
1/5	Wiener Neustadt	h	4-2	Janko 2 (1p), Dudić, Afolabi
4/5	Kapfenberg	a	0-2	
9/5	Austria Wien	h	0-1	
13/5	Sturm	a	2-0	Cziommer, Wallner

No	Name	Nat	DoB	Pos	Aps	(s)	Gls
5	Rabiu AFOLABI	NGA	18/4/80	D	29		4
33	Heinz ARZBERGER		27/8/72	G	5	(1)	
26	Alexander ASCHAUER		14/2/92	A		(1)	
28	René AUFHAUSER		21/6/76	M	2	(5)	
8	Thomas AUGUSTINUSSEN	DEN	20/3/81	M	5	(7)	
19	Simon CZIOMMER	GER	6/11/80	M	14	(12)	6
3	Milan DUDIĆ	SRB	1/11/79	D	11	(2)	1
1	Eddie GUSTAFSON	SWE	31/1/77	G	31		
22	Saša ILIĆ	SRB	30/12/77	M	1		
21	Marc JANKO		25/6/83	A	28	(6)	18
11	Patrik JEŽEK	CZE	28/12/76	M	1	(5)	
2	Christoph KRÖPFL		4/5/90	M		(1)	
24	Christoph LEITGEB		14/4/85	M	31	(2)	5
9	Robin NELISSE	ANT	25/1/78	A	1	(7)	1
29	Louis Clement NGWAT-MAHOP	CMR	16/9/87	A	1	(1)	
14	Barry OPDAM	NED	27/2/76	D	15	(8)	1
16	Karel PITÁK	CZE	28/1/80	M		(1)	
10	Nikola POKRIVAČ	CRO	26/11/85	M	16	(6)	4
15	Franz SCHIEMER		21/3/86	D	25		2
6	Christian SCHWEGLER	SUI	6/6/84	D	35		1
23	Ibrahim SEKAGYA	UGA	19/12/80	D	23	(1)	
18	Dušan ŠVENTO	SVK	1/8/85	A	34	(1)	5
13	Somen TCHOYI	CMR	29/3/83	M	33	(3)	8
17	Andreas ULMER		30/10/85	D	35	(1)	
25	Admir VLADAVIĆ	BIH	29/6/82	M	3	(12)	1
11	Roman WALLNER		4/2/82	A	10	(4)	5
7	Alexander ZICKLER	GER	28/2/74	A	7	(17)	4

SK STURM GRAZ
Coach – Franco Foda (GER)
Founded – 1909
Stadium – UPC-Arena (15,400)
MAJOR HONOURS:
Austrian League – (2) 1998, 1999;
Austrian Cup – (4) 1996, 1997, 1999, 2010.

2009

26/7	Wiener Neustadt	h	3-0	Beichler 2, Hölzl
2/8	Mattersburg	a	2-0	Hölzl, Hassler
9/8	Austria Kärnten	a	3-1	Lamotte, Hölzl, Jantscher
23/8	Austria Wien	h	0-1	
30/8	Ried	a	2-1	Muratović, Bukva
12/9	LASK	h	3-3	Hlinka, Weber, Beichler
23/9	Salzburg	a	2-4	Beichler 2

26/9	Kapfenberg	a	1-0	*Beichler*
4/10	Kapfenberg	h	0-0	
18/10	Rapid	h	1-0	*Beichler*
25/10	Wiener Neustadt	a	0-0	
28/10	Mattersburg	a	2-0	*Jantscher, Hölzl*
31/10	Austria Kärnten	h	4-0	*Jantscher 2, Hölzl, Beichler*
8/11	Austria Wien	a	0-1	
21/11	Ried	h	0-2	
25/11	Rapid	a	1-2	*Lavrič*
28/11	LASK	a	2-2	*Jantscher, Beichler*
6/12	Salzburg	h	0-0	
13/12	Austria Wien	h	2-2	*Hölzl, Jantscher*
2010				
14/2	Austria Kärnten	a	3-0	*Beichler 2, Lavrič*
20/2	Mattersburg	h	4-0	*Lavrič 3 (1p), Kienast*
27/2	LASK	a	2-1	*Lavrič, Weber*
6/3	Ried	h	1-0	*Lavrič*
13/3	Wiener Neustadt	a	0-0	
20/3	Rapid	h	1-1	*Lavrič (p)*
24/3	Salzburg	a	0-3	
27/3	Kapfenberg	a	3-0	*Schildenfeld, Jantscher, Hlinka*
3/4	Kapfenberg	h	1-1	*Kienast*
11/4	Austria Wien	a	0-1	
14/4	Austria Kärnten	h	3-2	*Kienast, Hlinka, Salmutter*
17/4	Mattersburg	a	0-0	
24/4	LASK	h	0-1	
1/5	Ried	a	2-1	*Haas, Kienzl*
5/5	Wiener Neustadt	h	1-0	*Kienast*
9/5	Rapid	a	1-4	*Kienast (p)*
13/5	Salzburg	h	0-2	

No	Name	Nat	DoB	Pos	Aps	(s)	Gls
28	Daniel BEICHLER		13/10/88	M	26	(3)	11
9	Haris BUKVA		15/3/88	M	4	(16)	1
17	Martin EHRENREICH		10/5/83	D	14	(6)	
5	Ferdinand FELDHOFER		23/10/79	D	16	(2)	
29	Sandro FODA	GER	28/12/89	M	9	(2)	
1	Christian GRATZEI		19/9/81	G	36		
11	Mario HAAS		16/9/74	A	5	(12)	1
12	Dominic HASSLER		30/3/81	A	1	(8)	1
7	Peter HLINKA	SVK	5/12/78	M	25	(1)	3
8	Andreas HÖLZL		16/3/85	M	29		6
13	Jakob JANTSCHER		8/1/89	A	32	(1)	7
18	Ilia KANDELAKI	GEO	26/12/81	D	24		
24	Roman KIENAST		29/3/84	A	9	(8)	5
19	Mario KIENZL		19/12/83	M	6	(3)	1
27	Christian KLEM		21/4/91	M	4	(2)	
2	Fabian LAMOTTE	GER	25/2/83	D	18	(2)	1
30	Klemen LAVRIČ	SVN	12/6/81	A	18	(8)	8
10	Samir MURATOVIĆ	BIH	22/1/76	M	18	(10)	1
20	Mark PRETTENTHALER		11/4/83	D	2	(3)	
16	Christian PRWADA		6/8/82	D	9	(2)	
39	Klaus SALMUTTER		3/1/84	A	5	(3)	1
23	Gordon SCHILDENFELD	CRO	18/3/85	D	33	(1)	1
4	Mario SONNLEITNER		8/10/86	D	27		
6	Manuel WEBER		28/8/85	M	26	(3)	2
26	Marvin WEINBERGER		4/4/89	A		(5)	

SC WIENER NEUSTADT

Coach – Helmut Kraft; (14/12/09) Peter Schöttel
Founded – 2008
Stadium – Stadion Wiener Neustadt (7,500)

2009				
17/7	Austria Kärnten	h	3-1	*Kuljic (p), Johana, Wolf*
26/7	Sturm	a	0-3	
31/7	Ried	h	2-1	*Diego Viana, Simkovic*
9/8	Austria Wien	a	1-2	*Aigner (p)*
22/8	Salzburg	h	1-1	*Aigner*
30/8	LASK	a	2-4	*Reiter, Johana*

12/9	Kapfenberg	h	2-3	*Kuljic 2*
22/9	Mattersburg	h	3-0	*Kurtisi 2, Koštál*
26/9	Rapid	a	1-3	*Kurtisi*
4/10	Rapid	h	0-4	
17/10	Austria Kärnten	a	0-0	
25/10	Sturm	h	0-0	
28/10	Ried	a	0-3	
31/10	Austria Wien	h	4-3	*Kuljic, Aigner (p), Ari, Wolf*
8/11	Salzburg	h	2-3	*Aigner, Reiter*
25/11	LASK	h	4-1	*Kuljic 4*
28/11	Kapfenberg	a	1-3	*Reiter*
4/12	Mattersburg	a	3-1	*Diego Viana, Kurtisi, og (Malić)*
12/12	LASK	h	4-0	*Kurtisi 2, Diego Viana, Niklas*
2010				
13/2	Mattersburg	a	0-1	
19/2	Rapid	h	2-2	*Reiter, Aigner*
27/2	Ried	a	1-0	*Aigner*
6/3	Salzburg	a	1-1	*Aigner*
13/3	Sturm	h	0-0	
19/3	Kapfenberg	a	3-2	*Aigner (p), Simkovic, Grünwald*
24/3	Austria Kärnten	h	2-1	*Simkovic, Aigner*
27/3	Austria Wien	a	0-1	
4/4	Austria Wien	h	0-1	
10/4	LASK	a	1-1	*Diego Viana*
14/4	Mattersburg	h	2-1	*Sadović, Johana*
17/4	Rapid	a	0-3	
24/4	Ried	h	2-0	*Aigner, Sadović*
1/5	Salzburg	a	2-4	*Grünwald, Kurtisi*
5/5	Sturm	a	0-1	
9/5	Kapfenberg	h	3-1	*Simkovic, Diego Viana 2*
13/5	Austria Kärnten	a	2-2	*Niklas, Ramsebner*

No	Name	Nat	DoB	Pos	Aps	(s)	Gls
20	Hannes AIGNER		16/3/81	A	23	(5)	10
12	Taner ARI		29/5/87	D	11		1
28	Bernd BESENLEHNER		24/11/86	M	1	(2)	
30	Guido BURGSTALLER		24/4/89	A	14	(16)	
18	DIEGO VIANA	BRA	5/5/83	A	14	(14)	6
6	Daniel DUNST		12/4/84	D	15	(5)	
32	Sašo FORNEZZI	SVN	11/12/82	G	34		
4	Ronald GERCALIU		12/2/86	D	23	(1)	
7	Alexander GRÜNWALD		1/5/89	M	23	(5)	2
22	Christian HASELBERGER		2/6/89	D	1	(3)	
17	Thomas HELLY		20/10/90	A	1		
19	Petr JOHANA	CZE	1/11/76	D	17	(3)	3
15	Tanju KAYHAN		22/7/89	D	7	(1)	
13	Wolfgang KLAPF		14/12/78	M	25		
21	Václav KOLOUŠEK	CZE	13/4/76	M	6	(4)	
2	Pavel KOŠTÁL	CZE	17/9/80	D	30	(1)	1
27	Sanel KULJIC		10/10/77	A	13	(1)	8
10	Mensur KURTISI	MKD	25/3/86	A	10	(13)	7
15	Sebastian MARTINEZ		4/12/77	M		(3)	
11	Patrick NIKLAS		13/11/87	M	1	(2)	2
24	Ihsan POYRAZ		5/3/88	G	1		
25	Christian RAMSEBNER		26/3/89	D	27	(3)	1
1	Manfred RAZENBÖCK		4/7/78	G	1		
23	Mario REITER		23/10/86	M	31	(1)	4
9	Mirnel SADOVIĆ	BIH	25/5/84	A	4	(4)	2
26	Yüksel SARIYAR		1/8/79	M	3	(2)	
8	Tomas SIMKOVIC		16/4/87	M	25	(6)	4
5	Michael STANISLAW		5/6/87	M	6	(5)	
33	Patrick WOLF		4/5/81	A	29	(3)	2

PROMOTED CLUB

FC WACKER INNSBRUCK
Coach - Walter Kogler
Founded - 1915
Stadium - Tivoli Neu (17,400)
MAJOR HONOURS:
Austrian League - (10) 1971, 1972, 1973, 1975, 1977, 1989, 1990, 2000, 2001, 2002;
Austrian Cup - (7) 1970, 1973, 1975, 1978, 1979, 1989, 1993.

SECOND LEVEL FINAL TABLE 2009/10

	Pld	W	D	L	F	A	Pts
FC Wacker Innsbruck	33	21	6	6	67	26	69
FC Admira/Wacker Mödling	33	20	7	6	68	22	67
SCR Altach	33	20	6	7	60	27	66
SKN St Pölten	33	14	9	10	44	42	51
SC Austria Lustenau	33	15	5	13	43	46	50
FC Salzburg Juniors	33	13	5	15	58	49	44
FC Gratkorn	33	11	10	12	57	51	43
FC Lustenau 07	33	12	5	16	42	52	41
TSV Hartberg	33	11	5	17	36	68	38
FK Austria Wien Amateure	33	9	8	16	42	57	35
First Vienna FC	33	8	6	19	37	57	30
FC Dornbirn 1913	33	6	4	23	24	81	22

NB FC Salzburg Juniors and FK Austria Wien Amateure relegated as reserve teams ineligible for this division in 2010/11.

DOMESTIC CUP 2009/10

ÖFB-CUP

FIRST ROUND

(14/8/09)
Admira Amateure 2, Mattersburg 0
Allerheiligen 2, Hard 0
Blau-Weiss Linz 3, St Pölten 2
Floridsdorfer AC Team für Wien 3, Fürstenfeld 1
Grazer AK 5, Gleisdorf 0
Grieskirchen 1, Wiener Neustadt 3
Horn 2, Austria Wien Amateure 2 *(aet; 6-7 on pens)*
Pasching 1, Altach 0
SAK Klagenfurt 2, St Andrä 1
Schwaz 0, Wattens 3
Schwechat 0, Austria Lustenau 1
Seekirchen 0, Vienna 1
Sierning 0, Lustenau 07 2
Stegersbach 2, Flavia Solva 4
Sturm Amateure 3, Kapfenberg 1
Zurndorf 2, Dornbirn 3
Zwettl 2, Hartberg 4

(15/8/09)
Ankerbrot 0, Admira/Wacker Mödling 5
Baumgarten 1, Salzburg Juniors 6
Gaflenz 1, Gratkorn 4
Hall 0, Kottingbrunn 2
Kufstein 1, Wacker Innsbruck 2
Lendorf 1, St. Veit 2
Parndorf 2, Rapid Wien 3 *(aet)*
Post Wien 1, LASK 4
Reichenau/Union Innsbruck 5, Wiener Neudorf 3 *(aet)*
Rennweg 2, Austria Kärnten 4
St Johann 2, Sturm 4 *(aet)*

Viktoria Bregenz 1, Grödig 3 *(aet)*
Vorwärts Steyr 1, Salzburg 7
Wels 0, Ried 3
Würmla 0, Austria Wien 4

SECOND ROUND

(18/9/09)
Admira Amateure 0, Vienna 2
Allerheiligen 1, Austria Kärnten 2
Blau-Weiss Linz 2, Austria Wien Amateure 2 *(aet; 5-4 on pens)*
Dornbirn 3, Hartberg 1 *(aet)*
Flavia Solva 1, Austria Lustenau 3
Grazer AK 0, Lustenau 07 3
Kottingbrunn 1, LASK 3
Pasching 2, Wiener Neustadt 2 *(aet; 2-4 on pens)*
Salzburg Juniors 2, Gratkorn 2 *(aet; 3-5 on pens)*
Sturm Amateure 1, Ried 2

(19/9/09)
SAK Klagenfurt 1, Admira/Wacker Mödling 3
Reichenau/Union Innsbruck 1, Wacker Innsbruck 4

(20/9/09)
Floridsdorfer AC Team für Wien 0, Austria Wien 6
Grödig 0, Salzburg 1
St Veit 1, Rapid Wien 7
Wattens 0, Sturm 1

THIRD ROUND

(10/2/10)
Sturm 2, Salzburg 0

(9/3/10)
Admira/Wacker Mödling 0, Gratkorn 0 *(aet; 4-2 on pens)*
Austria Kärnten 3, Vienna 2
Dornbirn 0, Ried 2
LASK 1, Austria Wien 0
Wacker Innsbruck 0, Austria Lustenau 1
Lustenau 07 1, Wiener Neustadt 3

(10/3/10)
Blau-Weiss Linz 1, Rapid Wien 2

QUARTER-FINALS

(30/3/10)
Sturm 1 *(Jantscher 118)*, Admira/Wacker Mödling 0 *(aet)*

(31/3/10)
Austria Kärnten 3 *(Kaufmann 40, Jelavić 56og, Hierländer 76)*, Rapid Wien 2 *(Heikkinen 44, Trimmel 54)*
Ried 1 *(Drechsel 50)*, Austria Lustenau 1 *(Salkic 89) (aet; 4-2 on pens)*
Wiener Neustadt 2 *(Aigner 90+2, Grünwald 100)*, LASK 1 *(Kragl 48) (aet)*

SEMI-FINALS

(20/4/10)
Austria Kärnten 0, Wiener Neustadt 4 *(Grünwald 18, Wolf 33, Sadović 45, Diego Viana 80)*

(21/4/10)
Ried 0, Sturm 1 *(Lavrič 19)*

FINAL

(16/5/10)
Hypo Group Arena, Klagenfurt
SK STURM GRAZ 1 *(Lavrič 81)*
SC WIENER NEUSTADT 0
Referee – Grobelnik
STURM – Gratzei, Lamotte, Schildenfeld, Sonnleitner, Kandelaki, Salmutter *(Beichler 56)*, Kienzl, Weber, Jantscher *(Haas 78)*, Kienast *(Muratović 74)*, Lavrič.
WIENER NEUSTADT – Fornezzi, Johana, Košťál *(Reiter 51)*, Ramsebner, Gercaliu, Stanislaw, Wolf *(Koloušek 83)*, Grünwald, Simkovic, Aigner, Sadović *(Diego Viana 60)*.

İnter emerge victorious from title scrap

t was the title that no team seemed to want, but in the end there had to be a winner and it was İnter Bakı PİK who eventually sneaked home to claim the Premyer Liqası crown for the second time in three years, a last-day victory over Qäbälä PFK proving sufficient to see them home by one point from Bakı FK and two from both Qarabağ FK and the leaders going into the last game, Xäzär Länkäran FK.

A new, complex two-tiered league system had been introduced for 2009/10, with the 12 clubs splitting into two groups after they had played each other once home and away. That was straightforward enough, but the unconventional aspect was that the clubs carried forward only the points they had obtained against the five teams that accompanied them into their second-phase pool.

If this was intended to condense the teams and induce a closely contested race for the title, it succeeded. The only problem was that none of the six teams involved in the championship pool were able to find form when it mattered. There was a preponderance of drawn matches, and incredibly only one team, defending champions Bakı, actually won more matches than they lost over that decisive ten-game stretch.

Poškus pops up

Indeed, it was Bakı's 1-0 win away to Xäzär Länkäran on the final day that effectively handed the title to their city rivals İnter. It meant that if İnter could end a seven-game winless streak and overcome bottom-of-the-section Qäbälä, the title would be theirs. They did just that, producing their best display of the season, with top scorer, veteran Lithuanian international striker Robertas Poškus, seeing them over the line with a very timely hat-trick in a 4-1 win.

There was relief mixed with joy for coach Kakhaber Tskhadadze and his players. İnter had led the league at the winter break, at the 22-match cut-off point and also after the re-calculations, taking 17 of their first-phase points forward – two more than Xäzär Länkäran and Qarabağ, and five more than Bakı. That they took the title despite winning only two play-off games was largely down to the failures of others. The team most pained by defeat were Xäzär Länkäran, who dropped from first to fourth with that last-day loss against Bakı and then, eight days later, succumbed once again to the same opponents in the final of the domestic cup, losing 2-1 after extra time. Bakı thus reclaimed the trophy they had last won in 2005.

Azärbaycan Futbol Federasiyaları Assosiasiyası (AFFA)

228 Nobel Prospekti
AZ-1025 Bakı
tel – +994 12 490 8721
fax – +994 12 490 8722
website – affa.az
email – info@affa.az
Year of Formation – 1992

President – Rövnaq Abdullayev
General Secretary – Elkhan Mämmädov
Media Officer – Mikayıl Quliyev
National Stadium – Tofiq Bähramov adına Respublika, Baku (29,858)

TOP FIVE ALL-TIME CAPS
Aslan Kärimov (79); Tärlan Ähmädov (73); Mahmud Qurbanov (72); Qurban Qurbanov (65); Emin Ağayev (64)
TOP FIVE ALL-TIME GOALS
Qurban Qurbanov (12); Elvin Mämmädov, Branimir Subašić & Zaur Tağızadä (6); Vaqif Cavadov, Färrux İsmayılov, Vyaçeslav Lıçkin, Vidadi Rzayev & Nazim Süleymanov (5)

Robertas Poškus – his last-day hat-trick brought İnter Bakı the Premyer Liqası title

The growth of the game in Azerbaijan – highlighted by the foreigners that now flock to the Premyer Liqası in increasing numbers – has yielded improved results in European club competition. Bakı and Qarabağ did the country proud in 2009 as they lasted three ties each before bowing out in the play-off round of the UEFA Europa League. Qarabağ, having defeated Scandinavian duo Rosenborg BK and FC Honka Espoo, were eliminated by FC Twente, but their talented young striker Vaqif Cavadov did enough to warrant a winter move to the Dutch club. The 20-year-old was also highly prominent as Azerbaijan ended a generally disappointing 2010 FIFA World Cup campaign on a positive note with a 2-0 win in Liechtenstein and a 1-1 draw at home to Russia – results that helped to earn head coach Berti Vogts a new two-year contract.

NATIONAL TEAM RESULTS 2009/10

Date	Opponent		Venue	Score	Scorers
12/8/09	Germany (WCQ)	H	Baku	0-2	
5/9/09	Finland (WCQ)	H	Lankaran	1-2	Mämmädov (49)
9/9/09	Germany (WCQ)	A	Hanover	0-4	
10/10/09	Liechtenstein (WCQ)	A	Vaduz	2-0	Cavadov (55), Mämmädov (82)
14/10/09	Russia (WCQ)	H	Baku	1-1	Cavadov (53)
15/11/09	Iraq	N	Al Ain (UAE)	0-1	
18/11/09	Czech Republic	N	Al Ain (UAE)	2-0	Cavadov (25), Abışov (89)
25/2/10	Jordan	A	Amman	2-0	Fábio (1), İsmayılov (31)
3/3/10	Luxembourg	A	Luxembourg	2-1	Quliyev (28), Mämmädov (37)
26/5/10	Moldova	N	Seekirchen (AUT)	1-1	Mämmädov (21)
29/5/10	FYROM	N	Bischofshofen (AUT)	1-3	Mämmädov (89)
2/6/10	Honduras	N	Zell am See (AUT)	0-0	

NATIONAL TEAM APPEARANCES 2009/10

Coach – Berti VOGTS (GER)	30/12/46		GER	FIN	GER	LIE	RUS	Irq	Cze	Jor	Lux	Mda	Mkd	Hon	Caps	Goals
Färhad VÄLİYEV	1/11/80	Qarabağ	G						G	s46	s22				32	-
Räşad F. SADIQOV	16/6/82	Qarabağ	D						D	D	D	D75	D		60	3
Rail MÄLİKOV	18/12/85	Neftçi	D		s94	D	D			s71	D	s74			30	-
Saşa YUNİSOĞLU	18/12/85	Bakı	D	M	D						s46			D 73*	23	-
Elnur ALLAHVERDİYEV	2/11/83	Qarabağ	D	D	D	D			D	D	D	D74	D	D	11	-
Mahir ŞÜKÜROV	12/12/82	İnter Bakı /Anzhi (RUS)	M	M	M	M	M	M	M	M	M	M	M	M	44	-
Aleksandr CHERTOGANOV	8/2/80	İnter Bakı	M		M	M	M	M32			M46	M	M	s68	35	-
Samir ABBASOV	1/2/78	İnter Bakı	M	D	M 50*		M			M	M46	M	s69	s75	43	-
Elvin MÄMMÄDOV	18/7/88	Qarabağ	M	M84	M67	M	M	s62	M90	s78	M	M69	s46	M77	21	6
Vüqar NADİROV	15/6/87	Qarabağ	M74	M72	M56	M46	s46	M85	s84	M64			M46		30	1
Vaqif CAVADOV	25/5/89	Qarabağ	A	A	A	A91	A			M					28	5
Daniel AXTYAMOV	26/3/85	unattached /Simurq	s74	s72		A		A							13	-
Kamran AĞAYEV	9/2/86	Xäzär Länkäran	G	G	G	G	G			G46	G22	G	G		15	-
Volodimir LEVIN	23/1/84	İnter Bakı	D	D	D	D	D	D	D			D46	D46		13	-
Ruslan ABISOV	10/10/87	Neftçi	D46		D	D	D	D	s46	D	D77	D			9	1
Räşad Ä. SADIQOV	8/10/83	Qarabağ	M	M	s46	M46	M62	s32	M						10	-
Cavid HÜSEYNOV	9/3/88	İnter Bakı /Neftçi	s46	s67	s91	s73						s62		s46	19	-
Rahid ÄMİRQULİYEV	1/9/89	Xäzär Länkäran	s84							s64	s77				6	-
ERNANI Pereira	22/1/78	Karvan		s56						s90					12	-
Maksim MEDVEDEV	29/9/89	Qarabağ				D94	D73		D	D	D	D62	D	D	8	-
FÁBIO Luis Ramin	10/4/81	Bakı					M75	A84	M71	s58		s75	s46		15	4

AZERBAIJAN
AFFA

NATIONAL TEAM APPEARANCES 2009/10 (contd.)

			GER	FIN	GER	LIE	RUS	Irq	Cze	Jor	Lux	Mda	Mkd	Hon	Caps	Goals
Zeynal ZEYNALOV	6/12/79	Standard						s75							14	1
Tural CÄLİLOV	28/11/86	Simurq						s85							4	-
Äfran İSMAYILOV	8/10/88	Qarabağ								M71					1	1
Färid QULİYEV	6/1/86	Standard									A78	A	A	A46	4	1
Rauf ÄLİYEV	12/2/89	Qarabağ								s71	A58	A	A75	A46	5	-
Vurğun HÜSEYNOV	5/4/88	Qäbälä										s46	s46		2	-
Amit QULUZADÄ	20/11/92	Neftçi											M	M68	2	-
Salähät AĞAYEV	4/11/91	İnter Bakı												G	1	-
Ruslan ÄMİRCANOV	1/2/85	Neftçi												s77	2	-

DOMESTIC LEAGUE 2009/10

PREMYER LİQASI FINAL TABLES
SECOND PHASE
Championship Pool

	Pld	Home					Away					Total					Pts
		W	D	L	F	A	W	D	L	F	A	W	D	L	F	A	
1 İnter Bakı PİK	20	6	3	1	15	8	1	5	4	7	11	7	8	5	22	19	29
2 Bakı FK	20	4	3	3	9	8	3	4	3	10	7	7	7	6	19	15	28
3 Qarabağ FK	20	4	5	1	10	8	2	4	4	6	10	6	9	5	16	18	27
4 Xäzär Länkäran FK	20	4	5	1	11	6	2	4	4	8	8	6	9	5	19	14	27
5 Neftçi PFK	20	3	6	1	7	5	1	5	4	4	7	4	11	5	11	12	23
6 Qäbälä PFK	20	3	4	3	9	9	1	4	5	9	18	4	8	8	18	27	20

Relegation Pool

	Pld	Home					Away					Total					Pts
		W	D	L	F	A	W	D	L	F	A	W	D	L	F	A	
7 Olimpik-Şüvälan PFK	20	4	4	2	16	9	6	2	2	11	6	10	6	4	27	15	36
8 Simurq Zaqatala PFK	20	5	3	2	10	10	3	4	3	11	11	8	7	5	21	21	31
9 Turan PFK	20	4	4	2	10	5	3	4	3	17	17	7	8	5	27	22	29
10 Muğan Salyan FK	20	5	2	3	12	9	2	4	4	5	7	7	6	7	17	16	27
11 Standard Sumqayıt FK	20	4	1	5	15	11	3	3	4	11	12	7	4	9	26	23	25
12 Karvan İK	20	1	5	4	10	15	1	2	7	4	20	2	7	11	14	35	13

FIRST PHASE

	Pld	Home					Away					Total					Pts
		W	D	L	F	A	W	D	L	F	A	W	D	L	F	A	
1 İnter Bakı PİK	22	9	2	0	21	10	6	2	3	15	8	15	4	3	36	18	49
2 Xäzär Länkäran FK	22	6	5	0	14	3	6	3	2	15	8	12	8	2	29	11	44
3 Qarabağ FK	22	7	4	0	12	5	4	5	2	9	7	11	9	2	21	12	42
4 Bakı FK	22	4	3	4	8	9	6	4	1	14	8	10	7	5	22	17	37
5 Qäbälä PFK	22	7	2	2	14	8	3	4	4	10	13	10	6	6	24	21	36
6 Neftçi PFK	22	4	5	2	9	6	5	3	3	11	8	9	8	5	20	14	35
7 Simurq Zaqatala PFK	22	4	5	2	12	8	5	2	4	14	13	9	7	6	26	21	34
8 Olimpik-Şüvälan PFK	22	3	3	5	11	12	3	4	4	9	11	6	7	9	20	23	25
9 Turan PFK	22	3	1	7	11	13	1	4	6	12	19	4	5	13	23	32	17
10 Muğan Salyan FK	22	2	3	6	8	16	1	4	6	4	11	3	7	12	12	27	16
11 Standard Sumqayıt FK	22	2	1	8	10	16	0	4	7	6	18	2	5	15	16	34	11
12 Karvan İK	22	2	5	4	14	16	0	0	11	3	20	2	5	15	17	36	11

NB League split into two halves after 22 matches, with each club playing ten further matches exclusively against clubs from its half of the table. Clubs carried forward head-to-head record against Second Phase opponents only.

TOP GOALSCORERS

16 Färid QULİYEV (Standard)
12 Robertas POŠKUS (İnter)
   Anatol DOROS (Olimpik-Şüvälan)
11 Adrian NEAGA (Neftçi)
10 JABÁ (Bakı)
   Nadir NÄBİYEV (Turan)
9 Allan LALÍN (Xäzär Länkäran)
   SOUZA (Xäzär Länkäran)
8 Girts KARLSONS (İnter)
7 Aleksandar ŠOLIĆ (Bakı)
   Xäqani MÄMMÄDOV (Karvan)
   Tomasz STOLPA (Qäbälä)
   Ruslan HUNCHAK (Simurq)
   Elşän MÄMMÄDOV (Simurq)
   Ivan TSVETKOV (Xäzär Länkäran)

CLUB-BY-CLUB

BAKI FK

Coach – Gjokica Hadzievski (MKD);
(24/9/09) (Nazim Süleymanov); (29/9/09) Bülent Korkmaz (TUR);
(22/3/10) (Mäqsäd Yaqubäliyev); (3/4/10) Cüneyt Biçer (TUR)
Founded – 1997
Stadium – Tofiq Bähramov adına Respublika stadionu (29,858)
MAJOR HONOURS:
Azerbaijan League - (2) 2006, 2009;
Azerbaijan Cup - (2) 2005, 2010.

2009
12/9	Simurq	h	1-2	*Šolić*
20/9	Olimpik-Şüvälan	a	1-0	*Skulić*
23/9	Standard	h	0-0	
26/9	Qarabağ	h	0-1	
17/10	Turan	a	1-0	*Jabá*
22/10	İnter	a	0-1	
25/10	Neftçi	h	0-2	
31/10	Qäbälä	a	2-0	*Soltanov, Šolić*
7/11	Karvan	h	1-0	*Jabá*
22/11	Muğan	a	1-0	*Jabá*
25/11	Xäzär Länkäran	a	1-1	*Tijani*
29/11	Xäzär Länkäran	h	0-3	
5/12	Standard	a	4-3	*Soltanov 2, Jabá, Šolić*
9/12	İnter	h	2-0	*Jabá, Skulić*
13/12	Simurq	a	2-1	*Fábio, Šolić*
20/12	Olimpik-Şüvälan	h	0-0	
24/12	Qarabağ	a	0-0	

2010
2/2	Turan	h	2-1	*Jabá, Kürşat*
9/2	Neftçi	a	1-1	*Jabá (p)*
13/2	Qäbälä	h	2-0	*Kürşat, Adriano*
17/2	Karvan	a	1-1	*Fábio*
20/2	Muğan	h	0-0	
12/3	Qarabağ	h	2-0	*Jabá, Fábio*
21/3	Neftçi	a	0-1	
28/3	Qäbälä	h	1-1	*Šolić*
4/4	İnter	a	1-1	*Jabá*
11/4	Xäzär Länkäran	h	1-0	*Fábio*
17/4	Qarabağ	a	4-1	*Sofroni, Jabá, Šolić, Wěnio*
23/4	Neftçi	h	1-1	*Skulić*
1/5	Qäbälä	a	0-1	
9/5	İnter	h	0-0	
15/5	Xäzär Länkäran	a	1-0	*Šolić*

No	Name	Nat	DoB	Pos	Aps	(s)	Gls
55	Giorgi ADAMIA	GEO	10/3/81	A	14	(2)	
34	ADRIANO Padilha Nascimento	BRA	20/6/80	A	3	(4)	1
	Hacı AHMÄDOV		23/11/93	D	1	(2)	
14	Elvin ÄLİYEV		21/8/84	D	23	(3)	
3	Rafael ÄMİRBÄYOV		23/2/76	D	1	(1)	
11	Adnan BARAKAT	NED	3/9/82	D	9	(1)	
5	Stevan BATES	SRB	29/11/81	D	26		
	Vadim BORET	MDA	5/9/76	D	27		
20	FÁBIO Luis Ramin		10/4/81	M	19	(2)	4
9	FELIPE Almeida Félix	BRA	20/4/85	A	3	(3)	
	Rähman HACIYEV		25/7/93	D	1	(2)	
22	Säbuhi HÄSÄNOV		8/7/87	D	1	(1)	
85	Silvino João de Carvalho "JABÁ"	BRA	20/5/81	A	28		10
6	KÜRŞAT Duymuş	TUR	1/2/79	D	10		2
15	Cämşid MÄHÄRRÄMOV		3/10/83	M	11	(9)	
10	Amiran MUJIRI	GEO	20/2/74	M	3	(6)	
29	Cristian Valentin MUSCALU	ROU	3/10/89	A		(1)	
11	Daniel Ionel OPRIŢA	ROU	10/8/81	A	2	(1)	
6	Mihai PANC	ROU	7/4/81	D	8	(2)	
12	Fernando Néstor PÉREZ	ARG	11/9/80	A	1		
29	Äziz QULİYEV		2/5/87	M	2	(5)	
7	Mahmud QURBANOV		10/5/73	M	2	(9)	

2	RAFAEL BARBOSA do Nascimento	BRA	10/8/83	D		(1)	
32	Alexei SAVINOV	MDA	19/4/79	D	18	(1)	
23	Khalidou SISSOKHO	SEN	28/8/78	G	8		
8	Ernad SKULIĆ	CRO	2/5/80	M	26	(3)	3
12	Veaceslav SOFRONI	MDA	30/4/84	A	7	(3)	1
27	Bäxtiyar SOLTANOV		21/6/89	A	21	(3)	3
1	Marko ŠARLIJA	CRO	31/1/82	G	24		
77	Aleksandar ŠOLIĆ	BIH	29/1/81	M	27	(1)	7
19	Ahmed TIJANI	NGA	10/10/87	A	7	(10)	1
21	Aleksandar TOMASH	BUL	2/9/78	D	3	(4)	
55	Allan Wetende WANGA	KEN	26/11/85	A		(6)	
21	WÊNIO Moraes Pio	BRA	9/9/79	M	9	(2)	1
33	Saşa YUNİSOĞLU		18/12/85	D	8	(4)	

İNTER BAKI PİK

Coach – Kakhaber Tskhadadze (GEO)
Founded – 2004
Stadium – Şäfa (7,852)
MAJOR HONOURS:
Azerbaijan League - (2) 2008, 2010.

2009
15/8	Karvan	h	1-0	*Karlsons*
21/8	Xäzär Länkäran	a	0-1	
13/9	Olimpik-Şüvälan	h	2-2	*Karlsons, Rubins*
19/9	Turan	a	1-0	*Červenka*
26/9	Qäbälä	h	3-2	*Levin, Leo Rocha, Karlsons*
18/10	Muğan	a	6-1	*Rubins 2, Leo Rocha, Abbasov, Poškus 2*
22/10	Bakı	h	1-0	*Leo Rocha*
25/10	Standard	h	4-2	*Abbasov, Zlatinov, Mzhanavadze, Gutiérrez*
31/10	Simurq	a	1-1	*Odikadze*
7/11	Qarabağ	h	2-1	*Poškus, Leo Rocha*
22/11	Neftçi	h	1-2	*Poškus*
29/11	Karvan	a	2-0	*Zlatinov, Poškus*
6/12	Xäzär Länkäran	h	1-1	*Leo Rocha*
9/12	Bakı	a	0-2	
13/12	Olimpik-Şüvälan	a	1-0	*Karlsons*
19/12	Turan	h	3-1	*Karlsons 3*
24/12	Qäbälä	a	1-0	*Zlatinov*

2010
3/2	Muğan	h	1-0	*Zlatinov*
9/2	Standard	a	1-0	*Odikadze*
13/2	Simurq	h	2-1	*Poškus, Navalovski*
17/2	Qarabağ	a	1-1	*Poškus*
21/2	Neftçi	a	1-0	*Karlsons*
13/3	Neftçi	h	1-1	*Červenka*
21/3	Xäzär Länkäran	h	1-0	*Zlatinov (p)*
27/3	Qarabağ	a	1-1	*Abbasov*
4/4	Bakı	h	1-1	*og (Yunisoğlu)*
10/4	Qäbälä	a	1-1	*Poškus (p)*
18/4	Neftçi	a	0-1	
23/4	Xäzär Länkäran	a	2-2	*Červenka, Poškus*
1/5	Qarabağ	h	0-1	
9/5	Bakı	a	0-0	
15/5	Qäbälä	h	4-1	*Zlatinov (p), Poškus 3*

No	Name	Nat	DoB	Pos	Aps	(s)	Gls
9	Samir ABBASOV		1/2/78	D	22	(3)	3
	Elnur ABDULOV		18/9/92	M		(1)	
4	Danildo José ACCIOLY Filho	BRA	30/3/81	D	24		
18	Goran ARNAUT	SRB	22/3/79	M	1	(1)	
17	Rövşän ÄMİRASLANOV		18/3/86	M		(2)	
8	Aleksandr CHERTOGANOV		8/2/80	M	21	(4)	
13	Branislav ČERVENKA	CZE	22/9/75	M	22	(9)	3
88	FILIPE José MACHADO	BRA	13/3/84	M		(2)	

AZERBAIJAN
AFFA

		Nat	DoB	Pos	Aps	(s)	Gls
7	Ángel Gustavo GUTIÉRREZ	URU	12/1/80	M	8	(10)	1
25	Cavid HÜSEYNOV		9/3/88	M	3	(1)	
6	Aliyar ISMAILOV	RUS	11/4/76	D		(2)	
20	Ģirts KARLSONS	LVA	7/6/81	A	12	(7)	8
27	Lubomír KUBICA	CZE	10/3/79	M	14	(4)	
22	LEOnardo da Silva ROCHA	BRA	7/3/85	M	18	(3)	5
15	Volodimir LEVIN		23/1/84	D	28	(1)	1
72	Giorgi LOMAIA	GEO	8/8/79	G	21	(1)	
11	Asif MÄMMÄDOV		5/8/86	M	6	(10)	
16	Tofiq MİKAYILOV		11/4/86	M		(1)	
12	Xäyal MUSTAFAYEV		22/12/80	D	4	(1)	
30	Kakhaber MZHAVANADZE	GEO	2/10/78	D	20		1
77	Giorgi NAVALOVSKI	GEO	28/6/86	D	13		1
19	David ODIKADZE	GEO	14/4/81	M	16	(9)	2
33	Paulius PAKNYS	LTU	10/5/84	D	6		
21	Robertas POŠKUS	LTU	5/5/79	A	21	(5)	12
2	Şähriyar RÄHİMOV		6/4/88	M		(1)	
24	Andrejs RUBINS	LVA	26/11/78	M	27	(3)	3
23	Mahir ŞÜKÜROV		12/12/82	D	15		
1	WILSON Raimundo JÚNIOR	BRA	27/10/76	G	11		
5	Milan ZAGORAC	SRB	15/6/80	D	2	(1)	
14	Petar ZLATINOV	BUL	13/3/81	M	17	(12)	6

KARVAN İK
Coach – Yunis Hüseynov; (8/5/10) (Firdovsi Mehdiyev)
Founded – 2004
Stadium – Yevlax şähär stadionu (4,980)

2009
15/8	İnter	a	0-1	
23/8	Olimpik-Şüvälan	h	2-3	og (Nduka), Leandro Gomes
12/9	Qäbälä	h	4-1	Leandro Gomes, Mämmädov İ., Ernani, Ataev
20/9	Muğan	a	0-1	
26/9	Standard	h	2-2	Marcos, Mämmädov İ.
17/10	Simurq	a	0-2	
21/10	Turan	a	1-2	Häsänov O.
25/10	Qarabağ	h	1-1	Ataev
1/11	Neftçi	a	0-1	
7/11	Bakı	a	0-1	
21/11	Xäzär Länkäran	h	0-2	
29/11	İnter	h	0-2	
4/12	Olimpik-Şüvälan	a	0-4	
8/12	Turan	h	0-0	
13/12	Qäbälä	a	0-1	
18/12	Muğan	h	1-1	Mämmädov İ. (p)
24/12	Standard	a	0-1	
2010				
3/2	Simurq	h	3-2	Mämmädov X. 2, Marcos
9/2	Qarabağ	a	2-3	Mämmädov X. 2
13/2	Neftçi	h	0-1	
17/2	Bakı	h	1-1	Mämmädov X.
21/2	Xäzär Länkäran	a	0-3	
12/3	Simurq	a	0-0	
20/3	Muğan	h	0-0	
28/3	Olimpik-Şüvälan	a	0-0	
4/4	Standard	h	1-2	Mämmädov X.
11/4	Turan	a	0-2	
17/4	Simurq	h	0-0	
24/4	Muğan	a	3-2	Rähimov, Marcos, Mämmädov X.
1/5	Olimpik-Şüvälan	h	0-1	
9/5	Standard	a	0-6	
16/5	Turan	h	1-4	Mämmädzadä

No	Name	Nat	DoB	Pos	Aps	(s)	Gls
19	Mehman ABDULLAYEV		16/8/89	M	2		
8	Samäddin ABDULLAYEV		25/9/81	M	2		
	Ceyhun ADIŞİRİNOV		30/6/86	M	2	(1)	
2	ANDRÉ Luiz LADAGA		19/2/75	D	1	(1)	
21	Dovletmurat ATAEV	TKM	16/3/83	M	16	(8)	2
	Rövşan ÄMİRASLANOV		18/3/86	M	12		
15	Yacouba BAMBA	CIV	16/12/75	A	9	(4)	

5	Omar BERDIYEV	TKM	25/6/79	D	2	(2)	
17	Vüqar CABBAROV		15/11/91	D	2		
4	Elxan CÄBRAYILOV		21/2/84	D	5	(4)	
17	Emin CÄFÄRQULİYEV		17/9/90	D	11	(2)	
12	ERNANI Pereira		22/1/78	D	21	(1)	1
	Murod HAMROEV	TKM	14/5/83	D	12		
7	Anar HÄSÄNOV		14/2/83	M	20	(4)	
19	Orxan HÄSÄNOV		18/12/91	M	9	(5)	1
9	Elnur HEYDÄROV		27/3/90	G	1	(1)	
10	Ruslan HÜSEYNOV		24/3/87	A	2		
12	Teyyub HÜSEYNOV		31/5/87	D	1		
10	Cavid İMAMVERDİYEV		1/8/90	M	17	(8)	
24	Aleksandre INTSKIRVELI	GEO	24/8/81	D	25	(1)	
	Däyanät KÄRİMOV		5/3/86	D		(1)	
79	Pavel KHARCHIK	TKM	5/4/74	G	7		
32	LEANDRO Melino GOMES		24/8/76	A	9		2
23	Edvinas LUKOŠEVIČIUS	LTU	22/5/78	D	8	(4)	
8	MARCOS Ferreira Javier	BRA	18/2/82	M	25		3
5	Anar MÄMMÄDOV		31/12/83	D	2		
	Füzuli MÄMMÄDOV		8/9/77	M	12		
18	İsmayıl MÄMMÄDOV		5/8/76	M	25	(1)	3
20	Ramin MÄMMÄDOV		13/8/92	A	2	(3)	
	Xäqani MÄMMÄDOV		29/9/76	A	13		7
6	Nicat MÄMMÄDZADÄ		20/11/89	M	1	(1)	1
	Rauf MEHDİYEV		17/10/76	G	10		
14	Béchir MOGAÄDİ	TUN	8/11/78	M	8		
	Elgün MUSAYEV		24/10/92	M		(1)	
3	Pärviz MUSAYEV		9/7/86	D	2		
27	Yuriy MUZIKA		10/8/82	M	1	(1)	
1	Amil ORUCOV		24/12/85	G	2		
28	Äziz QULİYEV		2/5/87	M	12	(2)	
	Emin QULİYEV		4/12/77	D	5		
	Zaur RAMAZANOV		27/7/76	A	7		
	Şähriyar RÄHİMOV		6/4/89	M	7	(5)	1
7	Süleyman SADIQOV		6/2/87	M	2		
13	Zamiq SALMANOV		21/2/90	A		(1)	
14	Asif SÄFÄROV		22/12/87	D	2		
	THIAGO Rocha dos Santos	BRA	22/3/82	D	1	(6)	
16	Ivan VASILYEV	RUS	31/1/91	G	13	(1)	
3	İlham YADULLAYEV		17/9/75	D	4		

MUĞAN SALYAN FK
Coach – Kemal Alispahić (BIH); (2/12/09) Almir Hurtić (BIH)
Founded – 2007
Stadium – Salyan Olimpiya İdman Kompleksi (2,000)

2009
14/8	Standard	h	1-0	og (Gvelesiani)
22/8	Simurq	a	0-0	
13/9	Neftçi	a	2-0	Hüseynov, Ćulov
20/9	Karvan	h	1-0	Ćulov
26/9	Xäzär Länkäran	a	0-2	
18/10	İnter	h	1-6	Yaméogo (p)
21/10	Qarabağ	h	0-1	
24/10	Olimpik-Şüvälan	a	0-0	
1/11	Turan	h	2-3	Hüseynov, Qafitullin
7/11	Qäbälä	a	0-3	
22/11	Bakı	h	0-1	
29/11	Standard	a	0-1	
6/12	Simurq	h	0-0	
10/12	Qarabağ	a	1-2	Hüseynov
13/12	Neftçi	h	2-2	Adilović, Hodžić
18/12	Karvan	a	1-1	İsmayılov
24/12	Xäzär Länkäran	h	1-2	Adilović
2010				
3/2	İnter	a	0-1	
9/2	Olimpik-Şüvälan	a	0-1	
13/2	Turan	a	0-1	
17/2	Qäbälä	h	0-0	
20/2	Bakı	a	0-0	
13/3	Turan	a	2-1	Hüseynov, İsmayılov
20/3	Karvan	a	0-0	
27/3	Standard	h	1-0	Cricimari

AFFA

3/4	Simurq	a	0-1	
10/4	Olimpik-Şüvälan	h	2-1	Hüseynov, İsmayılov
18/4	Turan	h	0-0	
24/4	Karvan	h	2-3	Samura, Abdullayev (p)
1/5	Standard	a	2-0	Samura, Axundov
9/5	Simurq	h	3-1	Zečević, Axundov, Jugo
16/5	Olimpik-Şüvälan	a	0-2	

No	Name	Nat	DoB	Pos	Aps	(s)	Gls
7	Elnur ABDULLAYEV		16/2/86	M	29	(1)	1
21	Eldin ADILOVIĆ	BIH	8/2/86	A	8	(5)	2
25	Amil AĞACANOV		24/7/87	G	3		
	Häsän ALLAHYAROV		14/9/92	A		(1)	
4	Tural AXUNDOV		1/8/88	D	4	(7)	2
19	Zaur ÄSÄDOV		14/2/82	M	11	(7)	
10	Vadim CRICIMARI	MDA	22/8/88	M	15		1
9	Adis ČULOV	BIH	18/7/87	M	14		2
14	Säbuhi HÄSÄNOV		8/7/87	D	5	(3)	
22	Ekrem HODŽIĆ	BIH	7/8/79	M	23	(1)	1
20	Vüsal HÜSEYNOV		9/8/82	M	19	(3)	5
10	Arif İSAYEV		28/7/85	A	11	(2)	
16	Färrux İSMAYILOV		30/8/78	A	16	(10)	3
9	Amir JUGO	BIH	5/12/82	M	12		1
1	Edis KURTANOVIĆ	BIH	25/11/81	G	29		
5	Novruz MÄMMÄDOV		20/3/90	D	28		
34	Cavad MİRZÄYEV		14/1/82	D	21	(1)	
6	Taqim NOVRUZOV		21/11/88	M	20	(7)	
11	Akeem PRIESTLY	JAM	13/4/85	A	4	(8)	
18	Ruslan QAFİTULLIN		5/8/79	D	10		1
	Nuran QURBANOV		10/8/93	M		(2)	
2	Mikayıl RÄHİMOV		11/5/87	D	2	(2)	
17	Rävi RÄHMANOV		22/7/86	M	4	(12)	
15	Kabba SAMURA	SLE	26/10/81	M	5	(8)	2
18	David SVANIDZE	GEO	14/10/79	D	12	(1)	
8	Narcisse YAMÉOGO	BFA	19/11/80	M	18	(10)	1
23	Miloš ZEČEVIĆ	SRB	17/5/83	D	29		

NEFTÇİ PFK

Coach – Böyükağa Ağayev; (29/9/09) Vaqif Sadıqov; (22/2/10) Arif Äsädov
Founded – 1937
Stadiums – İsmät Qayıbov adına Baxıxanov qäsäbä stadionu (2,000) & Tofiq Bähramov adına Respublika stadionu (29,858)
MAJOR HONOURS:
Azerbaijan League - (5) 1992, 1996, 1997, 2004, 2005;
Azerbaijan Cup - (5) 1995, 1996, 1999, 2002, 2004.

2009

16/8	Olimpik-Şüvälan	a	1-0	Naidin
22/8	Turan	h	2-0	Neaga (p), Guglielmone (p)
13/9	Muğan	h	0-2	
19/9	Standard	a	2-1	Abdullayev R., Neaga
27/9	Simurq	h	0-1	
18/10	Qarabağ	a	0-1	
21/10	Qäbälä	a	0-1	
25/10	Baxı	a	2-0	Neaga, Aliuță
1/11	Karvan	h	1-0	Kruglov
8/11	Xäzär Länkäran	h	0-0	
22/11	İnter	h	2-1	Guglielmone, Äliyev
29/11	Olimpik-Şüvälan	h	0-0	
5/12	Turan	a	3-2	Neaga 2, Atem
10/12	Qäbälä	h	1-1	Mälikov
13/12	Muğan	a	2-2	Neaga (p), Aliuță
20/12	Standard	h	2-0	Neaga (p), Aliuță
26/12	Simurq	a	0-0	

2010

3/2	Qarabağ	h	0-0	
9/2	Baxı	h	1-1	Neaga (p)
13/2	Karvan	a	1-0	Neaga (p)
17/2	Xäzär Länkäran	h	0-0	
21/2	İnter	a	0-1	
13/3	İnter	h	1-1	Neaga (p)
21/3	Baxı	h	1-0	Neaga

27/3	Xäzär Länkäran	a	0-0	
3/4	Qäbälä	h	1-2	Abdullayev R.
10/4	Qarabağ	a	0-2	
18/4	İnter	h	1-0	Hüseynov
23/4	Baxı	a	1-1	Voskoboinikov
1/5	Xäzär Länkäran	h	0-0	
9/5	Qäbälä	a	0-0	
15/5	Qarabağ	h	0-0	

No	Name	Nat	DoB	Pos	Aps	(s)	Gls
17	Araz ABDULLAYEV		18/4/92	M	6	(3)	
27	Räşad ABDULLAYEV		1/10/81	M	25	(1)	2
15	Ruslan ABIŞOV		10/10/87	D	25		
44	Valeri ABRAMIDZE	GEO	17/1/80	D	13		
10	Marian ALIUȚĂ	ROU	4/2/78	M	15	(9)	3
30	Valentine Fondongbeze ATEM	CMR	26/8/79	A	5	(10)	1
7	Samir ÄLİYEV		14/4/79	A	1	(12)	1
18	Ruslan ÄMİRCANOV		1/2/85	M	17	(4)	
26	Nazar BAIRAMOV	TKM	4/9/82	M	12	(2)	
8	Elmar BAXŞIYEV		30/8/80	M	14	(6)	
34	Paulius GRYBAUSKAS	LTU	2/6/84	G	22		
9	Walter Fernando GUGLIELMONE	URU	11/4/78	A	14	(8)	2
11	Cavid HÜSEYNOV		9/3/88	M	7	(4)	1
20	JOSÉ CARLOS dos Reis	BRA	11/2/88	A	1	(7)	
16	Dmitri KRUGLOV	EST	24/5/84	D	29		1
2	Rail MÄLİKOV		18/12/85	D	27		1
1	Vladimir MIČOVIĆ	SRB	11/10/75	G	9		
5	Leonard Toni NAIDIN	ROU	15/9/79	M	23	(2)	1
23	Tural NÄRİMANOV		27/10/89	D	3	(2)	
25	Adrian Constantin NEAGA	ROU	4/6/79	A	30		11
6	Eşqin QULİYEV		11/12/90	M	1	(4)	
	Tärlan QULİYEV		19/4/92	D	1		
	Amit QULUZADÄ		20/11/92	M	1		
4	Taavi RÄHN	EST	16/5/81	D	19		
	Elçin SADIQOV		14/6/89	G	1		
	Mirhüseyn SEYİDOV		10/8/92	M	1	(1)	
14	Andrei STEPANOV	EST	16/3/79	D	2		
3	SUAT Usta	TUR	3/8/81	D	17	(3)	
22	Zaur TAĞIZADÄ		21/2/79	M	6	(4)	
14	Vladimir VOSKOBOINIKOV	EST	2/2/83	A	5	(4)	1

OLİMPİK-ŞÜVÄLAN PFK

Coach – Äsgär Abdullayev; (23/11/09) Nazim Süleymanov
Founded – 1996
Stadium – Şäfa, Baku (7,852)

2009

16/8	Neftçi	h	0-1	
23/8	Karvan	a	3-2	Doros 2, Diano
13/9	İnter	a	2-2	Goginashvili, Doros
20/9	Baxı	h	0-1	
27/9	Turan	h	3-3	Goginashvili, Kvirtia, Doros
17/10	Qäbälä	a	1-2	Doros
21/10	Xäzär Länkäran	h	1-0	Doros
24/10	Muğan	h	0-0	
1/11	Standard	a	1-0	Xälilov
8/11	Simurq	h	0-3	
22/11	Qarabağ	a	0-1	
29/11	Neftçi	a	0-0	
4/12	Karvan	h	4-0	Mandić, Doros, og (Häsänov A.), Kvirtia
10/12	Xäzär Länkäran	a	1-2	Ibekoyi
13/12	İnter	h	0-1	
20/12	Baxı	a	0-0	
26/12	Turan	h	0-0	

2010

2/2	Qäbälä	h	0-2	
9/2	Muğan	a	1-0	Ismael Gaúcho
13/2	Standard	a	2-0	Ismael Gaúcho 2
17/2	Simurq	a	0-2	
20/2	Qarabağ	h	1-1	Qurbanov
12/3	Standard	h	1-2	Bunjevčević
20/3	Simurq	a	3-0	Ibekoyi, Diano, Doros

AZERBAIJAN
AFFA

28/3	Karvan	h	0-0	
3/4	Turan	h	4-1	Doros 3, Diano
10/4	Muğan	a	1-2	Doros
18/4	Standard	a	1-0	Ibekoyi
23/4	Simurq	h	0-0	
1/5	Karvan	a	1-0	Qurbanov
9/5	Turan	a	0-0	
16/5	Muğan	h	2-0	Xälilov, og (Svanidze)

No	Name	Nat	DoB	Pos	Aps	(s)	Gls
16	Samir ABDULOV		8/5/87	M	7	(3)	
15	Hüseyn AXUNDOV		30/4/88	M	6	(7)	
13	Näriman ÄZİMOV		29/9/86	A	1	(7)	
21	Mirko BUNJEVČEVIĆ	SRB	5/2/78	M	13		1
6	Abdoul Kader CAMARA	GUI	18/3/82	M	12	(2)	
5	Claudiano Alves dos Santos "DIANO"	BRA	7/10/81	D	28		3
9	Anatol DOROS	MDA	21/3/83	A	27	(1)	12
22	ENDER Günlü	TUR	9/5/84	M	2	(6)	
4	Roman GOGINASHVILI	GEO	23/1/84	D	9	(1)	2
14	Vasif HAQVERDİYEV		15/10/78	M	1	(6)	
12	Cahangir HÄSÄNZADÄ		4/8/79	G	11	(1)	
23	Viktor Kayode IBEKOYI	NGA	1/9/86	A	17	(3)	3
22	ISMAEL da Silva Francisco "GAÚCHO"	BRA	7/10/84	A	6	(5)	3
16	Ramaz JABNIDZE	RUS	25/11/79	A		(3)	
15	JUNIVAN Soares de Melo	BRA	20/11/77	A	3	(9)	
24	Nikolajs KOZAČUKS	LVA	7/8/85	M	5	(5)	
10	Nugzar KVIRTIA	GEO	16/9/84	M	25	(5)	2
2	Serghey LASCENCOV	MDA	24/3/80	D	25		
11	Dragan MANDIĆ	SRB	10/12/76	D	28		1
8	Füzuli MÄMMÄDOV		8/9/77	D	1	(4)	
7	Aqil NÄBİYEV		16/6/82	M	24		
20	Ramin NÄSİBOV		20/11/79	A		(1)	
3	Usim NDUKA		23/3/85	D	29		
1	Elşan POLADOV		30/11/79	G	21	(1)	
	Vüsal QARAYEV		8/7/86	M	4	(2)	
18	İlqar QURBANOV		26/4/86	M	17	(6)	2
	Orxan SÄFİYAROĞLU		22/2/90	M		(3)	
19	Artem VASKOV	BLR	21/10/88	M	5	(7)	
17	Tärlan XÄLİLOV		27/8/84	M	25	(2)	2

QARABAĞ FK
Coach – Qurban Qurbanov
Founded – 1987
Stadiums – Quzanlı Olimpiya İdman Kompleksi (2,000) &
Tofiq İsmayılov adına Suraxanı qäsäbä stadionu (2,800)
MAJOR HONOURS:
Azerbaijan League - (1) 1993;
Azerbaijan Cup - (3) 1993, 2006, 2009.

2009

13/9	Standard	h	1-0	Cavadov
16/9	Turan	a	2-1	Cavadov, Mämmädov E.
20/9	Simurq	a	0-1	
23/9	Qäbälä	h	0-0	
26/9	Bakı	a	1-0	Kärimov A.
18/10	Neftçi	h	1-0	Cavadov
21/10	Muğan	a	1-0	İsmayılov
25/10	Karvan	a	1-1	Äliyev
30/10	Xäzär Länkäran	h	1-0	Äliyev
7/11	İnter	a	1-2	Sadıqov R.Ä.
22/11	Olimpik-Şüvälan	h	1-0	İsmayılov
27/11	Turan	h	2-1	Nadirov 2
6/12	Qäbälä	a	1-1	Sadıqov R.Ä.
10/12	Muğan	h	2-1	İmamäliyev, Cavadov
13/12	Standard	a	1-0	İsmayılov
20/12	Simurq	h	0-0	
24/12	Bakı	h	0-0	

2010

3/2	Neftçi	a	0-0	
9/2	Karvan	h	3-2	İsmayılov, Allahverdiyev, İmamäliyev (p)

13/2	Xäzär Länkäran	a	0-0	
17/2	İnter	h	1-1	Kärimov R.
20/2	Olimpik-Şüvälan	a	1-1	Teli
12/3	Bakı	a	0-2	
21/3	Qäbälä	a	1-3	Adamia
27/3	İnter	h	1-1	Kärimov A.
3/4	Xäzär Länkäran	a	1-2	Adamia
10/4	Neftçi	h	2-0	Adamia, Äliyev
17/4	Bakı	h	1-4	İsmayılov
24/4	Qäbälä	h	1-1	Äliyev
1/5	İnter	a	1-0	Adamia
9/5	Xäzär Länkäran	h	2-1	Sadıqov R.F., Äliyev
15/5	Neftçi	a	0-0	

No	Name	Nat	DoB	Pos	Aps	(s)	Gls
15	Ayxan ABBASOV		25/8/81	M	6	(4)	
20	Giorgi ADAMIA	GEO	10/3/81	A	9	(1)	4
2	Elnur ALLAHVERDİYEV		2/11/83	D	24		1
11	Rauf ÄLİYEV		12/2/89	A	18	(9)	5
20	Vaqif CAVADOV		25/5/89	A	13	(3)	4
3	Aftandil HACIYEV		13/8/81	D	3	(5)	
4	Zaur HÄŞİMOV		24/10/81	D	22	(2)	
10	Emin İMAMÄLİYEV		7/8/80	M	12	(8)	2
23	Tural İSGÄNDÄROV		9/2/92	A	1	(4)	
22	Äfran İSMAYILOV		8/10/88	M	27		5
8	Aslan KÄRİMOV		1/1/73	M	17	(11)	2
16	Räşad KÄRİMOV		2/4/86	M	8	(3)	1
12	Sahil KÄRİMOV		22/1/79	G	3		
9	Elvin MÄMMÄDOV		18/7/88	M	20	(8)	1
21	Nodar MÄMMÄDOV		3/6/88	D	2	(3)	
5	Maksim MEDVEDEV		29/9/89	D	26		
19	Emin MUSTAFAYEV		2/1/90	M		(1)	
17	Vüqar NADİROV		15/6/87	A	17	(12)	2
13	Qara QARAYEV		12/10/92	D	1		
6	Räşad Ä.SADIQOV		8/10/83	M	23	(2)	2
14	Räşad F. SADIQOV		16/6/82	D	17	(3)	1
24	Admir TELI	ALB	2/6/81	D	29	(1)	1
1	Färhad VÄLİYEV		1/11/80	G	29		
7	Namiq YUSİFOV		14/8/86	M	25	(5)	

QÄBÄLÄ PFK
Coach – Ramiz Mämmädov
Founded – 2005
Stadium – Qäbälä şähär stadionu (2,000)

2009

16/8	Simurq	h	2-1	Kärimov K., Melnyk
12/9	Karvan	h	1-4	Antić
19/9	Xäzär Länkäran	h	1-1	Melnyk
23/9	Qarabağ	a	0-0	
26/9	İnter	a	2-3	Melnyk, Torres
17/10	Olimpik-Şüvälan	h	2-1	Kärimov K., og (Diano)
21/10	Neftçi	h	1-0	Torres
25/10	Turan	a	1-0	Hüseynov
31/10	Bakı	h	0-2	
7/11	Muğan	h	3-0	Stolpa 2, Beraia
20/11	Standard	a	2-1	Stolpa, Melnyk
28/11	Simurq	a	1-1	og (Malyhin)
6/12	Qarabağ	h	1-1	Stolpa (p)
10/12	Neftçi	a	1-1	Hüseynov
13/12	Karvan	h	1-0	Ţârlea
19/12	Xäzär Länkäran	a	0-1	
24/12	İnter	h	0-1	

2010

2/2	Olimpik-Şüvälan	a	2-0	Torres 2
9/2	Turan	h	1-0	Kärimov K. (p)
13/2	Bakı	a	0-2	
17/2	Muğan	a	0-0	
21/2	Standard	h	2-1	Torres, Hüseynov
12/3	Xäzär Länkäran	a	1-4	Antić
21/3	Qarabağ	h	3-1	Paulinho, Melnyk 2
28/3	Bakı	a	1-1	Paşayev
3/4	Neftçi	a	2-1	Antić, Stolpa

10/4	İnter	h	1-1	Kärimov K. (p)		
17/4	Xäzär Länkäran	h	1-2	Stolpa		
24/4	Qarabağ	a	1-1	Kärimov K. (p)		
1/5	Bakı	h	1-0	Paulinho		
9/5	Neftçi	h	0-0			
15/5	İnter	a	1-4	Stolpa		

No	Name	Nat	DoB	Pos	Aps	(s)	Gls
7	Yaşar ABUZÄROV		9/9/77	M	7	(9)	
14	Milan ANTIĆ	SRB	1/7/81	D	28	(1)	3
26	Namiq ÄLIYEV		29/9/80	M	6	(7)	
6	Ljubo BARANIN	SRB	25/8/86	D	29	(1)	
18	Goga BERAIA	RUS	26/1/84	D	28		1
17	Volodymyr BONDARCHUK	UKR	20/2/81	M	12	(2)	
16	Abdoul Kader CAMARA	GUI	18/3/82	M	13		
21	Arif DAŞDÄMİROV		10/2/87	M	13	(5)	
12	Pävels DOROŠEVS	LVA	9/10/80	G	29		
19	Revaz GETSADZE	GEO	11/1/85	M	12	(5)	
23	Azär HÄŞİMOV		6/11/84	M	1	(1)	
16	Mykola HIBALYUK	UKR	21/5/84	D	10	(1)	
3	Vurğun HÜSEYNOV		5/4/88	D	26	(1)	3
1	Elnar KÄRİMOV		5/4/85	G	3		
10	Känan KÄRİMOV		5/8/76	A	20	(3)	5
2	Milan MARINKOVIĆ	SRB	23/5/86	D		(1)	
4	Azär MÄMMÄDOV		7/2/76	D	3		
24	Ihor MELNYK	UKR	5/3/83	A	22	(5)	6
25	Rähman MUSAYEV		14/12/86	A		(2)	
11	Anatol OSTAP	MDA	22/11/79	M	14	(5)	
22	Pärvin PAŞAYEV		29/8/88	M	3	(9)	1
	Paulo Lopes Tavares "PAULINHO"	POR	10/12/84	M	7	(7)	2
8	Maxym SKOROKHODOV	UKR	3/12/86	M	6	(1)	
5	Sergey SOKOLOV		12/3/77	D	2	(3)	
9	Tomasz STOLPA	POL	18/3/83	A	15	(12)	7
15	Räzvan ŢÄRLEA	ROU	5/8/79	D	23	(2)	1
20	Cristian Damián TORRES	ARG	18/6/85	M	16	(12)	5
2	Velichko VELICHKOV	BUL	8/7/86	D	4		

SİMURQ ZAQATALA PFK
Coach – Roman Pokora (UKR)
Founded – 2005
Stadium – Zaqatala Olimpiya İdman Kompleksi (3,500)

2009

16/8	Qäbälä	a	1-2	Artyukh
22/8	Muğan	h	0-0	
12/9	Bakı	a	2-1	Mämmädov E., Hunchak
20/9	Qarabağ	h	1-0	Artyukh
27/9	Neftçi	a	1-0	Sokolov
17/10	Karvan	h	2-0	Mämmädov E., Hunchak
20/10	Standard	a	2-1	Bolkvadze, Bulychev
24/10	Xäzär Länkäran	a	0-3	
31/10	İnter	h	1-1	Chkhetiani
8/11	Olimpik-Şüvälan	h	3-0	Mämmädov E., Hunchak (p), Valev
21/11	Turan	h	2-1	Soloņicins, Chkhetiani
28/11	Qäbälä	h	1-1	Mämmädov E.
6/12	Muğan	a	0-0	
9/12	Standard	h	1-1	Valev
13/12	Bakı	h	1-2	Hunchak (p)
20/12	Qarabağ	a	0-0	
26/12	Neftçi	h	0-0	

2010

3/2	Karvan	a	2-3	Perišić, og (Intskiveli)
9/2	Xäzär Länkäran	h	1-2	Hunchak (p)
13/2	İnter	a	1-2	Hunchak (p)
17/2	Olimpik-Şüvälan	h	2-0	Hunchak, Golban
21/2	Turan	a	2-1	Bolkvadze 2
12/3	Karvan	h	0-0	
20/3	Olimpik-Şüvälan	h	0-3	
27/3	Turan	h	1-0	Mämmädov E.
3/4	Muğan	h	1-0	Mämmädov E.
10/4	Standard	a	1-3	Mämmädov E.
17/4	Karvan	a	0-0	

23/4	Olimpik-Şüvälan	a	0-0		
1/5	Turan	h	2-1	Golban, Mämmädov E.	
9/5	Muğan	a	1-3	Cälilov	
16/5	Standard	h	0-4		

No	Name	Nat	DoB	Pos	Aps	(s)	Gls
	Ramil AĞAYEV		7/8/81	M		(5)	
23	Roman AKHALKATSI	GEO	20/2/80	M	14	(4)	
14	Serhiy ARTYUKH	UKR	29/7/85	A	19		2
33	Daniel AXTYAMOV		26/3/85	A		(3)	
12	Fuad ÄHMÄDOV		14/1/88	G	2		
	Säbuhi ÄHMÄDOV		26/4/87	G	2		
33	Nenad BEGOVIĆ	SRB	6/1/80	D	2	(2)	
18	David BOLKVADZE	GEO	5/6/80	M	21	(8)	3
19	Yuriy BULYCHEV	UKR	12/10/82	D	30		1
15	Tural CÄLİLOV		28/11/86	M	17	(11)	1
17	Kakhaber CHKHETIANI	GEO	24/2/78	D	28		2
1	Taras CHOPIK	UKR	2/2/72	G	10		
32	Alexandru GOLBAN	MDA	28/2/79	A	15		2
2	Teimuraz GONGADZE	GEO	8/9/85	D	11	(1)	
8	Ruslan HUNCHAK	UKR	9/8/79	M	31		7
4	Olexandr MALYHIN	UKR	27/11/79	D	18	(1)	
88	Camal MÄMMÄDOV		26/12/83	M	4	(7)	
9	Elşän MÄMMÄDOV		4/5/80	A	25	(5)	7
11	Rüstäm MÄMMÄDOV		14/8/84	D	5	(5)	
	Ramin NÄSİBOV		20/11/79	A	1	(7)	
5	Dragan PERIŠIĆ	SRB	27/10/79	D	3	(1)	1
77	Vitaliy POSTRANSKIY	UKR	2/8/77	G	18		
	İlkin QIRTIMOV		4/11/90	M		(1)	
3	Rasim RAMALDANOV		24/1/86	D	11		
24	Andriy RASPOPOV	UKR	25/6/78	D	5		
25	Ramil SAYADOV		11/7/83	M	8	(5)	
29	Andrei SHERYAKOV	BLR	10/10/82	A	4	(3)	
32	Andriy SOKOLENKO	UKR	8/6/78	D	8	(1)	
5	Sergey SOKOLOV		12/8/77	D	16		1
7	Genädijs SOLONICINS	LVA	3/1/80	M	14	(4)	1
	Laçın ŞÄKÄROV		23/6/89	D		(2)	
21	Nikolai VALEV	BUL	24/4/81	A	10	(7)	2

STANDARD SUMQAYIT FK
Coach – Valdas Ivanauskas (LTU); (21/10/09) (Elbrus Mämmädov); (26/10/09) Böyükağa Hacıyev
Founded – 2006
Stadium – Mehdi Huseynzade adına şähär stadionu (12,000)

2009

14/8	Muğan	a	0-1	
13/9	Qarabağ	a	0-1	
19/9	Neftçi	h	1-2	Quliyev F.
23/9	Bakı	a	0-0	
26/9	Karvan	a	2-2	Zärgärov, El Zein
17/10	Xäzär Länkäran	h	1-2	Seturidze
20/10	Simurq	h	1-2	Quliyev F.
25/10	İnter	a	2-4	Quliyev F., Zärgärov
1/11	Olimpik-Şüvälan	h	0-1	
8/11	Turan	h	0-3	
20/11	Qäbälä	h	1-2	Zeynalov
29/11	Muğan	h	1-0	Quliyev F.
5/12	Bakı	h	3-4	Hugo Machado 2 (1p), Riquelme Chiapa
9/12	Simurq	a	1-1	Quliyev F.
13/12	Qarabağ	h	0-1	
20/12	Neftçi	a	0-2	
24/12	Karvan	h	1-0	Quliyev F.

2010

3/2	Xäzär Länkäran	a	0-0	
9/2	İnter	h	0-1	
13/2	Olimpik-Şüvälana	a	0-2	
17/2	Turan	h	1-1	Hugo Machado (p)
21/2	Qäbälä	a	1-2	Balamestnyi
12/3	Olimpik-Şüvälan	a	2-1	Riquelme Chiapa, Quliyev F.
20/3	Turan	h	2-3	Zärgärov, Mujiri
27/3	Muğan	a	0-1	

AZERBAIJAN
AFFA

4/4	Karvan	a	2-1	*Quliyev F., Seturidze*
10/4	Simurq	h	3-1	*Mazyar, Quliyev F., Riquelme Chiapa*
18/4	Olimpik-Şüvälan	h	0-1	
23/4	Turan	a	0-0	
1/5	Muğan	h	0-2	
9/5	Karvan	h	6-0	*Balamestnyi 2, Quliyev F. 4*
16/5	Simurq	a	4-0	*İsayev, Quliyev F. 3*

No	Name	Nat	DoB	Pos	Aps	(s)	Gls
33	ADRIANO da Silva	BRA	5/2/80	M	4		
9	Murad AĞAKİŞİYEV		13/6/85	M	17	(5)	
85	Natiq ÄKBÄROV		24/4/85	D	13	(2)	
28	Vasif ÄLİYEV		6/8/86	M		(3)	
18	Vitali BALAMESTNYI	RUS	28/7/80	A	7	(2)	3
5	David CHICHVEISHVILI	GEO	23/10/75	D	12	(4)	
1	Alexandru CHIRILOV	MDA	28/1/78	G	3		
30	Andrei CHIRSUL	MDA	20/11/81	D	5		
8	Omar EL ZEIN	LIB	12/8/85	A		(4)	1
7	Räcäb FÄRÄCZADÄ		19/12/80	M		(3)	
18	Eduard GROSSU	MDA	5/1/80	M		(1)	
17	Oleg GVELESIANI	GEO	16/9/80	D	1		
10	HUGO Miguel Alves MACHADO	POR	4/7/82	M	23	(2)	3
67	Ramal HÜSEYNOV		16/12/84	M	15		
17	Arif İSAYEV		28/7/85	M	6	(7)	1
1	Pavel KHARCHIK	TKM	5/4/79	G	11		
11	Aqil MÄMMÄDOV		12/4/72	M	11	(3)	
55	Volodymyr MAZYAR	UKR	28/9/77	A	5	(6)	1
99	Amiran MUJIRI	GEO	22/2/74	M	4	(6)	1
12	Anar NÄZİROV		8/9/85	G	18	(1)	
3	Sergo ORBELADZE	GEO	1/5/82	D	27	(1)	
20	Daniel Petru PISLA	MDA	14/6/86	M	2	(2)	
86	Färid QULİYEV		6/1/86	A	26	(3)	16
8	Kamal QULİYEV		14/11/76	D	10		
77	Ramin QULİYEV		22/6/81	D	28		
2	Vüqar QULİYEV		20/11/78	D	10	(1)	
50	Richard Gabriel RIQUELME CHIAPA	URU	6/9/80	M	23	(5)	3
99	RODRIGO SILVA dos Santos	BRA	16/11/82	A	2		
22	Giorgi SETURIDZE	GEO	8/4/85	D	25	(1)	2
4	Levan SILAGADZE	GEO	4/8/76	D	5		
30	Eduardo Moreira VARGAS Fernandes	CPV	21/8/77	M	6	(2)	
28	Marius Constantin VINTILA	ROU	9/1/82	M	4	(5)	
25	Samir ZÄRGÄROV		29/8/86	M	16	(7)	3
14	Zeynal ZEYNALOV		6/12/79	M	13	(2)	1

TURAN PFK
Coach – Nizami Sadıqov
Founded – 1992
Stadium – Tovuz şähär stadionu (6,350)
MAJOR HONOURS:
Azerbaijan League - (1) 1994.

2009
22/8	Neftçi	a	0-2	
12/9	Xäzär Länkäran	a	1-1	*Muammer*
16/9	Qarabağ	h	1-2	*Saiko*
19/9	İnter	h	0-1	
27/9	Olimpik-Şüvälan	a	3-3	*Häsänov 2, Kovalevskiy*
17/10	Bakı	h	0-1	
21/10	Karvan	h	2-1	*Näbiyev, Onila*
25/10	Qäbälä	h	0-1	
1/11	Muğan	a	3-2	*Musayev 3*
8/11	Standard	h	3-0	*Näbiyev, Musayev, Häsänov*
21/11	Simurq	h	1-2	*Abbasov*
27/11	Qarabağ	a	1-2	*Häsänov*
5/12	Neftçi	h	2-3	*Khromtsov, Tağıyev*
8/12	Karvan	a	0-0	
13/12	Xäzär Länkäran	h	1-2	*Abbasov*
19/12	İnter	a	1-3	*Onila (p)*
26/12	Olimpik-Şüvälan	h	0-0	

2010
2/2	Bakı	a	1-2	*Häsänov*
9/2	Qäbälä	a	0-1	
13/2	Muğan	h	1-0	*Onila*
17/2	Standard	a	1-1	*Saiko (p)*
21/2	Simurq	h	1-2	*Kolawole*
13/3	Muğan	h	1-2	*Näbiyev*
20/3	Standard	a	3-2	*Näbiyev 2, Kolawole*
27/3	Simurq	h	0-0	
3/4	Olimpik-Şüvälan	a	1-4	*Näbiyev*
11/4	Karvan	h	2-0	*Näbiyev, Kolawole*
18/4	Muğan	a	0-0	
23/4	Standard	h	0-0	
1/5	Simurq	a	1-2	*Mämmädov E.*
9/5	Olimpik-Şüvälan	h	0-0	
16/5	Karvan	a	4-1	*Näbiyev 3, Äliyev F.*

No	Name	Nat	DoB	Pos	Aps	(s)	Gls
3	Ruslan ABBASOV		1/6/80	D	27	(1)	2
7	Kamal ÄLÄKBÄROV		4/3/78	D	19	(4)	
	Tuqay ÄLHÜSEYNLİ		1993	A		(1)	
	Färmai ÄLİYEV		1990	M	1		1
18	Hafiz ÄLİYEV		17/2/83	M	25		
1	Kamal BAYRAMOV		19/8/85	G	16		
19	Räşid HASÄNOV	RUS	26/6/82	M	15	(5)	5
22	Qärib İBRAHİMOV		11/9/88	M	5	(3)	
2	Hüseyn İSGÄNDÄROV		19/7/90	D	30	(1)	
11	JUNIVAN Soares de Melo	BRA	20/11/77	A	10	(4)	
14	Bayram KÄRİMOV		21/3/89	D	16		
33	Oleg KHROMTSOV	MDA	30/5/81	A	2	(4)	1
	Peter KOLAWOLE	NGA	19/11/90	A	2	(7)	
8	Anton KOVALEVSKIY	UKR	2/8/84	A	22	(5)	1
	Azär MÄMMÄDOV		1990	A		(3)	
23	Elnur MÄMMÄDOV		10/8/84	M	24	(3)	1
78	MUAMMER Erdoğdu	TUR	7/7/87	D	23	(2)	1
9	Samir MUSAYEV		13/7/79	A	16	(8)	4
4	Ruslan NAMAZOV		15/2/85	D		(3)	
10	Nadir NÄBİYEV		18/7/80	A	22	(4)	10
25	Romuald ONANA	CMR	11/2/90	M	4	(2)	
84	Valeriu ONILA	MDA	14/4/84	M	16	(7)	3
	Räşad ORUCOV		1989	M	1	(2)	
17	Xäyal QARAYEV		8/7/86	M	3	(2)	
21	Asäf QÄDİRİ		17/8/84	M	14	(12)	
	Aqşin SADIQOV		1992	D		(1)	
16	Shamil SAIDOV	RUS	21/3/82	G	16	(2)	
6	Yevhen SAIKO	UKR	21/8/80	M	20	(6)	2
	Cavid TAĞIYEV		22/7/92	A	3	(1)	1
32	Mareks ZUNTNERS	LVA	12/3/83	M		(1)	

XÄZÄR LÄNKÄRAN FK
Coach – Ağasälim Mircavadov
Founded – 2004
Stadium – Xäzär Länkäran stadionu (15,000)
MAJOR HONOURS:
Azerbaijan League - (1) 2007;
Azerbaijan Cup - (2) 2007, 2008.

2009
21/8	İnter	h	1-0	*Calincov*
12/9	Turan	h	1-1	*Calincov*
19/9	Qäbälä	a	1-1	*Souza*
26/9	Muğan	h	2-0	*Lalín 2*
17/10	Standard	a	2-1	*Lalín 2*
21/10	Olimpik-Şüvälan	a	0-1	
24/10	Simurq	h	3-0	*Lalín, Calincov, Tsvetkov*
30/10	Qarabağ	a	0-1	
8/11	Neftçi	h	0-0	
21/11	Karvan	a	2-0	*Souza, Calincov*
25/11	Bakı	h	1-1	*Souza*
29/11	Bakı	a	3-0	*Tsvetkov 2 (1p), Souza*
6/12	İnter	a	1-1	*Souza*
10/12	Olimpik-Şüvälan	h	2-1	*Lalín, og (Camara)*
13/12	Turan	a	2-1	*Juninho, Tsvetkov*

19/12	Qäbälä	h	1-0	Ämirquliyev	
24/12	Muğan	a	2-1	Souza, Tsvetkov	

2010

3/2	Standard	h	0-0	
9/2	Simurq	a	2-1	Juninho, Cristian
13/2	Qarabağ	h	0-0	
17/2	Neftçi	a	0-0	
21/2	Karvan	h	3-0	Qurbanov, Opara, Souza
12/3	Qäbälä	h	4-1	Lalín 2, Opara, Calincov
21/3	İnter	a	0-1	
27/3	Neftçi	h	0-0	
3/4	Qarabağ	h	2-1	Tsvetkov (p), Souza
11/4	Bakı	a	0-1	
17/4	Qäbälä	a	2-1	Lalín, Opara
23/4	İnter	h	2-2	Tsvetkov (p), Opara
1/5	Neftçi	a	0-0	
9/5	Qarabağ	a	1-2	Souza
15/5	Bakı	h	0-1	

No	Name	Nat	DoB	Pos	Aps	(s)	Gls
17	Ramazan ABBASOV		22/9/83	M	3	(6)	
25	Kamran AĞAYEV		9/2/86	G	30		
14	Rahid ÄMİRQULİYEV		1/9/89	M	25	(2)	1
3	Elvin BEQIRI	ALB	27/9/80	D	14		
20	Denis CALINCOV	MDA	15/9/85	A	18	(7)	5
28	CRISTIAN Martins Cabral	BRA	28/8/79	M	10	(3)	1
72	DEVRAN Ayhan	TUR	25/3/78	M	20	(5)	
3	DÊNIS Silva Cruz	BRA	28/12/85	D	15	(1)	
5	DIEGO SOUZA Gusmão	BRA	12/9/88	M	9	(6)	
19	Kostadin DZHAMBAZOV	BUL	6/7/80	D	3	(1)	
2	FATİH Sonkaya	TUR	1/7/81	D	3		
23	Nizami HACIYEV		8/2/88	M	10	(9)	
6	Tomáš INEMAN	CZE	28/11/81	D	7	(3)	
8	Osvaldo José Martins Júnior "JUNINHO"	BRA	7/7/82	M	14	(7)	2
1	Dmitri KRAMARENKO		12/9/74	G	2		
12	Allan LALÍN	HON	5/1/81	A	21	(6)	9
15	Emeka OPARA	NGA	2/12/84	A	13	(1)	4
77	Ivan PECHA	SVK	23/1/86	D	31		
7	Ruslan POLADOV		30/11/79	D	14		
18	Alim QURBANOV		5/12/77	M	2	(8)	1
30	Mário Sérgio Aumarante Santana SOUZA	BRA	30/12/77	M	22	(6)	
10	Ceyhun SULTANOV		12/6/79	M	2	(10)	
4	Tihhon ŠIŠOV	EST	11/2/83	D	9		
21	Radomir TODOROV	BUL	11/8/80	D	30		
9	Ivan TSVETKOV	BUL	31/8/79	A	25	(4)	7

PROMOTED CLUBS

GÄNCÄ PFK
Coach – Fuad İsmayılov
Founded – 1959
Stadium – Gäncä şähär stadionu (25,000)
MAJOR HONOURS:
Azerbaijan League - (3) 1995, 1998, 1999;
Azerbaijan Cup - (4) 1994, 1997, 1998, 2000.

MOİK BAKI PFK
Coach – Ramil Äliyev; (7/4/10) Siyasät Äsgärov.
Founded – 1961
Stadium – Şäfa II (250) & Zabrat qäsäbä stadionu (100)

SECOND LEVEL FINAL TABLE 2009/10

		Pld	W	D	L	F	A	Pts
1	Gäncä PFK	22	14	5	3	51	15	47
2	MOİK Bakı PFK	22	15	2	5	48	25	47
3	Bakılı Bakı PFK	22	14	1	7	41	19	43
4	Neftçi İSM Bakı	22	12	3	7	38	26	39
5	MKT Araz İmişli FK	22	11	5	6	41	29	38
6	Rävan Bakı FK	22	11	4	7	32	28	37
7	ABN Bärdä FK	22	11	3	8	31	23	36
8	Şahdağ Qusar FK	22	8	8	6	33	24	32
9	ANŞAD-Petrol Neftçala FK	22	5	2	15	25	61	17
10	Energetik Mingäçevir PFK	22	3	6	13	24	51	15
11	Ädliyyä Bakı PFK	22	3	5	14	16	40	14
12	Göyäzän Qazax PFK	22	1	4	17	16	55	7

DOMESTIC CUP 2009/10

AZÄRBAYCAN KUBOKU

1/8 FINALS
(4/11/09 & 11/11/09)
Bakı v Bakılı Bakı 6-0; 0-0 *(6-0)*
İnter Bakı v Karvan 4-0; 3-2 *(7-2)*
Neftçi v Neftçi İSM Bakı 5-0; 2-0 *(7-0)*
Olimpik-Şüvälan v Qäbälä 2-0; 0-1 *(2-1)*
Qarabağ v Şahdağ Qusar 4-0; 0-0 *(4-0)*
Simurq v Gäncä 2-0; 1-0 *(3-0)*
Standard v Turan 3-1; 0-0 *(3-1)*
Xäzär Länkäran v Muğan 3-1; 1-0 *(4-1)*

QUARTER-FINALS
(6/3/10 & 16/3/10)
Bakı 1 *(Fábio 59)*, Standard 1 *(Mujiri 89)*
Standard 1 *(Quliyev F. 81)*, Bakı 3 *(Jabá 14, Šolić 24, 79)*
(Bakı 4-2)

(7/3/10 & 16/3/10)
Simurq 0, Olimpik-Şüvälan 0
Olimpik-Şüvälan 0, Simurq 0 *(aet)*
(0-0; Olimpik-Şüvälan 4-2 on pens)

(7/3/10 & 17/3/10)
Qarabağ 2 *(Sadiqov R.F. 59, Teli 90+3)*, Xäzär Länkäran 1 *(Opara 19)*
Xäzär Länkäran 1 *(Cristian 17)*, Qarabağ 0
(2-2; Xäzär Länkäran on away goal)

Neftçi 0, İnter Bakı 3 *(Poškus 49, 88, Odikadze 72)*
İnter Bakı 2 *(Mämmädov 27, Karlsons 54)*, Neftçi 1 *(Aliuţă 83p)*
(İnter Bakı 5-1)

SEMI-FINALS
(27/4/09 & 5/5/09)
Olimpik-Şüvälan 1 *(Qurbanov 73)*, Xäzär Länkäran 1 *(Calincov 23)*
Xäzär Länkäran 2 *(Lalín 6, Souza 81)*, Olimpik-Şüvälan 1 *(Bunjevčević 77)*
(Xäzär Länkäran 3-2)

Bakı 0, İnter Bakı 1 *(Mämmädov 61)*
İnter Bakı 1 *(Gutiérrez 51)*, Bakı 3 *(Sofroni 27, Jabá 56, Zagorac 66og)*
(Bakı 3-2)

FINAL
(23/5/09)
Tofiq Bähramov adına Respublika stadionu, Baku
BAKI FK 2 *(Skulić 100, Šolić 104)*
XÄZÄR LÄNKÄRAN FK 1 *(Beqiri 120)*
(aet)
Referee – Mämmädov
BAKI – Šarlija, Bates, Skulić, Barakat (Sofroni 64), Äliyev, Mähärrämov, Fábio (Wênio 83), Soltanov, Savinov, Šolić (Qurbanov 116), Jabá.
Sent off: Yunisoğlu (102 – on bench)
XÄZÄR LÄNKÄRAN – Ağayev, Beqiri, Diego Souza (Qurbanov 106), Poladov, Lalín (Calincov 62), Ämirquliyev, Opara, Todorov, Cristian (Souza 83), Devran, Pecha.

BATE Borisov continue to conquer

Belarusian football has discovered a worthy standard-bearer in FC BATE Borisov. A year after becoming the country's first participant in the group phase of the UEFA Champions League, the provincial club reached the same stage of the UEFA Europa League. They also won the domestic title for the fourth year in a row and, in the spring of 2010, added victory in the Belarusian Cup for good measure.

With the youthful Viktor Goncharenko at the helm, BATE cruised to the Premier League title. It was the sixth in the club's history, putting them one behind record champions FC Dinamo Minsk, who finished 12 points adrift of the champions in second place to take the runners-up berth for the fourth time in five years.

Dinamo eclipsed

If Dinamo remain the country's best known club internationally thanks to their achievements during the Soviet era – they won the USSR title in 1982 – BATE are pushing hard to eclipse them. As Dinamo bowed out along with Belarus's other two inaugural UEFA Europa League entrants, FC Naftan Novopolotsk and FC MTZ-RIPO Minsk, in the second qualifying round of the competition – the 4-1 defeat by Tromsø IL cost Dinamo's Serbian coach Slavoljub Muslin his job – BATE recovered from the disappointment of an away-goals defeat to Latvia's FK Ventspils in the third qualifying round of the UEFA Champions League to reach the group stage of the new-look secondary competition thanks to an amazing 4-0 extra-time win away to PFC Litex Lovech. There they not only took on three prestigious European opponents in SL Benfica, AEK Athens FC and Everton FC, but also performed with great credit, taking third place thanks to a 1-0 win on Merseyside.

Goncharenko's men were able to enjoy their European adventure because their fourth straight domestic crown was virtually assured after a blistering start that yielded maximum points from their opening seven fixtures (including a 3-1 win at Dinamo Minsk).

Although they lost at home to FC Shakhtyor Soligorsk and away to FC Dnepr Mogilev, those defeats were mere blips. Another string of wins in September in October carried them serenely home, and it was only after the title had been secured that they eased off, drawing three matches in succession including 0-0 against bottom club FC Smorgon – the only one of their 26 league games in which they failed to score.

The top-scoring team in the division with 55 goals, BATE were largely indebted for that handsome total to the contributions of star playmaker Sergei Krivets, who struck 14 times, and effervescent 19-year-old striker Maxim Skavysh, who emerged from nowhere to become the revelation of the season, scoring 12 goals. Other key contributors were goalkeeper Sergei Veremko, defender Igor Shitov and midfield pivot Dmitriy Likhtarovich – all locally produced talents in what was virtually an all-Belarusian team.

Sergei Krivets – a champion in Belarus with BATE Borisov and Poland with Lech Poznan

Young BATE Borisov striker Maxim Skavysh was the revelation of the 2009 Premier League season

Five-star performance

Krivets left to claim another domestic title in the spring with Polish club Lech Poznań, and his replacement, Brazilian import Renan from relegated FC Gomel, made a positive early impression by scoring twice in the 2010 Belarusian Cup final. Long-serving striker Vitaliy Rodionov also added a double as BATE secured their first victory in the competition for four years by hammering FC Torpedo Zhodino 5-0 in Minsk.

Zhodino had eliminated holders Naftan en route to the final and were rewarded with a place in the 2010/11 UEFA Europa League in the company of Dinamo Minsk and Dnepr, the latter finishing third in the league after many pundits had tipped them for

relegation. Smorgon, Gomel and FC Granit Mikashevichi were the three teams to go down, with just one, 2001 champions FC Belshina Bobruisk, travelling in the opposite direction to replace them.

Belarus's hopes of reaching the 2010 FIFA World Cup qualifying play-offs, not totally unrealistic at the start of the 2009/10 season, were destroyed by back-to-back defeats by Croatia. The team's veteran German coach, Bernd Stange, escaped censure, however, and was retained for the UEFA EURO 2012™ qualifying campaign, in which Belarus, who won two, drew two and lost two of their six post-World Cup qualifying friendlies, encounter France, Romania, Bosnia-Herzegovina, Albania and Luxembourg.

Belorusskaja Federacija Futbola (BFF)

Prospekt Pobediteli 20, korp. 3
BY-220020 Minsk
tel – +375 172 545 600
fax – +375 172 544 478
website – bff.by
email – info@bff.by
Year of Formation – 1989

President – Gennadiy Nevyglas
General Secretary – Leonid Dmitranitsa
Media Officer – Yulia Zenkovich
National Stadium – Dinamo, Minsk (40,000)

TOP FIVE ALL-TIME CAPS
Aleksandr Kulchiy (82); Sergei Gurenko (80); Sergei Shtanyuk (71); Maxim Romashchenko (64); Sergei Omelyanchuk (60)
TOP FIVE ALL-TIME GOALS
Maxim Romashchenko (20); Vitaliy Kutuzov (13); Valentin Belkevich & Roman Vasilyuk (10); Sergei Kornilenko (9)

NATIONAL TEAM RESULTS 2009/10

12/8/09	Croatia (WCQ)	H	Minsk	1-3	*Verkhovtsov (81)*
5/9/09	Croatia (WCQ)	A	Zagreb	0-1	
9/9/09	Ukraine (WCQ)	H	Minsk	0-0	
10/10/09	Kazakhstan (WCQ)	H	Brest	4-0	*Bordachev (23), Kalachev (69, 90+2), Kovel (86)*
14/10/09	England (WCQ)	A	Wembley	0-3	
14/11/09	Saudi Arabia	A	Dammam	1-1	*Bordachev (20)*
18/11/09	Montenegro	A	Podgorica	0-1	
3/3/10	Armenia	N	Antalya (TUR)	3-1	*Putilo (58), Hleb A. (73), Rodionov (85)*
27/5/10	Honduras	N	Villach (AUT)	2-2	*Putilo (56, 60)*
30/5/10	South Korea	N	Kufstein (AUT)	1-0	*Kislyak (53)*
2/6/10	Sweden	H	Minsk	0-1	

NATIONAL TEAM APPEARANCES 2009/10

Coach – Bernd STANGE (GER)	14/3/48		CRO	CRO	UKR	KAZ	ENG	Ksa	Mne	Arm	Hon	Kor	Swe	Caps	Goals
Yuriy ZHEVNOV	17/4/81	FC Moskva (RUS)	G	G	G	G	G	G 26*	G						
		/Zenit (RUS)										G	G	38	-
Aleksandr YUREVICH	8/8/79	BATE	D	D	D	D	D	D	D	D	D	D46	D86	24	-
Sergei OMELYANCHUK	8/8/80	Terek (RUS)	D	M	M	M	M	M75	M		M	M	M76	60	1
Sergei SOSNOVSKIY	14/8/81	BATE	D	D	D	D	D	D	s79	D46	D	D89	D69	14	-
Dmitriy VERKHOVTSOV	10/10/86	Naftan	D	D		D	D	s46 68*		s87			s69	15	2
		/Ventspils (LVA)							s87						
Nikolai KASHEVSKIY	5/10/80	Illychivets (UKR)	M54				s83							13	-
Aleksandr KULCHIY	1/11/73	Rostov (RUS)	M	M	M	M90	M	M						82	5
Timofei KALACHEV	1/5/81	Krylya Sovetov (RUS) /Rostov (RUS)	M	M	M	M	M	M	M79		M			41	7
Aleksandr HLEB	1/5/81	Stuttgart (GER)	M		M					M87				51	6
Sergei KORNILENKO	14/6/83	Zenit (RUS) /Tom (RUS)	A69	A77	A76	A	A76	A90	A67	A56	A76	A46	A46	41	9
Vitaliy KUTUZOV	20/3/80	Bari (ITA)	A85		A88	A73	A46							48	13
Leonid KOVEL	29/7/86	Saturn (RUS)	s54	s77	s76	s73	s76		s67	s87				15	3
Vitaliy RODIONOV	11/12/83	BATE	s69		s90	s46	A26	A46	s56	s46	A75		A46	21	4
Gennadiy BLIZNYUK	30/7/80	Sibir (RUS)	s85											12	4
Igor SHITOV	24/10/86	BATE		D	D	D	D	D	D	D		s46	s46	15	1
Maxim BORDACHEV	18/6/86	BATE		M55		M83	M83	M	M90				s86	7	2
Vyacheslav HLEB	12/2/83	Shanghai Shenhua (CHN)		M63	s88			s75	s46	s56			s46	33	8
Igor STASEVICH	21/10/85	BATE		s55										11	1
Sergei KRIVETS	8/6/86	BATE /Lech (POL)		s63	s83			s90		M46	M46	s46	s46	8	-
Pavel PLASKONNYI	29/1/85	Shakhtyor Soligorsk		D57										13	1
Dmitriy LENTSEVICH	20/6/83	Bohemians (CZE)			s57			D	D	D87		s89		14	-
Anton AMELCHENKO	27/3/85	FC Moskva (RUS) /Rostov (RUS)						s26			G46			3	-
Sergei KISLYAK	6/8/87	Dinamo Minsk						s90	M	M	M87	M	M	6	1
Aleksandr MARTYNOVICH	26/8/87	Dinamo Minsk							D46	s46	D	D	D	5	-
Sergei VEREMKO	16/10/82	BATE									G	s46		4	-
Yan TIGOREV	10/3/84	Metalurh Zaporizhya (UKR)								M56	M	M	M	13	-
Anton PUTILO	23/6/87	Dinamo Minsk								s46	M	M	M	12	3
Dmitriy MOLOSH	10/12/81	Sibir (RUS)									D	D	D46	8	-
Andrei VORONKOV	8/2/89	Dynamo Kyiv (UKR)									s76	s75		3	-
Mikhail SIVAKOV	16/1/88	Cagliari (ITA)											s76	1	-

DOMESTIC LEAGUE 2009

PREMIER LEAGUE FINAL TABLE

	Pld	W	D	L	F	A	W	D	L	F	A	W	D	L	F	A	Pts
			Home					**Away**					**Total**				
1 FC BATE Borisov	26	9	3	1	30	8	10	2	1	25	8	19	5	2	55	16	62
2 FC Dinamo Minsk	26	8	2	3	24	11	6	6	1	14	7	14	8	4	38	18	50
3 FC Dnepr Mogilev	26	7	2	4	20	12	5	2	6	11	14	12	4	10	31	26	40
4 FC Naftan Novopolotsk	26	9	0	4	18	16	3	2	8	10	23	12	2	12	28	39	38
5 FC Dinamo Brest	26	6	4	3	20	11	4	4	5	10	13	10	8	8	30	24	38
6 FC Shakhtyor Soligorsk	26	4	5	4	13	13	6	3	4	20	15	10	8	8	33	28	38
7 FC Neman Grodno	26	7	3	3	13	8	4	1	8	10	23	11	4	11	23	31	37
8 FC Torpedo Zhodino	26	5	3	5	18	12	5	4	4	13	10	10	7	9	31	22	37
9 FC Minsk	26	6	3	4	12	10	5	0	8	21	16	11	3	12	33	26	36
10 FC Vitebsk	26	6	1	6	12	14	4	1	8	14	23	10	2	14	26	37	32
11 FC MTZ-RIPO Minsk	26	4	3	6	16	17	4	3	6	18	21	8	6	12	34	38	30
12 FC Gomel	26	5	3	5	20	24	3	2	8	11	23	8	5	13	31	47	29
13 FC Granit Mikashevichi	26	4	2	7	15	22	2	5	6	12	17	6	7	13	27	39	25
14 FC Smorgon	26	1	5	7	7	21	1	4	8	10	25	2	9	15	17	46	15

TOP GOALSCORERS

15 MAICON (Gomel)
14 Sergei KRIVETS (BATE)
12 Maxim SKAVYSH (BATE)
11 Roman VASILYUK (Dinamo Brest)
 Givi KVARATSKHELIA (MTZ-RIPO)
9 Dmitriy MOZOLEVSKIY (Dinamo Brest)
 Andrei RAZIN (Minsk)
8 Aleksandr GAVRYUSHKO (Dinamo Minsk)
 Andrei LYASYUK (Dnepr)
7 Vitaliy RODIONOV (BATE)
 Stanislav DRAGUN (Dinamo Minsk)
 Sergei KISLYAK (Dinamo Minsk)
 Aleksandr SAZANKOV (Dnepr)
 Sergei KOSHEL (Minsk)
 Dmitriy OSIPENKO (Minsk)
 Ivan DENISEVICH (Neman)
 Andrei SHERYAKOV (Zhodino)

CLUB-BY-CLUB

FC BATE BORISOV
Coach – Viktor Goncharenko
Founded – 1996
Stadium – City Stadium (5,392)
MAJOR HONOURS: Belarus League - (6) 1999, 2002, 2006, 2007, 2008, 2009; Belarus Cup - (2) 2006, 2010.

2009

5/4	Dnepr	h	1-0	Skavysh
13/4	Minsk	a	1-0	Volodko A.
18/4	Smorgon	h	2-0	Krivets, Bulyga
26/4	Dinamo Minsk	a	3-1	Skavysh, Krivets 2 (1p)
2/5	Dinamo Brest	h	1-0	Krivets
6/5	Neman	h	6-0	Skavysh 2, Krivets 2 (1p), Stasevich, Nekhaichik (p)
10/5	Vitebsk	a	2-0	Pavlov, Krivets
16/5	Mikashevichi	h	1-1	Skavysh
23/5	Naftan	a	4-0	Radkov, Skavysh, Krivets, Pavlov
27/5	Shakhtyor	h	2-3	Radkov, Sosnovskiy
27/6	MTZ-RIPO	a	2-0	Skavysh 2
4/7	Zhodino	h	3-0	Krivets, Skavysh 2
10/7	Gomel	a	3-0	Krivets, Nekhaichik, Bordachev
1/8	Dnepr	a	1-3	Nekhaichik
16/8	Minsk	h	1-0	Krivets
31/8	Dinamo Minsk	h	1-1	Krivets
13/9	Dinamo Brest	a	2-1	Pavlov 2
19/9	Neman	a	2-1	Rodionov, Baga
24/9	Vitebsk	h	3-1	Rodionov 2, Goharyan (p)
27/9	Mikashevichi	a	3-1	Volodko A., Krivets, Skavysh
5/10	Naftan	h	4-0	Rodionov 2, Shitov, Krivets
18/10	Shakhtyor	a	1-0	Nekhaichik
25/10	MTZ-RIPO	h	2-2	Goharyan, Skavysh
28/10	Smorgon	a	0-0	
1/11	Zhodino	a	1-1	Alumona
8/11	Gomel	h	3-0	Radkov, Rodionov 2

No	Name	Nat	DoB	Pos	Aps	(s)	Gls
19	Kirill ALEKSIYAN		22/1/91	M		(1)	
11	Aleksandr ALUMONA	RUS	18/12/83	A	5	(6)	1
25	Dmitriy BAGA		4/1/90	M	5	(3)	1
18	Maxim BORDACHEV		18/6/86	D	24	(1)	1
7	Vitaliy BULYGA		12/1/80	A	5	(4)	1
88	Hovhannes GOHARYAN	ARM	18/3/88	A	6	(13)	2
30	Aleksandr GUTOR		18/4/89	G	5		
10	Sergei KRIVETS		8/6/86	M	22	(4)	14
2	Dmitriy LIKHTAROVICH		1/3/78	M	21	(2)	
13	Pavel NEKHAICHIK		15/7/88	M	18	(8)	4
17	Aleksandr PAVLOV		18/8/84	M	16	(9)	4
14	Artem RADKOV		26/8/85	D	9	(3)	3
20	Vitaliy RODIONOV		11/12/83	A	9	(3)	7
32	Vladimir RZHEVSKIY	RUS	19/7/87	D	3	(1)	
4	Igor SHITOV		24/10/86	D	21	(1)	1
15	Maxim SKAVYSH		13/11/89	A	19	(6)	12
3	Sergei SOSNOVSKIY		14/8/81	D	22		1
22	Igor STASEVICH		21/10/85	M	16	(3)	1
16	Sergei VEREMKO		16/10/82	G	21		
8	Aleksandr VOLODKO		18/6/86	M	18	(5)	2
24	Maxim VOLODKO		10/11/92	M		(2)	
5	Aleksandr YUREVICH		8/8/79	D	21	(3)	

BELARUS

FC DINAMO BREST
Coach – Yevgeniy Trotsyuk; (5/8/09) Sergei Kovalchuk;
(15/9/09) Yuriy Puntus
Founded – 1960
Stadium – GOSK Brestskiy (10,080)
MAJOR HONOURS: Belarus Cup – (1) 2007.

2009

5/4	Smorgon	a	1-0	Vasilyuk
13/4	Shakhtyor	h	1-1	Vasilyuk
18/4	Dinamo Minsk	a	0-2	
26/4	MTZ-RIPO	h	1-0	Baga
2/5	BATE	a	0-1	
6/5	Zhodino	h	2-2	Mozolevskiy, Demidovich
10/5	Neman	a	1-0	Vasilyuk
17/5	Gomel	h	3-1	Demidovich, Mozolevskiy, Vasilyuk
23/5	Vitebsk	a	2-0	Mozolevskiy, Vasilyuk
30/5	Dnepr	h	0-0	
27/6	Mikashevichi	a	1-1	Mozolevskiy
4/7	Minsk	h	1-2	Tsevan (p)
10/7	Naftan	a	0-1	
1/8	Smorgon	h	1-1	Papush
16/8	Shakhtyor	a	1-1	Sokol
23/8	Dinamo Minsk	h	0-1	
30/8	MTZ-RIPO	a	1-1	Mozolevskiy
13/9	BATE	h	1-2	Vasilyuk (p)
19/9	Zhodino	a	2-1	Vasilyuk 2
23/9	Neman	h	2-0	Mozolevskiy, Kozak
27/9	Gomel	a	1-3	Vasilyuk
4/10	Vitebsk	h	3-0	Mozolevskiy 2, Vasilyuk
17/10	Dnepr	a	0-0	
24/10	Mikashevichi	h	3-1	Mozolevskiy, Papush, Makar
1/11	Minsk	a	0-2	
8/11	Naftan	h	2-0	Vasilyuk, Kozak

No	Name	Nat	DoB	Pos	Aps	(s)	Gls
16	Aleksei BAGA		4/2/81	D	16	(1)	1
21	Vitaliy BEREZOVSKIY	UKR	11/4/84	D	9	(2)	
11	Andrei CHISTYI		30/3/83	M	2	(2)	
22	Aleksandr DEMESHKO		7/11/86	M		(3)	
6	Vadim DEMIDOVICH		20/9/85	M		(13)	2
24	Vitaliy GAIDUCHIK		12/7/89	D	24		
19	Alexei GONCEAROV	MDA	24/2/84	D	11		
26	Vladimir KHVASHCHINSKIY		10/5/90	A	1	(8)	
14	Sergei KOVALYUK		7/1/80	M	15	(5)	
8	Sergei KOZAK		17/10/81	M	16	(2)	2
20	Dmitriy MAKAR		1/1/81	M	5	(2)	1
9	Vladimir MOROZ		4/9/85	M	10		
18	Dmitriy MOZOLEVSKIY		30/4/85	A	26		9
23	Edgar OLEKHNOVICH		17/5/87	M	25	(1)	
7	Olexandr PAPUSH	UKR	14/1/85	M	18	(6)	2
1	Aleksandr PLOTNIKOV	RUS	17/2/79	G	26		
15	Vladimir SHCHERBO		1/4/86	D	21	(3)	
2	Aleksei SHCHIGOLEV	RUS	18/9/72	D	17	(1)	
13	Viktor SOKOL		9/5/81	M	10	(2)	1
17	Aleksei TARABANOV		3/5/84	M	6	(8)	
4	Andrei TSEVAN		15/3/86	M	4	(10)	1
10	Roman VASILYUK		23/11/78	A	24	(1)	11

FC DINAMO MINSK
Coach – Slavoljub Muslin (SRB); (28/7/09) Kirill Alshevskiy;
(21/8/09) Sergei Gurenko
Founded – 1927
Stadium – Dinamo (40,000)
MAJOR HONOURS: USSR League – (1) 1982;
Belarus League – (7) 1992, 1993, 1994, 1995 (spring), 1995 (autumn), 1997, 2004;
Belarus Cup – (3) 1992, 1994, 2003.

2009

5/4	Minsk	h	2-1	Zita, Kislyak
12/4	Smorgon	a	0-0	
18/4	Dinamo Brest	h	2-0	Putilo, Dragun
26/4	BATE	h	1-3	Gavryushko
2/5	Neman	a	0-0	
6/5	Vitebsk	h	2-1	Zita, Dragun
10/5	Mikashevichi	a	1-2	Kislyak
16/5	Naftan	h	2-0	Gavryushko 2
23/5	Shakhtyor	a	1-1	Kislyak
30/5	MTZ-RIPO	h	5-0	og (Kvaratskhelia), Gavryushko, Veretilo, Putilo, Lebedev
28/6	Zhodino	a	0-0	
5/7	Gomel	h	1-2	Dragun
12/7	Dnepr	a	1-0	Gavryushko
2/8	Minsk	a	0-0	
16/8	Smorgon	h	1-1	Gavryushko
23/8	Dinamo Brest	a	1-0	Rekish
31/8	BATE	a	1-1	Kislyak
13/9	Neman	h	2-0	Strakhanovich, Kislyak (p)
19/9	Vitebsk	a	3-2	Gavryushko 2, Kislyak
23/9	Mikashevichi	h	1-0	Jefferson
27/9	Naftan	a	2-0	Strakhanovich, Shkabara
4/10	Shakhtyor	h	0-1	
18/10	MTZ-RIPO	a	2-0	Strakhanovich, Putilo
25/10	Zhodino	h	0-0	
1/11	Gomel	a	2-1	Dragun 2
8/11	Dnepr	h	5-2	Dragun 2, Strakhanovich (p), Kislyak, Rekish

No	Name	Nat	DoB	Pos	Aps	(s)	Gls
13	Yuriy BROVCHENKO	UKR	25/1/88	A		(1)	
1	Aleksandar ČANOVIĆ	SRB	18/2/83	G	10	(1)	
9	Andrei CHUKHLEI		2/10/87	M	18	(1)	
2	Stanislav DRAGUN		4/6/88	M	21	(4)	7
6	Sergei GAVRILOVICH		5/1/90	D		(1)	
22	Aleksandr GAVRYUSHKO		23/1/86	A	20	(6)	8
8	Sergei GIGEVICH		26/1/87	M	5	(7)	
35	Andrei GORBUNOV		29/5/83	G	16		
41	Sergei GURENKO		30/9/72	M	14	(1)	
30	Filipp IVANOV		21/7/90	M		(2)	
12	JEFFERSON de Sousa Leite	BRA	7/1/89	M		(8)	1
10	Sergei KISLYAK		6/8/87	M	22	(3)	7
3	Sergei KONDRATIYEV		2/2/90	D	1	(1)	
7	Aleksandr LEBEDEV		14/4/85	A	2	(8)	1
23	Aleksandr MARTYNOVICH		26/8/87	D	24	(1)	
19	Aurélien MONTAROUP	FRA	19/12/85	D	25		
14	Sergei PAVLYUKOVICH		19/5/74	D	17		
16	Anton PUTILO		23/6/87	M	17	(5)	3
15	Dmitriy REKISH		14/9/88	M	5	(8)	2
26	Zdravko ŠARABA	BIH	15/5/80	D	8		
21	Oleg SHKABARA		15/2/83	M	8	(6)	1
33	Artem SOLOVEI		1/11/90	M		(2)	
11	Oleg STRAKHANOVICH		13/10/79	M	13	(2)	4
24	Kyrylo SYDORENKO	UKR	25/7/85	D	1		
20	Oleg VERETILO		10/7/88	D	24		1
5	Igor YASINSKIY		4/7/90	M	2	(1)	
4	Andrei ZALESKIY		20/1/91	D	1	(1)	
18	Ihor ZENKOVICH	UKR	17/9/87	A		(2)	
17	Bruno Mbanangoyé ZITA	GAB	15/7/80	M	12	(4)	2

FC DNEPR MOGILEV
Coach – Andrei Skorobogatko
Founded – 1960
Stadium – Spartak (7,300)
MAJOR HONOURS: Belarus League – (1) 1998.

2009

5/4	BATE	a	0-1	
13/4	Neman	a	1-0	Bondarev
18/4	Vitebsk	a	1-0	Tereshchenko
26/4	Mikashevichi	h	1-2	Berdnik
2/5	Naftan	a	1-2	Shuneiko
6/5	Shakhtyor	h	1-0	Sazankov
10/5	MTZ-RIPO	a	1-0	Sazankov
17/5	Zhodino	h	0-0	
23/5	Gomel	a	0-2	
30/5	Dinamo Brest	a	0-0	
27/6	Minsk	h	3-2	Lyasyuk 2, Zhevnerov
4/7	Smorgon	a	2-0	Berdnik, Sazankov
12/7	Dinamo Minsk	h	0-1	
1/8	BATE	h	3-1	Berdnik, Bychenok, Sazankov
16/8	Neman	h	1-2	Berdnik
22/8	Vitebsk	h	3-2	Sazankov, Matveyenko, Lyasyuk
30/8	Mikashevichi	a	0-1	
13/9	Naftan	h	2-1	Lyasyuk, Sazankov
19/9	Shakhtyor	a	2-1	Lyasyuk 2 (1p)
23/9	MTZ-RIPO	h	0-1	
27/9	Zhodino	a	0-0	
4/10	Gomel	h	2-0	Bychenok, Lyasyuk
17/10	Dinamo Brest	h	0-0	
24/10	Minsk	a	1-2	Berdnik
1/11	Smorgon	h	4-0	Sazankov, Bychenok, Chernykh 2
8/11	Dinamo Minsk	a	2-5	Lyasyuk, Bordok

No	Name	Nat	DoB	Pos	Aps	(s)	Gls
12	Eric Arsène BAYEMI Moamble	CMR	11/10/83	D	17	(1)	
18	Maksim BERDNIK	RUS	18/1/86	M	16	(6)	5
9	Vitaliy BONDAREV	UKR	15/6/85	A	5	(4)	1
8	Anton BORDOK		23/6/86	A	5	(7)	1
7	Aleksandr BYCHENOK		30/5/85	M	22		3
39	Fedor CHERNYKH	LTU	21/5/91	A		(2)	2
3	Andriy HONCHAR	UKR	15/3/85	D	25		
92	Dmitriy KALACHEV		16/6/78	M	24		
2	Yevgeniy KAPOV		30/1/77	D	26		
11	Tornike KHACHIDZE	GEO	3/6/89	A		(1)	
1	Ruslan KOPANTSOV		12/5/81	G	26		
17	Andrei LATYPOV		16/3/90	A		(2)	
32	Konstantin LEPIN		17/6/88	D		(1)	
32	Andrei LYASYUK		14/4/83	A	13	(7)	8
15	Pavel MARKOV		4/12/91	D		(1)	
10	Anton Yevgeniyevich MATVEYENKO		30/9/86	M	25	(1)	1
26	Gabriel NOAH	CMR	4/8/86	M	9	(4)	
4	Denis OBRAZOV		24/6/88	D	2	(7)	
15	Aleksandr RAYEVSKIY		19/6/88	M		(3)	
29	Aleksandr SAZANKOV		18/3/84	A	18	(2)	7
6	Vladimir SHUNEIKO		22/4/74	D	10	(3)	1
9	Aleksandr SHUPIKOV		27/9/90	M		(1)	
11	Dmytro TERESHCHENKO	UKR	4/4/87	M	16	(7)	1
20	Olexiy TUPCHIY	UKR	22/8/86	M	6	(9)	
14	Dmitriy TURLIN		8/9/85	M	3	(8)	
5	Eduard ZHEVNEROV		1/11/87	D	18		1

FC GOMEL
Coach – Andrei Yusipets; (20/8/09) Leonid Borsuk
Founded – 1995
Stadium – Centralnyi (14,307)
MAJOR HONOURS: Belarus League – (1) 2003;
Belarus Cup – (1) 2002.

2009

4/4	Neman	a	0-1	
12/4	Vitebsk	h	1-1	Linev
18/4	Mikashevichi	a	2-0	Maicon, Klimenko
26/4	Naftan	h	1-3	Maicon
2/5	Shakhtyor	a	1-1	Maicon
6/5	MTZ-RIPO	h	3-3	Klimenko, Renan, Maicon
10/5	Zhodino	h	2-1	Misyuk, Matveyenko
17/5	Dinamo Brest	a	1-3	Maicon
23/5	Dnepr	h	2-0	Matveichik, Maicon
30/5	Minsk	a	0-1	
26/6	Smorgon	h	3-2	Klimenko, Linev, Maicon
5/7	Dinamo Minsk	a	2-1	Renan 2
10/7	BATE	h	0-3	
2/8	Neman	h	0-3	
16/8	Vitebsk	a	0-1	
22/8	Mikashevichi	h	1-1	Maicon
30/8	Naftan	a	2-1	Maicon 2
13/9	Shakhtyor	h	2-1	Renan, Maicon
19/9	MTZ-RIPO	a	2-4	Maicon, Bredun
23/9	Zhodino	a	0-4	
27/9	Dinamo Brest	h	3-1	og (Kozak), Maicon 2
4/10	Dnepr	a	0-2	
17/10	Minsk	h	1-3	Maicon
24/10	Smorgon	a	1-1	Renan
1/11	Dinamo Minsk	h	1-2	Timoshenko
8/11	BATE	a	0-3	

No	Name	Nat	DoB	Pos	Aps	(s)	Gls
9	Andrei BARANOK		20/7/79	M	9	(6)	
23	Yevgeniy BARSUKOV		5/7/90	A	1	(3)	
26	Yevgeniy BERUN	RUS	18/8/82	D	3	(1)	
30	Yevhen BREDUN	UKR	10/9/82	M	4	(2)	1
14	Andrei DASHUK		14/8/87	A	3	(3)	
29	Vladimir GAYEV		28/10/77	G	23		
99	Aleksandr KLIMENKO		28/3/83	A	11	(5)	3
25	Igor KUZMENOK		7/6/90	D	14		
2	Yevgeniy LINEV		27/10/80	D	26		2
21	Pavlo LOBTSOV	UKR	8/1/88	M	2	(7)	
24	Igor LOGVINOV		23/8/83	G	3		
11	MAICON Rogério Silva Calijuri	BRA	6/6/86	M	22	(4)	15
3	Sergei MATVEICHIK		5/6/88	D	24		1
37	Anton Viktorovich MATVEYENKO		28/4/89	D	12	(4)	1
28	Alexandru MAXIM	MDA	19/1/86	A	3	(9)	
15	Denis MEDVEDEV		26/1/88	M	2	(3)	
7	Andrei MISYUK		20/3/81	M	21	(4)	1
10	RENAN Bardini Bressan	BRA	3/11/88	M	24		5
4	Anton RYABTSEV		19/2/84	D	9	(1)	
17	Dmitriy RYABTSEV		16/8/91	M		(5)	
22	Ilya RYLINSKIY		16/2/84	M	21		
8	Eduard SERGIENKO	KAZ	18/2/88	M	26		
6	Aleksandr SHAGOIKO		27/7/80	D	11		
19	Pavel SVIRIDENKO	RUS	20/1/85	D	1	(2)	
20	Aleksei TIMOSHENKO		9/12/86	M	11	(3)	1

FC GRANIT MIKASHEVICHI
Coach – Valeriy Bokhno
Founded – 1978
Stadium – Volna, Pinsk (3,136)

2009

4/4	MTZ-RIPO	h	1-2	Yanush
12/4	Zhodino	h	1-3	Yanush
18/4	Gomel	h	0-2	
26/4	Dnepr	a	2-1	Miceika 2
2/5	Minsk	h	1-4	Bylina
6/5	Smorgon	a	0-1	
10/5	Dinamo Minsk	h	2-1	Yanush, Kavaliauskas
16/5	BATE	a	1-1	Buloichik
23/5	Neman	h	3-0	(w/o; original game 1-1 Chalei)
30/5	Vitebsk	a	1-2	Miceika

BELARUS

27/6	Dinamo Brest	h	1-1	*Vágner (p)*
4/7	Naftan	h	0-2	
11/7	Shakhtyor	a	0-0	
2/8	MTZ-RIPO	a	2-2	*Loshankov, Vágner*
16/8	Zhodino	a	3-1	*Loshankov 2, Bylina*
22/8	Gomel	a	1-1	*Chalei*
30/8	Dnepr	h	1-0	*Loshankov*
13/9	Minsk	a	0-1	
19/9	Smorgon	h	1-1	*Poryvayev*
23/9	Dinamo Minsk	a	0-1	
27/9	BATE	h	1-3	*Sashcheko*
4/10	Neman	a	0-0	
17/10	Vitebsk	h	1-2	*Yanush*
24/10	Dinamo Brest	a	1-3	*Loshankov*
1/11	Naftan	a	1-3	*Goncharik*
8/11	Shakhtyor	h	2-1	*Yanush, Sashcheko*

No	Name	Nat	DoB	Pos	Aps	(s)	Gls
5	Pavel BEGANSKIY		9/1/81	A		(4)	
20	Andrei BOKHNO		19/11/73	D	26		
22	Aleksandr BULOICHIK		30/8/79	M	12	(7)	1
17	Dmitriy BUTRAMYEV		24/2/88	A		(1)	
3	Aleksandr BYLINA		26/3/81	D	23	(1)	2
9	Dmitriy CHALEI		14/2/78	M	23		2
2	Aleksandr GOLOVCHIK		17/10/79	D	1		
23	Artem GONCHARIK		13/4/80	M	4	(6)	1
7	Vyacheslav GRIGOROV		8/3/82	M	4	(8)	
26	Vitalijus KAVALIAUSKAS	LTU	2/7/83	A	8	(11)	1
28	Sergei KUZNETSOV		3/11/79	D	13		
18	Vadim LASOVSKIY		4/10/75	D	7	(5)	
1	Igor LOGVINOV		23/8/83	G	13		
11	Yevgeniy LOSHANKOV		2/1/79	M	22	(1)	5
4	Vladimir MAKOVSKIY		23/4/77	A	5	(11)	
8	Darius MICEIKA	LTU	22/2/83	M	13		3
30	Boris PANKRATOV		30/12/82	G	8	(1)	
1	Denis PARECHIN		17/11/79	G	5		
24	Andrei PORYVAYEV		3/1/82	D	19	(3)	1
	Andriy RASPOPOV	UKR	25/6/78	D	6		
19	Denis SASHCHEKO		3/10/81	M	24		2
28	Andrius ŠIDLAUSKAS	LTU	30/10/84	M	1		
27	Valeriy TARASENKO		1/9/81	M	17	(1)	
21	VÁGNER Pereira Costa	BRA	1/6/87	M	6	(10)	2
10	Nikolai YANUSH		9/9/84	A	26		5

FC MINSK
Coach – Sergei Yaromko; (9/10/09) Vitaliy Tarakanov
Founded – 2005
Stadium – Dinamo (40,000)

2009

5/4	Dinamo Minsk	a	1-2	*Osipenko (p)*
13/4	BATE	h	0-1	
18/4	Neman	a	1-2	*Makar*
26/4	Vitebsk	h	0-1	
2/5	Mikashevichi	a	4-1	*Razin, Koshel, Horbanenko,*
				Khachaturyan
6/5	Naftan	h	2-0	*Horbanenko, Razin*
10/5	Shakhtyor	a	5-0	*Razin 2, Koshel 2, Osipenko*
17/5	MTZ-RIPO	h	1-2	*Koshel*
23/5	Zhodino	a	0-1	
30/5	Gomel	h	1-0	*Osipenko*
27/6	Dnepr	a	2-3	*Razin, Koshel*
4/7	Dinamo Brest	a	2-1	*Razin, Koshel*
10/7	Smorgon	h	2-0	*Koshel, Osipenko*
2/8	Dinamo Minsk	h	0-0	
16/8	BATE	a	0-1	
22/8	Neman	h	0-0	
30/8	Vitebsk	a	0-1	

13/9	Mikashevichi	h	1-0	*Razin*
19/9	Naftan	a	0-1	
23/9	Shakhtyor	h	1-1	*Osipenko*
27/9	MTZ-RIPO	a	0-1	
4/10	Zhodino	h	0-4	
17/10	Gomel	a	3-1	*Khachaturyan 2, Soro*
24/10	Dnepr	h	2-1	*Osipenko, Makarov*
1/11	Dinamo Brest	h	2-0	*Osipenko (p), Razin*
8/11	Smorgon	a	3-1	*Razin, Khachaturyan, Navikas*

No	Name	Nat	DoB	Pos	Aps	(s)	Gls
22	Daniel AKHTYAMOV	RUS	26/3/85	A	1	(2)	
19	Yevgeniy BRANOVITSKIY		15/5/81	D	4	(5)	
3	David CHIGLADZE	GEO	22/2/84	M	7		
11	Vyacheslav HORBANENKO	UKR	22/2/84	M	18	(7)	2
9	Andrei KHACHATURYAN	ARM	2/9/87	M	25	(1)	4
25	Igor KHMELYUK		27/1/90	A		(1)	
18	Sergei KOSHEL		14/3/86	A	20	(3)	7
16	Aleksandr LENTSEVICH		2/5/79	G	9		
	David LOGUA	GEO	6/6/91	M		(1)	
77	Dmitriy MAKAR		1/10/81	M		(3)	1
7	Igor MAKAROV		26/2/85	M	4	(10)	1
25	Aleksandr MIKHNOVETS		24/11/82	M		(3)	
13	Donatas NAVIKAS	LTU	30/6/83	M	4		1
26	Dmitriy OSIPENKO		12/12/82	A	24	(1)	7
2	Yevgeniy PANKOV		24/11/83	D	17	(1)	
	Aleksei PANKOVETS		18/4/81	D	11		
4	Oleg PROTCHENKO		16/4/83	D		(2)	
10	Ionas PYATRAUSKAS		18/5/79	D	19	(5)	
24	Artem RAKHMANOV		10/7/90	D	6	(4)	
6	Andrei RAZIN		12/8/79	M	25	(1)	9
8	Pavel RYBAK		11/9/83	D	23		
20	Aleksandr SACHIVKO		5/1/86	M	25		
20	Aleksandr SOBOL		8/12/82	D	1	(2)	
30	Taina Adama SORO	CIV	20/12/81	M	25		1
1	Simas SKINDERIS	LTU	17/2/81	G	17		
3	Vyacheslav YAROSLAVSKIY		14/5/85	M	1	(2)	

FC MTZ-RIPO MINSK
Coach – Yuriy Puntus; (28/8/09) Ludas Rumbutis;
(13/9/09) Sergei Tsykalo
Founded – 1947
Stadium – Traktor (17,600)
MAJOR HONOURS: Belarus Cup – (2) 2005, 2008.

2009

4/4	Mikashevichi	a	2-1	*Ryndyuk 2*
13/4	Naftan	h	4-0	*Kvaratskhelia, Ryndyuk 2,*
				Rafael Ledesma
18/4	Shakhtyor	a	0-1	
26/4	Dinamo Brest	a	0-1	
2/5	Zhodino	a	0-0	
6/5	Gomel	a	3-3	*Kvaratskhelia, Ryndyuk, Lukša*
10/5	Dnepr	h	0-1	
17/5	Minsk	a	2-1	*Lukša, Kvaratskhelia*
23/5	Smorgon	a	2-1	*Kvaratskhelia 2*
30/5	Dinamo Minsk	a	0-5	
27/6	BATE	h	0-2	
5/7	Neman	a	1-2	*Kvaratskhelia*
12/7	Vitebsk	h	1-2	*Kvaratskhelia*
2/8	Mikashevichi	h	2-2	*Kvaratskhelia, Kharitonchik*
16/8	Naftan	a	1-2	*og (Gorbachev)*
23/8	Shakhtyor	h	1-2	*Kvaratskhelia*
30/8	Dinamo Brest	h	1-1	*Nicolas*
13/9	Zhodino	a	1-2	*Bubnov*
19/9	Gomel	h	4-2	*Nicolas 2 (1p), Zrnanović, Camara*
23/9	Dnepr	a	1-0	*Kvaratskhelia*
27/9	Minsk	h	1-0	*Camara*

4/10	Smorgon	a	4-0	Kvaratskhelia, Tolkanitsa, Nicolas, Shchegrikovich D.
18/10	Dinamo Minsk	h	0-2	
25/10	BATE	a	2-2	Lukša, Nicolas
1/11	Neman	h	0-2	
8/11	Vitebsk	a	1-1	Shchegrikovich D.

27/9	Dinamo Minsk	h	0-2	
5/10	BATE	a	0-4	
18/10	Neman	h	2-0	Rudik, Degterev
24/10	Vitebsk	a	0-1	
1/11	Mikashevichi	h	3-1	Degterev, Zyulev 2
8/11	Dinamo Brest	a	0-2	

No	Name	Nat	DoB	Pos	Aps	(s)	Gls
23	Anton BUBNOV		23/11/88	M	4	(14)	1
6	Aboubacar CAMARA	GUI	3/11/88	M	8	(12)	2
9	Mikhail GORNAK		9/3/89	A	1	(3)	
27	Yuriy KENDYSH		10/6/90	M	11	(1)	
19	Dmitriy KHARITONCHIK		11/6/86	A	1	(3)	1
7	Givi KVARATSKHELIA	GEO	11/5/79	M	22		11
10	Vitaliy LEDENEV		26/3/79	A	4	(4)	
9	Vytautas LUKŠA	LTU	14/8/84	M	18	(5)	3
22	Aleksandr MAKAS		8/10/91	A	1	(6)	
13	Igor MALTSEV		11/3/86	M	21	(3)	
20	Ivan MAYEVSKIY		5/5/88	M	2	(3)	
99	NICOLAS Ceolin	BRA	10/4/86	A	12		5
16	Nikolai OSIPOVICH		29/5/86	D	24	(1)	
17	Oleg POPEL		1/1/83	D	12	(4)	
21	RAFAEL Pompeo Rodrigues LEDESMA	BRA	31/12/82	M	4		1
31	Nikolai RYNDYUK		2/2/78	A	10	(1)	5
11	Dmitriy SHCHEGRIKOVICH		7/12/83	M	25	(1)	2
20	Sergei SHCHEGRIKOVICH		9/12/90	M		(2)	
14	Ivan SITKO		10/10/88	M		(4)	
2	Aleksandr SKSHYNETSKIY		28/2/90	D	3	(2)	
8	Aleksandr STASHCHENYUK		23/2/83	D	1		
77	Donatas STROCKIS	LTU	23/3/87	D	5		
1	Aleksandr SULIMA		1/8/79	G	26		
8	Aleksandr TOLKANITSA		9/5/89	M	24	(2)	1
22	Mikhail TYUFYAKOV	RUS	26/4/74	A	1		
15	Maxim VITUS		11/2/89	D	6		
25	Mikhail YEREMCHUK		14/11/90	M	25		
	Yuriy YURCHENKO		29/4/89	D	1		
4	Dilaver ZRNANOVIĆ	BIH	17/11/84	D	11	(2)	1
	Vygantas ZUBAVIČIUS	LTU	14/11/84	A	3	(3)	

FC NAFTAN NOVOPOLOTSK
Coach – Igor Kovalevich
Founded – 1995
Stadium – Atlant (5,300)
MAJOR HONOURS: Belarus Cup – (1) 2009.

2009

4/4	Shakhtyor	a	1-1	Zuyev
13/4	MTZ-RIPO	a	0-4	
18/4	Zhodino	h	1-0	Gorbachev
26/4	Gomel	a	3-1	Rudik (p), Komarovskiy, Gorbachev
2/5	Dnepr	h	2-1	Rudik, Zuyev
6/5	Minsk	a	0-2	
10/5	Smorgon	h	3-0	og (Khrapkovskiy), Zuyev 2
16/5	Dinamo Minsk	a	0-2	
23/5	BATE	h	0-4	
27/5	Neman	a	0-2	
28/6	Vitebsk	h	2-1	Trukhov, Rudik
4/7	Mikashevichi	a	2-0	Verkhovtsov 2
10/7	Dinamo Brest	h	1-0	Gorbachev
2/8	Shakhtyor	h	0-4	
16/8	MTZ-RIPO	h	2-1	Verkhovtsov, Degterev
22/8	Zhodino	a	1-0	Degterev
30/8	Gomel	h	1-2	Zyulev
13/9	Dnepr	a	1-2	Komarovskiy
19/9	Minsk	h	1-0	Politevich
23/9	Smorgon	a	2-2	Rudik, Zuyev

No	Name	Nat	DoB	Pos	Aps	(s)	Gls
15	Aleksei BELOUSOV		26/4/76	D	23	(1)	
88	Nikita BUKATKIN		7/3/88	M	10	(2)	
12	Aleksandr DEGTEREV		20/3/86	M	19	(5)	4
28	Dmitriy GINTOV		14/9/84	M	9	(1)	
2	Vyacheslav GOLIK		1/5/89	D		(1)	
4	Mikhail GORBACHEV		29/7/83	D	22	(1)	3
14	Maxim KARPOVICH		27/2/86	M	6		
11	Dmitriy KOMAROVSKIY		10/10/84	A	16	(5)	2
71	Anton KOVALEVSKIY		2/2/86	G	10		
22	Eduardas KURSKIS	LTU	17/10/76	G	7		
6	Sergei POLITEVICH		9/4/90	D	11		1
10	Maxim RAZUMOV		4/3/77	M	16	(1)	
1	Nikolai ROMANYUK		2/6/84	G	9		
7	Filipp RUDIK	RUS	22/3/87	M	23	(2)	5
13	Valeriy STRIPEIKIS		13/11/74	A	8	(10)	
8	Vitaliy TARASHCHIK		18/5/80	M	5	(9)	
21	Igor TRUKHOV		19/8/76	M	21		1
19	Ruslan USOV		4/8/79	A	3	(2)	
18	Dmitriy VERKHOVTSOV		10/10/86	D	26		3
17	Vitaliy VOLODENKOV		25/4/76	M	7	(1)	
9	Aleksandr YATSKEVICH		4/1/85	A	3	(14)	
5	Nikolai YEZERSKYI		17/6/84	D	8	(1)	
25	Valeriy ZHUKOVSKIY		21/5/84	M	7	(5)	
20	Yevgeniy ZUYEV		2/3/83	A	12	(10)	5
	Igor ZYULEV		5/1/84	M	5	(5)	3

FC NEMAN GRODNO
Coach – Oleg Radushko
Founded – 1964
Stadium – Central Sportkomplex Neman (9,000)
MAJOR HONOURS: Belarus Cup – (1) 1993.

2009

4/4	Gomel	h	1-0	Denisevich
13/4	Dnepr	h	0-1	
18/4	Minsk	h	2-1	Denisevich (p), Kovalenok
26/4	Smorgon	a	2-0	Nicolas, Kovalenok
2/5	Dinamo Minsk	h	0-0	
6/5	BATE	a	0-6	
10/5	Dinamo Brest	h	0-1	
16/5	Vitebsk	h	1-0	Denisevich
23/5	Mikashevichi	a	0-3	(w/o; original game 1-1 Nadiyevskiy)
27/5	Naftan	h	2-0	Denisevich 2
28/6	Shakhtyor	a	0-2	
5/7	MTZ-RIPO	h	2-1	Semenov, Yuzvovich
11/7	Zhodino	a	0-3	
2/8	Gomel	a	3-0	Suchkov, Gorbach, Semenov
16/8	Dnepr	a	2-1	Gorbach 2
22/8	Minsk	a	0-0	
30/8	Smorgon	h	1-1	Denisevich
13/9	Dinamo Minsk	a	0-2	
19/9	BATE	h	1-2	Kovalenok
23/9	Dinamo Brest	a	0-2	
27/9	Vitebsk	a	1-2	Kovalenok
4/10	Mikashevichi	h	0-0	
18/10	Naftan	a	0-2	
24/10	Shakhtyor	h	2-1	Gorbach, Suchkov (p)
1/11	MTZ-RIPO	a	0-2	Gorbach, Kovalenok
8/11	Zhodino	h	1-0	Denisevich (p)

No	Name	Nat	DoB	Pos	Aps	(s)	Gls
1	Andrei ASHIKHMIN		2/12/74	G	2		
29	Roman ASTAPENKO		10/3/80	G	16		
25	Dmitriy CHAKA		16/10/90	D		(1)	
77	Igor CHUMACHENKO		26/10/76	M	11	(9)	
9	Ivan DENISEVICH		9/11/84	D	25		7
13	Mohamed Seydou DERA	CIV	9/4/86	M	24		
90	Nikolai FASTOV		29/5/90	M		(1)	
17	Andrei GORBACH		20/5/85	D	17	(3)	5
5	Oleg ICHIM	MDA	27/10/79	D	24		
19	Andrei KAZARIN		27/10/84	M	2	(7)	
10	Dmitriy KOVALENOK		3/11/77	A	16	(9)	5
12	Vasiliy KUZNETSOV	RUS	24/8/78	G	8		
46	Aleksei LEGCHILIN		11/4/92	M		(3)	
6	Sergei LEVITSKIY		17/3/90	D	11	(9)	
4	Vitaliy NADIYEVSKIY		20/10/81	D	24		1
7	NICOLAS Ceolin	BRA	10/4/86	A	8	(3)	1
11	Artems OSIPOVS	LVA	8/1/89	A	2	(4)	
32	Kirill PAVLYUCHEK		27/6/84	D	5	(1)	
55	Dmitriy ROVNEIKO		12/5/80	D	25	(1)	
23	Yevgeniy SAVOSTYANOV		30/1/88	M	7	(3)	
33	Aleksandr SEMENOV	RUS	11/6/82	A	24	(2)	2
18	Vitaliy SHEPETOVSKIY		27/9/83	M	2	(1)	
8	Yuriy SHUMANSKIY		21/9/80	D	20	(2)	
	Aleksei SUCHOV		21/3/81	M	12		2
14	Artem VASKOV		21/10/88	M		(1)	
52	Dmitriy YUZVOVICH		25/1/89	A	1	(10)	1

16	Pāvels DAVYDOVS	LVA	30/12/80	G	7		
9	Aleksandr GRENKOV		20/1/78	M	21	(3)	4
12	Maxim GUKAILO		16/10/79	M	21	(1)	1
30	Roman KIRENKIN		20/2/81	D	13	(1)	1
20	Sergei KOVALCHUK		9/10/78	D	26		3
24	Dmitriy KOZLOV	RUS	22/10/84	A		(1)	
7	Andrei LEONCHIK		2/1/77	M	23	(2)	5
1	Vitaliy MAKAVCHIK		20/9/81	G	15		
11	Mikhail MARTINOVICH		14/9/79	M	9	(7)	
10	Sergei NIKIFORENKO		18/2/78	A	18	(4)	3
16	Andrejs PAVLOVS	LVA	22/2/79	G	4		
14	Aleksei PETROV		30/4/91	A	1	(1)	
21	Pavel PLASKONNYI		29/1/85	D	14	(1)	
26	Dmitriy PLATONOV		7/2/86	A	16	(8)	3
27	Pavel PLATONOV		7/2/86	M	1		
4	Serhiy PONOMARENKO	UKR	18/12/83	D	7		
17	Aleksei RIOS		14/5/87	M	10	(4)	1
28	Igor ROZHKOV		24/6/81	M	19	(1)	1
8	Nikolai RYNDYUK		2/2/78	A	7	(4)	1
77	Pavel SITKO		17/12/85	M	9	(2)	1
29	Aleksei SUCHKOV		21/3/81	M	5	(1)	
15	Aleksei YANUSHKEVICH		15/1/86	D	13	(1)	
5	Valeriy ZHUKOVSKIY		21/5/84	M	4	(8)	
18	Igor ZYULEV		5/1/84	A	5	(4)	3

FC SHAKHTYOR SOLIGORSK

**Coach – Yuriy Vergeichik; (23/5/09) Anatoliy Bogovik;
(14/9/09) Aleksei Vergeyenko**
Founded – 1963
Stadium – Stroitel (4,200)
*MAJOR HONOURS: Belarus League – (1) 2005;
Belarus Cup – (1) 2004.*

2009

4/4	Naftan	h	1-1	*Kovalchuk (p)*	
13/4	Dinamo Brest	a	1-1	*Platonov D.*	
18/4	MTZ-RIPO	h	1-0	*Grenkov*	
26/4	Zhodino	h	0-1		
2/5	Gomel	h	1-1	*Kovalchuk (p)*	
6/5	Dnepr	a	0-1		
10/5	Minsk	h	0-5		
16/5	Smorgon	a	2-2	*Balanovich, Kirenkin*	
23/5	Dinamo Minsk	h	1-1	*Zyulev*	
27/5	BATE	a	3-2	*Platonov D., Zyulev 2*	
28/6	Neman	h	2-0	*Nikiforenko, Grenkov*	
4/7	Vitebsk	a	1-0	*Leonchik*	
11/7	Mikashevichi	h	0-0		
2/8	Naftan	a	4-0	*Nikiforenko 2, Ryndyuk, Grenkov*	
16/8	Dinamo Brest	h	1-1	*Leonchik*	
23/8	MTZ-RIPO	a	2-1	*Leonchik 2*	
30/8	Zhodino	a	2-1	*Balanovich, Rozhkov*	
13/9	Gomel	a	1-2	*Leonchik*	
19/9	Dnepr	h	1-2	*Beganskiy*	
23/9	Minsk	a	1-1	*Sitko*	
27/9	Smorgon	h	2-0	*Platonov D., Gukailo*	
4/10	Dinamo Minsk	a	1-0	*Grenkov*	
18/10	BATE	h	0-1		
24/10	Neman	a	1-2	*Rios*	
1/11	Vitebsk	h	3-0	*Beganskiy 2, Balanovich*	
8/11	Mikashevichi	a	1-2	*Kovalchuk*	

No	Name	Nat	DoB	Pos	Aps	(s)	Gls
22	Sergei BALANOVICH		29/8/87	M	11	(12)	3
29	Pavel BEGANSKIY		9/1/81	A	3	(10)	3
8	Nikita BUKATKIN		7/3/88	M	4	(1)	

FC SMORGON

Coach – Aleksandr Lisovskiy; (22/7/09) Aleksandr Brazevich
Founded – 1987
Stadium – Yunost (3,200)

2009

5/4	Dinamo Brest	h	0-1		
12/4	Dinamo Minsk	h	0-0		
18/4	BATE	a	0-2		
26/4	Neman	h	0-2		
2/5	Vitebsk	a	1-2	*Lebedev*	
6/5	Mikashevichi	h	1-0	*Krot*	
10/5	Naftan	a	0-3		
16/5	Shakhtyor	h	2-2	*Litvinchuk, Lebedev*	
23/5	MTZ-RIPO	a	1-2	*Tarlovskiy*	
30/5	Zhodino	h	0-1		
26/6	Gomel	a	2-3	*Litvinchuk, Kazarin*	
4/7	Dnepr	h	0-2		
10/7	Minsk	a	0-2		
1/8	Dinamo Brest	a	1-1	*Martynets*	
16/8	Dinamo Minsk	a	1-1	*Kolodin*	
30/8	Neman	a	1-1	*Verstak*	
13/9	Vitebsk	h	0-3		
19/9	Mikashevichi	a	1-1	*Kolodin*	
23/9	Naftan	h	2-2	*Davidovich, Dukso*	
27/9	Shakhtyor	a	0-2		
4/10	MTZ-RIPO	h	0-4		
17/10	Zhodino	a	2-1	*Verstak, Martynets*	
24/10	Gomel	h	1-1	*Verstak*	
28/10	BATE	h	0-0		
1/11	Dnepr	a	0-4		
8/11	Minsk	h	1-3	*Kolodin*	

No	Name	Nat	DoB	Pos	Aps	(s)	Gls
9	Yuriy ALESHCHENKO		6/9/84	A	6	(4)	
18	Aleksandr ALKHOVIK		18/4/82	M	12	(2)	
84	Andrei ARKHIPTSEV		5/7/84	M	3	(4)	
7	Aleksandr BARANOV		27/11/74	M	14	(1)	
21	Nikolai BORSUKOV		30/11/82	D	11		
9	Sergei BUBNOV		13/4/89	A	6	(6)	
15	Aleksandr BUCHA		3/11/87	D	4	(2)	
19	Aleksandr DAVIDOVICH		13/2/81	D	6	(10)	1
1	Igor DOVGYALLO		17/7/85	G	7		

No	Name	Nat	DoB	Pos	Aps	(s)	Gls
3	Vladislav DUKSO		7/7/80	D	22		1
5	Aleksei DVORETSKIY		17/12/77	D	4	(2)	
17	Nikolai FASTOV		29/5/90	M		(1)	
22	Sergei IRKHA		25/3/84	M	5	(4)	
23	Andrei KAZARIN		27/10/84	M	9	(2)	1
33	Sergei KHALETSKIY		14/4/84	D	11		
84	Elmar KHEIROV	AZE	14/1/87	M	2	(1)	
13	Aleksandr KHRAPKOVSKIY		12/3/75	D	16	(3)	
10	Dmytro KOLODIN	UKR	12/4/78	M	12		3
10	Sergei KROT		27/6/80	A	6	(3)	1
	Ihor KRYVOBOK	UKR	28/7/78	A	4	(1)	
12	Eduardas KURSKIS	LTU	17/10/76	G	12		
17	Dmitriy LEBEDEV		13/5/86	M	10	(3)	2
11	Mikhail LITVINCHUK		21/6/80	A	5	(4)	2
2	Gennadiy MARDAS		12/6/70	D	1		
8	Vladimir MARGULETS		15/1/84	M	19	(5)	
21	Aleksei MARTYNETS		13/3/85	M	13		2
33	Vitaliy ROGOZHKIN		21/1/76	D	7	(1)	
22	Yuriy RYZHKO		10/10/89	D	13		
36	Vitaliy SHEPETOVSKIY		27/9/83	M	8	(3)	
6	Igor TARLOVSKIY		21/9/74	D	16		1
77	Nerijus VALSKIS	LTU	4/8/87	A	11	(1)	
23	Dmitriy VERSTAK		29/8/80	A	4	(7)	3
27	Aleksei ZHUK		6/3/83	G	7		

FC TORPEDO ZHODINO

Coach – Oleg Kubarev
Founded – 1961
Stadium – City Stadium, Borisov (5,392); City Stadium, Molodechno (4,800); Torpedo, Mogilev (3,500)

2009

4/4	Vitebsk	a	1-0	Boiko
12/4	Mikashevichi	a	3-1	Kovalenko, Boiko, Klimovich
18/4	Naftan	a	0-1	
26/4	Shakhtyor	a	1-0	Klimovich
2/5	MTZ-RIPO	h	0-0	
6/5	Dinamo Brest	a	2-2	Klimovich, Sheryakov
10/5	Gomel	a	1-2	og (Kuzmenok)
17/5	Dnepr	a	0-0	
23/5	Minsk	h	1-0	og (Pankov)
30/5	Smorgon	a	1-0	Sheryakov
28/6	Dinamo Minsk	h	0-0	
4/7	BATE	a	0-3	
11/7	Neman	h	3-0	Sheryakov 2 (1p), Vasiliyev
2/8	Vitebsk	h	3-0	Sheryakov 2, Brusnikin
16/8	Mikashevichi	h	1-3	Sheryakov (p)
22/8	Naftan	h	0-1	
30/8	Shakhtyor	h	1-2	Zubovich
13/9	MTZ-RIPO	h	2-1	Boiko, Voronkov
19/9	Dinamo Brest	h	1-2	Boiko
23/9	Gomel	h	4-0	Kovalenko, Levitskiy, Voronkov, Boiko
27/9	Dnepr	h	0-0	
4/10	Minsk	a	4-0	Kovalenko 2, Yevseyenko, Boiko (p)
17/10	Smorgon	h	1-2	Kontsevoi
25/10	Dinamo Minsk	a	0-0	
1/11	BATE	h	1-1	Zubovich
8/11	Neman	a	0-1	

No	Name	Nat	DoB	Pos	Aps	(s)	Gls
18	Ilya ALEKSIYEVICH		10/2/91	M		(1)	
9	Vadim BOIKO		3/12/78	A	18	(6)	6
9	Nikolai BORSUKOV		30/11/82	D	11		
5	Nikolai BRANFILOV		16/12/77	D	10	(1)	
8	Anton BRUSNIKIN	RUS	13/1/86	M	15	(8)	1
1	Vladimir BUSHMA		24/11/83	G	24		
28	Valeriy KARSHAKEVICH		15/2/88	D		(1)	
13	Dmitriy KLIMOVICH		9/2/84	M	23		3
26	Sergei KONTSEVOI		21/6/86	D	23		1
12	Sergei Sergeyevich KOVALENKO	RUS	12/1/89	D	20	(4)	4
17	Aleksei KOZLOV		11/7/89	M		(1)	
17	Sergei Sergeyevich KUZMINICH		20/1/77	D	5	(3)	
23	Artur LEVITSKIY		17/3/85	M	13	(8)	1
7	Nukri MANCHKAVA	GEO	5/1/82	D	17		
6	Andrei SHERYAKOV		10/11/82	A	11	(4)	7
19	Nikolai SHVYDAKOV		6/7/80	A	15	(8)	
30	Sergei SINEVICH		11/1/89	G	2		
21	Aleksandr TERENTIYEV		4/9/81	M	3	(13)	
20	Maxim VASILIYEV	RUS	31/1/87	D	8	(1)	1
2	Ihor VORONKOV	UKR	24/4/81	M	26		
10	Pavel YEVSEYENKO		30/10/80	M	26		1
14	Yegor ZUBOVICH		1/6/89	M	16	(6)	2

FC VITEBSK

Coach – Aleksandr Khatskevich; (31/7/09) Yuriy Konoplev
Founded – 1960
Stadium – Central Sportkomplex (CSK) (8,300)
MAJOR HONOURS: Belarus Cup – (1) 1998.

2009

4/4	Zhodino	h	0-1	
12/4	Gomel	a	1-1	Sitko
18/4	Dnepr	h	0-1	
26/4	Minsk	a	1-0	Tselykh
2/5	Smorgon	h	2-1	Shakov, Sokol
6/5	Dinamo Minsk	a	1-2	Shakov
10/5	BATE	h	0-2	
16/5	Neman	a	0-1	
23/5	Dinamo Brest	h	0-1	
30/5	Mikashevichi	h	2-1	Gorovtsov, Goncharik
28/6	Naftan	a	1-2	Kobets
4/7	Shakhtyor	a	0-1	
12/7	MTZ-RIPO	h	2-1	Sokol, Kobets
2/8	Zhodino	a	0-3	
16/8	Gomel	h	1-0	Shakov
22/8	Dnepr	a	2-3	Shakov, Kholodkov
30/8	Minsk	h	1-0	Sorokin
13/9	Smorgon	a	3-0	Kosak, Lebedev D., Shakov
19/9	Dinamo Minsk	h	2-3	Shakov, Gorovtsov
24/9	BATE	a	1-3	Lebedev D.
27/9	Neman	h	2-1	Kobets, og (Shumanskiy)
4/10	Dinamo Brest	a	0-3	
17/10	Mikashevichi	a	2-1	Lebedev D., Gospodars
24/10	Naftan	h	1-0	Lebedev D.
1/11	Shakhtyor	a	0-3	
8/11	MTZ-RIPO	h	1-1	Gorovtsov

No	Name	Nat	DoB	Pos	Aps	(s)	Gls
1	Pavel CHESNOVSKIY		4/3/86	G	5		
5	Andrei DIVAKOV		7/10/78	D	25		
4	Artem GONCHARIK		13/4/80	M	9	(2)	1
20	Andrei GOROVTSOV		2/4/81	D	17	(4)	3
14	Vadims GOSPODARS	LVA	25/12/83	M	11		1
27	Igor KHOLODKOV		19/4/91	A		(6)	1
37	Aleksandr KOBETS		11/6/81	M	20	(4)	3
15	Aleksandr KOLOTSEI		27/1/88	M	7	(11)	
12	Artem KOSAK		22/2/77	D	25		1
10	Pavel KOSINETS		2/2/89	A		(3)	
1	Anton KOVALEVSKIY		2/2/86	G	3		
17	Sergei KUZMINICH		20/1/77	D	9	(2)	
8	Andrei LEBEDEV		1/2/91	M	5	(3)	
11	Dmitriy LEBEDEV		13/5/86	M	9	(3)	4
33	Pavel LYUTKO		1/7/87	D	7		
22	Irakli MAISURADZE	GEO	22/8/88	M	2	(6)	

2	Simon OGAR Veron	NGA	24/4/87	M	18	(5)	
3	Vitaliy PANASYUK		9/2/80	D	22		
17	Aleksei SAVELIYEV	RUS	10/4/77	M	11	(1)	
9	Vladimir SHAKOV		28/8/84	A	19	(4)	6
7	Pavel SITKO		17/12/85	M	7	(2)	1
	Artem SKITOV		21/1/91	M		(2)	
13	Viktor SOKOL		9/5/81	M	11	(1)	2
	Roman SOROKIN	RUS	17/5/85	M	9	(2)	1
18	Yuriy TSELYKH	UKR	18/4/79	A	10	(1)	1
16	Yuriy VASYUTIN		20/7/78	G	18		
	Sergei VEKHTEV		8/5/71	M		(1)	
	Eduard ZATSEPIN	RUS	27/4/74	A	6	(2)	
21	Denis ZHUKOV		27/10/87	M	1	(4)	

PROMOTED CLUB
FC BELSHINA BOBRUISK
Coach – Oleg Volokh
Founded – 1976
Stadium – Spartak (3,700)
MAJOR HONOURS: Belarus League – (1) 2001;
Belarus Cup - (3) 1997, 1999, 2001.

SECOND LEVEL FINAL TABLE 2009

		Pld	W	D	L	F	A	Pts
1	FC Belshina Bobruisk	26	20	4	2	55	15	64
2	FC Volna Pinsk	26	16	3	7	52	31	51
3	FC DSK Gomel	26	13	9	4	34	18	48
4	FC Veras Nesvizh	26	12	7	7	33	26	43
5	FC SKVICH Minsk	26	11	6	9	37	29	39
6	FC Baranovichi	26	10	8	8	39	33	38
7	FC Khimik Svetlogorsk	26	9	9	8	33	28	36
8	FC Vedrich-97 Rechitsa	26	10	5	11	40	47	35
9	FC BelCard Grodno	26	8	5	13	23	34	29
10	FC Kommunalnik Slonim	26	7	8	11	20	32	29
11	FC Lida	26	6	8	12	19	31	26
12	FC Polotsk	26	6	4	16	29	46	22
13	FC Slaviya Mozyr	26	4	8	14	21	40	20
14	FC Spartak Shklov	26	4	8	14	21	46	20

DOMESTIC CUP 2009/10
KUBOK BELARUSII

SECOND ROUND

(7/8/09)
Molodechno 2, Neman Grodno 3

(8/8/09)
Belshina 1, Dinamo Brest 0
Baranovichi 0, BATE 4
BelCard 0, Zhodino 1
DSK Gomel 2, Smorgon 0
Gorodeya 1, Dnepr 2 *(aet)*
Kommunalnik 0, FC Gomel 2
Polotsk 3, Vitebsk 3 *(aet; 3-2 on pens)*
Rudensk 1, Minsk 3
Slaviya 2, Volna 0
Slutsksahar 1, MTZ-RIPO 2
Spartak Shklov 1, Veras 2 *(aet)*

Vedrich-97 2, Mikashevichi 5
Zhlobin 0, Naftan 2
Zvezda-BGU 1, Dinamo Minsk 7

(9/8/09)
Neman Mosty 0, Shakhtyor Soligorsk 5

THIRD ROUND

(28/10/09 & 4/11/09)
Dnepr v Dinamo Minsk 2-4; 0-3 *(2-7)*

(4/11/09 & 11/11/09)
Naftan v Slaviya 4-0; 3-1 *(7-1)*

(11/11/09 & 15/11/09)
Belshina v Shakhtyor Soligorsk 0-1; 2-2 *(2-3)*
FC Gomel v DSK Gomel 1-1; 2-3 *(3-4)*
Mikashevichi v Neman Grodno 0-1; 0-1 *(0-2)*
Zhodino v Veras 5-0; 3-0 *(8-0)*

(15/11/09 & 18/11/09)
MTZ-RIPO v Polotsk 5-2; 0-1 *(5-3)*

(22/11/09 & 27/11/09)
BATE v Minsk 1-0; 2-0 *(3-0)*

QUARTER-FINALS

(13/3/10 & 17/3/10)
BATE 7 *(Kontsevoi 5, 16, Nekhaichik 12, Olekhnovich 37, Renan 77, 83, Alumona 86)*, Partizan 0
Partizan 1 *(Makas 15)*, BATE 0
(BATE 7-1)

Naftan 0, Zhodino 2 *(Chelyadinskiy 41og, Kryvobok 89)*
Zhodino 3 *(Brusnikin 32, Kozlov 78, 85)*, Naftan 1 *(Stripeikis 28)*
(Zhodino 5-1)

Neman Grodno 1 *(Gorbach 14)*, Shakhtyor Soligorsk 2 *(Grenkov 87, Sitko 90+2)*
Shakhtyor Soligorsk 2 *(Rozhkov 86, Balanovich 90+4)*, Neman Grodno 0
(Shakhtyor Soligorsk 4-1)

(14/3/10 & 18/3/10)
DSK Gomel 0, Dinamo Minsk 2 *(Kislyak 18, Gavryushko 90)*
Dinamo Minsk 1 *(Kislyak 42)*, DSK Gomel 3 *(Zabolotskiy 55, 59, Dobrovolyanskiy 90+1)*
(3-3; DSK Gomel on away goals)

NB MTZ-RIPO changed name to Partizan for 2010 season.

SEMI-FINALS

(24/3/10 & 28/3/10)
DSK Gomel 1 *(Dobrovolyanskiy 84)*, Zhodino 2 *(Kontsevoi 29, Levitskiy 43)*
Zhodino 0, DSK Gomel 1 *(Zabolotskiy 39)*
(2-2; Zhodino on away goals)

Shakhtyor Soligorsk 1 *(Kirenkin 78)*, BATE 2 *(Alumona 24p, Baga 60)*
BATE 1 *(Kontsevoi 62)*, Shakhtyor Soligorsk 0
(BATE 3-1)

FINAL

(23/5/10)
Dinamo stadium, Minsk
FC BATE BORISOV 5 *(Renan 5, 64, Rodionov 22, 69, Kontsevoi 57p)*
FC TORPEDO ZHODINO 0
Referee – Sakharevich
BATE – Veremko, Likhtarovich *(Olekhnovich 69)*, Sosnovskiy, Shitov, Yurevich, Kontsevoi, Volodko A., Renan, Nekhaichik *(Alumona 68)*, Radkov *(Bordachev 58)*, Rodionov.
ZHODINO – Bushma, Solovei, Ostroukh, Ponomarenko, Branovitskiy *(Karshakevich 34)*, Brusnikin *(Kazarin 48)*, Levitskiy, Beganskiy, Ryzhko, Ogar, Krivobok *(Karolik 76)*.
Sent off: Beganskiy (45+1)

Anderlecht take 30th title with ease

A new play-off format was imposed on Belgium's elite clubs in 2009/10, but any hopes that the change would be for the better were dashed by the ease with which record champions RSC Anderlecht cruised to their 30th domestic championship title.

The 2008/09 season had required a play-off of a different kind as Anderlecht went head to head with arch-rivals R. Standard de Liège after the two teams ended the 18-club, 34-match campaign level on points. The title race could hardly have been tighter, but in their wisdom the Pro League organisers decided to lop off two teams and supplement the regular season - reduced mid-term from 30 matches to 28 with the expulsion of financially crippled R. Excelsior Mouscron - with three separate mini-leagues. One, containing the top six clubs, would yield the champions, and two others, containing four clubs apiece, would determine the two candidates to go forward to a further series of play-offs for UEFA Europa League qualification.

By the end of the regular season Anderlecht were 12 points clear of second-placed Club Brugge KV. As the points totals for championship pool participants were halved, that lead was duly trimmed to six, but it was not long before Ariël Jacobs' team had not only restored their previous advantage but stretched it still further. When they wrapped up the title with a 2-1 win at Club Brugge, their lead was 13 points with four games remaining. By the end of the campaign, their final margin of victory had soared to a whopping 18 points.

Convincing triumph

It was as convincing a championship triumph as any the Brussels giants had previously achieved and was a measure of the team's determination to atone

Romelu Lukaku - Anderlecht's boy wonder

for losing that 2008/09 play-off to Standard. Their dominance was reflected not only in the rows and columns of the final table but also in the end-of-season awards, with Jacobs taking the prize as Coach of the Year and playmaker Mbark Boussoufa retaining his Player of the Year gong. Also worthy of distinction was the incredible performance of 16-year-old striker Romelu Lukaku, who was officially declared as the Pro League's Golden Boot winner, his 15-goal tally topping the charts in the regular season (before Club Brugge's Cameroonian striker Dorge Kouemaha overtook him in the play-off round).

Although it ended in glory, Anderlecht's season had started horribly - with an 8-2 aggregate annihilation by Olympique Lyonnais in the UEFA Champions League play-off round and a savage injury to Polish defender Marcin Wasilewski (inflicted by Standard midfielder Axel Witsel). Denied access to the main European event, they took refuge in the UEFA Europa League and enjoyed a decent run, highlighted by a memorable 3-1 win at AFC Ajax (in which Lukaku struck twice).

Standard, who qualified for the UEFA Champions League proper but won only one group stage fixture, also switched to the UEFA Europa League thanks to a sensational last-gasp goal from goalkeeper Sinan Bolat against AZ Alkmaar, and they went one round further than Anderlecht, to the quarter-finals, before falling victim to the same opposition, Hamburger SV. László Bölöni, who had led Les Rouches to the 2008/09 Belgian title, was unable to avert a dramatic decline in the team's domestic form and left in February. His successor, Dominique D'Onofrio, could do little better as the champions failed to reach the top six for the play-offs and subsequently missed out on backdoor European qualification.

BELGIUM

Gent glory

Standard's 2007/08 title-winning boss, Michel Preud'homme, enjoyed a superb season with KAA Gent, earning himself a move to Dutch champions FC Twente. Before he left, he gave the Gent fans two glorious parting gifts – the first a 6-2 home win over Club Brugge that delivered a UEFA Champions League qualifying place as league runners-up; the second a 3-0 win in the Belgian Cup final over Cercle Brugge KSV that brought Gent their first major trophy since 1984.

Gent's second place in the league ensured that Cercle would qualify alongside their Bruges rivals for the UEFA Europa League. The third ticket for that competition was claimed in the play-offs by Frank Vercauteren's KRC Genk, who defeated first KVC Westerlo then the season's surprise package, newly promoted K. Sint-Truidense, who had confounded predictions by finishing fourth in the championship pool. With Mouscron withdrawn, and the results of their fixtures expunged, it was decided that there would be no automatic relegation, but bottom club KSV Roeselare went down anyway in the promotion/relegation play-offs. K. AS Eupen won that mini-league to go up with second tier champions K. Lierse SK as the Pro League restored its 16-team complement for 2010/11.

The disorder of the domestic league was mirrored in the comings and goings of the Belgian national team. Despite another qualifying failure – the Red Devils' fourth in succession – there was an upbeat mood when Dick Advocaat was appointed to replace the ill-starred Vercauteren as national coach in October 2009. Six months later, though, the Dutchman was gone, lured away by Russia, leaving the team in the hands once again of Georges Leekens, the man who had taken Belgium to the 1998 FIFA World Cup finals and who enjoyed an impressive 2009/10 season with KV Kortrijk.

Union Royale des Sociétés de Football Association (URBSFA) Koninklijke Belgische Voetbalbond (KBVB)

Houba de Strooperlaan 145
BE-1020 Bruxelles
tel – +32 2 477 1211
fax – +32 2 478 2391
website – footbel.com
email – urbsfa.kbvb@footbel.com
Year of Formation – 1895

President – François De Keersmaecker
Media Officer – Nicolas Cornu
National Stadium – Stade Roi Baudouin, Brussels (50,024)

INTERNATIONAL TOURNAMENT APPEARANCES
FIFA World Cup - (11) 1930, 1934, 1938, 1954, 1970, 1982 (2nd phase), 1986 (4th), 1990 (2nd round), 1994 (2nd round), 1998, 2002 (2nd round).
UEFA European Championship - (3) 1972 (3rd), 1980 (runners-up), 2000.
TOP FIVE ALL-TIME CAPS
Jan Ceulemans (96); Eric Gerets & Franky Van Der Elst (86); Vincenzo Scifo (84); Paul Van Himst (81)
TOP FIVE ALL-TIME GOALS
Paul Van Himst & Bernard Voorhoof (30); Marc Wilmots (28); Jef Mermans (27); Raymond Braine & Robert De Veen (26)

Gifted crop

Leekens has vowed to reintroduce a winning mentality and spirit to a gifted young crop of individuals featuring, among others, Lukaku, Witsel, Steven Defour, Marouane Fellaini and the 'new Enzo Scifo', Eden Hazard. The team's immediate target is for a strong showing in the UEFA EURO 2012 qualifiers, in which Belgium are grouped with Germany, Turkey, Austria, Kazakhstan and Azerbaijan and can realistically hope for a place in the play-offs.

NATIONAL TEAM RESULTS 2009/10

12/8/09	Czech Republic	A	Teplice	1-3	Vertonghen (11)
5/9/09	Spain (WCQ)	A	La Coruna	0-5	
9/9/09	Armenia (WCQ)	A	Yerevan	1-2	Van Buyten (90+2)
10/10/09	Turkey (WCQ)	H	Brussels	2-0	Mpenza (7, 84)
14/10/09	Estonia (WCQ)	A	Tallinn	0-2	
14/11/09	Hungary	H	Ghent	3-0	Fellaini (38), Vermaelen (55), Mirallas (61p)
17/11/09	Qatar	N	Sedan (FRA)	2-0	Witsel (21), Sonck (54)
3/3/10	Croatia	H	Brussels	0-1	
19/5/10	Bulgaria	H	Brussels	2-1	Lepoint (89), Kompany (90+1)

BELGIUM

NATIONAL TEAM APPEARANCES 2009/10

			Cze	ESP	ARM	TUR	EST	Hun	Qat	Cro	Bul	Caps	Goals
Coach – Frank VERCAUTEREN	28/10/56												
(1/10/09) Dick ADVOCAAT (NED)	27/9/47												
(11/5/10) Georges LEEKENS	18/5/49												
Stijn STIJNEN	7/4/81	Club Brugge	G									30	-
Anthony VANDEN BORRE	24/10/87	Portsmouth (ENG)	D	D								22	1
Daniel VAN BUYTEN	7/2/78	Bayern (GER)	D	D	D	D	D46	D	D			55	7
Thomas VERMAELEN	14/11/85	Arsenal (ENG)	D46	D		D	D	D	D	D84		28	1
Jelle VAN DAMME	10/10/83	Anderlecht	D80							D	D64	25	-
Marouane FELLAINI	22/11/87	Everton (ENG)	M46	M		M		M88	M			21	3
Steven DEFOUR	15/4/88	Standard	M	M	M						M84	24	1
Jan VERTONGHEN	24/4/87	Ajax (NED)	M86	D29		M	M	M	M	M	M46	22	1
Eden HAZARD	7/1/91	Lille (FRA)	A68	M58	s72	s74		A	A70	M76	A	12	-
Tom DE SUTTER	3/7/85	Anderlecht	A46		s53	s89	s76	A75	s78			14	-
Moussa DEMBÉLÉ	16/7/87	AZ (NED)	A	A	A	A	A			A70	A46	28	5
Émile MPENZA	4/7/78	Sion (SUI)	s46					A89	A			57	19
Timmy SIMONS	11/12/76	PSV (NED)	s46	M	D							74	3
Wesley SONCK	9/8/78	Club Brugge	s46	A70	A81			s75	A78	s46		55	24
Kevin MIRALLAS	5/10/87	St-Étienne (FRA)	s68	s58	M72	A74	M	A75	A78		s84	20	4
Olivier DESCHACHT	16/2/81	Anderlecht	s80	s29	D				D		s64	19	-
Toby ALDERWEIRELD	2/3/89	Ajax (NED)	s86				s46			s84	D64	6	-
Jean-François GILLET	31/5/79	Bari (ITA)	G	G				G	G		G	5	-
Igor DE CAMARGO	12/5/83	Standard	s70	M								4	-
Gill SWERTS	23/9/82	AZ (NED)				D	D	D76				17	1
Maarten MARTENS	2/7/84	AZ (NED)		M53					M46			9	-
Roland LAMAH	31/12/87	Le Mans (FRA)			s81	M78	M	s75	s70			5	-
Logan BAILLY	27/12/85	Mönchengladbach (GER)				G	G		G			3	-
Nicolas LOMBAERTS	20/3/85	Zenit (RUS)				D	D	D		s70	D	9	-
Gabi MUDINGAYI	1/10/81	Bologna (ITA)				s78	M46					17	-
Thomas BUFFEL	19/2/81	Genk				s46	s88			s76	M	34	6
Sepp DE ROOVER	12/11/84	Groningen (NED)					D	D				2	-
Karel GERAERTS	5/1/82	Club Brugge						M46	s78			20	4
Vincent KOMPANY	10/4/86	Man. City (ENG)						s46		D70	D	31	1
Axel WITSEL	12/1/89	Standard							M62	M		11	2
Mehdi CARCELA-GONZÁLEZ	1/7/89	Standard							s62	s70		2	-
Steve COLPAERT	13/9/86	Zulte Waregem								D		1	-
Romelu LUKAKU	13/5/93	Anderlecht								A76	A64	2	-
Jonathan BLONDEL	3/4/84	Club Brugge								s76		4	-
Christophe LEPOINT	24/10/84	Gent									s46	1	1
Bernd THIJS	28/6/78	Gent									s46	6	-
Christian BENTEKE	3/12/90	Kortrijk									s64	1	-
Laurent CIMAN	5/8/85	Kortrijk									s64	1	-

BELGIUM

DOMESTIC LEAGUE 2009/10

PRO LEAGUE FINAL TABLE

		Pld	Home					Away					Total					Pts
			W	D	L	F	A	W	D	L	F	A	W	D	L	F	A	
1	RSC Anderlecht	28	11	2	1	27	10	11	1	2	35	10	22	3	3	62	20	69
2	Club Brugge KV	28	10	3	1	24	12	7	3	4	28	21	17	6	5	52	33	57
3	KAA Gent	28	7	3	4	26	18	7	4	3	23	12	14	7	7	49	30	49
4	KV Kortrijk	28	9	1	4	21	14	3	8	3	18	16	12	9	7	39	30	45
5	K. Sint-Truidense VV	28	6	3	5	21	18	6	3	5	14	17	12	6	10	35	35	42
6	SV Zulte Waregem	28	7	5	2	23	13	3	6	5	16	19	10	11	7	39	32	41
7	KV Mechelen	28	8	2	4	21	18	4	1	9	15	28	12	3	13	36	46	39
8	R. Standard de Liège	28	6	5	3	20	16	4	4	6	18	18	10	9	9	38	34	39
9	Cercle Brugge KSV	28	8	2	4	24	16	3	3	8	21	24	11	5	12	45	40	38
10	KFC Germinal Beerschot Antwerpen	28	6	4	4	20	22	3	4	7	10	21	9	8	11	30	43	35
11	KRC Genk	28	4	7	3	16	13	4	3	7	17	18	8	10	10	33	31	34
12	KVC Westerlo	28	6	4	4	19	14	2	4	8	9	20	8	8	12	28	34	32
13	R. Charleroi SC	28	3	4	7	17	23	2	4	8	11	22	5	8	15	28	45	23
14	KSC Lokeren OV	28	4	3	7	14	21	1	0	13	8	33	5	3	20	22	54	18
15	KSV Roeselare	28	2	3	9	15	29	2	3	9	14	29	4	6	18	29	58	18

NB After 28 rounds top six clubs entered title play-off mini-league, carrying forward half of their points total (half points rounded upwards); clubs placed 7-14 entered two play-off groups; R. Excelsior Mouscron withdrew after Round 18; all their results were annulled.

PLAY-OFF 1 FINAL TABLE

		Pld	Home					Away					Total					Pts
			W	D	L	F	A	W	D	L	F	A	W	D	L	F	A	
1	RSC Anderlecht	10	4	1	0	15	5	3	2	0	9	4	7	3	0	24	9	59
2	KAA Gent	10	2	2	1	12	5	2	2	1	8	8	4	4	2	20	13	41
3	Club Brugge KV	10	3	1	1	10	3	0	2	3	4	12	3	3	4	14	15	41
4	K. Sint-Truidense VV	10	1	3	1	4	4	2	1	2	5	6	3	4	3	9	10	34
5	KV Kortrijk	10	2	0	3	7	7	1	1	3	2	6	3	1	6	9	13	33
6	SV Zulte Waregem	10	1	1	3	5	6	1	0	4	2	17	2	1	7	7	23	28

PLAY-OFF 2 A FINAL TABLE

		Pld	Home					Away					Total					Pts
			W	D	L	F	A	W	D	L	F	A	W	D	L	F	A	
1	KVC Westerlo	6	2	0	1	6	3	1	1	1	6	6	3	1	2	12	9	10
2	KV Mechelen	6	2	0	1	5	4	1	1	1	5	4	3	1	2	10	8	10
3	Cercle Brugge KSV	6	2	1	0	5	2	0	0	3	4	10	2	1	3	9	12	7
4	KSC Lokeren OV	6	1	2	0	10	8	0	1	2	2	6	1	3	2	12	14	6

PLAY-OFF 2 B FINAL TABLE

		Pld	Home					Away					Total					Pts
			W	D	L	F	A	W	D	L	F	A	W	D	L	F	A	
1	KRC Genk	6	3	0	0	6	0	2	1	0	6	3	5	1	0	12	3	16
2	R. Standard de Liège	6	2	1	0	6	1	0	1	2	2	4	2	2	2	8	5	8
3	KFC Germinal Beerschot Antwerpen	6	0	2	1	5	7	1	0	2	1	5	1	2	3	6	12	5
4	R. Charleroi SC	6	1	0	2	2	3	0	1	2	2	7	1	1	4	4	10	4

TOP GOALSCORERS
(excluding Play-offs)

15 Romelu LUKAKU (Anderlecht)

13 Dorge KOUEMAHA (Club Brugge)
   Ibrahim SIDIBÉ (Sint-Truiden)

12 Teddy CHEVALLIER (Zulte Waregem)
   Cyril THÉRÉAU (Charleroi)

11 Dawid JANCZYK (Lokeren/GBA)

10 Milan JOVANOVIĆ (Standard)

9 Mbark BOUSSOUFA (Anderlecht)
   Dominic FOLEY (Cercle Brugge)
   Elimane COULIBALY (Gent)
   Faris HAROUN (GBA)
   Christian BENTEKE (Kortrijk)

TOP GOALSCORERS
(including Play-offs)

16 Dorge KOUEMAHA (Club Brugge)

15 Romelu LUKAKU (Anderlecht)

14 Mbark BOUSSOUFA (Anderlecht)
   Dominic FOLEY (Cercle Brugge)
   Christian BENTEKE (Kortrijk)

13 Cyril THÉRÉAU (Charleroi)
   Ibrahim SIDIBÉ (Sint-Truiden)

12 Dawid JANCZYK (Lokeren/GBA)
   Teddy CHEVALIER (Zulte Waregem)

11 Matías SUÁREZ (Anderlecht)
   Elimane COULIBALY (Gent)
   Faris HAROUN (GBA)
   Julien GORIUS (Mechelen)

UEFA EUROPA LEAGUE QUALIFICATION PLAY-OFFS

FIRST ROUND

(2/5/10 & 7/5/10)
Genk 2 *(De Bruyne 85, Yeboah 90)*,
Westerlo 2 *(Yakovenko 23, Liliu 63)*
Westerlo 0,
Genk 3 *(João Carlos 4, Buffel 71, Ogunjimi 81)*
(Genk 5-2)

SECOND ROUND

(13/5/10 & 16/5/10)
Genk 2 *(Ogunjimi 21, Camus 61)*,
Sint-Truiden 1 *(Sidibé 42)*
Sint-Truiden 2 *(Sidibé 7p, Onana 80)*,
Genk 3 *(Ogunjimi 21, Barda 45, Buffel 58)*
(Genk 5-3)

CLUB-BY-CLUB

RSC ANDERLECHT
Coach – Ariël Jacobs
Founded – 1908
Stadium – Constant Vanden Stock (28,063)
MAJOR HONOURS:
UEFA Cup Winners' Cup - (2) 1976, 1978;
UEFA Cup - (1) 1983;
UEFA Super Cup - (2) 1976, 1978;
Belgian League - (30) 1947, 1949, 1950, 1951, 1954, 1955, 1956, 1959,
1962, 1964, 1965, 1966, 1967, 1968, 1972, 1974, 1981, 1985, 1986, 1987,
1991, 1993, 1994, 1995, 2000, 2001, 2004, 2006, 2007, 2010;
Belgian Cup - (9) 1965, 1972, 1973, 1975, 1976, 1988, 1989, 1994, 2008.

2009
1/8	Kortrijk	a	2-0	*Boussoufa, Wasilewski*
8/8	Cercle Brugge	h	3-2	*Suárez, og (Boi), Boussoufa*
15/8	Westerlo	h	3-0	*Van Damme, Suárez, Boussoufa*
22/8	Zulte Waregem	a	2-0	*Boussoufa, Lukaku*
30/8	Standard	h	1-1	*Gillet*
12/9	Sint-Truiden	a	1-2	*Juhász*
20/9	Gent	h	1-1	*Mazuch*
24/9	Mouscron	a	2-1	*Suárez (p), Lukaku (result annulled)*
27/9	GBA	h	1-0	*Lukaku*
4/10	Club Brugge	a	2-4	*De Sutter 2*
17/10	Charleroi	h	2-0	*Biglia, Lukaku*
25/10	Mechelen	a	2-0	*Lukaku, Boussoufa*
31/10	Lokeren	h	2-0	*Lukaku, Suárez*
8/11	Genk	a	2-0	*Mazuch, Lukaku*
21/11	Roeselare	h	3-1	*Juhász, og (Sierens), Lukaku*
27/11	Kortrijk	h	1-0	*Juhász*
6/12	Cercle Brugge	a	3-1	*Legear, Boussoufa, Frutos*
11/12	Westerlo	a	2-0	*Lukaku, Frutos*
27/12	Gent	a	2-2	*Legear, De Sutter*
30/12	Zulte Waregem	h	2-1	*De Sutter 2*

2010
17/1	Standard	a	4-0	*Legear, Lukaku, og (Traoré), og (Mangala)*
29/1	GBA	a	5-0	*Lukaku 2, Kanu, Legear, Boussoufa*
3/2	Club Brugge	h	3-2	*Juhász, Frutos, Boussoufa*
6/2	Sint-Truiden	h	1-2	*Van Damme*
21/2	Mechelen	a	2-0	*Gillet, Lukaku*
28/2	Roeselare	a	2-1	*Mazuch, Suárez*
6/3	Charleroi	a	2-0	*Suárez, De Sutter*
14/3	Genk	h	2-0	*Lukaku, De Sutter*
21/3	Lokeren	h	4-0	*Lukaku, Kouyaté, og (Gueye), Boussoufa*
28/3	Zulte Waregem	h	6-0	*Boussoufa 2, Suárez (p), Van Damme, De Sutter, Gillet*
31/3	Gent	a	3-1	*Boussoufa, Juhász, Gillet*
3/4	Club Brugge	h	2-2	*og (Donk), Suárez*
9/4	Sint-Truiden	a	1-1	*Boussoufa*
14/4	Kortrijk	h	1-0	*Mazuch*
18/4	Club Brugge	a	2-1	*Van Damme, Suárez*
25/4	Gent	h	4-2	*Van Damme, Suárez, Chatelle, Gillet*
30/4	Zulte Waregem	a	0-0	
5/5	Kortrijk	a	3-1	*Van Damme, Boussoufa, Badibanga*
8/5	Sint-Truiden	h	2-1	*Van Damme, Suárez*

No	Name	Nat	DoB	Pos	Aps	(s)	Gls
39	Ziguy BADIBANGA		26/11/91	A		(2)	1
26	Víctor BERNÁRDEZ	HON	24/5/82	D	3	(4)	
5	Lucas BIGLIA	ARG	30/1/86	M	34		1
11	Mbark BOUSSOUFA	MAR	15/8/84	M	35	(1)	14
12	Thomas CHATELLE		31/3/81	M	11	(12)	1
21	Tom DE SUTTER		3/7/85	A	16	(13)	8
3	Olivier DESCHACHT		16/2/81	D	37		
35	Christophe DIANDY	SEN	16/2/89	M		(6)	
19	Nicolás FRUTOS	ARG	10/5/81	A	1	(9)	3
30	Guillaume GILLET		9/3/84	M	35	(3)	5
23	Roland JUHÁSZ	HUN	1/7/83	D	38		5
10	Rubenilson dos Santos da Rocha "KANU"	BRA	23/9/87	A	8	(14)	1

16	Cheikhou KOUYATÉ	SEN	21/12/89	M	17	(4)	1
13	Jonathan LEGEAR		13/4/87	M	14	(10)	4
36	Romelu LUKAKU		13/5/93	A	21	(12)	15
18	Lukáš MAREČEK	CZE	17/4/90	M	2		
2	Ondřej MAZUCH	CZE	15/3/89	D	30		4
8	Jan POLÁK	POL	14/3/81	M	4	(3)	
24	Silvio PROTO		23/5/83	G	36		
37	REYNALDO dos Santos Silva	BRA	24/8/89	M		(3)	
44	Nemanja RNIĆ	SRB	30/9/84	D	4	(2)	
99	Bakary Bouba SARÉ	CIV	5/4/90	M	12	(6)	
22	Davy SCHOLLEN		28/2/78	G	2		
9	Matías SUÁREZ	ARG	9/5/88	A	29	(6)	11
6	Jelle VAN DAMME		10/10/83	D	34		7
27	Marcin WASILEWSKI	POL	9/6/80	D	5	(1)	1
1	Daniel ZÍTKA	CZE	20/6/75	G	1		

CERCLE BRUGGE KSV
Coach – Glen De Boeck
Founded – 1899
Stadium – Jan Breydel (29,042)
MAJOR HONOURS:
Belgian League - (3) 1911, 1927, 1930;
Belgian Cup - (2) 1927, 1985.

2009
2/8	Gent	h	1-3	*Foley*
8/8	Anderlecht	a	2-3	*Portier, Buffel*
15/8	Zulte Waregem	h	2-2	*Yashchuk (p), Foley*
22/8	Mouscron	a	1-0	*Foley (result annulled)*
30/8	Club Brugge	h	2-3	*Yashchuk, Buffel*
12/9	Charleroi	a	4-0	*Serebrennikov (p), Yashchuk, Vossen 2*
19/9	GBA	h	1-2	*Vossen*
23/9	Standard	a	1-1	*Evens*
28/9	Mechelen	h	1-0	*Vossen (p)*
3/10	Roeselare	a	2-3	*Boi, Evens*
17/10	Lokeren	a	1-1	*Božović*
24/10	Kortrijk	h	1-1	*Portier*
2/11	Genk	a	0-2	
7/11	Westerlo	h	2-1	*Božović, Serebrennikov*
21/11	Sint-Truiden	a	1-1	*Nyoni*
28/11	Gent	a	1-3	*Yashchuk*
6/12	Anderlecht	h	1-3	*Yashchuk*
13/12	Zulte Waregem	a	0-1	
26/12	Club Brugge	a	1-2	*Yashchuk*
29/12	Standard	h	2-0	*Foley, Cornelis*

2010
17/1	GBA	a	4-1	*Vossen, Foley 2, Kelhar*
30/1	Mechelen	a	2-1	*Foley, Reynaldo*
6/2	Roeselare	h	2-0	*Sergeant, Reynaldo*
20/2	Kortrijk	a	1-3	*Evens*
24/2	Charleroi	h	1-0	*Yashchuk*
27/2	Genk	h	1-0	*Foley*
6/3	Lokeren	h	4-0	*Boi 2, Yashchuk, Reynaldo*
14/3	Westerlo	a	1-2	*Foley*
21/3	Sint-Truiden	h	3-1	*Nyoni, Vossen, Reynaldo*
31/3	Lokeren	a	3-5	*Cornelis, Foley 2*
3/4	Westerlo	h	2-0	*Sergeant, Foley (p)*
10/4	Mechelen	a	0-1	
14/4	Mechelen	h	2-1	*Foley (p), Yashchuk*
17/4	Westerlo	a	1-4	*Foley*
24/4	Lokeren	h	1-1	*Boi*

No	Name	Nat	DoB	Pos	Aps	(s)	Gls
12	Frederik BOI		25/10/81	D	26	(7)	4
10	Bojan BOŽOVIĆ	MNE	3/2/85	A	11	(13)	2
8	Thomas BUFFEL		19/2/81	M	4	(1)	2
37	Olivier CLAESSENS		22/12/88	A		(8)	
37	Jo COPPENS		21/12/90	G	15		
8	Hans CORNELIS		23/10/82	D	23	(1)	2
1	Rubin DANTSCHOTTER		18/2/86	G	1		
4	Bernt EVENS		9/11/78	D	32		3

15	Dominic FOLEY	IRL	7/7/76	A	25	(5)	14
20	Igor GJUZELOV	MKD	2/4/76	D	5	(4)	
5	Honour GOMBAMI	ZIM	9/1/83	M	13		
16	Dejan KELHAR	SVN	5/4/84	D	26		1
22	Vusumuzi Prince NYONI	ZIM	21/4/84	D	23	(5)	2
26	Kevin PACKET		14/3/92	M		(1)	
3	Anthony PORTIER		1/6/82	D	14	(6)	2
18	REYNALDO dos Santos Silva	BRA	24/8/89	A	6	(9)	4
14	Serhiy SEREBRENNIKOV	UKR	1/9/76	M	20	(11)	2
17	Tony SERGEANT		6/6/77	M	15	(7)	2
30	Lukas VAN EENOO		6/2/91	M	7	(6)	
25	Bram VERBIST		5/3/83	G	19		
7	Deni VIANE		2/10/77	D	31		
6	Arnar Thór VIDARSSON	ISL	15/3/78	M	26	(2)	
21	Jelle VOSSEN		22/3/89	A	13	(4)	6
11	WANG Yang	CHN	26/7/89	A		(1)	
9	Oleh YASHCHUK	UKR	26/10/77	A	30	(1)	9

CLUB BRUGGE KV
Coach – Adrie Koster (NED)
Founded – 1891
Stadium – Jan Breydel (29,042)
MAJOR HONOURS:
*Belgian League - (13) 1920, 1973, 1976, 1977, 1978, 1980, 1988, 1990,
1992, 1996, 1998, 2003, 2005;*
Belgian Cup - (10) 1968, 1970, 1977, 1986, 1991, 1995, 1996, 2002, 2004, 2007.

2009
2/8	Charleroi	a	2-1	*Odjidja-Ofoe, Dirar*
9/8	Lokeren	h	2-0	*Geraerts, Chávez*
15/8	Mechelen	a	1-2	*Akpala*
23/8	Kortrijk	h	2-2	*Akpala, Odjidja-Ofoe (p)*
30/8	Cercle Brugge	a	3-2	*Sonck 2, Akpala*
13/9	Genk	h	1-1	*Perišić*
20/9	Westerlo	a	4-1	*Perišić, Akpala, Vargas, Kouemaha*
23/9	Zulte Waregem	h	3-1	*Geraerts, Odjidja-Ofoe, Kouemaha*
27/9	Mouscron	a	1-1	*Kouemaha (result annulled)*
4/10	Anderlecht	h	4-2	*Alcaraz, og (Van Damme), Sonck, Vargas*
18/10	Gent	h	1-0	*Chávez*
25/10	Roeselare	h	3-2	*Perišić, Vargas, Kouemaha*
31/10	Sint-Truiden	h	1-0	*Vargas*
8/11	Standard	a	1-3	*Geraerts*
21/11	GBA	h	1-2	*Dahmane*
28/11	Charleroi	h	1-0	*Kouemaha*
6/12	Lokeren	a	1-0	*Donk*
12/12	Mechelen	h	1-1	*Kouemaha*
26/12	Cercle Brugge	h	2-1	*Geraerts, Sonck*
30/12	Kortrijk	a	4-1	*Dirar, Perišić, Kouemaha, Geraerts*

2010
24/1	Genk	a	0-2	
30/1	Westerlo	h	2-1	*Perišić, Akpala*
3/2	Anderlecht	a	2-3	*Odjidja-Ofoe, Kouemaha*
7/2	Zulte Waregem	a	1-1	*Kouemaha*
14/2	Gent	a	1-1	*Kouemaha*
21/2	Standard	h	2-1	*Sonck (p), Kouemaha*
28/2	Sint-Truiden	a	1-1	*Sonck (p)*
14/3	Roeselare	a	1-0	*Kouemaha*
21/3	GBA	a	4-1	*Dahmane, Perišić, Kouemaha, Akpala*
27/3	Sint-Truiden	a	0-0	
31/3	Kortrijk	h	3-0	*Perišić 2, Lestienne*
3/4	Anderlecht	a	2-2	*Dirar, Donk*
11/4	Gent	h	1-1	*Dirar*
14/4	Zulte Waregem	a	0-2	
18/4	Anderlecht	h	1-2	*Sonck*
23/4	Kortrijk	a	0-2	
2/5	Sint-Truiden	h	2-0	*Kouemaha, Akpala*
5/5	Zulte Waregem	h	3-0	*og (Dachelet), Simaeys, Kouemaha*
8/5	Gent	a	2-6	*Perišić, Kouemaha*

No	Name	Nat	DoB	Pos	Aps	(s)	Gls
15	Joseph AKPALA	NGA	24/8/90	A	18	(13)	7
30	Antolín ALCARAZ	PAR	30/7/82	D	29		1
11	Jonathan BLONDEL		3/4/84	M	30	(1)	
19	Daniel CHÁVEZ	PER	8/1/88	A	1	(5)	2

7	Koen DAERDEN		8/3/82	M	8	(3)	
77	Mohamed DAHMANE	ALG	9/4/82	A	3	(12)	2
29	Gertjan DE METS		2/4/87	D	7	(5)	
13	Geert DE VLIEGER		16/10/71	G	3		
8	Nabil DIRAR	MAR	25/2/86	M	24	(5)	4
18	Ryan DONK	NED	30/3/86	D	20	(3)	2
22	Karel GERAERTS		5/1/82	M	31	(1)	5
4	Carl HOEFKENS		6/10/78	D	31		
5	Michael KLUKOWSKI	CAN	27/5/81	D	34	(1)	
40	Dorge Rostand KOUEMAHA	CMR	28/6/83	A	26	(7)	16
16	Maxime LESTIENNE		17/6/92	A	5	(7)	1
32	Vadis ODJIDJA-OFOE		21/2/89	M	32	(3)	4
44	Ivan PERIŠIĆ	CRO	2/2/89	M	29	(4)	9
14	Jeroen SIMAEYS		12/5/85	D	23	(2)	1
10	Wesley SONCK		9/8/78	A	11	(11)	7
1	Stijn STIJNEN		7/4/81	G	36		
3	Peter VAN DER HEYDEN		16/7/76	M	4	(5)	
24	Daan VAN GIJSEGHEM		2/3/88	D	2	(3)	
20	Ronald VARGAS	VEN	2/12/86	M	14	(12)	4
21	Jorn VERMEULEN		16/4/87	D	8		

R. CHARLEROI SC
**Coach – Stéphane Demol; (31/10/09) (Mario Notaro);
(20/11/09) Tommy Craig (SCO); (14/4/10) Tibor Balog (HUN)**
Founded – 1904
Stadium – Pays de Charleroi (22,000)

2009
2/8	Club Brugge	h	1-2	*Théréau*
8/8	Sint-Truiden	a	0-0	
16/8	GBA	h	1-0	*Théréau*
21/8	Standard	a	1-1	*Habibou*
29/8	Roeselare	a	3-1	*Théréau 2 (1p), Habibou*
12/9	Cercle Brugge	h	0-4	
18/9	Genk	a	2-1	*Christ, Mujangi-Bia*
23/9	Mechelen	h	1-2	*Théréau (p)*
26/9	Lokeren	a	1-4	*Brillault*
3/10	Kortrijk	h	3-3	*Cordaro, Théréau 2 (1p)*
17/10	Anderlecht	a	0-2	
24/10	Westerlo	h	1-1	*Oulmers*
31/10	Zulte Waregem	a	2-2	*Mujangi-Bia, Habibou*
6/11	Gent	h	0-2	
21/11	Mouscron	a	1-4	*Théréau (p) (result annulled)*
28/11	Club Brugge	a	0-1	
4/12	Sint-Truiden	h	0-0	
12/12	GBA	a	0-0	
26/12	Roeselare	h	3-0	*Habibou 2, Christ*
30/12	Mechelen	a	0-1	

2010
16/1	Genk	h	1-3	*Ciza*
4/2	Standard	h	2-3	*Théréau, Kéré*
7/2	Kortrijk	a	1-2	*Ederson*
20/2	Westerlo	a	0-4	
24/2	Cercle Brugge	a	0-1	
27/2	Zulte Waregem	h	0-0	
6/3	Anderlecht	h	0-2	
10/3	Lokeren	h	4-1	*Théréau 3, Oulmers*
14/3	Gent	a	1-2	*Ederson*
27/3	Standard	a	0-2	
3/4	GBA	h	0-1	
10/4	Genk	h	1-2	*Théréau (p)*
13/4	Genk	a	0-3	
18/4	GBA	a	2-2	*Christ, Serwy*
25/4	Standard	h	1-0	*Cordaro*

No	Name	Nat	DoB	Pos	Aps	(s)	Gls
20	Amad AL-HOSNI	OMA	18/7/84	A	3	(5)	
23	Cyprien BAGUETTE		12/5/89	G	16		
55	Michaël BLANC	FRA	11/9/88	D		(1)	
55	Maxime BRILLAULT	FRA	25/4/83	D	33		1
8	Sébastien CHABAUD	FRA	9/3/77	M	2		
5	Sébastien CHABBERT	FRA	15/5/78	G	19		
6	Mohamed CHAKOURI	FRA	21/5/86	D	18	(1)	
24	Grégory CHRIST	FRA	14/8/80	M	28	(4)	3
20	Cédric CIZA		2/2/90	M	5	(4)	1
29	Alessandro CORDARO		2/5/86	M	21	(9)	2

BELGIUM

KRC GENK

No	Name	Nat	DoB	Pos	Aps	(s)	Gls
33	Ibrahima DIALLO	GUI	26/9/86	D	22	(2)	
27	EDERSON Tormena	BRA	14/3/86	M	13		2
24	Samuel FABRIS		30/1/91	D	3	(4)	
19	Peter FRANQUART	FRA	4/1/85	D	18	(2)	
5	Adlène GUEDIOURA	ALG	12/11/85	M	11	(2)	
7	Mouhamadou Habib HABIBOU	FRA	16/4/87	A	13	(8)	5
9	Mouhcine IAJOUR	MAR	14/6/85	A	2	(11)	
26	Hervé KAGÉ	COD	10/4/89	M	22	(8)	
16	Mahamoudou KÉRÉ	BFA	2/1/82	D	30		1
22	Moussa KOÏTA	FRA	19/11/82	A	1	(4)	
17	Grégory LAZITCH		26/5/92	D	4		
2	Jan LELLA		6/11/89	M	11	(3)	
27	Ilombe MBOYO		27/4/87	A	12	(13)	
3	Massimo MOIA		9/3/87	D		(1)	
10	Geoffrey MUJANGI-BIA		12/8/89	M	6	(4)	2
22	ORLANDO dos Santos Costa	BRA	26/2/81	A	6	(2)	
21	Abdelmajid OULMERS	MAR	12/9/78	M	24	(1)	2
25	Pietro PERDICHIZZI		16/12/92	D	6		
25	Rahim SEBAH ABDUL	GHA	27/11/91	D		(1)	
8	Jérémy SERWY		4/6/91	A		(2)	1
26	Paul TAYLOR	ENG	4/10/87	A	3		
77	Cyril THÉRÉAU	FRA	24/4/83	A	32	(1)	13
18	David VANDENBROECK		12/7/85	D	1		

Coach – Hein Van Haezebrouck; (3/12/09) Frank Vercauteren
Founded – 1988
Stadium – Cristal Arena (25,010)
MAJOR HONOURS:
Belgian League - (2) 1999, 2002;
Belgian Cup - (3) 1998, 2000, 2009.

2009

1/8	Mouscron	h	1-2	João Carlos (result annulled)
8/8	Zulte Waregem	a	2-2	Tőzsér 2 (1p)
15/8	Gent	h	1-1	Koïta
23/8	Westerlo	a	1-0	Camus
30/8	GBA	h	1-1	Ogunjimi
13/9	Club Brugge	a	1-1	Buffel
18/9	Charleroi	h	1-2	Tőzsér
22/9	Sint-Truiden	a	4-2	Ogunjimi, Barda, Buffel, Koïta
26/9	Roeselare	h	1-1	Joneleit
4/10	Standard	a	0-1	
18/10	Mechelen	h	1-2	Tőzsér (p)
23/10	Lokeren	a	2-0	Joneleit, Camus
2/11	Cercle Brugge	h	2-0	og (Viane), og (Foley)
8/11	Anderlecht	h	0-2	
22/11	Kortrijk	a	1-2	Buffel
28/11	Mouscron	a	0-2	(result annulled)
4/12	Westerlo	h	0-0	
13/12	Gent	a	1-2	Joneleit
19/12	Zulte Waregem	h	2-2	Ogunjimi 2
26/12	GBA	a	0-1	
29/12	Sint-Truiden	h	0-0	

2010

16/1	Charleroi	a	3-1	Tőzsér, Ogunjimi, João Carlos
24/1	Club Brugge	h	2-0	Buffel (p), Camus
7/2	Standard	h	1-0	De Bruyne
19/2	Lokeren	h	3-1	Barda, Ogunjimi, Orlando
24/2	Roeselare	a	1-1	Barda
27/2	Cercle Brugge	a	0-1	
7/3	Mechelen	a	1-2	Yeboah
14/3	Anderlecht	a	0-2	
21/3	Kortrijk	h	1-1	Ogunjimi
30/3	GBA	a	3-1	Buffel, Barda, Yeboah
4/4	Standard	h	1-0	Barda
10/4	Charleroi	a	2-1	Ogunjimi, Barda
13/4	Charleroi	h	3-0	Ogunjimi, Matoukou, De Bruyne
18/4	Standard	a	1-1	Barda (p)
25/4	GBA	h	2-0	Camus (p), Yeboah

No	Name	Nat	DoB	Pos	Aps	(s)	Gls
22	Maurizio AQUINO		1/3/90	A	1	(1)	
11	Istvan BAKX	NED	20/1/86	A	2	(2)	
8	Elyaniv BARDA	ISR	15/12/81	A	26	(4)	7
29	Thomas BUFFEL		19/2/81	M	29	(1)	5

KAA GENT

No	Name	Nat	DoB	Pos	Aps	(s)	Gls
7	Fabien CAMUS	TUN	28/2/85	M	17	(10)	4
23	Hans CORNELIS		23/10/82	D	1		
2	Dimitri DAESELEIRE		18/5/90	D	15	(1)	
14	Kevin DE BRUYNE		28/6/94	M	15	(16)	2
21	Timothy DURWAEL		24/2/91	D	4	(1)	
3	David HUBERT		12/2/88	D	20	(1)	
17	Stein HUYSEGEMS		16/6/82	A	4	(10)	
3	JOÃO CARLOS Chaves Pinto	BRA	1/1/82	D	24	(1)	2
4	Torben JONELEIT	GER	17/5/87	D	24	(2)	3
9	Moussa KOÏTA	FRA	19/11/82	A	7	(13)	2
26	László KÖTELES	HUN	1/9/84	G	16		
5	Eric MATOUKOU	CMR	8/7/83	D	20	(4)	1
21	Dugary NDABASHINZE	BUR	8/10/89	M	1	(1)	
16	Calvin Anele NGCONGCA	RSA	20/10/87	D	30	(1)	
31	Marvin OGUNJIMI		12/10/87	A	24	(2)	9
32	ORLANDO dos Santos Costa	BRA	26/2/81	A	1	(6)	1
33	Daniel PUDIL	CZE	27/9/85	M	32	(1)	
27	TIAGO SILVA dos Santos	BUL	4/4/79	D	17		
20	Balász TÓTH	HUN	24/9/81	M	10	(8)	
8	Dániel TŐZSÉR	HUN	12/5/85	M	30	(4)	5
1	Davino VERHULST		25/11/87	G	20		
19	Jelle VOSSEN		22/3/89	A		(3)	
23	Samuel YEBOAH	GHA	8/8/86	A	6	(8)	3

Coach – Michel Preud'homme
Founded – 1898
Stadium – Jules Ottenstadion (12,919)
MAJOR HONOURS:
Belgian Cup - (3) 1964, 1984, 2010.

2009

2/8	Cercle Brugge	a	3-1	Ljubijankič, De Smet, Marić
9/8	Mechelen	h	2-1	Azofeifa 2
15/8	Genk	a	1-1	Ljubijankič
22/8	Lokeren	h	4-1	Čustović 2 (1p), Wils, Lepoint
29/8	Kortrijk	a	0-1	
12/9	Roeselare	h	5-1	Azofeifa, Leye 2, Ljubijankič, De Smet
20/9	Anderlecht	a	1-1	Leye
23/9	Westerlo	h	1-2	Leye (p)
26/9	Zulte Waregem	a	1-3	Marić
2/10	Mouscron	h	1-1	Azofeifa (result annulled)
18/10	Club Brugge	a	0-1	
24/10	Sint-Truiden	a	2-1	Rosales, Wils
1/11	GBA	h	0-1	
6/11	Charleroi	a	2-0	Wils, Čustović
21/11	Standard	h	2-1	Lepoint, Čustović (p)
28/11	Cercle Brugge	h	3-1	Marić (p), Rosales, Thijs
4/12	Mechelen	a	5-2	Coulibaly 2, Čustović, Rosales, Smolders
13/12	Genk	h	2-1	Marić 2 (1p)
19/12	Lokeren	a	1-0	De Smet
27/12	Anderlecht	h	2-2	Marić, Coulibaly
30/12	Roeselare	a	4-0	Wils, Coulibaly 3

2010

15/1	Kortrijk	h	2-2	Coulibaly, Azofeifa
23/1	Westerlo	a	0-0	
31/1	Zulte Waregem	h	0-2	
14/2	Club Brugge	h	1-1	Thijs
20/2	Sint-Truiden	h	0-1	
26/2	GBA	a	1-1	Coulibaly
14/3	Charleroi	h	2-1	Lepoint, Coulibaly
21/3	Standard	a	2-0	Leye, Pieroni
28/3	Kortrijk	a	2-1	Čustović, Lepoint
31/3	Anderlecht	h	1-3	Čustović
4/4	Zulte Waregem	a	2-1	Lepoint, Leye
11/4	Club Brugge	a	1-1	Coulibaly
14/4	Sint-Truiden	h	0-0	
18/4	Zulte Waregem	h	5-0	Čustović, Elghanassy, Pieroni (p), Ljubijankič, Azofeifa
25/4	Anderlecht	a	2-4	Coulibaly, Grondin
1/5	Kortrijk	h	0-0	
5/5	Sint-Truiden	a	1-1	Grondin
8/5	Club Brugge	h	6-2	Azofeifa, Leye, Elghanassy, Lepoint, Čustović, Thijs

BELGIUM

No	Name	Nat	DoB	Pos	Aps	(s)	Gls
13	ADRIANO DUARTE Mansur da Silva	BRA	29/1/80	D	8		
10	Randall AZOFEIFA	CRC	30/12/84	M	17	(6)	7
28	Ibrahima CONTÉ	SEN	3/4/91	M		(1)	
16	Elimane COULIBALY	SEN	15/3/80	A	19	(9)	11
14	Adnan ČUSTOVIĆ	BIH	14/4/78	A	17	(9)	9
19	Stijn DE SMET		27/3/85	A	6	(8)	3
11	Yassine ELGHANASSY	MAR	12/7/90	A	20	(16)	2
31	Christophe GRONDIN	FRA	2/9/83	M	12	(11)	2
5	Erlend HANSTVEIT	NOR	28/1/81	D	22	(3)	
29	Bojan JORGAČEVIĆ	SRB	12/2/82	G	39		
26	Christophe LEPOINT		24/10/84	M	25	(10)	6
9	Mbaye LEYE	SEN	1/12/82	A	28	(6)	7
30	Zlatan LJUBIJANKIČ	SVN	15/12/83	A	28	(4)	4
28	Miloš MARIĆ	SRB	5/3/82	M	12	(4)	6
4	Roy MYRIE	CRC	21/8/82	D	10	(1)	
25	Mamoutou N'DIAYE	MLI	15/3/90	D		(1)	
15	Adékanmi OLUFADÉ	TOG	7/1/80	A		(2)	
21	Luigi PIERONI		8/9/80	A	4	(4)	2
17	Roberto ROSALES	VEN	20/11/88	D	31	(1)	3
7	Tim SMOLDERS		26/8/80	M	25	(8)	1
3	Marko ŠULER	SVN	9/3/83	D	36		
8	Bernd THIJS		28/6/78	M	16	(2)	3
12	Kenny THOMPSON		26/4/85	D	17	(3)	
6	Stef WILS		2/8/82	D	37	(1)	4

No	Name	Nat	DoB	Pos	Aps	(s)	Gls
13	Jean ACOSTA SOARES	BRA	27/1/92	M	1	(1)	
7	Philippe CLEMENT		22/3/74	D	28		2
10	Daniel CRUZ	COL	9/5/81	M	12	(16)	3
6	Wim DE DECKER		6/4/82	M	32		
31	Mark DE MAN		27/4/83	D	5	(7)	
15	Tosin DOSUNMU	NGA	15/7/80	A	17	(14)	5
24	Guillaume FRANÇOIS		3/6/90	A	4	(3)	
3	Maxim GEURDEN		2/11/90	D	1		
44	Bart GOOR		9/4/73	M	20		5
9	Faris HAROUN		22/9/85	M	31		11
17	Nadjim HAROUN		10/6/88	M		(3)	
27	Dawid JANCZYK	POL	23/9/87	A	9	(2)	3
26	Thomas KAMINSKI		23/10/92	G	4		
18	Paul KPAKA	SLE	7/8/81	A		(1)	
78	Ivan LEKO	CRO	7/2/78	M	7	(7)	
8	Sherjill MacDONALD	NED	20/11/84	A	28	(1)	4
20	Kristof MAES		19/4/88	G	2		
24	Sanharib MALKI	SYR	1/3/84	A	2	(2)	1
15	Tomislav MIKULIĆ	CRO	4/1/82	D	21	(2)	1
22	Martijn MONTEYNE		12/11/84	D	31		
5	Pieterjan MONTEYNE		1/1/83	D	34		
1	Tomislav PACOVSKI	MKD	28/6/82	G	29		
86	Mats RITS		18/7/93	M	5	(7)	2
21	Bavon TSHIBUABUA	COD	17/7/91	A	9	(7)	1
4	Kurt VANDOOREN		3/8/78	D	17	(2)	
29	Justice WAMFOR	CMR	5/8/81	M	24	(1)	1
12	Victor WANYAMA	KEN	25/6/91	M	12	(8)	

KFC GERMINAL BEERSCHOT ANTWERPEN

Coach – Aimé Anthuenis; (3/9/09) Jos Daerden
Founded – 1999
Stadium – Olympisch Stadion (12,400)
MAJOR HONOURS:
Belgian Cup - (2) 1997, 2005.

2009

1/8	Roeselare	a	1-1	Cruz
7/8	Standard	h	1-1	Goor
16/8	Charleroi	a	0-1	
22/8	Mechelen	h	1-3	Malki
30/8	Genk	a	1-1	Haroun F.
13/9	Lokeren	h	2-1	Tshibuabua, Haroun F.
19/9	Cercle Brugge	a	2-1	MacDonald, Haroun F.
23/9	Kortrijk	h	1-0	MacDonald
26/9	Anderlecht	a	0-1	
3/10	Westerlo	h	3-1	Rits 2, Haroun F.
17/10	Zulte Waregem	a	0-4	
24/10	Mouscron	h	3-2	Clement 2, Goor (result annulled)
1/11	Gent	a	1-0	Haroun F.
7/11	Sint-Truiden	h	4-1	Dosunmu, Goor 2, Haroun F. (p)
21/11	Club Brugge	a	2-1	MacDonald, Dosunmu
28/11	Roeselare	h	3-0	MacDonald, Haroun F. 2
4/12	Standard	a	2-2	Goor, Dosunmu
12/12	Charleroi	h	0-0	
26/12	Genk	h	1-0	Dosunmu
30/12	Lokeren	a	0-2	

2010

17/1	Cercle Brugge	h	1-4	Dosunmu
23/1	Kortrijk	a	0-3	
29/1	Anderlecht	h	0-5	
2/2	Mechelen	a	0-1	
6/2	Westerlo	a	1-1	Janczyk
26/2	Gent	h	1-1	Janczyk
7/3	Zulte Waregem	h	1-1	Haroun F.
14/3	Sint-Truiden	a	0-2	
21/3	Club Brugge	h	1-1	Mikulić
30/3	Genk	h	1-3	Wamfor
3/4	Charleroi	a	1-0	Cruz
11/4	Standard	a	0-3	
15/4	Standard	h	2-2	Cruz, Haroun F.
18/4	Charleroi	h	2-2	Janczyk, Haroun F.
25/4	Genk	a	0-2	

KV KORTRIJK

Coach – Georges Leekens
Founded – 1971
Stadium – Guldensporenstadion (9,500)

2009

1/8	Anderlecht	h	0-2	
8/8	Westerlo	a	1-1	Belhocine
16/8	Mouscron	h	2-2	Benko (p), Belhocine (result annulled)
23/8	Club Brugge	a	2-2	Sawaneh 2
29/8	Gent	h	1-0	Benko
12/9	Zulte Waregem	a	2-0	Benko, Benteke
19/9	Sint-Truiden	h	0-1	
23/9	GBA	a	0-1	
26/9	Standard	h	0-2	
3/10	Charleroi	a	3-3	Vandenbroeck, Sawaneh, Hempte
17/10	Roeselare	h	2-0	Benteke, og (Vandenbussche)
24/10	Cercle Brugge	a	1-1	og (Portier)
31/10	Mechelen	h	2-0	Sawaneh, Messoudi
7/11	Lokeren	a	0-0	
22/11	Genk	a	2-1	Benteke, Pavlović
27/11	Anderlecht	a	0-1	
4/12	Zulte Waregem	h	1-0	Benko
12/12	Sint-Truiden	a	2-0	Benko, Benteke
19/12	Westerlo	h	1-1	Capon
30/12	Club Brugge	h	1-4	Benteke

2010

15/1	Gent	a	2-2	og (Rosales), Sawaneh
23/1	GBA	h	3-0	Sawaneh, Benteke, De Beule
31/1	Standard	a	1-3	De Beule
7/2	Charleroi	h	2-1	Kums, Benteke
13/2	Roeselare	a	2-0	Ciman, Vandenbroeck
20/2	Cercle Brugge	h	3-1	Benteke, De Beule, Messoudi
27/2	Mechelen	a	1-1	Ciman
14/3	Lokeren	h	3-1	Sawaneh 2, De Beule
21/3	Genk	a	1-1	
28/3	Gent	h	1-2	Vandenbroeck
31/3	Club Brugge	a	0-3	
4/4	Sint-Truiden	h	1-2	De Beule
10/4	Zulte Waregem	a	2-0	Benteke 2
14/4	Anderlecht	a	0-1	
17/4	Sint-Truiden	a	0-1	
23/4	Club Brugge	h	2-0	Benteke 2
1/5	Gent	a	0-0	
5/5	Anderlecht	h	1-3	Benteke
8/5	Zulte Waregem	a	2-1	De Beule 2

BELGIUM

No	Name	Nat	DoB	Pos	Aps	(s)	Gls
25	Salah BAKOUR	ALG	15/4/82	M	5	(7)	
5	Karim BELHOCINE	FRA	2/1/83	M	26	(5)	2
7	Leon BENKO	CRO	11/11/83	A	13	(13)	5
9	Christian BENTEKE		3/12/90	A	26	(8)	14
18	Daniel CALVO		11/7/79	M	1		
21	Brecht CAPON		22/4/88	A	25	(8)	1
26	Laurent CIMAN		5/8/85	D	34		2
22	Rob CLAEYS		24/4/87	M		(2)	
14	Davy DE BEULE		7/11/81	M	37	(1)	7
16	Bram DELY		21/1/84	D	4	(5)	
6	Jimmy HEMPTE		24/3/82	M	29	(6)	1
10	Sven KUMS		26/2/88	M	37	(1)	1
30	Damien LAHAYE		30/1/84	G	1		
23	Tristan LAHAYE	FRA	16/2/83	D		(1)	
4	Mladen LAZAREVIĆ	SRB	16/1/84	D	13	(1)	
20	Mohamed MESSOUDI		7/1/84	M	16	(10)	2
27	Mustapha OUSSALAH	MAR	19/2/82	M		(2)	
8	Nebojša PAVLOVIĆ	SRB	9/4/81	M	34		1
3	Loris REINA	FRA	10/6/80	D	1		
12	Ebrahima Ibou SAWANEH	GAM	7/9/86	A	31	(4)	8
11	Tom SOETAERS		21/7/80	M		(8)	
2	David VANDENBROECK		12/7/85	D	35	(1)	3
13	Glenn VERBAUWHEDE		19/5/85	G	38		
7	Brecht VERBRUGGHE		29/4/82	D	10	(6)	
23	Wouter VRANCKEN		3/2/79	M	6	(4)	
9	WILLIAM Xavier Barbosa	BRA	22/9/83	A		(1)	

No	Name	Nat	DoB	Pos	Aps	(s)	Gls
30	Boubacar "Copa" BARRY	CIV	30/12/79	G	19		
14	Ali BOUABÉ	MAR	7/3/79	D	1		
18	Mario CAREVIĆ	CRO	29/3/82	M	26	(2)	4
25	Kwinten CLAPPAERT		6/12/88	A		(1)	
28	Laurens DE BOCK		7/11/92	D	5		
20	Donovan DEEKMAN	NED	23/6/88	A	2	(8)	
1	Stefan DELOOSE		14/1/90	G	2		
29	Nill DE PAUW		6/1/90	A	9	(2)	
4	Olivier DOLL		9/6/73	D	26		2
16	Frédéric DUPRÉ		12/5/79	D	20		
3	Hassan EL MOUATAZ	MAR	21/9/81	D	20		1
15	Omer GOLAN	ISR	4/10/82	A	6	(12)	2
23	Ibrahima GUEYE	SEN	19/2/78	D	27	(1)	3
22	Baba IDDI	GHA	6/7/82	A		(3)	
17	Dawid JANCZYK	POL	23/9/87	A	13	(5)	9
12	Jugoslav LAZIĆ	SRB	12/12/79	G	15	(2)	
78	Ivan LEKO	CRO	7/2/78	M	12		2
21	Sanharib MALKI	SYR	1/3/84	A	21	(8)	3
10	Marcel MBAYO	COD	23/4/78	M	18	(8)	2
14	Benjamin MOKULU Tembe		11/10/89	A	4		1
11	Veldin MUHAREMOVIĆ	BIH	6/12/84	M	6	(9)	
7	Killian OVERMEIRE		6/12/85	M	30	(4)	2
9	Jérémy PERBET	FRA	12/12/84	A	4	(6)	1
8	Sulejman SMAJIĆ	BIH	13/4/84	M	20	(6)	4
27	Tomislav ŠOKOTA	CRO	8/4/77	A	20	(7)	5
5	Avi STRUL	ISR	18/9/90	D	23	(1)	
6	Tsholola Tshinyama TIKO	COD	12/12/80	M	19	(1)	
26	Derrick Katuku TSHIMANGA		6/11/88	A	5	(7)	1
2	Yoav ZIV	ISR	16/3/81	D	23	(1)	1

KSC LOKEREN OV
Coach – Aleksandar Janković (SRB); (25/10/09) Jacky Mathijssen; (28/1/10) Emilio Ferrera
Founded – 1970
Stadium – Daknamstadion (9,271)

2009

1/8	Zulte Waregem	h	1-1	Smajić
9/8	Club Brugge	a	0-2	
15/8	Sint-Truiden	h	1-2	Mbayo
22/8	Gent	a	1-4	Carević
29/8	Mouscron	h	4-1	Janczyk, Smajić 2, Šokota (result annulled)
13/9	GBA	a	1-2	Janczyk
19/9	Standard	h	1-3	Smajić
23/9	Roeselare	a	2-1	Malki, Janczyk
26/9	Charleroi	h	4-1	Janczyk 2, Carević (p), El Mouataz (p)
3/10	Mechelen	a	0-2	
17/10	Cercle Brugge	h	1-1	Carević
23/10	Genk	h	0-2	
31/10	Anderlecht	a	0-2	
7/11	Kortrijk	h	0-0	
21/11	Westerlo	a	0-1	
29/11	Zulte Waregem	a	0-1	
6/12	Club Brugge	h	0-1	
12/12	Mouscron	a	5-0	Janczyk 3, Carević, Doll (result annulled)
19/12	Gent	h	0-1	
26/12	Standard	a	0-2	
30/12	GBA	h	2-0	Mbayo, Janczyk
2010				
16/1	Sint-Truiden	a	1-2	Gueye
23/1	Roeselare	h	1-4	Ziv
6/2	Mechelen	h	2-1	Gueye, Doll
19/2	Genk	a	1-3	Malki
27/2	Westerlo	h	1-0	Šokota
6/3	Cercle Brugge	a	0-4	
10/3	Charleroi	a	1-4	Šokota
14/3	Kortrijk	a	1-3	Leko
21/3	Anderlecht	h	0-4	
31/3	Cercle Brugge	h	5-3	Malki, Gueye, Overmeire, Šokota, Leko
3/4	Mechelen	a	1-3	Overmeire
10/4	Westerlo	h	3-3	Mokulu, Golan, Tshimanga
14/4	Westerlo	a	0-2	
17/4	Mechelen	h	2-2	Šokota, Perbet
24/4	Cercle Brugge	a	1-1	Golan

KV MECHELEN
Coach – Peter Maes
Founded – 1904
Stadium – Veolia Stadion (13,123)
MAJOR HONOURS:
UEFA Cup Winners' Cup - (1) 1988;
UEFA Super Cup - (1) 1989;
Belgian League - (4) 1943, 1946, 1948, 1989;
Belgian Cup - (1) 1987.

2009

1/8	Westerlo	h	4-1	Nong, Destorme 2, Gorius (p)
9/8	Gent	a	1-2	Destorme
15/8	Club Brugge	h	2-1	Ivens, Gorius (p)
22/8	GBA	a	3-1	Gorius, Nong, Iddi A.-Y.
29/8	Sint-Truiden	h	0-2	
12/9	Standard	a	0-3	
19/9	Roeselare	h	3-2	Gorius (p), Destorme, Nong
23/9	Charleroi	a	2-1	Rossini, Diabang
28/9	Cercle Brugge	a	0-1	
3/10	Lokeren	h	2-0	Gorius (p), Nong
18/10	Genk	a	2-1	Mununga, Van Dessel
25/10	Anderlecht	h	0-2	
31/10	Kortrijk	a	0-2	
7/11	Mouscron	h	0-1	(result annulled)
22/11	Zulte Waregem	a	1-4	Nong
28/11	Westerlo	a	0-2	
4/12	Gent	h	2-5	Nong, Destorme
12/12	Club Brugge	a	1-1	Destorme
26/12	Sint-Truiden	a	2-5	Gorius, Mununga
30/12	Charleroi	h	1-0	Nong
2010				
16/1	Roeselare	a	2-1	Gorius, Nong
24/1	Standard	h	0-0	
30/1	Cercle Brugge	h	1-2	Destorme
2/2	GBA	h	1-0	Buyens
6/2	Lokeren	a	1-2	Van Dessel
21/2	Anderlecht	a	0-2	
27/2	Kortrijk	h	1-1	Soetaers
7/3	Genk	h	2-1	Gorius, Biset
21/3	Zulte Waregem	h	2-1	og (Colpaert), Biset
31/3	Westerlo	a	2-0	Dunković, Soetaers
3/4	Lokeren	h	3-1	Soetaers, Mununga, Gorius
10/4	Cercle Brugge	h	1-0	Gorius
14/4	Cercle Brugge	a	1-2	Biset
17/4	Lokeren	a	2-2	Mununga, Nong
24/4	Westerlo	h	1-3	Gorius (p)

No	Name	Nat	DoB	Pos	Aps	(s)	Gls
20	Wouter BIEBAUW		21/5/84	G	23		
19	Maxime BISET		26/3/86	M	16		3
17	Yoni BUYENS		10/3/88	M	29	(3)	1
8	Xavier CHEN		5/10/83	D	21	(1)	
18	David DESTORME		30/8/79	M	28	(3)	7
28	Boubacar DIABANG Dialiba	BIH	13/7/88	A	2	(10)	1
13	Antun DUNKOVIĆ	CRO	7/6/81	M	2	(6)	1
16	Kevin GEUDENS		2/12/80	M	9	(9)	
26	Antonio GHOMSY	CMR	22/4/86	D	30		
15	Julien GORIUS	FRA	17/3/85	M	28	(4)	11
24	Abdul-Ganiyu IDDI	GHA	8/1/90	A	1	(3)	
10	Abdul-Yakinu IDDI	GHA	25/5/86	M	9	(8)	1
3	Jonas IVENS		14/10/84	D	30		1
27	Tidiane Baba KOUROUMA	GUI	23/8/91	M		(1)	
4	Jeroen MELLEMANS		16/8/77	D	4		
2	Aymar Fabrice MORO-MVÉ	GAB	1/6/87	D		(2)	
11	Joachim MUNUNGA		30/6/88	A	29	(3)	4
14	Aloys NONG	CMR	16/10/83	A	28	(2)	9
6	Koen PERSOONS		12/7/83	M	31		
23	Olivier RENARD		24/5/79	G	12		
9	Giuseppe ROSSINI		23/8/86	A	5	(17)	1
21	Abdallah Khaled SALIM	JOR	10/3/87	A		(2)	
29	Tom SOETAERS		21/7/80	M	5		3
22	Romeo VAN DESSEL		9/4/89	D	9	(4)	2
7	Kenneth VAN GOETHEM		13/2/84	D	7	(9)	
5	Kenny VAN HOEVELEN		24/6/83	D	24	(6)	
25	Wouter VRANCKEN		3/2/79	M	3	(6)	

R. EXCELSIOR MOUSCRON
Coach – Miroslav Đukić (SRB); (30/10/09) Hans Galjé (NED)
Founded – 1964
Stadium – Le Canonnier (10,571)

2009

1/8	Genk	a	2-1	John 2
8/8	Roeselare	h	0-0	
16/8	Kortrijk	a	2-2	John 2
22/8	Cercle Brugge	h	0-1	
29/8	Lokeren	a	1-4	Maah
12/9	Westerlo	h	0-1	
19/9	Zulte Waregem	a	1-3	Lestienne
24/9	Anderlecht	h	1-2	El Araichi
27/9	Club Brugge	h	1-1	John
2/10	Gent	a	1-1	Lestienne
17/10	Sint-Truiden	h	2-1	Van Gijseghem, John (p)
24/10	GBA	a	2-3	Lestienne, François
30/10	Standard	h	0-0	
7/11	Mechelen	a	1-0	Jonathan Aspas
21/11	Charleroi	h	4-1	John 2, François, Maah
28/11	Genk	h	2-0	og (Matoukou), Jonathan Aspas (p)
4/12	Roeselare	a	2-1	Moreno 2
12/12	Lokeren	h	0-5	

NB All results annulled.

No	Name	Nat	DoB	Pos	Aps	(s)	Gls
8	Mathieu ASSOU-EKOTTO	FRA	8/4/78	M	16		
12	Cédric BERTHELIN	FRA	25/12/76	G	10		
3	Sylvain BERTON		8/4/88	M		(2)	
19	Bastien CHANTRY		22/12/84	D	2	(1)	
7	Alejandro CORTELL Palanca	ESP	8/11/90	A	1	(1)	
11	Zvonimir DERANJA	CRO	22/9/79	A	4	(3)	
4	Aliou DIA	FRA	30/5/90	D	1		
4	Mamadou DIAKITÉ	FRA	22/5/85	M	5	(7)	
6	Chemcedine EL ARAICHI	MAR	18/5/81	D	14		1
24	Kieran FELIX	FRA	9/8/90	M		(1)	
24	Guillaume FRANÇOIS		3/6/90	A	13	(3)	2
22	Thomas HOVINE		12/12/90	M	2	(3)	
9	Jaycee JOHN Okwunwanne	BHR	8/10/85	A	14	(2)	8
26	JONATHAN ASPAS Juncal	ESP	28/2/82	M	14	(1)	2
14	Maxime LESTIENNE		17/6/92	M	16	(2)	3
39	Robert MAAH	FRA	25/3/85	A	5	(7)	2
29	MANUel MICÓ Yebana	ESP	18/7/86	D	5	(1)	
2	Carlos Daniel MORENO Hernández	ESP	14/6/86	D	13		2
27	Idir OUALI	FRA	21/5/88	M	12	(2)	

No	Name	Nat	DoB	Pos	Aps	(s)	Gls
21	José Antonio SALCEDO	ESP	1/10/90	G	5		
25	Jérémy SAPINA	FRA	1/2/85	D	5		
40	Andréa SCHIFFANO		10/2/91	M	1	(2)	
80	Asanda SISHUBA	RSA	13/4/80	M	6	(7)	
23	Ján SLOVENČIAK	SVK	5/11/81	G	3		
22	Alexandre TEKLAK		16/8/75	D	3	(3)	
15	Daan VAN GIJSEGHEM		2/3/88	D	16		1
20	Gonzague VANDOOREN		17/8/79	D	12		
28	Jonathan WALASIAK		23/10/82	M		(2)	
80	Jean-Baptist YAKASSONGO		20/3/89	A		(1)	

KSV ROESELARE
Coach – Dennis van Wijk (NED)
Founded – 1999
Stadium – Schiervelde (9,036)

2009

1/8	GBA	h	1-1	Dissa
8/8	Mouscron	a	0-0	(result annulled)
15/8	Standard	h	1-5	El Gaaouri
22/8	Sint-Truiden	a	1-2	El Gaaouri
29/8	Charleroi	h	1-3	El Gaaouri (p)
12/9	Gent	a	1-5	Vidarsson
19/9	Mechelen	a	2-3	El Gaaouri (p), Dissa
23/9	Lokeren	h	1-2	Dissa
26/9	Genk	a	1-1	Dissa
3/10	Cercle Brugge	h	3-2	Dissa 2, Vidarsson
17/10	Kortrijk	a	0-2	
25/10	Club Brugge	h	2-3	Vidarsson (p), Dissa
31/10	Westerlo	a	2-2	Mirvić, Nikolić
7/11	Zulte Waregem	h	2-0	Vidarsson, Dequevy
21/11	Anderlecht	a	1-3	Vidarsson
28/11	GBA	a	0-3	
4/12	Mouscron	h	1-2	Vidarsson (result annulled)
12/12	Standard	a	1-0	Dequevy
19/12	Sint-Truiden	h	1-2	Nikolić
26/12	Charleroi	a	0-3	
30/12	Gent	h	0-4	

2010

16/1	Mechelen	h	1-2	Dequevy
23/1	Lokeren	a	4-1	Tomou, Rukavytsya 2, Dequevy
6/2	Cercle Brugge	a	0-2	
13/2	Kortrijk	h	0-2	
20/2	Zulte Waregem	a	1-1	Dissa
24/2	Genk	h	1-1	Rukavytsya
28/2	Anderlecht	h	1-2	Rukavytsya
14/3	Club Brugge	a	0-1	
21/3	Westerlo	h	0-0	

No	Name	Nat	DoB	Pos	Aps	(s)	Gls
28	Daan DE PEVER		17/1/89	M	7	(4)	
11	Joeri DEQUEVY		27/4/88	M	27	(1)	4
23	Mahamadou DISSA	MLI	18/5/79	A	25	(3)	8
22	Vadim DOTSENKO	RUS	3/7/88	A		(6)	
10	Samir EL GAAOURI	NED	28/5/84	M	12	(7)	4
2	Hólmar Örn EYJÓLFSSON	ISL	6/8/90	D	9		
16	Bert GOOSSENS		5/1/85	D		(3)	
5	Sergio HELLINGS	NED	11/10/84	D	9	(5)	
7	Thomas HOVINE		12/12/90	M		(1)	
14	Jérémy HUYGEBAERT		7/1/89	D	28		
17	Collins JOHN	NED	17/11/85	A	7	(4)	
25	Štěpán KUČERA	CZE	11/6/84	D	17	(2)	
3	Damir MIRVIĆ	BIH	30/11/82	D	28		1
7	Jimmy MULISA	RWA	24/4/84	A		(6)	
9	Stefan NIKOLIĆ	MNE	16/4/89	A	8	(13)	2
18	Vincent PROVOOST		7/2/84	M	27		
33	Anduele PRYOR	NED	26/4/85	M	2	(3)	
29	Nikita RUKAVYTSYA	AUS	22/6/87	A	8	(1)	4
1	Jurgen SIERENS		10/4/76	G	16		
8	Stefaan TANGHE		15/1/72	M	11	(3)	
78	Arturo TEN HEUVEL	NED	20/12/88	M	3	(1)	
30	Bertin TOMOU	CMR	8/8/78	A	6	(3)	1
21	Bram VANDENBUSSCHE		1/2/81	D	15	(3)	
1	Anthony VAN LOO		5/10/88	D	22		
15	Jeroen VANTHOURNOUT		29/6/89	D	7	(3)	
27	Bjarni Thór VIDARSSON	ISL	5/3/88	M	22	(1)	6

R. STANDARD DE LIÈGE

Coach – László Bölöni (ROU); (10/2/10) Dominique D'Onofrio
Founded – 1898
Stadium – Maurice Dufrasne (27,500)
MAJOR HONOURS:
Belgian League - (10) 1958, 1961, 1963, 1969, 1970, 1971, 1982, 1983,
2008, 2009;
Belgian Cup - (5) 1954, 1966, 1967, 1981, 1993.

2009

31/7	Sint-Truiden	h	2-2	*De Camargo 2*
7/8	GBA	a	1-1	*Jovanović*
15/8	Roeselare	a	5-1	*Jovanović 3 (1p),*
				Carcela-González, Mbokani
21/8	Charleroi	h	1-1	*Jovanović*
30/8	Anderlecht	a	1-1	*Mbokani*
12/9	Mechelen	h	3-0	*Carcela-González 2, Mangala*
19/9	Lokeren	a	3-1	*Carcela-González, Mbokani, Felipe*
23/9	Cercle Brugge	h	1-1	*Jovanović (p)*
26/9	Kortrijk	a	2-0	*Dalmat, Angeli*
4/10	Genk	h	1-0	*Jovanović (p)*
17/10	Westerlo	a	0-2	
24/10	Zulte Waregem	h	1-1	*Cyriac*
30/10	Mouscron	a	0-0	*(result annulled)*
8/11	Club Brugge	h	3-1	*Jovanović 2, Witsel*
21/11	Gent	a	1-2	*Cyriac*
29/11	Sint-Truiden	a	0-2	
4/12	GBA	h	2-2	*Jovanović, De Camargo*
12/12	Roeselare	h	0-1	
26/12	Lokeren	h	2-0	*Witsel, De Camargo*
29/12	Cercle Brugge	a	0-2	

2010

17/1	Anderlecht	h	0-4	
24/1	Mechelen	a	0-0	
31/1	Kortrijk	h	3-1	*Daerden, Witsel, Carcela-González*
4/2	Charleroi	a	3-2	*Dalmat, Defour (p), Witsel*
7/2	Genk	a	0-1	
14/2	Westerlo	h	1-0	*Pocognoli*
21/2	Club Brugge	a	1-2	*Mbokani*
14/3	Zulte Waregem	a	1-1	*Witsel*
21/3	Gent	h	0-2	
27/3	Charleroi	h	2-0	*Mbokani 2*
4/4	Genk	a	0-1	
11/4	GBA	h	3-0	*De Camargo 2, Witsel (p)*
15/4	GBA	a	2-2	*Mbokani, Traoré*
18/4	Genk	h	1-1	*Mutombo*
25/4	Charleroi	a	0-1	

No	Name	Nat	DoB	Pos	Aps	(s)	Gls
27	Arnor ANGELI		25/2/91	M	1	(7)	1
32	Jonathan BUATU		27/9/93	M	1		
4	Pape Abdou CAMARA	SEN	24/9/91	M		(1)	
33	Mehdi CARCELA-GONZÁLEZ		1/7/89	M	25	(7)	5
6	Cédric COLLET	FRA	7/3/84	M	3		
29	CYRIAC Gohi Bi Zoro Sede	CIV	15/8/90	A	3	(4)	2
15	Olivier DACOURT	FRA	25/9/74	M	3	(5)	
24	Koen DAERDEN		8/3/82	M	9	(1)	1
7	Wilfried DALMAT	FRA	17/7/82	M	15	(6)	2
10	Igor DE CAMARGO		12/5/83	A	23	(4)	6
8	Steven DEFOUR		15/4/88	M	12	(1)	1
11	Grégory DUFER		19/12/81	M	7	(7)	
5	FELIPE Trevizan Martins	BRA	15/5/87	D	16	(1)	1
25	Rami GERSHON	ISR	12/8/88	M	2		
2	Réginal GOREUX		31/12/87	D	7	(5)	
77	Gheorghe GROZAV	ROU	29/9/90	A	4	(1)	
23	Milan JOVANOVIĆ	SRB	18/4/81	A	23	(3)	10
22	Eliaquim MANGALA	FRA	13/2/91	M	28	(3)	1
17	MARCOS Camozzato	BRA	17/6/83	D	30	(2)	
9	Dieumerci MBOKANI	COD	22/11/85	A	23	(1)	7
15	Tomislav MIKULIĆ	CRO	4/1/82	D	1		
14	Landry MULEMO		17/9/86	D	14	(4)	
15	Andréa Mbuyi MUTOMBO		6/7/90	M	2		1
20	Benjamin NICAISE	FRA	28/9/80	M	11	(9)	

35	Sébastien POCOGNOLI		1/8/87	D	9	(1)	1
4	RICARDO Sérgio ROCHA						
	Azevedo	POR	3/10/78	D	7		
19	Mohamed Adama SARR	SEN	23/12/83	D	25		
38	SİNAN Bolat	TUR	3/9/88	G	31		
20	Moussa TRAORÉ	CIV	19/4/90	A	7	(15)	1
1	Kristof VAN HOUT		9/2/87	G	4		
	Christopher VERBIST		8/10/91	D		(1)	
3	VICTOR RAMOS Ferreira	BRA	5/5/89	D	13		
28	Axel WITSEL		12/1/89	M	25	(2)	6
21	Franco ZENNARO		1/4/93	D	1		

K. SINT-TRUIDENSE VV

Coach – Guido Brepoels
Founded – 1924
Stadium – Staayen (11,250)

2009

31/7	Standard	a	2-2	*Chimedza, Euvrard*
8/8	Charleroi	h	0-0	
15/8	Lokeren	a	2-1	*Sidibé, Chimedza*
22/8	Roeselare	h	2-1	*Wilmet, Sidibé*
29/8	Mechelen	a	2-0	*Wilmet, Sidibé*
12/9	Anderlecht	h	2-1	*Chimedza, Sidibé*
19/9	Kortrijk	a	1-0	*Sidibé*
22/9	Genk	h	2-4	*Euvrard, Alex*
26/9	Westerlo	a	0-2	
3/10	Zulte Waregem	h	1-2	*Sidibé*
17/10	Mouscron	a	1-2	*Odoi (result annulled)*
24/10	Gent	h	1-2	*Sidibé*
31/10	Club Brugge	a	0-1	
7/11	GBA	a	1-4	*Onana*
21/11	Cercle Brugge	h	1-1	*Delorge*
29/11	Standard	h	2-0	*Sidibé, Wilmet*
4/12	Charleroi	a	0-0	
12/12	Kortrijk	h	0-2	
19/12	Roeselare	a	2-1	*Wilmet, Wagemakers*
26/12	Mechelen	h	5-2	*Sidibé, Euvrard, Schouterden,*
				Charaï, Chimedza (p)
29/12	Genk	a	0-0	

2010

16/1	Lokeren	h	2-1	*Sidibé 2*
23/1	Zulte Waregem	a	0-2	
3/2	Westerlo	a	0-1	
6/2	Anderlecht	a	2-1	*Delorge, Chimedza (p)*
20/2	Gent	a	1-0	*Chimedza*
28/2	Club Brugge	h	1-1	*Sidibé*
14/3	GBA	h	2-0	*Sidibé, Onana*
21/3	Cercle Brugge	a	1-3	*Delorge*
27/3	Genk	h	0-0	
31/3	Zulte Waregem	a	2-1	*Delorge, Siani*
4/4	Kortrijk	a	2-1	*Delorge, Wilmet*
9/4	Anderlecht	h	1-1	*Schouterden*
14/4	Gent	a	0-0	
17/4	Kortrijk	h	1-0	*Buysens*
24/4	Zulte Waregem	h	1-2	*og (Dachelet)*
2/5	Club Brugge	a	0-2	
5/5	Gent	h	1-1	*Siani (p)*
8/5	Anderlecht	a	1-2	*Cantaluppi (p)*

No	Name	Nat	DoB	Pos	Aps	(s)	Gls
7	ALEXandre Afonso da Silva	BRA	15/8/83	M	13	(3)	1
23	Yorick ANTHEUNIS		26/6/91	A		(3)	
16	Jeroen APPELTANS		27/8/90	M	6	(6)	
6	Ludovic BUYSENS		13/3/86	D	18	(8)	1
5	Mario CANTALUPPI	SUI	11/4/74	D	32		1
11	Issame CHARAÏ		11/5/82	A	6	(5)	1
13	Cephas CHIMEDZA	ZIM	5/12/84	M	22	(8)	6
21	Benji COMMERS		18/12/92	D		(1)	
24	Giel DEFERM		30/6/88	D	10	(6)	
17	Peter DELORGE		19/4/80	M	32		5
3	Vincent EUVRARD		12/3/82	D	38		3
2	Wim MENNES		25/1/77	M	37		

BELGIUM

22	Simon MIGNOLET		6/3/88	G	37		
15	Massimo MOIA		9/3/87	D	3		
1	Tom MUYTERS		5/12/84	G	2		
15	Denis ODOI		27/5/88	D	35		1
12	Hervé Ndjana ONANA	CMR	1/6/87	A	13	(22)	2
18	Nils SCHOUTERDEN		14/12/88	M	22	(1)	2
9	Sébastien SIANI	CMR	21/12/86	A	9	(11)	2
19	Ibrahim SIDIBÉ	SEN	10/8/80	A	36		13
14	Marc WAGEMAKERS		7/6/78	M	28	(1)	1
10	Jonathan WILMET		7/1/86	A	30	(7)	5

23	Jarno MOLENBERGHS		11/12/89	M	4	(3)	1
14	Michael MODUBI	RSA	22/4/85	M	6	(1)	
27	Adnan MRAVAC	BIH	10/4/82	D	22		2
6	Obiora Emmanuel ODITA	NGA	14/5/83	A	9	(5)	
27	Nelinho Minzun QUINA	PER	11/5/87	D	11	(2)	
19	Jaime Alfonso RUIZ	COL	3/1/84	A	9	(3)	1
10	Emmanuel SARKI	NGA	26/12/87	M	4	(8)	
5	Wouter SCHEELEN		16/10/85	M	2	(6)	
9	Bertin TOMOU	CMR	8/8/78	A	10	(4)	3
12	Glenn VAN ASTEN		16/6/87	M	3	(12)	1
16	Joris VAN HOUT		10/11/77	D	19	(8)	2
11	Nico VAN KERCKHOVEN		14/12/70	D	26		1
32	Gunther VANAUDENAERDE		23/1/84	D	27		2
17	Olexandr YAKOVENKO	UKR	23/6/87	M	27		9
8	Lukáš ZELENKA	CZE	5/10/79	M	3		

KVC WESTERLO
Coach – Jan Ceulemans
Founded – 1933
Stadium – Het Kuipje (8,141)
MAJOR HONOURS:
Belgian Cup - (1) 2001.

2009

1/8	Mechelen	a	1-4	Tomou
8/8	Kortrijk	h	1-1	Tomou
15/8	Anderlecht	a	0-3	
23/8	Genk	h	0-1	
28/8	Zulte Waregem	h	1-2	Farssi
12/9	Mouscron	a	1-0	Mravac (result annulled)
20/9	Club Brugge	h	1-4	Yakovenko
23/9	Gent	a	2-1	Mravac (p), Tomou
26/9	Sint-Truiden	h	2-0	Yakovenko 2
3/10	GBA	a	1-3	Dekelver
17/10	Standard	h	2-0	Dekelver 2
24/10	Charleroi	a	1-1	Yakovenko
31/10	Roeselare	h	2-2	Dekelver, De Petter (p)
7/11	Cercle Brugge	a	1-2	Dekelver
21/11	Lokeren	h	1-0	og (Lazić)
28/11	Mechelen	h	2-0	Yakovenko, De Petter
4/12	Genk	a	0-0	
11/12	Anderlecht	h	0-2	
19/12	Kortrijk	a	1-1	Dekelver
26/12	Zulte Waregem	a	0-1	
2010				
23/1	Gent	h	0-0	
30/1	Club Brugge	a	1-2	Yakovenko
3/2	Sint-Truiden	a	1-0	Van Hout
6/2	GBA	h	1-1	Vanaudenaerde
14/2	Standard	a	0-1	
20/2	Charleroi	h	4-0	Yakovenko, De Petter, Molenberghs, Van Asten
27/2	Lokeren	a	0-1	
14/3	Cercle Brugge	h	2-1	Liliu, og (Cornelis)
21/3	Roeselare	a	0-0	
31/3	Mechelen	h	0-2	
3/4	Cercle Brugge	a	0-2	
10/4	Lokeren	a	3-3	Liliu, De Petter, Van Hout
14/4	Lokeren	h	2-0	Liliu, Vanaudenaerde
17/4	Cercle Brugge	h	4-1	Yakovenko, Annab, Van Kerckhoven (p), Liliu
24/4	Mechelen	a	3-1	Yakovenko, Ruiz, Annab

No	Name	Nat	DoB	Pos	Aps	(s)	Gls
20	Moses ADAMS	NGA	21/7/88	M	10	(7)	
24	Lens ANNAB		20/7/88	M	26	(1)	2
26	Soufiane BIDAOUI		20/4/90	A		(2)	
25	Momodou CEESAY	GAM	24/12/88	A	12	(8)	
8	Dragan ĆERAN	SRB	6/10/87	A	1	(2)	
22	Jo CHRISTIAENS		17/4/88	D	1	(1)	
4	Wouter CORSTJENS		13/2/87	D	13	(5)	
3	Steven DE PETTER		22/11/85	D	31		4
1	Yves DE WINTER		25/5/87	G	32		
30	Bart DEELKENS		25/4/78	G	3		
7	Dieter DEKELVER		17/8/79	A	17	(7)	6
18	Jef DELEN		29/6/76	M	30	(1)	
21	Rachid FARSSI		15/1/85	D	22	(2)	1
9	Ellinton Antonio Costa Morais "LILIU"	BRA	30/3/90	A	5	(2)	4

SV ZULTE WAREGEM
Coach – Francky Dury
Founded – 2001
Stadium – Regenboogstadion (8,500)
MAJOR HONOURS:
Belgian Cup - (1) 2006.

2009

1/8	Lokeren	a	1-1	Meert
8/8	Genk	h	2-2	D'Haene, Chevalier
15/8	Cercle Brugge	a	2-2	Chevalier, Berrier
22/8	Anderlecht	h	0-2	
28/8	Westerlo	a	2-1	Berrier, N'For
12/9	Kortrijk	h	0-2	
19/9	Mouscron	h	3-1	Makiese 2 (1p), Sadik (result annulled)
23/9	Club Brugge	a	1-3	Makiese
26/9	Gent	h	3-1	Makiese, Taravel, Chevalier
3/10	Sint-Truiden	a	2-1	Makiese, Chevalier
17/10	GBA	h	4-0	Chevalier 2, Roelandts, Makiese
24/10	Standard	a	1-1	Roelandts
31/10	Charleroi	h	2-2	Roelandts, Van Nieuwenhuyze
7/11	Roeselare	a	0-2	
22/11	Mechelen	h	4-1	Van Nieuwenhuyze, Ernemann 2, Chevalier
29/11	Lokeren	h	1-0	D'Haene
4/12	Kortrijk	a	0-1	
13/12	Cercle Brugge	h	1-0	Chevalier
19/12	Genk	a	2-2	og (Tiago Silva), Chevalier
26/12	Westerlo	h	1-0	Berrier
30/12	Anderlecht	a	1-2	Berrier
2010				
23/1	Sint-Truiden	h	2-0	D'Haene, Chevalier
31/1	Gent	a	2-0	Roelandts, Makiese
7/2	Club Brugge	h	1-1	Lyng
20/2	Roeselare	h	1-1	Roelandts
27/2	Charleroi	a	0-0	
7/3	GBA	a	1-1	Chevalier
14/3	Standard	h	1-1	Chevalier
21/3	Mechelen	a	1-2	Roelandts (p)
28/3	Anderlecht	a	0-6	
31/3	Sint-Truiden	h	1-2	Makiese
4/4	Gent	h	1-2	Roelandts
10/4	Kortrijk	a	0-2	
14/4	Club Brugge	h	2-0	Taravel, N'For (p)
18/4	Gent	a	0-5	
24/4	Sint-Truiden	a	2-1	N'For 2
30/4	Anderlecht	h	0-0	
5/5	Club Brugge	a	0-3	
8/5	Kortrijk	h	1-2	Roelandts

No	Name	Nat	DoB	Pos	Aps	(s)	Gls
16	Franck BERRIER	FRA	2/2/84	M	28		4
1	Sammy BOSSUT		11/8/85	G	39		
23	Bart BUYSSE		16/10/86	D	37		
9	Teddy CHEVALIER	FRA	28/6/87	A	32	(2)	12
3	Steve COLPAERT		13/9/86	D	30	(5)	

15	Miguel DACHELET		16/1/88	D	11	(2)	
24	Karel D'HAENE		5/9/80	D	32		3
17	Steffen ERNEMANN	DEN	26/4/82	M	15	(5)	2
21	Khaleem HYLAND	TRI	5/6/89	M	19	(8)	
5	Baddis LEBBIHI	FRA	14/3/90	D	2	(1)	
19	Emil LYNG	DEN	3/8/89	A	8	(6)	1
14	Chris MAKIESE	FRA	14/10/87	A	14	(15)	8
12	Thomas MATTON		24/10/85	M	14	(5)	
11	Stijn MEERT		6/4/78	M	9	(4)	1
2	Stijn MINNE		29/6/78	D	23		
10	Ernest N'FOR	CMR	28/4/86	A	27	(9)	4
9	Kevin ROELANDTS		27/8/82	M	34	(3)	8
18	Berat SADIK	FIN	14/9/86	A	1	(13)	1
7	Jérémy TARAVEL	FRA	17/1/87	D	24	(3)	2
6	Ludwin VAN NIEUWENHUYZE		25/2/78	M	30	(1)	2
4	Bart VAN ZUNDERT		30/11/80	D		(1)	
20	Jorgo WAEGHE		30/3/89	A		(3)	

PROMOTED CLUBS

K. LIERSE SK
Coach – Herman Helleputte; (21/2/10) Aimé Antheunis
Founded – 1906
Stadium – Herman Vanderpoortenstadion (14,538)
MAJOR HONOURS:
Belgian League - (4): 1932, 1942, 1960, 1997;
Belgian Cup - (2) 1969, 1999.

K. AS EUPEN
Coach – Dany Ost
Founded – 1945
Stadium – Am Kehrweg (6,000)

SECOND LEVEL FINAL TABLE 2009/10

		Pld	W	D	L	F	A	Pts
1	K. Lierse SK	36	21	12	3	75	32	75
2	KVSK United Overpelt-Lommel	36	20	10	6	55	27	70
3	RAEC Mons	36	19	9	8	56	32	66
4	K. AS Eupen	36	16	12	8	56	37	60
5	R. Boussu Dour	36	13	14	9	46	43	53
6	KV Red Star Waasland	36	13	13	10	46	49	52
7	KV Oostende	36	12	15	9	49	45	51
8	R. Antwerp FC	36	10	17	9	55	53	47
9	Oud-Heverlee Leuven	36	11	12	13	50	66	45
10	K. Standaard Wetteren	36	12	8	16	48	59	44
11	RFC Tournai	36	11	11	14	50	51	44
12	KVK Tienen	36	11	10	15	44	58	43
13	FCV Dender EH	36	10	13	13	45	49	43
14	FC Molenbeek Brussels	36	11	9	16	47	53	42
15	AFC Tubize	36	9	15	12	41	41	42
16	KV Turnhout	36	10	11	15	50	57	41
17	KSK Ronse	36	10	9	17	51	57	39
18	KSK Beveren	36	8	12	16	37	55	36
19	RFC de Liège	36	5	8	23	23	60	23

PROMOTION/RELEGATION PLAY-OFF FINAL TABLE

		Pld	W	D	L	F	A	Pts
1	K. AS Eupen	6	4	1	1	9	4	13
2	RAEC Mons	6	2	2	2	8	8	8
3	KVSK United Overpelt-Lommel	6	2	0	4	7	7	6
4	KSV Roeselare	6	1	3	2	5	10	6

DOMESTIC CUP 2009/10

COUPE DE BELGIQUE/BEKER VAN BELGIË

SIXTH ROUND

(27/10/09)
Cercle Brugge 2, Leuven 0
GBA 3, Deinze 0
Mons 2, Mouscron 1 *(aet)*
Sint-Truiden 0, Genk 1
Standard 2, Lierse 1 *(aet)*

Gent 3, White Star Woluwe 1
Lokeren 2, Tubize 0
Mechelen 2, Spouwen-
Mopertingen 0
Roeselare 2, Beveren 1 *(aet)*
Standaard Wetteren 1, Charleroi 2
(aet)

(28/10/09)
Anderlecht 2, Verviers 0
Antwerp 0, Dender 1
Club Brugge 5, Hamme 0

Virton 0, Kortrijk 1 *(aet)*
Westerlo 3, Eendracht Aalst 2 *(aet)*
Zulte Waregem 3, Ronse 0

SEVENTH ROUND

(23/12/09)
Anderlecht 3, Dender 0
Charleroi 2, Mechelen 5 *(aet)*
Club Brugge 2, Lokeren 1
Genk 1, Roeselare 2

Gent 1, GBA 0
Standard 1, Kortrijk 2
Westerlo 3, Mons 1

(20/1/10)
Zulte Waregem 1, Cercle Brugge 3

QUARTER-FINALS

(20/1/10 & 27/1/10)
Club Brugge 1 *(Akpala 17)*, Gent 4 *(Ćustović 49, 72, Leye 58, Smolders 85)*
Gent 1 *(Pieroni 44)*, Club Brugge 0
(Gent 5-1)

Kortrijk 3 *(Benteke 46, De Beule 63, Sawaneh 73)*, Roeselare 2 *(Dissa 74, Tomou 87)*
Roeselare 1 *(Dequevy 83)*, Kortrijk 0
(3-3; Roeselare on away goals)

Mechelen 3 *(Mununga 17, Gorius 19, 64p)*, Westerlo 2 *(Dekelver 15, Yakovenko 45)*
Westerlo 0, Mechelen 0
(Mechelen 3-2)

(23/1/10 & 26/1/10)
Anderlecht 2 *(Boussoufa 3p, Kouyaté 78)*, Cercle Brugge 1 *(Božović 66)*
Cercle Brugge 1 *(Božović 4)*, Anderlecht 0
(2-2; Cercle Brugge on away goal)

SEMI-FINALS

(9/2/10 & 25/3/10)
Mechelen 2 *(Gorius 35, Biset 46)*, Gent 2 *(Ljubijankič 8, Coulibaly 64)*
Gent 1 *(Coulibaly 38)*, Mechelen 0
(Gent 3-2)

(17/3/10 & 26/3/10)
Cercle Brugge 3 *(Vossen 29, Cornelis 36, Yashchuk 72)*, Roeselare 0
Roeselare 3 *(Dissa 33, 71, Huygebaert 57)*, Cercle Brugge 1 *(Vossen 3p)*
(Cercle Brugge 4-3)

FINAL

(15/5/10)
Stade Roi Baudouin, Brussels
KAA GENT 3 *(Coulibaly 35, Leye 85, Grondin 90+3)*
CERCLE BRUGGE KSV 0
Referee – Allaerts
GENT – Jorgačević, Rosales, Wils, Šuler, Thompson, Thijs, Lepoint, Azofeifa *(Grondin 83)*, Leye, Coulibaly *(De Smet 89)*, Elghanassy *(Ljubijankič 71)*.
CERCLE BRUGGE – Verbist, Cornelis, Viane *(Portier 34)*, Kelhar, Evens, Serebrennikov, Sergeant *(Van Eenoo 64)*, Yashchuk, Vossen, Boi *(Reynaldo 46)*, Foley.

BOSNIA-HERZEGOVINA

Osim returns title to Željezničar

After an eight-year wait, FK Željezničar reclaimed the Bosnian-Herzegovinian Premijer Liga title, an impressive run of victories during the spring hoisting them clear of fellow challengers NK Široki Brijeg, FK Borac Banja Luka and defending champions HŠK Zrinjski. There would be no domestic double for the Sarajevo club, however, as they were defeated on away goals in the Cup final by Borac.

Željezničar won the championship under the same coach who had steered them to two championships and two Cup wins at the start of the previous decade – Amar Osim. The 42-year-old son of Ivica Osim, the former head coach of Yugoslavia, enjoyed a triumphant return, not only by winning another trophy but by reinvigorating a club that had fallen on hard times. Inspired by his presence, the Željo fans began to congregate again in large numbers at the Grbavica stadium and there was a sense that the club was about to embark on an exciting new era.

The transformation of Željezničar's fortunes did not happen overnight. Having finished ninth in the 2008/09 Premijer Liga, they had a lot of ground to make up, and by the halfway point of the campaign they lay a mere fifth in the table seven points adrift of leaders Široki Brijeg. The three-month winter break was evidently used to good effect by Osim and his players, because on the resumption the team stormed decisively out of the blocks. A 2-0 win at Široki Brijeg's Pecara fortress, where Željezničar had lost on each of their previous nine visits, lit the fuse for an explosive run of form that would carry the Blues all the way through to the season's climax, the title being secured by a 4-1 home win over lowly FK Laktaši with one match to spare.

Show-stealer Bekrić

Fittingly, it was Željezničar's top performer, playmaker Samir Bekrić, who stole the show in that championship-clinching win, scoring two goals himself and assisting in both of the others. He would end up with 15 goals for the season – just one behind NK Travink's Feđa Dudić in the top scorer standings - and the title of Premijer Liga Player of the Year.

Four days before Željezničar wrapped up the league they suffered the disappointment of losing the Cup final to Borac. Both teams reached the two-legged showpiece undefeated, so it was perhaps no great surprise that both matches were drawn. Decisively, however, the champions-elect conceded two goals at home to Borac's one. Željezničar were actually 2-0 down at half-time of the second leg at the Grbavica, and although they drew level shortly after the interval, Borac bravely withstood a barrage of attacks to cling on to their slender advantage and claim their first major honour since they shocked FK Crvena zvezda to win the final of the Yugoslav Cup 22 years earlier. Victory also enabled Borac to represent Bosnia-Herzegovina in Europe for the first time. Having been denied a licence to compete a year earlier, they actually qualified twice over for the 2010/11 UEFA Europa League, their third place in the league also providing access.

Samir Bekrić of champions Željezničar – the Premijer Liga Player of the Year

Return to Europe

Runners-up Široki Brijeg and fourth-placed Zrinjski both booked an immediate return to European competition, from which they had made an early exit the previous summer. FK Sarajevo were the best of Bosnia-Herzegovina's four representatives, eliminating FC Spartak Trnava and Helsingborgs IF, the latter on penalties, before narrowly losing out on a place in the UEFA Europa League group stage to CFR 1907 Cluj. Sarajevo could only finish fifth in the Premijer Liga, their bid for a European return not helped by the misbehaviour of their followers, which forced their big derby with Željezničar to be played behind closed doors.

The team that succeeded Sarajevo as domestic champions in 2007/08, FK Modriča, suffered relegation after a calamitous spring campaign during which they lost 14 of their 15 matches. Laktaši also went down, with FK Budućnost Banovići, runaway winners of the Prva Liga FBiH, returning to the top flight after a four-year gap in the company of Srpska league champions FK Drina Zvornik.

Bosnia-Herzegovina's rising star Edin Džeko enjoyed another excellent season

Chances squandered

Bosnia-Herzegovina's valiant bid to qualify for the 2010 FIFA World Cup was ended by Portugal in the play-offs. Several chances to score a precious away goal were created but squandered in the first leg in Lisbon, and once Portugal went 2-0 up on aggregate in the Zenica return, all hope was lost. Star striker Edin Džeko had ended the group campaign with nine goals but he could not add to his tally when it mattered most against Portugal – a rare blip during another brilliant season in which the 24-year-old topped the German Bundeliga goal charts.

Miroslav Blažević stepped down as national coach after the play-offs, to be succeeded the following month by Bosnian football legend Safet Sušić. Twenty years Blažević's junior, the one-time Paris Saint-Germain FC midfield maestro came to the job after a lengthy, generally uninspiring spell as a coach in Turkey. The country will look to him for inspiration, though, as Bosnia-Herzegovina seek to make their long-awaited first major tournament appearance in Poland/Ukraine at UEFA EURO 2012. Luxembourg, Albania, Belarus, Romania and Sušić's former land of residence France are the five teams that stand in their way.

Nogometni/ Fudbalski savez Bosne i Hercegovine (NFSBiH)

Ulica Ferhadija 30
BA-71000 Sarajevo
tel – +387 33 276 660
fax – +387 33 444 332
website – nfsbih.ba
email – nsbih@bih.net.ba
Year of Formation – 1992

President – Sulejman Čolaković
General Secretary – Jasmin Baković
Media Officer – Slavica Pecikoza
National Stadium – Olimpijski Asim Ferhatović Hase, Sarajevo (34,630)

TOP FIVE ALL-TIME CAPS
Elvir Bolić (51); Zvjezdan Misimović (48); Sergej Barbarez (47); Vedin Musić (45); Hasan Salihamidžić (42)
TOP FIVE ALL-TIME GOALS
Elvir Bolić (22); Sergej Barbarez (17); Edin Džeko & Zvjezdan Misimović (15); Elvir Baljić (14)

BOSNIA-HERZEGOVINA

NATIONAL TEAM RESULTS 2009/10

Date	Opponent	H/A	Venue	Score	Scorers
12/8/09	Iran	H	Sarajevo	2-3	*Džeko (52, 65)*
5/9/09	Armenia (WCQ)	A	Yerevan	2-0	*Ibričić (6), Muslimović (75)*
9/9/09	Turkey (WCQ)	H	Zenica	1-1	*Salihović (25)*
10/10/09	Estonia (WCQ)	A	Tallinn	2-0	*Džeko (30), Ibišević (64)*
14/10/09	Spain (WCQ)	H	Zenica	2-5	*Džeko (90), Misimović (90+2)*
14/11/09	Portugal (WCQ)	A	Lisbon	0-1	
18/11/09	Portugal (WCQ)	H	Zenica	0-1	
3/3/10	Ghana	H	Sarajevo	2-1	*Ibišević (40), Pjanić (65)*
29/5/10	Sweden	A	Solna	2-4	*Salihović (47), Zec (90)*
3/6/10	Germany	A	Frankfurt	1-3	*Džeko (15)*

NATIONAL TEAM APPEARANCES 2009/10

Coach – Miroslav BLAŽEVIĆ (CRO) 10/2/35 /(28/12/09) Safet SUŠIĆ 13/4/55

Player	DOB	Club	Irn	ARM	TUR	EST	ESP	POR	POR	Gha	Swe	Ger	Caps	Goals
Nemanja SUPIĆ	12/1/82	unattached /Timişoara (ROU)	G63	G	G		G						8	-
Adnan MRAVAC	10/4/82	Mattersburg (AUT) /Westerlo (BEL)	D								D	D44	7	-
Safet NADAREVIĆ	30/8/80	Eskişehirspor (TUR)	D	D	D	D	D	D	D	D	s46	D	27	-
Emir SPAHIĆ	18/8/80	Montpellier (FRA)	D77	D	D	D	D	D		D	D67	D	40	2
Sanel JAHIĆ	10/12/81	Aris (GRE) /AEK (GRE)	M	D	D	D	D	D	D	D64	s67	D	15	1
Senijad IBRIČIĆ	26/9/86	Hajduk (CRO)	M	M84	M79	M		M	M	M46	s77	s44	25	3
Miralem PJANIĆ	2/4/90	Lyon (FRA)	M68	s65	s61		M	s87	M	M	M	M	16	1
Sejad SALIHOVIĆ	8/10/84	Hoffenheim (GER)	M	M	M	M	M73	M	M77*	M	M	M77	20	3
Zlatan BAJRAMOVIĆ	12/8/79	Eintracht (GER)	M73	s84			s46			M83			35	3
Vedad IBIŠEVIĆ	6/8/84	Hoffenheim (GER)	A	A69	A68	A	A	A	A	A79	s65	A74	23	5
Edin DŽEKO	17/3/86	Wolfsburg (GER)	A	A	A	A	A	A	A		A81	A	26	15
Adis NURKOVIĆ	28/4/86	Travnik	s63										1	-
Dario DAMJANOVIĆ	23/7/81	Kaiserslautern (GER)	s68										17	2
Boris PANDŽA	15/12/86	Hajduk (CRO)	s73						D		D46		9	-
Ivan RADELJIĆ	14/9/80	Energie (GER)	s77										10	-
Elvir RAHIMIĆ	4/4/76	CSKA Moskva (RUS)		M	M	M	M46	M		M46		M	21	-
Samir MURATOVIĆ	25/2/76	Sturm (AUT)		M65	M61	M85	M67	M87			s46	M46	23	-
Admir VLADAVIĆ	29/6/82	Salzburg (AUT)		M	s79		s67						12	-
Zlatan MUSLIMOVIĆ	6/3/81	PAOK (GRE)		s69	s68		s81	s46	s46	A65	s79		23	11
Zvjezdan MISIMOVIĆ	5/6/82	Wolfsburg (GER)			M	M	M	M81		M72	M	M79	48	15
Kenan HASAGIĆ	1/2/80	İstanbul BB (TUR)				G92		G	G	G46		G	32	-
Džemal BERBEROVIĆ	5/11/81	Denizlispor (TUR)					s85		s83	s64		s77	33	-
Asmir BEGOVIĆ	20/6/87	Portsmouth (ENG) /Stoke (ENG)				s92					s46	G	3	-
Mirko HRGOVIĆ	5/2/79	Fürth (GER)					s73						29	2
Haris MEDUNJANIN	8/3/85	Valladolid (ESP)							M46		s72	M77	3	-
Ermin ZEC	6/6/88	Šibenik (CRO)								s79	s81	s74	4	1
Mehmed ALISPAHIĆ	24/11/87	Šibenik (CRO)										s46	1	-

DOMESTIC LEAGUE 2009/10

PREMIJER LIGA FINAL TABLE

	Pld	Home W	D	L	F	A	Away W	D	L	F	A	Total W	D	L	F	A	Pts
FK Željezničar	30	12	2	1	35	10	6	5	4	17	12	18	7	5	52	22	61
NK Široki Brijeg	30	11	3	1	28	7	5	4	6	18	20	16	7	7	46	27	55
FK Borac Banja Luka	30	13	0	2	27	7	4	2	9	10	22	17	2	11	37	29	53
HŠK Zrinjski	30	11	3	1	32	7	4	3	8	14	26	15	6	9	46	33	51
FK Sarajevo	30	11	4	0	30	7	3	4	8	13	18	14	8	8	43	25	50
FK Olimpik Sarajevo	30	8	4	3	16	9	4	4	7	14	25	12	8	10	30	34	44
FK Velež	30	12	2	1	34	8	1	2	12	8	25	13	4	13	42	33	43
FK Sloboda Tuzla	30	12	1	2	20	8	1	2	12	10	26	13	3	14	30	34	42
NK Travnik	30	10	4	1	34	17	1	2	12	6	24	11	6	13	40	41	39
10 FK Rudar Prijedor	30	10	4	1	22	7	1	1	13	5	25	11	5	14	27	32	38
11 FK Leotar	30	9	3	3	23	14	2	2	11	9	34	11	5	14	32	48	38
12 NK Zvijezda	30	9	3	3	29	16	2	1	12	6	31	11	4	15	35	47	37
13 NK Čelik	30	9	2	4	24	13	1	3	11	9	24	10	5	15	33	37	35
14 FK Slavija Sarajevo	30	9.	3	3	23	14	1	2	12	9	32	10	5	15	32	46	35
15 FK Laktaši	30	8	2	5	22	11	2	2	11	16	35	10	4	16	38	46	34
16 FK Modriča	30	5	1	9	15	22	2	2	11	13	35	7	3	20	28	57	24

TOP GOALSCORERS

16 Feđa DUDIĆ (Travnik)
15 Samir BEKRIĆ (Željezničar)
14 Juan Manuel VAREA (Široki Brijeg)
13 Alen ŠKORO (Sarajevo)
   Adin DŽAFIĆ (Velež)
10 Elvir ČOLIĆ (Velež)
   Alen MEŠANOVIĆ (Željezničar)
   Krešimir KORDIĆ (Zrinjski)
9 Duško STAJIĆ (Modriča)
8 Vladimir KARALIĆ (Laktaši)
   Dalibor ŠILIĆ (Široki Brijeg)
   WAGNER (Široki Brijeg)
   Damir SMAJLOVIĆ (Sloboda)
   Lazar POPOVIĆ (Željezničar)
   Mario IVANKOVIĆ (Zrinjski)

CLUB-BY-CLUB

FK BORAC BANJA LUKA
Coach – Velimir Stojnić; (31/12/09) Zoran Marić (SRB)
Founded – 1926
Stadium – Gradski (10,000)
MAJOR HONOURS:
Yugoslav Cup – (1) 1988;
Bosnia-Herzegovina Cup – (1) 2010.

2009
1/8	Laktaši	a	2-0	Vranješ, Ljubojević
8/8	Leotar	h	2-0	Ćorić, Ljubojević
15/8	Čelik	a	1-0	Bilbija
22/8	Široki Brijeg	h	3-2	Bilbija, Maksimović 2 (1p)
29/8	Zvijezda	a	1-1	Bilbija
12/9	Zrinjski	h	3-0	Bilbija 2,Vranješ
19/9	Slavija	a	1-0	Vranješ
26/9	Željezničar	h	2-0	Maksimović, Vranješ
3/10	Prijedor	a	0-1	
17/10	Travnik	a	0-2	
24/10	Sloboda	h	1-0	Kajkut (p)
31/10	Modriča	a	0-1	
7/11	Velež	h	2-0	Vranješ, Kajkut
22/11	Olimpik	a	2-1	og (Suljević), Bilbija
29/11	Sarajevo	h	0-1	

2010
27/2	Laktaši	h	1-0	Jandrić
6/3	Leotar	a	1-2	Ćorić
17/3	Čelik	h	2-1	Vukelja 2
20/3	Široki Brijeg	a	0-0	
28/3	Zvijezda	h	2-0	Stupar, Stevanović
3/4	Zrinjski	a	0-3	
10/4	Slavija	h	3-1	Vukelja 2, og (Tadić)
17/4	Željezničar	a	2-4	og (Bogičević), Kajkut
21/4	Prijedor	h	1-0	Kajkut
25/4	Travnik	h	1-0	Kajkut (p)
30/4	Sloboda	a	0-2	
9/5	Modriča	h	4-0	Stevanović, Jandrić, Kajkut, Petrović
15/5	Velež	a	0-2	
23/5	Olimpik	h	0-2	
26/5	Sarajevo	a	0-3	

No	Name	Nat	DoB	Pos	Aps	(s)	Gls
23	Miloš BABIĆ		10/9/81	D	1	(5)	
10	Nemanja BILBIJA		2/10/90	A	13		6
14	Mladen BOJIĆ		2/10/82	A		(11)	
26	Josip CRNJAC		20/3/92	M		(2)	
5	Leonid ĆORIĆ		30/4/83	D	26		2
19	Nemanja DAMJANOVIĆ		27/9/86	M	12	(4)	
3	Ognjen DAMJANOVIĆ		19/11/87	D		(2)	
17	Siniša GAGULA		3/1/84	D	4	(1)	
11	Srđan GRAHOVAC		19/10/92	M	3	(6)	
7	Dario GRUJIĆ		24/9/89	M		(1)	
21	Oliver JANDRIĆ		21/12/74	M	27	(1)	2
9	Saša KAJKUT		7/7/84	M	25	(2)	6
12	Marko KNEŽEVIĆ	SRB	29/3/89	G	2		
2	Petar KUNIĆ		15/7/93	A		(1)	
14	Darko LJUBOJEVIĆ		8/1/75	M	8		2
15	Marko MAKSIMOVIĆ		13/8/84	M	12		3
26	Toni MARKIĆ		25/10/90	M	8	(1)	
16	Marko MAZALICA		14/8/87	D		(5)	
25	Miloš MILINOVIĆ	SRB	12/7/84	G	9		
27	Ozren PERIĆ		4/4/87	A		(3)	
4	Bojan PETRIĆ		29/11/84	D	15	(7)	
13	Aleksandar PETROVIĆ		8/6/89	M	5	(6)	1
7	Bojan PUZIGAĆA		10/5/85	M	9	(2)	
18	Duško SAKAN		3/3/89	M	14	(4)	
28	Perica STANCESKI	MKD	29/1/85	D	12	(4)	
23	Sreten STANIĆ	SRB	15/2/84	M	3	(3)	
24	Dragan STARČEVIČ	SRB	1/7/77	G	15		
24	Miroslav STEVANOVIĆ		29/7/90	A	15		2
27	Srđan STOJNIĆ		27/10/91	D		(1)	
6	Milan STUPAR	SRB	9/1/80	D	23	(1)	1
1	Marko SUŠAC		23/10/88	G	4	(1)	
26	Vule TRIVUNOVIĆ		13/3/83	D	11	(1)	
29	Stojan VRANJEŠ		11/10/86	M	14		5
20	Ljubiša VUKELJA	SRB	22/7/83	A	12		4
20	Dragomir VUKOBRATOVIĆ	SRB	12/5/88	M	8	(1)	
22	Draško ŽARIĆ		9/10/78	D	20	(1)	

BOSNIA-HERZEGOVINA

NK ČELIK

Coach – Ivo Ištuk; (25/8/09) Omer Kopić
Founded – 1945
Stadium – Bilino Polje (15,000)
MAJOR HONOURS:
Bosnia-Herzegovina League – (3) 1994, 1996, 1997;
Bosnia-Herzegovina Cup – (2) 1995, 1996.

2009				
1/8	Željezničar	h	0-1	
8/8	Prijedor	a	1-1	Isaković
15/8	Borac	h	0-1	
22/8	Sloboda	a	1-2	Vidović (p)
29/8	Modriča	h	1-0	Vidović
12/9	Velež	a	0-0	
19/9	Olimpik	h	1-2	Sánchez
26/9	Sarajevo	a	1-3	Vidović
3/10	Laktaši	h	2-1	Vidović, Šabić
17/10	Leotar	a	1-2	Sánchez
24/10	Travnik	h	2-1	Vidović, Nikić
31/10	Široki Brijeg	h	0-0	
7/11	Zvijezda	a	0-1	
21/11	Zrinjski	h	4-1	Puzigaća, Sánchez, Nikić, Šišić
29/11	Slavija	a	0-1	
2010				
27/2	Željezničar	a	1-4	Purić
6/3	Prijedor	h	3-0	Kapetan (p), Duro, Obuća
17/3	Borac	a	1-2	Obuća
20/3	Sloboda	h	2-1	Obuća, Jamak
27/4	Modriča	a	1-0	Purić
3/4	Velež	h	2-1	Obuća, Dilaver
11/4	Olimpik	a	0-0	
17/4	Sarajevo	h	0-0	
21/4	Laktaši	a	0-2	
24/4	Leotar	h	0-1	
30/4	Travnik	a	1-2	Duro
9/5	Široki Brijeg	a	1-2	Nikić
15/5	Zvijezda	h	4-2	Purić 3, Dilaver
23/5	Zrinjski	a	0-2	
26/5	Slavija	h	3-1	Kapetan 2, Purić

No	Name	Nat	DoB	Pos	Aps	(s)	Gls
12	Luka BILOBRK		8/12/85	G	30		
15	Zoran DEKET		12/11/85	M	7		
19	Haris DILAVER		6/2/90	M	7	(13)	2
6	Samir DURO		18/10/77	M	12		2
4	Almir HASANOVIĆ		6/11/81	D	15		
13	Kenan HORIĆ		13/9/90	M	3	(2)	
13	Armin IMAMOVIĆ		19/8/83	M	12	(1)	
18	Aladin ISAKOVIĆ		28/7/85	M	15	(9)	1
10	Nermin JAMAK		25/8/86	M	21	(5)	1
3	Goran JURIĆ		22/8/83	D	20	(3)	
17	Armin KAPETAN		11/3/86	A	19	(5)	3
20	Mahir KARIĆ		14/12/86	M	7	(2)	
15	Dženan KRAJIŠNIK		6/8/81	D	2	(3)	
22	Bojan MARKOVIĆ		12/11/85	M	21	(1)	
16	Kenan NEMELJAKOVIĆ		1/6/83	M	16	(5)	
11	Branislav NIKIĆ		15/8/83	M	14	(7)	3
9	Emir OBUĆA		11/12/78	A	13		4
8	Dario PURIĆ		18/5/86	M	14		6
7	Bojan PUZIGAĆA		10/5/85	M	15		1
14	Anto RADIĆ		21/11/86	D	1	(1)	
4	Danijel RIZVANOVIĆ		10/3/90	D	3	(1)	
21	Elvis SADIKOVIĆ		29/10/83	D	13	(1)	
8	Muamer SALIHBAŠIĆ		3/12/84	M	1	(2)	
21	Phil Jackson Ibarguen SÁNCHEZ	COL	2/2/85	M	12		3
20	Jasmin SMRIKO		20/1/91	A	1	(4)	
6	Ilija STOJANOV	MKD	21/7/78	D	5		
20	Kenan STUPAR		12/4/89	M		(1)	
10	Nermin ŠABIĆ		21/12/73	M	4		1
20	Aldin ŠIŠIĆ		3/12/84	M		(4)	1
9	Rajko VIDOVIĆ		4/3/75	A	14		5
5	Adnan ZAHIROVIĆ		23/3/90	D	13	(3)	

FK LAKTAŠI

Coach – Milan Milanović; (31/10/09) Miodrag Petković;
(31/12/09) Dragoslav Stjepanović (SRB)
Founded – 1974
Stadium – Gradski (2,500)

2009				
1/8	Borac	h	0-2	
8/8	Sloboda	a	4-2	Karalić 3, Mikić
15/8	Modriča	h	1-1	Karalić
22/8	Velež	a	1-4	Karalić
29/8	Olimpik	h	4-0	Petković 2, Stanojević, Karalić
12/9	Sarajevo	a	1-3	Karalić
19/9	Travnik	h	0-0	
26/9	Leotar	h	0-1	
3/10	Čelik	a	1-2	Petković
17/10	Široki Brijeg	h	1-2	Petković
24/10	Zvijezda	a	1-4	Petković
31/10	Zrinjski	h	0-1	
8/11	Slavija	a	1-3	Karalić
21/11	Željezničar	h	0-1	
29/11	Prijedor	a	0-2	
2010				
27/2	Borac	a	0-1	
6/3	Sloboda	h	2-0	Mikić, Novaković
17/3	Modriča	a	2-0	og (Alić), Mikić (p)
20/3	Velež	h	3-1	Cvetković, Novaković 2 (1p)
28/3	Olimpik	a	0-0	
3/4	Sarajevo	h	2-1	Mikić, Zečević
10/4	Travnik	a	2-2	Tosunović 2
17/4	Leotar	a	1-3	Đelmić
21/4	Čelik	h	2-0	Grujić (p), Popović
25/4	Široki Brijeg	a	0-3	
2/5	Zvijezda	h	1-0	Mikić
9/5	Zrinjski	a	1-2	Vranešević
15/5	Slavija	h	4-1	Mikić, Memišević, Popović, Grujić
23/5	Željezničar	a	1-4	Karalić
26/5	Prijedor	h	2-0	Novaković, Ljubojević

No	Name	Nat	DoB	Pos	Aps	(s)	Gls
15	Miljan BAJIĆ		16/9/82	D	24		
12	Božidar BAŠA		12/8/87	G	4	(1)	
16	Marko CVETKOVIĆ	MKD	13/2/87	D	4		1
2	Sari DENIZ	TUR	29/7/85	D		(1)	
14	Ljubiša DRLJAČA		8/10/79	D	11		
7	Ognjen ĐELMIĆ		18/8/88	M	12	(13)	1
8	Vladan GRUJIĆ		17/5/81	M	14		2
4	Nikola ILIĆ		9/4/84	M	9	(1)	
11	Jovica JOKIĆ	SRB	6/5/84	D	5	(3)	
23	Stefan KARADŽIĆ	SRB	8/5/83	D	1	(3)	
21	Vladimir KARALIĆ		17/1/78	A	15		8
19	Vladan KUJUNDŽIĆ		26/10/82	A	3	(4)	1
17	Darko LJUBOJEVIĆ	SRB	8/1/75	M	9	(1)	1
25	Njegoš MATIĆ		8/5/83	M		(6)	
16	Zlatko MATIĆ		4/11/84	M		(6)	
18	Damir MEMIŠEVIĆ		30/1/84	M	5	(7)	1
17	Borislav MIKIĆ		20/12/75	A	22		6
8	Igor MIRKOVIĆ		24/6/85	M	6	(12)	
1	Siniša MRKOBRADA		17/1/78	G	3		
5	Aleksandar NJEGOMIROVIĆ		7/7/81	D	12		
11	Zoran NOVAKOVIĆ		4/1/76	A	7	(4)	4
13	Branko OJDANIĆ		21/6/90	D	1	(2)	
3	Miša PETKOVIĆ	SRB	16/10/83	M	15		5
3	Goran POPOVIĆ		28/4/89	D	11	(3)	2
6	Darko RACA		21/5/77	D	12		
3	Dušan RADOJEVIĆ	SRB	14/3/83	G	4		
10	Aleksandar RADULOVIĆ		9/2/87	M		(6)	
2	Boris SAVIĆ		16/1/88	D	9		
20	Željko SEKULIĆ		6/9/76	M	15		
18	Marko STANOJEVIĆ	SRB	22/6/88	A	15		1
7	Nemanja STJEPANOVIĆ		7/2/84	M	13	(2)	

5	Zdravko ŠARABA		15/5/80	D	14		
1	Bojan ŠEJIĆ	SRB	14/7/83	G	11		
3	Nenad TANASIJEVIĆ	SRB	24/1/78	D	12	(1)	
16	Damir TOSUNOVIĆ		5/11/85	A	5	(4)	2
14	Duško VRANEŠEVIĆ		10/11/80	A	5	(4)	1
12	Nikola VUKLIŠ		24/9/87	G	8		
4	Saša ZEČEVIĆ	SRB	20/11/83	M	14		1

FK LEOTAR

Coach – Srđan Bajić; (30/8/09) Borče Sredojević; (31/12/09) Goran Skakić
Founded – 1925
Stadium – Police (9,000)
MAJOR HONOURS:
Bosnia-Herzegovina League – (1) 2003.

2009

1/8	Prijedor	h	1-0	*Jair*
8/8	Borac	a	0-2	
15/8	Sloboda	h	1-0	*Zečević N.*
22/8	Modriča	a	1-2	*Vico (p)*
29/8	Velež	h	0-1	
13/9	Olimpik	h	0-1	
19/9	Sarajevo	h	1-0	*Zečević N.*
26/9	Laktaši	a	1-0	*Vico*
3/10	Travnik	h	2-0	*Zečević N., Ramić*
17/10	Čelik	h	2-1	*Ristić 2*
25/10	Široki Brijeg	a	1-4	*Magazin*
31/10	Zvijezda	h	1-1	*Rašević*
8/11	Zrinjski	a	0-3	
21/11	Slavija	h	2-1	*Zečević N., Čorlija (p)*
29/11	Željezničar	a	1-3	*Vico (p)*

2010

27/2	Prijedor	a	0-0	
7/3	Borac	h	2-1	*Vico (p), Ristić*
17/3	Sloboda	a	0-1	
20/3	Modriča	h	3-1	*Ristić, Šešlija, Magazin*
27/3	Velež	a	2-6	*Ramić, Magazin (p)*
3/4	Olimpik	h	0-0	
10/4	Sarajevo	a	0-3	
17/4	Laktaši	h	3-1	*Krunić, Todorović 2*
21/4	Travnik	a	2-2	*Ristić, Andrić*
24/4	Čelik	a	1-0	*Zečević L.*
1/5	Široki Brijeg	h	0-1	
8/5	Zvijezda	a	0-5	
15/5	Zrinjski	h	2-3	*Ristić, Magazin*
23/5	Slavija	a	0-2	
26/5	Željezničar	h	3-3	*Krunić, Vučinić 2*

No	Name	Nat	DoB	Pos	Aps	(s)	Gls
4	Srđan ANDRIĆ		19/9/85	M	10	(4)	1
1	Novica BERAK		29/4/86	G	28		
10	Rade BOŠKOVIĆ		18/4/84	M		(4)	
5	Gojko CIMIROT	MNE	12/12/76	M		(1)	
3	Milorad CIMIROT		27/7/90	D	12	(1)	
18	Gavrilo ČORLIJA		29/10/79	M	24	(1)	1
6	Rajko ĆERANIĆ		7/2/73	M	17	(1)	
6	Oleg ĆURIĆ		28/2/78	D	3		
3	Darko DREČ		14/1/80	D	3	(5)	
9	JAIR Júnior Souto	BRA	26/2/87	M	2	(11)	1
2	Rajko KOMNENIĆ		15/7/84	D	20	(6)	
5	Dalibor KREZOVIĆ		15/1/84	D	1		
10	Branislav KRUNIĆ		28/1/79	M	7		2
31	Mladen KUKRIKA		11/1/91	G	2		
2	Božidar LALIĆ		31/10/92	M	2		
10	Zvjezdan LAZIĆ	SRB	10/7/86	M	6	(5)	
8	Bojan MAGAZIN		12/12/76	M	12	(11)	4
2	Radivoje MARIĆ	MNE	12/3/85	A	1		
8	Miljan MIJANOVIĆ		15/6/91	M	2		

5	Semjon MILOŠEVIĆ		21/10/79	D	9		
6	Nemanja MULINA		3/12/92	M	2		
16	Aleksandar MUMALO		7/1/92	M		(1)	
19	Radoš PROTIĆ	SRB	31/1/87	D	5	(2)	
11	Marko SPAIĆ		16/2/92	D	2		
4	Dragan SREDANOVIĆ		19/3/92	M		(1)	
14	Đorđe SULAVER		24/4/91	D	2		
5	Željko RADOVIĆ		12/12/76	D	10	(3)	
15	Anel RAMIĆ		5/4/87	M	20	(1)	2
7	Dejan RAŠEVIĆ		25/11/83	M	25	(2)	1
2	Dragan RISTIĆ		27/2/82	D	19	(5)	6
2	Marko ROGAN		11/5/91	M		(1)	
9	Branko ŠEŠLIJA		26/1/87	A	6	(7)	1
19	Vladimir TODOROVIĆ		8/12/86	D	14	(2)	2
14	Aleksandar TRNINIĆ	SRB	27/3/87	D	14		
11	Jovica VICO		27/2/78	A	18	(1)	4
17	Bojan VUČINIĆ		29/2/80	M	14	(1)	2
17	Jovan VUJOVIĆ		17/5/92	D	2		
4	Lazar ZEČEVIĆ		10/11/91	M		(3)	1
16	Nenad ZEČEVIĆ	SRB	7/3/78	A	16	(4)	4

FK MODRIČA

Coach – Zoran Čurguz; (30/9/09) Marko Stojić; (27/3/10) Dragan Savić; (3/5/10) Nikola Nikić
Founded – 1922
Stadium – Dr. Milan Jelić (2,500)
MAJOR HONOURS:
Bosnia-Herzegovina League – (1) 2008;
Bosnia-Herzegovina Cup – (1) 2004.

2009

1/8	Olimpik	a	2-2	*Vasiljević, Stajić*
9/8	Sarajevo	h	3-0	*Stajić 2 (1p), Kujundžić*
15/8	Laktaši	a	1-1	*Stajić*
22/8	Leotar	h	2-1	*Đorić, Rankić*
29/8	Čelik	a	0-1	
12/9	Široki Brijeg	h	2-4	*Bogičević, Stajić*
19/9	Zvijezda	a	1-0	*Stajić (p)*
26/9	Zrinjski	h	1-2	*Stajić (p)*
4/10	Slavija	a	1-4	*Kujundžić*
17/10	Željezničar	h	2-1	*Rankić, Kujundžić*
24/10	Prijedor	a	0-1	
31/10	Borac	h	1-0	*Stokić*
7/11	Sloboda	a	2-1	*Bogičević, Stajić*
21/11	Travnik	a	5-6	*Stokić 2, Rankić 2, Kujundžić*
29/11	Velež	h	1-1	*Stajić*

2010

27/2	Olimpik	h	0-1	
6/3	Sarajevo	a	0-2	
17/3	Laktaši	h	0-2	
20/3	Leotar	a	1-3	*Stokić*
27/3	Čelik	h	0-1	
3/4	Široki Brijeg	a	0-2	
10/4	Zvijezda	h	0-1	
17/4	Zrinjski	a	0-4	
21/4	Slavija	h	2-0	*Savkić, Simić*
24/4	Željezničar	a	0-3	
1/5	Prijedor	h	1-2	*Savkić*
9/5	Borac	a	0-4	
15/5	Sloboda	h	0-4	
23/5	Travnik	h	0-2	
26/5	Velež	a	0-1	

No	Name	Nat	DoB	Pos	Aps	(s)	Gls
24	Predrag ALIĆ	CRO	28/2/87	A	19	(1)	
9	Fatmir BAJRAMOVIĆ		18/1/83	M	7	(4)	
15	Jadranko BOGIČEVIĆ		11/3/83	D	12		2
9	Mladen BOJIĆ		2/10/82	A		(1)	
18	Nikola CEKINOVIĆ	CRO	11/11/83	M	3		
23	Dragan ĐAKOVIĆ		21/8/90	M	13	(3)	

BOSNIA-HERZEGOVINA

3	Zlatko ĐORIĆ	SRB	7/9/86	D	10	(2)	1
22	Ranko GALEŠIĆ		21/1/89	M	14		
7	Goran GAVRIĆ		13/5/86	M	7	(4)	
26	Igor JOKSIMOVIĆ		16/8/90	A	7		
8	Nedeljko JOKSIMOVIĆ		5/7/87	D	2	(1)	
5	Dragan JOLOVIĆ	SRB	30/3/76	D	25		
13	Jovo KOJIĆ		8/4/88	A	8	(1)	
11	Vladanko KOMLENOVIĆ	SRB	15/12/88	M	9	(1)	
11	Vladimir KUJUNDŽIĆ		26/10/82	M	12	(1)	4
26	Miloš KULJANIN		21/3/88	D		(1)	
3	Nenad KUTLAČIĆ		4/3/81	D	11		
6	Perica MAKSIMOVIĆ		2/12/92	M		(5)	
21	Nemanja MARINKOVIĆ		14/8/91	M		(2)	
11	Petar MATOVIĆ	SRB	17/5/83	M	8		
16	Vladimir MILJKOVIĆ	SRB	1/7/84	M	4	(8)	
12	Milan NIKIĆ		16/6/86	G	6	(1)	
14	Bojan PUPČEVIĆ		23/2/81	M	10	(7)	
16	Dragan RADIĆ		13/6/92	M	1	(9)	
6	Ognjen RADULOVIĆ		27/1/91	D	11	(3)	
10	Vladmir RANKIĆ		11/8/80	M	13		4
29	Đorđe SAVIĆ		9/12/82	M	17	(3)	
17	Spasoje SAVKIĆ		30/5/90	M	5	(14)	2
19	Jovan SIMIĆ		20/4/89	A	8	(2)	1
13	Duško STAJIĆ		11/7/82	A	15		9
4	Nemanja STJEPANOVIĆ		7/2/84	D	9		
16	Zvezdan STOILJKOV	SRB	4/6/83	A	1	(3)	
14	Joco STOKIĆ		7/4/87	M	14	(5)	4
7	Darjan TODOROVIĆ		26/9/87	M	9		
8	Stojan TOMIĆ		26/6/86	M	8	(4)	
1	Bojan TRIPIĆ		29/11/81	G	24		
21	Nikola VASILJEVIĆ		19/12/83	D	6		1
2	Jovan VUJANIĆ		9/1/92	M	2	(2)	

No	Name	Nat	DoB	Pos	Aps	(s)	Gls
12	Adi ADILOVIĆ		20/2/81	G	7		
11	Sabit ALIMANOVIĆ		21/7/87	A	15		5
21	Adis ĆULOV		18/7/87	A	5		
1	Irfan FEJZIĆ		1/7/86	G	11		
6	Stefan GAVARIĆ	SRB	19/7/81	M	10		
6	Adis HADŽANOVIĆ		3/1/93	D	3	(3)	
10	Adis HASAČIĆ		11/3/87	A		(2)	
13	Admir MAKIĆ		27/7/87	M	1		
4	Vedran JEŠE	CRO	3/2/81	M	20		1
8	Miloš JOKIĆ		7/6/87	M	11	(1)	
17	Semir KAPIĆ		28/6/86	M	11	(2)	2
2	Farik KEČO		3/6/85	D	1	(1)	
5	Nikola KOLAROV	SRB	14/3/83	D	27		
15	Muamer KURTO		15/4/80	A	6	(13)	2
14	Armin LULIĆ		2/7/79	D	2	(7)	
11	Mirko MARINKOVIĆ		7/6/87	A	4	(5)	
8	Muhamed MUJIĆ		26/1/91	M	6	(5)	1
20	Kliment NASTOVSKI		20/4/87	M	2	(3)	
7	Šaban PEHILJ		23/9/92	A	1	(6)	
7	Albin PELAK		1/1/81	M	13		1
16	Bruno PRLIĆ		11/3/83	D	13	(8)	1
18	Zoran RAJOVIĆ	CRO	28/10/79	M	8		2
20	Mladen RISTIĆ	SRB	30/3/82	M	11	(2)	2
3	Salem SALKIĆ		11/6/88	M	3	(3)	
2	Aleksandar SIMČEVIĆ	SRB	15/2/87	D	6	(1)	
17	Nermin SPAHOVIĆ		16/5/91	M		(1)	
9	Darko SPALEVIĆ	SRB	24/3/77	A	13		5
3	Mehmed SUBAŠIĆ		19/3/88	D	24	(3)	
22	Nihad SULJEVIĆ		5/11/80	D	26	(1)	
2	Smail ŠADIĆ		4/12/91	M		(6)	
9	Edin ŠARANOVIĆ		8/3/76	A	12		2
10	THIAGO de Andrade Lopes "CARIOCA"	BRA	8/2/88	M	7	(2)	2
22	Azur VELAGIĆ		20/10/91	M	20	(3)	
10	Miloš VIDOVIĆ	SRB	3/10/89	M	19		4
1	Dragan VRANIĆ	SRB	2/7/79	G	12		

FK OLIMPIK SARAJEVO

Coach – Husref Musemić; (20/8/09) Faik Kolar; (5/9/09) Vlatko Glavaš; (10/11/09) Edin Prljača
Founded – 1993
Stadium – Otoka (3,500)

2009

1/8	Modriča	h	2-2	Kurto, Spalević
8/8	Velež	a	1-4	Spalević
16/8	Travnik	h	1-0	Spalević
29/8	Laktaši	a	0-4	
13/9	Leotar	h	1-0	Vidović
19/9	Čelik	a	2-1	Ristić, Vidović
27/9	Široki Brijeg	h	0-1	
3/10	Zvijezda	a	4-3	Spalević, Rajović, Pelak, Ješe
13/10	Sarajevo	h	1-1	Spalević (p)
18/10	Zrinjski	h	1-0	Rajović (p)
25/10	Slavija	a	0-0	
1/11	Željezničar	h	0-2	
7/11	Prijedor	a	1-3	Kurto
22/11	Borac	h	1-2	Ristić
29/11	Sloboda	a	0-0	
2010				
27/2	Modriča	a	1-0	Vidović
6/3	Velež	h	1-0	Alimanović
17/3	Travnik	a	0-1	
20/3	Sarajevo	a	1-2	Šaranović
28/3	Laktaši	h	0-0	
3/4	Leotar	a	0-0	
11/4	Čelik	h	0-0	
18/4	Široki Brijeg	a	2-2	Kapić, Šaranović
22/4	Zvijezda	h	1-0	Prlić
25/4	Zrinjski	a	0-3	
2/5	Slavija	h	3-0	Alimanović 2, Vidović
9/5	Željezničar	a	0-2	
15/5	Prijedor	h	3-1	Alimanović 2, Mujić
23/5	Borac	a	2-0	Thiago Carioca, Kapić
26/5	Sloboda	h	1-0	Thiago Carioca

FK RUDAR PRIJEDOR

Coach – Darko Nestorović; (18/3/10) Boris Gavran
Founded – 1928
Stadium – Gradski stadion (5,000)

2009

1/8	Leotar	a	0-1	
8/8	Čelik	h	1-1	Kušljić
15/8	Široki Brijeg	a	0-1	
22/8	Zvijezda	h	3-0	Kušljić, Kovačević, Stijepić
30/8	Zrinjski	a	1-3	Stakić
12/9	Slavija	h	1-0	Kušljić
19/9	Željezničar	a	1-1	Golić
26/9	Travnik	a	0-1	
2/10	Borac	h	1-0	Dašić
17/10	Sloboda	a	0-1	
24/10	Modriča	h	1-0	Kušljić
1/11	Velež	a	0-1	
7/11	Olimpik	h	3-1	Žerić, Dašić, Stijepić
21/11	Sarajevo	a	0-3	
29/11	Laktaši	h	2-0	Kantar, Kušljić
2010				
27/2	Leotar	h	0-0	
7/3	Čelik	a	0-3	
17/3	Široki Brijeg	h	1-1	Kušljić
20/3	Zvijezda	a	0-1	
27/3	Zrinjski	h	2-0	Dašić, Stakić
3/4	Slavija	a	0-2	
10/4	Željezničar	h	0-2	
17/4	Travnik	h	2-0	Rankić, Žerić (p)
21/4	Borac	a	0-1	
24/4	Sloboda	h	1-0	Džafić

1/5	Modriča	a	2-1	Žerić, Dašić	
8/5	Velež	h	2-0	Džafić 2	
15/5	Olimpik	a	1-3	Džafić	
23/5	Sarajevo	h	2-2	Žerić, Džafić	
26/5	Laktaši	a	0-2		

9/5	Slavija	a	4-0	Škoro Al., Džakmić, Torlak, Handžić K.	
15/5	Željezničar	h	0-0		
23/5	Prijedor	a	2-2	Dudo, Jahovic	
26/5	Borac	h	3-0	Jahovic 2, Handžić H.	

No	Name	Nat	DoB	Pos	Aps	(s)	Gls
1	Asmir AVDUKIĆ		13/5/81	G	29		
13	Ognjen DAŠIĆ		7/2/78	D	18	(3)	4
2	Budimir DESPOTOVIĆ		22/2/85	D	8	(4)	
3	Slobodan DOBRIJEVIĆ		18/11/81	D	8	(6)	
15	Ljubiša DRLJAČA		6/1/79	D	8	(3)	
7	Mirza DŽAFIĆ		30/3/81	A	7	(2)	5
10	Igor GOLIĆ		4/2/85	M	11	(8)	1
5	Marko JEVTIĆ	SRB	21/5/82	D	19	(1)	
10	Momčilo KANTAR		31/3/85	M	24	(2)	1
11	Bojan KECMAN		23/1/83	M	6	(8)	
13	Aleksandar KIKIĆ		12/12/81	M	21	(3)	
16	Marko KOLUNDŽIJA		23/9/88	M		(3)	
	Milan KONDIĆ		12/3/84	G	1		
16	Goran KOTARAN		11/1/79	M	23	(1)	
6	Saša KOVAČEVIĆ		4/3/83	D	26		1
14	Goran KUŠLJIĆ		28/7/84	A	16	(3)	6
15	Boris MUZGONJA		27/8/84	M	12	(4)	
18	Nedeljko RADIVOJAC		16/6/91	D		(3)	
13	Vladimir RANKIĆ		11/8/80	M	6	(3)	1
4	Dragoslav STAKIĆ		20/9/85	D	26		2
9	Saša STJEPIĆ		11/7/83	A	15		2
2	Nebojša ŠODIĆ		15/7/85	D	17	(2)	
8	Nedžad ŽERIĆ		26/8/72	M	29		4

No	Name	Nat	DoB	Pos	Aps	(s)	Gls
22	Muhamed ALAIM		10/2/81	G	29		
9	Alen AVDIĆ		3/4/77	A	20	(2)	5
21	Zoran BELOŠEVIĆ	SRB	20/6/83	D	30		1
2	Jasmin ČAMPARA		8/5/90	M	1	(8)	
4	Fadil ČIZMIĆ		10/7/91	D		(1)	
17	Denis ČOMOR		3/1/90	M	6	(8)	
5	Edin DUDO		30/4/81	D	23	(1)	3
14	Muhamed DŽAKMIĆ		23/8/85	M	23		2
3	Adi Amar FOČIĆ		2/8/92	M		(1)	
11	Damir HADŽIĆ		2/10/78	M	19	(6)	2
16	Đenaldin HAMZAGIĆ		28/4/86	A	14	(6)	
12	Dino HAMZIĆ		22/1/88	G	1		
77	Haris HANDŽIĆ		20/6/90	A	3	(9)	1
13	Kemal HANDŽIĆ		23/1/91	M	2		1
7	Faruk IHTIJAREVIĆ		1/5/76	M	16	(3)	4
18	Adis JAHOVIC	MKD	18/3/87	A	11	(12)	5
33	Emir JANJOŠ		28/3/86	M	3	(4)	
2	Amar KADIĆ		6/8/90	D		(1)	
19	Ajdin MAKSUMIĆ		24/7/85	M	21		1
8	Milan MUMINOVIĆ		2/10/81	M	23		1
23	Almir PLISKA		12/8/87	A	8	(14)	
20	Mirza RIZVANOVIĆ		27/9/86	D	27		2
15	Nail ŠEHOVIĆ		18/1/90	M	1	(3)	
	Edin ŠEKO		12/2/92	A		(1)	
10	Alen ŠKORO		30/3/81	A	17	(3)	13
3	Anel ŠKORO		27/6/87	D	9	(4)	
6	Sedin TORLAK		12/1/85	D	23	(2)	1

FK SARAJEVO

Coach – Mehmed Janjoš; (28/3/10) Almir Turković;
(7/4/10) Mirza Varešanović
Founded – 1946
Stadium – Olimpijski Asim Ferhatović Hase (34,630)
MAJOR HONOURS:
Yugoslav League – (2) 1967, 1985;
Bosnia-Herzegovina League – (1) 2007;
Bosnia-Herzegovina Cup – (4) 1997, 1998, 2002, 2005.

2009

2/8	Sloboda	h	1-1	Hadžić
9/8	Modriča	a	0-3	
15/8	Velež	h	1-1	Ihtijarević
31/8	Travnik	h	2-1	Muminović, Maksumić
12/9	Laktaši	h	3-1	Ihtijarević, Jahovic, Škoro Al.
19/9	Leotar	a	0-1	
26/9	Čelik	h	3-1	Škoro Al. 3 (1p)
13/10	Olimpik	a	1-1	Dudo
17/10	Zvijezda	h	1-0	Avdić
25/10	Zrinjski	a	1-1	Avdić
31/10	Slavija	h	2-0	Škoro Al. 2
4/11	Široki Brijeg	a	0-2	
7/11	Željezničar	a	2-1	Škoro Al. (p), Jahovic
21/11	Prijedor	h	3-0	Škoro Al. 2 (1p), Rizvanović
29/11	Borac	a	1-0	Džakmić

2010

6/3	Modriča	h	2-0	Avdić, Rizvanović (p)
17/3	Velež	a	0-1	
20/3	Olimpik	h	2-1	Belošević, Ihtijarević
24/3	Sloboda	a	0-1	
27/3	Travnik	a	0-1	
3/4	Laktaši	a	1-2	Hadžić
10/4	Leotar	h	3-0	Škoro Al. 2, Avdić
17/4	Čelik	a	0-0	
21/4	Široki Brijeg	h	1-1	Ihtijarević
25/4	Zvijezda	a	1-2	Škoro Al.
1/5	Zrinjski	h	3-0	Avdić, Dudo, og (Ivanković)

NK ŠIROKI BRIJEG

Coach – Ivan Katalinić (CRO); (24/8/09) Toni Karačić
Founded – 1948
Stadium – Pecara (7,000)
MAJOR HONOURS:
Bosnia-Herzegovina League – (2) 2004, 2006;
Bosnia-Herzegovina Cup – (1) 2007.

2009

9/8	Željezničar	a	0-1	
15/8	Prijedor	h	1-0	Wagner
22/9	Borac	a	2-3	Šilić, Wagner
26/8	Slavija	h	0-0	
30/8	Sloboda	h	2-0	Wagner, Varea
12/9	Modriča	a	4-2	Varea, Ivanković, Šilić, Glavina
19/9	Velež	h	2-0	Varea, Mišić
27/9	Olimpik	a	1-0	Ivanković
17/10	Laktaši	a	2-1	Šilić, Mišić
25/10	Leotar	h	4-1	Varea, Mišić, Wagner 2
31/10	Čelik	a	0-0	
4/11	Sarajevo	h	2-0	Mišić, Wagner
8/11	Travnik	h	1-0	Varea
21/11	Zvijezda	h	5-0	Mišić 2, Ivanković, Varea, Šilić (p)
29/11	Zrinjski	a	1-4	Martinović

2010

28/2	Slavija	a	2-3	Wagner (p), Varea
7/3	Željezničar	h	0-2	
17/3	Prijedor	h	1-1	Karoglan
20/3	Borac	h	0-0	
28/3	Sloboda	a	0-1	
3/4	Modriča	h	2-0	Šilić, Varea
10/4	Velež	a	0-1	
18/4	Olimpik	h	2-2	Šilić, Ćutuk
21/4	Sarajevo	a	1-1	Wagner

25/4	Laktaši	h	3-0	*Šilić (p), Varea, Mišić*
1/5	Leotar	a	1-0	*Varea*
9/5	Čelik	h	2-1	*Varea 2*
15/5	Travnik	a	2-1	*Ivanković 2*
23/5	Zvijezda	a	1-1	*Varea*
26/5	Zrinjski	h	2-1	*Šilić, Varea*

No	Name	Nat	DoB	Pos	Aps	(s)	Gls
1	Dejan BANDOVIĆ		11/6/83	G	28		
6	Josip BARIŠIĆ		12/8/83	D	28		
16	Dino ĆORIĆ		30/6/90	M	1	(2)	
7	Josip ĆUTUK		4/5/84	M	22	(1)	1
13	DIOGO Souza dos Anjos	BRA	9/7/86	D	24		
24	Jure GLAVINA		4/1/89	M		(10)	1
11	Mirko HRGOVIĆ		5/2/79	M	13		
25	Vlado HRKAČ		31/8/82	D	2	(3)	
18	Jure IVANKOVIĆ		15/11/85	M	26	(1)	5
7	Mislav KAROGLAN		14/4/82	M	3	(7)	1
4	Danijel KOŽUL		1/8/84	M	5		
4	Mladen KRIŽANOVIĆ	CRO	24/9/77	D	5	(4)	
7	Mario LJUBIĆ		5/3/85	M	1		
12	Nikola MARIĆ		29/8/79	G	2		
2	Toni MARKIĆ		25/10/90	M	10		
5	Gonzalo Darío MARTÍNEZ	ARG	1/5/83	M	2	(3)	
21	Dejan MARTINOVIĆ		19/7/83	A	15	(8)	1
20	Hrvoje MIŠIĆ	CRO	17/8/87	A	18	(10)	7
11	Boško PERAICA		7/12/77	M	4	(6)	
9	Ante PINJUH		9/10/90	A		(3)	
2	Mario PINJUH		3/4/90	M		(9)	
3	RENATO Alves Gomides	BRA	12/5/84	M	13	(3)	
10	Dalibor ŠILIĆ		23/1/79	M	27	(1)	8
16	TIAGO Rodrigues	BRA	17/8/86	M	1	(3)	
8	Josip TOPIĆ		22/10/82	D	21	(1)	
14	Juan Manuel VAREA	ARG	23/3/86	M	29		14
15	WAGNER Santos Lago	BRA	1/1/78	M	29		8
19	Ivan ZOVKO		23/6/86	M		(2)	
22	Ante ZURAK		13/8/84	D	1		

FK SLAVIJA SARAJEVO
Coach – Zoran Erbez; (20/9/09) Milomir Odović; (4/5/10) Dragan Bjelica
Founded – 1908
Stadium – SC Slavija (4,500)
MAJOR HONOURS:
Bosnia-Herzegovina Cup – (1) 2009.

2009

8/8	Zvijezda	h	2-0	*Todorović, Radovanović*
16/8	Zrinjski	a	0-0	
22/8	Travnik	a	0-3	
26/8	Široki Brijeg	a	0-0	
30/8	Željezničar	h	1-1	*Regoje*
12/9	Prijedor	a	0-1	
19/9	Borac	h	0-1	
26/9	Sloboda	a	0-1	
4/10	Modriča	h	4-1	*Šćepanović, Jovanović, Todorović, Šešlija*
17/10	Velež	a	2-4	*Regoje, Radovanović*
25/10	Olimpik	h	6-0	
31/10	Sarajevo	a	0-2	
8/11	Laktaši	h	3-1	*Radovanović, Baković 2 (1p)*
21/11	Leotar	a	1-2	*Baković (p)*
29/11	Čelik	h	1-0	*Stanić*

2010

28/2	Široki Brijeg	h	3-2	*Todorović 2, Spalević (p)*
6/3	Zvijezda	a	3-2	*Spalević 2, Šćepanović*
17/3	Zrinjski	h	0-2	
21/3	Travnik	h	1-1	*Baković*
27/3	Željezničar	a	0-2	
3/4	Prijedor	h	2-0	*Regoje, Milinković*

10/4	Borac	a	1-3	*Spalević*
18/4	Sloboda	h	2-1	*Radovanović, Regoje*
21/4	Modriča	a	0-2	
25/4	Velež	h	2-0	*Jovanović, Oglečevac*
2/5	Olimpik	a	0-3	
9/5	Sarajevo	h	0-4	
15/5	Laktaši	a	1-4	*Pušara*
23/5	Leotar	h	2-0	*Stanković, Regoje*
26/5	Čelik	a	1-3	*Regoje*

No	Name	Nat	DoB	Pos	Aps	(s)	Gls
11	Branislav ARSENIJEVIĆ	SRB	2/8/82	M	14	(4)	
17	Branko BAKOVIĆ	SRB	31/8/81	A	3	(4)	4
6	Vukašin BENOVIĆ		31/7/86	D	18		
1	Ratko DUJKOVIĆ		16/3/73	G	9		
18	Dejan ĐERMANOVIĆ	SVN	17/6/88	A	7	(5)	
27	Vlastimir JOVANOVIĆ		3/4/85	M	18		2
25	Marko KOPRIVICA		6/6/91	M		(2)	
20	Levan KUTALIA	GEO	27/2/86	M	9	(2)	
3	Đorđe LACKANOVIĆ		26/10/88	D	5		
31	Mladen LUČIĆ		6/7/85	G	20	(1)	
2	Milan MILINKOVIĆ		15/1/90	M	5	(10)	1
22	Dragan NIKOLIĆ		15/1/91	A	1	(2)	
14	Veselko NJEGUŠ		20/4/88	D		(3)	
22	Nikola ODOVIĆ		26/5/91	M	3	(7)	
27	Nedim OGLEČEVAC		7/4/91	A	5	(3)	1
7	Predrag PAPAZ		20/1/87	D	19	(1)	
26	Čedomir PAUNOVIĆ	SRB	13/11/83	M	1	(1)	
16	Marko PERIŠIĆ		25/1/91	M	5	(3)	
8	Nemanja PUŠARA		21/8/91	A	1	(9)	1
10	Miljan RADONJA		3/6/84	M	3	(7)	
9	Igor RADOVANOVIĆ		2/8/85	M	14	(8)	4
8	Bojan REGOJE		2/12/81	D	26		6
8	Goran SIMIĆ		6/4/73	D	26	(1)	
9	Darko SPALEVIĆ	SRB	24/3/77	A	13		4
7	Zvjezdan STANIĆ		30/1/86	A	15	(6)	1
21	Ivan STANKOVIĆ		7/7/76	A	23	(2)	1
13	Vučina ŠĆEPANOVIĆ	SRB	17/11/82	M	21		2
16	Nemanja ŠEŠLIJA		30/7/88	M	6	(3)	1
11	Đorđe TADIĆ	SRB	16/2/83	D	13		
15	Ognjen TODOROVIĆ		24/3/89	M	24	(2)	4
23	Stefan TOMOVIĆ		15/1/91	G	1		
19	Sretko VUKSANOVIĆ		15/2/73	M	2	(1)	

FK SLOBODA TUZLA
Coach – Adnan Osmanhodžić; (5/9/09) Nermin Hadžiahmetović; (21/11/09) Adnan Osmanhodžić; (31/12/09) Vlatko Glavaš
Founded – 1919
Stadium – Tušanj (8,000)

2009

2/8	Sarajevo	a	1-1	*Mujić M.*
8/8	Laktaši	h	2-4	*Mujić S., Čehajić*
15/8	Leotar	a	0-1	
22/8	Čelik	h	2-1	*Okanović, Mujić S.*
30/8	Široki Brijeg	a	0-2	
12/9	Zvijezda	h	1-0	*Kuduzović (p)*
19/9	Zrinjski	a	0-2	
26/9	Slavija	h	1-0	*Joksimović*
3/10	Željezničar	a	1-4	*Hasić*
17/10	Prijedor	h	1-0	*Okanović (p)*
24/10	Borac	a	0-1	
31/10	Travnik	a	0-4	
7/11	Modriča	h	1-2	*Bekić Al.*
21/11	Velež	a	0-1	
29/11	Olimpik	h	0-0	

2010

6/3	Laktaši	a	0-2	
17/3	Leotar	h	1-0	*Milošević*
20/3	Čelik	a	1-2	*Mostarlić*

24/3	Sarajevo	h	1-0	Jogunčić	
28/3	Široki Brijeg	h	1-0	Milošević	
3/4	Zvijezda	a	2-2	Mujić S., Jogunčić	
10/4	Zrinjski	h	2-0	Smajlović, Jogunčić	
18/4	Slavija	a	1-2	Smajlović	
21/4	Željezničar	h	1-0	Smajlović	
24/4	Prijedor	a	0-1		
30/4	Borac	h	2-0	Okanović (p), Mostarlić	
8/5	Travnik	h	2-1	Smajlović 2	
15/5	Modriča	a	4-0	Smajlović 2, Okanović, Jogunčić	
23/5	Velež	h	2-0	Smajlović, Mujić S.	
26/5	Olimpik	a	0-1		

No	Name	Nat	DoB	Pos	Aps	(s)	Gls
21	Aleksandar ANĐIĆ		9/9/82	D	2	(1)	
3	Almir BEKIĆ		1/6/89	M	24		1
9	Amer BEKIĆ		5/8/92	M	2	(8)	
20	Emir CEKIĆ	MNE	30/12/84	D	1	(1)	
4	Gradimir CRNOGORAC		14/11/82	D	23	(1)	
17	Admir ČEHAJIĆ		12/8/86	M	3	(3)	1
5	Mirza ČEJVANOVIĆ		23/12/84	D	2	(1)	
12	Tino DIVKOVIĆ		7/2/91	G	3		
9	Samir EFENDIĆ		10/5/91	M	3	(2)	
8	Srefan GAVARIĆ	SRB	19/7/81	M	12		
13	Šerif HASIĆ		7/1/88	D	12		1
3	Maid JAGANJAC		11/6/92	M		(1)	
2	Samir JOGUNČIĆ		19/12/80	D	22	(1)	4
9	Igor JOKSIMOVIĆ	SRB	16/8/80	A	5	(1)	1
11	Marko JURIĆ		27/7/87	A		(3)	
17	Alvin KARADŽA		28/5/84	D	10	(2)	
19	Emir KASAPOVIĆ		21/5/86	M	4	(6)	
16	Ognjen KRASIĆ	SRB	9/4/88	D	19	(3)	
21	Elmir KUDUZOVIĆ		28/2/85	D	7		1
22	Mersed MALKIĆ		19/7/90	M	19	(5)	
23	Damir MEMIŠEVIĆ		22/1/84	D	9	(2)	
11	Jasmin MEŠANOVIĆ		6/1/92	M		(1)	
20	Semjon MILOŠEVIĆ		21/10/79	D	10		2
9	Igor MOSTARLIĆ	CRO	31/3/83	A	7	(3)	2
11	Muhamed MUJIĆ		26/9/91	M	11	(1)	1
18	Senad MUJIĆ		17/9/81	A	15	(4)	4
1	Denis MUJKIĆ		2/9/83	G	27		
15	Nenad NOVAKOVIĆ	SRB	23/3/86	D		(1)	
17	Ilija PRODANOVIĆ		16/10/79	D	9		
10	Tarik OKANOVIĆ		3/6/83	A	20	(3)	4
6	Amir REKIĆ		12/2/83	D	4		
29	Džemal SADIKOVIĆ		30/11/83	D	5	(6)	
9	Adnan SALIHOVIĆ		18/10/92	M		(1)	
8	Adnan SARAJLIĆ		6/1/81	M	5	(4)	
7	Semir SLOMIĆ		14/1/88	A	14	(11)	
11	Damir SMAJLOVIĆ		27/3/83	A	14		8
20	Bojan TRKULJA		20/10/82	D	2		
6	Muamer ZOLETIĆ		20/1/83	M	4	(2)	
13	Mirza ZONIĆ		6/4/91	D		(3)	
18	Adnan ZUKIĆ		29/8/91	M	1		

NK TRAVNIK

Coach – Nedžad Selimović
Founded – 1922
Stadium – Pirota (3,000)

2009

1/8	Velež	a	0-5		
9/8	Zrinjski	h	3-3	Dudić, Sarajčić, Dolić	
16/8	Olimpik	a	0-1		
22/8	Slavija	h	3-0	Dudić 2, Terzić Si.	
31/8	Sarajevo	a	1-2	Pranjković	
12/9	Željezničar	h	0-0		
19/9	Laktaši	a	0-0		
26/9	Prijedor	h	1-0	Bradarić	
3/10	Leotar	a	0-2		

17/10	Borac	h	2-0	Erić, Dudić	
24/10	Čelik	a	1-2	Dolić (p)	
31/10	Sloboda	h	4-0	Dudić 2, Varupa E. (p), Ćurić	
8/11	Široki Brijeg	a	0-1		
21/11	Modriča	h	6-5	Varupa E. (p), Sarajčić, Dudić 2, Ćurić, Šiljak	
29/11	Zvijezda	a	0-1		
2010					
27/2	Velež	h	2-1	Dudić, Ribić	
7/3	Zrinjski	a	0-2		
17/3	Olimpik	h	1-0	Brkić	
21/3	Slavija	a	1-1	og (Papaz)	
27/3	Sarajevo	h	1-0	Dudić	
3/4	Željezničar	a	0-2		
10/4	Laktaši	h	2-2	Šiljak, Dudić	
17/4	Prijedor	a	0-2		
21/4	Leotar	h	2-2	Fajić, Dudić	
25/4	Borac	a	0-1		
30/4	Čelik	h	2-1	Fajić, Ribić	
8/5	Sloboda	a	1-2	Ćurić	
15/5	Široki Brijeg	h	1-2	Dudić	
23/5	Modriča	a	2-0	Erić, Dudić	
26/5	Zvijezda	h	4-1	Dudić 2 (1p), Mujakić, Erić	

No	Name	Nat	DoB	Pos	Aps	(s)	Gls
19	Stjepan BADROV		1/12/87	D	14	(8)	
16	Nedžad BEGIĆ		15/7/87	D	4	(2)	
6	Ekrem BRADARIĆ		12/7/69	D	14		1
17	Arnes BRKIĆ		18/12/78	M	17	(3)	1
11	Anel ĆURIĆ		28/7/88	M	15	(11)	3
1	Alen DELIĆ		25/3/83	G	3	(5)	
10	Velimir DOLIĆ		21/7/81	A	2	(7)	2
13	Feđa DUDIĆ		1/2/83	A	27		16
2	Amir ĐURIĆ		25/2/89	D	1	(1)	
14	Nenad ERIĆ	CRO	30/8/89	M	21	(8)	3
16	Nusmir FAJIĆ		12/1/87	M	14	(4)	2
15	Armin HELVIDA		20/2/86	D	25		
9	Jasmin KOLAŠINAC		14/12/88	M	3	(9)	
7	Adin LIHOVAC		22/8/87	D	3	(7)	
21	Sanid MUJAKIĆ		19/4/88	A	2	(3)	1
12	Adis NURKOVIĆ		28/4/86	G	27		
22	Dario PRANJKOVIĆ		5/2/84	M	21	(3)	1
5	Nihad RIBIĆ		10/11/81	D	16	(3)	2
20	Midhet SARAJČIĆ		16/9/72	M	21	(1)	2
8	Mirsad ŠILJAK		22/2/81	M	22		2
15	Senad TABAKOVIĆ		26/9/91	D		(1)	
11	Sanel TERZIĆ		18/5/91	D		(1)	
2	Sinbad TERZIĆ		22/2/81	D	25	(1)	1
3	Elvedin VARUPA		16/11/75	M	24		2
21	Nermin VARUPA		18/4/91	M	6	(7)	
4	Seldin ZATAGIĆ		11/4/88	M	3	(2)	

FK VELEŽ

Coach – Abdulah Ibraković; (5/5/10) Veselin Đurasović
Founded – 1922
Stadium – Vrapčići (2,500)
MAJOR HONOURS:
Yugoslav Cup – (2) 1981, 1986.

2009

1/8	Travnik	h	5-0	Zaimović 2, Džafić, Velagić, Duraković	
8/8	Olimpik	h	4-2	Ćolić 2, Zaimović, Džafić	
15/8	Sarajevo	a	1-1	Džafić	
22/8	Laktaši	h	4-1	Džafić 2 (1p), Zaimović, Ćolić	
29/8	Leotar	a	1-0	Šećić	
12/9	Čelik	h	0-0		
19/9	Široki Brijeg	a	0-2		
26/9	Zvijezda	h	4-0	Džafić 3, Knežević	
4/10	Zrinjski	a	1-2	Zaimović	

BOSNIA-HERZEGOVINA

17/10	Slavija	h	4-2	Kadić, Majkić 2, Čolić
24/10	Željezničar	a	0-1	
1/11	Prijedor	h	1-0	Čolić
7/11	Borac	a	0-2	
22/11	Sloboda	h	1-0	Džafić (p)
29/11	Modriča	a	1-1	Džafić
2010				
27/2	Travnik	a	1-2	Velagić
7/3	Olimpik	a	0-1	
17/3	Sarajevo	h	1-0	Čolić
20/3	Laktaši	a	1-3	Salihović
27/3	Leotar	h	6-2	Velagić, Džafić 2, Čolić 3
3/4	Čelik	a	1-2	Aličić
10/4	Široki Brijeg	h	1-0	Čolić
17/4	Zvijezda	a	1-2	Osmanagić
21/4	Zrinjski	h	0-0	
25/4	Slavija	a	0-2	
1/5	Željezničar	h	0-2	
8/5	Prijedor	a	0-2	
15/5	Borac	h	2-0	Salihović, Džafić
23/5	Sloboda	a	0-2	
26/5	Modriča	h	1-0	og (Kutlačić)

No	Name	Nat	DoB	Pos	Aps	(s)	Gls
18	Jasmin ALIČIĆ		21/6/87	D	7	(3)	1
22	Sanel BORIĆ		23/7/87	G	6		
2	Elvir ČOLIĆ		17/7/86	M	18	(2)	10
28	Mirza ČEMALOVIĆ		6/7/93	M	3	(10)	
8	Rijad DEMIĆ		17/11/89	M	6	(8)	
83	Dženan DURAKOVIĆ		20/6/90	D	1	(15)	1
77	Adin DŽAFIĆ		21/5/89	A	27		13
1	Emir HADŽUĐULBIĆ		12/4/76	G	24		
19	Adis HALILHODŽIĆ		14/6/86	M		(1)	
14	Armin JAZVIN		11/10/90	M	2	(2)	
14	Marko JOVANOVIĆ	MNE	2/5/82	D	1	(3)	
7	Amer JUGO		15/12/82	M	11	(2)	
16	Nermin KADIĆ		12/5/82	D	21	(3)	1
13	Adnan KADRIĆ		7/4/76	D	1	(3)	
17	Adil KAJAN		20/6/90	D		(1)	
3	Admir KAJTAZ		30/3/78	D	22		
55	Zlatko KAZAZIĆ		10/2/89	M	8	(1)	
69	Milan KNEŽEVIĆ	SRB	6/5/88	M	21		1
11	Mustafa KODRO		29/8/81	M	1	(2)	
7	Amer MAHIMIĆ		2/6/90	D		(1)	
6	Danijel MAJKIĆ		16/12/87	M	28		2
10	Adis OBAD		12/5/71	A		(4)	
9	Amer OSMANAGIĆ		16/12/87	A	27		1
7	Mirnes SALIHOVIĆ		3/2/85	A	5	(7)	2
15	Arnel STUPAC		24/3/82	M		(1)	
23	Edin ŠEČIĆ	SVN	15/12/84	D	11		1
5	Asim ŠKALJIĆ		9/8/88	D	24		
9	Arnel ŠKALJIĆ		9/8/81	M	13	(9)	
11	Admir VELAGIĆ		19/10/75	M	18	(2)	3
4	Dženan ZAIMOVIĆ		25/9/73	D	24		5
21	Amir ZOLJ		24/11/89	D		(4)	

FK ŽELJEZNIČAR
Coach – Amar Osim
Founded – 1921
Stadium – Grbavica (14,000)
MAJOR HONOURS:
Yugoslav League – (1) 1972;
Bosnia-Herzegovina League – (4) 1998, 2001, 2002; 2010;
Bosnia-Herzegovina Cup – (3) 2000, 2001, 2003.

2009				
1/8	Čelik	a	1-0	Mešanović
9/8	Široki Brijeg	h	1-0	Mešanović
15/8	Zvijezda	a	1-2	Bekrić (p)
23/8	Zrinjski	h	1-1	Bekrić (p)

30/8	Slavija	a	1-1	Cocalić
12/9	Travnik	a	0-0	
19/9	Prijedor	h	1-1	Mešanović
26/9	Borac	a	0-2	
3/10	Sloboda	h	4-1	Cocalić, Stanić, Mešanović, Radovanović
17/10	Modriča	a	1-2	Bešlija M.
24/10	Velež	h	1-0	Mešanović
1/11	Olimpik	a	2-0	Mešanović, Bekrić (p)
7/11	Sarajevo	h	1-2	Bekrić
21/11	Laktaši	a	1-0	Popović
29/11	Leotar	h	3-1	Bekrić (p), Mešanović 2
2010				
27/2	Čelik	h	4-1	Mešanović 2, Bučan, Popović
7/3	Široki Brijeg	a	2-0	Kerla, Popović
17/3	Zvijezda	h	2-0	Šimić, Bekrić (p)
21/3	Zrinjski	a	1-1	Bajić
27/3	Slavija	h	2-0	Bekrić (p), Bajić
3/4	Travnik	h	2-0	Bekrić, Višća
10/4	Prijedor	a	2-0	Bešlija M., Bekrić (p)
17/4	Borac	h	4-2	Mešić, Bekrić, Popović 2
21/4	Sloboda	a	0-1	
24/4	Modriča	h	3-0	Popović 2, Bekrić
1/5	Velež	a	2-0	Kerla, Bučan
9/5	Olimpik	h	2-0	Popović, Višća
15/5	Sarajevo	a	0-0	
23/5	Laktaši	h	4-1	Bekrić 2 (1p), Bešlija M., Bešlija H.
26/5	Leotar	a	3-3	Bekrić 2, Svraka

No	Name	Nat	DoB	Pos	Aps	(s)	Gls
5	Delimir BAJIĆ		28/3/83	D	13	(2)	2
10	Samir BEKRIĆ		20/10/84	M	29	(1)	15
14	Haris BEŠLIJA		27/9/86	M	3	(4)	1
20	Mirsad BEŠLIJA		6/7/79	M	21	(1)	3
6	Jadranko BOGIČEVIĆ		11/3/83	G	11	(1)	
21	Sead BUČAN		8/3/81	M	17	(4)	2
6	Edin COCALIĆ		5/12/87	D	8		2
17	Benjamin ČOLIĆ		23/7/91	D	12	(3)	
16	Milan ČULUM	SRB	28/10/84	D	26		
33	Marko FARIĆ	CRO	18/6/90	M	1	(1)	
15	Semir KERLA		26/9/87	D	6		2
18	Slaven KOVAČEVIĆ	MNE	17/6/80	M	1	(5)	
25	Amar MEHIĆ		15/4/89	M	1	(5)	
19	Alen MEŠANOVIĆ		26/10/75	A	16	(1)	10
24	Elvis MEŠIĆ		12/9/80	M	28		1
26	Dino MUHAREMOVIĆ		25/10/85	M	4	(2)	
25	Goran PERAK		1/6/86	M		(3)	
29	Lazar POPOVIĆ	SRB	10/1/83	M	16	(7)	8
22	Božidar RADOŠEVIĆ	SRB	4/4/89	G	1		
3	Mirko RADOVANOVIĆ	SRB	5/4/86	D	27		1
9	Damir ROVČANIN		15/4/89	A	1	(9)	
44	Denis SELIMOVIĆ	SVN	22/08/79	M	8	(2)	
8	Nedžad SERDAREVIĆ		23/7/81	M	6	(6)	
2	Bajro SPAHIĆ		23/4/84	A		(6)	
11	Srđan STANIĆ		6/7/89	A	12	(8)	1
23	Muamer SVRAKA		14/2/88	M	15	(8)	1
12	Ibrahim ŠEHIĆ		2/9/88	G	29		
7	Predrag ŠIMIĆ		28/6/79	M	9	(5)	1
18	Edin VIŠĆA		17/2/90	M	9	(2)	2

HŠK ZRINJSKI
Coach – Dragan Jović
Founded – 1912
Stadium – Bijeli Brijeg (15,000)
MAJOR HONOURS:
Bosnia-Herzegovina League – (2) 2005, 2009;
Bosnia-Herzegovina Cup – (1) 2008.

2009

1/8	Zvijezda	a	0-2	
9/8	Travnik	a	3-3	Ivanković, Žuržinov, Selimović
16/8	Slavija	h	0-0	
23/8	Željezničar	a	1-1	Selimović
30/8	Prijedor	h	3-1	Ivanković (p), Žuržinov, Zadro
12/9	Borac	a	0-3	
19/9	Sloboda	h	2-0	Zadro, Kordić
26/9	Modriča	a	2-1	Ivanković (p), Žuržinov
4/10	Velež	h	2-1	Aničić M., Kordić
18/10	Olimpik	a	0-1	
25/10	Sarajevo	h	1-1	Kordić
31/10	Laktaši	a	1-0	Selimović
8/11	Leotar	h	3-0	Bobby, Zadro, Dragičević
21/11	Čelik	a	1-4	Selimović
29/11	Široki Brijeg	h	4-1	Bobby, Kordić, Afedzie, Dragičević

2010

28/2	Zvijezda	h	0-1	
7/3	Travnik	h	2-0	Ivanković 2 (1p)
17/3	Slavija	a	2-0	Dragičević, Kordić
21/3	Željezničar	h	1-1	Ivanković (p)
27//4	Prijedor	a	0-2	
3/4	Borac	h	3-0	Kordić 3
10/4	Sloboda	a	0-2	
17/4	Modriča	h	4-0	Ivanković (p), Zadro, Dragičević, Selimović
21/4	Velež	a	0-0	
25/4	Olimpik	h	3-0	Ivanković (p), Zadro, Kordić
1/5	Sarajevo	a	0-3	
9/5	Laktaši	h	2-1	Marković, Dragičević
15/5	Leotar	a	3-2	Žižović, Stojanović, Žuržinov
23/5	Čelik	h	2-0	Kordić, Selimović
26/5	Široki Brijeg	a	1-2	Žuržinov

No	Name	Nat	DoB	Pos	Aps	(s)	Gls
5	Stanley AFEDZIE	GHA	30/12/87	M	15	(3)	1
15	Josip ANIČIĆ		23/10/91	D	1	(1)	
27	Marin ANIČIĆ		17/8/89	M	21	(2)	1
20	Prince BOBBY	GHA	7/12/89	M	11	(6)	2
3	Stanko CVITKOVIĆ		1/7/90	D		(2)	
18	Mate DRAGIČEVIĆ	CRO	19/11/79	A	9	(8)	5
1	Adnan HADŽIĆ		15/1/88	G	11	(1)	
14	Mario IVANKOVIĆ		8/2/75	M	28		8
19	Krešimir KORDIĆ		3/9/81	A	25		10
15	Goran MARKOVIĆ		2/2/86	M	25	(1)	1
12	Igor MELHER		1/11/79	G	19		
10	Igor MUSA		18/10/73	M	17	(6)	
4	Mile PEHAR		1/2/91	D	1	(5)	
4	Ivan REZDAUŠEK		27/1/90	M		(4)	
9	Vernes SELIMOVIĆ		8/5/83	M	27		6
17	Danijel STOJANOVIĆ	CRO	18/8/84	M	16	(1)	1
16	Mateo SUŠIĆ		18/11/90	M	8	(17)	
13	Pavle SUŠIĆ		15/4/88	M	6	(11)	
7	Ivan ŠARAC		23/4/89	M	1	(6)	
2	Toni ŠUNJIĆ		15/12/88	D	28		
6	William Etchu TABI	CMR	13/11/82	M	4	(1)	
23	Vlado ZADRO		17/3/87	A	24	(5)	5
18	Mladen ŽIŽOVIĆ		27/12/80	M	11	(2)	1
11	Igor ŽURŽINOV	SRB	30/5/81	M	22		5

NK ZVIJEZDA

Coach – Ratko Ninković; (20/9/09) Amir Durgutović;
(31/12/09) Zoran Ćurguz
Founded – 1922
Stadium – Banja Ilidža (3,500)

2009

1/8	Zrinjski	h	2-0	Savić, Omeragić
8/8	Slavija	a	0-2	

15/8	Željezničar	h	2-1	Huseinbašić Ned., Delić A.
22/8	Prijedor	a	0-3	
29/8	Borac	h	1-1	Delić A.
12/9	Sloboda	a	0-1	
18/9	Modriča	h	0-1	
26/9	Velež	a	0-4	
3/10	Olimpik	h	3-4	Hamzić, Ćorić, Brković
17/10	Sarajevo	a	0-1	
24/10	Laktaši	h	4-1	Hamzić 2 (1p), Jusić, Ćorić
31/10	Leotar	a	1-1	Moranjkić
7/11	Čelik	h	1-0	Savić
21/11	Široki Brijeg	a	0-5	
29/11	Travnik	h	1-0	Brković

2010

28/2	Zrinjski	a	1-0	Savić
6/3	Slavija	h	2-3	Savić, Šest
17/3	Željezničar	a	0-2	
20/3	Prijedor	h	1-0	Delić A.
28/4	Borac	a	0-2	
3/4	Sloboda	h	2-2	Savić, Delić A.
10/4	Modriča	a	1-0	Hamzić
17/4	Velež	h	2-1	Hamzić, Prodanović
22/4	Olimpik	a	0-1	
24/4	Sarajevo	h	2-1	Savić, Hamzić
2/5	Laktaši	a	0-1	
8/5	Leotar	h	5-0	Kovačević, Hamzić (p), Omeragić, Savić, Prodanović
15/5	Čelik	a	2-4	Delić B., Đorić
23/5	Široki Brijeg	h	1-1	Huseinbašić Ner.
26/5	Travnik	a	1-4	Brković

No	Name	Nat	DoB	Pos	Aps	(s)	Gls
16	Rašid AVDIĆ	SRB	14/8/80	A		(2)	
24	Haris BEŠLIJA		27/9/86	M	9	(3)	
11	Zoran BRKOVIĆ		2/5/84	D	23	(2)	3
9	Elvis ĆORIĆ		7/7/81	A	11	(1)	2
18	Armin DELIĆ		19/6/83	M	28		4
22	Benjamin DELIĆ		7/3/91	A	1	(4)	1
6	Moussa DIABANG	SEN	6/8/80	M	1	(2)	
9	Zlatko ĐORIĆ	SRB	7/9/76	A	12	(1)	1
13	Fuad GAZIBEGOVIĆ	SVN	27/10/82	M	14	(5)	
17	Edin GENJAC		29/6/87	M		(2)	
20	Amar HAMZIĆ		5/1/75	M	25		7
7	Samir HAZNADAR		4/1/86	M	2	(1)	
14	Ermin HUSEINBAŠIĆ		15/8/88	D		(1)	
23	Nedim HUSEINBAŠIĆ		7/12/82	M	13	(2)	1
10	Nermin HUSEINBAŠIĆ		2/6/81	M	10	(9)	1
16	Senad HUSIĆ		12/4/90	A	9	(9)	
25	Alen HUSKIĆ		23/11/92	G		(1)	
8	Omer JAHIĆ		12/4/93	M	1		
15	Rusmir JUSIĆ		20/10/80	D	25		1
12	Elvis KARIĆ		21/5/80	G	26		
17	Milan KOVAČEVIĆ	SRB	26/5/77	M	7	(6)	1
14	Dženan KRAJIŠNIK		6/8/81	D		(4)	
3	Dragiša LAZIĆ		1/6/09	M	5	(2)	
4	Jasmin MORANJKIĆ		11/10/83	M	20	(1)	1
3	Muamer NEZIĆ		18/11/90	M	10	(5)	
21	Vedad OMERAGIĆ		31/7/91	A	7	(11)	2
1	Senedin OŠTRAKOVIĆ		13/4/87	G	3		
22	Denis PARAŠ		29/1/89	M	1	(1)	
6	Ilija PRODANOVIĆ		16/10/79	D	11	(1)	2
5	Srđan SAVIĆ		27/9/84	D	25		7
14	Rajko STANKOVIĆ	SRB	1/9/86	M	4	(7)	
10	Adnan SULJIĆ		16/5/92	D		(2)	
7	Sanel ŠEHRIĆ		12/11/90	D	1		
8	Saša ŠEST	CRO	5/12/85	M	2	(2)	1
19	Velibor VASILIĆ		19/11/90	D	23		
1	Damir ZUKIĆ		2/3/85	G	1	(1)	

PROMOTED CLUBS

FK BUDUĆNOST BANOVIĆI
Coach – Munever Rizvić
Founded – 1947
Stadium – Gradski (4,000)

FK DRINA ZVORNIK
Coach – Mile Milanović
Founded – 1945
Stadium – Gradski (3,000)

SECOND LEVEL FINAL TABLES 2009/10

Prva Liga FBiH	Pld	W	D	L	F	A	Pts
1 FK Budućnost Banovići	28	20	2	6	50	19	62
2 HNK Orašje	28	16	0	12	44	33	48
3 NK Iskra Bugojno	28	14	5	9	50	26	47
4 FK Rudar Kakanj	28	14	5	9	41	29	47
5 NK SAŠK Napredak Sarajevo	28	13	3	12	44	39	42
6 FK Bosna Visoko	28	13	2	13	47	41	41
7 GOŠK Gabela	28	13	1	14	36	31	40
8 NK Igman Konjic	28	12	4	12	40	36	40
9 NK Slaven Živinice	28	12	4	12	33	39	40
10 NK Krajišnik Velika Kladuša	28	12	4	12	36	49	40
11 NK Omladinac Mionica	28	12	2	14	37	49	38
12 FK Goražde	28	11	4	13	27	38	37
13 NK Jedinstvo Bihać	28	11	4	13	33	47	37
14 NK Vitez	28	11	3	14	36	38	36
15 NK Žepče	28	3	3	22	20	60	12

NB NK Posušje withdrew after round 15; all matches annulled.

Prva Liga RS	Pld	W	D	L	F	A	Pts
1 FK Drina Zvornik	26	12	11	3	39	18	47
2 FK Radnik Bijeljina	26	12	7	7	47	32	43
3 BSK Banja Luka	26	11	6	9	34	26	39
4 FK Proleter Teslić	26	9	10	7	27	22	37
5 FK Kozara Bos.Gradiška	26	9	9	8	35	22	36
6 FK Sutjeska Foča	26	9	9	8	31	30	36
7 FK Sloga Doboj	26	9	8	9	27	25	35
8 FK Sloboda Bos. Novi	26	9	8	9	29	28	35
9 FK Famos Vojkovići	26	10	5	11	29	34	35
10 FK Mladost Gacko	26	10	5	11	31	43	35
11 FK Drina Višegrad	26	8	10	8	28	30	34
12 FK Romanija Pale	26	8	8	10	32	33	32
13 FK Ljubić Prnjavor	26	6	7	13	26	52	25
14 FK Sloga Trn	26	4	9	13	24	44	21

DOMESTIC CUP 2009/10

KUP BOSNE I HERCEGOVINE

1/16 FINALS

(8/9/09)
Modriča 7, Sloboda Bosanski Novi/Novi Grad 1
(15/9/09)
Proleter Teslić 2, Leotar 3
Željezničar 1, Bosna Sarajevo 0
(16/9/09)
Borac Banja Luka 3, Posušje 0 *(w/o)*
Kozara Bosanska Gradiška 0, Široki Brijeg 4
Laktaši 0, Sloga Doboj 2

Olimpik Sarajevo 4, Radnik Lipnica 2
Rudar Kakanj 0, Sloboda Tuzla 2
Prijedor 4, Sutjeska Foča 1
Sarajevo 4, Radnik Hadžići 0
Slavija 2, Turbina Jablanica 0
Sloga Uskoplje/Gornji Vakuf 2, Zvijezda 2 *(5-4 on pens)*
Travnik 2, Jedinstvo Bihać 1
Velež 4, BSK Banja Luka 0
Zrinjski 4, Mladost Donji Svilaj 0
(23/9/09)
Čelik 4, Krajina Cazin 2

1/8 FINALS

(29/9/09 & 21/10/09)
Modriča v Sloga Doboj 1-2; 1-1 *(2-3)*
(30/9/09 & 21/10/09)
Borac Banja Luka v Široki Brijeg 2-0; 1-1 *(3-1)*
Čelik v Slavija 1-0; 0-3 *(1-3)*
Sarajevo v Zrinjski 1-1; 0-0 *(1-1; Zrinjski on away goal)*
Sloga Uskoplje/Gornji Vakuf v Prijedor 1-2; 0-1 *(1-3)*
Travnik v Sloboda Tuzla 1-1; 0-2 *(1-3)*
Velež v Željezničar 0-0; 1-2 *(1-2)*
(30/9/09 & 22/10/09)
Leotar v Olimpik Sarajevo 3-0; 1-0 *(4-0)*

QUARTER-FINALS

(28/10/09 & 11/11/09)
Leotar 0, Borac Banja Luka 3 *(Bilbija 25, Jandrić 84, Maksimović 90+2)*
Borac Banja Luka 1 *(Bilbija 65p)*, Leotar 0
(Borac Banja Luka 4-0)

Slavija 2 *(Regoje 24p, Jovanović 52)*, Sloboda Tuzla 0
Sloboda Tuzla 1 *(Kasapović 86)*, Slavija 0
(Slavija 2-1)

Sloga Doboj 0, Zrinjski 2 *(Kordić 36, 43)*
Zrinjski 1 *(Kordić 53)*, Sloga Doboj 0
(Zrinjski 3-0)

Željezničar 3 *(Stanić 11, Bekrić 25, Bučan 90)*, Prijedor 0
Prijedor 0, Željezničar 0
(Željezničar 3-0)

SEMI–FINALS

(23/3/10 & 14/4/10)
Željezničar 3 *(Bučan 14, 69, Mešanović 61)*, Zrinjski 1 *(Kordić 28)*
Zrinjski 1 *(Šunjić 78)*, Željezničar 1 *(Bučan 67)*
(Željezničar 4-2)

(24/3/10 & 14/4/10)
Slavija 2 *(Baković 53, Regoje 73p)*, Borac Banja Luka 2 *(Vukelja 87, Ćorić 88)*
Borac Banja Luka 1 *(Petrović 86)*, Slavija 0
(Borac Banja Luka 3-2)

FINAL

(5/5/10)
Gradski stadium, Banja Luka
FK BORAC BANJA LUKA 1 *(Vukelja 10)*
FK ŽELJEZNIČAR 1 *(Višća 83)*
Referee – Jakupović
BORAC BANJA LUKA – Sušac, Stupar, Trivunović, Ćorić, Žarić, Sakan, Stanceski, Stevanović, Jandrić (Vukobratović 66), Kajkut (Petrović 86), Vukelja.
ŽELJEZNIČAR – Šehić, Bajić, Radovanović, Mešić, Kerla, Ćulum, Svraka (Višća 46), Bučan (Stanić 65), Bekrić, Bešlija M. (Perak 86), Popović.

(19/5/10)
Grbavica, Sarajevo
FK ŽELJEZNIČAR 2 *(Višća 49, Bešlija M. 56)*
FK BORAC BANJA LUKA 2 *(Stevanović 6, Kajkut 36)*
Referee – Skakić
ŽELJEZNIČAR – Šehić, Šimić (Mešanović 72), Radovanović, Bajić (Višća 29), Mešić, Svraka, Bekrić, Bešlija M., Ćulum, Popović (Rovčanin 72), Bučan.
BORAC BANJA LUKA – Knežević, Stupar, Žarić, Petrić (Damjanović N. 17), Trivunović, Sakan, Stanceski, Jandrić (Ćorić 90), Stevanović, Vukelja, Kajkut (Vukobratović 83).
(3-3; BORAC BANJA LUKA on away goals)

BULGARIA

Provincials grab the prizes

For only the second time since the formation of a Bulgarian professional league in 1948, both major domestic trophies were won by clubs from outside the capital. With PFC CSKA Sofia and PFC Levski Sofia both having a season to forget, the prizes went to the provinces, PFC Litex Lovech winning the A PFG league title and PFC Beroe Stara Zagora enjoying a maiden triumph in the Bulgarian Cup.

Bulgarian champions twice before, in 1998 and 1999, Litex claimed their third crown in style, winning 22 of their 30 matches and finishing 12 points clear of the pack. They scored more goals (59) and conceded fewer (17) than every other team, boasted the best records home and away and also possessed the league's top scorer in 19-goal French striker Wilfried Niflore as well as its most dazzling technician, Brazilian playmaker Doka Madureira. Litex's star of stars, however, was 22-year-old captain Ivelin Popov. Once considered one of Bulgarian football's bad boys, he missed most of the autumn campaign with a foot injury but returned with a vengeance in the spring, scoring several crucial goals and inspiring the team to the title. His efforts earned him the Player of the Season vote from his fellow professionals.

Doubters silenced

Litex were led to victory by Angel Chervenkov, a 45-year-old whose previous job had been on the coaching staff of Heart of Midlothian FC. He was appointed in late August 2009 – six months after leaving Hearts - following the dismissal of Stanimir Stoilov, who paid the price for the team's ignominious exit from the UEFA Europa League against FC BATE Borisov. Stoilov, also the Bulgarian national coach, was considered a hard act to follow, but Chervenkov quickly silenced those who doubted his credentials, leading Litex to nine wins and a draw in his first ten matches.

Although Litex went into the winter break irked by a Cup defeat to CSKA, thus surrendering the trophy they had won in each of the previous two seasons, they

held a four-point lead in the league. That advantage grew and grew during the spring. Although they started to struggle on their travels, they remained peerless at home, winning every game in Lovech under Chervenkov. Ironically it was with a 3-0 win at PFC Lokomotiv Plovdiv 1936 - their first bona fide three-pointer away from home in six months (discounting the walkover over PFC Botev Plovdiv, who were excluded in mid-season for financial reasons) - that Litex clinched the title.

Beroe's Bulgarian Cup success was the Cinderella story of the season. Newly promoted to the A PFG, they performed creditably in the league under ex-Levski midfielder Ilian Iliev and surpassed themselves in the Cup. Fielding only Bulgarian players, they beat CSKA 1-0 at home before overcoming two second division teams by the same scoreline in the semi-final and final. It was only with a last-minute winner from Doncho Atanasov – who had not scored a league goal all season - that Beroe saw off plucky PFC Chernomorets

Ivelin Popov returned from injury to inspire Litex Lovech to the Bulgarian title

BULGARIA

Pomorie in the final, but it was a special victory nonetheless for a club whose only previous trophy success had been the league title in 1986.

Sofia gloom

More accustomed to taking home the silver are CSKA and Levski, but there was nothing for either the Reds or Blues to celebrate in 2009/10 with the possible exception of qualification for the group stage of the UEFA Europa League. Unfortunately, in a dozen group games the two Sofia giants managed just one win and one draw between them.

CSKA had reached the group stage by becoming the first Bulgarian club to eliminate a Russian team from Europe – they put out FC Dinamo Moskva – and they also made a bright start to the domestic campaign, winning eight of their opening nine league games. However, a 3-0 home defeat to struggling PFC Minyor Pernik in late October brusquely halted their charge and they were never the same again. Coach Luboslav Penev tendered his resignation in November after a fall-out with club directors. It was flatly rejected but the discontent simmered and two months later Penev duly departed. His replacement, Romanian Ioan Andone, lasted only six matches, and CSKA were eventually hauled back into second place by Adalbert Zafirov and Dimitar Penev.

Levski began the season dreaming of UEFA Champions League football and they remained optimistic after drawing Debreceni VSC in the play-off round. 2008/09 title-winning coach Emil Velev had been replaced by Ratko Dostanić to assist in that objective, but two defeats against the Hungarian champions left the Serbian on borrowed time, and as an awful run of results in the domestic league coincided with two defeats in the UEFA Europa

Bulgarski Futbolen Soyuz (BFS)

26 Tzar Ivan Assen II Street
BG-1124 Sofia
tel – +359 2 942 6202
fax – +359 2 942 6201
website – bfunion.bg
email – bfu@bfunion.bg

Year of Formation – 1923
President – Borislav Mihaylov
General Secretary – Borislav Popov
Media Officer – Pavel Kolev
National Stadium – Vasil Levski, Sofia (43,230)

INTERNATIONAL TOURNAMENT APPEARANCES
FIFA World Cup – (7) 1962, 1966, 1970, 1974, 1986 (2nd round), 1994 (4th), 1998.
UEFA European Championship – (2) 1996, 2004.
TOP FIVE ALL-TIME CAPS
Borislav Mihaylov (102); Hristo Bonev (96); Stilian Petrov (94); Krassimir Balakov (92); Dimitar Penev (90)
TOP FIVE ALL-TIME GOALS
Dimitar Berbatov (48); Hristo Bonev (47); Hristo Stoichkov (37); Emil Kostadinov (26); Lyubomir Angelov, Ivan Kolev & Petar Zhekov (25)

League, Dostanić was soon history. Club director Georgi Ivanov took charge for the remainder of the season – with Antoni Zdravkov officially installed as coach – and improbably steered Levski back into Europe as PFC Lokomotiv Sofia went to pieces in the run-in, taking just two points from their last seven games as resident goal machine Martin Kamburov suddenly and inexplicably lost his scoring touch.

Berbatov quits

Dimitar Berbatov, another ace Bulgarian marksman, made the headlines twice over in 2009/10 – firstly by scoring seven goals in five games for his country during the autumn to take his cumulative tally at

NATIONAL TEAM RESULTS 2009/10

12/8/09	Latvia	H	Sofia	1-0	Rangelov (54)
5/9/09	Montenegro (WCQ)	H	Sofia	4-1	Kishishev (45+1), Telkiyski (49), Berbatov (83p), Domovchiyski (90+1)
9/9/09	Italy (WCQ)	A	Turin	0-2	
10/10/09	Cyprus (WCQ)	A	Larnaca	1-4	Berbatov (44)
14/10/09	Georgia (WCQ)	H	Sofia	6-2	Berbatov (6, 23, 35), Petrov M. (14, 44), Angelov (31)
18/11/09	Malta	A	Paola	4-1	Bojinov (5), Berbatov (75, 83), Georgiev (80)
3/3/10	Poland	A	Warsaw	0-2	
19/5/10	Belgium	A	Brussels	1-2	Popov (31)
24/5/10	South Africa	A	Johannesburg	1-1	Bojinov (30)

international level to 48 and become Bulgaria's all-time top scorer; secondly by announcing, six months later, that he was retiring from international football at 29. To lose his captain and star striker on the eve of the UEFA EURO 2012 qualifying campaign was a bitter blow to coach Stoilov, who, short of emerging talent, will be hard pressed to take Bulgaria through to the finals from an awkward group.

NATIONAL TEAM APPEARANCES 2009/10

Coach –Stanimir STOILOV	13/2/67		Lva	MNE	ITA	CYP	GEO	Mlt	Pol	Bel	Rsa	Caps	Goals
Nikolay MIHAYLOV	28/6/88	Twente (NED)	G			s68	G	G46		G	G	7	-
Stanislav MANOLEV	16/12/85	PSV (NED)	D	D	D			D63		D	D	11	-
Alexander TUNCHEV	10/7/81	Leicester (ENG)	D46									26	1
Kiril KOTEV	18/4/82	CSKA Sofia	D	D46								6	-
Zhivko MILANOV	15/7/84	Levski /Vaslui (ROU)	D						D	D	D	16	-
Blagoy GEORGIEV	21/12/81	Terek (RUS)	M72	s76	s57	M	M	M84	M69	M	M90	42	5
Chavdar YANKOV	29/3/84	Duisburg (GER) /Metalurh Donetsk (UKR)	M46	M	M72			M	M77	M	M60	42	5
Stanislav ANGELOV	12/4/78	Energie (GER)	M	M	D	M	M78	D	D	D	D	33	1
Martin PETROV	15/1/79	Man. City (ENG)	M59	M76	M57	M	M					82	18
Ivelin POPOV	26/10/87	Litex	M23						A46	A66	A55	15	3
Dimitar BERBATOV	30/1/81	Man. United (ENG)	A46	A	A	A	A	A86	A46			78	48
Valeri DOMOVCHIYSKI	5/10/86	Hertha (GER)	s23	s82	s72	s62		s46				9	1
Plamen NIKOLOV	12/6/85	Litex	s46			D	D			s88	s90	5	-
Georgi SARMOV	7/9/85	Levski	s46		M			M	M			5	-
Dimitar RANGELOV	9/2/83	Dortmund (GER)	s46	A82	A57		A64	s86		s63	s55	15	1
Valeri BOJINOV	15/2/86	Parma (ITA)	s59		s57	A62	s78	A46	s46	A63	A55	29	5
Pavel VIDANOV	8/1/88	CSKA Sofia	s72								s88	2	-
Dimitar IVANKOV	30/10/75	Bursaspor (TUR)		G	G	G68		s46	G			64	-
Radostin KISHISHEV	30/7/74	Litex		D	D							83	1
Ilian STOYANOV	20/1/77	Sanfrecce (JPN)		D	D							37	-
Stilian PETROV	5/7/79	Aston Villa (ENG)		M	M	M68		M46	M	M88	M	94	8
Dimitar TELKIYSKI	5/5/77	Amkar (RUS)		s46								22	3
Ivan IVANOV	25/2/88	CSKA Sofia /Alania (RUS)				D	D		D77	D	D	8	-
Kostadin STOYANOV	26/5/86	CSKA Sofia				D	D46		s87			3	-
Veselin MINEV	14/10/80	Levski				D	D	D	D87		D	5	-
Kosta YANEV	27/4/83	CSKA Sofia				s68	M					3	-
Ivan BANDALOVSKI	23/11/86	Lokomotiv Sofia					s46	s46				2	-
Ivan STOYANOV	24/7/83	CSKA Sofia /Alania (RUS)					s64	s63	s77	s90		7	-
Ivo IVANOV	11/3/85	Beroe						s84				1	-
Velizar DIMITROV	13/4/79	Metalurh Donetsk (UKR)							s46			31	3
Martin KAMBUROV	13/10/80	Lokomotiv Sofia							s69	s66	s55	15	-
Jordan MILIEV	5/10/87	Levski							s77			1	-
Georgi PEEV	11/3/79	Amkar (RUS)								M90	M88	49	-
Nikolai DIMITROV	15/10/87	Levski									s60	2	-

DOMESTIC LEAGUE 2009/10

A PFG FINAL TABLE

			Home				Away					Total						
		Pld	W	D	L	F	A	W	D	L	F	A	W	D	L	F	A	Pts
1	PFC Litex Lovech	30	14	0	1	34	2	8	4	3	25	15	22	4	4	59	17	70
2	PFC CSKA Sofia	30	10	4	1	32	11	6	6	3	19	14	16	10	4	51	25	58
3	PFC Levski Sofia	30	10	2	3	34	9	7	4	4	23	17	17	6	7	57	26	57
4	PFC Lokomotiv Sofia	30	7	5	3	21	12	8	2	5	26	21	15	7	8	47	33	52
5	PSFC Chernomorets Burgas	30	9	3	3	26	14	6	3	6	18	15	15	6	9	44	29	51
6	PFC Slavia Sofia	30	9	3	3	23	14	5	5	5	11	14	14	8	8	34	28	50
7	PFC Cherno More Varna	30	9	6	0	27	8	4	3	8	13	20	13	9	8	40	28	48
8	PFC Minyor Pernik	30	6	3	6	17	12	7	3	5	21	14	13	6	11	38	26	45
9	PFC Pirin Blagoevgrad	30	8	4	3	22	11	3	6	6	12	21	11	10	9	34	32	43
10	PFC Beroe Stara Zagora	30	5	5	5	13	13	5	3	7	17	23	10	8	12	30	36	38
11	PFC Montana	30	5	4	6	15	15	4	5	6	15	22	9	9	12	30	37	36
12	PFC Lokomotiv Plovdiv 1936	30	6	2	7	22	27	3	4	8	14	25	9	6	15	36	52	33
13	OFC Sliven 2000	30	6	3	6	19	17	3	2	10	10	23	9	5	16	29	40	32
14	PFC Lokomotiv Mezdra	30	4	5	6	18	23	3	1	11	12	25	7	6	17	30	48	27
15	PFC Sportist Svoge	30	4	3	8	16	26	1	1	13	7	33	5	4	21	23	59	19
16	PFC Botev Plovdiv	30	1	2	12	6	35	0	2	13	6	43	1	4	25	12	78	1

NB PFC Botev Plovdiv – 6 pts deducted and excluded after round 15; their remaining matches awarded as 0-3 defeats.

TOP GOALSCORERS

19 Wilfried NIFLORE (Litex)
16 Martin KAMBUROV (Lokomotiv Sofia)
12 JOSÉ JÚNIOR (Slavia)
11 Hristo YOVOV (Levski)
10 Ismail ISA (Lokomotiv Mezdra)
   Deyan HRISTOV (Sliven)
9 Georgi ANDONOV (Beroe)
   Miroslav ANTONOV (Sportist/Levski)
8 Héctor GONZÁLEZ (Chernomorets)
   Ivan STOYANOV (CSKA)
   Yordan TODOROV (CSKA/Lokomotiv Plovdiv)
   Dimitar ILIEV (Lokomotiv Plovdiv/Minyor)
   Goran JANKOVIĆ (Minyor)

CLUB-BY-CLUB

PFC BEROE STARA ZAGORA

Coach – Ilian Iliev
Founded – 1916
Stadium – Beroe (15,000)
MAJOR HONOURS:
Bulgarian League - (1) 1986;
Bulgarian Cup - (1) 2010.

2009

7/8	Lokomotiv Sofia	h	2-1	Andonov, Zhekov
15/8	CSKA	a	0-3	
21/8	Chernomorets	h	1-1	Pisarov
28/8	Lokomotiv Plovdiv	a	3-1	Pisarov, Andonov 2
13/9	Cherno More	h	0-0	
19/9	Sportist	h	1-0	Ivanov
26/9	Lokomotiv Mezdra	a	1-2	Genchev (p)
5/10	Pirin	h	1-1	Dimitrov P.
18/10	Levski	a	1-0	Dimitrov P.
23/10	Montana	h	0-0	
2/11	Sliven	a	1-1	Andonov
7/11	Botev	h	3-1	Andonov 2 (1p), Pisarov
23/11	Minyor	a	0-3	
29/11	Litex	h	3-0	Ivanov, Dimitrov P., Andonov
4/12	Slavia	a	1-3	Dimitrov P.

2010

28/2	Lokomotiv Sofia	a	0-2	
6/3	CSKA	h	0-0	
15/3	Chernomorets	a	2-0	Andonov, Pisarov
19/3	Lokomotiv Plovdiv	h	0-1	
25/3	Cherno More	a	0-0	
28/3	Sportist Svoge	a	2-1	Hadzhivanov, Minchev
4/4	Lokomotiv Mezdra	h	1-0	Stankov
9/4	Pirin	a	2-2	Ivanov, Andonov
14/4	Levski	h	1-3	Ivanov
18/4	Montana	a	1-2	Genchev (p)
22/4	Sliven	h	0-1	
26/4	Botev	a	3-0	(w/o)
2/5	Minyor	h	0-3	
9/5	Litex	a	0-3	
16/5	Slavia	h	0-1	

No	Name	Nat	DoB	Pos	Aps	(s)	Gls
25	Alexander Emilov ALEXANDROV		30/7/86	D	14		
77	Georgi ANDONOV		28/6/83	A	25	(1)	9
27	Atanas APOSTOLOV		11/3/89	A	4	(11)	
15	Kostadin ARNAUDOV		13/11/86	M		(2)	
16	Atanas ATANASOV		14/7/85	D	18		
11	Doncho ATANASOV		2/4/83	A	16	(3)	
24	Stanislav BACHEV		3/1/78	D	15	(1)	
6	Georgi BOZHANOV		7/10/88	M		(3)	
9	Ivan CHERGEV		21/3/87	A	2	(4)	
8	Petar DIMITROV		28/2/82	A	8	(3)	4
9	Zahari DIMITROV		9/10/75	A	1	(7)	
25	Miroslav ENCHEV		8/8/91	D	5	(1)	
21	Dian GENCHEV		8/2/75	M	18	(5)	2
16	Antonio HADZHIVANOV		16/1/90	D	5	(7)	1
20	Ahmet HIKMET		5/10/84	M	2	(4)	
2	Zdravko ILIEV		19/10/84	D	14	(4)	
5	Ivo IVANOV		11/3/85	D	25		4
8	Ivan KANEV		21/12/84	M	4	(2)	

18	Petar KOSTADINOV		1/4/78	M	23	(1)	
30	Pavel KOVACHEV		27/7/87	D	8	(2)	
29	Simeon MINCHEV		28/6/82	M	5	(2)	1
20	Milen MITEV		27/12/90	M		(1)	
27	Dragan NIKOLIĆ	SRB	9/7/82	M		(2)	
14	Anton OGNYANOV		30/6/88	M	2		
14	Ivailo PARGOV		21/8/74	A	1	(2)	
22	Boyan PEIKOV		1/5/84	G	23		
17	Iskren PISAROV		5/10/85	M	21	(4)	4
29	Steliyan POPCHEV		8/4/76	D		(2)	
15	Emil RACHEV		10/11/89	M		(1)	
33	Teodor SKORCHEV		4/9/86	G	6	(1)	
20	Nikolai STANKOV		11/12/84	M	4	(7)	1
21	Milen TANEV		4/3/87	M	7	(4)	
3	Todor TODOROV		28/11/82	D	16	(1)	
4	Dimitar VAKAVLIEV		9/12/90	D	1		
10	Kostadin VIDOLOV		2/5/70	M	4	(2)	
7	Slavi ZHEKOV		21/8/76	M	22		1

13	Chudomir GRIGOROV		18/3/89	D	9	(3)	
4	Svetoslav ILIEV		24/6/89	M	4	(1)	
8	Eric KABU	GHA	21/12/89	M	6	(2)	
16	Ivan KARAMANOV		23/4/81	M	7	(1)	2
10	Vasil KOCHEV		11/11/89	M	6	(6)	1
21	Alfred MAPOKA	CMR	29/9/85	A	2	(1)	
10	Emanuele MORINI	ITA	31/1/82	A	10		6
5	Daniel OLA	GHA	23/11/82	D	6		
18	Asen POPOV		21/6/85	D		(1)	
12	Rumen POPOV		21/5/83	G	2		
18	Alberto REBECCA	ITA	30/5/85	A	6		
3	Ciro SIRAIGNANO	ITA	1/10/85	D	10		
9	Hristo STALEV		11/7/85	A	4	(2)	
17	Fabio TINAZZI	ITA	1/1/83	M	9		
17	Todor TODOROV		1/4/86	M		(1)	
17	Tsvetelin TONEV		3/1/92	A		(2)	
14	Petko VASILEV		16/1/90	A		(3)	
2	Vasil VASILEV		13/10/84	D	6	(2)	
1	Ventsislav VELINOV		2/1/81	G	6		
3	Anton VERGILOV		31/1/85	D	2	(2)	
19	Dimitar VITANOV		10/6/89	D	8	(3)	
11	Iliyan YORDANOV		1/1/89	A	3	(5)	1
15	Gilberto ZANOLETTI	ITA	2/1/80	M	9		1

PFC BOTEV PLOVDIV

Coach – Vladimir Chernev; (25/8/09) Enrico Piccioni (ITA)
Founded – 1912
Stadium – Hristo Botev (21,000)
MAJOR HONOURS:
Bulgarian League – (2) 1929, 1967;
Bulgarian Cup - (1) 1962 (as Soviet Army Cup).

2009
8/8	Levski	a	0-5	
15/8	Montana	h	2-3	*Etov, Kochev*
22/8	Sliven	a	0-3	
30/8	Cherno More	a	0-3	
14/9	Minyor	h	0-3	
20/9	Litex	a	1-2	*Morini*
26/9	Slavia	h	0-1	
3/10	Lokomotiv Sofia	a	2-2	*Karamanov, Morini*
17/10	CSKA	a	0-1	
24/10	Chernomorets	a	0-2	
31/10	Lokomotiv Plovdiv	h	1-0	*Morini*
7/11	Beroe	a	1-3	*Zanoletti*
21/11	Sportist	h	1-1	*Morini*
28/11	Lokomotiv Mezdra	a	2-2	*Karamanov, Yordanov*
5/12	Pirin	h	2-2	*Morini 2*

2010
27/2	Levski	h	0-3	*(w/o)*
6/3	Montana	a	0-3	*(w/o)*
12/3	Sliven	h	0-3	*(w/o)*
20/3	Cherno More	h	0-3	*(w/o)*
23/3	Minyor	a	0-3	*(w/o)*
27/3	Litex	h	0-3	*(w/o)*
2/4	Slavia	a	0-3	*(w/o)*
12/4	Lokomotiv Sofia	h	0-3	*(w/o)*
15/4	CSKA	a	0-3	*(w/o)*
18/4	Chernomorets	h	0-3	*(w/o)*
22/4	Lokomotiv Plovdiv	a	0-3	*(w/o)*
26/4	Beroe	h	0-3	*(w/o)*
2/5	Sportist	a	0-3	*(w/o)*
9/5	Lokomotiv Mezdra	h	0-3	*(w/o)*
16/5	Pirin	a	0-3	*(w/o)*

No	Name	Nat	DoB	Pos	Aps	(s)	Gls
15	Lyubomir ALEXANDROV		6/6/90	A		(1)	
80	ALExandre da Silva CERDEIRA	BRA	14/4/80	A	1		
5	Stoyan ANGELOV		5/11/83	D	4		
27	Gustave BAHOKEN	CMR	13/6/79	D	4		
20	Deyan BEKYAROV		1/6/90	D	3		
7	Boris BLAGOEV		4/5/83	M	4	(3)	
30	Luca BRIGNOLI	ITA	12/1/83	G	7		
23	Massimiliano BRIZZI	ITA	13/2/75	A	9		
36	Alan CARLET	ITA	12/1/77	M	7		
6	Marco D'ARGENIO	ITA	30/6/84	D	5	(1)	
4	Marco DI PAOLO	ITA	27/12/87	D		(3)	
6	Yordan ETOV		10/2/89	M	4	(1)	1
5	Sebastián FLORES	URU	9/9/83	D	2		

PFC CHERNO MORE VARNA

Coach – Nikola Spasov; (16/9/09) Velizar Popov
Founded – 1945
Stadium – Ticha (8,000)

2009
9/8	Chernomorets	a	1-2	*Yurukov*
15/8	Sliven	h	4-0	*Manolov 2, Georgiev Da., Bornosuzov*
24/8	Lokomotiv Plovdiv	a	0-1	
30/8	Botev	h	3-0	*Bornosuzov, Kakalov, Manolov*
13/9	Beroe	a	0-0	
20/9	Minyor	h	1-0	*Iliev*
26/9	Sportist	a	1-2	*Manolov*
3/10	Litex	h	0-0	
18/10	Lokomotiv Mezdra	a	2-1	*Manolov (p), Iliev*
26/10	Slavia	h	1-1	*Iliev*
30/10	Pirin	a	0-1	
7/11	Lokomotiv Sofia	h	4-2	*Georgiev Da. 2, Manolov (p), Domakinov*
21/11	Levski	a	0-3	
28/11	CSKA	h	0-0	
7/12	Montana	a	2-1	*Georgiev Da., Zakov*

2010
1/3	Chernomorets	h	2-0	*Dimov, Ademar Júnior*
8/3	Sliven	a	0-0	
14/3	Lokomotiv Plovdiv	h	3-2	*Iliev, Bozhilov, Ademar Júnior*
20/3	Botev	a	3-0	*(w/o)*
25/3	Beroe	h	0-0	
28/3	Minyor	a	0-1	
4/4	Sportist	h	3-0	*Kolev, Dyakov, Dimov*
11/4	Litex	a	0-4	
14/4	Lokomotiv Mezdra	h	2-0	*Nikolov, og (Pažin)*
17/4	Slavia	a	0-1	
21/4	Pirin	h	1-1	*Bozhilov*
25/4	Lokomotiv Sofia	a	2-1	*Ademar Júnior 2*
2/5	Levski	h	1-1	*Bozhilov*
9/5	CSKA	a	2-2	*Yurukov (p), Ademar Júnior*
16/5	Montana	h	2-1	*Zakov, Ratnikov*

No	Name	Nat	DoB	Pos	Aps	(s)	Gls
3	ADEMAR José Tavares JÚNIOR	BRA	20/9/80	D	13		5
15	Alexander Dragomirov ALEXANDROV		13/4/86	D	23		
25	Alexander Emilov ALEXANDROV		30/7/86	D	10		
10	Alexander Yordanov ALEXANDROV		19/1/75	M	3	(2)	
18	Georgi AVRAMOV		5/10/83	M	2	(1)	
4	Radoslav BACHEV		9/4/81	D	20	(2)	

No	Name	Nat	DoB	Pos	Aps	(s)	Gls
8	Atanas BORNOSUZOV		5/10/79	M	25		2
14	Georgi BOZHILOV		12/2/87	A	10		3
84	Mamoutou COULIBALY	MLI	23/2/84	D	14	(4)	
27	Daniel DIMOV		21/1/89	M	16	(1)	2
5	Nikolai DOMAKINOV		11/7/80	D	11		1
6	Tanko DYAKOV		18/8/84	D	20	(4)	1
28	ELIdiano MARQUES Lima	BRA	14/3/82	D	18	(4)	
23	Daniel GEORGIEV		6/11/82	M	13	(4)	4
8	Dilyan GEORGIEV		6/6/90	M	1		
1	Karamfil ILCHEV		7/1/79	G	1		
21	Georgi ILIEV		5/9/81	M	15	(1)	4
9	Georgi KAKALOV		18/7/84	A	4	(3)	1
13	Iliyan KAPITANOV		25/1/92	M		(1)	
58	Martin KERCHEV		22/10/84	M	2	(5)	
62	Todor KOLEV		22/9/89	A	7	(11)	1
5	Krasen KOSTOV		6/6/90	D		(1)	
20	Mihail LAZAROV		31/8/80	D	10	(6)	
11	Zdravko LAZAROV		20/12/76	A	4	(4)	
31	Miroslav MANOLOV		20/5/85	A	15		6
10	Rumen NIKOLOV		5/2/90	M	6	(3)	1
22	Milen PETKOV		12/1/74	M	10	(1)	
26	Ilko PIRGOV		23/5/86	G	28		
27	Daniil RATNIKOV	EST	10/2/88	M		(6)	1
7	Stanislav STOYANOV		10/9/76	M	8	(8)	
34	Kamen TRIFONOV		27/7/90	D	1		
77	Yordan YURUKOV		2/10/83	M	7	(3)	2
19	Gerasim ZAKOV		7/9/84	A	2	(9)	2
17	Georgi CHILIKOV		23/8/78	A	3	(3)	
32	DALMO Inácio da Silva	BRA	18/2/84	A	1		
30	Velin DAMYANOV		8/8/88	D	2	(1)	
11	Adalton Luís Juvenal "DUDU"	BRA	30/6/85	A	2	(8)	3
10	Kostadin DYAKOV		22/8/85	D	7	(11)	3
2	Trayan DYAKOV		21/6/76	D	18	(1)	2
9	Adrián FERNÁNDEZ	ARG	28/11/80	A	21		7
20	Héctor GONZÁLEZ	VEN	11/4/77	M	22	(2)	8
4	Enis HAJRI	TUN	6/3/83	M	13	(1)	
12	Stoyan KOLEV		3/2/76	G	3		
29	Emil KOPARANOV		14/6/83	D	2		
17	Branimir KOSTADINOV		4/3/89	M	1	(1)	
25	Plamen KRUMOV		23/1/75	A	9	(5)	2
5	Nikolai KRUSTEV		29/10/79	D	9	(1)	
8	MÁRCIO Nuno ABREU	POR	25/4/80	M	25	(1)	
23	MICHEL Platini Ferreira Mesquita	BRA	8/9/83	A	3	(1)	3
21	Matthias MORYS	GER	3/7/87	M	7	(13)	3
7	Cristian Valentin MUSCALU	ROU	3/10/89	M	3	(5)	
7	NILTON Rogério Cardoso Fernandes	CPV	7/3/79	M	7	(3)	
23	Pedro Ricardo Marques Monteiro "PEDRINHA"	POR	3/5/78	M	10	(1)	2
24	Shaner REMZI		18/9/86	M		(1)	
14	RICARDO ANDRÉ Duarte Pires	POR	24/10/82	M	14		1
18	Jochen SEITZ	GER	11/10/76	D	27		
16	Svetlin SIMEONOV		24/8/75	M	1	(1)	
6	Orlin STAROKIN		8/1/87	D	25		1
15	Aleksandar STOJMIROVIĆ	SRB	11/12/82	M	5		
26	Georgi TERZIEV		18/4/92	D	9	(4)	
13	Martin TOSHEV		15/8/90	A	11	(12)	2
22	Tsvetomir TSONKOV		25/6/81	M	15	(3)	

PSFC CHERNOMORETS BURGAS
Coach – Krassimir Balakov
Founded – 2005
Stadium – Lazur (18,000)

2009

9/8	Cherno More	h	2-1	González, Michel
17/8	Lokomotiv Plovdiv	h	2-1	Michel 2
21/8	Beroe	a	1-1	Dyakov
29/8	Sportist	h	3-0	González, Fernández, Carboni
12/9	Lokomotiv Mezdra	a	5-0	Toshev, Dyakov, Dyankov, Dudu 2
20/9	Pirin	h	2-1	Bonev, Dudu
27/9	Levski	a	1-0	Dyankov
3/10	Montana	h	1-1	Fernández
16/10	Sliven	a	1-0	Krumov
24/10	Botev	h	2-0	González (p), Dyakov
31/10	Minyor	a	0-2	
7/11	Litex	h	1-2	Fernández
22/11	Slavia	a	2-3	Morys, Carboni
29/11	Lokomotiv Sofia	h	0-2	
6/12	CSKA	a	0-0	

2010

1/3	Cherno More	a	0-2	
6/3	Lokomotiv Plovdiv	a	1-2	Toshev
15/3	Beroe	h	0-2	
20/3	Sportist	a	0-0	
24/3	Lokomotiv Mezdra	h	3-0	González 2 (1p), Pedrinha
29/3	Pirin	a	3-1	Ricardo André, Fernández, Morys
3/4	Levski	h	1-1	Krumov
9/4	Montana	a	0-2	
13/4	Sliven	h	2-0	Starokin, Morys
18/4	Botev	a	3-0	(w/o)
22/4	Minyor	h	3-1	Fernández 2, Pedrinha
25/4	Litex	a	0-2	
2/5	Slavia	h	2-2	Atz, González
9/5	Lokomotiv Sofia	a	1-0	González
16/5	CSKA	h	2-0	Fernández, González

No	Name	Nat	DoB	Pos	Aps	(s)	Gls
31	Gabriel Fernando ATZ	BRA	4/8/81	D	2		1
3	Ventsislav BONEV		8/5/80	D	6	(2)	1
28	Pascal BOREL	GER	26/9/78	G	26		
19	Roberto Eduardo CARBONI	ARG	8/4/85	M	10	(6)	2

PFC CSKA SOFIA
Coach – Luboslav Penev; (17/1/10) Ioan Andone (ROU); (31/3/10) Adalbert Zafirov; (22/4/10) Dimitar Penev
Founded – 1948
Stadium – Bulgarska Armia (22,000)
MAJOR HONOURS:
Bulgarian League – (31) 1948, 1951, 1952, 1954, 1955, 1956, 1957, 1958, 1959, 1960, 1961, 1962, 1966, 1969, 1971, 1972, 1973, 1975, 1976, 1980, 1981, 1982, 1983, 1987, 1989, 1990, 1992, 1997, 2003, 2005, 2008;
Bulgarian Cup – (19) 1951, 1954, 1955, 1961, 1965, 1969, 1972, 1973, 1974 (as Soviet Army Cup), 1981, 1983, 1985, 1987, 1988, 1989, 1993, 1997, 1999, 2006.

2009

9/8	Lokomotiv Plovdiv	a	5-0	Kotev, Stoyanov I. 2 (1p), Rui Miguel, Timonov
15/8	Beroe	h	3-0	Yanev, Todorov, Ivanov
23/8	Sportist	a	2-0	Marquinhos, Todorov
30/8	Lokomotiv Mezdra	h	4-0	Todorov, Stoyanov I. 2 (1p), Manchev V.
12/9	Pirin	a	0-0	
20/9	Levski	h	2-0	Stoyanov I., Stoyanov K.
26/9	Montana	a	2-1	Marquinhos, Michel
5/10	Sliven	h	1-0	Timonov
17/10	Botev	a	1-0	Stoyanov I.
25/10	Minyor	h	0-3	
1/11	Litex	a	0-2	
8/11	Slavia	h	2-0	Stoyanov I., Delev
21/11	Lokomotiv Sofia	a	2-2	Stoyanov I. (p), Michel
28/11	Cherno More	a	0-0	
6/12	Chernomorets	h	0-0	

2010

27/2	Lokomotiv Plovdiv	h	3-2	Rui Miguel 2, Pancu
6/3	Beroe	a	0-0	
13/3	Sportist	h	4-1	Grandin, Yanchev, Petre, Pancu (1p)
21/3	Lokomotiv Mezdra	a	0-4	(w/o; match abandoned after 70 mins at 0-1)
24/3	Pirin	h	1-1	Saidhodzha

27/3	Levski	a	0-0	
4/4	Montana	h	1-1	*Marquinhos*
10/4	Sliven	a	4-2	*Yanchev, Grandin, Popov, Trifonov*
15/4	Botev	h	3-0	*(w/o)*
18/4	Minyor	a	0-0	
21/4	Litex	h	1-0	*Yanchev*
24/4	Slavia	a	3-1	*Grandin (p), Delev, Yanchev*
2/5	Lokomotiv Sofia	h	5-1	*Marquinhos, Minev, Grandin, Yanchev, Branekov*
9/5	Cherno More	h	2-2	*Rui Miguel, og (Alexandrov A.D.)*
16/5	Chernomorets	a	0-2	

No	Name	Nat	DoB	Pos	Aps	(s)	Gls
34	Georgi AMZIN		2/3/92	M		(1)	
24	Hugo BÁEZ	PAR	24/7/83	D	2		
73	Vladimir BAHUROV		25/1/92	A		(1)	
13	Alexander BRANEKOV		31/5/87	D	6	(1)	1
1	Zdravko CHAVDAROV		28/5/80	G	10		
3	DAVID Mendes SILVA	POR	11/10/86	M		(2)	
77	Spas DELEV		22/9/89	A	18	(8)	2
18	Boris GALCHEV		31/10/83	M	6	(3)	
88	Elliot GRANDIN	FRA	17/10/87	A	10		4
15	Ivan IVANOV		5/2/88	D	10	(1)	1
12	Ivan KARADZHOV		12/6/89	G	17	(1)	
6	Kiril KOTEV		18/4/82	D	9		1
20	Nikolai MANCHEV		4/1/85	M	2	(8)	
7	Vladimir MANCHEV		6/10/77	A		(5)	1
28	Marcos Antônio Malachias Júnior "MARQUINHOS"	BRA	20/8/82	M	12	(1)	4
22	MICHEL Platini Ferreira Mesquita	BRA	8/9/83	A	13	(4)	2
52	Yordan MINEV		14/10/80	D	25		1
29	Igor MITRESKI	MKD	19/2/79	D	4		
32	Viktors MOROZS	LVA	30/7/80	M	4	(7)	
30	Borislav NIKOLOV		3/2/92	A	1		
11	Orlin ORLINOV		8/8/88	A		(3)	
23	Daniel Gabriel PANCU	ROU	17/8/77	A	7		2
29	Blagoi PASKOV		2/3/81	A		(3)	
17	Florentin PETRE	ROU	5/1/76	A	6	(2)	1
27	Ivailo PETROV		3/5/73	G	2		
14	Svetoslav PETROV		12/2/78	M	11	(1)	
19	Apostol POPOV		22/12/82	D	12	(1)	1
10	RUI MIGUEL Marinho Reis	POR	30/1/84	M	11	(7)	4
99	Dormushali SAIDHODZHA		16/5/85	A	4	(5)	1
36	Yanko SANDANSKI		23/11/88	M		(2)	
73	Ivan STOYANOV		24/7/83	A	13		8
4	Kostadin STOYANOV		26/5/86	D	22	(2)	1
8	Todor TIMONOV		3/9/86	M	3	(7)	2
30	Yordan TODOROV		27/7/81	M	10	(2)	3
8	Rumen TRIFONOV		21/2/85	M	11	(1)	1
33	Kristiyan VELINOV		10/10/91	D	1		
2	Pavel VIDANOV		8/1/88	D	19	(1)	
5	Todor YANCHEV		19/5/76	M	24	(1)	5
20	Kosta YANEV		27/4/83	M	14	(1)	1
29	Ivailo ZAFIROV		16/4/92	A		(1)	
18	Atanas ZEHIROV		13/2/89	M		(1)	

PFC LEVSKI SOFIA

Coach – Ratko Dostanić (SRB); (20/10/09) Antoni Zdravkov
Founded – 1914
Stadium – Georgi Asparuhov (29,000)
MAJOR HONOURS:
Bulgarian League – (26) 1933, 1937, 1942, 1946, 1947, 1949, 1950, 1953, 1965, 1968, 1970, 1974, 1977, 1979, 1984, 1985, 1988, 1993, 1994, 1995, 2000, 2001, 2002, 2006, 2009;
Bulgarian Cup – (26) 1942 (as Tsar's Cup), 1946, 1947, 1949, 1950, 1956, 1957, 1959, 1967, 1970, 1971, 1976, 1977, 1979 (as Soviet Army Cup), 1982, 1984, 1986, 1991, 1992, 1994, 1998, 2000, 2002, 2003, 2005, 2007.

2009

8/8	Botev	h	5-0	*Krastovchev, Miliev, Tasevski, Deniran 2*
15/8	Minyor	a	2-0	*Yovov, Deniran*
29/8	Slavia	a	3-1	*Bardon, Zé Soares, Dimitrov N.*
12/9	Lokomotiv Sofia	h	1-2	*Yovov*
20/9	CSKA	a	0-2	
27/9	Chernomorets	h	0-1	
5/10	Lokomotiv Plovdiv	a	2-2	*Bardon (p), Yovov*
18/10	Beroe	h	0-1	
25/10	Sportist	a	3-2	*Yovov, Sarmov, Krastovchev*
31/10	Lokomotiv Mezdra	h	3-1	*Bardon, Sarmov, Krastovchev*
8/11	Pirin	a	2-0	*Tasevski, Krastovchev*
21/11	Cherno More	h	3-0	*Joãozinho, Bardon (p), Dimitrov N.*
25/11	Litex	h	2-2	*Zé Soares, Yovov*
28/11	Montana	h	3-1	*og (Luiz Eduardo) Hristov, Joãozinho*
6/12	Sliven	a	0-1	
2010				
27/2	Botev	a	3-0	*(w/o)*
7/3	Minyor	h	3-1	*Joãozinho 2, Bardon (p)*
14/3	Litex	a	0-3	
20/3	Slavia	h	3-0	*og (Joseph-Reinette), Yovov, Dimitrov N.*
24/3	Lokomotiv Sofia	a	0-2	
27/3	CSKA	h	0-0	
3/4	Chernomorets	a	1-1	*Bardon (p)*
10/4	Lokomotiv Plovdiv	h	2-0	*Petráš, Antonov*
14/4	Beroe	a	3-1	*Dimitrov N., Antonov, Yovov*
17/4	Sportist	h	5-0	*Antonov 2, Alexandrov, Tasevski*
20/4	Lokomotiv Mezdra	a	1-1	*Baltanov*
24/4	Pirin	h	2-0	*Yovov 2*
2/5	Cherno More	a	1-1	*Gadzhev*
9/5	Montana	a	2-0	*Alexandrov, Yovov*
16/5	Sliven	h	2-0	*Yovov, Petráš*

No	Name	Nat	DoB	Pos	Aps	(s)	Gls
7	Alexander Yordanov ALEXANDROV		19/1/75	M	5	(5)	3
6	Georgi ANGELOV		12/11/90	M		(1)	
9	Miroslav ANTONOV		10/3/86	A	9	(4)	4
30	Luchezar BALTANOV		11/7/88	M	5	(6)	1
27	Cédric BARDON	FRA	15/10/76	M	21	(3)	6
15	Chakib BENZOUKANE	MAR	7/8/86	D	18	(1)	
17	Ortega DENIRAN	NGA	28/5/86	A	2	(5)	3
24	Nikolai DIMITROV		15/10/87	M	13	(9)	4
31	Tsvetan DIMITROV		10/2/87	G	3	(2)	
45	Vladimir GADZHEV		18/7/87	M	8	(2)	1
2	Viktor GENEV		27/10/88	D	7		
99	Georgi HRISTOV		10/1/85	A	7	(5)	1
20	João Natailton Ramos dos Santos "JOÃOZINHO"	BRA	25/12/88	M	22	(5)	4
7	Enyo KRASTOVCHEV		7/2/84	A	9	(2)	4
3	Zhivko MILANOV		15/7/84	D	10		
55	Yordan MILIEV		5/10/87	D	22		1
14	Veselin MINEV		14/10/80	D	22		
12	Bozhidar MITREV		31/3/87	G	7		
16	Mariyan OGNYANOV		30/7/88	M	2	(5)	
1	Georgi PETKOV		14/4/76	G	19		
21	Peter PETRÁŠ	SVK	7/5/79	D	9	(1)	2
5	Youssef RABEH	MAR	13/4/85	D	9		
8	Georgi SARMOV		7/9/85	M	19		2
70	Saša SIMONOVIĆ	SRB	20/7/75	M	2	(4)	
4	Stefan STANCHEV		26/4/89	D	6		
32	Boyan TABAKOV		2/2/90	A		(2)	
22	Darko TASEVSKI	MKD	20/5/84	M	9	(6)	3
18	Michael TAWIAH	GHA	1/12/90	M		(1)	
32	Dimitar TELKIYSKI		5/5/77	M	12	(2)	
11	Elin TOPUZAKOV		5/2/77	D	8	(4)	
19	Ivan TSACHEV		19/1/89	A		(3)	
25	Lúcio WAGNER		15/6/76	D	6	(1)	
10	Hristo YOVOV		4/11/77	A	20	(4)	11
21	José "ZÉ" SOARES da Silva Filho	BRA	26/7/83	M	8	(1)	2

BULGARIA

PFC LITEX LOVECH
Coach – Stanimir Stoilov; (29/8/09) Angel Chervenkov
Founded – 1921
Stadium – Gradski (7,000)
MAJOR HONOURS:
Bulgarian League – (3) 1998, 1999, 2010;
Bulgarian Cup – (4) 2001, 2004, 2008, 2009.

2009				
8/8	Lokomotiv Mezdra	a	5-0	Milanov G., Niflore 2, Petkov (p), Todorov
15/8	Pirin	h	0-1	
30/8	Montana	h	3-0	Venkov, Yanev, Milanov G.
13/9	Sliven	a	2-1	Niflore, Barthe
20/9	Botev	h	2-1	Niflore, Saidhodzha
27/9	Minyor	a	1-0	Niflore
3/10	Cherno More	a	0-0	
17/10	Slavia	h	1-0	Niflore
24/10	Lokomotiv Sofia	a	1-0	Wellington
1/11	CSKA	h	2-0	Niflore, Yanev
7/11	Chernomorets	a	2-1	Niflore, Yanev
21/11	Lokomotiv Plovdiv	h	5-0	Yanev, Niflore (p), Wellington, Doka Madureira, Sandrinho
25/11	Levski	a	2-2	Nikolov, Niflore
29/11	Beroe	a	0-3	
7/12	Sportist	h	2-0	Yanev, Popov
2010				
26/2	Lokomotiv Mezdra	h	3-0	Niflore 2 (1p), Wellington
7/3	Pirin	a	1-4	Popov
14/3	Levski	h	3-0	Doka Madureira, Popov, Yanev
20/3	Montana	a	0-0	
25/3	Sliven	h	1-0	Bodurov
27/3	Botev	a	3-0	(w/o)
5/4	Minyor	h	1-0	Popov
11/4	Cherno More	h	4-0	Barthe, Popov, Doka Madureira, Niflore
14/4	Slavia	a	1-1	Todorov (p)
18/4	Lokomotiv Sofia	h	2-0	Doka Madureira, Jelenković
21/4	CSKA Sofia	a	0-1	
25/4	Chernomorets	h	2-0	Popov, Niflore (p)
2/5	Lokomotiv Plovdiv	a	3-0	Niflore 2, Doka Madureira
9/5	Beroe	h	3-0	Bodurov, Doka Madureira, Popov
16/5	Sportist	a	4-2	Tsvetanov, Niflore 3 (1p)

No	Name	Nat	DoB	Pos	Aps	(s)	Gls
24	ADRIANO MIRANDA de Carvalho	BRA	22/6/89	M		(1)	
2	Alexandre BARTHE	FRA	5/3/86	D	27		2
33	Nikolai BODUROV		30/5/86	D	18		2
28	DIEGO Ferares Scheda	BRA	21/5/92	A	4	(5)	
15	Francisco Lima da Silva "DOKA MADUREIRA"	BRA	11/2/84	M	25	(1)	6
31	Rodrigo Jose GALLATO	BRA	10/3/83	G	12		
2	Dimitar GEORGIEV		9/2/92	A		(1)	
1	Uroš GOLUBOVIĆ	SRB	19/8/76	G	17	(2)	
23	Nebojša JELENKOVIĆ	SRB	26/5/78	M	20	(4)	1
25	Radostin KISHISHEV		30/7/74	M	16	(4)	
17	Georgi MILANOV		19/2/92	M	8	(19)	2
18	Iliya MILANOV		19/2/92	D	1		
19	Wilfried NIFLORE	FRA	29/4/81	A	25	(2)	19
22	Plamen NIKOLOV		12/6/85	D	27		1
60	Tsvetomir PANOV		17/4/89	D		(1)	
6	Ivailo PETKOV		4/3/76	D	9	(6)	1
32	Ivelin POPOV		26/10/87	A	14	(4)	7
99	Dormushali SAIDHODZHA		16/5/86	A	4	(7)	1
10	Alessandro Correa "SANDRINHO"	BRA	5/7/80	M	24	(1)	1
6	Maksim STOIKOV		13/1/91	M		(1)	
	Svetoslav TODOROV		30/8/78	A	2	(10)	2
27	Momchil TSVETANOV		12/3/90	A	1	(3)	1
21	Alexander TSVETKOV		31/8/90	D	1		
5	Mihail VENKOV		28/7/83	D	10		1
8	WELLINGTON Brito da Silva	BRA	23/7/85	M	13	(5)	3
7	Hristo YANEV		4/5/79	A	22	(4)	6
	Petar ZANEV		18/10/85	D	19		

PFC LOKOMOTIV MEZDRA
Coach – Voin Voinov
Founded – 1929
Stadium – Lokomotiv (3,000)

2009				
8/8	Litex	h	0-5	
15/8	Slavia	a	0-1	
23/8	Lokomotiv Sofia	h	1-2	Tawiah
30/8	CSKA	a	0-4	
12/9	Chernomorets	h	0-5	
21/9	Lokomotiv Plovdiv	a	1-0	Hazurov
26/9	Beroe	h	2-1	Isa, Bamba
3/10	Sportist	a	4-0	Isa 2, og (Todorov), Petkov
18/10	Cherno More	h	1-2	Isa
24/10	Pirin	h	4-0	Hazurov, Iliev, Isa 2
31/10	Levski	a	1-3	Hazurov
6/11	Montana	h	0-2	
21/11	Sliven	a	0-1	
28/11	Botev	h	2-2	Iliev (p), Isa
5/12	Minyor	a	0-1	
2010				
26/2	Litex	a	0-3	
5/3	Slavia	h	0-0	
13/3	Lokomotiv Sofia	a	1-2	Isa
21/3	CSKA	h	4-0	(w/o; match abandoned after 70 mins at 1-0 Isa)
24/3	Chernomorets	a	0-3	
27/3	Lokomotiv Plovdiv	h	0-0	
4/4	Beroe	a	0-1	
11/4	Sportist	h	2-1	Petkov, Iliev
14/4	Cherno More	a	0-2	
17/7	Pirin	a	1-3	Isa
20.4	Levski	h	1-1	Iliev
26/4	Montana	a	1-1	Kirov
2/5	Sliven	h	1-1	Petkov
9/5	Botev	a	3-0	(w/o)
16/5	Minyor	h	0-1	

No	Name	Nat	DoB	Pos	Aps	(s)	Gls
11	Borislav BALDZHIISKI		12/10/90	M	2	(3)	
26	Abudramae BAMBA	CIV	26/10/87	A	5	(10)	1
22	DANIEL Alexandre MORALES Batagello	BRA	6/12/75	M	12	(1)	
15	Martin DECHEV		12/4/90	D	1		
3	Kiril DZHOROV		12/8/75	D	11		
11	Boyan GAITANOV		2/12/89	A		(5)	
11	Georgi GEORGIEV		15/6/76	A		(1)	
24	Stanimir GOSPODINOV		3/3/75	D	17	(3)	
23	Yordan GOSPODINOV		15/6/78	G	9		
9	Borislav HAZUROV		4/10/85	A	10	(3)	3
4	Nikolai HRISTOZOV		6/3/82	D	28		
7	Strati ILIEV		15/10/74	M	25	(1)	4
10	Ismail ISA Mustafa		26/6/89	A	24	(1)	10
33	Hristo IVANOV		6/4/82	G	11		
19	Georgi KARANEICHEV		9/6/88	A	1	(2)	
2	Martin KAVDANSKI		13/2/87	D	10		
17	Martin KERCHEV		22/10/84	M	13		
8	Alexander KIROV		25/10/90	A	6	(3)	1
20	Milan KOPRIVAROV		20/7/83	A	5		
23	Yordan LINKOV		21/1/78	G	9		
3	Milcho MAKENDZHIEV		31/10/89	D	3	(4)	
10	Tsvetomir MATEV		22/6/86	A	1		
99	Predrag PAŽIN		14/3/73	D	17	(2)	
16	Dimitar PETKOV		24/8/87	A	19	(3)	3
77	Strahil POPOV		31/8/90	M	10	(4)	
12	Desislav RUSEV		27/4/79	A	5	(5)	
8	Viktor SOFRONIEV		4/4/81	M	18		
1	Zdravko STANKOV		1/4/77	G	16		
9	Boyan TABAKOV		2/2/90	A	2	(10)	
18	Michael TAWIAH	GHA	1/12/90	M	9	(1)	1
20	Anatoli TODOROV		24/4/85	A	8	(7)	
24	Lyubomir TODOROV		4/10/88	A	1	(12)	
19	Marco TÚLIO Lopes Silva	BRA	28/2/81	M	1	(2)	
11	Vladislav UZUNOV		25/5/91	M		(1)	
29	Tsvetan ZAREV		5/11/83	D	10		

PFC LOKOMOTIV PLOVDIV 1936

Coach – Ayan Sadakov; (13/8/09) Ivan Marinov;
(1/11/09) Stefan Genov; (7/1/10) Naji Shensoy;
(4/5/10) Hristo Bonev
Founded – 1936
Stadium – Lokomotiv (13,000)
MAJOR HONOURS:
Bulgarian League – (1) 2004.

2009

9/8	CSKA	h	0-5	
17/8	Chernomorets	a	1-2	Ton
24/8	Cherno More	h	1-0	Dakson
28/8	Beroe	h	1-3	Komljenović
12/9	Sportist	a	1-2	Trifonov
21/9	Lokomotiv Mezdra	h	0-1	
27/9	Pirin	a	0-0	
5/10	Levski	h	2-2	Iliev D., Dakson
17/10	Montana	a	3-2	Kiki, Dakson 2
24/10	Sliven	h	1-2	Rafael
31/10	Botev	a	0-1	
9/11	Minyor	h	3-3	Iliev D. 2, Danov
21/11	Litex	a	0-5	
30/11	Slavia	h	0-2	
5/12	Lokomotiv Sofia	a	0-3	
2010				
27/2	CSKA	a	2-3	Lazarov 2 (2p)
6/3	Chernomorets	h	2-1	Todorov, Dembélé
14/3	Cherno More	a	2-3	Bengelloun 2
19/3	Beroe	a	1-0	Todorov
23/3	Sportist	h	3-0	Dembélé, Lazarov (p), Todorov
27/3	Lokomotiv Mezdra	a	0-0	
2/4	Pirin	h	2-0	Dembélé, Todorov
10/4	Levski	a	0-2	
15/4	Montana	h	2-4	Dembélé, Kiki
19/4	Sliven	a	1-1	Todorov
22/4	Botev	h	3-0	(w/o)
26/4	Minyor	a	0-0	
2/5	Litex	h	0-3	
9/5	Slavia	a	3-1	Dembélé, Erős, Lazarov
16/5	Lokomotiv Sofia	h	2-1	Chipev, Lazarov

No	Name	Nat	DoB	Pos	Aps	(s)	Gls
21	Rangel ABUSHEV		26/5/89	M		(4)	
12	Kiril AKALSKI		17/10/85	G	15		
5	Youness BENGELLOUN	FRA	3/1/83	D	13		2
9	Georgi BOZHILOV		12/2/87	A	4	(1)	
5	Georgi BUCHVAROV		17/4/90	M		(1)	
17	Georgi CHILIKOV		23/8/78	A		(2)	
16	Nikolai CHIPEV		20/2/89	M	7	(5)	1
11	DAKSON Soares da Silva	BRA	11/6/87	M	20	(1)	4
19	Georgi DANOV		17/10/90	M	7	(6)	1
39	Garra DEMBÉLÉ	FRA	21/2/86	A	14		5
80	Gábor ERŐS	HUN	17/1/80	M	2	(6)	1
14	Kostadin GADZHALOV		10/7/89	D	3	(2)	
3	Valeri GEORGIEV		28/7/84	D	2		
15	Boyan ILIEV		21/8/82	D	9	(1)	
14	Dimitar ILIEV		25/9/88	M	13		3
88	Dani KIKI		8/1/88	M	10	(9)	2
17	Dejan KOMLJENOVIĆ	SVN	2/1/83	M	4	(5)	1
55	Kiril KOTEV		18/4/82	D	12		
28	Petar KYUMYURDZHIEV		15/12/81	D	15	(1)	
77	Zdravko LAZAROV		20/12/76	A	13	(1)	5
16	Veselin MARCHEV		7/2/90	A	3	(2)	
10	Milan MILUTINOVIĆ	SRB	20/4/83	M	13		
23	Georgi MECHECHIEV		27/4/78	D	25		
7	Lyudmil NIKOLOV		27/8/84	D	5	(2)	
21	Georgi PETROV		6/7/91	A		(1)	
7	Hristian POPOV		5/2/90	M	3	(4)	
6	RAFAEL Ribeiro Sciani	BRA	24/10/87	M	5	(2)	1
4	Martin SECHKOV		17/11/86	D	8	(1)	
3	Félicien SINGBO	BEN	25/10/80	D	12		
1	Stoyan STAVREV		7/12/75	G	14	(2)	
9	Emil STOEV		16/3/86	M	1	(4)	

6	Staiko STOICHEV		30/8/89	D		(1)	
3	THIAGO Barbosa Soares	BRA	11/12/89	D	4	(2)	
7	Yordan TODOROV		27/7/81	D	13		5
20	Éverton Fernando Gílio "TON"	BRA	18/3/86	M	18	(4)	1
18	Krasen TRIFONOV		5/12/83	M	10	(12)	1
25	Angel YOSHEV		1/1/85	D	22	(2)	

PFC LOKOMOTIV SOFIA

Coach – Dragomir Okuka (SRB); (26/4/10) Dimitar Vasev
Founded – 1929
Stadium – Lokomotiv (25,000)
MAJOR HONOURS:
Bulgarian League – (4) 1940, 1945, 1964, 1978;
Bulgarian Cup – (3) 1948, 1953 (as Soviet Army Cup), 1995.

2009

7/8	Beroe	a	1-2	Asamoah
14/8	Sportist	h	3-2	Kamburov 2 (1p), Zlatinski
23/8	Lokomotiv Mezdra	a	2-1	Kamburov 2
29/8	Pirin	h	1-0	Asamoah
12/9	Levski	a	2-1	Karadzhinov, Kamburov (p)
18/9	Montana	h	0-0	
25/9	Sliven	a	3-1	Kamburov, Špišić 2
3/10	Botev	h	2-2	Kamburov, Bandalovski
18/10	Minyor	a	2-1	Špišić, Dobrev
24/10	Litex	h	0-1	
1/11	Slavia	a	0-0	
7/11	Cherno More	a	2-4	Bandalovski, Dafchev
21/11	CSKA S	h	2-2	Kamburov (p), Mitev
29/11	Chernomorets	a	2-0	Baldovaliev 2
5/12	Lokomotiv Plovdiv	h	3-0	Kamburov, Mitev, Zlatinski
2010				
28/2	Beroe	h	2-0	Asamoah 2
7/3	Sportist	a	5-1	Kamburov 2 (1p), Genkov 2, Asamoah
13/3	Lokomotiv Mezdra	h	2-1	Atanasov, Kamburov
21/3	Pirin	a	1-1	Kamburov (p)
24/3	Levski	h	2-0	Atanasov, Genkov
29/3	Montana	a	1-0	Kamburov (p)
3/4	Sliven	h	2-0	Kamburov 2 (1p)
12/4	Botev	a	3-0	(w/o)
13/4	Minyor	h	1-1	Genkov
18/4	Litex	h	0-2	
21/4	Slavia	h	0-0	
25/4	Cherno More	h	1-2	og (Domakinov)
2/5	CSKA	a	1-5	Asamoah
9/5	Chernomorets	h	0-1	
16/5	Lokomotiv Plovdiv	a	1-2	Atanasov

No	Name	Nat	DoB	Pos	Aps	(s)	Gls
9	Derek ASAMOAH	GHA	1/5/81	A	17	(5)	6
30	Dimo ATANASOV		24/10/85	M	14	(11)	3
28	Zoran BALDOVALIEV	MKD	4/3/83	A	11	(2)	2
22	Ivan BANDALOVSKI		23/11/86	D	20	(1)	2
10	Marcho DAFCHEV		12/5/78	M	5	(10)	1
17	Ivailo DIMITROV		26/6/87	M	14		
11	Kristiyan DOBREV		23/9/78	D	20	(2)	1
20	Svetoslav DYAKOV		31/5/84	M	26	(1)	
13	Vanja DŽAFEROVIĆ	CRO	19/3/83	D	12	(1)	
84	Valentin GALEV		1/1/84	G	15		
3	Iliyan GAROV		24/11/86	D		(2)	
9	Tsvetan GENKOV		8/8/84	A	13		4
7	Rumen GORANOV		15/7/84	M	4	(10)	
23	Ivo IVANOV		30/4/85	M	3	(2)	
19	Martin KAMBUROV		13/10/80	A	29		16
18	Kaloyan KARADZHINOV		25/1/77	M	9	(1)	1
21	Yulian LEVASHKI		2/3/81	G	14		
5	Georgi MARKOV		20/1/72	D	18	(1)	
15	Danail MITEV		11/1/84	M	7	(13)	2
24	Ivan PASKOV		4/1/73	D	10	(4)	
12	Darko SAVIĆ	SRB	19/1/79	D	23		
8	Viktor ŠPIŠIĆ	CRO	8/6/82	M	17	(2)	3
25	Preslav YORDANOV		27/7/89	A		(9)	
16	Hristo ZLATINSKI		22/8/81	M	18	(8)	2

BULGARIA

PFC MINYOR PERNIK
Coach –Anton Velkov
Founded – 1945
Stadium – Minyor (15,000); Osogovo, Kyustendil (5,000)

2009
8/8	Pirin	a	1-0	Janković
15/8	Levski	h	0-2	
22/8	Montana	a	0-0	
29/8	Sliven	h	4-2	Gospodinov 2 (1p), Stankov, Petrov
14/9	Botev	a	3-0	Nikolov 3
20/9	Cherno More	a	0-1	
27/9	Litex	h	0-1	
2/10	Slavia	a	0-1	
18/10	Lokomotiv Sofia	h	1-2	Janković
25/10	CSKA	a	3-0	Trifonov 2, Zlatkov
31/10	Chernomorets	h	2-0	Nikolov, Olegov
9/11	Lokomotiv Plovdiv	a	3-3	Tsvetkov 2, Janković
23/11	Beroe	h	3-0	Janković 2, Trifonov
28/11	Sportist	a	1-0	Janković
5/12	Lokomotiv Mezdra	h	1-0	Janković

2010
27/2	Pirin	h	0-1	
7/3	Levski	a	1-3	Iliev
12/3	Montana	h	1-1	Iliev
21/3	Sliven	a	3-1	Krumov, Delibašić, Stoev
23/3	Botev	h	3-0	(w/o)
28/3	Cherno More	h	1-0	Delibašić (p)
5/4	Litex	a	0-1	
9/4	Slavia	h	0-1	
13/4	Lokomotiv Sofia	a	1-1	Janković (p)
18/4	CSKA	h	0-0	
22/4	Chernomorets	a	1-3	Iliev
26/4	Lokomotiv Plovdiv	h	0-0	
2/5	Beroe	a	3-0	og (Vakavliev), Iliev, Stoev
9/5	Sportist	h	1-2	Olegov
16/5	Lokomotiv Mezdra	a	1-0	Iliev

No	Name	Nat	DoB	Pos	Aps	(s)	Gls
26	Samet ASHIMOV		16/5/79	D	3	(2)	
2	Vasil BOZHIKOV		2/6/88	D	22	(1)	
91	Ivan ĆVOROVIĆ	SRB	15/6/85	G	5		
31	Pavle DELIBAŠIĆ	SRB	30/11/78	A	6	(5)	2
11	Anton EVTIMOV		27/6/73	A		(1)	
23	Hristo GOSPODINOV		19/1/79	M	14		2
23	Nikolai HARIZANOV		14/6/83	D	7	(1)	
21	Kostadin HAZUROV		5/8/85	A	7	(10)	
18	Goran JANKOVIĆ	SRB	10/12/78	A	21	(5)	8
41	Dimitar ILIEV		25/9/88	A	9	(5)	5
99	Ivailo IVANOV		8/12/74	G	24		
22	Yuri IVANOV		5/7/82	D	3	(1)	
28	Velimir IVANOVIĆ	SRB	22/11/78	M	20	(3)	
19	Plamen KRUMOV		4/11/85	M	13	(4)	1
32	Kostadin MARKOV		18/2/79	M	18	(1)	
88	Kiril MIHAILOV		13/2/85	M		(1)	
15	Dimitar MUTAFOV		25/11/73	D	8	(7)	
17	Atanas NIKOLOV		21/7/77	A	15	(4)	4
3	Adrian OLEGOV		1/5/85	D	28		2
10	Tomislav PAVLOV		28/6/91	M	1		
9	Petar PETROV		19/4/84	M	5	(7)	1
9	Stanislav RUMENOV		11/2/80	A	1	(8)	
20	Nikolai STANKOV		11/12/84	D	1	(2)	1
7	Mladen STOEV		26/1/84	M	5	(7)	2
13	Ivailo STOYANOV		13/7/90	A	1		
8	Rumen TRIFONOV		22/2/85	D	14		3
14	Ivailo TSVETKOV		28/8/79	M	26		2
7	Josué dos Santos "VALMIR"	BRA	11/4/79	M	1	(4)	
5	Ventsislav VASILEV		8/7/88	D	1		
24	Lyubomir VITANOV		11/5/81	M	22	(5)	
6	Daniel ZLATKOV		6/3/89	D	18	(1)	1

PFC MONTANA
Coach – Stevica Kuzmanovski (MKD);
(23/12/09) Atanas Dzhambazki
Founded – 1921
Stadium – Ogosta (4,000)

2009
8/8	Sliven	h	0-0	
15/8	Botev	a	3-2	Chepilov, Ivanov V. (p), Michev
22/8	Minyor	h	0-0	
30/8	Litex	a	0-3	
11/9	Slavia	h	2-0	Michev, Nikolov
18/9	Lokomotiv Sofia	a	0-0	
26/9	CSKA	h	1-2	Harlov
3/10	Chernomorets	a	1-1	Chepilov
17/10	Lokomotiv Plovdiv	h	2-3	Luiz Eduardo 2
23/10	Beroe	a	0-0	
31/10	Sportist	h	1-0	Ivanov M.
6/11	Lokomotiv Mezdra	a	2-0	Trifonov, Beto
20/11	Pirin	h	0-3	
28/11	Levski	a	1-3	Beto
7/12	Cherno More	h	1-2	Nikolov

2010
27/2	Sliven	a	0-1	
6/3	Botev	h	3-0	(w/o)
12/3	Minyor	a	1-1	Chepilov
20/3	Litex	h	0-0	
24/3	Slavia	a	0-4	
29/3	Lokomotiv Sofia	h	0-1	
4/4	CSKA	a	1-1	Kondev
10/4	Chernomorets	h	2-0	Michev, Luiz Eduardo
15/4	Lokomotiv Plovdiv	a	4-2	Ivanov V. 2 (1p), Chepilov, Petrov
18/4	Beroe	h	2-1	Luiz Eduardo, Hikmet
21/4	Sportist	a	1-0	Ivanov M.
26/4	Lokomotiv Mezdra	h	1-1	Ivanov V.
2/5	Pirin	a	0-2	
9/5	Levski	h	0-2	
16/5	Cherno More	a	1-2	Iliev

No	Name	Nat	DoB	Pos	Aps	(s)	Gls
9	Hristo BANCHEV		12/6/81	A		(4)	
19	Webert da Silva Miguel "BETO"	BRA	15/11/86	M	12	(1)	2
17	Slavcho BOICHEV		2/5/83	D	16	(2)	
11	Atanas CHEPILOV		6/2/87	A	24	(3)	4
20	Radoslav DIMITROV		12/8/88	M	13		
25	Atanas FIDANIN		9/8/86	D	13	(2)	
21	Daniel GADZHEV		21/6/85	M	18	(1)	
12	Viktor GEORGIEV		28/10/83	G	4		
13	Stefan HARLOV		16/1/83	A	3	(6)	1
5	Ahmet HIKMET		5/10/84	M	5	(4)	1
8	Dimitar ILIEV		27/7/86	D	17	(5)	1
3	Georgi IVANOV		13/3/80	D	8	(1)	
33	Hristo IVANOV		6/4/82	G	13		
20	Miroslav IVANOV		11/9/81	M	19	(4)	2
10	Ventsislav IVANOV		20/5/82	A	23	(3)	4
22	JÚLIO CÉSAR Mendes Moreira	BRA	19/1/83	M	7	(3)	
22	Svetlan KONDEV		23/1/76	A	2	(5)	1
9	Anton LICHKOV		5/8/80	A	17	(1)	
9	LUIZ EDUARDO Azevedo Dantas	BRA	24/5/85	A	18	(6)	4
5	Simeon MECHEV		16/3/90	D	2	(1)	
16	Vladimir MICHEV		20/11/85	M	14	(12)	3
5	Nikolai NIKOLOV		26/1/81	D	14		2
18	Miroslav PETROV		7/6/81	A	4	(10)	1
77	Strahil POPOV		31/8/90	M		(2)	
19	Igor TASKOVIĆ	SRB	10/9/81	M	2	(2)	
7	Yordan TODOROV		12/11/81	M	2	(5)	
6	Tihomir TRIFONOV		25/11/86	D	25		1
1	Tsvetomir TSANKOV		6/6/84	G	12		
4	Stanislav ZHEKOV		6/2/80	D	12		

PFC PIRIN BLAGOEVGRAD

Coach – Naji Shensoy; (30/10/09) Vasil Petrov;
(9/11/09) Stefan Grozdanov
Founded – 1931
Stadium – Hristo Botev (6,500); Osogovo, Kyustendil (5,000)

2009
8/8	Minyor	h	0-1	
15/8	Litex	a	1-0	Tsachev
22/8	Slavia	h	1-0	Tsachev
29/8	Lokomotiv Sofia	a	0-1	
12/9	CSKA	h	0-0	
20/9	Chernomorets	a	1-2	Kocev
27/9	Lokomotiv Plovdiv	h	0-0	
5/10	Beroe	a	1-1	Peev
17/10	Sportist	h	2-0	Mladenov 2
24/10	Lokomotiv Mezdra	a	0-4	
30/10	Cherno More	h	1-0	Peev
8/11	Levski	h	0-2	
20/11	Montana	a	3-0	Peev 2 (1p), Stoyanov
27/11	Sliven	h	2-0	Kondev, Galchev
5/12	Botev	a	2-2	Kondev, Mladenov

2010
27/2	Minyor	a	1-0	Kondev
7/3	Litex	h	4-1	Mladenov, Kocev, Kondev, Zlatkovski
13/3	Slavia	a	0-0	
21/3	Lokomotiv Sofia	h	1-1	Mladenov
24/3	CSKA	a	1-1	Zlatkovski
29/3	Chernomorets	h	1-3	og (Hajri)
2/4	Lokomotiv Plovdiv	a	0-2	
10/4	Beroe	h	2-2	Zlatkovski, Kondev
14/4	Sportist	a	1-1	Mladenov
17/4	Lokomotiv Mezdra	h	3-1	Zlatkovski 2, Kondev
21/4	Cherno More	a	1-1	Zlatkovski (p)
24/4	Levski	a	0-2	
2/5	Montana	h	2-5	Kondev, Kocev
9/5	Sliven	a	0-4	
16/5	Botev	h	3-0	(w/o)

No	Name	Nat	DoB	Pos	Aps	(s)	Gls
11	Radoslav ANEV		1/2/85	D	11	(2)	
21	Nikolai DIMIROV		6/6/85	D		(5)	
2	Alexander DYULGEROV		19/4/90	M	5	(1)	
18	Boris GALCHEV		31/10/83	M	15		1
22	Veselin GANEV		15/9/87	G	9		
6	Georgi GEORGIEV		25/2/81	D	26		
16	Kostadin KATSIMERSKI		7/2/87	D	1	(3)	
20	Dragi KOCEV	MKD	25/2/87	M	24	(2)	3
26	Boris KONDEV		29/8/79	A	20	(8)	7
12	Blagoi MAKENDZHIEV		11/7/88	D	20		
3	Ivan MIHOV		8/6/91	D	2	(3)	
27	Radoslav MITREVSKI		22/4/81	D	27		
17	Daniel MLADENOV		25/5/87	M	19	(7)	6
23	Diyan MOLDOVANOV		2/4/85	D	13	(3)	
8	Blagoi NAKOV		19/3/85	M	2	(9)	
10	Todor PALANKOV		13/1/84	M	27		
28	Daniel PEEV		6/10/84	M	15		4
26	Yulian POPEV		7/7/86	D	17	(3)	
25	Miroslav RIZOV		10/10/76	D	23		
14	Yanko SANDANSKI		23/11/88	M	12	(1)	
19	Todor SIMOV		26/1/85	A		(2)	
1	Stefan STANCHEV		26/4/89	D	8	(2)	
19	Kaloyan STOYANOV		2/11/86	A	1	(14)	1
13	Miroslav TODOROV		26/6/85	M		(2)	
9	Ivan TSACHEV		18/1/89	A	7	(5)	2
11	Dimitar VODENICHAROV		26/12/87	A	5	(1)	
18	Alexander YAKIMOV		27/4/89	M		(4)	
7	Zoran ZLATKOVSKI	MKD	5/4/87	A	10	(7)	6

PFC SLAVIA SOFIA

Coach – Velislav Vutsov
Founded – 1913
Stadium – Slavia (25,000)
MAJOR HONOURS:
Bulgarian League – (7) – 1928, 1930, 1936, 1939, 1941, 1943, 1996;
Bulgarian Cup – (7) 1952, 1963, 1964, 1966, 1975,
1980 (as Soviet Army Cup), 1996.

2009
10/8	Sportist	a	1-1	Kolev
15/8	Lokomotiv Mezdra	h	1-0	Mladenov (p)
22/8	Pirin	a	0-1	
29/8	Levski	h	1-3	José Júnior
11/9	Montana	a	0-2	
19/9	Sliven	h	2-1	José Júnior, Kolev
26/9	Botev	a	1-0	Kolev
2/10	Minyor	h	1-0	Didi González
17/10	Litex	a	0-1	
26/10	Cherno More	a	1-1	José Júnior
1/11	Lokomotiv Sofia	h	0-0	
8/11	CSKA	a	0-2	
22/11	Chernomorets	h	3-2	José Júnior 3 (1p)
30/11	Lokomotiv Plovdiv	a	2-0	José Júnior 2
4/12	Beroe	h	3-1	Santos Du Bala 2, Petkov

2010
27/2	Sportist	h	1-0	Alberoni
5/3	Lokomotiv Mezdra	a	0-0	
13/3	Pirin	h	0-0	
20/3	Levski	a	0-3	
24/3	Montana	h	4-0	José Júnior 2 (1p), Kolev, Ivanov
28/3	Sliven	a	2-1	José Júnior, Ivanov
2/4	Botev	h	3-0	(w/o)
9/4	Minyor	a	1-0	Kolev
14/4	Litex	h	1-1	Peev
17/4	Cherno More	h	1-0	Dyulgerov
21/4	Lokomotiv Sofia	a	0-0	
24/4	CSKA	h	1-3	Popara
2/5	Chernomorets	a	2-2	Kolev (p), Valev
9/5	Lokomotiv Plovdiv	h	1-3	Petkov
16/5	Beroe	a	1-0	José Júnior

No	Name	Nat	DoB	Pos	Aps	(s)	Gls
11	Francisco Terra ALBERONI	BRA	16/5/84	A	1		1
15	Galin BOGDANOV		6/9/90	M	4		
24	Didac "DIDI" Rodríguez GONZÁLEZ	ESP	20/2/85	M	3	(3)	1
	Petar DIMITROV		28/2/82	M	6	(3)	
20	Radoslav DIMITROV		12/8/88	M	8	(2)	
2	Atanas DRENOVICHKI		5/4/90	D	4	(6)	
21	Bogomil DYAKOV		12/4/84	D	19		
6	Nikolai DYULGEROV		10/3/88	M	15	(7)	1
8	Borislav GEORGIEV		17/7/74	D	21	(2)	
14	Stoyan GEORGIEV		15/6/86	D	2		
23	Yordan GOSPODINOV		15/6/78	G	2		
33	Galin IVANOV		15/4/88	M	20	(8)	2
11	JOSÉ Carlos Nogueira JÚNIOR	BRA	18/7/85	A	24	(4)	12
11	Steeve JOSEPH-REINETTE	FRA	2/12/83	D	18		
5	Martin KAVDANSKI		13/2/87	D	9	(1)	
9	Todor KOLEV		2/8/80	A	20	(3)	6
77	Milan KOPRIVAROV		20/7/83	A	1	(3)	
20	Raïs M'BOHLI	ALG	25/4/86	G	25		
7	Alexander MLADENOV		25/6/82	A	3	(4)	1
10	Asen NIKOLOV		5/8/76	M	4	(1)	
77	Daniel PEEV		6/10/84	M	13	(1)	1
35	Yordan PETKOV		11/3/76	D	19	(1)	2
12	Emil PETROV		22/7/83	G	2		
4	Nikolai PETROV		30/9/88	M	15	(3)	
22	Robert PETROV	MKD	2/6/78	D	17	(3)	
27	Pavle POPARA	SRB	20/5/87	M	21	(4)	1
18	Radoslav RANGELOV		18/9/85	D	1	(2)	
29	Tomasz SAJDAK	POL	11/10/84	M		(2)	
28	Eduardo Roberto dos Santos "SANTOS DU BALA"	BRA	2/8/81	A	4	(9)	2
28	Alexander TOMASH		2/9/78	D	9	(3)	
9	Nikolai VALEV		24/4/80	A	4	(5)	1
17	Dzhuneit YASHAR		30/12/82	M	5	(4)	
14	Ivan ZDRAVKOV		25/6/91	M			

OFC SLIVEN 2000
Coach – Diyan Petkov; (4/11/09) Dragoljub Simonović (SRB)
Founded – 2000
Stadium – Hadzhi Dimitar (14,000)

2009

8/8	Montana	a	0-0	
15/8	Cherno More	a	0-4	
22/8	Botev	h	3-0	Hristov, og (Vergilov), Iliev
29/8	Minyor	a	2-4	Kovachev, Hristov
13/9	Litex	h	1-2	Mindev
19/9	Slavia	a	1-2	Hristov
25/9	Lokomotiv Sofia	h	1-3	Kovachev
5/10	CSKA	a	0-1	
16/10	Chernomorets	h	0-1	
24/10	Lokomotiv Plovdiv	a	2-1	Hristov 2
2/11	Beroe	h	1-1	Ignatov
7/11	Sportist	a	0-1	
21/11	Lokomotiv Mezdra	h	1-0	Kikov
27/11	Pirin	a	0-2	
6/12	Levski	h	1-0	Hristov

2010

27/2	Montana	h	1-0	Hristov (p)
8/3	Cherno More	h	0-0	
12/3	Botev	a	3-0	(w/o)
21/3	Minyor	h	1-3	Hristov (p)
25/3	Litex	a	0-1	
28/3	Slavia	h	1-2	Hristov
3/4	Lokomotiv Sofia	a	0-2	
10/4	CSKA	h	2-4	Mindev, Kovachev
13/4	Chernomorets	a	0-2	
19/4	Lokomotiv Plovdiv	h	1-1	Tonev
22/4	Beroe	a	1-0	Hristov
25/5	Sportist	h	1-0	Yamukov
2/5	Lokomotiv Mezdra	a	1-1	Yamukov
9/5	Pirin	h	4-0	Mindev, Kikov, Adriano Miranda, Bakalov
16/5	Levski	a	0-2	

No	Name	Nat	DoB	Pos	Aps	(s)	Gls
24	ADRIANO MIRANDA de Carvalho	BRA	22/6/89	M	13		1
11	Atanas APOSTOLOV		11/3/89	A		(3)	
8	Dimo BAKALOV		19/12/88	M	2	(10)	1
6	Nikolai DIMITROV		12/6/90	D	7	(5)	
2	Zhivko DINEV		30/7/87	D	6	(5)	
1	Petar DENCHEV		16/3/89	G	5		
24	Filip FILIPOV		2/8/88	M	25	(3)	
1	Ivan GEORGIEV		20/5/85	G	5		
14	Deyan HRISTOV		28/2/82	A	27	(2)	10
19	Evgeni IGNATOV		4/6/88	M	5	(4)	1
10	Iliya ILIEV		20/12/74	M	12	(3)	1
25	Yavor IVANOV		11/9/91	D	2	(5)	
12	Evgeni KARAMANOV		26/3/86	G	7		
3	Stefan KIKOV		2/4/82	D	22	(1)	2
20	Ivan KOKONOV		17/8/91	A	1	(4)	
16	Martin KOVACHEV		12/3/82	D	26		3
30	Marko MARKOV		11/9/81	D	2	(5)	
7	Miroslav MINDEV		27/7/80	A	21	(3)	3
17	Viktor PETAKOV		27/1/89	M	3	(3)	
21	Ivailo PETROV		23/1/91	M	3	(7)	
28	Borislav STOICHEV		26/11/86	D	5		
22	Petar STOYANOV		15/8/85	D	27	(1)	
1	Todor TODOROV		9/5/82	G	12		
15	Alexander TONEV		3/2/90	A	20	(3)	1
20	Tsvetomir VALERIEV		16/8/83	M	5		
18	Yavor VANDEV		29/5/83	A	5	(6)	
13	Vasil VELEV		15/1/84	D	9	(8)	
25	Velichko VELICHKOV		8/7/86	D	2		
19	Valentin VESELINOV		15/6/92	M		(1)	
27	Vladislav YAMUKOV		22/3/80	D	18		2
23	Ivelin YANEV		23/11/86	D	21		
18	Atanas ZEHIROV		13/2/89	M	1	(4)	

PFC SPORTIST SVOGE
Coach – Alexandar Alexandrov; (1/9/09) Stefan Kolev;
(24/10/09) Ivan Atanasov; (24/12/09) Stoicho Stoev
Founded – 1924
Stadium – Gradski (5,000)

2009

10/8	Slavia	h	1-1	Semerdzhiev
14/8	Lokomotiv Sofia	a	2-3	Dimov, Antonov
23/8	CSKA	h	0-2	
29/8	Chernomorets	a	0-3	
12/9	Lokomotiv Plovdiv	h	2-1	Antonov (p), Dimitrov
19/9	Beroe	a	0-1	
26/9	Cherno More	h	2-1	Shopov, Antonov
3/10	Lokomotiv Mezdra	h	0-4	
17/10	Pirin	a	0-2	
25/10	Levski	h	2-3	Simov, Antonov (p)
31/10	Montana	a	0-1	
7/11	Sliven	h	1-0	Tsvetkov
21/11	Botev	a	1-1	Antonov
28/11	Minyor	h	0-1	
7/12	Litex	a	0-2	

2010

27/2	Slavia	a	0-1	
7/3	Lokomotiv Sofia	h	1-5	Pietrobon
13/3	CSKA	a	1-4	Petrov M. (p)
20/3	Chernomorets	h	0-0	
23/3	Lokomotiv Plovdiv	a	0-3	
28/3	Beroe	h	1-2	Tsvetkov (p)
4/4	Cherno More	a	0-3	
11/4	Lokomotiv Mezdra	a	1-2	Mladenov S.
14/4	Pirin	h	1-1	Nakov
17/4	Levski	a	0-5	
21/4	Montana	h	0-1	
25/4	Sliven	a	0-1	
2/5	Botev	h	3-0	(w/o)
9/5	Minyor	a	2-1	Mladenov S. 2
16/5	Litex	h	2-4	Dimitrov, Ignatov

No	Name	Nat	DoB	Pos	Aps	(s)	Gls
9	Miroslav ANTONOV		10/3/86	A	14	(1)	5
2	Danail BACHKOV		21/12/76	D	15		
20	Georgi BIZHEV		6/7/81	A	2	(4)	
14	Deyan BORISOV		1/3/89	M	5	(9)	
77	Georgi CHAKAROV		13/1/89	M	3	(1)	
20	Nikolai CHIPEV		20/2/89	M	2	(1)	
15	Victor DENIRAN	NGA	27/5/90	A	19	(2)	
7	Ivailo DIMITROV		26/3/89	A	15	(9)	2
33	Martin DIMOV		1/3/86	D	22	(1)	1
3	Diyan DONCHEV		8/1/74	D	14	(1)	
8	Kiril GEORGIEV		21/6/90	M		(1)	
20	Antoni GRIGOROV		9/10/90	A		(1)	
18	Grozdan GROZDANOV		19/6/84	M		(1)	
23	Nikolai HARIZANOV		14/6/83	D	7		
19	Evgeni IGNATOV		4/6/88	M	7	(6)	1
4	Borislav ILIEV		18/2/88	D	12	(5)	
8	Nikola IVANOV		11/8/88	D	1	(1)	
30	Georgi KORUDZHIEV		2/3/88	M	11	(6)	
18	Kiril KRUMOV		29/6/83	D	4	(1)	
27	Todor KYUCHUKOV		26/1/78	G	21		
11	Nikolai MARINOV		3/4/86	A	4	(2)	
6	Luchezar MLADENOV		19/3/82	D	26		
32	Stoicho MLADENOV		27/8/85	A	18	(3)	3
90	Dimitar NAKOV		18/10/80	M	7		1
28	Lyudmil NIKOLOV		27/8/84	D	1	(2)	
77	Marin PETROV		7/8/77	M	11	(2)	1
23	Svetoslav PETROV		20/8/88	M	1		
18	Germán Ariel PIETROBON	ARG	1/4/83	A	9	(3)	1
99	Georgi SEMERDZHIEV		7/8/86	M	2	(5)	1
90	Petar SHOPOV		14/1/78	A	4	(4)	1
12	Dimitar SIMEONOV		6/7/86	G	3		
19	Todor SIMOV		26/1/85	A	5	(1)	1
1	Alexander STOYANOV		25/7/86	G	4		
12	Denislav STOYANOV		16/4/86	G	1		
23	Kristiyan STOYANOV		13/5/90	D		(1)	
13	Stoyan TODOROV		9/8/82	D	21	(2)	
10	Nikolai TSVETKOV		10/8/87	M	19	(6)	2
28	Ivo VARBANOV		1/3/87	D	1		
5	Petar VASILEV		20/6/83	D	8	(4)	

PROMOTED CLUBS

PFC KALIAKRA KAVARNA
Coach – Radostin Trifonov; (5/10/10) Filip Filipov
Founded - 1922
Stadium – Gradski (3,000)

PFC VIDIMA-RAKOVSKI SEVLIEVO
Coach – Dimitar Todorov
Founded – 1997
Stadium – Rakovski (6,000)

PFC AKADEMIK SOFIA
Coach – Krasimir Borisov; (20/9/09) Samir Seliminski
Founded – 1947
Stadium – Akademik (5,000)

SECOND LEVEL FINAL TABLES 2009/10

ASTERN B PFG

	Pld	W	D	L	F	A	Pts
PFC Kaliakra Kavarna	28	17	6	5	44	20	57
PFC Nesebar	28	17	6	5	56	24	57
PFC Dunav Ruse	28	16	6	6	48	29	54
FC Spartak Plovdiv	28	13	8	7	36	24	47
Lyubimets 2007	28	12	9	7	39	24	45
PFC Brestnik 1948 Plovdiv	28	13	6	9	42	29	45
PFC Chernomorets Pomorie	28	13	4	11	46	36	43
PFC Chernomorets Balchik	28	12	6	10	37	30	42
PFC Spartak Varna	28	11	4	13	33	41	37
0 FC Panayot Volov	28	9	6	13	37	40	33
1 PFC Svetkavista Targovishte	28	8	8	12	28	31	32
2 FC Svilengrad 1921	28	10	1	17	36	58	31
3 PFC Dobrudzha 1919	28	8	6	14	27	39	30
4 PFC Minyor Radnevo	28	8	6	14	34	46	30
5 PFC Rodopa Smolyan	28	1	2	25	6	78	5

*NB PFC Lokomotiv Stara Zagora withdrew before the start of the season;
PFC Rodopa Smolyan withdrew after round 15 – their remaining
matches were awarded as 0-3 defeats.*

WESTERN B PFG

	Pld	W	D	L	F	A	Pts
PFC Vidima-Rakovski Sevlievo	30	19	3	8	53	32	60
2 PFC Akademik Sofia	30	18	5	7	49	37	59
3 FC Bansko 1951	30	17	8	5	50	22	59
4 PFC Vihren Sandanski	30	16	8	6	45	24	56
5 PFC Etar Veliko 1924 Tarnovo	30	13	8	9	47	38	47
6 OFC Botev Vratsa	30	11	12	7	39	26	45
7 FC Septemvri Simitli	30	13	4	13	40	34	43
8 PFC Chavdar Etropole	30	12	7	11	34	32	43
9 PFC Balkan Botevgrad	30	9	14	7	35	28	41
10 PFC Marek Dupnitsa	30	12	5	13	36	36	41
11 PFC Pirin Gotse Delchev	30	11	7	12	35	38	40
12 PFC Kom-Minyor Berkovista	30	10	8	12	36	43	38
13 FC Botev Krivodov	30	8	7	15	21	40	31
14 PFC Rilski Sportist Samokov	30	8	6	16	32	49	30
15 PFC Bdin Vidin	30	4	8	18	26	48	20
16 PFC Belite orli Pleven	30	2	4	24	20	71	10

*NB PFC Belite orli Pleven withdrew after round 15 – their remaining
matches were awarded as 0-3 defeats.*

PROMOTION PLAY-OFF
(23/5/10)
Nesebar 1, Akademik 2

DOMESTIC CUP 2009/10

KUPA NA BULGARIYA

SECOND ROUND

(24/11/09)
Sliven 1, Pirin Blagoevgrad 0

(25/11/09)
Botev Vratsa 2, Chernomorets Balchik 0
Chernomorets Burgas 0, Cherno More 2
Chernomorets Pomorie 3, Dunav 0
Kaliakra 2, Lokomotiv Plovdiv 0
Lokomotiv Mezdra 3, Sportist Svoge 0
Lokomotiv Sofia 2, Botev Plovdiv 1
Marek 2, Belite Orli 0
Maritsa 3, Minyor Radnevo 1
Rilski Sportist 0, Chavdar Etropole 2
Svilengrad 0, CSKA Sofia 1
Vihren 0, Slavia Sofia 0 *(aet; 3-4 on pens)*

(2/12/09)
Septemvri Simitli 0, Minyor Pernik 0 *(aet; 4-5 on pens)*

(3/12/09)
Pirin Gotse Delchev 0, Litex 4

(9/12/09)
Brestnik 0, Levski 2

(10/12/09)
Montana 0, Beroe 1

THIRD ROUND

(12/12/09)
Chernomorets Pomorie 1, Botev Vratsa 0
CSKA Sofia 1, Litex 0
Lokomotiv Sofia 1, Slavia Sofia 2
Marek 1, Kaliakra 5
Maritsa 0, Chavdar Etropole 1 *(aet)*
Minyor Pernik 1, Sliven 0

(13/12/09)
Cherno More 4, Levski 1
Lokomotiv Mezdra 0, Beroe 3

QUARTER-FINALS

(31/3/10)
Beroe 1 *(Pisarov 72)*, CSKA Sofia 0
Chavdar Etropole 0, Slavia Sofia 0 *(aet; 4-2 on pens)*
Chernomorets Pomorie 2 *(Pehlivanov 56, Petkov 88)*, Minyor Pernik 0
Kaliakra 0, Cherno More 0 *(aet; 3-2 on pens)*

SEMI-FINALS

(28/4/10)
Chavdar Etropole 0, Beroe 1 *(Atanasov A. 39)*
Chernomorets Pomorie 1 *(Filipov T. 33)*, Kaliakra 1 *(Stoilov 13)* *(aet; 3-0
on pens)*

FINAL

(5/5/10)
Gradski stadium, Lovech
PFC BEROE STARA ZAGORA 1 *(Atanasov D. 90)*
PFC CHERNOMORETS POMORIE 0
Referee – Yordanov
BEROE – Peikov, Iliev, Ivanov, Bachev, Atanasov A. (Todorov 46),
Kostadinov, Genchev (Stankov 71), Pisarov, Zhekov, Atanasov D.,
Andonov.
CHERNOMORETS POMORIE – Georgiev, Koev, Dimov P., Velkov,
Orachev, Manev, Kostadinov, Mitev, Chakarov (Dimov G. 89),
Pehlivanov, Filipov T. (Filipov V. 90).

Dinamo title triumph turns sour

NK Dinamo Zagreb showed no sign of abdicating their Croatian championship crown in 2009/10, leading from the front all season and securing their fifth successive title with a May Day goalless draw at home to HNK Hajduk Split. However, there would be no fourth straight domestic double, Hajduk defeating Dinamo in the Croatian Cup semi-final and going on to win their first trophy for five years.

Omnipotent for so long, Dinamo did not take kindly to surrendering the Cup to their bitter arch-rivals. In fact, their form in the league tailed off dramatically after that 1-0 aggregate defeat, and although they were too far in front to be caught, the season ended in dispiriting fashion for the club and their ever-demanding supporters. That 0-0 stalemate against Hajduk in the Maksimir – an identical result to the first leg of the Cup semi-final – was hardly the most illuminating way in which to seal the title. Furthermore, it sat in the middle of a five-game winless run, the consequences of which were a reduction of the team's margin of victory to just four points and, following reports of dressing-room unrest, the post-season resignation of coach Krunoslav Jurčić.

Krunoslav Jurčić left Dinamo Zagreb after leading them to three trophies during his 14-month reign

It was an undignified end to what, in general, had been a more than satisfactory season for the club. Although they failed to reach the promised land of the UEFA Champions League, going out to FC Salzburg after a second-leg home defeat in the third qualifying round, they did make it into the UEFA Europa League group stage and, following a memorable 1-0 win at RSC Anderlecht, were still in contention for a place in the round of 32 going into their last fixture. But a third home defeat out of three, against FC Timişoara, scuppered their hopes of extended European involvement. Dinamo had won the reverse fixture in Romania 3-0 but the misbehaviour of their travelling fans had led to the imposition of a three-point penalty, only for it to be waived by UEFA's Appeals Body.

Opening blitz

Domestically, Dinamo may have gone out like lambs, but they went in like lions, wresting control of the 1. HNL title race from day one. They hammered newly promoted NK Istra 7-1 in their opening game and took 28 points from their first ten, scoring 37 goals in the process – more than half of their final total. With the league having been controversially increased to accommodate 16 clubs, rather than the previous dozen, Dinamo responded by reducing many of their opponents to cannon fodder. By the winter break, with 17 of the 30 games completed, they had a six-point lead over surprise packages HNK Cibalia and HNK Šibenik. As for traditional pursuers Hajduk, they were out of the frame completely, 11 points adrift in seventh place.

Dinamo maintained their form in March to give themselves sufficient protection before the April/May slump. Their talented young central defender Dejan Lovren left for Olympique Lyonnais in January but the team's other key players all remained to collect their winner's medals, including young Croatian international striker Mario Mandžukić, who, with 14 goals, could not quite match his top-scoring tally of the previous season but still ended up as Dinamo's leading marksman, registering one goal more than Chilean playmaker Pedro

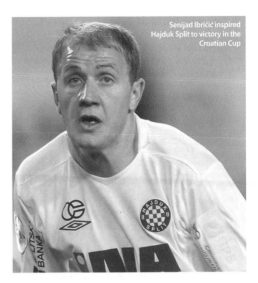
Senijad Ibričić inspired Hajduk Split to victory in the Croatian Cup

Morales, the pick of Dinamo's South American clan. Another homegrown youngster to impress was 21-year-old midfielder Milan Badelj, of whom comparisons were made with former Dinamo star Luka Modrić.

Top man Ibričić

The season's outstanding individual, however, was neither a Dinamo player nor a Croatian. Like his team, Hajduk's Bosnia-Herzegovina international playmaker Senijad Ibričić may have taken a while to get his season into gear, but once he did there was no stopping him. His efforts not only made him an inspirational figure for Hajduk's belligerent Torcida fan-base but also had a major impact on the club's dramatic form swing, which resulted in their Croatian Cup triumph and an astonishing rise up the league table to finish second.

Ibričić ended the season with 17 goals in the league – just one shy of the 1. HNL's leading marksman, NK Zagreb's Davor Vugrinec – and he was Hajduk's main man also in the Cup, scoring the only goal of the semi-final against Dinamo and one in each leg of the final against Šibenik, which Hajduk won 4-1 on aggregate to take the trophy for the fifth time, ending a seven-year wait. The man who led them to victory was 72-year-old Stanko Poklepović, Hajduk's fifth coach of the season.

A dreadful start to the domestic campaign – no wins in their first five matches – was exacerbated by European elimination. The UEFA Europa League qualifying tie with MŠK Žilina was a horror show from first to last, with uninvited Hajduk fans going on the rampage in Slovakia, coach Ivan Katalinić suffering a heart attack, the team losing 1-0 at the Poljud and, in consequence, the club's entire board of directors resigning.

Tasty welcome

A new president, Joško Svaguša, the owner of a chain of bakeries and pastry houses, came in – to be welcomed by unhappy Hajduk fans hurling doughnuts on to the pitch in protest at his appointment. He hired, at some expense, Italian coach Edoardo Reja to steer the club out of troubled waters, and although there were signs of improvement in the run-up to Christmas, Reja was no longer there when the league resumed in February, having returned to his homeland to become the new coach of S.S. Lazio. The call then went out to old-timer Poklepović, who thus took charge of his hometown club for the third time (after spells in 1984-86 and 1991-93). Happy to help on a fraction of his predecessor's salary, he finally brought some stability and Hajduk won

nine of their remaining 13 league games as well as lifting the Cup.

Šibenik fancied their chances of winning a first major trophy when they held Hajduk 1-1 going into the closing minutes of the first leg of the Cup final. Even at 2-1 down with the home leg to come, their supporters remained optimistic. But it was not to be, Hajduk's 2-0 win leaving Šibenik with the consolation of a first ever qualification for European football – a milestone attained by their unlikely fourth-place finish in the league. Also set for a European debut were Cibalia, who rose from eighth in 2008/09 to third in 2009/10, finishing just five points in arrears of champions Dinamo. But for a last-day defeat at NK Osijek, Stanko Mršić's side, who were unbeaten at home in Vinkovci, would have been runners-up.

Of the four newly promoted teams NK Karlovac did best, defying all pre-season predictions by finishing sixth. Great credit was due to their coach, ex-Croatia international striker Igor Pamić, who worked wonders with limited resources to create a team that were extremely tough to beat. NK Međimurje went straight back down, accompanied by bottom club NK Croatia Sesvete. RNK Split and NK Hrvatski Dragovoljac Zagreb came up from the second division, the latter only because second-placed NK Pomorac Kostrena were refused a licence to compete at the top level.

For the first time since Croatia seceded from Yugoslavia, a FIFA World Cup final tournament took place without them. Slaven Bilić's side were thumped twice by an

England side seeking – and obtaining – revenge for UEFA EURO 2008, and although back-to-back wins over Belarus kept alive Croatian hopes of reaching the qualifying play-offs, England's subsequent defeat in Ukraine extinguished them.

Positive run

Bilić had intended to call it quits and seek a club job, but he later changed his mind and decided to stay on for at least two more years. A positive run of results in post-qualification friendlies, with five games yielding four wins, one draw and no goals against, suggested that he could make amends for the World Cup failure by steering the team to UEFA EURO 2012. As the seeded team in a favourable section containing Greece, Israel, Latvia, Georgia and Malta, and with experienced, top-class performers such as Modrić, Niko Kranjčar, Ivan Rakitić and Ivica Olić to call upon, qualification for Poland/Ukraine may be viewed by some Croatian fans as an obligation rather than a challenge.

Hrvatski nogometni savez (HNS)

Rusanova 13
HR-10000 Zagreb
tel – +385 1 2361 555
fax – +385 1 2441 500
website – hns-cff.hr
email – info@hns-cff.hr
Year of Formation – 1912

President – Vlatko Marković
General Secretary – Zorislav Srebrić
Media Officer – Davor Gavran
National Stadium – Maksimir, Zagreb (38,079)

INTERNATIONAL TOURNAMENT APPEARANCES
FIFA World Cup – (3) 1998 (3rd), 2002, 2006.
UEFA European Championship – (3) 1996 (qtr-finals), 2004, 2008 (qtr-finals).
TOP FIVE ALL-TIME CAPS
Dario Šimić (100); Robert Kovač (84); Niko Kovač (83); Robert Jarni (81); Stipe Pletikosa (80)
TOP FIVE ALL-TIME GOALS
Davor Šuker (45); Eduardo da Silva & Darijo Srna (18); Goran Vlaović (15); Niko Kovač (14)

NATIONAL TEAM RESULTS 2009/10

Date	Opponent		Venue	Score	Scorers
12/8/09	Belarus (WCQ)	A	Minsk	3-1	*Olić (22, 85), Eduardo (69)*
5/9/09	Belarus (WCQ)	H	Zagreb	1-0	*Rakitić (24)*
9/9/09	England (WCQ)	A	Wembley	1-5	*Eduardo (71)*
8/10/09	Qatar	H	Rijeka	3-2	*Ćorluka (7), Klasnić (11), Jelavić (90)*
14/10/09	Kazakhstan (WCQ)	A	Astana	2-1	*Vukojević (10), Kranjčar (90+3)*
14/11/09	Liechtenstein	H	Vinkovci	5-0	*Bilić (1, 49), Srna (10), Eduardo (23, 47)*
3/3/09	Belgium	A	Brussels	1-0	*Kranjčar (63)*
19/5/10	Austria	A	Klagenfurt	1-0	*Bilić (86)*
23/5/10	Wales	H	Osijek	2-0	*Rakitić (45), Gabrić (82)*
26/5/10	Estonia	A	Tallinn	0-0	

NATIONAL TEAM APPEARANCES 2009/10

Coach – Slaven BILIĆ	11/9/68		BLR	BLR	ENG	Qat	KAZ	Lie	Bel	Aut	Wal	Est	Caps	Goals
Vedran RUNJE	10/2/76	Lens (FRA)	G	G	G	G	G		G				13	-
Vedran ĆORLUKA	5/2/86	Tottenham (ENG)	D	D 78*		D66	D		D				37	1
Ivica KRIŽANAC	13/4/79	Zenit (RUS)	D46	D	D	D		D46	D56				11	-
Josip ŠIMUNIĆ	18/2/78	Hoffenheim (GER)	D	D	D			D	D46	D	D		78	3
Danijel PRANJIĆ	2/12/81	Bayern (GER)	D	D	M	D46	D	D	s65			M	30	-
Darijo SRNA	1/5/82	Shakhtar (UKR)	M	M	D	M74	M94	M59	M91	D	D75		74	18
Luka MODRIĆ	9/9/85	Tottenham (ENG)	M						M65	M	M		39	7
Ognjen VUKOJEVIĆ	20/12/83	Dynamo Kyiv (UKR)	M	M	M	M90	M	M66	M83	M	M65	s80	23	2
Niko KRANJČAR	13/8/84	Portsmouth (ENG)/Tottenham (ENG)	M66	M	M	M	M	M78	M				55	10
Ivica OLIĆ	14/9/79	Bayern (GER)	A	A73	A46	A46			A55				69	13
EDUARDO da Silva	25/2/83	Arsenal (ENG)	A88	A81	A73		A59	s55					29	18

NATIONAL TEAM APPEARANCES 2009/10 (contd.)

Player	DOB	Club	BLR	BLR	ENG	Qat	KAZ	Lie	Bel	Aut	Wal	Est	Caps	Goals
Ivan RAKITIĆ	10/3/88	Schalke (GER)	s46	M65	s46	s46	M		s56		M77	A	27	8
Mario MANDŽUKIĆ	21/5/86	Dinamo Zagreb	s66	s65	M	s46	A63		s65	M	M90		13	1
Ivan JURIĆ	25/8/75	Genoa (ITA)	s88	s81									5	-
Mladen PETRIĆ	1/1/81	Hamburg (GER)		s73	s46					A60	A46		37	11
Nikola POKRIVAČ	26/11/85	Salzburg (AUT)			D46	M46	s94	s78		s78	s77	M	14	-
Ivan KLASNIĆ	29/1/80	Bolton (ENG)			s73	A64	A76	s59					39	12
Robert KOVAČ	6/4/74	Dinamo Zagreb					D	D					84	-
Dejan LOVREN	5/7/89	Dinamo Zagreb /Lyon (FRA)				s46	D			s46	D	D46	5	-
Nikica JELAVIĆ	27/8/85	Rapid Wien (AUT)				s64	s76	s74			A67	A46	5	1
Hrvoje ČALE	4/3/85	Trabzonspor (TUR)				s66				M		D46	5	-
Anas SHARBINI	21/2/87	Hajduk				s74							1	-
Jerko LEKO	9/4/80	Monaco (FRA)				s90							59	2
Mate BILIĆ	23/10/80	Sporting Gijón (ESP)						s63	A74	A65	s67	s46	5	3
Danijel SUBAŠIĆ	27/10/84	Hajduk							G	G		G	3	-
Mladen BARTULOVIĆ	5/10/86	Kryvbas (UKR)							D				2	-
Drago GABRIĆ	27/9/86	Trabzonspor (TUR)						M	s91	s60	s46	M	5	1
Dario KNEŽEVIĆ	20/4/82	Livorno (ITA)						s46					13	1
Gordon SCHILDENFELD	18/3/85	Sturm (AUT)							s59	D	D		3	-
Tomislav DUJMOVIĆ	26/2/81	Lokomotiv Moskva (RUS)						s66	s83	M78	s65	M80	5	-
Ivan STRINIĆ	17/7/87	Hajduk								D	D	s46	3	-
Stipe PLETIKOSA	8/1/79	Spartak Moskva (RUS)									G		80	-
Domagoj VIDA	29/4/89	Osijek									s75	D	2	-
Milan BADELJ	25/2/89	Dinamo Zagreb									s90	M88	2	-
Luka VUČKO	11/4/84	Eskişehirspor (TUR)										s46	1	-
Jurica BULJAT	19/9/86	Hajduk										s88	1	-

DOMESTIC LEAGUE 2009/10

1.HNL FINAL TABLE

		Pld	Home					Away					Total					Pts
			W	D	L	F	A	W	D	L	F	A	W	D	L	F	A	
1	NK Dinamo Zagreb	30	10	5	0	48	6	8	3	4	22	14	18	8	4	70	20	62
2	HNK Hajduk Split	30	11	2	2	30	8	6	5	4	20	13	17	7	6	50	21	58
3	HNK Cibalia	30	11	4	0	30	6	5	5	5	16	14	16	9	5	46	20	57
4	HNK Šibenik	30	7	6	2	16	10	7	2	6	18	27	14	8	8	34	37	50
5	NK Osijek	30	9	3	3	29	11	4	5	6	20	25	13	8	9	49	36	47
6	NK Karlovac	30	7	5	3	15	8	5	6	4	17	15	12	11	7	32	23	47
7	NK Slaven Koprivnica	30	9	3	3	34	19	2	7	6	10	26	11	10	9	44	45	43
8	NK Lokomotiva Zagreb	30	8	4	3	20	12	4	2	9	15	26	12	6	12	35	38	42
9	HNK Rijeka	30	8	5	2	37	18	2	5	8	12	26	10	10	10	49	44	40
10	NK Varteks	30	7	3	5	22	16	2	6	7	14	27	9	9	12	36	43	36
11	NK Istra	30	8	2	5	19	11	1	6	8	12	29	9	8	13	31	40	35
12	NK Zadar	30	7	5	3	17	12	2	2	11	10	29	9	7	14	27	41	34
13	NK Inter Zaprešić	30	7	1	7	20	21	3	2	10	16	29	10	3	17	36	50	33
14	NK Zagreb	30	7	4	4	27	21	2	2	11	16	28	9	6	15	43	49	33
15	NK Međimurje	30	6	5	4	25	24	2	0	13	12	37	8	5	17	37	61	29
16	NK Croatia Sesvete	30	2	3	10	20	37	1	2	12	10	44	3	5	22	30	81	14

TOP GOALSCORERS

18 Davor VUGRINEC (Zagreb)
17 Senijad IBRIČIĆ (Hajduk)
15 Asim ŠEHIĆ (Istra)
14 Mario MANDŽUKIĆ (Dinamo)
   Nino BULE (Lokomotiva)
13 Pedro MORALES (Dinamo)
   Bojan GOLUBOVIĆ (Međimurje)
11 Milan BADELJ (Dinamo)
   Ermin ZEC (Šibenik)
   Miljenko MUMLEK (Varteks)

 **CROATIA**

CLUB-BY-CLUB

HNK CIBALIA
Coach – Stanko Mršić
Founded – 1919
Stadium – HNK Cibalia (10,000)

2009

Date	Opp		Score	Scorers
25/7	Zadar	a	3-0	Kresinger, Baraban, Mazalović
2/8	Slaven	h	2-0	Parmaković, Baraban
7/8	Inter	a	0-1	
15/8	Rijeka	h	1-0	Pavličić
22/8	Lokomotiva	a	0-2	
29/8	Varteks	h	4-0	Pavličić 2 (1p), Kresinger, Milardović
11/9	Zagreb	a	1-0	Baraban
19/9	Istra	a	0-0	
27/9	Hajduk	h	0-0	
3/10	Šibenik	a	2-0	Malčić 2 (1p)
17/10	Karlovac	h	2-2	Husić, Prgomet
25/10	Dinamo	a	1-1	Kresinger
31/10	Međimurje	h	3-0	Prgomet, Kresinger, Husić
7/11	Croatia	a	3-0	Pavličić, Husić, Kresinger
21/11	Osijek	h	1-1	Pavličić
28/11	Zadar	h	2-0	Lukačević, Jurić
5/12	Slaven	a	1-1	Tomić

2010

Date	Opp		Score	Scorers
27/2	Inter	h	2-0	Jurić, Pavličić
6/3	Rijeka	a	1-1	Malčić
13/3	Lokomotiva	h	1-0	Malčić (p)
20/3	Varteks	a	1-1	Grgić
27/3	Zagreb	h	1-0	Bagarić
3/4	Istra	h	0-0	
10/4	Hajduk	a	1-2	Kresinger
14/4	Šibenik	h	4-3	Milardović 2 (1p), Kresinger, Tomić
17/4	Karlovac	a	0-3	
24/4	Dinamo	h	2-0	Kresinger, Baraban
1/5	Međimurje	a	2-0	Lukačević, Radotić
8/5	Croatia	h	5-0	Milardović 3 (1p), Pavličić, Kresinger
13/5	Osijek	a	0-2	

No	Name	Nat	DoB	Pos	Aps	(s)	Gls
1	Marijan ANTOLOVIĆ		7/5/89	G	30		
10	Davor BAGARIĆ		8/9/85	M	3	(5)	1
25	Ivica BARABAN		22/1/88	A	12	(12)	4
4	Josip DUVNJAK		11/4/86	D	2	(8)	
20	Ivan GRGIĆ		12/5/88	M	17	(7)	1
8	Edin HUSIĆ	BIH	10/11/85	M	13	(3)	3
21	Tomislav JURIĆ		8/4/90	D	6	(8)	2
7	Dino KRESINGER		20/3/82	A	24	(2)	9
	Luka KUJUNDŽIJA		3/3/87	M		(1)	
5	Boris LEUTAR		20/8/72	D	8	(2)	
30	Mario LUČIĆ		29/4/81	D	23		
3	Josip LUKAČEVIĆ	BIH	3/11/83	M	14	(6)	2
48	Željko MALČIĆ		15/11/81	A	14		4
13	Marijan MATIĆ		6/8/87	D		(1)	
28	Tomislav MAZALOVIĆ		10/6/90	M	15	(6)	1
26	Josip MILARDOVIĆ		10/1/82	D	27		6
15	Ninoslav PARMAKOVIĆ		24/11/82	D	27		1
9	Tomislav PAVLIČIĆ		6/12/83	M	25	(2)	7
19	Krešimir PRGOMET		20/6/86	M	10	(11)	2
16	Tomislav RADOTIĆ		13/12/81	M	16	(6)	1
24	Dario RUGAŠEVIĆ		29/1/91	D	16	(1)	
17	Vlatko ŠIMUNAC		1/2/90	A	1	(9)	
6	Petar TOMIĆ		29/10/82	D	27		2

NK CROATIA SESVETE
Coach – Anto Petrović; (1/9/09) Nenad Gračan;
(11/11/09) Anto Petrović; (22/11/09) (Ivica Zelenbrz);
(8/1/10) Adolf Pinter (AUT); (27/2/10) Goran Jerković
Founded – 1957
Stadium – ŠRC Sesvete (3,500)

2009

Date	Opp		Score	Scorers
25/7	Šibenik	h	1-2	Jurin
1/8	Karlovac	a	0-0	
8/8	Dinamo	h	2-5	Polozani, Guja
15/8	Međimurje	a	1-2	Polozani
22/8	Istra	h	2-2	Guja, Mus
29/8	Osijek	h	1-2	Čižmek
12/9	Zadar	a	0-2	
19/9	Slaven	h	1-1	Čižmek
26/9	Inter	a	2-1	Bošnjak, Celiščak
3/10	Rijeka	h	1-2	Celiščak
17/10	Lokomotiva	a	2-3	Polozani, Bošnjak
24/10	Varteks	h	2-2	Pokrajčić, Agić
31/10	Zagreb	a	2-4	Guja, Agić
7/11	Cibalia	h	0-3	
21/11	Hajduk	a	0-6	
28/11	Šibenik	a	0-2	
5/12	Karlovac	h	0-3	

2010

Date	Opp		Score	Scorers
27/2	Dinamo	a	0-6	
6/3	Međimurje	h	2-1	Pokrajčić, Zubak
13/3	Istra	a	0-1	
20/3	Osijek	a	0-0	
27/3	Zadar	h	1-2	Pokrajčić
3/4	Slaven	a	0-4	
10/4	Inter	h	3-1	Pokrajčić 3
14/4	Rijeka	a	2-4	Guja, Zubak
17/4	Lokomotiva	h	1-2	Čižmek
24/4	Varteks	a	1-4	Zubak (p)
30/4	Zagreb	h	1-4	Zubak
8/5	Cibalia	a	0-5	
13/5	Hajduk	h	2-5	Zubak, Pejić

No	Name	Nat	DoB	Pos	Aps	(s)	Gls
10	Jasmin AGIĆ		26/12/74	M	27	(1)	2
23	Ivan BABIĆ		29/4/84	A	9	(6)	
1	Ivan BANOVIĆ		1/12/84	G	13		
11	Igor BARKUČIĆ		5/4/82	M	2	(3)	
12	Franjo BERIŠIĆ		30/8/90	G	2	(1)	
22	Martin BLJAJIĆ		21/1/89	D	11	(1)	
24	Miljenko BOŠNJAK		11/4/87	M	26		2
28	Vedran CELIŠČAK		16/7/82	M	9		2
20	Ivan CRNOV		14/8/88	M	1		
15	Krunoslav ČIČAK		8/2/84	D	5	(3)	
8	Mario ČIŽMEK		23/12/75	M	9	(9)	3
16	Dino DIZDAREVIĆ		2/9/89	M		(2)	
18	Petar DUSPARA		2/6/87	A		(3)	
30	Marko GUJA		13/5/90	M	23	(4)	4
23	Luka JAKARA		4/3/91	D	2		
5	Vedran JERKOVIĆ		13/10/91	D		(2)	
9	Stjepan JUKIĆ		10/12/79	A	4	(4)	
20	Mario JURIN		10/8/86	M	1	(1)	1
19	Goran JUROŠ		9/1/86	D	9	(1)	
13	Matija KATANEC		4/5/90	D	4	(2)	
	Mihajl KOSTIL		16/11/85	M		(1)	
33	Tomislav LABUDOVIĆ		25/10/85	D	8		
22	Matthew LAM	CAN	10/9/89	M		(1)	
13	Mario LONČAR		22/6/88	D	10	(1)	
98	Marko Domagoj LONČAR		13/4/92	M		(3)	
5	Ivan LOVRIĆ		10/4/90	M	3	(6)	
2	Antonio MAMIĆ		21/9/85	D	2		
21	Saša MUS		19/7/86	D	27		1
23	Božo MUSA		15/9/88	D	1		
17	Antun PALIĆ		25/6/88	M	3	(4)	
27	Pero PEJIĆ		28/11/80	A	12	(1)	1
27	Renato PILIPOVIĆ		14/1/77	M	6	(1)	
9	Ante POKRAJČIĆ	BIH	28/9/85	A	19	(3)	6
18	Artim POLOZANI	MKD	25/6/82	M	13	(2)	3

4	Marko PUŠKARIĆ		1/9/89	D	7	(6)
1	Ivan RADOŠ		21/2/84	G	12	
77	Damir SMAJLOVIĆ	BIH	27/3/83	A	3	(1)
12	Josip ŠARIĆ		29/7/87	G	3	
3	Dario ŠUŠAK		17/6/87	D	18	(1)
26	Josip Juraj TOMINAC		14/4/89	M	4	(6)
17	Hrvoje TRUPAC		14/8/87	M	2	(4)
14	Nikola VASILJEVIĆ	BIH	19/12/83	D	3	
7	Matias ZUBAK		17/10/89	M	17	(2)	5

NK DINAMO ZAGREB
Coach – Krunoslav Jurčić
Founded – 1945
Stadium – Maksimir (38,079)
MAJOR HONOURS:
Inter Cities Fairs Cup - (1) 1967;
Yugoslavian League - (4) 1948, 1954, 1958, 1982;
Croatian League – (12) 1993, 1996, 1997, 1998, 1999, 2000, 2003, 2006,
2007, 2008 , 2009, 2010;
Yugoslavian Cup – (8) 1951, 1960, 1963, 1965, 1969, 1973, 1980, 1983;
Croatian Cup – (10) 1994, 1996, 1997, 1998, 2001, 2002, 2004, 2007, 2008, 2009.

2009

25/7	Istra	h	7-1	Slepička, Morales 2, Mandžukić 2, Sivonjić, Badelj
1/8	Međimurje	h	4-0	Kramarić 2, Slepička, Papadopoulos
8/8	Croatia	a	5-2	Papadopoulos, Mandžukić 2, Morales 2 (1p)
16/8	Osijek	h	5-0	Sammir 3 (2p), Mandžukić, Badelj
23/8	Zadar	a	0-0	
30/8	Slaven	h	6-0	Barbarić, Morales 2 (2p), Mandžukić, Sivonjić, Badelj
12/9	Inter	a	1-0	Morales
20/9	Rijeka	h	6-0	Morales 2, Sivonjić 2, Barbarić, Kramarić
26/9	Lokomotiva	a	1-0	Mandžukić
4/10	Varteks	h	2-1	Mandžukić, Badelj
17/10	Zagreb	a	0-1	
25/10	Cibalia	h	1-1	Morales (p)
31/10	Hajduk	a	1-2	Sivonjić
8/11	Šibenik	h	5-0	Morales, Sivonjić, Kramarić, Badelj, Barbarić
22/11	Karlovac	a	3-1	Badelj 2, Morales
28/11	Istra	a	0-0	
6/12	Međimurje	a	4-1	Morales, Slepička, Kramarić 2

2010

27/2	Croatia	h	6-0	Dodô, Mandžukić 3, Badelj, Tomečak
6/3	Osijek	a	1-0	Mandžukić
13/3	Zadar	h	0-0	
20/3	Slaven	a	1-0	Slepička
27/3	Inter	h	3-1	Mandžukić 2, Badelj
3/4	Rijeka	a	2-2	Sammir (p), Barbarić
10/4	Lokomotiva	h	1-0	Sammir (p)
14/4	Varteks	a	2-1	Dodô, Badelj
17/4	Zagreb	h	1-1	Badelj
24/4	Cibalia	a	0-2	
1/5	Hajduk	h	0-0	
8/5	Šibenik	a	1-2	Dodô
13/5	Karlovac	h	1-1	Kramarić

No	Name	Nat	DoB	Pos	Aps	(s)	Gls
18	Domagoj ANTOLIĆ		30/6/90	M	6	(4)	
16	Milan BADELJ		25/2/89	M	27		11
19	Tomislav BARBARIĆ		29/3/89	D	18	(4)	4
22	Igor BIŠĆAN		4/5/78	D	8		
1	Tomislav BUTINA		30/3/74	G	25		
5	Adrián Daniel CALELLO	ARG	14/5/87	M	9	(11)	
15	CARLOS SANTOS de Jesus	BRA	25/2/85	D	2		
	Mathias Dellgoue CHAGO de Confiance	CMR	13/3/83	M	1	(2)	
25	Leonardo Damián CUFRÉ	ARG	9/5/78	D	18		
23	Luiz Paulo Hilário "DODÔ"	BRA	16/10/87	A	8	(1)	3
7	Oélilton Araújo dos Santos "ETTO"	BRA	8/3/81	D	16	(5)	

11	Denis GLAVINA		3/3/86	D	2	(2)	
3	Luis Ezequiel IBÁÑEZ	ARG	15/7/88	D	15	(3)	
4	Robert KOVAČ		6/4/74	D	13	(1)	
9	Andrej KRAMARIĆ		19/6/91	A	6	(18)	7
30	Filip LONČARIĆ		6/12/86	G	4		
6	Dejan LOVREN		5/7/89	D	14		
17	Mario MANDŽUKIĆ		21/5/86	A	24		14
13	Frano MLINAR		30/3/92	M		(1)	
77	Pedro Andrés MORALES Flores	CHI	25/5/85	M	17	(4)	13
99	Dimitrios PAPADOPOULOS	GRE	20/10/81	A	7	(6)	2
99	Dominik PICAK		12/2/92	G	1		
15	Karlo PRIMORAC		1/6/84	A	3	(4)	
10	Jorge SAMMIR Cruz Campos	BRA	23/4/87	M	20	(6)	5
24	Ilija SIVONJIĆ		10/7/87	A	11		6
20	Miroslav SLEPIČKA	CZE	10/11/81	A	13	(2)	4
2	Ivan TOMEČAK		7/12/89	D	12	(5)	1
30	Ivan TURINA		3/10/80	G		(1)	
21	Ivica VRDOLJAK		19/9/83	M	21	(6)	
14	Šime VRSALJKO		10/1/92	M	9	(1)	

HNK HAJDUK SPLIT
Coach – Ante Miše; (3/8/09) Ivica Kalinić;
(7/8/09) (Joško Španjić); (17/8/09) Edoardo Reja (ITA);
(12/2/10) Stanko Poklepović
Founded – 1911
Stadium – Poljud (34,200)
MAJOR HONOURS:
Yugoslavian League – (9) 1927, 1929, 1950, 1952, 1955, 1971, 1974, 1975, 1979;
Croatian League – (6) 1992, 1994, 1995, 2001, 2004, 2005;
Yugoslavian Cup – (9) 1967, 1972, 1974, 1975, 1976, 1977, 1984, 1987, 1991;
Croatian Cup – (5) 1993, 1995, 2000, 2003, 2010.

2009

25/7	Osijek	a	1-1	og (Pranjić)
2/8	Zadar	h	0-1	
9/8	Slaven	a	1-2	Ibričić
15/8	Inter	h	2-2	Tičinović, Ibričić (p)
23/8	Rijeka	a	0-2	
29/8	Lokomotiva	h	1-0	Ibričić (p)
13/9	Varteks	a	3-0	Oremuš, Šerić, Sharbini An. (p)
19/9	Zagreb	h	2-0	Sharbini An., Pandža
27/9	Cibalia	a	0-0	
3/10	Istra	a	1-0	Vukušić
18/10	Šibenik	h	0-1	
24/10	Karlovac	a	0-1	
31/10	Dinamo	h	2-1	og (Lovren), Strinić
7/11	Međimurje	a	1-1	Ibričić
21/11	Croatia	h	6-0	Vejić, Ibričić 2, Rafael Paraíba, Vukušić, Sharbini An. (p)
28/11	Osijek	h	1-0	Ibričić (p)
5/12	Zadar	a	2-1	og (Skočibušić), Čop

2010

28/2	Slaven	h	5-0	Andrić, Tomasov, Vukušić, Strinić, Cernat
6/3	Inter	a	3-0	Strinić, Ibričić 2
13/3	Rijeka	h	1-1	Skoko
20/3	Lokomotiva	a	1-2	Vukušić
27/3	Varteks	h	2-0	Vukušić, Ibričić
2/4	Zagreb	a	1-1	Strinić
10/4	Cibalia	h	2-1	Tičinović, Vukušić
14/4	Istra	h	1-0	Ibričić
17/4	Šibenik	a	1-0	Ibričić
24/4	Karlovac	h	1-0	Ibričić (p)
1/5	Dinamo	a	0-0	
8/5	Međimurje	h	4-1	Jozinović, Tomasov, Čop, Ibričić
13/5	Croatia	a	5-2	Ibričić 3, Cernat, Čop

No	Name	Nat	DoB	Pos	Aps	(s)	Gls
11	Srđan ANDRIĆ		5/1/80	M	15		1
	Franko ANDRIJAŠEVIĆ		22/6/91	M		(1)	
5	Jurica BULJAT		19/9/86	D	15	(2)	
19	Marijan BULJAT		12/9/81	D	3	(3)	
50	Florin CERNAT	ROU	10/3/80	M	17	(8)	2

No	Name	Nat	DoB	Pos	Aps	(s)	Gls
90	Duje ČOP		1/2/90	A	3	(7)	3
15	Drago GABRIĆ		27/9/86	M	2		
10	Senijad IBRIČIĆ	BIH	26/9/85	M	29		17
29	Darijo JERTEC		4/10/85	M		(1)	
27	Matej JONJIĆ		29/1/91	D	2		
16	Goran JOZINOVIĆ		27/8/90	D	3	(2)	1
8	Krešo LJUBIČIĆ		26/9/88	M		(6)	
30	Marin LJUBIČIĆ		15/6/88	M	7	(2)	
22	Mario MALOČA		4/5/89	D	20		
2	Jure OBŠIVAČ		28/5/90	D		(1)	
18	Mirko OREMUŠ		6/9/88	M	18	(8)	1
28	Boris PANDŽA	BIH	15/12/86	D	16	(3)	1
3	Toni PEZO		14/2/87	M		(1)	
30	RAFAEL Alves Targino "PARAÍBA"	BRA	3/2/89	A	4	(3)	1
21	Ivan RODIĆ		11/11/85	A	3	(2)	
26	Goran RUBIL		9/3/81	D	19		
9	Ahmad SHARBINI		21/2/84	A	4	(5)	
99	Anas SHARBINI		21/2/87	M	19	(2)	3
20	Josip SKOKO	AUS	10/12/75	M	23		1
6	Ivo SMOJE		21/11/78	D	4		
25	Dante STIPICA		30/5/91	G	1		
17	Ivan STRINIĆ		17/7/87	D	22		4
1	Danijel SUBAŠIĆ		27/10/84	G	28		
4	Ante ŠERIĆ		15/1/79	D	11		1
24	Mario TIČINOVIĆ		20/8/91	M	6	(11)	2
14	Marin TOMASOV		31/8/87	M	9	(11)	2
12	Vjekoslav TOMIĆ		14/10/83	G	1		
7	Hrvoje VEJIĆ		8/6/77	D	12		1
13	Ante VUKUŠIĆ		4/6/91	A	14	(8)	6
11	Tomislav BOSEC		14/6/90	A	18	(8)	3
1	Goran BRAŠNIĆ	BIH	26/9/73	G	3		
3	Vinko BUDEN		18/1/86	D	12	(1)	
20	Marijan BUDIMIR		19/10/80	D	23		
17	Silvio CAVRIĆ		29/3/85	M	17	(2)	1
2	Tomislav CERAJ		4/1/79	M	12	(4)	
32	Ivan ČOVIĆ		17/9/90	G	4	(1)	
1	Matej DELAČ		20/8/92	G	23		
22	Luiz Paulo Hilário "DODÔ"	BRA	16/10/87	A	17		4
22	Emmanuel Gamarra FERNÁNDEZ	PAR	18/1/88	A	3	(4)	
5	Toni GOLEM		14/1/82	D	11	(2)	1
13	Mario GRGUROVIĆ		2/2/85	M	13	(5)	5
9	Bernard GULIĆ		9/4/80	A	12	(5)	1
10	Tomislav JONJIĆ		19/5/83	M	19	(5)	4
6	Damir KRZNAR		10/6/72	D	6	(2)	
5	Luka KUJUNDŽIJA		3/3/87	A		(5)	
5	Tomislav LABUDOVIĆ		25/10/85	D	8		
	Mislav ORŠIĆ		29/12/92	M	1	(7)	3
19	Antun PALIĆ		25/6/88	M	3	(4)	1
4	Srđan PECELJ	BIH	12/3/75	D	11	(2)	
8	Ilija SIVONJIĆ		13/1/87	A	13		3
7	Mladen STIPKOVIĆ		15/7/84	M	5	(5)	
21	Guillermo Alejandro SUÁREZ	ARG	9/6/85	M	4	(2)	
15	Miroslav ŠARIĆ		7/2/86	M	15	(6)	5
16	Tomislav ŠARIĆ		24/6/90	M	25	(1)	1
8	Armand Dubois YANKEP	CMR	17/12/85	M	8	(2)	
	Tomislav ŽIVKO	BIH	29/1/88	M	4	(2)	1

NK INTER ZAPREŠIĆ

Coach – Borimir Perković; (11/4/10) Ilija Lončarević
Founded – 1929
Stadium – ŠRC Zaprešić (4,500)
MAJOR HONOURS:
Croatian Cup – (1) 1992.

2009

24/7	Varteks	h	1-1	Bosec
31/7	Zagreb	a	3-0	Bosec, Jonjić 2 (1p)
7/8	Cibalia	h	1-0	Grgurović (p)
15/8	Hajduk	a	2-2	Jonjić, Šarić M.
21/8	Šibenik	h	0-1	
29/8	Karlovac	a	0-1	
12/9	Dinamo	a	0-1	
18/9	Međimurje	a	1-2	Grgurović
26/9	Croatia	h	1-2	Gulić
3/10	Osijek	a	2-4	Dodô, Grgurović
16/10	Zadar	h	4-3	Šarić M. 3, Dodô
23/10	Slaven	a	2-5	Grgurović, Batarelo
30/10	Istra	h	1-0	Golem
7/11	Rijeka	h	3-0	Cavrić, Šarić T., Barišić
21/11	Lokomotiva	a	1-0	Dodô
28/11	Varteks	a	1-2	Šarić M. (p)
4/12	Zagreb	h	1-3	Dodô

2010

27/2	Cibalia	a	0-2	
6/3	Hajduk	h	0-3	
13/3	Šibenik	a	0-0	
19/3	Karlovac	h	0-1	
27/3	Dinamo	a	1-3	Jonjić
2/4	Međimurje	h	2-1	Palić, Balić
10/4	Croatia	a	1-3	Sivonjić (p)
14/4	Osijek	h	0-3	
17/4	Zadar	a	1-0	Bosec
23/4	Slaven	h	2-0	Sivonjić (p), Živko
1/5	Istra	a	0-2	
8/5	Rijeka	a	1-3	Grgurović (p)
13/5	Lokomotiva	h	4-2	Oršić 3, Sivonjić

No	Name	Nat	DoB	Pos	Aps	(s)	Gls
3	Saša BALIĆ	MNE	29/1/90	D	10	(1)	1
14	Josip BARIŠIĆ		7/3/81	D	12		1
18	Marijan BATARELO		21/11/84	M	18	(8)	1

NK ISTRA

Coach – Elvis Scoria; (3/11/09) Valdi Šumberac; (28/2/10) Zoran Vulić
Founded – 1948
Stadium – ŠRC Uljanik Veruda (3,500)

2009

25/7	Dinamo	a	1-7	Župan
1/8	Lokomotiva	h	3-1	Šehić 2, Traoré
8/8	Međimurje	a	2-4	Roce, Šehić
15/8	Varteks	h	0-1	
22/8	Croatia	a	2-2	og (Mus), Šehić (p)
29/8	Zagreb	h	2-1	Šehić 2 (1p)
12/9	Osijek	a	0-3	
19/9	Cibalia	a	0-1	
26/9	Zadar	a	1-1	Bodrušić
3/10	Hajduk	h	0-1	
17/10	Slaven	a	0-3	
24/10	Šibenik	h	1-2	Roce
30/10	Inter	a	0-1	
7/11	Karlovac	h	2-0	Šehić (p), Traoré
22/11	Rijeka	a	0-2	
28/11	Dinamo	h	0-0	
5/12	Lokomotiva	a	1-2	Roce

2010

27/2	Međimurje	h	1-2	Stupić
6/3	Varteks	a	2-0	Anđelković, Šehić
13/3	Croatia	h	1-0	Župan
19/3	Zagreb	a	1-1	Chago
27/3	Osijek	h	1-3	Šehić
3/4	Cibalia	a	0-0	
10/4	Zadar	h	2-0	Traoré, Šehić
14/4	Hajduk	a	0-1	
17/4	Slaven	h	2-0	Traoré, Šehić
24/4	Šibenik	a	1-1	Traoré
1/5	Inter	h	2-0	Šehić 2 (1p)
8/5	Karlovac	a	1-1	Šehić
13/5	Rijeka	h	2-0	Anđelković, Šehić (p)

Name	Nat	DoB	Pos	Aps	(s)	Gls
Armend ALIMI	MKD	11/12/87	M	14	(3)	
Mislav ANĐELKOVIĆ		22/4/88	M	24	(3)	2
Goran BARIŠIĆ		12/12/85	D	18	(2)	
Dario BODRUŠIĆ		25/1/83	D	13	(7)	1

Gjergj BUSHAJ	ALB	8/3/91	M		(3)	
Mathias Dellgoue CHAGO de Confiance	CMR	13/3/83	M	12		1
Robert DEAK		31/1/90	D	5	(2)	
Paolo GRBAC		9/7/90	M		(1)	
Hasan KACIĆ		29/7/76	D	30		
Tonči KUKOČ		25/9/90	D	1	(4)	
Robert LISJAK		5/2/78	G	25		
Igor LOVRIĆ		7/10/87	G	5	(1)	
Marjan MARKOVIĆ	SRB	28/9/81	D	20	(1)	
Eldin MAŠIĆ	BIH	2/1/87	M	7	(3)	
Marijan NIKOLIĆ		31/10/83	A		(1)	
Ševo OKIĆ	BIH	26/7/88	A	4	(13)	
Dalibor PAULETIĆ		27/10/78	D	24		
Nikola PRELČEC		12/11/89	M	5	(6)	
Goran ROCE		12/4/86	M	22	(4)	3
Slobodan STRANATIĆ		27/11/85	D	12		
Boško STUPIĆ	BIH	26/7/84	A	7	(5)	1
Asim ŠEHIĆ	BIH	16/6/81	A	27	(2)	15
Andro ŠVRLJUGA		24/10/85	M	16	(5)	
Dragan TADIĆ		12/2/73	M	8	(7)	
Mohamed Kalilou TRAORÉ	MLI	9/9/87	M	21	(5)	5
Dragan ŽUPAN		26/5/82	M	10	(8)	2

NK KARLOVAC
Coach – Igor Pamić
Founded – 1919
Stadium – Branko Čavlović-Čavlek (12,000)

2009

Date	Opp		Score	Scorers
25/7	Međimurje	a	1-1	Lajtman
1/8	Croatia	h	0-0	
8/8	Osijek	a	1-0	Novinić
15/8	Zadar	h	2-0	Kovačević, Paracki
22/8	Slaven	a	3-1	Pamić 2, Paracki
29/8	Inter	h	1-0	Štefančić
12/9	Rijeka	a	1-1	Pamić
19/9	Lokomotiva	h	0-1	
26/9	Varteks	a	1-0	Tokić
3/10	Zagreb	h	0-0	
17/10	Cibalia	a	2-2	Novinić, Jerneić
24/10	Hajduk	h	1-0	Redžepi
31/10	Šibenik	a	0-1	
7/11	Istra	a	0-2	
22/11	Dinamo	h	1-3	Novinić
28/11	Međimurje	h	2-0	Novinić, Lajtman
5/12	Croatia	a	3-0	Jerneić, Karabatić, Pamić (p)
2010				
27/2	Osijek	h	1-0	Vukman
6/3	Zadar	a	1-1	Jerneić
13/3	Slaven	h	0-0	
19/3	Inter	a	1-0	Vukman
27/3	Rijeka	h	2-0	Paracki, Bunoza
3/4	Lokomotiva	a	0-0	
10/4	Varteks	h	1-1	Tokić
14/4	Zagreb	a	2-4	Tokić, Paracki
17/4	Cibalia	h	3-0	Lajtman 2 (1p), Pamić
24/4	Hajduk	a	0-1	
1/5	Šibenik	h	0-2	
8/5	Istra	h	1-1	Novinić
13/5	Dinamo	a	1-1	Štefančić

Name	Nat	DoB	Pos	Aps	(s)	Gls
Mario BARIĆ		15/4/85	D	26		
Gordan BUNOZA	BIH	5/2/88	M	27		1
David DUJANIĆ		28/10/85	M		(4)	
Ivan GRABOVAC		12/7/83	G	2		
Mahir IFTIĆ	BIH	17/3/80	D	3	(7)	
Josip JERNEIĆ		6/5/80	M	22	(2)	3
Jurica KARABATIĆ		22/7/78	D	29		1
Željko KOVAČEVIĆ		9/8/79	D	21	(3)	1
Ivan LAJTMAN		7/1/79	M	21	(3)	4
Mauro MATIKA		24/5/88	D	4	(2)	

Enes NOVINIĆ		18/7/85	A	23	(5)	5
Andrea OTTOCHIAN		28/6/88	M	1	(7)	
Zvonko PAMIĆ		4/2/91	M	30		5
Goran PARACKI		21/1/87	M	22	(2)	4
Ivan PARAZAJDER		14/4/88	G		(2)	
Borislav PILIPOVIĆ	BIH	25/3/84	M	25	(2)	
Haris REDŽEPI	BIH	20/7/88	M	2	(12)	1
Adis STAMBOLIJA	BIH	24/11/83	M	3	(2)	
Hrvoje SUNARA		4/8/79	G	28		
Matija ŠTEFANČIĆ		13/7/81	A	12	(13)	2
Niko TOKIĆ		7/6/88	A	9	(13)	3
Neven VUKMAN		14/10/85	D	20		2

NK LOKOMOTIVA ZAGREB
Coach – Roy Ferečina
Founded – 1914
Stadium – Kajzerica (1,000)

2009

Date	Opp		Score	Scorers
26/7	Rijeka	a	0-6	
1/8	Istra	a	1-3	Bule
8/8	Varteks	a	1-2	Bule
14/8	Zagreb	a	4-2	Bule 2 (1p), Martinac, Bagarić
22/8	Cibalia	h	2-0	Bule, Jelić
29/8	Hajduk	a	0-1	
12/9	Šibenik	h	0-0	
19/9	Karlovac	a	1-0	Martinac
26/9	Dinamo	h	0-1	
2/10	Međimurje	a	3-0	Sopić, Bule, Puljić
17/10	Croatia	h	3-2	Puljić 2, Antolić (p)
24/10	Osijek	a	0-3	
31/10	Zadar	h	1-0	Bule (p)
7/11	Slaven	a	0-1	
21/11	Inter	h	0-1	
28/11	Rijeka	h	3-0	Sopić, Bule, og (Pamić)
5/12	Istra	h	2-1	Puljić, Peko
2010				
25/2	Varteks	h	2-0	Bule, Havojić
6/3	Zagreb	h	1-0	Bule
13/3	Cibalia	a	0-1	
20/3	Hajduk	h	2-1	og (Rubil), Bule (p)
27/3	Šibenik	a	0-0	
3/4	Karlovac	h	0-0	
10/4	Dinamo	a	0-1	
14/4	Međimurje	h	1-3	Mesarić
17/4	Croatia	a	2-1	Peko, Bagarić
24/4	Osijek	h	2-2	Poljak, Bule (p)
1/5	Zadar	a	1-1	Poljak (p)
8/5	Slaven	h	1-1	Bule
13/5	Inter	a	2-4	Peko, Bule

No	Name	Nat	DoB	Pos	Aps	(s)	Gls
77	Gheorghe ANDRONIC	MDA	25/9/91	M	1	(7)	
77	Domagoj ANTOLIĆ		30/6/90	A	10	(1)	1
17	Matej BAGARIĆ		16/1/89	D	24		2
22	Boris BAJTO		26/3/85	M	3	(3)	
	Ivan BORAS		31/10/91	D	3	(1)	
9	Nino BULE		19/3/76	A	27		14
99	Denis CEROVEC		4/4/91	D	5	(1)	
21	Petar FRANJIĆ		31/8/91	M		(3)	
19	Tomislav HAVOJIĆ		10/3/89	M	16	(9)	1
24	Ivan HERCEG		10/2/90	D	20	(2)	
22	Ivor HORVAT		19/8/91	D	4	(6)	
18	Matej JELIĆ		5/11/90	A	14	(14)	1
1	Ivan KELAVA		20/2/88	G	27		
4	Mirko KRAMARIĆ		27/1/89	D		(4)	
	Diego Jorajurja LÓPEZ	ARG	1/10/90	M		(1)	
7	Mate MALEŠ		13/1/89	M	6	(5)	
10	Tomislav MARTINAC		27/6/83	M	24	(3)	2
4	Leonard MESARIĆ		10/8/83	D	12		1
20	Ivan MRŠIĆ	BIH	24/6/91	D	5		
3	Mario MUSA		6/7/90	D	10	(3)	
	Dalibor PANDŽA	BIH	23/3/91	A	1	(7)	

CROATIA

23	Ivan PEKO	5/1/90	M	19	(5)	3
11	Josip PIVARIĆ	30/1/89	D	8	(1)	
8	Mateo POLJAK	10/9/89	M	13		2
6	Tomislav PULJIĆ	21/3/83	D	23	(3)	4
13	Željko SOPIĆ	24/7/74	M	29		2
16	Filip ŠĆRBEC	3/6/91	M	2	(5)	
	Igor VIDAKOVIĆ	20/8/83	G	3		
21	Emiljano VILA	ALB 12/3/88	M	4	(4)	
	Šime VRSALJKO	10/1/92	M	17		

3	Franjo PINTARIĆ	5/7/88	D	4		
21	Mirko PLANTIĆ	15/1/85	M	6	(10)	1
23	Ante REŽIĆ	4/6/88	M	4	(1)	
24	Dejan SLUNJSKI	28/11/87	M	1	(2)	
24	Edvin ŠKRIJELJ	21/9/91	A		(1)	
23	Adrian VALENTIĆ	10/8/87	D	9		1
9	Marijan VUKA	10/1/80	A	8	(12)	7
22	Neven VULJANKO	19/3/87	G	9		
10	Ivica ŽULJEVIĆ	24/5/80	A	17	(6)	2

NK MEĐIMURJE

Coach – Mario Ćutuk; (9/10/09) Srećko Bogdan;
(2/4/10) Tomislav Ivković
Founded – 2003
Stadium – SRC Mladost (8,000)

2009

25/7	Karlovac	h	1-1	Cícero Lima
1/8	Dinamo	a	0-4	
8/8	Istra	h	4-2	Cícero Lima, Darmopil, Vuka, og (Kacić)
15/8	Croatia	h	2-1	Kovač, Eliomar
22/8	Osijek	a	1-3	Golubović
29/8	Zadar	h	3-0	Eliomar, Golubović, Vuka
12/9	Slaven	a	2-3	Golubović, Žuljević (p)
18/9	Inter	h	2-1	Golubović, Eliomar
26/9	Rijeka	a	0-4	
2/10	Lokomotiva	h	0-3	
17/10	Varteks	a	0-3	
24/10	Zagreb	h	4-2	Golubović 2, Plantić, Kovač
31/10	Cibalia	a	0-3	
7/11	Hajduk	h	1-1	Golubović
21/11	Šibenik	a	0-1	
28/11	Karlovac	a	0-2	
6/12	Dinamo	h	1-4	Vuka

2010

27/2	Istra	a	2-1	Vuka, Golubović
6/3	Croatia	a	1-2	Vuka (p)
13/3	Osijek	h	1-1	Vuka
20/3	Zadar	a	0-2	
27/3	Slaven	h	1-1	Žuljević
2/4	Inter	a	1-2	Amauri
10/4	Rijeka	h	1-5	Golubović
14/4	Lokomotiva	a	3-1	Golubović 2, Cícero Lima
17/4	Varteks	h	0-0	
23/4	Zagreb	a	1-2	Golubović
1/5	Cibalia	h	0-2	
8/5	Hajduk	a	1-4	Grgić
13/5	Šibenik	h	4-0	Valentić, Lesjak, Vuka, Golubović (p)

No	Name	Nat	DoB	Pos	Aps	(s)	Gls
11	Adnan AGANOVIĆ		3/10/87	D	16	(6)	
5	AMAURI Vicente de Jesus Júnior	BRA	7/3/83	D	19	(2)	1
19	ANDRÉ SILVA Batista	BRA	20/2/80	D	21	(2)	
12	Ivan BANOVIĆ		9/2/84	G	14		
15	Krunoslav BRATKOVIĆ		13/8/81	D	2		
4	Hrvoje BUBALO		30/12/77	D	12	(1)	
7	CÍCERO Paulo LIMA Pereira	BRA	16/4/81	M	21	(4)	3
13	Mario DARMOPIL		5/10/80	M	29		1
27	ELIOMAR dos Santos Silva	BRA	12/2/87	A	28	(1)	3
2	Daniel GEORGIEVSKI	MKD	17/2/88	D	24		
20	Bojan GOLUBOVIĆ	SRB	22/8/83	M	29		13
28	Marko GRGIĆ	BIH	30/6/87	M	8	(2)	1
	Nikola JURIN		3/11/87	G	1	(1)	
26	Joško KOVAČ		11/2/87	M	8	(9)	2
98	Domagoj KRAJAČIĆ		14/4/87	M		(3)	
6	Zoran LESJAK		19/5/88	M	4	(4)	1
5	Tomislav LEVAČIĆ		6/8/90	M		(1)	
99	Igor LOZO		2/3/84	D	3	(3)	
12	Danijel MAĐARIĆ		13/11/75	G	6		
6	Hrvoje MARKOVIĆ		11/11/84	D	5	(1)	
26	Nikola MELNJAK		6/9/81	D	22	(1)	
	Petar MILATOVIĆ		3/10/89	A		(1)	

NK OSIJEK

Coach – Tomislav Steinbruckner
Founded – 1945
Stadium – Gradski vrt (19,800)
MAJOR HONOURS:
Croatian Cup – (1) 1999.

2009

25/7	Hajduk	h	1-1	Jugović
1/8	Šibenik	a	2-2	Nikšić 2 (1p)
8/8	Karlovac	h	0-1	
16/8	Dinamo	a	0-5	
22/8	Međimurje	h	3-1	Barišić 2, Miličević
29/8	Croatia	a	2-1	Miličević 2
12/9	Istra	h	3-0	Miličević, Knežević, Jugović
19/9	Zadar	h	3-0	Pavličić, Miličević, Jugović
26/9	Slaven	a	2-5	Knežević, Hrničević
3/10	Inter	h	4-2	Barišić 2, Vida 2
17/10	Rijeka	a	1-1	Jugović
24/10	Lokomotiva	h	3-0	Knežević, Jugović, Nikšić
31/10	Varteks	a	2-1	Ibriks, Nikšić
7/11	Zagreb	h	5-3	og (Oršulić), Pranjić, Knežević 2, Miličević
21/11	Cibalia	a	1-1	Barišić
28/11	Hajduk	a	0-1	
5/12	Šibenik	h	3-0	Vida, Barišić, Nikšić

2010

27/2	Karlovac	a	0-1	
6/3	Dinamo	h	0-1	
13/3	Međimurje	a	1-1	Hrničević
20/3	Croatia	h	0-0	
27/3	Istra	a	3-1	Šorša, Pušić, Jugović
3/4	Zadar	a	1-2	Nikšić
10/4	Slaven	h	0-1	
14/4	Inter	a	3-0	Miličević (p), Barišić, Vida
17/4	Rijeka	h	1-0	Barišić
24/4	Lokomotiva	a	2-2	Nikšić, Gavrić
1/5	Varteks	h	1-1	Nikšić (p)
8/5	Zagreb	a	0-1	
13/5	Cibalia	h	2-0	Vidaković, Miličević

No	Name	Nat	DoB	Pos	Aps	(s)	Gls
28	ANDRÉ LUIZ Cardoso Ferreira	BRA	2/7/87	D	4		
20	Josip BARIŠIĆ		14/11/86	A	25	(5)	8
14	Andrej ČAUŠIĆ		19/2/90	D	10		
6	Mario ĐIKIĆ		27/4/86	D	12	(1)	
2	Dino GAVRIĆ		11/4/89	M	12		1
11	Antonio HRNIČEVIĆ		7/7/84	A	2	(11)	2
15	Ivan IBRIKS		6/10/87	D	21		1
17	Vedran JUGOVIĆ		10/9/89	M	27		6
12	Ivan KARDUM		18/7/87	G	30		
10	Josip KNEŽEVIĆ		3/10/88	M	14	(1)	5
4	Hrvoje KURTOVIĆ		6/10/83	M	20		
9	Anton MAGLICA		11/11/91	A		(1)	
26	Ivan MILIČEVIĆ		11/2/88	A	25	(3)	8
7	Vedran NIKŠIĆ		5/5/87	A	11	(14)	8
13	Saša NOVAKOVIĆ		27/5/91	M	1		
21	Milan PAVLIČIĆ		20/12/80	M	7	(6)	1
18	Antonio PEROŠEVIĆ		6/3/92	M		(1)	
9	Ivan PLUM		6/5/92	A		(1)	
3	Jurica PRANJIĆ		16/12/87	D	22	(1)	1
9	Karlo PRIMORAC		1/6/84	A	3	(2)	
5	Domagoj PUŠIĆ		24/10/91	M	3	(10)	1
27	Petar STOJKIĆ	BIH	9/12/86	D	11		

8	Mile ŠKORIĆ		19/6/91	M	3	(9)	
22	Tomislav ŠORŠA		11/5/89	A	21	(7)	1
16	Goran TODORCEV	MKD	21/1/84	M	9	(6)	
19	Domagoj VIDA		29/4/89	D	27		4
23	Srđan VIDAKOVIĆ		13/10/86	M	10	(10)	1

HNK RIJEKA

Coach – Robert Rubčić; (21/9/09) Zoran Vulić;
(10/11/09) Nenad Gračan
Founded – 1946
Stadium – Kantrida (11,000)
MAJOR HONOURS:
Yugoslavian Cup – (2) 1978, 1979;
Croatian Cup – (2) 2005, 2006.

2009

26/7	Lokomotiva	h	6-0	*Sharbini Ah. 3, Sharbini An. 3 (1p)*
2/8	Varteks	a	1-1	*Turkalj*
9/8	Zagreb	h	3-1	*Budicin, Gerc, Fernández (p)*
15/8	Cibalia	a	0-1	
23/8	Hajduk	h	2-0	*Fernández 2 (2p)*
29/8	Šibenik	a	0-1	
12/9	Karlovac	h	1-1	*Tadejević*
20/9	Dinamo	a	0-6	
26/9	Međimurje	h	4-0	*Matko 2, Fernández 2*
3/10	Croatia	a	2-1	*Turkalj, Fernández*
17/10	Osijek	h	1-1	*Čulina*
24/10	Zadar	a	1-1	*Đalović*
31/10	Slaven	h	2-3	*Pamić, og (Csizmadia)*
7/11	Inter	a	0-3	
21/11	Istra	h	2-0	*Štrok, Križman*
28/11	Lokomotiva	a	0-3	
5/12	Varteks	h	3-3	*Đalović 2, Križman*

2010

26/2	Zagreb	a	1-1	*Đalović*
6/3	Cibalia	h	1-1	*Križman*
13/3	Hajduk	a	1-1	*Kreilach*
20/3	Šibenik	h	0-1	
27/3	Karlovac	a	0-2	
3/4	Dinamo	h	2-2	*Štrok, Pamić*
10/4	Međimurje	a	5-1	*Gerc 3, Kreilach, Đalović (p)*
14/4	Croatia	h	4-2	*Đalović 2 (1p), Štrok 2*
17/4	Osijek	a	0-1	
24/4	Zadar	h	3-2	*Đalović, Budicin, Pamić*
1/5	Slaven	a	1-1	*Križman*
8/5	Inter	h	3-1	*Đalović 2 (1p), Gerc*
13/5	Istra	a	0-2	

No	Name	Nat	DoB	Pos	Aps	(s)	Gls
13	Ivan BIJELIĆ		15/1/90	M		(3)	
16	Fausto BUDICIN		1/5/81	D	26	(1)	2
22	Tarik CERIĆ	BIH	28/1/78	D	7	(1)	
5	Igor ČAGALJ		8/10/82	D	26		
9	Nastja ČEH	SVN	26/1/78	M	3	(4)	
6	Kenan ČEJVANOVIĆ	BIH	9/8/86	D	9	(5)	
15	Antonini ČULINA		27/1/92	M	2	(3)	1
	Niko DATKOVIĆ		21/4/93	M		(1)	
21	Radomir ĐALOVIĆ	MNE	29/10/82	A	20	(1)	10
20	Ramón Ignacio FERNÁNDEZ	ARG	14/2/86	M	18	(9)	6
9	Vedran GERC		14/2/86	A	8	(6)	5
	Jonathan Miguel GERMANO	ARG	1/1/88	M		(4)	
	Mislav KAROGLAN	BIH	14/4/82	M	2	(3)	
17	Damir KREILACH		16/4/89	M	16	(9)	2
15	Sandi KRIŽMAN		17/8/89	A	15	(2)	4
8	Davor LANDEKA	BIH	18/9/84	M	24		
4	Vlade LAZAREVSKI	MKD	9/6/83	D	10		
3	Denis LJUBOVIĆ		20/3/88	D	12	(2)	
12	Ivan MANCE		4/2/83	G	18		
11	Matija MATKO		20/9/82	A	11	(4)	2
19	Alen PAMIĆ		15/10/89	M	26		3
1	Velimir RADMAN		28/5/83	G	12		
	Dino RASPOR		4/1/92	G		(1)	
9	Ahmad SHARBINI		21/2/84	A	1		3

10	Anas SHARBINI		21/2/87	M	1		3
	Johann SMITH	USA	25/4/87	A		(5)	
23	Valentino STEPČIĆ		16/1/90	M	5	(4)	
14	Hrvoje ŠTROK		14/7/80	M	25	(4)	4
	Matej ŠUĆUROVIĆ		8/5/85	D		(1)	
23	Mario TADEJEVIĆ		28/8/89	M	12	(5)	1
26	Vedran TURKALJ		11/5/88	D	14	(2)	2
2	Mikael David YOURASSOWSKY	BEL	26/2/83	D	7		

HNK ŠIBENIK

Coach – Ivica Kalinić; (7/8/09) (Anđelko Godinić);
(11/8/09) Branko Karačić
Founded – 1932
Stadium – Šubićevac (12,000)

2009

25/7	Croatia	a	2-1	*og (Puškarić), Ademi*
1/8	Osijek	h	2-2	*Duro, Dajić*
8/8	Zadar	a	1-2	*Zec*
15/8	Slaven	h	0-0	
21/8	Inter	a	1-0	*Elez (p)*
29/8	Rijeka	h	1-0	*Alispahić*
12/9	Lokomotiva	a	0-0	
19/9	Varteks	h	2-1	*Zec 2 (1p)*
25/9	Zagreb	a	2-0	*Zec 2*
3/10	Cibalia	h	0-2	
18/10	Hajduk	a	1-0	*Zec*
24/10	Istra	a	2-1	*Zec, Budiša*
31/10	Karlovac	h	1-0	*Alispahić*
8/11	Dinamo	a	0-5	
21/11	Međimurje	h	1-0	*Alispahić*
28/11	Croatia	h	2-0	*Božić, Zec*
5/12	Osijek	a	0-3	

2010

27/2	Zadar	h	1-1	*Alispahić*
6/3	Slaven	a	2-2	*Alispahić, Medvid*
13/3	Inter	h	0-0	
20/3	Rijeka	a	1-0	*Alispahić*
27/3	Lokomotiva	h	0-0	
3/4	Varteks	a	1-5	*Zec*
10/4	Zagreb	h	3-1	*Bačelić-Grgić 2, Zec*
14/4	Cibalia	a	3-4	*Bačelić-Grgić 2, Ademi*
17/4	Hajduk	h	0-1	
24/4	Istra	a	1-1	*Dajić*
1/5	Karlovac	a	2-0	*Alispahić, Zec*
8/5	Dinamo	h	2-1	*Alispahić, Jakoliš*
13/5	Međimurje	a	0-4	

No	Name	Nat	DoB	Pos	Aps	(s)	Gls
20	Arijan ADEMI		29/5/91	D	27		2
10	Mehmed ALISPAHIĆ	BIH	24/11/87	M	27	(1)	8
14	Stipe BAČELIĆ-GRGIĆ		16/2/88	M	22	(2)	4
28	Ivan BAKOVIĆ	GER	3/9/90	M		(1)	
1	Goran BLAŽEVIĆ		7/6/86	G	29		
29	Sandro BLOUDEK	SVN	16/2/86	M	8	(5)	
21	Ivan BOŽIĆ	BIH	19/11/83	A	5	(16)	1
3	Igor BUDIŠA		23/9/77	D	23		1
24	Ante BULAT		6/1/85	A	8	(3)	
9	Jusuf DAJIĆ	BIH	21/8/84	A	12	(6)	2
16	Samir DURO	BIH	18/10/77	M	7	(4)	1
8	Ivan ELEZ		9/5/81	M	14	(11)	1
19	Ivan FUŠTAR		18/8/89	A	19	(2)	
5	Luka GUSIĆ		27/9/89	D	3	(2)	
11	Zeni HUSMANI		28/11/90	M	24	(3)	
17	Antonio JAKOLIŠ		28/2/92	M	2	(12)	1
25	Marko JORDAN		27/10/90	A	1	(1)	
6	Mladen JURČEVIĆ	BIH	4/3/83	D	14	(1)	
4	Ivan KARADŽA	BIH	28/5/84	D	5	(2)	
	Senid KULAČIĆ	BIH	8/3/88	A		(1)	
26	Adnan LIKIĆ	BIH	9/8/86	D	3		
23	Krešimir MAKARIN		7/1/87	A		(8)	
18	Ivan MEDVID	BIH	13/10/77	D	19	(1)	1
26	Anto RADELJIĆ		31/12/90	M		(1)	

CROATIA

12	Hrvoje SLAVICA		27/4/81	G	1	
27	Hrvoje SPAHIJA		23/3/88	D	6	(3)
4	Velimir VIDIĆ	BIH	12/4/79	D	25	
7	Ermin ZEC	BIH	6/6/88	A	22	11
2	Alen ZORČIĆ		19/9/89	D	4	(1)

NK SLAVEN KOPRIVNICA
Coach – Milivoj Bračun; (8/8/09) Zlatko Dalić
Founded – 1912
Stadium – Gradski stadion (3,800)

2009

26/7	Zagreb	h	2-0	Vručina, Maras
2/8	Cibalia	a	0-2	
9/8	Hajduk	h	2-1	Posavec, Jurić
15/8	Šibenik	a	0-0	
22/8	Karlovac	h	1-3	Jurić
30/8	Dinamo	a	0-6	
12/9	Međimurje	h	3-2	Kokalović, Vojnović, Delić (p)
19/9	Croatia	a	1-1	Maras
26/9	Osijek	h	5-2	Posavec, Delić, Vojnović, Tepurić 2
3/10	Zadar	a	0-1	
17/10	Istra	h	3-0	Delić, Papa, Tepurić
23/10	Inter	h	5-2	Delić, Maras, Posavec, Vručina 2 (1p)
31/10	Rijeka	a	3-2	Poredski, Csizmadia, Tepurić
7/11	Lokomotiva	h	1-0	Poredski
21/11	Varteks	h	0-0	
28/11	Zagreb	a	3-3	Posavec (p), Rogulj, Delić
5/12	Cibalia	h	1-1	Csizmadia

2010

28/2	Hajduk	a	0-5	
6/3	Šibenik	h	2-2	Tepurić, Rogulj
13/3	Karlovac	a	0-0	
20/3	Dinamo	h	0-1	
27/3	Međimurje	a	1-1	Šafarić
3/4	Croatia	h	4-0	Mujanović, Delić (p), Maras, Poredski
10/4	Osijek	a	1-0	Mujanović
14/4	Zadar	h	2-1	Maras, Jurić
17/4	Istra	a	0-2	
23/4	Inter	a	0-2	
1/5	Rijeka	h	1-1	Poldrugač
8/5	Lokomotiva	a	1-1	Mujanović
13/5	Varteks	h	2-3	og (Šimek) Jakšinić

No	Name	Nat	DoB	Pos	Aps	(s)	Gls
13	Mario BILEN		23/1/85	M	1	(2)	
3	Csaba CSIZMADIA	HUN	30/5/85	D	15		2
30	Kristijan ČAVAL		11/10/78	M	8	(6)	
14	Mateas DELIĆ		17/6/88	M	24	(2)	6
99	Stjepan GENG		2/3/93	D		(2)	
20	Mario GREGURINA		23/3/88	M	7	(10)	
15	Marin JAKŠINIĆ		15/5/89	M		(5)	1
	Krunoslav JAMBRUŠIĆ		7/2/84	A		(1)	
21	Mario JURIĆ	BIH	7/8/76	A	13	(9)	3
4	Elvis KOKALOVIĆ		17/7/88	D	26		1
26	Alen MARAS		27/2/82	M	26		5
	Filip MARČIĆ		22/2/85	D	1		
17	Goran MUJANOVIĆ		29/9/83	A	12	(1)	3
22	Nicolás Niverge NYNKEU	CMR	14/12/82	M	19	(4)	
11	Drago PAPA		9/2/84	M	14		1
1	Tomislav PELIN		26/3/81	G	17		
7	Dalibor POLDRUGAČ		23/4/75	D	15	(2)	1
5	Matija POREDSKI		9/11/88	A	11	(6)	3
10	Srebrenko POSAVEC		19/3/80	M	20	(4)	4
16	Vedran PURIĆ		13/6/86	M	12	(7)	
12	Silvio RODIĆ		25/7/87	G	13		
6	Kaja ROGULJ		15/6/86	D	29		2
8	Nikola ŠAFARIĆ		11/3/81	M	21	(4)	1
24	Franjo TEPURIĆ		10/2/90	A	4	(18)	5
9	Aljoša VOJNOVIĆ		24/10/85	A	16	(2)	2
17	Bojan VRUČINA		8/11/84	A	6	(4)	3

NK VARTEKS
Coach – Dražen Besek; (4/1/10) Damir Jagačić; (15/3/10) Samir Toplak
Founded – 1931
Stadium – Anđelko Herjavec (10,800)

2009

24/7	Inter	a	1-1	Mumlek
2/8	Rijeka	h	1-1	Mujanović
8/8	Lokomotiva	h	2-1	Vuk A., Prahić
15/8	Istra	a	1-0	Vuk A.
22/8	Zagreb	h	1-0	Mumlek (p)
29/8	Cibalia	a	0-4	
13/9	Hajduk	h	0-3	
19/9	Šibenik	a	1-2	Mujanović
26/9	Karlovac	h	0-1	
4/10	Dinamo	a	1-2	Smrekar
17/10	Međimurje	h	3-0	Hojski 2, Mumlek (p)
24/10	Croatia	a	2-2	Mujanović, Mumlek
31/10	Osijek	h	1-2	Prahić
7/11	Zadar	a	0-2	
21/11	Slaven	h	0-0	
28/11	Inter	h	2-1	Smrekar, Mumlek (p)
5/12	Rijeka	a	3-3	Punčec, Mumlek, Škvorc D.

2010

25/2	Lokomotiva	a	0-2	
6/3	Istra	h	0-2	
13/3	Zagreb	a	0-3	
20/3	Cibalia	h	1-1	Mumlek (p)
27/3	Hajduk	a	0-2	
3/4	Šibenik	h	5-1	Mumlek 2 (1p), Smrekar, Šimek, Glavica
10/4	Karlovac	a	1-1	Tkalčić
14/4	Dinamo	h	1-2	Mumlek
17/4	Međimurje	a	0-0	
24/4	Croatia	h	4-1	Mumlek, Smrekar 2, Škvorc F.
1/5	Osijek	a	1-1	Sačer
8/5	Zadar	h	1-0	Smrekar
13/5	Slaven	a	3-2	Škvorc D., Sačer, Škvorc F.

No	Name	Nat	DoB	Pos	Aps	(s)	Gls
16	Andrija BALAJIĆ		22/8/72	D	10	(8)	
29	Sandro BLOUDEK	SVN	16/2/86	M		(2)	
4	Josip BREZOVEC		21/12/86	M	12	(6)	
27	Ivan CONJAR		15/5/88	D	3	(7)	
1	Saša DREVEN		27/1/90	G	16		
13	Nikola FRLJUŽEC		29/6/89	A	1	(5)	
8	Dejan GLAVICA		20/8/91	M	6	(1)	1
99	Dominik GLAVINA		6/10/92	D		(2)	
20	Josip GOLUBAR		4/3/85	A	19	(2)	
30	Saša HOJSKI		11/5/90	M	11	(12)	2
2	Zoran IVANČIĆ		16/9/75	D	12		
5	Luka JAGAČIĆ		26/10/90	A	11	(3)	
9	Ivan JOLIĆ	BIH	18/5/80	A	5	(6)	
12	Denis KRKLEC		2/4/91	G	14		
19	Josip KVESIĆ	BIH	21/9/90	D	10	(2)	
23	Zoran LESJAK		19/5/88	M		(1)	
7	Goran MUJANOVIĆ		29/9/83	A	16		3
10	Miljenko MUMLEK		21/11/72	M	29		11
3	Adi MUSLI	BIH	5/5/84	M	1		
16	Igor PRAHIĆ		15/4/87	M	11		2
6	Roberto PUNČEC		27/10/91	M	18	(3)	1
3	Danijel RADIČEK		9/7/80	D	4	(2)	
7	Mario SAČER		17/11/90	A	3	(3)	2
17	Matija SMREKAR		8/4/89	A	18	(2)	6
17	Adam SUŠAC		20/6/89	D	10		
14	Karlo ŠIMEK		3/6/88	M	21	(2)	1
16	Dino ŠKVORC		2/2/90	D	27		2
28	Filip ŠKVORC		22/7/91	A	3	(1)	2
15	Nikola TKALČIĆ		3/12/89	D	26		1
26	Andrej VUK		22/3/89	M	11	(6)	2
11	Gordan VUK		26/5/87	A	2	(11)	

NK ZADAR
Coach – Dalibor Zebić
Founded – 1945
Stadium – Stanovi (12,000)

2009

Date			Score	Scorers
25/7	Cibalia	h	0-3	
2/8	Hajduk	a	1-0	Šaranović
8/8	Šibenik	h	2-1	Terkeš (p), Ćurjurić
15/8	Karlovac	a	0-2	
23/8	Dinamo	h	0-0	
29/8	Međimurje	a	0-3	
12/9	Croatia	h	2-0	Ćurjurić, Jozinović
19/9	Osijek	a	0-3	
26/9	Istra	h	1-1	Bilaver J.
3/10	Slaven	h	1-0	Ćurjurić
16/10	Inter	a	3-4	Mitrović, Terkeš, Šaranović
24/10	Rijeka	h	1-1	og (Tadejević)
31/10	Lokomotiva	a	0-1	
7/11	Varteks	h	2-0	Santini 2
20/11	Zagreb	a	0-4	
28/11	Cibalia	a	0-2	
5/12	Hajduk	h	1-2	Mršić

2010

Date			Score	Scorers
27/2	Šibenik	a	1-1	Santini
6/3	Karlovac	h	1-1	Santini (p)
12/3	Dinamo	a	0-0	
20/3	Međimurje	h	2-0	Terkeš, Santini (p)
27/3	Croatia	a	2-1	Ćurjurić, Mršić
3/4	Osijek	h	2-1	Santini, Terkeš
10/4	Istra	a	0-2	
14/4	Slaven	a	1-2	Mršić
17/4	Inter	h	0-1	
24/4	Rijeka	a	2-3	Mršić 2
1/5	Lokomotiva	h	1-1	Mršić (p)
8/5	Varteks	a	0-1	
13/5	Zagreb	h	1-0	Ćurjurić

No	Name	Nat	DoB	Pos	Aps	(s)	Gls
10	Sabit ALIMANOVIĆ	BIH	14/11/86	M	6		
4	Marko ANIĆ		26/6/88	M		(1)	
16	Igor BANOVIĆ		12/5/87	M	9	(1)	
3	Erdžan BEČIRI	SVN	24/8/85	D	10	(1)	
11	Luka BEGONJA		23/5/92	M	1	(1)	
9	Franko BILAVER		9/2/92	M	1	(2)	
2	Josip BILAVER		14/8/84	D	19		1
11	Semiran ÇELA	ALB	1/1/89	M	3	(3)	
5	Tomislav ČULJAK		25/5/87	M	9	(2)	
14	Ivan ĆURJURIĆ		30/11/88	M	12	(13)	5
12	Tomislav GLUIĆ		26/7/83	G	7		
21	Tomislav GLUMAC		14/5/91	M	13		
15	Jure JERBIĆ		28/6/90	D	16	(4)	
1	Antonio JEŽINA		5/6/89	G	23		
4	Matej JONJIĆ		29/1/91	D	13		
5	Goran JOZINOVIĆ		27/8/90	D	13	(1)	1
25	Marin LJUBIČIĆ		15/6/88	M	15	(1)	
22	Marin KURTIN		12/7/87	M		(5)	
13	Šime MARUNA		10/10/89	M	9	(5)	
7	Ferdo MILIN		15/12/77	M	16	(2)	
21	Ante MITROVIĆ		1/4/88	A	7	(10)	1
16	Antonio MRŠIĆ		5/6/87	A	8	(15)	6
10	Davor PIŠKOR		23/4/82	A	1	(6)	
18	Ante PULJIĆ		15/11/87	D	23		
19	Ivan SANTINI		21/5/89	A	14	(5)	6
26	Stjepan SKOČIBUŠIĆ		13/8/79	D	12		
8	Jakov SURAĆ		12/2/75	M	22	(1)	
9	Edin ŠARANOVIĆ	BIH	8/3/76	A	13	(3)	2
6	Bruno ŠIKLIĆ		14/3/83	D	6	(2)	
20	Želimir TERKEŠ	BIH	8/1/81	A	28	(1)	4
99	Ivan Anton VASILJ		5/4/81	M	1	(3)	

NK ZAGREB
Coach – Luka Pavlović; (14/9/09) Igor Štimac
Founded – 1903
Stadium – Kranjčevićeva (12,000)
MAJOR HONOURS:
Croatian League – (1) 2002.

2009

Date			Score	Scorers
26/7	Slaven	a	0-2	
31/7	Inter	h	0-3	
9/8	Rijeka	a	1-3	Pejić
14/8	Lokomotiva	h	2-4	Abdurahimi 2
22/8	Varteks	a	0-1	
29/8	Istra	a	1-2	Vugrinec (p)
11/9	Cibalia	h	0-1	
19/9	Hajduk	h	0-2	
25/9	Šibenik	h	0-2	
3/10	Karlovac	a	0-0	
17/10	Dinamo	h	1-0	Vugrinec
24/10	Međimurje	a	2-4	og (Georgievski), Vugrinec
31/10	Croatia	h	4-2	Krstanović, Vugrinec, Pejić, Šovšić
7/11	Osijek	a	3-5	Vugrinec 3
20/11	Zadar	h	4-0	Vugrinec 2, Krstanović, Kartelo
28/11	Slaven	h	3-3	Krstanović, Piškor, Jefthon
4/12	Inter	a	3-1	Vugrinec 2, Krstanović

2010

Date			Score	Scorers
26/2	Rijeka	h	1-1	Abdurahimi
6/3	Lokomotiva	a	0-1	
12/3	Varteks	h	3-0	Vugrinec, Abdurahimi 2
19/3	Istra	h	1-1	Ljubojević
27/3	Cibalia	a	0-1	
2/4	Hajduk	h	1-1	Ljubojević
10/4	Šibenik	a	1-3	Ljubojević
14/4	Karlovac	h	4-2	Ljubojević 2, Abdurahimi, Vugrinec
17/4	Dinamo	a	0-1	Vugrinec
23/4	Međimurje	h	2-1	Vugrinec, Abdurahimi
30/4	Croatia	a	4-1	Vugrinec 2, Ljubojević, Jefthon
8/5	Osijek	h	1-0	Vugrinec (p)
13/5	Zadar	a	0-1	

No	Name	Nat	DoB	Pos	Aps	(s)	Gls
16	Besart ABDURAHIMI		31/7/90	M	18	(9)	7
8	Stjepan BABIĆ		14/12/88	M	4	(3)	
2	Vedran CELJAK		13/8/91	D	16		
25	Sven DEDIĆ		15/4/91	M		(10)	
21	Ivica DŽOLAN	BIH	11/10/88	D		(1)	
25	Marko GRGIĆ		30/6/87	M	2	(7)	
15	Jakša HERCEG		15/2/89	G	2	(1)	
20	Vedran IVANKOVIĆ	BIH	3/5/83	D	20	(1)	
4	JEFTHON Ferreira de Sena	BRA	3/1/82	M	18		2
17	Igor JUGOVIĆ		23/1/89	M	18	(3)	
7	Josip JURENDIĆ		26/4/87	M	18	(5)	
18	Marko KARTELO		16/2/81	M	4	(3)	1
29	Ivan KRSTANOVIĆ	BIH	5/1/83	A	21	(3)	4
22	Goran LJUBOJEVIĆ		4/5/83	A	7	(5)	6
28	Lovro MEDIĆ		23/10/90	A	3	(2)	
23	Josip MIKULIĆ		12/4/86	D	5		
27	Valentino NOVOSEL		14/2/89	M	2	(5)	
13	Marin ORŠULIĆ		25/8/87	D	18	(3)	
10	Ivan PARLOV		3/4/84	M	21		
11	Mateo PAVLOVIĆ		9/6/90	D	10	(4)	
9	Miroslav PEJIĆ		16/2/86	D	15	(2)	2
24	Goran PETKOVIĆ		4/5/90	A		(1)	
8	Davor PIŠKOR		23/4/82	A	5	(4)	1
26	Kažimir POLJAK		13/8/91	D		(2)	
12	Marin SKENDER		1/1/80	G	13		
1	Josip ŠKORIĆ		13/2/81	G	15		
19	Damir ŠOVŠIĆ	BIH	5/2/90	M	20	(5)	1
14	Matija ŠPIČIĆ		24/2/88	M	18	(3)	
5	Mario TOKIĆ		23/7/75	D	12		
6	Marin VIDOŠEVIĆ		9/10/86	D	1		
30	Davor VUGRINEC		24/3/75	A	24	(2)	18

PROMOTED CLUBS

RNK SPLIT
Coach – Tonći Bašić
Founded – 1912
Stadium – Park mladeži (8,000)

NK HRVATSKI DRAGOVOLJAC ZAGREB
Coach – Albert Pobor
Founded – 1975
Stadium – NŠC Stjepan Spajić (5,000)

SECOND LEVEL FINAL TABLE 2009/10

		Pld	W	D	L	F	A	Pts
1	RNK Split	26	16	5	5	56	26	53
2	NK Pomorac Kostrena	26	14	5	7	39	22	47
3	NK Hrvatski dragovoljac Zagreb	26	11	9	6	33	21	42
4	NK Lučko	26	12	6	8	38	28	42
5	NK Solin	26	10	10	6	29	22	40
6	NK Vinograd Jastrebarsko	26	11	4	11	38	37	37
7	NK Rudeš	26	10	7	9	38	38	37
8	NK Junak Sinj	26	10	5	11	29	31	35
9	NK Imotski	26	10	4	12	40	49	34
10	NK Mosor Žrnovnica	26	9	6	11	26	34	33
11	HNK Suhopolje	26	8	7	11	29	31	31
12	NK Vukovar '91	26	7	10	9	31	39	31
13	HNŠK Moslavina	26	6	6	14	25	44	24
14	HNK Segesta Sisak	26	4	4	18	17	46	16

NB NK Pomorac Kostrena did not receive licence for top division.

DOMESTIC CUP 2009/10

HRVATSKI NOGOMETNI KUP

FIRST ROUND

(25/8/09)
Bjelovar 0, Split 1
Međimurje 2, Hrvatski dragovoljac 0
Rovinj 0, Moslavina 2

(26/8/09)
Gaj 2, Croatia Sesvete 5
Graničar 2, Podravec 0
Graničar Vodovod 0, Karlovac 6
Konavljanin 3, Dugo Selo 1
Koprivnica 0, Nehaj 0 *(aet; 2-4 on pens)*
Krka 0, Plitvica 1
Mladost Prelog 2, Lipik 4
Mladost Ždralovi 0, Slavonac 5
MV Croatia 5, Bistrica 1
Orijent 2, Podravina 1
Suhopolje 7, BSK Budaševo 0
Velebit 3, Olimpija 2
Vuteks 2, Rudar 4

SECOND ROUND

(22/9/09)
Croatia Sesvete 0, Istra 1
Orijent 1, Zagreb 2
Rudar Labin 5, Cibalia 2
Slavonac 1, Pomorac 5
Suhopolje 2, Inter Zaprešić 2 *(aet; 8-9 on pens)*

(23/9/09)
Graničar 1, Osijek 3
Karlovac 3, HAŠK 0
Lipik 3, Hajduk 5
Moslavina 2, Konavljanin 0
MV Croatia 0, Rijeka 2
Nehaj 0, Segesta 1 *(aet)*
Plitvica 0, Dinamo Zagreb 4
Split 0, Slaven Koprivnica 2
Velebit 0, Varteks 2
Vinogradar 4, Međimurje 1 *(aet)*

(29/09/09)
Belišće 0, Šibenik 3

THIRD ROUND

(27/10/09)
Istra 0, Slaven Koprivnica 1
Osijek 1, Inter Zaprešić 0
Šibenik 4, Rijeka 0
Varteks 2, Karlovac 1
Zagreb 3, Segesta 1

(28/10/09)
Hajduk 5, Moslavina 1
Pomorac 9, Rudar Labin 0
Vinogradar 1, Dinamo Zagreb 4

QUARTER-FINALS

(24/11/09 & 9/12/09)
Slaven Koprivnica 1 *(Vručina 64)*, Varteks 4 *(Csizmadia 10og, Šimek 18, Jagačić 30, Brezovec 54)*
Varteks 2 *(Golubar 61, Smrekar 72)*, Slaven Koprivnica 0
(Varteks 6-1)

(25/11/09 & 9/12/09)
Osijek 1 *(Šorša 68)*, Šibenik 1 *(Vidić 86)*
Šibenik 4 *(Budiša 37, Zec 59p, 77, Dajić 90)*, Osijek 0
(Šibenik 5-1)

Pomorac 0, Dinamo Zagreb 2 *(Papadopoulos 84, Badelj 90)*
Dinamo Zagreb 3 *(Kramarić 29, Ibáñez 45, Chago 57)*, Pomorac 2
(Ivičić 16, Nenadić 69)
(Dinamo Zagreb 5-2)

Zagreb 0, Hajduk 0
Hajduk 4 *(Tičinović 39, 53, Andrić 58, Ibričić 74)*, Zagreb 1 *(Jurendić 69)*
(Hajduk 4-1)

SEMI-FINALS

(24/3/10 & 7/4/10)
Dinamo Zagreb 0, Hajduk 0
Hajduk 1 *(Ibričić 51)*, Dinamo Zagreb 0
(Hajduk 1-0)

Šibenik 0, Varteks 0
Varteks 0, Šibenik 2 *(Zec 75, Fuštar 90)*
(Šibenik 2-0)

FINAL

(21/4/10)
Poljud, Split
HNK HAJDUK SPLIT 2 *(Tičinović 61, Ibričić 88)*
HNK ŠIBENIK 1 *(Zec 65p)*
Referee – *Kovačić*
HAJDUK – Subašić, Buljat J., Maloča, Oremuš *(Tičinović 61)*, Strinić, Skoko, Ljubičić M., Cernat *(Andrić 70)*, Sharbini An. *(Tomasov 83)*, Ibričić, Vukušić.
ŠIBENIK – Blažević, Vidić, Budiša, Bulat, Elez, Husmani, Ademi, Bačelić-Grgić *(Bloudek 88)*, Alispahić, Fuštar *(Božić 74)*, Jakoliš 90), Zec.

(5/5/10)
Šubićevac, Šibenik
HNK ŠIBENIK 0
HNK HAJDUK SPLIT 2 *(Vukušić 12, Ibričić 90+3p)*
Referee – *Vučkov*
ŠIBENIK – Blažević, Bulat, Vidić, Budiša, Medvid, Bloudek *(Elez 62)*, Bačelić-Grgić, Ademi, Husmani *(Jakoliš 71)*, Dajić *(Fuštar 46)*, Zec.
HAJDUK – Subašić, Strinić, Maloča, Buljat J., Oremuš *(Ljubičić M. 46)*, Andrić, Skoko *(Pandža 79)*, Rubil, Sharbini An. *(Tičinović 85)*, Ibričić, Vukušić.
(HAJDUK 4-1)

Omonia come in from the cold

After seven years of frustrating underachievement, AC Omonia finally gave their legions of fans what they had been waiting for – a 20th Cypriot championship.

The club's heavy investment paid off at last as Omonia recaptured the First Division crown, joining APOEL FC as the country's all-time record champions – a distinction they had conceded to their Nicosia rivals the previous season. Led by Panagiotis 'Takis' Lemonis, the former Olympiacos FC player and coach, the Greens fully merited their victory, displaying a season-long consistency that brought them 22 wins from their 32 matches and just two defeats.

Especially rewarding for the long-suffering Omonia fans was their domination of APOEL and the other two teams that made it into the six-game championship play-off group, Anorthosis Famagusta FC and Apollon Limassol FC. Not only did Omonia remain unbeaten throughout the play-off series, they did not lose to any of their main rivals during the regular campaign either, taking all six points from Apollon and four apiece off APOEL and Anorthosis.

Aloneftis on target

Omonia held a four-point lead going into the final phase. Three wins and three draws later their advantage had stretched to nine points – the second highest winning margin ever - with APOEL having leapfrogged both Anorthosis and Apollon to take the runners-up spot. Fittingly, it was at home to APOEL, in the penultimate match of the season, that Omonia made mathematically certain of the title, defeating the old enemy 1-0 with a 17th-minute strike from attacking midfielder Efstathios Aloneftis. It was the Cypriot international's 11th league goal of the season and his third in as many games against APOEL. On top of his game throughout the campaign, Aloneftis was arguably Omonia's most eye-catching performer. Other Cypriots to shine were skipper Ilias Charalambous, midfielder Constantinos Makrides and

dazzling 20-year-old newcomer Giorgos Efrem while Brazilian wing-back Davidson was the most assiduous of the club's overseas contingent.

Having taken the title, Omonia immediately knew there would be pressure on them to do well in the UEFA Champions League because earlier in the season APOEL had become the second Cypriot club in as many years to reach the group stage of Europe's flagship competition. The champions of Serbia – FK Partizan – and Denmark – FC København – were both despatched into the UEFA Europa League as APOEL emulated Anorthosis's achievement of 12 months earlier by joining Europe's elite 32. Ivan Jovanović's team did not win any of their six group games but they were never outclassed. Their three defeats were

Efstathios Aloneftis – a figure of great importance in Omonia's Cypriot championship triumph

CYPRUS

all by the odd goal and they drew twice with Club Atlético de Madrid before closing the campaign with a memorable 2-2 draw against Chelsea FC at Stamford Bridge. They only finished bottom of the group by virtue of the away goals rule in their head-to-head clashes with Atlético, who of course took full advantage of their third place by going on to win the UEFA Europa League.

Apollon lift Cup

If Europe was a case of what might have been for APOEL, then so too was the end-of-season Cypriot Cup final, in which they were surprisingly beaten by Apollon – a side APOEL had beaten home and away in the league and who were without their star player, leading scorer and semi-final match-winner, Argentine striker Gastón Sangoy. The underdogs from Limassol made the perfect start in a match officiated by Italian referee Roberto Rosetti, scoring the fastest goal in the history of the fixture when Sierra Leone striker Mustapha Bangura gave them the lead after just 45 seconds. APOEL equalised before half-time, through Polish striker Marcin Żewłakow, and subsequently dominated, only to be floored by a sucker punch when Argentina midfielder Giorgos Merkis – who had not scored all season in the league – headed in from a free-kick 17 minutes from time. It enabled Apollon's Slobodan Krčmarević to come out on top in the battle of the Serbian coaches and it also brought the club their sixth Cup win.

Apollon's Cup win earned them a later start in the 2010/11 UEFA Europa League, at the third qualifying round stage, with APOEL returning to Europe a round earlier and Anorthosis, as they had done the previous year, entering right at the start of the preliminary phase. Omonia's bid to bring more UEFA Champions League glory to the country was scheduled to begin in the second qualifying round.

Italian heartbreak

The impressive recent efforts of Cypriot football in the club arena have largely been matched by the improvement of the national team. Angelos Anastasiadis's charges finished their 2010 FIFA World Cup campaign with a real swagger, hammering Bulgaria 4-1 in their final home tie before giving reigning champions Italy an almighty fright four days later in Parma. Leading 2-0 with just 12 minutes to go, they were cruelly denied their glory when Alberto Gilardino turned the game around with a quickfire

Kypriaki Omospondia Podosfairon (KOP)/ Cyprus Football Association (CFA)

10 Achaion Street
2413-Engomi
PO Box 25071
CY-1306 Nicosia
tel - +357 22 352 341
fax - +357 22 590 544
website – cfa.com.cy
email – info@cfa.com.cy
Year of Formation – 1934

President - Costakis Koutsokoumnis
General Secretary – Phivos Vakis
Media Officer – Kyriacos Giorgallis
National Stadium – GSP, Nicosia (22,859)

TOP FIVE ALL-TIME CAPS
Yiannis Okkas (95); Pambos Pittas (82); Michalis Konstantinou (76); Nicos Panayiotou (75); Giorgos Theodotou (70)
TOP FIVE ALL-TIME GOALS
Michalis Konstantinou (29); Yiannis Okkas (23); Kostas Charalambides (11); Marios Agathokleous (10); Siniša Gogić, Andros Sotiriou, Milenko Spoljarić & Phivos Vrahimis (8)

hat-trick, his winning goal coming two minutes into stoppage time. It was a case of déjà vu for the heartbroken islanders, who had also lost their opening game of the campaign to an added-time Italian winner in Larnaca.

Cyprus coach Angelos Anastasiadis oversaw a positive end to the World Cup qualifying campaign

CYPRUS

NATIONAL TEAM RESULTS 2009/10

12/8/09	Albania	A	Tirana	1-6	Charalambides (37)
5/9/09	Republic of Ireland (WCQ)	H	Nicosia	1-2	Elia (30)
9/9/09	Montenegro (WCQ)	A	Podgorica	1-1	Okkas (63)
10/10/09	Bulgaria (WCQ)	H	Larnaca	4-1	Charalambides (11, 20), Konstantinou (58), Aloneftis (78)
14/10/09	Italy (WCQ)	A	Parma	2-3	Makrides (12), Michail (48)
3/3/10	Iceland	H	Larnaca	0-0	

NATIONAL TEAM APPEARANCES 2009/10

Coach – Angelos ANASTASIADIS (GRE) 3/10/53			Alb	IRL	MNE	BUL	ITA	Isl	Caps	Goals
Sofronis AVGOUSTI	9/3/77	Aris Limassol	G	G	G	G	G			
		/APOEL						G46	11	-
Ilias CHARALAMBOUS	25/9/80	Omonia	D	D	D		D		46	-
Paraskevas CHRISTOU	2/2/84	Omonia	D	D	D	D	D30	D	25	-
Marios ELIA	14/4/79	APOEL	D77	D		D75	D	D	43	2
Marios NICOLAOU	4/10/83	Panionios (GRE)	D59	D	D83	s75		D46	31	1
Marinos SATSIAS	24/5/78	APOEL	M46	M90	M	D	s30		53	-
Kostas CHARALAMBIDES	25/7/81	APOEL	M	M		M	M		50	11
Andreas AVRAAM	6/6/87	Apollon	M46	M	D	D	D	D46	11	1
Efstathios ALONEFTIS	29/3/83	Omonia	M56	M	s46	M86	M74	M	38	7
Yiannis OKKAS	11/2/77	Anorthosis	A	A91	A91		A85		95	23
Michalis KONSTANTINOU	19/2/78	Omonia	A46		A	A89	s74		76	29
Chrysis MICHAIL	26/5/77	APOEL	s46	M71	M	M	M	M46	62	7
Dimitris CHRISTOFI	28/9/88	Omonia	s46	s91				M	12	2
Alexandros GARPOZIS	5/9/80	Anorthosis	s46						36	1
Nektarios ALEXANDROU	19/12/83	APOEL	s56	s71	M46		s85		10	-
Christos MARANGOS	9/5/83	Anorthosis	s59	s90	s83			s46	18	1
Giorgos PANAGI	3/11/86	Omonia	s77					s80	11	-
Constantinos MAKRIDES	13/1/82	Omonia			M	M	M	M80	47	3
Giorgos EFREM	5/7/89	Omonia			s91	s86		s58	3	-
Siniša DOBRAŠINOVIĆ	17/2/77	Kavala (GRE)				A	A	A	3	-
Andreas PAPATHANASIOU	3/10/83	APOEL				s89		A58	4	-
Anastasios KISSAS	18/1/88	APOEL						s46	1	-
Savvas POURSAITIDIS	26/6/76	APOEL						s46	1	-
Giorgos MERKIS	30/7/84	Apollon						s46	2	-

CYPRUS

DOMESTIC LEAGUE 2009/10

FIRST DIVISION FINAL TABLE

	Pld	Home					Away					Total					Pts
		W	D	L	F	A	W	D	L	F	A	W	D	L	F	A	
1 AC Omonia	32	10	6	0	28	12	12	2	2	32	13	22	8	2	60	25	74
2 APOEL FC	32	11	3	2	29	9	8	5	3	24	15	19	8	5	53	24	65
3 Anorthosis Famagusta FC	32	11	3	2	31	13	8	4	4	20	14	19	7	6	51	27	64
4 Apollon Limassol FC	32	9	4	3	23	9	8	5	3	24	14	17	9	6	47	23	60
5 AEL Limassol FC	32	11	3	2	27	13	7	1	8	23	20	18	4	10	50	33	58
6 Enosis Neon Paralimni FC	32	6	4	6	25	22	4	6	6	15	20	10	10	12	40	42	40
7 Ethnikos Achnas FC	32	8	3	5	21	19	2	5	9	13	23	10	8	14	34	42	38
8 APOP/Kinyras Peyias FC	32	6	4	6	26	27	5	0	11	24	38	11	4	17	50	65	37
9 Ermis Aradippou FC	32	9	3	4	24	15	3	5	8	19	23	12	8	12	43	38	44
10 AEP Paphos FC	32	8	1	7	25	21	1	8	7	14	29	9	9	14	39	50	36
11 Doxa Katokopia FC	32	5	5	6	22	21	4	3	9	14	25	9	8	15	36	46	35
12 Aris Limassol FC	32	3	6	7	16	26	1	3	12	14	37	4	9	19	30	63	21
13 Nea Salamis FC	26	1	3	9	8	22	1	5	7	11	23	2	8	16	19	45	14
14 APEP Kyperounda FC	26	2	4	7	15	28	2	0	11	10	26	4	4	18	25	54	10

NB After 26 matches the top 12 clubs were split into three groups of four, after which they played exclusively against teams in their group.

APEP Kyperounda FC - 6 pts deducted

TOP GOALSCORERS

22 SEMEDO (APOP)
 JOEANO (Ermis)

13 Gastón SANGOY (Apollon)

12 Dieter VAN TORNHOUT (Paralimni)

11 Nenad MIROSAVLJEVIĆ (APOEL)
 Efstathios ALONEFTIS (Omonia)
 Michalis KONSTANTINOU (Omonia)

10 FREDDY (AEL)
 CAFÚ (Anorthosis)
 Christos MARANGOS (Anorthosis)
 Andreas AVRAAM (Apollon)
 HENRIQUE (Doxa)

CLUB-BY-CLUB

AEL LIMASSOL FC

Coach – Nir Klinger (ISR); (29/12/09) Dušan Uhrin Jr (CZE)
Founded – 1930
Stadium – Tsirion (13,000)
MAJOR HONOURS:
Cypriot League - (5) 1941, 1953, 1955, 1956, 1968;
Cypriot Cup - (6) 1939, 1940, 1948, 1985, 1987, 1989.

2009
29/8	Doxa	h	1-0	Vargas
13/9	Ethnikos	a	4-1	Freddy 2, González 2
20/9	APEP	h	2-0	Freddy, González
27/9	Anorthosis	a	0-1	
4/10	Apollon	h	0-0	
25/10	APOP	a	0-1	
31/10	Paralimni	h	2-1	Dossa Júnior, Kakoyiannis
8/11	Ermis	a	0-1	
15/11	Aris	h	1-0	González
23/11	Nea Salamis	a	3-1	Clayton 2, Vargas
30/11	APOEL	h	1-2	Freddy
5/12	Omonia	h	1-0	Kerkez
12/12	AEP	a	0-1	
19/12	Doxa	a	0-1	

2010
2/1	Ethnikos	h	2-2	Serjão, Rouga
10/1	APEP	a	1-0	Clayton
16/1	Anorthosis	h	0-1	
24/1	Apollon	a	2-0	Freddy 2
31/1	APOP	h	2-0	González, Freddy
6/2	Paralimni	a	2-1	og (Mertakas), Clayton
13/2	Ermis	h	2-1	Clayton, Kakoyiannis
21/2	Aris	a	0-0	
1/3	Nea Salamis	h	3-1	Ricardo Fernandes, Garpozis, Charalambous
7/3	APOEL	a	0-1	
14/3	Omonia	a	0-4	
21/3	AEP	h	3-1	Hélio Roque, Serjão, Clayton
27/3	Paralimni	a	3-1	Ricardo Fernandes, Clayton (p), Grozdanoski
10/4	APOP	h	4-2	Hélio Roque, Freddy, González 2
17/4	Ethnikos	a	3-4	og (Simov), Vargas, Garpozis
25/4	Omonia	h	1-0	Serjão
1/5	Pralimni	h	2-2	Hélio Roque, González
8/5	APOP	a	5-2	Freddy 2, González, Garpozis, Andrew

No	Name	Nat	DoB	Pos	Aps	(s)	Gls
18	Allie ANDREW	SLE	14/6/88	M		(1)	1
27	Balázs BORBÉLY	SVK	2/10/79	D	7	(5)	
8	Christos CHARALAMBOUS		3/10/81	M	5	(7)	1
17	Martinos CHRISTOFI		26/7/93	D	2	(1)	
10	CLAYTON Ferreira da Cruz	BRA	19/7/75	M	23	(4)	7
33	Kamil ČONTOFALSKÝ	SVK	3/6/78	G	13		
2	DOSSA Momade Omar Hassamo JÚNIOR	POR	28/7/86	M	27		1
80	Angelos EFTHYMIOU		18/11/84	M	6	(10)	
9	Frederico de Castro Roque dos Santos "FREDDY"	ANG	14/8/79	A	22	(2)	10
32	Alexandros GARPOZIS		5/9/80	M	10	(2)	3
19	Silvio Augusto GONZÁLEZ	ARG	8/6/80	A	24	(5)	9
77	Vlatko GROZDANOSKI	MKD	30/1/83	M	2	(1)	1
28	HÉLIO José Lopes ROQUE	POR	20/7/85	M	7	(7)	3
26	JEFISLEY André Caldeira	BRA	16/5/80	M	8	(3)	
3	Rui Paulo Silva JÚNIOR	POR	16/6/75	D	23	(1)	
87	Charalambos KAIRINOS		6/6/82	G	15	(1)	

81	Loizos KAKOYIANNIS		2/5/81	D	19	(1)	2
13	Dušan KERKEZ	BIH	1/5/79	M	19	(2)	1
1	Panos KONSTANTINOU		11/1/85	G	4		
30	Simos KRASSAS		10/7/82	M		(2)	
20	Maxim LARROQUE	FRA	20/2/89	M	4	(1)	
31	Hamad NDIKUMANA	RWA	5/10/78	D	22	(4)	
29	Edwin OUON	RWA	26/1/81	D	19	(2)	
14	Rafael PANAYIOTOU		18/6/91	D	1	(1)	
5	Stelios PARPAS		25/7/85	D	4	(1)	
6	Angelos PERIKLEOUS		5/1/90	M	1	(1)	
25	RICARDO Ribeiro FERNANDES	POR	21/4/78	M	12	(1)	2
21	Enrique Andrés ROUGA	VEN	2/3/82	D	8	(2)	1
50	Sérgio Luis Gardino da Silva "SERJÃO"	BRA	9/12/79	A	15	(12)	3
15	Nikolas THEODOROU		22/3/93	D		(1)	
22	Pedro Miguel Ferreira Silva TORRÃO	POR	12/3/77	M	9		
55	Miguel Rodrigo Pereira VARGAS	POR	18/11/78	M	21	(6)	3

AEP PAPHOS FC

Coach – Eyal Lahman (ISR); (8/9/09) Tasos Kyriakou; (4/2/10)
Savvas Kofidis (GRE); (29/3/10) Demetris Ioannou
Founded – 2000
Stadium – Pafiako (10,000)

2009

29/8	Omonia	a	2-3	Ba, Chailis
12/9	APOEL	a	0-0	
19/9	Doxa	h	1-2	Ba
26/9	Ethnikos	a	2-1	Tiquinho, Brahami
3/10	APEP	h	2-1	Ba 2
24/10	Anorthosis	a	0-3	
2/11	Apollon	h	1-2	Lima
7/11	APOP	a	0-0	
14/11	Paralimni	h	2-0	og (Fassotte), Vasconcelos
22/11	Ermis	a	0-0	
28/11	Aris	h	1-3	Brahami
12/12	AEL	h	1-0	Anderson do Ó
19/12	Omonia	h	1-3	Lukman
23/12	Nea Salamis	a	0-0	

2010

3/1	APOEL	h	0-1	
10/1	Doxa	a	2-2	Chailis, Mishaelov
16/1	Ethnikos	h	0-0	
23/1	APEP	a	3-3	Lukman, Chailis, Hugo Coelho
30/1	Anorthosis	h	0-2	
7/2	Apollon	a	0-0	
13/2	APOP	h	3-2	Eduardo Marques, Lukman 2
21/2	Paralimni	a	1-5	Chailis
27/2	Ermis	h	3-1	Vasconcelos 2, Eduardo Marques
6/3	Aris	a	1-2	Vasconcelos
13/3	Nea Salamis	h	0-1	
21/3	AEL	a	1-3	Sichone
27/3	Doxa	a	0-4	
11/4	Aris	h	3-2	Eduardo Marques, Vasconcelos, Sichone
17/4	Ermis	h	3-0	Chailis (p), Vasconcelos 2
24/4	Ermis	a	0-1	
1/5	Doxa	h	4-1	og (Nuno Rodrigues), Bezares, Eduardo Marques 2
8/5	Aris	a	2-2	Dimosthenous 2

No	Name	Nat	DoB	Pos	Aps	(s)	Gls
80	ANDERSON Oliveira Almeida DO Ó	BRA	14/12/80	D	15	(4)	1
32	Thanasis ATHANASIOU		6/4/92			(2)	
7	Ismaili BA	SEN	22/5/74	M	25	(2)	4
25	Juan José BEZARES Alarcón	ESP	17/5/81	M	7	(6)	1
10	Fodel BRAHAMI	ALG	27/6/78	M	9	(5)	2
22	José António CALADO da Silva	POR	1/3/74	D	8	(5)	
9	Kyriakos CHAILIS		23/2/78	A	22	(4)	5
46	Abdul Moktar DIALLO	BFA	23/12/85	A	1	(6)	

4	Alexandros DIMITRIOU		12/8/87	M	25	(1)	
21	Charalambos DIMOSTHENOUS		16/4/90	M	3	(3)	2
35	EDUARDO MARQUES de Jesus Passos	BRA	26/6/76	M	11		5
3	Dimitris FILIPOU		16/6/92	M		(1)	
23	Giorgos GEORGIOU		30/6/78	M	20	(1)	
11	Irakli GEPERIDZE	GEO	14/2/87	A		(4)	
2	Andreas HADJIZINOVIOU		30/4/90	D	1	(1)	
28	HUGO Nunes COELHO	POR	30/10/80	D	25	(1)	1
8	Romik KHACHATRYAN	ARM	23/8/78	M	5	(2)	'
38	Martin KOLÁŘ	CZE	18/9/83	M	17	(4)	
13	Gabriel LIMA	BRA	13/6/78	A	3	(10)	1
1	Florian LUCCHINI	FRA	13/2/81	G	15	(1)	
20	Imoro LUKMAN	GHA	4/10/84	D	23		4
55	Moshe MISHAELOV	ISR	14/9/83	D	5	(1)	1
12	Jane NIKOLOSKI	MKD	12/12/73	G	15		
15	Onisiforos PACHTALIAS		12/9/91	M	2	(1)	
33	Yiannis SAMPSON		6/12/81	D	3	(9)	
24	Ioannis SAVVA		18/8/91	D	3	(1)	
5	Moses SICHONE	ZAM	31/5/77	D	24		2
17	Giorgos SIELIS		23/10/86	M	5	(5)	
14	Almir TANJIČ	SVN	16/1/79	D	10	(2)	
6	Paulo Edson Nascimento Costa "TINGA"	BRA	15/5/81	D	22	(1)	
99	Fábio André Silva Ferraz "TIQUINHO"	POR	14/7/85	M	9	(8)	1
39	Artūrs VAIČULIS	LVA	16/2/90	G	2		
31	Ioannis VARNAVIDIS		9/8/92	M	1	(2)	
77	Bernardo Lino Castro Paes VASCONCELOS	POR	10/6/79	A	16	(2)	7

ANORTHOSIS FAMAGUSTA FC

Coach – Ernst Middendorp (GER); (7/8/09) Slavoljub Muslin (SRB); (18/2/10) Nikos Nicolaou
Founded – 1911
Stadium – Antonis Papadopoulos (9,782)
MAJOR HONOURS:
Cypriot League - (13) 1950, 1957, 1958, 1960, 1962, 1963, 1995, 1997, 1998, 1999, 2000, 2005, 2008;
Cypriot Cup - (10) 1949, 1959, 1962, 1964, 1971, 1975, 1998, 2002, 2003, 2007.

2009

30/8	Ermis	a	0-0	
14/9	Aris	h	3-1	Okkas, Katsavakis, Marangos
20/9	Nea Salamis	a	2-1	Café, Cristovão
27/9	AEL	h	1-0	Ricardo Fernandes
3/10	Omonia	a	1-1	Café
24/10	AEP	h	3-0	Tofas, Marangos, Okkas
31/10	Doxa	a	3-2	Café 2, Okkas
7/11	Ethnikos	h	2-1	Ocokoljić, Skopelitis
14/11	APEP	a	2-0	Marangos, Café
21/11	APOEL	a	0-2	
28/11	Apollon	h	1-1	Skopelitis
5/12	AEP	a	0-2	
12/12	Paralimni	h	2-0	Marangos, Laban
21/12	Ermis	h	1-0	Okkas

2010

3/1	Aris	a	3-0	Okkas (p), Marangos, Laban (p)
11/1	Nea Salamis	h	4-1	Leiwakabessy, Mantzios, Marangos (p), Buckley
16/1	AEL	a	1-0	Cristovão
23/1	Omonia	h	1-3	Okkas
30/1	AEP	a	2-0	Marangos 2 (1p)
6/2	Doxa	h	3-0	Marangos (p), Café, Mantzios
14/2	Ethnikos	a	3-1	Mantzios, Fotheringham, Okkas (p)
22/2	APEP	h	3-0	Mantzios, Okkas (p), Dellas
28/2	APOEL	h	0-0	
7/3	Apollon	a	0-2	
14/3	APOP	h	2-1	Cheyrou, Buckley
21/3	Paralimni	a	2-1	Café, Mantzios
28/3	Apollon	a	2-0	Mantzios, Marangos (p)
11/4	Omonia	a	1-1	Café

CYPRUS

18/4	APOEL	h	1-1	Cafú
24/4	APOEL	a	0-1	
2/5	Apollon	a	0-0	
8/5	Omonia	h	2-4	Cafú, Cheyrou

No	Name	Nat	DoB	Pos	Aps	(s)	Gls
1	Arjan BEQAJ	ALB	25/8/75	G	19		
27	Delron BUCKLEY	RSA	7/12/77	A	13	(7)	2
17	Arlindo Gomes Semedo "CAFÚ"	CPV	17/11/77	A	24	(5)	10
21	Bruno CHEYROU	FRA	10/5/78	M	10	(1)	2
16	CRISTÓVÃO da Silva Ramos	POR	25/3/83	M	16	(5)	2
5	Traianos DELLAS	GRE	31/1/76	D	15	(4)	1
34	Mark FOTHERINGHAM	SCO	22/10/83	M	4	(3)	1
11	Nikos FROUSOS	GRE	29/4/74	A		(5)	
19	Alexandros GARPOZIS		5/9/80	M	3	(6)	
28	Giorgos GEORGIOU	GRE	24/9/79	D	18	(1)	
22	JANÍCIO de Jesus Gomes Martins	CPV	30/11/79	D	14	(3)	
4	Nikos KATSAVAKIS	GRE	16/5/79	D	20		1
24	Andreas KONSTANTINOU		12/10/80	D	9	(1)	
12	Vincent LABAN	FRA	9/9/84	M	23	(3)	2
12	Jeffrey LEIWAKABESSY	NED	23/2/81	D	29		1
18	Vangelis MANTZIOS	GRE	22/4/83	A	9	(5)	6
6	Christos MARANGOS		9/5/83	M	24	(3)	10
70	MIGUEL António Teixeira Ferreira PEDRO	POR	6/11/83	A	9	(5)	
30	Zoltán NAGY	HUN	30/3/74	G	13	(2)	
35	Predrag OCOKOLJIĆ	SRB	29/7/77	D	21		1
33	Yiannis OKKAS		11/2/77	A	21	(7)	8
4	RICARDO Ribeiro FERNANDES	POR	21/4/78	M	7	(2)	1
8	Giannis SKOPELITIS	GRE	2/3/78	M	22	(4)	2
9	Łukasz SOSIN	POL	7/5/77	A	4	(7)	
29	Loukas STYLIANOU		7/5/84	D	2		
7	Giorgos TOFAS		17/6/89	A	3	(13)	1

APEP KYPEROUNDA FC
Coach – Marc Hodel (SUI); (3/9/10) Nikos Antronikou; (9/12/09) Venizelos Tziampazis; (5/1/10) Stephen Constantine (ENG)
Founded – 1979
Stadium – Kyperounda (6,000)

2009

31/8	Aris	a	0-2	
13/9	Nea Salamis	h	2-1	Maliqi, Kryeziu
20/9	AEL	a	0-2	
28/9	Omonia	h	1-1	Pantos
3/10	AEP	a	1-2	Guerrero
25/10	Doxa	h	0-0	
31/10	Ethnikos	a	0-1	
9/11	APOEL	a	1-3	Maliqi
14/11	Anorthosis	h	0-2	
21/11	Apollon	a	0-2	
28/11	APOP	h	2-3	Gelson, Nägelein
6/12	Paralimni	a	0-2	
13/12	Ermis	h	3-3	Gelson, Guerrero, Wilhelmsen
19/12	Aris	h	2-1	Guerrero, João Paulo

2010

3/1	Nea Salamis	a	2-1	Wilhelmsen, Gelson
10/1	AEL	h	0-1	
17/1	Omonia	a	3-4	García 2, Gelson
23/1	AEP	h	3-3	Konstanti, Maliqi, Gelson
31/1	Doxa	a	0-1	
8/2	Ethnikos	h	0-3	(w/o; original result 1-1 Gelson)
15/2	APOEL	h	1-4	Gelson
22/2	Anorthosis	a	0-3	
27/2	Apollon	h	0-4	
6/3	APOP	a	2-1	Pittakas, Gelson
13/3	Paralimni	h	1-2	Gelson
20/3	Ermis	a	1-2	Pittakas

No	Name	Nat	DoB	Pos	Aps	(s)	Gls
66	Onoufrios ANTONIOU		7/6/91	M	2		
30	Stefanos EROTOKRITOU		26/1/92	D		(2)	
6	Carlos Andrés GARCÍA Cuña	URU	6/11/79	D	23		2
16	GELSON Rodrigues de Souza	BRA	3/1/82	A	18	(2)	9
1	Luigi GENNAMO	ITA	7/2/80	G	25		
29	Rafael GIAGKOUDAKIS		15/8/90	M	8	(6)	
39	Peter GRAVESEN	DEN	11/2/79	M	17	(1)	
8	Francisco Gabriel GUERRERO	ARG	23/8/77	A	12	(3)	3
2	Marvin HAMILTON	ENG	8/10/88	D	1	(4)	
27	Pascal HEIJE	NED	2/10/79	M	2		
97	Christos IOANNOU		12/9/92	M	1		
20	JOÃO PAULO Lopes Caetano	POR	4/6/84	M	13	(10)	1
14	JORGE PRADO Rus	ESP	20/1/82	D	18	(1)	
59	Stelios KALOPAIDIS		30/9/88	D	1		
33	Giorgos KONSTANTI		19/9/80	D	15	(1)	1
23	Dániel KOVÁCS	HUN	27/7/90	M	14	(4)	
19	Clirim KRYEZIU	SUI	15/2/89	M	11	(6)	1
5	Xenios KYRIAKOU		1/12/79	M	4	(1)	
10	Sokol MALIQI	SUI	24/12/81	A	19	(3)	3
26	Gábor NAGY	HUN	30/9/81	D	22		
18	Andreas NÄGELEIN	GER	5/10/81	D	10		1
9	Stamatis PANTOS		22/3/90	A	6	(4)	1
7	Ali PARHIZI	GER	29/3/83	A	1	(9)	
99	Charalambos PITTAKAS		22/3/82	A	3	(3)	2
4	Pasquale SBARRA	ITA	4/6/88	D	9	(2)	
13	Djelaludin SHARITYAR	AFG	15/3/83	D	15	(3)	
21	Antonis STYLIANOU		31/1/87	A	2	(1)	
30	Daniel Andras TOTKA	HUN	5/10/87	G	1		
11	Fabian WILHELMSEN	GER	26/5/86	A	2	(9)	2
15	Kilian WITSCHI	SUI	9/11/85	D	11	(1)	

APOEL FC
Coach – Ivan Jovanović (SRB)
Founded – 1926
Stadium – GSP (22,859)
MAJOR HONOURS:
Cypriot League - (20) 1936, 1937, 1938, 1939, 1940, 1947, 1948, 1949, 1952, 1965, 1973, 1980, 1986, 1990, 1992, 1996, 2002, 2004, 2007, 2009;
Cypriot Cup - (19) 1937, 1941, 1947, 1951, 1963, 1968, 1969, 1973, 1976, 1978, 1979, 1984, 1993, 1995, 1996, 1997, 1999, 2006, 2008.

2009

30/8	APOP	a	3-4	Paulo Jorge, Haxhi, Mirosavljević (p)
12/9	AEP	h	0-0	
20/9	Paralimni	a	1-1	Michail (p)
26/9	Doxa	h	3-0	Sikora 2, Charalambides (p)
5/10	Ermis	a	2-1	Papathanasiou, Michail
26/10	Ethnikos	h	2-0	og (Luís Torres), Michail
30/10	Aris	a	2-0	Kontis, Charalambides (p)
9/11	APEP	h	3-1	Michail (p), Grncarov, Papathanasiou
15/11	Nea Salamis	a	3-0	(w/o; match abandoned at 1-0 Hélio Pinto)
21/11	Anorthosis	h	2-0	Mirosavljević, Alexandrou
30/11	AEL	a	2-1	Nono Morais, Mirosavljević
4/12	Apollon	h	1-1	Charalambides
13/12	Omonia	a	1-1	Żewłakow
20/12	APOP	h	3-1	Żewłakow, Michail, Mirosavljević (p)

2010

3/1	AEP	a	1-0	Michail
10/1	Paralimni	h	3-1	Mirosavljević 2, Jean Paulista
16/1	Doxa	a	2-1	Mirosavljević 2
23/1	Ermis	h	1-0	Kosowski
7/2	Aris	h	5-0	Mirosavljević, Kontis, Grncarov, Charalambides, Breška
15/2	APEP	a	4-1	Mirosavljević 2, Charalambides 2
20/2	Nea Salamis	h	0-0	
24/2	Ethnikos	a	0-0	
28/2	Anorthosis	a	0-0	
7/3	AEL	h	1-0	Michail

14/3	Apollon	a	0-2	
21/3	Omonia	h	1-2	Papathanasiou
28/3	Omonia	h	0-1	
11/4	Apollon	a	2-1	Żewłakow, Charalambides
18/4	Anorthosis	a	1-1	Kosowski
24/4	Anorthosis	h	1-0	Solomou
2/5	Omonia	a	0-1	
8/5	Apollon	h	3-2	Charalambides 2, Jean Paulista

No	Name	Nat	DoB	Pos	Aps	(s)	Gls
29	Nektarios ALEXANDROU		19/12/83	M	16	(6)	1
37	Mário BREŠKA	SVK	27/12/79	A	10	(10)	1
14	Joost BROERSE	NED	8/5/79	D	13	(6)	
10	Kostas CHARALAMBIDES		25/7/81	M	20	(7)	9
22	Dionissis CHIOTIS	GRE	4/6/77	G	23		
19	Marios ELIA		14/4/79	D	15	(1)	
5	Boban GRNCAROV	MKD	12/8/82	D	13	(4)	2
32	Altin HAXHI	ALB	17/6/75	D	13	(1)	1
23	HÉLIO José Ribiero PINTO	POR	29/2/84	M	17	(8)	1
20	JEAN Francisco Rodrigues PAULISTA	BRA	28/11/77	A	8	(10)	2
88	Anastasios KISSAS		18/1/88	G	8		
24	Christos KONTIS	GRE	13/5/75	D	27		2
11	Kamil KOSOWSKI	POL	30/8/77	M	19	(1)	2
44	Vangelis KOUTSOPOULOS	GRE	2/2/80	D	9		
81	Márcio Ivanildo da Silva "MARCINHO"	BRA	23/3/81	M	3	(5)	
33	Chrysis MICHAIL		26/5/77	M	23	(3)	7
30	Nenad MIROSAVLJEVIĆ	SRB	4/9/77	A	20	(3)	11
1	Michalis MORFIS		15/1/79	G	1		
26	NUNO Miguel Barbosa MORAIS	POR	29/1/84	M	27	(2)	1
9	Andreas PAPATHANASIOU		3/10/83	A	4	(11)	3
3	PAULO JORGE Soares Gomes	POR	16/6/80	D	11	(2)	1
7	Savvas POURSAITIDIS	GRE	23/6/76	D	24		
17	Marinos SATSIAS		24/5/78	M	11		
8	Adrian SIKORA	POL	19/3/80	A	2	(1)	2
77	Athos SOLOMOU		30/11/85	M		(7)	1
21	Marcin ŻEWŁAKOW	POL	22/4/76	A	15	(4)	3

APOLLON LIMASSOL FC
Coach – Thomas von Heesen (GER);
(2/2/10) Slobodan Krčmarević (SRB)
Founded – 1954
Stadium – Tsirion (13,000)
MAJOR HONOURS:
Cypriot League (3) 1991, 1994, 2006;
Cypriot Cup - (6) 1966, 1967, 1986, 1992, 2001, 2010.

2009

29/8	Paralimni	a	3-0	Sangoy, Avraam, Bangura
12/9	Ermis	h	2-1	Agogo, Bangura
19/9	Aris	a	1-1	Bangura
26/9	Nea Salamis	h	4-1	Sangoy 2, Toni, Avraam
4/10	AEL	a	0-0	
24/10	Omonia	h	0-1	
2/11	AEP	a	2-1	Avraam, Núñez
8/11	Doxa	h	2-0	Sangoy 2
15/11	Ethnikos	a	1-0	Avraam
21/11	APEP	h	2-0	Matušovič, Sangoy
28/11	Anorthosis	a	1-1	Sangoy
4/12	APOEL	a	1-1	Bangura
12/12	APOP	h	1-0	Avraam
20/12	Paralimni	h	1-1	Bangura

2010

3/1	Ermis	a	2-1	Adorno, Agogo
9/1	Aris	h	3-0	Agogo 2, Avraam (p)
17/1	Nea Salamis	a	1-0	Agogo
24/1	AEL	h	0-2	
30/1	Omonia	a	1-2	Oseni
7/2	AEP	h	0-0	
13/2	Doxa	a	1-0	Sangoy (p)
20/2	Ethnikos	h	3-1	Avraam, Sangoy 2

27/2	APEP	a	4-0	Adorno 2, Sangoy, Bangura
7/3	Anorthosis	h	2-0	Sangoy, og (Cafú)
14/3	APOEL	h	2-0	Agogo, Adorno
21/3	APOP	a	3-1	Avraam, Sangoy, Neva
28/3	Anorthosis	a	0-2	
11/4	APOEL	h	1-2	Lai
18/4	Omonia	h	0-0	
18/4	Omonia	a	1-1	Thiago Sales
2/5	Anorthosis	h	0-0	
8/5	APOEL	a	2-3	Avraam 2

No	Name	Nat	DoB	Pos	Aps	(s)	Gls
12	Aldo ADORNO	PAR	8/4/82	A	19	(2)	4
23	Manuel "Junior" AGOGO	GHA	1/8/79	A	20	(3)	6
30	Andreas AVRAAM		6/6/87	A	27	(4)	10
22	Mustapha BANGURA	SLE	24/10/89	A	10	(14)	6
17	Aleš CHVALOVSKÝ	CZE	29/5/79	G	28		
11	Klodian DURO	ALB	21/12/77	M	12	(12)	
3	JOVALDIR Ferreira Peris	BRA	9/1/82	D	5		
6	Valentino LAI	SWE	3/2/84	M	7	(3)	1
83	Ioannis MASMANIDIS	GER	9/3/83	M	3	(5)	
80	Miroslav MATUŠOVIČ	CZE	2/11/80	A	16	(6)	1
16	Giorgos MERKIS		30/7/84	M	25		
8	Moshe MISHAELOV	ISR	14/9/83	D	3	(2)	
99	Miljan MRDAKOVIĆ	SRB	6/5/82	A		(1)	
15	Samuel NEVA	FRA	15/5/81	D	24	(3)	1
27	Antonio NÚÑEZ Tena	ESP	15/1/79	M	9	(6)	1
4	Waheed OSENI	NGA	17/1/88	M	25	(3)	1
40	Nico PELLATZ	GER	8/7/86	G	4		
60	Daniel Eduardo QUINTEROS	ARG	10/3/76	M	25	(2)	
10	Gastón Maximiliano SANGOY	ARG	5/10/84	A	26	(1)	13
13	Gonzalo Alberto SEGARES Gonzalez	CRC	13/10/82	D	10	(2)	
5	Giannis SFAKIANAKIS	GRE	6/2/76	D	1	(1)	
26	Andreas STAVROU		27/10/88	M	4	(13)	
21	Christis THEOFILOU		30/4/80	D	12	(6)	
37	THIAGO Guimarães SALES	BRA	7/5/87	D	9	(5)	1
2	António Pedro de Brito Lopes "TONI"	POR	23/7/79	D	28	(1)	1

APOP/KINYRAS PEYIAS FC
Coach – Giorgos Polyviou
Founded – 2003
Stadium – Peyia Municipal (3,500)
MAJOR HONOURS:
Cypriot Cup - (1) 2009.

2009

30/8	APOEL	h	4-3	og (Hélio Pinto), Buyse, Željković (p), Semedo
12/9	Paralimni	h	1-2	Silva
21/9	Ermis	a	3-2	Željković, Semedo 2
27/9	Aris	h	1-1	Liri
4/10	Nea Salamis	a	2-1	Semedo, Tall
25/10	AEL	h	1-0	Tall
1/11	Omonia	a	0-1	
7/11	AEP	h	0-0	
14/11	Doxa	a	2-1	Semedo 2
22/11	Ethnikos	h	3-0	González 2, Semedo
28/11	APEP	a	3-2	González 2, Semedo
5/12	Anorthosis	h	2-0	Semedo 2
12/12	Apollon	a	0-1	
20/12	APOEL	a	1-3	Semedo (p)

2010

2/1	Paralimni	a	1-3	González
9/1	Ermis	h	1-1	Semedo (p)
17/1	Aris	a	4-2	Semedo 2, Galanis, González
23/1	Nea Salamis	h	2-1	Tall, González
31/1	AEL	a	0-2	
6/2	Omonia	h	1-3	González
13/2	AEP	a	2-3	Sfakianakis, Semedo (p)
20/2	Doxa	h	2-2	Mašek, Liri

1/3	Ethnikos	a	1-3	Semedo (p)
6/3	APEP	h	1-2	González
14/3	Anorthosis	a	1-2	Semedo (p)
21/3	Apollon	h	1-3	Semedo
27/3	Ethnikos	h	3-2	Paulo Costa, Fylaktou, Željković
10/4	AEL	a	2-4	Semedo, Vitali
17/4	Paralimni	h	1-2	Semedo
25/4	Paralimni	a	0-4	
30/4	Ethnikos	a	2-4	Žinko, Galanis
8/5	AEL	h	2-5	Semedo 2

No	Name	Nat	DoB	Pos	Aps	(s)	Gls
44	Michalis AGATHANGELOU		14/11/86	M	4	(3)	
1	Gábor BARDI	HUN	20/11/78	G	19		
17	Samir BENGELLOUN	FRA	7/2/85	M	14	(5)	
2	Fangio BUYSE	BEL	27/9/74	M	2		1
13	CARLOS Manuel de Oliveira MARQUES	POR	6/2/83	D	14	(3)	
3	Stavros CHRISTODOULOU		17/2/92	D		(2)	
31	Michalis FANI		4/2/81	G	7	(2)	
91	Lambros FYLAKTOU		16/6/91	M	4	(3)	1
6	Theodoros GALANIS	GRE	14/7/80	D	27		2
32	Sebastián Ignacio GONZÁLEZ Valdés	CHI	14/12/78	A	16	(8)	9
77	Dejan GRABIČ	SVN	21/9/80	M	15	(8)	
23	Sébastien GRIMALDI	FRA	10/9/79	D	22		
25	Šarūnas JUREVIČIUS	LTU	3/5/89	G	5		
29	Serge Alain LIRI	CIV	23/3/79	A	20	(6)	2
26	Jiří MAŠEK	CZE	5/10/78	A	3	(1)	1
9	Marios NEOPHYTOU		4/4/79	A	2	(7)	
24	Paulos NEOPHYTOU		2/1/87	D	5	(2)	
19	Roland OJONG	CMR	23/1/89	A	2	(7)	
12	Christos PALATES		13/7/90	A	4	(3)	
15	PAULO Sérgio Cardoso da COSTA	POR	5/12/79	M	8	(3)	1
80	Ioannis RETSAS		21/11/89	M	10	(3)	
18	Konstantinos SAMARAS		18/5/84	D	18		
99	Marios SAVVA		6/5/77	G	1	(1)	
11	João Filipe Correia SEMEDO	CPV	26/12/79	A	25	(2)	22
7	Giannis SFAKIANAKIS	GRE	6/2/76	D	12	(1)	1
8	Fillip Rodrigues da SILVA	BRA	23/11/81	M	6	(14)	1
85	Gora TALL	SEN	20/5/85	D	21		3
14	Martín Ariel VITALI	ARG	11/11/75	D	28		1
21	Zoran ŽELJKOVIĆ	SVN	9/5/80	M	16	(7)	3
16	Luka ŽINKO	SVN	23/3/83	D	22	(3)	1

ARIS LIMASSOL FC

Coach – Marios Konstantinou; (20/1/10) Stéphane Demol (BEL); (21/3/10) Tasos Kyriakou
Founded – 1930
Stadium – Tsirion (13,000)

2009

31/8	APEP	h	2-0	Stojanović, Eduardo Marques
14/9	Anorthosis	a	1-3	Mihalcea
19/9	Apollon	h	1-1	Stojanović
27/9	APOP	a	1-1	Mihalcea
3/10	Paralimni	h	1-1	Eduardo Marques
25/10	Ermis	a	3-5	Stojanović, McKenzie, Eduardo Marques
30/10	APOEL	h	0-2	
7/11	Nea Salamis	h	3-1	Stojanović, Mihalcea, Eduardo Marques
15/11	AEL	a	0-1	
22/11	Omonia	h	0-1	
28/11	AEP	a	3-1	Mihalcea, Dugić, Markou
7/12	Doxa	h	1-4	Mihalcea (p)
14/12	Ethnikos	a	0-0	
19/12	APEP	a	1-2	Stojanović

2010

3/1	Anorthosis	h	0-3	
9/1	Apollon	a	0-3	
17/1	APOP	h	2-4	Dugić 2
23/1	Paralimni	a	0-1	
30/1	Ermis	h	2-2	Mihalcea, Dugić
7/2	APOEL	a	0-5	
13/2	Nea Salamis	a	2-3	Woobay, Dugić
21/2	AEL	h	0-0	
28/2	Omonia	a	1-2	Bruno Pinheiro
6/3	AEP	h	2-1	Mihalcea, Kardanas
13/3	Doxa	a	0-0	
20/3	Ethnikos	h	0-0	
27/3	Ermis	h	0-2	
11/4	AEP	a	2-3	Mihalcea (p), Aguirre
17/4	Doxa	a	0-3	
24/4	Doxa	h	0-2	
1/5	Ermis	a	0-4	
8/5	AEP	h	2-2	Stojanović 2

No	Name	Nat	DoB	Pos	Aps	(s)	Gls
99	Francisco Ricardo AGUIRRE	ARG	1/9/77	A	4	(4)	1
55	Menelaos ARISTIDOU		22/2/86	M	5	(1)	
86	Nikolas ASPROGENIS		6/4/86	G	1		
33	Sofronis AVGOUSTI		9/3/77	G	10		
6	Daniel BĂLAN	ROU	18/9/79	D	6	(1)	
91	Gilbert BAYIHA N'DJEMA	FRA	9/8/79	G	20		
4	BRUNO Filipe Tavares PINHEIRO	POR	21/8/87	D	23	(3)	1
11	Slaviša DUGIĆ	SUI	17/1/85	A	7	(15)	5
5	Marc EBERLE	GER	3/6/80	D	24		
17	EDUARDO MARQUES de Jesus Passos	BRA	26/6/76	M	18	4	
18	Elias ELIA		6/11/85	D	5	(6)	
20	Andrew ESEALUKA	NGA	20/12/85	A	1	(6)	
2	Filippos FILIPPOU		24/6/75	D	8	(1)	
25	Panayiotis IOANNOU		25/3/83	D	6		
16	Dimitris KARDANAS		19/5/90	A	2	(5)	1
50	Gábor KOROLOVSZKY	HUN	11/7/79	M	18	(1)	
32	Nikos KOUNENAKIS	GRE	3/2/78	D	17		
69	Ognjen LEKIĆ	SRB	7/1/82	M		(3)	
69	Carl LOMBÉ	ARM	18/5/86	M	28	(1)	
31	MÁRCIO FERREIRA de Souza	BRA	3/7/77	D	21	(4)	
30	Kostas MARKOU		27/3/88	M	13	(15)	1
3	Jamie McKENZIE	SCO	8/5/86	D	3		1
9	Adrian MIHALCEA	ROU	24/5/76	A	27	(1)	8
8	PAULO Alexandre Monteiro dos SANTOS	BRA	11/7/77	M	1		
27	Vitālijs REČICKIS	LVA	8/9/86	M	6	(4)	
77	RICARDO Nuno dos Santos NUNES	POR	18/6/86	D	3	(4)	
14	Sebastián SALOMÓN	ARG	12/12/78	M	11	(1)	
1	Michalis SAVVIDIS		17/9/86	G	1		
10	Saša STOJANOVIĆ	SRB	21/1/83	M	19	(3)	7
23	Andreas THEOFANOUS		8/1/85	M	14	(5)	
19	Ventsislav VASILEV	BUL	8/8/87	D	10		
12	Giorgos VASILIOU		12/8/84	M	12	(4)	
12	Giorgos VOUREXAKIS		1/4/77	D	7		
88	Julius WOOBAY	SLE	17/5/84	M	1	(4)	1

DOXA KATOKOPIA FC

Coach – Charalambos Christodoulou
Founded – 1954
Stadium – Peristerona (4,000)

2009

29/8	AEL	a	0-1	
13/9	Omonia	h	2-4	Comboio, Malá
19/9	AEP	a	2-1	Henrique, Carlos André
26/9	APOEL	a	0-3	
3/10	Ethnikos	h	1-0	Margaça
25/10	APEP	a	0-0	
31/10	Anorthosis	h	2-3	Roma, Rodrigão
8/11	Apollon	a	0-2	
14/11	APOP	h	1-2	Nuno Rodrigues
21/11	Paralimni	h	1-1	Margaça

29/11	Ermis	h	1-1	Henrique
7/12	Aris	a	4-1	Rodrigão, Milton, Henrique 2 (2p)
13/12	Nea Salamis	h	0-0	
19/12	AEL	h	1-0	Carlos André
2010				
4/1	Omonia	a	0-3	
10/1	AEP	h	2-2	Eleftheriou 2
16/1	APOEL	h	1-2	Henrique
24/1	Ethnikos	a	0-1	
31/1	APEP	h	1-0	Carlos André
6/2	Anorthosis	a	0-3	
13/2	Apollon	h	0-1	
20/2	APOP	a	2-2	Margaça, Henrique
27/2	Paralimni	h	2-2	Roma, Henrique
6/3	Ermis	a	1-2	Carlos André
13/3	Aris	h	0-0	
20/3	Nea Salamis	a	1-0	Henrique (p)
27/3	AEP	h	4-0	Henrique, Roma 2, Eleftheriou
11/4	Ermis	a	0-1	
17/4	Aris	h	3-0	Roma 3
24/4	Aris	a	2-0	Paulo Sereno, Henrique
1/5	AEP	a	1-4	Roma
8/5	Ermis	h	1-4	Roma

No	Name	Nat	DoB	Pos	Aps	(s)	Gls
7	CARLOS ANDRÉ Filipe Martins	POR	15/4/82	M	27	(1)	4
24	Demetris CHADJISAVVAS		8/3/90	A	1		
23	Andreas CHATZIGEORGIOU		6/12/93	D	3		
31	João Manuel Dinis "COMBOIO"	POR	13/10/79	D	11	(4)	1
23	Giorgos ELEFTHERIOU		30/9/84	M	9	(10)	3
4	GILVAN Rosa da Lima	BRA	26/3/82	D	13	(4)	
22	Glaukos GLAFKOU		6/1/91	G	1		
20	José HENRIQUE Souto Esteves	POR	31/3/80	A	25	(2)	10
12	Giorgos KAKOULIS		14/1/85	G	5		
10	Giorgos KOSTIS		7/10/72	M	1	(1)	
1	Gabriel LIMA	BRA	13/6/78	A	2	(2)	
6	Muhamed Lamine Jabula Sanó "MALÁ"	GNB	6/12/79	M	7	(6)	1
18	Ricardo Jorge Marques Duarte "MANGUALDE"	POR	14/2/82	D	28	(2)	
29	MARCO Paulo Amaral BICHO	POR	7/3/80	M	18	(6)	
28	Renato João Inácio MARGAÇA	POR	17/7/85	M	25	(3)	3
9	MILTON Andrade Vaz Mendes	POR	7/10/79	A	8	(6)	1
33	Andreas NEOPHYTOU		8/8/91	D	1		
11	Nikos NICOLAOU		10/5/79	M	14	(4)	
17	NUNO Filipe Martins RODRIGUES	POR	14/11/79	D	17	(6)	1
40	Udochukwu NWOKO	MLT	15/10/84	M	6	(8)	
51	Márcio Henrique Silva PAIVA	POR	31/7/80	G	26		
50	PAULO Jorge Fernandes SERENO	POR	24/10/83	A	2	(5)	1
22	PEDRO Miguel Mimoso DUARTE	POR	22/4/78	M	20	(1)	
8	Kyriakos POLYKARPOU		17/3/80	M	16	(7)	
3	Rodrigo Rodrigues Ribeiro "RODRIGÃO"	BRA	18/7/78	D	27		2
30	Juliano Laurentino dos Santos "ROMA"	BRA	16/2/85	A	16	(12)	9
19	Carlos Manuel Dias SAAVEDRA	POR	1/2/81	M	23	(3)	

ENOSIS NEON PARALIMNI FC

Coach – Cedomir Janevski (MKD)
Founded – 1936
Stadium – Tasos Markou (8,000)

2009				
29/8	Apollon	h	0-3	
12/9	APOP	a	2-1	Trickovski, Van Tornhout
20/9	APOEL	h	1-1	Van Tornhout
26/9	Ermis	h	2-0	Krivokapić, Trickovski (p)
3/10	Aris	a	1-1	Fassotte

24/10	Nea Salamis	h	1-1	Van Tornhout (p)
31/10	AEL	a	1-2	Goumenos
7/11	Omonia	h	0-4	
14/11	AEP	a	0-2	
21/11	Doxa	h	1-1	Milenković
28/11	Ethnikos	a	0-1	
6/12	APEP	h	2-0	og (Nagy), Krivokapić
12/12	Anorthosis	a	0-2	
20/12	Apollon	a	1-1	González
2010				
2/1	APOP	h	3-1	Trickovski 2, Mertakas
10/1	APOEL	a	1-3	Van Tornhout
23/1	Aris	h	1-0	Peeters
1/2	Nea Salamis	a	0-0	
6/2	AEL	h	1-2	Markovski
14/2	Omonia	a	0-0	
17/2	Ermis	a	0-1	
21/2	AEP	h	5-1	De Wulf, Trickovski 2, Van Tornhout, Tarumbwa
27/2	Doxa	a	2-2	Van Tornhout, Krivokapić
6/3	Ethnikos	h	1-2	González
13/3	APEP	a	2-1	Krivokapić, Van Tornhout
21/3	Anorthosis	h	1-2	Trickovski
27/3	AEL	h	1-3	Van Tornhout
10/4	Ethnikos	a	1-0	Krivokapić
17/4	APOP	a	2-1	Krivokapić, Trickovski
25/4	APOP	h	4-0	Van Tornhout 2, Pierettis, Peeters
1/5	AEL	a	2-2	De Wulf, Van Tornhout
7/5	Ethnikos	h	1-1	Van Tornhout

No	Name	Nat	DoB	Pos	Aps	(s)	Gls
20	Armen AMBARTSUMYAN	ARM	18/2/78	G	4		
16	Matthew CASSIDY	IRL	2/10/88	M	8	(9)	
14	Jimmy DE WULF	BEL	9/6/80	D	26	(2)	2
10	EDMAR Lacerda da SILVA	BRA	19/4/82	A	3	(7)	
4	Laurent FASSOTTE	BEL	31/12/77	D	20	(2)	1
7	Raúl GONZÁLEZ	VEN	28/8/75	D	18	(6)	2
17	Dimos GOUMENOS		25/12/78	M	18	(6)	1
6	HUGO Miguel da Encarnação Pires FARIA	POR	15/2/83	M	26	(2)	
9	Radovan KRIVOKAPIĆ	SRB	14/8/78	M	29	(2)	6
40	Vasilis MANOLIS		22/3/91	M		(2)	
5	Bojan MARKOVSKI	MKD	8/8/83	D	21	(4)	1
30	Lefteris MERTAKAS		16/3/85	D	20	(1)	1
89	Ninoslav MILENKOVIĆ	BIH	31/12/77	D	20	(1)	1
1	Petar MILOSEVSKI	MKD	6/12/73	G	28		
25	Dimitris OIKONOMOU		10/11/92	D		(3)	
77	Rocky PEETERS	BEL	18/8/79	M	19	(7)	2
28	Christos PIERETTIS		12/6/89	M		(8)	1
19	Konstantinos PRIS		10/8/90	M	3	(11)	
33	Panikos SPYROU		17/10/76	D	24	(2)	
12	Obadiah TARUMBWA	ZIM	29/11/85	A	15	(10)	1
11	Ivan TRICKOVSKI	MKD	18/4/87	A	29		8
24	Nikolas TZIAMBOURIS		18/8/89	D		(2)	
23	Dieter VAN TORNHOUT	BEL	18/3/85	A	21	(4)	12

ERMIS ARADIPPOU FC

Coach – Yiannos Stavrinou; (30/9/09) Dušan Mitošević (SRB)
Founded – 1958
Stadium – Aradippou Municipal (4,500)

2009				
30/8	Anorthosis	h	0-0	
12/9	Apollon	a	1-2	Joeano
21/9	APOP	h	2-3	Miguel Oliveira, Suma
26/9	Paralimni	a	0-2	
5/10	APOEL	h	1-2	Joeano
25/10	Aris	h	5-3	Joeano 3, Lambrou, Wender (p)
31/10	Nea Salamis	a	3-0	Louka 2, Joeano
8/11	AEL	h	1-0	Pavlou
18/11	Omonia	a	0-1	
22/11	AEP	h	0-0	

CYPRUS

29/11	Doxa	a	1-1	*Joeano*
6/12	Ethnikos	h	1-0	*Joeano*
13/12	APEP	a	3-3	*og (García), Wender, Suma*
21/12	Anorthosis	a	0-1	
2010				
3/1	Apollon	h	1-2	*Joeano (p)*
9/1	APOP	a	1-1	*Joeano*
23/1	APOEL	a	0-1	
30/1	Aris	a	2-2	*Miguel Oliveira, Wender*
7/2	Nea Salamis	h	1-1	*Roncatto*
13/2	AEL	a	1-2	*Maghradze*
17/2	Paralimni	h	1-0	*Joeano*
21/2	Omonia	h	1-2	*Wender*
27/2	AEP	a	1-3	*Roncatto*
6/3	Doxa	h	2-1	*Bemba, Joeano*
13/3	Ethnikos	a	0-0	
20/3	APEP	h	2-1	*Joeano, Wender*
27/3	Aris	a	2-0	*Roncatto, Sebastião Nogueira*
11/4	Doxa	h	1-0	*Joeano*
17/4	AEP	a	0-3	
24/4	AEP	h	1-0	*Joeano*
1/5	Aris	h	4-0	*Joeano 4*
8/5	Doxa	a	4-1	*Joeano 3, Guilherme*

No	Name	Nat	DoB	Pos	Aps	(s)	Gls
2	Marko BARUN	SVN	7/1/78	D	24	(2)	
13	Kiran BECHAN	NED	12/9/82	M	2	(4)	
4	Mathieu Yannick BEMBA	FRA	3/3/88	M	22	(1)	1
40	Aleksandar ČANOVIĆ	SRB	18/2/83	G	9		
31	Athos CHRYSOSTOMOU		8/7/81	G	8		
20	Cheikh GADIAGA	SEN	30/11/79	M	27	(1)	
7	GILBERTO Manuel Pereira da Silva	POR	26/3/85	D	7	(6)	
9	Juan Cruz GILL	ARG	18/7/83	D	18	(4)	
58	Spyros GOGOLOS	GRE	11/4/78	D	7	(2)	
6	GUILHERME Weisheimer	BRA	22/1/81	A	9	(15)	1
8	JAÍLSON Alexandre Alves dos Santos	BRA	16/6/81	A		(2)	
23	Ricardo Jorge da Silva Pinto Ferreira "JOCA"	POR	4/3/81	M	10	(5)	
9	JOEANO Pinto Chaves	BRA	12/8/79	A	28	(1)	22
25	Abdelkarim KISSI	MAR	5/5/80	M	10	(4)	
3	Lambros LAMBROU		9/9/77	D	27		1
30	Charis LOIZOU		8/11/82	M	2	(2)	
44	Marios LOUKA		9/12/82	M	3	(2)	2
16	Levan MAGHRADZE	GEO	5/12/77	D	25	(2)	1
19	Loizos MICHAIL		14/4/90	1			
26	Pedro MIGUEL dos Santos OLIVEIRA	POR	18/8/83	D	27	(2)	2
12	Christos MYLONAS		19/10/90	M	1		
91	Giorgos PAPADOPOULOS		24/4/81	G	1		
86	Kyriakos PAVLOU		4/9/86	A	1	(5)	1
10	Eliseo Ortiz QUINTANILLA	SLV	5/2/83	M	10		
14	Nicolás RAIMONI	URU	5/9/84	A	1	(2)	
1	RODRIGO POSSO Moreno	BRA	16/5/76	G	14		
10	Evandro RONCATTO	BRA	24/5/86	A	13	(3)	3
77	SEBASTIÃO José Lopes de Melo e NOGUEIRA	POR	9/9/88	M	9	(3)	1
22	Sérgio Fernando Silva Rodrigues "SERGINHO"	POR	12/10/85	D	9	(5)	
11	Sheriff SUMA	SLE	12/10/86	A		(14)	2
15	WENDERson de Arruda Said	BRA	17/4/75	M	27	(2)	5

ETHNIKOS ACHNAS FC

Coach – Panikos Orfanidis; (29/9/09) Svetozar Šapurić (SRB)
Founded – 1968
Stadium – Dasaki (5,000)

2009				
29/8	Nea Salamis	a	1-1	*Siailis*
13/9	AEL	h	1-4	*Kebadze*
19/9	Omonia	a	0-2	
26/9	AEP	h	1-2	*Petrović*

3/10	Doxa	a	0-1	
26/10	APOEL	a	0-2	
31/10	APEP	h	1-0	*Alekou*
7/11	Anorthosis	a	1-2	*Petrović*
15/11	Apollon	h	0-1	
22/11	APOP	a	0-3	
28/11	Paralimni	h	1-0	*Poyiatzis (p)*
6/12	Ermis	a	0-1	
14/12	Aris	h	0-0	
19/12	Nea Salamis	h	2-1	*Belić, Poyiatzis (p)*
2010				
2/1	AEL	a	2-2	*Belić, Eduardo*
9/1	Omonia	h	2-1	*Sikov, Cássio*
16/1	AEP	a	0-0	
24/1	Doxa	h	1-0	*Mrdaković*
8/2	APEP	a	3-0	*(w/o; original result 1-1 Alekou)*
14/2	Anorthosis	h	1-3	*Mrdaković*
20/2	Apollon	a	1-3	*Sikov*
24/2	APOEL	h	0-0	
1/3	APOP	h	3-1	*Filaniotis, Kebadze, Poyiatzis*
6/3	Paralimni	a	2-1	*Kebadze, Petrović*
13/3	Ermis	h	0-0	
20/3	Aris	a	0-0	
27/3	APOP	a	2-3	*Mrdaković 2*
10/4	Paralimni	h	0-1	
17/4	AEL	h	4-3	*Kebadze, Mrdaković, Stjepanović, Petrović (p)*
25/4	AEL	a	0-1	
30/4	APOP	h	4-2	*Mrdaković 2, Elia 2*
7/5	Paralimni	a	1-1	*Mrdaković*

No	Name	Nat	DoB	Pos	Aps	(s)	Gls
9	Alekos ALEKOU		13/11/83	A	9	(13)	2
25	Milan BELIĆ	SRB	29/8/77	A	14	(9)	2
30	CÁSSIO Magalhães Fernandes	BRA	11/2/87	M	26	(1)	1
7	ÉDSON de Jesus Nobre	ANG	3/2/80	M	2		
21	EDUARDO Pinceli	BRA	23/4/83	M	17	(8)	1
16	Elpidoforos ELIA		5/8/85	M	4	(5)	2
33	Petros FILANIOTIS		13/4/80	M	17	(6)	1
28	Slavco GEORGIEVSKI	MKD	30/3/80	M	4	(2)	
3	JOÃO PEDRO Lima dos Santos	POR	15/8/80	D	12		
29	Levan KEBADZE	GEO	1/2/75	A	27	(1)	4
6	Christos KOTSONIS		13/6/76	M	21		
14	Sahr LAHAI	SLE	1/4/83	M	2	(9)	
2	LUÍS Filipe Baptista TORRES	POR	15/10/79	D	27		
27	MARCELO Costa Resende Siqueira	BRA	27/1/87	D	3	(2)	
99	Miljan MRDAKOVIĆ	SRB	6/5/82	A	14		8
17	Mickaël NIÇOISE	FRA	19/9/84	A	2	(6)	
1	Edin NUREDINOSKI	MKD	21/4/82	G	31		
18	Panagiotis ONISIFOROU		6/8/85	M	3	(2)	
20	Ivan PETROVIĆ	SRB	5/9/78	M	13	(8)	4
10	Christos POYIATZIS		12/4/78	M	23	(1)	3
8	Lars SCHLICHTING	GER	14/9/82	M	18	(2)	
4	Christos SIAILIS		30/10/79	D	6	(5)	1
5	Vance SIKOV	MKD	19/7/85	D	27	(2)	2
15	Dimitris SIMOV		9/4/82	D	24		
77	Zoran STJEPANOVIĆ	SRB	13/6/75	M	4	(5)	1
22	Dimitris STYLIANOU		5/7/84	G	1		
32	José Antonio VILLANUEVA Muñoz	ESP	16/8/85	M	1	(4)	

NEA SALAMIS FC

**Coach – Attila Supka (HUN); (2/11/09) Mirko Micić (SRB);
(22/12/09) (Louis Stefanis); (30/12/09) Nir Klinger (ISR)**
Founded – 1948
Stadium – Ammochostos (4,000)
MAJOR HONOURS:
Cypriot Cup – (1) 1990.

2009				
29/8	Ethnikos	h	1-1	*Mašek*
13/9	APEP	a	1-2	*Rui Lima (p)*

20/9	Anorthosis	h	1-2	Tsitaishvili
26/9	Apollon	a	1-4	Mašek
4/10	APOP	h	1-2	Tsitaishvili (p)
24/10	Paralimni	a	1-1	Voskaridis
31/10	Ermis	h	0-3	
7/11	Aris	a	1-3	Mašek
15/11	APOEL	h	0-3	(w/o; match abandoned at 0-1)
23/11	AEL	h	1-3	Ávalos
29/11	Omonia	a	1-1	Koulouris
13/12	Doxa	a	0-0	
19/12	Ethnikos	a	1-2	Therapontos
23/12	AEP	h	0-0	
2010				
3/1	APEP	h	1-2	Tsitaishvili
11/1	Anorthosis	a	1-4	Kyprianou
17/1	Apollon	h	0-1	
23/1	APOP	a	1-2	Voskaridis
1/2	Paralimni	h	0-0	
7/2	Ermis	a	1-1	Tsitaishvili
13/2	Aris	h	3-2	Tsitaishvili, Kyprianou, Rodrigo Silva
20/2	APOEL	a	0-0	
1/3	AEL	a	1-3	Voskaridis
7/3	Omonia	h	0-2	
13/3	AEP	a	1-0	Rodrigo Silva
20/3	Doxa	h	0-1	

No	Name	Nat	DoB	Pos	Aps	(s)	Gls
2	Louis ANIWETA	RWA	10/7/84	D	19	(1)	
4	Fernando Horácio ÁVALOS	ARG	31/3/78	D	22		1
10	Barukh DEGO	ISR	26/3/81	M	7		
19	EUGÉNIO André Calesso das Neves	POR	27/8/87	A	1	(1)	
78	Willy FONDJA	FRA	22/9/83	D	2		
27	Nikolas FOTIOU		11/11/89	D	7	(4)	
79	Eugénio Fernando Bila "GENITO"	MOZ	3/3/79	M	18	(1)	
12	Marcin JUSZCZYK	POL	23/1/85	G	8		
5	Theodoros KATSIARIS		9/8/86	M	11	(2)	
20	Andreas KOULOURIS		16/4/88	M	4	(5)	1
11	Andreas KYPRIANOU		5/12/88	A	7	(9)	2
8	Liasos LOUKA		1/2/80	M	16	(4)	
26	Jiří MAŠEK	CZE	5/10/78	A	10	(1)	3
25	Christos MODESTOU		3/7/88	M	4	(2)	
21	Nikos NICOLAOU		28/8/78	D	12	(1)	
30	Tomáš PEŠÍR	CZE	30/5/81	A	1	(5)	
30	Rafael Antonio PONZO García	VEN	18/10/78	G	10		
7	RODRIGO Jorge SILVA	BRA	12/1/80	A	3	(4)	2
15	Jérémie RODRIGUES	FRA	1/11/80	D	18	(2)	
10	RUI Manuel Pinto de LIMA	POR	25/3/78	M	12		1
23	Nordine SAM	ALG	25/3/82	D	14	(2)	
28	SEBASTIÃO José Lopes de Melo e NOGUEIRA	POR	9/9/88	M	4	(2)	
41	SÉRGIO Roberto VITORI	BRA	13/11/81	G	8		
18	Norbert SIPOS	HUN	21/3/81	M	4	(2)	
3	José de SOUZA Pereira	BRA	4/5/84	D	1		
52	Prodromos THERAPONTOS		23/3/89	M	3	(10)	1
17	Péter TÓTH	HUN	17/4/91	A	3	(6)	
9	Klimenti TSITAISHVILI	GEO	5/1/79	A	16	(6)	5
9	VÍTOR Simões da VINHA	POR	11/11/86	D	26		
1	Stefanos VOSKARIDIS		1/2/80	A	15	(5)	3

AC OMONIA
Coach – Takis Lemonis (GRE)
Founded – 1948
Stadium – GSP (22,859)
MAJOR HONOURS:
Cypriot League - (20) 1961, 1966, 1972, 1974, 1975, 1976, 1977, 1978, 1979, 1981, 1982, 1983, 1984, 1985, 1987, 1989, 1993, 2001, 2003, 2010;
Cypriot Cup - (12) 1965, 1972, 1974, 1980, 1981, 1982, 1983, 1988, 1991, 1994, 2000, 2005.

2009				
29/8	AEP	h	3-2	Aloneftis 2, Bruno Aguiar
13/9	Doxa	a	4-2	Efrem, Charalambous, Aloneftis, Alabi
19/9	Ethnikos	h	2-0	Charalambous, Efrem
28/9	APEP	a	1-1	Aloneftis
3/10	Anorthosis	h	1-1	Konstantinou
24/10	Apollon	a	1-0	Konstantinou
1/11	APOP	h	1-0	Efrem
7/11	Paralimni	a	4-0	Alabi, Makrides 2, Konstantinou
18/11	Ermis	h	1-0	Aloneftis
22/11	Aris	a	1-0	Žurawski (p)
29/11	Nea Salamis	h	1-1	Žurawski
5/12	AEL	a	0-1	
13/12	APOEL	h	1-1	Konstantinou
19/12	AEP	a	3-1	Charalambous, Žurawski, Konstantinou
2010				
4/1	Doxa	h	3-0	Efrem, Žlogar, Žurawski
9/1	Ethnikos	a	1-2	Charalambous
17/1	APEP	h	4-3	Wenzel, Konstantinou 3 (2p)
23/1	Anorthosis	a	3-1	Kaseke, Aloneftis, Efrem
30/1	Apollon	h	2-1	Konstantinou (p), Davidson
6/2	APOP	a	3-1	Makrides 2 (1p), Rengifo
14/2	Paralimni	h	0-0	
21/2	Ermis	a	2-1	Rengifo, Žurawski
28/2	Aris	h	2-1	Žurawski, Christofi
7/3	Nea Salamis	a	2-0	Efrem, Žurawski (p)
14/3	AEL	a	4-0	Efrem, Aloneftis 2, Rengifo
21/3	APOEL	a	2-1	Aloneftis, Konstantinou
28/3	APOEL	a	1-0	Aloneftis
11/4	Anorthosis	h	1-1	Konstantinou
18/4	Apollon	a	0-0	
25/4	Apollon	h	1-1	Charalambous
2/5	APOEL	h	1-0	Aloneftis
8/5	Anorthosis	a	4-2	Rengifo, Leandro, Katsis, Žurawski

No	Name	Nat	DoB	Pos	Aps	(s)	Gls
2	Rasheed ALABI	NGA	9/1/86	D	19	(2)	2
46	Efstathios ALONEFTIS		29/3/83	M	22	(4)	11
10	BRUNO João Morais AGUIAR	POR	24/2/81	M	13	(2)	1
33	Ilias CHARALAMBOUS		25/9/80	D	28		5
77	Dimitris CHRISTOFI		28/9/88	M	16	(12)	1
84	Paraskevas CHRISTOU		2/2/84	D	2	(3)	
3	DAVIDSON de Oliveira Morais	BRA	18/7/81	M	30		1
7	Giorgos EFREM		5/7/89	M	27	(1)	7
30	Antonis GEORGALLIDES		30/1/82	G	15		
14	Dimitris GRAMMOZIS	GRE	8/7/78	M	8	(7)	
28	Claudiano Bezerra da Silva "KAKÁ"	BRA	16/5/81	D	7		
5	Christos KARIPIDIS	GRE	2/12/82	D	16	(5)	
16	Noel KASEKE	ZIM	24/12/80	D	24	(2)	1
27	Antonis KATSIS		6/9/89	M		(2)	1
19	Michalis KONSTANTINOU		19/2/78	A	16	(5)	11
20	Stefanos KOTSOLIS	GRE	6/5/79	G	15		
21	Tassos KYRIAKOS	GRE	14/8/78	M		(4)	
44	LEANDRO Marcolini Pedroso de Almeida	HUN	19/3/82	D	10	(5)	1
13	Constantinos MAKRIDES		13/1/82	M	23	(4)	4
6	Giorgos PANAGI		3/11/86	M	4	(4)	
22	Christos PATSATZOGLOU	GRE	19/3/79	M	6		
23	Hernán RENGIFO Trigoso	PER	18/4/83	A	8	(5)	4
38	Mahamadou SIDIBÈ	MLI	8/10/78	G	2		
4	Timo WENZEL	GER	30/11/77	D	22	(2)	1
8	Anton ŽLOGAR	SVN	24/11/77	A	4	(13)	1
9	Maciej ŽURAWSKI	POL	12/9/76	A	15	(8)	8

 **CYPRUS**

PROMOTED CLUBS

ALKI LARNACA FC
Coach – Radmilo Ivančević (SRB); (21/3/10) Marios Konstantinou
Founded – 1948
Stadium – Ammochostos (4,000)

AEK LARNACA FC
Coach – Andreas Michaelidis
Founded – 1994
Stadium – Neo GSZ (13,032)
MAJOR HONOURS:
Cypriot Cup - (1) 2004.

OLYMPIAKOS NICOSIA FC
Coach – Andros Kouloumbris; (28/12/09) Saša Jovanović (SRB);
(14/2/10) Nicodemus Papavassiliou
Founded – 1931
Stadium – GSP (22,859)
MAJOR HONOURS:
Cypriot League – (3) 1967, 1969, 1971;
Cypriot Cup – (1) 1977.

SECOND LEVEL FINAL TABLE 2009/10

		Pld	W	D	L	F	A	Pts
1	Alki Larnaca FC	32	19	7	6	52	33	64
2	AEK Larnaca FC	32	17	6	9	49	27	57
3	Olympiakos Nicosia FC	32	14	9	9	55	43	51
4	Othellos Athienou FC	32	12	10	10	40	38	46
5	Atromitos Yeroskipou FC	26	10	7	9	35	31	37
6	Omonia Aradippou FC	26	9	9	8	26	28	36
7	PAEEK FC	26	9	9	8	24	27	36
8	Digenis Akritas Morphou FC	26	9	9	8	35	33	36
9	ASIL FC	26	8	11	7	29	29	35
10	Onisilos Sotira FC	26	9	6	11	30	31	33
11	Akritas Chloraka FC	26	7	11	8	25	26	32
12	Frenaros 2000 FC	26	7	7	12	26	32	28
13	Ayia Napa FC	26	5	5	16	19	41	20
14	MEAP Nisou FC	26	2	8	16	19	45	14

NB After 26 rounds top four clubs entered play-off round.

DOMESTIC CUP 2009/10

CYPRUS CUP

SECOND ROUND

(23/9/09 & 30/9/09)
Alki v Ethnikos 1-1; 0-0 *(1-1; Ethnikos on away goal)*
Ayia Napa v PAEEK 2-0; 0-0 *(2-0)*
Digenis v Nea Salamis 1-1; 0-1 *(1-2)*
Frenaros v AEK 2-2; 0-3 *(2-5)*
MEAP v Doxa 0-2; 1-0 *(1-2)*
Omonia Aradippou v AEP 1-0; 0-7 *(1-7)*
Othelos v Anorthosis 0-3; 1-5 *(1-8)*

(23/9/09 & 21/10/09)
Akritas v Paralimni 0-0; 0-3 (0-3)

(23/9/09 & 28/10/09)
ASIL v APEP 0-3; 2-1 *(2-4)*
Olympiakos v Omonia 1-3; 1-5 *(2-8)*

(30/9/09 & 21/10/09)
Atromitos v Ermis 2-2; 0-4 *(2-6)*
Onisilos v Aris 1-2; 0-1 *(1-3)*

THIRD ROUND

(25/11/09 & 2/12/09)
APOP v AEP 4-1; 2-4 *(6-5)*
Aris v AEK 0-0; 1-0 *(1-0)*
Ermis v Paralimni 4-0; 0-2 *(4-2)*

(25/11/09 & 9/12/09)
Anorthosis v Ayia Napa 6-0; 1-2 *(7-2)*

(2/12/09 & 16/12/09)
APEP v Doxa 1-1; 1-0 *(2-1)*

(9/12/09 & 16/12/09)
AEL v Omonia 0-1; 2-0 *(2-1)*
Nea Salamis v Apollon 1-0; 0-2 *(1-2)*

(6/1/10 & 27/1/10)
APOEL v Ethnikos 0-2; 4-0 (aet) (4-2)

QUARTER-FINALS

(27/1/10 & 18/2/10)
APEP 0, AEL 0
AEL 2 *(González 7, Kerkez 10)*, APEP 0
(AEL 2-0)

(3/2/10 & 10/2/10)
APOEL 5 *(Hélio Pinto 17, Mirosavljević 45, 75, 90, Koutsopoulos 59)*,
Ermis 0
Ermis 0, APOEL 1 *(Charalambides 76)*
(APOEL 6-0)

Aris 1 *(Mihalcea 90p)*, APOP 1 *(Semedo 73)*
APOP 0, Aris 1 *(Dugić 32)*
(Aris 2-1)

(10/2/10 & 17/2/10)
Apollon 3 *(Sangoy 6, 23, Agogo 77)*, Anorthosis 1 *(Cafú 63)*
Anorthosis 2 *(Cafú 54, Laban 64)*, Apollon 3 *(Sangoy 47, Avraam 72, Adorno 90)*
(Apollon 6-3)

SEMI-FINALS

(14/4/10 & 27/4/10)
APOEL 0, Aris 0
Aris 0, APOEL 2 *(Charalambides 41, Kosowski 76)*
(APOEL 2-0)

(14/4/10 & 28/4/10)
AEL 0, Apollon 1 *(Sangoy 82)*
Apollon 1 *(Sangoy 90)*, AEL 0
(Apollon 2-0)

FINAL

(15/5/10)
GSP stadium, Nicosia
APOLLON LIMASSOL FC 2 *(Bangura 1, Merkis 73)*
APOEL FC FC 1 *(Żewłakow 23)*
Refree – Rosetti *(ITA)*
APOLLON – Chvalovský, Toni, Segares, Merkis, Thiago Sales, Quinteros,
Oseni, Bangura (Stavrou 89), Adorno (Lai 76), Avraam (Neva 81),
Núñez.
APOEL – Chiotis, Poursaitidis, Haxhi (Alexandrou 81), Broerse
(Marcinho 88), Kontis, Michail (Jean Paulista 81), Nuno Morais, Hélio
Pinto, Kosowski, Charalambides, Żewłakow.

Unbeaten Sparta back where they belong

After a two-year hiatus, their longest wait for a national title in over a quarter of a century, AC Sparta Praha restored Czech football's natural order by recapturing the 1. Liga crown from their city rivals SK Slavia Praha. They did so by going through the entire 30-match campaign without defeat.

Coached by their former player and president, Jozef Chovanec, Sparta were always in the thick of the title race but they never commanded it. Three other clubs – FK Jablonec, FK Teplice and FC Baník Ostrava – were all heavily involved, with the outcome of a thrillingly unpredictable contest remaining uncertain right up until the final whistle of the final game.

Sparta knew that if they won their last fixture, at home to Teplice, a 35th national title – and a first in an even-numbered year for a decade - would almost certainly be theirs. Although Baník were level on points, Sparta's goal difference was superior; they also had a one-point advantage over Jablonec whereas their opponents on the day, having led at the winter break, had fallen out of contention. For the first time in the season Sparta's Letná stadium was sold out, and although the match was not one for the faint-hearted, the result was all that mattered, and, to the great delight of the vast majority present, Sparta claimed the three points they needed thanks to a headed goal just after half-time from their veteran captain, Tomáš Řepka.

Exemplary leader

It was a case of 'cometh the hour, cometh the man' as the 36-year-old defender had not scored a league goal for over two years. He fully deserved his moment of glory, though, because he had been an exemplary leader throughout the campaign, showing a greater level of discipline than usual and proving an inspiration to the many young players around him. Řepka was not the only golden oldie in the Sparta side. There were two other ex-Czech internationals of even more advanced years, and although Patrik Berger hardly played, 37-year-old goalkeeper Jaromír Blažek

was just as influential as Řepka in making Sparta's defence the tightest by far in the league, with just 14 goals conceded in their 30 games.

In a league where goals were at a premium, no Sparta player managed a personal haul in double figures. Ivory Coast striker Bony Wilfried came closest, with nine, and between them Jan Holenda (in the autumn, before he left for Russia) and Libor Sionko (in the spring, after he returned from Denmark) managed eight, while skilful Slovakian international midfielder Juraj Kucka posted five, including both goals in Sparta's crucial 2-2 draw at FC Slovan Liberec in the penultimate round. There were also half a dozen from 17-year-old boy wonder Václav Kadlec, who, despite his tender years, missed only one league game all season.

Sparta captain Tomáš Řepka led by example in the club's 1. Liga title triumph

Sparta may have avoided defeat in the league, but they were beaten home and away by Slavia in the quarter-finals of the Czech Cup – a rare ray of light in a season of gloom for the defending champions, who could finish no higher than seventh in the 1. Liga, 21 points behind Sparta, with as many defeats as victories. Title-winning boss Karel Jarolím was dismissed after a particularly bad run in March and replaced by František Cipro, who started his third spell at the club with that Cup win over Sparta but was unable to take Slavia into the final, an away-goals defeat by Jablonec in the semi-finals bringing to an end the club's long unbroken run of European qualifications.

Slavia and Sparta both began the 2009/10 European season in the UEFA Champions League, but neither made it into the group stage, Slavia exiting at the third qualifying round after a shock away-goals defeat against FC Sheriff and Sparta going out at the same stage after squandering a 3-1 first-leg lead against Panathinaikos FC. On the positive side, both teams subsequently came through the play-off round of the UEFA Europa League, against FK Crvena zvezda and NK Maribor respectively, to prolong their European involvement in the group stage. Slavia failed to win any of their six matches but Sparta fared better, doing the double over CFR 1907 Cluj yet ultimately failing to progress after conceding a last-gasp goal at PSV Eindhoven and then blowing their big night at home to FC København with a 3-0 defeat when victory would have taken them through.

Flu bug bites

The Czech Republic's three original UEFA Europa League entrants – Teplice, Liberec and SK Sigma Olomouc – all fell in the play-off round. Teplice,

Českomoravský fotbalový svaz (CMFS)

Diskarská 100
CZ-160 17 Praha 6
tel - +420 2 3302 9111
fax - +420 2 3335 3107
website - fotbal.cz
email - cmfs@fotbal.cz
Year of Formation - 1901

President – Ivan Hašek
General Secretary – Rudolf Řepka
Media Officer – Petr Svěcený

INTERNATIONAL HONOURS*
UEFA European Championship - (1) 1976.
INTERNATIONAL TOURNAMENT APPEARANCES*
FIFA World Cup - (9) 1934 (runners-up), 1938 (qtr-finals), 1954, 1958, 1962 (runners-up), 1970, 1982, 1990 (qtr-finals), 2006.
UEFA European Championship - (7) 1960 (3rd), 1976 (Winners), 1980 (3rd), 1996 (runners-up), 2000, 2004 (semi-finals), 2008.
TOP FIVE ALL-TIME CAPS (including Czechoslovakia)
Karel Poborský (118); Jan Koller & Pavel Nedvěd (91); Zdeněk Nehoda (90); Pavel Kuka (87)
TOP FIVE ALL-TIME GOALS (including Czechoslovakia)
Jan Koller (55); Milan Baroš (38); Antonín Puč (35); Zdeněk Nehoda (32); Oldřich Nejedlý & Pavel Kuka (29)

(* before 1996 as Czechoslovakia)

however, recovered well, reeling off a sequence of impressive displays in the domestic league. Unbeaten and top of the table after 14 matches, the club's bid for a first ever championship title was thrown off course by a bout of swine flu. Forced to fulfil their 15th fixture, in Olomouc, with barely half a squad, they lost their unbeaten record to a 6-2 defeat. Their next fixture, at home to FC Viktoria Plzeň, was duly postponed, and although they won it, in March, to stay top, a couple of defeats in quick succession against Baník and Liberec proved to be the beginning

NATIONAL TEAM RESULTS 2009/10

12/8/09	Belgium	H	Teplice	3-1	Hubník (28), Baroš (41p), Rozehnal (78)
5/9/09	Slovakia (WCQ)	A	Bratislava	2-2	Pudil (68), Baroš (84)
9/9/09	San Marino (WCQ)	H	Uherske Hradiste	7-0	Baroš (28, 44, 45+3p, 66), Svěrkoš (47, 90+4), Necid (86)
10/10/09	Poland (WCQ)	H	Prague	2-0	Necid (51), Plašil (72)
14/10/09	Northern Ireland (WCQ)	H	Prague	0-0	
15/11/09	United Arab Emirates	A	Al Ain	0-0	(2-3 on pens)
18/11/09	Azerbaijan	N	Al Ain (UAE)	0-2	
3/3/10	Scotland	A	Glasgow	0-1	
22/5/10	Turkey	N	Harrison (USA)	1-2	Černý M. (81)
25/5/10	United States	A	East Hartford	4-2	Sivok (44), Polák (58), Fenin (78), Necid (90+2)

NATIONAL TEAM APPEARANCES 2009/10

Coach – Ivan HAŠEK (20/10/09) Michal BÍLEK	6/9/63 13/4/65		Bel	SVK	SMR	POL	NIR	Uae	Aze	Sco	Tur	Usa	Caps	Goals
Petr ČECH	20/5/82	Chelsea (ENG)	G	G	G	G	G				G	G	74	-
Zdeněk GRYGERA	14/5/80	Juventus (ITA)	D46	D	D77								65	2
Michal KADLEC	13/12/84	Leverkusen (GER)	D	D	D46						D		15	1
Tomáš SIVOK	15/9/83	Beşiktaş (TUR)	D	D		D	D				D	D	12	1
Roman HUBNÍK	6/6/84	Sparta Praha	D46		D	D	D	D65		D			7	1
Jaroslav PLAŠIL	5/1/82	Bordeaux (FRA)	M	M	M	M	M			M79	M77	M90	55	4
Jan POLÁK	14/3/81	Anderlecht (BEL)	M								s46	M90	50	7
David JAROLÍM	17/5/79	Hamburg (GER)	M46	M65	s56	s78	M83						29	1
Jiří ŠTAJNER	27/5/76	Hannover (GER)	M88	M83	s77	s86	s72						32	4
Václav SVĚRKOŠ	1/11/83	Sochaux (FRA)	A66	s83	A					A67			11	3
Milan BAROŠ	28/10/81	Galatasaray (TUR)	A46	s55	A	A	A						78	38
David ROZEHNAL	5/7/80	Hamburg (GER)	s46	D				D	s81				60	1
Zdeněk POSPĚCH	14/12/78	København (DEN)	s46			D	D						18	1
Marek JANKULOVSKI	9/5/77	Milan (ITA)	s46	D		D	D						78	12
Daniel PUDIL	27/9/85	Genk (BEL)	s46	M	s46	M86		D	D46	s86	D	D	13	2
Tomáš NECID	13/8/89	CSKA Moskva (RUS)	s66	s65	A	s46	A59	A	s63	A67	A77	s67	15	5
Jan ŠIMŮNEK	20/2/87	Wolfsburg (GER)	s88						s65	D			4	-
Tomáš HÜBSCHMAN	4/9/81	Shakhtar (UKR)		M	M	M	M			M79	M	M	28	-
Jan KOLLER	30/3/73	Krylya Sovetov (RUS)		A55									91	55
Tomáš ROSICKÝ	4/10/80	Arsenal (ENG)			M56	M78	M72			M67			72	19
Michal PAPADOPULOS	14/4/85	Heerenveen (NED)			A46	s83		s62/83	A	s67			6	-
Adam HLOUŠEK	20/12/88	Slavia Praha				s59		A62	s46				3	-
Jaroslav DROBNÝ	18/10/79	Hertha (GER)						G	G				3	-
David LIMBERSKÝ	6/10/83	Plzeň						D	D			s90	4	-
Mario LIČKA	30/4/82	Baník						M79	M				2	-
Marek MATĚJOVSKÝ	20/12/81	Reading (ENG)						M	M75				15	1
Michal ŠVEC	19/3/87	Heerenveen (NED)						M	s75				2	-
Martin FILLO	7/2/86	Viking (NOR)						A62	s75				3	-
Jan BLAŽEK	20/3/88	Liberec /Larissa (GRE)						s62	A75	s67			3	-
Lukáš MAGERA	17/1/83	Timişoara (ROU)						s79	A63				3	-
Jan RAJNOCH	30/9/81	Mladá Boleslav /Ankaragücü (TUR)						s83	D	s79	D	D	7	-
Tomáš GRIGAR	1/2/83	Teplice							G				2	-
Mario HOLEK	28/10/86	Dnipro (UKR)							M81	M	M46	s90	4	-
Ondřej KUŠNÍR	5/4/84	Sparta Praha								D86	D	D	3	-
Rudolf SKÁCEL	17/7/79	Larissa (GRE)								s67	s77		7	1
Jan MORÁVEK	1/11/89	Schalke (GER)								s79		s85	2	-
Ondřej MAZUCH	15/3/89	Anderlecht (BEL)									D63		1	-
Jaroslav ČERNÝ	26/6/79	Slavia Praha									M46		2	-
Martin FENIN	16/4/87	Eintracht (GER)									A63	A79	12	2
Libor SIONKO	1/2/77	Sparta Praha									s46	M85	41	8
Milan ČERNÝ	16/3/88	Slavia Praha									s63	s79	2	1
David LAFATA	18/9/81	Jablonec									s63	A67	8	2
Tomáš PEKHART	26/5/89	Jablonec									s77		1	-

of the end of their title challenge. Ultimately, they would fail even to qualify for Europe.

There was end-of-season disappointment too for Jablonec, who, despite enjoying the best season in their history, finished second in both the 1. Liga and the Czech Cup. Furthermore, with the Czech Republic no longer benefiting from two UEFA Champions League places, there was no bumper consolation prize for them. Czech international striker David Lafata was on fire in the spring, scoring ten goals in the league and one each in the quarter-final and semi-final of the Cup. He was also on target in the final, against Plzeň, but the team that had taken five precious points off Jablonec in the league proved to be their bogey side again in Prague, winning an entertaining game 2-1 with goals from midfielder Milan Patržela and defender David Bystroň to claim their first major honour and book a return to European competition after an absence of 39 years.

Adventurous style

Both Pavel Vrba, the coach of Plzeň, and František Komňacký, the coach of Jablonec, had won league titles in neighbouring Slovakia – with MŠK Žilina (2007) and MFK Ružomberok (2006), respectively – and the latter had also been a Czech title-winner with Baník back in 2004. His former club came close to a repeat triumph six years on under Miroslav Koubek. Playing in an adventurous style with three forwards, including, from February onwards, dynamic 18-year-old revelation Matěj Vydra, the Ostrava club looked title-bound after a six-match winning run in March and April, but that sequence was ended by a 1-1 home draw with Sparta, and when they failed to win their next home game as well, drawing 2-2 with FK Mladá Boleslav, the initiative swung back to the serial champions from the capital.

At the bottom of the table, FC Bohemians Praha were effectively thrown out of the 1. Liga after being handed a 20-point punishment for failing to fulfil their spring fixture away to Bohemians 1905, the club with whom they had a long-running and unresolved feud over naming rights. On the way down anyway, they ended up with a minus points balance and were accompanied to the second flight by SK Kladno, enabling 14th-placed 1. FC Slovácko, who had bought their 1. Liga place the previous summer, to survive. FC Hradec Králové and FK Ústí nad Labem were promoted by a more conventional route, each winning 20 of their 30 matches to go up in both style and comfort.

The Czech national team failed to qualify for the 2010 FIFA World Cup, their hopes of a play-off place reduced by a 2-2 draw away to neighbours Slovakia then completely crushed when the Slovakians lost at home to Slovenia. Ivan Hašek, the Czech Football Association (CMFS) president who had taken it upon himself to coach the team through their last four qualifying fixtures, decided to return to his principal function after the campaign was over, handing the coaching baton over to his assistant – and former Czechoslovakia and Sparta team-mate – Michal Bílek.

Welcome win

Bílek, who led Sparta to the domestic double in 2006/07, began his reign with a couple of relatively low-key friendlies in the Gulf, neither of which went as planned. There were further defeats against Scotland – a forthcoming UEFA EURO 2012 qualifying rival – and Turkey before Bílek broke his duck with a welcome 4-2 win away to the United States. The Czech Republic have been UEFA European Championship ever-presents since they became an independent nation in 1993. It is a competition with which the country has a great affinity and a proud history, but with defending champions Spain heading the Czechs' qualifying group, it is not unreasonable to predict that the only way Petr Čech, Milan Baroš, Tomáš Necid and co will make it across the border to Poland – or Ukraine – will be via the play-offs.

Michal Bílek –
the Czech Republic's
fifth coach in
18 months

DOMESTIC LEAGUE 2009/10

1. LIGA FINAL TABLE

		Home					Away					Total					
	Pld	W	D	L	F	A	W	D	L	F	A	W	D	L	F	A	Pts
AC Sparta Praha	30	10	5	0	24	3	6	9	0	18	11	16	14	0	42	14	62
FK Jablonec	30	10	4	1	20	7	8	3	4	22	17	18	7	5	42	24	61
FC Baník Ostrava	30	10	4	1	28	13	7	5	3	19	12	17	9	4	47	25	60
FK Teplice	30	9	4	2	23	9	6	6	3	21	16	15	10	5	44	25	55
FC Viktoria Plzeň	30	7	7	1	27	17	5	5	5	15	16	12	12	6	42	33	48
SK Sigma Olomouc	30	9	3	3	30	11	5	2	8	19	25	14	5	11	49	36	47
SK Slavia Praha	30	7	4	4	23	14	4	4	7	14	21	11	8	11	37	35	41
FK Mladá Boleslav	30	6	2	7	24	17	5	4	6	23	24	11	6	13	47	41	39
FC Slovan Liberec	30	6	4	5	21	18	4	3	8	13	21	10	7	13	34	39	37
10 1. FK Příbram	30	9	4	2	26	17	1	2	12	9	24	10	6	14	35	41	36
11 1. FC Brno	30	5	4	6	19	19	4	4	7	12	21	9	8	13	31	40	35
12 Bohemians 1905	30	5	4	6	12	9	3	6	6	9	20	8	10	12	21	29	34
13 SK Dynamo České Budějovice	30	3	8	4	12	13	4	2	9	12	22	7	10	13	24	35	31
14 1. FC Slovácko	30	7	3	5	17	14	1	3	11	11	28	8	6	16	28	42	30
15 SK Kladno	30	4	0	11	14	28	3	4	8	10	22	7	4	19	24	50	25
16 FC Bohemians Praha	30	3	3	9	14	31	1	1	13	13	34	4	4	22	27	65	-4

JB FC Bohemians Praha – 20 pts deducted.

TOP GOALSCORERS

12 Michal ORDOŠ (Sigma)
11 David LAFATA (Jablonec)
Marek KULIČ (Mladá Boleslav)
9 Pavel ŠULTES (Sigma)
Bony WILFRIED (Sparta)
8 Mario LIČKA (Baník)
Daniel HUŇA (Příbram)
Aidin MAHMUTOVIĆ (Teplice)
7 Tomáš MIČOLA (Baník)
Jiří JESLÍNEK (Bohemians)
Ludovic SYLVESTRE (Mladá Boleslav)
Václav ONDŘEJKA (Slovácko)
Petr ŠVANCARA (Slovácko)
Marek BAKOŠ (Plzeň)

CLUB-BY-CLUB

FC BANÍK OSTRAVA

Coach – Miroslav Koubek
Founded – 1922
Stadium – Bazaly (17,372)
MAJOR HONOURS:
Czechoslovakian/Czech League - (4) 1976, 1980, 1981, 2004;
Czechoslovakian/Czech Cup - (4) 1973, 1978, 1991, 2005.

2009

25/7	Příbram	h	2-1	Zeher, Lukeš
2/8	Sigma	a	0-0	
8/8	Plzeň	h	1-0	Zeher
17/8	Jablonec	a	1-2	Lička
24/8	Brno	h	1-1	Lička
30/8	České Budějovice	a	2-1	Mičola, Lička
12/9	Bohemians	h	1-0	Bolf
21/9	Slavia	a	1-3	Lukeš
26/9	Teplice	h	2-2	Strnad, Lička
3/10	Slovácko	a	2-0	og (Němčický), Lička
17/10	Liberec	h	1-0	Mičola
24/10	Bohemians 1905	h	3-1	Lukeš, Strnad, Lička
31/10	Sparta	a	1-1	Tchuř
7/11	Kladno	h	2-0	Strnad, Řezník
22/11	Mladá Boleslav	a	1-3	Bolf
30/11	Sigma	h	2-0	Lička, Kraut

2010

1/3	Plzeň	a	0-0	
7/3	Jablonec	h	4-1	Vydra 2, Mičola, Varadi
15/3	Brno	a	1-1	Neuwirth
20/3	České Budějovice	h	0-1	
24/3	Bohemians	a	3-0	Varadi, Mičola, Zeher
29/3	Slavia	h	3-1	Vydra, Bolf, Mičola
5/4	Teplice	a	1-0	Vydra
10/4	Slovácko	h	3-2	Neves, Varadi, Neuwirth
19/4	Liberec	a	1-0	Neves
26/4	Bohemians 1905	a	1-0	Varadi
2/5	Sparta	h	1-1	og (Řepka)
5/5	Kladno	a	3-0	Lička, Mičola, Zeher
8/5	Mladá Boleslav	h	2-2	Mičola, Neves (p)
15/5	Příbram	a	1-1	Varadi

No	Name	Nat	DoB	Pos	Aps	(s)	Gls
16	Vít BARÁNEK		27/9/74	G	22	(1)	
5	René BOLF		25/2/74	D	20		3
1	Antonín BUČEK		24/2/84	G	8		
26	Michal FRYDRYCH		27/2/90	M	1		
11	Ján GREGUŠ	SVK	29/1/91	M	2	(10)	
7	Jan HABLE		4/1/89	M		(2)	
13	Dominik KRAUT		15/1/90	A	(13)		1
21	LEE Hyung-sang	KOR	6/5/85	M		(1)	
27	Mario LIČKA		30/4/82	M	29		8
4	Martin LUKEŠ		17/11/78	M	29		3
18	Tomáš MAREK		20/4/81	M	24	(1)	
24	František METELKA		8/4/80	M		(1)	
25	Tomáš MIČOLA		26/9/88	M	27		7
23	Aleš NEUWIRTH		4/1/85	D	25	(1)	2
2	Fernando Maria NEVES	CPV	9/6/78	D	25	(1)	3
9	Vít PŘECECHTĚL		29/9/88	A	1		
3	Radim ŘEZNÍK		20/1/89	D	24	(1)	1
28	Miloslav STRNAD		3/12/81	A	8	(12)	3
22	Daniel TCHUŘ		8/8/76	D	14	(1)	1
20	Petr TOMAŠÁK		20/2/86	D	8	(1)	
14	Adam VARADI		30/4/85	A	24	(5)	5
9	Matěj VYDRA		1/5/92	A	11	(3)	4
29	Petr WOJNAR		12/1/89	M	1	(13)	
12	Jan ZAWADA		6/6/88	D	8	(1)	
10	Róbert ZEHER	SVK	12/2/85	A	19	(9)	4

CZECH REPUBLIC

BOHEMIANS 1905
Coach – Pavel Hoftych
Founded – 1905
Stadium – Stadion Bohemians 1905 "Ďolíček" (7,500)
MAJOR HONOURS:
Czechoslovakian League - (1) 1983.

2009

Date	Opponent		Result	Scorers
27/7	Brno	h	0-0	
31/7	Sparta	a	0-0	
9/8	Jablonec	h	0-1	
16/8	Sigma	a	1-1	Štohanzl
23/8	Plzeň	h	0-1	
29/8	Mladá Boleslav	a	1-0	Štohanzl
13/9	České Budějovice	h	2-0	Škoda, Kaufman
20/9	Teplice	a	0-1	
26/9	Slavia	h	1-1	Štohanzl
4/10	Bohemians	a	0-0	
18/10	Slovácko	h	0-1	
24/10	Baník	a	1-3	Škoda
1/11	Liberec	h	0-1	
8/11	Příbram	h	1-0	Kaufman
21/11	Kladno	a	2-1	Cseh, Slezák
28/11	Sparta	h	0-2	

2010

Date	Opponent		Result	Scorers
28/2	Jablonec	a	0-3	
6/3	Sigma	h	2-0	Kaufman, Štohanzl
14/3	Plzeň	a	0-3	
21/3	Mladá Boleslav	h	2-0	Kaufman (p), Štohanzl
24/3	České Budějovice	a	0-0	
28/3	Teplice	h	1-1	og (Rosa)
5/4	Slavia	a	0-3	
10/4	Bohemians	h	3-0	(w/o)
17/4	Slovácko	a	1-1	Škoda
26/4	Baník	h	0-1	
1/5	Liberec	a	1-1	Bálek
5/5	Příbram	a	0-2	
8/5	Kladno	h	0-0	
15/5	Brno	a	2-1	Hartig, Bálek

No	Name	Nat	DoB	Pos	Aps	(s)	Gls
32	Lukáš ADAM		5/9/80	M	3		
31	Vladimír BÁLEK		8/3/81	A	7	(5)	2
5	David BARTEK		13/2/88	M	9	(4)	
20	Amadou CISSÉ	GUI	23/10/85	M	4	(5)	
27	Martin CSEH	SVK	22/8/88	D	21		1
33	Michal DIAN	SVK	13/11/81	M	6	(3)	
12	Lukáš HARTIG		28/10/76	A	15	(3)	1
8	Ivan HAŠEK		30/8/87	M	2	(3)	
30	Tomáš HRDLIČKA		17/2/82	M	8		
22	Aziz IBRAGIMOV	UZB	21/7/86	A	12	(11)	
17	Ivan JANEK	SVK	1/7/86	D	5	(4)	
4	Josef JINDŘÍŠEK		14/2/81	D	27		
15	Jiří KAUFMAN		28/11/79	A	18	(6)	4
25	Martin KOTYZA		1/10/84	M	2	(2)	
3	Pavel LUKÁŠ		20/11/75	D	17	(3)	
28	Václav MAREK		16/3/81	G	1		
16	Jan MORAVEC		13/7/87	M	4	(1)	
14	Martin NEŠPOR		5/6/90	A		(4)	
7	Marek NIKL		20/2/76	D	27		
24	Michal PÁVEK		13/2/85	D	14	(3)	
11	Ferenc RÓTH	HUN	24/12/78	M	14	(5)	
13	Jan RŮŽIČKA		26/8/84	D	1	(1)	
9	Jiří RYCHLÍK		24/11/77	D	28		
18	Jiří ŠISLER		24/11/84	M	1	(2)	
21	Milan ŠKODA		16/1/86	A	18	(4)	3
10	Dalibor SLEZÁK		28/1/70	A		(8)	1
1	Radek SŇOZÍK		17/10/75	G	28		
6	Jan ŠTOHANZL		20/3/85	M	24	(1)	5
23	Luděk ZELENKA		11/9/73	A	3	(5)	

FC BOHEMIANS PRAHA
Coach – Robert Žák; (18/8/09) Jaromír Jindráček
Founded – 1905
Stadium – Stadion Evžena Rošického (18,875)

2009

Date	Opponent		Result	Scorers
26/7	Sigma	h	0-2	
2/8	České Budějovice	h	0-2	
9/8	Slavia	a	1-3	Očovan
16/8	Teplice	h	1-3	Kincl
22/8	Slovácko	a	0-2	
30/8	Liberec	h	2-1	Kincl, Zoubek
12/9	Baník	a	0-1	
20/9	Příbram	h	1-0	Macháček
27/9	Kladno	a	2-3	Kincl, Ibe
4/10	Bohemians 1905	h	0-0	
18/10	Mladá Boleslav	a	2-4	Jeslínek, Andronic
25/10	Sparta	h	2-3	Ibe, Dobeš
1/11	Jablonec	a	0-1	
8/11	Brno	h	2-1	Jeslínek, Dobeš
21/11	Plzeň	a	2-3	Jeslínek 2
29/11	České Budějovice	a	0-3	

2010

Date	Opponent		Result	Scorers
27/2	Slavia	h	0-1	
6/3	Teplice	a	1-2	Ibe
14/3	Slovácko	h	1-1	Ibe
20/3	Liberec	a	3-2	Fenyk, Dobeš, Jeslínek
24/3	Baník	h	0-3	
28/3	Příbram	a	2-3	Jeslínek, Ibe
4/4	Kladno	h	1-4	Horáček
10/4	Bohemians 1905	a	0-3	(w/o)
18/4	Mladá Boleslav	h	2-4	Kincl (p), Ibe
24/4	Sparta	a	0-1	
2/5	Jablonec	h	0-4	
5/5	Brno	a	0-0	
8/5	Plzeň	h	2-2	Jeslínek, Flachbart
15/5	Sigma	a	0-3	

No	Name	Nat	DoB	Pos	Aps	(s)	Gls
24	Eric Kwame ADJEI	GHA	12/9/84	M	2	(1)	
26	Valeriu ANDRONIC	MDA	21/12/82	M	2	(8)	1
22	Jaroslav BELAŇ	SVK	21/5/81	G	25	(1)	
18	Michal DEMETER	SVK	15/5/82	M	14	(2)	
24	Jan DEVÁTÝ		17/6/78	M	1	(3)	
13	Jaroslav DITTRICH		8/3/82	M	20	(1)	
8	Roman DOBEŠ		29/7/78	M	19	(5)	3
3	Václav DROBNÝ		9/9/80	D	8		
7	Tomáš FENYK		30/1/79	M	15	(6)	1
5	Jan FLACHBART		3/1/75	D	13		1
15	Vladimir GERASIMOV	RUS	12/4/89	M		(1)	
19	Pavel GRZNÁR		16/3/79	D	9	(3)	
28	Jan HALAMA		14/7/88	D	6	(2)	
5	Jakub HEIDENREICH		27/2/85	D	5	(1)	
27	Martin HORÁČEK		21/6/80	D	17	(4)	1
16	Stanley IBE	NGA	19/7/84	A	10	(8)	6
9	Jiří JESLÍNEK		30/9/87	A	15	(2)	7
28	Václav JEŽDÍK		3/7/87	M	6	(2)	
10	Marek KINCL		3/4/73	A	13	(7)	4
17	Dmitriy LENTSEVICH	BLR	20/6/83	D	24	(2)	
6	Petr MACH		22/3/85	D	13	(2)	
2	Pavel MACHÁČEK		18/12/77	D	24	(1)	1
29	Jimmy MODESTE	CPV	8/7/81	A	10		
4	Miroslav OBERMAJER		5/10/73	D	5	(1)	
12	Peter OČOVAN	SVK	20/2/84	A	2	(8)	1
1	Peter PIŽANOWSKI		13/4/74	G	3	(1)	
14	Jakub PODANÝ		15/6/87	M	3	(2)	
11	Michal POSPÍŠIL		3/5/79	A	6	(2)	
30	Dominik RODINGER		17/8/87	G	1		
21	Marek SMOLA		7/4/75	D	1		
3	Vít TURTENWALD		5/3/80	D	10	(3)	
25	Hidetoshi WAKUI	JPN	12/2/83	A	3	(8)	
11	David ZOUBEK		3/2/74	M	14		1

1. FC BRNO

Coach – Miroslav Beránek
Founded – 1913
Stadium – Městský stadion Srbská (8,065)
MAJOR HONOURS:
Czechoslovakian League - (1) 1978.

2009

27/7	Bohemians 1905	a	0-0	
2/8	Slavia	h	2-0	*Rabušic, Došek*
9/8	Liberec	a	1-0	*Rabušic*
14/8	Slovácko	h	1-0	*Došek*
24/8	Baník	a	1-1	*Dalmo*
31/8	Teplice	h	2-3	*Došek, Rabušic*
13/9	Kladno	a	0-1	
21/9	Sparta	h	1-1	*Došek*
28/9	Mladá Boleslav	a	0-0	
2/10	Příbram	h	2-1	*Došek, Križko (p)*
18/10	Sigma	a	0-5	
24/10	Jablonec	h	0-1	
2/11	Plzeň	a	1-1	*Sus*
8/11	Bohemians	a	1-2	*Dalmo*
21/11	České Budějovice	h	0-3	
29/11	Slavia	a	1-3	*Polách*

2010

27/2	Liberec	h	1-0	*Polách*
6/3	Slovácko	a	2-0	*Hodek, Došek*
15/3	Baník	h	1-1	*Dostálek*
20/3	Teplice	a	1-0	*Jílek*
24/3	Kladno	h	3-0	*Dostálek 2, Rabušic*
28/3	Sparta	a	0-3	
3/4	Mladá Boleslav	h	2-3	*Kalabiška, Rabušic*
10/4	Příbram	a	1-3	*Kalabiška*
17/4	Sigma	h	1-2	*Dostálek (p)*
24/4	Jablonec	a	0-1	
1/5	Plzeň	h	2-2	*Rabušic, Dostálek*
5/5	Bohemians	h	0-0	
8/5	České Budějovice	a	3-1	*Pernica 2, Oklešťek*
15/5	Bohemians 1905	h	1-2	*Dostálek*

No	Name	Nat	DoB	Pos	Aps	(s)	Gls
27	Jaroslav BORÁK		9/11/89	A	3	(5)	
20	Tomáš BUREŠ		27/9/78	G	24		
18	Jakub ČERVÍNEK		4/6/87	D	1	(4)	
10	Filip CHLUP		10/6/85	M		(3)	
3	Petr ČOUPEK		10/5/82	D	4		
8	David CUPÁK		27/5/89	M	2	(3)	
19	DALMO Inácio da Silva	BRA	18/2/84	A	1	(11)	2
1	Martin DOLEŽAL		18/12/80	G	6		
26	Tomáš DOŠEK		12/9/78	A	25		6
7	Richard DOSTÁLEK		26/4/74	M	21	(6)	6
12	František DŘÍŽĎAL		8/8/78	D	13		
29	Josef DVORNÍK		24/3/78	D	25	(1)	
8	Andrej HODEK	SVK	24/5/81	A	2		1
30	Martin HUSÁR	SVK	1/2/85	D	12		
18	Jiří HUŠKA		27/1/88	D	8	(3)	
2	Martin JÍLEK		7/7/86	D	19	(2)	1
11	Jan KALABIŠKA		22/12/86	A	14		2
25	David KALIVODA		25/8/82	M		(1)	
19	Lukáš KŘEČEK		18/9/86	M	9		
13	Juraj KRIŽKO	SVK	20/9/85	D	18	(2)	1
10	LÉOnardo Fabrício Soares da Costa	BRA	3/3/86	M	4	(5)	
4	Elton Santiago dos Santos LIRA	BRA	21/9/86	M	10	(3)	
5	Lukáš MAREČEK		17/4/90	M	14		
15	Lukáš MICHNA		28/4/90	M	9		
9	Tomáš OKLEŠŤEK		21/2/87	D	2	(10)	1
3	Luděk PERNICA		16/6/90	D	5	(1)	2
21	Tomáš POLÁCH		16/1/77	M	23	(3)	2
14	Michael RABUŠIC		17/9/89	A	27	(1)	6
28	Rostislav ŠAMÁNEK		9/8/89	A		(3)	
24	Roman SMUTNÝ		22/4/85	M	1	(5)	
23	Josef ŠURAL		30/5/90	A	10	(9)	
27	Martin SUS		8/5/89	M	5		1
28	Róbert SZEGEDI	SVK	26/5/85	M		(1)	
22	Jan TROUSIL		9/4/76	D	13		

SK DYNAMO ČESKÉ BUDĚJOVICE

Coach – Pavel Tobiáš; (15/10/09) Jaroslav Šilhavý
Founded – 1905
Stadium – E.ON (6,746)

2009

26/7	Jablonec	h	1-1	*Meszáros*
2/8	Bohemians	a	2-0	*Meszáros, Ondrášek*
9/8	Teplice	a	0-3	
15/8	Slavia	h	0-1	
23/8	Liberec	a	0-3	
30/8	Baník	h	1-2	*Stráský*
13/9	Bohemians 1905	a	0-2	
20/9	Slovácko	h	0-0	
27/9	Příbram	a	1-3	*Ondrášek*
4/10	Kladno	h	0-0	
17/10	Sparta	a	1-1	*Hudson*
25/10	Plzeň	a	0-0	
1/11	Sigma	a	0-2	
8/11	Mladá Boleslav	h	1-3	*Ondrášek*
21/11	Brno	a	3-0	*Doležal 2 (1p), Mezlík*
29/11	Bohemians	h	3-0	*Leština, Stráský, Meszáros*

2010

28/2	Teplice	h	0-0	
8/3	Slavia	a	2-3	*Černák, Ondrášek*
14/3	Liberec	h	1-1	*Otepka*
20/3	Baník	a	1-0	*Hořejš*
24/3	Bohemians 1905	h	0-0	
28/3	Slovácko	a	0-1	
4/4	Příbram	h	2-1	*Hořejš 2*
11/4	Kladno	a	1-2	*Otepka*
18/4	Sparta	h	0-0	
24/4	Plzeň	a	0-0	
2/5	Sigma	h	2-1	*Otepka, Volešák*
5/5	Mladá Boleslav	a	1-0	*Volešák*
8/5	Brno	h	1-3	*Sedláček*
15/5	Jablonec	a	0-2	

No	Name	Nat	DoB	Pos	Aps	(s)	Gls
7	Petr BENÁT		20/5/80	M	14		
21	Peter ČERNÁK	SVK	21/1/76	M	23		1
9	Petr DOLEJŠ		1/4/86	M	3	(7)	
11	Michal DOLEŽAL		19/8/77	M	9		2
22	ÉVERSON Alan da Lima	BRA	1/7/86	D	1	(2)	
4	David HOMOLÁČ		12/10/73	D	6		
3	David HOŘEJŠ		19/5/77	D	14		3
18	Fernando Tobias de Carvalho "HUDSON"	BRA	18/7/86	M	17	(11)	1
2	Tomáš HUNAL		1/6/73	D	18	(1)	
16	Marián JARABICA	SVK	27/4/89	D	13	(1)	
6	Martin JASANSKÝ		4/8/89	M	1	(2)	
20	Michal KAŇÁK		16/7/88	A		(1)	
4	Jan KROB		27/4/87	M	19	(2)	
1	Pavel KUČERA		2/7/76	G	30		
20	Josef LAŠTOVKA		20/2/82	D	8		
19	Martin LEŠTINA		25/4/81	D	16	(2)	1
17	Ľubomír MESZÁROŠ	SVK	23/3/79	A	16	(11)	3
10	Pavel MEZLÍK		25/6/83	M	10	(7)	1
5	Pavel NOVÁK		30/11/89	D	2		
13	Zdeněk ONDRÁŠEK		22/12/88	A	12	(11)	4
9	Rudolf OTEPKA		13/11/73	M	13		3
13	Michal RAKOVAN		15/4/89	M		(1)	
15	Jan RIEGEL		3/8/80	M	23	(1)	
28	Tomáš SEDLÁČEK		29/8/80	A	14	(8)	2

CZECH REPUBLIC

20	Ronald ŠIKLIĆ	CRO	24/11/80	D		(1)	
25	Petr ŠÍMA		25/2/83	M	10	(3)	
14	Tomáš STRÁSKÝ		15/4/87	A	9	(3)	2
23	Jan SVÁTEK		24/5/83	A		(1)	
11	Marián TIMM	SVK	7/1/90	A		(2)	
23	Ladislav VOLEŠÁK		7/4/84	M	7	(4)	2
12	Michael ŽIŽKA		23/5/81	D	22	(3)	

FK JABLONEC
Coach – František Komňacký
Founded –1945
Stadium – Chance Arena (6,280)
MAJOR HONOURS: Czech Cup - (1) 1998.

2009

26/7	České Budějovice	a	1-1	Huber
3/8	Slovácko	h	3-2	Pavlík (p), Vošahlík, Drsek
9/8	Bohemians 1905	a	1-0	Vošahlík
17/8	Baník	h	2-1	Pavlík, Drsek
23/8	Kladno	a	2-1	og (Šilhan), Drsek
30/8	Příbram	h	0-0	
12/9	Sparta	a	0-2	
19/9	Liberec	h	2-1	Zábojník, Lafata
27/9	Sigma	a	1-0	Jarolím
4/10	Mladá Boleslav	h	1-0	Haurdić
19/10	Plzeň	h	0-1	
24/10	Brno	a	1-0	Vošahlík
1/11	Bohemians	h	1-0	Huber
7/11	Teplice	a	0-1	
21/11	Slavia	h	1-1	Čížek
28/11	Slovácko	a	1-1	Pavlík

2010

28/2	Bohemians 1905	h	3-0	Pavlík (p), Lafata, Kovařík
7/3	Baník	a	1-4	Lafata
14/3	Kladno	h	1-0	Jarolím
20/3	Příbram	a	2-1	Pavlík, Pekhart
24/3	Sparta	h	0-0	
28/3	Liberec	a	2-4	Lafata 2
3/4	Sigma	h	3-1	Jarolím, Eliáš, Haurdić
11/4	Mladá Boleslav	a	2-1	Kovařík, Lafata
17/4	Plzeň	h	1-1	Lafata
24/4	Brno	h	1-0	Lafata
2/5	Bohemians	a	4-0	Pekhart 2, Krejčí, Lafata
5/5	Teplice	h	0-0	
8/5	Slavia	a	3-0	Pekhart, Jarolím, Lafata
15/5	České Budějovice	h	2-0	Drsek, Lafata

No	Name	Nat	DoB	Pos	Aps	(s)	Gls
11	Tomáš ČÍŽEK		27/11/87	M	7		1
25	Pavel DRSEK		22/9/76	D	29		4
13	Pavel ELIÁŠ		24/11/86	M	12	(7)	1
26	Michal FARKAŠ	SVK	10/3/85	D	1		
20	Luděk FRYDRYCH		3/1/87	G	2		
3	Anes HAURDIĆ	BIH	1/3/90	M	21	(4)	2
27	Tomáš HUBER		29/8/85	D	19	(1)	2
10	Tomáš JABLONSKÝ		21/6/87	D	23	(1)	
22	Marek JAROLÍM		21/5/85	M	20	(9)	4
12	Filip KLAPKA		20/6/81	M		(1)	
9	Daniel KOCOUREK		12/12/86	A		(2)	
16	Jan KOVAŘÍK		19/6/88	M	23	(5)	2
18	Jiří KREJČÍ		22/3/86	D	18	(6)	1
21	David LAFATA		18/9/81	A	27		11
15	Luboš LOUČKA		25/8/82	M	24		
23	Tomáš MICHÁLEK		27/11/77	M	1	(18)	
24	Petr PAVLÍK		17/7/78	M	29		5
11	Tomáš PEKHART		26/5/89	A	7	(7)	4
1	Michal ŠPIT		9/4/75	G	28		
7	Jiří VALENTA		14/2/88	M		(5)	
17	Jan VOŠAHLÍK		8/3/89	A	16	(6)	3
19	Milan VUKOVIĆ	CRO	28/4/88	A	1	(13)	
5	Petr ZÁBOJNÍK		3/10/80	D	22		1

SK KLADNO
Coach – Martin Hřídel; (1/4/10) (Stanislav Procházka);
(26/4/10) Stanislav Hejkal
Founded – 1903
Stadium – Františka Kloze (4,000)

2009

25/7	Liberec	a	1-1	Szabo
2/8	Příbram	h	0-2	
10/8	Mladá Boleslav	h	1-3	Bartoš
15/8	Sparta	a	0-2	
23/8	Jablonec	h	1-2	Bartoš
29/8	Plzeň	a	0-1	
13/9	Brno	h	1-0	Tatanashvili
20/9	Sigma	a	2-1	Procházka, Holub
27/9	Bohemians	h	3-2	Tatanashvili, Zoubele, Szabo (p)
4/10	České Budějovice	a	0-0	
18/10	Slavia	h	0-2	
24/10	Slovácko	a	0-2	
1/11	Teplice	h	0-2	
7/11	Baník	a	0-2	
21/11	Bohemians 1905	h	1-2	Zachariáš
28/11	Příbram	a	2-3	Strnad, Zoubele

2010

28/2	Mladá Boleslav	a	1-0	Strnad
7/3	Sparta	h	0-1	
14/3	Jablonec	a	0-1	
20/3	Plzeň	h	1-3	Lička
24/3	Brno	a	0-3	
28/3	Sigma	h	2-3	Procházka, Holub
4/4	Bohemians	a	4-1	Zoubek 2, Beneš, Novotný
11/4	České Budějovice	h	2-1	Holub, Tatanashvili
18/4	Slavia	a	0-0	
25/4	Slovácko	h	1-0	Tatanashvili
1/5	Teplice	a	0-5	
5/5	Baník	h	0-3	
8/5	Bohemians 1905	a	0-0	
15/5	Liberec	h	1-2	Gross

No	Name	Nat	DoB	Pos	Aps	(s)	Gls
3	Pavel BARTOŠ		17/8/79	D	26		2
23	Vít BENEŠ		12/8/88	D	23		1
13	Jan BROSCHINSKÝ		1/9/85	D	1		
10	Tomáš CIGÁNEK		30/11/78	M	10	(8)	
16	Patrik GROSS		6/5/78	D	24	(1)	1
4	Lukáš HAJNÍK		24/9/85	D	10	(3)	
18	David HLAVA		28/6/80	M	2	(2)	
8	Antonín HOLUB		8/3/86	M	23	(1)	3
7	Tomáš KLINKA		24/4/77	A	13	(3)	
1	Peter KOSTOLANSKÝ	SVK	8/9/85	G	5		
17	Marcel LIČKA		17/7/77	M	2	(10)	1
32	Tomáš MAŠANSKÝ		11/7/85	A	1	(2)	
17	Jan MORAVEC		13/7/87	M	1	(5)	
24	Peter MRÁZ	SVK	4/5/85	D	30		
18	Jan NOVOTNÝ		15/4/82	M	10		1
30	Roman PAVLÍK		17/1/76	G	19		
14	Jan PROCHÁZKA		2/12/78	D	28		2
15	Zdeněk RADA		1/1/90	D		(2)	
11	Jaromír ŠILHAN		10/4/83	A	7	(11)	
2	Tomáš STRNAD		8/12/80	M	26		2
9	Patrik SVOBODA		13/4/94	A	1	(4)	
6	Ondřej SZABO		23/2/79	M	17	(5)	2
21	Dimitri TATANASHVILI	GEO	19/10/83	A	19	(3)	4
22	Jaroslav TESAŘ		25/5/86	G	6		
12	Michal ZACHARIÁŠ		25/5/84	A	4	(13)	1
20	David ZOUBEK		3/2/74	M	12		2
19	Lukáš ZOUBELE		20/12/85	M	10	(3)	2

FK MLADÁ BOLESLAV

Coach – Dušan Uhrin jr.; (1/1/10) Karel Stanner
Founded – 1902
Stadium – Městský (5,000)

2009

26/7	Slavia	a	1-1	*Mendy*
2/8	Liberec	h	4-1	*Pecka 2, Kulič, Procházka*
10/8	Kladno	a	3-1	*Táborský, Sylvestre, Kulič*
16/8	Příbram	h	2-0	*Kulič, Rajnoch*
23/8	Sparta	a	0-1	
29/8	Bohemians 1905	h	0-1	
14/9	Sigma	h	2-2	*Kulič, Táborský (p)*
19/9	Plzeň	a	1-2	*Kulič*
28/9	Brno	h	0-0	
4/10	Jablonec	a	0-1	
18/10	Bohemians	h	4-2	*Chramosta, Sylvestre (p), Rajnoch, Poláček*
24/10	Teplice	a	2-2	*Sylvestre, Chramosta*
1/11	Slovácko	h	3-2	*Rolko, Mendy, Kulič*
8/11	České Budějovice	a	3-1	*Kulič 2, Fabián*
22/11	Baník	h	3-1	*Sylvestre (p), Kulič, Rajnoch*
28/11	Liberec	a	0-3	

2010

28/2	Kladno	h	0-1	
14/3	Sparta	h	1-2	*Kulič*
21/3	Bohemians 1905	a	0-2	
24/3	Sigma	a	2-1	*Chramosta, Kalina*
27/3	Plzeň	h	4-0	*Táborský, Sylvestre (p), Sedláček, Poláček*
3/4	Brno	a	3-2	*Sedláček 2, Kalina*
11/4	Jablonec	h	1-2	*Chramosta*
14/4	Příbram	a	2-2	*Kúdela, Hrdlička*
18/4	Bohemians	a	4-2	*Sylvestre 2 (1p), Kulič, Chramosta*
25/4	Teplice	h	0-1	
30/4	Slovácko	a	0-1	
5/5	České Budějovice	h	0-1	
8/5	Baník	a	2-2	*Chramosta, Táborský*
15/5	Slavia	h	0-1	

No	Name	Nat	DoB	Pos	Aps	(s)	Gls
22	Jan BOŘIL		11/1/91	A	2	(8)	
17	David BRUNCLÍK		17/4/85	M	4	(1)	
19	Jan CHRAMOSTA		12/10/90	A	16	(8)	6
2	Marko ĐALOVIĆ	SRB	19/5/86	D	12	(1)	
3	Tomáš FABIÁN		10/9/89	M	7	(3)	1
23	Tomáš HRDLIČKA		17/2/82	D	12	(1)	1
5	Tomáš JANÍČEK		7/9/82	D	10	(4)	
6	Václav KALINA		15/7/79	D	18	(1)	2
11	Ondřej KÚDELA		26/3/87	M	22	(3)	1
10	Marek KULIČ		11/10/75	A	22	(1)	11
20	Jan KYSELA		17/12/85	M	3	(4)	
21	Fikru-Teferra LEMESSA	ETH	24/1/86	A	3	(6)	
18	Alexandre Noël MENDY	FRA	14/12/83	M	27	(2)	2
27	Miroslav MILLER		19/8/80	G	9		
30	Radim NEČAS		12/1/88	M		(1)	
33	Lukáš OPIELA	SVK	13/1/86	M	5	(10)	
16	Luboš PECKA		19/2/78	A	6	(2)	2
13	Tomáš POLÁČEK		29/8/80	M	8	(7)	2
26	Václav PROCHÁZKA		8/5/84	D	26		1
17	Jan RAJNOCH		30/9/81	D	16		3
7	Jakub ŘEZNÍČEK		26/5/88	A		(1)	
4	Adrian ROLKO		14/9/78	D	23		1
12	Jan ŠEDA		17/12/85	G	14		
28	Michal SEDLÁČEK		27/10/88	M	11		3
14	Ludovic SYLVESTRE	FRA	5/2/84	M	24	(3)	7
8	Ivo TÁBORSKÝ		10/5/85	A	17	(10)	4
15	Libor TAFAT		12/12/86	A		(4)	
1	Michal VOREL		27/6/75	G	7		
21	Ondřej ZAHUSTĚL		18/6/91	M	6		

1. FK PŘÍBRAM

Coach – Karol Marko
Founded – 1948
Stadium – Na Litavce (9,100)

2009

26/7	Baník	a	1-2	*Cafú*
2/8	Kladno	a	2-0	*Huňa, Cafú*
8/8	Sparta	h	1-1	*Cafú*
16/8	Mladá Boleslav	a	0-2	
23/8	Sigma	h	2-1	*Pleško, Šmejkal*
30/8	Jablonec	a	0-0	
12/9	Plzeň	h	1-0	*Huňa*
20/9	Bohemians	a	0-1	
27/9	České Budějovice	h	3-1	*Štochl J., Dort, Paulo*
2/10	Brno	a	1-2	*Paulo*
17/10	Teplice	h	0-3	
25/10	Liberec	a	0-1	
31/10	Slavia	h	1-0	*Plašil*
8/11	Bohemians 1905	a	0-1	
21/11	Slovácko	h	2-0	*Huňa, Hušbauer*
28/11	Kladno	h	3-2	*Hušbauer 2, Wágner*

2010

27/2	Sparta	a	1-1	*Wágner*
14/3	Sigma	a	1-3	*Hušbauer*
20/3	Jablonec	h	1-2	*Pilík*
24/3	Plzeň	a	1-3	*Wágner*
28/3	Bohemians	h	3-2	*Huňa, Pleško, Šmejkal*
4/4	České Budějovice	a	1-2	*Huňa*
11/4	Brno	h	3-1	*Klesa, Šmejkal, Huňa*
14/4	Mladá Boleslav	h	2-2	*Klesa, Huňa*
18/4	Teplice	a	0-1	
24/4	Liberec	h	1-1	*Huňa*
2/5	Slavia	a	0-3	
5/5	Bohemians 1905	h	2-0	*Šmejkal, Fantiš*
8/5	Slovácko	a	1-2	*Paulo*
15/5	Baník	h	1-1	*Pilík*

No	Name	Nat	DoB	Pos	Aps	(s)	Gls
23	Tomáš BOREK		4/4/86	M	8	(4)	
19	Filipe dos Santos "CAFÚ"	BRA	24/7/87	A	3	(4)	3
24	Filip DORT		27/7/80	M	6	(3)	1
10	Antonín FANTIŠ		15/4/92	A	14	(5)	1
11	Daniel HUŇA		25/6/79	A	23	(1)	8
5	Josef HUŠBAUER		16/3/90	M	20	(2)	4
18	Martin JIROUŠ		27/11/86	A	3	(2)	
27	Michal KLESA		13/5/83	M	26		2
22	Lukáš KRBEČEK		27/10/85	G	30		
15	Martin MÜLLER		6/11/70	D	12		
17	Stanislav NOHÝNEK		2/8/83	D	24	(2)	
9	PAULO Rodrigues da Silva	BRA	10/11/86	A	18	(8)	3
25	Tomáš PILÍK		20/12/88	M	12	(14)	2
20	Marek PLAŠIL		19/12/85	D	24		1
7	Lukáš PLEŠKO		21/5/77	D	22	(3)	2
13	František SCHNEIDER		21/4/87	M	3	(1)	
13	Martin ŠLAPÁK		25/3/87	A		(2)	
8	Zdeněk ŠMEJKAL		29/6/88	D	21	(4)	4
4	Jakub ŠTOCHL		2/2/87	D	28		1
18	Matěj ŠTOCHL		4/5/89	A		(2)	
6	Daniel TARCZAL		22/3/85	M	26	(2)	
12	Claude Roland VIDEGLA	TOG	14/5/90	M	2	(3)	
16	Tomáš WÁGNER		6/3/90	A	5	(12)	3

CZECH REPUBLIC

SK SIGMA OLOMOUC
Coach – Zdeněk Psotka
Founded – 1919
Stadium – Andrův (12,072)

2009

Date	Opponent	H/A	Score	Scorers
26/7	Bohemians	a	2-0	Daniel Rossi, Janotka
2/8	Baník	h	0-0	
9/8	Slovácko	a	0-2	
16/8	Bohemians 1905	h	1-1	Ordoš
23/8	Příbram	a	1-2	Dreksa
31/8	Sparta	h	1-1	Ordoš
14/9	Mladá Boleslav	a	2-2	Petr, Janotka
20/9	Kladno	h	1-2	Bajer (p)
27/9	Jablonec	h	0-1	
3/10	Plzeň	a	0-1	
18/10	Brno	h	5-0	Ordoš 2, Šultes, Petr, Hořava
26/10	Slavia	a	2-1	Hořava, Šultes
1/11	České Budějovice	h	2-0	Ordoš, Hubník
7/11	Liberec	a	4-0	Šultes 2, Ordoš, Daniel Rossi
23/11	Teplice	h	6-2	Ordoš 2, Dreksa 2, Šultes, Janotka (p)
30/11	Baník	a	0-2	

2010

Date	Opponent	H/A	Score	Scorers
28/2	Slovácko	h	1-0	Ordoš
6/3	Bohemians 1905	a	0-2	
14/3	Příbram	h	3-1	Šultes 2, og (Nohýnek)
20/3	Sparta	a	0-4	
24/3	Mladá Boleslav	h	1-2	og (Rolko)
28/3	Kladno	a	3-2	Šultes, Schulmeister, Daniel Rossi
3/4	Jablonec	a	1-3	Petr
11/4	Plzeň	h	1-0	Hubník
17/4	Brno	a	2-1	Navrátil 2
25/4	Slavia	h	3-1	Hubník 2, Šultes
2/5	České Budějovice	a	1-2	Petr
5/5	Liberec	h	2-0	Hubník, Ordoš (p)
8/5	Teplice	a	1-1	Navrátil
15/5	Bohemians	h	3-0	Ordoš 2, Navrátil

No	Name	Nat	DoB	Pos	Aps	(s)	Gls
16	Lukáš BAJER		15/12/84	M	17	(10)	1
1	Martin BLAHA		8/8/85	G	4		
11	Esis Steines CAIHAME	BRA	11/2/87	A	1	(4)	
8	DANIEL ROSSI da Silva	BRA	4/1/81	D	25	(1)	3
3	Pavel DREKSA		17/9/89	D	22	(1)	3
18	Petr DROBISZ		14/7/76	G	10		
15	Jakub HEIDENREICH		27/4/89	D	6	(1)	
17	Tomáš HOŘAVA		29/5/88	M	20	(2)	2
10	Michal HUBNÍK		1/6/83	A	18	(1)	5
23	Tomáš JANOTKA		4/3/82	M	26	(3)	3
28	Tomáš KALAS		15/5/93	D	1		
5	Marek KAŠČÁK	SVK	22/5/82	M	20	(1)	
4	Martin KOMÁREK		14/10/84	D	13	(3)	
20	Tomáš LOVÁSIK	SVK	31/7/74	G	16		
2	Milan MACHALICKÝ		1/6/91	D	6	(1)	
19	Ondřej MURIN		15/2/91	D	1		
25	Jan NAVRÁTIL		13/4/90	M	5	(4)	4
24	Tomáš NUC		9/3/89	D	1	(5)	
6	Ladislav ONOFREJ	SVK	20/9/77	D	16	(4)	
7	Michal ORDOŠ		27/1/83	A	23	(5)	12
9	Rudolf OTEPKA		13/11/73	M	9	(3)	
22	Jakub PETR		10/4/90	A	22	(8)	4
11	Jan SCHULMEISTER		11/3/86	A	3	(6)	1
12	Aleš ŠKERLE		14/6/82	D	23		
14	Vojtěch ŠTĚPÁN		8/6/85	M	3	(13)	
27	Vít ŠTĚTINA		29/9/89	M		(1)	
29	Pavel ŠULTES		15/9/85	A	17	(3)	9
26	Václav VAŠÍČEK		10/2/91	A		(2)	
21	Michal VEPŘEK		17/6/85	D	2	(3)	

SK SLAVIA PRAHA
Coach – Karel Jarolím; (31/3/10) František Cipro
Founded – 1892
Stadium – Multifunkční areál Eden (20,800)
MAJOR HONOURS:
Czechoslovakian/Czech League - (12) 1925, 1929, 1930, 1931, 1933, 1934, 1935, 1937, 1947, 1996, 2008, 2009;
Czech Cup - (3) 1997, 1999, 2002.

2009

Date	Opponent	H/A	Score	Scorers
25/7	Mladá Boleslav	h	1-1	Jarolím
2/8	Brno	a	0-2	
9/8	Bohemians	h	3-1	Šenkeřík 3
15/8	České Budějovice	a	1-0	Černý J.
23/8	Teplice	a	1-1	Černý J.
31/8	Slovácko	h	3-0	Šenkeřík, Čelůstka, og (Kubáň)
12/9	Liberec	a	1-1	Belaid
21/9	Baník	h	3-1	Hloušek 2, Grajciar
26/9	Bohemians 1905	h	1-1	Belaid (p)
5/10	Sparta	h	0-1	
18/10	Kladno	a	2-0	Naumov 2
1-2	Sigma	h	1-2	Hloušek
31/10	Příbram	a	0-1	
9/11	Plzeň	h	0-0	
21/11	Jablonec	a	1-1	Naumov
29/11	Brno	h	3-1	Skácel 3

2010

Date	Opponent	H/A	Score	Scorers
27/2	Bohemians	a	1-0	Grajciar
8/3	České Budějovice	h	3-2	Vlček 2, Janda
13/3	Teplice	h	0-0	
22/3	Slovácko	a	1-3	Trapp
25/3	Liberec	h	0-2	
29/3	Baník	a	1-3	Trapp
5/4	Bohemians 1905	h	3-0	Grajciar 2, Trapp
12/4	Sparta	a	0-1	
18/4	Kladno	h	0-0	
25/4	Sigma	a	1-3	Ivanovski
2/5	Příbram	h	3-0	Zákostelský, Krajčík, Dens
5/5	Plzeň	a	2-4	Ivanovski 2
8/5	Jablonec	h	0-3	
15/5	Mladá Boleslav	a	1-0	Černý J. (p)

No	Name	Nat	DoB	Pos	Aps	(s)	Gls
21	Tijani BELAID	TUN	6/9/87	M	9	(5)	2
5	Ondřej ČELŮSTKA		18/6/89	D	12	(1)	1
26	Jaroslav ČERNÝ		26/6/79	M	11	(3)	3
13	Milan ČERNÝ		16/3/88	M	8	(5)	
33	James DENS da Silva	BRA	14/8/86	D	4		1
18	Filip DURANSKI	MKD	17/7/91	M		(1)	
27	Peter GRAJCIAR	SVK	17/7/83	M	15	(6)	4
1	Jan HANUŠ		28/4/88	G	4		
9	Adam HLOUŠEK		20/12/88	M	15		3
25	Jan HOŠEK		1/4/89	D	5		
4	David HUBÁČEK		23/2/77	D	22		
23	Martin HURKA		20/4/93	A		(1)	
11	Mirko IVANOVSKI	MKD	31/10/89	A	4	(6)	3
8	Petr JANDA		5/1/87	M	16	(4)	1
10	Marek JAROLÍM		21/5/84	M		(1)	
29	Josef KAUFMAN		27/3/84	D		(2)	
3	Milan KOPIC		23/11/85	D	9		
20	Štěpán KOREŠ		14/2/89	M	3	(1)	
19	Matej KRAJČÍK	SVK	19/3/78	D	25	(2)	1
10	Jan KYSELA		17/12/85	M	7	(1)	
16	Kevin Pierre LAFRANCE	FRA	13/1/90	D	4	(2)	
15	Petr MAREŠ		17/11/91	D	1		
18	Riste NAUMOV	MKD	14/4/81	A	9	(5)	3
6	Hocine RAGUED	TUN	4/4/81	M	21	(2)	
31	Deniss ROMANOVS	LVA	2/9/78	G	4		
34	Štefan SENECKÝ	SVK	6/1/80	G	4		

14	Zdeněk ŠENKEŘÍK		19/12/80	A	11	(14)	4
30	Rudolf SKÁCEL		17/7/79	M	5		3
11	Vladimír ŠMICER		24/5/73	M	1	(2)	
12	Jaroslav STARÝ		9/2/88	D	2		
17	Marek SUCHÝ		29/3/88	D	16		
15	Libor TAFAT		12/12/86	A		(1)	
11	Stanislav TECL		1/9/90	A	2	(2)	
2	Petr TRAPP		6/12/85	M	17		3
24	Vitaliy TRUBILA	BLR	7/1/85	M	5	(4)	
32	Ondřej VANĚK		5/7/90	M	1	(1)	
28	Martin VANIAK		4/10/70	G	18	(1)	
12	Dušan VASILJEVIĆ	SRB	7/5/82	M	5	(4)	
7	Stanislav VLČEK		26/2/76	A	16	(7)	2
23	Ladislav VOLEŠÁK		7/4/84	M	6	(2)	
22	Benjamin VOMÁČKA		27/6/78	D	12		
17	Jan ZÁKOSTELSKÝ		25/11/91	A	1	(1)	1

17	Martin KUNCL		1/4/84	D	13		1
10	Radim NEČAS		12/1/88	M	1	(4)	
12	Pavel NĚMČICKÝ		13/8/77	D	19	(4)	
20	Ilija NESTOROSKI	MKD	1/1/90	A	5	(6)	1
18	Václav ONDŘEJKA		30/4/88	A	20	(7)	7
15	Jiří PERŮTKA		22/2/88	M	12	(3)	
11	Filip RACKO		22/7/85	M	6	(3)	
24	Tomáš RANDA		23/12/74	D	12	(2)	
23	Jan ŠIMÁČEK		29/11/82	D	4		
26	Ondřej SMETANA		4/9/82	A	3	(8)	2
23	Václav STRÁNÍK		13/11/92	A		(1)	
25	Peter STRUHÁR	SVK	17/1/84	D	9	(1)	
9	Petr ŠVANCARA		5/11/77	A	19	(5)	7
26	Jakub SVÍZELA		9/1/92	M	5	(1)	
21	Aleš URBÁNEK		25/5/80	D	20		
2	Vít VALENTA		4/1/84	M	16	(9)	
27	Petr VAŠEK		9/4/79	G	10		
7	Lukáš ZELENKA		5/10/79	M	13	(4)	2

1. FC SLOVÁCKO

Coach – Josef Mazura; (18/4/10) Miroslav Soukup
Founded – 2000
Stadium – Městský fotbalový stadion Stonky (8,000)

2009

25/7	Plzeň	h	2-3	Švancara 2 (1p)
3/8	Jablonec	a	2-3	Švancara, Chmelíček
9/8	Sigma	h	2-0	Švancara (p), Chmelíček
14/8	Brno	a	0-1	
22/8	Bohemians	h	2-0	Švancara (p), Ondřejka
31/8	Slavia	a	0-3	
13/9	Teplice	h	0-2	
20/9	České Budějovice	a	0-0	
26/9	Liberec	a	0-2	
3/10	Baník	a	0-2	
18/10	Bohemians 1905	a	1-0	Kordula
2410	Kladno	h	2-0	Zelenka, Abrahám
1/11	Mladá Boleslav	a	2-3	Ondřejka, Smetana
9/11	Sparta	h	0-1	
21/11	Příbram	a	0-2	
28/11	Jablonec	h	1-1	Smetana
2010				
28/2	Sigma	a	0-1	
6/3	Brno	h	0-2	
14/3	Bohemians	a	1-1	Fujerik
22/3	Slavia	h	3-1	Fujerik, Nesteroski, Ondřejka
25/3	Teplice	a	1-2	Fujerik
28/3	České Budějovice	h	1-0	Ondřejka
3/4	Liberec	h	0-0	
10/4	Baník	a	2-3	Kuncl, Fujerik
17/4	Bohemians 1905	h	1-1	Ondřejka
25/4	Kladno	a	0-1	
30/4	Mladá Boleslav	h	1-0	Ondřejka
5/5	Sparta	a	0-4	
8/5	Příbram	h	2-1	Ondřejka, Zelenka
15/5	Plzeň	a	2-2	Švancara 2

No	Name	Nat	DoB	Pos	Aps	(s)	Gls
6	Tomáš ABRAHÁM		18/4/79	M	15	(7)	1
19	Aleš CHMELÍČEK		24/2/80	A	12	(1)	2
4	CLÉBER Nascimento da Silva	BRA	13/6/86	M	18	(7)	
30	Miroslav FILIPKO	SVK	23/9/73	G	19		
13	René FORMÁNEK		9/1/75	D	9		
8	Lukáš FUJERIK		9/12/83	M	15	(2)	4
10	Michal GONDA	SVK	29/8/82	M		(5)	
8	Filip HLÚPIK		30/4/91	M		(1)	
16	Milan KERBR		10/9/89	A		(1)	
5	Michal KORDULA		11/2/78	M	22		1
22	Tomáš KOŠÚT	SVK	13/1/90	D	12		
3	Lukáš KUBÁŇ		22/6/87	D	20	(1)	
29	Josef KUBÁSEK		6/5/85	G	1		

FC SLOVAN LIBEREC

Coach – Ladislav Škorpil; (8/11/09) Josef Petřík
Founded – 1921
Stadium – U Nisy (9,900)
MAJOR HONOURS:
Czech League - (2) 2002, 2006;
Czech Cup - (1) 2000.

2009

25/7	Kladno	h	1-1	Gecov
2/8	Mladá Boleslav	a	1-4	Nezmar
9/8	Brno	h	0-1	
16/8	Plzeň	a	3-2	Čorić 2, Blažek
23/8	České Budějovice	h	3-0	Vácha, Dočkal, Nezmar
30/8	Bohemians	a	1-2	Blažek
12/9	Slavia	h	1-1	Gebre Selassie
19/9	Jablonec	a	1-2	Bosančić
26/9	Slovácko	h	2-0	Gebre Selassie, Blažek
3/10	Teplice	a	0-2	
17/10	Baník	a	0-1	
25/10	Příbram	h	1-0	Kelić
1/11	Bohemians 1905	a	1-0	Blažek
7/11	Sigma	h	0-4	
21/11	Sparta	a	0-2	
28/11	Mladá Boleslav	h	3-0	Nezmar, Kerić, Bosančić
2010				
27/2	Brno	a	0-1	
6/3	Plzeň	h	0-2	
14/3	České Budějovice	a	1-1	Vulin
20/3	Bohemians	h	2-3	Vulin, Kerić
25/3	Slavia	a	2-0	Vulin, Kerić
28/3	Jablonec	h	4-2	Nezmar, Dočkal, Kerić, og (Zábojník)
3/4	Slovácko	a	0-0	
11/4	Teplice	h	1-0	Dočkal (p)
19/4	Baník	h	0-1	
24/4	Příbram	a	1-1	Dočkal
1/5	Bohemians 1905	h	1-1	Kelić
5/5	Sigma	a	0-2	
8/5	Sparta	h	2-2	Vulin, Papoušek
15/5	Kladno	a	2-1	Dočkal, Kerić

No	Name	Nat	DoB	Pos	Aps	(s)	Gls
28	Jan BLAŽEK		20/3/88	A	9	(3)	4
12	Miloš BOSANČIĆ	SRB	22/5/88	M	11	(9)	2
22	Josip ČORIĆ	BIH	9/11/88	M	2	(4)	2
21	Radek DEJMEK		2/2/88	D	23	(1)	
14	Jaroslav DIVIŠ		9/7/86	A	2	(9)	
18	Bořek DOČKAL		30/9/88	M	25	(4)	5
20	Tomáš FREJLACH		24/11/85	M	11	(4)	
32	Theodor GEBRE SELASSIE		24/12/86	D	16	(2)	2

No	Name	Nat	DoB	Pos	Aps	(s)	Gls
10	Marcel GECOV		1/1/88	M	19	(2)	1
1	Zbyněk HAUZR		20/4/73	G	24		
11	Miroslav HOLEŇÁK		10/2/76	D	20	(4)	
17	Tomáš JANŮ		17/9/73	D	19	(1)	
2	Renato KELIĆ	CRO	31/3/91	D	16	(2)	2
15	Andrej KERIĆ	CRO	11/2/86	A	23	(2)	5
9	Tomáš KRBEČEK		27/10/85	A	2	(2)	
8	Jiří LIŠKA		13/3/82	D	11	(4)	
26	Ladislav MARTAN		8/10/89	A		(1)	
7	Jan NEZMAR		5/7/77	A	15	(8)	4
23	Petr PAPOUŠEK		7/5/77	M	13	(9)	1
13	Jan POLÁK		26/3/89	D	9	(3)	
5	Dario PURIĆ	BIH	18/5/86	M		(1)	
16	Daniel ŘEHÁK		2/4/85	D		(1)	
9	Ondřej SMETANA		4/9/82	A	4	(4)	
27	Lukáš SUK		31/3/90	M		(2)	
6	Lukáš VÁCHA		13/5/89	M	23	(2)	1
3	Jakub VOJTA		19/4/91	M	1	(5)	
19	Lovre VULIN	CRO	2/9/84	D	17		4
5	Michal ZEMAN		18/8/84	M	9		
16	Lukáš ZICH		10/1/85	G	4		
16	Zdeněk ZLÁMAL		5/11/85	G	2		

AC SPARTA PRAHA

Coach – Jozef Chovanec
Founded – 1893
Stadium – Letná (20,558)
MAJOR HONOURS:
Czechoslovakian/Czech League League - (30) 1926, 1927, 1932, 1936, 1938, 1946, 1948, 1952, 1954, 1965, 1967, 1984, 1985, 1987, 1988, 1989, 1990, 1991, 1993, 1994, 1995, 1997, 1998, 1999, 2000, 2001, 2003, 2005, 2007, 2010; Czechoslovakian/Czech Cup - (13) 1964, 1972, 1976, 1980, 1984, 1988, 1989, 1992, 1996, 2004, 2006, 2007, 2008.

2009

24/7	Teplice	a	0-0	
31/7	Bohemians 1905	h	0-0	
8/8	Příbram	a	1-1	Kadlec
15/8	Kladno	h	2-0	Vacek, Wilfried
23/8	Mladá Boleslav	h	1-0	Kadlec
31/8	Sigma	a	1-1	Hubník
12/9	Jablonec	h	2-0	Kušnír, Wilfried
21/9	Brno	a	1-1	Holenda
26/9	Plzeň	h	0-0	
5/10	Slavia	a	1-0	Wilfried
17/10	České Budějovice	h	1-1	Wilfried
25/10	Bohemians	a	3-2	Zeman, Vacek, Kušnír
31/10	Baník	h	1-1	Žofčák (p)
9/11	Slovácko	a	1-0	Holenda
21/11	Liberec	h	2-0	Holenda, Kadlec
28/11	Bohemians 1905	a	2-0	Holenda, Žofčák

2010

27/2	Příbram	h	1-1	Wilfried
7/3	Kladno	a	1-0	Žofčák (p)
14/3	Mladá Boleslav	a	2-1	Kušnír, Sionko
20/3	Sigma	h	4-0	Sionko 2, Žofčák (p), Wilfried
24/3	Jablonec	a	0-0	
28/3	Brno	h	3-0	Kucka 2, Kadlec
5/4	Plzeň	a	2-2	Wilfried, Kucka
12/4	Slavia	h	1-0	Sionko
18/4	České Budějovice	a	0-0	
24/4	Bohemians	h	1-0	Kadlec
2/5	Baník	a	1-1	Kadlec
5/5	Slovácko	h	4-0	Wilfried 2, Žofčák, Kušnír
8/5	Liberec	a	2-2	Kucka 2
15/5	Teplice	h	1-0	Řepka

No	Name	Nat	DoB	Pos	Aps	(s)	Gls
8	Patrik BERGER		10/11/73	M	2		
29	Jaromír BLAŽEK		29/12/72	G	23		
21	Erich BRABEC		24/2/77	D	13		
28	Zdeněk FOLPRECHT		1/7/91	M	1		
30	Lukáš HEJDA		9/3/90	D	2	(2)	
4	Niklas HOHENEDER	AUT	17/8/86	D	14	(7)	
17	Jan HOLENDA		22/8/85	A	7	(4)	4
6	Roman HUBNÍK		6/6/84	D	15		1
27	Luboš HUŠEK		26/1/84	M	9		
10	Martin JIROUŠ		27/11/86	A	1	(3)	
9	Milan JURDÍK		8/11/91	A		(1)	
14	Václav KADLEC		20/5/92	A	19	(10)	6
19	Luboš KALOUDA		20/5/87	M	5	(11)	
15	Jiří KLADRUBSKÝ		19/11/85	D	2	(4)	
23	Denis KOVBA	BLR	6/9/79	M	7	(1)	
24	Matúš KOZÁČIK	SVK	27/12/83	G	7		
5	Ladislav KREJČÍ		5/7/92	M	1	(2)	
20	Juraj KUCKA	SVK	26/2/87	M	16	(4)	5
13	Ondřej KUŠNÍR		5/4/84	D	29		4
6	Miloš LAČNÝ		8/3/88	A	4	(6)	
3	Manuel PAMIĆ	CRO	20/8/86	D	26		
9	Alexander PRUDNIKOV	RUS	24/2/89	A	2	(6)	
2	Tomáš ŘEPKA		2/1/74	D	28		1
7	Libor SIONKO		1/2/77	M	14		4
7	Marek STŘEŠTÍK		1/2/87	M	3	(2)	
17	Lukáš TŘEŠŇÁK		3/5/88	A		(5)	
25	Kamil VACEK		18/5/87	M	23	(3)	2
12	Bony WILFRIED	CIV	10/12/88	A	26	(3)	9
22	Martin ZEMAN		28/3/89	M	11	(9)	1
11	Igor ŽOFČÁK	SVK	10/4/83	M	20	(5)	5

FK TEPLICE

Coach – Jiří Plíšek
Founded – 1945
Stadium – Na Stínadlech (18,221)
MAJOR HONOURS: Czech Cup - (2) 2003, 2009.

2009

24/7	Sparta	h	0-0	
1/8	Plzeň	a	2-2	Vachoušek, Vidlička
9/8	České Budějovice	h	3-0	Stožický, Mahmutović, Vidlička
16/8	Bohemians	a	3-1	Mareš, og (Kincl), Verbíř
23/8	Slavia	h	1-1	Stožický
31/8	Brno	a	3-2	Merzić, Mahmutović, Mareš
13/9	Slovácko	a	2-0	Vondrášek, Mahmutović
20/9	Bohemians 1905	h	1-0	Smejkal
26/9	Baník	a	2-2	Vachoušek, Kalivoda
3/10	Liberec	h	2-0	Vidlička, Mahmutović
17/10	Příbram	a	3-0	Mareš 2, Verbíř
24/10	Mladá Boleslav	h	2-2	og (Miller), Stožický
1/11	Kladno	a	2-0	Vondrášek, Kalivoda
7/11	Jablonec	h	1-0	og (Špit)
23/11	Sigma	a	2-6	Mahmutović, Klein

2010

28/2	České Budějovice	a	0-0	
6/3	Bohemians	h	2-1	Došek, Stožický
10/3	Plzeň	a	2-1	Siva, Mahmutović
13/3	Slavia	a	0-0	
20/3	Brno	h	0-1	
25/3	Slovácko	h	2-1	Došek 2
28/3	Bohemians 1905	a	1-1	Vondrášek
5/4	Baník	h	0-1	
11/4	Liberec	a	0-1	
18/4	Příbram	h	1-0	Mahmutović
25/4	Mladá Boleslav	a	1-0	Vachoušek (p)
1/5	Kladno	h	5-0	Vachoušek 2, Rosa, Mahmutović, Kalivoda
5/5	Jablonec	a	0-0	

8/5	Sigma	h	1-1	Vachoušek (p)
15/5	Sparta	a	0-1	

No	Name	Nat	DoB	Pos	Aps	(s)	Gls
12	Michal DOLEŽAL		19/8/77	M		(9)	
18	Libor DOŠEK		24/4/78	A	8	(5)	3
23	Osama ELSAMNI	JPN	29/9/88	A	1	(3)	
7	Michal GAŠPARÍK	SVK	19/12/81	M	1	(4)	
30	Tomáš GRIGAR		1/2/83	G	15		
11	Andrej HESEK	SVK	12/6/81	A	1	(7)	
27	David KALIVODA		25/8/82	M	5	(14)	3
4	Martin KLEIN		2/7/84	D	25		1
5	Admir LJEVAKOVIĆ	BIH	7/8/84	M	26		
15	Petr LUKÁŠ		24/4/78	D	22		
25	Aidin MAHMUTOVIĆ	BIH	6/4/86	A	26	(3)	8
19	Jakub MAREŠ		26/1/87	M	10	(3)	4
20	Milan MATULA		22/4/84	D	21		
14	Samir MERZIĆ	BIH	29/6/84	D	4	(2)	1
24	Jakub PÍCHA		21/7/91	M		(1)	
22	Antonín ROSA		12/11/86	D	15	(2)	1
2	Matej SIVA	SVK	10/10/84	D	13	(1)	1
1	Martin SLAVÍK		21/9/79	G	15		
18	Michal SMEJKAL		21/2/86	A	7	(1)	1
10	Vlastimil STOŽICKÝ		19/8/83	M	22	(5)	4
8	Štěpán VACHOUŠEK		26/7/79	A	27		6
9	Pavel VERBÍŘ		13/11/72	M	18	(8)	2
24	Richard VEVERKA		16/12/87	A	1	(7)	
6	Vlastimil VIDLIČKA		2/7/81	D	27		3
17	Tomáš VONDRÁŠEK		26/10/87	A	15	(6)	3
11	Lukáš ZOUBELE		20/12/85	M	5	(6)	

FC VIKTORIA PLZEŇ
Coach – Pavel Vrba
Founded – 1911
Stadium – Města Plzně (7,425)
MAJOR HONOURS:
Czech Cup - (1) 2010.

2009

25/7	Slovácko	a	3-2	Střihavka, Petržela, Rýdel
1/8	Teplice	h	2-2	Jiráček, Lecjaks
8/8	Baník	a	0-1	
16/8	Liberec	h	2-3	Bakoš, Horváth (p)
23/8	Bohemians 1905	a	1-0	Střihavka
29/8	Kladno	h	1-0	og (Strnad)
12/9	Příbram	a	0-1	
19/9	Mladá Boleslav	h	2-1	Horváth (p) og (Rolko)
26/9	Sparta	a	0-0	
3/10	Sigma	h	1-0	Bakoš
19/10	Jablonec	a	1-0	Rajtoral
25/10	České Budějovice	a	0-0	
2/11	Brno	h	1-1	Bakoš
9/11	Slavia	a	0-0	
21/11	Bohemians	h	3-2	Horváth, Rajtoral, Rada

2010

1/3	Baník	h	0-0	
6/3	Liberec	a	2-0	Rezek, Kolář
10/3	Teplice	a	1-2	Bakoš
14/3	Bohemians 1905	h	3-0	og (Jindříšek), Ševinský, Krbeček
20/3	Kladno	a	3-1	Bakoš, Limberský, Navrátil
24/3	Příbram	h	3-1	Kolář, Bakoš, Horváth
27/3	Mladá Boleslav	a	0-4	
5/4	Sparta	h	2-2	Bakoš, Rajtoral
11/4	Sigma	a	0-1	
17/4	Jablonec	h	1-1	Střihavka
24/4	České Budějovice	h	0-0	
1/5	Brno	a	2-2	Rezek, Kolář
5/5	Slavia	h	4-2	Kolář, Rezek, Střihavka, Horváth
8/5	Bohemians	a	2-2	Rada, Bystroň
15/5	Slovácko	h	2-2	Střihavka, Kolář

No	Name	Nat	DoB	Pos	Aps	(s)	Gls
6	Marek BAKOŠ	SVK	15/4/83	A	19	(5)	7
18	David BYSTROŇ		18/11/82	D	24		1
25	Michal DANĚK		6/7/83	G	25		
16	Vladimír DARIDA		8/8/90	M		(3)	
3	Tomáš HÁJOVSKÝ	SVK	10/12/82	D	9	(3)	
10	Pavel HORVÁTH		22/4/75	M	28		5
20	Petr JIRÁČEK		2/3/86	M	11	(15)	1
26	Daniel KOLÁŘ		27/10/85	M	20	(6)	5
9	Tomáš KRBEČEK		27/10/85	A		(8)	1
13	Jan LECJAKS		9/8/90	D	15	(7)	1
8	David LIMBERSKÝ		6/10/83	D	24	(2)	1
23	Jiří MLIKA		18/7/80	A		(5)	
21	Jakub NAVRÁTIL		1/2/84	D	20	(7)	1
11	Milan PETRŽELA		19/6/83	M	28	(1)	1
4	Tomáš RADA		28/9/83	D	26		2
27	František RAJTORAL		12/3/86	M	20	(9)	3
17	Jan REZEK		5/5/82	A	17	(5)	3
24	Filip RÝDEL		30/3/84	M	9	(4)	1
15	František ŠEVINSKÝ		31/3/79	D	14	(2)	1
7	David STŘIHAVKA		4/3/83	A	16	(5)	5
30	Martin TICHÁČEK		15/9/81	G	5	(1)	
6	David VANĚČEK		9/3/91	M		(2)	

PROMOTED CLUBS

FC HRADEC KRÁLOVÉ
Coach – Václav Kotal
Founded – 1905
Stadium – Všesportovní stadion (17,504)
MAJOR HONOURS:
Czechoslovakian League - (1) 1960.

FK ÚSTÍ NAD LABEM
Coach – Svatopluk Habanec
Founded – 1927
Stadium – Městský stadion (1,170)

SECOND LEVEL FINAL TABLE 2009/10

		Pld	W	D	L	F	A	Pts
1	FC Hradec Králové	30	20	8	2	47	18	68
2	FK Ústí nad Labem	30	20	5	5	52	27	65
3	FC Zlín	30	17	5	8	49	33	56
4	FC Vysočina Jihlava	30	15	7	8	57	37	52
5	FK Viktoria Žižkov	30	13	7	10	42	41	46
6	FK Dukla Praha	30	12	8	10	45	41	44
7	FC Vlašim	30	11	7	12	40	41	40
8	MFK OKD Karviná	30	11	6	13	44	36	39
9	FK Fotbal Třinec	30	10	8	12	34	38	38
10	FK Baník Sokolov	30	9	10	11	37	43	37
11	FK Baník Most	30	8	12	10	35	38	36
12	AC Sparta Praha B	30	6	11	13	33	50	29
13	FC Hlučín	30	6	11	13	27	43	29
14	FC Zenit Čáslav	30	7	8	15	28	49	29
15	SFC Opava	30	6	11	13	30	37	29
16	FC Vitkovice	30	4	6	20	23	51	18

DOMESTIC CUP 2009/10

POHÁR ČMFS

SECOND ROUND

(25/8/09)
Valašské Meziříčí 0, Vítkovice 2

(26/8/09)
Slavoj Řevnice 0, Písek 0 *(2-4 on pens)*
Sokol Protivanov 1, Uničov 1 *(6-5 on pens)*

(1/9/09)
ČAFC Židenice 1, Břeclav 1 *(5-6 on pens)*
FRAMOZ Rousínov 0, Zlín 3

(2/9/09)
1. HFK Olomouc 1, Karviná 4
ARSENAL Česká Lípa 2, Slavia Praha 4
ELSEREMO Brumov 0, Třinec 5
FK Kunice 1, Náchod-Deštné 3
FK Tachov 1, Buldoci Karlovy Vary 1 *(15-16 on pens)*
FRC Zábřeh 1, FC Hlučín 2
Horácký Třebíč 2, Slovácko 2 *(4-1 on pens)*
HS Kroměříž 0, Baník 3
Králův Dvůr 0, Dukla Praha 0 *(1-4 on pens)*
Meteor Praha 1, Příbram 1 *(2-4 on pens)*
Most 1, Kladno 1 *(6-7 on pens)*
Mutěnice 0, SFC Opava 2
Pěnčín-Turnov 0, Slovan Varnsdorf 2
SK Hlavice 0, Jablonec 3
Sokol Ovčáry 2, Bohemians 1905 2 *(3-4 on pens)*
Sokol Živanice 1, Mladá Boleslav 0
Spartak Sezimovo Ústí 0, České Budějovice 2
Union Čelákovice 1, Bohemians 4
Vlašim 1, Plzeň 3
Znojmo 2, Vysočina Jihlava 0
Žižkov 2, Baník Sokolov 1

(3/9/09)
Admira Praha 0, Hradec Králové 3
Líšeň 1, Sigma 3
FK Ústí nad Labem 1, Teplice 4
Fotbal Frýdek-Místek 1, Brno 2
Jiskra Ústí nad Orlicí 0, Sparta Praha 4

(16/9/09)
Dvůr Králové 2, Liberec 7

THIRD ROUND

(16/9/09)
SFC Opava 1, Baník 1 *(3-5 on pens)*

(22/9/09)
Zlín 1, Liberec 1 *(1-3 on pens)*
Dukla Praha 1, Plzeň 4

(23/9/09)
Břeclav 0, Kladno 1
FC Hlučín 1, Teplice 3
Horácký Třebíč 0, Znojmo 1
Hradec Králové 2, Bohemians 1
Písek 1, Jablonec 1 *(1-4 on pens)*
Slovan Varnsdorf 0, Příbram 1
Sokol Protivanov 0, Sigma 5
Třinec 0, Bohemians 1905 1
Žižkov 0, České Budějovice 1

(29/9/09)
Sokol Živanice 1, Vítkovice 0

(8/10/09)
Buldoci Karlovy Vary 1, Slavia Praha 1 *(4-5 on pens)*
Karviná 1, Brno 1 *(5-4 on pens)*
Náchod-Deštné 0, Sparta Praha 6

FOURTH ROUND

(7/10/09 & 13/10/09)
Kladno v Plzeň 0-3; 1-1 *(1-4)*

(7/10/09 & 27/10/09)
Příbram v Baník 2-0; 0-0 *(2-0)*

(7/10/09 & 28/10/09)
Bohemians 1905 v Liberec 1-2; 1-1 *(2-3)*
Sokol Živanice v Jablonec 3-6; 1-5 *(4-11)*

(7/10/09 & 11/11/09)
Hradec Králové v Teplice 1-2; 1-2 *(2-4)*

(8/10/09 & 28/10/09)
Znojmo v Sigma 1-3; 0-0 *(1-3)*

(13/10/09 & 12/11/09)
České Budějovice v Sparta Praha 0-5; 0-1 *(0-6)*

(14/10/09 & 25/11/09)
Karviná v Slavia Praha 1-0; 0-2 *(1-2)*

QUARTER-FINALS

(31/3/10 & 7/4/10)
Liberec 0, Sigma 2 *(Šultes 30, 36)*
Sigma 1 *(Komárek 21)*, Liberec 0
(Sigma 3-0)

(31/3/10 & 8/4/10)
Plzeň 1 *(Bakoš 44)*, Příbram 0
Příbram 1 *(Tarczal 90+1)*, Plzeň 1 *(Petržela 71)*
(Plzeň 2-1)

Teplice 1 *(Vondrášek 32)*, Jablonec 3 *(Jarolím 22, Krejčí 31, Lafata 40)*
Jablonec 0, Teplice 0
(Jablonec 3-1)

(1/4/10 & 15/4/10)
Slavia Praha 1 *(Černý M. 16)*, Sparta Praha 0
Sparta Praha 0, Slavia Praha 1 *(Černý J. 8p)*
(Slavia 2-0)

SEMI-FINALS

(21/4/10 & 28/4/10)
Jablonec 1 *(Jarolím 90p)*, Slavia 0
Slavia 2 *(Černý J. 57p, Trapp 88)*, Jablonec 1 *(Lafata 37)*
(2-2; Jablonec on away goal)

Plzeň 2 *(Horváth 29, Kolář 38)*, Sigma 2 *(Ordoš 31, Janotka 66p)*
Sigma 1 *(Navrátil 81)*, Plzeň 3 *(Rezek 18p, Střihavka 23, Petržela 49)*
(Plzeň 5-3)

FINAL

(18/5/10)
Letná, Prague
FC VIKTORIA PLZEŇ 2 *(Petržela 2, Bystroň 68)*
FK JABLONEC 1 *(Lafata 60)*
Referee – Jílek
PLZEŇ – Daněk, Rajtoral, Navrátil, Bystroň, Limberský, Petržela (Rýdel 89), Kolář (Ševinský 90+2), Horváth, Rada, Rezek, Střihavka (Bakoš 83).
JABLONEC – Špit, Zábojník, Pavlík, Drsek, Jablonský, Jarolím, Eliáš (Vošahlík 75), Loučka, Kovařík, Pekhart, Lafata.

Olsen's unlikely lads fall short

Denmark's fourth appearance at the FIFA World Cup finals will historically go down as their worst. On their previous participations – in 1986, 1998 and 2002 – they had always passed the first round, but in 2010 that feat proved beyond them as they were well beaten in their 'must-win' last group game by Japan.

In truth, given the comparatively modest quality of the collection of players available to him, Morten Olsen, the Denmark coach, overachieved simply by steering the team to South Africa. Absent from both the 2006 finals and UEFA EURO 2008, little was expected of the Danes in a qualifying section that also contained Portugal and Sweden, two countries that had been present at every major tournament since the turn of the century. Yet Denmark won the group, with a game to spare, clinching their ticket in the sweetest way imaginable with a hard-fought victory over Sweden in Copenhagen.

Low expectations

Despite that improbable success, the general level of expectation for the finals was low, with a place in the last 16 considered by most Danes to be the limit of the

Denmark trio Lars Jacobsen, Jakob Poulsen and Dennis Rommedahl take in the disappointment of their World Cup defeat by Japan

team's abilities – especially after an uninspiring build-up. Things did not start well with a stodgy 2-0 defeat to the Netherlands in Johannesburg, Olsen's men failing to recover from a comical own-goal conceded just after half-time. There was a major improvement in the second game – one of the most entertaining of the group stage – as Denmark came from behind to beat Cameroon 2-1 in Pretoria with two sumptuous goals from Nicklas Bendtner and Dennis Rommedahl, the latter producing one of his finest displays - in his 98th international.

The veteran winger was unable to reach his century of caps in South Africa because Denmark, requiring all three points against Japan in Rustenburg to reach the last 16, were beaten 3-1 on a night that long-serving goalkeeper Thomas Sørensen will not wish to recall in a hurry. Two first-half free-kick goals from Japan effectively ended the game as a contest, and although Jon Dahl Tomasson reduced the arrears when he finally scored his record-equalling 52nd international goal – almost two and a half years after his 51st – it was not a pretty sight, his mis-hit rebound sneaking in after he had missed a penalty. A late third Japanese goal was the final seal on a disappointing campaign, after which both Martin Jørgensen – the only Danish player to operate at three World Cups – and Jesper Grønkjær announced their international retirement.

Jørgensen and Grønkjær travelled to South Africa as representatives not just of Denmark but of the Danish Superliga. The two players could hardly have headed south in more contrasting moods, however, with Jørgensen, who had returned to his homeland in January after 13 years in Italy, suffering relegation with AGF Århus and Grønkjær celebrating a third league title in four years with FC København.

FCK triumph

For FCK, by far the wealthiest and most resourceful club in Denmark, it was a seventh championship win in ten years – and eighth in all. Astutely led once again by Norwegian coach Ståle Solbakken, they paced

DENMARK

themselves perfectly over the 33-match campaign. European commitments in the autumn left them trailing Odense BK by a point at the winter break, but once they resumed with a thumping 5-0 win over AGF that sent them to the top of the table, they took command. A 2-0 victory over OB at Parken, watched by 24,076 spectators, corrected a brief wobble, and after that there was no looking back.

The title was all but secured in round 30, with a 2-0 win at arch-rivals Brøndby IF. This gave København a nine-point lead with three games to go, which, supplemented by a vastly superior goal difference, made them uncatchable. The 4-0 home win over relegated HB Køge three days later simply iced the celebration cake, with the club's top scorer, Senegalese striker Dame N'Doye, adding the cherry as he maintained his rich vein of scoring form with another couple of goals.

Dame N'Doye scored goals galore in domestic and European football for FC København

Dansk Boldspil-Union (DBU)

House of Football
DBU Allé 1
DK-2605 Brøndby
tel – +45 43 262 222
fax – +45 43 262 245
website – dbu.dk
email – dbu@dbu.dk
Year of Formation – 1889

President – Allan Hansen
General Secretary – Jim Stjerne Hansen
Press Officer – Lars Berendt
National Stadium – Parken, København (38,010)

INTERNATIONAL HONOURS
UEFA European Championship – (1) 1992.
INTERNATIONAL TOURNAMENT APPEARANCES
FIFA World Cup – (4) 1986 (2nd round), 1998 (qtr-finals), 2002 (2nd round), 2010.
UEFA European Championship – (7) 1964 (4th), 1984 (semi-finals), 1988, 1992 (Winners), 1996, 2000, 2004 (qtr-finals).
TOP FIVE ALL-TIME CAPS
Peter Schmeichel (129); Jon Dahl Tomasson (112); Thomas Helveg (108); Michael Laudrup (104); Morten Olsen (102,
TOP FIVE ALL-TIME GOALS
Poul "Tist" Nielsen & Jon Dahl Tomasson (52); Pauli Jørgensen (44); Ole Madsen (42); Preben Elkjær (38)

By the end of the campaign, N'Doye had 14 Superliga goals and FCK a winning margin of nine points. OB, despite a disappointing spring, during which they picked up only 21 points from the 45 on offer, finished runners-up for the second successive season. They boasted a powerful and prolific African striker of their own in 26-year-old Nigerian Peter Utaka, whose 18 goals earned him the Golden Boot, and were also ably served by a couple of former Manchester United FC players in goalkeeper Roy Carroll and midfielder Eric Djemba-Djemba as well as 38-year-old ex-AC Milan veteran Thomas Helveg.

NATIONAL TEAM RESULTS 2009/10

12/8/09	Chile	H	Brondby	1-2	*Schøne (63)*
5/9/09	Portugal (WCQ)	H	Copenhagen	1-1	*Bendtner (43)*
9/9/09	Albania (WCQ)	A	Tirana	1-1	*Bendtner (40)*
10/10/09	Sweden (WCQ)	H	Copenhagen	1-0	*Poulsen J. (78)*
14/10/09	Hungary (WCQ)	H	Copenhagen	0-1	
14/11/09	South Korea	H	Esbjerg	0-0	
18/11/09	United States	H	Aarhus	3-1	*Absalonsen (46), Rieks (51), Bernburg (54)*
3/3/10	Austria	A	Vienna	1-2	*Bendtner (17)*
27/5/10	Senegal	H	Aalborg	2-0	*Poulsen C. (27), Enevoldsen (92)*
1/6/10	Australia	N	Roodepoort (RSA)	0-1	
5/6/10	South Africa	A	Atteridgeville (RSA)	0-1	
14/6/10	Netherlands (WCF)	N	Johannesburg (RSA)	0-2	
19/6/10	Cameroon (WCF)	N	Pretoria (RSA)	2-1	*Bendtner (33), Rommedahl (61)*
24/6/10	Japan (WCF)	N	Rustenburg (RSA)	1-3	*Tomasson (81)*

NATIONAL TEAM APPEARANCES 2009/10

Coach – Morten OLSEN 14/8/49

Name	DOB	Club	Chi	POR	ALB	SWE	HUN	Kor	Usa	Aut	Sen	Aus	Rsa	NED	CMR	JPN	Caps	Goals
Stephan ANDERSEN	26/11/81	Brøndby	G46	G							G	G					7	-
Lars JACOBSEN	20/9/79	Blackburn (ENG)	D68	D	D	D	D	D	D			D	D	D	D	D	34	-
Simon KJÆR	26/3/89	Palermo (ITA)	D	D	D	D		D	D	D	D			D	D		11	-
Anders Møller CHRISTENSEN	26/7/77	OB	D	D	D		D										6	-
Michael JAKOBSEN	2/1/86	AaB	D46					D	D								5	-
Martin JØRGENSEN	6/10/75	Fiorentina (ITA) /AGF	M55	A61	A69	M46			M80		s46	s79	M	A	M46	M34	99	12
Jakob POULSEN	7/7/83	AGF	M	M88	M54	M	M	M	A			M61	s46	M46	s86	s34	15	1
Christian POULSEN	28/2/80	Juventus (ITA)	M	M	M	M	M	M	M46		M46	M79	M72	M	M	M	77	6
Dennis ROMMEDAHL	22/7/78	Ajax (NED)	M	A	A	A	A71			A46	A72	s46	A57	A	A	A	99	17
Jon Dahl TOMASSON	29/8/76	Feyenoord (NED)	A79	M	M73	A	M62					A	A64	A57	M86	M	112	52
Nicklas BENDTNER	16/1/88	Arsenal (ENG)	A62	A	A	A	A			A61				A62	A	A	35	12
Jesper CHRISTIANSEN	24/4/78	København	s46								s46						11	-
William Kvist JØRGENSEN	24/2/85	København	s46	s66	D				s46	M75	D	s70					14	-
Jesper GRØNKJÆR	12/8/77	København	s55	s88	s54			s80	A46			s62	A	s56	A67		80	5
Lasse SCHØNE	27/5/86	NEC (NED)	s62														1	1
Kris STADSGAARD	1/8/85	Rosenborg (NOR)	s68														1	-
Hjalte Bo NØRREGAARD	8/4/81	København	s79	s61	s69												4	-
Michael SILBERBAUER	7/7/81	Utrecht (NED)		D66		s46	s71			D							14	1
Thomas SØRENSEN	12/6/76	Stoke (ENG)		G	G	G	G	G	G					G	G	G	89	-
Søren LARSEN	6/9/81	Duisburg (GER)			s73		s46					s64	s72			s56	20	11
Daniel AGGER	12/12/84	Liverpool (ENG)			D	D					D	D	D70	D	D	D	35	3
Thomas ENEVOLDSEN	27/7/87	Groningen (NED)					A46	s63	s90		s61	A62	s57	M56			7	1
Daniel JENSEN	25/6/79	Werder (GER)						s62	M70	M46	M56	M46	s46		s46		50	3
Per KRØLDRUP	31/7/79	Fiorentina (ITA)						D	D	D		D	D			D56	31	-
Leon JESSEN	11/6/86	Midtjylland						D	D46								2	-
Søren RIEKS	7/4/87	Esbjerg							A80	s46	s46						3	1
Thomas KAHLENBERG	20/3/83	Wolfsburg (GER)						A63		M	A	A82		M73	s67	A63	34	3
Morten "Duncan" RASMUSSEN	31/1/85	Brøndby							A74	A35							3	-
Johan ABSALONSEN	16/9/85	OB							s70	s46							2	1
Martin BERNBURG	26/12/85	Brøndby							s74	s35 /90							4	1
Michael LUMB	9/1/88	AGF /Zenit (RUS)							D		s46						2	-
Jesper BECH	25/5/82	Silkeborg							s80								2	-
Michael KROHN-DEHLI	6/6/83	Brøndby							A	s67							5	-
Christian ERIKSEN	14/2/92	Ajax (NED)								s56	s72	M46		s73		s63	5	-
Rajko LEKIC	3/7/81	Silkeborg								s61							1	-
Peter NYMANN Mikkelsen	22/8/82	Esbjerg								s75							1	-
Kim CHRISTENSEN	16/7/79	Göteborg (SWE)									G46						1	-
Simon Busk POULSEN	7/10/84	AZ (NED)									D46		D34	D	D	D	8	-
Mikkel BECKMANN	24/10/83	Randers									M67	s82	s57	s62			6	-
Patrick MTILIGA	28/1/81	Málaga (ESP)									s46	D	s34				4	-

For a long time it seemed unlikely that Brøndby would match their third-place finish of the previous season, especially after they sold leading marksman Morten "Duncan" Rasmussen to Celtic FC in January, but a change of coach in late March, with former women's team boss Henrik Jensen replacing Kent Nielsen, turned things around and they came through to snatch a UEFA Europa League place from Esbjerg fB on the final day of the season with a 3-1 win at Randers FC.

Randers rescue act

Although Randers lost, they too had much to celebrate. With AGF simultaneously losing 3-0 at home to OB, it meant the Jutland club had pulled off one of the most remarkable escapes from relegation that Danish football – perhaps even European football – had ever witnessed. Rooted to the bottom of the table with just two points from their first 11 games, coach John Jensen, the former Arsenal FC and Denmark midfielder, was sacked and replaced by Ove Christensen. The switch did not immediately have the desired effect, but after registering their first win in the last game before the winter break – which lifted them off the bottom of the table but still left them 13 points from safety – Randers displayed championship-winning form for the last third of the campaign. Points were collected in every one of their spring matches as the team stitched together a 16-game unbeaten run that lasted right up to that final-day defeat against Brøndby, by which stage they had hauled themselves above AGF and out of the relegation zone. It was a miraculous comeback, and, just to add to the jubilation, Randers were rewarded with a Fair Play place in the 2010/11 UEFA Europa League. Furthermore, the driving force of their spring recovery, striker Mikkel Beckmann, earned himself a place in Denmark's World Cup squad.

Randers had also reached the 2009/10 UEFA Europa League via the Fair Play route. They went as far as the third qualifying round before bowing out to Hamburger SV – though not before a consolation 1-0 win in Germany. None of Denmark's three conventional qualifiers made it through the qualifying maze, either. Aalborg BK, European trailblazers in 2008/09, fell embarrassingly at the first hurdle to unsung FK Slavija Sarajevo, while OB and Brøndby, rather more predictably, came unstuck against Italian and German opposition, respectively, in the play-off round.

That left København to carry the Danish flag alone into the group stage, although they did so despondently after having wasted a glorious opportunity to follow in

the footsteps of AaB and reach the UEFA Champions League equivalent when they lost to Cypriot underdogs APOEL FC in the play-off round. FCK would qualify impressively for the UEFA Europa League round of 32 with a 3-0 win at AC Sparta Praha – in which N'Doye scored his eighth and ninth European goals of the season – before they lost home and away to Olympique de Marseille in February.

Debut Cup win

FCK were left to concentrate on the Superliga in the spring because they also exited the Danish Cup early, their defence of the trophy lasting only until the fourth round. With both Brøndby and AaB also going out at the same stage, the competition was left wide open, and it was FC Nordsjælland, coached by ex-Denmark international Morten Wieghorst, who seized the opportunity to claim their first major trophy – and a place in Europe - when they went on to win the final at Parken, beating FC Midtjylland 2-0 after extra-time with goals from Bajram Fetai and Nicolai Stokholm. It was a joyous day for the Farum club but a miserable one for their opponents, whose third appearance in the final had ended like the previous two – in defeat.

Nordsjælland's Nicolai Stokholm – a goalscorer in the club's Danish Cup final win over Midtjylland

DOMESTIC LEAGUE 2009/10

SUPERLIGA FINAL TABLE

	Pld	Home					Away					Total					Pts
		W	D	L	F	A	W	D	L	F	A	W	D	L	F	A	
FC København	33	13	2	2	40	10	8	3	5	21	12	21	5	7	61	22	68
Odense BK	33	9	4	4	20	14	8	4	4	26	20	17	8	8	46	34	59
Brøndby IF	33	6	5	6	30	27	9	2	5	27	23	15	7	11	57	50	52
Esbjerg fB	33	8	5	3	27	20	5	6	6	21	23	13	11	9	48	43	50
Aalborg BK	33	8	5	3	15	10	5	4	8	21	20	13	9	11	36	30	48
FC Midtjylland	33	10	3	4	28	20	4	2	10	17	28	14	5	14	45	48	47
FC Nordsjælland	33	5	4	7	17	20	7	3	7	23	21	12	7	14	40	41	43
Silkeborg IF	33	6	3	7	29	25	6	4	7	18	26	12	7	14	47	51	43
SønderjyskE	33	7	2	7	16	15	4	6	7	16	22	11	8	14	32	37	41
0 Randers FC	33	6	4	7	21	22	4	6	6	16	21	10	10	13	37	43	40
1 AGF Århus	33	4	6	7	17	27	6	2	8	19	20	10	8	15	36	47	38
2 HB Køge	33	2	3	11	13	32	2	4	11	17	37	4	7	22	30	69	19

TOP GOALSCORERS

18 Peter UTAKA (OB)
15 Tim JANSSEN (Esbjerg)
14 Dame N'DOYE (København)
13 Rajko LEKIC (Silkeborg)
12 Morten "Duncan" RASMUSSEN (Brøndby)
11 CÉSAR SANTIN (København)
   Christian HOLST (Silkeborg)
10 Mikkel BECKMANN (Randers)
   Kenneth FABRICIUS (SønderjyskE)
9 Frank KRISTENSEN (Midtjylland)

CLUB-BY-CLUB

AALBORG BK

Coach – Magnus Pehrsson (SWE)
Founded – 1885
Stadium – Energi Nord Arena (13,800)
MAJOR HONOURS:
Danish League - (3) 1995, 1999, 2008;
Danish Cup - (2) 1966, 1970.

2009
20/7	AGF	a	0-1	
2/8	Køge	a	5-0	*Curth, Schwartz, Johansson, Wæhler, Fredheim Holm*
9/8	Brøndby	a	2-0	*Johansson, Due*
15/8	SønderjyskE	h	1-0	*Chanko*
19/8	Nordsjælland	h	1-0	*Johansson*
23/8	Esbjerg	a	0-2	
30/8	Midtjylland	h	1-0	*Fredheim Holm*
14/9	Randers	a	3-0	*Curth, Nielsen L., Schwartz*
19/9	Silkeborg	h	0-1	
27/9	København	h	1-2	*Fredheim Holm*
5/10	OB	a	1-2	*Curth*
18/10	Randers	h	1-1	*Due*
25/10	Brøndby	h	1-2	*Kristensen*
2/11	OB	a	1-1	*Johansson*
8/11	København	h	1-0	*Tracy*
23/11	AGF	h	0-0	
28/11	Esbjerg	a	1-1	*Jakobsen*
5/12	SønderjyskE	a	0-2	

2010
8/3	Nordsjælland	h	2-1	*Chanko, Jakobsen (p)*
14/3	Midtjylland	a	0-2	
21/3	Køge	a	3-0	*Schwartz 2, Jakobsen (p)*
24/3	Silkeborg	h	1-0	*Johansson*
27/3	Nordsjælland	a	1-1	*Schwartz*
2/4	SønderjyskE	h	1-1	*Curth*
5/4	Silkeborg	a	1-1	*Chanko*
10/4	AGF	a	2-0	*Nielsen L, Johansson*
14/4	OB	h	1-0	*Rolfe*
19/4	Esbjerg	h	0-0	

25/4	København	a	0-2	
2/5	Midtjylland	h	3-2	*Johansson, Jakobsen (p), Petersen*
5/5	Randers	a	1-3	*Johansson*
9/5	Brøndby	a	0-2	
16/5	Køge	h	0-0	

No	Name	Nat	DoB	Pos	Aps	(s)	Gls
16	Kasper BØGELUND		8/10/80	D	28	(1)	
6	Louay CHANKO	SYR	29/11/79	M	25	(3)	3
36	Daniel CHRISTENSEN		19/9/88	M		(9)	
10	Jeppe CURTH		21/3/84	A	20	(6)	4
20	Henrik DALSGAARD		27/7/89	A	13	(12)	
7	Anders DUE		17/3/82	M	21	(6)	2
23	Thomas ENEVOLDSEN		27/7/87	M	5	(1)	
9	Daniel FREDHEIM HOLM	NOR	30/7/85	A	7	(6)	3
22	Thomas GAARDSØE		23/11/79	D	2	(4)	
28	Emil HAUCKE		17/1/89	D		(2)	
2	Michael JAKOBSEN		2/1/86	D	29		4
28	Nicklas Helenius JENSEN		8/5/91	A		(1)	
8	Andreas JOHANSSON	SWE	5/7/78	M	31	(1)	8
27	Patrick KRISTENSEN		28/4/87	M	22	(10)	1
15	Dennis MARSHALL	CRC	9/8/85	M		(1)	
26	Jakob Ahlmann NIELSEN		18/1/91	D		(1)	
31	Lasse NIELSEN		8/1/88	D	25	(1)	2
5	Kenneth Emil PETERSEN		15/1/85	D	18	(2)	1
17	Chris ROLFE	USA	17/1/83	M	4	(3)	1
32	Ronnie SCHWARTZ		29/8/89	A	15	(7)	5
24	Jens-Kristian SØRENSEN		21/3/87	M	3	(8)	
19	Marcus TRACY	USA	2/10/86	A	4	(4)	1
30	Mathias WICHMANN		6/8/91	M	1	(2)	
14	Rasmus WÜRTZ		18/9/83	M	30		
3	Kjetil WÆHLER	NOR	16/3/76	D	27		1
1	Karim ZAZA	MAR	9/1/75	G	33		

DENMARK

AGF ÅRHUS
Coach – Erik Rasmussen
Founded – 1880
Stadium – NRGi Park (20,032)
MAJOR HONOURS:
Danish League - (5) 1955, 1956, 1957, 1960, 1986;
Danish Cup - (9) 1955, 1957, 1960, 1961, 1965, 1987, 1988, 1992, 1996.

2009
20/7	AaB	h	1-0	Graulund
27/7	Randers	a	3-2	Howard, Rafael, Feilhaber
3/8	OB	h	2-2	Poulsen (p), Rafael
9/8	Køge	h	2-1	Devdariani, Poulsen (p)
15/8	København	a	1-0	Graulund
22/8	Silkeborg	h	2-2	Rafael, og (Larsen)
29/8	Nordsjælland	a	2-0	Rafael, Williams
13/9	Brøndby	a	0-1	
21/9	Midtjylland	h	2-4	Rafael, Graulund
28/9	Esbjerg	a	2-3	og (Vendelbo), Poulsen
3/10	SønderjyskE	h	2-1	og (Egholm), Graulund
19/10	SønderjyskE	a	0-1	
26/10	Nordsjælland	h	0-2	
31/10	Midtjylland	h	2-2	Graulund, og (Reid)
7/11	Køge	a	1-1	Krabbe
23/11	AaB	a	0-0	
29/11	Brøndby	h	1-0	Graulund
7/12	Esbjerg	h	1-1	Williams

2010
7/3	København	a	0-5	
15/3	Silkeborg	h	1-2	Kapidžić
21/3	OB	a	0-2	
25/3	Randers	a	1-2	Thomassen
28/3	København	h	0-0	
31/3	Esbjerg	a	4-0	Petersen 2, Devdariani, Høegh
4/4	Randers	h	0-0	
10/4	AaB	h	0-2	
14/4	Midtjylland	a	0-1	
18/4	Brøndby	a	0-1	
25/4	Køge	h	0-3	
1/5	Silkeborg	a	4-1	Graulund, Poulsen (p), Sloth 2
6/5	SønderjyskE	h	1-2	Graulund
9/5	Nordsjælland	a	1-0	Petersen
16/5	OB	h	0-3	

No	Name	Nat	DoB	Pos	Aps	(s)	Gls
20	Dennis CAGARA		19/2/85	D	13	(1)	
30	David DEVDARIANI	GEO	28/10/87	M	16	(8)	2
17	Benny FEILHABER	USA	19/1/85	M	21	(5)	1
19	Jens GJESING		13/1/86	M	12	(7)	
11	Peter GRAULUND		20/9/76	A	18	(2)	8
3	Mark HOWARD	ENG	29/1/86	D	8	(1)	1
35	Dennis HØEGH		21/2/89	A	3	(4)	1
10	Martin JØRGENSEN		6/10/75	M	12	(1)	
32	Sanel KAPIDŽIĆ		14/4/90	A	7	(4)	1
2	Frederik KRABBE		10/3/88	D	30	(1)	1
27	Anders KURE		12/9/85	D	15	(4)	
21	Jerry LUCENA		11/8/80	M	30	(1)	
28	Michael LUMB		9/1/88	D	17		
4	Kim MADSEN		13/2/78	D	1		
22	Alexander Jackson MØLLER		21/1/90	D	1	(1)	
5	Anders NIELSEN		28/9/86	D	3	(3)	
7	Stephan PETERSEN		15/11/85	M	10	(3)	3
14	Jakob POULSEN		7/7/83	M	22	(2)	4
25	Kasper POVLSEN		26/9/89	M	21	(5)	
10	Nando RAFAEL	GER	10/1/84	A	12	(4)	5
23	Anders RASMUSSEN		1/6/76	G	2	(1)	
1	Steffen RASMUSSEN		30/9/82	G	31		
38	Casper SLOTH		26/3/92	M	7	(7)	2
16	Dan THOMASSEN		24/3/81	D	30		1
15	Jeremiah WHITE	USA	4/4/82	M	6	(7)	
9	Dioh WILLIAMS	LBR	8/10/84	A	15	(11)	2

BRØNDBY IF
Coach – Kent Nielsen; (26/3/10) Henrik Jensen
Founded – 1964
Stadium – Brøndby Stadion (29,000)
MAJOR HONOURS:
Danish League - (10) 1985, 1987, 1988, 1990, 1991, 1996, 1997, 1998, 2002, 2005;
Danish Cup - (6) 1989, 1994, 1998, 2003, 2005, 2008.

2009
19/7	OB	h	2-2	Jallow (p), Jönsson
26/7	Esbjerg	a	1-2	Wass
2/8	Midtjylland	h	3-1	Holmén, Von Schlebrügge, Rasmussen T.
9/8	AaB	h	0-2	
16/8	Randers	a	3-1	Krohn-Dehli, Madsen, og (Jepsen)
23/8	Køge	h	6-1	Rasmussen M. 2 (1p), Farnerud, Jensen, Krohn-Dehli, Kanstrup
30/8	København	a	1-1	Rasmussen M.
13/9	AGF	h	1-0	Holmén
20/9	SønderjyskE	a	4-2	Rasmussen M. 2, Von Schlebrügge, Madsen (p)
27/9	Silkeborg	a	1-4	Kristiansen
4/10	Nordsjælland	h	6-3	Rasmussen M. 4 (1p), og (Novaković), Madsen
18/10	Midtjylland	h	1-1	Rasmussen M.
25/10	AaB	a	2-1	Jensen, Rasmussen M.
1/11	Nordsjælland	a	1-0	Bernburg
8/11	Esbjerg	h	2-4	Bernburg, og (Conboy)
22/11	OB	h	1-3	Rasmussen M.
29/11	AGF	a	0-1	
6/12	Silkeborg	a	0-3	

2010
7/3	SønderjyskE	h	1-1	Farnerud (p)
14/3	København	a	0-2	
22/3	Randers	h	1-1	Farnerud
25/3	Køge	h	1-3	Holmén
28/3	SønderjyskE	a	3-1	Nilsson, Jallow 2
1/4	Silkeborg	h	2-2	Jönsson, Krohn-Dehli (p)
4/4	Køge	a	2-1	Holmén, Wass
11/4	OB	a	1-0	Kristiansen
15/4	Nordsjælland	h	0-1	
18/4	AGF	h	1-0	Holmén
25/4	Esbjerg	a	1-1	Jallow
2/5	København	h	0-2	
5/5	Midtjylland	a	4-2	Krohn-Dehli (p), Kristiansen, Farnerud 2
9/5	AaB	h	2-0	Jallow, Kristiansen
16/5	Randers	a	3-1	Farnerud, Kristiansen 2

No	Name	Nat	DoB	Pos	Aps	(s)	Gls
18	Nicolaj AGGER		23/10/88	A	1	(1)	
16	Stephan ANDERSEN		26/11/81	G	31		
10	Martin BERNBURG		26/12/85	A	14	(5)	2
24	Mikkel BISCHOFF		3/2/82	D	25	(1)	
9	Alexander FARNERUD	SWE	1/5/84	A	21	(8)	6
5	Jan FREDERIKSEN		20/6/82	D	5	(4)	
20	Stefán GÍSLASON	ISL	15/3/80	M	6	(6)	
6	Samuel HOLMÉN	SWE	28/6/84	M	27		5
22	Ousman JALLOW	GAM	21/10/88	A	14	(9)	5
28	Paul JATTA	GAM	21/2/91	M	6		
26	Mike JENSEN		19/2/88	M	29	(1)	2
15	Jon JÖNSSON	SWE	8/7/83	D	7	(3)	2
34	Pierre KANSTRUP		21/2/89	D	1	(2)	1
27	Jan KRISTIANSEN		4/8/81	M	16	(14)	6
23	Michael KROHN-DEHLI		6/6/83	M	30	(2)	4
39	Jens LARSEN		21/2/91	M	8	(7)	
17	Peter MADSEN		26/4/78	A	3	(16)	3
32	Brent McGRATH	AUS	18/6/91	A		(6)	
8	Mikael NILSSON	SWE	24/6/78	D	30		1

2	Anders RANDRUP		16/7/88	D	15	(5)	
11	Morten "Duncan" RASMUSSEN		31/1/85	A	14	(1)	12
21	Thomas RASMUSSEN		16/4/77	D	16	(1)	1
1	Michael TØRNES		8/1/86	G	2		
4	Remco VAN DER SCHAAF	NED	28/2/79	D	14		
3	Max VON SCHLEBRÜGGE	SWE	1/2/77	D	19		2
29	Daniel WASS		31/5/89	D	9	(3)	2

ESBJERG FB
Coach – Ove Pedersen
Founded – 1924
Stadium – Blue Water Arena (18,000)
MAJOR HONOURS:
Danish League – (5) 1961, 1962, 1963, 1965, 1979;
Danish Cup – (2) 1964, 1976.

2009
18/7	Midtjylland	a	0-0	
26/7	Brøndby	h	2-1	*Nymann 2*
1/8	SønderjyskE	a	1-1	*Høgh*
9/8	OB	h	1-2	*Janssen*
16/8	Silkeborg	a	3-2	*Janssen, Rieks, Lange*
23/8	AaB	h	2-0	*Jørgensen (p), Mehl*
30/8	Randers	a	1-0	*Mehl*
13/9	Køge	h	3-2	*Janssen, Høgh, Lange*
20/9	Nordsjælland	a	4-0	*Vendelbo, Janssen, Rieks 2*
28/9	AGF	h	3-2	*Janssen 2, Jørgensen*
4/10	København	a	1-2	*Rieks*
18/10	Silkeborg	a	2-2	*Jørgensen (p), Björck*
25/10	SønderjyskE	h	2-0	*Mehl, Vendelbo*
1/11	København	h	0-0	
8/11	Brøndby	a	4-2	*Björck, Janssen, Rieks 2*
21/11	Midtjylland	a	0-3	
28/11	AaB	h	1-1	*Janssen*
7/12	AGF	a	1-1	*Lange*

2010
7/3	Randers	h	0-0	
14/3	Køge	h	2-1	*Janssen, Mehl*
21/3	Nordsjælland	a	0-1	
25/3	OB	h	1-2	*Vendelbo*
28/3	Randers	a	0-4	
31/3	AGF	a	0-4	
5/4	OB	a	0-0	
11/4	Midtjylland	h	2-1	*Vendelbo, Lange*
14/4	København	a	2-3	*Vendelbo, Janssen*
19/4	AaB	a	0-0	
25/4	Brøndby	h	1-1	*Vendelbo*
2/5	Køge	a	2-1	*Lange, Janssen*
6/5	Silkeborg	h	4-0	*Janssen 3, Mehl*
9/5	SønderjyskE	a	0-1	
16/5	Nordsjælland	h	3-3	*Mehl, Janssen, Nymann*

No	Name	Nat	DoB	Pos	Aps	(s)	Gls
21	Sebastian Lykke ANDERSEN		23/12/88	M	2	(1)	
19	Peter ANKERSEN		22/9/90	D		(1)	
21	Fredrik BJÖRCK	SWE	22/10/79	D	17		2
32	Martin BRAITHWAITE	CAN	5/6/91	A		(10)	
4	Adrian CANN	CAN	19/9/80	D		(5)	
20	Kennie CHOPART		1/6/90	A		(3)	
4	Morten CHRISTENSEN		11/5/79	D		(1)	
13	Kevin CONBOY		15/10/87	D	23		
5	Thomas GAARDSØE		23/11/79	D	12		
19	Kian HANSEN		3/3/89	D	9	(4)	
1	Lukáš HRÁDECKÝ	FIN	24/11/89	G	3	(2)	
24	Nicolai HØGH		9/11/83	D	31		2
10	Tim JANSSEN	NED	6/3/86	A	31	(1)	15
7	Jesper JØRGENSEN		9/5/84	M	31		3
15	Andreas KLARSTRÖM	SWE	23/12/77	D	30	(1)	
23	Jonas KNUDSEN		16/9/92	D	4	(3)	
14	Jones KUSI-ASARE	SWE	21/5/80	A	1	(4)	

22	Jesper LANGE		11/1/86	A	18	(13)	5
18	Jeppe MEHL		21/9/86	M	31	(1)	6
11	Peter NYMANN Mikkelsen		22/8/82	M	31	(2)	3
31	Søren RIEKS		7/4/87	M	29	(1)	6
6	Mikael RYNELL	SWE	25/2/82	M	5	(11)	
9	Gunnar Heidar THORVALDSSON	ISL	1/4/82	A		(2)	
17	Kevin Bechmann TIMM		9/7/89	A		(2)	
12	Emmanuel UKPAI	NGA	11/10/87	A		(15)	
26	Mikkel VENDELBO		15/8/87	M	25		6
16	Lars WINDE		3/12/75	G	30		

FC KØBENHAVN
Coach – Ståle Solbakken (NOR)
Founded – 1992
Stadium – Parken (38,010)
MAJOR HONOURS:
Danish League- (8) 1993, 2001, 2003, 2004, 2006, 2007, 2009, 2010;
Danish Cup - (4) 1995, 1997, 2004, 2009.

2009
18/7	Nordsjælland	a	0-2	
25/7	Køge	h	7-1	*Jørgensen M., Pospěch, Aílton,*
				César Santin, Nordstrand,
				N'Doye, Vingaard
1/8	Silkeborg	h	1-1	*Nordstrand (p)*
9/8	SønderjyskE	a	1-0	*Nørregaard*
15/8	AGF	h	0-1	
22/8	Midtjylland	a	4-1	*Jørgensen M., N'Doye, Vingaard,*
				Jørgensen W.K.
30/8	Brøndby	h	1-1	*Aílton*
12/9	OB	a	1-1	*Vingaard (p)*
20/9	Randers	h	3-0	*Pospěch 2, Vingaard*
27/9	AaB	a	2-1	*Hutchinson 2*
4/10	Esbjerg	h	2-1	*César Santin (p), Wendt*
18/10	Køge	a	2-0	*Antonsson, Grønkjær*
25/10	Silkeborg	h	1-0	*César Santin*
1/11	Esbjerg	a	0-0	
8/11	AaB	a	0-1	
22/11	Randers	h	2-0	*Aílton 2*
29/11	Midtjylland	h	2-0	*Hutchinson, N'Doye*
6/12	OB	a	2-0	*N'Doye 2*

2010
7/3	AGF	h	5-0	*César Santin 3 (1p), Vingaard,*
				Jørgensen M.
14/3	Brøndby	h	2-0	*Vingaard, Jørgensen W.K.*
21/3	SønderjyskE	a	2-0	*César Santin, og (Østli)*
24/3	Nordsjælland	h	2-0	
28/3	AGF	a	0-0	
1/4	OB	h	2-0	*N'Doye, Grønkjær*
5/4	Nordsjælland	a	3-0	*Pospěch, Wendt, César Santin*
11/4	Randers	a	0-1	
14/4	Esbjerg	h	3-2	*Nørregaard, César Santin,*
				N'Doye 2
17/4	Midtjylland	a	2-3	*N'Doye 2*
25/4	AaB	h	2-0	*César Santin (p), Pospěch*
2/5	Brøndby	a	2-0	*Jørgensen M., N'Doye*
5/5	Køge	h	4-0	*N'Doye 2, Pospěch, Nørregaard*
9/5	Silkeborg	a	0-2	
16/5	SønderjyskE	h	3-1	*N'Doye 2, César Santin*

No	Name	Nat	DoB	Pos	Aps	(s)	Gls
7	AÍLTON José Almeida	BRA	20/8/84	A	15	(10)	4
15	Mikael ANTONSSON	SWE	31/5/81	D	26		1
11	CÉSAR SANTIN	BRA	24/2/81	A	22	(5)	11
1	Jesper CHRISTIANSEN		24/4/78	G	10	(1)	
27	Thomas DELANEY		3/9/91	M	1	(8)	
10	Jesper GRØNKJÆR		12/8/77	M	20	(9)	2
13	Atiba HUTCHINSON	CAN	8/2/83	M	30		3
25	Mathias "Zanka" JØRGENSEN		23/4/90	D	20	(4)	4
8	William Kvist JØRGENSEN		24/2/85	M	32	(1)	2

DENMARK

16	Thomas KRISTENSEN		17/4/83	M	5	(18)	
12	Peter LARSSON	SWE	30/4/84	D	9	(3)	
5	Ulrik LAURSEN		28/2/76	D	11	(2)	
14	Dame N'DOYE	SEN	21/2/85	A	24	(8)	14
9	Morten NORDSTRAND		8/6/83	A	1	(4)	2
4	Hjalte Bo NØRREGAARD		8/4/81	M	28	(3)	3
19	Bryan OVIEDO	CRC	18/2/90	D		(3)	
28	Saban ÖZDOGAN		14/3/90	M		(2)	
2	Zdeněk POSPĚCH	CZE	14/12/78	D	30	(1)	6
24	Libor SIONKO	CZE	1/2/77	M	1	(3)	
20	Martin VINGAARD		20/3/85	M	22	(10)	6
17	Oscar WENDT	SWE	24/10/85	D	33		2
21	Johan WILAND	SWE	24/1/81	G	23	(1)	
18	Kenneth Dahrup ZOHORE		31/1/94	A		(1)	

HB KØGE
Coach – Aurelijus Skarbalius (LTU)
Founded – 2009
Stadium – SEAS-NVE Park (8,000)

2009

19/7	Silkeborg	h	1-1	Nielsen M.
25/7	København	a	1-7	Ake
2/8	AaB	h	0-5	
9/8	AGF	a	1-2	Fabinho
16/8	Nordsjælland	h	1-1	Fabinho
23/8	Brøndby	a	1-6	Toft (p)
30/8	SønderjyskE	h	1-0	Nielsen S.
13/9	Esbjerg	a	2-3	Ake 2
20/9	OB	h	1-3	Fabinho
27/9	Randers	a	1-1	Ake
4/10	Midtjylland	a	1-2	Andersen
18/10	København	h	0-2	
25/10	Midtjylland	a	1-2	Ake
1/11	SønderjyskE	a	0-0	
7/11	AGF	h	1-1	og (Gjesing)
21/11	Nordsjælland	h	1-2	Christoffersen S.
30/11	OB	a	0-1	
6/12	Randers	a	1-2	Nielsen S.

2010

7/3	Silkeborg	h	1-4	Antipas
14/3	Esbjerg	a	1-2	Toft
21/3	AaB	h	0-3	
25/3	Brøndby	a	3-1	Laudrup, Sørensen K., Pedersen
28/3	Silkeborg	a	0-3	
1/4	Randers	h	1-2	Toft
4/4	Brøndby	h	1-2	Storm
12/4	Nordsjælland	a	1-1	Toft
15/4	SønderjyskE	h	1-2	Toft
18/4	OB	h	1-2	Toft
25/4	AGF	a	3-0	Rømer, Madsen, Antipas
2/5	Esbjerg	h	1-2	Toft
5/5	København	a	0-4	
9/5	Midtjylland	h	1-0	Antipas
16/5	AaB	a	0-0	

No	Name	Nat	DoB	Pos	Aps	(s)	Gls
19	Emmanuel AKE	KEN	11/6/80	A	12	(1)	5
2	Martin ALTOFELT		25/1/85	D	15	(1)	
8	Sebastian Lykke ANDERSEN		23/12/88	M	10	(6)	1
11	Quincy ANTIPAS	ZIM	20/4/84	A	9	(4)	3
1	Lars BJERRING		30/11/81	G	33		
4	Thomas Guldborg CHRISTENSEN		20/1/84	D	17		
18	Mikkel CHRISTOFFERSEN		10/8/83	D	16	(5)	
21	Simon Makienok CHRISTOFFERSEN		21/11/90	A		(10)	1
28	Alexander DIGE		21/4/92	D		(2)	
30	Martin DUE		27/11/92	A		(1)	
22	Fábio Trindade da Silveira "FABINHO"	BRA	26/5/77	A	17	(7)	3

24	Patrick HANSEN		15/4/91	M		(2)	
5	Stefan HANSEN		18/5/89	D	13	(2)	
28	Ömer KARATAS		31/10/90	A		(1)	
3	Lasse KRONBORG		3/4/86	M	14	(6)	
10	Mads LAUDRUP		9/2/89	M	13		1
9	Rytis LELIŪGA	LTU	4/1/87	M	7	(6)	
15	Nicolaj MADSEN		16/7/88	M	15	(4)	1
16	Arman MEHAKOVIĆ	BIH	9/3/88	A	1	(14)	
23	Morten NIELSEN		14/8/82	D	22		1
26	Søren NIELSEN		14/8/82	M	28	(1)	2
14	Mark Leth PEDERSEN		17/8/89	A	6	(6)	1
11	ROBERTO SARAIVA Fagundas	BRA	5/2/83	M	4	(5)	
27	Marcel RØMER		8/8/91	M	13	(5)	1
12	Anders SIMONSEN		9/3/83	M	3	(2)	
30	Nicklas SVENDSEN		11/12/86	D	8	(1)	
7	Bo STORM		3/2/87	A	13		1
6	Kenneth SØRENSEN		14/3/82	M	16	(1)	1
17	Thomas SØRENSEN		1/8/84	D	25	(1)	
13	Henrik TOFT		15/4/81	A	33		7

FC MIDTJYLLAND
Coach – Thomas Thomasberg; (12/8/09) Allan Kuhn
Founded – 1999
Stadium – MCH Arena (11,809)

2009

18/7	Esbjerg	h	0-0	
26/7	Silkeborg	a	0-4	
2/8	Brøndby	a	1-3	Olsen
9/8	Randers	h	4-1	Kristensen F., Olsen, Borring, Sivebæk
17/8	OB	a	0-1	
22/8	København	h	1-4	Olsen
30/8	AaB	a	0-1	
12/9	Nordsjælland	h	0-2	
21/9	AGF	a	4-2	Ilsø, Hübertz, Borring, Kristensen F.
27/9	SønderjyskE	h	0-2	
4/10	Køge	a	2-1	Kristensen F. 2
18/10	Brøndby	a	1-1	Kristensen F.
25/10	Køge	h	2-1	Borring, Olsen
31/10	AGF	a	2-2	Olsen, og (Gjesing)
8/11	Randers	a	2-1	Thygesen, Ilsø
21/11	Esbjerg	h	3-0	Ipša, Borring, Thygesen
29/11	København	a	0-2	
6/12	Nordsjælland	a	0-3	

2010

6/3	OB	h	2-2	Kristensen F. 2
14/3	AaB	h	2-0	Borring, Kristensen F.
20/3	Silkeborg	a	2-0	Ilsø, Babatunde
25/3	SønderjyskE	h	0-0	
29/3	OB	a	2-1	Afriyie, Babatunde
1/4	Nordsjælland	h	1-0	Sivebæk
5/4	SønderjyskE	a	2-0	Ilsø, Thygesen
11/4	Esbjerg	a	1-2	Borring
14/4	AGF	h	1-0	Sviatchenko
17/4	København	h	3-2	Borring 2, Ilsø
26/4	Randers	a	0-2	
2/5	AaB	a	2-3	Albrechtsen, Babatunde
5/5	Brøndby	h	2-4	Babatunde, Ilsø
9/5	Køge	a	0-1	
16/5	Silkeborg	h	3-0	Uzochukwu, Afriyie, Kristensen F.

No	Name	Nat	DoB	Pos	Aps	(s)	Gls
3	Kolja AFRIYIE	GER	6/4/82	D	18	(3)	2
5	Martin ALBRECHTSEN		31/3/80	D	22		1
17	Mads Winther ALBÆK		14/1/90	M	16	(12)	
30	Babajide Collins BABATUNDE	NGA	2/1/88	A	8	(3)	4
8	Jonas BORRING		4/1/85	M	32		8
26	Jesper BØGE		22/2/90	D		(1)	
4	Danny CALIFF	USA	17/3/80	D	4	(1)	

No	Name	Nat	DoB	Pos	Aps	(s)	Gls
12	Kim CHRISTENSEN		8/5/80	A	3	(1)	
24	Ken FAGERBERG	SWE	9/1/89	A		(1)	
9	George FLORESCU	ROU	21/5/84	M	15	(2)	
21	Kasper HANSEN		15/2/91	M		(1)	
36	Rilwan Olanrewaju HASSAN	NGA	9/2/91	M		(4)	
28	Poul HÜBERTZ		21/9/76	A	2	(5)	1
22	Mads HVILSOM		23/8/92	A		(1)	
44	Sylvester IGBOUN	NGA	8/9/90	A		(1)	
7	Ken ILSØ		2/12/86	A	23	(2)	6
20	Kristijan IPŠA	CRO	4/4/86	D	21	(2)	1
19	Leon JESSEN		11/6/86	D	27	(1)	
23	Frank KRISTENSEN		10/3/77	A	14	(7)	9
6	Jesper Juelsgård KRISTENSEN		26/1/89	D	6	(1)	
49	Jonas LÖSSL		1/2/89	G	12		
18	Filip MARČIĆ	CRO	22/2/85	D	1	(1)	
39	Jude Ikechukwu NWORUH	NGA	9/6/89	A	4	(9)	
26	Sekou OLISEH	NGA	5/6/90	M		(1)	
11	Danny OLSEN		11/6/85	M	16	(8)	5
25	Arkadiusz ONYSZKO	POL	12/1/74	G	13		
15	Christopher POULSEN		11/9/81	D	2	(2)	
16	Martin RAŠKA	CZE	31/1/77	G	8		
29	Winston REID	NZL	3/7/88	D	29		
27	Adigun Taofeek SALAMI	NGA	6/5/88	M	9	(4)	
34	Christian SIVEBÆK		19/2/88	M	9	(14)	2
18	Erik SVIATCHENKO		4/10/91	D	3	(2)	1
10	Mikkel THYGESEN		22/10/84	M	31	(1)	3
43	Izunna Arnest UZOCHUKWU	NGA	11/4/90	M	15	(5)	1

FC NORDSJÆLLAND
Coach – Morten Wieghorst
Founded – 2003
Stadium – Farum Park (10,100)
MAJOR HONOURS:
Danish Cup - (1) 2010.

2009

18/7	København	h	2-0	Petersen, Bernburg
2/8	Randers		2-2	Petersen, Stokholm
8/8	Silkeborg	h	3-0	Lawan, Petersen, Bernburg
16/8	Køge	a	1-1	Lawan
19/8	AaB	a	0-1	
23/8	SønderjyskE	a	0-1	
29/8	AGF	h	0-2	
12/9	Midtjylland	a	2-0	Nielsen N.B., Lawan
20/9	Esbjerg	h	0-4	
26/9	OB	a	0-2	
4/10	Brøndby	a	3-6	Petersen, Lawan, Nielsen N.B.
17/10	OB	h	0-2	
26/10	AGF	a	2-0	Christensen, Nielsen N.B.
1/11	Brøndby	h	0-2	
8/11	SønderjyskE	a	1-0	Zuma
21/11	Køge	a	2-1	Lawan 2
29/11	Silkeborg	h	0-1	
6/12	Midtjylland	h	3-0	Stokholm, Nielsen N.B., Lawan

2010

8/3	AaB	a	1-2	Nielsen N.B.
14/3	Randers	a	0-0	
21/3	Esbjerg	h	1-0	og (Hansen)
24/3	København	a	2-0	Bernier, Nielsen N.B.
27/3	AaB	h	1-1	Laudrup
1/4	Midtjylland	a	0-1	
5/4	København	h	0-3	
12/4	Køge	h	1-1	Nielsen N.B.
15/4	Brøndby	a	1-0	Fetai
18/4	Silkeborg	a	4-1	Fetai 2, Nielsen N.B., Bernier
25/4	SønderjyskE	h	3-1	Granskov 2, Fetai
2/5	Randers	h	1-1	Mikkelsen
6/5	OB	a	1-2	Bengtsson
9/5	AGF	h	0-1	
16/5	Esbjerg	a	3-3	Bjelland, Granskov, Mikkelsen

No	Name	Nat	DoB	Pos	Aps	(s)	Gls
27	Pierre BENGTSSON	SWE	12/4/88	D	19	(1)	1
9	Martin BERNBURG		26/12/85	A	1	(2)	2
8	Patrice BERNIER	CAN	23/9/79	M	22	(5)	2
5	Andreas BJELLAND		11/7/88	D	22		1
3	Dennis CAGARA		19/2/85	D	11	(2)	
17	Søren CHRISTENSEN		29/6/86	M	18	(7)	1
15	Bajram FETAI		7/9/85	A	21	(10)	4
24	Andreas GRANSKOV		5/3/89	A	3	(6)	3
19	Mark GUNDELACH		7/1/92	D		(1)	
1	Jesper HANSEN		31/3/85	G	21		
23	Daniel JENSEN		8/5/85	D	2		
6	Morten KARLSEN		25/3/79	M	11	(1)	
2	Benjamin KIBEBE	SWE	13/8/81	D	26		
4	Henrik KILDENTOFT		18/3/85	D	28		
22	Andreas LAUDRUP		10/11/90	M	6	(9)	1
12	Rawez LAWAN	SWE	4/10/87	A	24	(6)	7
9	Tobias MIKKELSEN		18/9/86	M	6	(11)	2
20	Matti Lund NIELSEN		8/5/88	M	10	(3)	
16	Nicki Bille NIELSEN		7/2/88	A	25	(7)	8
25	Nenad NOVAKOVIĆ	SRB	14/7/82	G	12		
18	Michael PARKHURST	USA	24/1/84	D	23		
20	Stephan PETERSEN		15/11/85	M	13	(2)	4
33	Philip RASMUSSEN		12/1/89	M	4	(12)	
26	Jonathan RICHTER		16/1/85	M		(1)	
7	Nicolai STOKHOLM		1/4/76	M	29	(1)	2
13	Mads THOMSEN		15/3/89	A		(1)	
10	Sibusiso ZUMA	RSA	23/6/75	A	6	(7)	1

ODENSE BK
Coach – Lars Olsen
Founded – 1887
Stadium – Fionia Park (15,790)
MAJOR HONOURS:
Danish League - (3) 1977, 1982, 1989;
Danish Cup - (5) 1983, 1991, 1993, 2002, 2007.

2009

19/7	Brøndby	a	2-2	Sørensen (p), Demba-Nyrén
25/7	SønderjyskE	h	3-1	Absalonsen, Håland, Utaka
3/8	AGF	a	2-2	Utaka, Demba-Nyrén
9/8	Esbjerg	a	2-1	Cacá, Utaka
17/8	Midtjylland	h	1-0	Utaka
24/8	Randers	h	1-0	Hansen H.
31/8	Silkeborg	a	1-3	Utaka
12/9	København	a	1-1	Utaka
20/9	Køge	a	3-1	Sørensen (p), og 2 (Svendsen 2)
26/9	Nordsjælland	h	2-0	Gíslason, Absalonsen
5/10	AaB	h	2-1	Utaka 2
17/10	Nordsjælland	a	2-0	Ruud, Utaka
24/10	Randers	a	1-1	Utaka
2/11	AaB	a	1-1	Utaka
7/11	Silkeborg	a	1-0	og (Larsen)
22/11	Brøndby	a	3-1	Utaka, Sørensen (p), Absalonsen
30/11	Køge	h	1-0	Utaka
6/12	København	h	0-2	

2010

6/3	Midtjylland	a	2-2	Gíslason, Sørensen
13/3	SønderjyskE	h	1-1	Hansen H.
21/3	AGF	h	2-0	Utaka, Cacá
25/3	Esbjerg	a	2-1	Sørensen, Gíslason
29/3	Midtjylland	h	1-2	Utaka
1/4	København	a	0-2	
5/4	Esbjerg	h	0-0	
11/4	Brøndby	h	0-1	
14/4	AaB	a	0-1	
18/4	Køge	a	2-1	Håland, Andreasen
24/4	Silkeborg	h	1-0	Utaka
3/5	SønderjyskE	a	0-2	
6/5	Nordsjælland	h	2-1	Utaka 2
9/5	Randers	h	1-3	Cacá
16/5	AGF	a	3-0	Demba-Nyrén 2, Andreasen

No	Name	Nat	DoB	Pos	Aps	(s)	Gls
11	Johan ABSALONSEN		16/9/85	M	26		3
4	Hans Henrik ANDREASEN		10/1/79	M	29	(2)	2
17	Lucas de Deus Santos "CACÁ"	BRA	9/10/82	A	17	(15)	3
30	Roy CARROLL	NIR	30/9/77	G	28		
5	Anders Møller CHRISTENSEN		26/7/77	D	30	(1)	
22	Njogu DEMBA-NYRÉN	SWE	26/6/79	A	15	(15)	4
19	Eric DJEMBA-DJEMBA	CMR	4/5/81	M	18	(1)	
33	Rasmus FALK		15/1/92	M		(1)	
25	Oliver FELDBALLE		3/4/90	A	1	(6)	
21	Rúrik GÍSLASON	ISL	25/2/88	M	24	(4)	3
30	Alexander Lund HANSEN	NOR	6/10/82	G	1	(2)	
14	Esben HANSEN		10/8/81	M	9	(9)	
8	Henrik HANSEN		28/7/79	M	11	(17)	2
6	Thomas HELVEG		24/6/71	D	14	(5)	
3	Atle Roar HÅLAND	NOR	26/7/77	D	28		2
28	Anders Kvindebjerg JACOBSEN		27/10/89	A		(1)	
1	Anders LINDEGAARD		13/4/84	G	4		
10	Björn RUNSTRÖM	SWE	1/3/84	A		(2)	
2	Espen RUUD	NOR	28/2/84	M	30	(2)	1
15	Chris SØRENSEN		27/7/77	D	32		5
18	Jonas TROEST		4/3/85	D	13	(2)	
7	Peter UTAKA	NGA	12/2/84	A	33		18

RANDERS FC

Coach – John "Faxe" Jensen; (7/10/09) Ove Christensen
Founded – 1898
Stadium – Essex Park (12,000)
MAJOR HONOURS:
Danish Cup - (4) 1967, 1968, 1973, 2006.

2009

19/7	SønderjyskE	a	0-1	
27/7	AGF	h	2-3	*Pedersen K.M., Lorentzen*
2/8	Nordsjælland	a	2-2	*Beckmann, Berg*
9/8	Midtjylland	a	1-4	*Pedersen K.M. (p)*
16/8	Brøndby	h	1-3	*Berg*
24/8	OB	a	0-1	
30/8	Esbjerg	h	0-1	
14/9	AaB	h	0-3	
20/9	København	a	0-3	
27/9	Køge	h	1-1	*Sane*
4/10	Silkeborg	h	1-2	*Pedersen K.M.*
18/10	AaB	a	1-1	*Júnior*
24/10	OB	h	1-1	*Berg*
1/11	Silkeborg	h	0-2	
8/11	Midtjylland	a	1-2	*Beckmann*
22/11	København	a	0-2	
29/11	SønderjyskE	h	0-0	
6/12	Køge	h	2-1	*Beckmann, Berg*

2010

7/3	Esbjerg	a	0-0	
14/3	Nordsjælland	h	0-0	
22/3	Brøndby	a	1-1	*Fischer*
25/3	AGF	h	2-1	*Olsen, Jensen*
28/3	Esbjerg	h	4-0	*Pedersen, Beckmann, Berg, Movsisyan (p)*
1/4	Køge	a	2-1	*Jensen, Beckmann*
4/4	AGF	a	0-0	
11/4	København	h	1-0	*Beckmann*
14/4	Silkeborg	a	3-1	*Movsisyan 2, Beckmann*
18/4	SønderjyskE	a	1-0	*Egholm*
26/4	Midtjylland	h	2-0	*Movsisyan 2*
2/5	Nordsjælland	a	1-1	*Beckmann*
5/5	AaB	h	3-1	*og (Bøgelund), Movsisyan, Beckmann*
9/5	OB	a	3-1	*Berg, Beckmann, Movsisyan*
16/5	Brøndby	h	1-3	*og (Bischoff)*

No	Name	Nat	DoB	Pos	Aps	(s)	Gls
7	David ADDY	GHA	21/2/90	M	10	(2)	
4	Issah AHMED	GHA	24/5/82	D	5		
24	Robert ARZUMANYAN	ARM	24/7/86	D	10	(6)	
11	Mikkel BECKMANN		24/10/83	A	29	(2)	10
10	Søren BERG		15/5/76	M	29		6
35	Michael BYSKOV		20/2/88	M	1	(3)	
40	Nicolas BØGILD		23/2/88	A	2	(2)	
18	Nathan COE	AUS	1/6/84	G	4		
39	Mikkel CRAMER		25/1/92	D		(1)	
12	Jonas DAMBORG		17/4/86	M	21	(4)	
5	Anders EGHOLM		15/5/83	D	14		1
1	Kevin Stuhr ELLEGAARD		23/5/83	G	29		
36	Mads FENGER		10/9/90	D	25		
21	Alexander FISCHER		16/9/86	D	13	(5)	2
3	Bobbie FRIBERG DA CRUZ	SWE	16/2/82	D	12		
20	Christopher GEERTSEN		24/1/93	M		(1)	
9	Tobias GRAHN	SWE	5/3/80	M	3	(5)	
14	Esben HANSEN		10/8/81	M	2	(2)	
16	Søren JENSEN		1/3/84	D	14	(1)	2
6	Allan Kierstein JEPSEN		4/7/77	D	12		
90	José Luiz Guimarães Sanabio "JÚNIOR"	BRA	15/6/76	A	7	(3)	1
7	Morten KARLSEN		25/3/79	M	14		
17	Danni KÖNIG		17/12/86	A		(7)	
6	Kasper LORENTZEN		19/11/85	M	23	(9)	1
9	Yura MOVSISYAN	ARM	2/8/87	A	13		7
30	Marc NYGAARD		1/9/76	A	10	(12)	
15	Ricki OLSEN		21/10/88	M	3	(15)	1
14	Kenneth Møller PEDERSEN		18/4/73	M	15	(3)	3
8	Søren PEDERSEN		2/11/78	D	32		
31	Tidiane SANE	SEN	10/7/85	M	11	(7)	1

SILKEBORG IF

Coach – Troels Bech
Founded – 1917
Stadium – Silkeborg Stadion (9,200)
MAJOR HONOURS:
Danish League - (1) 1994;
Danish Cup - (1) 2001.

2009

19/7	Køge	a	1-1	*Bech*
26/7	Midtjylland	h	4-0	*Lekic 3, Nielsen*
1/8	København	a	1-1	*Bech*
8/8	Nordsjælland	a	0-3	
16/8	Esbjerg	h	2-3	*Lekic, Saag*
22/8	AGF	a	2-2	*Holst, Bech*
31/8	OB	h	3-1	*Saag, Bech 2*
13/9	SønderjyskE	h	1-1	*Degn*
19/9	AaB	a	1-0	*Lekic*
27/9	Brøndby	h	4-1	*Holst 2, Larsen, Lekic (p)*
4/10	Randers	a	2-1	*Nielsen, Svensson*
18/10	Esbjerg	h	2-2	*Holst, Lekic*
25/10	København	a	0-1	
1/11	Randers	a	2-0	*Hansen F., Lekic*
7/11	OB	h	0-1	
22/11	SønderjyskE	h	1-2	*Lekic*
29/11	Nordsjælland	a	1-0	*Holst*
6/12	Brøndby	h	3-0	*Lekic, Svensson, Bech*

2010

7/3	Køge	a	4-1	*Bech, Degn 2, Holst*
15/3	AGF	a	2-1	*Flinta, Lekic*
20/3	Midtjylland	h	0-2	
24/3	AaB	a	0-1	
28/3	Køge	h	3-0	*Holst 3*
1/4	Brøndby	a	2-2	*Degn, Bech*
5/4	AaB	h	1-1	*Lekic (p)*
11/4	SønderjyskE	a	0-4	
14/4	Randers	h	1-3	*Nielsen*
18/4	Nordsjælland	h	1-4	*Holst*

24/4	OB	a	0-1	
1/5	AGF	h	1-4	*Flinta*
6/5	Esbjerg	a	0-4	
9/5	København	h	2-0	*Lekic, Holst*
16/5	Midtjylland	a	0-3	

No	Name	Nat	DoB	Pos	Aps	(s)	Gls
10	Jesper BECH		25/5/82	A	30		8
15	Thomas BÆLUM		5/6/78	D	4	(3)	
7	Peter DEGN		6/4/77	M	22	(4)	4
14	Dennis FLINTA		14/11/83	M	19	(11)	2
20	Frank HANSEN		23/2/83	D	32		1
16	Thomas HANSEN		18/1/83	D	23	(7)	
30	Lasse HEINZE		3/4/86	G	32		
18	Christian Lamhauge HOLST	FRO	25/12/81	M	28	(5)	11
24	Lars HULDGAARD		1/2/89	A		(8)	
4	Jim LARSEN		6/11/85	D	31		1
8	Rajko LEKIC		3/7/81	A	32		13
2	Steven LUSTÜ		13/4/71	D	17		
6	Martin Ørnskov NIELSEN		10/10/85	M	31	(1)	3
31	Thomas NØRGAARD		7/1/87	G	1		
11	Henrik "Tømrer" PEDERSEN		10/6/75	D	14	(5)	
9	Simon Azoulay PEDERSEN		14/12/82	A	6	(13)	
5	Christopher POULSEN		11/9/81	D	13	(2)	
26	Thorbjørn Holst RASMUSSEN		21/3/87	M	18	(2)	
17	Kaimar SAAG	EST	5/8/88	A	4	(15)	2
22	Martin SVENSSON		10/8/89	M	5	(15)	2
28	Mathias VALENTIN		29/3/89	D	1	(1)	

SØNDERJYSKE
Coach – (Michael Hemmingsen); (14/9/09) Frank Andersen
Founded – 2004
Stadium – Haderslev Fodboldstadion (10,000)

2009

19/7	Randers	h	1-0	*Fabricius*
25/7	OB	a	1-3	*Frederiksen*
1/8	Esbjerg	h	1-1	*Thomson*
9/8	København	h	0-1	
15/8	AaB	a	0-1	
23/8	Nordsjælland	h	1-0	*Fabricius*
30/8	Køge	a	0-1	
13/9	Silkeborg	a	1-1	*Østli*
20/9	Brøndby	h	2-4	*Fabricius, Kjærulff*
27/9	Midtjylland	a	2-0	*Egholm, Fabricius*
3/10	AGF	a	1-2	*Agger*
19/10	AGF	h	1-0	*Fabricius*
25/10	Esbjerg	a	0-2	
1/11	Køge	h	0-0	
8/11	Nordsjælland	h	0-1	
22/11	Silkeborg	a	2-1	*Sidorenkov, Fabricius*
29/11	Randers	a	0-0	
5/12	AaB	h	2-0	*Hansen, Frederiksen*

2010

7/3	Brøndby	a	1-1	*Ottesen*
13/3	OB	a	1-1	*Fabricius*
21/3	København	h	0-2	
25/3	Midtjylland	a	0-0	
28/3	Brøndby	h	1-3	*Thomson*
2/4	AaB	a	1-1	*Bødker*
5/4	Midtjylland	h	0-2	
11/4	Silkeborg	h	4-0	*Jessen 2, Fabricius, Kjærulff*
15/4	Køge	a	2-1	*Fabricius, Kjærulff*
18/4	Randers	h	0-1	
25/4	Nordsjælland	a	1-3	*Frederiksen*
3/5	OB	h	2-0	*Ottesen, Frederiksen*
6/5	AGF	a	2-1	*og (Poulsen), Skúlason*
9/5	Esbjerg	h	1-0	*Skúlason*
16/5	København	a	1-3	*Fabricius*

No	Name	Nat	DoB	Pos	Aps	(s)	Gls
18	Nicolaj AGGER		23/10/88	A	7		1
23	Sedin ALIC		31/5/89	M	1	(4)	
7	Morten AVNSKJOLD		26/8/79	M	1		
12	Morten BERTOLT		12/2/84	M	16	(8)	
24	Henrik BØDKER		6/6/83	M	17	(10)	1
14	Anders EGHOLM		15/5/83	D	15	(2)	1
11	Kenneth FABRICIUS		3/11/81	A	33		10
29	Søren FREDERIKSEN		8/7/89	A	17	(13)	4
20	Martin HALLE		16/10/81	D	6	(1)	
18	Rasmus Grønborg HANSEN		12/4/86	M	33		1
25	Anders HOSTRUP		13/4/90	A		(8)	
10	Ken ILSØ		2/12/86	A	4		
1	Henrik IPSEN		30/6/73	G		(1)	
19	Mads JESSEN		14/10/89	M	12	(9)	2
8	Jesper KJÆRULFF		7/10/83	A	17	(14)	3
4	Jesper KRISTOFFERSEN		2/2/84	D		(2)	
13	Michael LARSEN		6/2/83	D	13		
5	Sölvi Geir OTTESEN	ISL	18/2/84	D	27		2
16	David OUSTED		1/2/85	G	33		
30	Bjørn PAULSEN		2/7/91	A		(1)	
26	Andrei SIDORENKOV	EST	12/2/84	M	17	(6)	1
22	Ólafur Ingi SKÚLASON	ISL	1/4/83	M	13		2
3	Michael STRYGER		15/4/83	D	19	(3)	
6	Johnny THOMSEN		26/2/82	M	30		2
2	Anders ØSTLI	NOR	8/1/83	D	32		1

PROMOTED CLUBS

AC HORSENS
Coach – Johnny Mølby
Founded – 1994
Stadium – CASA Arena (10,400)

LYNGBY BK
Coach – Niels Frederiksen
Founded – 1921
Stadium – Lyngby Stadion (9,000)
MAJOR HONOURS:
Danish League - (2) 1983, 1992;
Danish Cup - (3) 1984, 1985, 1990.

SECOND LEVEL FINAL TABLE 2009/10

		Pld	W	D	L	F	A	Pts
1	AC Horsens	30	21	3	6	67	27	66
2	Lyngby BK	30	19	5	6	59	39	62
3	FC Fredericia	30	18	5	7	56	22	59
4	Akademisk BK	30	15	9	6	47	30	54
5	FC Vestsjælland	30	14	8	8	56	46	50
6	Næstved BK	30	13	5	12	44	34	44
7	Viborg FF	30	10	14	6	30	26	44
8	FC Fyn	30	12	6	12	42	51	42
9	Skive IK	30	13	2	15	44	52	41
10	Vejle BK	30	7	12	11	33	34	33
11	FC Roskilde	30	9	6	15	37	51	33
12	Hvidovre IF	30	7	11	12	37	43	32
13	Kolding FC	30	8	7	15	41	59	31
14	Thisted FC	30	8	6	16	33	57	30
15	BK Frem	30	7	7	16	38	59	28
16	Brabrand IF	30	1	10	19	18	52	13

DENMARK

DOMESTIC CUP 2009/10

LANDSPOKALTURNERINGEN

SECOND ROUND

(26/8/09)
Aabenraa 0, Brabrand 2
Aalborg Chang 1, Marstal 3
AIK Strøby 3, Avedøre 2
Assens 1, Fredericia 5
B1908 1, Brønshøj 3
Djursland 3, Aarhus Fremad 3 *(aet; 3-5 on pens)*
Fyn 1, AaB 3
Frem 0, HB Køge 3
Greve 3, SønderjyskE 4
Helsingør 3, Skjold 1
Hjørring 0, Silkeborg 2
Hobro 2, Kolding 1 *(aet)*
Holstebro 3, Thisted 5 *(aet)*
Horsens 0, Vejle 1
Lindholm 1, Blokhus 5
Lolland-Falster Alliancen 1, Lyngby 2
Ringsted 0, Nordsjælland 9
Rishøj 2, Stenløse 0
Svebølle 1, Allerød 2
Søllerød 0, AB 3
Tved 1, Odder 0 *(aet)*
Tårnby 1, Avarta 0
Vejen 2, Varde 2 *(aet; 4-3 on pens.)*
Vestsjælland 1, Esbjerg 2
Viborg 1, AGF 0
Værløse 1, FB 3 *(aet)*

(2/9/09)
Lejre 1, HIK 4

(9/9/09)
Otterup 0, Randers 5

Byes – Brøndby, København, Midtjylland, OB

THIRD ROUND

(16/9/09)
Brønshøj 1, Midtjylland 3

(23/9/09)
Aarhus Fremad 0, Brabrand 0 *(aet; 3-4 on pens)*
AB 1, Nordsjælland 4
AIK Strøby 5, Tårnby 4
Allerød, 0, Hobro 2
Blokhus 0, Brøndby 2
FB 0, Vejle 4
Fredericia 3, OB 5
Helsingør 1, København 2
HIK 2, SønderjyskE 4
Marstal 1, Silkeborg 3
Rishøj 0, Viborg 4
Thisted 0, AaB 3
Tved 0, HB Køge 2
Vejen 0, Randers 9

(1/10/09)
Lyngby 1, Esbjerg 2

FOURTH ROUND

(21/10/09)
AIK Strøby 1, Nordsjælland 5
Brabrand 0, HB Køge 2

(27/10/09)
Randers 1, OB 2

(28/10/09)
Esbjerg 0, Midtjylland 5
Vejle 1, Brøndby 0
Viborg 1, Silkeborg 3

(29/10/09)
Hobro 2, AaB 1
SønderjyskE 5, København 0

QUARTER-FINALS

(8/4/10)
HB Køge 1 *(Mehaković 80)*, OB 3 *(Hansen H. 23, Utaka 60, 81)*
Hobro 1 *(Christensen 72)*, Midtjylland 2 *(Babatunde 55, 60)*
Silkeborg 1 *(Pedersen H. 43)*, Nordsjælland 3 *(Larsen 90og, Granskov 105, Stokholm 111)* *(aet)*
Vejle 2 *(Borre 52, Nielsen 61)*, SønderjyskE 1 *(Hostrup 5)*

SEMI-FINALS

(21/4/10 & 29/4/10)
Midtjylland 2 *(Sivebæk 44, Thygesen 83)*, OB 0
OB 2 *(Hansen H. 67, Utaka 74)*, Midtjylland 2 *(Sørensen 11og, Albrechtsen 64)*
(Midtjylland 4-2)

(22/4/10 & 28/4/10)
Nordsjælland 2 *(Bernier 79, Granskov 90)*, Vejle 0
Vejle 0, Nordsjælland 2 *(Nielsen N.B. 5, 47)*
(Nordsjælland 4-0)

FINAL

(13/5/10)
Parken, Copenhagen
FC NORDSJÆLLAND 2 *(Stokholm 97, Fetai 106)*
FC MIDTJYLLAND 0
(aet)
Referee – Vollquartz
NORDSJÆLLAND – Hansen, Kildentoft, Kibebe, Bjelland, Bengtsson, Stokholm, Parkhurst, Fetai, Nielsen M.L. (Zuma 60), Mikkelsen (Laudrup 66), Nielsen N.B (Granskov 99).
MIDTJYLLAND – Lössl, Afriyie, Albrechtsen, Reid, Jessen, Thygesen, Uzochukwu, Albæk (Sivebæk 100), Borring, Ilsø (Olsen 73), Babatunde (Kristensen F. 73).

Another crushing anti-climax

England travelled to the 2010 FIFA World Cup with high hopes of winning the trophy. They returned home from South Africa not just empty-handed but with the reputations of their coach and leading players in shreds. Almost everything that could go wrong did go wrong. It was a painful experience for the Three Lions from start to finish and, in particular, a crushing disappointment to the legions of long-suffering supporters who had invested so much expectation in them.

The remarkably poor quality of England's football throughout their four-match stay suggested that the pre-tournament optimism which had accompanied them on their journey south had been misplaced. Yet this was a team that had not only cruised through qualification with nine wins out of ten, hammering Croatia 4-1 in Zagreb and 5-1 at Wembley, but was also blessed with several seasoned internationals of lofty standing in European club football circles, such as Steven Gerrard (Liverpool FC), John Terry, Ashley Cole and Frank Lampard (Chelsea FC) and Wayne Rooney (Manchester United FC). Plus, the man leading them into battle was Fabio Capello, one of the finest coaches of the modern era and with a CV to prove it.

Heaviest defeat

Armed with such attributes, there was no reason, certainly no excuse, for England to fail. The pre-tournament hype was not baseless. They should have been contenders. Yet, as had happened so often to England in previous major tournaments, they were unable to transform potential into reality, or expectation into fulfilment. In South Africa, they didn't even come close. Mishaps and calamities repeatedly thwarted them, and they exited the tournament after their heaviest ever World Cup defeat, the final nails in their coffin coming in the shape of four goals from, of all teams, arch-rivals Germany.

That England ended up facing Joachim Löw's vibrant young side as early as the second round was a consequence of their inability to live up to their seeded status and top a first-round group containing the United States, Algeria and Slovenia. Even a mildly out-of-sorts England should have accomplished that task in comfort, but a stoppage-time winner for the Americans against Algeria meant that even their only success of the tournament, a 1-0 win over Slovenia in Port Elizabeth that secured their berth in the last 16, could not be fully savoured. The feeling after the other three matches ranged from disappointment to utter dejection.

The opening game against the United States was scarred by a gruesome goalkeeping error from Robert Green. His inexplicable failure to field a tame long-range shot from Clint Dempsey cancelled out a fine early opening strike from Gerrard, who was standing in as captain for Rio Ferdinand, ruled out of the tournament with an injury sustained in the team's first

England manager Fabio Capello looks on in frustration during the World Cup

training session on South African soil. An average display in Rustenburg was followed six days later by an abject one against Algeria in Cape Town – on Capello's 64th birthday - after which Rooney, England's most ineffective player, blamed the fans for their hostile reaction, for which he later apologised.

Bittersweet victory

Although England had not lost, the two draws left them having to beat Slovenia simply to remain in the competition. To top the group they were obliged to win by a bigger margin than the United States should they overcome Algeria. Capello made changes to personnel, but he stuck defiantly to the 4-4-2 system, with Gerrard on the left of midfield, that had received a cascade of criticism after the first two games. To his credit, James Milner and Jermain Defoe, two of the new starters, combined to put England ahead, but the team's failure to score a second goal, which their improved overall play warranted, not only led to some anxious moments at the other end but also left them vulnerable – in terms of the group leadership – to events in Pretoria. It was after the final whistle in Port Elizabeth, as the normally reserved but visibly relieved Capello joined in a mass celebratory huddle with his players, that news of Landon Donovan's late winner filtered through.

Later that evening England discovered that their next opponents would indeed be old foes Germany – a team that, discounting the 1966 final, they had never outlasted in any previous World Cup. The talk in the camp was of a new spirit forged in victory – albeit a nervous one – over Slovenia, but when push came to shove, and the match got underway in Bloemfontein, that fighting talk rang hollow. England's shaky rearguard was punctured twice as Germany took total command in the first half. Against the run of the play England pulled one back, through Matthew Upson's header, and moments later, remarkably, they had a second goal – only for celebrations to be cut short by the dreadful realisation that neither the Uruguayan referee nor his touchline assistant had spotted that Lampard's shot off the underside of the crossbar had clearly bounced over the line. What should have been 2-2 remained 2-1 to Germany. England, understandably angered by the injustice, tried to force their way back into the game in the second half but left themselves open to Germany's swift, incisive counterattacks, two of which brought goals for Thomas Müller, leaving Capello's team comprehensively beaten and out of the tournament.

Jermain Defoe scores the winning goal against Slovenia to put England through to the knockout phase of the World Cup

The Italian looked as dazed and confused as the England supporters in the immediate aftermath of elimination. Indeed, the difficulty he faced in having to express himself in a foreign tongue left his precise feelings about what had gone wrong shrouded in mystery. The media post-mortem focused on a variety of factors behind the team's premature demise – fatigue, lack of fitness, boredom, outdated tactics – but the stark reality was that, once again, an England team had failed to deliver when it really mattered. Individually and collectively, they had underperformed. Rooney, of whom so much had been expected, was the biggest disappointment, but none of the team's other supposed 'world-class' players – Gerrard, Lampard, Terry – rose sufficiently to the occasion, and there was little of distinction from anyone else. Positive contributions were patchy and unsustained, with moments of inspiration invariably followed by errors. England had been outstanding as an attacking force in qualification, registering more goals than any other team, but in South Africa they passed the ball inaccurately, shot waywardly and seldom looked like scoring. No wonder Capello was so flummoxed.

Capello's challenge

Having already agreed a lucrative new two-year contract extension before the tournament, it was never likely that Capello would be dismissed by the Football Association – despite the World Cup flop. Whether he learns from the experience and stirs England back into life in time for UEFA EURO 2012 remains to be seen, but, with many of the team's stalwarts now over 30 and precious few superior-quality individuals standing by to replace them, the Italian faces one of the toughest challenges of his career. Furthermore, he and his players have to regain the respect and support of a nation. It will not be an easy ride.

If 2010 was a bad year for the national team, it was also a largely forgettable one for England's top clubs. Having provided three of the four UEFA Champions League semi-finalists in each of the previous three seasons, the Premier League was entirely unrepresented in 2009/10. It was quite a fall from grace. Not since 2002/03 had there been a complete absence of English clubs from the last four, and at least one of them had appeared in every final since 2005.

The rot set in when Liverpool failed to make it through their opening group – the first time in four years that any of the Premier League's big guns had been spiked prior to the knockout phase. Chelsea were the next to fall, losing twice to FC Internazionale Milano – and

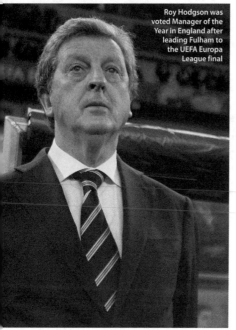

Roy Hodgson was voted Manager of the Year in England after leading Fulham to the UEFA Europa League final

former boss José Mourinho – in the last 16, before Arsenal FC and Manchester United both came a cropper in the quarter-finals, the Gunners coming off a distant second-best to FC Barcelona while United's bid for a third successive final appearance was ended agonisingly on the away-goals rule by FC Bayern München.

Fabulous Fulham

Happier tidings were provided in the UEFA Europa League, where Liverpool made the most of their second chance by reaching the semi-finals, only to be eclipsed by the extraordinary endeavours of European flyweights Fulham FC, who, brilliantly led by Roy Hodgson, progressed all the way from the third qualifying round to the final, eliminating en route a succession of illustrious adversaries - trophy holders FC Shakhtar Donetsk, Italian giants Juventus (with a never-to-be-forgotten 4-1 win at Craven Cottage), German champions VfL Wolfsburg and final hosts Hamburger SV. Unfortunately, the west Londoners could not get their hands on what would have been the first major trophy in the club's history, going down 2-1 after extra time to Liverpool's conquerors Club Atlético de Madrid in the final, but the remarkable run, during which players such as Bobby Zamora, Zoltán Gera and Brede Hangeland took their careers to a new level, provided English football with a timely ray of sunshine. It also reminded everybody of the talent and virtues of Hodgson. Shrewd, dignified and articulate, he might even have become the next manager of England had Liverpool not stepped in first and whipped him off to Anfield.

If Fulham's UEFA Europa League's exploits provided the most pleasant surprise of the season, Liverpool's metamorphosis from Premier League contenders to also-rans was arguably the most unexpected. A close second to Manchester United in the 2008/09 title race, the Merseysiders were widely tipped to go one better in 2009/10 and become champions of England again for the first time in 20 years. But two defeats in their opening three games – including their first at home in the league since December 2007, 1-3 against Aston Villa FC – forced them to play catch-up from the very start. Three successive away defeats in October not only eliminated Rafael Benítez's side from the title race but also raised serious questions about their ability to re-qualify for the UEFA Champions League, from which they crashed out prematurely after finishing third in their group behind ACF Fiorentina and Olympique Lyonnais, both of whom scored last-minute goals in 2-1 wins at Anfield.

ENGLAND

By the end of the season Liverpool had restored some credit in Europe by reaching the last four of the UEFA Europa League – thanks to a couple of Fernandes Torres-inspired Anfield comebacks against LOSC Lille Métropole and SL Benfica – but with their Spanish striker injured for a large portion of the season and captain Gerrard struggling to make an impact without him, the best they could manage in the Premier League was seventh place. Beaten also in the third round of the FA Cup, by Championship (second division) opponents Reading FC, it was a season to forget for the Merseysiders and the last in the six-year reign of Benítez.

One piece of good news for Kopites was the failure of Manchester United to win the Premier League for a record fourth year in a row and thus unseat Liverpool as England's all-time record champions. Sir Alex Ferguson's side gave it their best shot, but with the brilliant Cristiano Ronaldo having debunked to Real Madrid CF for a world-record fee, a gaping hole was left in the United attack, and although Rooney did his very best to fill it, enjoying the finest season of his career and scoring 26 league goals, collectively the team were a reduced force. That they lost seven matches and still finished just one point from the summit was a credit to their gutsy endeavour as well as the evergreen skills of their veteran manager.

United were beaten five times in the first half of the Premier League campaign, but a familiar post-Christmas charge, spearheaded by the irrepressible Rooney, enabled them to claw back lost ground and keep pace with leaders Chelsea. Although, like Liverpool, they suffered a shock third-round defeat to

The Football Association (FA)

Wembley Stadium
PO Box 1966
GB-London SW1P 9EQ
tel – +44 844 980 8200
fax – +44 844 980 8201
website – thefa.com
email – info@thefa.com
Year of Formation – 1863

President – Roger Burden (acting)
General Secretary – Alex Horne
Media Officer – Julian Eccles
National Stadium – Wembley, London (90,000)

INTERNATIONAL HONOURS
FIFA World Cup – (1) 1966.
INTERNATIONAL TOURNAMENT APPEARANCES
FIFA World Cup – (13) 1950, 1954 (qtr-finals), 1958, 1962 (qtr-finals), 1966 (Winners), 1970 (qtr-finals), 1982 (2nd phase), 1986 (qtr-finals), 1990 (4th), 1998 (2nd round), 2002 (qtr-finals), 2006 (qtr-finals), 2010 (2nd round).
UEFA European Championship – (7) 1968 (3rd), 1980, 1988, 1992, 1996 (semi-finals), 2000, 2004 (qtr-finals).
TOP FIVE ALL-TIME CAPS
Peter Shilton (125); David Beckham (115); Bobby Moore (108); Bobby Charlton (106); Billy Wright (105)
TOP FIVE ALL-TIME GOALS
Bobby Charlton (49); Gary Lineker (48); Jimmy Greaves (44); Michael Owen (40); Alan Shearer, Nat Lofthouse & Tom Finney (30)

lower-league opposition in the FA Cup, losing 1-0 at home to Leeds United AFC, they came through a highly charged League Cup semi-final against Manchester City FC and went on to retain the trophy by beating Aston Villa FC in the final. They were in even better form in Europe, trouncing AC Milan 7-2 on aggregate with a brace of goals in each leg from Rooney.

NATIONAL TEAM RESULTS 2009/10

12/8/09	Netherlands	A	Amsterdam	2-2	Defoe (49, 76)
5/9/09	Slovenia	H	Wembley	2-1	Lampard (31p), Defoe (63)
9/9/09	Croatia (WCQ)	H	Wembley	5-1	Lampard (7p, 59), Gerrard (18, 67), Rooney (77)
10/10/09	Ukraine (WCQ)	A	Dnipropetrovsk	0-1	
14/10/09	Belarus (WCQ)	H	Wembley	3-0	Crouch (4, 76), Wright-Phillips (60)
14/11/09	Brazil	N	Doha (QAT)	0-1	
3/3/10	Egypt	H	Wembley	3-1	Crouch (56, 80), Wright-Phillips (75)
24/5/10	Mexico	H	Wembley	3-1	King (17), Crouch (34), Johnson G. (47)
30/5/10	Japan	N	Graz (AUT)	2-1	Tanaka (72og), Nakazawa (83og)
12/6/10	United States (WCF)	N	Rustenburg (RSA)	1-1	Gerrard (4)
18/6/10	Algeria (WCF)	N	Cape Town (RSA)	0-0	
23/6/10	Slovenia (WCF)	N	Port Elizabeth (RSA)	1-0	Defoe (23)
27/6/10	Germany (WCF)	N	Bloemfontein (RSA)	1-4	Upson (37)

NATIONAL TEAM APPEARANCES 2009/10

Coach – Fabio CAPELLO (ITA)	18/6/46		Ned	Svn	CRO	UKR	BLR	Bra	Egy	Mex	Jpn	USA	ALG	SVN	GER	Caps	Goals
Robert GREEN	18/1/80	West Ham	G	G	G	G 12*			G	G46		G				11	-
Glen JOHNSON	23/8/84	Liverpool	D	D	D	D	D			D	D46	D	D	D	D87	26	1
Rio FERDINAND	7/11/78	Man. United	D			D	D			D46	D					78	3
John TERRY	7/12/80	Chelsea	D	D	D	D	D		D		D	D	D	D	D	64	6
Ashley COLE	20/12/80	Chelsea	D84	D	D	D					D	D	D	D	D	82	-
David BECKHAM	2/5/75	LA Galaxy (USA)	M46		s81		s58									115	17
Frank LAMPARD	20/6/78	Chelsea	M	M46	M	M	M			M46	M	M	M	M	M	82	20
Gareth BARRY	23/2/81	Man. City	M46	M	M		M	M82	M				M84	M	M	39	2
Ashley YOUNG	9/7/85	Aston Villa	M68				s87									7	-
Emile HESKEY	11/1/78	Aston Villa	A46	A46	A59	A72					s77	A79	A74	s86	s71	62	7
Wayne ROONEY	24/10/85	Man. United	A58	A80	A	A		A	A86	A	A	A	A	A72	A	64	25
Shaun WRIGHT-PHILLIPS	25/10/81	Man. City	s46	M46			M	M82	s57		s46	s31	s63		s87	34	6
Michael CARRICK	28/7/81	Man. United	s46	s46		M				s46	M62					22	-
Jermain DEFOE	7/10/82	Tottenham	s46	s46	s59			s54	A46	s46		s74	A86	A71		43	12
Carlton COLE	12/11/83	West Ham	s58	s80		s72	s66	s86								7	-
James MILNER	4/1/86	Aston Villa	s68	s46	s81	s46	s78	M87	s73	M84		M31		M	M64	11	-
Wayne BRIDGE	5/8/80	Man. City	s84			D78	D									36	1
Matthew UPSON	18/4/79	West Ham		D64	D			D	D					D	D	21	2
Steven GERRARD	30/5/80	Liverpool	M46	M81	M46			M73	M		s46	M	M	M	M	84	17
Aaron LENNON	16/4/87	Tottenham		s46	M81	M12	M58				s77	M77	M	M63		19	-
Joleon LESCOTT	16/8/82	Man. City	s64				D									9	-
David JAMES	1/8/70	Portsmouth				s12					G46		G	G	G	53	-
Ben FOSTER	3/4/83	Man. United						G	G							4	-
Peter CROUCH	30/1/81	Tottenham						A	s82	s46	A46	s79	s84			40	21
Gabriel AGBONLAHOR	13/10/86	Aston Villa					A66									3	-
Wes BROWN	13/10/79	Man. United						D	D							23	1
Jermaine JENAS	18/2/83	Tottenham						M								21	1
Darren BENT	6/2/84	Sunderland						A54		A46						6	-
Tom HUDDLESTONE	28/12/86	Tottenham						s82		s62	M46					3	-
Leighton BAINES	11/12/84	Everton						D	D							2	-
Theo WALCOTT	16/3/89	Arsenal						M57	M77	M46						11	3
Ledley KING	12/10/80	Tottenham								D	D46					21	2
Joe HART	19/4/87	Birmingham								s46	s46					3	-
Jamie CARRAGHER	28/1/78	Liverpool								s46	s46	s46	D			38	-
Adam JOHNSON	14/7/87	Man. City								s84						1	-
Joe COLE	8/11/81	Chelsea									s46			s72	s64	56	10

Bad week

All was looking good until United's season unravelled during a catastrophic week in late-March/early-April. Holding Bayern 1-1 in Munich as the first leg of the European quarter-final entered its final seconds, Rooney, battling for possession in the centre circle, twisted his ankle, and from the ensuing move Bayern snatched a winner. Four days later, without their injured centre-forward, United lost 2-1 at Old Trafford to Chelsea in the Premier League, a result that enabled the Londoners to turn a one-point deficit at the top of the table into a two-point lead. The following Wednesday, with Rooney back in the starting line-up but far from fully fit, United blitzed their way back into the UEFA Champions League tie, taking a 3-0 lead, but just before half-time Bayern pulled a goal back and, with United down to ten men, eventually scored again to take the tie.

Out of Europe, United were not quite done in the domestic title race, but a goalless draw four days later at Blackburn Rovers FC ultimately left them with too much to do to catch Chelsea. They were still in contention, one point in arrears, going into the final day, but as they beat Stoke City FC 4-0 at Old Trafford, the league leaders ran up double that number of goals to annihilate Wigan Athletic FC at Stamford Bridge and reclaim the title – only the fourth in their history - after a four-year wait. A week later, with a 1-0 win over Portsmouth FC at Wembley in the FA Cup final, Chelsea clinched the double, the first in their 105-year history.

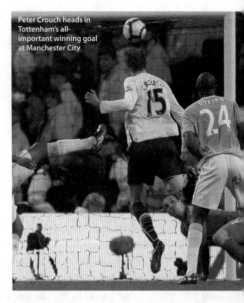

Peter Crouch heads in Tottenham's all-important winning goal at Manchester City

Architect Ancelotti

The architect of Chelsea's historic success was Carlo Ancelotti, the ex-Milan coach achieving the feat in his first season. Owner Roman Abramovich might have felt short-changed by the club's early elimination from the UEFA Champions League, but he could have no complaints about the dash and adventure that Ancelotti added to Chelsea's play. Although they lost six times in the league, including once at Stamford Bridge, where Manchester City routed them 4-2, the Blues were victorious on 27 occasions and scored a club-record tally of 103 goals – the first time a team had reached a century in the English top flight for 47 years – with 68 of them coming in front of their home supporters, 41 in the last nine matches. Didier Drogba alone accounted for 29 of them, although his only hat-trick came in that title-clinching 8-0 win over Wigan, the three goals enabling him to soar past Rooney and win the Premier League's Golden Boot. The Ivory Coast striker also scored the only goal in the FA Cup final, from a trademark free-kick, as Chelsea lifted football's most recognisable domestic club trophy for the third time in four years and the sixth time in all.

If Drogba was Chelsea's Player of the Year, he had close competition from Lampard, who scored 22 league goals from midfield, and French international Florent Malouda, a model of consistency all season long. Ashley Cole was also back to his best before he sustained an ankle injury, while Branislav Ivanović firmly established himself as Chelsea's first-choice right-back in the absence of José Bosingwa, ruled out from October onwards. The influential Michael Essein also missed the second half of the season, while skipper Terry battled wholeheartedly through a personal crisis that saw him stripped of the England armband.

As Chelsea celebrated their two-trophy triumph, Arsenal, third in the league, were left to contemplate a fifth straight season without silverware. Rocked by a long-term injury to in-form striker Robin van Persie, the Gunners were unable to mount a credible title challenge without him. Beaten home and away by both Manchester United and Chelsea, they were also found badly wanting against Barcelona, who teased and toyed with them for the first half-hour in London before the Catalans' matador-in-chief Lionel Messi mercilessly gored them at Camp Nou. New signing Thomas Vermaelen was a success, as much for his goals as his defending, while skipper Cesc Fàbregas enjoyed another terrific season, finding the net 15 times in the Premier League to become the club's top scorer.

Spurs go fourth

An intriguing battle for fourth place was won by Arsenal's north London rivals Tottenham Hotspur FC, who, astutely managed by Harry Redknapp, edged out the nouveaux riches of Manchester City into the highly-prized UEFA Champions League qualifying slot thanks to a 1-0 win at the home of their direct rivals in the penultimate game of the season. Spurs had not appeared in Europe's premier competition for almost half a century, and never before had three teams from one city appeared in it together, so there was much riding on their August play-off tie.

City's failure to reach Europe's heights was a major blow to the club's wealthy Arab owners, who had replaced Welshman Mark Hughes with suave Italian Roberto Mancini in December. However, that setback simply

triggered another wave of heavy spending in the summer – a luxury denied to most other English clubs, not least Portsmouth, who reached the FA Cup final despite going into administration and being docked nine points for their sins. Pompey's financial disarray also prevented them from obtaining a licence to compete in Europe, which meant that their place was passed on to Liverpool. Aston Villa FC, who reached Wembley twice and finished sixth in the league, joined City and Liverpool in the 2010/11 UEFA Europa League.

Portsmouth would have been relegated even without their handicap, and they were escorted down to the Championship by the play-off winners of the previous two seasons, Burnley FC and Hull City AFC. A quick return to the second tier will also be expected of 2010 play-off winners Blackpool FC, who made it back to the top flight after a 39-year wait thanks to a 3-2 win over Cardiff City FC at Wembley. The automatic promotion places went, as expected, to Newcastle United FC and West Bromwich Albion FC, who, 12 months after relegation, both bounced back to the Premier League at the first attempt.

DOMESTIC LEAGUE 2009/10

PREMIER LEAGUE FINAL TABLE

		Pld	Home					Away					Total					Pts
			W	D	L	F	A	W	D	L	F	A	W	D	L	F	A	
1	Chelsea FC	38	17	1	1	68	14	10	4	5	35	18	27	5	6	103	32	86
2	Manchester United FC	38	16	1	2	52	12	11	3	5	34	16	27	4	7	86	28	85
3	Arsenal FC	38	15	2	2	48	15	8	4	7	35	26	23	6	9	83	41	75
4	Tottenham Hotspur FC	38	14	2	3	40	12	7	5	7	27	29	21	7	10	67	41	70
5	Manchester City FC	38	12	4	3	41	20	6	9	4	32	25	18	13	7	73	45	67
6	Aston Villa FC	38	8	8	3	29	16	9	5	5	23	23	17	13	8	52	39	64
7	Liverpool FC	38	13	3	3	43	15	5	6	8	18	20	18	9	11	61	35	63
8	Everton FC	38	11	6	2	35	21	5	7	7	25	28	16	13	9	60	49	61
9	Birmingham City FC	38	8	9	2	19	13	5	2	12	19	34	13	11	14	38	47	50
10	Blackburn Rovers FC	38	10	6	3	28	18	3	5	11	13	37	13	11	14	41	55	50
11	Stoke City FC	38	7	6	6	24	21	4	8	7	10	27	11	14	13	34	48	47
12	Fulham FC	38	11	3	5	27	15	1	7	11	12	31	12	10	16	39	46	46
13	Sunderland AFC	38	9	7	3	32	19	2	4	13	16	37	11	11	16	48	56	44
14	Bolton Wanderers FC	38	6	6	7	26	31	4	3	12	16	36	10	9	19	42	67	39
15	Wolverhampton Wanderers FC	38	5	6	8	13	22	4	5	10	19	34	9	11	18	32	56	38
16	Wigan Athletic FC	38	6	7	6	19	24	3	2	14	18	55	9	9	20	37	79	36
17	West Ham United FC	38	7	5	7	30	29	1	6	12	17	37	8	11	19	47	66	35
18	Burnley FC	38	7	5	7	25	30	1	1	17	17	52	8	6	24	42	82	30
19	Hull City AFC	38	6	6	7	22	29	0	6	13	12	46	6	12	20	34	75	30
20	Portsmouth FC	38	5	3	11	24	32	2	4	13	10	34	7	7	24	34	66	19

N.B. Portsmouth FC – 9 pts deducted.

TOP GOALSCORERS

29 Didier DROGBA (Chelsea)
26 Wayne ROONEY (Man. United)
24 Darren BENT (Sunderland)
23 Carlos TÉVEZ (Man. City)
22 Frank LAMPARD (Chelsea)
18 FERNANDO TORRES (Liverpool)
   Jermain DEFOE (Tottenham)
15 Cesc FÀBREGAS (Arsenal)
14 Emmanuel ADEBAYOR (Man. City)
13 Gabriel AGBONLAHOR (Aston Villa)
   Louis SAHA (Everton)

CLUB-BY-CLUB

ARSENAL FC
Manager – Arsène Wenger (FRA)
Founded – 1886
Stadium – Emirates Stadium (60,361)
MAJOR HONOURS:
UEFA Cup Winners' Cup - (1) 1994;
Inter Cities Fairs Cup - (1) 1970;
English League - (13) 1931, 1933, 1934, 1935, 1938, 1948, 1953, 1971,
1989, 1991, 1998, 2002, 2004;
FA Cup - (10) 1930, 1936, 1950, 1971, 1979, 1993, 1998, 2002, 2003, 2005;
League Cup - (2) 1987, 1993.

2009
15/8	Everton	a	6-1	Denílson, Vermaelen, Gallas, Fàbregas 2, Eduardo
22/8	Portsmouth	h	4-1	Diaby 2, Gallas, Ramsey
29/8	Man. United	a	1-2	Arshavin
12/9	Man. City	a	2-4	Van Persie, Rosický
19/9	Wigan	h	4-0	Vermaelen 2, Eboué, Fàbregas
26/9	Fulham	a	1-0	Van Persie
4/10	Blackburn	h	6-2	Vermaelen, Van Persie, Arshavin, Fàbregas, Walcott, Bendtner
17/10	Birmingham	h	3-1	Van Persie, Diaby, Arshavin
25/10	West Ham	a	2-2	Van Persie, Gallas
31/10	Tottenham	h	3-0	Van Perise 2, Fàbregas
7/11	Wolves	a	4-1	og (Zubar), og (Craddock), Fàbregas, Arshavin
21/11	Sunderland	a	0-1	
29/11	Chelsea	h	0-3	
5/12	Stoke	h	2-0	Arshavin, Ramsey
13/12	Liverpool	a	2-1	og (Johnson), Arshavin
16/12	Burnley	h	1-1	Fàbregas
19/12	Hull	h	3-0	Denílson, Eduardo, Diaby
27/12	Aston Villa	h	3-0	Fàbregas 2, Diaby
30/12	Portsmouth	a	4-1	Eduardo, Nasri, Ramsey, Song
2010				
9/1	Everton	h	2-2	Denílson, Rosický
17/1	Bolton	a	2-0	Fàbregas, Fran Mérida
20/1	Bolton	h	4-2	Rosický, Fàbregas, Vermaelen, Arshavin
27/1	Aston Villa	a	0-0	
31/1	Man. United	h	1-3	Vermaelen
7/2	Chelsea	a	0-2	
10/2	Liverpool	h	1-0	Diaby
20/2	Sunderland	h	2-0	Bendtner, Fàbregas (p)
27/2	Stoke	a	3-1	Bendtner, Fàbregas (p), Vermaelen
6/3	Burnley	h	3-1	Fàbregas, Walcott, Arshavin
13/3	Hull	a	2-1	Arshavin, Bendtner
20/3	West Ham	h	2-0	Denílson, Fàbregas (p)
27/3	Birmingham	a	1-1	Nasri
3/4	Wolves	h	1-0	Bendtner
14/4	Tottenham	a	1-2	Bendtner
18/4	Wigan	a	2-3	Walcott, Silvestre
24/4	Man. City	h	0-0	
3/5	Blackburn	a	1-2	Van Persie
9/5	Fulham	h	4-0	Arshavin, Van Persie, og (Baird), Vela

No	Name	Nat	DoB	Pos	Aps	(s)	Gls
1	Manuel ALMUNIA	ESP	16/5/77	G	29		
23	Andrei ARSHAVIN	RUS	29/5/81	A	25	(5)	10
52	Nicklas BENDTNER	DEN	16/1/88	A	13	(10)	6
31	Sol CAMPBELL		18/9/74	D	10	(1)	
22	Gaël CLICHY	FRA	26/7/85	D	23	(1)	
15	DENÍLSON Pereira Neves	BRA	16/2/88	M	19	(1)	4
2	Abou DIABY	FRA	11/5/86	M	26	(3)	6
20	Johan DJOUROU	SUI	18/1/87	D		(1)	
37	Craig EASTMOND		9/12/90	M	2	(2)	
27	Emmanuel EBOUÉ	CIV	4/6/83	D	17	(8)	1
9	EDUARDO Alves da Silva	CRO	25/2/83	A	13	(11)	3
21	Łukasz FABIAŃSKI	POL	18/4/85	G	4		
4	Francesc "Cesc" FÀBREGAS i Soler	ESP	4/5/87	M	26	(1)	15
32	FRANcisco MÉRIDA Pérez	ESP	4/3/90	M		(4)	1
10	William GALLAS	FRA	17/8/77	D	26		3
28	Kieran GIBBS		26/9/89	D	3		
45	Henri LANSBURY		12/10/90	M		(1)	
24	Vito MANNONE	ITA	2/3/88	G	5		
8	Samir NASRI	FRA	26/6/87	M	22	(4)	2
16	Aaron RAMSEY	WAL	26/12/90	M	7	(11)	3
7	Tomáš ROSICKÝ	CZE	4/10/80	M	14	(11)	3
3	Bacary SAGNA	FRA	14/2/83	D	31	(4)	
18	Mikaël SILVESTRE	FRA	9/8/77	D	9	(3)	1
17	Alex SONG	CMR	9/9/87	M	25	(1)	1
30	Armand TRAORÉ	FRA	8/10/89	D	9		
11	Robin VAN PERSIE	NED	6/8/83	A	14	(2)	9
12	Carlos VELA	MEX	1/3/89	A	1	(10)	1
5	Thomas VERMAELEN	BEL	14/11/85	D	33		7
14	Theo WALCOTT		16/3/89	A	12	(11)	3
19	Jack WILSHERE		1/1/92	M		(1)	

ASTON VILLA FC
Manager – Martin O'Neill (NIR)
Founded – 1874
Stadium – Villa Park (42,640)
MAJOR HONOURS:
European Champion Clubs' Cup - (1) 1982;
UEFA Super Cup - (1) 1982;
English League - (7) 1894, 1896, 1897, 1899, 1900, 1910, 1981;
FA Cup - (7) 1887, 1895, 1897, 1905, 1913, 1920, 1957;
League Cup - (5) 1961, 1975, 1977, 1994, 1996.

2009
15/8	Wigan	h	0-2	
24/8	Liverpool	a	3-1	og (Lucas), Davies, Young A. (p)
30/8	Fulham	h	2-0	og (Pantsil), Agbonlahor
13/9	Birmingham	a	1-0	Agbonlahor
19/9	Portsmouth	h	2-0	Milner (p), Agbonlahor
26/9	Blackburn	a	1-2	Agbonlahor
5/10	Man. City	h	1-1	Dunne
17/10	Chelsea	h	2-1	Dunne, Collins
24/10	Wolves	a	1-1	Agbonlahor
31/10	Everton	a	1-1	Carew
4/11	West Ham	a	1-2	Young A.
7/11	Bolton	h	5-1	Young A., Agbonlahor, Carew, Milner, Cuéllar
21/11	Burnley	a	1-1	Heskey
28/11	Tottenham	a	1-1	Agbonlahor
5/12	Hull	h	3-0	Dunne, Milner, Carew (p)
12/12	Man. United	a	1-0	Agbonlahor
15/12	Sunderland	a	2-0	Heskey, Milner
19/12	Stoke	h	1-0	Carew
27/12	Arsenal	a	0-3	
29/12	Liverpool	h	0-1	
2010				
17/1	West Ham	h	0-0	
27/1	Arsenal	h	0-0	
30/1	Fulham	a	2-0	Agbonlahor 2
6/2	Tottenham	a	0-0	
10/2	Man. United	h	1-1	Cuéllar
21/2	Burnley	h	5-2	Young A., Downing 2, Heskey, Agbonlahor
13/3	Stoke	a	0-0	
16/3	Wigan	a	2-1	og (McCarthy), Milner
20/3	Wolves	h	2-2	Carew 2
24/3	Sunderland	h	1-1	Carew

27/3	Chelsea	a	1-7	Carew
3/4	Bolton	a	1-0	Young A.
14/4	Everton	h	2-2	Agbonlahor, og (Jagielka)
18/4	Portsmouth	a	2-1	Carew, Delfouneso
21/4	Hull	a	2-0	Agbonlahor, Milner (p)
25/4	Birmingham	h	1-0	Milner (p)
1/5	Man. City	a	1-3	Carew
9/5	Blackburn	h	0-1	

No	Name	Nat	DoB	Pos	Aps	(s)	Gls
11	Gabriel AGBONLAHOR		13/10/86	A	35	(1)	13
12	Marc ALBRIGHTON		18/11/89	M		(3)	
23	Habib BEYE	SEN	19/10/77	D	5	(1)	
10	John CAREW	NOR	5/9/79	A	22	(11)	10
47	Ciaran CLARK		26/9/89	D	1		
29	James COLLINS	WAL	23/8/83	D	26	(1)	1
24	Carlos Javier CUÉLLAR Jiménez	ESP	23/8/81	D	36		2
15	Curtis DAVIES		15/3/85	D	2		1
14	Nathan DELFOUNESO		2/2/91	A		(9)	1
16	Fabian DELPH		21/11/89	M	4	(4)	
6	Stewart DOWNING		22/7/84	M	23	(2)	2
5	Richard DUNNE	IRL	21/9/79	D	35		3
1	Brad FRIEDEL	USA	18/5/71	G	38		
26	Craig GARDNER		25/11/86	M		(1)	
8	Emile HESKEY		11/1/78	A	16	(15)	3
8	James MILNER		4/1/86	M	36		7
19	Stilian PETROV	BUL	5/7/79	M	37		
20	Nigel REO-COKER		14/5/84	M	6	(4)	
21	Nicky SHOREY		19/2/81	D	3		
4	Steve SIDWELL		14/12/82	M	12	(13)	
25	Stephen WARNOCK		12/12/81	D	30		
7	Ashley YOUNG		9/7/85	M	37		5
2	Luke YOUNG		19/7/79	D	14	(2)	

24/3	Blackburn	a	1-2	McFadden
27/3	Arsenal	h	1-1	Phillips
4/4	Liverpool	h	1-1	Ridgewell
11/4	Man. City	a	1-5	Jerome
17/4	Hull	h	0-0	
25/4	Aston Villa	a	0-1	
1/5	Burnley	h	2-1	og (Jensen), Benítez
9/5	Bolton	a	1-2	McFadden

No	Name	Nat	DoB	Pos	Aps	(s)	Gls
11	Cristian "Chucho" BENÍTEZ	ECU	1/5/86	A	21	(9)	3
4	Lee BOWYER		3/1/77	M	34	(1)	5
2	Stephen CARR	IRL	29/8/76	D	35		
26	Lee CARSLEY	IRL	28/2/74	M	3	(4)	
15	Scott DANN		14/2/87	D	30		
18	Keith FAHEY	IRL	15/1/83	M	18	(16)	
12	Barry FERGUSON	SCO	2/2/78	M	37		
33	Craig GARDNER		25/11/86	M	10	(3)	1
25	Joe HART		19/4/87	G	36		
10	Cameron JEROME		14/8/86	A	32		10
22	Damien JOHNSON	NIR	18/11/78	M		(1)	
14	Roger JOHNSON		28/4/83	D	38		
7	Sebastian LARSSON	SWE	6/6/85	M	26	(7)	4
16	James McFADDEN	SCO	14/4/83	A	32	(4)	5
19	Gary McSHEFFREY		13/8/82	M	1	(4)	
17	Miguel Marcos Madera "MÍCHEL"	ESP	8/11/85	M	3	(6)	
8	Garry O'CONNOR	SCO	7/5/83	A	5	(5)	1
24	Jay O'SHEA	IRL	10/8/88	M		(1)	
21	Stuart PARNABY		19/7/82	D	6	(2)	
9	Kevin PHILLIPS		25/7/73	A	2	(17)	4
20	Franck QUEUDRUE	FRA	25/8/78	D	6		
6	Liam RIDGEWELL		21/7/84	D	30	(1)	3
28	Teemu TAINIO	FIN	27/11/79	M	5	(1)	
1	Maik TAYLOR	NIR	4/9/71	G	2		
27	Grégory VIGNAL	FRA	19/7/81	D	6	(2)	

BIRMINGHAM CITY FC
Coach – Alex McLeish (SCO)
Founded – 1875
Stadium – St Andrews (30,079)
MAJOR HONOURS: League Cup – (1) 1963.

2009

16/8	Man. United	a	0-1	
19/8	Portsmouth	h	1-0	McFadden (p)
22/8	Stoke	h	0-0	
29/8	Tottenham	a	1-2	Bowyer
13/9	Aston Villa	h	0-1	
19/9	Hull	a	1-0	O'Connor
26/9	Bolton	h	1-2	Phillips
3/10	Burnley	a	1-2	Larsson
17/10	Arsenal	a	1-3	Bowyer
24/10	Sunderland	h	2-1	Ridgewell, McFadden
1/11	Man. City	h	0-0	
9/11	Liverpool	a	2-2	Benítez, Jerome
21/11	Fulham	h	1-0	Bowyer
29/11	Wolves	a	1-0	Bowyer
5/12	Wigan	a	3-2	Larsson 2, Benítez
12/12	West Ham	h	1-0	Bowyer
15/12	Blackburn	h	2-1	Jerome 2
20/12	Everton	a	1-1	Larsson
26/12	Chelsea	h	0-0	
28/12	Stoke	a	1-0	Jerome

2010

9/1	Man. United	h	1-1	Jerome
27/1	Chelsea	a	0-3	
30/1	Tottenham	h	1-1	Ridgewell
7/2	Wolves	h	2-1	Phillips 2
10/2	West Ham	a	0-2	
21/2	Fulham	a	1-2	og (Baird)
27/2	Wigan	h	1-0	McFadden (p)
9/3	Portsmouth	a	2-1	Jerome 2
13/3	Everton	a	2-2	Jerome, Gardner
20/3	Sunderland	a	1-3	Jerome

BLACKBURN ROVERS FC
Manager – Sam Allardyce
Founded – 1875
Stadium – Ewood Park (31,154)
MAJOR HONOURS: English League - (3) 1912, 1914, 1995; FA Cup - (6) 1884, 1885, 1886, 1890, 1891, 1928; League Cup - (1) 2002.

2009

15/8	Man. City	h	0-2	
22/8	Sunderland	a	1-2	Givet
29/8	West Ham	h	0-0	
12/9	Wolves	h	3-1	Diouf, Roberts, Dunn
20/9	Everton	a	0-3	
26/9	Aston Villa	h	2-1	Samba, Dunn (p)
4/10	Arsenal	a	2-6	N'Zonzi, Dunn
18/10	Burnley	h	3-2	Dunn, Di Santo, Chimbonda
24/10	Chelsea	a	0-5	
31/10	Man. United	a	0-2	
7/11	Portsmouth	h	3-1	Roberts 2, Nelsen
22/11	Bolton	a	2-0	Dunn, og (Ricketts)
25/11	Fulham	a	0-3	
28/11	Stoke	h	0-0	
5/12	Liverpool	h	0-0	
12/12	Hull	a	0-0	
15/12	Birmingham	a	1-2	Nelsen
19/12	Tottenham	h	0-2	
26/12	Wigan	a	1-1	McCarthy
28/12	Sunderland	h	2-2	Gamst Pedersen, Diouf

2010

11/1	Man. City	a	1-4	Gamst Pedersen
17/1	Fulham	h	2-0	Samba, Nelsen
27/1	Wigan	h	2-1	Gamst Pedersen, Kalinić
30/1	West Ham	a	0-0	
6/2	Stoke	a	0-3	
10/2	Hull	h	1-0	og (Myhill)

ENGLAND

21/2	Bolton	h	3-0	Kalinić, Roberts, Givet	
28/2	Liverpool	a	1-2	Andrews (p)	
13/3	Tottenham	a	1-3	Samba	
21/3	Chelsea	h	1-1	Diouf	
24/3	Birmingham	h	2-1	Dunn 2	
28/3	Burnley	a	1-0	Dunn (p)	
3/4	Portsmouth	a	0-0		
11/4	Man. United	h	0-0		
17/4	Everton	h	2-3	N'Zonzi, Roberts	
24/4	Wolves	a	1-1	Nelsen	
3/5	Arsenal	h	2-1	Dunn, Samba	
9/5	Aston Villa	a	1-0	og (Dunne)	

No	Name	Nat	DoB	Pos	Aps	(s)	Gls
17	Keith ANDREWS	IRL	13/9/80	M	22	(10)	1
20	Yıldıray BAŞTÜRK	TUR	24/12/78	M	1		
32	Jason BROWN	WAL	18/5/82	G	3	(1)	
39	Pascal CHIMBONDA	FRA	21/2/79	D	22	(2)	1
18	El-Hadji DIOUF	SEN	15/1/81	A	24	(2)	3
26	Franco DI SANTO	ARG	7/4/89	A	15	(7)	1
8	David DUNN		27/12/79	M	20	(3)	9
7	Brett EMERTON	AUS	22/2/79	M	17	(7)	
15	Paul GALLAGHER	SCO	9/8/84	A		(1)	
5	Morten GAMST PEDERSEN	NOR	8/9/81	M	27	(6)	3
5	Gaël GIVET	FRA	9/10/81	D	33	(1)	2
11	Vince GRELLA	AUS	5/10/79	M	10	(5)	
31	Grant HANLEY	SCO	20/1/91	D	1		
23	David HOILETT	CAN	5/6/90	A	8	(15)	
2	Lars JACOBSEN	DEN	20/9/79	D	11	(2)	
28	Phil JONES		21/2/92	D	7	(2)	
22	Nikola KALINIĆ	CRO	5/1/88	A	14	(12)	2
14	Amine LINGANZI	ALG	16/11/89	M	1		
10	Benni McCARTHY	RSA	12/11/77	A	7	(7)	1
27	Miguel Ángel "MÍCHEL" SALGADO Fernández	ESP	22/10/75	D	16	(5)	
6	Ryan NELSEN	NZL	18/10/77	D	25	(3)	4
15	Steven N'ZONZI	FRA	15/12/88	M	33		2
21	Martin OLSSON	SWE	17/5/88	D	19	(2)	
16	Steven REID	IRL	10/3/81	M	1	(3)	
9	Jason ROBERTS	GRN	25/1/78	A	15	(14)	5
1	Paul ROBINSON		15/10/79	G	35		
4	Christopher SAMBA	CGO	28/3/84	D	30		4
3	Stephen WARNOCK		12/12/81	D	1		

BOLTON WANDERERS FC
Manager – Gary Megson;
(30/12/09) (Chris Evans & Steve Wigley);
(8/1/10) Owen Coyle (IRL)
Founded – 1874
Stadium – Reebok Stadium (28,101)
MAJOR HONOURS: FA Cup – (4) 1923, 1926, 1929, 1958.

2009

15/8	Sunderland	h	0-1	
22/8	Hull	a	0-1	
29/8	Liverpool	h	2-3	Davies K., Cohen
12/9	Portsmouth	a	3-2	Cohen, Taylor (p), Cahill
19/9	Stoke	h	1-1	Taylor (p)
26/9	Birmingham	a	2-1	Cohen, Lee
3/10	Tottenham	h	2-2	Gardner, Davies K.
17/10	Man. United	a	1-2	Taylor
25/10	Everton	h	3-2	Lee, Cahill, Klasnić
31/10	Chelsea	h	0-4	
7/11	Aston Villa	a	1-5	Elmander
22/11	Blackburn	h	0-2	
28/11	Fulham	a	1-1	Klasnić
5/12	Wolves	a	1-2	Elmander
12/12	Man. City	h	3-3	Klasnić 2, Cahill
15/12	West Ham	h	3-1	Lee, Klasnić, Cahill
26/12	Burnley	h	1-1	Taylor
29/12	Hull	h	2-2	Klasnić, Davies K.

2010

17/1	Arsenal	h	0-2	
20/1	Arsenal	a	2-4	Cahill, Taylor (p)
26/1	Burnley	h	1-0	Lee
30/1	Liverpool	a	0-2	
6/2	Fulham	h	0-0	
9/2	Man. City	a	0-2	
17/2	Wigan	a	0-0	
21/2	Blackburn	a	0-3	
27/2	Wolves	h	1-0	Knight
6/3	West Ham	a	2-1	Davies K., Wilshere
9/3	Sunderland	a	0-4	
13/3	Wigan	h	4-0	Elmander, Davies K. (p), Muamba, Taylor
20/3	Everton	a	0-2	
27/3	Man. United	h	0-4	
3/4	Aston Villa	h	0-1	
13/4	Chelsea	a	0-1	
17/4	Stoke	a	2-1	Taylor 2
24/4	Portsmouth	h	2-2	Klasnić, Davies K.
1/5	Tottenham	a	0-1	
9/5	Birmingham	h	2-1	Davies K., Klasnić

No	Name	Nat	DoB	Pos	Aps	(s)	Gls
30	Chris BASHAM		20/7/88	M	2	(6)	
5	Gary CAHILL		19/12/85	D	29		5
21	Tamir COHEN	ISR	4/3/84	M	26	(1)	3
14	Kevin DAVIES		26/3/77	A	37		7
16	Mark DAVIES		18/2/88	M	5	(12)	
23	Sean DAVIS		20/9/79	M	3		
9	Johan ELMANDER	SWE	27/5/81	A	15	(10)	3
11	Ricardo GARDNER	JAM	25/9/78	M	11	(10)	1
25	Stuart HOLDEN	USA	1/8/85	M	1	(1)	
22	Jussi JÄÄSKELÄINEN	FIN	19/4/75	G	38		
17	Ivan KLASNIĆ	CRO	29/1/80	A	12	(15)	8
12	Zat KNIGHT		2/5/80	D	35		1
27	LEE Chung-yong	KOR	2/7/88	M	27	(7)	3
19	Gavin McCANN		10/1/78	M	5	(6)	
6	Fabrice MUAMBA		6/4/88	M	35	(1)	1
31	Andy O'BRIEN	IRL	26/6/79	D	6		
18	Sam RICKETTS	WAL	11/10/81	D	25	(2)	
10	Mustapha RIGA	NED	10/8/91	A		(1)	
4	Paul ROBINSON		14/12/78	D	24	(1)	
3	Jlloyd SAMUEL		29/3/81	D	12	(1)	
15	Grétar Rafn STEINSSON	ISL	9/1/82	D	25	(2)	
7	Matthew TAYLOR		27/11/81	M	29	(8)	8
33	Danny WARD		11/12/91	M		(2)	
40	Vladimír WEISS	SVK	30/11/89	M	3	(10)	
32	Jack WILSHERE		1/1/92	M	13	(1)	1

BURNLEY FC
Manager – Owen Coyle (IRL); (13/1/10) Brian Laws
Founded – 1882
Stadium – Turf Moor (21,973)
MAJOR HONOURS: English League – (2) 1921, 1960; FA Cup – (1) 1914.

2009

15/8	Stoke	a	0-2	
19/8	Man. United	h	1-0	Blake
23/8	Everton	h	1-0	Elliott
29/8	Chelsea	a	0-3	
12/9	Liverpool	a	0-4	
19/9	Sunderland	h	3-1	Alexander (p), Nugent 2
26/9	Tottenham	a	0-5	
3/10	Birmingham	h	2-1	Fletcher, Bikey
18/10	Blackburn	a	2-3	Blake, Eagles
24/10	Wigan	h	1-3	Fletcher
31/10	Hull	h	2-0	Alexander 2 (1p)
7/11	Man. City	a	3-3	Alexander (p), Fletcher, McDonald
21/11	Aston Villa	h	1-1	Caldwell
28/11	West Ham	a	3-5	Fletcher 2, Eagles
5/12	Portsmouth	a	0-2	
12/12	Fulham	h	1-1	Elliott

16/12	Arsenal	h	1-1	Alexander (p)
20/12	Wolves	a	0-2	
26/12	Bolton	h	1-1	Nugent
28/12	Everton	a	0-2	

2010

16/1	Man. United	a	0-3	
26/1	Bolton	a	0-1	
30/1	Chelsea	h	1-2	Fletcher
6/2	West Ham	h	2-1	Nugent, Fox
9/2	Fulham	a	0-3	
21/2	Aston Villa	a	2-5	Fletcher, Paterson
27/2	Portsmouth	h	1-2	Paterson
6/3	Arsenal	a	1-3	Nugent
10/3	Stoke	h	1-1	Nugent
13/3	Wolves	h	1-2	Thompson
20/3	Wigan	a	0-1	
28/3	Blackburn	h	0-1	
3/4	Man. City	h	1-6	Fletcher
10/4	Hull	a	4-1	Paterson, Alexander 2 (2p), Elliott
17/4	Sunderland	a	1-2	Thompson
25/4	Liverpool	h	0-4	
1/5	Birmingham	a	1-2	Thompson
9/5	Tottenham	h	4-2	Elliott, Cork, Paterson, Thompson

No	Name	Nat	DoB	Pos	Aps	(s)	Gls
2	Graham ALEXANDER	SCO	10/10/71	M	33		7
21	André BIKEY	CMR	8/1/85	D	26	(2)	1
20	Robbie BLAKE		4/3/76	M	20	(11)	2
6	Stephen CALDWELL	SCO	12/9/80	D	12	(1)	1
5	Clarke CARLISLE		14/10/79	D	27		
42	Jack CORK		25/6/89	M	8	(3)	1
18	Leon CORT		11/9/79	D	15		
4	Michael DUFF	NIR	11/1/78	D	10	(1)	
33	Chris EAGLES		19/11/85	M	20	(14)	2
15	David EDGAR	CAN	19/5/87	D	2	(2)	
11	Wade ELLIOTT		14/12/78	M	34	(4)	4
9	Steven FLETCHER	SCO	26/3/87	A	35		8
34	Danny FOX		29/5/86	D	13	(1)	1
8	Jóhannes Karl "Joey" GUDJÓNSSON	ISL	25/5/80	M	1	(9)	
32	Fernando GUERRERO	ECU	30/9/89	M		(7)	
12	Brian JENSEN	DEN	8/6/75	G	38		
23	Stephen JORDAN		6/3/82	D	23	(2)	
3	Christian KALVENES	NOR	8/3/77	D	3	(3)	
16	Chris McCANN	IRL	21/7/87	M	7		
7	Kevin McDONALD	SCO	4/11/88	M	15	(11)	1
14	Tyrone MEARS		18/2/83	D	38		
29	Frédéric NIMANI	FRA	8/10/88	A		(2)	
22	David NUGENT		2/5/85	A	20	(10)	6
10	Martin PATERSON	NIR	10/5/87	A	17	(6)	4
1	Diego PENNY	PER	22/4/84	G		(1)	
30	Steven THOMPSON	SCO	14/10/78	A	1	(19)	4

CHELSEA FC

Manager – Carlo Ancelotti (ITA)
Founded – 1905
Stadium – Stamford Bridge (41,841)
MAJOR HONOURS: UEFA Cup Winners' Cup - (2) 1971, 1998;
UEFA Super Cup - (1) 1998;
English League - (4) 1955, 2005, 2006, 2010;
FA Cup - (6) 1970, 1997, 2000, 2007, 2009, 2010;
League Cup - (4) 1965, 1998, 2005, 2007.

2009

15/8	Hull	h	2-1	Drogba 2
18/8	Sunderland	a	3-1	Ballack, Lampard (p), Deco
23/8	Fulham	a	2-0	Drogba, Anelka
29/8	Burnley	h	3-0	Anelka, Ballack, Cole A.
12/9	Stoke	a	2-1	Drogba, Malouda
20/9	Tottenham	h	3-0	Cole A., Ballack, Drogba
26/9	Wigan	a	1-3	Drogba
4/10	Liverpool	h	2-0	Anelka, Malouda
17/10	Aston Villa	a	1-2	Drogba
24/10	Blackburn	h	5-0	og (Givet), Lampard 2 (1p), Essien, Drogba
31/10	Bolton	a	4-0	Lampard (p), Deco, og (Knight), Drogba
8/11	Man. United	h	1-0	Terry
21/11	Wolves	h	4-0	Malouda, Essien 2, Cole J.
29/11	Arsenal	a	3-0	Drogba 2, og (Vermaelen)
5/12	Man. City	a	1-2	og (Adebayor)
12/12	Everton	h	3-3	Drogba 2, Anelka
16/12	Portsmouth	h	2-1	Anelka, Lampard (p)
20/12	West Ham	h	1-1	Lampard (p)
26/12	Birmingham	a	0-0	
28/12	Fulham	h	2-1	Drogba, og (Smalling)

2010

16/1	Sunderland	h	7-2	Anelka 2, Malouda, Cole A., Lampard 2, Ballack
27/1	Birmingham	h	3-0	Malouda, Lampard 2
30/1	Burnley	a	2-1	Anelka, Terry
2/2	Hull	a	1-1	Drogba
7/2	Arsenal	h	2-0	Drogba 2
10/2	Everton	a	1-2	Malouda
20/2	Wolves	a	2-0	Drogba 2
27/2	Man. City	h	2-4	Lampard 2 (1p)
13/3	West Ham	a	4-1	Alex, Drogba 2, Malouda
21/3	Blackburn	a	1-1	Drogba
24/3	Portsmouth	a	5-0	Drogba 2, Malouda 2, Lampard
27/3	Aston Villa	h	7-1	Lampard 4 (2p), Malouda 2, Kalou
3/4	Man. United	a	2-1	Cole J., Drogba
13/4	Bolton	h	1-0	Anelka
17/4	Tottenham	a	1-2	Lampard
24/4	Stoke	h	7-0	Kalou 3, Lampard 2 (1p), Sturridge, Malouda
2/5	Liverpool	a	2-0	Drogba, Lampard
9/5	Wigan	h	8-0	Anelka 2, Lampard (p), Kalou, Drogba 3 (1p), Cole A.

No	Name	Nat	DoB	Pos	Aps	(s)	Gls
33	ALEX Rodrigo Dias da Costa	BRA	17/6/82	D	13	(3)	1
39	Nicolas ANELKA	FRA	14/3/79	A	31	(2)	11
13	Michael BALLACK	GER	26/9/76	M	26	(6)	4
35	Juliano Haus BELLETTI	BRA	20/6/76	D	4	(7)	
45	Fabio BORINI	ITA	23/3/91	A		(4)	
17	José BOSINGWA da Silva	POR	24/8/82	D	8		
43	Jeffrey BRUMA	NED	13/11/91	D		(2)	
1	Petr ČECH	CZE	20/5/82	G	34		
3	Ashley COLE		20/12/80	D	25	(2)	4
10	Joe COLE		8/11/81	M	14	(12)	2
20	Anderson Luís de Souza "DECO"	POR	27/8/77	M	14	(5)	2
11	Didier DROGBA	CIV	11/3/78	A	31	(1)	29
5	Michael ESSIEN	GHA	3/12/82	M	13	(1)	3
40	Henrique HILÁRIO Meireles Alves Sampaio	POR	21/10/75	G	2	(1)	
41	Sam HUTCHINSON		3/8/89	D		(2)	
2	Branislav IVANOVIĆ	SRB	22/2/84	D	25	(3)	
44	Gaël KAKUTA	FRA	21/6/91	M		(1)	
21	Salomon KALOU	CIV	5/8/85	A	11	(12)	5
8	Frank LAMPARD		20/6/78	M	36		22
15	Florent MALOUDA	FRA	13/6/80	M	26	(7)	12
24	Nemanja MATIĆ	SRB	1/8/88	M		(2)	
12	John Obi MIKEL	NGA	22/4/87	M	21	(4)	
19	PAULO Renato Rebocho FERREIRA	POR	18/1/79	D	11	(2)	
6	RICARDO Alberto Silveira CARVALHO	POR	18/5/78	D	22		
7	Andriy SHEVCHENKO	UKR	29/9/76	A		(1)	
23	Daniel STURRIDGE		1/9/89	A	2	(11)	1
26	John TERRY		7/12/80	D	37		2
22	Ross TURNBULL		4/1/85	G	2		
52	Patrick VAN AANHOLT	NED	29/8/90	D		(2)	
18	Yuriy ZHIRKOV	RUS	20/8/83	M	10	(7)	

EVERTON FC

Manager – David Moyes (SCO)
Founded – 1878
Stadium – Goodison Park (40,157)
MAJOR HONOURS: UEFA Cup Winners' Cup - (1) 1985;
English League - (9) 1891, 1915, 1928, 1932, 1939, 1963, 1970, 1985, 1987;
FA Cup - (5) 1906, 1933, 1966, 1984, 1995.

2009

15/8	Arsenal	h	1-6	Saha
23/8	Burnley	a	0-1	
30/8	Wigan	h	2-1	Saha, Baines (p)
13/9	Fulham	a	1-2	Cahill
20/9	Blackburn	h	3-0	Saha 2, Yobo
26/9	Portsmouth	a	1-0	Saha
4/10	Stoke	h	1-1	Osman
17/10	Wolves	h	1-1	Bilyaletdinov
25/10	Bolton	a	2-3	Saha, Fellaini
31/10	Aston Villa	h	1-1	Bilyaletdinov
8/11	West Ham	a	2-1	Saha, Gosling
21/11	Man. United	a	0-3	
25/11	Hull	a	2-3	og (Zayatte), Saha (p)
29/11	Liverpool	h	0-2	
6/12	Tottenham	h	2-2	Saha, Cahill
12/12	Chelsea	a	3-3	og (Čech), Yakubu, Saha
20/12	Birmingham	h	1-1	Bilyaletdinov
26/12	Sunderland	a	1-1	Fellaini
28/12	Burnley	h	2-0	Vaughan, Pienaar

2010

9/1	Arsenal	a	2-2	Osman, Pienaar
16/1	Man. City	h	2-0	Pienaar, Saha (p)
27/1	Sunderland	h	2-0	Cahill, Donovan
30/1	Wigan	a	1-0	Cahill
6/2	Liverpool	a	0-1	
10/2	Chelsea	h	2-1	Saha 2
20/2	Man. United	h	3-1	Bilyaletdinov, Gosling, Rodwell
28/2	Tottenham	a	1-2	Yakubu
7/3	Hull	h	5-1	Arteta 2, og (Garcia), Donovan, Rodwell
13/3	Birmingham	a	2-2	Anichebe, Yakubu
20/3	Bolton	h	2-0	Arteta, Pienaar
24/3	Man. United	a	2-0	Cahill, Arteta
27/3	Wolves	a	0-0	
4/4	West Ham	h	2-2	Bilyaletdinov, Yakubu
14/4	Aston Villa	a	2-2	Cahill 2
17/4	Blackburn	a	3-2	Arteta (p), Yakubu, Cahill
25/4	Fulham	h	2-1	og (Smalling), Arteta (p)
1/5	Stoke	a	0-0	
9/5	Portsmouth	h	1-0	Bilyaletdinov

No	Name	Nat	DoB	Pos	Aps	(s)	Gls
35	Kieran AGARD		10/10/89	A		(1)	
28	Victor ANICHEBE	NGA	23/4/88	A	6	(5)	1
10	Mikel ARTETA Amatriain	ESP	26/3/82	M	11	(2)	6
3	Leighton BAINES		11/12/84	D	37		1
37	Jose BAXTER		7/2/92	M		(2)	
7	Diniyar BILYALETDINOV	RUS	27/2/85	M	16	(7)	6
17	Tim CAHILL	AUS	6/12/79	M	33		8
31	Séamus COLEMAN	IRL	11/10/88	D		(3)	
15	Sylvain DISTIN	FRA	16/12/77	D	29		
9	Landon DONOVAN	USA	4/3/82	A	7	(3)	2
25	Marouane FELLAINI	BEL	22/11/87	M	20	(3)	2
19	Dan GOSLING		2/2/90	M	3	(8)	2
5	John HEITINGA	NED	15/11/83	D	29	(2)	
2	Tony HIBBERT		20/2/81	D	17	(3)	
24	Tim HOWARD	USA	6/3/79	G	38		
6	Phil JAGIELKA		17/8/82	D	11	(1)	
11	João Alves de Assis Silva "JÔ"	BRA	20/3/87	A	6	(9)	
5	Joleon LESCOTT		16/8/82	D	1		
23	Lucas NEILL	AUS	9/3/78	D			
18	Phil NEVILLE		21/1/77	D	22	(1)	
21	Leon OSMAN		17/5/81	M	25	(1)	2
20	Steven PIENAAR	RSA	17/3/82	M	30		4

26	Jack RODWELL		11/3/91	M	17	(9)	2
8	Louis SAHA	FRA	8/8/78	A	26	(7)	13
23	Philippe SENDEROS	SUI	14/2/85	D	1	(1)	
14	James VAUGHAN		14/7/88	A		(8)	1
22	YAKUBU Aiyegbeni	NGA	22/11/82	A	9	(16)	5
4	Joseph YOBO	NGA	6/9/80	D	14	(3)	1

FULHAM FC

Manager – Roy Hodgson
Founded – 1879
Stadium – Craven Cottage (25,478)

2009

15/8	Portsmouth	a	1-0	Zamora
23/8	Chelsea	h	0-2	
30/8	Aston Villa	a	0-2	
13/9	Everton	h	2-1	Konchesky, Duff
20/9	Wolves	a	1-2	Murphy (p)
26/9	Arsenal	h	0-1	
4/10	West Ham	a	2-2	Murphy (p), Gera
19/10	Hull	h	2-0	Zamora, Kamara
25/10	Man. City	a	2-2	Duff, Dempsey
31/10	Liverpool	h	3-1	Zamora, Nevland, Dempsey
8/11	Wigan	a	1-1	Dempsey (p)
21/11	Birmingham	a	0-1	
25/11	Blackburn	h	3-0	Nevland, Dempsey 2
28/11	Bolton	h	1-1	Duff
6/12	Sunderland	h	1-0	Zamora
12/12	Burnley	a	1-1	Zamora
19/12	Man. United	h	3-0	Murphy, Zamora, Duff
26/12	Tottenham	h	0-0	
28/12	Chelsea	a	1-2	Gera

2010

5/1	Stoke	a	2-3	Duff, Dempsey
17/1	Blackburn	a	0-2	
26/1	Tottenham	a	0-2	
30/1	Aston Villa	h	0-2	
3/2	Portsmouth	h	1-0	Greening
6/2	Bolton	a	0-0	
9/2	Burnley	h	3-0	Murphy, Elm, Zamora
21/2	Birmingham	h	2-1	Duff, Zamora
28/2	Sunderland	a	0-0	
14/3	Man. United	a	0-3	
21/3	Man. City	h	1-2	Murphy (p)
27/3	Hull	a	0-2	
4/4	Wigan	h	2-1	Okaka Chuka, Hangeland
11/4	Liverpool	a	0-0	
17/4	Wolves	h	0-0	
25/4	Everton	a	1-2	Nevland
2/5	West Ham	h	3-2	Dempsey, og (Cole), Okaka Chuka
5/5	Stoke	h	0-1	
9/5	Arsenal	a	0-4	

No	Name	Nat	DoB	Pos	Aps	(s)	Gls
6	Chris BAIRD	NIR	25/2/82	D	29	(3)	
29	Simon DAVIES	WAL	23/10/79	M	12	(5)	
23	Clint DEMPSEY	USA	9/3/83	M	27	(2)	7
34	Kagisho DIKGACOI	RSA	24/11/84	M	7	(5)	
16	Damien DUFF	IRL	2/3/79	M	30	(2)	6
35	David ELM	SWE	10/1/83	A	3	(7)	1
20	Dickson ETUHU	NGA	8/6/82	M	14	(6)	
27	Zoltán GERA	HUN	22/4/79	M	19	(8)	2
5	Jonathan GREENING		2/1/79	M	15	(8)	1
5	Brede Paulsen HANGELAND	NOR	20/6/81	D	32		1
18	Aaron HUGHES	NIR	8/11/79	D	34		
8	Andrew JOHNSON		10/2/81	A	7	(1)	
21	Eddie JOHNSON	USA	31/3/84	A		(2)	
32	Toni KALLIO	FIN	9/8/78	D		(1)	
15	Diomansy KAMARA	SEN	8/11/80	A	5	(4)	1
2	Stephen KELLY	IRL	6/9/83	D	7	(1)	
3	Paul KONCHESKY		15/5/81	D	27		1
13	Danny MURPHY		18/3/77	M	25		5
10	Erik NEVLAND	NOR	10/11/77	A	12	(11)	3

9	Stefano OKAKA CHUKA	ITA	9/8/89	A	3	(8)	2	
4	John PANTSIL	GHA	15/6/81	D	22			
17	Bjørn Helge RIISE	NOR	21/6/83	M	5	(7)		
1	Mark SCHWARZER	AUS	6/10/72	G	37			
7	SEOL Ki-hyeon	KOR	8/1/79	A		(2)		
7	Nicky SHOREY		19/2/81	D	9			
26	Chris SMALLING		22/11/89	D	9	(3)		
12	David STOCKDALE		20/9/85	G	1			
22	Fredrik STOOR	SWE	28/2/84	D		(2)		
25	Bobby ZAMORA		16/1/81	A	27		8	

HULL CITY FC
Manager – Phil Brown; (17/3/10) Iain Dowie (NIR)
Founded – 1904
Stadium – KC Stadium (25,417)

2009

15/8	Chelsea	a	1-2	*Hunt*
19/8	Tottenham	h	1-5	*Hunt*
22/8	Bolton	h	1-0	*Ghilas*
29/8	Wolves	a	1-1	*Geovanni*
12/9	Sunderland	a	1-4	*Zayatte*
19/9	Birmingham	h	0-1	
26/9	Liverpool	a	1-6	*Geovanni*
3/10	Wigan	h	2-1	*Vennegoor of Hesselink, Geovanni*
19/10	Fulham	a	0-2	
24/10	Portsmouth	h	0-0	
31/10	Burnley	a	0-2	
8/11	Stoke	h	2-1	*Olofinjana, Vennegoor of Hesselink*
21/11	West Ham	h	3-3	*og (Cole), Zayatte, Bullard (p)*
25/11	Everton	h	3-2	*Hunt, Dawson, Marney*
28/11	Man. City	a	1-1	*Bullard (p)*
5/12	Aston Villa	a	0-3	
12/12	Blackburn	h	0-0	
19/12	Arsenal	a	0-3	
27/12	Man. United	h	1-3	*Fagan (p)*
29/12	Bolton	a	2-2	*Hunt 2*

2010

16/1	Tottenham	a	0-0	
23/1	Man. United	a	0-4	
30/1	Wolves	h	2-2	*Vennegoor of Hesselink, Hunt (p)*
2/2	Chelsea	h	1-1	*Mouyokolo*
6/2	Man. City	h	2-1	*Altidore, Boateng*
10/2	Blackburn	a	0-1	
20/2	West Ham	a	0-3	
7/3	Everton	a	1-5	*Cairney*
13/3	Arsenal	h	1-2	*Bullard (p)*
20/3	Portsmouth	a	2-3	*Folan 2*
27/3	Fulham	h	2-0	*Bullard (p), Fagan*
3/4	Stoke	a	0-2	
10/4	Burnley	h	1-4	*Kilbane*
17/4	Birmingham	h	0-0	
21/4	Aston Villa	h	0-2	
24/4	Sunderland	a	0-1	
3/5	Wigan	a	2-2	*Atkinson, Cullen*
9/5	Liverpool	h	0-0	

No	Name	Nat	DoB	Pos	Aps	(s)	Gls
9	Jozy ALTIDORE	USA	6/11/89	A	16	(12)	1
31	Will ATKINSON		14/10/88	M	2		1
8	Nick BARMBY		11/2/74	M	6	(14)	
20	George BOATENG	NED	5/9/75	M	26	(3)	1
21	Jimmy BULLARD		23/10/78	M	13	(1)	4
45	Tom CAIRNEY		20/1/91	M	10	(1)	1
35	Liam COOPER	SCO	3/8/91	D	1	(1)	
25	Daniel COUSIN	GAB	7/2/77	A	1	(2)	
13	Mark CULLEN		24/4/92	A	2	(1)	1
3	Andy DAWSON		20/10/78	D	35		1
12	Matt DUKE		16/7/77	G	11		
7	Craig FAGAN		11/12/82	A	20	(5)	2
18	Caleb FOLAN	IRL	26/10/82	A	7	(1)	2
14	Richard GARCIA	AUS	4/9/81	M	14	(4)	
2	Anthony GARDNER		19/9/80	D	24		

10	GEOVANNI Deiberson							
	Maurício Gómez	BRA	11/1/80	M	16	(10)	3	
23	Kamel GHILAS	ALG	9/3/84	A	6	(7)	1	
11	Stephen HUNT	IRL	1/8/81	M	27		6	
17	Kevin KILBANE	IRL	1/2/77	M	15	(6)	1	
22	Dean MARNEY		31/1/84	M	15	(1)	1	
6	Paul McSHANE	IRL	6/1/86	D	26	(1)		
15	Bernard MENDY	FRA	20/8/81	D	15	(6)		
19	Steven MOUYOKOLO	FRA	24/1/87	D	19	(2)	1	
1	Boaz MYHILL	WAL	9/11/82	G	27			
44	Seyi OLOFINJANA	NGA	30/6/80	M	11	(8)	1	
28	Ibrahima SONKO	SEN	22/1/81	D	9			
6	Michael TURNER		9/11/83	D	4			
29	Jan VENNEGOOR of HESSELINK	NED	7/11/78	A	17	(14)	3	
30	Amr ZAKI	EGY	1/4/83	A	2	(4)		
24	Kamil ZAYATTE	GUI	7/3/85	D	21	(2)	2	

LIVERPOOL FC
Manager – Rafael Benítez (ESP)
Founded – 1892
Stadium – Anfield (45,362)
MAJOR HONOURS:
European Champion Clubs' Cup/UEFA Champions League - (5) 1977, 1978, 1981, 1984, 2005;
UEFA Cup - (3) 1973, 1976, 2001;
UEFA Super Cup - (3) 1977, 2001, 2005;
English League - (18) 1901, 1906, 1922, 1923, 1947, 1964, 1966, 1973, 1976, 1977, 1979, 1980, 1982, 1983, 1984, 1986, 1988, 1990;
FA Cup - (7) 1965, 1974, 1986, 1989, 1992, 2001, 2006;
League Cup - (7) 1981, 1982, 1983, 1984, 1995, 2001, 2003.

2009

16/8	Tottenham	a	1-2	*Gerrard (p)*
19/8	Stoke	h	4-0	*Fernando Torres, Johnson, Kuyt, N'Gog*
24/8	Aston Villa	h	1-3	*Fernando Torres*
29/8	Bolton	a	3-2	*Johnson, Fernando Torres, Gerrard*
12/9	Burnley	h	4-0	*Benayoun 3, Kuyt*
19/9	West Ham	h	3-2	*Fernando Torres 2, Kuyt*
26/9	Hull	h	6-1	*Fernando Torres 3, Gerrard, Babel 2*
4/10	Chelsea	a	0-2	
17/10	Sunderland	a	0-1	
25/10	Man. United	h	2-0	*Fernando Torres, N'Gog*
31/10	Fulham	a	1-3	*Fernando Torres*
9/11	Birmingham	h	2-2	*N'Gog, Gerrard (p)*
21/11	Man. City	h	2-2	*Škrtel, Benayoun*
29/11	Everton	a	2-0	*og (Yobo), Kuyt*
5/12	Blackburn	a	0-0	
13/12	Arsenal	h	1-2	*Kuyt*
16/12	Wigan	h	2-1	*N'Gog, Fernando Torres*
19/12	Portsmouth	a	0-2	
26/12	Wolves	h	2-0	*Gerrard, Benayoun*
29/12	Aston Villa	h	1-0	*Fernando Torres*

2010

16/1	Stoke	a	1-1	*Kyrgiakos*
20/1	Tottenham	h	2-0	*Kuyt 2 (1p)*
26/1	Wolves	a	0-0	
30/1	Bolton	h	2-0	*Kuyt, og (Davies K.)*
6/2	Everton	h	1-0	*Kuyt*
10/2	Arsenal	a	0-1	
21/2	Man. City	a	0-0	
28/2	Blackburn	h	2-1	*Gerrard, Fernando Torres*
8/3	Wigan	a	0-1	
15/3	Portsmouth	h	4-1	*Fernando Torres 2, Babel, Aquilani*
21/3	Man. United	a	1-2	*Fernando Torres*
28/3	Sunderland	h	3-0	*Fernando Torres 2, Johnson*
4/4	Birmingham	a	1-1	*Gerrard*
11/4	Fulham	h	0-0	
19/4	West Ham	h	3-0	*Benayoun, N'Gog, og (Green)*
25/4	Burnley	a	4-0	*Gerrard 2, Maxi Rodríguez, Babel*
2/5	Chelsea	a	0-2	
9/5	Hull	a	0-0	

ENGLAND

No	Name	Nat	DoB	Pos	Aps	(s)	Gls
5	Daniel AGGER	DEN	12/12/84	D	23		
4	Alberto AQUILANI	ITA	7/7/84	M	9	(9)	1
19	Ryan BABEL	NED	19/12/86	M	9	(16)	4
15	Yossi BENAYOUN	ISR	5/5/80	M	19	(11)	6
23	Jamie CARRAGHER		28/1/78	D	37		
47	DANIel PACHECO Lobato	ESP	5/1/91	A		(4)	
32	Stephen DARBY		6/10/88	D		(1)	
27	Philipp DEGEN	SUI	15/2/83	D	3	(4)	
38	Andrea DOSSENA	ITA	11/9/81	D	1	(1)	
39	Nathan ECCLESTON		30/12/90	A		(1)	
31	Nabil EL ZHAR	MAR	27/8/86	A	1	(2)	
12	FÁBIO AURÉLIO Rodrigues	BRA	24/9/79	D	8	(6)	
9	FERNANDO José TORRES Sanz	ESP	20/3/84	A	20	(2)	18
8	Steven GERRARD		30/5/80	M	32	(1)	9
22	Emiliano INSÚA	ARG	7/1/89	D	30	(1)	
2	Glen JOHNSON		23/8/84	D	24	(1)	3
34	Martin KELLY		27/4/90	D		(1)	
18	Dirk KUYT	NED	22/7/80	A	35	(2)	9
16	Sotirios KYRGIAKOS	GRE	23/7/79	D	13	(1)	1
21	LUCAS Pezzini Leiva	BRA	9/1/87	M	32	(3)	
20	Javier MASCHERANO	ARG	8/6/84	M	31	(3)	
17	MAXImiliano Rubén RODRÍGUEZ	ARG	2/1/81	M	14	(3)	1
24	David N'GOG	FRA	1/4/89	A	10	(14)	5
25	José Manuel "Pepe" REINA	ESP	31/8/82	G	38		
11	Albert RIERA Ortega	ESP	15/4/82	M	9	(3)	
49	Jack ROBINSON		1/9/93	D		(1)	
40	Daniel SÁNCHEZ AYALA	ESP	7/11/90	D	2	(3)	
37	Martin ŠKRTEL	SVK	15/12/84	D	16	(3)	1
26	Jay SPEARING		25/11/88	M	1	(2)	
10	Andriy VORONIN	UKR	21/7/79	A	1	(7)	

MANCHESTER CITY FC

Manager – Mark Hughes (WAL);
(19/12/09) Roberto Mancini (ITA)
Founded – 1894
Stadium – City of Manchester Stadium (47,715)
MAJOR HONOURS:
UEFA Cup Winners' Cup - (1) 1970;
English League - (2) 1937, 1968;
FA Cup - (4) 1904, 1934, 1956, 1969;
League Cup - (2) 1970, 1976.

2009
15/8	Blackburn	a	2-0	Adebayor, Ireland
22/8	Wolves	h	1-0	Adebayor
30/8	Portsmouth	a	1-0	Adebayor
12/9	Arsenal	h	4-2	og (Almunia), Bellamy, Adebayor, Wright-Phillips
20/9	Man. United	a	3-4	Barry, Bellamy 2
28/9	West Ham	h	3-1	Tévez 2, Petrov
5/10	Aston Villa	a	1-1	Bellamy
18/10	Wigan	a	1-1	Petrov
25/10	Fulham	h	2-2	Lescott, Petrov
1/11	Birmingham	a	0-0	
7/11	Burnley	h	3-3	Wright-Phillips, Touré, Bellamy
21/11	Liverpool	a	2-2	Adebayor, Ireland
28/11	Hull	h	1-1	Wright-Phillips
5/12	Chelsea	h	2-1	Adebayor, Tévez
12/12	Bolton	a	3-3	Tévez 2, Richards
16/12	Tottenham	a	0-3	
19/12	Sunderland	h	4-3	Santa Cruz 2, Tévez (p), Bellamy
26/12	Stoke	h	2-0	Petrov, Tévez
28/12	Wolves	a	3-0	Tévez 2, Garrido
2010				
11/1	Blackburn	h	4-1	Tévez 3, Richards
16/1	Everton	a	0-2	
31/1	Portsmouth	h	2-0	Adebayor, Kompany
6/2	Hull	a	1-2	Adebayor
9/2	Bolton	h	2-0	Tévez (p), Adebayor
16/2	Stoke	a	1-1	Barry
21/2	Liverpool	h	0-0	

27/2	Chelsea	a	4-2	Tévez 2 (1p), Bellamy 2
14/3	Sunderland	a	1-1	Johnson A.
21/3	Fulham	a	2-1	Santa Cruz, Tévez
24/3	Everton	h	0-2	
29/3	Wigan	h	3-0	Tévez 3
3/4	Burnley	a	6-1	Adebayor 2, Bellamy, Tévez, Vieira, Kompany
11/4	Birmingham	h	5-1	Tévez 2 (1p), Adebayor 2, Onuoha
17/4	Man. United	h	0-1	
24/4	Arsenal	a	0-0	
1/5	Aston Villa	h	3-1	Tévez (p), Adebayor, Bellamy
5/5	Tottenham	h	0-1	
9/5	West Ham	a	1-1	Wright-Phillips

No	Name	Nat	DoB	Pos	Aps	(s)	Gls
25	Emmanuel ADEBAYOR	TOG	26/2/84	A	25	(1)	14
18	Gareth BARRY		23/2/81	M	34		2
39	Craig BELLAMY	WAL	13/1/79	A	26	(6)	10
27	Benjamin Mwaruwari "BENJANI"	ZIM	13/8/78	A	1	(1)	
44	Dedryck BOYATA	BEL	28/11/90	D	1	(2)	
3	Wayne BRIDGE		5/8/80	D	23		
45	Greg CUNNINGHAM	IRL	31/1/91	D		(2)	
34	Nigel DE JONG	NED	30/11/84	M	30	(4)	
22	Richard DUNNE	IRL	21/9/79	D	2		
38	Márton FÜLÖP	HUN	3/5/83	G	3		
15	Javier GARRIDO Behobide	ESP	15/3/85	D	7	(2)	1
1	Shay GIVEN	IRL	24/6/76	G	35		
48	Abdisalam IBRAHIM	NOR	8/2/91	M		(1)	
7	Stephen IRELAND	IRL	22/8/86	M	16	(6)	2
11	Adam JOHNSON		14/7/87	M	14	(2)	1
6	Michael JOHNSON		24/2/88	M		(1)	
33	Vincent KOMPANY	BEL	10/4/86	D	21	(4)	2
19	Joleon LESCOTT		16/8/82	D	17	(1)	1
37	Gunnar NIELSEN	FRO	7/10/86	G		(1)	
52	Alex NIMELY		11/5/91	A		(1)	
4	Nedum ONUOHA		12/11/86	D	5	(5)	1
17	Martin PETROV	BUL	15/1/79	M	8	(8)	4
2	Micah RICHARDS		24/6/88	D	19	(4)	2
10	Robson de Souza "ROBINHO"	BRA	25/1/84	A	6	(4)	
14	Roque SANTA CRUZ	PAR	16/8/81	A	6	(13)	3
16	Sylvio Mendes Campos Júnior "SYLVINHO"	BRA	12/4/74	D	6	(4)	
32	Carlos TÉVEZ	ARG	5/2/84	A	32	(3)	23
28	Kolo TOURÉ	CIV	19/3/81	D	31		1
24	Patrick VIEIRA	FRA	23/6/76	M	8	(5)	1
8	Shaun WRIGHT-PHILLIPS		25/10/81	M	19	(11)	4
5	Pablo ZABALETA	ARG	16/1/85	D	23	(4)	

MANCHESTER UNITED FC

Manager – Sir Alex Ferguson (SCO)
Founded – 1878
Stadium – Old Trafford (76,212)
MAJOR HONOURS: European Champion Clubs' Cup/UEFA Champions League - (3) 1968, 1999, 2008;
UEFA Cup Winners' Cup - (1) 1991;
UEFA Super Cup - (1) 1991;
World Club Cup - (2) 1999, 2008;
English League - (18) 1908, 1911, 1952, 1956, 1957, 1965, 1967, 1993, 1994, 1996, 1997, 1999, 2000, 2001, 2003, 2007, 2008, 2009;
FA Cup - (11) 1909, 1948, 1963, 1977, 1983, 1985, 1990, 1994, 1996, 1999, 2004;
League Cup - (4) 1992, 2006, 2009, 2010.

2009
16/8	Birmingham	h	1-0	Rooney
19/8	Burnley	a	0-1	
22/8	Wigan	a	5-0	Rooney 2, Berbatov, Owen, Nani
29/8	Arsenal	h	2-1	Rooney (p), og (Diaby)
12/9	Tottenham	a	3-1	Giggs, Anderson, Rooney
20/9	Man. City	a	4-3	Rooney, Fletcher 2, Owen
26/9	Stoke	a	2-0	Berbatov, O'Shea

3/10	Sunderland	h	2-2	Berbatov, og (Ferdinand)
17/10	Bolton	h	2-1	og (Knight), Valencia
25/10	Liverpool	a	0-2	
31/10	Blackburn	h	2-0	Berbatov, Rooney
8/11	Chelsea	a	0-1	
21/11	Everton	h	3-0	Fletcher, Carrick, Valencia
28/11	Portsmouth	a	4-1	Rooney 3 (2p), Giggs
5/12	West Ham	a	4-0	Scholes, Gibson, Valencia, Rooney
12/12	Aston Villa	h	0-1	
15/12	Wolves	h	3-0	Rooney (p), Vidić, Valencia
19/12	Fulham	a	0-3	
27/12	Hull	a	3-1	Rooney, og (Dawson), Berbatov
30/12	Wigan	h	5-0	Rooney, Carrick, Rafael, Berbatov, Valencia

2010

9/1	Birmingham	a	1-1	og (Dann)
16/1	Burnley	h	3-0	Berbatov, Rooney, Diouf
23/1	Hull	h	4-0	Rooney 4
31/1	Arsenal	a	3-1	og (Almunia), Rooney, Park
6/2	Portsmouth	h	5-0	Rooney, og (Vanden Borre), og (Hughes), Berbatov, og (Wilson)
10/2	Aston Villa	a	1-1	og (Collins)
20/2	Everton	a	1-3	Berbatov
23/2	West Ham	h	3-0	Rooney 2, Owen
6/3	Wolves	a	1-0	Scholes
14/3	Fulham	h	3-0	Rooney 2, Berbatov
21/3	Liverpool	h	2-1	Rooney, Park
27/3	Bolton	a	4-0	og (Samuel), Berbatov 2, Gibson
3/4	Chelsea	h	1-2	Macheda
11/4	Blackburn	a	0-0	
17/4	Man. City	a	1-0	Scholes
24/4	Tottenham	h	3-1	Giggs 2 (2p), Nani
2/5	Sunderland	a	1-0	Nani
9/5	Stoke	h	4-0	Fletcher, Giggs, og (Higginbotham), Park

No	Name	Nat	DoB	Pos	Aps	(s)	Gls
8	ANDERSON Luís de Abreu Oliveira	BRA	13/4/88	M	10	(4)	1
9	Dimitar BERBATOV	BUL	30/1/81	A	24	(9)	12
6	Wes BROWN		13/10/79	D	18	(1)	
16	Michael CARRICK		28/7/81	M	22	(8)	2
30	Ritchie DE LAET	BEL	28/11/88	D	2		
32	Mame Biram DIOUF	SEN	16/12/87	A		(5)	1
23	Jonny EVANS	NIR	3/1/88	D	18		
3	Patrice EVRA	FRA	15/5/81	D	37	(1)	
20	FÁBIO Pereira da Silva	BRA	9/7/90	D	1	(4)	
5	Rio FERDINAND		7/11/78	D	12	(1)	
24	Darren FLETCHER	SCO	1/2/84	M	29	(1)	4
12	Ben FOSTER		3/4/83	G	9		
28	Darron GIBSON	IRL	25/10/87	M	6	(9)	2
11	Ryan GIGGS	WAL	29/11/73	M	20	(5)	5
29	Owen HARGREAVES		20/1/81	M		(1)	
29	Tomasz KUSZCZAK	POL	20/3/82	G	8		
27	Federico MACHEDA	ITA	22/8/91	A	1	(4)	1
17	Luís Carlos Almeida da Cunha "NANI"	POR	17/11/86	M	19	(4)	3
2	Gary NEVILLE		18/2/75	D	15	(2)	
26	Gabriel OBERTAN	FRA	26/2/89	A	1	(6)	
22	John O'SHEA	IRL	30/4/81	D	12	(3)	1
7	Michael OWEN		14/12/79	A	5	(14)	3
13	PARK Ji-sung	KOR	25/2/81	M	10	(7)	3
21	RAFAEL Pereira da Silva	BRA	9/7/90	D	8		1
10	Wayne ROONEY		24/10/85	A	32		26
18	Paul SCHOLES		16/11/74	M	24	(4)	3
25	Luis Antonio VALENCIA	ECU	4/8/85	M	29	(5)	5
1	Edwin VAN DER SAR	NED	29/10/70	G	21		
15	Nemanja VIDIĆ	SRB	21/10/81	D	24		1
19	Danny WELBECK		26/11/90	A	1	(4)	

PORTSMOUTH FC

Manager – Paul Hart; (26/11/09) Avram Grant (ISR)
Founded – 1898
Stadium – Fratton Park (20,338)
*MAJOR HONOURS: English League - (2) 1949, 1950;
FA Cup - (2) 1939, 2008.*

2009

15/8	Fulham	h	0-1	
19/8	Birmingham	a	0-1	
22/8	Arsenal	a	1-4	Kaboul
30/8	Man. City	h	0-1	
12/9	Bolton	h	2-3	Kaboul, Boateng
19/9	Aston Villa	a	0-2	
26/9	Everton	h	0-1	
3/10	Wolves	a	1-0	Yebda
17/10	Tottenham	h	1-2	Boateng
24/10	Hull	a	0-0	
31/10	Wigan	h	4-0	Dindane 3 (1p), Piquionne
7/11	Blackburn	a	1-3	O'Hara
22/11	Stoke	a	0-1	
28/11	Man. United	h	1-4	Boateng (p)
5/12	Burnley	h	2-0	Hreidarsson, Dindane
12/12	Sunderland	a	1-1	Kaboul
16/12	Chelsea	a	1-2	Piquionne
19/12	Liverpool	h	2-0	Belhadj, Piquionne
26/12	West Ham	a	0-2	
30/12	Arsenal	h	1-4	Belhadj

2010

26/1	West Ham	h	1-1	Webber
31/1	Man. City	a	0-2	
3/2	Fulham	a	0-1	
6/2	Man. United	a	0-5	
9/2	Sunderland	h	1-1	Dindane
20/2	Stoke	a	1-2	Piquionne
27/2	Burnley	a	2-1	Piquionne, Yebda (p)
9/3	Birmingham	h	1-2	Kanu
15/3	Liverpool	a	1-4	Belhadj
20/3	Hull	h	3-2	Smith, O'Hara, Kanu
24/3	Chelsea	h	0-5	
27/3	Tottenham	a	0-2	
3/4	Blackburn	h	0-0	
14/4	Wigan	a	0-0	
18/4	Aston Villa	h	1-2	Brown
24/4	Bolton	a	2-2	Dindane 2
1/5	Wolves	h	3-1	Dindane, Utaka, Brown
9/5	Everton	a	0-1	

No	Name	Nat	DoB	Pos	Aps	(s)	Gls
21	Jamie ASHDOWN		30/11/80	G	5	(1)	
33	Angelos BASINAS	GRE	3/1/76	M	7	(5)	
31	Asmir BEGOVIĆ	BIH	20/6/87	G	8	(1)	
39	Nadir BELHADJ	ALG	18/6/82	D	16	(3)	3
26	Tal BEN HAIM	ISR	31/3/82	D	21	(1)	
23	Kevin-Prince BOATENG	GHA	6/3/87	M	20	(2)	3
11	Michael BROWN		25/1/77	M	22	(2)	2
24	Aruna DINDANE	CIV	26/11/80	A	18	(1)	8
8	Pape Bouba DIOP	SEN	28/1/78	M	9	(3)	
15	Sylvain DISTIN	FRA	16/12/77	D	3		
16	Steve FINNAN	IRL	20/4/76	D	20	(1)	
7	Hermann HREIDARSSON	ISL	11/7/74	D	17		1
22	Richard HUGHES	SCO	25/6/79	M	9	(1)	
1	David JAMES		1/8/70	G	25		
3	Younes KABOUL	FRA	4/1/86	D	19		3
27	Nwankwo KANU	NGA	1/8/76	A	6	(17)	2
19	Niko KRANJČAR	CRO	13/8/84	M	4		
4	Aaron MOKOENA	RSA	25/11/80	M	21	(2)	
6	Hayden MULLINS		27/3/79	M	15	(3)	
10	David NUGENT		2/5/85	A	3	(3)	
5	Jamie O'HARA		25/9/86	M	25	(1)	2
14	Quincy OWUSU-ABEYIE	GHA	15/4/86	A	3	(7)	
9	Frédéric PIQUIONNE	FRA	8/12/78	A	26	(8)	5
3	RICARDO Sérgio ROCHA Azevedo	POR	3/10/78	D	10		

No	Name	Nat	DoB	Pos	Aps	(s)	Gls
41	Matt RITCHIE		10/9/89	M	1	(1)	
20	Tommy SMITH		22/5/80	A	12	(4)	1
46	Lennard SOWAH	GER	23/8/92	D	3	(2)	
17	John UTAKA	NGA	8/1/82	M	10	(8)	1
18	Anthony VANDEN BORRE	BEL	24/10/87	D	15	(4)	
40	Joel WARD		29/10/89	D	1	(2)	
19	Danny WEBBER		28/12/81	A	4	(13)	1
35	Marc WILSON	IRL	17/8/87	D	28		
32	Hassan YEBDA	ALG	14/5/84	M	15	(3)	2

STOKE CITY FC
Manager – Tony Pulis (WAL)
Founded – 1868
Stadium – Britannia Stadium (28,218)
MAJOR HONOURS:
League Cup – (1) 1972.

2009

15/8	Burnley	h	2-0	Shawcross, og (Jordan)
19/8	Liverpool	a	0-4	
22/8	Birmingham	a	0-0	
29/8	Sunderland	h	1-0	Kitson
12/9	Chelsea	h	1-2	Faye
19/9	Bolton	a	1-1	Kitson
26/9	Man. United	h	0-2	
4/10	Everton	a	1-1	Huth
17/10	West Ham	h	2-1	Beattie 2 (1p)
24/10	Tottenham	a	1-0	Whelan
31/10	Wolves	h	2-2	og (Elokobi), Etherington
8/11	Hull	a	1-2	Etherington
22/11	Portsmouth	h	1-0	Fuller
28/11	Blackburn	a	0-0	
5/12	Arsenal	a	0-2	
12/12	Wigan	h	2-2	Tuncay, Shawcross
19/12	Aston Villa	a	0-1	
26/12	Man. City	a	0-2	
28/12	Birmingham	h	0-1	

2010

5/1	Fulham	h	3-2	Tuncay, Faye, Sidibé
16/1	Liverpool	h	1-1	Huth
1/2	Sunderland	a	0-0	
6/2	Blackburn	h	3-0	Higginbotham, Sidibé, Etherington
9/2	Wigan	a	1-1	Tuncay
16/2	Man. City	h	1-1	Whelan
20/2	Portsmouth	a	2-1	Huth, Diao
27/2	Arsenal	h	1-3	Pugh
10/3	Burnley	a	1-1	Tuncay
13/3	Aston Villa	h	0-0	
20/3	Tottenham	h	1-2	Etherington (p)
27/3	West Ham	a	1-0	Fuller
3/4	Hull	h	2-0	Fuller, Lawrence
11/4	Wolves	a	0-0	
17/4	Bolton	h	1-2	Kitson
24/4	Chelsea	a	0-7	
1/5	Everton	h	0-0	
5/5	Fulham	a	1-0	Etherington
9/5	Man. United	a	0-4	

No	Name	Nat	DoB	Pos	Aps	(s)	Gls
9	James BEATTIE		27/2/78	A	11	(11)	2
27	Asmir BEGOVIĆ	BIH	20/6/87	G	3	(1)	
22	Danny COLLINS	WAL	6/8/80	D	22	(3)	
16	Richard CRESSWELL		20/9/77	A	1	(1)	
24	Rory DELAP	IRL	6/7/76	M	34	(2)	
15	Salif DIAO	SEN	10/2/77	M	11	(5)	1
26	Matthew ETHERINGTON		14/8/81	M	33	(1)	5
25	Abdoulaye FAYE	SEN	26/2/78	D	30	(1)	2
10	Ricardo FULLER	JAM	31/10/79	A	22	(13)	3
3	Danny HIGGINBOTHAM		29/12/78	D	23	(1)	1

No	Name	Nat	DoB	Pos	Aps	(s)	Gls
4	Robert HUTH	GER	18/8/84	D	30	(2)	3
12	Dave KITSON		21/1/80	A	10	(8)	3
7	Liam LAWRENCE	IRL	14/12/81	M	14	(11)	1
42	Louis MOULT		14/5/92	A		(1)	
14	Danny PUGH		19/10/82	M	1	(6)	1
17	Ryan SHAWCROSS		4/10/87	D	27	(1)	2
11	Mamady SIDIBÉ	MLI	18/12/79	A	19	(5)	2
1	Steve SIMONSEN		3/4/79	G	2	(1)	
29	Thomas SØRENSEN	DEN	12/6/76	G	33		
20	TUNCAY Şanlı	TUR	16/1/82	A	13	(17)	4
6	Glenn WHELAN	IRL	13/1/84	M	25	(8)	2
18	Dean WHITEHEAD		12/1/82	M	33	(3)	
28	Andy WILKINSON		6/8/84	D	21	(4)	

SUNDERLAND AFC
Manager – Steve Bruce
Founded – 1879
Stadium – Stadium of Light (49,000)
MAJOR HONOURS:
English League – (6) 1892, 1893, 1895, 1902, 1913, 1936;
FA Cup – (2) 1937, 1973.

2009

15/8	Bolton	a	1-0	Bent
18/8	Chelsea	h	1-3	Bent
22/8	Blackburn	h	2-1	Jones 2
29/8	Stoke	a	0-1	
12/9	Hull	h	4-1	Bent 2 (1p), Reid, og (Zayatte)
19/9	Burnley	a	1-3	Bent
27/9	Wolves	h	5-2	Bent (p), Jones 2 (1p), Turner, og (Mancienne)
3/10	Man. City	a	2-2	Bent, Jones
17/10	Liverpool	h	1-0	Bent
24/10	Birmingham	a	1-2	og (Dann)
31/10	West Ham	h	2-2	Reid, Richardson
7/11	Tottenham	a	0-2	
21/11	Arsenal	h	1-0	Bent
28/11	Wigan	a	0-1	
6/12	Fulham	a	0-1	
12/12	Portsmouth	h	1-1	Bent
15/12	Aston Villa	h	0-2	
19/12	Man. City	a	3-4	Mensah, Henderson, Jones
26/12	Everton	h	1-1	Bent
28/12	Blackburn	a	2-2	Bent 2

2010

16/1	Chelsea	a	2-7	Zenden, Bent
27/1	Everton	a	0-2	
1/2	Stoke	h	0-0	
6/2	Wigan	h	1-1	Jones
9/2	Portsmouth	a	1-1	Bent (p)
20/2	Arsenal	a	0-2	
28/2	Fulham	h	0-0	
9/3	Bolton	h	4-0	Campbell, Bent 3 (1p)
14/3	Man. City	h	1-1	Jones
20/3	Birmingham	h	3-1	Bent 2, Campbell
24/3	Aston Villa	h	1-1	Campbell
28/3	Liverpool	a	0-3	
3/4	Tottenham	h	3-1	Bent 2 (1p), Zenden
10/4	West Ham	a	0-1	
17/4	Burnley	h	2-1	Campbell, Bent
24/4	Hull	a	1-0	Bent
2/5	Man. United	h	0-1	
9/5	Wolves	a	1-2	Jones

No	Name	Nat	DoB	Pos	Aps	(s)	Gls
2	Phil BARDSLEY		28/6/85	D	18	(8)	
28	Benjamin Mwaruwari "BENJANI"	ZIM	13/8/78	A	1	(7)	
11	Darren BENT		6/2/84	A	38		24
9	Fraizer CAMPBELL		13/9/87	A	19	(12)	4

No	Name	Nat	DoB	Pos	Aps	(s)	Gls
19	Lorik CANA	ALB	27/7/83	M	29	(2)	
39	Lee CATTERMOLE		21/3/88	M	19	(3)	
29	Jack COLBACK		24/10/89	M		(1)	
15	Danny COLLINS	WAL	6/8/80	D	3		
22	Paulo DA SILVA	PAR	1/2/80	D	12	(4)	
5	Anton FERDINAND		18/2/85	D	19	(5)	
32	Márton FÜLÖP	HUN	3/5/83	G	12	(1)	
1	Craig GORDON	SCO	31/12/82	G	26		
23	David HEALY	NIR	5/8/79	A		(3)	
16	Jordan HENDERSON		17/6/90	M	23	(10)	1
6	Alan HUTTON	SCO	30/11/84	D	11		
17	Kenwyne JONES	TRI	5/10/84	A	24	(8)	9
27	Matthew KILGALLON		8/1/84	D	6	(1)	
18	Grant LEADBITTER		7/1/86	M		(1)	
8	Steed MALBRANQUE	FRA	6/1/80	M	30	(1)	
3	George McCARTNEY	NIR	29/4/81	D	20	(5)	
12	John MENSAH	GHA	29/11/82	D	14	(2)	1
18	David MEYLER	IRL	29/5/89	M	9	(1)	
14	Daryl MURPHY	IRL	15/3/83	M	2	(1)	
6	Nyron NOSWORTHY	JAM	11/10/80	D	7	(3)	
20	Andy REID	IRL	29/7/82	M	18	(3)	2
10	Kieran RICHARDSON		21/10/84	M	28	(1)	1
4	Michael TURNER		9/11/83	D	29		1
7	Boudewijn ZENDEN	NED	15/8/76	M	1	(19)	2

TOTTENHAM HOTSPUR FC

Manager – Harry Redknapp
Founded – 1882
Stadium – White Hart Lane (36,310)
MAJOR HONOURS:
UEFA Cup Winners' Cup - (1) 1963;
UEFA Cup - (2) 1972, 1984;
English League - (2) 1951, 1961;
FA Cup - (8) 1901, 1921, 1961, 1962, 1967, 1981, 1982, 1991;
League Cup - (4) 1971, 1973, 1999, 2008.

2009

Date	Opponent		Score	Scorers
16/8	Liverpool	h	2-1	Assou-Ekotto, Bassong
19/8	Hull	a	5-1	Defoe 3, Palacios, Keane
23/8	West Ham	a	2-1	Defoe, Lennon
29/8	Birmingham	h	2-1	Crouch, Lennon
12/9	Man. United	h	1-3	Defoe
20/9	Chelsea	a	0-3	
26/9	Burnley	h	5-0	Keane 4 (1p), Jenas
3/10	Bolton	a	2-2	Kranjčar, Čorluka
17/10	Portsmouth	a	2-1	King, Defoe
24/10	Stoke	h	0-1	
31/10	Arsenal	a	0-3	
7/11	Sunderland	h	2-0	Keane, Huddlestone
22/11	Wigan	h	9-1	Crouch, Defoe 5, Lennon, og (Kirkland), Kranjčar
28/11	Aston Villa	a	1-1	Dawson
6/12	Everton	a	2-2	Defoe, Dawson
12/12	Wolves	h	0-1	
16/12	Man. City	h	3-0	Kranjčar 2, Defoe
19/12	Blackburn	a	2-0	Crouch 2
26/12	Fulham	a	0-0	
28/12	West Ham	h	2-0	Modrić, Defoe

2010

Date	Opponent		Score	Scorers
16/1	Hull	h	0-0	
20/1	Liverpool	a	0-2	
26/1	Fulham	h	2-0	Crouch, Bentley
30/1	Birmingham	a	1-1	Defoe
6/2	Aston Villa	h	0-0	
10/2	Wolves	a	0-1	
21/2	Wigan	h	3-0	Defoe, Pavlyuchenko 2
28/2	Everton	h	2-1	Pavlyuchenko, Modrić
13/3	Blackburn	h	3-1	Defoe, Pavlyuchenko 2
20/3	Stoke	a	2-1	Gudjohnsen, Kranjčar
27/3	Portsmouth	h	2-0	Crouch, Kranjčar
3/4	Sunderland	a	1-3	Crouch
14/4	Arsenal	h	2-1	Rose, Bale
17/4	Chelsea	h	2-1	Defoe (p), Bale
24/4	Man. United	a	1-3	King
1/5	Bolton	h	1-0	Huddlestone
5/5	Man. City	a	1-0	Crouch
9/5	Burnley	a	2-4	Bale, Modrić

No	Name	Nat	DoB	Pos	Aps	(s)	Gls
27	Ben ALNWICK		1/1/87	G	1		
32	Benoît ASSOU-EKOTTO	CMR	24/3/84	D	29	(1)	1
3	Gareth BALE	WAL	16/7/89	D	18	(5)	3
19	Sébastien BASSONG	CMR	9/7/86	D	25	(3)	1
5	David BENTLEY		27/8/84	M	11	(4)	1
22	Vedran ČORLUKA	CRO	5/2/86	D	29		1
15	Peter CROUCH		30/1/81	A	21	(17)	8
23	Carlo CUDICINI	ITA	6/9/73	G	6	(1)	
20	Michael DAWSON		18/11/83	D	25	(4)	2
18	Jermain DEFOE		7/10/82	A	31	(3)	18
17	GIOVANI dos Santos Ramírez	MEX	11/5/89	M		(1)	
1	Heurelho da Silva GOMES	BRA	15/2/81	G	31		
17	Eidur Smári GUDJOHNSEN	ISL	15/9/78	A	3	(8)	1
6	Tom HUDDLESTONE		28/12/86	M	33		2
2	Alan HUTTON	SCO	30/11/84	D	1	(7)	
8	Jermaine JENAS		18/2/83	M	9	(10)	1
4	Younes KABOUL	FRA	4/1/86	D	8	(2)	
10	Robbie KEANE	IRL	8/7/80	A	15	(5)	6
26	Ledley KING		12/10/80	D	19	(1)	2
21	Niko KRANJČAR	CRO	13/8/84	M	19	(5)	6
7	Aaron LENNON		16/4/87	M	20	(2)	3
29	Jake LIVERMORE		14/11/89	M		(1)	
14	Luka MODRIĆ	CRO	9/9/85	M	21	(4)	3
16	Kyle NAUGHTON		11/11/88	D		(1)	
24	Jamie O'HARA		25/9/86	M		(2)	
12	Wilson PALACIOS	HON	29/7/84	M	29	(4)	1
9	Roman PAVLYUCHENKO	RUS	15/12/81	A	8	(8)	5
25	Danny ROSE		2/6/90	M	1		1
28	Kyle WALKER		28/5/90	D	2		
39	Jonathan WOODGATE		22/1/80	D	3		

WEST HAM UNITED FC

Manager – Gianfranco Zola (ITA)
Founded – 1900
Stadium – Upton Park (35,303)
MAJOR HONOURS:
UEFA Cup Winners' Cup – (1) 1965;
FA Cup – (3) 1964, 1975, 1980.

2009

Date	Opponent		Score	Scorers
15/8	Wolves	a	2-0	Noble, Upson
23/8	Tottenham	h	1-2	Cole
29/8	Blackburn	a	0-0	
12/9	Wigan	a	0-1	
19/9	Liverpool	h	2-3	Diamanti (p), Cole
28/9	Man. City	a	1-3	Cole
4/10	Fulham	h	2-2	Cole, Stanislas
17/10	Stoke	a	1-2	Upson
25/10	Arsenal	h	2-2	Cole, Diamanti (p)
31/10	Sunderland	a	2-2	Franco, Cole
4/11	Aston Villa	h	2-1	Noble (p), Hines
8/11	Everton	h	1-2	og (Hibbert)
21/11	Hull	a	3-3	Franco, Collison, Da Costa
28/11	Burnley	h	5-3	Collison, Stanislas, Cole (p), Franco, Jiménez (p)
5/12	Man. United	h	0-4	
12/12	Birmingham	a	0-1	
15/12	Bolton	a	1-3	Diamanti
20/12	Chelsea	h	1-1	Diamanti (p)
26/12	Portsmouth	h	2-0	Diamanti (p), Kováč
28/12	Tottenham	a	0-2	

2010

Date	Opponent		Score	Scorers
17/1	Aston Villa	a	0-0	
26/1	Portsmouth	a	1-1	Upson
30/1	Blackburn	h	0-0	
6/2	Burnley	a	1-2	Ilan
10/2	Birmingham	h	2-0	Diamanti, Cole
20/2	Hull	a	3-0	Behrami, Cole, Faubert
23/2	Man. United	a	0-3	
6/3	Bolton	h	1-2	Diamanti
13/3	Chelsea	a	1-4	Parker
20/3	Arsenal	a	0-2	
23/3	Wolves	h	1-3	Franco
27/3	Stoke	h	0-1	
4/4	Everton	a	2-2	Da Costa, Ilan
10/4	Sunderland	h	1-0	Ilan
19/4	Liverpool	a	0-3	
24/4	Wigan	h	3-2	Ilan, Kováč, Parker
2/5	Fulham	a	2-3	Cole, Franco
9/5	Man. City	h	1-1	Boa Morte

No	Name	Nat	DoB	Pos	Aps	(s)	Gls
21	Valon BEHRAMI	SUI	19/4/85	M	24	(3)	1
13	Luís BOA MORTE Pereira	POR	4/8/77	M	1		1
12	Carlton COLE		12/10/83	A	26	(4)	10
19	James COLLINS	WAL	23/8/83	D	3		
31	Jack COLLISON	WAL	2/10/88	M	19	(3)	2
22	Manuel DA COSTA	POR	6/5/86	D	12	(3)	2
33	Fabio DAPRELÀ	SUI	19/2/91	D	4	(3)	
32	Alessandro DIAMANTI	ITA	2/5/83	A	18	(9)	7
7	Kieron DYER		29/12/78	M	4	(6)	
20	Julien FAUBERT	FRA	1/8/83	D	32	(1)	1
10	Guillermo FRANCO	MEX	3/11/76	A	16	(7)	5
4	Danny GABBIDON	WAL	8/8/79	D	8	(2)	
1	Robert GREEN		18/1/80	G	38		
41	Zavon HINES	JAM	27/12/88	A	5	(8)	1
9	ILAN Araújo dall'Igna	BRA	18/9/80	A	6	(5)	4
3	Hérita ILUNGA	COD	25/2/82	D	16		
17	Luis Antonio JIMÉNEZ	CHI	17/6/84	M	6	(5)	1
14	Radoslav KOVÁČ	CZE	27/11/79	D	27	(4)	2
28	Péter KURUCZ	HUN	30/5/88	G		(1)	
17	Benni McCARTHY	RSA	12/11/77	A	2	(3)	
11	Ahmed Hossam Hussein Abdelhamid "MIDO"	EGY	23/2/83	A	5	(4)	
16	Mark NOBLE		8/5/87	M	25	(2)	2
24	Frank NOUBLE		24/9/91	A	3	(5)	
8	Scott PARKER		13/10/80	M	30	(1)	2
19	Freddie SEARS		27/11/89	A		(1)	
18	Jonathan SPECTOR	USA	1/3/86	D	22	(5)	
42	Jordan SPENCE		24/5/90	D		(1)	
46	Junior STANISLAS		26/11/89	M	11	(15)	1
30	James TOMKINS		29/3/79	D	22	(1)	
15	Matthew UPSON		18/4/79	D	33		3

WIGAN ATHLETIC FC
Manager – Roberto Martínez (ESP)
Founded – 1932
Stadium – DW Stadium (25,138)

2009

Date	Opponent		Score	Scorers
15/8	Aston Villa	a	2-0	Rodallega, Koumas
18/8	Wolves	h	0-1	
22/8	Man. United	h	0-5	
30/8	Everton	a	1-2	Scharner
12/9	West Ham	h	1-0	Rodallega
19/9	Arsenal	a	0-4	
26/9	Chelsea	h	3-1	Bramble, Rodallega (p), Scharner
3/10	Hull	a	1-2	Sinclair
18/10	Man. City	h	1-1	N'Zogbia
24/10	Burnley	a	3-1	Rodallega 2, Boyce
31/10	Portsmouth	a	0-4	
8/11	Fulham	h	1-1	Boyce
22/11	Tottenham	a	1-9	Scharner
28/11	Sunderland	h	1-0	Rodallega
5/12	Birmingham	h	2-3	N'Zogbia, Jordi Gómez
12/12	Stoke	a	2-2	Boyce, Figueroa
16/12	Liverpool	a	1-2	N'Zogbia
26/12	Blackburn	h	1-1	Rodallega
30/12	Man. United	a	0-5	

2010

Date	Opponent		Score	Scorers
16/1	Wolves	a	2-0	McCarthy, N'Zogbia
27/1	Blackburn	a	1-2	Caldwell
30/1	Everton	h	0-1	
6/2	Sunderland	a	1-1	Diamé
9/2	Stoke	h	1-1	Scharner
17/2	Bolton	h	0-0	
21/2	Tottenham	h	0-3	
27/2	Birmingham	a	0-1	
8/3	Liverpool	h	1-0	Rodallega
13/3	Bolton	a	0-4	
16/3	Aston Villa	h	1-2	Caldwell
20/3	Burnley	h	1-0	Rodallega
29/3	Man. City	a	0-3	
4/4	Fulham	a	1-2	Scotland
14/4	Portsmouth	a	0-0	
18/4	Arsenal	h	3-2	Watson, Bramble, N'Zogbia
24/4	West Ham	a	2-3	og (Spector), Rodallega
3/5	Hull	h	2-2	Moses, Gohouri
9/5	Chelsea	a	0-8	

No	Name	Nat	DoB	Pos	Aps	(s)	Gls
17	Emmerson BOYCE	BRB	24/9/79	D	23	(1)	3
19	Titus BRAMBLE		21/7/81	D	35		2
11	Michael BROWN		25/1/77	M	2		
5	Gary CALDWELL	SCO	12/4/82	D	16		2
5	CHO Won-hee	KOR	17/4/83	M	1	(3)	
27	Mohamed DIAMÉ	FRA	14/6/87	M	34		1
3	Erik EDMAN	SWE	11/11/78	D	2	(1)	
31	Maynor FIGUEROA	HON	2/5/83	D	35		1
2	Steve GOHOURI	CIV	8/2/81	D	4	(1)	1
15	JORDI GÓMEZ Garcia-Penche	ESP	24/5/85	M	11	(12)	1
23	Olivier KAPO	FRA	27/9/80	M		(1)	
30	Marlon KING	JAM	26/4/80	A		(3)	
1	Chris KIRKLAND		2/5/81	G	32		
10	Jason KOUMAS	WAL	25/9/79	M	6	(2)	1
18	MARCELO MORENO Martins	BOL	18/6/87	A	9	(3)	
24	James McCARTHY	SCO	12/11/90	M	19	(1)	1
25	Mario MELCHIOT	NED	4/11/76	D	32		
11	Victor MOSES		12/12/90	A	2	(12)	1
14	Charles N'ZOGBIA	FRA	28/5/86	M	35	(1)	1
12	Mike POLLITT		29/2/72	G	2	(2)	
20	Hugo RODALLEGA	COL	25/7/85	A	38		10
7	Paul SCHARNER	AUT	11/3/80	M	30	(8)	4
9	Jason SCOTLAND	TRI	18/2/79	A	14	(18)	1
16	Scott SINCLAIR		25/3/89	A	1	(17)	1
29	Vladimir STOJKOVIĆ	SRB	28/7/83	G	4		
6	Hendry THOMAS	HON	23/2/85	M	27	(4)	
8	Ben WATSON		9/7/85	M	4	(1)	1

WOLVERHAMPTON WANDERERS FC
Manager – Mick McCarthy (IRL)
Founded – 1877
Stadium – Molineux (28,576)
MAJOR HONOURS:
English League – (3) 1954, 1958, 1959;
FA Cup – (4) 1893, 1908, 1949, 1960;
League Cup – (2) 1974, 1980.

2009

Date	Opponent		Score	Scorers
15/8	West Ham	h	0-2	
18/8	Wigan	a	1-0	Keogh

22/8	Man. City	a	0-1	
29/8	Hull	h	1-1	Stearman
12/9	Blackburn	a	1-3	Maierhofer
20/9	Fulham	h	2-1	Doyle, Edwards
27/9	Sunderland	a	2-5	og (Mensah), Doyle
3/10	Portsmouth	h	0-1	
17/10	Everton	a	1-1	Doyle
24/10	Aston Villa	h	1-1	Ebanks-Blake (p)
31/10	Stoke	a	2-2	Craddock 2
7/11	Arsenal	h	1-4	Craddock
21/11	Chelsea	a	0-4	
29/11	Birmingham	h	0-1	
5/12	Bolton	h	2-1	Craddock, Milijaš
12/12	Tottenham	a	1-0	Doyle
15/12	Man. United	a	0-3	
20/12	Burnley	h	2-0	Milijaš, Doyle
26/12	Liverpool	a	0-2	
28/12	Man. City	h	0-3	
2010				
16/1	Wigan	h	0-2	
26/1	Liverpool	h	0-0	
30/1	Hull	a	2-2	og (Gardner), Jarvis
7/2	Birmingham	a	1-2	Doyle
10/2	Tottenham	h	1-0	Jones
20/2	Chelsea	h	0-2	
27/2	Bolton	a	0-1	
6/3	Man. United	h	0-1	
13/3	Burnley	a	2-1	Jarvis, og (Carlisle)
20/3	Aston Villa	a	2-2	Craddock, og (Milner)
23/3	West Ham	a	3-1	Doyle, Zubar, Jarvis
27/3	Everton	h	0-0	
3/4	Arsenal	a	0-1	
11/4	Stoke	h	0-0	
17/4	Fulham	a	0-0	
24/4	Blackburn	h	1-1	Ebanks-Blake
1/5	Portsmouth	a	1-3	Doyle
9/5	Sunderland	h	2-1	Doyle (p), Guedioura

No	Name	Nat	DoB	Pos	Aps	(s)	Gls
16	Christophe BERRA	SCO	31/1/85	D	32		
35	Segundo CASTILLO	ECU	15/5/82	M	7	(1)	
6	Jody CRADDOCK		25/7/75	D	33		5
29	Kevin DOYLE	IRL	18/9/83	A	33	(1)	9
9	Sylvan EBANKS-BLAKE		29/3/86	A	12	(11)	2
4	David EDWARDS	WAL	3/2/86	M	16	(4)	1
3	George ELOKOBI	CMR	31/1/86	D	17	(5)	
32	Kevin FOLEY	IRL	1/11/84	D	23	(2)	
28	George FRIEND		19/10/87	M	1		
34	Adlène GUEDIOURA	ALG	12/11/85	M	7	(7)	1
1	Marcus HAHNEMANN	USA	15/6/72	G	25		
15	Greg HALFORD		8/12/84	D	12	(3)	
1	Wayne HENNESSEY	WAL	24/1/87	G	13		
8	Karl HENRY		26/11/82	M	34		
26	Matthew HILL		26/3/81	D	2		
19	Chris IWELUMO	SCO	1/8/78	A	2	(13)	
17	Matthew JARVIS		22/5/86	M	30	(4)	3
14	David JONES		4/11/84	M	16	(4)	1
10	Andrew KEOGH	IRL	16/5/86	A	8	(5)	1
7	Michael KIGHTLY		24/1/86	M	3	(6)	
33	Stefan MAIERHOFER	AUT	16/8/82	A	1	(7)	1
27	Michael MANCIENNE		8/1/88	D	22	(8)	
20	Nenad MILIJAŠ	SRB	30/4/83	M	12	(7)	2
25	Geoffrey MUJANGI BIA	BEL	12/8/89	M	1	(2)	
5	Richard STEARMAN		19/8/87	D	12	(4)	1
12	Andrew SURMAN		20/8/86	M	3	(4)	
18	Sam VOKES	WAL	21/10/89	A		(5)	
11	Stephen WARD	IRL	20/8/85	D	18	(4)	
2	Ronald ZUBAR	FRA	20/9/85	D	23		1

PROMOTED CLUBS

NEWCASTLE UNITED FC
Manager – Chris Hughton (IRL)
Founded – 1881
Stadium – St. James' Park (52,387)
MAJOR HONOURS: Inter Cities Fairs Cup - (1) 1969; English League - (4) 1905, 1907, 1909, 1927; FA Cup - (6) 1910, 1924, 1932, 1951, 1952, 1955.

WEST BROMWICH ALBION FC
Manager – Roberto Di Matteo (ITA)
Founded – 1878
Stadium – The Hawthorns (27,877)
MAJOR HONOURS: English League – (1) 1920; FA Cup – (5) 1888, 1892, 1931, 1954, 1968; League Cup – (1) 1966.

BLACKPOOL FC
Manager – Ian Holloway
Founded – 1887
Stadium – Bloomfield Road (12,555)
MAJOR HONOURS: FA Cup – (1) 1953.

SECOND LEVEL FINAL TABLE 2009/10

		Pld	W	D	L	F	A	Pts
1	Newcastle United FC	46	30	12	4	90	35	102
2	West Bromwich Albion FC	46	26	13	7	89	48	91
3	Nottingham Forest FC	46	22	13	11	65	40	79
4	Cardiff City FC	46	22	10	14	73	54	76
5	Leicester City FC	46	21	13	12	61	45	76
6	Blackpool FC	46	19	13	14	74	58	70
7	Swansea City FC	46	17	18	11	40	37	69
8	Sheffield United FC	46	17	14	15	62	55	65
9	Reading FC	46	17	12	17	68	63	63
10	Bristol City FC	46	15	18	13	56	65	63
11	Middlesbrough FC	46	16	14	16	58	50	62
12	Doncaster Rovers FC	46	15	15	16	59	58	60
13	Queens Park Rangers FC	46	14	15	17	58	65	57
14	Derby County FC	46	15	11	20	53	63	56
15	Ipswich Town FC	46	12	20	14	50	61	56
16	Watford FC	46	14	12	20	61	68	54
17	Preston North End FC	46	13	15	18	58	73	54
18	Barnsley FC	46	14	12	20	53	69	54
19	Coventry City FC	46	13	15	18	47	64	54
20	Scunthorpe United FC	46	14	10	22	62	84	52
21	Crystal Palace FC	46	14	17	15	50	53	49
22	Sheffield Wednesday FC	46	11	14	21	49	69	47
23	Plymouth Argyle FC	46	11	8	27	43	68	41
24	Peterborough United FC	46	8	10	28	46	80	34

NB Crystal Palace FC – 10 pts deducted.

PROMOTION PLAY-OFFS

(8/5/10 & 11/5/10)
Blackpool 2, Nottingham Forest 1
Nottingham Forest 3, Blackpool 4
(Blackpool 6-4)

(9/5/10 & 12/5/10)
Leicester 0, Cardiff 1
Cardiff 2, Leicester 3 (aet)
(3-3; Cardiff 4-3 on pens)

(22/5/10)
Blackpool 3, Cardiff 2

ENGLAND

DOMESTIC CUPS 2009/10

FA CUP

THIRD ROUND

(2/1/10)
Aston Villa 3, Blackburn 1
Blackpool 1, Ipswich 2
Bolton 4, Lincoln 0
Everton 3, Carlisle 1
Fulham 1, Swindon 0
Huddersfield 0, West Brom 2
Leicester 2, Swansea 1
Middlesbrough 0, Man. City 1
Millwall 1, Derby 1
MK Dons 1, Burnley 2
Nottingham Forest 0, Birmingham 0
Plymouth 0, Newcastle 0
Portsmouth 1, Coventry 1
Preston 7, Colchester 0
Reading 1, Liverpool 1
Scunthorpe 1, Barnsley 0
Sheffield Wednesday 1, Crystal Palace 2
Southampton 1, Luton 0
Stoke 3, York 1
Sunderland 3, Barrow 0
Torquay 0, Brighton 1
Tottenham 4, Peterborough 0
Wigan 4, Hull 1

(3/1/10)
Chelsea 5, Watford 0
Man. United 0, Leeds 1
Sheffield United 1, QPR 1
Tranmere 0, Wolves 1
West Ham 1, Arsenal 2

(12/1/10)
Bristol City 1, Cardiff 1

(19/1/10)
Accrington 1, Gillingham 0
Brentford 0, Doncaster 1
Notts County 2, Forest Green 1

Replays

(12/1/10)
Birmingham 1, Nottingham Forest 0
Coventry 1, Portsmouth 2 *(aet)*
Derby 1, Millwall 1 *(aet; 5-3 on pens)*
QPR 2, Sheffield United 3

(13/1/10)
Liverpool 1, Reading 2 *(aet)*
Newcastle 3, Plymouth 0

(19/1/10)
Cardiff 1, Bristol City 0

FOURTH ROUND

(23/1/10)
Accrington 1, Fulham 3
Aston Villa 3, Brighton 2
Bolton 2, Sheffield United 0
Cardiff 4, Leicester 2
Derby 1, Doncaster 0
Everton 1, Birmingham 2
Notts County 2, Wigan 2
Portsmouth 2, Sunderland 1
Preston 0, Chelsea 2
Reading 1, Burnley 0
Southampton 2, Ipswich 1
Tottenham 2, Leeds 2
West Brom 4, Newcastle 2
Wolves 2, Crystal Palace 2

(24/1/10)
Scunthorpe 2, Man. City 4
Stoke 3, Arsenal 1

Replays

(2/2/10)
Crystal Palace 3, Wolves 1
Wigan 0, Notts County 2

(3/2/10)
Leeds 1, Tottenham 3

FIFTH ROUND

(13/2/10)
Chelsea 4, Cardiff 1
Derby 1, Birmingham 2
Man. City 1, Stoke 1
Reading 2, West Brom 2
Southampton 1, Portsmouth 4

(14/2/10)
Bolton 1, Tottenham 1
Crystal Palace 2, Aston Villa 2
Fulham 4, Notts County 0

Replays

(24/2/10)
Aston Villa 3, Crystal Palace 1
Stoke 3, Man. City 1 *(aet)*
Tottenham 4, Bolton 0
West Brom 2, Reading 3 *(aet)*

QUARTER-FINALS

(6/3/10)
Fulham 0, Tottenham 0
Portsmouth 2 *(Piquionne 67, 70)*, Birmingham

(7/3/10)
Chelsea 2 *(Lampard 35, Terry 67)*, Stoke 0
Reading 2 *(Long 27, 42)*, Aston Villa 4 *(Young A. 47, Carew 51, 57, 90+3p)*

Replay

(24/3/10)
Tottenham 3 *(Bentley 47, Pavlyuchenko 60, Gudjohnsen 66)*, Fulham 1 *(Zamora 17)*

SEMI-FINALS

(10/4/10)
Chelsea 3 *(Drogba 68, Malouda 89, Lampard 90+5)*, Aston Villa 0

(11/4/10)
Portsmouth 2 *(Piquionne 99, Boateng 117p)*, Tottenham 0 *(aet)*

FINAL

(15/5/10)
Wembley Stadium, London
CHELSEA FC 1 *(Drogba 59)*
PORTSMOUTH FC 0
Referee – Foy
CHELSEA – Čech, Ivanović, Alex, Terry, Cole A., Lampard, Ballack (Belletti 44), Malouda, Kalou (Cole J. 71), Drogba, Anelka (Sturridge 90).
PORTSMOUTH – James, Finnan, Ricardo Rocha, Mokoena, Mullins (Belhadj 81), Dindane, Brown, Diop (Kanu 81), Boateng (Utaka 73), O'Hara, Piquionne.

LEAGUE CUP

QUARTER-FINALS

(1/12/09)
Man. United 2 *(Gibson 16, 38)*, Tottenham 0
Portsmouth 2 *(Petrov 10og, Kanu 87)*, Aston Villa 4 *(Heskey 12, Milner 27, Downing 74, Young A. 89)*

(2/12/09)
Blackburn 3 *(Kalinić 9, Emerton 64, McCarthy 93p)*, Chelsea 3 *(Drogba 48, Kalou 52, Paulo Ferreira 120+2) (aet; 4-3 on pens)*
Man. City 3 *(Tévez 50, Wright-Phillips 69, Weiss 89)*, Arsenal 0

SEMI-FINALS

(14/1/10 & 20/1/10)
Blackburn 0, Aston Villa 1 *(Milner 23)*
Aston Villa 6 *(Warnock 30, Milner 40p, N'Zonzi 53og, Agbonlahor 58, Heskey 62, Young A. 90+3)*, Blackburn 4 *(Kalinić 10, 26, Olsson 63, Emerton 84) (Aston Villa 7-4)*

(19/1/0 & 27/1/10)
Man. City 2 *(Tévez 42p, 65)*, Man. United 1 *(Giggs 17)*
Man. United 3 *(Scholes 52, Carrick 71, Rooney 90+2)*, Man. City 1 *(Tévez 76) (Man. United 4-3)*

FINAL

(28/2/10)
Wembley Stadium, London
MANCHESTER UNITED FC 2 *(Owen 12, Rooney 7*
ASTON VILLA FC 1 *(Milner 5p)*
Referee – Dowd
MAN. UNITED – Kuszczak, Rafael (Neville 66), Evans, Vidić, Evra, Valencia, Fletcher, Carrick, Pa (Gibson 85), Owen (Rooney 42), Berbatov.
ASTON VILLA – Friedel, Cuéllar (Carew 80), Dunne, Collins, Warnock, Young A., Petrov, Milne Downing, Agbonlahor, Heskey.

ESTONIA

Levadia in a league of their own

FC Levadia Tallinn collected their fourth successive Meistriliiga crown at a canter. Pressed hard by city rivals FC Flora Tallinn the previous season, they had it all their own way in 2009, securing the title with four games to spare and finishing 21 points clear of second-placed JK Sillamäe Kalev.

In the year that Estonian football celebrated its Centenary, Levadia fell agonisingly short of marking the occasion with 100 league points. They fell just three short, the consequence of a 2-1 defeat away to JK Trans Narva in their penultimate fixture. It was the only match they lost all season and brought a 61-game unbeaten run in the Meistriliiga to a rather inopportune end. All things considered, however, it

was but a minor scar on a thoroughly memorable season for the club in which they knocked Polish champions Wisła Kraków out of the UEFA Champions League and their reserve team also lifted the Esiliiga, the nation's second division. There would be yet more success around the corner, too, as Levadia beat Flora 3-0 to win the final of the 2010 Estonian Cup.

Early burst

The league triumph was a foregone conclusion from very early on as Igor Prins' side racked up maximum points from their first 11 fixtures and reached the halfway point of the season with just four points squandered. The goals flowed from all quarters, with young Russian striker Nikita Andreev proving especially prolific (17 goals in 17 games) before he was sold in mid-season to Spanish club UD Almería. Former Estonian international Tarmo Neemelo returned from Belgium to take his place, and by the end of the season Levadia had put 121 goals past their opponents (16 more than in 2008), with Vitali Gussev's individual haul of 26 placing him on top of the Meistriliiga's scorer charts. Midfielders Vitali Leitan (13 goals) and Konstantin Nahk (12) also joined him and Andreev in the top ten.

Levadia also defended well, conceding just 23 goals and keeping 17 clean sheets. That was largely to the credit of goalkeeper Martin Kaalma, who decided, at the relatively young age of 32, to hang up his gloves at the end of the season and become the club's goalkeeping coach. Another legendary figure of Estonian football to quit at the season's end was Indrek Zelinski, although there was a rather sad climax to a memorable career when he was red-carded in his final game.

Two other key players who were no longer at the club when Levadia won the Estonian Cup six months later were Estonian internationals Sander Puri, who left during the winter for Greek club Larissa FC, and defender Tihhon Šišov, who decided to try his luck in

Estonian legend Indrek Zelinski bowed out for club and country in 2009/10

Azerbaijan with Xäzär Länkäran FK. There was still enough talent left at the club, however, to see off holders Flora with relative ease at the Kadriorg stadium and reclaim the Cup after a three-year gap.

Reim replaces Rüütli

Flora went into that final under a new coach, record Estonian international cap-holder Martin Reim having replaced national team boss Tarmo Rüütli at the beginning of 2010. Rüütli's position at Flora was under threat after a desperately disappointing 2009 Meistriliiga campaign. Although Flora won the Cup that year, their league form fell way below expectations. Crippled by a bad start, they never recovered. They lost all four of their matches against Levadia, and although they finished the season with a bang, winning their last seven games, that was not enough to lift them higher than fourth place.

Sillamäe Kalev and Trans both finished four points above Flora, with the former already secure of taking the runners-up spot on the head-to-head rule before they lost 2-0 to the latter on the final day (they had won all three previous meetings). There were UEFA Europa League places for both clubs as well as for Flora, who looked like causing a sensation in the second qualifying round of the 2009/10 competition when they won the first leg 1-0 away to Danish heavyweights Brøndby IF – only to suffer a 4-1 home defeat in the return.

A few weeks later Rüütli oversaw another home defeat, this time in his other guise as Estonia's head coach, but as it was only by one goal to nil against a star-studded Brazil team in a specially arranged

Eesti Jalgpalli Liit (EJL)

A. Le Coq Arena
Asula 4c
EE-11312 Tallinn
tel - +372 627 9960
fax - +372 627 9969
website - jalgpall.ee
email - efa@jalgpall.ee
Year of Formation – 1921

President – Aivar Pohlak
General Secretary - Tõnu Sirel
Media Officer – Mihkel Uiboleht
National Stadium - A. Le Coq Arena, Tallinn (9,692)

TOP FIVE ALL-TIME CAPS
Martin Reim (157); Marko Kristal (143); Mart Poom (120); Andres Oper (116); Kristen Viikmäe (114)
TOP FIVE ALL-TIME GOALS
Andres Oper (36); Indrek Zelinski (27); Eduard Ellmen-Eelma (21); Arnold Pihlak (17); Richard Kuremaa (16)

Centenary match, it hardly mattered. In fact, Estonia had much to be proud of that day and there was even more to celebrate a couple of months later when Rüütli's team closed a generally substandard 2010 FIFA World Cup qualifying campaign with a memorable 2-0 home win over Belgium.

Oper on target

There was another prized scalp for Estonia in May 2010 when they beat northern neighbours Finland 2-0 in a Tallinn friendly. Record marksman Andres Oper ended a 20-month drought by opening the scoring early on with his 36th international goal, and ten minutes later there was warm applause for his long-time strike partner Zelinski as he left the field on the occasion of his 103rd and final international appearance.

NATIONAL TEAM RESULTS 2009/10

Date	Opponent		Venue	Score	Scorers
12/8/09	Brazil	H	Tallinn	0-1	
5/9/09	Turkey (WCQ)	A	Kayseri	2-4	*Voskoboinikov (7), Vassiljev (52)*
9/9/09	Spain (WCQ)	A	Merida	0-3	
10/10/09	Bosnia-Herzegovina (WCQ)	H	Tallinn	0-2	
14/10/09	Belgium (WCQ)	H	Tallinn	2-0	*Piiroja (30), Vassiljev (67)*
14/11/09	Albania	H	Tallinn	0-0	
30/12/09	Angola	N	Vila Real (POR)	1-0	*Saag (79)*
3/3/10	Georgia	A	Tbilisi	1-2	*Purje (83)*
21/5/10	Finland	H	Tallinn	2-0	*Oper (5), Post (55)*
26/5/10	Croatia	H	Tallinn	0-0	
19/6/10	Latvia	N	Kaunas (LTU)	0-0	
20/6/10	Lithuania	A	Kaunas	0-2	

NATIONAL TEAM APPEARANCES 2009/10

Coach – Tarmo RÜÜTLI	11/8/54		Bra	TUR	ESP	BIH	BEL	Alb	Ang	Geo	Fin	Cro	Lva	Ltu	Caps	Goals
Sergei PAREIKO	31/1/77	Tom (RUS)	G	G	G	G	G	G			G46	G			18	-
Raio PIIROJA	11/7/79	Fredrikstad (NOR)	D	D	D		D63	D 87*		D 45*	D	D	D		96	7
Ragnar KLAVAN	30/10/85	AZ (NED)	D	D	D	D		s46							62	1
Enar JÄÄGER	18/11/84	Ascoli (ITA)	D	D	s64	D	D	s46							69	-
Alo BÄRENGRUB	12/2/84	Bodø/Glimt (NOR)	D	D		D		s89	D	D	s90			D	32	-
Aleksandr DMITRIJEV	18/2/82	Hønefoss (NOR)	M61	M73			M	M	M	s46	M	M	M	M	56	-
Sander PURI	7/5/88	Levadia /Larissa (GRE)	M89				M		s60	M	M90	M	M78	s58	22	2
Tarmo KINK	6/10/85	Győr (HUN)	M73	s74	M71	M73	M60		M64	A59		A78			42	3
Joel LINDPERE	5/10/81	Tromsø (NOR)	M61	M	s71		M	M	s46						74	5
Konstantin VASSILJEV	16/8/84	Nafta (SVN)	M	M	M	M	M	M	M	M46	M	M	M	M67	32	3
Sergei ZENJOV	20/4/89	Karpaty (UKR)	A61	s54	A46										11	3
Dmitri KRUGLOV	24/5/84	Neftçi (AZE)	s61 87*	D	D	D	D	D46		D 90*	D46		D	s67	52	1
Vladimir VOSKOBOINIKOV	2/2/83	Syrianska (SWE) /Luch-Energia (RUS) /Neftçi (AZE)	s61	M54	s46	A60	s72	s60	A46	A59					25	3
Martin VUNK	21/8/84	Flora /Syrianska (SWE)	s61	s73	M		M				M	M78			26	-
Kristen VIIKMÄE	10/2/79	Jönköping (SWE)	s73					A	s64						114	15
Ats PURJE	3/8/85	Inter Turku (FIN) /unattached	s89		s73		M89	M			s59	s62	s78		19	2
Andres OPER	7/11/77	Shanghai Shenhua (CHN) /Den Haag (NED)		A74	A							A62	A60		116	36
Tihhon ŠIŠOV	11/2/83	Levadia /Xäzär Länkäran (AZE)			D64		D46		D	D			D	D	23	-
Taavi RÄHN	16/5/81	Neftçi (AZE)			D	D	D	D46			s46	D	D		52	-
Kaimar SAAG	5/8/88	Silkeborg (DEN)				s60	A72	A60	s46			s60	A65	s68	22	1
Igor MOROZOV	27/5/89	Levadia					s63		D						5	-
Andrei SIDORENKOV	12/2/84	SønderjyskE (DEN)						s46	M	M46	M	D			17	-
Mihkel AKSALU	7/11/84	Flora /Sheffield United (ENG)							G		G46			G46	8	-
Taijo TENISTE	31/1/88	Levadia								D51				D	6	-
Eino PURI	7/5/88	Levadia								M46			s78		3	-
Gert KAMS	25/5/85	Flora								s51	s59	D85	M73	s58	14	-
Artur KOTENKO	20/8/81	Viking (NOR)									s46	s46	G		22	-
Andrei STEPANOV	16/3/79	Khimki (RUS)									D	D			81	1
Indrek ZELINSKI	13/11/75	unattached									A15				103	27
Oliver KONSA	4/3/85	Flora									s15		s65	M	15	-
Sander POST	10/9/84	Go Ahead Eagles (NED)									s46	s78	A65	A68	5	1
Karl PALATU	5/12/82	Flora									s85		D		2	-
Sergei MOŠNIKOV	7/1/88	Flora											s73	M58	2	-
Alo DUPIKOV	5/11/85	Flora											s65	A58	3	-
Pavel LONDAK	14/5/80	Bodø/Glimt (NOR)												s46	17	-

 **ESTONIA**

DOMESTIC LEAGUE 2009

MEISTRILIIGA FINAL TABLE

		Pld	Home W	D	L	F	A	Away W	D	L	F	A	Total W	D	L	F	A	Pts
1	FC Levadia Tallinn	36	17	1	0	72	11	14	3	1	49	12	31	4	1	121	23	97
2	JK Sillamäe Kalev	36	12	2	4	45	14	12	2	4	40	26	24	4	8	85	40	76
3	JK Trans Narva	36	11	3	4	39	14	12	4	2	43	15	23	7	6	82	29	76
4	FC Flora Tallinn	36	11	4	3	38	16	11	2	5	41	15	22	6	8	79	31	72
5	JK Nõmme Kalju	36	7	5	6	42	25	8	4	6	23	22	15	9	12	65	47	54
6	JK Tulevik Viljandi	36	8	2	8	30	25	7	4	7	25	24	15	6	15	55	49	51
7	JK Tammeka Tartu	36	3	1	14	9	41	4	2	12	20	45	7	3	26	29	86	24
8	FC Kuressaare	36	4	1	13	11	42	3	2	13	10	57	7	3	26	21	99	24
9	Paide Linnameeskond	36	5	2	11	13	44	1	2	15	8	53	6	4	26	21	97	22
10	JK Tallinna Kalev	36	1	4	13	15	44	3	0	15	17	45	4	4	28	32	89	16

NB FC Kuressaare v JK Nõmme Kalju - defeat for both teams.

TOP GOALSCORERS

26 Vitali GUSSEV (Levadia)
21 FELIPE (Kalju)
17 Nikita ANDREEV (Levadia)
14 Jüri JEVDOKIMOV (Tulevik)
13 Alo DUPIKOV (Flora)
   Vjatšeslav ZAHOVAIKO (Flora)
   Vitali LEITAN (Levadia)
   Aleksei NAUMOV (Sillamäe Kalev)
   Aleksandr TARASSENKOV (Trans)
12 Konstantin NAHK (Levadia)
   Tõnis KAUKVERE (Kalju)

CLUB-BY-CLUB

FC FLORA TALLINN
Coach – Tarmo Rüütli
Founded – 1990
Stadium – A. Le Coq Arena (9,692)
MAJOR HONOURS:
Estonian League - (7) 1994, 1995, 1998, 1998 (autumn), 2001, 2002, 2003;
Estonian Cup - (4) 1995, 1998, 2008, 2009.

2009

7/3	Kalju	a	1-0	Reintam
14/3	Levadia	h	1-3	Zahovaiko
17/3	Trans	a	2-1	Kasimir (p), Zahovaiko
21/3	Paide	h	4-0	Kams, Kasimir, Zahovaiko (p), Konsa
4/4	Kuressaare	a	0-1	
11/4	Sillamäe Kalev	a	2-3	Dupikov, Zahovaiko
18/4	Tallinna Kalev	h	1-0	Zahovaiko
25/4	Tulevik	a	1-1	Konsa
2/5	Tammeka	h	2-1	Vunk 2 (1p)
9/5	Tammeka	a	4-0	Dupikov, Kallaste, Tamm, Anier He.
16/5	Tulevik	h	1-0	Dupikov
23/5	Tallinna Kalev	a	2-0	Dupikov, Luts
13/6	Paide	a	6-0	Dupikov 3, Zahovaiko 2, Vunk
16/6	Trans	h	1-1	Dupikov
20/6	Levadia	a	2-3	Dupikov, Vunk
11/7	Tammeka	h	2-1	Dupikov, Palatu
28/7	Sillamäe Kalev	h	4-1	Dupikov, Mošnikov, Anniste (p), Zahovaiko
1/8	Sillamäe Kalev	a	3-1	Jürgenson, Kasimir, Vunk
4/8	Kalju	h	0-0	
8/8	Kuressaare	a	3-0	Anier He. 2, Palatu
15/8	Paide	h	0-0	
18/8	Kuressaare	h	3-0	Kasimir (p), Mošnikov, Vunk (p)
22/8	Trans	a	0-0	
12/9	Kalju	a	2-3	Konsa, Mošnikov
15/9	Levadia	h	1-3	Zahovaiko
19/9	Kalju	h	2-2	Palatu, Vunk
26/9	Levadia	a	0-1	
29/9	Tulevik	a	1-0	Konsa
3/10	Trans	h	1-2	Konsa
17/10	Paide	a	6-0	Mošnikov 2, Kasimir (p), Kams, Konsa, Kuresoo
20/10	Tallinna Kalev	h	4-1	Mošnikov, Kams, Konsa, Stüf
24/10	Kuressaare	h	3-0	Stüf, Kams, Reintam
31/10	Sillamäe Kalev	h	4-0	Konsa, Allas, Palatu, Zahovaiko
3/11	Tallinna Kalev	a	2-1	Kasimir, Dupikov
7/11	Tulevik	h	4-1	Jürgenson, Palatu, Vunk, Dupikov
10/11	Tammeka	a	4-0	Zahovaiko 3, Mošnikov

Name	Nat	DoB	Pos	Aps	(s)	Gls
Mihkel AKSALU		7/11/84	G	31		
Teet ALLAS		2/6/77	D	12	(4)	1
Hannes ANIER		16/1/93	A	1	(1)	
Henri ANIER		17/12/90	A	7	(3)	3
Aivar ANNISTE		18/2/80	M	19	(6)	1
Alo DUPIKOV		5/11/85	A	24	(4)	13
Andre FROLOV		18/4/88	D	5	(2)	
Markus JÜRGENSON		9/9/87	D	26		2
Ken KALLASTE		31/8/88	M	18	(5)	1
Gert KAMS		25/5/85	M	22	(3)	4
Siksten KASIMIR		23/7/80	M	28	(5)	6
Oliver KONSA		4/3/85	M	26	(5)	8
Jürgen KURESOO		11/2/87	M	8	(8)	1
Siim LUTS		12/3/89	M	5	(3)	1
Sergei MOŠNIKOV		7/1/88	M	23	(8)	7
Karl MÖÖL		4/3/92	M		(1)	
Karl PALATU		5/12/82	D	26	(2)	5
Stanislav PEDÕK		6/6/88	G	5		
Meelis PEITRE		27/3/90	M		(1)	
Mikk REINTAM		22/5/90	M	21		2
Urmas ROOBA		8/7/78	D	7	(5)	
Henri RÜÜTLI		16/3/87	M	16	(12)	
Edvin STÜF		30/7/89	M	1	(4)	
Joonas TAMM		2/2/92	A	7	(2)	1
Tõnis VANNA		5/6/84	D	23	(1)	
Martin VUNK		21/8/84	M	22	(6)	8
Vjatšeslav ZAHOVAIKO		29/12/81	A	13	(10)	13

ESTONIA

FC KURESSAARE

Coach – Jan Važinski; (15/9/09) Sergei Zamogilnõi
Founded – 1997
Stadium – Kuressaare Linnastaadion (2,000)

2009

7/3	Levadia	a	0-3	
14/3	Trans	h	0-5	
17/3	Paide	a	0-0	
21/3	Sillamäe Kalev	a	1-0	Kuusik
4/4	Flora	h	1-0	Pukk
11/4	Tallinna Kalev	a	1-1	Kluge
18/4	Tulevik	h	0-3	
25/4	Tammeka	a	0-2	
2/5	Kalju	h	1-2	Aljas
9/5	Kalju	a	1-6	Kuusik
16/5	Tammeka	h	0-0	
23/5	Tulevik	a	0-3	
26/5	Tallinna Kalev	h	0-1	
13/6	Sillamäe Kalev	h	0-1	
16/6	Paide	h	1-0	Laht
20/6	Trans	a	0-2	
7/7	Levadia	h	1-7	Laht (p)
14/7	Kalju	h	0-0	(w/o; defeat for both sides; original game 2-3 Skiperskiy 2)
18/7	Tammeka	a	2-1	Skiperskiy 2
25/7	Tulevik	h	0-4	
1/8	Tallinna Kalev	h	4-1	Skiperskiy 3, Pukk
8/8	Flora	h	0-3	
15/8	Sillamäe Kalev	a	1-5	Kuusik
18/8	Flora	a	0-3	
22/8	Paide	a	0-2	
29/8	Trans	h	0-7	
12/9	Levadia	a	0-8	
19/9	Levadia	h	1-3	Rajaver U.
26/9	Trans	a	0-10	
3/10	Paide	h	4-1	Skiperskiy, Pukk, Švets, Kriska
17/10	Sillamäe Kalev	h	0-3	
24/10	Flora	a	0-3	
31/10	Tallinna Kalev	h	2-0	Skiperskiy 2
3/11	Tulevik	a	0-6	
7/11	Tammeka	h	0-2	
10/11	Kalju	a	0-1	

Name	Nat	DoB	Pos	Aps	(s)	Gls
Argo AAVA		29/3/86	D	33	(1)	
Rene ALJAS		18/12/86	A	22	(1)	1
Taavi AZAROV		20/4/80	M	14	(7)	
Rait HANSEN		12/11/88	G	3		
Tõnu ILVES		13/1/91	A		(9)	
Endrik JÄGER		13/1/90	M	27	(5)	
Märt KLUGE		8/3/84	D	25	(6)	1
Jaanis KRISKA		23/6/82	D	21	(6)	1
Reijo KUUSIK		24/6/87	A	25	(5)	3
Roland KÜTT		22/4/87	G	33		
Sander LAHT		26/9/91	A	12	(15)	2
Aivo LAUL		1/1/84	M	28	(3)	
Kalle LEPP		29/1/89	M	17	(2)	
Amor LUUP		18/2/92	A	2	(8)	
Kristen MERE		27/10/91	A		(1)	
Pelle POHLAK		31/12/88	M	16	(3)	
Mario PRUUL		10/9/90	A		(1)	
Martti PUKK		20/2/77	A	28	(5)	3
Margus RAJAVER		16/7/89	M	2	(7)	
Urmas RAJAVER		3/1/88	D	30	(1)	1
Kristo SALUMAA		6/3/88	M		(1)	
Sander SEEMAN		12/9/92	M	1	(3)	
Dmitriy SKIPERSKIY	RUS	29/4/73	A	24	(6)	10

Mark ŠVETS		1/10/76	M	12	(1)	1
Elari VALMAS		2/7/88	D	2	(7)	
Sander VIIRA		29/8/89	D	19		

FC LEVADIA TALLINN

Coach – Igor Prins
Founded – 1998
Stadium – Kadriorg (4,700)
MAJOR HONOURS:
Estonian League - (7) 1999, 2000, 2004, 2006, 2007, 2008, 2009;
Estonian Cup - (6) 1999, 2000, 2004, 2005, 2007, 2010.

2009

7/3	Kuressaare	h	3-0	Andreev, Leitan, Zelinski
14/3	Flora	a	3-1	Gussev, Leitan, Nahk
17/3	Tallinna Kalev	h	4-1	Malov 2, Andreev, Gussev
21/3	Tulevik	a	7-0	Andreev 3, Gussev, Leitan, Nahk (p), Puri S.
4/4	Tammeka	h	8-0	Gussev 3, Andreev, Puri S., Teniste, Aristov, Marmor
11/4	Kalju	a	2-1	Malov, Nahk (p)
18/4	Sillamäe Kalev	h	3-1	Andreev, Nahk, Gussev
25/4	Trans	h	2-0	Andreev, Gussev
2/5	Paide	a	3-0	Andreev 2, Puri S.
9/5	Paide	h	2-0	Gussev, Andreev
16/5	Trans	a	3-0	Andreev, Gussev, Puri S.
23/5	Sillamäe Kalev	a	1-1	Puri S.
13/6	Tulevik	h	5-0	Leitan 2, Gussev, Malov, Nahk
16/6	Tallinna Kalev	a	2-2	Andreev 2 (1p)
20/6	Flora	h	3-2	Puri S. 2, Andreev
7/7	Kuressaare	a	7-1	Puri S. 2, Kalimullin, Gussev, Nahk, Andreev, og (Lepp)
11/7	Paide	a	5-1	Gussev 2, Puri S., Ivanov, Andreev
1/8	Kalju	h	3-1	Zelinski, Ivanov, Saarelma
8/8	Tammeka	h	6-1	Zelinski 3 (1p), Neemelo, Saarelma, Nahk
15/8	Tulevik	a	0-0	
23/8	Tallinna Kalev	h	5-1	Gussev, Ivanov (p), Neemelo, Mones, Zelinski
1/9	Sillamäe Kalev	h	6-1	Leitan 2, Gussev 2, Saarelma, Neemelo
12/9	Kuressaare	h	8-0	Gussev 2, Neemelo 2, Saarelma, Zelinski, Leitan, og (Kriska)
15/9	Flora	a	3-1	Neemelo, Gussev, Leitan
19/9	Kuressaare	a	3-1	Leitan, Gussev, Neemelo
26/9	Flora	h	1-0	Nahk (p)
29/9	Kalju	a	3-1	Nahk, Gussev, Šišov
3/10	Tallinna Kalev	a	1-0	Malov
6/10	Trans	h	1-1	Neemelo
17/10	Tulevik	h	3-0	Nahk, Gussev, Teniste
20/10	Tammeka	a	2-0	Nahk, Malov
24/10	Tammeka	a	2-0	Leitan, og (Aristov)
31/10	Kalju	h	5-0	Nahk, Leitan, Ivanov, Marmor, Gussev
3/11	Sillamäe Kalev	a	1-0	Kalimullin
7/11	Trans	a	1-2	Teniste
10/11	Paide	h	4-2	Gussev 2 (1p), Leitan, Neemelo

Name	Nat	DoB	Pos	Aps	(s)	Gls
Nikita ANDREEV	RUS	22/9/88	A	17		17
Anton ARISTOV		22/8/86	D		(5)	1
Yaroslav DMITRIEV	RUS	25/6/88	A		(3)	
Vitali GUSSEV		16/3/83	A	34	(1)	26
Vladislav IVANOV	RUS	24/1/86	A	7	(5)	4
Martin KAALMA		14/4/77	G	32		
Andrei KALIMULLIN		6/10/77	D	33		2
Kert KÜTT		9/10/80	G	1		

 **ESTONIA**

Vitali LEITAN	1/12/78	M	29		13
Sergei LEPMETS	5/4/87	G	3		
Deniss MALOV	8/6/80	M	29	(3)	6
Kristian MARMOR	27/2/87	M	31	(1)	2
Aleks MONES	27/6/90	M	2	(9)	1
Igor MOROZOV	27/5/89	D	32		
Konstantin NAHK	10/2/75	M	35		12
Tarmo NEEMELO	2/10/82	A	13	(4)	9
Maksim PODHULJUZIN	13/11/92	M	1		
Eino PURI	7/5/88	M	11	(11)	
Sander PURI	7/5/88	M	16	(3)	10
Tomi Tapani SAARELMA	FIN 30/11/88	M	14	(1)	4
Tõnis STARKOPF	10/1/85	A		(1)	
Igor SUBBOTIN	26/6/90	M	2	(6)	
Tihhin ŠIŠOV	11/2/83	D	22	(7)	1
Taijo TENISTE	31/1/88	D	24		3
Indrek ZELINSKI	13/11/74	A	8	(18)	7

JK NÕMME KALJU
Coach – Fredo Getúlio Aurélio (BRA)
Founded – 1923
Stadium – Hiiu (600)

2009

7/3	Flora	h	0-1	
14/3	Tallinna Kalev	a	2-1	Mitt (p), Hurt
17/3	Tulevik	h	1-1	Maccari
21/3	Tammeka	a	2-1	Maccari, Felipe
4/4	Sillamäe Kalev	h	1-3	Tükk
11/4	Levadia	h	1-2	Kägo
18/4	Trans	a	0-3	
25/4	Paide	h	3-0	Felipe 2, Smirnov
2/5	Kuressaare	a	2-1	Tükk, Felipe
9/5	Kuressaare	h	6-1	Rõškevitš 3, Smirnov, Felipe, Kaukvere
16/5	Paide	a	3-0	Felipe 2, Kaukvere
23/5	Trans	h	1-2	Smirnov
30/5	Sillamäe Kalev	a	0-2	
13/6	Tammeka	h	4-0	Felipe 4 (1p)
16/6	Tulevik	a	2-0	Kaukvere 2
20/6	Tallinna Kalev	h	2-1	Tükk, Hurt
14/7	Kuressaare	a	0-0	(w/o; defeat for both sides; original game 3-2 Kaukvere, Shuhanau, Felipe)
18/7	Paide	h	10-0	Felipe 3, Kaukvere 3, Tükk 2, Diego, Rafael
25/7	Trans	a	0-0	
1/8	Levadia	a	1-3	og (Kalimullin)
4/8	Flora	a	0-0	
8/8	Sillamäe Kalev	h	1-1	Felipe
15/8	Tammeka	a	1-0	Rõškevitš
22/8	Tulevik	h	1-1	Hurt
29/8	Tallinna Kalev	a	2-0	Rõškevitš (p), Kaukvere
12/9	Flora	h	3-2	Shuhanau, Diego, og (Vanna)
19/9	Flora	a	2-2	Maccari, Felipe
26/9	Tallinna Kalev	a	3-4	Felipe 2 (1p), Shuhanau
29/9	Levadia	h	1-3	Felipe
3/10	Tulevik	a	2-3	Kaukvere, Tšegodajev
17/10	Tammeka	h	1-1	Rõškevitš
24/10	Sillamäe Kalev	a	1-1	Terehhov
31/10	Levadia	a	0-5	
3/11	Trans	h	2-2	Shuhanau, Alan Arruda
7/11	Paide	a	3-0	Kaukvere 2, Haavistu
10/11	Kuressaare	h	1-0	Felipe

Name	Nat	DoB	Pos	Aps	(s)	Gls
ALAN Monken ARRUDA	BRA	12/9/81	D	32		1
DIEGO Douglas Balbinot	BRA	7/1/84	D	22	(1)	2

FELIPE de Araújo Nunes	BRA	2/3/81	M	34	(1)	21
Mikk HAAVISTU		27/3/85	D	25		1
Janno HERMANSON		27/6/81	G	8	(1)	
Martin HURT		27/6/84	M	33		3
Rene KAAS		16/1/82	G	15		
Kristofer KASK		6/3/86	A	1	(3)	
Tõnis KAUKVERE		19/3/86	M	24	(7)	12
Sami-Sander KIVI		11/5/90	D		(3)	
Anti KÕLU		19/7/91	A	1	(4)	
Risto KÄGO		4/8/89	D	12	(2)	1
Liivo LEETMA		20/1/77	M	3	(4)	
Murilo MACCARI	BRA	12/9/87	M	20	(1)	3
MARCÍO Cardoso Pimentel	BRA	29/11/80	D	17	(1)	
Andrus MITT		19/1/81	A	4		1
Marek MÄEKALA		24/11/91	A		(2)	
Jevgeni NOVIKOV		28/6/80	M	21		
Ranner PAK		17/2/89	M		(3)	
RAFAEL Amaral do Nascimento	BRA	10/10/88	M	5		1
Miroslav RÕŠKEVITŠ		21/6/86	M	15	(9)	6
Aleksander SAHAROV		22/4/82	M	2	(1)	
Daniil SAVITSKI		4/5/89	G	13	(1)	
Vitaliy SHUHANAU	BLR	19/10/84	A	15	(2)	4
Maksim SMIRNOV		28/12/79	M	10	(19)	3
Ingemar TEEVER		24/2/83	A	3	(3)	
Sergei TEREHHOV		18/4/75	M	29	(2)	1
Martin TŠEGODAJEV		30/11/90	A	10	(8)	1
Janar TÜKK		1/2/85	M	20	(8)	5
Salvador Jesus VASQUEZ	SWE	3/8/90	M	2	(1)	

PAIDE LINNAMEESKOND
Coach – Viktor Mets
Founded – 1999
Stadium – Paide Ühisgümnaasium (500)

2009

7/3	Trans	a	0-3	
14/3	Sillamäe Kalev	a	0-6	
17/3	Kuressaare	h	0-0	
21/3	Flora	a	0-4	
4/4	Tallinna Kalev	h	1-0	Laurits
11/4	Tulevik	a	0-1	
18/4	Tammeka	h	3-1	Laurits 2, Saar
25/4	Kalju	a	0-3	
2/5	Levadia	a	0-3	
9/5	Levadia	h	0-2	
16/5	Kalju	h	0-3	
23/5	Tammeka	a	2-0	Ellram, og (Kiidron)
26/5	Tulevik	h	0-1	
30/5	Tallinna Kalev	h	0-0	
13/6	Flora	h	0-6	
16/6	Kuressaare	a	0-1	
20/6	Sillamäe Kalev	h	0-2	
11/7	Levadia	h	1-5	Ellram
18/7	Kalju	a	0-10	
25/7	Tammeka	h	2-1	Rooba (p), Pebre
28/7	Trans	h	0-5	
1/8	Tulevik	a	0-4	
8/8	Tallinna Kalev	h	3-2	Voolaid, Rooba, Köll
15/8	Flora	a	0-3	
22/8	Kuressaare	h	2-0	Varendi, Pebre
29/8	Sillamäe Kalev	a	0-3	
12/9	Trans	a	1-4	Pebre
19/9	Trans	h	1-1	Rooba
26/9	Sillamäe Kalev	h	0-1	
3/10	Kuressaare	a	1-4	Rooba
17/10	Tulevik	h	0-6	
24/10	Tallinna Kalev	a	2-3	Rooba (p), Rikberg
31/10	Tulevik	h	0-4	

3/11	Tammeka	a	0-1	
7/11	Kalju	h	0-3	
10/11	Levadia	a	2-4	Lomp, Kõll (p)

Name	Nat	DoB	Pos	Aps	(s)	Gls
Marion ADUSOO		13/10/84	A		(1)	
Lauri ELLRAM		18/2/84	A	24	(6)	2
Rauno KALD		11/3/91	M	5	(14)	
Sander KOOSER		24/9/88	D	11		
Ervin KÕLL		18/3/89	M	17		2
Romet KÖHLER		22/12/90	M	1	(7)	
Rauno KÖÖP		18/8/89	D	16	(6)	
Kristo KÜLLJASTINEN		16/2/85	D	2	(3)	
Taavi LAURITS		23/1/90	M	12		3
Liivo LEETMA		20/1/77	M	11		
Timo LOMP		26/7/88	D	12	(2)	1
Andre MÄGI		14/1/88	D	35		
Artur MÜÜR		19/1/85	A	5		
Silver NEEMELO		28/11/78	A	13	(11)	
Keio OJA		13/8/88	D	6	(6)	
Herkki ORRO		12/2/88	M	4	(2)	
Andero PEBRE		7/8/91	M	14	(1)	3
Priit RAAL		9/2/89	M	19	(4)	
Margus REINARU		12/11/86	D	2	(6)	
Rauno RIKBERG		30/7/88	A	11	(4)	1
Meelis ROOBA		20/4/77	M	26		5
Sten RÕNGELEP		31/1/88	A	1	(5)	
Martin SAAR		28/9/88	A	26	(3)	1
Karlis SEIRE		23/10/89	M	7	(3)	
Viljo TIBU		25/5/90	M		(1)	
Allar TOOM		23/11/89	G	19		
Carl TUBARIK		31/7/81	D	33		
Rauno UUS		23/9/77	M	3	(4)	
Lauri VARENDI		29/12/88	D	25		1
Allan VENTSEL		2/9/88	G	17	(1)	
Karel VOOLAID		4/7/77	M	12		1
Tanel VÕTTI		16/5/88	D	7	(1)	

JK SILLAMÄE KALEV
Coach – Vadym Dobizha (UKR);
(30/4/09) Anatoliy Ushanov (UKR)
Founded – 1951
Stadium – Sillamäe Kalevi (500)

2009

7/3	Tulevik	a	3-1	Kulik A., Lipartov, Gruznov
14/3	Paide	h	6-0	Lapeikis 2 (2p), Stankevičius, Naumov, Gruznov, Lipartov
17/3	Tammeka	a	8-0	Kulik A., Gruznov, Lipartov, Dubõkin, Grigas, Lapeikis (p), Vihrov, Ametov
21/3	Kuressaare	h	0-1	
4/4	Kalju	a	3-1	Lipartov, Gruznov, Naumov
11/4	Flora	h	3-2	Gruznov, Mačiulis, Lipartov
18/4	Levadia	a	1-3	Naumov
25/4	Tallinna Kalev	h	2-0	Kulik A. 2
2/5	Trans	a	2-1	Stankevičius, Naumov
9/5	Trans	h	2-1	Lapeikis (p), Mačiulis
16/5	Tallinna Kalev	a	1-1	Lipartov
23/5	Levadia	h	1-1	Lipartov
30/5	Kalju	h	2-0	Kulik A., Dubõkin
13/6	Kuressaare	a	1-0	og (Kriska)
16/6	Tammeka	h	5-0	Naumov 2 (1p), Kulik A., Lipartov, Kulik V.
20/6	Paide	a	2-0	Kulik A., Naumov
4/7	Tulevik	h	1-0	Kabaev
14/7	Trans	a	1-0	Kulik A.

18/7	Tallinna Kalev	h	7-0	Gruznov 2, Naumov, Dubõkin, Lipartov, Boyko, Rogov
28/7	Flora	a	1-4	Dubõkin
1/8	Flora	h	1-3	Kulik A.
8/8	Kalju	a	1-1	Lipartov
15/8	Kuressaare	h	5-1	Dubõkin 3, Gnedojus, Kulik A.
22/8	Tammeka	a	2-1	Naumov (p), og (Aristov)
29/8	Paide	h	3-0	Dubõkin, Kulik V., Gnedojus
1/9	Levadia	a	1-6	Kabaev
12/9	Tulevik	a	3-1	Valaitis, Naumov, Kabaev
19/9	Tulevik	h	3-1	Naumov (p), Lipartov, Gruznov
26/9	Paide	a	1-0	Užkuraitis
3/10	Tammeka	h	3-0	Kabaev 2, Gnedojus
17/10	Kuressaare	a	3-0	Naumov, Vihrov, Dubõkin
24/10	Kalju	h	1-1	Naumov
31/10	Flora	a	0-4	
3/11	Levadia	h	0-1	
7/11	Tallinna Kalev	a	6-2	Stankevičius 2, Vihrov 2, Dubõkin, Boyko
10/11	Trans	h	0-2	

Name	Nat	DoB	Pos	Aps	(s)	Gls
Irfan AMETOV	UKR	3/2/80	M	4	(5)	1
Dmytro BOYKO	UKR	30/9/81	M	12	(3)	2
Aleksandr BÕKOV		19/10/92	M		(1)	
Roman DANILJUK		22/12/89	M		(2)	
Aleksandr DJATŠENKO		3/2/81	G	11	(1)	
Aleksandr DUBÕKIN		6/5/83	M	30	(1)	10
Kazimieras GNEDOJUS	LTU	28/2/86	D	16	(1)	3
Andrei GORNEV		28/7/88	M		(1)	
Gvidas GRIGAS	LTU	19/1/80	D	17	(4)	1
Maksim GRUZNOV		21/4/74	A	23	(7)	8
Evgeniy KABAEV	RUS	28/2/88	A	15	(13)	5
Aleksandr KULIK		23/7/81	A	28	(6)	10
Vassili KULIK		20/12/86	D	6	(15)	2
Vilius LAPEIKIS	LTU	30/6/83	M	12		4
Ivan LIHHATŠOV		23/6/91	M	1		
Dmitriy LIPARTOV	RUS	2/4/73	A	29	(5)	11
Nerijus MAČIULIS	LTU	1/4/83	M	5	(5)	2
Aleksandr MUTIK	RUS	3/9/86	M	5	(9)	
Aleksei NAUMOV	RUS	2/2/72	M	33		13
Roman NESTEROVSKI		9/6/89	D	29	(2)	
Igor ROGOV		27/1/90	M		(6)	1
Dmitri SMIRNOV		10/9/89	M	1	(7)	
Vitalis STANKEVIČIUS	LTU	23/6/82	A	29	(2)	4
Mihhail STARODUBTSEV		14/8/82	G	25		
Evaldas UŽKURAITIS	LTU	29/6/85	D	7	(7)	1
Eimantas VALAITIS	LTU	3/6/82	M	34		1
Roman VEDEHHOV		20/7/81	D		(1)	
Sergei VIHROV		2/3/86	M	24	(3)	4

JK TALLINNA KALEV
Coach – Aavo Sarap; (26/8/09) Daniel Meijel
Founded – 1911
Stadium – Tallinna Kalevi (6,000)
MAJOR HONOURS:
Estonian League - (2) 1923, 1930.

2009

7/3	Tammeka	a	3-0	Tšurilkin 2, Stüf Ed.
14/3	Kalju	h	1-2	Stüf Ed.
17/3	Levadia	a	1-4	Stüf Ed.
21/3	Trans	h	2-4	Vahtramäe, Tomson
4/4	Paide	a	0-1	
11/4	Kuressaare	h	1-1	Nõmme
18/4	Flora	a	0-1	
25/4	Sillamäe Kalev	a	0-2	

2/5	Tulevik	h	0-1	
9/5	Tulevik	a	1-2	Oja
16/5	Sillamäe Kalev	h	1-1	Nõmme
23/5	Flora	h	0-2	
26/5	Kuressaare	a	1-0	Tomson
30/6	Paide	h	0-0	
13/6	Trans	a	1-3	Vahtramäe (p)
16/6	Levadia	h	2-2	Tiismann (p), Nõmme
20/6	Kalju	a	1-2	Nõmme
4/7	Tammeka	h	0-4	
11/7	Tulevik	h	0-2	
18/7	Sillamäe Kalev	a	0-7	
1/8	Kuressaare	h	1-4	Vahtramäe (p)
8/8	Paide	a	2-3	Karpõtšev, Vahtramäe (p)
15/8	Trans	h	0-2	
23/8	Levadia	a	1-5	Vahtramäe (p)
29/8	Kalju	h	0-2	
12/9	Tammeka	a	0-1	
19/9	Tammeka	h	1-6	Kiis
26/9	Kalju	a	4-3	Kõlu 2, Paponov, Tomson
3/10	Levadia	h	0-1	
17/10	Trans	a	0-1	
20/10	Flora	a	1-4	Vahtramäe
24/10	Paide	h	3-2	Kõrtsmik 2, Tšurilkin
31/10	Kuressaare	a	0-2	
3/11	Flora	h	1-2	Paponov
7/11	Sillamäe Kalev	h	2-6	Savitski, Tomson
10/11	Tulevik	a	1-4	Külm

Name	Nat	DoB	Pos	Aps	(s)	Gls
Andrei AFANASOV		19/12/77	A		(1)	
Priidu AHVEN		30/6/89	A	2	(5)	
Aleksei DEMUTSKI		24/10/84	M	16	(1)	
Janno HERMANSON		27/6/81	G	17		
Marek KAHR		9/12/81	D	9	(3)	
Mart KALJUSTE		11/9/90	G	1		
Aleksandr KARPÕTŠEV		16/8/82	D	6	(1)	1
Vahur KIIS		17/6/80	A	16	(6)	1
Margus KORJU		19/3/81	A	4		
Igor KOROLJOV		19/8/88	D	1		
Johannes KUKEBAL		19/7/93	M	1	(4)	
Aleksandr KUSLAP		25/3/84	D		(2)	
Anti KÕLU		19/7/91	A	13	(3)	2
Cristian KÕRTSMIK		7/2/91	A	25	(4)	2
Henri KÜLM		18/10/90	D	23	(3)	1
Mati LEMBER		21/7/85	M	16	(10)	
Rameš MAMEDOV		30/1/83	M	6	(3)	
Mario MÕISTLIK		1/9/86	M	12	(5)	
Martin NORMANN		25/2/89	A	1		
Mait NÕMME		1/7/83	D	10	(10)	4
Reimo OJA		23/11/82	A	13	(9)	1
Grigori OŠOMKOV		10/11/85	G	1	(1)	
Maksim PAPONOV		11/1/90	M	14	(2)	2
Priit PÄSTLANE		5/12/90	A		(1)	
Sander REELO		10/3/85	G	17	(1)	
Aleksei SAVITSKI		3/10/85	D	31		1
Edwin STÜF		30/7/89	A	14	(4)	3
Ervin STÜF		3/12/90	M	1	(6)	
Andrei ŠADRIN		18/7/86	M		(1)	
Jüri TIISMANN		23/5/80	M	10	(3)	1
Rasmus TOMSON		13/8/85	M	28	(6)	4
Vladislav TŠURILKIN		30/5/89	D	21	(2)	3
Vahur VAHTRAMÄE		24/9/76	M	32	(1)	6
Jesper VEBER		1/9/84	D	10		
Taavi VIIKNA		14/2/93	D	25	(2)	
Tanel VÄHESOO		3/7/92	M		(2)	

JK TAMMEKA TARTU
Coach – Norbert Hurt
Founded – 1989
Stadium – Tamme (800)

2009

7/3	Tallinna Kalev	h	0-3	
14/3	Tulevik	a	0-3	
17/3	Sillamäe Kalev	h	0-8	
21/3	Kalju	h	1-2	Tamm (p)
4/4	Levadia	a	0-8	
11/4	Trans	h	1-4	Paapsi
18/4	Paide	a	1-3	Mikheim
25/4	Kuressaare	h	2-0	Kiidron, Laabus
2/5	Flora	a	1-2	Laas
9/5	Flora	h	0-4	
16/5	Kuressaare	a	0-0	
23/5	Paide	h	0-2	
26/5	Trans	a	1-3	Tamm (p)
13/6	Kalju	a	0-4	
16/6	Sillamäe Kalev	a	0-5	
20/6	Tulevik	h	1-1	Torop
4/7	Tallinna Kalev	a	4-0	Hansi, Tamm, Valtna, Prosa
11/7	Flora	a	1-2	Laas
18/7	Kuressaare	h	1-2	Schachner
25/7	Paide	a	1-2	Teniste (p)
1/8	Trans	h	0-1	
8/8	Levadia	a	1-6	Paapsi
15/8	Kalju	h	0-1	
22/8	Sillamäe Kalev	h	1-2	Konal
29/8	Tulevik	a	1-0	Hansi
12/9	Tallinna Kalev	h	1-0	Prosa
19/9	Tallinna Kalev	a	6-1	Prosa 2, Schachner, Artjunin, Laas, Vouis (p)
26/9	Tulevik	h	0-3	
3/10	Sillamäe Kalev	a	0-3	
17/10	Kalju	a	1-1	Tamm (p)
20/10	Levadia	h	0-2	
24/10	Levadia	h	0-2	
31/10	Trans	a	0-2	
3/11	Paide	h	1-0	Sonn
7/11	Kuressaare	a	2-0	Prosa 2
10/11	Flora	h	0-4	

Name	Nat	DoB	Pos	Aps	(s)	Gls
Fidèle Eric AFIMA OLÉMÉ	CMR	10/10/85	D	13		
Anton ARISTOV		22/8/86	D	15		
Artjom ARTJUNIN		24/1/90	D	12	(1)	1
Martin HALJAK		16/5/90	D	10	(2)	
Badr HAMDOUCHI	MAR	16/2/83	A	6	(2)	
Mario HANSI		21/5/87	M	16	(4)	2
Tanel JOOSEP		8/8/90	D	10	(1)	
Kennet JÄDAL		8/5/90	M	21	(3)	
Kaspar KALDOJA		1/1/90	M	4		
Kaarel KALLANDI		22/3/89	M	3	(6)	
Kaarel KIIDRON		30/4/90	D	19	(3)	1
Kaspar KOHLER		17/3/90	G	5		
Sercan KONAL	GER	29/3/88	D	9		1
Ats KUTTER		28/3/91	G		(1)	
Reio LAABUS		14/3/90	M	12	(14)	1
Mikk LAAS		30/9/80	A	10	(19)	3
Marek LAASIK		7/8/90	D	11		
Mihkel MIKHEIM		14/7/88	A	2	(6)	1
Kristjan PAAPSI		30/7/87	A	14	(3)	2
Olari PERLIN		28/2/90	D		(2)	
Albert PROSA		1/10/90	M	28	(2)	6
Eldar RASSULOV		25/2/87	D	11	(1)	
Bernhard SCHACHNER	AUT	3/10/87	M	13	(2)	2
Marko SONN		29/10/88	D	11	(1)	1

ESTONIA

Moritz STEHLING	GER	25/5/87	G	14		
Heiko TAMM		18/3/87	M	20	(7)	4
Timo TENISTE		27/10/85	D	17		1
Siim TENNO		4/8/90	M	32	(2)	
Mait TOOM		7/5/90	G	17		
Kaarel TOROP		20/9/92	A	10	(4)	1
Siim VALTNA		31/7/87	M	10	(1)	1
Erik VARES		6/7/90	M	2	(1)	
Panagiotis VOUIS	GRE	23/10/85	M	6	(5)	1
Jaanus VÕRNO		17/1/90	D	13	(1)	

JK TRANS NARVA
Coach – Sergei Ratnikov
Founded – 1979
Stadium – Kreenholm (1,000)
MAJOR HONOURS:
Estonian Cup - (1) 2001.

2009
7/3	Paide	h	3-0	*Ratnikov D., Bazyukin, Leontovitš*
14/3	Kuressaare	a	5-0	*Ivanov 2, Rimas, Ratnikov E., Lõsanov*
17/3	Flora	h	1-2	*Ratnikov E. (p)*
21/3	Tallinna Kalev	a	4-2	*Ivanov, Ratnikov D., Čepauskas, Tiirik*
4/4	Tulevik	h	1-1	*Bazyukin*
11/4	Tammeka	a	4-1	*Rimas, Tarassenkov, Ratnikov E., Bazyukin*
18/4	Kalju	h	3-0	*Kitto 2, Bazyukin*
25/4	Levadia	a	0-2	
2/5	Sillamäe Kalev	h	1-2	*Ratnikov D.*
9/5	Sillamäe Kalev	a	1-2	*Tarassenkov (p)*
16/5	Levadia	h	0-3	
23/5	Kalju	a	2-1	*Tarassenkov, Kazakov*
26/5	Tammeka	h	3-1	*Kitto, Tarassenkov (p), Leontovitš*
30/5	Tulevik	a	2-1	*Lõsanov, Ratnikov D.*
13/6	Tallinna Kalev	h	3-1	*Lõsanov 2, Tarassenkov (p)*
16/6	Flora	a	1-1	*Tarassenkov (p)*
20/6	Kuressaare	h	2-0	*Ratnikov D., Ratnikov E.*
14/7	Sillamäe Kalev	h	0-1	
25/7	Kalju	h	0-0	
28/7	Paide	a	5-0	*Ratnikov D. 2, Kazakov, Leontovitš, Dmitrijev*
1/8	Tammeka	a	1-0	*Dmitrijev*
8/8	Tulevik	h	3-1	*Mandinho 2, Tarassenkov*
15/8	Tallinna Kalev	a	2-0	*Starovoitov 2*
22/8	Flora	h	0-0	
29/8	Kuressaare	a	7-0	*Breytveyt 2, Leontovitš, Rimas, Starovoitov, Kazakov, og (Laul)*
12/9	Paide	h	4-1	*Kazakov 2, Rimas, Leontovitš*
19/9	Paide	a	1-1	*Ratnikov D.*
26/9	Kuressaare	h	10-0	*Tarassenkov 3 (1p), Breytveyt 2, Ratnikov D. 2, Leontovitš 2, Kazakov*
3/10	Flora	a	2-1	*Tarassenkov (p), og (Reintam)*
6/10	Levadia	a	1-1	*Ratnikov E.*
17/10	Tallinna Kalev	h	1-0	*Volodin*
24/10	Tulevik	a	1-0	*Starovoitov*
31/10	Tammeka	h	2-0	*Breytveyt, Tarassenkov (p)*
3/11	Kalju	a	2-2	*Starovoitov, Tarassenkov*
7/11	Levadia	h	2-1	*Breytveyt, Starovoitov*
10/11	Sillamäe Kalev	a	2-0	*Kazakov, Bazyukin*

Name	Nat	DoB	Pos	Aps	(s)	Gls
Maksim BAZYUKIN	RUS	18/6/83	M	18	(7)	5
Philipp BREYTVEYT	RUS	20/12/90	A	18	(9)	6
Vitoldas ČEPAUSKAS	LTU	17/3/79	D	11	(6)	1

Artjom DMITRIJEV		14/11/88	M	4	(3)	2
Kirill EDER		20/1/87	M		(3)	
Vladislav FJODOROV		31/7/92	A		(2)	
Aleksei GORŠKOV		13/2/85	D	25	(2)	
Vladislav IVANOV	RUS	24/1/86	M	9		3
Sergei KAZAKOV		2/1/80	M	24	(9)	7
Stanislav KITTO		30/11/72	M	32	(3)	3
Sergei LEONTOVITŠ		4/3/87	M	15	(14)	7
Oleg LEPIK		1/8/73	D	26	(4)	
Nikolai LÕSANOV		9/5/83	A	5	(6)	4
Armando Tarlazis Viera dos Santos "MANDINHO"	BRA	28/4/84	M	7	(5)	2
Nikolaj MISIUK	LTU	4/1/87	A	1	(3)	
Daniil RATNIKOV		10/2/88	M	22	(7)	10
Eduard RATNIKOV		13/9/83	M	29	(2)	5
Tomas RIMAS	LTU	2/5/78	D	33		4
Rustam RUSTAMOV		31/10/82	A		(1)	
Jüris SAHKUS		12/9/90	G	1	(1)	
Sergei STAROVOITOV		26/7/81	D	25	(4)	6
Modestas STONYS	LTU	17/1/80	G	19	(1)	
Aleksandr TARASSENKOV		29/9/80	M	31	(1)	13
Timo TENISTE		27/10/85	D	7	(1)	
Kristjan TIIRIK		25/8/82	A	8	(5)	1
Sergei USSOLTSEV		2/4/75	G	16		
Aleksandr VOLODIN		29/3/88	D	10	(2)	1

JK TULEVIK VILJANDI
Coach – Marko Lelov
Founded – 1912
Stadium – Viljandi Linnastaadion (1,000)

2009
7/3	Sillamäe Kalev	h	1-3	*Taar*
14/3	Tammeka	h	3-0	*Tutk, Jevdokimov, Frolov*
17/3	Kalju	a	1-1	*Jevdokimov*
21/3	Levadia	h	0-7	
4/4	Trans	a	1-1	*Jevdokimov*
11/4	Paide	h	1-0	*Kureso*
18/4	Kuressaare	a	3-0	*Jevdokimov 2, Toomet*
25/4	Flora	h	1-1	*Kureso*
2/5	Tallinna Kalev	a	1-0	*Jevdokimov*
9/5	Tallinna Kalev	h	2-1	*Kureso, Tutk*
16/5	Flora	a	0-1	
23/5	Kuressaare	h	3-0	*Frolov, Jevdokimov, og (Kluge)*
26/5	Paide	a	1-0	*Jevdokimov*
30/5	Trans	h	1-2	*Frolov*
13/6	Levadia	a	0-5	
16/6	Kalju	h	0-2	
20/6	Tammeka	a	1-1	*Kalda*
4/7	Sillamäe Kalev	a	0-1	
11/7	Tallinna Kalev	a	2-0	*Frolov 2 (1p)*
25/7	Kuressaare	a	4-0	*Alliku, Kulatšenko, Luts, Kureso*
1/8	Paide	h	4-0	*Luts 2, Kulatšenko, Koogas*
8/8	Trans	a	1-3	*Kulatšenko*
15/8	Levadia	h	0-0	
22/8	Kalju	a	1-1	*Jevdokimov*
29/8	Tammeka	h	0-1	
12/9	Sillamäe Kalev	h	1-3	*Jevdokimov*
19/9	Sillamäe Kalev	a	1-3	*Kulatšenko*
26/9	Tammeka	h	3-0	*Alliku 2, Jegorov*
29/9	Flora	h	0-1	
3/10	Kalju	h	3-2	*Jevdokimov, Alliku, og (Tšegodajev)*
17/10	Levadia	a	0-3	
24/10	Trans	h	0-1	
31/10	Paide	a	4-0	*Luts, Koogas, Jevdokimov (p), Alliku*
3/11	Kuressaare	h	6-0	*Kulatšenko, Koogas, Taska, Jevdokimov, Luts, Alliku*

7/11	Flora	a	1-4	*Kulatšenko*	
10/11	Tallinna Kalev	h	4-1	*Taar, Kulatšenko, Jevdokimov, Sillaste A.*	

Name	Nat	DoB	Pos	Aps	(s)	Gls
Rauno ALLIKU		2/3/90	M	16	(3)	6
Andre FROLOV		18/4/88	D	20		5
Aleksei JAHHIMOVITŠ		30/3/90	M	14	(2)	
Sergei JEGOROV		1/1/89	M	2	(3)	1
Jüri JEVDOKIMOV		3/6/88	A	34	(1)	14
Janek KALDA		13/9/78	M	4	(10)	1
Rait KASTERPALU		1/9/87	M	1		
Andres KOOGAS		5/9/87	D	30		3
Kaido KOPPEL		9/5/88	G	3	(2)	
Markko KUDU		23/7/83	A	3	(4)	
Aleksandr KULATŠENKO		25/5/87	M	16	(6)	7
Jürgen KURESOO		11/2/87	M	18	(1)	4
Ervin KÕLL		18/3/89	M	5	(6)	
Rasmus LUHAKOODER		8/12/88	M	12	(7)	
Karl-Eerik LUIGEND		15/1/93	M		(2)	
Siim LUTS		12/3/89	M	16	(1)	5
Armand NARIS		6/10/88	D	7	(7)	
Aiko OGRLA		24/5/87	G	33		
Eerik REINSOO		12/5/88	M	7	(9)	
Siim ROOPS		4/3/86	D	3		
Ats SILLASTE		8/4/88	D	25	(7)	1
Mikk SILLASTE		1/3/87	D	17	(3)	
Sander SINILAID		7/10/90	D	1	(6)	
Albert TAAR		15/1/90	M	26	(7)	2
Martin TASKA		9/12/86	D	30		1
Janar TOOMET		10/8/89	M	1	(8)	1
Rauno TUTK		10/4/88	D	27	(1)	2
Andrei VEIS		6/4/90	D	16	(4)	
Tanel VÕTTI		16/5/88	D	9	(1)	

PROMOTED CLUB

FC LOOTUS KOHTLA-JÄRVE
Coach – Aleksei Zhukov
Founded – 1998
Stadium – Spordikeskuse Staadion (2,200)

SECOND LEVEL FINAL TABLE 2009

		Pld	W	D	L	F	A	Pts
1	FC Levadia II Tallinn	36	26	8	2	96	21	86
2	FC Lootus Kohtla-Järve	36	24	2	10	88	48	74
3	FC Warrior Valga	36	21	2	13	68	63	65
4	FC Ajax Lasnamäe	36	20	4	12	75	53	64
5	Kiviõli Tamme Auto	36	17	2	17	77	77	50
6	Tallinna JK Legion	36	13	5	18	63	76	44
7	JK Vaprus Pärnu	36	11	6	19	64	77	39
8	JK Tulevik II Viljandi	36	10	6	20	49	79	36
9	FC Flora II Tallinn	36	9	5	22	35	64	32
10	FC Flora Rakvere	36	2	2	26	48	105	20

NB FC Levadia II Tallinn ineligible for promotion; FC Lootus Kohtla-Järve promoted directly; FC Warrior Valga entered play-offs; FC Flora Rakvere – 6 pts deducted; Kiviõli Tamme Auto – 3 pts deducted.

PROMOTION/RELEGATION PLAY-OFFS
(15/11/09)
FC Warrior Valga 0, Paide Linnameeskond 1
(21/11/09)
Paide Linnameeskond 1, FC Warrior Valga 1
(Paide Linnameeskond 2-1)

DOMESTIC CUP 2009/10

EESTI KARIKAS

SECOND ROUND

Lootus w/o Navi
(4/8/09)
Kose 0, Kuressaare 8
(5/8/09)
Ajax w/o Hell Hunt
Elva II 0, Trans 9
Järva-Jaani 0, Flora II 2
Kalju III 0, Tammeka 3
Koeru 4, Igiliikur 0
Kristiine 1, Tabasalu 2
Lootos 5, Noorus 96 1
Metec 1, Võru 5
Sillamäe Kalev w/o Keskerakond
Sillamäe Kalev II 1, Rakvere Flora 0
Soccernet 1, Olympic 3
Tallinna Kalev 3, aaMeraaS 1
Tartu Ülikooli Fauna 0, Tamme Auto 10
Tulevik 5, Esteve 1
Warrior 8, Elva 3
(11/8/09)
Kalju II 10, Püsivus 1

Quattromed 1, Atletik 3
Alko 0, Levadia 3
HansaNet.ee w/o Keskerakond II
(13/8/09)
A&A Kinnisvara 2, Orbiit 7
(19/8/09)
Ganvix 3, Velldoris 0
Haiba 2, Rada 1
Sörve 0, EMÜ 1
(25/8/09)
Kalju 6, Kotkad 0
Paide 2, Otepää 3
Rada II 0, Flora 9
Toompea 3, Nõmme United 3 *(aet)*
3-4 on pens)
(26/8/09)
Eston Villa 4, Aspen 0
Tulevik II 13, Twister 0
(2/9/09)
Toompea 1994 0, Piraaja 4

THIRD ROUND

(1/9/09)
Lootos 2, Kuressaare 5
(2/9/09)
Ajax 0, Lootus 3
EMÜ 0, Flora II 5
Kalju 5, Tulevik II 0
Tallinna Kalev 8, Koeru 1
Trans 13, Haiba 0
Võru w/o HansaNet.ee
(8/9/09)
Olympic 2, Tammeka 3
Sillamäe Kalev II 0, Levadia 5

Warrior 1, Kalju II 0
(9/9/09)
Atletik 2, Eston Villa 1 *(aet)*
Orbiit 1, Ganvix 3
(16/9/09)
Sillamäe Kalev 3, Tulevik 1 *(aet)*
(30/9/09)
Nõmme United 5, Tamme Auto 1
Piraaja 5, Tabasalu 3 *(aet)*
(6/10/09)
Flora 4, Otepää 1

1/8 FINALS

(6/10/09)
Kalju 3, Tallinna Kalev 1
(7/10/09)
Lootus 6, Atletik 0
(8/10/09)
Ganvix 4, Võru 2
(10/10/09)
Sillamäe Kalev 3, Piraaja 0

(28/10/09)
Flora II 0, Warrior 1
Tammeka 4, Nõmme United 0
(14/11/09)
Trans 0, Levadia 3
(21/11/09)
Kuressaare 0, Flora 4

QUARTER-FINALS

(13/4/10)
Flora 2 *(Dupikov 105, Luts 109)*, Kalju 0 *(aet)*
(14/4/10)
Lootus 5 *(Kulik 19, Mamontov 61, Bolšakov 73, Škaleta 83, 90+2)*, Ganvix 0
Sillamäe Kalev 0, Levadia 1 *(Kalimullin 19)*
Tammeka 4 *(Kiidron 14, Haljak 18, Torop 47, Anderson 73)*, Warrior 1 *(Karpov 84,*

SEMI-FINALS

(27/4/10)
Flora 4 *(Dupikov 15, Konsa 33, Allas 47, Alliku 86)*, Tammeka 1 *(Prosa 45+1)*
(28/4/10)
Levadia 2 *(Ivanov 19, 32)*, Lootos 0

FINAL

(11/5/10)
Kadriorg stadium, Tallinn
FC LEVADIA TALLINN 3 *(Pebre 33, Leitan 61, Dmitrijev 72)*
FC FLORA TALLINN 0
Referee – Kotter
LEVADIA – Lepmets, Teniste, Morozov, Kalimullin, Volodin, Nahk, Malov, Saarelma (Subbotin 33), Dmitrijev (Ivanov 89), Leitan, Pebre.
FLORA – Pedõk, Kams, Palatu, Jahhimovitš, Jürgenson, Mašitšev (Beglarishvili 71), Kasimir, Minkenen, Luts (Mošnikov 63), Konsa, Alliku.

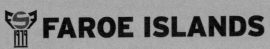
HB make their mark

HB Tórshavn, the Faroe Islands' most decorated club, recorded their 20th domestic championship title in 2009, returning to power after a three-year absence. It was a sad season, however, for the country's only other top-flight ever-presents, KÍ Klaksvik, who were relegated for the first time in their history.

Indeed, it was with a 4-2 home win over their long-time rivals, in the penultimate round of the campaign, that HB secured the title – and effectively sent KÍ down. Having failed to win any of their previous four fixtures, the team from the capital were looking edgy going into that fixture, but in the event KÍ offered little resistance as HB raced into a four-goal lead, the visitors' two replies coming too late to dampen the home team's celebrations.

Inspirational skipper

HB coach Sámal Erik Hentze thus took the top prize at the end of his first season in charge. He had operated in conjunction with Rúni Nolsøe as the club ended the 2008 season as runners-up to EB/Streymur. Now, in sole charge, he returned HB to the summit in fine style. They started the season strongly, winning seven of their opening nine fixtures, and at one stage held a ten-point lead at the top of the table. Do-it-all skipper Fróði Benjaminsen, a regular Faroe Islands international, was the team's stand-out performer, both in defence and attack, and the inspirational 31-year-old fully deserved the Player of the Year crown that came his way at the end of the season.

Benjaminsen's ten goals were supplemented by 14 from the club's top scorer, Andrew av Fløtum, another Faroe Islands international, but the Golden Boot for the Formuladeildin's leading marksman was won, with 19 goals, by 20-year-old Finnur Justinussen of Víkingur, a player who had never previously scored in the top flight. The youngster's season was made even more memorable by the goal he scored to seal his team's victory in the Faroese Cup final – a 3-2 victory over

holders EB/Streymur in Torshavn. He was also on target in each leg of the semi-final, won 6-0 on aggregate against ÍF Fuglafjørdur.

Whereas the 2008 season had belonged to EB/Streymur, victors in both league and cup, the merger club from the north could only manage runners-up spots in both competitions in 2009. Coach Sigfríður Clementsen was dismissed two days after the Cup final defeat but Arnbjørn Theodor Hansen, the league's top scorer with 20 goals in 2008, remained a potent force up front under new boss Hedin Askham, finishing second in the 2009 standings to Justinussen on 17. The prolific 23-year-old also distinguished himself by scoring the winning goal for the Faroe Islands in their final home 2010 FIFA World Cup qualifier, against Lithuania.

Faroe Islands international Fróði Benjaminsen inspired HB to their title triumph

FAROE ISLANDS

Fitting farewell

That 2-1 victory in Toftir was the country's first in a World Cup game for eight years and provided an early confidence boost for the team's new head coach, former Republic of Ireland manager Brian Kerr, appointed only five months earlier. The campaign would close with a couple of predictable away defeats to France (0-5) and Romania (1-3), but the win over Lithuania, which quadrupled the Faroes' points total in the group, provided a fitting farewell to home fans for the team's veteran goalkeeper Jakúp Mikkelsen on the day that he equalled his predecessor Jens Martin Knudsen's total of 65 caps. Mikkelsen moved to 67 by playing against France and Romania before retiring from international football, after 14 years of service, at the age of 39.

Fótbóltssamband Føroya (FSF)

Gundadalur
PO Box 3028
FO-110 Tórshavn
tel – +298 351979
fax – +298 319079
website – football.fo
email – fsf@football.fo
Year of Formation – 1979

President – Christian Andreasen
General Secretary – Virgar Hvidbro
National Stadium – Tórsvøllur, Torshavn (6,040)

TOP FIVE ALL-TIME CAPS
Óli Johannesen (83); Jákup Mikkelsen (67); Jens Martin Knudsen (65); Julian Johnsson (62); Jákup á Borg (60)
TOP FIVE ALL-TIME GOALS
Rógvi Jacobsen (10); Todi Jónsson (9); Uni Arge (8); John Petersen (6); Julian Johnsson & Jan Allan Müller (4)

NATIONAL TEAM RESULTS 2009/10

12/8/09	France (WCQ)	H	Torshavn	0-1	
5/9/09	Austria (WCQ)	A	Graz	1-3	Olsen A. (82)
9/9/09	Lithuania (WCQ)	H	Toftir	2-1	Olsen S. (15), Hansen A. (35)
10/10/09	France (WCQ)	A	Guingamp	0-5	
14/10/09	Romania (WCQ)	A	Piatra Neamt	1-3	Bø (83)
21/3/10	Iceland	A	Kopavogur	0-2	
4/6/10	Luxembourg	A	Hesperange	0-0	

NATIONAL TEAM APPEARANCES 2009/10

Coach – Brian KERR (IRL)	3/3/53		FRA	AUT	LTU	FRA	ROU	Isl	Lux	Caps	Goals
Jákup MIKKELSEN	14/8/70	KÍ	G	G	G	G	G			67	-
Jónas Tór NÆS	27/12/86	Frem (DEN)	D	D	s64	D	D		D	13	-
Jóhan Troest DAVIDSEN	31/1/88	NSÍ	D		D	D			D	15	-
Atli GREGERSEN	15/6/82	Víkingur	D	D	D	D	D	s65	D	8	
Egil á BØ	2/4/74	EB/Streymur	D	D		D	D	D65		12	1
Atli DANIELSEN	15/8/83	KÍ /Roskilde (DEN)	M42	M		D	D	M46		36	-
Fródi BENJAMINSEN	14/12/77	HB	M	M80		M	M81	M	M	58	3
Simun SAMUELSEN	21/5/85	Keflavík (ISL) /HB	M	M	M		M	M79	A	29	1
Súni OLSEN	7/3/81	Víkingur	M85	M67	M	M90	M	s46	M	41	3
Bogi LØKIN	22/10/88	NSÍ /Frem (DEN)	M	M		M	s70	M72	s70	13	1
Christian Lamhauge HOLST	25/12/81	Silkeborg (DEN)	A28	A71	M		M70		M80	19	2
Jóan Símun EDMUNDSSON	26/7/91	B68 /Newcastle (ENG)	s28					A79	s81	3	
Jann Ingi PETERSEN	7/1/84	NSÍ	s42	s80	M	M64				16	

NATIONAL TEAM APPEARANCES 2009/10 (contd.)

			FRA	AUT	LTU	FRA	ROU	Isl	Lux	Caps	Goals
Jákup á BORG	26/10/79	B36	s85		M90		M			60	2
Einar T. HANSEN	2/4/88	NSÍ			D	D		s72	D	10	-
Levi HANSSEN	24/2/88	EB/Streymur	s67							2	-
Andreas Lava OLSEN	9/10/87	Víkingur	s71		s68		s79			6	1
Bartal ELIASEN	23/8/76	ÍF					D			6	-
Arnbjørn Theodor HANSEN	27/2/86	EB/Streymur					A68	s73		7	1
Brian OLSEN	22/8/85	EB/Streymur			s90	s90				2	-
Christian Høgni JACOBSEN	12/5/80	NSÍ					M	s81	s80	50	2
Rógvi JACOBSEN	5/3/79	ÍF					A79	A73		54	10
Gunnar NIELSEN	7/10/86	Man. City (ENG)						G	G	3	-
Høgni ZACHARIASSEN	26/8/82	ÍF						D72		1	-
Vagnur Mohr MORTENSEN	10/2/83	HB						D		4	-
Rógvi POULSEN	31/10/89	HB						M	M70	2	-
Andrew av FLØTUM	13/6/79	HB						s72		34	1
Bárdur OLSEN	5/12/85	B36						s79		3	-
Christian R. MOURITSEN	3/12/88	B36						s79	M81	3	-

DOMESTIC LEAGUE 2009

PREMIER DIVISION FINAL TABLE 2009

		Home					Away					Total					Pts
	Pld	W	D	L	F	A	W	D	L	F	A	W	D	L	F	A	
1 HB Tórshavn	27	9	4	1	34	17	7	3	3	25	20	16	7	4	59	37	55
2 EB/Streymur	27	8	3	3	34	18	7	2	4	22	16	15	5	7	56	34	50
3 Víkingur	27	9	1	4	35	21	5	4	4	16	15	14	5	8	51	36	47
4 NSÍ Runavík	27	7	2	5	27	18	6	3	4	29	28	13	5	9	56	46	44
5 B68 Toftir	27	8	4	1	28	14	4	3	7	20	27	12	7	8	48	41	43
6 AB Argír	27	5	3	5	17	18	4	4	6	12	17	9	7	11	29	35	34
7 ÍF Fuglafjørður	27	7	1	5	27	16	1	5	8	18	32	8	6	13	45	48	30
8 B36 Tórshavn	27	6	3	5	22	21	1	4	8	15	32	7	7	13	37	53	28
9 KÍ Klaksvík	27	3	5	5	16	21	3	1	10	14	36	6	6	15	30	57	24
10 07 Vestur	27	3	5	5	21	25	1	2	11	18	38	4	7	16	39	63	19

TOP GOALSCORERS

19 Finnur JUSTINUSSEN (Víkingur)
17 Arnbjørn Theodor HANSEN (EB/Streymur)
15 Ahmed KEITA (B68)
14 Andrew av FLØTUM (HB)
   Károly POTEMKIN (NSÍ)
11 Hjalgrím ELTTØR (NSÍ/KÍ)
   Jens Erik RASMUSSEN (Vestur)
10 Fródi BENJAMINSEN (HB)
9 Rógvi POULSEN (HB)
  Andy OLSEN (ÍF)
  Christian Høgni JACOBSEN (NSÍ)
  Bogi LØKIN (NSÍ)

CLUB-BY-CLUB

AB ARGÍR
Coach – John Petersen
Founded – 1973
Stadium - í Vika (2,000)

2009

Date	Opp		Score	Scorers
5/4	B36	a	2-3	Eriksen, Olsen
13/4	B68	a	0-1	
19/4	ÍF	h	2-0	Nielsen, Hansen
26/4	KÍ	a	1-0	Nielsen
3/5	Vestur	h	2-2	Jacobsen, Eriksen
10/5	HB	a	0-4	
17/5	EB/Streymur	h	1-1	Joensen J.
21/5	Víkingur	h	0-1	
24/5	NSÍ	a	1-0	Drangastein
1/6	B36	h	3-1	Aristide, Joensen J. (p), og (Jacobsen H.)
13/6	B68	h	0-3	
17/6	ÍF	a	0-3	
21/6	KÍ	h	0-2	
24/6	Vestur	a	0-0	
27/6	HB	h	0-0	

FAROE ISLANDS

2/8	Víkingur	a	0-1	
5/8	EB/Streymur	a	3-0	Splidt, Søbstad, Nielsen
9/8	NSÍ	h	3-1	Splidt, Søbstad, Jacobsen
15/8	B36	a	2-0	Nielsen, Søbstad
19/8	B68	a	0-0	
23/8	ÍF	h	4-2	Eriksen 2, Overgaard, Søbstad
30/8	KÍ	a	1-1	Sigurdsson
13/9	Vestur	h	2-1	Søbstad, Eriksen
16/9	HB	a	1-1	Mellemgaard
20/9	EB/Streymur	h	0-3	
27/9	NSÍ	a	1-3	Eriksen
3/10	Víkingur	h	0-1	

No	Name	Nat	DoB	Pos	Aps	(s)	Gls
3	Tehe ARISTIDE	CIV	31/12/86	D	25		1
7	Evrard BLE	CIV	2/1/82	M	22	(1)	
14	Jákup DAM		28/9/89	A		(1)	
6	Rói DANIELSEN		18/2/89	D	16	(2)	
19	Jobin Schrøter DRANGASTEIN		1/11/90	M	9	(11)	1
11	Nikolai Lindholm ERIKSEN	DEN	1/8/86	A	18	(2)	6
8	John HANSEN		14/11/88	M	18	(1)	1
14	Mortan úr HØRG		21/9/80	D	11		
20	Kenneth JACOBSEN		11/5/81	M	25		2
5	Teitur JÓANNESARSSON		18/6/89	D	1	(4)	
15	Høgni Mouritsarson JOENSEN		4/5/82	D	11	(4)	
4	Janus JOENSEN		8/6/76	D	17		2
2	Tummas JUSTINUSSEN		10/3/90	M	10	(9)	
14	Liam KILLA	WAL	4/10/88	M	1	(2)	
18	Alex MELLEMGAARD		27/11/91	D	9	(1)	1
9	Allan MØRKØRE		22/11/71	A		(1)	
12	Rasmus NIELSEN		22/9/89	M	23	(2)	4
17	Dánjal Rói OLSEN		4/8/90	A	5	(7)	1
4	Morten OVERGAARD	DEN	24/5/87	D	11		1
11	Dan PETERSEN		2/7/90	A		(1)	
17	John PETERSEN		22/4/72	A		(1)	
11	Thomas Hans Lamain RUBEKSEN		13/6/86	A	3	(7)	
9	Tróndur SIGURDSSON		16/12/88	A	5	(6)	1
10	Dion SPLIDT		5/6/89	M	16	(4)	2
1	Hedin STENBERG		14/1/89	G	9	(1)	
13	Jónas STENBERG		7/4/87	D	2	(3)	
6	Sakaris Ludvík SÚNASON		17/8/92	D		(1)	
13	Stig-Roar SØBSTAD	NOR	12/3/82	A	12		5
1	Tórdur THOMSEN		11/6/86	G	18		

B36 TÓRSHAVN
Coach – Milan Čimburović (SRB); (17/4/09) Mikkjal Thomassen
Founded – 1936
Stadium - Gundadalur (5,000)
MAJOR HONOURS:
Faroe Islands League - (8) 1946, 1948, 1950, 1959, 1962, 1997, 2001, 2005;
Faroe Islands Cup - (5) 1965, 1991, 2001, 2003, 2006.

2009

5/4	AB	h	3-2	Koroma, Malsom, Borg
13/4	ÍF	a	2-1	Matras, Borg
19/4	KÍ	h	1-0	Jacobsen R.
26/4	Vestur	a	2-4	Malsom, Ellingsgaard
3/5	HB	h	2-2	Koroma, Jacobsen R.
10/5	EB/Streymur	a	0-0	
17/5	NSÍ	h	2-3	Malsom 2
21/5	B68	h	0-2	
25/5	Víkingur	a	1-3	og (Gregersen)
1/6	AB	a	1-3	Eysturoy
14/6	ÍF	h	0-0	
17/6	KÍ	a	2-2	Koroma, Jacobsen R.
20/6	Vestur	h	2-1	Olsen, Hermansen
25/6	HB	a	2-2	Midjord, Olsen
26/7	NSÍ	a	0-3	
2/8	B68	a	0-3	
9/8	Víkingur	h	1-3	Midjord
15/8	AB	h	0-2	
19/8	ÍF	a	1-1	Olsen
23/8	KÍ	h	3-0	Borg, Jacobsen R., Midjord

26/8	EB/Streymur	h	1-3	Koroma
30/8	Vestur	a	0-2	
13/9	HB	h	1-0	Mouritsen
16/9	EB/Streymur	a	1-4	Mouritsen
20/9	NSÍ	h	5-2	Koroma 3, Holmberg, Midjord
27/9	Víkingur	a	3-4	Midjord, Færø, Thomasen
3/10	B68	h	1-1	Borg

No	Name	Nat	DoB	Pos	Aps	(s)	Gls
9	Jákup á BORG		26/10/79	A	19	(3)	4
8	Fródi CLEMENTSEN		30/11/78	D	4	(1)	
12	Jóhan ELLINGSGAARD		12/5/89	M	24	(1)	1
23	Høgni EYSTUROY		14/7/90	M	4	(16)	1
5	Odmar FÆRØ		1/11/89	M	12	(1)	1
19	Christian í GARDI		2/12/90	D	1	(1)	
24	Ásbjørn Viderø GUNNARSSON		1/9/87	M	4	(3)	
17	Bogi HERMANSEN		3/6/86	A	1	(5)	1
6	Dennis HOLMBERG	DEN	24/8/87	M	11		1
13	Súni úr HØRG		24/12/82	D	4	(2)	
28	Herbert í Lon JACOBSEN		1/12/79	D	25		
4	Poul Arni JACOBSEN		27/9/85	D	15	(5)	
10	Róaldur JACOBSEN		23/1/91	M	26	(1)	4
1	Jóan Pauli Dahl JAKOBSEN		26/8/89	G	18		
14	Brima KOROMA	SLE	8/7/84	A	21	(4)	7
23	Sam Andrew MALSOM	ENG	10/11/87	A	12		4
22	Klæmint MATRAS		20/5/81	M	26		1
7	Bergur MIDJORD		20/4/85	A	20	(1)	5
11	Christian Restorff MOURITSEN		3/12/88	M	9		2
19	Janus MORTENSEN		21/12/90	M		(6)	
18	Magnus Hendriksson OLSEN		26/10/86	M	20	(6)	3
2	Atli PETERSEN		21/5/85	D	1	(1)	
23	André RIEL	DEN	21/10/89	M		(5)	
19	Sjúrdur THOMASEN		15/4/90	A		(10)	1
6	Hanus THORLEIFSSON		19/12/85	M	11	(1)	
1	Tróndur VATNHAMAR		12/1/80	G	9		

B68 TOFTIR
Coach – Bill McLeod Jacobsen
Founded – 1962
Stadium - Svangarskard (1,200)
MAJOR HONOURS:
Faroe Islands League - (3) 1984, 1985, 1992.

2009

4/4	HB	a	1-3	Højgaard D.
13/4	AB	h	1-0	Keita
19/4	EB/Streymur	a	0-3	
26/4	ÍF	a	2-3	Edmundsson, Keita
3/5	NSÍ	a	2-2	Guéye, Olsen Ó.
10/5	KÍ	h	2-0	Keita, Joensen
17/5	Víkingur	a	3-3	Keita, Edmundsson, Hansen
21/5	B36	a	2-0	Guéye, Olsen Ó.
24/5	Vestur	h	2-1	Edmundsson, Keita
1/6	HB	h	3-3	Keita, Justinussen, Højgaard Jón.
13/6	AB	a	3-0	Justinussen, Højgaard D., Keita
17/6	EB/Streymur	h	3-2	Keita, Guéye, Edmundsson
21/6	ÍF	h	2-1	Edmundsson 2
25/6	NSÍ	h	2-2	Keita, Joensen
19/7	KÍ	a	4-2	Keita, Joensen 2, Olsen Ó.
2/8	B36	h	3-0	Keita, Justinussen, Stanković
5/8	Víkingur	h	2-2	Guéye, Hansen (p)
9/8	Vestur	a	0-1	
16/8	HB	a	1-3	Poulsen J.
19/8	AB	h	0-0	
23/8	EB/Streymur	h	0-4	
30/8	ÍF	h	5-2	Keita 3, Olsen Ó. (p), Danielsen
13/9	NSÍ	a	1-0	Olsen Ó.
16/9	KÍ	h	0-1	
20/9	Víkingur	a	0-2	
27/9	Vestur	h	3-0	Olsen Ó. (p), Stanković, Poulsen J.
3/10	B36	a	1-1	Keita

No	Name	Nat	DoB	Pos	Aps	(s)	Gls
19	Debes DANIELSEN		12/8/86	M	6	(10)	1
14	Jóan Símun EDMUNDSSON		26/7/91	M	22	(3)	6
1	Vlada FILIPOVIĆ	SRB	18/3/78	G	26		
17	Bogi GREGERSEN		4/8/80	A	4	(3)	
6	Ndende Adama GUÉYE	SEN	5/1/83	M	24		4
5	Øssur HANSEN		7/1/71	M	11		2
9	Dánial Pauli HØJGAARD		27/12/83	D	23	(4)	2
20	Jóhan Dávur HØJGAARD		11/6/82	D	26		
15	Jónleif HØJGAARD		26/10/88	D	2	(18)	1
16	Oddur Árnason HØJGAARD		12/9/89	D		(6)	
32	Niklas Fridrikur JOENSEN		12/9/89	D	12	(6)	4
2	Pól Jóhannus JUSTINUSSEN		13/1/89	D	26		3
18	Ahmed KEITA	SEN	12/5/87	A	26	(1)	15
17	Remi LANGAARD		16/12/91	M	1	(2)	
12	Petur Meinhard MAGNUSSEN		26/3/90	G	1		
23	André OLSEN		23/10/90	A	8	(14)	
8	Óli Højgaard OLSEN		24/11/85	A	20	(2)	6
11	Jóhan Petur POULSEN		8/5/86	M	8	(5)	2
17	Niklas POULSEN		30/3/89	M	1		
10	Poul Narvi POULSEN		22/9/86	D	24	(1)	
7	Nenad STANKOVIĆ	SRB	8/8/77	M	26		2

EB/STREYMUR

Coach – Sigfríður Clementsen; (31/7/09) Hedin Askham
Founded – 1993
Stadium - Vid Margáir (1,000)
MAJOR HONOURS:
Faroe Islands League - (1) 2008; Faroe Islands Cup - (2) 2007, 2008.

2009

Date	Opp		Res	Scorers
5/4	Vestur	h	2-1	Hansen A. 2
13/4	HB	a	0-1	
19/4	B68	h	3-0	Hanssen, Hansen A., Niclasen
26/4	NSÍ	h	3-4	Olsen Br., Olsen Bá., Anghel
4/5	Víkingur	a	2-0	Hanssen 2
10/5	B36	h	0-0	
17/5	AB	a	1-1	og (Danielsen)
21/5	KÍ	a	0-0	
24/5	ÍF	h	2-2	Hanssen, Olsen Br.
1/6	Vestur	a	5-3	Anghel, Hanssen, Alex, Hansen A., Samuelsen
14/6	HB	h	2-3	Alex, Hansen A.
17/6	B68	a	2-3	Bø, Alex (p)
20/6	NSÍ	a	2-1	Samuelsen, Olsen Bá.
24/6	Víkingur	h	1-0	Jacobsen
2/8	KÍ	h	7-0	Anghel 2, Hansen A. 2, Samuelsen, Alex, Niclasen
5/8	AB	h	0-3	
9/8	ÍF	a	1-3	Hansen A.
16/8	Vestur	h	1-0	Hansen A.
19/8	HB	a	1-0	og (Nolsøe R.)
23/8	B68	h	4-0	Hansen A. 2, Samuelsen, Anghel
26/8	B36	a	3-1	Bø, og (Olsen), Samuelsen
31/8	NSÍ	h	2-2	Davidsen, Hansen A.
13/9	Víkingur	a	0-3	
16/9	B36	h	4-1	Alex (p), Olsen Br., Anghel, Hansen A.
20/9	AB	a	3-0	Hansen A. 2, Hanssen
27/9	ÍF	h	3-2	Hansen A., Hansen P., Samuelsen
3/10	KÍ	a	2-0	Hansen A., Anghel

No	Name	Nat	DoB	Pos	Aps	(s)	Gls
2	ALEX José dos Santos	BRA	28/3/81	D	16	(6)	5
10	Sorin Vasile ANGHEL	ROU	16/7/79	A	25	(1)	7
8	Egil á BØ		2/4/74	D	23	(1)	2
9	Arnar DAM		18/10/91	M		(1)	
5	Dánjal DAVIDSEN		17/4/88	D	15	(5)	1
12	Marni DJURHUUS		6/9/85	D	26		
22	Arnbjørn Theodor HANSEN		27/2/86	A	24	(3)	17
4	Gert Åge HANSEN		25/7/84	D		(3)	
16	Pauli Gregersen HANSEN		9/4/80	M	9	(8)	1
12	Levi HANSSEN		24/2/88	M	27		6

6	Pætur Dam JACOBSEN		5/12/82	M	11	(14)	1
23	Leif NICLASEN		1/10/86	D	20	(7)	2
27	Gudmund NIELSEN		10/10/87	M	11	(6)	
15	Bárdur OLSEN		5/12/85	M	25	(2)	2
18	Brian OLSEN		22/8/85	M	12	(13)	3
11	Hans Pauli SAMUELSEN		18/10/84	M	26	(1)	6
24	Gunnar á STEIG		20/12/76	G	14		
1	René TÓRGARD		3/8/79	G	13		

HB TÓRSHAVN

Coach – Sámal Erik Hentze
Founded – 1904
Stadium - Gundadalur (5,000)
MAJOR HONOURS:
Faroe Islands League - (20) 1955, 1960, 1963, 1964, 1965, 1971, 1973, 1974, 1975, 1978, 1981, 1982, 1988, 1990, 1998, 2002, 2003, 2004, 2006, 2009; Faroe Islands Cup - (26) 1955, 1957, 1959, 1962, 1963, 1964, 1968, 1969, 1971, 1972, 1973, 1975, 1976, 1978, 1979, 1980, 1981, 1982, 1984, 1987, 1988, 1989, 1992, 1995, 1998, 2004.

2009

Date	Opp		Res	Scorers
4/4	B68	h	3-1	Kuljić, Poulsen, Fløtum (p)
13/4	EB/Streymur	h	1-0	Kuljić
20/4	NSÍ	a	1-2	Poulsen
26/4	Víkingur	h	2-1	Benjaminsen, Kuljić
3/5	B36	a	2-2	og (Clementsen), Lag
10/5	AB	h	4-0	Nolsøe R., Joensen, Benjaminsen, Jørgensen B.
17/5	ÍF	a	3-1	Benjaminsen, Kuljić, Poulsen
21/5	Vestur	a	3-2	Benjaminsen 2 (1p), Kuljić
24/5	KÍ	h	4-2	Lag, Fløtum 2, Joensen
1/6	B68	a	3-3	Fløtum, Benjaminsen, Poulsen
14/6	EB/Streymur	a	3-2	Jørgensen B. 2, Fløtum
17/6	NSÍ	h	5-2	Jørgensen B., Poulsen, Fløtum 3
21/6	Víkingur	a	3-2	Hørg, Jørgensen B., Fløtum
25/6	B36	h	2-2	Poulsen, Fløtum
27/6	AB	a	0-0	
26/7	ÍF	h	0-0	
2/8	Vestur	h	4-3	Kuljić, Jørgensen B., Benjaminsen, Poulsen
6/8	KÍ	a	2-0	Fløtum (p), Thorleifsson
16/8	B68	h	3-1	Fløtum 2 (1p), Jørgensen B.
19/8	EB/Streymur	h	0-1	
23/8	NSÍ	a	2-0	Kuljić, Lag
30/8	Víkingur	h	1-1	Poulsen
13/9	B36	a	0-1	
16/9	AB	h	1-1	Benjaminsen
20/9	ÍF	a	0-3	
27/9	KÍ	h	4-2	Lag, Fløtum, Benjaminsen, Poulsen
3/10	Vestur	a	3-2	Kuljić, Benjaminsen (p), Mouritsen J.

No	Name	Nat	DoB	Pos	Aps	(s)	Gls
7	Fróði BENJAMINSEN		14/12/77	M	27		10
15	Rani Debes CHRISTIANSEN		8/3/84	D	2		
17	Poul Thomas DAM		28/10/87	D	18	(4)	
21	Jógvan Rói DAVIDSEN		9/10/91	M		(2)	
1	Marcin DAWID	POL	28/1/80	G	9		
10	Andrew av FLØTUM		13/6/79	A	21	(4)	14
16	Símun Rógvi HANSEN		10/4/87	G	18		
3	Mortan úr HØRG		21/9/80	D	7	(2)	1
2	Svenn Fuglø JACOBSEN		18/2/86	M	4		
23	Rókur av Fløtum JESPERSEN		16/3/85	M	3		
24	Páll Mohr JOENSEN		29/6/86	A	16	(8)	2
11	Bjarni JØRGENSEN		9/8/84	A	24	(2)	7
22	Pætur Tórstein JØRGENSEN		12/4/88	D	25		
14	Milan KULJIĆ	SRB	24/12/75	D	18	(6)	8
4	Hans á LAG		26/9/74	D	24	(1)	4
20	Vagnur Mohr MORTENSEN		10/2/83	D	6	(4)	
19	Christian Restorff MOURITSEN		3/12/88	M		(5)	
12	Johan Eyvind Restorff MOURITSEN		20/3/86	A	3	(14)	1
21	Kristin Restorff MOURITSEN		23/4/91	M		(1)	
2	Jón NIELSEN		20/5/80	M	1		

FAROE ISLANDS

8	Kári NIELSEN	3/3/81	M	22	(3)	
15	Jógvan Andrias Skeel NOLSØE	20/5/92	M		(1)	
5	Rasmus NOLSØE	25/1/85	D	20		1
6	Ólavur Sakarisson i ÓLAVSSTOVU	14/6/88	M		(2)	
18	Rógvi POULSEN	31/10/89	M	27		9
9	Tróndur SIGURDSSON	16/12/88	A	1	(9)	
9	Hanus THORLEIFSSON	19/12/85	M	1	(3)	1

ÍF FUGLAFJØRDUR
Coach – Jón Simonsen
Founded – 1946
Stadium - Fløtugerdi (3,000)
MAJOR HONOURS:
Faroe Islands League - (1) 1979.

2009

3/4	Víkingur	a	0-2	
13/4	B36	h	1-2	*Eliasen B.*
19/4	AB	a	0-2	
26/4	B68	h	3-2	*Zachariassen, Poulsen, Olsen*
3/5	KÍ	h	1-0	*Sinkó*
10/5	Vestur	a	1-1	*Sarić*
17/5	HB	h	1-3	*Olsen*
21/5	NSÍ	h	1-2	*Olsen (p)*
24/5	EB/Streymur	a	2-2	*Olsen (p), Lakjuni*
1/6	Víkingur	h	1-2	*Eliasen H.*
14/6	B36	a	0-0	
17/6	AB	h	3-0	*Eliasen B., Olsen, Jacobsen V.*
21/6	B68	a	1-2	*Jovević*
24/6	KÍ	a	2-3	*Sarić, Sinkó*
19/7	Vestur	h	3-0	*Lakjuni, Olsen (p), og (Petersen)*
26/7	HB	a	0-0	
3/8	NSÍ	a	1-4	*Sinkó*
6/8	EB/Streymur	h	3-1	*Poulsen, Jacobsen R. 2*
16/8	Víkingur	a	3-2	*Dalbúd 2, Sinkó*
19/8	B36	h	1-1	*Olsen*
23/8	AB	a	2-4	*Sarić, Sinkó (p)*
30/8	B68	a	2-5	*Olsen, Jacobsen R.*
12/9	KÍ	h	5-0	*Jacobsen R. 2, Dalbúd, Sarić, Olsen*
16/9	Vestur	a	2-2	*Dalbúd, Lakjuni*
20/9	HB	h	3-0	*Poulsen (p), Jacobsen R., Lakjuni*
27/9	EB/Streymur	a	2-3	*Jacobsen R., Jovević*
3/10	NSÍ	h	1-3	*Ennigard P.*

No	Name	Nat	DoB	Pos	Aps	(s)	Gls
25	Øssur DALBÚD		28/3/89	A	12	(1)	4
6	Bartal ELIASEN		23/8/76	D	18	(1)	2
10	Hanus ELIASEN		9/5/84	A	1	(9)	1
21	Ari Ólavsson ELLINGSGAARD		3/2/93	M		(6)	
3	Jan ELLINGSGAARD		26/6/90	D	24	(2)	
12	Kaj ENNIGARD		6/3/84	D	1	(4)	
15	Poul ENNIGARD		29/7/77	D	18	(2)	1
1	András GÁNGÓ	HUN	2/3/84	G	27		
9	Rógvi JACOBSEN		5/3/79	A	6	(7)	7
18	Vincent JACOBSEN		23/12/89	A		(6)	1
12	Viggo JOHANNESEN		5/6/79	D	8	(2)	
7	Aleksandar JOVEVIĆ	SRB	10/4/78	M	21		2
14	Dánjal á LAKJUNI		22/9/90	M	13	(8)	4
8	Fritleif í LAMBANUM		13/4/86	M	15	(5)	
23	Andy OLSEN		3/12/84	A	25		9
2	Áki PETERSEN		1/12/84	D	17	(3)	
13	Hans Paule PETERSEN		29/7/80	D	1	(3)	
24	Hilmar PETERSEN		5/10/89	M		(2)	
11	Frank POULSEN		3/12/84	M	22	(1)	3
4	Nenad SARIĆ	SRB	5/7/81	M	24	(1)	4
17	Balázs SINKÓ	HUN	9/2/79	M	18	(5)	5
5	Jonn Sólheim THOMSEN		26/12/81	D	3		
22	Høgni ZACHARIASSEN		26/8/82	M	23		1

KÍ KLAKSVÍK
Coach – Aleksandar Đorđević (SRB); (25/8/09) Petur Mohr
Founded – 1904
Stadium - Djúpumýri (4,000)
MAJOR HONOURS:
Faroe Islands League - (17) 1942, 1945, 1952, 1953, 1954, 1956, 1957, 1958,
1961, 1966, 1967, 1968, 1969, 1970, 1972, 1991, 1999;
Faroe Islands Cup - (5) 1966, 1967, 1990, 1994, 1999.

2009

4/4	NSÍ	a	1-1	*Jacobsen K.*
13/4	Víkingur	h	2-2	*Joensen I., Lervig*
19/4	B36	a	0-1	
26/4	AB	h	0-1	
3/5	ÍF	a	0-1	
10/5	B68	a	0-2	
17/5	Vestur	h	2-2	*Jacobsen K. 2*
21/5	EB/Streymur	h	0-0	
24/5	HB	a	2-4	*Jacobsen K., Kalsø Sø.*
1/6	NSÍ	h	0-2	
13/6	Víkingur	a	1-4	*Jacobsen K.*
17/6	B36	h	2-2	*Joensen I., Isaksen*
21/6	AB	a	2-0	*Jacobsen K., Danielsen E.*
24/6	ÍF	h	3-2	*Kalsø St., Hammer, Isaksen*
19/7	B68	h	2-4	*Jónsson, Klettskard*
26/7	Vestur	a	3-1	*Danielsen A., Elttør, Klettskard*
2/8	EB/Streymur	a	0-7	
6/8	HB	h	0-2	
16/8	NSÍ	a	2-3	*Lakjuni O., Kalsø St.*
19/8	Víkingur	h	2-0	*Elttør 2*
23/8	B36	a	0-3	
30/8	AB	h	1-1	*Danielsen A.*
12/9	ÍF	a	0-5	
16/9	B68	a	1-0	*og (Højgaard Jóh.)*
20/9	Vestur	h	2-1	*Elttør, Kalsø Sø.*
27/9	HB	a	2-4	*Elttør 2 (1p)*
3/10	EB/Streymur	h	0-2	

No	Name	Nat	DoB	Pos	Aps	(s)	Gls
4	Jan ANDREASEN		14/11/72	D	17	(3)	
16	Eilif ARGE		12/5/91	G	1		
19	Leon BJARTALÍÐ		13/9/80	D	6	(4)	
12	Álvur CHRISTIANSEN		29/5/89	M	1	(3)	
8	Atli DANIELSEN		15/8/83	M	12	(1)	2
7	Erland Berg DANIELSEN		16/5/90	M	15	(2)	1
3	Niels Pauli DANIELSEN		18/1/89	M	3	(6)	
23	Hjalgrím ELTTØR		3/3/83	A	12		6
2	Rudolf ELIASEN		23/2/87	D	15	(2)	
20	John HAMMER		17/2/89	D	21	(3)	1
13	Jógvan ISAKSEN		25/4/90	D	20		2
5	Jón JACOBSEN		26/7/86	M	1	(6)	
10	Kristoffur JACOBSEN		7/11/88	M	21	(4)	6
6	Allan JOENSEN		3/1/74	M	1	(4)	
9	Arnold JOENSEN		11/12/74	M	2	(4)	
11	Ivan JOENSEN		20/2/92	M	8	(5)	2
5	Símin JOENSEN		12/7/83	M	6	(1)	
11	Todi JÓNSSON		2/2/72	A	7	(1)	1
17	Steffan KALSØ		8/9/87	M	20	(4)	2
6	Sørmund KALSØ		20/1/92	D	21	(2)	2
9	Páll KLETTSKARD		17/5/90	M	4	(3)	2
18	Hedin á LAKJUNI		19/2/78	A	19		
22	Oddmar á LAKJUNI		17/10/86	D	13	(5)	1
21	Tórdur LERVIG		18/5/85	M	1	(2)	1
19	Høgni MADSEN		4/2/85	M	7	(1)	
1	Jákup MIKKELSEN		14/8/70	G	26		
6	Ovi NYSTED		30/3/80	D		(1)	
13	Ári SAMSON		9/6/89	M		(1)	
14	Eli SIMONSEN		3/9/90	M	13	(4)	
8	Adrian STAUSS		11/2/84	M	3	(4)	
15	Bjarki VÁGSTÚN		31/8/88	M	1	(1)	

NSÍ RUNAVÍK

Coach – Pauli Poulsen
Founded – 1957
Stadium - Runavík (4,000)
MAJOR HONOURS:
Faroe Islands League - (1) 2007; Faroe Islands Cup - (2) 1986, 2002.

2009

4/4	KÍ	h	1-1	*Elttør*
13/4	Vestur	a	4-1	*Løkin, Hansen Ó., Elttør, Potemkin*
20/4	HB	h	2-1	*Potemkin 2*
26/4	EB/Streymur	a	4-3	*Potemkin 3, Hansen E.*
3/5	B68	h	2-2	*Potemkin, Hansen J.*
9/5	Víkingur	h	1-2	*Potemkin*
17/5	B36	a	3-2	*Elttør, Olsen, Petersen*
21/5	ÍF	a	2-1	*Mortensen, Løkin*
24/5	AB	h	0-1	
1/6	KÍ	a	2-0	*Potemkin 2*
14/6	Vestur	h	5-1	*Løkin 3, Potemkin, Hansen Ó. (p)*
17/6	HB	a	2-5	*Elttør 2*
20/6	EB/Streymur	h	1-2	*Hansen Ó.*
25/6	B68	a	2-2	*Olsen, Løkin*
18/7	Víkingur	a	0-1	
26/7	B36	h	3-0	*Jacobsen C. 2, Petersen*
3/8	ÍF	h	4-1	*Petersen, Hansen Ó., Hansen E., Olsen*
9/8	AB	a	1-3	*Jacobsen C.*
16/8	KÍ	h	3-2	*Jacobsen C., Petersen, Potemkin*
19/8	Vestur	a	2-2	*Hansen Ó. (p), Jacobsen C.*
23/8	HB	h	0-2	
31/8	EB/Streymur	a	2-2	*Jacobsen C. 2*
13/9	B68	h	0-1	
16/9	Víkingur	h	2-1	*Jacobsen C. 2*
20/9	B36	a	2-5	*Jacobsen S., Potemkin (p)*
27/9	AB	h	3-1	*Potemkin, Løkin 2*
3/10	ÍF	a	3-1	*Davidsen, og (Poulsen), Løkin*

No	Name	Nat	DoB	Pos	Aps	(s)	Gls
16	Øssur DALBÚD		28/3/89	A		(11)	
8	Jóhan Troest DAVIDSEN		31/1/88	D	23		1
15	Bergur DJURHUUS		22/11/82	D		(2)	
10	Hjalgrím ELTTØR		3/3/83	A	15		5
17	Jónhard FREDERIKSBERG		27/8/80	A	23		
12	Einar Tróndargjógv HANSEN		2/4/88	D	26		2
6	Jústinus Ragnarson HANSEN		22/1/86	M	20	(4)	1
3	Óli HANSEN		26/11/77	D	26	(1)	5
10	Christian Høgni JACOBSEN		12/5/80	A	13		9
19	Monrad Holm JACOBSEN		23/4/91	D		(1)	
18	Sjúrdur JACOBSEN		29/8/76	D		(8)	1
4	Jens JOENSEN		17/5/89	D	10	(5)	
1	Meinhardt JOENSEN		27/11/79	G	27		
14	Bogi LØKIN		22/10/88	M	27		9
7	Høgni MADSEN		4/2/85	M	12	(1)	
5	Jann Martin MORTENSEN		18/7/89	M	18	(8)	1
13	Klæmint Andrasson OLSEN		17/7/90	M	10	(13)	3
11	Jann Ingi PETERSEN		7/1/84	M	25	(1)	4
9	Károly POTEMKIN	HUN	19/6/77	A	22	(3)	14

07 VESTUR

Coach – Piotr Krakowski (POL)
Founded – 2007
Stadium - Sørvágur (1,000)

2009

5/4	EB/Streymur	a	1-2	*Rasmussen*
13/4	NSÍ	h	1-4	*Rubeksen*
17/4	Víkingur	a	2-6	*Pejčić, Akselsen*
26/4	B36	h	4-2	*Ellefsen H., Pejčić, Rasmussen 2 (1p)*
3/5	AB	a	2-2	*Akselsen, Stongum*
10/5	ÍF	h	1-1	*Rubeksen*
17/5	KÍ	a	2-2	*Rasmussen 2 (1p)*
21/5	HB	h	2-3	*Pejčić, Akselsen*
24/5	B68	a	1-2	*Rasmussen (p)*
1/6	EB/Streymur	h	3-5	*Rasmussen 2, Akselsen*

14/6	NSÍ	a	1-5	*Rasmussen*
17/6	Víkingur	h	0-0	
20/6	B36	a	1-2	*Akselsen*
24/6	AB	h	0-0	
19/7	ÍF	a	0-3	
26/7	KÍ	h	1-3	*Akselsen*
2/8	HB	a	3-4	*Yarjah 2, Rasmussen*
9/8	B68	h	1-0	*Pejčić*
16/8	EB/Streymur	a	0-1	
19/8	NSÍ	h	2-2	*Akselsen, Stongum*
22/8	Víkingur	a	3-2	*Yarjah 2, Nielsen J.*
30/8	B36	h	2-0	*og (Midjord), Stongum*
13/9	AB	a	1-2	*Pejčić (p)*
16/9	ÍF	h	2-2	*Pejčić, Rasmussen*
20/9	KÍ	a	1-2	*Haraldsen*
27/9	B68	a	0-3	
3/10	HB	h	2-3	*Pandurović, og (Lag)*

No	Name	Nat	DoB	Pos	Aps	(s)	Gls
21	Tór-Ingar AKSELSEN		1/5/81	M	26		7
1	Trygvi ASKHAM		28/3/88	G	27		
11	Holgar DJURHUUS		29/10/92	M	1	(14)	
7	Karl Johan DJURHUUS		18/10/85	A		(1)	
2	Hans Arni ELLEFSEN		25/8/87	D	8	(6)	1
14	Sjúrdur ELLEFSEN		22/10/81	D	12	(8)	
7	Gunnar HARALDSEN		21/11/87	D	25		1
18	Jógvan HOLM		21/12/85	A		(2)	
19	Ingi Ole JACOBSEN		13/2/88	M		(2)	
3	Henning Svabo JOENSEN		12/12/91	M		(1)	
4	Torkil KOLLSKER		11/7/89	D	19	(3)	
11	Morris LEWIS	SLE	26/12/82	A	7	(2)	
5	Ragnar NICLASEN		1/2/86	D	14	(6)	
17	Eli Falkvard NIELSEN		23/9/92	M	10	(12)	
18	Jón NIELSEN		20/5/80	M	12		1
8	Rógvi Egilstoft NIELSEN		7/12/92	M	3	(1)	
19	Rúni NOLSØE		21/5/71	M	2		
5	Aco PANDUROVIĆ	SRB	5/8/81	D	12		1
22	Jovan Radinović PANIĆ	SRB	8/11/79	M	2		
10	Milan PEJČIĆ	SRB	20/10/73	M	27		6
3	Sigtór Asbjørn PETERSEN		6/4/88	D	9	(4)	
22	Kim POULSEN		17/7/79	A		(3)	
6	Jens Erik RASMUSSEN		2/6/68	M	24	(1)	11
20	RICARDO da Silva Braga	BRA	2/6/68	M	15	(7)	
8	Hendrik RUBEKSEN		1/11/83	A	18	(1)	2
13	Jóhan Petur á STONGUM		12/4/85	D	12	(3)	3
19	Tamba YARJAH	SLE	6/6/84	M	12		4

VÍKINGUR

Coach – Jógvan Martin Olsen
Founded – 2008
Stadium - Sarpugerdi (2,000)
MAJOR HONOURS:
Faroe Islands League - (6) 1983, 1986, 1993, 1994, 1995, 1996 (as GÍ Gøta);
Faroe Islands Cup - (7) 1983, 1985, 1996, 1997, 2000, 2005 (as GÍ Gøta), 2009.

2009

3/4	ÍF	h	2-0	*Skordalíd, Djurhuus*
13/4	KÍ	a	2-2	*Olsen S., Justinussen*
17/4	Vestur	h	6-2	*Justinussen, Djurhuus, Olsen S., Olsen A. 2, Petersen Á.*
26/4	HB	a	1-2	*Djurhuus*
4/5	EB/Streymur	h	0-2	
9/5	NSÍ	a	2-1	*Justinussen, Olsen M.*
17/5	B68	h	3-3	*Jacobsen Sv., Djurhuus, Justinussen*
21/5	AB	a	1-0	*Justinussen*
25/5	B36	h	3-1	*Jacobsen Sv., Justinussen 2*
1/6	ÍF	a	2-1	*Olsen S., Olsen A.*
13/6	KÍ	h	4-1	*Gregersen, Bükszegi, Olsen S., Jacobsen Sv.*
17/6	Vestur	a	0-0	
21/6	HB	h	2-3	*Justinussen 2*
24/6	EB/Streymur	a	0-1	

FAROE ISLANDS

18/7	NSÍ	h	1-0	*Vatnhamar*
2/8	AB	h	1-0	*Justinussen*
5/8	B68	a	2-2	*Justinussen 2*
9/8	B36	a	3-1	*Bükszegi, Justinussen 2*
15/8	ÍF	h	2-3	*Olsen A., Olsen S. (p)*
19/8	KÍ	a	0-2	
22/8	Vestur	h	2-3	*Olsen A. 2*
30/8	HB	a	1-1	*Vatnhamar*
13/9	EB/Streymur	h	3-0	*Bükszegi, Olsen A., Justinussen*
16/9	NSÍ	a	1-2	*Gregersen*
20/9	B68	h	2-0	*Jacobsen H., Justinussen*
27/9	B36	h	4-3	*Justinussen 3, Vatnhamar*
3/10	AB	a	1-0	*Petersen Á.*

No	Name	Nat	DoB	Pos	Aps	(s)	Gls
8	Zoltán BÜKSZEGI	HUN	16/12/75	A	17	(2)	3
15	Hans Jørgin DJURHUUS		29/11/78	D	19	(2)	4
5	Kaj ENNIGARD		6/3/84	D		(1)	
4	Atli GREGERSEN		15/6/82	D	20		2
20	Bardur Jógvansson HANSEN		13/3/92	D	4	(9)	
25	Hjartvard HANSEN		17/9/88	M	4	(7)	
5	Erling JACOBSEN		13/2/90	M	1		
3	Hanus JACOBSEN		25/5/85	D	25		1
14	Sam JACOBSEN		24/2/88	M	14		
11	Símun Louis JACOBSEN		11/6/86	M	7	(8)	
12	Sverri JACOBSEN		29/3/86	A	27		3
17	Finnur JUSTINUSSEN		30/3/89	M	23	(2)	19
23	Niclas NICLASEN		26/7/79	D	26		
2	Andreas Lava OLSEN		9/10/87	A	24	(1)	7
19	Martin OLSEN		22/12/89	M	1	(12)	1
9	Súni OLSEN		7/3/81	M	25	(1)	5
6	Áslakur Reinert PETERSEN		9/4/78	D	4	(12)	2
7	Hans Paule PETERSEN		29/7/80	D	2	(5)	
13	Magnus SKORDALÍD		10/2/85	M	3	(10)	1
1	Géza TURI	HUN	11/3/74	G	27		
10	Sølvi VATNHAMAR		5/5/86	M	24	(2)	3

PROMOTED CLUBS

VB/SUMBA VÁGUR
Coach – Jón Pauli Olsen
Founded – 1905
Stadium – Vesturi á Eidinum (3,300)
MAJOR HONOURS
Faroe Islands League – (1) 2000;
Faroe Islands Cup – (1) 1974.

B71 SANDOY
Coach – Frankie Jensen; (6/8/09) Eli Hentze
Founded – 1970
Stadium – Inni í Dal (1,000)
MAJOR HONOURS
Faroe Islands League – (1) 1989;
Faroe Islands Cup – (1) 1993.

SECOND LEVEL FINAL TABLE 2009

		Pld	W	D	L	F	A	Pts
1	VB/Sumba Vágur	27	16	6	5	67	40	54
2	B71 Sandoy	27	15	7	5	63	36	52
3	TB Tvøroyri	27	14	5	8	58	48	47
4	HB Tórshavn II	27	13	6	8	56	39	45
5	Víkingur II	27	9	10	8	46	39	37
6	B68 Toftir II	27	10	6	11	68	59	36
7	FC Hoyvík	27	11	1	15	36	53	34
8	NSÍ Runavík II	27	9	6	12	45	57	33
9	Skála	27	9	5	13	38	41	32
10	MB Midvágur	27	2	2	23	27	92	8

DOMESTIC CUP 2009

LØGMANSSTEYPID

SECOND ROUND

(9/4/09)
AB 3, B68 2
B71 0, ÍF 1
HB 2, NSÍ 1
Hoyvík 4, Undri 0
KÍ 0, Vestur 3
TB 0, B36 0 (aet; 8-7 on pens)
VB/Sumba 0, EB/Streymur 4
Víkingur 5, MB 0

QUARTER-FINALS

(29/4/09)
Vestur 0, ÍF 3 (Ennigard P. 5, Zachariassen 38, Niclasen 82og)
EB/Streymur 1 (Samuelsen 86), Hoyvík 0
TB 1 (Mortensen Ha. 47), AB 1 (Joensen H. 75) (aet; 3-4 on pens)
Víkingur 2 (Olsen A. 9, Jacobsen H. 71), HB 1 (Lag 74)

SEMI-FINALS

(13/5/09 & 28/5/09)
AB 1 (Jacobsen 68), EB/Streymur 1 (Davidsen 53)
EB/Streymur 4 (Olsen Bá. 2, Olsen Br. 63, Hansen A. 74, Anghel 88), AB 1 (Nielsen 61)
(EB/Streymur 5-2)

ÍF 0, Víkingur 1 (Justinussen 67)
Víkingur 5 (Djurhuus 24, Justinussen 44, Olsen S. 59, Skordalíd 76, Vatnhamar 80), ÍF 0
(Víkingur 6-0)

FINAL

(29/7/09)
Gundadalur stadium, Torshavn
VÍKINGUR 3 (Djurhuus 7, Olsen A. 48, Justinussen 88)
EB/STREYMUR 2 (Hansen P. 16, Hansen A. 89)
Referee – Augustinussen
VÍKINGUR – Turi, Djurhuus (Jacobsen E. 71), Gregersen, Jacobsen H., Niclasen, Olsen S., Vatnhamar (Jacobsen Sí. 85), Jacobsen Sv., Justinussen, Bükszegi, Olsen A. (Petersen Á. 80).
EB/STREYMUR – Steig, Davidsen, Djurhuus, Niclasen, Olsen Bá. (Olsen Br. 71), Hanssen (Jacobsen 84), Nielsen (Alex 52), Samuelsen, Anghel, Hansen A.

HJK end six-year title drought

The 2009 Veikkausliiga season heralded the return of HJK Helsinki, who ended a six-year wait by claiming a record-extending 22nd Finnish championship title.

Billed as pre-season favourites, Antti Muurinen's men recovered from a slow start to set the pace at the halfway stage. However, a sequence of five successive draws slowed down their title march, enabling closest pursuers TPS Turku and FC Honka Espoo to revive their challenge. With two matches remaining, HJK led TPS by three points and Honka by five. In the penultimate round HJK managed only a nervous away draw at outgoing champions FC Inter Turku, but TPS did likewise at Myllykosken Pallo-47 while Honka routed RoPS Rovaniemi 9-0.

Antti Muurinen led HJK to the Veikkausliiga title

HJK's final fixture was at home to FF Jaro while TPS and Honka met in Turku. Jaro shocked the Finnair Stadium faithful by taking an early lead, but HJK's Gambian striker Dawda Bah scored a 61st-minute equaliser to earn his team the one point they needed as TPS and Honka fought out a goalless draw.

Strength in depth

"Klubi" were far from flamboyant but had strength in depth, boasting several players who had returned to Finnish football after spells abroad, the most influential of whom were right-winger Sebastian Sorsa and ex-Finland midfielder Aki Riihilahti. Their key players in defence were goalkeeper Ville Wallén,

centre-back Pyry Kärkkäinen and young left-back Jukka Raitala, who departed for Germany in the autumn. Up front Juho Mäkelä and Bah contributed eight goals apiece.

As in 2008, the most entertaining team on show were Honka. They scored 65 goals – 20 more than HJK – with the league's top two marksmen, Hermanni Vuorinen (16) and Jami Puustinen (12), leading the way. Too many points were frittered away in the early part of the season, however, so Honka finished runners-up for the second season running.

Brown shines

By common consent the best player in the league was young English midfielder Wayne Brown, loaned by former Finland coach Roy Hodgson from Fulham FC's reserves to TPS. Other talents to shine under firebrand coach Pasi Rautiainen at the Turku club were goalkeeper Jukka Lehtovaara and midfielder Kasper Hämäläinen, who both earned frequent national team call-ups. TPS's challenge for the title restored bragging rights over city rivals and 2008 champions Inter, who never really recovered from the departure of key players Jos Hooiveld and Dominic Chatto and finished fifth.

There was controversy at the foot of the table. Struggling KuPS Kuopio signed three Nigerians, including talented striker Dickson Nwakaeme, who powered KuPS to victory over RoPS in his first match. RoPS subsequently protested that Nwakaeme's registration had broken transfer rules. The result was annulled and victory awarded to RoPS, only for the decision to be overturned later by a court of arbitration. KuPS were already safe by then, but the verdict doomed RoPS to last place on goal difference behind JJK Jyväskylä and automatic relegation. RoPS went down unlamented, ending the season in complete disarray, but the promotion of AC Oulu ensured there would be top-flight representation from northern Finland in 2010. JJK saved themselves by defeating KPV Kokkola in the play-off.

FINLAND

The best Finnish showing in Europe came surprisingly from FC Lahti. The club struggled domestically, but inspired performances from 38-year-old Jari Litmanen carried them through two UEFA Europa League qualifiers and almost past Club Brugge KV. Inter, Honka and HJK, by contrast, had their European adventures disappointingly cut short by teams from Moldova, Azerbaijan and Lithuania, respectively. Litmanen's hopes of returning to Europe with his hometown club in 2010/11 were dashed by Inter in the Finnish Cup semi-final. In the final, Inter came from behind to defeat Tampere United 2–1 with goals from Nigerian striker Kennedy Nwanganga and Timo Furuholm.

Youngsters blooded

With hopes of 2010 FIFA World Cup qualification already dashed, Stuart Baxter's Finland side played for pride only in the autumn qualifiers. The topsy-turvy nature of their campaign was encapsulated by two 1-1 away draws - a hapless one in Liechtenstein, an honourable one in Germany. In the spring, Baxter tested young players in low-key friendlies, which produced unconvincing results. The only newcomer to break through was Tim Sparv, Finland's captain at the

Suomen Palloliitto – Finlands Bollförbund (SPL-FBF)

Urheilukatu 1, PO Box 191
FI-00251 Helsinki
tel – +358 9 742 151
fax – +358 9 454 3352
website – palloliitto.fi
email – sami.terava@palloliitto.fi
Year of Formation – 1907

President – Sauli Niinisto
General Secretary – Kimmo J. Lipponen
Media Officer – Sami Terävä
National Stadium – Olympic Stadium, Helsinki (37,500)

TOP FIVE ALL-TIME CAPS
Jari Litmanen (133); Sami Hyypiä & Jonatan Johansson (103); Ari Hjelm (100); Joonas Kolkka (98)
TOP FIVE ALL-TIME GOALS
Jari Litmanen (31); Jonatan Johansson (22); Ari Hjelm (20); Mikael Forssell (19); Mika-Matti Paatelainen (18)

2009 UEFA European Under-21 Championship. Meanwhile, Litmanen took his record cap-total to 133 and was joined in the hundred-club by Sami Hyypiä and Jonatan Johansson, the latter celebrating his century with a goal against Germany.

NATIONAL TEAM RESULTS 2009/10

12/8/09	Sweden	A	Solna	0-1	
5/9/09	Azerbaijan (WCQ)	A	Lankaran	2-1	Tihinen (74), Johansson (85)
9/9/09	Liechtenstein (WCQ)	A	Vaduz	1-1	Litmanen (74p)
10/10/09	Wales (WCQ)	H	Helsinki	2-1	Porokara (5), Moisander (77)
14/10/09	Germany (WCQ)	A	Hamburg	1-1	Johansson (11)
18/1/10	South Korea	N	Malaga (ESP)	0-2	
3/3/10	Malta	A	Ta'Qali	2-1	Eremenko R. (66p), Väyrynen (70)
21/5/10	Estonia	A	Tallinn	0-2	
29/5/10	Poland	A	Kielce	0-0	

NATIONAL TEAM APPEARANCES 2009/10

Coach – Stuart BAXTER (ENG)	16/8/53		Swe	AZE	LIE	WAL	GER	Kor	Mlt	Est	Pol	Caps	Goals
Otto FREDRIKSON	30/11/81	Lillestrøm (NOR) /Spartak Nalchik (RUS)	G					G	s46		G	6	-
Veli LAMPI	18/7/84	Zürich (SUI) /Aarau (SUI)	D	D			D		D	D	D82	19	-
Petri PASANEN	24/9/80	Werder (GER)	D	D	D	D						57	1
Sami HYYPIÄ	7/10/73	Leverkusen (GER)	D		D	D	D					103	5
Niklas MOISANDER	29/9/85	AZ (NED)	D	D	D	D	D		D	D	D	11	1
Tim SPARV	20/2/87	Halmstad (SWE) /Groningen (NED)	M83			M	M		M46	D	D	8	-
Roman EREMENKO	19/3/87	Dynamo Kyiv (UKR)	M83	M	M	M	M		M	s46	M90	27	1

NATIONAL TEAM APPEARANCES 2009/10 (contd.)

			Swe	AZE	LIE	WAL	GER	Kor	Mlt	Est	Pol	Caps	Goals
Roni POROKARA	12/12/83	Örebro (SWE)	M65			M	M72	M68	M	M	M66	13	2
Joonas KOLKKA	28/9/74	NAC (NED)	M46	s83	s59	M68	s66		s76			98	11
Jari LITMANEN	20/2/71	Lahti /unattached	M46	s45	M82	M90	M87	M60	M46	M46	M71	133	31
Mikael FORSSELL	15/3/81	Hannover (GER)	A77							s81	s66	67	19
Alexei EREMENKO Jr.	24/3/83	Metalist (UKR)	s46	M	M	s90						43	13
Perparim HETEMAJ	12/12/86	AEK (GRE)	s46									2	-
Kasper HÄMÄLÄINEN	8/8/86	TPS /Djurgården (SWE)	s65				s68	M66	s60	M76	M80	7	-
Berat SADIK	14/9/86	Arminia (GER) /Zulte Waregem (BEL)	s77		A59							4	-
Teemu TAINIO	27/11/79	Sunderland (ENG) /Birmingham (ENG)	s83	M45						s46		51	6
Markus HEIKKINEN	13/10/78	Rapid Wien (AUT)	s83	M	M		D			s46	D	52	-
Jussi JÄÄSKELÄINEN	19/4/75	Bolton (ENG)		G	G	G	G					55	-
Hannu TIHINEN	1/7/76	Zürich (SUI)		D	D	D						76	5
Jonatan JOHANSSON	16/8/75	unattached /TPS		A	A	A88	A	A60	A83		A	103	22
Shefki KUQI	10/11/76	Koblenz (GER)		A72	s82	s88	s72					60	7
Daniel SJÖLUND	22/4/83	Djurgården (SWE)	s72 /83									22	2
Ari NYMAN	7/2/84	Inter Turku					s87	D		D		22	-
Jani LYYSKI	16/3/83	Djurgården (SWE)						D	s57			2	-
Markus HALSTI	19/3/84	Malmö (SWE)						D				3	-
Joni AHO	12/4/86	Inter Turku						D				2	-
Joel PEROVUO	11/8/85	Djurgården (SWE)						M84			s80	2	-
Juska SAVOLAINEN	1/9/83	Haugesund (NOR)						M		M46		2	-
Hermanni VUORINEN	27/1/85	Honka						A74				1	-
Sebastian SORSA	25/1/84	HJK Helsinki						s60				1	-
Mika OJALA	21/6/88	Inter Turku						s68				1	-
Timo FURUHOLM	11/10/87	Inter Turku						s74				1	-
Paulus ARAJUURI	15/6/88	Kalmar (SWE)						s84				1	-
Peter ENCKELMAN	10/3/77	Cardiff (WAL)						G46				12	-
Toni KALLIO	9/8/78	Sheffield United (ENG)						D57				49	2
Jukka RAITALA	15/9/88	Hoffenheim (GER)						D				2	-
Mika VÄYRYNEN	28/12/81	Heerenveen (NED)						s46		s46		43	4
Teemu PUKKI	29/3/90	Sevilla (ESP)						s83		s46		3	-
Jukka LEHTOVAARA	15/3/88	TPS						G46				1	-
Mehmet HETEMAJ	8/12/87	AlbinoLeffe (ITA)						M46				2	-
Mika ÄÄRITALO	25/7/85	TPS								A81		1	-
Juho MÄKELÄ	23/6/83	HJK Helsinki								A46		7	-
Lukas HRADECKY	24/11/89	Esbjerg (DEN)								s46		1	-
Kalle PARVIAINEN	3/10/82	Haka									D	1	-
Paulus ROIHA	3/8/80	Åtvidaberg (SWE)									s71	19	4
Ville JALASTO	19/4/86	Aalesund (NOR)									s82	1	-
Tuomo TURUNEN	30/8/87	Göteborg (SWE)									s90	2	-

FINLAND

DOMESTIC LEAGUE 2009

VEIKKAUSLIIGA FINAL TABLE

			Home				Away				Total				
	Pld	W	D	L	F	A	W	D	L	F	A	W	D	L	F	A	Pts
1 HJK Helsinki	26	8	5	0	26	9	6	5	2	19	12	14	10	2	45	21	52
2 FC Honka Espoo	26	7	5	1	37	12	6	5	2	28	17	13	10	3	65	29	49
3 TPS Turku	26	7	5	1	22	9	6	5	2	24	11	13	10	3	46	20	49
4 IFK Mariehamn	26	8	5	0	20	7	2	8	3	10	14	10	13	3	30	21	43
5 FC Inter Turku	26	6	4	3	21	13	5	3	5	17	17	11	7	8	38	30	40
6 Haka Valkeakoski	26	5	3	5	23	18	5	4	4	17	17	10	7	9	40	35	37
7 Tampere United	26	8	1	4	16	12	3	3	7	15	19	11	4	11	31	31	37
8 VPS Vaasa	26	4	2	7	15	21	6	3	4	15	15	10	5	11	30	36	35
9 Myllykosken Pallo-47	26	4	4	5	20	16	5	3	5	12	14	9	7	10	32	30	34
10 FF Jaro	26	5	3	5	17	14	3	5	5	16	20	8	8	10	33	34	32
11 FC Lahti	26	5	3	5	20	20	3	4	6	13	20	8	7	11	33	40	31
12 KuPS Kuopio	26	3	4	6	19	25	3	1	9	10	28	6	5	15	29	53	23
13 JJK Jyväskylä	26	2	5	6	12	18	1	2	10	13	34	3	7	16	25	52	16
14 RoPS Rovaniemi	26	4	3	6	14	22	0	1	12	7	44	4	4	18	21	66	16

TOP GOALSCORERS

16 Hermanni VUORINEN (Honka)
12 Jami PUUSTINEN (Honka)
11 Timo FURUHOLM (Inter)
9 Wayne BROWN (TPS)
   Mikko PAATELAINEN (TPS)
   Babatunde WUSU (TPS)
8 Dawda BAH (HJK)
   Juho MÄKELÄ (HJK)
   NAM Ik-kyung (JJK)
   Drilon SHALA (Lahti)
   Tamás GRUBOROVICS (Mariehamn)
   Maksim VOTINOV (MyPa)

CLUB-BY-CLUB

HAKA VALKEAKOSKI

Coach – Olli Huttunen; (8/9/09) Sami Ristilä

Founded – 1934

Stadium – Tehtaan kenttä (3,500)

MAJOR HONOURS:

Finnish League – (9) 1960, 1962, 1965, 1977, 1995, 1998, 1999, 2000, 2004;
Finnish Cup – (12) 1955, 1959, 1960, 1963, 1969, 1977, 1982, 1985, 1988,
1997, 2002, 2005.

2009

18/4	TPS	a	2-1	Holopainen, Corpache
22/4	VPS	a	1-0	Holopainen
29/4	HJK	h	1-2	Holopainen
4/5	Honka	h	1-1	Bäckman
7/5	JJK	a	0-0	
14/5	Tampere United	h	1-0	Innanen
17/5	RoPS	h	3-1	Strandvall, Holopainen 2
23/5	Inter	a	2-0	Ristilä, Mäkitalo
31/5	KuPS	h	3-0	Strandvall (p), Hynynen, Ikävalko (p)
17/6	Mariehamn	a	1-2	Hynynen
24/6	Lahti	h	3-0	Ikävalko, Mäkitalo, Innanen
28/6	Jaro	h	0-0	
5/7	MyPa	a	2-0	Hynynen 2
13/7	TPS	h	0-3	
18/7	VPS	h	0-1	
26/7	HJK	a	3-3	Strandvall 2, Mattila
2/8	JJK	h	2-4	Ikävalko, Ristilä
7/8	Tampere United	a	1-1	Strandvall (p)
16/8	RoPS	a	0-0	
22/8	Inter	h	2-2	Strandvall, Hynynen
13/9	KuPS	a	1-5	Kauppila
20/9	Honka	a	0-2	
23/9	Mariehamn	h	5-1	Hynynen, og (Gustavsson), Innanen 2, Mäkitalo
27/9	Lahti	a	4-2	Innanen, Multanen, Strandvall, Mäkitalo
4/10	Jaro	a	0-1	
17/10	MyPa	h	2-3	Hynynen, Multanen

No	Name	Nat	DoB	Pos	Aps	(s)	Gls
16	Jani BÄCKMAN		20/3/88	A		(8)	1
26	Jhon Patricio CAGUA	ECU	25/9/79	D	5		
2	Diego CORPACHE	ARG	21/5/76	D	15		1
28	Hans DENISSEN	NED	9/3/84	M	1	(4)	
26	Antti HAKALA		3/2/85	A	1		
21	Pietari HOLOPAINEN		26/9/82	D	22		5
11	Antti HYNYNEN		30/5/84	M	18	(6)	7
9	Niko IKÄVALKO		24/4/88	A	17	(1)	3
7	Mikko INNANEN		8/9/82	M	26		5
4	Markus JOENMÄKI		11/2/88	D	15		
8	Jani KAUPPILA		16/1/80	M	24		1
15	Nicolas KIVISTÖ		27/3/88	M	1	(5)	
1	Janne KORHONEN		28/11/79	G	26		
10	Mika MÄKITALO		12/6/85	M	20	(3)	4
22	Jarno MATTILA		10/11/84	A	17	(6)	1
41	Valeri MINKENEN		9/4/89	M	6	(9)	
17	Kalle MULTANEN		7/4/89	A	3	(2)	2
20	Joni NIEMINEN		3/4/90	A		(3)	
18	Jari NIKKILÄ		16/8/89	D	17	(3)	
25	Maido PAKK	EST	23/11/89	A		(1)	
5	Kalle PARVIAINEN		3/10/82	D	3	(1)	
20	Sami RISTILÄ		15/8/74	A	14	(2)	2
19	Juuso SALONEN		28/7/91	D	2	(3)	
6	Sebastian STRANDVALL		16/9/86	M	23	(2)	7
3	Petri VILJANEN		3/2/87	D	10	(8)	

HJK HELSINKI

Coach – Antti Muurinen

Founded – 1907

Stadium – Finnair Stadium (10,800)

MAJOR HONOURS:

Finnish League – (22) 1911, 1912, 1917, 1918, 1919, 1923, 1925,
1936, 1938, 1964, 1973, 1978, 1981, 1985, 1987, 1988, 1990, 1992,
1997, 2002, 2003, 2009;
Finnish Cup – (10) 1966, 1981, 1984, 1993, 1996, 1998, 2000, 2003,
2006, 2008.

2009

18/4	KuPS	h	5-1	Kärkkäinen, Popovich 2, Parikka, Mäkelä
23/4	TPS	h	2-2	Bah, Kamara
29/4	Haka	a	2-1	Popovich, Sorsa
6/5	Mariehamn	h	2-0	Mäkelä 2
11/5	MyPa	a	0-1	
14/5	Honka	h	1-1	Bah
17/5	JJK	a	1-1	Kamara
25/5	Lahti	h	1-0	Kärkkäinen
28/5	Tampere United	h	1-0	Sorsa
31/5	RoPS	a	0-1	
28/6	Inter	h	2-0	Mäkelä, Parikka
1/7	VPS	a	4-3	Sorsa, Fowler, Pelvas 2
5/7	Jaro	a	2-0	Parikka, og (Mannström)
12/7	KuPS	a	3-0	Pelvas, Sorsa, Bah
19/7	TPS	a	1-1	og (Cleaver)
26/7	Haka	h	3-3	Bah 2, Pelvas
2/8	Mariehamn	a	0-0	
9/8	Honka	a	1-1	Kamara
16/8	JJK	h	1-1	Riihilahti
23/8	Lahti	a	2-1	og (Toivomäki), Pelvas
13/9	RoPS	h	4-0	Riihilahti, Mäkelä 2, Sorsa
20/9	VPS	h	2-0	Bah, Mäkelä
23/9	Tampere United	a	2-1	Sorsa, Riihilahti
27/9	MyPa	h	1-0	Mäkelä
4/10	Inter	a	1-1	Bah
17/10	Jaro	h	1-1	Bah

No	Name	Nat	DoB	Pos	Aps	(s)	Gls
17	Dawda BAH	GAM	12/11/83	A	25		8
6	Cheyne FOWLER	RSA	8/3/82	M	9	(8)	1
7	Tuomas HAAPALA		20/4/79	M	5	(1)	
3	Mikko HAUHIA		3/9/84	D	25		
4	Mohamed "Medo" KAMARA	SLE	16/11/87	M	23		3
2	Tuomas KANSIKAS		15/5/81	D	8	(3)	
13	Pyry KÄRKKÄINEN		10/11/86	D	26		2
11	Mathias LINDSTRÖM		14/1/81	D	4		
10	Juho MÄKELÄ		23/6/83	A	16	(10)	8
18	Juhani OJALA		19/6/89	D	2	(2)	
21	Petri ORAVAINEN		26/1/83	M	1	(14)	
16	Jarno PARIKKA		21/7/86	A	15	(9)	3
31	Akseli PELVAS		8/2/89	A	10	(9)	5
14	Valeriy POPOVICH	RUS	10/5/70	M	10	(7)	3
3	Jukka RAITALA		15/9/88	D	19	(1)	
19	Aki RIIHILAHTI		9/9/76	M	9	(1)	3
15	Paulus ROIHA		3/8/80	A	1	(4)	
5	Jukka SAUSO		20/6/82	D	20		
9	Sebastian SORSA		25/1/84	M	25		6
27	Mikko SUMUSALO		12/3/90	D		(1)	
8	Ville TAULO		14/8/85	M	6	(6)	
1	Ville WALLÉN		26/6/76	G	26		
26	Johannes WESTÖ		1/4/91	A	1	(1)	

FC HONKA ESPOO
Coach – Mika Lehkosuo
Founded – 1957
Stadium – Tapiolan urheilupuisto (5,000)

2009

19/4	Lahti	h	2-2	Vuorinen, Hakanpää
23/4	Mariehamn	a	2-2	Weckström, Vuorinen
27/4	VPS	a	5-2	Vuorinen 4, Otaru
4/5	Haka	a	1-1	Perovuo
7/5	MyPa	h	0-0	
14/5	HJK	a	1-1	Turunen
17/5	Tampere United	a	0-1	
23/5	JJK	a	3-2	Otaru, Savage, Puustinen
27/5	Jaro	h	5-1	Puustinen 2, Lepola, Vuorinen, Perovuo
1/6	Inter	a	1-2	Lepola
24/6	KuPS	h	4-1	Savage, Schüller, Vuorinen, Lepola
28/6	RoPS	a	2-1	Vasara, Vuorinen
6/7	TPS	h	0-0	
12/7	Lahti	a	1-1	Koskimaa
19/7	Mariehamn	h	1-1	Vuorinen (p)
26/7	VPS	h	3-0	Vuorinen, Lepola, Puustinen
2/8	MyPa	a	3-1	Vasara, Perovuo, Savage
9/8	HJK	h	1-1	Savage
15/8	Tampere United	h	3-1	Hakanpää, Schüller, Vasara
23/8	JJK	h	5-2	Vuorinen 3, Vasara 2
12/9	Inter	h	2-3	Puustinen, Heilala
20/9	Haka	h	2-0	Kokko, Vasara
23/9	Jaro	a	5-3	Puustinen 3 (1p), Vuorinen, Vasara
26/9	KuPS	a	4-0	Otaru, Puustinen 3 (2p)
4/10	RoPS	h	9-0	Hakanpää, Vuorinen, Savage, Koskimaa 2, Perovuo, Puustinen (p), Weckström, Kokko
17/10	TPS	a	0-0	

No	Name	Nat	DoB	Pos	Aps	(s)	Gls
5	Henri AALTO		20/4/89	D	10	(3)	
22	Jani BÄCKMAN		20/3/88	A		(1)	
11	Hannu HAARALA		15/8/81	D	15	(2)	
19	Rami HAKANPÄÄ		9/10/78	D	24		3
3	Roope HEILALA		13/8/80	D	15	(2)	1
12	Janne HENRIKSSON		5/8/81	G	6		
15	Aleksandr KOKKO		4/6/87	A	6	(13)	2
13	Ville KOSKIMAA		21/5/83	D	13	(2)	3
2	Sampo KOSKINEN		1/3/79	D	19		
26	Jaakko LEPOLA		14/3/90	M	10	(6)	4
20	Nicholas OTARU		15/7/86	M	20	(3)	3
1	Tuomas PELTONEN		20/10/77	G	20	(1)	
21	Joel PEROVUO		11/8/85	M	24	(1)	4
10	Jami PUUSTINEN		9/1/87	A	18	(7)	12
27	Konsta RASIMUS		15/12/90	M		(1)	
17	Demba SAVAGE	GAM	17/6/88	M	19	(5)	5
28	Rasmus SCHÜLLER		18/6/91	M	16	(3)	2
22	Tuomo TURUNEN		30/8/87	D	10	(1)	1
14	Jussi VASARA		14/5/87	M	10	(16)	7
6	Hermanni VUORINEN		27/1/85	A	26		16
7	John WECKSTRÖM		26/12/80	M	5	(8)	2

FC INTER TURKU
Coach – Job Dragtsma (NED)
Founded – 1990
Stadium – Veritas Stadion (9,300)
MAJOR HONOURS:
Finnish League – (1) 2008;
Finnish Cup – (1) 2009.

2009

20/4	Mariehamn	a	0-2	
23/4	MyPa	h	2-0	Kauko, Grot
29/4	Jaro	h	1-0	Grot
2/5	MyPa	a	0-0	
7/5	RoPS	a	2-0	Grot, Ojala
14/5	TPS	h	2-0	Nwanganga, Furuholm
18/5	KuPS	a	2-0	Furuholm, Verino
23/5	Haka	h	0-2	
28/5	VPS	h	0-1	
1/6	Honka	h	2-1	Ojala, Purje
28/6	HJK	a	0-2	
1/7	Tampere United	a	2-3	Furuholm, Ramírez

FINLAND

5/7	Lahti	h	1-1	Furuholm
11/7	Mariehamn	h	1-1	Furuholm
18/7	JJK	a	0-1	
25/7	Jaro	a	1-0	Kauko
1/8	RoPS	h	4-0	Purje 2, Furuholm 2
9/8	TPS	a	0-2	
14/8	KuPS	h	2-3	Furuholm 2
22/8	Haka	a	2-2	Lehtonen, Aho (p)
12/9	Honka	a	3-2	Ojala, Furuholm, Nwanganga
20/9	JJK	h	3-0	Furuholm, Ojala (p), Aho
23/9	VPS	a	2-2	Ojala, Pertot
26/9	Tampere United	h	2-2	Ojala 2
4/10	HJK	h	1-1	Kauko
17/10	Lahti	a	3-1	Civit, Grot, Purje

No	Name	Nat	DoB	Pos	Aps	(s)	Gls
14	Joni AHO		12/4/86	D	23		2
26	Felix ÅKERLUND		12/2/90	M		(1)	
1	Patrick BANTAMOI	SLE	24/5/86	G	18		
30	Martín CIVIT	ARG	25/9/85	M	1		1
11	Timo FURUHOLM		11/10/87	A	19	(4)	11
21	Pablo GOMEZ-MARTTILA		9/10/88	M		(1)	
9	Guilliano GROT	NED	15/3/83	A	8	(9)	4
6	Jermu GUSTAFSSON		22/6/86	D	7	(1)	
24	Joni KAUKO		12/7/90	M	16	(3)	3
29	Henri LEHTONEN		28/7/80	D	23		1
12	David MONSALVE	CAN	21/12/88	G	7		
23	Ville NIKKARI		5/11/88	D	8	(6)	
27	Kennedy NWANGANGA	NGA	15/8/90	M	15	(6)	2
7	Ari NYMAN		7/2/84	M	25		
17	Mika OJALA		21/6/88	A	19	(3)	7
15	Severi PAAJANEN		23/10/86	M	23	(3)	
19	Arístides PERTOT	ARG	24/9/76	M	14	(4)	1
18	Ats PURJE	EST	3/8/85	A	9	(12)	4
5	Alberto RAMÍREZ	MEX	1/2/86	D	20	(3)	1
13	Eemeli REPONEN		6/6/90	G	1	(1)	
22	Sami SANEVUORI		20/2/86	M	10	(9)	
20	Arttu SEPPÄLÄ		18/3/87	A		(1)	
8	Touko TUMANTO		6/3/82	M	6	(8)	
2	Claudio VERINO	ARG	31/1/84	D	14		1

FF JARO
Coach – Mika Laurikainen; (18/8/09) Alexei Eremenko
Founded – 1965
Stadium – Centralplan (5,000)

2009
23/4	Tampere United	a	2-0	Niang, Meyer
29/4	Inter	a	0-1	
4/5	TPS	a	1-1	Mannström
7/5	KuPS	h	1-1	Laurikainen
13/5	VPS	a	2-1	Matrone, Kojola
17/5	Lahti	a	1-2	Mannström
24/5	MyPa	h	3-0	Laurikainen, Mannström, Kojola
27/5	Honka	a	1-5	Hyyrynen (p)
31/5	JJK	h	5-1	Hyyrynen, Niang, Emet, Mannström, Koivisto
14/6	RoPS	h	2-0	Tanska, Emet
24/6	Mariehamn	h	0-0	
28/6	Haka	a	0-0	
5/7	HJK	h	0-2	
12/7	RoPS	a	3-5	Hyyrynen, Laurikainen, Emet
20/7	Tampere United	h	0-0	
25/7	Inter	h	0-1	
2/8	KuPS	a	2-2	Meyer, Sundqvist
6/8	VPS	h	1-3	Meyer
17/8	Lahti	h	0-1	
21/8	MyPa	a	0-0	

12/9	JJK	a	2-0	Niang, Meyer
20/9	TPS	h	1-0	Meyer
23/9	Honka	h	3-5	Meyer, Hyyrynen, Koivisto (p)
27/9	Mariehamn	a	1-2	Koivisto (p)
4/10	Haka	h	1-0	Koivisto
17/10	HJK	a	1-1	Grove

No	Name	Nat	DoB	Pos	Aps	(s)	Gls
3	Heikki AHO		16/3/83	D	8	(1)	
10	Jonas EMET		13/2/88	M	20	(5)	3
21	Daniel FELLMAN		26/1/90	A		(8)	
20	Tillmann GROVE	GER	3/9/88	D	4		1
26	Tommi HAANPÄÄ		21/4/90	A		(2)	
18	Mikko HYYRYNEN		1/11/77	A	21	(2)	4
11	Jani KOIVISTO		25/2/85	A	7	(8)	4
5	Kristian KOJOLA		12/9/86	D	20	(6)	2
1	Markus KOLJANDER		25/10/83	G	18		
23	Joonas LAURIKAINEN		19/5/83	M	23	(3)	3
19	Sebastian MANNSTRÖM		29/10/88	M	23	(2)	4
7	Marco MATRONE		2/7/87	M	17	(3)	1
17	Petter MEYER		21/2/85	A	23	(2)	6
16	Papa NIANG	SEN	15/12/88	A	12	(11)	3
22	Jens PORTIN		13/12/84	D	24	(1)	
4	Jonas PORTIN		30/9/86	D	9		
27	Urmas ROOBA	EST	8/7/78	D	5	(1)	
13	Jani SARAJÄRVI		9/9/79	D	4	(5)	
9	Björn-Erik SUNDQVIST		5/3/88	A		(12)	1
2	Jani TANSKA		29/7/88	D	20		1
12	Vitali TELEŠ	EST	17/10/83	G	8	(1)	
6	Janne VELLAMO		28/9/84	M	20	(3)	

JJK JYVÄSKYLÄ
Coach – Ville Priha
Founded – 1992
Stadium – Harjun stadion (4,600)

2009
27/4	TPS	a	0-0	
7/5	Haka	h	0-0	
10/5	KuPS	a	0-2	
14/5	RoPS	h	1-1	Lahtinen
17/5	HJK	h	1-1	Nam
23/5	Honka	h	2-3	Nam, Kari
27/5	Mariehamn	h	0-2	
31/5	Jaro	a	1-5	Kari
17/6	Lahti	h	2-1	Kari, Lahtinen
25/6	VPS	a	2-3	Nam, Kari
1/7	RoPS	a	1-2	Nam
4/7	Tampere United	a	0-1	
13/7	MyPa	h	0-1	
18/7	Inter	h	1-0	Lahtinen
27/7	TPS	h	1-1	Sinisalo
2/8	Haka	a	4-2	og (Viljanen), Nam 2, Sund
5/8	KuPS	h	1-2	Hristov
16/8	HJK	a	1-1	Nam
23/8	Honka	a	2-5	Lahtinen, Poutiainen
4/9	MyPa	a	0-4	
12/9	Jaro	h	0-2	
20/9	Inter	a	0-3	
23/9	Lahti	a	1-3	Kari
26/9	VPS	h	1-2	Lahtinen
4/10	Mariehamn	a	1-3	Latikka
17/10	Tampere United	h	2-2	Nam, Kari (p)

No	Name	Nat	DoB	Pos	Aps	(s)	Gls
18	Zakaria ABAHASSINE		23/7/88	M	6	(12)	
22	Shkumbin ARSLLANI	MKD	27/2/80	M	5	(2)	
25	Dejan BRANKOVIĆ	SRB	29/8/80	D	3	(2)	

3	Janne HANNULA		3/1/82	D	15	(3)	
11	Georgi HRISTOV	MKD	30/1/76	A	9		1
10	Tommi KARI		22/9/86	A	18	(5)	6
31	Antti-Jussi KARNIO		14/3/78	G	2	(1)	
17	KIM Hyun-kwan	KOR	20/4/85	M		(4)	
21	Toni KOSKELA		16/2/83	M	17		
8	Matti LÄHITIE		13/2/85	M	15	(4)	
9	Mika LAHTINEN		30/4/85	A	24	(2)	5
13	Tuomas LATIKKA		20/9/85	D	24	(1)	1
20	LEE Ho-jin	KOR	9/3/83	M		(1)	
16	Niko MARKKULA		27/6/90	M	5	(5)	
5	NAM Ik-kyung	KOR	26/1/83	A	23		8
4	Markus PAIJA		6/5/74	D	5	(2)	
23	Patrick POUTIAINEN		14/6/91	M	7	(5)	1
14	Jukka SINISALO		21/5/82	D	25		1
19	Christian SUND		28/12/78	M	21	(2)	1
30	Mihály SZERÖVAY	HUN	14/4/82	G	24		
15	Antto TAPANINEN		16/6/89	D	2	(2)	
6	Jukka-Pekka TUOMANEN		14/12/85	M	13	(3)	
7	Anssi VIREN		10/4/77	D	23	(1)	

19	Juho KARPPINEN		8/3/90	M	3	(1)	2
11	Pele KOLJONEN		25/7/88	A	20	(1)	5
6	Tuomas KUPARINEN		7/8/79	M	15	(5)	1
2	Joni NISSINEN		21/4/91	D		(1)	
26	Dickson NWAKAEME	NGA	21/4/86	A	10	(1)	4
15	Patrice OLLO Ndoumba	CMR	10/1/86	M	18	(1)	2
12	Joonas PÖNTINEN		19/3/90	G	6		
19	Tuomas RANNANKARI		21/5/91	M	10	(2)	
3	Janne REINIKAINEN		23/10/81	D	16	(4)	
23	Jussi-Pekka SAVOLAINEN		25/6/86	M	12	(8)	
18	Ville STRANDMAN		20/4/90	A	1	(4)	
8	Tero TAIPALE		14/12/72	M	26		
7	Miikka TURUNEN		18/8/79	M	17	(7)	3
4	Patrik TURUNEN		1/7/88	D	11	(6)	
28	Raphael UDAH	NGA	1/9/89	M	9	(1)	
10	Ilja VENÄLÄINEN		27/9/80	A	24		7
14	Harri YLÖNEN		21/12/71	D	2	(1)	

FC LAHTI
Coach – Ilkka Mäkelä
Founded – 1996
Stadium – Lahden stadion (7,400)

2009

19/4	Honka	a	2-2	Huuhka, og (Koskimaa)
23/4	KuPS	h	1-0	Kemppinen
29/4	RoPS	h	4-1	Fofana, Korte, Shala, Länsitalo
7/5	VPS	h	0-0	
14/5	MyPa	a	2-2	Shala 2
17/5	Jaro	h	2-1	Rafael, Fofana
25/5	HJK	a	0-1	
31/5	TPS	h	2-4	Shala 2
14/6	Mariehamn	h	1-1	Rafael
17/6	JJK	a	1-2	Fofana
24/6	Haka	a	0-3	
27/6	Tampere United	h	2-1	Haara, Korte
5/7	Inter	a	1-1	Kemppinen
12/7	Honka	h	1-1	Länsitalo
19/7	KuPS	a	1-1	og (Ollo)
26/7	RoPS	a	1-0	Rafael
2/8	VPS	a	0-1	
9/8	MyPa	h	0-1	
17/8	Jaro	a	1-0	Vanninen (p)
23/8	HJK	h	1-2	Fofana
13/9	TPS	a	2-5	Shala, Rafael
20/9	Mariehamn	a	0-2	
23/9	JJK	h	3-1	Eerola, Litmanen 2
27/9	Haka	h	2-4	Shala, og (Cagua)
4/10	Tampere United	a	2-0	Shala, Eerola
17/10	Inter	h	1-3	Kemppinen

No	Name	Nat	DoB	Pos	Aps	(s)	Gls
6	Kalle EEROLA		1/11/83	D	19	(2)	2
8	Mohamed FOFANA	GUI	21/10/85	M	16	(7)	4
2	Heikki HAARA		20/11/82	D	18		1
5	Juho-Matti HEIKARI		14/2/91	D	1	(3)	
16	Jussi HEIKKINEN		19/7/88	D	2		
19	Riku HEINI		9/12/90	M	11	(6)	
14	Konsta HIETANEN		20/7/84	M	21	(3)	
5	Jari HOLOPAINEN		31/3/90	A	1		
12	Toni HUUHKA		4/8/89	D	20	(1)	1
20	Janne KEMPPINEN		25/8/81	M	12	(8)	3
17	Eero KORTE		20/9/87	M	24	(2)	2
13	Jussi LÄNSITALO		30/6/90	A	5	(10)	1
10	Jari LITMANEN		20/2/71	M	5	(8)	2
4	Janne MOILANEN		24/6/78	D	7	(1)	
9	RAFAEL Pires Vieira	BRA	1/8/78	A	19	(5)	4
21	Kaarlo RANTANEN		14/12/88	M	5	(7)	

KUPS KUOPIO
Coach – Kai Nyyssönen; (14/6/09) Esa Pekonen
Founded – 1923
Stadium – Magnum Areena (3,700)
MAJOR HONOURS:
Finnish League – (5) 1956, 1958, 1966, 1974, 1976;
Finnish Cup – (2) 1968, 1989.

2009

18/4	HJK	a	1-5	Venäläinen
23/4	Lahti	a	0-1	
29/4	Mariehamn	a	0-3	
7/5	Jaro	a	1-1	Balogh
10/5	JJK	h	2-0	Koljonen, Venäläinen
18/5	Inter	h	0-2	
24/5	Tampere United	a	0-2	
28/5	TPS	h	0-3	
31/5	Haka	a	0-3	
13/6	MyPa	h	0-2	
17/6	VPS	a	0-1	
24/6	Honka	a	1-4	Venäläinen
4/7	RoPS	h	3-0	Turunen M. 2, Nwakaeme
12/7	HJK	h	0-3	
19/7	Lahti	h	1-1	Koljonen
26/7	Mariehamn	h	2-2	Ilo, Koljonen
2/8	Jaro	h	2-2	Koljonen, Venäläinen (p)
5/8	JJK	a	2-1	Ollo 2
14/8	Inter	a	3-2	Koljonen, og (Nyman), Kuparinen
22/8	Tampere United	h	1-2	Venäläinen
13/9	Haka	h	5-1	Ilo 2, Karppinen, Venäläinen, Nwakaeme
20/9	MyPa	a	2-1	Nwakaeme, Karppinen
23/9	TPS	a	0-3	
26/9	Honka	h	0-4	
4/10	VPS	h	3-3	Turunen M., Nwakaeme, Venäläinen
17/10	RoPS	a	0-1	

No	Name	Nat	DoB	Pos	Aps	(s)	Gls
13	Betim ALIJU	MKD	17/3/89	M	2	(7)	
9	Balázs BALOGH	HUN	21/7/82	D	19		1
3	Jani HARTIKAINEN		16/9/75	D	9	(1)	
24	Atte HOIVALA		10/2/92	M	8	(4)	
1	Ville IISKOLA		26/4/85	G	20	(1)	
27	Segun IKUDEHINBU	NGA	16/8/89	M	7	(2)	
11	Miikka ILO		9/5/82	A	21	(4)	3
22	Jyrki JUVONEN		20/1/90	M		(1)	

FINLAND

11	Drilon SHALA		20/3/87	A	22	(4)	8
1	Viktor SZENTPÉTERI	HUN	1/11/79	G	15	(1)	
3	Henri TOIVOMÄKI		21/2/91	D	24		
22	Juha TUOMI		7/11/89	G	11		
15	Jukka VANNINEN		31/1/77	M	23		1
23	Jarkko VÄRTTÖ		24/2/89	D	4	(2)	
7	Jukka VELTHEIM		18/6/84	M	1	(1)	

IFK MARIEHAMN
Coach – Pekka Lyyski
Founded – 1919
Stadium – Wiklöf Holding Arena (4,000)

2009

20/4	Inter	h	2-0	Gruborovics, Šimunac
23/4	Honka	h	2-2	Anttilainen, Ingves
29/4	KuPS	h	3-0	Arajuuri, Gruborovics, Niskala
6/5	HJK	a	0-2	
10/5	RoPS	a	0-0	
17/5	MyPa	h	0-0	
24/5	TPS	a	0-0	
27/5	JJK	a	2-0	Gruborovics, Šimunac
31/5	Tampere United	h	1-0	Gashi
14/6	Lahti	a	1-1	Gruborovics
17/6	Haka	h	2-1	Dujilo, Olofsson
24/6	Jaro	a	0-0	
5/7	VPS	h	0-0	
11/7	Inter	a	1-1	Gruborovics
19/7	Honka	a	1-1	Ingves
26/7	KuPS	a	2-2	Ingves, Gustavsson
2/8	HJK	h	0-0	
9/8	RoPS	h	2-1	Olofsson, Šimunac
16/8	MyPa	a	2-1	Olofsson, Gustavsson
22/8	TPS	h	1-1	Carlsson
12/9	Tampere United	a	0-1	
20/9	Lahti	h	2-0	Ekhalie, Gruborovics
23/9	Haka	a	1-5	Šimunac
27/9	Jaro	h	2-1	Gruborovics 2
4/10	JJK	h	3-1	Rikama, Ingves, Olofsson
17/10	VPS	a	0-0	

No	Name	Nat	DoB	Pos	Aps	(s)	Gls
30	Sasha ANTTILAINEN		19/12/86	A	14	(1)	1
23	Paulus ARAJUURI		15/6/88	D	21		1
4	Johan CARLSSON	SWE	1/8/81	M	14	(5)	1
24	Mate DUJILO	CRO	30/11/81	D	19	(3)	1
15	Amos EKHALIE	KEN	8/7/88	M	7	(7)	1
14	Arsim GASHI	SWE	6/12/83	M	18	(5)	1
10	Tamás GRUBOROVICS		3/7/84	M	25		8
8	Kenneth GUSTAVSSON	SWE	10/8/82	D	16	(7)	2
26	Wilhelm INGVES		10/1/90	A	11	(13)	4
29	Gustav LÅNGBACKA		8/5/84	G	25		
11	Mika NISKALA		28/3/81	M	22	(1)	1
1	Willis OCHIENG	KEN	10/10/81	G	1	(1)	
6	Marcus OLOFSSON	SWE	4/8/82	M	20	(5)	4
22	Alexandros PAPPAS	SWE	13/2/78	D	23		
18	Dmytro PRONEVYCH	UKR	19/11/84	M	4	(2)	
3	Patrik RIKAMA		8/2/83	D	20	(3)	1
9	Ante ŠIMUNAC	CRO	12/1/84	M	18	(3)	4
31	Jimmy SUNDMAN		7/3/89	M		(1)	
2	Dmytro VOLOSHYN	UKR	29/4/86	D	8	(3)	

MYLLYKOSKEN PALLO-47
Coach – Janne Lindberg
Founded – 1947
Stadium – Saviniemen jalkapallostadion (4,100)
MAJOR HONOURS:
Finnish League – (1) 2005;
Finnish Cup – (3) 1992, 1995, 2004.

2009

23/4	Inter	a	1-2	Äijälä
29/4	Tampere United	h	4-1	Äijälä 2, Ady, Votinov
2/5	Inter	h	0-0	
7/5	Honka	a	0-0	
11/5	HJK	h	1-0	Ricketts
14/5	Lahti	h	2-2	Huttunen, Ady (p)
17/5	Mariehamn	a	0-0	
24/5	Jaro	a	0-3	
31/5	VPS	h	0-2	
13/6	KuPS	a	2-0	Ricketts, Votinov
27/6	TPS	a	1-3	Ricketts
5/7	Haka	h	0-2	
13/7	JJK	a	1-0	Lindberg
19/7	RoPS	h	4-0	Ricketts 2, Mustafi, Lindberg
26/7	Tampere United	a	0-2	
2/8	Honka	h	1-3	Puhakainen
9/8	Lahti	a	1-0	Oksanen
16/8	Mariehamn	h	1-2	Äijälä
21/8	Jaro	h	0-0	
4/9	JJK	h	4-0	Huttunen, Könönen, Puhakainen, Votinov
11/9	VPS	a	2-0	Uimaniemi, Cleiton
20/9	KuPS	h	1-2	Äijälä
23/9	RoPS	a	1-1	Votinov
27/9	HJK	a	0-1	
4/10	TPS	h	2-2	Votinov 2
17/10	Haka	a	3-2	Votinov 2, Äijälä

No	Name	Nat	DoB	Pos	Aps	(s)	Gls
8	Adaílton Pereira dos Santos "ADY"	TUN	18/4/73	M	11	(6)	2
18	Tuomas AHO		27/5/81	D	25		
11	Ilari ÄIJÄLÄ		30/9/86	D	17	(5)	6
26	José CLEITON Ferreira Júnior	BRA	6/4/86	A	2	(4)	1
20	FELIPE de Oliveira BENEVIDES	BRA	3/1/89	A	1	(6)	
16	Toni HUTTUNEN		12/1/73	D	26		2
12	Mika JOHANSSON		13/3/84	G	2		
6	Tuomo KÖNÖNEN		29/12/77	D	24	(1)	1
1	Antti KUISMALA		20/1/76	G	24		
17	Einari KURITTU		27/9/89	A		(1)	
13	Toni LINDBERG		23/9/85	D	12	(5)	2
2	Miikka MULTAHARJU		9/10/77	M	12	(5)	
24	Nebi MUSTAFI	MKD	21/8/76	M	8	(5)	1
23	Niko NAKARI		6/4/84	A	2	(4)	
25	Antti OKKONEN		6/6/82	M	7		
15	Ville OKSANEN		25/2/87	M	11	(12)	1
9	Saku PUHAKAINEN		14/1/75	A	15	(11)	2
14	Tosaint RICKETTS	CAN	6/6/87	A	13	(3)	5
3	Sampsa TIMOSKA		12/2/79	D	6	(3)	
5	Jarno TUUNAINEN		5/11/77	D	11		
4	Antti UIMANIEMI		30/1/86	D	24	(1)	1
19	Maksim VOTINOV	RUS	29/8/88	A	14	(5)	8
7	Ben WEBSTER	ENG	28/3/86	M	19	(1)	

ROPS ROVANIEMI
Coach – Valeri Bondarenko (EST); (27/5/09) Mika Lumijärvi; (6/10/09) Zeddy Saileti (ZAM)
Founded – 1950
Stadium – Keskuskenttä (3,400)
MAJOR HONOURS:
Finnish Cup – (1) 1986.

2009

29/4	Lahti	a	1-4	Musonda
7/5	Inter	h	0-2	
10/5	Mariehamn	h	0-0	
14/5	JJK	a	1-1	Saileti

17/5	Haka	a	1-3	Chibwe
24/5	VPS	a	0-2	
31/5	HJK	h	1-0	Pires
14/6	Jaro	a	0-2	
17/6	Tampere United	a	1-3	Okodugha
24/6	TPS	a	2-3	Ikäläinen, Musonda
28/6	Honka	h	1-2	Mwaba
1/7	JJK	h	2-1	Maisonvaara (p), Musonda
4/7	KuPS	a	0-3	
12/7	Jaro	h	5-3	Ikäläinen, Chibwe, Okodugha 3
19/7	MyPa	a	0-4	
26/7	Lahti	h	0-1	
1/8	Inter	a	0-4	
9/8	Mariehamn	a	1-2	Okodugha
16/8	Haka	h	0-0	
23/8	VPS	h	2-3	Ani 2
13/9	HJK	a	0-4	
20/9	Tampere United	h	1-5	Mweetwa
23/9	MyPa	h	1-1	Musonda
27/9	TPS	h	0-4	
4/10	Honka	a	0-9	
17/10	KuPS	h	1-0	Okodugha

No	Name	Nat	DoB	Pos	Aps	(s)	Gls
23	Jeremiah ANI	NGA	12/2/85	A	5	(1)	2
14	Jerry BJÖRKBERG		23/12/92	M		(1)	
2	Godfrey CHIBANGA	ZAM	16/2/89	M	15	(6)	
11	Chileshe CHIBWE	ZAM	13/5/85	A	20	(4)	2
6	Joonas IKÄLÄINEN		5/1/82	D	25		2
20	Juha-Pekka INKERÖINEN		23/11/88	M	1	(10)	
3	Marko KOIVURANTA		10/3/78	D	3	(5)	
5	Stephen KUNDA	ZAM	17/8/84	D	25		
1	KWON Jung-hyuk	KOR	8/2/78	G	20		
15	Mika-Matti MAISONVAARA		11/3/91	M	12	(10)	1
18	Christopher MUSONDA	ZAM	24/1/86	A	25		4
10	Chanda MWABA	ZAM	2/10/88	M	22		1
8	Nchimunya MWEETWA	ZAM	23/3/84	A	5	(12)	1
30	Echiabhi OKODUGHA	NGA	12/10/88	D	26		6
16	Jeferson Luiz PIRES da Silva	BRA	19/5/78	A	2	(5)	1
9	Zeddy SAILETI	ZAM	16/1/69	A	11	(5)	1
5	Whiteson SIMWANZA	ZAM	11/12/84	M	19	(2)	
5	Kari-Pekka SYVÄJÄRVI		26/11/87	G	6	(2)	
17	Ville SYVÄJÄRVI		23/6/83	D	16		
7	Jarno TENKULA		16/6/82	M	5	(2)	
19	Janne TURPEENNIEMI		17/5/89	D	20		
13	Jukka YRJÄNHEIKKI		23/9/88	D	3	(5)	

TAMPERE UNITED
Coach – Ari Hjelm
Founded – 1998
Stadium – Ratinan stadion (16,800)
MAJOR HONOURS:
Finnish League – (3) 2001, 2006, 2007;
Finnish Cup – (1) 2007.

2009

23/4	Jaro	h	0-2	
29/4	MyPa	a	1-4	Savolainen J.
2/5	VPS	h	1-0	Pohja
8/5	TPS	h	0-2	
14/5	Haka	a	0-1	
17/5	Honka	h	1-0	og (Koskimaa)
24/5	KuPS	h	2-0	Kujala, Scheweleff
28/5	HJK	a	0-1	
31/5	Mariehamn	a	0-1	
17/6	RoPS	h	3-1	Lindström, Ojanperä, Rafinha
27/6	Lahti	a	1-2	Hjelm
1/7	Inter	h	3-2	Kangaskolkka, James (p), Rafinha

4/7	JJK	h	1-0	Rafinha
12/7	VPS	a	1-0	Kangaskolkka
20/7	Jaro	a	0-0	
26/7	MyPa	h	2-0	Kangaskolkka, Petrescu
31/7	TPS	a	0-1	
7/8	Haka	h	1-1	Kujala
15/8	Honka	a	1-3	Hjelm
22/8	KuPS	a	2-1	Rafinha, Kangaskolkka
12/9	Mariehamn	h	1-0	Hjelm
20/9	RoPS	a	5-1	Kangaskolkka 2, Rafinha 2, Niemi (p)
23/9	HJK	h	1-2	Petrescu
26/9	Inter	a	2-2	Petrescu, Rafinha
4/10	Lahti	h	0-2	
17/10	JJK	a	2-2	Hjelm, Kangaskolkka (p)

No	Name	Nat	DoB	Pos	Aps	(s)	Gls
21	Jonne HJELM		14/1/88	A	23	(3)	4
23	Chris JAMES	NZL	4/7/87	M	1	(1)	1
11	Aleksei KANGASKOLKKA		29/10/88	A	16	(9)	7
14	Jusu KARVONEN		17/1/93	M	1	(11)	
1	Mikko KAVÉN		19/2/75	G	15		
7	Jussi KUJALA		4/4/83	D	19		2
4	Jesse-Juho KUUSISTO		27/3/91	D	1	(7)	
25	Aapo LAPPALAINEN		3/11/89	A	1	(1)	
3	Mathias LINDSTRÖM		14/1/81	D	20		1
27	Johannes MONONEN		4/5/91	D	5		
30	Jari NIEMI		2/2/77	A	22	(2)	1
5	Antti OJANPERÄ		6/4/83	D	18	(3)	
10	Tomi PETRESCU		24/7/86	A	10	(3)	3
9	Juha PIRINEN		22/10/91	M	4	(7)	
8	Antti POHJA		11/1/77	A	8	(2)	1
18	Rafael Scapini de Almeida "RAFINHA"	BRA	29/6/82	A	25		7
28	Jaakko RUUSKANEN		26/8/90	A		(2)	
16	Ilari RUUTH		27/8/90	D	11	(3)	
13	Sakari SAARINEN		18/7/78	M	23	(1)	
20	Juska SAVOLAINEN		1/9/83	M	15		1
17	Vili SAVOLAINEN		25/10/85	M	21	(2)	
22	Henri SCHEWELEFF		15/4/83	A	16	(9)	1
12	Juha SOUKIALA		12/2/83	G	11		

TPS TURKU
Coach – Pasi Rautiainen
Founded – 1922
Stadium – Veritas Stadion (9,300)
MAJOR HONOURS:
Finnish League – (8) 1928, 1939, 1941, 1949, 1968, 1971, 1972, 1975;
Finnish Cup – (2) 1991, 1994.

2009

18/4	Haka	h	1-2	Brown
23/4	HJK	a	2-2	Nyberg, Paatelainen
27/4	JJK	h	0-0	
4/5	Jaro	h	1-1	Nyberg
8/5	Tampere United	a	2-0	Andreasen, Brown
14/5	Inter	a	0-2	
17/5	VPS	h	2-0	Riski, Andreasen
24/5	Mariehamn	h	0-0	
28/5	KuPS	a	3-0	Andreasen, Wusu 2
31/5	Lahti	a	4-2	Wusu, Andreasen, Riski 2
24/6	RoPS	h	3-2	Paatelainen, Riski, Andreasen
27/6	MyPa	h	3-1	Wusu, Brown, og (Huttunen)
6/7	Honka	a	0-0	
13/7	Haka	a	3-0	Wusu, Paatelainen, Ääritalo
19/7	HJK	h	1-1	Ääritalo
27/7	JJK	a	1-1	Wusu
31/7	Tampere United	h	1-0	Brown (p)

FINLAND

9/8	Inter	h	2-0	Brown (p), Ääritalo	
16/8	VPS	a	2-0	Paatelainen, Brown	
22/8	Mariehamn	a	1-1	Paatelainen	
13/9	Lahti	h	5-2	Kujala, Wusu, Paatelainen, Manninen, Brown	
20/9	Jaro	a	0-1		
23/9	KuPS	h	3-0	Brown, Paatelainen 2	
27/9	RoPS	a	4-0	Brown, Wusu, Paatelainen, Riski	
4/10	MyPa	a	2-2	Wusu, Manninen	
17/10	Honka	h	0-0		

No	Name	Nat	DoB	Pos	Aps	(s)	Gls
2	Iiro AALTO		19/7/77	D	23		
11	Mika ÄÄRITALO		25/7/85	A	1	(14)	3
16	Christian ANDREASEN	DEN	18/5/88	A	4	(4)	5
21	Wayne BROWN	ENG	6/8/88	A	26		9
18	Chris CLEAVER	ENG	24/3/79	M	21	(1)	
14	Kasper HÄMÄLÄINEN		8/8/86	M	22	(3)	
8	Jarno HEINIKANGAS		5/3/79	D	26		
29	Yll HOXHA	SRB	26/12/87	M		(10)	
4	Igor JOVANOVIĆ	GER	3/5/89	M	2	(3)	
34	Jussi KUJALA		4/4/83	D	6		1
23	Juho LÄHDE		11/2/91	M		(1)	
12	Jukka LEHTOVAARA		15/3/88	G	25		
19	Patrik LOMSKI		3/2/89	A	1	(5)	
13	Samu-Petteri MÄKELÄ		9/11/86	A	1	(7)	
9	Mikko MANNINEN		25/5/85	M	24		2
6	Jaakko NYBERG		19/12/80	D	23		2
28	Mikko PAATELAINEN		24/11/80	A	21	(5)	9
7	Sami RÄHMÖNEN		19/4/87	D	24	(2)	
10	Riku RISKI		16/8/89	M	7	(15)	5
1	Jani TUOMALA		3/2/77	G	1		
5	Simo VALAKARI		28/4/73	M	7		
20	Babatunde WUSU	NGA	18/4/84	A	21	(4)	9

VPS VAASA
Coach – Tomi Kärkkäinen; (15/5/09) Petri Vuorinen & Juha Reini
Founded – 1924
Stadium – Hietalahden jalkapallostadion (4,600)
MAJOR HONOURS:
Finnish League – (2) 1945, 1948.

2009

22/4	Haka	h	0-1	
27/4	Honka	h	2-5	Nygård, Saranpää
2/5	Tampere United	a	0-1	
7/5	Lahti	a	0-0	
13/5	Jaro	h	1-2	Hietaharju
17/5	TPS	a	0-2	
24/5	RoPS	h	2-0	Björk, Inutile
28/5	Inter	a	1-0	Smith
31/5	MyPa	a	2-0	Nygård, Aalto
17/6	KuPS	h	1-0	Forsell
25/6	JJK	h	3-2	Nygård, Koskela, Lindroos
1/7	HJK	h	3-4	Inutile 2, Lyyski
5/7	Mariehamn	a	0-0	
12/7	Tampere United	h	0-1	
18/7	Haka	a	1-0	Smith
26/7	Honka	a	0-3	
2/8	Lahti	h	1-0	Lyyski
6/8	Jaro	a	3-1	Björk, Inutile, Lindroos
16/8	TPS	h	0-2	
23/8	RoPS	a	3-2	Seppälä, Smith, Lyyski
11/9	MyPa	h	0-2	
20/9	HJK	a	0-2	
23/9	Inter	h	2-2	Björk, Kainu
26/9	JJK	a	2-1	Hietaharju 2 (1p)
4/10	KuPS	a	3-3	Inutile, Björk, Koskela
17/10	Mariehamn	h	0-0	

No	Name	Nat	DoB	Pos	Aps	(s)	Gls
9	Jussi AALTO		28/7/83	A	8	(8)	1
4	Jussi ÄIJÄLÄ		27/11/88	D	19	(2)	
17	Juho ALASUUTARI		6/11/90	M		(4)	
19	Jan BERG		22/5/85	D	21	(4)	
22	Tony BJÖRK		25/10/83	M	26		4
6	Petteri FORSELL		16/10/90	M	4	(8)	1
11	Toni HAHTO		7/4/82	M	7	(8)	
23	Jyri HIETAHARJU		23/4/81	M	25		3
10	Antonio INUTILE		12/5/85	A	25		5
25	Pekka KAINU		20/12/79	A	13	(8)	1
7	Tero KOSKELA		13/10/76	M	24		2
20	Rikard LINDROOS		12/7/85	M	5	(12)	2
8	Jani LYYSKI		16/3/83	M	26		3
12	Henrik MOISANDER		29/9/85	G	6	(2)	
14	Jens NYGÅRD		8/1/78	M	25		3
16	Jyrki SARANPÄÄ		30/8/83	A	14	(2)	1
21	Arttu SEPPÄLÄ		18/3/87	A	3	(1)	1
1	Henri SILLANPÄÄ		4/6/79	G	20	(1)	
3	Lawrence SMITH	USA	16/3/85	A	15	(7)	3
5	Joacim TUURI		16/10/89	M		(1)	

PROMOTED CLUB

AC OULU
Coach – Juha Malinen
Founded – 2002
Stadium – Oulu-lehti Areena (4,000)

SECOND LEVEL FINAL TABLE 2009

		Pld	W	D	L	F	A	Pts
1	AC Oulu	26	16	5	5	57	24	53
2	KPV Kokkola	26	15	6	5	32	25	51
3	FC Viikingit	26	15	5	6	48	19	50
4	PoPa Pori	26	11	8	7	53	39	41
5	FC KooTeePee	26	11	6	9	23	21	39
6	FC Hämeenlinna	26	10	8	8	36	33	38
7	PS Kemi	26	12	2	12	36	46	38
8	Klubi 04	26	10	7	9	46	45	37
9	PK-35 Vantaa	26	10	5	11	31	30	35
10	JIPPO Joensuu	26	8	5	13	28	39	29
11	TPV Tampere	26	7	7	12	28	38	28
12	TP-47 Tornio	26	7	6	13	29	41	27
13	Atlantis FC	26	6	3	17	26	50	21
14	FC Kiisto Vaasa	26	5	5	16	25	48	20

PROMOTION/RELEGATION PLAY-OFFS
(21/10/09)
KPV 2, JJK 3
(25/10/09)
JJK 2, KPV 1
(JJK 5-3)

DOMESTIC CUP 2009

SUOMEN CUP

FIFTH ROUND

(2/6/09)
Pöxyt 4, GrIFK 0

(3/6/09)
BET 0, Gnistan 7
City Stars 2, KTP 0
Honka/U20 2, KuPS 3
KTP/JKKI-35 0, JJK 8
MPS 1, JIPPO 3 *(aet)*

(4/6/09)
MasKi 0, Pallohonka 5
TPK/U20 1, Tampere United 10

(5/6/09)
KalK/TePa 0, VPS 5
VPS-j 0, RoPS 4

(8/6/09)
Naseva 0, MyPa 9

(9/6/09)
BK-46 0, Viikingit 2
Real Kokkola JKKI-35 2, FC SantaClaus 1
Tervarit 0, Jaro 5
AC Vantaa 2, EIF 2 *(aet; 4-3 on pens)*

(10/6/09)
Spartak Kajaani 2, YPA 1 *(aet)*

(11/6/09)
FC Futura 2, LoPa 0
KaVo 1, PoPa 4
Ilves 1, TPV 5
FC Tampere 0, Haka 7
TOVE 0, Pirkkala JK 6

(12/6/09)
PP-70 3, FC Jazz-j 3 *(aet; 0-3 on pens)*
SC Riverball 1, PK-35 3
Viikingit/2 1, FC Espoo 2

(13/6/09)
HDS 0, KooTeePee 4

(14/6/09)
PK-37 0, GBK 4

(17/6/09)
Karhu 0, JBK 8
MaPS 1, TPS 6

SIXTH ROUND

(8/7/09)
FC Espoo 0, HJK Helsinki 1
FC Futura 1, VPS 4
Gnistan 5, JBK 0
Inter Turku 2, RoPS 0
MyPa 1, KuPS 3
PoPa 3, PK-35 1
Real Kokkola JKKI-35 2, Pallohonka 6
TPV 3, JIPPO 1

(9/7/09)
City Stars 3, Pirkkala JK 1
GBK 0, FC Jazz-j 1
KooTeePee 0, Honka 2
Pöxyt 0, TPS 2

Spartak Kajaani 0, Haka 5
Tampere United 2, Jaro 0
AC Vantaa 2, JJK 3

(12/8/09)
Viikingit 1, Lahti 2 *(aet)*

SEVENTH ROUND

(29/8/09)
Haka 2, JJK 1
TPS 2, Honka 6 *(aet)*
TPV 2, Tampere United 3 *(aet)*

(30/8/09)
City Stars 2, Pallohonka 0
Gnistan 1, Lahti 2
Inter Turku 1, PoPa 0
KuPS 1, HJK Helsinki 0
VPS 0, FC Jazz-j 2

QUARTER-FINALS

(30/9/09)
City Stars 0, Honka 3 *(Puustinen 68, 89, 90)*

(1/10/09)
Haka 1 *(Minkenen 82p)*, Tampere United 3 *(Hjelm 26, Rafinha 34, 36)*
KuPS 0, Inter Turku 2 *(Kauko 2, Nwanganga 22)*
Lahti 4 *(Shala 13, Hietanen 65, Rafael 78, Rantanen 86)*, FC Jazz-j 0

SEMI-FINALS

(25/10/09)
Lahti 3 *(Rafael 11, 55, Kemppinen 67)*, Inter Turku 4 *(Ojala 15p, 53, 86, Nwanganga 45)*
Tampere United 1 *(Niemi 94p)*, Honka 1 *(Puustinen 119)* *(aet; 4-3 on pens)*

FINAL

(31/10/09)
Finnair Stadium, Helsinki
FC INTER TURKU 2 *(Nwanganga 45, Furuholm 77)*
TAMPERE UNITED 1 *(Hjelm 11)*
Referee – Järvenpää
INTER TURKU – Monsalve, Aho, Nyman, Sanevuori, Lehtonen, Ramírez, Ojala, Pertot (Paajanen 76), Kauko, Nwanganga (Purje 79), Furuholm.
TAMPERE UNITED – Kavén, Ojanperä, Mononen, Savolainen V., Ruuth, Niemi, Scheweleff (Petrescu 64), Saarinen, Hjelm (Pohja 54), Rafinha, Kangaskolkka.

World Cup disruption ends Domenech era

For France, the 2010 FIFA World Cup was an experience that will live long in the memory for all the wrong reasons. Wracked by deep divisions within the camp, the team performed without unity or spirit and were sent packing with just one point and one goal from their three games. They returned home to a national outcry, their sorry performances on the field exacerbated by unresolvable tension between some of the players and the coaching staff.

The whole affair was deemed an embarrassment to the nation, leading to direct intervention from the French president and a government inquiry into what had gone on, and gone wrong, in South Africa. For Raymond Domenech, the longest serving coach in Les Bleus' history, it was a last stand that probably confirmed him as also the least popular. Essentially it was his squabbles with the players over tactics, discipline and team selection – many of them leaked to the media – that lay at the source of the problem.

Training boycott

The sparks flew out of control after Nicolas Anelka was sent home by the French Football Federation (FFF) for a foul-mouthed outburst at Domenech at half-time during the second of France's three games, against Mexico in Polokwane. The players, led by newly appointed captain Patrice Evra, rallied around their departed colleague and refused to take part in a training session prior to the final group game against South Africa. That they lost that match, 2-1, and were therefore eliminated was hardly surprising in the circumstances, although Domenech's last act as France coach – pointedly refusing to shake the hand of his opposite number, Carlos Alberto Parreira, after the game – scarcely improved the situation.

As the tournament bid France farewell, the size of the rebuilding task awaiting Domenech's already installed successor, Laurent Blanc, was plain for all to see. Away from all the personal, off-the-field issues, the harsh fact was that none of the players had really performed. It had been a similar tale at UEFA EURO 2008 and during the big games of the World Cup qualifying campaign, notably in the second leg of the play-off against the Republic of Ireland at the Stade de France when the pressure of the occasion got to them and they had to rely on a highly fortuitous extra-time goal – created by Thierry Henry's infamous sleight of hand – to book their place in South Africa. Although marginally the better side in their opening game of the finals, 0-0 against Uruguay, Domenech's team were well beaten by both Mexico and South Africa as key players such as Franck Ribéry, Yoann Gourcuff, Anelka and Evra all failed to deliver.

Blanc on a mission

It could be argued that France are still trying to get used to life without Zinédine Zidane. Since the great man retired after the 2006 World Cup, Les Bleus have

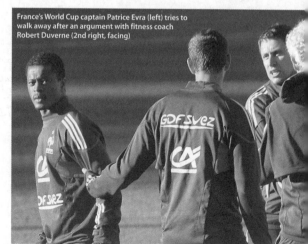

France's World Cup captain Patrice Evra (left) tries to walk away after an argument with fitness coach Robert Duverne (2nd right, facing)

always struggled on the major occasions. With record goalscorer Henry, another all-time great and the last survivor of the 1998 World Cup-winning squad, having also now departed the scene, a new era beckons under Blanc, whose first mission is to ensure that France can be re-generated in time to qualify for UEFA EURO 2012. As the seeded team in a group containing no other 2010 World Cup finals participants, they will be fully expected to do so – whatever the extent of the fall-out from the team's South African misadventure.

Blanc's credentials for the France job – over and above the respect he earned as a player in winning 97 caps, the World Cup and UEFA EURO 2000 - were cemented by his success in leading FC Girondins de Bordeaux to the 2008/09 Ligue 1 title in only his second season as a coach. His third season was not quite so memorable as Bordeaux's hopes of a successful championship defence, very much alive for two thirds of the campaign, shrivelled and died during a dramatic end-of-season collapse following the team's quarter-final exit from the UEFA Champions League at the hands of domestic rivals Olympique Lyonnais.

Bordeaux enjoyed themselves for a long time in Europe, emphatically topping a group containing Juventus and FC Bayern München – they did the double over the Germans - before seeing off Greek champions Olympiacos FC in the first knockout round. The pain, however, of losing to Lyon – narrowly, 3-2 on aggregate, and somewhat controversially – seemed to leave the team so empty that they were unable to rouse themselves for the Ligue 1 run-in. Top of the table going into that European quarter-final, albeit by a much reduced margin from the nine-point lead they had held at Christmas, their form disintegrated to such an extent after it that they collected just eight points from their last ten matches and dropped all the way down to sixth place in the final standings, leaving the club - and Blanc's successor, Jean Tigana - with only domestic football to look forward to in 2010/11.

Marseille wait over

As Bordeaux collapsed, the team they had pipped to the previous season's title, Olympique de Marseille, raised their game, staging a superb 15-match unbeaten run – including 12 victories – to break out of an increasingly congested title-chasing pack and claim their first championship crown since the halcyon days of the early 1990s. The club's 18-year wait for the title was brought to an end by the iconic figure of Didier

Marseille coach Didier Deschamps brandishes the Ligue 1 trophy

Deschamps. Marseille's captain when the club made it four French championship wins in a row in 1992, and again a year later when they won the inaugural UEFA Champions League, he returned to the Stade Vélodrome as coach in the summer of 2009, replacing the departed Eric Gerets, and restored Marseille to the pinnacle of the French game at the first attempt.

Like Bordeaux the season before, Marseille did not restrict themselves to one trophy, preceding their charge to the championship with victory in the League Cup. The final, at the Stade de France on the last Saturday in March, offered a foretaste of the imminent transition of power as Deschamps' team relieved Blanc's of their trophy with a comprehensive 3-1 win, the first of Marseille's three goals symbolically being scored by Souleymane Diawara, who had left Bordeaux for the Mediterranean port club the previous summer.

With the burden of a 17-year wait for a major trophy finally lifted, Marseille were noticeably more relaxed as they set about chasing the bigger prize. With four wins out of four in February supplemented by a vital 2-1 win at home to Lyon, their Ligue 1 title bid was already firmly back on track, but there had been

FRANCE

several previous instances in which Marseille had blown their hopes with an untimely form dip in the closing weeks, so nobody at the Vélodrome was counting any chickens. But Deschamps, so experienced at handling similar circumstances as a player, successfully maintained the team's forward momentum during a busy month of April in which they were obliged to play seven matches. Impressively they won the first six of them, then drew the seventh – a Friday night goalless stalemate at closest pursuers AJ Auxerre that was of much greater use to them than their opponents.

With a five-point advantage and three games remaining, Marseille were virtually home and dry. Five days later the club's ninth French title – one behind record champions AS Saint-Étienne – was safely under lock and key, Auxerre's 2-1 defeat at Lyon enabling OM to take an unassailable lead at the top of the table with a 3-1 win at home to Stade Rennais FC, two goals in as many minutes late in the second half, from skipper Mamadou Niang and playmaker Lucho González, sending the 55,377 spectators in the Vélodrome into a state of delirious joy.

Decisive figures

With goals in each of the club's last two games taking his final tally for the season to 18, Niang would lift the Golden Boot as well as the Ligue 1 trophy, while Lucho would officially be credited with the division's highest number of assists, 11. Both players, evidently, were

Fédération Française de Football (FFF)

87 boulevard de Grenelle
FR-75738 Paris Cedex 15
tel – +33 1 44 31 7300
fax – +33 1 4431 7373
website – fff.fr
email – webmaster@fff.fr
Year of formation – 1919

President - Fernand Duchaussoy
General Secretary – Jacques Lambert
Media Officer – Pierre-Jean Golven
National Stadium – Stade de France, Saint-Denis (76,474)

INTERNATIONAL HONOURS
FIFA World Cup – (1) 1998.
UEFA European Championship – (2) 1984, 2000.
FIFA Confederations Cup – (2) 2001, 2003.
INTERNATIONAL TOURNAMENT APPEARANCES
FIFA World Cup – (12) 1930, 1938 (2nd round), 1954, 1958 (3rd), 1966, 1978, 1982 (4th), 1986 (3rd), 1998 (Winners), 2002, 2006 (runners-up), 2010.
UEFA European Championship – (7) 1960 (4th), 1984 (Winners), 1992, 1996 (semi-finals), 2000 (Winners), 2004 (qtr-finals), 2008.
TOP FIVE ALL-TIME CAPS
Lilian Thuram (142); Thierry Henry (123); Marcel Desailly (116); Zinedine Zidane (108); Patrick Vieira (107)
TOP FIVE ALL-TIME GOALS
Thierry Henry (51); Michel Platini (41); David Trezeguet (34); Zinedine Zidane (31); Just Fontaine & Jean-Pierre Papin (30)

decisive figures in Marseille's triumph, the latter shaking off a succession of niggling injuries following his high-profile arrival from FC Porto to become the team's master conductor during their drive for the

NATIONAL TEAM RESULTS 2009/10

12/8/09	Faroe Islands (WCQ)	A	Torshavn	1-0	Gignac (41)
5/9/09	Romania (WCQ)	H	Saint-Denis	1-1	Henry (48)
9/9/09	Serbia (WCQ)	A	Belgrade	1-1	Henry (35)
10/10/09	Faroe Islands (WCQ)	H	Guingamp	5-0	Gignac (34, 39), Gallas (53), Anelka (85), Benzema (87)
14/10/09	Austria (WCQ)	H	Saint-Denis	3-1	Benzema (18), Henry (26p), Gignac (66)
14/11/09	Republic of Ireland (WCQ)	A	Dublin	1-0	Anelka (72)
18/11/09	Republic of Ireland (WCQ)	H	Saint-Denis	1-1	Gallas (103) (aet)
3/3/10	Spain	H	Saint-Denis	0-2	
26/5/10	Costa Rica	H	Lens	2-1	Sequeira (22og), Valbuena (83)
30/5/10	Tunisia	A	Rades	1-1	Gallas (62)
4/6/10	China	N	Saint-Pierre (Reunion)	0-1	
11/6/10	Uruguay (WCF)	N	Cape Town (RSA)	0-0	
17/6/10	Mexico (WCF)	N	Polokwane (RSA)	0-2	
22/6/10	South Africa (WCF)	A	Bloemfontein	1-2	Malouda (70)

FRANCE

NATIONAL TEAM APPEARANCES 2009/10

Coach – Raymond DOMENECH	24/1/52		FRO	ROU	SRB	FRO	AUT	IRL	IRL	Esp	Crc	Tun	Chn	URU	MEX	RSA	Caps	Goals
Hugo LLORIS	26/12/86	Lyon	G	G	G 12*		G	G	G	G		G	G	G	G	G	14	-
Bacary SAGNA	14/2/83	Arsenal (ENG)	D	D	D	D		D	D	D	D	D	D46	D	D	D	23	-
William GALLAS	17/8/77	Arsenal (ENG)	D	D	D	D		D	D		D46	D63	D	D	D	D	84	5
Julien ESCUDÉ	17/8/79	Sevilla (ESP)	D	D			D			D9	D						13	-
Patrice EVRA	15/5/81	Man. United (ENG)	D	D	D	D		D	D	D	D	D63	D	D	D		32	-
Jérémy TOULALAN	10/9/83	Lyon	M	M	M	M62					M	M46	M	M	M	M	36	-
Lassana DIARRA	10/3/85	Real Madrid (ESP)	M	M	M	M		M	M	M							27	-
Nicolas ANELKA	14/3/79	Chelsea (ENG)	M	M	M	A		M	M	A77	A46	A63	A62	A72	A46		69	14
Yoann GOURCUFF	11/7/86	Bordeaux	M	M73	M85			M	M88	M		M	M63	M	M75	M 25*	22	1
Florent MALOUDA	13/6/80	Chelsea (ENG)	M65		s62	M	s91	s88	s74	M77	M	M62	s75	M		s46	57	4
André-Pierre GIGNAC	5/12/85	Toulouse	A	A57	A12	A73	s51	A91	A57		s84	s63	s62	s85	s46	A46	16	4
Franck RIBÉRY	1/4/83	Bayern (GER)	s65	s57	s77					M74	M84	M46	M62	M	M	M	48	7
Thierry HENRY	17/8/77	Barcelona (ESP)			M	M77	M	A51	M	M	M65	s46	s46	s62	s72	s55	123	51
Karim BENZEMA	19/12/87	Real Madrid (ESP)		s73		s73	A79										27	8
Éric ABIDAL	11/9/79	Barcelona (ESP)			D	D				D		D	D46	D	D	D	50	-
Steve MANDANDA	28/3/85	Marseille			s12	G					G						13	-
Alou DIARRA	15/7/81	Bordeaux			s85			M	M	M	s46				M82		26	-
Sidney GOVOU	27/7/79	Lyon				M62	M		s57	s65	M65	M75	M71	M85	M69	s82	49	10
Moussa SISSOKO	16/8/89	Toulouse				s62	M										2	-
Rod FANNI	6/12/81	Rennes					D										4	-
Sébastien SQUILLACI	11/8/80	Sevilla (ESP)					D			s9	s46	s63				D	21	-
Gaël CLICHY	26/7/85	Arsenal (ENG)					D					s63	D				5	-
Bafétimbi GOMIS	6/8/85	Lyon				s79											5	2
Michaël CIANI	6/4/84	Bordeaux								D							1	-
Djibril CISSÉ	12/8/81	Panathinaikos (GRE)									s77	s75	A55				40	9
Mathieu VALBUENA	28/9/84	Marseille									s65			s71	s69		3	1
Abou DIABY	11/5/86	Arsenal (ENG)									s77	s63	s62	M	M	M	8	-
Marc PLANUS	7/3/82	Bordeaux										s46					1	-
Anthony RÉVEILLÈRE	10/11/79	Lyon												s46			6	-

FRANCE

title. It was a season of two halves for many Marseille players. Others to have come to the fore in the spring after a modest autumn included Cameroonian international Stéphane Mbia, who was switched successfully from anchorman to central defence; Edouard Cissé and Charles Kaboré, who formed a fine partnership in central midfield; and Mathieu Valbuena, who came off the bench – and the transfer list - to produce the finest form of his career.

Whereas Bordeaux had reacted badly to European elimination, Marseille, conversely, grew stronger after they were knocked out of the UEFA Europa League by SL Benfica – victims of a stoppage-time heartbreaker in the Vélodrome. Unable to finish higher than third in a UEFA Champions League group containing the competition's two most decorated clubs, Real Madrid CF and AC Milan, they made light work of seeing off FC København on their introduction to the secondary competition before losing out to the Portuguese champions-elect in the round of 16.

Europe, however, proved to be the saving grace for Lyon – and their coach, Claude Puel – as, for the very first time, the perennial UEFA Champions League quarter-final fallers made it through to the semis. They had to eliminate another French team to do it, but the victory over Bordeaux enabled Puel to do what no other Lyon coach had previously managed and, in terms of his job security, make amends for a second

successive season without a trophy on the domestic front. The highlight of Lyon's European run was their elimination of Real Madrid in the first knockout round – although a smash-and-grab 2-1 win over Liverpool FC at Anfield in the group stage ran it close. Their most emphatic performance came right at the start when they demolished RSC Anderlecht 8-2 on aggregate, with new record signing Lisandro López announcing himself with a terrific hat-trick in Brussels.

Player of the Year

Lisandro, who was brought in to replace Real-bound Karim Benzema, scored three further goals in the UEFA Champions League proper, plus another 15 in Ligue 1, and was rewarded for his combined efforts with France's Player of the Year award. Neither he nor any of his team-mates could find the net against Bayern, however, as the Germans ran Lyon ragged in both legs of the European semi-final, but a strong finish in the league, in which the club took eight points from a four-match sequence against fellow contenders LOSC Lille Métropole, Bordeaux, Montpellier Hérault SC and Auxerre and another six from their last two games, ensured direct access to Europe's premier club competition in 2010/11. Lisandro apart, Lyon's most consistent performer was Hugo Lloris, who once again upstaged Marseille's Steve Mandanda as the country's No1 goalkeeper. His fellow French international Jérémy Toulalan also performed with consistency, while Bosnian teenager Miralem Pjanić, though erratic, hinted that he could become a worthy successor to former skipper Juninho in the playmaking role, not least with his memorable tie-winning strike against Real in the Santiago Bernabéu.

Auxerre's third-place finish in Ligue 1 was a remarkable achievement for a team that lost their opening three games of the season and failed to score in their first four. Coach Jean Fernandez eventually sorted things out, though, and after a seven-match winning streak lifted them from the bottom of the table to near the top during the autumn, they emerged as genuine title contenders during the spring. An incredible 5-0 thrashing by basement club Grenoble Foot 38 in early February was followed by a long unbeaten run that did not end until that defeat to Lyon on the day that Marseille won the title. Defence was the team's strong point – indeed, Auxerre conceded fewer goals than any other team in the division (29) – so it was perhaps appropriate that one of the most prominent members of the back four, right-back Cédric Hengbart, should sign off the season

Cameroon international Stéphane Mbia was a key figure in Marseille's Ligue 1 triumph

Lyon's record signing Lisandro López was voted Player of the Year by his fellow Ligue 1 professionals

with the vital last-minute winner away to FC Sochaux-Montbéliard that earned the Burgundy club a UEFA Champions League qualifying place. Swiss international centre-back Stéphane Grichting was a tower of strength throughout the season, as was inspirational captain Benoît Pedretti, while Polish striker Ireneusz Jeleń weighed in with 14 goals, a third of the team's total.

Rampant Lille

Unlike Auxerre, Lille, who finished one point behind them in fourth after a last-day defeat at FC Lorient, were much stronger in attack than in defence. Given licence to go forward in every game by adventurous coach Rudi Garcia, the unleashed Dogues made the most of their freedom. Brilliantly prompted by Belgian teenager Eden Hazard, the Lille attacking trident of Yohan Cabaye, Pierre-Alain Frau and Ivory Coast wing wizard Gervinho cut through the Ligue 1 defences at will. Each of them bagged 13 goals, with Hazard contributing five and Brazilian reserve striker Túlio de Melo six in a league-best club total of 72. The Lille attack was especially rampant in the run-up to Christmas, scoring 23 goals in six successive victories, and there was also a strong showing from the team in

the UEFA Europa League, where they struck 29 goals in 14 games, the only blank being drawn in the second leg of their last-16 tie, a 3-0 defeat at Liverpool that knocked them out of the competition.

Montpellier's fifth place was the surprise of the season. Freshly promoted from Ligue 2 and with a new coach in René Girard, they were widely tipped for a relegation struggle but a team short of star individuals bonded brilliantly and actually looked like genuine title contenders shortly after the New Year when they strung together five successive wins, in the midst of which was a 2-0 victory over Marseille – the champions' last defeat of the season. The two clubs that had accompanied Montpellier up, RC Lens and US Boulogne CO, experienced contrasting fortunes, with the former enjoying mid-table tranquility while the latter went straight back down. The Channel port club were joined in relegation by Le Mans UC 72 and bottom-of-the-pile Grenoble, whose fate was already decided in the autumn when they lost every one of their opening 11 fixtures.

PSG prevail

Ligue 1 expanded its geographical spread for 2010/11 with the promotion of teams from Normandy (SM Caen), Brittany (Stade Brestois 29) and Provence (merger club AC Arles-Avignon). The capital city also had something to celebrate as Paris Saint-Germain FC made up for a disappointing league campaign under new coach Antoine Kombouaré by winning the French Cup. Their eighth victory in the competition – just two short of Marseille's record haul – was secured with an extra-time winner from Guillaume Hoarau in a drab Stade de France showpiece against AS Monaco FC. It was the second Cup final defeat in as many years for Monaco boss Guy Lacombe, who had suffered the same fate with Rennes 12 months earlier. He had, however, led PSG to victory in their previous Coupe de France triumph, against Marseille in the 2006 final.

Although PSG and Monaco contested the final, it was amateur club US Quevilly, from France's fourth tier, who made the biggest waves in the competition, going further than every one of the six teams contesting the Ligue 1 title as they progressed all the way from the regional qualifying rounds to the semi-final, eliminating top-flight clubs Rennes and Boulogne en route. It was a tale to gladden the heart in a season tainted by the tragic deaths of two fans – one from PSG, another from Toulouse FC – and France's shameful shenanigans at the World Cup.

FRANCE

DOMESTIC LEAGUE 2009/10

LIGUE 1 FINAL TABLE

		Pld	Home					Away					Total					Pts
			W	D	L	F	A	W	D	L	F	A	W	D	L	F	A	
1	Olympique de Marseille	38	14	3	2	37	14	9	6	4	32	22	23	9	6	69	36	78
2	Olympique Lyonnais	38	12	4	3	32	17	8	8	3	32	21	20	12	6	64	38	72
3	AJ Auxerre	38	11	5	3	24	14	9	6	4	18	15	20	11	7	42	29	71
4	LOSC Lille Métropole	38	14	3	2	44	15	7	4	8	28	25	21	7	10	72	40	70
5	Montpellier Hérault SC	38	12	4	3	24	12	8	5	6	26	28	20	9	9	50	40	69
6	FC Girondins de Bordeaux	38	12	4	3	34	13	7	3	9	24	27	19	7	12	58	40	64
7	FC Lorient	38	10	7	2	36	19	6	3	10	18	23	16	10	12	54	42	58
8	AS Monaco FC	38	11	5	3	26	14	4	5	10	13	31	15	10	13	39	45	55
9	Stade Rennais FC	38	10	4	5	31	18	4	7	8	21	23	14	11	13	52	41	53
10	Valenciennes FC	38	7	7	5	23	21	7	3	9	27	29	14	10	14	50	50	52
11	RC Lens	38	9	7	3	27	17	3	5	11	13	27	12	12	14	40	44	48
12	AS Nancy-Lorraine	38	6	4	9	20	26	7	5	7	26	27	13	9	16	46	53	48
13	Paris Saint-Germain FC	38	9	5	5	32	20	3	6	10	18	26	12	11	15	50	46	47
14	Toulouse FC	38	8	4	7	19	16	4	7	8	17	20	12	11	15	36	36	47
15	OGC Nice	38	7	7	5	23	23	4	4	11	18	34	11	11	16	41	57	44
16	FC Sochaux-Montbéliard	38	8	1	10	18	29	3	7	9	10	23	11	8	19	28	52	41
17	AS Saint-Étienne	38	5	7	7	13	16	5	3	11	14	29	10	10	18	27	45	40
18	Le Mans UC 72	38	6	6	7	22	25	2	2	15	14	34	8	8	22	36	59	32
19	US Boulogne CO	38	4	5	10	19	31	3	5	11	12	31	7	10	21	31	62	31
20	Grenoble Foot 38	38	4	5	10	24	28	1	3	15	7	33	5	8	25	31	61	23

TOP GOALSCORERS

18 Mamadou NIANG (Marseille)

17 Kevin GAMEIRO (Lorient)

15 LISANDRO LÓPEZ (Lyon)
MEVLÜT Erdinç (PSG)

14 Ireneusz JELEŃ (Auxerre)
NENÊ (Monaco)
Loïc RÉMY (Nice)

13 Yohan CABAYE (Lille)
Pierre-Alain FRAU (Lille)
GERVINHO (Lille)
Asamoah GYAN (Rennes)

CLUB-BY-CLUB

AJ AUXERRE
Coach – Jean Fernandez
Founded – 1905
Stadium – Stade Abbé-Deschamps (24,493)
MAJOR HONOURS:
French League - (1) 1996;
French Cup - (4) 1994, 1996, 2003, 2005.

2009
8/8	Sochaux	h	0-1	
15/8	Lens	a	0-2	
22/8	Lyon	h	0-3	
29/8	Boulogne	a	0-0	
13/9	Nice	h	2-0	*Hengbart, Niculae*
19/9	St-Étienne	a	1-1	*Lejeune*
26/9	Grenoble	h	2-0	*Pedretti, Hengbart*
3/10	Rennes	a	1-0	*Pedretti*
17/10	Bordeaux	h	1-0	*Birsa (p)*
25/10	Lille	h	3-2	*Jeleń 2, Niculae*
31/10	Montpellier	h	2-1	*Jeleń 2*
7/11	Le Mans	a	1-0	*og (Andrade)*
21/11	Monaco	h	2-0	*Coulibaly, Ndinga*
28/11	PSG	a	0-1	
6/12	Nancy	h	1-3	*Birsa*
12/12	Lorient	a	0-0	
15/12	Valenciennes	a	0-0	
20/12	Toulouse	h	1-1	*Contout*
23/12	Marseille	a	2-0	*Oliech 2*

2010
16/1	Boulogne	h	0-0	
20/1	Nice	a	1-0	*Jeleń*
31/1	St-Étienne	h	1-0	*Mignot*
6/2	Grenoble	a	0-5	
14/2	Rennes	h	1-0	*Jeleń*
23/2	Lille	a	2-1	*Contout 2*
6/3	Valenciennes	h	1-0	*Jeleń*
10/3	Bordeaux	a	2-1	*Jeleń 2*
13/3	Montpellier	a	1-1	*Oliech*
20/3	Le Mans	h	2-1	*Jeleń, Pedretti*
29/3	Monaco	a	0-0	
4/4	PSG	h	1-1	*Niculae*
11/4	Nancy	a	1-0	*Niculae*
17/4	Lorient	h	4-1	*Oliech, Jeleń, Birsa, Hengbart (p)*
25/4	Toulouse	a	3-0	*Pedretti, Jeleń 2*
30/4	Marseille	h	0-0	
5/5	Lyon	a	1-2	*Jeleń*
8/5	Lens	h	0-0	
15/5	Sochaux	a	2-1	*Hengbart 2*

No	Name	Nat	DoB	Pos	Aps	(s)	Gls
23	Jérémy BERTHOD		24/4/84	D	13	(6)	
9	Valter BIRSA	SVN	7/8/86	A	24	(11)	3
25	Maxime BOURGEOIS		3/2/91	A		(5)	
11	Aurélien CAPOUE		28/2/82	M	16	(5)	
7	Kamel CHAFNI	MAR	11/6/82	M	16	(9)	

No	Name	Nat	DoB	Pos	Aps	(s)	Gls
18	Roy CONTOUT		11/2/85	M	18	(15)	3
6	Adama COULIBALY	MLI	9/10/80	D	33		1
5	Dariusz DUDKA	POL	9/12/83	D	17	(2)	
4	Stéphane GRICHTING	SUI	30/3/79	D	37		
2	Cédric HENGBART		13/7/80	D	37		5
22	Ireneusz JELEŃ	POL	9/4/81	A	28	(1)	14
13	Kévin LEJEUNE		22/1/85	A	1	(7)	1
32	Kevin MALAGA		24/6/87	D		(1)	
12	Jean-Pascal MIGNOT		26/2/81	D	28	(4)	1
3	Moussa NARRY	GHA	19/4/86	M	2	(1)	
29	Delvin NDINGA	CGO	3/4/88	M	23	(3)	1
21	Daniel NICULAE	ROU	6/10/82	A	28	(5)	4
14	Dennis OLIECH	KEN	2/2/85	A	23	(10)	4
17	Benoît PEDRETTI		12/11/80	M	36		4
11	Julien QUERCIA		17/8/86	A		(10)	
16	Rémy RIOU		6/8/87	G	3		
19	Yaya SANOGO		27/1/93	A		(1)	
1	Olivier SORIN		16/4/81	G	35		
27	Alain TRAORÉ	BFA	31/12/88	M		(1)	

FC GIRONDINS DE BORDEAUX

Coach – Laurent Blanc
Founded – 1881
Stadium – Stade Chaban-Delmas (34,198)
MAJOR HONOURS:
French League – (6) 1950, 1984, 1985, 1987, 1999, 2009;
French Cup – (3) 1941, 1986, 1987;
League Cup – (3) 2002, 2007, 2009.

2009

Date	Opp		Score	Scorers
9/8	Lens	h	4-1	Wendel, Gourcuff 2, Chamakh
15/8	Sochaux	a	3-2	Chamakh 2, og (Stevanović)
23/8	Nice	h	4-0	Jussié, Gourcuff 2, Diarra
30/8	Marseille	a	0-0	
12/9	Grenoble	h	1-0	Gouffran
19/9	Boulogne	a	2-0	Gouffran, og (Lachor)
27/9	Rennes	h	1-0	Wendel
3/10	St-Étienne	a	1-3	Jussié (p)
17/10	Auxerre	a	0-1	
24/10	Le Mans	h	3-0	og (Ovono), Chamakh, Bellion
31/10	Monaco	h	1-0	Planus
8/11	Lille	a	0-2	
21/11	Valenciennes	h	0-1	
29/11	Nancy	a	3-0	Fernando, Wendel, Gouffran
5/12	PSG	h	1-0	Plašil
13/12	Lyon	a	1-0	Chamakh
16/12	Montpellier	a	1-0	Jussié
19/12	Lorient	h	4-1	Bellion 2, Cavenaghi, Gourcuff
23/12	Toulouse	a	2-1	Chamakh, Wendel

2010

Date	Opp		Score	Scorers
17/1	Marseille	h	1-1	og (Mandanda)
20/1	Grenoble	a	3-1	Gouffran, Chamakh, Cavenaghi
30/1	Boulogne	h	0-0	
6/2	Rennes	a	2-4	Gouffran, Wendel
14/2	St-Étienne	h	3-1	Chamakh, Wendel 2
7/3	Montpellier	h	1-1	Chamakh
10/3	Auxerre	h	1-2	Trémoulinas
13/3	Monaco	a	0-0	
21/3	Lille	h	3-1	Ciani, Jussié (p), Gourcuff
3/4	Nancy	h	1-2	Cavenaghi
10/4	PSG	a	1-3	Sané
14/4	Le Mans	a	1-2	Henrique
17/4	Lyon	h	2-2	Chamakh, Plašil
24/4	Lorient	a	0-1	
28/4	Valenciennes	a	0-2	
2/5	Toulouse	h	1-0	Ciani
5/5	Nice	a	1-1	Wendel
8/5	Sochaux	h	2-0	Wendel (p), Trémoulinas
15/5	Lens	a	3-4	Wendel 2 (2p), og (Bedimo)

No	Name	Nat	DoB	Pos	Aps	(s)	Gls
11	David BELLION		27/11/82	A	6	(14)	3
1	Cédric CARRASSO		30/12/81	G	29		
9	Fernando CAVENAGHI	ARG	21/9/83	A	14	(16)	3
21	Mathieu CHALMÉ		7/10/80	D	33		
29	Marouane CHAMAKH	MAR	10/1/84	A	32	(6)	10
2	Michaël CIANI		6/4/84	D	29	(1)	2
4	Alou DIARRA		15/7/81	M	30		1
5	FERNANDO Menegazzo	BRA	3/5/81	M	20	(9)	1
7	Yoan GOUFFRAN		25/5/86	A	22	(10)	5
8	Yoann GOURCUFF		11/7/86	M	26	(3)	6
3	Carlos HENRIQUE dos Santos Souza	BRA	2/5/83	D	11	(2)	1
6	Franck JURIETTI		30/3/75	D	2	(1)	
10	JUSSIÉ Ferreira Vieira	BRA	19/9/83	A	13	(17)	4
30	Abdoulaye KEITA		16/8/90	G		(1)	
13	Diego PLACENTE	ARG	24/4/77	D	3		
27	Marc PLANUS		7/3/82	D	26		1
18	Jaroslav PLAŠIL	CZE	5/1/82	M	27	(7)	2
16	Ulrich RAMÉ		19/9/72	G	9	(1)	
20	Henri SAIVET		26/10/90	A	1	(2)	
25	Ludovic SANÉ		22/3/87	D	14	(3)	1
22	Grégory SERTIC		5/8/89	M	7	(5)	
24	Abdou TRAORÉ	MLI	17/1/88	M	4	(6)	
28	Benoît TRÉMOULINAS		28/12/85	D	35		2
17	WENDEL Geraldo Maurício da Silva	BRA	8/4/82	M	25	(6)	11

US BOULOGNE CO

Coach – Laurent Guyot
Founded – 1898
Stadium – Stade de la Libération (15,004)

2009

Date	Opp		Score	Scorers
8/8	Rennes	a	0-3	
16/8	Grenoble	h	2-1	Thil 2
22/8	St-Étienne	a	1-0	Cuvillier
29/8	Auxerre	h	0-0	
12/9	Valenciennes	a	1-1	Moreira
19/9	Bordeaux	h	0-2	
26/9	Montpellier	a	0-1	
4/10	Lille	h	2-3	Dembélé, Blayac
17/10	Le Mans	a	1-1	Robert
24/10	Monaco	a	1-3	Blayac
31/10	Nancy	h	1-2	Cuvillier
7/11	Lorient	a	0-5	
28/11	Toulouse	a	0-1	
2/12	PSG	h	2-5	Ducatel, Ramaré (p)
6/12	Lens	h	2-1	Karuru, og (Sartre)
12/12	Marseille	a	0-2	
16/12	Lyon	a	0-2	
23/12	Nice	a	2-2	Perrinelle, Blayac

2010

Date	Opp		Score	Scorers
13/1	Sochaux	h	0-0	
16/1	Auxerre	a	0-0	
20/1	Valenciennes	h	0-2	
30/1	Bordeaux	a	0-0	
6/2	Montpellier	h	0-2	
13/2	Lille	a	1-3	Adefemi
20/2	Le Mans	h	1-3	Yatabaré
27/2	Monaco	a	0-1	
6/3	Nancy	h	0-0	
13/3	Nancy	a	3-1	Agouazi, Moussilou, Cuvillier
20/3	Lorient	h	2-0	Marcq, og (Koscielny)
28/3	PSG	a	0-3	
4/4	Toulouse	h	1-1	Kapo
10/4	Lens	a	0-3	
17/4	Marseille	h	1-2	Blayac
24/4	Sochaux	a	3-0	Thil, Yatabaré, Blayac
2/5	Nice	h	3-3	Blayac, Kapo, Cuvillier
5/5	St-Étienne	h	0-1	
8/5	Grenoble	a	0-2	
15/5	Rennes	h	1-0	Thil (p)

No	Name	Nat	DoB	Pos	Aps	(s)	Gls
13	Olubayo ADEFEMI	NGA	13/8/85	D	11	(2)	1
4	Laurent AGOUAZI		16/3/84	M	20	(5)	1
1	Florian BAGUE		27/7/84	G	1		
30	Jean-François BÉDENIK		2/11/78	G	25		
31	Habib BELLAÏD	ALG	28/3/86	D	9		
14	Jérémy BLAYAC		13/6/83	A	14	(8)	6
12	Guillaume BORNE		12/2/88	D	16	(1)	
27	Lakhdar BOUSSAHA		18/7/87	A	1	(1)	
19	Alexandre CUVILLIER		17/6/86	M	28	(6)	4
9	Frédéric DA ROCHA		16/9/74	M	18	(12)	
6	Kévin DAS NEVES		8/5/86	D	8		
23	Bira DEMBÉLÉ		22/3/88	D	15	(7)	1
11	Guillaume DUCATEL		21/1/79	M	19	(8)	1
20	Olivier KAPO		27/9/80	M	15	(1)	2
15	Ovidy KARURU	ZIM	23/1/89	M	9	(5)	1
16	Ibrahim KONÉ	CIV	5/12/89	G	3		
3	Yoann LACHOR		17/1/76	D	29		
22	Antony LECOINTE		5/10/80	D	19	(3)	
21	Dorian LEVÊQUE		22/11/89	M	6		
26	Juan Gonzalo LORCA	CHI	15/1/85	A	2	(2)	
25	Damien MARCQ		8/12/88	D	33	(1)	1
7	Daniel MOREIRA		8/8/77	A	4	(2)	1
20	Matt MOUSSILOU		1/6/82	A	8	(7)	1
28	Mame N'DIAYE	SEN	11/1/86	M	4		
5	Damien PERRINELLE		12/9/83	D	8	(3)	1
2	Nicolas RABUEL		15/1/78	D	23		
8	Johann RAMARÉ		5/6/84	M	6	(11)	1
17	Fabien ROBERT		6/1/89	A	3	(13)	1
18	Bakary SOUMARÉ	MLI	9/11/85	D	18	(2)	
10	Grégory THIL		15/3/80	A	12	(3)	4
29	Zargo TOURÉ	SEN	11/11/89	M	13	(1)	
40	Matthieu VALVERDE		14/5/83	G	9		
32	Mustapha YATABARÉ	MLI	26/1/86	A	9	(8)	2

GRENOBLE FOOT 38
Coach – Mehmed Baždarević (BIH)
Founded – 1997
Stadium – Stade des Alpes (20,068)

2009

8/8	Marseille	h	0-2	
16/8	Boulogne	a	1-2	Ljuboja
23/8	Lens	h	1-2	Ljuboja
29/8	St-Étienne	a	0-1	
12/9	Bordeaux	a	0-1	
19/9	Rennes	h	0-4	
26/9	Auxerre	a	0-2	
3/10	Montpellier	h	2-3	Ljuboja, Dieuze
17/10	Valenciennes	a	0-2	
24/10	Nancy	h	1-2	Ljuboja
31/10	Lille	h	0-2	
7/11	Monaco	a	0-0	
21/11	Lyon	h	1-1	Ljuboja
28/11	Lorient	a	2-2	Matsui, Juan
6/12	Toulouse	h	1-0	Dieuze
13/12	Sochaux	a	0-1	
16/12	Le Mans	a	0-1	
19/12	Nice	h	1-1	Dieuze
23/12	PSG	a	0-4	

2010

16/1	St-Étienne	h	1-2	og (Varrault)
20/1	Bordeaux	h	1-3	Batlles
30/1	Rennes	a	0-4	
6/2	Auxerre	h	5-0	Ljuboja, Akrour 2, Matsui 2
13/2	Montpellier	a	0-1	
20/2	Valenciennes	h	0-1	
27/2	Nancy	a	2-0	Ravet 2
7/3	Le Mans	h	1-1	Akrour
14/3	Lille	a	0-1	
20/3	Monaco	h	0-0	
27/3	Lyon	a	0-2	

3/4	Lorient	h	1-2	Akrour
10/4	Toulouse	a	0-4	
17/4	Sochaux	h	2-2	Ljuboja, Matsui
24/4	Nice	a	1-2	Akrour
27/4	PSG	h	4-0	Batlles, Dieuze, Akrour, Ljuboja
5/5	Lens	a	1-1	Courtois
8/5	Boulogne	h	2-0	Ljuboja 2
15/5	Marseille	a	0-2	

No	Name	Nat	DoB	Pos	Aps	(s)	Gls
17	Nassim AKROUR	ALG	10/7/74	A	26	(12)	6
10	Laurent BATLLES		23/9/75	M	33	(1)	2
33	Mehdi BOURABIA		7/8/91	M		(2)	
19	Pierre BOYA	CMR	16/1/84	A	10	(7)	
21	Jean CALVÉ		30/4/84	D	20	(4)	
12	Boštjan CESAR	SVN	9/7/82	D	25		
25	Hugo CIANCI		9/6/89	D	2	(6)	
2	Laurent COURTOIS		11/9/78	M	23	(4)	1
7	Nicolas DIEUZE		7/2/79	M	27	(5)	4
8	Sofiane FEGHOULI		26/12/89	M	4	(1)	
20	Sho ITO	JPN	24/7/88	A		(1)	
14	David JEMMALI	TUN	13/12/74	D	8		
21	Jimmy JUAN		10/6/83	M	11	(7)	1
31	Mustafa KUCUKOVIC	GER	5/11/86	A		(4)	
30	Ronan LE CROM		13/7/74	G	15	(1)	
28	Danijel LJUBOJA	SRB	4/9/76	A	30	(4)	10
18	Laurent MACQUET		11/8/79	M	6	(1)	
29	Jimmy MAINFROI		28/3/83	D	10	(4)	
4	François MARQUE		31/7/83	D	5	(1)	
22	Daisuke MATSUI	JPN	11/5/81	M	25	(4)	4
16	Brice MAUBLEU		1/12/89	G	2		
3	Sandy PAILLOT		27/2/87	D	16		
26	Yoric RAVET		12/9/89	M	5	(11)	2
15	Zoran RENDULIĆ	SRB	22/5/84	D	5	(4)	
5	Martial ROBIN		27/8/77	M	14	(3)	
6	Alaixys ROMAO	TOG	18/1/84	M	29		
23	David SAUGET		23/11/79	D	25	(2)	
33	Saphir SLITI TAÏDER		29/2/92	M	1		
9	Josip TADIĆ	CRO	22/8/87	A	6	(8)	
28	Jonathan TINHAN		1/6/89	M		(6)	
27	Milivoje VITAKIĆ	SRB	16/5/77	D	14	(1)	
1	Jody VIVIANI		25/1/82	G	21		

LE MANS UC 72
Coach – Paulo Duarte (POR); (10/12/09) Arnaud Cormier
Founded – 1985
Stadium – Stade Léon-Bollée (16,674)

2009

8/8	Lyon	h	2-2	Maïga, Coutadeur (p)
15/8	PSG	a	1-3	Helstad
22/8	Nancy	h	2-1	Helstad, Le Tallec
29/8	Lorient	a	0-1	
12/9	Marseille	h	1-2	Maïga
20/9	Toulouse	a	0-2	
27/9	Lens	h	3-0	Thomas 2, Le Tallec
3/10	Sochaux	a	0-1	
17/10	Boulogne	h	1-1	Lamah
24/10	Bordeaux	a	0-3	
1/11	Nice	a	0-1	
7/11	Auxerre	h	0-1	
21/11	Rennes	a	1-2	Lamah
29/11	St-Étienne	h	1-1	Le Tallec
5/12	Montpellier	a	1-2	Le Tallec
12/12	Valenciennes	h	2-1	Corchia, Le Tallec
16/12	Grenoble	h	1-0	Helstad
20/12	Lille	a	0-3	
23/12	Monaco	h	1-1	Le Tallec

2010

16/1	Lorient	h	0-3	
20/1	Marseille	a	1-2	Le Tallec
30/1	Toulouse	h	1-3	Ouali

6/2	Lens	a	1-2	*Maïga*
13/2	Sochaux	h	0-0	
20/2	Boulogne	a	3-1	*Dossevi, Cerdan, Maïga*
7/3	Grenoble	a	1-1	*Maïga*
13/3	Nice	h	0-1	
20/3	Auxerre	a	1-2	*Helstad*
28/3	Rennes	h	1-3	*Dossevi*
3/4	St-Étienne	a	0-2	
10/4	Montpellier	h	2-2	*Lamah 2*
14/4	Bordeaux	h	2-1	*Le Tallec, Dossevi*
17/4	Valenciennes	a	1-0	*Corchia*
24/4	Lille	h	1-2	*Maïga*
27/4	Monaco	a	1-1	*Dossevi*
5/5	Nancy	a	2-3	*Maïga, Dossevi*
8/5	PSG	h	1-0	*og (Armand)*
15/5	Lyon	a	0-2	

No	Name	Nat	DoB	Pos	Aps	(s)	Gls
27	Almen ABDI	SUI	21/10/86	M	9	(4)	
23	João Paulo ANDRADE	POR	6/6/81	D	18	(2)	
24	Ludovic BAAL		24/5/86	M	35	(3)	
3	Saber BEN FREJ	TUN	3/7/79	D		(1)	
18	Samuel BOUHOURS		26/6/87	D	5		
29	Ibrahima CAMARA	GUI	1/7/85	D	3		
5	Grégory CERDAN		28/7/82	D	30		1
33	Fousseyni CISSÉ		17/7/89	A	3	(7)	
28	Sébastien CORCHIA		1/11/90	D	31	(4)	2
22	Mathieu COUTADEUR		20/6/86	M	4		1
14	Mathieu DOSSEVI		12/2/88	M	19	(12)	5
11	Marcelo Alejandro ESTIGARRIBIA	PAR	21/9/87	M	1	(4)	
2	António Malta Camila GÉDER	BRA	23/4/78	D	14		
	Pierre GIBAUD		22/4/88	D		(1)	
26	Darry Herold GOULON		12/6/88	M	22	(4)	
22	Thorstein HELSTAD	NOR	28/4/77	A	15	(16)	4
15	Alphousseyni KEITA	MLI	13/11/85	M	5	(2)	
25	Roland LAMAH	BEL	31/12/87	A	22	(9)	4
39	Guy-Michel LANDEL	GUI	3/7/90	M		(1)	
10	Anthony LE TALLEC		3/10/84	A	33	(3)	8
21	Guillaume LORIOT		21/5/86	M	18	(3)	
13	Cyriaque LOUVION		24/7/87	D	17	(2)	
9	Modibo MAÏGA	MLI	3/9/86	A	23	(9)	7
30	Giorgi MAKARIDZE	GEO	31/3/90	G	2		
21	MARCOS PAULO Gelmini Gomes	BRA	13/7/88	M	3		
3	Moussa NARRY	GHA	19/4/86	M	12		
6	Idir OUALI		21/5/88	M	2	(8)	1
1	Didier OVONO	GAB	23/1/83	G	32		
16	Rodolphe ROCHE		14/6/79	G	4		
19	Badara SÈNE	SEN	19/11/84	M	1	(4)	
7	Fredrik STRØMSTAD	NOR	20/1/82	M		(3)	
8	Frédéric THOMAS		10/8/80	M	30		2
11	Olivier THOMERT		28/3/80	A	4		
33	Mamadou WAGUE		19/8/90	M	1	(1)	

RC LENS

Coach – Jean-Guy Wallemme
Founded – 1906
Stadium – Félix-Bollaert (41,233)
MAJOR HONOURS:
French League – (1) 1998;
League Cup – (1) 1999.

2009

9/8	Bordeaux	a	1-4	*Jemaa*
15/8	Auxerre	h	2-0	*Monnet-Paquet, Boukari*
23/8	Grenoble	a	2-1	*Eduardo, Boukari*
29/8	Rennes	h	2-2	*Demont (p), Jemaa*
12/9	Montpellier	a	0-1	
20/9	Lille	h	1-1	*Boukari*
27/9	Le Mans	a	0-3	
3/10	Lyon	h	0-2	

18/10	Monaco	a	0-2	
25/10	Toulouse	h	0-2	
31/10	Lorient	h	1-1	*Eduardo*
7/11	Sochaux	a	2-1	*Sartre, Boukari*
21/11	Nancy	h	2-1	*Jemaa, Monnet-Pacquet*
28/11	Marseille	h	1-0	*Eduardo*
6/12	Boulogne	a	1-2	*og (Dembélé)*
12/12	Nice	h	2-0	*Akalé, Maoulida*
16/12	PSG	a	1-1	*Maoulida*
19/12	Valenciennes	a	0-0	
22/12	St-Étienne	h	1-0	*Eduardo (p)*
2010				
16/1	Rennes	a	1-1	*Monnet-Pacquet*
20/1	Montpellier	h	0-1	
30/1	Lille	a	0-1	
6/2	Le Mans	h	2-1	*Monnet-Pacquet, Eduardo*
13/2	Lyon	a	0-1	
20/2	Monaco	h	3-0	*Jemaa, Roudet, Bedimo (p)*
27/2	Toulouse	a	0-1	
6/3	PSG	h	1-1	*Roudet*
13/3	Lorient	a	0-1	
20/3	Sochaux	h	0-0	
28/3	Nancy	a	1-5	*Jemaa*
4/4	Marseille	a	0-1	
10/4	Boulogne	h	3-0	*Maoulida 3*
17/4	Nice	a	0-0	
24/4	Valenciennes	h	1-1	*Roudet*
2/5	St-Étienne	a	4-1	*Akalé, Jemaa, Maoulida 2*
5/5	Grenoble	h	1-1	*Maoulida*
8/5	Auxerre	a	0-0	
15/5	Bordeaux	h	4-3	*Maoulida 2, Sow, Jemaa (p)*

No	Name	Nat	DoB	Pos	Aps	(s)	Gls
28	Kanga AKALÉ	CIV	7/3/81	M	17	(11)	2
33	Serge AURIER		5/12/93	M	5		
6	Henri BEDIMO	CMR	4/6/84	D	12	(3)	1
7	Razak BOUKARI	TOG	25/4/87	M	20	(7)	4
24	Éric CHELLE	MLI	11/11/77	D	31		
26	Yohan DEMONT		15/5/78	M	37		1
11	EDUARDO Ribeiro dos Santos	BRA	5/8/80	A	18	(13)	5
20	Adil HERMACH	MAR	27/6/86	D	30	(4)	
22	Issam JEMAA	TUN	28/1/84	A	18	(11)	7
25	Steven JOSEPH-MONROSE		20/7/90	M		(2)	
16	Hamdi KASRAOUI	TUN	18/1/83	G	6		
23	Nenad KOVAČEVIĆ	SRB	11/11/80	M	24	(2)	
15	Fabien LAURENTI		6/1/83	D	3	(2)	
9	Toifilou MAOULIDA		8/6/79	A	11	(13)	10
10	Dejan MILOVANOVIĆ	SRB	21/1/84	M	8	(8)	
14	Kévin MONNET-PACQUET		19/8/88	A	23	(9)	4
2	Marco RAMOS	POR	26/4/83	D	27	(3)	
18	Sébastien ROUDET		16/6/81	M	28	(2)	3
1	Vedran RUNJE	CRO	10/2/76	G	32		
19	Romain SARTRE		12/11/82	D	12	(6)	1
27	Samba SOW	MLI	29/4/89	M	22	(9)	1
34	Alassane TOURÉ		9/2/89	D		(1)	
5	Alaeddine YAHIA	TUN	26/9/81	D	34		

LOSC LILLE MÉTROPOLE

Coach – Rudi Garcia
Founded – 1944
Stadium – Stadium Lille Métropole (21,803)
MAJOR HONOURS:
French League - (2) 1946, 1954;
French Cup - (5) 1946, 1947, 1948, 1953, 1955.

2009

9/8	Lorient	h	1-2	*og (Monterrubio)*
16/8	Marseille	a	0-1	
23/8	Toulouse	h	1-1	*Vittek*
30/8	PSG	a	0-3	
12/9	Sochaux	h	1-0	*Frau*
20/9	Lens	a	1-1	*Rami*

27/9	Nice	h	1-1	*Frau*
4/10	Boulogne	a	3-2	*Gervinho, Frau 2*
17/10	Rennes	h	0-0	
25/10	Auxerre	a	2-3	*Gervinho, Frau*
31/10	Grenoble	a	2-0	*Cabaye, Gervinho*
8/11	Bordeaux	h	2-0	*Cabaye, Balmont (p)*
22/11	Montpellier	a	0-2	
28/11	Valenciennes	h	4-0	*Frau, Gervinho 2, Cabaye (p)*
6/12	Lyon	h	4-3	*Frau, Gervinho 2, Cabaye (p)*
10/12	St-Étienne	h	4-0	*Frau, Cabaye (p), Gervinho, Rami*
13/12	Monaco	a	4-0	*Túlio de Melo 2, Cabaye (p), Aubameyang*
20/12	Le Mans	h	3-0	*Chedjou, Gervinho, Hazard*
23/12	Nancy	a	4-0	*Hazard, Gervinho 2, Frau (p)*
2010				
16/1	PSG	h	3-1	*Obraniak, Balmont, Béria*
20/1	Sochaux	a	1-2	*Vittek*
30/1	Lens	h	1-0	*Hazard*
6/2	Nice	a	1-1	*Túlio de Melo*
13/2	Boulogne	h	3-1	*Obraniak 2, Rami*
21/2	Rennes	a	2-1	*Frau, Aubameyang*
28/2	Auxerre	h	1-2	*Hazard*
6/3	St-Étienne	a	1-1	*Dumont*
14/3	Grenoble	h	1-0	*og (Cesar)*
21/3	Bordeaux	a	1-3	*Hazard*
28/3	Montpellier	h	4-1	*Gervinho, Cabaye (p), Frau, Touré*
3/4	Valenciennes	a	0-1	
11/4	Lyon	a	1-1	*Frau*
18/4	Monaco	h	4-0	*Chedjou, Cabaye 2 (1p), Túlio de Melo*
24/4	Le Mans	a	2-1	*Túlio de Melo, Cabaye (p)*
2/5	Nancy	h	3-1	*Cabaye, Gervinho, Frau*
5/5	Toulouse	a	2-0	*Cabaye, Obraniak*
8/5	Marseille	h	3-2	*Cabaye (p), Túlio de Melo, Debuchy*
15/5	Lorient	a	1-2	*Ricardo Costa*

No	Name	Nat	DoB	Pos	Aps	(s)	Gls
11	Pierre-Emerick AUBAMEYANG	GAB	18/6/89	A	4	(10)	2
4	Florent BALMONT		2/2/80	M	35		2
18	Franck BÉRIA		23/5/83	D	31	(2)	1
1	Ludovic BUTELLE		3/4/83	G	10		
7	Yohan CABAYE		14/1/86	M	30	(2)	13
22	Aurélien CHEDJOU	CMR	20/6/85	M	28	(3)	2
2	Mathieu DEBUCHY		28/7/85	M	30	(1)	1
29	Stéphane DUMONT		6/9/82	M	9	(14)	1
15	EMERSON da Conceição	BRA	23/2/86	D	14	(9)	
17	Pierre-Alain FRAU		15/4/80	A	25	(9)	13
27	Gervais Yao Kouassi "GERVINHO"	CIV	27/5/87	A	28	(4)	13
26	Eden HAZARD	BEL	7/1/91	M	31	(6)	5
16	Michaël LANDREAU		14/5/79	G	28		
24	Rio MAVUBA		8/3/84	M	34	(1)	
10	Ludovic OBRANIAK	POL	10/11/84	M	17	(12)	4
25	Nicolas PLESTAN		2/6/81	D	5		
23	Adil RAMI		27/12/85	D	34		3
8	RICARDO Miguel Moreira da COSTA	POR	16/5/81	D	9	(1)	1
35	Arnaud SOUQUET		12/2/92	M	1		
20	Larsen TOURÉ	GUI	20/7/84	A	1	(13)	1
9	TÚLIO Vinícius Fróes DE MELO	BRA	31/1/85	A	9	(11)	6
3	Jerry VANDAM		8/12/88	M	1	(7)	
14	Róbert VITTEK	SVK	1/4/82	A	4	(8)	2

FC LORIENT

Coach – Christian Gourcuff
Founded – 1926
Stadium – Stade du Moustoir (15,870)
MAJOR HONOURS:
French Cup – (1) 2002.

2009				
9/8	Lille	a	2-1	*Gameiro, Vahirua*
15/8	Montpellier	h	2-2	*Gameiro, Koscielny*
22/8	Monaco	a	0-2	
29/8	Le Mans	h	1-0	*Vahirua*
12/9	Lyon	a	0-1	
19/9	Nancy	h	3-1	*Diarra, Gameiro, Monterrubio (p)*
26/9	PSG	h	1-1	*Mvuemba*
4/10	Toulouse	a	1-0	*Monterrubio (p)*
18/10	Nice	h	4-1	*Mvuemba, Vahirua, Diarra, Gameiro*
24/10	Sochaux	a	0-1	
31/10	Lens	h	1-1	*Sosa*
7/11	Boulogne	h	5-0	*Gameiro 2, Vahirua 2, Amalfitano*
22/11	St-Étienne	a	2-0	*Vahirua, Sosa*
28/11	Grenoble	h	2-2	*og (Cesar), Gameiro*
5/12	Rennes	a	0-1	
12/12	Auxerre	h	0-0	
16/12	Marseille	h	1-2	*Vahirua (p)*
19/12	Bordeaux	a	1-4	*Gameiro*
23/12	Valenciennes	h	3-2	*Amalfitano 2, Sosa*
2010				
16/1	Le Mans	a	3-0	*Koscielny, Monterrubio 2*
20/1	Lyon	h	1-3	*Ducasse*
30/1	Nancy	a	0-1	
6/2	PSG	a	3-0	*Vahirua (p), Gameiro, Amalfitano*
14/2	Toulouse	h	1-1	*Gameiro*
20/2	Nice	a	0-1	
27/2	Sochaux	h	1-0	*Diarra*
7/3	Marseille	a	1-1	*Koscielny*
13/3	Lens	h	1-0	*Marchal*
20/3	Boulogne	a	0-2	
28/3	St-Étienne	h	4-0	*Amalfitano, Gameiro 2, Dubarbier*
3/4	Grenoble	a	2-1	*Gameiro, Fanchone*
10/4	Rennes	h	1-1	*Diarra*
17/4	Auxerre	a	1-4	*Gameiro*
24/4	Bordeaux	h	1-0	*Gameiro*
2/5	Valenciennes	a	0-0	
5/5	Monaco	h	2-2	*Amalfitano, Gameiro*
8/5	Montpellier	a	1-2	*Bourillon*
15/5	Lille	h	2-1	*Gameiro, Jouffre*

No	Name	Nat	DoB	Pos	Aps	(s)	Gls
18	Morgan AMALFITANO		20/3/85	M	37		6
16	Fabien AUDARD		28/3/78	G	35		
17	Maxime BACA		2/6/83	D	12	(3)	
22	Maxime BARTHELME		8/9/88	M		(1)	
6	Grégory BOURILLON		1/7/84	D	8	(2)	1
1	Lionel CAPPONE		8/2/79	G	3		
11	Sigamary DIARRA		10/1/84	A	33	(5)	4
13	Sebastián DUBARBIER	ARG	19/2/86	A	6	(6)	1
19	Pierre DUCASSE		7/5/87	M	27	(3)	1
12	James FANCHONE		21/2/90	A	6	(18)	1
9	Kevin GAMEIRO		9/5/87	A	34	(1)	17
5	Benjamin GENTON		20/5/80	D	3	(5)	
8	Yann JOUFFRE		23/7/84	M	3	(5)	1
4	Laurent KOSCIELNY		10/9/85	D	35		3
14	Arnaud LE LAN		22/3/78	D	17	(3)	
23	Yazid MANSOURI	ALG	25/2/78	M	9	(11)	
29	Sylvain MARCHAL		10/2/80	D	31		1
10	Olivier MONTERRUBIO		8/8/76	M	7	(12)	4
15	Jérémy MOREL		2/4/84	D	18	(1)	

7	Arnold MVUEMBA		28/1/85	M	34	(3)	2
6	Gabriel PEÑALBA	ARG	23/9/84	M	2	(6)	
25	Jonas SAKUWAHA	ZAM	22/7/83	M	1	(13)	
2	Franco Sebastián SOSA	ARG	4/4/81	D	29		3
19	Marama VAHIRUA		12/5/80	A	28	(4)	8

OLYMPIQUE LYONNAIS
Coach – Claude Puel
Founded – 1950
Stadium – Stade de Gerland (43,051)
MAJOR HONOURS:
French League - (7) 2002, 2003, 2004, 2005, 2006, 2007, 2008;
French Cup - (4) 1964, 1967, 1973, 2008;
League Cup - (1) 2001.

2009

8/8	Le Mans	a	2-2	Bodmer, Lisandro López
15/8	Valenciennes	h	1-0	Gomis
22/8	Auxerre	a	3-0	Boumsong, Makoun, Pjanić
29/8	Nancy	h	3-1	Gomis, Lisandro López, Michel Bastos
12/9	Lorient	h	1-0	Michel Bastos
20/9	PSG	a	1-1	Gomis
26/9	Toulouse	h	2-1	Tafer, Gomis
3/10	Lens	a	2-0	Govou, Källström
17/10	Sochaux	h	0-2	
24/10	Nice	a	1-4	Ederson
31/10	St-Étienne	a	1-0	Gomis
8/11	Marseille	h	5-5	Pjanić, Govou, Lisandro López 2 (1p), Michel Bastos
21/11	Grenoble	a	1-1	Delgado
29/11	Rennes	h	1-1	Lisandro López
6/12	Lille	a	3-4	Lisandro López 3 (1p)
13/12	Bordeaux	h	0-1	
16/12	Boulogne	h	2-0	Pjanić, Delgado
20/12	Monaco	a	1-1	Michel Bastos
23/12	Montpellier	h	1-2	Gomis

2010

16/1	Nancy	a	2-0	Cris, Gonalons
20/1	Lorient	a	3-1	Lisandro López, Källström 2
31/1	PSG	h	2-1	Gomis, Cris
7/2	Toulouse	a	0-0	
13/2	Lens	h	1-0	Delgado
21/2	Sochaux	a	4-0	Michel Bastos 3, Lisandro López
27/2	Nice	h	2-0	Lisandro López, og (Apam)
6/3	Boulogne	a	0-0	
13/3	St-Étienne	h	1-1	Lisandro López
21/3	Marseille	a	1-2	Gomis
27/3	Grenoble	h	2-0	Michel Bastos, Delgado
3/4	Rennes	a	2-1	Michel Bastos, Lisandro López
11/4	Lille	h	1-1	Cris
17/4	Bordeaux	a	2-2	Ederson, Cris
2/5	Montpellier	a	1-0	Michel Bastos
5/5	Auxerre	h	2-1	Lisandro López (p), Pjanić
8/5	Valenciennes	a	2-2	Källström, og (Baldé)
12/5	Monaco	h	3-0	Pjanić, Gomis, Lisandro López
15/5	Le Mans	h	2-0	Gomis, Pjanić

No	Name	Nat	DoB	Pos	Aps	(s)	Gls
39	Ishak BELFODIL		12/1/92	A		(3)	
5	Mathieu BODMER		22/11/82	D	10	(4)	1
4	Jean-Alain BOUMSONG		14/12/79	D	19		1
20	Aly CISSOKHO		15/9/87	D	31		
2	François CLERC		18/4/83	D	5	(2)	
3	CRIStiano Marques Gomes	BRA	3/6/77	D	34		4
19	César DELGADO	ARG	18/8/81	A	13	(14)	4
10	EDERSON Honorato Campos	BRA	13/1/86	M	11	(13)	2
32	Lamine GASSAMA		20/10/89	D	5	(1)	
18	Bafétimbi GOMIS		6/8/85	A	22	(15)	10
41	Maxime GONALONS		10/3/89	M	12	(3)	1
14	Sidney GOVOU		27/7/79	A	22	(8)	2
22	Clément GRENIER		7/1/91	M		(3)	

11	Fabio GROSSO	ITA	28/11/77	D	1		
6	Kim KÄLLSTRÖM	SWE	24/8/82	M	28	(4)	4
12	Timothée KOLODZIEJCZAK		1/10/91	D	1	(1)	
38	Alexandre LACAZETTE		28/5/91	A		(1)	
9	LISANDRO LÓPEZ	ARG	2/3/83	A	27	(6)	15
1	Hugo LLORIS		26/12/86	G	36		
26	Dejan LOVREN	CRO	5/7/89	D	8		
17	Jean II MAKOUN	CMR	29/5/83	M	25	(3)	1
7	MICHEL Fernandes BASTOS	BRA	2/8/83	M	22	(10)	10
27	Anthony MOUNIER		27/9/87	M	1		
8	Miralem PJANIĆ	BIH	2/4/90	M	27	(10)	6
13	Anthony RÉVEILLÈRE		10/11/79	D	29	(1)	
29	Yannis TAFER		11/2/91	A		(7)	1
28	Jérémy TOULALAN		10/9/83	M	27	(4)	
30	Rémy VERCOUTRE		26/6/80	G	2		

OLYMPIQUE DE MARSEILLE
Coach – Didier Deschamps
Founded – 1899
Stadium – Stade Vélodrome (60,031)
MAJOR HONOURS:
UEFA Champions League – (1) 1993;
French League – (9) 1937, 1948, 1971, 1972, 1989, 1990, 1991, 1992, 2010;
French Cup - (10) 1924, 1926, 1927, 1935, 1938, 1943, 1969, 1972, 1976, 1989;
League Cup – (1) 2010.

2009

8/8	Grenoble	a	2-0	Niang, Cheyrou
16/8	Lille	h	1-0	Brandão
22/8	Rennes	a	1-1	Niang
30/8	Bordeaux	h	0-0	
12/9	Le Mans	a	2-1	Niang, Brandão
19/9	Montpellier	h	4-2	Lucho González, Niang, Cissé, Diawara
26/9	Valenciennes	a	2-3	Morientes, Niang
4/10	Monaco	h	1-2	Niang
17/10	Nancy	a	3-0	Valbuena, Brandão, Abriel
31/10	Toulouse	h	1-1	Brandão
8/11	Lyon	a	5-5	Diawara, Cheyrou, Koné, Brandão, og (Toulalan)
20/11	PSG	h	1-0	Heinze
28/11	Lens	a	0-1	
5/12	Nice	a	3-1	Niang, Lucho González, Koné
12/12	Boulogne	h	2-0	Heinze, Taiwo (p)
16/12	Lorient	a	2-1	Ayew, Diawara
19/12	St-Étienne	a	0-0	
23/12	Auxerre	h	0-2	

2010

17/1	Bordeaux	a	1-1	Cheyrou
20/1	Le Mans	h	2-1	Niang 2 (1p)
30/1	Montpellier	a	0-2	
7/2	Valenciennes	h	5-1	Lucho González, Brandão, Cheyrou, Valbuena, Niang
13/2	Monaco	a	2-1	Niang, og (N'Koulou)
21/2	Nancy	h	3-1	Niang 3
28/2	PSG	a	3-0	Ben Arfa, Lucho González, Cheyrou
7/3	Lorient	h	1-1	Niang
14/3	Toulouse	a	1-1	Brandão
21/3	Lyon	h	2-1	Kaboré, Taiwo
4/4	Lens	h	1-0	Brandão
7/4	Sochaux	h	3-0	Heinze, Ben Arfa (p), Koné
11/4	Nice	a	4-1	Koné, Mbia, Valbuena, Diawara
14/4	Sochaux	a	1-0	Mbia
17/4	Boulogne	a	2-1	Valbuena, Taiwo (p)
25/4	St-Étienne	h	1-0	Valbuena
30/4	Auxerre	a	0-0	
5/5	Rennes	h	3-1	Heinze, Niang, Lucho González
8/5	Lille	a	2-3	Niang, Hilton
15/5	Grenoble	h	2-0	Niang (p), Ben Arfa

FRANCE

No	Name	Nat	DoB	Pos	Aps	(s)	Gls
18	Fabrice ABRIEL		6/7/79	M	18	(14)	1
40	Elinton ANDRADE	BRA	30/3/79	G	2	(1)	
15	Jordan AYEW		11/9/91	M		(4)	1
10	Hatem BEN ARFA		7/3/87	M	17	(12)	3
2	Garry BOCALY		19/4/88	D	3	(1)	
24	Laurent BONNART		25/12/79	D	30	(1)	
9	Evaeverson Lemos da Silva "BRANDÃO"	BRA	16/6/80	A	27	(3)	8
7	Benoît CHEYROU		3/5/81	M	27	(5)	5
6	Edouard CISSÉ		30/3/78	M	27	(5)	1
21	Souleymane DIAWARA	SEN	24/12/78	D	37		4
19	Gabriel HEINZE	ARG	19/4/78	D	26	(1)	4
5	Vittorino HILTON da Silva	BRA	13/9/77	D	9	(3)	1
12	Charles KABORÉ	BFA	9/2/88	M	17	(8)	1
14	Bakari KONÉ	CIV	17/9/81	A	11	(16)	4
8	Luis Óscar "LUCHO" GONZÁLEZ	ARG	19/1/81	M	28	(4)	5
30	Steve MANDANDA		28/3/85	G	36		
17	Stéphane MBIA	CMR	20/5/86	M	26	(1)	2
27	Pape M'BOW	SEN	22/5/88	D		(3)	
23	Fernando MORIENTES	ESP	5/4/76	A	4	(8)	1
11	Mamadou NIANG	SEN	13/10/79	A	29	(3)	18
22	Cyril ROOL		15/4/75	D	1	(1)	
3	Taye TAIWO	NGA	16/4/85	D	24	(3)	3
28	Mathieu VALBUENA		28/9/84	M	19	(12)	5

AS MONACO FC

Coach – Guy Lacombe
Founded – 1919
Stadium – Stade Louis II (18,523)
MAJOR HONOURS:
French League - (7) 1961, 1963, 1978, 1982, 1988, 1997, 2000;
French Cup - (5) 1960, 1963, 1980, 1985, 1991;
League Cup - (1) 2003.

2009
8/8	Toulouse	h	1-0	*Nenê*
15/8	Nancy	a	0-4	
22/8	Lorient	h	2-0	*Nimani, Nenê*
29/8	Sochaux	a	0-1	
13/9	PSG	h	2-0	*Park, Nenê*
19/9	Nice	a	3-1	*Nenê (p), Alonso 2*
26/9	St-Étienne	h	1-2	*Puygrenier*
4/10	Marseille	a	2-1	*Nenê, Park*
18/10	Lens	h	2-0	*Nenê 2 (1p)*
24/10	Boulogne	a	3-1	*Park, Nenê 2*
31/10	Bordeaux	a	0-1	
7/11	Grenoble	h	0-0	
21/11	Auxerre	a	0-2	
5/12	Valenciennes	a	1-3	*Nenê (p)*
13/12	Lille	h	0-4	
16/12	Rennes	h	1-0	*Park*
20/12	Lyon	h	1-1	*Park*
23/12	Le Mans	a	1-1	*Park*

2010
13/1	Montpellier	h	4-0	*Puygrenier, Haruna 2, og (El-Kaoutari)*
16/1	Sochaux	h	2-0	*Nenê 2*
20/1	PSG	a	1-0	*og (Édel)*
30/1	Nice	h	3-2	*Park 2, Nenê*
7/2	St-Étienne	a	0-3	
13/2	Marseille	h	1-2	*Maazou*
20/2	Lens	a	0-3	
27/2	Boulogne	h	1-0	*Maazou*
6/3	Rennes	a	0-1	
13/3	Bordeaux	h	0-0	
20/3	Grenoble	a	0-0	
29/3	Auxerre	h	0-0	
3/4	Montpellier	a	0-0	
10/4	Valenciennes	h	2-1	*Nenê, Maazou*
18/4	Lille	a	0-4	
27/4	Le Mans	h	1-1	*Maazou*

5/5	Lorient	a	2-2	*Haruna, Maazou*
8/5	Nancy	h	2-1	*og (Lotiès), Maazou*
12/5	Lyon	a	0-3	
15/5	Toulouse	a	0-0	

No	Name	Nat	DoB	Pos	Aps	(s)	Gls
12	ADRIANO Pereira da Silva	BRA	3/4/82	D	15	(1)	
8	Alejandro ALONSO	ARG	3/3/82	M	27		2
11	Djamel BAKAR		6/4/89	A	4		
22	Mathieu COUTADEUR		20/6/86	M	11	(8)	
5	DIEGO Fernando PÉREZ Aguado	URU	18/5/80	M	20	(3)	
24	EDUARDO Nascimento da COSTA	BRA	23/9/82	M	14	(1)	
17	Serge GAKPÉ	TOG	7/5/87	A		(3)	
19	Jean-Jacques GOSSO	CIV	15/3/83	M	7	(1)	
9	Eidur Smári GUDJOHNSEN	ISL	15/9/78	A	6	(3)	
25	Lukman HARUNA	NGA	4/12/90	M	16	(7)	3
23	Jerko LEKO	CRO	9/4/80	M		(4)	
32	Igor LOLO	CIV	22/7/82	D	8	(7)	
31	Moussa MAAZOU	NIG	25/8/88	A	10	(8)	6
15	Thomas MANGANI		29/4/87	D	10	(4)	
4	François-Joseph MODESTO		19/8/78	D	23	(1)	
26	Yohan MOLLO		18/7/89	M	7	(11)	
2	Cédric MONGONGU	COD	22/6/89	D	33		
13	Vincent MURATORI		3/8/87	D	12	(4)	
11	Anderson Luís de Carvalho "NENÊ"	BRA	19/7/81	A	34		14
27	Frédéric NIMANI		8/10/88	A	2	(6)	1
3	Nicolas N'KOULOU N'Doubena	CMR	27/3/90	D	21	(3)	
10	PARK Chu-young	KOR	10/7/85	A	26	(1)	8
20	Juan Pablo PINO	COL	30/3/87	A	9	(5)	
28	Sébastien PUYGRENIER		28/1/82	D	36		2
16	Stéphane RUFFIER		27/9/86	G	37		
9	Yannick SAGBO		12/4/88	A	1	(14)	
1	Yohann THURAM-ULIEN		31/10/88	G	1		
18	Djimi TRAORÉ	MLI	1/3/80	D	28	(1)	

MONTPELLIER HÉRAULT SC

Coach – René Girard
Founded – 1974
Stadium – Stade de la Mosson (32,500)
MAJOR HONOURS:
French Cup – (1) 1990.

2009
8/8	PSG	h	1-1	*Spahić*
15/8	Lorient	a	2-2	*Costa, Spahić*
22/8	Sochaux	h	2-0	*Costa (p), Aït-Fana*
29/8	Nice	a	3-0	*Dernis, Montaño, Compan*
12/9	Lens	h	1-0	*Costa (p)*
19/9	Marseille	a	2-4	*Belhanda, Camara (p)*
26/9	Boulogne	h	1-0	*Džodić*
3/10	Grenoble	a	3-2	*Montaño, Džodić 2*
17/10	St-Étienne	h	2-1	*Aït-Fana, Camara*
24/10	Rennes	a	0-3	
31/10	Auxerre	a	1-2	*Džodić*
7/11	Valenciennes	a	1-1	*Montaño*
22/11	Lille	h	2-0	*Montaño 2*
5/12	Le Mans	h	2-1	*Aït-Fana, Compan*
13/12	Toulouse	a	1-0	*Camara*
16/12	Bordeaux	h	0-1	
19/12	Nancy	h	0-2	
23/12	Lyon	a	2-1	*Montaño, Marveaux*

2010
13/1	Monaco	a	0-4	
16/1	Nice	h	1-0	*Camara*
20/1	Lens	a	1-0	*Montaño*
30/1	Marseille	h	2-0	*Aït-Fana, og (Cheyrou)*
6/2	Boulogne	a	2-0	*Camara, Montaño*
13/2	Grenoble	h	1-0	*Montaño*
20/2	St-Étienne	a	0-1	

27/2	Rennes	h	3-1	Marveaux 2, Camara
7/3	Bordeaux	a	1-1	Costa
13/3	Auxerre	h	1-1	Costa
21/3	Valenciennes	h	2-1	Montaño, Marveaux
28/3	Lille	a	1-4	Camara
3/4	Monaco	h	0-0	
10/4	Le Mans	a	2-2	Aït-Fana, Camara (p)
18/4	Toulouse	h	1-1	Costa
24/4	Nancy	a	0-0	
2/5	Lyon	h	0-1	
5/5	Sochaux	a	1-0	Costa
8/5	Lorient	h	2-1	Montaño (p), Camara (p)
15/5	PSG	a	3-1	Dernis 2, Compan

No	Name	Nat	DoB	Pos	Aps	(s)	Gls
18	Karim AÏT-FANA		25/2/89	M	24	(9)	5
29	Younes BELHANDA		25/2/90	M	19	(14)	1
14	Mourad BENHAMIDA		18/1/86	D		(3)	
2	Garry BOCALY		19/4/88	D	8	(4)	
19	Souleymane CAMARA	SEN	22/12/82	A	30	(8)	9
25	Xavier COLLIN		17/8/74	D	9	(10)	
10	Lilian COMPAN		30/4/77	A	3	(10)	3
20	Alberto Facundo COSTA	ARG	9/1/85	M	31		7
33	Bryan DABO		18/2/92	M		(1)	
8	Philippe DELAYE		26/6/75	M	3	(1)	
12	Geoffrey DERNIS		24/12/80	M	9	(6)	3
4	Nenad DŽODIĆ	SRB	4/1/77	D	17		4
21	Abdelhamid EL-KAOUTARI		17/3/90	D	20	(5)	
27	Cyril JEUNECHAMP		18/12/75	D	28		
16	Geoffrey JOURDREN		4/2/86	G	38		
24	Bengali Fodé KOÏTA		21/10/90	A		(6)	
7	Grégory LACOMBE		11/1/82	M	2	(6)	
6	Joris Steve MARVEAUX		15/8/82	D	31		4
11	Víctor MONTAÑO	COL	1/5/84	A	33	(3)	11
17	Romain PITAU		8/8/77	M	36		
23	Jamel SAIHI		27/1/87	D	7	(19)	
5	Emir SPAHIĆ	BIH	18/8/80	D	34		2
3	Mapou YANGA M'BIWA		15/5/89	D	36		

AS NANCY-LORRAINE
Coach – Pablo Correa (URU)
Founded – 1967
Stadium – Stade Marcel-Picot (20,085)
MAJOR HONOURS:
French Cup – (1) 1978;
League Cup – (1) 2006.

2009

8/8	Valenciennes	a	3-1	Féret, Brison, Traoré (p)
15/8	Monaco	h	4-0	Dia, André Luiz (p), Alo'o Efoulou 2
22/8	Le Mans	a	1-2	Macaluso
29/8	Lyon	a	1-3	Hadji
12/9	Toulouse	h	0-0	
19/9	Lorient	a	1-3	Alo'o Efoulou
26/9	Sochaux	h	2-1	Hadji 2 (1p)
3/10	PSG	a	1-1	Hadji
17/10	Marseille	h	0-3	
24/10	Grenoble	a	2-1	og (Jemmali), Hadji (p)
31/10	Boulogne	a	2-1	Dia, Hadji
7/11	St-Étienne	h	0-1	
21/11	Lens	a	1-2	Alo'o Efoulou
29/11	Bordeaux	h	0-3	
6/12	Auxerre	a	3-1	André Luiz, Ouaddou, Hadji
12/12	Rennes	h	1-2	Féret
16/12	Nice	h	2-0	Féret, Malonga
19/12	Montpellier	a	2-0	Bakar, Bérenguer
23/12	Lille	h	0-4	

2010

16/1	Lyon	h	0-2	
20/1	Toulouse	a	0-0	
30/1	Lorient	h	1-0	Hadji
6/2	Sochaux	a	1-1	Dia
13/2	PSG	h	0-0	
21/2	Marseille	a	1-3	André Luiz
27/2	Grenoble	h	0-2	
6/3	Nice	a	3-2	Bakar, Brison, Dia
13/3	Boulogne	h	1-3	Malonga
20/3	St-Étienne	a	0-0	
28/3	Lens	h	5-1	Dia 3, Hadji, Bérenguer
3/4	Bordeaux	a	2-1	Hadji, Dia
11/4	Auxerre	h	0-1	
17/4	Rennes	a	0-0	
24/4	Montpellier	h	0-0	
2/5	Lille	a	1-3	Malonga
5/5	Le Mans	h	3-2	Féret 2, Malonga
8/5	Monaco	a	1-2	Sami
15/5	Valenciennes	h	1-1	Hadji

No	Name	Nat	DoB	Pos	Aps	(s)	Gls
14	Paul ALO'O EFOULOU	CMR	12/11/83	A	13	(10)	4
5	ANDRÉ LUIZ Silva do Nascimento	BRA	27/1/80	D	31	(1)	3
28	Floyd AYITÉ	TOG	15/2/88	M	4	(2)	
11	Djamel BAKAR		6/4/89	A	13	(19)	2
6	Pascal BÉRENGUER		20/5/81	M	29	(1)	2
1	Gennaro BRACIGLIANO		1/3/80	G	32		
23	Jonathan BRISON		7/2/83	M	23	(3)	2
7	Bocundji CA	GNB	28/12/86	M	10	(7)	
33	Aatif CHAHÉCHOUCHE		2/7/86	M		(2)	
20	Michaël CHRÉTIEN	MAR	10/7/84	D	18	(2)	
10	Issiar DIA		8/6/87	A	28	(5)	8
26	Cheick DIABATÉ	MLI	25/4/88	A		(2)	
19	Samba DIAKITÉ		24/1/89	M	2	(1)	
18	Julien FÉRET		5/7/82	M	35	(2)	5
24	Benjamin GAVANON		9/8/80	M		(2)	
16	Damien GRÉGORINI		2/3/79	G	6		
15	Youssouf HADJI	MAR	25/2/80	M	24	(2)	11
25	Reynald LEMAÎTRE		28/6/83	M	22	(3)	
8	Jordan LOTIÈS		5/8/84	M	19	(3)	
13	Damian MACALUSO	URU	9/3/80	D	11	(1)	1
4	Francis Chris MALONGA		11/7/87	M	17	(8)	4
22	Florian MARANGE		3/3/86	D	12	(4)	
29	Alfred N'DIAYE		6/3/90	M	17	(6)	
27	Abdeslam OUADDOU	MAR	1/11/78	D	20	(1)	1
3	Joël SAMI	COD	13/11/84	D	19	(4)	1
12	Bakaye TRAORÉ	MLI	6/3/85	M	13	(9)	1

OGC NICE
Coach – Didier Ollé-Nicolle; (9/3/10) Éric Roy
Founded – 1904
Stadium – Stade municipal du Ray (18,696)
MAJOR HONOURS:
French League - (4) 1951, 1952, 1956, 1959;
French Cup - (3) 1952, 1954, 1997.

2009

8/8	St-Étienne	a	2-0	Traoré, Rémy
16/8	Rennes	h	1-1	Ben Saada
23/8	Bordeaux	a	0-4	
29/8	Montpellier	a	0-3	
13/9	Auxerre	a	0-2	
19/9	Monaco	h	1-3	Rémy
27/9	Lille	h	1-1	Rémy
3/10	Valenciennes	h	3-2	Ben Saada, Echouafni, og (Ducourtioux)
18/10	Lorient	a	1-4	Rémy
24/10	Lyon	h	4-1	Bagayoko, og (Cissokho), Hellebuyck, Rémy
1/11	Le Mans	h	1-0	Gace
7/11	PSG	a	1-0	Rémy
22/11	Toulouse	h	1-0	Rémy (p)
28/11	Sochaux	a	0-1	
5/12	Marseille	h	1-3	Coulibaly
12/12	Lens	a	0-2	

FRANCE

16/12	Nancy	a	0-2	
19/12	Grenoble	a	1-1	*Ben Saada*
23/12	Boulogne	h	2-2	*Poté 2*
2010				
16/1	Montpellier	a	0-1	
20/1	Auxerre	h	0-1	
30/1	Monaco	a	2-3	*Ben Saada, Digard*
6/2	Lille	h	1-1	*Ben Saada*
13/2	Valenciennes	a	1-2	*Rémy*
20/2	Lorient	h	1-0	*Rémy (p)*
27/2	Lyon	a	0-2	
6/3	Nancy	h	2-3	*Civelli, Ben Saada*
13/3	Le Mans	a	1-0	*Rémy*
20/3	PSG	h	1-0	*Rémy*
28/3	Toulouse	a	2-0	*Mounier, Mouloungui*
3/4	Sochaux	h	0-0	
11/4	Marseille	a	1-4	*Faé*
17/4	Lens	h	0-0	
24/4	Grenoble	h	2-1	*Mouloungui, Faé*
2/5	Boulogne	a	3-3	*Rémy 2, Hellebuyck*
5/5	Bordeaux	h	1-1	*Faé*
8/5	Rennes	a	2-2	*Mounier, Faé*
15/5	St-Étienne	h	1-1	*Rémy*

No	Name	Nat	DoB	Pos	Aps	(s)	Gls
4	Onyekachi APAM	NGA	30/12/86	D	23		
20	Mamadou BAGAYOKO	MLI	21/5/79	A	18	(5)	1
21	Habib BAMOGO	BFA	8/5/82	A	2	(11)	
17	Chaouki BEN SAADA	TUN	1/7/84	A	18	(10)	6
37	Julien BERTHOMIER		10/4/90	D		(1)	
3	Alain CANTAREIL		15/8/83	D	5	(5)	
24	Gérald CID		17/2/83	D	10	(3)	
2	Renato CIVELLI	ARG	14/10/83	D	17		1
15	Kafoumba COULIBALY	CIV	26/10/85	M	24	(3)	1
23	Drissa DIAKITÉ	MLI	18/2/85	M	28	(3)	
22	Didier DIGARD		12/7/86	M	11	(1)	1
6	Olivier ECHOUAFNI		13/9/72	M	13	(7)	1
14	Emerse FAÉ	CIV	24/1/84	M	26	(3)	4
18	Ismaël GACE		19/9/86	D	19	(1)	1
8	David HELLEBUYCK		12/5/79	M	27	(2)	2
16	Lionel LETIZI		28/5/73	G	1	(1)	
5	Larrys MABIALA	COD	8/10/87	D	19		
30	Jérémie MOREAU		22/7/80	G		(1)	
11	Eric MOULOUNGUI	GAB	1/4/84	A	5	(12)	2
27	Anthony MOUNIER		27/9/87	M	23	(7)	2
1	David OSPINA	COL	31/8/88	G	37		
28	Grégory PAISLEY		7/5/77	D	28	(1)	
9	Mickaël POTÉ	BEN	24/9/84	A	5	(7)	2
12	Abeiku QUANSAH	GHA	2/11/90	A		(2)	
7	Loïc RÉMY		2/1/87	A	33	(1)	14
27	Julien SABLÉ		11/9/80	M	19	(4)	
10	Mahamane TRAORÉ	MLI	31/8/88	M	7	(9)	1

PARIS SAINT-GERMAIN FC
Coach – Antoine Kombouaré
Founded – 1970
Stadium – Parc des Princes (48,712)
MAJOR HONOURS:
UEFA European Cup-Winners' Cup - (1) 1996;
French League - (2) 1986, 1994;
French Cup - (8) 1982, 1983, 1993, 1995, 1998, 2004, 2006, 2010;
League Cup - (3) 1995, 1998, 2008.

2009				
8/8	Montpellier	a	1-1	*Giuly*
15/8	Le Mans	h	3-1	*Mevlüt, og (Thomas), Giuly*
22/8	Valenciennes	a	3-2	*Luyindula, Mevlüt, Jallet*
30/8	Lille	h	3-0	*Clément, Luyindula, Jallet*
13/9	Monaco	a	0-2	
20/9	Lyon	h	1-1	*Giuly*
26/9	Lorient	a	1-1	*Hoarau*
3/10	Nancy	h	1-1	*Sessegnon*

18/10	Toulouse	a	0-1	
1/11	Sochaux	a	4-1	*Clément, Chantôme, Mevlüt, Luyindula*
7/11	Nice	h	0-1	
20/11	Marseille	a	0-1	
28/11	Auxerre	h	1-0	*Clément*
2/12	Boulogne	a	5-2	*Chantôme, Luyindula (p), Mevlüt 2, Maurice*
5/12	Bordeaux	a	0-1	
13/12	St-Étienne	h	3-0	*Luyindula, Sessegnon, Mevlüt*
16/12	Lens	h	1-1	*Makelele*
19/12	Rennes	a	0-1	
23/12	Grenoble	h	4-0	*Luyindula, Armand, Mevlüt, Jallet*
2010				
16/1	Lille	a	1-3	*Mevlüt*
20/1	Monaco	h	0-1	
31/1	Lyon	a	1-2	*Mevlüt*
6/2	Lorient	h	0-3	
13/2	Nancy	a	0-0	
20/2	Toulouse	h	1-0	*Hoarau (p)*
28/2	Marseille	h	0-3	
6/3	Lens	a	1-1	*Sessegnon*
13/3	Sochaux	h	4-1	*Hoarau, Mevlüt 3*
20/3	Nice	a	0-1	
28/3	Boulogne	h	3-0	*og (Lecointe), Hoarau (p), Kežman*
4/4	Auxerre	a	1-1	*Sankharé*
10/4	Bordeaux	h	3-1	*Armand, Mevlüt, Hoarau*
18/4	St-Étienne	a	0-0	
24/4	Rennes	h	1-1	*Hoarau*
27/4	Grenoble	a	0-4	
5/5	Valenciennes	h	2-2	*Mevlüt, Kežman*
8/5	Le Mans	a	0-1	
15/5	Montpellier	a	1-3	*Mevlüt*

No	Name	Nat	DoB	Pos	Aps	(s)	Gls
22	Sylvain ARMAND		1/8/80	D	33		2
6	Grégory BOURILLON		1/7/84	D	2	(4)	
15	Zoumana CAMARA		3/4/79	D	22	(1)	
2	Marcos Venâncio de Albuquerque "CEARÁ"	BRA	18/6/80	D	26	(3)	
20	Clément CHANTÔME		11/9/87	M	11	(13)	2
23	Jérémy CLÉMENT		26/8/84	M	33	(1)	3
1	Grégory COUPET		31/12/72	G	16		
30	Apoula Edima ÉDEL	ARM	17/6/86	G	22	(1)	
7	Ludovic GIULY		10/7/76	M	25	(6)	3
9	Guillaume HOARAU		5/3/84	A	17	(5)	6
26	Christophe JALLET		31/10/83	D	24	(11)	3
14	Mateja KEŽMAN	SRB	12/4/79	A	3	(10)	2
8	Péguy LUYINDULA		25/5/79	A	23	(5)	6
4	Claude MAKELELE		18/2/73	M	31		1
24	Tripy MAKONDA		24/1/90	M	1		
21	Jean-Eudes MAURICE		21/6/86	A	3	(20)	1
11	MEVLÜT Erdinç	TUR	25/2/87	A	30	(1)	15
17	Granddi NGOYI		17/5/88	M	8	(8)	
3	Mamadou SAKHO		13/2/90	D	32		
27	Younousse SANKHARÉ		10/9/89	M	7	(15)	1
10	Stéphane SESSEGNON	BEN	1/6/84	M	27	(2)	3
13	Sammy TRAORÉ	MLI	25/2/76	D	22	(1)	

STADE RENNAIS FC
Coach – Frédéric Antonetti
Founded – 1901
Stadium – Stade de la Route-de-Lorient (29,778)
MAJOR HONOURS:
French Cup - (2) 1965, 1971.

2009				
8/8	Boulogne	h	3-0	*Bangoura, Mangane, Leroy*
16/8	Nice	a	1-1	*Gyan (p)*
22/8	Marseille	h	1-1	*Leroy (p)*

29/8	Lens	a	2-2	Bangoura, Gyan	
13/9	St-Étienne	h	1-0	Marveaux	
19/9	Grenoble	a	4-0	Gyan 2 (1p), Marveaux, Mangane	
27/9	Bordeaux	a	0-1		
3/10	Auxerre	h	0-1		
17/10	Lille	a	0-0		
24/10	Montpellier	h	3-0	Marveaux, Sow, Gyan	
1/11	Valenciennes	h	0-3		
8/11	Toulouse	a	2-3	Gyan, Mangane	
21/11	Le Mans	h	2-1	Mangane, Gyan	
29/11	Lyon	a	1-1	Gyan	
5/12	Lorient	h	1-0	Sow	
12/12	Nancy	a	2-1	og (Traoré), Marveaux	
16/12	Monaco	a	0-1		
19/12	PSG	h	1-0	Bangoura	
23/12	Sochaux	a	0-2		
2010					
16/1	Lens	h	1-1	Sow	
19/1	St-Étienne	a	0-0		
30/1	Grenoble	h	4-0	Danzé, Marveaux 2, Bangoura	
6/2	Bordeaux	h	4-2	Marveaux, Briand (p), Bangoura, Gyan	
14/2	Auxerre	a	0-1		
21/2	Lille	h	1-2	Leroy	
27/2	Montpellier	a	1-3	Briand	
6/3	Monaco	h	1-0	Bocanegra	
14/3	Valenciennes	a	2-0	Marveaux, Gyan	
20/3	Toulouse	h	4-1	Hansson, Gyan 2, Kembo-Ekoko	
28/3	Le Mans	a	3-1	Bangoura (p), Briand 2	
3/4	Lyon	h	1-2	Gyan	
10/4	Lorient	a	1-1	Danzé	
17/4	Nancy	h	0-0		
24/4	PSG	a	3-1	Leroy	
2/5	Sochaux	h	1-2	Marveaux (p)	
5/5	Marseille	a	1-3	Briand	
8/5	Nice	h	2-2	Leroy, Marveaux	
15/5	Boulogne	a	0-1		

No	Name	Nat	DoB	Pos	Aps	(s)	Gls
25	Lucien AUBEY		24/5/84	D	3		
21	Ismaël BANGOURA	GUI	2/1/85	A	21	(14)	6
3	Carlos BOCANEGRA	USA	25/5/79	D	24	(2)	1
19	Jimmy BRIAND		2/8/85	A	17	(6)	5
14	Bruno CHEYROU		10/5/78	M	5	(3)	
29	Romain DANZÉ		3/7/86	M	19	(13)	2
33	Abdoulaye DIALLO		30/3/92	G	1		
1	Nicolas DOUCHEZ		22/4/80	G	37		
28	Tongo Hamed DOUMBIA		6/8/89	M		(3)	
12	Rod FANNI		6/12/81	D	38		
10	Asamoah GYAN	GHA	22/11/85	A	27	(2)	13
13	Petter HANSSON	SWE	14/12/76	D	34		1
6	Junichi INAMOTO	JPN	18/9/79	M	3	(2)	
20	Jirès KEMBO-EKOKO		8/1/88	A	4	(20)	1
18	Fabien LEMOINE		13/3/87	M	28	(3)	
7	Jérôme LEROY		4/11/74	M	26	(6)	5
5	Abdou Kader MANGANE	SEN	23/3/83	D	34		4
8	Sylvain MARVEAUX		15/4/86	M	33	(2)	10
15	Yann M'VILA		29/6/90	M	33	(2)	
9	Mickaël PAGIS		17/8/73	A		(3)	
23	Moussa SOW		19/1/86	A	9	(15)	3
4	Alexander TETTEY	NOR	4/4/86	M	20	(4)	
26	Kévin THÉOPHILE-CATHERINE		28/10/89	D	1	(1)	
11	Olivier THOMERT		28/3/80	A	1	(1)	

AS SAINT-ÉTIENNE
Coach – Alain Perrin; (15/12/09) Christophe Galtier
Founded – 1933
Stadium – Stade Geoffroy-Guichard (35,616)
MAJOR HONOURS:
French League - (10) 1957, 1964, 1967, 1968, 1969, 1970, 1974, 1975, 1976, 1981;
French Cup - (6) 1962, 1968, 1970, 1974, 1975, 1977.

2009				
8/8	Nice	h	0-2	
15/8	Toulouse	a	1-3	Rivière
22/8	Boulogne	h	0-1	
29/8	Grenoble	h	1-0	Landrin
13/9	Rennes	a	0-1	
19/9	Auxerre	h	1-1	Bergessio
26/9	Monaco	a	2-1	Sanogo, Bergessio
3/10	Bordeaux	h	3-1	Fernández, Ilan, Payet
17/10	Montpellier	a	1-2	Bergessio (p)
24/10	Valenciennes	h	0-2	
31/10	Lyon	h	0-1	
7/11	Nancy	a	1-0	Payet
22/11	Lorient	h	0-2	
29/11	Le Mans	a	1-1	Ilan
5/12	Sochaux	h	0-0	
10/12	Lille	a	0-4	
13/12	PSG	a	0-3	
19/12	Marseille	h	0-0	
22/12	Lens	a	0-1	
2010				
16/1	Grenoble	a	2-1	Perrin, Rivière
19/1	Rennes	h	0-0	
31/1	Auxerre	a	0-1	
7/2	Monaco	h	3-0	Matuidi, Bergessio, Rivière
14/2	Bordeaux	a	1-3	Sako
20/2	Montpellier	h	1-0	Rivière
27/2	Valenciennes	a	0-1	
6/3	Lille	h	1-1	Rivière
13/3	Lyon	a	1-1	Rivière
20/3	Nancy	h	0-0	
28/3	Lorient	a	0-4	
3/4	Le Mans	h	2-0	Varrault, Benalouane
10/4	Sochaux	a	2-0	Perrin, Bergessio
18/4	PSG	h	0-0	
25/4	Marseille	a	0-1	
2/5	Lens	h	1-4	Diakhaté
5/5	Boulogne	a	1-0	Rivière
8/5	Toulouse	h	0-1	
15/5	Nice	a	1-1	Rivière

No	Name	Nat	DoB	Pos	Aps	(s)	Gls
15	Yohann ANDREU		3/5/89	D	8	(4)	
26	Mustapha BAYAL SALL	SEN	30/11/85	D	8	(1)	
28	Yohan BENALOUANE		28/3/87	D	27	(2)	1
9	Gonzalo Rubén BERGESSIO	ARG	20/7/84	A	26	(5)	5
21	Mouhamadou DABO		28/11/86	D	23	(2)	
3	Pape DIAKHATÉ	SEN	21/6/84	D	18		1
27	Helton DOS REIS		1/5/88	A	2	(2)	
31	Maodo Malick FAYE	SEN	13/12/87	A		(4)	
22	Gelson FERNANDES	SUI	2/9/86	M	29	(4)	
5	Augusto Matías FERNÁNDEZ	ARG	10/4/86	M	8	(4)	1
13	David GIGLIOTTI		30/5/85	A		(1)	
35	Josua GUILAVOGUI		19/9/90	M	1	(1)	
17	Yohan HAUTCOEUR		30/10/81	M	5	(4)	
8	ILAN Araújo Dall'Igna	BRA	18/9/80	A	9	(3)	2
16	Jérémie JANOT		11/10/77	G	38		
14	Christophe LANDRIN		30/6/77	M	15	(3)	1
20	Boubacar MANSALY	SEN	4/2/88	M	1		
12	Blaise MATUIDI		9/4/87	M	35	(1)	1
10	Kevin MIRALLAS	BEL	5/10/87	A	14	(9)	
6	Sylvain MONSOREAU		23/3/81	D	3	(5)	
18	Guirane NDAW	SEN	24/4/84	M	29	(5)	
7	Dimitri PAYET		29/3/87	A	25	(10)	2
24	Loïc PERRIN		7/8/85	A	15	(3)	2
29	Emmanuel RIVIÈRE		3/3/90	A	19	(11)	8
11	Bakary SAKO		26/4/88	M	17	(13)	1
14	Boubacar SANOGO	CIV	17/12/82	A	14	(3)	1
4	Efstathios TAVLARIDIS	GRE	25/1/80	D	6		
2	Cédric VARRAULT		30/1/80	D	23		1

FRANCE

FC SOCHAUX-MONTBÉLIARD
Coach – Francis Gillot
Founded – 1928
Stadium – Stade Auguste-Bonal (20,005)
MAJOR HONOURS:
French League - (2) 1935, 1938;
French Cup - (2) 1937, 2007;
League Cup - (1) 2004.

2009

8/8	Auxerre	a	1-0	Svêrkoš
15/8	Bordeaux	h	2-3	Davies 2
22/8	Montpellier	a	0-2	
29/8	Monaco	h	1-0	Svêrkoš (p)
12/9	Lille	a	0-1	
19/9	Valenciennes	h	2-5	Bréchet, Boudebouz
26/9	Nancy	a	1-2	Martin
3/10	Le Mans	h	1-0	Martin
17/10	Lyon	a	2-0	Faty, Privat
24/10	Lorient	h	1-0	Perquis
1/11	PSG	h	1-4	Dalmat
7/11	Lens	h	1-2	Privat
28/11	Nice	h	1-0	Mikari
5/12	St-Étienne	a	0-0	
10/12	Toulouse	a	0-2	
13/12	Grenoble	h	1-0	Mikari
23/12	Rennes	h	2-0	Dalmat, Butin
2010				
13/1	Boulogne	a	0-0	
16/1	Monaco	a	0-2	
20/1	Lille	h	2-1	Perquis, Dalmat
31/1	Valenciennes	a	1-1	Perquis
6/2	Nancy	h	1-1	Dalmat
13/2	Le Mans	a	0-0	
21/2	Lyon	h	0-4	
27/2	Lorient	a	0-1	
6/3	Toulouse	h	1-0	Boudebouz
13/3	PSG	a	1-4	Boudebouz (p)
20/3	Lens	a	0-0	
3/4	Nice	a	0-0	
7/4	Marseille	a	0-3	
10/4	St-Étienne	h	0-2	
14/4	Marseille	h	0-1	
17/4	Grenoble	a	2-2	Brown, Bréchet
24/4	Boulogne	h	0-3	
2/5	Rennes	a	2-1	og (Briand), Gavanon
5/5	Montpellier	h	0-1	
8/5	Bordeaux	a	0-2	
15/5	Auxerre	h	1-2	Brown

No	Name	Nat	DoB	Pos	Aps	(s)	Gls
10	Ryad BOUDEBOUZ	ALG	19/2/90	M	20	(11)	3
13	Jérémie BRÉCHET		14/8/79	D	33		2
12	Ideye Aide BROWN	NGA	10/10/88	A	17		2
20	Edouard BUTIN		16/6/88	A	4	(18)	1
8	Carlos Roberto Da Cruz Júnior "CARLÃO"	BRA	19/1/86	D	9	(7)	
18	Stéphane DALMAT		16/2/79	M	29		4
9	Charlie DAVIES	USA	25/6/86	A	6	(2)	2
4	Boukary DRAMÉ	SEN	22/7/85	D	22	(1)	
30	Mathieu DREYER		20/3/89	G	7	(1)	
2	Frédéric DUPUIS		7/4/90	D	8	(2)	
5	Jacques FATY		25/2/84	D	33		1
24	Benjamin GAVANON		9/8/80	M	19	(8)	1
14	Bojan JOKIČ	SVN	17/5/86	D	5	(1)	
1	Maxime JOSSE		21/3/87	D	3	(4)	
26	Marvin MARTIN		10/6/88	M	34	(2)	2
28	Nicolas MAURICE-BELAY		19/4/85	A	34	(3)	
14	Yassine MIKARI	TUN	9/1/83	D	29	(1)	2
21	Vincent NOGUEIRA		16/1/88	M	8	(5)	
30	Damien PERQUIS		10/4/84	D	34		3
29	Mathieu PEYBERNES		21/10/90	D		(1)	
27	Loïc POUJOL		27/2/89	M	8	(8)	
11	Sloan PRIVAT		24/7/89	A	1	(13)	2
33	RAFAEL DIAS Lucas Brito		29/1/91	M		(2)	
16	Teddy RICHERT		21/9/74	G	31		
15	SERDAR Gürler	TUR	14/9/91	A		(1)	
3	Ivan STEVANOVIĆ	SRB	24/6/83	D	5	(1)	
25	Václav SVÊRKOŠ	CZE	1/11/83	A	19	(6)	2
7	Geoffrey TULASNE		24/2/88	M		(4)	

TOULOUSE FC
Coach – Alain Casanova
Founded – 1970
Stadium – Stadium de Toulouse (35,472)

2009

8/8	Monaco	a	0-1	
15/8	St-Étienne	h	3-1	Paulo Machado, Gignac, Sissoko
23/8	Lille	a	1-1	M'Bengué
30/8	Valenciennes	h	0-1	
12/9	Nancy	a	0-0	
20/9	Le Mans	h	2-0	Didot, Sissoko
26/9	Lyon	a	1-2	Sissoko
4/10	Lorient	h	0-1	
18/10	PSG	h	1-0	Ebondo
25/10	Lens	a	2-0	Sissoko, Gignac
31/10	Marseille	a	1-1	Sissoko
8/11	Rennes	h	3-2	Sissoko, Braaten, Gignac
22/11	Nice	a	0-1	
28/11	Boulogne	h	1-0	Fofana
6/12	Grenoble	a	0-1	
10/12	Sochaux	h	2-0	Gignac 2
13/12	Montpellier	h	0-1	
20/12	Auxerre	a	1-1	Luan
23/12	Bordeaux	h	1-2	Paulo Machado
2010				
16/1	Valenciennes	a	3-1	Tabanou 2, Sissoko
20/1	Nancy	h	0-0	
30/1	Le Mans	a	3-1	Paulo Machado, Gignac, Kazım Kazım
7/2	Lyon	h	0-0	
14/2	Lorient	a	1-1	Braaten
20/2	PSG	a	0-1	
27/2	Lens	h	1-0	Dupuis
6/3	Sochaux	a	0-1	
14/3	Marseille	h	1-1	Paulo Machado
20/3	Rennes	a	1-4	Braaten
28/3	Nice	h	0-2	
4/4	Boulogne	a	1-1	Braaten
10/4	Grenoble	h	4-0	Paulo Machado, Tabanou 2, Gignac
18/4	Montpellier	a	1-1	Kazım Kazım
25/4	Auxerre	h	0-3	
2/5	Bordeaux	a	0-1	
5/5	Lille	h	0-2	
8/5	St-Étienne	a	1-0	Gignac
15/5	Monaco	h	0-0	

No	Name	Nat	DoB	Pos	Aps	(s)	Gls
20	Mathieu BERSON		23/2/80	M	14	(2)	
16	Olivier BLONDEL		9/7/79	G	11	(2)	
25	Daniel Omoya BRAATEN	NOR	25/5/82	M	24	(8)	4
29	Étienne CAPOUE		11/7/88	M	30	(3)	
4	Mauro CETTO	ARG	14/4/82	D	16		
3	Daniel CONGRÉ		5/4/85	D	33		
6	Antoine DEVAUX		21/2/85	M	1	(2)	
8	Étienne DIDOT		24/7/83	M	22	(4)	1
18	Kévin DUPUIS		14/1/87	A	2	(4)	1
23	Albin EBONDO		23/2/84	D	27	(1)	1
2	Mohamed FOFANA		7/3/85	D	16	(1)	1
10	André-Pierre GIGNAC		5/12/85	A	30	(1)	8
9	Colin Kazim-Richards "KAZIM KAZIM"	TUR	26/8/86	M	10	(5)	2
33	Anthony LOUSTALLOT		30/3/92	G	1		

FRANCE

11	LUAN Michel De Louzã	BRA	21/9/88	M	6	(8)	1
12	Cheikh M'BENGUÉ		23/7/88	D	30		1
7	Fodé MANSARÉ	GUI	3/9/81	M	2	(6)	
34	Alexandre N'GADI KAKOU		28/11/90	A		(1)	
13	Dany NOUNKEU	CMR	11/4/86	D	17		
5	PAULO Ricardo Ribeiro de Jesus MACHADO	POR	31/3/86	M	27	(5)	5
30	Yohann PELÉ		4/11/82	G	18		
19	Xavier PENTECÔTE		13/8/86	A		(6)	
17	Jean-Joël PERRIER-DOUMBÉ	CMR	27/9/78	D	2	(1)	
26	Adrien REGATTIN		22/8/91	M		(5)	
14	François SIRIEIX		7/10/80	M	10	(8)	
28	Moussa SISSOKO		16/8/89	M	35	(2)	7
28	Ahmed SOUKOUNA		13/1/90	A		(3)	
27	Franck TABANOU		30/1/89	M	26	(7)	4
1	Matthieu VALVERDE		14/5/83	G	7	(1)	
33	Marc VIDAL		3/6/91	G	1		

VALENCIENNES FC
Coach – Philippe Montanier
Founded – 1913
Stadium – Stade Nungesser (16,547)

2009

8/8	Nancy	h	1-3	Samassa
15/8	Lyon	a	0-1	
22/8	PSG	h	2-3	Tiéné, Mater
30/8	Toulouse	a	1-0	Samassa
12/9	Boulogne	h	1-1	Pujol
19/9	Sochaux	a	5-2	Sánchez, Pujol 2, Audel, Ben Khalfallah
26/9	Marseille	h	3-2	Biševac, Ducourtioux, Schmitz
3/10	Nice	a	2-3	Samassa (p), Sánchez
17/10	Grenoble	h	2-0	Samassa, Ben Khalfallah
24/10	St-Étienne	a	2-0	Audel, Ducourtioux
1/11	Rennes	a	3-0	Baldé, Ben Khalfallah, Pujol
7/11	Montpellier	h	1-1	Sánchez
21/11	Bordeaux	a	1-0	Samassa
28/11	Lille	a	0-4	
5/12	Monaco	h	3-1	Ducourtioux, Samassa, Ben Khalfallah
12/12	Le Mans	a	1-2	Danic
15/12	Auxerre	h	0-0	
19/12	Lens	h	0-0	
23/12	Lorient	a	2-3	Audel, Danic

2010

16/1	Toulouse	h	1-3	Audel
20/1	Boulogne	a	2-0	Bong, Ben Khalfallah
31/1	Sochaux	h	1-1	Audel
7/2	Marseille	h	1-5	Sánchez
13/2	Nice	h	2-1	Mater, Šebo
20/2	Grenoble	a	1-0	Sánchez
27/2	St-Étienne	h	1-0	Audel
6/3	Auxerre	a	0-1	
14/3	Rennes	h	0-2	
21/3	Montpellier	a	1-2	Ben Khalfallah
3/4	Lille	h	1-0	Samassa
10/4	Monaco	a	1-2	Biševac
17/4	Le Mans	h	0-1	
25/4	Lens	a	1-1	Pujol
28/4	Bordeaux	h	2-0	Pujol, Kadir
2/5	Lorient	h	0-0	
5/5	PSG	a	2-2	Bong, Ben Khalfallah
8/5	Lyon	h	2-2	Audel, Cohade (p)
15/5	Nancy	a	1-1	Angoua

No	Name	Nat	DoB	Pos	Aps	(s)	Gls
3	Jacques ABARDONADO		27/5/78	D	13	(2)	
20	Benjamin ANGOUA	CIV	28/11/86	D	15		1
7	Johan AUDEL		12/12/83	A	20	(6)	7
4	Bobo BALDÉ	GUI	5/10/75	D	6	(4)	1
8	Amara Karba BANGOURA	GUI	10/6/86	M		(1)	

10	Fahid BEN KHALFALLAH	TUN	9/10/82	M	24	(12)	7
6	Milan BIŠEVAC	SRB	31/8/83	D	31		2
24	Gaëtan BONG	CMR	25/4/88	D	20	(9)	2
26	Renaud COHADE		29/9/84	M	28	(4)	1
8	Gaël DANIC		19/11/81	M	20	(9)	2
2	David DUCOURTIOUX		11/4/78	D	26	(2)	3
12	Rémi GOMIS		14/2/84	M	31	(5)	
14	Foued KADIR	ALG	5/12/83	A	14	(4)	1
30	Jean-Louis LECA		21/9/85	G	1		
25	Rudy MATER		13/10/80	D	28		2
19	NAM Tae-hee	KOR	3/7/91	M		(6)	
40	Guy Roland N'DY ASSEMBÉ	CMR	28/2/86	G	17		
1	Nicolas PENNETEAU		20/2/81	G	19		
11	Luigi PIERONI	BEL	8/9/80	A		(2)	
28	Grégory PUJOL		25/1/80	A	21	(9)	6
23	José SAEZ		7/5/82	M	10	(5)	
27	Mamadou SAMASSA	MLI	1/5/86	A	11	(6)	7
17	Carlos SÁNCHEZ	COL	6/2/86	M	28		5
5	Rafael SCHMITZ	BRA	17/12/80	D	8		1
9	Filip ŠEBO	SVK	24/2/84	A		(11)	1
15	Siaka TIÉNÉ	CIV	22/2/82	M	26	(2)	1
40	Grégory WIMBEE		19/8/71	G	1		

PROMOTED CLUBS

SM CAEN
Coach – Franck Dumas
Founded – 1919
Stadium – Michel-d'Ornano (21,500)

STADE BRESTOIS 29
Coach – Alex Dupont
Founded – 1950
Stadium – Francis-Le Blé (10,508)

AC ARLES-AVIGNON
Coach – Michel Estevan
Founded – 1913
Stadium – Parc des Sports d'Avignon (7,000)

SECOND LEVEL FINAL TABLE 2009/10

		Pld	W	D	L	F	A	Pts
1	SM Caen	38	18	15	5	52	30	69
2	Stade Brestois 29	38	20	7	11	53	34	67
3	AC Arles-Avignon	38	16	12	10	43	39	60
4	FC Metz	38	14	14	10	43	39	56
5	Angers SCO	38	15	10	13	46	43	55
6	Clermont Foot Auvergne	38	15	9	14	48	41	54
7	Le Havre AC	38	14	10	14	45	50	52
8	Stade Lavallois MFC	38	11	18	9	49	41	51
9	Dijon FCO	38	12	15	11	52	46	51
10	Nîmes Olympique	38	13	12	13	37	43	51
11	Tours FC	38	11	16	11	47	46	49
12	CS Sedan Ardennes	38	11	16	11	46	46	49
13	AC Ajaccio	38	13	9	16	41	42	48
14	Vannes OC	38	11	13	14	40	49	46
15	FC Nantes	38	12	9	17	43	54	45
16	La Berrichonne de Châteauroux	38	10	14	14	50	54	44
17	FC Istres	38	11	11	16	34	52	44
18	En Avant Guingamp	38	9	16	13	35	40	43
19	RC Strasbourg	38	9	15	14	42	49	42
20	SC Bastia	38	10	9	19	40	48	39

FRANCE

DOMESTIC CUPS 2009/10

COUPE DE FRANCE

1/32 FINALS

(8/1/10)
Pau 0, Évian-Thonon 2

(9/1/10)
AC Ajaccio 3, Cannes 0
Bordeaux 1, Rodez 0
Chauray 0, Agen 1
Laval 1, Vesoul 2 *(aet)*
Le Mans 1, Valenciennes 0
Les Herbiers 0, Toulouse 1
Monaco 0, Tours 0 *(aet; 4-3 on pens)*
Rennes 2, Caen 0
Saint-Dizier 0, Raon-l'Étape 4
Seclin 1, Boulogne 4
Strasbourg 1, Lyon 3
Vannes 1, Troyes 1 *(aet; 8-7 on pens)*

(10/1/10)
Aubervilliers 0, PSG 5
Bonchamps-Laval 0, Guingamp 2
Lattes 0, Angers 1
Plabennec 2, Nice 1
Trélissac 0, Marseille 2
Versailles 0, Beauvais 3

(11/1/10)
Amiens 1, Auxerre 1

(16/1/10)
Avranches 0, Saumur 1 *(aet)*
La Grande Motte 0, Villefranche 2
Marquette 1, Mulhouse 2
Quevilly 6, Saint-Quentin 0

(23/1/10)
Colmar 0, Lille 0 *(aet; 10-9 on pens)*
Compiègne 0, Lens 1
Grenoble 3, Montpellier 2 *(aet)*
Pontivy 0, Brest 1 *(aet)*
Saint-Louis Neuweg 0, Sochaux 1
Saint-Ouen l'Aumône 0, Sedan 3

(24/1/10)
St-Étienne 4, Lorient 1
Thiers 1, Nancy 1 *(aet; 2-3 on pens)*

1/16 FINALS

(22/1/10)
Saumur 0, Rennes 4

(23/1/10)
Beauvais 3, Agen 0
Bordeaux 5, AC Ajaccio 1
Quevilly 1, Angers 0
Raon-l'Étape 0, Vesoul 1

(24/1/10)
Monaco 2, Lyon 1
Mulhouse 0, Guingamp 1
PSG 3, Évian-Thonon 1

(26/1/10)
Auxerre 1, Sedan 1 *(aet; 3-0 on pens)*
Vannes 4, Grenoble 3 *(aet)*

(27/1/10)
Colmar 1, Boulogne 2
Nancy 0, Plabennec 2

(3/2/10)
Sochaux 3, Le Mans 0
Villefranche 2, St-Étienne 2 *(aet; 1-3 on pens)*

(10/2/10)
Lens 3, Marseille 1
Toulouse 0, Brest 2

1/8 FINALS

(9/2/10)
Beauvais 1, Sochaux 4
Boulogne 1, Guingamp 0
Quevilly 1, Rennes 0
Vesoul 0, PSG 1

(10/2/10)
Auxerre 4, Plabennec 0
Bordeaux 0, Monaco 2
St-Étienne 2, Vannes 0

(17/2/10)
Lens 2, Brest 1 *(aet)*

QUARTER-FINALS

(23/3/10)
Auxerre 0, PSG 0 *(aet; 5-6 on pens)*
Quevilly 3 *(Coquio 12, Laup 29, Ouahbi 67)*,
Boulogne 1 *(Marcq 45)*

(24/3/10)
Lens 3 *(Eduardo 35, Yahia 75, Roudet 90)*,
St-Étienne 1 *(Mirallas 1)*
Monaco 4 *(Puygrenier 34, Haruna 38, Pino 90, Maazou 95)*, Sochaux 3 *(Boudebouz 29, Dalmat 48, Brown 71)* *(aet)*

SEMI-FINALS

(13/4/10)
Monaco 1 *(Maazou 110)*, Lens 0 *(aet)*

(14/4/10)
Quevilly 0, PSG 1 *(Mevlüt 51)*

FINAL

(1/5/10)
Stade de France, Saint-Denis
PARIS SAINT-GERMAIN FC 1 *(Hoarau 107)*
AS MONACO FC 0
(aet)
Referee – *Jaffredo*
PSG – Edel, Jallet *(Traoré 117)*, Camara,
Sakho, Armand, Makelele, Clément, Giuly
(Luyindula 77), Sessegnon, Hoarau, Mevlüt
(Ceará 105).
MONACO – Ruffier, Modesto, Mongongu,
Puygrenier, Traoré, Eduardo Costa *(Sagbo 110)*, Mangani *(Haruna 55)*, Pino *(Maazou 86)*, Alonso, Nenê, Park.

COUPE DE LA LIGUE

QUARTER-FINALS

(27/1/10)
Guingamp 0, Toulouse 1 *(Ebondo 54)*
Lorient 1 *(Gameiro 4)*, Lyon 0
Marseille 2 *(Lucho González 9, Valbuena 81)*, Lille 1 *(Túlio de Melo 4)*

(2/2/10)
Bordeaux 1 *(Gouffran 50)*, Sedan 0

SEMI-FINALS

(3/2/10)
Toulouse 1 *(Gignac 60)*, Marseille 2 *(Brandão 86, 105)* *(aet)*

(17/2/10)
Lorient 1 *(Koscielny 12)*, Bordeaux 4 *(Wendel 24p, 81, Chamakh 28, Gouffran 88)*

FINAL

(27/3/10)
Stade de France, Saint-Denis
OLYMPIQUE DE MARSEILLE 3 *(Diawara 61, Valbuena 68, Chalmé 77og)*
FC GIRONDINS DE BORDEAUX 1 *(Sané 85)*
Referee – *Lannoy*
MARSEILLE – Mandanda, Bonnart, Diawara, Mbia, Taiwo, Lucho
González *(Abriel 74)*, Cissé, Kaboré, Ben Arfa *(Heinze 66)*, Niang
(Valbuena 52), Brandão.
BORDEAUX – Ramé, Chalmé, Sané, Ciani, Trémoulinas, Plašil, Fernando
(Jussiê 66), Diarra, Gourcuff *(Gouffran 70)*, Wendel, Chamakh
(Cavenaghi 70).

Olimpi benefit from Brazilian blend

A turbulent season for Georgian football ended with FC Olimpi Rustavi being crowned as Umaglesi Liga champions and FC WIT Georgia, the team they succeeded, coming good in the other domestic competition to win the Georgian Cup, defeating holders FC Dinamo Tbilisi 1-0 in the first final between two clubs from the capital.

Olimpi's title triumph – their second in four seasons – was largely attributable to their bold pre-season recruitment of six Brazilian players on loan from CA Paranaense. Some were better than others and one of them, striker Anderson Aquino, was outstanding. He found the defences of Georgia's top division very much to his liking, notching five goals in his first five games and going on to maintain a steady supply throughout the season. By the end of the campaign the 24-year-old had struck 26 times in 31 matches and become the first foreigner to win the Umaglesi Liga's Golden Boot, scoring ten goals more than the runner-up, FC Zestafoni's Nikoloz Gelashvili, who had won the trophy the previous season.

Irresistible surge

Powered by the boy from Brazil, Olimpi proved irresistible, going unbeaten for six months – an 18-game sequence interrupted only by a disciplinary defeat, after an ugly on-pitch brawl between players and fans forced their match at Zestafoni to be abandoned – and taking the title with three games to spare after a 1-1 draw at home to second-placed Dinamo gave them an unassailable 11-point lead. A stuttering finish meant that the margin of victory over Dinamo was down to five points by the close of the campaign, but that could not detract from the achievement of a team that had used as many as 39 players over the 36-match campaign and had undergone two changes of coach.

Varlam Kilasonia was dismissed on the eve of the league campaign after Olimpi's UEFA Europa League elimination by Legia Warszawa. His replacement, Otar Korgalidze, lasted only three months before he was replaced by Temur Makharadze, and it was under the veteran journeyman coach that Olimpi enjoyed the fabulous mid-season run that propelled them to victory.

Defending champions WIT had to make do without their long-serving, title-winning coach Nestor Mumladze, who suddenly announced his retirement in August, but with Merab Kochiashvili, his replacement, returning for a second spell in charge at the tail-end of the campaign, the club made up for a disappointing title defence by winning the Georgian Cup for the first time, a bitterly contested derby against Dinamo being decided by Pavle Datunaishvili's near-post header just before half-time.

As a team WIT did not fire on all cylinders in 2009/10, but their young blond attacking midfielder Irakli Klimiashvili did, emerging as the country's brightest young star – an Under-21 international blessed with the kind of natural talent that his country have been crying out for at senior level. He won his first full international cap three days before his 20th birthday, in May 2008, and although by the end of the 2009/10 season he had yet to start a game for Georgia, it can safely be assumed that he will be called upon for the UEFA EURO 2012 qualifiers.

Ketsbaia comes in

Georgia go into that campaign with a new coach, national icon Temur Ketsbaia, who was appointed in November 2009 – a couple of months after walking away from a plum club job at Greek giants Olympiacos FC. The appointment of the 42-year-old ex-international midfielder, who proved his international coaching credentials by taking Cypriot club Anorthosis

Temur Ketsbaia –
a popular choice as Georgia's
new national team coach

GEORGIA

Famagusta FC into the group stage of the 2008/09 UEFA Champions League, was warmly received in his homeland.

Whatever Ketsbaia goes on to achieve, he can do no worse than his predecessor, Héctor Cúper, who oversaw a wretched 2010 FIFA World Cup qualifying campaign, from which Georgia plundered a mere three points. The Argentine's sorry reign ended with five straight defeats, the last of them a 6-2 thumping by Bulgaria in Sofia. Ketsbaia, by contrast, started with a 2-1 win against Estonia and a goalless draw against Cameroon. With Croatia, Greece, Israel, Latvia and Malta to face on the road to Poland/Ukraine, a mid-table position has to be the very least of Georgia's objectives. And if Ketsbaia can instruct and inspire his charges as the nation hopes, a challenge for second place – and the play-offs - is not entirely out of the question.

Georgian Football Federation (GFF)

76a Chavchavadze Ave.
GE-0162 Tbilisi
tel – +995 32 912 680
fax – +995 32 915 995
website – gff.ge
email – gff@gff.ge

Year of Formation – 1990
President – Domenti Sichinava
General Secretary – Revaz Arveladze
Media Officer – Lasha Dvalishvili
National Stadium – Boris Paichadze, Tbilisi (53,284)

TOP FIVE ALL-TIME CAPS
Levan Kobiashvili (82); Giorgi Nemsadze (69); Kakha Kaladze (65); Gocha Jamarauli (62); Shota Arveladze (61).
TOP FIVE ALL-TIME GOALS
Shota Arveladze (26); Temur Ketsbaia (17); Aleksandre Iashvili (13); Giorgi Demetradze (12); Mikheil Kavelashvili & Levan Kobiashvili (9).

NATIONAL TEAM RESULTS 2009/10

12/8/09	Malta	A	Ta'Qali	0-2	
5/9/09	Italy (WCQ)	H	Tbilisi	0-2	
9/9/09	Iceland	A	Reykjavik	1-3	Dvalishvili (33)
10/10/09	Montenegro (WCQ)	A	Podgorica	1-2	Dvalishvili (45)
14/10/09	Bulgaria (WCQ)	A	Sofia	2-6	Dvalishvili (34), Kobiashvili (51p)
3/3/10	Estonia	H	Tbilisi	2-1	Kobiashvili (45p), Siradze (90+4)
25/5/10	Cameroon	N	Linz (AUT)	0-0	

NATIONAL TEAM APPEARANCES 2009/10

Coach – Héctor CÚPER (ARG) /(6/11/09) Temur KETSBAIA	16/11/55 18/3/68		Mlt	ITA	Isl	MNE	BUL	Est	Cmr	Caps	Goals
Giorgi LOMAIA	8/8/79	İnter Bakı (AZE)	G	G		G	G29	G		45	-
Mate GVINIANIDZE	10/12/86	1860 München (GER)	D82							7	-
Guram KASHIA	4/7/87	Dinamo Tbilisi	D		D			s84		5	-
Zurab KHIZANISHVILI	6/10/81	Blackburn (ENG) /Newcastle (ENG) /Reading (ENG)	D	D		D	D	M56	D	66	1
Giorgi POPKHADZE	25/9/86	Viborg (DEN)	D85		D	s79				7	-
Giorgi SETURIDZE	8/4/85	Olimpi /Standard (AZE)	M68		M					5	-
Levan KOBIASHVILI	10/7/77	Schalke (GER) /Hertha (GER)	M	M		M		M	M	87	11
Levan TSKITISHVILI	10/10/76	unattached	M64	s73	M60					58	1
Levan KHMALADZE	6/4/85	Dinamo Tbilisi	M	M	s60	M	M 58*			10	-
Levan KENIA	18/10/90	Schalke (GER)	M	M			M88			18	3
Vladimer DVALISHVILI	20/4/86	M. Haifa (ISR)	A	A	A	A	A	A46	A69	9	4
David DEVDARIANI	28/10/87	AGF (DEN)	s64		M					4	-
Giorgi MEREBASHVILI	15/8/86	Dinamo Tbilisi /Vojvodina (SRB)	s68		M76	s78		s46	s76	12	-

NATIONAL TEAM APPEARANCES 2009/10 (contd.)

			Mlt	ITA	Isl	MNE	BUL	Est	Cmr	Caps	Goals
Teimuraz GONGADZE	8/9/85	Simurq (AZE)	s82	D73						2	-
Amiran SANAIA	3/9/89	Le Mans (FRA)	s85	D		D79	D78			6	-
Micha LOBJANIDZE	23/2/87	Zestafoni /Dnipro (UKR)	D	s73	D	D			D	15	-
Kakha KALADZE	27/2/78	Milan (ITA)	D		D	D	D			69	1
Luka RAZMADZE	30/12/83	WIT	M73	M	M	M				11	-
Zhano ANANIDZE	10/10/92	Spartak Moskva (RUS)	M59						M58	2	-
Mate VATSADZE	17/12/88	Dinamo Tbilisi	s59						s46	2	-
Zurab MAMALADZE	2/10/82	Zestafoni					G		s29	3	-
Aleksandre KVAKHADZE	17/8/84	WIT					D			11	-
Nikoloz GELASHVILI	5/8/85	Zestafoni					A	A67	s58	5	-
Aleksandre IASHVILI	23/10/77	Karlsruhe (GER)			M	M		M66	M76	55	13
Jaba LIPARTIA	16/11/87	WIT						s67		1	-
David ODIKADZE	14/4/81	İnter Bakı (AZE)						s76	s88	14	-
Lasha SALUKVADZE	21/12/81	Rubin (RUS)						D66		29	1
Malkhaz ASATIANI	4/8/81	Lokomotiv Moskva (RUS)						D	M	37	4
David KVIRKVELIA	27/6/80	Anzhi (RUS)						D		38	-
Otar MARTSVALADZE	14/7/84	Volga N. Novgorod (RUS)						M46		13	2
Gogita GOGUA	4/10/83	Spartak Nalchik (RUS)						M84		20	1
Zurab MENTESHASHVILI	30/1/80	H. Tel-Aviv (ISR)						s56	M58	40	1
Giorgi SHASHIASHVILI	1/9/79	Ergotelis (GRE)						s66	s89	32	1
David SIRADZE	21/10/81	Spartak Nalchik (RUS)						s66		19	5
Nukri REVISHVILI	2/3/87	Anzhi (RUS)							G	9	-
Aleksandre AMISULASHVILI	20/8/82	Spartak Nalchik (RUS)							D	11	1
Ilia KANDELAKI	26/12/81	Sturm (AUT)							D89	14	-
Tornike APTSIAURI	28/11/79	Zestafoni							s58	3	-
Revaz BARABADZE	4/10/88	Anzhi (RUS)							s69	2	-

DOMESTIC LEAGUE 2009/10

UMAGLESI LIGA FINAL TABLE

		Pld	Home					Away					Total					Pts
			W	D	L	F	A	W	D	L	F	A	W	D	L	F	A	
1	FC Olimpi Rustavi	36	14	4	0	39	5	11	3	4	30	21	25	7	4	69	26	79
2	FC Dinamo Tbilisi	36	14	2	2	38	6	8	6	4	24	13	22	8	6	62	19	74
3	FC Zestafoni	36	11	4	3	37	16	8	6	4	21	17	19	10	7	58	33	67
4	FC WIT Georgia	36	9	7	2	30	15	8	6	4	18	16	17	13	6	48	31	64
5	FC Spartaki Tskhinvali	36	7	7	4	27	21	4	3	11	17	37	11	10	15	44	58	43
6	FC Sioni Bolnisi	36	4	7	7	14	21	4	7	7	13	22	8	14	14	27	43	38
7	FC Samtredia	36	9	2	7	24	24	1	5	12	19	44	10	7	19	43	68	37
8	FC Baia Zugdidi	36	5	7	6	20	23	2	4	12	9	25	7	11	18	29	48	32
9	FC Lokomotivi Tbilisi	36	3	5	10	11	27	2	6	10	8	23	5	11	20	19	50	26
10	FC Gagra	36	5	5	8	18	16	0	4	14	12	43	5	9	22	30	59	24

NB FC Olimpi Rustavi – 3 pts deducted. Zestafoni v Olimpi was awarded as a 0-3 defeat to both sides.

TOP GOALSCORERS

26 ANDERSON AQUINO (Olimpi)
16 Nikoloz GELASHVILI (Zestafoni)
13 Jaba DVALI (Zestafoni)
12 Vakhtang KVARATSKHELIA (WIT)
11 Georges AKIEREMY (Dinamo)
   Zaur KHACHIPERADZE (Samtredia)
10 Mate VATSADZE (Dinamo)
   Giorgi GABEDAVA (Gagra)
8 Guram KASHIA (Dinamo)
  Giorgi CHEDIA (Olimpi)
  David IMEDASHVILI (Olimpi)
  Giorgi BERIASHVILI (WIT)

CLUB-BY-CLUB

FC BAIA ZUGDIDI
Coach – Besik Sherozia; (12/2/10) Elguja Kometiani
Founded – 2005
Stadium – G. Tutberidze (4,200)

2009
1/8	Olimpi	h	1-2	Kiria D.
8/8	Spartaki	a	0-1	
15/8	Lokomotivi	h	2-1	Kiria D. 2
22/8	Samtredia	a	0-1	
30/8	Gagra	h	2-2	Jikia, Khutsidze
12/9	Sioni	a	0-1	
19/9	Dinamo	h	0-6	
25/9	WIT	a	1-2	Jikia
29/9	Zestafoni	h	0-1	
4/10	Olimpi	a	0-2	
17/10	Spartaki	h	4-1	Jikia 2, Ekhvaia, Vartagava
24/10	Lokomotivi	a	0-0	
30/10	Samtredia	h	2-2	Dzalamidze 2
8/11	Gagra	a	0-1	
22/11	Sioni	h	2-0	Guguchia, Oniani
28/11	Dinamo	a	0-1	
6/12	WIT	h	0-1	
12/12	Zestafoni	a	1-2	Guguchia

2010
12/2	Spartaki	h	0-2	
17/2	Lokomotivi	h	0-0	
21/2	Samtredia	a	1-0	Oniani
26/2	Gagra	h	2-1	Akobia 2
6/3	Sioni	a	0-0	
10/3	Olimpi	a	0-1	
14/3	Dinamo	h	1-1	Oniani
19/3	WIT	a	2-2	Pipia, Ekhvaia
27/3	Zestafoni	h	0-1	
3/4	Olimpi	h	1-1	Lungu
10/4	Spartaki	a	0-2	
18/4	Lokomotivi	a	3-1	Pipia, Ekhvaia, Oniani
25/4	Samtredia	h	2-0	Sakhokia, Bakarandze
30/4	Gagra	a	1-1	Ekhvaia
5/5	Sioni	h	0-0	
9/5	Dinamo	a	0-3	
15/5	WIT	h	1-1	Ekhvaia
20/5	Zestafoni	a	0-4	

Name	Nat	DoB	Pos	Aps	(s)	Gls
Levan AKOBIA		11/2/80	D	17		2
Makar AKUBARDIA		20/1/88	D	22		
Nikoloz APAKIDZE		4/4/92	M		(1)	
Paata BAKARANDZE		20/3/82	A	10	(1)	1
Mamuka CHKADUA		15/11/85	M		(4)	
Nika DZALAMIDZE		6/1/92	M	9	(2)	2
Irakli EKHVAIA		9/1/91	A	11	(13)	5
Zurab EKONIA		7/6/84	D	14	(2)	
Valter GUCHUA		6/7/75	M	13		
Luka GUGUCHIA		10/12/91	D	11	(7)	2
Rezo JIKIA		1/9/80	A	12		4
Giga JVANIA		16/1/82	D	12	(1)	
Irakli KHUTSIDZE		16/4/90	A	4	(3)	1
David KIRIA		8/2/82	M	8	(3)	3
Giorgi KIRIA		10/5/83	M	11	(8)	
Lasha KUKAVA		12/1/92	M	2	(2)	
David KUTALIA		5/12/89	M	2	(10)	
Nika KVEKVESKIRI		29/5/92	D	17	(5)	
Amiran KVELASHVILI		10/2/85	D	14		
Giorgi KVESIESHVILI		1/12/85	D	17		
Shota LOMIA		13/2/84	M	5	(3)	
Chisamba LUNGU	ZAM	31/1/91	A	27	(2)	1
Archil MAKATSARIA		19/3/92	G	14		
Roin ONIANI		14/6/75	D	30		4

Giorgi PACHKORIA	29/5/89	M	2	(1)	
Gogi PIPIA	4/2/85	A	12	(4)	2
Data RAPAVA	10/10/91	D		(2)	
Zaza SAKHOKIA	12/2/84	A	5	(4)	1
Guram SAMADASHVILI	5/2/86	A	1	(5)	
Guram SAMUSHIA	5/9/94	M		(1)	
Koba SHONIA	12/12/88	M		(1)	
Nika SHONIA	12/12/88	M	1	(1)	
Zviad SIKHARULIA	1/8/92	M	3	(9)	
Giorgi SOMKHISHVILI	27/11/80	G	17		
Lasha SVIRAVA	8/3/89	D	3		
Sevasti TODUA	13/5/76	D	17		
Levan TSURTSUMIA	28/1/89	A	17	(7)	
Levan VARTAGAVA	10/8/81	M	31	(3)	1
Tornike ZARKUA	1/9/90	G	5		

FC DINAMO TBILISI
Coach –Kakha Kacharava
Founded – 1925
Stadium – Boris Paichadze (53,284)
MAJOR HONOURS:
UEFA Cup Winners' Cup – (1) 1981;
USSR League – (2) 1964, 1978;
Georgian League - (13) 1990, 1991, 1992, 1993, 1994, 1995, 1996, 1997,
1998, 1999, 2003, 2005, 2008;
USSR Cup - (2) 1976, 1979;
Georgian Cup - (9) 1992, 1993, 1994, 1995, 1996, 1997, 2003, 2004, 2009.

2009
16/8	Spartaki	h	5-0	Kashia S., Pirtskhalava, Vatsadze, Akieremy, Nergadze
22/8	WIT	h	0-0	
25/8	Gagra	h	2-0	Merebashvili 2
29/8	Zestafoni	a	1-4	Akieremy
13/9	Olimpi	h	4-0	Koshkadze 2, Digmelashvili, Kashia G.
19/9	Baia	a	6-0	Merebashvili 2, Koshkadze 2, Vatsadze 2
22/9	Sioni	a	0-0	
25/9	Lokomotivi	h	1-0	Merebashvili (p)
30/9	Samtredia	a	1-3	Vatsadze
4/10	Gagra	a	0-0	
18/10	Sioni	h	0-2	
25/10	Spartaki	a	1-1	Koshkadze
30/10	WIT	a	0-0	
7/11	Zestafoni	h	2-0	Koshkadze, Kashia G.
22/11	Olimpi	a	0-1	
28/11	Baia	h	1-0	Merebashvili
6/12	Lokomotivi	a	3-0	Akieremy, Kashia G., Merebashvili
12/12	Samtredia	h	2-0	Kashia G., Mamuchashvili

2010
8/2	Gagra	h	4-1	Vatsadze 2, Kashia S., Chikviladze
17/2	Spartaki	h	2-0	Akieremy, Kashia G. (p)
21/2	WIT	h	1-2	Kashia G. (p)
26/2	Zestafoni	a	1-0	Kashia G.
6/3	Olimpi	h	0-0	
10/3	Sioni	a	1-0	Vatsadze
14/3	Baia	a	1-1	Krsteski
19/3	Lokomotivi	h	1-0	Krsteski
27/3	Samtredia	a	1-0	Chikviladze
3/4	Gagra	a	1-0	Kashia G.
10/4	Sioni	h	4-0	Chikviladze 2, Akieremy, Vatsadze
18/4	Spartaki	a	1-2	Akieremy
24/4	WIT	a	2-0	Akieremy 2
1/5	Zestafoni	h	2-0	Akieremy 2
5/5	Olimpi	a	1-1	Chikviladze
9/5	Baia	h	3-0	Akieremy, Kashia S. (p), Chikviladze
15/5	Lokomotivi	a	3-0	Vatsadze 2, Robertinho
20/5	Samtredia	h	4-1	Lekvtadze 2, Sikharulidze 2

Name	Nat	DoB	Pos	Aps	(s)	Gls
Georges Edouard AKIEREMY Owondo	GAB	23/4/82	A	23	(5)	11
Elguja AVSAJANISHVILI		15/9/90	M		(1)	
Lasha CHADUNELI		14/1/90	D	3	(3)	
Tengiz CHIKVILADZE		12/8/83	D	16		6
David DIGMELASHVILI		18/1/80	M	10		1
Donald Dering DJOUSSE	CMR	18/3/90	A	8	(6)	
EDNILSON Pedro Rocha Andrade Mendes	POR	25/9/82	M	16	(1)	
Giorgi GETIASHVILI		7/3/90	D	3		
Giorgi ICHKITI		29/4/90	M		(1)	
Nikoloz JISHKARIANI		4/6/90	M		(2)	
Giorgi KAKHELISHVILI		22/5/87	M	16		
Levan KAKUBAVA		15/10/90	D	22	(5)	
Zviad KANTARIA		3/6/90	A		(3)	
Guram KASHIA		4/7/87	D	33		8
Shota KASHIA		22/10/84	D	34	(1)	3
Giorgi KAVTARADZE		1/1/89	M	1	(4)	
Saba KHAZALIA		21/3/91	M		(1)	
Levan KHMALADZE		6/4/85	M	13		
Aleksandre KOSHKADZE		4/12/81	M	24		6
Aleksandar KRSTESKI	MKD	3/9/83	D	14	(1)	2
Irakli LEKVTADZE		30/8/91	M	3	(4)	2
Shota LOMIA		13/2/84	M	1	(5)	
Giorgi LORIA		27/1/86	G	34		
Giorgi MAMUCHASHVILI		12/4/90	M	13	(5)	1
Giorgi MEREBASHVILI		15/8/86	A	14	(2)	7
Guram MINDORASHVILI		16/2/90	D	1		
Vaja NEMSADZE		7/12/90	M	15	(6)	
Giorgi NERGADZE		20/8/82	D	11		1
Giorgi OTARISHVILI		12/12/90	M	1		
Nikoloz PIRTSKHALAVA		15/5/87	M	8	(5)	1
Roberto Soares Anghinetti "ROBERTINHO"	BRA	13/6/88	M	1	(7)	1
Beka SHEKRILADZE		28/11/83	G	1		
Irakli SIKHARULIDZE		18/7/90	A	1	(11)	2
Giorgi SOMKHISHVILI		27/11/80	G	1		
Giorgi TEKTURMANIDZE		17/9/90	M	9	(1)	
Gulverd TOMASHVILI		13/10/88	D	30	(2)	
Giga TSENGUASHVILI		5/1/91	M	1		
Mate VATSADZE		17/12/88	A	14	(13)	10
Giorgi ZVIADADZE		15/9/91	A	1		

FC GAGRA

Coach – Kakha Karanadze; (3/4/10) Anatoly Piskovets
Founded – 2004
Stadium – Ameri, Tbilisi (900)

2009

8/8	WIT	h	4-0	Gabedava 4
16/8	Zestafoni	a	0-1	
22/8	Olimpi	h	0-1	
25/8	Dinamo	a	0-2	
30/8	Baia	a	2-2	Totadze, Pavliashvili
12/9	Lokomotivi	h	2-0	Gogichaishvili, Gabedava
20/9	Samtredia	a	3-4	Gabedava, Pavliashvili, og (Kvesieshvili)
26/9	Spartaki	a	1-3	Gabedava
30/9	Sioni	h	1-1	Owonikoko
4/10	Dinamo	h	0-0	
18/10	WIT	a	1-5	Pavliashvili
25/10	Zestafoni	h	0-1	
31/10	Olimpi	a	0-5	
8/11	Baia	h	1-0	Gabedava
22/11	Lokomotivi	a	0-1	
27/11	Samtredia	h	1-1	Koberidze
6/12	Spartaki	h	1-2	Koberidze
12/12	Sioni	a	1-1	Gabedava (p)

2010

8/2	Dinamo	a	1-4	Gabedava
17/2	Zestafoni	a	1-4	Chkhetiani
21/2	Olimpi	h	0-2	
26/2	Baia	a	1-2	Pavliashvili
6/3	Lokomotivi	h	0-1	
10/3	WIT	h	0-1	
14/3	Samtredia	a	0-1	
19/3	Spartaki	a	0-0	
26/3	Sioni	h	1-2	Gedenidze
3/4	Dinamo	h	0-1	
10/4	WIT	a	0-2	
17/4	Zestafoni	h	0-0	
25/4	Olimpi	a	0-3	
30/4	Baia	h	1-1	Tkeshelashvili
5/5	Lokomotivi	a	1-1	Kvantaliani
9/5	Samtredia	h	2-1	Kvantaliani, Koberidze
14/5	Spartaki	h	4-1	Kvantaliani 2, Tkeshelashvili, Okriashvili
20/5	Sioni	a	0-2	

No	Name	Nat	DoB	Pos	Aps	(s)	Gls
	Giorgi BAGALISHVILI		2/1/91	M		(2)	
	Serhiy BERBAT	UKR	11/11/80	M	4		
	Giorgi CHAAVA		27/11/91	D	12	(2)	
	Zviad CHKHETIANI		17/10/83	M	11	(4)	1
	Giorgi CHOKHONELIDZE		19/9/91	M		(2)	
	Giorgi ELBAKIDZE		28/6/88	D	1	(3)	
	Giorgi GABEDAVA		3/10/89	A	19	(10)	10
	Jemal GABUNIA		9/11/89	D	20	(2)	
	Bichiko GEDENIDZE		11/11/91	M	4	(2)	1
	David GIGAURI		15/1/86	D	11	(3)	
	Guram GOGICHAISHVILI		8/2/89	M	6	(3)	1
	Vasil GRYGOROVYCH	UKR	14/10/84	D	2		
	Giorgi GULORDAVA		6/4/87	M	2	(3)	
	Mikheil JISHKARIANI		31/10/92	A		(1)	
	Nikoloz JISHKARIANI		4/6/90	M	16		
	Noshrevan JISHKARIANI		24/1/92	D	3	(1)	
	Lasha KALANDADZE		17/6/91	M		(1)	
	Tsotne KHARABADZE		16/5/93	D	13		
	Pavle KHORGUASHVILI		13/8/87	M	10		
	Valter KHORGUASHVILI		13/8/87	M	5	(1)	
	Irakli KIKNADZE		1/2/87	M	3	(2)	
	Mikheil KOBERIDZE		4/5/87	M	15	(5)	3
	Ika KORTUA		5/10/87	D	12	(2)	
	Zurab KURDOBADZE		31/5/91	D	1		
	Akaki KUPREISHVILI		1/4/83	D	9	(1)	
	Shalva KVANTALIANI		26/3/91	A	5	(3)	4
	Nika KVASKHVADZE		15/4/88	M	7	(1)	
	MOISES Antônio da Silva	BRA	1/1/86	M	8	(1)	
	Tornike MOSIASHVILI		9/10/91	M	4	(5)	
	Lado NADIRASHVILI		12/2/84	G	5		
	Mykola NAKONECHNIY	UKR	10/9/81	D	8		
	Tornike OKRIASHVILI		12/2/92	M	20	(2)	1
	Olexandr OMELYANOV	UKR	10/11/79	M	4		
	Abayomi OWONIKOKO Seun	NGA	13/9/92	M	7	(18)	1
	Ilia PAVLIASHVILI		12/8/89	A	23	(8)	4
	Teimuraz RAKVIASHVILI		15/10/83	D	11		
	Irakli SHALIKASHVILI		24/10/90	M	5	(3)	
	Tornike SHALIKASHVILI		24/10/90	D	25		
	Levan SHARIKADZE		16/7/89	A	20	(2)	
	Nemo SHELIA		6/5/91	M	2	(1)	
	Zviad STURUA		25/4/78	G	5		
	Arnaud TCHUENSU	CMR	28/10/91	D	1		
	Revaz TEVDORADZE		14/2/88	G	26	(2)	
	Giorgi TKESHELASHVILI		24/8/85	M	18	(3)	2
	Lasha TOTADZE		24/8/88	D	11	(3)	1
	Giorgi TSAAVA		27/11/91	M		(1)	
	Tornike TUKHARELI		11/9/91	M	2	(8)	

GEORGIA

FC LOKOMOTIVI TBILISI
Coach – Gela Sanaia
Founded – 1936
Stadium – Mikheil Meskhi (24,455)
MAJOR HONOURS:
Georgian Cup - (3) 2000, 2002, 2005.

2009

2/8	Zestafoni	a	0-0	
8/8	Olimpi	h	1-2	Gusharashvili
15/8	Baia	a	1-2	Modebadze
22/8	Spartaki	a	0-2	
30/8	Samtredia	h	0-3	
12/9	Gagra	a	0-2	
19/9	Sioni	h	0-0	
25/9	Dinamo	a	0-1	
29/9	WIT	h	1-3	Kebadze (p)
3/10	Zestafoni	h	0-1	
17/10	Olimpi	a	1-3	og (Abramidze)
24/10	Baia	h	0-0	
30/10	Spartaki	h	0-0	
08/11	Samtredia	a	0-2	
22/11	Gagra	h	1-0	Kachakhidze
27/11	Sioni	a	0-0	
6/12	Dinamo	h	0-3	
12/12	WIT	a	1-1	Chikvaidze

2010

8/2	Zestafoni	a	1-1	Metreveli
17/2	Baia	a	0-0	
21/2	Spartaki	a	1-1	Gotsiridze
26/2	Samtredia	h	3-2	Metreveli, Gotsiridze, Chagelishvili D.
6/3	Gagra	a	1-0	Chelidze
14/3	Sioni	h	0-1	
19/3	Dinamo	a	0-1	
24/3	Olimpi	a	0-2	
28/3	WIT	h	0-1	
2/4	Zestafoni	h	1-1	Chelidze (p)
12/4	Olimpi	h	0-2	
18/4	Baia	h	1-3	Chelidze (p)
25/4	Spartaki	h	2-1	Gusharashvili, Metreveli
1/5	Samtredia	a	2-1	Makharadze B., Chikvaidze
5/5	Gagra	h	1-1	Metreveli
9/5	Sioni	a	0-1	
15/5	Dinamo	h	0-3	
20/5	WIT	a	0-3	

Name	Nat	DoB	Pos	Aps	(s)	Gls
Iakob APKHAZAVA		30/4/91	A	3	(9)	
Giorgi BARBAKADZE		6/5/89	M	1	(1)	
Beka BEBUA		26/9/89	D	2	(1)	
Zakaria BEGLARISHVILI		30/4/90	M	1		
Giorgi BOCHORMELI		26/1/90	M	10	(3)	
David CHAGELISHVILI		10/1/87	A	9	(14)	1
Levan CHAGELISHVILI		10/1/87	D	28		
Lasha CHAGIASHVILI		17/2/81	D	2		
Giorgi CHELIDZE		29/4/84	M	18		3
Giorgi CHIKVAIDZE		11/9/89	M	14	(10)	2
Konstantine DARSANIA		29/10/84	M	1	(2)	
Zamora DATUNASHVILI		31/7/88	A	1		
Irakli DGEBUADZE		4/5/90	G	1		
Giorgi DIAKVNISHVILI		21/11/87	M	28	(1)	
Ilia GADELIA		19/12/90	D	7		
Ioseb GILAURI		11/10/88	M	6	(5)	
Irakli GONADZE		2/9/90	A	9	(4)	
Bondo GOTSIRIDZE		15/4/86	M	11	(6)	2
Nika GUSHARASHVILI		25/7/83	D	28		2
Amiran GVENTSADZE		10/4/87	G	1		
Erekle KACHAKHIDZE		19/1/91	M	9	(4)	1
David KAKULIA		5/1/91	M	2	(3)	
Lasha KEBADZE		27/8/83	M	23	(6)	1
Giorgi KHATIASHVILI		7/1/88	D	31		
Giorgi KHUMARASHVILI		24/8/89	D	3		
Levan KURDADZE		3/9/90	D	2	(2)	
Giorgi KVANTALIANI		6/8/89	D	4		
Lasha KVARATSKHELIA		29/1/94	M		(1)	
Maksime KVILITAIA		17/9/85	G	34		
Boris MAKHARADZE		8/11/90	M	8	(14)	1
Giorgi MAKHARADZE		6/1/90	M		(2)	
Zviad METREVELI		28/11/85	A	16	(1)	4
Giorgi MODEBADZE		27/3/83	A	6	(2)	1
Levan SARALIDZE		8/4/86	D	27		
Aleksandre SHENGELIA		27/6/89	M	10	(6)	
Giorgi SOSELIA		1/1/91	M	7	(1)	
Anzor SUKHIASHVILI		27/10/88	M	1		
Giorgi TIKURISHVILI		15/3/89	M	9		
Revaz TSULADZE		20/1/89	M	16	(6)	
Ilia VEKUA		20/12/89	D	7	(3)	

FC OLIMPI RUSTAVI
Coach – Otar Korgalidze; (25/10/09) Temur Makharadze
Founded – 1991
Stadium – Poladi (4,656)
MAJOR HONOURS:
Georgian League - (2) 2007, 2010.

2009

1/8	Baia	a	2-1	Todua G., Anderson Aquino
8/8	Lokomotivi	a	2-1	Anderson Aquino, Gerônimo
15/8	Samtredia	h	5-0	Jonatas 2, Anderson Aquino 2 (1p), Rekhviashvili
22/8	Gagra	a	1-0	Machavariani
30/8	Sioni	h	3-0	Anderson Aquino, Jonatas (p), Gerônimo
13/9	Dinamo	a	0-4	
19/9	WIT	h	0-0	
25/9	Zestafoni	a	2-2	Abramidze, Chedia
30/9	Spartaki	h	1-1	Anderson Aquino
4/10	Baia	h	2-0	Anderson Aquino (p), Babunashvili
17/10	Lokomotivi	h	3-1	Salles, Anderson Aquino 2 (2p)
25/10	Samtredia	a	4-0	Imedashvili, Anderson Aquino 2 (1p), Chedia
31/10	Gagra	h	5-0	Anderson Aquino 3 (1p), Chedia, Gerônimo
8/11	Sioni	a	6-0	Imedashvili 2, Alex, Chedia, Babunashvili, Salles
22/11	Dinamo	h	1-0	Anderson Aquino
27/11	WIT	a	2-1	Chedia 2
5/12	Zestafoni	h	1-0	Anderson Aquino (p)
12/12	Spartaki	a	2-1	Anderson Aquino 2 (1p)

2010

17/2	Samtredia	h	3-1	Kvaratskhelia, Iashvili, Anderson Aquino
21/2	Gagra	a	2-0	Imedashvili, Chedia
26/2	Sioni	h	0-0	
6/3	Dinamo	a	0-0	
10/3	Baia	h	1-0	Anderson Aquino
14/3	WIT	h	1-0	Anderson Aquino (p)
20/3	Zestafoni	a	0-3	(w/o; match abandoned at 1-1 Jikia)
24/3	Lokomotivi	h	2-0	Anderson Aquino 2
28/3	Spartaki	h	4-0	Jikia, Anderson Aquino 2 (1p), Kvaratskhelia
3/4	Baia	a	1-1	Anderson Aquino
12/4	Lokomotivi	a	2-0	Iashvili 2
17/4	Samtredia	a	1-0	Imedashvili
25/4	Gagra	h	3-0	Iashvili, Imedashvili 2
1/5	Sioni	a	2-1	Imedashvili, Iashvili
5/5	Dinamo	h	1-1	Kvaratskhelia
9/5	WIT	a	0-2	
15/5	Zestafoni	h	3-1	Chedia, Kvaratskhelia 2
20/5	Spartaki	a	1-4	Rekhviashvili

Name	Nat	DoB	Pos	Aps	(s)	Gls
Valeri ABRAMIDZE		17/1/80	D	11		1
Mikheil Alavidze		5/11/87	G	1	(1)	
ALEX José de Oliveira Fraga	BRA	22/5/86	D	31		1
Besik AMASHUKELI		16/9/92	M	1		
ANDERSON Angus AQUINO	BRA	18/12/86	A	31		26
Vasil APTSIAURI		9/9/90	M		(1)	
Shota BABUNASHVILI		17/11/80	M	18		2
Grigol CHANTURIA		25/9/73	G	34		
Giorgi CHEDIA		28/8/88	A	24	(4)	8
Zaza CHELIDZE		12/1/87	M	6	(6)	
Pavle DATUNAISHVILI		25/8/83	M	9	(7)	
Denis DOBROVOLSKI		10/10/85	M	31	(4)	
Emanuel EGWARE ELOH	NGA	3/4/90	D		(3)	
GERÔNIMO dos Santos Oliveira	BRA	1/7/89	M	17		3
David GIGAURI		15/1/86	D	5	(5)	
Akvsenti GILAURI		6/8/79	M	2	(1)	
Temur GONGADZE		21/5/85	D	14		
Gaga GUGUNASHVILI		25/1/88	M		(1)	
João GUILHERME Estevão da Silva	BRA	4/1/90	M	3	(3)	
Oleg GVELESIANI		16/9/80	M	8	(5)	
Sandro IASHVILI		23/1/85	A	8	(5)	5
David IMEDASHVILI		15/12/84	M	31		8
Rezo JIKIA		1/9/80	A	8	(2)	2
JONATAS Oliveira Cardoso	BRA	30/8/88	M	6	(3)	3
David KAKULIA		5/1/91	M		(3)	
Valeri KAZAISHVILI		29/1/93	M	1	(1)	
Giorgi KHIDESHELI		21/11/85	M	5	(10)	
Gela KHUBUA		25/1/84	M	15	(1)	
Givi KVARATSKHELIA		11/5/79	M	15		5
Vakhtang LOBJANIDZE		18/11/92	G	1		
Nodar MACHAVARIANI		14/1/87	D	18	(6)	1
Mirza MERLANI		5/10/80	G		(1)	
Lasha PARUNASHVILI		14/2/93	A	1	(1)	
Dachi POPKHADZE		27/1/84	D	4	(5)	
Giorgi REKHVIASHVILI		1/2/88	D	15	(12)	2
Eduardo Faria Machado SALLES Filho	BRA	6/4/90	A	3	(3)	2
Giorgi SETURIDZE		1/4/85	M	3		
Gia TODUA		7/6/82	A		(8)	1
Sevasti TODUA		13/5/76	D	16		

FC SAMTREDIA

Coach – Valerian Chkhartishvili; (4/10/09) Mamuka Mesiachenko
& Levan Anjaparidze; (27/3/10) Levan Anjaparidze
Founded – 1936
Stadium – Erosi Manjgaladze (2,000)

2009

2/8	WIT	a	1-2	Bakarandze
8/8	Zestafoni	h	0-2	
15/8	Olimpi	a	0-5	
22/8	Baia	h	1-0	Kakaladze
30/8	Lokomotivi	a	3-0	Kakaladze 2 (1p), Tkemaladze
12/9	Spartaki	a	0-2	
20/9	Gagra	h	4-3	Vashakidze (p), Khachiperadze Z., og (Rakviashvili), Pirtskhalava
26/9	Sioni	a	0-3	
30/9	Dinamo	h	3-1	Tkemaladze, Kvesieshvili, Khachiperadze Z.
4/10	WIT	h	2-2	Bakarandze, Vashakidze
18/10	Zestafoni	a	2-4	Kakaladze, Khachiperadze Z.
25/10	Olimpi	h	0-4	
30/10	Baia	a	2-2	Khachiperadze Z. 2
8/11	Lokomotivi	h	2-0	Bakarandze, Chomakhidze
22/11	Spartaki	h	2-1	Koridze, Khachiperadze Z.
27/11	Gagra	a	1-1	Tkemaladze
6/12	Sioni	h	1-1	Kvesieshvili
12/12	Dinamo	a	0-2	
2010				
13/2	Zestafoni	h	2-3	Tkemaladze, Jvania
17/2	Olimpi	a	1-3	Samseishvili
21/2	Baia	h	0-1	

26/2	Lokomotivi	a	2-3	Samseishvili (p), Tkemaladze		
2/3	WIT	a	1-1	og (Kvakhadze)		
6/3	Spartaki	a	1-1	Khachiperadze Z.		
14/3	Gagra	h	1-0	Samseishvili (p)		
20/3	Sioni	a	2-2	Khachiperadze Z., Pirtskhalava		
27/3	Dinamo	h	0-1			
2/4	WIT	h	1-0	Bakuradze		
9/4	Zestafoni	a	1-5	Tkemaladze		
17/4	Olimpi	h	0-1			
25/4	Baia	a	0-2			
1/5	Lokomotivi	h	1-2	Khachiperadze Z.		
5/5	Spartaki	h	2-1	Chaladze, Khachiperadze Z.		
9/5	Gagra	a	1-2	Khachiperadze Z.		
15/5	Sioni	h	2-1	Samseishvili (p), Tkemaladze		
20/5	Dinamo	a	1-4	Baramidze		

Name	Nat	DoB	Pos	Aps	(s)	Gls
Paata BAKARANDZE		20/3/82	A	13	(2)	3
Levan BAKURADZE		18/1/86	M	24	(3)	1
Teimuraz BARAMIDZE		16/8/87	M	6	(10)	1
Lasha CHALADZE		5/11/87	M	13		1
Giorgi CHANTURIA		30/6/89	M		(1)	
Besik CHKHAIDZE		14/7/90	M		(3)	
Shota CHOMAKHIDZE		17/11/78	M	35		1
Giorgi DARBAIDZE		24/12/89	M	1	(4)	
Akaki DVALISHVILI		30/6/91	D	4	(1)	
Zurab ENDELADZE		23/4/91	D	1		
Zurab ETSADEISHVILI		6/10/85	A	9	(13)	
Spartak GOGIA		11/12/78	D	34		
Murad GOGISHVILI		15/6/92	M		(2)	
Aleksandre GUBELADZE		21/3/86	M		(1)	
Giorgi ILURIDZE		19/10/76	M	11	(1)	
Lasha JANGIDZE		11/5/83	M	6		
Levan JIKIDZE		30/3/86	D	1	(5)	
Kakhaber JINCHARADZE		25/3/85	G	2		
Giga JVANIA		16/1/82	D	4		1
Mikheil KAKALADZE		6/6/82	A	10		4
Tornike KAPANADZE		4/6/92	M		(1)	
Besik KHACHIPERADZE		19/11/84	D	2	(7)	
Zaur KHACHIPERADZE		19/9/86	A	16	(12)	11
David KHARDZEISHVILI		30/11/80	G	16		
David KIRKITADZE		3/9/92	D	1	(2)	
Kakhaber KIRTADZE		28/7/86	D	23	(3)	
Vaja KORIDZE		5/1/87	D	27		1
Akaki KUPREISHVILI		1/4/83	D	14		
Giorgi KVAGINIDZE		6/3/87	M	1	(1)	
Giorgi KVESIESHVILI		1/12/85	D	17		2
Gocha LOMIDZE		5/4/86	M	1	(1)	
Eric Francis MBENE	CMR	20/9/87	M	2		
Buba NIKURADZE		11/3/87	M	1		
Rezo NINUA		3/1/86	M	16	(9)	
Shalva PIRTSKHALAVA		18/9/84	M	15	(12)	2
Demur SAMSEISHVILI		3/5/85	A	12	(3)	4
Irakli SHENGELIA		25/7/87	G	18	(2)	
Valiko TKEMALADZE		14/11/87	M	25	(1)	7
Lasha VASHAKIDZE		19/11/85	M	15	(1)	2

FC SIONI BOLNISI

Coach – Teimuraz Makharadze; (25/10/09) Giorgi Kipshidze;
(5/2/10) Khvicha Kasrashvili
Founded – 1936
Stadium – T. Stepania (3,500)
MAJOR HONOURS:
Georgian League - (1) 2006.

2009

1/8	Spartaki	h	1-4	Bobokhidze
16/8	WIT	a	1-2	Gogoberishvili
22/8	Zestafoni	h	0-0	
30/8	Olimpi	a	0-3	
12/9	Baia	h	1-0	Khidesheli
19/9	Lokomotivi	a	0-0	

GEORGIA

22/9	Dinamo	h	0-0
26/9	Samtredia	h	3-0 *Kiknadze, Svanidze, Gogoberishvili (p)*
30/9	Gagra	a	1-1 *Kobauri*
4/10	Spartaki	a	1-1 *Chikviladze*
18/10	Dinamo	a	2-0 *Khubua, Khidesheli*
25/10	WIT	h	0-1
30/10	Zestafoni	a	0-3
8/11	Olimpi	h	0-6
22/11	Baia	a	0-2
27/11	Lokomotivi	h	0-0
6/12	Samtredia	a	1-1 *Chimakadze*
12/12	Gagra	h	1-1 *Gogoberishvili (p)*
2010			
5/2	Spartaki	h	0-1
16/2	WIT	a	0-0
21/2	Zestafoni	h	0-1
26/2	Olimpi	a	0-0
6/3	Baia	h	0-0
10/3	Dinamo	h	0-1
14/3	Lokomotivi	a	1-0 *Shengelia*
20/3	Samtredia	h	2-2 *Gogoberishvili (p), Ugrekhelidze*
26/3	Gagra	a	2-1 *Chelidze, Ugrekhelidze*
3/4	Spartaki	a	3-1 *Melkadze L., Gogoberishvili (p), Ugrekhelidze*
10/4	Dinamo	a	0-4
18/4	WIT	h	2-2 *Chelidze, og (Maisashvili)*
25/4	Zestafoni	a	0-1
1/5	Olimpi	h	1-2 *Melkadze G.*
5/5	Baia	a	0-0
9/5	Lokomotivi	h	1-0 *Gogoberishvili*
15/5	Samtredia	a	1-2 *Melkadze G.*
20/5	Gagra	h	2-0 *Ugulava J., Melkadze L.*

Name	Nat	DoB	Pos	Aps	(s)	Gls
Archil ALAVIDZE		6/10/85	M	1		
Levan BAJELIDZE		2/10/78	M	1	(4)	
Mindia BOBGIASHVILI		2/8/83	G	25		
Mikheil BOBOKHIDZE		23/11/81	A	4	(1)	1
Lasha CHELIDZE		13/3/85	D	16		2
Tengiz CHIKVILADZE		12/8/83	D	14	(2)	1
Besik CHIMAKADZE		24/6/88	A	14	(2)	1
Levan CHKHETIANI		17/8/87	M	4	(3)	
Suliko DAVITASHVILI		11/12/77	A	1	(6)	
Giorgi DEKANOSIDZE		21/1/81	M	13	(1)	
Givi DIDAVA		21/3/76	D	14		
Shota GABRICHIDZE		21/12/89	M	1	(1)	
Aleksandre GOGOBERISHVILI		26/2/77	M	29		6
Vili ISIANI		22/3/91	M	1	(4)	
Giorgi JOKHADZE		24/3/90	M	1	(2)	
Revaz KEMOKLIDZE		13/3/79	D	29		
Giorgi KHIDESHELI		21/11/85	M	16	(2)	2
Gela KHUBUA		25/1/84	M	8		1
Irakli KIKNADZE		1/2/87	M	3	(7)	1
Mikheil KOBAURI		11/6/82	D	21		1
Murman KURASBEDIANI		11/4/88	M	3	(8)	
Giorgi KVANTALIANI		6/8/89	D	3	(1)	
Giorgi MAISURADZE		29/12/91	M	8	(5)	
Mikheil MAKHVILADZE		22/7/78	D	9	(3)	
Giorgi MELKADZE		24/11/84	M	12	(1)	2
Levan MELKADZE		12/12/79	A	13	(2)	2
Levan MEREBASHVILI		22/2/79	D	3	(4)	
Otar NAKOPIA		29/1/87	M	2		
Beka NOZADZE		9/2/82	M	2		
Lasha NOZADZE		18/3/80	M	25	(2)	
Giorgi OKROPIRIDZE		1/3/86	M	1	(4)	
Manuchar OKROPIRIDZE		19/2/90	M		(1)	
Gogi PIPIA		4/2/85	A	3	(6)	
Teimuraz RAKVIASHVILI		15/10/83	D	15		
Lasha RUSIESHVILI		10/1/90	M	1	(4)	
Irakli SHENGELIA		13/4/81	A	9	(6)	1
Giorgi SILAGAVA		26/5/84	M	1	(2)	
Zviad STURUA		25/4/78	G	1		

David SVANIDZE	14/10/79	D	17		1
Tornike TARKHNISHVILI	30/6/90	M	4		
Vladimer UGREKHELIDZE	24/11/85	M	17	(6)	3
Jaba UGULAVA	8/4/92	M	7	(8)	1
Levan UGULAVA	15/7/88	M		(1)	
Irakli VASHAKIDZE	13/3/76	D	14		
Vladimer ZUKHBAIA	31/1/86	G	10		

FC SPARTAKI TSKHINVALI
Coach – Vladimer Khachidze; (18/4/10) Gocha Chikovani
Founded – 2007
Stadium – Kartli, Gori (400)

2009			
1/8	Sioni	a	4-1 *Gotsiridze 2, Datunaishvili, Chaladze*
8/8	Baia	h	1-0 *Odikadze*
16/8	Dinamo	a	0-5
22/8	Lokomotivi	h	2-0 *Tskhadadze, Boyomo*
30/8	WIT	a	0-2
12/9	Samtredia	h	2-0 *Kbiltsetskhlashvili, Tskhadadze (p)*
19/9	Zestafoni	a	1-4 *Kbiltsetskhlashvili*
26/9	Gagra	h	3-1 *Chivadze, Shalamberidze, Maisuradze*
30/9	Olimpi	h	1-1 *Shalamberidze*
4/10	Sioni	h	1-1 *Boyomo*
17/10	Baia	a	1-4 *Maisuradze*
25/10	Dinamo	h	1-1 *Chirikashvili*
30/10	Lokomotivi	a	0-0
8/11	WIT	h	1-2 *Maisuradze*
22/11	Samtredia	a	1-2 *Datunaishvili*
27/11	Zestafoni	h	3-3 *Tskhadadze, Mantskava, Kvakhadze*
6/12	Gagra	a	2-1 *Gotsiridze 2*
12/12	Olimpi	h	1-2 *Datunaishvili*
2010			
5/2	Sioni	a	1-0 *Chirikashvili*
12/2	Baia	a	2-0 *Maisuradze, Dekanoidze*
17/2	Dinamo	a	0-2
21/2	Lokomotivi	h	1-1 *Chirikashvili*
25/2	WIT	a	1-3 *Clovis*
6/3	Samtredia	h	1-1 *Chirikashvily (p)*
14/3	Zestafoni	a	0-0
19/3	Gagra	h	0-0
28/3	Olimpi	a	0-4
3/4	Sioni	h	1-3 *Clovis*
10/4	Baia	h	2-0 *Shonia, Chivadze*
18/4	Dinamo	h	2-1 *Dekanoidze, Burjanadze*
25/4	Lokomotivi	a	1-2 *Med Nalo*
1/5	WIT	h	0-0
5/5	Samtredia	a	1-2 *Demetradze*
9/5	Zestafoni	h	1-4 *Burduli*
14/5	Gagra	a	1-4 *Shonia*
20/5	Olimpi	h	4-1 *Shonia 2, Clovis, Tarkhnishvili*

Name	Nat	DoB	Pos	Aps	(s)	Gls
Giorgi ALAVIDZE		28/11/89	M		(1)	
David BAKRADZE		6/6/79	D	21		
Zurab BATIASHVILI		6/2/80	G	25		
Fridolin BOYOMO	CMR	4/8/82	D	28		2
Vladimer BURDULI		26/10/80	M	6	(2)	1
Giga BURJANADZE		19/5/87	M	1	(1)	1
Ilia BUZALADZE		29/2/92	A	3	(4)	
Lasha CHALADZE		5/11/87	D		(8)	1
Irakli CHIRIKASHVILI		10/1/87	M	24	(2)	4
Giorgi CHIVADZE		14/6/84	M	17	(8)	2
Thierry CLOVIS	CIV	15/8/93	M	9	(14)	3
Pavle DATUNAISHVILI		25/8/83	M	15		3
Nika DAUSHVILI		16/10/89	G	1	(2)	
Besik DEKANOIDZE		1/3/92	M	10	(6)	2
Lasha DEKANOSIDZE		9/7/87	D	7	(1)	
Giorgi DEMETRADZE		26/9/76	A	6		1
Givi DIDAVA		21/3/76	D	7		
Akvsenti GILAURI		6/8/79	M	10		
Revaz GOTSIRIDZE		17/1/81	A	14	(1)	4

Name						
Amiran GVENTSADZE	10/4/87	G	1	(1)	
Giorgi IASHVILI	18/12/88	M		(1)	
Shota JISHKARIANI	14/1/86	M		(1)	
Ivane KANDELAKI	2/1/90	M	8	(7)	
Giorgi KBILTSETSKHLASHVILI	21/5/89	A	1	(10)	2
Erekle KHACHVANI	31/12/91	M	1	(1)	
Giorgi KVAKHADZE	16/8/81	D	20	(4)	1
Nikoloz MAISURADZE	29/5/89	M	25	(8)	4
Giorgi MANTSKAVA	25/10/81	M	4		1
Patrick MED NALO	FRA 16/8/87	M	15	(2)	1
Nodar MGALOBLISHVILI	2/8/86	D	8	(3)	
Nika MGELADZE	16/8/87	D	14	(1)	
Lasha NINIKASHVILI	23/10/88	M	4		
Jules Andre NONOS Mbog	CMR 4/8/91	G	1		
David ODIKADZE	14/4/81	M	5		1
Dachi POPKHADZE	27/1/84	D	12	(1)	
Giorgi SEPIASHVILI	29/9/90	M		(1)	
Koba SHALAMBERIDZE	15/10/84	M	11	(4)	2
Beka SHEKRILADZE	28/11/83	G	8		
Teimuraz SHONIA	28/5/90	M	30		4
Tornike TARKHNISHVILI	30/6/90	M	12		1
Bachana TSKHADADZE	23/10/87	A	12	(3)	3
Tornike UKHURGUNASHVILI	28/1/89	A		(2)	
ZOHI Gbagodai Melec	CIV 20/12/90	M		(2)	

FC WIT GEORGIA
Coach – Nestor Mumladze; (22/8/09) Merab Kochlashvili; (6/12/09) Gela Gomelauri; (10/4/10) Merab Kochlashvili
Founded – 1968
Stadium – T. Burjanadze, Gori (4,000)
MAJOR HONOURS:
Georgian League - (2) 2004, 2009;
Georgian Cup - (1) 2010.

2009
2/8	Samtredia	h	2-1	*Bechvaia, Beriashvili*
8/8	Gagra	a	0-4	
16/8	Sioni	h	2-1	*Lipartia, Razmadze (p)*
22/8	Dinamo	a	0-0	
30/8	Spartaki	h	2-0	*Kvaratskhelia 2*
13/9	Zestafoni	h	1-1	*Kvaratskhelia*
19/9	Olimpi	a	0-0	
25/9	Baia	h	2-1	*Kvaratskhelia 2*
29/9	Lokomotivi	a	3-1	*Kvaratskhelia 2 (1p), Razmadze*
4/10	Samtredia	a	2-2	*Lomaia, Kvaratskhelia*
18/10	Gagra	h	5-1	*Kvaratskhelia 2, Razmadze, Beriashvili, Bechvaia*
25/10	Sioni	a	1-0	*Lipartia*
30/10	Dinamo	h	0-0	
8/11	Spartaki	a	2-1	*Kvakhadze 2*
22/11	Zestafoni	a	1-2	*Kvakhadze*
27/11	Olimpi	h	1-2	*Razmadze (p)*
6/12	Baia	a	1-0	*Kvaratskhelia*
12/12	Lokomotivi	h	1-1	*Lipartia*

2010
16/2	Sioni	h	0-0	
21/2	Dinamo	a	2-1	*Beriashvili, Janelidze*
25/2	Spartaki	h	3-1	*Beriashvili 2, Lipartia*
2/3	Samtredia	h	1-1	*og (Kirtadze)*
6/3	Zestafoni	h	1-1	*Japaridze*
10/3	Gagra	a	1-0	*Klimiashvili*
14/3	Olimpi	a	0-1	
19/3	Baia	h	2-2	*Vasadze 2*
28/3	Lokomotivi	a	1-0	*Razmadze*
2/4	Samtredia	a	0-1	
10/4	Gagra	h	2-0	*Beriashvili 2*
18/4	Sioni	a	2-2	*Chimakadze 2*
24/4	Dinamo	h	0-2	
1/5	Spartaki	a	0-0	
5/5	Zestafoni	a	1-0	*Datunaishvili*
9/5	Olimpi	h	2-0	*Klimiashvili, Razmadze (p)*
15/5	Baia	a	1-1	*Datunaishvili*
20/5	Lokomotivi	h	3-0	*Beriashvili, Lomaia, Kvaratskhelia*

Name	Nat	DoB	Pos	Aps	(s)	Gls
Guram ADAMADZE		31/8/88	D	14	(1)	
Giga BECHVAIA		29/8/86	D	23	(3)	2
Grigol BEDIASHVILI		7/2/80	G	29		
Giorgi BERIASHVILI		10/9/86	A	22	(8)	8
Besik CHIMAKADZE		24/6/88	A	2	(3)	2
Giorgi DATUNAISHVILI		9/2/85	M	34		2
Guram GURESHIDZE		8/10/89	M	2	(9)	
Giorgi JANELIDZE		25/9/89	M	5	(15)	1
Lasha JAPARIDZE		16/4/85	D	32		1
Giorgi KAKHELISHVILI		22/5/87	M	12	(4)	
Lasha KASRADZE		26/7/89	M		(1)	
David KHURTSILAVA		9/3/88	D	18	(3)	
Irakli KLIMIASHVILI		30/5/88	M	26	(3)	2
Giorgi KORIFADZE		10/3/89	M	2	(3)	
Aleksandre KVAKHADZE		17/8/84	D	33		3
Vakhtang KVARATSKHELIA		30/3/88	A	18	(8)	12
Amiran KVELASHVILI		10/2/85	D		(2)	
Jaba LIPARTIA		16/11/87	A	33	(1)	4
David LOMAIA		18/5/85	D	27	(2)	2
David MAISASHVILI		18/2/89	M	1	(5)	
Giorgi MELKADZE		24/11/84	M	1	(5)	
Nika MGELADZE		20/12/85	D	2	(1)	
Ardalion MIKABERIDZE		2/6/86	G	7	(1)	
Luka RAZMADZE		30/12/83	M	33		6
Mikheil ROSTIASHVILI		21/9/90	A		(7)	
Giorgi VASADZE		14/6/89	M	19	(7)	2
Beka ZAKRADZE		30/5/90	M	1	(2)	

FC ZESTAFONI
Coach – Giorgi Geguchadze
Founded – 1936
Stadium – Central (5,000)
MAJOR HONOURS:
Georgian Cup - (1) 2008.

2009
2/8	Lokomotivi	h	0-0	
8/8	Samtredia	a	2-0	*Khidesheli, Dvali*
16/8	Gagra	h	1-0	*Gelashvili*
22/8	Sioni	a	0-0	
29/8	Dinamo	h	4-1	*Eliava, Dvali 2, Gelashvili*
13/9	WIT	a	1-1	*Dzaria*
19/9	Spartaki	h	4-1	*Grigalashvili, Gelashvili 2 (1p), Aptsiauri*
25/9	Olimpi	h	2-2	*Gelashvili 2*
29/9	Baia	a	1-0	*Gelashvili*
3/10	Lokomotivi	a	1-0	*Oniani*
18/10	Samtredia	h	4-2	*Gelashvili 2, Korgalidze, Benashvili*
25/10	Gagra	a	1-0	*Gelashvili*
30/10	Sioni	h	3-0	*Dvali 2, Aptsiauri*
7/11	Dinamo	a	0-2	
22/11	WIT	h	2-1	*Korgalidze, Daushvili*
27/11	Spartaki	a	3-3	*Dvali, Gelashvili 2*
5/12	Olimpi	a	0-1	
12/12	Baia	h	2-1	*Korgalidze, Gelashvili*

2010
8/2	Lokomotivi	h	1-1	*Khidesheli*
13/2	Samtredia	a	3-2	*Dvali 2, Dzaria*
17/2	Gagra	h	4-1	*Dzaria, Gelashvili 2, Korgalidze*
21/2	Sioni	a	1-0	*Dvali*
26/2	Dinamo	h	0-1	
6/3	WIT	a	1-1	*Korgalidze*
14/3	Spartaki	h	0-0	
20/3	Olimpi	h	0-3	*(w/o; match abandoned at 1-1 Dvali)*
27/3	Baia	a	1-0	*Gorgiashvili*
2/4	Lokomotivi	a	1-1	*Chikhladze*
9/4	Samtredia	h	5-1	*Dzaria, Benashvili, Dvali, Gorgiashvili*
17/4	Gagra	a	0-0	
25/4	Sioni	h	1-0	*Tsinamdzgvrishvili*
1/5	Dinamo	a	0-2	

5/6	WIT	h	0-1	
9/5	Spartaki	a	4-1	*Gelashvili (p), Dvali 2, Chikhladze*
15/5	Olimpi	a	1-3	*Gorgiashvili*
20/5	Baia	h	4-0	*Benashvili 2, Chankotadze, Chikhladze*

Name	Nat	DoB	Pos	Aps	(s)	Gls
Tornike APTSIAURI		28/11/79	M	29	(1)	2
Aleksi BENASHVILI		20/3/89	M	23	(11)	4
Giorgi CHANKOTADZE		6/5/91	M		(2)	1
Nikoloz CHIKHLADZE		8/2/91	A		(8)	3
Murtaz DAUSHVILI		1/5/89	M	32		1
Jaba DVALI		8/2/85	A	33		13
Irakli DZARIA		1/12/87	M	31	(2)	4
Zaal ELIAVA		2/1/85	D	35	(1)	1
David GAMEZARDASHVILI		7/5/82	D	5	(4)	
Nikoloz GELASHVILI		5/8/85	A	29	(2)	16
Tornike GORGIASHVILI		27/4/88	M	11	(7)	3
Shota GRIGALASHVILI		21/6/86	M	22	(2)	1
Zurab IONANIDZE		2/12/71	A		(1)	
Giorgi KHIDESHELI		23/1/88	D	32	(1)	2
Mamuka KOBAKHIDZE		23/8/92	D	8	(4)	
Levan KORGALIDZE		21/2/80	M	12	(16)	6
Nika KVASKHVADZE		15/4/88	M		(12)	
Roin KVASKHVADZE		31/5/89	G	18		
Ucha LOBJANIDZE		23/2/87	D	15		
Saba LOMIA		7/7/90	M	3	(3)	
Karen MAKARIANI		3/3/88	M	1	(1)	
Zurab MAMALADZE		2/10/82	G	18		
Giorgi MIKABERIDZE		17/2/88	M	2	(6)	
Giorgi ONIANI		23/11/83	D	32		1
Rati TSINAMDZGVRISHVILI		22/3/88	A	3	(8)	1
Giorgi TSKHADAIA		23/4/88	M	2	(11)	

PROMOTED CLUB

FC TORPEDO 2008 KUTAISI
Coach – Gia Gigatadze
Founded – 2008
Stadium – Givi Kiladze (11,000)

FC KOLKHETI-1913 POTI
Coach – Zaza Iniashvili; (28/2/10) Besik Sherozia
Founded – 2006
Stadium – Fazisi (6,000)

SECOND LEVEL FINAL TABLES 2009/10

		Pld	W	D	L	F	A	Pts
1	FC Torpedo 2008 Kutaisi	28	22	4	2	70	12	70
2	FC Kolkheti-1913 Poti	28	19	4	5	63	21	61
3	FC Merani Martvili	28	17	2	9	44	31	53
4	FC Guria Lanchkhuti	28	16	5	7	53	32	53
5	FC Dinamo Batumi	28	15	8	5	44	17	53
6	FC Chikhura Sachkhere	28	14	7	7	41	28	49
7	FC IBSU Tbilisi	28	9	7	12	45	40	34
8	FC Norchi Dinamo Tbilisi	28	9	5	14	38	57	32
9	FC Mertskhali Ozurgeti	28	9	4	15	29	45	31
10	FC Chiatura	28	9	3	16	36	58	30
11	FC Kolkheti Khobi	28	9	3	16	36	52	30
12	FC Meshakhte Tkibuli	28	6	7	15	36	68	25
13	FC 35 Football Club Tbilisi	28	6	6	16	30	49	24
14	FC Hereti Lagodekhi	28	6	5	17	27	60	23
15	FC Meskheti Akhaltsikhe	28	7	4	17	26	48	22

NB FC Meskheti Akhaltsikhe – 3 pts deducted.

DOMESTIC CUP 2009/10

SAKARTVELOS TASI

FIRST ROUND

(25/8/09)
35-Football Club 2, Meskheti 1
Dinamo Batumi 1, Chikhura 2
Imereti 2, Kolkheti-1913 Poti 3 *(aet)*
Kolkheti Khobi 0, Merani Martvili 2

(26/8/09)
Adeli 1, Torpedo 2008 3
Guria 1, Baia Zugdidi 3
Hereti 1, Lokomotivi Tbilisi 2
IBSU 0, Spartaki Tskhinvali 2
Mertskhali 2, Chiatura 1
Meshakhte 0, Samtredia 2
Norchi Dinamo 0, Sioni 1

(16/9/09)
Dusheti 1, Gagra 2 *(aet)*

Byes: Dinamo Tbilisi, Olimpi, WIT, Zestafoni.

SECOND ROUND

(21/10/09)
35-Football Club 0, Dinamo Tbilisi 1
Baia Zugdidi 3, Sioni 0
Chikhura 1, Olimpi 0
Kolkheti-1913 Poti 2, Gagra 1 *(aet)*
Lokomotivi Tbilisi 1, WIT 3
Merani Martvili 2, Samtredia 0
Mertskhali 0, Spartaki Tskhinvali 6
Torpedo 2008 0, Zestafoni 2

QUARTER-FINALS

(3/11/09 & 1/12/09)
Merani Martvili 0, Kolkheti-1913 Poti 0
Kolkheti-1913 Poti 1 *(Gvalia 48)*, Merani Martvili 1 *(Giorgobiani 41)*
(1-1; Merani Martvili on away goal)

Zestafoni 3 *(Dvali 6, Daushvili 38, Grigalashvili 40)*, WIT 0
WIT 4 *(Bechvaia 7, Lipartia 52, Japaridze 61, Kvaratskhelia 117)*, Zestafoni 0 *(aet)*
(WIT 4-3)

(3/11/09 & 2/12/09)
Baia Zugdidi 1 *(Kvekveskiri 5)*, Spartaki Tskhinvali 1 *(Boyomo 67)*
Spartaki Tskhinvali 2 *(Tskhadadze 20, Gilauri 83)*, Baia Zugdidi 1 *(Jikia 24)*
(Spartaki Tskhinvali 3-2)

Chikhura 1 *(Enukidze G. 67)*, Dinamo Tbilisi 1 *(Kashia G. 22)*
Dinamo Tbilisi 0 Chikhura 0
(1-1; Dinamo Tbilisi on away goal)

SEMI-FINALS

(23/3/10 & 14/4/10)
Merani Martvili 1 *(Iobashvili 51)*, WIT 0
WIT 2 *(Khurtsilava 35, Adamadze 62)*, Merani Martvili 0
(WIT 2-1)

Spartaki Tskhinvali 0, Dinamo Tbilisi 0
Dinamo Tbilisi 3 *(Chikviladze 39, Vatsadze 82, 90)*, Spartaki Tskhinvali 0
(Dinamo Tbilisi 3-0)

FINAL

(26/5/10)
Boris Paichadze National stadium, Tbilisi
FC WIT GEORGIA 1 *(Datunaishvili 40)*
FC DINAMO TBILISI 0
Referee – *Silagava*
WIT – Bediashvili, Khurtsilava, Lomaia, Kvakhadze, Lipartia (Bechvaia 79), Vasadze, Razmadze, Japaridze, Klimiashvili (Gureshidze 90), Beriashvili (Kvaratskhelia 68), Datunaishvili.
DINAMO TBILISI – Loria, Chikviladze, Tomashvili, Kashia G., Krsteski (Tekturmanidze 76), Ednilson, Koshkadze, Kakubava, Kashia S. (Robertinho 67), Kakhelishvili (Djousse 58), Vatsadze.

Löw's young guns make their mark

ermany did not bring the FIFA World Cup back with them from South Africa, but Joachim Löw and his team illuminated the tournament with the quality of their football. Young, vibrant and full of adventure, the new-look, multi-ethnic Nationalmannschaft scored more goals at the finals than any other team and, unlike most of their fellow-competitors, were attractive and exciting to watch. Flair, mobility and variety were added to the traditional German strengths of discipline, organisation and ruthless efficiency, Third place was the very least they deserved.

It is always, of course, a nonsense to write off Germany's chances before any major tournament, but with so many players having been lost to injury this time, including key first-choice personnel in goalkeeper René Adler and inspirational skipper Michael Ballack, and the two main attackers, Miroslav Klose and Lukas Podolski, struggling for goals and form at their clubs, it was understandable that, despite

The World Cup bronze medals belong to Germany after Sami Khedira (right, with Per Mertesacker) scores the winning goal against Uruguay

the country's remarkable World Cup roll of honour, they were not listed among the pre-tournament favourites. On the other hand, Germany had finished second at UEFA EURO 2008 under Löw and followed that up by qualifying for South Africa with an unbeaten record, defeating European semi-finalists Russia home and away. Furthermore, the team's large FC Bayern München contingent were still buoyant after an outstanding season at club level.

Dynamic start

The popular consensus was that Germany had been drawn in a difficult first-round group, but any concerns about their well-being in the company of Australia, Serbia and Ghana were quickly dismissed with a dynamic opening display against the Aussies, in which senior major tournament debutants Thomas Müller, Mesut Özil, Sami Khedira and Manuel Neuer – the last three all members of Germany's 2009 UEFA European Under-21 Championship-winning squad – proved beyond doubt that they could perform at the highest level. That thrilling 4-0 win was only partly negated by the team's subsequent 1-0 defeat by Serbia – a match which, despite the scoreline and Klose's first-half dismissal, Germany largely dominated.

A place in the knockout phase was duly secured when Özil's superb strike brought a 1-0 win over Ghana. Although victory was required to guarantee their safe passage, a draw would have given Germany an easier route to the final. No matter, Löw's men went out and put four goals past both England and Argentina to book a semi-final date with Spain. Although fortune favoured them in the last-16 clash when a legitimate England equaliser – which would have made the score 2-2 at the interval - was missed by the match officials, overall Germany were much the better team. Exceptional on the breakaway against Fabio Capello's side, they reprised those virtues against Diego Maradona's highly fancied Argentina, with the last of their four goals, Klose's 14th at the World Cup finals (matching the great Gerd Müller), a counterattacking classic.

Germany could not, alas, sustain their form against Spain. Paying a little too much respect to their UEFA EURO 2008 final conquerors, they nevertheless played their part in an excellent match and, despite being pegged back for long periods by Xavi and co, came close to conjuring a win. Instead, the outcome would be the same as in Vienna two years earlier – 1-0 to Spain.

Müller's Golden Boot

A lively 3-2 win in the third place play-off against Uruguay – in which Müller, badly missed through suspension against Spain, scored his fifth goal of the tournament to take the Golden Boot (thanks to his additional three assists) – ensured, as in 2006, that Germany departed with the bronze medals. Of greater satisfaction, perhaps, to Löw and his players was the way they had performed over the seven games and the admiration that their positive brand of football had drawn from far and wide.

Müller, Özil, Khedira and Neuer had come of age as international-class footballers, Klose and Podolski had continued to supply goals, while stand-in skipper Philipp Lahm and his Bayern team-mate Bastian Schweinsteiger had once again confirmed their reputations as big-game, big-tournament stars. With only Klose and defender Arne Friedrich – another who excelled – the wrong side of 30, this team looks set for more good times ahead, especially as Löw, after initial speculation to the contrary, will be there to oversee their further development - at least in the short term – after extending his contract to take in UEFA EURO 2012.

Germany's strong showing in South Africa capped a season in which the country's leading club side also re-emerged as an international force, Bayern reaching the final of the UEFA Champions League – the first Bundesliga side since 2002 to do so – in addition to winning their fifth domestic double in eight years. The pride of Bavaria were led to the brink of an unprecedented treble by Dutch coach Louis van Gaal in his first season at the club.

FC Internazionale Milano got the better of Bayern in Madrid, beating them 2-0, but while Van Gaal came off second best to José Mourinho, his team could not be accused of failing to rise to the occasion. They were on top for much of a well balanced contest but could not find the necessary firepower to storm the barricades of Inter's impenetrable defence. Thus Mourinho, rather than Van Gaal, became only the third coach to win the trophy with two different clubs.

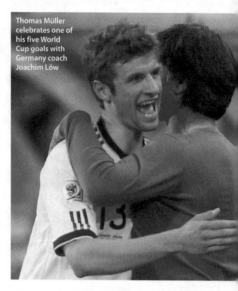
Thomas Müller celebrates one of his five World Cup goals with Germany coach Joachim Löw

Victorious Van Gaal

Losing at the Santiago Bernabéu was painful, but it could not take the shine off a fabulous debut season for the experienced, outspoken Dutchman. His arrival from AZ Alkmaar, with whom he had just won the Eredivisie title, did not meet with universal approval, and indeed for much of the autumn the Bayern players struggled to get to grips with the idiosyncratic methods of the former AFC Ajax and FC Barcelona boss. But once the corner was turned with a majestic 4-1 victory over Juventus in Turin – a game Bayern had to win to remain in the UEFA Champions League – there was no stopping them, either on the road to Madrid or in their quest for domestic glory.

Off the pace early on in the Bundesliga campaign, during which they collected only five wins from 13 matches and were flapping about rather nervously in seventh place, Bayern improved as the temperatures dropped. Four straight wins before Christmas lifted them into third place, two points behind halfway leaders Bayer 04 Leverkusen, and with the mid-season shutdown shorter than normal Bayern were able to maintain their momentum and plough their way to the Bundesliga summit with another five wins in January and early February.

The return of European competition coincided with a temporary dip in their domestic form, but as Bayern edged past both ACF Fiorentina and Manchester

United FC in identical fashion – winning 2-1 at home, losing 3-2 away and progressing on away goals thanks to a brilliant deciding strike from Dutch winger Arjen Robben – they also recovered from two successive Bundesliga defeats by beating FC Schalke 04, who had dislodged them from the top of the table, 2-1 in Gelsenkirchen – where they had also won a German Cup semi-final 11 days earlier - and cementing their return to the summit with a 1-1 draw at Leverkusen.

The title celebrations would be two-tiered. The first came in the Allianz-Arena after a 3-1 home win over VfL Bochum. Although, strictly speaking, Bayern were not mathematically home and dry, their advantage over Schalke of three points and 17 goals – with one game left - was enough to generate a party. The official presentation of the Bundesliga shield was delayed until a week later when Bayern defeated relegated Hertha BSC Berlin 3-1.

Another Bayern double

If Bayern fans knew what was coming on that visit to the Olympiastadion, they travelled north to the same venue seven days later unsure what to expect in the German Cup final against a Werder Bremen side that had finished the Bundesliga campaign strongly enough to oust Leverkusen from third place and snatch the UEFA Champions League qualifying spot. Furthermore, Thomas Schaaf's side had a trophy to defend. But Bayern

Bayern coach Louis van Gaal holds aloft the Bundesliga championship shield

warmed up for their big Madrid date with Inter by taking the holders apart, goals from Robben, Ivica Olić, Franck Ribéry and Schweinsteiger ensuring that for the fifth time in a row a Bayern victory in the Bundesliga would be accompanied by success in the DFB-Pokal.

If Van Gaal was the architect of Bayern's triumph, Robben was the constructor-in-chief. Expensively acquired from Real Madrid CF, the gifted Dutch winger got off to a flying start, scoring twice on his Bundesliga debut against defending champions VfL Wolfsburg, and although his autumn campaign was disturbed by all-too-familiar injury problems, his form in the spring was astonishing. While his two goals against Fiorentina and Manchester United stood out, there were many more in the Bundesliga and he ended the season as Bayern's top scorer, with 16.

Müller, just 20 years old and the revelation of the season, managed 13 goals, and there were 11 for the indefatigable Olić, who also bagged seven in Europe, including two of vital importance against United and a brilliant hat-trick in the semi-final against Olympique Lyonnais. Despite being fielded in unfamiliar positions, Schweinsteiger – switched from the flanks to central midfield - and Lahm - moved to right-back from left – repeatedly demonstrated their class, and there were impressive contributions also from veteran goalkeeper Hans-Jörg Butt, captain Mark van Bommel and homegrown youngster Holger Badstuber, who, effective both at left-back and in central defence, started every league game bar one. Like Müller, the 21-year-old would end a remarkable first season with a trip to the World Cup. Less celebrated were Ribéry (injured and unsettled), Klose (benched), Luca Toni (offloaded to AS Roma) and new signings Danijel Pranjić, Anatoliy Tymoshchuk and Mario Gómez, none of whom fitted in with Van Gaal's plans.

Schalke second

Schalke's second place prolonged the popular Ruhr club's long wait for a first Bundesliga title – and a first championship win since 1958. They gave it their best shot but did not quite possess Bayern's class and conviction. Even so, a guaranteed UEFA Champions League place was no mean achievement for a club that had finished eighth the previous season. Felix Magath, who arrived in Gelsenkirchen fresh from taking Wolfsburg to the title, made all the difference, imbibing the team with self-belief and a positive attitude to hard work. Neuer's fine goalkeeping enabled the Blues to match Bayern's league-best

GERMANY

defensive figures – 31 goals conceded – while up front Kevin Kuranyi redeemed himself with the Schalke faithful by scoring 18 goals.

Leverkusen led the title race from early October to late February but ran out of steam in the final weeks, spoiling their record 24-match unbeaten start. Jupp Heynckes had spent the last few weeks of the 2008/09 season as Jürgen Klinsmann's temporary replacement at Bayern, leading the Bavarians into the UEFA Champions League. Sadly he could not repeat that feat over a full season with the Rhinelanders, although the newly refurbished Bay-Arena did play host to some memorable matches and a cascade of goals. With 2008/09 top scorer Patrick Helmes laid low by injury, Stefan Kiessling rose impressively to the challenge, ably supported by Swiss striker Eren Derdiyok. Youngster Toni Kroos, on loan from Bayern, also starred, while veteran Finnish defender Sami Hyypiä, over 16 years his senior, proved emphatically that there was life after Liverpool FC.

Playmaker Özil and striker Claudio Pizarro were the men chiefly responsible for lifting Werder above Leverkusen and reaching the Cup final. There was no second successive European final for Schaaf's free-scoring team, however, as they fell to Valencia CF after a fabulous 4-4 draw in the last 16 of the UEFA Europa League. Hamburger SV seemed destined to play in the final of that competition, in their home stadium, until they encountered Fulham FC in the semis. Remarkably, Hamburg went into the second leg of that evenly

Deutscher Fussball-Bund (DFB)

Otto-Fleck-Schneise 6
Postfach 710265
D-60492 Frankfurt am Main
tel – +49 69 67 880
fax – +49 69 67 88266
website – dfb.de
email – info@dfb.de
Year of Formation – 1900

President – Theo Zwanziger
General Secretary – Wolfgang Niersbach
Media Officer – Harald Stenger

INTERNATIONAL HONOURS*
FIFA World Cup – (3) 1954, 1974, 1990.
UEFA European Championship – (3) 1972, 1980, 1996.
INTERNATIONAL TOURNAMENT APPEARANCES*
FIFA World Cup – (17) 1934 (3rd), 1938, 1954 (Winners), 1958 (4th), 1962 (qtr-finals), 1966 (runners-up), 1970 (3rd), 1974 (Winners), 1978 (2nd phase), 1982 (runners-up), 1986 (runners-up), 1990 (Winners), 1994 (qtr-finals), 1998 (qtr-finals), 2002 (runners-up), 2006 (3rd), 2010 (3rd).
UEFA European Championship – (10) 1972 (Winners), 1976 (runners-up), 1980 (Winners), 1984, 1988 (semi-finals), 1992 (runners-up), 1996 (Winners), 2000, 2004, 2008 (runners-up).
TOP FIVE ALL-TIME CAPS
Lothar Matthäus (150); Jürgen Klinsmann (108); Jürgen Kohler (105); Franz Beckenbauer (103); Thomas Hässler & Miroslav Klose (101)
TOP FIVE ALL-TIME GOALS
Gerd Müller (68); Miroslav Klose (52); Jürgen Klinsmann & Rudi Völler (47); Karl-Heinz Rummenigge (45)
(* before 1992 as West Germany)

NATIONAL TEAM RESULTS 2009/10

12/8/09	Azerbaijan (WCQ)	A	Baku	2-0	Schweinsteiger (11), Klose (53)
5/9/09	South Africa	H	Leverkusen	2-0	Gómez (35), Özil (77)
9/9/09	Azerbaijan (WCQ)	H	Hanover	4-0	Ballack (15p), Klose (55, 66), Podolski (71)
10/10/09	Russia (WCQ)	A	Moscow	1-0	Klose (35)
14/10/09	Finland (WCQ)	H	Hamburg	1-1	Podolski (90)
18/11/09	Ivory Coast	H	Gelsenkirchen	2-2	Podolski (11p, 90+3)
3/3/10	Argentina	H	Munich	0-1	
13/5/10	Malta	H	Aachen	3-0	Cacau (16, 58), Scicluna (61og)
29/5/10	Hungary	A	Budapest	3-0	Podolski (5p), Gómez (69), Cacau (72)
3/6/10	Bosnia-Herzegovina	H	Frankfurt	3-1	Lahm (50), Schweinsteiger (73p, 77p)
13/6/10	Australia (WCF)	N	Durban (RSA)	4-0	Podolski (8), Klose (26), Müller (68), Cacau (70)
18/6/10	Serbia (WCF)	N	Port Elizabeth (RSA)	0-1	
23/6/10	Ghana (WCF)	N	Johannesburg (RSA)	1-0	Özil (60)
27/6/10	England (WCF)	N	Bloemfontein (RSA)	4-1	Klose (20), Podolski (32), Müller (67, 70)
3/7/10	Argentina (WCF)	N	Cape Town (RSA)	4-0	Müller (3), Klose (68, 89), Friedrich (74)
7/7/10	Spain (WCF)	N	Durban (RSA)	0-1	
10/7/10	Uruguay (WCF)	N	Port Elizabeth (RSA)	3-2	Müller (19), Jansen (56), Khedira (82)

NATIONAL TEAM APPEARANCES 2009/10

Coach – Joachim LÖW	3/2/60		AZE	Rsa	AZE	RUS	FIN	Civ	Arg	Mlt	Hun	Bih	AUS	SRB	GHA	ENG	ARG	ESP	URU	Caps	Goals
Robert ENKE	24/8/77	Hannover	G																	8	-
Philipp LAHM	11/11/83	Bayern	D	D	D	D	D	D	D			D	D	D	D	D	D	D		71	4
Per MERTESACKER	29/9/84	Werder	D		D	D		D	D		D	D	D	D	D	D	D	D	D	69	1
Serdar TAŞÇI	24/4/87	Stuttgart	D	D46				D	D46			s86							s91	13	-
Marcel SCHÄFER	7/6/84	Wolfsburg	D	D	D46			s86												7	-
Michael BALLACK	26/9/76	Chelsea (ENG)	M	M80	M	M	M46	M												98	42
Thomas HITZLSPERGER	5/4/82	Stuttgart	M	M		M46	M													51	6
Bastian SCHWEINSTEIGER	1/8/84	Bayern	M	M84	M65	M				M80	M76	M87	M	M	M81	M	M	M	M	81	21
Piotr TROCHOWSKI	22/3/84	Hamburg	M76	s84	s65	s85		M	M86		M	M61	M46		s67	s72	s84	M62		35	2
Miroslav KLOSE	9/6/78	Bayern	A71	s46	s46	A89	s77		A46		A61	A46	A68	A 37*		A72	A	A		101	52
Mario GÓMEZ	10/7/85	Bayern	A83	A46	A46	s89	A77	s70	s46		s61	s80	s74	s77		s72		s81		38	12
Jerónimo da Silva "CACAU"	27/3/81	Stuttgart	s71					M	s67	M	s46	s46	s68	s70	A				A73	12	4
Marcell JANSEN	4/11/85	Bayern/Hamburg	s76								s61				s73		s72	s52	M81	35	3
Mesut ÖZIL	15/10/88	Werder	s83	M	M	M72	s46	M	M67		M46	M80	M74	M70	M	M83	M	M	M91	17	2
René ADLER	15/1/85	Leverkusen		G	G	G	G		G											9	-
Arne FRIEDRICH	29/5/79	Hertha	D		s72	D				D72	D71	D86	D	D	D	D	D	D	D	79	1
Simon ROLFES	21/1/82	Leverkusen	M73			M														21	1
Marko MARIN	13/3/89	Werder	M46								s61		s70	s81	s70					11	1
Lukas PODOLSKI	4/6/85	Köln	s46	M	M85	M	A	M	M	M	M	M70	M81	M	M	M	M	M		79	40
Heiko WESTERMANN	14/8/83	Schalke	s46	D	D	D	D		s72		D									19	2
Sami KHEDIRA	4/4/87	Stuttgart	s73						s76		M72	M46	M	M	M	M	M77	M81	M	12	1
Christian GENTNER	14/8/85	Wolfsburg	s80			s46														4	-
Andreas BECK	13/3/87	Hoffenheim		s46			D	s65	D57											7	-
Jérôme BOATENG	3/9/88	Hamburg				D 69*		D65	D	s79	D				D73	D	D72	D52	D	10	-
Tim WIESE	17/12/81	Werder						G46												2	-
Stefan KIESSLING	25/1/84	Leverkusen						A70		A				s83				s73		6	-
Manuel NEUER	27/3/86	Schalke						s46		G	G	G	G	G	G	G	G			11	-
Aaron HUNT	4/9/86	Werder						s80												1	-
Thomas MÜLLER	13/9/89	Bayern							M67		s46			M	M70	M67	M72	M84	M	8	5
Toni KROOS	4/1/90	Leverkusen						s67		M57	M61	s87			s81		s77	s62	s81	8	-
Dennis AOGO	14/1/87	Hamburg								D79	s46							D		3	-
Mats HUMMELS	16/12/88	Dortmund							s46											1	-
Kevin GROSSKREUTZ	19/7/88	Dortmund							s57											1	-
Christian TRÄSCH	1/9/87	Stuttgart							s57											2	-
Stefan REINARTZ	1/1/89	Leverkusen							s72											1	-
Holger BADSTUBER	13/3/89	Bayern								s71	D	D	D77							4	-
Hans-Jörg BUTT	28/5/74	Bayern																	G	4	-

balanced tie without a coach, having just dismissed Bruno Labbadia.

Seventh place for Hamburg meant no return to the European arena in 2010/11. Joining Leverkusen in the UEFA Europa League instead were Jürgen Klopp's BV Borussia Dortmund - who, fired by the 19 goals of their razor-sharp South American striker Lucas Barrios, took fifth place – and Stuttgart – a team totally transformed by the mid-term arrival of Christian Gross, who succeeded Markus Babbel as coach after a dreadful autumn and lifted the Swabian club 11 places up the table to sixth. Aside from beating southern rivals Bayern in Munich – the only Bundesliga team to do so - they also gave FC Barcelona a fright in the UEFA Champions League.

Despite another fine season for Edin Džeko, who topped the Bundesliga score charts with 22 goals, Wolfsburg were never in the hunt for a repeat title triumph after a shaky start under Magath-replacement Armin Veh. The man who led Stuttgart to the 2006/07 title lasted only until January. Lorenz-Günther Köstner improved things in the spring but the cash-rich club chose to replace him for 2010/11 with Englishman Steve McClaren, who had just won the Eredivisie title with FC Twente – the

thinking perhaps being that whatever a Dutch title-winning coach could do at Bayern …

Enke tragedy

Tragedy struck at Wolfsburg's local rivals Hannover 96 in November when Robert Enke, the club's goalkeeper and a regular German international, committed suicide. His death, aged 32, stunned the whole of German football and beyond, but the impact was felt most keenly at his club, where he was universally adored. Inevitably Hannover's form slumped horribly during a lengthy period of mourning, but a degree of happiness was restored at the end of the campaign when the club dramatically escaped relegation with a 3-0 win at Bochum. As a consequence, their vanquished opponents went down instead, alongside hapless Hertha, the two relegated teams between them managing a paltry three wins at home. 1. FC Nürnberg, who had come up via the promotion/relegation play-off a year before, won the fixture again, beating FC Augsburg home and away and thus leaving second division champions 1. FC Kaiserslautern and runners-up FC St Pauli as the only two teams to savour the joys of promotion.

DOMESTIC LEAGUE 2009/10

BUNDESLIGA FINAL TABLE

		Pld	Home					Away					Total					Pts
			W	D	L	F	A	W	D	L	F	A	W	D	L	F	A	
1	FC Bayern München	34	12	4	1	39	13	8	6	3	33	18	20	10	4	72	31	70
2	FC Schalke 04	34	11	2	4	29	15	8	6	3	24	16	19	8	7	53	31	65
3	Werder Bremen	34	8	6	3	34	21	9	4	4	37	19	17	10	7	71	40	61
4	Bayer 04 Leverkusen	34	11	5	1	37	14	4	9	4	28	24	15	14	5	65	38	59
5	BV Borussia Dortmund	34	10	4	3	29	14	6	5	6	25	28	16	9	9	54	42	57
6	VfB Stuttgart	34	8	5	4	28	21	7	5	5	23	20	15	10	9	51	41	55
7	Hamburger SV	34	8	6	3	25	12	5	7	5	31	29	13	13	8	56	41	52
8	VfL Wolfsburg	34	7	2	8	39	39	7	6	4	25	19	14	8	12	64	58	50
9	1. FSV Mainz 05	34	9	6	2	22	14	3	5	9	14	28	12	11	11	36	42	47
10	Eintracht Frankfurt	34	7	5	5	25	26	5	5	7	22	28	12	10	12	47	54	46
11	TSG 1899 Hoffenheim	34	5	6	6	26	20	6	3	8	18	22	11	9	14	44	42	42
12	VfL Borussia Mönchengladbach	34	8	5	4	25	22	2	4	11	18	38	10	9	15	43	60	39
13	1. FC Köln	34	3	6	8	18	29	6	5	6	15	13	9	11	14	33	42	38
14	SC Freiburg	34	5	4	8	14	26	4	4	9	21	33	9	8	17	35	59	35
15	Hannover 96	34	5	4	8	27	33	4	2	11	16	34	9	6	19	43	67	33
16	1. FC Nürnberg	34	5	4	8	18	23	3	3	11	14	35	8	7	19	32	58	31
17	VfL Bochum 1848	34	2	6	9	18	35	4	4	9	15	29	6	10	18	33	64	28
18	Hertha BSC Berlin	34	1	6	10	10	26	4	3	10	24	30	5	9	20	34	56	24

TOP GOALSCORERS

22 Edin DŽEKO (Wolfsburg)
21 Stefan KIESSLING (Leverkusen)
19 Lucas BARRIOS (Dortmund)
18 Kevin KURÁNYI (Schalke)
16 Arjen ROBBEN (Bayern)
   Claudio PIZARRO (Bremen)
13 Thomas MÜLLER (Bayern)
   CACAU (Stuttgart)
12 Eren DERDIYOK (Leverkusen)
   Vedad IBIŠEVIĆ (Hoffenheim)
   Albert BUNJAKU (Nürnberg)

CLUB-BY-CLUB

BAYER 04 LEVERKUSEN
Coach – Jupp Heynckes
Founded – 1904
Stadium – Bay-Arena (22,500)
MAJOR HONOURS:
UEFA Cup – (1) 1988;
German Cup – (1) 1993.

2009
8/8	Mainz	a	2-2	Derdiyok, Kiessling
15/8	Hoffenheim	h	1-0	Kiessling
22/8	Freiburg	a	5-0	Kiessling, Barnetta 2, Derdiyok 2
29/8	Bochum	h	2-1	Friedrich, Kiessling
12/9	Wolfsburg	a	3-2	Rolfes 2 (1p), Kiessling
20/9	Werder	h	0-0	
26/9	Köln	a	1-0	Rolfes
3/10	Nürnberg	h	4-0	Kroos, Rolfes (p), Derdiyok, Kiessling
17/10	Hamburg	a	0-0	
23/10	Dortmund	h	1-1	Friedrich
31/10	Schalke	a	2-2	Kroos, Kiessling
6/11	Eintracht	h	4-0	Kiessling, Reinartz, Kroos, Bender
22/11	Bayern	a	1-1	Kiessling
29/11	Stuttgart	h	4-0	Kiessling 3 (1p), Derdiyok
5/12	Hannover	a	0-0	
11/12	Hertha	a	2-2	Kroos, Kaplan
19/12	Mönchengladbach	h	3-2	Kroos 2, Derdiyok

2010
16/1	Mainz	h	4-2	Kadlec, Barnetta, Kroos, Derdiyok
24/1	Hoffenheim	a	3-0	Hyypiä, Kroos, Barnetta
31/1	Freiburg	h	3-1	Kiessling, Derdiyok, Hyypiä
6/2	Bochum	a	1-1	Derdiyok
13/2	Wolfsburg	h	2-1	Reinartz, Derdiyok
21/2	Werder	a	2-2	Derdiyok, Kroos
27/2	Köln	h	0-0	
7/3	Nürnberg	a	2-3	Kiessling, Helmes
14/3	Hamburg	h	4-2	Kiessling 2, Derdiyok, Castro
20/3	Dortmund	a	0-3	
27/3	Schalke	h	0-2	
3/4	Eintracht	a	2-3	Kiessling 2
10/3	Bayern	h	1-1	Vidal
17/4	Stuttgart	a	1-2	Kiessling
24/4	Hannover	h	3-0	Kiessling 2 (1p), Kaplan
1/5	Hertha	a	1-1	Friedrich
8/5	Mönchengladbach	a	1-1	Helmes

No	Name	Nat	DoB	Pos	Aps	(s)	Gls
1	René ADLER		15/1/85	G	31		
7	Tranquillo BARNETTA	SUI	22/5/85	M	31	(1)	4
8	Lars BENDER		27/4/89	M	6	(14)	1
27	Gonzalo CASTRO		11/6/87	D	27	(2)	1
19	Eren DERDIYOK	SUI	12/6/88	A	32	(1)	12
5	Manuel FRIEDRICH		13/9/79	D	31		3
29	Theofanis GEKAS	GRE	23/5/80	A	1	(5)	
36	Fabian GIEFER		17/5/90	G	3		
9	Patrick HELMES		1/3/84	A	2	(10)	2
24	Sami HYYPIÄ	FIN	7/10/73	D	32		2
24	Michal KADLEC	CZE	13/12/84	D	17	(6)	1
28	Burak KAPLAN	TUR	1/2/90	M	2	(2)	2
11	Stefan KIESSLING		25/1/84	A	33		21
39	Toni KROOS		4/1/90	M	26	(7)	9
3	Stefan REINARTZ		1/1/89	D	23	(4)	2
10	RENATO Soares de Oliveira AUGUSTO	BRA	8/2/88	M	11	(6)	
6	Simon ROLFES		21/1/82	M	8	(3)	4
15	Hans SARPEI	GHA	28/6/76	D	2	(10)	

2	Daniel SCHWAAB		23/8/88	D	24	(3)	
20	Lukas SINKIEWICZ		9/10/85	D	1	(6)	
26	Assimiou TOURÉ	TOG	1/1/88	D		(1)	
23	Arturo VIDAL	CHI	22/5/87	M	31		1
18	Tomasz ZDEBEL	POL	25/5/73	M		(8)	

FC BAYERN MÜNCHEN
Coach – Louis van Gaal (NED)
Founded – 1900
Stadium – Allianz-Arena (69,000)
MAJOR HONOURS:
European Champion Clubs' Cup/UEFA Champions League - (4) 1974, 1975,
1976, 2001;
UEFA Cup - (1) 1996;
World Club Cup - (2) 1976, 2001;
German League - (22) 1932, 1969, 1972, 1973, 1974, 1980, 1981, 1985,
1986, 1987, 1989, 1990, 1994, 1997, 1999, 2000, 2001, 2003, 2005, 2006,
2008, 2010;
German Cup - (15) 1957, 1966, 1967, 1969, 1971, 1982, 1984, 1986, 1998,
2000, 2003, 2005, 2006, 2008, 2010.

2009
8/8	Hoffenheim	a	1-1	Olić
15/8	Werder	h	1-1	Gómez
22/8	Mainz	a	1-2	og (Noveski)
28/8	Wolfsburg	h	3-0	Gómez, Robben 2
12/9	Dortmund	a	5-1	Gómez, Schweinsteiger, Ribéry, Müller 2
19/9	Nürnberg	h	2-1	Olić, Van Buyten
26/9	Hamburg	a	0-1	
3/10	Köln	h	0-0	
17/10	Freiburg	a	2-1	Müller, og (Cha)
24/10	Eintracht	h	2-1	Robben, Van Buyten
31/10	Stuttgart	a	0-0	
7/11	Schalke	h	1-1	Van Buyten
22/11	Leverkusen	h	1-1	Gómez
29/11	Hannover	a	3-0	Müller, Olić, Gómez
4/12	Mönchengladbach	h	2-1	Gómez, Badstuber
12/12	Bochum	a	5-1	Gómez, og (Mavraj), Olić 2, Pranjić
19/12	Hertha	h	5-2	Van Buyten, Gómez, Robben, Müller, Olić

2010
15/1	Hoffenheim	h	2-0	Demichelis, Klose
23/1	Werder	a	3-2	Müller, Olić, Robben
30/1	Mainz	h	3-0	Van Buyten, Gómez, Robben
6/2	Wolfsburg	a	3-1	Robben, Van Buyten, Ribéry
13/2	Dortmund	h	3-1	Van Bommel, Robben, Gómez
20/2	Nürnberg	a	1-1	Müller
28/2	Hamburg	h	1-0	Ribéry
6/3	Köln	a	1-1	Schweinsteiger
13/3	Freiburg	h	2-1	Robben 2 (1p)
20/3	Eintracht	a	1-2	Klose
27/3	Stuttgart	h	1-2	Olić
3/4	Schalke	a	2-1	Ribéry, Müller
10/4	Leverkusen	a	1-1	Robben (p)
17/4	Hannover	h	7-0	Olić 2, Robben 3, Müller 2
24/4	Mönchengladbach	a	1-1	Klose
1/5	Bochum	h	3-1	Müller 3
8/5	Hertha	a	3-1	Olić, Robben 2

No	Name	Nat	DoB	Pos	Aps	(s)	Gls
27	David ALABA	AUT	24/6/92	M	2	(1)	
28	Holger BADSTUBER		13/3/89	D	33		1
19	Alexander BAUMJOHANN		23/1/87	M	1	(2)	
4	Edson BRAAFHEID	NED	8/4/83	D	5	(4)	
15	BRENO Vinícius Rodrigues Borges	BRA	13/10/89	D	1	(2)	

GERMANY

22	Hans-Jörg BUTT		28/5/74	G	31		
26	Diego CONTENTO		1/5/90	D	8	(1)	
6	Martín DEMICHELIS	ARG	20/12/80	D	17	(4)	1
33	Mario GÓMEZ		10/7/85	A	21	(8)	10
8	HAMIT Altıntop	TUR	8/12/82	M	7	(8)	
18	Miroslav KLOSE		9/6/78	A	11	(14)	3
21	Philipp LAHM		11/11/83	D	34		
25	Thomas MÜLLER		13/9/89	A	29	(5)	13
11	Ivica OLIĆ	CRO	14/9/79	A	23	(6)	11
16	Andreas OTTL		1/3/85	M	1	(3)	
23	Danijel PRANJIĆ	CRO	2/12/81	M	14	(6)	1
1	Michael RENSING		14/5/84	G	3	(1)	
7	Franck RIBÉRY	FRA	7/4/83	M	10	(9)	4
10	Arjen ROBBEN	NED	23/1/84	M	18	(6)	16
31	Bastian SCHWEINSTEIGER		1/8/84	M	33		2
20	José Ernesto SOSA	ARG	19/6/85	M	2	(1)	
9	Luca TONI	ITA	26/5/77	A	3	(1)	
44	Anatoliy TYMOSHCHUK	UKR	30/3/79	M	11	(10)	
17	Mark VAN BOMMEL	NED	22/4/77	M	25		1
5	Daniel VAN BUYTEN	BEL	7/2/78	D	31		6

5	Joël EPALLE	CMR	20/2/78	M	24	(3)	1
30	Patrick FABIAN		11/10/87	D	1		
7	Paul FREIER		26/7/79	M	15	(13)	2
6	Christian FUCHS	AUT	7/4/86	D	29	(2)	4
19	Dennis GROTE		9/8/86	M	5	(5)	1
16	Vahid HASHEMIAN	IRN	21/7/76	A	5	(20)	2
18	Philipp HEERWAGEN		13/4/83	G	30		
17	Lewis HOLTBY		18/9/90	M	11	(3)	2
15	Daniel IMHOF	CAN	22/11/77	M	6		
8	Andreas JOHANSSON	SWE	10/3/82	M	7	(9)	
14	Diego Fernando KLIMOWICZ	ARG	6/7/74	A	9	(6)	3
26	Andreas LUTHE		10/3/87	G	3		
4	Marcel MALTRITZ		2/10/78	D	29		
23	Miloš MARIĆ	SRB	5/3/82	M	13		
20	Mergim MAVRAJ		9/6/86	D	24	(3)	
23	Shinji ONO	JPN	27/9/79	M	7	(2)	
21	Marc PFERTZEL	FRA	21/5/81	D	18		
29	Roman PROKOPH		6/8/85	A	11	(4)	
9	Stanislav ŠESTÁK	SVK	16/12/82	A	28	(1)	6
25	Antar YAHIA	ALG	21/3/82	D	17	(1)	1

VFL BOCHUM 1848
**Coach – Marcel Koller (SUI); (20/9/09) Frank Heinemann;
(27/10/09) Heiko Herrlich; (29/4/10) Dariusz Wosz
Founded – 1938
Stadium – Rewirpower-Stadion (31,328)**

2009
9/8	Mönchengladbach	h	3-3	Azaouagh 2, Šesták
16/8	Schalke	a	0-3	
23/8	Hertha	h	1-0	Yahia
29/8	Leverkusen	a	1-2	og (Friedrich)
12/9	Hoffenheim	a	0-3	
19/9	Mainz	h	2-3	Azaouagh, Klimowicz
25/9	Nürnberg	a	1-0	Klimowicz
3/10	Wolfsburg	h	1-1	Hashemian
18/10	Dortmund	a	0-2	
25/10	Werder	h	1-4	Šesták
1/11	Eintracht	a	1-2	og (Franz)
7/11	Freiburg	h	1-2	Klimowicz
22/11	Hamburg	a	1-0	Grote
27/11	Köln	h	0-0	
5/12	Stuttgart	a	1-1	Fuchs
12/12	Bayern	h	1-5	Fuchs
19/12	Hannover	a	3-2	Freier, Epalle, Fuchs

2010
16/1	Mönchengladbach	a	2-1	Šesták, Dedič
23/1	Schalke	h	2-2	Hashemian, Šesták
30/1	Hertha	a	0-0	
6/2	Leverkusen	h	1-1	Dedič
13/2	Hoffenheim	h	2-1	Šesták, Dedič
20/2	Mainz	a	0-0	
27/2	Nürnberg	h	0-0	
6/2	Wolfsburg	a	1-4	Freier
13/3	Dortmund	h	1-4	Holtby
20/3	Werder	a	2-3	Šesták, Dedič
26/3	Eintracht	h	1-2	Holtby
3/4	Freiburg	a	1-1	Dabrowski
11/4	Hamburg	h	1-2	Dedič
16/4	Köln	a	0-2	
23/4	Stuttgart	h	0-2	
1/5	Bayern	a	1-3	Fuchs
8/5	Hannover	h	0-3	

No	Name	Nat	DoB	Pos	Aps	(s)	Gls
32	Mirkan AYDIN		8/7/87	M		(1)	
22	Mimoun AZAOUAGH		17/11/82	M	12	(5)	3
24	Philipp BÖNIG		20/3/80	D	10		
2	Matias CONCHA	SWE	31/3/80	D	18	(3)	
5	Christoph DABROWSKI		26/3/78	M	26	(3)	1
1	DANIEL Márcio FERNANDES	POR	25/9/83	G	1		
11	Zlatko DEDIČ	SVN	5/10/84	A	15	(12)	5

BV BORUSSIA DORTMUND
**Coach – Jürgen Klopp
Founded – 1909
Stadium – Signal-Iduna-Park (80,552)
MAJOUR HONOURS:
UEFA Champions League - (1) 1997;
UEFA Cup Winners' Cup - (1) 1966;
World Club Cup - (1) 1997;
German League - (6) 1956, 1957, 1963, 1995, 1996, 2002;
German Cup - (2) 1965, 1989.**

2009
8/8	Köln	h	1-0	og (Matip)
15/8	Hamburg	a	1-4	Valdez
22/8	Stuttgart	h	1-1	Zidan
29/8	Eintracht	a	1-1	Zidan
12/9	Bayern	h	1-5	Hummels
19/9	Hannover	a	1-1	Nuri
26/9	Schalke	h	0-1	
3/10	Mönchengladbach	a	1-0	Barrios
18/10	Bochum	h	2-0	Barrios, Subotić
23/10	Leverkusen	a	1-1	Barrios
30/10	Hertha	h	2-0	Nuri (p), Barrios
8/11	Werder	a	1-1	Barrios
21/11	Mainz	h	0-0	
28/11	Hoffenheim	a	2-1	Błaszczykowski, Nuri (p)
5/12	Nürnberg	h	4-0	Grosskreutz, Barrios, Zidan, Hummels
13/12	Wolfsburg	a	3-1	Barrios 2, Owomoyela
19/12	Freiburg	h	1-0	Barrios

2010
17/1	Köln	a	3-2	Hummels 2, Grosskreutz
23/1	Hamburg	h	1-0	Valdez
31/1	Stuttgart	a	1-4	Barrios
7/2	Eintracht	h	2-3	Hummels, Barrios
13/2	Bayern	a	1-3	Zidan
20/2	Hannover	h	4-1	Subotić, og (Eggimann), Valdez, Grosskreutz
26/2	Schalke	a	1-2	Nuri
6/3	Mönchengladbach	h	3-0	Grosskreutz, Zidan 2
13/3	Bochum	a	4-1	Kehl, Zidan, Barrios 2
20/3	Leverkusen	h	3-0	Barrios 2, Rangelov
3/4	Hertha	a	0-0	
3/4	Werder	h	2-1	Grosskreutz, Subotić
10/4	Mainz	a	0-1	
18/4	Hoffenheim	h	1-1	Valdez
24/4	Nürnberg	h	3-2	Barrios 3
1/5	Wolfsburg	h	1-1	Stiepermann
8/5	Freiburg	a	1-3	Barrios

No	Name	Nat	DoB	Pos	Aps	(s)	Gls
18	Lucas BARRIOS	PAR	13/11/84	A	30	(3)	19
22	Sven BENDER		27/4/89	M	17	(2)	
16	Jakub BŁASZCZYKOWSKI	POL	14/12/85	M	30	(2)	1
17	Leonardo de Déus Santos "DEDÉ"	BRA	18/4/78	D	11	(16)	
27	FELIPE Augusto SANTANA	BRA	17/3/86	D	13	(12)	
14	Markus FEULNER		12/2/82	M	1	(8)	
31	Mario GÖTZE		3/6/92			(5)	
19	Kevin GROSSKREUTZ		19/7/88	A	21	(11)	5
30	Tamás HAJNAL	HUN	15/3/81	M	10	(11)	
15	Mats HUMMELS		16/12/88	D	27	(3)	5
21	Uwe HÜNEMEIER		9/1/86	D		(1)	
5	Sebastian KEHL		13/2/80	M	5	(1)	1
45	Julian KOCH		11/11/90	D		(2)	
13	Damien LE TALLEC	FRA		A	1	(3)	
8	NURİ Şahin	TUR	5/9/88	M	33		4
25	Patrick OWOMOYELA		5/11/79	D	33		1
11	Dimitar RANGELOV	BUL	9/2/83	A	1	(9)	1
29	Marcel SCHMELZER		22/1/88	D	24	(4)	
39	Marco STIEPERMANN		9/2/91	A		(3)	1
4	Neven SUBOTIĆ	SRB	10/12/88	D	34		3
7	Paulo César Fonseca "TINGA"	BRA	13/1/78	M	7		
9	Nelson Haedo VALDEZ	PAR	28/11/83	A	18	(10)	5
1	Roman WEIDENFELLER		6/8/80	G	30		
10	Mohamed ZIDAN	EGY	11/12/81	A	24	(3)	6
20	Marc ZIEGLER		13/6/76	G	4	(1)	

No	Name	Nat	DoB	Pos	Aps	(s)	Gls
29	Fabian BÄCKER		28/5/90	A		(2)	1
30	Logan BAILLY	BEL	27/12/85	G	29		
10	Raúl Marcelo BOBADILLA	ARG	18/6/87	A	25	(5)	4
26	Michael BRADLEY	USA	31/7/87	M	28	(1)	2
4	Roel BROUWERS	NED	28/11/81	D	34		8
9	Roberto COLAUTTI	ISR	24/5/82	A	15	(8)	5
3	Filip DAEMS	BEL	31/10/78	D	18		1
31	DANTE Bonfim Costa Santos	BRA	18/10/83	D	32		3
16	Rob FRIEND	CAN	23/1/81	A	11	(15)	3
1	Christofer HEIMEROTH		1/8/81	G	5		
42	Patrick HERRMANN		12/12/91	M	3	(1)	1
24	Tony JANTSCHKE		7/4/90	M	2	(4)	
20	Jean-Sébastien JAURÈS	FRA	30/9/77	D	14	(2)	
18	JUAN Fernando ARANGO Sáenz	VEN	17/5/80	M	33	(1)	2
15	Thomas KLEINE		28/12/77	D	2	(12)	
25	Moses LAMIDI		5/1/88	A	1	(2)	
22	Tobias LEVELS		22/11/86	D	32		
14	Thorben MARX		1/6/81	M	28		
40	Karim MATMOUR	ALG	25/6/85	A	18	(7)	1
8	Marcel MEEUWIS	NED	31/10/80	M	14	(4)	
13	Roman NEUSTÄDTER		18/2/88	M		(2)	
27	Oliver NEUVILLE		1/5/73	A	1	(11)	
11	Marco REUS		31/5/89	M	27	(6)	8
7	Paul STALTIERI	CAN	18/10/77	D	2	(1)	

VFL BORUSSIA MÖNCHENGLADBACH
Coach – Michael Frontzeck
Founded – 1900
Stadium – Borussia-Park (54,067)
MAJOR HONOURS:
UEFA Cup – (2) 1975, 1979;
German League – (5) 1970, 1971, 1975, 1976, 1977;
German Cup – (3) 1960, 1973, 1995.

2009

9/8	Bochum	a	3-3	Juan Arango, Colautti, Brouwers
16/8	Hertha	h	2-1	Brouwers, Matmour
22/8	Werder	a	0-3	
28/8	Mainz	h	2-0	Bobadilla, Reus
12/9	Nürnberg	a	0-1	
19/9	Hoffenheim	h	2-4	Juan Arango, Colautti
27/9	Freiburg	a	0-3	
3/10	Dortmund	h	0-1	
18/10	Wolfsburg	a	1-2	Bradley
24/10	Köln	h	0-0	
31/10	Hamburg	a	3-2	Reus, Dante, Friend
7/11	Stuttgart	h	0-0	
21/11	Eintracht	a	2-1	og (Nikolov), Brouwers
28/11	Schalke	h	1-0	Reus
4/12	Bayern	a	1-2	Brouwers
12/12	Hannover	h	5-3	og 2 (Haggui 2), Friend, og (Djakpa), Bradley
19/12	Leverkusen	a	2-3	Brouwers, Dante

2010

16/1	Bochum	h	1-2	Bäcker
23/1	Hertha	a	0-0	
30/1	Werder	h	4-3	Reus, Colautti, Bobadilla 2
7/2	Mainz	a	0-1	
12/2	Nürnberg	h	2-1	Colautti, Friend
19/2	Hoffenheim	a	2-2	Daems (p), Colautti
27/2	Freiburg	h	1-1	Brouwers
6/3	Dortmund	a	0-3	
13/3	Wolfsburg	h	0-4	
19/3	Köln	a	1-1	Reus
28/3	Hamburg	h	1-0	Brouwers
3/4	Stuttgart	a	1-2	Reus
9/4	Eintracht	h	2-0	Reus, Dante
17/4	Schalke	a	1-3	Bobadilla
24/4	Bayern	h	1-1	Reus
1/5	Hannover	a	1-6	Herrmann
8/5	Leverkusen	h	1-1	Brouwers

EINTRACHT FRANKFURT
Coach – Michael Skibbe
Founded – 1899
Stadium – Commerzbank-Arena (51,500)
MAJOR HONOURS:
UEFA Cup - (1) 1980;
German League - (1) 1959;
German Cup - (4) 1974, 1975, 1981, 1988.

2009

8/8	Werder	a	3-2	Amanatidis 2, Fenin
15/8	Nürnberg	h	1-1	Caio
22/8	Köln	a	0-0	
29/8	Dortmund	h	1-1	Amanatidis
12/9	Freiburg	a	2-0	Franz, Meier
20/9	Hamburg	h	1-1	Russ
26/9	Stuttgart	h	0-3	
2/10	Schalke	a	0-2	
17/10	Hannover	h	2-1	Liberopoulos, Meier
24/10	Bayern	a	1-2	Meier
1/11	Bochum	h	2-1	Caio, Franz
6/11	Leverkusen	a	0-4	
21/11	Mönchengladbach	h	1-2	Schwegler (p)
28/11	Hertha	a	3-1	Ochs, Franz, Meier
5/12	Mainz	h	2-0	Franz, Meier
12/12	Hoffenheim	a	1-1	Schwegler
19/12	Wolfsburg	h	2-2	Franz, Meier

2010

16/1	Werder	h	1-0	Russ
23/1	Nürnberg	a	1-1	Köhler
30/1	Köln	h	1-1	Chris
7/2	Dortmund	a	3-2	Köhler, Jung, Meier
14/2	Freiburg	h	2-1	Köhler, Halil Altıntop
20/2	Hamburg	a	0-0	
27/2	Stuttgart	a	1-2	Köhler
6/3	Schalke	h	1-4	Meier
13/3	Hannover	a	1-2	Halil Altıntop
20/3	Bayern	h	2-1	Tsoumou, Fenin
26/3	Bochum	a	2-1	Russ, Caio
3/4	Leverkusen	h	3-2	Teber (p), Caio, Franz
9/4	Mönchengladbach	a	0-2	
17/4	Hertha	h	2-2	Korkmaz, Russ
24/4	Mainz	a	3-3	Meier 2, Korkmaz
1/5	Hoffenheim	h	1-2	Schwegler
8/5	Wolfsburg	a	1-3	Halil Altıntop

No	Name	Nat	DoB	Pos	Aps	(s)	Gls
18	Ioannis AMANATIDIS	GRE	3/12/81	A	7	(1)	3
8	Zlatan BAJRAMOVIĆ	BIH	12/8/79	M	7	(4)	
30	CAIO César Alves dos Santos	BRA	29/5/86	M	15	(11)	4
29	CHRIStian Maicon Hening	BRA	25/8/78	D	29		1
13	Ricardo CLARK	USA	10/2/83	M	3		
22	Ralf FÄHRMANN		27/9/88	G	3		
17	Martin FENIN	CZE	16/4/87	A	2	(15)	2
4	Maik FRANZ		5/8/81	D	25	(2)	6
19	HALIL Altıntop	TUR	8/12/82	A	15		3
25	Marcel HELLER		12/2/86	M	2	(7)	
24	Sebastian JUNG		22/6/90	D	12	(2)	1
7	Benjamin KÖHLER		4/8/80	M	21	(10)	4
11	Ümit KORKMAZ	AUT	17/9/85	A	10	(8)	2
10	Nikos LIBEROPOULOS	GRE	4/8/75	A	14	(7)	1
14	Alexander MEIER		17/1/83	M	34		10
1	Oka NIKOLOV	MKD	25/5/74	G	31		
2	Patrick OCHS		14/5/84	D	28		1
3	Nikola PETKOVIĆ	SRB	28/3/86	D		(2)	
20	Christoph PREUSS		4/7/81	M		(3)	
23	Marco RUSS		4/8/85	D	30		4
27	Pirmin SCHWEGLER	SUI	9/3/87	M	25		3
16	Christoph SPYCHER	SUI	30/3/78	D	27		
13	Marcus STEINHÖFER		7/3/86	M	3	(2)	
6	Selim TEBER		7/3/81	M	24	(5)	1
34	Cenk TOSUN		7/6/91	M		(1)	
26	Juvhel TSOUMOU		27/12/90	A		(4)	1
5	Aleksandar VASOSKI	MKD	21/11/79	D	7		
28	Jan ZIMMERMANN		19/4/85	G		(1)	

No	Name	Nat	DoB	Pos	Aps	(s)	Gls
10	Yacine ABDESSADKI	MAR	1/1/81	M	20	(3)	2
20	Ivica BANOVIĆ	CRO	2/8/80	M	22	(3)	4
15	Oliver BARTH		6/10/79	D	12	(4)	
3	Felix BASTIANS		9/5/88	D	33	(1)	1
37	Oliver BAUMANN		2/6/90	G	1		
13	Tommy BECHMANN	DEN	22/12/81	A	10	(11)	1
34	Squipon BEKTASI		14/9/90	A		(1)	
5	Heiko BUTSCHER		28/7/80	D	29		1
40	Daniel CALIGIURI		15/1/88	M	9	(7)	
6	CHA Du-ri	KOR	25/7/80	D	19	(4)	1
9	Papiss Demba CISSÉ	SEN	3/6/85	A	13	(3)	6
18	Johannes FLUM		14/12/87	M	22	(3)	1
19	Andreas GLOCKNER		25/2/88	M		(2)	
8	Mohamadou IDRISSOU	CMR	8/3/80	A	30		9
11	Jonathan JÄGER	FRA	23/5/78	A	20	(5)	
2	Pavel KRMAŠ	CZE	3/3/80	D	15	(2)	
7	Cédric MAKIADI	COD	23/4/84	A	27	(6)	3
39	Jackson MENDY	FRA	25/5/87	D	6		
24	Mensur MUJDŽA	BIH	28/3/84	D	9	(5)	
14	Hamed NAMOUCHI	TUN	14/2/84	M	1		
1	Simon POUPLIN	FRA	28/5/85	G	30		
27	Stefan REISINGER		14/9/81	A	9	(16)	
26	Manuel SALZ		6/8/85	G	3		
23	Julian SCHUSTER		15/4/85	M	18	(10)	2
30	David TARGAMADZE	GEO	22/8/89	M		(2)	
38	Ömer TOPRAK		21/7/89	D	10	(4)	
22	Eke UZOMA	NGA	11/8/89	M	1	(3)	
28	Daniel WILLIAMS		8/3/89	M	5	(1)	

SC FREIBURG

Coach – Robin Dutt
Founded – 1904
Stadium – Badenova–Stadion (25,000)

2009

9/8	Hamburg	h	1-1	Bechmann
15/8	Stuttgart	a	2-4	Idrissou 2
22/8	Leverkusen	h	0-5	
29/8	Schalke	a	1-0	Cha
12/9	Eintracht	h	0-2	
20/9	Hertha	a	4-0	Banović 2, Makiadi, Idrissou
27/9	Mönchengladbach	h	3-0	Idrissou, Abdessadki, Schuster
3/10	Hannover	a	2-5	Banović, Schuster
17/10	Bayern	h	1-2	Reisinger
24/10	Mainz	a	0-3	
1/11	Hoffenheim	h	0-1	
7/11	Bochum	a	2-1	Butscher, Reisinger
21/11	Werder	h	0-6	
28/11	Nürnberg	a	1-0	Reisinger
5/12	Wolfsburg	a	2-2	Idrissou, Banović (p)
12/12	Köln	h	0-0	
19/12	Dortmund	a	0-1	

2010

16/1	Hamburg	a	0-2	
22/1	Stuttgart	h	0-1	
31/1	Leverkusen	a	1-3	Bastians
6/2	Schalke	h	0-0	
14/2	Eintracht	a	1-2	Cissé
21/2	Hertha	h	0-3	
27/2	Mönchengladbach	a	1-1	Cissé
6/3	Hannover	h	1-2	Abdessadki
13/3	Bayern	a	1-2	Makiadi
20/3	Mainz	h	1-0	Flum
28/3	Hoffenheim	a	1-1	Idrissou
1/4	Bochum	h	1-1	Cissé
10/4	Werder	a	0-4	
17/4	Nürnberg	h	2-1	og (Maroh), Cissé
25/4	Wolfsburg	h	1-0	Makiadi
1/5	Köln	a	2-2	Idrissou 2
8/5	Dortmund	h	3-1	Idrissou, Cissé 2

HAMBURGER SV

Coach – Bruno Labbadia; (26/4/10) (Ricardo Moniz (NED))
Founded – 1919
Stadium – HSH-Nordbank-Arena (57,000)
MAJOR HONOURS:
European Champion Clubs' Cup - (1) 1983;
UEFA Cup Winners' Cup - (1) 1977;
German League - (6) 1923, 1928, 1960, 1979, 1982, 1983;
German Cup - (3) 1963, 1976, 1987.

2009

9/8	Freiburg	a	1-1	Pitroipa
15/8	Dortmund	h	4-1	Demel, Zé Roberto, Guerrero, Berg
23/8	Wolfsburg	a	4-2	Guerrero, Elia, Petrić, Castelen
30/8	Köln	h	3-1	Guerrero 2, Trochowski (p)
12/9	Stuttgart	h	3-1	Petrić, Elia, Zé Roberto
20/9	Eintracht	a	1-1	Zé Roberto
26/9	Bayern	h	1-0	Petrić
4/10	Hertha	a	3-1	og (Kaká), Jarolím, Zé Roberto
17/10	Leverkusen	h	0-0	
25/10	Schalke	a	3-3	Berg 2, Trochowski
31/10	Mönchengladbach	h	2-3	Trochowski, Zé Roberto
8/11	Hannover	a	2-2	Jansen, Elia
22/11	Bochum	h	0-1	
28/11	Mainz	a	1-1	Torun
5/12	Hoffenheim	h	0-0	
12/12	Nürnberg	a	4-0	Elia 2, Jansen, Torun
20/12	Werder	h	2-1	Mathijsen, Jansen

2010

16/1	Freiburg	h	2-0	Jansen, Petrić
23/1	Dortmund	a	0-1	
29/1	Wolfsburg	h	1-1	Trochowski
6/2	Köln	a	3-3	Jansen, Petrić 2
13/2	Stuttgart	a	3-1	Berg, Van Nistelrooy 2
20/2	Eintracht	h	0-0	
28/2	Bayern	a	0-1	
6/3	Hertha	h	1-0	Jansen
14/3	Leverkusen	a	2-4	Zé Roberto, Rozehnal
21/3	Schalke	h	2-2	Van Nistelrooy, Pitroipa
28/3	Mönchengladbach	a	0-1	
4/4	Hannover	h	0-0	

11/4	Bochum	a	2-1	Tesche, og (Johansson)
17/4	Mainz	h	0-1	
25/4	Hoffenheim	a	1-5	Tesche
1/5	Nürnberg	h	4-0	Pitroipa, Petrić 2, Van Nistelrooy
8/5	Werder	a	1-1	Van Nistelrooy

No	Name	Nat	DoB	Pos	Aps	(s)	Gls
6	Dennis AOGO		14/1/87	D	31		
19	Tolgay ARSLAN		16/8/90	M	2	(3)	
31	Maximillian BEISTER		6/9/90	A		(2)	
16	Marcus BERG	SWE	17/8/86	A	16	(14)	4
27	Sören BERTRAM		5/6/91	M		(2)	
17	Jérôme BOATENG		3/9/88	D	26	(1)	
18	Romeo CASTELEN	NED	3/5/83	M		(2)	1
20	Guy DEMEL	CIV	13/6/81	D	22	(4)	1
11	Eljero ELIA	NED	13/2/87	M	20	(4)	5
9	José Paolo GUERRERO	PER	1/1/84	A	4	(2)	4
12	Wolfgang HESL		13/1/86	G		(1)	
7	Marcell JANSEN		4/11/85	D	15	(3)	6
14	David JAROLÍM	CZE	17/5/79	M	33		1
5	Joris MATHIJSEN	NED	5/4/80	D	33		1
10	Mladen PETRIĆ	CRO	1/1/81	A	25	(1)	8
21	Jonathan PITROIPA	BFA	12/4/86	M	7	(13)	3
4	Bastian REINHARDT		19/11/75	D		(1)	
25	Tomás Eduardo RINCÓN	VEN	13/1/88	M	14	(3)	
1	Frank ROST		30/6/73	G	34		
3	David ROZEHNAL	CZE	5/7/80	D	19	(4)	1
28	Mickaël TAVARES	SEN	25/10/82	M		(3)	
13	Robert TESCHE		27/5/87	M	6	(10)	2
35	Tunay TORUN	TUR	21/4/90	A	12	(7)	2
15	Piotr TROCHOWSKI		22/3/84	M	25	(8)	4
22	Ruud VAN NISTELROOY	NED	1/7/76	A	7	(4)	5
8	José Roberto da Silva Júnior "ZÉ ROBERTO"	BRA	6/7/74	M	23		6

HANNOVER 96
Coach – Dieter Hecking; (20/8/09) Andreas Bergmann;
(19/1/10) Mirko Slomka
Founded – 1896
Stadium – AWD-Arena (49,000)
MAJOR HONOURS:
German League - (2) 1938, 1954;
German Cup - (1) 1992.

2009
8/8	Hertha	a	0-1	
15/8	Mainz	h	1-1	Štajner (p)
22/8	Nürnberg	a	2-0	Štajner 2
28/8	Hoffenheim	h	0-1	
13/9	Werder	a	0-0	
19/9	Dortmund	h	1-1	Konan Ya
26/9	Wolfsburg	a	2-4	Balitsch, og (Madlung)
3/10	Freiburg	h	5-2	Chahed, Bruggink, Haggui, Konan Ya, Pinto
17/10	Eintracht	a	1-2	Štajner
24/10	Stuttgart	h	1-0	Konan Ya
31/3	Köln	a	1-0	Rosenthal
8/11	Hamburg	h	2-2	Konan Ya, Štajner (p)
21/11	Schalke	a	0-2	
29/11	Bayern	h	0-3	
5/12	Leverkusen	a	0-4	
12/12	Mönchengladbach	a	3-5	Konan Ya 2, Schulz
19/12	Bochum	h	2-3	Schlaudraff 2

2010
16/1	Hertha	h	0-3	
23/1	Mainz	a	0-1	
30/1	Nürnberg	h	1-3	Štajner
6/2	Hoffenheim	a	1-2	Koné
13/2	Werder	h	1-5	Schulz
20/2	Dortmund	a	1-4	Koné
28/2	Wolfsburg	h	0-1	
6/3	Freiburg	a	2-1	Élson, og (Cissé)

13/3	Eintracht	h	2-1	Andreasen, Pinto
20/3	Stuttgart	a	0-2	
27/3	Köln	h	1-4	Cherundolo
4/4	Hamburg	a	0-0	
10/4	Schalke	h	4-2	og (Westermann), Konan Ya 2, Balitsch
17/4	Bayern	a	0-7	
24/4	Leverkusen	a	0-3	
1/5	Mönchengladbach	h	6-1	Haggui, Pinto, Konan Ya, Hanke, Chahed, Bruggink
8/5	Bochum	a	3-0	Bruggink, Hanke, Pinto

No	Name	Nat	DoB	Pos	Aps	(s)	Gls
3	Leon ANDREASEN	DEN	23/4/83	M	7		1
14	Hanno BALITSCH		2/1/81	M	25	(2)	2
28	Leon BALOGUN		28/6/88	D	1	(1)	
10	Arnold BRUGGINK	NED	24/7/77	M	21	(5)	3
41	Florian BÜCHLER		23/10/88	A		(1)	
23	Sofian CHAHED	TUN	18/4/83	D	9	(7)	2
6	Steve CHERUNDOLO	USA	19/2/79	D	23	(3)	1
15	Constant DJAKPA	CIV	17/10/86	D	20	(4)	
4	Ján ĎURICA	SVK	10/12/81	D	8	(1)	
5	Mario EGGIMANN	SUI	24/1/81	D	12	(7)	
25	ÉLSON Falcão da Silva	BRA	16/11/81	M	7		1
1	Robert ENKE		24/8/77	G	6		
41	Henrik ERNST		2/9/86	M		(2)	
32	Mikael FORSSELL	FIN	15/3/81	A	2		
27	Florian FROMLOWITZ		2/7/86	G	28		
17	Rubic GHASEMI-NOBAKHT	IRN	27/7/87	A		(1)	
21	Karim HAGGUI	TUN	20/1/84	D	30		2
9	Mike HANKE		5/11/83	A	5	(13)	2
11	Didier KONAN YA	CIV	22/5/84	A	24	(1)	9
18	Arouna KONÉ	CIV	11/11/83	A	8		2
20	Jacek KRZYNÓWEK	POL	15/5/76	M	3	(8)	
8	Altin LALA	ALB	18/11/75	M	3	(1)	
38	Jarosław LINDNER	POL	28/6/88	A		(1)	
7	Sérgio PINTO		16/10/80	M	20	(6)	4
22	Valdet RAMA	ALB	20/11/87	M	4	(11)	
34	Konstantin RAUSCH		15/3/90	D	20	(6)	
26	Jan ROSENTHAL		7/4/86	M	13	(3)	1
13	Jan SCHLAUDRAFF		18/7/83	A	5	(5)	2
33	Manuel SCHMIEDEBACH		5/12/88	D	11	(3)	
19	Christian SCHULZ		1/4/83	D	33		2
24	Jiří ŠTAJNER	CZE	27/5/76	A	26	(4)	6
37	Salvatore ZIZZO	USA	3/4/87	M		(1)	

HERTHA BSC BERLIN
Coach – Lucien Favre (SUI); (29/9/09) (Karsten Heine);
(3/10/09) Friedhelm Funkel
Founded – 1892
Stadium – Olympiastadion (74,400)
MAJOR HONOURS:
German League - (2) 1930, 1931.

2009
8/8	Hannover	h	1-0	Kačar
16/8	Mönchengladbach	a	1-2	Kačar
23/8	Bochum	a	0-1	
30/8	Werder	h	2-3	Piszczek, Ebert
12/9	Mainz	a	1-2	Nicu
20/9	Freiburg	h	0-4	
27/9	Hoffenheim	a	1-5	Raffael
4/10	Hamburg	h	1-3	Friedrich
17/10	Nürnberg	a	0-3	
25/10	Wolfsburg	h	0-0	
30/10	Dortmund	a	0-2	
8/11	Köln	h	0-1	
21/11	Stuttgart	a	1-1	Ramos
28/11	Eintracht	h	1-3	Ramos
6/12	Schalke	a	0-2	
11/12	Leverkusen	h	2-2	Ramos 2
19/12	Bayern	a	2-5	Ramos, Raffael

GERMANY

2010

16/1	Hannover	a	3-0	Piszczek, Raffael, Gekas
23/1	Mönchengladbach	h	0-0	
30/1	Bochum	h	0-0	
5/2	Werder	a	1-2	Gekas
13/2	Mainz	h	1-1	Ramos
21/2	Freiburg	a	3-0	Ramos, Cícero 2
27/2	Hoffenheim	h	0-2	
6/3	Hamburg	a	0-1	
13/3	Nürnberg	h	1-2	Gekas
21/3	Wolfsburg	a	5-1	Gekas 3, Ramos 2
27/3	Dortmund	h	0-0	
3/4	Köln	a	3-0	Raffael 2, Cícero
10/4	Stuttgart	h	0-1	
17/4	Eintracht	a	2-2	Kačar, Raffael
24/4	Schalke	h	0-1	
1/5	Leverkusen	a	1-1	Raffael
8/5	Bayern	h	1-3	Ramos

No	Name	Nat	DoB	Pos	Aps	(s)	Gls
22	Rasmus BENGTSSON	SWE	26/6/86	D	3	(3)	
29	Sascha BIGALKE		8/1/90	M	1		
40	Sascha BURCHERT		30/10/89	G	2	(1)	
27	Clederson CÉSAR de Souza	BRA	14/7/79	M		(3)	
7	CÍCERO Santos	BRA	26/8/84	M	28	(2)	3
8	Pál DÁRDAI	HUN	16/3/76	M	10	(7)	
23	Valeri DOMOVCHIYSKI	BUL	5/10/86	A	4	(12)	
1	Jaroslav DROBNÝ	CZE	18/10/79	G	30		
20	Patrick EBERT		17/3/87	M	12	(4)	1
3	Arne FRIEDRICH		29/5/79	D	31		1
17	Theofanis GEKAS	GRE	23/5/80	A	15	(2)	6
36	Lennart HARTMANN		3/4/91	M	1	(1)	
16	Roman HUBNÍK	CZE	6/6/84	D	7		
6	Christoph JANKER		14/2/85	D	8	(7)	
44	Gojko KAČAR	SRB	26/1/87	M	18	(4)	3
2	Claudiano Bezerra da Silva "KAKÁ"	BRA	16/5/81	D	2		
21	Levan KOBIASHVILI	GEO	10/7/77	M	16		
11	Florian KRINGE		18/8/82	M	10	(2)	
28	Fabian LUSTENBERGER	SUI	2/5/88	M	23		
25	Maximilian NICU	ROU	25/11/82	M	12	(3)	1
12	Timo OCHS		17/10/81	G	2		
5	Nemanja PEJČINOVIĆ	SRB	4/11/87	D	16		
26	Łukasz PISZCZEK	POL	3/6/85	M	28	(3)	2
10	RAFFAEL Caetano de Araújo	BRA	28/3/85	A	30	(1)	7
9	Adrián RAMOS	COL	22/1/86	A	23	(6)	10
13	Marc STEIN		7/7/85	D	9	(1)	
4	Steve VON BERGEN	SUI	10/6/83	D	24	(1)	
18	Artur WICHNIAREK	POL	28/2/77	A	9	(10)	

TSG 1899 HOFFENHEIM

Coach – Ralf Rangnick
Founded – 1899
Stadium – Rhein-Neckar-Arena, Sinsheim (30,164)

2009

8/8	Bayern	h	1-1	Obasi
15/8	Leverkusen	a	0-1	
21/8	Schalke	h	0-0	
28/8	Hannover	a	1-0	Carlos Eduardo
12/9	Bochum	h	3-0	Ba, Obasi, Compper
19/9	Mönchengladbach	a	4-2	Salihović, Maicosuel, Obasi, Ba
27/9	Hertha	h	5-1	Ibišević 3, Obasi, Carlos Eduardo (p)
3/10	Mainz	a	1-2	Ibertsberger
17/10	Werder	a	0-2	
24/10	Nürnberg	h	3-0	Eichner, Ibišević, Zuculini
1/11	Freiburg	a	1-0	Maicosuel
7/11	Wolfsburg	h	1-2	Ibišević
21/11	Köln	a	4-0	Carlos Eduardo, Obasi, Ba, Ibišević (p)
28/11	Dortmund	h	1-2	Ba

5/12	Hamburg	a	0-0	
12/12	Eintracht	h	1-1	Salihović
19/12	Stuttgart	a	1-3	Maicosuel

2010

15/1	Bayern	a	0-2	
24/1	Leverkusen	h	0-3	
30/1	Schalke	a	0-2	
6/2	Hannover	h	2-1	Carlos Eduardo, Salihović (p)
13/2	Bochum	a	1-2	Ibišević
19/2	Mönchengladbach	h	2-2	Ibišević, Carlos Eduardo (p)
27/2	Hertha	a	2-0	Ba, Ibišević
7/3	Mainz	h	0-1	
14/3	Werder	h	0-1	
20/3	Nürnberg	a	0-0	
28/3	Freiburg	h	1-1	Šimunić
4/4	Wolfsburg	a	0-4	
10/4	Köln	h	0-2	
18/4	Dortmund	a	1-1	Ibišević
25/4	Hamburg	h	5-1	Ibišević 2, Obasi 2, Salihović
1/5	Eintracht	a	2-1	Tagoe 2
8/5	Stuttgart	h	1-1	Vukčević

No	Name	Nat	DoB	Pos	Aps	(s)	Gls
9	Demba BA	SEN	25/5/85	A	12	(5)	5
2	Andreas BECK		13/3/87	D	24	(1)	
10	CARLOS EDUARDO Marques	BRA	18/7/87	M	32	(1)	5
5	Marvin COMPPER		14/6/85	D	32		1
8	Christian EICHNER		24/11/82	D	22	(3)	1
39	Pascal GROSS		15/6/91	M		(1)	
37	Manuel GULDE		12/2/91	D	2	(4)	
1	Daniel HAAS		1/8/83	G	6		
16	Kai HERDLING		27/6/84	A		(1)	
28	Timo HILDEBRAND		5/4/79	G	28		
26	Andreas IBERTSBERGER	AUT	27/7/82	D	23		1
19	Vedad IBIŠEVIĆ	BIH	6/8/84	A	30	(4)	12
29	Adam JABIRI		3/6/84	A		(1)	
31	Andreas LUDWIG		11/9/90	A		(1)	
21	LUIZ GUSTAVO Dias	BRA	23/7/87	M	26	(1)	
7	MAICOSUEL Reginaldo de Matos	BRA	16/6/86	A	17	(10)	3
24	Per NILSSON	SWE	15/9/82	D	5	(3)	
20	Chinedu OBASI	NGA	1/6/86	A	21	(2)	7
22	Jukka RAITALA	FIN	15/9/89	D	1	(1)	
23	Sejad SALIHOVIĆ	BIH	8/10/84	M	31	(1)	4
14	Josip ŠIMUNIĆ	CRO	18/2/78	D	31		1
18	Prince TAGOE	GHA	9/11/86	A	1	(11)	2
11	Marco TERRAZZINO		15/4/91	A		(8)	
25	Isaac VORSAH	GHA	21/6/88	D	11	(5)	
34	Boris VUKČEVIĆ		16/3/90	M	6	(22)	1
17	Tobias WEIS		30/7/85	M	11	(4)	
12	WELLINGTON Luís de Sousa	BRA	11/2/88	A		(1)	
36	Franco ZUCULINI	ARG	5/9/90	M	2	(5)	1

1. FC KÖLN

Coach – Zvonimir Soldo (CRO)
Founded – 1948
Stadium – Rhein-Energie-Stadion (50,000)
MAJOR HONOURS:
German League - (3) 1962, 1964, 1978;
German Cup - (4) 1968, 1977, 1978, 1983.

2009

8/8	Dortmund	a	0-1	
15/8	Wolfsburg	h	1-3	Ehret
22/8	Eintracht	h	0-0	
30/8	Hamburg	a	1-3	Chihi
13/9	Schalke	h	1-2	Podolski
19/9	Stuttgart	a	2-0	Freis, Sanou
26/9	Leverkusen	h	0-1	
3/10	Bayern	a	0-0	
17/10	Mainz	h	1-0	Novaković
24/10	Mönchengladbach	a	0-0	

31/3	Hannover	h	0-1	
8/11	Hertha	a	1-0	*Novakovič*
21/11	Hoffenheim	h	0-4	
27/11	Bochum	a	0-0	
6/12	Werder	h	0-0	
12/12	Freiburg	a	0-0	
20/12	Nürnberg	h	3-0	*Geromel, Novakovič 2*
2010				
17/1	Dortmund	h	2-3	*McKenna, Mohamad*
24/1	Wolfsburg	a	3-2	*Pezzoni, Freis, Chihi*
30/1	Eintracht	a	2-1	*Maniche, og (Russ)*
6/2	Hamburg	h	3-3	*Mohamad, Novakovič, Chihi*
14/2	Schalke	a	0-2	
20/2	Stuttgart	h	1-5	*Schorch*
27/2	Leverkusen	a	0-0	
6/3	Bayern	h	1-1	*Podolski*
13/3	Mainz	a	0-1	
19/3	Mönchengladbach	h	1-1	*Maniche*
27/3	Hannover	a	4-1	*Tošić 2, Petit, Novakovič (p)*
3/4	Hertha	h	0-3	
10/4	Hoffenheim	a	2-0	*Matuszczyk 2*
16/4	Bochum	h	2-0	*Tošić 2*
24/4	Werder	a	0-1	
1/5	Freiburg	h	2-2	*Tošić, Freis*
8/5	Nürnberg	a	0-1	

No	Name	Nat	DoB	Pos	Aps	(s)	Gls
2	Mišo BREČKO	SVN	1/5/84	D	31	(1)	
13	Daniel BROSINSKI		17/7/88	M		(8)	
20	Adil CHIHI	MAR	21/2/88	M	12	(3)	3
28	Carsten CULLMANN		5/3/76	D	1	(2)	
22	Fabrice EHRET	FRA	28/9/79	M	21	(8)	1
7	Sebastian FREIS		23/4/85	A	20	(11)	3
21	Pedro Tonon GEROMEL	BRA	21/9/85	D	29		1
9	Manasseh ISHIAKU	NGA	9/1/83	A	6	(9)	
18	Thomas KESSLER		20/1/86	G	2		
12	Nuno Ricardo de Oliveira Ribeiro "MANICHE"	POR	11/11/77	M	26		2
4	Marvin MATIP		25/9/85	D		(4)	
25	Adam MATUSZCZYK	POL	14/2/89	M	9		2
23	Kevin McKENNA	CAN	21/1/80	D	11	(14)	1
3	Youssef MOHAMAD	LIB	1/7/80	D	31		2
1	Faryd Aly Camilo MONDRAGÓN	COL	21/6/71	G	32		
11	Milivoje NOVAKOVIČ	SVN	18/5/79	A	26	(4)	6
8	Armando Gonçalves Teixeira "PETIT"	POR	25/9/76	M	32		1
17	Kevin PEZZONI		22/3/89	M	18	(3)	1
10	Lukas PODOLSKI		4/6/85	A	27		2
14	Wilfried SANOU	BFA	16/3/84	M	1	(5)	1
16	Christopher SCHORCH		30/1/89	D	13	(4)	1
14	Zoran TOŠIĆ	SRB	28/4/87	M	9	(4)	5
6	Pierre WOMÉ	CMR	26/3/79	D	11	(1)	
37	Reinhold YABO		10/2/92	D		(1)	
19	Taner YALÇIN		18/2/90	M	6	(1)	1
29	Sebastian ZIELINSKY		21/2/88	A		(2)	

1. FSV MAINZ 05

Coach – Jørn Andersen (NOR); (3/8/09) Thomas Tuchel
Founded – 1905
Stadium – Bruchwegstadion (20,300)

2009				
8/8	Leverkusen	h	2-2	*Hoogland, Gunkel*
15/8	Hannover	a	1-1	*Bancé*
22/8	Bayern	h	2-1	*Ivanschitz, Bancé*
28/8	Mönchengladbach	a	0-2	
12/9	Hertha	a	2-1	*Ivanschitz (p), Bancé*
19/9	Bochum	a	3-2	*Ivanschitz, Schürrle 2*
26/9	Werder	a	0-3	
3/10	Hoffenheim	h	2-1	*Ivanschitz, Bancé*
17/10	Köln	a	0-1	

24/10	Freiburg	h	3-0	*Ivanschitz, Hoogland 2*
31/10	Wolfsburg	a	3-3	*Amri, Ivanschitz, Hoogland*
7/11	Nürnberg	h	1-0	*Soto*
21/11	Dortmund	a	0-0	
28/11	Hamburg	h	1-1	*Hoogland*
5/12	Eintracht	a	0-2	
13/12	Stuttgart	h	1-1	*Polanski (p)*
18/12	Schalke	a	0-1	
2010				
16/1	Leverkusen	a	2-4	*Hoogland, Bungert*
23/1	Hannover	h	1-0	*Schürrle*
30/1	Bayern	a	0-3	
7/2	Mönchengladbach	h	1-0	*Svensson*
13/2	Hertha	a	1-1	*Bancé*
20/2	Bochum	h	0-0	
27/2	Werder	h	1-2	*Bancé*
7/3	Hoffenheim	a	1-0	*Bancé*
13/3	Köln	h	1-0	*Schürrle*
20/3	Freiburg	a	0-1	
27/3	Wolfsburg	h	0-2	
3/4	Nürnberg	a	0-2	
10/4	Dortmund	h	1-0	*Szalai*
7/4	Hamburg	a	1-0	*Bancé*
24/4	Eintracht	h	3-3	*Bancé 2, Šimák*
1/5	Stuttgart	a	2-2	*Fathi, Schürrle*
8/5	Schalke	h	0-0	

No	Name	Nat	DoB	Pos	Aps	(s)	Gls
22	Chadli AMRI	ALG	14/12/84	A	6	(13)	1
8	Srđan BALJAK	SRB	25/11/78	A	1	(3)	
23	Aristide BANCÉ	BFA	19/9/84	A	28	(2)	10
9	Félix Alexander BORJA	ECU	19/9/84	A		(1)	
32	Dragan BOGAVAC	MNE	7/4/80	A		(1)	
26	Niko BUNGERT		24/10/86	D	21	(6)	1
3	Malik FATHI		29/10/83	D	14		1
5	Eugen GOPKO		5/1/91	M		(1)	
34	Adriano GRIMALDI	ITA	5/4/91	A		(6)	
27	Daniel GUNKEL		7/6/80	M		(4)	1
16	Florian HELLER		10/3/82	M	26	(4)	
6	Tim HOOGLAND		11/6/85	D	19	(2)	6
18	Jahmir HYKA	ALB	8/3/88	M	2	(6)	
25	Andreas IVANSCHITZ	AUT	10/10/83	M	24	(3)	6
21	Miroslav KARHAN	SVK	21/6/76	M	30		
24	Zsolt LÖW	HUN	29/4/79	M	14	(1)	
33	Heinz MÜLLER		30/5/78	G	30		
4	Nikolce NOVESKI	MKD	28/4/79	D	33		
13	Milorad PEKOVIĆ	MNE	5/8/77	M	4	(7)	
7	Eugen POLANSKI		17/3/86	M	14	(7)	1
14	André SCHÜRRLE		6/11/90	A	25	(8)	5
10	Jan ŠIMÁK	CZE	13/10/78	M	5	(3)	1
19	Elkin SOTO	COL	4/8/80	M	28	(2)	1
2	Bo SVENSSON	DEN	4/8/79	D	20	(6)	1
28	Ádám SZALAI	HUN	9/12/87	A	8	(7)	1
11	Filip TROJAN	CZE	21/2/83	M	3	(2)	
3	Peter VAN DER HEYDEN	BEL	16/7/76	D	4	(4)	
29	Christian WETKLO		11/1/80	G	4	(1)	
8	Radoslav ZABAVNÍK	SVK	16/9/80	D	11	(1)	

1. FC NÜRNBERG

Coach – Michael Oenning; (22/12/09) Dieter Hecking
Founded – 1900
Stadium – Easycredit-Stadion (46,780)
MAJOR HONOURS:
German League - (9) 1920, 1921, 1924, 1925, 1927, 1936, 1948, 1961, 1968;
German Cup - (4) 1935, 1939, 1962, 2007.

2009				
8/8	Schalke	h	1-2	*Mintál*
15/8	Eintracht	a	1-1	*Bunjaku*
22/8	Hannover	h	0-2	
29/8	Stuttgart	a	0-0	
12/9	Mönchengladbach	h	1-0	*Kluge*

19/9	Bayern	a	1-2	Choupo-Moting
25/9	Bochum	h	0-1	
3/10	Leverkusen	a	0-4	
17/10	Hertha	h	3-0	Gygax, Bunjaku 2
24/10	Hoffenheim	a	0-3	
31/10	Werder	h	2-2	Eigler, Bunjaku
7/11	Mainz	a	0-1	
21/11	Wolfsburg	a	3-2	Bunjaku 2, Kluge
28/11	Freiburg	h	0-1	
5/12	Dortmund	a	0-4	
12/12	Hamburg	h	0-4	
20/12	Köln	a	0-3	
2010				
17/1	Schalke	a	0-1	
23/1	Eintracht	h	1-1	Eigler
30/1	Hannover	a	3-1	Bunjaku 3
6/2	Stuttgart	h	1-2	Bunjaku
12/2	Mönchengladbach	a	1-2	Bunjaku
20/2	Bayern	h	1-1	Gündoğan
27/2	Bochum	a	0-0	
7/3	Leverkusen	h	3-2	Choupo-Moting 2, Tavares
13/3	Hertha	a	2-1	Bunjaku, Charisteas
20/3	Hoffenheim	h	0-0	
27/3	Werder	a	2-4	Frantz, Choupo-Moting
3/4	Mainz	h	2-0	Frantz, Choupo-Moting
11/4	Wolfsburg	h	0-2	
17/4	Freiburg	a	1-2	Maroh
24/4	Dortmund	h	2-3	Frantz, Eigler
1/5	Hamburg	a	0-4	
8/5	Köln	h	1-0	Ottl

No	Name	Nat	DoB	Pos	Aps	(s)	Gls
20	Pascal BIELER		26/2/86	D	3		
19	Isaac BOAKYE	GHA	26/11/81	A	4	(5)	
3	BRENO Vinícius Rodrigues Borges	BRA	13/10/83	D	7		
26	Thomas BROICH		29/1/81	M	2	(5)	
10	Albert BUNJAKU	SUI	29/11/83	A	25	(3)	12
9	Angelos CHARISTEAS	GRE	9/2/80	A	7	(11)	1
14	Eric Maxim CHOUPO-MOTING	CMR	23/3/89	A	13	(12)	5
2	Dennis DIEKMEIER		20/10/89	D	30		
8	Christian EIGLER		1/1/84	A	18	(6)	3
17	Mike FRANTZ		14/10/86	M	20	(4)	3
22	İlkay GÜNDOĞAN		24/10/90	M	19	(3)	1
7	Daniel GYGAX	SUI	28/8/81	M	8	(2)	1
16	Juri JUDT		24/7/86	M	8	(10)	
24	Peer KLUGE		22/11/80	M	17		2
6	Dominic MAROH	SVN	4/3/87	D	24	(3)	1
11	Marek MINTÁL	SVK	2/9/77	M	15	(7)	1
36	Jawhar MNARI	TUN	8/11/76	M	3		
4	Håvard NORDTVEIT	NOR	21/6/90	D	14	(5)	
23	Andreas OTTL		1/3/85	M	17		1
25	Javier Horacio PINOLA	ARG	24/2/83	D	33		
12	Marcel RISSE		17/12/89	M	10	(10)	
1	Raphael SCHÄFER		30/1/79	G	30		
23	Matthew SPIRANOVIC	AUS	27/6/88	D	1		
30	Alexander STEPHAN		15/9/86	G	4	(1)	
21	Mickaël TAVARES	SEN	25/10/82	M	9	(2)	1
21	Dario VIDOSIC	AUS	8/4/87	A	4	(5)	
5	Andreas WOLF		12/6/82	D	29		

FC SCHALKE 04
Coach – Felix Magath
Founded – 1904
Stadium – Veltins-Arena (61,673)
MAJOR HONOURS:
UEFA Cup - (1) 1997;
German League - (7) 1934, 1935, 1937, 1939, 1940, 1942, 1958;
German Cup - (4) 1937, 1972, 2001, 2002.

2009				
8/8	Nürnberg	a	2-1	Kuranyi 2
18/8	Bochum	h	3-0	Moritz, Westermann, Farfán
21/8	Hoffenheim	a	0-0	
29/8	Freiburg	h	0-1	
13/9	Köln	a	2-1	Farfán, Kobiashvili
18/9	Wolfsburg	h	1-2	Höwedes
26/9	Dortmund	a	1-0	Farfán
2/10	Eintracht	h	2-0	Asamoah, Farfán (p)
17/10	Stuttgart	a	2-1	Rakitić, Kuranyi
25/10	Hamburg	h	3-3	Kuranyi 2, Schmitz
31/10	Leverkusen	h	2-2	Kuranyi, Sánchez
7/11	Bayern	a	1-1	Matip
21/11	Hannover	h	2-0	Farfán, Morávek
28/11	Mönchengladbach	a	0-1	
6/12	Hertha	h	2-0	Kuranyi, Rafinha
12/12	Werder	a	2-0	Kuranyi, Morávek
18/12	Mainz	h	1-0	Farfán
2010				
17/1	Nürnberg	h	1-0	Kuranyi
23/1	Bochum	a	2-2	Sánchez, Kuranyi
30/1	Hoffenheim	h	2-0	Kuranyi, Schmitz
6/2	Freiburg	a	0-0	
14/2	Köln	h	2-0	Matip, Fárfan
21/2	Wolfsburg	a	1-2	Kuranyi
26/2	Dortmund	h	2-1	Höwedes, Rakitić
6/3	Eintracht	a	4-1	Matip, Höwedes, Rakitic, Kuranyi
12/3	Stuttgart	h	2-1	Edu, Kuranyi
21/3	Hamburg	a	2-2	Kuranyi, Rakitić (p)
27/3	Leverkusen	a	2-0	Kuranyi 2
3/4	Bayern	h	1-2	Kuranyi
10/4	Hannover	a	2-4	Edu, Rakitić (p)
17/4	Mönchengladbach	h	3-1	Rakitić 2 (1p), Fárfan
24/4	Hertha	a	1-0	Westermann
1/5	Werder	h	0-2	
8/5	Mainz	a	0-0	

No	Name	Nat	DoB	Pos	Aps	(s)	Gls
14	Gerald ASAMOAH		3/10/78	A	2	(6)	1
11	Alexander BAUMJOHANN		23/1/87	M	1	(10)	
5	Marcelo José BORDON	BRA	7/1/87	D	30		
9	EDUardo Gonçalves de Oliveira	BRA	30/11/81	A	7	(6)	2
17	Jefferson FARFÁN	PER	26/10/84	A	32	(1)	8
19	Mario GAVRANOVIĆ	SUI	24/11/89	A		(2)	
29	Ľuboš HANZEL	SVK	7/5/87	D		(1)	
7	HAO Junmin	CHN	24/3/87	M	5	(3)	
17	Lewis HOLTBY		18/9/90	M	4	(5)	
4	Benedikt HÖWEDES		29/2/88	D	32	(1)	3
34	Besart IBRAIMI	MKD	17/12/86	A		(2)	
30	Levan KENIA	GEO	18/10/90	M	4	(6)	
12	Peer KLUGE		22/11/80	M	13		
3	Levan KOBIASHVILI	GEO	10/7/77	M	3	(1)	1
22	Kevin KURÁNYI		2/3/82	A	31	(2)	18
43	Joël MATIP	CMR	8/8/91	D	17	(3)	3
8	Carlos Luciano da Silva "MINEIRO"	BRA	2/8/75	M	5	(2)	
16	Jan MORÁVEK	CZE	1/11/89	M		(7)	2
28	Christoph MORITZ		27/1/90	M	18	(10)	1
1	Manuel NEUER		27/3/86	G	34		
20	Vasilios PLIATSIKAS	GRE	14/4/88	M	4	(4)	
18	Márcio Rafael Ferreira de Souza "RAFINHA"	BRA	7/9/85	D	30	(1)	1
10	Ivan RAKITIĆ	CRO	10/3/88	M	25	(4)	7
3	Tore REGINIUSSEN	NOR	10/4/86	D		(1)	
27	Vicente SÁNCHEZ	URU	7/12/79	A	7	(7)	2
21	Lukas SCHMITZ		13/10/88	M	27	(2)	2
2	Heiko WESTERMANN		14/8/83	D	27	(2)	2
25	Carlos ZAMBRANO	PER	10/7/89	D	14	(2)	

VFB STUTTGART
Coach – Markus Babbel; (6/12/09) Christian Gross (SUI)
Founded – 1893
Stadium – Mercedes-Benz-Arena (55,896)
MAJOR HONOURS:
German League - (5) 1950, 1952, 1984, 1992, 2007;
German Cup - (3), 1954, 1958, 1997.

2009

7/8	Wolfsburg	a	0-2
15/8	Freiburg	h	4-2 *Pogrebnyak, Élson 2 (1p), Schieber*
22/8	Dortmund	a	1-1 *Niedermeier*
29/8	Nürnberg	h	0-0
12/9	Hamburg	a	1-3 *Pogrebnyak*
19/9	Köln	h	0-2
26/9	Eintracht	a	3-0 *Schieber 2, Hitzlsperger*
4/10	Werder	h	0-2
17/10	Schalke	h	1-2 *Cacau*
24/10	Hannover	a	0-1
31/10	Bayern	h	0-0
7/11	Mönchengladbach	a	0-0
21/11	Hertha	h	1-1 *Kuzmanović*
29/11	Leverkusen	a	0-4
5/12	Bochum	h	1-1 *Taşçı*
13/12	Mainz	a	1-1 *Pogrebnyak*
19/12	Hoffenheim	h	3-1 *Marica (p), Cacau, Khedira*
16/1	Wolfsburg	h	3-1 *Hilbert, Pogrebnyak, Gebhart*

2010

22/1	Freiburg	a	1-0 *Marica*
31/1	Dortmund	h	4-1 *og (Felipe Santana), Kuzmanović, Marica, Träsch*
6/2	Nürnberg	a	2-1 *Gebhart, Hilbert*
13/2	Hamburg	h	1-3 *Träsch*
20/2	Köln	a	5-1 *Cacau 4, Pogrebnyak*
27/2	Eintracht	h	2-1 *Cacau 2*
6/3	Werder	a	2-2 *Pogrebnyak, Khedira*
12/3	Schalke	a	1-2 *Taşçı*
20/3	Hannover	h	2-0 *Marica 2*
27/3	Bayern	a	2-1 *Träsch, Marica*
3/4	Mönchengladbach	h	2-1 *Marica, Kuzmanović*
10/4	Hertha	a	1-0 *Cacau*
17/4	Leverkusen	h	2-1 *Cacau 2*
23/4	Bochum	a	2-0 *Cacau, Marica*
1/5	Mainz	h	2-2 *Marica 2*
8/5	Hoffenheim	a	1-1 *Cacau*

No	Name	Nat	DoB	Pos	Aps	(s)	Gls
10	Yıldıray BAŞTÜRK	TUR	24/12/78	M		(1)	
15	Arthur BOKA	CIV	2/4/83	D	12	(2)	
4	Khalid BOULAHROUZ	NED	28/12/81	D	5	(1)	
18	Jerónimo Maria Barreto Claudemir da Silva "CACAU"		27/3/81	A	19	(6)	13
27	Stefano CELOZZI		2/11/88	D	18	(3)	
17	Matthieu DELPIERRE	FRA	26/4/81	D	27		
25	ÉLSON Falcão da Silva	BRA	16/11/81	M	2	(9)	2
13	Timo GEBHART		12/4/89	M	23	(5)	2
19	Roberto HILBERT		16/10/84	M	12	(11)	2
11	Thomas HITZLSPERGER		5/4/82	M	11	(1)	1
23	Aleksandr HLEB	BLR	1/5/81	M	24	(3)	
28	Sami KHEDIRA		4/4/87	M	24	(1)	2
32	Zdravko KUZMANOVIĆ	SRB	22/9/87	M	14	(12)	3
7	Martin LANIG		11/7/84	M		(1)	
1	Jens LEHMANN		10/11/69	G	31		
21	Ludovic MAGNIN	SUI	20/4/79	D	5	(1)	
9	Ciprian MARICA	ROU	2/10/85	A	18	(7)	10
21	Cristian MOLINARO	ITA	30/7/83	D	17		
2	Georg NIEDERMEIER		26/2/86	D	12		1
3	Ricardo OSORIO	MEX	30/3/80	D	6	(1)	
9	Pavel POGREBNYAK	RUS	8/11/83	A	23	(5)	6
16	Sebastian RUDY		28/2/90	M	5	(8)	
39	Julian SCHIEBER		13/2/89	A	6	(13)	3

8	Jan ŠIMÁK	CZE	13/10/78	M	1	(1)	
5	Serdar TAŞÇI		24/4/87	D	27		2
35	Christian TRÄSCH		1/9/87	D	28	(1)	3
24	Sven ULREICH		3/8/88	G	3	(1)	
38	Clemens WALCH	AUT	10/7/87	M	1	(1)	

WERDER BREMEN
Coach – Thomas Schaaf
Founded – 1899
Stadium – Weserstadion (42,100)
MAJOR HONOURS:
UEFA Cup Winners' Cup - (1) 1992;
German League - (4) 1965, 1988, 1993, 2004;
German Cup - (6) 1961, 1991, 1994, 1999, 2004, 2009.

2009

8/8	Eintracht	h	2-3 *Özil (p), Sanogo*
15/8	Bayern	a	1-1 *Özil*
22/8	Mönchengladbach	h	3-0 *Pizarro 2, Naldo*
30/8	Hertha	a	3-2 *Özil, Borowski, Naldo*
13/9	Hannover	h	0-0
20/9	Leverkusen	a	0-0
26/9	Mainz	h	3-0 *Hunt, Pizarro 2*
4/10	Stuttgart	a	2-0 *Pizarro, Hunt*
17/10	Hoffenheim	h	2-0 *Pizarro, Mertesacker*
25/10	Bochum	a	4-1 *Hunt, Marin, Borowski, Özil*
31/10	Nürnberg	a	2-2 *Hunt 2*
8/11	Dortmund	h	1-1 *Özil*
21/11	Freiburg	a	6-0 *Hugo Almeida 2, Marin, Özil, Naldo (p), Rosenberg*
28/11	Wolfsburg	h	2-2 *Hugo Almeida, Mertesacker*
6/12	Köln	a	0-0
12/12	Schalke	h	0-2
20/12	Hamburg	a	1-2 *Naldo*

2010

16/1	Eintracht	a	0-1
23/1	Bayern	h	2-3 *Hunt, Hugo Almeida*
30/1	Mönchengladbach	a	3-4 *Özil, Pizarro, Frings (p)*
5/2	Hertha	h	2-1 *Marin, Pizarro*
13/2	Hannover	a	5-1 *Niemeyer, Naldo, og (Andreasen), Hunt, Pizarro*
21/2	Leverkusen	h	2-2 *Pizarro, Mertesacker*
27/2	Mainz	a	2-1 *Borowski, Prödl*
6/3	Stuttgart	h	2-2 *Hugo Almeida, Frings (p)*
14/3	Hoffenheim	a	1-0 *Pizarro*
20/3	Bochum	h	3-2 *Pizarro, Marin, Frings*
27/3	Nürnberg	h	4-2 *Mertesacker 2, Borowski, Fritz*
3/4	Dortmund	a	1-2 *Hunt*
10/4	Freiburg	h	4-0 *Pizarro 2, Hunt, Özil*
17/4	Wolfsburg	a	4-2 *Frings 2 (1p), Pizarro, Hugo Almeida*
24/4	Köln	h	1-0 *Frings (p)*
1/5	Schalke	a	2-0 *Özil, Hugo Almeida*
8/5	Hamburg	h	1-1 *Pizarro*

No	Name	Nat	DoB	Pos	Aps	(s)	Gls
16	Aymen ABDENNOUR	TUN	6/8/89	D	5	(1)	
46	Onur AYIK	TUR	28/1/90	A		(1)	
44	Philipp BARGFREDE		3/3/89	M	20	(3)	
2	Sebastian BOENISCH		1/2/87	D	16	(1)	
6	Tim BOROWSKI		2/5/80	M	20	(8)	4
22	Torsten FRINGS		22/11/76	M	29	(1)	6
8	Clemens FRITZ		7/12/80	D	30		1
23	HUGO Miguel Pereira de ALMEIDA	POR	23/5/84	A	13	(13)	7
14	Aaron HUNT		4/9/86	A	26	(6)	9
17	Said HUSEJINOVIĆ	BIH	13/5/88	M		(3)	
20	Daniel JENSEN		25/6/79	M	5	(8)	
39	MARCELO MORENO Martins	BOL	18/6/87	A		(5)	
10	Marko MARIN		13/3/89	M	30	(2)	4
29	Per MERTESACKER		29/9/84	D	33		5
21	Sebastian MIELITZ		18/7/89	G	2		

4	Ronaldo Aparecido Rodrigues "NALDO"	BRA	10/9/82	D	31		5
25	Peter NIEMEYER		22/11/83	M	4	(7)	1
11	Mesut ÖZIL		15/10/88	M	29	(2)	9
3	Petri PASANEN	FIN	24/9/80	D	16	(3)	
24	Claudio PIZARRO	PER	3/10/78	A	23	(3)	16
15	Sebastian PRÖDL	AUT	21/6/87	D	5	(4)	1
9	Markus ROSENBERG	SWE	27/9/82	A	3	(14)	1
18	Boubacar SANOGO	CIV	17/12/82	A	2		1
5	Duško TOŠIĆ	SRB	19/1/85	D		(1)	
33	Christian VANDER		24/10/80	G	1	(1)	
1	Tim WIESE		17/12/81	G	31		

VFL WOLFSBURG
Coach – Armin Veh; (25/1/10) Lorenz-Günther Köstner
Founded – 1945
Stadium – Volkswagen-Arena (30,000)
MAJOR HONOURS:
German League - (1) 2009.

2009

7/8	Stuttgart	h	2-0	*Misimović, Grafite*
15/8	Köln	a	3-1	*Džeko, og (Womé), Martins*
23/8	Hamburg	h	2-4	*Misimović, Martins*
28/8	Bayern	a	0-3	
12/9	Leverkusen	h	2-3	*Misimović, Grafite (p)*
18/9	Schalke	a	2-1	*Džeko 2*
26/9	Hannover	h	4-2	*Misimović, Gentner, Hasebe, Džeko*
3/10	Bochum	a	1-1	*Martins*
18/10	Mönchengladbach	h	2-1	*Madlung, Gentner*
25/10	Hertha	a	0-0	
31/10	Mainz	h	3-3	*Martins 2, Misimović*
7/11	Hoffenheim	a	2-1	*Misimović, Grafite*
21/11	Nürnberg	h	2-3	*Dejagah, Grafite (p)*
28/11	Werder	a	2-2	*Džeko 2*
5/12	Freiburg	h	2-2	*og (Bastians), Johnson*
13/12	Dortmund	h	1-3	*Grafite*
19/12	Eintracht	a	2-2	*Džeko, Josué*
2010				
16/1	Stuttgart	a	1-3	*Džeko*
24/1	Köln	h	2-3	*Gentner, Ricardo Costa*
29/1	Hamburg	a	1-1	*Džeko*
6/2	Bayern	h	1-3	*Grafite*
13/2	Leverkusen	a	1-2	*Džeko*
21/2	Schalke	h	2-1	*Grafite 2*
28/2	Hannover	a	1-0	*Misimović*
6/3	Bochum	h	4-1	*Džeko 2 (1p), Martins, Santana*
13/3	Mönchengladbach	a	4-0	*Misimović, Džeko 2 (1p), Gentner*
21/3	Hertha	h	1-5	*Grafite*
27/3	Mainz	a	2-0	*Džeko 2*
4/4	Hoffenheim	h	4-0	*Džeko 2, Barzagli, Misimović*
11/4	Nürnberg	a	2-0	*Džeko, Grafite*
17/4	Werder	h	2-4	*Džeko, Grafite*
24/4	Freiburg	a	0-1	
1/5	Dortmund	a	1-0	*Džeko*
8/5	Eintracht	h	3-1	*Misimović, Riether, Džeko*

No	Name	Nat	DoB	Pos	Aps	(s)	Gls
28	Daniel BAIER		18/5/84	M		(1)	
43	Andrea BARZAGLI	ITA	8/5/81	D	24		1
1	Diego BENAGLIO	SUI	8/9/83	G	22		
24	Ashkan DEJAGAH		5/7/86	M	4	(20)	1
9	Edin DŽEKO	BIH	17/3/86	A	33	(1)	22
27	Alexander ESSWEIN		25/3/90	A		(4)	
25	Christian GENTNER		14/8/85	M	34		4
23	Edinaldo Batista Libano "GRAFITE"	BRA	2/4/79	A	27	(3)	11
13	Makoto HASEBE	JPN	18/1/84	M	19	(5)	1
35	Marwin HITZ	SUI	18/9/87	G	5		
16	Fabian JOHNSON		11/12/87	D	4	(6)	1

7	JOSUÉ Anunciado de Oliveira	BRA	19/7/79	M	31		1
8	Thomas KAHLENBERG	DEN	20/3/83	M	3	(9)	
12	André LENZ		19/11/73	G	7	(1)	
17	Alexander MADLUNG		11/7/82	D	26	(2)	1
11	Obafemi MARTINS	NGA	28/10/84	A	7	(9)	6
10	Zvjezdan MISIMOVIĆ	BIH	5/6/82	M	31		10
19	Peter PEKARÍK	SVK	30/10/86	D	10	(6)	
5	RICARDO Miguel Moreira da COSTA	POR	16/5/81	D	10	(1)	1
20	Sascha RIETHER		23/3/83	D	33		1
14	Jonathan SANTANA	PAR	19/10/81	M	2	(5)	1
4	Marcel SCHÄFER		7/6/84	D	32		
32	Sebastian SCHINDZIELORZ		21/1/79	M	1	(1)	
6	Jan ŠIMŮNEK	CZE	20/2/87	D	4	(1)	
2	Cristian ZACCARDO	ITA	21/12/81	D		(1)	
15	Karim ZIANI	ALG	17/8/82	M	5	(5)	

PROMOTED CLUBS

1. FC KAISERSLAUTERN
Coach – Marco Kurz
Founded – 1900
Stadium – Fritz-Walter-Stadion (48,500)
MAJOR HONOURS:
German League – (4) 1951, 1953, 1991, 1998;
German Cup – (2) 1990, 1996.

FC ST PAULI
Coach – Holger Stanislawski
Founded – 1910
Stadium – Millerntor-Stadion (23,201)

SECOND LEVEL FINAL TABLE 2009/10

		Pld	W	D	L	F	A	Pts
1	1. FC Kaiserslautern	34	19	10	5	56	28	67
2	FC St Pauli	34	20	4	10	72	37	64
3	FC Augsburg	34	17	11	6	60	40	62
4	Fortuna Düsseldorf	34	17	8	9	48	31	59
5	SC 07 Paderborn	34	14	9	11	49	49	51
6	MSV Duisburg	34	14	8	12	51	46	50
7	DSC Arminia Bielefeld	34	16	5	13	48	41	49
8	TSV 1860 München	34	14	6	14	43	45	48
9	FC Energie Cottbus	34	13	8	13	55	49	47
10	Karlsruher SC	34	13	7	14	43	45	46
11	SpVgg Greuther Fürth	34	12	8	14	51	50	44
12	1. FC Union Berlin	34	11	11	12	42	45	44
13	Alemannia Aachen	34	11	10	13	37	41	43
14	Rot-Weiss Oberhausen	34	12	5	17	38	52	41
15	FSV Frankfurt	34	9	11	14	29	50	38
16	FC Hansa Rostock	34	10	6	18	33	45	36
17	TuS Koblenz	34	7	10	17	35	60	31
18	Rot-Weiss Ahlen	34	5	7	22	19	55	22

NB DSC Arminia Bielefeld – 4 pts deducted.

PROMOTION/RELEGATION PLAY-OFFS

(13/5/10)
Nürnberg 1, Augsburg 0
(16/5/10)
Augsburg 0, Nürnberg 2
(Nürnberg 3-0)

DOMESTIC CUP 2009/10

DFB-POKAL

FIRST ROUND

(31/7/09)
Babelsberg 0, Leverkusen 1
Braunschweig 0, Kaiserslautern 1
Ingolstadt 1, Augsburg 2
Lübeck 2, Mainz 1 *(aet)*
Osnabrück 2, Rostock 1
Wehen Wiesbaden 1, Wolfsburg 4

(1/8/09)
Burghausen 1, Ahlen 1 *(aet; 4-5 on pens)*
Dresden 0, Nürnberg 3
Elversberg 0, Freiburg 2
Emden 0, Köln 3
FSV Frankfurt 1, Mönchengladbach 2
Grossaspach 1, Stuttgart 4
Magdeburg 1, Energie 3
Münster 1, Hertha 3 *(aet)*
Paderborn 0, 1860 München 1
TB Berlin 0, Karlsruhe 2
Unterhaching 0, Arminia 3
Weiden 1, Dortmund 3
Windeck 0, Schalke 4

(2/8/09)
Concordia Hamburg 0, Koblenz 4
Erfurt 1, Duisburg 2
Lotte 0, Bochum 1
Neckarelz 1, Bayern 3
Oberneuland 0, Hoffenheim 2
Offenbach 0, Eintracht 3
Speldorf 0, Oberhausen 3
Torgelow 1, Aachen 4
Trier 3, Hannover 1
Union Berlin 0, Werder 5
Villingen 0, St Pauli 2 *(aet)*
Worms 0, Greuther Fürth 1 *(aet)*

(3/8/09)
Düsseldorf 3, Hamburg 3 *(aet; 1-4 on pens)*

SECOND ROUND

(22/9/09)
Ahlen 2, Greuther Fürth 3 *(aet)*
Bayern 5, Oberhausen 0
Bochum 0, Schalke 3
Karlsruhe 0, Dortmund 3
Koblenz 4, Energie 2 *(aet)*
Mönchengladbach 0, Duisburg 1
Nürnberg 0, Hoffenheim 1
Trier 4, Arminia 2 *(aet)*

(23/9/09)
Augsburg 1, Freiburg 0
Eintracht 6, Aachen 4
Kaiserslautern 2, Leverkusen 1
Köln 3, Wolfsburg 2
Lübeck 1, Stuttgart 3 *(aet)*
1860 München 2, Hertha 2 *(aet; 4-1 on pens)*
Osnabrück 3, Hamburg 3 *(aet; 4-2 on pens)*
Werder 2, St Pauli 1

THIRD ROUND

(27/10/09)
Augsburg 5, Duisburg 0
Greuther Fürth 1, Stuttgart 0
Osnabrück 3, Dortmund 2
Trier 0, Köln 3

(28/10/09)
Eintracht 0, Bayern 4
Hoffenheim 4, Koblenz 0
1860 München 0, Schalke 3
Werder 3, Kaiserslautern 0

QUARTER-FINALS

(9/2/10)
Werder 2 *(Naldo 27, Hugo Almeida 75)*, Hoffenheim 1
(Tagoe 73)

(10/2/10)
Augsburg 2 *(Thurk 3, Raffael 87)*, Köln 0
Bayern 6 *(Müller 5, 82, Robben 58, Ribéry 60, Lahm 64, Allagui 89og)*, Greuther Fürth 2 *(Nöthe 10, Allagui 40)*
Osnabrück 0, Schalke 1 *(Kurányi 59)*

SEMI-FINALS

(23/3/10)
Bremen 2 *(Marin 30, Pizarro 84)*, Augsburg 0

(24/3/10)
Schalke 0, Bayern 1 *(Robben 112) (aet)*

FINAL

(15/5/10)
Olympiastadion, Berlin
FC BAYERN MÜNCHEN 4 *(Robben 35p, Olić 51, Ribéry 63, Schweinsteiger 83)*
WERDER BREMEN 0
Referee – *Kinhöfer*
BAYERN – *Butt, Lahm, Van Buyten, Demichelis, Badstuber, Van Bommel, Schweinsteiger, Robben (Hamıt 86), Müller (Tymoshchuk 77), Ribéry, Olić (Klose 80).*
WERDER – *Wiese, Fritz, Mertesacker, Naldo, Boenisch, Frings, Bargfrede (Marin 54), Hunt (Hugo Almeida 46), Borowski (Jensen 70), Özil, Pizarro.*
Sent off: *Frings (77).*

GREECE

Rehhagel era comes to uneventful end

Greece's second appearance at the FIFA World Cup finals was more rewarding than the first, in 1994, when they lost all three games without scoring, but although there was something for the team and their supporters to celebrate in South Africa – a welcome 2-1 victory over Nigeria – the outcome was the same, with Greece catching an early flight home after being eliminated at the end of the first round.

Otto Rehhagel, at 71 the oldest coach at the finals, decided that, after almost nine years in charge, it was time for him to step down. The longest-serving Greece national team coach in history, he bowed out after 106 matches, winning precisely half of them. The German will forever be remembered for his miraculous triumph at UEFA EURO 2004, when he led the pre-tournament 100/1 outsiders to the European title, but although he subsequently led the country to UEFA EURO 2008 and the 2010 World Cup, that stunning effort in Portugal, though eternally uplifting for all Greek football followers, remained an isolated success.

Qualification for South Africa came via the play-offs, in which Rehhagel's team, as had become their custom, defended for their lives against Ukraine, keeping two clean sheets and nicking a 1-0 aggregate victory with a superb counterattacking goal – created with a sublime pass by Georgios Samaras and converted with an adroit finish by his strike partner Dimitris Salpingidis.

Shortage of flair

There would be precious little attacking flair of that quality from Greece in South Africa. Winless in their three warm-up matches, the team's lack of form and confidence was evident in their opening game against South Korea. Behind early, they seldom threatened to open their World Cup goal account and were deservedly beaten 2-0. A second defeat, against Nigeria, would have spelt elimination, but after another woeful start, in which they again conceded an early goal, they got lucky when the Africans had a player stupidly sent off. That enabled them to break

their scoring duck – with a heavily deflected Salpingidis effort – and go on to dominate and eventually register that historic first World Cup win through Vassilis Torosidis's tap-in.

Greece's final game, against a virtually-qualified Argentina team that saw fit to rest several first-choice players, provided an opportunity to join the South Americans in the next round, yet from the outset, with Salpingidis and the European qualifying zone's top scorer, Theofanis Gekas, both dropped, Greece's strategy seemed to be to gamble on aiming for a draw – which might or might not be good enough. For most of the game Argentina were duly stifled, with Sokratis Papastathopoulos successfully carrying out an old-fashioned man-for-man marking job on Lionel Messi, but when the scoreline in the other game

Greece players trudge off the field after losing their opening World Cup game to South Korea

swung against them and they had to score, Greece were unable to shift into a different gear. Argentina's two late goals were the final nails in the coffin of a team that, in truth, could have no real complaints about the outcome.

Rehhagel's legacy has been passed on to another foreigner, Fernando Santos. The 55-year-old from Portugal is very familiar with Greek football and Greek footballers having spent the best part of the past decade working in the country. One of the few coaches to have led all of the Big Three clubs in his homeland, his CV also includes two spells with AEK Athens FC and, latterly, three fine years with PAOK FC.

His parting gift from the Salonika club – six weeks before he was named as Rehhagel's successor – was to steer them into the UEFA Champions League. That was achieved after a resounding display in the Greek Super League's six-match play-off series, in which PAOK finished well clear of the other three participants – AEK, Aris Thessaloniki FC and defending champions Olympiacos FC. Although the fans' joy was immediately tempered by Fernando Santos's decision to leave, PAOK had much to be proud of at the end of a 2009/10 campaign in which their multi-national, if relatively starless, squad had won 16 of their 18 home games and conceded only 19 goals.

Nikolaos Nioplias joined Panathinaikos midway through the season and steered them to the Greek double

Panathinaikos double

PAOK's pleasure bore little comparison, however, to that of Panathinaikos FC, who ended a six-year trophy drought by repeating their 2003/04 feat of capturing both domestic trophies. The Greens had made it their pre-season mission to bring Olympiacos's long run of Super League triumphs to an end. In preparation they made a raft of summer signings, the most expensive of whom, French international striker Djibril Cissé, was to go on and justify both his large transfer fee and club-record salary with a plethora of goals – 23 in 28 games – that would not only leave him as the runaway winner of the Super League's Golden Boot but also prove to be the decisive factor in his new club's title success.

For much of the autumn Panathinaikos were neck and neck with Olympiacos, the two traditional rivals turning the title race into a private joust with a succession of early wins. It was Olympiacos, though, who drew first blood, beating Panathinaikos 2-0 in the big head-to-head at the Karaiskakis stadium at the end of November. That defeat prompted the dismissal of Pana coach Henk ten Cate. The Dutchman's earlier

sin had been to fail to take the Greens into the UEFA Champions League – they were beaten home and away by Club Atlético de Madrid in the play-off round. The club's powerful start to the Super League campaign had bought him more time, but club president Nikos Pateras eventually chose to wield the axe and bring in ex-player Nikolaos Nioplias, who had been making a name for himself with the Greek Under-21 side.

Nioplias settled quickly and proved to be an inspired choice. As Panathinaikos began to build a lead in the league that they would not surrender – despite another defeat to Olympiacos in March – they also demonstrated their prowess on the European stage with a pair of thrilling 3-2 victories over AS Roma in the UEFA Europa League. Pana's hopes of European glory would end in the next round, against R. Standard de Liège, but their long-awaited 20th Greek championship title was duly secured in their penultimate fixture with a 2-0 win over Iraklis FC, goals from the inevitable Cissé – after just 34 seconds – and 20-year-old starlet Sotirios Ninis sending 65,000 fans at the OACA Spyro Louis stadium into raptures of delight.

A fortnight later Panathanaikos were back at their adopted home to make it a double as they beat Aris 1-0 in the final of the Greek Cup. The winning goal was

scored by Argentine winger Sebastián Leto, who had also won the double while on loan at Olympiacos (from Liverpool FC) the previous season, joining Antonios Nikopolidis as the only player to have achieved the feat in successive seasons with different clubs.

Olympiacos ousted

If two trophies were not enough, further evidence of Greek football's new pecking order was supplied by Rehhagel's World Cup squad, in which eight of the 14 home-based players selected were from Panathinaikos, with no more than two from any other Greek club, Olympiacos included. The perennial champions may have won both of the so-called 'derbies of the eternal enemies' but otherwise theirs was a fairly wretched season, in which neither Temur Ketsbaia nor Zico, two expensively acquired high-profile coaches, lasted long and which concluded, under unsung former head scout Božidar Bandović, with last place in the European qualifying play-offs, resulting in their lowest finish since 1988. Olympiacos had reached the knockout phase of the 2009/10 UEFA Champions League but their 2010/11 continental adventure, under new coach Ewald Lienen, would have to commence in the second qualifying round of the UEFA Europa League.

Later entrants in that competition would be Aris and AEK. The latter were one of only four Super League clubs to stay loyal to their coach throughout the campaign – PAOK, Atromitos FC and Ergotelis FC were the others – but Dušan Bajević's team had a very discreet season on all fronts, an uneventful UEFA Europa League campaign adding to disappointment on the domestic front. It was a season of frustration too for

OFI Crete FC, the islanders failing to win back their top flight place after falling just short of an immediate return both in the regular second division and the promotion play-offs. The latter mini-league was won by Panserraikos FC, the Greek Cup conquerors of Olympiacos, who thus went up with Olympiacos Volou FC and Kerkyra FC to replace the relegated threesome of Panthrakikos FC, PAS Giannina FC and Levadiakos FC.

Ellinikos Podosfairikos Omospondia (EPO)

Goudi Park
PO Box 14161
GR-11510 Athens
tel - +30 210 930 6000
fax - +30 210 935 9666
website - epo.gr
email - epo@epo.gr
Year of Formation – 1926

President – Sofoklis Pilavios
General Secretary - Ioannis Economides
Media Officer – Michael Tsapidis
National Stadium – OACA Spyro Louis, Athens (72,080)

INTERNATIONAL HONOURS
UEFA European Championship – (1) 2004.
INTERNATIONAL TOURNAMENT APPEARANCES
FIFA World Cup – (2) 1994, 2010.
UEFA European Championship – (3) 1980, 2004 (Winners), 2008.
TOP FIVE ALL-TIME CAPS
Theodoros Zagorakis (120); Angelos Basinas (100); Efstratios Apostolakis & Georgios Karagounis (96); Antonis Nikopolidis (90)
TOP FIVE ALL-TIME GOALS
Nikolaos Anastopoulos (29); Angelos Charisteas (24); Dimitrios Saravakos (22); Theofanis Gekas & Dimitrios "Mimis" Papaioannou (20)

NATIONAL TEAM RESULTS 2009/10

12/8/09	Poland	A	Bydgoszcz	0-2	
5/9/09	Switzerland (WCQ)	A	Basel	0-2	
9/9/09	Moldova (WCQ)	A	Chisinau	1-1	Gekas (33)
10/10/09	Latvia (WCQ)	H	Athens	5-2	Gekas (4, 47p, 57, 90+1), Samaras (73)
14/10/09	Luxembourg (WCQ)	H	Athens	2-1	Torosidis (30), Gekas (33)
14/11/09	Ukraine (WCQ)	H	Athens	0-0	
18/11/09	Ukraine (WCQ)	A	Donetsk	1-0	Salpingidis (31)
3/3/10	Senegal	H	Volos	0-2	
25/5/10	North Korea	N	Altach (AUT)	2-2	Katsouranis (2), Charisteas (49)
2/6/10	Paraguay	N	Winterthur (SUI)	0-2	
12/6/10	South Korea (WCF)	N	Port Elizabeth (RSA)	0-2	
17/6/10	Nigeria (WCF)	N	Bloemfontein (RSA)	2-1	Salpingidis (44), Torosidis (71)
22/6/10	Argentina (WCF)	N	Polokwane (RSA)	0-2	

NATIONAL TEAM APPEARANCES 2009/10

			Pol	SUI	MDA	LVA	LUX	UKR	UKR	Sen	Prk	Par	KOR	NGA	ARG	Caps	Goals
Coach – Otto REHHAGEL (GER)	9/8/38																
Kostas CHALKIAS	30/5/74	PAOK	G	G	G					s46						27	-
Loukas VINTRA	5/2/81	Panathinaikos	D	D 42*			D83	D	D	D	D46	s46	D	D	M	32	-
Nikolaos SPIROPOULOS	10/10/83	Panathinaikos	D	D	D		D	D	D	D	D	s75		s46		20	-
Sokratis PAPASTATHOPOULOS	9/6/88	Genoa (ITA)	D46	D		D		D	D29					M37	M	12	-
Vangelis MORAS	26/8/81	Bologna (ITA)	D46	D	D58	D	s43	D	D	D69	D				D	12	-
Alexandros TZIOLIS	13/2/85	Panathinaikos /Siena (ITA)	M79		M	M46				s71 M	M	M	M	M	M	22	-
Kostas KATSOURANIS	21/6/79	Panathinaikos	M	M	M	M		M	M	M	M	M58	M	M	M54	72	8
Georgios KARAGOUNIS	6/3/77	Panathinaikos	M63		M76	M89	M	M	M	M46	M62	s46	M46	M	M46	96	6
Dimitris SALPINGIDIS	18/8/81	Panathinaikos	A46	A46		A46	A	A71	A	s46	A	A46	s59	A		38	4
Georgios SAMARAS	21/2/85	Celtic (SCO)	A	s46	A	A		A	A63	A66	A46	A	A59	s37	A	37	5
Angelos CHARISTEAS	9/2/80	Nürnberg (GER)	A46	A73	A			s65	A71	A46	s46	s46	A61			85	24
Avraam PAPADOPOULOS	3/12/84	Olympiacos	s46	s73	s58		D			s46	s46	D	D	D	D	17	-
Sotirios KYRGIAKOS	23/7/79	AEK /Liverpool (ENG)	s46	D	D		D43	D	D	D	D46	D46		D	D	60	4
Ioannis AMANATIDIS	3/12/81	Eintracht (GER)	s46	A81	s76	s46										35	3
Theofanis GEKAS	23/5/80	Leverkusen (GER) /Hertha (GER)	s46	s81	A	A	A	A65	s63	s46	A46			A	A79	49	20
Christos PATSATZOGLOU	19/3/79	Omonia (CYP)	s63	M	D	s46	M			s62	s58	s46			s55	45	1
Nikos LIBEROPOULOS	4/8/75	Eintracht (GER)	s79													67	13
Alexandros TZORVAS	12/8/82	Panathinaikos					G		G	G	G46	s46	G	G	G	11	-
Giourkas SEITARIDIS	4/6/81	Panathinaikos					D			s46	D	D				70	1
Vassilis TOROSIDIS	10/6/85	Olympiacos					D	M				D	D	D	D55	29	3
Vassilis PLIATSIKAS	14/4/88	Schalke (GER)					s89	s46		s29						4	-
Mihail SIFAKIS	9/9/84	Aris					G					G46				1	-
Georgios FOTAKIS	29/10/81	PAOK					M46									1	-
Sotirios NINIS	3/4/90	Panathinaikos					s83						M46	s79	s54	6	1
Konstantinos MITROGLOU	12/3/88	Olympiacos							s71							1	-
Pantelis KAPETANOS	8/6/83	Steaua (ROU)								A46	s46	A75	s61			4	-
Lazaros HRISTODOULOPOULOS	19/12/86	Panathinaikos								s66						3	-
Grigorios MAKOS	18/1/87	AEK								s69						3	-

GREECE

DOMESTIC LEAGUE 2009/10

SUPER LEAGUE FINAL TABLE

		Pld	Home					Away					Total					Pts
			W	D	L	F	A	W	D	L	F	A	W	D	L	F	A	
1	Panathinaikos FC	30	11	2	2	31	10	11	2	2	23	7	22	4	4	54	17	70
2	Olympiacos FC	30	9	4	2	26	10	10	3	2	21	8	19	7	4	47	18	64
3	PAOK FC	30	13	0	2	26	6	6	5	4	15	10	19	5	6	41	16	62
4	AEK Athens FC	30	11	2	2	29	14	4	6	5	14	17	15	8	7	43	31	53
5	Aris Thessaloniki FC	30	9	4	2	17	8	3	6	6	18	20	12	10	8	35	28	46
6	FC Kavala	30	6	7	2	21	16	4	2	9	10	16	10	9	11	31	32	39
7	Atromitos FC	30	8	3	4	16	12	2	5	8	18	24	10	8	12	34	36	38
8	Larissa FC	30	7	4	4	17	17	3	3	9	14	25	10	7	13	31	42	37
9	Panionios GSS	30	5	5	5	20	19	4	5	6	14	16	9	10	11	34	35	37
10	Iraklis FC	30	6	5	4	19	18	4	2	9	20	23	10	7	13	39	41	37
11	Ergotelis FC	30	6	6	3	19	16	3	3	9	18	25	9	9	12	37	41	36
12	Asteras Tripolis FC	30	7	3	5	20	18	3	3	9	9	18	10	6	14	29	36	36
13	Xanthi FC	30	9	1	5	19	16	1	4	10	8	20	10	5	15	27	36	35
14	Levadiakos FC	30	7	3	5	17	15	2	4	9	14	29	9	7	14	31	44	34
15	PAS Giannina FC	30	6	4	5	17	14	1	3	11	10	32	7	7	16	27	46	28
16	Panthrakikos FC	30	1	3	11	11	27	2	0	13	10	35	3	3	24	21	62	12

TOP GOALSCORERS

23 Djibril CISSÉ (Panathinaikos)

11 Javier Edgardo CÁMPORA (Aris)
   Victoraş Constantin IACOB (Iraklis)
   Georgios BARKOGLOU (Levadiakos)

10 Danijel CESAREC (Tripolis)
   Benjamin ONWUACHI (Kavala)

9 Konstantinos MITROGLOU
  (Olympiacos)

8 Ismael BLANCO (AEK)
  Ignacio Martín SCOCCO (AEK)
  Ilias ANASTASAKOS (Atromitos)
  Emanuel PERRONE (Atromitos)
  Konstantinos KATSOURANIS
  (Panathinaikos)
  Boško BALABAN (Panionios)

UEFA CHAMPIONS LEAGUE QUALIFICATION PLAY-OFFS

(28/4/10)
AEK 0, PAOK 0
Aris 2 *(Johnson 39, 90)*, Olympiacos 0

(1/5/10)
Olympiacos 2 *(Mellberg 10, Maresca 43)*, AEK 1 *(Djebbour 22p)*
PAOK 2 *(Ivić 26, Savini 36)*, Aris 0

(6/5/10)
AEK 4 *(Djebbour 27, Leonardo 75, 84, Scocco 77p)*, Aris 2 *(Cámpora 56p, Johnson 72)*
PAOK 1 *(Muslimović 11)*, Olympiacos 0

(12/5/10)
Aris 1 *(Prittas 47)*, AEK 1 *(Leonardo 90)*
Olympiacos 0, PAOK 1 *(Ivić 33)*

(16/5/10)
Olympiacos 0, Aris 0
PAOK 1 *(Muslimović 52)*, AEK 0

(19/5/10)
AEK 2 *(Manolas 6, Blanco 54)*, Olympiacos 1 *(Papadopoulos I. 11)*
Aris 3 *(Malezas 11og, Javito 32, Cámpora 63p)*, PAOK 2 *(Papazoglou 22, Cirillo 45p)*

		Pld	Home					Away					Total					Pts
			W	D	L	F	A	W	D	L	F	A	W	D	L	F	A	
2	PAOK FC	6	3	0	0	4	0	1	1	1	3	3	4	1	1	7	3	16
3	AEK Athens FC	6	2	1	0	6	3	0	1	2	2	4	2	2	2	8	7	9
4	Aris Thessaloniki FC	6	2	1	0	6	3	0	1	2	2	6	2	2	2	8	9	8
5	Olympiacos FC	6	1	1	1	2	2	0	0	3	1	5	1	1	4	3	7	8

NB Points carried forward from regular league - Olympiacos 4 pts, PAOK 3 pts, AEK 1 pt, Aris 0 pts.

CLUB-BY-CLUB

AEK ATHENS FC

Coach – Dušan Bajević (SRB)
Founded – 1924
Stadium – OACA Spyro Louis (72,080)
MAJOR HONOURS:
Greek League – (11) 1939, 1940, 1963, 1968, 1971, 1978, 1979, 1989, 1992, 1993, 1994;
Greek Cup – (13) 1932, 1939, 1949, 1950, 1956, 1964, 1966, 1978, 1983, 1996, 1997, 2000, 2002.

2009
30/8	Atromitos	a	1-0	*Blanco*
13/9	Iraklis	h	1-0	*Kafes*

20/9	Giannina	a	1-1	*Németh*
23/9	Olympiacos	h	1-2	*Németh*
27/9	Panathinaikos	h	0-1	
5/10	Xanthi	a	0-1	
18/10	Panthrakikos	h	3-2	*Majstorović, og (Đokić), Scocco*
25/10	Aris	a	1-1	*Scocco*
1/11	Ergotelis	a	2-2	*Manduca, Blanco (p)*
9/11	Larissa	h	3-1	*Majstorović, Blanco (p), Németh*
21/11	Kavala	a	1-2	*Gentsoglou*
28/11	PAOK	h	1-0	*Manduca*
6/12	Panionios	a	1-3	*Leonardo*
13/12	Levadiakos	h	3-2	*Tahtsidis, Manduca 2*
20/12	Tripolis	a	0-2	

ARIS THESSALONIKI FC

2010

Date	Opponent		Score	Scorers
6/1	Olympiacos	a	2-1	Scocco 2
10/1	Atromitos	h	3-3	Gentsoglou, Scocco, Blanco
16/1	Iraklis	a	1-1	Djebbour
24/1	Giannina	h	3-1	Djebbour, Kafes 2
31/1	Panathinaikos	a	1-1	Scocco
6/2	Xanthi	h	3-1	Blanco 2 (1p), Leonardo
13/2	Panthrakikos	a	2-1	Scocco, Hersi
21/2	Aris	h	1-0	Kafes
27/2	Ergotelis	h	1-0	Djebbour
6/3	Larissa	a	0-1	
13/3	Kavala	h	3-0	Blanco (p), Jahić, Manduca
21/3	PAOK	a	1-0	Blanco
28/3	Panionios	h	1-1	Scocco
11/4	Levadiakos	a	0-0	
18/4	Tripolis	h	2-0	Djebbour, Kafes

No	Name	Nat	DoB	Pos	Aps	(s)	Gls
22	Ioannis ARABATZIS		28/5/84	G	8		
2	Carlos Luciano ARAUJO	ARG	19/11/81	D	26		
87	Nicolás Bianchi ARCE	ARG	28/1/87	D	3		
18	Ismael BLANCO	ARG	19/1/83	A	27	(2)	8
10	Rafik DJEBBOUR	ALG	8/3/84	A	14		4
90	Savvas GENTSOGLOU		19/9/90	M	10	(3)	2
31	Nikolaos GEORGEAS		27/12/76	D	11	(2)	
4	GERALDO Washington Regufe ALVES	POR	8/11/80	D	11	(2)	
5	Youssouf HERSI	NED	20/8/82	M	9	(11)	1
30	Ilie IORDACHE	ROU	23/3/86	M		(3)	
12	Sanel JAHIĆ	BIH	10/12/81	D	19	(1)	1
7	JUAN FRANcisco García García	ESP	15/7/76	D	5	(1)	
1	Pantelis KAFES		24/6/78	M	23	(2)	5
15	Nikolaos KARABELAS		20/12/84	D	16	(4)	
19	Panagiotis LAGOS		18/7/85	M	1	(8)	
9	LEONARDO Rodrigues Pereira	BRA	22/9/86	M	14	(9)	2
5	Daniel MAJSTOROVIĆ	SWE	5/4/77	D	28		2
14	Grigorios MAKOS		18/1/87	D	13	(5)	
11	Gustavo MANDUCA	BRA	8/6/80	M	19	(7)	5
24	Kostas MANOLAS		14/6/91	D	5		
29	Krisztián NÉMETH	HUN	5/1/89	A	7	(5)	3
8	Tamandani NSALIWA	CAN	28/1/82	M	5		
21	Mihail PAVLIS		29/9/89	A	1	(7)	
16	ROGER Guerreiro	POL	25/5/82	M	5	(9)	
23	Diego Sebastián SAJA	ARG	5/6/79	G	22		
32	Ignacio Martín SCOCCO	ARG	29/5/85	A	23	(1)	8
34	Panagiotis TAHTSIDIS		15/2/91	M	3	(6)	1
26	Seydou YAHAYA	GHA	31/12/89	M	2	(1)	

ARIS THESSALONIKI FC

Coach – Iomar Mazinho (BRA); (3/11/09) (Dimitrios Bougiouklis);
(8/11/09) Héctor Cúper (ARG)
Founded – 1914
Stadium – Kleanthis Vikelidis (22,800)
MAJOR HONOURS:
Greek League – (3) 1928, 1932, 1946;
Greek Cup – (1) 1970.

2009

Date	Opponent		Score	Scorers
22/8	Atromitos	h	1-0	Nasuti
29/8	Iraklis	a	2-2	Cámpora 2
12/9	Giannina	h	1-0	Nafti
20/9	Panathinaikos	a	1-2	Ronaldo
26/9	Xanthi	h	1-0	Abreu
3/10	Panthrakikos	a	1-1	Flávio
17/10	Ergotelis	a	0-0	
25/10	AEK	h	1-1	Abreu
31/10	Larissa	a	2-2	Abreu, Koke
7/11	Kavala	h	0-0	
22/11	PAOK	a	1-0	Neto
29/11	Panionios	h	1-1	Neto
5/12	Levadiakos	a	2-0	Cámpora, Nafti
12/12	Tripolis	h	0-1	
20/12	Olympiacos	h	1-0	Cámpora

2010

Date	Opponent		Score	Scorers
5/1	Atromitos	a	3-0	Toni Calvo, Cámpora 2
10/1	Iraklis	h	4-2	Cámpora 2, Toni Calvo 2
17/1	Giannina	a	1-0	Nafti
24/1	Panathinaikos	h	0-0	
31/1	Xanthi	a	1-2	Johnson
7/2	Panthrakikos	h	0-2	
14/2	Ergotelis	h	2-1	Koke, Adu
21/2	AEK	a	0-1	
28/2	Larissa	h	2-0	Nafti, Cámpora
6/3	Kavala	a	1-1	Toni Calvo
14/3	PAOK	h	2-0	Cámpora 2
21/3	Panionios	a	1-1	Johnson
28/3	Levadiakos	h	1-0	Neto
11/4	Tripolis	a	1-2	Koke
18/4	Olympiacos	h	1-2	Toni Calvo (p)

No	Name	Nat	DoB	Pos	Aps	(s)	Gls
13	Washington Sebastián ABREU Gallo	URU	17/10/76	A	8		3
11	Freddy ADU	USA	2/6/89	M	4	(1)	1
3	Carlos Andrés ARANO	ARG	6/5/80	D	25		
23	Christos ARAVIDIS		13/3/87	A	1	(5)	
18	Javier Edgardo CÁMPORA	ARG	7/1/80	A	19	(7)	11
25	CÉSAR Ortiz Puenteneva	ESP	30/10/89	D	2		
99	Ian DALY	IRL	20/3/90	A	1	(2)	
9	Darío Ezequiel FERNÁNDEZ	ARG	24/9/78	M	15	(3)	
25	FLÁVIO Pinto de Souza	BRA	12/3/80	D	6	(3)	1
11	Leandro GRACIÁN	ARG	6/8/82	M	9	(3)	
20	Francisco Javier Peral Periane "JAVITO"	ESP	4/11/83	A	12	(12)	
14	Eddie JOHNSON	USA	31/3/84	A	6	(6)	2
10	Sergio Contreras Pardo "KOKE"	ESP	27/4/83	A	25	(4)	3
4	Efthimios KOULOUHERIS		10/3/81	D	12	(3)	
33	Stavros LAMBRIAKOS		30/11/75	A		(10)	
17	Camel MERIEM	FRA	18/10/89	M	3	(2)	
8	Ronald Lazaro "NACHO" GARCÍA Justiniano	BOL	17/12/80	M	8	(5)	
6	Mehdi NAFTI	TUN	28/11/78	M	21	(1)	4
15	Cristian Javier NASUTI	ARG	6/9/82	D	22	(1)	1
2	Darcy Dolce NETO	BRA	7/2/81	D	26	(1)	3
28	Michal PEŠKOVIČ	SVK	8/2/82	G	5	(1)	
19	Miguel Sebastián García "PITU"	ARG	27/1/84	M	5	(5)	
55	Athanasios PRITTAS		9/1/79	M	13	(2)	
21	Valentin ROBERGE	FRA	9/6/87	D	3	(2)	
5	RONALDO Guiaro	BRA	18/2/74	D	21		1
12	Vasilios ROVAS		6/1/84	M	2	(3)	
1	Mihail SIFAKIS		9/9/84	G	25		
7	Antonio "TONI" CALVO Arandes	ESP	28/3/87	M	24	(4)	5
32	Kristi VANGJELI	ALB	5/9/85	D	7	(2)	

ASTERAS TRIPOLIS FC

Coach – Roberto Mario Gómez (ARG);
(25/10/09) Evangelos Vlahos
Founded – 1931
Stadium – Asteras Tripolis (6,000)

2009

Date	Opponent		Score	Scorers
23/8	Larissa	h	0-0	
29/8	Kavala	a	1-0	Cesarec
13/9	PAOK	h	1-1	Cesarec
19/9	Panionios	a	3-1	Cesarec, Éder 2
27/9	Levadiakos	h	2-1	Bastía, Cesarec
5/10	Ergotelis	h	2-4	Marcelão, Cesarec
17/10	Olympiacos	a	0-3	
24/10	Atromitos	h	1-2	Kaounos
1/11	Iraklis	a	0-1	
8/11	Giannina	h	3-0	Cesarec 3
22/11	Panathinaikos	a	1-1	Udoji
28/11	Xanthi	h	0-0	
6/12	Panthrakikos	a	0-0	
12/12	Aris	a	1-0	Udoji
20/12	AEK	h	2-0	Éder, Cesarec

2010				
5/1	Larissa	a	0-1	
10/1	Kavala	h	1-0	*Marcelão*
16/1	PAOK	a	0-1	
23/1	Panionios	h	2-0	*Wilchez 2*
31/1	Levadiakos	a	0-1	
7/2	Ergotelis	a	3-4	*Lazaridis, Carrera 2*
14/2	Olympiacos	h	1-3	*Éder*
21/2	Atromitos	a	0-0	
27/2	Iraklis	h	0-4	
7/3	Giannina	a	0-1	
14/3	Panathinaikos	h	0-1	
21/3	Xanthi	a	0-2	
28/3	Panthrakikos	h	3-1	*Fitanidis, Cesarec (p), Udoji*
11/4	Aris	h	2-1	*Éder, Bartolini*
18/4	AEK	a	0-2	

No	Name	Nat	DoB	Pos	Aps	(s)	Gls
79	Nikolaos ANASTASOPOULOS		5/8/79	G	16		
13	Leonidas ARGIROPOULOS		29/5/90	D	17	(2)	
34	Anastasios BAKASETAS		28/6/93	A		(1)	
22	Sebastián BARTOLINI	ARG	1/2/82	D	9	(6)	1
14	Adrián Jesús BASTÍA	ARG	20/12/78	M	24	(1)	1
8	Horacio Ramón CARDOZO	ARG	29/11/79	M	18		
18	Sebastián CARRERA	ARG	25/5/78	M	21	(4)	2
9	Danijel CESAREC	CRO	8/1/83	A	29	10	
7	Israel Alejandro DAMONTE	ARG	6/1/82	M		(2)	
32	Matías Omar DEGRA	ARG	18/6/83	G	14		
10	ÉDER Luiz Limade Sousa	BRA	9/1/87	A	18	(8)	5
5	Sokratis FITANIDIS		25/5/84	D	24	(2)	1
11	JEAN CARLOS Dondé	BRA	12/8/83	D	2	(6)	
99	Evagelos KAOUNOS		29/10/77	A	2	(12)	1
84	Antonios LADAKIS		25/1/82	M	7	(6)	
4	Vasilios LAMBROPOULOS		31/3/90	D	4	(5)	
20	Nikolaos LAZARIDIS		12/7/79	M	27		1
33	Anderson Marcelo da Silva "MARCELÃO"	BRA	13/1/81	D	23		2
25	RICARDO Filipe dos Santos ESTEVES	POR	16/9/79	D	4	(4)	
30	Leonel RÍOS	ARG	17/11/82	M	4	(8)	
21	Efstathios ROKAS		18/9/84	M	4	(8)	
23	Shikoze UDOJI	NGA	16/7/86	M	17	(9)	3
6	Bruno Saul URRIBARRI	ARG	6/11/86	D	25	(1)	
31	Lucas Antonio WILCHEZ	ARG	31/8/83	M	21	(5)	2

ATROMITOS FC

Coach – Georgios Donis

Founded – 1923

Stadium – Dimotiko Peristeriou (9,000)

2009				
22/8	Aris	a	0-1	
30/8	AEK	h	0-1	
12/9	Larissa	a	2-2	*Kalantzis, Favalli*
19/9	Kavala	a	1-2	*Favalli*
27/9	PAOK	h	0-0	
5/10	Panionios	a	1-2	*Perrone (p)*
18/10	Levadiakos	h	3-0	*Anastasakos 2, Popović*
24/10	Tripolis	a	2-1	*Anastasakos, Perrone*
31/10	Olympiacos	h	0-1	
8/11	Ergotelis	h	0-0	
22/11	Iraklis	a	2-2	*Brito, Perrone*
29/11	Giannina	h	2-1	*Brito, Perrone*
6/12	Panathinaikos	a	1-3	*Melissas*
13/12	Xanthi	h	1-0	*Favalli*
20/12	Panthrakikos	a	3-0	*Anastasakos 3*
2010				
5/1	Aris	h	0-3	
10/1	AEK	a	3-3	*Nebegleras, Perrone 2 (1p)*
17/1	Larissa	h	2-1	*Anastasakos, Baszczyński*
24/1	Kavala	h	2-0	*Nebegleras, Perrone*
30/1	PAOK	a	0-1	
7/2	Panionios	h	1-0	*Brito*
14/2	Levadiakos	a	1-1	*Sfakianakis*
21/2	Tripolis	h	0-0	
28/2	Olympiacos	a	0-2	
7/3	Ergotelis	a	1-1	*Sfakianakis*
13/3	Iraklis	h	2-1	*Karagounis, Saganowski*
21/3	Giannina	a	0-1	
28/3	Panathinaikos	h	0-3	
11/4	Xanthi	a	1-2	*Saganowski*
26/4	Panthrakikos	h	3-1	*Anastasakos (p), Karalis, Perrone*

No	Name	Nat	DoB	Pos	Aps	(s)	Gls
7	Ilias ANASTASAKOS		3/3/78	A	23	(4)	8
5	Vasilios APOSTOLOPOULOS		13/8/88	D	9	(2)	
30	Jean-Hugues ATEBA Bilayi	CMR	1/4/81	D	2	(1)	
4	Marcin BASZCZYŃSKI	POL	7/6/77	D	19	(1)	1
2	Juan Carlos BLENGIO	ARG	26/6/80	D	10	(3)	
11	Luiz Eduardo de Santana BRITO	BRA	21/9/82	M	20	(4)	3
10	Lucas Gabriel FAVALLI	ARG	16/7/85	M	24	(2)	3
21	Hristos KALANTZIS		1/12/82	A	7	(11)	1
14	Ilias KAMBAS		13/2/74	A	4	(3)	
12	Fotios KARAGIOLIDIS		28/8/87	G	1		
25	Athanasios KARAGOUNIS		25/9/91	A	4	(7)	1
40	Ioannis KARALIS		6/11/88	M	1	(4)	1
1	Fotios KIPOUROS		9/8/75	G	1	(1)	
3	Evangelos KOUTSOPOULOS		2/2/80	D	11	(2)	
26	MARCELO José de OLIVEIRA	BRA	5/9/81	D	17	(2)	
33	Stergos MARINOS		17/9/87	D	2		
8	Pashalis MELISSAS		9/3/82	M	17	(3)	1
23	Hristostomos MIHAILIDIS		15/1/75	G	28		
13	Evangelos NASTOS		13/9/80	D	27	(1)	
6	Konstantinos NEBEGLERAS		14/4/75	M	26		2
9	Emanuel PERRONE	ARG	14/6/83	A	18	(7)	8
18	Zdravko POPOVIĆ	CRO	2/1/83	A		(5)	1
20	Marek SAGANOWSKI	POL	31/10/78	A	6	(3)	2
17	Marcelo SARMIENTO	ARG	3/11/79	M	28		
19	Stilianos SFAKIANAKIS		19/3/76	M	6	(16)	2
32	Ioannis SKONDRAS		21/2/90	D	5	(2)	
22	Andreas TATOS		11/5/89	M	14	(6)	

ERGOTELIS FC

Coach – Nikolaos Karageorgiou

Founded – 1929

Stadium – Pagrition (27,574)

2009				
22/8	Panathinaikos	h	0-3	
29/8	Panionios	a	1-1	*Romano*
13/9	Xanthi	h	1-0	*Leal*
20/9	Levadiakos	a	2-2	*Hieblinger, Budimir,*
27/9	Panthrakikos	h	4-0	*Júnior (p), Budimir, Beto, Leal*
5/10	Tripolis	a	4-2	*Verpakovskis 2, Orfanos, Česnauskis*
17/10	Aris	h	0-0	
24/10	Olympiacos	a	1-2	*Shashiashvili*
1/11	AEK	h	2-2	*Leal 2*
8/11	Atromitos	a	0-0	
28/11	Iraklis	a	2-0	*Orfanos, Budimir*
2/12	Larissa	h	0-0	
6/12	Kavala	h	1-0	*Verpakovskis*
12/12	Giannina	a	0-1	
19/12	PAOK	h	0-2	
2010				
6/1	Panathinaikos	a	1-4	*Fragoulakis*
9/1	Panionios	h	0-0	
16/1	Xanthi	a	0-1	
23/1	Levadiakos	h	1-0	*Orfanos*
31/1	Panthrakikos	a	2-3	*Orfanos, Kordonouris*
7/2	Tripolis	h	4-3	*Fragoulakis (p), Budimir, Hieblinger, Beto*
14/2	Aris	a	1-2	*Beto*
20/2	Olympiacos	h	1-1	*Budimir*
27/2	AEK	a	0-1	

7/3	Atromitos	h	1-1	og (Saganowski)
14/3	Larissa	a	0-1	
21/3	Iraklis	h	1-3	Leal
28/3	Kavala	a	3-1	Česnauskis, Budimir, Fragoulakis
11/4	Giannina	h	3-1	Leal 2 (1p), Fragoulakis
18/4	PAOK	a	1-4	Chrisofakis

No	Name	Nat	DoB	Pos	Aps	(s)	Gls
84	Grigorios ATHANASIOU		9/3/84	G	6		
19	Sotirios BALAFAS		19/8/86	M	6	(2)	
18	Mateo BERTOŠA	CRO	10/8/88	D	2		
11	Gilberto Galdino dos Santos "BETO"	BRA	20/11/76	M	20	(4)	3
25	Mario BUDIMIR	CRO	13/2/86	A	19	(5)	6
33	Deividas ČESNAUSKIS	LTU	30/6/81	M	21	(2)	2
24	Hristos CHRISOFAKIS		18/1/90	M		(2)	1
1	Iosif DASKALAKIS		7/8/82	G	16	(1)	
31	Mihail FRAGOULAKIS		15/7/83	M	17	(4)	4
3	Dimitrios GELADARIS		6/11/74	D	20	(1)	
27	Eleftherios GIALOUSIS		18/7/85	D	4	(2)	
5	Mario HIEBLINGER	AUT	5/7/77	D	22	(2)	2
15	Manuel Oliveira Silva "JÚNIOR"	BRA	24/9/76	M	27		1
14	Nikolaos KARELIS		24/2/92	A		(6)	
23	Dimitrios KILIARAS		23/3/86	M	1	(9)	
6	Panagiotis KORDONOURIS		8/11/75	D	18	(5)	1
10	Sergio LEAL	URU	25/9/82	A	15	(11)	7
99	Patrick Babatunde OGUNSOTO	NGA	19/4/83	A	1	(5)	
12	Dimitrios ORFANOS		2/11/82	M	14	(11)	4
30	Zsolt POSZA	HUN	11/5/77	G	8		
8	Diego Sebastián ROMANO	ARG	2/3/80	M	22	(2)	1
7	Emmanouil ROUMBAKIS		6/1/79	M	23	(1)	
89	Georgios SARRIS		8/9/89	D	1		
37	Giorgi SHASHIASHVILI	GEO	1/9/79	D	27		1
20	Georgios SIAKKAS		23/3/88	D		(1)	
9	Māris VERPAKOVSKIS	LVA	15/10/79	A	13	(9)	3
4	Tomasz WISIO	POL	20/1/82	D	7		

21/3	Atromitos	h	1-0	Bakayoko
28/3	Iraklis	a	0-2	
11/4	Ergotelis	a	1-3	Arrache
26/4	Panathinaikos	h	0-1	

No	Name	Nat	DoB	Pos	Aps	(s)	Gls
16	Paraskevas ANDRALAS		2/12/78	M	12	(4)	1
82	Salim ARRACHE	ALG	14/7/82	M	3	(1)	1
20	Ibrahima BAKAYOKO	CIV	31/12/76	A	13	(11)	4
13	Sotirios BALAFAS		19/8/86	M	11		
18	Esteban Santiago BUJÁN	ARG	13/7/79	M	7	(3)	
2	Georgios DASIOS		12/5/83	D	23		
23	Patrick DIMBALA	BEL	20/9/82	A	16	(10)	2
33	Dimitrios ELEFTHEROPOULOS		7/8/76	G	16		
88	Nikolaos GEORGIADIS		23/3/83	D	4	(1)	
6	Petros KANAKOUDIS		16/4/84	M	12	(4)	
17	Konstantinos KAZNAFERIS		22/6/87	M	6	(2)	
11	Evangelos KONTOGOULIDIS		13/7/81	M	3	(4)	1
5	Ilias KOTSIOS		25/4/77	D	26		1
4	Georgios KOUSAS		12/8/82	D	22	(1)	1
19	Ivica MAJSTOROVIĆ	CRO	20/9/81	M	26		
8	Konstantinos MENDRINOS		28/5/85	M	19	(5)	1
7	Ilias MIHALOPOULOS		15/10/85	M	7	(10)	
66	Vasilios ROVAS		6/1/84	M	8	(2)	
9	Georgios SAITIOTIS		25/7/81	A	19	(6)	6
28	Nicolás Andrés SCHENONE	URU	24/4/86	A		(1)	
10	Dimitrios SIALMAS		19/6/86	A	3	(2)	
30	Georgios SIKALIAS		25/3/86	G	8	(1)	
81	Mirnes ŠIŠIĆ	SVN	8/8/81	M	14	(1)	2
3	Ioannis STATHIS		20/5/87	D	5	(5)	
22	Hristos TZANIS		22/4/85	A	16	(10)	5
27	VANDERSON Scardovelli	BRA	27/9/84	D	23		
21	Lambros VANGELIS		10/2/82	M	1	(3)	
32	Pavlos VARTZIOTIS		27/1/81	M	1		
1	Nikolaos ZAFIROPOULOS		8/1/74	G	6	(2)	

PAS GIANNINA FC

Coach – Georgios Parashos; (7/1/10) (Efthimios Georgoulis); (13/1/10) Nikolaos Anastopoulos
Founded – 1966
Stadium – Oi Zosimades (7,652)

2009

22/8	Xanthi	a	1-1	Tzanis
30/8	Panthrakikos	h	2-0	Kotsios, Tzanis
12/9	Aris	a	0-1	
20/9	AEK	h	1-1	Kontogoulidis
26/9	Larissa	a	0-0	
3/10	Kavala	h	2-1	Saitiotis 2
17/10	PAOK	a	0-2	
24/10	Panionios	a	1-3	Dimbala
1/11	Levadiakos	h	1-1	Andralas
8/11	Tripolis	a	0-3	
21/11	Olympiacos	h	2-2	Tzanis, Bakayoko
29/11	Atromitos	a	1-2	Dimbala
6/12	Iraklis	h	2-3	Saitiotis 2 (1p)
12/12	Ergotelis	h	1-0	Kousas
19/12	Panathinaikos	a	0-4	

2010

6/1	Xanthi	h	0-0	
10/1	Panthrakikos	a	2-1	Tzanis 2
17/1	Aris	h	0-1	
24/1	AEK	a	1-3	Saitiotis
30/1	Larissa	h	2-0	Šišić 2
6/2	Kavala	a	0-1	
13/2	PAOK	h	0-1	
21/2	Panionios	h	2-3	Mendrinos, Saitiotis (p)
28/2	Levadiakos	a	1-4	Bakayoko
7/3	Tripolis	h	1-0	Bakayoko
13/3	Olympiacos	a	2-2	og (Papadopoulos A.), og (Mellberg)

IRAKLIS FC

Coach – Oleh Protasov (UKR); (30/10/09) Savvas Kofidis; (25/1/10) Jozef Bubenko (SVK)
Founded – 1908
Stadium – Kaftanzoglion (29,080)
MAJOR HONOURS:
Greek Cup – (1) 1976.

2009

23/8	Panthrakikos	a	2-1	Dică 2
29/8	Aris	h	2-2	Iacob, Epstein (p)
13/9	AEK	a	0-1	
19/9	Larissa	h	2-1	Epstein, Iacob
27/9	Kavala	a	0-1	
5/10	PAOK	a	0-1	
18/10	Panionios	h	0-2	
25/10	Levadiakos	a	0-1	
1/11	Tripolis	h	1-0	Iacob
7/11	Olympiacos	a	1-1	Vellios
22/11	Atromitos	h	2-2	Iacob, Vellios
28/11	Ergotelis	h	0-2	
6/12	Giannina	a	3-2	Epstein (p), Dică, Kone
12/12	Panathinaikos	h	0-1	
20/12	Xanthi	a	3-4	Voutsias, Sarakatsanos, Milano

2010

6/1	Panthrakikos	h	3-1	Iliadis, Iacob, Milano
10/1	Aris	a	2-4	Epstein, Milano
16/1	AEK	h	1-1	Kone
23/1	Larissa	a	1-2	Giantsis
30/1	Kavala	h	1-0	Iacob
7/2	PAOK	h	1-1	Giantsis
14/2	Panionios	a	0-0	
20/2	Levadiakos	h	1-1	Kone
27/2	Tripolis	a	4-0	Iacob 2, Kone, Milano (p)
7/3	Olympiacos	h	1-0	Mara (p)
13/3	Atromitos	a	1-2	Papazaharias

GREECE

21/3	Ergotelis	a	3-1	og (Budimir), Iacob, Papazaharias
28/3	Giannina	h	2-0	Iacob, Iliadis
11/4	Panathinaikos	a	0-2	
18/4	Xanthi	h	2-4	Kone, Iacob

No	Name	Nat	DoB	Pos	Aps	(s)	Gls
6	ANDRÉ Filipe Farias MARQUES	POR	1/8/87	D	1		
1	Georgios BANDIS		30/4/85	G	6		
12	Ivan BOŠNJAK	CRO	6/2/79	A	8	(5)	
11	Carlos César Matheus "CARLINHOS"	BRA	2/8/84	M	5	(1)	
24	Samuele DALLA BONA	ITA	6/2/81	M		(2)	
66	DANIEL Márcio FERNANDES	POR	25/9/83	G	10		
10	Nicolae Constantin DICĂ	ROU	9/5/80	M	12	(1)	3
6	Serge DIÉ	CIV	4/10/77	M	14		
21	Denis EPSTEIN	GER	2/7/86	M	23	(3)	4
13	Konstantinos FOUFOULAS		25/10/84	D		(2)	
18	Konstantinos GIANNOULIS		9/12/87	D	19	(3)	
19	Dimitrios GIANTSIS		4/3/88	A	4	(11)	2
20	Victoraş Constantin IACOB	ROU	14/10/80	A	22	(1)	11
88	Stilianos ILIADIS		3/6/86	M	16	(2)	2
16	Georgios IOANNIDIS		4/5/88	M	3	(2)	
4	Anastasios KATSABIS		30/7/73	D	27		
5	Georgios KATSIKAS		14/6/90	D		(1)	
80	Daigo KOBAYASHI	JPN	19/2/83	M	6	(2)	
99	Panagiotis KONE		26/7/87	M	11	(13)	5
30	Wojciech KOWALEWSKI	POL	11/5/77	G	14		
27	Matías LEQUI	ARG	13/5/81	D	14		
10	Bogdanlon MARA	ROU	29/9/77	M	10	(2)	1
8	Francisco Javier MARTOS Espigares	ESP	4/1/84	D	24	(2)	
32	Mauro MILANO	ARG	18/1/84	M	10	(10)	4
17	Emmanouil PAPASTERIANOS		15/8/87	M	19	(3)	
2	Grigorios PAPAZAHARIAS		20/3/85	D	17	(3)	2
23	Haralambos PERPERIDIS		29/4/86	D	5	(1)	
84	Miguel Sebastián García "PITU"	ARG	27/1/84	M	9	(1)	
29	Lucas Roberto RIMOLDI	ARG	7/8/80	M	1	(2)	
33	Achilleas SARAKATSANOS		3/11/82	D	10	(4)	1
7	Sharbel TOUMA	SWE	25/3/79	A	7	(1)	
9	Apostolos VELLIOS		8/1/92	A		(9)	2
36	Pashalis VOUTSIAS		23/3/90	M	3	(3)	1

FC KAVALA

Coach – Giannis Papakostas; (15/11/09) (Evangelos Goutis); (1/2/10) Aad de Mos (NED); (2/4/10) (Konstantinos Tsalikis)
Founded – 1965
Stadium – Dimotiko Stadio Anthi Karagianni (12,600)

2009
23/8	Levadiakos	a	1-0	Dobrasinović
29/8	Tripolis	h	0-1	
12/9	Olympiacos	a	0-0	
19/9	Atromitos	h	2-1	Onwuachi, Soultanidis
27/9	Iraklis	h	1-0	Douglão
3/10	Giannina	a	1-2	Ioannou
18/10	Panathinaikos	h	2-2	Onwuachi 2
25/10	Xanthi	a	1-2	Ioannou
1/11	Panthrakikos	h	3-0	Siontis, Ioannou, Onwuachi
7/11	Aris	a	0-0	
21/11	AEK	h	2-1	Dobrasinović (p), Giannou
29/11	Larissa	a	0-1	
6/12	Ergotelis	a	0-1	
13/12	PAOK	h	0-0	
20/12	Panionios	a	2-1	Diogo Rincón (p), Onwuachi

2010
5/1	Levadiakos	h	2-2	Onwuachi 2
10/1	Tripolis	a	0-1	
17/1	Olympiacos	h	0-0	
24/1	Atromitos	a	0-2	
30/1	Iraklis	a	0-1	
6/2	Giannina	h	1-0	og (Kotsios)

14/2	Panathinaikos	a	2-0	Smolarek 2
20/2	Xanthi	h	2-1	Onwuachi 2
28/2	Panthrakikos	a	3-1	Smolarek, Onwuachi, Diogo Rincón
6/3	Aris	h	1-1	Dié
13/3	AEK	a	0-3	
21/3	Larissa	h	3-3	Dié, og (Katsiaros), Diogo Rincón
28/3	Ergotelis	h	1-3	Moore (p)
11/4	PAOK	a	0-1	
18/4	Panionios	h	1-1	Diogo Rincón

No	Name	Nat	DoB	Pos	Aps	(s)	Gls
6	Serge DIÉ	CIV	4/10/77	M	9		2
15	DIOGO Augusto Pachecoda Fontoura RINCÓN	BRA	18/4/80	M	12	(12)	4
6	Siniša DOBRASINOVIĆ	CYP	17/2/77	M	17	(3)	2
40	Douglas Ferreira "DOUGLÃO"	BRA	15/8/86	D	23	(1)	1
14	Pierre DUCROCQ	FRA	18/12/76	M	20	(3)	
29	Apostolos GIANNOU		25/1/90	A	1	(4)	1
17	Ivan GVOZDENOVIĆ	SRB	19/8/78	D	4		
88	Evangelos IKONOMOU		18/7/87	D	25		
44	Ilias IOANNOU		23/10/79	A	13	(11)	3
1	Charles ITANDJE	FRA	2/11/82	G	19		
60	Željko KALAC	AUS	16/12/72	G	9		
16	Željko KALAJDŽIĆ	SRB	11/5/78	M	2	(1)	
13	Theofanis KATERGIANNAKIS		16/2/74	G	2	(1)	
23	Vasilios LAKIS		10/9/76	M	9	(8)	
8	Sotirios LEONDIOU		17/7/84	M	1	(2)	
11	Frédéric MENDY	SEN	6/11/81	A	13	(6)	
3	Craig MOORE	AUS	12/12/75	D	11		1
80	Benjamin ONWUACHI	NGA	9/4/84	A	28	10	
10	Wilson ORUMA	NGA	30/12/76	M	20	(3)	
2	Savo PAVIĆEVIĆ	MNE	11/12/80	D	25		
21	Dimitrios PETKAKIS		1/8/83	M	8	(2)	
7	Aleksandar POPOVIĆ	AUT	2/11/83	M	1	(6)	
22	Emmanouil PSOMAS		11/11/78	D	15	(1)	
5	Stefanos SIONTIS		4/9/87	D	12	(4)	1
9	Euzebiusz SMOLAREK	POL	9/1/81	A	8	(7)	3
20	Łukasz SOSIN	POL	7/5/77	A	8	(3)	
33	Nikolaos SOULTANIDIS		2/1/77	A	7	(9)	1
88	Lazaros THEODORELIS		14/1/82	D	8	(3)	

LARISSA FC

Coach – Marinos Ouzounidis; (22/2/10) Giannis Papakostas
Founded – 1964
MAJOR HONOURS:
Greek League – (1) 1988;
Greek Cup – (2) 1985, 2007.

2009
23/8	Tripolis	a	0-0	
30/8	Olympiacos	h	0-2	
12/9	Atromitos	a	2-2	Tümer, Romeu
19/9	Iraklis	a	1-2	Abuhazeira
26/9	Giannina	h	0-0	
5/10	Panathinaikos	a	0-4	
18/10	Xanthi	h	2-0	Tümer, Abuhazeira
25/10	Panthrakikos	a	3-1	Melissis, Abuhazeira, Simić
31/10	Aris	h	2-2	Simić, Toama
9/11	AEK	a	1-3	Romeu
29/11	Kavala	h	1-0	Casas
2/12	Ergotelis	a	0-0	
5/12	PAOK	a	0-1	
13/12	Panionios	h	2-2	Tümer 2 (1p)
19/12	Levadiakos	a	0-3	

2010
5/1	Tripolis	h	1-0	Casas
10/1	Olympiacos	a	1-2	Romeu
17/1	Atromitos	a	1-2	Dabizas
23/1	Iraklis	h	2-1	Ricardo Jesus, Romeu
30/1	Giannina	a	0-2	

7/2	Panathinaikos	h	0-3	
13/2	Xanthi	a	1-0	*Blažek*
21/2	Panthrakikos	h	0-2	
28/2	Aris	a	0-2	
6/3	AEK	h	1-0	*Blažek*
14/3	Ergotelis	h	1-0	*Romeu*
21/3	Kavala	a	3-3	*Tümer 2 (1p), Ricardo Jesus*
28/3	PAOK	h	2-1	*Cousin, Puri*
11/4	Panionios	a	3-0	*Tümer, Toama, Cousin*
18/4	Levadiakos	h	1-2	*Kiriakidis*

No	Name	Nat	DoB	Pos	Aps	(s)	Gls
19	Naïm AARAB	BEL	7/2/88	D	12	(4)	
99	Shimon ABUHAZEIRA	ISR	10/10/86	A	12	(1)	3
88	Jan BLAŽEK	CZE	20/3/88	A	9		2
2	Mihail BOUKOUVALAS		14/1/88	D	15	(1)	
20	Ángel Gastón CASAS	ARG	10/1/78	A	5	(8)	2
7	Daniel COUSIN	GAB	7/2/77	A	8	(1)	2
4	Nikos DABIZAS		3/8/73	D	25		1
9	Antonio DE NIGRIS	MEX	1/4/78	A	6	(1)	
6	DELSON Ferreira	BRA	26/7/80	M	6	(3)	
15	FLÁVIO Pinto de Souza	BRA	12/3/80	D	10	(1)	
7	Stelios GIANNAKOPOULOS		12/7/74	M	4	(6)	
42	Walter Matías IGLESIAS	ARG	18/4/85	M	13	(5)	
77	Panagiotis KATSIAROS		8/5/78	D	20	(2)	
5	Ilias KIRIAKIDIS		5/8/85	M	11	(8)	1
26	Dimitrios KOLOVETSIOS		16/10/91	D	1		
18	Arkadiusz MALARZ	POL	19/6/80	G	15		
45	Hristos MELISSIS		1/12/82	D	26	(1)	1
28	Sander PURI	EST	7/5/88	A	3	(8)	1
13	Aleksandar RADOSAVLJEVIĆ	SVN	25/4/79	M	4	(3)	
14	RICARDO JESUS da Silva	BRA	16/5/85	A	4	(6)	2
21	ROMEU Pereira dos Santos	BRA	13/2/85	M	24	(2)	5
1	Dino SEREMET	SVN	16/8/80	G		(1)	
92	Savvas SIATRAVANIS		24/11/92	M	1	(4)	
17	Aleksandar SIMIĆ	SRB	31/1/80	M	7	(3)	2
30	Rudolf SKÁCEL	CZE	17/7/79	M	5	(2)	
25	Dimitrios SOTIRIOU		13/9/87	G	1		
10	Salim TOAMA	ISR	9/8/79	M	13	(10)	2
22	Theodoros TRIPOTSERIS		4/3/86	D	3	(2)	
11	TÜMER Metin	TUR	14/10/74	M	22	(4)	7
23	Juan VELASCO Damas	ESP	15/5/77	D	13		
3	Stilianos VENETIDIS		19/11/76	D	17	(1)	
83	Mario Sebastián VIERA Galain	URU	7/3/83	G	14		
8	Nikolaos VLASSOPOULOS		30/5/88	M	1	(1)	

LEVADIAKOS FC

Coach – Momčilo Vukotić (SRB); (24/9/09) Quique Hernández (ESP); (16/2/10) (Dimitrios Farantos)
Founded – 1961
Stadium – Dimotiko Livadias (6,200)

2009

23/8	Kavala	h	0-1	
30/8	PAOK	a	0-3	
13/9	Panionios	h	1-0	*Barkoglou*
20/9	Ergotelis	h	2-2	*Barkoglou 2*
27/9	Tripolis	a	1-2	*Napoleoni*
3/10	Olympiacos	h	0-3	
18/10	Atromitos	a	0-3	
25/10	Iraklis	h	1-0	*Moulopoulos*
1/11	Giannina	a	1-1	*Barkoglou*
8/11	Panathinaikos	h	0-2	
21/11	Xanthi	a	0-1	
29/11	Panthrakikos	a	2-0	*Napoleoni 2*
5/12	Aris	h	0-2	
13/12	AEK	a	2-3	*Barkoglou, Agali*
19/12	Larissa	h	3-0	*Taralidis, Barkoglou, Napoleoni*

2010

5/1	Kavala	a	2-2	*Balvorín, Agali*
9/1	PAOK	h	0-2	
17/1	Panionios	a	2-2	*Napoleoni, Barkoglou*

23/1	Ergotelis	a	0-1	
31/1	Tripolis	h	1-0	*Kike Sola*
7/2	Olympiacos	a	1-5	*Taralidis*
14/2	Atromitos	h	1-1	*Barkoglou*
20/2	Iraklis	a	1-1	*Nacho González*
28/2	Giannina	h	4-1	*Barkoglou, Agali 2, Nacho González*
7/3	Panathinaikos	a	0-3	
14/3	Xanthi	h	2-1	*Barkoglou 2*
21/3	Panthrakikos	h	2-0	*Abubakari, Napoleoni*
28/3	Aris	a	0-1	
11/4	AEK	h	0-0	
18/4	Larissa	a	2-1	*Serginho, Agali*

No	Name	Nat	DoB	Pos	Aps	(s)	Gls
28	Mohammed ABUBAKARI	GHA	15/2/86	M	7	(5)	1
15	Victor AGALI	NGA	29/12/78	A	13	(6)	5
24	Ioannis ALEXIOU		8/12/84	D	7	(6)	
11	Gustavo Alberto BALVORÍN	ARG	6/9/77	A	7	(7)	1
21	Georgios BARKOGLOU		8/7/78	M	29	(1)	11
1	Srđan BLAŽIĆ	MNE	26/11/82	G	9		
14	Serge BRANCO	CMR	11/10/80	M	15	(3)	
8	Alban BUSHI	ALB	20/8/73	A	1	(7)	
77	Argirios GATSOS		2/9/88	M		(1)	
22	Dimitrios HALOULOS		2/5/87	D	3	(1)	
44	IKER BEGOÑA Zubiaur	ESP	15/11/76	M	13	(1)	
19	Mihail KAPSIS		18/10/73	D	2		
76	Nikolaos KARAKOSTAS		22/9/76	G	5		
50	Enrique "KIKE" SOLA Clemente	ESP	25/2/86	A	6	(4)	1
20	Georgios KOLTSIS		22/10/74	D		(2)	
3	Georgios KOLTZOS		13/9/76	D	24		
52	Javier LÓPEZ VALLEJO	ESP	22/9/75	G	10		
5	Luis Fernando MACHADO	URU	26/9/79	D	21	(1)	
6	Dimitrios MAHERAS		16/8/90	M		(4)	
4	Federico MARTORELL	ARG	16/3/81	D	11	(3)	
2	Athanasios MOULOPOULOS		9/6/85	D	26		1
40	Ignacio María "NACHO" GONZÁLEZ Gatti	URU	14/5/82	M	13		2
27	Stefano NAPOLEONI	ITA	26/6/86	A	26	(1)	6
10	PAULO Sérgio Cardosoda COSTA	POR	5/12/79	A	5	(5)	
7	Sérgio Dias Ribeiro "SERGINHO"	POR	16/6/85	M	9	(13)	1
31	Diogo Rodrigues SISTON	BRA	25/1/81	M	3	(2)	
29	Kiriakos STRATILATIS		5/1/88	G	6	(1)	
17	Ioannis TARALIDIS		17/5/81	M	26	(1)	2
12	Mihail TZORBATZAKIS		2/7/82	D	1		
9	Stilianos VASILIOU		29/4/91	A	2	(13)	
13	Georgios ZISOPOULOS		23/5/84	M	30		

OLYMPIACOS FC

Coach – Temuri Ketsbaia (GEO); (15/9/09) (Božidar Bandović (SRB)); (21/9/09) Zico (BRA); (19/1/10) Božidar Bandović (SRB)
Founded – 1925
Stadium – Georgios Karaiskakis (32,130)
MAJOR HONOURS:
Greek League – (37) 1931, 1933, 1934, 1936, 1937, 1938, 1947, 1948, 1951, 1954, 1955, 1956, 1957, 1958, 1959, 1966, 1967, 1973, 1974, 1975, 1980, 1981, 1982, 1983, 1987, 1997, 1998, 1999, 2000, 2001, 2002, 2003, 2005, 2006, 2007, 2008, 2009;
Greek Cup – (24) 1947, 1951, 1952, 1953, 1954, 1957, 1958, 1959, 1960, 1961, 1963, 1965, 1968, 1971, 1973, 1975, 1981, 1990, 1992, 1999, 2005, 2006, 2008, 2009.

2009

30/8	Larissa	a	2-0	*Leonardo, Maresca*
12/9	Kavala	h	0-0	
20/9	PAOK	a	2-1	*Diogo, Papadopoulos A.*
23/9	AEK	a	2-1	*Torosidis 2*
26/9	Panionios	h	1-0	*Zairi*
3/10	Levadiakos	a	3-0	*Óscar, Dudu Cearense (p), Diogo*
17/10	Tripolis	h	3-0	*Mellberg, Mitroglou, Zairi*

24/10	Ergotelis	h	2-1	Dudu Cearense, Mitroglou
31/10	Atromitos	a	1-0	Óscar
7/11	Iraklis	h	1-1	Maresca
21/11	Giannina	a	2-2	Żewłakow, Mitroglou
29/11	Panathinaikos	h	2-0	Mitroglou 2
5/12	Xanthi	a	1-0	Leonardo
13/12	Panthrakikos	h	3-0	Galletti, Dudu Cearense 2
20/12	Aris	a	0-1	
2010				
6/1	AEK	h	1-2	Papadopoulos A.
10/1	Larissa	h	2-1	Maresca, Galletti
17/1	Kavala	a	0-0	
24/1	PAOK	h	0-1	
31/1	Panionios	a	1-0	Derbyshire
7/2	Levadiakos	h	5-1	Mellberg, Derbyshire 2, Mitroglou 2
14/2	Tripolis	a	3-1	LuaLua 2, Stoltidis
20/2	Ergotelis	a	1-1	Torosidis
28/2	Atromitos	h	2-0	Derbyshire, Mitroglou
7/3	Iraklis	a	0-1	
13/3	Giannina	h	2-2	Derbyshire, LuaLua
21/3	Panathinaikos	a	1-0	Derbyshire
28/3	Xanthi	h	0-0	
11/4	Panthrakikos	a	2-0	Torosidis, Mitroglou
18/4	Aris	h	2-1	Żewłakow, Maresca (p)

No	Name	Nat	DoB	Pos	Aps	(s)	Gls
19	Jesús Alberto DÁTOLO	ARG	19/5/84	M	6	(1)	
9	Matt DERBYSHIRE	ENG	14/4/86	A	10	(4)	6
10	DIOGO Luís Santo	BRA	26/5/87	A	9	(7)	2
3	Didier DOMI	FRA	2/5/78	D	4	(5)	
20	Alexandro Silva de Souza "DUDU CEARENSE"	BRA	15/4/83	M	15	(1)	4
18	Ioannis FETFATZIDIS		21/12/90	M	1	(1)	
5	Georgios GALITSIOS		6/7/86	D	13	(7)	
7	Luciano Martín GALLETTI	ARG	9/4/80	A	8	(1)	2
88	Georgios KATSIKOGIANNIS		5/9/88	M	2	(1)	
50	Pavel KOVÁČ	SVK	12/8/74	G		(1)	
28	Cristian Raúl LEDESMA	ARG	29/12/78	M	10	(4)	
24	LEONARDO de Jesus Geraldo	BRA	4/8/85	D	13	(6)	2
32	Lomana Trésor LUALUA	COD	28/12/80	A	10	(2)	3
25	Enzo MARESCA	ITA	10/2/80	M	19	(1)	4
4	Olof MELLBERG	SWE	3/9/77	D	25		2
22	Konstantinos MITROGLOU		12/3/88	A	18	(8)	9
23	Georgios NIKLITSIOTIS		23/3/91	A	1		
71	Antonios NIKOPOLIDIS		14/1/71	G	28		
8	ÓSCAR González Marcos	ESP	12/11/82	M	15	(4)	2
30	Anastasios PANTOS		5/5/76	D	4	(5)	
21	Avraam PAPADOPOULOS		3/12/84	D	23	(1)	2
33	Ioannis PAPADOPOULOS		9/3/89	M	4	(7)	
2	Kiriakos PAPADOPOULOS		23/2/92	D	2	(1)	
15	RAÚL BRAVO Sanfélix	ESP	14/4/81	D	26		
31	Aristidis SOILEDIS		8/2/91	A	1	(1)	
6	Ieroklis STOLTIDIS		2/2/75	M	13	(5)	1
35	Vasilios TOROSIDIS		10/6/85	D	19	(3)	4
78	Rafael URKO PARDO Goas	ESP	28/1/83	G	2		
81	Georgios VALERIANOS		13/2/92	D		(1)	
11	Jaouad ZAIRI	MAR	14/4/82	A	13	(6)	2
14	Michał ŻEWŁAKOW	POL	22/4/76	D	16	(3)	2

13/9	Panthrakikos	a	1-0	Leto
20/9	Aris	h	2-1	og (Abreu), Katsouranis
27/9	AEK	a	1-0	Salpingidis
5/10	Larissa	h	4-0	Vintra, Katsouranis, Cissé 2
18/10	Kavala	a	2-2	Katsouranis, Cissé
25/10	PAOK	h	2-1	Katsouranis 2
1/11	Panionios	h	2-1	Cissé 2 (1p)
8/11	Levadiakos	a	2-0	og (Karakostas), Cissé
22/11	Tripolis	h	1-1	Cissé
29/11	Olympiacos	a	0-2	
6/12	Atromitos	h	3-1	Katsouranis 2, Cissé
12/12	Iraklis	a	1-0	Ninis
19/12	Giannina	h	4-0	Cissé 2 (1p), Vintra, Hristodoulopoulos
2010				
6/1	Ergotelis	h	4-1	Cissé 2, Karagounis, Leto
9/1	Xanthi	a	2-1	Cissé 2
17/1	Panthrakikos	h	2-0	Karagounis, Salpingidis
24/1	Aris	a	0-0	
31/1	AEK	h	1-1	Salpingidis
7/2	Larissa	a	3-0	Cissé 2, Ninis
14/2	Kavala	h	0-2	
21/2	PAOK	a	1-2	Cissé
28/2	Panionios	a	2-0	Cissé 2 (1p)
7/3	Levadiakos	h	3-0	Salpingidis, Leto, Cissé
14/3	Tripolis	a	1-0	Vintra
21/3	Olympiacos	h	0-1	
28/3	Atromitos	a	3-0	Salpingidis, Cissé (p), Leto
11/4	Iraklis	h	2-0	Cissé, Ninis
18/4	Giannina	a	1-0	Gabriel

No	Name	Nat	DoB	Pos	Aps	(s)	Gls
18	Mattias BJÄRSMYR	SWE	3/1/86	D	13	(4)	
9	Djibril CISSÉ	FRA	12/8/81	A	27	(1)	23
38	Alexandre Henri Marco CLEYTON Silva	BRA	8/3/83	M		(4)	
21	Filippos DARLAS		23/10/83	D	5		
46	Xenofon FETSIS		5/5/91	M		(1)	
19	GABRIEL Rodrigues dos Santos	BRA	5/6/81	D	7	(6)	1
1	Mario GALINOVIĆ	CRO	15/11/76	G	3		
15	GILBERTO Aparecido da SILVA	BRA	7/10/76	M	22	(2)	
17	Lazaros HRISTODOULOPOULOS		19/12/86	M	5	(12)	1
8	Cédric KANTÉ	MLI	6/7/79	D	21		
26	Georgios KARAGOUNIS		6/3/77	M	21	(3)	2
27	Orestis KARNEZIS		11/7/85	G	1		
29	Konstantinos KATSOURANIS		21/6/79	M	28		8
11	Sebastián Eduardo LETO	ARG	30/8/86	M	21	(4)	6
22	Stergos MARINOS		17/9/87	D	4	(6)	
7	Sotirios NINIS		3/4/90	M	14	(12)	3
28	Antonios PETROPOULOS		28/1/86	A	2	(4)	
5	Ante RUKAVINA	CRO	18/6/86	A	3	(8)	
14	Dimitrios SALPINGIDIS		18/8/81	A	25	(3)	5
3	Josu SARRIEGI Zumárraga	ESP	19/1/79	D	21		
25	Giourkas SEITARIDIS		4/6/81	D	7	(1)	
23	SIMÃO Mate Júnior	MOZ	23/7/88	M	12	(6)	
31	Nikolaos SPIROPOULOS		10/10/83	D	19	(2)	
37	Alexandros TZIOLIS		13/2/85	M		(2)	
30	Alexandros TZORVAS		12/8/82	G	26		
24	Loukas VINTRA		5/2/81	D	23	(1)	3

PANATHINAIKOS FC

Coach – Henk ten Cate (NED); (8/12/09) Nikolaos Nioplias
Founded – 1908
Stadium – OACA Spyro Louis (72,080)
MAJOR HONOURS:
Greek League – (20) 1930, 1949, 1953, 1960, 1961, 1962, 1964, 1965, 1969, 1970, 1972, 1977, 1984, 1986, 1990, 1991, 1995, 1996, 2004, 2010;
Greek Cup – (17) 1940, 1948, 1955, 1967, 1969, 1977, 1982, 1984, 1986, 1988, 1989, 1991, 1993, 1994, 1995, 2010.

2009				
22/8	Ergotelis	a	3-0	Cissé, Leto 2
30/8	Xanthi	h	1-0	Katsouranis

PANIONIOS GSS

Coach – Emilio Ferrera (BEL); (26/1/10) (Apostolos Mantzios); (3/2/10) Georgios Parashos
Founded – 1890
Stadium – Panionios GSS (16,800)
MAJOR HONOURS:
Greek Cup – (2) 1979, 1998.

2009				
29/8	Ergotelis	h	1-1	Yao Kumordzi
13/9	Levadiakos	a	0-1	
19/9	Tripolis	h	1-3	Suleiman Omo
23/9	PAOK	h	0-0	

26/9	Olympiacos	a	0-1	
5/10	Atromitos	h	2-1	Skoufalis, Suleiman Omo
18/10	Iraklis	a	2-0	Balaban, Maniatis
24/10	Giannina	h	3-1	Goundoulakis, Balaban, Casteglione
1/11	Panathinaikos	a	1-2	Sito Riera
8/11	Xanthi	a	2-1	Balaban 2
22/11	Panthrakikos	h	3-1	Estoyanoff (p), Suleiman Omo, Sito Riera
29/11	Aris	a	1-1	Yao Kumordzi
6/12	AEK	h	3-1	Maniatis, Sito Riera, Balaban
13/12	Larissa	a	2-2	Goundoulakis 2
20/12	Kavala	h	1-2	Balaban (p)
2010				
6/1	PAOK	a	0-1	
9/1	Ergotelis	a	0-0	
17/1	Levadiakos	h	2-2	Balaban, Latka
23/1	Tripolis	a	0-2	
31/1	Olympiacos	h	0-1	
7/2	Atromitos	a	0-1	
14/2	Iraklis	h	0-0	
21/2	Giannina	a	3-2	Cocalić, Sito Riera, Maniatis
28/2	Panathinaikos	h	0-2	
7/3	Xanthi	h	3-0	Yao Kumordzi, Latka, Balaban
14/3	Panthrakikos	a	1-0	Latka
21/3	Aris	h	1-1	Kukec
28/3	AEK	a	1-1	Goundoulakis
11/4	Larissa	h	0-3	
18/4	Kavala	a	1-1	Goundoulakis

No	Name	Nat	DoB	Pos	Aps	(s)	Gls
24	Dimitrios ANASTASOPOULOS		11/4/90	M	5	(6)	
12	Konstantinos ANDRIOLAS		1/5/85	G	9		
9	Boško BALABAN	CRO	15/10/78	A	24		8
1	Tomáš BELIC	SVK	2/7/78	G	18		
21	Bédi BUVAL	FRA	16/6/86	A	3	(6)	
13	Carlos Damián CASTEGLIONE	ARG	9/5/80	D	14	(1)	1
26	Edin COCALIĆ	BIH	5/12/87	M	7		1
11	Fabián Larry ESTOYANOFF	URU	27/9/82	A	8	(3)	1
20	Fanourios GOUNDOULAKIS		13/7/83	M	15	(8)	5
30	ISAAC Becerra Alguacil	ESP	18/6/88	G	3	(1)	
4	Markus JONSSON	SWE	9/3/81	D	6		
25	Ioannis KONTOES		24/5/86	D	16	(4)	
18	Davor KUKEC	CRO	16/3/86	M	6	(9)	1
5	Martin LATKA	CZE	28/9/84	D	19	(2)	3
19	Ioannis LOUKINAS		20/9/91	A		(2)	
32	Hristos MANIATIS		6/5/91	D		(1)	
2	Ioannis MANIATIS		12/10/86	D	25		3
28	Marios NICOLAOU	CYP	4/10/83	M	20	(3)	
10	Álvaro RECOBA	URU	17/3/76	A	5		
22	Andreas SAMARIS		13/6/89	M	1	(1)	
17	Ioannis SIMOSIS		13/3/91	A	1	(3)	
23	Dimitrios SIOVAS		16/9/88	D	11	(4)	
8	Lorenç "SITO" RIERA Ortega	ESP	5/1/87	A	25		4
7	Emmanouil SKOUFALIS		21/8/78	M	8	(13)	1
4	Dario SMOJE	CRO	19/9/78	D		(1)	
6	SULEIMAN Akim OMOlade	NGA	15/12/85	D	24		3
31	Georgios TZAVELAS		26/11/87	D	24		
3	WELLINGTON Baroni	BRA	1/4/89	D	6	(8)	
14	Bernard YAO KUMORDZI	GHA	21/3/85	M	27	(1)	3

PANTHRAKIKOS FC

**Coach – Ilie Dumitrescu (ROU); (27/8/09) (Leonidas Bilis);
(31/8/09) Albert Cartier (FRA); (12/1/10) Pavlos Dermitzakis**
Founded – 1963
Stadium – Dimotiko Komotinis (3,000)

2009				
23/8	Iraklis	h	1-2	Mitu
30/8	Giannina	a	0-2	
13/9	Panathinaikos	h	0-1	
20/9	Xanthi	a	0-1	

27/9	Ergotelis	a	0-4	
3/10	Aris	h	1-1	João Fajardo (p)
18/10	AEK	a	2-3	Buval, Robert
25/10	Larissa	h	1-3	Robert (p)
1/11	Kavala	a	0-3	
7/11	PAOK	h	1-2	Buval
22/11	Panionios	a	1-3	Robert
29/11	Levadiakos	h	0-2	
6/12	Tripolis	h	0-0	
13/12	Olympiacos	a	0-3	
20/12	Atromitos	h	0-3	
2010				
6/1	Iraklis	a	1-3	João Fajardo
10/1	Giannina	h	1-2	Buval
17/1	Panathinaikos	a	0-2	
24/1	Xanthi	h	1-1	Papoulis
31/1	Ergotelis	h	3-2	Kazakis, Manuel Lopes, Arsenijević
7/2	Aris	a	2-0	Papoulis, Robert (p)
13/2	AEK	h	1-2	Beleck
21/2	Larissa	a	2-0	Beleck 2
28/2	Kavala	h	1-3	Beleck
6/3	PAOK	a	0-3	
14/3	Panionios	h	0-1	
21/3	Levadiakos	a	0-2	
28/3	Tripolis	a	1-3	Papoulis
12/4	Olympiacos	h	0-2	
18/4	Atromitos	a	1-3	Beleck (p)

No	Name	Nat	DoB	Pos	Aps	(s)	Gls
27	Anestis ARGIRIOU		4/1/88	D	22	(3)	
7	Filip ARSENIJEVIĆ	SRB	2/9/83	A	1	(7)	1
33	Nikolaos BACHARIDIS		20/10/76	D	8	(4)	
8	Steve Leo BELECK	CMR	10/2/93	A	13		5
11	Periklis BOUSINAKIS		23/4/86	M		(5)	
9	Bedi BUVAL	FRA	16/6/86	A	15	(2)	3
12	Ludovic CLÉMENT	FRA	5/12/76	D	13	(2)	
40	Abdul Moktar DIALLO	BFA	23/12/85	A	4	(6)	
4	Željko ĐOKIĆ	SRB	10/5/82	D	20		
14	Pashalis DRAGANIDIS		11/8/92	M		(2)	
35	Lazaros HARITONIDIS		18/12/89	D	3	(1)	
24	Konstantinos IASONIDIS		1/10/85	D	9	(1)	
17	JOÃO Paulo Silva Freitas FAJARDO	POR	27/10/78	M	18		2
13	Ioannis KANOTIDIS		2/5/79	M	16	(3)	
21	Konstantinos KAPETANOS		27/10/84	M	5	(2)	
34	Vlassios KAZAKIS		17/6/83	A	26	(2)	1
15	Fotios KONSTANTINIDIS		25/7/78	M	2	(4)	
31	MANUEL Jesus LOPES	POR	19/8/82	M	13		1
5	MARCELO Rodrigues Alves "GOIANIRA"	BRA	6/8/80	M	24	(1)	
22	Spiridon MATENTZIDIS		23/7/90	D	11	(2)	
99	Marius MITU	ROU	10/9/76	M	1	(6)	1
88	Juan Manuel MUNAFO	ARG	20/3/88	M	1	(2)	
32	Alexis N'GAMBI	CMR	20/1/82	D	5	(1)	
10	Udochukwu NWOKO	MLT	15/10/84	A		(1)	
8	Egutu OLISEH	NGA	18/11/80	M	4	(5)	
11	Daniel ORAC	ROU	6/4/85	M	6		
16	PABLO CASAR Bustillo	ESP	17/9/78	D	2		
2	Theodoros PAPADOPOULOS		11/8/87	D	3	(3)	
25	Fotios PAPOULIS		22/1/85	A	11	(2)	3
39	Hristos PENTSAS		31/5/88	A		(2)	
15	Georgios PITHAROULIS		4/6/90	D	1	(3)	
15	Bertrand ROBERT	FRA	16/11/83	M	23	(2)	4
1	José Manuel ROCA Cases	ESP	28/2/76	G	20	(1)	
45	Zlatko RUNJE	CRO	10/2/79	G	1	(1)	
3	Eleftherios SAKELLARIOU		17/2/87	D	12	(4)	
20	Athanasios STOIKOS		28/1/88	M	1	(8)	
3	Dimitrios TAIRIS		3/12/89	G	5		
6	Emanuele TROISE	ITA	10/2/79	D	3		
24	Juan VELASCO Damas	ESP	15/5/77	D	4		
18	Spiridon VRONDARAS		11/12/84	G	4	(1)	

GREECE

PAOK FC

Coach – Fernando Santos (POR)
Founded – 1926
Stadium – Toumbas (31,060)
MAJOR HONOURS:
Greek League – (2) 1976, 1985;
Greek Cup – (4) 1972, 1974, 2001, 2003.

2009

30/8	Levadiakos	h	3-0	*Vieirinha, Filomeno,*
				Koutsianikoulis
13/9	Tripolis	a	1-1	*Fotakis*
20/9	Olympiacos	h	1-2	*Vieirinha*
23/9	Panionios	a	0-0	
27/9	Atromitos	a	0-0	
5/10	Iraklis	h	1-0	*Ivić*
17/10	Giannina	h	2-0	*Lino, Arabatzis*
25/10	Panathinaikos	a	1-2	*Vieirinha*
31/10	Xanthi	h	1-0	*Ivić*
7/11	Panthrakikos	a	2-1	*Vieirinha, Pablo García*
22/11	Aris	h	4-1	*Ivić (p), Muslimović 2, Vitolo (p)*
28/11	AEK	a	0-1	
5/12	Larissa	h	1-0	*Ivić (p)*
13/12	Kavala	a	0-0	
19/12	Ergotelis	a	2-0	*Arabatzis, Vieirinha*

2010

6/1	Panionios	h	1-0	*Ivić*
9/1	Levadiakos	a	2-0	*Ivić, Lino*
16/1	Tripolis	h	1-0	*Koutsianikoulis*
24/1	Olympiacos	a	1-0	*Edinho*
30/1	Atromitos	h	1-0	*Papazoglou*
7/2	Iraklis	a	1-1	*Muslimović*
13/2	Giannina	a	1-0	*Fotakis*
21/2	Panathinaikos	h	2-1	*Pablo García, Muslimović*
27/2	Xanthi	a	3-0	*Vieirinha 2, Ivić*
6/3	Panthrakikos	h	3-0	*Malezas, Sorlin, Lino*
14/3	Aris	a	0-2	
21/3	AEK	h	0-1	
28/3	Larissa	a	1-2	*Contreras*
11/4	Kavala	h	1-0	*Muslimović*
18/4	Ergotelis	h	4-1	*Sorlin, Muslimović, Cirillo,*
				Papazoglou

No	Name	Nat	DoB	Pos	Aps	(s)	Gls
28	Mohammed ABUBAKARI	GHA	15/2/86	M	1		
2	Nikolaos ARABATZIS		10/3/84	D	19	(1)	2
23	Joe Émerson BIZERA	URU	17/5/80	D	1		
1	Konstantinos CHALKIAS		30/5/74	G	28		
8	Bruno CIRILLO	ITA	21/3/77	D	17	(2)	1
15	Pablo CONTRERAS	CHI	11/9/78	D	15	(4)	1
80	CRISTIANO Morães de Oliveira	BRA	28/9/83	A	4	(4)	
9	Arnaldo Edi Lopes da Silva "EDINHO"	POR	7/7/82	A	5	(5)	1
31	Lucio Alejo FILOMENO	ARG	8/5/80	A	2	(7)	1
18	Georgios FOTAKIS		29/10/81	M	14	(7)	2
21	Vladimir IVIĆ	SRB	7/5/77	M	23	(3)	7
9	Vasilios KOUTSIANIKOULIS		9/8/88	M	8	(18)	2
91	Dario KREŠIĆ	CRO	11/1/84	G	2	(2)	
16	DorvaLINO Alves Maciel	BRA	1/7/77	D	28		3
13	Stilianos MALEZAS		11/3/85	D	21		1
3	Bryce MOON	RSA	6/4/86	D	1	(5)	
11	Zlatan MUSLIMOVIĆ	BIH	6/3/81	A	15	(4)	6
5	PABLO Gabriel GARCÍA Pérez	URU	11/5/77	M	24	(1)	2
14	Athanasios PAPAZOGLOU		30/3/88	A	8	(11)	2
36	Mirko SAVINI	ITA	11/3/79	D	8	(4)	
7	SÉRGIO Paulo Marceneiro CONCEIÇÃO	POR	15/11/74	M	4	(2)	
10	Olivier SORLIN	FRA	9/4/79	M	22	(2)	2
27	Mirosław SZNAUCNER	POL	9/5/79	D	11	(1)	
22	Ricardo Matías VERÓN	ARG	22/1/81	M		(1)	
20	Adelino André Vieira Freitas "VIEIRINHA"	POR	14/1/86	A	28		7
6	Víctor José Añino Bermúdez "VITOLO"	ESP	9/9/83	M	21		1

XANTHI FC

Coach – Wolfgang Wolf (GER); (15/9/09) (Panagiotis Goutsidis);
(21/9/09) Ioannis Matzourakis; (23/2/10) Nikolaos Kehagias
Founded – 1967
Stadium – Skoda Xanthi Arena (7,500)

2009

22/8	Giannina	h	1-1	*Marcelinho*
30/8	Panathinaikos	a	0-1	
13/9	Ergotelis	a	0-1	
20/9	Panthrakikos	h	1-0	*Štrba*
26/9	Aris	a	0-1	
5/10	AEK	h	1-0	*Poy*
18/10	Larissa	a	0-2	
25/10	Kavala	h	2-1	*Štrba, Vallas*
31/10	PAOK	a	0-1	
8/11	Panionios	h	1-2	*Zieńczuk*
21/11	Levadiakos	h	1-0	*Poy*
28/11	Tripolis	h	0-0	
5/12	Olympiacos	h	0-1	
13/12	Atromitos	a	0-1	
20/12	Iraklis	h	4-3	*Zieńczuk, Poy, Štrba, Luciano (p)*

2010

6/1	Giannina	a	0-0	
9/1	Panathinaikos	h	1-2	*Souanis*
16/1	Ergotelis	h	1-0	*Ellington*
24/1	Panthrakikos	a	1-1	*Štrba*
31/1	Aris	h	2-1	*Marcelinho, Ellington*
6/2	AEK	a	1-3	*Buga*
13/2	Larissa	h	0-1	
20/2	Kavala	a	1-2	*Poy*
27/2	PAOK	h	0-3	
7/3	Panionios	a	0-3	
14/3	Levadiakos	a	1-2	*Buga*
21/3	Tripolis	h	2-0	*Souanis, Buga*
28/3	Olympiacos	a	0-0	
11/4	Atromitos	h	2-1	*Quintana, Ellington*
18/4	Iraklis	a	4-2	*Bertos, Buga, Poy, Ellington (p)*

No	Name	Nat	DoB	Pos	Aps	(s)	Gls
85	Martin ABENA	CMR	14/6/86	M		(1)	
10	Odai ALSAIFY	JOR	26/4/86	A	5	(1)	
35	Emmanouil BERTOS		13/5/89	D	6		1
29	Mugurel Mihai BUGA	ROU	16/12/77	A	10	(2)	4
99	Nathan ELLINGTON	ENG	2/7/81	A	6	(4)	4
21	Konstantinos FLISKAS		22/12/80	D	20	(3)	
24	Michael GSPURNING	AUT	2/5/81	G	29		
15	Kim JAGGY	SUI	14/11/82	D	27	(1)	
28	Athanasios KOSTOULAS		24/3/76	D	28		
77	Mariusz KUKIEŁKA	POL	7/11/76	D	3	(1)	
6	Emmanouil LIAPAKIS		11/6/84	D		(1)	
33	Sotirios LIBEROPOULOS		29/6/77	G	1	(1)	
8	LUCIANO de Souza	BRA	21/8/72	M	9	(6)	1
20	Petros MANTALOS		31/8/91	M	1		
11	Marcelo Leite Pereira "MARCELINHO"	BRA	22/6/87	M	10	(9)	2
17	Marko MARIĆ	CRO	25/4/83	M		(3)	
32	Iván MORENO Y FABIANESI	ESP	4/6/79	M	5	(3)	
5	Ioannis PAPADIMITRIOU		15/5/76	D	24		
7	Mauro POY	ARG	7/2/81	A	28		5
9	Diego QUINTANA	ARG	24/4/78	M	23		1
14	Pantelis RIZOGIANNIS		1/2/88	D	1	(6)	
30	Dimitrios SOUANIS		17/11/85	A	6	(16)	2
30	Florin Cornel STÂNGĂ	ROU	22/6/78	M	10	(1)	
18	Stavros STATHAKIS		30/11/87	D	11	(5)	
66	Zdeno ŠTRBA	SVK	9/6/76	M	23	(4)	4
41	Peter ŠTYVAR	SVK	13/8/80	A		(4)	
4	Nabil TAÏDER	TUN	26/5/83	M	2	(3)	
4	Stavros TZIORTZOPOULOS		15/8/78	D	2	(3)	
12	Georgios VAKOUFTSIS		31/8/80	M	1	(2)	
25	Spiridon VALLAS		26/8/81	D	26		1
14	Theodoros VASILAKAKIS		20/7/88	M	2	(8)	
27	Marek ZIEŃCZUK	POL	24/9/78	M	11	(2)	2

PROMOTED CLUBS

OLYMPIACOS VOLOU FC
Coach – Athanasios Tsiolis
Founded – 1937
Stadium – Dimotiko Volou (9,000)

KERKYRA FC
Coach – Haralampos Tennes
Founded – 1967
Stadium – Ethniko Athlitiko Kentro (EAK) Kerkyras (2,685)

PANSERRAIKOS FC
oach – Guillermo Hoyos (ARG); (2/2/10) Dragan Kokotović (SRB)
Founded – 1964
Stadium – Dimotiko Serron (9,500)

SECOND LEVEL FINAL TABLE 2009/10

	Pld	W	D	L	F	A	Pts
Olympiacos Volou FC	34	21	5	8	73	36	68
Kerkyra FC	34	18	9	7	45	25	63
OFI Crete FC	34	18	8	8	44	35	62
Ethnikos Piraeus FC	34	14	11	9	43	30	53
Panserraikos FC	34	14	10	10	37	35	52
Pierikos FC	34	12	14	8	41	31	50
Panetolikos FC	34	13	11	10	43	36	50
Diagoras FC	34	14	6	14	43	42	48
GS Ilioupoli	34	12	10	12	33	35	46
Agrotikos Asteras FC	34	10	15	9	36	31	45
Ethnikos Asteras FC	34	12	9	13	39	37	45
Anagennisi Karditsas FC	34	10	14	10	29	28	44
Thrasivoulos Fylis FC	34	9	14	11	42	42	41
Doxa Dramas FC	34	10	10	14	37	49	40
Ionikos FC	34	10	9	15	32	45	39
Rodos FC	34	9	7	18	31	46	34
Kalamata FC	34	6	10	18	21	50	28
Ilisiakos FC/Egaleo FC	34	5	6	23	19	55	21

PROMOTION PLAY-OFF FINAL TABLE

	Pld	W	D	L	F	A	Pts
Panserraikos FC	6	4	1	1	9	3	14
OFI Crete FC	6	2	3	1	9	8	12
Ethnikos Piraeus FC	6	2	2	2	11	11	9
Pierikos FC	6	0	2	4	6	13	2

B Points carried forward from regular league - OFI 3 pts, Panserraikos
pt, Ethnikos 1 pt, Pierikos 0 pts.

DOMESTIC CUP 2009/10

KYPELLO ELLADOS

FORTH ROUND
(27/10/09)
Egaleo 0, Tripolis 3
Kalamata 0, Giannina 3
Panetolikos 0, Panionios 0 *(aet; 7-8 on pens)*
Panserraikos 3, Olympiacos 1
(28/10/09)
Agrotikos Asteras 0, Kavala 3
Aspropirgos 3, Aris 4
Eordaikos 0, Panathinaikos 3
Ethnikos Piraeus 1, Xanthi 2
Ionikos 1, Levadiakos 2
Kallithea 1, Panthrakikos 0
OFI 0, PAOK 1
Olympiacos Volou 2, Larissa 1
Pierikos 2, Ergotelis 2 *(aet; 4-2 on pens)*
Visaltiakos Nigritas 0, Atromitos 0 *(aet; 4-5 on pens)*
(29/10/09)
Thrasivoulos 1, AEK 0 *(aet)*
Trikala 1, Iraklis 0

FIFTH ROUND
(13/1/10)
Aris 2, Tripolis 0
Kallithea 1, Trikala 1 *(aet; 4-3 on pens)*
Levadiakos 0, Kavala 0 *(aet; 2-4 on pens)*
Panathinaikos 2, Pierikos 1
(20/1/10)
Atromitos 0, Giannina 1 *(aet)*
Panserraikos 0, PAOK 2
Thrasivoulos 0, Panionios 1
Xanthi 2, Olympiacos Volou 0

QUARTER-FINALS
(2/2/10)
Giannina 4 *(Dimbala 7, 81, Kousas 24, Sznaucner 43og)*, PAOK 0
Panathinaikos 2 *(Salpingidis 51, Arkoudas 88og)*, Kallithea 0
(10/2/10)
Xanthi 1 *(Stângâ 70)*, Aris 1 *(Neto 90+4)*
(11/2/10)
Kavala 0, Panionios 0

Replays
(17/2/10)
Aris 3 *(Cámpora 17, Adu 23, Koke 65)*, Xanthi 0
Panionios 1 *(Sito Riera 47)*, Kavala 2 *(Dobrasinović 83, Onwuachi 97)* *(aet)*

SEMI-FINALS
(17/3/10 & 25/3/10)
Aris 3 *(Koke 26p, 68, Javito 84)*, Kavala 1 *(Onwuachi 45)*
Kavala 1 *(Dié 57)*, Aris 1 *(Koke 44)*
(Aris 4-2)
(24/3/10 & 7/4/10)
Panathinaikos 3 *(Kotsios 13og, Ninis 44, Cissé 85)*, Giannina 1 *(Kousas 89)*
Giannina 0, Panathinaikos 0
(Panathinaikos 3-1)

FINAL
(24/4/10)
OACA Spyro Louis, Athens
PANATHINAIKOS FC 1 *(Leto 63)*
ARIS FC 0
Referee – Kakos
PANATHINAIKOS – Tzorvas, Vintra, Spiropoulos, Kanté, Katsouranis, Gilberto
Silva, Simão, Ninis *(Marinos 65)*, Leto *(Hristodoulopoulos 78)*, Salpingidis
(Karagounis 62), Cissé.
ARIS – Sifakis, Neto, Vangjeli, Nasuti, Ronaldo, Nafti *(Fernández 72)*, Prittas,
Meriem *(Javito 66)*, Toni Calvo *(Adu 83)*, Koke, Cámpora.

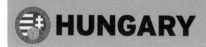

HUNGARY

Dominant Debrecen sweep the board

Debreceni VSC started the new decade as they finished the old one – as the pre-eminent force in Hungarian football. The 2009/10 season brought the club a first taste of UEFA Champions League football, and although living the European high life proved to be a somewhat deflating experience, András Herczeg's team responded to continental disappointment by making a clean sweep of the domestic trophies.

Jubilant Debrecen players look forward to the UEFA Champions League group stage after knocking out Levski Sofia

For the first time in 14 years Hungary had representation in the group stage of Europe's flagship club competition. Debrecen had to come through three qualifying ties to achieve that feat, but after the champions of Sweden, Estonia and Bulgaria had all been successfully slain, the latter with an impressive 4-1 aggregate victory in the play-off round, Hungary's finest found the challenge presented by three non-champions from Europe's elite leagues – Liverpool FC, Olympique Lyonnais and ACF Fiorentina – considerably more taxing. The dream of keeping such company turned into a nightmare as Debrecen lost all six matches, conceding a record-equalling tally of 19 goals in the process. Other than the revenue the club collected from sell-out crowds in Budapest's Ferenc Puskás stadium, the only consolation was that they scored as many goals in their six matches as Liverpool (five).

Fixture backlog

The extended European campaign left Debrecen having to play catch-up on the domestic front as they ran up a backlog of fixtures. It also had an adverse effect on their form, with three successive defeats in the league – to their principal NB I title rivals Videoton FC, Újpest FC and Győri ETO FC – temporarily upsetting their rhythm. By the winter break, however, they had hoisted themselves back up the table by winning each of their three games in hand and trailed leaders Videoton by just two points.

The second half of the season developed into a straight two-way title tussle between Videoton and Debrecen. The former, led by wily veteran coach

György Mezey, appeared to have the edge as they entered May – and a six-game run-in – with a two-point lead and the confidence gained from a series of 18 league games without defeat. But that run ended with a shock home loss to MTK Budapest and three days later, with the doubts starting to creep in, Videoton lost again – in the potential title-decider to Debrecen, 3-2, enabling the defending champions to go four points clear with three games left.

They thought it was all over…but it wasn't. Debrecen lost their next game 2-1 at Újpest and held a slender one-point lead going into their final fixture – away to lowly Kecskemét. Videoton had a much tougher engagement – away to a Győr side that boasted the best defence in the league and had not conceded a goal in their three previous clashes with the two title challengers – and never more than one in any game since the previous August. Sure enough, Attila Pintér's third-placed side proved difficult to break down once

again, but with that game goalless going into the final ten minutes and Debrecen unexpectedly 1-0 down against Kecskemét, a championship play-off beckoned. But then came the season's final dramatic twist as Győr's Serbian defender Lazar Stanišić scored to put his team 1-0 up. Videoton pressed hard thereafter but could not find a reply. The title – despite their defeat – thus belonged to Debrecen.

Entertaining win

It was not the way Debrecen would have wished to retain their crown. Indeed, with eight defeats and six points fewer than the previous season, it was hardly the most convincing of title defences, but the relief of the 'Loki' fans turned to wholehearted jubilation three days later when the club completed the double with an entertaining 3-2 victory over Janos Csánk's fifth-placed Zalaegerszegi TE in the final of the Hungarian Cup. Having also won the League Cup earlier in the season – 2-1 in the final against Paksi SE – Debrecen completed the set of major domestic trophies.

Two goals against ZTE from Debrecen's leading marksman, Adamo Coulibaly, paved the way for the club's second Cup win in three seasons – and fourth in all. The French striker was the pick of the team's foreign contingent, scoring steadily throughout a season in which Loki's leading man, Hungarian international striker Gergely Rudolf, was often unavailable through injury. Videoton, whose powerful young defender Gábor Horváth was voted the NB I Player of the Year, also possessed two reliable goalgetters in Brazilian André Alves and Serbian Nemanja Nikolić. The latter arrived in mid-season from Kaposvári Rákóczi FC, for whom he had scored ten goals in the autumn, and added another eight for Videoton to claim the NB I's Golden Boot, nudging ZTE's Latvian striker Artjoms Rudņevs – a scorer also in the Cup final – into second place.

The highest-placed Hungarian in the listings was Újpest's veteran skipper Péter Kabát, with 14 goals. Újpest finished fourth – the highest placed of the NB I's five Budapest clubs in what proved to be a thoroughly degrading season for the capital city, with not one of them qualifying for Europe. The return of Ferencváros, the country's most popular club, to the top flight was something of an anti-climax, with the man who brought them back up, Bobby Davison, losing his job after a poor start and being replaced by his compatriot Craig Short – another sharing the Sheffield United FC connections of Fradi's English owner Kevin McCabe.

Fall from grace

Budapest's fall from grace was echoed by that of the Hungarian national team, who endured an abject season, losing seven of their nine fixtures. Two home defeats in four days against Sweden and Portugal in September extinguished all hopes of 2010 FIFA World Cup qualification, which, had the results gone the other way, would have been an attainable target. Hungary closed that campaign by defeating group winners Denmark 1-0 in Copenhagen but in a sense the victory only rubbed salt into the team's World Cup wounds. It certainly didn't spark a revival because Hungary then lost three of their next four friendlies, culminating in a 6-1 thrashing by the Netherlands in Amsterdam – not a happy homecoming for coach Erwin Koeman, who was subsequently dismissed and replaced by Sándor Egervári. The 60-year-old, promoted from the Under-21s, will hope to draw improved performances in the UEFA EURO 2012 qualifiers from a decent group of players containing well-established foreign-based talents such as Balázs Dzsudzsák, Szabolcs Huszti, Roland Juhász and Fulham FC's 2009/10 UEFA Europa League hero Zoltán Gera.

Magyar Labdarúgó Szövetség (MLSZ)

Kőérberek Tóváros Kánai út 314/24 hrsz.
H-1112 Budapest
tel – +36 1 577 9500
fax – +36 1 577 9503
website – mlsz.hu
email – mlsz@mlsz.hu
Year of Formation – 1901

General Secretary – Géza Róka
Media Officer – László Pajor-Gyulai
National Stadium – Puskás Ferenc, Budapest (39,111)

INTERNATIONAL TOURNAMENT APPEARANCES
FIFA World Cup – (9) 1934 (2nd round), 1938 (runners-up), 1954 (runners-up), 1958, 1962 (qtr-finals), 1966 (qtr finals), 1978, 1982, 1986.
UEFA European Championship – (2)
1964 (3rd), 1972 (4th).
TOP FIVE ALL-TIME CAPS
József Bozsik (101); László Fazekas (92); Gyula Grosics (86); Ferenc Puskás (85); Imre Garaba (82)
TOP FIVE ALL-TIME GOALS
Ferenc Puskás (84); Sándor Kocsis (75); Imre Schlosser (59); Lajos Tichy (51); György Sárosi (42)

HUNGARY

NATIONAL TEAM RESULTS 2009/10

12/8/09	Romania	H	Budapest	0-1	
5/9/09	Sweden (WCQ)	H	Budapest	1-2	*Huszti (79p)*
9/9/09	Portugal (WCQ)	H	Budapest	0-1	
10/10/09	Portugal (WCQ)	A	Lisbon	0-3	
14/10/09	Denmark (WCQ)	A	Copenhagen	1-0	*Buzsáky (35)*
14/11/09	Belgium	A	Ghent	0-3	
3/3/10	Russia	H	Gyor	1-1	*Vanczák (39)*
29/5/10	Germany	H	Budapest	0-3	
5/6/10	Netherlands	A	Amsterdam	1-6	*Dzsudzsák (6)*

NATIONAL TEAM APPEARANCES 2009/10

Coach – Erwin KOEMAN (NED)	20/9/61		Rou	SWE	POR	POR	DEN	Bel	Rus	Ger	Ned	Caps	Goals
Gábor BABOS	24/10/74	NEC (NED)	G	G	G	G	G					27	-
Vilmos VANCZÁK	20/6/83	Sion (SUI)	D			D	D	D	D	D	D	47	1
Gábor GYEPES	26/6/81	Cardiff (WAL)	D74	D	D	D						26	1
Roland JUHÁSZ	1/7/83	Anderlecht (BEL)	D	D64	D	D	D	D	D	M71	D	53	5
Boldizsár BODOR	27/4/82	Roda (NED)	D83					s46	M62	D46	M	24	-
Pál DÁRDAI	16/3/76	Hertha (GER)	M76	M46	M65				s72			61	5
Péter HALMOSI	25/9/79	Hull (ENG)	M	D	D		D	D				30	-
Szabolcs HUSZTI	18/4/83	Zenit (RUS)	M46	A	M65	M67	s76		M89	M71	M68	49	7
Tamás HAJNAL	15/3/81	Dortmund (GER)	M	M85	s65				s62			34	4
Balázs DZSUDZSÁK	23/12/86	PSV (NED)	M46	M	M	M84	M89	A88		M	M	26	2
Sándor TORGHELLE	5/5/82	Augsburg (GER)	A78	s46	A	A	A	A	A	A62	A58	42	11
Zoltán GERA	22/4/79	Fulham (ENG)	s46	M		M						63	18
Gergely RUDOLF	9/3/85	Debrecen	s46				A87	A46	M79			11	1
Csaba FEHÉR	2/9/75	NAC (NED)	s74									41	-
Balázs TÓTH	24/9/81	Genk (BEL)	s76		M83	M	M	M64				33	-
Tamás PRISKIN	27/9/86	Ipswich (ENG)	s78		s65	s56	s89	s46		s71	A	26	7
Krisztián VADÓCZ	30/5/85	Osasuna (ESP)	s83	M	M	M56	s87	s88		M	s80	28	2
Zoltán SZÉLESI	22/11/81	Debrecen		D					M	s71	M	26	-
Krisztián TÍMÁR	4/10/79	Plymouth (ENG)		s64								4	-
Ákos BUZSÁKY	7/5/82	QPR (ENG)		s85	s83	s67	M76	M46	M46			19	2
László BODNÁR	25/2/79	Debrecen			D	D	D	D46	D	D86	D80	46	-
József VARGA	6/6/88	Debrecen					s84	M				2	-
Gábor KIRÁLY	1/4/76	1860 München (GER)						G46	G	G		73	-
György SÁNDOR	20/3/84	Újpest						M				4	-
Márton FÜLÖP	3/5/83	Sunderland (ENG)						s46			G	21	-
Gábor HORVÁTH	4/7/85	Videoton						s46	D72	D	D80	4	-
Dániel TŐZSÉR	12/5/85	Genk (BEL)						s64	s46	s46		18	1
Ádám SZALAI	9/12/87	Mainz (GER)							s79			2	-
Tamás KOLTAI	30/4/87	Győr							s89			2	-
Vladimir KOMAN	16/3/89	Bari (ITA)								M88		1	-
Krisztián NÉMETH	5/1/89	AEK (GRE)								s62		1	-
Zsolt LACZKÓ	18/12/86	Debrecen								s86	s80	2	-
János LÁZOK	4/10/84	MTK								s88	s68	2	-
Ákos ELEK	21/7/88	Videoton									s58	1	-

DOMESTIC LEAGUE 2009/10

NB I FINAL TABLE

	Pld	Home					Away					Total					Pts
		W	D	L	F	A	W	D	L	F	A	W	D	L	F	A	
1 Debreceni VSC	30	13	1	1	37	14	7	1	7	26	23	20	2	8	63	37	62
2 Videoton FC	30	10	3	2	27	8	8	4	3	32	23	18	7	5	59	31	61
3 Győri ETO FC	30	9	6	0	22	9	6	6	3	16	9	15	12	3	38	18	57
4 Újpest FC	30	11	0	4	28	20	6	4	5	21	19	17	4	9	49	39	55
5 Zalaegerszegi TE	30	9	3	3	34	22	6	5	4	25	23	15	8	7	59	45	53
6 MTK Budapest	30	5	6	4	27	17	7	1	7	25	24	12	7	11	52	41	43
7 Ferencvárosi TC	30	7	6	2	19	13	3	5	7	15	22	10	11	9	34	35	41
8 Szombathelyi Haladás	30	7	4	4	28	22	3	5	7	18	27	10	9	11	46	49	39
9 Budapest Honvéd FC	30	4	7	4	21	17	5	4	6	17	18	9	11	10	38	35	38
10 Kecskeméti TE	30	6	6	3	33	28	4	1	10	17	28	10	7	13	50	56	37
11 Lombard-Pápa FC	30	8	0	7	22	20	2	5	8	17	30	10	5	15	39	50	35
12 Kaposvári Rákóczi FC	30	6	6	3	24	19	2	2	11	14	31	8	8	14	38	50	32
13 Vasas SC	30	5	3	7	23	26	3	4	8	16	35	8	7	15	39	61	31
14 Paksi SE	30	7	3	5	19	16	0	7	8	12	28	7	10	13	31	44	31
15 Nyíregyháza Spartacus FC	30	4	5	6	26	29	2	4	9	15	31	6	9	15	41	60	27
16 Diósgyőri VTK	30	3	2	10	15	22	1	3	11	16	34	4	5	21	31	56	17

TOP GOALSCORERS

18 Nemanja NIKOLIĆ (Kaposvár/Videoton)

16 Artjoms RUDŅEVS (ZTE)

15 ANDRÉ ALVES (Videoton)

14 Adamo COULIBALY (Debrecen)
Péter KABÁT (Újpest)

13 Tibor MONTVAI (Kecskemét)
János LÁZOK (Vasas/MTK)
Darko PAVIĆEVIĆ (ZTE)

12 Tarmo KINK (Győr)

11 Csaba CSORDÁS (Kecskemét)
Attila TÖKÖLI (Paks)

CLUB-BY-CLUB

BUDAPEST HONVÉD FC

Coach – Tibor Sisa; (27/10/09) Massimo Morales (ITA)
Founded – 1909
Stadium – Bozsik József (13,500)
MAJOR HONOURS:
Hungarian League – (13) 1950, 1950 (autumn), 1952, 1954, 1955, 1980,
1984, 1985, 1986, 1988, 1991, 1993;
Hungarian Cup – (7) 1926, 1964, 1985, 1989, 1996, 2007, 2009.

2009

25/7	Kaposvár	h	3-1	Hajdu, Abraham, Hrepka
2/8	MTK	a	1-2	Hajdu
15/8	Videoton	a	0-2	
23/8	Újpest	h	1-1	Hrepka
30/8	Győr	a	0-2	
12/9	Kecskemét	h	0-1	
19/9	Diósgyőr	a	2-1	Hrepka, Macko (p)
26/9	Pápa	h	1-3	Hajdu
2/10	Vasas	h	3-3	Cséke, Bajner, Hrepka
17/10	Haladás	a	2-2	Botiş, Hrepka
23/10	ZTE	h	0-1	
31/10	Nyíregyháza	a	1-0	Nagy
7/11	Paks	h	1-1	Palásthy
13/11	Ferencváros	a	0-0	
20/11	Debrecen	h	1-2	Abraham

2010

27/2	Kaposvár	a	0-1	
6/3	MTK	h	4-1	Abass, Botiş, Vaccaro, Pablo Coira
13/3	Debrecen	a	1-2	Abraham
20/3	Videoton	h	0-0	
27/3	Újpest	a	1-0	Diego
3/4	Győr	h	0-0	
10/4	Kecskemét	a	2-2	Botiş, Hrepka
17/4	Diósgyőr	h	4-2	Abraham, Bajner, Diego 2 (1p)
24/4	Pápa	a	3-0	Abraham, Diego, Bajner
1/5	Vasas	a	2-2	Fernando, Hajdu
5/5	Haladás	h	0-0	
8/5	ZTE	a	1-0	og (Panikvar)
15/5	Nyíregyháza	h	1-1	Fernando
19/5	Paks	a	1-2	Vaccaro (p)
22/5	Ferencváros	h	2-0	Pablo Coira, Vaccaro

No	Name	Nat	DoB	Pos	Aps	(s)	Gls
17	Dieng Cheikh ABASS	SEN	1/1/85	A	13	(9)	1
18	Guie Gneki ABRAHAM	CIV	25/7/86	A	22	(5)	5
15	Jean-Baptiste AKASSOU Akra	CIV	5/11/85	M	10	(1)	
99	Bálint BAJNER		18/11/90	A	9	(4)	3
5	Angoua Brou BENJAMIN	CIV	28/11/86	D	13		
85	László BOJTOR		17/9/85	A	2	(2)	
6	Sorin BOTIŞ	ROU	14/4/78	D	22	(1)	3
4	György CSÉKE		7/4/83	D	2	(1)	1
14	András DEBRECENI		21/4/89	D	17		
19	DIEGO Rigonato Rodrigues	BRA	9/3/88	M	20		4
2	Géza FAZAKAS		18/1/90	D		(1)	
20	FERNANDO Cuerda Peña	ESP	6/3/84	D	5	(1)	2
15	Attila FRITZ		17/7/86	M	1		
21	Gergő GOHÉR		16/6/87	D	1		
27	GUILHERME Rodrigues Moreira	BRA	11/4/87	A	7	(9)	
8	Norbert HAJDU		1/10/82	M	25	(1)	4
26	Patrik HIDI		27/11/90	M	5	(3)	
24	Adrián HORVÁTH		20/11/87	M	8	(7)	
13	Ádám HREPKA		15/4/87	A	13		6
71	Szabolcs KEMENES		18/5/86	G	1		
9	Viliam MACKO	SVK	22/10/81	M	19		1
22	Zoltán NAGY		25/10/85	D	17	(3)	1
33	Gábor NÉMETH		21/5/75	G	22	(6)	
28	PABLO COIRA Lojo	ESP	18/10/79	M	9	(3)	2
3	Norbert PALÁSTHY		10/2/81	A	7	(8)	1
16	Milan PASTVA	SVK	1/7/80	D	4		
29	Ákos TAKÁCS		14/2/82	M	19		
22	Gary TAVARS	FRA	15/7/84	D	1		

HUNGARY

1	Iván TÓTH		22/3/71	G	7	(2)	
23	Angelo VACCARO	ITA	4/10/81	A	1	(5)	3
7	Roland VÖLENT		23/9/92	A		(2)	
55	Dragan VUKMIR	SRB	2/8/78	D	16	(4)	
5	Pavlo YANCHUK	UKR	12/7/86	D	5	(1)	
11	Róbert ZSOLNAI		11/4/82	A	7	(6)	

DEBRECENI VSC

Coach – András Herczeg
Founded – 1902
Stadium – Oláh Gábor utcai (11,500)
MAJOR HONOURS:
Hungarian League – (5) 2005, 2006, 2007, 2009, 2010;
Hungarian Cup – (4) 1999, 2001, 2008, 2010.

2009

25/7	Diósgyőr	a	0-1	
1/8	Pápa	h	2-0	Oláh, Coulibaly
14/8	Haladás	h	2-1	Leandro, Czvitkovics
29/8	Nyíregyháza	h	3-1	Rudolf 2, Coulibaly
11/9	Paks	a	1-0	Szakály
20/9	Ferencváros	h	2-1	Szakály, Coulibaly
25/9	Kaposvár	a	4-4	Czvitkovics 2 (1p), Szakály, Rezes
16/10	Vasas	a	4-2	Coulibaly 2, Kiss, Leandro
25/10	Videoton	a	0-3	
30/10	Újpest	h	1-2	Rudolf (p)
8/11	Győr	a	0-1	
17/11	Kecskemét	h	1-0	Czvitkovics
20/11	Honvéd	a	2-1	Leandro, Rudolf
29/11	ZTE	h	5-3	Varga, Oláh, Szakály, Komlósi, Coulibaly
3/12	MTK	h	2-0	Coulibaly, Szakály

2010

26/2	Diósgyőr	h	3-1	Laczkó, Rudolf, Mijadinoski
7/3	Pápa	a	5-1	Rudolf, og (Tóth), Mijadinoski, Szakály, Coulibaly
13/3	Honvéd	h	2-1	Feczesin, Coulibaly
19/3	Haladás	a	2-0	Czvitkovics, Feczesin
27/3	ZTE	a	1-4	Coulibaly
10/4	Paks	h	3-1	Coulibaly 2, Feczesin (p)
16/4	Ferencváros	a	0-1	
20/4	Nyíregyháza	a	3-0	Mijadinoski, Feczesin, Coulibaly (p)
23/4	Kaposvár	h	5-1	Czvitkovics, Feczesin, Rudolf, Mészáros, Coulibaly
1/5	MTK	a	3-2	Feczesin 2, Czvitkovics
4/5	Vasas	h	3-0	Yannick 2, Czvitkovics
7/5	Videoton	h	3-2	Szakály, Czvitkovics, Coulibaly
15/5	Újpest	a	1-2	Feczesin
19/5	Győr	h	0-0	
23/5	Kecskemét	a	0-1	

No	Name	Nat	DoB	Pos	Aps	(s)	Gls
22	Csaba BERNÁTH		26/3/79	D	10	(1)	
27	Ádám BÓDI		18/10/90	M	1		
10	László BODNÁR		25/2/79	D	15		
39	Adamo COULIBALY	FRA	14/8/81	A	21	(9)	14
60	Károly CZANÍK	SVK	13/9/84	M	1		
77	Péter CZVITKOVICS		10/2/83	M	26	(2)	10
7	Tibor DOMBI		11/11/73	M	1	(19)	
99	MacPherlin DUDU Omagbeni	NGA	18/7/85	A	4	(1)	
46	Awoundza Etogo ESSEMA	CMR	9/10/88	A		(1)	
11	Róbert FECZESIN		22/2/86	A	13	(3)	8
21	Marcell FODOR		27/10/87	D	14	(1)	
88	Tamás HUSZÁK		2/10/88	M	1		
81	Attila KATONA		16/6/81	D	2	(2)	
30	Zoltán KISS		18/8/80	M	13	(4)	1
16	Ádám KOMLÓSI		6/12/77	D	13	(1)	1
69	Mihály KORHUT		1/12/88	D	2		
86	Zsolt LACZKÓ		18/12/86	M	19	(4)	1
4	LEANDRO de Almeida		19/3/82	M	11	(2)	3
18	Péter MÁTÉ		2/12/84	D	1		
17	Norbert MÉSZÁROS		19/8/80	D	17		1
24	Mirsad MIJADINOSKI	MKD	1/10/81	D	11	(1)	3
5	Dávid MOHL		28/4/85	D	1		
28	Zoltán NAGY		25/10/85	D	2		

41	Lóránt OLÁH		23/11/79	A	8	(1)	2
12	Đorđe PANTIĆ	SRB	27/1/80	G	7		
1	Vukašin POLEKSIĆ	MNE	30/8/82	G	20	(1)	
6	Luis Arcangel RAMOS	HON	11/4/85	M	10	(4)	
15	László REZES		12/8/87	M	4	(6)	1
14	Gergely RUDOLF		9/3/85	A	11	(2)	7
69	Mihály SPITZMÜLLER		14/5/86	M	1		
55	Péter SZAKÁLY		17/8/86	M	21	(5)	7
25	Zoltán SZÉLESI		22/11/81	D	14	(3)	
23	Péter SZILÁGYI		26/1/88	A		(3)	
2	István SZŰCS		3/5/85	D	4	(1)	
33	József VARGA		6/6/88	M	18	(1)	1
87	István VERPECZ		4/2/87	G	3		
19	VINÍCIUS Galvão Leal	BRA	12/8/89	A	1	(5)	
20	Mbengono Ondoa YANNICK	CMR	11/6/87	A	9	(4)	2

DIÓSGYŐRI VTK

Coach – Zoltán Aczél; (1/1/10) Barnabás Tornyi;
(7/4/10) László Tóth
Founded – 1910
Stadium – Borsodi (12,000)
MAJOR HONOURS:
Hungarian Cup – (2) 1977, 1980.

2009

25/7	Debrecen	h	1-0	Lippai
1/8	Videoton	a	2-3	Lippai, Horváth
9/8	Újpest	h	1-2	Balajti
15/8	Győr	a	1-3	Balajti
22/8	Kecskemét	h	4-1	Balajti 2, Miličić, Szabó
29/8	Vasas	h	0-1	
12/9	Pápa	a	1-2	Ivancsics
19/9	Honvéd	h	1-2	Miličić
26/9	Haladás	a	1-2	Lipusz
3/10	ZTE	h	1-1	Ivancsics (p)
17/10	Nyíregyháza	a	1-1	Ivancsics (p)
24/10	Paks	h	0-0	
31/10	Ferencváros	a	3-0	(w/o; abandoned at 3-1 Huszák, Jeknić, Lippai)
7/11	Kaposvár	h	1-3	Huszák
21/11	MTK	a	0-4	

2010

26/2	Debrecen	a	1-3	Bognár
6/3	Videoton	h	0-1	
14/3	Újpest	a	1-4	Menougong
20/3	Győr	a	0-1	
27/3	Kecskemét	a	1-1	Balajti
3/4	Vasas	a	0-1	
10/4	Pápa	h	3-0	Lippai, Brnović, Burány
17/4	Honvéd	a	2-4	Bajzát 2
25/4	Haladás	h	1-3	Menougong
2/5	ZTE	a	0-3	
5/5	Nyíregyháza	h	0-1	
8/5	Paks	a	0-1	
15/5	Ferencváros	h	0-1	
20/5	Kaposvár	a	2-2	Somorjai, Lippai
23/5	MTK	h	2-5	Gal, Somorjai

No	Name	Nat	DoB	Pos	Aps	(s)	Gls
82	Radu Bogdan APOSTU	ROU	20/4/82	A	2	(3)	
92	Patrik BACSA		3/6/92	A	2	(2)	
22	Péter BAJZÁT		22/6/81	A	9	(1)	2
91	Ádám BALAJTI		7/3/91	A	18	(4)	5
2	Gyula BIHARI		17/5/91	D		(1)	
13	Zsolt BOGNÁR		28/3/79	D	13		1
59	Károly BOGYÓ		18/2/90	A		(2)	
17	Tibor BOKROS		28/8/89	D		(2)	
11	Bojan BRNOVIĆ	MNE	10/2/79	A	9		1
15	Zoltán BURÁNY		26/7/89	M	21	(1)	1
99	Attila DOBOS		24/11/78	M	5	(6)	
11	Milán FAGGYAS		1/6/89	A		(3)	
5	Igor GAL	CRO	20/1/83	D	13		1
25	Tamás GIÁK		2/4/90	G	1		
9	Gergő GÓHÉR		16/6/87	D	11		
23	Gábor HORVÁTH		10/7/83	D	9	(1)	1

HUNGARY

No	Name	Nat	DoB	Pos	Aps	(s)	Gls
8	Tamás HUSZÁK		2/10/88	M	9	(5)	2
22	Richárd ILLÉS		15/2/91	M		(1)	
20	Gellért IVANCSICS		23/2/87	M	11		3
2	Vlado JEKNIĆ	MNE	14/8/83	D	11	(1)	1
5	Norbert KÁLLAI		6/3/84	D	4	(1)	
7	Bence KOVÁCS		23/8/91	M		(1)	
19	Szilárd KOVÁCS		25/6/91	A	1	(1)	
29	Zoltán KOVÁCS		29/10/84	G	9		
1	László KÖTELES		1/9/84	G	4		
7	Béla LAKATOS		26/9/84	M	11		
79	Ákos LIPPAI		13/6/79	M	22	(2)	5
19	Norbert LIPUSZ		23/4/86	M	11	(2)	1
27	Mindaugas MALINAUSKAS	LTU	11/8/83	G	10		
21	George MENOUGONG	CMR	18/5/85	M	4	(4)	2
4	Boris MILIČIĆ	SRB	4/4/79	D	11	(2)	2
77	Róbert NAGY		26/11/87	M		(8)	
58	Gábor POLÉNYI		2/7/91	D	4		
1	Ivan RADOS	CRO	21/2/84	G	4		
4	Rohan RICKETTS	ENG	22/12/82	M		(1)	
9	Róbert ROSZEL		30/1/83	M	8	(1)	
17	Haman SADJO	CMR	28/11/84	D	5	(6)	
22	Bence SOMODI		25/11/88	G	2		
28	Tamás SOMORJAI		12/1/80	M	4	(3)	2
26	Zoran ŠUPIĆ	SRB	21/7/84	D	12	(3)	
14	Viktor SZABÓ		23/7/86	A	6	(7)	1
10	Péter TAKÁCS		25/1/90	M	18	(4)	
12	Despot VISKOVIĆ	SRB	3/3/80	D	6	(1)	
88	Dejan VUKADINOVIĆ	SRB	3/9/82	D	21		
7	Bence ZÁMBÓ		17/8/89	D	5	(4)	
20	Norbert ZSIVÓCZKY		16/2/88	M	4	(4)	

FERENCVÁROSI TC
Coach – Bobby Davison (ENG); (29/10/09) Craig Short (ENG)
Founded – 1899
Stadium – Albert Flórián (18,100)
MAJOR HONOURS:
Inter Cities Fairs Cup - (1) 1965;
Hungarian League - (28) 1903, 1905, 1907, 1909, 1910, 1911, 1912, 1913, 1926, 1927, 1928, 1932, 1934, 1938, 1940, 1941, 1949, 1963, 1964, 1967, 1968, 1976, 1981, 1992, 1995, 1996, 2001, 2004;
Hungarian Cup - (20) 1913, 1922, 1927, 1928, 1933, 1935, 1942, 1943, 1944, 1958, 1972, 1974, 1976, 1978, 1991, 1993, 1994, 1995, 2003, 2004.

2009
1/8	ZTE	h	4-1	Shaw, Dragóner, Pölöskey 2
7/8	Nyíregyháza	a	1-3	Wedgbury
15/8	Paks	h	1-1	Ashmore
21/8	Vasas	a	2-3	Rósa, Joaquín
26/8	Haladás	a	0-0	
29/8	Kaposvár	a	0-0	
13/9	MTK	h	1-2	Ferenczi, Rósa
20/9	Debrecen	a	1-2	Ferenczi
25/9	Videoton	h	2-2	Ferenczi, Wolfe
3/10	Újpest	a	1-2	Fitos
24/10	Kecskemét	a	1-3	Ferenczi
31/10	Diósgyőr	h	0-3	(w/o; abandoned at 1-3 Tóth)
4/11	Győr	h	1-0	Ferenczi
7/11	Pápa	a	1-0	Wolfe
13/11	Honvéd	h	0-0	

2010
27/2	Haladás	h	2-1	Ferenczi (p), Elding
6/3	ZTE	a	3-3	Elding 2, og (Todorović)
12/3	Nyíregyháza	h	0-0	
20/3	Paks	a	2-1	Elding, Ferenczi
28/3	Vasas	h	1-1	Elding
3/4	Kaposvár	h	0-0	
10/4	MTK	a	1-1	Elding
16/4	Debrecen	h	1-0	Tóth
24/4	Videoton	a	0-0	
30/4	Újpest	h	0-1	
4/5	Győr	a	1-2	Abdi
8/5	Kecskemét	h	3-2	Ferenczi (p), Elding, Morrison
15/5	Diósgyőr	a	1-0	Tutorić
18/5	Pápa	h	2-0	Elding, Gárdos
22/5	Honvéd	a	0-2	

No	Name	Nat	DoB	Pos	Aps	(s)	Gls
19	Liban ABDI	SOM	5/10/88	A	7	(3)	1
7	Adnan AHMED	PAK	7/6/84	M	12	(2)	
3	Carlos ALCÁNTARA	ESP	1/2/85	D	8		
8	James ASHMORE	ENG	2/3/86	M	10	(3)	1
78	Zoltán BALOG		22/2/78	D	21	(2)	
85	Csaba CSIZMADIA		30/5/85	D	14		
14	Thomas DOHERTY	ENG	17/3/79	M	11		
26	Attila DRAGÓNER		15/11/74	D	15		1
9	Anthony ELDING	ENG	16/4/82	A	15		8
13	István FERENCZI		14/9/77	A	29		8
87	László FITOS		27/2/87	M	3	(7)	1
29	Noel FÜLÖP		29/1/88	D	3		
38	András GÁRDOS		9/1/91	M		(1)	1
23	Justin HABER	MLT	9/6/81	G	2		
16	Ádám HOLCZER		28/3/88	G	4		
5	JOAQUÍN Pastor Martínez	ESP	26/10/87	D	6	(3)	1
88	Dávid KULCSÁR		25/2/88	M	18	(4)	
6	Péter LIPCSEI		28/3/72	M	12	(13)	
14	Matthew LOWTON	ENG	9/6/89	D	4	(1)	
11	Bojan MAMIĆ	SRB	13/9/81	A	0	(4)	
42	Balázs MEGYERI		31/3/90	G	24		
25	Jason MORRISON	JAM	7/6/84	M	23	(1)	1
36	Igor PISANJUK	CAN	28/10/89	A		(3)	
60	Péter PÖLÖSKEY		11/8/88	A	1	(3)	2
20	Dénes RÓSA		7/4/77	M	16	(8)	2
27	André SCHEMBRI	MLT	27/5/86	M	4	(5)	
10	Paul SHAW	ENG	4/9/73	A	6	(4)	1
32	Sam STOCKLEY	ENG	5/9/77	D	14	(1)	
30	Bence TÓTH		27/7/89	M	12	(3)	2
15	Đorđe TUTORIĆ	SRB	5/3/83	D	13		1
17	Sam WEDGBURY	ENG	26/2/89	M	6		1
39	Rafe WOLFE	JAM	19/12/85	D	17	(3)	2

GYŐRI ETO FC
Coach – Attila Pintér
Founded – 1904
Stadium – ETO Park (16,000)
MAJOR HONOURS:
Hungarian League – (3) 1963 (autumn), 1982, 1983;
Hungarian Cup – (4) 1965, 1966, 1967, 1979.

2009
26/7	Újpest	h	0-0	
31/7	Vasas	a	2-0	Józsi, Kink
8/8	Kecskemét	a	0-2	
15/8	Diósgyőr	h	3-1	Brnović, Kink, Copa
22/8	Pápa	a	0-1	
30/8	Honvéd	h	2-0	Kink, Đorđević
12/9	Haladás	a	2-1	Nicorec, Józsi
18/9	ZTE	h	1-1	Babić
26/9	Nyíregyháza	a	3-1	Kink 2, Aleksidze
3/10	Paks	h	3-1	Nicorec, Kink, Józsi (p)
24/10	Kaposvár	h	1-1	Aleksidze
31/10	MTK	a	0-0	
4/11	Ferencváros	a	0-1	
8/11	Debrecen	h	1-0	Pilibaitis
21/11	Videoton	a	0-0	

2010
27/2	Újpest	a	3-0	Koltai 2, Aleksidze
6/3	Vasas	h	1-1	Nicorec (p)
13/3	Kecskemét	h	1-0	Aleksidze
20/3	Diósgyőr	a	1-0	Józsi (p)
27/3	Pápa	h	1-1	Kink
3/4	Honvéd	a	0-0	
10/4	Haladás	h	1-1	Józsi (p)
18/4	ZTE	a	1-1	Koltai
24/4	Nyíregyháza	h	2-1	Kink 2
1/5	Paks	a	1-1	Nicorec
4/5	Ferencváros	h	1-2	Tokody, Kink
8/5	Kaposvár	a	3-1	Nicorec, Kink 2
15/5	MTK	h	2-0	Józsi, Koltai
19/5	Debrecen	a	0-0	
23/5	Videoton	h	1-0	Stanišić

HUNGARY

No	Name	Nat	DoB	Pos	Aps	(s)	Gls
7	Eldin ADILOVIĆ	BIH	8/2/86	A		(5)	
10	Rati ALEKSIDZE	GEO	3/8/78	A	25		4
22	Valentin BABIĆ	CRO	6/7/81	D	18	(1)	1
19	Péter BAJZÁT		22/6/81	A		(1)	
49	István BERDE		24/12/88	M		(2)	
12	Mário BICÁK	SVK	21/10/79	M	3	(2)	
11	Bojan BRNOVIĆ	MNE	10/2/79	A	1	(11)	1
33	Arsène COPA	GAB	7/6/88	A	3	(8)	1
5	Marko DINJAR	CRO	21/5/86	M	4	(11)	
28	Vladimir ĐORĐEVIĆ	SRB	25/12/82	D	15	(1)	1
7	Ádám DUDÁS		12/2/89	M	6	(2)	
32	Chemcedine EL ARACHI	BEL	18/5/81	D		(1)	
6	Zoltán FEHÉR		12/6/81	D	23	(2)	
2	Eugène FOMUMBOD	CMR	22/2/85	M	14		
30	Giorgi GANUGRAVA	GEO	21/2/88	M		(4)	
8	György JÓZSI		31/1/83	M	27		6
16	Tarmo KINK	EST	6/10/85	A	27	(1)	12
35	Máté KISS		30/4/91	M	6	(3)	
29	Tamás KOLTAI		30/4/87	M	15	(9)	4
31	Péter MOLNÁR	SVK	14/12/83	G	1		
1	NICOLAS Ceolin	BRA	10/4/86	A		(5)	
20	Onişor Mihai NICOREC	ROU	28/3/86	A	18	(5)	5
14	Vakhtang PANTSKHAVA	GEO	8/10/89	A	1	(4)	
17	Linas PILIBAITIS	LTU	5/6/85	M	26	(1)	1
24	András SÁNTA		6/4/85	G	1		
25	Teimuraz SHARASHENIDZE	GEO	21/1/92	A		(1)	
4	Lazar STANIŠIĆ	SRB	21/7/82	D	16	(1)	1
1	Saša STEVANOVIĆ	SRB	4/8/74	G	28		
9	Ottó SZABÓ	SVK	1/3/81	M	27		
23	Tibor TOKODY		1/9/80	M	20	(5)	1
15	Lasha TOTADZE	GEO	24/8/88	D		(1)	
14	Dániel VÖLGYI		7/6/87	M	5	(1)	
5	István BANK		14/4/84	M	9		1
25	Gábor BOGDÁN		30/8/80	D	5	(4)	
4	Lukács BÖLE		27/3/90	M	1	(8)	
11	Danijel CULUM	BIH	19/8/89	A	1	(6)	
3	Gabriele FABRIS	ITA	28/4/88	D		(1)	
9	Krisztián FARKAS		15/4/79	A	5	(2)	1
20	Zoltán FARKAS		7/10/89	M	5	(6)	
9	Ukwoma Egejuru GODSLOVE	NGA	4/12/86	A	8	(3)	
21	Károly GRASZL		8/1/85	D		(1)	
26	Tamás GRÚZ		8/11/85	D	23		
7	Boris GUJIĆ	BIH	9/7/86	D	27	(1)	2
24	Dávid HEGEDŰS		6/6/85	M	1	(5)	
22	Zoltán JOVÁNCZAI		8/12/84	A	2	(2)	
6	Róbert KOVÁCSEVICS		19/3/79	D	8	(1)	
8	Kornél KULCSÁR		11/11/91	M	2	(10)	
11	Igor LAMBULIĆ	MNE	21/8/88	A		(1)	
21	Slobodan MARKOVIĆ	SRB	4/12/87	D		(2)	
27	Béla MARÓTI		7/5/79	M	23	(3)	6
32	Árpád MILINTE		4/5/76	G	30		
10	Nemanja NIKOLIĆ	SRB	31/12/87	A	15		10
14	Lóránt OLÁH		23/11/79	A	15		3
9	Krisztián PEST		7/5/75	M	15	(5)	
17	Viktor PETRÓK		3/4/81	D	27		1
3	László PINTÉR		6/12/83	D	1		
16	Gábor RESZLI		20/1/88	A	5	(8)	2
30	Srđan STANIĆ	SRB	7/6/82	M	23	(2)	2
14	Róbert SZEPESSY		12/8/85	A	7	(3)	2
28	Krisztián ZAHORECZ		28/10/75	D	29		8

KAPOSVÁRI RÁKÓCZI FC

Coach – László Prukner
Founded – 1923
Stadium – Városi (7,000)

2009

25/7	Honvéd	a	1-3	Farkas K.
2/8	Haladás	h	3-0	Petrók, Reszli, Zahorecz
8/8	ZTE	a	3-0	Zahorecz 3 (1p)
15/8	Nyíregyháza	h	1-1	Nikolić
22/8	Paks	a	0-2	
29/8	Ferencváros	h	0-0	
12/9	Vasas	a	0-1	
19/9	MTK	a	0-4	
25/9	Debrecen	h	4-4	Bank, Nikolić, Zahorecz (p), Reszli
3/10	Videoton	a	0-2	
17/10	Újpest	h	2-0	Nikolić 2
24/10	Győr	a	1-1	Nikolić
31/10	Kecskemét	h	2-1	Maróti 2
7/11	Diósgyőr	a	3-1	Nikolić 3
22/11	Pápa	h	3-1	Nikolić 2, Maróti

2010

27/2	Honvéd	h	1-0	Oláh
5/3	Haladás	a	1-2	Stanić
13/3	ZTE	h	1-1	Gujić
20/3	Nyíregyháza	a	1-2	Gujić
27/3	Paks	h	1-1	Zahorecz (p)
3/4	Ferencváros	a	0-0	
10/4	Vasas	h	1-0	Oláh
17/4	MTK	h	1-2	Maróti
23/4	Debrecen	a	1-5	Maróti
1/5	Videoton	h	1-3	Zahorecz (p)
5/5	Újpest	a	1-2	Zahorecz (p)
8/5	Győr	h	1-3	Stanić
17/5	Kecskemét	a	1-3	Szepessy
20/5	Diósgyőr	h	2-2	Oláh, Szepessy
23/5	Pápa	a	1-3	Maróti

No	Name	Nat	DoB	Pos	Aps	(s)	Gls
13	AÍLTON José Pereira Junior	BRA	23/7/87	A	25	(1)	
15	Dragan ANTANASIJEVIĆ	SRB	10/6/87	M	1	(4)	
18	Benjámin BALÁZS		26/4/90	M	17	(7)	

KECSKEMÉTI TE

Coach – Tomislav Sivić (SRB); (28/10/09) László Czéh; (22/11/09) Aurél Csertői; (8/4/10) István Urbányi
Founded – 1911
Stadium – Széktói (6,500)

2009

25/7	Videoton	h	3-6	Litsingi, Gyagya, Yannick
2/8	Újpest	a	1-3	Yannick
8/8	Győr	h	2-0	Csordás, Rakić
15/8	Vasas	h	5-1	Csordás, Alempijević, Yannick, Montvai 2
22/8	Diósgyőr	a	1-4	Csordás
29/8	Pápa	a	0-2	
12/9	Honvéd	a	1-0	Savić
19/9	Haladás	h	3-3	Csordás, Yannick, Bertus
26/9	ZTE	a	2-3	Csordás, Koller
4/10	Nyíregyháza	h	2-2	Montvai, Csordás
17/10	Paks	h	1-2	Montvai
24/10	Ferencváros	h	3-1	Litsingi 2, Montvai
31/10	Kaposvár	a	1-2	Montvai
7/11	MTK	a	2-5	Némedi 2 (2p)
17/11	Debrecen	a	0-1	

2010

27/2	Videoton	a	0-2	
6/3	Újpest	h	2-1	Montvai, Simon (p)
13/3	Győr	a	0-1	
20/3	Vasas	a	1-0	Simon
27/3	Diósgyőr	h	1-1	Čukić
3/4	Pápa	h	2-2	Montvai, Csordás
10/4	Honvéd	h	2-2	Montvai, Némedi (p)
17/4	Haladás	h	2-3	Farkas, Némedi
24/4	ZTE	h	2-2	Montvai, Csordás
1/5	Nyíregyháza	a	3-2	Farkas, Montvai, Čukić
5/5	Paks	h	1-1	Némedi (p)
8/5	Ferencváros	a	2-3	Montvai, Csordás
17/5	Kaposvár	h	3-1	Litsingi, Csordás, Montvai
20/5	MTK	a	1-0	Némedi
23/5	Debrecen	h	1-0	Csordás

No	Name	Nat	DoB	Pos	Aps	(s)	Gls
17	Aleksandar ALEMPIJEVIĆ	SRB	25/7/88	M	20	(2)	1
22	István BAGI		23/3/89	D	6	(9)	
26	Lajos BERTUS		26/9/90	M	4	(6)	1
21	Gábor BORI		16/1/84	A	15		
11	Csaba CSORDÁS		9/8/77	A	23	(5)	11
14	Vladan ČUKIĆ	SRB	27/6/80	M	14		2

9	MacPherlin DUDU Omagbeni	NGA	18/7/85	A	1	(4)	
5	István FARKAS		16/1/84	D	18	(2)	2
15	Attila GYAGYA	ROU	30/3/82	D	18	(2)	1
23	Ádám HEGEDŰS		29/3/88	A	1	(1)	
1	Ádám HOLCZER		28/3/88	G	7		
16	Ales KOKOT	SVN	23/10/79	D	3	(1)	
21	Ákos KOLLER		4/9/74	D	9	(2)	1
8	Zsolt KONCZ		18/9/77	M	11	(2)	
2	Balázs KOSZÓ		20/3/88	D	7	(1)	
19	Mladen LAMBULIĆ	SRB	9/7/72	D	15		
33	Filip LĂZĂREANU	ROU	5/7/81	G	12	(2)	
18	Francis LITSINGI	CGO	9/10/86	A	18	(6)	4
6	Dario MEMIĆ	BIH	21/3/90	D	1	(1)	
30	Romeo MITROVIĆ	BIH	12/7/79	G	11		
7	Tibor MONTVAI		23/11/78	A	24	(4)	13
12	Norbert NÉMEDI		1/6/77	M	22	(4)	6
19	Goran PERAK	CRO	1/6/86	M	1		
4	Milan RAKIČ	SVN	2/9/81	M	1	(3)	1
3	ROBSON de SOUSA Vasconcelos Goes	BRA	20/1/86	D	5	(1)	
10	Vladan SAVIĆ	MNE	26/7/79	M	16	(4)	1
36	Szabolcs SCHINDLER		26/10/74	D	17	(1)	
27	Attila SIMON		4/2/83	A	2	(12)	2
4	István SZŰCS		3/5/85	D	2		
6	Viktor TÖLGYESI		23/11/78	M		(2)	
20	Uroš VESELIČ	SVN	20/5/87	A	6	(3)	
20	Péter VÖRÖS		14/12/77	M	6	(1)	
27	Mbengono Ondoa YANNICK	CMR	11/6/87	A	14	(1)	4

LOMBARD-PÁPA FC
Coach – György Véber
Founded – 2004
Stadium – Perutz (8000)

2009

25/7	MTK	h	0-1	
1/8	Debrecen	a	0-2	
8/8	Videoton	h	0-1	
16/8	Újpest	a	3-0	Bali, Farkas (p), Rebryk
22/8	Győr	h	1-0	Bali
29/8	Kecskemét	h	2-0	Heffler, Tóth
12/9	Diósgyőr	h	2-1	Heffler, Bali
19/9	Vasas	h	4-1	Bali, Bárányos, Rebryk, Mészáros
26/9	Honvéd	a	3-1	Bárányos, Orosz 2
3/10	Haladás	h	1-3	Gyömbér
16/10	ZTE	a	0-3	
24/10	Nyíregyháza	h	5-1	Bárányos, Alex 2, Bali, Gyömbér
31/10	Paks	a	2-2	Bali, Alex
7/11	Ferencváros	h	0-1	
22/11	Kaposvár	a	1-3	Bárányos
2010				
27/2	MTK	a	0-0	
7/3	Debrecen	h	1-5	Farkas (p)
13/3	Videoton	a	0-2	
21/3	Újpest	h	1-0	Tóth
27/3	Győr	a	1-1	Orosz
3/4	Kecskemét	a	2-2	Varga, Bárányos
10/4	Diósgyőr	a	0-3	
17/4	Vasas	a	2-2	Abwo 2
24/4	Honvéd	h	0-3	
1/5	Haladás	a	2-4	Jovánczai, og (Simon Á.)
5/5	ZTE	h	1-2	Rebryk
8/5	Nyíregyháza	a	1-3	Gyömbér
15/5	Paks	h	1-0	og (Éger)
18/5	Ferencváros	a	0-2	
23/5	Kaposvár	h	3-1	Szabó, Jovánczai, Abwo

No	Name	Nat	DoB	Pos	Aps	(s)	Gls
10	David Salomon ABWO	NGA	10/5/86	M	8	(5)	3
10	ALEX José de Paula	BRA	13/9/81	A	4	(4)	3
39	Péter BALI		6/1/84	A	23	(1)	6
20	Zsolt BÁRÁNYOS		15/12/75	M	29		5
11	Ferenc BÉRES		15/4/82	A	1	(2)	
16	Attila CSÁSZÁR		23/4/84	D		(2)	
5	András DLUSZTUS		22/7/88	D	10	(3)	
23	Attila FARKAS		5/10/78	D	27		2

3	Gergely FŰZFA		18/7/88	M	3		
22	Balázs GRANÁTH		24/5/85	A	1	(14)	
13	Gábor GYÖMBÉR		27/2/88	M	29		3
8	Norbert HEFFLER		24/5/90	M	23	(1)	2
12	Zoltán JOVÁNCZAI		8/12/84	A	5	(6)	2
88	Márk MÉSZÁROS		26/2/88	D	6	(7)	1
19	Sándor NAGY		1/1/88	D	10	(2)	
89	Gahwagi NEBIL		20/8/89	A		(1)	
21	Péter OROSZ		19/8/81	A	11	(6)	3
30	César Alexander QUINTERO Jiménez	COL	9/11/88	D	7	(2)	
14	Attila RAJNAY		3/6/79	D	24		
17	Denys REBRYK	UKR	4/4/85	A	14	(7)	3
7	Balázs SARUS		9/12/88	M		(5)	
26	Tamás SIPOS		6/3/88	D	1		
9	Zsolt SZABÓ		30/4/86	A	3	(6)	1
27	Lajos SZŰCS		8/8/73	G	30		
1	Tamás TAKÁCS		5/9/79	G		(1)	
4	Gábor TÓTH		26/3/87	D	24	(1)	2
18	Gábor VARGA		20/8/85	D	23	(1)	1
6	Balázs VENCZEL		6/9/86	M	12	(3)	
15	Vadims ŽUĻEVS	LVA	1/3/88	M	2	(6)	

MTK BUDAPEST
Coach – József Garami
Founded – 1888
Stadium – Hidegkuti Nándor (7,702)
MAJOR HONOURS:
Hungarian League – (23) 1904, 1908, 1914, 1917, 1918, 1919, 1920, 1921, 1922, 1923, 1924, 1925, 1929, 1936, 1937, 1951, 1953, 1958, 1987, 1997, 1999, 2003, 2008;
Hungarian Cup – (12) 1910, 1911, 1912, 1914, 1923, 1925, 1932, 1952, 1968, 1997, 1998, 2000.

2009

25/7	Pápa	a	1-0	Lencse
2/8	Honvéd	h	2-1	Molnár, Lencse
9/8	Haladás	a	4-2	Lencse 2, Könyves, Gosztonyi
15/8	ZTE	h	1-0	Balogh
22/8	Nyíregyháza	a	1-1	Gosztonyi
29/8	Paks	h	1-1	Melczer (p)
13/9	Ferencváros	a	1-2	Lencse
19/9	Kaposvár	h	4-0	Lencse 2, Pátkai, Könyves
26/9	Vasas	a	0-2	
18/10	Videoton	h	2-2	Szatmári L., Lencse
24/10	Újpest	a	2-3	Gosztonyi, Vági
31/10	Győr	h	0-0	
7/11	Kecskemét	a	5-2	Könyves 2, Zsidai, Gosztonyi, Lencse
21/11	Diósgyőr	h	4-0	Szatmári L., Vadnai, Gosztonyi (p), Pál
3/12	Debrecen	a	0-2	
2010				
27/2	Pápa	h	0-0	
6/3	Honvéd	a	1-4	Lázok (p)
13/3	Haladás	h	0-0	
20/3	ZTE	a	0-1	
27/3	Nyíregyháza	h	4-0	Kulcsár, Könyves, Pál, Lázok (p)
3/4	Paks	a	2-0	Hidvégi, Lázok
10/4	Ferencváros	h	1-1	Szatmári L.
17/4	Kaposvár	a	2-1	Lázok, Kulcsár
24/4	Vasas	h	2-3	Vadnai, Zsidai
1/5	Debrecen	a	2-3	Lázok, Szatmári L.
4/5	Videoton	h	1-0	Szatmári L.
9/5	Újpest	a	4-5	Pál 4
15/5	Győr	a	0-2	
20/5	Kecskemét	h	0-1	
23/5	Diósgyőr	a	5-2	Pál 2, Kulcsár, Zsidai, Szabó

No	Name	Nat	DoB	Pos	Aps	(s)	Gls
5	Béla BALOGH		30/12/84	D	24		1
21	Gábor BORI		16/1/84	M	8		
20	Nenad FILIPOVIĆ	SRB	24/4/87	G	9		
30	András GOSZTONYI		7/11/90	M	13		5
3	Dávid HAUSER		22/8/86	D		(3)	
7	Sándor HIDVÉGI		9/4/83	D	30		1

19	József KANTA	24/3/84	M	1	(2)	
77	Tamás KULCSÁR	10/6/89	M	15		3
15	Norbert KÖNYVES	10/6/89	A	7	(18)	5
10	János LÁZOK	4/10/84	A	12	(2)	5
12	László LENCSE	2/7/88	A	14		9
11	Vilmos MELCZER	25/2/86	M	1	(10)	1
31	Marcell MOLNÁR	26/8/90	A	4	(5)	1
25	Márk NIKHÁZI	2/2/89	M		(7)	
9	András PÁL	19/8/85	A	16	(5)	8
2	Máté PÁTKAI	6/3/88	M	14	(6)	1
27	Ádám PINTÉR	12/6/88	D	25	(1)	
22	István RODENBÜCHER	22/2/84	D	26		
6	Ádám SZABÓ	2/1/88	M	4	(5)	1
26	Levente SZÁNTAI	15/11/82	G	7	(1)	
32	Lóránd SZATMÁRI	3/10/88	M	21		5
23	Zoltán SZATMÁRI	2/5/79	G	13		
3	Adrián SZEKERES	21/4/89	D	17	(1)	
33	Viktor SZENTPÉTERI	1/11/79	G	1		
30	Patrik TISCHLER	30/7/91	A		(3)	
4	Dániel VADNAI	19/2/88	D	16	(4)	2
2	András VÁGI	25/12/88	D	12	(1)	1
17	László ZSIDAI	16/7/86	M	20	(1)	3

NYÍREGYHÁZA SPARTACUS FC

Coach – Lázár Szentes
Founded – 1959
Stadium – Városi (13,500)

2009

24/7	Vasas	h	5-1	Andorka, Miskolczi, Homma 2, Bogdanović
1/8	Paks	a	0-1	
7/8	Ferencváros	h	3-1	Dosso, Homma 2
15/8	Kaposvár	a	1-1	Homma
22/8	MTK	h	1-1	Bogdanović
29/8	Debrecen	a	1-3	Homma
12/9	Videoton	h	2-3	Dosso (p), Homma
19/9	Újpest	a	1-3	Goia
26/9	Győr	h	1-3	Pákolicz
4/10	Kecskemét	a	2-2	Andorka, Pákolicz
17/10	Diósgyőr	h	1-1	og (Lakatos)
24/10	Pápa	a	1-5	Andorka
31/10	Honvéd	h	0-1	
7/11	Haladás	a	0-2	
21/11	ZTE	h	0-4	

2010

28/2	Vasas	a	3-2	Struhár, og (Hrepka), Kovačević
6/3	Paks	h	1-1	Fekete
12/3	Ferencváros	a	0-0	
20/3	Kaposvár	h	2-1	Bouguerra, Homma
27/3	MTK	a	0-4	
11/4	Videoton	a	0-1	
17/4	Újpest	h	2-2	Bošnjak, Andorka
20/4	Debrecen	h	0-3	
24/4	Győr	a	1-2	Kovačević
1/5	Kecskemét	h	2-3	Bouguerra 2 (1p)
5/5	Diósgyőr	a	1-0	Bouguerra
8/5	Pápa	h	3-1	Andorka, Miskolczi (p), Abdelali
15/5	Honvéd	a	1-1	Struhár
19/5	Haladás	h	3-3	Bouguerra 3 (1p)
22/5	ZTE	a	3-4	Bouguerra 3

No	Name	Nat	DoB	Pos	Aps	(s)	Gls
19	Nacim Mustapha ABDELALI	ALG	19/12/81	A	14		1
14	Árpád AMBRUSZ		2/7/80	D	4	(1)	
99	Péter ANDORKA		19/7/84	A	22	(5)	5
92	Balázs BATIZI-PÓCSI		20/4/92	A	2	(6)	
10	Igor BOGDANOVIĆ	SRB	25/9/74	A	13		2
35	Predrag BOŠNJAK	SRB	13/11/85	D	10	(1)	1
99	Fouad BOUGUERRA	ALG	7/5/81	A	10	(2)	10
29	Alfi CONTEH-LACALLE	SLE	18/1/85	A		(3)	
3	Claudiu CORNACI	ROU	19/7/75	D	5		
27	Károly CZANÍK	SVK	13/9/84	M		(5)	
14	Milan DAVIDOV	SRB	1/6/79	M	12		
3	DIEGO Douglas Balbinot	BRA	7/1/84	D	9		
67	Sindou DOSSO	CIV	23/4/86	A	10	(4)	2

88	Ádám FEKETE		22/1/88	M	1	(6)	1
29	Sabin Cosmin GOIA	ROU	16/2/82	M	13		1
45	Kazuo HOMMA	JPN	17/3/80	A	28	(1)	8
25	Martin HURT	EST	27/6/84	D	8		
86	Zoltán KISS		12/7/86	D	11		
44	Željko KOVAČEVIĆ	SRB	30/10/81	D	7	(1)	2
43	Zoltán KOVÁCS		16/12/86	D	1		
7	István LAKATOS		24/10/80	D	10	(3)	
11	Tibor MÁRKUS		10/10/78	A		(1)	
18	Yves Simplice MBOUSSI	CMR	30/5/87	D	12		
23	Tibor MINCZÉR		23/6/84	M	7	(5)	
12	László MISKOLCZI		12/3/86	D	29		2
8	Zsolt MÜLLER		8/4/84	M	6	(6)	
4	Balázs NÁNÁSI		22/4/89	D	4	(4)	
33	Volodymyr OVSIYENKO	UKR	30/10/78	G	13		
9	Dávid PÁKOLICZ		13/9/84	M	8	(13)	2
24	Szabolcs Mihály PERÉNYI		5/7/82	D		(1)	
27	Luis Arcangel RAMOS	HON	11/4/85	M		(1)	
42	Gergely SIMON		21/9/87	A		(1)	
11	Petar STANIŠIĆ	SRB	23/9/84	D	4	(1)	
9	Aco STOJKOV	MKD	29/4/83	A	2		
13	Peter STRUHÁR	SVK	17/1/84	M	15		2
21	Tamás SZÉLPÁL		11/7/87	M		(4)	
25	Norbert SZILÁGYI		14/10/85	A		(1)	
37	Krisztián VARGA		23/10/89	M	5	(6)	
1	Draško VOJINOVIĆ	SRB	3/12/84	G	17	(1)	
5	Attila ZABOS		21/8/80	M	18	(4)	

PAKSI SE

Coach – Imre Gellei; (12/4/10) Károly Kiss
Founded – 1952
Stadium – Városi (5,000)

2009

25/7	ZTE	a	1-2	Böde
1/8	Nyíregyháza	h	1-0	Tököli (p)
8/8	Vasas	a	1-3	Tököli
15/8	Ferencváros	a	1-1	Lisztes
22/8	Kaposvár	h	2-0	Éger, Böde
29/8	MTK	a	1-1	Böde
11/9	Debrecen	h	0-1	
19/9	Videoton	a	0-3	
27/9	Újpest	h	1-0	Kiss
3/10	Győr	a	1-3	og (Babić)
17/10	Kecskemét	h	2-1	Tököli, Böde
24/10	Diósgyőr	a	0-0	
31/10	Pápa	h	2-2	Böde, Tököli
7/11	Honvéd	a	1-1	Kiss
21/11	Haladás	h	2-0	Böde, Éger

2010

6/3	Nyíregyháza	a	1-1	Tököli
13/3	Vasas	h	2-2	Tököli, Kiss
20/3	Ferencváros	h	1-2	Vayer
27/3	Kaposvár	a	1-1	Tököli
31/3	ZTE	h	1-2	Nagy
3/4	MTK	h	0-2	
10/4	Debrecen	a	1-3	Böde
17/4	Videoton	h	1-2	Tököli
24/4	Újpest	a	2-3	Tököli 2
1/5	Győr	h	1-1	Tököli
5/5	Kecskemét	a	1-1	Vayer
8/5	Diósgyőr	h	1-0	Lisztes
15/5	Pápa	a	0-1	
19/5	Honvéd	h	2-1	Kiss, Böde
23/5	Haladás	a	0-4	

No	Name	Nat	DoB	Pos	Aps	(s)	Gls
7	Tamás BÁLÓ		12/1/84	M	3	(4)	
39	László BARTA		9/2/87	A	5	(5)	
8	Roland BOHNER		6/7/84	A		(2)	
13	Dániel BÖDE		24/10/86	A	27	(1)	8
77	Norbert CSERNYÁNSZKI		1/2/76	G	8		
73	László ÉGER		7/5/77	D	29		2
18	Attila FIOLA		17/2/90	D	12	(2)	
5	Zsolt GÉVAY		19/11/87	D	8	(4)	
16	Tibor HEFFLER		17/5/87	M	17	(10)	

15	Levente HORVÁTH	13/4/82	D	28	
49	Sándor HORVÁTH	10/9/73	G		(3)
10	Tamás KISS	27/9/79	A	25	4
1	Attila KOVÁCS	17/2/81	G	21	
33	Krisztián LISZTES	2/7/76	M	17	(6)	2
2	István NAGY	16/5/86	M	7	(5)	1
25	Balázs NIKOLOV	4/7/77	M	14	(5)	
11	Attila PINTÉR	8/9/78	D	2	(2)	
28	Péter POKORNI	21/11/89	G	1		
22	István SIPEKI	17/2/79	M	19	(4)	
30	János SZABÓ	11/7/89	D	18	(2)	
26	Gábor TAMÁSI	26/8/81	M	1	(5)	
21	Attila TÖKÖLI	14/5/76	A	27		11
17	Balázs TÓTH	14/7/86	M	1	(2)	
9	Gábor URBÁN	30/12/84	A	3	(11)	
68	László VARGA	28/8/68	A		(1)	
87	Barnabás VÁRI	15/9/87	A	10	(2)	
11	Gábor VAYER	18/5/77	M	11	(3)	2
20	Dániel VÖLGYI	7/6/87	M	6	(1)	
24	Ádám WEITNER	9/9/82	M		(2)	
6	János ZOVÁTH	5/2/77	A	10	(3)	

SZOMBATHELYI HALADÁS
Coach – Aurél Csertői; (15/9/09) Antal Róth
Founded – 1919
Stadium – Rohonci úti (12,500)

2009
2/8	Kaposvár	a	0-3	
9/8	MTK	h	2-4	Tóth, Lattenstein
14/8	Debrecen	a	1-2	Ugrai
23/8	Videoton	h	4-3	Schimmer, Kenesei (p), Oross, Nagy
26/8	Ferencváros	h	0-0	
30/8	Újpest	a	1-3	Rajos
12/9	Győr	h	1-2	Kenesei (p)
19/9	Kecskemét	h	3-3	Lattenstein, Nagy, Kuttor
26/9	Diósgyőr	h	2-1	Oross, Irhás
3/10	Pápa	a	3-1	Lattenstein, Oross, Rácz
17/10	Honvéd	h	2-2	Oross, Simon A.
24/10	Vasas	h	0-1	
31/10	ZTE	a	0-3	
7/11	Nyíregyháza	h	2-0	Simon Á., Tóth
21/11	Paks	a	0-2	

2010
27/2	Ferencváros	a	1-2	Halmosi
5/3	Kaposvár	h	2-1	Bogdanović 2 (1p)
13/3	MTK	a	0-0	
19/3	Debrecen	h	0-2	
26/3	Videoton	a	2-4	Tóth (p), Oross
3/4	Újpest	h	1-0	Nagy
10/4	Győr	a	1-1	Tóth (p)
17/4	Kecskemét	h	3-2	Sipos, Nagy 2
25/4	Diósgyőr	a	3-1	Nagy, Oross, Guzmics
1/5	Pápa	h	4-2	Tóth (p), Halmosi, Kenesei 2 (1p)
5/5	Honvéd	a	0-0	
8/5	Vasas	a	0-0	
16/5	ZTE	h	1-1	Kenesei
19/5	Nyíregyháza	a	3-3	Simon Á., Simon A., Molnár (p)
23/5	Paks	h	4-0	Lengyel, Halmosi, Oross, Irhás

No	Name	Nat	DoB	Pos	Aps	(s)	Gls
55	Igor BOGDANOVIĆ	SRB	25/9/74	M	6	(4)	2
18	Victor Pony CARR	LBR	12/3/88	A		(2)	
2	Zoltán CSONTOS		30/5/86	D	6	(6)	
25	El Hadji DIOUF	SEN	20/8/88	M		(3)	
22	Richárd GUZMICS		16/4/87	D	29		1
13	Péter HALMOSI		25/9/79	M	15		3
11	Ignác IRHÁS		18/3/85	A	4	(12)	2
90	Bence ISZLAI		29/5/90	D	3	(12)	
20	Krisztián KENESEI		7/1/77	A	5	(5)	5
10	István KOVÁCS		27/3/92	M		(1)	
77	Attila KUTTOR		29/5/70	D	15		1
84	Norbert LATTENSTEIN		13/2/84	M	12	(9)	3
6	Dániel LENGYEL		1/3/89	D	15		1
5	Balázs MOLNÁR		1/7/77	M	24		1

8	Gábor NAGY	16/10/85	M	28		6
9	Márton OROSS	3/3/81	A	28	(1)	7
27	Jean-Baptiste PATERNOTTE	FRA	4/1/81	D	1	
32	Ferenc RÁCZ	28/3/91	A	1	(4)	1
4	Gábor RAJOS	17/3/84	M	16	(2)	1
66	Dániel RÓZSA	24/11/84	G	30		
23	Szabolcs SCHIMMER	24/2/84	M	26		1
46	Ádám SIMON	30/3/90	M	15	(1)	2
17	Attila SIMON	23/9/88	A	9	(8)	2
18	Norbert SIPOS	21/3/81	M	11	(1)	1
16	Máté SKRIBA	13/3/92	A	3	(11)	
15	Péter TÓTH	25/6/77	M	28		5
14	Roland UGRAI	13/11/92	A		(2)	1

ÚJPEST FC
Coach – Willie McStay (SCO); (4/4/10) Géza Mészöly
Founded – 1885
Stadium – Szusza Ferenc (13,500)
MAJOR HONOURS:
Hungarian League – (20) 1930, 1931, 1933, 1935, 1939, 1945, 1946, 1947, 1960, 1969, 1970, 1971, 1972, 1973, 1974, 1975, 1978, 1979, 1990, 1998; Hungarian Cup – (8) 1969, 1970, 1975, 1982, 1983, 1987, 1992, 2002.

2009
26/7	Győr	a	0-0	
2/8	Kecskemét	h	3-1	Kabát, Tisza, Simon A.
9/8	Diósgyőr	a	2-1	og (Miličić), Tisza
16/8	Pápa	h	0-3	
23/8	Honvéd	a	1-1	Foxi
30/8	Haladás	h	3-1	Kabát, Foxi, Sándor
12/9	ZTE	a	4-1	Kabát 3, Foxi
19/9	Nyíregyháza	h	3-1	Kabát 2 (1p), Foxi
27/9	Paks	a	0-1	
3/10	Ferencváros	h	2-1	Kabát, Rajczi
17/10	Kaposvár	a	0-2	
24/10	MTK	h	3-2	Rajczi, Simek, Takács
30/10	Debrecen	a	2-1	Kabát 2 (2p)
6/11	Videoton	h	0-1	
21/11	Vasas	a	2-1	Tóth, Rajczi

2010
27/2	Győr	h	0-3	
6/3	Kecskemét	a	1-2	Millar
14/3	Diósgyőr	h	4-1	Rajczi, Kabát 2, Varga
21/3	Pápa	a	0-1	
27/3	Honvéd	h	0-1	
3/4	Haladás	a	0-1	
9/4	ZTE	h	2-1	Barczi, Kabát
17/4	Nyíregyháza	a	2-2	Vermes, Foxi
24/4	Paks	h	3-2	Rajczi, Barczi, Simek
30/4	Ferencváros	a	1-0	Kabát
5/5	Kaposvár	h	2-1	Rajczi 2
9/5	MTK	a	5-4	Vasiljević 3 (2p), Korcsmár, Vaskó
15/5	Debrecen	h	2-1	Korcsmár, Barczi
19/5	Videoton	a	1-1	Vasiljević
23/5	Vasas	h	1-0	Korcsmár

No	Name	Nat	DoB	Pos	Aps	(s)	Gls
1	Szabolcs BALAJCZA		14/7/79	G	28		
31	Dávid BARCZI		1/2/89	M	9	(3)	3
23	Dániel BORDÁS		20/8/90	G		(1)	
16	Gábor DEMJÉN		1/3/86	M		(2)	
2	Ivan DUDIĆ	SRB	13/2/77	D	13	(1)	
25	Gábor DVORSCHÁK		14/9/89	D	1	(1)	
20	FOXI Kethevoama	CTA	30/5/86	M	14	(10)	5
36	Tamás HORVÁTH		18/6/87	G	2		
28	JUCEMAR Décio Ribeiro da Silva	BRA	10/8/86	M	1	(7)	
22	Péter KABÁT		25/9/77	A	22	(2)	14
15	Zoltán KISS		12/7/86	D	1	(3)	
21	Zsolt KORCSMÁR		9/1/89	D	24	(1)	3
27	Dániel KOVÁCS		16/6/90	M	1	(8)	
14	Mladen LAMBULIĆ	SRB	9/7/72	D	5	(1)	
9	Gary John MARTIN	ENG	10/10/90	A		(2)	
3	Mark MILLAR	SCO	23/2/88	M	13	(1)	1
24	Zoltán POLLÁK		13/1/84	D	23	(1)	
8	Péter RAJCZI		3/4/81	A	20	(3)	7

HUNGARY

5	György SÁNDOR		20/3/84	M	13	(1)	1
11	Péter SIMEK		30/1/80	M	23	(5)	2
9	Attila SIMON		4/2/83	A	2	(6)	1
7	Krisztián SIMON		10/6/91	M		(1)	
6	Tony STOKES	ENG	7/1/87	M	7	(4)	
26	Zsolt SZOKOL		16/3/90	D	11	(1)	
4	Zoltán TAKÁCS		26/11/83	D	15	(1)	1
10	Tibor TISZA		10/11/84	A	3	(1)	2
17	Norbert TÓTH		11/8/76	M	15	(7)	1
14	Roland VARGA		23/1/90	A	6	(6)	1
5	Dušan VASILJEVIĆ	SRB	7/5/82	M	13	(2)	4
19	Tamás VASKÓ		20/2/84	D	17		1
18	Krisztián VERMES		7/7/85	D	28		1

3	Dušan MILEUSNIĆ	SRB	10/4/84	D	14		
37	Đorđe MRĐANIN	SRB	26/2/81	D	5	(1)	1
31	Roland MUNDI		9/6/88	M	2	(3)	
10	Ćedomir PAVIĆEVIĆ	SRB	23/5/78	M	23	(2)	
32	József PILLER		16/8/88	M	7	(9)	
77	Mohamed REMILI		30/5/86	M	20		4
38	Péter SZILÁGYI		26/1/88	A	1	(3)	2
5	Péter SZŰCS		12/10/90	A	3	(3)	
14	Tamás TANDARI		21/1/88	M		(1)	
7	Balázs TÓTH		14/7/86	M	11	(3)	
1	Ákos TULIPÁN		16/11/90	G	2		
30	Zoltán VÉGH		7/4/71	G	28		
2	Balázs VILLÁM		2/6/89	D	3	(2)	

VASAS SC

Coach – Géza Mészöly; (21/12/09) Giovanni Dellacasa (ITA)
Founded – 1911
Stadium – Illovszky Rudolf (18,000)
MAJOR HONOURS:
Hungarian League – (6) 1957, 1961, 1962, 1965, 1966, 1977;
Hungarian Cup – (4) 1955, 1973, 1981, 1986.

2009
24/7	Nyíregyháza	a	1-5	Lázok
31/7	Győr	h	0-2	
8/8	Paks	h	3-1	Remili 2, Divić
15/8	Kecskemét	a	1-5	Remili
21/8	Ferencváros	h	3-2	Divić, Lázok 2
29/8	Diósgyőr	a	1-0	Lázok
12/9	Kaposvár	h	1-0	Szilágyi
19/9	Pápa	a	1-4	Divić
26/9	MTK	h	2-0	Mrđanin, Szilágyi
2/10	Honvéd	a	3-3	Lázok 3 (1p)
16/10	Debrecen	h	2-4	Dobrić 2
24/10	Haladás	a	1-0	Balog
1/11	Videoton	h	2-4	Remili, Dobrić
7/11	ZTE	a	1-4	Dobrić
21/11	Újpest	h	1-2	Lázok (p)

2010
28/2	Nyíregyháza	h	2-3	Divić (p), Hrepka
6/3	Győr	a	1-1	Hrepka
13/3	Paks	a	2-2	Hrepka, Divić
20/3	Kecskemét	h	0-1	
28/3	Ferencváros	a	1-1	Benounes (p)
3/4	Diósgyőr	h	1-0	Benounes
10/4	Kaposvár	a	0-1	
17/4	Pápa	h	2-2	Benounes, Hrepka
25/4	MTK	a	3-2	Beliczky 3
1/5	Honvéd	h	2-2	Bakos, Benounes
4/5	Debrecen	a	0-3	
8/5	Haladás	h	0-0	
14/5	Videoton	a	0-3	
19/5	ZTE	h	2-3	Benounes (p), og (Bogunović)
23/5	Újpest	a	0-1	

VIDEOTON FC

Coach – György Mezey
Founded – 1941
Stadium – Sóstói (15,000)
MAJOR HONOURS:
Hungarian Cup – (1) 2006.

2009
25/7	Kecskemét	a	6-3	Elek 2, Nagy, Lipták, Sitku, Horváth
1/8	Diósgyőr	h	3-2	Vujović, André Alves 2
8/8	Pápa	a	1-0	André Alves
15/8	Honvéd	h	2-0	André Alves (p), Présinger
23/8	Haladás	a	3-4	Andić, Sitku 2
28/8	ZTE	h	1-2	Sitku
12/9	Nyíregyháza	h	3-2	André Alves 2, Sitku
19/9	Paks	h	3-0	Szakály 2, Nagy
25/9	Ferencváros	a	2-2	Polonkai, Sitku
3/10	Kaposvár	a	2-0	Polonkai, André Alves
18/10	MTK	a	2-2	Andić, Sitku
25/10	Debrecen	h	3-0	Lipták, Polonkai, Andić
1/11	Vasas	a	4-2	André Alves 3, Farkas (I)
6/11	Újpest	a	1-0	Nagy
21/11	Győr	h	0-0	

2010
27/2	Kecskemét	h	2-0	Polonkai, André Alves
6/3	Diósgyőr	a	1-0	Nikolić
13/3	Pápa	h	2-0	André Alves, Nikolić
20/3	Honvéd	a	0-0	
26/3	Haladás	h	4-2	og 2 (Guzmics 2), Nikolić 2
4/4	ZTE	a	2-2	André Alves, Elek
11/4	Nyíregyháza	h	1-0	Sándor
17/4	Paks	a	2-1	Sándor, Nikolić
24/4	Ferencváros	h	0-0	
1/5	Kaposvár	a	3-1	Nikolić, André Alves 2 (1p)
4/5	MTK	h	0-1	
7/5	Debrecen	a	2-3	Elek, Lipták
14/5	Vasas	h	3-0	Nikolić 2, Sándor
19/5	Újpest	h	1-1	Elek
23/5	Győr	a	0-1	

No	Name	Nat	DoB	Pos	Aps	(s)	Gls
8	Szabolcs BAKOS		4/2/87	M	21	(9)	1
27	Zsolt BALOG		10/11/78	D	28		
11	Gergő BELICZKY		3/7/90	A	3	(5)	3
59	Karim BENOUNES	ALG	9/2/84	M	9	(4)	5
22	BRUNO dos Santos BOSI	BRA	13/9/87	M	4	(3)	
20	Mamadou DANFA	FRA	24/7/90	M	1	(1)	
19	Petar DIVIĆ	SRB	11/7/75	A	19	(5)	5
25	Saša DOBRIĆ	SRB	21/1/82	M	25		4
36	József GÁSPÁR	SVK	23/8/77	D	11	(1)	
7	Ádám HREPKA		15/4/87	A	12		4
24	László IMRIK		15/4/85	M	2	(4)	
15	Máté KATONA		16/2/90	M	11		
23	Péter KINCSES		23/5/80	M	2	(8)	
6	Gábor KOVÁCS		4/9/87	D	28		
9	Zsolt LACZKÓ		18/12/86	M	6		
11	János LÁZOK		4/10/84	M	15		8
9	Árpád MAJOROS		21/12/83	M	8	(6)	
34	Attila MARTON		2/4/89	A		(3)	
4	Óscar Velázquez Basilio MENDOZA	PAR	19/4/90	D	6	(2)	

No	Name	Nat	DoB	Pos	Aps	(s)	Gls
17	ALISON Moreira Silva	BRA	1/6/88	A		(5)	
2	Marko ANDIĆ	SRB	14/12/83	D	25	(1)	3
21	ANDRÉ ALVES dos Santos	BRA	15/10/83	A	30		15
27	Gábor DEMJÉN		1/3/86	M		(1)	
10	Zsolt DVÉRI		12/8/76	M		(5)	
25	Ákos ELEK		21/7/88	M	24	(4)	5
14	Balázs FARKAS (I)		15/10/79	M	29		1
29	Balázs FARKAS (II)		24/4/88	A	7	(6)	
3	Gábor HORVÁTH		4/7/85	D	29		1
20	Pál LÁZÁR		11/3/88	D	13		
19	László LENCSE		2/7/88	A		(9)	
5	Zoltán LIPTÁK		10/12/84	D	28		3
26	Damir MILANOVIĆ	CRO	19/7/82	M	2	(4)	
28	Tamás MÓRI		1/9/78	A		(1)	
15	Dániel NAGY		22/11/84	A	23	(2)	3
17	Nemanja NIKOLIĆ	SRB	31/12/87	A	13	(2)	8
8	Attila POLONKAI		12/6/79	M	23	(6)	4
24	Csaba PONCZÓK		29/1/92	M		(2)	
16	Ádám PRÉSINGER		26/1/89	D	1	(1)	1
11	Milan PUROVIĆ	MNE	7/5/85	A		(7)	

HUNGARY

13	Ilija RADOVIĆ	MNE	9/5/85	D	3	
11	György SÁNDOR		20/3/84	M	15	3
1	Zsolt SEBŐK		3/4/79	G	29	
9	Illés SITKU		5/2/78	A	15	(7)	7
7	Dénes SZAKÁLY		15/3/88	M	11	(14)	2
12	Tomáš TUJVEL	SVK	19/9/83	G	1	
4	Róbert VARGA		25/11/86	D	6	
18	Goran VUJOVIĆ	MNE	3/5/87	A	3	(4)	1

ZALAEGERSZEGI TE
Coach – János Csank
Founded – 1920
Stadium – Városi (16,000)
MAJOR HONOURS:
Hungarian League – (1) 2002.

2009

25/7	Paks	h	2-1	Rudņevs, Balázs
1/8	Ferencváros	a	1-4	Máté
8/8	Kaposvár	h	0-3	
15/8	MTK	a	0-1	
28/8	Videoton	a	2-1	Bogunović, Balázs
12/9	Újpest	h	1-4	Magasföldi
18/9	Győr	a	1-1	Szalai
26/9	Kecskemét	h	3-2	Pavićević, Magasföldi, Miljatovič
3/10	Diósgyőr	a	1-1	Rudņevs
16/10	Pápa	h	3-0	Magasföldi, Rudņevs, Kamber
23/10	Honvéd	a	1-0	Magasföldi
31/10	Haladás	h	3-0	Rudņevs 2, Pavićević (p)
7/11	Vasas	h	4-1	Magasföldi, Rudņevs 2 (1p), Balázs
21/11	Nyíregyháza	a	4-0	Rudņevs 3, Pavićević
29/11	Debrecen	a	3-5	Balázs, Rudņevs, Todorović (p)

2010

6/3	Ferencváros	h	3-3	Pavićević, Illés, Miljatovič
13/3	Kaposvár	h	1-1	Pavićević
20/3	MTK	h	1-0	Pavićević
27/3	Debrecen	h	4-1	Sluka, Pavićević, Illés, Szalai
31/3	Paks	a	2-1	Sluka, Illés
4/4	Videoton	h	2-2	Balázs, Pavićević (p)
9/4	Újpest	a	1-2	Pavićević
18/4	Győr	h	1-1	Illés
24/4	Kecskemét	a	2-2	Rudņevs, Magasföldi
2/5	Diósgyőr	h	3-0	Rudņevs 2, Magasföldi
5/5	Pápa	a	2-1	Balázs, Horváth
8/5	Honvéd	h	0-1	
16/5	Haladás	a	1-1	Rudņevs
19/5	Vasas	a	3-2	Kamber, Pavićević, Horváth
22/5	Nyíregyháza	h	4-3	Rudņevs, Pavićević 3

No	Name	Nat	DoB	Pos	Aps	(s)	Gls
17	Zsolt BALÁZS		11/8/88	A	13	(12)	6
13	Zsolt BARNA		10/9/87	M		(2)	
3	Milan BOGUNOVIĆ	SRB	31/5/83	D	25		1
29	András HORVÁTH		6/8/80	M	15	(7)	2
7	Gyula ILLÉS		10/7/82	M	11	(7)	4
14	Đorđe KAMBER	SRB	20/11/83	M	28	(1)	2
2	Gergely KOCSÁRDI		24/11/75	D	26	(3)	
18	Gergő KOVÁCS		30/10/89	D	5	(8)	
6	József MAGASFÖLDI		10/11/84	M	26	(3)	7
16	Péter MÁTÉ		15/11/79	M	29		1
22	Matej MILJATOVIČ	SVN	23/6/79	D	25	(1)	2
8	Leon PANIKVAR	SVN	28/1/83	D	16	(1)	
5	Darko PAVIĆEVIĆ	MNE	24/6/85	A	13	(7)	13
15	Márk PETNEHÁZI		4/10/88	M		(2)	
12	Krisztián POGACSICS		17/10/85	G	2		
25	Prince RAJCOMAR	NED	25/4/85	A	5	(5)	
11	Artjoms RUDŅEVS	LVA	13/1/88	A	24	(1)	16
10	Levente SCHULTZ		22/3/77	M	2	(11)	
20	Marián SLUKA	SVK	22/7/79	M	16	(5)	2
1	Tamás SZALAI		10/1/80	M	8	(8)	2
4	Nenad TODOROVIĆ	SRB	26/5/82	D	13	(6)	1
1	Géza VLASZÁK		3/9/73	G	28		

PROMOTED CLUBS

BFC SIÓFOK
Coach – Zoltán Hagymási; (15/1/10) Károly Horváth
Founded – 1921
Stadium – Városi (10,500)
MAJOR HONOURS:
Hungarian Cup – (1) 1984.

SZOLNOKI MÁV FC
Coach – Attila Vágó
Founded – 1910
Stadium – Tiszaligeti (6,500)

SECOND LEVEL FINAL TABLES 2009/10

EAST		Pld	W	D	L	F	A	Pts
1	BFC Siófok	28	20	3	5	49	20	63
2	Gyirmót SE	28	19	5	4	56	25	62
3	Pécsi MFC	28	16	7	5	56	25	55
4	FC Ajka	28	14	5	9	47	45	47
5	FC Tatabánya	28	14	3	11	49	41	45
6	Kozármisleny SE	28	11	8	9	42	35	41
7	Győri ETO FC II	28	9	12	7	43	31	39
8	Szigetszentmiklósi TK	28	10	9	9	43	45	38
9	Videoton FC II	28	10	6	12	41	43	36
10	Budaörsi SC	28	9	6	13	38	47	33
11	Kaposvölgye VSC	28	8	7	13	36	44	31
12	Budapest Honvéd FC II	28	6	9	13	29	54	27
13	Barcsi SC	28	6	5	17	25	45	23
14	Zalaegerszegi TE II	28	4	8	16	29	51	20
15	Hévíz FC	28	5	5	18	23	55	20

NB Szigetszentmiklósi TK – 1 pt deducted.

WEST		Pld	W	D	L	F	A	Pts
1	Szolnoki MÁV FC	28	18	6	4	54	28	60
2	Debreceni VSC II	28	17	4	7	53	26	55
3	Dunakanyar-Vác FC	28	15	7	6	47	36	52
4	Rákospalotai EAC	28	15	5	8	76	36	50
5	Mezőkövesdi SE	28	11	9	8	37	35	42
6	Vecsési FC	28	11	8	9	45	32	41
7	Makói FC	28	11	5	12	46	46	38
8	BKV Előre SC	28	9	11	8	38	39	38
9	Bőcs KSC	28	9	11	8	33	36	38
10	Hajdúböszörményi TE	28	10	7	11	33	36	37
11	MTK Budapest II	28	10	5	13	53	48	35
12	Kazincbarcika SC	28	9	5	14	35	50	32
13	Békéscsaba Előre SE	28	7	7	14	31	44	28
14	Ceglédi VSE	28	6	9	13	40	53	27
15	Baktalórántházi VSE	28	1	3	24	21	97	0

NB Baktalórántházi VSE – 6 pts deducted.

HUNGARY

DOMESTIC CUP 2009/10

MAGYAR KUPA

THIRD ROUND

(9/9/09)
Putnok 2, DVSC DEAC 3

(15/9/09)
Hévíz 0, ZTE 3
Mosonmagyaróvár 0, Győr 7

(16/9/09)
Baja 2, Makó 1
Balassagyarmat 1, REAC 7
Cegléd 1, Békéscsaba 0
Győr II. 0, Pápa 2
Győrszemere 1, Tatabánya 5
Harta 1, Szolnok 7
Jánoshida 0, Szigetszentmiklós 2
Kozármisleny 0, Paks 1
Lébény 0, Gyirmót 6
Lövő 1, Ajka 8
Mándok 1, Diósgyőr 2
Mátészalka 0, Mezőkövesd 6
MTK II. 2, Ferencváros 0
Nyírbátor 2, Baktalórántháza 1 *(aet)*
Nyírmada 2, Nyíregyháza 0
Orosháza 0, Kecskemét 3
Pálhalma 2, Siófok 1
Szabadegyháza 0, Kaposvölgye 3
Tököl 2, Barcs 1
Tura 5, Vasas 4 *(aet)*
Vác 2, Budaörs 0
Vecsés 0, MTK 5
Videoton II. 0, Videoton 3
ZTE II. 1, Pécs 5

(30/9/09)
Veszprém 1, Kaposvár 2

Byes - Debrecen, Haladás, Honvéd, Újpest

FOURTH ROUND

(29/9/09)
Pécs 0, ZTE 1 *(aet)*

(30/9/09)
Ajka 1, Győr 5
Baja 0, Haladás 1
Cegléd 1, Kecskemét 3
Kaposvölgye 1, Paks 0
Mezőkövesd 4, DVSC-DEAC 2
MTK II. 0, Újpest 4
Nyírbátor 0, Diósgyőr 4
Pálhalma 1, Videoton 4 *(aet)*
REAC 1, Szolnok 4
Tatabánya 1, Pápa 2 *(aet)*
Tököl 0, Szigetszentmiklós 1
Tura 0, MTK 6

(7/10/09)
Gyirmót 1, Kaposvár 1 *(aet; 3-4 on pens)*
Nyírmada 2, Debrecen 8
Vác 0, Honvéd 2

FIFTH ROUND

(20/10/09 & 27/10/09)
Kecskemét v Újpest 2-5; 2-6 *(4-11)*
Szolnok v Honvéd 4-1; 0-3 *(4-4; Honvéd on away goal)*

(20/10/09 & 28/10/09)
Haladás v ZTE 0-2; 1-1 *(1-3)*

(21/10/09 & 27/10/09)
MTK v Diósgyőr 3-0; 3-0 *(6-0)*

(21/10/09 & 28/10/09)
Győr v Kaposvár 1-1; 2-0 *(3-1)*
Kaposvölgye v Szigetszentmiklós 2-2; 2-3 *(4-5)*
Videoton v Pápa 3-0; 0-0 *(3-0)*

(22/10/09 & 28/10/09)
Mezőkövesd v Debrecen 1-4; 3-4 *(4-8)*

QUARTER-FINALS

(11/11/09 & 17/11/09)
Szigetszentmiklós 0, ZTE 3 *(Pavićević 6, 27, Rajcomar 80)*
ZTE 3 *(Kamber 33, Máté 62, Pavićević 88),*
Szigetszentmiklós 1 *(Riedl 30)*
(ZTE 6-1)

(17/11/09 & 25/11/09)
Honvéd 1 *(Guilherme 64),* Győr 1 *(Aleksidze 70)*
Győr 0, Honvéd 1 *(Diego 9)*
(Honvéd 2-1)

Videoton 0, Újpest 1 *(Kabát 42p)*
Újpest 1 *(Sándor 73),* Videoton 0
(Újpest 2-0)

(13/12/09 & 17/12/09)
Debrecen 2 *(Feczesin 44, Czvitkovics 50),* MTK 0
MTK 2 *(Pál 77, Zsidai 80),* Debrecen 0 *(aet)*
(2-2; Debrecen 5-4 on pens)

SEMI-FINALS

(23/3/10 & 13/4/10)
Honvéd 1 *(Abraham 88),* Debrecen 1 *(Szilágyi 80)*
Debrecen 2 *(Yannick 34, Laczkó 85),* Honvéd 1 *(Abraham 83)*
(Debrecen 3-2)

(24/3/10 & 14/4/10)
Újpest 0, ZTE 1 *(Balázs 88)*
ZTE 0, Újpest 0
(ZTE 1-0)

FINAL

(26/5/10)
Puskás Ferenc stadium, Budapest
DEBRECENI VSC 3 *(Coulibaly 24, 68, Yannick 30)*
ZALAEGERSZEGI TE 2 *(Pavićević 41, Rudņevs 70)*
Referee – Vad
DEBRECEN – Verpecz, Laczkó, Bernáth, Mijadinoski,
Komlósi, Yannick (Rezes 44), Czvitkovics (Kiss 83), Szélesi,
Bódi (Varga 90), Szakály, Coulibaly.
ZTE – Vlaszák, Kocsárdi (Rajcomar 77), Miljatovič,
Bogunović, Máté, Sluka (Balázs 61), Horváth, Kamber, Illés,
Pavićević, Rudņevs.

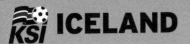

FH find strength in adversity

Beset by injuries for much of the season, FH Hafnarfjördur managed to hold off a late challenge from KR Reykjavík and win the Icelandic Úrvalsdeild title for the fifth time in six years.

It was a second championship win in two attempts by FH's young coach Heimir Gudjónsson. The second proved less dramatic than the first, when FH had belatedly snatched victory from a faltering Keflavík. Although they opened the 2009 campaign with a 1-0 defeat by Keflavík, ten straight victories followed thereafter – six in a row without conceding a goal – as FH took firm control of the title race.

Points in reserve

It was only as an injury crisis mounted during the summer that FH began to flag. An early exit from Europe, against FC Aktobe of Kazakhstan, coupled with a quarter-final elimination from the Icelandic Cup – at the hands of the ever-vengeful Keflavík – induced concerns about the team's ability to hang on to their big lead in the Úrvalsdeild. But although KR ran hard at them, FH had too many points in reserve and eventually clinched the title with a 2-0 home win over Valur Reykjavík in the penultimate round. Fittingly it was the team's star performer, Atli Gudnason, who scored both goals. The 25-year-old teacher would end the season with the league's Player of the Year crown.

The defence of their title confirmed FH as Iceland's team of the decade. Since claiming their maiden championship victory in 2004 they had won the title every year bar one – in 2007, when they consoled themselves by winning the Icelandic Cup.

The 2009 winners of that competition were Breidablik, who, like FH two years earlier, took the trophy for the first time. In fact, it was the Kopavogur club's first major trophy of any description and was claimed after a thrilling end-of-season final against Fram Reykjavík. Level at 1-1 after full time and 2-2 after extra time, the game went to penalties and then to sudden-death, with Fram's Scottish import Paul McShane missing the decisive kick. Added to the joy of Breidablik's victory was the knowledge that they had qualified for a first ever crack at European football.

The other two 2010/11 UEFA Europa League places went to KR and Fylkir, second and third respectively in the Úrvalsdeild. The former, champions of Iceland a record 24 times but without a league title since 2003, enjoyed a splendid season under former national team

Atli Gudnason of FH – Iceland's Player of the Year

Knattspyrnusamband Íslands (KSÍ)

Laugardal
IS-104 Reykjavík
tel – +354 5 102 900
fax – +354 5 6897 93
website – ksi.is
email – ksi@ksi.is
Year of Formation – 1947

President – Geir Thorsteinsson
General Secretary – Thórir Hákonarson
Media Officer – Ómar Smárason
National Stadium – Laugardalsvöllur, Reykjavik (9,800)

TOP FIVE ALL-TIME CAPS
Rúnar Kristinsson (104); Hermann Hreidarsson (85); Gudni Bergsson (80); Brynjar Björn Gunnarsson & Birkir Kristinsson (74)
TOP FIVE ALL-TIME GOALS
Eidur Smári Gudjohnsen (24); Ríkhardur Jónsson (17); Ríkhardur Dadason & Arnór Gudjohnsen (14); Thórdur Gudjónsson (13)

ICELAND

coach Logi Ólafsson. Impressive in Europe, where they defeated Larissa FC and held FC Basel 1893 at home, they won nine of their last ten league games. Striker Björgólfur Takefusa also poached the league's top scorer prize by bagging all five of KR's goals in a final-day 5-2 win at Valur, enabling him to leapfrog FH's Atli Vidar Björnsson to the top of the standings.

Remarkable sequence

The Icelandic national team ended a disappointing 2010 FIFA World Cup qualifying campaign with a frustrating 1-1 draw against Norway in Reykjavik that left them bottom of the group table. Over the next nine months, however, Ólafur Jóhannesson's side lost only one of eight friendlies. A 4-0 victory over Andorra prolonged to 27 matches a remarkable sequence in which Iceland had not conceded more than two goals in any game, and with the Under-21 side also performing creditably, there was no shortage of encouragement for the team as the UEFA EURO 2012 qualifiers approached.

NATIONAL TEAM RESULTS 2009/10

12/8/09	Slovakia	H	Reykjavik	1-1	Sigurdsson K. (59)
5/9/09	Norway (WCQ)	H	Reykjavik	1-1	Gudjohnsen (29)
9/9/09	Georgia	H	Reykjavik	3-1	Jóhannsson (14), Skúlason Ó. (17), Gunnarsson V. (54)
13/10/09	South Africa	H	Reykjavik	1-0	Gunnarsson V. (50)
10/11/09	Iran	A	Tehran	0-1	
14/11/09	Luxembourg	A	Luxembourg	1-1	Jóhannsson (63)
3/3/10	Cyprus	A	Larnaca	0-0	
21/3/10	Faroe Islands	H	Kopavogur	2-0	Vilhjálmsson (10), Sigthórsson (37)
24/3/10	Mexico	N	Charlotte (USA)	0-0	
29/5/10	Andorra	H	Reykjavik	4-0	Helguson (32p, 51), Gunnarsson V. (87p), Sigthórsson (89)

NATIONAL TEAM APPEARANCES 2009/10

Coach – Ólafur JÓHANNESSON	30/6/57		Svk	NOR	Geo	Rsa	Irn	Lux	Cyp	Fro	Mex	And	Caps	Goals
Gunnleifur GUNNLEIFSSON	14/7/75	HK /FH	G	G	G				s38	G46	G	G	17	-
Grétar Rafn STEINSSON	9/1/82	Bolton (ENG)	D	D	D35	D		D					38	4
Kristján Örn SIGURDSSON	7/10/80	Brann (NOR)	D	D	D	D46	D	D					44	4
Sölvi Geir OTTESEN	18/2/84	SønderjyskE (DEN)	D50	D92	s46				D	D		D	11	-
Indridi SIGURDSSON	12/10/81	Viking (NOR)	D	D	D	D	D	D	D	D		D76	53	2
Pálmi Rafn PÁLMASON	9/11/84	Stabæk (NOR)	M89		s46	s66			s83				18	-
Brynjar Björn GUNNARSSON	16/10/75	Reading (ENG)	M	M		M82		M					74	4
Eidur Smári GUDJOHNSEN	15/9/78	Barcelona (ESP) /Monaco (FRA)	M77	M				M					61	24
Ólafur Ingi SKÚLASON	1/4/83	Helsingborg (SWE) /SønderjyskE (DEN)	M		M85	s82	M85			M74		M46	12	1
Emil HALLFREDSSON	29/6/84	Reggina (ITA) /Barnsley (ENG)	M	M88	M85	M		M		M83			29	1
Heidar HELGUSON	22/8/77	QPR (ENG) /Watford (ENG)	A86	A			A66			A		A72	48	10
Aron Einar GUNNARSSON	22/4/89	Coventry (ENG)	s50	M81		M		M70	M				17	-
Stefán GÍSLASON	15/3/80	Brøndby (DEN)	s77	s81	M85								32	-
Gardar JÓHANNSSON	1/4/80	Fredrikstad (NOR)	s86		A75	A66	s66	s46					6	2
Atli Vidar BJÖRNSSON	4/1/80	FH	s89		s75	s87	s85						4	-
Rúrik GÍSLASON	25/2/88	OB (DEN)		M		M			M46	M		A60	6	-
Veigar Páll GUNNARSSON	21/3/80	Nancy (FRA) /Stabæk (NOR)		s88	M	M87		A				s60	30	6
Ragnar SIGURDSSON	19/6/86	Göteborg (SWE)		s92	D					D66			14	-
Bjarni Ólafur EIRÍKSSON	28/3/82	Valur		D46									16	-

NATIONAL TEAM APPEARANCES 2009/10 (contd.)

			Svk	NOR	Geo	Rsa	Irn	Lux	Cyp	Fro	Mex	And	Caps	Goals
Helgi Valur DANÍELSSON	13/7/81	Elfsborg (SWE) /Hansa (GER)			M		M	s70	M				15	-
Birkir Már SÆVARSSON	11/11/84	Brann (NOR)					s35	D					18	-
Davíd Thór VIDARSSON	24/4/84	FH					s85						8	-
Baldur SIGURDSSON	24/4/85	KR					s85		s77		s49		3	-
Björgólfur TAKEFUSA	11/5/80	KR					s85		s85				3	-
Árni Gautur ARASON	7/5/75	Odd Grenland (NOR)							G	G	G	G38	70	-
Ari Freyr SKÚLASON	14/5/87	Sundsvall (SWE)							D77				1	-
Steinthór Freyr THORSTEINSSON	29/7/85	Stjarnan							M85	M77	M87	s79	4	-
Jónas Gudni SÆVARSSON	28/11/83	Halmstad (SWE)						M76					7	2
Atli GUDNASON	28/9/84	FH						M46			s77	s84	3	-
Arnór Sveinn ADALSTEINSSON	26/1/86	Breidablik						s46	s66	D	D	s76	5	-
Matthías VILHJÁLMSSON	30/1/87	FH						s76			M49	M	4	1
Kári ÁRNASON	13/10/82	Plymouth (ENG)							D				17	1
Bjarni Eggerts GUDJÓNSSON	26/2/79	KR							s74				23	1
Skúli Jón FRIDGEIRSSON	30/7/88	KR								D89	D	D	3	-
Jón Gudni FJÓLUSON	10/4/89	Fram								D	D	D	3	-
Valur Fannar GÍSLASON	8/9/77	Fylkir								D	D	D	5	-
Jóhann Berg GUDMUNDSSON	27/10/90	AZ (NED)								M65	M84	A79	6	-
Gudmundur KRISTJÁNSSON	1/3/89	Breidablik									M	M	3	-
Kolbeinn SIGTHÓRSSON	14/3/90	AZ (NED)								A84	A	s72	3	2
Fjalar THORGEIRSSON	18/1/77	Fylkir									s46		5	-
Óskar Örn HAUKSSON	22/8/84	KR									s65		2	-
Alfred FINNBOGASON	1/2/89	Breidablik									s84		1	-
Gudmundur Reynir GUNNARSSON	21/1/89	GAIS (SWE)									s89		3	-
Gunnar Örn JÓNSSON	30/4/85	KR										s87	1	-
Gylfi Thór SIGURDSSON	8/9/89	Reading (ENG)										M60	1	-
Birkir BJARNASON	27/5/88	Viking (NOR)										M	1	-
Eggert Gunnthór JÓNSSON	18/8/88	Hearts (SCO)										s46	5	-
Arnór SMÁRASON	7/9/88	Heerenveen (NED)										s60	8	1

DOMESTIC LEAGUE 2009

ÚRVALSDEILD FINAL LEAGUE TABLE

		Home					Away					Total					
	Pld	W	D	L	F	A	W	D	L	F	A	W	D	L	F	A	Pts
1 FH Hafnarfjördur	22	8	1	2	30	14	8	2	1	27	7	16	3	3	57	21	51
2 KR Reykjavík	22	7	1	3	30	18	8	2	1	28	13	15	3	4	58	31	48
3 Fylkir	22	7	3	1	22	11	6	1	4	19	15	13	4	5	41	26	43
4 Fram Reykjavík	22	6	2	3	22	12	4	2	5	18	20	10	4	8	40	32	34
5 Breidablik	22	4	3	4	20	19	6	1	4	18	14	10	4	8	38	33	34
6 Keflavík	22	8	1	2	21	10	0	8	3	17	27	8	9	5	38	37	33
7 Stjarnan	22	6	3	2	24	13	1	2	8	21	31	7	5	10	45	44	26
8 Valur Reykjavík	22	3	3	5	16	24	4	1	6	10	19	7	4	11	26	43	25
9 Grindavík	22	3	3	5	15	21	3	1	7	19	23	6	4	12	34	44	22
10 ÍBV Vestmannaeyjar	22	4	3	4	14	14	2	1	8	10	31	6	4	12	24	45	22
11 Thróttur Reykjavík	22	2	3	6	13	26	2	1	8	10	22	4	4	14	23	48	16
12 Fjölnir	22	3	1	7	17	25	0	5	6	10	22	3	6	13	27	47	15

TOP GOALSCORERS

16 Björgólfur TAKEFUSA (KR)

14 Atli Vidar BJÖRNSSON (FH)

13 Alfred FINNBOGASON (Breidablik)

11 Atli GUDNASON (FH)
   Gilles Mbang ONDO (Grindavík)

10 Matthías VILHJÁLMSSON (FH)

9 Arnar Már BJÖRGVINSSON (Stjarnan)

8 Kristinn STEINDÓRSSON (Breidablik)
  Albert Brynjar INGASON (Fylkir)
  Gunnar Örn JÓNSSON (KR)

 **ICELAND**

CLUB-BY-CLUB

BREIDABLIK
Coach – Ólafur H. Kristjánsson
Founded – 1950
Stadium – Kópavogsvöllur (5,039)
MAJOR HONOURS:
Icelandic Cup - (1) 2009.

2009
10/5	Thróttur	h	2-1	Steindórsson, Finnbogason
13/5	ÍBV	a	1-0	Finnbogason
18/5	FH	h	2-3	Kristjánsson, Finnbogason
24/5	Fylkir	a	1-3	Finnbogason
28/5	Keflavík	h	4-4	Baldvinsson 2, Finnbogason, Steindórsson
1/6	Fram	a	1-1	Ársælsson
15/6	Valur	h	0-1	
22/6	Stjarnan	h	2-1	Finnbogason, Steindórsson
29/6	KR	a	2-3	Finnbogason, Sigurgeirsson
2/7	Fjölnir	h	0-0	
13/7	Grindavík	a	1-0	Steindórsson
20/7	Thróttur	a	0-4	
23/7	ÍBV	h	3-4	Steindórsson, Pétursson, Thórisson
26/7	FH	a	1-2	Finnbogason
6/8	Fylkir	h	1-0	Grétarsson
9/8	Keflavík	a	3-0	Steindórsson, Gunnarsson Á., Finnbogason
16/8	Fram	h	3-3	Kristjánsson 3 (1p)
22/8	Valur	a	3-0	Pétursson 2, Kristjánsson
31/8	Stjarnan	a	3-1	Finnbogason 2, Ársælsson
16/9	KR	h	0-2	
20/9	Fjölnir	a	2-0	Steindórsson, Pétursson
26/9	Grindavík	h	3-0	Finnbogason 2, Steindórsson

No	Name	Nat	DoB	Pos	Aps	(s)	Gls
22	Arnór Sveinn ADALSTEINSSON		26/1/86	D	16	(1)	
6	Kári ÁRSÆLSSON		2/7/85	D	20	(1)	2
9	Haukur BALDVINSSON		5/5/90	A	3	(12)	2
10	Alfred FINNBOGASON		1/2/89	A	17	(1)	13
8	Arnar GRÉTARSSON		20/2/72	M	15		1
2	Árni Kristinn GUNNARSSON		10/4/80	D	15	(2)	1
17	Gudjón GUNNARSSON		5/1/88	M	1	(2)	
13	Elfar Freyr HELGASON		27/7/89	D	12	(3)	
19	Kristinn JÓNSSON		4/8/90	D	19		
1	Ingvar Thór KALE		8/12/83	G	21		
16	Gudmundur KRISTJÁNSSON		1/3/89	M	16	(3)	5
29	Reynir MAGNÚSSON		20/10/92	D		(1)	
3	Finnur Orri MARGEIRSSON		8/3/91	M	21		
24	Gudmundur PÉTURSSON		24/11/86	A	8	(2)	4
4	Evan SCHWARTZ	USA	27/10/87	M		(3)	
25	Sigmar SIGURDARSON		25/6/83	G	1	(1)	
14	Arnar SIGURDSSON		24/11/81	M	1	(2)	
11	Olgeir SIGURGEIRSSON		22/10/82	M	16	(4)	1
18	Aron Már SMÁRASON		26/4/84	M		(4)	
7	Kristinn STEINDÓRSSON		29/4/90	A	22		8
15	Gudmann THÓRISSON		30/1/87	D	12	(4)	1
30	Andri Rafn YEOMAN		18/4/92	M	6	(4)	

FH HAFNARFJÖRDUR
Coach – Heimir Gudjónsson
Founded – 1929
Stadium – Kaplakriki (6,390)
MAJOR HONOURS:
Icelandic League - (5) 2004, 2005, 2006, 2008, 2009;
Icelandic Cup - (1) 2007.

2009
11/5	Keflavík	a	0-1	
14/5	Fram	h	2-1	Gudmundsson T., Gudnason

18/5	Breidablik	a	3-2	Vilhjálmsson, Gudnason, Søderlund
23/5	Stjarnan	h	5-1	Søderlund 2, Björnsson, Ásgeirsson, Vidarsson D. (p)
28/5	KR	a	2-1	Vilhjálmsson, Gudnason
1/6	Fjölnir	h	3-0	Sverrisson 2, Björnsson
14/6	Grindavík	a	3-0	Björnsson 2, Vilhjálmsson
21/6	Thróttur	h	4-0	Vilhjálmsson 2, Gudnason, Björnsson
25/6	Fram	a	2-0	Gudmundsson T. 2
28/6	ÍBV	a	3-0	Björnsson, Vilhjálmsson, Ásgeirsson
2/7	Valur	a	5-0	Gudmundsson T. 2 (1p), Björnsson, Ásgeirsson, Vidarsson D.
9/7	Fylkir	h	3-2	Björnsson 2, Vilhjálmsson
18/7	Keflavík	h	2-2	Vidarsson D., Gudnason
26/7	Breidablik	h	2-1	Gudmundsson M., Gudmundsson T.
6/8	Stjarnan	a	4-1	Vilhjálmsson 2, Valgardsson, Björnsson
9/8	KR	h	2-4	Gudnason 2
15/8	Fjölnir	a	4-1	Björnsson 2, Gudmundsson T. (p), Sverrisson
22/8	Grindavík	h	0-3	
31/8	Thróttur	a	0-0	
13/9	ÍBV	h	5-0	Björnsson 2, Vilhjálmsson, Gudnason, Sverrisson
20/9	Valur	h	2-0	Gudnason 2
26/9	Fylkir	a	1-1	Gudnason

No	Name	Nat	DoB	Pos	Aps	(s)	Gls
6	Ásgeir Gunnar ÁSGEIRSSON		3/6/80	M	10	(1)	3
23	Brynjar BENEDIKTSSON		7/2/90	A		(5)	
5	Freyr BJARNASON		30/6/77	D	7	(5)	
17	Atli Vidar BJÖRNSSON		4/1/80	A	20	(1)	14
18	Kristján Gauti EMILSSON		26/4/93	M	1	(2)	
20	Sverrir GARDARSSON		15/9/84	D	6	(2)	
16	Matthías GUDMUNDSSON		1/8/80	A	7	(3)	1
9	Tryggvi GUDMUNDSSON		30/7/74	M	14	(6)	7
26	Viktor Örn GUDMUNDSSON		9/11/89	D	2	(2)	
11	Atli GUDNASON		28/9/84	A	19	(1)	11
19	Hákon Atli HALLFREDSSON		30/3/90	M	2	(5)	
13	Gudni Páll KRISTJÁNSSON		13/2/89	D	3		
1	Dadi LÁRUSSON		19/6/73	G	19		
4	Tommy NIELSEN	DEN	11/6/72	D	17	(3)	
12	Gunnar SIGURDSSON		14/8/75	G	3		
3	Dennis SIIM	DEN	10/4/76	M	5	(2)	
22	Ólafur Páll SNORRASON		22/4/82	M	7		
21	Björn Daníel SVERRISSON		29/5/90	M	7	(10)	4
14	Gudmundur SÆVARSSON		31/7/78	D	11		
2	Alexander SØDERLUND	NOR	3/8/87	A	7	(11)	3
27	Hjörtur Logi VALGARDSSON		27/9/88	D	18		1
8	Davíd Thór VIDARSSON		24/4/84	M	19		
7	Pétur VIDARSSON		25/11/87	D	16	(1)	
10	Matthías VILHJÁLMSSON		30/1/87	M	22		10

FJÖLNIR
Coach – Ásmundur Arnarsson
Founded – 1988
Stadium – Fjölnisvöllur (1,038)

2009
10/5	KR	a	1-2	Gardarsson
14/5	Valur	a	1-3	Leifsson
18/5	Grindavík	h	3-2	Gardarsson, Gunnarsson G., Gudmundsson G.M. (p)

23/5	Þróttur	a	1-1	Gunnarsson R.
28/5	ÍBV	h	1-3	og (Mwesigwa)
1/6	FH	a	0-3	
13/6	Fylkir	h	1-3	Gunnarsson I.
21/6	Keflavík	a	1-3	Gudmundsson G.M.(p)
28/6	Fram	h	1-2	Gardarsson
2/7	Breidablik	a	0-0	
9/7	Stjarnan	h	3-1	Ívarsson, Gardarsson, Gudmundsson G.M.(p)
19/7	KR	h	1-2	Ívarsson
23/7	Valur	h	2-0	Gunnarsson I., Gudmundsson G.M.
27/7	Grindavík	a	1-1	Gardarsson
5/8	Þróttur	h	1-3	Gardarsson
9/8	ÍBV	a	1-3	Ívarsson
15/8	FH	h	1-4	Jóhannsson
22/8	Fylkir	a	2-2	og (Óskarsson I.), Gunnarsson I.
29/8	Keflavík	h	3-3	Leifsson 2, Gardarsson
15/9	Fram	a	1-3	Gudmundsson G.M.(p)
20/9	Breidablik	h	0-2	
26/9	Stjarnan	a	1-1	Gudmundsson G.M.

No	Name	Nat	DoB	Pos	Aps	(s)	Gls
28	Hermann ADALGEIRSSON		4/4/85	M	1	(5)	
17	Ágúst Thór AGÚSTSSON		3/11/84	M	6	(7)	
10	Ásgeir Aron ÁSGEIRSSON		12/6/86	M	12	(2)	
27	Andri Steinn BIRGISSON		23/12/83	M	8		
12	Hrafn DAVÍDSSON		30/10/84	G	9		
22	Eythór Atli EINARSSON		13/7/83	D	3	(2)	
8	Magnús Ingi EINARSSON		14/12/81	D	21		
9	Jónas Grani GARDARSSON		15/3/73	A	19		7
29	Gudmundur Karl GUDMUNDSSON		30/3/91	A	2	(8)	
4	Gunnar Már GUDMUNDSSON		15/12/83	M	21		6
16	Heimir Snær GUDMUNDSSON		13/6/84	M	7		
2	Gunnar Valur GUNNARSSON		16/2/82	D	20		1
20	Illugi Thór GUNNARSSON		22/6/88	D	19	(1)	3
14	Ragnar Heimir GUNNARSSON		20/2/83	D	6	(4)	1
7	Ágúst Thór GYLFASON		1/8/71	M	2		
1	Thórdur INGASON		30/3/88	G	13		
23	Andri Valur ÍVARSSON		4/9/80	A	8	(4)	3
19	Marinó Thór JAKOBSSON		6/2/90	M		(1)	
6	Ólafur Páll JOHNSON		22/1/85	D	10	(3)	
13	Aron JÓHANNSSON		10/11/90	M	9	(7)	1
24	Vigfús Arnar JÓSEPSSON		15/8/84	D	11	(1)	
25	Geir KRISTINSSON		27/11/90	D	6	(2)	
26	Kolbeinn KRISTINSSON		27/11/90	M		(1)	
11	Tómas LEIFSSON		1/5/85	A	18		3
3	Olgeir ÓSKARSSON		28/1/89	M		(5)	
18	Kristinn Freyr SIGURDSSON		25/12/91	M	4	(10)	
15	Marinko SKARIĆIĆ	CRO	28/5/80	D	7		

FRAM REYKJAVÍK
Coach – Thorvaldur Örlygsson
Founded – 1908
Stadium – Laugardalsvöllur (9,800)
MAJOR HONOURS:
Icelandic League - (18) 1913, 1914, 1915, 1916, 1917, 1918, 1921, 1922, 1923, 1925, 1939, 1946, 1947, 1962, 1972, 1986, 1988, 1990;
Icelandic Cup - (7) 1970, 1973, 1979, 1980, 1985, 1987, 1989.

2009

10/5	ÍBV	h	2-0	Júlíusson, Thórarinsson H.
14/5	FH	a	1-2	og (Gudnason)
18/5	Fylkir	h	0-0	
23/5	Keflavík	a	0-1	
28/5	Valur	h	1-2	McShane
1/6	Breidablik	h	1-1	Thórarinsson H.
14/6	Stjarnan	a	1-4	Ólason
21/6	KR	h	3-0	Thórarinsson H. 2, Ormarsson
25/6	FH	h	0-2	
28/6	Fjölnir	a	2-1	Björnsson, Ormarsson
13/7	Þróttur	a	3-1	Gudmundsson, Thórarinsson H., Júlíusson (p)

20/7	ÍBV	a	1-1	Björnsson
27/7	Fylkir	a	1-2	Magnússon G.
6/8	Keflavík	h	5-0	Jónsson 2, Fjóluson, Tillen J., Magnússon G.
9/8	Valur	a	2-1	Tillen J., Ormarsson
16/8	Breidablik	a	3-3	Tillen S. (p), Júlíusson, Fjóluson
22/8	Stjarnan	h	3-2	Magnússon G., Thórarinsson H., Fjóluson
26/8	Grindavík	a	4-3	Ormarsson 2, Helgason, Thórarinsson H.
30/8	KR	a	1-3	Ormarsson
15/9	Fjölnir	h	3-1	og (Ásgeirsson), Tillen J., Fjóluson
20/9	Grindavík	a	3-1	Fjóluson, Björnsson, Júlíusson (p)
26/9	Þróttur	h	0-1	

No	Name	Nat	DoB	Pos	Aps	(s)	Gls
22	Ívar BJÖRNSSON		12/1/85	A	9	(4)	3
23	Jón Gudni FJÓLUSON		10/4/89	D	12	(5)	5
17	Grímur Björn GRÍMSSON		17/3/88	A		(3)	
13	Vidar GUDJÓNSSON		14/7/80	M		(2)	
7	Dadi GUDMUNDSSON		11/2/81	D	17		1
5	Hannes Thór HALLDÓRSSON		27/4/84	G	22		
4	Kristján HAUKSSON		3/2/86	D	20		
5	Audun HELGASON		18/6/74	D	17		1
16	Björn Orri HERMANNSSON		17/3/89	D		(2)	
6	Halldór Hermann JÓNSSON		1/10/84	M	20		2
8	Heidar Geir JÚLÍUSSON		16/8/87	M	16	(5)	4
30	Ögmundur KRISTINSSON		19/6/89	G		(1)	
21	Gudmundur MAGNÚSSON		10/6/91	A	2	(9)	3
14	Hlynur Atli MAGNÚSSON		11/9/90	M	2	(6)	
25	Hördur Björgvin MAGNÚSSON		11/2/93	A		(3)	
2	Paul McSHANE	SCO	13/4/78	M	15	(1)	1
11	Almarr ORMARSSON		25/2/88	M	20	(2)	6
26	Jón Orri ÓLAFSSON		11/3/85	D	6	(1)	
3	Ingvar ÓLASON		24/10/92	M	12	(3)	1
28	Rúrik THORFINNSSON		21/4/92	A		(1)	
20	Alexander THÓRARINSSON		14/12/88	M		(4)	
10	Hjálmar THÓRARINSSON		16/2/86	A	21	(1)	7
29	Joseph TILLEN	ENG	15/12/86	M	14	(5)	5
9	Samuel TILLEN	ENG	16/4/85	D	17	(1)	1

FYLKIR
Coach – Ólafur Thórdarson
Founded – 1967
Stadium – Fylkisvöllur (2,832)
MAJOR HONOURS:
Icelandic Cup - (2) 2001, 2002.

2009

10/5	Valur	h	1-0	Breiddal
14/5	Keflavík	h	2-0	Gíslason 2 (2p)
18/5	Fram	a	0-0	
24/5	Breidablik	h	3-1	Breiddal, Gíslason, Hilmisson
28/5	Stjarnan	a	1-2	Gíslason (p)
1/6	KR	h	2-2	Gíslason (p), Hannesson
13/6	Fjölnir	a	3-1	Óskarsson I. 2, Breiddal
21/6	Grindavík	h	2-3	Óskarsson I., Ingason
28/6	Þróttur	a	2-1	Hilmisson, Thórhallsson
1/7	ÍBV	h	3-0	Hilmisson, Breiddal, Ingason
9/7	FH	a	2-3	Óskarsson I., Breiddal
20/7	Valur	a	1-0	Baldvinsson
23/7	Keflavík	a	0-1	
27/7	Fram	h	2-1	Óskarsson I., Gíslason (p)
6/8	Breidablik	a	0-1	
9/8	Stjarnan	h	2-1	Stígsson, Ingason (p)
17/8	KR	a	4-2	Óskarsson I. 2, og (Rutgers), Ingason
21/8	Fjölnir	h	2-2	Ingason (p), Pétursson
31/8	Grindavík	a	3-2	Breiddal, Pétursson, Ingason (p)
13/9	Þróttur	h	2-0	Ingason, Faye

ICELAND

19/9	ÍBV	a	3-2	Ingason, Hannesson, Stígsson
26/9	FH	h	1-1	Breiddal

No	Name	Nat	DoB	Pos	Aps	(s)	Gls
17	Ásgeir Örn ARNTHÓRSSON		2/5/90	M		(1)	
30	Davið Thór ÁSBJÖRNSSON		24/2/92	M	1	(4)	
21	Ásgeir Börkur ÁSGEIRSSON		16/4/87	M	18	(2)	
19	Kjartan Andri BALDVINSSON		6/5/88	A		(17)	1
11	Kjartan Ágúst BREIDDAL		20/3/86	M	21		7
10	Pape Mamadou FAYE		6/3/91	A	9	(10)	1
4	Valur Fannar GÍSLASON		8/9/77	M	18		6
25	Ólafur Thór GUNNARSSON		25/10/77	G	8		
6	Thórir HANNESSON		8/10/86	D	11	(3)	2
22	Halldór Arnar HILMISSON		20/6/77	M	20	(1)	3
28	Felix HJÁLMARSSON		8/3/90	M		(3)	
14	Albert Brynjar INGASON		16/1/86	A	12	(3)	8
8	Andrés Már JÓHANNESSON		21/12/88	D	18		
1	Daníel KARLSSON		15/5/83	G	1		
7	Ingimundur ÓSKARSSON		4/2/86	A	20		7
3	Theódór ÓSKARSSON		17/5/80	A	4	(5)	
23	Einar PÉTURSSON		8/2/86	D	17		2
5	Ólafur STÍGSSON		16/12/75	M	13	(6)	2
18	Fjalar THORGEIRSSON		18/1/77	G	13		
16	Tómas THORSTEINSSON		8/12/88	D	12	(2)	
9	Jóhann THÓRHALLSSON		7/1/80	A	3	(8)	1
20	Arnar Thór ÚLFARSSON		29/4/80	D	1	(1)	
2	Kristján VALDIMARSSON		12/5/84	D	22		

GRINDAVÍK
Coach – Milan Stefán Jankovic; (20/5/09) Lúkas Kostic
Founded – 1935
Stadium – Grindavíkurvöllur (1,750)

2009

10/5	Stjarnan	a	1-3	Ondo
14/5	KR	h	0-4	
18/5	Fjölnir	a	2-3	Ondo, Jónasson
25/5	Valur	a	1-1	Ramsay
28/5	Thróttur	h	2-1	Helgason J., Hjaltalín
1/6	ÍBV	a	1-3	Ondo (p)
14/6	FH	h	0-3	
21/6	Fylkir	a	3-2	Helgason J., Ramsay, Ondo
25/6	KR	a	0-2	
28/6	Keflavík	h	1-1	Jósefsson
13/7	Breidablik	h	0-1	
19/7	Stjarnan	h	4-2	Bjarnason, Ondo, Stamenić, Ramsay
27/7	Fjölnir	h	1-1	Bjarnason
6/8	Valur	h	3-1	Einarsson, Gudmundsson, Ondo
9/8	Thróttur	a	5-1	Ramsay 2, Bjarnason, Gudmundsson, Jósefsson
22/8	FH	a	3-0	Ramsay, Ondo, Helgason J.
26/8	Fram	a	3-4	Hjaltalín, Helgason J., Ondo (p)
31/8	Fylkir	h	2-3	Hjaltalín, Ondo
3/9	ÍBV	h	1-1	Ondo
16/9	Keflavík	a	0-1	
20/9	Fram	h	1-3	Ondo
26/9	Breidablik	a	0-3	

No	Name	Nat	DoB	Pos	Aps	(s)	Gls
25	Jóhann Helgi ADALGEIRSSON		16/3/80	D		(1)	
21	Gudmundur BERGSTEINSSON		26/4/92	M		(2)	
2	Óli Baldur BJARNASON		31/10/89	M	10	(9)	3
17	Bogi Rafn EINARSSON		22/6/88	D	12		1
27	Óli Stefán FLÓVENTSSON		7/12/75	D	11		
8	Páll GUDMUNDSSON		22/10/86	M	2	(10)	2
8	Eysteinn HAUKSSON		12/8/74	M	7	(3)	
16	Helgi Már HELGASON		18/1/83	G	1		
7	Jóhann HELGASON		19/4/84	M	20	(1)	4
11	Orri Freyr HJALTALÍN		1/7/80	M	20		3
6	Sveinbjörn JÓNASSON		17/7/86	A	8	(5)	1

3	Ray Anthony JÓNSSON		3/2/79	D	21		
23	Jósef Kristinn JÓSEFSSON		12/9/89	D	21		2
9	Thórarinn KRISTJÁNSSON		30/12/80	A	6	(12)	
22	Ben LONG	ENG	16/4/90	D	3	(1)	
30	Óttar Steinn MAGNÚSSON		8/2/89	M	1	(2)	
28	Tor Erik MOEN	NOR	3/10/83	M	7	(1)	
19	Gilles Mbang ONDO	GAB	10/10/85	A	21		11
1	Óskar PÉTURSSON		26/1/89	G	21		
4	Scott RAMSAY	SCO	2/10/75	M	20		6
26	Emil Dadi SÍMONARSON		2/6/88	M	2	(6)	
18	Sylvain SOUMARE	FRA	25/8/82	M	4		
14	Zoran STAMENIĆ	BIH	3/8/77	D	18		1
5	Marko Valdimar STEFÁNSSON		18/9/90	D	6	(1)	
15	Gunnar THORSTEINSSON		1/2/94	M		(2)	

ÍBV VESTMANNAEYJAR
Coach – Heimir Hallgrímsson
Founded – 1945
Stadium – Hásteinsvöllur (2,834)
MAJOR HONOURS:
Icelandic League – (3) 1979, 1997, 1998; Icelandic Cup - (4) 1968, 1972, 1981, 1998.

2009

10/5	Fram	a	0-2	
13/5	Breidablik	h	0-1	
17/5	Stjarnan	a	0-3	
23/5	KR	h	0-1	
28/5	Fjölnir	a	3-1	Mawejje, Leitch-Smith, Ólafsson An.
1/6	Grindavík	h	3-1	Thorvardarson, Leitch-Smith, Kjartansson
14/6	Thróttur	a	1-2	Valdimarsson
22/6	Valur	a	0-2	
28/6	FH	h	0-3	
1/7	Fylkir	a	0-3	
12/7	Keflavík	h	2-2	Sigurbjörnsson, Ólafsson An.
20/7	Fram	h	1-1	Leitch-Smith
23/7	Breidablik	a	4-3	Leitch-Smith, Clements, Garner, Nsumba
26/7	Stjarnan	h	1-0	Ólafsson An.
9/8	Fjölnir	h	3-1	Kjartansson, Ólafsson An., Mawejje
23/8	Thróttur	h	1-0	Nsumba
26/8	KR	a	0-3	
29/8	Valur	h	1-1	Leitch-Smith
3/9	Grindavík	a	1-1	Nsumba
13/9	FH	a	0-5	
19/9	Fylkir	h	2-3	Ólafsson An., Sigurbjörnsson
26/9	Keflavík	a	1-6	Borgthórsson

No	Name	Nat	DoB	Pos	Aps	(s)	Gls
26	Elías Ingi ÁRNASON		12/8/83	A		(3)	
20	Eythór Helgi BIRGISSON		24/2/89	A		(2)	
11	Anton BJARNASON		25/7/87	M		(2)	
8	Yngvi Magnús BORGTHÓRSSON		26/3/75	M	16		1
2	Chris CLEMENTS	ENG	6/2/90	M	13	(2)	1
16	Bjarni Rúnar EINARSSON		6/9/83	M	8	(8)	
3	Matt GARNER	ENG	9/4/84	D	17		1
20	Atli GUDJÓNSSON		25/2/88	D		(1)	
23	Ingi Rafn INGIBERGSSON		30/11/83	M	1	(6)	
17	Egill JÓHANNSSON		18/7/88	M	1	(2)	
12	Vidar Örn KJARTANSSON		11/3/90	A	10	(7)	2
28	Ajay LEITCH-SMITH	ENG	6/3/90	A	16	(2)	5
15	Tony MAWEJJE	UGA	15/12/86	M	20	(1)	2
14	Andrew MWESIGWA	UGA	24/4/84	D	15		
21	Augustine NSUMBA	UGA	18/8/87	A	11	(8)	3
6	Andri ÓLAFSSON		26/6/85	M	20		5
19	Arnór Eyvar ÓLAFSSON		27/11/89	D	13	(3)	
9	Pétur RUNÓLFSSON		20/11/81	M	18	(1)	
24	Eidur Aron SIGURBJÖRNSSON		26/2/90	D	19		2

30	Elías Fannar STEFNISSON	17/10/90	G	4	(1)	
7	Albert SÆVARSSON	18/10/73	G	18		
22	Gauti THORVARDARSON	19/2/89	A	8	(9)	1
5	Thórarinn Ingi VALDIMARSSON	23/4/90	M	14	(5)	1

KEFLAVÍK

Coach – Kristján Gudmundsson;
(28/9/09) (Willum Thór Thórsson)
Founded – 1929
Stadium – Keflavíkurvöllur (2,872)
MAJOR HONOURS:
Icelandic League – (4) 1964, 1969, 1971, 1973;
Icelandic Cup - (4) 1975, 1997, 2004, 2006.

2009

11/5	FH	h	1-0	*Rúnarsson*
14/5	Fylkir	a	0-2	
18/5	Valur	h	3-0	*Sveinsson 2, Antoníusson*
23/5	Fram	h	1-0	*Gudmundsson J.*
28/5	Breidablik	a	4-4	*Gudnason, Thorsteinsson, Matthíasson, Adalsteinsson*
1/6	Stjarnan	h	1-1	*Sveinsson*
14/6	KR	a	1-4	*Sutej*
21/6	Fjölnir	h	3-1	*Matthíasson, Thorsteinsson, Gudnason*
25/6	Thróttur	h	3-2	*Arnarson, Thorsteinsson (p), Sveinsson*
28/6	Grindavík	a	1-1	*Thorsteinsson (p)*
12/7	ÍBV	a	2-2	*Gudnason 2*
18/7	FH	a	2-2	*Antoníusson, Thorsteinsson*
23/7	Fylkir	h	1-0	*Rúnarsson*
27/7	Valur	a	2-2	*Gudnason, Gudmundsson J.*
6/8	Fram	a	0-5	
9/8	Breidablik	h	0-3	
17/8	Stjarnan	a	0-0	
22/8	KR	h	1-2	*Steinarsson (p)*
29/8	Fjölnir	a	3-3	*Samuelsen, Thorsteinsson, Eysteinsson*
16/9	Grindavík	h	1-0	*Thorsteinsson*
20/9	Thróttur	a	2-2	*Gudmundsson J., Rúnarsson*
26/9	ÍBV	h	6-1	*Steinarsson 2, Samuelsen 2, Sutej, Gudmundsson H.*

No	Name	Nat	DoB	Pos	Aps	(s)	Gls
20	Bjarni Hólm ADALSTEINSSON		5/10/84	D	20		1
3	Gudjón Árni ANTONÍUSSON		3/9/83	D	20		2
29	Stefán Örn ARNARSON		8/10/81	A	1	(4)	1
13	Einar Orri EINARSSON		28/10/90	M	11	(7)	
7	Jón Gunnar EYSTEINSSON		3/7/86	M	16	(3)	1
16	Brynjar Örn GUDMUNDSSON		9/10/82	M	16	(1)	
8	Haraldur Freyr GUDMUNDSSON		14/12/81	M	8		1
14	Jóhann Birnir GUDMUNDSSON		5/12/77	M	10	(4)	3
4	Haukur Ingi GUDNASON		8/9/78	A	15	(5)	5
26	Viktor GUDNASON		13/12/89	M		(2)	
1	Ómar JÓHANNSSON		2/3/81	G	1		
21	Lasse JØRGENSEN	DEN	23/4/84	G	21		
6	Nicolai JØRGENSEN	DEN	15/1/80	D	6	(2)	
5	Tómas Karl KJARTANSSON		23/10/90	D		(2)	
15	Bojan Stefán LJUBICIC		22/6/92	M		(4)	
22	Magnús Thór MAGNÚSSON		20/2/92	A		(2)	
18	Magnús Thórir MATTHÍASSON		22/1/90	A	5	(9)	2
25	Hólmar Örn RÚNARSSON		10/12/81	M	13		3
10	Símon SAMUELSEN	FRO	21/5/85	M	17	(1)	3
9	Gudmundur STEINARSSON		20/10/79	A	8	(2)	3
2	Alen SUTEJ	SVN	10/9/85	D	21		2
27	Hördur SVEINSSON		24/3/83	A	9	(4)	4
30	Sverrir Thór SVERRISSON		23/5/75	A		(2)	
24	Sigurdur Gunnar SÆVARSSON		25/7/90	D	1		
11	Magnús THORSTEINSSON		22/9/82	A	22		7
1	Bessi VÍDISSON		11/10/90	M	1	(3)	

KR REYKJAVÍK

Coach – Logi Ólafsson
Founded – 1899
Stadium – KR-völlur (2,781)
MAJOR HONOURS:
Icelandic League – (24) 1912, 1919, 1926, 1927, 1928, 1929, 1931, 1932, 1934, 1941, 1948, 1949, 1950, 1952, 1955, 1959, 1961, 1963, 1965, 1968, 1999, 2000, 2002, 2003;
Icelandic Cup - (11) 1960, 1961, 1962, 1963, 1964, 1966, 1967, 1994, 1995, 1999, 2008.

2009

10/5	Fjölnir	h	2-1	*Takefusa, Sævarsson*
14/5	Grindavík	a	4-0	*Jónsson, og (Ramsay), Rajcomar, Takefusa (p)*
17/5	Thróttur	h	0-0	
23/5	ÍBV	a	1-0	*Sigurdsson B.*
28/5	FH	h	1-2	*Gudjónsson*
1/6	Fylkir	a	2-2	*Jónsson, Hauksson*
14/6	Keflavík	h	4-1	*Benediktsson, Sævarsson, Hauksson, Sigurdsson B.*
21/6	Fram	a	0-3	
25/6	Grindavík	h	2-0	*Sigurdsson B. 2*
29/6	Breidablik	h	3-2	*Hauksson, Sigurdarson, Rutgers*
2/7	Stjarnan	a	1-1	*Takefusa (p)*
11/7	Valur	h	3-4	*Benediktsson, og (Hreidarsson), Sigurdsson B.*
19/7	Fjölnir	a	2-1	*Takefusa, Rajcomar*
27/7	Thróttur	a	5-1	*Sigurdarson, Takefusa (p), Jónsson, Jóhannsson, Sigurdsson B.*
9/8	FH	a	4-2	*Jónsson 2, Takefusa, Sigurdsson B.*
17/8	Fylkir	h	2-4	*Benediktsson, Takefusa (p)*
22/8	Keflavík	a	2-1	*Jónsson, Takefusa*
26/8	ÍBV	h	3-0	*Takefusa, og (Sigurbjörnsson), Sigurdsson I.*
30/8	Fram	h	3-1	*Takefusa, Rutgers, Fridgeirsson*
16/9	Breidablik	a	2-0	*Jónsson, Sigurdarson*
20/9	Stjarnan	h	7-3	*Hauksson 3, Benediktsson, Gudjónsson, Jónsson, Takefusa*
26/9	Valur	a	5-2	*Takefusa 5*

No	Name	Nat	DoB	Pos	Aps	(s)	Gls
11	Gudmundur BENEDIKTSSON		3/9/74	A	11	(9)	4
30	Jordão da Encarnação Tackey DIOGO	POR	12/11/85	D	20		
25	Eggert Rafn EINARSSON		28/1/90	D			
7	Skúli Jón FRIDGEIRSSON		30/7/88	D	21		1
4	Bjarni Eggerts GUDJÓNSSON		26/2/79	M	21		2
23	Gudmundur R. GUNNARSSON		21/1/89	D	2	(5)	
29	André HANSEN	NOR	17/12/89	G	8		
9	Óskar Örn HAUKSSON		22/8/84	M	17	(4)	6
8	Atli JÓHANNSSON		5/10/82	M	9	(8)	1
13	Atli JÓNASSON		12/3/88	G	1		
20	Gunnar Örn JÓNSSON		30/4/85	M	18	(2)	8
12	Gunnar KRISTJÁNSSON		2/3/87	D	1	(11)	
22	Stefán Logi MAGNÚSSON		5/9/80	G	13		
17	Ásgeir Örn ÓLAFSSON		12/1/88	D		(1)	
3	Gudmundur PÉTURSSON		24/11/86	A		(10)	
21	Prince RAJCOMAR	NED	25/4/85	A	9	(6)	2
18	Mark RUTGERS	NED	29/6/86	D	17	(1)	2
2	Grétar SIGURDARSON		9/10/82	D	22		3
16	Baldur SIGURDSSON		24/4/85	M	21		7
19	Ingólfur SIGURDSSON		12/2/93	M	(3)		1
6	Jónas Gudni SÆVARSSON		28/11/83	M	13		2
10	Björgólfur TAKEFUSA		11/5/80	A	17	(2)	16

STJARNAN
Coach – Bjarni Jóhannsson
Founded – 1960
Stadium – Stjörnuvöllur (1,080)

2009

10/5	Grindavík	h 3-1	Helgason G., Laxdal J., Björnsson
14/5	Thróttur	a 6-0	Björgvinsson A. 2, Laxdal J., Björnsson, Thorsteinsson, Björgvinsson M.
17/5	ÍBV	h 3-0	Björgvinsson A. 2, Bjarnason
23/5	FH	a 1-5	Helgason H.
28/5	Fylkir	h 2-1	Thorsteinsson, Pálsson
1/6	Keflavík	a 1-1	Björnsson
14/6	Fram	h 4-1	Björnsson 2, Björgvinsson A. 2
22/6	Breidablik	a 1-2	Björgvinsson A.
25/6	Valur	h 3-0	Hreinsson 2, Björgvinsson A.
2/7	KR	h 1-1	Bjarnason
9/7	Fjölnir	a 1-3	Björgvinsson M.
19/7	Grindavík	a 2-4	Laxdal J., Björgvinsson A.
23/7	Thróttur	h 5-1	Hreinsson 2, Helgason H., Bjarnason, Björnsson
26/7	ÍBV	a 0-1	
6/8	FH	h 1-4	Hreinsson
9/8	Fylkir	a 1-2	Björnsson
17/8	Keflavík	h 0-0	
22/8	Fram	a 2-3	Björgvinsson M., Laxdal J.
31/8	Breidablik	h 1-3	Bjarnason
13/9	Valur	a 3-3	Árnason 2, Birgisson
20/9	KR	a 3-7	Árnason 2, Thorsteinsson
26/9	Fjölnir	h 1-1	Laxdal J.

No	Name	Nat	DoB	Pos	Aps	(s)	Gls
28	Thorvaldur ÁRNASON		25/6/80	A	10	(2)	4
14	Birgir Hrafn BIRGISSON		6/10/85	M	18		1
3	Tryggvi Sveinn BJARNASON		16/1/83	D	20		4
18	Arnar Már BJÖRGVINSSON		10/2/90	A	8	(7)	9
7	Magnús BJÖRGVINSSON		12/9/87	A	3	(11)	3
10	Halldór Orri BJÖRNSSON		2/3/87	M	21		7
19	Heiðar Atli EMILSSON		14/3/90	M	3	(4)	
11	Bjarki Páll EYSTEINSSON		1/4/86	D	7	(5)	
26	Grétar Atli GRÉTARSSON		5/11/86	D		(3)	
25	Davíd GUDJÓNSSON		21/3/93	G		(1)	
30	Baldvin GUDMUNDSSON		20/6/64	G		(1)	
4	Bjarni HALLDÓRSSON		26/7/83	G	21		
6	Gudni Rúnar HELGASON		16/7/76	D	18	(1)	1
23	Hafsteinn Rúnar HELGASON		9/6/85	D	22		2
22	Ellert HREINSSON		12/10/86	A	9	(2)	5
16	Richard HURLIN	WAL	14/1/84	M	(4)		
24	Alfred Elías JÓHANNSSON		12/8/76	A	4	(1)	
9	Daníel LAXDAL		22/9/86	D	21		
12	Jóhann LAXDAL		27/1/90	M	18	(2)	5
1	Kjartan ÓLAFSSON		7/10/85	G	1		
5	Björn PÁLSSON		28/12/86	M	21		1
8	Andri SIGURJÓNSSON		11/4/90	M	3	(6)	
2	Sindri Már SIGURTHÓRSSON		8/4/86	M		(1)	
21	Baldvin STURLUSON		9/4/89	D	1	(7)	
20	Steinthór Freyr THORSTEINSSON		29/7/85	M	13	(1)	3

THRÓTTUR REYKJAVÍK
Coach – Gunnar Oddsson; (28/7/09) Thorsteinn Halldórsson; (26/9/09) Páll Einarsson
Founded – 1949
Stadium – Valbjarnarvöllur (3,102)

2009

10/5	Breidablik	a 1-2	Hjartarson
14/5	Stjarnan	h 0-6	
17/5	KR	a 0-0	
23/5	Fjölnir	h 1-1	Smidt

28/5	Grindavík	a	1-2	Haraldsson
1/6	Valur	a	1-2	Danry (p)
14/6	ÍBV	h	2-1	Hjartarson, Danry
21/6	FH	a	0-4	
25/6	Keflavík	a	2-3	Lúdvíksson (p), Sigurdsson
28/6	Fylkir	h	1-2	Sigurdsson
13/7	Fram	h	1-3	Smidt
20/7	Breidablik	h	4-0	Sigurdsson 2, Danry, Smidt
23/7	Stjarnan	a	1-5	Sigurdsson
27/7	KR	h	1-5	Malsom
5/8	Fjölnir	a	3-1	Sigurdsson, Malsom, Vilhjálmsson A.
9/8	Grindavík	h	1-5	Gudmundsson
17/8	Valur	h	0-1	
23/8	ÍBV	a	0-1	
31/8	FH	h	0-0	
13/9	Fylkir	a	0-2	
20/9	Keflavík	h	2-2	Malsom, Björnsson O.
26/9	Fram	a	1-0	Malsom

No	Name	Nat	DoB	Pos	Aps	(s)	Gls
22	Kristján Ómar BJÖRNSSON		14/11/80	D	20	(1)	
16	Oddur BJÖRNSSON		18/11/91	M	2	(2)	1
1	Henrik BØDKER	DEN	23/6/81	G	6	(1)	
21	Dennis DANRY	DEN	5/12/78	D	22		3
29	Trausti EIRÍKSSON		12/5/88	M	1	(3)	
8	Oddur Ingi GUDMUNDSSON		28/1/89	M	9	(3)	1
3	Hallur HALLSSON		10/3/80	M	16	(1)	
19	Rafn Andri HARALDSSON		10/4/89	M	18		1
9	Hjörtur Júlíus HJARTARSON		31/10/74	A	6	(3)	2
4	Thórdur HREIDARSSON		13/12/86	D	8	(2)	
28	Dušan IVKOVIĆ	SRB	31/1/80	D	10		
12	Sindri Snær JENSSON		12/8/86	G	16		
24	Jón Ragnar JÓNSSON		30/10/85	D	17	(2)	
13	Skúli JÓNSSON		29/4/88	M	2	(2)	
26	Kristinn Steinar KRISTINSSON		31/3/89	M	1	(1)	
20	Magnús Már LÚDVÍKSSON		30/5/81	M	12	(1)	1
14	Samuel MALSOM	ENG	10/11/87	A	10		4
25	Vilhjálmur PÁLMASON		1/11/91	M		(2)	
5	Birkir PÁLSSON		1/2/83	D	10	(4)	
11	Davíð Thór RÚNARSSON		9/10/78	A	4	(6)	
2	Runólfur SIGMUNDSSON		21/6/89	D	8		
7	Haukur Páll SIGURDSSON		5/8/87	M	15		6
10	Morten SMIDT	DEN	27/10/89	A	14	(4)	3
18	Ingvi SVEINSSON		19/2/79	D	1	(7)	
15	Miloš TANASIĆ	SRB	18/11/88	M	1		
17	Andrés VILHJÁLMSSON		12/12/83	M	6	(14)	1
30	Hafthór Ægir VILHJÁLMSSON		29/9/86	M	7	(1)	

VALUR REYKJAVÍK
Coach – Willum Thór Thórsson; (3/7/09) Atli Edvaldsson; (27/9/09) Gunnlaugur Jónsson.
Founded – 1911
Stadium – Vodafonevöllurinn ad Hlídarenda (2,225)
MAJOR HONOURS:
Icelandic League – (20) 1930, 1933, 1935, 1936, 1937, 1938, 1940, 1942, 1943, 1944, 1945, 1956, 1966, 1967, 1976, 1978, 1980, 1985, 1987, 2007;
Icelandic Cup – (9) 1965, 1974, 1976, 1977, 1988, 1990, 1991, 1992, 2005.

2009

10/5	Fylkir	a 0-1	
14/5	Fjölnir	h 3-1	Sigurdsson, Snorrason, Baldvinsson
18/5	Keflavík	a 0-3	
25/5	Grindavík	h 1-1	Baldvinsson
28/5	Fram	a 2-1	Eiríksson, Baldvinsson
1/6	Thróttur	h 2-1	Snorrason, Hreidarsson
15/6	Breidablik	a 1-0	Bett
22/6	ÍBV	h 2-0	Markan, Snorrason
25/6	Stjarnan	a 0-3	
2/7	FH	h 0-5	

11/7	KR	a	4-3	Thórarinsson, Markan, Sigurdsson (p), Illugason
20/7	Fylkir	h	0-1	
23/7	Fjölnir	a	0-2	
27/7	Keflavík	h	2-2	Markan, Sigurdsson
6/8	Grindavík	a	1-3	Thórarinsson
9/8	Fram	h	1-2	Sigurdsson
17/8	Thróttur	a	1-0	Sigurdsson
22/8	Breidablik	h	0-3	
29/8	ÍBV	a	1-1	Hreidarsson (p)
13/9	Stjarnan	h	3-3	Sigurdsson, Geirsson, Hreidarsson (p)
20/9	FH	a	0-2	
26/9	KR	h	2-5	Sigurdsson (p), Hafsteinsson

No	Name	Nat	DoB	Pos	Aps	(s)	Gls
16	Baldur ADALSTEINSSON		12/2/80	M	9	(5)	
30	Marel BALDVINSSON		18/12/80	A	15	(4)	3
8	Baldur BETT		12/4/80	M	12	(1)	1
23	Haraldur BJÖRNSSON		11/1/89	G	9		
21	Bjarni Ólafur EIRÍKSSON		28/3/82	D	21		1
18	Arnar Sveinn GEIRSSON		30/8/91	A	3	(4)	1
3	Steinthór GÍSLASON		27/12/83	D	11		
11	Matthías GUDMUNDSSON		1/8/80	M	7		
13	Arnar GUNNLAUGSSON		6/3/73	A	4		
14	Bjarki GUNNLAUGSSON		6/3/73	M		(1)	
17	Gudmundur HAFSTEINSSON		14/6/89	A	5	(8)	1
7	Sigurbjörn HREIDARSSON		25/11/75	M	17		3
19	Viktor Unnar ILLUGASON		25/1/90	A	3	(14)	1
20	Ian JEFFS	ENG	12/10/82	M	18	(2)	
4	Reynir LEÓSSON		20/8/79	D	20		
6	Pétur Georg MARKAN		16/2/81	M	9	(6)	3
12	Einar MARTEINSSON		22/4/89	D	4	(5)	
2	Gudmundur Vidar METE		4/2/81	D	7	(5)	
10	Helgi SIGURDSSON		17/9/74	A	17	(2)	7
22	Ólafur Páll SNORRASON		22/4/82	M	12		3
1	Kjartan STURLUSON		27/12/75	G	13		
5	Atli Sveinn THÓRARINSSON		24/1/80	D	20		2
9	Hafthór Ægir VILHJÁLMSSON		29/9/86	M	6	(1)	

PROMOTED CLUBS

SELFOSS
Coach – Gunnlaugur Jónsson; (30/9/09) Gudmundur Benediktsson
Founded – 1936
Stadium – Selfossvöllur (1,500)

HAUKAR
Coach – Andri Marteinsson
Founded – 1931
Stadium – Ásvellir (1,400)

SECOND LEVEL FINAL TABLE 2009

		Pld	W	D	L	F	A	Pts
1	Selfoss	22	15	2	5	53	26	47
2	Haukar	22	13	5	4	44	28	44
3	HK Kópavogur	22	11	3	8	36	28	36
4	Fjardabyggd	22	11	3	8	32	33	36
5	KA Akureyri	22	10	5	7	32	24	35
6	Thór Akureyri	22	10	1	11	33	35	31
7	Leiknir Reykjavík	22	7	8	7	32	33	29
8	ÍR Reykjavík	22	9	2	11	40	46	29
9	ÍA Akranes	22	7	7	8	26	27	28
10	Víkingur Reykjavík	22	7	5	10	36	34	26
11	Afturelding	22	3	7	12	25	45	16
12	Víkingur Ólafsvík	22	3	4	15	24	54	13

DOMESTIC CUP 2009

BIKAR

THIRD ROUND

(17/6/09)
Fram 2, Njardvík 1
Haukar 0, Fjardabyggd 1 *(aet)*
Reynir S. 2, KV 1
Selfoss 2, Höttur 2 *(aet; 1-3 on pens)*
Thór 3, Víkingur Ó. 1

(18/6/09)
Carl 0, FH 3
Fjölnir 0, HK 2
Fylkir 7, Stjarnan 3
Grindavík 3, ÍA 1
Grótta 0, KR 2
Hvöt 0, Breidablik 2
ÍBV 3, Víkingur R. 2
KA 3, Afturelding 1
Keflavík 2, Einherji 0
Valur 3, Álftanes 0
Vídir 0, Thróttur R. 0 *(aet; 3-2 on pens)*

FOURTH ROUND

(5/7/09)
Breidablik 3, Höttur 1 *(aet)*
Fram 1, Grindavík 0 *(aet)*
Fylkir 6, Fjardabyggd 1
ÍBV 2, FH 3 *(aet)*
Keflavík 2, Thór 1

(6/7/09)
HK 5, Reynir S. 2 *(aet)*
Valur 3, KA 2 *(aet)*
Vídir 0, KR 2

QUARTER-FINALS

(30/7/09)
Fram 2 *(Tillen S. 85p, Fjóluson 90)*, Fylkir 0
HK 0, Breidablik 1 *(Pétursson 35)*
Keflavík 3 *(Nielsen 20og, Samuelsen 48, 58)*, FH 1 *(Gudnason 71)*

(2/8/09)
Valur 1 *(Eiríksson 43)*, KR 3 *(Takefusa 60, 87, Benediktsson 77p)*

SEMI-FINALS

(12/9/09)
Fram 1 *(Tillen J. 78)*, KR 0

(13/9/09)
Breidablik 3 *(Helgason 8, Jónsson 12, Pétursson 66p)*, Keflavík 2 *(Antoníusson 22, Samuelsen 26)*

FINAL

(3/10/09)
Laugardalsvöllur, Reykjavik
BREIDABLIK 2 *(Finnbogason 60, 102p)*
FRAM REYKJAVÍK 2 *(Ólason 73, Tillen S. 98p)*
(aet; 5-4 on pens)
Referee – Valgeirsson
BREIDABLIK – Kale, Gunnarsson A., Helgason, Ársælsson, Jónsson *(Adalsteinsson 99)*, Grétarsson *(Yeoman 99)*, Margeirsson, Kristjánsson *(Sigurgeirsson 106)*, Pétursson, Finnbogason, Steindórsson.
FRAM – Halldórsson, Ólafsson, Helgason, Hauksson, Tillen S., Júlíusson *(McShane 69)*, Ólason, Jónsson, Fjóluson *(Tillen J. 69)*, Ormarsson *(Magnússon G. 106)*, Thórarinsson H.

Fairytale finish for Hapoel Tel-Aviv

srael's Ligat Ha'al has had some tight, tense finishes in its time but nothing as sensationally dramatic as the ending to the 2009/10 season, in which Hapoel Tel-Aviv FC, reduced to ten men, scored a winning goal two minutes into added time of their final fixture to snatch the title away from defending champions and long-time front-runners Maccabi Haifa FC on goal difference.

One of the main motives behind the decision to increase Israel's top division to a 16-team, two-tier format was to stoke up late-season interest. In that respect the experiment could hardly have produced a more successful outcome. The fans of Maccabi Haifa did not quite see it like that, however, many of them vehemently suggesting that Israel Football Association (IFA) president Avi Luzon, the man behind the league revamp, had robbed them of the title given that their club had actually won three points more than Hapoel Tel-Aviv over the full campaign – only to have a six-point lead at the 30-match split reduced to three. The truth, however, was that the rules and regulations were known to all and sundry at the start and that Haifa surrendered the title by failing to win their last game.

The contest should never have become so close. At one stage Haifa held a 12-point lead. While simultaneously struggling in the UEFA Champions League – they reached the group stage impressively with a fine win over FC Salzburg but failed to register any points or goals in the main event – Elisha Levi's side were taking out their frustrations at home. They won their first ten games and by mid-February had yielded only five points. A 12th league title seemed assured, but Hapoel Tel-Aviv - who also had to cope with a weighty extra-curricular schedule in the UEFA Europa League, in which they sensationally topped a group containing Celtic FC, Hamburger SV and SK Rapid Wien before being frozen out, almost literally, in Kazan - refused to go away.

Long unbeaten run

The Reds, expertly coached by the experienced Eli Gutman, went 31 league matches unbeaten following a 2-1 defeat to Maccabi Haifa in September. They won the big clash at Bloomfield in late April to replace their rivals at the top of the table, and although they subsequently handed the initiative back to Haifa with a 0-0 draw against Maccabi Tel-Aviv FC, they did what they had to on decision-day, Eran Zhavi striking in the dying seconds to bring them a 2-1 win at Beitar Jerusalem FC while Haifa could only manage a 1-1 draw at Bnei Yehuda Tel-Aviv FC.

Hapoel Tel-Aviv's league triumph – their first in a decade – completed a domestic double, because four days earlier they had inscribed their name on the State Cup for the 12th time with a 3-1 win over Bnei Yehuda in the final at Ramat-Gan. Diminutive midfielder Gil Vermouth, the Reds' Player of the Season, scored twice, with the other goal going to the club's regular penalty-taker, goalkeeper Vincent Enyeama, an entertaining

Israel Football Association (IFA)

Ramat-Gan Stadium
299 Aba Hilell Street
PO Box 3591
IL-52134 Ramat-Gan
tel – +972 3 617 1500
fax - +972 3 570 2044
website – football.org.il
email – info@football.org.il
Year of Formation - 1928

President – Avraham Luzon
General Secretary – Ori Shilo
Media Officer – Gil Lebanony
National Stadium – Ramat-Gan (41,583)

INTERNATIONAL TOURNAMENT APPEARANCES
FIFA World Cup - (1) 1970.
TOP FIVE ALL-TIME CAPS
Arik Benado (94); Alon Harazi (88); Amir Shelache (85); Mordechay Shpiegler (84); Nir Klinger (83)
TOP FIVE ALL-TIME GOALS
Mordechay Shpiegler (33); Yehushua Feigenboim (24); Ronen Harazi (23); Nahum Stelmach (22); Gideon Damti (21)

tay Shechter (right) leads the celebrations after scoring for Hapoel Tel-Aviv against Rapid Wien in the UEFA Europa League

maverick who would go on to distinguish himself for Nigeria at the FIFA World Cup. Another star turn was striker Itay Shechter, Hapoel's top scorer in the league

with 22 goals – six shy of the Ligat Ha'al's most prolific marksman, Maccabi Haifa's Shlomi Arbeitman.

Shechter, 23, and Arbeitman, 25, have the potential to become a potent strike partnership at international level for Israel. Both were included by the national team's new coach, Luis Fernandez, in his first couple of squads, and although neither impressed as the Frenchman's reign got off to a false start with two heavy defeats in South America against World Cup-bound Uruguay and Chile, the pair should get the chance to shine in the UEFA EURO 2012 qualifying campaign, in which Israel have the opportunity to avenge both Greece and Latvia for ruining their chances of going to South Africa under previous coach Dror Kashtan.

NATIONAL TEAM RESULTS 2009/10

12/8/09	Northern Ireland	A	Belfast	1-1	Barda (82)
5/9/09	Latvia (WCQ)	H	Tel-Aviv	0-1	
9/9/09	Luxembourg (WCQ)	H	Tel-Aviv	7-0	Barda (9, 21, 43), Baruchyan (15), Golan (58), Sahar (63, 84)
10/10/09	Moldova (WCQ)	H	Tel-Aviv	3-1	Barda (21, 70), Ben Dayan (65)
14/10/09	Switzerland (WCQ)	A	Basel	0-0	
3/3/10	Romania	A	Timisoara	2-0	Benayoun (45), Barda (83p)
26/5/10	Uruguay	A	Montevideo	1-4	Refaelov (30)
30/5/10	Chile	A	Concepcion	0-3	

NATIONAL TEAM APPEARANCES 2009/10

Coach – Dror KASHTAN /(17/2/10) (Eli OHANA) /(21/3/10) Luis FERNÁNDEZ (FRA)	1/10/44 1/2/64 2/10/59		Nir	LVA	LUX	MDA	SUI	Rou	Uru	Chi	Caps	Goals
Dudu AWAT	17/10/77	Mallorca (ESP)	G46	G	G46	G	G	G46	G	G	51	-
Eyal MESHUMAR	10/8/83	M. Haifa	D								4	-
Dekel KEINAN	15/9/84	M. Haifa	D46	D			s53	D			15	-
Avi STRUL	18/9/80	Lokeren (BEL)	D70	D	D	D	D	D53		D46	15	-
Dedi BEN DAYAN	27/11/78	H. Tel-Aviv	D	D	D	D					23	1
Tamir COHEN	4/3/84	Bolton (ENG)	M46	s46	M	M	M	s46			16	-
Avihai YADIN	26/10/86	H. Tel-Aviv	M68			M	M	M46 60*	M54	M	6	-
Aviram BARUCHYAN	20/3/85	Beitar Jerusalem	M	s67	M						10	2
Yossi BENAYOUN	5/5/80	Liverpool (ENG)	M54	M67	M	M	M	M80			78	20
Roberto COLAUTTI	24/5/82	Mönchengladbach (GER)	A		s72	A68	A46	A59	s66		19	6
Elyaniv BARDA	15/12/81	Genk (BEL)	A	A	A59	A72	A85	s46	s73	A53	22	11
Nir DAVIDOVICH	17/12/76	M. Haifa	s46		s46			s46			51	-
Tal BEN HAIM	31/3/82	Man. City (ENG) /Portsmouth (ENG)	s46		D	D	D	D70			54	-
Biram KAYAL	2/5/88	M. Haifa	s46	M	M		M	M90			13	-
Salim TOAMA	9/8/79	Larissa (GRE)	s54								13	1
Yoav ZIV	16/3/81	Lokeren (BEL)	s68		D	D29	D	D	D	D	26	-
Din MORI	8/11/88	Bnei Yehuda	s70					s70			2	-

ISRAEL

NATIONAL TEAM APPEARANCES 2009/10 (contd.)

			Nir	LVA	LUX	MDA	SUI	Rou	Uru	Chi	Caps	Goals
Yuval SHPUNGIN	3/4/87	M. Tel-Aviv	D								9	-
Gal ALBERMAN	17/4/83	Mönchengladbach (GER)	M46								26	1
Yaniv KATAN	27/1/81	M. Haifa	A								31	5
Omer GOLAN	4/10/82	Lokeren (BEL)	A63	A67					s80	s52	37	8
Ben SAHAR	10/8/89	Espanyol (ESP)	s63	s59	A61				A64		19	5
Barak ITZHAKI	25/9/84	Beitar Jerusalem		s67							11	1
Gil VERMOUTH	5/8/85	H. Tel-Aviv				M	s85	M70	M61	M52	6	-
Klimi SABAN	17/2/80	M. Netanya				s29	D	D	D78	D52	25	1
Itay SHECHTER	22/2/87	H. Tel-Aviv				s61	s68	A46	s64	A59	6	-
Shlomi ARBEITMAN	14/5/85	M. Haifa						s46	s59	s53	8	3
Bibras NATCHO	18/2/88	H. Tel-Aviv /Rubin (RUS)						s70	M73	M	3	-
Roni GAFNI	11/3/80	M. Tel-Aviv						s90			2	-
Shai MAYMON	18/3/86	M. Haifa							D	D66	2	-
Lior REFAELOV	26/4/86	M. Haifa							M	s59	3	1
Nir BITON	30/10/91	Ashdod							s54	M	2	-
Maor MELIKSSON	30/10/84	H. Beer-Sheva							s61		1	-
Ali OSMAN	8/2/87	M. Haifa							s78	s46	2	-
Eliran DANIN	29/3/84	Beitar Jerusalem								s52	1	-

DOMESTIC LEAGUE 2009/10

LIGAT HA'AL FINAL TABLE

		Pld	Home					Away					Total					Pts
			W	D	L	F	A	W	D	L	F	A	W	D	L	F	A	
1	Hapoel Tel-Aviv FC	35	13	4	1	52	17	12	5	0	35	9	25	9	1	87	26	49
2	Maccabi Haifa FC	35	15	2	1	35	8	13	1	3	37	8	28	3	4	72	16	49
3	Maccabi Tel-Aviv FC	35	10	5	3	29	17	7	4	6	23	18	17	9	9	52	35	34
4	Bnei Yehuda Tel-Aviv FC	35	7	5	5	21	17	7	6	5	22	17	14	11	10	43	34	31
5	Beitar Jerusalem FC	35	9	3	5	26	15	5	4	9	24	29	14	7	14	50	44	26
6	FC Ashdod	35	8	4	5	23	19	3	6	9	13	26	11	10	14	36	45	22
7	Bnei Sakhnin FC	33	8	5	4	21	17	5	3	8	10	14	13	8	12	31	31	27
8	Maccabi Petach-Tikva FC	33	4	5	7	19	22	6	6	5	25	25	10	11	12	44	47	24
9	Hapoel Beer-Sheva FC	33	9	2	6	27	24	2	8	6	22	31	11	10	12	49	55	23
10	Maccabi Netanya FC	33	7	4	5	24	17	3	5	9	20	30	10	9	14	44	47	21
11	Hapoel Haifa FC	35	5	5	8	22	25	5	4	8	22	25	10	9	16	44	50	23
12	Hapoel Akko FC	35	3	9	5	17	23	4	5	9	21	29	7	14	14	38	52	23
13	Hapoel Petach-Tikva FC	35	5	10	3	18	18	3	4	10	10	30	8	14	13	28	48	23
14	Hapoel Ramat-Gan FC	35	4	7	7	13	27	5	4	8	21	22	9	11	15	34	49	22
15	Hapoel Ra'anana FC	35	5	4	8	21	27	1	6	11	12	31	6	10	19	33	58	18
16	Maccabi Ahi Nazareth FC	35	4	2	11	17	40	3	5	10	16	41	7	7	21	33	81	16

NB After 30 matches clubs were split into three groups, after which they played exclusively against teams in their group. Points obtained during the regular season were halved (and rounded upwards).

TOP GOALSCORERS

28 Shlomi ARBEITMAN (M. Haifa)

22 Itay SHECHTER (H. Tel-Aviv)

16 Barak ITZHAKI (Beitar Jerusalem)
   Vladimer DVALISHVILI (M. Haifa)

13 Dimitar MAKRIEV (Ashdod)

12 Toto TAMUZ (Beitar Jerusalem)
   Pedro GALVÁN (Bnei Yehuda)

11 Dedi BEN DAYAN (H. Tel-Aviv)
   Eran ZHAVI (H. Tel-Aviv)
   Idan SHRIKI (Ashdod)
   Eran LEVI (H. Haifa)

CLUB-BY-CLUB

FC ASHDOD
Coach – Yossi Mizrahi
Founded – 1999
Stadium – Yud Alef (7,420)

2009

23/8	Bnei Yehuda	h	0-3	(w/o; original result 1-1 Makriev)
29/8	H. Haifa	a	1-0	Makriev
12/9	H. Akko	h	1-0	Ohayon Mo.
26/9	H. Ra'anana	a	1-1	Shriki
3/10	H. Ramat-Gan	h	0-0	
17/10	H. Tel-Aviv	a	2-2	Makriev 2
24/10	M. Petach-Tikva	h	1-1	Checkul
2/11	H. Beer-Sheva	a	0-1	
9/11	M. Haifa	h	0-1	
21/11	M. Netanya	a	1-0	Shriki
28/11	Beitar	h	2-0	Ohayon Mo., Shriki
6/12	M. Ahi Nazareth	h	2-1	Sade, Ohayon Mo.
14/12	M. Tel-Aviv	a	0-2	
19/12	Bnei Sakhnin	h	0-0	
26/12	H. Petach-Tikva	a	1-1	Shriki

2010

2/1	Bnei Yehuda	a	3-2	Makriev 2, Shriki
9/1	H. Haifa	h	1-0	Makriev
16/1	H. Akko	a	1-1	Makriev
23/1	H. Ra'anana	h	0-0	
30/1	H. Ramat-Gan	a	1-0	Makriev
7/2	H. Tel-Aviv	h	0-4	
13/2	M. Petach-Tikva	a	1-1	Weitzman
20/2	H. Beer-Sheva	h	5-2	Shriki 2, Makriev 2, Biton
28/2	M. Haifa	a	0-1	
6/3	M. Netanya	h	3-0	Makriev, Shriki, Sade
13/3	Beitar	a	0-2	
20/3	M. Ahi Nazareth	a	0-1	
27/3	M. Tel-Aviv	h	3-1	Sade (p), Shriki, Nachum
3/4	Bnei Sakhnin	a	0-1	
10/4	H. Petach-Tikva	h	2-1	Shriki, Makriev
17/4	M. Haifa	a	1-3	Sade (p)
24/4	Beitar	h	1-2	Shriki
1/5	H. Tel-Aviv	a	0-4	
8/5	Bnei Yehuda	h	2-3	Mizrahi 2
15/5	M. Tel-Aviv	a	0-2	

No	Name	Nat	DoB	Pos	Aps	(s)	Gls
11	Barak BADASH		30/8/82	A	5	(9)	
28	Eden BATIT		14/8/90	M		(2)	
12	Nenad BEGOVIĆ	SRB	6/1/80	M		(3)	
20	Itzhak BEN SALOMON		3/10/85	M		(1)	
4	Nir BITON		30/10/91	M	15	(4)	1
3	Ben BUTBOL		22/5/90	M		(4)	
8	Rahamim CHECKUL		8/5/88	D	26	(1)	1
10	Barukh DEGO		26/3/81	M	3	(6)	
25	Cristian GONZÁLEZ	URU	19/12/76	D	32		
6	Stéphane KINGUE	CMR	2/6/85	M	26	(1)	
20	Amir LAVIE		8/9/89	M	5	(11)	
7	Dimitar Ivanov MAKRIEV	BUL	7/1/84	A	33	(1)	13
1	Offir MARCIANO		7/10/89	G	2		
19	Nevo MIZRAHI		26/7/87	A	2	(4)	2
18	Nir NACHUM		9/9/83	A	12	(14)	1
17	Mattan OHAYON		25/2/86	D	27		
9	Moshe OHAYON		24/5/83	M	30	(2)	3
13	Maor PERETZ		18/11/83	D	6	(3)	
21	Marko POPOVIĆ	SRB	25/8/82	D	12		
15	Shay REVIVO		13/12/86	M	14	(10)	
2	Isreal ROSH		5/3/88	D	12		
27	Idan SADE		8/5/88	D	19	(13)	4
14	Idan SHRIKI		30/11/81	A	29	(5)	11
22	Dragan STOJKIĆ	BIH	7/10/75	G	33		
16	Adir TOBUL		3/6/79	D	11	(5)	
3	Idan TZION		24/5/88	D	8		
28	Ori UZAN		27/12/78	D	9	(1)	
5	Idan WEITZMAN		20/4/85	M	14	(5)	1

BEITAR JERUSALEM FC
Coach – Itzhak Shum; (20/2/10) David Amsalem
Founded – 1939
Stadium – Teddy (21,600)
MAJOR HONOURS:
Israeli League - (6) 1987, 1993, 1997, 1998, 2007, 2008;
Israeli Cup - (7) 1976, 1979, 1985, 1986, 1989, 2008, 2009.

2009

24/8	H. Tel-Aviv	h	0-0	
31/8	Bnei Sakhnin	a	0-0	
12/9	M. Petach-Tikva	a	3-1	Vered, Tamuz 2
26/9	H. Petach-Tikva	h	3-0	Tal, Itzhaki, Ben Shoshan
5/10	H. Beer-Sheva	a	2-3	Itzhaki, Tamuz
19/10	Bnei Yehuda	h	1-0	Ben Shoshan
26/10	M. Haifa	a	1-2	Vered
31/10	H. Haifa	h	3-1	Itzhaki 2 (2p), Tamuz
7/11	M. Netanya	a	0-3	
21/11	H. Akko	h	1-1	Tamuz
28/11	Ashdod	a	0-2	
5/12	H. Ra'anana	h	3-1	Baruchyan A., Tamuz 2
12/12	M. Ahi Nazareth	a	1-0	Ben Shoshan
19/12	H. Ramat-Gan	h	1-0	Tamuz
26/12	M. Tel-Aviv	a	3-4	Tamuz, Itzhaki 2

2010

4/1	H. Tel-Aviv	a	3-4	Itzhaki, Rikan, Baruchyan A.
11/1	Bnei Sakhnin	h	1-0	og (Abu Ria Ma.)
16/1	M. Petach-Tikva	h	1-2	Itzhaki
23/1	H. Petach-Tikva	a	0-0	
30/1	H. Beer-Sheva	h	1-1	Ben Yossef
6/2	Bnei Yehuda	a	0-0	
14/2	M. Haifa	h	0-3	
20/2	H. Haifa	a	2-3	Itzhaki, Benado
27/2	M. Netanya	h	3-1	Itzhaki 3
6/3	H. Akko	a	3-0	Tal, Baruchyan A., Azriel
13/3	Ashdod	h	2-0	Ben Shoshan, Tamuz
20/3	H. Ra'anana	a	3-1	Itzhaki 3
27/3	M. Ahi Nazareth	h	5-0	Azriel, Tamuz, Ben Shoshan, Einbinder, Elihen
3/4	H. Ramat-Gan	a	0-0	
10/4	M. Tel-Aviv	h	0-1	
17/4	M. Haifa	a	0-3	
24/4	Ashdod	a	2-1	Ben Shoshan, Tamuz
1/5	Bnei Yehuda	h	0-2	
8/5	M. Haifa	a	1-2	Benado
15/5	H. Tel-Aviv	h	1-2	Itzhaki

No	Name	Nat	DoB	Pos	Aps	(s)	Gls
14	Chen AZRIEL		26/6/88	A	17	(7)	2
8	Aviram BARUCHYAN		20/3/85	M	19	(2)	3
16	Evitar BARUCHYAN		24/8/89	D	1	(3)	
7	Amit BEN SHOSHAN		23/5/85	A	26	(7)	6
6	Tomer BEN YOSSEF		2/9/79	D	17	(6)	1
4	Arik BENADO		5/12/73	D	26	(5)	2
3	Eliran DANIN		29/3/84	D	16	(2)	
25	Paolo DE LA HAZA	PER	30/11/83	M	19		
15	Dan EINBINDER		16/8/89	M	1	(5)	1
17	Tzahi ELIHEN		3/4/91	A		(6)	1
5	Shimon GERSHON		6/10/77	D	28		
23	David GOMES Pimenta	BRA	5/9/88	A		(5)	
1	Ariel HAROSH		25/5/88	G	35		
9	Barak ITZHAKI		25/9/84	A	31	(2)	16
2	Shmoel KOZOKIN		23/7/87	D	3	(3)	
19	Barak MOSHE		19/3/91	A	1		
21	Kobi MOYAL		12/6/87	M	23	(5)	
18	Avi RIKAN		10/9/88	D	25	(3)	1
10	Idan TAL		13/9/75	M	27	(5)	2
10	Toto TAMUZ		1/4/88	A	26	(6)	12
28	Eitan TIBI		16/11/87	D	18	(3)	
23	Sebastián VÁZQUEZ Maidana	URU	4/11/80	D	1	(7)	
20	Idan VERED		25/5/89	M	16	(5)	2
27	César Junior VIZA	PER	3/4/85	M	9	(10)	

ISRAEL

BNEI SAKHNIN FC
Coach – Eran Kulik; (21/10/09) Marko Balbul
Founded – 1993
Stadium – Doha (6,000)
MAJOR HONOURS:
Israeli Cup - (1) 2004.

2009

22/8	M. Tel-Aviv	a	1-3	*Kasum*
31/8	Beitar	h	0-0	
12/9	H. Petach-Tikva	h	2-0	*Djako 2*
26/9	Bnei Yehuda	a	1-2	*Hen (p)*
3/10	H. Haifa	h	0-3	
18/10	H. Akko	a	0-0	
24/10	H. Ra'anana	h	1-1	*Cadu*
31/10	H. Ramat-Gan	a	0-1	
8/11	H. Tel-Aviv	h	1-2	*Halaila Ha.*
21/11	M. Petach-Tikva	a	2-1	*Kasum, Cadu*
28/11	H. Beer-Sheva	h	1-1	*Abu Ria Ma.*
5/12	M. Haifa	a	0-1	
13/12	M. Netanya	h	0-3	
19/12	Ashdod	a	0-0	
26/12	M. Ahi Nazareth	h	1-1	*Djako*

2010

2/1	M. Tel-Aviv	h	0-0	
11/1	Beitar	a	0-1	
17/1	H. Petach-Tikva	a	0-0	
23/1	Bnei Yehuda	h	2-0	*Cadu, Halaila Ha. (p)*
30/1	H. Haifa	a	1-0	*Kasum*
6/2	H. Akko	h	1-0	*Cohen L.*
13/2	H. Ra'anana	a	1-0	*Ganaym H.*
21/2	H. Ramat-Gan	h	3-1	*og (Levi), Cadu, Čeh*
28/2	H. Tel-Aviv	a	0-1	
6/3	M. Petach-Tikva	h	3-4	*Cadu, Cohen L., Yeye*
14/3	H. Beer-Sheva	a	0-1	
21/3	M. Haifa	h	2-1	*Cohen L., Ganaym H.*
27/3	M. Netanya	a	2-1	*Hen, Ganaym H.*
3/4	Ashdod	h	1-0	*Hen*
10/4	M. Ahi Nazareth	a	2-0	*Ganaym H. 2*
17/4	M. Petach-Tikva	h	2-0	*Kasum, Itzhak*
24/4	H. Beer-Sheva	h	1-0	*Itzhak*
1/5	M. Netanya	a	0-2	

No	Name	Nat	DoB	Pos	Aps	(s)	Gls
25	Ibrahem ABO SALEM		20/2/89	M	6	(1)	
23	Amir ABU ARAR		23/4/85	A	1	(1)	
27	Mahran ABU RIA		22/1/83	D	30	(1)	1
24	Mohamad ABU RIA		2/9/88	A		(2)	
38	Ala'a ABU SALAH		25/6/87	M	18	(1)	
27	Mohammed BADRANY		8/5/90	M		(1)	
14	Haim BANOON		26/7/80	M	30	(2)	
5	Emad BDARNH		18/3/89	M		(2)	
18	Eli BITTON		25/1/82	M		(8)	
20	Carlos Eduardo Castro da Silva "CADU"	BRA	23/4/82	A	17	(12)	5
10	Nastja ČEH	SVN	26/1/78	M	13		1
21	Jair Edson CÉSPEDES	PER	22/5/84	M	3	(1)	
19	Đorđije ĆETKOVIĆ	MNE	3/1/83	M	1	(7)	
18	Liran COHEN		4/2/83	M	11	(2)	3
1	Meir COHEN		8/6/72	G	31		
11	Arafat DJAKO	TOG	30/6/91	A	21	(6)	3
12	Basem GANAYM		27/1/76	D	11	(5)	
17	Hamed GANAYM		8/7/87	M	20	(11)	5
12	Haled HALAILA		16/12/82	M	26	(2)	2
5	Hilal HALAILA		24/1/88	D	1		1
3	Tal HEN		4/8/79	M	32		2
9	Ran ITZHAK		2		(10)		2
22	Mahmod KANDALI		11/8/88	G	2		
9	Ahmed KASUM		25/1/85	A	25	(3)	4
18	Ali OSMAN		8/2/87	D	1		
10	Reuven OVED		28/11/83	M	4	(5)	
19	Scott SEALY	TRI	4/6/81	A	6	(4)	
8	Abbas SUAN		27/1/76	M	15	(1)	
23	Cherifou YACOUBOU-FOUSSEND	TOG	31/12/88	A	1	(2)	
6	Lenkebe Paty YEYE	COD	2/2/82	D	32		1

23	Obada ZBEDAT		30/7/90	A	2	(2)	
16	Liran ZERKO		23/1/81	D		(1)	
7	Muhammad ZVIDATH		15/11/91	D	1		

BNEI YEHUDA TEL-AVIV FC
Coach – Guy Luzon
Founded – 1936
Stadium – Bloomfield (15,700)
MAJOR HONOURS:
Israeli League - (1) 1990;
Israeli Cup - (2) 1968, 1981.

2009

23/8	Ashdod	a	3-0	*(w/o; original result 1-1 Amsis)*
31/8	M. Ahi Nazareth	h	2-0	*Galván 2*
14/9	M. Tel-Aviv	a	0-0	
26/9	Bnei Sakhnin	h	2-1	*Afek, Cohen*
3/10	H. Petach-Tikva	a	1-1	*Atar*
19/10	Beitar	a	0-1	
24/10	H. Haifa	h	2-0	*Atar, Biton*
31/10	H. Akko	a	1-1	*Zairi*
7/11	H. Ra'anana	h	2-1	*Galván 2*
21/11	H. Ramat-Gan	a	2-0	*Amsis, Galván*
28/11	H. Tel-Aviv	h	0-1	
5/12	M. Petach-Tikva	a	1-0	*Galván*
12/12	H. Beer-Sheva	h	2-2	*Atar 2*
20/12	M. Haifa	a	0-2	
27/12	M. Netanya	h	2-1	*Galván 2*

2010

2/1	Ashdod	h	2-3	*Galván, Biton*
9/1	M. Ahi Nazareth	a	2-2	*Atar, Galván*
16/1	M. Tel-Aviv	h	0-1	
23/1	Bnei Sakhnin	a	0-2	
30/1	H. Petach-Tikva	h	1-1	*Baldut*
6/2	Beitar	h	0-0	
15/2	H. Haifa	a	3-0	*Radi, Galván, Atar*
20/2	H. Akko	h	2-1	*Biton, Galván*
27/2	H. Ra'anana	a	3-0	*Baldut (p), Radi, Amsis*
7/3	H. Ramat-Gan	h	1-2	*Atar (p)*
13/3	H. Tel-Aviv	a	0-4	
20/3	M. Petach-Tikva	h	2-0	*Biton, Zairi*
27/3	H. Beer-Sheva	h	0-0	
5/4	M. Haifa	h	0-2	
10/4	M. Netanya	a	1-1	*Linić*
17/4	H. Tel-Aviv	a	0-1	
24/4	M. Tel-Aviv	h	0-0	
1/5	Beitar	a	2-0	*og (Moyal), Biton*
8/5	Ashdod	a	3-2	*Levi, Radi, Atar*
15/5	M. Haifa	h	1-1	*Zairi*

No	Name	Nat	DoB	Pos	Aps	(s)	Gls
7	Hassan ABU ZEID		4/4/91	M	14	(7)	
18	Omri AFEK		31/3/79	M	17	(8)	1
1	Bamidele AIYENUGBA	NGA	20/11/83	G	29		
15	George AMSIS		17/12/90	M	7	(9)	3
11	Eliran ATAR		17/2/87	A	31	(2)	8
17	Itzhak AZOZ		30/11/85	D	9	(6)	
8	Asi BALDUT		21/10/81	M	17	(8)	2
14	Moshe BITON		18/11/82	A	14	(16)	5
25	Liran COHEN		4/2/83	M	3	(6)	1
23	Kfir EDRI		12/10/76	D	34		
20	Pedro Joaquín GALVÁN	ARG	18/8/85	M	28	(1)	12
6	Iván Alonso GARRIDO	COL	2/6/81	D	31		
13	Nitzan HA'ARONOVIC		8/9/89	D	3		
16	Aviv HADAD		4/2/84	D	5	(2)	
22	Ran KADOSH		4/10/85	G	6	(1)	
25	Shlomi LEVI		29/7/91	A	1	(2)	1
12	Siniša LINIĆ	CRO	4/3/83	M	25	(4)	1
30	Tal MISHAN		1/7/90	M	1	(1)	
4	Din MORI		8/11/88	D	31		
9	Maharan RADI		1/7/82	M	25	(7)	3
27	Oz RALI		22/12/87	D	28	(2)	
19	Omer REPS		5/3/85	A		(1)	
10	Liroy ZAIRI		2/3/89	M	18	(10)	3
19	Michael ZANDBERG		16/4/80	M	8	(4)	

HAPOEL AKKO FC
Coach – Yaron Hochenboym
Founded – 1946
Stadium – Green Nazareth Ilit (3,000)

2009

22/8	M. Haifa	a	1-2	Elmaliah
29/8	M. Netanya	h	1-1	Barkai
12/9	Ashdod	a	0-1	
26/9	M. Ahi Nazareth	h	0-1	
3/10	M. Tel-Aviv	a	1-1	Barkai
18/10	Bnei Sakhnin	h	0-0	
24/10	H. Petach-Tikva	a	1-1	Simantov (p)
31/10	Bnei Yehuda	h	1-1	Cohen
7/11	H. Haifa	a	4-2	Simantov (p), Dayan, Elmaliah, Gita
21/11	Beitar	a	1-1	Gita
29/11	H. Ra'anana	h	1-1	Ben Nahum
5/12	H. Ramat-Gan	a	1-1	Simantov (p)
19/12	M. Petach-Tikva	h	3-2	Gita, Barkai, Elmakies
26/12	H. Beer-Sheva	h	1-3	Elmakies
29/12	H. Tel-Aviv	h	1-1	Cohen

2010

2/1	M. Haifa	h	0-3	
10/1	M. Netanya	a	0-1	
16/1	Ashdod	h	1-1	Fadlon
23/1	M. Ahi Nazareth	a	0-1	
30/1	M. Tel-Aviv	h	2-3	Mba, Simantov
6/2	Bnei Sakhnin	a	0-1	
13/2	H. Petach-Tikva	h	0-0	
20/2	Bnei Yehuda	a	1-2	Dayan
27/2	H. Haifa	h	2-2	Simantov (p), Abdul Razak Ib.
7/3	Beitar	h	0-3	
13/3	H. Ra'anana	a	1-0	Elmaliah
20/3	H. Ramat-Gan	h	1-0	Dayan
27/3	H. Tel-Aviv	a	3-5	Abdul Razak Ib. 2, Dayan
3/4	M. Petach-Tikva	h	2-2	Martins, Awudu
10/4	H. Beer-Sheva	a	2-3	Gita 2
17/4	H. Petach-Tikva	a	2-1	Awudu, Cohen
24/4	H. Haifa	a	0-4	
1/5	M. Ahi Nazareth	h	3-1	Awudu, Simantov, Dayan
8/5	H. Ramat-Gan	a	0-0	
15/5	H. Haifa	h	1-0	Tenenbaum

No	Name	Nat	DoB	Pos	Aps	(s)	Gls
11	Omar ABDUL AZIZ	NGA	26/12/85	A	7	(4)	
11	Ibrahim ABDUL RAZAK	GHA	18/4/83	A	16		3
5	Ismail ABDUL RAZAK	GHA	7/3/89	M	2		
6	Avi ALFASI		18/12/80	M	8	(18)	
13	Emmanuel AMUNGWA	CMR	6/9/83	M	24		
8	Hay ATIAS		26/4/87	M		(2)	
7	Samed Abdul AWUDU	GHA	15/9/84	A	14	(1)	3
24	Geva BARKAI		29/6/78	D	32		3
12	Ron BEN NAHUM		7/12/82	D	24	(4)	1
19	Ben BENJAMIN		17/12/85	M	24		
33	Yaniv CHICIAN		15/8/79	D	(2)		
3	Itzhak COHEN		22/4/83	D	24	(3)	3
9	Roei DAYAN		19/9/84	A	19	(9)	5
10	Omri ELMAKIES		21/7/87	A	6	(10)	2
20	Liad ELMALIAH		21/2/89	M	15	(6)	3
2	Ilay ERLIKH		14/1/89	D		(6)	
25	Dudu FADLON		16/9/76	D	26		1
15	Oshri GITA		2/7/85	A	13	(14)	5
1	Dudu GORESH		1/2/80	G	35		
77	Sharon GORMEZANO		14/8/87	A		(1)	
15	Moshe HALFON		24/11/86	M		(1)	
23	Lior LEVI		26/10/87	D	8	(3)	
5	Ben McCarthy MARTINS	LBR	16/1/86	A	4	(8)	1
14	Adeck Akah MBA	CMR	4/3/79	M	12	(5)	1
17	Ardijan NUHIJI	MKD	12/7/87	A	2	(1)	
18	Lior REUBEN		12/12/80	D	24	(1)	
10	Elior SAIDER		17/11/91	A		(2)	
7	Shachar SIMANTOV		18/4/79	M	23	(9)	6
29	Jonatan TENENBAUM		1/9/79	D	23	(3)	1

HAPOEL BEER-SHEVA FC
Coach – Guy Azori; (3/3/10) Victor Hadad
Founded – 1949
Stadium – Artur Vasermil (12,000)
MAJOR HONOURS:
Israeli League - (2) 1975, 1976;
Israeli Cup - (1) 1997.

2009

22/8	H. Ra'anana	h	2-1	Asulin L. 2
29/8	H. Ramat-Gan	a	2-2	Ilouz, Kadusi
13/9	H. Tel-Aviv	h	1-3	Asulin L.
26/9	M. Petach-Tikva	a	0-3	
5/10	Beitar	h	3-2	Asulin L., Meliksson, Revivo
17/10	M. Haifa	h	1-3	Kadusi
24/10	M. Netanya	a	2-2	Asulin L., Pergl
2/11	Ashdod	h	1-0	Meliksson
7/11	M. Ahi Nazareth	a	4-1	Offir 2, Pergl, Kadusi
23/11	M. Tel-Aviv	h	1-3	Meliksson (p)
28/11	Bnei Sakhnin	a	1-1	Kadusi
5/12	H. Petach-Tikva	h	2-0	Meliksson, Naser
12/12	Bnei Yehuda	a	2-2	Asulin L., Meliksson
19/12	H. Haifa	h	2-3	Fadida, Kadusi
26/12	H. Akko	a	3-1	Revivo, Fadida, Danilo

2010

2/1	H. Ra'anana	a	2-2	Offir, Naser
9/1	H. Ramat-Gan	h	1-0	Revivo
18/1	H. Tel-Aviv	a	1-4	Revivo
24/1	M. Petach-Tikva	h	0-1	
30/1	Beitar	a	1-1	Fadida
6/2	M. Haifa	a	1-4	Meliksson (p)
13/2	M. Netanya	h	2-0	Badash, Meliksson (p)
20/2	Ashdod	a	2-5	Badash 2
27/2	M. Ahi Nazareth	h	2-2	Meliksson, Offir
6/3	M. Tel-Aviv	a	1-1	Ilouz
14/3	Bnei Sakhnin	h	1-0	Badash (p)
20/3	H. Petach-Tikva	a	0-1	
27/3	Bnei Yehuda	h	0-0	
3/4	H. Haifa	a	0-0	
10/4	H. Akko	h	3-2	Naser, Badash, Kale
17/4	M. Netanya	h	4-0	Meliksson, Adeleye, Badash, Harosh
24/4	Bnei Sakhnin	a	0-1	
2/5	M. Petach-Tikva	h	1-4	Badash

No	Name	Nat	DoB	Pos	Aps	(s)	Gls
28	Ryan ADELEYE	USA	28/4/87	D	7	(1)	1
3	Lior ASULIN		6/10/80	A	13	(1)	6
21	Moshe ASULIN		11/10/88	M	8	(4)	
20	Barak BADASH		30/8/82	A	11	(2)	7
23	James BISSUE	GHA	15/6/91	A	3		
25	Gil BLUMENSHTIEN		21/5/90	A	5	(9)	
2	DANILO Moreira Serrano	BRA	19/8/80	D	28		1
13	Ofir DAVIDAZE		5/5/91	D	11		
22	Dor DAVIDI		20/10/87	G	2	(1)	
5	Yossi ELKAYAM		26/3/89	M		(4)	
7	Hanan FADIDA		1/12/81	A	11	(10)	3
3	Marcos Adrián GALARZA	ARG	3/4/84	D	8		
29	Shimon HAROSH		20/2/87	D	22	(1)	1
14	Aviatar ILOUZ		4/11/83	D	21	(3)	2
26	Hagai ITZHAK		8/10/90	A		(1)	
20	Ziv KABEDA		10/12/78	M		(1)	
11	Ohad KADUSI		24/9/85	A	14	(15)	5
1	Tvrtko KALE	CRO	5/6/74	G	31		1
4	Nadav KEDAR		9/1/87	D	15	(7)	
24	Maor MELIKSSON		30/10/84	M	28	(2)	9
17	Erez MESIKA		20/12/79	M	5		
16	Adamu MOHAMMED	GHA	24/3/83	D	7	(2)	
19	Siraj NASER		2/9/90	M	5	(18)	3
12	Yossi OFFIR		18/11/76	M	26	(4)	4
23	Dandi OKOGO	NGA	13/5/81	M	1	(4)	
27	Pavel PERGL	CZE	14/11/77	D	13		2
10	David REVIVO		5/12/77	M	28	(2)	4
15	Eyal SHEN		29/1/80	M	28	(1)	
25	Joseph TACHIE-MENSAH	GHA	28/3/85	M		(1)	
3	WILLIAM Ribeiro Soares	BRA	7/2/85	M	12		

ISRAEL

HAPOEL HAIFA FC
Coach – Shlomi Dora
Founded – 1924
Stadium – Kiriat Eliezer (17,000)
MAJOR HONOURS:
Israeli League - (1) 1999;
Israeli Cup - (3) 1963, 1966, 1974.

2009
22/8	M. Netanya	a	2-1	*Abu-El-Nir, Arel*
29/8	Ashdod	h	0-1	
12/9	M. Ahi Nazareth	a	3-1	*Levi E., Bello, Abu-El-Nir*
26/9	M. Tel-Aviv	h	3-1	*Bello, Tartazki, Gerzicich*
3/10	Bnei Sakhnin	a	3-0	*Abukarat, Bello, Arel*
17/10	H. Petach-Tikva	h	1-2	*Levi E.*
24/10	Bnei Yehuda	a	0-2	
31/10	Beitar	a	1-3	*Lipenia*
7/11	H. Akko	h	2-4	*Abukarat, Ben Basat (p)*
22/11	H. Ra'anana	a	1-2	*Lipenia*
28/11	H. Ramat-Gan	h	1-1	*Ben Basat*
7/12	H. Tel-Aviv	a	0-2	
12/12	M. Petach-Tikva	h	2-0	*Lipenia, Levi E.*
19/12	H. Beer-Sheva	a	3-2	*Levi E. 2, Tartazki*
28/12	M. Haifa	h	0-1	
2010				
2/1	M. Netanya	h	0-0	
9/1	Ashdod	a	0-1	
16/1	M. Ahi Nazareth	h	2-2	*Levi E., Tartazki*
23/1	M. Tel-Aviv	a	0-1	
30/1	Bnei Sakhnin	h	0-1	
7/2	H. Petach-Tikva	a	2-2	*Bello 2*
15/2	Bnei Yehuda	h	0-3	
20/2	Beitar	h	3-2	*Lipenia, Bello 2*
27/2	H. Akko	a	2-2	*Levi E., Abukarat*
6/3	H. Ra'anana	h	3-1	*Ben Basat 3*
13/3	H. Ramat-Gan	a	2-3	*Bello, Ben Basat (p)*
20/3	H. Tel-Aviv	h	1-2	*Ben Basat*
27/3	M. Petach-Tikva	a	2-2	*Levi E. 2*
3/4	H. Beer-Sheva	h	0-0	
10/4	M. Haifa	a	0-0	
17/4	M. Ahi Nazareth	h	2-2	*Ben Basat, Bello*
25/4	H. Ramat-Gan	a	1-0	*Levi E. (p)*
1/5	H. Ra'anana	h	1-0	*Levi E.*
8/5	H. Petach-Tikva	h	1-2	*Ben Basat*
15/5	H. Akko	a	0-1	

No	Name	Nat	DoB	Pos	Aps	(s)	Gls
23	Amir ABU-EL-NIR		27/2/89	A	14	(12)	2
20	Ran ABUKARAT		14/12/88	M	25	(8)	3
29	Omri ALON		29/8/83	G	3	(2)	
6	Gal AREL		9/7/89	M	17	(10)	2
14	Yero BELLO	NGA	11/12/87	A	25	(5)	9
11	Eden BEN BASAT		8/9/86	A	23	(7)	9
28	Hai BEN LOLO		28/1/82	D	18		
22	Galil BEN SENAN		27/6/82	G	17		
1	Ohad COHEN		10/6/75	G	15		
19	Ahemd DIAB		22/1/85	A		(4)	
26	Yossi DORA		25/8/81	M	25		
11	Adel ELBISHER		15/6/89	A		(1)	
5	Oded ELKAYAM		9/2/88	D	20	(2)	
9	Yossi GANAH		13/7/77	A		(3)	
18	Bryan Paul GERZICICH	USA	20/3/84	M	28	(1)	1
16	Levan KHMALADZE	GEO	6/4/85	M	2		
8	Hiasham KIWAN		17/5/87	M	13	(18)	
10	Eran LEVI		4/8/85	M	31	(2)	11
17	Sharon LEVI		1/6/87	D	7	(4)	
24	Savity LIPENIA	COD	17/4/79	D	33		4
15	Hanan MAMAN		28/8/89	M	3	(10)	
12	Emmanuel PAPPOE	GHA	3/3/81	D	4		
21	Oshri ROASH		25/7/88	D	30	(1)	
25	RUI Manuel Pinto de LIMA	POR	25/3/78	M	1	(2)	
7	Shai SIBONI		6/4/83	M		(1)	
13	Eyal TARTAZKI		13/9/77	D	31	3	

HAPOEL PETACH-TIKVA FC
Coach – Dani Niron; (22/10/09) Shvit Elimekech;
(16/12/09) Eli Mahpud
Founded – 1935
Stadium – Municipal (7,500)
MAJOR HONOURS:
Israeli League - (6) 1955, 1959, 1960, 1961, 1962, 1963;
Israeli Cup - (2) 1957, 1992.

2009
22/8	M. Ahi Nazareth	a	2-1	*Balilti, Salami*
29/8	M. Tel-Aviv	h	0-2	
12/9	Bnei Sakhnin	a	0-2	
26/9	Beitar	a	0-3	
3/10	Bnei Yehuda	h	1-1	*Bashiru*
17/10	H. Haifa	a	2-1	*Salami, Hanun*
24/10	H. Akko	h	1-1	*Bashiru*
31/10	H. Ra'anana	a	1-2	*Bashiru*
7/11	H. Ramat-Gan	h	0-0	
21/11	H. Tel-Aviv	a	1-7	*Salami*
28/11	M. Petach-Tikva	h	1-1	*Salami*
5/12	H. Beer-Sheva	a	0-2	
12/12	M. Haifa	h	0-4	
19/12	M. Netanya	a	0-1	
26/12	Ashdod	h	1-1	*Cohen G.*
2010				
2/1	M. Ahi Nazareth	h	3-0	*Salami, Bashiru, Sror*
9/1	M. Tel-Aviv	a	0-1	
17/1	Bnei Sakhnin	h	0-0	
23/1	Beitar	h	0-0	
30/1	Bnei Yehuda	a	1-1	*Ben Naim*
7/2	H. Haifa	h	2-2	*Tzarfati, Basit*
13/2	H. Akko	a	0-0	
20/2	H. Ra'anana	h	2-1	*Oved (p), Assous*
1/3	H. Ramat-Gan	a	0-0	
8/3	H. Tel-Aviv	h	1-1	*Tzarfati*
13/3	M. Petach-Tikva	a	0-0	
20/3	H. Beer-Sheva	h	1-0	*Addo*
28/3	M. Haifa	a	0-3	
3/4	M. Netanya	h	2-1	*Basit, Cohen G.*
10/4	Ashdod	a	1-2	*Basit*
17/4	H. Akko	h	1-2	*Tzarfati*
24/4	M. Ahi Nazareth	a	0-3	
1/5	H. Ramat-Gan	h	2-1	*Salami, Bashiru*
8/5	H. Haifa	a	2-1	*Bashiru, Basit*
15/5	H. Ra'anana	h	0-0	

No	Name	Nat	DoB	Pos	Aps	(s)	Gls
10	Eli ABARBANEL		22/2/76	M	7	(1)	
11	Aiman ABU SALH		23/11/83	A	4	(10)	
33	Salem ABU SIAM		8/3/83	D	11	(1)	
27	Daniel ADDO	GHA	6/3/84	D	17		1
4	Jonathan ASSOUS	FRA	2/9/86	M	23		1
19	Shahar BALILTI		20/3/90	A		(5)	1
4	Tomo BARLECAJ	CRO	6/7/82	A	2		
21	Osman BASHIRU	GHA	5/5/89	A	29	(3)	6
23	Ibrahim BASIT	GHA	13/10/90	A	6	(5)	4
18	Tomer BEN HAIM		2/1/88	M	7	(4)	
8	Armon BEN NAIM		6/2/90	M	14	(11)	1
11	Eli BITON		25/1/82	M	12	(4)	
30	Efraim BUGLA		4/4/92	M		(1)	
12	Almog BUZAGLO		8/12/92	A		(1)	
20	Asi BUZAGLE		3/12/82	M	1	(4)	
6	Gal COHEN		14/8/82	D	33		2
17	Sagiv COHEN		20/9/87	D	12	(2)	
99	Rafael DAHAN		28/9/89	M	4	(9)	
7	Kobi DAJANI		5/11/84	M	13		
15	Kfir DAR		9/8/89	M	2	(3)	
13	Snir DORI		4/8/87	G	9		
12	Austin EJIDE	NGA	8/4/84	G	5		
16	Or FISHBEIN		20/6/89	A		(1)	
17	George GEBRO	LBR	13/9/81	M	15		
19	Mark GORMAN		9/2/89	D	1	(1)	
23	Revaz GOTSIRIDZE	GEO	17/1/81	A	2	(1)	
33	Dor HALEVI		5/2/86	M	3	(2)	
23	Udi HANUN		28/2/87	D	9	(2)	1

ISREAL

22	Tzlil HATUKA	6/8/89	G	4		
29	Elad KHOTABA	20/11/87	M	12	(3)	
12	Guy LEVI	25/10/91	A		(1)	
12	James LOMELL	LBR 16/10/85	M	2	(3)	
3	Emmanuel MATHIAS	TOG 3/4/86	D	30		
7	Reuven OVED	28/11/83	M	6	(3)	1
9	Elnatan SALAMI	5/4/86	A	23	(8)	6
13	Youssi SHEKEL	24/9/84	G	17	(1)	
16	Amiran SHKALIM	23/3/88	D	3		
16	Idan SROR	5/10/86	A	23	(7)	1
5	Guy TZARFATI	28/4/79	M	24	(5)	3

HAPOEL RA'ANANA FC
Coach – Eli Cohen; (14/2/10) Ami Vazana;
(31/3/10) Zvika Tzemach
Founded – 1972
Stadium – Ori Karni (2,500)

2009

22/8	H. Beer-Sheva	a	1-2	Atia
29/8	M. Haifa	h	1-3	For
12/9	M. Netanya	a	1-1	Cristiano
26/9	Ashdod	h	1-1	Cohen S.
3/10	M. Ahi Nazareth	a	1-2	Biton
17/10	M. Tel-Aviv	h	0-3	
24/10	Bnei Sakhnin	a	1-1	Cristiano
31/10	H. Petach-Tikva	h	2-1	Toaf (p), Cohen S.
7/11	Bnei Yehuda	a	1-2	Sofer
22/11	H. Haifa	h	2-1	Cohen S., Cristiano
29/11	H. Akko	a	1-1	Koper
5/12	Beitar	a	1-3	Cohen S.
12/12	H. Ramat-Gan	h	0-1	
21/12	H. Tel-Aviv	a	0-5	
26/12	M. Petach-Tikva	h	3-1	For, Biton 2

2010

2/1	H. Beer-Sheva	h	2-2	Knafo, Cohen S.
9/1	M. Haifa	a	0-3	
16/1	M. Netanya	h	1-1	Biton
23/1	Ashdod	a	0-0	
31/1	M. Ahi Nazareth	h	1-1	Cohen S.
6/2	M. Tel-Aviv	a	0-2	
13/2	Bnei Sakhnin	h	0-1	
20/2	H. Petach-Tikva	a	1-2	Zohar
27/2	Bnei Yehuda	h	0-3	
6/3	H. Haifa	a	1-3	Biton
13/3	H. Akko	h	0-1	
20/3	Beitar	h	1-3	Biton
27/3	H. Ramat-Gan	a	0-1	
3/4	H. Tel-Aviv	h	1-4	Cohen S.
10/4	M. Petach-Tikva	h	3-2	Beniušis 3
17/4	H. Ramat-Gan	a	0-0	
24/4	H. Akko	h	4-0	Knafo 2, Sofer, Biton
1/5	H. Haifa	a	0-1	
8/5	M. Ahi Nazareth	h	2-0	Biton 2
15/5	H. Petach-Tikva	h	0-0	

No	Name	Nat	DoB	Pos	Aps	(s)	Gls
12	Omri ATIA		28/10/85	D	29	(1)	1
14	Moshe BALBILIA		1/1/88	M		(1)	
29	Ričardas BENIUŠIS	LTU	23/4/80	A	8	(4)	3
21	Dudu BITON		1/3/88	A	21	(9)	9
18	Raz COHEN		10/3/90	A	12	(12)	
10	Steven COHEN	FRA	27/2/86	M	30	(2)	7
11	CRISTIANO Pinto dos Santos	BRA	12/3/82	A	23	(9)	3
23	Davit DIGMELASHVILI	GEO	18/1/81	M	3	(1)	
4	Itai ELKASLASI		15/6/88	M	15	(8)	
7	Tamir FOR		19/8/82	D	26	(3)	2
13	Haim FUNTREMOLI		9/8/81	D	11	(2)	
9	Avi KNAFO		4/8/82	A	20	(5)	3
17	Gil KOPER		22/3/85	D	15	(5)	1
2	Guy KOWAZ		26/4/84	D	4	(4)	
24	Armando René LESCANO	ARG	25/2/88	M	6	(8)	
15	Roei LEVI		4/9/87	D	28	(1)	
6	Lirodiou Gonçalves "LIRA"	BRA	25/4/83	D	7	(1)	
8	Snir SHOKER		8/5/89	A	8	(17)	

1	Shaul SMADJA	2/10/72	G	35	
5	Avi SOFER	29/3/86	D	27	2
19	Itai TOAF	5/12/83	D	35	1
25	Irmantas ZELMIKAS	LTU 3/1/80	D	16	(1)
55	Maor ZOHAR	9/6/85	D	6	(8)	1

HAPOEL RAMAT-GAN FC
Coach – Yuval Naim
Founded – 1927
Stadium – Winter (4,000)
MAJOR HONOURS:
Israeli League - (1) 1964;
Israeli Cup - (1) 2003.

2009

22/8	M. Petach-Tikva	a	1-1	Hadad S.
29/8	H. Beer-Sheva	h	2-2	Hadad B., Datoru
12/9	M. Haifa	a	1-3	Kovačević
26/9	M. Netanya	h	1-0	Hasan (p)
3/10	Ashdod	a	0-0	
17/10	M. Ahi Nazareth	h	2-3	Datoru, Hasan
24/10	M. Tel-Aviv	a	1-3	William
31/10	Bnei Sakhnin	h	1-0	Golan
7/11	H. Petach-Tikva	a	0-0	
21/11	Bnei Yehuda	h	0-2	
28/11	H. Haifa	a	1-1	Aylei
5/12	H. Akko	h	1-1	Aylei
12/12	H. Ra'anana	a	1-0	Tayar
19/12	Beitar	a	0-1	
26/12	H. Tel-Aviv	h	0-3	

2010

3/1	M. Petach-Tikva	h	0-3	
9/1	H. Beer-Sheva	a	0-1	
16/1	M. Haifa	h	0-5	
23/1	M. Netanya	a	3-2	Datoru, Peretz 2
30/1	Ashdod	h	1-1	Hermon
6/2	M. Ahi Nazareth	a	1-0	Hadad S.
13/2	M. Tel-Aviv	h	1-4	Aylei
21/2	Bnei Sakhnin	a	1-3	Hadad S.
1/3	H. Petach-Tikva	h	0-0	
7/3	Bnei Yehuda	a	2-1	Golan, Hadad S.
13/3	H. Haifa	h	3-2	Aylei 2, Datoru
20/3	H. Akko	a	0-1	
27/3	H. Ra'anana	h	1-0	Hadad B.
3/4	Beitar	h	0-0	
10/4	H. Tel-Aviv	a	1-3	Hadad B.
17/4	H. Ra'anana	a	0-0	
25/4	M. Haifa	h	0-1	
1/5	H. Petach-Tikva	a	1-2	Aylei
8/5	H. Akko	h	0-0	
15/5	M. Ahi Nazareth	a	7-0	Datoru, Hermon 2, Aylei (p), og (Amaria), Lotati, Chacana

No	Name	Nat	DoB	Pos	Aps	(s)	Gls
22	Itai ARKIN		7/7/88	G	8		
9	Eliran ASAO		3/2/85	A		(2)	
11	Serge AYLEI	CIV	23/8/81	A	23	(2)	7
30	Tamir BEN AMI		28/2/79	M	15	(8)	
12	Ori BIBI		27/7/91	M	1		
10	Omer BUKSENBAUM		12/11/82	M	9		
14	Carlos CHACANA	ARG	23/6/76	A	21	(8)	1
1	Rafi COHEN		28/11/70	G	27		
20	George DATORU	NGA	25/6/77	A	22	(12)	5
16	Hezi DILMONI		7/5/89	D		(2)	
32	Asi DOMB		27/2/74	D	13		
10	Eyal-Elyaho GANALI		22/8/92	A	1	(1)	
9	Mor GOLAN		23/6/83	A	16	(7)	2
17	Benny HADAD		4/8/77	D	31		3
15	Shay HADAD		2/7/87	D	30	(2)	4
5	Asaf HAKAK		16/5/89	D		(1)	
10	Kobi HASAN		26/9/78	M	14	(2)	2
25	Golan HERMON		26/9/77	D	24	(1)	3
26	JEFISLEY André Caldeira	BRA	16/5/80	M	14	(1)	
21	Hrvoje KOVAČEVIĆ	CRO	21/7/82	M	10	(1)	1
8	Eli LEVI		15/5/75	D	14	(12)	

ISRAEL

21	Matan LOTATI		29/1/90	A	1	(4)	1
12	Benzion LUZ		18/2/78	M	1	(5)	
5	Haim MALKA		12/8/80	D	10	(1)	
7	Kobi MUSA		18/4/82	A	33		
24	Amit OHANA		12/10/87	A	9	(8)	
19	Omer PERETZ		26/1/86	A	3	(4)	2
23	Pavel PERGL	CZE	14/11/77	D	8	(1)	
26	Vladimir ROZENFELD		06/051989	M		(6)	
30	Tommer TAYAR		15/1/83	M	10	(8)	1
23	WILLIAM Ribeiro Soares	BRA	7/2/85	M	17		1

HAPOEL TEL-AVIV FC
Coach – Eli Gutman
Founded – 1927
Stadium – Bloomfield (15,700)
MAJOR HONOURS:
Israeli League - (14) 1934, 1935, 1936, 1938, 1940, 1943, 1957, 1966, 1969, 1981, 1986, 1988, 2000, 2010;
Israeli Cup - (12) 1928, 1934, 1937, 1938, 1939, 1960, 1972, 1999, 2000, 2006, 2007, 2010.

2009

24/8	Beitar	a	0-0	
30/8	M. Petach-Tikva	h	1-1	Ben Dayan
13/9	H. Beer-Sheva	a	3-1	Vučićević, Zandberg, Yadin
21/9	M. Haifa	h	1-2	Shechter
4/10	M. Netanya	a	3-0	Shechter 2, Yeboah
17/10	Ashdod	h	2-2	Vučićević, Enyeama (p)
25/10	M. Ahi Nazareth	a	4-0	Shechter 2, Vučićević, Ben Dayan
1/11	M. Tel-Aviv	h	1-0	Douglas
8/11	Bnei Sakhnin	a	2-1	Douglas, Shechter
21/11	H. Petach-Tikva	h	7-1	Shechter 3, Ben Dayan, Lala, Zhavi, Vermouth
28/11	Bnei Yehuda	a	1-0	Shechter
7/12	H. Haifa	h	2-0	Shechter, Yadin
21/12	H. Ra'anana	h	5-0	Yeboah, Ben Dayan 2, Zhavi, Shechter
26/12	H. Ramat-Gan	a	3-0	Ben Dayan, Enyeama (p), Douglas
29/12	H. Akko	a	1-1	Lala
2010				
4/1	Beitar	h	4-3	Lala, Ben Dayan (p), Zhavi, Shechter
9/1	M. Petach-Tikva	a	0-0	
18/1	H. Beer-Sheva	h	4-1	Ben Dayan, Vermouth 2 (1p), Zhavi
25/1	M. Haifa	a	0-0	
30/1	M. Netanya	h	3-3	Vermouth 2, Badir
7/2	Ashdod	a	4-0	Zhavi, Shechter 2, Ben Dayan
13/2	M. Ahi Nazareth	h	4-0	Shechter, Enyeama (p), Maree, Lala
22/2	M. Tel-Aviv	a	4-2	Lala, Shechter 2, Douglas
28/2	Bnei Sakhnin	h	1-0	Zhavi
8/3	H. Petach-Tikva	a	1-1	Douglas
13/3	Bnei Yehuda	h	4-0	Yadin, Shechter, Zhavi, Vermouth
20/3	H. Haifa	a	2-1	Vermouth, Zhavi
27/3	H. Akko	h	5-3	Badir, Zhavi, Maree, Shechter, Ben Dayan.
3/4	H. Ra'anana	a	4-1	Vermouth, Enyeama (p), Vručina, Shechter
10/4	H. Ramat-Gan	h	3-1	Enyeama (p), Zhavi, Shechter (p)
17/4	Bnei Yehuda	h	1-0	De Ridder
26/4	M. Haifa	a	1-0	Lala
1/5	Ashdod	h	4-0	Ben Dayan, Badir, De Ridder, Douglas
8/5	M. Tel-Aviv	h	0-0	
15/5	Beitar	a	2-1	Vermouth, Zhavi

No	Name	Nat	DoB	Pos	Aps	(s)	Gls
22	Nhil ABARBANEL		19/6/87	G	6		
18	Shay ABUTBOL		16/1/83	M	2	(9)	
10	Walid BADIR		12/3/74	D	32		3
19	Dedi BEN DAYAN		27/11/78	D	31		11

4	Dani BONDARV		7/2/87	D	20	(3)	
8	Daniel DE RIDDER	NED	6/3/84	M	5	(6)	2
3	DOUGLAS da Silva	BRA	7/3/84	D	34		6
1	Vincent ENYEAMA	NGA	29/8/82	G	29		5
24	Yehuda HUTA		19/2/89	D	3	(2)	
23	Omri KENDA		6/7/86	D	14	(8)	
17	Ma'aran LALA		7/3/82	A	21	(9)	6
27	Victor MAREE		31/5/89	A	2	(21)	2
15	Zurab MENTESHASHVILI	GEO	30/1/80	M	8	(17)	
6	Bibras NATCHO		18/2/88	M	24		
9	Itay SHECHTER		22/2/87	A	34		22
25	Gal SHISH		28/1/89	D	4	(1)	
14	Gil VERMOUTH		5/8/85	M	34		9
20	Bojan VRUČINA	CRO	8/11/84	M	3	(7)	1
7	Nemanja VUČIĆEVIĆ	SRB	11/8/79	M	9		3
26	Avihai YADIN		26/10/86	M	34		3
11	Samuel YEBOAH	GHA	8/8/86	A	9	(2)	2
5	Michael ZANDBERG		16/4/80	M	2	(12)	1
16	Eran ZHAVI		25/7/87	A	25	(8)	11

MACCABI AHI NAZARETH FC
Coach – Eli Mahpud; (8/12/09) John Gregory (ENG)
Founded – 1967
Stadium – Ilut (5,000)

2009

22/8	H. Petach-Tikva	h	1-2	Shina
31/8	Bnei Yehuda	a	0-2	
12/9	H. Haifa	h	1-3	Luzon
26/9	H. Akko	a	1-0	N'Toya-Zoa
3/10	H. Ra'anana	h	2-1	Hemed, Kiel
17/10	H. Ramat-Gan	a	3-2	Luzon 2, Hemed
25/10	H. Tel-Aviv	h	0-4	
31/10	M. Petach-Tikva	a	0-1	
7/11	H. Beer-Sheva	h	1-4	Djida
21/11	M. Haifa	a	1-4	Kiel
28/11	M. Netanya	h	1-3	Dayan
6/12	Ashdod	a	1-2	Luzon
12/12	Beitar	h	0-1	
19/12	M. Tel-Aviv	h	3-3	Hemed, Luzon, og (Kapiloto)
26/12	Bnei Sakhnin	a	1-1	N'Toya-Zoa
2010				
2/1	H. Petach-Tikva	a	0-3	
9/1	Bnei Yehuda	h	2-2	Amer, Hemed
16/1	H. Haifa	a	2-2	Tukura, Hemed
23/1	H. Akko	h	1-0	Hemed
31/1	H. Ra'anana	a	1-1	Luzon
6/2	H. Ramat-Gan	h	0-1	
13/2	H. Tel-Aviv	a	0-4	
20/2	M. Petach-Tikva	h	1-2	Paser (p)
27/2	H. Beer-Sheva	a	2-2	Hemed, Djida
6/2	M. Haifa	h	0-5	
13/3	M. Netanya	h	0-5	
20/3	Ashdod	h	1-0	Luzon
27/3	Beitar	a	0-5	
3/4	M. Tel-Aviv	a	1-0	Luzon
10/4	Bnei Sakhnin	h	0-2	
17/4	H. Haifa	a	2-2	Hemed, Mayebi
24/4	H. Petach-Tikva	h	3-0	Hemed, Luzon, Kiel
1/5	H. Akko	a	1-3	Dayan
8/5	H. Ra'anana	a	0-2	
15/5	H. Ramat-Gan	a	0-7	

No	Name	Nat	DoB	Pos	Aps	(s)	Gls
19	Tarek AABS		15/11/83	D	1		
7	Ahmed ABED		30/3/90	M	1	(7)	
23	Saleh ABU AYASH		17/1/88	M		(3)	
20	Shlomi ADREI		29/5/82	M		(5)	
25	Eric AKOTO	TOG	20/7/80	D	9		
15	Mohamad AMARIA		8/2/89	M	14	(5)	
3	Ismaail AMER		30/3/77	D	19	(3)	1
77	Dabor ANAS		29/4/91	A		(4)	
8	Assaf BRAUN		20/4/86	D	4	(3)	
12	Jair Edson CÉSPEDES	PER	22/5/84	M	1		

No	Name	Nat	DoB	Pos	Aps	(s)	Gls
10	Moanes DABOR		14/5/92	M	1	(3)	
4	Mor DAHAN		19/3/89	D	13	(3)	
20	Guy DAYAN		20/8/86	A	21	(2)	2
11	Yves DJIDA	CMR	14/7/88	A	11	(8)	2
6	Ram DUANI		24/5/87	D	12	(2)	
19	Mark GORMAN		9/2/89	D	29		
20	Adham HADIA		12/2/85	M	13		
14	Shlomi HANOKA		15/8/85	M	26	(4)	
9	Tomer HEMED		02/051987	A	32	(1)	9
88	Lohab KIEL		3/5/88	M	26	(6)	3
99	Yaniv LUZON		26/8/81	M	26	(5)	9
1	Joslain Leonel MAYEBI	CMR	14/10/86	G	17		1
1	Ruslan NIGMATULLIN	RUS	7/10/74	G	9		
10	Tcham N'TOYA-ZOA	COD	3/11/83	A	19	(5)	2
7	Abu-Rabia OBEIDA		10/2/90	M		(2)	
1	Gil OFEK		9/1/86	G	9		
23	Naor PASER		18/10/85	D	4	(1)	1
8	Amjad SALIMAN		7/5/87	M	2	(6)	
6	Hani SHAHIN		8/5/90	A	2	(3)	
5	Yakir SHINA		25/9/85	D	2		1
12	Michael TUKURA	NGA	19/8/88	M	22	(1)	1
6	Baracat WAHAB		20/4/80	D	9		
5	Anderson WEST	NGA	31/8/89	D	5		
7	Amjed YUNESS		15/3/89	D	26	(2)	

No	Name	Nat	DoB	Pos	Aps	(s)	Gls
19	Shlomi ARBEITMAN		14/5/85	A	23	(11)	28
7	Gustavo BOCCOLI	BRA	16/2/78	M	15	(11)	2
11	Sadat BUKARI	GHA	12/4/89	A	1	(10)	
8	John Jairo CULMA	COL	17/3/81	M	24	(3)	
1	Nir DAVIDOVICH		17/12/76	G	35		
9	Vladimer DVALISHVILI	GEO	20/4/86	A	30	(5)	16
16	Muhammad GHDIR		21/1/91	M	14	(17)	3
15	Eyal GOLASA		7/10/91	M	11	(5)	5
3	Alon HARAZI		13/2/71	D	1	(2)	
5	JORGE Filipe Avelino TEIXEIRA	POR	27/8/86	D	27		1
14	Mohamd KALEBAT		15/6/90	A		(1)	
20	Yaniv KATAN		27/1/81	A	34		7
23	Biram KAYAL		2/5/88	M	25	(2)	1
21	Dekel KEINAN		15/9/84	D	34		1
17	Tsepo MASILELA	RSA	5/5/85	D	31		1
4	Shai MAYMON		18/3/86	D	9	(4)	
27	Eyal MESHUMAR		10/8/83	D	28	(2)	
18	Ali OSMAN		8/2/87	D	13	(13)	
26	Lior REFAELOV		26/4/86	M	28	(6)	7
12	Sintiyahu SALALIK		1/1/91	A		(1)	
13	Taleb TAWATHA		21/6/92	D	2	(1)	
14	TIAGO da Silva DUTRA	BRA	17/9/90	M		(2)	
24	Israel ZAGURI		29/1/90	M		(7)	

MACCABI HAIFA FC

Coach – Elisha Levi
Founded – 1913
Stadium – Kiriat Eliezer (17,000)
MAJOR HONOURS:
Israeli League - (11) 1984, 1985, 1989, 1991, 1994, 2001, 2002, 2004, 2005, 2006, 2009;
Israeli Cup - (5) 1962, 1991, 1993, 1995, 1998.

2009

22/8	H. Akko	h	2-1	Katan, Arbeitman
29/8	H. Ra'anana	a	3-1	Arbeitman 2, Dvalishvili
12/9	H. Ramat-Gan	h	3-1	Golasa, Dvalishvili, Arbeitman
21/9	H. Tel-Aviv	a	2-1	Katan (p), Golasa
3/10	M. Petach-Tikva	h	2-0	Arbeitman, Dvalishvili
17/10	H. Beer-Sheva	a	3-1	Dvalishvili 2, Arbeitman
26/10	Beitar	h	2-1	Ghdir, Dvalishvili
31/10	M. Netanya	h	2-0	Arbeitman 2
9/11	Ashdod	a	1-0	Arbeitman
21/11	M. Ahi Nazareth	h	4-1	Katan (p), Dvalishvili, Arbeitman, Kayal
30/11	M. Tel-Aviv	a	0-1	
5/12	Bnei Sakhnin	h	1-0	Arbeitman
12/12	H. Petach-Tikva	a	4-0	Golasa, Refaelov, Arbeitman 2
20/12	Bnei Yehuda	h	2-0	Arbeitman, Golasa
28/12	H. Haifa	a	1-0	Golasa

2010

2/1	H. Akko	a	3-0	Katan, Dvalishvili 2
9/1	H. Ra'anana	h	3-0	Dvalishvili 2, Refaelov
16/1	H. Ramat-Gan	a	5-0	Refaelov 2, Dvalishvili 2, Arbeitman
25/1	H. Tel-Aviv	h	0-0	
1/2	M. Petach-Tikva	a	1-0	Dvalishvili
6/2	H. Beer-Sheva	h	4-1	Arbeitman 3, Masilela
14/2	Beitar	a	3-0	Ghdir, Arbeitman, Boccoli
20/2	M. Netanya	a	0-1	
28/2	Ashdod	h	1-0	Ghdir
6/3	M. Ahi Nazareth	a	5-0	Arbeitman 3 (1p), Katan, Refaelov
15/3	M. Tel-Aviv	h	1-0	Arbeitman (p)
21/3	Bnei Sakhnin	a	1-2	Arbeitman (p)
28/3	H. Petach-Tikva	h	3-0	Katan, Arbeitman, Refaelov
5/4	Bnei Yehuda	a	2-0	Arbeitman, Katan (p)
10/4	H. Haifa	h	0-0	
17/4	Ashdod	h	3-1	Boccoli, Dvalishvili, Arbeitman
26/4	H. Tel-Aviv	a	0-1	
1/5	M. Tel-Aviv	a	2-0	Arbeitman, Refaelov
8/5	Beitar	h	2-1	Dvalishvili, Keinan
15/5	Bnei Yehuda	a	1-1	Jorge Teixeira

MACCABI NETANYA FC

Coach – Nati Azaria; (29/9/09) Reuven Atar
Founded – 1934
Stadium – Sar-Tov (7,500)
MAJOR HONOURS:
Israeli League - (5) 1971, 1974, 1978, 1980, 1983;
Israeli Cup - (1) 1978.

2009

22/8	H. Haifa	h	1-2	Saba'a
29/8	H. Akko	a	1-1	Ezra
12/9	H. Ra'anana	h	1-1	Awudu
26/9	H. Ramat-Gan	a	0-1	
4/10	H. Tel-Aviv	h	0-3	
17/10	M. Petach-Tikva	a	3-0	Saba'a, Menashe 2
24/10	H. Beer-Sheva	h	2-2	Saba'a, Gazal
31/10	M. Haifa	a	0-2	
7/11	Beitar	h	3-0	Menashe, Goata, Gazal
21/11	Ashdod	h	1-0	
28/11	M. Ahi Nazareth	a	3-1	Cohen (p), Goata, Awudu
5/12	M. Tel-Aviv	h	1-0	Saba'a
13/12	Bnei Sakhnin	a	3-0	Cohen, Menashe, Goata
19/12	H. Petach-Tikva	h	1-0	Menashe
27/12	Bnei Yehuda	a	1-2	Gazal

2010

2/1	H. Haifa	a	0-0	
10/1	H. Akko	h	1-0	Cohen
16/1	H. Ra'anana	a	1-1	Goata
23/1	H. Ramat-Gan	h	2-3	Dgani, Fransman
30/1	H. Tel-Aviv	a	3-3	Ben Harush, Saba'a 2
6/2	M. Petach-Tikva	h	2-2	Fabrício, Fransman
13/2	H. Beer-Sheva	a	0-2	
20/2	M. Haifa	h	1-0	Menashe
27/2	Beitar	a	1-3	Cohen
6/3	Ashdod	a	0-3	
13/3	M. Ahi Nazareth	h	5-0	Cohen, Gomes, Genish, Yampolski, Menashe
20/3	M. Tel-Aviv	a	2-2	Cohen, Saba'a
27/3	Bnei Sakhnin	h	1-2	Gomes
3/4	H. Petach-Tikva	a	1-2	Gomes
10/4	Bnei Yehuda	h	1-1	Saba'a
17/4	H. Beer-Sheva	h	0-4	
24/4	M. Petach-Tikva	a	1-3	Cohen (p)
1/5	Bnei Sakhnin	h	2-0	Saba'a, Ben Harush

No	Name	Nat	DoB	Pos	Aps	(s)	Gls
22	Guy ABEND		8/11/90	M		(1)	
20	Igal ANTEBI		1/8/74	D	9	(2)	
7	Samed Abdul AWUDU	GHA	15/9/84	A	12	(3)	2
18	Omri BEN HARUSH		7/3/90	D	11	(3)	2

ISRAEL

8	Almog COHEN		1/9/88	M	30	(1)	7
12	Orel DGANI		8/1/89	D	28	(1)	1
22	Hen EZRA		19/1/89	M	7	(3)	1
23	FABRÍCIO Silva Cabral	BRA	16/9/81	A	4	(8)	1
17	Bevan FRANSMAN	RSA	31/10/83	D	31		2
6	Ravid GAZAL		9/6/82	M	23	(1)	3
14	Gal GENISH		16/12/91	M	5	(3)	1
10	Snir GOATA		7/1/88	M	20	(7)	4
2	Guy GOMBERG		24/9/90			(1)	
7	David GOMES Pimenta	BRA	5/9/88	A	11	(5)	3
2	Leonid KRUPNIK	UKR	15/7/79	D	9	(3)	
1	Dniel LIFSHITZ		24/4/88	G	14	(1)	
21	Tal MA'ABI		15/5/85	D	18	(2)	
14	Feras MAGHARBEH		24/7/91	A	12	(15)	
26	Shalev MENASHE		23/5/82	M	29	(3)	7
24	Reef MESSIKA		15/6/89	M	1	(4)	
33	Tarek NATOUR		18/8/90	G	3		
25	Adi NIMNI		27/8/91	D		(2)	
28	Stephen OFEI	GHA	14/1/86	D	2	(1)	
9	Ahmed SABA'A		24/5/80	A	15	(11)	9
5	Klimi SABAN		17/2/80	D	31		
25	Maoz SAMYA		14/12/87	D	1		
19	Taras SHOLLKOVSKY		28/12/89	D		(1)	
15	Amaya TAGA		4/2/85	M	1	(4)	
18	Alon VAYSBERG		26/4/89	A		(1)	
11	Bamidele YAMPOLSKI		28/7/88	A	20	(6)	1
16	Aristide ZOGBO	CIV	30/12/81	G	16		
17	Tomislav BUŠIĆ	CRO	2/2/86	A	13	(6)	1
22	Ohad COHEN		10/6/75	G	14		
5	Nitzan DAMARI		13/1/87	D	27	(2)	2
10	Omer DAMARI		24/3/89	A	21	(11)	10
25	Tomer ELBAZ		6/7/89	D	1	(3)	
9	Dovev GABAY		1/4/87	A	4	(22)	6
12	Kobi GANON		17/5/76	D	27		
2	Hagai GOLDENBERG		15/9/90	D	2		
3	Amer GRE		21/12/90	A		(2)	
22	Dragoslav JEVRIĆ	SRB	8/7/84	G	18		
24	Marwan KABAHA		23/2/91	M	2	(2)	
1	Robi LEVKOVICH		31/8/88	G	1		
8	Ori LOZON		11/8/84	M	1	(3)	
24	Asi MASHIACH		10/10/81	M	21	(3)	1
28	Haim MAGRELASHVILI		4/6/82	D	6	(6)	
28	Sameh MAREEV		8/1/91	A		(1)	
8	Nebojša MARINKOVIĆ	SRB	19/6/86	M	5	(6)	3
4	Merad MEGAMADOV		25/9/73	D	30		
28	Naor PASER		18/10/85	D	6	(1)	
36	Dani PRADA		1/4/87	M	19	(9)	3
7	Dan ROMANN		27/8/82	M	21	(7)	1
6	Sébastien SANSONI	FRA	30/1/78	D	12		
11	Rubil SARSOR		18/7/83	A	7	(1)	2
15	Vanco TRAJANOV	MKD	9/8/78	M	16	(5)	
26	Jonathan TURGEMAN		15/3/90	M		(1)	
20	Ori UZAN		27/12/78	D	17	(1)	
30	Avi YEHIEL		26/9/79	D	32		2

MACCABI PETACH-TIKVA FC
Coach – Roni Levi; (22/11/09) Fredi David
Founded – 1912
Stadium – Municipal (7,500)
MAJOR HONOURS:
Israeli Cup - (2) 1935, 1952.

2009
22/8	H. Ramat-Gan	h	1-1	Bušić
30/8	H. Tel-Aviv	a	1-1	Ben Haim
12/9	Beitar	h	1-3	Gabay
26/9	H. Beer-Sheva	h	3-0	Ben Haim 2 (1p), Buksenbaum
3/10	M. Haifa	a	0-2	
17/10	M. Netanya	h	0-3	
24/10	Ashdod	a	1-1	Romann
31/10	M. Ahi Nazareth	h	1-0	Sarsor
7/11	M. Tel-Aviv	a	1-1	Damari O.
21/11	Bnei Sakhnin	h	1-2	Buksenbaum (p)
28/11	H. Petach-Tikva	a	1-1	Sarsor
5/12	Bnei Yehuda	h	0-1	
12/12	H. Haifa	a	0-2	
19/12	H. Akko	h	2-3	Prada, Damari N.
26/12	H. Ra'anana	a	1-3	Gabay

2010
3/1	H. Ramat-Gan	a	3-0	Damari O. 2, Ganon
9/1	H. Tel-Aviv	h	0-0	
16/1	Beitar	a	2-1	Damari O., Mashiach
24/1	H. Beer-Sheva	a	1-0	Damari N.
1/2	M. Haifa	h	0-1	
6/2	M. Netanya	a	2-2	Ben Haim (p), Marinković
13/2	Ashdod	h	1-1	Ben Haim (p)
20/2	M. Ahi Nazareth	a	2-1	Damari O., Prada
27/2	M. Tel-Aviv	h	2-1	Yehiel, Gabay
6/3	Bnei Sakhnin	a	4-3	Damari O., Ben Haim 2, Marinković
13/3	H. Petach-Tikva	h	0-0	
20/3	Bnei Yehuda	a	0-2	
27/3	H. Haifa	h	2-2	Damari O. Yehiel
3/4	H. Akko	a	2-2	Damari O. 2
10/4	H. Ra'anana	h	2-2	Damari O., Marinković
17/4	Bnei Sakhnin	a	0-2	
24/4	M. Netanya	h	3-1	Prada, Gabay 2
2/5	H. Beer-Sheva	a	4-1	Gabay, og (Kedar), Ben Haim 2

No	Name	Nat	DoB	Pos	Aps	(s)	Gls
18	Reinaldo Andrés ALDERETE	ARG	17/1/83	D	3		
14	Tal BEN HAIM		5/8/89	A	22	(7)	9
20	Omer BUKSENBAUM		12/11/82	M	15		2

MACCABI TEL-AVIV FC
Coach – Avi Nimni
Founded – 1906
Stadium – Bloomfield (15,700)
MAJOR HONOURS:
Israeli League – (18) 1937, 1939, 1941, 1947, 1950, 1952, 1954, 1956, 1958, 1968, 1970, 1972, 1977, 1979, 1992, 1995, 1996, 2003;
Israeli Cup – (22) 1929, 1930, 1933, 1941, 1946, 1947, 1954, 1955, 1958, 1959, 1964, 1965, 1967, 1970, 1977, 1987, 1988, 1994, 1996, 2001, 2002, 2005.

2009
22/8	Bnei Sakhnin	h	3-1	Yavruyan 2, Yeini
29/8	H. Petach-Tikva	a	2-0	Yavruyan, Shivhon
14/9	Bnei Yehuda	h	0-0	
26/9	H. Haifa	a	1-3	Yavruyan (p)
3/10	H. Akko	h	1-1	Tzemach
17/10	H. Ra'anana	a	3-0	Iliev, Shivhon, Yeini
24/10	H. Ramat-Gan	h	3-1	Israilevich, Iliev (p), Mayuka
1/11	H. Tel-Aviv	a	0-1	
7/11	M. Petach-Tikva	h	1-1	Kahlon
23/11	H. Beer-Sheva	a	3-1	Yeini, Mayuka, Israilevich
30/11	M. Haifa	h	1-0	Mayuka
5/12	M. Netanya	a	0-1	
14/12	Ashdod	h	2-0	Mayuka, Avidor
19/12	M. Ahi Nazareth	a	3-3	Israilevich, Shivhon, Iliev
26/12	Beitar	h	4-3	Yeini, Kahlon, Shivhon, Mayuka

2010
2/1	Bnei Sakhnin	a	0-0	
9/1	H. Petach-Tikva	h	1-0	og (Cohen S.)
16/1	Bnei Yehuda	a	1-0	Shivhon
23/1	H. Haifa	h	1-0	Avidor
30/1	H. Akko	a	3-2	Yavruyan 2, Shivhon
6/2	H. Ra'anana	h	2-0	Yavruyan, Shivhon
13/2	H. Ramat-Gan	a	4-1	og (Levi), Israilevich, Avidor, Kahlon
22/2	H. Tel-Aviv	h	2-4	Avidor, Buzaglo
27/2	M. Petach-Tikva	a	1-2	Shivhon
6/3	H. Beer-Sheva	h	1-1	Shivhon
15/3	M. Haifa	a	0-1	
20/3	M. Netanya	h	2-2	Buzaglo, Israilevich
27/3	Ashdod	a	1-3	Yavruyan
3/4	M. Ahi Nazareth	h	0-1	
10/4	Beitar	a	1-0	Mayuka
17/4	Beitar	h	3-0	Buzaglo, Avidor, Shitrit
24/4	Bnei Yehuda	a	0-0	
1/5	M. Haifa	h	0-2	
8/5	H. Tel-Aviv	a	0-0	
15/5	Ashdod	h	2-0	Buzaglo, Mayuka

No	Name	Nat	DoB	Pos	Aps	(s)	Gls
10	Yuval AVIDOR		19/10/86	A	17	(16)	5
11	Maor BUZAGLO		14/1/88	M	10	(7)	4
18	Ronni GAFNI		11/3/80	D	33		
20	Lior GAN		21/8/86	D	28	(1)	
25	Maor HALABI		30/5/90	M		(1)	
27	Ivica ILIEV	SRB	27/10/79	A	16	(1)	3
7	Guillermo ISRAILEVICH	ARG	10/9/82	M	25	(6)	5
28	Tamir KAHLON		29/10/87	M	20	(7)	3
5	Nisso KAPILOTO		10/1/89	D	19	(2)	
6	Andrej KOMAC	SVN	4/12/79	M	9	(9)	
19	Dor MALUL		30/4/89	D	15	(7)	
24	Emmanuel MAYUKA	ZAM	21/11/90	A	19	(10)	7
29	Reef PERETZ		25/2/91	M	2		
32	Ronald Belcázar RALDES	BOL	20/4/81	D	24		
26	Uri SHITRIT		21/1/86	D	2	(4)	1
14	Yossi SHIVHON		22/3/82	M	26	(7)	9
4	Yuval SHPUNGIN		3/4/87	D	21	(2)	
22	Guy SOLOMON		23/9/77	G	1		
1	Liran STRAUBER		20/8/74	G	34		
13	Igor TOMAŠIĆ	BUL	14/12/76	D	19	(2)	
23	Tzhion TZEMACH		19/1/90	M	2	(10)	1
9	Yeghia YAVRUYAN	ARM	18/10/81	A	15	(11)	8
21	Sherran YEINI		8/12/86	M	28	(2)	4

PROMOTED CLUBS

HAPOEL KIRYAT SHMONA FC
Coach – Ran Ben Shimon
Founded – 2000
Stadium – Municipal (5,300)

HAPOEL ASHKELON FC
Coach – Uri Malmilian
Founded – 1955
Stadium – Sala Stadium (10,000)

SECOND LEVEL FINAL TABLE 2009/10

		Pld	W	D	L	F	A	Pts
	Hapoel Kiryat Shmona FC	35	21	9	5	51	22	41
	Hapoel Ashkelon FC	35	15	11	9	47	42	34
8	Hapoel Kfar-Saba FC	35	16	9	10	56	47	32
4	Sektzya Ness Ziona FC	35	13	15	7	45	29	31
5	Ironi Ramat Hasharon FC	35	13	11	11	50	37	27
6	Maccabi Bat-Yam FC	35	14	7	14	43	41	27
7	Hapoel Nazareth Ilit FC	33	12	14	7	38	24	29
8	Hapoel Rishon Letzion FC	33	13	7	13	39	31	26
9	Ahva Arabe FC	33	12	9	12	37	37	23
0	Maccabi Herzliya FC	33	10	12	11	31	28	22
1	Hakoah Amidar Ramat-Gan FC	35	11	14	10	44	42	28
2	Beitar Shimshon Tel-Aviv FC	35	10	13	12	31	47	27
3	Hapoel Bnei Lod FC	35	10	15	10	37	34	26
3	Maccabi Beer-Sheva FC	35	12	6	17	42	53	24
5	Hapoel Jerusalem FC	35	6	11	18	40	66	18
6	Hapoel Marmorek FC	35	9	21	21	72	8	

NB After 30 matches clubs were split into three groups, after which they played exclusively against teams in their group. Points obtained during the regular season were halved (and rounded upwards); Ahva Arabe FC – 1 pt deducted.

PROMOTION/RELEGATION PLAY-OFF
(22/5/10)
H. Ramat-Gan 1, H. Kfar-Saba 0

DOMESTIC CUP 2009/10

G'VIAA HAMEDINA (STATE CUP)

THIRD ROUND

(8/2/10)
H. Kiryat Shmona 0, M. Kabilio Yaffo 1
H. Marmorek 0, H. Bnei Lod 2

(9/2/10)
B. Kfar-Saba 0, Ironi Ramat Hasharon 1
Carmiel Tzfat 0, H. Ramat-Gan 1
H. Arad 1, H. Nazareth Ilit 1 *(aet; 4-5 on pens)*
H. Beer-Sheva 1, Irony Netivot 0
H. Um El Fahen 0, Bnei Sakhnin 2 *(aet)*
M. Haifa 5, H. Kfar-Saba 0
M. Petach-Tikva 5, M. Ahi Nazareth 1
M. Tel-Aviv 3, M. Netanya 1

(10/2/10)
Bnei Yehuda 2, H. Akko 0
Hakoah Amidar 0, Ashdod 1
H. Ashkelon 2, Ness Ziona 1
H. Haifa 1, H. Tel-Aviv 3
H. Petach-Tikva 1, H. Ra'anana 1 *(aet; 8-7 on pens)*
M. Beer-Sheva 1, Beitar Jerusalem 4

FOURTH ROUND

(23/3/10)
Bnei Yehuda 1, H. Ashkelon 0
H. Bnei Lod 1, M. Petach-Tikva 3
H. Petach-Tikva 0, H. Nazareth Ilit 0 *(aet; 0-3 on pens)*
M. Kabilio Yaffo 0, H. Tel-Aviv 5

(24/3/10)
Ashdod 2, Bnei Sakhnin 1
Beitar Jerusalem 1, M. Tel-Aviv 1 *(aet; 9-8 on pens)*
H. Ramat-Gan 2, M. Haifa 1 *(aet)*
Ironi Ramat Hasharon 3, H. Beer-Sheva 1

QUARTER-FINALS

(13/4/10)
H. Tel-Aviv 2 *(Ben Dayan 56, Vermouth 73)*, Beitar Jerusalem 0
Ironi Ramat Hasharon 2 *(Ben Lulu 27, Avraham 68)*, M. Petach-Tikva 1 *(Ben Haim 35)*

(14/4/10)
Ashdod 3 *(Makriev 61, 83, Checkul 90)*, H. Nazareth Ilit 0
H. Ramat-Gan 0, Bnei Yehuda 1 *(Zandberg 27)*

SEMI-FINALS

(4/5/10)
Bnei Yehuda 1 *(Zairi 37)*, Ashdod 1 *(Kingue 52)* *(aet; 4-3 on pens)*
H. Tel-Aviv 3 *(Shechter 26, Vermouth 39, Enyeama 58p)*, Ironi Ramat Hasharon 1 *(Avraham 44)*

FINAL

(11/5/10)
Ramat Gan stadium, Ramat Gan
HAPOEL TEL-AVIV FC 3 *(Vermouth 25, 75, Enyeama 42p)*
BNEI YEHUDA TEL-AVIV FC 1 *(Douglas 38og)*
Referee – Tabrizi
H. TEL-AVIV – Enyeama, Kenda, Badir, Douglas, Ben Dayan, Yadin, Zhavi, Vermouth, De Ridder (Abutbol 74), Shechter (Menteshashvili 88), Al Lala (Vručina 70).
BNEI YEHUDA – Aiyenugba, Rali (Radi 86), Mori (Kadosh 42), Hadad, Garrido, Edri, Zairi, Azoz, Baldut, Zandberg (Biton 65), Atar.
Sent off: Aiyenugba (42)

ITALY

Aged Azzurri upstaged by Mourinho's Inter

Italy's defence of the FIFA World Cup they won in Germany in 2006 came to an end in the first round of the 2010 tournament in South Africa. Three matches yielded no wins and just two points, leaving Marcello Lippi's titleholders in the humiliating position of finishing bottom of a group from which they had been widely expected to qualify at a canter. It was agony on the grandest scale for the Azzurri fans as they endured one of the country's most embarrassing World Cup exits of all time.

There had been concerns among the Italian public that Lippi would be over-reliant in South Africa on the players who had served him so well four years earlier – and, indeed, again during the qualifying competition for the 2010 finals, from which the team emerged as unbeaten group winners, fending off the challenge of a Republic of Ireland side led by ex-Azzurri boss Giovanni Trapattoni. Loyalty often brings its rewards in football, but on this occasion the heroes of 2006 were seen to be collectively and individually over the hill, their decline symbolised by their captain, Fabio Cannavaro, who, four years after giving one of the greatest sustained performances of top-class defending the World Cup had ever witnessed, suddenly looked out of his depth.

Short of inspiration

With little or no inspiration from their struggling skipper and all-time record cap-holder, and with goalkeeper Gianluigi Buffon lasting just 45 minutes of the opening game, Italy suddenly lost the ability to defend – the bedrock of their 2006 triumph. Furthermore, with the unavailability of playmaker-in-chief Andrea Pirlo, another highly polished performer in Germany, depriving the team of creativity and invention in midfield, and nobody making a positive impression up front, the class of 2010 had very little going for it.

Even so, while the lack of star individuals suggested that a successful title defence was highly unlikely, few

could have foreseen how badly Italy would struggle in a group that seemed almost hand-picked to guarantee their safe passage into the last 16. Drawing 1-1 with Paraguay in Cape Town was no disaster, but for the team to do no better in their second game, against New Zealand in Nelspruit, was more than unsettling. Italy had survived similar such setbacks early on in previous World Cups, though, so all was not lost for the notoriously slow starters. But that was before they encountered Slovakia in Johannesburg and started to give goals away in a manner that almost defied belief. Only in the final 15 minutes, with Pirlo at last introduced to the fray, did Italy begin to feature as an attacking force. They scored two goals and might have added a couple more, but Slovakia, for

A disconsolate Fabio Cannavaro hangs his head after Italy's World Cup elimination by Slovakia

whom journeyman striker Róbert Vittek scored twice, held firm for a historic 3-2 victory and Italy, shame-faced, limped out of the tournament.

Lippi had walked away after the 2006 triumph as a hero. Now, he departed with his previous reputation somewhat frayed, to say the least. Commendably, and not untypically, he put himself first in the firing line, claiming full responsibility for the team's poor showing and confessing that he had not prepared them properly. Other observers claimed that he had not selected the right personnel, the brunt of the argument being that he had chosen players on reputation rather than form.

Charitable defending

While much-touted mavericks such as Antonio Cassano, Fabrizio Miccoli, Mario Balotelli and Giuseppe Rossi would undoubtedly have added some variety and urgency to Italy's attack, there is not much they could have done to shore up an uncharacteristically charitable defence that shipped five goals in three games – three more than were conceded during the whole of the team's run to victory in 2006. The harsh reality was that Italy's best players were getting old and that Lippi still picked them because he felt there were no viable alternatives. It remains to be seen how his replacement, ex-ACF Fiorentina boss Cesare Prandelli, will cope with the task of reviving and regenerating the team in time for the 2014 World Cup. His more immediate objective is UEFA EURO 2012, for which Italy will have to see off the dual threat of Serbia and Slovenia if they are to claim automatic qualification for Poland/Ukraine.

If Prandelli is to be thwarted by the lack of young Italian talent coming through the ranks, then that will hardly be a surprise given that the FC Internazionale Milano team which won an unprecedented treble of Coppa Italia, Serie A and UEFA Champions League in 2009/10 was almost wholly made up of foreigners. They were also coached by one, too, in the formidable figure of José Mourinho.

In his second season at Inter, the self-proclaimed Special One lived up to that billing as he achieved a clean sweep of trophies that peaked with the club's long-awaited return to the pinnacle of European football after a 2-0 win over FC Bayern München in the UEFA Champions League final in Madrid. Mourinho could hardly have scripted it better, his last game as Inter boss taking place in the very stadium where he

José Mourinho raises the UEFA Champions League trophy as Inter celebrate in Madrid

was due to take up new employment. Although nothing had been signed and sealed in advance of the Nerazzurri's big day at the Santiago Bernabéu, it had long been an open secret that Mourinho would be leaving Italy for Spain at the season's end and signing up as the new head coach of Real Madrid CF.

Perfect parting gift

Before he left, though, Mourinho gave the Inter fans the best parting gift imaginable – their first European Cup win in 45 years. It was the reason he had been brought to the San Siro by president Massimo Moratti, and he did not fail. Indeed, his class and authority were stamped all over the club from the day he arrived to the day he left, during which time he brought in four major trophies, including the biggest, most cherished of all – a prize only he and two other coaches before him, Ernst Happel and Ottmar Hitzfeld, had claimed with two different clubs

Bayern were beaten in the Bernabéu by a typically shrewd tactical display from the ex-FC Porto coach and by two beautifully taken goals, one in each half, from the ever-reliable Diego Milito, the same man who had also scored the winning goals in the final of the Coppa Italia – against AS Roma – and the must-win final game of the Serie A campaign – against AC Siena. A new arrival from Genoa CFC, the Argentine striker enjoyed a campaign, and a climax to it, that he will surely never rival, but Milito was just one of many contributors to a remarkable annus mirabilis that all Interistas will forever recall with great pride and affection.

In a season of constant highs, the deliverance in Madrid inevitably outranked everything else, but the intensity of that occasion was matched by the team's earlier European successes against Chelsea FC and FC Barcelona. Eliminating the Londoners with a 1-0 win at Stamford Bridge, to consolidate a 2-1 first-leg lead taken in Milan, was a particularly sweet victory for Mourinho, who had spent over three years at the club before falling out with owner Roman Abramovich, but even that was eclipsed by the semi-final triumph against the holders as Inter came from behind to beat Barça 3-1 in the San Siro before defending with outrageous endeavour in Camp Nou and taking the tie 3-2 on aggregate. While Mourinho's safety-first strategy of all-out defence may have displeased the purists, it got the job done, taking Inter into the final of Europe's premier club competition for the first time in 36 years.

Inter overtake Milan

Inter had found domestic success rather easier to come by in recent times, and in 2009/10 they claimed their fifth Serie A title in a row. It was also the 18th in the club's history, which carried special local significance as it put the Nerazzurri one ahead of their Rossoneri neighbours, AC Milan, in the all-time roll of honour, with only Juventus, on 27, ahead of them. It also made it two scudetti out of two for Mourinho, though the second would eventually prove much tougher to obtain than the first, with Inter being taken to the wire by Roma before they prevailed.

Late-season drama in the title race seemed unlikely when, at Christmas, Inter held a commanding eight-point lead over Milan, with Roma three points further back in fourth place. But even the most resilient and resourceful teams can find the burden of competing for glory on two high-pressure fronts overtaxing, and a run of just one win in seven games during the early spring opened the gate for the chasing pack to hunt Inter down. When Mourinho's men then lost 2-1 at a resurgent Roma, their lead had been whittled down to

Diego Milito scored crucial goals in every competition to help Inter claim an unprecedented hat-trick of trophies

just one point. A fortnight later, after a 2-2 draw at ACF Fiorentina, Roma actually moved above them, but as the Giallorossi subsequently fell to an unexpected home defeat against UC Sampdoria, Inter re-seized the initiative and won each of their last five matches to retain the title.

The narrow last-day win at already-relegated Siena saw them home with a two-point advantage over Roma. For much of that final afternoon the team from the capital sat in the driving seat. As they led AC Chievo Verona, their head-to-head advantage over Inter – with whom they had drawn 1-1 at the San Siro in November – meant that, with the leaders being held in Tuscany, the scudetto was heading for Rome. But cometh the hour, cometh Milito, and his 57th-minute strike, brilliantly set up by his compatriot, Inter captain Javier Zanetti, was to prove decisive. It was the second time in 11 days that Milito had thrust a knife into Giallorossi hearts, another one of his timely and beautifully converted strikes having already seen Inter to a 1-0 win over Roma in the final of the Coppa Italia – a game played in Roma's own Stadio Olimpico.

If the Italian contribution to Inter's tripletta triumph was negligible – Balotelli, Davide Santon and Marco Materazzi, the only locals in the squad, started just 28 Serie A games between them – the South American influence was huge. Besides Milito, there were three other Argentinians, and they were all of crucial importance – Zanetti, the indefatigable, versatile veteran; Esteban Cambiasso, the doughty midfield conduit; and rock-hard central defender Walter Samuel. The Brazilian contingent was no less effective, especially in defence where Júlio César furthered his claims to be considered as the world's best goalkeeper and Lúcio, a new arrival from Bayern, and Maicon cemented theirs as the planet's foremost centre-back and right-back, respectively. Thiago Motta also added strength and industry in midfield, where much of the creativity was supplied by dazzling Dutchman Wesley Sneijder. Hastily offloaded by Real Madrid, the 25-year-old was especially prominent in the big European ties, while another newcomer, Samuel Eto'o, though outshone by Milito in the goalscoring department, gave Inter arguably the better of the exchange deal that saw Zlatan Ibrahimović transferred in the opposite direction to Barcelona. Eastern European trio Dejan Stanković, Cristian Chivu and mid-season signing Goran Pandev also played their part in a vintage season for the Nerazzurri that Mourinho's replacement, Rafael Benítez, will find almost impossible to match.

Leonardo dismissed

As Inter lost their coach, Milan got rid of theirs, saying thanks but no thanks to popular but inexperienced former playing icon Leonardo after his one and only season in charge brought only disappointment. The Brazilian's efforts were severely handicapped by a spate of injuries, but a bad start and an even worse finish could not make up for much of the good work that he achieved in between. On the plus side, Ronaldinho rediscovered some of his form of old, especially during a glorious spell in January; and there were strong performances from ex-Italy defender Alessandro Nesta as well as fit-again striker Marco Borriello, who deputised well for the injured Pato. In the season after Carlo Ancelotti, Paolo Maldini and Kaká, three club legends, had all departed, Milan were always likely to struggle, but their comprehensive 7-2 aggregate thrashing by Manchester United FC in the first knockout round of the UEFA Champions League was a shattering blow to morale from which the team, and particularly their coach, never fully recovered.

Still, third place meant that Leonardo's successor, ex-Cagliari Calcio boss Massimiliano Allegri, would have the pleasure of steering Milan back into the UEFA Champions League in 2010/11. Not so new Juventus coach Luigi Del Neri, who swapped the prospect of elite European football with Sampdoria for a UEFA Europa League campaign when he headed inland from Genoa to Turin during the summer. While Del Neri's Samp confounded the pundits by taking fourth place after a battle royale with the Sicilians of US Città di Palermo – neither of the two clubs, like champions Inter, were beaten at home - Juve endured a wretched 2009/10 campaign, finishing in a lowly seventh spot.

Juve fall flat

The 2008/09 Serie A runners-up started brightly, under Ciro Ferrara, winning their first four league games, but a miserable winter period, during which they suffered two fateful 4-1 defeats in Europe (against Bayern and Fulham FC) and also coughed up points on a regular basis in Serie A, accelerated their demise. Ferrara was replaced by Alberto Zaccheroni, whose short reign brought more league defeats than wins. The performances of new Brazilian signings Diego and Felipe Melo were surprisingly flat, while veterans like Alessandro Del Piero, David Trezeguet and Cannavaro discovered that they could no longer trade on former glories.

Claudio Ranieri took over at hometown club Roma and led the Giallorossi to second place in Serie A

ITALY

It was the man who had led Juventus for most of the previous season, Claudio Ranieri, who steered Roma to the brink of their first scudetto for nine years. Appointed in early September to replace long-serving Luciano Spalletti, the native Roman thus rejoined the club where he had kicked off his playing career in the early 1970s. It proved to be a marriage made in heaven as Ranieri oversaw a club-record run of 24 Serie A matches without defeat that enabled the Giallorossi to claw back a large deficit and temporarily dislodge Inter – until that harrowing 2-1 home defeat by Sampdoria, in which Giampaolo Pazzini's two goals effectively shredded their title hopes.

Costly defeat

Roma, whose European ambitions also came to grief on home turf, against Panathinaikos FC in the UEFA Europa League, had cause to reflect ruefully on an even costlier defeat at the Stadio Olimpico, 1-0 by AS Livorno Calcio, back in October. The club promoted via the play-offs had taken only three points from eight games – all from 0-0 draws – before that shock win in Rome. It would prove to be of little long-term value, however, as Livorno ended the season propping up the table and returning whence they had come, in the company of Siena and an Atalanta BC side that went through four coaches.

Just three places above Atalanta, surprisingly, were Udinese Calcio. They were rescued from relegation almost single-handedly by Italian international Antonio Di Natale, whose capocannoniere-winning tally of 29 goals accounted for more than half of his team's total. A cluster of other Italian strikers – Pazzini,

Federazione Italiana Giuoco Calcio (FIGC)

Via Gregorio Allegri 14
CP 2450
IT-00198 Roma
tel – +39 06 84 911
fax – +39 06 84 912 526
website – figc.it
email – international@figc.it
Year of Formation – 1898

President – Giancarlo Abete
General Secretary – Antonio Di Sebastiano
Media Officer – Antonello Valentini
National Stadium – Stadio Olimpico, Rome (73,095)

INTERNATIONAL HONOURS
FIFA World Cup – (4) 1934, 1938, 1982, 2006.
UEFA European Championship – (1) 1968.
INTERNATIONAL TOURNAMENT APPEARANCES
FIFA World Cup – (17) 1934 (Winners), 1938 (Winners), 1950, 1958, 1962, 1966, 1970 (runners-up), 1974, 1978 (4th), 1982 (Winners), 1986 (2nd round), 1990 (3rd), 1994 (runners-up), 1998 (qtr-finals), 2002 (2nd round), 2006 (Winners), 2010.
UEFA European Championship – (7) 1968 (Winners), 1980 (4th), 1988 (semi-finals), 1996, 2000 (runners-up), 2004, 2008 (qtr-finals), 2010.
TOP FIVE ALL-TIME CAPS
Fabio Cannavaro (136); Paolo Maldini (126); Dino Zoff (112); Gianluigi Buffon (102); Gianluca Zambrotta (97)
TOP FIVE ALL-TIME GOALS
Luigi Riva (35); Giuseppe Meazza (33); Silvio Piola (30); Roberto Baggio & Alessandro Del Piero (27)

Miccoli, Fiorentina's Alberto Gilardino and Roma's Francesco Totti – also scored abundantly for their clubs, but it was the decisive goals of an Argentinian – or perhaps of a Slovakian - that would linger longest in the memory from a season of bittersweet fortunes for Italian football.

NATIONAL TEAM RESULTS 2009/10

Date	Opponent		Venue	Score	Scorers
12/8/09	Switzerland	A	Basle	0-0	
5/9/09	Georgia (WCQ)	A	Tbilisi	2-0	Kaladze (56og, 66og)
9/9/09	Bulgaria (WCQ)	H	Turin	2-0	Grosso (11), Iaquinta (40)
10/10/09	Republic of Ireland (WCQ)	A	Dublin	2-2	Camoranesi (26), Gilardino (90)
14/10/09	Cyprus (WCQ)	H	Parma	3-2	Gilardino (78, 81, 90+2)
14/11/09	Netherlands	H	Pescara	0-0	
18/11/09	Sweden	H	Cesena	1-0	Chiellini (29)
3/3/10	Cameroon	N	Monaco (FRA)	0-0	
3/6/10	Mexico	N	Brussels (BEL)	1-2	Bonucci (89)
5/6/10	Switzerland	A	Geneva	1-1	Quagliarella (14)
14/6/10	Paraguay (WCF)	N	Cape Town (RSA)	1-1	De Rossi (63)
20/6/10	New Zealand (WCF)	N	Nelspruit (RSA)	1-1	Iaquinta (29p)
24/6/10	Slovakia (WCF)	N	Johannesburg (RSA)	2-3	Di Natale (73), Quagliarella (90+2)

NATIONAL TEAM APPEARANCES 2009/10

Coach – Marcello LIPPI	11/4/48		Sui	GEO	BUL	IRL	CYP	Ned	Swe	Cmr	Mex	Sui	PAR	NZL	SVK	Caps	Goals
Gianluigi BUFFON	28/1/78	Juventus	G	G	G	G		G			G		G46			102	-
Gianluca ZAMBROTTA	19/2/77	Milan	D46	D	D	D		D			D63	D81	D	D	D	97	2
Fabio CANNAVARO	13/9/73	Juventus	D	D	D		D	D		D81	D89		D	D	D	136	1
Giorgio CHIELLINI	14/8/84	Juventus	D	D	D	D		D	D	D		D	D	D	D	32	2
Domenico CRISCITO	30/12/86	Genoa	D	D				s80	D55	M46	D	s81	D	D	D46	10	-
Mauro CAMORANESI	4/10/76	Juventus	M30	M71	M	M	s46	M86	s77				s59	s46		55	5
Andrea PIRLO	19/5/79	Milan	M61	M	M	M		M		M46	M82				s56	67	9
Angelo PALOMBO	25/9/81	Sampdoria	M	M		M89		M71	s65		s82	M88				17	-
Claudio MARCHISIO	19/1/86	Juventus	M72		M73					s46	M		M59	M61		6	-
Alberto GILARDINO	5/7/82	Fiorentina	A46		A58	s76	A	A76			A64	s78	A72	A46		43	16
Giuseppe ROSSI	1/2/87	Villarreal (ESP)	A61	A57	s58		A46	s55	s46							14	3
Simone PEPE	30/8/83	Udinese	s30		s73	s89	M46			s46	s46	M	M46	A		18	-
Davide SANTON	2/1/91	Inter	s46	s71				D								5	-
Vincenzo IAQUINTA	21/11/79	Juventus	s46	A	A83	A				M	s86	M	A	A		40	6
Fabio QUAGLIARELLA	31/1/83	Napoli	s61	s57			A			s61	s75	A66		s46		21	5
Gaetano D'AGOSTINO	3/6/82	Udinese	s61	s57	s83		M66									5	-
Fabio GROSSO	28/11/77	Lyon (FRA) /Juventus	s72		D	D76		D80								48	4
Marco MARCHIONNI	22/7/80	Fiorentina		M57				s86	A77							6	-
Daniele DE ROSSI	24/7/83	Roma				M	M	s66		M46	M75	s88	M	M	M	57	9
Nicola LEGROTTAGLIE	20/10/76	Juventus				D		D								16	1
Antonio DI NATALE	13/10/77	Udinese				M76	s46		A	A61	M46	s66	s72	s46	A	36	10
Salvatore BOCCHETTI	30/11/86	Genoa				s76	D		s55		s89	D				5	-
Federico MARCHETTI	7/2/83	Cagliari					G		G	G		G	s46	G	G	8	-
Alessandro GAMBERINI	27/8/81	Fiorentina					D									7	-
Gennaro GATTUSO	9/1/78	Milan					M			s46	M86				M46	73	1
Antonio CANDREVA	28/2/87	Livorno						M76	M46							2	-
Raffaele PALLADINO	17/4/84	Genoa						M55								3	-
Davide BIONDINI	24/1/83	Cagliari						s71	M46							2	-
Riccardo MONTOLIVO	18/1/85	Fiorentina						s76	M65	s46		M	M	M	M56	16	-
Giampaolo PAZZINI	2/8/84	Sampdoria						s76	A	s46	s64	A78		s61		9	1
Christian MAGGIO	11/2/82	Napoli						D46	M	s63	D				s46	6	-
Mattia CASSANI	26/8/83	Palermo						s46	s81							2	-
Daniele GALLOPPA	15/5/85	Parma						s46								2	-
Leonardo BONUCCI	1/5/87	Bari								D	D					2	1
Andrea COSSU	3/5/80	Cagliari								A		A46				2	-
Marco BORRIELLO	18/6/82	Milan								A46						4	-

DOMESTIC LEAGUE 2009/10

SERIE A FINAL TABLE

		Pld	Home					Away					Total					Pts
			W	D	L	F	A	W	D	L	F	A	W	D	L	F	A	
1	FC Internazionale Milano	38	15	4	0	42	15	9	6	4	33	19	24	10	4	75	34	82
2	AS Roma	38	15	1	3	36	17	9	7	3	32	24	24	8	6	68	41	80
3	AC Milan	38	12	5	2	37	20	8	5	6	23	19	20	10	8	60	39	70
4	UC Sampdoria	38	13	6	0	31	10	6	4	9	18	31	19	10	9	49	41	67
5	US Città di Palermo	38	13	6	0	34	14	5	5	9	25	33	18	11	9	59	47	65
6	SSC Napoli	38	9	8	2	26	16	6	6	7	24	27	15	14	9	50	43	59
7	Juventus	38	9	4	6	32	26	7	3	9	23	30	16	7	15	55	56	55
8	Parma FC	38	10	4	5	24	17	4	6	9	22	34	14	10	14	46	51	52
9	Genoa CFC	38	11	5	3	42	28	3	4	12	15	33	14	9	15	57	61	51
10	AS Bari	38	11	4	4	30	15	2	7	10	19	34	13	11	14	49	49	50
11	ACF Fiorentina	38	9	3	7	28	20	4	5	10	20	27	13	8	17	48	47	47
12	S.S. Lazio	38	5	6	8	19	21	6	7	6	20	22	11	13	14	39	43	46
13	Calcio Catania	38	8	7	4	25	15	2	8	9	19	30	10	15	13	44	45	45
14	AC Chievo Verona	38	6	5	8	20	21	6	3	10	17	21	12	8	18	37	42	44
15	Udinese Calcio	38	10	5	4	38	25	1	6	12	16	34	11	11	16	54	59	44
16	Cagliari Calcio	38	7	7	5	37	29	4	4	11	19	29	11	11	16	56	58	44
17	Bologna FC	38	7	5	7	25	27	3	7	9	17	28	10	12	16	42	55	42
18	Atalanta BC	38	7	5	7	24	20	2	3	14	13	33	9	8	21	37	53	35
19	AC Siena	38	4	7	8	17	25	3	3	13	23	42	7	10	21	40	67	31
20	AS Livorno Calcio	38	5	5	9	19	25	2	3	14	8	36	7	8	23	27	61	29

TOP GOALSCORERS

29 Antonio DI NATALE (Udinese)

22 Diego MILITO (Inter)

19 Fabrizio MICCOLI (Palermo)
Giampaolo PAZZINI (Sampdoria)

15 Alberto GILARDINO (Fiorentina)

14 BARRETO (Bari)
Marco BORRIELLO (Milan)
Francesco TOTTI (Roma)
Mirko VUČINIĆ (Roma)

13 Alessandro MATRI (Cagliari)
Edinson CAVANI (Palermo)

CLUB-BY-CLUB

ATALANTA BC

Coach – Angelo Gregucci; (21/9/09) Antonio Conte;
(7/1/10) (Walter Bonacina); (11/1/10) Bortolo Mutti
Founded – 1907
Stadium – Atleti Azzurri d'Italia (26,393)
MAJOR HONOURS:
Italian Cup – (1) 1963.

2009

23/8	Lazio	a	0-1	
30/8	Genoa	h	0-1	
13/9	Sampdoria	h	0-1	
20/9	Bari	a	1-4	*Bellini*
23/9	Catania	h	0-0	
27/9	Chievo	a	1-1	*Tiribocchi*
4/10	Milan	h	1-1	*Tiribocchi*
18/10	Udinese	a	3-1	*Tiribocchi, Valdés, De Ascentis*
25/10	Parma	h	3-1	*Valdés (p), Tiribocchi, Peluso*
28/10	Livorno	a	0-1	
1/11	Cagliari	a	0-3	
7/11	Juventus	h	2-5	*Valdés, Ceravolo*
22/11	Siena	a	2-0	*Tiribocchi, Acquafresca (p)*
29/11	Roma	h	1-2	*Ceravolo*
6/12	Fiorentina	a	0-2	
13/12	Inter	h	1-1	*Tiribocchi*

2010

6/1	Napoli	h	0-2	
10/1	Palermo	a	0-1	
17/1	Lazio	h	3-0	*Doni 2, Padoin*
20/1	Bologna	a	2-2	*Manfredini, Chevantón*
24/1	Genoa	a	0-2	
31/1	Sampdoria	a	0-2	
7/2	Bari	h	1-0	*Tiribocchi*
14/2	Catania	a	0-0	
21/2	Chievo	h	0-1	
28/2	Milan	a	1-3	*Valdés*
7/3	Udinese	h	0-0	
14/3	Parma	a	0-1	
21/3	Livorno	h	3-0	*Padoin, Chevantón, Ferreira Pinto*
24/3	Cagliari	h	3-1	*Tiribocchi, Valdés 2 (1p)*
28/3	Juventus	a	1-2	*Amoruso*
3/4	Siena	h	2-0	*Valdés, Ferreira Pinto*
11/4	Roma	a	1-2	*Tiribocchi*
18/4	Fiorentina	h	2-1	*Ferreira Pinto, Tiribocchi*
24/4	Inter	a	1-3	*Tiribocchi*
2/5	Bologna	h	1-1	*Guarente*
9/5	Napoli	a	0-2	
16/5	Palermo	h	1-2	*Ceravolo*

No	Name	Nat	DoB	Pos	Aps	(s)	Gls
9	Robert ACQUAFRESCA		11/9/87	A	10	(2)	1
9	Nicola AMORUSO		29/8/74	A	12	(3)	1
16	Edgar Osvaldo BARRETO	PAR	15/7/84	M	3	(1)	
6	Gianpaolo BELLINI		27/3/80	D	29		1
77	Paolo BIANCO		20/8/77	D	20	(1)	
28	Giacomo BONAVENTURA		22/8/89	M		(1)	
4	Daniele CAPELLI		20/6/86	D	10		
18	Fabio CASERTA		24/9/78	M	5	(9)	

70	Fabio Giovanni CERAVOLO		5/3/87	A	9	(18)	3
19	Ernesto Javier CHEVANTÓN	URU	12/8/80	A	3	(9)	2
1	Andrea CONSIGLI		27/1/87	G	31		
32	Ferdinando COPPOLA		10/6/78	G	7	(1)	
15	Diego DE ASCENTIS		31/7/76	M	14	(3)	1
72	Cristiano DONI		1/4/73	M	23	(7)	2
79	Adriano FERREIRA PINTO	BRA	10/12/79	M	21	(2)	3
38	Manolo GABBIADINI		26/11/91	A		(2)	
8	György GARICS	AUT	8/3/84	D	28	(2)	
17	Tiberio GUARENTE		1/11/85	M	32		1
19	Miguel Ángel LAYÚN Prado	MEX	25/6/88	M		(2)	
7	Nicola MADONNA		31/10/86	M	2	(4)	
5	Thomas MANFREDINI		27/5/80	D	26		1
22	Simone PADOIN		18/3/84	M	36		2
26	Maximiliano PELLEGRINO	ARG	26/1/80	D	6		
13	Federico PELUSO		20/1/84	D	17	(7)	1
21	Ivan RADOVANOVIĆ	SRB	29/8/88	M	3	(9)	
2	Leonardo José TALAMONTI	ARG	12/11/81	D	15	(2)	
11	Christian TIBONI		6/4/88	A		(1)	
90	Simone TIRIBOCCHI		31/1/78	A	28	(9)	11
20	Jaime Andrés VALDÉS Zapata	CHI	11/1/81	A	25	(8)	7
74	Sergio VOLPI		2/2/74	M	1	(4)	
25	Paolo ZANETTI		16/12/82	M	2		

AS BARI
Coach – Giampiero Ventura
Founded – 1908
Stadium – San Nicola (58,270)

2009

23/8	Inter	a	1-1	Kutuzov
29/8	Bologna	h	0-0	
13/9	Palermo	a	1-1	Allegretti
20/9	Atalanta	h	4-1	Rivas, Barreto, Álvarez, Donati
23/9	Cagliari	h	0-1	
27/9	Milan	a	0-0	
3/10	Catania	h	0-0	
18/10	Chievo	a	2-1	Almirón, Ranocchia
25/10	Lazio	h	2-0	Barreto, Meggiorini
28/10	Parma	a	0-2	
1/11	Sampdoria	a	0-0	
8/11	Livorno	h	1-0	Allegretti
22/11	Roma	a	1-3	og (Andreolli)
29/11	Siena	h	2-1	Masiello A., Greco
6/12	Napoli	a	2-3	Barreto, Ranocchia
12/12	Juventus	h	3-1	Meggiorini, Barreto (p), Almirón
2010				
6/1	Udinese	h	2-0	Meggiorini, Barreto
10/1	Fiorentina	a	1-2	Barreto
16/1	Inter	h	2-2	Barreto 2 (2p)
20/1	Genoa	a	1-1	Barreto
24/1	Bologna	a	1-2	Barreto
30/1	Palermo	h	4-2	Bonucci, Álvarez, Barreto (p), Koman
7/2	Atalanta	a	0-1	
14/2	Cagliari	a	1-3	Masiello S.
21/2	Milan	h	0-2	
27/2	Catania	a	0-4	
7/3	Chievo	h	1-0	Castillo
14/3	Lazio	a	2-0	Almirón, Álvarez
21/3	Parma	h	1-1	Masiello A.
24/3	Sampdoria	h	2-1	Meggiorini, Barreto
28/3	Livorno	a	1-1	Allegretti
3/4	Roma	h	0-1	
11/4	Siena	a	2-3	Rivas, Castillo
18/4	Napoli	h	1-2	Almirón
25/4	Juventus	a	0-3	
2/5	Genoa	h	3-0	Meggiorini, Castillo, Barreto
9/5	Udinese	a	3-3	Barreto, Koman, Almirón
16/5	Fiorentina	h	2-0	Stellini, Rivas

No	Name	Nat	DoB	Pos	Aps	(s)	Gls
30	Riccardo ALLEGRETTI		15/2/78	M	14	(2)	3
4	Sergio Bernardo ALMIRÓN	ARG	7/11/80	M	20	(7)	5
90	Edgar Anthony ÁLVAREZ	HON	18/1/80	M	37		3
8	Filippo Agomeri ANTONELLI		13/7/78	M	1	(3)	
10	Paulo Vítor BARRETO de Souza	BRA	12/7/85	A	30	(1)	14
15	Nicola BELMONTE		15/4/87	D	17	(1)	
19	Leonardo BONUCCI		1/5/87	D	38		1
6	José Ignacio CASTILLO	ARG	4/11/75	A	11	(5)	3
9	Daniele DE VEZZE		9/1/80	M	5	(4)	
3	Souleymane DIAMONTÈNE	MLI	30/1/83	D	3		
16	Massimo DONATI		26/3/81	M	26	(6)	1
14	Alessandro Carlo GAZZI		28/1/83	M	25	(7)	
1	Jean-François GILLET	BEL	31/5/79	G	37		
8	András GOSZTONYI	HUN	7/11/90	A		(2)	
18	Giuseppe GRECO		6/8/83	A		(6)	1
88	Pedro KAMATA	FRA	6/9/81	M	1	(13)	
11	Vladimir KOMAN	HUN	16/3/89	M	11	(5)	2
20	Vitaliy KUTUZOV	BLR	20/3/80	A	10	(2)	1
23	Antonio LANGELLA		30/3/77	A	2	(7)	
5	Andrea MASIELLO		5/2/86	D	37		2
17	Salvatore MASIELLO		31/1/82	M	25	(2)	1
69	Riccardo MEGGIORINI		4/9/85	A	23	(8)	5
25	Daniele PADELLI		25/10/85	G	1		
21	Alessandro PARISI		15/4/77	D	13	(2)	
26	Marco PISANO		13/8/81	D		(1)	
13	Andrea RANOCCHIA		16/2/88	D	17		2
7	Emanuel Benito RIVAS	ARG	17/3/83	M	10	(10)	3
77	Alessio SESTU		29/9/83	M		(3)	
99	Ferdinando SFORZINI		4/12/84	A	1	(7)	
27	Cristian STELLINI		27/4/74	D	3	(6)	1

BOLOGNA FC
Coach – Giuseppe Papadopulo; (20/10/09) Franco Colomba
Founded – 1909
Stadium – Renato Dall'Ara (39,444)
MAJOR HONOURS:
Italian League - (7) 1925, 1929, 1936, 1937, 1939, 1941, 1964;
Italian Cup - (2) 1970, 1974.

2009

22/8	Fiorentina	h	1-1	Osvaldo
29/8	Bari	a	0-0	
13/9	Chievo	h	0-2	
20/9	Milan	a	0-1	
23/9	Livorno	h	2-0	Portanova, Di Vaio
27/9	Juventus	a	1-1	Adaílton
4/10	Genoa	h	1-3	Di Vaio (p)
18/10	Napoli	a	1-2	Adaílton
24/10	Sampdoria	a	1-4	Osvaldo
28/10	Siena	h	2-1	Adaílton, Osvaldo
1/11	Roma	a	1-2	Adaílton
8/11	Palermo	h	3-1	Zalayeta 2, Di Vaio
21/11	Inter	h	1-3	Zalayeta
29/11	Lazio	h	0-0	
6/12	Udinese	h	2-1	Adaílton, Di Vaio (p)
13/12	Parma	a	1-2	Mudingayi
2010				
6/1	Catania	a	0-1	
10/1	Cagliari	h	0-1	
17/1	Fiorentina	a	2-1	Giménez, Di Vaio
20/1	Atalanta	h	2-2	Di Vaio 2
24/1	Bari	h	2-1	Giménez 2
31/1	Chievo	a	1-1	Di Vaio
7/2	Milan	h	0-0	
14/2	Livorno	a	1-0	Di Vaio
21/2	Juventus	h	1-2	Buscè
28/2	Genoa	a	4-3	Buscè, Adaílton 3 (1p)
7/3	Napoli	h	2-1	Zalayeta, Adaílton
14/3	Sampdoria	h	1-1	Raggi
21/3	Siena	a	0-1	
24/3	Roma	h	0-2	

ITALY

27/3	Palermo	a	1-3	*Adaílton*
3/4	Inter	a	0-3	
11/4	Lazio	h	2-3	*Guana, Portanova*
18/4	Udinese	a	1-1	*og (Zapata)*
25/4	Parma	h	2-1	*Di Vaio 2*
2/5	Atalanta	a	1-1	*og (Peluso)*
9/5	Catania	h	1-1	*Di Vaio*
16/5	Cagliari	a	1-1	*Adaílton*

No	Name	Nat	DoB	Pos	Aps	(s)	Gls
85	ADAÍLTON Martins Bolzan	BRA	24/1/77	A	24	(7)	11
4	Stephen APPIAH	GHA	24/12/80	M	1	(1)	
50	Alessandro BASSOLI		19/6/90	D		(1)	
10	Davide BOMBARDINI		21/6/74	M	4	(5)	
6	Miguel Ángel BRITOS	URU	17/7/85	D	21	(2)	
24	Antonio BUSCÈ		12/12/75	M	16	(1)	2
32	Federico CASARINI		7/8/89	M	10	(9)	
15	Roberto COLOMBO		24/8/75	G	4		
9	Marco DI VAIO		15/7/76	A	28	(2)	12
20	Henry Damián GIMÉNEZ	URU	13/3/86	A	4	(14)	3
14	Roberto GUANA		21/1/81	M	33	(1)	1
23	Salvatore LANNA		31/7/76	D	33		
41	Massimo MARAZZINA		16/7/74	A		(4)	
8	Nicola MINGAZZINI		13/8/80	M	18	(6)	
30	Francesco MODESTO		16/2/82	D	11	(2)	
18	Vangelis MORAS	GRE	26/8/81	D	17	(3)	
26	Gaby MUDINGAYI	BEL	1/10/81	M	21	(7)	1
5	Massimo MUTARELLI		13/1/78	M	3	(4)	
89	Savio NSEREKO	GER	27/7/89	A		(2)	
22	Pablo Daniel OSVALDO		12/1/86	A	4	(9)	3
7	Andrea PISANU		7/1/82	M	1	(1)	
13	Daniele PORTANOVA		17/12/78	D	36		2
3	RAFAEL Alves dos Santos	BRA	10/11/84	D	2		
84	Andrea RAGGI		24/6/84	D	30	(1)	1
11	Davide SUCCI		11/10/81	A	2	(8)	
19	Giacomo TEDESCO		2/2/76	M	5	(3)	
7	Francesco VALIANI		29/10/80	M	15	(4)	
11	Luca VIGIANI		25/8/76	M	6	(5)	
1	Emiliano VIVIANO		1/12/85	G	34		
25	Marcelo ZALAYETA	URU	5/12/78	A	23	(6)	4
21	Cristian ZENONI		23/4/77	D	12	(4)	

CAGLIARI CALCIO
Coach – Massimiliano Allegri; (13/4/10) (Giorgio Melis)
Founded – 1920
Stadium – Sant'Elia (23,486)
MAJOR HONOURS:
Italian League - (1) 1970.

2009
23/8	Livorno	a	0-0	
30/8	Siena	h	1-3	*Jeda (p)*
13/9	Fiorentina	a	0-1	
20/9	Inter	h	1-2	*Jeda (p)*
23/9	Bari	a	1-0	*Nenê*
27/9	Parma	a	2-0	*Jeda, Dessena*
4/10	Chievo	h	1-2	*Matri*
18/10	Catania	a	1-2	*Dessena*
25/10	Genoa	h	3-2	*Biondini, Nenê (p), Lazzari*
28/10	Lazio	a	1-0	*Matri*
1/11	Atalanta	h	3-0	*Nenê 2, Matri (p)*
8/11	Sampdoria	h	2-0	*Conti, Matri*
22/11	Milan	a	3-4	*Matri, Lazzari, Nenê*
29/11	Juventus	h	2-0	*Nenê, Matri*
6/12	Palermo	a	1-2	*Matri*
12/12	Napoli	h	3-3	*Larrivey, Matri, Jeda*
2010				
6/1	Roma	h	2-2	*Diego López, Conti*
10/1	Bologna	a	1-0	*Matri*
16/1	Livorno	h	3-0	*Larrivey 2, Jeda*
24/1	Siena	a	1-1	*Matri (p)*

31/1	Fiorentina	h	2-2	*Lazzari, Astori*
7/2	Inter	a	0-3	
14/2	Bari	h	3-1	*Conti, Nenê, og (Gazzi)*
21/2	Parma	h	2-0	*og (Zaccardo), Matri*
24/2	Udinese	a	1-2	*Jeda*
28/2	Chievo	a	1-2	*Astori*
7/3	Catania	h	2-2	*Lazzari, Cossu*
14/3	Genoa	a	3-5	*Dessena, Conti, Matri (p)*
21/3	Lazio	h	0-2	
24/3	Atalanta	a	1-3	*Conti*
28/3	Sampdoria	a	1-1	*Nenê*
3/4	Milan	h	2-3	*Ragatzu, Matri*
11/4	Juventus	a	0-1	
18/4	Palermo	h	2-2	*Cossu, Jeda*
25/4	Napoli	a	0-0	
2/5	Udinese	h	2-2	*Lazzari, Jeda*
9/5	Roma	a	1-2	*Lazzari*
16/5	Bologna	h	1-1	*Ragatzu*

No	Name	Nat	DoB	Pos	Aps	(s)	Gls
25	Michael AGAZZI		3/7/84	G	3		
31	Alessandro AGOSTINI		23/7/79	D	38		
3	Lorenzo ARIAUDO		11/6/89	D	8	(1)	
13	Davide ASTORI		7/1/87	D	34		2
20	Simone BARONE		30/4/78	M	5	(11)	
8	Davide BIONDINI		24/1/83	M	32	(4)	1
21	Michele CANINI		5/6/85	D	30		
5	Daniele CONTI		9/1/79	M	32		5
7	Andrea COSSU		3/5/80	M	31	(2)	2
4	Daniele DESSENA		10/5/87	M	19	(10)	3
6	Luis DIEGO LÓPEZ Breijo	URU	22/8/74	D	18		1
29	Mattia GALLON		30/5/92	A		(1)	
27	Jedaias Capucho Neves "JEDA"	BRA	15/4/79	A	21	(11)	8
23	Joaquín LARRIVEY	ARG	20/8/84	A	12	(15)	3
10	Andrea LAZZARI		3/12/84	M	24	(9)	6
24	Cristiano LUPATELLI		21/6/78	G	1	(1)	
22	Federico MARCHETTI		7/2/83	G	33		
15	Lino MARZORATTI		12/10/86	D	12	(1)	
32	Alessandro MATRI		19/8/84	A	30	(8)	13
28	Radja NAINGGOLAN	BEL	4/5/88	M	2	(5)	
9	Ânderson Miguel da Silva "NENÊ"	BRA	28/7/83	A	14	(19)	8
18	Andrea PAROLA		22/4/79	M	7	(7)	
14	Francesco PISANO		29/4/86	D	7	(2)	
30	Daniele RAGATZU		21/9/91	A	4	(4)	2
16	Mikhail SIVAKOV	BLR	16/1/88	M		(1)	
16	Enrico VERACHI		18/1/90	M		(1)	
1	Mauro VIGORITO		22/5/90	G	1	(1)	

CALCIO CATANIA
Coach – Gianluca Atzori; (8/12/09) Siniša Mihajlović (SRB)
Founded – 1946
Stadium – Angelo Massimino (23,420)

2009
23/8	Sampdoria	h	1-2	*Morimoto*
30/8	Parma	a	1-2	*Biagianti*
13/9	Udinese	a	2-4	*Morimoto, Mascara (p)*
20/9	Lazio	h	1-1	*Martínez*
23/9	Atalanta	a	0-0	
27/9	Roma	h	1-1	*Morimoto*
3/10	Bari	a	0-0	
18/10	Cagliari	h	2-1	*Ricchiuti, Martínez*
24/10	Inter	a	1-2	*Mascara (p)*
28/10	Chievo	h	1-2	*Mascara (p)*
1/11	Fiorentina	a	1-3	*Mascara*
7/11	Napoli	h	0-0	
22/11	Palermo	a	1-1	*Martínez*
29/11	Milan	h	0-2	
6/12	Siena	a	2-3	*Martínez 2*
13/12	Livorno	h	0-1	
20/12	Juventus	a	2-1	*Martínez (p), Izco*

2010

6/1	Bologna	h	1-0	Spolli
10/1	Genoa	a	0-2	
17/1	Sampdoria	a	1-1	Llama
23/1	Parma	h	3-0	Mascara, Martínez, Morimoto
31/1	Udinese	h	1-1	Biagianti
7/2	Lazio	a	1-0	Maxi López
14/2	Atalanta	h	0-0	
21/2	Roma	a	0-1	
27/2	Bari	h	4-0	Ricchiuti, Llama, Morimoto, Martínez
7/3	Cagliari	a	2-2	Mascara (p), Maxi López
12/3	Inter	h	3-1	Maxi López, Mascara (p), Martínez
21/3	Chievo	a	1-1	Maxi López (p)
24/3	Fiorentina	h	1-0	Mascara
28/3	Napoli	a	0-1	
3/4	Palermo	h	2-0	Maxi López 2
11/4	Milan	a	2-2	Maxi López, Ricchiuti
18/4	Siena	h	2-2	Maxi López, Biagianti
25/4	Livorno	a	1-3	Maxi López
2/5	Juventus	h	1-1	Silvestre
9/5	Bologna	a	1-1	Maxi López
16/5	Genoa	h	1-0	Maxi López

No	Name	Nat	DoB	Pos	Aps	(s)	Gls
22	Pablo Sebastián ÁLVAREZ	ARG	17/4/84	D	23	(2)	
21	Mariano Gonzalo ANDÚJAR	ARG	30/7/83	G	35		
18	Błażej AUGUSTYN	POL	26/1/88	D	6	(4)	
10	Pablo César BARRIENTOS	ARG	17/1/85	M		(2)	
14	Giuseppe BELLUSCI		21/8/89	D	7	(5)	
27	Marco BIAGIANTI		19/4/84	M	35	(1)	3
30	Andrea CAMPAGNOLO		17/6/78	G	3		
33	Ciro CAPUANO		10/7/81	D	29	(1)	
5	Ezequiel Alejo CARBONI	ARG	4/4/79	M	26	(2)	
4	Gennaro DELVECCHIO		25/3/78	M	7	(10)	
13	Mariano Julio IZCO	ARG	13/3/83	M	24	(8)	1
1	Tomáš KOŠICKÝ	SVK	11/3/86	G		(1)	
8	Pablo Martín LEDESMA	ARG	4/2/84	M	6	(10)	
16	Cristian Ezequiel LLAMA	ARG	26/6/86	M	18	(5)	2
12	Giovanni MARCHESE		17/10/84	D	2	(2)	
25	Jorge Andrés MARTÍNEZ	URU	5/4/83	A	19	(6)	9
7	Giuseppe MASCARA		22/8/79	A	33	(1)	8
11	MAXImiliano Gastón LÓPEZ	ARG	3/4/84	A	17		11
17	Federico MORETTI		28/10/88	M		(2)	
15	Takayuki MORIMOTO	JPN	7/5/88	A	16	(11)	5
24	Simone PESCE		10/7/82	M	1	(3)	
9	Gianvito PLASMATI		28/1/83	A	1	(12)	
2	Alessandro POTENZA		8/3/84	D	14	(5)	
19	Adrián RICCHIUTI		30/6/78	A	22	(5)	3
20	Orazio RUSSO		6/10/73	M		(1)	
20	Gennaro SARDO		26/1/88	D	1		
26	Fabio SCIACCA		16/5/89	M	1	(3)	
6	Matías Agustín SILVESTRE	ARG	25/9/84	D	35		1
3	Nicolás Federico SPOLLI	ARG	20/2/83	D	22	(4)	1
23	Christian TERLIZZI		10/7/81	D	15	(2)	

AC CHIEVO VERONA
Coach – Domenico Di Carlo
Founded – 1929
Stadium – Marc'Antonio Bentegodi (39,211)

2009

23/8	Juventus	a	0-1	
30/8	Lazio	h	1-2	Pellissier
13/9	Bologna	a	2-0	Pinzi, Pellissier
20/9	Genoa	h	3-1	Marcolini (p), Bogdani, Pellissier
23/9	Siena	a	0-0	
27/9	Atalanta	h	1-1	Pellissier
4/10	Cagliari	a	2-1	Marcolini 2
18/10	Bari	h	1-2	Bogdani
25/10	Milan	h	1-2	Pinzi
28/10	Catania	a	2-1	Mantovani, Marcolini

1/11	Udinese	h	1-1	Yepes
8/11	Parma	a	0-2	
22/11	Sampdoria	a	1-2	Mantovani
29/11	Palermo	h	1-0	Abbruscato
6/12	Livorno	a	2-0	Rigoni, Bentivoglio
13/12	Fiorentina	h	2-1	Pinzi, Sardo
20/12	Napoli	a	0-2	

2010

6/1	Inter	h	0-1	
9/1	Roma	a	0-1	
17/1	Juventus	a	1-0	Sardo
24/1	Lazio	h	1-1	Pellissier
31/1	Bologna	h	1-1	Pellissier
7/2	Genoa	a	0-1	
14/2	Siena	a	0-1	
21/2	Atalanta	a	1-0	Pellissier
28/2	Cagliari	h	2-1	Marcos, Granoche
7/3	Bari	a	0-1	
14/3	Milan	a	0-1	
21/3	Catania	h	1-1	Pellissier
24/3	Udinese	a	0-0	
28/3	Parma	h	0-0	
3/4	Sampdoria	h	1-2	Mantovani
11/4	Palermo	a	1-3	Marcos
17/4	Livorno	h	2-0	Pellissier, Abbruscato
25/4	Fiorentina	a	2-0	Pellissier, Sardo
2/5	Napoli	h	1-2	Granoche
9/5	Inter	a	3-4	og (Thiago Motta), Granoche, Pellissier
16/5	Roma	h	0-2	

No	Name	Nat	DoB	Pos	Aps	(s)	Gls
22	Elvis ABBRUSCATO		14/4/81	A	9	(6)	2
19	Luca ARIATTI		27/12/78	M	8	(23)	
9	Simone BENTIVOGLIO		29/5/85	M	13	(22)	1
23	Erjon BOGDANI	ALB	14/4/77	A	12	(9)	2
21	Nicolas FREY	FRA	6/3/84	D	20	(4)	
11	Pablo Mariano GRANOCHE	URU	5/9/83	A	10	(20)	3
90	Yonese HANINE		20/2/90	M		(1)	
15	Manuel IORI		12/3/82	M	14	(1)	
17	Bojan JOKIČ	SVN	17/5/86	D	5	(4)	
10	LUCIANO Siqueira de Oliveira	BRA	3/12/75	M	31	(2)	
8	Marco MALAGÒ		30/12/78	D		(2)	
5	Davide MANDELLI		28/6/77	D	19	(2)	
4	Andrea MANTOVANI		22/6/84	D	36		3
7	Michele MARCOLINI		2/10/75	M	28	(2)	4
83	MARCOS Ariel de Paula	BRA	19/12/83	A	10	(6)	2
2	Santiago Eduardo MORERO	ARG	18/4/82	D	23	(1)	
27	Fabio MORO		13/7/75	D		(1)	
31	Sergio PELLISSIER		12/4/79	A	35		11
6	Giampiero PINZI		11/3/81	M	31	(1)	3
16	Luca RIGONI		7/12/84	M	24		1
20	Gennaro SARDO		8/5/79	D	19	(3)	3
14	Alessandro SBAFFO		27/8/90	M		(2)	
3	Francesco SCARDINA		11/12/81	D	2	(1)	
28	Stefano SORRENTINO		28/3/79	G	37		
18	Lorenzo SQUIZZI		20/6/74	G	1		
33	Mario Alberto YEPES	COL	13/1/76	D	31		1

ACF FIORENTINA
Coach – Cesare Prandelli
Founded – 1926
Stadium – Artemio Franchi (47,282)
MAJOR HONOURS:
UEFA Cup Winners' Cup - (1) 1961;
Italian League - (2) 1956, 1969;
Italian Cup - (6) 1940, 1961, 1966, 1975, 1996, 2001.

2009

22/8	Bologna	a	1-1	Mutu
30/8	Palermo	h	1-0	Jovetić
13/9	Cagliari	h	1-0	Gilardino

ITALY

20/9	Roma	a	1-3	Gilardino
23/9	Sampdoria	h	2-0	Jovetić, Gilardino
26/9	Livorno	a	1-0	Jovetić (p)
4/10	Lazio	h	0-0	
17/10	Juventus	a	1-1	Vargas
25/10	Napoli	h	0-1	
28/10	Genoa	a	1-2	Marchionni
1/11	Catania	h	3-1	Marchionni 2, Gilardino
8/11	Udinese	a	1-0	Vargas
21/11	Parma	h	2-3	Gilardino 2
29/11	Inter	a	0-1	
6/12	Atalanta	h	2-0	Vargas, Gilardino
13/12	Chievo	a	1-2	Montolivo
2010				
6/1	Siena	a	5-1	Krøldrup, Santana, Gilardino 2, Mutu
10/1	Bari	h	2-1	Mutu, Castillo
17/1	Bologna	h	1-2	Mutu
24/1	Palermo	a	0-3	
31/1	Cagliari	a	2-2	Marchionni, Jovetić
7/2	Roma	h	0-1	
13/2	Sampdoria	a	0-2	
21/2	Livorno	h	2-1	Vargas, Gilardino
24/2	Milan	h	1-2	Gilardino
27/2	Lazio	a	1-1	Keirrison
6/3	Juventus	h	1-2	Marchionni
13/3	Napoli	a	3-1	Gilardino 2, Jovetić
20/3	Genoa	h	3-0	Santana, Gilardino (p), Babacar
24/3	Catania	a	0-1	
28/3	Udinese	h	4-1	Vargas, Gilardino, Santana, Jovetić
3/4	Parma	a	1-1	De Silvestri
10/4	Inter	h	2-2	Keirrison, Krøldrup
18/4	Atalanta	a	1-2	Montolivo
25/4	Chievo	h	0-2	
1/5	Milan	a	0-1	
9/5	Siena	h	1-1	Marchionni
16/5	Bari	a	0-2	

No	Name	Nat	DoB	Pos	Aps	(s)	Gls
26	Daniel Kofi AGYEI	GHA	1/1/92	M		(1)	
35	Vlada AVRAMOV	SRB	5/4/79	G	2		
21	BABACAR El Hadji Khouma	SEN	17/3/93	A		(4)	1
28	Mario Ariel BOLATTI	ARG	17/2/85	M	9	(3)	
45	Federico CARRARO		23/6/92	M		(1)	
9	José Ignacio CASTILLO	ARG	4/11/75	A		(6)	1
25	Gianluca COMOTTO		16/10/78	D	22	(4)	
3	Dario DAINELLI		9/6/79	D	11		
29	Lorenzo DE SILVESTRI		23/5/88	D	17	(9)	1
4	Marco DONADEL		21/4/83	M	20	(8)	
19	FELIPE Dias da Silva dal Belo	BRA	31/7/84	D	16	(2)	
1	Sébastien FREY	FRA	18/3/80	G	36		
5	Alessandro GAMBERINI		27/8/81	D	16	(2)	
11	Alberto GILARDINO		5/7/82	A	32	(4)	15
19	Massimo GOBBI		31/10/80	M	19	(6)	
8	Stevan JOVETIĆ	MNE	2/11/89	A	26	(3)	6
20	Martin JØRGENSEN	DEN	6/10/75	M	2	(11)	
39	KEIRRISON de Souza Carneiro	BRA	3/12/88	A	2	(8)	2
2	Per KRØLDRUP	DEN	31/7/79	D	24	(1)	2
22	Adem LJAJIĆ	SRB	29/9/91	M	3	(6)	
32	Marco MARCHIONNI		22/7/80	M	23	(5)	6
18	Riccardo MONTOLIVO		18/1/85	M	33	(3)	2
10	Adrian MUTU	ROU	8/1/79	A	9	(2)	4
14	Cesare NATALI		5/4/79	D	14	(3)	
23	Manuel PASQUAL		13/3/82	D	18	(3)	
24	Mario Alberto SANTANA	ARG	23/12/81	M	21	(5)	3
6	Juan Manuel VARGAS	PER	5/10/83	M	27	(2)	5
15	Cristiano ZANETTI		14/4/77	M	16	(7)	

GENOA CFC

Coach – Gian Piero Gasperini
Founded – 1893
Stadium – Luigi Ferraris (36,685)
MAJOR HONOURS:
Italian League – (9) 1898, 1899, 1900, 1902, 1903, 1904, 1915, 1923, 1924;
Italian Cup – (1) 1937.

2009				
23/8	Roma	h	3-2	Criscito, Zapater, Biava
30/8	Atalanta	a	1-0	Moretti
13/9	Napoli	h	4-1	Floccari (p), Mesto, Crespo, Kharja (p)
20/9	Chievo	a	1-3	Floccari (p)
24/9	Juventus	h	2-2	Mesto, Crespo
27/9	Udinese	a	0-2	
4/10	Bologna	a	3-1	Kharja (p), Sculli, Zapater
17/10	Inter	h	0-5	
25/10	Cagliari	a	2-3	Mesto, Floccari
28/10	Fiorentina	h	2-1	Palladino, Mesto
1/11	Palermo	a	0-0	
8/11	Siena	h	4-2	Crespo 2, Palladino, Floccari
22/11	Livorno	a	1-2	Criscito
28/11	Sampdoria	h	3-0	Milanetto (p), Rossi, Palladino (p)
6/12	Parma	h	2-2	Palacio, Palladino
13/12	Lazio	a	0-1	
2010				
6/1	Milan	a	2-5	Sculli, Suazo
10/1	Catania	h	2-0	Mesto, Sculli
17/1	Roma	a	0-3	
20/1	Bari	h	1-1	Milanetto
24/1	Atalanta	h	2-0	Palacio, Crespo
30/1	Napoli	a	0-0	
7/2	Chievo	h	1-0	Rossi
14/2	Juventus	a	2-3	Rossi 2
20/2	Udinese	h	3-0	Acquafresca 2 (1p), Palacio
28/2	Bologna	h	3-4	Suazo 2, Sculli
7/3	Inter	a	0-0	
14/3	Cagliari	h	5-3	Zapater (p), Palacio, Sculli, Rossi, Milanetto
20/3	Fiorentina	a	0-3	
24/3	Palermo	h	2-2	Bocchetti, Kharja (p)
28/3	Siena	a	0-0	
3/4	Livorno	h	1-1	Boakye
11/4	Sampdoria	a	0-1	
18/4	Parma	h	3-2	Palacio 2, Fatić
25/4	Lazio	h	1-2	Palacio
2/5	Bari	a	0-3	
9/5	Milan	h	1-0	Sculli
16/5	Catania	a	0-1	

No	Name	Nat	DoB	Pos	Aps	(s)	Gls
9	Robert ACQUAFRESCA		11/9/87	A	8	(2)	2
33	Danijel ALEKSIĆ	SRB	30/4/91	A		(1)	
32	Marco AMELIA		2/4/82	G	30		
25	Giuseppe BIAVA		8/5/77	D	17	(2)	1
18	Richmond Yiadom BOAKYE	GHA	28/1/93	A		(3)	1
26	Salvatore BOCCHETTI		30/11/86	D	25	(3)	1
31	Isaac COFIE	GHA	5/4/91	M		(1)	
9	Hernán Jorge CRESPO	ARG	5/7/75	A	6	(10)	5
4	Domenico CRISCITO		30/12/86	D	28	(1)	2
3	Dario DAINELLI		9/6/79	D	9	(1)	
11	Stephan EL SHAARAWI		27/10/92	M		(2)	
16	Andrea ESPOSITO		17/5/86	D	2	(3)	
13	Ivan FATIĆ	MNE	21/8/88	D	3	(7)	1
30	Luciano Gabriel FIGUEROA	ARG	19/5/81	A	1	(1)	
33	Sergio FLOCCARI		12/11/81	A	7	(4)	4
17	Bosko JANKOVIĆ	SRB	1/3/84	M		(3)	
28	Ivan JURIĆ	CRO	25/8/75	M	15	(4)	
5	Houssine KHARJA	MAR	9/11/82	M	3	(4)	3
27	Dejan LAZAREVIĆ	SVN	15/2/90	M		(2)	
20	Giandomenico MESTO		25/5/82	M	32	(4)	5

77	Omar MILANETTO		30/11/75	M	31	(1)	3
23	Francesco MODESTO		16/2/82	M	8	(2)	
24	Emiliano MORETTI		11/6/81	D	28	(1)	1
8	Rodrigo Sebastián PALACIO	ARG	5/2/82	A	23	(8)	7
10	Raffaele PALLADINO		17/4/84	M	18	(7)	4
15	Sokratis PAPASTATHOPOULOS	GRE	9/6/88	D	25	(5)	
7	Marco ROSSI		1/4/78	M	26	(2)	5
73	Alessio SCARPI		19/4/73	G	8		
14	Giuseppe SCULLI		23/3/81	A	27	(10)	6
19	David SUAZO	HON	5/11/79	A	11	(5)	3
40	Nenad TOMOVIĆ	SRB	30/8/87	D	8	(6)	
21	Alberto ZAPATER	ESP	13/6/85	M	19	(9)	3

FC INTERNAZIONALE MILANO
Coach – José Mourinho (POR)
Founded – 1908
Stadium – Giuseppe Meazza (82,955)
MAJOR HONOURS:
European Champion Clubs' Cup/UEFA Champions League - (3) 1964, 1965, 2010;
UEFA Cup - (3) 1991, 1994, 1998;
World Club Cup - (2) 1964, 1965;
Italian League - (18) 1910, 1920, 1930, 1938, 1940, 1953, 1954, 1963, 1965, 1966, 1971, 1980, 1989, 2006, 2007, 2008, 2009, 2010;
Italian Cup - (6) 1939, 1978, 1982, 2005, 2006, 2010.

2009
23/8	Bari	h	1-1	Eto'o (p)
29/8	Milan	a	4-0	Thiago Motta, Milito (p), Maicon, Stanković
13/9	Parma	h	2-0	Eto'o, Milito
20/9	Cagliari	a	2-1	Milito 2
23/9	Napoli	h	3-1	Eto'o, Milito, Lúcio
26/9	Sampdoria	a	0-1	
3/10	Udinese	h	2-1	Stanković, Sneijder
17/10	Genoa	a	5-0	Cambiasso, Balotelli, Stanković, Vieira, Maicon
24/10	Catania	h	2-1	Muntari, Sneijder
29/10	Palermo	h	5-3	Eto'o 2 (1p), Balotelli 2, Milito
1/11	Livorno	a	2-0	Milito, Maicon
8/11	Roma	h	1-1	Eto'o
21/11	Bologna	a	3-1	Milito, Balotelli, Cambiasso
29/11	Fiorentina	h	1-0	Milito (p)
5/12	Juventus	a	1-2	Eto'o
13/12	Atalanta	a	1-1	Milito
20/12	Lazio	h	1-0	Eto'o
2010				
6/1	Chievo	a	1-0	Balotelli
9/1	Siena	h	4-3	Milito, Sneijder 2, Samuel
16/1	Bari	a	2-2	Pandev, Milito (p)
24/1	Milan	h	2-0	Milito, Pandev
7/2	Cagliari	a	3-0	Pandev, Samuel, Milito
10/2	Parma	a	1-1	Balotelli
14/2	Napoli	a	0-0	
20/2	Sampdoria	h	0-0	
28/2	Udinese	a	3-2	Balotelli, Maicon, Milito
7/3	Genoa	h	0-0	
12/3	Catania	a	1-3	Milito
20/3	Palermo	a	1-1	Milito (p)
24/3	Livorno	h	3-0	Eto'o 2, Maicon
27/3	Roma	a	2-1	Milito
3/4	Bologna	h	3-0	Thiago Motta 2, Balotelli
10/4	Fiorentina	a	2-2	Milito, Eto'o
16/4	Juventus	h	2-0	Maicon, Eto'o
24/4	Atalanta	h	3-1	Milito, Muntari, Chivu
2/5	Lazio	a	2-0	Samuel, Thiago Motta
9/5	Chievo	h	4-3	og (Mantovani), Cambiasso, Milito, Balotelli
16/5	Siena	a	1-0	Milito

No	Name	Nat	DoB	Pos	Aps	(s)	Gls
89	Marko ARNAUTOVIĆ	AUT	19/4/89	A		(3)	
45	Mario Barwuah BALOTELLI		12/8/90	A	13	(13)	9

19	Esteban Matías CAMBIASSO	ARG	18/8/80	M	26	(4)	3
26	Cristian Eugen CHIVU	ROU	26/10/80	D	16	(4)	1
2	Iván Ramiro CÓRDOBA	COL	11/8/76	D	15	(6)	
9	Samuel ETO'O	CMR	10/3/81	A	27	(5)	12
12	JÚLIO CÉSAR Soares Espindola	BRA	3/9/79	G	38		
15	René KRHIN	SVN	21/5/90	M	1	(4)	
6	Lucimar Ferreira da Silva "LÚCIO"	BRA	8/5/78	D	30	(1)	1
13	MAICON Douglas Sisenando	BRA	26/7/81	D	33		6
30	Alessandro Faiolhe Amantino "MANCINI"	BRA	1/8/80	M	1	(5)	
17	McDonald MARIGA	KEN	4/4/87	M	3	(5)	
23	Marco MATERAZZI		19/8/73	D	7	(5)	
22	Diego Alberto MILITO	ARG	12/6/79	A	33	(2)	22
11	Sulley Ali MUNTARI	GHA	27/8/84	M	16	(11)	2
27	Goran PANDEV	MKD	27/7/83	A	13	(6)	3
7	RICARDO Andrade QUARESMA	POR	26/9/83	M	3	(8)	
25	Walter Adrián SAMUEL	ARG	23/3/78	D	25	(3)	3
39	Davide SANTON		2/1/91	D	8	(4)	
10	Wesley SNEIJDER	NED	9/6/84	M	24	(2)	4
5	Dejan STANKOVIĆ	SRB	11/9/78	M	24	(5)	3
28	Alen STEVANOVIĆ	SRB	7/1/91	M		(1)	
18	David SUAZO	HON	5/11/79	A		(1)	
8	THIAGO MOTTA	BRA	28/8/82	M	18	(8)	4
14	Patrick VIEIRA	FRA	23/6/76	M	7	(5)	1
4	Javier ZANETTI	ARG	10/8/73	D	37		

JUVENTUS
Coach – Ciro Ferrara; (29/1/10) Alberto Zaccheroni
Founded – 1897
Stadium – Olimpico (27,500)
MAJOR HONOURS: European Champion Clubs' Cup/UEFA Champions League - (2) 1985, 1996;
UEFA Cup Winners' Cup - (1) 1984;
UEFA Cup - (3) 1977, 1990, 1993;
UEFA Super Cup - (2) 1984, 1997;
World Club Cup - (2) 1985, 1996;
Italian League - (27) 1905, 1926, 1931, 1932, 1933, 1934, 1935, 1950, 1952, 1958, 1960, 1961, 1967, 1972, 1973, 1975, 1977, 1978, 1981, 1982, 1984, 1986, 1995, 1997, 1998, 2002, 2003;
Italian Cup - (9) 1938, 1942, 1959, 1960, 1965, 1979, 1983, 1990, 1995.

2009
23/8	Chievo	h	1-0	Iaquinta
30/8	Roma	a	3-1	Diego 2, Felipe Melo
12/9	Lazio	a	2-0	Cáceres, Trezeguet
19/9	Livorno	h	2-0	Iaquinta, Marchisio
24/9	Genoa	a	2-2	Iaquinta, Trezeguet
27/9	Bologna	h	1-1	Trezeguet
4/10	Palermo	a	0-2	
17/10	Fiorentina	h	1-1	Amauri
25/10	Siena	a	1-0	Amauri
28/10	Sampdoria	h	5-1	Amauri 2, Chiellini, Camoranesi, Trezeguet
31/10	Napoli	a	2-3	Trezeguet, Giovinco
7/11	Atalanta	a	5-2	Camoranesi 2, Felipe Melo, Diego, Trezeguet
22/11	Udinese	h	1-0	Grosso
29/11	Cagliari	a	0-2	
5/12	Inter	h	2-1	Chiellini, Marchisio
12/12	Bari	a	1-3	Trezeguet
20/12	Catania	h	1-2	Salihamidžić
2010				
6/1	Parma	a	2-1	Salihamidžić, og (Castellini)
10/1	Milan	h	0-3	
17/1	Chievo	a	0-1	
23/1	Roma	h	1-2	Del Piero
31/1	Lazio	h	1-1	Del Piero (p)
6/2	Livorno	a	1-1	Legrottaglie
14/2	Genoa	h	3-2	Amauri, Del Piero 2 (1p)
21/2	Bologna	a	2-1	Diego, Candreva
28/2	Palermo	h	0-2	
6/3	Fiorentina	a	2-1	Diego, Grosso

14/3	Siena	h	3-3	Del Piero 2, Candreva
21/3	Sampdoria	a	0-1	
25/3	Napoli	a	1-3	Chiellini
28/3	Atalanta	h	2-1	Del Piero, Felipe Melo
3/4	Udinese	a	0-3	
11/4	Cagliari	h	1-0	Chiellini
16/4	Inter	a	0-2	
25/4	Bari	h	3-0	Iaquinta 2, Del Piero (p)
2/5	Catania	a	1-1	Marchisio
9/5	Parma	h	2-3	Del Piero, Iaquinta
15/5	Milan	a	0-3	

No	Name	Nat	DoB	Pos	Aps	(s)	Gls
11	AMAURI Carvalho de Oliveira	BRA	3/6/80	A	24	(6)	5
1	Gianluigi BUFFON		28/1/78	G	27		
2	José Martín CÁCERES Silva	URU	7/4/87	D	11	(4)	1
16	Mauro Germán CAMORANESI		4/10/76	M	14	(10)	3
26	Antonio CANDREVA		28/2/87	M	8	(8)	2
5	Fabio CANNAVARO		13/9/73	D	27		
3	Giorgio CHIELLINI		14/8/84	D	32		4
12	Antonio CHIMENTI		30/6/70	G	2		
29	Paolo DE CEGLIE		17/9/86	D	14	(11)	
10	Alessandro DEL PIERO		9/11/74	A	18	(5)	9
28	DIEGO Ribas da Cunha	BRA	28/2/85	M	31	(2)	5
4	FELIPE MELO de Carvalho	BRA	26/6/83	M	28	(1)	3
36	Manuel GIANDONATO		10/10/91	M		(1)	
20	Sebastian GIOVINCO		26/1/87	M	5	(10)	1
6	Fabio GROSSO		28/11/77	D	22	(4)	2
21	Zdeněk GRYGERA	CZE	14/5/80	D	15	(4)	
9	Vincenzo IAQUINTA		21/11/79	A	12	(3)	6
40	Ciro IMMOBILE		20/2/90	A		(2)	
33	Nicola LEGROTTAGLIE		20/10/76	D	18	(1)	1
13	Alexander MANNINGER	AUT	4/6/77	G	9	(2)	
8	Claudio MARCHISIO		19/1/86	M	27	(1)	3
39	Luca MARRONE		28/3/90	M		(2)	
19	Cristian MOLINARO		30/7/83	D	4	(1)	
27	Michele PAOLUCCI		6/2/86	A	1	(3)	
18	Christian POULSEN	DEN	28/2/80	M	19	(6)	
7	Hasan SALIHAMIDŽIĆ	BIH	1/1/77	M	6	(8)	2
22	Mohamed Lamine SISSOKO	MLI	22/1/85	M	14	(3)	
30	TIAGO Cardoso Mendes	POR	2/5/81	M	4	(3)	
17	David TREZEGUET	FRA	15/10/77	A	13	(6)	7
15	Jonathan ZEBINA	FRA	19/7/78	D	13	(3)	

S.S. LAZIO

Coach – Davide Ballardini; (10/2/10) Edoardo Reja
Founded – 1900
Stadium – Olimpico (73,095)
MAJOR HONOURS:
UEFA Cup Winners' Cup - (1) 1999;
UEFA Super Cup - (1) 1999;
Italian League - (2) 1974, 2000;
Italian Cup - (5) 1958, 1998, 2000, 2004, 2009.

2009

23/8	Atalanta	h	1-0	Rocchi
30/8	Chievo	a	2-1	Cruz 2 (1p)
12/9	Juventus	h	0-2	
20/9	Catania	a	1-1	Cruz
23/9	Parma	h	1-2	Zárate (p)
27/9	Palermo	h	1-1	Zárate
4/10	Fiorentina	a	0-0	
18/10	Sampdoria	h	1-1	Matuzalém
25/10	Bari	a	0-2	
28/10	Cagliari	h	0-1	
1/11	Siena	a	1-1	Mauri
8/11	Milan	h	1-2	og (Thiago Silva)
22/11	Napoli	a	0-0	
29/11	Bologna	h	0-0	
6/12	Roma	a	0-0	
13/12	Genoa	h	1-0	Kolarov
20/12	Inter	a	0-1	

2010

6/1	Livorno	h	4-1	Floccari 2, Rocchi, Kolarov (p)
10/1	Udinese	a	1-1	Floccari
17/1	Atalanta	a	0-3	
24/1	Chievo	h	1-1	Stendardo
31/1	Juventus	a	1-1	Mauri
7/2	Catania	h	0-1	
14/2	Parma	a	2-0	Stendardo, Zárate
21/2	Palermo	a	1-3	Kolarov
27/2	Fiorentina	h	1-1	Siviglia
7/3	Sampdoria	a	1-2	Floccari
14/3	Bari	h	0-2	
21/3	Cagliari	a	2-0	Rocchi, Floccari
24/3	Siena	h	2-0	Lichtsteiner, Cruz
28/3	Milan	a	1-1	Lichtsteiner
3/4	Napoli	h	1-1	Floccari
11/4	Bologna	a	3-2	Mauri, André Dias, Rocchi
18/4	Roma	h	1-2	Rocchi
25/4	Genoa	a	2-1	André Dias, Floccari
2/5	Inter	h	0-2	
9/5	Livorno	a	2-1	Rocchi, Brocchi
15/5	Udinese	h	3-1	Hitzlsperger, Floccari, Brocchi

o	Name	Nat	DoB	Pos	Aps	(s)	Gls
80	ANDRÉ Gonçalves DIAS	BRA	15/5/79	D	12		2
33	Roberto BARONIO		11/12/77	M	22	(2)	
88	Tommaso BERNI		6/3/83	G	2		
25	Giuseppe BIAVA		8/5/77	D	10	(3)	
32	Cristian BROCCHI		30/1/76	M	25	(2)	2
25	Emílson Sánchez CRIBARI	BRA	6/3/80	D	7	(3)	
74	Julio Ricardo CRUZ	ARG	10/10/74	A	8	(17)	4
6	Ousmane DABO	FRA	8/2/77	M	6	(6)	
81	Simone DEL NERO		4/8/81	A	6	(1)	
87	Modibo DIAKITÉ	FRA	2/3/87	D	11	(8)	
7	ELISEU Pereira dos Santos	POR	1/10/83	M		(2)	
4	Fabio FIRMANI		26/5/78	M	8	(4)	
20	Sergio FLOCCARI		12/11/81	A	17		8
17	Pasquale FOGGIA		3/6/83	M	9	(7)	
15	Thomas HITZLSPERGER	GER	5/4/82	M	2	(4)	1
21	Simone INZAGHI		5/4/76	A		(3)	
11	Aleksandar KOLAROV	SRB	10/11/85	D	33		3
24	Cristian Daniel LEDESMA	ARG	24/9/82	M	13		
2	Stephan LICHTSTEINER	SUI	16/1/84	D	28	(5)	2
52	Alessio LUCIANI		16/1/90	D		(1)	
18	Stephen Ayodele MAKINWA	NGA	26/7/83	A		(2)	
8	MATUZALÉM Francelino da Silva	BRA	10/6/80	M	14	(4)	1
5	Stefano MAURI		8/1/80	M	29	(6)	3
23	Mourad MEGHNI	ALG	16/4/84	M	3	(4)	
86	Néstor Fernando MUSLERA	URU	16/6/86	G	36		
99	Riccardo PERPETUINI		4/8/90	M	1	(1)	
26	Ştefan Andrei RADU	ROU	22/10/86	D	28		
9	Tommaso ROCCHI		19/9/77	A	23	(9)	6
3	Lionel Sebastián SCALONI	ARG	16/5/78	D	1	(4)	
13	Sebastiano SIVIGLIA		29/3/73	D	18	(2)	1
28	Guglielmo STENDARDO		6/5/81	D	19		2
10	Mauro Matías ZÁRATE	ARG	18/3/87	A	27	(5)	3

AS LIVORNO CALCIO

Coach – Vittorio Russo; (21/10/09) Serse Cosmi; (5/4/10) Gennaro Ruotolo
Founded – 1915
Stadium – Armando Picchi (19,238)

2009

23/8	Cagliari	h	0-0	
30/8	Napoli	a	1-3	Lucarelli
12/9	Milan	h	0-0	
19/9	Juventus	a	0-2	
23/9	Bologna	a	0-2	
26/9	Fiorentina	h	0-1	
4/10	Siena	a	0-0	

18/10	Palermo	h	1-2	*Danilevičius*
25/10	Roma	a	1-0	*Tavano*
28/10	Atalanta	h	1-0	*Miglionico*
1/11	Inter	h	0-2	
8/11	Bari	a	0-1	
22/11	Genoa	h	2-1	*Lucarelli, Pulzetti*
28/11	Udinese	a	0-2	
6/12	Chievo	h	0-2	
13/12	Catania	a	1-0	*Danilevičius*
20/12	Sampdoria	h	3-1	*Rivas, Danilevičius 2*
2010				
6/1	Lazio	a	1-4	*Bergvold*
10/1	Parma	h	2-1	*Tavano, Lucarelli*
16/1	Cagliari	a	0-3	
24/1	Napoli	h	0-2	
31/1	Milan	a	1-1	*Lucarelli*
6/2	Juventus	h	1-1	*Filippini*
14/2	Bologna	h	0-1	
21/2	Fiorentina	a	1-2	*Rivas*
28/2	Siena	h	1-2	*Lucarelli (p)*
7/3	Palermo	a	0-1	
14/3	Roma	h	3-3	*Lucarelli 3 (1p)*
21/3	Atalanta	a	0-3	
24/3	Inter	a	0-3	
28/3	Bari	h	1-1	*Tavano*
3/4	Genoa	a	1-1	*Tavano*
11/4	Udinese	h	0-2	
17/4	Chievo	a	0-2	
25/4	Catania	h	3-1	*Lucarelli (p), Bellucci, Bergvold*
2/5	Sampdoria	a	0-2	
9/5	Lazio	h	1-2	*Lucarelli*
16/5	Parma	a	1-4	*Danilevičius*

No	Name	Nat	DoB	Pos	Aps	(s)	Gls
92	Francesco BARDI		18/1/92	G	1		
20	Claudio BELLUCCI		31/5/75	A	12	(2)	1
11	Francesco BENUSSI		15/10/81	G	4	(1)	
8	Martin BERGVOLD	DEN	20/2/84	M	16	(7)	2
44	Alessandro BERNARDINI		21/8/87	D	4	(1)	
83	Antonio CANDREVA		28/2/87	M	16	(3)	
15	Gastón CELLERINO	ARG	27/6/86	A		(6)	
9	Tomas DANILEVIČIUS	LTU	18/7/78	A	8	(18)	5
1	Alfonso DE LUCIA		12/11/83	G	22	(1)	
23	Alessandro DIAMANTI		2/5/83	A	1		
19	Davide DI GENNARO		16/6/88	M	6	(5)	
18	Federico DIONISI		16/6/87	A		(3)	
16	Andrea ESPOSITO		17/5/86	D	3		
3	Antonio FILIPPINI		3/7/73	M	20	(4)	1
6	Fabio GALANTE		20/11/73	D	5	(4)	
22	Alessandro GRANDONI		22/7/77	D	1		
13	Dario KNEŽEVIĆ	CRO	20/4/82	D	25	(2)	
26	Matteo LIGNANI		7/9/91	M	1	(1)	
99	Cristiano LUCARELLI		4/10/75	A	28		10
5	Davide MARCHINI		23/2/81	M	4	(12)	
59	MARCUS Plínio DINIZ Paixão	BRA	1/8/87	D	15	(6)	
17	Leonardo Martín MIGLIONICO	URU	31/1/80	D	12	(1)	1
91	Samuele MODICA		5/7/91	D	1	(1)	
21	Davide MORO		2/1/82	M	22	(6)	
24	MOZART Santos Batista Júnior	BRA	8/11/79	M	21	(4)	
30	Welle OSSOU	SEN	11/3/91	D		(1)	
2	Romano PERTICONE		13/8/86	D	26	(1)	
46	Mirko PIERI		24/7/78	D	23	(1)	
22	Jürgen PRUTSCH	AUT	22/9/89	M	5	(1)	
7	Nico PULZETTI		13/2/84	M	25	(4)	1
77	Cristian RAIMONDI		30/4/81	M	32		
4	Nelson Enrique RIVAS	COL	25/3/83	D	16		2
25	Rubens Fernando Moedim "RUBINHO"	BRA	4/8/83	G	11		
90	Luca SIMEONI		22/2/90	A		(2)	
10	Francesco TAVANO		2/3/79	A	18	(6)	4
87	Luigi VITALE		5/10/87	M	14	(8)	

AC MILAN

Coach – Leonardo (BRA)
Founded – 1899
Stadium – Giuseppe Meazza (82,955)
MAJOR HONOURS:
European Champion Clubs' Cup/UEFA Champions League - (7) 1963, 1969,
1989, 1990, 1994, 2003, 2007;
UEFA Cup Winners' Cup - (2) 1968, 1973;
UEFA Super Cup - (5) 1989, 1990, 1995, 2003, 2007;
World Club Cup - (4) 1969, 1989, 1990, 2007;
Italian League - (17) 1901, 1906, 1907, 1951, 1955, 1957, 1959, 1962, 1968,
1979, 1988, 1992, 1993, 1994, 1996, 1999, 2004;
Italian Cup - (5) 1967, 1972, 1973, 1977, 2003.

2009				
22/8	Siena	a	2-1	*Pato 2*
29/8	Inter	h	0-4	
12/9	Livorno	a	0-0	
20/9	Bologna	h	1-0	*Seedorf*
23/9	Udinese	a	0-1	
27/9	Bari	h	0-0	
4/10	Atalanta	a	1-1	*Ronaldinho*
18/10	Roma	h	2-1	*Ronaldinho (p), Pato*
25/10	Chievo	a	2-1	*Nesta 2*
28/10	Napoli	a	2-2	*Inzaghi, Pato*
31/10	Parma	h	2-0	*Borriello 2*
8/11	Lazio	a	2-1	*Thiago Silva, Pato*
22/11	Cagliari	h	4-3	*Seedorf, Borriello, Pato, Ronaldinho (p)*
29/11	Catania	a	2-0	*Huntelaar 2*
5/12	Sampdoria	h	3-0	*Borriello, Seedorf, Pato*
13/12	Palermo	h	0-2	
2010				
6/1	Genoa	h	5-2	*Ronaldinho (p), Thiago Silva, Borriello 2, Huntelaar (p)*
10/1	Juventus	a	3-0	*Nesta, Ronaldinho 2*
17/1	Siena	h	4-0	*Ronaldinho 3 (1p), Borriello*
24/1	Inter	a	0-2	
31/1	Livorno	h	1-1	*Ambrosini*
7/2	Bologna	a	0-0	
12/2	Udinese	h	3-2	*Huntelaar 2, Pato*
21/2	Bari	a	2-0	*Borriello, Pato*
24/2	Fiorentina	a	2-1	*Huntelaar, Pato*
28/2	Atalanta	h	3-1	*Pato 2, Borriello*
6/3	Roma	a	0-0	
14/3	Chievo	h	1-0	*Seedorf*
21/3	Napoli	h	1-1	*Inzaghi*
24/3	Parma	a	0-1	
28/3	Lazio	h	1-1	*Borriello (p)*
3/4	Cagliari	a	3-2	*Borriello, Huntelaar, og (Astori)*
11/4	Catania	h	2-2	*Borriello 2*
18/4	Sampdoria	a	1-2	*Borriello*
24/4	Palermo	a	1-3	*Seedorf*
1/5	Fiorentina	h	1-0	*Ronaldinho (p)*
9/5	Genoa	a	0-1	
15/5	Juventus	h	3-0	*Antonini, Ronaldinho 2*

No	Name	Nat	DoB	Pos	Aps	(s)	Gls
20	Ignazio ABATE		12/11/86	M	22	(8)	
12	Christian ABBIATI		8/7/77	G	8	(1)	
23	Massimo AMBROSINI		29/5/77	M	26	(4)	1
77	Luca ANTONINI		4/8/82	D	20	(2)	1
32	David BECKHAM	ENG	2/5/75	M	7	(4)	
25	Daniele BONERA		31/5/81	D	6	(1)	
22	Marco BORRIELLO		18/6/82	A	27	(2)	14
56	Andrea DE VITO		27/11/91	D		(1)	
1	Nélson de Jesus Silva "DIDA"	BRA	7/10/73	G	23		
19	Giuseppe FAVALLI		8/1/72	D	15	(1)	
16	Mathieu FLAMINI	FRA	7/3/84	M	14	(11)	
8	Gennaro Ivan GATTUSO		9/1/78	M	20	(2)	
11	Klaas Jan HUNTELAAR	NED	12/8/83	A	11	(14)	7
9	Filippo INZAGHI		9/8/73	A	4	(20)	2

ITALY

18	Marek JANKULOVSKI	CZE	9/5/77	D	5	(7)	
4	Kakhaber KALADZE	GEO	27/2/78	D	5	(1)	
30	Alessandro Faiolhe Amantino "MANCINI"	BRA	1/8/80	M	3	(4)	
13	Alessandro NESTA		19/3/76	D	22	(1)	3
44	Massimo ODDO		14/6/76	D	9	(5)	
7	Alexandre Rodrigues da Silva "PATO"	BRA	2/9/89	A	20	(3)	12
21	Andrea PIRLO		19/5/79	M	33	(1)	
80	Ronaldo de Assis Moreira "RONALDINHO"	BRA	21/3/80	A	34	(2)	12
10	Clarence SEEDORF	NED	1/4/76	M	25	(4)	5
30	Marco STORARI		7/1/77	G	7		
51	Rodney STRASSER	SLE	30/3/90	M		(1)	
33	THIAGO Emiliano da SILVA	BRA	22/9/84	D	33		2
15	Gianluca ZAMBROTTA		19/2/77	D	19	(5)	
17	Gianmarco ZIGONI		10/5/91	A		(1)	

SSC NAPOLI
Coach – Roberto Donadoni; (6/10/09) Walter Mazzarri
Founded – 1926
Stadium – San Paolo (60,240)
MAJOR HONOURS:
UEFA Cup – (1) 1989 ;
Italian League – (2) 1987, 1990;
Italian Cup – (3) 1962, 1976, 1987.

2009
23/8	Palermo	a	1-2	Hamšík
30/8	Livorno	h	3-1	Quagliarella 2, Hamšík
13/9	Genoa	a	1-4	Hamšík
19/9	Udinese	h	0-0	
23/9	Inter	a	1-3	Lavezzi
27/9	Siena	h	2-1	Hamšík 2
4/10	Roma	a	1-2	Lavezzi
18/10	Bologna	h	2-1	Quagliarella, Maggio
25/10	Fiorentina	a	1-0	Maggio
28/10	Milan	h	2-2	Cigarini, Denis
31/10	Juventus	a	3-2	Hamšík 2, Dátolo
7/11	Catania	a	0-0	
22/11	Lazio	h	0-0	
29/11	Parma	a	1-1	Denis
6/12	Bari	h	3-2	Quagliarella 2, Maggio
12/12	Cagliari	a	3-3	Lavezzi, Pazienza, Bogliacino
20/12	Chievo	h	2-0	Hamšík (p), Quagliarella

2010
6/1	Atalanta	a	2-0	Quagliarella, Pazienza
10/1	Sampdoria	h	1-0	Denis
17/1	Palermo	h	0-0	
24/1	Livorno	a	2-0	Maggio, Cigarini
30/1	Genoa	h	0-0	
7/2	Udinese	a	1-3	Maggio
14/2	Inter	h	0-0	
21/2	Siena	a	0-0	
28/2	Roma	h	2-2	Denis, Hamšík (p)
7/3	Bologna	a	1-2	Rinaudo
13/3	Fiorentina	h	1-3	Lavezzi
21/3	Milan	a	1-1	Campagnaro
25/3	Juventus	h	3-1	Hamšík, Quagliarella, Lavezzi
28/3	Catania	h	1-0	Cannavaro
3/4	Lazio	a	1-1	Hamšík
10/4	Parma	h	2-3	Quagliarella, Hamšík
18/4	Bari	a	2-1	Lavezzi 2
25/4	Cagliari	h	0-0	
2/5	Chievo	a	2-1	Denis, Lavezzi
9/5	Atalanta	h	2-0	Quagliarella 2
16/5	Sampdoria	a	0-1	

No	Name	Nat	DoB	Pos	Aps	(s)	Gls
6	Salvatore ARONICA		20/1/78	D	24	(2)	
18	Mariano Adrián BOGLIACINO	URU	2/6/80	M	2	(16)	1

14	Hugo Armando CAMPAGNARO	ARG	27/6/80	D	28		1
28	Paolo CANNAVARO		26/6/81	D	32	(1)	1
21	Luca CIGARINI		20/6/86	M	11	(17)	2
96	Matteo CONTINI		16/4/80	D	12	(1)	
15	Jesús Alberto DÁTOLO	ARG	19/5/84	M	6	(7)	1
26	Morgan DE SANCTIS		26/3/77	G	38		
19	Germán Gustavo DENIS	ARG	10/9/81	A	16	(13)	5
8	Andrea DOSSENA		11/9/81	D	3	(7)	
23	Walter Alejandro GARGANO	URU	23/7/84	M	35	(1)	
2	Gianluca GRAVA		7/3/77	D	22	(2)	
17	Marek HAMŠÍK	SVK	27/7/87	M	37		12
9	Erwin HOFFER	AUT	14/4/87	A		(8)	
12	João Batista INÁCIO PIÁ	BRA	22/3/82	A	1	(1)	
34	Lorenzo INSIGNE		4/6/91	M		(1)	
7	Ezequiel Iván LAVEZZI	ARG	3/5/85	A	27	(3)	8
11	Christian MAGGIO		11/2/82	M	33	(1)	5
91	Raffaele MAIELLO		10/7/91	M		(1)	
5	Michele PAZIENZA		5/8/82	M	27	(6)	2
27	Fabio QUAGLIARELLA		31/1/83	A	32	(2)	11
77	Leandro RINAUDO		9/5/83	D	13	(7)	1
33	Erminio RULLO		19/2/84	D		(1)	
13	Fabiano SANTACROCE		24/8/86	D	4		
16	Juan Camilo ZÚÑIGA Mosquera	COL	14/12/85	D	15	(7)	

US CITTÀ DI PALERMO
Coach – Walter Zenga; (23/11/09) Delio Rossi
Founded – 1900
Stadium – Renzo Barbera (37,242)

2009
23/8	Napoli	h	2-1	Cavani, Miccoli (p)
30/8	Fiorentina	a	0-1	
13/9	Bari	h	1-1	Budan
20/9	Parma	a	0-1	
23/9	Roma	h	3-3	Budan, Miccoli, Nocerino
27/9	Lazio	a	1-1	Cavani
4/10	Juventus	h	2-0	Cavani, Fábio Simplício
18/10	Livorno	a	2-1	Miccoli, Balzaretti
25/10	Udinese	h	1-0	Bovo
29/10	Inter	a	3-5	Miccoli 2, Hernández
1/11	Genoa	h	0-0	
8/11	Bologna	a	1-3	Kjær
22/11	Catania	h	1-1	Migliaccio
29/11	Chievo	a	0-1	
6/12	Cagliari	h	2-1	Budan, Kjær
13/12	Milan	a	2-0	Miccoli, Bresciano
20/12	Siena	h	1-0	Cavani

2010
6/1	Sampdoria	a	1-1	Cavani
10/1	Atalanta	h	1-0	Cavani (p)
17/1	Napoli	a	0-0	
24/1	Fiorentina	h	3-0	Hernández 2, Budan
30/1	Bari	a	2-4	Cavani, Pastore
6/2	Parma	h	2-1	Cavani, Fábio Simplício
13/2	Roma	a	1-4	Miccoli (p)
21/2	Lazio	h	3-1	Hernández, Miccoli (p), Nocerino
28/2	Juventus	a	2-0	Miccoli, Budan
7/3	Livorno	h	1-0	Miccoli
14/3	Udinese	a	2-3	Fábio Simplício, Cavani
20/3	Inter	h	1-1	Cavani
24/3	Genoa	a	2-2	Hernández, Pastore
27/3	Bologna	h	3-1	Miccoli 3 (1p)
3/4	Catania	a	0-2	
11/4	Chievo	h	3-1	Pastore, Miccoli 2 (1p)
18/4	Cagliari	a	2-2	Miccoli, Hernández
24/4	Milan	h	3-1	Bovo, Hernández, Miccoli
2/5	Siena	a	2-1	Cavani, Miccoli
9/5	Sampdoria	h	1-1	Miccoli (p)
16/5	Atalanta	a	2-1	Cavani 2 (1p)

724 - The European Football Yearbook 2010/11

No	Name	Nat	DoB	Pos	Aps	(s)	Gls
42	Federico BALZARETTI		6/12/81	D	34		1
14	Nicolás Santiago BERTOLO	ARG	2/1/86	M	5	(16)	
88	Manuele BLASI		17/8/80	M	4	(10)	
5	Cesare BOVO		14/1/83	D	29		2
23	Mark BRESCIANO	AUS	11/2/80	M	18		1
20	Igor BUDAN	CRO	22/4/80	A	5	(25)	5
27	Marco CALDERONI		18/2/89	D	1		
16	Mattia CASSANI		26/8/83	D	37		
7	Edinson CAVANI	URU	14/2/87	A	31	(3)	13
89	Ondřej ČELŮSTKA	CZE	18/6/89	D		(1)	
30	FÁBIO Henrique SIMPLÍCIO	BRA	23/9/79	M	21	(6)	3
3	Dorin Nicolae GOIAN	ROU	12/12/80	D	12	(2)	
90	Abel Mathías HERNÁNDEZ	URU	8/8/90	A	8	(13)	7
24	Simon KJÆR	DEN	26/3/89	D	35		2
11	Fabio LIVERANI		29/4/76	M	20	(1)	
99	Levan MCHEDLIDZE	GEO	24/3/90	A		(2)	
21	Cristian Costel MELINTE	ROU	9/5/88	D	1	(1)	
10	Fabrizio MICCOLI		27/6/79	A	32	(3)	19
8	Giulio MIGLIACCIO		23/6/81	M	28	(2)	1
9	Antonio NOCERINO		9/4/85	M	32	(3)	2
6	Javier PASTORE	ARG	20/6/89	M	27	(7)	3
83	Rubens Fernando Moedim "RUBINHO"	BRA	4/8/83	G	6		
46	Salvatore SIRIGU		12/1/87	G	32		
19	Davide SUCCI		11/10/81	A		(6)	
4	Giovanni TEDESCO		13/5/72	M		(4)	

PARMA FC

Coach – Francesco Guidolin
Founded – 1913
Stadium – Ennio Tardini (27,906)
MAJOR HONOURS:
UEFA Cup Winners' Cup - (1) 1993;
UEFA Cup - (2) 1995, 1999;
UEFA Super Cup - (1) 1994;
Italian Cup - (3) 1992, 1999, 2002.

2009
23/8	Udinese	a	2-2	*Paloschi, Lucarelli*
30/8	Catania	h	2-1	*Galloppa, Paloschi*
13/9	Inter	a	0-2	
20/9	Palermo	h	1-0	*Zaccardo*
23/9	Lazio	a	2-1	*Bojinov, Amoruso (p)*
27/9	Cagliari	h	0-2	
4/10	Sampdoria	a	1-1	*Galloppa*
18/10	Siena	h	1-0	*Bojinov*
25/10	Atalanta	a	1-3	*Paloschi*
28/10	Bari	h	2-0	*Bojinov, Paloschi*
31/10	Milan	a	0-2	
8/11	Chievo	h	2-0	*Zaccardo, Lanzafame*
21/11	Fiorentina	a	3-2	*Amoruso, Bojinov, Lanzafame*
29/11	Napoli	h	1-1	*Amoruso (p)*
6/12	Genoa	a	2-2	*Biabiany 2*
13/12	Bologna	h	2-1	*Panucci, Amoruso*
20/12	Roma	a	0-2	

2010
6/1	Juventus	h	1-2	*Amoruso*
10/1	Livorno	a	1-2	*Zaccardo*
17/1	Udinese	h	0-0	
23/1	Catania	a	0-3	
6/2	Palermo	a	1-2	*Biabiany*
10/2	Inter	h	1-1	*Bojinov*
14/2	Lazio	h	0-2	
21/2	Cagliari	a	0-2	
28/2	Sampdoria	h	1-0	*Zaccardo*
7/3	Siena	a	1-1	*Biabiany*
14/3	Atalanta	h	1-0	*Bojinov*
21/3	Bari	a	1-1	*og (Belmonte)*
24/3	Milan	h	1-0	*Bojinov*
28/3	Chievo	a	0-0	
3/4	Fiorentina	h	1-1	*Bojinov*

10/4	Napoli	a	3-2	*Antonelli, Lucarelli, Jiménez*
18/4	Genoa	h	2-3	*Zaccardo, og (Bocchetti)*
25/4	Bologna	a	1-2	*Biabiany*
1/5	Roma	h	1-2	*Lanzafame*
9/5	Juventus	a	3-2	*Lanzafame 2, Biabiany*
16/5	Livorno	h	4-1	*Lanzafame 2, Morrone, Crespo*

No	Name	Nat	DoB	Pos	Aps	(s)	Gls
23	Nicola AMORUSO		29/8/74	A	10	(7)	5
3	Luca ANTONELLI		11/2/87	D	13	(11)	1
20	Jonathan Ludovic BIABIANY	FRA	28/4/88	M	25	(4)	6
86	Valeri BOJINOV	BUL	15/2/86	A	15	(15)	8
32	Alessandro BUDEL		25/2/81	M		(1)	
7	Paolo CASTELLINI		25/3/79	D	20	(8)	
77	Hernán Jorge CRESPO	ARG	5/7/75	A	10	(3)	1
15	Hernán Paolo DELLAFIORE		2/2/85	D	22	(1)	
10	Blerim DZEMAILI	SUI	12/4/86	M	17	(2)	
14	Daniele GALLOPPA		15/5/85	M	33	(1)	2
34	Abel GIGLI		16/8/90	D		(1)	
11	Luis Antonio JIMÉNEZ	CHI	17/6/84	M	10	(2)	1
9	Davide LANZAFAME		9/2/87	M	14	(13)	7
6	Alessandro LUCARELLI		22/7/77	D	33		2
8	Francesco LUNARDINI		3/11/84	M	7	(11)	
21	Alessio MANZONI		10/4/87	M		(1)	
17	McDonald MARIGA	KEN	4/4/87	M	8	(1)	
83	Antonio MIRANTE		8/7/83	G	37		
4	Stefano MORRONE		26/10/78	M	30	(1)	1
24	Massimo PACI		9/5/78	D	23	(4)	
43	Alberto PALOSCHI		4/1/90	A	9	(8)	4
2	Christian PANUCCI		12/4/73	D	19		1
90	Riccardo PASI		27/8/90	M		(1)	
1	Nicola PAVARINI		24/2/74	G	1	(1)	
80	Francesco VALIANI		29/10/80	M	14		
5	Cristian ZACCARDO		21/12/81	D	34		5
19	Damiano ZENONI		23/4/77	D	14	(5)	

AS ROMA

Coach – Luciano Spalletti; (2/9/09) Claudio Ranieri
Founded – 1927
Stadium – Olimpico (73,095)
MAJOR HONOURS:
Inter Cities Fairs Cup - (1) 1961;
Italian League - (3) 1942, 1983, 2001;
Italian Cup - (9) 1964, 1969, 1980, 1981, 1984, 1986, 1991, 2007, 2008.

2009
23/8	Genoa	a	2-3	*Taddei, Totti*
30/8	Juventus	h	1-3	*De Rossi*
13/9	Siena	a	2-1	*Mexès, Riise*
20/9	Fiorentina	h	3-1	*Totti 2 (1p), De Rossi*
23/9	Palermo	a	3-3	*Brighi, Burdisso, Totti (p)*
27/9	Catania	a	1-1	*De Rossi*
4/10	Napoli	h	2-1	*Totti 2*
18/10	Milan	a	1-2	*Ménez*
25/10	Livorno	h	0-1	
28/10	Udinese	h	1-2	*De Rossi*
1/11	Bologna	h	2-1	*Vučinić, Perrotta*
8/11	Inter	a	1-1	*Vučinić*
22/11	Bari	h	3-1	*Totti 3 (1p)*
29/11	Atalanta	a	2-1	*Vučinić, Perrotta*
6/12	Lazio	h	1-0	*Cassetti*
13/12	Sampdoria	a	0-0	
20/12	Parma	h	2-0	*Burdisso, Brighi*

2010
6/1	Cagliari	a	2-2	*Pizarro (p), Perrotta*
9/1	Chievo	h	1-0	*De Rossi*
17/1	Genoa	h	3-0	*Perrotta, Toni 2*
23/1	Juventus	a	2-1	*Totti (p), Riise*
31/1	Siena	h	2-1	*Riise, Okaka Chuka*
7/2	Fiorentina	a	1-0	*Vučinić*
13/2	Palermo	h	4-1	*Brighi 2, Júlio Baptista, Riise*
21/2	Catania	a	1-0	*Vučinić*

28/2	Napoli	a	2-2	Júlio Baptista (p), Vučinić	
6/3	Milan	h	0-0		
14/3	Livorno	a	3-3	Perrotta, Toni, Pizarro	
20/3	Udinese	h	4-2	Toni, Vučinić 3 (1p)	
24/3	Bologna	a	2-0	Riise, Júlio Baptista	
27/3	Inter	h	2-1	De Rossi, Toni	
3/4	Bari	a	1-0	Vučinić	
11/4	Atalanta	h	2-1	Vučinić, Cassetti	
18/4	Lazio	a	2-1	Vučinić 2 (1p)	
25/4	Sampdoria	h	1-2	Totti	
1/5	Parma	a	2-1	Totti, Taddei	
9/5	Cagliari	h	2-1	Totti 2 (1p)	
16/5	Chievo	a	2-0	Vučinić, De Rossi	

No	Name	Nat	DoB	Pos	Aps	(s)	Gls
3	Marco ANDREOLLI		10/6/86	D	4	(4)	
25	ARTUR Guilherme Morais Gusmão	BRA	25/1/81	G	1		
33	Matteo BRIGHI		14/2/81	M	15	(9)	4
29	Nicolás Andrés BURDISSO	ARG	12/4/81	D	32	(1)	2
77	Marco CASSETTI		29/5/77	D	26	(3)	2
24	Alessio CERCI		23/7/87	M	2	(7)	
2	Cicero João de Cézare "CICINHO"	BRA	24/6/80	D		(2)	
16	Daniele DE ROSSI		24/7/83	M	33		7
32	DONIéber Alexander Marangon	BRA	22/10/79	G	7		
14	Ricardo FATY	FRA	4/8/86	M	2	(6)	
21	Stefano GUBERTI		6/11/84	M	3	(3)	
4	JUAN Silveira dos Santos	BRA	1/2/79	D	28	(1)	
19	JÚLIO César BAPTISTA	BRA	1/10/81	A	4	(19)	3
27	JÚLIO SÉRGIO Bertagnoli	BRA	8/11/78	G	30		
1	Bogdan Ionuţ LOBONŢ	ROU	18/1/78	G		(2)	
94	Jérémy MÉNEZ	FRA	7/5/87	M	18	(5)	1
5	Philippe MEXÈS	FRA	30/3/82	D	16	(3)	1
13	Marco MOTTA		14/5/86	D	13	(3)	
89	Stefano OKAKA CHUKA		9/8/89	A		(7)	1
20	Simone PERROTTA		17/9/77	M	31	(1)	5
42	Stefano PETTINARI		27/1/92	M		(1)	
26	Adrian Florin PIŢ	ROU	16/7/83	M		(2)	
7	David PIZARRO	CHI	11/9/79	M	31		2
17	John Arne RIISE	NOR	24/9/80	D	34	(2)	5
11	Rodrigo TADDEI		6/3/80	M	25	(8)	2
22	Max TONETTO		18/11/74	D		(4)	
30	Luca TONI		26/5/77	A	10	(5)	5
10	Francesco TOTTI		27/9/76	A	21	(2)	14
9	Mirko VUČINIĆ	MNE	1/10/83	A	32	(2)	14

UC SAMPDORIA

Coach – Luigi Del Neri
Founded – 1946
Stadium – Luigi Ferraris (36,685)
MAJOR HONOURS:
UEFA Cup Winners' Cup - (1) 1990;
Italian League - (1) 1991;
Italian Cup - (4) 1985, 1988, 1989, 1994.

2009

23/8	Catania	a	2-1	Pazzini, Gastaldello	
30/8	Udinese	h	3-1	Pazzini, Mannini, Cassano	
13/9	Atalanta	a	1-0	Mannini	
20/9	Siena	h	4-1	Palombo, Mannini, Padalino 2	
23/9	Fiorentina	a	0-2		
26/9	Inter	h	1-0	Pazzini	
4/10	Parma	h	1-1	Pazzini	
18/10	Lazio	a	1-1	Pazzini	
24/10	Bologna	h	4-1	Pazzini, Mannini 2, Ziegler	
28/10	Juventus	a	1-5	Pazzini	
1/11	Bari	h	0-0		
8/11	Cagliari	a	0-2		
22/11	Chievo	h	2-1	Rossi, Pazzini	

28/11	Genoa	a	0-3		
5/12	Milan	a	0-3		
13/12	Roma	h	0-0		
20/12	Livorno	a	1-3	Cassano	
2010					
6/1	Palermo	h	1-1	Cassano	
10/1	Napoli	a	0-1		
17/1	Catania	h	1-1	Pazzini (p)	
24/1	Udinese	a	3-2	Pazzini (p), Pozzi, Semioli	
31/1	Atalanta	h	2-0	Palombo, Pazzini	
7/2	Siena	a	2-1	Gastaldello, Pozzi	
13/2	Fiorentina	h	2-0	Semioli, Pazzini	
20/2	Inter	a	0-0		
28/2	Parma	a	0-1		
7/3	Lazio	h	2-1	Guberti, Pazzini	
14/3	Bologna	a	1-1	Gastaldello	
21/3	Juventus	h	1-0	Cassano	
24/3	Bari	a	1-2	Cassano	
28/3	Cagliari	h	1-1	Guberti	
3/4	Chievo	a	2-1	Cassano, Pazzini	
11/4	Genoa	h	1-0	Cassano	
18/4	Milan	h	2-1	Cassano (p), Pazzini	
25/4	Roma	a	2-1	Pazzini 2	
2/5	Livorno	h	2-0	Cassano, Ziegler	
9/5	Palermo	a	1-1	Pazzini (p)	
16/5	Napoli	h	1-0	Pazzini	

No	Name	Nat	DoB	Pos	Aps	(s)	Gls
5	Pietro ACCARDI		12/9/82	D	5	(9)	
11	Claudio BELLUCCI		31/5/75	A	3	(5)	
22	Fabrizio CACCIATORE		8/10/86	D	5	(5)	
99	Antonio CASSANO		12/7/82	A	30	(2)	9
1	Luca CASTELLAZZI		19/7/75	G	19		
90	Vincenzo FIORILLO		13/1/90	G		(1)	
19	Daniele FRANCESCHINI		13/1/76	M	1	(5)	
28	Daniele GASTALDELLO		25/6/83	D	33		3
18	Stefano GUBERTI		6/11/84	M	12	(4)	2
6	Stefano LUCCHINI		2/10/80	D	25	(1)	
7	Daniele MANNINI		25/10/83	M	25	(11)	5
20	Marco PADALINO	SUI	8/12/83	M	6	(14)	2
17	Angelo PALOMBO		25/9/81	M	36		2
10	Giampaolo PAZZINI		2/8/84	A	37		19
16	Andrea POLI		29/9/89	M	26	(5)	
9	Nicola POZZI		30/6/86	A	7	(11)	2
13	Marco ROSSI		30/9/87	D	17	(3)	1
30	Paolo SAMMARCO		17/3/83	M		(1)	
11	Stefan ŠĆEPOVIĆ	SRB	10/1/90	A	1	(1)	
77	Franco SEMIOLI		20/6/80	M	25	(1)	2
23	Marius STANKEVIČIUS	LTU	15/7/81	D	14		
30	Marco STORARI		7/1/77	G	19		
90	Emanuele TESTARDI		31/12/90	A	1	(4)	
12	Fernando Damián TISSONE	ARG	24/7/86	M	15	(14)	
8	Luciano ZAURI		20/1/78	M	25	(7)	
3	Reto ZIEGLER	SUI	16/1/86	D	31	(6)	2

AC SIENA

Coach – Marco Giampaolo; (29/10/09) Marco Baroni;
(23/11/09) Alberto Malesani
Founded – 1904
Stadium – Artemio Franchi (15,373)

2009

22/8	Milan	h	1-2	Ghezzal	
30/8	Cagliari	a	3-1	Calaiò 2, Reginaldo	
13/9	Roma	h	1-2	Maccarone	
20/9	Sampdoria	a	1-4	Fini	
23/9	Chievo	h	0-0		
27/9	Napoli	a	1-2	Maccarone	
4/10	Livorno	h	0-0		
18/10	Parma	a	0-1		
25/10	Juventus	h	0-1		

28/10	Bologna	a	1-2	Calaiò
1/11	Lazio	h	1-1	Maccarone
8/11	Genoa	a	2-4	Paolucci, Maccarone
22/11	Atalanta	h	0-2	
29/11	Bari	a	1-2	Vergassola
6/12	Catania	h	3-2	Calaiò, Terzi, Paolucci
13/12	Udinese	h	2-1	Maccarone, Ghezzal
20/12	Palermo	a	0-1	
2010				
6/1	Fiorentina	h	1-5	Maccarone (p)
10/1	Inter	a	3-4	Maccarone 2, Ekdal
17/1	Milan	a	0-4	
24/1	Cagliari	h	1-1	Calaiò
31/1	Roma	a	1-2	Vergassola
7/2	Sampdoria	h	1-2	Maccarone
14/2	Chievo	a	1-0	Reginaldo
21/2	Napoli	h	0-0	
28/2	Livorno	a	2-1	Calaiò, Maccarone
7/3	Parma	h	1-1	Vergassola
14/3	Juventus	a	3-3	Maccarone, Ghezzal 2 (1p)
21/3	Bologna	h	1-0	Larrondo
24/3	Lazio	a	0-2	
28/3	Genoa	h	0-0	
3/4	Atalanta	a	0-2	
11/4	Bari	h	3-2	Ghezzal 2, Rosi
18/4	Catania	a	2-2	Maccarone, Vergassola
25/4	Udinese	a	1-4	Calaiò
2/5	Palermo	h	1-2	Calaiò
9/5	Fiorentina	a	1-1	Vergassola
16/5	Inter	h	0-1	

No	Name	Nat	DoB	Pos	Aps	(s)	Gls
15	Gonçalo Jardim BRANDÃO	POR	9/10/86	D	20	(1)	
11	Emanuele CALAIÒ		8/1/82	A	13	(20)	8
10	Paul Costantin CODREA	ROU	4/4/81	M	22	(2)	
29	Emílson Sánchez CRIBARI	BRA	6/3/80	D	18		
85	Gianluca CURCI		12/7/85	G	36		
3	Cristiano DEL GROSSO		24/3/83	D	34	(2)	
12	Albin EKDAL	SWE	28/7/89	M	20	(6)	1
77	Daniele FICAGNA		23/2/81	D	10	(1)	
17	Michele FINI		14/6/74	M	11	(6)	1
19	Agostino GAROFALO		29/9/84	M		(3)	
2	Gaël GENEVIER	FRA	26/6/82	M	4		
18	Abdelkader GHEZZAL	ALG	5/12/84	A	26	(4)	6
24	Mato JAJALO	CRO	25/5/88	M	14	(11)	
23	Lukáš JAROLÍM	CZE	29/7/76	M	6	(12)	
63	Marcelo Alejandro LARRONDO	ARG	5/10/88	A	5	(10)	1
32	Massimo MACCARONE		6/9/79	A	37		12
9	Marco MALAGÒ		30/12/78	D	4	(2)	
88	Michael ODIBE	NGA	31/3/88	D	4	(1)	
9	Michele PAOLUCCI		6/2/86	A	2	(8)	2
5	Francesco PARRAVICINI		31/1/82	M	1		
31	Gianluca PEGOLO		25/3/81	G	2	(2)	
50	Francesco PRATALI		17/1/79	D	12		
7	REGINALDO Ferreira da Silva	BRA	31/7/83	A	18	(11)	2
87	Aleandro ROSI		17/5/87	M	28	(2)	1
13	Luca ROSSETTINI		9/5/85	D	2		
21	Andrea ROSSI		7/11/86	D	5	(3)	
6	Claudio TERZI		19/6/84	D	17	(2)	1
22	Alexandros TZIOLIS	GRE	13/2/85	M	13		
8	Simone VERGASSOLA		24/1/76	M	34		5

UDINESE CALCIO

Coach – Pasquale Marino; (22/12/09) Gianni De Biasi;
(21/2/10) Pasquale Marino
Founded – 1896
Stadium – Friuli (41,652)

2009				
23/8	Parma	h	2-2	Di Natale 2 (1p)
30/8	Sampdoria	a	1-3	Di Natale
13/9	Catania	h	4-2	Floro Flores, Di Natale 3 (1p)
19/9	Napoli	a	0-0	
23/9	Milan	h	1-0	Di Natale
27/9	Genoa	h	2-0	Di Natale, Pepe
3/10	Inter	a	1-2	Di Natale
18/10	Atalanta	h	1-3	Lodi
25/10	Palermo	a	0-1	
28/10	Roma	h	2-1	Floro Flores 2
1/11	Chievo	a	1-1	Floro Flores
8/11	Fiorentina	h	0-1	
22/11	Juventus	a	0-1	
28/11	Livorno	h	2-0	Di Natale, Floro Flores
6/12	Bologna	a	1-2	Di Natale
13/12	Siena	a	1-2	D'Agostino
2010				
6/1	Bari	a	0-2	
10/1	Lazio	h	1-1	Di Natale
17/1	Parma	a	0-0	
24/1	Sampdoria	h	2-3	Di Natale (p), Isla
31/1	Catania	a	1-1	Floro Flores
7/2	Napoli	h	3-1	Di Natale 3
12/2	Milan	a	2-3	Floro Flores, Di Natale
20/2	Genoa	a	0-3	
24/2	Cagliari	h	2-1	Sánchez, Di Natale
28/2	Inter	h	2-3	Pepe, Di Natale (p)
7/3	Atalanta	a	0-0	
14/3	Palermo	h	3-2	Floro Flores 2, Asamoah
20/3	Roma	a	2-4	Di Natale 2 (1p)
24/3	Chievo	h	0-0	
28/3	Fiorentina	a	1-4	Pepe
3/4	Juventus	h	3-0	Sánchez, Pepe, Di Natale
11/4	Livorno	a	2-0	Sánchez, Di Natale
18/4	Bologna	h	1-1	Di Natale
25/4	Siena	h	4-1	Pepe 2, Sánchez, Di Natale (p)
2/5	Cagliari	a	2-2	Di Natale, Sánchez
9/5	Bari	h	3-3	Di Natale 2, Pepe
15/5	Lazio	a	1-3	Di Natale

No	Name	Nat	DoB	Pos	Aps	(s)	Gls
19	Emmanuel AGYEMANG-BADU	GHA	2/12/90	M		(5)	
20	Kwadwo ASAMOAH	GHA	9/12/88	M	24	(1)	1
8	Dušan BASTA	SRB	18/8/84	M	14	(2)	
13	Andrea CODA		25/4/85	D	24	(2)	
9	Bernardo CORRADI		30/3/76	A	2	(17)	
4	Juan Guillermo CUADRADO	COL	26/5/88	D	4	(7)	
21	Gaetano D'AGOSTINO		3/6/82	M	18	(2)	1
10	Antonio DI NATALE		13/10/77	A	33	(2)	29
80	Maurizio DOMIZZI		28/6/80	D	13		
19	FELIPE Dias da Silva dal Belo	BRA	31/7/84	D	3		
32	Damiano FERRONETTI		1/11/84	D	8	(4)	
83	Antonio FLORO FLORES		18/6/83	A	25	(7)	9
27	Alexandre GEIJO Pazos	SUI	11/3/82	A		(4)	
22	Samir HANDANOVIĆ	SVN	14/7/84	G	37		
88	Gökhan INLER	SUI	27/6/84	M	32	(1)	
3	Mauricio Aníbal ISLA	CHI	12/6/88	M	27	(3)	1
23	JAIME Romero Gómez	ESP	31/7/90	M	1	(3)	
84	Francesco LODI		23/3/84	M	4	(15)	1
24	Aleksandar LUKOVIĆ	SRB	23/10/82	D	31	(2)	
5	Christian OBODO	NGA	11/5/84	M		(1)	
26	Giovanni PASQUALE		5/1/82	D	19	(3)	
7	Simone PEPE		30/8/83	A	25	(7)	7
1	Rafael Enrique ROMO Pérez	VEN	25/2/90	G	1		
14	Paolo SAMMARCO		17/3/83	M	17	(9)	
11	Alexis Alejandro SÁNCHEZ	CHI	19/12/88	A	25	(7)	5
86	Guilherme Madalena SIQUEIRA	BRA	28/4/86	M		(3)	
2	Cristián ZAPATA Valencia	COL	30/9/86	D	30	(1)	
28	Niki ZIMLING	DEN	19/4/85	M	1		

PROMOTED CLUBS

US LECCE
Coach – Luigi De Canio
Founded – 1908
Stadium – Via del Mare (36,285)

AC CESENA
Coach – Pierpaolo Bisoli
Founded – 1940
Stadium – Dino Manuzzi (23,860)

BRESCIA CALCIO
Coach – Alberto Cavasin; (4/10/09) Giuseppe Iachini
Founded – 1911
Stadium – Mario Rigamonti (27,547)

SECOND LEVEL FINAL TABLE 2009/10

		Pld	W	D	L	F	A	Pts
1	US Lecce	42	20	15	7	66	47	75
2	AC Cesena	42	20	14	8	55	29	74
3	Brescia Calcio	42	21	9	12	60	44	72
4	US Sassuolo Calcio	42	18	15	9	60	42	69
5	Torino FC	42	19	11	12	53	36	68
6	AS Cittadella	42	18	12	12	62	43	66
7	US Grosseto	42	14	19	9	66	63	61
8	FC Crotone	42	17	11	14	53	50	60
9	Ascoli Calcio	42	15	12	15	57	57	57
10	Empoli FC	42	15	11	16	66	56	56
11	UC Albinoleffe	42	14	13	15	59	56	55
12	Modena FC	42	14	12	16	39	47	54
13	Reggina Calcio	42	15	9	18	51	56	54
14	Vicenza Calcio	42	12	17	13	40	41	53
15	Piacenza Calcio	42	13	14	15	40	45	53
16	Frosinone Calcio	42	15	8	19	50	67	53
17	AC Ancona	42	15	9	18	55	56	52
18	US Triestina Calcio	42	13	12	17	41	51	51
19	Calcio Padova	42	12	15	15	44	48	51
20	AC Mantova	42	10	18	14	46	58	48
21	Gallipoli Calcio	42	10	10	22	43	74	40
22	Salernitana Calcio	42	5	8	29	40	80	17

NB Salernitana Calcio – 6 pts deducted;
AC Ancona & FC Crotone – 2 pts deducted.

PROMOTION PLAY-OFFS

(2/6/10 & 6/6/10)
Cittadella 0, Brescia 1
Brescia 0, Cittadella 1
(1-1; Brescia on higher position in regular season)

Torino 1, Sassuolo 1
Sassuolo 1, Torino 2
(Torino 3-2)

(9/6/10 & 13/6/10)
Torino 0, Brescia 0
Brescia 2, Torino 1
(Brescia 2-1)

DOMESTIC CUP 2009/10

COPPA ITALIA

THIRD ROUND
(14/8/09)
Livorno 2, Torino 0
Parma 1, Novara 2
Sassuolo 2, Verona 0

Cesena 0, Atalanta 1
Chievo 3, Mantova 0
Cittadella 2, Ascoli 1 *(aet)*
Palermo 4, Spal 2

(15/8/09)
Ancona 2, Lumezzane 3
Bari 1, Empoli 1 *(aet; 5-6 on pens)*
Bologna 0, Frosinone 0 *(aet; 6-7 on pens)*
Brescia 0, Reggina 1
Catania 1, Cremonese 0

(16/8/09)
Napoli 3, Salernitana 0
Sampdoria 6, Lecce 2
Triestina 1, Cagliari 0

(12/11/09)
Siena 2, Grosseto 0

FOURTH ROUND
(25/11/09)
Chievo 2, Frosinone 0
Siena 0, Novara 2

(26/11/09)
Atalanta 0, Lumezzane 1
Napoli 1, Cittadella 0

Palermo 4, Reggina 1

(1/12/09)
Sampdoria 1, Livorno 2
Triestina 1, Sassuolo 0

(2/12/09)
Catania 2, Empoli 0

FIFTH ROUND
(16/12/09)
Inter 1, Livorno 0

Juventus 3, Napoli 0
Milan 2, Novara 1

(12/1/10)
Roma 3, Triestina 1

(13/1/10)
Genoa 1, Catania 2

(14/1/10)
Fiorentina 3, Chievo 2
Lazio 2, Palermo 0
Udinese 2, Lumezzane 0

QUARTER-FINALS
(20/1/10)
Fiorentina 3 *(Mutu 9, 44, Krøldrup 59)*, Lazio 2 *(Zárate 51, Rocchi 68)*

(26/1/10)
Roma 1 *(De Rossi 74)*, Catania 0

(27/1/10)
Milan 0, Udinese 1 *(Inler 56)*

(28/1/10)
Inter 2 *(Lúcio 72, Balotelli 90)*, Juventus 1 *(Diego 10)*

SEMI-FINALS
(3/2/10 & 13/4/10)
Inter 1 *(Milito 34)*, Fiorentina 0
Fiorentina 0, Inter 1 *(Eto'o 57)*
(Inter 2-0)

(4/2/10 & 21/4/10)
Roma 2 *(Vučinić 13, Mexès 41)*, Udinese 0
Udinese 1 *(Sánchez 81)*, Roma 0
(Roma 2-1)

FINAL
(5/5/10)
Stadio Olimpico, Roma
FC INTERNAZIONALE MILANO 1 *(Milito 40)*
AS ROMA 0
Referee – Rizzoli
INTER – Júlio César, Maicon, Córdoba *(Samuel 39)*, Materazzi, Chivu, Zanetti, Cambiasso, Thiago Motta, Sneijder *(Balotelli 5; Muntari 90+3)*, Eto'o, Milito.
ROMA – Júlio Sérgio, Burdisso *(Motta 46)*, Mexès, Juan, Riise, De Rossi, Pizarro *(Totti 46)*, Taddei, Perrotta , Vučinić, Toni *(Ménez 63)*.
Sent off: Totti *(88)*.

KAZAKHSTAN

Superleague hat-trick for Aktobe

FC Aktobe maintained their Premier Liga supremacy by becoming champions of Kazakhstan for the third year in a row, finishing five points clear of newly formed FC Lokomotiv Astana.

Ably led once again by Russian coach Vladimir Mukhanov and captain Samat Smakov, the team from the country's north-western corner, some 2,000 kilometres distant from the capital of Almaty, saw off all pretenders to their crown with a powerful and consistent title defence. Taken to the wire in 2008, when only a penalty shoot-out victory in a title play-off against FC Tobol Kostanay saw them home, Aktobe seemed empowered by that experience and seldom wavered in pursuit of their title hat-trick.

Positive response

Although they were defeated three times, they always responded with a run of positive results. As impressive on their travels as they were at home – and their journeys were never short – they ended the season with 21 victories from their 26 games, the 20th of them, 5-2 at home to a Tobol side unbeaten in their previous 16 matches, securing the title with one match to spare. Murat Tleshev, Aktobe's leading marksman, was on target twice in that championship-clinching win to take his cumulative tally for the season to 20, a figure that would earn him a share of the Premier Liga's top-scorer prize alongside Tobol's Russian striker Vladimir Bayramov, who moved alongside him with a penalty on the final day of the season. Tleshev had won the Golden Boot alone in 2008 with just 13 goals.

Tleshev was also on target in each leg of Aktobe's UEFA Champions League second qualifying round tie against Icelandic champions FH Hafnarfjördur, which they won 6-0. In the next round Aktobe looked set for a sensational victory over Maccabi Haifa FC when they went 3-0 up early on in the second leg in Israel – after a 0-0 draw at home – but their opponents came back to win 4-3, sending Mukhanov's men into the play-off round of the UEFA Europa League, where they

predictably struggled against the might of Werder Bremen, losing 8-3 overall.

The country's three original UEFA Europa League participants – Tobol, FC Irtysh Pavlodar and FC Okzhetpes Kokshetau – had all gone out of the competition at the first time of asking, further strengthening Aktobe's status as Kazakhstan's number one club. However, there would be no repeat domestic double for the team in 2009. A fortnight after securing the championship they were surprisingly knocked out of the Kazakhstan Cup in a thrilling two-legged semi-final by FC Shakhter Karagandy.

Atyrau's Cup

Shakhter, who had rebuilt under coach Vladimir Cherubin after a scandal-filled 2008 campaign, were the season's surprise package, taking third place in the Premier Liga, but they were unable to cap off a

Kazakhstanning Futbol Federatsiyasi (KFF)

29 Syganak Street
6th floor, section 21
KZ-010000 Astana
tel – +7 7172 790780
fax – +7 7172 790788
website – kff.kz
email - kfo@mail.online.kz
Year of Formation – 1992

President – Adilbek Dzhaksybekov
General Secretary – Sayan Khamitzhanov
Media Officer – Timur Kamashev
National Stadium – Astana Arena, Astana (30,000)

TOP FIVE ALL-TIME CAPS
Ruslan Baltiyev (73); Samat Smakov (56); Nurbol Zhumaskaliev (47); Andrei Karpovich (45); Aleksandr Kuchma (37)
TOP FIVE ALL-TIME GOALS
Ruslan Baltiyev (13); Viktor Zubarev (12); Dmitry Byakov (8); Oleg Litvinenko & Igor Avdeev (6)

memorable campaign by winning a first major trophy. That honour went instead to FC Atyrau, the club from the banks of the Caspian Sea, who overcame Shakhter 1-0 in the final in the newly built Astana Arena with a first-half goal from their veteran Russian captain Denis Zubko.

The residents of the Astana Arena in 2009 were Lokomotiv, the 'superclub' newly created out of the remnants of two clubs from the capital, FC Alma-Ata and FC MegaSport Almaty. Coached by Ukrainian-born former Russian international striker Sergei Yuran and boasting ex-FC Spartak Moskva veterans Andrei Tikhonov and Yegor Titov among their playing staff, they claimed the runners-up spot in the Premier Liga,

winning 20 of their 26 matches (but, oddly, drawing none of them). Tikhonov, at 39, was especially prominent, scoring 12 goals and supplying 19 assists, while another high-profile import, ex-FC Dynamo Kyiv striker Maksim Shatskikh, made an impact with nine goals in 15 appearances.

Club mergers, financial problems and point deductions had distorted the relegation picture in 2008, and it was a similar story in 2009 as the Premier Liga reduced its number from 14 teams to 12 for the 2010 season. FC Vostok, who escaped relegation by two points and the play-offs by one, ultimately withdrew from the 2010 campaign, which rendered the promotion/relegation

NATIONAL TEAM RESULTS 2009/10

9/9/09	Andorra (WCQ)	A	Andorra la Vella	3-1	Khizhnichenko (13, 34), Baltiyev (28p)
10/10/09	Belarus (WCQ)	A	Brest	0-4	
14/10/09	Croatia (WCQ)	H	Astana	1-2	Khizhnichenko (26)
3/3/10	Moldova	N	Antalya (TUR)	0-1	

NATIONAL TEAM APPEARANCES 2009/10

Coach - Bernd STORCK (GER)	25/1/63		AND	BLR	CRO	Mda	Caps	Goals
Aleksandr MOKIN	19/6/81	Ordabasy	G	G	G		11	-
Yuri LOGVINENKO	22/7/88	Aktobe	D	D	D	D	9	-
Aleksandr KISLITSIN	8/3/86	Shakhter Karagandy	D	D	D	D	9	-
Aleksandr KIROV	4/6/84	Atyrau	D	D	D		7	-
Renat ABDULIN	14/4/82	Lokomotiv Astana	D	D	D	s78	11	1
Ruslan BALTIYEV	16/9/78	Tobol	M	M61	s90		73	13
Andrei KARPOVICH	18/1/81	Lokomotiv Astana /Aktobe	M	M		M	45	2
Zhambyl KUKEEV	20/9/88	Lokomotiv Astana	M87	M	s54	M78	20	1
Yevgeny AVERCHENKO	6/4/82	Aktobe	M	M	M	M	6	-
Sergei KHIZHNICHENKO	17/7/91	Vostok /Lokomotiv Astana	A92	A	A	A87	5	3
Andrei FINONCHENKO	21/6/82	Shakhter Karagandy	A78			s87	13	2
Sergei SKORYKH	25/5/84	Tobol /Shakhter Karagandy	s78	M79	M	s85	26	-
Azat NURGALIEV	30/6/86	Tobol	s87		M54	M	4	-
Vyacheslav ERBES	14/1/88	Vostok /Lokomotiv Astana	s92	s79	D90	D85	7	-
Tanat NUSERBAYEV	1/1/88	Ordabasy		s61	A76		7	1
Denis MALININ	11/6/83	Irtysh			s76		1	-
Andrei SIDELNIKOV	8/3/80	Aktobe				G	1	-
Farhadbek IRISMETOV	10/8/81	Tobol				D	32	-
Mikhail ROZHKOV	27/12/83	Lokomotiv Astana				D	1	-

play-off, in which second tier runners-up FC Akzhaiyk Uralsk defeated Okzhetpes 3-2, redundant. Already secure of their place in the 2010 Premier Liga were First Division winners FC Kairat Almaty - the same club that earlier in the year had withdrawn from the top division after filing for bankruptcy.

Wonderboy Khizhnichenko

Vostok's withdrawal led to the transfer of their highly promising young forward Sergei Khizhnichenko to Lokomotiv. Handed his international debut for Kazakhstan at the age of 17 in a FIFA World Cup qualifier against Ukraine, he scored twice on his next appearance – a 3-1 win in Andorra – and another goal in the final qualifier at home to Croatia. Kazakhstan played only one further international in 2009/10, a friendly against Moldova in the Turkish city of Antalya which they lost 1-0, but, with Khizhnichenko leading the attack, hopes are high that the qualifying series for UEFA EURO 2012 will provide an improvement on the 2010 World Cup campaign in which Kazakhstan failed to pick up points from any opponents other than Andorra.

Hot prospect Sergei Khizhnichenko (No9) in World Cup qualifying action for Kazakhstan

DOMESTIC LEAGUE 2009

PREMIER LIGA FINAL TABLE

		Pld	Home					Away					Total					Pts
			W	D	L	F	A	W	D	L	F	A	W	D	L	F	A	
1	FC Aktobe	26	10	1	2	34	12	11	1	1	31	7	21	2	3	65	19	65
2	FC Lokomotiv Astana	26	11	0	2	29	10	9	0	4	25	14	20	0	6	54	24	60
3	FC Shakhter Karagandy	26	11	1	1	27	8	7	2	4	23	10	18	3	5	50	18	57
4	FC Tobol Kostanay	26	9	4	0	33	5	5	5	3	21	18	14	9	3	54	23	51
5	FC Zhetysu Taldykorgan	26	9	2	2	18	8	4	3	6	15	18	13	5	8	33	26	44
6	FC Atyrau	26	8	3	2	24	13	3	4	6	13	16	11	7	8	37	29	40
7	FC Ordabasy Shymkent	26	5	3	5	16	15	5	3	5	17	15	10	6	10	33	30	36
8	FC Taraz	26	5	3	5	21	18	4	3	6	16	18	9	6	11	37	36	33
9	FC Irtysh Pavlodar	26	4	3	6	9	13	4	2	7	15	18	8	5	13	24	31	29
10	FC Vostok	26	6	1	6	15	20	1	4	8	17	36	7	5	14	32	56	23
11	FC Okzhetpes Kokshetau	26	3	3	7	12	29	3	1	9	10	19	6	4	16	22	48	22
12	FC Kazakhmys	26	3	3	7	19	31	4	0	9	13	30	7	3	16	32	61	21
13	FC Kaisar Kyzylorda	26	1	3	9	7	23	2	2	9	8	22	3	5	18	15	45	14
14	FC Kyzylzhar Petropavlovsk	26	2	2	9	8	25	1	2	10	6	31	3	4	19	14	56	6

NB FC Vostok and FC Kazakhmys – 3 pts deducted; FC Kyzylzhar Petropavlovsk – 7 pts deducted; FC Vostok withdrew from 2010 Superleague.

TOP GOALSCORERS

20 Murat TLESHEV (Aktobe)
   Vladimir BAYRAMOV (Tobol)

14 Danilo BELIĆ (Zhetysu)

12 Andrei TIKHONOV (Lokomotiv)

11 Konstantin GOLOVSKOY (Aktobe)
   Sergei KOSTYUK (Shakhter)

10 Geysar ALEKPERZADE
   (Kazakhmys/Tobol)
   Ivan PERIĆ (Shakhter)

9 Sergei STRUKOV (Aktobe)
   Denis ZUBKO (Atyrau)
   Maksim SHATSKIKH (Lokomotiv)
   Dmitriy PARKHACHEV (Ordabasy)

CLUB-BY-CLUB

FC AKTOBE

Coach – Vladimir Mukhanov (RUS)
Founded – 1967
Stadium – Aktobe Central Stadium (13,500)
MAJOR HONOURS:
Kazakhstan League - (4) 2005, 2007, 2008, 2009;
Kazakhstan Cup - (1) 2008.

2009

7/3	Kaisar	a	1-0	Tleshev (p)
14/3	Taraz	a	3-1	Tleshev, Golovskoy, Smakov
21/3	Irtysh	h	3-1	Kenzhesariev 2, Tleshev
6/4	Ordabasy	h	1-0	Tleshev
12/4	Vostok	a	4-0	Tleshev 2, Asanbaev, Khairullin
19/4	Okzhetpes	h	1-2	Tleshev
30/4	Kyzylzhar	a	1-0	Golovskoy
10/5	Atyrau	h	2-1	Kenzhesariev, Smakov
16/5	Tobol	a	0-0	
24/5	Shakhter	h	2-1	Tleshev 2
15/6	Zhetysu	a	2-0	Golovskoy, Tleshev
19/6	Lokomotiv	a	2-0	Tleshev 2
28/6	Kazakhmys	h	4-0	Strukov 3, Kenzhesariev
10/7	Kazakhmys	a	4-2	Golovskoy 3, Smakov
15/8	Atyrau	a	0-1	
24/8	Kyzylzhar	h	6-1	Strukov 2, Khairullin, Asanbaev, Kenzhesariev, Golovskoy
31/8	Okzhetpes	a	7-1	Khairullin 3, Smakov (p), Tleshev, Strukov, Averchenko
14/9	Vostok	h	4-0	Khairullin, Golovskoy, Tleshev 2
21/9	Ordabasy	a	2-1	Smakov (p), Strukov
25/9	Lokomotiv	h	0-1	
29/9	Irtysh	a	2-1	Tleshev 2
3/10	Zhetysu	h	1-1	Tleshev
22/10	Shakhter	a	3-0	Golovskoy 3
25/10	Taraz	h	2-1	Averchenko, Khokhlov
29/10	Tobol	h	5-2	Tleshev 2, Strukov 2, Smakov
2/11	Kaisar	h	3-1	Lavrik, Smakov 2 (1p)

No	Name	Nat	DoB	Pos	Aps	(s)	Gls
22	Pyotr ASANBAEV		13/9/78	M	17	(5)	2
30	Yevgeny AVERCHENKO		6/4/82	M	13	(1)	2
5	Pyotr BADLO		24/5/76	D	11	(5)	
77	Andrei BOGOMOLOV		11/4/77	M		(5)	
29	Sergei BOYCHENKO		27/9/77	G	1		
6	Anton CHICHULIN		27/10/84	D	5	(8)	
18	Azat ERSALIMOV		19/7/88	M		(1)	
17	Konstantin GOLOVSKOY		25/4/75	M	21	(4)	11
20	Emil KENZHESARIEV		26/3/87	D	25		5
10	Marat KHAIRULLIN	RUS	26/4/84	M	24	(1)	6
24	Nikita KHOKHLOV		27/10/83	M	3	(8)	1
14	Aleksandr KIROV		4/6/84	D	6		
32	Maksat KURMASHEV		14/8/91	A	1		
33	Andrei LAVRIK	BLR	7/12/74	M	23	(1)	1
91	Sergei LISENKOV		17/6/91	A	1	(1)	
23	Yuri LOGVINENKO		22/7/88	D	25		
9	Aleksandr MITROFANOV		1/11/77	M	3	(7)	
69	Sergei OSTAPENKO		23/2/86	A		(9)	
25	Maxim SEMENYOV		2/9/88	M	22	(3)	
55	Andrei SIDELNIKOV		8/3/80	G	25		
8	Samat SMAKOV		8/12/78	D	25		8
27	Sergei STRUKOV	RUS	17/9/82	A	9	(15)	9
19	Murat TLESHEV		12/4/80	A	23	(2)	20
11	Nikolay ZABRODIN		23/7/90	M	4		

FC ATYRAU

Coach – Anton Shokh; (14/3/09) (Igor Vostrikov);
(21/3/09) Vakhid Masudov
Founded – 1980
Stadium – Munayshi (8,660)
MAJOR HONOURS:
Kazakhstan Cup - (1) 2009.

2009

7/3	Vostok	a	2-2	Zubko 2 (1p)
14/3	Kyzylzhar	a	0-1	
21/3	Okzhetpes	h	2-0	Shakin 2
6/4	Lokomotiv	a	1-2	Shakin
12/4	Tobol	h	2-2	Uzdenov, Tatishev
19/4	Shakhter	h	2-0	Kostrub, Zubko (p)
30/4	Zhetysu	h	0-2	
10/5	Aktobe	a	1-2	Zubko
16/5	Kazakhmys	h	2-1	Peikrishvili, Tatishev
24/5	Kaisar	a	1-1	Borovskoy
15/6	Irtysh	h	2-0	Zubko, Shakin
19/6	Taraz	a	1-1	Zubko (p)
28/6	Ordabasy	h	0-0	
12/7	Ordabasy	a	3-1	Aliyev, Uzdenov, Shakin
19/7	Taraz	h	1-1	Zubko (p)
26/7	Irtysh	a	0-1	
2/8	Kaisar	h	3-2	Abuov, Uzdenov 2
8/8	Kazakhmys	a	2-1	Shakin, Kirov
15/8	Aktobe	h	1-0	Zubko (p)
23/8	Zhetysu	a	1-2	Shumeyko
30/8	Shakhter	a	0-0	
14/9	Tobol	a	0-0	
20/9	Lokomotiv	h	1-2	Zubko
27/9	Okzhetpes	a	1-0	Kirov
25/10	Kyzylzhar	h	4-1	Sarkisyan, Shakin, Peikrishvili, Uzdenov
2/11	Vostok	h	4-2	Peikrishvili, Buleshev, Larin, Zununov

No	Name	Nat	DoB	Pos	Aps	(s)	Gls
14	Almat ABDRAMANOV		12/3/90	M	7	(5)	
17	Bakhyt ABUOV		24/1/89	D	25		1
7	Piraly ALIYEV		13/1/84	D	13	(1)	1
2	Alibek BAKIBAEV		3/4/90	M		(1)	
13	Vadim BOROVSKOY		30/10/86	M	3	(3)	1
77	Alibek BULESHEV		9/4/81	A	2	(7)	1
8	Valentin CHUREEV		29/8/86	D	4	(4)	
2	Roman DUPLYAKIN		23/6/87	D		(1)	
35	Artem KIRBYATEV		16/8/84	G	2		
84	Aleksandr KIROV		4/6/84	D	10	(1)	2
23	Yevgeny KOSTRUB		27/8/82	M	22	(2)	1
7	Marat KSANAEV	RUS	5/3/81	M	1	(1)	
86	Sergei LARIN		22/7/86	M	4	(5)	1
10	Giorgi PEIKRISHVILI	GEO	28/2/83	M	17	(1)	3
44	Mamadi SANGARÉ	GUI	4/12/82	D	17	(1)	
75	Albert SARKISYAN	ARM	15/5/75	M	7	(1)	1
1	Andrei SHABANOV		17/11/86	G	24		
6	Alexei SHAKIN		6/8/84	M	25		7
5	Vitaliy SHUMEYKO	UKR	6/10/81	D	5	(3)	1
5	Igor SOLTANICI	MDA	4/5/84	D	8		
9	Beybit TATISHEV		24/7/84	A	3	(11)	2
11	Roman UZDENOV		10/3/79	A	9	(7)	5
4	Ilya VOROTNIKOV		1/2/86	D	25		
	Baurzhan ZHOLCHIEV		8/5/90	M	3	(4)	

KAZAKHSTAN

3	Abzal ZHUMABAEV		28/5/86	D	12	(2)	
74	Denis ZUBKO	RUS	7/11/74	A	21	(4)	9
15	Telman ZUNUNOV		17/8/89	M	17	(7)	1

6	Denis TSCHETKIN		14/9/82	D	2	(5)	
30	Anton TSIRIN		10/8/87	G	1	(1)	
9	Igor YURIN		3/7/82	M	22	(4)	2
12	Konstantin ZARECHNI		14/2/84	M	9	(6)	
16	Eduard ZATSEPIN	RUS	27/7/74	A	3	(3)	
5	Konstantin ZOTOV		14/1/86	M	11	(2)	

FC IRTYSH PAVLODAR

Coach – Oyrat Saduov; (16/5/09) (Talgat Baysufinov);
(24/5/09) Leonid Nazarenko (RUS)
Founded – 1965
Stadium – Pavlodar Centralny (12,000)
MAJOR HONOURS:
Kazakhstan League - (5) 1993, 1997, 1999, 2002, 2003;
Kazakhstan Cup - (1) 1998.

2009

7/3	Zhetysu	h	0-2	
14/3	Kazakhmys	h	0-2	
21/3	Aktobe	a	1-3	Shomko
6/4	Kaisar	a	1-0	Gumar (p)
12/4	Lokomotiv	h	0-1	
19/4	Taraz	h	0-0	
30/4	Ordabasy	a	0-2	
10/5	Vostok	h	1-1	Gumar (p)
16/5	Okzhetpes	a	4-1	Andreev, Maltsev 2, Yurin
24/5	Kyzylzhar	h	1-0	Goloveshkin
15/6	Atyrau	a	0-2	
19/6	Tobol	h	1-2	Gumar (p)
27/6	Shakhter	a	0-1	
13/7	Shakhter	h	1-1	Shomko
26/7	Atyrau	h	1-0	Daskalov
31/7	Kyzylzhar	a	3-0	Daskalov 3
4/8	Tobol	a	1-1	Shabalin
9/8	Okzhetpes	h	1-0	Rimavičius
16/8	Vostok	a	3-1	Daskalov, Shabalin, Chernyshov
23/8	Ordabasy	h	1-2	Chernyshov
31/8	Taraz	a	1-1	Ivanov
14/9	Lokomotiv	a	0-2	
20/9	Kaisar	h	1-0	Chernyshov
29/9	Aktobe	h	1-2	Yurin
25/10	Kazakhmys	a	1-2	Shabalin
2/11	Zhetysu	a	0-2	

FC KAISAR KYZYLORDA

Coach – Khazret Dyshekov (RUS); (19/4/09) Sultan Abuildayev;
(31/8/09) Teleukhan Turmagambetov
Founded – 1968
Stadium – Gany Muratbayev (7,300)
MAJOR HONOURS:
Kazakhstan Cup - (1) 1999.

2009

7/3	Aktobe	h	0-1	
14/3	Lokomotiv	h	0-4	
21/3	Kazakhmys	a	1-1	Tazhimbetov
6/4	Irtysh	h	0-1	
12/4	Taraz	a	1-2	Khromtsov
19/4	Ordabasy	h	1-1	Khromtsov
30/4	Vostok	a	0-1	
10/5	Okzhetpes	h	2-1	Moldakarayev, Tazhimbetov
16/5	Kyzylzhar	a	1-1	Ovshinov
24/5	Atyrau	h	1-1	Tazhimbetov
15/6	Tobol	a	0-3	
19/6	Shakhter	h	0-3	
28/6	Zhetysu	a	1-0	Borantaev
12/7	Zhetysu	h	2-3	Bogatyrev, Urazbakhtin
19/7	Shakhter	a	0-2	
28/7	Tobol	h	1-1	Tazhimbetov (p)
2/8	Atyrau	a	2-3	Menlikhoza, Gorkun
8/8	Kyzylzhar	h	0-1	
16/8	Okzhetpes	a	1-0	Gorkun
23/8	Vostok	h	0-2	
31/8	Ordabasy	a	0-2	
14/9	Taraz	h	0-2	
20/9	Irtysh	h	0-1	
27/9	Kazakhmys	h	0-2	
25/10	Lokomotiv	a	0-3	
2/11	Aktobe	a	1-3	Gorkun

No	Name	Nat	DoB	Pos	Aps	(s)	Gls
	Eldos AKHMETOV		1/6/90	D	3	(4)	
27	Aleksandr ANDREEV		9/9/86	A	3	(6)	1
	Timur BAYZHANOV		30/3/90	A	1	(1)	
3	Vladislav CHERNYSHOV		16/3/81	D	22		3
40	Georgi DASKALOV	BUL	3/8/81	A	11	(1)	5
	Anton DERKACH		3/5/91	M	1		
	Vitaliy GOLOVESHKIN		7/11/87	A	3	(11)	1
2	Ruslan GUMAR		18/11/73	D	7		3
11	Sergei IVANOV		30/5/80	A	23		1
	Nikita KALMYKOV		24/8/89	G	2		
10	Sergei KIROV		4/2/78	D	5	(3)	
4	Yuriy KOLOMYTS	RUS	30/4/79	D	25		
10	Boris KONDEV	BUL	20/8/79	A	2		
22	Denis MALININ		11/6/83	A	4	(4)	
7	Gleb MALTSEV		7/3/88	A	6	(3)	2
37	Dimitar NAKOV	BUL	18/10/80	D	18	(1)	
8	Vladimir NOSKOV		28/1/86	A	6	(7)	
24	Dmitriy PARKHAMCHUK		7/3/87	M	3	(1)	
1	Daniil RIKHARD		27/2/74	G	23		
31	Laurynas RIMAVIČIUS	LTU	21/10/85	D	18	(1)	1
18	Pavel SHABALIN		23/10/88	A	23	(1)	3
13	Andrei SHETLE		27/4/91	M	1		
15	Dmitriy SHOMKO		19/3/90	D	19		2
14	Vyacheslav SOBOLEV		13/10/84	D	9	(4)	

No	Name	Nat	DoB	Pos	Aps	(s)	Gls
1	Akhmet ALAYDAROV		19/8/83	G	4		
3	Aldan BALTAEV		15/1/89	D	17	(2)	
11	Aydos BAYTENOV		8/1/88	M	5	(1)	
4	Victor BERCO	MDA	20/4/79	M	9	(3)	
45	Abumuslim BOGATYREV	RUS	28/8/84	M	9	(1)	1
21	Askhat BORANTAEV		22/8/78	D	21	(3)	1
30	Dmitriy DENISENYA		14/2/88	D	2		
	Timur DOSHANOV		25/2/88	A	12	(1)	
78	Dmitriy EPIFANOV	RUS	31/1/78	G	22		
46	Valentyn GORKUN	UKR	19/7/82	A	9	(4)	3
35	Bagdat ISMAILOV		23/2/91	M		(1)	
39	Oleg KHROMTSOV	MDA	30/5/83	A	3	(5)	2
24	Suyndyk KUSHEKOV		7/5/90	A	1	(1)	
20	Sergei KUTSOV		23/4/77	D	6	(3)	
19	Aset MENLIKHOZA		13/3/89	M	19	(2)	1
17	Zhaslan MOLDAKARAYEV		7/5/87	A	8	(12)	1
5	Aleksandr MOSKALENKO		18/9/76	D	21		
8	Yevgeny OVSHINOV		17/10/80	M	25		1
9	Vladimir SHIPILOV	RUS	5/12/72	M	15	(7)	
2	Yerlan SHOYTYMOV		6/4/80	D	3	(1)	
47	Denis STOYAN	UKR	24/8/81	D	7		
10	Talgat SYZDYKOV		23/2/78	M	21		

KAZAKHSTAN

27	Askhat TAGYBERGEN		9/8/90	M	2	(9)	
36	Chingiz TANATKANOV		25/1/90	G		(1)	
18	Daurenbek TAZHIMBETOV		2/7/85	A	22	(3)	4
25	Galymzhan UMBETBAYEV		4/2/90	A	1	(3)	
	Rafael URAZBAKHTIN		20/11/78	A	9	(3)	1
23	Igor VOZNESENSKIY	RUS	28/5/85	M	4	(2)	
7	Islam ZHUNISBEKOV		26/12/81	M	9	(3)	

FC KAZAKHMYS

Coach – Vladimir Dogaylo (UKR); (24/5/09) Vladimir Golovlev;
(14/6/09) Altay Bitusupov; (28/6/09) Aleksandr Arefyev;
(20/9/09) Altay Bitusupov; (27/9/09) Eduard Glazunov
Founded – 2006
Stadium – SOK Kazakhmys (2,300)

2009

7/3	Lokomotiv	h	3-4	Serikzhanov, Alekperzade, Siminidi
14/3	Irtysh	a	2-0	Iskulov, Alekperzade
21/3	Kaisar	h	1-1	Serikzhanov
6/4	Taraz	h	1-0	Alekperzade
12/4	Ordabasy	a	2-1	Alekperzade, Boziev
19/4	Vostok	h	3-2	Boziev, Alekperzade (p), Serikzhanov
30/4	Okzhetpes	a	1-3	Alekperzade
10/5	Kyzylzhar	h	1-1	Burdiyan
16/5	Atyrau	a	1-2	Alekperzade
24/5	Tobol	h	0-1	
14/6	Shakhter	a	1-3	Alekperzade (p)
19/6	Zhetysu	h	2-2	Khamzin, Alekperzade
28/6	Aktobe	a	0-4	
10/7	Aktobe	h	2-4	Gavrish, Iskulov
19/7	Zhetysu	a	1-2	Ivanov
26/7	Shakhter	h	1-5	Solomatin
31/7	Tobol	a	0-5	
8/8	Atyrau	h	1-2	Iskulov
16/8	Kyzylzhar	a	2-0	Ivanov, Maksymyuk
23/8	Okzhetpes	h	1-4	Serikzhanov
30/8	Vostok	a	1-2	Khamzin
14/9	Ordabasy	h	1-4	Siminidi (p)
20/9	Taraz	a	0-5	
27/9	Kaisar	a	2-0	Serikzhanov, Ivanov
25/10	Irtysh	h	2-1	Serikzhanov, Iskulov (p)
2/11	Lokomotiv	a	0-3	

No	Name	Nat	DoB	Pos	Aps	(s)	Gls
11	Geysar ALEKPERZADE		2/12/84	A	13		9
8	Kasim BOZIEV		9/6/88	M	10	(6)	2
6	Andriy BURDIYAN	UKR	18/1/86	M	8		1
31	Aleksei CHEREDNIKOV	RUS	14/10/86	G	2		
7	DOUGLAS de Souza Ferreira	BRA	7/10/85	M	13	(7)	
5	Marlen ERALIYEV		14/4/91	M		(1)	
18	Yerzhan ISKAKOV		21/11/85	D	3	(2)	
88	Marat ISKULOV		11/4/82	M	26		4
11	Vladimir IVANOV		10/2/86	A	11	(2)	3
25	Yevgeniy GAVRISH		4/2/87	M	7	(12)	1
77	Arsen KANAPIYA		11/10/84	M		(3)	
4	Maxim KAZNACHEEV		30/1/86	D	5		
87	Dias KHAMZIN		24/6/87	M	11	(8)	2
1	Vyacheslav KOTLYAR	UKR	3/3/82	G	24	(1)	
2	Ayan KUSAINOV		10/6/90	D	10	(3)	
12	Roman MAKSYMYUK	UKR	14/6/74	D	23		1
24	Alexei MIKHAYLUK		23/7/82	D	17	(1)	
6	Daulet NURASYLOV		3/11/84	M	1	(3)	
28	Zhandos ORAZALIYEV		3/10/85	M	1	(10)	
22	Zhomart RSALIYN		3/2/91	M	9	(3)	

10	Akzhol SERIKZHANOV		6/5/90	A	23	(2)	6
27	Andrei SHABAEV		15/2/87	D	25		
20	Fedor SIMINIDI		14/3/85	M	24		2
19	Sergei SOLOMATIN		24/4/85	D	20	(4)	1

FC KYZYLZHAR PETROPAVLOVSK

Coach – Bolat Yesmagambetov
Founded – 1968
Stadium – Avangard (11,000)

2009

7/3	Okzhetpes	a	0-0	
14/3	Atyrau	h	1-0	Keker
21/3	Lokomotiv	a	0-1	
6/4	Tobol	a	0-3	
12/4	Shakhter	h	0-1	
19/4	Zhetysu	a	0-4	
30/4	Aktobe	h	0-1	
10/5	Kazakhmys	a	1-1	Mukhametzhanov
16/5	Kaisar	h	1-1	Sagyndykov
24/5	Irtysh	a	0-1	
15/6	Taraz	h	1-2	Solomin (p)
19/6	Ordabasy	a	0-1	
26/6	Vostok	h	4-1	Vereshak, Mukhametzhanov 2, Solomin
12/7	Vostok	a	1-3	Aitov
19/7	Ordabasy	h	0-1	
26/7	Taraz	a	0-5	
31/7	Irtysh	h	0-3	
8/8	Kaisar	a	1-0	Shulyak
16/8	Kazakhmys	h	0-2	
24/8	Aktobe	a	1-6	Ustinov
31/8	Zhetysu	h	1-4	Bogdanov
14/9	Shakhter	a	1-2	Saltaev
20/9	Tobol	h	0-7	
29/9	Lokomotiv	h	0-2	
25/10	Atyrau	a	1-4	Arslanov
2/11	Okzhetpes	h	0-0	

No	Name	Nat	DoB	Pos	Aps	(s)	Gls
40	Ildar AITOV		2/3/90	M	12	(3)	1
12	Ramil AKBAROV		17/1/87	M	10	(6)	
20	Akhmetzhan AKHMETZHANOV		16/1/86	M	3	(3)	
19	Dmitriy ARSLANOV	RUS	10/2/90	M	9		1
10	Yevgeny AVERCHENKO		6/4/82	A	10		
21	Bulat BAYKENOV		22/5/89	D	2	(3)	
11	Stanislav BOGDANOV		17/1/88	A	11	(4)	1
6	Aleksei GORELKIN	RUS	8/11/83	M	14		
2	Kirill KEKER		22/6/79	D	10		1
3	Aleksandr KUDRYASHOV	RUS	3/8/74	D	9		
32	Yevgeny KUSKOV		11/11/88	D	8	(4)	
1	Vladimir LOGINOVSKY		8/10/85	G	21		
9	Yuriy MARKHEL	BLR	9/1/79	A	7		
47	Nikolay MATVEEV		16/3/91	A	1	(2)	
33	Pavel MAZUROV		27/3/87	D	7		
	Ruslan MUKHAMETZHANOV		25/1/89	M	10	(1)	3
5	Adil MUSABAYEV		19/5/90	D	23		
13	Vladimir NIKLEVICH		8/10/85	G	5	(1)	
4	Denis PROSKURIN		3/4/79	D	9		
16	Serik SAGYNDYKOV		9/1/84	D	19	(3)	1
14	Anatoliy SALTAEV	RUS	19/10/89	A	9	(14)	1
48	Nikolay SARAYEV		20/5/90	D	7	(5)	
17	Bekseyut SHULANBEKOV		23/6/88	A	4	(3)	
15	Stanislav SHULYAK		9/11/87	D	11	(2)	1
22	Nikolay SOLOMIN		6/4/85	A	13	(3)	2
4	Aleksei TYSHKEVICH	RUS	17/2/91	M	2	(3)	

No	Name	Nat	DoB	Pos	Aps	(s)	Gls
7	Vitaliy USHAKOV		12/9/74	M	9		
18	Alexei USTINOV		21/1/87	D	13	(1)	1
3	Dmitriy VAVILOV	RUS	2/2/86	D	12		
8	Alexei VERESHAK		2/12/76	A	6	(6)	1

No	Name	Nat	DoB	Pos	Aps	(s)	Gls
99	Murat SUYUMAGAMBETOV		14/10/83	A	4	(4)	1
11	Andrei TIKHONOV	RUS	16/10/70	M	25		12
9	Yegor TITOV	RUS	29/5/76	M	24		6
33	Eduard VALUTA	MDA	9/4/79	D	1	(1)	

FC LOKOMOTIV ASTANA
Coach – Sergei Yuran (RUS)
Founded – 2009
Stadium – Astana Arena (30,000)

2009

7/3	Kazakhmys	a	4-3	Shatskykh 2, Abdulin, Khasenov
14/3	Kaisar	a	4-0	Tikhonov 2 (1p), Khasenov, Titov
21/3	Kyzylzhar	h	1-0	Tikhonov (p)
6/4	Atyrau	h	2-1	Tikhonov 2 (1p)
12/4	Irtysh	a	1-0	Kukeev
19/4	Tobol	h	4-0	Tikhonov (p), Suyumagambetov, Kukeev, Karpovich
30/4	Taraz	a	2-1	Avdeev, Tikhonov
10/5	Shakhter	h	1-2	Beysebekov
16/5	Ordabasy	a	0-1	
24/5	Zhetysu	h	1-0	Tikhonov
15/6	Vostok	a	2-1	Dautov, Sakhalbayev
19/6	Aktobe	h	0-2	
28/6	Okzhetpes	h	2-1	og (Nurgaliyev), Tikhonov (p)
13/7	Okzhetpes	a	5-1	Kukeev, Tikhonov 2, Karpovich, Shatskikh
26/7	Vostok	h	3-2	Shatskikh 2, Titov
2/8	Zhetysu	a	0-1	
8/8	Ordabasy	h	3-1	Muminov, Shakhmetov, Ashirbekov
16/8	Shakhter	a	2-4	Shatskikh, Tikhonov
23/8	Taraz	h	4-1	Titov, Pakholyuk 2, Ovie
30/8	Tobol	a	0-1	
14/9	Irtysh	h	2-0	Muminov, Shatskikh
20/9	Atyrau	a	2-1	Titov 2
25/9	Aktobe	a	1-0	Shatskikh
29/9	Kyzylzhar	a	2-0	Kukeev, Muminov
25/10	Kaisar	h	3-0	Pakholyuk, Shatskikh 2
2/11	Kazakhmys	h	3-0	Shatskikh, Ashirbekov, Titov

No	Name	Nat	DoB	Pos	Aps	(s)	Gls
19	Renat ABDULIN		14/4/82	D	14	(3)	1
77	Talgat ADYRBEKOV		26/1/89	A		(3)	
8	Kayrat ASHIRBEKOV		21/10/81	M	6	(5)	2
5	Igor AVDEEV		10/1/73	D	8	(2)	1
2	Maksat BAYZHANOV		6/8/84	M	8	(11)	
40	Abzal BEYSEBEKOV		30/11/92	A	4	(5)	1
55	Damir DAUTOV		3/3/90	D	16	(3)	1
20	Andrei KARPOVICH		18/1/81	M	23		2
10	Daniyar KHASENOV		1/8/76	A	3	(1)	2
	Zakhar KOROBOV		15/5/88	D	3		
21	Zhambyl KUKEEV		20/9/88	M	18	(3)	4
14	Sergei LARIN		22/7/86	M		(1)	
	David LORIA		31/10/81	G	12		
12	Marko MITROVIĆ	SRB	8/7/78	M	15	(4)	
80	Madiyar MUMINOV		18/10/80	M	11	(2)	3
32	Roman NESTERENKO		22/3/77	G	14	(1)	
	Patrick OVIE	NGA	2/6/78	D	16	(1)	1
37	Roman PAKHOLYUK		3/10/79	M	13	(3)	3
7	Ruslan SAKHALBAYEV		27/6/84	M	1	(17)	1
70	Maxim SAMCHENKO		5/5/79	D	18		
6	Marat SHAKHMETOV		30/8/78	M	12	(1)	1
16	Maksim SHATSKIKH	UZB	30/8/78	A	15		9
15	Aleksandr SHATSKYKH		21/1/74	A	2		2

FC OKZHETPES KOKSHETAU
Coach – Eduard Glazunov; (23/8/09) Valeriy Shapovalov
Founded – 1968
Stadium – Torpedo (6,000)

2009

7/3	Kyzylzhar	h	0-0	
14/3	Tobol	h	1-1	Chonkayev
21/3	Atyrau	a	0-2	
6/4	Shakhter	a	0-2	
12/4	Zhetysu	h	1-0	Osipenco (p)
19/4	Aktobe	a	2-1	Dosmagambetov 2
30/4	Kazakhmys	h	3-1	Malkov, Dosmanbetov, Chudinov
10/5	Kaisar	a	1-2	Dosmagambetov
16/5	Irtysh	h	1-4	Aliyev
24/5	Taraz	a	1-0	Dosmanbetov
15/6	Ordabasy	a	0-4	
19/6	Vostok	a	0-1	
28/6	Lokomotiv	a	1-2	Krutskevich
13/7	Lokomotiv	h	1-5	Malkov (p)
19/7	Vostok	h	1-0	Dosmanbetov (p)
24/7	Ordabasy	h	2-2	Krutskevich
2/8	Taraz	h	2-2	Dosmagambetov, Malkov
9/8	Irtysh	a	0-1	
16/8	Kaisar	h	0-1	
23/8	Kazakhmys	a	4-1	Karakulov 2 (2p), Malkov, Chonkayev
31/8	Aktobe	h	1-7	Malkov
14/9	Zhetysu	a	0-1	
20/9	Shakhter	h	0-5	
27/9	Atyrau	h	0-1	
25/10	Tobol	a	1-2	Sabalakov
2/11	Kyzylzhar	a	0-0	

No	Name	Nat	DoB	Pos	Aps	(s)	Gls
17	Kanat ALIYEV		2/9/85	M	20	(3)	1
	Aslanmurad AMANOV		28/3/91	D	1		
25	Yerlen BEKMUKHAYEV		25/2/85	M	13	(5)	
20	Gakharman CHONKAYEV	TKM	19/10/83	A	10	(11)	2
32	Maxim CHUDINOV		12/9/88	M	18	(2)	1
2	Serghey CUZNETSOV	MDA	20/8/74	D	20	(1)	
23	Timur DOSMAGAMBETOV		1/5/89	M	21	(2)	4
10	Serik DOSMANBETOV		3/3/82	A	21	(4)	3
5	Yuri DYAK		4/7/84	M	11	(1)	
21	Bahyt GAYNULIN		27/9/86	D	7	(2)	
24	Rasim GUSEYNOV		21/4/83	A	1	(5)	
7	Kuanysh KARAKULOV		20/6/77	M	19	(4)	2
12	Kirill KEKER		22/6/79	D	8	(3)	
18	Oleg KHAN		27/8/86	M		(2)	
26	Olexandr KRUTSKEVICH	UKR	13/11/80	D	14		2
22	Denis LEDENEV		22/12/87	A	1	(3)	
16	Konstantin LEDOVSKIKH	RUS	12/7/72	G	5		
15	Anatoliy MALKOV	RUS	8/7/81	A	18		5
6	Nurbolat MAYMAKOV		27/4/82	A	1	(5)	
9	Yuri MOKROUSOV		21/4/89	M	14	(2)	
13	Yuri NURGALIYEV		8/8/86	M	16	(3)	
30	Nursultan NURZHIGIT		3/8/89	A	1	(1)	
8	Iurie OSIPENCO	MDA	6/7/74	M	8	(3)	1
3	Pavel PISCHULIN		23/11/78	D	9	(4)	
11	Talgat SABALAKOV		9/7/86	A	8	(5)	1

52	Yevgeniy SAMOKHIN		3/9/90	A		(3)
77	Arslan SATYBALDIN		14/8/84	G	18	(1)
1	Ivan SIVOZHELEZOV		12/3/85	G	3	
42	Zhadyger TYCHTYBAYEV		24/10/88	M		(1)
40	Aleksandr ULCHYIN		15/10/92	M		(1)

FC ORDABASY SHYMKENT
Coach – Vladimir Nikitenko
Founded – 1998
Stadium – Kazhimukan (17,000)

2009

7/3	Tobol	h	1-1	Parkhachev
14/3	Zhetysu	h	0-0	
6/4	Aktobe	a	0-1	
12/4	Kazakhmys	h	1-2	Parkhachev
19/4	Kaisar	a	1-1	Nuserbayev (p)
30/4	Irtysh	h	2-0	Nuserbayev 2
10/5	Taraz	a	5-0	Buleshev 2, Uchurov, Zhantleyov, Nuserbayev
16/5	Lokomotiv	h	1-0	Mukhtarov
24/5	Vostok	h	1-1	Parkhachev
15/6	Okzhetpes	h	4-0	Parkhachev, Zhantleyov 2, Shkred
19/6	Kyzylzhar	h	1-0	Mukhtarov
28/6	Atyrau	a	0-0	
3/7	Shakhter	a	0-3	
12/7	Atyrau	h	1-3	Mizigurskis
19/7	Kyzylzhar	a	1-0	Suyumagambetov
24/7	Okzhetpes	a	2-1	Parkhachev, Mizigurskis
2/8	Vostok	a	0-1	
8/8	Lokomotiv	a	1-3	Nuserbayev
16/8	Taraz	h	1-4	Suyumagambetov (p)
23/8	Irtysh	a	2-1	Parkhachev 2
31/8	Kaisar	h	2-0	Zhikrizov, Kozulin
14/9	Kazakhmys	a	4-1	Nuserbayev 2, Parkhachev 2
21/9	Aktobe	h	1-2	Zhikrizov
27/9	Shakhter	h	0-2	
25/10	Zhetysu	a	1-1	Suyumagambetov
2/11	Tobol	a	0-2	

No	Name	Nat	DoB	Pos	Aps	(s)	Gls
21	Zhandos AMETOV		8/2/80	M	10	(6)	
18	Maxim AZOVSKI		4/6/86	A		(4)	
8	Bekzat BEYSENOV		18/2/88	M	5	(9)	
10	Alibek BULESHEV		9/4/81	A	3	(3)	2
20	Dauren KENZHEBEK		14/3/88	D	24	(1)	
2	Sergei KOZULIN		2/8/80	D	23		1
3	Aleksandr KUCHMA		9/12/80	D	25		
44	Yevgeniy LEVIN		12/7/92	A	1	(5)	
9	Valerijus MIZIGURSKIS	LTU	22/4/83	M	3	(5)	2
1	Aleksandr MOKIN		19/6/81	G	26		
4	Mukhtar MUKHTAROV		6/1/86	D	18	(1)	2
7	Tanat NUSERBAYEV		1/1/88	A	15	(5)	7
11	Dmitriy PARKHACHEV	BLR	2/1/85	M	24	(1)	9
5	Dmitriy PROTORCHIN		2/7/78	D	10		
9	Andrei SALNIKOV	RUS	13/3/82	A	7	(2)	
15	Azamat SEYTBEKOV		22/11/88	D		(1)	
14	Oleh SHKRED	UKR	1/10/82	M	20	(5)	1
10	Murat SUYUMAGAMBETOV		14/10/83	A	13	(1)	3
13	Eduard UCHUROV	RUS	20/12/79	M	16	(3)	1
27	Abzal YESHMANOV		5/2/90	M	2	(6)	
6	Vladimir ZELENBABA	CRO	6/2/82	M	16	(6)	
17	Malik ZHANTLEYOV		2/2/89	M	23	(3)	3
42	Yevgeniy ZHIKRIZOV		30/7/90	A	2	(5)	2
22	Nursayun ZHOLDASOV		11/5/91	M	(2)		

FC SHAKHTER KARAGANDY
Coach – Vladimir Cheburin
Founded – 1958
Stadium – Shakhter (19,500)

2009

7/3	Taraz	a	0-1	
14/3	Vostok	a	3-1	Darabaev, Perić, Shaff
6/4	Okzhetpes	h	2-0	Kostyuk, Perić
12/4	Kyzylzhar	a	1-0	Shaff
19/4	Atyrau	a	0-2	
30/4	Tobol	a	0-0	
10/5	Lokomotiv	a	2-1	Darabaev, Mangutkin
16/5	Zhetysu	h	1-0	Danaev
24/5	Aktobe	a	1-2	og (Chichulin)
14/6	Kazakhmys	h	3-1	Kenetaev, Kostyuk, Lunev
19/6	Kaisar	a	3-0	Kostyuk 2, Shaff
27/6	Irtysh	h	1-0	Đorđević
3/7	Ordabasy	h	3-0	Kostyuk 2 (1p), Shaff
13/7	Irtysh	a	1-1	Shaff
19/7	Kaisar	h	2-0	Shaff, Kostyuk
26/7	Kazakhmys	a	5-1	Perić 2, Finonchenko 2, Kostyuk
8/8	Zhetysu	a	0-1	
16/8	Lokomotiv	h	4-2	Bogdanov, Finonchenko, Kostyuk (p), Shevchenko
23/8	Tobol	h	1-1	Kenetaev
30/8	Atyrau	h	2-0	Kostyuk, Perić
14/9	Kyzylzhar	h	2-1	Perić, Mangutkin
20/9	Okzhetpes	a	5-0	Perić 3, Kostyuk, Kislitsyn
27/9	Ordabasy	a	2-0	Perić, Shaff
22/10	Aktobe	h	0-3	
26/10	Vostok	h	5-0	Đorđević, Finonchenko 2, Mangutkin, Glushko
2/11	Taraz	h	1-0	Darabaev

No	Name	Nat	DoB	Pos	Aps	(s)	Gls
23	Vitaliy ARTEMOV		16/2/79	D		(1)	
15	Anatoly BOGDANOV		7/8/81	A	26		1
4	Alexei DANAEV		1/9/79	D	23		1
36	Aslan DARABAEV		21/1/89	M	23	(3)	3
2	Saša ĐORĐEVIĆ	SRB	4/8/81	D	25		2
14	Andrei FINONCHENKO		21/6/82	A	13	(4)	5
19	Mikhail GLUSHKO		3/1/84	M	13	(2)	1
20	Samson GODWIN	NGA	11/11/83	A	1	(1)	
1	Aleksandr GRIGORENKO		6/2/85	G	24		
7	Ruslan KENETAEV		21/3/88	M	9	(10)	2
5	Aleksandr KISLITSYN		8/3/86	D	21	(3)	1
8	Sergei KOSTYUK		30/11/78	M	23	(2)	11
	Zhasylan KUSAINOV		23/12/89	M		(2)	
9	Yevgeny LUNEV		26/4/76	M	2	(11)	1
6	Ilnur MANGUTKIN		16/9/86	M	12	(9)	3
20	Nikolay PENGRIN		7/8/84	A		(1)	
55	Ivan PERIĆ	SRB	9/5/82	A	20	(5)	10
	Igor PIKALKIN		19/3/92	M		(3)	
16	Sergei SARANA		7/12/78	G	2		
10	Sergei SHAFF		15/4/88	A	20	(4)	7
30	Ivan SHEVCHENKO		10/9/87	D	12	(6)	1
3	Igor SOLOSHENKO		22/5/79	D	1	(2)	
29	Yevgeny TARASOV		16/4/85	D	16		

FC TARAZ
Coach – Vladimir Fomichev
Founded – 1961
Stadium – Taraz Centralny (12,000)
MAJOR HONOURS:
Kazakhstan League - (1) 1996; Kazakhstan Cup - (1) 2004.

2009

7/3	Shakhter	h	1-0	Nedashkovsky	
14/3	Aktobe	h	1-3	og (Ostapenko)	
6/4	Kazakhmys	a	0-1		
12/4	Kaisar	h	2-1	Yevstigneev V., Nedashkovsky	
19/4	Irtysh	a	0-0		
30/4	Lokomotiv	h	1-2	Bagayev	
10/5	Ordabasy	h	0-5		
16/5	Vostok	a	2-0	Kurgulin, Konysbayev	
24/5	Okzhetpes	h	0-1		
15/6	Kyzylzhar	a	2-1	Nedashkovsky, Iepureanu	
19/6	Atyrau	h	1-1	Ilin	
27/6	Tobol	a	1-4	Konysbayev	
3/7	Zhetysu	a	0-1		
9/7	Tobol	h	0-1		
19/7	Atyrau	a	1-1	Iepureanu	
26/7	Kyzylzhar	h	5-0	Essomba 3, Nedashkovsky, Konysbayev	
2/8	Okzhetpes	a	2-2	Yevstigneev V. (p), Essomba	
8/8	Vostok	h	2-2	Iepureanu 2	
16/8	Ordabasy	a	4-1	Iepureanu 2, Essomba, Yevstigneev V.	
23/8	Lokomotiv	a	1-4	Anarmetov	
31/8	Irtysh	h	1-1	Iepureanu (p)	
14/9	Kaisar	a	2-0	Baytana, Yevstigneev V.	
20/9	Kazakhmys	h	5-0	Nedashkovsky, Baytana, Yevstigneev V., Bagayev, Konysbayev	
27/9	Zhetysu	h	2-1	Essomba, Anarmetov	
25/10	Aktobe	a	1-2	Yevstigneev D.	
2/11	Shakhter	a	0-1		

No	Name	Nat	DoB	Pos	Aps	(s)	Gls
23	Galymzhan ALIMBAEV		9/5/89	M	5	(5)	
20	Maksat AMIRKHANOV		10/2/92	D		(1)	
22	Aziz ANARMETOV		30/7/82	M	22	(3)	2
9	Aleksandr BAGAYEV	RUS	17/4/85	A	9	(11)	2
18	Aziz BAYSHAKOV		30/7/85	A		(1)	
30	Baurzhan BAYTANA		6/6/92	M	4	(4)	2
12	David DAVIDSON	GHA	17/10/86	M	1	(5)	
11	Martin DIMITROV	BUL	6/12/80	A	5	(3)	
50	Titi ESSOMBA	CMR	18/8/87	A	14		6
4	Ilya FOMICHEV		14/8/82	D	24		
25	Serghei IEPUREANU	MDA	12/9/76	M	25		7
24	Ilya ILIN	UZB	29/9/85	D	22	(2)	1
38	Bakhyt IMANMUSAYEV		14/10/88	D		(1)	
13	Rustam ISLAMOV		5/3/91	M		(4)	
2	Alik KHAYDAROV		27/4/81	D	17	(4)	
7	Turarkhan KONYSBAYEV		28/5/89	A	23	(3)	4
5	Nurtas KURGULIN		20/9/86	D	12	(5)	1
12	Sergei LOBADOVSKY		14/1/82	A	1	(2)	
20	Murat MUKASHEV		18/9/82	G	26		
17	Oleg NEDASHKOVSKY		9/9/87	M	21	(1)	5
10	Kayrat SULEY		26/10/85	A		(2)	
14	Vaid TALGAEV		21/12/90	M	12	(6)	
11	Irakli TSIKOLIA	UKR	26/5/87	M	12	(1)	
19	Dmitriy YEVSTIGNEEV		27/11/86	D	9	(5)	1
8	Vitaliy YEVSTIGNEEV		8/8/85	M	14	(1)	5
6	Amangeldy ZHUSUPOV		18/7/88	D	8	(5)	

FC TOBOL KOSTANAY
Coach – Dmitriy Ogai
Founded – 1967
Stadium – Kostanay Centralny (5,720)
MAJOR HONOURS:
Kazakhstan Cup - (1) 2007.

2009

7/3	Ordabasy	a	1-1	Nurdauletov	
14/3	Okzhetpes	a	1-1	Skorykh	
21/3	Vostok	a	2-1	Bayramov, Romanov	
6/4	Kyzylzhar	h	3-0	Bayramov, Chilikov, Golban	
12/4	Atyrau	a	2-2	Skorykh, Bayramov	
19/4	Lokomotiv	a	0-4		
30/4	Shakhter	h	0-0		
10/5	Zhetysu	a	0-1		
16/5	Aktobe	h	0-0		
24/5	Kazakhmys	a	1-0	Bayramov	
15/6	Kaisar	h	3-0	Bayramov 2, Kharabara	
19/6	Irtysh	a	2-1	Serdyukov, Zhumaskaliyev	
27/6	Taraz	h	4-1	Bayramov 2, Zhumaskaliyev, Kharabara	
9/7	Taraz	a	1-0	Bayramov	
28/7	Kaisar	a	1-1	Bayramov	
31/7	Kazakhmys	h	5-0	Lotov, Kharabara 2, Zhumaskaliyev, Alekperzade	
4/8	Irtysh	h	1-1	Bayramov	
16/8	Zhetysu	h	6-0	Bayramov 3, Nurgaliev, Skorykh, Zhumaskaliyev	
23/8	Shakhter	a	1-1	Skorykh	
30/8	Lokomotiv	h	1-0	Zhumaskaliyev	
14/9	Atyrau	h	0-0		
20/9	Kyzylzhar	a	7-0	Skorykh, Zhumaskaliyev 2, Nurgaliev 2, Bayramov 2	
27/9	Vostok	h	6-2	Zhumaskaliyev, Bayramov 2, Ibraev, Nurgaliev, Baltiyev (p)	
25/10	Okzhetpes	a	2-1	Baltiyev 2	
29/10	Aktobe	a	2-5	Bayramov, Baltiyev	
2/11	Ordabasy	h	2-0	Bayramov (p), Nurgaliev	

No	Name	Nat	DoB	Pos	Aps	(s)	Gls
20	Geysar ALEKPERZADE		2/12/84	A	1	(7)	1
11	Azamat AUBAKIROV		10/11/87	M		(8)	
1	Yaroslav BAGINSKY		3/10/87	G	8	(1)	
25	Ruslan BALTIYEV		16/9/78	M	17	(3)	4
32	Vladimir BAYRAMOV	RUS	2/8/80	A	19	(3)	20
2	Artem CHELYADINSKIY	BLR	29/12/77	D	10		
19	Georgi CHILIKOV	BUL	23/8/78	A	7	(2)	1
3	Stanimir DIMITROV	BUL	24/4/72	M	9		
23	Alexandru GOLBAN	MDA	28/2/79	A	4	(13)	1
22	Sabyrkhan IBRAEV		22/3/88	M	16	(7)	1
14	Farhadbek IRISMETOV		10/8/81	D	18	(4)	
13	Andrei KHARABARA		1/9/85	M	12	(9)	4
15	Oleg LOTOV		21/11/75	D	2		1
18	Daniyar MUKANOV		26/9/76	D	13	(3)	
5	Kayrat NURDAULETOV		6/11/82	M	15		1
7	Azat NURGALIEV		30/6/86	M	19	(4)	5
35	Aleksandr PETUKHOV		11/1/85	G	18	(1)	
8	Yevgeny ROMANOV		14/3/90	M	4	(3)	1
6	Vyacheslav SERDYUKOV		16/8/89	A	9	(5)	1
4	Aleksandr SHKOT		15/5/89	D	23	(1)	
10	Sergei SKORYKH		25/5/84	M	23		5
17	Vladimir YAKOVLEV		2/8/84	M	16	(1)	
9	Nurbolat ZHUMASKALIYEV		11/5/81	M	23	(1)	8

KAZAKHSTAN

FC VOSTOK

Coach – Andrey Miroshnichenko; (30/4/09) Pavel Yevteev;
(12/7/09) Oyrat Saduov
Founded – 1963
Stadium – Vostok (8,500)
MAJOR HONOURS:
Kazakhstan Cup - (1) 1994.

2009

7/3	Atyrau	h	2-2	Salhi, Khizhnichenko
14/3	Shakhter	h	1-3	Erbes
21/3	Tobol	h	1-2	Khizhnichenko
6/4	Zhetysu	a	2-2	Erbes, Gavrilenko
12/4	Aktobe	h	0-4	
19/4	Kazakhmys	a	2-3	Pastukhov, Salhi (p)
30/4	Kaisar	h	1-0	Salhi
10/5	Irtysh	a	1-1	Udalov
16/5	Taraz	h	0-2	
24/5	Ordabasy	a	1-1	Moltusinov
15/6	Lokomotiv	h	1-2	Moltusinov
19/6	Okzhetpes	h	1-0	Prosekov
26/6	Kyzylzhar	a	1-4	Kenzhekhanov
12/7	Kyzylzhar	h	3-1	Salhi 2 (1p), Erbes
19/7	Okzhetpes	a	0-1	
26/7	Lokomotiv	a	2-3	Rogaciov, Erbes
2/8	Ordabasy	h	1-0	Rogaciov
8/8	Taraz	a	2-2	Salhi, Rogaciov
16/8	Irtysh	h	1-3	Khizhnichenko
23/8	Kaisar	a	2-0	Khizhnichenko, Rogaciov
30/8	Kazakhmys	h	2-1	Rogaciov, Salhi
14/9	Aktobe	a	0-4	
22/9	Zhetysu	h	1-0	Khizhnichenko
27/9	Tobol	a	2-6	Salhi, Kenzhekhanov
26/10	Shakhter	a	0-5	
2/11	Atyrau	a	2-4	Rogaciov, Khizhnichenko

No	Name	Nat	DoB	Pos	Aps	(s)	Gls
77	Dauren AITKAZINOV		13/5/86	A		(1)	
16	Dmitriy DRALOV		22/6/84	G	3		
88	Yerkin EDIGENOV		20/7/88	M	2		
4	Vyacheslav ERBES		14/1/88	M	25		4
36	Mikhail GABYCHEV		2/1/90	D	4	(1)	
25	Artem GAVRILENKO		26/3/84	D	4	(1)	1
3	Zviad JELADZE	GEO	16/12/73	D	9		
9	Daniyar KENZHEKHANOV		20/1/83	A	4	(10)	2
91	Sergei KHIZHNICHENKO		17/7/91	A	16	(8)	6
88	Roman KISMETOV		17/6/87	M	7	(3)	
8	Anton MOLTUSINOV		18/5/88	M	17	(3)	2
85	Serghei NAMASCO	MDA	19/6/84	M	11	(6)	
	Aslan OMARBEKOV		2/7/90	M		(1)	
22	Igor OSIPCHUK		2/8/75	G	13	(1)	
83	Valeriy PASTUKHOV		17/12/83	M	2	(6)	1
5	Vasiliy PROSEKOV		31/10/83	A	5	(6)	1
83	Denis PROSKURIN		3/4/79	D	4		
12	Serghei ROGACIOV	MDA	20/5/77	A	12	(1)	6
13	Oleg SABIROV		13/3/81	D	23	(1)	
23	Toafik SALHI	TUN	21/8/79	M	24	(1)	8
27	Dmitriy SLASTNIKOV		25/7/89	M		(1)	
84	Vitaliy TIKHONOV	RUS	31/1/84	D	17	(1)	
12	Serhiy TSGURA	UKR	3/11/77	M	12		
16	Yuriy TSYGALKO	BLR	27/5/83	G	10		
10	Pavel UDALOV		25/1/83	A	10	(6)	1
3	Vitaliy USHAKOV		12/9/74	M	10		
32	Darkhan YUSUPOV		10/1/87	M		(1)	
17	Serik ZHEYLITBAYEV		23/8/74	M	20	(1)	
	Sanat ZHUMAKHANOV		30/1/87	A	6	(4)	
20	Maxim ZUEV		27/4/83	D	16	(1)	

FC ZHETYSU TALDYKORGAN

Coach – Voit Talgayev
Founded – 1981
Stadium – Zhetysu (4,000)

2009

7/3	Irtysh	a	2-0	Belić, Kenbaev
14/3	Ordabasy	a	0-0	
6/4	Vostok	h	2-2	Belić 2 (1p)
12/4	Okzhetpes	a	0-1	
19/4	Kyzylzhar	h	4-0	Belić 3 (1p), Mamonov
30/4	Atyrau	a	2-0	Daskalov, Mamonov
10/5	Tobol	h	1-0	Daskalov
16/5	Shakhter	a	0-1	
24/5	Lokomotiv	a	0-1	
15/6	Aktobe	h	0-2	
19/6	Kazakhmys	a	2-2	Zhalmagambetov, Tintor
28/6	Kaisar	h	0-1	
3/7	Taraz	h	1-0	Mamonov
12/7	Kaisar	a	3-2	Stanišić, Chelidze 2
19/7	Kazakhmys	h	2-1	Belić, Azovski Y.
2/8	Lokomotiv	h	1-0	Azovski M.
8/8	Shakhter	h	1-0	Belić
16/8	Tobol	a	0-6	
23/8	Atyrau	h	2-1	Belić, Stanišić
31/8	Kyzylzhar	a	4-1	Belić 2, Stanišić, Mamonov
14/9	Okzhetpes	h	1-0	Belić
22/9	Vostok	a	0-1	
27/9	Taraz	a	1-2	Kumisbekov
3/10	Aktobe	a	1-1	Rodionov
25/10	Ordabasy	h	1-1	Belić
2/11	Irtysh	h	2-0	Belić, og (Rimavičius)

No	Name	Nat	DoB	Pos	Aps	(s)	Gls
88	Kuanysch ABDUALIEV		4/11/88	M	3	(1)	
55	Piraly ALIYEV		13/1/84	D		(1)	
7	Maxim AZOVSKI		4/6/86	A	9	(2)	1
15	Yegor AZOVSKI		10/1/85	M	22	(2)	1
20	Ruslan BARZUKAYEV		5/12/87	M	1		
13	Danilo BELIĆ	SRB	10/11/80	A	23	(1)	14
27	Vladimir BERIKBAEV		27/2/88	D	13	(1)	
23	Siniša BRANKOVIĆ	SRB	30/1/79	M	22	(1)	
21	Alexei BULUCHEVSKIY		8/8/87	G	(1)		
5	Lasha CHELIDZE	GEO	13/3/85	D	16		2
33	Serghei GRIDIN		20/5/87	A	(3)		
19	Georgi DASKALOV	BUL	3/8/81	A	11		2
10	Yerzat KENBAEV		24/4/88	A	5	(12)	1
55	Zakhar KOROBOV		18/5/88	D	12	(2)	
24	Viktor KOVALEV		25/8/80	D	17		
2	Aydar KUMISBEKOV		9/2/79	D	19	(2)	1
8	Dmitriy MAMONOV		26/4/78	M	21	(4)	4
25	Ruslan MUKHAMEDZHANOV		25/1/89	A	(3)		
32	Serikzhan MUZHIKOV		17/6/89	D	21	(3)	
1	Kirill PRYADKIN		6/7/77	G	19	(1)	
19	Denis RODIONOV		26/7/85	M	7	(1)	1
11	Andrei SALNIKOV	RUS	13/3/82	A	3	(6)	
6	Petar STANIŠIĆ	SRB	23/9/84	D	22	(1)	3
25	Vladimir TINTOR	SRB	1/9/79	M	1	(3)	1
9	Andrei TRAVIN		27/4/79	M	13	(3)	
16	Ilya YUROV		10/9/81	G	7	(2)	
3	Maxim ZABELIN		4/2/77	D	5	(3)	
4	Maxim ZHALMAGAMBETOV		11/7/83	D	4	(4)	1

PROMOTED CLUBS

FC KAIRAT ALMATY

Coach – Sergei Volgin
Founded – 1954
Stadium – Almaty Centralny (25,057)
MAJOR HONOURS:
Kazakhstan League - (2) 1992, 2004;
Kazakhstan Cup - (5) 1992, 1996, 2000, 2001 (autumn), 2003.

FC AKZHAIYK URALSK

Coach – Viktor Kablov
Founded – 1968
Stadium – Pyotr Atoyan (8,320)

SECOND LEVEL FINAL TABLES 2009

		Pld	W	D	L	F	A	Pts
1	FC Kairat Almaty	26	19	4	3	63	21	61
2	FC Akzhaiyk Uralsk	26	16	4	6	46	29	52
3	FC Namys Astana	26	16	3	7	57	27	51
4	FC Sunkar Kaskelen	26	15	6	5	49	23	51
5	FC Ilie-Saupet Almatinskaya oblast	26	12	9	5	53	24	45
6	FC Bolat-AMT Temirtau	26	11	6	9	36	37	39
7	FC Spartak Semey	26	12	2	12	35	41	38
8	FC Ekibastuz	26	10	5	11	37	43	35
9	FC Gefest Karagandy	26	8	5	13	26	34	29
10	FC Kaspiy Aktau	26	5	8	13	26	40	23
11	FC Aktobe-Jas	26	5	5	16	25	42	20
12	OSSHIOSD Taraz	26	5	11	10	31	56	19
13	FC Ayiarik Shymkent	26	7	3	16	36	62	18
14	FC Turkestan	26	5	1	20	25	66	7

NB FC Ayiarik Shymkent withdrew after round 18. FC Turkestan withdrew after round 23. Their remaining matches were awarded as 0-3 defeats.

FC Turkestan – 9 pts deducted; OSSHIOSD Taraz – 7 pts deducted; FC Ayiarik Shymkent – 6 pts deducted.

PROMOTION/RELEGATION PLAY-OFF

(8/11/09)
Okzhetpes 2, Akzhaiyk 3

N.B. Okzhetpes subsequently remained at first level as Vostok withdrew from 2010 Superleague.

DOMESTIC CUP 2009

KUBOK KAZAKHSTANA

FIRST ROUND

(4/4/09)
Shakhter Karagandy 3, Ekibastuz 1

(5/4/09)
Aktobe-Jas 0, Kaisar 3
Akzhaiyk 2, Atyrau 3
Ayiarik 1, Zhetysu 2

Bolat-AMT 0, Kazakhmys 5
Gefest 0, Lokomotiv Astana 2
Ilie-Saulet 0, Vostok 2
Kairat 0, Kyzylzhar 1
Kaspiy 1, Aktobe 5
Namys 0, Okzhetpes 0 *(aet; 4-5 on pens)*
OSSHIOSD 1, Ordabasy 2
Spartak 1, Irtysh 4
Sunkar 0, Tobol 1
Turkestan 0, Taraz 4

SECOND ROUND

20/5/09 & 23/6/09)
Aktobe v Lokomotiv Astana 1-0; 1-2 *(2-2; Aktobe on away goal)*
Irtysh v Ordabasy 3-0; 0-1 *(3-1)*
Kazakhmys v Kaisar 1-3; 0-2 *(1-5)*
Shakhter Karagandy v Okzhetpes 4-1; 5-1 *(9-2)*
Taraz v Tobol 1-1; 2-2 *(3-3; Taraz on away goals)*
Vostok v Kyzylzhar 0-1; 4-1 *(4-2)*

Byes – Zhetysu & Atyrau

QUARTER-FINALS

(27/8/09 & 18/10/09)
Irtysh 1 *(Daskalov 36p)*, Shakhter Karagandy 1 *(Kolomyts 45og)*
Shakhter Karagandy 3 *(Perić 55, Mangutkin 81, Finonchenko 83)*, Irtysh 0
(Shakhter Karagandy 4-1)

Taraz 0, Zhetysu 1 *(Korobov 51)*
Zhetysu 1 *(Belić 36)*, Taraz 0
(Zhetysu 2-0)

(17/9/09 & 18/10/09)
Aktobe 2 *(Khairullin 56, Strukov 82)*, Vostok 1 *(Erbes 16)*
Vostok 0, Aktobe 4 *(Kenzhesariev 21, Golovskoy 45, Khairullin 70, Tleshev 89)*
(Aktobe 6-1)

(3/10/09 & 18/10/09)
Kaisar 0, Atyrau 1 *(Tatishev 11)*
Atyrau 4 *(Shumeyko 11, Tatishev 24, 45, Shakin 88)*, Kaisar 0
(Atyrau 5-0)

SEMI-FINALS

(7/11/09 & 11/11/09)
Aktobe 1 *(Tleshev 13)*, Shakhter Karagandy 0
Shakhter Karagandy 2 *(Finonchenko 46, Shaff 115)*, Aktobe 0 *(aet)*
(Shakhter Karagandy 2-1)

Zhetysu 0, Atyrau 2 *(Shumeyko 49, Kostrub 86)*
Atyrau 2 *(Zubko 79, Zholchiev 83)*, Zhetysu 1 *(Kenbaev 71)*
(Atyrau 4-1)

FINAL

(15/11/09)
Astana Arena, Astana
FC ATYRAU 1 *(Zubko 34)*
FC SHAKHTER KARAGANDY 0
Referee – Rakhimbayev
ATYRAU – Shabanov, Aliyev, Vorotnikov, Shumeyko, Kirov *(Sangaré 78)*, Kostrub, Zununov, Peikrishvili, Larin, Zholchiev *(Abdramanov 87)*, Zubko *(Shakin 72)*.
SHAKHTER KARAGANDY – Grigorenko, Đorđević, Kislitsyn, Mangutkin *(Tarasov 17)*, Shevchenko, Kostyuk, Bogdanov, Finonchenko, Kenetaev *(Shaff 68)*, Darabaev, Perić *(Glushko 56)*.

Dethroned champions prosper in Europe

FK Ventspils' three-year monopoly of the Virsliga title came to an end as they surrendered their crown to western rivals SK Liepājas Metalurgs, but there was more than adequate consolation for the deposed champions as they flew the flag for Latvia in Europe by reaching the group stage of the UEFA Europa League.

No Latvian club had ever previously extended their European participation until December, and although Ventspils failed to win any of their six group matches, they did the country proud by claiming impressive away draws against Hertha BSC Berlin and Sporting Clube de Portugal and were competitive in every game until the last one away to sc Heerenveen, when fatigue finally took its toll at the end of a long season and they were comprehensively beaten 5-0.

Access to the secondary European competition had come after Ventspils reached the UEFA Champions League play-off round thanks to an unlikely away-goals success over FC BATE Borisov of Belarus – group stage participants only a year previously. The team had been led to that victory by their long-standing and successful Ukrainian coach Roman Grigorchuk, but in a shock move the man who had led Ventspils to each of their three successive Virsliga triumphs was replaced

before the play-off round against FC Zürich by little-known Italian Nunzio Zavettieri, a former youth coach at Udinese Calcio and FC Internazionale Milano.

Metalurgs triumph

Zavettieri was unable to make it four straight domestic titles for Ventspils although, in his defence, the extra workload and travel required in Europe was a contributory factor. A 2-0 home defeat to Skonto FC at the end of October effectively handed the title to Liepājas Metalurgs, who thus held a five-point lead with two games remaining. Ventspils' next fixture was away to the leaders, and although they still had a mathematical chance of retaining the title – their final fixture guaranteed them three points as a walkover after the mid-season exclusion from the league of FC Dinaburg for alleged match-fixing - Zavettieri, with one eye on Europe and a high-profile trip to Lisbon to face Sporting, fielded a weakened team. The match ended 1-1 and Liepājas Metalurgs, thanks to an equalising penalty from their top scorer, Kristaps Grebis, duly sealed their second league title.

The Virsliga victory – the second for the club after their maiden triumph in 2005 - was a splendid achievement for coach Rüdiger Abramczik at the end of his first full season in charge. Although the former West Germany striker orchestrated an impressive team effort, with Liepājas Metalurgs winning 25 of their 32 matches and losing just three, the goals of Grebis were vital. The 28-year-old Latvian international registered 30 times in 28 starts to win the league's Golden Boot by a landslide, with the holder of the trophy for each of the previous two seasons, Ventspils veteran Vīts Rimkus, trailing 13 goals behind him in second place.

Liepājas Metalurgs coach Rüdiger Abramczik gets his hands on the Virsliga trophy

Latvijas Futbola Federācija (LFF)

Olympic Sports Centre
Grostonas Street 6b
LV-1013 Rīga
Tel – +371 67 292988
Fax – +371 67 315604
website – lff.lv
email – futbols@lff.lv
Year of Formation – 1921

President – Guntis Indriksons
General Secretary – Jānis Mežeckis
Media Officer – Martins Hartmanis
National Stadium – Skonto, Riga (9,500)

INTERNATIONAL TOURNAMENT APPEARANCES
UEFA European Championship – (1) 2004.
TOP FIVE ALL-TIME CAPS
Vitālijs Astafjevs (162); Andrejs Rubins (108); Imants Bleidelis (106); Mihails Zemļinskis (105); Juris Laizāns (103)
TOP FIVE ALL-TIME GOALS
Māris Verpakovskis (26); Eriks Pétersons (24); Vitālijs Astafjevs (16); Juris Laizāns & Marians Pahars (15)

The champions scored 96 goals in total – an average of three per game – and that figure was matched by Skonto, who finished six points off the pace in third place. It was the fifth successive season that the former serial champions had failed to win a trophy. In charge throughout that barren run was English coach Paul Ashworth, who left at the end of the season, to be replaced by Aleksandrs Starkovs - the man who had overseen the majority of Skonto's world record-breaking run of 14 successive national titles from 1991-2004.

Starkovs was voted Latvia's Coach of the Year once again in 2009 after steering the Latvian national team to some impressive results in the 2010 FIFA World Cup qualifying campaign. Latvia finished third in their group and were firmly in contention for a place in the play-offs after beating Israel 1-0 in Tel-Aviv and holding Switzerland 2-2 in Riga during four memorable days in September. But all hopes of a second major tournament

appearance in six years were dashed in their next outing against Greece in Athens where, despite taking the lead with a couple of goals from Greece-based Māris Verpakovskis – a double that made the diminutive striker his country's all-time record scorer – Starkovs' men ultimately crashed to a 5-2 defeat.

Record breaker Astafjevs

Missing for that game was Latvia's veteran skipper Vitālijs Astafjevs, but he returned for the team's final qualifier, a 3-2 home win over Moldova, and a month later he was to create history by becoming Europe's most capped international footballer of all time, overtaking Estonia's Martin Reim, when he made his 158th appearance in a friendly in Honduras. By the following summer the 39-year-old was still active, stretching his haul to 162 with a couple of appearances at the Baltic Cup.

While Astafjevs was continuing to break records on the international stage, the domestic headlines in the spring of 2010 were written by FK Jelgava, who, having been promoted to the Virsliga as second-tier champions the previous autumn, celebrated their return to the top division by winning three successive penalty shoot-outs to lift the Latvian Cup. Previous winners of the trophy twice in the 1990s when they were known as RAF Jelgava, they saw off champions Liepājas Metalurgs in the quarter-finals thanks to a late extra-time equaliser and a 5-4 spot-kicks success, then overcame Skonto by the same method after a 1-1 draw. They lived even more precariously in the final, against fellow outsiders FK Jūrmala, falling behind twice. But a regulation penalty five minutes from time led to another examination of their nerve from 11 metres. Again Jelgava prevailed, with goalkeeper Marks Bogdanovs proving to be the hero of the hour with the decisive save from Jūrmala's Gatis Kalniņš after the spot-kick contest had gone to sudden-death.

NATIONAL TEAM RESULTS 2009/10

Date	Opponent		Venue	Score	Scorers
12/8/09	Bulgaria	A	Sofia	0-1	
5/9/09	Israel (WCQ)	A	Tel-Aviv	1-0	Gorkšs (59)
9/9/09	Switzerland (WCQ)	H	Riga	2-2	Cauņa (62), Astafjevs (75)
10/10/09	Greece (WCQ)	A	Athens	2-5	Verpakovskis (12, 40)
14/10/09	Moldova (WCQ)	H	Riga	3-2	Rubins (32, 44), Grebis (76)
14/11/09	Honduras	A	Tegucigalpa	1-2	Koļesničenko (45p)
22/1/10	South Korea	N	Malaga (ESP)	0-1	
3/3/10	Angola	A	Luanda	1-1	Karlsons (45)
5/6/10	Ghana	N	Milton Keynes (ENG)	0-1	
18/6/10	Lithuania	A	Kaunas	0-0	
19/6/10	Estonia	N	Kaunas (LTU)	0-0	

LATVIA

NATIONAL TEAM APPEARANCES 2009/10

Coach - Aleksandrs STARKOVS	26/7/55		Bul	ISR	SUI	GRE	MDA	Hon	Kor	Ang	Gha	Ltu	Est	Caps	Goals
Andris VAŅINS	30/4/80	Sion (SUI)	G	G	G	G	G	G	G46		G46			31	-
Oskars KĻAVA	8/8/83	Liepājas Metalurgs	D88	D	D	D	D			D	D	D	D	40	1
Deniss IVANOVS	11/1/84	Liepājas Metalurgs /Ajax Cape Town (RSA)	D	D	D	D	D	D			D	D	D	D	35	2
Pāvels MIHADJUKS	27/5/80	Ventspils /Dundee United (SCO)	D						D		D	D	D	D	6	-
Deniss KAČANOVS	27/11/79	Ventspils	D83	D	D	D	D	D	D						28	-
Jurijs ŽIGAJEVS	14/11/85	Ventspils	M61	s82				s77	s65	s69	s72	s65	M90	16	1
Vitālijs ASTAFJEVS	3/4/71	Ventspils /Skonto	M	M	M		M	M		M73	M80	M	s90	162	16
Vladimirs KOĻESNIČENKO	4/5/80	unattached /Skonto /Chornomorets (UKR)	M61	M	M86		M	M74	M90	M		s80		47	6
Aleksandrs CAUŅA	19/1/88	Skonto	M76	M82	M89	M	M							16	2
Andrejs RUBINS	26/11/78	İnter Bakı (AZE)	A	M82	M	M78	M63	A	M81	M82				108	10
Ģirts KARLSONS	7/6/81	İnter Bakı (AZE)	A66	A	A85	A71	A69	s62	s64	A				44	9
Genādijs SOLOŅICINS	3/1/80	Simurq (AZE) /Liepājas Metalurgs	s61			s78	s63	M79	M65	M69	M	M	s55	43	1
Maksims RAFAĻSKIS	14/5/84	Liepājas Metalurgs	s61		s86			M77			s46	M	M	6	-
Kristaps GREBIS	13/12/80	Liepājas Metalurgs	s66		s85	s71	s69	A62		A72	A	A		11	2
Kristaps BLANKS	30/1/86	Skonto	s76					s81	s65					21	-
Dzintars ZIRNIS	25/4/77	Liepājas Metalurgs	s83	s82	s89		D		D80	D				65	-
Ritus KRJAUKLIS	23/4/86	Dinaburg /Ventspils	s88					D	D	s82	s84	D	D	7	-
Kaspars GORKŠS	6/11/81	QPR (ENG)		D	D	D	D	D						30	2
Māris VERPAKOVSKIS	15/10/79	Ergotelis (GRE)		A92	A	A84	A							80	26
Andrejs PEREPĻOTKINS	27/12/84	Skonto		s92		s84		s90	A64	A65	M84	M75	M65	23	3
Juris LAIZĀNS	6/1/79	Ventspils /unattached /Skonto			M	s74			M		M46		M65	103	15
Aleksandrs FERTOVS	16/6/87	Skonto							s79	s70	s80				3	-
Jevgenijs KOSMAČOVS	18/2/88	Ventspils							M70					3	-
Artjoms RUDŅEVS	13/1/88	ZTE (HUN)							A64		A58			4	-
Aleksandrs KOĻINKO	18/6/75	Ventspils							s46		s46	G	G	86	-
Ivans LUKJANOVS	24/1/87	Lechia Gdańsk (POL)							s64					1	-
Deniss ROMANOVS	2/9/78	Slavia Praha (CZE)								G				3	-
Igors TARASOVS	16/1/88	Skonto								s73				1	-
Arturs KARAŠAUSKAS	29/1/92	Skonto									s58		s65	2	-
Oļegs MALAŠENOKS	27/4/86	Jelgava										A65		1	-
Deniss RAKEĻS	20/8/92	Liepājas Metalurgs										s75	A55	2	-
Artis LAZDIŅŠ	3/5/86	Jelgava											s65	1	-

DOMESTIC LEAGUE 2009

VIRSLĪGA FINAL TABLE

		Home					Away					Total					
	Pld	W	D	L	F	A	W	D	L	F	A	W	D	L	F	A	Pts
SK Liepājas Metalurgs	32	13	2	1	50	8	12	2	2	46	15	25	4	3	96	23	79
FK Ventspils	32	11	3	2	48	14	12	2	2	41	7	23	5	4	89	21	74
Skonto FC	32	11	2	3	44	19	12	2	2	52	11	23	4	5	96	30	73
FK Jūrmala	32	5	2	9	16	30	7	2	7	26	30	12	4	16	42	60	40
Olimps/RFS	32	5	3	8	27	34	6	2	8	26	26	11	5	16	53	60	38
SK Blāzma Rēzekne	32	5	1	10	19	32	2	4	10	11	39	7	5	20	30	71	26
FC Tranzīts	32	1	7	8	11	25	1	3	12	11	40	2	10	20	22	65	16
FK Daugava Rīga	32	3	2	11	15	58	0	3	13	11	58	3	5	24	26	116	14
FC Dinaburg	32	9	1	6	16	19	6	3	7	15	20	15	4	13	31	39	49

NB FC Dinaburg excluded after round 26; remaining matches awarded 3-0 to opponents.

TOP GOALSCORERS

30 Kristaps GREBIS (Liepājas Metalurgs)
17 Vits RIMKUS (Ventspils)
15 Jurģis KALNS (Jūrmala)
   Ģirts KARLSONS (Liepājas Metalurgs)
14 Ivans LUKJANOVS (Skonto)
13 Vladimer DVALISHVILI (Skonto)
11 Maksims RAFAĻSKIS (Liepājas Metalurgs)
   Andrejs PEREPĻOTKINS (Skonto)
10 Artūrs KARAŠAUSKAS (Olimps)
9 Deniss RAKEĻS (Liepājas Metalurgs)
   Grigoriy CHIRKIN (Ventspils)
   Jurijs ŽIGAJEVS (Ventspils)

CLUB-BY-CLUB

SK BLĀZMA RĒZEKNE
Coach – Žanis Ārmanis
Founded – 2004
Stadium – RSP (2,000)

2009

14/3	Skonto	h	0-7	
21/3	Liepājas Metalurgs	a	0-4	
5/4	Ventspils	a	1-5	Jukšs
9/4	Daugava	a	1-1	Ryzhevskiy
12/4	Olimps	h	0-1	
26/4	Tranzīts	a	0-0	
29/4	Jūrmala	h	1-2	Borisovs
4/5	Dinaburg	a	0-1	
10/5	Skonto	a	0-4	
14/5	Liepājas Metalurgs	h	0-3	
28/5	Ventspils	h	0-3	
31/5	Daugava	h	4-3	Ryzhevskiy, Rečickis 2 (1p), Ivanovs
11/6	Olimps	a	1-1	Rečickis
18/6	Tranzīts	h	1-0	Rečickis (p)
22/6	Jūrmala	a	0-3	
26/6	Dinaburg	h	1-2	Bogdaškins
1/7	Skonto	h	0-1	
4/7	Liepājas Metalurgs	a	0-6	
8/7	Ventspils	a	0-5	
1/8	Daugava	a	3-0	Novožilovs 2, Ivanovs
15/8	Olimps	h	3-1	Rečickis 2, Volkovs
29/8	Jūrmala	h	0-3	
5/9	Tranzīts	a	1-1	Rečickis (p)
10/9	Dinaburg	a	0-1	
17/9	Skonto	a	0-4	
26/9	Ventspils	h	0-2	
30/9	Tranzīts	h	1-1	Ivanovs
3/10	Daugava	h	4-0	Volkovs 2, Borisovs 2
11/10	Dinaburg	h	3-0	(w/o)
18/10	Olimps	a	2-3	Ivanovs, Ryzhevskiy
24/10	Liepājas Metalurgs	h	1-3	Ryzhevskiy
1/11	Jūrmala	a	2-0	Rečickis (p), Borisovs

No	Name	Nat	DoB	Pos	Aps	(s)	Gls
13	Konstantins AFANASJEVS		25/6/90	M		(3)	
8	Ilja ANTONOVS		12/1/87	M	1	(9)	
4	Jevgenijs BELOVS		21/5/90	D	11	(5)	
9	Ivars BILINSKIS		7/7/89	D		(10)	
7	Boriss BOGDAŠKINS		21/12/90	M	23	(1)	1
11	Dmitrijs BORISOVS		20/12/87	A	11	(6)	4
22	Dmitrijs ČUGUNOVS		5/6/82	D	9		
2	Aleksandrs IVANOVS		16/11/85	D	31		4
16	Armands JERMAKOVS		18/3/90	M	2	(4)	
10	Jānis JUKŠS		18/1/89	A	15	(4)	1
6	Valdis KAĻVA		3/4/91	D	21	(1)	
3	Ilja KIRILOVS		12/1/85	D	12	(7)	
19	Aleksejs KLAPINS		3/2/91	M		(1)	
14	Edgars KLEINS		14/2/90	D	6	(5)	
5	Ervins KRAINIS		19/2/85	M	22	(2)	
12	Igors LABUTS		7/6/90	G		(2)	
1	Vitālijs MEĻNIČENKO		11/11/87	G	10		
18	Aleksandrs NOVOŽILOVS		20/12/89	M	6	(2)	2
9	Vadims PEREPEĻICA		20/7/88	M	3		
26	Edgars PORTNOJS		9/8/89	G	1		
15	Mihails PROPUSTINS		4/5/88	M	21		
19	Rolands PUTĀNS		12/12/88	D		(4)	
17	Māris RANCĀNS		21/9/86	M	24		
20	Vitālijs REČICKIS		8/9/86	M	27		8
23	Pavel RYZHEVSKIY	BLR	3/3/81	A	28		4
12	Aigars SEĻECKIS		13/5/92	G	1		
25	Oļegs SEMJONOVS		1/4/84	A	18	(1)	
21	Dmitrijs SILOVS		7/6/85	A	9	(12)	
13	Dmitrijs SUVOROVS		13/6/92	M	1	(6)	
1	Aleksandrs VLASOVS		7/5/86	G	19		
25	Vladimirs VOLKOVS		10/8/84	A	9	(1)	3

FK DAUGAVA RĪGA
Coach – Vladimirs Beļajevs
Founded – 2005
Stadium – Salaspils pilsētas (300)

2009

15/3	Ventspils	h	1-5	Gomaa
5/4	Olimps	a	0-4	
9/4	Blāzma	h	1-1	Tarasovs D.
13/4	Tranzīts	a	3-3	Ševeļovs 2, Tarasovs D.
17/4	Jūrmala	h	1-1	Mišins

LATVIA

26/4	Dinaburg	a	0-1	
30/4	Skonto	h	1-7	Hačatrjans
4/5	Liepājas Metalurgs	a	0-1	
10/5	Ventspils	a	2-4	Tarasovs D., Priedens
28/5	Olimps	h	1-5	Zotovs
31/6	Blāzma	a	3-4	Agafonovs R., Žuļovs, Tarasovs D. (p)
11/6	Tranzīts	h	2-0	Priedens, og (Baimatov)
14/6	Jūrmala	a	1-1	Priedens
18/6	Dinaburg	h	0-3	
22/6	Skonto	a	0-6	
26/6	Liepājas Metalurgs	h	1-4	Ševeļovs
30/6	Ventspils	h	0-5	
8/7	Olimps	a	0-7	
1/8	Blāzma	h	0-3	
15/8	Tranzīts	a	1-1	Priedens
20/8	Jūrmala	h	0-3	
24/8	Dinaburg	a	0-1	
29/8	Skonto	h	0-7	
13/9	Liepājas Metalurgs	a	0-3	
26/9	Olimps	h	0-5	
3/10	Blāzma	a	0-4	
15/10	Ventspils	a	0-8	
18/10	Tranzīts	h	2-1	Hačatrjans, Tarasovs D.
24/10	Jūrmala	a	1-3	Tarasovs M.
25/10	Dinaburg	h	3-0	(w/o)
1/11	Skonto	a	0-7	
8/11	Liepājas Metalurgs	h	2-8	og (Jemeļins), Fjodorovs

No	Name	Nat	DoB	Pos	Aps	(s)	Gls
18	Ruslans AGAFONOVS		18/4/89	M	11	(3)	1
15	Timurs AGAFONOVS		24/7/91	M		(3)	
1	Kristaps DZELME		30/1/90	G	24		
12	Artūrs FJODOROVS		8/3/91	M	12	(10)	1
3	Sergejs GOLOVINS		10/5/90	D	20	(1)	
10	Karim GOMAA	EGY	10/9/81	A	2		1
20	Arevšat HAČATRJANS		24/7/90	D	16	(9)	2
11	Jurijs HLIBOVS		1/4/90	D	21	(1)	
2	Vitālijs JAGODINSKIS		28/2/92	D	1		
22	Edgars JERMOLAJEVS		16/1/92	D		(1)	
23	Tomass JEVDOKIMOVS		9/2/87	A	9		
17	Jurijs KAMERILOVS		5/6/92	M	2	(5)	
17	Ilič KANDOV	GER	26/6/88	M	9	(1)	
2	Oļegs KĻUŠKINS		1/10/92	M		(2)	
6	Igors KORABĻOVS		23/11/74	D	24	(3)	
21	Deniss KOROTKEVIČS		3/2/93	M	1	(6)	
9	Vitālijs MAKSIMENKO		8/12/90	M	9		
24	Sergejs MIŠINS		4/6/87	A	17	(4)	1
27	Alexis NGAMBI	CMR	20/1/82	M	6		
16	Andrejs PIEDELS		17/9/70	G	5		
13	Vladislavs POŅAKOVS		26/1/90	D	11	(3)	
14	Kristaps PRIEDĒNS		12/1/90	A	23	(2)	4
21	Germans RAKĻINSKIS		14/5/90	M		(3)	
17	Alekss REGŽA		16/7/94	M		(1)	
16	Renats SABIROVS		18/12/91	G	2	(4)	
15	Valērijs ŠABALA		12/10/94	A		(2)	
26	Viktors ŠEKOVS		22/1/86	M	5		
4	Kirils ŠEVEĻOVS		2/6/90	D	24		3
15	Aleksejs TARASOVS		24/6/93	A	8	(3)	
7	Deniss TARASOVS		14/9/90	M	25	(2)	5
25	Maksims TARASOVS		29/3/87	M	23	(3)	1
5	Artjoms ZOTOVS		16/1/91	M	14	(11)	1
22	Vladislavs ŽDAŅKO		25/12/91	A	4	(3)	
15	Vadims ŽUĻOVS		1/3/88	A	13		1

FC DINABURG

Coach – Tamaz Pertia (GEO)
Founded – 1990
Stadium – Celtnieks (3,000)
MAJOR HONOURS:
Latvian Cup – (1) 1991.

2009

14/3	Tranzīts	a	1-1	Vorobjovs
21/3	Jūrmala	h	1-2	Vorobjovs
8/4	Skonto	a	2-3	Sokolovs (p), Logins
12/4	Liepājas Metalurgs	h	0-3	
18/4	Ventspils	h	0-0	
26/4	Daugava	h	1-0	Hong
4/5	Blāzma	h	1-0	Sokolovs (p)
10/5	Tranzīts	h	2-0	Hong, Danilin
13/5	Jūrmala	a	0-1	
25/5	Olimps	h	2-1	Afanasjevs, Danilin
31/5	Skonto	h	1-1	Žavoronkovs
11/6	Liepājas Metalurgs	a	1-3	Guchashvili
14/6	Ventspils	h	1-0	Afanasjevs
18/6	Daugava	h	3-0	Sokolovs, Afanasjevs, Vorobjovs
22/6	Olimps	a	1-1	Krjauklis
26/6	Blāzma	a	2-1	Sokolovs, Danilin (p)
26/7	Jūrmala	h	2-0	Guchashvili, Danilin
30/7	Tranzīts	a	2-0	Kovaļovs, Kortua
3/8	Skonto	a	1-0	Afanasjevs
16/8	Liepājas Metalurgs	h	1-2	Afanasjevs
24/8	Daugava	h	1-0	Kuzņecovs
30/8	Olimps	a	1-0	Guchashvili
10/9	Blāzma	h	1-0	Kovaļovs
13/9	Ventspils	a	0-1	
17/9	Tranzīts	h	2-1	Koļcovs, Sokolovs (p)
20/9	Jūrmala	a	1-0	Logins
11/10	Blāzma	a	0-3	(w/o)
21/10	Liepājas Metalurgs	a	0-3	(w/o)
25/10	Daugava	a	0-3	(w/o)
1/11	Olimps	h	0-3	(w/o)
5/11	Skonto	h	0-3	(w/o)
8/11	Ventspils	h	0-3	(w/o)

No	Name	Nat	DoB	Pos	Aps	(s)	Gls
19	Valērijs AFANASJEVS		20/9/82	M	26		5
7	Vyacheslav DANILIN	RUS	14/3/84	M	14	(3)	4
9	Maksims DAŅILOVS		2/8/86	M	5	(2)	
77	Pāvels DAVIDOVS		30/12/80	G	12		
2	Maksims DEŅISEVIČS		2/1/87	M	3	(6)	
1	Vadims FJODOROVS		14/3/77	G	14		
24	Vladislavs GABOVS		13/7/87	D	16	(5)	
16	Vasili GUCHASHVILI	GEO	26/1/85	A	9	(2)	3
36	HONG Kum-song	PRK	3/1/90	M	13	(3)	2
17	Eriks KOKINS		11/1/91	A		(3)	
4	Pāvels KOĻCOVS		1/9/82	D	20	(2)	1
3	Ika KORTUA	GEO	5/10/87	D	8	(9)	1
6	Andrejs KOVAĻOVS		23/3/89	A	9		2
26	Ritus KRJAUKLIS		23/4/86	D	21	(1)	1
10	Vladimir KULESHOV	RUS	18/5/86	D	20		
21	Aleksejs KUPLOVS-OGINSKIS		21/1/88	M	1	(3)	
5	Artjoms KUZŅECOVS		5/3/86	D	2		1
25	Vadims LOGINS		30/12/81	D	22	(2)	2
36	Jans RADEVIČS		14/3/89	M	2	(2)	
20	RI Myong-jun	PRK	16/8/90	A	7	(6)	
22	Jevgeņijs SIMONOVS		29/3/84	M	16	(4)	
11	Jurijs SOKOLOVS		12/9/83	M	25		5
2	Oļegs TIMOFEJEVS		28/11/88	M	3	(1)	
15	Vladimirs VOLKOVS		10/8/84	A	2	(4)	
17	Dmitrijs VOROBJOVS		31/3/90	A	4	(7)	3
8	Artyom YASHKIN	RUS	29/4/75	A	2		
9	Mihails ZIZIĻEVS		27/12/73	M	8		
32	Vladimirs ŽAVORONKOVS		25/11/76	D	2	(2)	1

FK JŪRMALA

Coach – Vladimirs Babičevs
Founded – 2003
Stadium – Sloka (2,000)

2009

21/3	Dinaburg	a	2-1	Kalns, Torres
5/4	Skonto	a	0-3	
8/4	Liepājas Metalurgs	a	2-2	Koļesņikovs, Ņesterenko
12/4	Ventspils	h	0-3	
17/4	Daugava	a	1-1	Koļesņikovs
25/4	Olimps	h	0-1	
29/4	Blāzme Rēzekne	a	2-1	Žatkins, Bezzubovs
6/5	Tranzīts	h	4-2	Baspalovs, Kuzņecovs, Torres, Kalns
13/5	Dinaburg	h	1-0	Bespalovs
27/5	Skonto	h	0-3	
31/5	Liepājas Metalurgs	h	1-1	Bezzubovs
11/6	Ventspils	a	0-3	
14/6	Daugava	h	1-1	Kalns (p)
19/6	Olimps	a	3-2	Kalns (p), Torres, Gospodars
22/6	Blāzma	h	3-0	Kalns 3
28/6	Tranzīts	a	2-1	Kalns 2 (1p)
8/7	Skonto	h	0-5	
26/7	Dinaburg	a	0-2	
2/8	Liepājas Metalurgs	a	1-4	Kalns
15/8	Ventspils	h	0-4	
20/8	Daugava	a	3-0	Paplavskis, Bespalovs 2
23/8	Olimps	h	1-0	Kalns
29/8	Blāzma	a	3-0	Ņesterenko, Čistjakovs, Kalns (p)
13/9	Tranzīts	h	1-2	Matsion
20/9	Dinaburg Daigavpils	h	0-1	
26/9	Skonto	a	2-3	Kalns, Bezzubovs
30/9	Olimps	a	0-2	
3/10	Liepājas Metalurgs	h	1-4	Kalns (p)
18/10	Ventspils	a	1-4	Bezzubovs
24/10	Daugava	a	3-1	Bezzubovs, Žatkins, Kalns
1/11	Blāzma	h	0-2	
8/11	Tranzīts	h	4-1	Matsion, Kalniņš 3

No	Name	Nat	DoB	Pos	Aps	(s)	Gls
18	Alberts BARBALIS		5/3/88	D	12	(3)	
11	Romans BESPALOVS		18/10/88	A	25	(4)	4
8	Romans BEZZUBOVS		15/5/79	M	29	(1)	5
21	Artūrs BIEZAIS		8/11/86	G	13		
1	Marks BOGDANOVS		2/12/86	G	19	(1)	
12	Aleksandrs ČEKULAJEVS		2/8/85	A		(6)	
14	Valērijs ČISTJAKOVS		27/11/92	M	5	(3)	1
7	Vadims GOSPODARS		25/12/83	M	7	(5)	1
5	Aleksandrs GUBINS		16/5/88	D	19	(5)	
24	Gaga GUGUNASHVILI	GEO	25/1/88	A	16	(8)	
4	Vitālijs JAGODINSKIS		28/2/92	M	7		
3	Kirils JEĻKINS		1/9/87	D	12	(4)	
22	Edgars JERMOLAJEVS		16/1/92	M		(2)	
23	Gatis KALNIŅŠ		12/8/81	A	3	(5)	3
9	Jurģis KALNS		5/10/82	A	31		15
15	Aleksejs KOĻESŅIKOVS		5/10/81	A	6	(4)	2
16	Jurijs KSENZOVS		5/6/81	D	13	(2)	
4	Artjoms KUZŅECOVS		5/3/86	D	17		1
2	Kostyantyn MATSION	UKR	9/2/82	M	22	(3)	2
23	Filips MIHAILOVSKIS		18/3/86	M		(2)	
14	Bogdans ŅESTERENKO		16/5/84	D	28		2
2	Marians PAHARS		5/8/76	A		(1)	
19	Dmitrijs PAPLAVSKIS		10/4/88	M	7	(6)	1
17	Vadims SIŅICINS		17/6/78	D	17	(1)	
20	Cristian TORRES	ARG	18/6/85	M	14	(1)	3
14	Mareks ZUNTNERS		13/2/83	A	1	(7)	
10	Oļegs ŽATKINS		13/4/87	A	29	(2)	2

SK LIEPĀJAS METALURGS

Coach – Rüdiger Abramczik (GER)
Founded – 1997
Stadium – Daugava (6,000)
MAJOR HONOURS:
Latvian League – (2) 2005, 2009;
Latvian Cup – (1) 2006.

2009

14/3	Olimps	a	2-1	Rafaļskis, Grebis
21/3	Blāzma	h	4-0	Grebis 2 (1p), Karlsons, Kastner
5/4	Tranzīts	a	1-0	Surņins
8/4	Jūrmala	h	2-2	Kastner, Grebis (p)
12/4	Dinaburg	a	3-0	Grebis 2, Karlsons
18/4	Skonto	h	4-0	Kļava, Tamošauskas, Karlsons, Rafaļskis
30/4	Ventspils	a	1-1	Surņins
4/5	Daugava	h	1-0	Kastner
10/5	Olimps	h	5-1	Grebis 2 (1p), Karlsons 3
14/5	Blāzma	a	3-0	Karlsons, Kastner, Rafaļskis
27/5	Tranzīts	h	5-0	Grebis 2, Karlsons, Rafaļskis, Kirhners
31/5	Jūrmala	a	1-1	Kastner
11/6	Dinaburg	h	3-1	Karlsons, Grebis 2
14/6	Skonto	a	1-2	og (Gaiļus)
22/6	Ventspils	h	2-1	Rafaļskis, Karlsons
26/6	Daugava	a	4-1	Kastner, Karlsons 3
1/7	Olimps	a	5-1	Grebis 3 (2p), Karlsons 2
4/7	Blāzma	h	6-0	Grebis 3, Rafaļskis, Kastner, Prohorenkovs
8/7	Tranzīts	a	0-1	
2/8	Jūrmala	h	4-1	Surņins, Ivanovs, Grebis (p), Rakeļs
16/8	Dinaburg	a	2-1	Grebis 2 (1p)
19/8	Skonto	h	0-1	
30/8	Ventspils	a	2-1	Grebis, Kirhners
13/9	Daugava	h	3-0	Grebis 2, Prohorenkovs
17/9	Olimps	h	3-0	Rakeļs, Kļava, Jemeļins
26/9	Tranzīts	h	4-0	Rakeļs 3, Grebis
3/10	Jūrmala	a	4-1	Prohorenkovs, Rafaļskis 2, Grebis
18/10	Skonto	a	6-1	Prohorenkovs 2, Rakeļs 3, Grebis
21/10	Dinaburg	h	3-0	(w/o)
24/10	Blāzma	a	3-1	Rafaļskis, Prohorenkovs, Kamešs
1/11	Ventspils	h	1-1	Grebis (p)
8/11	Daugava	a	8-2	Grebis 2, Rafaļskis 2, Kamešs, Rakeļs, Dobrecovs, Kalniņš

No	Name	Nat	DoB	Pos	Aps	(s)	Gls
27	Igors AĻEKSEJEVS		31/7/88	M	9	(4)	
15	Andrei COJOCARI	MDA	21/1/87	M	9	(16)	
10	Viktors DOBRECOVS		9/1/77	M	1	(5)	1
15	Jevgenijs GOLOVINS		6/3/89	M		(3)	
23	Kristaps GREBIS		13/12/80	A	28		30
6	Deniss IVANOVS		11/1/84	D	18	(1)	1
28	Antons JEMEĻINS		19/2/84	D	18	(6)	1
6	Raivo KALNIŅŠ		19/2/89	D		(3)	1
22	Vladimirs KAMEŠS		28/10/88	A		(11)	2
20	Ģirts KARLSONS		7/6/81	A	17	(1)	15
5	Daniel KASTNER	AUT	3/11/81	A	18	(2)	7
14	Intars KIRHNERS		9/4/83	M	18	(5)	2
3	Oskars KĻAVA		8/8/83	D	27		2
21	Jevgenijs KORŠAKOVS		17/4/89	M		(2)	
25	Toms MEŽS		7/9/89	M		(7)	
17	Andrejs PROHORENKOVS		5/2/77	M	24	(5)	6
7	Maksims RAFAĻSKIS		14/5/84	M	30		11
8	Deniss RAKEĻS		20/8/92	A	10	(4)	9
16	Roberts SAVAĻNIEKS		6/5/87	M	1	(1)	
10	Genādijs SOLOŅICINS		3/1/80	M	4	(9)	
31	Viktors SPOLE		5/7/72	G	25		
13	Pāvels SURŅINS		4/8/85	M	18		3
27	Pāvels ŠTEINBORS		21/9/85	G	6		
9	Tomas TAMOŠAUSKAS	LTU	22/5/83	D	29		1
4	Dzintars ZIRNIS		25/4/77	D	29		
2	Andrejs ŽURAVĻOVS		10/7/84	D	2	(3)	

OLIMPS/RFS

Coach – Anton Joore (NED)
Founded – 2005
Stadium – Daugava (2,000)

2009

14/3	Liepājas Metalurgs	h	1-2	Perepechko
21/3	Ventspils	a	0-1	
5/4	Daugava	h	4-0	Perepechko, Pētersons, Štolcers 2
12/4	Blāzma	a	1-0	Miholaps (p)
18/4	Tranzīts	a	0-0	
25/4	Jūrmala	a	1-0	Miholaps
6/5	Skonto	a	0-2	
10/5	Liepājas Metalurgs	a	1-5	og (Kļava)
13/5	Ventspils	h	1-5	Astafjevs
25/5	Dinaburg	a	1-2	Cepurītis
28/5	Daugava	a	5-1	Kļimovs 2, Petrenko, Miholaps, Pētersons
11/6	Blāzma	h	1-1	Karašauskas
14/6	Tranzīts	h	1-1	Miholaps
19/6	Jūrmala	h	2-3	Štolcers, Miholaps (p)
22/6	Dinaburg	h	1-1	Kļimovs
27/6	Skonto	h	1-8	Pētersons
1/7	Liepājas Metalurgs	h	1-5	Turkovs
4/7	Ventspils	a	3-5	Karašauskas, Sputajs 2
8/7	Daugava	h	7-0	Rode, Turkovs, Karašauskas 3, Perepechko, Pētersons
19/7	Tranzīts	a	2-0	Turkovs, Siņicins
15/8	Blāzma	a	1-3	Turkovs (p)
23/8	Jūrmala	a	0-1	
26/8	Tranzīts	h	2-1	Daņilovs, Štolcers
30/8	Dinaburg	h	0-1	
13/9	Skonto	h	0-2	
17/9	Liepājas Metalurgs	a	0-3	
20/9	Ventspils	h	0-2	
26/9	Daugava	a	5-0	Turkovs, Pētersons, Karašauskas 2, Kļimovs
30/9	Jūrmala	h	2-0	Dubra, Karašauskas
18/10	Blāzma	h	3-2	Karašauskas, Pētersons, Turkovs
1/11	Dinaburg	a	3-0	(w/o)
8/11	Skonto	a	3-3	Pētersons, Turkovs (p), Karašauskas

Name	Nat	DoB	Pos	Aps	(s)	Gls
Vitālijs ASTAFJEVS		3/4/71	M	14		1
Reinis BRODERS		17/7/92	M		(1)	
Konstantins BUDILOVS		21/3/91	A	6	(4)	
Harijs CEPURĪTIS		12/6/91	M	2	(5)	1
Dmitrijs DAŅILOVS		25/1/91	D	19	(3)	1
Oskars DARĢIS		6/3/93	G	2	(1)	
Kaspars DUBRA		20/12/90	D	9		1
Kirils GRIGOROVS		19/10/92	M		(1)	
Kaspars IKSTENS		5/6/88	G	23		
Artūrs KARAŠAUSKAS		29/1/92	A	13	(5)	10
Jevgeņijs KAZURA		24/1/88	D	16		
Artūrs KĻIMOVIČS		31/8/91	D	16	(1)	
Aleksandrs KĻIMOVS		16/11/91	A	7	(7)	4
Aleksandrs KOĻINKO		18/6/75	G	6		
Andrejs KOSTJUKS		17/2/88	M	5	(3)	
Jurijs LAIZĀNS		6/1/79	M	9	(1)	
Artūrs MAGEJENKOVS		19/3/90	A	9	(2)	
Mihails MIHOLAPS		24/8/74	A	12	(3)	5
Deniss OSTROVSKIS		5/2/92	M		(2)	
Aleksandr PEREPECHKO	BLR	7/4/89	A	12	(6)	3
Armands PĒTERSONS		5/12/90	A	28	(1)	7
Deniss PETRENKO		14/3/88	D	18		1
Renārs RODE		6/4/89	M	13	(2)	1
Alans SIŅEĻŅIKOVS		14/5/90	A	10		
Andrejs SIŅICINS		30/1/91	M	20	(3)	1
Ivans SPUTAJS		9/2/88	M	22	(5)	2
Igors STEPANOVS		21/1/76	D	7		

Dmitrijs ŠIĻUKS		21/6/87	D	21	
Aleksandrs ŠKOĻŅIKOVS		7/3/91	A	2	(2)
Aleksandrs ŠPEĻS		11/4/91	D	2	(1)
Andrejs ŠTOLCERS		8/7/74	M	5	(12)	4
Danils TURKOVS		17/2/88	A	12		7
Dmitrijs VAĻEGŽAŅINS		14/7/89	M	1	(4)

SKONTO FC

Coach – Paul Ashworth (ENG)
Founded – 1991
Stadium – Skonto (9,500)
MAJOR HONOURS:
Latvian League – (14) 1991, 1992, 1993, 1994, 1995, 1996, 1997, 1998, 1999, 2000, 2001, 2002, 2003, 2004;
Latvian Cup - (7) 1992, 1995, 1997, 1998, 2000, 2001, 2002.

2009

14/3	Blāzma	a	7-0	Lukjanovs 2, Dvalishvili 3, Hščanovičs (p), Perepļotkins
21/3	Tranzīts	h	1-0	Dvalishvili
5/4	Jūrmala	h	3-0	Dvalishvili, Lukjanovs, Gamezardashvili
8/4	Dinaburg	h	3-2	Kozlovs, Perepļotkins, Dvalishvili
18/4	Liepājas Metalurgs	a	0-4	
26/4	Ventspils	h	1-3	Semjonovs
30/4	Daugava	a	7-1	Kožans, Hščanovičs (p), Lukjanovs 4, Perepļotkins
6/5	Olimps	h	2-0	Kozlovs, og (Petrenko)
10/5	Blāzma	h	4-0	Lukjanovs, Kozlovs, Blanks 2
13/5	Tranzīts	a	1-1	Hščanovičs
27/5	Jūrmala	a	3-0	Semjonovs, Blanks 2
31/5	Dinaburg	a	1-1	Dvalishvili
14/6	Liepājas Metalurgs	h	2-1	Lukjanovs 2 (1p)
18/6	Ventspils	h	1-2	Lukjanovs
22/6	Daugava	h	6-0	Blanks, Lukjanovs 3 (1p), Semjonovs, Dvalishvili
27/6	Olimps	a	8-1	Dvalishvili 4, Blanks, Laizāns, Perepļotkins, Semjonovs
1/7	Blāzma	a	1-0	Dvalishvili
4/7	Tranzīt Ventspils	h	4-1	Blanks 2, Smirnovs, Hščanovičs (p)
8/7	Jūrmala	a	5-0	Júnior 2, Mingazov, og (Kuzņecovs), Tarasovs
3/8	Dinaburg	h	0-1	
19/8	Liepājas Metalurgs	a	1-0	Kozlovs
29/8	Daugava	a	7-0	Perepļotkins 3, Cauņa 2, Tarasovs, Hščanovičs (p)
13/9	Olimps	a	2-0	Perepļotkins 2
17/9	Blāzma	h	4-0	Gamezardashvili, og (Ivanovs), Laizāns, Semjonovs
20/9	Tranzīts	a	3-1	Laizāns, Perepļotkins, Gamezardashvili
26/9	Jūrmala	h	3-2	Cauņa, Mingazov, Laizāns (p)
4/10	Ventspils	h	0-0	
18/10	Liepājas Metalurgs	h	1-6	Koļesņičenko (p)
26/10	Ventspils	a	2-0	Cauņa, Koļesņičenko
1/11	Daugava	h	7-0	Júnior 3, Perepļotkins, Kozlovs 3
5/11	Dinaburg	a	3-0	(w/o)
8/11	Olimps	h	3-3	Koļesņičenko (p), Kozlovs, Laizāns

No	Name	Nat	DoB	Pos	Aps	(s)	Gls
17	Andrei AGAFONOV	RUS	29/1/79	M	1	(8)	
9	Kristaps BLANKS		30/1/86	A	11	(10)	8
23	Aleksandrs CAUŅA		19/1/88	M	9	(2)	4
14	Kaspars DUBRA		20/12/90	D		(1)	
10	Vladimer DVALISHVILI	GEO	20/4/86	A	12	(3)	13
7	Aleksandrs FERTOVS		16/6/87	M	19	(3)	
22	Vadims GAIĻUS		27/5/88	D	4	(4)	
4	David GAMEZARDASHVILI	GEO	7/5/82	D	28		3
2	Sergejs GOLUBEVS		24/2/85	D	19		
3	Raivis HŠČANOVIČS		15/2/87	D	26		5

12	Nathan Soares Carvalho JÚNIOR	BRA	10/3/89	A	14	(5)	5
20	Vladimirs KOĻESŅIČENKO		4/5/80	M	10		3
6	Igors KOZLOVS		26/3/87	M	23	(2)	8
5	Sergejs KOŽANS		18/2/86	D	7	(1)	1
8	Oļegs LAIZĀNS		28/3/87	M	13	(12)	5
17	Ivans LUKJANOVS		24/1/87	A	14	(1)	14
1	Hermanis MĀLIŅŠ		12/10/87	G	19		
16	Vitālijs MEĻNIČENKO		11/11/87	G	2		
13	Ruslan MINGAZOV	TKM	23/11/91	A	9	(11)	2
21	Aleksandr PEREPECHKO	BLR	7/4/89	A	2	(3)	
11	Andrejs PEREPĻOTKINS		27/12/84	A	28		11
5	Deniss PETRENKO		14/3/88	D	1	(1)	
15	Igors SEMJONOVS		3/7/85	M	10	(8)	5
21	Alans SIŅEĻŅIKOVS		14/5/90	A		(3)	
18	Vitālijs SMIRNOVS		28/6/86	D	24	(1)	1
19	Igors TARASOVS		16/1/88	M	26	(4)	2
16	Aleksandrs VLASOVS		7/5/86	G	10		

FC TRANZĪTS
Coach – Igor Kichigin (RUS)
Founded – 2006
Stadium – 2. pamatskolas (500)

2009
14/3	Dinaburg	h	1-1	Kārkļiņš
21/3	Skonto	a	0-1	
5/4	Liepājas Metalurgs	h	0-1	
8/4	Ventspils	a	1-1	Mukins
13/4	Daugava	h	3-3	Malašenoks 3 (1p)
18/4	Olimps	h	0-0	
26/4	Blāzma	h	0-0	
6/5	Jūrmala	a	2-4	Kuzmickis, Malašenoks (p)
10/5	Dinaburg	a	0-2	
13/5	Skonto	h	1-1	Bulvitis
27/5	Liepājas Metalurgs	a	0-5	
31/5	Ventspils	h	0-3	
11/6	Daugava	a	0-2	
14/6	Olimps	a	1-1	Gramovičs
18/6	Blāzma	a	0-1	
28/6	Jūrmala	h	1-2	Višņakovs
4/7	Skonto	a	1-4	Višņakovs
8/7	Liepājas Metalurgs	h	1-0	Višņakovs
19/7	Olinps Rīga	a	0-2	
30/7	Dinaburg	h	0-2	
8/8	Ventspils	a	0-7	
15/8	Daugava	h	1-1	Hohlovs
26/8	Olimps	a	1-2	Malašenoks
5/9	Blāzma	h	1-1	Rjumšins
13/9	Jūrmala	a	2-1	Kārkļiņš, Chamkhanov
17/9	Dinaburg	a	1-2	Ignatāns
20/9	Skonto	h	1-3	og (Smirnovs)
23/9	Ventspils	a	0-1	
26/9	Liepājas Metalurgs	a	0-4	
30/9	Blāzma	a	1-1	Dimčuks
18/10	Daugava	a	1-2	Zjuzins
8/11	Jūrmala	a	1-4	Stols (p)

No	Name	Nat	DoB	Pos	Aps	(s)	Gls
17	Toms AIZGRĀVIS		30/4/89	M	12		
4	Deniss BABUĻS		1/2/91	M	5	(5)	
3	Azamat BAIMATOV	KGZ	3/12/89	M	13	(1)	
18	Igors BARINOVS		1/6/94	M	1	(2)	
22	Vitālijs BARINOVS		4/5/93	M	18	(1)	
15	Aleksandrs BATURINSKIS		15/12/91	D	11	(4)	
7	Nauris BULVITIS		8/3/91	D	17		1
9	Imran CHAMKHANOV	FRA	14/6/91	D	8	(1)	1
20	Aleksejs DIMČUKS		7/2/91	M	22	(4)	1
8	Aleksandrs GRAMOVIČS		25/3/89	M	24	(1)	1
10	Pāvels HOHLOVS		19/12/89	M	13	(3)	1
7	Visvaldis IGNATĀNS		3/8/91	M	11	(1)	1

15	David JANELIDZE	GEO	12/9/89	A	8	(2)	
3	Edgars KĀRKĻIŅŠ		21/7/91	A	8	(9)	2
6	Aleksandrs KUZMICKIS		8/7/90	M	16	(2)	1
18	Dmitrijs KUZMINS		19/8/91	M	3	(8)	
11	Oļegs MALAŠENOKS		27/4/86	A	19	(5)	5
16	Mindaugas MALINAUSKAS	LTU	8/11/83	G	20	(1)	
19	Vladimirs MUKINS		29/1/93	M	18	(4)	1
11	Jojo OGUNNUPE	NGA	23/2/92	A	1	(1)	
1	Valentins RAĻKEVIČS		8/3/91	G	4	(2)	
7	Vladas RIMKUS		28/5/93	A		(1)	
13	Mihails RJUMŠINS		28/2/90	D	7	(5)	1
21	Julien RULLIER	FRA	4/4/90	D	9	(1)	
8	Sergejs SAĻEIKO		27/5/92	M		(1)	
1	Jevgenijs SAZONOVS		31/7/88	G	6		
2	Roland SOLOMIN	LTU	25/3/91	D	6	(3)	
7	Aleksandrs SOLOVJOVS		25/2/88	M	8	(3)	
21	Vitālijs STOLS		1/6/91	D	21	(2)	1
14	Kaspars SVĀRUPS		28/1/94	A		(2)	
19	Dario TORBIĆ	CRO	26/10/90	A	2	(1)	
15	Daniel VASILJEVS		7/4/93	M		(2)	
14	Edgars VĒRDIŅŠ		29/3/93	A	6	(3)	
9	Eduards VIŠŅAKOVS		10/5/90	A	17	(2)	3
26	Andris ZABUSOVS		5/9/93	G	2		
5	Artūrs ZJUZINS		18/6/91	M	16	(2)	1

FK VENTSPILS
Coach – Roman Grigorchuk (UKR);
(10/8/09) Nunzio Zavettieri (ITA)
Founded – 1997
Stadium – OSC Ventspils (3,200)
MAJOR HONOURS:
Latvian League – (3) 2006, 2007, 2008;
Latvian Cup - (4) 2003, 2004, 2005, 2007.

2009
15/3	Daugava	a	5-1	Menteshashvili, Chirkin, Žigajevs, Butriks, Rugins
21/3	Olimps	h	1-0	Rimkus
5/4	Blāzma	h	5-1	Chirkin 2, Rimkus (p), Višņakovs A., Mysikov
8/4	Tranzīts	h	1-1	Rimkus
12/4	Jūrmala	a	3-0	Tigirlas, Chirkin 2
18/4	Dinaburg	h	0-0	
26/4	Skonto	a	3-1	Menteshashvili, Žigajevs, Rimkus (p)
30/4	Liepājas Metalurgs	h	1-1	Kosmačovs
10/5	Daugava	h	4-2	Tigirlas, Rimkus, Chirkin, Mysikov
13/5	Olimps	a	5-1	Žigajevs 2, Rimkus 2 (1p), Višņakovs A.
28/5	Blāzma	a	3-0	Butriks 2, Rimkus
31/5	Tranzīts	a	3-0	Tigirlas 2, Butriks (p)
11/6	Jūrmala	h	3-0	Kačanovs, Višņakovs A., Dedov
14/6	Dinaburg	a	0-1	
18/6	Skonto	h	2-1	Tigirlas, Rimkus
22/6	Liepājas Metalurgs	h	1-2	Chirkin
30/6	Daugava	a	5-0	Rimkus 3, Višņakovs A., og (Poņakovs)
4/7	Olimps	h	5-3	Tigirlas 2, Višņakovs A., Chirkin, Rimkus (p)
8/7	Blāzma	h	5-0	Žigajevs 2, Shpakov, Rimkus (p), Dedov
8/8	Tranzīts	h	7-0	Shpakov (p), Višņakovs A. 2, Jõao Martins, Rimkus 2 (1p), Chirkin
15/8	Jūrmala	a	4-0	Ndeki, Shpakov, Žigajevs, Rimkus
30/8	Liepājas Metalurgs	h	1-2	Žigajevs
13/9	Dinaburg	h	5-0	Shpakov
20/9	Olimps	a	2-0	Višņakovs E. 2
23/9	Tranzīts	h	1-0	Shpakov
26/9	Blāzma	a	2-0	Žigajevs, Butriks (p)
4/10	Skonto	a	0-0	
15/10	Daugava	h	8-0	Višņakovs E. 2, Jõao Martins 2, Rugins, Mysikov, Shpakov 2

 **LATVIA**

18/10	Jūrmala	h	4-1	Gauračs, Višņakovs A.,			
				Višņakovs E., Iheruome			
26/10	Skonto	h	0-2				
1/11	Liepājas Metalurgs	a	1-1	Butriks			
8/11	Dinaburg	a	3-0	(w/o)			

No	Name	Nat	DoB	Pos	Aps	(s)	Gls
3	Vitālijs ASTAFJEVS		3/4/71	M	2	(3)	
24	Azamat BAIMATOV	KGZ	3/12/89	M	3	(2)	
36	Aleksandrs BATURINSKIS		15/12/91	D	3		
32	Andrejs BUTRIKS		20/12/82	A	13	(7)	6
1	Pavel CHESNOVSKIY	BLR	4/3/86	G	5		
15	Grigoriy CHIRKIN	RUS	26/2/86	M	18	(4)	9
7	Saša CILINŠEK	SRB	28/1/82	D	10		
20	Alexandru DEDOV	MDA	26/7/89	A	11	(10)	2
30	Māris ELTERMANIS		16/10/81	G	5		
27	Edgars GAURAČS		10/3/88	A	5	(1)	1
31	Ronny HODEL	SUI	27/10/82	D	4	(1)	

PROMOTED CLUBS

FK JELGAVA
Coach - Dainis Kazakevičs
Founded - 2004
Stadium - Ozolnieki (800)
MAJOR HONOURS:
Latvian Cup – (3) 1993, 1996, 2010.

FK JAUNĪBA RĪGA
Coach - Sergejs Davidovs
Founded - 2006
Stadium - Daugava (5,500)

FC DAUGAVA DAUGAVPILS
Coach - Sergejs Pogodins
Founded - 1944
Stadium - Daugava (2,000)
MAJOR HONOURS:
Latvian Cup (1) – 2008.

SECOND LEVEL FINAL TABLE 2009

		Pld	W	D	L	F	A	Pts
1	FK Jelgava	26	19	5	2	57	21	62
2	FK Jaunība Rīga	26	18	6	2	59	24	60
3	SK Liepājas Metalurgs II	26	18	2	6	65	30	56
4	FC Jūrmala	26	15	5	6	46	18	50
5	JFC Kauguri/PLBC	26	14	6	6	66	40	48
6	FS Metta/Latvijas Universitāte Rīga	26	13	6	7	47	19	45
7	FK Auda Rīga	26	10	7	9	45	33	37
8	Skonto FC II	26	10	4	12	36	38	34
9	FC Daugava Daugavpils	26	9	7	10	38	43	34
10	FK Tukums-2000	26	8	3	15	42	55	27
11	FK Valmiera/LFKA	26	6	5	15	26	51	23
12	FK Spartaks Jūrmala	26	4	2	20	26	70	14
13	Preiļu BJSS	26	2	5	19	26	87	11
14	JRC/JRSS Jēkabpils	26	2	5	19	25	75	11

NB FC Daugava Daugavpils invited to 2010 Virslīga.

PROMOTION/RELEGATION PLAY-OFFS
(11/11/09)
Daugava Rīga 1, Jaunība 1
(15/11/09)
Jaunība 0, Daugava Rīga 0
(1-1; Jaunība on away goal)

3	Visvaldis IGNATĀNS		3/8/91	M	1	(2)	
29	Uche IHERUOME		14/4/87	A		(4)	1
33	JOÃO Pedro Pinto MARTINS	POR	20/6/82	A	3	(1)	3
8	Deniss KAČANOVS		27/11/79	D	19	(1)	1
16	Aleksandrs KOĻIŅKO		18/6/75	G	4		
5	Jevgenijs KOSMAČOVS		18/2/88	M	23	(1)	1
10	Jurijs LAIZĀNS		6/1/79	M	5		
6	Artis LAZDIŅŠ		3/5/86	M	13	(5)	
10	Zurab MENTESHASHVILI	GEO	30/1/80	M	11	(3)	2
18	Pāvels MIHADJUKS		27/5/80	D	11	(2)	
19	Aleksandr MYSIKOV	RUS	13/8/88	A	9	(10)	3
17	Jean-Paul NDEKI	CMR	27/10/82	D	7	(3)	1
30	Andrejs PAVLOVS		22/2/79	G	4		
9	Vits RIMKUS		21/6/73	A	16	(3)	17
25	Ritvars RUGINS		17/10/89	A	8	(6)	2
12	Igors SAVČENKOVS		3/11/82	D	11	(1)	
14	Ivan SHPAKOV	RUS	8/6/86	A	15	(3)	7
12	Māris SMIRNOVS		2/6/76	D	4	(1)	
34	Aleksandrs SOLOVJOVS		25/2/88	M	6		
2	Aleksejs SOĻEIČUKS		12/8/80	D	10		
22	Igor TIGIRLAS	MDA	24/2/84	M	25		7
16	Andris VANIŅS		30/4/80	G	13		
11	Aleksejs VIŠŅAKOVS		3/2/84	M	17	(7)	8
28	Eduards VIŠŅAKOVS		10/5/90	A	5	(3)	5
21	Alessandro ZAMPERINI	ITA	15/8/82	D	4		
4	Jurijs ŽIGAJEVS		14/11/85	M	16	(7)	9
35	Tomislav ŽIVKO	CRO	29/1/88	A	2	(2)	

DOMESTIC CUP 2009/10

LATVIJAS KAUSS

THIRD ROUND

(2/4/10)
Daugava Daugavpils 1, Liepājas
Metalurgs 4
Jūrmala 0, Ventspils 4

(4/4/10)
ColdGel/Varaviksne 0, Olimps 2
Skonto w/o Kauguri-PBLC
Upesciems 0, Blāzma 5
Valka 0, Jūrmala 13

(3/4/10)
Jelgava 2, Tranzīts 1
Metta/LU Rīga 1, Daugava Rīga 3

QUARTER-FINALS

(14/4/10)
Daugava Rīga 0, Olimps 4 (Kostjuks 27, Šabala 73, 90p, Magejenkovs 80)
Jūrmala 4 (Stepanovs 20, Bezzubovs 57p, Melnyk 72, Krjauklis 87), Blāzma
Liepājas Metalurgs 3 (Spasojević 81, 95, Rakeļs 108), Jelgava 3 (Malašeno
38, Ķeris 110, Kazura 118) (aet; 4-5 on pens)
Ventspils 0, Skonto 0 (aet; 6-7 on pens)

SEMI-FINALS

(28/4/10)
Olimps 1 (Šabala 19), Jūrmala 3 (Žatkins 47, Stepanovs 61, Paplavskis 72)
Skonto 1 (Júnior 14), Jelgava 1 (Malašenoks 50) (aet; 3-5 on pens)

FINAL

(19/5/10)
Skonto stadium, Riga
FK JELGAVA 2 (Lapkovskis I. 55, Redjko 85p)
FK JŪRMALA 2 (Paplavskis 14, Čistjakovs 76)
(aet; 6-5 on pens)
Referee – Sipailo
JELGAVA – Bogdanovs, Gubins (Weiss 78), Kazura, Redjko, Lapkovskis V.,
Lapkovskis I., Lazdiņš, Bogdaškins, Bormakovs (Pelcis 78), Kozlovs (Medeck
90+1), Malašenoks.
JŪRMALA – Biezais, Jagodinskis, Stepanovs (Golubevs 85), Kolokoļenkins,
Matsion (Zuntners 59), Bezzubovs, Žatkins, Nagumanov, Bārbaļis, Paplavs
(Čistjakovs 65), Kalniņš.

Vaduz taken to the limit

There are few certainties in football, but it is practically an annual ritual that FC Vaduz will win the Liechtenstein Cup and therefore qualify to be the country's sole representative in Europe the following season. In 2009/10, however, their quest for a 13th successive victory in the competition very nearly came unstuck.

Having scored a dozen goals without reply in the two games that earned them a place in the final – 8-0 against FC Balzers' second team in the quarter-finals, 4-0 against FC Balzers' first team in the semis – Vaduz prepared for a mid-May date in the Rheinparkstadion (their home ground) with USV Eschen/Mauren, the team that had run them close a year earlier, losing 2-1.

Penalty triumph

Eschen/Mauren were on a mission to end a 23-year wait for the trophy. Led once again by ex-FC Bayern München striker Uwe Wegmann, they actually took the lead against the perennial Cup winners, newly coached by Dutchman Eric Orie, with a goal from Francesco Clemente ten minutes into the second half. But a Vaduz side containing five regular Liechtenstein internationals, including Franz Burgmeier and

National team goalkeeper Peter Jehle helped Vaduz to victory in the Liechtenstein Cup

Liechtensteiner Fussballverband (FLV)

Landstrasse 149
FL-9494 Schaan
tel - +423 237 4747
fax - +423 237 4748
website – lfv.li
email – info@lfv.li
Year of Formation – 1934

President – Reinhard Wasler
General Secretary – Roland Ospelt
Media Officer – Judith Frommelt
Stadium – Rheinpark, Vaduz (7,789)

TOP FIVE ALL-TIME CAPS
Mario Frick (92); Martin Stocklasa (86); Peter Jehle (79); Daniel Hasler (78); Martin Telser (74)
TOP FIVE ALL-TIME GOALS
Mario Frick (14); Franz Burgmeier (7); Thomas Beck & Martin Stocklasa (5); Manfred Moser, Fabio D'Elia & Benjamin Fischer (2)

goalkeeper Peter Jehle, fought back to equalise through their Swiss defender Pascal Cerrone and take the game into extra time. No further goals meant penalties and a first shoot-out in the fixture since 1983, when Eschen/Mauren had lost to Balzers. They would be unlucky losers again, going down 4-2 as a relieved Vaduz claimed the Cup for the 39th time.

Burgmeier and Jehle had marked their return to Liechtenstein the previous summer, from England and France respectively, by playing leading roles in helping Vaduz, newly demoted back to Switzerland's second tier, to knock Falkirk FC out of the UEFA Europa League. The Scottish club thus became only the fifth team vanquished by Vaduz in 15 years of European participation. There was also a positive result for the Liechtenstein national team as Hans-Peter Zaugg's side doubled their points tally in the 2010 FIFA World Cup qualifying campaign to two with a 1-1 draw at home to Finland.

LIECHTENSTEIN

NATIONAL TEAM RESULTS 2009/10

12/8/09	Portugal	H	Vaduz	0-3	
5/9/09	Russia (WCQ)	A	St Petersburg	0-3	
9/9/09	Finland (WCQ)	H	Vaduz	1-1	*Polverino (75)*
10/10/09	Azerbaijan (WCQ)	H	Vaduz	0-2	
14/10/09	Wales (WCQ)	H	Vaduz	0-2	
14/11/09	Croatia	A	Vinkovci	0-5	

NATIONAL TEAM APPEARANCES 2009/10

Coach – Hans-Peter ZAUGG (SUI) 2/12/52			Por	RUS	FIN	AZE	WAL	Cro	Caps	Goals
Peter JEHLE	22/1/82	Vaduz	G	G	G	G	G	G	79	-
Yves OEHRI	15/3/87	St Gallen (SUI)	D	D	D	D	D	D	19	-
Michael STOCKLASA	2/12/80	Eschen/Mauren	D	D	D				60	1
Martin STOCKLASA	29/5/79	Ried (AUT)	D					D	86	5
Franz-Josef VOGT	30/10/85	Balzers	D46	M82				s84	22	-
Franz BURGMEIER	7/4/82	Vaduz	M73	D	D	D		M67	58	7
Ronny BÜCHEL	19/3/82	Eschen/Mauren	M	M	M	M	M70	M	69	-
Michele POLVERINO	26/9/84	Aarau (SUI)	M82	s65		s70			15	1
Marco RITZBERGER	27/12/86	Vaduz	M46	M	M	M82	M	M84	29	-
Mario FRICK	7/9/74	St Gallen (SUI)	A64	A	A		A	A37	92	14
Thomas BECK	21/2/81	Hard (AUT)	A46	M57	s79	s68			72	5
Martin RECHSTEINER	15/2/89	Vaduz	s46	D	D	D	D	D	7	-
Mathias CHRISTEN	18/8/87	Gossau (SUI) /Vaduz	s46	A72		s82	s72	s37	12	-
Raphael ROHRER	31/5/85	Eschen/Mauren	s46		M85	M60	M36		44	1
David HASLER	4/5/90	Basel (SUI)	s64	s57	A79	A	A72	A	9	-
Roger BECK	3/8/83	Balzers	s73	s72	s85	s60	s36		43	1
Stefan BÜCHEL	30/6/86	Eschen/Mauren	s82	s82	M68				9	-
Martin BÜCHEL	19/2/87	Zürich (SUI)		M65 75*				M70	29	-
Fabio D'ELIA	19/1/83	Eschen/Mauren				D	D		47	2
Wolfgang KIEBER	22/7/84	BW Feldkirch (AUT)				M	M	s70	8	-
Lucas EBERLE	13/10/90	Balzers				D	D		2	-
Philippe ERNE	14/12/86	Eschen/Mauren						s67	1	-

DOMESTIC CUP 2009/10

FL1 CUP

FIRST ROUND
(18/8/09)
Balzers III 2, Vaduz Portugues 1
Eschen/Mauren II 3, Triesen 2
Ruggell II 2, Triesen II 4
(19/8/09)
Triesenberg II 0, Schaan Azzurri 6
Eschen/Mauren III 4, Vaduz II 6
Vaduz IV 0, Triesenberg 3
SECOND ROUND
(15/9/09)
Schaan Azzurri 0, Triesenberg 3
Triesen II 0, Balzers II 3

(16/9/09)
Vaduz II 1, Ruggell 9
(23/9/09)
Balzers III 0, Eschen/Mauren II 6
QUARTER-FINALS
(20/10/09)
Balzers II 0, Vaduz 8
(21/10/09)
Eschen/Mauren II 1, Schaan 0
(27/10/09)
Ruggell 2, Balzers 4
(28/10/09)
Triesenberg 0, Eschen/Mauren 3

SEMI-FINALS
(6/4/10)
Eschen/Mauren II 2,
Eschen/Mauren 6
Balzers 0, Vaduz 4
FINAL
(13/5/10)
Rheinparkstadion, Vaduz
FC VADUZ 1 *(Cerrone 71)*
USV ESCHEN/MAUREN 1 *(Clemente F. 55)*
(aet ; 4-2 on pens)

Referee – Sperenda
VADUZ – Jehle, Bellón, Stuckmann, Bader (Steil 69), Stegmayer, Rechsteiner, Burgmeier (Akdemir 78), Ritzberger (Colocci 46), Christen, Cerrone, Proschwitz.
ESCHEN/MAUREN – Büchel B., Sturzenegger, Frrokaj, Müller, Stocklasa, Büchel R., Clemente G., Büchel S., Clemente F. (Memeti 97), Erne (Biedermann 76), D'Elia (Domuzeti 29).

Ekranas retain title in last-day thriller

The 2009 A Lyga championship featured eight clubs, the same number as in 2008, but only half of them competed in both campaigns and, not surprisingly, it was the surviving quartet that occupied the top four positions, with FK Ekranas retaining their title ahead of, respectively, FK Vėtra, FK Sūduva and FC Šiauliai.

With FBK Kaunas, FK Atlantas and FK Žalgiris having been excluded for non-footballing reasons, the league authorities were obliged to dig deep into the second-tier 1 Lyga to make up the numbers. Inevitably, the four newcomers, particularly debutants FK LKKA ir Teledema Kaunas and FK Kruoja, found top-flight football a struggle, but theirs would ultimately be a season free of stress as it was decided during the course of the campaign that, due to a re-expansion of the A Lyga to 11 clubs in 2010, there would be no relegation.

Expedient emergency measures may have curbed interest at the bottom of the league, but there was plenty of excitement at the other end, with everybody's title favourites Ekranas surprisingly being taken to the final round of the 28-game campaign before they retained their championship crown.

Enthralling climax

In fact, the league could hardly have had a more enthralling climax as Ekranas's final fixture was away to Vėtra, who, just three points in arrears of the Panevezys club, would force a championship play-off with a victory. Vėtra had not lost to Ekranas in any of their previous three meetings but, against that, the defending champions were on a 20-match unbeaten run, their only defeat of the campaign having come five months earlier, 2-3 at home to Vėtra.

It was a tense occasion and the home side had the better of the first half before the A Lyga's leading marksman, Lithuanian international striker Valdas Trakys, converted Ekranas captain Deimantas Bička's cross after 52 minutes to put the visitors 1-0 up. Vėtra

replied with an equaliser from Evaldas Grigaitis, the match-winner in the earlier win against Ekranas, but Trakys struck again ten minutes from time with his 20th goal of the season to give Ekranas victory and secure the club's fourth national title.

With 18 wins, one defeat, 58 goals scored and 20 conceded, Ekranas ended the season with the best figures in every significant statistical category, making them more than worthy champions. The club's inexperienced coach, 41-year-old Valdas Urbonas, deserved great credit for winning the title in each of his two seasons at the helm, and high praise was also due to skipper Bička, at 37 the oldest outfield player in the league but still one of its most consistently productive midfielders. Trakys, whose goal tally was both a personal best and the highest by far in the league, was voted A Lyga Player of the Year for his exploits, while Vytautas Černiauskias, the team's goalkeeper, took the Young Player of the Year award.

Valdas Trakys took the A Lyga Player of the Year award after scoring 20 goals for champions Ekranas

LITHUANIA

Cup final repeat

Trakys left Ekranas for Greek club Panserraikos FC in January 2010, so he was not around when, in May, the club added victory in the LFF Tauré, the Lithuanian Cup, to their league triumph. Once again they overcame Vėtra on the big occasion, winning the final 2-1 in Kaunas thanks to a late headed goal from substitute Egidijus Varnas after they had fallen behind to a strike from Vėtra's veteran ex-Lithuania international Tomas Ražanauskas just before half-time. It was Ekranas's first victory in the competition for ten years.

Vėtra's defeat denied them a first major trophy but, with 2009 Coach of the Year Virginijus Liubšys at the helm, the previously unsung club from the capital had made giant strides. The A Lyga title might well have been theirs but for a couple of costly defeats to Šiauliai – their only losses prior to the last-day showdown against Ekranas – and in ever-present young goalkeeper Povilas Valinčius, who kept six straight clean sheets in August and September, they possessed a potential star of the future.

Vėtra may have come off second best to Ekranas domestically, but they outshone their rivals in Europe. While Ekranas lasted just one round of the UEFA Champions League, coming unstuck against Bakı FK of Azerbaijan, Vėtra eliminated CS Grevenmacher and Finnish champions-elect HJK Helsinki in the UEFA Europa League before falling to eventual finalists Fulham FC.

Star man Stankevičius

Lithuania's hit-and-miss 2010 FIFA World Cup qualifying campaign reached a low with a 2-1 defeat in the Faroe Islands before concluding the following month with a victory by the same scoreline at home to South Africa-bound group winners Serbia. The winning goal in that game in Marijampole was scored,

Lietuvos futbolo federacija (LFF)

Seimyniskiu Street 15
LT-09312 Vilnius
tel – +370 5 2638741
fax – +370 5 2638740
website – lff.lt
email – info@lff.lt
Year of Formation – 1922

President – Liutauras Varanavičius
General Secretary – Julius Kvedaras
Media Officer – Jurga Chomskyte-McGeever
National Stadium – S. Darius ir S. Girėnas, Kaunas (9,180)

TOP FIVE ALL-TIME CAPS
Andrius Skerla (75); Deividas Šemberas (67); Aurelijus Skarbalius (65); Gintaras Staučė (61); Tomas Danilevičius (60)
TOP FIVE ALL-TIME GOALS
Tomas Danilevičius (19); Antanas Lingis (12); Edgaras Jankauskas & Robertas Poškus (10); Virginijus Baltušnikas (9)

from the penalty spot, by full-back Marius Stankevičius, who would go on to retain his Lithuanian Footballer of the Year title, beating PFC CSKA Moskva midfielder Deividas Šemberas into second place. Stankevičius joined Sevilla FC from UC Sampdoria in January 2010 and, curiously, his new team would be eliminated from the UEFA Champions League in the first knockout round by Šemberas's CSKA.

The win over Serbia was the last game of José Couceiro's reign as Lithuania coach. He departed in December and was replaced a couple of months later by 37-year-old Raimondas Žutautas, a former Lithuanian international who had played in the UEFA Champions League for both Maccabi Haifa FC and Panathinaikos FC but who had no previous head coaching experience. The new man began with a heavy defeat away to Ukraine but steadied the ship by leading Lithuania to victory in the Baltic Cup, a 2-0 win over Estonia giving them the trophy after an opening 0-0 draw against Latvia. Much tougher challenges lay ahead, however, in a UEFA EURO 2012 qualifying group containing Scotland, the Czech Republic and defending champions Spain.

NATIONAL TEAM RESULTS 2009/10

Date	Opponent		Venue	Score	Scorers
12/8/09	Luxembourg	A	Luxembourg	1-0	Danilevičius (40)
9/9/09	Faroe Islands (WCQ)	A	Toftir	1-2	Danilevičius (23p)
10/10/09	Austria (WCQ)	A	Innsbruck	1-2	Stankevičius (66)
14/10/09	Serbia (WCQ)	H	Marijampole	2-1	Kalonas (20p), Stankevičius (68p)
25/5/10	Ukraine	A	Kharkiv	0-4	
18/6/10	Latvia	H	Kaunas	0-0	
20/6/10	Estonia	H	Kaunas	2-0	Savėnas (31p), Rimkevičius (90+2)

NATIONAL TEAM APPEARANCES 2009/10

Coach – José COUCEIRO (POR) 4/10/62
/(9/2/10) Raimondas ŽUTAUTAS 4/9/72

Player	DOB	Club	Lux	FRO	AUT	SRB	Ukr	Lva	Est	Caps	Goals
Žydrūnas KARČEMARSKAS	24/5/83	Dinamo Moskva (RUS)	G	G	G	G					
		/Gaziantepspor (TUR)						s46		48	-
Marius STANKEVIČIUS	15/7/81	Sampdoria (ITA)	D	D	D	D					
		/Sevilla (ESP)					D			50	4
Ignas DEDURA	1/6/78	Spartak Moskva (RUS)	D	D	D	D					
		/Salyut Belgorod (RUS)					D	D64		47	1
Andrius SKERLA	29/4/77	Jagiellonia (POL)	D	D						75	1
Arūnas KLIMAVIČIUS	5/10/82	Ural (RUS)	D88	D60			D				
		/Sibir (RUS)						D	D	28	2
Kęstutis IVAŠKEVIČIUS	17/4/85	Kryvbas (UKR)	M66	M82	M		M	M70	M	13	-
Linas PILIBAITIS	5/4/85	Győr (HUN)	M59	M60	M					16	-
Deividas ŠEMBERAS	2/8/78	CSKA Moskva (RUS)	M	M	M					67	-
Saulius MIKOLIŪNAS	2/5/84	Arsenal Kyiv (UKR)	M81	s60		M67		M		38	2
Deividas ČESNAUSKIS	30/6/81	Ergotelis (GRE)	M73					M62	M	39	4
Tomas DANILEVIČIUS	18/7/78	Livorno (ITA)	A	A	A		A			60	19
Darvydas ŠERNAS	22/7/84	Widzew (POL)	s59	M	M	A89	M63	A72	A71	16	1
Mindaugas PANKA	1/5/84	Widzew (POL)	s66		M89	M				6	-
Valdas TRAKYS	20/3/79	Ekranas	s73	s60	s89	s89				11	2
Vytautas LUKŠA	14/8/84	MTZ-RIPO (BLR)	s81			s82	s67				
		/Illychivets (UKR)					M82	s46	M77	8	-
Vidas ALUNDERIS	27/3/79	LASK (AUT)	s88				D82	D		21	-
Edgaras ČESNAUSKIS	5/2/84	FC Moskva (RUS)	M	M						26	1
Mindaugas KALONAS	28/2/84	Metalurh Zaporizhya (UKR)	s82	s46	M82	s63				34	2
Tadas KIJANSKAS	6/9/85	Vėtra					D	D			
		/Sūduva						D	D	4	-
Tomas RAŽANAUSKAS	7/1/76	Vėtra					M46	s82		40	7
Giedrius ARLAUSKIS	1/12/87	Unirea Urziceni (ROU)					G46	G		4	-
Ramūnas RADAVIČIUS	20/1/81	Ekranas					D	D	D	3	-
Dominykas GALKEVIČIUS	16/10/86	Ekranas					M	M	M80	3	-
Arvydas NOVIKOVAS	18/12/90	Hearts (SCO)					M55			1	-
Robertas POŠKUS	5/5/79	İnter Bakı (AZE)					s55	s62		45	10
Vitalijus KAVALIAUSKAS	2/7/83	Liepājas Metalurgs (LVA)					s82	s70	s77	15	3
Mantas SAVĖNAS	27/8/82	Sibir (RUS)						M46	M81	33	5
Artūras RIMKEVIČIUS	14/4/83	Vėtra						s72	s71	2	1
Paulius GRYBAUSKAS	2/6/84	Neftçi (AZE)							G	6	-
Irmantas ZELMIKAS	3/1/80	unattached							s64	12	-
Andrius ARLAUSKAS	16/1/86	Ekranas							s80	1	-
Ričardas BENIUŠIS	23/4/80	Sūduva							s81	24	2

LITHUANIA

DOMESTIC LEAGUE 2009

A LYGA FINAL LEAGUE TABLE

		Pld	Home					Away					Total					Pts
			W	D	L	F	A	W	D	L	F	A	W	D	L	F	A	
1	FK Ekranas	28	11	2	1	35	10	7	7	0	23	10	18	9	1	58	20	63
2	FK Vėtra	28	10	3	1	33	11	6	6	2	22	11	16	9	3	55	22	57
3	FK Sūduva	28	8	6	0	33	9	6	5	3	22	13	14	11	3	55	22	53
4	FC Šiauliai	28	7	3	4	17	10	6	0	8	23	24	13	3	12	40	34	42
5	FK Tauras	28	6	5	3	12	7	4	3	7	14	15	10	8	10	26	22	38
6	FK Banga	28	4	3	7	15	22	3	3	8	10	27	7	6	15	25	49	27
7	FK LKKA ir Teledema Kaunas	28	2	1	11	10	35	2	2	10	9	28	4	3	21	19	63	15
8	FK Kruoja	28	2	5	7	15	28	0	2	12	9	42	2	7	19	24	70	13

NB No relegation – 2010 A Lyga extended to 11 clubs;
FK LKKA ir Teledema Kaunas renamed FK Atletas Kaunas for 2010 season.

TOP GOALSCORERS

20 Valdas TRAKYS (Ekranas)

11 Mantas KUKLYS (Šiauliai)
   Ričardas BENIUŠIS (Sūduva)
   Tadas KIJANSKAS (Vėtra)

10 Egidijus VARNAS (Ekranas)

9 Povilas LUKŠYS (Sūduva)
  Mindaugas GRIGALEVIČIUS (Vėtra)

8 Israel Awenayeri DOUGLAS (Banga)
  Igoris MORINAS (Kruoja)
  Andrius URBŠYS (Sūduva)

CLUB-BY-CLUB

FK BANGA
Coach – Valdas Ivanauskas; (20/7/09) Vytautas Jančiauskas
Founded – 1966
Stadium – Gargždai (1,000)

2009

4/4	Sūduva	a	0-4	
11/4	Vėtra	h	0-5	
18/4	Ekranas	a	0-1	
26/4	LKKA	h	1-0	Kura
2/5	Kruoja	a	0-2	
9/5	Tauras	a	0-0	
17/5	Šiauliai	h	3-2	Vaitkūnas, Lipskis (p), Bačanskis
26/5	Sūduva	h	0-0	
10/6	Vėtra	a	2-2	Staponka 2
14/6	Ekranas	h	1-2	Douglas
17/6	LKKA	a	2-0	Douglas, Lipskis
21/6	Kruoja	h	3-0	Douglas 3
28/6	Tauras	h	1-1	Douglas
5/7	Šiauliai	a	0-4	
26/7	Sūduva	a	1-1	Douglas (p)
2/8	Vėtra	h	0-1	
9/8	Ekranas	h	0-3	
16/8	LKKA	h	0-1	
23/8	Kruoja	h	4-2	Douglas, Staponka, Kožikis, Remeza
29/8	Tauras	h	0-2	
5/9	Šiauliai	h	1-2	Lipskis
13/9	Sūduva	h	1-1	Staponka
20/9	Vėtra	a	0-2	
27/9	Ekranas	a	1-5	Staponka
3/10	LKKA	a	2-1	Lipskis (p), Arlauskis
18/10	Kruoja	a	2-1	Staponka 2
25/10	Tauras	a	0-1	
31/10	Šiauliai	a	0-3	

No	Name	Nat	DoB	Pos	Aps	(s)	Gls
14	Davydas ARLAUSKIS		18/11/86	D	11	(1)	1
8	Algimantas BAČANSKIS		30/10/90	A	3	(8)	1
20	Marius BIRŠKYS		16/7/87	M	3		
27	Edvinas BRAČKUS		11/9/90	D	9		
90	Aivaras BRAŽINSKAS		1/11/90	G	7		
22	Rimantas CEPOVAS		22/1/80	M	5		

22	Sergei CHELOKHSAYEV	RUS	21/9/83	A	1	(1)	
24	Israel Awenayeri DOUGLAS	NGA	24/7/84	A	18	(7)	8
15	Gytis GAILIUS		20/11/90	M	2	(3)	
30	Žygimantas GEDRIMAS		16/6/91	M		(1)	
7	Rimvydas GRUDYS		20/9/82	M	17	(4)	
13	Mantas GUDAUSKAS		4/1/89	D	26		
12	Aleksandras IVANAUSKAS		5/12/87	D	15	(2)	
30	Giedrius KOŽIKIS		29/3/89	M	7	(2)	1
10	Mikas KURA		1/4/89	M	8	(12)	1
9	Andrius LIPSKIS		16/2/88	M	27	(1)	4
28	Donatas REMEZA		12/5/88	M	16	(2)	1
17	Aurimas ŠLUŠNYS		21/6/84	D	13		
99	Igor SPIRIDONOV		27/8/88	G	19		
21	Aurelijus STAPONKA		9/11/83	A	25	(1)	7
19	Darius TAMAŠAUSKAS		29/6/87	D	8		
11	Julius TRIUŠKA		22/3/89	M	4	(2)	
5	Karolis URBAITIS		12/12/90	D	19	(2)	
25	Egidijus VAITKŪNAS		8/8/88	D	13	(1)	1
23	Germanas VANIUCHINAS		15/11/89	M		(12)	
16	Mindaugas VIJEIKIS		15/6/80	M	13	(4)	
4	Darius ŽUTAUTAS		30/9/78	D	17	(3)	
77	Vaidas ŽUTAUTAS		18/7/71	G	2		

FK EKRANAS
Coach – Valdas Urbonas
Founded – 1964
Stadium – Aukštaitija (4,000)
MAJOR HONOURS:
Lithuanian League - (4) 1993, 2005, 2008, 2009;
Lithuanian Cup - (3) 1998, 2000, 2010.

2009

4/4	Kruoja	h	4-0	Trakys 2, Banys 2
11/4	LKKA	a	1-1	Gleveckas
18/4	Banga	h	1-0	Pogreban
26/4	Tauras	a	1-0	Gleveckas
2/5	Šiauliai	h	2-0	Varnas, Trakys
9/5	Sūduva	a	1-1	Bička
23/5	Vėtra	h	2-3	Galkevičius, Trakys
26/5	Kruoja	a	2-2	Varnas, Bička
10/6	LKKA	h	3-0	Varnas, Bička (p), Arlauskas
14/6	Banga	a	2-1	Ademolu, Galkevičius

17/6	Tauras	h	2-1	Trakys, Varnas	
21/6	Šiauliai	a	1-0	Galkevičius	
28/6	Sūduva	h	2-2	Varnas, Gleveckas	
26/7	Kruoja	h	3-0	Galkevičius, Aranđelović (p), Varnas	
2/8	LKKA	a	3-0	Trakys 2, Varnas	
9/8	Banga	a	3-0	Varnas, Trakys 2	
16/8	Tauras	a	1-1	Varnas	
23/8	Šiauliai	h	2-0	Bička (p), Trakys (p)	
29/8	Sūduva	a	1-1	Trakys	
13/9	Kruoja	a	2-2	Trakys 2	
16/9	Vėtra	a	0-0		
20/9	LKKA	h	3-0	Trakys 2, Bička	
27/9	Banga	h	5-1	Gleveckas, Ademolu 2, Varnas, Galkevičius	
30/9	Vėtra	h	1-1	Bička (p)	
4/10	Tauras	h	1-0	Trakys	
18/10	Šiauliai	a	3-0	Trakys 2, Šidlauskas	
25/10	Sūduva	h	4-2	Galkevičius, Šidlauskas, Tomkevičius, Bička	
31/10	Vėtra	a	2-1	Trakys 2	

No	Name	Nat	DoB	Pos	Aps	(s)	Gls
7	Stephen ADEMOLU	CAN	20/11/82	A	20	(3)	3
32	Darko ARANĐELOVIĆ	SRB	3/1/81	M	5	(1)	
17	Andrius ARLAUSKAS		16/1/86	M	19	(3)	1
10	Žilvinas BANYS		25/2/86	M	5	(17)	2
22	Deimantas BIČKA		19/2/72	M	27		7
1	Vytautas ČERNIAUSKAS		12/3/89	G	25		
88	Dominykas GALKEVIČIUS		16/10/86	M	28		6
3	Dainius GLEVECKAS		5/3/77	D	26		4
16	Paulius JANUŠAUSKAS		28/2/89	M		(7)	
12	Tadas KAUNECKAS		31/3/86	G	3		
25	Aurimas MARCINKEVIČIUS		17/1/90	A		(2)	
58	Dušan MATOVIĆ	SRB	8/7/87	D	28		
2	Deividas PADAIGIS		2/2/86	D		(6)	
37	Serghei POGREBAN	MDA	13/5/78	A	12	(6)	1
5	Taavi RÄHN	EST	16/5/81	D	7	(2)	
6	Povilas ŠARŪNAS		14/11/85	D	8	(11)	
15	Nerijus SASNAUSKAS		20/4/80	D	15	(4)	
14	Dainius SAULĖNAS		13/3/79	A		(5)	
11	Adrius ŠIDLAUSKAS		30/10/84	M	11	(3)	2
77	Giedrius TOMKEVIČIUS		29/2/84	M	26	(1)	1
9	Valdas TRAKYS		20/3/79	A	26	(1)	20
19	Egidijus VARNAS		31/7/75	A	17	(6)	10

FK KRUOJA

Coach – Aidas Dambrauskas
Founded – 2001
Stadium – Pakruojis (1,000)

2009

4/4	Ekranas	a	0-4	
11/4	Šiauliai	a	1-2	Mykolaitis
18/4	LKKA	h	1-1	Mykolaitis
26/4	Sūduva	a	0-6	
2/5	Banga	h	2-0	Januš6evičius, Vilėniškis
9/5	Vėtra	a	1-6	Vilėniškis (p)
23/5	Tauras	h	2-2	Mykolaitis, Janušsevičius
26/5	Ekranas	h	2-2	Janušsevičius, Zeniauskas
10/6	Šiauliai	h	0-5	
14/6	LKKA	a	2-3	Vilėniškis, Šimkus
17/6	Sūduva	h	0-1	
21/6	Banga	a	0-3	
28/6	Vėtra	h	0-3	
5/7	Tauras	a	0-2	
26/7	Ekranas	a	0-3	
2/8	Šiauliai	a	0-0	
9/8	LKKA	h	2-1	Morinas 2
16/8	Sūduva	a	1-3	Morinas

23/8	Banga	a	2-4	Morinas, Vilėniškis (p)
29/8	Vėtra	a	0-3	
5/9	Tauras	h	0-3	
13/9	Ekranas	h	2-2	Šimkus, Morinas (p)
20/9	Šiauliai	h	1-3	Šimkus
27/9	LKKA	a	1-2	Morinas
4/10	Sūduva	h	0-1	
18/10	Banga	h	1-2	Jakštas
25/10	Vėtra	h	2-2	Morinas, Mykolaitis
31/10	Tauras	a	1-1	Morinas

No	Name	Nat	DoB	Pos	Aps	(s)	Gls
17	Gediminas BUTAVIČIUS		5/6/83	A	10	(2)	
5	Marius BUTĖNAS		22/3/81	D	26	(1)	
1	Raimondas ČEGINSKAS		2/1/78	G	21		
33	Piotr DUBROVSKIJ		19/6/87	G	6		
7	Mindaugas JAKŠTAS		3/1/86	M	5	(11)	1
12	Lauras JANUŠEVIČIUS		6/7/83	D	21	(3)	3
17	Dalius KIŠLA		25/8/87	M		(1)	
40	Giedrius KVEDARAS		9/7/91	G	1		
11	Igoris MORINAS		21/2/75	M	14		8
19	Kęstutis MYKOLAITIS		4/7/83	M	22	(2)	4
24	Deividas PADAIGIS		2/2/86	D	14		
20	Donatas PAULAUSKAS		20/2/87	D	3	(13)	
11	Viktor RASKOV	UKR	8/5/84	A	7	(1)	
21	Ovidijus ŠIDLAUSKAS		7/1/91	A		(1)	
23	Paulius ŠIDLAUSKAS		29/6/86	M	10	(5)	
13	Virginijus ŠIMKUS		25/7/83	A	18	(6)	3
15	Ernestas STANIKAITIS		23/7/87	D	10	(1)	
16	Evaldas STANIKAITIS		14/10/89	G		(1)	
14	Tomas STATKEVIČIUS		19/12/89	D	14		
9	Arūnas ŠTEINAS		6/7/81	A	15	(4)	
4	Aurimas STROLĖ		26/8/82	D		(1)	
3	Aidas TUMĖNAS		20/4/86	D	11	(6)	
10	Mantas USELIS		28/11/80	A	20	(4)	
2	Mindaugas VALYS		26/1/86	D	6	(5)	
25	Arvydas VEIKUTIS		19/3/87	M	9	(2)	
22	Raimondas VILĖNIŠKIS		10/6/76	M	20		4
8	Kęstutis ZENIAUSKAS		29/6/86	M	25		1

FK LKKA IR TELEDEMA KAUNAS

Coach – Viačeslavas Novikovas
Founded – 2005
Stadium – LŽŪU (500)

2009

4/4	Vėtra	a	1-3	Bezykornovas
11/4	Ekranas	h	1-1	Macevičius G.
18/4	Kruoja	a	1-1	Petkevičius
26/4	Banga	a	0-1	
2/5	Tauras	h	0-3	
9/5	Šiauliai	a	1-0	Bezykornovas (p)
23/5	Sūduva	h	2-7	Bezykornovas, Urbelionis
26/5	Vėtra	h	0-2	
10/6	Ekranas	a	0-3	
14/6	Kruoja	h	3-2	Mikalauskas, Rūškys, Grušauskas
17/6	Banga	h	0-2	
21/6	Tauras	a	0-1	
28/6	Šiauliai	h	0-2	
5/7	Sūduva	a	0-2	
26/7	Vėtra	a	1-4	Venckus
2/8	Ekranas	h	0-3	
9/8	Kruoja	a	1-2	Rūškys
16/8	Banga	a	1-0	Bezykornovas (p)
23/8	Tauras	h	0-1	
29/8	Šiauliai	a	1-1	Bezykornovas
13/9	Vėtra	h	0-1	
20/9	Ekranas	a	0-3	
27/9	Kruoja	h	2-1	Smaryginas, Bezykornovas

LITHUANIA

3/10	Banga	h	1-2	*Bezykornovas (p)*
7/10	Sūduva	h	0-4	
18/10	Tauras	a	0-3	
25/10	Šiauliai	h	1-4	*Rūškys*
31/10	Sūduva	a	2-4	*Vasiliauskas, Jefišovas*

No	Name	Nat	DoB	Pos	Aps	(s)	Gls
15	Donatas BENDINSKAS		27/4/89	D	18	(2)	
8	Marius BEZYKORNOVAS		22/8/76	M	26		7
19	Vitoldas ČEPAUSKAS		17/3/79	D	6		
7	Eivinas ČERNIAUSKAS		24/9/84	M	15	(2)	
19	Eringas DEGUTIS		25/4/87	D		(2)	
27	Tomas DOMARKAS		5/2/86	A		(1)	
22	Justinas GASIŪNAS		21/4/85	G	6		
1	Mantas GINTALAS		4/4/88	G	9		
14	Mindaugas GRUŠAUSKAS		16/1/88	A	5	(16)	1
36	Arnold GUDALEVIČ		7/3/90	G		(1)	
20	Aleksandras JEFIŠOVAS		24/11/84	M	10	(5)	1
4	Audrius JUOZAITIS		13/8/86	D	9		
33	Mantas JUOZAPAITIS		13/3/92	M		(1)	
2	Dainius KUNEVIČIUS		30/7/78	D	3		
4	Gediminas MACEVIČIUS		27/11/86	D	12	(2)	1
39	Paulius MACEVIČIUS		9/5/89	D	13		
12	Kostas MAKAREVUČIUS		20/4/88	G	9		
18	Armando Tarlazis Viera dos Santos "MANDINHO"	BRA	28/1/84	M	4		
10	Jaunius MIKALAUSKAS		12/9/83	A	10	(12)	1
6	Aurimas MOCKUS		22/1/85	D	8	(5)	
11	Vladas PETKEVIČIUS		2/8/89	A	22	(4)	1
21	Kęstutis PETKUS		22/7/88	D		(7)	
17	Erikas RŪŠKYS		12/9/87	M	19	(5)	3
2	Vitalijus SAVICKAS		2/6/89	D	9	(1)	
13	Paulius SMARYGINAS		30/10/86	M	11		1
28	Artūras ŠNEKUTIS		30/6/84	D		(1)	
1	Andrius STRUKAS		10/8/86	G	4		
5	Darius URBELIONIS		30/9/78	M	17	(2)	1
16	Eisvinas UTYRA		14/9/90	M	9	(10)	
13	Mindaugas VALANČIUS		7/5/86	D	2	(1)	
9	Karolis VASILIAUSKAS		8/5/89	D	27		1
38	Deivydas VENCKUS		2/3/86	A	11		1
3	Gediminas ZABORSKIS		4/4/88	D	14	(2)	

FC ŠIAULIAI
Coach – Deivis Kančelskis
Founded – 1995
Stadium – Šiauliai Municipal (3,000)

2009

4/4	Tauras	h	1-0	*Špukas*
11/4	Kruoja	h	2-1	*Kuklys 2*
18/4	Sūduva	a	0-1	
26/4	Vėtra	h	2-1	*Kuklys, Romašovas*
2/5	Ekranas	a	0-2	
9/5	LKKA	h	0-1	
17/5	Banga	a	2-3	*Šilėnas, Romašovas*
26/5	Tauras	a	0-1	
10/6	Kruoja	a	5-0	*Šilėnas, Romašovas, Špukas, Marozas, Lunskis*
14/6	Sūduva	h	0-1	
17/6	Vėtra	a	1-2	*Marozas*
21/6	Ekranas	h	0-1	
28/6	LKKA	a	2-0	*Romašovas, Kuklys*
5/7	Banga	h	4-0	*Kuklys 2 (1p), Marozas, Urbelis*
26/7	Tauras	h	2-0	*Jasaitis 2*
2/8	Kruoja	h	0-0	
9/8	Sūduva	a	1-5	*Viktoravičius*
16/8	Vėtra	h	1-0	*Marozas*
23/8	Ekranas	a	0-2	
29/8	LKKA	h	1-1	*Viktoravičius*
5/9	Banga	a	2-1	*Kuklys, Romašovas*
13/9	Tauras	a	1-0	*Špukas*

20/9	Kruoja	a	3-1	*Špukas, Šilėnas, Kuklys (p)*
27/9	Sūduva	h	1-1	*Lunskis*
4/10	Vėtra	a	2-5	*Burkšaitis, Lapeikis*
18/10	Ekranas	h	0-3	
25/10	LKKA	a	4-1	*Viktoravičius, Šilėnas, Kuklys 2 (1p)*
31/10	Banga	h	3-0	*Kuklys, Lunskis, Viktoravičius*

No	Name	Nat	DoB	Pos	Aps	(s)	Gls
10	Saimonas BURKŠAITIS		21/1/90	M	15	(5)	1
23	Paulius DRUBLIONIS		17/12/91	D	6	(8)	
18	Tautvydas ELIOŠIUS		3/11/91	M		(3)	
17	Aurimas GARUCKAS		5/6/86	D	10	(4)	
4	Klimas GUSOČENKO		9/3/89	D	2	(8)	
28	Edvinas JASAITIS		11/4/90	M	17	(5)	2
1	Šarūnas JUREVIČIUS		3/5/89	G	21		
5	Tomas KANČELSKIS		19/8/75	D	19		
13	Justinas KUIZINAS		9/10/91	A		(4)	
8	Mantas KUKLYS		10/6/87	M	27		11
25	Vilius LAPEIKIS		30/6/83	D	14		1
15	Deivydas LUNSKIS		12/7/77	D	26		3
14	Eimantas MAROZAS		28/12/85	A	17	(5)	4
66	Ernestas PILYPAS		17/5/90	D	9	(1)	
19	Edvardas PŠELENSKIS		11/2/88	M	21	(1)	
30	Aivaras RENUSAS		27/3/92	M		(2)	
27	Aleksandras ROMAŠOVAS		28/9/85	A	13	(10)	5
20	Vaidas ŠILĖNAS		10/7/85	M	24		4
88	Tadas SIMAITIS		29/12/90	G	7		
6	Rolandas SLEPAKOVAS		29/8/86	D	19	(2)	
22	Tadas ŠPUKAS		31/7/86	A	21	(3)	4
77	Donatas STROCKIS		23/3/87	D	6		
99	Rokas URBELIS		27/1/90	M		(15)	1
11	Vaidas VIKTORAVIČIUS		8/5/87	A	14	(6)	4

FK SŪDUVA
Coach – Gedas Jarmalavičius
Founded – 1968
Stadium – Marijampolė FC (6,250)
MAJOR HONOURS:
Lithuanian Cup - (2) 2006, 2009.

2009

4/4	Banga	h	4-0	*Lukšys 2, Urbšys, Radavičius*
11/4	Tauras	a	2-0	*Urbšys, Slavickas G.*
18/4	Šiauliai	h	1-0	*Gardzijauskas (p)*
26/4	Kruoja	h	6-0	*Urbšys, Lukšys, Gardzijauskas 2 (1p), Brokas, Radavičius*
2/5	Vėtra	a	0-0	
9/5	Ekranas	h	1-1	*Lukšys*
23/5	LKKA	a	7-2	*og (Macevičius G.), Urbšys 2, Gardzijauskas, Lukšys, Radavičius, og (Mockus)*
26/5	Banga	a	0-0	
10/6	Tauras	h	3-0	*Lukšys 2, Slavickas V.*
14/6	Šiauliai	a	1-0	*Krasnovskis*
17/6	Kruoja	a	1-0	*Krasnovskis*
21/6	Vėtra	h	1-1	*Radavičius*
28/6	Ekranas	a	2-2	*Skroblas, Lukšys*
5/7	LKKA	h	2-0	*Brokas, Gardzijauskas*
26/7	Banga	h	1-1	*Lukšys*
2/8	Tauras	a	0-1	
9/8	Šiauliai	h	5-1	*Urbšys, Klevinskas G., Brokas, Esaú, Gardzijauskas*
16/8	Kruoja	h	3-1	*Esaú 2, Radavičius (p)*
23/8	Vėtra	a	0-2	
29/8	Ekranas	h	1-1	*Beniušis*
13/9	Banga	a	1-1	*Beniušis (p)*
20/9	Tauras	h	0-0	
27/9	Šiauliai	a	1-1	*Beniušis*
4/10	Kruoja	a	1-0	*Leimonas*
7/10	LKKA	h	4-0	*Beniušis 4*

18/10	Vėtra	h	1-1	Leimonas
25/10	Ekranas	a	2-4	Beniušis, Urbšys
31/10	LKKA	h	4-2	Beniušis 3, Urbšys

No	Name	Nat	DoB	Pos	Aps	(s)	Gls
88	Ričardas BENIUŠIS		23/4/80	A	10		11
14	Brunas BISKYS		31/3/91	A		(3)	
39	Ernestas BISKYS		31/3/90	M		(3)	
16	Audrius BROKAS		20/8/90	M	7	(18)	3
44	Karolis CHVEDUKAS		21/4/91	M	2	(4)	
23	ESAÚ García Álvarez	ESP	2/1/87	A	10	(2)	3
51	Mindaugas GARDZIJAUSKAS		28/9/78	M	19	(3)	6
4	Kazimieras GNEDUJUS		28/2/86	D	4	(1)	
4	Jevgenijs KAZURA	LVA	24/1/88	D	1		
5	Giedrius KLEVINSKAS		4/10/81	D	14	(1)	1
55	Saulius KLEVINSKAS		2/4/84	G	27		
10	Serhiy KOZYUBERDA	UKR	21/3/80	M	3	(1)	
29	Povilas KRASNOVSKIS		29/4/89	M	3	(13)	2
12	Povilas LEIMONAS		16/11/87	D	27		2
11	Povilas LUKŠYS		7/7/79	A	15		9
7	Ramūnas RADAVIČIUS		20/1/81	D	24		5
18	Mantas SAMUSIOVAS		8/9/78	D	11		
3	Marius SKINDERIS		13/10/84	D	21	(2)	
8	Alfredas SKROBLAS		11/3/84	D	24	(1)	1
9	Giedrius SLAVICKAS		13/10/82	M	22	(1)	1
19	Vaidas SLAVICKAS		26/2/86	D	24		1
34	Gytis URBA		1/1/91	D	1		
17	Andrius URBŠYS		22/8/86	M	24	(2)	8
1	Armantas VITKAUSKAS		31/5/86	G	1		
15	Eivinas ZAGURSKAS		9/9/89	M	4	(17)	
4	Irmantas ZELMIKAS		3/1/80	D	10		

FK TAURAS

Coach – Edvardas Malkevičius;
(14/6/09) Aleksandr Brazevich (BLR);
(26/7/09) Jurijs Popkovs (LVA)
Founded – 1922
Stadium – Vytautas (1,600)

2009

4/4	Šiauliai	a	0-1	
11/4	Sūduva	h	0-2	
18/4	Vėtra	a	0-1	
26/4	Ekranas	h	0-1	
2/5	LKKA	a	3-0	Chelokhsayev 2, Puotkalis
9/5	Banga	h	0-0	
23/5	Kruoja	a	2-2	Mižigurskis, Rimkevičius
26/5	Šiauliai	h	1-0	Mockus
10/6	Sūduva	a	0-3	
14/6	Vėtra	h	1-1	Ngapounou
17/6	Ekranas	a	1-2	Rimkevičius
21/6	LKKA	h	1-0	Rimkevičius
28/6	Banga	a	1-1	Jasaitis
5/7	Kruoja	h	2-0	Jasaitis, Puotkalis
26/7	Šiauliai	a	0-2	
2/8	Sūduva	h	1-2	Laurišas
9/8	Vėtra	a	1-2	Semjonovs
16/8	Ekranas	h	1-1	Regelskis
23/8	LKKA	a	1-0	Irkha
29/8	Banga	a	2-0	Irkha, Semjonovs
5/9	Kruoja	a	3-0	Straleckas 3
13/9	Šiauliai	h	0-1	
20/9	Sūduva	a	0-0	
27/9	Vėtra	h	0-0	
4/10	Ekranas	a	0-0	
18/10	LKKA	h	3-0	Žavoronkovs 2, Irkha
25/10	Banga	h	1-0	Vaitkūnas
31/10	Kruoja	h	1-1	Žavoronkovs

No	Name	Nat	DoB	Pos	Aps	(s)	Gls
32	Egidijus AURYLA		26/7/92	D	1		
15	Lukas BIELSKIS		11/5/92	M		(5)	
76	Iulian BURSUC	MDA	23/9/76	M	10		
16	Sergei CHELOKHSAYEV	RUS	21/9/83	A	4	(1)	2
77	Besik CHIGLADZE	GEO	23/7/81	M	5	(1)	
70	David CHIGLADZE	GEO	22/2/84	D	11	(1)	
7	Vytautas DRAGŪNEVIČIUS		9/1/76	M	4	(10)	
4	Robertas FREIDGEIMAS		21/2/89	D	9		
21	Dalius GIRDVAINIS		4/2/87	M	8	(12)	
35	Sergei IRKHA	BLR	25/3/84	M	13	(1)	3
29	Karolis JASAITIS		1/11/82	M	4	(2)	2
9	Giedrius KOŽIKIS		29/3/89	M	1	(5)	
34	Aivaras LAURIŠAS		5/4/77	A	4		1
3	Mantas LĖKIS		15/11/86	D	24		
78	Pavel LEUS		15/9/78	G	3		
14	Nerijus MAČIULIS		1/4/83	M	13	(1)	
23	Martynas MATUZAS		28/8/89	G	1		
99	Valerijus MIŽIGURSKIS		22/4/83	A	9	(1)	1
18	Jaunius MOCKUS		1/1/85	D	26		1
5	Bertrand NGAPOUNOU	CMR	20/11/82	D	10		1
17	Valdas POCEVIČIUS		16/5/86	D	14		
13	Eimantas PODERIS		13/9/73	M	9	(1)	
14	Andrius PUOTKALIS		6/10/80	A	14		2
8	Darius REGELSKIS		15/4/76	D	26		1
20	Artūras RIMKEVIČIUS		14/4/83	A	4		3
17	Arvydas RUDŽIONIS		18/4/87	M	2	(4)	
36	Olegs SEMJONOVS	LVA	1/4/84	A	14		2
1	Ernestas ŠETKUS		25/5/85	G	24		
20	Tomas SIREVIČIUS		23/3/79	D	6		
11	Paulius SMARYGINAS		30/10/86	M	6	(4)	
42	Tadas STRALECKAS		4/3/83	A	1	(5)	3
10	Sigitas TAROZA		4/6/82	A		(8)	
5	Egidijus VAITKŪNAS		8/8/88	D	10		1
13	Jānis VAITKUS	LVA	24/10/84	M	7	(3)	
41	Vladimirs ŽAVORONKOVS	LVA	25/11/76	D	11		3

FK VĖTRA

Coach – Virginijus Liubšys
Founded – 1996
Stadium – Vėtra (5,900)

2009

4/4	LKKA	h	3-1	Kulbis, Dmitrijev, Žulpa
11/4	Banga	a	5-0	Grigalevičius 2, Mašitšev, Kijanskas 2
18/4	Tauras	h	1-0	Kijanskas (p)
26/4	Šiauliai	a	1-2	Kijanskas
2/5	Sūduva	h	0-0	
9/5	Kruoja	h	6-1	Vasiliauskas, Kijanskas 3 (3p), Grigalevičius, Moroz
23/5	Ekranas	a	3-2	og (Rähn), Eliošius, Grigaitis
26/5	LKKA	a	2-0	Grigaitis, Kijanskas (p)
10/6	Banga	h	2-2	Mikuckis, Kijanskas (p)
14/6	Tauras	a	1-1	Jankauskas
17/6	Šiauliai	h	2-1	Moroz, Eliošius
21/6	Sūduva	a	1-1	Grigalevičius
28/6	Kruoja	a	3-0	Mašitšev, Grigalevičius 2
26/7	LKKA	h	4-1	Veževičius 2, Vasiliauskas, Kijanskas (p)
2/8	Banga	a	1-0	Vasiliauskas
9/8	Tauras	h	2-1	Stanaitis, Grigaitis
16/8	Šiauliai	a	0-1	
23/8	Sūduva	h	2-0	Jankauskas, Grigaitis
29/8	Kruoja	h	3-0	Ražanauskas, Paulauskas, Grigaitis
13/9	LKKA	a	1-0	Jankauskas
16/9	Ekranas	h	0-0	
20/9	Banga	h	2-0	Ngapounou, Kijanskas
27/9	Tauras	a	0-0	
30/9	Ekranas	a	1-1	Mikuckis

 # LITHUANIA

4/10	Šiauliai	h	5-2	Borovskij, Grigalevičius 2 (1p),	
				Vėževičius, Mašitšev	
18/10	Sūduva	a	1-1	Grigalevičius	
25/10	Kruoja	a	2-2	Vasiliauskas, Jankauskas	
31/10	Ekranas	h	1-2	Grigaitis	

No	Name	Nat	DoB	Pos	Aps	(s)	Gls
3	Valdemar BOROVSKIJ		2/5/84	D	23	(2)	1
2	Janusz BUCHOLC	POL	18/6/85	D	4	(1)	
77	Artjom DMITRIJEV	EST	14/11/88	A	6		1
20	Tadas ELIOŠIUS		1/3/90	M	16	(7)	2
11	Evaldas GRIGAITIS		28/9/87	A	20	(5)	6
44	Mindaugas GRIGALEVIČIUS		3/12/81	A	17	(1)	9
5	Algis JANKAUSKAS		27/9/82	D	27		4
4	Tadas KIJANSKAS		6/9/85	D	26		11
10	Gajus KULBIS		5/7/89	M	4	(8)	1
12	Nikolai MAŠITŠEV	EST	5/12/88	M	22	(2)	3
25	Tomas MIKUCKIS		13/1/89	D	9	(2)	2
7	Jevgenij MOROZ		20/1/90	M	8	(17)	2
6	Bertrand NGAPOUNOU	CMR	20/11/82	D	6	(3)	1
13	Gediminas PAULAUSKAS		27/10/82	D	24		1
33	Tomas RAŽANAUSKAS		7/1/76	M	22		1
26	Marius STANAITIS		26/12/87	M	20	(2)	1
23	Tautvydas ŠVELNA		13/5/91	A		(1)	
30	Povilas VALINČIUS		16/5/89	G	28		
14	Nerijus VASILIAUSKAS		20/6/77	A	11	(9)	4
19	Robertas VĖŽEVIČIUS		5/1/86	M	12	(9)	3
27	Aleksander VOLODIN	EST	29/3/88	D	2	(1)	
8	Artūras ŽULPA		10/6/90	M	1	(9)	1

PROMOTED CLUBS

FK MAŽEIKIAI
Coach – Nerijus Gudaitis
Founded – 1947
Stadium – Mažeikiai (748)
MAJOR HONOURS:
Lithuanian League - (1) 1994.

FK KLAIPĖDA
Coach – Saulius Mikalajūnas
Founded – 2005
Stadium – Klaipėda (4,940)

VMFD ŽALGIRIS
Coach – Igoris Pankratjevas
Founded – 1947
Stadium – Sportima (3,200)
MAJOR HONOURS:
Lithuanian League (3) 1991, 1992, 1999;
Lithuanian Cup - (5) 1991, 1993, 1994, 1997, 2003 (autumn).

SECOND LEVEL FINAL TABLE 2009

Second Phase	Pld	W	D	L	F	A	Pts
1 FK Šilutė	24	17	5	2	55	14	56
2 FK Alytis	24	14	2	8	41	27	44
3 FK Mažeikiai	24	12	4	8	40	32	40
4 FK Nevėžis	24	10	7	7	41	34	37
5 FK Glestum	24	8	3	13	31	40	27
6 VMFD Žalgiris	24	7	5	12	27	35	26
7 FK Lietava	24	2	2	20	20	73	8

NB FK Šilutė and FK Alytis declined promotion to A Lyga;
FK Mažeikiai, FK Klaipėda (formerly FK Glestum) & VMFD Žalgiris were
invited to 2010 A Lyga.

DOMESTIC CUP 2009/10

LFF TAURÉ

FIFTH ROUND

(21/10/09)
Banga 0, Kaunas 4
Kruoja 1, Šilutė 2
Sakuona 2, Žalgiris 1 *(aet)*
Tauras 2, LKKA 1

QUARTER-FINALS

(7/11/09)
Kaunas 3 *(Pehlić 47, 89p, Macežinskas 51)*, Šiauliai 0
Šilutė 1 *(Juška 39)*, Ekranas 1 *(Gleveckas 74p) (aet; 5-6 on pens)*
Tauras 1 *(Vaitkus 90)*, Vėtra 1 *(Mikuckis 88) (aet; 3-4 on pens)*

(8/11/09)
Sakuona 2 *(Dančenka 14, Stonys 90)*, Sūduva 8 *(Urbšys 38, 43, Radavičius 51, 59, Beniušis 57, Slavickas V. 66, Esaú 74, Chvedukas 86)*

SEMI-FINALS

(31/3/10 & 14/4/10)
Kaunas 1 *(Činikas 79)*, Ekranas 2 *(Banys 43, Radavičius 45p)*
Ekranas 2 *(Pogreban 50, Galkevičius 72)*, Kaunas 0
(Ekranas 4-1)

Vėtra 1 *(Gogberashvili 72)*, Sūduva 1 *(Kijanskas 12p)*
Sūduva 2 *(Lukšys 28, Liu 95)*, Vėtra 2 *(Ražanauskas 62, Gogberashvili 104) (aet)*
(3-3; Vėtra 4-2 on pens)
N.B. Away-goals rule was not applied after extra time.

FINAL

(15/5/10)
Darius & Girėnas stadium, Kaunas
FK EKRANAS 2 *(Galkevičius 69, Varnas 89)*
FK VĖTRA 1 *(Ražanauskas 45)*
Referee – Gaigalas
EKRANAS – Černiauskas, Matović, Gleveckas, Tomkevičius, Pogreban, Radavičius *(Markevičius 90)*, Arlauskas, Galkevičius, Kučys, Ademolu, Rimkus *(Varnas 65)*.
VĖTRA – Valinčius, Usachev, Jankauskas, Veikutis, Borovskij, Eliošius, Gogberashvili *(Žulpa 90)*, Lyakh *(Stanaitis 46)*, Ražanauskas, Vėževičius *(Freidgeimas G. 67)*, Rimkevičius.

Jeunesse roll back the years

The five-year reign of F91 Dudelange was brought to an end in 2009/10 as AS Jeunesse Esch, Luxembourg's most decorated club, revived memories of their halcyon days by reclaiming the National Division championship from their near neighbours on the French border.

Jeunesse's record-extending 28th title was sealed on the final day of the 26-match campaign with a resounding 4-0 win against relegated US Rumelange in the Stade de la Frontière, leaving them four points clear of Dudelange, who were simultaneously held 3-3 by Jeunesse's local rivals AS Fola Esch.

Although Dudelange had made a bold bid to win a sixth successive title, they clearly missed the man who had led them to the previous five, Michel Leflochmoan. The Frenchman's departure – to the third tier of the Belgian league – was felt early on as Dudelange went five games without a win under new boss Marc Grosjean, allowing Jeunesse, coached by Jacques Muller, to take charge with a six-match winning run that straddled the winter break. A 4-0 defeat by Dudelange – a team Jeunesse had not beaten for six years – brought that sequence to a shuddering halt, but Muller's men held their nerve sufficiently in the run-in to keep the defending champions at bay.

Team effort

Whereas Dudelange, as ever, were a squad predominantly made up of foreigners, Jeunesse were helped to the title by a number of Luxembourg internationals, chief among them Dan Collette, Eric Hoffmann and René Peters. Their victory was very much a team effort, with the goals shared around and no individual consistently taking centre stage. The title might have been secured earlier had Jeunesse possessed a consistent marksman up front like CS Grevenmacher's Daniel Huss, who struck 22 league goals – two more than the previous season – to claim both the Golden Boot and the National Division's Player of the Year vote.

Huss also struck four times in the semi-final of the Luxembourg Cup, against Fola, but in the final against FC Differdange 03 he had a rare off-day and Grevenmacher's bid for a fifth win in the competition was shattered in the 89th minute when Differdange's Argentine midfielder Dario Soraire, who had only just come on as a substitute, struck his first goal of the season to give the merger club a 1-0 victory and their first major silverware since they came into being seven years earlier.

Differdange were the only Luxembourg club to register a win in Europe at the start of the season when a goal from the 2008/09 National Division top scorer, Pierre Piskor, gave them a 1-0 first leg lead against HNK Rijeka. Somewhat predictably, however, they went down 3-0 in the return in Croatia and

Luxembourg's national team coach Guy Hellers

LUXEMBOURG

therefore joined all of the other three Grand Duchy representatives as first-hurdle fallers. There was better news on the international front for Guy Hellers' national team, however, as Luxembourg concluded their 2010 FIFA World Cup qualifying campaign with a fighting display against Greece and, moreover, a respectable tally of five points – a total that put them ahead of Moldova in the final Group 2 table.

Goalless draws home and away against Moldova proved to be precious but it was the remarkable 2-1 victory against eventual group winners Switzerland in Zurich at the start of the campaign that made the campaign so memorable. Indeed, that result acquired even greater kudos at the World Cup finals in South Africa, where Switzerland defeated Spain, who then went on to become the new world champions. Logical conclusions, alas, seldom paint the whole picture in football…

Fédération Luxembourgeoise de Football (FLF)

BP5
Rue de Limpach
LU-3901 Mondercange
tel – +352 488 665 1
fax – +352 488665 82
website – football.lu
email – flf@football.lu
Year of Formation – 1908

President – Paul Philipp
General Secretary – Joël Wolff
Media Officer – Marc Diederich
National Stadium – Josy Barthel, Luxembourg (8,000)

TOP FIVE ALL-TIME CAPS
Jeff Strasser (97); Carlo Weis (88); François Konter (77);
Roby Langers & René Peters (73)
TOP FIVE ALL-TIME GOALS
Leon Mart (16); Gusty Kemp (15); Camille Libar (14); Nicolas
Kettel (13); François Müller (12)

NATIONAL TEAM RESULTS 2009/10

12/8/09	Lithuania	H	Luxembourg	0-1	
5/9/09	Moldova (WCQ)	A	Chisinau	0-0	
9/9/09	Israel (WCQ)	A	Tel-Aviv	0-7	
10/10/09	Switzerland (WCQ)	H	Luxembourg	0-3	
14/10/09	Greece (WCQ)	A	Athens	1-2	Papadopoulos (89og)
14/11/09	Iceland	H	Luxembourg	1-1	Kintziger (75)
3/3/10	Azerbaijan	H	Luxembourg	1-2	Strasser (34)
4/6/10	Faroe Islands	H	Hesperange	0-0	

NATIONAL TEAM APPEARANCES 2009/10

Coach –Guy HELLERS (Ronny BONVINI)	10/10/64 17/3/71		Ltu	MDA	ISR	SUI	GRE	Isl	Aze	Fro	Caps	Goals
Jonathan JOUBERT	12/9/79	Dudelange	G	G		G	G		G	G	34	-
Eric HOFFMANN	21/6/84	Jeunesse Esch	D	D	D		D		D67	s59	62	-
Mario MUTSCH	3/9/84	Metz (FRA)	D72		M	D	D	D	M	M	40	1
Jeff STRASSER	5/10/74	Fola /Grasshoppers (SUI)	D	D		D	D	D	D	D	97	7
Mathias JÄNISCH	27/8/90	Differdange	D46	D58	D50	s73	M46	s85	M		9	-
Guy BLAISE	12/12/80	Virton (BEL)	M	M	M	D	D	D81	D	M59	8	-
Gilles BETTMER	31/3/89	Freiburg (GER) /Trier (GER)	M	M	M	M	M	M	M54		32	-
René PETERS	15/6/81	Jeunesse Esch	M	M	M	M	M	M	M	M	73	3
Ben PAYAL	8/9/88	Dudelange	M76	M	D46	M	M 58*	M92	s67	M	31	-
Claudio LOMBARDELLI	4/10/87	Jeunesse Esch	M46	M79	M62						25	-
Stefano BENSI	11/8/88	Dudelange	A46								5	-
Massimo MARTINO	18/9/90	Wuppertal (GER)	s46				s80		s64		5	-
Daniel DA MOTA	11/9/85	Dudelange	s46	s84					A85	s54	M71	19	-

NATIONAL TEAM APPEARANCES 2009/10 (contd.)

			Ltu	MDA	ISR	SUI	GRE	Isl	Aze	Fro	Caps	Goals
Dan COLLETTE	2/4/85	Jeunesse Esch	s46	s58	s50	M73				s71	24	-
Kim KINTZIGER	2/4/87	Differdange	s72	D	D	D	D80	D	D64	D	35	1
Joël PEDRO de Almeida	10/4/92	Sedan (FRA)	s76		s46						2	-
Sergio PUPOVAC	5/7/79	Jeunesse Esch				A84	A	s60	s73	s90	5	-
Alphonse LEWECK	16/12/81	Etzella				s79	s62	s46	s46		52	4
Marc OBERWEIS	6/11/82	Jeunesse Esch				G			G		7	-
Tom LATERZA	9/5/92	Sedan (FRA)					M46		s81		2	-
Joël KITENGE	12/11/87	Fola				A60	A73	A90	A	A77	22	1
Ante BUKVIC	14/11/87	Differdange							D		1	-
Carlos FERREIRA	24/8/80	Etzella							s92		20	-
Tom SCHNELL	8/10/85	Racing Union							D	D	10	-
Kevin MALGET	15/1/91	Aachen (GER)							D		1	-
Amel COSIC	19/11/89	Wiltz								s77	1	-

DOMESTIC LEAGUE 2009/10

NATIONAL DIVISION FINAL TABLE

	Pld	Home					Away					Total					Pts
		W	D	L	F	A	W	D	L	F	A	W	D	L	F	A	
1 AS Jeunesse Esch	26	10	2	1	26	7	7	4	2	19	13	17	6	3	45	20	57
2 F91 Dudelange	26	9	4	0	32	8	7	2	4	30	15	16	6	4	62	23	54
3 CS Grevenmacher	26	9	1	3	27	18	4	3	6	19	22	13	4	9	46	40	43
4 FC Differdange 03	26	9	2	2	30	12	3	4	6	11	18	12	6	8	41	30	42
5 FC RM Hamm Benfica	26	7	4	2	31	15	4	4	5	19	14	11	8	7	50	29	41
6 CS Fola Esch	26	6	4	3	27	20	5	4	4	22	18	11	8	7	49	38	41
7 Racing FC Union Lëtzebuerg	26	7	2	4	20	15	5	3	5	19	32	12	5	9	39	47	41
8 FC Etzella Ettelbruck	26	3	5	5	18	18	5	3	5	24	25	8	8	10	42	43	32
9 CS Pétange	26	4	3	6	19	20	5	2	6	17	22	9	5	12	36	42	32
10 FC Swift Hesper	26	3	3	7	15	23	5	2	6	18	19	8	5	13	33	42	29
11 FC Progrès Niedercorn	26	3	5	5	18	22	3	5	5	21	22	6	10	10	39	44	28
12 UN Käerjéng 97	26	3	4	6	9	15	4	3	6	19	21	7	7	12	28	36	28
13 US Rumelange	26	2	0	11	10	34	5	1	7	17	29	7	1	18	27	63	22
14 FC Mondercange	26	1	4	8	10	36	1	3	9	8	22	2	7	17	18	58	13

TOP GOALSCORERS

22 Daniel HUSS (Grevenmacher)

15 Joris DI GREGORIO (Fola)
   Romain ZEWE (Käerjéng)

12 Anel PJANIĆ (Pétange)
   Nicolas CALDIERI (Progrès)

11 Tomasz GRUSZCZYŃSKI (Dudelange)
   Antonio NSANGU (Progrès)

10 Daniel DA MOTA (Dudelange)
   Aouëd AOUAÏCHIA (Hamm)
   Djilali KEHAL (Hamm)
   Johan Carlos SAMPAIO (Hesper)

CLUB-BY-CLUB

FC DIFFERDANGE 03
Coach – Dan Theis
Founded – 2003
Stadium – Thillenberg (6,000)
MAJOR HONOURS:
Luxembourg Cup - (1) 2010.

2009

2/8	Racing Union	a	1-0	Joachim	
8/8	Käerjéng	h	2-1	Siebenaler, Pace	
16/8	Grevenmacher	a	0-2		
23/8	Mondercange	h	1-0	*Albanese*	
30/8	Fola	a	1-1	*Albanese*	
13/9	Hamm	h	1-0	*Mendes*	
20/9	Dudelange	a	1-3	*Lebresne*	
27/9	Progrès	h	1-1	*Piskor*	
4/10	Etzella	a	0-1		
18/10	Hesper	h	1-1	*May*	
25/10	Pétange	h	4-1	*Piskor, Joachim, Pedro Ribeiro, Kintziger*	

31/10	Jeunesse	a	1-2	Albanese
8/11	Rumelange	h	4-0	Kettenmeyer, Joachim 2, Pedro Ribeiro
22/11	Grevenmacher	h	2-0	Piskor, Albanese
29/11	Mondercange	a	1-1	Piskor
6/12	Käerjéng	a	4-1	Albanese 2, Wagner, Joachim
2010				
7/3	Fola	h	0-5	
14/3	Hamm	a	0-3	
21/3	Dudelange	h	0-1	
28/3	Progrès	a	0-0	
11/4	Etzella	h	2-0	Albanese, Joachim
18/4	Hesper	a	0-3	
25/4	Pétange	a	0-0	
9/5	Jeunesse	h	5-2	Lebresne, Piskor, Jänisch, Siebenaler, Pedro Ribeiro
16/5	Rumelange	a	2-1	Jänisch, Albanese
21/5	Racing Union	h	7-0	Piskor 3, Joachim 2, Alunni, Wagner (p)

No	Name	Nat	DoB	Pos	Aps	(s)	Gls
19	Mirko ALBANESE		4/9/89	A	12	(10)	8
17	Alessandro ALUNNI		19/12/91	M	1	(3)	1
7	BRUNO RIBEIRO Alves	POR	21/6/83	M		(1)	
15	Ante BUKVIĆ		14/11/87	D	17	(1)	
25	Ibrahim DIOP	FRA	20/11/86	D	4	(8)	
20	Thomas HYM	FRA	29/8/87	G	4	(1)	
16	Mathias JÄNISCH		27/8/90	M	22	(2)	2
11	Aurélien JOACHIM		10/8/86	A	21	(2)	8
12	Michel KETTENMEYER		7/2/89	M	19	(2)	1
2	Kim KINTZIGER		2/4/87	D	25	(1)	1
23	Daniel LARA COSTA	POR	14/4/87	M	2	(5)	
8	Philippe LEBRESNE	FRA	29/7/78	M	19	(3)	2
22	Andy MAY		2/9/89	D	12	(4)	1
21	Alain MENDES	FRA	9/9/76	M	11	(2)	1
18	Carlo PACE		7/4/78	A	2	(3)	1
6	PEDRO RIBEIRO Alves		17/1/89	M	11	(9)	3
24	Igor PEREIRA		6/7/87	D		(1)	
9	Pierre PISKOR	FRA	2/5/87	A	16	(4)	8
13	André RODRIGUES Almeida		6/12/87	D	12	(2)	
5	Tom SIEBENALER		28/9/90	D	18	(2)	2
10	Dario SORAIRE	ARG	31/3/78	M	17	(6)	
3	Jean WAGNER		3/12/69	D	19	(3)	2
1	Julien WEBER	FRA	12/10/85	G	22		

F91 DUDELANGE
Coach – Marc Grosjean (BEL)
Founded – 1991
Stadium – Jos Nosbaum (4,500)
MAJOR HONOURS:
Luxembourg League - (8) 2000, 2001, 2002, 2005, 2006, 2007, 2008, 2009;
Luxembourg Cup - (4) 2004, 2006, 2007, 2009.

2009				
2/8	Fola	a	3-1	Da Mota Dan. 2, Remy
8/8	Hamm	h	3-0	Françoise 2, Gruszczyński
16/8	Pétange	h	2-0	Ronny, Da Mota Dan.
23/8	Progrès	a	2-4	Defays, Hareau
30/8	Etzella	h	1-3	Bendaha
13/9	Hesper	a	2-0	Hammami, Françoise
20/9	Differdange	h	3-1	Françoise, Molnar, Da Mota Dan.
27/9	Jeunesse	a	1-1	Molnar
4/10	Rumelange	h	0-0	
18/10	Racing Union	a	2-2	Bensi, Guthleber
25/10	Käerjéng	h	1-1	Defays
31/10	Grevenmacher	a	0-1	
8/11	Mondercange	h	1-0	Ronny
22/11	Pétange	a	1-0	Da Mota Dan.
29/11	Progrès	h	2-1	Bensi, Guthleber
6/12	Hamm	a	2-4	Da Cruz 2
2010				
7/3	Etzella	a	2-1	Karaca, Da Mota Dan.
14/3	Hesper	h	4-1	Da Mota Dan. 2, Bensi, Karaca

21/3	Differdange	a	1-0	Remy
28/3	Jeunesse	h	4-0	Karaca, Gruszczyński 3
11/4	Rumelange	a	5-0	Gruszczyński 2, Da Mota Dan. 2, Toppmöller
18/4	Racing Union	h	3-0	(w/o)
25/4	Käerjéng	a	0-1	
9/5	Grevenmacher	h	5-0	Hammami, Gruszczyński 2, Karaca, Bensi
16/5	Mondercange	a	9-0	Karaca 2, Gruszczyński, Hammami, Toppmöller, Molnar 2 (1p), og (Jager), Bensi
21/5	Fola	h	3-3	Gruszczyński 2 (1p), Toppmöller

No	Name	Nat	DoB	Pos	Aps	(s)	Gls
27	Arnaud ANASTASSOWA	FRA	23/1/88	D	3		
13	Romain ANDRES	FRA	20/1/88	M	1	(1)	
7	Bareck BENDAHA	FRA	30/12/83	M	4	(4)	1
11	Stefano BENSI		11/8/88	A	7	(13)	5
4	Ricardo CENTRONE	ITA	3/6/90	M		(5)	
24	Stéphane DA CRUZ	FRA	1/3/88	A		(4)	2
9	Daniel DA MOTA		11/9/85	A	20	(4)	10
28	David DA MOTA	POR	5/12/89	D	4		
2	Frank DEFAYS	FRA	23/2/74	D	8		2
26	Abdoul DIAKITE	FRA	11/1/86	D	12	(1)	
5	Emmanuel FRANÇOISE	FRA	8/6/87	M	13	(4)	4
20	Tomasz GRUSZCZYŃSKI	FRA	4/12/80	A	9	(4)	11
19	Laurent GUTHLEBER	FRA	26/10/80	D	18		2
15	Nasreddine HAMMAMI	TUN	5/12/81	D	20		3
10	Sébastien HAREAU	FRA	25/9/81	M	18	(5)	1
21	Yann HEIL		5/9/90	G	5		
1	Jonathan JOUBERT		12/9/79	G	20		
14	Emko KALABIĆ	BIH	30/3/83	M	1	(2)	
29	Yasin KARACA	TUR	16/12/83	A	9		6
12	Grégory MOLNAR	FRA	10/7/83	A	8	(5)	4
3	Loïc MOUNY	FRA	28/3/81	D	16		
6	Ben PAYAL		8/9/88	M	25		
16	Sébastien REMY		19/4/74	M	14	(6)	2
25	Walder Alves Souto Amado "RONNY"	CPV	7/12/78	M	20		2
30	Dino TOPPMÖLLER	GER	23/11/80	A	3	(2)	3
31	Taïmo Mustafa VAZ DJASSI		9/3/88	M		(2)	
8	Christophe WALTER	FRA	26/1/83	M	4		
23	Lehit ZEGHDANE	FRA	3/10/77	D	13	(2)	

FC ETZELLA ETTELBRUCK
Coach – Jeannot "Benny" Reiter
Founded – 1917
Stadium – Deich (4,500)
MAJOR HONOURS:
Luxembourg Cup - (1) 2001.

2009				
2/8	Grevenmacher	a	1-3	Plein
8/8	Mondercange	h	0-0	
16/8	Fola	a	4-5	Camara, Nilton 2, André Bastos (p)
23/8	Hamm	h	1-1	André Bastos
30/8	Dudelange	a	1-1	Leweck A.
13/9	Progrès	h	2-2	Pietrasik, Leweck A.
20/9	Pétange	h	2-4	Leweck A. 2
27/9	Hesper	a	2-2	Da Luz 2
4/10	Differdange	h	1-0	Da Luz
18/10	Jeunesse	a	2-1	Camara, Belli
25/10	Rumelange	h	1-2	Camara
31/10	Racing Union	a	4-3	Da Luz, Nilton 2, Camara
8/11	Käerjéng	h	1-1	Da Luz
22/11	Fola	h	0-1	
29/11	Hamm	a	1-3	Camara
6/12	Mondercange	a	1-2	Da Luz
2010				
7/3	Dudelange	h	1-2	André Bastos
14/3	Progrès	a	3-1	Remacle 2 (1p), Camara
21/3	Pétange	a	1-1	Mendes Gomes

28/3	Hesper	h	1-0	Cleudir
11/4	Differdange	a	0-2	
18/4	Jeunesse	h	1-1	Nilton
25/4	Rumelange	a	3-1	Nilton 2, Belli
9/5	Racing Union	h	6-1	Cleudir 2, Camara 2 (1p), Pietrasik, Da Luz
16/5	Käerjéng	a	1-0	Pietrasik
21/5	Grevenmacher	h	1-3	Leweck C.

No	Name	Nat	DoB	Pos	Aps	(s)	Gls
10	ANDRÉ BASTOS Silva	POR	18/3/91	M	13	(8)	3
23	Noël BARKLEY	FRA	28/10/84	G	2		
11	Anouar BELLI	BEL	21/4/80	M	10	(8)	2
18	Soriba CAMARA	GUI	5/2/74	A	18	(4)	8
25	CLEUDIR Lopes	CPV	4/1/83	M	5	(3)	3
19	Claudio DA LUZ		27/5/79	A	21	(4)	7
4	Gilles ENGELDINGER		4/5/84	D	15	(1)	
3	Jorge FERNANDES		8/1/77	D	15	(6)	
12	Carlos FERREIRA		24/8/80	M	19	(5)	
1	Joé FLICK		16/7/79	G	16		
22	Philippe HAHM		13/1/90	G	7	(1)	
8	Tom KOPECKY		16/5/82	D	5	(2)	
14	Alphonse 'Fons' LEWECK		16/12/81	M	8	(4)	4
13	Charles LEWECK		19/7/83	M	21	(1)	1
15	Bobby MENDES GOMES	BEL	7/6/88	M	17	(7)	1
21	Didier NILTON Rocha	CPV	19/1/79	A	21	(2)	7
21	Didier NILTON Rocha (same player)	CPV	19/1/79	G	1		
9	François PAPIER	BEL	27/3/90	M	3	(5)	
2	Bartlomiej PIETRASIK	POL	25/5/84	D	22		3
7	Jacques PLEIN		17/2/87	D	11	(2)	1
6	Claude REITER		2/7/81	D	12		
17	Gauthier REMACLE	BEL	26/5/77	M	24	(1)	2
24	SYDNEY do Rosário	CPV	19/1/90	M		(1)	

No	Name	Nat	DoB	Pos	Aps	(s)	Gls
37	Jean-Baptiste ANDRADE	POR	6/3/92	M	2	(5)	
2	Billy BERNARD		29/4/91	D	15	(2)	1
1	Alija BEŠIĆ		30/3/75	G	22		
16	Paul BOSSI		22/7/91	M	10	(6)	
35	Steve CABRAL Antunes	POR	28/3/91	M		(1)	
17	Luciano CRAPA	ITA	10/1/74	M	6		2
36	Jakob DALLEVEDOVE	BEL	21/11/87	A	10		6
25	Joris DI GREGORIO	FRA	4/9/82	A	24		15
12	Claus Oktay GRESZKOWIAK	GER	30/12/73	D	4	(2)	
26	Mustapha HADJI	MAR	16/11/71	A	1	(1)	1
8	Carlos Silva HELENA	POR	6/11/74	D	23	(1)	2
37	HUGO Miguel Gonçalves FERNANDES	POR	1/1/90	D		(2)	
19	Tarik KHARIF	FRA	16/9/77	M	5	(5)	
27	Joël KITENGE		12/11/87	A	20	(3)	5
4	Benoît LANG		19/12/83	D	8	(1)	
5	Yannick LOOSE		17/9/84	D	4	(2)	
3	Sébastien MAZURIER	FRA	13/4/81	M	20	(3)	5
32	Joé MEYERS		8/12/91	M	1		
21	Tom NILLES		1/3/92	M	1	(1)	
22	Johanna OMOLO	KEN	13/5/88	M	24	(1)	6
23	Christophe PAZOS DE MATOS	ESP	19/5/90	M	14	(6)	
6	Jérémie PEIFFER		19/5/81	D	18		
15	João Bartolomeu Lopes "PEPE"	POR	20/7/88	M	1	(3)	
28	Marco PIRES		13/12/82	A	5	(13)	2
7	Bruno POMPIÈRE	FRA	10/6/80	D	14	(2)	
33	Mourad SAIDI	FRA	6/8/90	D	11	(4)	1
29	Charly SCHINKER		5/11/87	G	4		
14	Alex SEMEDO BORGES		22/8/89	D	17	(3)	
9	Jeff STRASSER		5/10/74	D	2		1
10	Dany TANA		4/2/87	M		(5)	1

CS FOLA ESCH
Coach – Pascal Welter; (27/10/09) Philippe Guerard (BEL)
Founded – 1906
Stadium – Emile Mayrisch (6,000)
MAJOR HONOURS:
Luxembourg League – (5) 1918, 1920, 1922, 1924, 1930;
Luxembourg Cup - (3) 1923, 1924, 1955.

2009
2/8	Dudelange	h	1-3	Di Gregorio (p)
7/8	Progrès	a	1-1	Strasser
16/8	Etzella	h	5-4	Di Gregorio 3, Bernard, Helena
23/8	Hesper	a	1-0	Di Gregorio (p)
30/8	Differdange	h	1-1	Di Gregorio
13/9	Jeunesse	a	0-1	
20/9	Rumelange	h	4-2	Mazurier, Saidi, Pires 2
27/9	Racing Union	a	2-2	Mazurier, Kitenge
4/10	Käerjéng	h	0-0	
18/10	Grevenmacher	a	0-2	
25/10	Mondercange	h	1-1	Omolo
31/10	Pétange	a	3-1	Kitenge 2, Helena
8/11	Hamm	a	0-3	
22/11	Etzella	a	1-0	Crapa
29/11	Hesper	h	4-1	Di Gregorio 2, Kitenge, Tana
6/12	Progrès	h	4-1	Crapa, Hadji, Omolo, Di Gregorio

2010
7/3	Differdange	a	5-0	Omolo, Di Gregorio 2, Mazurier, Dallevedove
14/3	Jeunesse	h	0-1	
21/3	Rumelange	a	4-2	Kitenge, og (Da Silva), Dallevedove, Di Gregorio
28/3	Racing Union	h	1-2	Di Gregorio
11/4	Käerjéng	a	0-1	
18/4	Grevenmacher	h	2-2	Mazurier 2, Di Gregorio
25/4	Mondercange	a	2-2	Di Gregorio, Dallevedove
9/5	Pétange	h	2-1	Omolo 2
16/5	Hamm	h	1-1	Omolo
21/5	Dudelange	a	3-3	Dallevedove 3 (1p)

CS GREVENMACHER
Coach – Claude Osweiler
Founded – 1909
Stadium – Op Flohr (4,000)
MAJOR HONOURS:
Luxembourg League - (1) 2003;
Luxembourg Cup - (4) 1995, 1998, 2003, 2008.

2009
2/8	Etzella	h	3-1	Müller, Huss (p), Traoré
8/8	Hesper	a	3-1	Marić, Huss 2
16/8	Differdange	h	2-0	Müller, Huss
23/8	Jeunesse	a	0-2	
30/8	Rumelange	h	4-1	Müller, Boussi 2, Huss (p)
13/9	Racing Union	a	1-2	Habte
20/9	Käerjéng	h	5-2	Huss 3, Müller, Lorig
27/9	Pétange	a	0-2	
4/10	Mondercange	a	5-1	Huss, Müller 2, Hoffmann 2
18/10	Fola	h	2-0	Huss 2
25/10	Hamm	a	2-2	Hartung, Hoffmann
31/10	Dudelange	h	1-0	Huss
8/11	Progrès	a	0-0	
22/11	Differdange	a	0-2	
29/11	Jeunesse	h	2-5	Marić, Di Domenico
6/12	Hesper	h	2-1	Müller, Traoré

2010
7/3	Rumelange	a	2-0	Huss 2
14/3	Racing Union	h	1-1	Hoffmann
21/3	Käerjéng	a	1-1	Huss
28/3	Pétange	h	0-3	
11/4	Mondercange	h	0-1	
18/4	Fola	a	2-3	Huss, Hoffmann
25/4	Hamm	h	3-2	Huss 2 (1p), Boussi
9/5	Dudelange	a	0-5	
16/5	Progrès	h	2-1	Huss 2 (1p)
21/5	Etzella	a	3-1	Huss 2, Hartung

LUXEMBOURG

No	Name	Nat	DoB	Pos	Aps	(s)	Gls
19	Ahmed BOUSSI	GER	23/10/88	A	19	(5)	3
27	Christian BRAUN		12/8/86	M	14	(4)	
28	Dariusz BRZYSKI		6/9/86	M	3	(2)	
7	Sven DI DOMENICO		15/3/82	M	2	(6)	1
12	Christophe DIEDERICH		2/4/84	G	16		
4	Ben FEDERSPIEL		18/5/81	D	14	(5)	
5	Sammy HABTE	GER	14/10/83	D	14	(4)	1
14	Sebastian HARTUNG	GER	16/12/80	M	22		2
22	Tim HEINZ		5/2/84	D	24	(1)	
17	Sébastien HOFFMANN	FRA	7/9/81	A	25		5
8	Daniel HUSS		4/10/79	A	26	22	
23	Tobias LORIG	GER	12/2/81	D	18	(4)	1
15	Dario MARIĆ		11/12/81	D	14	(3)	2
16	Samir MERIEM	FRA	16/6/82	M	1	(2)	
21	Christian MÜLLER	GER	17/1/81	A	22	(2)	7
6	Adis OMEROVIĆ		6/6/80	M	17	(4)	
29	Marc PLEIMLING		11/6/89	G	10		
3	Volker SCHMITT	GER	24/2/78	M	1	(4)	
13	Igor STOJADINOVIĆ		18/11/85	D	13	(7)	
11	David Lautaro TEJERINA	ARG	6/9/83	M	3	(4)	
10	Luc THIMMESCH		20/9/80	M	4	(7)	
24	Malick TRAORÉ	GER	21/1/87	A	2	(7)	2
30	Thorsten WITTEK	GER	31/12/76	D	2	(4)	

FC RM HAMM BENFICA
Coach – Fernando Gutiérrez (ARG)
Founded – 2004
Stadium – Cents (3,000)

2009

2/8	Pétange	a	1-0	Milak
8/8	Dudelange	a	0-3	
16/8	Progrès	h	3-3	Kehal 2, Ramires
23/8	Etzella	a	1-1	Ramires
30/8	Hesper	h	0-0	
13/9	Differdange	a	0-1	
20/9	Jeunesse	h	0-1	
27/9	Rumelange	a	6-0	Kehal 2, Aouaïchia 2 (1p), Milak 2
4/10	Racing Union	h	1-1	Aouaïchia
18/10	Käerjéng	a	1-0	Belabed
25/10	Grevenmacher	h	2-2	Aouaïchia, Ramires
31/10	Mondercange	a	5-1	Ramires, Kehal 2, Aouaïchia, Kitenge
8/11	Fola	h	3-0	Belabed, Ramires, Milak
22/11	Progrès	a	2-2	Eriton Sousa, Kehal
29/11	Etzella	h	3-1	Naguez 2, Aouaïchia
6/12	Dudelange	h	4-2	og (Hammami), Aouaïchia 2, Kehal
2010				
7/3	Hesper	a	0-0	
14/3	Differdange	h	3-0	Alomerović Ass., Aouaïchia, Kitenge
21/3	Jeunesse	a	0-1	
28/3	Rumelange	h	0-3	
11/4	Racing Union	a	0-1	
18/4	Käerjéng	h	3-0	Milak 2, Kitenge
25/4	Grevenmacher	a	2-3	Kehal, Belabed
9/5	Mondercange	h	2-0	Carlos Lima, Kehal
16/5	Fola	a	1-1	Ramires
21/5	Pétange	h	7-2	Ramires, Carlos Lima, Aouaïchia, Eriton Sousa 2, Kitenge 2

No	Name	Nat	DoB	Pos	Aps	(s)	Gls
9	Asmir ALOMEROVIĆ		24/11/80	M		(2)	
2	Assim ALOMEROVIĆ		25/1/83	D	22		1
11	Aouëd AOUAÏCHIA	FRA	20/6/77	A	23		10
10	Rachid BELABED	BEL	20/10/80	M	24		3
19	Abdellah BETTAHAR	FRA	31/10/79	M	22		
21	Jailson Emanuel da Pina Duarte Moreira "CADABRA"	CIV	26/6/94	G	9		
12	CARLOS LIMA dos Santos	POR	2/10/77	M	12	(1)	2
3	Christopher COLITO PEREIRA	CPV	4/10/85	D		(11)	
20	Sven DI DOMENICO		15/3/82	M	8		
16	ERITON SOUSA Lacerda	BRA	31/10/79	M	13	(5)	3

4	Evariste KABONGO Kalonji	COD	15/6/69	D	24		
17	Djilali KEHAL	FRA	1/10/78	A	26		10
18	Dimitri KITENGE		2/1/91	A	2	(21)	5
5	Miguel António LOPES RODRIGUES	POR	23/10/91	D	1	(1)	
7	David LOPEZ	FRA	10/10/75	D	26		
6	Jérôme MARCOLINO RODRIGUES		27/3/89	D	10	(6)	
19	Alen MILAK		23/5/84	A	7	(10)	6
14	Mohamed NAGUEZ	TUN	26/1/87	M	20	(1)	2
15	Ricardo RAMIRES Santos Lopes	POR	22/3/76	M	19	(4)	7
8	RICARDO TEIXEIRA Carvalho	POR	26/1/88	D		(2)	
22	Aderito VAZ dos Reis	CIV	4/1/80	M	1		
1	Jérôme WINCKEL		20/12/85	G	17		

AS JEUNESSE ESCH
Coach – Jacques Muller
Founded – 1907
Stadium – Stade de la Frontière (7,000)
MAJOR HONOURS:
Luxembourg League - (28) 1921, 1937, 1951, 1954, 1958, 1959, 1960, 1963, 1967, 1968, 1970, 1973, 1974, 1975, 1976, 1977, 1980, 1983, 1985, 1987, 1988, 1995, 1996, 1997, 1998, 1999, 2004, 2010;
Luxembourg Cup - (12) 1935, 1937, 1946, 1954, 1973, 1974, 1976, 1981, 1988, 1997, 1999, 2000.

2009

2/8	Rumelange	a	1-0	Cantonnet (p)
8/8	Racing Union	h	5-1	Collette 2, Gonçalves Fernandes, Cantonnet (p), Fullenwarth
16/8	Käerjéng	a	0-0	
23/8	Grevenmacher	h	2-0	Cantonnet (p), Gonçalves Fernandes
30/8	Mondercange	a	1-1	Collette
13/9	Fola	h	1-0	Pupovac
20/9	Hamm	a	1-0	Cantonnet (p)
27/9	Dudelange	h	1-1	Pupovac
4/10	Progrès	a	2-0	Rougeaux, Pupovac
18/10	Etzella	h	1-2	Piron
25/10	Hesper	a	0-0	
31/10	Differdange	h	2-1	Cantonnet 2
8/11	Pétange	h	0-0	
22/11	Käerjéng	h	2-0	De Sousa, Piron
29/11	Grevenmacher	a	5-2	Pupovac 2, Piron 2, Peters
6/12	Racing Union	a	2-0	Piron, Leoni
2010				
7/03	Mondercange	h	2-0	Pupovac, og (Niabaly)
14/03	Fola	a	1-0	Fullenwarth
21/03	Hamm	h	1-0	Piron
28/03	Dudelange	a	0-4	
11/04	Progrès	h	2-1	Collette, De Sousa
18/04	Etzella	a	1-1	Rougeaux
25/04	Hesper	h	3-1	Pupovac, Peters, Piron
9/05	Differdange	a	2-5	Gonçalves Fernandes, Peters
17/05	Pétange	a	3-0	Gonçalves Fernandes, Cantonnet, Hoffmann
21/05	Rumelange	h	4-0	Gonçalves Fernandes 2, Piron, Martin

No	Name	Nat	DoB	Pos	Aps	(s)	Gls
24	Cédric ANTON	FRA	20/2/88	M	3	(6)	
3	Almin BABAČIĆ		16/1/84	D	8	(2)	
4	Benjamin BOUSSELIN	FRA	28/3/88	D	3	(5)	
9	Loïc CANTONNET	FRA	6/9/80	M	18	(4)	7
11	Dan COLLETTE		2/4/85	D	24	(1)	4
2	Clayton DE SOUSA Moreira		24/2/88	D	18	(5)	2
5	Thomas FULLENWARTH	FRA	27/1/87	D	22	(3)	2
10	Keiven GONÇALVES FERNANDES	POR	26/8/86	A	5	(10)	6
7	Eric HOFFMANN		21/6/84	D	24	(1)	1
19	Jérémy LAROCHE	FRA	19/10/80	A	6	(6)	
13	Mickaël LEONI	FRA	22/4/89	M	3	(10)	1
16	Claudio LOMBARDELLI		4/10/87	M	6	(7)	

No	Name	Nat	DoB	Pos	Aps	(s)	Gls
14	Kevin MARTIN	FRA	17/2/80	M	24		1
1	Marc OBERWEIS		6/11/82	G	25		
15	René PETERS		15/6/81	M	25		3
21	Stéhane PIRON	BEL	17/1/84	A	17	(4)	8
8	Adrien PORTIER	FRA	2/2/88	D	22		
22	Sergio PUPOVAC		5/7/79	A	20	(3)	7
12	Meris RAMDEDOVIĆ	BIH	3/10/90	D		(1)	
23	Lévy ROUGEAUX	FRA	8/5/85	A	12	(6)	2
25	Sébastien SCHERER	FRA	17/6/79	G	1	(1)	
17	Jeff TREMONT		3/8/90	M		(1)	

UN KÄERJÉNG 97

Coach – Claude Heinz; (15/12/09) Roland Schaack
Founded – 1997
Stadium – Bëchel (3,000)

2009

Date	Opp	H/A	Score	Scorers
2/8	Hesper	h	0-2	
8/8	Differdange	a	1-2	Boulahfari
16/8	Jeunesse	h	0-0	
23/8	Rumelange	a	3-2	Zewe 3
30/8	Racing Union	h	1-3	Zewe
13/9	Pétange	a	1-3	Zewe
20/9	Grevenmacher	a	2-5	Boulahfari, Barton
27/9	Mondercange	h	1-1	Cleyton
4/10	Fola	a	0-0	
18/10	Hamm	h	0-1	
25/10	Dudelange	a	1-1	Zewe (p)
31/10	Progrès	h	2-0	og (Ghin), Rolandi
8/11	Etzella	a	1-1	Zewe
22/11	Jeunesse	a	0-2	
29/11	Rumelange	h	1-2	Zewe
6/12	Differdange	h	1-4	Zewe

2010

Date	Opp	H/A	Score	Scorers
7/3	Racing Union	a	0-1	
14/3	Pétange	h	0-0	
21/3	Grevenmacher	h	1-1	Heller
28/3	Mondercange	a	4-0	Rolandi 2, Zewe, Imessad
11/4	Fola	h	1-0	Zewe (p)
18/4	Hamm	a	0-3	
25/4	Dudelange	h	1-0	Zewe
9/5	Progrès	a	2-0	Boulahfari, Shoffner
16/5	Etzella	h	0-1	
21/5	Hesper	a	4-1	Zewe 3, Regulant

No	Name	Nat	DoB	Pos	Aps	(s)	Gls
7	Marc-Olivier BARTON	GER	1/8/78	M	16	(6)	1
28	Morgan BETORANGAL	FRA	28/8/88	D	1		
19	Rachid BOULAHFARI	FRA	17/4/84	M	23	(1)	3
24	Christoph CARL	GER	22/3/85	A	2	(3)	
1	Fabiano CASTELLANI		11/5/89	G	24		
10	CLEYTON Santos Pires	CPV	20/8/90	M	12	(3)	1
15	Paulo DA COSTA	POR	24/4/81	D	17		
22	Steve DUNKEL		9/7/76	G	2		
20	Alessandro FIORANI	ITA	19/2/89	M	1	(8)	
2	Lars HELLER	GER	2/4/77	D	25		1
25	Samir IMESSAD	FRA	30/4/84	A	6	(7)	1
16	Mutamba Kinda KIVUNGHE	BEL	17/5/73	M	14	(1)	
3	Kevin LEITE		15/2/89	D	11	(6)	
18	Zarko LUKIĆ		22/5/83	A	4	(1)	
17	Vito MARINELLI		7/8/90	A	23	(1)	
4	Gilles MARTINS DA SILVA		3/6/82	M	7	(2)	
11	Rémy 'Snoop' MUKENGE	FRA	6/5/75	D	1	(2)	
14	Ben POLIDORI		13/11/89	M	4	(7)	
13	Henid RAMDEDOVIĆ		20/7/87	D	14	(3)	
29	Mickaël REGULANT	FRA	16/4/90	M	2	(4)	1
8	Julien ROLANDI	FRA	28/3/86	M	24	(2)	3
26	Chris SAGRAMOLA		25/2/88	A	3	(7)	
12	Romain SANTARELLI	FRA	20/4/90	M	2	(1)	
5	Christophe SCHOLER		12/9/89	D	4		
6	Jamath SHOFFNER	USA	10/7/78	D	13	(2)	1
21	Fabiano SPINELLI		30/11/87	M	9	(4)	
27	Romain ZEWE	FRA	21/4/88	A	23		15

FC MONDERCANGE

Coach – Olivier Ciancanelli (POL); (6/10/09) Claude Campos;
(26/3/10) Olivier Ciancanelli (POL); (18/4/10) Alijaj Florim
Founded – 1933
Stadium – Stade Communal (3,300)

2009

Date	Opp	H/A	Score	Scorers
2/8	Progrès	h	1-1	Chaillou
8/8	Etzella	a	0-0	
16/8	Hesper	h	0-2	
23/8	Differdange	a	0-1	
30/8	Jeunesse	h	1-1	Cerullo
13/9	Rumelange	a	0-2	
20/9	Racing Union	h	1-2	Prieur
27/9	Käerjéng	a	1-1	Cerullo
4/10	Grevenmacher	h	1-5	Chaillou
18/10	Pétange	a	2-5	Cerullo, Niabaly
25/10	Fola	a	1-1	Deidda
31/10	Hamm	h	1-5	Prieur
8/11	Dudelange	a	0-1	
22/11	Hesper	a	1-2	Fus
29/11	Differdange	h	1-1	Kamouni
6/12	Etzella	h	2-1	Kamouni, Even

2010

Date	Opp	H/A	Score	Scorers
7/3	Jeunesse	a	0-2	
14/3	Rumelange	h	0-2	
21/3	Racing Union	a	0-1	
28/3	Käerjéng	h	0-4	
11/4	Grevenmacher	a	1-0	Winter
18/4	Pétange	h	0-1	
25/4	Fola	h	2-2	Winter, Cerullo
9/5	Hamm	a	0-2	
16/5	Dudelange	h	0-9	
21/5	Progrès	a	2-4	Hégué, Winter

No	Name	Nat	DoB	Pos	Aps	(s)	Gls
9	ANDRÉ Neves Fitas	POR	14/8/91	D	1	(3)	
10	Adrien CERULLO	FRA	29/4/88	A	22	(2)	4
21	Didier CHAILLOU	FRA	10/12/74	M	8	(2)	2
13	Geoffrey CROUGHS		1/8/90	M	11	(6)	
17	Ilario DEIDDA	ITA	12/12/89	A	2	(14)	1
22	Marc DEPIENNE		12/9/91	G	1		
3	Gilles EVEN		5/11/85	D	12	(6)	1
4	Alexandre FUS	FRA	8/12/82	D	19		1
11	Benjamin HÉGUÉ	FRA	16/3/89	A	12	(9)	1
18	Frank HOUSSOU	FRA	14/7/78	D	16	(2)	
15	Franck JAGER	FRA	26/8/76	M	22	(2)	
23	Tarek KAMOUNI	FRA	17/10/78	M	17	(1)	2
5	Kader MEKTOUB	FRA	22/6/73	D		(2)	
28	Sacha MERSCH		16/1/92	G	3	(1)	
14	Gilles MEURISSE		12/12/85	D	22		
16	Ousmane NIABALY	FRA	25/6/79	D	22		1
29	Jeff NITSCHAEFF		9/7/93	M		(1)	
30	Mathieu NOWICKI	FRA	11/4/88	M		(1)	
8	Stéphane PASQUALETTO	FRA	6/8/77	M	23	(1)	
24	PAULO PINTO Henriques		14/2/84	M	2	(4)	
9	Franklin PRIEUR	FRA	3/2/86	A	10	(4)	2
6	Aldin RAMČILOVIĆ		20/6/91	M		(2)	
2	RICARDO Filipe FERREIRA Gomes	POR	27/6/82	M	1	(4)	
19	Kevin RUPPERT		16/8/91	D	2		
25	Michael SIMON		11/5/90	M		(1)	
26	Bartosz STEPIEN	FRA	19/6/90	M	1		
1	Pit THEIS		25/1/79	G	22		
7	Ricardo THOM		12/7/90	M	15	(5)	
6	David VEIGA	POR	12/6/91	M	11	(3)	
31	Désiré-Patrick WINTER	FRA	17/5/80	A	9	(1)	3

CS PÉTANGE

Coach – Carlo Weis
Founded – 1910
Stadium – Stade Municipal (2,400)
MAJOR HONOURS:
Luxembourg Cup - (1) 2005.

2009

2/8	Hamm	h	0-1	
8/8	Rumelange	h	1-3	Steger
16/8	Dudelange	a	0-2	
23/8	Racing Union	h	4-1	Pjanić 2, Steger, Wang
30/8	Progrès	a	1-0	Pjanić (p)
13/9	Käerjéng	h	3-1	Steger, Wang, David Teixeira
20/9	Etzella	a	4-2	Pjanić 2, Kirchen, Dione E.
27/9	Grevenmacher	h	2-0	Pjanić, Kirchen
4/10	Hesper	a	3-1	Pjanić 3 (1p)
18/10	Mondercange	h	5-2	David Teixeira, Pjanić 2, Steger 2
25/10	Differdange	a	1-4	Wang
31/10	Fola	h	1-3	og (Di Gregorio)
8/11	Jeunesse	a	0-0	
22/11	Dudelange	h	0-1	
29/11	Racing Union	a	1-3	Pjanić
6/12	Rumelange	a	0-1	
2010				
7/3	Progrès	h	1-1	Steger
14/3	Käerjéng	a	0-0	
21/3	Etzella	h	1-1	David Teixeira
28/3	Grevenmacher	a	3-0	Thonon, Steger, David Teixeira
11/4	Hesper	h	1-3	Thonon
18/4	Mondercange	a	1-0	Thill
25/4	Differdange	h	0-0	
9/5	Fola	a	1-2	og (Silva Helena)
17/5	Jeunesse	h	0-3	
21/5	Hamm	a	2-7	Dione P., Ericson Santos

No	Name	Nat	DoB	Pos	Aps	(s)	Gls
7	ADAÍLTON de Oliveira Rodrigues	BRA	11/6/77	M	12	(8)	
25	Claudio BERETTA		1/1/85	M		(6)	
17	Mustapha BERRIH	FRA	14/9/75	M		(1)	
6	CARLO Dinis ANTUNES do Carmo	POR	12/10/82	M	26		
22	Nedim CIRIKOVIĆ		13/6/88	A	3	(7)	
1	Christophe CUM		10/9/86	G	15		
10	DAVID TEIXEIRA Caçador		17/12/86	M	13	(6)	4
18	Aldi DERVIŠEVIĆ	SRB	19/8/89	M	4		
8	Jasmin DERVIŠEVIĆ		1/7/69	M	3		
2	El Hadji DIONE	GER	25/3/73	D	20		1
3	Papa Aye DIONE	SEN	8/3/86	D	25		1
21	ERICSON SANTOS Duarte	POR	4/1/85	M		(9)	1
12	Jens KIRCHEN	GER	13/2/89	A	17	(4)	2
26	Björn KLOS	GER	1/11/83	M	2	(1)	
4	Tim LEHNEN		15/6/05	D	25		
27	Steven MARTINS	POR	15/6/05	M		(1)	
19	Manuel MOROCUTTI		22/10/81	M	4	(7)	
28	Jérémy NEVES	POR	15/6/05	D	3	(1)	
9	Dylan NISSAN	IRQ	7/11/88	M	19	(2)	
13	Anel PJANIĆ	BIH	26/12/83	A	16	(1)	12
24	Samin REDZEPAGIĆ	SRB	1/10/91	G	10		
5	Benoît SCHNEIDER	FRA	20/10/80	D	12	(5)	
14	André STEGER	GER	27/5/86	A	22		7
29	Sébastien THILL		1/2/94	M	10		1
23	Thibaut THONON	FRA	5/2/87	A	8	(4)	2
30	Alain WALAS		3/10/89	G	1		
11	Juncai WANG		5/4/90	M	16	(3)	3

FC PROGRÈS NIEDERCORN

Coach – Manuel Peixoto (FRA); (14/3/10) Giovanni Barnabo
Founded – 1919
Stadium – Jos Haupert (4,000)
MAJOR HONOURS:
Luxembourg League – (3) 1953, 1978, 1981;
Luxembourg Cup – (4) 1933, 1945, 1977, 1978.

2009

2/8	Mondercange	a	1-1	Proietti
8/8	Fola	h	1-1	Kabran
16/8	Hamm	a	3-3	Rigo, Nsangu, Proietti (p)
23/8	Dudelange	h	4-2	Caldieri, Nsangu 2, Proietti
30/8	Pétange	h	0-1	
13/9	Etzella	a	2-2	Caldieri, Rigo
20/9	Hesper	h	1-4	Caldieri
27/9	Differdange	a	1-1	Caldieri
4/10	Jeunesse	h	0-2	
18/10	Rumelange	a	3-0	Caldieri 2, Nsangu
25/10	Racing Union	h	2-2	Proietti, Caldieri
31/10	Käerjéng	a	0-2	
8/11	Grevenmacher	h	0-0	
22/11	Hamm	h	2-2	Caldieri, Nsangu
29/11	Dudelange	a	1-2	Colleatte
6/12	Fola	a	1-4	Nsangu
2010				
7/3	Pétange	a	1-1	Kabran
14/3	Etzella	h	1-3	Caldieri
21/3	Hesper	a	4-1	Caldieri 2, Colleatte, Nsangu
28/3	Differdange	h	0-0	
11/4	Jeunesse	a	1-2	Kabran
18/4	Rumelange	h	3-1	Caldieri, Proietti, De Sousa
25/4	Racing Union	a	2-1	Colleatte, De Sousa
9/5	Käerjéng	h	0-2	
16/5	Grevenmacher	a	1-2	Nsangu
21/5	Mondercange	h	4-2	Nsangu 3, Rigo

No	Name	Nat	DoB	Pos	Aps	(s)	Gls
28	Jérémie BANDEL	FRA	3/4/85	G	9		
10	Nelson de Jesus Silva CABRAL		24/9/87	M		(5)	
20	Nicolas CALDIERI	FRA	1/12/82	A	24		12
29	David CASTELLANI		3/7/87	G	1		
21	François COLLEATTE	FRA	25/2/85	A	24	(1)	3
11	Marco DE SOUSA		17/8/86	M	4	(13)	2
3	Ivan FAUSTINO		10/6/89	D	3	(1)	
1	Philippe FELGEN		8/10/75	G	16		
30	Aquiles da Silva FERREIRA	POR	26/3/84	D		(1)	
31	Diafara GARY	FRA	30/3/89	M	4	(3)	
4	Enzo GHIN	FRA	21/2/75	D	26		
5	Thomas GILGEMANN	FRA	15/9/83	D	22		
6	Stéphane HERGOTT	FRA	20/7/83	D	12		
18	JORGE Manuel RIBEIRO Magalhães	POR	24/10/92	M	9	(8)	
24	Lambert KABRAN Anguoa	CPV	18/10/89	A	7	(16)	3
13	Eric LAROCHE	BEL	16/12/86	M	5		
15	David MARQUES Soares	POR	20/2/91	M	14	(9)	
14	Maurizio MASI		2/6/80	M		(3)	
16	Tarek NOUIDRA	FRA	9/5/87	M	22		
25	Antonio NSANGU	FRA	11/4/84	A	21	(4)	11
31	Michael OLIVEIRA MARTINS	POR	21/9/93	M		(1)	
7	Thierry PICARD	FRA	13/10/86	D	15		
17	Jonathan PROIETTI		17/7/82	M	18	(7)	5
9	Jonathan RIGO	FRA	16/9/87	D	23		3
26	Bruno RONDINELLI	ITA	8/4/87	A	7	(3)	

RACING FC UNION LËTZEBUERG

Coach – Sébastien Allieri (FRA)
Founded – 2005
Stadium – Achille Hammerel (6,000)

2009

2/8	Differdange	h	0-1	
8/8	Jeunesse	a	1-5	Bilon (p)
16/8	Rumelange	h	3-0	Bilon 2, Lider
23/8	Pétange	a	1-4	Molinero
30/8	Käerjéng	h	3-1	Martine 2, Schnell
13/9	Grevenmacher	a	2-1	D'Exelle 2
20/9	Mondercange	a	2-1	Martine, Schnell
27/9	Fola	h	2-2	Zennane, D'Exelle
4/10	Hamm	a	1-1	Feller
18/10	Dudelange	h	2-2	Schnell, Martine
25/10	Progrès	a	2-2	Lider, Muhović

31/10	Etzella	h	3-4	Schnell 2, Molinero
8/11	Hesper	a	2-0	Molinero, Bellini
22/11	Rumelange	a	3-0	Martine, Zennane, Bellini
29/11	Pétange	h	3-1	Carvalho, Rani, Lider
6/12	Jeunesse	h	0-2	
2010				
7/3	Käerjéng	h	1-0	Martine
14/3	Grevenmacher	a	1-1	Bellini
21/3	Mondercange	h	1-0	Zennane
28/3	Fola	a	2-1	Rani, Martine
11/4	Hamm	h	1-0	Zennane
18/4	Dudelange	a	0-3	(w/o)
25/4	Progrès	h	1-2	Bilon
9/5	Etzella	a	1-6	Martine (p)
16/5	Hesper	h	1-0	Bellini
21/5	Differdange	a	0-7	

No	Name	Nat	DoB	Pos	Aps	(s)	Gls
4	Olivier BAUDRY	FRA	13/4/70	D	4		
13	Johan BELLINI	FRA	2/6/83	M	24		4
16	Yannick BIANCHINI		13/11/80	A		(2)	
28	Jérôme BIGARD		16/2/85	M	1		
12	Sully BILON	BEL	15/10/80	A	11		4
11	Michael CARVALHO Gonçalves	POR	5/8/86	M	2	(12)	1
27	Chris CLEMENT		25/12/91	G	1		
25	Matthew DE CAE		2/1/89	M	3	(3)	
14	Kris D'EXELLE	BEL	13/7/89	A	9	(8)	3
15	Jeff FELLER		18/4/85	D	15	(4)	1
8	Sami FONTES		1/2/89	M	2	(3)	
29	Raoul HOFFMANN		29/5/86	G	5	(1)	
7	Gaël HUG	FRA	8/1/80	M	23		
9	Gabin LIDER	FRA	2/5/90	A	8	(13)	3
10	Stéphane MARTINE	FRA	5/3/78	M	17	(5)	8
5	Kevin MOLINERO	FRA	9/1/85	M	9	(1)	3
21	Gilles MOLITOR		6/10/90	M		(1)	
6	Damir MUHOVIĆ		19/2/85	M	11	(7)	1
1	Jeff OSTER		8/7/89	G	4		
17	Laurent PELLEGRINO	FRA	20/1/73	D	18	(1)	
20	Ahmed RANI	FRA	20/8/87	M	18	(5)	2
22	Marc RAUS		31/10/87	D	16	(3)	
30	Steeve ROUILLON	FRA	15/12/73	G	15		
24	Tom SCHNELL		8/10/85	D	22		5
3	Marco SIMOES		1/8/86	D	21	(1)	
26	TIAGO da Silva Teixeira	POR	3/10/92	M		(1)	
2	Saber ZENNANE	MAR	27/7/76	D	16		4

US RUMELANGE
Coach – Marc Thomé; (26/4/10) Manuel Cardoni
Founded – 1908
Stadium – Municipal (4,000)
MAJOR HONOURS:
Luxembourg Cup - (2) 1968, 1975.

2009				
2/8	Jeunesse	h	0-1	
8/8	Pétange	a	3-1	Furst (p), Soares, Pesce
16/8	Racing Union	a	0-3	
23/8	Käerjéng	h	2-3	Bastos, Bitti
30/8	Grevenmacher	a	1-4	Pesce (p)
13/9	Mondercange	h	2-0	Pesce, Furst
20/9	Fola	a	2-4	Pesce 2 (1p)
27/9	Hamm	h	0-6	
4/10	Dudelange	a	0-0	
18/10	Progrès	h	0-3	
25/10	Etzella	a	2-1	Soares, Furst
31/10	Hesper	h	1-2	Bastos
8/11	Differdange	a	0-4	
22/11	Racing Union	h	0-3	
29/11	Käerjéng	a	2-1	Kleber, Dall'o
6/12	Pétange	h	1-0	Pupovac
2010				
7/3	Grevenmacher	h	0-2	
14/3	Mondercange	a	2-0	Pace, Pesce

21/3	Fola	h	2-4	Furst 2
28/3	Hamm	a	3-0	Dall'o, Goettling, Pace
11/4	Dudelange	h	0-5	
18/4	Progrès	a	1-3	Pace
25/4	Etzella	h	1-3	Pace
9/5	Hesper	a	1-4	Pace (p)
16/5	Differdange	h	1-2	Pace
21/5	Jeunesse	a	0-4	

No	Name	Nat	DoB	Pos	Aps	(s)	Gls
11	Cédric BASTOS		7/5/89	M	9	(13)	2
25	Jamel BITTI	FRA	4/7/83	A	6	(5)	1
5	Ronny BODRI		2/10/83	D	21	(2)	
26	CARLOS FERREIRA Doria	POR	4/6/83	A	4	(7)	
2	Serge DA COSTA Ribeiro		18/5/76	D	6		
13	Jonathan DA SILVA	FRA	7/5/87	M	18	(2)	
14	Joffrey DALL'O	FRA	17/5/76	M	19	(3)	2
32	EDGAR TAVARES Mascarenhas	CPV	5/1/78	D	2		
15	Jonathan FURST	FRA	23/3/87	M	21		5
3	Kevin GOETTLING	FRA	25/9/89	D	24		1
16	Anthony GUERRA	FRA	6/7/88	M		(3)	
7	Xavier HELLENBRAND		16/10/79	D	1		
1	Bob KIRSCH		18/2/87	G	16	(1)	
17	Kim KLEBER	FRA	4/12/87	M	8	(5)	1
27	Pierre LE BAIL	FRA	4/8/88	A		(2)	
24	Mario Barbosa LOURENÇO	POR	8/6/81	A	3	(8)	
10	Anis MEHOVIĆ		5/12/88	D	21		
29	Carlo PACE		7/4/78	A	9	(1)	6
18	Laurent PESCE	FRA	17/3/80	M	20	(5)	6
28	Nikola PUPOVAC	FRA	12/6/84	A	11	(8)	1
19	Pedro RAMIRES ROCHA	POR	31/1/81	M	1	(1)	
31	Raphaël RODRIGUES	POR	16/2/89	M	9	(1)	
22	Kim ROHMANN		21/1/84	G	10		
4	Sacha ROHMANN		3/8/80	D	4		
21	Miguel SANTOS de Sousa		13/1/77	M	18		
23	Sérgio Teixeira SOARES		3/1/92	M	16	(7)	2
6	Marc WIRTH		8/5/84	D	9	(1)	

FC SWIFT HESPER
Coach – Théo Scholten; (31/3/10) Angelo Fioruccio
Founded – 1916
Stadium – Alphonse Theis (5,000)
MAJOR HONOURS:
Luxembourg Cup - (1) 1990.

2009				
2/8	Käerjéng	a	2-0	Casafina, Rodrigues Pinto
8/8	Grevenmacher	h	1-3	Sampaio
16/8	Mondercange	a	2-0	Sampaio 2
23/8	Fola	h	0-1	
30/8	Hamm	a	0-0	
13/9	Dudelange	h	0-2	
20/9	Progrès	a	4-1	Schiltz 2, Sözen 2
27/9	Etzella	h	2-2	Sampaio 2 (1p)
4/10	Pétange	h	1-3	Sözen
18/10	Differdange	a	1-1	Sözen
25/10	Jeunesse	h	0-0	
31/10	Rumelange	a	2-1	Munoz, Sampaio
8/11	Racing Union	h	0-2	
22/11	Mondercange	a	2-1	Sampaio 2
29/11	Fola	a	1-4	Heinz B.
6/12	Grevenmacher	a	1-2	Munoz
2010				
7/3	Hamm	h	0-0	
14/3	Dudelange	a	1-4	Hilbert
21/3	Progrès	h	1-4	Nuno Miguel
28/3	Etzella	a	0-1	
11/4	Pétange	a	3-1	Casafina 2, Nuno Miguel
18/4	Differdange	h	3-0	Casafina 2, Munoz
25/4	Jeunesse	a	1-3	Sözen
9/5	Rumelange	h	4-1	Munoz, Casafina, Sampaio 2
16/5	Racing Union	a	0-1	
21/5	Käerjéng	h	1-4	Schiltz

LUXEMBOURG

No	Name	Nat	DoB	Pos	Aps	(s)	Gls
10	Patrick AQUARO		5/6/91	M		(8)	
1	Alex BOUKHETAIA	FRA	19/11/79	G	23		
15	Anton BOZIC		15/2/86	A	14	(2)	
7	Denis CABRILLON		22/5/90	M	15	(2)	
8	Antonio CASAFINA		15/1/91	M	14	(8)	6
9	Mounir DJAAFRI	FRA	24/3/82	M		(9)	
16	Michael GRILO MONHO		13/2/90	A	3	(1)	
11	Bernard HEINZ		14/7/69	M		(1)	1
24	David HEINZ	GER	9/4/83	M	1	(1)	
12	Pit HILBERT		18/2/90	M	24		1
26	Edvin HUMEROVIC		15/10/92	D		(1)	
2	Olivier LICKES		27/6/88	D	22	(2)	
25	Celso Gabriel MALHEIRO GONÇALVES	POR	25/2/86	G	3		
27	Hugo MARTINS ALVES	POR	16/2/93	D	1	(2)	
28	Jordan MOROCUTTI		26/9/92	M		(1)	
18	Tom MUNOZ		2/8/81	A	14	(6)	4
3	NUNO MIGUEL Mendes Batista	POR	17/1/83	D	21		2
29	Larson Sergio PEREIRA LIMA	POR	15/6/90	D	1	(4)	
14	Pedro RODRIGUES PINTO	POR	3/1/84	M	24		1
30	Ernad SABOTIĆ		23/10/79	M	8	(1)	
19	Johan Carlos SAMPAIO Miranda	POR	20/7/80	A	17	(4)	10
4	Anibal SANTOS da Graça		24/11/83	D	11	(1)	
21	Laurent SCHILTZ		17/2/82	A	16	(2)	3
22	Fatih SÖZEN	GER	7/5/82	A	16	(7)	5
5	Damian STOKLOSA	GER	30/8/79	D	15		
6	Armando TAVARES	CPV	26/10/76	D	20		
23	Naby TWIMUMU		24/8/90	A	3	(6)	

PROMOTED CLUBS

FC WILTZ 71
Coach – Steve Majerus
Founded – 1971
Stadium – Géitzt (2,000

FC JEUNESSE CANACH
Coach – Patrick Maurer
Founded – 1930
Stadium – rue de Lenningen (1,000)

SECOND LEVEL FINAL TABLE 2009/10

		Pld	W	D	L	F	A	Pts
1	FC Wiltz 71	26	17	4	5	66	38	55
2	FC Jeunesse Canach	26	14	9	3	53	29	51
3	CS Obercorn	26	14	6	6	52	27	48
4	Sporting Club Steinfort	26	14	4	8	53	32	46
5	FC Erpeldange 72	26	12	7	7	53	40	43
6	FC Victoria Rosport	26	11	6	9	48	40	39
7	FC Koeppchen Wormeldange	26	10	6	10	43	42	36
8	FC Young Boys Diekirch	26	10	5	11	52	50	35
9	FC Avenir Beggen	26	8	10	8	36	37	34
10	FC Union 05 Kayl/Tétange	26	10	4	12	48	50	34
11	FC Minerva Lintgen	26	9	5	12	42	46	32
12	US Hostert	26	9	3	14	41	57	30
13	FC Jeunesse Schieren	26	4	4	18	32	60	16
14	AS Colmar-Berg	26	3	1	22	15	86	10

PROMOTION/RELEGATION PLAY-OFF
(28/5/10)
Käerjéng 3, Obercorn 1

DOMESTIC CUP 2009/10

COUPE DE LUXEMBOURG

1/16 FINALS

(26/2/10)
Schifflange 1, Käerjéng 3

(27/2/10)
Beggen 1, Fola 2
Bissen 1, Differdange 6
Canach 2, Racing Union 1
Diekirch 3, Jeunesse Esch 2
Erpeldange 1, Dudelange 3
Lintgen 1, Pétange 3 *(aet)*
Mondorf 0, Hamm 2
Steinfort 0, Etzella 1
US Esch 0, Hesper 1
Wiltz 0, Rumelange 0 *(aet; 6-7 on pens)*

(17/3/10)
Clemency 2, Schieren 0
Echternach 2, Mondercange 4 *(aet)*
Gasperich 0, Progrès 7
Mertert/Wasserbillig 0, Obercorn 1
Mertzig 2, Grevenmacher 4

SIXTH ROUND

(2/4/10)
Etzella 2, Pétange 1 *(aet)*
Mondercange 0, Progrès 0 *(aet; 4-3 on pens)*

(3/4/10)
Canach 0, Rumelange 0 *(aet; 4-3 on pens)*
Clemency 1, Grevenmacher 4 *(aet)*
Diekirch 1, Hesper 2
Fola 4, Käerjéng 2 *(aet)*
Hamm 1, Dudelange 2
Obercorn 0, Differdange 3

QUARTER-FINALS

(1/5/10)
Differdange 3 *(Kettenmeyer 66, Piskor 73, Alunni 75)*, Mondercange 0

(2/5/10)
Dudelange 2 *(Gruszczyński 78, 119p)*, Fola 2 *(Di Gregorio 69, Greszkowiak 11¢ (aet; 9-10 on pens)*
Etzella 2 *(Nilton 4, Leweck C. 23)*, Hesper 1 *(Casafina 66)*
Grevenmacher 4 *(Tejerina 40, Hoffmann 47, Müller 53, Hartung 90 + 3)*, Canach 2 *(Borges 19, Amrane 24)*

SEMI-FINALS

(25/5/10)
Grevenmacher 5 *(Huss 32, 42, 59, 90+4, Hoffmann 88)*, Fola 1 *(Dallevedove 2*

(26/5/10)
Differdange 3 *(Albanese 17, Lebresne 60, Joachim 65)*, Etzella 1 *(Camara 43p*

FINAL

(30/5/10)
Stade Josy Barthel, Luxembourg
FC DIFFERDANGE 03 1 *(Soraire 89)*
CS GREVENMACHER 0
Referee – Parage
DIFFERDANGE – Hym, Kintziger, Siebenaler, Wagner, Rodrigues, Lebresne *(Soraire 85)*, Kettenmeyer, Jänisch *(Diop 90+3)*, Albanese *(Alunni 74)*, Piskor, Joachim.
GREVENMACHER – Pleimling, Braun, Heinz, Brzyski, Federspiel *(Thimmesch 90+2)*, Hartung, Omerović, Stojadinović *(Tejerina 63)*, Boussi *(Lorig 83)*, Hoffmann, Huss.

Village champions emerge from disruption

The 2009/10 season in the Former Yugoslav Republic of Macedonia (FYROM) was unlike any that had preceded it. For the most part it was one of disorder and disruption, with the Prva Liga tainted by boycotts, bans and points deductions and only nine of the original dozen participants seeing out the season. The good news was provided by village club FK Renova, who benefited from the chaos by claiming their first league title, and by the country's star player, Goran Pandev, who won the UEFA Champions League with FC Internazionale Milano.

Everything appeared to be progressing smoothly in the Prva Liga until a third of the way through the season, in November, when the outcome of the Football Federation of Macedonia (FFM) presidential elections led to an announcement from four clubs that they would be withdrawing from the league. Two of them, FK Pelister and FK Turnovo, went back on their original decision, but the other two, FK Sloga

Goran Pandev – his mid-season move from Lazio to Inter paid rich dividends

Jugomagnat and reigning champions FK Makedonija GP Skopje, followed their boycott through and, having failed to fulfil two consecutive fixtures, were subsequently expelled by the FFM.

Far-reaching consequences

The consequences of this move were far-reaching for the league as a whole. A decision to ratify the results of the two departed teams for the first ten rounds but to annul them thereafter led to a full-scale recalculation of points and positions in the table. By the winter break, however, it was Renova, led by coach Vlatko Kostov, who sat proudly on top of the standings with 13 wins from their 17 games and a five-point lead over second-placed FK Rabotnicki.

But that was not the end of the story. Further mathematical adjustments would be enforced just a few weeks before the end of the season when FK Pobeda were expelled from the league – with all results annulled – following a FIFA ruling on UEFA's original judgment of a year earlier regarding the club's alleged illegal manipulation of results in European competition. Furthermore, Pobeda were banned from all competitions for eight years.

With all points accrued against Pobeda thus removed, the season eventually came to a close, with just three quarters of its original cast remaining, at the end of May. Renova had surrendered the six points they won against Pobeda and were also defeated in each of their final two games, but the club from Dzepciste, a hamlet of just 4,200 inhabitants in the country's north-western corner, were still able to claim their maiden title by a five-point margin from Rabotnicki, the team who destroyed Renova's perfect home record by beating them 1-0 in Tetovo – the town in which they play – on the final day.

Renova's excellence at home was supplemented by a strong attack, especially before the mid-season departure, to German club FC Schalke 04, of powerful young striker Besart Ibraimi, who scored 12 goals in 16

games. The experienced Boban Jancevski also found the net 11 times before Christmas, but the most consistent marksman over the whole campaign was Rabotnicki's skilful attacking midfielder Bobi Bozinovski, who added 14 goals to a multitude of assists.

Second in the league, Rabotnicki also finished runners-up in the domestic cup, thus surrendering a trophy they had won in each of the previous two seasons. Their conquerors in the final were FK Teteks, the other club from Tetovo, who raced into a 3-0 lead at the Philip II Arena with three goals in the third quarter of the game. Rabotnicki responded with two goals of their own to ensure a tense finish but Teteks survived to claim their first major trophy and win an unexpected place in the UEFA Europa League alongside Rabotnicki and European debutants FK Metalurg Skopje, who finished third in the league despite the dismissal of two former Macedonian national team coaches – Gjore Jovanonski and Nikola Ilievski – in the late autumn. The less experienced Zikica Tasevski took over and proved to be an inspired choice, leading Metalurg unbeaten through the spring, during which they twice got the better of champions Renova.

Pandev conquers Europe

FYROM's four European representatives in 2009/10 did very little of note, with only Rabotnicki actually winning a tie, but the country's interest in continental competition was refuelled in mid-season when Pandev left S.S. Lazio, where he had fallen out of favour in a contract dispute and was banished from the team, and joined Inter. He would emerge as a key figure for José Mourinho's side as the Nerazzurri went on to win the the Serie A/Coppa Italia double and also become champions of Europe for the first time in 45 years. After Darko Pancev and Ilija Najdoski, who both featured in FK Crvena zvezda's 1991 Champion Clubs' Cup win,

Fudbalska Federatsija na Makedonija (FFM)

8-ma Udarna Brigada 31 A
PO Box 84
NK-1000 Skopje
tel – +389 3 222 603
fax – +389 3 165 448
website - ffm.com.mk
email - ffm@ffm.com.mk
Year of Formation – 1948

President – Haralampie Hadzi-risteski
General Secretary – Igor Klimper
Media Officer – Zoran Nikolovski
National Stadium – Philip II Arena, Skopje (32,000)

TOP FIVE ALL-TIME CAPS
Goce Sedloski (100); Artim Sakiri (73); Velice Sumulikoski (66); Igor Mitreski (62); Petar Milosevski (59)
TOP FIVE ALL-TIME GOALS
Goran Pandev (23); Georgi Hristov (16); Artim Sakiri (15); Goran Maznov (10); Sasa Ciric & Goce Sedloski (8)

Pandev became only the third Macedonian to win Europe's top club prize.

Pandev also hit top form for his country, scoring six goals in four successive friendly internationals, three of which – against Qatar, Canada and Montenegro – yielded victories and the other – against Iran – a draw. In fact, further wins (without Pandev) in the late spring, against Azerbaijan – in which defender Goce Sedloski became the first Macedonian footballer to win 100 caps – and Romania, enabled Mirsad Jonuz's side to stretch their unbeaten run to a record-breaking six matches. Unfortunately, there were no points at stake in any of those games, but the results provided plenty of encouragement ahead of the UEFA EURO 2012 qualifying campaign, in which the team were set to do battle with Russia, Slovakia, the Republic of Ireland, Armenia and Andorra.

NATIONAL TEAM RESULTS 2009/10

12/8/09	Spain	H	Skopje	2-3	*Pandev (7, 33)*
5/9/09	Scotland (WCQ)	A	Glasgow	0-2	
9/9/09	Norway (WCQ)	A	Oslo	1-2	*Grncarov (79)*
11/10/09	Qatar	H	Skopje	2-1	*Pandev (25, 40)*
14/11/09	Canada	H	Strumica	3-0	*Sedloski (48), Pandev (61p, 90+4p)*
18/11/09	Iran	A	Tehran	1-1	*Pandev (49)*
3/3/10	Montenegro	H	Skopje	2-1	*Naumoski (27), Pandev (31)*
29/5/10	Azerbaijan	N	Bischofshofen (AUT)	3-1	*Trickovski (8), Despotovski (65), Djurovski (88)*
2/6/10	Romania	N	Villach (AUT)	1-0	*Sikov (28)*

NATIONAL TEAM APPEARANCES 2009/10

Coach – Mirsad JONUZ	9/4/62		Esp	SCO	NOR	Qat	Can	Irn	Mne	Aze	Rou	Caps	Goals
Jane NIKOLOSKI	12/12/73	AEP (CYP)	G62	G								27	-
Goce SEDLOSKI	10/4/74	Mattersburg (AUT)	D46	D	D	s46	s46	D	s46	s54		100	8
Igor MITRESKI	19/2/79	Energie (GER) /CSKA Sofia (BUL)	D	D	D	D70	D46		D46	D54	D	62	1
Nikolce NOVESKI	28/4/79	Mainz (GER)	D57	D		D46	D66	D	D46	s46	D	37	2
Goran POPOV	2/10/84	Heerenveen (NED)	M	M	M	M	D	M46	M	D	D	32	2
Filip DESPOTOVSKI	18/11/82	Vorskla (UKR)	M65	M		M	M	M71	M	M	M60	10	1
Velice SUMULIKOSKI	24/4/81	Preston (ENG)	M	M	M	M	M	M	M	M	M58	66	1
Slavco GEORGIEVSKI	30/3/80	Ulsan Hyundai (KOR) /Ethnikos Achnas (CYP)	M60	M69	M		M77	M79	M	M72	M	14	-
Goran PANDEV	27/7/83	Lazio (ITA) /Inter (ITA)	A82	M	M	A68	A	A86	A75			53	23
Ilco NAUMOSKI	29/7/83	Mattersburg (AUT)	A58	A64	A75	A46	A46		A46			36	7
Aco STOJKOV	29/4/83	Aarau (SUI)	A	A79	A60	A46	A59	s46	A46			39	5
Vlade LAZAREVSKI	9/6/83	Karpaty (UKR) /Rijeka (CRO)	s46			D46	D46	s46		D75	D71	37	-
Daniel MOJSOV	25/12/87	Makedonija Skopje	s57			s70	s66	s79				6	-
Filip IVANOVSKI	1/5/85	Polonia Warszawa (POL)	s58		s75	s46		A46				5	-
Vlatko GROZDANOSKI	30/1/83	Vojvodina (SRB) /AEL (CYP)	s60	s69							s60	48	4
Tome PACOVSKI	28/6/82	GBA (BEL)	s62		G	G81	G86	G	G65	G	s79	18	-
Darko TASEVSKI	20/5/84	Levski (BUL)	s65	s64	M65							32	-
Agim IBRAIMI	29/8/88	Olimpija (SVN)	s82								A46	2	-
Besart IBRAIMI	17/12/86	Renova /Schalke (GER)		s79	s60	M	s46	s46	s46			6	-
Boban GRNCAROV	12/8/82	APOEL (CYP)					D		s46	D46		16	1
Armend ALIMI	11/12/87	Istra (CRO)				s65	s46	s77	s71	s75	s58	6	-
Robert POPOV	16/4/82	Auxerre (FRA)				s46	s46	D				17	-
Dusan SAVIC	1/10/85	Rabotnicki /Braşov (ROU)				s68	s59	A46	s46	A64		6	-
Edin NUREDINOSKI	21/4/82	Ethnikos Achnas (CYP)				s81			s65		G79	3	-
Kristijan NAUMOVSKI	17/9/88	Rabotnicki						s86				1	-
Gligor GLIGOROV	5/3/87	Sileks								s86		1	-
Aleksandar TODOROVSKI	26/2/84	Rad (SRB)								s75	s71	2	-
Mensur KURTISI	25/3/86	Wiener Neustadt (AUT)								M46	s64	2	-
Stevica RISTIC	23/5/82	Bunyodkor (UZB)								A61		9	1
Ivan TRICKOVSKI	18/4/87	Paralimni (CYP)								A	A68	2	1
Blaze ILIJOSKI	9/7/84	Metalurg Skopje								s46	s68	4	1
Mario DJUROVSKI	11/12/85	Vojvodina (SRB)								s61	s46	2	1
Vance SIKOV	19/7/85	Ethnikos Achnas (CYP)								s72	D	4	1

DOMESTIC LEAGUE 2009/10

PRVA LIGA FINAL TABLE

		Pld	Home					Away					Total					Pts
			W	D	L	F	A	W	D	L	F	A	W	D	L	F	A	
1	FK Renova	26	13	0	1	30	9	4	4	4	15	12	17	4	5	45	21	55
2	FK Rabotnicki	26	7	4	2	23	12	8	1	4	15	8	15	5	6	38	20	50
3	FK Metalurg Skopje	26	8	4	1	27	7	4	7	2	8	9	12	11	3	35	16	47
4	FK Pelister	26	8	4	1	17	6	3	2	8	11	21	11	6	9	28	27	39
5	FK Sileks	26	6	4	3	16	11	2	4	7	13	22	8	8	10	29	33	32
6	FK Vardar	26	6	3	3	16	9	3	3	8	15	19	9	6	11	31	28	30
7	FK Teteks	26	4	5	4	15	9	4	1	8	16	21	8	6	12	31	30	30
8	FK Turnovo	26	4	2	7	14	17	4	3	6	13	18	8	5	13	27	35	26
9	FK Milano	26	1	2	10	9	35	0	1	12	5	46	1	3	22	14	81	6
10	FK Makedonija GP Skopje	10	4	1	0	19	1	1	3	1	4	4	5	4	1	23	5	0
11	FK Sloga Jugomagnat	10	2	1	2	3	5	1	1	3	6	9	3	2	5	9	14	0
12	FK Pobeda	0	0	0	0	0	0	0	0	0	0	0	0	0	0	0	0	0

NB FK Makedonija GP Skopje and FK Sloga Jugomagnat were excluded after round 15; results from rounds 1-10 stood but points annulled. FK Pobeda were excluded after round 28, with all results annulled. FK Vardar & FK Turnovo – 3 pts deducted.

TOP GOALSCORERS

14 Bobi BOZINOVSKI (Rabotnicki)
12 Dusan SAVIC (Rabotnicki)
   Besart IBRAIMI (Renova)
11 Dragan DIMITROVSKI (Pelister/Pobeda)
   Boban JANCEVSKI (Renova)
10 Ilija NESTOROVSKI (Pobeda)
9 Baze ILIJOSKI (Metalurg)
8 WANDEIR (Rabotnicki)
7 Ivica GLIGOROVSKI (Makedonija/Teteks)
   Mile KRSTEV (Metalurg)
   Marjan ALTIPARMAKOVSKI (Pelister)
   Ilber ALI (Renova)
   Dragan GEORGIEV (Turnovo)
   Boško STUPIĆ (Vardar)

CLUB-BY-CLUB

FK MAKEDONIJA GP SKOPJE
Coach – Ilco Gjorgioski
Founded – 1932
Stadium – Gjorce Petrov (5,000)
MAJOR HONOURS:
Macedonian League – (1) 2009;
Macedonian Cup – (1) 2006.

2009

1/8	Teteks	a	2-2	Ivanovski, Kleckarovski
9/8	Renova	a	0-1	
16/8	Vardar	h	5-0	Gligorovski 3, Kleckarovski, Ivanovski
23/8	Pobeda	a	0-0	(match annulled)
13/9	Sloga	h	4-1	Lena, Brnjarcevski, Mojsov 2
20/9	Metalurg	a	0-0	
26/9	Milano	h	8-0	Jakimovski, Gligorovski 2, Ivanovski 2, Kralevski, Nastevski, Gjurgjevic
3/10	Rabotnicki	a	1-1	Lena
18/10	Pelister	h	0-0	
24/10	Turnovo	a	1-0	Gligorovski
1/11	Sileks	h	2-0	Nastevski, Ilievski
4/11	Teteks	h	1-0	Mitrev (match annulled)
8/11	Renova	h	0-1	(match annulled)
22/11	Vardar	a	0-3	(w/o) (match annulled)
29/11	Pobeda	h	0-3	(w/o) (match annulled)

No	Name	Nat	DoB	Pos	Aps	(s)	Gls
3	Georges AMBOUROUET	GAB	1/5/86	D	4	(1)	
26	Daniel ATANASOVSKI		18/7/90	A		(1)	
9	Toni BRNJARCEVSKI		7/6/85	A	7	(4)	1
17	CARLOS AUGUSTO Farias	BRA	12/2/86	M	1		
6	FELIPE Moreira MONTENARI	BRA	19/8/87	D	13		
27	Fahrudin GJURGJEVIC		17/2/92	A		(7)	1
19	Ivica GLIGOROVSKI		15/4/81	A	8	(5)	6
7	Milan ILIEVSKI		21/7/82	D	9	(2)	1
16	Mirko IVANOVSKI		31/10/89	A	11	(1)	4
14	Nikola JAKIMOVSKI		26/2/90	A	1	(3)	1
13	Daniel JOVANOVSKI		12/11/83	D	6	(2)	
18	Beni Popol KIENDE	GAB	10/3/86	A	2	(2)	
10	Nikolce KLECKAROVSKI		17/5/83	A	10	(2)	2
23	Igor KRALEVSKI		11/10/78	D	3	(2)	1
8	Nijaz LENA		25/6/86	M	8		2
12	Marjan MADZAROSKI		30/7/86	G	1		
4	Blagoja MILEVSKI		25/3/71	D	11		
20	Vasko MITREV		23/5/84	M	12		1
5	Daniel MOJSOV		25/12/87	D	11		2
24	Ivan NASTEVSKI		30/7/91	D	3	(5)	2
22	Danilo PUSTINJAKOVIĆ	SRB	12/3/77	G	12		
	Goran SILJANOVSKI		1/7/90	D	1		
15	Dusan SIMOVSKI		1/5/88	D	9		

FK METALURG SKOPJE
Coach – Gjore Jovanovski; (22/11/09) Nikola Ilievski; (13/12/09) Zikica Tasevski
Founded – 1964
Stadium – Zelezarnica (3,000)

2009

2/8	Rabotnicki	a	1-1	Gesoski
9/8	Pelister	h	1-2	Rutevski
16/8	Turnovo	a	1-1	Đurić
23/8	Sileks	h	2-2	Ilijoski 2
13/9	Teteks	a	0-0	
20/9	Makedonija	h	0-0	
27/9	Vardar	a	0-0	
4/10	Pobeda	h	2-1	Stefanovic, Velkovski (match annulled)
18/10	Sloga	a	1-0	Ilijoski

24/10	Renova	a	1-3	Krstev	
1/11	Milano	h	4-0	Shabani, Đurić, Neno, Tadić	
4/11	Rabotnicki	h	1-1	Stefanovic	
8/11	Pelister	a	0-3		
22/11	Turnovo	h	3-0	(w/o)	
29/11	Sileks	a	1-0	Velkovski	
6/12	Teteks	h	4-0	Krstev 3, Dimitrovski	
13/12	Vardar	h	3-0	(w/o)	
2010					
28/2	Pobeda	a	1-0	Ilijoski (match annulled)	
21/3	Renova	h	3-1	Krstev 2 (1p), Ilijoski	
24/3	Milano	a	0-0		
28/3	Turnovo	h	1-1	Ilijoski	
3/4	Vardar	a	0-0		
11/4	Milano	h	3-0	Krstev, Ejupi, Kostencoski	
18/4	Sileks	a	1-0	Ilijoski	
25/4	Pelister	h	1-0	Ilijoski	
2/5	Pobeda	h	3-0	Ilijoski, Ejupi, Kostencoski (match annulled)	
9/5	Rabotnicki	a	2-1	Ejupi 2	
12/5	Renova	h	1-0	Kralevski	
15/5	Teteks	a	0-0		

No	Name	Nat	DoB	Pos	Aps	(s)	Gls
6	Betim ALIU		17/3/89	D		(1)	
6	Omer BISEVAC		2/9/83	D	10	(1)	
	Goran BOGDANOVIC		9/6/90	D	2	(1)	
4	Gjoko CVETANOVSKI		16/7/82	M	13	(6)	
27	Vladimir DIMITROVSKI		30/11/88	D	16	(1)	1
2	Aleksandar DONEV		26/4/82	D	3	(3)	
5	Milan ĐURIĆ	SRB	3/10/87	M	14	(7)	2
16	Muzafer EJUPI		16/9/88	A	5	(6)	4
1	Jorde GEORGIEVSKI		3/1/82	G	10		
16	Blagoja GESOSKI		28/4/81	A	4	(7)	1
9	Blaze ILIJOSKI		9/7/84	A	20	(3)	9
23	Zoran JOVANOSKI		21/8/72	D	2		
22	Miodrag JOVANOVIĆ	SRB	10/7/86	D	1	(3)	
8	Marko KOSTENCOSKI		8/10/89	M	9	(2)	2
9	Jovan KOSTOVSKI		19/4/87	A	8	(4)	
23	Igor KRALEVSKI		11/10/78	D	10	(2)	1
20	Mile KRSTEV		13/5/79	M	17	(4)	7
29	Dimitrija LAZAREVSKI		23/9/82	D	20		
25	Vance MANCEVSKI		3/9/82	G	10		
18	Bojan MIHAJLOVIĆ	SRB	16/12/73	M	15		
17	Aleksandar MILUSEV		5/4/88	D	2		
10	Carlos Adélsio Abrilio "NENO"	BRA	10/10/79	M	7	(1)	1
1	Trajce NIKOV		20/8/87	G	7		
21	Mile PETKOVSKI		19/9/88	D	16	(1)	
14	Aleksandar POPOVSKI		3/2/81	A	1	(7)	
19	Blagojce RUTEVSKI		28/3/80	A	3	(9)	1
7	Emir SHABANI		2/1/90	M	3	(2)	1
22	Jovan STEFANOVIC		2/5/84	M	6	(3)	2
	Mirce STOJANOV		7/3/93	M		(1)	
21	Đorđe TADIĆ	SRB	16/2/83	D	7	(1)	1
24	Aleksandar TENEKEDZIEV		13/3/86	M	4		
11	Jovica TRAJCEV		9/1/81	M	19		
28	Miroslav VAJS		27/7/79	D	19		
8	Krste VELKOVSKI		20/2/88	A	14		2

FK MILANO

Coach – Erkan Jusuf; (1/9/09) Dzemail Zekiri;
(29/9/09) Kenan Ameti; (10/1/10) Dragan Antić (SRB)
Founded – 1990
Stadium – Milano Arena (5,000)

2009					
1/8	Renova	h	0-2		
12/8	Rabotnicki	h	0-2		
16/8	Pelister	a	1-3	Alimi	
23/8	Turnovo	h	0-2		
13/9	Sileks	a	0-4		

19/9	Teteks	h	1-5	Beluli	
26/9	Makedonija	a	0-8		
4/10	Vardar	h	0-4		
18/10	Pobeda	a	1-4	Sulimani A. (match annulled)	
26/10	Sloga	h	0-3		
1/11	Metalurg	a	0-4		
4/11	Renova	a	0-4		
7/11	Rabotnicki	a	1-5	Limani	
22/11	Pelister	h	3-0	(w/o)	
29/11	Turnovo	a	1-3	Limani	
6/12	Sileks	h	1-4	Maliqi D.	
9/12	Teteks	a	0-6		
2010					
27/2	Vardar	a	0-2		
7/3	Pobeda	h	3-2	Bogoslovski, Erdogan, Bajlozov (match annulled)	
24/3	Metalurg	h	0-0		
28/3	Sileks	a	1-1	Bogoslovski	
3/4	Pelister	h	2-2	Aliji, Bogatinov	
11/4	Metalurg	a	0-3		
18/4	Rabotnicki	h	0-2		
25/4	Renova	a	0-1		
30/4	Teteks	h	2-4	Aliji, Ermedin	
9/5	Turnovo	a	1-2	Milić	
12/5	Vardar	h	0-5		

Name	Nat	DoB	Pos	Aps	(s)	Gls
Llokman ABAZI		27/2/90	D	1	(1)	
Nderim ABDULI		21/4/82	G	13	(1)	
Burhan ALIJI		29/7/89	M	12		2
Armend ALIMI		11/12/87	M	4		1
Erkan ALIU		15/1/91	D	9		
Orhan ALIU		30/11/93	D	6	(1)	
Fatlum AQIFOVIC			M		(1)	
Ziba ARIJETON		8/4/88	M	3	(2)	
Dzokica ARSOVSKI		29/4/92	M	1		
Avni AZIRI		20/12/81	M	5		
Sasko BAJLOZOV		31/8/82	A	10	(1)	1
Valmir BELULI		16/3/91	M	13	(6)	1
Sedat BERISA		3/9/89	D	6	(3)	
Liman BILALI		15/4/89	D	3	(1)	
Omer BISEVAC		2/9/83	D	11		
Antonio BOGATINOV		19/6/85	D	7		1
Nikola BOGOSLOVSKI	SRB	3/10/86	M	11		2
Faton CECELIA		22/8/83	M	4		
Aleksandar DANIĆ	SRB	27/10/80	G	10		
Kadri EMINI		8/4/92	D	8	(1)	
Brando ERDOGAN		19/5/84	M	6		1
Adem ERMEDIN		7/7/90	A	8	(3)	1
Bunjamin FAZLIU		18/5/91	A	8	(3)	
Dijamant FAZLIU		3/10/91	M	8	(2)	
Argjend FETAHI			D		(2)	
Durim HIDA		15/4/91	M		(3)	
Gezim IBRAIM		8/8/92	M		(1)	
Edon JASAREVIC		11/1/90	M	6	(2)	
Leonid KALABA		3/5/86	M	9	(1)	
Rilind KAMBERI		3/6/93	M		(3)	
Sase KOSTADINOVSKI		26/9/90	M	2	(3)	
Ivica LAZAREV		7/7/83	A	3		
Adnan LIMANI		14/10/90	A	7		2
Dijamant MALIQI		31/12/89	A	6	(2)	1
Fejzi MALIQI		25/3/89	M	12	(2)	
Ivan MARINKOVIĆ	SRB	31/8/92	M	8		
Zoran MARKOVSKI		18/6/80	G	2		
Cristian Trabanino MAYORGA	GUA	22/2/90	M	3	(1)	
Shpetim MEMETI			A	2	(5)	
Nikola MILIĆ	SRB	27/9/87	A	5	(1)	1
Ivan PUZOVIĆ	SRB	18/10/80	D	9		
Suat RAMADANI			M		(1)	
Burim SHABANI		3/2/86	D	4		
Fuad SHABANI		2/1/90	D	9	(1)	

Lulzim SHABANI	10/10/87	M		(3)		Blagoja LJAMCESKI		7/4/87	M	26	(1)	1
Jovan SEKOVSKI	18/8/83	M	2	(1)		Stefan MAGLOVSKI		17/7/90	M	4	(8)	
Igor STANOJEVIC	5/9/89	M		(1)		Ljupco MICEVSKI		9/6/87	D	2		
Zvezdan STEFANOVIĆ	SRB 19/9/84	M	1			Goran MIROVIĆ	SRB	18/5/82	M	12	(2)	2
Saša STOJANOVIĆ	SRB 24/8/78	M	2			Igor PAVLOVIĆ	SRB	24/2/82	G	17		
Aleksandar STOJANOVSKI	16/2/83	A	4	(6)		Mile PETKOVSKI		19/9/88	D	3		
Arijan SULIMANI	20/4/90	A	5	(2)	1	Nikola PETKOVSKI		14/12/86	M	14	(3)	1
Fidan SULIMANI	20/10/90	M	12	(3)		Ilce PETROVSKI		22/7/89	G	10	(1)	
Dragan TRAJKOVSKI	11/10/88	M	14	(1)		Toni PITOSKA		24/7/82	A		(3)	
Filip TRAJKOVSKI	6/4/91	M	1	(4)		Kire RISTESKI		22/10/90	D	23	(2)	
Goran TRAJKOVSKI	18/10/92	G	2	(1)		Zoran SIMONOVSKI		13/3/89	M		(12)	
						Stefan SPIROVSKI		23/8/90	M	14	(2)	
						Jovan STEFANOVIC		2/5/84	M	6	(1)	1

FK PELISTER

Blagoja LJAMCESKI / Aleksandar VELJANOVSKI — 9/8/91 D 15 (4) 2

Coach – Alekso Mackov; (29/9/09) Gjoko Ilievski;
(6/10/09) Naum Ljamcevski

Saso VELJANOVSKI 16/1/90 A 2 (2)
Toni VELJANOVSKI 12/4/84 D 23 (1) 2

Founded – 1945

Stadium – Tumbe Kafe (10,000)

MAJOR HONOURS:
Macedonian Cup - (1) 2001.

FK POBEDA

Coach – Goran Todorovski

2009

1/8	Sloga	h	0-0	
9/8	Metalurg	a	2-1	Dimitrovski, Lazarevski
16/8	Milano	h	3-1	Dimitrovski, Lazarevski 2
23/8	Rabotnicki	a	0-3	
13/9	Renova	h	1-1	Veljanovski A.
20/9	Turnovo	h	1-2	Dimitrovski
27/9	Sileks	a	0-1	
4/10	Teteks	h	3-1	Dimitrovski 2, Altiparmakovski
18/10	Makedonija	a	0-0	
25/10	Vardar	h	1-0	Altiparmakovski
1/11	Pobeda	a	0-0	(match annulled)
4/11	Sloga	a	3-1	Dimitrovski, Mirović,
				Kleckarovski (match annulled)
8/11	Metalurg	h	3-0	Mirović, Altiparmakovski,
				Dimitrovski
22/11	Milano	a	0-3	(w/o)
29/11	Rabotnicki	h	1-0	Altiparmakovski
6/12	Renova	a	0-1	
9/12	Turnovo	a	3-4	Ljamceski, Dimitrovski,
				Altiparmakovski
13/12	Sileks	h	1-1	Dimitrovski

2010

28/2	Teteks	a	2-1	Iliev, Petkovski N.
21/3	Vardar	a	0-1	
24/3	Pobeda	h	1-0	Stefanovic (match annulled)
28/3	Vardar	h	1-0	Veljanovski A.
3/4	Milano	a	2-2	Altiparmakovski, Iliev
11/4	Sileks	h	1-0	Altiparmakovski
18/4	Pobeda	h	1-0	Veljanovski T. (match annulled)
25/4	Metalurg	a	0-1	
30/4	Rabotnicki	h	1-0	Iliev
9/5	Renova	a	1-3	Veljanovski T.
12/5	Teteks	h	0-0	
15/5	Turnovo	a	1-0	Bujcevski

Founded – 1941

Stadium – Goce Delcev (10,000)

MAJOR HONOURS:
Macedonian League – (2) 2004, 2007;
Macedonian Cup - (1) 2002.

2009

3/8	Turnovo	a	1-3	Nestorovski
9/8	Sileks	h	2-2	Nestorovski, Veljanovski V.
16/8	Teteks	a	1-3	Nestorovski
23/8	Makedonija	h	0-0	
13/9	Vardar	a	0-0	
19/9	Renova	a	1-2	Curlinov
27/9	Sloga	h	2-0	Nestorovski 2
4/10	Metalurg	a	1-2	Marković
18/10	Milano	h	4-1	Curlinov 2, Nestorovski, Mirceski
24/10	Rabotnicki	a	2-6	Petrović, Nestorovski
1/11	Pelister	h	0-0	
4/11	Turnovo	h	1-0	Curlinov
8/11	Sileks	a	1-0	Aceski
22/11	Teteks	h	2-0	Nestorovski, Dameski
29/11	Makedonija	a	3-0	(w/o)
6/12	Vardar	h	2-1	Nestorovski 2
9/12	Renova	h	0-4	

2010

28/2	Metalurg	h	0-1	
7/3	Milano	a	2-3	Rutevski, Stojanovski
21/3	Rabotnicki	h	4-2	Veljanovski V., Rutevski,
				Dameski 2 (1p)
24/3	Pelister	a	0-1	
28/3	Renova	a	1-2	Dimitrovski
3/4	Sileks	a	0-3	
11/4	Teteks	h	2-0	Rutevski, Dimitrovski
18/4	Pelister	a	0-1	
25/4	Turnovo	h	0-1	
2/5	Metalurg	a	0-3	

NB All matches annulled.

Name	Nat	DoB	Pos	Aps	(s)	Gls
Marijan ALTIPARMAKOVSKI		18/7/91	A	19	(6)	7
Dejan APOSTOLOVSKI		6/8/90	G	2		
Nemanja BRADARIĆ	SRB	3/8/87	M	19	(2)	
Vladica BRDAROVSKI		7/2/90	D	14		
Antonio BUJCEVSKI		24/1/90	A	4	(5)	1
Mihael CVETKOVSKI		21/11/87	D	20	(2)	
Dragan DIMITROVSKI		26/7/77	A	16		9
Vladimir DOKNIĆ	SRB	2/2/84	D	5	(2)	
Hristijan DRAGARSKI		16/4/92	D	2	(2)	
Goran GANCEV		4/8/83	D	23		
Lazar ILIEV		25/3/87	A	8	(2)	3
Milan IVANOVIC		21/7/88	M	2	(6)	
Igor KLECKAROVSKI		4/3/87	A	2	(7)	1
Sasko LAZAREVSKI		24/3/78	M	12	(2)	3

Name	Nat	DoB	Pos	Aps	(s)	Gls
Nove ACESKI		26/5/87	M	16	(2)	1
Vangel ALTIPARMAKOVSKI		1/3/88	M	2	(2)	
Cvetan CURLINOV		24/7/86	M	10	(3)	4
Blagojce DAMESKI		17/10/81	D	23		3
Zlatko DELOVSKI		10/4/79	M	4	(7)	
Dragan DIMITROVSKI		26/7/77	A	8	(1)	2
Stojance DUNIMAGLOSKI		29/9/91	M	3	(4)	
Hristijan GJORGIESKI		16/2/90	D		(1)	
Uros JANKOVIĆ	MNE	22/9/85	D	4		
Aleksandar JEFTIMOV		22/12/91	G	3	(1)	
Miodrag JOVANOVIĆ	SRB	10/7/86	D		(1)	
Bektas JUSUFOVSKI		17/10/89	D	1	(1)	

Zoran KOTESKI	13/11/91	D		(1)	
Vlado MARKOVIĆ	BIH 26/8/85	D	15		1
Toni MEGLENSKI	22/5/81	M	19		
Filip MIRCESKI	15/3/89	D	25		1
Risto MITREVSKI	5/10/91	M	8	(3)	
Ilija NESTOROVSKI	12/3/90	A	15		10
Goran PASOVSKI	15/2/80	G	23		
Milovan PETROVIĆ	SRB 23/1/90	D	24	(1)	1
Robert PLASTINOVSKI	6/2/85	M	1	(5)	
Bruno PRESILSKI	25/12/72	M	7		
Blagojce RISTEVSKI	12/7/90	A	3	(5)	
Nikola RISTOV	12/10/88	M	14	(4)	
Blagojce RUTEVSKI	28/3/80	A	6		3
Emir SHABANI	2/1/90	M	9	(1)	
Filip SPIRKOSKI	6/6/91	D	7	(3)	
Hristijan SRKESKI	7/1/92	G		(1)	
Nikolce STISNIOVSKI	19/7/78	M	3	(8)	
Aleksandar STOJANOVSKI	14/11/84	M	19	(3)	1
Hristijan TODOROVSKI	22/11/93	A	1		
Bobi VELJANOVSKI	13/7/88	D	7	(3)	
Viktor VELJANOVSKI	25/10/86	A	4	(3)	2
Aleksandar ZOJCESKI	8/7/90	M	2	(7)	

	Toni BRNJARCEVSKI		7/6/85	M	3	(5)	1
18	CARLOS ROBERTO da Silva	BRA	24/10/88	M	7	(11)	1
5	Goran DIMOVSKI		14/10/82	D	24	(1)	
	Adem EMIR		21/10/86	D	3	(1)	
15	FÁBIO Gilvan da Nascimento Silva	BRA	13/9/83	A	5	(5)	2
7	FERNANDO Alcantro Lopes	BRA	28/3/87	D	16		
16	Nikola GLIGOROV		15/8/83	M	24		2
9	MÁRCIO Francisco da Silva	BRA	4/3/82	M	5	(6)	3
21	Filip MISEVSKI		1/11/91	D	3		
	Risto MITREVSKI		5/10/91	M	1		
8	Muarem MUAREM		22/10/88	M	17	(2)	
12	Kristijan NAUMOVSKI		17/9/88	G	20		
20	Filip PETKOVSKI		24/5/90	A	5	(20)	2
2	Saško RISTOV		19/5/83	M	3	(2)	
10	Dusan SAVIC		1/10/85	A	17		12
3	Vladimir SEKULOVSKI		7/10/80	D	17		
	Kristijan SINKOVIĆ	CRO	2/4/87	M	1	(4)	
13	Goce TODOROVSKI		13/9/82	M	15	(4)	1
19	Vladimir TUNESKI		8/3/83	M	11	(4)	
23	WANDEIR Oliveira dos Santos		15/5/80	A	16	(2)	8
11	José "ZÉ" CARLOS Gomes Filho	BRA	4/10/79	A	10	(2)	

FK RABOTNICKI
Coach – Zoran Stratev
Founded – 1937
Stadium – Philip II Arena (25,000)
MAJOR HONOURS:
Macedonian League - (3) 2005, 2006, 2008;
Macedonian Cup - (2) 2008, 2009.

2009

2/8	Metalurg	h	1-1	*Todorovski*
12/8	Milano	a	2-0	*Bozinovski B. 2*
16/8	Renova	h	2-1	*Savic, Carlos Roberto*
23/8	Pelister	h	3-0	*Gligorov, Bozinovski B. 2*
13/9	Turnovo	a	2-0	*Savic, Bozinovski B.*
18/9	Sileks	h	1-1	*Savic*
27/9	Teteks	a	1-0	*Petkovski*
3/10	Makedonija	h	1-1	*Savic*
18/10	Vardar	a	2-1	*Savic, Bozinovski B.*
24/10	Pobeda	h	6-2	*Savic 3, Bozinovski B. 2, Wandeir (match annulled)*
1/11	Sloga	a	3-0	*Wandeir 2, Bozinovski B.*
4/11	Metalurg	a	1-1	*Savic*
7/11	Milano	h	5-1	*Savic, Márcio, Bozinovski B., Petkovski, Wandeir*
22/11	Renova	a	0-2	
29/11	Pelister	a	0-1	
5/12	Turnovo	h	1-0	*Wandeir (p)*
9/12	Sileks	a	0-2	
12/12	Teteks	h	3-1	*Bozinovski B., Savic 2 (1p)*
2010				
6/3	Vardar	h	1-0	*Bozinovski B. (p)*
21/3	Pobeda	a	2-4	*Fábio, Márcio (match annulled)*
28/3	Teteks	h	2-1	*Wandeir, Gligorov*
3/4	Turnovo	a	1-0	*Wandeir*
11/4	Vardar	h	1-1	*Bozinovski B.*
18/4	Milano	a	2-0	*Wandeir (p), Bozinovski B.*
25/4	Sileks	h	1-2	*Brnjarcevski*
30/4	Pelister	a	0-1	
9/5	Metalurg	h	1-2	*Márcio*
15/5	Renova	a	1-0	*Fábio*

FK RENOVA
Coach – Vlatko Kostov
Founded – 2003
Stadium – City, Tetovo (15,000)
MAJOR HONOURS:
Macedonian League - (1) 2010.

2009

1/8	Milano	a	2-0	*Nuhiu, Jancevski*
9/8	Makedonija	h	1-0	*Todorovski*
16/8	Rabotnicki	a	1-2	*Ibraimi*
30/8	Vardar	h	3-2	*Jancevski 2, Todorovski*
13/9	Pelister	a	1-1	*Jancevski*
19/9	Pobeda	h	2-1	*Ali, Ibraimi (match annulled)*
27/9	Turnovo	a	2-2	*Ibraimi, Bajrami*
4/10	Sloga	h	3-1	*Jancevski 2, og (Kalaba)*
18/10	Sileks	a	5-0	*Ibraimi 2, Ali, Todorovski, Ismaili*
24/10	Metalurg	h	3-1	*Ibraimi, Memedi A., Todorovski*
1/11	Teteks	a	1-0	*Ibraimi*
4/11	Milano	h	4-0	*Jancevski 4*
8/11	Makedonija	a	1-0	*Ali (match annulled)*
22/11	Rabotnicki	h	2-0	*Ibraimi, Angelovski*
29/11	Vardar	a	1-1	*Ibraimi*
6/12	Pelister	h	1-0	*Ibraimi*
9/12	Pobeda	a	4-0	*Ali, Todorovski, Bajrami, Gasi (match annulled)*
13/12	Turnovo	h	3-2	*Ibraimi 2 (1p), Jancevski*
2010				
7/3	Sileks	h	3-1	*Nuhiu, Emini, Todorovski*
21/3	Metalurg	a	1-3	*Ali*
24/3	Teteks	h	1-0	*Ismaili*
28/3	Pobeda	h	2-1	*Ali 2 (1p) (match annulled)*
3/4	Teteks	a	1-0	*Toleski*
11/4	Turnovo	h	2-0	*Toleski, Nuhiu*
18/4	Vardar	a	0-2	
25/4	Milano	h	1-0	*Emini*
2/5	Sileks	a	0-0	
9/5	Pelister	h	3-1	*Emini 2, Osmani*
12/5	Metalurg	a	0-1	
15/5	Rabotnicki	h	0-1	

No	Name	Nat	DoB	Pos	Aps	(s)	Gls
7	Eftim AKSENTIEV		17/8/85	A	1	(6)	
	Bunjamin ASANI		10/8/88	M	10		
1	Martin BOGATINOV		26/4/86	G	8		
4	Radenko BOJOVIĆ	SRB	26/12/80	D	24		
6	Bobi BOZINOVSKI		24/2/81	M	26		14
22	Vasko BOZINOVSKI		11/3/75	D	16		

No	Name	Nat	DoB	Pos	Aps	(s)	Gls
	Festim ADEMI		10/9/77	M	1	(5)	
9	Ilber ALI		7/5/79	A	20	(6)	7
18	Aleksandar ANGELOVSKI		11/7/86	M	6	(7)	1
29	Muharem BAJRAMI		29/11/85	M	12	(9)	2
6	Vladimir DESPOTOVSKI		5/10/77	D	26		
12	Armend ELEZI		20/4/80	G		(1)	

No	Name	Nat	DoB	Pos	Aps	(s)	Gls
7	Vulnet EMINI		10/9/78	M	21	(1)	4
15	Argent GAFURI		1/2/89	M	1	(7)	
19	Fisnik GASI		22/11/84	D	20	(1)	1
8	Besart IBRAIMI		17/12/86	A	16		12
21	Darko IGNJATOVSKI		19/5/81	D	4	(1)	
11	Ismail ISMAILI		24/11/81	A	1	(19)	2
20	Boban JANCEVSKI		30/4/78	A	14	(10)	11
1	Ljubo KOVAČEVIĆ	SRB	8/9/78	G	30		
4	Agron MEMEDI		5/12/80	M	29		1
22	Bajram MEMEDI		3/6/91	A		(1)	
24	Marjan MICKOV		10/2/87	M	12	(8)	
10	Fisnik NUHIU		26/11/83	M	26	(1)	3
	Minas OSMANI		22/2/85	M	4	(7)	1
3	Burim SADIKI		5/8/89	M		(1)	
14	Faruk STATOVCI		29/11/79	D	24	(1)	
23	Igorce STOJANOV		12/2/76	D	27		
13	Blagoja TODOROVSKI		11/6/85	M	28	(1)	6
	Goce TOLESKI		5/5/77	A	8	(1)	2

Name	Nat	DoB	Pos	Aps	(s)	Gls
Gligor GLIGOROV		5/3/87	M	21	(1)	2
Dejan KOSTURANOV		9/8/86	G	9		
Daniel LAMPEVSKI		3/9/88	D	19	(1)	
Blagojce MARKOVSKI		12/12/87	A	24	(1)	3
Nikola MISOVSKI		22/10/85	D	28		
Tomce MIZOROV		19/10/85	M		(4)	
Angel NACEV		10/10/89	A	8	(11)	3
Stojance NASEVSKI		12/2/91	A		(5)	
Martin PETROV		5/4/85	D	12	(5)	
Nikola SAKIĆ	SRB	6/1/87	A	2	(8)	1
Zoran SALEVSKI		24/7/86	D	5	(5)	
Borjan STOJANOVSKI		15/1/90	M	7	(13)	
Aleksandar TEMELKOV		6/10/87	M	26	(3)	6
Darko TRAJCEV		19/3/88	M	27		3
Vanco TRAJCOV		5/7/75	M	26		2
Haris UKIĆ	BIH	11/8/86	M	3	(1)	
Georgi ZAREVSKI		30/1/89	A	7	(1)	5

FK SILEKS
Coach – Ane Andovski
Founded – 1965
Stadium – Sileks (5,000)
MAJOR HONOURS:
Macedonian League - (3) 1996, 1997, 1998;
Macedonian Cup - (2) 1994, 1997.

FK SLOGA JUGOMAGNAT
Coach – Mensur Nedzipi; (27/10/09) Nedzat Sabani
Founded – 1927
Stadium – Cair, Skopje (4,500)
MAJOR HONOURS:
Macedonian League - (3) 1999, 2000, 2001;
Macedonian Cup - (3) 1996, 2000, 2004.

2009

1/8	Vardar	h	1-1	Boskovski
9/8	Pobeda	a	2-2	Zarevski, Trajcev (match annulled)
16/8	Sloga	h	2-1	Temelkov, Trajcov
23/8	Metalurg	a	2-2	Temelkov 2
13/9	Milano	h	4-0	Zarevski 2, Sakić, Andonov
18/9	Rabotnicki	a	1-1	Zarevski
27/9	Pelister	h	1-0	Markovski
4/10	Turnovo	a	0-2	
18/10	Renova	h	0-5	
25/10	Teteks	h	1-0	Markovski
1/11	Makedonija	a	0-2	
4/11	Vardar	a	1-3	Zarevski
8/11	Pobeda	h	0-1	(match annulled)
22/11	Sloga	a	3-0	(w/o) (match annulled)
29/11	Metalurg	h	0-1	
6/12	Milano	a	4-1	Gligorov 2, Nacev, Temelkov
9/12	Rabotnicki	h	2-0	Nacev, Andonov
13/12	Pelister	a	1-1	Markovski

2010

28/2	Turnovo	h	3-0	Trajcev, Đurić 2
7/3	Renova	a	1-3	Temelkov
21/3	Teteks	a	1-1	Trajcev
28/3	Milano	h	1-1	Boskovski
3/4	Pobeda	h	3-0	Đurić, Nacev, Boskovski (match annulled)
11/4	Pelister	a	0-1	
18/4	Metalurg	h	0-1	
24/4	Rabotnicki	a	2-1	Boskovski, Trajcov
2/5	Renova	h	0-0	
9/5	Teteks	a	0-2	
12/5	Turnovo	h	1-1	Temelkov
15/5	Vardar	a	0-2	

2009

1/8	Pelister	a	0-0	
9/8	Turnovo	h	1-1	Muminovic
16/8	Sileks	a	1-2	Idai
30/8	Teteks	h	1-0	Sulejmani Ju.
13/9	Makedonija	a	1-4	Alomerovic
21/9	Vardar	h	1-0	Idrizi
27/9	Pobeda	a	0-2	(match annulled)
4/10	Renova	a	1-3	Idrizi
18/10	Metalurg	h	0-1	
26/10	Milano	a	3-0	Nedzipi, Idrizi 2
1/11	Rabotnicki	h	0-3	
4/11	Pelister	h	1-3	Biljali (match annulled)
8/11	Turnovo	a	0-2	(match annulled)
22/11	Sileks	h	0-3	(w/o) (match annulled)
29/11	Teteks	a	0-3	(w/o) (match annulled)

No	Name	Nat	DoB	Pos	Aps	(s)	Gls
	Veton AJDINI		13/7/89	D	4	(5)	
	Sabri ALI		4/9/89	A	1		
	Kemal ALOMEROVIC		8/12/80	M	8		1
	Bujamin ASANI		10/8/88	M	10		
	Sedat BERISA		23/9/89	D	8	(3)	
	Zekirija BILJALI		13/3/89	D	3		1
	Ferdi DZELADINI		30/10/86	A	2	(2)	
	Sali DZUNEJ		3/9/86	D	8	(1)	
	Adem EMIR		21/10/86	D	12		
	Adem ERMADIN		7/7/90	M	9		
	Faruk GURU		20/12/89	A	2	(6)	
	Blerim GUDZUFI		28/8/86	G	12		
	Burim GUDZUFI		28/6/86	A	3		
	Bajram IDAI		7/11/86	D	10		1
	Mentor IDRIZI		15/11/85	A	11		4
	Eridin KAIL		17/2/89	M	1		
	Leonid KALABA		14/5/87	M	6		
	Senat MUMINOVIC		18/3/85	D	10		1
	Burhan MUSTAFA		22/7/90	G	1		
	Armen NEDZIPI		11/8/86	M	10		1
	Fitim RAMADANI		7/7/90	A	1	(1)	
	Admir SHABANI		19/2/87	M		(4)	
	Mendim SHABANI		19/7/90	D	1	(2)	
	Jasim SULEJMAN		21/2/89	M	1	(1)	
	Saban SULEJMAN		1/2/88	D	1	(3)	
	Besnik SULEJMAN		10/1/90	M	1	(6)	
	Jusif SULEJMANI		7/7/87	A	7	(1)	1

Name	Nat	DoB	Pos	Aps	(s)	Gls
Duško ANDONOV		6/2/87	D	17	(4)	2
Zlatko BOSKOVSKI		10/8/86	D	23		4
Daniel BOZINOVSKI		8/7/89	G	20		
Naum DZALESKI		18/6/88	M	2	(12)	
Boban DZANGAROVSKI		17/6/83	D	17		
Amir ĐURIĆ	BIH	25/2/89	A	9	(2)	3
Stole GJORGIEV		18/2/82	D	6	(3)	
Krste GJORGOV		15/8/87	M	1	(3)	

FK TETEKS

Coach – Toni Jakimovski
Founded – 1953
Stadium – City (15,000)
MAJOR HONOURS:
Macedonian Cup – (1) 2010.

2009

1/8	Makedonija	h	2-2	Jovanovski Mi., Urosevic
9/8	Vardar	a	1-3	Radonjić
16/8	Pobeda	h	3-1	Savevski D., Jovanovski Mi., Postolov (match annulled)
30/8	Sloga	a	0-1	
13/9	Metalurg	h	0-0	
19/9	Milano	a	5-1	Ristevski 2 (1p), Redzepi, Stojanovski 2
27/9	Rabotnicki	h	0-1	
4/10	Pelister	a	1-3	Redzepi
18/10	Turnovo	h	1-0	Levkov
25/10	Sileks	a	0-1	
1/11	Renova	h	0-1	
4/11	Makedonija	a	0-1	(match annulled)
8/11	Vardar	h	1-0	Stojanovski (p)
22/11	Pobeda	a	0-2	(match annulled)
29/11	Sloga	h	3-0	(w/o) (match annulled)
6/12	Metalurg	a	0-4	
9/12	Milano	h	6-0	Radonjić 3, Savevski D. (p), Redzepi, Aliji
12/12	Rabotnicki	a	1-3	Stojanovski

2010

28/2	Pelister	h	1-2	Jovanovski Mi.
7/3	Turnovo	a	2-0	Stojanovski 2
21/3	Sileks	h	1-1	Ristov
24/3	Renova	a	0-1	
28/3	Rabotnicki	a	1-2	Urosevic
3/4	Renova	h	0-1	
11/4	Pobeda	a	0-2	(match annulled)
18/4	Turnovo	a	1-0	Ristevski
25/4	Vardar	h	1-1	Radonjić
30/4	Milano	a	4-2	Radonjić, Iseni 2, Ristevski (p)
9/5	Sileks	h	2-0	Gligorovski, Iseni
12/5	Pelister	a	0-0	
15/5	Metalurg	h	0-0	

No	Name	Nat	DoB	Pos	Aps	(s)	Gls
	Burhan ALIJI		29/7/89	D	1	(7)	1
	Marjan BELCEV		22/10/82	M	7	(2)	
3	Bojan BOGOJEVSKI	SRB	11/6/89	D	5	(2)	
22	Aguinaldo de Jesús BRAGA		9/8/74	D	1	(1)	
14	Elias da Silva DEILSON	BRA	25/8/88	M	2	(4)	
19	Stole GEORGIEV		18/2/82	D	14	(1)	
	Ivica GLIGOROVSKI		15/4/81	A	10	(3)	1
5	Toni GORGEVSKI		15/9/86	D	6		
	Genc ISENI		28/3/83	A	6		3
	Daniel JOVANOVSKI		12/11/83	D	6	(1)	
	Marko JOVANOVSKI		24/7/88	G	17		
6	Miroslav JOVANOVSKI		13/5/91	M	21	(4)	3
1	Ljupco KMETOVSKI		8/7/72	G	1	(1)	
12	Ljupco KOLEV		6/12/78	G	12		
17	Blagoj LEVKOV		7/2/82	A	7	(4)	1
18	Nenad MISKOVSKI		26/12/86	D	27	(1)	
2	Dragan NAUMOVSKI		19/7/84	M	20	(1)	
	Mustapha Kamal NDAW	GAM	15/11/81	A	4	(4)	
	Oliver PEEV		8/7/87	M	6	(2)	
4	Borče POSTOLOV		30/4/81	A	8	(4)	1
9	Živorad RADONJIĆ	SRB	2/10/84	A	11	(12)	6
8	Elmedin REDZEPI		30/9/88	M	18	(5)	3
13	Dimce RISTEVSKI		6/11/82	M	17	(5)	4
	Sasko RISTOV		19/5/83	M	11		1
10	Darko SAVEVSKI		21/6/71	M	16	(5)	2
15	Igor SAVEVSKI		21/3/83	D	7		
11	Aleksandar STOJANOVSKI		4/4/84	A	17	(7)	6

20	Dalibor STOJKOVIC		10/9/77	D	20	(1)	
	TIAGO Rodrigues	BRA	24/7/81	A	1	(1)	
7	Aleksandar UROSEVIC		14/9/90	M	9	(8)	2
21	Srgan ZAHARIEVSKI		12/9/73	M	22	(3)	

FK TURNOVO

Coach – Ace Stojanov; (28/3/10) Ratko Janusev
Founded – 1950
Stadium – Kukus (3,000)

2009

3/8	Pobeda	h	3-1	Pandev 2, Georgiev (match annulled)
9/8	Sloga	a	1-1	Georgiev
16/8	Metalurg	h	1-1	Mitrev
23/8	Milano	a	2-0	Milošević, Todorov
13/9	Rabotnicki	h	0-2	
20/9	Pelister	a	2-1	Andonov, Milošević (p)
27/9	Renova	h	2-2	Tasev M. 2
4/10	Sileks	h	2-0	Tenekedziev, Andonov
18/10	Teteks	a	0-1	
24/10	Makedonija	h	0-1	
1/11	Vardar	a	3-1	Georgiev, Pandev, Andonov
4/11	Pobeda	a	0-1	(match annulled)
8/11	Sloga	h	2-0	Petrov, Milošević (match annulled)
22/11	Metalurg	a	0-3	(w/o)
29/11	Milano	h	3-1	Milošević (p), Siskov, Georgiev
5/12	Rabotnicki	a	0-1	
9/12	Pelister	h	4-3	Georgiev 2, Andonov, Milusev
13/12	Renova	a	2-3	Milošević, Georgiev

2010

28/2	Sileks	a	0-3	
7/3	Teteks	h	0-2	
24/3	Vardar	a	0-1	
28/3	Metalurg	a	1-1	Curlinov
3/4	Rabotnicki	h	0-1	
11/4	Renova	a	0-2	
18/4	Teteks	h	0-1	
25/4	Pobeda	a	1-0	Curlinov (match annulled)
2/5	Vardar	a	1-0	Tasev M.
9/5	Milano	h	2-1	Pandev, Kovacev
12/5	Sileks	h	1-1	Stojanov (p)
15/5	Pelister	h	0-1	

No	Name	Nat	DoB	Pos	Aps	(s)	Gls
9	Marjan ANDONOV		20/12/85	A	14		4
	Cvetan CURLINOV		24/7/86	A	12		2
1	Stojan DIMOVSKI		19/9/82	G	27		
10	Dragan GEORGIEV		16/12/90	A	19	(5)	7
5	Robert HRISTOVSKI		27/11/78	D	16	(5)	
11	Daniel KOVACEV		3/3/90	A	8	(15)	1
21	Robert LAZAREVSKI		19/9/90	M	8	(1)	
15	Danco MASEV		16/12/83	A	5		
17	Mitko MAVROV		8/4/91	D	5	(9)	
21	Miroslav MILOŠEVIĆ	SRB	12/1/74	M	16		5
	Aleksandar MILUSEV		5/4/88	D	20		1
	Mitko MITEV		20/12/89	G	1		
6	Dejan MITREV		20/7/88	D	24		1
19	Sasko PANDEV		1/5/87	A	20	(3)	4
4	Tomica PETROV		16/7/90	D	24		1
22	Ilce POCEV		31/7/81	D	12	(1)	
16	Martin SISKOV		1/7/86	A	17	(1)	1
3	Ljupco STOILOV		22/1/75	D	6	(8)	
23	Pance STOJANOV		23/6/75	D	25	(1)	1
2	Krste TANCEV		6/1/90	A	1	(2)	
2	Marjan TASEV		2/5/85	M	21	(2)	3
12	Pance TASEV		29/6/91	G	1		
7	Aleksandar TENEKEDZIEV		13/3/86	M	13		1
8	Krste TODOROV		24/12/87	M	2	(9)	1
27	Aleksandar TRAJKOVSKI		17/2/90	D		(3)	
	Aleksandar VASILEV		3/7/85	D	2		

FK VARDAR

Coach – Pane Blazevski; (1/9/09) Mario Vujovic;
(20/11/09) Gjorgi Todorovski; (28/2/10) Ilco Gjorgioski
Founded – 1947
Stadium – Philip II Arena (32,000)
MAJOR HONOURS:
Macedonian League - (5) 1993, 1994, 1995, 2002, 2003;
Yugoslav Cup - (1) 1961;
Macedonian Cup - (5) 1993, 1995, 1998, 1999, 2007.

2009

1/8	Sileks	a	1-1	*Stupić*
9/8	Teteks	h	3-1	*Ejupi, Stupić, Ristevski*
16/8	Makedonija	a	0-5	
30/8	Renova	a	2-3	*Stupić, Ejupi*
13/9	Pobeda	h	0-0	*(match annulled)*
21/9	Sloga	a	0-1	
27/9	Metalurg	h	0-0	
4/10	Milano	a	4-0	*Idrizi 2, Petrov 2*
18/10	Rabotnicki	h	1-2	*Peev*
25/10	Pelister	a	0-1	
1/11	Turnovo	h	1-3	*Petrov*
4/11	Sileks	h	3-1	*Stupić 2, Petrov*
8/11	Teteks	a	0-1	
22/11	Makedonija	h	3-0	*(w/o) (match annulled)*
29/11	Renova	h	1-1	*Stupić*
6/12	Pobeda	a	1-2	*Stupić (match annulled)*
13/12	Metalurg	a	0-3	*(w/o)*

2010

27/2	Milano	h	2-0	*Ilievski, Gjurgjevic*
6/3	Rabotnicki	a	0-1	
21/3	Pelister	h	1-0	*Hristov*
24/3	Turnovo	a	1-0	*Nastevski*
28/3	Pelister	a	0-1	
3/4	Metalurg	h	0-0	
11/4	Rabotnicki	a	1-1	*Polozani (p)*
18/4	Renova	h	2-0	*Siljanovski, Polozani*
25/4	Teteks	a	1-1	*Nuhiu Ard.*
2/5	Turnovo	h	0-1	
12/5	Milano	a	5-0	*Nuhiu Ard. 2, Pandovski, Gjurgjevic, Blazevski*
15/5	Sileks	h	2-0	*Polozani, Nuhiu Ard.*

Name	Nat	DoB	Pos	Aps	(s)	Gls
Marjan BELCEV		22/10/82	M	14		
Boban BLAZEVSKI		22/11/91	M		(1)	1
Bozidar DIMITROVSKI		5/2/87	D		(1)	
Toni DZANGAROVSKI		17/6/85	D	8	(4)	
Muzafer EJUPI		16/9/88	A	11		2
Bojan GEORGIEVSKI		25/1/92	D	9	(1)	
Fahrudin GJURGJEVIC		17/2/92	M	4	(8)	2
Darko GLISIC		23/9/91	D	4		
Goce GOCEVSKI		1/1/93	G	5		
Simeon HRISTOV		6/4/92	A	2	(8)	1
Mensur IDRIZI		3/8/83	M	7	(5)	2
Milan ILIEVSKI		21/7/82	D	11		1
Dragan JAKOVLEVSKI		5/5/85	M		(9)	
Marko JOVANOVSKI		24/7/88	G	2		
Nikola KARCEV		31/3/81	D	11		
Marko KOSTENCOSKI		8/10/89	M	13		
Aleksandar KRSTESKI		3/9/83	D	12		
Dragan LJUBISAVLJEVIĆ	SRB	22/12/79	D	9		
Filip MADZOVSKI		1/1/84	G	8		
Blagoja MILEVSKI		25/3/71	D	10		
Vladan MILOSAVLJEVIĆ	SRB	4/3/80	M	1		
Vasko MITREV		23/5/84	M	10		
Daniel MOJSOV		25/12/87	D	7		
Dino NAJDOSKI		8/5/92	D	4		
Ivan NASTEVSKI		30/7/91	M	9	(2)	1
Goran NAUMOVSKI		30/11/85	A		(1)	
Arben NUHIU		27/2/72	M		(5)	
Ardijan NUHIU		12/7/78	A	8	(1)	4
Aleksandar PANDOVSKI		13/8/91	A	5	(9)	1

Oliver PEEV		8/6/87	M	12		1
Filip PETROV		23/2/89	A	12	(1)	4
Artim POLOZANI		25/7/82	M	9		3
Zekirija RAMADAN		21/1/78	D	2		
Stefan RISTEVSKI		12/2/92	A	8	(3)	1
Zlatko RISTOV		13/6/79	D	6	(1)	
Goran SILJANOVSKI		1/7/90	D	7		1
Goran SIMOV	SRB	31/3/75	G	12		
Dusan SIMOVSKI		1/5/88	M	8		
Filip SPASESKI		5/5/88	M	7	(7)	
Dimitar STOJANOVSKI		21/3/89	D		(1)	
Boško STUPIĆ	BIH	27/6/84	A	12		7
Redzep SULEJMANI		8/1/91	A		(1)	
Nikola TRIPUNOVSKI		19/12/82	M	18	(8)	
Perica VASILEVSKI		28/8/89	A		(1)	

PROMOTED CLUBS

FK SKENDIJA 79
Coach – Catip Osmani
Founded – 1979
Stadium – City (15,000)

FK SKOPJE
Coach – Zarko Serafimovski
Founded – 1960
Stadium – Zelezarnica (3,000)

FK NAPREDOK
Coach – Baze Lazarevski; (6/3/10) Dragan Boceski
Founded – 1928
Stadium – City (5,000)

FK BREGALNICA STIP
Coach – Dragan Hristovski
Founded – 1921
Stadium – City (6,000)

SECOND LEVEL FINAL TABLE 2009/10

		Pld	W	D	L	F	A	Pts
1	FK Skendija 79	26	20	3	3	57	15	57
2	FK Skopje	26	17	6	3	49	22	57
3	FK Napredok	26	17	3	6	55	32	54
4	FK Bregalnica Stip	26	15	7	4	49	20	52
5	FK Drita	26	12	5	9	36	34	41
6	FK Miravci	26	11	3	12	31	31	36
7	FK 11 Oktomvri	26	10	4	12	30	34	34
8	FK Belasica	26	10	3	13	27	40	33
9	FK Novaci 2005	26	8	7	11	26	37	31
10	FK Lokomotiva Skopje	26	8	5	13	29	30	29
11	FK Vlaznimi	26	7	7	12	26	42	28
12	FK Cementarnica 55	26	7	5	14	21	40	26
13	FK Vlazrimi	26	3	5	18	16	49	14
14	FK Ohrid 2004	26	5	1	20	26	52	13

NB FK Skendija 79 – 6 pts deducted; FK Ohrid 2004 – 3 pts deducted.

PROMOTION/RELEGATION PLAY-OFF

(30/5/10)

Milano 1, Bregalnica Stip 2

DOMESTIC CUP 2009/10
KUP NA MAKEDONIJA

FIRST ROUND

(26/8/09)
11 Oktomvri 3, Vardar 1
Babuna 1, Metalurg Skopje 3
Belasica 3, Milano 1
Bregalnica Delcevo 0, Pobeda 2
Dobrusevo 1, Sileks 13
Drita 1, Napredok 0
Gostivar 0, Lokomotiva 3 *(w/o)*
Karbinci 1, Makedonija Skopje 4
Kozuf 0, Rabotnicki 5
Lepenec 0, Fortuna 3 *(w/o)*
Mirce Acev 0, Renova 11
Ohrid 3, Turnovo 0
Prevalec 0, Teteks 4
Skopje 2, Sloga 1
Vlazerimi 0, Pelister 3
Vlaznimi 0, Bregalnica Stip 0 *(4-3 on pens)*

SECOND ROUND

(22/9/09 & 29/9/09)
Skopje v 11 Oktomvri 3-1, 0-1 *(3-2)*

(23/9/09 & 30/9/09)
Belasica v Teteks 1-3, 0-1 *(1-4)*
Fortuna v Rabotnicki 0-6, 0-3 w/o *(0-9)*
Renova w/o Lokomotiva
Metalurg Skopje v Pobeda 1-0, 0-1 *(1-1; 4-3 on pens)*
Pelister v Ohrid 2-0, 3-0 w/o *(5-0)*
Sileks v Makedonija Skopje 1-1, 1-2 *(2-3)*
Vlaznimi v Drita 0-1, 1-1 *(1-2)*

QUARTER-FINALS

(28/10/09 & 25/11/09)
Pelister 2 *(Kleckarovski 7, Gancev 87)*, Drita 2 *(Aliji 55, Ramadani 74)*
Drita 0, Pelister 1 *(Dimitrovski 45)*
(Pelister 3-2)

Rabotnicki 4 *(Wandeir 38p, Bojović 45, Gligorov 77, Petkovski 90+2)*, Renova 0
Renova 0, Rabotnicki 1 *(Gligorov 59)*
(Rabotnicki 5-0)

Skopje 0, Metalurg Skopje 0
Metalurg Skopje 2 *(Ilijoski 4, Krstev 6)*, Skopje 2 *(Mojsovski 11, Nakovski 90+3)*
(2-2; Skopje on away goals)

(28/10/09 & 26/11/09)
Makedonija Skopje 2 *(Brnjarcevski 63, Ilievski 65)*, Teteks 0
Teteks 3, Makedonija Skopje 0 *(w/o)*
(Teteks 3-2)

SEMI-FINALS

(7/4/10 & 5/5/10)
Pelister 1 *(Veljanovski A. 7)*, Rabotnicki 0
Rabotnicki 1 *(Bojović 37)*, Pelister 0
(1-1; Rabotnicki 5-4 on pens)

Teteks 0, Skopje 0
Skopje 1 *(Mojsovski 87)*, Teteks 2 *(Radonjić 13, Ristov 33)*
(Teteks 2-1)

FINAL

(26/5/10)
Philip II Arena, Skopje
FK TETEKS 3 *(Zaharievski 47p, Iseni 49, Stojanovski 65)*
FK RABOTNICKI 2 *(Gligorov 70, Petkovski 83)*
Referee – Kiprijanovski
TETEKS – Jovanovski Ma., Jovanovski D., Ristov, Miskovski, Ristovski, Belcev, Ristevski *(Savevski D. 65)*, Zaharievski, Peev *(Stojanovski 46)*, Radonjić, Iseni *(Jovanovski Mi. 77)*.
RABOTNICKI – Naumovski, Bojović, Dimovski *(Todorovski 78)*, Bozinovski B. *(Petkovski 61)*, Fernando, Muarem, Emir, Fábio, Gligorov, Tuneski, Brnjarcevski *(Sinković 46)*.

MALTA

Sweet revenge for Birkirkara boss

Jettisoned by Valletta FC at the end of a 2008/09 season in which the club he coached finished second in both league and cup, Paul Zammit gained sweet revenge for his dismissal as he led his new club Birkirkara FC to victory in the 2009/10 Maltese Premier League, edging out his old club by a single point. Valletta did, however, win the FA Trophy for the first time in nine years after a 2-1 victory in the final over the season's principal over-achievers, Qormi FC, who also finished third in the league.

Valletta defeated Birkirkara 4-2 on the final day of the season, but it was too little too late for the star-studded pre-season favourites from the capital. Their opponents had already claimed the title five days earlier with a 1-0 win against Tarxien Rainbows FC that concluded a storming 11-match unbeaten run in which they had only been denied victory once – in an earlier 3-3 draw with Tarxien.

Although the final table showed Birkirkara and Valletta with identical records for games won, drawn and lost, the Stripes were ahead because they had accumulated one point more in the ten-match play-off series. Valletta had been a point in front of Birkirkara at the end of the regular 18-match season, but their rivals benefited from the rule that allows odd-numbered points to be rounded up before they are halved for the second phase.

Lucky or not, Zammit's side deserved their triumph for that powerful surge to the finishing line, during which 27-year-old Trevor Cilia proved to be the central figure, not least with his winning goal in a pivotal 1-0 victory over Valletta. The Citizens would make amends by beating Birkirkara 3-1 in

the quarter-final of the FA Trophy a few days later. After overcoming Hamrun Spartans FC on penalties, they were hot favourites to win the final against a Qormi side they had defeated in all four league encounters and who had just parted company with their impressive coach, Jesmond Zerafa, after a contract wrangle.

Mifsud record

There would be no upset, although Qormi ran Valletta close, a late penalty from the league's top scorer, Brazilian striker Camilo, ensuring an exciting finish after Valletta had swept into an early two-goal lead. The scorer of the game's opening goal was Michael Mifsud, recently crowned Malta's all-time top scorer at international level, his consolation goal in a friendly defeat by Finland having lifted his cumulative tally to 24 and taken him past previous record-holder Carmel Busuttil.

Malta Football Association (MFA)

Millennium Stand
Floor 2
National Stadium
MT-Ta' Qali ATD 4000
tel – +356 21 232 581
fax – +356 21 245 136
website – mfa.com.mt
email – info@mfa.com.mt
Year of Formation – 1900

President – Norman Darmanin Demajo
General Secretary – Joseph Gauci
Media Officer – Alex Vella
National Stadium – National, Ta' Qali (17,797)

TOP FIVE ALL-TIME CAPS
David Carabott (121); Gilbert Agius (120); Carmel Busuttil (111); Joe Brincat (103); John Buttigieg (95)
TOP FIVE ALL-TIME GOALS
Michael Mifsud (24); Carmel Busuttil (23); David Carabott (12); Gilbert Agius & Hubert Suda (8)

Paul Zammit – Birkirkara's title-winning coach

NATIONAL TEAM RESULTS 2009/10

12/8/09	Georgia	H	Ta'Qali	2-0	Mifsud (64, 73)
4/9/09	Cape Verde Islands	H	Ta'Qali	0-2	
9/9/09	Sweden (WCQ)	H	Ta'Qali	0-1	
10/10/09	Angola	N	Vila Real (POR)	1-2	Cohen (13)
14/10/09	Portugal (WCQ)	A	Guimaraes	0-4	
18/11/09	Bulgaria	H	Paola	1-4	Mifsud (46)
3/3/10	Finland	H	Ta'Qali	1-2	Mifsud (17)
13/5/10	Germany	A	Aachen	0-3	

NATIONAL TEAM APPEARANCES 2009/10

Coach – John BUTTIGIEG 5/10/63

			Geo	Cpv	SWE	Ang	POR	Bul	Fin	Ger	Caps	Goals
Mario MUSCAT	18/8/76	Hibernians	G46								68	-
Andrei AGIUS	12/8/86	Cassino (ITA) /Melfi (ITA)	D	s82				D	D	D	12	-
Alex MUSCAT	14/12/84	Sliema	D		D61				D	D	12	-
Ian AZZOPARDI	12/8/82	Sliema	D60	D	s70	D					42	1
Brian SAID	15/3/73	Marsaxlokk /Floriana	D		D67	D	D24	D	D		91	5
Jamie PACE	1/1/77	Valletta	M	M75	M	M57	M	M81	M82	M9	36	2
Gilbert AGIUS	21/2/74	Valletta	M90		M	s57		s71			120	8
Kevin SAMMUT	26/5/81	Valletta	M60	s75		s64	s88	M57			35	-
Andrew COHEN	13/5/81	Hibernians	M82	M	M	M70	M23		M65	M	35	1
Michael MIFSUD	17/4/81	unattached /Valletta	A	A	A	A	A	A	A86	A83	74	24
Andre SCHEMBRI	27/5/86	Austria Kärnten (AUT)	A46	A46							30	3
Andrew HOGG	2/3/85	Valletta	s46	G46	G	G	G	G			14	-
Ivan WOODS	31/12/76	Sliema	s46						s65	s75	44	1
Roderick BRIFFA	24/8/81	Valletta	s60	D	s61	D64	D88	M	M76	M	49	-
Clayton FAILLA	8/1/86	Sliema	s60	D	s72	D	s23	D46	D51	s67	10	-
Shaun BAJADA	19/10/83	Birkirkara	s82	s46	M72	M70	M73	s46	s86	D	19	-
Ryan FENECH	20/4/86	Sliema	s90	M		s57	s73	M61	M	M67	16	-
Kenneth SCICLUNA	15/6/79	Valletta		D	D	s24	D		D58	D	27	-
Emmanuel MUSCAT	7/12/84	Wellington Phoenix (NZL)				M82	M	M	M		6	-
Justin HABER	9/6/81	Ferencváros (HUN)	s46						G	G	38	-
Jonathan CARUANA	24/7/86	Hibernians	s67				D		s58		10	-
John HUTCHINSON	29/12/79	Central Coast Mariners (AUS)						M57	M		4	-
George MALLIA	10/10/78	Birkirkara					s70		s81		65	5
Steven BEZZINA	5/1/87	Valletta							D	s51	2	-
Daniel BOGDANOVIC	26/3/80	Barnsley (ENG)						A71	A	s83	28	1
Edward HERRERA	14/9/86	Hibernians							s57		1	-
Paul FENECH	20/12/86	Birkirkara							s61	s82	2	-
Trevor CILIA	2/1/83	Birkirkara							s76	s9	4	-
Massimo GRIMA	5/7/79	Qormi								M75	12	-

MALTA

DOMESTIC LEAGUE 2009/10

PREMIER LEAGUE FINAL TABLES

SECOND PHASE

Championship Pool	Pld	W	D	L	F	A	Pts
1 Birkirkara FC	28	20	4	4	64	32	45
2 Valletta FC	28	20	4	4	71	25	44
3 Qormi FC	28	15	2	11	53	36	30
4 Sliema Wanderers FC	28	14	2	12	41	37	30
5 Tarxien Rainbows FC	28	10	6	12	41	50	23
6 Hibernians FC	28	8	6	14	40	51	17

Relegation Pool	Pld	W	D	L	F	A	Pts
7 Floriana FC	24	10	6	8	35	41	25
8 Hamrun Spartans FC	24	10	4	10	41	39	24
9 Dingli Swallows FC	24	2	0	22	23	71	5
10 Msida St Joseph FC	24	4	4	16	24	51	1

NB Msida St Joseph FC – 10 pts deducted.

FIRST PHASE

	Pld	W	D	L	F	A	Pts
1 Valletta FC	18	12	4	2	45	15	40 (20)
2 Birkirkara FC	18	12	3	3	40	18	39 (20)
3 Qormi FC	18	11	2	5	37	22	35 (18)
4 Sliema Wanderers FC	18	9	2	7	29	21	29 (15)
5 Hibernians FC	18	7	6	5	31	28	27 (14)
6 Tarxien Rainbows FC	18	7	5	6	30	29	26 (13)
7 Floriana FC	18	6	5	7	23	35	23 (12)
8 Hamrun Spartans FC	18	6	3	9	24	31	21 (11)
9 Msida St Joseph FC	18	3	2	13	12	34	11 (6)
10 Dingli Swallows FC	18	1	0	17	13	51	3 (2)

*NB Figures in brackets indicate points carried forward to the Second Phase.
Marsaxlokk FC excluded after two matches – results annulled; Vittoriosa
Stars FC excluded after one match – result annulled.*

UEFA EUROPA LEAGUE QUALIFICATION PLAY-OFF

(1/6/10)
Qormi 0, Sliema 2 *(Dronca 62p, Mifsud Triganza 90+5)*

STADIUMS

Ta' Qali National Stadium (17,797)
Centenary Stadium (2,000)
Hibernians Ground (2,000)
Victor Tedesco Stadium (2,000)

TOP GOALSCORERS

24	CAMILO (Qormi)
20	Terence SCERRI (Valletta)
17	Ryan DARMANIN (Floriana)
15	Sylvano COMVALIUS (Birkirkara)
	MARCELO (Hamrun)
	DENNI (Tarxien)
14	Michael GALEA (Birkirkara)
13	Joseph OKONKWO (Dingli)
	Jean Pierre MIFSUD TRIGANZA (Sliema)
12	Trevor CILIA (Birkirkara)
	Alfred EFFIONG (Qormi)

CLUB-BY-CLUB

BIRKIRKARA FC
Coach – Paul Zammit
Founded – 1950
MAJOR HONOURS:
Maltese League – (3) 2000, 2006, 2010;
Maltese Cup – (4) 2002, 2003, 2005, 2008.

2009

21/8	Valletta	1-3	*Comvalius*
30/8	Tarxien	2-0	*Galea M., Mallia*
26/9	Hamrun	2-1	*Comvalius, Mallia*
2/10	Dingli	3-1	*Galea M. 2, Fenech*
18/10	Hibernians	2-2	*Cilia, Pulo*
24/10	Floriana	0-1	
23/11	Sliema	3-0	*Cilia, Galea M., Comvalius*
29/11	Msida	4-1	*Cilia, Comvalius, Mallia, Buhagiar*
12/12	Qormi	5-2	*Bajada, Comvalius, Mallia, og (Wellman), Cilia*
19/12	Valletta	1-1	*Comvalius*
27/12	Tarxien	5-1	*Vukanac, Comvalius 2 (2p), Galea M Pulo*

2010

3/1	Hamrun	2-0	*Bajada, Galea M.*
9/1	Dingli	2-0	*Comvalius 2*
18/1	Hibernians	2-2	*Nišević, Pulo*
25/1	Floriana	2-1	*og (Ciantar), Galea M.*
30/1	Sliema	0-1	
7/2	Msida	2-1	*Galea M., Pulo*
13/2	Qormi	2-0	*Pulo, Cilia*
26/2	Sliema	2-1	*Comvalius, Cilia*
6/3	Qormi	2-0	*Galea M., Mallia*
13/3	Hibernians	2-1	*Comvalius, Galea M.*
20/3	Tarxien	3-3	*Bajada 2, Galea M.*
28/3	Valletta	1-0	*Cilia*
9/4	Sliema	3-0	*Vukanac, Cilia 2*
15/4	Qormi	3-1	*Comvalius, Cilia 2*
25/4	Hibernians	5-4	*Galea M. 2, Comvalius, Bajada, Cilia*
30/4	Tarxien	1-0	*Bajada*
5/5	Valletta	2-4	*Galea M., Comvalius*

No	Name	Nat	DoB	Pos	Aps	(s)	Gls
18	Shaun BAJADA		19/10/83	M	27		6
22	Omar BORG		12/2/81	G	2	(2)	
11	Angus BUHAGIAR		29/4/87	A	16	(6)	1
23	Michael CAMILLERI		23/3/93	D		(2)	
7	Trevor CILIA		2/1/83	A	26	(1)	12
17	Sylvano COMVALIUS	NED	10/8/87	A	26	(2)	15
6	Paul FENECH		20/12/86	M	26		1
15	Andreas GALEA		23/4/91	D		(1)	
9	Michael GALEA		1/2/79	A	28		14
12	Ronny HARTVIG	DEN	26/5/78	D	2		
21	George MALLIA		10/10/78	M	13	(6)	5
24	Carlo MAMO		23/4/79	D	10		
1	Jorge MORA	ESP	3/6/82	G	26		
2	Rowen MUSCAT		5/6/91	M	17	(4)	
5	Branko NIŠEVIĆ	SRB	31/8/71	D	24		1
8	Thomas PARIS		15/11/86	A	11	(8)	
16	Karl PULO		30/7/89	A	4	(14)	5
14	Andrew SCICLUNA		17/6/90	D	4	(5)	
10	Alan TABONE		31/10/81	A	6	(18)	
15	Nikola VUKANAC	SRB	14/1/86	D	26		2
19	Joseph ZERAFA		31/5/88	D	14	(9)	

DINGLI SWALLOWS FC
Coach – Jesmond Zammit
Founded – 1948

2009

22/8	Tarxien	1-4	Okonkwo
19/8	Marsaxlokk	0-1	(result annulled)
27/9	Hibernians	1-2	Okonkwo
2/10	Birkirkara	1-3	og (Tabone)
18/10	Floriana	2-1	Okonkwo 2
25/10	Sliema	0-2	
4/11	Hamrun	0-3	
21/11	Msida	1-2	Okonkwo
27/11	Qormi	1-4	Okonkwo (p)
13/12	Valletta	1-4	Borg K.
20/12	Tarxien	1-2	Okonkwo
28/12	Hamrun	1-3	og (Bonnici)

2010

2/1	Hibernians	1-2	Okonkwo
9/1	Birkirkara	0-2	
17/1	Floriana	0-2	
24/1	Sliema	1-3	André
31/1	Msida	1-2	Okonkwo
5/2	Qormi	0-4	
15/2	Valletta	0-6	
27/2	Msida	2-3	Cachia, Okonkwo
14/3	Hamrun	0-6	
20/3	Floriana	0-3	
11/4	Msida	5-2	Zarb 2, André, Okonkwo 2
16/4	Hamrun	1-2	Spiteri
24/4	Floriana	2-4	Zarb, Okonkwo

No	Name	Nat	DoB	Pos	Aps	(s)	Gls
	Jeremy AGIUS		19/5/75	A	3		
19	ANDRÉ Rocha da Silva	BRA	24/3/79	M	17		2
22	Christopher AZZOPARDI		10/3/88	M	2	(11)	
17	Kevin BORG		5/1/82	M	19	(1)	1
18	Matthew BORG		3/5/87	M	12		
2	Roderick BRIFFA		26/9/83	D	15	(2)	
15	Dino CACHIA		13/12/76	M	16	(1)	1
4	David CAMILLERI		9/4/79	M		(1)	
3	Clint CARUANA		12/4/80	M	5	(4)	
24	Ivan CASSAR		3/4/82	G	4	(1)	
9	Haruna DODA	NGA	16/1/75	M	8	(9)	
16	Etienne FARRUGIA		7/1/92	M	6	(13)	
1	Jeffrey FARRUGIA		18/10/88	G	21		
14	Victor FITENI		7/9/77	D	13	(3)	
10	Kurt FORMOSA		8/12/79	M	24	(1)	
13	Christian MUSCAT		1/4/79	M	19		
8	Justin MUSCAT		27/5/90	D		(3)	
20	Joseph OKONKWO	NGA	27/9/89	A	24	(1)	13
21	Tyrone PACE		10/3/92	D		(1)	
5	RENATO Garcia da Conceição	BRA	14/6/81	D	19		
12	Charlon SAMMUT		6/8/92	D	2	(4)	
7	Roderick SPITERI		13/3/80	M	17	(3)	1
6	Shawn TELLUS		26/8/83	D	21		
23	Dylan ZARB		13/5/88	M	8	(10)	3

FLORIANA FC
Coach – Zoran Popović (SRB); (20/12/09) Roddy Collins (IRL)
Founded – 1894
MAJOR HONOURS:
Maltese League – (25) 1910, 1912, 1913, 1921, 1922, 1925, 1927, 1928, 1929, 1931, 1935, 1937, 1950, 1951, 1952, 1953, 1955, 1958, 1962, 1968, 1970, 1973, 1975, 1977, 1993;
Maltese Cup – (18) 1938, 1945, 1947, 1949, 1950, 1953, 1954, 1955, 1957, 1958, 1961, 1966, 1967, 1972, 1976, 1981, 1993, 1994.

2009

23/8	Qormi	1-1	Anonam
29/8	Valletta	0-6	
27/9	Tarxien	1-1	Wasiu
4/10	Hamrun	1-0	Simmonds
18/10	Dingli	1-2	Wasiu
24/10	Birkirkara	1-0	Caruana

21/11	Hibernians	3-2	Ciantar, Darmanin, og (Herrera)
29/11	Sliema	1-1	Wasiu
13/12	Msida	2-1	Darmanin, Anonam
18/12	Qormi	2-6	Darmanin 2
26/12	Valletta	0-4	

2010

4/1	Tarxien	1-2	Darmanin
10/1	Hamrun	1-1	Briffa M.
17/1	Dingli	2-0	Caruana, Darmanin
25/1	Birkirkara	1-2	Darmanin
30/1	Hibernians	1-1	Doffo
7/2	Sliema	0-3	
16/2	Msida	4-2	Darmanin 3, Zlydarev
7/3	Hamrun	1-2	Darmanin
14/3	Msida	2-1	Darmanin, Caruana
20/3	Dingli	3-0	Darmanin, Ghebru, Ciantar
10/4	Hamrun	1-0	Darmanin
16/4	Msida	1-1	Darmanin
24/4	Dingli	4-2	Said, Caruana, Darmanin 2

No	Name	Nat	DoB	Pos	Aps	(s)	Gls
27	Alan ABELA		5/1/90	M		(1)	
19	Luke AGIUS		6/3/88	M	3	(6)	
13	Orosco ANONAM		15/6/79	M	20		2
22	Clyde BORG		20/3/92	D	5	(7)	
17	Joseph BORG		26/1/87	M	18	(4)	
11	Sasha BORG		27/5/93	D	9	(2)	
4	Julian BRIFFA		11/8/81	D	13	(2)	
7	Marlon BRIFFA		31/10/83	M	10	(1)	1
6	Jermain BRINCAT		20/9/86	D	7	(4)	
2	Roberto BRINCAT		14/1/87	A	2	(4)	
14	Owen BUGEJA		20/2/90	D	11	(5)	
10	Christian CARUANA		21/10/86	M	10	(5)	4
8	Christian CASSAR		20/6/83	M	2		
3	Clifton CIANTAR		26/5/81	D	17	(4)	2
18	Ryan DARMANIN		12/12/85	A	19	(3)	17
23	Pablo César DOFFO	ARG	6/3/83	M	19	(1)	1
5	Sunday EBOH	NGA	30/9/81	D	2		
20	Michael GHEBRU	ETH	7/11/87	M	4	(2)	1
15	Stefano GRIMA		13/6/78	M	5	(2)	
26	Mauro GRIOLI		23/2/92	D	2		
25	Goran JOVANOVIĆ	SRB	8/5/77	G	1		
24	Stefan LIJESKIĆ	SRB	26/1/90	M	7		
19	Greg MARNEY		27/5/92	A		(1)	
12	Jurgen MICALLEF		29/7/88	G	5		
1	Bernard PARIS		7/2/85	G	18		
16	Duncan PISANI		25/5/88	D	11	(1)	
2	Brian SAID		15/3/73	D	18		1
9	Donovan SIMMONDS	ENG	12/10/88	A	5		1
21	Mark SPITERI		11/5/73	D	6	(8)	
11	Akanni-Sunday WASIU	NGA	18/3/84	A	13		3
9	Victor ZLYDAREV	RUS	8/12/80	A	2	(2)	1

HAMRUN SPARTANS FC
Coach – Steve D'Amato
Founded – 1907
MAJOR HONOURS:
Maltese League – (7) 1914, 1918, 1947, 1983, 1987, 1988, 1991;
Maltese Cup – (6) 1983, 1984, 1987, 1988, 1989, 1992.

2009

26/9	Birkirkara	1-2	Marcelo
30/9	Hibernians	2-4	Spiteri 2
4/10	Floriana	0-1	
17/10	Sliema	0-5	
24/10	Msida	1-0	Fenech
4/11	Dingli	3-0	Mawete, Marcelo, Spiteri
22/11	Qormi	0-2	
28/11	Valletta	2-3	Marcelo 2 (1p)
11/12	Tarxien	1-0	og (Magro)
19/12	Hibernians	2-2	Cucciardi, Marcelo
28/12	Dingli	3-1	Micallef 2, Cucciardi

 **MALTA**

2010		
3/1	Birkirkara	0-2
10/1	Floriana	1-1 *Marcelo*
15/1	Sliema	3-0 *Marcelo, Mawete 2*
22/1	Msida	2-0 *Marcelo (p), Fenech*
1/2	Qormi	1-2 *Fenech*
6/2	Valletta	0-4
16/2	Tarxien	2-2 *Zammit (p), Mawete*
7/3	Floriana	2-1 *Spiteri, Fenech*
14/3	Dingli	6-0 *Obiefule, Marcelo 4 (1p), Mifsud*
27/3	Msida	5-3 *Fenech, Marcelo 2 (2p), Spiteri, Zammit (p)*
10/4	Floriana	0-1
16/4	Dingli	2-1 *Marcelo, Obiefule*
25/4	Msida	2-2 *Mifsud, Zammit*

No	Name	Nat	DoB	Pos	Aps	(s)	Gls
18	Lee James AGIUS		8/12/90	M	9	(3)	
5	Aaron ATTARD		19/9/83	D	6	(5)	
15	Mark BARBARA		31/3/86	M	8	(10)	
2	Mark Anthony BONNICI		17/1/80	D	15		
30	Mauro BUSUTTIL		19/12/87	A	2	(4)	
16	Christian CACCIATTOLO		11/3/89	M		(3)	
29	Clyde CAIMON		31/7/87	M	17	(1)	
31	Chris CARDONA		19/4/92	M		(1)	
4	Dalton CARUANA		6/11/89	D		(2)	
1	Ivan CASHA		21/6/78	G	20		
12	Andrea CASSAR		19/12/92	G	4		
3	Diego Armando CUCCIARDI		18/12/86	M	6	(6)	2
13	John DEBATTISTA		12/1/82	D		(1)	
8	Roderick FENECH		19/12/87	D	21		5
20	Timothy FLERI SOLER		30/3/90	D	5	(1)	
17	Neville GALEA		7/2/80	D	7	(1)	
19	Jonathan HOLLAND		15/7/78	M	8	(3)	
23	Martin HRUBSA	CZE	9/10/84	D	24		
6	Karl MAGRO		30/8/74	D	2		
7	Rupert MANGION		31/3/75	M	20		
19	MARCELO Pereira	BRA	6/4/81	A	21		15
28	João Batista MAWETE	ANG	4/5/83	A	13		4
99	Manolito MICALLEF		16/11/83	A	17		2
14	Mead MIFSUD		9/6/88	D	6	(10)	2
9	Polycrap Obinna OBIEFULE	NGA	7/1/88	A	6		2
21	Gaetan SPITERI		5/6/81	A	20	(1)	5
90	Ian ZAMMIT		9/12/86	A	7		3
24	Daniel ZERAFA		8/4/94	D		(2)	

HIBERNIANS FC

Coach – Mark Miller (ENG)
Founded – 1922
MAJOR HONOURS:
Maltese League – (10) 1961, 1967, 1969, 1979, 1981, 1982, 1994, 1995, 2002, 2009.
Maltese Cup – (8) 1962, 1970, 1971, 1980, 1982, 1998, 2006, 2007.

2009		
23/8	Marsaxlokk	3-1 *Barbara 3 (result annulled)*
27/9	Dingli	2-1 *Caruana J., og (Renato)*
30/9	Hamrun	4-2 *Cauchi E., Herrera, Barbara, og (Fenech)*
4/10	Qormi	1-3 *Galabov*
18/10	Birkirkara	2-2 *Galabov, Malašenoks*
23/10	Valletta	1-0 *Herrera*
4/11	Msida	1-0 *Malašenoks*
21/11	Floriana	2-3 *Malašenoks 2*
28/11	Tarxien	2-1 *Cohen (p), Pulis*
12/12	Sliema	0-1
19/12	Hamrun	2-2 *Callejas, Caruana J.*
27/12	Msida	3-0 *Callejas, Camilleri B., Cohen*
2010		
2/1	Dingli	2-1 *Galabov, Cohen (p)*
8/1	Qormi	2-2 *Barbara, Cohen*
18/1	Birkirkara	2-2 *Pulis 2*
23/1	Valletta	2-4 *Caruana J., Cohen*
30/1	Floriana	1-1 *Callejas*
6/2	Tarxien	0-1

13/2	Sliema	2-2 *Cohen (p), Barbara*
26/2	Qormi	1-0 *Miguel*
6/3	Valletta	1-2 *Camilleri B.*
13/3	Birkirkara	1-2 *Caruana J.*
19/3	Sliema	1-2 *Miguel*
28/3	Tarxien	0-2
11/4	Qormi	0-3
16/4	Valletta	1-3 *og (Hogg)*
25/4	Birkirkara	4-5 *Farrugia, Caruana T. 2, Herrera*
30/4	Sliema	0-3
4/5	Tarxien	0-1

No	Name	Nat	DoB	Pos	Aps	(s)	Gls
16	Ayrton AZZOPARDI		19/9/92	M		(2)	
13	Daniel BALZAN		8/5/91	G	3		
9	Etienne BARBARA		10/7/82	A	19	(1)	6
8	Christian Fabián CALLEJAS	URU	17/5/78	M	20	(1)	3
7	Ben CAMILLERI		16/8/88	M	12	(9)	2
12	Christopher CAMILLERI		2/10/79	M	8	(4)	
27	Ryan CAMILLERI		22/5/88	D	13	(4)	
2	Jonathan CARUANA		24/7/86	D	25		4
17	Triston CARUANA		15/9/91	M	12	(11)	2
13	Kevin CASSAR		22/6/79	D	3	(1)	
15	Elkien CAUCHI		23/7/91	D	3	(7)	1
18	Yan CAUCHI		23/7/91	D	6	(5)	
26	Ndubisi CHUKUNYERE	NGA	23/12/79	A	1	(1)	
10	Andrew COHEN		13/5/81	M	23	(2)	6
19	Rene DUCA		30/11/92	D	1	(2)	
25	ELTON Aparecido Crepaldi Morelato	BRA	13/8/88	A	11	(1)	
23	Jean Paul FARRUGIA		22/8/90	A	1	(5)	1
22	Rumen Angelov GALABOV	BUL	29/7/78	M	13		3
20	Leighton GRECH		20/3/90	M	2	(3)	
21	Matthew HAMMETT		16/8/92	A		(2)	
3	Edward HERRERA		14/9/86	D	27		3
11	Olegs MALAŠENOKS	LVA	27/4/86	A	14		4
18	MIGUEL Martins Nimes Lopes de Pina	POR	4/2/83	A	8		2
1	Mario MUSCAT		18/8/76	G	26		
6	Jonathan PEARSON		13/1/87	D	24		
4	Adrian PULIS		30/3/79	D	22		3
28	Dylan SAMMUT		11/12/90	M		(2)	
14	Matthew TABONE		29/4/92	D	3	(7)	
24	Keith TANTI		11/5/93	D		(2)	
5	Aaron XUEREB		3/10/79	D	19	(2)	

MSIDA ST JOSEPH FC

Coach – Keith Gouder; (23/1/10) Mark Marlow
Founded – 1906

2009		
26/9	Qormi	0-3
30/9	Sliema	0-2
3/10	Valletta	0-0
17/10	Tarxien	1-1 *Aganun*
24/10	Hamrun	0-1
4/11	Hibernians	0-1
21/11	Dingli	2-1 *Spiteri, Farrugia T.*
29/11	Birkirkara	1-4 *Lattes*
13/12	Floriana	1-2 *Farrugia T.*
22/12	Sliema	1-0 *Spiteri*
27/12	Hibernians	0-3
2010		
2/1	Qormi	0-3
9/1	Valletta	0-1
17/1	Tarxien	1-3 *Lattes*
22/1	Hamrun	0-2
31/1	Dingli	2-1 *Farrugia T., Formosa*
7/2	Birkirkara	1-2 *Kalenga*
16/2	Floriana	2-4 *Farrugia T., Lattes*
27/2	Dingli	3-2 *Kalenga 2, Ciantar*
14/3	Floriana	1-2 *Sciberras*
27/3	Hamrun	3-5 *Levnaić, Bartolo (p), Ciantar*
11/4	Dingli	2-5 *Farrugia T., Formosa*
16/4	Floriana	1-1 *Curmi*
25/4	Hamrun	2-2 *Farrugia T. 2*

No	Name	Nat	DoB	Pos	Aps	(s)	Gls
20	Olushola Olumuyiwa AGANUN	NGA	4/5/84	A	4		1
5	Larson AGIUS		24/4/90	D	2	(2)	
15	Neville ARPA		22/11/82	A	1	(1)	
11	Roderick BALDACCHINO		7/10/75	D	19		
1	Manuel BARTOLO		11/9/82	G	23		1
24	Charlie BLACK		19/2/91	M	2	(1)	
12	Matthew BORDA		29/5/89	D	11	(1)	
23	Dassier BORG		7/5/82	M	4		
21	Vincenzo BRINCAT		4/3/89	D		(3)	
6	Miguel CIANTAR		17/10/90	A	14	(1)	2
19	Iro CURMI		23/5/81	M	6	(10)	1
15	Joseph DAMATO		18/8/91	M	5	(6)	
20	Damian DEBONO		24/12/90	M		(1)	
9	Karl EBEJER		26/5/86	M	7	(1)	
7	Adrian FARRUGIA		20/9/81	M	13	(6)	
22	Tyrone FARRUGIA		22/2/89	D	22		7
16	Andrew FORMOSA		19/7/84	A	7	(14)	2
10	Kurt GRECH		1/9/90	D		(1)	
4	Stefano GRIMA		13/6/78	D	10	(1)	
7	N'Dayi KALENGA	COD	29/9/78	A	5		3
10	Emiliano LATTES	ARG	28/1/85	A	19		3
14	Zoran LEVNAIĆ	SRB	11/10/80	M	17		1
17	Lydon MICALLEF		22/9/85	M	20	(1)	
18	Gallen MIFSUD		30/1/88	G	1		
8	Kevin MIFSUD		14/3/66	M	16	(1)	
26	Matthew MULHOLLAND		16/6/91	G		(1)	
13	Sakchai PHIRAM Nong		22/2/91	M		(2)	
14	Luke SALIBA		30/11/90	A		(3)	
5	Cedric SCIBERRAS		22/3/81	D	17		1
6	Adam SPITERI		18/2/89	M	15	(3)	2
2	Gabriels WINDELL	CRC	1/2/85	A	3		
3	Ryan XUEREB		3/12/92	A	1		

QORMI FC
Coach – Jesmond Zerafa; (28/4/10) (Vince Carbonaro)
Founded – 1961

2009

23/8	Floriana	1-1	Chetcuti
30/8	Sliema	1-0	Camilo
26/9	Msida	3-0	Camilo 3
4/10	Hibernians	3-1	Camilo 3
19/10	Valletta	0-2	
25/10	Tarxien	2-1	Camilo, Effiong
22/11	Hamrun	2-0	Grima, Camilo
27/11	Dingli	4-1	Camilo 2, Effiong, Grima
12/12	Birkirkara	2-5	Camilo, Deguara
18/12	Floriana	6-2	Camilo 4, Effiong, Farrugia J. (p)
26/12	Sliema	2-1	Wellman, Meilak

2010

2/1	Msida	3-0	Effiong 3
8/1	Hibernians	2-2	Effiong, Camilo (p)
16/1	Valletta	0-1	
24/1	Tarxien	0-2	
1/2	Hamrun	2-1	Bartolo, Grima
5/2	Dingli	4-0	Deguara, Bartolo, Giglio, Effiong
13/2	Birkirkara	0-2	
26/2	Hibernians	0-1	
6/3	Birkirkara	0-2	
12/3	Tarxien	2-0	Effiong, Camilo
19/3	Valletta	0-3	
27/3	Sliema	4-0	Camilo 4
11/4	Hibernians	3-0	Effiong 2, Camilo
15/.4	Birkirkara	1-3	Grima
24/4	Tarxien	2-3	Grima, Effiong
29/4	Valletta	1-2	Grima
4/5	Sliema	3-0	Camilo, Farrugia J., Giglio

No	Name	Nat	DoB	Pos	Aps	(s)	Gls
7	Matthew BARTOLO		14/6/86	M	12	(2)	
22	Jonathan BONDIN		11/10/82	D	25		
3	Gabriel BUTTIGIEG		10/9/91	M		(5)	
5	Malcolm BUTTIGIEG		3/10/86	M		(5)	
21	Matthew CAMILLERI		4/9/79	G		(1)	

No	Name			Nat	DoB	Pos	Aps	(s)	Gls
17	CAMILO da Silva Sanvezzo			BRA	21/7/88	A	21	(1)	24
10	Joseph CHETCUTI				16/8/82	M	7	(3)	1
9	George CHIRCOP				18/7/92	M		(2)	
19	Ryan DEGUARA				19/5/86	M	12	(15)	2
99	Alfred EFFIONG			NGA	29/11/84	A	27		12
80	Joseph FARRUGIA				26/7/81	M	26		2
1	Matthew FARRUGIA				17/4/81	G	28		
8	Keith FENECH				28/2/76	M	22	(2)	
2	Stefan GIGLIO				26/2/79	M	9	(5)	2
6	Massimo GRIMA				5/7/79	M	27		6
18	Steven MEILAK				17/5/86	A	2	(14)	1
29	Sharlon PACE				29/2/80	D	4	(2)	
11	Duncan PISANI				25/5/88	D	11	(2)	
4	Lucas RAMON dos Santos			BRA	28/6/85	D	28		
55	Roderick SAMMUT				7/12/83	D	17	(2)	
23	Kenneth SPITERI				22/3/86	D	4	(13)	
12	Jurgen STANYER				19/6/92	A		(1)	
31	Stephen WELLMAN				31/8/82	D	26		1

SLIEMA WANDERERS FC
Coach – Mark Marlow; (23/1/10) Stephen Azzopardi
Founded – 1909
MAJOR HONOURS:
Maltese League – (26) 1920, 1923, 1924, 1926, 1930, 1933, 1934, 1936,
1938, 1939, 1940, 1949, 1954, 1956, 1957, 1964, 1965, 1966, 1971, 1972,
1976, 1989, 1996, 2003, 2004, 2005;
Maltese Cup – (20) 1935, 1936, 1937, 1940, 1946, 1948, 1951, 1952, 1956,
1959, 1963, 1965, 1968, 1969, 1974, 1979, 1990, 2000, 2009.

2009

30/8	Qormi	0-1	
25/8	Valletta	0-1	
22/8	Vittoriosa	3-0	Fenech, Woods, Ciantar M.
			(result annulled)
30/9	Msida	2-0	og (Farrugia T.), Mintoff
3/10	Tarxien	1-3	Isaac
17/10	Hamrun	5-0	Mifsud Triganza 3, Bartolo, Failla
25/10	Dingli	2-0	Dronca (p), Bartolo
23/11	Birkirkara	0-3	
29/11	Floriana	1-1	Mifsud Triganza
12/12	Hibernians	1-0	Mifsud Triganza
22/12	Msida	0-1	
26/12	Qormi	1-2	Woods

2010

3/1	Valletta	3-1	Woods, Mifsud Triganza 2
10/1	Tarxien	4-2	Woods, Pedrinho, Dronca (p), Alcorsé
15/1	Hamrun	0-3	
24/1	Dingli	3-1	Mifsud Triganza, Woods (p), Azzopardi
30/1	Birkirkara	1-0	Mifsud Triganza
7/2	Floriana	3-0	Fenech, Dronca (p), Mifsud Triganza
13/2	Hibernians	2-2	Woods 2
26/2	Birkirkara	1-2	Woods
7/3	Tarxien	2-0	Dronca, Alcorsé
13/3	Valletta	2-1	Azzopardi, Mifsud Triganza
19/3	Hibernians	2-1	Mifsud Triganza 2
27/3	Qormi	0-4	
9/4	Birkirkara	0-3	
15/4	Tarxien	2-0	Fenech, Alcorsé
23/4	Valletta	0-2	
30/4	Hibernians	3-0	Dronca, Woods, Failla
4/5	Qormi	0-3	

No	Name	Nat	DoB	Pos	Aps	(s)	Gls
12	Simon AGIUS		12/4/78	G	29		
17	Julio Cesar ALCORSÉ	ARG	17/9/81	A	9	(5)	3
16	Jeremy ALDEN		5/10/90	G		(1)	
20	Ray ATTARD		25/11/91	M		(1)	
3	Ian AZZOPARDI		12/8/82	D	29		2
11	Matthew BARTOLO		14/6/86	M	3	(6)	2
19	Ian CIANTAR		19/12/75	D	10	(8)	
10	Miguel CIANTAR		17/10/90	A	1	(4)	1

MALTA

15	Lucian Florin DRONCA	ROU	30/5/73	D	26		5
77	Clayton FAILLA		8/1/86	M	25	(2)	2
6	Ryan FENECH		20/4/86	M	24		3
13	Clifford GATT BALDACCHINO		9/2/88	D	16	(5)	
21	Henry ISAAC Osaro Nwosu Kanu	NGA	14/2/80	A	1	(5)	1
24	Michael Gustavo Siscoutto LIMA	BRA	18/12/83	G		(2)	
4	Luca MARTINELLI	ITA	20/12/88	M		(2)	
22	Amadeo MERCIECA		22/7/91	A		(6)	
5	Josef MIFSUD		7/9/84	D	26	(1)	
9	Jean Pierre MIFSUD TRIGANZA		20/11/81	A	24	(3)	13
23	John MINTOFF		23/8/88	M	13	(7)	1
2	Alexander MUSCAT		14/12/84	D	22	(1)	
18	Pedro Henrique dos Santos Calçado "PEDRINHO"	BRA	4/8/86	M	11	(2)	1
8	Mark SCERRI		16/1/90	D	21	(1)	
7	Noel TURNER		9/12/74	M	4	(13)	
14	Ivan WOODS		31/12/76	A	25	(1)	9

TARXIEN RAINBOWS FC
Coach – Noel Coleiro
Founded – 1944

2009

22/8	Dingli	4-1	Denni, Anderson Ribeiro 2, Shead
30/8	Birkirkara	0-2	
27/9	Floriana	1-1	Calabretta
3/10	Sliema	3-1	Anderson Ribeiro, Éverton, Denni
17/10	Msida	1-1	Denni
25/10	Qormi	1-2	Calabretta
24/11	Valletta	2-2	Anderson Ribeiro 2
28/11	Hibernians	1-2	Anderson Ribeiro
11/12	Hamrun	0-1	og (Magro)
20/12	Dingli	2-1	Tanti, Denni
27/12	Birkirkara	1-5	Denni

2010

4/1	Floriana	2-1	Denni, Anderson Ribeiro
10/1	Sliema	2-4	og (Gatt Baldacchino), Denni
17/1	Msida	3-1	Decesare, Anderson Ribeiro 2
24/1	Qormi	2-0	Denni (p), Tanti
31/1	Valletta	2-2	Anderson Ribeiro, Camilleri
6/2	Hibernians	1-0	Denni (p)
16/2	Hamrun	2-2	Denni 2
27/2	Valletta	2-6	Decesare 2
7/3	Sliema	0-2	
12/3	Qormi	0-2	
20/3	Birkirkara	3-3	Calabretta 2, Anderson Ribeiro
28/3	Hibernians	2-0	Denni 2
10/4	Valletta	0-3	
15/4	Sliema	0-2	
24/4	Qormi	3-2	Denni 2, Decesare
30/4	Birkirkara	0-1	
4/5	Hibernians	1-0	Grech

No	Name	Nat	DoB	Pos	Aps	(s)	Gls
9	ANDERSON RIBEIRO Mendes	BRA	2/7/81	A	21		11
7	Gianluca CALABRETTA		14/10/87	M	18	(8)	4
11	David CAMILLERI		21/8/74	M	24	(1)	1
4	Manuel CARUANA		17/2/85	D	22	(3)	
12	David CASSAR		24/11/87	G	10		
13	Warren CHIRCOP		15/9/88	A	3	(5)	
1	Anthony CURMI		20/11/82	G	18	(1)	
3	Andrew DECESARE		4/3/84	A	18	(2)	4
17	DENNI Rocha dos Santos	BRA	21/8/82	M	27		15
8	ÉVERTON António Pereira	BRA	15/11/79	M	26		1
5	Clive FENECH		13/4/91	M		(1)	
66	Lee GALEA		14/2/88	D	10	(9)	
6	Ryan GRECH		3/4/85	M	5	(5)	1
9	Justin GRIOLI		20/9/87	D	12	(3)	
77	Kurt MAGRO		4/6/86	M	8	(13)	
20	Ryan MINTOFF		3/7/83	D	23		
10	Ryan PREVI		4/2/90	D		(1)	

2	Steven Marc SADOWSKI		21/1/82	D	24	(1)	
18	James SHEAD		2/2/90	M	1	(8)	1
10	Mark TANTI		20/4/81	M	22	(5)	2
16	Luke VELLA CRITIEN		19/3/86	M	16	(5)	
14	Warren ZERAFA		24/2/92	A		(3)	

VALLETTA FC
Coach – Tom Caanen (NED)
Founded – 1943
MAJOR HONOURS:
Maltese League – (19) 1915, 1932, 1945, 1946, 1948, 1959, 1960, 1963, 1974, 1978, 1980, 1984, 1990, 1992, 1997, 1998, 1999, 2001, 2008;
Maltese Cup – (12) 1960, 1964, 1975, 1977, 1978, 1991, 1995, 1996, 1997, 1999, 2001, 2010.

2009

21/8	Birkirkara	3-1	Den Ouden, Scerri 2
29/8	Floriana	6-0	Cruyff, Priso 2 (1p), Scerri 2, Zammit
25/9	Sliema	1-0	Scerri
3/10	Msida	0-0	
19/10	Qormi	2-0	Sammut, Pace
23/10	Hibernians	0-1	
24/11	Tarxien	2-2	Pace, Priso
28/11	Hamrun	3-2	Cruyff, Priso 2 (2p)
13/12	Dingli	4-1	Zammit, Scerri, Cruyff 2
19/12	Birkirkara	1-1	Agius G.
26/12	Floriana	4-0	Briffa, Agius G., Sammut, Scerri

2010

3/1	Sliema	1-3	Priso
9/1	Msida	1-0	Scerri
16/1	Qormi	1-0	Scerri
23/1	Hibernians	4-2	Agius G. 2, Sammut, Priso
31/1	Tarxien	2-2	Scerri, Pace
6/2	Hamrun	4-0	Pace, Agius G., Scerri 2
15/2	Dingli	6-0	O'Brien 4, Cruyff 2
27/2	Tarxien	6-2	Cruyff 3 (2p), Scerri, O'Brien 2
6/3	Hibernians	2-1	Scerri 2
13/3	Sliema	1-2	Agius G.
19/3	Qormi	3-0	Scerri, Agius G., Mifsud
28/3	Birkirkara	0-1	
10/4	Tarxien	3-0	Mifsud 3
16/4	Hibernians	3-1	Mifsud, Scerri, Cruyff
23/4	Sliema	2-0	Mifsud, Priso
29/4	Qormi	2-1	Bezzina, Mifsud
5/5	Birkirkara	4-2	Scerri 3, Agius E.

No	Name	Nat	DoB	Pos	Aps	(s)	Gls
8	Edmond AGIUS		23/2/87	M	9	(8)	1
7	Gilbert AGIUS		21/2/74	A	22	(2)	7
13	Steven BEZZINA		5/1/87	D	25	(2)	1
4	Steve BORG		15/5/88	D	17	(3)	
10	Roderick BRIFFA		24/8/81	M	24		1
5	Adrian CARABOTT		4/1/91	A		(1)	
77	Jordi CRUYFF	NED	9/2/74	M	17	(2)	10
16	Geert DEN OUDEN	NED	24/7/76	A	4	(1)	1
66	Luke DIMECH		11/1/77	D	23		
20	Dyson FALZON		9/3/86	M	11	(12)	
11	Cleavon FRENDO		1/7/85	A		(6)	
6	Clifford GAUCI		8/4/92	A		(1)	
26	Stephen GIGLIO		26/2/79	M		(4)	
19	Dylan GRIMA		18/7/90	M		(9)	
2	Justin GRIOLI		20/9/87	M	2	(2)	
24	Andrew HOGG		2/3/85	G	28		
12	Michael MIFSUD		17/4/81	A	7		7
14	Declan O'BRIEN	IRL	16/6/79	A	5	(8)	6
18	Jamie PACE		1/1/77	M	23	(1)	4
30	Njongo Lobe PRISO Doding	CMR	24/12/88	A	23	(1)	8
23	Kevin SAMMUT		26/5/81	M	18	(8)	3
21	Terence SCERRI		3/4/84	A	24	(1)	20
17	Kenneth SCICLUNA		15/6/79	D	25		
9	Ian ZAMMIT		9/12/86	A	1	(7)	2

EXCLUDED CLUBS

MARSAXLOKK FC

2009

23/8	Hibernians	1-3 *Deyanov (result annulled)*
29/8	Dingli	1-0 *Licari (result annulled)*

No	Name	Nat	DoB	Pos	Aps	(s)	Gls
19	Roderick BAJADA		4/1/83	M	2		
16	Clive BRINCAT		31/5/83	M	1		
11	William CAMENZULI		11/2/79	D	2		
10	Chris CAMILLERI		2/10/79	M		(2)	
7	Martin DEYANOV	BUL	17/1/80	A	2		1
22	Dylan KOKAVESSIS		14/1/89	A	1	(1)	
9	Malcolm LICARI		18/4/78	A	1	(1)	1
3	Carlo MAMO		23/4/79	D	2		
8	Peter PULLICINO		17/6/76	M	2		
35	Florent RAIMY	BEN	7/2/86	M	2		
6	Brian SAID		15/5/73	D	1		
4	Gareth SCIBBERRAS		29/3/83	M	2		
81	Trevor TEMPLEMAN		25/11/81	M		(2)	
24	Emil YANCHEV	BUL	15/9/74	D	2		
21	Glenn ZAMMIT		5/8/87	G	2		

VITTORIOSA STARS FC

2009

22/8	Sliema	0-3 *(result annulled)*

Name	Nat	DoB	Pos	Aps	(s)	Gls
Pierre AQUILINA		3/11/77	D	1		
Henry BONELLO		13/10/88	G	1		
Mauro BRINCAT		3/6/84	M	1		
Justin CAMILLERI		23/11/81	D		(1)	
Jeffrey CHETCUTI		24/4/74	D	1		
Kurt FORMOSA		4/4/86	D	1		
Martin HRUSBA	CZE	9/10/84	D	1		
Henry ISAAC Osaro Nwosu Kanu	NGA	14/2/80	A	1		
Clayton MICALLEF		21/2/84	M	1		

Beppe MUSCAT	13/4/89	D	1
Lucian SCERRI	28/11/81	M	(1)
Johann SPITERI	2/4/83	M	(1)
Elton VELLA	28/4/83	A	1
Nikola VUKANAC	SRB 14/1/86	D	1

NB For further details of these two clubs, see below.

PROMOTED CLUBS

MARSAXLOKK FC
Coach – Patrick Curmi
Founded – 1949
MAJOR HONOURS:
Maltese League – (1) 2007.

VITTORIOSA STARS FC
Coach – Wiston Muscat
Founded - 1906

SECOND LEVEL FINAL TABLE 2009/10

		Pld	W	D	L	F	A	Pts
1	Marsaxlokk FC	18	12	5	1	42	14	41
2	Vittoriosa Stars FC	18	11	3	4	28	13	36
3	Balzan Youths FC	18	9	4	5	26	18	31
4	St George's FC	18	9	2	7	28	32	29
5	Mosta FC	18	7	6	5	31	28	27
6	Mqabba FC	18	5	6	7	30	30	21
7	Melita FC	18	5	4	9	21	31	19
8	Pietà Hotspurs FC	18	4	5	9	14	25	17
9	St Patrick FC	18	5	2	11	14	34	17
10	San Gwann FC	18	2	5	11	21	30	11

DOMESTIC CUP 2009/10

FA TROPHY

PRELIMINARY ROUND

(28/10/09)
Vittoriosa 1, Melita 0 *(aet)*

FIRST ROUND

(31/10/09)
Hamrun 3, St George´s 0
Mosta 1, Tarxien 5
Mqabba 0, Qormi 3
Msida 0, Balzan 5

(1/11/09)
Floriana 4, San Gwann 0
Marsaxlokk 1, Pietà 0 *(aet)*
Sannat 1, St Patrick 2
Vittoriosa 2, Dingli 2 *(aet; 4-5 on pens)*

SECOND ROUND

(20/2/10)
Marsaxlokk 0, Hamrun 1
St Patrick 1, Qormi 5

(21/2/10)
Balzan 2, Dingli 1 *(aet)*
Floriana 1, Tarxien 4 *(aet)*

QUARTER-FINALS

(3/4/10)
Hamrun 5 *(Mifsud 1og, Spiteri 4, Fenech 29, Obiefule 62, 71)*, Sliema 2 *(Pedrinho 10, Woods 71)*
Valletta 3 *(Pace 6, Mifsud 21, O'Brien 90+3)*, Birkirkara 1 *(Galea M. 81)*

(5/4/10)
Hibernians 1 *(Pearson 74)*, Qormi 1 *(Camilo 62p) (aet; 3-4 on pens)*
Tarxien 2 *(Anderson Ribeiro 15, Denni 33)*, Balzan 0

SEMI-FINALS

(17/5/10)
Hamrun 0, Valletta 0 *(aet; 5-6 on pens)*

(18/5/10)
Qormi 2 *(Camilo 55, Bartolo 82)*, Tarxien 0

FINAL

(23/5/10)
National Stadium, Ta'Qali
VALLETTA FC 2 *(Mifsud 8, Scerri 21)*
QORMI FC 1 *(Camilo 78p)*
Referee – Pisani
VALLETTA – Hogg, Borg, Scicluna, Agius G., Agius E., Briffa, Falzon *(Grima 86)*, Sammut, Mifsud, Scerri, Priso.
QORMI – Farrugia M., Pisani *(Meilak 89)*, Ramon, Bondin, Wellman, Grima, Bartolo *(Giglio 60)*, Fenech *(Deguara 60)*, Farrugia J., Camilo, Effiong.

Sheriff strengthen their grip

FC Sheriff prolonged their march towards a world-record haul of successive national titles by claiming their tenth Divizia Nationala championship win in a row. Their total domination of Moldovan football in the 21st century was further confirmed by a third consecutive Cup win and, in consequence, a hat-trick of domestic doubles.

Eager to export their winning habit into Europe, Sheriff made good ground in 2009/10. For the first time ever they managed to win back-to-back UEFA Champions League qualifying ties, and although a play-off round defeat by Olympiacos FC denied them access to the promised land of the competition's group stage, their last-gasp away-goals success against SK Slavia Praha in the previous round had at least guaranteed them an extended run of games in the UEFA Europa League, where they were able to welcome heavyweight opposition in the shape of Fenerbahçe SK, FC Twente and FC Steaua Bucureşti to their elegant stadium in Tiraspol. They did not disgrace themselves either. On the contrary, Twente were famously beaten 2-0, ending a 17-match run without defeat in all competitions for the Dutch club, while Steaua were twice held to draws, enabling Sheriff to finish above the winless Romanians in the final Group H table.

Strong squad

Domestic rivals hoping that Sheriff's extended European participation might lead to a drain on their resources and a diminished effort on the home front were to be seriously disappointed. The club's large squad, replete with foreigners from far and wide, had more than enough in reserve to withstand the extra workload. A run of seven wins and a draw in the lead-up to the winter break maintained Sheriff's firm grip on the title race, giving them a handsome advantage to carry forward into the spring.

The biggest threat to Sheriff's title charge came in January when long-serving coach Leonid Kuchuk announced that he would be leaving, after six and a half trophy-packed years, to join Russian second-tier club FC Salyut Belgorod. Seeking continuity, Sheriff appointed Kuchuk's assistant, Andrei Sosnitskiy, another Belarusian, to succeed him, and although his opening match in charge, a 1-0 defeat at FC Olimpia Balti, did not bode well, it was no indication of what was to come as Sheriff dropped only two points and conceded just two goals over the next 14 matches, securing the title with four matches to spare and ending up with a 19-point victory margin over surprise runners-up FC Iskra-Stal.

The difference between first and last place in the 12-team division was a whopping 73 points as FC Nistru Otaci's financial struggles got the better of them, ten of their 11 points being accrued before the end of September. They would be spared relegation at

Sheriff's top-scoring Brazilian striker Jymmy in UEFA Europa League action

Federatia Moldoveneasca de Fotbal (FMF)

Str. Tricolorului 39
MD-2012 Chisinau
tel – +373 22 210 413
fax – +373 22 210 432
website – fmf.md
email – fmf@fmf.md
Year of Formation – 1990

President – Pavel Cebanu
General Secretary – Nicolai Cebotari
Media Officer – Victor Daghi
National Stadium – Zimbru, Chisinau (10,500)

TOP FIVE ALL-TIME CAPS
Radu Rebeja (74); Serghey Clescenco (69); Ivan Testimitanu (56); Valeriu Catinsus (55); Serghey Rogaciov (52)
TOP FIVE ALL-TIME GOALS
Serghey Clescenco (11); Serghey Rogaciov (9); Iurie Miterev (8); Serghey Dadu (7); Igor Bugaiov & Viorel Frunza (6)

Defeat for Dacia left the club from the capital still seeking their first trophy. They finished fifth in the league, one point behind city rivals FC Zimbru Chisinau and two behind Olimpia, the team they overcame impressively in the Cup semi-finals to book an immediate return to the UEFA Europa League. Olimpia qualified for the same competition, reaching Europe for the first time thanks to their highest placing in the Divizia Nationala for 15 years. Iskra-Stal's runners-up spot bettered anything the club had achieved before – although the fact that they lost all three of their games against Sheriff without scoring was a measure of the gulf in class between first and second.

As usual, the man who made Sheriff tick more than any other was their evergreen skipper, Vaja Tarkhnishvili. Sheriff's tenth straight title was also the 38-year-old Georgian's, and yet again he spent more minutes on the field than any of his team-mates, starting 29 of the 33 league games and also appearing from first whistle to last in all 12 of the club's European games. At the other end of the age scale in Sheriff's squad was 18-year-old Serghei Gheorghiev, a midfielder of high promise who appears to have a bright international future with Moldova if he can go on to fulfil his considerable potential.

the end of their horrendous losing streak, however, as the Divizia Nationala was increased in number to 14 for 2010/11, with second division champions FC Costuleni being accompanied up not by runners-up RS Lilcora, who were refused a licence to compete at the top level, but third-placed CF Gagauziya Comrat.

Jymmy joy

As other clubs considered their futures, Sheriff concluded another flawless domestic campaign by defeating FC Dacia Chisinau 2-0 in the final of the Moldovan Cup. They had not had an easy path to the final, requiring an extra-time winner to see off FC Academia UTM Chisinau in the quarter-final and then another late strike, from their top-scoring Brazilian striker Jymmy, to get past Iskra-Stal on the away-goals rule in the semis. The early stages of the final were also something of a struggle for the holders until Jymmy secured the club's seventh victory in the competition – and a repeat of the previous season's scoreline, against the same opponents – with a goal in each half.

Balint appointed

The country could certainly do with an injection of fresh talent following a miserable 2010 FIFA World Cup qualifying campaign that yielded just three points and no wins. Finishing below Luxembourg was clearly unacceptable, and head coach Igor Dobrovolsky paid the price with his job. His replacement, appointed in January on a two-year contract, was former Romanian international striker Gavril Balint, whose preparations for the UEFA EURO 2012 qualifiers began with a trio of low-key friendlies that brought one win, one draw and one defeat.

NATIONAL TEAM RESULTS 2009/10

12/8/09	Armenia	A	Yerevan	4-1	Golovatenco (34, 64), Andronic (82), Epureanu (90+3)
5/9/09	Luxembourg (WCQ)	H	Chisinau	0-0	
9/9/09	Greece (WCQ)	H	Chisinau	1-1	Andronic (90)
10/10/09	Israel (WCQ)	A	Tel-Aviv	1-3	Calincov (90+2)
14/10/09	Latvia (WCQ)	A	Riga	2-3	Ovseannicov (25), Sofroni (90)
3/3/10	Kazakhstan	N	Antalya (TUR)	1-0	Epureanu (65)
26/5/10	Azerbaijan	N	Seekirchen (AUT)	1-1	Cojocari (81)
29/5/10	United Arab Emirates	N	Anif (AUT)	2-3	Tigirlas (14), Bulgaru (80)

MOLDOVA

NATIONAL TEAM APPEARANCES 2009/10

Coach – Igor DOBROVOLSKY 27/8/67 /(20/1/10) Gavril BALINT (ROU) 3/1/63			Arm	LUX	GRE	ISR	LVA	Kaz	Aze	Uae	Caps	Goals
Stanislav NAMASCO	10/11/86	Sheriff	G	G	G	G	G					
		/Kuban (RUS)						G90	G		19	-
Igor ARMAS	14/7/87	Hammarby (SWE)	D	D	D		D81					
		/Kuban (RUS)						D			14	-
Serghey LASCENCOV	24/3/80	Olimpik-Şüvälan (AZE)	D73	D	D	D	D				37	-
							30*					
Alexandru EPUREANU	27/9/86	FC Moskva (RUS)	D		M	M	M					
		/Dinamo Moskva (RUS)						D	D	D	33	3
Victor GOLOVATENCO	28/4/84	Khimki (RUS)	D	D		D	D					
		/unattached						D			29	3
Vasile CARAUS	6/8/88	Metalurh Zaporizhya (UKR)	M46								1	-
Evgheny CEBOTARI	16/10/84	Ceahlăul (ROU)	M46			M67		M86	M71	D81	15	-
Victor BULAT	5/1/85	Dacia Chisinau	M77		M	M					8	-
Alexandru ONICA	29/7/84	Dacia Chisinau	M	M								
		/Vorskla (UKR)						s86		M68	10	-
Georgy OVSEANNICOV	12/10/85	Olimpia Balti	A46		s79	A76					11	1
Igor BUGAIOV	26/6/84	Metalurh Zaporizhya (UKR)	A46	A77	A46	A74	A70					
		/unattached						A89			28	6
Alexandru SUVOROV	2/2/87	Sheriff	s46	s77		s74	s70					
		/Cracovia (POL)						s46	s71	s68	22	-
Alexei SAVINOV	19/4/79	Bakı (AZE)	s46		D79	D	D	D	s71	D63	33	-
Veaceslav SOFRONI	30/4/84	Zimbru	s46	A	s46	A79	s76					
		/Bakı (AZE)							s55	s75	9	2
Denis CALINCOV	15/9/85	Academia	s46									
		/Xäzär Länkäran (AZE)			M	M	M	M		M46	s58	19	2
Serghey NAMASCO	19/6/84	Vostok (KAZ)	s73		M56		M				18	2
Valeriu ANDRONIC	21/12/82	Bohemians (CZE)	s77	s81	s79	s67	s81	s72			27	4
Valeriu CATINSUS	27/4/78	Tom (RUS)			D	D	D	D			55	-
Alexandru GATCAN	27/3/84	Rostov (RUS)			M	M					20	1
Victor COMLEONOC	23/2/79	Obolon (UKR)			M81	s56					19	-
Vadim BORET	5/9/76	Bakı (AZE)						M89			35	1
Igor TIGIRLAS	24/2//84	Metalurh Zaporizhya (UKR)						M	M66	M	13	1
Anatol DOROS	21/3/83	Olimpik-Şüvälan (AZE)						A72	A55		5	-
Alexandru GOLBAN	28/2/79	Simurq (AZE)						A46			15	4
Vadim BOLOHAN	15/8/86	Zakarpattya (UKR)						s89	D	D	3	-
Eugeniu GORCEAC	10/3/87	Academia						s89			3	-
Artiom GAIDUCHEVICI	22/4/87	Iskra-Stal						s90		G	2	-
Semion BULGARU	26/5/85	Viborg (DEN)							D	s63	7	-
Alexandru CHELTUIALA	5/2/83	Olimpia Balti							D80		1	-
Nicolai JOSAN	18/9/83	Anzhi (RUS)							M71	M76	11	1
Serghey DADU	23/1/81	Alania (RUS)							A	A75	28	7
Andrei COJOCARI	21/1/87	CSCA-Rapid							s46	M58	3	-
Eugen SIDORENCO	19/3/89	Zimbru							s66		1	-
Oleg ICHIM	27/10/79	Neman (BLR)							s80		1	-
Denis ZMEU	8/5/85	Vaslui (ROU)								M	15	-
Alexandru ANTONIUC	23/5/89	Zimbru								s76	1	-
Serghey GAFINA	10/11/84	Iskra-Stal								s81	1	-

DOMESTIC LEAGUE 2009/10

DIVIZIA NATIONALA FINAL TABLE

		Pld	Home W	D	L	F	A	Away W	D	L	F	A	Total W	D	L	F	A	Pts
1	FC Sheriff	33	16	1	0	46	2	11	2	3	29	6	27	3	3	75	8	84
2	FC Iskra-Stal	33	12	4	1	31	5	7	4	5	19	20	19	8	6	50	25	65
3	FC Olimpia Balti	33	12	2	3	25	10	5	7	4	20	13	17	9	7	45	23	60
4	FC Zimbru Chisinau	33	11	3	3	29	16	6	5	5	18	13	17	8	8	47	29	59
5	FC Dacia Chisinau	33	9	5	3	26	15	7	5	4	28	15	16	10	7	54	30	58
6	CSCA-Rapid Chisinau	33	7	4	6	22	18	5	5	6	18	21	12	9	12	40	39	45
7	FC Academia UTM Chisinau	33	6	6	4	19	14	5	3	9	17	23	11	9	13	36	37	42
8	FC Viitorul Orhei	33	6	4	6	17	25	4	2	11	15	20	10	6	17	32	45	36
9	FC Tiraspol	33	6	5	5	12	12	2	5	10	8	22	8	10	15	20	34	34
10	FC Dinamo Bender	33	7	3	6	22	29	2	2	13	14	37	9	5	19	36	66	32
11	FC Sfintul Gheorghe Suruceni	33	4	4	8	14	30	2	2	13	15	37	6	6	21	29	67	24
12	FC Nistru Otaci	33	1	3	12	7	31	1	2	14	6	43	2	5	26	13	74	11

NB No relegation.

TOP GOALSCORERS

13 JYMMY (Sheriff)
Alexandru MAXIMOV (Viitorul)
12 Olexandr ZGURA (Dacia)
11 Aleksandr EROKHIN (Sheriff)
10 Daniil NIKOLAEV (Academia)
9 Eric SACKEY (Dacia)
Alexandru POPOVICI (Dinamo/Iskra-Stal)
Georgy OVSEANNICOV (Olimpia)
8 Stanislav LUCA (CSCA-Rapid)
Nicolai RUDAC (Iskra-Stal)
Mykola GLEGA (Olimpia)
Vladimir VOLKOV (Sheriff)

CLUB-BY-CLUB

FC ACADEMIA UTM CHISINAU
Coach – Igor Dobrovolsky
Founded – 2006
Stadium – Dinamo (2,500)

2009
5/7	Dacia	h	1-1	Leuca
11/7	Tiraspol	a	1-1	Slivca
19/7	Viitorul	h	0-2	
25/7	Nistru	a	2-1	Gorceac, Nikolaev
2/8	Zimbru	h	2-2	Ilescu, Nikolaev
7/8	CSCA-Rapid	a	1-4	Nikolaev
22/8	Sfintul Gheorghe	a	3-1	Ginsari, Cascaval, Nikolaev
30/8	Olimpia	h	2-1	Cascaval 2
13/9	Iskra-Stal	a	0-2	
20/9	Dinamo	h	1-1	Leuca
26/9	Dacia	a	0-1	
4/10	Tiraspol	h	1-1	Nikolaev
18/10	Viitorul	a	0-2	
24/10	Nistru	h	1-0	Ginsari
28/10	Zimbru	a	1-4	og (Hvorosteanov)
1/11	CSCA-Rapid	h	0-1	
10/11	Sheriff	a	0-1	
17/11	Sfintul Gheorghe	h	3-0	Leuca 2, Nikolaev
26/11	Sheriff	h	0-0	

2010
10/3	Olimpia	a	2-2	Bludnov 2
13/3	Iskra-Stal	h	1-1	Lambarschi (p)
17/3	Dinamo	a	4-1	Potirnica, Nikolaev 2, Bludnov
21/3	CSCA-Rapid	a	1-0	Bludnov
26/3	Nistru	a	2-0	Nikolaev, Ginsari
3/4	Viitorul	h	3-0	Lambarschi, Nikolaev, Ginsari
10/4	Tiraspol	a	0-0	
18/4	Dinamo	h	1-0	Cascaval
24/4	Sfintul Gheorghe	a	0-1	
2/5	Sheriff	h	0-1	
8/5	Iskra-Stal	a	0-1	
15/5	Dacia	h	3-1	Cascaval, Lambarschi, Bludnov
19/5	Olimpia	a	0-1	
23/5	Zimbru	h	0-2	

No	Name	Nat	DoB	Pos	Aps	(s)	Gls
17	Artem BLUDNOV	RUS	5/9/88	A	14	(1)	5
22	Firuz BOBIEV	TJK	18/6/92	M	1	(6)	
15	Denis CALINCOV		15/9/85	A	3		
7	Vasile CARAUS		6/8/88	M	2		
2	Adrian CASCAVAL		10/6/87	D	23	(2)	5
5	Alexandru CHICIUC		7/11/88	D	28	(1)	
21	Valeri CIUPERCEA		12/6/92	M	13	(11)	
26	Efim COJUHARI		19/3/88	M	2	(2)	
12	Maxim COPELCIUC		6/8/88	G	15	(1)	
2	Serghei CUZNETOV		20/8/74	D	12	(1)	
23	Victor DIMOV		19/1/90	G	18	(0)	
14	Radu GINSARI		10/12/91	A	31		4
10	Eugeniu GORCEAC		10/3/87	M	17	(1)	1
6	Denis ILESCU		20/1/87	D	17		1
11	Daniel INDOITU		8/9/90	D	22	(6)	
8	Igor LAMBARSCHI		26/11/92	M	26	(3)	3
19	Petru LEUCA		19/7/90	A	15	(10)	4
17	Victor LISA		10/3/91	A		(3)	
4	Serhiy LYUBCHAK	UKR	15/4/86	D	28		
26	Andrei MARINA		21/2/90	M	6	(13)	
20	Daniil NIKOLAEV	RUS	14/10/91	A	25	(5)	10
21	Maxim POTIRNICA		13/6/89	D	17	(3)	1
35	Zalimhan SAADUEV	RUS	11/3/88	M	3		
13	Eugeniu SLIVCA		13/7/89	M	25	(2)	1

CSCA-RAPID CHISINAU
Coach – Pavel Irichuk (UKR); (25/8/09) Serghey Secu; (30/9/09) Spiridon Niculescu (ROU); (20/3/10) Serghey Sirbu
Founded – 1992
Stadium – Ghidigici (1,500)

2009
5/7	Dinamo	h	2-1	Luca, Istrati
10/7	Sheriff	h	0-6	
18/7	Sfintul Gheorghe	a	3-0	Grosu (l), Oanta, Luca (p)
25/7	Olimpia	h	0-0	
2/8	Iskra-Stal	a	0-5	
7/8	Academia	h	4-1	Bugneac 2, Luca, Jardan
16/8	Dacia	a	0-4	

MOLDOVA

22/8	Tiraspol	h	1-2	*Luca*
30/8	Viitorul	a	2-2	*Bugneac, Istrati*
13/9	Nistru	h	1-0	*Grosu (I)*
20/9	Zimbru	a	1-0	*Grosu (I)*
26/9	Dinamo	a	1-2	*Grosu (I)*
6/10	Sheriff	a	0-1	
18/10	Sfintul Gheorghe	h	1-1	*Bugneac*
24/10	Olimpia	a	2-0	*Luca 2*
28/10	Iskra-Stal	h	0-2	
1/11	Academia	a	1-0	*Bugneac*
7/11	Dacia	h	0-2	
18/11	Tiraspol	a	0-0	
2010				
7/3	Viitorul	h	1-0	*Maxim*
13/3	Nistru	a	0-0	
17/3	Zimbru	h	0-1	
21/3	Academia	h	0-1	
27/3	Viitorul	a	0-1	
3/4	Tiraspol	h	4-1	*Manaliu, Maxim, Rusu V., Luca*
10/4	Dinamo	a	4-0	*Maxim, Seul, Frantuz (p), Livandovschi*
18/4	Sfintul Gheorghe	h	2-0	*Rusu V., Frantuz (p)*
24/4	Sheriff	a	1-3	*Livandovschi*
2/5	Iskra-Stal	h	0-0	
8/5	Dacia	a	2-2	*Frantuz 2 (1p)*
15/5	Olimpia	h	0-0	
19/5	Zimbru	a	1-1	*Frantuz*
23/5	Nistru	h	6-0	*Manaliu, Bugneac 2, Frantuz (p), Luca, Grosu (II)*

No	Name	Nat	DoB	Pos	Aps	(s)	Gls
19	Manuel AMARANDEI	ROU	17/5/79	D	5		
13	Dumitru BERBINSCHI		23/2/88	D	31		
23	Andrei BEREGHICI		9/12/86	M	14		
16	Anatoli BUCSANU		16/10/89	M	3	(13)	
25	Andrei BUGNEAC		30/3/88	A	15	(8)	7
22	Maxim CEBOTARI		16/11/82	M	11	(2)	
78	Alexandru CHIRILOV		28/1/78	G	15		
14	Marcel CIORTAN		19/1/83	M	14	(3)	
8	Serghei CIUICO		2/2/83	A		(2)	
17	Andrei COJOCARI		21/1/87	M	10		
1	Vasili COSELEV		12/2/72	G		(1)	
18	Vadim CRAVCESCU		7/3/85	M	12		
7	Maxim FRANTUZ		4/5/86	M	8	(2)	6
11	Alexandru GROSU (I)		16/6/86	A	5	(16)	4
8	Alexandru GROSU (II)		18/4/88	M	28		1
20	Sergiu ISTRATI		7/8/88	A	14	(3)	2
15	Ion JARDAN		10/1/90	M	7	(11)	1
3	Alexandru LEU		4/5/91	D	6	(2)	
19	Iurie LIVANDOVSCHI		17/2/88	A	5	(5)	2
10	Stanislav LUCA		28/8/86	M	30	(2)	8
14	Vitalie MANALIU		23/3/85	A	11	(3)	2
11	Alexandru MAXIM		19/1/86	A	11		3
27	Ionel MIRCIU		27/2/91	M		(2)	
30	Eugen NACUL		2/9/87	G	2		
5	Stefan OANTA		10/1/90	D	9		1
4	Ghenadie OCHINCA		1/3/84	D	11	(1)	
18	Denis RASSULOV		2/1/90	D	12	(1)	
21	Vladimir RASSULOV		11/11/92	M		(1)	
33	Denis ROMANENCO		18/11/74	G	11		
15	Iurie ROMANIUC		27/11/78	M	2	(1)	
30	Denis RUSU		2/8/90	G	5	(2)	
5	Vasile RUSU		28/7/85	M	13		2
6	Dumitru SEUL		31/3/87	M	18	(6)	1
5	Igor SOLTANICI		4/5/84	D	11		
9	Tudor STARCIUC		1/2/90	A	4	(8)	
9	Anatol STAVILA		28/5/81	M	4	(1)	
21	Timur VALCU		16/1/91	D	4		
6	Andrei VERBITSCHI		21/7/89	D	2	(1)	

FC DACIA CHISINAU
Coach – Roman Pylypchuk (UKR); (1/9/09) Serghey Botnaras; (23/12/09) Veaceslav Semionov
Founded – 1999
Stadium – Dinamo (2,500); Zimbru (10,500)

2009				
5/7	Academia	a	1-1	*Zgura*
11/7	Dinamo	a	3-2	*Arabadji, Sackey, Onica*
29/7	Viitorul	a	5-1	*Sackey 3, Orbu (p), Onica (p)*
2/8	Nistru	h	1-1	*Sackey*
7/8	Zimbru	a	1-2	*Zgura*
16/8	CSCA-Rapid	h	4-0	*Sackey 4 (1p)*
22/8	Sheriff	a	0-0	
26/8	Tiraspol	h	1-0	*Zgura*
30/8	Sfintul Gheorghe	h	1-0	*Zgura*
12/9	Olimpia	a	1-0	*Arabadji*
20/9	Iskra-Stal	h	1-2	*Orbu*
26/9	Academia	h	1-0	*Zgura*
4/10	Dinamo	h	3-2	*Zgura 2, Popovici*
18/10	Tiraspol	a	3-0	*Arabadji, Boestean, Onica*
24/10	Viitorul	h	2-0	*Boestean, Arabadji*
28/10	Nistru	a	6-0	*Orbu (p), Bulat, Onica, Boestean, og (Orlovschi), Zgura*
1/11	Zimbru	h	1-0	*Zgura*
7/11	CSCA-Rapid	a	2-0	*Zgura (p), Popovici*
18/11	Sheriff	h	1-2	*Zgura*
2010				
7/3	Sfintul Gheorghe	a	0-0	
13/3	Olimpia	h	1-1	*Bursuc*
17/3	Iskra-Stal	a	1-3	*Mekang*
21/3	Dinamo	h	0-0	
27/3	Sfintul Gheorghe	a	2-2	*Akhilgov, Orbu*
3/4	Sheriff	h	0-0	
10/4	Iskra-Stal	a	0-0	
19/4	Nistru	h	3-0	*og (Klimakov), Guchashvili, Zgura*
23/4	Olimpia	h	2-4	*Akhilgov, Mekang*
2/5	Zimbru	a	0-1	
8/5	CSCA-Rapid	h	2-2	*Bulat, Guchashvili*
15/5	Academia	a	1-3	*Bursuc*
19/5	Viitorul	h	2-1	*Molla, Akhilgov*
23/5	Tiraspol	a	2-0	*Bulat, Gorceac*

No	Name	Nat	DoB	Pos	Aps	(s)	Gls
5	Abdulkhamid AKHILGOV	RUS	31/8/80	M	5	(2)	3
15	Ion ARABADJI		31/7/84	D	22	(1)	4
23	Dumitru BACAL		28/11/84	D	4	(4)	
4	Anatolie BOESTEAN		26/3/85	D	12	(4)	3
6	Aleksei BONDAREV	RUS	5/8/87	D	1		
13	Victor BULAT		5/1/85	M	24		3
20	Iulian BURSUC		23/9/76	M	8	(3)	2
19	Eugen BUZA		9/3/90	M	1	(10)	
20	Stefan CARAULAN		2/2/89	D	21	(3)	
11	Andrei DEMCHENKO	RUS	20/8/76	D	1		
24	Kum Maka Ernest DEZIRE	NGA	16/5/85	M	3	(3)	
8	Eugeniu GORCEAC		10/3/87	M	8		1
18	Iurie GROSEV		16/5/76	D	21	(4)	
10	Olexandr GROZOV	UKR	1/4/82	A	5	(2)	
16	Vasili GUCHASHVILI	GEO	25/1/85	A	5	(6)	2
3	Mykola HIBALYUK	UKR	21/5/84	D	2		
12	Adam ISMAILOV	RUS	1/5/76	G	1		
13	Magomed KHASHANOV	RUS	27/6/75	D	5		
10	Levan KORGALIDZE	GEO	21/2/80	M	1		
22	Yuri KOTYKOV	RUS	21/2/84	A	6		
25	Evghenii MATIUGHIN		31/10/81	G	12		
2	Anatoliy MATKEVYCH	UKR	17/6/77	D	4	(1)	
5	Serghei MAXIMOV		6/7/89	M		(1)	
2	Gock Habib MEKANG	CMR	23/4/82	D	21	(2)	2
11	Oleg MOLLA		22/2/86	A	3	(4)	1

MOLDOVA

1	Ghenadie MOSNEAGA	25/4/85	G	20	(2)	
16	Igor NEGRESCU	17/4/79	D	12	(1)	
8	Alexandru ONICA	29/7/84	M	17		4
9	Ghenadie ORBU	8/7/82	A	28	(4)	4
5	Dumitru POPOVICI	5/8/83	D	24	(2)	2
10	Eric SACKEY	GHA 20/8/87	A	11	(1)	9
18	Iurie SOIMU	18/3/84	M	13	(10)	
23	Aleksei TRINITATSKIY	RUS 10/1/85	M	18		
11	Andrei TURCU	26/5/86	M		(3)	
17	Olexandr ZGURA	UKR 20/8/85	A	24	(4)	12

FC DINAMO BENDER
Coach – Iuri Hodichin
Founded – 1950
Stadium – Dinamo (5,000)

2009

5/7	CSCA-Rapid	a	1-2	*Dizov*
11/7	Dacia	h	2-3	*Chiriliuc, og (Grosev)*
25/7	Tiraspol	h	2-1	*Zacon, Chiriliuc*
2/8	Sfintul Gheorghe	a	1-2	*Chiriliuc*
7/8	Viitorul	h	1-0	*Dragan*
16/8	Olimpia	a	1-3	*Popovici (p)*
22/8	Nistru	h	1-2	*Golubovschi*
30/8	Iskra-Stal	a	0-2	
7/9	Sheriff	a	0-5	
12/9	Zimbru	h	3-1	*Chiriliuc, Tofan, Bidirlan*
20/9	Academia	a	1-1	*Dizov*
26/9	CSCA-Rapid	h	2-1	*Popovici 2 (1p)*
4/10	Dacia	a	2-3	*og (Arabadji), Boicenco*
18/10	Sheriff	h	0-5	
24/10	Tiraspol	a	1-4	*Chiriliuc*
28/10	Sfintul Gheorghe	h	0-2	
1/11	Viitorul	a	2-3	*Chiriliuc, Titucenco*
7/11	Olimpia	h	1-1	*Popovici*
18/11	Nistru	a	1-0	*Titucenco*
2010				
7/3	Iskra-Stal	h	2-1	*Zacon, Tiverenco*
13/3	Zimbru	a	1-3	*Pascenco*
17/3	Academia	h	1-4	*Pascenco*
21/3	Dacia	a	0-0	
27/3	Olimpia	h	0-0	
3/4	Zimbru	a	0-2	
10/4	CSCA-Rapid	h	0-4	
18/4	Academia	a	0-1	
24/4	Viitorul	h	1-0	*Pascenco*
2/5	Tiraspol	a	0-2	
8/5	Nistru	a	3-1	*Tiverenco, Dizov 2*
15/5	Sfintul Gheorghe	h	5-3	*Pascenco 2 (1p), Agafonov, Tiverenco, Namasco*
19/5	Sheriff	a	0-3	
23/5	Iskra-Stal	h	1-1	*Tiverenco*

No	Name	Nat	DoB	Pos	Aps	(s)	Gls
14	Veaceslav AGAFONOV		29/5/85	M	29	(4)	1
19	Dumitru BAILEVICI		3/1/85	A		(2)	
3	Igor BARDUC		6/5/85	D	10	(2)	
2	Alexandr BICOV		15/11/86	M	16	(1)	
18	Alexandr BIDIRLAN			M		(6)	1
7	Alexei BOBU		23/9/88	M	22	(4)	
16	Evgheny BOICENCO		28/10/79	M	21		1
77	Pavel CALININ		15/2/89	G	20		
19	Alexei CASIAN		10/1/87	M	3	(1)	
18	Vadim CEMIRTAN		21/7/87	A		(8)	
10	Denis CHIRILIUC		5/8/87	A	17	(1)	6
11	Alexei DIZOV		20/3/88	A	23	(6)	4
5	Vladimir DRAGAN		10/4/79	D	6	(10)	1
9	Evgheny GOLUBOVSCHI		19/3/91	A	4	(20)	1
8	Alexandru HODICHIN		16/7/84	D	24	(2)	

1	Evgheny NACUL	2/9/87	G	1		
15	Serghei NAMASCO	19/6/86	M	12	(1)	1
12	Mihai PAIUS	6/2/83	G	12		
9	Alexandr PASCENCO	28/5/89	M	8	(3)	5
9	Alexandru POPOVICI	9/4/77	M	13	(3)	4
2	Timur ROMANET		D	5	(1)	
5	Victor SEVCENCO	8/9/91	D	4	(2)	
16	Artur SPINU	14/1/87	M	13	(9)	
4	Alexandru SVET	29/10/82	D	30	(1)	
6	Nicolai TITUCENCO	1/9/81	D	28		2
10	Eugen TIVERENCO	18/4/87	M	14	(1)	4
15	Leonid TOFAN	6/4/82	M	16	(1)	1
18	Andrei TONTICI	15/9/86	M		(3)	
17	Sergey ZACON	13/10/87	M	12	(15)	2
16	Alan ZUZI		D		(4)	

FC ISKRA-STAL
Coach – Vlad Goian
Founded – 2002
Stadium – Municipal (3,800)

2009

5/7	Tiraspol	h	1-0	*Osipenco*
11/7	Viitorul	a	3-0	*Hauşi, Manaliu, Rudac*
29/7	Zimbru	a	1-3	*Kilikevych*
2/8	CSCA-Rapid	h	5-0	*Onofrei 2, Rudac, Osipenco, Kilikevych*
10/8	Sheriff	a	0-5	
18/8	Sfintul Gheorghe	h	1-0	*Onofrei*
22/8	Olimpia	a	1-0	*Rudac*
26/8	Nistru	h	2-1	*Hauşi, Picus*
30/8	Dinamo	h	2-0	*Rudac (p), Taranu*
13/9	Academia	h	2-0	*og (Chiciuc), Hauşi*
20/9	Dacia	a	2-1	*Gafina, Taranu*
26/9	Tiraspol	a	0-0	
18/10	Nistru	a	2-1	*Osipenco (p), og (Antonii)*
24/10	Zimbru	h	1-1	*Osipenco*
28/10	CSCA-Rapid	a	2-0	*Rudac, Taranu*
1/11	Sheriff	h	0-1	
7/11	Sfintul Gheorghe	a	1-0	*Rudac*
11/11	Viitorul	a	1-0	*Hauşi*
18/11	Olimpia	h	1-1	*Hauşi*
2010				
7/3	Dinamo	a	1-2	*Cucovei*
13/3	Academia	a	1-1	*Rudac*
17/3	Dacia	h	3-1	*Taranu, Kilikevych 2*
21/3	Sfintul Gheorghe	h	5-0	*Popovici, Svitlichniy, Rudac (p), Burcovschi, Osipenco*
26/3	Sheriff	a	0-3	
3/4	Nistru	h	3-0	*Popovici, Osipenco (p), Onofrei*
10/4	Dacia	h	0-0	
18/4	Olimpia	a	1-2	*Novicov*
24/4	Zimbru	h	0-0	
2/5	CSCA-Rapid	a	0-0	
8/5	Academia	h	1-0	*Svitlichniy*
15/5	Viitorul	a	3-1	*Kilikevych, Yemelyanov, Popovici*
19/5	Tiraspol	h	3-0	*Popovici 2, Chiriliuc*
23/5	Dinamo	a	1-1	*Novicov*

No	Name	Nat	DoB	Pos	Aps	(s)	Gls
21	Andrei BURCOVSCHI		7/8/79	M	28	(3)	1
3	Alexei CASIAN		10/1/87	M	6	(2)	
1	Anatol CEBOTARI		29/3/88	G	1		
11	Denis CHIRILIUC		5/8/87	A	4	(8)	1
4	Vadim CRAVCESCU		7/3/85	D	1		
4	Andrian CUCOVEI		21/4/82	D	13	(3)	1
17	Olexandr FESHCHENKO	UKR	2/1/85	D	19	(1)	
2	Serghey GAFINA		10/11/84	D	26	(2)	1
22	Artiom GAIDUCHEVICI		22/4/87	G	32		

MOLDOVA

16	Kaloyan GENCHEV	BUL	5/11/80	M	2	(4)	
9	Bogdan HAUŞI	ROU	29/9/85	D	17		5
18	Oleh JURCA	UKR	4/11/77	D	19		
15	Volodymyr KILIKEVYCH	UKR	30/11/83	A	26	(4)	5
14	Vitali MANALIU		23/3/85	A		(2)	1
25	Maxim MIHALIOV		22/8/86	A	10	(4)	
5	Andrei NOVICOV		24/4/86	D	9	(1)	2
25	Ghenadie OCHINCA		1/3/84	D	2	(1)	
11	Octavian ONOFREI	ROU	16/5/91	A	4	(19)	4
8	Iurie OSIPENCO		6/7/74	M	20	(6)	6
23	Igor PICUS		7/5/90	M		(12)	1
9	Alexandru POPOVICI		9/4/77	M	9	(1)	5
11	Claudio RODOLFO Leão Costa	BRA	13/10/84	M		(7)	
20	Iurie ROMANIUC		28/11/78	M	1	(1)	
10	Nicolai RUDAC		23/3/86	M	30	(3)	8
19	Olexandr STAHIV	UKR	13/1/81	D	3	(5)	
7	Petru STINGA		17/4/87	M	8	(10)	
23	Roman SVITLICHNIY	UKR	4/1/86	M	20	(5)	2
20	Vladimir TARANU		27/6/82	A	23	(3)	4
13	Alexandru TOFAN		19/8/87	M	19	(8)	
14	Fedir YEMELYANOV	UKR	23/8/84	M	11	(8)	1

FC NISTRU OTACI
Coach – Lilian Popescu; (13/2/10) Ivan Caras
Founded – 1953
Stadium – Calarasauca (1,000)
MAJOR HONOURS:
Moldovan Cup – (1) 2005.

2009

5/7	Sfintul Gheorghe	a	0-3	(w/o; original result 0-0)
11/7	Olimpia	h	0-6	
25/7	Academia	h	1-2	Belle (p)
2/8	Dacia	a	1-1	Belle
7/8	Tiraspol	h	1-1	Repinetschii
16/8	Viitorul	a	0-0	
22/8	Dinamo	a	2-1	Soppo, Repinetschii
26/8	Iskra-Stal	a	1-2	Vdovicenco
30/8	Zimbru	h	0-0	
13/9	CSCA-Rapid	a	0-1	
22/9	Sheriff	h	0-1	
26/9	Sfintul Gheorghe	h	2-0	Belle (p), Maliarenko
4/10	Olimpia	a	0-3	
18/10	Iskra-Stal	h	1-2	Orlovschi
24/10	Academia	a	0-1	
28/10	Dacia	h	0-6	
1/11	Tiraspol	a	0-1	
7/11	Viitorul	h	0-2	
18/11	Dinamo	h	0-1	

2010

7/3	Zimbru	a	1-4	Maliarenko
13/3	CSCA-Rapid	h	0-0	
17/3	Sheriff	a	0-5	
21/3	Sheriff	a	0-4	
26/3	Academia	h	0-2	
3/4	Iskra-Stal	a	0-3	
10/4	Viitorul	h	0-1	
19/4	Dacia	a	0-3	
24/4	Tiraspol	h	0-1	
2/5	Olimpia	a	0-3	
8/5	Dinamo	h	1-3	Repinetschii
15/5	Zimbru	a	1-2	Maliarenko
19/5	Sfintul Gheorghe	h	1-3	Belle
23/5	CSCA-Rapid	a	0-6	

No	Name	Nat	DoB	Pos	Aps	(s)	Gls
8	Vitalie ANDRIES		5/9/87	D	2		
4	Victor ANTONII		26/6/89	M	20	(1)	
13	Iduelos APEZTEGUIA	CUB	17/12/83	D	1	(1)	

10	Titi BELLE	CMR	10/3/85	M	28		4
11	Vitaly BONDARENCO		5/12/88	D	4	(1)	
2	Vadim CAMINSCHI			M		(1)	
14	Oleg COLTUNOVSCHI		9/2/85	D	1	(1)	
16	Artiom COZACENCO		25/7/92	M	2	(3)	
14	Maxim CRUPENIN		29/4/92	M	13	(1)	
13	Sergiu CUSCEAC		18/6/87	A	4	(11)	
12	Olexandr DEADIK	UKR	17/1/88	G	12	(2)	
5	Gheorghe EREMIA		20/8/87	D	1		
31	Evgeni HMARUC		13/6/77	G	19		
9	Andriy HORDEI	UKR	18/7/88	M	17	(1)	
1	Ivan ILENKIV	UKR	25/5/87	G	1		
2	Petro KLIMAKOV	UKR	26/10/92	D	8		
8	Felix KUIPOU	CMR	8/9/87	D	4	(5)	
10	Lilian LAMBARSCHI			M		(2)	
23	Evghenii LAVRINOVICI		13/10/88	M	21	(6)	
21	Igor LEONOV		28/3/89	M	1	(2)	
18	Evgheny LIVITSCHI		12/10/89	M	12	(3)	
7	Ihor MALIARENKO	UKR	9/10/89	A	24	(5)	3
13	Taras MALIUC		26/10/92	M		(1)	
21	Ilie MOSTOVEI		26/10/89	D	21		
21	Ilie MOSTOVEI		26/10/89	G	1		
11	Renat MURGULET		18/4/89	M	7	(1)	
14	Sergiu ONOFREI		26/11/89	M	2	(1)	
8	Serghei ORLOV		12/8/84	A	3	(1)	
20	Nikolai ORLOVSCHI		1/4/85	D	16		1
11	Veaceslav OZIUM		9/3/92	M	3	(5)	
9	Oleh PAVLIV	UKR	17/1/92	M	11		
18	Ivan PETRUK	UKR	10/8/89	D	3	(16)	
18	Igor POPOV		18/5/88	D	1	(1)	
16	Andrei PRAPORSCIC		24/10/88	D	3	(5)	
11	Maxim REPINETSCHII		2/7/89	D	22		3
3	Andrei RILSCHII		17/10/88	M	10	(7)	
14	Anatoli ROMANCIUC			M		(4)	
19	Vadym SMOLEAK	UKR		M	13	(4)	
6	Alphonse Denis SOPPO	CMR	15/5/85	M	21		1
2	Vladimir SURUCEANU		27/7/85	M	2		
16	François TAMBELL	CMR	25/7/92	M	1		
14	Vadim UCRAINET		9/9/92	M	17	(3)	
11	Alexandru VDOVICENCO		29/6/83	M	11	(2)	1

FC OLIMPIA BALTI
Coach – Valery Pogorelov; (29/7/09) Emil Caras;
(17/8/09) Nicolai Bunea
Founded – 1984
Stadium – Olimpia (7,000)

2009

5/7	Viitorul	h	1-0	Ovseannicov
11/7	Nistru	a	6-0	Ovseannicov 3, Gritiuc, Glega, Tcaciuc
25/7	CSCA-Rapid	a	0-0	
7/8	Sfintul Gheorghe	a	0-0	
16/8	Dinamo	h	3-1	Sosnovschi, Ovseannicov 2
22/8	Iskra-Stal	h	0-1	
30/8	Academia	a	1-2	Gritiuc (p)
12/9	Dacia	h	0-1	
16/9	Zimbru	h	0-0	
20/9	Tiraspol	a	1-0	Somide
26/9	Viitorul	a	1-0	Adaramola
4/10	Nistru	h	3-0	Adaramola, Glega, Somide
18/10	Zimbru	a	4-1	Ovseannicov 3, Glega
24/10	CSCA-Rapid	h	0-2	
28/10	Sheriff	a	0-2	
1/11	Sfintul Gheorghe	h	4-2	Sischin 2 (1p), Glega 2
7/11	Dinamo	a	1-1	Jerome
18/11	Iskra-Stal	a	1-1	Somide

2010				
27/2	Sheriff	h	1-0	Pasecniuc
7/3	Academia	h	2-2	Sischin, Cheltuiala
13/3	Dacia	a	1-1	Jerome
17/3	Tiraspol	h	1-0	Somide
21/3	Tiraspol	h	1-0	Somide
27/3	Dinamo	a	0-0	
3/4	Sfintul Gheorghe	h	2-0	Tcaciuc, Adaramola
10/4	Sheriff	a	0-1	
18/4	Iskra-Stal	h	2-1	Adaramola, Glega
23/4	Dacia	a	4-2	Glega, Sischin 2 (1p), Cheltuiala
2/5	Nistru	h	3-0	Gritiuc 2, Somide
8/5	Zimbru	h	1-0	Glega
15/5	CSCA-Rapid	a	0-0	
19/5	Academia	h	1-0	Tcaciuc
23/5	Viitorul	a	0-2	

No	Name	Nat	DoB	Pos	Aps	(s)	Gls
30	Julius Olumide ADARAMOLA	NGA	4/4/90	M	28	(3)	4
11	Vitaliy BAZAN	UKR	11/10/85	M	5	(2)	
20	Victor BERCO		20/4/79	M	2	(6)	
18	Evgheny BERUN		18/8/80	M		(1)	
21	Ibrahima Sory CAMARA	GUI	6/10/92	M	15	(6)	
15	Alexandru CHELTUIALA		5/2/83	M	23	(2)	2
1	Denis CRISTOFOVICI		26/11/86	G	1		
16	Volodymyr DRON	UKR	6/8/85	M	2	(8)	
7	Mykola GLEGA	UKR	19/6/89	M	28	(5)	8
17	Sergiu GRADINARU		22/1/88	M	1	(3)	
22	Serghei GRITIUC		6/4/84	A	20	(12)	4
4	Serghei GUSACOV		6/4/86	D	22	(1)	
20	Evgheny HOROLSKY	UKR	31/8/88	M	1	(3)	
17	Maxim HOVANSCHII		24/2/90	D	10	(1)	
13	Jean-Robens JEROME	HAI	1/1/81	M	13	(10)	2
6	Thomas KOUROUMA	GUI	26/6/92	D	12	(11)	
19	Denis NACONECNII		28/1/89	M	5	(5)	
2	Jude Iloba OGADA	NGA	15/12/89	M	26	(3)	
16	David OGOAZI	NGA	15/12/90	M	1		
5	Nicolai ORLOVSCHI		1/4/85	D	8		
9	Georgy OVSEANNICOV		12/10/85	A	16	(2)	9
32	Mihail PAIUS		6/2/83	G	14		
20	Mihail PASECNIUC		9/3/91	M	4	(13)	1
8	Oleg SISCHIN		7/1/75	M	19		5
25	Oluwawunmi SOMIDE	NGA	16/5/91	A	11	(15)	6
5	Andrian SOSNOVSCHI		13/6/77	D	11		1
14	Andrei TCACIUC		10/2/82	M	16	(11)	3
18	Eduard VALUTA		9/4/79	D	9		
3	Victor VERBETSCHI		3/7/83	D	22	(2)	
32	Mykola ZBARAKH	UKR	25/2/75	G	18		

FC SFINTUL GHEORGHE SURUCENI
Coach – Sergiu Caraman
Founded – 2003
Stadium – Sfintul Gheorghe (1,000)

2009				
5/7	Nistru	h	3-0	(w/o; original result 0-0)
18/7	CSCA-Rapid	h	0-3	
25/7	Sheriff	a	0-2	
2/8	Dinamo	h	2-1	Cricmari, Plamadeala
7/8	Olimpia	h	0-0	
16/8	Iskra-Stal	a	0-1	
22/8	Academia	h	1-3	Plamadeala (p)
26/8	Zimbru	a	1-2	Cricmari
30/8	Dacia	a	0-1	
13/9	Tiraspol	h	2-0	Bogdan, Cricmari
20/9	Viitorul	a	0-1	
26/9	Nistru	a	0-2	
18/10	CSCA-Rapid	a	1-1	Livandovschi
24/10	Sheriff	h	2-5	Vremea, Livandovschi

28/10	Dinamo	a	2-0	Cricmari, Platica
1/11	Olimpia	a	2-4	Platica 2
7/11	Iskra-Stal	h	0-1	
18/11	Academia	a	0-3	
2010				
27/2	Zimbru	h	0-1	
7/3	Dacia	h	0-0	
13/3	Tiraspol	a	0-2	
17/3	Viitorull	h	0-7	
21/3	Iskra-Stal	a	0-5	
27/3	Dacia	h	2-2	Posmac, Bogdan
3/4	Olimpia	a	0-2	
10/4	Zimbru	h	1-5	Vremea
18/4	CSCA-Rapid	a	0-2	
24/4	Academia	h	1-0	Platica
2/5	Viitorul	a	3-3	Platica, Stinga, Plamadeala
8/5	Tiraspol	h	0-0	
15/5	Dinamo	a	3-5	Istrati S. 2, Platica
19/5	Nistru	a	3-1	Stinga, Railean, Istrati S.
23/5	Sheriff	h	0-2	

No	Name	Nat	DoB	Pos	Aps	(s)	Gls
6	Firuz BOBIEV	TJK	18/6/86	M	6	(1)	
19	Dmitrii BOGDAN		4/3/89	D	25		2
16	Sergiu BUGA		1/6/90	D		(5)	
17	Mihai BUZDUGAN		7/5/90	M		(1)	
18	Alexandr CARABULEA		23/9/88	A	7	(9)	
5	Vadim CRICMARI		22/8/88	A	17		4
3	Gheorghe EREMIA		20/8/87	D	20	(5)	
17	Valentin FURDUI		1/9/87	M	2	(4)	
6	Vadym GOSTIEV	UKR	19/1/87	A	7	(8)	
11	Sergiu ISTRATI		7/8/88	A	7	(6)	3
22	Vadim ISTRATI		7/8/88	G	17	(4)	
9	Iurie LIVANDOVSCHI		17/2/88	A	6		2
9	Andrei MARTIN		27/6/74	M	11	(2)	
2	Andrei MOCAN			M	1	(1)	
11	Oleg MOLLA		22/2/86	A	18		
9	Petr OJOG		17/8/90	M	5	(9)	
18	Stanislav PANUTA		15/7/89	M	3	(4)	
7	Vitalie PLAMADEALA		21/1/85	M	30		3
10	Mihai PLATICA		15/3/90	M	28		6
21	Veaceslav POSMAC		7/11/90	D	25	(2)	1
18	Andrei PREPELITA		24/7/89	D	5	(2)	
14	Alexandr RAILEAN		4/10/90	A	3	(13)	1
12	Ion RINBU		3/10/87	G	2	(1)	
3	Dorin ROTARU		23/10/90	M	28		
9	Sergiu RUSU		17/1/89	M	7	(12)	
6	Petru STINGA		17/4/87	M	12	(3)	2
15	Valentin TERNAVSCHI		16/7/88	D	25	(3)	
20	Andrei TODOROV		6/6/89	D	3	(4)	
8	Alexandru VREMEA		3/11/91	M	29	(2)	2
30	Vitaliy ZHEREBKIN	UKR	2/1/87	G	14		

FC SHERIFF
Coach – Leonid Kuchuk (BLR); (9/1/10) Andrei Sosnitskiy (BLR)
Founded – 1997
Stadium – Sheriff (14,000)
MAJOR HONOURS:
Moldovan League – (10) 2001, 2002, 2003, 2004, 2005, 2006, 2007, 2008, 2009, 2010;
Moldovan Cup – (7) 1999, 2001, 2002, 2006, 2008, 2009, 2010.

2009				
10/7	CSCA-Rapid	a	6-0	Bulat, Erokhin 3, Mandricenco, Balima
25/7	Sfintul Gheorghe	h	2-0	Truhanov, Volkov (p)
10/8	Iskra-Stal	h	5-0	Corneencov, Rouamba, Jymmy 2, Balima
22/8	Dacia	h	0-0	

MOLDOVA

30/8	Tiraspol	a	0-1	
7/9	Dinamo	h	5-0	Kuchuk 3, Volkov, Diedhiou
13/9	Viitorul	h	3-0	Erokhin, Volkov, Da Costa
22/9	Nistru	a	1-0	Erokhin
26/9	Zimbru	a	0-1	
6/10	CSCA-Rapid	h	1-0	Erokhin
11/10	Sfintul Gheorghe	a	5-2	Kuchuk 2, Diedhiou 2, Bulat
18/10	Dinamo	a	5-0	Erokhin, Diedhiou, Kuchuk 2 (1p), Jymmy
28/10	Olimpia	h	2-0	Balima, Suvorov
1/11	Iskra-Stal	a	1-0	Erokhin
10/11	Academia	h	1-0	Branković
18/11	Dacia	a	2-1	Nádson, Jymmy
26/11	Academia	a	0-0	
7/12	Zimbru	h	3-0	Branković, Volkov, Arbănaş
2010				
27/2	Olimpia	a	0-1	
7/3	Tiraspol	h	2-0	og (Iastrebov), Gheorghiev
13/3	Viitorul	a	3-0	Diedhiou, Bulat, Jymmy
17/3	Nistru	h	5-0	Adamović, Volkov 3, Erokhin
21/3	Nistru	h	4-0	Jymmy 3 (1p), Adamović
26/3	Iskra-Stal	h	3-0	Jymmy, Bulat, Đurović
3/4	Dacia	a	0-0	
10/4	Olimpia	h	1-0	Jymmy
18/4	Zimbru	a	1-0	Rouamba
24/4	CSCA-Rapid	h	3-1	Erokhin, Gheorghiev, Nikolić
2/5	Academia	a	1-0	Erokhin
8/5	Viitorul	h	3-1	Jymmy, Hoderean, Volkov
15/5	Tiraspol	a	2-0	og (Celeadnic), Nádson
19/5	Dinamo	h	3-0	Jymmy 2 , Diedhiou
23/5	Sfintul Gheorghe	a	2-0	Branković, Nádson

No	Name	Nat	DoB	Pos	Aps	(s)	Gls
44	Miloš ADAMOVIĆ	SRB	19/6/88	M	13	(1)	2
18	Constantin Dorian ARBĂNAŞ	ROU	28/7/83	D	12	(8)	1
14	Wilfried Benjamin BALIMA	BFA	20/3/85	M	14	(4)	3
30	Vladimir BRANKOVIĆ	SRB	22/9/85	D	20	(2)	3
27	Vitalie BULAT		14/9/87	M	13	(7)	4
7	Andrei CORNEENCOV		1/4/82	M	9	(1)	1
23	Vadim COSTANDACHI		22/9/91	M	1	(0)	
2	Sérgio Rafael DA COSTA	BRA	17/9/85	D	9	(3)	1
21	Amath André DIEDHIOU	SEN	19/11/89	A	17	(9)	6
13	Serghei DULGHIER		21/3/91	D	3	(2)	
19	Marko ĐUROVIĆ	MNE	2/5/88	M	2	(6)	1
10	Aleksandr EROKHIN	RUS	13/10/89	A	23	(5)	11
26	Serghei GHEORGHIEV		20/10/91	M	11	(3)	2
16	Artem HACATUROV		18/6/92	M	8	(5)	
23	Eduard HODEREAN		7/1/90	M	1	(7)	1
9	JYMMY Douglas França	BRA	15/4/84	A	16	(5)	13
15	Igor KARPOVICH	BLR	2/8/88	D	5	(3)	
11	Žarko KORAĆ	MNE	11/6/87	A	3	(5)	
88	Aleksei KUCHUK	BLR	9/9/86	A	7	(7)	7
24	Abdul Gafar MAMAH	TOG	24/8/85	D	7	(1)	
8	Constantin MANDRICENCO		19/2/91	A	1	(1)	1
25	Alexandru MELENCIUC		20/3/79	G	11		
28	José NÁDSON Fereira	BRA	18/10/84	D	20	(1)	3
1	Stanislav NAMASCO		10/11/86	G	7		
7	Baćo NIKOLIĆ	MNE	19/1/86	M	2	(5)	1
22	Luis Antonio RODRÍGUEZ	ARG	4/3/85	D	12	(2)	
17	Florent ROUAMBA	BFA	31/12/86	M	16	(6)	2
26	Miral SAMARDŽIĆ	SVN	17/2/87	D	5	(2)	
6	Alexandru SCRIPCENCO		13/1/91	D	3	(2)	
1	Dumitru STAJILA		2/8/91	G	6		
25	Vladislav STOYANOV	BUL	8/6/87	G	9		
11	Alexandru SUVOROV		2/2/87	M	8	(5)	1
5	Vaja TARKHNISHVILI	GEO	25/8/71	D	29		
19	Victor TRUHANOV		30/1/91	M	2	(2)	1
20	Rustam TSYNYA	UKR	17/6/91	D	12	(4)	
4	Andrei VERBETCHI		21/7/89	D	8	(5)	
5	Vladimir VOLKOV	SRB	6/6/86	M	18	(10)	8

FC TIRASPOL

Coach – Iury Blonari
Founded – 2001
Stadium – Sheriff (14,000)

2009				
5/7	Iskra-Stal	a	0-1	
11/7	Academia	h	1-1	Fred
26/8	Dacia	a	0-1	
25/7	Dinamo	a	1-2	Cheptine
2/8	Viitorul	h	0-0	
7/8	Nistru	a	1-1	Vornisel
18/8	Zimbru	h	1-0	Pascenco
22/8	CSCA-Rapid	a	2-1	Vornisel, Bondarciuc
30/8	Sheriff	h	1-0	Pascenco
12/9	Sfintul Gheorghe	a	0-2	
20/9	Olimpia	h	0-1	
26/9	Iskra-Stal	h	0-0	
4/10	Academia	a	1-1	Fred
18/10	Dacia	h	0-3	
24/10	Dinamo	h	4-1	Hoderean 2, Fred, Procopiev
28/10	Viitorul	a	0-1	
1/11	Nistru	h	1-0	Vornisel
7/11	Zimbru	a	1-1	Cheptine
18/11	CSCA-Rapid	h	0-0	
2010				
7/3	Sheriff	a	0-2	
13/3	Sfintul Gheorghe	h	2-0	Cheptine, Radiola
17/3	Olimpia	a	0-1	
21/3	Olimpia	h	0-1	
27/3	Zimbru	h	0-2	
3/4	CSCA-Rapid	a	1-4	Bondarciuc
10/4	Academia	h	0-0	
18/4	Viitorul	a	0-0	
24/4	Nistru	a	1-0	Bondarciuc
2/5	Dinamo	h	2-0	Vornisel, Bridnea
8/5	Sfintul Gheorghe	a	0-0	
15/5	Sheriff	h	0-2	
19/5	Iskra-Stal	a	0-3	
23/5	Dacia	h	0-0	

No	Name	Nat	DoB	Pos	Aps	(s)	Gls
16	Maxim ALACEV		6/10/90	D	24	(7)	
19	Iury BONDARCIUC		25/2/89	A	13	(12)	3
18	Igor BRIDNEA		20/8/88	A	13	(1)	1
24	Evgheni CELEADNIC		9/10/90	D	4	(3)	
10	Anatoli CHEPTINE		20/5/90	M	26	(5)	3
6	Dmitri CONDARIUC		16/2/90	D	10	(3)	
24	Nélson FRED de Oliveira	BRA	22/7/86	M	32	(1)	3
14	Eduard HODEREAN		7/1/90	M	6	(6)	2
2	Oleg IASTREBOV		30/10/90	D	7	(13)	
21	Vitaliy IEZHOV	UKR	30/8/90	M		(8)	
1	Serghei JURIC		3/3/84	G	23		
11	Gheorghe NICOLOGLO		2/1/91	A	18	(9)	
4	Dmitri NICOLOV		28/1/88	D	9	(1)	
3	Andrei NOVICOV		24/4/86	D	19		
22	Artem OSIPOVS	LVA	8/1/89	A	1	(7)	
7	Alexandr PASCENCO		28/5/89	M	15	(1)	2
13	Djibril PAYE	GUI	26/2/90	D	24		
20	Andrei PORFIREANU		11/5/83	A	13		
9	Alexei PROCOPIEV		15/7/91	A		(15)	1
23	Andrei RADIOLA		13/1/90	D	32		1
8	Eugen SIDORENCO		19/3/89	M	1		
5	Iurii SINITCHIN		9/2/91	D	6	(17)	
15	Ilya SOSHNIN	RUS	10/6/90	D	10	(3)	
12	Victor TRUHANOV		30/1/91	M	3	(6)	
15	Victor VERBETSCHI		3/7/83	D	12		
22	Dmitri VORNISEL		2/2/90	A	32	(1)	4
25	Alexandr ZVEAGHINTEV		26/7/87	G	10		

FC VIITORUL ORHEI
Coach – Igor Oprea
Founded – 2005
Stadium – Municipal (1,000)

2009

5/7	Olimpia	a	0-1	
11/7	Iskra-Stal	h	0-3	
19/7	Academia	a	2-0	Maximov S. 2
25/7	Dacia	h	1-5	Maximov A.
2/8	Tiraspol	a	0-0	
7/8	Dinamo	a	0-1	
16/8	Nistru	h	0-0	
22/8	Zimbru	a	1-1	Maximov A.
30/8	CSCA-Rapid	h	2-2	Maximov A. 2 (1p)
13/9	Sheriff	a	0-3	
20/9	Sfintul Gheorghe	h	1-0	Maximov A.
26/9	Olimpia	h	0-1	
18/10	Academia	h	2-0	Maximov A., Cucu
24/10	Dacia	a	0-2	
28/10	Tiraspol	h	1-0	Maximov A. (p)
1/11	Dinamo	h	3-2	Bacal, Maximov A., Cabac
7/11	Nistru	a	2-0	Maximov A., Josan
11/11	Iskra-Stal	a	0-1	
18/11	Zimbru	h	0-3	

2010

7/3	CSCA-Rapid	a	0-1	
13/3	Sheriff	h	0-3	
17/3	Sfintul Gheorghe	a	7-0	Maximov A., Marian, Cucu 3, Gonta 2
21/3	Zimbru	a	0-1	
27/3	CSCA-Rapid	h	1-0	Cabac
3/4	Academia	a	0-3	
10/4	Nistru	a	1-0	Maximov A. (p)
18/4	Tiraspol	h	0-0	
24/4	Dinamo	a	0-1	
2/5	Sfintul Gheorghe	h	3-3	Maximov A. 2 (1p), Castravet
8/5	Sheriff	a	1-3	Dragovozov
15/5	Iskra-Stal	h	1-3	Marian
19/5	Dacia	a	1-2	Gliga
23/5	Olimpia	h	2-0	Dragovozov, Gonta

No	Name	Nat	DoB	Pos	Aps	(s)	Gls
7	Dumitru BACAL		28/11/84	M	14	(4)	1
1	Gheorghe BANTIS		19/6/89	G	7		
20	Andrei BEREGHICI		9/12/86	M	10	(3)	
5	Mihail CABAC		9/2/86	M	13	(9)	2
15	Ivan CASTRAVET		18/5/88	D	19	(3)	1
22	Andrei COVALIOV		24/5/81	M	1	(9)	
13	Igor CUCERENCO		18/1/89	M		(3)	
6	Alexandru CUCU		28/9/87	M	32		4
16	Vladimir DRAGOVOZOV		1/1/84	A	20	(4)	2
16	Sergiu DUBAC		15/8/85	A		(3)	
12	Vadim GHERASIMOV		22/12/92	A		(9)	
23	Dumitru GLIGA		29/8/84	M	8	(7)	1
18	Victor GONTA		21/9/88	A	2	(10)	3
16	Serghei IEPUREANU		12/9/76	M	14		
11	Alexei JOSAN		28/6/88	M	10	(17)	1
20	Aurel MARDARE		21/8/89	M	1	(1)	
2	Vitalie MARDARI		28/7/79	D	30		
20	Victor MARIAN		10/9/84	M	21	(2)	2
9	Alexandru MAXIMOV		8/7/82	A	29		13
10	Sergiu MAXIMOV		6/7/89	M	5	(13)	2
19	Serghei MOCANU		24/10/87	M	22	(7)	
21	Mihai MORARU		22/10/78	G	13		
1	Adrian PATRAS		28/9/84	G	11		
22	Serghei POJAR		16/4/84	G	2		
20	Vladimir POTLOG		4/4/88	A	4	(2)	
24	Ghenadie SINGUREANU		4/8/86	D	1	(1)	
18	Sergiu SIRBU		1/4/86	D	17		

8	Alexandru STADIICIUC	14/7/81	D	32	
3	Vasile TUGUTSCHI	14/1/87	D	12	
9	Mihai TURCAN	20/8/89	A	4	(10)
4	Alexandr ZISLIS	14/3/86	A	9	(6)

FC ZIMBRU CHISINAU
Coach – Ivan Tabanov
Founded – 1947
Stadium – Zimbru (10,500)
MAJOR HONOURS:
Moldovan League – (8) 1992, 1993, 1994, 1995, 1996, 1998, 1999, 2000;
Moldovan Cup – (5) 1997, 1998, 2003, 2004, 2007.

2009

29/7	Iskra-Stal	h	3-1	Sofroni, Antoniuc A., Catan
2/8	Academia	a	2-2	Andronic O. (p), Demerji
7/8	Dacia	h	2-1	Catan 2
18/8	Tiraspol	a	0-1	
22/8	Viitorul	h	1-1	Catan
26/8	Sfintul Gheorghe	h	2-1	Andronic O., Chirsul
30/8	Nistru	a	0-0	
12/9	Dinamo	a	1-3	Sofroni
16/9	Olimpia	a	0-0	
20/9	CSCA-Rapid	h	0-1	
26/9	Sheriff	h	1-0	Andronic G.
18/10	Olimpia	h	1-4	Antoniuc M.
24/10	Iskra-Stal	a	1-1	Hvorosteanov
28/10	Academia	h	4-1	Andronic G. 2, Antoniuc A., Secrieru
1/11	Dacia	a	0-1	
7/11	Tiraspol	h	1-1	Sofroni
18/11	Viitorul	a	3-0	Sidorenco, Antoniuc A., Sofroni
7/12	Sheriff	a	0-3	

2010

27/2	Sfintul Gheorghe	a	1-0	Secrieru
7/3	Nistru	h	4-1	Bezimov, Secrieru, Nosenco, Andronic O.
13/3	Dinamo	h	3-1	Bezimov, Sosnovschi, Secrieru
17/3	CSCA-Rapid	a	1-0	Sosnovschi
21/3	Viitorul	h	1-0	Andronic O.
27/3	Tiraspol	a	2-0	Hvorosteanov, Sosnovschi (p)
3/4	Dinamo	h	2-0	Bezimov, Secrieru
10/4	Sfintul Gheorghe	a	5-1	Secrieru, Sosnovschi (p), Bezimov, Cojocari, Antoniuc M.
18/4	Sheriff	h	0-1	
24/4	Iskra-Stal	a	0-0	
2/5	Dacia	h	1-0	Sidorenco
8/5	Olimpia	a	0-1	
15/5	Nistru	h	2-1	Antoniuc A., Secrieru
19/5	CSCA-Rapid	h	1-1	Sidorenco
23/5	Academia	a	2-0	Furdui, Nosenco

No	Name	Nat	DoB	Pos	Aps	(s)	Gls
24	Gheorghe ANDRONIC		25/9/91	M	7	(3)	3
6	Igor ANDRONIC		11/3/88	D	7		
10	Oleg ANDRONIC		6/2/89	A	14	(11)	4
11	Kaloyan ANGELOV	BUL	5/8/89	M	4	(8)	
9	Alexandru ANTONIUC		23/5/89	A	26	(3)	4
11	Maxim ANTONIUC		15/1/91	A		(14)	2
16	Eduard AVRAM		5/1/90	M		(1)	
26	Alexandr BELIUGA		2/10/91	D	2	(1)	
10	Victor BERCO		20/4/79	A	6	(1)	
11	Alexandr BEZIMOV		8/2/84	A	10	(5)	4
3	Maxim BOGHIU		24/5/91	D	4	(3)	
3	Ion BOJII		6/4/90	D	3	(2)	
1	Nicolae CALANCEA		29/8/86	G	24		
8	Radu CATAN		30/5/89	M	7	(3)	4
22	Anatol CHIRINCIUC		4/2/89	G	9		
2	Andrei CHIRSUL		20/11/81	D	9		1

MOLDOVA

18	Oleg CLONIN		2/4/88	M	23	(2)	
6	Sergiu COJOCARI		15/5/89	D	9	(7)	1
7	Ion DEMERJI		28/4/89	M	19	(11)	1
14	Iulian ERHAN		1/7/86	D	16		
7	Valentin FURDUI		1/9/87	M	5	(6)	1
15	Piotr HVOROSTEANOV		28/8/86	M	32	(1)	2
5	Vitalie MARDARI		28/7/89	D	1		
7	Sergiu MATEI		23/4/92	A		(1)	
17	Ovidiu MENDIZOV	ROU	9/8/86	M	10	(2)	
8	Maxim MIHALACHI		20/12/90	M		(2)	
5	Denis MOISEI		31/1/91	M		(1)	
1	Adrian NEGAI		28/1/85	G		(1)	
4	Victor NOSENCO		10/5/87	D	14		2
23	Valeriu ONILA		14/4/84	M	3	(3)	
25	Ion POPUSOI		2/2/90	D	1	(2)	
19	Andrei SECRIERU		7/6/84	M	27	(3)	7
20	Eugen SIDORENCO		19/3/89	A	21	(7)	3
14	Sergiu SIRBU		1/4/86	M	9	(3)	
17	Veaceslav SOFRONI		30/4/84	A	14	(4)	4
25	Andrian SOSNOVSCHI		13/6/77	D	13	(4)	4
13	Valentin TERNAVSCHI		16/7/88	D	2		
4	Ivan TESTIMITANU		27/4/74	D	12		
18	Pavel TROFIN		18/11/91	A		(4)	

PROMOTED CLUBS

FC COSTULENI
Coach – Ilie Vieru
Stadium – Municipial, Orhei (3,000)

CF GAGAUZIYA COMRAT
Coach – Oleg Petrov
Stadium – UTM, Chisinau (3,000)

SECOND LEVEL FINAL TABLE 2009/10

		Pld	W	D	L	F	A	Pts
1	FC Costuleni	30	24	2	4	90	27	74
2	RS Lilcora	30	22	6	2	77	32	72
3	CF Gagauziya Comrat	30	18	4	8	62	32	58
4	FC Cahul-2005	30	16	5	9	44	33	53
5	FC Intersport-Aroma Cobusca Noua	30	15	7	8	43	26	52
6	FC Sheriff-2	30	15	6	9	38	26	51
7	FC Zimbru-2 Chisinau	30	14	5	11	44	34	47
8	FC Podis Inesti	30	12	10	8	37	28	46
9	CF Locomotiv	30	13	2	15	47	58	41
10	FC Dinamo-2 Bender	30	10	8	12	42	40	38
11	CS MIPAN Chisinau	30	9	9	12	38	41	36
12	CSCA-Buiucani	30	7	9	14	46	50	30
13	FC Olimp Ungheni	30	6	6	18	34	66	24
14	FC Sfintul Gheorghe-2 Suruceni	30	5	5	20	33	60	20
15	FC Olimpia-2 Tiligul	30	5	4	21	36	82	19
16	FC Academia UTM-2 Chisinau	30	5	0	25	26	102	15

NB RS Lilcora did not receive licence for top division; CF Gagauziya Comrat promoted instead.

DOMESTIC CUP 2009/10

CUPA MOLDOVEI

SECOND ROUND

(16/9/09)
Cahul-2005 1, Sfintul Gheorghe 0
Costuleni 0, CSCA-Rapid 2
Cricova 2, Intersport Aroma 1 *(aet)*
Dava 0, Academia 3
Olimp 1, Locomotiv 1 *(aet; 7-6 on pens)*
Universitatea Agrara 2, Fortuna 1
Victoria 1, Lilcora 3 *(aet)*
Viisoara 1, Viitorul Orhei 2

1/8 FINALS

(30/9/09)
Cricova 0, Dinamo Bender 1
Nistru 0, Academia 2
Olimp 0, Iskra-Stal 1
Olimpia Balti 2, Lilcora 1
Tiraspol 3, Cahul-2005 2 *(aet)*
Viitorul Orhei 0, Dacia Chisinau 2
Zimbru 8, Universitatea Agrara 0

(22/11/09)
Sheriff 5, CSKA-Rapid 0

QUARTER-FINALS

(22/11/09 & 28/11/09)
Dinamo Bender 0, Iskra-Stal 2 *(Svitlichniy 50, 59)*
Iskra-Stal 3 *(Stahiv 45, Burcovschi 80, Svitlichniy 84)*, Dinamo Bender 0
(Iskra-Stal 5-0)

Olimpia Balti 3 *(Ovseannicov 28, Cheltuiala 45, Pasecniuc 60)*, Zimbru 1
(Demerji 1)
Zimbru 0, Olimpia Balti 0
(Olimpia Balti 3-1)

Tiraspol 0, Dacia Chisinau 0
Dacia Chisinau 3 *(Onica 39, Orbu 44, Mekang 81)*, Tiraspol 1 *(Vornisel 87)*
(Dacia Chisinau 3-1)

(23/2/10 & 30/3/10)
Sheriff 0, Academia 0
Academia 0, Sheriff 1 *(Rouamba 94) (aet)*
(Sheriff 1-0)

SEMI-FINALS

(14/4/10 & 28/4/10)
Dacia Chisinau 4 *(Matkevych 38, Guchashvili 41, Orbu 76p, Grozov 79)*,
Olimpia Balti 2 *(Orlovschi 45, Camara 71)*
Olimpia Balti 0, Dacia Chisinau 1 *(Bulat 40)*
(Dacia Chisinau 5-2)

Sheriff 0, Iskra-Stal 0
Iskra-Stal 1 *(Kilikevych 43)*, Sheriff 1 *(Jymmy 83)*
(1-1; Sheriff on away goal)

FINAL

(30/5/10)
Zimbru stadium, Chisinau
FC SHERIFF 2 *(Jymmy 27, 52)*
FC DACIA CHISINAU 0
Referee – Banari
SHERIFF – Stoyanov, Branković, Samardžić, Tarkhnishvili, Volkov (Nikolić 90+3), Gheorghiev, Balima, Rouamba, Bulat (Haciaturov 46), Jymmy (Đurović 65), Erokhin (Adamović 90).
DACIA CHISINAU – Matiughin, Mekang (Molla 80), Popovici, Caraulan, Negrescu, Gorceac, Soimu (Akhilgov 67), Grosev (Bursuc 76), Bulat, Orbu (Dezire 67), Guchashvili.

Redoubtable Rudar land historic double

The fourth staging of Montenegro's Prva Liga produced a fourth different champion as FK Rudar Pljevlja succeeded FK Zeta, FK Budućnost Podgorica and FK Mogren on to the winner's podium. It was a particularly momentous season for the small-town club from the north as they added victory in the Montenegrin Cup to become the newly formed nation's first double winners.

A mere fifth in 2008/09, 33 points in arrears of champions Mogren, Rudar recruited ex-FK Grbalj coach Nebojša Vignjević, and with his fellow Serbian Predrag Ranđelović, the club captain, consistently finding the net in the early rounds, Rudar established a firm foothold in the title race. By the end of the autumn schedule they had won 13 of their 17 games and were level at the top of the table alongside pre-season title favourites Budućnost, with the rest of the field, led by Mogren, too far adrift to contend.

Record-setting run

Budućnost, also led by a Serbian, Mihailo Ivanović, had rattled off a new league record of nine successive victories following a 1-0 away defeat to Rudar, but they could only draw the re-match with their rivals 0-0 in Podgorica and when the competition resumed after the winter break, with financial constraints beginning to bite, they looked edgy and short of confidence, losing their first game back at home to lowly FK Mornar and, a month later, going down 2-1 in Pljevlja in their third meeting with Rudar – a result that enabled their victors to go five points clear.

Rudar lost 3-2 to Zeta four days later but thereafter they proved to be redoubtable front-runners. Budućnost, increasingly feeling the pinch on and off the field, changed their coach, replacing Ivanović with newcomer Nenad Vukčević, but they were unable to keep pace with the leaders and when they fell to their first defeat under Vukčević, 0-2 at FK Sutjeska, the race was over. Rudar, despite losing themselves, 0-2 at FK Berane, had an unassailable seven-point lead with two games to go. The title was theirs.

Four days later the two title rivals met again, in the Montenegrin Cup final. It was the perfect opportunity for Budućnost to get their revenge, particularly as the game took place in their home stadium, but whereas the team from the capital were under pressure to save their season, the newly crowned champions were relaxed and fearless. The outcome was effectively decided in the first five minutes as Budućnost skipper Goran Perišić was red-carded for a foul in the penalty area and his Rudar counterpart Ranđelović converted the ensuing spot-kick. Rudar went on to win 2-1 and regain the trophy they had won three years earlier, making them the first club in Montenegro to win three trophies.

Top man Ranđelović

The only member of Rudar's starting line-up to have survived from the 2007 Cup final win was their outstanding young centre-back Mijuško Bojović – arguably the club's second most important contributor to the double triumph after Ranđelović, whose final tally of league goals came to 19 – one short of the Prva Liga's 2009 Player of the Year Ivan Vuković, who struck 20 times for Budućnost, and nine behind the hyper-prolific Ivan Bošković of Grbalj.

Four of Bošković's Golden Boot-winning haul came in the final day as Grbalj sent relegated FK Kom packing with an 11-0 rout. Kom took the field with a second-string team, raising the number of players used during their campaign to over 50. Berane joined them in the second division after losing their promotion/relegation play-off against OFK Bar, who thus went up with automatically promoted FK Mladost

Rudar skipper and top scorer Predrag Ranđelović

MONTENEGRO

Podgorica. Mornar won the other-play-off, against FK Bratstvo, to retain their top-flight status.

Montenegro's 2010 FIFA World Cup qualifying campaign ended with a couple of positive results – a first competitive victory, 2-1 at home to Georgia, followed by a 0-0 draw in Dublin – but it was not enough to keep coach Zoran Filipović in his job. Montenegrin Football Association (FSCG) president Dejan Savićević decided it was time for a change and appointed Zlatko Kranjčar, the ex-Croatia coach, as his replacement. The 53-year-old, who led his homeland to the 2006 World Cup, did not get off to the best of starts, losing each of his first three games, against the Former Yugoslav Republic of Macedonia (FYROM), Albania and Norway – although, in his defence, he was without two key men in midfielder Nikola Drinčić and the 2009 Montenegrin Footballer of the Year Stevan Jovetić.

Futbalski savez Crne Gore (FSCG)

Ulica 19. dicembra bb
ME-81000 Podgorica
tel - +382 20 445 600
fax - +382 20 445 660
website – fscg.co.me
email – info@fscg.co.me
Year of Formation – 1931

President – Dejan Savićević
General Secretary – Momir Đurđevac
Media Officer – Ivan Radović
National Stadium – Gradski, Podgorica (12,000)

TOP FIVE ALL-TIME CAPS
Vukašin Poleksić (22); Savo Pavićević & Simon Vukčević (20); Radoslav Batak & Vladimir Božović (19)
TOP FIVE ALL-TIME GOALS
Mirko Vučinić (9); Stevan Jovetić (6); Radomir Đalović (4); Igor Burzanović & Dejan Damjanović (2)

NATIONAL TEAM RESULTS 2009/10

12/8/09	Wales	H	Podgorica	2-1	Jovetić (31p), Đalović (45)
5/9/09	Bulgaria (WCQ)	A	Sofia	1-4	Jovetić (9)
9/9/09	Cyprus (WCQ)	H	Podgorica	1-1	Vučinić (56p)
10/9/09	Georgia (WCQ)	H	Podgorica	2-1	Batak (14), Delibašić (78)
14/10/09	Ireland (WCQ)	A	Dublin	0-0	
18/11/09	Belarus	H	Podgorica	1-0	Vučinić (80)
3/3/10	FYROM	A	Skopje	1-2	Baša (62)
25/5/10	Albania	H	Podgorica	0-1	
29/5/10	Norway	A	Oslo	1-2	Vučinić (81)

NATIONAL TEAM APPEARANCES 2009/10

Coach – Zoran FILIPOVIĆ 6/2/53
/(5/2/10) Zlatko KRANJČAR (CRO) 15/11/56

			Wal	BUL	CYP	GEO	IRL	Blr	Mkd	Alb	Nor	Caps	Goals
Vukašin POLEKSIĆ	30/8/82	Debrecen (HUN)	G46	G	G	G	G		G46		G	22	-
Savo PAVIĆEVIĆ	11/12/80	Energie (GER) /Kavala (GRE)	D		D	D		D		D	D70	20	-
Miodrag DŽUDOVIĆ	6/9/79	Spartak Nalchik (RUS)	D	D		s31	D90		D	D		8	1
Radoslav BATAK	15/8/77	Antalyaspor (TUR)	D65		D	D31	D46		D	D46		19	1
Milan JOVANOVIĆ	21/7/83	Rapid Wien (AUT)	D		s46	D	D	D	D	D67		18	-
Nikola DRINČIĆ	7/9/84	Amkar (RUS)	M	M	M	M	M	M				18	1
Milorad PEKOVIĆ	5/8/77	Mainz (GER) /Fürth (GER)	M59	M66	M70		M	M78	M	s62	M	17	-
Vladimir BOŽOVIĆ	13/11/81	Rapid Bucureşti (ROU)	M67	M58					M62	M87		19	-
Simon VUKČEVIĆ	29/1/86	Sporting (POR)	M80	M	M	M	M	M90	M60	M	M59	20	-
Radomir ĐALOVIĆ	29/10/82	Rapid Bucureşti (ROU) /Rijeka (CRO)	A68						s46	s46	A70	A	14	4
Stevan JOVETIĆ	2/11/89	Fiorentina (ITA)	A	A	A	A						13	6
Mladen BOŽOVIĆ	1/8/84	Partizan (SRB)	s46						G46	s46	G	8	-
Mladen KAŠĆELAN	13/2/83	Łódź (POL) /Karpaty (UKR) /Jagiellonia (POL)	s59			s62	s71	s81	s86	M65	M46	s70	9	-
Luka PEJOVIĆ	31/7/85	Mogren	s65	D	D	D46			s46	D77		s67	18	-
Nemanja NIKOLIĆ	1/1/88	Crvena zvezda (SRB)	s67									1	-

NATIONAL TEAM APPEARANCES 2009/10 (contd.)

			Wal	BUL	CYP	GEO	IRL	Blr	Mkd	Alb	Nor	Caps	Goals
Fatos BEĆIRAJ	5/5/88	Budućnost Podgorica	s68							s70	s87	5	-
Mitar NOVAKOVIĆ	27/9/81	Amkar (RUS)	s80			M71	M			M74	M56	12	-
Marko BAŠA	29/12/82	Lokomotiv Moskva (RUS)	D73	D	D	D			D			7	1
Dejan DAMJANOVIĆ	27/7/86	FC Seoul (KOR)	A	s70	A61	s69				A46		7	2
Branko BOŠKOVIĆ	21/6/80	Rapid Wien (AUT)	s58	M62	M	M81	M46	M				18	1
Mirko VUČINIĆ	1/10/83	Roma (ITA)	s66	A					A83	A	A	18	9
Ivan FATIĆ	21/8/88	Genoa (ITA)	s73	D							s83	4	-
Elsad ZVEROTIĆ	31/10/86	Luzern (SUI)				D	D	M86	D83	s46	s56	15	-
Andrija DELIBAŠIĆ	24/4/81	Hércules (ESP)				s61	A69		s60	s74	s59	5	1
Srđan BLAŽIĆ	26/11/82	Levadiakos (GRE)							s46			1	-
Ivan VUKOVIĆ	9/2/87	Budućnost Podgorica							s78			1	-
Vladimir GLUŠČEVIĆ	21/10/79	Mogren							s90			1	-
Nikola VUKČEVIĆ	22/3/84	Budućnost Podgorica							s90			1	-
Dejan OGNJANOVIĆ	21/6/78	Smederevo (SRB)								s65		5	-
Slobodan LAKIĆEVIĆ	12/1/88	Budućnost Podgorica								s77		1	-
Ivan DELIĆ	15/2/86	Budućnost Podgorica								s83		2	-
Žarko TOMAŠEVIĆ	22/2/90	Nacional (POR)									s46	1	-

DOMESTIC LEAGUE 2009/10

PRVA LIGA FINAL TABLE

		Pld	Home					Away					Total					Pts
			W	D	L	F	A	W	D	L	F	A	W	D	L	F	A	
1	FK Rudar Pljevlja	33	13	2	2	31	12	9	3	4	25	14	22	5	6	56	26	71
2	FK Budućnost Podgorica	33	13	2	2	41	16	8	4	4	26	19	21	6	6	67	35	69
3	FK Mogren	33	8	6	3	25	12	8	3	5	24	22	16	9	8	49	34	57
4	FK Zeta	33	11	3	3	25	15	6	3	7	18	18	17	6	10	43	33	57
5	FK Grbalj	33	10	3	4	44	19	5	5	6	22	23	15	8	10	66	42	53
6	FK Lovćen	33	10	4	3	18	15	5	3	8	14	22	15	7	11	32	37	52
7	FK Sutjeska	33	10	3	3	26	11	1	4	12	7	25	11	7	15	33	36	40
8	OFK Petrovac	33	5	1	10	19	27	5	5	7	19	22	10	6	17	38	49	36
9	FK Dečić	33	5	5	6	15	18	3	6	8	12	17	8	11	14	27	35	35
10	FK Mornar	33	5	5	6	16	20	4	3	10	13	29	9	8	16	29	49	34
11	FK Berane	33	5	4	7	17	17	3	2	12	11	32	8	6	19	28	49	30
12	FK Kom	33	4	3	9	8	17	1	0	16	8	42	5	3	25	16	59	18

NB FK Mornar - 1 pt deducted.

TOP GOALSCORERS

28 Ivan BOŠKOVIĆ (Grbalj)
20 Ivan VUKOVIĆ (Budućnost)
19 Predrag RANĐELOVIĆ (Rudar)
16 Vladimir GLUŠČEVIĆ (Mogren)
12 Božo MILIĆ (Mogren/Petrovac)
11 Žarko KORAĆ (Zeta)
10 Fatos BEĆIRAJ (Budućnost)
9 Marko LALEVIĆ (Berane)
  Igor MATIĆ (Grbalj)
7 Nenad VASIĆ (Grbalj)
  Marko ĐUROVIĆ (Lovćen)
  Ivan JABLAN (Lovćen)
  Miloš ĐALAC (Mornar/Berane)
  Aleksandar MADŽAR (Mornar)
  Luka ROTKOVIĆ (Petrovac)
  Krsto ZVICER (Sutjeska)

CLUB-BY-CLUB

FK BERANE
Coach – Dragan Lacmanović; (30/3/10) Predrag Pejović
Founded – 1920
Stadium – Gradski (7,000)

2009

8/8	Sutjeska	h	2-1	Lutovac (p), Lalević
15/8	Dečić	a	1-2	Aković
21/8	Budućnost	h	1-3	Ćulafić
29/8	Rudar	h	0-1	
10/9	Mornar	a	2-0	Žižić, Lalević
19/9	Grbalj	h	2-2	Lalević, Radović
26/9	Lovćen	a	1-2	Šćekić A.
30/9	Zeta	h	1-2	Lalević
3/10	Mogren	a	0-4	
17/10	Kom	h	3-0	Zejnilović, Ćulafić 2
24/10	Petrovac	a	2-1	Bulić, Lalević
31/10	Sutjeska	a	0-1	
7/11	Dečić	h	1-0	Zejnilović
21/11	Budućnost	a	1-2	Lalević
28/11	Rudar	a	0-1	
5/12	Mornar	h	1-2	Ćulafić
12/12	Grbalj	a	0-5	

MONTENEGRO

2010

27/2	Lovćen	h	1-2	Đalac
6/3	Zeta	a	0-1	
13/3	Mogren	h	0-0	
17/3	Kom	a	3-2	Lalević 2, Peličić
20/3	Petrovac	h	1-1	Vukićević
27/3	Mogren	a	0-2	
31/3	Lovćen	h	1-0	Lalević
3/4	Grbalj	a	0-5	
10/4	Dečić	h	1-1	Đalac
17/4	Sutjeska	a	0-0	
24/4	Kom	a	0-0	
1/5	Petrovac	h	0-1	
8/5	Mornar	a	1-2	Radović
15/5	Rudar	h	2-0	Tintor 2
22/5	Budućnost	a	0-2	
29/5	Zeta	h	0-1	

Name	Nat	DoB	Pos	Aps	(s)	Gls
Slobodan AKOVIĆ		4/7/77	M	31		1
Igor ASANOVIĆ		6/9/92	G	1		
Kosta BAJOVIĆ		16/8/80	M		(1)	
Radosav BULIĆ		2/1/76	M	10	(4)	1
Mijat ČAJEVIĆ		31/3/90	D	9	(1)	
Emir ČEKIĆ		30/12/84	M	8	(4)	
Boris CIMBALJEVIĆ		23/10/88	D	20	(5)	
Danilo ĆULAFIĆ		1/8/86	M	15	(2)	4
Miloš ĐALAC		17/10/82	A	13	(2)	2
Saša JANAČKOVIĆ		17/2/91	A	6	(6)	
Marko LALEVIĆ		31/7/82	A	28		9
Stefan LUTOVAC		10/5/86	D	7		1
Đuro MILANOVIĆ		7/7/91	D	1	(1)	
Nikola MILIĆ		20/7/90	M	4	(8)	
Saša MIŠIĆ		24/8/87	G	13		
Haris PAČARIZ		25/9/90	D	1	(2)	
Miljan PAUNOVIĆ		19/7/92	A	3	(1)	
Vladan PELIČIĆ		24/7/89	D	13		1
Ranko PEŠIĆ		12/1/78	D	18	(1)	
Bojan PETROVIĆ	SRB	24/7/84	G	11		
Vladan RADOVIĆ		8/3/91	A	7	(15)	2
Mihailo RADULOVIĆ		8/3/87	G	8		
Novak RAJKOVIĆ		24/7/90	A	1	(5)	
Branislav ROSIĆ	SRB	24/2/82	M	4	(1)	
Armin RUGOVAC		2/10/91	D		(1)	
Aleksandar ŠĆEKIĆ		12/12/91	M	21	(1)	1
Milan ŠĆEKIĆ		25/9/92	D	2	(1)	
Goran STOJKOVIĆ	SRB	6/12/83	D	14		
Vladimir TINTOR	SRB	1/9/79	M	13	(2)	2
Nikola TOMOVIĆ		30/6/92	M	22	(8)	
Bojan VEKOVIĆ		20/8/87	M		(1)	
Darko VUČETIĆ		24/7/90	D	16	(2)	
Nikola VUČINIĆ		23/6/93	M	5	(6)	
Dragoslav VUKIĆEVIĆ		5/4/90	A	11	(7)	1
Branko VUKOVIĆ		13/12/91	D		(1)	
Admir ZEJNILOVIĆ		25/11/86	M	13	(1)	2
Gojko ŽIŽIĆ		17/4/89	D	14	(1)	1

FK BUDUĆNOST PODGORICA
Coach – Mihailo Ivanović (SRB);
(2/4/10) Nenad Vukčević & Radislav Dragićević
Founded – 1925
Stadium – Gradski (12,000)
MAJOR HONOURS:
Montenegrin League - (1) 2008.

2009

8/8	Dečić	a	1-0	Kudemor
14/8	Zeta	h	4-2	Vukčević P., Vuković (p), Ćetković 2
21/8	Berane	a	3-1	Vuković, Delić, Ajković
28/8	Mogren	h	1-2	Bećiraj
11/9	Rudar	a	0-1	
19/9	Kom	h	3-0	Kudemor 2, Vuković
26/9	Mornar	a	3-2	Vuković, Vukčević N. 2
30/9	Petrovac	h	3-2	Ćetković, Vuković, Delić
4/10	Grbalj	a	4-0	Vuković 2, Delić, Bećiraj
17/10	Sutjeska	h	2-1	Vuković 2 (1p)

24/10	Lovćen	a	2-1	Vuković 2 (1p)
31/10	Dečić	h	2-1	Ćetković, Bećiraj
8/11	Zeta	a	4-2	Bećiraj, Vukčević N. 2, Vešović
21/11	Berane	h	2-1	Vuković, Ćetković
29/11	Mogren	a	0-0	
5/12	Rudar	h	0-0	
12/12	Kom	a	1-0	Bećiraj

2010

27/2	Mornar	h	0-2	
6/3	Petrovac	a	1-1	Vuković (p)
13/3	Grbalj	h	4-1	Delić, og (Čabarkapa), Vuković, Đurišić
17/3	Sutjeska	a	1-3	Vuković
20/3	Lovćen	h	3-1	Kudemor 2, Vuković
27/3	Mornar	h	4-0	Delić 2, Bećiraj 2
31/3	Rudar	a	1-2	Mazić
3/4	Kom	h	3-1	Radulović Milan, Vuković, Bošković
10/4	Zeta	h	3-1	Bećiraj 2, Vuković
18/4	Mogren	a	2-2	Đokaj, Nikač
24/4	Lovćen	h	4-0	Stolica 3 (1p), Bećiraj
1/5	Grbalj	a	1-1	Đokaj (p)
8/5	Dečić	h	1-1	Mazić
15/5	Sutjeska	a	0-2	
22/5	Berane	h	2-0	Bošković, Golubović
29/5	Petrovac	a	2-1	Vuković 2

No	Name	Nat	DoB	Pos	Aps	(s)	Gls
5	Goran ADAMOVIĆ	SRB	24/4/87	D	19	(2)	
6	Dražen AJKOVIĆ		25/8/85	M	17	(3)	1
25	Fatos BEĆIRAJ		5/5/88	A	25	(5)	10
20	Dragan BOŠKOVIĆ		27/12/85	A	13	(11)	2
10	Nenad BRNOVIĆ		18/1/80	M	27	(1)	
42	Đorđije ĆETKOVIĆ		3/1/83	A	5	(10)	5
7	Ivan DELIĆ		15/2/86	M	17	(3)	6
1	Miloš DRAGOJEVIĆ		2/2/89	G	1	(1)	
8	Ardian ĐOKAJ		25/3/79	A	5	(4)	2
11	Milan ĐURIŠIĆ		11/4/87	M	7	(12)	1
21	Radivoje GOLUBOVIĆ		22/4/90	D	4	(4)	1
23	Abraham KUDEMOR	GHA	25/2/85	M	24		5
3	Slobodan LAKIĆEVIĆ		12/1/88	D	10	(1)	
3	Slobodan MAZIĆ	SRB	15/11/77	D	29		2
27	Stefan MUGOŠA		26/2/92	A	4	(4)	
28	Darko NIKAČ		15/9/90	A	3	(7)	1
22	Jovan NIKOLIĆ		21/7/91	M	2	(2)	
30	Adnan ORAHOVAC		15/1/91	D		(1)	
4	Goran PERIŠIĆ		6/12/76	D	9	(5)	
17	Milan RADULOVIĆ		18/8/81	D	22	(1)	1
16	Mileta RADULOVIĆ		29/1/81	G	18		
9	Ilija STOLICA	SRB	7/7/79	A	9	(1)	3
29	Marko VEŠOVIĆ		28/8/91	M		(5)	1
15	Marko VIDOVIĆ		30/6/88	D		(1)	
36	Nenad VIŠNJIĆ	SRB	25/4/83	D	4	(2)	
21	Miroslav VUJADINOVIĆ		22/4/83	G	14		
2	Nikola VUKOVIĆ		22/3/84	D	23	(1)	4
14	Petar VUKČEVIĆ		15/8/87	M	25	(3)	1
24	Ivan VUKOVIĆ		9/2/87	M	27	(1)	20

FK DEČIĆ
Coach – Ivan Čančarević; (26/12/09) Aleksandar Miljenović;
(5/1/10) Slaviša Božičić
Founded – 1920
Stadium – Tuzi (1,000)

2009

8/8	Budućnost	h	0-1	
15/8	Berane	h	2-1	Grbović, Kuč
22/8	Rudar	a	1-1	Tomić
29/8	Mornar	h	0-0	
12/9	Grbalj	h	0-0	
19/9	Lovćen	h	2-1	Lekić (p), Spnulović
26/9	Zeta	a	1-2	Idrizović
30/9	Mogren	h	1-1	Spnulović
3/10	Kom	a	1-0	Idrizović
17/10	Petrovac	h	0-0	
24/10	Sutjeska	a	0-2	
31/10	Budućnost	a	1-2	Đoković Ed.

7/11	Berane	a	0-1	
21/11	Rudar	h	0-1	
28/11	Mornar	a	0-0	
5/12	Grbalj	h	1-3	Lekić
12/12	Lovćen	a	1-1	Ljumić
2010				
27/2	Zeta	h	0-2	
6/3	Mogren	a	2-0	Krstović (p), Čarapić
13/3	Kom	h	2-1	Todorović, Lekić
17/3	Petrovac	a	3-1	Živković, Grbović, Ljumić
20/3	Sutjeska	h	0-0	
27/3	Grbalj	a	0-1	
31/3	Kom	a	0-1	
3/4	Sutjeska	h	1-0	Čarapić
10/4	Berane	a	1-1	Mihailović
17/4	Petrovac	h	2-3	Lekić, Ljumić
24/4	Mornar	a	0-2	
1/5	Rudar	h	2-2	Mihailović, Đoković A.
8/5	Budućnost	a	1-1	Ljumić
15/5	Zeta	h	2-1	Popović, Mihailović
22/5	Mogren	a	0-1	
29/5	Lovćen	h	0-1	

Name	Nat	DoB	Pos	Aps	(s)	Gls
Ivan ČARAPIĆ		8/2/82	D	12	(1)	2
Vedad DREŠEVIĆ		22/8/80	G	28		
Adis ĐOKOVIĆ		25/8/91	A	5	(16)	1
Edin ĐOKOVIĆ		14/12/84	M	12		1
Enis ĐOKOVIĆ		27/2/87	G	5	(1)	
Hasim ĐOKOVIĆ		20/5/78	D	4	(9)	
Ikechukwu EZEH	NGA	20/12/87	A	8	(7)	
Boris GRBOVIĆ		31/1/80	D	26	(1)	2
Ferid IDRIZOVIĆ	BIH	10/9/82	M	14	(1)	2
Kristijan KRSTOVIĆ		9/7/89	M	13	(1)	1
Igor KUČ		10/7/84	D	16		1
Edin LEKIĆ		23/6/79	M	21	(1)	4
Mirza LJUMIĆ		5/8/81	A	9	(13)	4
Minja LJUMOVIĆ		12/9/82	M	2	(2)	
Nikola MIHAILOVIĆ		15/9/84	D	22		3
Vladimir MILJKOVIĆ	SRB	1/7/84	M	9	(5)	
Amar NUHODŽIĆ		12/9/90	M	14	(3)	
Njazim PADOVIĆ		19/11/87	D	23	(1)	
Rijad PEPIĆ		19/9/91	M		(6)	
Davor POPOVIĆ		18/7/85	D	22	(3)	1
Miladin RADOVIĆ		1/9/82	M	9	(6)	
Demir RAMOVIĆ		3/1/81	D	17	(1)	
Nikola ROGOŠIĆ		22/5/80	D	18	(3)	
Predrag SPNULOVIĆ	SRB	17/9/84	M	14	(1)	2
Mirko TODOROVIĆ	SRB	22/8/85	D	14		1
Željko TOMIĆ		26/8/84	M	6	(3)	1
Miloš VRANJEŠ		27/7/88	M	8	(4)	
Marko ŽIVKOVIĆ	SRB	1/6/83	M	12		1

FK GRBALJ
Coach – Saša Petrović
Founded – 1970
Stadium – Radanovici (1,500)

2009				
7/8	Mogren	h	2-4	Bošković I., Grujić
15/8	Kom	a	0-1	
22/8	Petrovac	h	2-0	Bošković I. 2 (1p)
29/8	Sutjeska	a	2-2	Matić, Bošković I.
12/9	Dečić	h	0-0	
19/9	Berane	a	2-2	Vasić, Bošković I.
26/9	Rudar	h	4-2	Bošković I. 2, Matić 2
30/9	Mornar	a	3-3	Bošković I., Matić, Radulović
4/10	Budućnost	h	0-4	
17/10	Lovćen	h	4-0	Matić 2, Bošković I. (p), Kajević
24/10	Zeta	a	0-1	
1/11	Mogren	a	2-0	Bošković I. 2
7/11	Kom	h	1-0	Simunović
21/11	Petrovac	a	2-0	Matić, Radusinović
28/11	Sutjeska	h	0-0	
5/12	Dečić	a	3-1	Popović, Bošković I. 2 (1p)
12/12	Berane	h	5-0	Bošković I. 3 (1p), Matić, Kasom

2010				
27/2	Rudar	a	0-1	
6/3	Mornar	h	2-0	Bošković I. 2 (2p)
13/3	Budućnost	a	1-4	Vasić
17/3	Lovćen	a	0-0	
20/3	Zeta	h	0-2	
27/3	Dečić	h	1-0	Franišković
31/3	Sutjeska	a	2-0	Radulović, Nikezić
3/4	Berane	h	5-0	Bošković I. 3 (1p), Radusinović, Franišković
10/4	Petrovac	a	2-1	Bošković I., Franišković (p)
17/4	Mornar	h	3-1	Nikezić, Vasić 2
24/4	Rudar	a	0-3	
1/5	Budućnost	h	1-1	Simunović
8/5	Zeta	a	2-2	Vasić, Bošković I.
15/5	Mogren	h	3-5	Kasom, Matić, Vasić
22/5	Lovćen	a	1-2	Bošković I.
29/5	Kom	h	11-0	Vasić, Bošković I. 4 (1p), Simunović 2, Nikezić 2, Bošković N., Kajević

Name	Nat	DoB	Pos	Aps	(s)	Gls
Luka BAKOČ		20/9/91	A	2	(6)	
Ivan BOŠKOVIĆ		1/1/81	M	30		28
Nenad BOŠKOVIĆ		17/11/89	M	1	(3)	1
Milan CAREVIĆ		27/2/91	D		(1)	
Boban ČABARKAPA		1/12/87	D	12		
Dalibor ĐUKIĆ		16/9/86	M	9	(4)	
Ivica FRANCIŠKOVIĆ	SRB	28/9/78	M	15	(4)	3
Ilija GLAVAN	BIH	22/11/90	M	1		
Bojan GOLUBOVIĆ		28/11/86	M	30	(1)	
Goran GRUJIĆ	SRB	27/11/82	D	15		1
Milan IVANOVIĆ		6/7/76	D	2	(2)	
Branislav JANKOVIĆ		30/4/91	A	1		
Aleksandar JOVANOVIĆ		1/6/92	D	5	(1)	
Demir KAJEVIĆ		20/4/89	M	24	(4)	2
Nenad KAŠĆELAN		24/8/90	M		(1)	
Petar KASOM		21/12/81	A	1	(17)	2
Nemanja KLJAJEVIĆ		5/3/87	D	6		
Marko KNEŽEVIĆ		18/10/85	G	27		
Miodrag KOPRIVICA		9/4/90	M	1	(4)	
Dušan KOSTIĆ		13/5/90	G	4	(2)	
Stefan LATKOVIĆ		19/4/91	M		(1)	
Lazar MARTINOVIĆ		3/7/89	M	5	(4)	
Vuk MARTINOVIĆ		19/9/89	D	21	(1)	
Igor MATIĆ	SRB	22/7/81	M	25	(2)	9
Zoran MIKIJELJ		23/2/91	D	1		
Dražen MILIĆ		14/9/80	A		(7)	
Bojan MLADENOVIĆ	SRB	5/1/89	D	4	(9)	
Zvonko NEDELJKOVIĆ	SRB	17/11/79	M	3		
Miloš NIKEZIĆ		2/3/87	A	7	(12)	4
Saša POPOVIĆ	SRB	9/9/81	D	12	(2)	1
Nikola RADULOVIĆ		17/12/85	D	25	(4)	2
Igor RADUSINOVIĆ		15/3/84	D	23		2
Nikola ŠEVALJEVIĆ		16/4/83	G	2	(3)	
Andrija SIMUNOVIĆ		21/3/91	M	21		4
Nenad VASIĆ	SRB	28/7/79	A	26	(2)	7
Predrag VIDEKANIĆ		23/8/86	M	2		

FK KOM
Coach – Milija Savović; (5/11/2009) Duško Globarević;
(23/3/10) Milorad Nedović & Filip Jovićević
Founded – 1958
Stadium – na Zlatici (1,000)

2009				
8/8	Mornar	a	3-0	(w/o; original result 0-0)
15/8	Grbalj	h	1-0	Cicmil
22/8	Lovćen	a	0-1	
29/8	Zeta	h	1-0	Tuzović
12/9	Mogren	a	1-3	Novović
19/9	Budućnost	a	0-3	
26/9	Petrovac	h	1-2	og (Mikijelj)
30/9	Sutjeska	a	0-1	
3/10	Dečić	a	0-1	
17/10	Berane	a	0-3	
24/10	Rudar	h	0-2	
31/10	Mornar	h	0-2	

MONTENEGRO

7/11	Grbalj	a	0-1
21/11	Lovćen	h	0-0
28/11	Zeta	a	0-2
5/12	Mogren	h	0-2
12/12	Budućnost	h	0-1
2010			
28/2	Petrovac	a	0-2
7/3	Sutjeska	h	1-0 Petrović
13/3	Dečić	a	1-2 Vemić
17/3	Berane	h	2-3 Bulatović, Vemić
20/3	Rudar	a	0-1
27/3	Rudar	a	0-3
31/3	Dečić	h	1-0 Nelević
3/4	Budućnost	a	1-3 Petrović
10/4	Sutjeska	h	0-1
17/4	Zeta	a	0-2
24/4	Berane	h	0-0
1/5	Mogren	a	1-2 Račić
8/5	Petrovac	h	0-2
15/5	Lovćen	a	1-2 Jovanović S.
22/5	Mornar	h	1-1 Račić
29/5	Grbalj	a	0-11

Name	Nat	DoB	Pos	Aps	(s)	Gls
Zlatan ADROVIĆ		30/11/89	G	12		
Jovan BAOŠIĆ		15/8/92	D		(2)	
Ljubomir BELOJEVIĆ		20/7/85	G	7	(1)	
Nebojsa BRAKOVIĆ		21/11/90	D	5		
Nemanja BULATOVIĆ	SRB	13/8/91	A	3	(4)	1
Boban ČABARKAPA		1/12/87	D	17		
Đorđije ČARAPIĆ		23/8/91	D	1	(1)	
Stefan CICMIL		16/8/90	M	15		1
Mirko ČOLAKOVIĆ		22/9/92	M	9		
Elvis ĆOROVIĆ		19/7/89	D	13	(2)	
Aleksandar DABETIĆ		9/4/91	A	2	(1)	
Željko DAŠIĆ		10/3/88	D	2	(2)	
Nikola DOBROVIĆ		26/2/91	M	1		
Đorđije DRAKULOVIĆ		23/2/85	G	3	(1)	
Mirko DURUTOVIĆ		13/3/89	M	10		
Marko ĐURETIĆ		17/2/86	M	1	(5)	
Igor IVANOVIĆ		5/7/92	D	4	(2)	
Predrag JAREDIĆ		5/10/85	M	9	(1)	
Luka JOVANOVIĆ		27/10/91	D	5		
Stefan JOVANOVIĆ		24/8/90	M	6	(2)	1
Miodrag KARADŽIĆ		20/1/87	M	4		
Srđan KLJAJEVIĆ		23/11/74	G	10		
Veljko KOLINOVIĆ		31/7/91	D	7	(1)	
Kristijan KRSTOVIĆ		9/7/89	M	12	(3)	
Đorđe LUKETA		17/9/92	M		(2)	
Ivan MILIĆ		26/10/84	M	16	(1)	
Luka MILIĆ		9/3/89	A	11	(4)	
Jasmin MUHOVIĆ		27/4/91	M	3	(1)	
Miladin NELEVIĆ		15/3/86	D	17	(1)	1
Vladimir NIKITOVIĆ	SRB	14/12/80	D	10		
Milivoje NOVOVIĆ		29/2/84	D	12	(1)	1
Nikola OSMAJIĆ		18/10/92	A		(4)	
Miloš PAVIĆEVIĆ		16/5/90	A	4	(1)	
Rade PETROVIĆ		21/9/82	M	11		2
Blagota POPOVIĆ		10/2/82	M	9	(4)	
Stefan RAČIĆ		2/7/90	A	11	(10)	2
Dejan RADEVIĆ		15/1/90	M	6		
Ranko RADONJIĆ		6/6/75	M	2	(4)	
Miladin RADOVIĆ		1/9/82	M	5	(1)	
Stefan RADUNOVIĆ		13/9/90	G	1		
Vladimir RAIČKOVIĆ		11/8/84	D	13	(1)	
Dejan SAVIĆ		10/10/93	M	1	(2)	
Milivoje ŠESTOVIĆ		10/2/92	M		(2)	
Đorđije STRUNJAŠ		7/4/90	A	2	(8)	
Filip ŠUNDIĆ		7/3/90	M	24	(3)	
Balša TOMANOVIĆ		15/2/87	M		(2)	
Denis TUZOVIĆ		12/2/88	A	12	(3)	1
Uroš VEMIĆ	SRB	22/1/87	A	7	(1)	2
Nikola VUJISIĆ		16/3/87	M	3	(2)	
Danilo VUKOVIĆ		1/4/89	D		(3)	
Radule ŽIVKOVIĆ		22/5/90	D	24	(5)	
Rajko ŽIVKOVIĆ		8/8/81	M	1		

FK LOVĆEN
Coach – Branislav Milačić
Founded – 1913
Stadium – Obilica poljana (1,500)

2009			
8/8	Zeta	h	2-1 Đurović, Stanojević
15/8	Mogren	a	3-1 Stevović 2, Jablan
22/8	Kom	h	1-0 Đurović
29/8	Petrovac	a	2-0 Đurović 2
12/9	Sutjeska	h	0-0
19/9	Dečić	a	1-2 Stevović
26/9	Berane	h	2-1 Đurović 2
30/9	Rudar	a	1-0 Jablan
3/10	Mornar	h	1-0 Perutović
17/10	Grbalj	a	0-4
24/10	Budućnost	h	1-2 Đurović
31/10	Zeta	a	1-2 Popović
7/11	Mogren	h	0-0
21/11	Kom	a	0-0
29/11	Petrovac	h	1-0 Jablan (p)
5/12	Sutjeska	a	1-1 Radunović M.
12/12	Dečić	h	1-1 Bogdanović
2010			
27/2	Berane	a	2-1 Perutović 2
7/3	Rudar	h	0-3
13/3	Mornar	a	1-1 Jablan
17/3	Grbalj	h	0-0
20/3	Budućnost	a	1-3 Perutović
27/3	Sutjeska	h	3-2 Jablan, Perutović (p), Bogdanović (p)
31/3	Berane	a	0-1
3/4	Petrovac	h	1-0 Tatar
10/4	Mornar	a	0-1
17/4	Rudar	h	0-3
24/4	Budućnost	a	0-4
1/5	Zeta	h	1-0 Pejaković A.
8/5	Mogren	a	0-1
15/5	Kom	h	2-1 Radunović V., Jablan
22/5	Grbalj	h	2-1 Jablan, Tatar
29/5	Dečić	a	1-0 Adrović (p)

Name	Nat	DoB	Pos	Aps	(s)	Gls
Zijad ADROVIĆ		17/2/86	M	30	(1)	1
Dejan BOGDANOVIĆ		8/8/80	M	12	(11)	2
Saša ĆETKOVIĆ		29/5/82	D	26	(1)	
Marko ĐUROVIĆ		8/5/88	A	12	(1)	7
Ivan JABLAN		18/7/79	A	31	(1)	7
Andrija KALUĐEROVIĆ		29/10/93	D	3	(8)	
Marko MARKOVIĆ		5/9/87	A		(3)	
Dušan MARTINOVIĆ		7/8/90	M	1	(5)	
Adnan MAŠIĆ	BIH	12/12/81	M	1	(3)	
Andrija MIRKOVIĆ		13/12/83	M	26		
Luka MIRKOVIĆ		1/11/90	M	5	(4)	
Baćo NIKOLIĆ		19/1/86	M	16	(1)	
Andrija PEJAKOVIĆ		22/2/86	D	11	(11)	1
Ivan PEJAKOVIĆ		28/9/92	M	4	(4)	
Jovan PEROVIĆ		28/12/89	G	25		
Blažo PERUTOVIĆ		8/12/83	A	17	(6)	5
Bracan POPOVIĆ		31/3/82	D	29		1
Mirko RADIŠIĆ		1/9/90	D	4	(5)	
Mihailo RADULOVIĆ		8/3/87	G	8		
Miloš RADUNOVIĆ		7/7/90	D	7	(3)	1
Vladan RADUNOVIĆ		2/1/89	A	6	(11)	1
Miodrag STANOJEVIĆ		19/7/81	D	27		1
Miloš STEVOVIĆ		14/9/89	M	20	(3)	3
Vladan TATAR		28/1/84	D	29		2
Nenad VUJOVIĆ		2/1/89	M	1	(1)	
Stevan VUJOVIĆ		13/12/89	A		(4)	
Luka VUŠUROVIĆ		24/2/90	D	12	(3)	

FK MOGREN

Coach – Dejan Vukićević; (11/4/10) Stevan Mojsilović (SRB)
Founded – 1920
Stadium – Lugovi (3,000)
MAJOR HONOURS:
Montenegrin League - (1) 2009;
Montenegrin Cup - (1) 2008.

2009

7/8	Grbalj	a	4-2	Milić 3, Radonjić
15/8	Lovćen	h	1-3	Milić
22/8	Zeta	a	3-0	Radonjić, Gluščević 2
28/8	Budućnost	a	2-1	Gluščević, Ćetković
12/9	Kom	h	3-1	Janičić 2, Gluscević
19/9	Petrovac	a	2-1	Radonjić 2
26/9	Sutjeska	h	4-0	Gluščević 2, Nuhi, Ćetković
30/9	Dečić	a	1-1	Božović B.
3/10	Berane	h	4-0	Milić 2, Božović D., Gluščević
18/10	Rudar	a	0-2	
24/10	Mornar	h	4-0	Radonjić 2 (1p), Gluščević, Sekulić
1/11	Grbalj	h	0-2	
7/11	Lovćen	a	0-0	
21/11	Zeta	h	0-0	
29/11	Budućnost	h	0-0	
5/12	Kom	a	2-0	Vujović, Gluščević
12/12	Petrovac	h	1-1	Milić

2010

28/2	Sutjeska	a	0-4	
6/3	Dečić	h	0-2	
13/3	Berane	a	0-0	
17/3	Rudar	h	0-0	
20/3	Mornar	a	2-1	Simović, Gluščević
27/3	Berane	h	2-0	Grbić, Jovanović G.
31/3	Petrovac	a	2-1	Grbić, og (Lakić)
3/4	Mornar	h	0-0	
10/4	Rudar	a	1-3	Gluščević (p)
18/4	Budućnost	h	2-2	Božović B., Gluščević
24/4	Zeta	a	0-1	
1/5	Kom	h	2-1	Ćetković, Martinović
8/5	Lovćen	h	1-0	Božović D.
15/5	Grbalj	a	5-3	Nuhi, Grbić, Gluščević 3 (1p)
22/5	Dečić	h	1-0	Gluščević
29/5	Sutjeska	a	0-2	

No	Name	Nat	DoB	Pos	Aps	(s)	Gls
23	Dejan BOLJEVIĆ		5/6/90	M	2	(4)	
28	Balša BOŽOVIĆ		1/5/87	M	15	(14)	2
8	Draško BOŽOVIĆ		30/6/88	M	23		2
31	Nebojša BOŽOVIĆ		5/2/93	M	1		
12	Ivan BUTOROVIĆ		19/8/92	G	1		
30	Marko ĆETKOVIĆ		10/7/86	M	25	(3)	3
9	Vladimir GLUŠČEVIĆ		21/10/79	A	28		16
7	Petar GRBIĆ		7/8/88	M	18	(5)	3
32	Goran IVANOVIĆ		24/9/92	M		(1)	
6	Nemanja JANIČIĆ	BIH	13/7/86	D	24		3
22	Ivan JANJUŠEVIĆ		11/7/87	G	19		
14	Goran JOVANOVIĆ	SRB	8/5/77	M	23		1
29	Miloš JOVANOVIĆ		29/1/88	A	2	(6)	
11	Bojan KALEZIĆ		11/3/88	M	5	(14)	
24	Aleksandar KAPISODA		17/8/89	D	11	(3)	
18	Okica KARADŽIĆ		15/12/92	A	1	(1)	
34	Srđan KOSOVIĆ		2/5/92	M	1		
20	Lazar MARTINOVIĆ		3/7/89	M	2	(9)	1
21	Božo MILIĆ		10/10/81	A	9	(3)	7
40	Dušan MOJSILOVIĆ		26/9/92	M		(1)	
35	Milenko NERIĆ		9/2/88	A	8	(4)	
25	Milko NOVAKOVIĆ		21/1/88	D	4	(2)	
13	Ajazdin NUHI	SRB	10/10/79	M	27	(1)	2
3	Luka PEJOVIĆ		31/7/85	D	29		
1	Nemanja POPOVIĆ		20/5/84	G	13	(2)	
19	Srđan RADONJIĆ		8/5/81	A	13	(2)	6
39	Argzim REDŽOVIĆ		26/2/92	D	1		
17	Radislav SEKULIĆ		27/9/85	A		(10)	1
5	Janko SIMOVIĆ		2/4/87	D	26	(1)	1
36	Merlin SKENDERI		13/1/90	M		(2)	
10	Luka TIODOROVIĆ		21/1/86	M	18	(11)	
26	Vladimir VUJOVIĆ		23/7/82	M	14		1

FK MORNAR

Coach – Mladen Vukićević; (5/1/10) Brajan Nenezić
Founded – 1931
Stadium – Topolica (2,000)

2009

8/8	Kom	h	0-3	(w/o; original result 0-0)
15/8	Petrovac	a	2-4	Madžar, Šofranac
22/8	Sutjeska	h	1-0	Mešter
28/8	Dečić	a	0-0	
10/9	Berane	h	0-2	
19/9	Rudar	a	0-1	
26/9	Budućnost	h	2-3	Rašović 2
30/9	Grbalj	h	3-3	Mirković 2, Mešter
3/10	Lovćen	a	0-1	
17/10	Zeta	h	0-0	
24/10	Mogren	a	0-4	
31/10	Kom	a	2-0	Đalac 2
7/11	Petrovac	h	1-3	Đalac
21/11	Sutjeska	a	2-1	Madžar, Đalac
28/11	Dečić	h	0-0	
5/12	Berane	a	2-1	Đalac, Mirković
12/12	Rudar	h	0-1	

2010

27/2	Budućnost	a	2-0	Jelenić, Marković
6/3	Grbalj	a	0-2	
13/3	Lovćen	h	1-1	Madžar (p)
17/3	Zeta	a	0-1	
20/3	Mogren	h	1-2	Rašović
27/3	Budućnost	a	0-4	
31/3	Zeta	h	0-0	
3/4	Mogren	a	0-0	
10/4	Lovćen	h	1-0	Šofranac
17/4	Grbalj	a	1-3	Madžar
24/4	Dečić	a	2-0	Madžar, Peričić
1/5	Sutjeska	a	0-3	
8/5	Berane	h	2-1	Peričić, Madžar
15/5	Petrovac	a	1-3	Nenezić D.
22/5	Kom	a	1-1	Peričić
29/5	Rudar	h	2-1	Madžar, Peričić

Name	Nat	DoB	Pos	Aps	(s)	Gls
Zlatan ADROVIĆ		27/7/89	G	7		
Nikola ALEKSIĆ		28/3/88	G	11		
Miloš BOKAN		10/7/88	M		(9)	
Igor BUKILIĆ		22/8/87	A	3	(6)	
Valento CAMAJ		17/9/77	A	17	(5)	
Boško DOPUĐ		9/12/90	D	7	(4)	
Miloš ĐALAC		17/10/82	A	12	(2)	5
Aleksandar JELENIĆ		6/12/89	D	10	(12)	1
Benjamin KACIĆ		28/6/91	A	1	(6)	
Srđan KLJAJEVIĆ		23/11/74	G	3		
Igor KUČ		10/6/84	D	6	(1)	
Ilija LALEVIĆ		26/11/87	A	12	(5)	
Aleksandar MADŽAR		23/7/88	A	17	(6)	7
Bogdan MARJANOVIĆ	SRB	3/11/80	D	20		
Danijel MARKOLOVIĆ		21/7/90	A		(1)	
Stevan MARKOVIĆ		31/1/88	D	27		1
Dragan MASONČIĆ		1/11/88	G	12	(1)	
Milan MEŠTER		23/10/75	M	31		2
Borko MILENKOVIĆ	SRB	10/7/84	D	8		
Vuk MIRANOVIĆ		24/4/89	M		(4)	
Ivan MIRKOVIĆ		9/8/81	M	27	(1)	3
Dejan NENEZIĆ		17/11/80	M	15	(6)	1
Marko NENEZIĆ		27/4/82	M	7	(2)	
Ervin PERIČIĆ		7/9/88	M	6	(8)	4
Mihailo PETROVIĆ		12/12/89	D	14	(6)	
Miloš RAŠOVIĆ		4/4/86	A	25	(5)	3
Nenad ŠOFRANAC		20/4/83	M	29		2
Željko TOMAŠEVIĆ		5/4/88	D	24	(1)	
Aleksandar VUJAČIĆ		9/7/90	A		(2)	
Zoran VUKOVIĆ		7/7/79	D	12		

MONTENEGRO

OFK PETROVAC

Coach – Milan Vraneš; (4/12/09) (Minja Prelević);
(25/12/09) Milorad Malovrazić
Founded – 1969
Stadium – Pod Malim brdom (1,500)
MAJOR HONOURS:
Montenegrin Cup - (1) 2009.

2009				
9/8	Rudar	a	1-3	*Divanović (p)*
15/8	Mornar	h	4-2	*Lakić 2, Đurasković, Rotković*
22/8	Grbalj	a	0-2	
29/8	Lovćen	h	0-2	
12/9	Zeta	a	0-2	
19/9	Mogren	h	1-2	*Đurasković*
26/9	Kom	a	2-1	*Radović 2*
30/9	Budućnost	a	2-3	*Divanović, Radović*
3/10	Sutjeska	h	1-0	*Barać*
17/10	Dečić	a	0-0	
24/10	Berane	h	1-2	*Divanović (p)*
31/10	Rudar	h	0-4	
7/11	Mornar	a	3-1	*Dragićević, Barać 2*
21/11	Grbalj	h	0-2	
29/11	Lovćen	a	0-1	
5/12	Zeta	h	0-1	
12/12	Mogren	a	1-1	*Dragićević*
2010				
28/2	Kom	h	2-0	*Milić 2*
6/3	Budućnost	h	1-1	*Graovac*
13/3	Sutjeska	a	0-1	
17/3	Dečić	h	1-3	*Mitić*
20/3	Berane	a	1-1	*Mitić*
27/3	Zeta	a	1-1	*Mikijelj*
31/3	Mogren	h	1-2	*Milić*
3/4	Lovćen	a	0-1	
10/4	Grbalj	h	1-2	*Novović*
17/4	Dečić	a	3-2	*Milić, Rotković 2*
24/4	Sutjeska	h	2-1	*Rotković 2 (1p)*
1/5	Berane	a	1-0	*Barać*
8/5	Kom	a	2-0	*Lakić, Rotković (p)*
15/5	Mornar	h	3-1	*Raičević, Mitić, Milić*
22/5	Rudar	a	2-2	*Mitić, Lopičić*
29/5	Budućnost	h	1-2	*Rotković (p)*

Name	Nat	DoB	Pos	Aps	(s)	Gls
Vladimir BARAĆ	SRB	29/8/81	M	12	(10)	4
Dejan BOLJEVIĆ		30/5/90	M		(4)	
Aleksandar BRAIĆ		19/2/85	G	11		
Miloš DELIĆ		22/5/83	M	1	(2)	
Mehmet DIVANOVIĆ		3/12/84	M	22	(4)	3
Zdravko DRAGIĆEVIĆ		17/6/86	A	23	(2)	2
Stefan ĐORĐEVIĆ		16/11/90	M	2	(4)	
Zoran ĐURAŠKOVIĆ	SRB	7/7/75	A	11	(3)	2
Siniša GRAOVAC		1/9/84	D	25	(2)	1
Miloš LAKIĆ		21/12/85	D	28	(2)	3
Srđan LOPIČIĆ		20/11/83	D	20	(7)	1
Marko LUKATELI		22/10/92	A		(1)	
Goran MARINKOVIĆ	SRB	8/1/79	M	13		
Marko MARKOVIĆ		5/9/87	M	1	(4)	
Aleksandar MIKIJELJ		5/2/79	D	23	(2)	1
Božo MILIĆ		10/10/81	A	13	(1)	5
Saša MITIĆ	SRB	7/12/78	A	11	(3)	4
Dejan MUSTUR		2/12/86	G	14		
Milivoje NOVOVIĆ		29/2/84	D	9	(1)	1
Boban OBRADOVIĆ	BIH	4/6/79	D	17	(6)	
Ervin PERIČIĆ		9/7/88	D		(3)	
Miljan RADOVIĆ		18/10/75	M	29		3
Marko RADULOVIĆ		17/6/85	M	24	(1)	
Marko RAIČEVIĆ		31/5/88	M	16	(8)	1
Luka ROTKOVIĆ		5/7/88	M	12	(12)	7
Merlin SKENDERI		13/1/90	M		(1)	
Ilija ŠOLJAGA		21/10/87	A		(1)	
Pavle VELIMIROVIĆ		4/11/90	G	8		
Milan VUČKOVIĆ		23/1/87	M	18	(3)	

FK RUDAR PLJEVLJA

Coach – Nebojša Vignjević (SRB)
Founded – 1914
Stadium – Pod Golubinjom (8,000)
MAJOR HONOURS:
Montenegrin League - (1) 2010;
Montenegrin Cup - (2) 2007, 2010.

2009				
9/8	Petrovac	h	3-1	*Vlahović, Ranđelović 2*
14/8	Sutjeska	a	2-1	*Ranđelović (p), Zec*
22/8	Dečić	h	1-1	*Ranđelović*
29/8	Berane	a	1-0	*Jovanović*
11/9	Budućnost	h	1-0	*Ranđelović*
19/9	Mornar	h	1-0	*Nestorović*
26/9	Grbalj	a	2-4	*Adžić, Ranđelović*
30/9	Lovćen	h	0-1	
3/10	Zeta	a	1-0	*Nestorović*
18/10	Mogren	h	2-0	*Zec, Vlahović*
24/10	Kom	a	2-0	*Jovanović 2*
31/10	Petrovac	a	4-0	*Zec 2, Sekulić, Ranđelović*
7/11	Sutjeska	h	3-1	*Ranđelović, Brnović, Minić*
21/11	Dečić	a	1-0	*Bojović*
28/11	Berane	h	1-0	*Bojić*
5/12	Budućnost	a	0-0	
12/12	Mornar	a	1-0	*Brnović*
2010				
27/2	Grbalj	h	1-0	*Lutovac*
7/3	Lovćen	a	3-0	*Useni, Ranđelović 2*
13/3	Zeta	h	2-4	*Useni, Bojić*
17/3	Mogren	a	0-0	
20/3	Kom	h	1-0	*Bojić*
27/3	Kom	h	3-0	*Ranđelović 2, Jovanović*
31/3	Budućnost	h	2-1	*Brnović, Ranđelović*
4/4	Zeta	a	2-3	*Ranđelović 2 (1p)*
10/4	Mogren	h	3-1	*Ranđelović, Vlahović, og (Janičić)*
17/4	Lovćen	a	3-0	*Bojić, Jovanović, Ranđelović*
24/4	Grbalj	h	3-0	*Bojić, Brnović, Ranđelović*
1/5	Dečić	a	2-2	*Vlahović, Jovanović*
9/5	Sutjeska	h	2-0	*Vlahović, Ranđelović (p)*
15/5	Berane	a	0-2	
22/5	Petrovac	h	2-2	*og (Barać), Minić*
29/5	Mornar	a	1-2	*Brnović*

Name	Nat	DoB	Pos	Aps	(s)	Gls
Vladan ADŽIĆ		5/7/87	D	12		1
Mihailo ALEKSIĆ	SRB	12/2/90	D	1	(1)	
Adi BAMBUR		21/5/91	A	1		
Fadil BAŠIĆ		13/11/80	D	1		
Veselin BOJIĆ		16/6/77	D	24	(2)	5
Mijuško BOJOVIĆ		9/8/88	D	31		1
Predrag BRNOVIĆ		22/10/86	M	28	(5)	5
Ferid IDRIZOVIĆ	BIH	10/9/82	M	7	(5)	
Blažo IGUMANOVIĆ		19/1/86	D	19	(8)	
Bojan IVANOVIĆ		3/12/81	M	23	(1)	
Miroje JOVANOVIĆ		10/3/87	A	20	(10)	6
Saša JOVOVIĆ		6/9/86	A	2	(4)	
Nikola LEKIĆ		20/11/92	M		(1)	
Stefan LUTOVAC		15/4/86	D	5		1
Armin MAHMUTOVIĆ		15/10/91	M	1	(2)	
Dušan MIĆIĆ	SRB	29/11/84	M	9	(6)	
Milan MIJATOVIĆ		26/7/87	G	6		
Aleksandar MINIĆ		13/11/75	A	7	(17)	2
Milivoje MRDAK		2/12/92	A		(1)	
Dušan NESTOROVIĆ	SRB	26/6/86	M	15	(1)	2
Miloš RADANOVIĆ		5/11/80	G	27		
Predrag RANĐELOVIĆ	SRB	13/9/76	A	30		19
Stevan RELJIĆ		31/3/86	M	12	(2)	
Nikola SEKULIĆ		10/4/81	M	24	(4)	1
Danilo TOMIĆ		23/6/86	M	5	(7)	
Nermin USENI	SRB	13/3/80	M	22	(3)	2
Lorenzo VALAGA	SUR	28/5/84	M	1	(1)	
Nedjeljko VLAHOVIĆ		15/1/84	M	15	(6)	5
Miloš VRANEŠ		27/7/88	M		(2)	
Zoran VUKOVIĆ		7/7/79	D		(2)	
Miodrag ZEC		4/10/82	A	15	(5)	4

FK SUTJESKA

Coach – Nikola Rakojević
Founded – 1927
Stadium – Kraj Bistrice (8,000)

2009

8/8	Berane	a	1-2	Zvicer
14/8	Rudar	h	1-2	Međedović
22/8	Mornar	a	0-1	
29/8	Grbalj	h	2-2	Vuković, Međedović
12/9	Lovćen	a	0-0	
19/9	Zeta	h	2-1	Zvicer, Adrović
26/9	Mogren	a	0-4	
30/9	Kom	h	1-0	Zvicer (p)
3/10	Petrovac	a	0-1	
17/10	Budućnost	a	1-2	Kasalica
24/10	Dečić	h	2-0	Dževerdanović M., Adrović
31/10	Berane	h	1-0	Dževerdanović M.
7/11	Rudar	a	1-3	Međedović
21/11	Mornar	h	1-2	Đikanović
28/11	Grbalj	a	0-0	
5/12	Lovćen	h	1-1	Međedović (p)
13/12	Zeta	a	0-3	

2010

28/2	Mogren	h	4-0	Adrović 2, Međedović (p), Ćulafić
7/3	Kom	a	0-1	
13/3	Petrovac	h	1-0	Đikanović
17/3	Budućnost	h	3-1	Merdović 2, Zvicer
20/3	Dečić	a	0-0	
27/3	Lovćen	a	2-3	Zvicer, Adrović
31/3	Grbalj	h	0-2	
3/4	Dečić	a	0-1	
10/4	Kom	a	1-0	Bulatović
17/4	Berane	h	0-0	
24/4	Petrovac	a	1-2	Ćiraković
1/5	Mornar	h	3-0	Merdović 2, Zvicer
9/5	Rudar	a	0-2	
15/5	Budućnost	h	2-0	Ćiraković, Merdović
22/5	Zeta	a	0-0	
29/5	Mogren	h	2-0	Međedović, Zvicer

No	Name	Nat	DoB	Pos	Aps	(s)	Gls
9	Admir ADROVIĆ		8/5/88	A	24	(1)	5
7	Sead BANDA		16/6/90	A	4	(8)	
18	Boris BULAJIĆ		27/4/88	M	30		
5	Darko BULATOVIĆ		5/9/89	D	19		1
11	Tomislav ĆIRAKOVIĆ		10/10/84	M	22	(5)	2
7	Danilo ĆULAFIĆ		1/8/86	M	14	(1)	1
2	Milivoje DELIĆ		14/5/88	D	7	(1)	
26	Aleksandar DUBLJEVIĆ		9/3/85	D	31		
15	Mirko DURUTOVIĆ		13/3/89	M	2	(2)	
20	Marko DŽEVERDANOVIĆ		3/11/81	D	11	(6)	2
30	Nikola DŽEVERDANOVIĆ		23/10/80	D	27	(1)	
6	Đorđe ĐIKANOVIĆ		18/8/84	D	26	(1)	2
13	Vukajlo ĐUKIĆ		12/10/83	D	1		
23	Vladan GILJEN		7/12/89	G	32		
29	Marko KASALICA		13/10/86	A	12	(14)	1
12	Boris LAKIĆEVIĆ		24/10/88	G	1		
9	Božo MARKOVIĆ		26/10/89	A	3	(10)	
10	Dražen MEĐEDOVIĆ		15/10/82	M	26	(1)	6
21	Luka MERDOVIĆ		14/3/89	M	11	(5)	5
16	Andrija PEJOVIĆ		1/12/91	A		(11)	
17	Vido SJEKLOĆA		14/5/86	M		(6)	
14	Marko SPASOJEVIĆ		3/7/88	M		(2)	
22	Miroslav TODOROVIĆ		29/3/87	M	11	(6)	
27	Ivan VUJAČIĆ		22/6/85	D	13	(5)	
3	Danilo VUKOVIĆ	SRB	1/4/89	D	10	(2)	1
99	Krsto ZVICER		10/6/87	A	26	(2)	7

FK ZETA

Coach – Velibor Matanović; (12/11/09) Dragoljub Đuretić
Founded – 1927.
Stadium – Tresnjica (4,000)
MAJOR HONOURS:
Montenegrin League - (1) 2007.

2009

8/8	Lovćen	a	1-2	Gutić
14/8	Budućnost	a	2-4	Knežević, Kaluđerović (p)
22/8	Mogren	h	0-3	
29/8	Kom	a	0-1	
12/9	Petrovac	h	2-0	Knežević, Kaluđerović
19/9	Sutjeska	a	1-2	Korać
26/9	Dečić	h	2-1	Korać, Knežević
30/9	Berane	a	2-1	Korać 2
3/10	Rudar	h	0-1	
17/10	Mornar	a	0-0	
24/10	Grbalj	h	1-0	Korać
31/10	Lovćen	h	2-1	Korać 2 (1p)
8/11	Budućnost	h	2-4	Knežević, Korać
21/11	Mogren	a	0-0	
28/11	Kom	h	2-0	Korać, Knežević
5/12	Petrovac	a	1-0	Petrović
13/12	Sutjeska	h	3-0	Novović, Korać 2

2010

27/2	Dečić	a	2-0	Lađić, Krkotić
6/3	Berane	h	1-0	Kojašević
13/3	Rudar	a	4-2	Boljević 2, Krkotić, Kojašević
17/3	Mornar	h	1-0	Krkotić
20/3	Grbalj	a	2-0	Peličić, Burzanović
27/3	Petrovac	h	1-1	Boljević
31/3	Mornar	a	0-0	
4/4	Rudar	h	3-2	Boljević, Jugović 2
10/4	Budućnost	a	1-3	Simović
17/4	Kom	h	2-0	Jugović, Zlatičanin
24/4	Mogren	a	1-0	Zlatičanin
1/5	Lovćen	a	0-1	
8/5	Grbalj	h	2-2	Petrović 2
15/5	Dečić	h	1-2	Petrović
22/5	Sutjeska	h	0-0	
29/5	Berane	a	1-0	Lambulić

Name	Nat	DoB	Pos	Aps	(s)	Gls
Vladimir BOLJEVIĆ		17/1/88	M	24	(3)	4
Davor BRNOVIĆ		17/1/88	G	2		
Miloš BULATOVIĆ		17/5/89	G	3		
Goran BURZANOVIĆ		4/8/84	M	13	(11)	1
Marko ČOLAKOVIĆ		20/7/80	M	16		
Boris DOŠLJAK		4/6/89	M	4	(15)	
Marko ĐURETIĆ		17/2/86	D	7	(5)	
Vuk ĐURIĆ		30/8/88	M	13		
Hilmo GUTIĆ		3/11/80	D	22	(1)	1
Damir HAVERIĆ		8/3/88	M	1		
Saša IVANOVIĆ		26/6/84	G	28		
Dušan JOVIĆEVIĆ		16/8/88	A		(5)	
Marjan JUGOVIĆ	SRB	26/8/83	A	13	(2)	3
Momčilo KALEZIĆ		14/6/89	M		(3)	
Miroslav KALUĐEROVIĆ		4/2/86	D	30		2
Ivan KNEŽEVIĆ		22/2/86	A	16	(1)	5
Damir KOJAŠEVIĆ		3/6/87	M	7	(5)	2
Žarko KORAĆ		11/6/87	A	13	(2)	11
Miloš KRKOTIĆ		29/9/87	M	24	(5)	3
Aleksa LAĐIĆ		7/7/86	A	2	(7)	1
Igor LAMBULIĆ		21/8/88	A	1	(5)	1
Nenad MATIĆ		20/11/91	D	5	(5)	
Ivan NOVOVIĆ		26/4/89	M	28	(2)	1
Petar ORLANDIĆ		6/8/90	M		(1)	
Zarija PELIČIĆ		22/1/89	M	21	(5)	1
Gavrilo PETROVIĆ		21/5/84	D	28	(1)	4
Miloš RADULOVIĆ		23/2/90	D	5	(1)	
Miloš RADULOVIĆ		6/8/90	D	1	(1)	
Janko SIMOVIĆ		4/2/87	M	20	(5)	1
Miroslav ZLATIČANIN		7/11/90	D	16	(5)	2

MONTENEGRO

PROMOTED CLUBS

FK MLADOST PODGORICA
Coach – Slobodan Šćepanović
Founded – 1950
Stadium – Cvijetin Brijeg (1,500)

OFK BAR
Coach – Slavoljub Bubanja
Founded – 2001
Stadium – FK Bar (1,000)

SECOND LEVEL FINAL TABLE 2009/10

		Pld	W	D	L	F	A	Pts
1	FK Mladost Podgorica	33	21	8	4	75	32	71
2	OFK Bar	33	18	11	4	40	10	65
3	FK Bratstvo	33	15	11	7	35	24	56
4	FK Bokelj	33	13	12	8	52	25	51
5	FK Zabjelo	33	12	9	12	33	34	45
6	FK Jedinstvo Bijelo Polje	33	11	10	12	42	43	43
7	FK Jezero	33	11	7	15	41	50	40
8	FK Čelik Nikšić	33	11	6	16	36	51	39
9	FK Ibar	33	10	7	16	27	44	37
10	FK Otrant	33	8	12	13	28	35	36
11	FK Crvena stijena	33	9	9	15	30	44	36
12	FK Gusinje	33	5	6	22	19	66	21

PROMOTION/RELEGATION PLAY-OFFS

(2/6/10 & 6/6/10)
Bratstvo 0, Mornar 1
Mornar 2, Bratstvo 1
(Mornar 3-1)

Bar 1, Berane 1
Berane 1, Bar 1 *(aet)*
(1-1; Bar 5-4 on pens)

DOMESTIC CUP 2009/10

KUP CRNE GORE

FIRST ROUND

(16/9/09)
Arsenal 1, Bokelj 1 *(aet; 1-3 on pens)*
Bar 1, Zabjelo 0
Budućnost Podgorica 2, Otrant 1
Čelik 0, Mogren 0 *(aet; 5-3 on pens)*
Crvena stijena 0, Grbalj 2
Drezga 0, Ibar 0 *(aet; 5-3 on pens)*
Gusinje 0, Dečić 2
Iskra 2, Sutjeska 3
Jedinstvo 2, Berane 0
Kom 1, Jezero 2
Mornar 1, Bratstvo 0
Petnjica 0, Mladost 5
Pljevlja 1997 1, Zeta 2
Sloga 0, Rudar Pljevlja 7

Byes – Lovćen, Petrovac

SECOND ROUND

(21/10/09 & 3/11/09)
Zeta v Bar 0-2; 1-0 *(1-2)*

(21/10/09 & 4/11/09)
Bokelj v Grbalj 0-4; 1-4 *(1-8)*
Budućnost Podgorica v Lovćen 2-0; 2-0 *(4-0)*
Čelik v Mornar 1-3; 0-2 *(1-5)*
Dečić v Sutjeska 0-1; 0-2 *(0-3)*
Drezga v Petrovac 0-3; 0-4 *(0-7)*
Jedinstvo v Rudar Pljevlja 0-2; 1-1 *(1-3)*
Jezero v Mladost 1-4; 3-6 *(4-10)*

QUARTER-FINALS

(25/11/09 & 9/12/09)
Budućnost Podgorica 1 *(Ćetković 46)*, Sutjeska 1 *(Dževerdanović M. 62)*
Sutjeska 0, Budućnost Podgorica 1 *(Vuković 5)*
(Budućnost Podgorica 2-1)

Mladost 1 *(Merdović 60)*, Grbalj 2 *(Radusinović 23, Nikezić 48)*
Grbalj 4 *(Kajević 6, 9, 83, Popović 57)*, Mladost 3 *(Merdović 25, Vučić 45, Šćepanović 80)*
(Grbalj 6-4)

Mornar 0, Rudar Pljevlja 0
Rudar Pljevlja 6 *(Ranđelović 9, 20, 56, Useni 6, Minić 68, 87)*, Mornar 1 *(Mešter 36)*
(Rudar Pljevlja 6-1)

Petrovac 1 *(Lopičić 27)*, Bar 1 *(Jovović 48)*
Bar 1 *(Nedović 90)*, Petrovac 3 *(Radulović 67p, Rotković 74, Lopičić 77)*
(Petrovac 4-2)

SEMI-FINALS

(14/4/10 & 28/4/10)
Grbalj 0, Budućnost Podgorica 1 *(Delić 55)*
Budućnost Podgorica 3 *(Stolica 40, 45+1, 83)*, Grbalj 2 *(Bošković I. 19, Matić 26)*
(Budućnost Podgorica 4-2)

Rudar Pljevlja 2 *(Ranđelović 21, 65)*, Petrovac 1 *(Mitić 87)*
Petrovac 0, Rudar Pljevlja 0
(Rudar Pljevlja 2-1)

FINAL

(19/5/10)
Stadion pod Goricom, Podgorica
FK RUDAR PLJEVLJA 2 *(Ranđelović 4p, Igumanović 36)*
FK BUDUĆNOST PODGORICA 1 *(Stolica 83)*
Referee – Kaluđerović
RUDAR PLJEVLJA – Radanović, Ivanović, Bojović, Bojić, Igumanović, Sekulić, Vlahović, Brnović *(Mićić 68)*, Useni, Ranđelović, Jovanović *(Tomić 40; Idrizović 90)*.
BUDUĆNOST PODGORICA – Radulović Mileta, Lakićević *(Vukčević N. 32)*, Perišić, Radulović Milan, Mazić, Kudemor, Ajković, Delić *(Vuković 43)*, Vukčević P., Bošković *(Stolica 70)*, Bećiraj.
Sent off: Perišić (4).

So near yet so far in South Africa

The Netherlands did not win many new friends and admirers at the 2010 FIFA World Cup, but they went home to a welcome fit for heroes, an estimated 700,000 of their orange-clad supporters lining the streets of Amsterdam to salute the team's performance in South Africa, where they reached the final and came within a few minutes of taking Spain to a penalty shoot-out.

Despite winning every one of their six previous matches – to add to the 100 per cent success rate they carried forward from the qualifying campaign – Bert van Marwijk's team would not have been hailed as popular champions had they prolonged that remarkable run with a spot-kick success at Soccer City. Their negative, over-aggressive display in the final, in which they sought to destabilise their opponents' slick passing game by whatever means possible, fair and foul, led to a sorry spectacle, and while Andrés Iniesta's late winning goal induced sympathy for the country after their third defeat in three World Cup finals, there was very little for the team.

Clear strategy

And yet the Dutch reached the final on merit. Denmark, Japan, Cameroon, Slovakia, Brazil and Uruguay all fell to them, and all within the regulation 90 minutes. Van Marwijk's side were efficient, ruthlessly so, and supremely well drilled in what they had to do. There was a clear strategy for every game, and the players, united in their objective, worked prodigiously to carry it through. This collective endeavour did not bring spectator-friendly football but it did bring results, and at the end of the tournament there were 30 other teams that would have loved to swap places with the Netherlands.

The approach in South Africa was a far cry from the classic 'Total Football' of yesteryear; or indeed from the exuberant football the Netherlands played in the group stage of UEFA EURO 2008 when, with Marco van Basten in charge, the Oranje hammered Italy and

France before going out to Russia in the quarter-final. Van Basten's bold adventure was replaced by Van Marwijk's calculated pragmatism, and with a perfect record in competitive internationals and a 25-match unbeaten run going into the World Cup final, nobody could dispute that the former Feyenoord and BV Borussia Dortmund coach had hit on a successful formula. It is one he will doubtless carry forward into the qualifying campaign for UEFA EURO 2012, for which another straightforward passage into the finals can be anticipated from a group containing San Marino, Moldova, Hungary, Finland and Sweden.

The Netherlands enjoyed the advantage of a settled side in South Africa, with even the traditional numbers 1-11 being worn by the starting XI in the final. There had been pre-tournament doubts about goalkeeper Maarten Stekelenburg, but he dismissed those with a number of super-athletic saves. Gregory van der Wiel, John Heitinga, Joris Mathijsen and captain Giovanni van Bronckhorst also proved more reliable as a defensive unit than expected, although they were helped by the indefatigable (sometimes illegal)

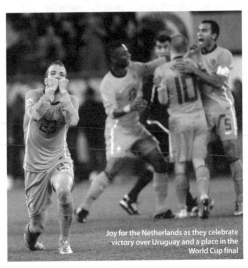

Joy for the Netherlands as they celebrate victory over Uruguay and a place in the World Cup final

shielding work of holding midfielders Mark van Bommel and Nigel de Jong. Dirk Kuyt was another who, true to his reputation, never gave less than his all, while Arjen Robben's introduction for the knockout games – after he had missed most of the group stage with a hamstring injury picked up in the final warm-up game – gave the team some much-needed flair, speed and directness.

Steve McClaren raises the Eredivisie trophy after leading FC Twente to the Dutch title

Superstar Sneijder

The ace in the Oranje's pack, though, was unquestionably Wesley Sneijder. A couple of the five goals with which he was officially credited were hardly works of art, but as the creative linchpin of the team he was consistently outstanding. His sublime pass through the centre for Robben in the final would have been talked about for years to come had the winger not spurned the glorious one-on-one opportunity that it presented to him. But if Sneijder was a resounding success, Robin van Persie was – like so many top-class forwards at the tournament – a major disappointment. Having missed most of the season through injury, he should have been fired up and fresh, but instead he looked laboured and short of confidence, and it was a surprise that Van Marwijk persevered with him to the detriment of Klaas Jan Huntelaar, particularly for the full 120 minutes of the final. More opportunities might also have been given to Eljero Elia, who, with his jinks and twists, transformed the game when he came on for Rafael van der Vaart (Robben's stand-in) in the opener against Denmark.

The Netherlands' South African adventure was preceded by a season in which Sneijder and Robben both excelled for their new clubs, FC Internazionale Milano and FC Bayern München respectively, after leaving Real Madrid CF – the pair coming face to face in the UEFA Champions League final after each winning domestic doubles – and in which the top prize in Dutch football, the Eredivisie championship, was claimed for the second year running by a provincial outsider, AZ Alkmaar being succeeded on to the victory podium by FC Twente.

The Enschede club were led to their first ever title by former England manager Steve McClaren. It was a brilliant achievement. Pursued all the way by a rampant AFC Ajax side that scored over a hundred goals, Twente held firm under enormous pressure, sealing the title on the final day amidst much jubilation with a 2-0 victory at NAC Breda. It was the club's 27th win in 34 matches. They were beaten just twice – by Ajax at the Amsterdam ArenA in early February and by outgoing champions AZ in Alkmaar two rounds before the end. It was a once-in-a-lifetime opportunity for McClaren and his players to make history, and they seized it, their enormous haul of 86 points leaving Ajax and all the other 16 Eredivisie teams trailing in their formidable wake.

Terrific Twente

Over and above the team's terrific resolve, there was much to admire. Runners-up in both league and cup in 2008/09, they were determined from the outset to show that they could go one better in 2009/10. An early setback in Europe, where they were eliminated from the UEFA Champions League by Sporting Clube de Portugal after conceding a stoppage-time own goal, was hastily digested and dismissed. The team's progress through to the last 32 of the UEFA Europa League was rendered of little consequence beside the team's fabulous efforts in the Eredivisie. After reaching the end of August with a respectable tally of 11 points, the Tukkers embarked on a sensational autumn run that brought them 12 consecutive victories. Even more extraordinarily, the last ten of those, including a 1-0 win at home to Ajax, all featured a goal from the club's new record signing Bryan Ruiz.

The Costa Rican striker, newly arrived from KAA Gent, ended the season with 24 goals, most of them decisive.

Long-serving striker Blaise Nkufo may have suffered in comparison, scoring only half that number, but the Swiss international also played his part – as did on-loan Slovakian winger Miroslav Stoch, whose tenth goal of the campaign wrapped up the title. Veteran goalkeeper Sander Boschker, a survivor from Twente's previous trophy triumph, in the 2001 Dutch Cup, was a reliable ever-present, his life made easier by a resolute back line in which young Brazilian centre-back Douglas, ably supported by Ronnie Stam, Peter Wisgerhof and Dwight Tiendalli, was immense. The irascible Theo Janssen was the key man in midfield, with the experienced Dane Kenneth Perez – once of AZ, Ajax and PSV Eindhoven but never a Dutch champion with any of them – providing solid support.

McClaren was rewarded for his fine work with a lucrative contract to coach VfL Wolfsburg. It was an offer he could not refuse and it meant that for the second successive year the Eredivisie's championship-winning coach had been lured across the border to Germany. Twelve months earlier Louis van Gaal had left AZ for FC Bayern München, but while he would go on to enjoy a magnificent first season in Munich, his replacement, Ronald Koeman, failed to deliver in Alkmaar and was sacked in December following a poor showing in both the Eredivisie and the UEFA Champions League, in which AZ, making their first appearance, finished bottom of their group. Another big name, Dick Advocaat, came in to salvage European qualification as the team finished the league campaign strongly, with a 14-match unbeaten run, to take fifth place.

Entertainment in Amsterdam

Ajax topped that by winning all of their last 14 matches, but it would not be enough to bring them their first Dutch championship in six years, a relatively disappointing autumn, in which they lost at PSV, Twente and FC Utrecht, leaving them with just that little bit too much ground to make up in the spring. While Twente were happy to win games by the odd goal, Ajax liked to pummel their opponents into submission and beyond. Entertainment was the name of the game for the Amsterdammers, and the leader of their goal-charge was captain Luis Suárez, who equalled the Eredivisie record for a foreigner by scoring 35 times in his 33 appearances. He was also credited with 17 assists, and there were substantial offerings from him also in both the UEFA Europa League, in which Ajax reached the last 32, and the Dutch Cup, which they won.

For security reasons the Cup final was switched from a one-off showpiece to a two-legged affair. This was because Ajax's opponents were Feyenoord, the residents of De Kuip, the fixture's traditional venue, and the Amsterdam club's hostile arch-rivals. Visiting fans were banned from both matches, and the outcome was an anti-climactic affair as Ajax won the first leg 2-0 at home before cruising to a 4-1 victory in Rotterdam. Suárez left his imprint on proceedings with two of Ajax's goals but on this occasion he was outgunned by his young in-form team-mate, Siem de Jong, who supplied the other four. The second leg was a sad club swansong for Feyenoord skipper Van Bronckhorst – though it probably paled into significance compared to what he would go through a couple of months later in the World Cup final, the very last match of his career. It was also the last hurrah for ex-Netherlands striker Roy Makaay, who, four days earlier, had marked his final league game with a hat-trick.

PSV fade

Like Feyenoord, PSV ended the season without a trophy. It was the first time in a decade that they had gone two successive seasons without winning the league. For much of the campaign, with ex-Twente boss Fred Rutten back from Germany to replace Huub Stevens, they looked title-bound, matching Twente all

Ajax captain Luis Suárez could not stop scoring in 2009/10

NETHERLANDS

the way and even lasting longer before they suffered their first defeat, in Breda in early March. But that loss was immediately followed by another – 1-4 at Ajax – and when they could only draw 1-1 at home to Twente six days later, their season was effectively over, defeats by Feyenoord (in the Dutch Cup) and Hamburger SV (in the UEFA Europa League) having already ended their interest elsewhere. With the honourable exception of Hungarian winger Balázs Dzsudzsák, too many PSV players failed to perform in the big games. One of them, Brazilian striker Jonathan Reis, was even sacked in mid-season for failing a drugs test.

Twente, Ajax, PSV, Feyenoord and AZ were joined in 2010/11 European competition by Utrecht, who, despite finishing one place below overachieving Heracles Almelo, won through the UEFA Europa League qualifying play-offs, demolishing Roda JC 6-1 on aggregate in the final. A post-season play-off series also resolved the issue of promotion and relegation. The Eredivisie's bottom club, RKC Waalwijk, had already been replaced by Eredivisie (second level) champions De Graafschap before the season ended in extraordinary fashion as SBV Excelsior scored deep into stoppage-time against city rivals Sparta Rotterdam in their play-off decider to go up on the away goals rule and simultaneously send their opponents down for only the second time in their history.

Koninklijke Nederlandse Voetbalbond (KNVB)

Woudenbergseweg 56-58
Postbus 515
NL-3700 AM Zeist
tel - +31 343 499 201
fax - +31 343 499 189
website - knvb. nl
email - concern@knvb.nl
Year of Formation – 1889

President – Michael van Praag
General Secretary - Harry Been
Media Officer – Rob de Leede

INTERNATIONAL HONOURS
UEFA European Championship – (1) 1988.
INTERNATIONAL TOURNAMENT APPEARANCES
FIFA World Cup – (9) 1934, 1938, 1974 (runners-up), 1978 (runners-up), 1990 (2nd round), 1994 (qtr-finals), 1998 (4th), 2006 (2nd round), 2010 (runners-up).
UEFA European Championship – (8) 1976 (3rd), 1980, 1988 (Winners), 1992 (semi-finals), 1996 (qtr-finals), 2000 (semi-finals), 2004 (semi-finals), 2008 (qtr-finals).
TOP FIVE ALL-TIME CAPS
Edwin van der Sar (130); Frank de Boer (112); Giovanni van Bronckhorst (106); Phillip Cocu (101); Clarence Seedorf (87)
TOP FIVE ALL-TIME GOALS
Patrick Kluivert (40); Dennis Bergkamp (37); Faas Wilkes (35); Johan Cruijff, Abe Lenstra & Ruud van Nistelrooy (33)

NATIONAL TEAM RESULTS 2009/10

12/8/09	England	H	Amsterdam	2-2	Kuyt (10), Van der Vaart (37)
5/9/09	Japan	H	Enschede	3-0	Van Persie (69), Sneijder (73), Huntelaar (87)
9/9/09	Scotland (WCQ)	A	Glasgow	1-0	Elia (82)
10/10/09	Australia	A	Sydney	0-0	
14/11/09	Italy	A	Pescara	0-0	
18/11/09	Paraguay	H	Heerenveen	0-0	
3/3/10	United States	H	Amsterdam	2-1	Kuyt (40p), Huntelaar (73)
26/5/10	Mexico	N	Freiburg (GER)	2-1	Van Persie (17, 41)
1/6/10	Ghana	H	Rotterdam	4-1	Kuyt (30), Van der Vaart (72), Sneijder (80), Van Persie (87p)
5/6/10	Hungary	H	Amsterdam	6-1	Van Persie (21), Sneijder (56), Robben (64, 78), Van Bommel (71), Elia (74)
14/6/10	Denmark (WCF)	N	Johannesburg (RSA)	2-0	Agger (46og), Kuyt (85)
19/6/10	Japan (WCF)	N	Durban (RSA)	1-0	Sneijder (53)
24/6/10	Cameroon (WCF)	N	Cape Town (RSA)	2-1	Van Persie (36), Huntelaar (83)
28/6/10	Slovakia (WCF)	N	Durban (RSA)	2-1	Robben (18), Sneijder (84)
2/7/10	Brazil (WCF)	N	Port Elizabeth (RSA)	2-1	Sneijder (53, 68)
6/7/10	Uruguay (WCF)	N	Cape Town (RSA)	3-2	Van Bronckhorst (18), Sneijder (70), Robben (73)
11/7/10	Spain (WCF)	N	Johannesburg (RSA)	0-1	(aet)

NATIONAL TEAM APPEARANCES 2009/10

Coach – Bert VAN MARWIJK 19/5/52

Player	DOB	Club	Eng	Jpn	SCO	Aus	Ita	Par	Usa	Mex	Gha	Hun	DEN	JPN	CMR	SVK	BRA	URU	ESP	Caps	Goals
Maarten STEKELENBURG	22/9/82	Ajax	G			G	G	G	G	G		G	G	G	G	G	G	G	G	34	-
John HEITINGA	15/11/83	Atlético (ESP)/Everton (ENG)	D			D	D	D	D	D	D	D61	D	D	D	D	D	D	D	61	6
Joris MATHIJSEN	5/4/80	Hamburg (GER)	D	D	D	D	D	D	D46	D	D	D	D	D	D	D		D	D	62	3
André OOIJER	11/7/74	PSV	D		D								s61					D		55	3
Edson BRAAFHEID	8/4/83	Bayern (GER)/Celtic (SCO)	D			s77	s46		s67	D46									s105	8	-
Stijn SCHAARS	11/1/84	AZ	M82			M64			M46											12	-
Nigel DE JONG	30/11/84	Man. City (ENG)	M	M	M		M	M46	M60			M	M	M88	M	M	M	M	M99	48	1
Rafael VAN DER VAART	11/2/83	Real Madrid (ESP)	M46	s78	s77	s64	M76	M85	s60	M71	s63	A80	M67	M72	M73			s46	s99	83	16
Robin VAN PERSIE	6/8/83	Arsenal (ENG)	M46	M	M84	A15			A64	A		A68	A77	A88	A59	A80	A85	A	A	51	19
Arjen ROBBEN	23/1/84	Real Madrid (ESP)/Bayern (GER)	M55	M46	M73				M46			s46			s73	M71		M89	M	52	15
Dirk KUYT	22/7/80	Liverpool (ENG)	A77	A64	A	A46	M	A62	A80	M	M73	A46	M	M	M66	M	M	M	M71	70	16
Ryan BABEL	19/12/86	Liverpool (ENG)	s46			s46	s72	s46	s80			s73								39	5
Wesley SNEIJDER	9/6/84	Real Madrid (ESP)/Inter (ITA)	s46	M78	M77	M70			M		M83	M73	M	M83	M	M92	M	M	M	68	19
Ibrahim AFELLAY	2/4/86	PSV	s55				s76	M	s74	M	M63	s80	s77	s83		s92				26	-
Klaas Jan HUNTELAAR	12/8/83	Milan (ITA)	s77	s64	s84	A	s15	s62	s46	s64		s68		s88	s59	s80	s85			36	16
David MENDES DA SILVA	4/8/82	AZ	s82	M64		s84														7	-
Michel VORM	20/10/83	Utrecht	G46	G					G46											4	-
Gregory VAN DER WIEL	3/2/88	Ajax	D	D		D	D	D				D	D	D	D	D	D		D	15	-
Giovanni VAN BRONCKHORST	5/2/75	Feyenoord	D	D	D77	D	D46	D67			D	D	D	D	D	D	D	D	D105	106	6
Glenn LOOVENS	22/9/83	Celtic (SCO)	D																	1	-
Eljero ELIA	13/2/87	Hamburg (GER)	s46	s73	M	M72	M46	M	s71	s83	s73	s67	s72	s66	s71			s89	s71	15	2
Piet VELTHUIZEN	3/11/86	Vitesse	s46																	1	-
Demy DE ZEEUW	26/5/83	Ajax	s64	M	M84				M				s79	s88				M46		27	-
Khalid BOULAHROUZ	28/12/81	Stuttgart (GER)				D			D						D			D		31	-
Orlando ENGELAAR	24/8/79	PSV					s70		s46	s46										14	-
Mark VAN BOMMEL	22/4/77	Bayern (GER)					M	M70	M74		M	M79	M	M	M	M	M	M	M	63	10
Wout BRAMA	21/8/86	Twente					s70													1	-
Otman BAKKAL	27/2/85	PSV					s85													1	-
Ron VLAAR	16/2/85	Feyenoord						s46												3	-
Vurnon ANITA	4/4/89	Ajax						s46												1	-
Sander BOSCHKER	20/10/70	Twente							s46											1	-

HEITINGA: 109*

NETHERLANDS
KNVB

DOMESTIC LEAGUE 2009/10

EREDIVISIE FINAL TABLE

		Pld	Home					Away					Total					Pts
			W	D	L	F	A	W	D	L	F	A	W	D	L	F	A	
1	FC Twente	34	16	1	0	37	10	11	4	2	26	13	27	5	2	63	23	86
2	AFC Ajax	34	16	1	0	64	4	11	3	3	42	16	27	4	3	106	20	85
3	PSV Eindhoven	34	13	4	0	40	13	10	5	2	32	16	23	9	2	72	29	78
4	Feyenoord	34	9	6	2	32	14	8	6	3	22	17	17	12	5	54	31	63
5	AZ Alkmaar	34	11	2	4	33	16	8	3	6	31	18	19	5	10	64	34	62
6	Heracles Almelo	34	11	1	5	36	25	6	4	7	18	24	17	5	12	54	49	56
7	FC Utrecht	34	8	7	2	21	12	6	4	7	18	21	14	11	9	39	33	53
8	FC Groningen	34	9	3	5	25	15	5	4	8	23	32	14	7	13	48	47	49
9	Roda JC	34	9	3	5	37	28	5	2	10	19	32	14	5	15	56	60	47
10	NAC Breda	34	8	5	4	26	17	4	5	8	16	32	12	10	12	42	49	46
11	sc Heerenveen	34	7	4	6	25	19	4	0	13	19	45	11	4	19	44	64	37
12	VVV-Venlo	34	7	6	4	30	23	1	5	11	13	34	8	11	15	43	57	35
13	NEC Nijmegen	34	5	5	7	20	27	3	4	10	15	32	8	9	17	35	59	33
14	Vitesse	34	5	5	7	22	28	3	3	11	16	34	8	8	18	38	62	32
15	ADO Den Haag	34	4	3	10	21	28	3	6	8	17	31	7	9	18	38	59	30
16	Sparta Rotterdam	34	5	4	8	18	26	1	4	12	12	40	6	8	20	30	66	26
17	Willem II	34	6	2	9	23	29	1	0	16	13	41	7	2	25	36	70	23
18	RKC Waalwijk	34	4	0	13	18	30	1	0	16	12	50	5	0	29	30	80	15

TOP GOALSCORERS

35 Luis SUÁREZ (Ajax)
24 Bryan RUIZ (Twente)
21 Mads JUNKER (Roda)
20 Mounir EL HAMDAOUI (AZ)
16 Marko PANTELIĆ (Ajax)
14 Bas DOST (Heracles)
   EVERTON (Heracles)
   Balázs DZSUDZSÁK (PSV)
13 Tim MATAVŽ (Groningen)
   Ola TOIVONEN (PSV)

UEFA EUROPA LEAGUE QUALIFICATION PLAY-OFFS

FIRST ROUND

(6/5/10 & 9/5/10)
Roda JC 1 *(Junker 40)*, Heracles 1 *(Dost 77)*
Heracles 1 *(Douglas 62)*, Roda 2 *(Van der Linden 80og, Bodor 90+2)*
(Roda JC 3-2)

Utrecht 3 *(Van Wolfswinkel 22, Asare 23, Granqvist 90og)*, Groningen 1 *(Matavž 40)*
Groningen 0, Utrecht 2 *(Van Wolfswinkel 38, Asare 81)*
(Utrecht 5-1)

SECOND ROUND

(13/5/10 & 16/5/10)
Roda 0, Utrecht 2 *(Cornelisse 2, Mertens 41)*
Utrecht 4 *(Van Wolfswinkel 2, 47, Mulenga 59, 71)*, Roda 1 *(Junker 21)*
(Utrecht 6-1)

CLUB-BY-CLUB

ADO DEN HAAG
Coach – Raymond Atteveld; (30/3/10) Maurice Steijn
Founded – 1971
Stadium – ADO Den Haag (15,000)
MAJOR HONOURS:
Dutch Cup - (1) 1975.

2009
2/8	NAC	h	1-2	Horváth
9/8	VVV	a	2-2	Verhoek, Van den Bergh (p)
15/8	Twente	h	0-1	
22/8	Vitesse	a	3-1	Milić, Horváth, Soltani
28/8	RKC	a	2-0	Milić, Verhoek
12/9	AZ	h	2-1	Verhoek, Immers
20/9	Utrecht	h	0-1	
27/9	Ajax	a	0-3	
3/10	Groningen	h	1-1	og (Sankoh)
18/10	NEC	a	1-1	Milić
24/10	Sparta	h	2-3	Buijs, Vicento
31/10	Heerenveen	a	0-3	
8/11	PSV	h	1-5	Soltani
22/11	Willem II	a	1-1	Soltani
29/11	Feyenoord	h	0-2	
4/12	Roda	a	1-1	Soltani
13/12	Heracles	h	1-4	og (Looms)
19/12	AZ	a	0-3	

2010
24/1	Sparta	a	0-0	
30/1	Heerenveen	h	2-1	Verhoek, Milić
3/2	Groningen	a	0-2	
6/2	PSV	a	0-2	
13/2	Willem II	h	3-0	Van den Bergh 2, Hulst
21/2	Feyenoord	a	2-2	og (Van Bronckhorst), Buijs
26/2	Roda	h	1-2	Luijckx
6/3	Vitesse	h	1-1	Kum
12/3	Twente	a	1-3	Verhoek
21/3	VVV	h	0-0	
26/3	NAC	a	0-3	
4/4	Ajax	h	0-1	
11/4	Utrecht	a	2-0	Buijs, Verhoek
14/4	NEC	h	2-3	og (Nuytinck), Verhoek
18/4	RKC	h	4-0	Derijck, Luijckx (p), Oper, Buijs
2/5	Heracles	a	2-4	Derijck, og (Van der Linden)

No	Name	Nat	DoB	Pos	Aps	(s)	Gls
2	Ahmed AMMI	MAR	19/1/81	D	21	(2)	
12	Ricky VAN DEN BERGH		17/11/80	M	15	(9)	3

18	Pascal BOSSCHAART		28/2/80	M	24	(5)
8	Danny BUIJS		21/6/82	M	30	4
17	Yuri CORNELISSE		8/5/75	M	3	(4)
26	Gino COUTINHO		5/8/82	G	4	
4	Timothy DERIJCK		25/5/87	D	32	2
16	Barry DITEWIG		14/10/77	G	18	(2)
21	Kai VAN HESE		15/6/89	D	10	(3)
20	Csaba HORVÁTH	SVK	2/5/82	D	20	(3) 2
27	Santy HULST		27/10/87	A	4	(5) 1
13	Raily IGNACIO		4/6/87	A		(4)
28	Lex IMMERS		8/6/86	M	20	(6) 1
10	Richard KNOPPER		29/8/77	M	4	(9)
3	Christian KUM		13/9/85	D	24	(1) 1
14	Kees LUIJCKX		11/2/86	M	16	2
9	Bogdan MILIĆ	MNE	24/11/87	A	18	(11) 4
19	Andres OPER	EST	7/11/77	A	5	(7) 1
41	Lorenzo PIQUÉ		17/9/90	D	9	(4)
14	Berry POWEL		2/5/80	A	2	(1)
6	Aleksandar RANKOVIĆ	SRB	31/8/78	M	1	
24	Leroy RESODIHARDJO		14/3/87	M	1	(1)
40	Levi SCHWIEBBE		13/9/86	M	2	(4)
7	Karim SOLTANI	FRA	29/8/84	A	27	(2) 4
37	Jens TOORNSTRA		1/1/89	M	16	(2)
11	Wesley VERHOEK		25/9/86	A	28	(4) 7
36	Charlton VICENTO		19/1/91	A	8	(6) 1
1	Robert ZWINKELS		4/5/83	G	12	

AFC AJAX

Coach – Martin Jol
Founded – 1900
Stadium – Amsterdam ArenA (51,638)
MAJOR HONOURS:
European Champion Clubs' Cup/UEFA Champions League - (4) 1971, 1972, 1973, 1995;
UEFA Cup Winners' Cup - (1) 1987; UEFA Cup - (1) 1992;
UEFA Super Cup - (3) 1972, 1973, 1995;
World Club Cup - (2) 1972, 1995;
Dutch League - (29) 1918, 1919, 1931, 1932, 1934, 1937, 1939, 1947, 1957, 1960, 1966, 1967, 1968, 1970, 1972, 1973, 1977, 1979, 1980, 1982, 1985, 1990, 1994, 1995, 1996, 1998, 2002, 2004;
Dutch Cup - (18) 1917, 1943, 1961, 1967, 1970, 1971, 1972, 1979, 1983, 1986, 1987, 1993, 1998, 1999, 2002, 2006, 2007, 2010.

2009
2/8	Groningen	a	2-0	Sulejmani, Rommedahl
8/8	RKC	h	4-1	Van der Wiel, Suárez 3 (1p)
16/8	PSV	a	3-4	Suárez 2, Emanuelson
23/8	Sparta	h	0-0	
30/8	Heracles	a	3-0	Alderweireld, Cvitanich, Aissati
13/9	NAC	h	6-0	Cvitanich 3, Vertonghen, Suárez, Bakircioglü
20/9	VVV	a	4-0	Suárez 4
27/9	Den Haag	h	3-0	De Zeeuw, Pantelić, De Jong
4/10	Roda	a	2-2	Suárez 2 (1p)
17/10	Willem II	h	4-0	Enoh, Sulejmani, Pantelić, Suárez
25/10	AZ	a	4-2	Emanuelson, Suárez 2, Van der Wiel
1/11	Feyenoord	h	5-1	De Zeeuw 2, Emanuelson, Van der Wiel, Suárez (p)
8/11	Twente	a	0-1	
22/11	Heerenveen	h	5-1	De Zeeuw 2, Pantelić, Suárez (p), Aissati
29/11	Vitesse	a	5-1	Pantelić 3, Bakircioglü, Aissati
6/12	Utrecht	a	0-2	
11/12	NEC	h	3-0	Suárez, De Jong, Donald

2010
17/1	NAC	a	1-1	Lindgren
24/1	AZ	h	1-0	Van der Wiel
31/1	Feyenoord	a	1-1	Pantelić
3/2	Roda	h	4-0	Suárez 4 (2p)
7/2	Twente	h	3-0	De Zeeuw, Pantelić, Rommedahl
13/2	Heerenveen	a	2-0	Rommedahl, Suárez
21/2	Vitesse	h	4-0	De Jong 2, Suárez, og (Verhaegh)
28/2	Utrecht	h	4-0	Suárez 2, Van der Wiel, Rommedahl
7/3	Sparta	a	3-0	De Jong, Van der Wiel, Rommedahl
14/3	PSV	h	4-1	De Jong, Emanuelson, Pantelić, Suárez
21/3	RKC	a	5-1	Suárez 2, De Jong, og (Mulder H.), Rommedahl
28/3	Groningen	h	3-0	Vertonghen 2, De Jong
04/4	Den Haag	a	1-0	Alderweireld
11/4	VVV	h	7-0	Suárez 3 (1p), Pantelić 3, Emanuelson
14/4	Willem II	a	2-0	Suárez (p), Pantelić
18/4	Heracles	h	4-0	De Jong 2, Pantelić 2
2/5	NEC	a	4-1	Suárez 2, De Zeeuw, Pantelić

No	Name	Nat	DoB	Pos	Aps	(s)	Gls
11	Ismael AISSATI		16/8/88	M	13	(1)	3
19	Toby ALDERWEIRELD	BEL	2/3/89	D	31		2
23	Vurnon ANITA		4/4/89	D	23	(3)	
7	Thimothée ATOUBA	CMR	17/2/82	D	1		
34	Kennedy BAKIRCIOGLÜ	SWE	2/11/80	A	4	(5)	2
20	Darío CVITANICH	ARG	16/5/84	A	4	(2)	4
29	Mitchell DONALD		10/12/88	M	1	(4)	1
8	Urby EMANUELSON		16/6/86	M	28	(3)	5
21	Eyong ENOH	CMR	23/3/86	M	25	(2)	1
51	Christian ERIKSEN	DEN	14/2/92	M	5	(10)	
18	GABRIel García de la Torre	ESP	10/2/79	M	4	(9)	
22	Siem DE JONG		28/1/89	M	16	(6)	10
6	Rasmus LINDGREN	SWE	29/11/84	M	5	(1)	1
45	Nicolás LODEIRO	URU	21/3/89	M		(8)	
3	OLEGUER Presas Renom	ESP	2/2/80	D	4	(2)	
9	Marko PANTELIĆ	SRB	15/9/78	A	23	(2)	16
28	Dennis ROMMEDAHL	DEN	22/7/78	A	16	(12)	6
1	Maarten STEKELENBURG		22/9/82	G	33		
16	Luis SUÁREZ	URU	24/1/87	A	33		35
39	SUK Hyun-jun	KOR	29/6/91	A		(3)	
10	Miralem SULEJMANI	SRB	5/12/88	A	3	(14)	2
12	Kenneth VERMEER		10/1/86	G	1		
5	Jan VERTONGHEN	BEL	24/4/87	D	32		3
2	Gregory VAN DER WIEL		3/2/88	D	34		6
17	Rob WIELAERT		29/12/78	D	3		
43	Marvin ZEEGELAAR		12/8/90	A		(2)	
40	Demy DE ZEEUW		26/5/83	M	32		7

AZ ALKMAAR

Coach – Ronald Koeman; (6/12/09) Dick Advocaat
Founded – 1967
Stadium – DSB (17,150)
MAJOR HONOURS:
Dutch League - (2) 1981, 2009;
Dutch Cup - (3) 1978, 1981, 1982.

2009
1/8	Heracles	a	2-3	Pellè, El Hamdaoui
7/8	Sparta	h	2-0	Dembélé, El Hamdaoui
15/8	RKC	a	6-0	El Hamdaoui 2, Dembélé, Martens 2, Lens
23/8	Heerenveen	a	2-0	og (Lejsal), El Hamdaoui
29/8	Willem II	h	2-1	Holman, Moreno
12/9	Den Haag	a	1-2	Lens
19/9	NEC	h	0-1	
26/9	Utrecht	a	0-1	
3/10	NAC	h	0-0	
17/10	Twente	a	2-3	El Hamdaoui, og (Wisgerhof)

25/10	Ajax	h	2-4	*El Hamdaoui, Pellè*
31/10	Groningen	a	1-0	*Lens*
8/11	Feyenoord	h	1-1	*Holman*
21/11	Roda	a	4-2	*Lens 2, Elm, Jonathas*
28/11	VVV	h	2-0	*Lens, Holman*
4/12	Vitesse	h	1-2	*Dembélé*
12/12	PSV	a	0-1	
19/12	Den Haag	h	3-0	*Elm, Pocognoli, Martens*
2010				
24/1	Ajax	a	0-1	
30/1	Groningen	h	0-1	
2/2	NAC	a	1-1	*Moisander*
7/2	Feyenoord	a	2-1	*El Hamdaoui, Moreno*
13/2	Roda	h	2-0	*og (Kah), Elm*
20/2	VVV	a	3-3	*Wernbloom, Poulsen, El Hamdaoui*
27/2	Vitesse	a	3-0	*El Hamdaoui 3*
6/3	Heerenveen	h	4-1	*Martens, El Hamdaoui, Lens, Holman*
13/3	RKC	h	6-2	*El Hamdaoui 3, Dembélé, Moreno, Lens*
21/3	Sparta	a	1-0	*Mendes da Silva*
27/3	Heracles	h	3-2	*Lens 3*
3/4	Utrecht	h	2-0	*Martens, El Hamdaoui (p)*
10/4	NEC	a	0-0	
13/4	Twente	h	1-0	*El Hamdaoui*
18/4	Willem II	a	3-0	*Moreno, Holman, El Hamdaoui*
2/5	PSV	h	1-1	*El Hamdaoui*

No	Name	Nat	DoB	Pos	Aps	(s)	Gls
9	ARlclenes da Silva Ferreira	BRA	11/12/85	A	2	(4)	
18	Moussa DEMBÉLÉ	BEL	16/7/87	A	28	(1)	4
1	Joey DIDULICA	CRO	14/10/77	G	7	(2)	
10	Mounir EL HAMDAOUI	MAR	14/7/84	A	26	(1)	20
20	Rasmus ELM	SWE	17/3/88	M	15	(8)	3
27	Brett HOLMAN	AUS	27/3/84	M	13	(10)	5
2	Kew JALIENS		15/9/78	D	22	(2)	
49	JONATHAS Cristian de Jesus Maurício	BRA	6/3/89	A		(4)	1
14	Ragnar KLAVAN	EST	30/10/85	D	4	(7)	
7	Jeremain LENS		24/11/87	A	20	(12)	12
19	Kees LUIJCKX		11/2/86	M	1	(2)	
11	Maarten MARTENS	BEL	2/7/84	M	27	(4)	5
6	David MENDES DA SILVA		4/8/82	M	29		1
25	Niklas MOISANDER	FIN	29/9/85	D	28		1
4	Héctor MORENO	MEX	17/1/88	D	30		4
26	Celso ORTÍZ	PAR	26/1/89	M	3	(3)	
29	Graziano PELLÈ	ITA	15/7/85	A	3	(10)	2
5	Sébastien POCOGNOLI	BEL	1/8/87	D	10	(1)	1
15	Simon Busk POULSEN	DEN	7/10/84	D	23	(3)	1
22	Sergio ROMERO	ARG	22/2/87	G	27		
8	Stijn SCHAARS		11/1/84	M	29		
28	Gill SWERTS	BEL	23/9/82	D	11	(6)	
23	Nick VAN DER VELDEN		16/12/81	M		(5)	
16	Pontus WERNBLOOM	SWE	25/6/86	M	16	(7)	1

FEYENOORD
Coach – Mario Been
Founded – 1908
Stadium – De Kuip (51,137)
MAJOR HONOURS:
European Champion Clubs' Cup - (1) 1970;
UEFA Cup - (2) 1974, 2002;
World Club Cup - (1) 1970;
Dutch League - (14) 1924, 1928, 1936, 1938, 1940, 1961, 1962, 1965, 1969, 1971, 1974, 1984, 1993, 1999;
Dutch Cup - (11) 1930, 1935, 1965, 1969, 1980, 1984, 1991, 1992, 1994, 1995, 2008.

2009				
2/8	NEC	h	2-0	*Tomasson, Fer (p)*
9/8	Vitesse	a	0-0	
16/8	Heracles	a	1-0	*Tomasson*
23/8	Roda	h	4-0	*Cissé, Tomasson, De Guzmán 2*
30/8	Twente	h	1-1	*Makaay (p)*
13/9	Willem II	a	3-2	*Tomasson 2, De Guzmán*
20/9	PSV	h	1-3	*Slory*
27/9	NAC	a	2-0	*Slory, Fer*
3/10	RKC	h	3-0	*Slory, og (Varela), Wijnaldum*
18/10	Sparta	a	1-2	*Bahia*
24/10	VVV	h	1-0	*Landzaat*
1/11	Ajax	a	1-5	*Landzaat*
8/11	AZ	a	1-1	*Cissé*
22/11	Utrecht	h	0-0	
29/11	Den Haag	a	2-0	*Vlaar, Slory*
6/12	Groningen	h	3-1	*Babović, Makaay, Tomasson*
12/12	Heerenveen	a	2-0	*Hofland, Tomasson*
19/12	Willem II	h	1-0	*Cissé*
2010				
24/1	VVV	a	1-1	*og (Paauwe)*
31/1	Ajax	h	1-1	*Wijnaldum*
4/2	RKC	a	1-0	*Tomasson*
7/2	AZ	h	1-2	*og (Wernbloom)*
14/2	Utrecht	a	0-0	
21/2	Den Haag	h	2-2	*Wijnaldum, Tomasson*
28/2	Groningen	a	3-2	*Bahia, Biseswar, Vlaar*
7/3	Roda	a	4-2	*Cissé 2, Bruins, Makaay*
14/3	Heracles	h	1-1	*Vlaar*
28/3	NEC	a	0-0	
31/3	Vitesse	h	2-1	*Vlaar, Makaay (first half played 20/3)*
4/4	NAC	h	0-0	
11/4	PSV	a	0-0	
14/4	Sparta	h	3-0	*Wijnaldum, Bruins, Tomasson*
18/4	Twente	a	0-2	
2/5	Heerenveen	h	6-2	*Makaay 3, De Vrij, Tomasson, Bahia*

No	Name	Nat	DoB	Pos	Aps	(s)	Gls
15	Stefan BABOVIĆ	SRB	7/1/87	M	3	(7)	1
4	André Luiz BAHIA dos Santos Viana	BRA	24/11/83	D	32		3
37	Diego BISESWAR		8/3/88	A	14	(15)	1
8	Giovanni VAN BRONCKHORST		5/2/75	D	29		
10	Luigi BRUINS		9/3/87	M	9	(12)	2
30	Luc CASTAIGNOS		27/2/92	A	1	(2)	
23	Sekou CISSÉ	CIV	23/5/85	A	21	(3)	5
5	Tim DE CLER		8/11/78	D	4	(3)	
16	DARLEY Ramon Torres	BRA	15/12/89	G	5		
18	Rob VAN DIJK		15/1/69	G	22	(1)	
6	Karim EL AHMADI	MAR	27/1/85	M	24	(2)	
14	Leroy FER		5/1/90	M	31		2
21	Daniel FERNÁNDEZ Artola	ESP	20/1/83	D	5		
23	Jonathan DE GUZMÁN		13/9/87	M	12	(1)	3
26	Ricky VAN HAAREN		21/1/91	M		(1)	
3	Kevin HOFLAND		7/6/79	D	3	(5)	1
7	Denny LANDZAAT		6/5/76	M	17	(3)	2
27	Kelvin LEERDAM		24/6/90	D	13	(4)	
9	Roy MAKAAY		9/3/75	A	12	(12)	7
17	Erwin MULDER		3/3/89	G	7	(3)	
28	Bart SCHENKEVELD		28/8/91	D	4	(1)	
24	Mitchell SCHET		28/1/88	A		(2)	
22	Andwelé SLORY		27/9/82	A	11	(2)	4
11	Jon Dahl TOMASSON	DEN	29/8/76	A	22	(2)	11
10	Ron VLAAR		16/2/85	D	32		4
29	Stefan DE VRIJ		5/2/92	D	15	(2)	1
25	Georginio WIJNALDUM		11/11/90	M	26	(5)	4

NETHERLANDS
KNVB

FC GRONINGEN
Coach – Ron Jans
Founded – 1926
Stadium – Euroborg (22,329)

2009

2/8	Ajax	h	0-2	
8/8	Roda	a	1-1	Lovre
16/8	NAC	h	1-2	Van de Laak
22/8	VVV	a	2-2	Pedersen, Granqvist
30/8	PSV	h	0-2	
12/9	Heerenveen	a	1-0	Nordstrand
18/9	Willem II	a	1-2	Van de Laak
27/9	Vitesse	h	1-0	Holla
3/10	Den Haag	a	1-1	Pedersen
18/10	Utrecht	h	0-0	
25/10	Twente	a	0-4	
31/10	AZ	h	0-1	
6/11	Heracles	h	4-1	Bacuna, Granqvist (p), Matavž 2
21/11	RKC	a	1-3	Matavž
29/11	NEC	h	2-2	Matavž, Pedersen
6/12	Feyenoord	a	1-3	Van de Laak
13/12	Sparta	a	4-2	Enevoldsen 3, Matavž

2010

20/1	Heerenveen	h	2-0	Matavž, Granqvist
24/1	Twente	h	0-0	
30/1	AZ	a	1-0	Matavž
3/2	Den Haag	h	2-0	Granqvist (p), Holla
6/2	Heracles	a	3-4	Enevoldsen 2, Nordstrand
14/2	RKC	h	2-1	Stenman, Granqvist (p)
20/2	NEC	a	2-0	Lovre, Matavž
28/2	Feyenoord	h	2-3	Matavž, Granqvist
7/3	VVV	h	1-0	Matavž
13/3	NAC	a	3-0	Oluwafemi 2, Van de Laak
21/3	Roda	h	1-0	Oluwafemi
28/3	Ajax	a	0-3	
3/4	Vitesse	a	0-3	
11/4	Willem II	h	4-0	Enevoldsen, Pedersen, Matavž, Bacuna
14/4	Utrecht	a	1-1	Pedersen
18/4	PSV	a	1-3	Matavž
2/5	Sparta	h	3-1	Van de Laak, Matavž, Stenman

No	Name	Nat	DoB	Pos	Aps	(s)	Gls
43	Leandro BACUNA		21/8/91	A	19	(1)	2
18	Daley BLIND		9/3/90	M	16	(1)	
23	Thomas ENEVOLDSEN	DEN	27/7/87	M	29		6
8	GONZALO Manuel García García	ESP	3/10/83	A		(6)	
7	Andreas GRANQVIST	SWE	16/4/85	D	32		6
24	Tom HIARIEJ		25/7/88	D	10	(5)	
21	Danny HOLLA		31/12/87	M	19	(3)	2
4	Michael JANSEN		10/6/84	D	2		
16	Serhat KOÇ		18/7/90	A	3	(9)	
13	Koen VAN DE LAAK		3/9/82	M	22	(4)	5
48	Darryl LACHMAN		11/11/89	D		(1)	
10	Brian VAN LOO		2/4/75	G	15	(3)	
10	Goran LOVRE	SRB	23/3/82	M	29	(4)	2
26	LUCIANO José Pereira da Silva	BRA	16/3/80	G	19	(1)	
17	Theo LUCIUS		19/12/76	D	3	(1)	
11	Tim MATAVŽ	SVN	13/1/89	A	22	(10)	13
51	Danny MENTING		5/5/90	A		(3)	
9	Morten NORDSTRAND	DEN	8/6/83	A	10	(2)	2
47	Frank OLIJVE		7/3/89	M	(2)		
15	Ajilore OLUWAFEMI	NGA	18/1/85	M	22	(3)	3
14	Nicklas PEDERSEN	DEN	10/10/87	A	15	(11)	5
35	Jeffrey RIJSDIJK		12/9/87	M		(1)	
2	Sepp DE ROOVER	BEL	12/11/84	D	14		
3	Gibril SANKOH	SLE	15/5/83	D	25	(1)	
8	Tim SPARV	FIN	20/2/87	M	4	(5)	

5	Fredrik STENMAN	SWE	2/6/83	D	29		2
12	Ondrej ŠVEJDÍK	CZE	3/12/82	D	5		
6	Mike ZONNEVELD		27/10/80	M	10	(11)	

SC HEERENVEEN
Coach – Trond Sollied (NOR); (12/9/09) Jan de Jonge;
(6/2/10) Jan Everse
Founded – 1920
Stadium – Abe Lenstra (26,100)
MAJOR HONOURS:
Dutch Cup - (1) 2009.

2009

31/7	Roda	h	0-0	
7/8	NEC	a	1-4	Papadopulos
15/8	Vitesse	h	1-0	Losada
23/8	AZ	h	0-2	
30/8	NAC	a	0-2	
12/9	Groningen	h	0-1	
20/9	Twente	h	0-2	
27/9	Sparta	a	2-0	Paulo Henrique, Elm
4/10	VVV	h	1-1	Papadopulos
17/10	PSV	a	0-1	
25/10	Willem II	a	1-4	Papadopulos
31/10	Den Haag	h	3-0	Beerens, Papadopulos 2
8/11	Utrecht	a	3-2	Elm, Papadopulos 2
22/11	Ajax	a	1-5	Popov
28/11	RKC	h	3-1	Elm 2, Beerens
6/12	Heracles	a	1-3	Assaidi
12/12	Feyenoord	h	0-2	

2010

20/1	Groningen	a	0-2	
23/1	Willem II	h	4-2	Breuer, Paulo Henrique 2, Losada
30/1	Den Haag	a	1-2	Sibon
2/2	VVV	a	1-3	Sibon (p)
6/2	Utrecht	h	2-0	Sibon 2 (1p)
13/2	Ajax	h	0-2	
20/2	RKC	a	2-1	Sibon 2 (1p)
27/2	Heracles	h	1-2	Sibon
6/3	AZ	a	1-4	Đuričić
14/3	Vitesse	a	1-0	Beerens
19/3	NEC	h	4-1	Sibon 2 (1p), Breuer (p), Fazli
27/3	Roda	a	2-4	Breuer (p), Väyrynen
3/4	Sparta	h	4-1	Losada 2, Sibon (p), Beerens
10/4	Twente	a	0-2	
14/4	PSV	h	2-2	Sibon, Wojciechowski
18/4	NAC	h	0-0	
2/5	Feyenoord	a	2-6	Grindheim, Elm

No	Name	Nat	DoB	Pos	Aps	(s)	Gls
22	Oussama ASSAIDI		5/8/88	A	11	(9)	1
3	Kristian BAK NIELSEN	DEN	20/10/82	D	26	(1)	
27	Diederik BANGMA		22/5/90	G		(1)	
8	Roy BEERENS		22/12/87	A	29		4
4	Michel BREUER		25/5/80	D	31		3
5	Michael DINGSDAG		18/10/82	D	17	(3)	
14	Filip ĐURIČIĆ	SRB	30/1/92	A	9		1
7	Viktor ELM	SWE	13/11/85	M	26	(2)	5
13	Tarik ELYOUNOUSSI	NOR	23/2/88	A	2	(7)	
40	Samir FAZLI	MKD	22/4/91	A		(6)	1
17	Christian GRINDHEIM	NOR	17/7/83	M	27	(1)	1
18	Philip HAGLUND	SWE	22/3/87	M	8	(4)	
14	Patrik INGELSTEN	SWE	25/1/82	A	2	(4)	
19	Daryl JANMAAT		22/7/89	D	26	(2)	
21	Bonaventure KALOU	CIV	12/1/78	A	2	(2)	
37	Gerry KONING		3/1/80	D	4	(5)	
2	Milan KOPIC	CZE	13/11/85	D		(1)	
24	Martin LEJSAL	CZE	16/9/82	G	10		
23	Hernán LOSADA	ARG	9/5/82	M	20	(9)	4
43	Luciano NARSINGH		13/9/90	A		(2)	

NETHERLANDS
KNVB

11	Michal PAPADOPULOS	CZE	14/4/85	A	15	(8)	7
12	PAULO HENRIQUE Carneiro Filho	BRA	13/3/89	A	9	(7)	3
20	Goran POPOV	MKD	2/10/84	D	26	(1)	1
9	Geert Arend ROORDA		2/3/88	M	3	(1)	
35	Gerald SIBON		19/4/74	A	23	(8)	11
31	Arnór SMÁRASON	ISL	7/9/88	A		(2)	
32	Richard STOLTE		8/1/90	M	1		
15	Michal ŠVEC	CZE	19/3/87	M	17	(1)	
26	Henk TIMMER		3/12/71	G	9		
25	Brian VANDENBUSSCHE	BEL	24/9/81	G	15		
10	Mika VÄYRYNEN	FIN	28/12/81	M	4	(6)	1
44	Paweł WOJCIECHOWSKI	POL	29/4/90	A	2	(4)	1

HERACLES ALMELO
Coach – Gertjan Verbeek
Founded – 1903
Stadium – Polman (8,500)

2009

1/8	AZ	h	3-2	Everton, Overtoom, Fledderus
9/8	NAC	a	0-0	
16/8	Feyenoord	h	0-1	
22/8	Willem II	a	1-0	Dost
30/8	Ajax	h	0-3	
13/9	VVV	a	0-1	
19/9	Sparta	h	1-1	Douglas
27/9	NEC	a	2-0	Everton, Dost
4/10	Twente	a	1-3	Everton
18/10	RKC	a	1-0	Dost
24/10	Vitesse	a	2-0	Overtoom, Steur
1/11	Utrecht	h	3-1	Overtoom, Everton, Douglas
6/11	Groningen	a	1-4	Dost
22/11	PSV	a	0-4	
28/11	Roda	h	3-2	Everton, Dost, Overtoom
6/12	Heerenveen	h	3-1	Looms, Overtoom (p), Dost
13/12	Den Haag	a	4-1	Dost 2, Vejinović, Overtoom
18/12	VVV	h	1-0	Everton

2010

23/1	Vitesse	h	1-2	Steur
31/1	Utrecht	a	0-0	
3/2	Twente	a	0-2	
6/2	Groningen	h	4-3	Dost 2, Overtoom, Maertens
14/2	PSV	h	0-1	
19/2	Roda	a	1-2	Everton
27/2	Heerenveen	a	2-1	Dost, Everton
6/3	Willem II	h	3-2	Douglas, Vejinović, Everton
14/3	Feyenoord	a	1-1	Everton
20/3	NAC	h	3-0	Dost, Overtoom, Everton
27/3	AZ	a	2-3	Douglas, Armenteros
4/4	NEC	h	2-0	Armenteros 2
10/4	Sparta	a	1-1	Dost
13/4	RKC	h	4-1	Van der Linden, Everton 2, Dost
18/4	Ajax	a	0-4	
2/5	Den Haag	h	4-2	Vejinović, Everton, Maertens, Douglas

No	Name	Nat	DoB	Pos	Aps	(s)	Gls
18	Samuel ARMENTEROS	SWE	27/5/90	A		(14)	3
22	Tim BREUKERS		4/11/87	D	34		
12	Bas DOST		31/5/89	A	34		14
21	Darl DOUGLAS		5/10/79	A	27	(6)	5
11	EVERTON Ramos da Silva	BRA	8/6/83	A	34		14
8	Mark-Jan FLEDDERUS		14/12/82	M	18	(8)	1
19	Juha Pekka HAKOLA	FIN	27/10/87	A	7	(11)	
2	Olivier TER HORST		6/4/89	D	4	(1)	
28	Gaby JALLO		1/1/89	D	1	(4)	
4	Antoine VAN DER LINDEN		17/3/76	D	33		1
5	Mark LOOMS		24/3/81	D	33		1
3	Birger MAERTENS	BEL	28/6/80	D	30		2
7	Andrew ORNOCH	CAN	21/8/85	M		(1)	

23	Willie OVERTOOM		2/9/86	A	33		8
1	Martin PIECKENHAGEN	GER	15/11/71	G	33		
17	Kwame QUANSAH	GHA	24/11/82	M	32		
15	Peter REEKERS		2/6/81	D	2		
9	Vojtěch SCHULMEISTER	CZE	9/9/83	A		(9)	
6	Resit SCHUURMAN		31/3/79	M		(2)	
30	Qays SHAYESTEH		22/3/88	M	1		
20	Sebastiaan STEUR		8/3/84	A		(8)	2
26	Dennis TELGENKAMP		9/5/87	G	1	(1)	
10	Marko VEJINOVIĆ		3/2/90	M	17	(9)	3

NAC BREDA
Coach – Robert Maaskant
Founded – 1912
Stadium – Rat Verlegh (17,254)
MAJOR HONOURS:
Dutch League - (1) 1921;
Dutch Cup - (1) 1973.

2009

2/8	Den Haag	a	2-1	Lurling, Amoah
9/8	Heracles	h	0-0	
16/8	Groningen	a	2-1	De Graaf, Kwakman
23/8	PSV	a	1-3	De Graaf
30/8	Heerenveen	h	2-0	Kwakman, Amoah
13/9	Ajax	a	0-6	
19/9	Roda	a	0-2	
27/9	Feyenoord	h	0-2	
3/10	AZ	a	0-1	
17/10	Vitesse	h	4-0	De Graaf (p), Kwakman, Lurling 2
24/10	RKC	h	1-0	Lurling
30/10	VVV	a	1-1	Leonardo
8/11	Willem II	h	4-0	Elshot, Kwakman, Amoah, Leonardo
21/11	NEC	h	3-3	og (Wellenberg), Amoah 2
29/11	Utrecht	a	1-3	Amoah
4/12	Sparta	h	2-2	Leonardo, Zwaanswijk
12/12	Twente	a	1-3	De Graaf

2010

17/1	Ajax	h	1-1	Cairo
23/1	RKC	a	1-0	Leonardo
30/1	VVV	h	2-0	Zwaanswijk, Lurling
2/2	AZ	h	1-1	Kwakman
5/2	Willem II	a	2-1	De Graaf, Amoah
12/2	NEC	a	2-4	Snoyl, Lurling
20/2	Utrecht	h	0-2	
28/2	Sparta	a	2-2	Amoah, Fehér
6/3	PSV	h	2-1	Gorter, Schilder
13/3	Groningen	h	0-3	
20/3	Heracles	a	0-3	
26/3	Den Haag	h	3-0	Lurling, Kwakman, Amoah
4/4	Feyenoord	a	0-0	
10/4	Roda	h	1-0	Gorter (p)
13/4	Vitesse	a	1-1	De Graaf
18/4	Heerenveen	a	0-0	
2/5	Twente	h	0-2	

No	Name	Nat	DoB	Pos	Aps	(s)	Gls
14	Matthew AMOAH	GHA	24/10/80	A	25	(1)	9
31	Omer BAYRAM		27/9/91	A		(4)	
20	Ellery CAIRO		3/8/78	A	3	(19)	1
2	Kurt ELSHOT		3/7/77	D	12	(6)	1
12	Csaba FEHÉR	HUN	2/9/75	M	25	(3)	1
6	Tim GILISSEN		4/6/82	M	25	(1)	
18	Donny GORTER		15/6/88	M	19	(10)	2
7	Edwin DE GRAAF		30/4/80	M	28	(2)	6
32	Tim HOFSTEDE		6/9/89	D		(1)	
9	Fouad IDABDELHAY		2/5/88	A		(2)	
11	Joonas KOLKKA	FIN	28/9/74	A	22	(9)	
5	Kees KWAKMAN		10/6/83	M	33	(1)	6

NETHERLANDS

8	Tommie VAN DER LEEGTE		27/3/77	M	4	(6)	
19	LEONARDO Vítor Santiago	BRA	9/3/83	A	12	(5)	4
28	Tyrone LORAN	ANT	29/6/81	D	8	(1)	
10	Anthony LURLING		22/4/77	A	29	(2)	7
3	Rob PENDERS		31/12/75	D	23		
15	Martijn REUSER		1/2/75	M	3	(13)	
1	Jelle TEN ROUWELAAR		24/12/80	G	34		
23	Robbert SCHILDER		18/4/86	M	30		1
29	Ferne SNOYL		8/3/85	D	9	(4)	1
22	Enric VALLÈS PRAT	ESP	1/3/90	M		(1)	
4	Patrick ZWAANSWIJK		17/1/75	D	30		2

NEC NIJMEGEN
Coach – Dwight Lodeweges; (26/10/09) (Wim Rip);
(16/11/09) Wiljan Vloet
Founded – 1900
Stadium – Goffert (12,500)

2009

2/8	Feyenoord	a	0-2
7/8	Heerenveen	h	4-1 Vleminckx 2, Fejzullahu, El Akchaoui
16/8	Roda	a	0-1
29/8	VVV	h	1-1 Zomer
13/9	Vitesse	a	2-2 Zomer, og (Van Diermen)
19/9	AZ	a	1-0 Davids
27/9	Heracles	h	0-2
30/9	Utrecht	h	1-1 Fejzullahu
3/10	Willem II	a	1-1 Fejzullahu
18/10	Den Haag	h	1-1 Goossens
25/10	PSV	h	0-4
1/11	Sparta	a	0-2
7/11	RKC	h	0-1
21/11	NAC	a	3-3 Vleminckx, Ntibazonkiza 2
29/11	Groningen	a	2-2 Vleminckx, El Akchaoui (p)
6/12	Twente	h	3-4 Goossens, Vleminckx 2
11/12	Ajax	a	0-3

2010

17/1	Vitesse	h	2-1 Ntibazonkiza, Zomer
22/1	PSV	a	0-3
30/1	Sparta	h	1-0 Ntibazonkiza
7/2	RKC	a	1-0 Sibum
12/2	NAC	h	4-2 Nuytinck 2, Radomski, Pothuizen
17/2	Willem II	h	2-1 Zomer, Vleminckx
20/2	Groningen	h	0-2
28/2	Twente	a	1-2 Vleminckx
7/3	Utrecht	a	0-1
13/3	Roda	h	0-2
19/3	Heerenveen	a	1-4 Goossens
28/3	Feyenoord	h	0-0
4/4	Heracles	a	0-2
10/4	AZ	h	0-0
14/4	Den Haag	a	3-2 Ten Voorde, og (Kum), Pothuizen
18/4	VVV	a	0-2
2/5	Ajax	h	1-4 Ntibazonkiza

No	Name	Nat	DoB	Pos	Aps	(s)	Gls
31	Shapoul ALI		15/7/90	A		(1)	
25	Rein BAART		13/4/72	G		(1)	
1	Gábor BABOS	HUN	24/10/74	G	34		
19	Mitchell BURGZORG		25/7/87	D	17	(3)	
8	Lorenzo DAVIDS		4/9/86	M	27	(4)	1
3	Rens VAN EIJDEN		3/3/88	D	18	(5)	
5	Youssef EL AKCHAOUI	MAR	18/2/81	D	17		2
21	Moestafa EL KABIR		5/10/88	A	9	(2)	
11	Erton FEJZULLAHU	SWE	9/4/88	A	23	(6)	3
20	John GOOSSENS		25/7/88	M	16	(5)	3
37	Sherwin GROT		27/7/90	A		(1)	
22	Jeroen HEUBACH		24/9/74	D	4	(1)	

4	Dominique KIVUVU	ANG	16/9/87	M	5	(6)	
17	Saidi NTIBAZONKIZA	BDI	1/5/87	A	19	(3)	5
35	Bram NUYTINCK		4/5/90	D	12	(1)	2
13	Mark OTTEN		2/9/85	D		(1)	
6	Patrick POTHUIZEN		15/5/72	D	19	(10)	2
23	Arek RADOMSKI	POL	27/6/77	M	30		1
9	Jeffrey SARPONG		3/8/88	M	15		
10	Lasse SCHØNE	DEN	27/5/86	M	4	(1)	
16	Bas SIBUM		26/12/82	M	15		1
18	Björn VLEMINCKX	BEL	1/12/85	A	32		8
14	Rick TEN VOORDE		20/6/91	A	1	(6)	1
36	Bastian WEISER	GER	19/6/90	D	1		
15	Niels WELLENBERG		9/8/82	D	20		
7	Rutger WORM		1/2/86	M	5	(17)	
2	Ramon ZOMER		13/4/83	D	31		4

PSV EINDHOVEN
Coach – Fred Rutten
Founded – 1913
Stadium – Philips (35,000)
MAJOR HONOURS:
European Champion Clubs' Cup - (1) 1988;
UEFA Cup - (1) 1978;
Dutch League - (21) 1929, 1935, 1951, 1963, 1975, 1976, 1978, 1986, 1987,
1988, 1989, 1991, 1992, 1997, 2000, 2001, 2003, 2005, 2006, 2007, 2008;
Dutch Cup - (8) 1950, 1974, 1976, 1988, 1989, 1990, 1996, 2005.

2009

2/8	VVV	h	3-3 Amrabat, Toivonen 2
9/8	Twente	a	1-2 Dzsudzsák
16/8	Ajax	h	4-3 Dzsudzsák 2, Bakkal 2
23/8	NAC	h	3-1 Koevermans 2, Afellay
30/8	Groningen	a	2-0 Koevermans 2
12/9	Roda	h	3-0 Dzsudzsák, Manolev, Bakkal
20/9	Feyenoord	a	3-1 Koevermans 2, Bakkal
26/9	Willem II	h	3-1 Bakkal, Lazović, Afellay
4/10	Utrecht	a	0-0
17/10	Heerenveen	h	1-0 Lazović
25/10	NEC	a	4-0 Dzsudzsák, Reis, Bakkal, Lazović (p)
31/10	Vitesse	h	1-0 Dzsudzsák
8/11	Den Haag	a	5-1 Toivonen 4, Bakkal
22/11	Heracles	h	4-0 Afellay, Dzsudzsák, Toivonen, Vuković
27/11	Sparta	a	3-2 Lazović, Reis, Dzsudzsák
6/12	RKC	a	2-0 Reis, Lazović
12/12	AZ	h	1-0 Toivonen

2010

19/1	Roda	a	1-0 Koevermans
22/1	NEC	h	3-0 Toivonen 2, Amrabat
31/1	Vitesse	a	0-0
3/2	Utrecht	h	2-1 Toivonen, Engelaar
6/2	Den Haag	h	2-0 Rodríguez, Toivonen
14/2	Heracles	a	1-0 Toivonen
21/2	Sparta	h	1-1 Bakkal
28/2	RKC	h	5-1 Dzsudzsák, Afellay, Koevermans 2, Amrabat
6/3	NAC	a	1-2 Engelaar
14/3	Ajax	a	1-4 Dzsudzsák (p)
20/3	Twente	h	1-1 Koevermans
28/3	VVV	a	4-2 Bakkal 2, Dzsudzsák, Koevermans
4/4	Willem II	a	1-0 Dzsudzsák
11/4	Feyenoord	h	0-0
14/4	Heerenveen	a	2-2 Dzsudzsák, Manolev
18/4	Groningen	h	3-1 Labyad 2, Dzsudzsák
2/5	AZ	a	1-1 Bakkal

NETHERLANDS
KNVB

No	Name	Nat	DoB	Pos	Aps	(s)	Gls
20	Ibrahim AFELLAY		2/4/86	M	29		4
11	Nordin AMRABAT		31/3/87	A	9	(16)	3
28	Otman BAKKAL		27/2/85	M	30	(1)	11
22	Balázs DZSUDZSÁK	HUN	23/12/86	A	32		14
18	Orlando ENGELAAR		24/8/79	M	26	(2)	2
1	Andreas ISAKSSON	SWE	3/10/81	G	34		
10	Danny KOEVERMANS		1/11/78	A	13	(9)	11
2	Jan KROMKAMP		17/8/80	D	1	(1)	
52	Zakaria LABYAD		9/3/93	M	2	(4)	2
9	Danko LAZOVIĆ	SRB	17/5/83	A	22	(2)	5
25	Stanislav MANOLEV	BUL	16/12/85	D	30		2
24	Dirk MARCELLIS		13/4/88	D	2	(9)	
36	Funso OJO	BEL	28/8/91	D	1	(2)	
23	André OOIJER		11/7/74	D	20	(5)	
14	Erik PIETERS		7/8/88	D	27		
42	Jonathan REIS	BRA	6/6/89	A	5	(7)	3
4	Francisco Javier RODRÍGUEZ	MEX	20/10/81	D	25	(4)	1
3	Carlos Arnoldo SALCIDO	MEX	2/4/80	D	25	(2)	
6	Timmy SIMONS	BEL	11/12/76	M	16	(9)	
7	Ola TOIVONEN	SWE	3/7/86	A	22	(11)	13
5	Jagoš VUKOVIĆ	SRB	10/6/88	D	2	(3)	1
15	Stijn WUYTENS	BEL	8/10/89	M	1	(5)	

No	Name	Nat	DoB	Pos	Aps	(s)	Gls
28	Kemy AGUSTIEN		2/8/86	M	15	(4)	1
9	Charlison BENSCHOP		21/8/89	A	24	(8)	6
14	Fred BENSON		10/4/84	A	10	(9)	4
10	Ruud BERGER		18/2/80	M	21	(6)	1
11	Derk BOERRIGTER		16/10/86	A	28	(3)	7
7	Benjamin DE CEULAER	BEL	19/12/83	A	21	(3)	4
40	Jurgen COLIN		20/1/81	D	22	(1)	
20	Alexandre DI GREGORIO	BEL	12/2/80	M	8	(2)	
3	Wouter GUDDE		5/8/84	D	22		
16	Roald VAN HOUT		23/4/88	A	2	(4)	
19	Fouad IDABDELHAY		2/5/88	A	14	(11)	3
15	Anton JONGSMA		13/1/83	M		(1)	
36	Ohad LEVITA	ISR	17/2/86	G	24		
21	Gérard LIFONDJA		2/3/89	M	4	(5)	
5	Gijs LUIRINK		12/9/83	D	12	(2)	
32	Shkodran METAJ		5/2/88	M	26	(3)	
4	Frank VAN MOSSELVELD		2/1/84	D	23	(1)	
2	Dustley MULDER		27/1/85	D	32		1
6	Hans MULDER		27/4/87	M	27		1
8	Anthony OBODAI	GHA	6/8/82	M	13	(7)	
12	Toni VARELA		13/6/86	D	15	(5)	
17	Kevin VINK		30/7/84	A	1	(10)	
25	Eddy VORM		4/6/89	A		(6)	
1	Jurgen WEVERS		12/1/79	G	10		

RKC WAALWIJK
Coach – Ruud Brood
Founded – 1940
Stadium – Mandemakers (7,500)

2009				
1/8	Utrecht	h	0-1	
8/8	Ajax	a	1-4	De Ceulaer
15/8	AZ	h	0-6	
23/8	Twente	a	1-2	Benschop
28/8	Den Haag	h	0-2	
13/9	Sparta	a	0-1	
19/9	Vitesse	a	1-3	Idabdelhay
26/9	Roda	h	4-1	Idabdelhay, Benschop, Boerrigter, Benson
3/10	Feyenoord	a	0-3	
18/10	Heracles	h	0-1	
24/10	NAC	a	0-1	
1/11	Willem II	h	0-1	
7/11	NEC	a	1-0	Boerrigter
21/11	Groningen	h	3-1	Benschop 2, Berger
28/11	Heerenveen	a	1-3	Benson
6/12	PSV	h	0-2	
12/12	VVV	a	0-3	
19/12	Sparta	h	4-1	Boerrigter 2, Agustien, Benson
2010				
23/1	NAC	h	0-1	
29/1	Willem II	a	1-2	Benson
4/2	Feyenoord	h	0-1	
7/2	NEC	h	0-1	
14/2	Groningen	a	1-2	Boerrigter
20/2	Heerenveen	h	1-2	De Ceulaer
28/2	PSV	a	1-5	Benschop
7/3	Twente	h	0-1	
13/3	AZ	a	2-6	De Ceulaer, Boerrigter
21/3	Ajax	h	1-5	og (Pantelić)
28/3	Utrecht	a	0-2	
3/4	Roda	a	1-5	Benschop
9/4	Vitesse	h	4-1	og (Jong-A-Pin), Boerrigter, Mulder D., De Ceulaer
13/4	Heracles	a	1-4	Idabdelhay
18/4	Den Haag	a	0-4	
2/5	VVV	h	1-2	Mulder H.

RODA JC
Coach – Harm van Veldhoven
Founded – 1962
Stadium – Parkstad Limburg (19,979)
MAJOR HONOURS:
Dutch Cup - (2) 1997, 2000.

2009				
31/7	Heerenveen	a	0-0	
8/8	Groningen	h	1-1	Hadouir
16/8	NEC	h	1-0	Junker
23/8	Feyenoord	a	0-4	
28/8	Vitesse	h	3-4	Junker, og (Van der Struijk), Hadouir
12/9	PSV	a	0-3	
19/9	NAC	h	2-0	Junker 2
26/9	RKC	a	1-4	Janssen
4/10	Ajax	h	2-2	Sutchuin, Bodor
18/10	VVV	a	1-1	Skoubo
23/10	Utrecht	a	1-2	Janssen
31/10	Twente	h	1-2	Yulu-Matondo
7/11	Sparta	a	2-1	Junker, Bodor
21/11	AZ	h	2-4	Kah, Yulu-Matondo
28/11	Heracles	a	2-3	Junker, Kah
4/12	Den Haag	h	1-1	Junker
13/12	Willem II	a	3-1	Junker 2, Vormer
2010				
19/1	PSV	h	0-1	
23/1	Utrecht	h	2-0	Janssen, Saeijs
31/1	Twente	a	0-2	
3/2	Ajax	a	0-4	
6/2	Sparta	h	2-1	Janssen, Junker
13/2	AZ	a	0-2	
19/2	Heracles	h	2-1	De Fauw, De Jong
26/2	Den Haag	a	2-1	Junker, Hadouir
7/3	Feyenoord	h	2-4	Yulu-Matondo, Bodor
13/3	NEC	a	2-0	Janssen, Junker
21/3	Groningen	a	0-1	
27/3	Heerenveen	h	4-2	Junker 2, De Jong, Bodor
3/4	RKC	h	5-1	Skoubo 2, Junker 3
10/4	NAC	a	0-1	
14/4	VVV	h	4-2	Janssen, Saeijs, Junker, Skoubo
18/4	Vitesse	a	5-2	Janssen 2, Skoubo, Junker 2
2/5	Willem II	h	3-2	Bodor, Junker (p), De Fauw

No	Name	Nat	DoB	Pos	Aps	(s)	Gls
3	Eric ADDO	GHA	12/11/78	D	12		
27	Boldizsár BODOR	HUN	27/4/82	M	27	(6)	5
1	Bram CASTRO	BEL	30/9/82	G	18		
26	Laurent DELORGE	BEL	21/7/79	M	16	(8)	
2	Davy DE FAUW	BEL	8/7/81	D	33		2
10	Anouar HADOUIR	MAR	14/9/82	A	26	(1)	3
8	Willem JANSSEN		4/7/86	M	34		8
17	Marcel DE JONG	CAN	15/10/86	M	30	(1)	2
9	Mads JUNKER	DEN	21/4/81	A	32	(2)	21
4	Pa Modou KAH	NOR	30/7/80	D	16	(7)	2
15	Arnold KRUISWIJK		2/11/84	D	17		
5	Vincent LACHAMBRE	BEL	6/11/80	D	10		
7	Edwin LINSSEN		28/8/80	M	8		
14	Rihairo MEULENS		3/6/88	A		(4)	
20	Jan-Paul SAEIJS		20/6/78	D	21		2
23	Adnan SEČEROVIĆ	BIH	1/12/91	M		(1)	
11	Morten SKOUBO	DEN	30/6/80	A	13	(10)	5
24	Aleksandar STANKOV	MKD	19/2/91	D		(1)	
18	Arnaud SUTCHUIN	BEL	2/5/89	M	12	(15)	1
7	Sebastian SVÄRD	DEN	15/1/83	M	2	(4)	
23	Dieter VAN TORNHOUT	BEL	18/3/85	A	1	(2)	
22	Przemysław TYTOŃ	POL	4/1/87	G	16		
16	Jamaïque VANDAMME	BEL	1/8/85	A		(1)	
6	Ruud VORMER		11/5/88	M	24	(6)	1
12	Kris DE WREE	BEL	21/5/81	D	1	(1)	
34	Jeanvion YULU-MATONDO	BEL	5/1/86	A	5	(15)	3

SPARTA ROTTERDAM

Coach – Frans Adelaar; (4/4/10) Aad de Mos
Founded – 1888
Stadium – Sparta (11,026)
MAJOR HONOURS:
Dutch League – (6) 1909, 1911, 1912, 1913, 1915, 1959;
Dutch Cup – (3) 1958, 1962, 1966.

2009

1/8	Twente	h	0-2	
7/8	AZ	a	0-2	
15/8	Willem II	h	2-1	*Strootman, Poepon*
23/8	Ajax	a	0-0	
29/8	Utrecht	a	0-2	
13/9	RKC	h	1-0	*Poepon*
19/9	Heracles	a	1-1	*Adeleye*
27/9	Heerenveen	h	0-2	
2/10	Vitesse	a	0-2	
18/10	Feyenoord	h	2-1	*Poepon, Strootman*
24/10	Den Haag	a	3-2	*Falkenburg 3*
1/11	NEC	h	2-0	*Falkenburg 2*
7/11	Roda	h	1-2	*Poepon (p)*
22/11	VVV	a	0-5	
27/11	PSV	h	2-3	*Poepon 2*
4/12	NAC	a	2-2	*Falkenburg, Poepon*
13/12	Groningen	h	2-4	*Falkenburg, Van Gessel*
19/12	RKC	a	1-4	*Bodul*

2010

24/1	Den Haag	h	0-0	
30/1	NEC	a	0-1	
3/2	Vitesse	h	1-1	*Falkenburg*
6/2	Roda	a	1-2	*Falkenburg*
14/2	VVV	h	2-0	*John, Duplan*
21/2	PSV	a	1-1	*Poepon*
28/2	NAC	h	2-2	*Koenders, Poepon*
7/3	Ajax	h	0-3	
14/3	Willem II	a	1-3	*Poepon (p)*
21/3	AZ	h	0-1	
27/3	Twente	a	0-3	
3/4	Heerenveen	a	1-4	*Falkenburg*

10/4	Heracles	h	1-1	*Duplan*
14/4	Feyenoord	a	0-3	
18/4	Utrecht	h	0-3	
2/5	Groningen	a	1-3	*John*

No	Name	Nat	DoB	Pos	Aps	(s)	Gls
25	David ABDUL		17/8/89	A	2		
3	Ayodele ADELEYE	NGA	25/12/88	D	28		1
13	Tim BAKENS		2/11/82	D	7	(3)	
26	Anthony BENTEM		19/3/90	D	1		
2	Emmanuel BOAKYE	GHA	25/3/85	D	11		
10	Darko BODUL	CRO	11/1/89	A	18	(6)	1
6	Edwin VAN BUEREN		4/4/80	M	11	(8)	
7	Romano DENNEBOOM		29/1/81	A	6	(4)	
11	Charles DISSELS		21/12/84	A	2	(14)	
32	Lerin DUARTE		11/8/90	M	1	(8)	
17	Édouard DUPLAN	FRA	13/5/83	A	28	(3)	2
20	Erik FALKENBURG		5/5/88	M	27	(3)	10
4	Sander VAN GESSEL		4/11/76	M	16	(9)	1
15	Joey GODEE		2/3/89	A		(7)	
24	Joshua JOHN		1/10/88	A	16	(12)	2
5	Ruud KNOL		13/3/81	D	10	(2)	
19	Milano KOENDERS		31/7/87	D	13		1
36	Marcellino VAN DER LEEUW		15/6/90	D		(1)	
9	Rydell POEPON		28/7/88	A	26	(7)	10
44	Marten DE ROON		29/3/91	M	3		
7	Yuri ROSE		8/5/79	A		(1)	
28	Nathan RUTJES		1/12/83	M	19	(2)	
1	Aleksander ŠELIGA	SVN	1/2/80	G	32		
8	Donovan SLIJNGARD		28/8/87	D	33		
14	Kevin STROOTMAN		13/2/90	M	27	(1)	2
16	Karim TOUZANI		11/9/80	M	6	(1)	
21	Cor VARKEVISSER		14/5/82	G	2		
22	Nick VIERGEVER		3/8/89	D	28	(1)	
36	Bjorn VLASBLOM		28/1/90	M	1		

FC TWENTE

Coach – Steve McClaren (ENG)
Founded – 1965
Stadium – De Grolsch Veste (24,244)
MAJOR HONOURS:
Dutch League – (1) 2010;
Dutch Cup - (2) 1977, 2001.

2009

1/8	Sparta	a	2-0	*Nkufo, Ruiz*
9/8	PSV	h	1-1	*Douglas*
15/8	Den Haag	a	1-0	*Nkufo*
23/8	RKC	h	2-1	*Ruiz, Nkufo*
30/8	Feyenoord	a	1-1	*Kuiper*
12/9	Utrecht	h	3-2	*Nkufo, Kuiper, Ruiz*
20/9	Heerenveen	a	2-0	*Stoch 2*
26/9	VVV	h	2-1	*Ruiz, Douglas*
4/10	Heracles	a	3-1	*Ruiz, Nkufo, Janssen*
17/10	AZ	h	3-2	*Perez, Ruiz, Nkufo*
25/10	Groningen	h	4-0	*Stoch, Tiendalli, Nkufo, Ruiz*
31/10	Roda	a	2-1	*Ruiz, Stoch*
8/11	Ajax	h	1-0	*Ruiz*
21/11	Vitesse	h	1-0	*Ruiz*
28/11	Willem II	a	3-1	*Brama, Stoch, Ruiz*
6/12	NEC	a	4-3	*Perez, Nkufo, Stoch, Ruiz*
12/12	NAC	h	3-1	*Stoch 2 (1p), Ruiz*

2010

17/1	Utrecht	a	0-0	
24/1	Groningen	a	0-0	
31/1	Roda	h	2-0	*Perez, Ruiz*
3/2	Heracles	h	2-0	*Ruiz, Nkufo*
7/2	Ajax	a	0-3	

NETHERLANDS

13/2	Vitesse	a	2-1	Ruiz, Stam
21/2	Willem II	h	1-0	Wisgerhof
28/2	NEC	h	2-1	De Jong, Ruiz
7/3	RKC	a	1-0	Perez
12/3	Den Haag	h	3-1	Ruiz 2 (1p), Perez
20/3	PSV	a	1-1	Nkufo
27/3	Sparta	h	3-0	Ruiz 3
3/4	VVV	a	2-0	Nkufo, Ruiz
10/4	Heerenveen	h	2-0	Tioté, De Jong
13/4	AZ	a	0-1	
18/4	Feyenoord	h	2-0	Nkufo, Stoch
2/5	NAC	a	2-0	Ruiz, Stoch

No	Name	Nat	DoB	Pos	Aps	(s)	Gls
23	Nashat AKRAM	IRQ	12/9/84	M		(10)	
1	Sander BOSCHKER		20/10/70	G	34		
6	Wout BRAMA		21/8/86	M	30	(1)	1
2	David CARNEY	AUS	30/11/83	D		(8)	
7	Romano DENNEBOOM		29/1/81	A		(1)	
19	DOUGLAS Franco Teixeira	BRA	12/1/88	D	31		2
24	Theo JANSSEN		27/7/81	M	27	(1)	1
20	Luuk DE JONG		27/8/90	A	3	(9)	2
3	Nicky KUIPER		7/6/89	D	7	(9)	2
9	Blaise NKUFO	SUI	25/5/75	A	31	(1)	12
16	Cees PAAUWE		3/11/77	G		(1)	
14	Bernard PARKER	RSA	16/3/86	A	2	(12)	
10	Kenneth PEREZ	DEN	29/8/74	M	31		5
5	Slobodan RAJKOVIĆ	SRB	3/2/89	D	8	(2)	
25	Andrej RENDLA	SVK	13/10/90	A		(2)	
22	Bryan RUIZ	CRC	18/8/85	A	34		24
11	Nikita RUKAVYTSYA	AUS	22/6/87	A		(2)	
8	Ronnie STAM		18/6/84	D	33		1
15	Miroslav STOCH	SVK	19/10/89	A	31	(1)	10
26	Dwight TIENDALLI		21/10/85	D	25	(1)	1
18	Cheik TIOTÉ	CIV	21/6/86	M	10	(18)	1
17	WELLINGTON Luís de Sousa	BRA	11/2/86	A		(3)	
4	Peter WISGERHOF		19/11/79	D	33		1
27	Dario VUJIČEVIĆ	CRO	1/4/90	M	4	(12)	

FC UTRECHT
Coach – Ton du Chatinier
Founded – 1970
Stadium – Galgenwaard (24,500)
MAJOR HONOURS:
Dutch Cup - (3) 1985, 2003, 2004.

2009

1/8	RKC	a	1-0	Van Wolfswinkel
9/8	Willem II	h	1-0	Dickoh
16/8	VVV	h	2-2	Mertens 2
29/8	Sparta	h	2-0	Lensky, Van Dijk (p)
12/9	Twente	a	2-3	Van Wolfswinkel 2
20/9	Den Haag	a	1-0	Mertens
26/9	AZ	h	1-0	Keller
30/9	NEC	a	1-1	Lensky
4/10	PSV	h	0-0	
18/10	Groningen	a	0-0	
23/10	Roda	h	2-1	Mulenga, Van Wolfswinkel
1/11	Heracles	a	1-3	Silberbauer
8/11	Heerenveen	h	2-3	Cornelisse, Mulenga
22/11	Feyenoord	a	0-0	
29/11	NAC	h	3-1	Vandenbergh, Nijholt, Mulenga
6/12	Ajax	h	2-0	Mulenga, Wuytens
13/12	Vitesse	a	2-2	Van Wolfswinkel, Mulenga

2010

17/1	Twente	h	0-0	
23/1	Roda	a	0-2	
31/1	Heracles	h	0-0	

3/2	PSV	a	1-2	Keller
6/2	Heerenveen	a	0-2	
14/2	Feyenoord	h	0-0	
20/2	NAC	a	2-0	Asare, Mertens
28/2	Ajax	a	0-4	
7/3	NEC	h	1-0	Van Wolfswinkel
13/3	VVV	a	1-0	Lensky
20/3	Willem II	a	3-0	Mulenga, Wuytens, Schut
28/3	RKC	h	2-0	Mertens, Silberbauer
3/4	AZ	a	0-2	
11/4	Den Haag	h	0-2	
14/4	Groningen	h	1-1	Mulenga
18/4	Sparta	a	3-0	Lensky, Van Wolfswinkel, Danso
2/5	Vitesse	h	2-2	Mertens, Mulenga

No	Name	Nat	DoB	Pos	Aps	(s)	Gls
15	Nana ASARE	GHA	11/7/86	M	26	(2)	1
2	Tim CORNELISSE		3/4/78	D	15	(2)	1
33	Erixon DANSO		22/7/89	A	1	(8)	1
5	Francis DICKOH	GHA	13/12/82	D	10	(3)	1
6	Gregoor VAN DIJK		16/11/81	M	17	(2)	1
21	Leroy GEORGE		21/4/87	A	1	(6)	
22	Sander KELLER		18/9/79	D	21	(2)	2
36	Jacob LENSKY	CAN	16/12/88	D	27	(1)	4
7	Loïc LOVAL	FRA	28/9/81	A	4	(14)	
35	Mark VAN DEN MAAREL		12/8/89	D	17	(1)	
18	Barry MAGUIRE		27/10/89	M	2	(5)	
11	Dries MERTENS	BEL	6/5/87	M	34		6
26	Ken VAN MIERLO		5/8/87	M		(4)	
25	Jacob MULENGA	ZAM	12/2/84	A	29		8
3	Mihai Mircea NEȘU	ROU	19/2/83	D	20	(4)	
27	Gianluca NIJHOLT		14/2/90	M	16	(6)	1
17	Alje SCHUT		18/2/81	D	8		1
8	Michael SILBERBAUER	DEN	7/7/81	M	30		2
19	Khalid SINOUH	MAR	2/5/75	G	1		
23	Hans SOMERS	BEL	9/3/78	M		(1)	
12	Kevin VANDENBERGH	BEL	16/5/83	A	4	(5)	1
1	Michel VORM		20/10/83	G	33		
9	Ricky VAN WOLFSWINKEL		27/1/89	A	27	(4)	7
29	Jan WUYTENS	BEL	9/6/85	D	31		2
41	Frank VAN DER ZWAN		27/7/88	A		(2)	

VITESSE
Coach – Theo Bos
Founded – 1892
Stadium – Gelredome (26,600)

2009

1/8	Willem II	a	1-3	Sinan
9/8	Feyenoord	h	0-0	
15/8	Heerenveen	a	0-1	
22/8	Den Haag	h	1-3	Sprockel
28/8	Roda	a	4-3	Nilsson, Hofs, Sinan, Kolk
13/9	NEC	h	2-2	Kolk, Claudemir
19/9	RKC	h	3-1	Nilsson, Kolk (p), Verhaegh
27/9	Groningen	a	0-1	
2/10	Sparta	h	2-0	Nilsson, Pluim
17/10	NAC	a	0-4	
24/10	Heracles	h	0-2	
31/10	PSV	a	0-1	
7/11	VVV	h	2-0	Stevanović, Claudemir
21/11	Twente	a	0-1	
29/11	Ajax	h	1-5	Stevanović
4/12	AZ	a	2-1	Nilsson, Stevanović
13/12	Utrecht	h	2-2	Nilsson (p), Claudemir

2010

17/1	NEC	a	1-2	Nilsson (p)
23/1	Heracles	a	2-1	Kaya 2

31/1	PSV	h	0-0	
3/2	Sparta	a	1-1	Greene
7/2	VVV	a	0-2	
13/2	Twente	h	1-2	Verhaegh
21/2	Ajax	a	0-4	
27/2	AZ	h	0-3	
6/3	Den Haag	a	1-1	Nilsson
14/3	Heerenveen	h	0-1	
27/3	Willem II	h	2-1	Greene, Kolk
31/3	Feyenoord	a	1-2	Pluim (first half played 20/3)
3/4	Groningen	h	3-0	Claudemir, Kolk, Büttner
9/4	RKC	a	1-4	og (Mulder D.)
13/4	NAC	h	1-1	Kolk
18/4	Roda	h	2-5	Kaya, Büttner
2/5	Utrecht	a	2-2	Kaya, Kolk

No	Name	Nat	DoB	Pos	Aps	(s)	Gls
22	Alexander BÜTTNER		11/2/89	M	11	(16)	2
7	CLAUDEMIR Domingues de Souza	BRA	27/3/88	M	34		4
3	Kevin VAN DIERMEN		3/7/89	D	19	(4)	
5	Jeroen DROST		21/1/87	D	14	(1)	
25	Gino FELIXDAAL		5/1/90	M	2		
35	Marco VAN GINKEL		1/12/92	M	1	(3)	
36	Giovanni GRAVENBEEK		11/5/88	A	5	(4)	
15	Serginho GREENE		23/2/82	D	17	(1)	2
30	Nicky HOFS		17/5/83	M	25	(6)	1
14	Julian JENNER		28/2/84	A	2	(2)	
20	Calvin JONG-A-PIN		18/7/86	D	28	(2)	
18	Onur KAYA	BEL	20/4/86	M	11	(8)	4
32	Cagri KODALAK		12/1/91	M		(1)	
10	Santi KOLK		2/10/81	A	23	(3)	7
8	Rogier MOLHOEK		22/7/81	M	15		
9	Lasse NILSSON	SWE	3/1/82	A	25	(5)	7
26	Wiljan PLUIM		4/1/89	A	17	(2)	2
24	Davy PRÖPPER		2/9/91	A	2	(9)	
29	Eloy ROOM		6/2/89	G	1	(2)	
40	Roy DE RUITER		19/8/89	A		(1)	
11	SİNAN Kaloğlu	TUR	10/6/81	A	1	(7)	2
17	Genaro SNIJDERS		29/7/89	A		(6)	
4	Civard SPROCKEL		10/5/83	D	29		1
16	Dalibor STEVANOVIČ	SVN	27/9/84	M	14	(9)	3
6	Frank VAN DER STRUIJK		28/3/85	D	15	(1)	
1	Piet VELTHUIZEN		3/11/86	G	33		
2	Paul VERHAEGH		1/9/83	D	30		2

VVV-VENLO
Coach – Jan van Dijk
Founded – 1903
Stadium – Seacon (7,500)
MAJOR HONOURS:
Dutch Cup - (1) 1959.

2009

2/8	PSV	a	3-3	Ahahaoui, Honda, Schaken
9/8	Den Haag	h	2-2	Honda 2
16/8	Utrecht	a	2-2	Calabro, Honda
22/8	Groningen	h	2-2	Honda, Calabro
29/8	NEC	a	1-1	Calabro
13/9	Heracles	h	1-0	Calabro
20/9	Ajax	h	0-4	
26/9	Twente	a	1-2	Ahahaoui
4/10	Heerenveen	a	1-1	Calabro
18/10	Roda	h	1-1	Leemans
24/10	Feyenoord	a	0-1	
30/10	NAC	h	1-1	Van Kouwen
7/11	Vitesse	a	0-2	

22/11	Sparta	h	5-0	Auassar, Ahahaoui, Calabro 2, Van Dessel
28/11	AZ	a	0-2	
4/12	Willem II	h	2-1	Auassar, Honda (p)
12/12	RKC	h	3-0	Auassar, Timisela, Leemans
18/12	Heracles	a	0-1	

2010

24/1	Feyenoord	h	1-1	De Regt
30/1	NAC	a	0-2	
2/2	Heerenveen	h	3-1	De Regt, Gonzalo, Calabro
7/2	Vitesse	h	2-0	og (Sprockel), Paauwe
14/2	Sparta	a	0-2	
20/2	AZ	h	3-3	Auassar, Schaken, Uchebo
27/2	Willem II	a	1-2	Gonzalo
7/3	Groningen	a	0-1	
13/3	Utrecht	h	0-1	
21/3	Den Haag	a	0-0	
28/3	PSV	h	2-4	Schaken, Boymans
3/4	Twente	h	0-2	
11/4	Ajax	a	0-7	
14/4	Roda	a	2-4	Nkume, Gonzalo
18/4	NEC	h	2-0	Boymans 2
2/5	RKC	a	2-1	Calabro, Boymans

No	Name	Nat	DoB	Pos	Aps	(s)	Gls
15	Achmed AHAHAOUI		6/2/83	A	31	(3)	3
18	Adil AUASSAR		6/10/86	M	31	(2)	4
16	Kevin BEGOIS	BEL	13/5/82	G	19	(1)	
30	Ruud BOFFIN	BEL	5/11/87	G	5		
22	Robert BÖHM	GER	28/3/88	G	3		
20	Ruud BOYMANS		28/4/89	A	6	(10)	4
9	Sandro CALABRO		11/4/83	A	27	(4)	9
24	Soufiane DADDA		18/6/90	A	1	(9)	
8	Kevin VAN DESSEL	BEL	9/4/79	M	11	(17)	1
21	DIOGO Filipe Guerreiro VIANA	POR	22/1/90	A	4	(19)	
26	Henrico DROST		21/1/87	D	1		
5	Niels FLEUREN		1/11/86	D	25	(2)	
1	Dennis GENTENAAR		30/9/75	G	7		
10	GONZALO Manuel García García	ESP	13/10/83	A	14		3
10	Keisuke HONDA	JPN	13/6/86	M	18		6
4	Frank VAN KOUWEN		2/7/80	D	21	(1)	1
6	Ken LEEMANS	BEL	5/1/83	M	30	(1)	2
19	Alex NKUME	NGA	1/1/90	D	7	(1)	1
27	Patrick PAAUWE		27/12/75	M	31		1
17	Ferry DE REGT		29/8/88	D	15	(6)	2
7	Ruben SCHAKEN		3/4/82	A	31	(1)	3
25	Jasar TAKAK		4/3/82	M	1	(6)	
2	Michael TIMISELA		5/5/86	D	24	(2)	1
14	Michael Okechukwu UCHEBO	NGA	27/9/90	A	1	(6)	1
23	Rick VERBEEK		14/12/88	A		(1)	
3	Sjors VERDELLEN		29/11/81	D	10	(5)	

WILLEM II
Coach – Alfons Groenendijk; (19/2/10) Mark Schenning; (27/2/10) Arno Pijpers; (26/4/10) Theo de Jong
Founded – 1896
Stadium – Willem II (14,700)
MAJOR HONOURS:
Dutch League - (3) 1916, 1952, 1955;
Dutch Cup - (2) 1944, 1963.

2009

1/8	Vitesse	h	3-1	Grégoire, Boutahar, Swinkels
9/8	Utrecht	a	0-1	
15/8	Sparta	a	1-2	Biemans
22/8	Heracles	h	0-1	
29/8	AZ	a	1-2	Zijler

NETHERLANDS
KNVB

13/9	Feyenoord	h	2-3	*Boutahar, Biemans*
18/9	Groningen	h	2-1	*Zijler, Grégoire (p)*
26/9	PSV	a	1-3	*Demouge*
3/10	NEC	h	1-1	*Boutahar*
17/10	Ajax	a	0-4	
25/10	Heerenveen	h	4-1	*Zijler, Boutahar, Demouge 2*
1/11	RKC	a	1-0	*Grégoire*
8/11	NAC	a	0-4	
22/11	Den Haag	h	1-1	*Demouge*
28/11	Twente	h	1-3	*Grégoire (p)*
4/12	VVV	a	1-2	*Swinkels*
13/12	Roda	h	1-3	*Grégoire (p)*
19/12	Feyenoord	a	0-1	
2010				
23/1	Heerenveen	a	2-4	*Demouge, Nijland*
29/1	RKC	h	2-1	*Nijland, Zijler*
5/2	NAC	h	1-2	*Donald*
13/2	Den Haag	a	0-3	
17/2	NEC	a	1-2	*Nijland*
21/2	Twente	a	0-1	
27/2	VVV	h	2-1	*Van der Heijden, Demouge*
6/3	Heracles	a	2-3	*Sheotahul 2*
14/3	Sparta	h	3-1	*Demouge, og (Adeleye), Nijland (p)*
20/3	Utrecht	h	0-3	
27/3	Vitesse	a	1-2	*Boutahar*
4/4	PSV	h	0-1	
11/4	Groningen	a	0-4	
14/4	Ajax	h	0-2	
18/4	AZ	h	0-3	
2/5	Roda	a	2-3	*Pereira, Boutahar*

No	Name	Nat	DoB	Pos	Aps	(s)	Gls
1	Maikel AERTS		26/6/76	G	28		
6	Mehmet AKGÜN	GER	6/8/86	M	3	(1)	
12	Bart BIEMANS	BEL	14/3/88	D	31		2
10	Saïd BOUTAHAR	MAR	12/8/82	M	32		6
25	Marciano BRUMA		7/3/84	D	16	(2)	
9	Frank DEMOUGE		25/6/82	A	29	(1)	7
7	Boy DEUL		30/8/87	M		(3)	
21	Daan VAN DINTER		12/1/89	D	1	(3)	
23	Mitchell DONALD		10/12/88	M	13	(1)	1
8	Christophe GRÉGOIRE	BEL	20/4/80	M	15	(5)	5
24	Jan-Arie VAN DER HEIJDEN		3/3/88	M	22	(4)	1
2	Jens JANSE		1/7/86	D	17	(1)	
22	Ibrahim KARGBO	SLE	10/4/82	M	19	(3)	
5	LÉOnardo Henrique VELOSO	BRA	29/5/87	D	10	(3)	
17	Josimar LIMA	CPV	2/8/89	D	1		
27	Junior LIVRAMENTO		12/12/87	M	4	(10)	
30	Bas VAN LOON		21/11/90	D	3		
16	Niki MÄENPÄÄ	FIN	23/1/85	G	6		
11	George MOURAD	SWE	18/9/82	A	1	(3)	
29	Stefan NIJLAND		10/8/88	A	16		4
28	Marlon PEREIRA		26/3/87	M	14	(6)	1
15	Ronnie RENIERS		8/11/87	A	1	(10)	
3	Danny SCHENKEL		1/4/78	D	17	(3)	
23	Sidney SCHMELTZ		8/6/89	A		(1)	
19	Gerson SHEOTAHUL		19/4/87	A	13	(10)	2
31	Frank VAN DER STRUIJK		28/3/85	D	11		
4	Arjan SWINKELS		15/10/84	D	22	(1)	2
20	Jasper WAALKENS		13/2/89	M	1	(9)	
14	Sergio ZIJLER		8/7/87	A	28	(3)	4

PROMOTED CLUBS

DE GRAAFSCHAP
Coach – Darije Kalezić (BIH)
Founded – 1954
Stadium – De Vijverberg (12,600)

SBV EXCELSIOR
Coach – Alex Pastoor
Founded – 1902
Stadium – Woudestein (3,527)

SECOND LEVEL FINAL TABLE 2009/10

		Pld	W	D	L	F	A	Pts
1	De Graafschap (*4)	36	25	6	5	85	34	81
2	SC Cambuur Leeuwarden	36	21	8	7	78	48	71
3	SBV Excelsior (*2)	36	20	5	11	77	49	65
4	FC Zwolle	36	19	8	9	59	37	65
5	Go Ahead Eagles (*1)	36	18	9	9	53	33	63
6	AGOVV Apeldoorn	36	16	9	11	63	52	55
7	FC Den Bosch	36	14	12	10	66	54	54
8	Helmond Sport	36	16	6	14	63	54	54
9	BV Veendam	36	14	11	11	57	48	52
10	MVV Maastricht	36	14	7	15	59	67	48
11	RBC Roosendaal	36	12	10	14	47	53	46
12	FC Eindhoven (*3)	36	13	7	16	63	81	46
13	FC Dordrecht	36	13	4	19	54	59	43
14	FC Omniworld	36	11	7	18	40	65	40
15	FC Emmen	36	10	8	18	51	79	38
16	FC Volendam	36	8	11	17	61	81	35
17	Fortuna Sittard	36	7	9	20	31	57	30
18	Telstar	36	7	8	21	45	65	29
19	FC Oss	36	6	11	19	54	65	29

N.B. (*) period champions; HFC Haarlem withdrew after round 23 - their results were annulled; AGOVV Apeldoorn - 2 pts deducted; MVV Maastricht & BV Veendam - 1 pt deducted

PROMOTION/RELEGATION PLAY-OFFS

FIRST ROUND	SECOND ROUND	THIRD ROUND
(26/4/10 & 29/4/10) Helmond Sport 1, Den Bosch 2 Den Bosch 1, Helmond Sport 2 *(3-3; Helmond Sport 5-3 on pens)*	*(6/5/10 & 9/5/10)* Eindhoven 1, Willem II 2 Willem II 1, Eindhoven 1 *(Willem II 3-2)*	*(13/5/10 & 16/5/10)* Go Ahead Eagles 1, Willem II 0 Willem II 3, Go Ahead Eagles 0 *(aet)* *(Willem II 3-1)*
(26/4/10 & 1/5/10) Eindhoven 1, AGOVV 0 AGOVV 2, Eindhoven 3 *(Eindhoven 4-2)*	Go Ahead Eagles 2, Cambuur 0 Cambuur 1, Go Ahead Eagles 0 *(Go Ahead Eagles 2-1)* Helmond Sport 2, Sparta 1 Sparta 2, Helmond Sport 0 *(Sparta 3-2)*	Excelsior 0, Sparta 0 Sparta 1, Excelsior 1 *(1-1; Excelsior on away goal)*
	Zwolle 0, Excelsior 1 Excelsior 4, Zwolle 3 *(Excelsior 5-3)*	

DOMESTIC CUP 2009/10

KNVB BEKER

SECOND ROUND

(22/9/09)
AFC 34 1, Emmen 6
ASWH 2, GVVV 1
AZ 2, Jong Ajax 0 *(aet)*
Dordrecht 3, Fortuna Sittard 2
Eindhoven 2, NEC 3
Excelsior Maassluis 4, Bennekom 2
Haaglandia 6, Excelsior 6 *(aet; 12-13 on pens)*
Heracles 1, RKC 0
Jong De Graafschap 1, Cambuur 0
LRC 1, RBC 5
Omniworld 1, Helmond Sport 3 *(aet)*
Spakenburg 3, MVV 1
Telstar 1, Haarlem 3
Vitesse 5, Oss 2
Volendam 1, Sparta 2 *(aet)*

(23/9/09)
AFC 0, WHC 1
Baronie 1, Barendrecht 1 *(aet; 7-6 on pens)*
Capelle 4, Westlandia 0
De Treffers 2, Veendam 0
IJsselmeervogels 1, Roda 2
Joure 0, Twente 8
Lisse 0, Den Bosch 4
PSV 2, De Graafschap 1
Rijnsburgse Boys 1, Go Ahead Eagles 4 *(aet)*
SDC Putten 0, Heerenveen 7
Sparta Nijkerk 2, Zwolle 2 *(aet; 4-6 on pens)*
Utrecht 2, Groningen 4
VVV 3, Den Haag 0
Willem II 2, NAC 3

(24/9/09)
Achilles 29 0, Gemert 1
AGOVV 1, Ajax 2
Harkemase Boys 0, Feyenoord 5

THIRD ROUND

(27/10/09)
De Treffers 1, NAC 6
Feyenoord 2, Den Bosch 0
Go Ahead Eagles 4, Emmen 2 *(aet)*
Helmond Sport 5, ASWH 0
Heracles 3, Haarlem 0
Jong De Graafschap 1, Zwolle 0 *(aet)*
Sparta 1, VVV 1 *(aet; 6-5 on pens)*

(28/10/09)
AZ 5, Spakenburg 2 *(aet)*
Baronie 1, Excelsior Maassluis 0 *(aet)*
Gemert 2, WHC 2 *(aet; 5-6 on pens)*
Heerenveen 4, RBC 2
NEC 2, Excelsior 1 *(aet)*
Roda 0, PSV 2
Twente 3, Capelle 0
Vitesse 1, Groningen 5

(29/10/09)
Dordrecht 1, Ajax 2 *(aet)*

FOURTH ROUND

(21/12/09)
Heracles 0, Go Ahead Eagles 2

(22/12/09)
Baronie 0, Sparta 5
Feyenoord 1, AZ 0

(23/12/09)
Groningen 0, NEC 2
Jong De Graafschap 0, NAC 2 *(aet)*
Twente 3, Helmond Sport 0
WHC 1, Ajax 14

(16/1/10)
Heerenveen 1, PSV 3

QUARTER-FINALS

(27/1/10)
Ajax 3 *(De Zeeuw 43, Alderweireld 112, De Jong 114)*, NEC 2
(Vleminckx 83, Van Eijden 93) (aet)
NAC 1 *(Gorter 72p)*, Go Ahead Eagles 2 *(De Groot 65, 76)*
PSV 0, Feyenoord 3 *(El Ahmadi 20, 87, Van Bronckhorst 34)*
Sparta 0, Twente 4 *(Perez 23, Nkufo 38, 81, Ruiz 85)*

SEMI-FINALS

(24/3/10)
Feyenoord 2 *(Van Bronckhorst 53, Makaay 84)*, Twente 1 *(Ruiz 42)*

(25/3/10)
Go Ahead Eagles 0, Ajax 6 *(De Zeeuw 11, Pantelić 38, De Jong 75,
Eriksen 77, Rommedahl 78, Lodeiro 85)*

FINAL

(25/4/10)
Amsterdam ArenA, Amsterdam
AFC AJAX 2 *(De Jong 6, 7)*
FEYENOORD 0
Referee – Braamhaar
AJAX – Stekelenburg, Van der Wiel, Alderweireld, Vertonghen, Anita, De
Zeeuw, De Jong, Enoh, Suárez, Pantelić *(Rommedahl 70)*, Emanuelson
(Eriksen 80).
FEYENOORD – Mulder, De Vrij, Vlaar *(Schenkeveld 72)*, Bahia, Van
Bronckhorst, Landzaat, El Ahmadi *(Leerdam 85)*, Fer, Wijnaldum,
Tomasson *(Cissé 73)*, Bruins.

(6/5/10)
De Kuip, Rotterdam
FEYENOORD 1 *(Tomasson 72)*
AFC AJAX 4 *(Suárez 4, 82, De Jong 64, 77)*
Referee – Luinge *(Blom 89)*
FEYENOORD – Mulder, De Vrij *(Schenkeveld 46)*, Vlaar, Bahia, De Cler
(Hofland 75), Landzaat *(De Guzmán 46)*, El Ahmadi, Fer, Wijnaldum,
Tomasson, Makaay.
AJAX – Stekelenburg, Van der Wiel, Alderweireld, Vertonghen, Anita, De
Zeeuw, De Jong *(Lodeiro 84)*, Enoh, Suárez, Pantelić *(Rommedahl 78)*,
Emanuelson *(Eriksen 63)*.

(AJAX 6-1)

Fourth double in five years for Linfield

After a rare trophyless campaign in 2008/09, Linfield FC restored their honour and pride by regaining both the Irish League and Cup. It was the Belfast Blues' fourth domestic double in five years and brought their all-time tally of league titles to a tantalising 49.

Although there was a happy end to the season, it was not all plain sailing for long-serving coach David Jeffrey and his players. Belfast rivals Crusaders FC, Cliftonville FC and defending champions Glentoran FC all headed the Premiership table at one point, and in the run-up to Christmas a shocking sequence of results, during which Linfield took just one point from four games, led to calls for Jeffrey to resign.

The Blues entered the New Year in third spot five points behind surprise leaders Crusaders – albeit with three games in hand. Jeffrey, who was about to enter his 14th year in charge, pulled off a masterstroke by re-recruiting former Linfield favourite Peter Thompson on loan from Stockport County FC. The Northern Ireland international striker's impact was immediate as he bagged five goals in his first four matches to help the club return to the top of the table.

Smooth ride

From that moment on, with their rivals' challenges all fading and Glentoran even deciding to part company with their championship-winning manager of the previous season, Alan McDonald, Linfield were able to freewheel their way to the title. There were a couple of bumps along the way but generally it was a smooth ride, and when they beat Cliftonville 1-0 at Windsor Park in the penultimate round – three days after veteran defender Noel Bailie had reached the incredible milestone of 1,000 games for his one and only club - the race was over. They could even afford to lose their final match, away to Portadown FC, and still boast a five-point victory margin, with Cliftonville taking the runners-up spot and Glentoran, under new boss Scott Young, finishing third.

A week after their league meeting, Linfield and Portadown met again – in the Irish Cup final. An early Thompson strike gave the champions the perfect start and they made it 2-0 not long afterwards. Portadown reduced the deficit, but there were no further goals and Linfield's 40th victory in the competition was complete.

While Jeffrey duly received the Manager of the Year award, his strongest rival was arguably former Newcastle United FC and Northern Ireland goalkeeper Tommy Wright. Handed what seemed to be a poisoned chalice when he was appointed as the new manager of rock bottom Lisburn Distillery FC in September, he took a few months to make his mark, but once he did the Whites staged an astonishing recovery, taking 25 points from their last 11 matches to overtake Institute FC and pull clear of a seemingly inevitable relegation.

Noel Bailie played his 1,000th match for Linfield in April 2010

Irish Football Association (IFA)

20 Windsor Avenue
GB-Belfast BT9 6EG
tel - +44 2890 669 458
fax - +44 2890 667 620
website - irishfa.com
email - info@irishfa.com
Year of Formation – 1880

General Secretary – Patrick Nelson
Media Officer – Sueann Harrison
National Stadium - Windsor Park, Belfast (13,500)

INTERNATIONAL TOURNAMENT APPEARANCES
FIFA World Cup - (3) 1958 (qtr-finals), 1982 (2nd phase), 1986.
TOP FIVE ALL-TIME CAPS
Pat Jennings (119), Mal Donaghy (91), Sammy McIlroy (88),
Keith Gillespie (86), Maik Taylor (83)
TOP FIVE ALL-TIME GOALS
David Healy (35), Colin Clarke (13), Billy Gillespie (13), Gerry Armstrong, Joe Bambrick, Ian Dowie & Jimmy Quinn (12)

Lisburn's great escape was assisted by the fact that with only one club in the IFA Championship (second division), Donegal Celtic FC, equipped with a licence to compete at the higher level, there was no automatic relegation. That left bottom-placed Institute with the chance to stay up, but they lost to Donegal Celtic in a two-legged play-off, a missed penalty in the last minute of the first leg proving very costly as the

Belfast club made amends for their play-off defeat 12 months earlier.

Prolific Patterson

The outstanding individual of the season was Coleraine FC's 25-year-old striker Rory Patterson, who hit 41 goals in all competitions for the Bannsiders, 30 of them in the Premiership. A former journeyman in English non-league football, he was set to join Glentoran in the summer of 2010, having signed a pre-contract with the club after scoring four times against them in a 6-0 romp, but, seduced by his season-long goalscoring streak, Plymouth Argyle FC gazumped the Glens and took him back to England. He returned as a Northern Ireland international, having started both of his country's end-of-season friendlies against Turkey and Chile.

A nation's hopes of a return to the world stage after a 24-year absence were crushed as Northern Ireland lost their penultimate 2010 FIFA World Cup qualifier at home to Slovakia. A terrific goal from Kyle Lafferty in a 1-1 draw in Poland four days earlier had given Nigel Worthington's men a genuine chance of qualification, but it was not to be, and the team headed towards the UEFA EURO 2012 qualifying campaign, and tough encounters against Italy, Serbia and Slovenia, in a state of uncertainty and transition.

NATIONAL TEAM RESULTS 2009/10

12/8/09	Israel	H	Belfast	1-1	McCann (18)
5/9/09	Poland (WCQ)	A	Chorzow	1-1	Lafferty (38)
9/9/09	Slovakia (WCQ)	H	Belfast	0-2	
14/10/09	Czech Republic (WCQ)	A	Prague	0-0	
14/11/09	Serbia	H	Belfast	0-1	
3/3/10	Albania	A	Tirana	0-1	
26/5/10	Turkey	N	New Britain (USA)	0-2	
30/5/10	Chile	A	Chillan	0-1	

NATIONAL TEAM APPEARANCES 2009/10

Coach – Nigel WORTHINGTON	4/11/61		Isr	POL	SVK	CZE	Srb	Alb	Tur	Chi	Caps	Goals
Maik TAYLOR	4/9/71	Birmingham (ENG)	G46	G	G	G	G77	G72			83	-
Chris BAIRD	25/2/82	Fulham (ENG)	D		s70	M	M				44	-
George McCARTNEY	29/4/81	Sunderland (ENG)	D				D	D			34	1
Aaron HUGHES	8/11/79	Fulham (ENG)	D46	D	D	D	D				71	-
Stephen CRAIGAN	29/10/76	Motherwell (SCO)	D46	D	D	D	D	D	D	D46	48	-
Damien JOHNSON	18/11/78	Birmingham (ENG)	M	M	M	M83					56	-
Grant McCANN	15/4/80	Scunthorpe (ENG)	M	M	M70	M80	s46	M			28	4
Sammy CLINGAN	13/1/84	Coventry (ENG)	M70	M	M70						24	-
Chris BRUNT	14/12/84	West Brom (ENG)	M46		s76		M65				26	1

NATIONAL TEAM APPEARANCES 2009/10 (contd.)

			Isr	POL	SVK	CZE	Srb	Alb	Tur	Chi	Caps	Goals
David HEALY	5/8/79	Sunderland (ENG)	A59	A	A	A69	s65	A78			80	35
Kyle LAFFERTY	16/9/87	Rangers (SCO)	A	A54				A71	A64		24	7
Jonathan TUFFEY	20/1/87	Partick (SCO)	s46				s77	s72			5	-
Niall McGINN	20/7/87	Celtic (SCO)	s46		s70		M	M71	M46		7	-
Gareth McAULEY	5/12/79	Ipswich (ENG)	s46	D	D	D			D	D	22	1
Steve DAVIS	1/1/85	Rangers (SCO)	s46	M	M	M	M	M			40	2
Martin PATERSON	10/5/87	Burnley (ENG)	s59	s54	A76						11	-
Ryan McGIVERN	8/1/90	Man. City (ENG) /Leicester (ENG)	s70				D	D	D76	D55	11	-
Jonny EVANS	3/1/88	Man. United (ENG)			D	D		D46			20	1
Warren FEENEY	17/1/81	Cardiff (WAL)					s69	A65			34	5
Michael O'CONNOR	6/10/87	Scunthorpe (ENG)					s80	s65	M46		9	-
Andy KIRK	29/5/79	Dunfermline (SCO)					s83	s71	s78		11	-
Patrick McCOURT	16/12/83	Celtic (SCO)						s71			3	-
Andrew LITTLE	12/5/89	Rangers (SCO)						D	D	D	5	-
Corry EVANS	30/7/90	Man. United (ENG)						s46	M	M	4	-
Dean SHIELS	1/2/85	Doncaster (ENG)						s46			9	-
Rory PATTERSON	16/7/84	Coleraine						s64	A60	A	3	-
Alan BLAYNEY	9/10/81	Linfield							G	G46	3	-
Robert GARRETT	5/5/88	Linfield							M80	M46	3	-
Jamie MULGREW	5/6/86	Linfield							M	M	2	-
Kevin BRANIFF	4/3/83	Portadown							M61	s46	2	-
John GORMAN	26/10/92	Wolves (ENG)							M66	M73	2	-
Josh MAGENNIS	15/8/90	Cardiff (WAL)							s60	s73	2	-
Rory McARDLE	1/5/87	Rochdale (ENG)							s61	s46	2	-
Michael BRYAN	21/2/90	Watford (ENG)							s66	M46	2	-
Colin COATES	26/10/85	Crusaders							s76	s55	3	-
James LAWRIE	18/12/90	Port Vale (ENG)							s80	s46	3	-
Michael McGOVERN	12/7/84	Ross County (SCO)								s46	1	-

DOMESTIC LEAGUE 2009/10

PREMIERSHIP FINAL TABLE

	Pld	Home					Away					Total					Pts
		W	D	L	F	A	W	D	L	F	A	W	D	L	F	A	
1 Linfield FC	38	13	2	4	41	16	9	6	4	37	21	22	8	8	78	37	74
2 Cliftonville FC	38	12	1	6	35	19	9	5	5	34	23	21	6	11	69	42	69
3 Glentoran FC	38	9	5	5	22	20	10	3	6	36	26	19	8	11	58	46	65
4 Crusaders FC	38	8	4	7	35	31	9	5	5	22	21	17	9	12	57	52	60
5 Dungannon Swifts FC	38	7	7	4	28	27	9	2	9	28	31	16	9	13	56	58	57
6 Portadown FC	38	10	4	5	35	21	5	6	8	35	34	15	10	13	70	55	55
7 Coleraine FC	38	10	4	4	41	29	6	5	9	35	33	16	9	13	76	62	57
8 Glenavon FC	38	6	6	8	28	34	6	1	11	19	33	12	7	19	47	67	43
9 Newry City FC	38	6	5	9	22	33	4	7	7	16	30	10	12	16	38	63	42
10 Ballymena United FC	38	7	2	10	23	25	4	5	10	23	31	11	7	20	46	56	40
11 Lisburn Distillery FC	38	4	5	10	22	43	7	1	11	23	33	11	6	21	45	76	39
12 Institute FC	38	3	7	9	18	28	3	6	10	18	34	6	13	19	36	62	31

NB League split into top and bottom halves after 33 games, with each team playing a further five matches exclusively against clubs from its half of the table.

TOP GOALSCORERS

30 Rory PATTERSON (Coleraine)
17 George McMULLAN (Cliftonville)
   Darren BOYCE (Coleraine)
16 Liam BOYCE (Cliftonville)
14 David RAINEY (Crusaders)
   Glenn FERGUSON (Lisburn)
   Kevin BRANIFF (Portadown)
   Richard LECKY (Portadown)
13 Timmy ADAMSON (Dungannon)
12 Gary McCUTCHEON (Portadown)

CLUB-BY-CLUB

BALLYMENA UNITED FC
Manager – Roy Walker
Founded – 1928
Stadium – The Showgrounds (4,390)
MAJOR HONOURS:
Irish Cup – (6) 1929, 1940, 1958, 1981, 1984, 1989.

2009
8/8	Cliftonville	h	0-1
15/8	Dungannon	a	1-2 McConnell
18/8	Coleraine	a	2-3 Watson Aid., Kelbie
22/8	Crusaders	h	1-2 Watson Alb.
26/8	Glentoran	a	2-1 Kelbie 2
1/9	Glenavon	h	0-3
5/9	Institute	a	1-0 Kelbie (p)
12/9	Newry	h	1-2 McConnell
15/9	Lisburn	a	2-0 Cushley, Lockhart
19/9	Portadown	h	2-1 Cushley, Kelbie
26/9	Linfield	a	0-1
6/10	Cliftonville	a	2-0 McConnell, Smith A.
10/10	Dungannon	h	0-1
17/10	Coleraine	h	3-2 Smith A., Anderson, og (Beverland)
24/10	Crusaders	h	2-0 Smith M., Cushley
27/10	Glentoran	h	2-3 McConnell 2
7/11	Glenavon	a	2-2 Stewart A., Smith M.
14/11	Institute	h	1-1 Kelbie
28/11	Lisburn	h	0-1
3/12	Newry	a	2-3 Colligan, Smith A.
12/12	Portadown	a	0-2
19/12	Linfield	h	2-0 Lockhart, Kelbie
2010			
23/1	Glentoran	a	0-3
26/1	Coleraine	a	1-3 Cushley
6/2	Institute	a	2-2 Lockhart, Muir G.
9/2	Cliftonville	h	2-1 Kelbie, Surgenor
16/2	Glenavon	h	1-0 Kelbie (p)
23/2	Dungannon	a	1-2 Surgenor
27/2	Newry	h	0-0
13/3	Portadown	h	0-1
20/3	Linfield	a	0-1
25/3	Crusaders	a	2-2 Smith A., Taggart
3/4	Lisburn	a	2-2 Muir G., Kelbie
6/4	Coleraine	h	2-4 Lockhart, Smith A.
17/4	Institute	h	3-0 Surgenor, Colligan, Smith A.
20/4	Newry	a	0-1
24/4	Lisburn	h	1-2 Anderson
1/5	Glenavon	a	1-1 Kelbie

Name	Nat	DoB	Pos	Aps	(s)	Gls
Noel ANDERSON		1/3/82	M	16	(7)	2
Philip CARSON		6/1/88	M	17	(1)	
Lee COLLIGAN		11/2/89	D	34	(1)	2
David CUSHLEY		22/7/89	M	15	(14)	4
Gary HAVERON		6/3/81	M	15	(2)	
Kevin KELBIE	SCO	24/2/85	A	26	(2)	11
Aaron KERR		8/12/82	G	2		
Aaron LEMON		13/7/89	M	1	(2)	
Darren LOCKHART		12/11/73	M	24	(3)	4
Lee McCAUGHERN		16/4/91	A		(2)	
Nathan McCONNELL		31/7/82	A	14	(8)	5
James McLAUGHLIN		6/3/90	A		(7)	
Paul McNEILL		7/6/88	A		(8)	
Gary MUIR	SCO	15/12/85	M	12	(1)	2
Paul MUIR		18/10/85	D	1		
Dwayne NELSON		5/9/84	G	25		
Ross NELSON		23/5/92	A		(1)	
Sean O'NEILL		11/4/88	G	11		
Orman OKUNAIYA		16/4/86	M	7	(6)	
Chris RAMSEY		24/5/90	D	22	(2)	
Andy SMITH		25/9/80	A	29	(1)	6
Michael SMITH		4/9/88	D	37		2
Aaron STEWART		3/12/89	D	25	(7)	1
George STEWART		19/6/90	M	3	(5)	
Mark SURGENOR		19/12/85	D	23	(9)	3

Gavin TAGGART		15/11/84	M	18	(4)	1
Aidan WATSON		16/8/86	M	14	(3)	1
Albert WATSON		8/9/85	D	27		1
George YOUNG		23/11/89	M		(2)	

CLIFTONVILLE FC
Manager – Eddie Patterson
Founded – 1879
Stadium – Solitude (2,552)
MAJOR HONOURS:
Irish League – (3) 1906 (shared), 1910, 1998;
Irish Cup - (8) 1883, 1888, 1897, 1900, 1901, 1907, 1909, 1979.

2009
8/8	Ballymena	a	1-0 Boyce
15/8	Coleraine	h	0-1
18/8	Crusaders	a	3-2 Murphy, Boyce, McMullan
22/8	Glentoran	h	1-2 Caldwell
25/8	Glenavon	a	2-3 Boyce 2
1/9	Institute	a	1-1 Dunlop
6/9	Newry	a	2-1 McMullan, Clarke
12/9	Lisburn	a	5-0 Boyce, McMullan 3, Donaghy
15/9	Portadown	a	2-2 Scannell C. 2
21/9	Linfield	h	4-0 Scannell R., Scannell C., McMullan 2
26/9	Dungannon	a	1-1 McMullan (p)
6/10	Ballymena	h	0-2
10/10	Coleraine	a	3-3 McMullan 2 (1p), Scannell C.
17/10	Crusaders	h	1-2 Scannell C.
24/10	Glentoran	a	1-2 Clarke
27/10	Glenavon	h	3-2 og (Magee), og (McDonagh), Scannell R.
15/11	Newry	h	3-2 Scannell R., McMullan (p), O'Connor
28/11	Portadown	h	2-1 O'Connor, Scannell C.
12/12	Linfield	a	2-1 Caldwell, Boyce
19/12	Dungannon	h	1-0 O'Connor
26/12	Crusaders	a	2-1 Boyce (p), Fleming
2010			
23/1	Glenavon	a	2-0 Boyce 2
30/1	Institute	h	3-0 Boyce, Scannell C., O'Connor
2/2	Institute	h	4-1 Scannell C., og (Seydak), Donaghy, O'Connor
6/2	Newry	a	1-1 McMullan (p)
9/2	Ballymena	h	1-2 og (Watson Alb.)
16/2	Lisburn	h	3-0 Boyce, Scannell C., McMullan
20/2	Portadown	a	0-2
23/2	Coleraine	h	0-1
2/3	Lisburn	h	1-0 McMullan
16/3	Linfield	h	1-1 Boyce
20/3	Dungannon	a	2-0 Scannell C., Boyce
23/3	Glentoran	h	1-2 Scannell C.
8/4	Crusaders	h	1-0 Boyce
17/4	Portadown	h	2-1 Boyce, McMullan (p)
24/4	Dungannon	h	4-1 Scannell R., Hutton, O'Connor, Boyce
27/4	Linfield	a	0-1
1/5	Glentoran	a	3-0 McMullan 2 (1p), Scannell R.

No	Name	Nat	DoB	Pos	Aps	(s)	Gls
16	Liam BOYCE		8/4/91	A	31	(3)	16
15	Ciaran BOYD		29/9/88	D		(5)	
26	Stephen BRENNAN		26/6/91	D		(2)	
21	Mark BURNS		16/1/88	M		(1)	
14	Ciaran CALDWELL		10/10/89	D	21	(7)	2
17	Ryan CATNEY		17/2/87	M	32	(1)	
24	Mark CLARKE		23/8/89	M	16	(3)	2
1	John CONNOLLY	IRL	1/2/77	G	35		
6	Ciaran DONAGHY		26/2/82	D	37		2
10	Conor DOWNEY		12/3/82	M	2	(2)	
22	Ryan DUNLOP		4/5/88	D	1	(7)	1
2	Liam FLEMING		2/7/81	D	23	(4)	1
4	Barry HOLLAND		10/5/84	D	28	(2)	
7	Mark HOLLAND		20/7/78	M	5	(10)	

30	Peter HUTTON	2/3/73	D	17		1
23	Martin JONES	16/1/88	A	1	(8)	
13	Paul McKANE	16/3/87	G	3		
8	George McMULLAN	4/8/81	M	34	(1)	17
11	Francis MURPHY	28/6/79	M	15	(11)	1
18	Kieran O'CONNOR	29/8/81	M	29	(4)	6
5	Declan O'HARA	4/2/83	D	15	(2)	
19	Mark PATTERSON	9/10/89	M	4	(5)	
9	Chris SCANNELL	7/9/77	A	32		11
3	Ronan SCANNELL	11/5/79	D	31	(1)	5
12	Aaron SMYTH	25/5/87	D	6	(5)	
25	Kevin TRAINOR	25/1/89	M		(1)	

6	Paddy McLAUGHLIN	10/10/79	D	18	(4)	
5	Kyle McVEY	7/7/86	D	34	(3)	
	Stuart MILLAR	5/12/91	M	2	(2)	
	Sammy MORROW	3/3/85	A	3	(1)	
15	Mark MUKENDI	IRL 25/6/87	D	24	(1)	1
18	John NEILL	20/7/81	D	2		
1	Davy O'HARE	19/3/76	G	34		
24	Eunan O'KANE	10/7/90	M	12	(1)	4
8	Rory PATTERSON	16/7/84	A	32	(1)	30
	Garrett QUINN	15/2/91	A		(1)	
9	Jody TOLAN	5/10/77	A	13	(15)	4
16	Gareth TOMMONS	18/5/89	M	17	(11)	2
14	John WATT	20/3/86	M	13	(2)	

COLERAINE FC
Manager – David Platt
Founded – 1927
Stadium – The Showgrounds (3,960)
MAJOR HONOURS:
Irish League – (1) 1974;
Irish Cup – (5) 1965, 1972, 1975, 1977, 2003.

2009

8/8	Linfield	h	2-2	*Boyce, Patterson*
15/8	Cliftonville	a	1-0	*Carson*
18/8	Ballymena	h	3-2	*Patterson 3*
22/8	Dungannon	a	0-1	
25/8	Crusaders	a	0-1	
1/9	Glentoran	h	0-1	
5/9	Glenavon	a	2-3	*O'Kane, Tolan*
12/9	Institute	h	3-1	*Tolan, Tommons, Patterson*
15/9	Newry	a	1-2	*og (Munster)*
22/9	Lisburn	h	2-1	*McClements, og (Thompson S.)*
26/9	Portadown	a	0-4	
10/10	Cliftonville	h	3-3	*Boyce 2, Harkin*
17/10	Ballymena	a	2-3	*O'Kane, Patterson (p)*
24/10	Dungannon	h	2-1	*Harkin, Patterson*
27/10	Crusaders	h	4-1	*Boyce 2, Patterson (p), Carson*
7/11	Glentoran	a	6-0	*Boyce, Patterson 4, Carson*
16/11	Glenavon	h	3-0	*Patterson, O'Kane 2*
21/11	Institute	a	2-2	*Patterson, Boyce*
28/11	Newry	h	3-0	*Carson, Boyce, Patterson*
12/12	Lisburn	a	2-3	*McCallion, Carson*
2010				
23/1	Crusaders	a	5-2	*Patterson 4 (2p), Boyce*
26/1	Ballymena	h	3-1	*Boyce, Carson, Dooley*
30/1	Glentoran	h	4-3	*Patterson 3, Tolan*
6/2	Glenavon	a	1-2	*Patterson*
9/2	Linfield	h	1-3	*Dooley*
16/2	Linfield	a	4-2	*Patterson 2, Gibson 2*
23/2	Cliftonville	a	1-0	*Patterson*
2/3	Institute	h	1-1	*Boyce*
6/3	Lisburn	h	1-3	*Boyce*
16/3	Newry	a	0-0	
19/3	Portadown	a	1-3	*Boyce*
23/3	Dungannon	a	1-1	*Boyce*
3/4	Portadown	h	3-3	*Boyce, Patterson, Mukendi*
6/4	Ballymena	a	4-2	*Boyce 2, Tolan, Patterson*
13/4	Newry	h	2-3	*Gibson 2 (1p)*
20/4	Glenavon	h	1-0	*Patterson*
23/4	Institute	a	1-1	*Tommons*
1/5	Lisburn	a	1-1	*Patterson*

No	Name	Nat	DoB	Pos	Aps	(s)	Gls
2	Howard BEVERLAND		30/3/90	D	24	(2)	
7	Darren BOYCE		25/1/86	M	25	(7)	17
	Sam BOYLAN		23/11/93	A		(1)	
21	Aaron CANNING		7/3/92	D	9	(3)	
11	Stephen CARSON		6/10/80	M	25	(3)	6
3	Matthew CROSSAN	IRL	28/4/92	D	6	(4)	
	Ryan DOHERTY		28/4/92	A		(1)	
22	Stephen DOOLEY		19/10/91	M	9	(9)	2
19	Richard GIBSON		11/1/85	A	7	(14)	4
17	Gareth HARKIN		19/12/87	M	30	(2)	2
4	Michael HEGARTY		9/12/83	M	30	(4)	
25	Stephen LOWRY		14/10/86	M	13	(1)	
10	Tommy McCALLION		18/1/77	M	29	(7)	1
12	David McCLEMENTS		14/1/89	M	3	(2)	1
20	Laurence McCORMICK		25/8/86	G	4		

CRUSADERS FC
Manager – Stephen Baxter
Founded – 1898
Stadium – Seaview (3,330)
MAJOR HONOURS:
Irish League – (4) 1973, 1976, 1995, 1997;
Irish Cup – (3) 1967, 1968, 2009.

2009

8/8	Portadown	h	3-1	*Donnelly (p), Rainey 2*
15/8	Linfield	a	1-0	*Coates*
18/8	Cliftonville	h	2-3	*Rainey, Arthurs*
22/8	Ballymena	a	2-1	*Rainey, Coates*
25/8	Coleraine	h	1-0	*Rainey*
29/8	Dungannon	a	2-1	*Owens, Rainey*
12/9	Glenavon	h	3-0	*Morrow (p), Rainey, McCann*
15/9	Institute	a	0-1	
19/9	Newry	h	1-1	*Rainey*
26/9	Lisburn	a	1-0	*Rainey*
3/10	Portadown	a	2-1	*Caddell, Rainey*
6/10	Glentoran	a	1-0	*Rainey*
10/10	Linfield	h	0-4	
17/10	Cliftonville	a	2-1	*Morrow 2*
24/10	Ballymena	h	0-2	
27/10	Coleraine	a	1-4	*Dickson*
7/11	Dungannon	a	1-1	*Melly*
14/11	Glentoran	h	1-1	*Owens*
21/11	Glenavon	a	1-1	*Black*
28/11	Institute	h	1-2	*Owens*
12/12	Newry	a	1-0	*Black*
19/12	Lisburn	h	2-0	*Rainey, Coates*
26/12	Cliftonville	h	1-2	*Owens*
2010				
2/1	Portadown	h	3-2	*McMaster, og (Convery), Owens*
23/1	Coleraine	h	2-5	*Collins, Morrow*
30/1	Dungannon	h	2-3	*Arthurs, Morrow (p)*
6/2	Glentoran	a	0-0	
23/2	Linfield	a	0-2	
1/3	Glenavon	h	3-0	*Donnelly, Arthurs, McCann*
13/3	Newry	h	4-1	*Arthurs, Owens, McKeown, Black*
16/3	Institute	a	3-1	*McMaster, Doherty, Donnelly*
20/3	Lisburn	a	2-2	*Owens, Arthurs*
25/3	Ballymena	h	2-2	*Donnelly, Faulkner*
8/4	Cliftonville	a	0-1	
17/4	Glentoran	h	2-1	*Coates, Donnelly*
20/4	Portadown	a	2-2	*Rainey 2*
24/4	Linfield	h	0-0	
1/5	Dungannon	a	2-3	*Owens, Arthurs*

No	Name	Nat	DoB	Pos	Aps	(s)	Gls
16	Ross ARTHURS		13/10/89	M	10	(13)	6
	David BELL		13/5/85	D	1		
4	Aaron BLACK		19/12/83	M	13	(13)	3
15	Declan CADDELL		13/4/88	M	10	(11)	1
6	Colin COATES		26/10/85	D	34		4
30	Michael COLLINS		6/9/77	M	9		1
7	Mark DICKSON		12/12/81	A	9	(5)	1
8	Eamon DOHERTY		4/1/74	M	25	(6)	1
11	Martin DONNELLY		28/8/88	M	35	(2)	5
	Willie FAULKNER		18/1/90	M	1	(5)	1
	David GIBSON		15/2/90	D	5		
25	Aaron HOGG		14/1/88	G		(1)	
1	Chris KEENAN		11/7/87	G	38		
19	Jonathan MAGEE		27/9/88	D	5	(1)	

5	David MAGOWAN	4/10/83	D	34		
17	Jamie MARKS	18/3/77	D	1		
3	Stephen McBRIDE	6/4/83	D	35		
7	Ryan McCANN	15/9/82	M	28	(7)	2
2	Gareth McKEOWN	14/7/83	D	32		1
21	David McMASTER	29/12/88	M	12	(7)	2
14	Dominic MELLY	19/7/87	A	2	(5)	1
12	Chris MORROW	20/9/85	M	25	(2)	5
20	Jordan OWENS	9/7/89	A	28	(4)	8
10	David RAINEY	6/4/76	A	26	(7)	14

DUNGANNON SWIFTS FC
Manager – Dixie Robinson
Founded – 1949
Stadium – Stangmore Park (2,154)

2009

8/8	Institute	a	1-0	*McCafferty (p)*
15/8	Ballymena	h	2-1	*Coney, McIlmoyle*
18/8	Newry	a	1-0	*McCafferty (p)*
22/8	Coleraine	h	1-0	*McIlmoyle*
25/8	Lisburn	a	0-0	
29/8	Crusaders	h	1-2	*Coney*
5/9	Portadown	a	4-1	*Mullan, McCafferty 2 (1p), Coney*
12/9	Glentoran	h	1-1	*McCann*
15/9	Linfield	a	0-1	
19/9	Glenavon	a	2-3	*Adamson, Ward*
26/9	Cliftonville	h	1-1	*Ward*
3/10	Institute	h	2-1	*McIlmoyle, McCafferty (p)*
10/10	Ballymena	a	1-0	*McCafferty (p)*
17/10	Newry	h	0-0	
24/10	Coleraine	a	1-2	*McCafferty*
27/10	Lisburn	h	2-1	*Hamilton, Adamson*
7/11	Crusaders	h	1-1	*Lavery*
14/11	Portadown	h	2-8	*McIlmoyle, Hamilton*
28/11	Linfield	h	2-2	*Coney, Adamson*
8/12	Glentoran	a	0-0	
12/12	Glenavon	h	4-0	*Ward, Adamson 2, McCafferty (p)*
19/12	Cliftonville	a	0-1	

2010

20/1	Newry	a	0-4	
23/1	Lisburn	a	5-2	*Morgan C., Emerson, Adamson, Mullan, Ward*
30/1	Crusaders	a	3-2	*Adamson, McIlmoyle, McCafferty*
6/2	Portadown	h	4-4	*Ward, Adamson, McMinn, Coney*
9/2	Institute	a	0-2	
23/2	Ballymena	h	2-1	*McIlmoyle 2*
27/2	Glentoran	h	2-0	*McCafferty (p), McCaffrey*
9/3	Linfield	a	1-4	*Ward (p)*
13/3	Glenavon	a	3-1	*McCaffrey, Emerson, Adamson*
20/3	Cliftonville	h	0-2	
23/3	Coleraine	h	1-1	*Adamson*
3/4	Glentoran	a	0-1	
6/4	Portadown	a	2-1	*og (Mackle), McCafferty*
10/4	Linfield	h	0-1	
24/4	Cliftonville	a	1-4	*Adamson*
1/5	Crusaders	a	3-2	*Adamson 2, Slater*

Name	Nat	DoB	Pos	Aps	(s)	Gls
Timmy ADAMSON		5/1/83	A	33		13
Aaron ARKINSON		4/10/90	M		(1)	
Jimmy CALLACHER		11/6/91	M	8	(3)	
Shane CONEY		2/11/78	A	12	(12)	5
Alain EMERSON		13/8/79	M	18	(8)	2
Andy FERGUSON		22/2/89	D	14	(2)	
Gary FITZPATRICK		27/1/77	D		(1)	
Terry FITZPATRICK		23/3/82	M	18	(5)	
Conor FORKER		10/4/82	A		(11)	
Andy HAMILTON		21/6/84	M	2	(6)	2
Stefan LAVERY		20/7/93	A	1	(3)	1
Fergal McALISKEY		29/6/89	D	13	(5)	
Rod McAREE		19/8/74	M	6	(5)	
Neil McCAFFERTY	IRL	11/6/84	M	30	(2)	11
Dermot McCAFFREY		29/3/86	D	11		2
Marc McCANN		6/8/80	M	27	(8)	1
Craig McCLEAN		6/7/85	D	36		

	Ryan McILMOYLE	12/12/84	M	38		7
	Adam McMINN	15/1/84	D	22	(3)	1
	Johnny MONTGOMERY	6/4/74	D	30	(1)	
	Calvin MOONEY	27/9/74	A		(9)	
	Chris MORGAN	11/1/76	A	9	(3)	1
	Niall MORGAN	17/7/91	G	2	(1)	
	Ryan MULLAN	11/11/88	D	21	(1)	2
	Darren MURPHY	23/1/75	D	4	(5)	
	Alvin ROUSE	BRB	18/2/76	A		(2)	1
	Jamie SLATER		17/4/84	A	27	(2)	6
	Michael WARD					

GLENAVON FC
Manager – Marty Quinn
Founded – 1889
Stadium – Mourneview Park (4,160)
MAJOR HONOURS:
Irish League – (3) 1952, 1957, 1960;
Irish Cup - (5) 1957, 1959, 1961, 1992, 1997.

2009

8/8	Newry	h	1-1	*Costello*
15/8	Lisburn	a	3-2	*Grant, King 2*
18/8	Portadown	h	2-2	*Grant, McDonagh*
22/8	Linfield	a	1-4	*Costello*
25/8	Cliftonville	h	3-2	*Molloy, Grant, Dickson*
1/9	Ballymena	a	3-0	*Molloy, Grant, King*
5/9	Coleraine	h	3-2	*Walsh 2, Molloy*
12/9	Crusaders	a	0-3	
15/9	Glentoran	h	2-2	*McDonagh, og (Morris)*
19/9	Dungannon	h	3-2	*Costello, Harpur, Grant*
26/9	Institute	a	1-0	*Molloy*
2/10	Newry	a	3-0	*Molloy, McDonagh 2*
10/10	Lisburn	h	2-1	*Molloy, Magee*
17/10	Portadown	a	0-2	
24/10	Linfield	h	1-2	*Liggett*
27/10	Cliftonville	a	2-3	*McDonagh 2 (1p)*
7/11	Ballymena	h	2-2	*Molloy, Magee*
16/11	Coleraine	a	0-3	
21/11	Crusaders	h	1-1	*McDonagh*
28/11	Glentoran	a	0-2	
12/12	Dungannon	a	0-4	
19/12	Institute	h	0-1	

2010

19/1	Lisburn	a	0-0	
23/1	Cliftonville	h	0-2	
2/2	Newry	h	1-0	*Dickson*
6/2	Coleraine	h	2-1	*Costello, Walsh*
16/2	Ballymena	a	0-1	
20/2	Glentoran	h	1-3	*Grant*
26/2	Portadown	h	0-1	
1/3	Crusaders	a	0-3	
13/3	Dungannon	h	1-3	*Finlay*
20/3	Institute	a	2-1	*Molloy, Liggett*
23/3	Linfield	a	2-1	*Harpur, Hamill*
6/4	Institute	h	1-2	*Molloy*
17/4	Lisburn	h	1-3	*Harpur*
20/4	Coleraine	a	0-1	
24/4	Newry	a	2-3	*Harpur (p), King*
1/5	Ballymena	h	1-1	*King*

No	Name	Nat	DoB	Pos	Aps	(s)	Gls
2	Shea CAMPBELL		30/4/81	D	20	(1)	
14	Paul CARVILL		20/8/85	D	23	(3)	
17	James COSTELLO		9/6/86	A	24	(10)	4
22	Hugh DAVEY		31/3/84	D	12		
5	Hugh DICKSON		28/8/81	D	13		2
16	Joe FINLAY		22/10/90	M		(2)	1
15	Mark GRACEY		30/1/75	D	22	(1)	
9	Tony GRANT	IRL	20/8/76	A	23	(4)	6
20	Rory HAMILL		4/5/76	A	7	(2)	1
6	Adrian HARPER	IRL	4/5/85	M	4	(9)	
24	Ryan HARPUR		1/12/88	M	30	(2)	4
16	Mark HAUGHEY		23/1/91	D	19	(2)	
23	Barry JOHNSTON		28/10/80	M	11		
11	Stuart KING		20/3/81	A	21	(13)	5
18	Gary LIGGETT		28/9/87	A	7	(14)	2
4	Jay MAGEE		4/5/88	D	33		2

No	Name	Nat	DoB	Pos	Aps	(s)	Gls
12	Will McDONAGH	IRL	14/3/83	M	29	(4)	7
10	Trevor MOLLOY	IRL	14/4/77	A	36		9
25	Ryan MURPHY		19/5/86	M		(1)	
13	Tuda MURPHY	CAY	4/11/80	G	10		
7	Eamon MURRAY		11/5/88	M	11	(12)	
1	Andrew PLUMMER	ENG	13/10/89	G	28		
30	Brendan SHANNON		27/9/88	D	7		
3	Mark TURKINGTON		20/3/84	D	3	(3)	
8	Conor WALSH		11/3/83	M	25	(4)	3

No	Name	Nat	DoB	Pos	Aps	(s)	Gls
6	Shane McCABE		21/12/81	M	19	(6)	
25	Jamie McGOVERN		29/5/89	M	9		
1	Elliott MORRIS		4/5/81	G	23		
3	Kyle NEILL		30/3/78	D	24	(4)	5
2	Colin NIXON		8/9/78	D	36	(1)	4
18	James TAYLOR		12/5/84	G	15	(1)	
15	Johnny TAYLOR		30/6/84	D	22	(1)	5
7	Sean WARD		12/4/84	D	21	(3)	
11	Andrew WATERWORTH		11/4/86	A	15	(16)	7

GLENTORAN FC
Manager – Alan McDonald; (4/3/10) Scott Young
Founded – 1882
Stadium – The Oval (9,400)
MAJOR HONOURS:
Irish League – (23) 1894, 1897, 1905, 1912, 1913, 1921, 1925, 1931, 1951, 1953, 1964, 1967, 1968, 1970, 1972, 1977, 1981, 1988, 1992, 1999, 2003, 2005, 2009; Irish Cup – (20) 1914, 1917, 1921, 1932, 1933, 1935, 1951, 1966, 1973, 1983, 1985, 1986, 1987, 1988, 1990, 1996, 1998, 2000, 2001, 2004.

2009
8/8	Lisburn	a	4-0	Leeman, Clarke (p), Hamilton, Taylor Jon.
15/8	Portadown	a	2-1	Taylor Jon., Hamilton
18/8	Linfield	h	2-2	Leeman, Halliday
22/8	Cliftonville	a	2-1	Neill (p), Nixon
26/8	Ballymena	h	1-2	Taylor Jon.
1/9	Coleraine	a	1-0	Waterworth
12/9	Dungannon	a	1-1	Fordyce
15/9	Glenavon	a	2-2	Clarke, Taylor Jon.
22/9	Institute	h	1-1	Gillespie
26/9	Newry	a	2-1	Halliday, Fordyce
3/10	Lisburn	h	1-0	Halliday
6/10	Crusaders	h	0-1	
10/10	Portadown	h	1-0	Hamilton
17/10	Linfield	a	1-2	Waterworth
24/10	Cliftonville	h	2-1	Halliday, Fitzgerald
27/10	Ballymena	h	3-2	Waterworth, Nixon 2
7/11	Coleraine	h	0-6	
14/11	Crusaders	a	1-1	Hamilton (p)
28/11	Glenavon	h	2-0	Neill 2
8/12	Dungannon	h	0-0	
12/12	Institute	a	3-0	Waterworth, Hamilton, Fordyce
19/12	Newry	h	0-1	

2010
23/1	Ballymena	h	3-0	Gillespie, Burrows, Hamilton
26/1	Linfield	h	2-2	Fordyce, Hamilton
30/1	Coleraine	a	3-4	Martyn, Black, Waterworth
6/2	Crusaders	h	0-0	
9/2	Lisburn	h	2-0	Leeman, Burrows
20/2	Glenavon	a	3-1	Halliday, Hill, Hamilton
23/2	Portadown	a	1-2	Nixon
27/2	Dungannon	a	0-2	
9/3	Institute	h	2-1	Hamilton (p), Clarke
20/3	Newry	a	3-0	Fitzgerald, og (O'Connor), Waterworth
23/3	Cliftonville	a	2-1	Neill, Waterworth
3/4	Dungannon	h	1-0	Martyn
6/4	Linfield	a	1-3	Hamilton
17/4	Crusaders	a	1-2	Neill
24/4	Portadown	h	2-0	Taylor Jon., Burrows
1/5	Cliftonville	h	0-3	

No	Name	Nat	DoB	Pos	Aps	(s)	Gls
16	Johnny BLACK		26/2/88	D	20	(2)	1
12	Matty BURROWS		15/10/85	A	6	(6)	3
11	Jimmy CALLACHER		11/6/91	M	4		
4	Richard CLARKE		28/11/85	M	21	(11)	3
14	Dean FITZGERLAD	IRL	20/12/75	M	26	(11)	2
8	Daryl FORDYCE		2/1/87	M	21	(11)	4
17	Grant GARDINER		13/9/88	M	2	(1)	
33	Kyle GILLESPIE		14/2/75	M	33		2
21	Andrew HALL		19/9/89	M	1	(2)	
9	Michael HALLIDAY		28/5/79	A	18	(18)	5
10	Kyle HAMILTON		6/10/80	A	33	(4)	10
24	Jason HILL		24/2/82	D	19	(1)	1
5	Paul LEEMAN		21/1/78	D	26		3
26	Ciaran MARTYN	IRL	25/3/80	M	4	(6)	2

INSTITUTE FC
Manager – John Gregg
Founded – 1905
Stadium – Riverside (1,570)

2009
8/8	Dungannon	h	0-1	
15/8	Newry	a	1-3	Ogilby
18/8	Lisburn	h	2-1	og (Rogers), Brown (p)
22/8	Portadown	a	0-0	
25/8	Linfield	h	1-2	Blackburn
1/9	Cliftonville	h	1-1	Friel
5/9	Ballymena	h	0-1	
12/9	Coleraine	a	1-3	Friel
15/9	Crusaders	h	1-0	Blackburn
22/9	Glentoran	a	1-1	Ramsey
26/9	Glenavon	h	0-1	
3/10	Dungannon	a	1-2	Divin
10/10	Newry	h	0-0	
17/10	Lisburn	a	1-2	Ramsey
24/10	Portadown	h	1-1	Brown (p)
27/10	Linfield	a	2-2	McLaughlin, Lowry
14/11	Ballymena	a	1-1	Scoltock
21/11	Coleraine	h	2-2	Friel, Parkhouse
28/11	Crusaders	a	2-1	Lowry 2
5/12	Glentoran	h	0-3	
19/12	Glenavon	a	1-0	Parkhouse

2010
30/1	Cliftonville	a	0-3	
2/2	Cliftonville	a	1-4	Boyle
6/2	Ballymena	h	2-2	Ogilby 2 (2p)
9/2	Dungannon	h	2-0	Ogilby, og (McMinn)
23/2	Newry	a	0-0	
2/3	Coleraine	a	1-1	McCready
9/3	Glentoran	a	1-2	Semple
13/3	Lisburn	h	2-3	Ramsey 2 (1p)
16/3	Crusaders	a	1-3	og (Owens)
20/3	Glenavon	h	1-2	McLaughlin
23/3	Portadown	a	1-3	Shields
26/3	Linfield	h	0-3	
6/4	Glenavon	a	2-1	Semple, Ogilby
10/4	Lisburn	a	1-2	McLaughlin
17/4	Ballymena	a	0-3	
23/4	Coleraine	h	1-1	McLaughlin
1/5	Newry	h	1-1	McLaughlin

Name	Nat	DoB	Pos	Aps	(s)	Gls
Jason BLACKBURN		5/8/86	M	4	(16)	2
Tom BONNER		20/10/85	M	1	(1)	
Ruairi BOYLE		3/11/78	D	26	(1)	1
Pau BROWN		20/1/80	A	16		2
Graham CROWN		2/3/92	D	14	(4)	
Gavin CULLEN	IRL	21/11/80	G	36		
Conor DEANE		8/10/91	M		(1)	
Declan DIVIN		3/4/80	M	35		1
Sean FRIARS		15/5/79	M	23	(3)	
Austin FRIEL		16/7/81	A	14	(2)	3
Shaun HOLMES		27/12/80	D	33	(1)	
Paul LOWRY		18/7/89	M	3	(15)	3
Ruairi McCLEAN		5/2/85	M	29		
David McCLEMENTS		14/1/89	M	7	(4)	
Ryan McCREADIE		10/12/80	A	2	(6)	
Joe McCREADY		24/7/90	A	14	(2)	1
Gary McFADDEN		23/10/89	M	1	(1)	
Paddy McLAUGHLIN		23/7/75	D	22	(2)	5
Liam McMENAMIN		10/4/89	D		(2)	
Conor MULLAN		6/8/86	M		(2)	
David OGILBY		2/6/84	D	34	(1)	5

Stephen PARKHOUSE	1/8/82	A	1	(3)	2
James QUIGLEY	21/9/76	M	4	(3)	
Kevin RAMSEY	18/9/84	A	17	(2)	4
Alan RYAN	18/9/84	G	2	(1)	
Mark SCOLTOCK	25/3/85	D	14		1
Ryan SEMPLE	2/7/77	M	16	(4)	2
Eamon SEYDAK	25/12/86	D	14	(4)	
Tony SHIELDS	4/6/80	M	10		1
Gareth SMITH	7/2/91	M	1		
Thomas WRAY	25/10/83	D	25	(2)	

LINFIELD FC
Manager – David Jeffrey
Founded – 1886
Stadium – Windsor Park (13,500)
MAJOR HONOURS:
Irish League – (49) 1891, 1892, 1893, 1895, 1898, 1902, 1904, 1907, 1908, 1909, 1911, 1914, 1922, 1923, 1930, 1932, 1934, 1935, 1949, 1950, 1954, 1955, 1956, 1959, 1961, 1962, 1966, 1969, 1971, 1975, 1978, 1979, 1980, 1982, 1983, 1984, 1985, 1986, 1987, 1989, 1993, 1994, 2000, 2001, 2004, 2006, 2007, 2008, 2010;
Irish Cup – (40) 1891, 1892, 1893, 1895, 1898, 1899, 1902, 1904, 1912, 1913, 1915, 1916, 1919, 1922, 1923, 1930, 1931, 1934, 1936, 1939, 1942, 1945, 1946, 1948, 1950, 1953, 1960, 1962, 1963, 1970, 1978, 1980, 1982, 1994, 1995, 2002, 2006, 2007, 2008, 2010.

2009

8/8	Coleraine	a	2-2	Mulgrew, Carvill
15/8	Crusaders	h	0-1	
18/8	Glentoran	a	2-2	Ervin (p) Tomelty
22/8	Glenavon	h	4-1	McAllister, Carvill, Ervin, Lowry
25/8	Institute	a	2-1	McAllister, Ervin (p)
29/8	Newry	h	3-0	Carvill 2, Tomelty
12/9	Portadown	h	1-1	Carvill
15/9	Dungannon	h	1-0	Gault
21/9	Cliftonville	a	0-4	
26/9	Ballymena	h	1-0	Miskimmon
6/10	Lisburn	a	2-1	og (Callaghan), Munster
10/10	Crusaders	a	4-0	Munster 3, Lowry
17/10	Glentoran	h	2-1	Ervin (p), Miskimmon
24/10	Glenavon	a	2-1	Munster, Tomelty
27/10	Institute	h	2-2	Mulgrew, Miskimmon
3/11	Lisburn	h	2-0	Lindsay, Burns B.
7/11	Newry	a	6-0	Allen 3, Ervin 2 (2p), Lindsay
21/11	Portadown	a	0-1	
28/11	Dungannon	a	2-2	Munster, Douglas
12/12	Cliftonville	h	1-2	Munster
19/12	Ballymena	a	0-2	
2010				
26/1	Glentoran	a	2-2	og (Ward), Tomelty
30/1	Newry	h	5-0	Tomelty, Allen 2, Thompson 2
6/2	Lisburn	a	5-0	Allen, Carvill, Thompson 2, McAllister
9/2	Coleraine	a	3-1	Lowry, Mulgrew, Thompson
16/2	Coleraine	h	2-4	Ervin (p), McAllister
23/2	Crusaders	h	2-0	Lowry, Allen (p)
2/3	Portadown	h	5-0	Allen 2, Lowry, Burns B., Tomelty
9/3	Dungannon	h	4-1	Burns B., Allen 2, Lowry
16/3	Cliftonville	a	1-1	McAllister
20/3	Ballymena	h	1-0	Lowry
23/3	Glenavon	h	1-2	Gault
26/3	Institute	a	3-0	Murphy, og (Seydak), Curran
6/4	Glentoran	h	3-1	Burns B., Munster, Garrett
10/4	Dungannon	a	1-0	Munster
24/4	Crusaders	a	0-0	
27/4	Cliftonville	h	1-0	Garrett
1/5	Portadown	a	0-1	

No	Name	Nat	DoB	Pos	Aps	(s)	Gls
18	Stuart ADDIS		5/7/79	G	11		
17	Curtis ALLEN		22/2/88	A	14	(7)	11
11	Noel BAILIE		23/2/71	D	16	(3)	
1	Alan BLAYNEY		9/10/81	G	27		
14	Aaron BURNS		29/5/92	D	7	(6)	
12	Billy Joe BURNS		24/4/89	D	25	(1)	4
	Joshua CAHOON		26/6/91	A		(1)	
10	Michael CARVILL		3/4/88	A	21	(4)	6
28	Chris CASEMENT		12/1/88	D	4	(3)	

7	Damien CURRAN		17/10/81	M	21	(8)	1
2	Stephen DOUGLAS		27/9/77	D	23	(4)	1
21	Jim ERVIN		5/6/85	D	23	(1)	7
27	John GALLAGHER		28/7/82	D	17		
20	Robert GARRETT		5/5/88	M	23	(4)	2
4	Michael GAULT		15/4/83	M	21	(8)	2
6	Conor HAGAN		31/3/82	D		(1)	
31	Marcus KANE		8/12/91	M	1		
13	Kris LINDSAY		5/2/84	D	14		2
8	Philip LOWRY		15/7/89	M	31	(4)	7
25	Mark McALLISTER		26/4/88	A	16	(10)	5
24	Brian McCAUL		6/8/90	M	1		
	Andrew McGRORY		15/12/91	M		(1)	
26	Kevin McHUGH	IRL	19/1/80	A	1	(3)	
15	Mark MISKIMMON		11/6/88	A	8	(3)	3
22	Jamie MULGREW		5/6/86	M	26		3
23	Paul MUNSTER		9/2/82	A	17	(13)	9
5	William MURPHY		29/1/74	D	17	(1)	1
16	Aidan O'KANE		24/11/79	D	2	(1)	
	Mark SHEARER		23/1/92	M	1		
9	Peter THOMPSON		2/5/84	A	13		5
19	Jamie TOMELTY		16/9/83	M	17	(8)	6
	Carl WINCHESTER		12/4/93	M		(1)	

LISBURN DISTILLERY FC
Manager – Jimmy Brown; (26/9/09) Tommy Wright
Founded – 1879
Stadium – New Grosvenor (2,220)
MAJOR HONOURS:
Irish League – (6) 1896, 1899, 1901, 1903, 1906 (shared), 1963;
Irish Cup – (12) 1884, 1885, 1886, 1889, 1894, 1896, 1903, 1905, 1910, 1925, 1956, 1971.

2009

8/8	Glentoran	h	0-4	
15/8	Glenavon	h	2-3	Gawley, Ferguson
18/8	Institute	a	1-2	Ferguson (p)
22/8	Newry	h	2-4	Ferguson, Melaugh
25/8	Dungannon	h	0-0	
28/8	Portadown	a	1-6	Ferguson
12/9	Cliftonville	h	0-5	
15/9	Ballymena	h	0-2	
22/9	Coleraine	a	1-2	Browne
26/9	Crusaders	h	0-1	
3/10	Glentoran	a	0-1	
6/10	Linfield	h	1-2	Whelan
10/10	Glenavon	a	1-2	Gawley
17/10	Institute	h	2-1	Walsh, Shaw
24/10	Newry	a	1-0	Ferguson (p)
27/10	Dungannon	a	1-2	Ferguson
3/11	Linfield	a	0-2	
7/11	Portadown	h	0-3	
28/11	Ballymena	a	1-0	Ferguson
12/12	Coleraine	h	3-2	McCann 2, Ferguson (p)
19/12	Crusaders	a	0-2	
2010				
19/1	Glenavon	h	0-0	
23/1	Dungannon	a	2-5	McDonnell J., Browne (p)
6/2	Linfield	h	0-5	
9/2	Glentoran	a	0-2	
16/2	Cliftonville	a	0-3	
2/3	Cliftonville	a	0-1	
6/3	Coleraine	a	3-1	Melaugh, Gawley, Curran
13/3	Institute	a	3-2	Gawley, Thompson G. 2
16/3	Portadown	a	3-1	Browne, Ferguson 2
20/3	Crusaders	h	2-2	Ferguson, Muir
23/3	Newry	h	3-0	Ferguson, Thompson G., Friel
3/4	Ballymena	h	2-2	Cooling, McCann
10/4	Institute	h	2-1	Ferguson, Gawley
17/4	Glenavon	a	3-1	Thompson G., Gawley, Friel
24/4	Ballymena	a	2-1	Browne 2
27/4	Newry	a	2-2	Thompson G., Curran
1/5	Coleraine	h	1-1	Ferguson

Name	Nat	DoB	Pos	Aps	(s)	Gls
Tony ANDERSON		1/9/82	M		(11)	
Darren ARMOUR		30/6/75	A	1		
Gary BROWNE		17/1/83	A	17	(8)	5

Aaron CALLAGHAN	1/7/86	D	28	(1)	
Mark COOLING	27/2/89	M	14	(4)	1
Gareth COREY	13/3/87	M	6	(11)	
John CURRAN	17/5/82	D	9		2
Glenn FERGUSON	10/7/69	A	30	(2)	14
Austin FRIEL	16/7/81	A	5	(5)	2
Neal GAWLEY	20/2/86	M	26	(8)	6
Rory HAMILL	4/5/76	A	6	(5)	
David HUME	11/12/91	D	1	(1)	
Andy KILMARTIN	18/1/83	M	34	(2)	
Chris KINGSBERRY	10/9/85	M	8	(3)	
Philip MATTHEWS	26/3/74	G	33		
David McALINDEN	28/9/83	D	10	(1)	
Niall McALLISTER	13/11/89	M	1	(1)	
Peter McCANN	18/1/81	D	26	(1)	3
Mark McCHRYSTAL	25/6/84	D	3		
Chris McCLUSKEY	20/7/89	G	1		
Joe McDONNELL	5/1/87	M	4	(2)	1
Seamus McDONNELL	22/8/90	M		(2)	
Pat McSHANE	28/11/74	D	32		
Gavin MELAUGH	9/7/81	M	17	(8)	2
Jason MOK	IRL 5/10/90	D	1	(1)	
Paul MUIR	18/10/75	D	13		1
Paul MURPHY	IRL 28/3/85	G	3		
Aaron NASH	22/2/89	A		(2)	
Mark PATTON	21/6/89	M	4	(8)	
Dave ROGERS	IRL 25/8/75	D	8	(2)	
Stephen SHAW	4/4/82	M	5	(3)	1
Philip SIMPSON	21/10/86	D	16	(2)	
Chris STEWART	17/6/91	G	1		
Gary THOMPSON	26/5/90	M	22	(6)	5
Stuart THOMPSON	9/7/85	D	21	(3)	
Davitt WALSH	27/6/86	A	3	(9)	1
Gavin WHELAN	IRL 28/10/83	M	9	(2)	1

NEWRY CITY FC
Manager – Gerry Flynn; (23/9/09) Jonny McDonnell;
(14/3/10) Gerry Flynn
Founded – 1923
Stadium – The Showgrounds (2,822)

2009

8/8	Glenavon	a	1-1	Feeney
15/8	Institute	h	3-1	Morgan 3
18/8	Dungannon	h	0-1	
22/8	Lisburn	a	4-2	Garrett 2 (1p), Feeney, Morgan
25/8	Portadown	h	0-0	
29/8	Linfield	a	0-3	
6/9	Cliftonville	h	1-2	Davidson
12/9	Ballymena	a	2-1	Friars, Morgan
15/9	Coleraine	h	2-1	Graham, Hazley
19/9	Crusaders	a	1-1	Friars
26/9	Glentoran	h	1-2	Friars (p)
2/10	Glenavon	h	0-3	
10/10	Institute	a	0-0	
17/10	Dungannon	a	0-0	
24/10	Lisburn	h	0-1	
27/10	Portadown	a	0-0	
7/11	Linfield	h	0-6	
15/11	Cliftonville	a	2-3	Morgan, Garrett (p)
28/11	Coleraine	a	0-3	
3/12	Ballymena	h	3-2	Morgan, Garrett 2 (1p)
12/12	Crusaders	h	0-1	
19/12	Glentoran	a	1-0	Garrett (p)

2010

20/1	Dungannon	h	4-0	Garrett (p), Davidson, Graham, Devlin
23/1	Portadown	h	1-5	Friars
30/1	Linfield	a	0-5	
2/2	Glenavon	a	0-1	
6/2	Cliftonville	h	1-1	Davidson
23/2	Institute	h	0-0	
27/2	Ballymena	a	0-0	
13/3	Crusaders	a	1-4	Garrett (p)
16/3	Coleraine	h	0-0	
20/3	Glentoran	h	0-3	
23/3	Lisburn	a	0-3	
13/4	Coleraine	a	3-2	Keenan, Davidson 2

20/4	Ballymena	h	1-0	Keenan
24/4	Glenavon	h	3-2	Rowe, Garrett (p), Graham
27/4	Lisburn	h	2-2	Garrett, Henderson
1/5	Institute	a	1-1	Graham

Name	Nat	DoB	Pos	Aps	(s)	Gls
Stephen ACHESON		12/8/90	D		(1)	
Łukasz ADAMCZYK	POL	24/12/82	A		(9)	
Jonny BLACK		2/9/82	M	1	(1)	
Ross BLACK		10/5/88	D	36	(2)	
Ciaran BOYD		29/9/88	D	6	(3)	
Darren CASSIDY		6/7/83	M	2	(5)	
Andy COLEMAN		13/6/85	G	27		
Alan DAVIDSON		19/3/88	M	27	(1)	5
Ruairi DEVLIN		2/5/90	A	5	(9)	1
Cullen FEENEY		17/8/80	D	27	(1)	2
Steven FERGUSON		25/2/83	M	11	(1)	
Emmett FRIARS		14/9/85	D	21	(1)	4
Neil GALLAGHER	IRL	20/1/85	G	11	(1)	
Stephen GARRETT		13/4/87	A	35		10
Andy GRAHAM		9/12/88	A	11	(23)	4
Matthew HAZLEY		30/12/87	M	15	(11)	1
Niall HENDERSON		7/2/88	M	25	(3)	1
Kevin KEEGAN		2/1/80	M	19	(5)	
Paul KEENAN		3/12/84	A	5	(5)	2
Darren KING		16/10/85	M	28	(1)	
Gavin McDONNELL	IRL	16/6/78	D	35		
Patrick MOONEY		2/5/91	D		(1)	
Chris MORGAN		11/1/76	A	20	(2)	7
Darren MUNSTER		24/2/79	D	35		
Danny O'CONNOR	IRL	28/9/80	M	10	(1)	
David RICHMOND		10/8/92	M		(1)	
Gerard ROWE	IRL	3/8/84	A	6	(4)	1

PORTADOWN FC
Coach – Ronnie McFall
Founded – 1924
Stadium – Shamrock Park (15,800)
MAJOR HONOURS:
Irish League – (4) 1990, 1991, 1996, 2002;
Irish Cup – (3) 1991, 1999, 2005.

2009

8/8	Crusaders	a	1-3	Mouncey
15/8	Glentoran	h	1-2	O'Hara
18/8	Glenavon	a	2-2	Convery, Braniff
22/8	Institute	h	0-0	
25/8	Newry	a	0-0	
28/8	Lisburn	h	6-1	Teggart N., Braniff, Boyle, og (Thompson S.), McCutcheon, McCullough
5/9	Dungannon	h	1-4	McCullough
12/9	Linfield	a	1-1	McCutcheon
15/9	Cliftonville	h	2-2	McCutcheon, Convery
19/9	Ballymena	a	1-2	McCullough
26/9	Coleraine	h	4-0	Braniff 2, Kelly, Teggart A.
3/10	Crusaders	h	1-2	Haire
10/10	Glentoran	a	0-1	
17/10	Glenavon	h	2-0	Mouncey, Lecky
24/10	Institute	a	1-1	McCutcheon (p)
27/10	Newry	h	0-0	
7/11	Lisburn	a	3-0	Braniff, Lecky, McCutcheon
14/11	Dungannon	a	8-2	Lecky 4, McCutcheon 2, Braniff, Boyle
21/11	Linfield	h	1-0	Braniff
28/11	Cliftonville	a	1-2	Mouncey
12/12	Ballymena	h	2-0	O'Hara, Lecky

2010

2/1	Crusaders	a	2-3	Braniff, Mouncey
23/1	Newry	a	5-1	Lecky 3, Braniff, McCutcheon
6/2	Dungannon	a	4-4	Topley, Baker, McCutcheon, Kelly
20/2	Cliftonville	h	2-0	Hunter, Lecky
23/2	Glentoran	h	2-1	Baker, McCutcheon
26/2	Glenavon	a	1-0	Hunter
2/3	Linfield	a	0-5	
13/3	Ballymena	a	1-0	Clarke
16/3	Lisburn	h	1-3	Lecky
19/3	Coleraine	h	3-1	Braniff, Baker, McCutcheon (p)

NORTHERN IRELAND

23/3	Institute	h	3-1	Lecky, Braniff 2
3/4	Coleraine	a	3-3	Braniff 2, McCutcheon
6/4	Dungannon	h	1-2	Lecky
17/4	Cliftonville	a	1-2	og (Holland B.)
20/4	Crusaders	h	2-2	Topley 2
24/4	Glentoran	a	0-2	
1/5	Linfield	h	1-0	Teggart A.

No	Name	Nat	DoB	Pos	Aps	(s)	Gls
13	Neil ARMSTRONG		18/12/75	G	10		
18	Jordan BAKER		18/4/89	A	11	(2)	3
7	Wesley BOYLE		30/3/79	M	19	(1)	2
10	Kevin BRANIFF		4/3/83	A	30	(1)	14
	Matthew BROWN		29/2/92	A		(1)	
4	Richard CLARKE		29/5/79	M	28	(5)	1
16	Chris COLEMAN		11/12/90	D	3	(1)	
5	John CONVERY		1/4/80	D	24	(1)	2
28	Chris CURRAN		15/1/91	M		(1)	
17	Aaron HAIRE		27/11/90	A	1	(14)	1
19	Andy HUNTER		19/1/81	D	16	(4)	2
6	Darren KELLY		30/6/79	D	31		2
21	Richard LECKY		13/5/84	M	9	(15)	14
24	Sean MACKLE	SCO	10/4/88	D	11	(4)	
8	Ryan McCLUSKEY		2/6/81	M	17	(10)	
12	David McCULLOUGH		24/4/87	M	16	(3)	3
15	Gary McCUTCHEON	SCO	8/10/78	A	27	(4)	12
1	David MISKELLY		3/9/79	G	28		
20	Owen MORRISON		8/12/81	M	5	(6)	
11	Tim MOUNCEY		27/4/82	M	25		4
2	Keith O'HARA		3/2/81	D	26	(1)	2
	Matthew PAGET		14/9/90	D	1		
23	Gareth PORTER		14/12/89	D	4		
3	Ross REDMAN		23/11/89	D	24		
14	Alan TEGGART		24/11/86	M	26	(5)	2
9	Neil TEGGART		16/9/84	A	17	(1)	1
22	Johnny TOPLEY		12/7/80	M	9	(6)	3

PROMOTED CLUB

DONEGAL CELTIC FC
Coach – Patrick McAllister
Founded – 1970
Stadium – Suffolk Road (4,200)

SECOND LEVEL FINAL TABLE 2009/10

		Pld	W	D	L	F	A	Pts
1	Loughgall FC	26	19	3	4	60	24	60
2	Donegal Celtic FC	26	19	2	5	59	21	59
3	Limavady United FC	26	18	3	5	56	29	57
4	Ards FC	26	13	6	7	49	27	45
5	Carrick Rangers FC	26	12	5	9	37	39	41
6	Ballinamallard United FC	26	10	8	8	36	29	38
7	Ballymoney United FC	26	10	8	8	39	33	38
8	Larne FC	26	11	4	11	34	37	37
9	Banbridge Town FC	26	8	3	15	33	48	27
10	Glebe Rangers FC	26	7	6	13	30	56	27
11	Bangor FC	26	7	5	14	36	48	26
12	Ballyclare Comrades FC	26	7	5	14	34	46	26
13	Coagh United FC	26	6	4	16	38	62	22
14	Armagh City FC	26	2	4	20	20	62	10

NB Loughgall FC ineligible for promotion.

PROMOTION/RELEGATION PLAY-OFFS

(11/5/10)
Donegal Celtic 0, Institute 0

(14/5/10)
Institute 0, Donegal Celtic 1
(Donegal Celtic 1-0)

DOMESTIC CUP 2009/10

IRISH CUP

FIFTH ROUND

(16/1/10)
Ballyclare 5, Islandmagee 1
Ballymena 0, Ards 0
Carrick 1, Portadown 1
Coagh 1, Tobermore 0
Crusaders 5, Bangor 1
Donegal Celtic 0, Linfield 1
Dundela 0, Coleraine 2
Dungannon 6, Malachians 0
Glenavon 5, Harlan & Wolff Welders 1
Glentoran 5, Omagh United 0
Institute 1, Ballymoney 1
Lisburn 0, Cliftonville 2
Loughgall 3, Ards Rangers 1
Newry 2, Larne 1

Nortel 2, Bryansburn Rangers 2

(19/1/10)
Glebe 0, Ballinamallard 3

Replays

(19/1/10)
Ballymena 1, Ards 0
Portadown 1, Carrick 0

(20/1/10)
Ballymoney 0, Institute 1

(27/1/10)
Bryansburn Rangers 2, Nortel 2
(aet; 3-5 on pens)

SIXTH ROUND

(13/2/10)
Ballyclare 1, Glentoran 2
Ballymena 5, Ballinamallard 2
Coleraine 6, Nortel 0
Crusaders 4, Coagh 0
Glenavon 2, Institute 1
Linfield 4, Dungannon 0
Portadown 2, Cliftonville 1

(27/3/10)
Loughgall 1, Newry 1

Replay

(7/4/10)
Newry 1, Loughgall 0

QUARTER-FINALS

(6/3/10)
Crusaders 1 *(Owens 29)*, Portadown 1 *(Braniff 27)*
Glenavon 3 *(Molloy 14p, 75, Costello 84)*, Ballymena 3 *(Kelbie 42p, Smith M. 71, Smith A. 73)*
Glentoran 1 *(Gillespie 63)*, Linfield 3 *(Garrett 14, Lowry 40, Mulgrew 50)*

(10/4/10)
Coleraine 3 *(Dooley 28, Patterson 29, 47)*, Newry 2 *(King 53, Davidson 57)*

Replays

(9/3/10)
Ballymena 2 *(Smith A. 64, Anderson 89)*, Glenavon 0
Portadown 1 *(Braniff 83p)*, Crusaders 0

SEMI-FINALS

(10/4/10)
Portadown 1 *(Baker 36)*, Ballymena 1 *(Smith A. 65) (aet; 4-3 on pens)*

(17/4/10)
Linfield 4 *(Thompson 45, Murphy 81, Carvill 89, Munster 90)*, Coleraine 2
(Carson 30, Patterson 63)

FINAL

(8/5/10)
Windsor Park, Belfast
LINFIELD FC 2 *(Thompson 2, Lowry 10)*
PORTADOWN FC 1 *(Braniff 13)*
Referee – Courtney
LINFIELD – Blayney, Burns B., Gallagher, Gault, Murphy, Garrett, Curran, Lowry (Mulgrew 71), Thompson, McAllister (Munster 46), Bailie.
PORTADOWN – Miskelly, Mackle, Redman, Clarke (Teggart A. 82), Kelly, Hunter (McCluskey 57), Boyle, Baker (Lecky 66), Braniff, Mouncey, Topley.

Rosenborg roar back to summit

The Tippeligaen title returned to Trondheim in 2009 as record champions Rosenborg BK re-emerged from two years in the shadows to claim their 21st Norwegian domestic crown.

There was a new look to Norway's top flight, with 16 teams competing instead of the usual 14, and Rosenborg found the expansion very much to their liking. Led by Swedish coach Erik Hamrén, who had joined midway through the 2008 season after winning the Danish title with Aalborg BK, the country's best supported club gave their fans a season to remember, dominating the title race to such an extent that they had it wrapped up with four matches to spare – and with an unbeaten record, to boot.

Record-breaking run

Rosenborg secured the championship in late September with a 2-0 win away to the team that had thrashed them 5-0 in the quarter-final of the Norwegian Cup, and would ultimately finish 13 points behind them as Tippeligaen runners-up, Molde FK. It was their 26th consecutive league game without defeat – a new record, breaking Molde's 21-game unbeaten run in 1998 – and their 20th victory of a campaign that had peaked during the months of June and July when they reeled off eight wins on the trot.

Hamrén stamped his authority on the team by switching from the club's traditional 4-3-3 model to a more pragmatic and modern, albeit less captivating, 4-2-3-1. The team's style of play, considered too defence-oriented by some diehards at the Lerkendal, nevertheless proved highly successful, and although Rosenborg were beaten in their first match as newly crowned champions – courtesy of a last-minute penalty by IK Start – that would be their only defeat of the entire 26-match Tippeligaen campaign.

Among Rosenborg's key performers were two new signings, strikers Rade Prica and Trond Olsen. The former, a Swede who had previously worked with

Hamrén at AaB, shook off the disappointment of a forgettable spell in England with Sunderland AFC to become the Tippeligaen's top scorer with 17 goals. In midfield, Slovakian international Marek Sapara pulled the creative strings while Ghanaian Anthony Annan proved to be an outstanding anchorman. Veteran midfielder Roar Strand, who made his Rosenborg debut in 1989, celebrated his 20th season at the club (he had just one year away, with Molde in 1993) by winning his 15th championship title. He also extended his all-time appearance record in Norway's top division to 423 matches while simultaneously passing the 600-game mark in all competitions.

After disappointing fifth-place finishes in each of the previous two seasons, Rosenborg were back where they belonged with a bang. Hamrén, however, had become hot property and in early November it was announced that he was to become the new head coach of the Swedish national team. The deal was that he would continue to serve Rosenborg through to the start of the UEFA EURO 2012 qualifiers in August 2010, but in the event he would leave Trondheim three months early.

Rade Prica of Rosenborg – the Tippeligaen's top scorer with 17 goals

Norges Fotballforbund (NFF)

Serviceboks 1, Ullevaal stadion,
NO-0840 Oslo
tel - +47 210 29300
fax - +47 210 29301
website - fotball.no
email - nff@fotball.no
Year of Formation – 1902

President – Yngve Hallén
General Secretary – Paul Glomsaker
Media Officer – Svein Graff
National Stadium – Ullevaal, Oslo (25,300)

INTERNATIONAL TOURNAMENT APPEARANCES
FIFA World Cup - (3) 1938, 1994, 1998 (2nd round).
UEFA European Championship - (1) 2000.
TOP FIVE ALL-TIME CAPS
Thorbjørn Svenssen (103); Henning Berg (100); Erik Thorstvedt (97); John Arne Riise (87); Øyvind Leonhardsen (86)
TOP FIVE ALL-TIME GOALS
Jørgen Juve (33); Einar Gundersen (26); Harald Hennum (25); Tore André Flo & Ole Gunnar Solskjær (23)

Sensational Senegalese

Molde's second place in the league was a pleasant surprise. Like Rosenborg, they were indebted to a Swedish coach, Kjell Jonevret, who made some clever signings. Foremost among these was Senegalese midfield general El Hadji Makhtar Thioune, who arrived largely unnoticed from second-tier Sarpsborg 08 FF but would go on to win the Tippeligaen Player of the Year award at the end of a sensational campaign during which he linked up brilliantly with his compatriot strikers Mame Biram Diouf and Pape Patè Diouf, who scored 27 league goals between them. The former was bought in mid-season by English giants Manchester United FC but allowed to stay on at Molde and see out the rest of the campaign.

Molde's Senegalese trio were also highly instrumental in leading the club into the final of the Norwegian Cup with high-scoring wins over Rosenborg and holders Vålerenga Fotball. Their opponents in the end-of-season Ullevaal showpiece were local rivals Aalesunds FK, led by former Molde legend Kjetil Rekdal. Molde were hotly fancied to take the trophy for the third time, but although they led twice through Mame Diouf – once in normal time, once in extra time – they could not see off resilient opponents who had been reduced to ten men after 51 minutes, and they ultimately paid the price in a penalty shoot-out – the first in the 107-year history of the fixture – as Aalesund prevailed by converting all five of their spot-kicks, the last of them, decisively, via the inside of the post, from captain Amund Skiri.

Stabæk, the 2008 champions, joined Molde and Aalesund in the 2010/11 UEFA Europa League by finishing third in the Tippeligaen. It was the third year in a row that coach Jan Jönsson – another Swede – had steered the Oslo club to a top-three finish, and with two of their stars from the title-winning campaign, Alanzinho and Veigar Páll Gunnarsson, having departed, it was no mean feat. 2008 top scorer Daniel Nannskog found his form in the second half of the campaign to finish up with 15 goals, and he was ably assisted by Pontus Farnerud and Henning Hauger, arguably the league's best midfield pairing. Newly housed in the spectacular, multi-purpose, indoor Telenor Arena, Stabæk were beaten there only twice – by Molde and Rosenborg.

2009 was a tough season for some of Norway's major clubs, not least Fredrikstad FK. Runners-up to Stabæk in 2008, they dropped to 14th spot and were relegated after losing their play-off semi-final to Sarpsborg. FC Lyn Oslo and FK Bodø/Glimt were both burdened by financial disarray and filled the two automatic relegation berths, enabling all three of the newly promoted clubs, Odd Grenland, Sandefjord Fotball and Start, to survive. FK Haugesund won the Adeccoligaen (second division) after a last-day home win over Sarpsborg and were promoted directly alongside Hønefoss BK, who had never previously competed at the highest level. Kongsvinger IL subsequently came up via the play-offs – a cruel twist of fate for former coach Tom Nordlie who had left Kongsvinger for Fredrikstad a few weeks earlier.

Fortunes revived

Seven points from their final three fixtures enabled Norway to rise from the bottom of their 2010 FIFA World Cup qualifying group to second place. However, as they had the worst record of the nine group runners-up, they failed to make it to the play-offs. Nevertheless, the revival of the team's fortunes under caretaker head coach Egil Olsen was plain for all to see, and there were no complaints when the man who had led Norway so successfully during the 1990s was handed a permanent contract to take the team through the UEFA EURO 2012 qualifiers. A run of four successive friendly wins substantiated this decision to go back to the future - though the international season ended in disappointment when Norway lost under Olsen at the Ullevaal for the very first time as they went down 1-0 to Ukraine.

NORWAY

NATIONAL TEAM RESULTS 2009/10

Date	Opponent	H/A	Venue	Score	Scorers
12/8/09	Scotland (WCQ)	H	Oslo	4-0	Riise J.A. (35), Gamst Pedersen (45+1, 90+2), Huseklepp (60)
5/9/09	Iceland (WCQ)	A	Reykjavik	1-1	Riise J.A. (11)
9/9/09	FYROM (WCQ)	H	Oslo	2-1	Helstad (2), Riise J.A. (25)
10/10/09	South Africa	H	Oslo	1-0	Wæhler (48)
14/11/09	Switzerland	A	Geneva	1-0	Carew (48p)
3/3/10	Slovakia	A	Zilina	1-0	Moldskred (67)
29/5/10	Montenegro	H	Oslo	2-1	Grindheim (44), Gamst Pedersen (89)
2/6/10	Ukraine	H	Oslo	0-1	

NATIONAL TEAM APPEARANCES 2009/10

Coach – (Egil OLSEN) 22/4/42
/(3/11/09) Egil OLSEN 22/4/42

Player	DOB	Club	SCO	ISL	MKD	Rsa	Sui	Svk	Mne	Ukr	Caps	Goals
Jon KNUDSEN	20/11/74	Stabæk	G	G	G	G	G46	G		G	14	-
Tom HØGLI	20/2/74	Tromsø	D	D		D	D	D	D46	D	12	-
Kjetil WÆHLER	16/3/76	AaB (DEN)	D	D	D	D		D	D	D	15	1
Brede HANGELAND	20/6/81	Fulham (ENG)	D	D	D		D	D74	D	D	60	-
John Arne RIISE	24/9/80	Roma (ITA)	D	D	D	D	D	D		D	87	12
Bjørn Helge RIISE	21/6/83	Fulham (ENG)	M84	s78	M	M70		M62		M66	22	1
Christian GRINDHEIM	17/7/83	Heerenveen (NED)	M	M	M71	M		M90	M90	M79	34	2
Magne HOSETH	13/10/80	Molde	M	M46							22	1
Morten GAMST PEDERSEN	8/9/81	Blackburn (ENG)	M	M	M	M46	M	M	M	M	58	13
Erik HUSEKLEPP	5/9/84	Brann	A76	A78		A78	M40	s87	M78	M75	11	1
John CAREW	5/9/79	Aston Villa (ENG)	A84	A	A84	A70	A78		A		83	22
Steffen IVERSEN	10/11/76	Rosenborg	s76								77	21
Per Ciljan SKJELBRED	16/6/87	Rosenborg	s84				M90	s62	s56	s66	15	-
Thorstein HELSTAD	28/4/77	Le Mans (FRA)	s84	s87	A77						37	10
Morten MOLDSKRED	13/6/80	Tromsø /Rosenborg		M87	s77	s78	s40	M85	s78	s75	7	1
Simen BRENNE	17/3/81	Odd Grenland		s46				s70	s90	s79	7	1
Jon Inge HØILAND	20/9/77	Stabæk					D	s59	D	s46	25	1
Henning HAUGER	17/7/85	Stabæk			M	M83	M87	M	M	M79	11	-
Fredrik WINSNES	28/12/75	Strømsgodset					s71				19	-
Daniel Omoya BRAATEN	25/5/82	Toulouse (FRA)					s84	s70	s78	A87	26	2
Tore REGINIUSSEN	10/6/86	Tromsø					D59				8	1
Knut Olav RINDARØY	17/7/85	Molde					s46				1	-
Kristofer HÆSTAD	9/12/83	Vålerenga					s83	M65			27	1
Rune Almenning JARSTEIN	29/9/84	Rosenborg /Viking					s46		G89		8	-
Alexander TETTEY	4/4/86	Rennes (FRA)						s65	s90		6	-
Jan Gunnar SOLLI	19/4/81	Brann						s87			38	1
Espen RUUD	26/2/84	OB (DEN)						s90	s85		2	-
Vadim DEMIDOV	10/10/86	Rosenborg							s74	s79	3	-
Jonathan PARR	21/10/88	Aalesund								D	1	-
Ruben YTTERGÅRD JENSSEN	4/5/88	Tromsø								M56	1	-
Espen Bugge PETTERSEN	10/5/80	Sandefjord								s89	1	-
Mohammed ABDELLAOUE	23/10/85	Vålerenga								A	5	-

DOMESTIC LEAGUE 2009

TIPPELIGAEN FINAL TABLE 2009

		Pld	Home					Away					Total					Pts
			W	D	L	F	A	W	D	L	F	A	W	D	L	F	A	
1	Rosenborg BK	30	10	4	1	29	10	10	5	0	31	12	20	9	1	60	22	69
2	Molde FK	30	10	2	3	39	16	7	3	5	23	19	17	5	8	62	35	56
3	Stabæk Fotball	30	10	3	2	35	15	5	5	5	17	19	15	8	7	52	34	53
4	Odd Grenland	30	9	3	3	33	18	3	7	5	20	26	12	10	8	53	44	46
5	SK Brann	30	8	4	3	30	21	4	4	7	21	28	12	8	10	51	49	44
6	Tromsø IL	30	7	5	3	19	13	3	5	7	16	23	10	10	10	35	36	40
7	Vålerenga Fotball	30	6	2	7	22	23	6	2	7	25	27	12	4	14	47	50	40
8	Sandefjord Fotball	30	6	5	4	22	19	4	5	6	17	25	10	10	10	39	44	40
9	IK Start	30	6	6	3	26	16	4	4	7	20	36	10	10	10	46	52	40
10	Viking FK	30	6	6	3	26	20	3	5	7	12	20	9	11	10	38	40	38
11	Lillestrøm SK	30	6	5	4	26	22	3	5	7	17	28	9	10	11	43	50	37
12	Strømsgodset IF	30	9	3	3	28	15	1	3	11	12	27	10	6	14	40	42	36
13	Aalesunds FK	30	5	6	4	19	17	4	3	8	15	26	9	9	12	34	43	36
14	Fredrikstad FK	30	8	1	6	23	18	2	3	10	16	26	10	4	16	39	44	34
15	FK Bodø/Glimt	30	5	5	5	16	20	1	5	9	13	33	6	10	14	29	53	28
16	FC Lyn Oslo	30	1	7	7	16	25	1	3	11	13	34	2	10	18	29	59	16

TOP GOALSCORERS

17 Rade PRICA (Rosenborg)

16 Mame Biram DIOUF (Molde)
   Péter KOVÁCS (Odd Grenland)

15 Erik HUSEKLEPP (Brann)
   Daniel NANNSKOG (Stabæk)

11 Arild SUNDGOT (Lillestrøm)
   Pape Patè DIOUF (Molde)
   Erik MJELDE (Sandefjord)
   Bengt SÆTERNES (Vålerenga)

10 Mads STOKKELIEN (Start)
   Marcus PEDERSEN (Strømsgodset)

CLUB-BY-CLUB

AALESUNDS FK

Coach – Kjetil Rekdal
Founded – 1914
Stadium – Color Line (10,778)
MAJOR HONOURS:
Norwegian Cup – (1) 2009.

2009

Date	Opponent	H/A	Result	Scorers
15/3	Tromsø	h	1-1	*Carlsen*
21/3	Vålerenga	a	1-1	*Kopteff*
5/4	Lillestrøm	h	3-1	*Aarøy 2, Skiri*
13/4	Odd Grenland	a	2-4	*Skiri, Aarøy*
19/4	Start	h	1-1	*Arneng (p)*
26/4	Fredrikstad	a	1-0	*Parr*
2/5	Molde	h	0-2	
6/5	Strømsgodset	a	0-2	
16/5	Lyn	h	2-0	*Diego Silva, Mathisen*
21/5	Bodø/Glimt	a	0-3	
25/5	Stabæk	h	1-0	*Stephenson*
1/6	Sandefjord	a	2-1	*Kopteff, Aarøy*
14/6	Viking	h	0-1	
20/6	Rosenborg	h	0-3	
25/6	Brann	a	1-2	*Aarøy*
28/6	Tromsø	a	1-3	*Stephenson*
5/7	Vålerenga	h	3-2	*Mathisen 2, Arneng*
12/7	Lillestrøm	a	1-1	*Kopteff*
27/7	Fredrikstad	h	1-1	*Parr*
2/8	Stabæk	a	0-3	
16/8	Odd Grenland	h	1-2	*Fløtre*
22/8	Molde	a	1-3	*Stephenson (p)*
30/8	Bodø/Glimt	h	1-1	*og (Bjørdal)*
13/9	Lyn	a	2-0	*Aarøy, Roberts*
19/9	Brann	h	3-0	*Herrera, og (Bjarnason), Mathisen*
27/9	Viking	a	1-1	*Stephenson*
4/10	Sandefjord	h	1-1	*Herrera*
18/10	Start	a	1-0	*Roberts*
25/10	Rosenborg	a	1-2	*Diego Silva*
1/11	Strømsgodset	h	1-1	*Diego Silva*

No	Name	Nat	DoB	Pos	Aps	(s)	Gls
8	Tor Hogne AARØY		20/3/77	A	22	(4)	6
15	Daniel ARNEFJORD	SWE	21/3/79	D	28		
10	Johan ARNENG	SWE	14/6/79	M	27		2
22	Fredrik CARLSEN		1/12/89	M	18	(1)	1
25	DIEGO SILVA	BRA	26/5/80	A	11	(13)	3
20	Didrik FLØTRE		31/12/91	A		(4)	1
7	Trond FREDRIKSEN		21/5/77	M	4	(12)	
1	Sten GRYTEBUST		25/10/89	G	1		
11	Pablo HERRERA Barrantes	CRC	14/2/87	D	6	(2)	2
16	Enar JÄÄGER	EST	18/11/84	D	16		
5	Ville JALASTO	FIN	19/4/86	D	19	(4)	
33	Peter KOPTEFF	FIN	10/4/79	A	8	(4)	3
19	Peter Orry LARSEN		25/2/89	M	19	(9)	
12	Andreas LIE		31/8/87	G	3		
13	Anders LINDEGAARD	DEN	13/4/84	G	26		
21	Alexander MATHISEN		14/11/86	A	15	(7)	4
31	Reiniery MAYORQUÍN	HON	13/7/87	M		(4)	
14	Jonathan PARR		21/10/88	A	23	(4)	2
17	Demar PHILLIPS	JAM	23/8/86	M	20	(1)	
9	Glenn ROBERTS		26/6/88	A	5	(7)	2
2	Amund SKIRI		25/2/78	D	24	(1)	2
18	Khari STEPHENSON	JAM	18/1/81	M	17	(6)	4
4	Jonatan TOLLÅS		1/7/90	D	18	(3)	
26	Sverre ØKLAND		19/6/93	M		(1)	

 **NORWAY**

FK BODØ/GLIMT
Coach – Kåre Ingebrigtsen
Founded – 1916
Stadium – Aspmyra (7,300)
MAJOR HONOURS:
Norwegian Cup – (2) 1975, 1993.

2009
15/3	Fredrikstad	h 1-1	Martins
22/3	Molde	a 1-3	Vågan Rønning
5/4	Lyn	h 0-2	
13/4	Strømsgodset	h 1-0	Vågan Rønning
19/4	Sandefjord	a 1-1	Johansen Sti.
27/4	Brann	h 0-2	
3/5	Viking	a 2-3	Johansen Sti. 2
6/5	Stabæk	h 2-1	Ludvigsen, Johansen Sti.
16/5	Tromsø	a 0-0	
21/5	Aalesund	h 3-0	Rønning, Ludvigsen, Sørensen
24/5	Start	a 0-4	
1/6	Rosenborg	h 0-4	
14/6	Odd Grenland	a 0-4	
21/6	Lillestrøm	h 1-1	Stensland
24/6	Vålerenga	a 1-2	Martins
28/6	Fredrikstad	a 2-2	Hamoud, Konradsen
5/7	Molde	h 2-4	Martins, Konradsen
12/7	Lyn	a 1-0	og (Sigurdsson)
26/7	Brann	a 2-4	Martins, Johansen Sti.
2/8	Sandefjord	h 1-0	Bärengrub
15/8	Rosenborg	a 0-2	
23/8	Viking	h 2-0	Berg C., Vågan Rønning
30/8	Aalesund	a 1-1	Bjørdal
13/9	Start	h 1-1	Johansen Sti.
20/9	Lillestrøm	a 2-2	Rønning, Johansen Sti.
27/9	Vålerenga	h 0-2	
3/10	Strømsgodset	a 0-3	
18/10	Tromsø	h 1-1	Johansen Sti.
25/10	Stabæk	a 0-2	
1/11	Odd Grenland	h 1-1	Hamoud

No	Name	Nat	DoB	Pos	Aps	(s)	Gls
28	Alo BÄRENGRUB	EST	12/2/84	D	6	(4)	1
18	Christian BERG		17/5/78	M	26		1
7	Runar BERG		7/10/70	M	21	(3)	
4	Johan Lædre BJØRDAL		5/5/86	D	13		1
2	Karl Morten EEK		25/6/88	D		(2)	
5	Willis FORKO	LBR	12/11/83	D	23		
11	Mounir HAMOUD		1/2/85	D	28		2
26	André HANSSEN		31/1/81	M	6	(3)	
17	Ruben IMINGEN		4/12/86	D	8	(6)	
27	Stefan JOHANSEN		8/1/91	A	1	(3)	
16	Stig JOHANSEN		13/6/72	A	15	(9)	8
12	Jonas Ueland KOLSTAD		21/9/76	G	2	(1)	
23	Anders KONRADSEN		18/7/90	A	20	(6)	2
1	Pavel LONDAK	EST	14/5/80	G	28		
14	Trond Fredrik LUDVIGSEN		22/6/82	A	17	(7)	2
9	Thiago MARTINS	BRA	4/9/76	A	15	(6)	4
15	Akwasi Qwakeye ODURO	BEL	8/2/87	A	6	(9)	
29	Thomas RØNNING		16/7/85	M	20	(3)	2
19	Håvard SAKARIASSEN		28/8/76	A	6	(2)	
21	Daniel STENSLAND		24/9/89	A	9	(9)	1
10	Jan Derek SØRENSEN		28/12/71	A	18	(5)	1
6	Stian THETING		21/10/76	D	18	(3)	
3	Per Verner VÅGAN RØNNING		9/1/83	D	24		3

SK BRANN
Coach – Steinar Nilsen
Founded – 1908
Stadium – Brann (17,317)
MAJOR HONOURS:
Norwegian League – (3) 1962, 1963, 2007;
Norwegian Cup – (6) 1923, 1925, 1972, 1976, 1982, 2004.

2009
16/3	Sandefjord	a 1-3	Bjarnason (p)
22/3	Stabæk	h 1-1	Solli
5/4	Rosenborg	a 1-1	Sigurdsson
13/4	Tromsø	h 2-4	Bjarnason 2 (2p)
19/4	Vålerenga	a 1-1	Solli
27/4	Bodø/Glimt	a 2-0	Nielsen 2
30/4	Lillestrøm	h 3-1	Nielsen, Huseklepp, Vaagan Moen
9/5	Odd Grenland	a 1-3	Huseklepp
16/5	Start	h 1-1	Vaagan Moen
21/5	Fredrikstad	a 4-2	Einarsson, Karadas, Vaagan Moen, Bakke
28/5	Molde	h 2-0	Jaiteh, Karadas
2/6	Strømsgodset	a 1-2	Nielsen
14/6	Lyn	h 2-1	Huseklepp 2
21/6	Viking	a 1-1	Sigurdsson
25/6	Aalesund	h 2-1	Huseklepp, Bakke
29/6	Stabæk	a 1-2	Huseklepp
6/7	Fredrikstad	h 2-1	Karadas, Björnsson
12/7	Molde	a 2-5	Huseklepp, Björnsson
26/7	Bodø/Glimt	h 4-2	Bjarnason (p), Austin, Huseklepp, Vaagan Moen
3/8	Lyn	a 2-2	Huseklepp, og (Simonsen)
16/8	Strømsgodset	h 4-2	Huseklepp 2, Vaagan Moen, Guastavino
24/8	Sandefjord	h 0-1	
30/8	Start	a 1-0	Sævarsson
14/9	Viking	h 1-1	og (Steenslid)
19/9	Aalesund	a 0-3	
28/9	Odd Grenland	h 4-2	Huseklepp 3, Sævarsson
4/10	Tromsø	a 2-0	Huseklepp, Solli
18/10	Vålerenga	h 1-2	Vaagan Moen
25/10	Lillestrøm	a 1-3	Austin
1/11	Rosenborg	h 1-1	Guastavino

No	Name	Nat	DoB	Pos	Aps	(s)	Gls
5	Rodolph AUSTIN	JAM	1/6/85	M	18	(2)	2
17	Eirik BAKKE		13/9/77	M	17	(1)	2
18	Ólafur Örn BJARNASON	ISL	15/5/75	D	28		4
28	Armann Smári BJÖRNSSON	ISL	7/1/81	A		(9)	2
3	Bjørn DAHL		17/4/78	D	3	(2)	
8	Gylfi EINARSSON	ISL	27/10/78	M	7	(17)	1
7	Hassan EL FAKIRI		18/4/77	D	24	(3)	
15	Diego GUASTAVINO	URU	26/7/84	A	6	(2)	2
4	Cato GUNTVEIT		6/8/75	D	3	(2)	
19	Cato HANSEN		26/5/88	A	1	(5)	
16	Bjarte HAUGSDAL		9/3/90	M		(1)	
26	Bjørnar HOLMVIK		2/6/85	D	17	(5)	
13	Erik HUSEKLEPP		5/9/84	A	29	(1)	15
14	Tijan JAITEH	GAM	31/12/88	M	22	(3)	1
6	Azar KARADAS		9/8/81	A	9	(10)	3
27	Matias MØVIK		16/5/91	A		(1)	
10	David NIELSEN	DEN	1/12/76	A	11	(12)	4
20	Kristian Flittie ONSTAD		9/5/84	D	5	(3)	
12	Håkon André OPDAL		11/6/82	G	20		
21	Kristján Örn SIGURDSSON	ISL	7/10/80	D	28		2
9	Jan Gunnar SOLLI		19/4/81	M	24	(4)	3
2	Birkir Már SÆVARSSON	ISL	11/11/84	D	25	(1)	2
1	Johan THORBJØRNSEN		19/8/83	G	1	(1)	
24	Kenneth UDJUS		2/7/83	G	9		
11	Petter VAAGAN MOEN		5/2/84	M	23	(2)	6

FREDRIKSTAD FK

**Coach – Anders Grönhagen (SWE); (23/3/09) (Tom Freddy Aune);
(22/4/09) Anders Grönhagen (SWE);
(17/6/09) (Tom Freddy Aune); (27/8/09) Tom Nordlie**
Founded – 1903
Stadium – Nye Fredrikstad (12,500)
MAJOR HONOURS:
*Norwegian League – (9) 1938, 1939, 1949, 1951, 1952, 1954, 1957, 1960,
1961; Norwegian Cup – (11) 1932, 1935, 1936, 1938, 1940, 1950, 1957,
1961, 1966, 1984, 2006.*

2009

15/3	Bodø/Glimt	a	1-1	*Shabani*
22/3	Strømsgodset	h	2-0	*Ramberg, Tegström*
5/4	Sandefjord	a	1-1	*Wehrman (p)*
14/4	Stabæk	h	0-1	
19/4	Viking	a	2-1	*Gashi, Kvisvik*
26/4	Aalesund	h	0-1	
3/5	Rosenborg	a	0-1	
7/5	Tromsø	h	3-0	*Ramberg, Borges, Martinsen*
16/5	Vålerenga	a	1-2	*Barsom*
21/5	Brann	h	2-4	*Jóhannsson 2*
24/5	Odd Grenland	a	0-2	
1/6	Start	h	1-0	*Askar*
14/6	Lillestrøm	a	2-4	*Borges, Éverton*
21/6	Molde	a	0-2	
24/6	Lyn	h	2-1	*Borges, Éverton*
28/6	Bodø/Glimt	h	2-2	*Wehrman (p), Borges*
6/7	Brann	a	1-2	*og (Sævarsson)*
12/7	Sandefjord	h	1-2	*Piiroja*
27/7	Aalesund	a	1-1	*Éverton*
2/8	Viking	h	1-0	*Borges*
16/8	Start	a	0-1	
21/8	Rosenborg	h	1-4	*Piiroja*
30/8	Tromsø	a	0-2	
12/9	Vålerenga	h	3-1	*Andersson, Éverton, Wallace*
20/9	Strømsgodset	a	1-4	*Borges*
26/9	Lillestrøm	h	1-0	*Andersson*
4/10	Stabæk	a	1-2	*Askar*
19/10	Odd Grenland	h	3-0	*Andersson, Éverton, Askar*
25/10	Molde	h	1-2	*Gashi (p)*
1/11	Lyn	a	5-0	*Borges, Valencia, Jóhannsson, Wass (p), Czwartek*

No	Name	Nat	DoB	Pos	Aps	(s)	Gls
10	Dominic ADIYIAH	GHA	10/7/89	A	2	(2)	
23	Mattias ANDERSSON	SWE	7/10/81	A	6		3
18	Amin ASKAR		1/10/85	M	26	(1)	3
77	Abgar BARSOM	SWE	4/7/77	M	17	(5)	1
22	Celso BORGES	CRC	27/5/88	M	20	(2)	7
25	Erik BRÅTHEN		16/9/87	G	4	(1)	
2	Pål André CZWARTEK		24/4/75	D	9	(3)	1
16	Martin ELVESTAD		26/7/89	D		(3)	
11	ÉVERTON Santos da Costa	BRA	6/1/86	A	23	(3)	5
21	Ardian GASHI		20/6/81	M	26	(2)	2
3	Patrik GERRBRAND	SWE	27/4/81	D	1		
27	Gardar JÓHANNSSON	ISL	1/4/80	A	7	(11)	3
14	Raymond KVISVIK		8/11/74	M	21	(5)	1
26	Atakora LALAWELE	TOG	9/11/90	M		(2)	
4	Vidar MARTINSEN		11/3/82	D	23	(1)	1
24	Jan Tore OPHAUG		25/3/77	D	12	(1)	
20	Levon PACHAJYAN	ARM	20/9/83	M	3	(2)	
9	Raio PIIROJA	EST	11/7/79	D	25		2
6	Hans Erik RAMBERG		8/8/76	M	20	(4)	2
5	Agim SHABANI		14/2/88	D	4		1
1	Kenny STAMATOPOULOS	CAN	28/8/79	G	11		
12	Lasse STAW		1/1/88	G	15		
19	Andreas TEGSTRÖM	SWE	18/1/79	A	5	(9)	1

15	Joachim THOMASSEN		4/5/88	D	17	(7)	
29	Michael TRULSEN		28/12/89	A		(5)	
7	Alex VALENCIA		22/9/79	A	4	(2)	1
17	WALLACE Fernando Pereira	BRA	29/10/86	D	12	(1)	1
20	Daniel WASS	DEN	31/5/89	D	2	(1)	1
7	Kasey WEHRMAN	AUS	16/8/77	M	15	(3)	2

LILLESTRØM SK

Coach – Henning Berg
Founded – 1917
Stadium – Åråsen (12,000)
MAJOR HONOURS:
*Norwegian League – (5) 1959, 1976, 1977, 1986, 1989;
Norwegian Cup – (5) 1977, 1978, 1981, 1985, 2007.*

2009

14/3	Stabæk	a	1-1	*Sundgot*
22/3	Viking	h	1-1	*Occean*
5/4	Aalesund	a	1-3	*Riise*
13/4	Vålerenga	h	1-2	*Kippe*
18/4	Tromsø	a	1-1	*Eziyodawe*
26/4	Rosenborg	h	1-2	*Riise*
30/4	Brann	a	1-3	*Riise*
6/5	Start	a	0-3	
16/5	Odd Grenland	h	1-1	*Sundgot*
21/5	Strømsgodset	a	2-1	*Igiebor, Sundgot*
24/5	Sandefjord	h	2-1	*Sundgot 2*
1/6	Lyn	a	1-1	*Johnsen*
14/6	Fredrikstad	h	4-2	*Søgård, Eziyodawe 2, Kippe*
21/6	Bodø/Glimt	a	1-1	*Riise*
25/6	Molde	h	0-1	
1/7	Start	h	3-2	*Sundgot (p), Riise, Myklebust*
5/7	Viking	a	2-4	*Sundgot, Riise*
12/7	Aalesund	h	1-1	*Eziyodawe*
26/7	Rosenborg	a	1-2	*Eziyodawe*
2/8	Tromsø	h	2-2	*Occean, Sundgot*
16/8	Vålerenga	a	1-0	*Kippe*
22/8	Strømsgodset	h	2-1	*Pedersen, Eziyodawe*
31/8	Stabæk	h	1-2	*Johnsen*
13/9	Odd Grenland	a	3-2	*og (Hansén), Kippe, Sundgot (p)*
20/9	Bodø/Glimt	h	2-2	*Igiebor, Sigurdarson*
26/9	Fredrikstad	a	0-1	
4/10	Lyn	h	2-1	*Sundgot, og (Risser)*
18/10	Sandefjord	a	2-2	*Igiebor, Sundgot (p)*
25/10	Brann	h	3-1	*Pedersen, Kippe, Søgård*
1/11	Molde	a	0-3	

No	Name	Nat	DoB	Pos	Aps	(s)	Gls
23	Pål Steffen ANDRESEN		19/5/82	D	3		
5	John Anders BJØRKØY		8/1/79	M	12	(2)	
26	Mathis BOLLY		14/11/90	M	3	(7)	
6	Alhassane DOSSO	CIV	27/12/89	M	9	(2)	
3	Lars-Kristian ERIKSEN		28/6/83	D	15		
21	Karim ESSEDIRI	TUN	29/7/79	D	19	(3)	
14	Edwin EZIYODAWE	NGA	9/5/88	A	11	(13)	6
1	Otto FREDRIKSON	FIN	30/11/81	G	18	(1)	
28	Lunan Ruben GABRIELSEN		10/3/92	D	3	(3)	
19	Fredrik GULBRANDSEN		10/9/92	M		(5)	
29	André HANSEN		17/12/89	G	2		
17	Martin HUSÁR	SVK	1/2/85	M	1		
16	Emanuell NOSA IGIEBOR	NGA	9/11/90	A	19	(3)	3
15	Marius JOHNSEN		28/8/81	D	15	(2)	2
13	Frode KIPPE		17/1/78	D	28		5
12	Stefán Logi MAGNÚSSON	ISL	5/9/80	G	10		
25	Khaled MOUELHI	TUN	13/2/81	M	22		
11	Magnus MYKLEBUST		8/7/85	A	23	(4)	1
4	Håvard NORDTVEIT		21/6/90	D	17		
30	Olivier OCCEAN	CAN	23/10/81	A	11	(3)	2

2	Steinar PEDERSEN		6/6/75	D	10		2
10	Bjørn Helge RIISE		21/6/83	M	14	(1)	6
20	Stian RINGSTAD		29/8/91	D	7		
9	Vidar RISETH		21/4/72	D	7	(3)	
8	Björn Bergmann SIGURDARSON	ISL	26/2/91	A	3	(9)	1
18	Arild SUNDGOT		17/4/78	A	20	(3)	11
7	Espen SØGÅRD		10/10/79	M	22	(2)	2
22	Kristoffer TOKSTAD		5/7/91	M	6	(4)	

FC LYN OSLO
Coach – Kent Bergersen; (3/8/09) (Gunnar Halle)
Founded – 1896
Stadium – Ullevaal (25,300)
MAJOR HONOURS:
Norwegian League – (2) 1964, 1968;
Norwegian Cup – (8) 1908, 1909, 1910, 1911, 1945, 1946, 1967, 1968.

2009

15/3	Molde	h	0-1	
22/3	Start	a	1-1	Guastavino (p)
5/4	Bodø/Glimt	a	2-0	Berget, Knudtzon
13/4	Viking	h	0-0	
19/4	Strømsgodset	a	1-1	Berget
26/4	Sandefjord	h	1-2	Dahm F.
3/5	Stabæk	a	0-0	
6/5	Rosenborg	h	1-1	Guastavino
16/5	Aalesund	a	0-2	
21/5	Vålerenga	h	4-4	Obiefule, Pratto 2, Guastavino
24/5	Tromsø	a	0-1	
1/6	Lillestrøm	h	1-1	Pratto
14/6	Brann	a	1-2	Guastavino
21/6	Odd Grenland	h	1-1	Guastavino
24/6	Fredrikstad	a	1-2	Angan
28/6	Molde	a	0-4	
5/7	Stabæk	h	2-2	Angan, Berget
12/7	Bodø/Glimt	h	0-1	
26/7	Viking	a	2-5	Guastavino 2
3/8	Brann	h	2-2	Angan, Obiefule
16/8	Sandefjord	a	1-2	Obiefule
23/8	Start	h	4-1	Berget 2, Angan, Holmen
31/8	Rosenborg	a	1-4	Angan (p)
13/9	Aalesund	h	0-2	
20/9	Vålerenga	a	1-4	Dahm F.
27/9	Tromsø	h	0-1	
4/10	Lillestrøm	a	1-2	Burgt
18/10	Strømsgodset	h	0-1	
25/10	Odd Grenland	a	1-4	Angan
1/11	Fredrikstad	h	0-5	

No	Name	Nat	DoB	Pos	Aps	(s)	Gls
19	Davy Claude ANGAN	CIV	20/9/87	A	18	(1)	6
18	Jo Inge BERGET		11/9/90	A	24	(3)	5
22	Tommy BERNTSEN		18/12/73	D	16	(2)	
8	Theódór Elmar BJARNASON	ISL	4/3/87	M	15	(1)	
6	Christian BRINK		17/3/83	D		(2)	
17	Gøran van den BURGT		1/1/90	M	7	(3)	1
24	Johan DAHLIN	SWE	8/9/86	G	13		
20	Fredrik DAHM		29/10/82	M	9	(7)	2
21	Mads DAHM		21/10/88	D	14	(2)	
28	Adama DIOMANDE		14/2/90	A		(1)	
10	Petter FURUSETH		14/8/78	A	2		
13	Vegar GJERMUNDSTAD		14/3/90	D	14	(3)	
11	Diego GUASTAVINO	URU	26/7/84	A	17	(1)	7
29	Alexander HASSUM		2/1/92	D		(1)	
14	Kim Kristian HOLMEN		14/7/82	A	11	(13)	1
23	Stanley Chinedu IHUGBA	NGA	19/11/87	M	16	(5)	
16	Thomas JACOBSEN		16/9/83	D	5	(3)	
7	Edwin KJELDNER		1/3/90	D		(1)	

26	Endre Fotland KNUDSEN		9/7/88	M	1	(3)	
15	Erling KNUDTZON		15/12/88	M	17	(10)	1
1	Tyrel LACEY	USA	8/2/86	G	6		
5	Rikard NILSSON	SWE	24/5/83	D	7	(4)	
25	Paul OBIEFULE	NGA	15/5/86	M	22		3
1	Tarjei Aase OMENÅS		2/2/92	G		(1)	
30	Arnar Darri PÉTURSSON	ISL	16/3/91	G	5		
9	Lucas PRATTO	ARG	4/6/88	A	9	(6)	3
6	Oliver RISSER	NAM	19/9/80	D	4	(3)	
4	Indridi SIGURDSSON	ISL	12/10/81	D	15		
27	Magne SIMONSEN		13/7/88	D	29		
12	Kenny STAMATOPOULOS	CAN	28/8/79	G	6		
3	Shane STEFANUTTO	AUS	12/1/80	D	18	(1)	
2	Jimmy TAMANDI	SWE	12/5/80	D	5		
9	Kasey WEHRMAN	AUS	16/8/77	M	5		
8	Jean Stéphane YAO YAO	CIV	6/10/90	M		(3)	

MOLDE FK
Coach – Kjell Jonevret (SWE)
Founded – 1911
Stadium – Aker (11,167)
MAJOR HONOURS:
Norwegian Cup – (2) 1994, 2005.

2009

15/3	Lyn	a	1-0	Ertsås
22/3	Bodø/Glimt	h	3-1	Thioune, Diouf P., Diouf M.
5/4	Strømsgodset	a	2-0	Diouf P., Diouf M.
13/4	Sandefjord	h	1-1	Diouf M.
19/4	Stabæk	h	3-2	og (Olsen), Thioune, Mota
25/4	Viking	h	1-2	Diouf M.
2/5	Aalesund	a	2-0	Diouf M., Hoseth
6/5	Vålerenga	h	0-3	
16/5	Rosenborg	h	2-2	Forren, og (Tettey)
21/5	Tromsø	h	1-1	Mota
28/5	Brann	a	0-2	
1/6	Odd Grenland	h	2-1	Diouf M., Skjølsvik
15/6	Start	a	2-2	Diouf P. 2
21/6	Fredrikstad	h	2-0	Mota, Hoseth (p)
25/6	Lillestrøm	a	1-0	Ertsås
28/6	Lyn	h	4-0	Diouf P., Diouf M., Thioune (p), Mota
5/7	Bodø/Glimt	a	4-2	Diouf P., Diouf M., Hoseth, Ertsås
12/7	Brann	h	5-2	Diouf M. 4, Diouf P.
26/7	Sandefjord	a	1-1	Mota
1/8	Start	h	8-1	Forren, Mota 2, Hoseth 3 (1p), Diouf M., Ertsås
19/8	Viking	a	1-2	Skjølsvik
22/8	Aalesund	h	3-1	Diouf P. 2, Moström
29/8	Vålerenga	a	1-2	Diouf M.
13/9	Strømsgodset	h	2-1	Steen 2
20/9	Tromsø	a	0-1	
27/9	Rosenborg	h	0-2	
3/10	Odd Grenland	a	1-2	Rindarøy
17/10	Stabæk	h	4-0	Diouf M., Moström, Diouf P. 2
25/10	Fredrikstad	a	2-1	Thioune, Mota
1/11	Lillestrøm	h	3-0	Diouf M., Hoseth, Forren

No	Name	Nat	DoB	Pos	Aps	(s)	Gls
3	Marcus ANDREASSON	SWE	13/7/78	D	12	(9)	
6	Daniel BERG HESTAD		30/7/75	M	27		
32	Mame Biram DIOUF	SEN	16/12/87	A	27	(2)	16
42	Pape Patè DIOUF	SEN	4/4/86	A	28		11
20	Rune ERTSÅS		24/5/87	A	2	(19)	4
24	Vegard FORREN		16/2/88	D	25	(2)	3
5	Øyvind GJERDE		18/3/77	D	1	(6)	
4	Thomas HOLM		19/2/81	M	12	(3)	

10	Magne HOSETH		13/10/80	M	19	(7)	7
22	Jan Kjell LARSEN		24/6/83	G	11		
1	Knut Dørum LILLEBAKK		27/4/78	G	19		
16	Jacob Falch MEIDELL		11/10/90	M		(1)	
9	Mattias MOSTRÖM	SWE	25/2/83	A	21	(5)	2
19	José Roberto Rodrigues MOTA	BRA	10/5/79	A	11	(15)	8
2	Kristoffer PAULSEN VATSHAUG		3/6/81	D	25	(1)	
23	Knut Olav RINDARØY		17/7/85	D	29		1
15	Aksel Berget SKJØLSVIK		15/5/87	M	8	(9)	2
14	Christian STEEN		2/7/77	D	28	(1)	2
21	Kristian STRANDHAGEN		26/7/89	M		(1)	
8	El Hadji Makhtar THIOUNE	SEN	5/8/84	M	25	(1)	4
18	Valter TOMAZ JÚNIOR	BRA	25/7/78	D		(2)	

ODD GRENLAND
Coach – Dag-Eilev Fagermo
Founded – 1894
Stadium – Skagerak Arena (13,500)
MAJOR HONOURS:
Norwegian Cup – (12) 1903, 1904, 1905, 1906, 1913, 1915, 1919, 1922, 1924, 1926, 1931, 2000.

2009

15/3	Viking	a	0-3	
22/3	Sandefjord	h	2-0	Akabueze, Storbæk
5/4	Stabæk	a	3-3	Kovács 2, Brenne
13/4	Aalesund	h	4-2	Rambekk, Kovács, Brenne, Valencia
19/4	Rosenborg	a	1-1	Kovács
26/4	Vålerenga	h	2-2	Akabueze 2
3/5	Tromsø	a	1-1	Sørensen
9/5	Brann	h	3-1	Brenne, Akabueze, Kovács
16/5	Lillestrøm	a	1-1	Akabueze
21/5	Start	a	1-1	Dokken
24/5	Fredrikstad	h	2-0	Kovács, Gulsvik
1/6	Molde	a	1-2	og (Steen)
14/6	Bodø/Glimt	h	4-0	Lekven, Storbæk, Fevang 2 (1p)
21/6	Lyn	a	1-1	og (Simonsen)
24/6	Strømsgodset	h	2-1	Brenne, Sørensen
28/6	Viking	h	2-2	Brenne, Kovács
4/7	Sandefjord	a	2-1	og (Raščić), Fevang (p)
12/7	Start	h	1-2	Brenne
26/7	Vålerenga	a	3-0	Brenne, Kovács 2
2/8	Rosenborg	h	1-1	Akabueze
16/8	Aalesund	a	2-1	Brenne, Sørensen
23/8	Tromsø	h	1-0	Kovács
30/8	Strømsgodset	a	1-3	Fevang (p)
13/9	Lillestrøm	h	2-3	Kovács, Fevang (p)
19/9	Stabæk	h	1-2	Kovács
28/9	Brann	a	2-4	Børven, Gulsvik
3/10	Molde	h	2-1	Gulsvik (p), Kovács
19/10	Fredrikstad	a	0-3	
25/10	Lyn	h	4-1	Brenne, Hagen, Kovács 2
1/11	Bodø/Glimt	a	1-1	Kovács

No	Name	Nat	DoB	Pos	Aps	(s)	Gls
26	Chukwuma AKABUEZE	NGA	6/5/89	A	29		6
1	Árni Gautur ARASON	ISL	7/5/75	G	29		
14	Fredrik Semb BERGE		6/2/90	D	1	(4)	
20	John Anders BJØRKØY		8/1/79	M	2	(2)	
6	Simen BRENNE		17/3/81	M	27		9
22	Torgeir BØRVEN		3/12/91	A		(2)	1
33	Kenneth DOKKEN		10/10/78	M	17	(2)	1
4	Morten FEVANG		6/3/75	D	29		5
23	Fredrik GULSVIK		29/8/89	A	9	(11)	3
21	Steffen HAGEN		8/3/86	D	30		1
5	Torjus HANSÉN		29/10/73	D	27	(1)	
36	Søren JENSEN	DEN	1/3/84	D	4	(12)	

9	Péter KOVÁCS	HUN	7/2/78	A	29		16
10	Magnus LEKVEN		13/1/88	M	21	(8)	1
20	MARCELO Miorando	BRA	9/10/85	D	1		
3	Anders RAMBEKK		17/8/76	D	27		1
2	Håvard STORBÆK		25/5/86	M	11	(16)	2
7	Tommy SVINDAL LARSEN		11/8/73	M	13	(9)	
19	Jacob SØRENSEN	DEN	12/2/83	A	11	(15)	3
28	Dag Ole THOMASSEN		26/8/86	G	1	(1)	
8	Alex VALENCIA		22/9/79	A	12	(3)	1

ROSENBORG BK
Coach – Erik Hamrén (SWE)
Founded – 1917
Stadium – Lerkendal (21,166)
MAJOR HONOURS:
Norwegian League – (21) 1967, 1969, 1971, 1985, 1988, 1990, 1992, 1993, 1994, 1995, 1996, 1997, 1998, 1999, 2000, 2001, 2002, 2003, 2004, 2006, 2009;
Norwegian Cup – (9) 1960, 1964, 1971, 1988, 1990, 1992, 1995, 1999, 2003.

2009

15/3	Vålerenga	h	3-0	Iversen, Olsen, Tettey
23/3	Tromsø	a	4-2	Tettey, Sapara, og (Haugen), Demidov
5/4	Brann	h	1-1	og (Dahl)
8/4	Start	a	2-1	Prica, Tettey
19/4	Odd Grenland	h	1-1	Prica
26/4	Lillestrøm	a	2-1	Prica, Sapara
3/5	Fredrikstad	h	1-0	Prica
6/5	Lyn	a	1-1	Sapara
16/5	Molde	h	2-2	Olsen, Iversen
19/5	Sandefjord	a	2-2	Olsen, Prica
24/5	Viking	h	1-0	Lustig
1/6	Bodø/Glimt	a	4-0	Sapara, Olsen, Tettey 2
13/6	Strømsgodset	h	3-0	Iversen 2, Prica
20/6	Aalesund	a	3-0	Konan Ya, Olsen, Prica
24/6	Stabæk	h	1-0	Skjelbred
28/6	Vålerenga	a	2-1	og (Muri), Prica
12/7	Strømsgodset	a	1-0	Prica
26/7	Lillestrøm	h	2-1	Lustig, Iversen (p)
2/8	Odd Grenland	a	1-1	Strand
15/8	Bodø/Glimt	h	2-0	Lustig, Iversen
21/8	Fredrikstad	a	4-1	Demidov, Prica 2, Iversen (p)
31/8	Lyn	h	4-1	Iversen (p), Prica 3
13/9	Stabæk	a	2-1	Sapara, Demidov
20/9	Sandefjord	h	4-0	Lustig, Prica, og (Gabrielsen), Olsen
23/9	Tromsø	h	0-0	
27/9	Molde	a	2-0	Iversen, og (Lillebakk)
4/10	Start	h	2-3	Olsen 2
18/10	Viking	a	0-0	
25/10	Aalesund	h	2-1	Traoré, Prica
1/11	Brann	a	1-1	Prica

No	Name	Nat	DoB	Pos	Aps	(s)	Gls
4	Anthony ANNAN	GHA	21/7/86	M	25		
34	Mushaga BAKENGA		8/8/92	A		(3)	
11	Vadim DEMIDOV		10/10/86	D	26	(2)	3
3	Mikael DORSIN	SWE	6/10/81	D	27		
17	Pål André HELLAND		4/1/90	M		(1)	
28	Markus HENRIKSEN		25/7/92	M		(3)	
14	Steffen IVERSEN		10/11/76	A	24	(5)	9
12	Rune Almenning JARSTEIN		29/9/84	G	28		
36	Michael KARLSEN		3/2/90	A		(3)	
8	Didier KONAN YA	CIV	22/5/84	A	1	(7)	1
18	Alejandro LAGO	URU	28/6/79	D	21	(3)	
1	Alexander LUND HANSEN		6/10/82	G	2	(1)	
5	Mikael LUSTIG	SWE	13/12/86	D	25		4
24	Roy MILLER	CRC	24/11/84	D		(3)	

NORWAY

22	Andreas NORDVIK		18/3/87	D	3	(2)	
7	Trond OLSEN		5/2/84	A	21	(8)	8
30	Rade PRICA	SWE	30/6/80	A	25	(3)	17
27	Marek SAPARA	SVK	31/7/82	M	19	(2)	5
19	Juska SAVOLAINEN	FIN	1/9/83	M	3	(2)	
25	Kjell Rune SELLIN		1/6/89	A		(8)	
15	Per Ciljan SKJELBRED		16/6/87	M	27		1
13	Kris STADSGAARD	DEN	1/8/85	D	20		
6	Roar STRAND		2/2/70	M	13	(9)	1
10	Alexander TETTEY		4/4/86	M	16	(1)	5
20	Abdou Razack TRAORÉ	CIV	28/12/88	M	3	(7)	1
26	Simen WANGBERG		6/5/91	D	1	(2)	
29	Dario ZAHORA	CRO	3/3/82	A		(5)	

21	Admir RAŠČIĆ	BIH	16/9/81	A	13	(10)	3
13	Ørjan RØYRANE		10/7/88	M	15	(10)	3
24	Fenan SALČINOVIĆ	BIH	26/6/87	M	23	(3)	3
9	Samir ŠARIĆ	BIH	27/5/84	A	7	(7)	1
15	Ebrima SOHNA	GAM	8/3/88	M	24	(2)	1
17	Olav ZANETTI		29/4/76	D	22	(1)	

STABÆK FOTBALL
Coach – Jan Jönsson (SWE)
Founded – 1912
Stadium – Telenor Arena (15,600)
MAJOR HONOURS:
Norwegian League – (1) 2008: Norwegian Cup – (1) 1998.

2009

14/3	Lillestrøm	h	1-1	*Pálmason*
22/3	Brann	a	1-1	*Diskerud*
5/4	Odd Grenland	h	3-3	*Nannskog 3 (1p)*
14/4	Fredrikstad	a	1-0	*Diskerud*
19/4	Molde	h	2-3	*Kobayashi, Farnerud*
26/4	Strømsgodset	a	0-1	
3/5	Lyn	h	0-0	
6/5	Bodø/Glimt	a	1-2	*Nannskog (p)*
16/5	Sandefjord	h	4-1	*Berglund, og (Marciano), Pálmason, Farnerud*
21/5	Viking	a	2-2	*Hedenstad, Kobayashi*
25/5	Aalesund	a	0-1	
1/6	Tromsø	h	2-0	*Kobayashi, Diskerud*
14/6	Vålerenga	h	1-0	*Nannskog*
21/6	Start	h	5-0	*Berglund, Kobayashi 2, Nannskog 2*
24/6	Rosenborg	a	0-1	
29/6	Brann	h	2-1	*Keller, Farnerud*
5/7	Lyn	a	2-2	*Keller, Nannskog*
11/7	Viking	h	2-0	*Berglund 2*
25/7	Start	a	2-2	*Rogne, Pálmason*
2/8	Aalesund	h	3-0	*Berglund, Farnerud, Hoff*
15/8	Tromsø	a	0-0	
23/8	Vålerenga	h	3-2	*Nannskog, Kobayashi, Høiland*
31/8	Lillestrøm	a	2-1	*Høiland 2*
13/9	Rosenborg	h	1-2	*Andersen Aase*
19/9	Odd Grenland	a	2-1	*Andersson, Berglund*
27/9	Strømsgodset	a	3-1	*Nannskog 2, Kobayashi (p)*
4/10	Fredrikstad	h	2-1	*Nannskog, og (Martinsen)*
17/10	Molde	a	0-4	
25/10	Bodø/Glimt	h	2-0	*Kobayashi, Nannskog*
1/11	Sandefjord	a	3-1	*Andersson, Nannskog 2 (1p)*

No	Name	Nat	DoB	Pos	Aps	(s)	Gls
27	Torstein ANDERSEN AASE		24/10/91	A	1	(5)	1
19	Johan ANDERSSON	SWE	22/8/83	A	5	(2)	2
25	Fredrik BERGLUND	SWE	21/3/79	A	23	(3)	6
21	Mikkel DISKERUD		2/10/90	M	5	(16)	3
17	Pontus FARNERUD	SWE	4/6/80	M	28		4
16	Tor Marius GROMSTAD		8/7/89	M		(3)	
7	Henning HAUGER		17/7/85	M	29		
23	Vegar Eggen HEDENSTAD		26/6/91	M	21	(1)	1
8	Espen HOFF		20/11/81	A	13	(15)	1
3	Jon Inge HØILAND		20/9/77	D	23	(1)	3
9	Christian KELLER	DEN	17/8/80	M	13	(3)	2
1	Jon KNUDSEN		20/11/74	G	30		
10	Daigo KOBAYASHI	JPN	19/2/83	M	28	(1)	8
11	Daniel NANNSKOG	SWE	22/5/74	A	28	(1)	15
20	Inge Andrè OLSEN		21/1/78	D	14	(1)	
13	Pálmi Rafn PÁLMASON	ISL	19/11/84	M	14	(11)	3
2	Fredrik RISP	SWE	15/12/80	D	6	(2)	
18	Thomas ROGNE		29/6/90	D	6	(4)	1

SANDEFJORD FOTBALL
Coach – Patrick Walker (IRL)
Founded – 1998
Stadium – Komplett.no Arena (9,000)

2009

16/3	Brann	h	3-1	*Mjelde, Mane 2*
22/3	Odd Grenland	a	0-2	
5/4	Fredrikstad	h	1-1	*Mjelde*
13/4	Molde	a	1-1	*Šarić*
19/4	Bodø/Glimt	h	1-1	*Nystuen*
26/4	Lyn	a	2-1	*Mjelde, Hansen*
3/5	Strømsgodset	h	1-0	*Mjelde (p)*
6/5	Viking	h	3-1	*Sohna, Salčinović, Raščić*
16/5	Stabæk	a	1-4	*Marciano*
19/5	Rosenborg	h	2-2	*Raščić, Isaksen*
24/5	Lillestrøm	a	1-2	*Mjelde*
1/6	Aalesund	h	1-2	*Madsen*
14/6	Tromsø	a	1-1	*Mane*
20/6	Vålerenga	h	0-2	
24/6	Start	a	2-3	*og (Høie), Mjelde*
28/6	Strømsgodset	a	1-1	*Raščić*
4/7	Odd Grenland	h	1-2	*Røyrane*
12/7	Fredrikstad	a	2-1	*Mjelde, Lamøy*
26/7	Molde	h	1-1	*Salčinović*
2/8	Bodø/Glimt	a	0-1	
16/8	Lyn	h	2-1	*Mjelde, Finnbogason*
24/8	Brann	a	1-0	*Røyrane*
30/8	Viking	a	2-2	*Mane, Salčinović*
13/9	Tromsø	h	2-0	*Mane 2*
20/9	Rosenborg	a	0-4	
27/9	Start	h	1-0	*Jensen*
4/10	Aalesund	a	1-1	*Mane*
18/10	Lillestrøm	h	2-2	*Røyrane, Mane*
25/10	Vålerenga	a	2-1	*Mjelde 2 (1p)*
1/11	Stabæk	h	1-3	*Mjelde (p)*

No	Name	Nat	DoB	Pos	Aps	(s)	Gls
23	Samuel CAMAZZOLA	BRA	30/8/82	M	8	(2)	
4	Victor DEMBA BINDIA	SEN	6/8/89	D	4	(8)	
10	Kjartan FINNBOGASON	ISL	9/7/86	A	4	(4)	1
2	Alexander GABRIELSEN		18/11/85	D	21	(1)	
6	Rune HANSEN	DEN	4/6/85	D	7	(8)	1
16	Samuel ISAKSEN		14/4/82	M	3	(6)	1
3	Martin JENSEN	DEN	27/7/78	D	29		1
19	Eirik André LAMØY		4/11/84	M	5	(9)	1
7	Rocky LEKAJ		12/10/89	M		(3)	
5	Birger MADSEN		23/4/82	D	20		1
14	Malick MANE	SEN	14/10/88	A	21	(7)	8
20	MARCIANO José do Nascimento	BRA	12/7/80	M	20	(5)	1
18	Erik MJELDE		6/3/84	A	29		11
8	Espen NYSTUEN		19/12/81	D	25	(2)	1
12	Espen Bugge PETTERSEN		10/5/80	G	30		

5	Pontus SEGERSTRÖM	SWE	17/2/81	D	13	(1)
14	Zdeněk ŠENKEŘÍK	CZE	19/12/80	A		(2)
24	Jørgen SKJELVIK		5/7/91	M		(4)
15	Morten Morisbak SKJØNSBERG		12/2/83	D	23	(4)
6	Tom STENVOLL		27/3/78	D	7	(4)

IK START
Coach – Knut Tørum
Founded – 1905
Stadium – Sør Arena (14,563)
MAJOR HONOURS:
Norwegian League – (2) 1978, 1980.

2009

15/3	Strømsgodset	a	3-3	*Bolaños 2, Hulsker*
22/3	Lyn	h	1-1	*Goodson*
4/4	Viking	a	1-0	*Hulsker*
8/4	Rosenborg	h	1-2	*Fevang (p)*
19/4	Aalesund	a	1-1	*Bolaños*
26/4	Tromsø	h	3-1	*Bolaños, Hulsker 2*
3/5	Vålerenga	a	3-2	*Fevang, Hulsker, Bolaños*
6/5	Lillestrøm	h	3-0	*og (Bjørkøy), Hulsker, Khalili*
16/5	Brann	a	1-1	*Stokkelien*
21/5	Odd Grenland	h	1-1	*Stokkelien*
24/5	Bodø/Glimt	h	4-0	*Goodson, Fevang, Stokkelien 2*
1/6	Fredrikstad	a	0-1	
15/6	Molde	h	2-2	*Fevang, Hulsker*
21/6	Stabæk	a	0-5	
24/6	Sandefjord	h	3-2	*Borgersen, Stokkelien, Fevang (p)*
1/7	Lillestrøm	a	2-3	*Stokkelien, Hulsker*
5/7	Strømsgodset	h	2-2	*Fevang, Børufsen*
12/7	Odd Grenland	a	2-1	*Freeman, Stokkelien*
25/7	Stabæk	h	2-2	*Borgersen, Bolaños*
1/8	Molde	a	1-8	*og (Lillebakk)*
16/8	Fredrikstad	h	1-0	*Stokkelien*
23/8	Lyn	a	1-4	*Stokkelien*
30/8	Brann	h	0-1	
13/9	Bodø/Glimt	a	1-1	*Vikstøl*
21/9	Viking	h	1-1	*Børufsen*
27/9	Sandefjord	a	0-1	
4/10	Rosenborg	a	3-2	*Stokkelien, Hulsker, Bolaños (p)*
18/10	Aalesund	h	0-1	
25/10	Tromsø IL	a	1-3	*Fevang*
1/11	Vålerenga	h	2-0	*og (Perkins), Goodson*

No	Name	Nat	DoB	Pos	Aps	(s)	Gls
9	Cristian BOLAÑOS	CRC	17/5/84	M	23	(2)	7
20	Bård BORGERSEN		20/5/72	D	22	(2)	2
14	Espen BØRUFSEN		4/3/88	A	26	(4)	2
11	Geir Ludvig FEVANG		17/11/80	A	29		7
2	Hunter FREEMAN	USA	8/1/85	D	27		1
4	Clarence GOODSON	USA	17/5/82	D	21		3
15	Petter Bruer HANSSEN		8/1/86	M	26		
19	Knut Henry HARALDSEN		14/12/76	D	4		
16	Bernt HULSKER		9/9/77	A	17	(10)	9
27	Morten HÆSTAD		11/3/87	M	5	(11)	
24	Kenneth HØIE		11/9/79	G	30		
8	Aram KHALILI		28/7/89	A	1	(6)	1
30	Christer KLEIVEN		9/4/88	M	8	(14)	
26	Jesper MATHISEN		11/3/87	D	12	(5)	
3	Branislav MILIČEVIĆ	SRB	23/7/83	D	24	(1)	
7	Erik MYKLAND		21/7/71	M	7	(1)	
5	Oladapo OLUFEMI	NGA	5/11/88	M	4	(5)	
10	Solomon James OWELLO	NGA	13/1/85	D	19	(2)	
22	Leif Otto PAULSEN		13/1/85	D	1	(6)	
13	Tommy RUNAR		25/4/82	G		(1)	
18	Mads STOKKELIEN		15/3/90	A	16	(7)	10
28	Rolf Daniel VIKSTØL		22/2/89	D	6	(1)	1
25	Ole Martin ÅRST		19/7/74	A	2		

STRØMSGODSET IF
Coach – Ronny Deila
Founded – 1907
Stadium – Marienlyst (8,500)
MAJOR HONOURS:
Norwegian League – (1) 1970;
Norwegian Cup – (4) 1969, 1970, 1973, 1991.

2009

15/3	Start	h	3-3	*Andersen, Pedersen M. 2*
22/3	Fredrikstad	a	0-2	
5/4	Molde	h	0-2	
13/4	Bodø/Glimt	a	0-1	
19/4	Lyn	h	1-1	*Sankoh*
26/4	Stabæk	h	1-0	*Keita*
3/5	Sandefjord	a	0-1	
6/5	Aalesund	h	2-0	*Winsnes (p), Nystrøm*
16/5	Viking	a	1-1	*Pedersen M.*
21/5	Lillestrøm	h	1-2	*Nordkvelle*
24/5	Vålerenga	a	0-1	
2/6	Brann	h	2-1	*Pedersen M. 2*
13/6	Rosenborg	a	0-3	
21/6	Tromsø	h	2-1	*Kamara, Storflor*
24/6	Odd Grenland	a	1-2	*Storflor*
28/6	Sandefjord	h	1-1	*Kamara*
5/7	Start	a	2-2	*Andersson, Storflor*
12/7	Rosenborg	h	0-1	
26/7	Tromsø	a	1-2	*Pedersen M.*
2/8	Vålerenga	h	3-0	*Nordkvelle, Pedersen M., Amewou*
16/8	Brann	a	2-4	*Andersson, Nordkvelle*
22/8	Lillestrøm	a	1-2	*Storflor*
30/8	Odd Grenland	h	3-1	*Pedersen M., Riddez, Nordkvelle*
13/9	Molde	a	1-2	*Kamara*
20/9	Fredrikstad	h	4-1	*Keita 2, Pedersen M., Storflor*
27/9	Stabæk	a	1-3	*Keita*
3/10	Bodø/Glimt	h	3-0	*og (Vågan Rønning), Nordkvelle, Winsnes*
18/10	Lyn	a	1-0	*Winsnes*
25/10	Viking	h	2-1	*Aas, Pedersen M.*
1/11	Aalesund	a	1-1	*Keita*

No	Name	Nat	DoB	Pos	Aps	(s)	Gls
6	Alexander AAS		14/9/78	D	24	(1)	1
7	Komlan AMEWOU	TOG	15/12/83	M	10	(8)	1
2	Glenn ANDERSEN		5/4/80	D	28	(1)	1
20	Mattias ANDERSSON	SWE	7/10/81	A	10	(3)	2
15	Marius BOLDT		3/2/88	D	2	(2)	
5	Samir FAZLAGIC		21/10/82	D	4	(6)	
13	Christer GEORGE		11/8/79	M	3		
35	Mergim HEREQI		12/11/92	A		(1)	
17	Ola KAMARA		15/10/89	A	6	(9)	3
23	Muhamed KEITA		2/9/90	A	15	(9)	5
12	Adam LARSEN		12/12/87	G	4		
28	Kjetil LUNDEBAKKEN		6/6/90	A		(2)	
24	Kim André MADSEN		12/3/89	D	12	(3)	
1	Lars Ivar MOLDSKRED		30/11/81	G	26		
14	Fredrik NORDKVELLE		13/9/85	M	25	(2)	5
8	Ousman NYAN		5/8/75	M	6	(5)	
22	Steffen NYSTRØM		1/7/84	A	11	(1)	1
10	Stian OHR		4/1/78	A	3	(22)	
19	Marcus PEDERSEN		8/6/90	A	24		10
3	Steinar PEDERSEN		6/6/75	D	17		
25	Joel RIDDEZ	SWE	21/5/80	D	28		1
3	Vidar RISETH		21/4/72	D	7		
27	Alfred SANKOH	SLE	22/10/88	M	15	(4)	1
9	Øyvind STORFLOR		18/12/79	A	21	(1)	5
39	Lars SÆTRA		24/7/91	D	1	(1)	
21	Fredrik WINSNES		28/12/75	M	28		3

NORWAY

TROMSØ IL
Coach – Per-Mathias Høgmo
Founded – 1920
Stadium – Alfheim (10,000)
MAJOR HONOURS:
Norwegian Cup – (2) 1986, 1996.

2009

15/3	Aalesund	a	1-1	Rushfeldt
23/3	Rosenborg	h	2-4	Koppinen, Rushfeldt (p)
6/4	Vålerenga	a	4-2	Moldskred 2, Rushfeldt, Strand
13/4	Brann	a	4-2	Moldskred 2, Rushfeldt 2
18/4	Lillestrøm	h	1-1	Strand
26/4	Start	a	1-3	Lindpere
3/5	Odd Grenland	h	1-1	Lindpere
7/5	Fredrikstad	a	0-3	
16/5	Bodø/Glimt	h	0-0	
21/5	Molde	a	1-1	Knarvik
24/5	Lyn	h	1-0	Moldskred
1/6	Stabæk	a	0-2	
14/6	Sandefjord	h	1-1	Koppinen
21/6	Strømsgodset	a	1-2	Moldskred
24/6	Viking	h	0-1	
28/6	Aalesund	h	3-1	Adriano Munoz, Moldskred, og (Jääger)
13/7	Vålerenga	h	2-0	Knarvik, Rushfeldt
26/7	Strømsgodset	h	2-1	Rushfeldt, Reginiussen T.
2/8	Lillestrøm	a	2-2	Reginiussen T., Strand
15/8	Stabæk	h	0-0	
23/8	Odd Grenland	a	0-1	
30/8	Fredrikstad	h	2-0	Rushfeldt, Larsen
13/9	Sandefjord	a	0-2	
20/9	Molde	h	1-0	Reginiussen T.
23/9	Rosenborg	a	0-0	
27/9	Lyn	a	1-0	Strand
4/10	Brann	h	0-2	
18/10	Bodø/Glimt	a	1-1	Knarvik
25/10	Start	h	3-1	Rushfeldt, Knarvik, Johansen
1/11	Viking	a	0-1	

No	Name	Nat	DoB	Pos	Aps	(s)	Gls
30	ADRIANO Afonso Thiel MUNOZ	BRA	23/7/78	A	6	(4)	1
20	Mohammed AHAMED Jama		5/8/85	A	1	(6)	
6	Helge HAUGEN		15/2/82	M	17	(11)	
26	Tom HØGLI		20/2/74	D	27	(1)	
15	Yngvar HÅKONSEN		29/1/78	D		(1)	
13	Espen ISAKSEN		16/1/79	G	1		
17	Remi JOHANSEN		4/9/90	M	4	(4)	1
18	Tommy KNARVIK		1/11/79	M	25	(2)	4
19	Martin KNUDSEN		4/1/78	M	10	(10)	
7	Miika KOPPINEN	FIN	5/7/78	D	23		2
5	Kevin LARSEN		10/5/86	D	11	(6)	1
22	Joel LINDPERE	EST	5/10/81	M	25	(2)	2
4	Morten MOLDSKRED		13/6/80	A	28	(2)	7
12	Sead RAMOVIĆ	BIH	14/3/79	G	26		
8	Mads REGINIUSSEN		2/1/88	M	1	(5)	
3	Tore REGINIUSSEN		10/6/86	D	21	(1)	3
10	Sigurd RUSHFELDT		11/12/72	A	22	(3)	9
1	Marcus SAHLMAN	SWE	2/1/85	G	3	(1)	
27	Douglas SEQUEIRA	CRC	23/8/77	D	8	(6)	
14	Lars Iver STRAND		7/5/83	M	15	(11)	4
24	Dominique TABOGA	AUT	6/11/82	D	5		
16	Hans Åge YNDESTAD		24/7/80	D	21	(5)	
11	Ruben YTTERGÅRD JENSSEN		4/5/88	M	30		

VIKING FK
Coach – Uwe Rösler (GER)
Founded – 1899
Stadium – Viking (16,600)
MAJOR HONOURS:
Norwegian League – (8) 1958, 1972, 1973, 1974, 1975, 1979, 1982, 1991;
Norwegian Cup – (5) 1953, 1959, 1979, 1989, 2001.

2009

15/3	Odd Grenland	h	3-0	Niang 2, Soma (p)
22/3	Lillestrøm	a	1-1	Skogseid
4/4	Start	h	0-1	
13/4	Lyn	a	0-0	
20/4	Fredrikstad	h	1-2	Soma (p)
25/4	Molde	a	2-1	Bjarnason, Nisja
3/5	Bodø/Glimt	h	3-2	Soma (p), Danielsen, Nisja
6/5	Sandefjord	a	1-3	Steenslid
16/5	Strømsgodset	h	1-1	Fillo
21/5	Stabæk	h	2-2	Ijeh 2
24/5	Rosenborg	a	0-1	
1/6	Vålerenga	h	0-3	
14/6	Aalesund	a	1-0	Fillo
21/6	Brann	h	1-1	Bertelsen
24/6	Tromsø	a	1-0	Bjarnason
28/6	Odd Grenland	a	2-2	Ijeh 2
5/7	Lillestrøm	h	4-2	Bjarnason 2, Skogseid, Sokolowski
11/7	Stabæk	a	0-2	
26/7	Lyn	h	5-2	Bjarnason, Nisja 2, Ødegaard, Danielsen
2/8	Fredrikstad	a	0-1	
19/8	Molde	h	2-1	Bjarnason, Fillo
23/8	Bodø/Glimt	a	0-2	
30/8	Sandefjord	h	2-2	Skogseid, Ijeh
14/9	Brann	a	1-1	Ijeh
21/9	Start	a	1-1	Ijeh
27/9	Aalesund	h	1-1	Steenslid
5/10	Vålerenga	a	1-3	Ijeh
18/10	Rosenborg	h	0-0	
25/10	Strømsgodset	a	1-2	Ijeh
1/11	Tromsø	h	1-0	Bjarnason

No	Name	Nat	DoB	Pos	Aps	(s)	Gls
18	Andreas Ulland ANDERSEN		6/5/89	M		(11)	
11	Joakim Rune AUSTNES		20/2/83	A		(4)	
2	Trond Erik BERTELSEN		5/6/84	D	25	(1)	1
21	Birkir BJARNASON	ISL	27/5/88	M	28	(2)	7
14	André DANIELSEN		20/1/85	M	19		2
24	Aslak FALCH		25/5/92	G		(1)	
16	Martin FILLO	CZE	7/2/86	A	23	(2)	3
9	Peter IJEH	NGA	28/3/77	A	22	(4)	9
28	Jørgen HORN		7/6/87	D	5	(2)	
19	Tommy HØILAND		11/4/89	A	7	(14)	
12	Artur KOTENKO	EST	20/8/81	G	1		
13	Christian LANDU LANDU		25/1/92	M	1	(3)	
1	Thomas MYHRE		16/10/73	G	28		
27	Mame NIANG	SEN	30/3/84	A	8	(14)	2
24	Kristian NICHT	GER	3/4/82	G	1	(1)	
8	Vidar NISJA		21/8/86	A	19	(9)	4
5	Thomas PEREIRA		12/6/73	D	1	(2)	
99	Jone SAMUELSEN		25/6/85	M	13	(4)	
20	Indridi SIGURDSSON	ISL	12/10/81	D	10		
6	Håkon SKOGSEID		14/1/88	D	30		3
7	Tomasz SOKOLOWSKI		25/6/85	M	20	(1)	1
15	Ragnvald SOMA		10/11/79	D	24		2
3	Børre STEENSLID		25/6/85	D	30		2
10	Alexander ØDEGAARD		13/9/80	A	19	(6)	1

VÅLERENGA FOTBALL

Coach – Tor Ole Skullerud; (26/8/09) Martin Andresen
Founded – 1913
Stadium – Ullevaal (25,300)
MAJOR HONOURS:
Norwegian League – (5) 1965, 1981, 1983, 1984, 2005;
Norwegian Cup – (4) 1980, 1997, 2002, 2008.

2009

15/3	Rosenborg	a	0-3	
21/3	Aalesund	h	1-1	*Sæternes*
6/4	Tromsø	h	2-4	*Andresen, Fredheim Holm*
13/4	Lillestrøm	a	2-1	*og (Occean), Abdellaoue Mos.*
19/4	Brann	h	1-1	*Abdellaoue Moh.*
26/4	Odd Grenland	a	2-2	*Abdellaoue Moh., Sæternes*
3/5	Start	h	2-3	*Abdellaoue Moh., Hæstad*
6/5	Molde	a	3-0	*Leigh, dos Santos, Zajić*
16/5	Fredrikstad	h	2-1	*Zajić, Muri*
21/5	Lyn	a	4-4	*Hæstad 2, Sæternes, Abdellaoue Mos.*
24/5	Strømsgodset	h	1-0	*Sæternes*
1/6	Viking	a	3-0	*Zajić, Hæstad, Muri*
14/6	Stabæk	h	0-1	
20/6	Sandefjord	a	2-0	*Sæternes, Abdellaoue Moh.*
24/6	Bodø/Glimt	h	2-1	*Zajić (p), Abdellaoue Moh.*
28/6	Rosenborg	h	1-2	*Muri*
5/7	Aalesund	a	2-3	*Muri, Fellah*
13/7	Tromsø	a	0-2	
26/7	Odd Grenland	h	0-3	
2/8	Strømsgodset	a	0-3	
16/8	Lillestrøm	h	0-1	
23/8	Stabæk	a	2-3	*Sæternes 2*
29/8	Molde	h	2-1	*Shelton, Storbæk*
12/9	Fredrikstad	a	1-3	*Berre*
20/9	Lyn	h	4-1	*Sæternes 2, Fellah, Shelton*
27/9	Bodø/Glimt	a	2-0	*Zajić, Singh*
5/10	Viking	h	3-1	*Sæternes, Madsen, Abdellaoue Moh.*
18/10	Brann	a	2-1	*Shelton, Sæternes*
25/10	Sandefjord	h	1-2	*Storbæk*
1/11	Start	a	0-2	

No	Name	Nat	DoB	Pos	Aps	(s)	Gls
25	Mohammed ABDELLAOUE		23/10/85	A	22	(2)	6
20	Mostafa ABDELLAOUE		1/8/88	A	5	(10)	2
8	Martin ANDRESEN		2/2/77	M	16	(1)	1
11	Morten BERRE		10/8/75	A	18	(7)	1
30	Øyvind André BOLTHOF		30/3/77	G	2		
31	Kristian BRIX		12/6/90	A		(5)	
17	Mohammed FELLAH		24/5/89	M	8	(15)	2
7	Daniel FREDHEIM HOLM		30/7/85	A	6	(1)	1
18	Juan FUENMAYOR	VEN	5/9/79	D	4	(4)	
5	Erik HAGEN		20/7/75	D	19	(2)	
23	Kristofer HÆSTAD		9/12/83	M	28		4
3	Allan Kierstein JEPSEN	DEN	4/10/77	D	2	(1)	
34	Gudmund Taksdal KONGSHAVN		23/1/91	G	1		
19	Dawda LEIGH		27/6/86	A	15	(6)	1
22	Birger MADSEN		23/4/82	D	5	(1)	1
9	Mario Roberto MARTÍNEZ	HON	30/7/89	M		(2)	
4	André MURI		22/4/81	D	21		4
10	Håvard NIELSEN		15/7/93	A		(1)	
3	Andreas NORDVIK		18/3/87	D	9		
33	Amin NOURI		10/1/90	D	19	(1)	
1	Troy PERKINS	USA	29/7/81	G	27		
6	Freddy dos SANTOS		2/10/76	D	8	(1)	1
21	Luton SHELTON	JAM	11/11/85	A	6	(3)	3
28	Harmeet SINGH		12/11/90	M	18	(7)	1
13	Jarl-André STORBÆK		21/9/78	D	29		2
24	Stefan STRANDBERG		25/7/90	D	3	(2)	
14	Bengt SÆTERNES		1/1/75	A	24	(4)	11
26	Bojan ZAJIĆ	SRB	17/6/80	M	15	(7)	5

PROMOTED CLUBS

FK HAUGESUND
Coach – Jostein Grindhaug
Founded – 1993
Stadium – Haugesund (5,200)

HØNEFOSS BK
Coach – Ole Bjørn Sundgot
Founded – 1895
Stadium – AKA Arena (3,500)

KONGSVINGER IL
Coach – Tom Nordlie; (27/8/09) (Øyvind Eide);
(4/9/09) Øyvind Eide; (20/11/09) Trond Amundsen
Founded – 1892
Stadium – Gjemselund (2,750)

SECOND LEVEL FINAL TABLE 2009

		Pld	W	D	L	F	A	Pts
1	FK Haugesund	30	18	4	8	67	37	58
2	Hønefoss BK	30	16	8	6	61	32	56
3	Kongsvinger IL	30	18	2	10	52	37	56
4	Sogndal IL Fotball	30	14	12	4	46	29	54
5	Sarpsborg 08 FF	30	15	5	10	47	38	47
6	Alta IF	30	12	6	12	50	49	42
7	Moss FK	30	12	5	13	47	53	41
8	Bryne FK	30	10	10	10	41	39	40
9	Nybergsund IL-Trysil	30	11	7	12	49	54	40
10	Løv-Ham Fotball	30	11	7	12	44	50	40
11	Mjøndalen IF	30	10	9	11	38	39	39
12	Tromsdalen UIL	30	11	6	13	38	54	39
13	HamKam Fotball	30	11	4	15	56	48	37
14	Notodden FK	30	9	2	19	38	55	29
15	Stavanger IF	30	6	11	13	35	55	29
16	Skeid Fotball	30	4	6	20	26	66	18

N.B. Sarpsborg 08 FF – 3 pts deducted.

PROMOTION/RELEGATION PLAY-OFFS

(6/11/09)
Fredrikstad 0, Sarpsborg 2
Kongsvinger 3, Sogndal 1
(9/11/09 & 12/11/09)
Sarpsborg 3, Kongsvinger 2
Kongsvinger 3, Sarpsborg 1
(Kongsvinger 5-4)

 **NORWAY**

DOMESTIC CUP 2009

NORGESMESTERSKAP

FIRST ROUND

(9/5/09)
Asker 2, Tønsberg 1
Bossekop 0, Tromsdalen 1
Eidsvold Turn 2, Valdres 0
Fjøra 0, Løv-Ham 1
Flisa 0, Kongsvinger 0 *(aet; 4-5 on pens)*
Klepp 1, Bryne 5
Mysen 1, Follo 5
Raufoss 3, Ullern 1
Redalen 0, Nybergsund 1
Skjetten 1, Kjelsås 2 *(aet)*
Strømmen 2, Korsvoll 0
Verdal 1, Vålerenga 6
Vindbjart 1, Randaberg 3
Ørn Horten 3, Sarpsborg 08 4

(10/5/09)
Brattvåg 0, Aalesund 5
Egersund 3, Kopervik 3 *(aet; 3-5 on pens)*
Elnesvågen og Omegn 1, Skarbøvik 2
Elverum 1, HamKam 4 *(aet)*
Fjellhamar 1, Lørenskog 2
Fløya 0, Tromsø 4
Follese 1, Fyllingen 2
Fram Larvik 1, Drammen 2 *(aet)*
Frigg 0, Lyn 4
Frøyland 1, Haugesund 4
Gjøvik 0, Rosenborg 4
Grüner 2, Ullensaker/Kisa 5
Hasle-Løren 0, Drøbak/Frogn 2
Jevnaker 1, Mjøndalen 1 *(aet; 3-4 on pens)*
Kattem 1, Levanger 5
KIL/Hemne 0, Byåsen 2
Kolstad 2, Ranheim 3
Konnerud 2, Strømsgodset 4 *(aet)*
Kristiansund 5, Nardo 2
Kvik Halden 2, Skeid 1
Lillehammer 1, KFUM Oslo 1 *(aet; 4-1 on pens)*
Lyngbø 1, Fana 0
Lyngdal 1, Stavanger 6
Mjølner 2, Harstad 2 *(aet; 9-8 on pens)*
Mo 1, Stålkameratene 2
Nordstrand 0, Fredrikstad 7
Odd 1, Viking 6
Pors Grenland 1, Notodden 2
Rakkestad 0, Moss 6
Røa 3, Manglerud Star 1
Sandar 0, Bærum 3
Sander 0, Stabæk 5
Sandnes Ulf 4, Mandalskameratene 2
Senja 0, Bodø/Glimt 1
Skarp 1, Alta 2
Smørås 0, Sogndal 4
Stathelle og Omegn 2, Sandefjord 4
Steinkjer 8, Charlottenlund 2
Stord 0, Nest-Sotra 2
Strindheim 5, Tiller 0
Tornado Måløy 1, Molde 8
Trauma 1, Start 4
Træff 3, Hødd 4
Vadmyra 1, Åsane 2 *(aet)*
Vard Haugesund 0, Vidar 4
Østsiden 2, Lillestrøm 3
Ålgård 3, Flekkerøy 2 *(aet)*
Årvoll 0, Hønefoss 3

(13/5/09)
Høyang 0, Brann 6
Vestfossen 0, Odd Grenland 4

SECOND ROUND

(24/5/09)
Lyngbø 0, Brann 2
Hødd 0, Molde 2

(27/5/09)
Drammen 1, Mjøndalen 5
Kjelsås 1, Odd Grenland 2
Kopervik 1, Bryne 5
Kvik Halden 1, Stabæk 4
Lillehammer 0, HamKam 4
Løv-Ham 3, Fyllingen 0
Randaberg 2, Haugesund 2 *(aet; 3-4 on pens)*
Ranheim 6, Steinkjer 0
Stavanger 3, Ulf Sandnes 2
Strømmen 1, Lillestrøm 2 *(aet)*
Vidar 1, Start 3

(28/5/09)
Byåsen 3, Alta 4
Drøbak/Frogn 1, Fredrikstad 2
Follo 0, Vålerenga 2
Hønefoss 1, Raufoss 1 *(aet; 6-5 on pens)*
Kristiansund 0, Aalesund 2
Levanger 0, Rosenborg 5
Lørenskog 0, Notodden 1
Mjølner 1, Bodø/Glimt 3
Røa 0, Lyn 6
Stålkameratene 2, Tromsø 3
Tromsdalen 2, Strindheim 3
Ullensaker/Kisa 1, Sandefjord 0
Ålgård 2, Viking 3

(4/6/09)
Nest-Sotra 2, Moss 1
Sarpsborg 08 2, Eidsvold Turn 3 *(aet)*
Sogndal 2, Åsane 1

(10/6/09)
Bærum 3, Strømsgodset 4
Kongsvinger 4, Skarbøvik 0
Nybergsund 1, Asker 3

THIRD ROUND

(17/6/09)
Aalesund 2, Stavanger 1
Alta 3, Bodø/Glimt 0
Asker 0, Lillestrøm 3
Bryne 0, Viking 0 *(aet; 3-2 on pens)*
Eidsvold Turn 1, Stabæk 2
HamKam 0, Lyn 2
Haugesund 1, Sogndal 2
Mjøndalen 3, Bærum 1
Nest-Sotra 2, Brann 4
Notodden 0, Odd Grenland 2
Strindheim 1, Rosenborg 7
Tromsø 4, Hønefoss 0
Vålerenga 5, Ullensaker/Kisa 3

(18/6/09)
Fredrikstad 5, Ranheim 3 *(aet)*
Molde 1, Kongsvinger 0
Start 2, Løv-Ham 2 *(aet; 13-14 on pens)*

FOURTH ROUND

(5/7/09)
Rosenborg 2, Løv-Ham 0
Tromsø 2, Bryne 0

(8/7/09)
Alta 0, Molde 1
Sogndal 0, Aalesund 1
Stabæk 4, Lillestrøm 0
Vålerenga 3, Mjøndalen 1

(9/7/09)
Brann 1, Lyn 0
Odd Grenland 3, Fredrikstad 1

QUARTER-FINALS

(8/8/09)
Aalesund 3 *(Parr 35, Jalasto 78, Stephenson 85)*, Stabæk 1 *(Pálmason 8)*
Odd Grenland 5 *(Akabueze 15, Kovács 33, 82, Lekven 55, Berge 90)*, Brann 1 *(Solli 73)*

(9/8/09)
Vålerenga 4 *(Sæternes 21, 85, Hæstad 74, Koppinen 90og)*, Tromsø 3 *(Rushfeldt 8, Moldskred 25, 38)*
Molde 5 *(Diouf M. 10, Berg Hestad 52, Hoseth 57, Diouf P. 74, Mota 83)*, Rosenborg 0

SEMI-FINALS

(23/9/09)
Molde 6 *(Hoseth 78p, Diouf P. 83, 95, Thioune 105, 120, Moström 120)*, Vålerenga 3 *(Singh 45, Abdellaoue Moh. 81, 117)* *(aet)*

(24/9/09)
Aalesund 1 *(Aarøy 60)*, Odd Grenland 0

FINAL

(8/11/09)
Ullevaal stadion, Oslo
AALESUNDS FK 2 *(Roberts 54, Aarøy 115)*
MOLDE FK 2 *(Diouf M. 27, 96)*
(aet; 5-4 on pens)
Referee – Helgerud
AALESUND – Lindegaard, Jalasto, Tollås, Skiri, Parr, Fredriksen *(Phillips 103)*, Carlsen, Arneng, Diego Silva *(Aarøy 102)*, Stephenson, Roberts *(Herrera 60)*.
Sent off: Carlsen *(51)*.
MOLDE – Lillebakk, Paulsen Vatshaug, Steen, Forren, Gjerde *(Andreasson 37)*, Berg Hestad, Hoseth *(Mota 90)*, Thioune, Moström *(Holm 62)*, Diouf M., Diouf P.

POLAND

Minute of madness transforms title race

The Ekstraklasa title looked set go to Wisła Kraków for the third season running until they fell victims to a devastating double whammy in the last minute of the season's penultimate round of fixtures. Wisła's loss was Lech Poznań's gain as the Railwaymen from the west took advantage and claimed their first Polish title for 17 years.

The outcome of the championship swung on one momentous minute. Wisła, who had topped the table for practically the entire season, led Lech by one point going into their local derby with MKS Cracovia Kraków. Their rivals, meanwhile, faced a tough assignment away to the season's surprise package KS Ruch Chorzów. With a minute to go the reigning champions looked likely to increase their advantage to three points, but after an extraordinary turnaround it was Lech who emerged at the final whistle as the league leaders.

Last-gasp goals

One-nil up with full-time approaching, Wisła gifted Cracovia a last-gasp equaliser when veteran defender Mariusz Jop put through his own net. At virtually the same time in Chorzow, Lech snatched a sensational winning goal through their mid-season signing Sergei Krivets. It was Lech's first victory away to Ruch for 21 years and it could hardly have come at a more opportune moment because they now found themselves topping the table with a one-point advantage over Wisła.

Four days later Lech duly wrapped up the title with a tension-free 2-0 home win over mid-table Zagłębie Lubin. Coached by 49-year-old Jacek Zieliński – not the more famous former Polish international defender of the same name – and inspired from the front by their outstanding young striker Robert Lewandowski, who topped the Ekstraklasa score charts with 18 goals, Lech were worthy champions. They lost only three matches

Robert Lewandowski's goals drove Lech to the Polish title

and none at all after September, going 22 unbeaten through to the end of the campaign. Lewandowski was unquestionably the ace in their pack but Krivets' arrival in the spring from Belarusian champions FC BATE Borisov also had an extremely positive impact and there were consistent performances too from veteran former international defender Bartosz Bosacki (Poland's only goalscorer at the 2006 FIFA World Cup) and 25-year-old midfield all-rounder Sławomir Peszko.

Lech had been impressive performers in the UEFA Cup under their previous coach Franciszek Smuda in 2008/09, reaching the round of 32, but their hopes of a repeat performance in the UEFA Europa League under Zieliński were dashed by a cruel penalty shoot-out defeat against Club Brugge KV in the play-off round. Nevertheless, Lech were once again the last Polish team standing in Europe. The two clubs from the capital, Legia Warszawa and KSP Polonia Warszawa, had both exited the same competition a round earlier and Wisła's ambition to reach the group stage of the UEFA Champions League was strangled at birth with a shock early elimination by FC Levadia Tallinn.

Kasperczak returns

Wisła's title-winning coach of the previous two seasons, Maciej Skorża, survived the axe on that occasion but when his team looked set to lose their lead at the top of the Ekstraklasa table after a dreadful start to the spring campaign – one point out of nine and no goals – he was duly dismissed by club owner Bogusław Cupiał, who then sprung a major surprise by replacing him with veteran coach Henryk Kasperczak – a man sacked by Cupiał six years earlier and in dispute with him for a long time afterwards over financial compensation for breach of contract. Under the 63-year-old, Wisła duly rediscovered their rhythm, and although the club were forced to play home games in

POLAND

Sosnowiec due to unfinished construction work on their own stadium, a seventh league title in ten years seemed to be on its way to Krakow…until that extraordinary minute of madness.

Wisła's most consistent performer was Brazilian defender Marcelo, but other foreign signings flattered to deceive and it was a disappointing season for resident netbuster Paweł Brożek who, after top-scoring tallies of 23 and 19 goals in the previous two campaigns, struggled to reach double figures. Takesure Chinyama, the Zimbabwean striker who shared the Ekstaklasa Golden Boot with Brożek in 2008/09, suffered a serious injury in the autumn and was badly missed by Legia, who never challenged for the title and, after replacing coach Jan Urban with Stefan Białas, eventually limped home in fourth. Their best player by some distance was Slovakian international goalkeeper Ján Mucha, whose dexterity and bravery repeatedly saved the team's blushes.

Joy for Jagiellonia

Legia were edged out of the European places by Ruch. At the start of the season the cash-strapped Chorzow club were expected to struggle, but under the resolute leadership of their former player and club icon Waldemar Fornalik they proved a tough nut to crack. They might even have won their first trophy for 14 years but for an unforeseen away-goals defeat by second division MKS Pogoń Szczecin in the semi-finals of the Polish Cup. Victory in the final went to Pogoń's opponents, Jagiellonia Bialystok, who claimed the trophy – and European qualification – for the first time thanks to a solitary goal from Lithuanian international Andrius Skerla. There was further cause for celebration at the club as Jagiellonia also maintained their Ekstraklasa status despite the handicap of a ten-point deduction. The goals of veteran striker Tomasz Frankowski, who scored 11 to take his all-time Ekstraklasa tally to 133, proved to be of great benefit in both league and cup.

The arrival of new owners and sponsors came too late to save MKS Odra Wodzisław Śląski from relegation but Polonia Warszawa were rescued from the drop by former Spanish international José María Bakero. Odra went down with GKS Piast Gliwice, while there was a welcome return to the top division for fallen giants RTS Widzew Łódź

and Górnik Zabrze, the former running away with the First League (second division) under ex-Poland coach Paweł Janas, the latter squeezing home in second place a year after their shock relegation.

EURO preparations begin

Janas's successor as national team coach, Leo Beenhakker, was sacked by Polish Football Association (PZPN) president Grzegorz Lato in September 2009 – after three years in the job – following a dismal 3-0 defeat in a World Cup qualifier against Slovenia, a result that all but ended Poland's hopes of reaching South Africa. Stefan Majewski took over temporarily for the final two qualifiers – both lost – before 61-year-old Smuda was given the job of preparing Poland for UEFA EURO 2012, from which, as co-hosts, they are exempt from qualification. Smuda began the long countdown to the finals by trying out an assortment of players in a series of low-key friendlies before the team travelled to south-east Spain to face the European champions in their final World Cup warm-up fixture. A defeat was expected, but the humbling 6-0 scoreline highlighted the extent of Smuda's task as he bids to build a team that will do the country proud in two summers' time.

Franciszek Smuda has the task of preparing Poland for UEFA EURO 2012

Polski Związek Piłki Nożnej (PZPN)

Bitwy Warszawskiej 1920 r.7
PL-02 366 Warszawa
tel – +48 22 551 2300
fax – +48 22 551 2240
website – pzpn.pl
email – pzpn@pzpn.pl
Year of Formation – 1919

President – Grzegorz Lato
General Secretary – Zdzisław Kręcina
Media Officer – Agnieszka Olejkowska
National Stadium – Śląski-Narodowy, Chorzow (47,246)

INTERNATIONAL TOURNAMENT APPEARANCES
FIFA World Cup - (7) 1938, 1974 (3rd), 1978 (2nd phase), 1982 (3rd), 1986 (2nd round), 2002, 2006.
UEFA European Championship – (1) 2008.
TOP FIVE ALL-TIME CAPS
Grzegorz Lato (100); Kazimierz Deyna (97); Jacek Bąk, Jacek Krzynówek & Michał Żewłakow (96)
TOP FIVE ALL-TIME GOALS
Włodzimierz Lubański (48); Grzegorz Lato (45); Kazimierz Deyna (41); Ernest Pol (39); Andrzej Szarmach (32)

NATIONAL TEAM RESULTS 2009/10

Date	Opponent		Venue	Score	Scorers
12/8/09	Greece	H	Bydgoszcz	2-0	Obraniak (47, 79)
5/9/09	Northern Ireland (WCQ)	H	Chorzow	1-1	Lewandowski M. (80)
9/9/09	Slovenia (WCQ)	A	Maribor	0-3	
10/10/09	Czech Republic (WCQ)	A	Prague	0-2	
14/10/09	Slovakia (WCQ)	H	Chorzow	0-1	
14/11/09	Romania	H	Warsaw	0-1	
18/11/09	Canada	H	Bydgoszcz	1-0	Rybus (18)
17/1/10	Denmark B	N	Nakhon Ratchasima (THA)	1-3	Peszko (26)
20/1/10	Thailand	A	Nakhon Ratchasima	3-1	Glik (43), Małecki (52), Robak (87)
23/1/10	Singapore	N	Nakhon Ratchasima (THA)	6-1	Lewandowski R. (26p, 37), Iwański (45p), Brożek Pi. (69), Małecki (80), Nowak T. (88p)
3/3/10	Bulgaria	H	Warsaw	2-0	Błaszczykowski (42), Lewandowski R. (63)
29/5/10	Finland	H	Kielce	0-0	
2/6/10	Serbia	N	Kufstein (AUT)	0-0	
8/6/10	Spain	A	Murcia	0-6	

NATIONAL TEAM APPEARANCES 2009/10

Coach – Leo BEENHAKKER (NED) 2/8/42
/(18/9/09) (Stefan MAJEWSKI) 31/1/56
/(29/10/09) Franciszek SMUDA 22/6/48

Player	DOB	Club	Gre	NIR	SVN	CZE	SVK	Rou	Can	Den	Tha	Sin	Bul	Fin	Srb	Esp	Caps	Goals
Artur BORUC	20/2/80	Celtic (SCO)	G	G	G												44	-
Marcin WASILEWSKI	9/6/80	Anderlecht (BEL)	D														38	1
Michał ŻEWŁAKOW	22/4/76	Olympiacos (GRE)	D	D	D			D89	D				D	D46		D	96	3
Dariusz DUDKA	9/12/83	Auxerre (FRA)	D	D	D			M	M				D	D	M	D	47	2
Jacek KRZYNÓWEK	15/5/76	Hannover (GER)	D	D	M												96	15
Jakub BŁASZCZYKOWSKI	14/12/85	Dortmund (GER)	M83	M	M	M68	M	M78					M79	M85	M89	M82	31	3
Mariusz LEWANDOWSKI	18/5/79	Shakhtar (UKR)	M	M	M	M	M										64	6
ROGER Guerreiro	25/5/82	Legia / AEK (GRE)	M75	M	M			M60	s78								22	4
Rafał MURAWSKI	9/10/81	Rubin (RUS)	M75	M61										M85		M	23	1
Euzebiusz SMOLAREK	9/1/81	unattached	M46	s46	s61												43	19
Robert LEWANDOWSKI	21/8/88	Lech	A54	s61	s61	s63	s68	A70	A	A70	A89	A46	A75	A90	A90	A67	23	6
Ludovic OBRANIAK	10/11/84	Lille (FRA)	s46	M46	M46	M	M	M78		M88			M46				8	2
Paweł BROŻEK	21/4/83	Wisła Kraków	s54	A	A61	A86											20	3
Tomasz JODŁOWIEC	22/3/85	Polonia Warszawa	s75							D	D	D	s58	M	s68	s78	12	-
Wojciech ŁOBODZIŃSKI	20/10/82	Wisła Kraków	s75		s46												23	2
Marek SAGANOWSKI	31/10/78	Southampton (ENG)	s83														33	5
Paweł GOLAŃSKI	12/10/82	Steaua (ROU)			D												14	1
Bartosz BOSACKI	20/12/75	Lech				D											20	-
Seweryn GANCARCZYK	22/11/81	Lech				D61	D	D		D							7	-
Wojciech KOWALEWSKI	11/5/77	Iraklis (GRE)					G										11	-
Jakub RZEŹNICZAK	26/10/86	Legia						D	D	D65							6	-
Arkadiusz GŁOWACKI	13/3/79	Wisła Kraków						D	D								21	-
Piotr POLCZAK	25/8/86	Cracovia						D									5	-
Maciej IWAŃSKI	7/5/81	Legia			M						M85	M83	M70	s46			8	2

POLAND

NATIONAL TEAM APPEARANCES 2009/10 (contd.)

Name	DOB	Club	Gre	NIR	SVN	CZE	SVK	Rou	Can	Den	Tha	Sin	Bul	Fin	Srb	Esp	Caps	Goals
Ireneusz JELEŃ	9/4/81	Auxerre (FRA)				A63	A68	A						A89			25	4
Kamil GROSICKI	8/6/88	Jagiellonia				A81											3	-
Sławomir PESZKO	19/2/85	Lech				s68	s60	s78	M	M77	M84*		M58	s61	M77	M78	13	1
Dawid JANCZYK	23/9/87	Lokeren (BEL)				s81	s86										5	-
Jerzy DUDEK	23/3/73	Real Madrid (ESP)				G											59	-
Jarosław BIENIUK	4/6/79	Widzew				D											8	1
Tomasz KUSZCZAK	20/3/82	Man. United (ENG)							G	G46			G			G	10	-
Marcin KOWALCZYK	9/4/85	Dinamo Moskva (RUS)							D	s65			D				6	-
Adam KOKOSZKA	6/10/86	Empoli (ITA)							D								10	2
Piotr BROŻEK	21/4/83	Wisła Kraków							D		M46	s79	s63				5	1
Kamil KOSOWSKI	30/8/77	APOEL (CYP)						M75	M66								52	4
Patryk MAŁECKI	1/8/88	Wisła Kraków						s70	s88	s85	A70	s63	s79	s90			7	2
Maciej RYBUS	19/8/89	Legia						s75	M76	A85	M89	M63	s46	s75	s77	s46	9	1
Maciej SADLOK	29/6/89	Ruch						s89	D	D	D	D	s85	s46	D	s46	9	-
Wojciech SZCZĘSNY	18/4/90	Arsenal (ENG)							s46								1	-
Janusz GANCARCZYK	19/6/84	Śląsk							s66								1	-
Radosław MAJEWSKI	15/12/86	Nottingham Forest (ENG)									s76			M46			7	-
Mariusz PAWEŁEK	17/3/81	Wisła Kraków									G						4	-
Łukasz MIERZEJEWSKI	31/8/82	Cracovia								D	D	D70					3	-
Jakub TOSIK	21/5/87	Bełchatów								D59		s70					2	-
Tomasz BANDROWSKI	18/9/84	Lech								M	M	M					6	-
Tomasz BRZYSKI	10/1/82	Ruch								s46	s89						2	-
Dawid NOWAK	30/11/84	Bełchatów									s59	A63	s75	s85	A71	s46	7	-
Marcin ROBAK	29/11/82	Widzew									s70	s70	s46				3	1
Jacek KIEŁB	10/1/88	Korona									s77			M46			2	-
Tomasz NOWAK	30/10/85	Polonia Bytom										s85	s89	s70			3	1
Janusz GOL	11/11/85	Bełchatów											s83	s46			2	-
Sebastian PRZYROWSKI	30/11/81	Polonia Warszawa											G	G			9	-
Kamil GLIK	3/2/88	Piast									D79	D	D		D	D46	5	1
Przemysław TYTOŃ	4/1/87	Roda (NED)												G			1	-
Łukasz PISZCZEK	3/6/85	Hertha (GER)												D	D68		8	-
Grzegorz WOJTKOWIAK	26/1/84	Lech												D	D	D	5	-
Adrian MIERZEJEWSKI	6/11/86	Polonia Warszawa												M75	M	M46	3	-
Adam MATUSZCZYK	14/2/89	Köln (GER)												M61	s89	s46	3	-
Artur SOBIECH	12/6/90	Ruch												s89	s90	s67	3	-
Łukasz FABIAŃSKI	18/4/85	Arsenal (ENG)													G		15	-
Mateusz CETNARSKI	6/7/88	Bełchatów													s71	s82	2	-

DOMESTIC LEAGUE 2009/10

EKSTRAKLASA FINAL TABLE

		Pld	Home					Away					Total					Pts
			W	D	L	F	A	W	D	L	F	A	W	D	L	F	A	
1	Lech Poznań	30	12	2	1	28	10	7	6	2	23	10	19	8	3	51	20	65
2	Wisła Kraków	30	8	3	4	18	9	11	2	2	30	11	19	5	6	48	20	62
3	KS Ruch Chorzów	30	10	2	3	22	12	6	3	6	18	18	16	5	9	40	30	53
4	Legia Warszawa	30	9	4	2	26	11	6	3	6	10	11	15	7	8	36	22	52
5	GKS Bełchatów	30	9	3	3	23	11	4	6	5	14	16	13	9	8	37	27	48
6	Korona Kielce	30	6	5	4	23	20	3	5	7	12	21	9	10	11	35	41	37
7	KS Polonia Bytom	30	7	5	3	19	12	2	5	8	10	19	9	10	11	29	31	37
8	KS Lechia Gdańsk	30	4	6	5	12	14	5	4	6	18	18	9	10	11	30	32	37
9	WKS Śląsk Wrocław	30	7	4	4	19	14	1	8	6	13	19	8	12	10	32	33	36
10	Zagłębie Lubin	30	3	8	4	14	16	5	3	7	16	22	8	11	11	30	38	35
11	Jagiellonia Białystok	30	9	5	1	18	6	2	6	7	11	21	11	11	8	29	27	34
12	MKS Cracovia Kraków	30	5	3	7	18	23	4	4	7	7	16	9	7	14	25	39	34
13	KSP Polonia Warszawa	30	6	3	6	13	15	3	3	9	12	23	9	6	15	25	39	33
14	Arka Gdynia	30	4	5	6	14	17	3	2	10	14	22	7	7	16	28	39	28
15	MKS Odra Wodzisław Śląski	30	5	3	7	15	20	2	3	10	12	25	7	6	17	27	45	27
16	GKS Piast Gliwice	30	4	4	7	17	23	3	2	10	13	27	7	6	17	30	50	27

NB Jagiellonia Białystok – 10 pts deducted.

TOP GOALSCORERS

18	Robert LEWANDOWSKI (Lech)
14	Ilian MITSANSKI (Zagłębie)
11	Tomasz FRANKOWSKI (Jagiellonia)
10	Artur SOBIECH (Ruch)
	Paweł BROŻEK (Wisła)
9	Dawid NOWAK (Bełchatów)
	Vuk SOTIROVIĆ (Śląsk)
8	Sławomir PESZKO (Lech)
	Łukasz JANOSZKA (Ruch)
	Patryk MAŁECKI (Wisła)

CLUB-BY-CLUB

ARKA GDYNIA

Coach – Marek Chojancki; (19/8/09) Dariusz Pasieka
Founded – 1929
Stadium – GOSiR (12,000); Narodowy Stadion Rugby (3,000)
MAJOR HONOURS:
Polish Cup – (1) 1979.

2009
31/7	Lechia	a	1-2	Wachowicz
9/8	Legia	h	0-1	
14/8	Ruch	a	0-1	
21/8	Wisła	h	0-1	
30/8	Zagłębie	a	2-0	Trytko, Ława
12/9	Cracovia	a	1-1	Ława
19/9	Polonia Warszawa	h	0-0	
27/9	Polonia Bytom	a	1-3	Wachowicz
4/10	Lech	h	1-1	Szmatiuk
17/10	Korona	a	2-1	Lubenov, Mrowiec
23/10	Jagiellonia	h	0-0	
31/10	Odra	h	2-0	Trytko 2
7/11	Bełchatów	a	0-1	
21/11	Piast	a	2-2	Wilczyński, Budziński
25/11	Lechia	h	1-2	Wachowicz
29/11	Śląsk Wrocław	h	1-1	Trytko
13/12	Legia	a	0-1	

2010
27/2	Ruch	h	0-3	
5/3	Wisła	a	1-0	Tshibamba
14/3	Zagłębie	h	0-2	
19/3	Cracovia	a	2-0	Tshibamba, Labukas
27/3	Polonia Warszawa	a	1-2	Ława
31/3	Polonia Bytom	h	2-2	og (Sawala), Labukas (p)
9/4	Lech	a	0-2	
23/4	Korona	h	1-2	Trytko

28/4	Jagiellonia	a	1-2	Tshibamba
1/5	Odra	a	1-2	Ława
6/5	Bełchatów	h	2-1	Tshibamba, Szmatiuk
11/5	Piast	h	2-1	Wilczyński, Trytko
15/5	Śląsk Wrocław	a	1-2	Tshibamba

No	Name	Nat	DoB	Pos	Aps	(s)	Gls
29	Robert BEDNAREK		23/2/79	D	18		
1	Andrzej BLEDZEWSKI		2/7/77	G	20		
19	Miroslav BOŻOK	SVK	19/10/84	M	13		
27	Marcin BUDZIŃSKI		6/7/90	M	21	(5)	1
22	Krzysztof BUŁKA		3/7/90	M		(1)	
25	Filip BURKHARDT		23/3/87	M	6	(10)	
31	Paweł CZOSKA		31/7/90	M		(5)	
13	Bartosz KARWAN		13/1/76	M	1		
3	Łukasz KOWALSKI		1/12/80	D	28	(1)	
11	Tadas LABUKAS	LTU	10/1/84	A	19	(8)	2
10	Lubomir LUBENOV	BUL	25/8/80	M	14	(6)	1
20	Bartosz ŁAWA		26/2/79	M	29		4
21	Joseph Désiré MAWAYE	CMR	14/5/86	A	1	(5)	
4	Adrian MROWIEC		1/12/83	M	25		1
16	Grzegorz NICIŃSKI		16/5/73	A		(4)	
8	Michał PŁOTKA		11/6/88	D	11	(2)	
77	Piotr ROBAKOWSKI		1/5/90	D		(1)	
15	Stoiko SAKALIEV	BUL	25/3/79	A	8	(5)	
17	Mateusz SIEBERT		4/4/89	D	16	(1)	
6	Tomasz SOKOŁOWSKI		27/4/77	D	9	(5)	
23	Maciej SZMATIUK		9/5/80	D	28		2
9	Przemysław TRYTKO		26/8/87	A	18	(7)	6
22	Joël Omari TSHIBAMBA	COD	22/9/88	A	11	(1)	5
7	Dariusz ULANOWSKI		3/3/71	M	7	(4)	
18	Marcin WACHOWICZ		14/2/81	A	10	(6)	3
37	Wojciech WILCZYŃSKI		18/3/90	D	7	(4)	2
33	Norbert WITKOWSKI		5/8/81	G	10	(1)	

 **POLAND**

GKS BEŁCHATÓW
Coach – Rafał Ulatowski
Founded – 1977
Stadium – GKS (5,238)

2009

31/7	Polonia Bytom	a	0-1	
8/8	Jagiellonia	h	1-1	Ujek
15/8	Wisła	a	0-3	
22/8	Piast	h	0-1	
30/8	Lech	a	2-2	Popek, Cetnarski
12/9	Ruch	h	2-1	Tosik, Ujek
18/9	Zagłębie	a	1-1	Pietrasiak (p)
26/9	Odra	a	1-0	Cetnarski
3/10	Korona	h	1-0	Popek
16/10	Śląsk Wrocław	h	2-0	Korzym, Tosik
24/10	Polonia Warszawa	h	3-0	Wróbel, Costly, Popek (p)
30/10	Cracovia	a	1-0	Korzym
7/11	Arka	h	1-0	Nowak
21/11	Lechia	a	2-0	Małkowski, Nowak
28/11	Legia	h	0-1	
5/12	Polonia Bytom	h	2-2	Pietrasiak (p), Lačić
13/12	Jagiellonia	a	1-2	Kuświk

2010

27/2	Wisła	h	1-0	Nowak
7/3	Piast	a	2-1	Rachwał, Gol
14/3	Lech	h	1-1	Wróbel
19/3	Ruch	a	0-1	
26/3	Zagłębie	h	1-3	Kuświk
1/4	Odra	h	3-0	Nowak 2, Cetnarski
20/4	Korona	a	1-1	Cetnarski
24/4	Śląsk Wrocław	a	0-0	
27/4	Polonia Warszawa	a	0-0	
30/4	Cracovia	h	3-0	Cetnarski, Nowak 2
6/5	Arka	a	1-2	Korzym
11/5	Lechia	h	2-1	Nowak 2 (1p)
15/5	Legia	a	2-2	Zakrzewski, Bartosiak

No	Name	Nat	DoB	Pos	Aps	(s)	Gls
45	Bartłomiej BARTOSIAK		26/2/91	M		(3)	1
51	Łukasz BOCIAN		29/5/88	M		(2)	
6	Edward CECOT		1/7/74	D	3	(1)	
10	Mateusz CETNARSKI		6/7/88	M	18	(10)	5
13	Carlos Yair COSTLY Molina	HON	18/7/82	A	6	(4)	1
28	Marcin DRZYMONT		16/9/81	D	4	(1)	
22	Grzegorz FONFARA		8/6/83	D	7	(4)	
5	Janusz GOL		11/11/85	M	23	(3)	1
7	Karol GREGOREK		26/1/83	A		(3)	
21	Krzysztof JANUS		25/3/86	M	7	(11)	
18	Maciej KORZYM		2/5/88	A	15	(5)	3
17	Grzegorz KUŚWIK		23/5/87	A	2	(7)	2
14	Mate LAČIĆ	CRO	12/9/80	D	25	(1)	1
33	Paweł MAGDOŃ		13/11/79	D	2		
8	Maciej MAŁKOWSKI		19/3/85	M	22	(2)	1
9	Dawid NOWAK		30/11/84	A	14	(6)	9
61	Krystian PIECZARA		12/4/89	A		(1)	
15	Dariusz PIETRASIAK		12/2/80	D	28		2
4	Jacek POPEK		20/8/78	D	22		3
19	Kamil POŹNIAK		11/12/89	M	1	(7)	
20	Patryk RACHWAŁ		27/1/81	M	30		1
12	Łukasz SAPELA		21/9/82	G	30		
2	Marek SZYNDROWSKI		30/10/80	D	7	(1)	
24	Jakub TOSIK		21/5/87	M	23	(2)	2
25	Mariusz UJEK		6/12/77	A	14	(2)	2
23	Tomasz WRÓBEL		10/7/82	M	23	(1)	2
11	Zbigniew ZAKRZEWSKI		26/1/81	A	4	(5)	1

MKS CRACOVIA KRAKÓW
Coach – Artur Płatek; (12/8/09) Orest Lenczyk
Founded – 1906
Stadium – Ludowy Stadion, Sosnowiec (7,500); Hutnik Kraków
(5,500); Marszałek Piłsudski (6,500)
MAJOR HONOURS:
Polish League – (5) 1921, 1930, 1932, 1937, 1948.

2009

1/8	Śląsk Wrocław	a	0-2	
7/8	Lechia	h	2-6	Polczak, Kaszuba
15/8	Legia	a	0-0	
23/8	Lech	h	1-0	Sasin
29/8	Korona	a	1-1	Matusiak
12/9	Arka	h	1-1	Pawlusiński
19/9	Ruch	a	0-2	
26/9	Jagiellonia	a	0-0	
2/10	Zagłębie	h	1-1	Sacha
17/10	Polonia Bytom	h	1-2	Sacha
25/10	Odra	a	0-1	
30/10	Bełchatów	a	0-1	
7/11	Polonia Warszawa	a	1-0	Sacha
22/11	Wisła	a	1-0	Goliński
28/11	Piast	h	3-2	Matusiak, Goliński, Klich
5/12	Śląsk Wrocław	h	1-0	Sacha
12/12	Lechia	a	0-1	

2010

26/2	Legia	h	1-2	Pawlusiński
6/3	Lech	a	1-3	Suvorov
13/3	Korona	h	3-0	Matusiak 2, Goliński
19/3	Arka	a	0-2	
27/3	Ruch	h	1-4	Sacha
1/4	Jagiellonia	h	0-1	
9/4	Zagłębie	a	0-0	
24/4	Polonia Bytom	a	2-1	Matusiak (p), Ślusarski
27/4	Odra	h	1-0	Wasiluk (p)
30/4	Bełchatów	h	0-3	
7/5	Polonia Warszawa	h	1-2	Matusiak
11/5	Wisła	h	1-1	og (Jop)
15/5	Piast	a	1-0	Ślusarski

No	Name	Nat	DoB	Pos	Aps	(s)	Gls
8	Arkadiusz BARAN		9/11/79	M	17	(4)	
33	Marcin CABAJ		23/5/80	G	21		
19	Konrad CEBULA		22/3/83	M	3	(6)	
23	Łukasz DERBICH		23/10/83	D	20	(2)	
41	Dawid DYNAREK		9/3/89	M		(2)	
77	Michał GOLIŃSKI		17/3/81	M	13	(2)	3
22	Jakub GRZEGORZEWSKI		16/4/82	A	1	(1)	
23	Mateusz JELEŃ		18/9/88	M	1	(1)	
11	Krzysztof KALICIAK		21/3/86	A		(3)	
6	Kamil KARCZ		19/8/86	M		(1)	
39	Jakub KASZUBA		28/1/88	A		(11)	1
43	Mateusz KLICH		13/6/90	M	18	(3)	1
10	Dariusz KŁUS		11/10/81	M	4	(4)	
10	Wojciech ŁUCZAK		28/7/89	A	1	(1)	
7	Radosław MATUSIAK		1/1/82	A	21	(4)	6
35	Łukasz MERDA		4/5/80	G	9		
24	Łukasz MIERZEJEWSKI		31/8/82	D	20	(3)	
18	Tomasz MOSKAŁA		5/4/77	A	13	(3)	
40	Georgy OVSEANNICOV	MDA	12/10/85	A	5	(4)	
9	Dariusz PAWLUSIŃSKI		24/11/77	M	23	(3)	2
16	Piotr POLCZAK		25/8/86	D	29		1
14	Mariusz SACHA		19/7/87	M	16	(5)	5
15	Paweł SASIN		2/10/83	M	16	(6)	1
19	Alexandru SUVOROV	MDA	2/2/87	M	6	(5)	1
23	Łukasz SZCZOCZARZ		19/1/84	A	1		
21	Sławomir SZELIGA		17/7/82	D	23	(5)	
20	Bartosz ŚLUSARSKI		11/12/81	A	10	(2)	2
17	Łukasz TUPALSKI		4/9/80	D	16	(2)	
5	Marek WASILUK		3/6/87	D	20	(3)	1
11	Kamil WITKOWSKI		9/12/84	A	1	(2)	

JAGIELLONIA BIAŁYSTOK
Coach – Michał Probierz
Founded – 1932
Stadium – Stadion Miejski (10,000)
MAJOR HONOURS:
Polish Cup – (1) 2010.

2009

1/8	Odra	h	2-1	*Frankowski, Grosicki*
8/8	Bełchatów	a	1-1	*Bruno*
15/8	Korona	h	2-0	*Lewczuk, Frankowski*
22/8	Śląsk Wrocław	h	2-0	*Bruno, Reich*
29/8	Wisła	a	1-2	*og (Pawełek)*
12/9	Lech	h	2-3	*Frankowski, Jezierski*
20/9	Piast	a	0-0	
26/9	Cracovia	h	0-0	
3/10	Legia	h	2-0	*Grosicki 2*
18/10	Zagłębie	a	0-0	
23/10	Arka	a	0-0	
31/10	Polonia Warszawa	h	1-0	*Frankowski*
8/11	Ruch	a	2-5	*Jezierski, Reich*
20/11	Polonia Bytom	a	1-1	*Frankowski*
28/11	Lechia	h	0-0	
5/12	Odra	a	2-2	*Frankowski 2 (2p)*
13/12	Bełchatów	h	2-1	*Frankowski, Staňo*

2010

27/2	Korona	a	0-1	
6/3	Śląsk Wrocław	a	2-1	*Lato, Jezierski*
12/3	Wisła	h	0-0	
21/3	Lech	a	0-2	
28/3	Piast	h	2-0	*Frankowski 2*
1/4	Cracovia	a	1-0	*Jezierski*
19/4	Legia	a	1-2	*Thiago Rangel*
24/4	Zagłębie	a	0-0	
28/4	Arka	h	2-1	*Grosicki, Frankowski (p)*
1/5	Polonia Warszawa	a	0-2	
7/5	Ruch	h	1-0	*Skerla*
11/5	Polonia Bytom	h	0-0	
15/5	Lechia	a	0-2	

No	Name	Nat	DoB	Pos	Aps	(s)	Gls
32	BRUNO Coutinho Martins	BRA	21/6/86	M	26	(3)	2
23	Marcin BURKHARDT		25/9/83	M	5	(3)	
28	Jacek FALKOWSKI		10/10/84	M		(2)	
25	Michał FIDZIUKIEWICZ		8/2/91	A		(1)	
21	Tomasz FRANKOWSKI		16/8/74	A	28	(2)	11
7	Vahan GEVORGYAN		19/12/81	M	5	(5)	
33	Rafał GIKIEWICZ		26/10/87	G	8		
10	Kamil GROSICKI		8/6/88	A	22	(8)	4
22	Rafał GRZYB		16/1/83	M	10	(2)	
11	HERMES Neves Soares	BRA	19/9/74	M	27		
14	Neil HLAVATY	USA	27/12/86	M		(2)	
24	Dariusz JARECKI		23/3/81	M	10	(7)	
9	Remigiusz JEZIERSKI		19/1/76	A	13	(13)	4
7	Piotr KLEPCZAREK		13/8/82	M	1	(1)	
23	Krzysztof KRÓL		6/2/87	D	4	(2)	
22	Gustavo Adolfo LAMOS Cardenas	COL	23/1/90	M		(1)	
13	Jarosław LATO		17/6/77	M	11	(1)	1
4	Igor LEWCZUK		30/5/85	D	23	(3)	1
30	MAICON Rogério Silva Calijuri	BRA	6/6/86	A	3	(5)	
20	Andrzej NIEWULIS		21/4/89	D	1	(1)	
17	Alexis Patricio NORAMBUENA Ruz	CHI	31/3/84	D	22	(3)	
16	Jan PAWŁOWSKI		18/11/92	A		(1)	
27	Marco REICH	GER	30/12/77	M	7	(8)	2
6	Michał RENUSZ		18/10/87	M	2		
12	Grzegorz SANDOMIERSKI		5/9/89	G	19		
14	El Mehdi SIDQY	MAR	6/1/84	D	10		
5	Andrius SKERLA	LTU	29/4/77	D	26		1
3	Pavol STAŇO	SVK	29/9/77	D	11	(4)	1
30	Michał STEĆ		6/10/91	A	1		

KORONA KIELCE
**Coach – Marek Motyka; (24/11/09) Marcin Gawron;
(29/11/09) Marcin Sasal**
Founded – 1973
Stadium – Stadion Miejski Arena Kielc (15,550)

2009

2/8	Polonia Warszawa	h	4-0	*Andradina, Gajtkowski, Markiewicz, Wilk*
9/8	Lech	h	0-5	
15/8	Jagiellonia	a	0-2	
22/8	Polonia Bytom	a	0-1	
29/8	Cracovia	h	1-1	*Andradina*
11/9	Odra	a	2-0	*Sobolewski, Édson*
19/9	Śląsk Wrocław	h	1-1	*Andradina*
26/9	Piast	h	3-2	*Andradina, Vuković, Wilk*
3/10	Bełchatów	a	0-1	
17/10	Arka	h	1-2	*Kiełb*
24/10	Legia	a	2-5	*Gajtkowski, Sobolewski*
30/10	Wisła	h	2-3	*Konon, Gawęcki*
6/11	Lechia	a	1-1	*Wilk*
20/11	Zagłębie	h	3-3	*Markiewicz, Wilk, Sobolewski*
28/11	Ruch	a	0-0	
6/12	Polonia Warszawa	a	1-1	*Hernâni*
12/12	Lech	a	0-2	

2010

27/2	Jagiellonia	h	1-0	*Staňo*
5/3	Polonia Bytom	h	1-0	*Staňo*
13/3	Cracovia	a	0-3	
20/3	Odra	h	1-1	*Tataj*
27/3	Śląsk Wrocław	a	1-1	*Staňo*
3/4	Piast	a	0-1	
20/4	Bełchatów	h	1-1	*Andradina (p)*
23/4	Arka	a	2-1	*Kiełb, Andradina*
26/4	Legia	h	0-1	
30/4	Wisła	a	1-0	*Kiełb*
8/5	Lechia	h	1-0	*Jędrzejczyk*
11/5	Zagłębie	a	2-2	*Tataj 2*
15/5	Ruch	h	3-0	*Tataj 2, og (Pilarz)*

No	Name	Nat	DoB	Pos	Aps	(s)	Gls
16	Edi Carlo Dias Marçal "ANDRADINA"	BRA	13/9/74	A	23	(3)	6
19	Paweł BUŚKIEWICZ		18/3/83	A	7	(3)	
8	Łukasz CICHOS		2/6/82	A	1	(4)	
1	Radosław CIERZNIAK		24/4/83	G	14		
37	ÉDSON Luis da Silva	BRA	15/3/77	D	8	(3)	1
17	Krzysztof GAJTKOWSKI		26/9/80	A	14	(7)	2
14	Piotr GAWĘCKI		24/5/89	A		(3)	1
4	HERNÂNI José da Rosa	BRA	3/2/84	D	29		
20	Artur JĘDRZEJCZYK		4/11/87	D	11		1
18	Paweł KACZMAREK		1/7/85	M	5	(6)	
9	Paweł KAL		9/7/89	M	3	(2)	
27	Jacek KIEŁB		10/1/88	M	16	(10)	1
30	Ernest KONON		16/3/74	A	6	(5)	1
3	Kamil KUZERA		11/3/83	D	7		
22	Grzegorz LECH		10/1/83	M	4	(2)	
2	Dariusz ŁATKA		14/9/78	M	11	(4)	
34	Piotr MALARCZYK		1/8/91	D	6		
21	Łukasz MALISZEWSKI		27/4/85	M	4	(3)	
33	Zbigniew MAŁKOWSKI		19/1/78	G	16		
15	Jacek MARKIEWICZ		18/4/76	D	19	(3)	2
7	Nikola MIJAILOVIĆ	SRB	15/2/82	D	23		
20	Łukasz NAWOTCZYŃSKI		30/3/82	D	5	(1)	
21	Tomasz NOWAK		30/10/85	M	1	(4)	
6	Paulius PAKNYS	LTU	10/5/84	D	3	(3)	
29	Paweł SOBOLEWSKI		20/6/79	M	23	(4)	3

1 Grzegorz SZAMOTULSKI 13/5/76 G 3
15 THIAGO RANGEL Cionek BRA 21/4/86 D 25 (2) 1
31 Łukasz TUMICZ 1/3/85 A (2)
8 Paweł ZAWISTOWSKI 4/6/84 M 7 (4)

17	Pavol STAŇO	SVK	29/9/77	D	13		3
31	Maciej TATAJ		9/1/80	A	6	(7)	5
5	Aleksandar VUKOVIĆ	SRB	25/8/79	M	21		1
28	Cezary WILK		12/2/86	M	21	(2)	4
10	Mariusz ZGANIACZ		31/1/84	M	9	(4)	
19	Michał ZIELIŃSKI		6/5/84	A	1	(7)	

LECH POZNAŃ
Coach – Jacek Zieliński
Founded – 1922
Stadium – Amica, Wronki (5,500); Stadion Miejski (17,000)
MAJOR HONOURS:
Polish League – (6) 1983, 1984, 1990, 1992, 1993, 2010;
Polish Cup – (5) 1982, 1984, 1988, 2004, 2009.

2009
2/8	Piast	a	3-1	Peszko, Rengifo, Wilk	
9/8	Korona	a	5-0	og (Nawotczyński), Peszko, Wilk, Lewandowski 2	
16/8	Polonia Warszawa	h	2-4	Rengifo, Peszko	
23/8	Cracovia	a	0-1		
30/8	Bełchatów	h	2-2	Lewandowski, Rengifo	
12/9	Jagiellonia	a	3-2	Lewandowski, Peszko, Arboleda	
19/9	Odra	h	1-0	Wilk	
25/9	Legia	a	0-2		
4/10	Arka	a	1-1	Lewandowski	
18/10	Wisła	h	1-0	Lewandowski	
25/10	Lechia	a	0-0		
31/10	Śląsk Wrocław	h	1-0	Bosacki (p)	
7/11	Polonia Bytom	a	1-1	Lewandowski	
21/11	Ruch	h	3-1	Lewandowski 2, Đurđević	
27/11	Zagłębie	a	1-0	Peszko	
5/12	Piast	h	1-1	Peszko	
12/12	Korona	h	2-0	Mikołajczak 2	

2010
28/2	Polonia Warszawa	a	3-0	Lewandowski 2, Mikołajczak	
6/3	Cracovia	h	3-1	Krivets, Lewandowski, Peszko	
14/3	GKS Bełchatów	a	1-1	Krivets	
21/3	Jagiellonia	h	2-0	Lewandowski, Mikołajczak	
28/3	Odra	a	0-0		
3/4	Legia	h	1-0	Štilić	
9/4	Arka	h	2-0	Štilić, Wojtkowiak	
24/4	Wisła	a	0-0		
28/4	Lechia	h	2-1	Bosacki (p), Peszko	
2/5	Śląsk Wrocław	a	3-0	Lewandowski 2, Injac	
8/5	Polonia Bytom	h	3-0	og (Skaba), Arboleda, Lewandowski	
11/5	Ruch	a	2-1	Lewandowski, Krivets	
15/5	Zagłębie	h	2-0	og (Kędziora), Lewandowski	

No	Name	Nat	DoB	Pos	Aps	(s)	Gls
5	Manuel Santos ARBOLEDA Sánchez	COL	2/8/79	D	17		2
6	Tomasz BANDROWSKI		18/9/84	M	21	(4)	
11	Bartosz BERESZYŃSKI		12/7/92	A		(2)	
19	Bartosz BOSACKI		20/12/75	D	27	(1)	2
30	Jasmin BURIĆ	BIH	18/2/87	G	15		
24	Krzysztof CHRAPEK		7/10/85	A	1	(11)	
20	Anderson Denyro CUETO Sánchez	PER	24/5/89	M	1	(5)	
3	Ivan ĐURĐEVIĆ	SRB	5/2/77	D	21		1
2	Seweryn GANCARCZYK		22/11/81	D	21	(2)	
29	Gordan GOLIK	CRO	4/3/85	M	2		
15	Haris HANDŽIĆ	BIH	20/6/90	A		(1)	
25	Luis Alfonso HENRÍQUEZ Ledezma	PAN	23/11/81	D	2		
21	Dimitrije INJAC	SRB	12/8/80	M	29		1
35	Marcin KAMIŃSKI		15/1/92	D	2	(2)	
1	Grzegorz KASPRZIK		20/9/83	G	8		
23	Marcin KIKUT		25/6/83	D	13	(4)	
27	Krzysztof KOTOROWSKI		12/9/76	G	7		
10	Sergei KRIVETS	BLR	8/6/86	M	13		3

8	Robert LEWANDOWSKI		21/8/88	A	28		18
26	Tomasz MIKOŁAJCZAK		11/12/87	A	6	(18)	4
32	Mateusz MOŻDŻEŃ		14/3/91	M	5	(7)	
17	Sławomir PESZKO		19/2/85	M	28		8
11	Hernán Trigoso RENGIFO	PER	18/4/83	A	5	(3)	3
14	Semir ŠTILIĆ	BIH	8/10/87	M	24	(2)	2
4	Mateusz SZAŁEK		16/10/91	M		(1)	
18	Zlatko TANEVSKI	MKD	3/8/83	D	1	(1)	
7	Jakub WILK		11/7/85	M	14	(6)	3
22	Grzegorz WOJTKOWIAK		26/1/84	D	17	(1)	1
13	Ján ZÁPOTOKA	SVK	23/3/88	M	2	(11)	

KS LECHIA GDAŃSK
Coach – Tomasz Kafarski
Founded – 1945
Stadium – GOSiR (15,000)
MAJOR HONOURS:
Polish Cup – (1) 1983.

2009
31/7	Arka	h	2-1	Piątek 2 (1p)	
7/8	Cracovia	a	6-2	Kaczmarek, Wiśniewski, Wołąkiewicz (p), Rogalski, Nowak 2	
16/8	Odra	h	0-2		
22/8	Polonia Warszawa	a	1-0	Mysona	
29/8	Śląsk Wrocław	h	1-1	Rogalski (p)	
13/9	Wisła	h	0-1		
18/9	Legia	a	0-2		
25/9	Zagłębie	h	1-0	og (Łabędzki)	
3/10	Polonia Bytom	a	1-1	Wiśniewski	
16/10	Ruch	a	0-1		
25/10	Lech	h	0-0		
30/10	Piast	a	2-0	Bąk K., Wiśniewski	
6/11	Korona	h	1-1	Kaczmarek	
21/11	Bełchatów	h	0-2		
25/11	Arka	a	2-1	Zabłocki, Lukjanovs	
28/11	Jagiellonia	a	0-0		
12/12	Cracovia	h	1-0	Dawidowski	

2010
26/2	Odra	a	0-0		
6/3	Polonia Warszawa	h	1-1	Laizāns	
13/3	Śląsk Wrocław	a	2-1	Lukjanovs, Wołąkiewicz (p)	
20/3	Wisła	a	0-3		
26/3	Legia	h	2-3	Nowak, Wołąkiewicz (p)	
3/4	Zagłębie	a	2-2	Bąk K., Buzała	
20/4	Polonia Bytom	h	0-0		
25/4	Ruch	h	1-1	og (Baran)	
28/4	Lech	a	1-2	Kožans	
1/5	Piast	h	0-1		
8/5	Korona	a	0-1		
11/5	GKS Bełchatów	a	1-2	Bajić	
15/5	Jagiellonia	h	2-0	Wołąkiewicz (p), Buzała	

No	Name	Nat	DoB	Pos	Aps	(s)	Gls
23	Marko BAJIĆ	SRB	28/9/85	M	13	(8)	1
5	Krzysztof BĄK		22/6/82	D	24		2
24	Mateusz BĄK		24/2/83	G	7		
20	Paweł BUZAŁA		27/12/85	A	12	(11)	2
19	Peter ČVIRIK	SVK	13/6/79	D	10		
32	Tomasz DAWIDOWSKI		4/2/78	A	8	(5)	1
29	Marcin KACZMAREK		3/12/79	M	22	(3)	2
1	Paweł KAPSA		24/7/82	G	22	(1)	
30	Rafał KOSZNIK		17/12/83	D	4	(1)	
28	Maciej KOWALCZYK		6/3/77	A	2	(6)	
4	Sergejs KOŽANS	LVA	18/2/86	D	18		1
7	Olegs LAIZĀNS	LVA	28/3/87	M	6	(2)	1
11	Ivans LUKJANOVS	LVA	24/1/87	A	24	(5)	2
33	Sebastian MAŁKOWSKI		2/3/87	G	1		
7	Marcin MANUSZEWSKI		8/12/73	D	5	(1)	
3	Arkadiusz MYSONA		11/5/81	D	18		1
22	Paweł NOWAK		27/1/79	M	26	(1)	3

6	Karol PIĄTEK	4/7/82	M	6	(3)	2
17	Marcin PIETROWSKI	1/3/88	M	11	(12)	
9	Maciej ROGALSKI	21/5/80	M	10	(9)	2
10	Andrzej RYBSKI	11/3/85	A	1	(1)	
8	Łukasz SURMA	28/6/87	M	28	(1)	
26	Damian SZUPRYTOWSKI	25/6/89	M		(2)	
14	Piotr WIŚNIEWSKI	11/8/82	M	17	(11)	3
21	Hubert WOŁĄKIEWICZ	21/10/85	D	27		4
18	Jakub ZABŁOCKI	14/7/84	A	8	(6)	1

LEGIA WARSZAWA
Coach – Jan Urban; (14/3/10) Stefan Białas
Founded – 1916
Stadium – Stadion Wojska Polskiego im. Marszałka Józefa
Piłsudskiego (6,000)
MAJOR HONOURS:
Polish League – (8) 1955, 1956, 1969, 1970, 1994, 1995, 2002, 2006;
Polish Cup – (13) 1955, 1956, 1964, 1966, 1973, 1980, 1981, 1989, 1990,
1994, 1995, 1997, 2008.

2009
2/8	Zagłębie	h	4-0	*og (Kapias), Paluchowski 2,*
				Jędrzejczyk
9/8	Arka	a	1-0	*Rybus*
15/8	Cracovia	h	0-0	
23/8	Odra	a	0-1	
28/8	Polonia Bytom	h	1-0	*Szałachowski*
12/9	Śląsk Wrocław	a	0-0	
18/9	Lechia	h	2-0	*Chinyama, Radović*
25/9	Lech	h	2-0	*Grzelak, Chinyama*
3/10	Jagiellonia	a	0-2	
17/10	Piast	a	1-1	*Iwański*
24/10	Korona	h	5-2	*Grzelak, Mięciel 2, Szałachowski,*
				Smoliński
31/10	Ruch	h	2-0	*Mięciel 2*
6/11	Wisła	a	1-0	*Radović*
20/11	Polonia Warszawa	h	1-1	*Grzelak*
28/11	Bełchatów	a	1-0	*Iwański*
4/12	Zagłębie	a	0-0	
13/12	Arka	h	1-0	*Iwański (p)*
2010				
26/2	Cracovia	a	2-1	*Szałachowski, Grzelak*
7/3	Odra	h	0-1	
13/3	Polonia Bytom	a	0-1	
20/3	Śląsk Wrocław	h	1-1	*Choto*
26/3	Lechia	a	3-2	*Rybus, Kiełbowicz, Iñaki Astiz*
3/4	Lech	a	0-1	
19/4	Jagiellonia	h	2-1	*Kiełbowicz, Grzelak*
23/4	Piast	h	3-0	*Mięciel, Iwański, Grzelak*
26/4	Korona	a	1-0	*Wawrzyniak*
1/5	Ruch	a	0-1	
8/5	Wisła	h	0-3	
11/5	Polonia Warszawa	a	0-1	
15/5	GKS Bełchatów	h	2-2	*Iwański 2*

No	Name	Nat	DoB	Pos	Aps	(s)	Gls
27	Adam BANASIAK		7/12/89	M		(1)	
16	Ariel BORYSIUK		29/7/91	M	15	(8)	
19	Takesure CHINYAMA	ZIM	30/9/82	A	5	(2)	2
4	Dickson CHOTO	ZIM	19/3/81	D	19		1
14	DONG Fangzhuo	CHN	23/1/85	A	1	(1)	
7	Piotr GIZA		28/2/80	M	11	(8)	
23	Maciej GÓRSKI		1/3/90	A		(2)	
9	Bartłomiej GRZELAK		9/8/81	A	18	(2)	6
15	IÑAKI ASTIZ Ventura	ESP	5/11/83	D	25		1
8	Maciej IWAŃSKI		7/5/81	M	30		6
78	Tomasz JARZĘBOWSKI		16/11/78	M	11	(4)	
2	Artur JĘDRZEJCZYK		4/11/87	D	4		1
11	Tomasz KIEŁBOWICZ		21/2/76	D	18	(2)	2
17	Marcin KOMOROWSKI		17/4/84	D	9	(1)	
22	Jakub KOSECKI		29/8/90	M		(2)	
26	Pance KUMBEV	MKD	25/12/79	D	5	(4)	

21	Marcin MIĘCIEL	22/12/75	A	17	(6)	5
82	Ján MUCHA	SVK	5/12/82	G	30		
14	Adrian PALUCHOWSKI	19/8/87	A	1	(8)	2
32	Miroslav RADOVIĆ	SRB	16/1/84	M	21	(5)	2
6	ROGER Guerreiro	25/5/82	M		(3)	
31	Maciej RYBUS	19/8/89	M	24	(5)	2
25	Jakub RZEŹNICZAK	26/10/86	D	23		
28	Marcin SMOLIŃSKI	5/4/85	M	8	(11)	1
3	Wojciech SZALA	27/1/76	D	12		
20	Sebastian SZAŁACHOWSKI	21/1/84	M	16	(10)	3
24	Jakub WAWRZYNIAK	7/7/83	D	7	(1)	1
33	Michał ŻYRO	20/9/92	M		(1)	

MKS ODRA WODZISŁAW ŚLĄSKI
Coach – Ryszard Wieczorek; (1/10/09) Martin Pulpit (CZE);
(5/10/09) Robert Moskal; (3/12/09) Marcin Brosz
Founded – 1922
Stadium – MOSiR (5,835)

2009
1/8	Jagiellonia	a	1-2	*Piechniak*
8/8	Polonia Bytom	h	0-1	
16/8	Lechia	a	2-0	*Daniel Bueno, Radzinevičius*
23/8	Legia	h	1-0	*Piechniak*
28/8	Piast	a	1-2	*Wodecki*
11/9	Korona	h	0-2	
19/9	Lech	a	0-1	
26/9	Bełchatów	h	0-1	
3/10	Ruch	h	1-3	*Kwiek*
17/10	Polonia Warszawa	a	1-2	*Wodecki*
25/10	Cracovia	h	1-0	*Kowalczyk*
31/10	Arka	a	0-2	
6/11	Zagłębie	h	1-2	*Mójta*
21/11	Śląsk Wrocław	a	0-4	
29/11	Wisła	h	1-3	*Radzinevičius*
5/12	Jagiellonia	h	2-2	*Daniel Bueno 2*
12/12	Polonia Bytom	a	1-1	*Wodecki*
2010				
26/2	Lechia	h	0-0	
7/3	Legia	a	1-0	*Piechniak*
12/3	Piast	h	2-0	*Daniel Bueno, Dymkowski*
20/3	Korona	a	1-1	*og (Hernâni)*
28/3	Lech	h	0-0	
1/4	GKS Bełchatów	a	0-3	
20/4	Ruch	a	2-3	*Brasília, Kwiek*
24/4	Polonia Warszawa	h	2-1	*Piechniak, og (Jodłowiec)*
27/4	Cracovia	a	0-1	
1/5	Arka	h	2-1	*Piechniak, Dymkowski*
8/5	Zagłębie	a	1-2	*Kwiek (p)*
11/5	Śląsk Wrocław	h	2-4	*Dymkowski, Daniel Bueno*
15/5	Wisła	h	1-1	*Daniel Bueno*

No	Name	Nat	DoB	Pos	Aps	(s)	Gls
11	Cristiano Pereira da Souza						
	"BRASÍLIA"	BRA	28/7/77	A	13		1
29	Michał BUCHALIK		3/2/89	G	4		
8	Roberto Mauro CANTORO	ARG	1/9/76	M	12		
39	Marcin CHMIEST		12/2/79	A	1	(7)	
14	Bartłomiej CHWALIBOGOWSKI		7/8/82	M	8	(7)	
10	DANIEL Mariano BUENO	BRA	15/12/83	A	22	(3)	6
3	Marcin DYMKOWSKI		10/3/81	D	22	(1)	3
28	Jakub GRZEGORZEWSKI		16/4/82	A	1	(8)	
2	Szymon JARY		26/5/88	M	3	(1)	
26	Robert KŁOS		4/2/82	D	15	(1)	
15	Marcin KOKOSZKA		23/2/84	D	6		
21	Robert KOLENDOWICZ		26/9/80	M	4	(5)	
16	Jacek KOWALCZYK		12/8/81	D	24		1
5	Jacek KUKURYK		6/2/78	M	11	(2)	
27	Aleksander KWIEK		13/1/83	M	19	(7)	3
2	Filip LUKŠIK	SVK	3/2/85	M	8	(1)	
5	Paweł MAGDOŃ		13/11/79	D	2	(2)	
9	Marcin MALINOWSKI		6/11/75	M	29		

30	Krzysztof MARKOWSKI		24/9/79	D	5	(2)
24	Deivydas MATULEVIČIUS	LTU	8/4/89	A	5	(4)
6	Adam MÓJTA		30/6/86	D	6	(3) 1
25	Arkadiusz ONYSZKO		12/1/74	G	13	
20	Piotr PIECHNIAK		9/3/77	M	27	(1) 5
23	Łukasz PIELORZ		23/5/83	D	13	(2)
8	Tomas RADZINEVIČIUS	LTU	5/6/81	A	5	(9) 2
21	Rodrigo da Silva Moledo "RODRIGÃO"	BRA	27/10/87	D	3	
22	Daniel RYGEL	CZE	16/11/79	M		(1)
2	Mateusz SŁODOWY		8/8/91	M		(2)
12	Adam STACHOWIAK		18/12/86	G	13	
13	Koba SZALAMBERIDZE	GEO	15/10/84	M	3	(3)
22	Stanislav VELICKÝ	SVK	16/4/81	M	12	
11	Marcin WODECKI		14/1/88	A	14	(3) 3
7	Jan WOŚ		17/2/74	M	7	(14)

GKS PIAST GLIWICE
Coach – Dariusz Fornalak; (15/3/10) Ryszard Wieczorek
Founded – 1945
Stadium – Stadion Piast (6,000)

2009

2/8	Lech	h	1-3	Maciejak
8/8	Ruch	a	0-2	
15/8	Zagłębie	h	4-1	Wilczek 2, Glik, Olszar
22/8	Bełchatów	a	1-0	Iwan D.
28/8	Odra	h	2-1	Olszar, Gamla
11/9	Polonia Bytom	a	0-4	
20/9	Jagiellonia	h	0-0	
26/9	Korona	a	2-3	Olszar, Muszalik
4/10	Polonia Warszawa	a	2-0	Olszar, Smektała
17/10	Legia	h	1-1	Gamla
24/10	Wisła	a	1-2	Biskup
30/10	Lechia	h	0-2	
7/11	Śląsk Wrocław	a	1-2	Krzycki
21/11	Arka	h	2-2	Olszar, Gamla
28/11	Cracovia	a	2-3	Łudziński, Kowalski
5/12	Lech	a	1-1	Szary
11/12	Ruch	h	1-2	Biskup

2010

28/2	Zagłębie	a	1-1	Wilczek
7/3	GKS Bełchatów	h	1-2	Gamla
12/3	Odra	a	0-2	
21/3	Polonia Bytom	h	1-0	Wilczek
28/3	Jagiellonia	a	0-2	
3/4	Korona	h	1-0	Wilczek
19/4	Polonia Warszawa	h	0-2	
23/4	Legia	a	0-3	
27/4	Wisła	h	1-4	Muszalik
1/5	Lechia	a	1-0	Iwan B.
8/5	Śląsk Wrocław	h	2-2	Olszar 2
11/5	Arka	a	1-2	Glik
15/5	Cracovia	h	0-1	

No	Name	Nat	DoB	Pos	Aps	(s)	Gls
24	Jakub BISKUP		8/5/83	M	20	(6)	2
22	Daniel CHYLASZEK		25/9/82	M	7	(6)	
5	Paweł GAMLA		6/8/76	D	23	(2)	4
25	Kamil GLIK		3/2/88	D	28		2
18	Bartosz IWAN		18/4/84	M	3	(6)	1
26	Daniel IWAN		27/7/89	M	1	(2)	1
93	Tomasz KASPRZIK		2/1/93	G	1	(1)	
8	Jarosław KASZOWSKI		24/5/78	M	5		
4	Mateusz KOWALSKI		30/9/86	D	17		1
15	Łukasz KRZYCKI		10/1/84	D	3	(4)	1
12	Rafał KWAPISZ		7/4/86	G	12		
6	Artur LENARTOWSKI		17/3/88	M		(1)	
18	Przemysław ŁUDZIŃSKI		3/2/83	A	5	(6)	1
13	Roman MACIEJAK		23/10/88	A	1	(18)	1
29	Szymon MATUSZEK		7/1/89	D	3	(6)	
26	Maciej MICHNIEWICZ		28/9/77	D	25	(1)	

11	Mariusz MUSZALIK		23/9/79	M	27	2
31	Maciej NALEPA		31/3/78	G	9	
9	Sebastian OLSZAR		16/12/81	A	27	(1) 7
21	Adrian PALUCHOWSKI		19/8/87	A	3	(8)
30	Marcin PIETROŃ		24/1/86	M	6	(6)
17	Tomasz PODGÓRSKI		30/12/85	M	2	
14	Lumír SEDLÁČEK	CZE	13/6/78	D	3	(6)
19	Damian SEWERYN		30/9/79	M		(1)
7	Jakub SMEKTAŁA		26/8/87	A	26	(4) 1
16	Sławomir SZARY		31/8/79	A	26	1
1	Jakub SZMATUŁA		22/3/81	G	8	
10	Kamil WILCZEK		14/1/88	M	26	5
6	Mariusz ZGANIACZ		31/1/84	M	13	

KS POLONIA BYTOM
Coach – Yuriy Shatalov (UKR)
Founded – 1945
Stadium – Stadion im. Edwarda Szymkowiaka (5,500)
MAJOR HONOURS:
Polish League – (2) 1954, 1962.

2009

31/7	Bełchatów	h	1-0	Sawala
8/8	Odra	a	1-0	Barčík
14/8	Śląsk Wrocław	a	1-2	Podstawek
22/8	Korona	h	1-0	Podstawek
28/8	Legia	a	0-1	
11/9	Piast	h	4-0	Podstawek 2, Trzeciak 2 (1p)
20/9	Wisła	a	1-1	Bažík
27/9	Arka	h	3-1	Nowak, og (Szmatiuk), Barčík
3/10	Lechia	h	1-1	Bažík
17/10	Cracovia	a	2-1	Podstawek, og (Polczak)
23/10	Ruch	h	0-1	
29/10	Zagłębie	a	0-2	
7/11	Lech	h	1-1	Radzewicz
20/11	Jagiellonia	a	1-1	Sawala
27/11	Polonia Warszawa	a	0-1	
5/12	Bełchatów	a	2-2	Bažík, Zieliński
12/12	Odra	h	1-1	Grzyb

2010

27/2	Śląsk Wrocław	h	0-0	
5/3	Korona	a	0-1	
13/3	Legia	h	1-0	Bažík
21/3	Piast	a	0-1	
27/3	Wisła	h	1-3	Kotrys
31/3	Arka	a	2-2	Bažík, Podstawek
20/4	Lechia	a	0-0	
24/4	Cracovia	h	1-2	Sawala
28/4	Ruch	a	1-2	Telichowski
2/5	Zagłębie	h	2-1	Sawala, Telichowski
8/5	Lech	a	0-3	
11/5	Jagiellonia	a	0-0	
15/5	Polonia Warszawa	h	1-0	Telichowski

No	Name	Nat	DoB	Pos	Aps	(s)	Gls
12	Juraj BALÁŽ	SVK	12/6/80	G	1		
7	Miroslav BARČÍK	SVK	9/2/76	M	23	(6)	2
19	Marek BAŽÍK	SVK	9/2/76	M	27	(1)	5
33	Maciej BYKOWSKI		22/2/77	A	7	(5)	
25	Adrian CHOMIUK		23/6/88	D	7		
30	Szymon GĄSIŃSKI		8/7/83	G	1		
24	Rafał GRZYB		16/1/83	M	17		1
8	Peter HRICKO	SVK	25/7/81	D	23		
2	Lukáš KILLAR	CZE	5/8/81	D	28		
14	Adrian KLEPCZYŃSKI		1/4/81	D	26		
18	David KOTRYS	CZE	3/6/77	D	20	(1)	1
15	Ireneusz KOWALSKI		17/3/79	M		(1)	
16	Piotr KULPAKA		12/9/84	D	7		
27	Jacek KURANTY		6/2/78	M	8		
9	Povilas LUKŠYS	LTU	7/7/79	A		(2)	
11	Vladimir MILENKOVIĆ	SRB	22/6/82	A	1	(4)	
26	Tomasz NOWAK		30/10/85	M	18	(5)	1

POLAND

10	Grzegorz PODSTAWEK	25/6/79	A	18	(9)	6
33	Vasilije PRODANOVIĆ	SRB 24/11/85	M		(1)	
20	Marcin RADZEWICZ	30/6/80	M	24	(4)	1
15	Wojciech REIMAN	5/8/88	M	1		
21	Szymon SAWAŁA	25/9/82	M	24	(2)	4
1	Wojciech SKABA	9/4/84	G	28		
22	Łukasz ŚLIFIRCZYK	9/6/87	A		(1)	
23	Błażej TELICHOWSKI	6/6/84	D	3	3	
17	Piotr TOMASIK	31/10/87	M	6	(21)	
6	Jacek TRZECIAK	26/12/71	M	6	(16)	2
4	Łukasz TYMIŃSKI	8/11/90	M	4	(1)	
25	Michał ZIELIŃSKI	6/5/84	A	6	(6)	1

KSP POLONIA WARSZAWA
Coach – Jacek Grembocki; (25/8/09) Dušan Radolský (SVK);
(3/11/09) Michał Libich; (15/11/09) José María Bakero (ESP)
Founded – 1911
Stadium – Stadion Polonii (7,000)
MAJOR HONOURS:
Polish League – (2) 1946, 2000;
Polish Cup – (2) 1952, 2001.

2009				
2/8	Korona	a	0-4	
9/8	Śląsk Wrocław	h	3-2	*Ivanovski, Gołębiewski, Marcelo Sarvas*
16/8	Lech	a	4-2	*Marcelo Sarvas, Jodłowiec, Nikolić, Ivanovski*
22/8	Lechia	h	0-1	
29/8	Ruch	a	0-2	
13/9	Zagłębie	h	0-1	
19/9	Arka	a	0-0	
26/9	Wisła	a	1-2	*og (Pawełek)*
4/10	Piast	h	0-2	
17/10	Odra	h	2-1	*Chałbiński, Nikolić*
24/10	Bełchatów	a	0-3	
31/10	Jagiellonia	a	0-1	
7/11	Cracovia	h	0-1	
20/11	Legia	a	1-1	*Piątek*
27/11	Polonia Bytom	h	1-0	*Trałka*
6/12	Korona	h	1-1	*Ivanovski*
12/12	Śląsk Wrocław	a	0-1	
2010				
28/2	Lech	h	0-3	
6/3	Lechia	a	1-1	*Gołębiewski*
13/3	Ruch	a	1-1	*Mierzejewski*
20/3	Zagłębie	a	0-2	
27/3	Arka	h	2-1	*Piątek, Gołębiewski*
3/4	Wisła	h	0-1	
19/4	Piast	a	2-0	*Piątek, Mierzejewski*
24/4	Odra	a	1-2	*Gołębiewski*
27/4	GKS Bełchatów	h	0-0	
1/5	Jagiellonia	h	2-0	*Gołębiewski, Jodłowiec*
7/5	Cracovia	a	2-1	*Gołębiewski, Brzyski*
11/5	Legia	h	1-0	*Andreu*
15/5	Polonia Bytom	a	0-1	

No	Name	Nat	DoB	Pos	Aps	(s)	Gls
16	ANDREU Guerao Mayoral	ESP	17/6/83	M	12		1
32	Tomasz BRZYSKI		10/1/82	D	13		1
9	Michał CHAŁBIŃSKI		16/10/76	A	3	(5)	1
33	Daniel CIACH		21/3/90	D	1		
10	César Alexis CORTÉS Pinto	CHI	9/1/84	A		(4)	
5	Piotr DZIEWICKI		26/6/79	D	21	(1)	
26	Krystian FERCIUCH		18/4/89	M		(3)	
20	Janusz GANCARCZYK		19/6/84	M	10	(2)	
1	Michał GLIWA		8/4/88	G	5		
19	Daniel GOŁĘBIEWSKI		15/7/87	A	15	(4)	6
8	Filip IVANOVSKI	MKD	1/5/85	A	10	(7)	4
17	Damian JAROŃ		9/4/90	A	4	(2)	
6	Tomasz JODŁOWIEC		22/3/85	D	21		2
24	Daniel KOKOSIŃSKI		25/7/85	D	2	(1)	

10	Jacek KOSMALSKI	4/9/76	A	3	(4)	
15	Igor KOZIOŁ	2/1/76	M	6	(1)	
77	Tamás KULCSÁR	HUN 13/10/82	A	3	(3)	
20	Jarosław LATO	17/6/77	M	6		
4	Dominik LEMANEK	3/1/89	M	1		
99	Radosław MAJDAN	10/5/72	G	2	(1)	
70	MARCELO Fazzio SARVAS	BRA 16/10/81	M	15	(9)	2
22	Daniel MĄKA	30/4/88	A		(10)	
7	Adrian MIERZEJEWSKI	6/11/86	M	29	(1)	2
2	Radek MYNÁŘ	CZE 22/11/74	D	23		
44	Milan NIKOLIĆ	SRB 21/6/87	A	7	(12)	2
28	Łukasz PIĄTEK	21/9/85	M	19	(2)	3
12	Sebastian PRZYROWSKI	30/11/81	G	23		
13	Łukasz SKRZYŃSKI	31/1/78	D	18	(2)	
11	Marek SOKOŁOWSKI	11/3/78	M	11	(6)	
3	Błażej TELICHOWSKI	6/6/84	D	8		
18	Łukasz TRAŁKA	11/5/84	M	27	(1)	1
22	Mariusz ZASADA	8/9/82	M	12	(6)	

KS RUCH CHORZÓW
Coach – Waldemar Fornalik
Founded – 1920
Stadium – Stadion Ruchu (10,000)
MAJOR HONOURS:
Polish League – (14) 1933, 1934, 1935, 1936, 1938, 1951, 1952, 1953, 1960, 1968, 1974, 1975, 1979, 1989;
Polish Cup – (3) 1951, 1974, 1996.

2009				
1/8	Wisła	a	0-2	
8/8	Piast	h	2-0	*Grodzicki, Sobiech*
14/8	Arka	h	1-0	*Sobiech*
21/8	Zagłębie	a	1-0	*Grzyb (p)*
29/8	Polonia Warszawa	h	2-0	*Sobiech, Niedzielan*
12/9	Bełchatów	a	1-2	*Brzyski*
19/9	Cracovia	a	2-0	*Grzyb, Niedzielan*
27/9	Śląsk Wrocław	a	0-0	
3/10	Odra	a	3-1	*Janoszka 2, Niedzielan*
16/10	Lechia	h	1-0	*Niedzielan*
23/10	Polonia Bytom	a	1-0	*Grzyb*
31/10	Legia	a	0-2	
8/11	Jagiellonia	h	5-2	*Sobiech 2, Janoszka, Niedzielan 2*
21/11	Lech	a	1-3	*Sobiech*
28/11	Korona	h	0-0	
6/12	Wisła	h	1-3	*Niedzielan*
11/12	Piast	a	2-1	*Sobiech, Stawarczyk*
2010				
27/2	Arka	a	3-0	*Sobiech, Zając, Piech*
6/3	Zagłębie	h	0-2	
13/3	Polonia Warszawa	a	1-1	*Zając*
19/3	GKS Bełchatów	h	1-0	*Grzyb (p)*
27/3	Cracovia	a	4-1	*Zając, Sobiech 2, Janoszka*
3/4	Śląsk Wrocław	h	0-0	
20/4	Odra	h	3-2	*Janoszka 3*
25/4	Lechia	a	1-1	*Janoszka*
28/4	Polonia Bytom	h	2-1	*Świerblewski 2*
1/5	Legia	h	1-0	*Piech*
7/5	Jagiellonia	a	0-1	
11/5	Lech	h	1-2	*Pulkowski*
15/5	Korona	a	0-3	

No	Name	Nat	DoB	Pos	Aps	(s)	Gls
20	Pavol BALÁŽ	SVK	1/4/84	M	6	(5)	
3	Grzegorz BARAN		23/12/82	D	29		
16	Michał BRZOZOWSKI		26/3/88	M		(1)	
22	Tomasz BRZYSKI		10/1/82	D	17		1
24	Martin FABUŠ	SVK	11/11/76	A		(2)	
11	Grzegorz GONCERZ		27/4/88	M		(1)	
15	Rafał GRODZICKI		28/10/83	D	24	(1)	1
6	Wojciech GRZYB		21/12/74	M	30		4
29	Ariel JAKUBOWSKI		7/9/77	D	12	(7)	
14	Łukasz JANOSZKA		18/3/87	A	24	(4)	8

POLAND

32	Piotr KIERUZEL	12/11/88	D	1	(1)	
31	Paweł LISOWSKI	8/10/91	M		(3)	
23	Andrzej NIEDZIELAN	27/2/79	A	17	(1)	7
11	Marcin NOWACKI	12/3/81	M	2	(2)	
8	Krzysztof NYKIEL	8/8/82	D	24	(1)	
18	Arkadiusz PIECH	7/6/85	A	2	(10)	2
80	Krzysztof PILARZ	9/11/80	G	30		
17	Michał PULKOWSKI	1/1/79	M	11	(12)	1
21	Maciej SADLOK	29/6/89	D	29		
13	Maciej SCHERFCHEN	24/2/79	M	5	(8)	
19	Artur SOBIECH	12/6/90	A	24	(4)	10
2	Piotr STAWARCZYK	29/9/83	D	11	(4)	1
4	Patryk STEFAŃSKI	12/3/90	M	1	(5)	
28	Gábor STRAKA	SVK 18/12/81	M	22	(1)	
26	Damian ŚWIERBLEWSKI	17/1/84	A	2	(6)	2
9	Marcin ZAJĄC	19/5/75	M	7	(7)	3

WKS ŚLĄSK WROCŁAW
Coach – Ryszard Tarasiewicz
Founded – 1947
Stadium – Stadion Piłkarski (8,273)
MAJOR HONOURS:
Polish League – (1) 1977;
Polish Cup – (2) 1976, 1987.

2009
1/8	Cracovia	h	2-0	*Dudek, Wołczek*
9/8	Polonia Warszawa	a	2-3	*Gancarczyk M., Dudek (p)*
14/8	Polonia Bytom	h	2-1	*Szewczuk, Wołczek*
22/8	Jagiellonia	a	0-2	
29/8	Lechia	a	1-1	*Gancarczyk M.*
12/9	Legia	h	0-0	
19/9	Korona	a	1-1	*Sotirović*
27/9	Ruch	h	0-0	
2/10	Wisła	h	1-3	*Dudek (p)*
16/10	Bełchatów	a	0-2	
24/10	Zagłębie	h	2-0	*Sotirović, Gancarczyk J.*
31/10	Lech	a	0-1	
7/11	Piast	h	2-1	*Sotirović 2*
21/11	Odra	h	4-0	*Spahić, Mila 2 (1p), Sotirović*
29/11	Arka	a	1-1	*Mila*
5/12	Cracovia	a	0-1	
12/12	Polonia Warszawa	h	1-0	*Łukasiewicz*

2010
27/2	Polonia Bytom	a	0-0	
6/3	Jagiellonia	h	1-2	*Celeban*
13/3	Lechia	h	1-2	*Madej*
20/3	Legia	a	1-1	*Dudek (p)*
27/3	Korona	h	1-1	*Celeban*
3/4	Ruch	a	0-0	
20/4	Wisła	a	0-1	
24/4	GKS Bełchatów	h	0-0	
27/4	Zagłębie Lubin	a	1-1	*Mila*
2/5	Lech	h	0-3	
8/5	Piast	a	2-2	*Sotirović, Szewczuk*
11/5	Odra	a	4-2	*Mila 2, Sotirović 2*
15/5	Arka	h	2-1	*Pawelec, Sotirović*

No	Name	Nat	DoB	Pos	Aps	(s)	Gls
31	Kamil BILIŃSKI		23/1/88	A	1	(10)	
3	Piotr CELEBAN		25/6/85	D	25		2
86	Piotr ĆWIELONG		23/4/86	A	12		
7	Sebastian DUDEK		19/1/80	M	20	(7)	4
16	Jarosław FOJUT		17/10/87	D	9	(1)	
18	Janusz GANCARCZYK		19/6/84	M	15	(1)	1
9	Marek GANCARCZYK		19/2/83	M	7	(5)	2
21	Dariusz GÓRAL		20/4/91	A		(1)	
1	Wojciech KACZMAREK		29/3/83	G	10		
15	Bartosz KAŚNIKOWSKI		31/7/89	D		(1)	
25	Marián KELEMEN	SVK	7/12/79	G	13		
5	Patryk KLOFIK		15/5/86	M	1	(3)	

28	Przemysław ŁUDZIŃSKI	3/2/83	A		(2)	
22	Antoni ŁUKASIEWICZ	26/6/83	D	22	(4)	1
8	Łukasz MADEJ	14/4/82	M	15	(7)	1
11	Sebastian MILA	10/7/82	M	22	(4)	6
17	Mariusz PAWELEC	14/4/86	D	29		1
24	Tadeusz SOCHA	15/2/88	D	16	(3)	
10	Vuk SOTIROVIĆ	SRB 13/7/82	A	11	(5)	9
4	Amir SPAHIĆ	BIH 13/9/83	D	20	(1)	1
6	Tomasz SZEWCZUK	3/12/78	A	25	(2)	2
19	Dariusz SZTYLKA	2/5/78	M	13	(3)	
15	Damian SZYDZIAK	15/3/89	M		(1)	
14	Krzysztof ULATOWSKI	25/7/80	M	18	(5)	
12	Ivo VAZGEČ	SWE 6/2/86	G	7		
2	Krzysztof WOŁCZEK	17/4/79	D	19	(2)	2

WISŁA KRAKÓW
Coach – Maciej Skorża; (15/3/10) Henryk Kasperczak
Founded – 1906
Stadium – Ludowy Stadion, Sosnowiec (7,500);
Hutnik Kraków (5,500);
Stadion Miejski im. Henryka Reymana (11,380)
MAJOR HONOURS:
Polish League – (12) 1927, 1928, 1949, 1950, 1978, 1999, 2001, 2003, 2004,
2005, 2008, 2009;
Polish Cup – (4) 1926, 1967, 2002, 2003.

2009
1/8	Ruch	h	2-0	*Głowacki, Łobodziński*
7/8	Zagłębie	a	4-1	*Marcelo, Małecki 2, og (Jasiński)*
15/8	Bełchatów	h	3-0	*Głowacki (p), Brożek Pa., Marcelo*
21/8	Arka	a	1-0	*og (Mrowiec)*
29/8	Jagiellonia	h	2-1	*Díaz, Brożek Pa.*
13/9	Lechia	a	1-0	*Małecki*
20/9	Polonia Bytom	h	1-1	*Ćwielong*
26/9	Polonia Warszawa	h	2-1	*Małecki, Brożek Pa.*
2/10	Śląsk Wrocław	a	3-1	*Brozek Pa., Ćwielong, Małecki*
18/10	Lech	a	0-1	
24/10	Piast	h	2-1	*Brożek Pa., Marcelo*
30/10	Korona	a	3-2	*Kirm, Marcelo, Jirsák*
6/11	Legia	h	0-1	
22/11	Cracovia	a	0-1	
29/11	Odra	a	3-1	*Kirm 2, Małecki*
6/12	Ruch	a	3-1	*Brożek Pi., Marcelo, Małecki*
11/12	Zagłębie	h	1-0	*Marcelo*

2010
27/2	GKS Bełchatów	a	0-1	
5/3	Arka	h	0-1	
12/3	Jagiellonia	h	0-0	
20/3	Lechia	h	3-0	*Marcelo, Jirsák, Boguski*
27/3	Polonia Bytom	a	3-1	*Brożek Pi., Boguski, Díaz*
3/4	Polonia Warszawa	h	1-0	*og (Przyrowski)*
20/4	Śląsk Wrocław	h	1-0	*Brożek Pa.*
24/4	Lech	h	0-0	
27/4	Piast	a	4-1	*Boguski 2, Brożek Pa., Sobolewski*
30/4	Korona	h	0-1	
8/5	Legia	a	3-0	*Brożek Pa. 3*
11/5	Cracovia	a	1-1	*Boguski*
15/5	Odra	h	1-1	*Małecki*

No	Name	Nat	DoB	Pos	Aps	(s)	Gls
11	Pablo ÁLVAREZ Menéndez	URU	7/2/85	D	26		
80	Issa BA	SEN	7/10/81	M	7	(3)	
9	Rafał BOGUSKI		9/6/84	A	10	(8)	5
23	Paweł BROŻEK		21/4/83	A	25		10
8	Piotr BROŻEK		21/4/83	D	28		2
30	Łukasz BURLIGA		15/5/88	M	2	(4)	
20	Roberto Mauro CANTORO	ARG	1/9/76	M	6	(8)	
1	Ilie Pavel CEBANU	MDA	29/12/86	G	4	(1)	
28	Michał CHRAPEK		3/4/92	M		(1)	
86	Piotr ĆWIELONG		23/4/86	A	4	(13)	2
15	Júnior Enrique DÍAZ Campbell	CRC	12/9/83	M	27		2

10	Łukasz GARGUŁA		25/2/81	M		(2)	
6	Arkadiusz GŁOWACKI		13/3/79	D	23		2
14	Georgi HRISTOV	BUL	10/1/85	A	1	(1)	
16	Tomáš JIRSÁK	CZE	29/6/84	M	12	(15)	2
22	Mariusz JOP		3/8/78	D	10	(2)	
1	Marcin JUSZCZYK		23/1/85	G	6		
17	Andraž KIRM	SVN	6/9/84	M	22	(8)	3
32	Sebastian LESZCZAK		20/1/92	A		(3)	
21	Wojciech ŁOBODZIŃSKI		20/10/82	M	19	(8)	1
19	Patryk MAŁECKI		1/8/88	M	29		8
3	MARCELO Antônio Guedes Filho	BRA	20/5/87	D	28		7
29	Krzysztof MĄCZYŃSKI		23/5/87	M		(6)	
81	Mariusz PAWEŁEK		17/3/81	G	20		
2	Peter ŠINGLÁR	SVK	24/7/79	D	1	(1)	
7	Radosław SOBOLEWSKI		13/12/76	M	20		1

ZAGŁĘBIE LUBIN

Coach – Andrzej Lesiak; (27/8/09) (Marcin Broniszewski);
(1/9/09) Franciszek Smuda; (17/12/09) Marek Bajor
Founded – 1945
Stadium – Dialog Arena (10,000)
MAJOR HONOURS:
Polish League – (2) 1991, 2007.

2009
2/8	Legia	a	0-4	
7/8	Wisła	h	1-4	David Caiado
15/8	Piast	a	1-4	Mitsanski
21/8	Ruch	h	0-1	
30/8	Arka	h	0-2	
13/9	Polonia Warszawa	a	1-0	Jackiewicz
18/9	Bełchatów	h	1-1	Ekwueme
25/9	Lechia	a	0-1	
2/10	Cracovia	a	1-1	Traoré
18/10	Jagiellonia	h	0-0	
24/10	Śląsk Wrocław	a	0-2	
29/10	Polonia Bytom	h	2-0	og (Skaba), Traoré
6/11	Odra	a	2-1	Traoré 2
20/11	Korona	a	3-3	Mitsanski 2, Nhamoinesu
27/11	Lech	h	0-1	
4/12	Legia	h	0-0	
11/12	Wisła	a	0-1	

2010
28/2	Piast	h	1-1	Hanzel
6/3	Ruch	a	2-0	Mitsanski 2
14/3	Arka	a	2-0	Mitsanski 2 (1p)
20/3	Polonia Warszawa	h	2-0	Mitsanski, Kędziora
26/3	GKS Bełchatów	a	3-1	Traoré, Kędziora, Mitsanski
3/4	Lechia	h	2-2	Mitsanski, Traoré
9/4	Cracovia	h	0-0	
24/4	Jagiellonia	a	0-0	
27/4	Śląsk Wrocław	h	1-1	Mitsanski
2/5	Polonia Bytom	a	1-2	Mitsanski (p)
8/5	Odra	h	2-1	Mitsanski, Fernando Dinis
11/5	Korona	h	2-2	Kędziora, Mitsanski
15/5	Lech	a	0-2	

No	Name	Nat	DoB	Pos	Aps	(s)	Gls
19	Grzegorz BARTCZAK		21/6/85	D	18		
8	Mateusz BARTCZAK		15/8/79	M	19		
24	Adrian BLĄD		16/4/91	M	4	(6)	
87	DAVID CAIADO Dias	POR	2/5/87	M	3	(6)	1
14	Damian DĄBROWSKI		27/8/92	M		(2)	
85	Martins EKWUEME	NGA	2/10/85	M	23		1
5	FERNANDO Alberto Morais DINIS	POR	25/7/82	D	11	(8)	1
17	Karol FRYZOWICZ		27/3/91	D		(1)	
77	Michał GOLIŃSKI		17/3/81	M	3		
25	Łukasz HANZEL		16/9/86	M	28	(1)	1
50	Bojan ISAILOVIĆ	SRB	25/3/80	G	10		

14	Dariusz JACKIEWICZ		2/12/73	M	5	(9)	1
3	Łukasz JASIŃSKI		13/10/85	D	12	(1)	
9	Szymon KAPIAS		12/6/84	D	7	(1)	
27	Wojciech KĘDZIORA		20/12/80	A	9	(6)	3
15	Przemysław KOCOT		31/1/86	D	8	(4)	
20	Robert KOLENDOWICZ		26/9/80	M	3	(5)	
1	Yevhen KOPYL	UKR	25/5/86	G	1		
16	Michał ŁABĘDZKI		24/9/80	D	7	(1)	
22	Ilian MITSANSKI	BUL	20/12/85	A	22	(6)	14
33	Costa NHAMOINESU	ZIM	6/1/86	D	24		1
23	Szymon PAWŁOWSKI		4/11/86	M	7	(1)	
7	Dawid PLIZGA		17/11/85	A	10	(10)	
30	Aleksander PTAK		4/11/77	G	19		
13	Sergio Mauricio REINA Piedrahíta	COL	26/1/85	D	12		
21	Bartosz RYMANIAK		13/11/89	D	4	(3)	
13	Sreten SRETENOVIĆ	SRB	12/1/85	D	2		
4	Michał STASIAK		12/3/81	D	22		
37	Piotr ŚWIERCZEWSKI		8/4/72	M	13		
99	Mouhamadou TRAORÉ	SEN	16/4/86	A	24		6
11	Arkadiusz WOŹNIAK		1/6/90	M		(2)	

PROMOTED CLUBS

RTS WIDZEW ŁÓDŹ

Coach – Paweł Janas
Founded – 1922
Stadium – Widzew (9,500)
MAJOR HONOURS:
Polish League – (4) 1981, 1982, 1996, 1997;
Polish Cup – (1) 1985.

GÓRNIK ZABRZE

Coach – Ryszard Komornicki; (23/12/09) Adam Nawałka
Founded – 1948
Stadium – Ernesta Pohla (9,000)
MAJOR HONOURS:
Polish League – (14) 1957, 1959, 1961, 1963, 1964, 1965, 1966, 1967,
1971, 1972, 1985, 1986, 1987, 1988;
Polish Cup – (6) 1965, 1968, 1969, 1970, 1971, 1972.

SECOND LEVEL FINAL TABLE 2009/10

		Pld	W	D	L	F	A	Pts
1	RTS Widzew Łódź	34	23	8	3	62	17	77
2	Górnik Zabrze	34	18	7	9	47	30	61
3	MKS Sandecja Nowy Sącz	34	17	8	9	55	42	59
4	ŁKS Łódź	34	16	7	11	51	45	55
5	MKS Pogoń Szczecin	34	13	12	9	46	35	51
6	MKS Kluczbork	34	12	10	12	43	37	46
7	MKS Flota Świnoujście	34	12	10	12	33	36	46
8	KSZO Ostrowiec Świętokrzyski	34	13	7	14	37	46	46
9	GKP Gorzów Wielkopolski	34	11	12	11	34	33	45
10	KS Warta Poznań	34	12	8	14	49	45	44
11	GKS Górnik Łęczna	34	11	11	12	38	45	44
12	TS Podbeskidzie Bielsko-Biała	34	10	14	10	45	38	44
13	GKS Katowice	34	11	10	13	41	41	43
14	MKS Dolcan Ząbki	34	10	12	12	37	43	42
15	Wisła Płock	34	9	13	12	43	51	40
16	MKS Znicz Pruszków	34	11	6	17	32	48	39
17	ZKS Stal Stalowa Wola	34	5	10	19	32	58	25
18	LKP Motor Lublin	34	4	11	19	27	62	23

 **POLAND**

DOMESTIC CUP 2009/10

PUCHAR POLSKI

FIRST ROUND

(25/8/09)
Bytovia II Bytów 1, Tur Turek 0
MKS Kluczbork 0, GKP Gorzów Wielkopolski 0 *(aet; 2-3 on pens)*
Nielba Wągrowiec 3, Znicz Pruszków 1
Pogoń Szczecin 2, Motor Lublin 0
Polonia Słubice 3, GKS Katowice 1
Ruch Radzionków 0, Korona Kielce 1
Ruch Zdzieszowice 0, Dolcan Ząbki 3
Zagłębie Sosnowiec 2, Flota Świnoujście 0

(26/8/09)
GKS Jastrzębie 3, Widzew Łódź 4
GKS Tychy 1, Górnik Łęczna 1 *(aet; 3-2 on pens)*
Hetman Zamość 1, Warta Poznań 1 *(aet; 5-4 on pens)*
Olimpia Grudziądz 3, Kmita Zabierzów 0 *(w/o)*
Piast Kobylin 3, Zagłębie Lubin 1
Stal Stalowa Wola 2, Wisła Płock 1
Start Otwock 2, Podbeskidzie Bielsko-Biała 1

Bye - Okocimski Brzesko

SECOND ROUND

(23/9/09)
Bytovia II Bytów 2, Polonia Bytom 1
Dolcan Ząbki 1, Śląsk Wrocław 1 *(aet; 5-4 on pens)*
GKS Tychy 0, Jagiellonia Białystok 1 *(aet)*
Hetman Zamość 0, Wisła Kraków 3
Korona Kielce 3, GKS Bełchatów 1
Okocimski Brzesko 1, Arka Gdynia 2
Olimpia Grudziądz 1, Odra Wodzisław Śląski 2
Piast Kobylin 1, Cracovia Kraków 1 *(aet; 2-4 on pens)*
Polonia Słubice 1, Piast Gliwice 2
Start Otwock 3, ŁKS Łódź 2
Widzew Łódź 0, Ruch Chorzów 1
Zagłębie Sosnowiec 2, Górnik Zabrze 0

(29/9/09)
GKP Gorzów Wielkopolski 0, Legia Warszawa 2
Nielba Wągrowiec 1, Lechia Gdańsk 3
Stal Stalowa Wola 0, Lech Poznań 0 *(aet; 4-1 on pens)*

(7/10/09)
Pogoń Szczecin 2, Polonia Warszawa 0

1/8 FINALS

(27/10/09)
Bytovia II Bytów 0, Wisła Kraków 2
Dolcan Ząbki 3, Korona Kielce 4 *(aet)*
Pogoń Szczecin 2, Piast Gliwice 0
Zagłębie Sosnowiec 3, Stal Stalowa Wola 0

(28/10/09)
Start Otwock 0, Ruch Chorzów 1

(3/11/09)
Arka Gdynia 0, Jagiellonia Białystok 2 *(aet)*

(11/11/09)
Lechia Gdańsk 1, Odra Wodzisław Śląski 0

(25/11/09)
Legia Warszawa 2, Cracovia Kraków 0 *(aet)*

QUARTER-FINALS

(16/3/09 & 23/3/09)
Ruch Chorzów 1 *(Sobiech 73)*, Legia Warszawa 0
Legia Warszawa 2 *(Grzelak 66, Jarzębowski 120)*, Ruch Chorzów 1 *(Janoszka 108) (aet)*
(2-2; Ruch Chorzów on away goal)

(16/3/09 & 24/3/09)
Zagłębie Sosnowiec 0, Pogoń Szczecin 3 *(Lebedyński 67, 83, Zawadzki 90)*
Pogoń Szczecin 1 *(Dziuba 16)*, Zagłębie Sosnowiec 1 *(Pajączkowski 65)*
(Pogoń Szczecin 4-1)

(17/3/09 & 23/3/09)
Lechia Gdańsk 0, Wisła Kraków 0
Wisła Kraków 1 *(Małecki 22p)*, Lechia Gdańsk 3 *(Surma 1, Brożek Pi. 100g, Ljukanovs 37)*
(Lechia Gdańsk 3-1)

(17/3/09 & 24/3/09)
Korona Kielce 3 *(Mijailović 28, Zieliński 33, Tataj 40)*, Jagiellonia Białystok 1 *(Frankowski 20)*
Jagiellonia Białystok 3 *(Klepczarek 16, Jezierski 56, Hermes 68p)*, Korona Kielce 0
(Jagiellonia Białystok 4-3)

SEMI-FINALS

(6/4/10 & 4/5/10)
Lechia Gdańsk 1 *(Wółąkiewicz 90+3p)*, Jagiellonia Białystok 2 *(Grzyb 6, Bruno 28)*
Jagiellonia Białystok 1 *(Frankowski 73)*, Lechia Gdańsk 1 *(Bajić 88)*
(Jagiellonia Białystok 3-2)

Ruch Chorzów 1 *(Sobiech 49)*, Pogoń Szczecin 1 *(Mysiak 84)*
Pogoń Szczecin 0, Ruch Chorzów 0
(1-1; Pogoń Szczecin on away goal)

FINAL

(22/5/10)
Stadion Miejski im. Zdzisława Krzyszkowiaka, Bydgoszcz
JAGIELLONIA BIAŁYSTOK 1 *(Skerla 49)*
MKS POGOŃ SZCZECIN 0
Referee – Małek
JAGIELLONIA – Gikiewicz, Lewczuk (Burkhardt 66), Skerla, Sidąy (Jezierski 73), Norambuena, Bruno, Grzyb, Hermes, Lato, Grosicki, Frankowski (Jarecki 81).
POGOŃ – Janukiewicz, Nowak (Lebedyński 60), Hrymowicz, Jarun, Woźniak, Rogalski, Mandrysz (Wólkiewicz 82), Mysiak, Pietruszka, Bojarski (Dziuba 68), Moskalewicz.

Early elimination not unexpected

Portugal's participation at the 2010 FIFA World Cup, for which they qualified only via the play-offs, ran along fairly predictable lines. They survived the 'Group of Death', finishing runners-up in their group to Brazil, before going out in the second round to Spain.

Elimination at the last-16 stage maintained a rather disturbing downward trend for the team – runners-up at UEFA EURO 2004, semi-finalists at the 2006 World Cup and quarter-finalists at UEFA EURO 2008 – but the general feeling was that Carlos Queiroz's team went about as far as they were expected to, and deserved to, in South Africa.

In three of their four games they failed to score a goal. Against that they conceded just one – 333 minutes into their tournament – but it was to prove fatal. David Villa's strike not only knocked Portugal out, it also prevented them from extending to 20 matches an 18-month unbeaten run in which the team's defence had been breached on only three occasions.

Strategic success

Strategically, Queiroz got things spot on until that goal went in against Spain. Each of the group games went largely to plan, the goalless draws against Ivory Coast and Brazil serving Portugal's purpose because of the 7-0 trouncing of North Korea in between. That goalfest in the Cape Town rain was fun to watch, and it gave Portugal the biggest win of the competition, but one or two of the goals would have been better saved up for later.

A more committed attacking effort against Brazil could have brought victory and first place in the group, but Portugal appeared unconcerned at facing Spain and, in any case, for the first hour against their Iberian neighbours they were the better team, with Queiroz winning the tactical battle - albeit without a goal to show for it. Once Spain scored, however, Portugal were unable to respond. Cristiano Ronaldo

was isolated up front, and Spain finished much the stronger team.

Ronaldo was one of the many big stars who failed to shine in South Africa. He had his moments but there were not nearly enough of them, and the same could be said about Portugal's other forwards. The team's two most consistently impressive performers were goalkeeper Eduardo and attacking left-back Fábio Coentrão, both of them making their major tournament debut, while Ricardo Carvalho confirmed his class in central defence and Raul Meireles and Tiago both worked diligently and tirelessly, if with limited attacking intent, in midfield.

Having finished second to Denmark in their World Cup qualifying group, Portugal now have the opportunity to make amends as they take on the same opponents – plus Norway, Iceland and Cyprus – in their UEFA EURO 2012 qualifying group. There was enough evidence in South Africa to suggest that Portugal

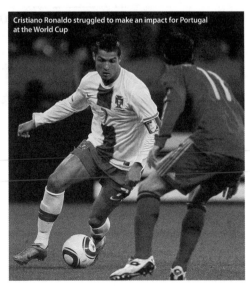

Cristiano Ronaldo struggled to make an impact for Portugal at the World Cup

PORTUGAL

should qualify quite comfortably for their fifth successive European finals.

Jesus delivers

Portuguese internationals were few and far between in the SL Benfica team that won the 2009/10 Liga. In fact, Fábio Coentrão was the only Eagle represented in Queiroz's original World Cup 23 before Rúben Amorim received a surprise late call-up to replace the injured Nani. The team was, however, led by a Portuguese coach, and Jorge Jesus, recruited from SC Braga, enjoyed a formidable first season in charge. The 55-year-old roused the great Lisbon giant from its slumber, producing not just a winning team but an entertaining, high-scoring one besides. So often seduced – like many big clubs – into employing a high-profile foreigner, Benfica discovered their saviour in a relatively unknown local who had served his dues with a succession of smaller clubs.

Jesus led Benfica to their 32nd Portuguese title, but it was the club's first in five years and only their second in 14. The rapport between the new coach and his players was virtually instantaneous. They kicked off the Liga campaign in imperious form, stringing together seven straight wins, most of them replete with goals, before they lost 2-0 in Braga at the end of October. Indeed, it was Braga – rather than traditional rivals FC Porto and Sporting Clube de Portugal – who would provide Benfica with their sternest challenge.

Federação Portuguesa de Futebol (FPF)

Rua Alexandre Herculano 58
CP 24013
PT-1250-012 Lisboa
tel - +351 21 325 2700
fax - +351 21 325 2780
website - fpf.pt
email - info@fpf.pt
Year of Formation – 1914

President – Gilberto Madaíl
General Secretary – Angelo Brou
Media Officer – Onofre Costa
National Stadium – Estádio Nacional, Lisbon (37,000)

IINTERNATIONAL TOURNAMENT APPEARANCES
FIFA World Cup - (5) 1966 (3rd), 1986, 2002, 2006 (4th), 2010 (2nd round).
UEFA European Championship - (5) 1984 (semi-finals), 1996 (qtr-finals), 2000 (semi-finals), 2004 (runners-up), 2008 (qtr-finals).
TOP FIVE ALL-TIME CAPS
Luís Figo (127); Fernando Couto (110); Rui Costa (94); Pedro Resendes "Pauleta" (88); Simão Sabrosa (85)
TOP FIVE ALL-TIME GOALS
Pedro Resendes "Pauleta" (47); Eusébio Ferreira Silva (41); Luís Figo (32); Nuno Gomes (29); Rui Costa (26)

Benfica and Braga shared top spot at Christmas with 33 points from 14 games, and there would be little to separate them thereafter until the underdogs crashed to a 5-1 defeat at Porto then lost the big head-to-head at the Estádio da Luz, enabling Benfica to go six points clear with six games remaining. Even then, Braga did not abandon hope, winning each of their next five games to

NATIONAL TEAM RESULTS 2009/10

Date	Opponent		Venue	Score	Scorers
12/8/09	Liechtenstein	A	Vaduz	3-0	Hugo Almeida (15, 26), Raul Meireles (23)
5/9/09	Denmark (WCQ)	H	Copenhagen	1-1	Liedson (86)
9/9/09	Hungary (WCQ)	A	Budapest	1-0	Pepe (10)
10/10/09	Hungary (WCQ)	H	Lisbon	3-0	Simão (18, 79), Liedson (74)
14/10/09	Malta (WCQ)	H	Guimaraes	4-0	Nani (14), Simão (45), Miguel Veloso (52), Edinho (90)
14/11/09	Bosnia-Herzegovina (WCQ)	H	Lisbon	1-0	Bruno Alves (31)
18/11/09	Bosnia-Herzegovina (WCQ)	A	Zenica	1-0	Raul Meireles (56)
3/3/10	China	H	Coimbra	2-0	Hugo Almeida (36), Liedson (90)
24/5/10	Cape Verde Islands	H	Covilha	0-0	
1/6/10	Cameroon	H	Covilha	3-1	Raul Meireles (32, 47), Nani (81)
8/6/10	Mozambique	N	Johannesburg (RSA)	3-0	Danny (52), Hugo Almeida (75, 83)
15/6/10	Ivory Coast (WCF)	N	Port Elizabeth (RSA)	0-0	
21/6/10	North Korea (WCF)	N	Cape Town (RSA)	7-0	Raul Meireles (29), Simão (53), Hugo Almeida (56), Tiago (60, 89), Liedson (81), Cristiano Ronaldo (87)
25/6/10	Brazil (WCF)	N	Durban (RSA)	0-0	
29/6/10	Spain (WCF)	N	Cape Town (RSA)	0-1	

NATIONAL TEAM APPEARANCES 2009/10

Coach – Carlos QUEIROZ	1/3/53		Lie	DEN	HUN	HUN	MLT	BIH	BIH	Chn	Cpv	Cmr	Moz	CIV	PRK	BRA	ESP	Caps	Goals
EDUARDO Carvalho	19/9/82	Braga	G62	G	G	G	G	G	G	G46	G	G	G	G	G	G	G	19	-
José BOSINGWA	24/8/82	Chelsea (ENG)	D	D	D	D	D											23	-
RICARDO CARVALHO	18/5/78	Chelsea (ENG)	D62	D	D	D	D	D	D	D46		D	D	D	D	D	D	67	4
BRUNO ALVES	27/11/81	Porto	D73	D	D	D		D	D	D64	D	D63	D	D	D	D	D	35	5
Sérgio Valente "DUDA"	27/6/80	Málaga (ESP)	D54	D	D	D		D	D	D46		D63	s86		s74	M54		18	1
Képler Ferreira "PEPE"	26/2/83	Real Madrid (ESP)	M	M	M		D	M	M					s76		M64	M72	27	2
RAUL MEIRELES	17/3/83	Porto	M	M80	M	M	M62	M	M	M	s46	M	M60	M85	M70	M84	M	37	6
TIAGO Mendes	2/5/81	Juventus (ITA) /Atlético (ESP)	M54	M46	M89			s84	M		M46	s57	s60	s62	M	M	M	55	3
Anderson Souza "DECO"	27/8/77	Chelsea (ENG)	M	M	M49	M	M	M84	s80		M57	M	M60	M62				75	5
SIMÃO Sabrosa	31/10/79	Atlético (ESP)	A62	A70	s49	A81	A	A88	A80	A46		A46	A63	s55	A74	s54	A72	85	22
HUGO ALMEIDA	23/5/84	Werder (GER)	A					s88		A	s46		s46		A77		A58	28	10
MIGUEL Monteiro	4/1/80	Valencia (ESP)	s54							s46	s69	s46	D		D			58	1
JOÃO MOUTINHO	8/9/86	Sporting	s54				s73			s46								26	1
ROLANDO Fonseca	31/8/85	Porto	s62		s89							D		s63				8	-
José MOREIRA	20/3/82	Benfica	s62															1	-
ELISEU Santos	1/10/83	Lazio (ITA)	s62															2	-
Luís Cunha "NANI"	17/11/86	Man. United (ENG)	s73	s70	s81	s27	A73	A69	A73	A62	A	s46						36	7
CRISTIANO RONALDO	5/2/85	Real Madrid (ESP)		A	A	A27				A46	A	A	s63	A	A	A	A	76	23
LIEDSON Muniz	17/12/77	Sporting	s46	A81	A83	A62	A	A91	s46	A46	A46	A46	A	s77		s72		13	4
NUNO GOMES	5/7/76	Benfica		s80			s83											76	29
PEDRO MENDES	26/2/79	Rangers (SCO) /Sporting						M	M	s46	M57	M73	M76	M	M	s64	s72	12	-
MIGUEL VELOSO	11/5/86	Sporting						s81	D	s91		M46		s60		s70	s84	14	1
Arnaldo Silva "EDINHO"	7/7/82	Málaga (ESP)						s62		s73								5	1
NUNO ASSIS	25/11/77	Guimarães						s62										5	-
PAULO FERREIRA	18/1/79	Chelsea (ENG)								D	D	D	D69	D46		D		62	-
FÁBIO COENTRÃO	11/3/88	Benfica						s69			D	s63	D	D	D	D	D	8	-
HILÁRIO Sampaio	21/10/75	Chelsea (ENG)								s46								1	-
Silvestre VARELA	2/2/85	Porto								s62								1	-
António Sousa "TONEL"	13/4/80	Sporting								s64								2	-
RICARDO COSTA	16/5/81	Lille (FRA)								s46	s73					D	D	10	-
"DANNY" Miguel Alves Gomes	7/8/83	Zenit (RUS)									s57	s46	A86	A55		M	s58	14	2
RÚBEN AMORIM	27/1/85	Benfica											s85					1	-

take the title race to the very last day, on which Benfica, needing a draw at home to Rio Ave FC, delivered all three points in front of a sell-out 65,000 crowd.

South American influence

Óscar Cardozo, fittingly, scored both goals in that 2-1 win, the second of them lifting his Liga tally for the season to 26 and securing the Golden Boot. The tall Paraguayan striker had a memorable campaign on all fronts and was also the joint-leading marksman in the UEFA Europa League, in which Benfica also put in some dynamic displays before they were eliminated in the quarter-final by Liverpool FC. Cardozo benefited hugely from the attacking brio of his three Argentine accomplices, Javier Saviola, Pablo Aimar and Ángel Di María, the latter proving particularly pleasing on the eye with his sumptuous left-footed skills. There was a strong South American influence at the back, too, where the experienced Luisão and the highly promising David Luiz formed an excellent partnership. Another Brazilian, Ramires, also earned a World Cup place with some quality displays in midfield.

In most seasons Braga's final tally of 71 points would have been enough to win the title, but it was still five short of Benfica's haul. Both clubs won 14 of their 15 home games and drew the other, and although the champions scored 30 goals more than the runners-up, the goals-against figures were identical. Braga's 'keeper Eduardo was as impressive for his club as he would be at the World Cup for his country, just that one bad night in Porto spoiling an outstanding record. Braga's success was largely a collective effort, but fallen star Hugo Viana was another to stand out, reviving his career with a plethora of assists for the front three of Alan, Paulo César and top scorer Albert Meyong. Having lost Jesus to Benfica, Braga struck lucky with his replacement, ex-Porto and Portugal striker Domingos Paciência, who, despite early European embarrassment against IF Elfsborg, confidently led the northerners to the highest position in their history and prospective qualification for the UEFA Champions League.

Portugal had only one team in the group stages of Europe's top competition in 2009/10. With Sporting losing on a goals to ACF Fiorentina in the play-off round and dropping into the UEFA Europa League – where th would reach the round of 16 before the away-goa rule denied them once again (against eventual winners Club Atlético de Madrid) – it was up to Po to fly the flag. Despite two 1-0 defeats to Chelsea they got through their group, but English opposit again proved their nemesis as Arsenal FC crushed them 5-0 in the first knockout round.

Fabulous Falcao

Porto's bid to win a fifth successive Portuguese tit went awry relatively early. Shorn of stalwarts Luch González and Lisandro López, who had both left fo France, they struggled to live with the pace set by Braga and Benfica, and defeats away to both club before Christmas left them with too much ground make up. A long domestic ban for Brazilian winge Hulk did not help, and although new centre-forwa Radamel Falcao enjoyed a magnificent debut campaign, scoring 34 goals, his, and his club's, onl tangible reward came in the Portuguese Cup, whe the prolific 24-year-old scored the winner in the fi against second division GD Chaves. That victory provided a fitting farewell for coach Jesualdo Ferre whose highly successful four-year spell at the club thus ended with a fifth major trophy.

Sporting had sacked their long-serving coach, Paulo Bento, back in the autumn after a wretched start to th season. The team's fortunes scarcely improved followi the arrival of his replacement, Carlos Carvalhal, and b end of the season the Lions were 28 points adrift of Benfica in fourth place – their low final position since 1999. Sportin only consolation was a return tic to the UEFA Europa League, whe they were joined by Porto – out the UEFA Champions League for first time in seven years – and CS Marítimo, who, having sacked Carvalhal at the start of the campaign, did well under Dutchr Mitchell van der Gaag and just ec out Vitória SC and their Madeira CD Nacional to take fifth place. Leixões SC finished last and were relegated with CF Os Belenenses be replaced in the top division fo 2010/11 by promoted SC Beira-N and Portmonense SC.

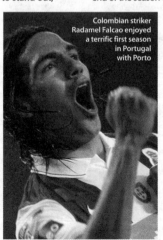

Colombian striker Radamel Falcao enjoyed a terrific first season in Portugal with Porto

DOMESTIC LEAGUE 2009/10

LIGA FINAL TABLE

		Pld	Home					Away					Total					Pts
			W	D	L	F	A	W	D	L	F	A	W	D	L	F	A	
1	SL Benfica	30	14	1	0	46	6	10	3	2	32	14	24	4	2	78	20	76
2	SC Braga	30	14	1	0	27	6	8	4	3	21	14	22	5	3	48	20	71
3	FC Porto	30	12	3	0	40	13	9	2	4	30	13	21	5	4	70	26	68
4	Sporting Clube de Portugal	30	8	3	4	24	13	5	6	4	18	13	13	9	8	42	26	48
5	CS Marítimo	30	7	3	5	22	20	4	5	6	20	23	11	8	11	42	43	41
6	Vitória SC	30	7	4	4	21	15	4	4	7	10	19	11	8	11	31	34	41
7	CD Nacional	30	7	6	2	20	16	3	3	9	16	30	10	9	11	36	46	39
8	A. Naval 1º Maio	30	6	3	6	12	17	4	3	8	8	18	10	6	14	20	35	36
9	UD Leiria	30	5	5	5	19	19	4	3	8	16	22	9	8	13	35	41	35
10	FC Paços de Ferreira	30	4	7	4	17	18	4	4	7	15	19	8	11	11	32	37	35
11	A. Académica de Coimbra	30	4	5	6	20	20	4	4	7	17	22	8	9	13	37	42	33
12	Rio Ave FC	30	3	7	5	10	14	3	6	6	12	19	6	13	11	22	33	31
13	SC Olhanense	30	4	5	6	12	18	1	9	5	19	28	5	14	11	31	46	29
14	Vitória FC	30	3	6	6	13	22	2	4	9	16	35	5	10	15	29	57	25
15	CF Os Belenenses	30	2	4	9	12	28	2	7	6	11	16	4	11	15	23	44	23
16	Leixões SC	30	4	5	6	18	23	1	1	13	7	28	5	6	19	25	51	21

TOP GOALSCORERS

26 Óscar CARDOZO (Benfica)
25 Radamel FALCAO (Porto)
13 LIEDSON (Sporting)
12 Albert MEYONG (Braga)
    EDGAR SILVA (Nacional)
    DJALMIR (Olhanense)
    CÁSSIO (Leiria)
11 Javier SAVIOLA (Benfica)
10 WILLIAM (Paços Ferreira)
    Ladji KEITA (Setúbal)

CLUB-BY-CLUB

A. ACADÉMICA DE COIMBRA
Coach – Rogério Gonçalves; (4/10/09) (Zé Nando); (13/10/09) André Vilas Boas
Founded – 1876
Stadium – Cidade de Coimbra (30,075)
MAJOR HONOURS:
Portuguese Cup - (1) 1939.

2009
15/8	Braga	a	0-1	
22/8	Paços Ferreira	h	1-1	*Miguel Fidalgo*
30/8	Sporting	h	0-2	
13/9	Olhanense	a	1-2	*Lito (p)*
20/9	Belenenses	h	1-1	*Miguel Pedro*
26/9	Rio Ave	a	0-0	
2/10	Marítimo	h	2-4	*Miguel Fidalgo, Modou Sougou*
25/10	Porto	a	2-3	*Miguel Fidalgo, Modou Sougou*
2/11	Guimarães	h	2-0	*Modou Sougou, Éder*
8/11	Leiria	a	1-1	*Cris*
29/11	Setúbal	h	3-0	*Modou Sougou 2 (1p), Tiero*
6/12	Benfica	a	0-4	*Lito, Orlando*
13/12	Leixões	h	2-0	*Rafael, Lito*
20/12	Nacional	a	3-4	*Tiero, Modou Sougou, Miguel Fidalgo*

2010
10/1	Naval	h	2-0	*Lito, Modou Sougou*
17/1	Braga	h	0-2	
31/1	Paços Ferreira	a	1-2	*Berger*
6/2	Sporting	a	2-1	*Orlando, João Ribeiro*
14/2	Olhanense	h	1-1	*Tiero (p)*
22/2	Belenenses	a	2-1	*Vouho, Berger*
28/2	Rio Ave	h	0-1	
7/3	Marítimo	a	0-0	
13/3	Porto	h	1-2	*Modou Sougou*
27/3	Guimarães	a	0-1	
3/4	Leiria	h	0-0	
12/4	Setúbal	a	1-1	*Henrique*
18/4	Benfica	h	2-3	*Diogo, Tiero*

25/4	Leixões	a	3-1	*Modou Sougou, Diogo, Éder*
2/5	Nacional	h	3-3	*Hélder Cabral, Miguel Fidalgo, Éder*
9/5	Naval	a	1-0	*Bruno Amaro*

No	Name	Nat	DoB	Pos	Aps	(s)	Gls
6	AMESSAN Niamien Rodolph	CIV	27/9/90	A		(1)	
2	Euripedes Daniel Adão AMOREIRINHA		5/8/84	D	7	(3)	
20	ANDRÉ Filipe Pereira FONTES		27/5/85	M	4	(1)	
31	João Gabriel Silva Ferreira "BARROCA"		29/7/86	G	2		
5	Markus BERGER	AUT	21/1/85	D	22		2
7	Amaury Armindo BISCHOFF		31/3/87	M	1	(1)	
28	Jonathan Pierre BRU	FRA	2/5/85	M		(3)	
61	BRUNO AMARO de Sousa Barros		17/12/83	M	1	(2)	1
17	Bruno CRIStiano da Carvalho Santos		17/1/84	M	23	(2)	1
85	DIOGO Soares Gomes	BRA	12/9/85	M	9	(3)	2
21	ÉDERzito António Macedo Lopes	GNB	22/12/87	A	17	(5)	3
55	HÉLDER José Vaz CABRAL		7/5/84	D	1	(5)	1
25	JOÃO Rocha RIBEIRO		13/8/87	A	19	(3)	1
16	Luís Carlos Pereira Carneiro "LICA"		8/9/88	A	2	(5)	
11	Cláudio Zélito Fernandes Aguiar "LITO"	CPV	3/2/75	M	11	(13)	3
4	LUIZ Fernando NUNES Duarte	BRA	4/12/80	D	7	(2)	
14	Nuno MIGUEL FIDALGO dos Santos		19/3/82	A	2	(10)	5
10	MIGUEL António Ferreira PEDRO		11/6/83	A	5	(4)	1
18	Papa Amodou "MODOU" SOUGOU	SEN	18/12/84	A	26	(3)	9
66	NUNO Miguel Prata COELHO		23/11/87	M	25	(2)	
15	Rui ORLANDO Ribeiro Santos Neto		24/10/79	D	24		2
8	PAULO SÉRGIO Ferreira Gomes	BRA	21/7/81	M	6	(8)	
19	Pedro Miguel da Silva Rocha "PEDRINHO"		6/3/85	D	26		(1)

PORTUGAL

No	Name	Nat	DoB	Pos	Aps	(s)	Gls
30	PEDRO Miguel de Brandão COSTA		21/11/81	D	8		
22	Emídio RAFAEL Augusto da Silva		24/1/86	D	26	1	
12	RICARDO Jorge Novo Nunes		6/7/82	G	14		
1	RUI Miguel NEREU de Batista		4/2/86	G	14	(1)	
33	William Kwabena TIERO	GHA	3/12/74	A	22	(2)	4
27	Djilli Arsène Dit Patrick VOUHO	CIV	25/6/87	A	6	(9)	1

CF OS BELENENSES
Coach – João Carlos Pereira; (23/12/09) António Conceição "Toni"
Founded – 1919
Stadium – Restelo (19,980)
MAJOR HONOURS:
Portuguese League - (1) 1946;
Portuguese Cup - (6) 1927, 1929, 1933, 1942, 1960, 1989.

2009
14/8	Leixões	a	0-0	
24/8	Naval	h	2-0	Yontcha, Ivan
30/8	Braga	a	1-3	Yontcha
13/9	Benfica	h	0-4	
20/9	Académica	a	1-1	Diakité
4/10	Sporting	a	0-0	
12/10	Nacional	h	0-1	
23/10	Olhanense	h	0-0	
30/10	Porto	a	1-1	Lima
6/11	Paços Ferreira	h	0-3	
29/11	Marítimo	h	2-2	Lima 2 (1p)
5/12	Rio Ave	a	0-0	
12/12	Guimarães	h	0-1	
20/12	Leiria	a	0-1	

2010
11/1	Setúbal	h	0-0	
17/1	Leixões	h	1-3	Yontcha
30/1	Naval	a	0-1	
8/2	Braga	h	1-3	Yontcha
13/2	Benfica	a	0-1	
22/2	Académica	h	1-2	Yontcha
1/3	Nacional	a	0-1	
7/3	Sporting	h	0-4	
14/3	Olhanense	a	3-1	Lima 2, Barge
28/3	Porto	h	0-3	
3/4	Paços Ferreira	a	0-0	
11/4	Marítimo	a	3-3	Miguelito, Lima, Dević
18/4	Rio Ave	h	0-0	
26/4	Guimarães	a	0-2	
2/5	Leiria	h	5-2	Lima, José Pedro, Mustafá, Miguelito, Pires
8/5	Setúbal	a	2-1	Romário, André Almeida

No	Name	Nat	DoB	Pos	Aps	(s)	Gls
25	Freddy ADU	USA	2/6/89	A	1	(2)	
14	ANDRÉ Gomes Magalhães de ALMEIDA		13/9/90	M	11	(9)	1
1	ASSIS Giovanaz	BRA	4/10/89	G	1	(1)	
4	Sérgio Filipe da Silva BARGE		4/1/84	M	26	(1)	1
33	Roberto Luís Gaspar Deus Severo "BETO"		3/5/76	D	10		
16	BRUNO Miguel Esteves VALE		8/4/83	G	16		
27	CÂNDIDO Alves Moreira da COSTA		30/5/81	A	8	(3)	
10	Pedro CELESTINO Silva Soares		2/1/87	M	22	(6)	
19	DANIel Afonso Fernandes Pinto		1/6/90	A		(4)	
15	Vukašin DEVIĆ	SRB	15/3/84	D	3	(4)	1
80	Mourtala DIAKITÉ	MLI	1/10/80	A	15		1
55	João Paulo Silva Freitas FAJARDO		27/10/78	M	4	(6)	
20	FELLIPE Ramos Ignez BASTOS	BRA	1/2/90	M	2	(6)	
23	FILIPE Manuel Carvalho PAIVA		10/5/91	M		(1)	
22	Alfredo Kulembe Ribeiro"FREDY"		27/3/90	A	13	(11)	
6	Gabriel Enrique GÓMEZ Giron	PAN	29/5/84	M	25	(1)	
17	IGOR Siqueira Pessanha	BRA	14/6/88	D		(3)	
26	IVAN Carlos de Souza Santos	BRA	8/6/82	M	6	(4)	1
11	JOSÉ PEDRO Alves Salazar		18/10/78	M	15	(8)	1
90	Rodrigo José LIMA Santos	BRA	11/5/83	A	26	(1)	7
7	Luís Miguel Lopes Mendes "MANO"		9/4/87	M	28		
28	MARCOS ANTÓNIO Elias Santos	BRA	25/5/83	D	14		
81	José Miguel Organista Simões Aguiar "MIGUELITO"		4/2/81	D	12		2

No	Name	Nat	DoB	Pos	Aps	(s)	Gls
18	Daniel Kabir MUSTAFÁ	ARG	2/8/84	D	10		1
3	NÉLSON Alexandre Gomes Pereira		20/10/75	G	13		
56	Judilson Mamadu Tuncara Gomes "PELÉ"		20/9/91	M	7	(6)	
21	André Ferro PIRES		7/2/90	D	8		1
13	RODRIGO António Magalhães Alves Pereira "ARROZ"	BRA	21/3/84	D	8	(1)	
89	ROMÁRIO Paula Ribeiro	BRA	6/9/89	A		(2)	1
5	TIAGO Henrique Damil GOMES		29/7/86	D	13		
9	Jean Paul YONTCHA	CMR	14/5/83	A	13	(6)	5

SL BENFICA
Coach – Jorge Jesus
Founded – 1904
Stadium – Luz (65,647)
MAJOR HONOURS:
European Champion Clubs' Cup – (2) 1961, 1962;
Portuguese League - (32) 1936, 1937, 1938, 1942, 1943, 1945, 1950, 1955, 1957, 1960, 1961, 1963, 1964, 1965, 1967, 1968, 1969, 1971, 1972, 1973, 1975, 1976, 1977, 1981, 1983, 1984, 1987, 1989, 1991, 1994, 2005, 2010;
Portuguese Cup - (27) 1930, 1931, 1935, 1940, 1943, 1944, 1949, 1951, 1952, 1953, 1955, 1957, 1959, 1962, 1964, 1969, 1970, 1972, 1980, 1981, 1983, 1985, 1986, 1987, 1993, 1996, 2004.

2009
16/8	Marítimo	h	1-1	Weldon
23/8	Guimarães	a	1-0	Ramires
31/8	Setúbal	h	8-1	Javi García, Luisão, Cardozo 3 (1p), Aimar, Ramires, Nuno Gomes
13/9	Belenenses	a	4-0	Saviola, Cardozo, Javi García, Ramires
20/9	Leiria	a	2-1	Saviola, Cardozo (p)
26/9	Leixões	h	5-0	David Luiz, Cardozo 2 (1p), Ramires, Maxi Pereira
5/10	Paços Ferreira	a	3-1	David Luiz, Carlos Martins, Cardozo
26/10	Nacional	h	6-1	Cardozo 3 (2p), Saviola 2, Nuno Gomes
31/10	Braga	a	0-2	
9/11	Naval	h	1-0	Javi García
28/11	Sporting	a	0-0	
6/12	Académica	h	4-0	Cardozo 3, Saviola
12/12	Olhanense	a	2-2	Saviola, Nuno Gomes
20/12	Porto	h	1-0	Saviola

2010
9/1	Rio Ave	a	1-0	Saviola
17/1	Marítimo	a	5-0	Saviola, Maxi Pereira, Cardozo, og (Roberto Sousa), Luisão
30/1	Guimarães	h	3-1	Pablo Aimar, Carlos Martins 2
3/2	Leiria	h	3-0	Cardozo, Saviola, Rúben Amorim
6/2	Setúbal	a	1-1	og (Ricardo Silva)
13/2	Belenenses	h	1-0	Cardozo
27/2	Leixões	a	4-0	Éder Luis, Di María 3
7/3	Paços Ferreira	h	3-1	Rúben Amorim, Saviola, Cardozo
14/3	Nacional	a	1-0	Cardozo
27/3	Braga	h	1-0	Luisão
5/4	Naval	a	4-2	Weldon 2, Di María, Cardozo
13/4	Sporting	h	2-0	Cardozo, Aimar
18/4	Académica	h	3-2	Weldon 2, Rúben Amorim
24/4	Olhanense	h	5-0	Cardozo 3 (1p), Di María, Aimar
2/5	Porto	a	1-3	Luisão
9/5	Rio Ave	h	2-1	Cardozo 2

No	Name	Nat	DoB	Pos	Aps	(s)	Gls
10	Pablo César AIMAR	ARG	3/11/79	M	21	(4)	4
2	AÍRTON Ribeiro Santos	BRA	21/2/90	M	3	(1)	
31	ALAN KARDEC Souza Pereira Júnior	BRA	12/1/89	A		(8)	
7	Óscar René CARDOZO	PAR	20/5/83	A	28	(1)	26
17	CARLOS Jorge Neto MARTINS		29/4/82	M	11	(6)	3
25	Paulo CÉSAR Silva PEIXOTO		12/5/80	M	10	(5)	
33	DAVID LUIZ Moreira Marinho	BRA	22/4/87	D	29		2
20	Ángel Fabián DI MARÍA	ARG	14/2/88	A	26		5
32	ÉDER LUIS Oliveira	BRA	19/4/85	A	2	(4)	1
18	FÁBIO Alexandre da Silva COENTRÃO		11/3/88	M	18	(8)	
24	FELIPE MENEZES Jácomo	BRA	20/1/88	M		(5)	

6	Francisco JAVIer GARCÍA Fernández	SPA	8/2/87	M	26		3
11	KEIRRISON de Souza Carneiro	BRA	3/12/88	A	1	(4)	
22	LUÍS FILIPE Angelo Rodrigues Fernandes		14/6/79	D		(1)	
4	Anderson Luís da Silva "LUISÃO"	BRA	13/2/81	D	28		4
14	Victorio MAXImiliano PEREIRA Páez	URU	8/6/84	D	21	(4)	2
28	MIGUEL Angelo Leonardo VÍTOR		30/6/89	D	1	(1)	
21	NUNO Miguel Soares Ribeiro GOMES		5/7/76	A	1	(12)	3
12	Joaquim Manuel Sampaio Gonçalves "QUIM"		20/3/82	G	30		
8	RAMIRES Santos do Nascimento	BRA	24/3/87	M	23	(3)	4
5	RÚBEN Filipe Marques AMORIM		27/1/85	M	14	(10)	3
30	Javier Pedro SAVIOLA	ARG	11/12/81	A	26	(1)	11
3	José Alberto SHAFFER	ARG	16/12/85	D	4		
27	SIDNEI Rechel da Silva Júnior	BRA	23/6/89	D	3	(2)	
16	Jonathan Matias URRETAvizcaya da Luz	URU	19/3/90	A	1		
19	WELDON Santos de Andrade	BRA	6/8/80	A	3	(9)	5

SC BRAGA
Coach – Domingos Paciência
Founded – 1921
Stadium – Municipal de Braga (30,286)
MAJOR HONOURS:
Portuguese Cup – (1) 1966.

2009

15/8	Académica	h	1-0	Meyong
22/8	Sporting	a	2-1	Alan, Meyong
30/8	Belenenses	h	3-1	og (Diakité), Hugo Viana 2
13/9	Marítimo	a	2-1	João Pereira, Meyong (p)
19/9	Porto	h	1-0	Alan
25/9	Olhanense	a	1-0	Alan
3/10	Setúbal	h	2-0	Paulo César, Hugo Viana
24/10	Rio Ave	a	1-0	Evaldo
31/10	Benfica	h	2-0	Hugo Viana, Paulo César
7/11	Guimarães	a	0-1	
30/11	Leiria	h	2-0	Paulo César, Matheus
5/12	Leixões	a	1-1	Alan
13/12	Naval	h	0-0	
18/12	Paços Ferreira	a	1-0	Meyong

2010

8/1	Nacional	h	2-0	Vandinho, André Leone
17/1	Académica	a	2-0	Meyong (p), Matheus
29/1	Sporting	h	1-0	Paulo César
8/2	Belenenses	h	3-1	Paulo César, Matheus, Rentería
14/2	Marítimo	h	2-1	Meyong, Luís Aguiar
21/2	Porto	a	1-5	Alan
27/2	Olhanense	h	3-1	Meyong 2, Evaldo
6/3	Setúbal	a	0-0	
13/3	Rio Ave	h	1-0	Andrés Madrid
27/3	Benfica	a	0-1	
2/4	Guimarães	h	3-2	Alan (p), Meyong 2 (2p)
10/4	Leiria	a	2-1	Meyong, Rentería
17/4	Leixões	h	3-1	Alan 2, Moisés
25/4	Naval	a	4-0	Luís Aguiar 2, Matheus, Paulão
2/5	Paços Ferreira	h	1-0	Meyong
9/5	Nacional	a	1-1	Rentería

No	Name	Nat	DoB	Pos	Aps	(s)	Gls
81	ADRIANO Vieira Louzada	BRA	3/1/79	A		(7)	
30	ALAN Osório da Costa Silva	BRA	19/9/79	A	30		8
4	ANDRÉ Augusto LEONE	BRA	12/2/79	D	10	(2)	1
23	ANDRÉS David MADRID	ARG	29/7/81	M	12	(4)	1
11	DIOGO Jorge Moreno VALENTE		23/9/84	M	2	(6)	
1	EDUARDO dos Reis Carvalho		19/9/82	G	30		
6	EVALDO dos Santos Fabiano	BRA	18/3/82	D	30		2
16	FERNANDO José Ribeiro ALEXANDRE		2/8/85	M		(1)	
27	FILIPE Vilaça OLIVEIRA		27/5/84	D	15	(2)	
45	HUGO Miguel Ferreira VIANA		15/1/83	M	22	(6)	4
47	JOÃO Pedro da Silva PEREIRA		25/2/84	D	13		1

10	LUÍS Bernardo AGUIAR Burgos	URU	17/11/85	M	10	(4)	3
8	José MÁRCIO Costa "MOSSORÓ"	BRA	4/7/83	A	20	(1)	
99	MATHEUS Leite do Nascimento	BRA	15/1/83	A	8	(22)	4
19	Albert MEYONG Zé	CMR	19/10/80	A	24	(5)	12
15	MIGUEL Ângelo Moita GARCIA		4/2/83	D	3	(1)	
5	MOISÉS Moura Pinheiro	BRA	25/7/79	D	28		1
68	Uedson NEY dos Santos	BRA	23/2/81	D	1		
13	OLBERDAM Oliveira Serra	BRA	6/2/85	M	2	(1)	
7	OSVALDO Lourenço Filho	BRA	11/4/87	A		(4)	
3	Paulo Afonso Santos Júnior "PAULÃO"	BRA	6/8/82	D	4	(3)	1
9	PAULO CÉSAR Rocha Rosa	BRA	5/1/80	A	26	(1)	5
29	Louis Angelo PEÑA	VEN	25/12/89	A		(1)	
22	RAFAEL BASTOS	BRA	1/1/85	M	1	(7)	
18	Wason Libardo RENTERÍA Cuesta	COL	4/7/85	A	5	(7)	3
2	Alberto Junior RODRÍGUEZ Valdelomar	PER	31/3/84	D	18	(2)	
88	Vanderson Valter de Almeida "VANDINHO"	BRA	15/1/78	M	16		1
14	YAZALDE Gomes Pinto		21/9/88	A		(3)	

LEIXÕES SC
Coach – José Mota; (9/2/10) Fernando Castro Santos (ESP)
Founded – 1907
Stadium – Mar (9,821)
MAJOR HONOURS:
Portuguese Cup - (1) 1961.

2009

15/8	Belenenses	h	0-0	
23/8	Marítimo	a	0-1	
30/8	Rio Ave	h	0-0	
12/9	Porto	h	1-4	Pouga
18/9	Guimarães	h	3-1	Laranjeiro (p), Pouga, Zé Manel
26/9	Benfica	a	0-5	
4/10	Leiria	h	3-2	Léo, Zé Manel, Hugo Morais
25/10	Setúbal	a	0-1	
31/10	Naval	a	0-1	
8/11	Nacional	h	2-4	Pouga, Hugo Morais (p)
29/11	Paços Ferreira	a	1-1	Hugo Morais (p)
5/12	Braga	h	1-1	og (Moisés)
13/12	Académica	h	0-2	
21/12	Olhanense	h	2-2	Pouga, Tiago Cintra

2010

9/1	Sporting	a	0-1	
17/1	Belenenses	a	3-1	Hugo Morais (p), Pouga, Didi
1/2	Marítimo	h	1-2	Hugo Morais
7/2	Rio Ave	a	0-2	
13/2	Porto	h	0-0	
20/2	Guimarães	a	0-2	
27/2	Benfica	h	0-4	
5/3	Leiria	a	1-2	Zé Manel
14/3	Setúbal	h	1-2	João Paulo
28/3	Naval	h	1-0	Hugo Morais (p)
2/4	Nacional	a	0-1	
11/4	Paços Ferreira	h	2-0	Zé Manel, Pouga
17/4	Braga	a	1-3	Pouga
25/4	Académica	a	1-3	Hugo Morais (p)
1/5	Olhanense	a	0-1	
8/5	Sporting	h	1-2	João Paulo

No	Name	Nat	DoB	Pos	Aps	(s)	Gls
5	Vitorino Gabriel Pacheco ANTUNES		1/4/87	D	10	(1)	
3	Nelson Pablo BENÍTEZ	ARG	24/5/84	D	6		
1	Hans Peter BERGER	AUT	28/9/81	G	7		
9	Bruno Manuel Araújo BRAGA		17/6/83	A	9	(6)	
14	BRUNO Manuel Rodrigues Silva "CHINA"		5/8/82	M	2		
18	CAUÊ Cecílio da Silva	BRA	24/5/89	M	8	(3)	
29	Lê CÔNG VINH	VIE	10/12/85	A	1	(3)	
99	Cleidimar Magalhães Silva "DIDI"	BRA	10/9/82	A	3	(3)	1
25	DIEGO Costa da Silva	BRA	11/5/79	G	23		
10	FÁBIO Ricardo Gomes Fonseca "ESPINHO"		18/8/85	M	6	(7)	

PORTUGAL

No	Name	Nat	DoB	Pos	Aps	(s)	Gls
11	Alexandre FAIOLI	BRA	22/11/83	A	4	(4)	
16	FERNANDO José Ribeiro ALEXANDRE		2/8/85	M	22		
33	FERNANDO Silva CARDOZO	BRA	13/3/79	D	12		
6	Bruno Vieira GALLO de Oliveira	BRA	7/5/88	M	10	(2)	
7	HUGO Eduardo dos Santos MORAIS		12/2/78	M	28	(1)	7
28	JEAN SONY Alcenat	CRC	23/1/86	A	17	(5)	
80	JOÃO PAULO Pinto Ribeiro		8/4/80	A	4	(7)	2
13	Ricardo JOEL dos Santos Dias		15/6/80	D	11	(3)	
20	Nuno Filipe Rodrigues LARANJEIRO		18/1/83	D	12		1
26	LÉOnardo Augusto Gomes Aro	BRA	14/12/83	A	7	(4)	1
22	NÉLSON Ricardo Cerqueira Lenho		22/3/84	D	6	(1)	
27	NUNO Miguel da Costa SILVA		27/10/75	D	21	(1)	
19	PAULO Daniel Fernandes TAVARES		9/12/85	M	3	(1)	
15	Christian POUGA	CMR	19/6/86	A	20	(7)	7
2	RUBEN Tiago Rodrigues RIBEIRO		1/8/87	D	4	(5)	
23	Pedro Miguel Costa SEABRA		11/11/87	A	19		
21	TIAGO Manuel Pinto CINTRA		5/7/89	A	9	(8)	1
30	Christian Damián TROMBETTA	ARG	15/10/86	A	4	(2)	
4	Roberto Raúl TUCKER	ARG	27/6/83	D	19	(1)	
17	WÉNIO Moraes Pio	BRA	9/9/79	M	10	(1)	
8	José Manuel Silva Fernandes "ZÉ MANEL"		22/2/75	A	13	(14)	4

CS MARÍTIMO

Coach – Carlos Carvalhal; (28/9/09) Mitchell van der Gaag (NED)
Founded – 1910
Stadium – Barreiros (8,922)
MAJOR HONOURS:
Portuguese Cup - (1) 1926.

2009

16/8	Benfica	a	1-1	Alonso (p)
23/8	Leixões	h	1-0	og (Hugo Morais)
30/8	Leiria	a	0-0	
13/9	Braga	h	1-2	Miguel Ângelo
20/9	Nacional	a	1-2	Djalma
26/9	Naval	h	1-2	Baba Diawara
2/10	Académica	a	4-2	Marcinho, Baba Diawara 2, Bruno
25/10	Paços Ferreira	h	3-1	og (Ozéia), Djalma 2
1/11	Sporting	a	1-1	Manú
8/11	Porto	h	1-0	og (Rolando)
29/11	Belenenses	a	2-2	og (Beto), Manú
6/12	Olhanense	h	5-2	Djalma, Bruno, Alonso (p), Baba Diawara 2
13/12	Rio Ave	h	0-1	
20/12	Setúbal	a	2-3	Alonso (p), João Guilherme

2010

9/1	Guimarães	h	0-1	
17/1	Benfica	h	0-5	
1/2	Leixões	a	2-1	Diakité, Kléber
7/2	Leiria	h	1-0	Kléber
14/2	Braga	a	1-2	Djalma
19/2	Nacional	h	1-1	Kléber
27/2	Naval	a	1-2	Kléber
7/3	Académica	h	0-0	
15/3	Paços Ferreira	a	0-1	
26/3	Sporting	h	3-2	Tchô, og (Sinama-Pongolle), Cláudio Pitbull
3/4	Porto	a	1-4	Soma
11/4	Belenenses	h	3-3	Rafael Miranda, Djalma, Soma
16/4	Olhanense	a	2-1	Baba Diawara, Kléber
23/4	Rio Ave	a	0-0	
2/5	Setúbal	h	2-0	Tchô, Kléber
9/5	Guimarães	a	2-1	Kléber 2

No	Name	Nat	DoB	Pos	Aps	(s)	Gls
2	ALONSO Ferreira de Matos	BRA	11/8/80	D	22	(1)	3
35	Papa BABAcar DIAWARA	SEN	5/1/88	A	20	(10)	6
21	Nuno Miguel Pereira Souza "BRIGUEL"		8/3/79	D	9	(10)	

No	Name	Nat	DoB	Pos	Aps	(s)	Gls
10	BRUNO Marcelo Pereira Fernandes		30/6/74	M	16	(2)	2
16	Abdelmalek CHERRAD	FRA	14/1/81	A		(1)	
9	CLÁUDIO Mejolaro "PITBULL"	BRA	8/1/82	A	6	(9)	1
80	Mourtala DIAKITÉ	MLI	10/10/80	D	6	(3)	1
17	DJALMA Braume Manuel Abel Campos	ANG	30/5/87	A	24	(4)	6
33	Dylan Ludovic DUVENTRU Huret	FRA	3/1/89	A		(1)	
14	FERNANDO Dinarte Santos Silva		3/10/80	D	9	(4)	
3	FERNANDO Silva CARDOZO	BRA	17/3/79	D	6		
31	Philipe FIDELIS dos Santos	BRA	14/6/89	M		(2)	
44	JOÃO GUILHERME Leme Amorin	BRA	21/4/86	M	24	(2)	1
20	JOÃO LUIZ Ramires Vieira	BRA	24/6/85	M	3	(3)	
11	Elias de Oliveira Rosa "KANU"	BRA	8/2/83	A	4	(1)	
22	Kléber Laube Pinheiro	BRA	2/5/90	A	14	(6)	8
18	LUÍS Miguel OLIM Andrade		22/8/81	D	1	(1)	
15	Emanuel de Jesus Bonfim Evaristo "MANÚ"		20/8/82	A	25	(2)	2
1	MARCELO Boeck	BRA	28/11/84	G	1	(2)	
28	Márcio Ivanildo da Silva "MARCINHO"	BRA	25/3/81	A	12	(1)	1
4	MIGUEL ÂNGELO Ferreira de Castro		10/10/84	D	2		1
5	José Miguel Simões Aguiar "MIGUELITO"		4/2/81	D	5	(1)	
13	OLBERDAM de Oliveira Serra	BRA	6/2/85	M	9		
8	PAULO JORGE Vieira Alves		5/5/81	D	26	(2)	
24	Peterson dos Santos PEÇANHA	BRA	11/1/80	G	29		
25	RAFAEL MIRANDA Conceição	BRA	11/8/84	M	9		1
26	ROBERTO de SOUSA Resende	BRA	18/1/85	M	24		
6	ROBSON Severino da Silva	BRA	10/7/83	D	13	(4)	
40	Leocísio Júlio SAMI		18/12/88	A		(1)	
7	Takahito SOMA	JPN	10/12/81	D	9	(8)	2
23	Valdecir Souza Júnior "TCHÔ"	BRA	21/4/87	M	2	(8)	2
59	YTALO José Oliveira Santos	BRA	12/1/88	A		(1)	

CD NACIONAL

Coach – Manuel Machado; (30/11/09) (José Augusto Araujo); (13/12/09) (Predrag Jokanović) (SRB); (26/1/10) Manuel Machado
Founded – 1910
Stadium – Madeira (5,132)

2009

15/8	Sporting	h	1-1	João Aurélio
23/8	Porto	a	0-3	
31/8	Olhanense	h	1-1	João Aurélio
12/9	Rio Ave	a	0-2	
20/9	Marítimo	h	2-1	Edgar Silva 2
12/10	Belenenses	a	1-0	Anselmo
5/10	Guimarães	h	2-0	Edgar Silva 2 (2p)
26/10	Benfica	a	1-6	Edgar Costa
1/11	Setúbal	h	2-1	Pečnik, Anselmo
8/11	Leixões	a	4-2	Edgar Silva 3 (2p), Anselmo
29/11	Naval	h	1-1	Mateus
7/12	Leiria	a	2-1	Edgar Silva, Felipe Lopes
11/12	Paços Ferreira	a	1-2	Amuneke
20/12	Académica	h	4-3	Mateus, Rúben Micael, Edgar Silva, Amuneke

2010

8/1	Braga	a	0-2	
16/1	Sporting	a	2-3	Rúben Micael, Edgar Silva
30/1	Porto	h	0-4	
7/2	Olhanense	a	0-1	
14/2	Rio Ave	h	1-1	Pedro Oldoni
19/2	Marítimo	a	1-1	Felipe Lopes
1/3	Belenenses	h	1-0	João Aurélio
8/3	Guimarães	a	0-2	
14/3	Benfica	h	0-1	
28/3	Setúbal	a	1-2	Pečnik
2/4	Leixões	h	1-0	Edgar Costa
9/4	Naval	a	0-0	
18/4	Leiria	h	2-0	Pedro Oldoni, Diego Barcellos
25/4	Paços Ferreira	h	1-1	Diego Barcellos

2/5	Académica	a	3-3	Diego Barcellos, Edgar Silva, João Aurélio		
9/5	Braga	h	1-1	Edgar Silva		

No	Name	Nat	DoB	Pos	Aps	(s)	Gls
34	ALEX BRUNO Costa Fernandes	BRA	9/5/82	D	5		
11	Kevin Onyekachi AMUNEKE	NGA	5/10/86	M	9	(7)	2
18	ANSELMO Gonçalves Cardoso		6/1/84	A	2	(12)	3
44	Cléber Oliveira "CLEBÃO"	BRA	9/7/85	D	7		
6	CLÉBER Monteiro de Oliveira	BRA	23/5/80	M	28		
19	DIEGO Lima BARCELOS	BRA	5/4/85	A	5	(2)	3
17	José EDGAR Andrade COSTA		14/4/87	A	5	(9)	2
9	EDGAR Bruno da SILVA	BRA	3/1/87	A	18	(6)	12
3	FELIPE Aliste LOPES	BRA	7/8/87	D	26		2
20	Abdou GUIRASSY	SEN	12/1/89	M	2	(2)	
4	Rafik HALLICHE	ALG	2/9/86	D	10	(6)	
23	JOÃO Miguel Coimbra AURÉLIO		17/8/88	A	22	(5)	4
88	JULIANO Mineiro Fernandes	BRA	14/2/86	M	4	(4)	
30	LEANDRO SALINO do Carmo	BRA	22/4/85	M	21	(3)	
8	LUÍS ALBERTO Silva dos Santos	BRA	17/11/83	M	21	(1)	
31	MATEUS Galiano da Costa	ANG	19/6/84	A	6	(2)	2
55	NUNO Miguel Sousa PINTO		6/8/86	D	22	(1)	
27	Pedro Miguel PACHECO de Melo		27/6/84	M	1	(4)	
2	Bruno Alexandre dos Santos PATACAS		30/11/77	D	28		
10	Nejc PEČNIK	SVN	3/1/86	M	14	(10)	2
99	PEDRO Henrique OLDONI Nascimento	BRA	26/9/85	A	8	(3)	2
1	RAFAEL Wibhi BRACALI	BRA	5/5/81	G	30		
29	RODRIGO Silva	BRA	15/6/83	A		(2)	
14	RÚBEN MICAEL Freitas Ressurreição		19/8/86	M	16		2
77	THIAGO GENTIL	BRA	8/4/80	M	4	(1)	
25	Ivan TODOROVIĆ	SRB	29/7/83	M		(4)	
33	Žarko TOMAŠEVIĆ	MNE	22/2/90	D	14	(3)	
5	José WELLINGTON da Silva Santos	BRA	3/9/89	D	2	(3)	

A. NAVAL 1º MAIO
Coach – Ulisses Morais; (31/8/09) (Fernando Mira); (12/9/09) Augusto Inácio
Founded – 1893
Stadium – Municipal José Bento Pessoa (9,116)

2009				
16/8	Olhanense	h	0-0	
24/8	Belenenses	a	0-2	
29/8	Porto	h	1-3	og (Rolando)
13/9	Guimarães	a	0-3	
20/9	Setúbal	h	0-1	
26/9	Marítimo	a	2-1	Kerrouche 2
3/10	Rio Ave	h	3-2	Diego Ângelo, Kerrouche 2
24/10	Leiria	a	0-2	
31/10	Leixões	h	1-0	Kerrouche
9/11	Benfica	a	0-1	
29/11	Nacional	a	1-1	Camora
5/12	Paços Ferreira	h	1-0	Diego Ângelo
13/12	Braga	h	0-0	
19/12	Sporting	h	0-1	
2010				
10/1	Académica	a	0-2	
16/1	Olhanense	a	0-1	
30/1	Belenenses	h	1-0	Godemèche
7/2	Porto	a	0-3	
15/2	Guimarães	h	0-0	
21/2	Setúbal	a	1-0	Bolívia
27/2	Marítimo	h	2-1	Hauw, Márinho
6/3	Rio Ave	a	0-0	
12/3	Leiria	h	1-0	Diego Ângelo
28/3	Leixões	a	0-1	
5/4	Benfica	h	2-4	Fábio Júnior, Bolívia
9/4	Nacional	h	0-0	
17/4	Paços Ferreira	a	3-1	Fábio Júnior, João Real, og (Kelly)
25/4	Braga	h	0-4	
2/5	Sporting	a	1-0	Fábio Júnior
9/5	Académica	h	0-1	

No	Name	Nat	DoB	Pos	Aps	(s)	Gls
19	Sekou BARADJI	FRA	24/4/84	M	6	(6)	
11	Edvaldo Rojas Hermoza "BOLÍVIA"	BRA	17/11/85	A	20	(5)	2
45	Mário Jorge Malico Paulino "CAMORA"		10/11/86	M	27	(2)	1
7	Carlos Pereira Rodrigues "CARLITOS"		5/12/81	D	23	(1)	
6	DANIEL Lopes CRUZ	BRA	1/6/82	D	17		
10	DAVIDE Alexandre Pinto Dias		12/4/83	M	6	(10)	
4	DIEGO ÂNGELO de Oliveira	BRA	12/2/86	D	30		3
28	FÁBIO JÚNIOR dos Santos	BRA	6/10/82	A	10	(3)	3
30	GIULIANO Dias AMARAL	BRA	8/9/80	M	5	(2)	
25	Nicolas GODEMÈCHE	FRA	22/6/84	M	28		1
26	Kevin GOMIS	FRA	20/1/89	M	23		
15	Alexandre HAUW	FRA	22/1/82	M	19	(7)	1
13	JOÃO Daniel Mendes REAL		13/5/83	D	9		1
1	JORGE Carlos Santos Moreira BAPTISTA		2/4/77	G	2		
31	JOSÉ MÁRIO Pinto dos Santos		16/7/89	D	4	(1)	
39	Mehdi KERROUCHE	ALG	11/10/85	M	11	(7)	5
5	Bruno Amorim LAZARONI	BRA	13/9/80	M	24	(1)	
3	Ulick LUPÉDE	FRA	6/1/84	D	2		
77	Mário Rui Correia Tomás "MÁRINHO"		26/4/83	A	17	(11)	1
9	MICHEL SIMPLÍCIO Rossetto	BRA	26/3/86	A	7	(18)	
8	William Moses NKAKE	CMR	13/7/85	M	1		
17	Bourama OUATTARA	FRA	13/9/84	M	3	(6)	
16	Romuald PEISER	FRA	3/8/79	G	28		
22	Aboubacar TANDIA	FRA	3/10/83	A	4	(7)	
2	TIAGO da Silva Rannow	BRA	3/9/82	D	4		

SC OLHANENSE
Coach – Jorge Costa
Founded – 1912
Stadium – José Arcanjo (11,622)

2009				
16/8	Naval	a	0-0	
21/8	Leiria	h	0-0	
31/8	Nacional	a	1-1	Carlos Fernandes
13/9	Académica	h	2-1	Castro, Toy
21/9	Sporting	a	2-3	Rabiola, Castro
25/9	Braga	h	0-1	
4/10	Porto	h	0-3	
23/10	Belenenses	a	0-0	
1/11	Rio Ave	h	0-1	
7/11	Setúbal	h	0-0	
27/11	Guimarães	h	0-2	
6/12	Marítimo	a	2-5	Djalmir, Tengarrinha
12/12	Benfica	h	2-2	Carlos Fernandes, Toy
21/12	Leixões	a	2-2	Rabiola, Castro
2010				
10/1	Paços Ferreira	h	1-1	Zéquinha
16/1	Naval	h	1-0	Castro
30/1	Leiria	a	0-2	
7/2	Nacional	h	1-0	Toy
14/2	Académica	a	1-1	Djalmir
20/2	Sporting	h	0-0	
27/2	Braga	a	1-3	Djalmir
6/3	Porto	a	2-2	Djalmir 2
14/3	Belenenses	h	1-3	Castro
28/3	Rio Ave	a	5-1	Tengarrinha, Djalmir 2 (1p), Yazalde, Rabiola (p)
3/4	Setúbal	h	2-2	Djalmir, Castro
11/4	Guimarães	a	1-1	Ukra (p)
16/4	Marítimo	h	1-2	Djalmir
24/4	Benfica	a	0-5	
2/5	Leixões	h	1-0	Djalmir
9/5	Paços Ferreira	a	2-2	Djalmir 2

No	Name	Nat	DoB	Pos	Aps	(s)	Gls
2	ANSELMO França Almeida	BRA	10/6/81	D	15		
1	BRUNO Miguel Ribeiro VERÍSSIMO		7/4/76	G	2	(2)	
13	CARLOS Miguel Brandão FERNANDES		5/5/78	D	26		2

PORTUGAL

No	Name		DoB	Pos	Aps	(s)	Gls
10	André CASTRO Pereira		2/4/88	A	28		6
27	DELSON Ferreira	BRA	26/7/80	M	9	(2)	
11	DJALMIR Vieira de Andrade	BRA	22/3/76	A	15	(2)	12
4	ÉDER Luiz de Carvalho "BAIANO"	BRA	14/5/84	D	5	(2)	
21	FÁBIO Bruno Assunção Marques		8/10/87	A		(2)	
30	José Augusto Santana dos Santos "GUGA"	BRA	30/4/88	M	1	(3)	
18	JOÃO Pedro Espírito Santo GONÇALVES		18/1/88	M	10		
25	Rodrigo Andrés LAMARDO	ARG	30/4/82	M		(1)	
26	José LIONN Barbosa Lucena	BRA	29/1/89	D	5	(3)	
8	Georges Parfait Mbida MESSI	CMR	8/12/80	M	1	(4)	
49	MIGUEL ÁNGELO Ferreira de Castro		10/10/84	D	13		
15	MIGUEL Ângelo Moita GARCIA		4/2/83	D	11		
19	Greg NWOKOLO	NGA	3/1/86	A	2	(11)	
23	PAULO SÉRGIO Moreira Gonçalves		24/1/84	A	18	(2)	
5	Juan Martín PIETRAVALLO	ARG	7/12/81	M	1	(1)	
29	Tiago André Coelho Lopes "RABIOLA"		25/7/89	A	14	(12)	3
12	RICARDO Abel Barbosa Ferreira		3/12/89	G	1		
7	RUI Miguel Marques BAIÃO		4/9/80	M	22	(1)	
16	RUI Pedro Viegas Silva Gomes DUARTE		16/9/78	M	20		
3	SANDRO Luiz da Silva	BRA	13/3/83	D	16	(1)	
20	STÉPHANE Agbre Dasse	BFA	1/11/89	D	4		
6	Bernardo David Mendes Salgueiro Campos TENGARRINHA		17/2/89	D	20	(3)	2
9	Vítor Manuel Andrade Gomes Costa "TOY"		15/6/77	A	9	(12)	3
17	André Filipe Alves Monteiro "UKRA"		16/3/88	A	28		1
24	Hugo VENTURA Ferreira Moura Guedes		14/1/88	G	27		
22	José Egas dos Santos Branco "ZÉQUINHA"		7/1/87	A	5	(12)	1
14	YAZALDE Gomes Pinto		21/9/88	A	2	(12)	1

FC PAÇOS DE FERREIRA

Coach – Paulo Sérgio; (16/10/09) Ulisses Morais
Founded – 1950
Stadium – Mata Real (5,172)

2009

16/8	Porto	h	1-1	og (Fucile)
22/8	Académica	a	1-1	Pedrinha
29/8	Guimarães	h	0-0	
13/9	Sporting	a	0-1	
19/9	Rio Ave	h	1-1	William
26/9	Setúbal	a	1-0	Maykon
5/10	Benfica	h	1-3	Maykon
25/10	Marítimo	a	1-3	Leonel Olímpio
1/11	Leiria	h	0-1	
6/11	Belenenses	a	3-0	Cristiano 2, William
29/11	Leixões	h	1-1	William
5/12	Naval	a	0-1	
11/12	Nacional	h	2-1	William 2
18/12	Braga	h	0-1	

2010

10/1	Olhanense	a	1-1	William
16/1	Porto	a	1-1	Maykon
31/1	Académica	h	2-1	Ricardo, Romeu
7/2	Guimarães	a	2-1	Ozéia, Maykon
12/2	Sporting	h	0-0	
21/2	Rio Ave	a	2-1	William, Ricardo
28/2	Setúbal	h	5-3	Pizzi, William 2 (1p), Maykon, Danielson
7/3	Benfica	a	1-3	William
15/3	Marítimo	h	1-0	Bruno di Paula
28/3	Leiria	a	1-2	Kelly
3/4	Belenenses	h	0-0	
11/4	Leixões	a	0-2	
17/4	Naval	h	1-3	og (João Real)
25/4	Nacional	a	1-1	Maykon

1/5	Braga	a	0-1	
9/5	Olhanense	h	2-2	Romeu, Candeias

No	Name		Nat	DoB	Pos	Aps	(s)	Gls
50	ANDRÉ Filipe Ribeiro LEÃO			20/5/85	M	1	(4)	
15	Wanderson de Souza Carneiro "BAIANO"		BRA	23/2/87	D	25		
30	BRUNO Flávio DI PAULA		BRA	5/2/89	M	13		1
32	Daniel João Santos CANDEIAS			25/2/88	A	6	(7)	1
37	Carlos Miguel Gomes de Andrade "CARLITOS"			24/9/88	A	1	(15)	
1	CÁSSIO Abuquerque dos Anjos		BRA	12/8/80	G	18		
21	JoCIEL Ferreira da Silva		BRA	31/3/82	M	5	(5)	
84	Júlio Manuel Pires COELHO			18/7/84	G	12		
10	CRISTIANO Moraes de Oliveira		BRA	28/9/83	A	9	(2)	2
4	DANIELSON Ferreira Trindade		BRA	9/1/81	D	28		1
3	Jason Alan DAVIDSON		AUS	29/6/91	D	2	(3)	
28	Abdramane Ladji DIARRA		BFA	9/7/88	A		(1)	
25	FÁBIO José Ferreira PACHECO			26/5/88	M	1	(7)	
96	FILIPE Alexandre Dias ANUNCIAÇÃO			27/5/79	D	25	(1)	
14	Jorge Manuel Amador Galufo "JORGINHO"			29/5/78	D	14		
77	JOSÉ Manuel Barbosa Alves "COELHO"			4/2/90	M		(3)	
17	KELLY Mathurin Berville		FRA	5/1/78	D	8	(3)	1
11	Leandro Barrios Rita dos Mártires "LEANDRINHO"		BRA	6/6/86	A	3	(4)	
16	LEONEL OLÍMPIO		BRA	7/7/82	M	29		1
84	António Fernando Amaro LIVRAMENTO			3/3/82	M	3	(5)	
81	MANUEL JOSÉ Azevedo Vieira			4/2/81	A	13	(2)	
7	MAYKON Daniel Elias Araújo		BRA	20/4/84	D	23	(2)	6
13	Berlin NLOME NDEBI		CMR	28/10/87	A		(3)	
5	OZÉIA de Paula Maciel		BRA	2/1/82	D	15		1
81	José PAULO SOUSA da Silva			13/5/75	M		(2)	
8	Pedro Ricardo Pereira Monteiro "PEDRINHA"			3/5/78	M	12	(2)	1
31	Luís Miguel Afonso Fernandes "PIZZI"			6/10/89	A	10	(5)	1
19	RICARDO Jorge Ferreira Pinto da Silva			19/8/80	D	26		2
20	ROMEU Freitas Torres			7/9/86	M	3	(7)	2
29	Evandro RONCATTO		BRA	24/5/86	A	2	(5)	
18	Mario Junior RONDON Fernández		VEN	26/3/86	A	2	(2)	
9	WILLIAM Artur Conceição dos Santos		BRA	27/7/82	A	21		10

FC PORTO

Coach – Jesualdo Ferreira
Founded – 1893
Stadium – Dragão (50,476)
MAJOR HONOURS:
European Champion Clubs' Cup/UEFA Champions League - (2) 1987, 2004;
UEFA Cup - (1) 2003;
UEFA Super Cup - (1) 1987;
World Club Cup - (2) 1987, 2004;
Portuguese League - (24) 1935, 1939, 1940, 1956, 1959, 1978, 1979, 1985, 1986, 1988, 1990, 1992, 1993, 1995, 1996, 1997, 1998, 1999, 2003, 2004, 2006, 2007, 2008, 2009;
Portuguese Cup - (19) 1922, 1925, 1932, 1937, 1956, 1958, 1968, 1977, 1984, 1988, 1991, 1994, 1998, 2000, 2001, 2003, 2006, 2009, 2010.

2009

16/8	Paços Ferreira	a	1-1	Falcao
23/8	Nacional	h	3-0	Falcao (p), Rolando, Rodríguez
29/8	Naval	a	3-1	Falcao, Varela, Farías
12/9	Leixões	h	4-1	Varela, Hulk (p), Rolando, Falcao
19/9	Braga	a	0-1	
26/9	Sporting	h	1-0	Falcao
4/10	Olhanense	a	3-0	Falcao 2, Bruno Alves
25/10	Académica	h	3-2	Mariano González, Farías 2
30/10	Belenenses	h	1-1	Farías
8/11	Marítimo	a	0-1	
29/11	Rio Ave	h	2-1	Hulk, Varela

4/12	Guimarães	a	4-1	Varela, Falcao, Bruno Alves, Rodríguez
13/12	Setúbal	h	2-0	Farías, Varela
20/12	Benfica	a	0-1	

2010

10/1	Leiria	h	3-2	Falcao 2, Bruno Alves
16/1	Paços Ferreira	h	1-1	Falcao
30/1	Nacional	a	4-0	Varela 2 (1p), Falcao 2
7/2	Naval	h	3-0	Tomás Costa, Falcao, Varela
13/2	Leixões	a	0-0	
21/2	Braga	h	5-1	Raul Meireles, Álvaro Pereira, Falcao 2, Belluschi
28/2	Sporting	a	0-3	
6/3	Olhanense	h	2-2	Falcao, Guarín
13/3	Académica	a	2-1	Bruno Alves, Rodríguez
28/3	Belenenses	a	3-0	Rolando, Hulk, Falcao
3/4	Marítimo	h	4-1	Falcao 2, Raul Meireles, Hulk
10/4	Rio Ave	a	1-0	Farías
18/4	Guimarães	h	3-0	Hulk, Guarín, Falcao
24/4	Setúbal	a	5-2	Falcao 2, Maicon, Guarín, Belluschi
2/5	Benfica	h	3-1	Bruno Alves, Farías, Belluschi
8/5	Leiria	a	4-1	Guarín, Falcao 2, Rodríguez

No	Name	Nat	DoB	Pos	Aps	(s)	Gls
15	ÁLVARO Daniel PEREIRA Barragán	URU	28/11/85	D	28		1
7	Fernando Daniel BELLUSCHI	ARG	10/9/83	M	21	(6)	3
24	António Alberto Bastos Pimparel "BETO"		1/5/82	G	6		
2	BRUNO Eduardo Regufe ALVES		27/11/81	D	27		5
9	Radamel FALCAO García Zárate	COL	10/2/86	A	26	(2)	25
19	Ernesto António FARÍAS	ARG	29/5/80	A	4	(14)	7
25	FERNANDO Francisco Reges	BRA	25/7/87	M	25		
13	Jorge Ciro FUCILE Perdomo	URU	19/11/84	D	21		
6	Freddy Alejandro GUARÍN Vásquez	COL	30/6/86	M	9	(10)	4
1	HÉLTON da Silva Arruda	BRA	18/5/78	G	24		
12	Givanildo Vieira de Souza "HULK"	BRA	25/7/86	A	18	(1)	5
16	MAICON Pereira Roque	BRA	14/9/88	D	4		1
11	MARIANO Nicolás GONZÁLEZ	ARG	5/5/81	A	12	(6)	1
22	Hugo MIGUEL Almeida Costa LOPES		19/12/86	D	8	(4)	
18	NUNO André da Silva COELHO		7/1/86	D	1		
29	ORLANDO Carlos Braga SÁ		26/5/88	A		(2)	
3	RAUL José Trindade MEIRELES		17/3/83	M	24	(1)	2
10	Cristian Gabriel RODRÍGUEZ Barroti	URU	30/9/85	A	10	(8)	4
14	ROLANDO Jorge Pires da Fonseca		31/8/85	D	28		3
28	RÚBEN MICAEL Freitas da Ressurreição		19/8/86	M	10		
21	Ionuț Cristian SĂPUNARU	ROU	5/4/84	D	3	(2)	
20	TOMÁS COSTA	ARG	30/1/85	M	5	(14)	1
8	Diego Hernán VALERI	ARG	1/5/86	M	2	(10)	
17	Silvestre Manuel Gonçalves VARELA		2/2/85	A	14	(4)	8

RIO AVE FC
Coach – Carlos Brito
Founded – 1939
Stadium – Rio Ave (12,815)

2009

16/8	Leiria	a	1-1	Wires (p)
23/8	Setúbal	h	1-0	Bruno Gama
30/8	Leixões	a	0-0	
12/9	Nacional	h	2-0	João Tomás, Vítor Gomes
19/9	Paços Ferreira	a	1-1	Adriano
26/9	Académica	h	0-0	
3/10	Naval	a	2-3	Wires (p), Sidnei
24/10	Braga	h	1-1	João Tomás
1/11	Olhanense	a	1-0	João Tomás
8/11	Sporting	h	2-2	João Tomás 2
29/11	Porto	a	1-2	João Tomás
5/12	Belenenses	h	0-0	
13/12	Marítimo	a	1-0	Gaspar
19/12	Guimarães	a	0-1	

2010

9/1	Benfica	h	0-1	
17/1	Leiria	h	0-2	
31/1	Setúbal	a	2-2	Chidi 2
7/2	Leixões	h	2-0	Bruno Gama 2
14/2	Nacional	a	1-1	Wires
21/2	Paços Ferreira	h	1-2	Fábio Faria
28/2	Académica	h	1-0	Wires
6/3	Naval	h	0-0	
13/3	Braga	a	0-1	
28/3	Olhanense	h	1-5	Vítor Gomes
2/4	Sporting	a	0-5	
10/4	Porto	h	0-1	
18/4	Belenenses	a	0-0	
23/4	Marítimo	h	0-0	
2/5	Guimarães	h	0-0	
9/5	Benfica	a	1-2	Ricardo Chaves

No	Name	Nat	DoB	Pos	Aps	(s)	Gls
17	ADRIANO José de Lara	BRA	9/12/87	A	1	(17)	1
14	ANDRÉ Filipe Monteiro VILAS BOAS		4/6/83	M	24		
11	BRUNO França FOGAÇA	BRA	17/11/81	A	2	(5)	
77	BRUNO Alexandre Vilela GAMA		15/11/87	A	29	(1)	3
20	BRUNO Miguel Sousa Oliveira MENDES		15/3/76	D	1	(1)	
99	BRUNO dos Santos MORAES	BRA	7/7/84	A	4	(4)	
13	CARLOS Alberto Fernandes	ANG	18/12/79	G	28		
15	Philip CHIDI Onyemah	NGA	20/2/84	A	14	(12)	2
4	EVANDRO Carlos Escardalete	BRA	12/2/74	A	1	(5)	
23	FÁBIO do Passo FARIA		24/4/89	D	26	(1)	1
12	FELIPE ALBERTO Silva Anjos		1/1/89	A		(2)	
2	José GASPAR da Silva Azevedo		1/6/75	D	30		1
5	JEFERSON da Silva	BRA	15/1/86	D	3		
9	JOÃO Henrique Pataco TOMÁS		27/5/75	A	15		6
32	MAGNO Machado dos Santos	BRA	16/10/84	D	1		
74	Miguel Abrón Morales	ESP	3/6/74	G	2	(2)	
21	NÉLSON Miguel Castro OLIVEIRA		8/8/91	A	5	(5)	
3	RICARDO Alberto Medeiro CHAVES		27/10/77	M	16	(1)	1
19	SIDNEI Sciola Moraes	BRA	2/11/86	A	18	(6)	1
25	SÍLVIO Manuel Azevedo Ferreira Sá Pereira		28/9/87	D	27		
83	Ricardo José Vaz Monteiro "TARANTINI"		7/10/83	M	9	(13)	
16	TIAGO André Ramos TERROSO		13/1/88	M		(3)	
55	Hugo VALDIR Romão Cardoso		1/1/84	D	1		
10	VÍTOR Hugo GOMES da Silva		25/12/87	M	20	(4)	2
7	António WESLLEM Sousa Monteiro	BRA	21/4/85	M	1	(5)	
30	WIRES José de Souza	BRA	30/12/82	M	25	(2)	4
18	José Manuel "ZÉ" GOMES da Silva		24/9/76	D	27		

SPORTING CLUBE DE PORTUGAL
Coach – Paulo Bento; (6/11/09) (Leonel Pontes);
(15/11/09) Carlos Carvalhal
Founded – 1906
Stadium – José Alvalade (50,466)
MAJOR HONOURS:
UEFA Cup Winners' Cup - (1) 1964;
Portuguese League - (18) 1941, 1944, 1947, 1948, 1949, 1951, 1952, 1953, 1954, 1958, 1962, 1966, 1970, 1974, 1980, 1982, 2000, 2002;
Portuguese Cup - (19) 1923, 1934, 1936, 1938, 1941, 1945, 1946, 1948, 1954, 1963, 1971, 1973, 1974, 1978, 1982, 1995, 2002, 2007, 2008.

2009

15/8	Nacional	a	1-1	og (João Aurélio)
22/8	Braga	h	1-2	Yannick Djaló
30/8	Académica	a	2-0	Liedson, Yannick Djaló
13/9	Paços Ferreira	h	1-0	Liedson
21/9	Olhanense	h	3-2	Daniel Carriço, João Moutinho (p), Vukčević
26/9	Porto	a	0-1	
4/10	Belenenses	h	0-0	
27/10	Guimarães	a	1-1	Matías Fernández
1/11	Marítimo	h	1-1	Matías Fernández

PORTUGAL

8/11	Rio Ave	a	2-2	Matías Fernández, João Moutinho (p)	
28/11	Benfica	h	0-0		
7/12	Setúbal	a	2-0	Liedson 2	
12/12	Leiria	h	0-1		
19/12	Naval	a	1-0	Carlos Saleiro	
2010					
9/1	Leixões	h	1-0	Tonel	
16/1	Nacional	h	3-2	Miguel Veloso, Liedson 2	
29/1	Braga	a	0-1		
6/2	Académica	h	1-2	João Moutinho	
12/2	Paços Ferreira	a	0-0		
20/2	Olhanense	a	0-0		
28/2	Porto	h	3-0	Yannick Djaló, Izmailov, Miguel Veloso	
7/3	Belenenses	a	4-0	Liedson 4	
14/3	Guimarães	h	3-1	Grimi, Liedson, Carlos Saleiro	
26/3	Marítimo	a	2-3	João Pereira, Sinama-Pongolle (p)	
2/4	Rio Ave	h	5-0	Yannick Djaló 3, Liedson, João Moutinho	
13/4	Benfica	a	0-2		
19/4	Setúbal	h	2-1	João Moutinho (p), Hélder Postiga	
25/4	Leiria	a	1-1	Liedson	
2/5	Naval	h	0-1		
8/5	Leixões	a	2-1	Miguel Veloso, Pedro Silva	

No	Name	Nat	DoB	Pos	Aps	(s)	Gls
78	ABEL Fernando Moreira Ferreira		22/12/78	D	18		
6	ADRIEN Sebastian Perruchet SILVA		15/3/89	M	9	(4)	
4	ANDERSON Corrêa POLGA	BRA	9/2/79	D	13	(2)	
55	ANDRÉ Filipe Faria MARQUES		1/8/87	D	6		
17	Miguel Ángel ANGULO Valderrey	ESP	23/6/77	A	3	(1)	
11	Filipe Salvador CAICEDO Corozo	ECU	5/9/88	A	1	(6)	
9	CARLOS Miguel Mondim SALEIRO		25/2/86	A	9	(8)	2
3	DANIEL Filipe Martins CARRIÇO		4/8/88	D	25		1
8	FÁBIO ROCHEMBACK	BRA	10/12/81	M	1		
18	Leandro Damián Marcelo GRIMI	ARG	2/9/85	D	19	(1)	1
23	HÉLDER Manuel Marques POSTIGA		2/8/82	A	11	(11)	1
7	Marat IZMAILOV	RUS	21/9/82	A	12	(1)	1
28	JOÃO Filipe Iria dos Santos MOUTINHO		8/9/86	M	28		5
21	JOÃO Pedro da Silva PEREIRA		25/2/84	D	11	(1)	1
31	LIEDSON da Silva Muniz		17/12/77	A	27	(1)	13
12	MARCO António Simões CANEIRA		9/2/79	D	4	(3)	
14	MATÍAS Ariel FERNÁNDEZ Fernández	CHI	15/5/86	M	13	(15)	3
24	MIGUEL Luís Pinto VELOSO		11/5/86	M	25		3
2	PEDRO Miguel da Silva MENDES		26/2/79	M	11		
5	PEDRO Alves da SILVA	BRA	25/4/81	D	4	(3)	1
25	Bruno Alexandre Marques PEREIRINHA		2/3/88	M	2	(15)	
46	RENATO Cardoso Porto NETO	BRA	27/9/91	M		(1)	
1	RUI Pedro dos Santos PATRÍCIO		15/2/88	G	30		
22	Florent SINAMA-PONGOLLE	FRA	20/10/84	A	2	(3)	1
13	António Leonel Vilar Nogueira de Sousa "TONEL"		13/4/80	D	22	(1)	1
10	Simon VUKČEVIĆ	MNE	29/1/86	A	11	(3)	1
20	YANNICK dos Santos DJALÓ		5/5/86	A	13	(5)	6

UD LEIRIA
Coach – Manuel Fernandes; (21/10/09) Lito Vidigal (ANG)
Founded – 1966
Stadium – Dr. Magalhães Pessoa (23,850)

2009					
16/8	Rio Ave	h	1-1	Carlão	
21/8	Olhanense	a	0-0		
30/8	Marítimo	h	0-0		

13/9	Setúbal	a	4-0	Carlão, Silas, Panandétiguiri (p), Kalaba	
20/9	Benfica	h	1-2	og (David Luiz)	
28/9	Guimarães	a	2-2	Carlão, Vinícius	
4/10	Leixões	a	2-3	Carlão, og (Benítez)	
24/10	Naval	h	2-0	Carlão, Cássio	
1/11	Paços Ferreira	a	1-0	Cássio	
8/11	Académica	h	1-1	Diego Gaúcho	
30/11	Braga	a	0-2		
7/12	Nacional	h	1-2	Pateiro	
12/12	Sporting	a	1-0	Vinícius	
20/12	Belenenses	h	1-0	Cássio	
2010					
10/1	Porto	a	2-3	Diego Gaúcho, Ronny	
17/1	Rio Ave	a	2-0	Cássio, Ronny	
30/1	Olhanense	h	2-0	Silas, Vítor Moreno	
3/2	Benfica	a	0-3		
7/2	Marítimo	a	0-1		
14/2	Setúbal	h	3-3	Cássio 2, Ronny	
26/2	Guimarães	h	0-1		
5/3	Leixões	h	2-1	Marco Soares (p), Carlão	
12/3	Naval	a	0-1		
28/3	Paços Ferreira	h	2-1	Cássio 2	
3/4	Académica	a	0-0		
10/4	Braga	h	1-2	Cássio	
18/4	Nacional	a	0-2		
25/4	Sporting	h	1-1	Cássio	
2/5	Belenenses	a	2-5	Cássio, Marco Soares	
8/5	Porto	h	1-4	Cássio	

No	Name	Nat	DoB	Pos	Aps	(s)	Gls
8	ANDRÉ Filipe Bernardo SANTOS		2/3/89	M	30		
28	Rúben Luís Maurício BRÍGIDO		23/6/91	M	1		
13	BRUNO MIGUEL Moreira de Sousa		24/9/82	D	16		
83	Carlos Alexandre Souza Silva "CARLÃO"	BRA	1/8/86	A	27	(2)	6
99	CÁSSIO Vargas Barbosa	BRA	25/11/83	A	24	(3)	12
81	Pedro Nuno Coelho CERVANTES		13/7/81	A	4	(7)	
3	DIEGO Goldim GAÚCHO	BRA	15/11/81	D	24	(1)	2
24	Andelko ĐURIČIĆ	SRB	21/11/80	G	26		
16	ELIAS Alves da Silva	BRA	4/9/81	M	6	(3)	
1	HELDER Manuel Teles GODINHO		8/9/77	G	4	(1)	
25	HUGO André Viriato dos Santos GOMES		11/10/79	D	15	(2)	
77	JOSÉ ANTÓNIO Santos Silva		14/3/77	D	12	(2)	
75	Rainford KALABA	ZAM	14/8/86	M		(3)	1
9	Seydou KONÉ	CIV	28/2/83	M		(1)	
20	MARCO Paulo da Silva SOARES		16/6/84	M	14	(3)	2
91	MICHAEL Simões Domingues		8/3/91	G		(1)	
7	MIGUEL José PAIXÃO dos Santos		14/3/85	A		(1)	
88	Issouf OUATTARA	BFA	7/10/88	M	1	(11)	
26	Saïdou Mady PANANDÉTIGUIRI	BFA	22/3/84	M	8	(1)	1
4	Ricardo da Costa PATEIRO		31/5/80	M	24		1
80	PATRICK Fabionn Lopes	BRA	20/8/80	D	4		
50	RAFAEL Felipe Bitencourt	BRA	13/4/87	A	2	(5)	
12	RONNY Herberson Furtado de Araújo	BRA	11/5/86	D	10	(7)	3
11	Jorge Manuel Rebelo Fernandes "SILAS"		1/9/76	M	27	(1)	2
23	STÉLVIO Rosa da Cruz	ANG	24/1/89	M	1	(1)	
30	Mamadou TALL	BFA	4/12/82	D	11		
7	TIAGO LUÍS Martins	BRA	13/3/91	A	5	(17)	
5	Paulo VINÍCIUS de Souza Nascimento	BRA	12/8/84	D	29	(1)	2
32	VÍTOR Manuel Borges MORENO		29/11/80	M	5	(9)	1
14	Vjatseslav ZAHOVAIKO	EST	29/12/81	A		(6)	

VITÓRIA FC (SETÚBAL)
Coach – Carlos Azenha; (17/9/09) [Joaquim Serafim]; (21/10/09) Manuel Fernandes
Founded – 1910
Stadium – Bonfim (18,694)
MAJOR HONOURS:
Portuguese Cup - (3) 1965, 1967, 2005.

2009

17/8	Guimarães	h	0-0
23/8	Rio Ave	a	0-1
31/8	Benfica	a	1-8	Hélder Barbosa
13/9	Leiria	h	0-4
20/9	Naval	a	1-0	Kaźmierczak
26/9	Paços Ferreira	h	0-1
3/10	Braga	a	0-2
25/10	Leixões	h	1-0	Keita
1/11	Nacional	a	1-2	Keita (p)
7/11	Olhanense	h	0-0
29/11	Académica	a	0-3
7/12	Sporting	h	0-2
13/12	Porto	a	0-2
20/12	Marítimo	h	3-2	André Pinto, Keita 2

2010

11/1	Belenenses	a	0-0
16/1	Guimarães	a	2-2	Keita, Collin
31/1	Rio Ave	h	2-2	Kaźmierczak (p), Neca
6/2	Benfica	h	1-1	og (David Luiz)
14/2	Leiria	a	3-3	Collin, Kaźmierczak, Henrique
21/2	Naval	h	0-1
28/2	Paços Ferreira	a	3-5	Keita, Hélder Barbosa, Regula
6/3	Braga	h	0-0
14/3	Leixões	a	2-1	Sandro, Keita
28/3	Nacional	h	2-1	Neca, Keita
3/4	Olhanense	a	2-2	Keita 2
12/4	Académica	h	1-1	Henrique
19/4	Sporting	a	1-2	Collin
24/4	Porto	h	2-5	Henrique 2
2/5	Marítimo	a	0-2
8/5	Belenenses	h	1-2	Kaźmierczak (p)

No	Name	Nat	DoB	Pos	Aps	(s)	Gls
31	ALAN Maciel Francisquini	BRA	27/1/83	D	7	(2)	
22	ANDRÉ Almeida PINTO		5/10/89	D	21	(1)	1
20	Adul BALDÉ	GNB	9/4/89	A	1	(2)	
13	Filipe Manuel Nunes BRIGUES		24/7/90	D	1	(1)	
27	BRUNO André Freitas MONTEIRO		5/10/84	M	3	(1)	
11	BRUNO Miguel Fernandes RIBEIRO		22/10/75	M	4	(3)	
2	Aurélien Marcel COLLIN	FRA	8/3/86	D	19		3
12	El Hadji DIOUF	SEN	20/8/88	A		(3)	
14	Mamadou DJIKINÉ	MLI	16/5/87	D	25		
24	Mário Jorge Quintas FELGUEIRAS	G	12/12/86	G	14		
21	Álvaro FERNÁNDEZ Gay	URU	11/10/85	M	6	(3)	
88	GUILHERME Paula Lucrécio	BRA	9/11/86	A	1	(2)	
10	HÉLDER Jorge Leal Rodrigues BARBOSA		25/5/87	A	24	(2)	2
91	HENRIQUE Jesus Bernardo	BRA	19/1/87	A	9	(5)	4
30	IVO Daniel Ferreira Mendonça PINTO		7/1/90	D		(2)	
89	João António Justino dos Santos "JOÃOZINHO"	BRA	3/3/90	A	1	(3)	
5	Przemysław KAŹMIERCZAK	POL	5/5/82	M	20	(8)	4
99	Ladji KEITA	SEN	29/4/83	A	25		10
18	LOURENÇO Miguel Ribeiro Baptista Oliveira Almeida		4/12/79	M	3	(5)	
23	LUÍS CARLOS Teixeira de Oliveira		25/12/82	D	11	(8)	
1	Ricardo Filipe Rodrigues MATOS		15/2/79	G	1		
79	João Alexandre Duarte Ferreira Fernandes "NECA"		31/12/79	M	10	(1)	2
68	Uédson NEY dos Santos	BRA	23/2/81	D	12	(1)	
17	NUNO Filipe Oliveira SANTOS		9/7/78	G	15		
8	Paulo Roberto Costa REGULA		12/3/89	M	4	(7)	1
33	RICARDO Emídio Ramalho SILVA		26/9/75	D	12		
3	RUBEN Alexandre Rocha LIMA		22/10/75	D	22	(2)	
28	RUI Pedro da Rocha FONTE		23/4/90	A	1	(12)	
6	SANDRO Miguel Laranjeira Mendes		4/2/77	M	25	(1)	1
19	Adama François SENE	SEN	30/11/89	D	1	(1)	
55	VASCO Filipe Pinto Quintíno VARÃO		28/7/81	M	3	(4)	
26	Kheireddine ZARABI	ALG	18/2/82	D	16	(3)	
4	Marc André ZORO	CIV	27/12/83	D	13	(7)	

VITÓRIA SC (GUIMARÃES)

Coach – Nelo Vingada; (8/10/09) (Basílio Marques);
(13/10/09) Paulo Sérgio
Founded – 1922
Stadium – D. Afonso Henriques (30,146)

2009

17/8	Setúbal	a	0-0
23/8	Benfica	h	0-1
29/8	Paços Ferreira	a	0-0
13/9	Naval	h	3-0	Roberto, Gustavo, Flávio Meireles
18/9	Leixões	a	1-3	Nuno Assis
28/9	Leiria	h	2-2	Nuno Assis, Roberto
5/10	Nacional	a	0-2
27/10	Sporting	h	1-1	Rui Miguel
2/11	Académica	a	0-2
7/11	Braga	h	1-0	Desmarets
27/11	Olhanense	a	2-0	Nuno Assis, Tiago Targino
4/12	Porto	h	1-4	Andrézinho
14/12	Belenenses	a	1-0	Roberto
19/12	Rio Ave	h	1-0	Andrézinho

2010

9/1	Marítimo	a	1-0	Sereno
16/1	Setúbal	h	2-2	Marquinho, Tiago Targino
30/1	Benfica	a	1-3	Nuno Assis
7/2	Paços Ferreira	h	1-2	Valdomiro
15/2	Naval	a	0-0
20/2	Leixões	h	2-0	Valdomiro, Rui Miguel
26/2	Leiria	a	1-0	Andrézinho (p)
8/3	Nacional	h	2-0	Roberto, Desmarets
14/3	Sporting	a	1-3	Valdomiro
27/3	Académica	h	1-0	Rui Miguel
2/4	Braga	a	2-3	Rui Miguel, Andrézinho (p)
11/4	Olhanense	h	1-1	Rui Miguel
18/4	Porto	a	0-3
26/4	Belenenses	h	2-0	Andrézinho(p), Nuno Assis
2/5	Rio Ave	a	0-0
9/5	Marítimo	h	1-2	Valdomiro

No	Name	Nat	DoB	Pos	Aps	(s)	Gls
79	Domingos ALEXandre Martins Costa		6/9/79	D	20	(2)	
31	André Ricardo Soares "ANDRÉZINHO"	BRA	9/10/81	D	25		
99	BRUNO Martins TELES		1/5/86	D	5	(1)	
7	Carlos Manuel da Silva Cunha "CARLITOS"		6/3/77	A		(4)	
27	CUSTÓDIO Miguel Dias de Castro		24/5/83	M	10	(5)	
20	Yves Hadlei DESMARETS	FRA	17/9/79	M	28		2
99	DOUGLAS de Oliveira	BRA	30/1/86	A	16	(5)	
81	FÁBIO Alexandre Duarte FELÍCIO		2/5/82	A	1	(7)	
26	FLÁVIO Miguel Magalhães de Sousa MEIRELES		3/10/76	M	14	(7)	1
22	GUSTAVO Lazzzaretti Araújo	BRA	9/3/84	D	26		1
80	JOÃO Artur Rocha ALVES		18/8/80	M	19	(3)	
13	JORGE Miguel Dias GONÇALVES		31/10/83	A	6	(11)	
34	LEANDRO da Silva	BRA	11/1/89	D	5		
89	José LIONN Barbosa Lucena	BRA	29/1/90	D		(1)	
39	Marco Aurélio Lubel "MARQUINHO"	BRA	8/7/86	A	8	(11)	1
25	Carlos Alberto Lourenço MILHAZES		17/3/81	D	3	(3)	
18	João Miguel Cunha Teixeira "MORENO"		19/8/81	D	23		
1	NILSON Corrêa Júnior	BRA	26/2/81	G	29		
10	NUNO ASSIS Lopes de Almeida		25/11/77	M	26		5
11	RENAN Fernandes Garcia	BRA	19/6/86	D	3	(2)	
9	ROBERTO Calmon Filho	BRA	2/8/79	A	15	(12)	4
17	RUI MIGUEL Melo Rodrigues		15/11/83	M	12	(9)	5
23	José da Silva SANTANA Carlos	ANG	15/6/83	A		(1)	
4	Henrique SERENO Fonseca		18/5/85	D	8	(1)	1
52	Sérgio Gabriel da Silva Andrade "SERGINHO"		6/12/82	G	1		
8	TIAGO João TARGINO da Silva		6/6/86	A	14	(2)	2
5	VALDOMIRO Duarte Macedo	BRA	6/2/79	D	13		4

PORTUGAL

PROMOTED CLUBS

SC BEIRA-MAR
Coach – José Jardim
Founded – 1922
Stadium – Municipal Aveiro (30,000)
MAJOR HONOURS:
Portuguese Cup - (1) 1998.

PORTIMONENSE SC
Coach – Lito Vidigal; (23/10/09) Luis Carvalho "Litos"
Founded – 1914
Stadium – Municipal (4,961)

SECOND LEVEL FINAL TABLE 2009/10

		Pld	W	D	L	F	A	Pts
1	SC Beira-Mar	30	16	6	8	44	30	54
2	Portimonense SC	30	16	6	8	43	34	54
3	CD Feirense	30	14	10	6	37	24	52
4	CD Santa Clara	30	13	12	5	45	29	51
5	UD Oliveirense	30	14	7	9	38	27	49
6	CD Trofense	30	13	6	11	44	45	45
7	FC Penafiel	30	10	11	9	35	34	41
8	CD Fátima	30	8	14	8	31	31	38
9	CD Aves	30	9	11	10	33	33	38
10	Gil Vicente FC	30	9	11	10	36	32	38
11	GD Estoril Praia	30	7	14	9	26	29	35
12	SC Freamunde	30	9	8	13	43	50	35
13	Varzim SC	30	6	13	11	25	38	31
14	SC Covilhã	30	7	9	14	35	49	30
15	GD Chaves	30	6	10	14	28	37	28
16	AD Carregado	30	6	6	18	26	47	24

DOMESTIC CUP 2009/10

TAÇA DE PORTUGAL
THIRD ROUND
(17/10/09)
Monsanto 0, Benfica 6
Porto 4, Sertanense 0
Sporting Covilhã 0, Braga 1
Valenciano 1, Olhanense 1 *(aet; 4-2 on pens)*
Varzim 1, Nacional 2
(18/10/09)
Académica 2, Portimonense 1
Aliados Lordelo 2, Machico 0 *(aet)*
Atlético 0, Setúbal 2
Beira Mar 4, Torre Moncorvo 0
Belenenses 3, Oriental 1
Camacha 3, Paredes 1
Cruzado Canicense 1, Vigor Mocidade 4
Fátima 3, Vila Meã 0
Freamunde 3, Carregado 0
Gil Vicente 6, Nelas 1
Guimarães 3, Feirense 1
Guinfães 1, Pescadores Caparica 3
Leça 0, Chaves 3
Leixões 2, Casa Paia 1
Merelinense 1, Leiria 2
Naval 1, Padroense 0 *(aet)*
Oeiras 6, Operário 1
Paços Ferreira 3, Aljustrelense 1
Rio Ave 2, Esmoriz 1

Santa Clara 2, Marítimo 1
Sintrense 1, Pinhalnovense 1 *(aet; 2-3 on pens)*
Sporting 3, Penafiel 0
Tirsense 1, Oliveira do Bairro 0
Tondela 1, Oliveirense 2
União da Serra 3, Coimbrões 2
União Madeira 2, Alcians 0
(4/11/09)
Vieira 0, Mafra 1
FOURTH ROUND
(22/11/09)
Académica 1, Beira Mar 1 *(aet; 2-4 on pens)*
Aliados Lordelo 1, Leixões 0
Benfica 0, Guimarães 1
Braga 3, Setúbal 0
Camacha 1, Vigor Mocidade 0
Chaves 2, União da Serra 0
Freamunde 2, Leiria 2 *(aet; 5-4 on pens)*
Mafra 1, União Madeira 1 *(aet; 3-2 on pens)*
Nacional 0, Fátima 0 *(aet; 4-3 on pens)*
Naval 3, Gil Vicente 2 *(aet)*
Oeiras 1, Pinhalnovense 2
Pescadores Caparica 1, Sporting 4
Rio Ave 1, Santa Clara 0
Tirsense 0, Paços Ferreira 0 *(aet; 9-10 on pens)*
Valenciano 0, Belenenses 1
(2/1/10)
Oliveirense 0, Porto 2
FIFTH ROUND
(20/1/10)
Aliados Lordelo 0, Naval 1
Belenenses 2, Porto 2 *(aet; 9-10 on pens)*
Camacha 0, Pinhalnovense 1
Freamunde 1, Braga 3
Nacional 1, Paços Ferreira 2
Rio Ave 2, Guimarães 2 *(aet; 4-2 on pens)*
Sporting 4, Mafra 3
(24/1/10)
Chaves 1, Beira Mar 0
QUARTER-FINALS
(2/2/10)
Porto 5 *(Rolando 18, Falcao 34, 42, Varela 48, Mariano González 58)*,
Sporting 2 *(Izmailov 22, Liedson 90)*
(3/2/10)
Braga 0, Rio Ave 0 *(aet; 5-6 on pens)*
Pinhalnovense 1 *(Diego 7)*, Naval 3 *(Fábio Júnior 58, Bolívia 82, Tandia 88)*
(4/2/10)
Paços Ferreira 1 *(William 64)*, Chaves 2 *(Diop 2, Carlos Pinto 10)*
SEMI-FINALS
(23/3/10 & 13/4/10)
Chaves 1 *(Ricardo Rocha 90)*, Naval 0
Naval 1 *(Fábio Júnior 15)*, Chaves 2 *(Edu 109, 119)* *(aet)*
(Chaves 3-1)
(24/3/10 & 14/4/10)
Rio Ave 1 *(Bruno Moraes 37)*, Porto 3 *(Rúben Micael 20, Raúl Meireles 54, Guarín 77)*
Porto 4 *(Belluschi 21, Guarín 79, Rúben Micael 86, Falcao 90)*, Rio Ave 0
(Porto 7-1)
FINAL
(16/5/10)
Estádio Nacional, Lisbon
FC PORTO 2 *(Guarín 13, Falcao 23)*
GD CHAVES 1 *(Clemente 85)*
Referee – Pedro Proença
PORTO – Hélton, Miguel Lopes *(Rodríguez 62)*, Rolando, Bruno Alves,
Álvaro Pereira, Fernando, Belluschi, Raúl Meireles *(Tomás Costa 46)*,
Guarín *(Valeri 72)*, Hulk, Falcao.
Sent off: Bruno Alves *(90)*.
CHAVES – Rui Rego, Danilo, Lameirão, Ricardo Rocha, Eduardo, Bamba,
Edu, Bruno Magalhães, Castanheira *(Flávio Igor 61)*, Samson *(Diego 61)*, Diop *(Clemente78)*.
Sent off: Ricardo Rocha *(90)*.

Tight title race eclipsed by controversy

Controversy and scandal hit Irish football hard in 2009, not least with the elimination of the national team from the 2010 FIFA World Cup after an aggregate defeat in the qualifying play-off by France decided by an extra-time goal in Paris that will forever be referred to as the 'Hand of Henry'. On the domestic front, the big story was the sad demise of two of the country's most successful and popular clubs, Cork City FC and Derry City FC.

On the positive side, League of Ireland fans were treated to a good old-fashioned title race between Dublin rivals Bohemian FC and Shamrock Rovers FC. Although Rovers got off to a slow start, their season was kick-started in May when two late Gary Twigg goals overturned a 1-0 deficit at home to Bohemians. It was the catalyst for a 22-game unbeaten run which, driven by the goals of Scotsman Twigg, kept Rovers in touch. Bohemians, with the goals of Jason Byrne, the excellence of goalkeeper Brian Murphy and the quality of defenders Conor Powell and Ken Oman and midfielders Paul Keegan and Gary Deegan, continued to set the pace. Rovers sneaked a 1-0 win over their rivals in October to leapfrog temporarily into first place, but a home defeat to Cork allowed Bohs to retake the lead and, eventually, to retain the title.

Five for Fenlon

Bohemians' triumph – the first time the club had ever won two titles in a row - brought manager Pat Fenlon his fifth title in seven seasons (three of them with Shelbourne FC), promoting interest from – but ultimately no move to - Scottish Premier League side Dundee United FC. Although they finished second, Shamrock Rovers were entitled to be pleased with their first season at their long-awaited permanent new home in Tallaght. The community-owned club enjoyed strong attendances, a high-profile visit from Real Madrid CF, and a genuine title challenge.

No sooner had the league season ended than Derry City, who had finished fourth, were expelled for illegally holding dual contracts with their players. This affected the relegation battle. Bray Wanderers AFC, who had struggled all season, thus moved out of the automatic relegation slot and competed instead in the play-off against Drogheda United FC (sparing Galway United FC the ordeal). Drogheda won 2-0, and Bray went on to lose to First Division Sporting Fingal FC in the subsequent promotion/relegation play-off. But that was not the end of the story.

At the other end of the country Cork City stumbled from one crisis to the next. Taken into receivership in late 2008, the season became a series of failed payments to players and court cases from creditors. Owner Tom Coughlan was banned as the Football Association of Ireland (FAI) sought to engineer a solution that could keep Premier Division football in the second city. The sorry tale finally came to an end weeks before the start of the 2010 season when the club were wound up by the courts. Bray were thus given a last-minute reprieve and replaced Cork in the Premier Division.

Republic of Ireland goalkeeper Shay Given leads the protests as the 'Hand of Henry' strikes in the Stade de France

 **REPUBLIC OF IRELAND**

Dundalk benefit

2009 top-flight newcomers Dundalk FC achieved an unwanted record as they collected a remarkable 20 red cards. The physical, committed nature of Sean Connor's side was exemplified in one game against Sligo Rovers FC, when they played half an hour with eight men but still held out for a draw. Finishing fifth, Dundalk benefited from Derry's and Cork's troubles, inheriting a UEFA Europa League place.

A thrilling First Division title race went to the wire, with University College Dublin AFC's fine football under manager Martin Russell eventually seeing them to the title. Shelbourne and Sporting Fingal, who had both pushed UCD all the way, faced off in an all-Dublin play-off. Fingal did not allow the prospect of an upcoming FAI Cup final appearance to distract them, defeating Shelbourne then Bray to clinch promotion just two seasons after their formation. Liam Buckley's side then completed a remarkable double, coming from behind to beat Sligo in the Cup final. Two goals in the last seven minutes gave Fingal a 2-1 win, the FAI Cup and a place in the UEFA Europa League.

The League of Ireland's 2009/10 European representatives put on a spirited show, with Bohemians coming within two minutes of knocking FC Salzburg out of the UEFA Champions League and Saint Patrick's Athletic FC putting their domestic troubles aside to enjoy a wonderful run in the UEFA Europa League, highlighted by a captivating away-goals success against Russia's PFC Krylya Sovetov Samara.

The Republic of Ireland's seemingly inevitable run to the World Cup qualifying play-offs was confirmed in their penultimate group game at home to Italy. After a laboured 2-1 win in Cyprus, Giovanni Trapattoni's side retained some hope of topping the group, but an

Cumann Peile na hÉireann/Football Association of Ireland (FAI)

National Sports Campus
Abbotstown
IE-Dublin 15
tel - +353 1 8999500
fax - +353 1 8999501
website - fai.ie
email - info@fai.ie
Year of Formation - 1921

Chairman - David Blood
General Secretary - John Delaney
Media Officer - Peter Sherrard
National Stadium - Dublin Arena, Dublin (50,000)

INTERNATIONAL TOURNAMENT APPEARANCES
FIFA World Cup - (3) 1990 (qtr-finals),
1994 (2nd round), 2002 (2nd round).
UEFA European Championship - (1) 1988.
TOP FIVE ALL-TIME CAPS
Shay Given & Kevin Kilbane (103); Stephen Staunton (102);
Robbie Keane (99); Niall Quinn (91)
TOP FIVE ALL-TIME GOALS
Robbie Keane (43); Niall Quinn (21); Frank Stapleton (20);
John Aldridge, Tony Cascarino & Don Givens (19)

entertaining 2-2 draw with the world champions at Croke Park, in which the visitors grabbed a last-gasp equaliser, saw Italy through and Ireland into the play-offs. With the late announcement by FIFA that teams would be seeded, Ireland found themselves paired with 2006 runners-up France.

Agonising exit

Raymond Domenech's team had the better of the first leg in Dublin, winning 1-0. Consequently, there was no place for Trapattoni's usual safety-first tactics in the return at the Stade de France. Forced on to the offensive, Ireland rose splendidly to the challenge. Record scorer Robbie Keane's fine strike levelled the tie, but chances were

NATIONAL TEAM RESULTS 2009/10

12/8/09	Australia	H	Limerick	0-3	
5/9/09	Cyprus (WCQ)	A	Nicosia	2-1	Doyle (5), Keane (83)
8/9/09	South Africa	H	Limerick	1-0	Lawrence (37)
10/10/09	Italy (WCQ)	H	Dublin	2-2	Whelan (8), St Ledger (87)
14/10/09	Montenegro (WCQ)	H	Dublin	0-0	
14/11/09	France (WCQ)	H	Dublin	0-1	
18/11/09	France (WCQ)	A	Saint-Denis	1-1	Keane (33) (aet)
2/3/10	Brazil	N	London (ENG)	0-2	
25/5/10	Paraguay	H	Dublin	2-1	Doyle (7), Lawrence (39)
28/5/10	Algeria	H	Dublin	3-0	Green (31), Keane (52, 85p)

NATIONAL TEAM APPEARANCES 2009/10

Coach – Giovanni TRAPATTONI (ITA) 17/3/39			Aus	CYP	Rsa	ITA	MNE	FRA	FRA	Bra	Par	Alg	Caps	Goals
Shay GIVEN	20/4/76	Man. City (ENG)	G68	G		G	G	G	G	G			103	-
John O'SHEA	30/4/81	Man. United (ENG)	D	D		D	s40	D	D67		D	D36	62	1
Sean ST LEDGER	28/12/84	Preston (ENG)	D	D	D	D	D	D	D	D	D	D	12	1
Richard DUNNE	21/9/79	Man. City (ENG)	D											
		/Aston Villa (ENG)		D		D	D	D	D				58	7
Kevin KILBANE	1/2/77	Hull (ENG)	D63	D		D	D	D	D				103	7
Damien DUFF	2/3/79	Newcastle (ENG)	M46											
		/Fulham (ENG)		M	s78	M	M76	M	M57	M77	M65		83	7
Glenn WHELAN	13/1/84	Stoke (ENG)	M	M		M70		M	M63	M57	M69	M75	20	2
Darron GIBSON	25/10/87	Man. United (ENG)	M63	M						s63	s57		9	-
Aiden McGEADY	4/4/86	Celtic (SCO)	M82	s67		M78		s76	s107	s57			32	-
Robbie KEANE	8/7/80	Tottenham (ENG)	A	A		A	A	A	A	A63		A	99	43
		/Celtic (SCO)									A			
Kevin DOYLE	18/9/83	Wolves (ENG)	A46	A75	A59	A67		A71	A	A78	A87	A72	35	8
Caleb FOLAN	26/10/82	Hull (ENG)	s46	s75	A								7	-
Stephen HUNT	1/8/81	Reading (ENG)	s46											
		/Hull (ENG)		M67			s78	M88	s80				25	1
Keith ANDREWS	13/9/80	Blackburn (ENG)	s63	M	M	M		M	M	M	M	s75	15	1
Eddie NOLAN	5/8/88	Preston (ENG)	s63		D								3	-
Keiren WESTWOOD	23/10/84	Coventry (ENG)	s68		G						G	G86	5	-
Shane LONG	22/1/87	Reading (ENG)	s82								s87	s86	13	3
Stephen KELLY	6/9/83	Fulham (ENG)		D						D	D	D	18	-
Paul McSHANE	6/1/86	Hull (ENG)		D62		D		s67		D	D		22	-
Liam LAWRENCE	14/12/81	Stoke (ENG)		M		M		M80	M107	M69	M82	M86	8	2
Andy KEOGH	16/5/86	Wolves (ENG)				M78	s88						13	1
Leon BEST	19/9/86	Coventry (ENG)				s59	s67	s69	s71					
		/Newcastle (ENG)								s78			7	-
Darren O'DEA	4/2/87	Reading (ENG)				s62								
		/Celtic (SCO)										s36	2	-
Martin ROWLANDS	8/2/79	QPR (ENG)					s70	M40					5	-
Liam MILLER	13/2/81	Hibernian (SCO)					M						21	1
Noel HUNT	26/12/82	Reading (ENG)						A69					3	-
James McCARTHY	12/11/90	Wigan (ENG)								s69			1	-
Cillian SHERIDAN	23/2/89	Celtic (SCO)									s63	s72	2	-
Paul GREEN	10/4/83	Derby (ENG)									s69	M	2	1
Keith FAHEY	15/1/83	Birmingham (ENG)									s77	s65	2	-
Kevin FOLEY	1/11/84	Wolves (ENG)									s82		2	-
Greg CUNNINGHAM	31/1/91	Man. City (ENG)										D	1	-
Joe MURPHY	21/8/81	Scunthorpe (ENG)										s86	2	-

squandered thereafter to wrap up the tie against strangely subdued opponents, and with the team's momentum stalling in extra time, there was an air of inevitability about the outcome - if not about the manner of the goal that would decide the tie, French striker Thierry Henry twice handling the ball (out of sight of the match officials) before setting up a close-range header for William Gallas. It was an awful way to be eliminated, with the players involved all but inconsolable. However, subsequent attempts by the Irish authorities, including the government, to right the apparent wrong with FIFA did the country no favours, diluting much of the widespread international sympathy that had accompanied the team's agonising exit.

DOMESTIC LEAGUE 2009

LEAGUE OF IRELAND PREMIER DIVISION FINAL TABLE

		Pld	Home					Away					Total					Pts
			W	D	L	F	A	W	D	L	F	A	W	D	L	F	A	
1	Bohemian FC	36	14	2	2	39	8	10	3	5	23	13	24	5	7	62	21	77
2	Shamrock Rovers FC	36	11	4	3	29	16	10	6	2	22	11	21	10	5	51	27	73
3	Cork City FC	36	9	4	5	16	11	8	5	5	26	17	17	9	10	42	28	60
4	Derry City FC	36	8	3	7	21	16	10	2	6	28	15	18	5	13	49	31	59
5	Dundalk FC	36	7	3	8	22	19	5	5	8	24	32	12	8	16	46	51	44
6	Sligo Rovers FC	36	7	3	8	21	26	4	7	7	20	25	11	10	15	41	51	43
7	Saint Patrick's Athletic FC	36	7	3	8	18	25	6	1	11	11	21	13	4	19	29	46	43
8	Galway United FC	36	7	3	8	19	25	5	3	10	17	32	12	6	18	36	57	42
9	Drogheda United FC	36	3	7	8	18	23	4	4	10	14	27	7	11	18	32	50	32
10	Bray Wanderers AFC	36	3	7	8	20	26	3	3	12	10	30	6	10	20	30	56	28

N.B. Derry City FC were expelled from the league at the end of the season for holding dual contracts with their players. As a result Bray Wanderers AFC were saved from automatic relegation and Galway United FC were saved from the relegation playoffs. Cork City FC were subsequently denied a Premier Division licence for the 2010 season. As a result Bray Wanderers AFC were once again saved from relegation.

TOP GOALSCORERS

24 Gary TWIGG (Shamrock Rovers)
22 Jason BYRNE (Bohemians)
15 Rafael CRETARO (Sligo)
12 Chris TURNER (Dundalk)
10 Mark FARREN (Derry)
8 Fahrudin KUDOZOVIĆ (Cork)
  Dessie BAKER (Shamrock Rovers)
7 Killian BRENNAN (Bohemians)
  Billy DENNEHY (Cork)
  Gareth McGLYNN (Derry)
  James CHAMBERS (Drogheda)
  Alex WILLIAMS (Dundalk)
  Ryan GUY (St Patrick's)

CLUB-BY-CLUB

BOHEMIAN FC

Manager – Pat Fenlon
Founded – 1890
Stadium – Dalymount Park (7,955)
MAJOR HONOURS:
League of Ireland – (11) 1924, 1928, 1930, 1934, 1936, 1975, 1978, 2001, 2003 (spring), 2008, 2009;
Irish Cup – (1) 1908;
FAI Cup – (7) 1928, 1935, 1970, 1976, 1992, 2001, 2008.

2009

6/3	Dundalk	a	1-0	Ndo
13/3	Derry	h	1-1	Brennan
20/3	Shamrock Rovers	h	2-0	Byrne J. 2 (1p)
27/3	Drogheda	a	1-0	Murphy A.
3/4	Cork	h	0-1	
7/4	Galway	a	2-0	Byrne J. 2
11/4	St Patrick's	h	3-0	Crowe, Carey, Byrne J.
18/4	Sligo	a	0-0	
24/4	Bray	h	2-0	Brennan, Byrne J.
1/5	Dundalk	h	5-0	Crowe, Byrne J. 4 (1p)
8/5	Derry	a	2-3	Keegan, Murphy A.
16/5	Shamrock Rovers	a	1-2	Byrne J. (p)
22/5	Drogheda	h	1-0	Hughes
29/5	Cork	a	1-0	Byrne J.
2/6	Galway	h	2-0	Oman, Byrne J. (p)
5/6	St Patrick's	a	1-3	Heary
19/6	Sligo	h	2-0	Deegan, Byrne J. (p)
3/7	Bray	a	3-1	Deegan, Byrne J. (p), Brennan
10/7	Dundalk	a	2-0	Crowe, Brennan
19/7	Derry	h	1-0	Byrne J.
26/7	Shamrock Rovers	h	0-0	
31/7	Drogheda	a	1-1	Fenn
7/8	Cork	h	1-0	Brennan
11/8	St Patrick's	a	2-0	Oman 2
21/8	Galway	h	5-0	Murphy A., Oman, Crowe, Brennan (p), Shelley
1/9	Sligo	a	0-1	
4/9	Bray	h	1-2	Crowe
18/9	Dundalk	h	3-2	Keegan, Byrne J. 2
29/9	Derry	a	1-0	Madden
2/10	Shamrock Rovers	a	0-1	
9/10	Drogheda	h	4-0	Byrne J., Ndo, Powell, Crowe
16/10	Cork	a	2-0	Oman, og (Long)
20/10	St Patrick's	h	3-1	Byrne J., Oman, Brennan
23/10	Galway	a	2-0	Madden 2
30/10	Sligo	h	3-1	Madden, Ndo, Byrne J.
6/11	Bray	a	1-1	Byrne J.

Name	Nat	DoB	Pos	Aps	(s)	Gls
Killian BRENNAN		31/1/84	M	27	(7)	7
Jason BYRNE		23/2/78	A	32	(2)	22
Sean BYRNE		13/7/89	D		(2)	
Graham CAREY		2/5/89	M	10	(5)	1
Glenn CRONIN		14/9/81	M	22	(4)	
Glen CROWE		25/12/77	A	18	(12)	6

Gary DEEGAN	28/9/87	M	19	(4)	2
Neale FENN	18/1/77	A	6	(15)	1
Matt GREGG	ENG 30/11/78	G	1	(1)	
Owen HEARY	4/10/76	D	17	(3)	1
Mark HUGHES	15/12/89	A		(3)	1
Paul KEEGAN	5/7/84	M	32	(2)	2
Patrick MADDEN	4/3/90	A	13	(5)	4
Ryan McEVOY	19/7/90	M		(1)	
Jason McGUINNESS	8/8/82	D	11	(3)	
Anto MURPHY	1/8/82	M	22	(8)	3
Brian MURPHY	7/5/83	G	35		
Joseph NDO	CMR 28/4/76	M	28	(2)	3
Ken OMAN	29/7/82	D	25	(1)	6
Conor POWELL	26/8/87	D	28	(1)	1
Mark ROSSITER	27/5/83	D	16	(6)	
Brian SHELLEY	15/11/81	M	34		1

BRAY WANDERERS AFC
Manager – Eddie Gormley
Founded – 1942
Stadium – Carlisle Grounds (7,000)
MAJOR HONOURS:
FAI Cup – (2) 1990, 1999.

2009

6/3	Shamrock Rovers	h	0-0	
13/3	Drogheda	a	0-0	
20/3	Galway	h	2-2	Kavanagh, McCabe (p)
27/3	Cork	a	1-2	Mulcahy
3/4	St Patrick's	h	2-1	Kelly (p), Byrne
7/4	Sligo	a	1-2	Byrne
10/4	Dundalk	h	1-1	Kelly (p)
17/4	Derry	h	1-1	McCabe
24/4	Bohemians	a	0-2	
2/5	Shamrock Rovers	a	1-0	Massey
8/5	Drogheda	h	0-1	
15/5	Galway	a	0-3	
22/5	Cork	h	0-2	
29/5	St Patrick's	a	1-1	Mulcahy
2/6	Sligo	h	3-1	Doyle, Coughlan, McCabe (p)
5/6	Dundalk	a	0-3	
19/6	Derry	a	0-2	
3/7	Bohemians	h	1-3	Shields
10/7	Shamrock Rovers	h	1-2	Mulcahy
17/7	Drogheda	a	2-1	og (Ryan), McCabe
24/7	Galway	h	1-2	O'Neill S.
31/7	Cork	a	0-1	
11/8	Dundalk	a	0-0	
21/8	Sligo	h	2-2	Massey, McCabe
28/8	Derry	h	0-1	
4/9	Bohemians	a	2-1	Flood, McCabe
19/9	Shamrock Rovers	a	1-3	Webster
25/9	Drogheda	h	1-2	Massey
28/9	St Patrick's	h	0-1	
2/10	Galway	a	1-3	Massey
9/10	Cork	h	3-2	Kelly (p), Mulcahy 2
13/10	Sligo	a	0-1	
16/10	St Patrick's	a	0-2	
20/10	Dundalk	h	1-1	Kelly (p)
30/10	Derry	a	0-3	
6/11	Bohemians	h	1-1	Reyes

No	Name	Nat	DoB	Pos	Aps	(s)	Gls
	Stephen BRENNAN		26/3/83	D	26	(1)	
	Paul BYRNE		19/5/86	A	21	(3)	2
	Gareth COUGHLAN		2/5/90	M	13	(10)	1
	Gary CRONIN		16/3/79	M	6		
	Chris DEANS		5/1/85	D	23	(1)	
	Daire DOYLE		18/10/80	M	18	(4)	1
	John FLOOD		16/1/84	A	17	(2)	1
	Derek FORAN		9/10/89	D	24	(1)	

Darren FORSYTH	21/2/88	A	3	(6)	
Brian KANE	6/7/90	G	1		
Patrick KAVANAGH	29/12/85	M	12	(1)	1
Jake KELLY	18/6/90	A	18	(10)	4
Philip KNIGHT	18/9/90	D	5	(2)	
Dane MASSEY	17/4/88	D	28	(6)	4
Gary McCABE	1/8/88	M	29	(1)	6
Ian McNEILL	6/7/90	M		(2)	
Dave MULCAHY	28/1/78	M	25	(2)	5
John MULROY	27/12/87	A	4	(24)	
Chris O'CONNOR	AUS 7/5/85	G	35		
David O'NEILL	17/8/90	M	7	(5)	
Shane O'NEILL	9/1/89	A	3	(3)	1
Derek PENDER	2/10/84	D	23		
Alejandro REYES	MEX 16/6/88	D	2		1
Daryl ROBSON	ENG 18/2/89	M	3		
Chris SHIELDS	27/12/90	D	24	(6)	1
Colm TRESSON	29/6/71	D	1	(5)	
Ian TUOHY	18/6/90	D	1	(2)	
Dave WEBSTER	8/9/89	D	24	(5)	1

CORK CITY FC
Manager – Paul Doolin
Founded – 1984
Stadium – Turner's Cross (7,485)
MAJOR HONOURS:
League of Ireland – (2) 1993, 2005;
FAI Cup – (2) 1998, 2007.

2009

7/3	Sligo	a	1-1	Dennehy
13/3	St Patrick's	h	0-1	
20/3	Derry	a	1-2	Silagailis
27/3	Bray	h	2-1	Silagailis 2
3/4	Bohemians	a	1-0	O'Neill
7/4	Drogheda	h	1-0	Behan
10/4	Shamrock Rovers	a	1-1	Healy
17/4	Dundalk	a	2-1	Dennehy, Behan
24/4	Galway	h	1-0	Dennehy
1/5	Sligo	h	1-0	Kudozović
9/5	St Patrick's	a	3-0	Behan, O'Halloran, Kudozović
15/5	Derry	h	1-0	Murray
22/5	Bray	a	2-0	Behan, Healy
29/5	Bohemians	h	0-1	
2/6	Drogheda	a	1-2	Murray
5/6	Shamrock Rovers	h	0-0	
19/6	Dundalk	h	1-2	Behan
3/7	Galway	a	2-0	Silagailis, Kudozović
7/7	St Patrick's	h	0-1	
12/7	Sligo	a	3-0	Murphy, Kudozović, Sullivan
26/7	Derry	a	1-1	Duggan S.
31/7	Bray	h	1-0	Kudozović (p)
7/8	Bohemians	a	0-1	
11/8	Shamrock Rovers	h	0-0	
21/8	Drogheda	a	1-2	og (McGill E.)
4/9	Galway	h	4-2	O'Neill 2, Dennehy, Cambridge
12/9	Dundalk	a	0-1	
25/9	St Patrick's	a	1-1	O'Neill
29/9	Sligo	h	0-0	
6/10	Derry	h	2-0	Kudozović (p), Dennehy
9/10	Bray	a	2-3	Murray, Kudozović (p)
16/10	Bohemians	h	0-2	
20/10	Shamrock Rovers	a	2-1	Dennehy, Duggan S.
23/10	Drogheda	h	0-0	
30/10	Dundalk	h	2-1	Long, Kudozović (p)
6/11	Galway	a	2-2	O'Neill, Dennehy

No	Name	Nat	DoB	Pos	Aps	(s)	Gls
21	Denis BEHAN		2/1/84	A	17	(3)	5
27	Gareth CAMBRIDGE		5/4/88	A	9	(2)	1
15	Dan CONNOR		31/1/81	G	28		

11	Billy DENNEHY	17/2/87	M	27	(2)	7
22	Craig DUGGAN	5/4/90	A		(3)	
18	Shane DUGGAN	3/1/89	M	6	(8)	2
8	Joe GAMBLE	14/1/82	M	22	(1)	
7	Colin HEALY	14/3/80	M	20	(2)	2
2	Neal HORGAN	29/11/79	D	17	(3)	
17	Tim KIELY	7/3/89	A	4	(9)	
10	Fahrudin KUDOZOVIĆ	BIH 10/10/84	M	26	(6)	8
26	Kevin LONG	18/8/90	M	15	(1)	1
14	Cillian LORDAN	6/7/82	M	23	(3)	
16	Mark McNULTY	13/10/80	G	8		
4	Roberts MEŽECKIS	LVA 29/1/81	D	3		
4	Stephen MULCAHY	9/7/87	M	4	(2)	
3	Danny MURPHY	4/12/82	D	32		1
6	Dan MURRAY	ENG 16/5/82	D	33		3
19	Alan O'CONNOR	18/8/83	M	1	(3)	
24	Stephen O'DONNELL	15/1/86	M	16	(4)	
5	Greg O'HALLORAN	6/9/80	D	29	(1)	1
25	Davin O'NEILL	22/6/83	M	16	(5)	5
9	Guntars SILAGAILIS	LVA 31/8/84	A	23	(7)	4
23	Pat SULLIVAN	30/10/82	D	17		1

DERRY CITY FC
Manager – Stephen Kenny
Founded – 1928
Stadium – The Brandywell (8,200)
MAJOR HONOURS:
Irish League – (1) 1965;
League of Ireland – (2) 1989, 1997;
Irish Cup – (3) 1949, 1954, 1964;
FAI Cup – (4) 1989, 1995, 2002 (autumn), 2006.

2009

6/3	Drogheda	h	1-0	*Farren*
13/3	Bohemians	a	1-1	*Stewart*
20/3	Cork	h	2-1	*Martyn, Nash*
27/3	Shamrock Rovers	a	2-1	*Stewart, Martyn*
3/4	Galway	h	1-1	*Stewart*
7/4	St Patrick's	a	3-0	*Stewart, McGlynn, Martyn*
10/4	Sligo	h	1-2	*McGlynn*
17/4	Bray	a	1-1	*Martyn*
24/4	Dundalk	h	0-1	
1/5	Drogheda	a	3-0	*Farren 3*
8/5	Bohemians	h	3-2	*Stewart, Farren, Molloy*
15/5	Cork	a	0-1	
22/5	Shamrock Rovers	h	0-0	
28/5	Galway	a	3-0	*Morrow 2 (1p), Scullion*
2/6	St Patrick's	h	1-0	*McGlynn*
5/6	Sligo	a	1-0	*Morrow*
19/6	Bray	h	2-0	*Deery, Farren*
3/7	Dundalk	a	0-1	
10/7	Drogheda	h	0-1	
19/7	Bohemians	a	0-1	
26/7	Cork	h	1-1	*og (Murray)*
2/8	Shamrock Rovers	a	1-2	*McManus*
11/8	Sligo	a	4-0	*Scullion, Hutton, Farren 2*
23/8	St Patrick's	h	1-0	*Martyn*
28/8	Bray	a	1-0	*McGlynn*
1/9	Galway	h	1-3	*McClean*
4/9	Dundalk	h	3-0	*Stewart, McManus, Kearney*
18/9	Drogheda	a	3-1	*Farren 2, McManus*
29/9	Bohemians	h	0-1	
6/10	Cork	a	0-2	
9/10	Shamrock Rovers	h	0-1	
16/10	Galway	a	1-3	*McGlynn*
20/10	Sligo	h	1-2	*McDaid*
23/10	St Patrick's	a	2-0	*McGlynn, McDaid*
30/10	Bray	h	3-0	*McDaid, Delaney, og (Mulcahy)*
6/11	Dundalk	a	2-1	*McGlynn (p), Delaney*

No	Name	Nat	DoB	Pos	Aps	(s)	Gls
15	Kevin DEERY		6/12/84	M	17	(1)	1
21	Clive DELANEY		2/1/80	D	19	(1)	2
16	Gerard DOHERTY	NIR	24/8/81	G	35		
18	Mark FARREN		21/5/81	A	23	(6)	10
6	Steven GRAY		19/10/81	D	22		
25	Ruairí HARKIN		11/10/89	M	1	(2)	
7	Ruaidhri HIGGINS	NIR	23/10/84	M	25	(7)	
4	Peter HUTTON	NIR	2/3/73	D	29	(1)	1
1	Patrick JENNINGS	ENG	24/9/79	G	1		
11	Liam KEARNEY		10/1/83	M	14	(4)	1
8	Ciaran MARTYN		25/3/80	M	18	(9)	5
2	Eddie McCALLION	NIR	25/1/79	D	26	(1)	
5	Mark McCHRYSTAL	NIR	26/6/84	D	11	(2)	
19	James McCLEAN	NIR	22/4/89	M	11	(15)	1
29	David McDAID		3/12/90	A	4	(1)	3
26	Shane McELENEY	NIR	31/1/91	D	1	(2)	
14	Gareth McGLYNN		29/10/82	M	30		7
23	Tam McMANUS	SCO	28/2/81	A	12	(11)	3
17	Barry MOLLOY	NIR	28/11/83	M	20	(6)	1
9	Sammy MORROW	NIR	3/3/85	A	15	(4)	3
27	Aaron NASH	NIR	14/10/88	A	2	(8)	1
12	Ger O'BRIEN		2/7/84	D	27	(2)	
20	David SCULLION	NIR	27/4/84	M	10	(9)	2
10	Thomas STEWART	NIR	12/11/86	A	23	(3)	6

DROGHEDA UNITED FC
Manager – Alan Mathews
Founded – 1919
Stadium – United Park (5,400)
MAJOR HONOURS:
League of Ireland – (1) 2007;
FAI Cup – (1) 2005.

2009

6/3	Derry	a	0-1	
13/3	Bray	h	0-0	
20/3	Dundalk	a	0-3	
27/3	Bohemians	h	0-1	
3/4	Shamrock Rovers	h	2-2	*Shiels, Farrell*
7/4	Cork	a	0-1	
10/4	Galway	h	0-1	
17/4	St Patrick's	a	1-2	*Duggan*
24/4	Sligo	h	0-0	
1/5	Derry	h	0-3	
8/5	Bray	a	1-0	*King*
15/5	Dundalk	h	1-1	*Kenna*
22/5	Bohemians	a	0-1	
30/5	Shamrock Rovers	a	1-1	*Duffy*
2/6	Cork	h	2-1	*Kenna, O'Connor*
5/6	Galway	a	1-0	*King*
19/6	St Patrick's	h	1-0	*Barrett*
5/7	Sligo	a	2-2	*Barrett 2 (1p)*
10/7	Derry	a	1-0	*King*
17/7	Bray	h	1-2	*Barrett*
24/7	Dundalk	a	2-4	*Kenna, Chambers*
31/7	Bohemians	h	1-1	*Chambers*
7/8	Shamrock Rovers	h	0-1	
11/8	Galway	a	2-0	*Kenna, Duffy*
21/8	Cork	h	0-1	
30/8	St Patrick's	a	0-1	
4/9	Sligo	h	2-2	*Chambers, Gibb*
18/9	Derry	h	1-3	*Duffy*
25/9	Bray	a	2-1	*Duffy, Chambers*
2/10	Dundalk	h	2-2	*Chambers 2*
9/10	Bohemians	a	0-4	
17/10	Shamrock Rovers	a	0-2	
20/10	Galway	h	4-0	*McGill B., Crowley, Ryan, Shiels*
23/10	Cork	a	0-0	
30/10	St Patrick's	h	1-2	*Chambers*
6/11	Sligo	a	1-3	*Gaynor*

Name	Nat	DoB	Pos	Aps	(s)	Gls
Shane BARRETT		23/11/81	A	13	(2)	4
Guy BATES	ENG	31/10/85	A	4	(9)	
James CHAMBERS		14/2/87	M	30	(3)	7
Mick CLARKE		19/6/89	D	5		
Robbie CLARKE		16/9/84	D	27	(1)	
Paul CROWLEY		13/8/80	M	20	(1)	1
Jamie DUFFY		20/11/83	M	27	(4)	4
Mark DUGGAN		22/9/86	M	6	(1)	1
Robbie FARRELL		16/1/78	A	2	(9)	1
Michael FOLEY		9/3/83	M		(1)	
Ross GAYNOR		9/9/87	A	13	(1)	1
Scott GIBB	NIR	16/9/88	D	10	(1)	1
John Paul KELLY		16/6/87	M	5		
Conor KENNA		21/8/84	D	33		4
Brian KING	NIR	8/1/87	M	21	(7)	3
Robbie MARTIN		27/7/82	A	18	(6)	
Austin McCANN		20/12/84	M		(1)	
Brendan McGILL		22/3/81	M	14	(2)	1
Eric McGILL		16/10/87	M	10	(2)	
Alan McNALLY		15/9/82	D	31	(1)	
Darragh McNAMARA		16/6/90	A		(1)	
Davie O'CONNOR		8/12/85	M	6	(8)	1
Eoghan OSBOURNE		25/3/92	D	4	(2)	
Ian RYAN		9/6/87	D	23	(4)	1
Mark SALMON		31/10/88	M		(3)	
Paul SHIELS		19/4/80	M	24	(4)	2
Paul SKINNER		3/2/89	G	13		
Gavin WHELAN		28/10/83	M	12		
Steve WILLIAMS	WAL	16/10/74	G	23		
William WOODS		5/7/91	A	2	(4)	

DUNDALK FC

Manager – Sean Connor
Founded – 1903
Stadium – Oriel Park (6,000)
MAJOR HONOURS:
League of Ireland – (9) 1933, 1963, 1967, 1976, 1979, 1982, 1988, 1991, 1995;
FAI Cup – (9) 1942, 1949, 1952, 1958, 1977, 1979, 1981, 1988, 2002 (spring).

2009

6/3	Bohemians	h	0-1	
13/3	Galway	a	0-1	
20/3	Drogheda	h	3-0	*Turner 2 (2p), Mansaram*
27/3	St Patrick's	a	0-2	
4/4	Sligo	a	3-1	*Mansaram, Burns, Turner*
7/4	Shamrock Rovers	h	0-1	
10/4	Bray	a	1-1	*O'Brien*
17/4	Cork	h	1-2	*Turner*
24/4	Derry	a	1-0	*Mansaram*
1/5	Bohemians	a	0-5	
8/5	Galway	h	1-0	*O'Brien*
15/5	Drogheda	a	1-1	*Turner (p)*
22/5	St Patrick's	h	0-1	
29/5	Sligo	h	0-2	
2/6	Shamrock Rovers	a	1-3	*Daly*
5/6	Bray	h	3-0	*Turner, Rowe, Mulvenna*
19/6	Cork	a	2-1	*Turner (p), Daly*
3/7	Derry	h	1-0	*Williams*
10/7	Bohemians	h	0-2	
17/7	Galway	a	3-0	*Collins 2, Williams*
24/7	Drogheda	h	4-2	*Rowe, Williams 2, Turner (p)*
2/8	St Patrick's	a	0-1	
8/8	Sligo	a	4-3	*McGowan Mi., Mulvenna, Turner 2*
11/8	Bray	h	0-0	
22/8	Shamrock Rovers	a	2-2	*Williams, Burns*
4/9	Derry	a	0-3	
12/9	Cork	h	1-0	*Mulvenna*
18/9	Bohemians	a	2-3	*Rowe, McGowan Mi.*
25/9	Galway	h	3-0	*Williams, McGowan Mi., Mansaram*

2/10	Drogheda	a	2-2	*Rowe, Mansaram*
9/10	St Patrick's	h	0-0	
16/10	Sligo	h	2-2	*McGowan Mi., Turner (p)*
20/10	Bray	a	1-1	*Daly*
23/10	Shamrock Rovers	h	2-4	*Turner, Williams*
30/10	Cork	a	1-2	*Kelly Sh.*
6/11	Derry	h	1-2	*McGowan Mi.*

No	Name	Nat	DoB	Pos	Aps	(s)	Gls
15	Dwight BARNETT	JAM	3/1/82	A		(1)	
1	Chris BENNION	SCO	30/8/80	G	19		
5	Liam BURNS	NIR	30/10/78	D	30		2
20	Peter CHERRIE	SCO	1/10/83	G	16		
15	Michael COBURN		8/10/85	D	14	(7)	
4	Michael COLLINS	NIR	6/9/77	M	8	(2)	2
25	Ryan COULTER		8/2/89	G	1		
16	Michael DALY		18/10/89	M	27	(1)	3
24	Philip DUFFY		8/9/91	D		(1)	
22	Mark GRIFFIN		16/7/91	M		(1)	
6	Thomas HEARY		14/2/79	D	29	(2)	
2	Shaun KELLY		15/10/89	D	30	(1)	1
19	Simon KELLY		4/7/84	D	22	(4)	
14	Sean MACKLE	SCO	10/4/88	M		(2)	
9	Darren MANSARAM	ENG	25/6/84	A	24	(7)	5
14	Paul McAREAVEY	NIR	3/12/80	M	6	(4)	
12	Michael McGINLAY	ENG	10/12/87	A		(8)	
21	Martin McGOWAN		30/6/90	M		(2)	
11	Michael McGOWAN	SCO	22/2/85	M	16		5
3	Kevin McKINLAY	SCO	28/2/86	M	12	(1)	
7	Tiarnán MULVENNA		10/12/88	M	17	(12)	3
17	Nathan MURPHY		1/11/92	A	6	(2)	
10	Declan O'BRIEN		16/6/79	A	10	(5)	2
23	George O'CALLAGHAN		5/9/79	M	11		
3	Dave ROGERS	ENG	25/8/75	D	11		
18	Ger ROWE		3/8/84	A	22	(5)	4
11	Harpal SINGH	ENG	15/9/81	M	11	(1)	
19	Billy SMITH		26/7/89	A		(1)	
17	Michael SYNNOTT		20/1/87	D	8	(3)	
8	Chris TURNER	NIR	3/1/87	M	31		12
10	Alex WILLIAMS	SCO	15/1/83	A	15		7

GALWAY UNITED FC

Manager – Ian Foster (ENG)
Founded – 1937
Stadium – Terryland Park (5,000)
MAJOR HONOURS:
FAI Cup – (1) 1991.

2009

6/3	St Patrick's	a	3-0	*O'Brien 2, Faherty*
13/3	Dundalk	h	1-0	*Breen*
20/3	Bray	a	2-2	*Faherty, McBrien*
27/3	Sligo	h	0-0	
3/4	Derry	a	1-1	*Conneely*
7/4	Bohemians	h	0-2	
10/4	Drogheda	a	1-0	*Edwards*
17/4	Shamrock Rovers	h	1-3	*Faherty*
24/4	Cork	a	0-1	
1/5	St Patrick's	h	2-1	*Breen, O'Shea*
8/5	Dundalk	a	0-1	
15/5	Bray	h	3-0	*O'Shea, McBrien, Molloy*
24/5	Sligo	a	0-2	
28/5	Derry	h	0-3	
2/6	Bohemians	a	0-2	
5/6	Drogheda	h	1-1	*Faherty*
20/6	Shamrock Rovers	a	0-1	
3/7	Cork	h	0-2	
10/7	St Patrick's	a	2-1	*O'Shea, Kelly*
17/7	Dundalk	h	0-3	
24/7	Bray	a	2-1	*Breen, O'Shea*
31/7	Sligo	h	1-0	*Russell*

REPUBLIC OF IRELAND

11/8	Drogheda	h	0-2	
21/8	Bohemians	a	0-5	
28/8	Shamrock Rovers	h	0-1	
1/9	Derry	a	3-1	Cooke, Green, Murphy
4/9	Cork	a	2-4	og (Long), Murphy
18/9	St Patrick's	h	2-1	Conneely, Russell
25/9	Dundalk	a	0-3	
2/10	Bray	h	3-1	Green 2, Russell
9/10	Sligo	a	0-2	
16/10	Derry	h	3-1	McBrien, Green, Molloy
20/10	Drogheda	a	0-4	
23/10	Bohemians	h	0-2	
30/10	Shamrock Rovers	a	1-1	Green
6/11	Cork	h	2-2	Faherty 2

No	Name	Nat	DoB	Pos	Aps	(s)	Gls
5	Garry BREEN		17/3/89	D	32		3
2	Séamus CONNEELY		9/7/88	D	34		2
4	David COOKE		5/10/85	M	19	(7)	1
21	Iarfhlaith DAVOREN		12/5/86	D	28	(1)	
19	Declan EDWARDS		23/12/89	M	2	(12)	1
9	Vinny FAHERTY		13/6/87	A	33	(2)	6
14	Shane FITZGERALD		12/1/87	M	2	(6)	
19	Aaron GREEN		2/1/90	A	11	(3)	5
6	Shane GUTHRIE		11/12/84	D	30	(1)	
16	Seán KELLY		9/7/87	D	26		1
17	Cian McBRIEN		19/6/89	M	25	(6)	3
18	Michael McGRATH	ENG	4/9/85	M	17		
13	Liam McKENNA		6/8/86	D	1		
20	Jason MOLLOY		22/9/88	M	3	(18)	2
10	Alan MURPHY		3/10/81	M	15	(9)	2
11	Derek O'BRIEN		14/11/79	M	26	(1)	2
7	Jay O'SHEA		10/8/88	M	19		4
3	Mark O'TOOLE		6/9/89	D	11	(6)	
8	John RUSSELL		18/5/85	M	18	(2)	3
1	Barry RYAN		29/8/78	G	36		
15	Paul SINNOTT		24/7/86	D	8	(6)	
12	Niall WALSH		23/1/92	D		(1)	

SAINT PATRICK'S ATHLETIC FC
Manager – Jeff Kenna
Founded – 1929
Stadium – Richmond Park (5,340)
MAJOR HONOURS:
League of Ireland – (7) 1952, 1955, 1956, 1990, 1996, 1998, 1999;
FAI Cup – (2) 1959, 1961.

2009

6/3	Galway	h	0-3	
13/3	Cork	a	1-0	Ryan D.
21/3	Sligo	a	1-0	Moran
27/3	Dundalk	h	2-0	Leech, Moran
3/4	Bray	a	1-2	Byrne
7/4	Derry	h	0-3	
11/4	Bohemians	a	0-3	
17/4	Drogheda	h	2-1	Haran, Byrne
25/4	Shamrock Rovers	a	0-2	
1/5	Galway	a	1-2	Quigley (p)
9/5	Cork	h	0-3	
15/5	Sligo	h	2-2	O'Connor, Cawley
22/5	Dundalk	a	1-0	Quigley
29/5	Bray	h	1-1	Partridge
2/6	Derry	a	0-1	
5/6	Bohemians	h	3-1	Guy 2, Lester
19/6	Drogheda	a	0-1	
4/7	Shamrock Rovers	h	1-2	Cawley (p)
7/7	Cork	a	1-0	Guy
10/7	Galway	h	1-2	Guy
26/7	Sligo	a	0-2	
2/8	Dundalk	h	1-0	O'Connor

11/8	Bohemians	h	0-2	
23/8	Derry	a	0-1	
30/8	Drogheda	h	1-0	Byrne
4/9	Shamrock Rovers	a	0-1	
18/9	Galway	a	1-2	Gavin
25/9	Cork	h	1-1	Quigley
28/9	Bray	h	1-0	O'Brien
6/10	Sligo	h	0-2	
9/10	Dundalk	a	0-0	
16/10	Bray	h	2-0	Guy, Lynch
20/10	Bohemians	a	1-3	Quigley
23/10	Derry	h	0-2	
30/10	Drogheda	a	2-1	O'Brien, Guy
6/11	Shamrock Rovers	h	1-0	Guy

No	Name	Nat	DoB	Pos	Aps	(s)	Gls
7	Stuart BYRNE		4/11/76	M	26	(4)	3
10	Alan CAWLEY		3/1/82	M	17	(8)	2
20	Brendan CLARKE		17/10/85	G	9		
8	Gary DEMPSEY		15/1/81	M	12	(2)	
24	Dave FAGAN		29/1/89	D		(1)	
12	Glenn FITZPATRICK		26/1/81	A	6	(8)	
24	Gints FREIMANIS	LVA	9/5/85	M	2		
18	Jason GAVIN		14/3/80	D	32		1
21	Ryan GUY	USA	5/9/85	M	30	(2)	7
16	Andrew HARAN		25/6/89	A	3	(6)	1
5	Jamie HARRIS	WAL	28/6/79	D	19	(4)	
19	Noel HAVERTY		24/2/89	D	7	(2)	
9	Mark LEECH		9/12/85	A	5	(4)	1
25	John LESTER		5/8/82	M	6	(7)	1
6	Damien LYNCH		31/7/79	D	25	(1)	1
2	Stephen MAHER		3/3/88	D	20	(1)	
15	Kyle MORAN		7/6/87	A	9	(6)	2
23	Declan O'BRIEN		16/6/79	A	10	(2)	2
17	Garreth O'CONNOR		10/11/78	M	19	(6)	2
4	David PARTRIDGE	WAL	26/11/78	D	26		1
11	Mark QUIGLEY		27/10/85	A	23	(2)	4
1	Gary ROGERS		25/9/81	G	27		
14	Bobby RYAN		1/5/79	M	16	(6)	
3	Darragh RYAN		21/5/80	D	20	(2)	1
22	Enda STEVENS		9/7/90	D	27	(3)	

SHAMROCK ROVERS FC
Manager – Michael O'Neill (NIR)
Founded – 1901
Stadium – Tallaght Stadium (6,000)
MAJOR HONOURS:
League of Ireland – (15) 1923, 1925, 1927, 1932, 1938, 1939, 1954, 1957,
1959, 1964, 1984, 1985, 1986, 1987, 1994;
FAI Cup – (24) 1925, 1929, 1930, 1931, 1932, 1933, 1936, 1940, 1944, 1945,
1948, 1955, 1956, 1962, 1964, 1965, 1966, 1967, 1968, 1969, 1978, 1985,
1986, 1987.

2009

6/3	Bray	a	0-0	
13/3	Sligo	h	2-1	Twigg, Baker
20/3	Bohemians	a	0-2	
27/3	Derry	h	1-2	Baker
3/4	Drogheda	a	2-2	Twigg, Amond
7/4	Dundalk	a	1-0	Rice
10/4	Cork	h	1-1	Twigg
17/4	Galway	a	3-1	Twigg 3
25/4	St Patrick's	h	2-0	Twigg 2
2/5	Bray	h	0-1	
9/5	Sligo	a	3-0	Amond 2, Robinson
16/5	Bohemians	h	2-1	Twigg 2
22/5	Derry	a	0-0	
30/5	Drogheda	h	1-1	Twigg
2/6	Dundalk	h	3-1	Twigg 2, Baker
5/6	Cork	a	0-0	

20/6	Galway	h	1-0	Baker	
4/7	St Patrick's	a	2-1	Twigg 2	
10/7	Bray	a	2-1	Baker, Twigg	
18/7	Sligo	h	3-1	Purcell, Price, Rice	
26/7	Bohemians	a	0-0		
2/8	Derry	h	2-1	O'Connor, Purcell	
7/8	Drogheda	a	1-0	Twigg	
11/8	Cork	a	0-0		
22/8	Dundalk	h	2-2	Rice, Twigg	
28/8	Galway	a	1-0	Bradley	
4/9	St Patrick's	h	1-0	Twigg	
19/9	Bray	h	3-1	Rice, Twigg 2	
26/9	Sligo	a	2-1	Twigg (p), og (Peers)	
2/10	Bohemians	h	1-0	Amond	
9/10	Derry	a	1-0	Baker	
17/10	Drogheda	h	2-0	Baker, Barrett	
20/10	Cork	h	1-2	Sullivan	
23/10	Dundalk	a	4-2	Robinson, Maguire, Twigg, Baker	
30/10	Galway	h	1-1	Twigg	
6/11	St Patrick's	a	0-1		

No	Name	Nat	DoB	Pos	Aps	(s)	Gls
21	Pádraig AMOND		23/4/88	A	8	(12)	4
18	Dessie BAKER		25/8/77	M	25	(7)	8
22	Graham BARRETT		6/10/81	A	4	(6)	1
3	Ian BERMINGHAM		8/1/89	D	15	(1)	
10	Stephen BRADLEY	SCO	19/11/84	M	24	(6)	1
14	Ollie CAHILL		29/9/75	M	30	(3)	
17	Greg CAMERON	SCO	10/4/88	M	10	(4)	
15	Ross CHISHOLM	SCO	14/1/88	M	5	(4)	
17	Don COWEN		16/11/89	A		(5)	
19	Eoin DOYLE		12/3/88	A		(2)	
16	Robert DUGGAN		1/4/87	G	7		
20	Pat FLYNN		13/1/85	D	12	(3)	
17	Barry JOHNSTON	NIR	28/10/79	M	2	(2)	
13	Patrick KAVANAGH		29/12/85	M	2	(5)	
2	Simon MADDEN		1/5/88	D	8	(2)	
4	Darragh MAGUIRE		6/2/76	D	16		1
23	Alan MANNUS	NIR	19/5/82	G	11		
13	Eric McGILL		16/10/87	M		(4)	
1	Barry MURPHY		8/6/85	G	18		
11	Sean O'CONNOR		21/10/83	M	19	(9)	1
5	Aidan PRICE		8/12/81	D	28		1
22	Tadhg PURCELL		2/9/85	A	8	(16)	2
8	Stephen RICE		6/10/84	M	34		4
7	Shane ROBINSON		17/12/80	M	29	(3)	2
6	Craig SIVES	SCO	9/4/86	D	17		
19	Pat SULLIVAN		30/10/82	D	12		1
15	Corie TREACY		11/1/89	D	9		
9	Gary TWIGG	SCO	19/3/84	A	33	(1)	24
6	Seán WEBB	NIR	4/1/83	D	10		

SLIGO ROVERS FC

Manager – Paul Cook (ENG)
Founded – 1928
Stadium – The Showgrounds (5,500)
MAJOR HONOURS:
League of Ireland – (2) 1937, 1977;
FAI Cup – (2) 1983, 1994.

2009

7/3	Cork	h	1-1	Parkhouse	
13/3	Shamrock Rovers	a	1-2	Peers	
21/3	St Patrick's	h	0-1		
27/3	Galway	a	0-0		
4/4	Dundalk	h	1-3	Cretaro	
7/4	Bray	h	2-1	Cretaro 2	
10/4	Derry	a	2-1	Boco, Cretaro	
18/4	Bohemians	h	0-0		
24/4	Drogheda	a	0-0		

1/5	Cork	a	0-1		
9/5	Shamrock Rovers	h	0-3		
15/5	St Patrick's	a	2-2	Peers, Keane	
24/5	Galway	h	2-0	Holmes, Keane (p)	
29/5	Dundalk	a	2-0	Keane, O'Grady	
2/6	Bray	a	1-3	Cretaro	
5/6	Derry	h	0-1		
19/6	Bohemians	a	0-2		
5/7	Drogheda	h	2-2	Cretaro, O'Grady	
12/7	Cork	h	0-3		
18/7	Shamrock Rovers	a	1-3	Holmes	
26/7	St Patrick's	h	2-0	Doyle, Blinkhorn	
31/7	Galway	a	0-1		
8/8	Dundalk	h	3-4	Blinkhorn 2, Cretaro	
11/8	Derry	h	0-4		
21/8	Bray	a	2-2	Cretaro 2	
1/9	Bohemians	h	1-0	Keane (p)	
4/9	Drogheda	a	2-2	Ventre, Morrison	
26/9	Shamrock Rovers	h	1-2	Cretaro	
29/9	Cork	a	0-0		
6/10	St Patrick's	a	2-0	Cretaro 2	
9/10	Galway	h	2-0	Cretaro, Marshall	
13/10	Bray	h	1-0	Doyle	
16/10	Dundalk	a	2-2	Cretaro, Keane (p)	
20/10	Derry	a	2-1	Cretaro, Boco	
30/10	Bohemians	a	1-3	Marshall	
6/11	Drogheda	h	3-1	Doyle, Peers, Blinkhorn	

Name	Nat	DoB	Pos	Aps	(s)	Gls
Mauro ALMEIDA	POR	29/1/82	D	2	(1)	
Matthew BLINKHORN	ENG	2/3/85	A	16	(1)	4
Romuald BOCO	BEN	8/7/85	A	29		2
Richard BRUSH	ENG	26/11/84	G	29		
Martín Nicolás CAMANO	ESP	20/4/85	D	4		
Brian CASH		24/11/82	M	21	(7)	
Rafael CRETARO		15/10/81	M	30	(1)	15
Paul CURRY		23/8/86	A	1		
Sean DOHERTY	ENG	10/2/85	M	8	(2)	
Eoin DOYLE		12/3/88	A	15		3
Danny FALLON		9/3/90	A		(1)	
Steve FEENEY		16/5/84	D	8	(7)	
Shaun HOLMES	NIR	27/12/80	D	17		2
Alan KEANE		23/9/84	D	34		5
Christopher KELLY		11/4/85	M	2	(2)	
Ciarán KELLY		14/3/80	G	6		
Joe KENDRICK		26/6/83	D	15		
Danny KEOHANE		16/3/87	D	4	(5)	
Dean MARSHALL		15/3/90	M	3	(10)	2
Michael McGRATH	ENG	4/9/85	M	4		
Ross McLOUGHLIN		4/5/89	A		(2)	
Paul McTIERNAN		17/12/82	A		(6)	
Darren MEENAN	NIR	16/11/86	M	1	(4)	
Owen MORRISON	NIR	8/12/81	M	21	(4)	1
Jason NOCTOR		7/6/89	D	4		
Conor O'GRADY		27/5/80	M	31		2
Stephen PARKHOUSE	NIR	1/8/82	A	4	(3)	1
Gavin PEERS		10/11/85	D	26	(1)	3
Gerard RAFTER		14/7/90	D	1		
Richie RYAN		6/1/85	M	23	(8)	
Michael SCHLINGERMANN		8/11/88	G	1		
Eoin TORPEY		1/4/89	M	4	(7)	
Rob TURNER	ENG	29/9/89	A	3	(9)	
Danny VENTRE	ENG	23/1/86	D	29		1

PROMOTED CLUBS

UNIVERSITY COLLEGE DUBLIN AFC
Manager – Martin Russell
Founded – 1895
Stadium – Belfield Bowl (2,500)
MAJOR HONOURS:
FAI Cup – (1) 1984.

SPORTING FINGAL FC
Manager – Liam Buckley
Founded – 2007
Stadium – Morton Stadium (4,000)
MAJOR HONOURS:
FAI Cup – (1) 2009.

SECOND LEVEL FINAL TABLE 2009

		Pld	W	D	L	F	A	Pts
1	University College Dublin AFC	33	23	5	5	63	21	74
2	Shelbourne FC	33	22	7	4	66	31	73
3	Sporting Fingal FC	33	21	6	6	68	28	69
4	Waterford United FC	33	20	6	7	51	21	66
5	Monaghan United FC	33	16	7	10	58	48	55
6	Wexford Youths FC	33	15	5	13	27	31	50
7	Limerick 37 FC	33	12	8	13	49	43	44
8	Finn Harps FC	33	8	9	16	35	51	33
9	Longford Town FC	33	8	4	21	46	62	28
10	Athlone Town FC	33	6	9	18	32	63	27
11	Mervue United FC	33	6	5	22	28	64	23
12	Kildare County FC	33	4	3	26	25	85	15

NB Kildare County FC withdrew at the end of the season.

PROMOTION/RELEGATION PLAY-OFFS

SEMI FINALS (10/11/09)
Drogheda 2, Bray 0
Shelbourne 1, Fingal 2

FINAL (13/11/09 & 16/11/09)
Fingal 2, Bray 0
Bray 2, Fingal 2
(Fingal 4-2)

DOMESTIC CUP 2009

FAI CUP

THIRD ROUND

(9/6/09)
Crumlin 1, Shelbourne 1

(12/6/09)
Blarney 0, Fingal 2
Bohemians 8, Mayfield 1
Bray 2, Bluebell 1
Cork 2, Sligo 2
Derry 6, Ballymun 0
Limerick 0, St Patrick's 1
Mervue 1, Dundalk 3
UCD 3, Arklow 1

(13/6/09)
Finn Harps 0, Galway 3
Kildare 1, Athlone 2

Shamrock Rovers 1, Drogheda 1
Tralee 2, Salthill 1
Waterford 6, Carrigaline 0

(14/6/09)
Cherry Orchard 2, Monaghan 2
Wexford 2, Longford 2

Replays

(15/6/09)
Shelbourne 0, Crumlin 1

(16/6/09)
Drogheda 0, Shamrock Rovers 3
Monaghan 4, Cherry Orchard 0
Sligo 2, Cork 1 *(aet)*

(17/6/09)
Longford 3, Wexford 2 *(aet)*

FOURTH ROUND

(14/8/09)
Bray 2, Tralee 0
Crumlin 0, Waterford 0
Dundalk 0, Bohemians 0
Fingal 4, Athlone 1
Galway 0, Longford 1
Monaghan 0, St Patrick's 0

(15/8/09)
Shamrock Rovers 3, UCD 1
Sligo 1, Derry 0

Replays

(18/8/09)
Bohemians 0, Dundalk 0 *(aet; 4-2 on pens)*
Waterford 2, Crumlin 0

(7/9/09)
St Patrick's 1, Monaghan 0

QUARTER-FINALS

(11/9/09)
Bohemians 0, Sligo 0

(12/9/09)
Fingal 2 *(Williams 54, Maher 59)*, Shamrock Rovers 2 *(Baker 27, Chisholm 30)*
Longford 0, Bray 0
Waterford 1 *(Kiely 17)*, St Patrick's 1 *(Dempsey 70)*

Replays

(15/9/09)
Bray 2 *(Flood 12, Shields 26)*, Longford 1 *(Glynn 90)*
Shamrock Rovers 1 *(Bradley 46p)*, Fingal 2 *(Kirby 8, 115p) (aet)*
Sligo 2 *(O'Grady 67, Doyle 71)*, Bohemians 1 *(Cronin 43)*
St Patrick's 0, Waterford 2 *(Carey 25, Kiely 39)*

SEMI-FINALS

(23/10/09)
Sligo 1 *(Blinkhorn 75)*, Waterford 0

(25/10/09)
Fingal 4 *(Zayed 4, 11, Kirby 21, Bayly 83)*, Bray 2 *(McCabe 74, Mulroy 90)*

FINAL

(22/11/09)
Tallaght stadium, Dublin
SPORTING FINGAL FC 2 *(James 84p, O'Neill 90)*
SLIGO ROVERS FC 1 *(Doyle 57)*
Referee – Kelly
FINGAL – Quigley, James, Maher, Paisley, Fitzgerald, Williams, Bayly, McFaul, Byrne C., O'Neill, Zayed.
SLIGO – Kelly Ci., Boco, Peers, Keane, Kendrick, Ventre, Cash (Morrison 55), Ryan, Doyle, Blinkhorn, Cretaro (Meenan 70).

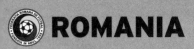

CFR Cluj continue to conquer

The 2009/10 Romanian season continued the recent trend for provincial success, with CFR 1907 Cluj, the well funded, foreigner-friendly club from Transylvania, maintaining their status as fashion leaders by winning all three domestic trophies open to them – the Super Cup, the Romanian Cup and, best of all, the Liga I title.

It was another bad year for Bucharest, with none of the capital's three major clubs – FC Steaua Bucureşti, FC Dinamo Bucureşti and FC Rapid Bucureşti – managing to finish among the top three in the league and only Dinamo reaching the latter stages of the cup. Steaua and Dinamo did both manage to accede to the group stage of the UEFA Europa League, but then so too did two of their provincial rivals, Cluj and FC Timişoara. FC Unirea Urziceni entered that competition in the spring – after all the other Romanian clubs had exited – thanks to a third-place finish in their UEFA Champions League group.

Unirea's European adventure, the highlight of which was a 4-1 win at Rangers FC in front of a crowd three times bigger than the population of their home town, eventually ended at the hands of Liverpool FC, but they went into that tie without their title-winning coach, Dan Petrescu, who, having stayed on to oversee the UEFA Champions League campaign, took up an offer to take charge of FC Kuban Krasnodar, a club just relegated from Russia's Premier-Liga. It seemed a puzzling career move for the former Chelsea FC and Romania right-back but he left a good legacy at Unirea, and although the club struggled initially under his successor, Roni Levi, they eventually rediscovered their old form and pursued Cluj all the way to the finish in a fascinating Liga I title race before ultimately surrendering their title in the penultimate round.

Italian influence

Unirea's 16-match unbeaten run in the spring earned them a runners-up spot and, with it, a place in the third qualifying round of the 2010/11 UEFA Champions League, Cluj, as champions, secured a direct passage into the group stage, in which they had participated in 2008/09, defeating AS Roma at the Stadio Olimpico in their opening game. It was an Italian, Maurizio Trombetta, who had led Cluj to that famous win in the Eternal City, and it was another Italian, Andrea Mandorlini who steered Cluj back to Europe's premier club competition by seeing them through to their second Romanian title in three seasons.

A purposeful midfielder with FC Internazionale Milano, Mandorlini's reputation as a coach in his homeland was no more than modest, but after replacing Portuguese coach Toni at Cluj in November he turned the team into an efficient, well-drilled unit that, in traditional Italian style, defended in depth and struck rapidly on the counterattack. Cluj's assortment of Africans, Argentinians, Brazilians and Portuguese – plus the odd Romanian – adapted well to Mandorlini's modus operandi. At the winter break Cluj were on top of the table, and although at that stage they were level on points with both Unirea and Steaua and only four points above seventh-placed FC Vaslui – with Steaua, Timişoara and Rapid in between – their form in the spring remained so consistent that they were never unseated from their perch.

Andrea Mandorlini led CFR Cluj to the Romanian league and cup double

ROMANIA

Shoot-out triumph

For the second season running Cluj were unbeaten at home, where they conceded a mere eight goals in 17 games. They won several tight games by the odd goal, and although their football was not always pretty to watch, it was highly effective. This was encapsulated by their Romanian Cup triumph – their third in as many years - where they edged out Dinamo in the semi-finals with a late goal from Ivorian striker Lacine Traoré before overcoming Vaslui on penalties in the final after a 0-0 draw.

Vaslui had been the only one of Romania's six 2009/10 European representatives eliminated in the qualifying stage – they lost to AEK Athens FC in the play-off round – but on reflection that was probably a blessing in disguise because the previously unheralded small-town club from the Moldovan border region proved to be the revelation of the domestic campaign. Owned by former FIFA referee Adrian Porumboiu, they maintained their consistent upwardly mobile progress since winning promotion in 2005 by finishing third in Liga I as well as reaching the Cup final. Marius Lăcătuş, the former Romanian international winger, was brought in as coach in late September and he made a stunning start, winning his first six matches. Back-to-back home wins over Steaua and Dinamo at the end of the season secured third place for a club whose significant investment in foreign players, not least Honduran striker Carlos Costly and Brazilian marksman Wesley, paid handsome dividends.

Lăcătuş's former club Steaua completed a fourth successive season without a trophy, their longest barren run in a quarter of a century. Italian coach Cristiano Bergodi was fired early on by the club's charismatic if controversial owner Gigi Becali, and although his replacement Mihai Stoichiţă had the

Federaţia Română de Fotbal (FRF)

Casa Fotbalului
Str. Serg. Serbanica Vasile 12
RO-022186 Bucureşti
tel - +40 21 325 0678
fax - +40 21 325 0679
website - frf.ro
email - frf@frf.ro
Year of Formation – 1909

President - Mircea Sandu
General Secretary - Adalbert Kassai
Media Officer – Paul Daniel Zaharia
National Stadium – Naţional - Lia Manoliu, Bucharest (55,000)

INTERNATIONAL TOURNAMENT APPEARANCES
FIFA World Cup - (7) 1930, 1934, 1938, 1970,
1990 (2nd round), 1994 (qtr-finals), 1998 (2nd round).
UEFA European Championship - (4) 1984, 1996,
2000 (qtr-finals), 2008.
TOP FIVE ALL-TIME CAPS
Dorinel Munteanu (134); Gheorghe Hagi (124); Gheorghe Popescu (115); László Bölöni (102); Dan Petrescu (95)
TOP FIVE ALL-TIME GOALS
Gheorghe Hagi (35); Iuliu Bodola (30); Adrian Mutu (29); Viorel Moldovan (25); László Bölöni (23)

opportunity to bring the club a 24th league crown, his ambitions were effectively blitzed by a harrowing 5-1 defeat to rivals Rapid in mid-April. A final placing of fourth was ultimately all Steaua could muster, and the disappointment continued when their top-scoring striker Pantelis Kapetanos missed out on the Golden Boot – denied by Dinamo's Andrei Cristea, who finished up with 16 goals to the Greek international's 15.

Best and worst

Thanks to Romania's strong collective European showing in recent years, Dinamo's sixth place in Liga I, one above

NATIONAL TEAM RESULTS 2009/10

12/8/09	Hungary	A	Budapest	1-0	Ghioane (42)
5/9/09	France (WCQ)	A	Saint-Denis	1-1	Escudé (55og)
9/9/09	Austria (WCQ)	H	Bucharest	1-1	Bucur (54)
10/10/09	Serbia (WCQ)	A	Belgrade	0-5	
14/10/09	Faroe Islands (WCQ)	H	Piatra Neamt	3-1	Apostol (16), Bucur (65), Mazilu (87)
14/11/09	Poland	A	Warsaw	1-0	Niculae D. (59)
3/3/10	Israel	H	Timisoara	0-2	
29/5/10	Ukraine	A	Lviv	2-3	Tamaş (56), Niculae D. (65)
2/6/10	FYROM	N	Villach (AUT)	0-1	
5/6/10	Honduras	N	St Veit an der Glan (AUT)	3-0	Niculae D. (20), Florescu (45), Radoi (76p)

NATIONAL TEAM APPEARANCES 2009/10

Coach – Răzvan LUCESCU   17/2/69

Player	DOB	Club	Hun	FRA	AUT	SRB	FRO	Pol	Isr	Ukr	Mkd	Hon	Caps	Goalss
Dănuț Dumitru COMAN	28/3/79	Brașov	G	G	G	G							14	-
Ovidiu Liviu DĂNĂNAE	26/8/85	Univ Craiova	D37								D	D	3	-
Mirel Matei RĂDOI	22/3/81	Al Hilal (KSA)	D59	D	D	D	D	D	D	M	M	M	63	2
Cristian Eugen CHIVU	26/10/80	Inter (ITA)	D81	D	D	D 85*		D			D	D	71	3
Mihai Mircea NEȘU	19/2/83	Utrecht (NED)	D							D87			8	-
Bogdan Ion MARA	29/9/77	CFR Cluj	M73	M61					M				11	1
Iulian Cătălin APOSTOL	3/12/80	Unirea Urziceni	M	M		M	M	M					6	1
Tiberiu GHIOANE	18/6/81	Dynamo Kyiv (UKR)	M	M	M	M60		s52	s85	M46	s52	s46	21	2
Maximilian Johannes NICU	25/11/82	Hertha (GER)	M59	M77									3	-
Ionel Daniel DĂNCIULESCU	6/12/76	Dinamo București	A46										8	2
Ciprian Andrei MARICA	2/10/85	Stuttgart (GER)	A	A	A78	A60	A82	A61	A56				39	12
Vasile MAFTEI	1/1/81	Unirea Urziceni	s37	D	D					D78	D	D	10	1
Romeo Constantin SURDU	12/1/84	Steaua	s46	A87	s86								3	-
Dorin Nicolae GOIAN	12/12/80	Palermo (ITA)	s59				s60	D25	s70	D46	s46	D	34	5
Paul Constantin CODREA	4/4/81	Siena (ITA)	s59	s87	M70					M52	M72		44	1
Mihai ROMAN	16/11/84	Brașov	s73	s61	M					M46	M46	M76	7	-
Marius Marcel CONSTANTIN	25/10/84	Rapid București	s81										4	-
Răzvan RAȚ Dincă	26/5/81	Shakhtar (UKR)		D	D	D	D	D		D	D	D84	65	1
Gheorghe BUCUR	8/4/80	Timișoara /Kuban (RUS)					s77	A	s60	A76	s61	s56	19	4
Ionuț Cristian SĂPUNARU	5/4/84	Porto (POR)							s78				6	-
Adrian CRISTEA	30/11/83	Dinamo București					M86	M					8	-
Costin LAZĂR	24/4/81	Rapid București					s70						9	-
Ionuț Costinel MAZILU	9/2/82	Arsenal Kyiv (UKR)							s78	s82	s84	A46	14	3
Dacian Șerban VARGA	15/10/84	Unirea Urziceni								M	M		3	-
Adrian MUTU	8/1/79	Fiorentina (ITA)							A75				67	29
Andrei CRISTEA	15/5/84	Dinamo București						s75	s76	s79	A46	s67	10	-
Costel Fane PANTILIMON	1/2/87	Timișoara						G	G	G			6	-
Cristian Călin PANIN	9/6/78	CFR Cluj						D					2	-
Nicolae GRIGORE	19/7/83	Brașov						M					1	-
George Daniel GALAMAZ	5/4/81	Unirea Urziceni						s25				s79	2	-
Cristian TĂNASE	18/2/87	Steaua							M70		M86	M52	7	-
Daniel George NICULAE	6/10/82	Auxerre (FRA)						A	A56	s46	A62	A66	31	7
Bănel NICOLIȚĂ	7/1/85	Steaua							s46	M79			29	1
George FLORESCU	21/5/84	Midtjylland (DEN) /Alania (RUS)						M85			M		2	-
Gabriel Sebastian TAMAȘ	9/11/83	West Brom (ENG)							s46	D	D46	D79	46	-
Ciprian Ioan DEAC	16/2/86	CFR Cluj							s46	s76	M67	M82	4	-
Marius Constantin NICULAE	16/5/81	Dinamo București						s56					38	13
Răzvan PĂDUREȚU	19/6/81	Unirea Urziceni						s72					1	-
Laszlo SEPSI	7/6/86	Timișoara						s87				s84	3	-
Bogdan Ionuț LOBONȚ	18/1/78	Roma (ITA)								G		G84	76	-
Marius Ioan BILAȘCO	13/7/81	Unirea Urziceni								A84	s62	A	3	-
Răzvan COCIȘ	19/2/83	Timișoara							s46	M	M46		35	2
Mihai Cosmin RĂDUȚ	18/3/90	Internațional Curtea								s86		s82	2	-
Nicolae Constantin DICĂ	9/5/80	CFR Cluj									s46	s66	32	9
Silviu LUNG jr.	4/6/89	Univ Craiova										s84	1	-

ROMANIA

Rapid, was high enough to earn them admission to the UEFA Europa League. It was in Europe that they enjoyed their best and worst moments of the season, all in one remarkable play-off round tie against FC Slovan Liberec. Handed a 3-0 defeat by UEFA's disciplinary body after crowd disturbances in the home leg, there seemed no way through to the group stage, but Dinamo dug in for the second encounter in the Czech Republic, won 3-0 themselves, then took the tie 9-8 on penalties.

Romania national team coach Răzvan Lucescu survived a fraught World Cup qualifying campaign

Romania's worst ever qualifying campaign for a major tournament – they finished fifth in their 2010 FIFA World Cup group – was not deemed a sackable offence for coach Răzvan Lucescu, who, after all, had only been in charge for the second half of it, having replaced Victor Pițurcă in April 2009. He did, however, oversee the team's 5-0 capitulation to Serbia in Belgrade, and there was little noticeable improvement in the spring when Romania lost

Bucharest had its number of Liga I participants increased to four in 2010/11 by the promotion of FC Sportul Studențesc București. They were accompanied up by three other teams, two of them new to the top flight – FC Victoria Brănești and FCM Târgu Mureș. Room was made for them by the relegation of FC Unirea Alba Iulia, FC Ceahlăul Piatra Neamț, FC Politehnica Iași and, ultimately, FC Internațional Curtea de Argeș, who withdrew from the 2010/11 Liga I campaign, enabling CS Pandurii Lignitul Târga Jiu to survive.

three successive friendlies to Israel, Ukraine and the Former Yugoslav Republic of Macedonia (FYROM). They did end the season on a brighter note by defeating World Cup-bound Honduras 3-0, but with star striker Adrian Mutu serving a nine-month ban for doping and very few talented young Romanian footballers coming through to supplement stalwart servants like Răzvan Raţ, Ciprian Marica and UEFA Champions League winner Cristian Chivu, the prospects for a successful UEFA EURO 2012 qualification do not look overly-encouraging.

DOMESTIC LEAGUE 2009/10

LIGA I FINAL TABLE

		Pld	Home					Away					Total					Pts
			W	D	L	F	A	W	D	L	F	A	W	D	L	F	A	
1	CFR 1907 Cluj	34	12	5	0	24	8	8	4	5	22	15	20	9	5	46	23	69
2	FC Unirea Urziceni	34	10	5	2	30	13	8	7	2	23	13	18	12	4	53	26	66
3	FC Vaslui	34	11	3	3	25	12	7	5	5	19	16	18	8	8	44	28	62
4	FC Steaua București	34	10	4	3	26	16	8	4	5	23	20	18	8	8	49	36	62
5	FC Timișoara	34	8	5	4	24	10	7	9	1	31	17	15	14	5	55	27	59
6	FC Dinamo București	34	6	8	3	20	15	7	6	4	28	22	13	14	7	48	37	53
7	FC Rapid București	34	10	3	4	35	20	4	7	6	18	18	14	10	10	53	38	52
8	FC Oțelul Galați	34	8	5	4	23	16	6	3	8	15	22	14	8	12	38	38	50
9	FC Brașov	34	9	5	3	25	9	3	5	9	15	21	12	10	12	40	30	46
10	CS Gaz Metan Mediaș	34	5	8	4	17	17	4	7	6	16	20	9	15	10	33	37	42
11	ACF Gloria 1922 Bistrița	34	8	5	4	24	17	2	6	9	11	29	10	11	13	35	46	41
12	FC Internațional Curtea de Argeș	34	4	1	12	14	29	6	5	6	18	20	10	6	18	32	49	36
13	FC Universitatea Craiova	34	8	1	8	33	27	3	2	12	11	25	11	3	20	44	52	36
14	FC Astra Ploiești	34	6	7	4	20	19	2	5	10	13	26	8	12	14	33	45	36
15	CS Pandurii Lignitul Târgu Jiu	34	4	10	3	12	11	3	3	11	7	19	7	13	14	19	30	34
16	FC Politehnica Iași	34	6	6	5	15	16	1	4	12	13	34	7	10	17	28	50	31
17	FC Ceahlăul Piatra Neamț	34	4	5	8	16	28	2	5	10	12	29	6	10	18	28	57	28
18	FC Unirea Alba Iulia	34	7	3	7	24	21	0	2	15	9	41	7	5	22	33	62	26

NB FC Internațional Curtea de Argeș withdrew for 2010/11 season; CS Pandurii Lignitul Târgu Jiu remain at first level.

TOP GOALSCORERS

16 Andrei CRISTEA (Dinamo)

15 Pantelis KAPETANOS (Steaua)

12 Dorin GOGA (Timișoara)
   Marius BILAȘCO (Unirea Urziceni)
   WESLEY (Vaslui)

11 Liviu GANEA (Astra)

10 Cristian BUD (Gaz Metan/CFR Cluj)
   JÚNIOR MORAES (Gloria Bistrița)
   Alexandru IONIȚĂ (Rapid)

9 Lukáš MAGERA (Timișoara)
   Florin COSTEA (Univ Craiova)

CLUB-BY-CLUB

FC ASTRA PLOIEŞTI

Coach – Ion Moldovan; (20/8/09) Nicolò Napoli (ITA);
(20/4/10) Marin Barbu
Founded – 1937
Stadium – Astra (7,000)

2009

2/8	Pandurii	h	0-1	
8/8	Braşov	a	0-0	
15/8	Gloria Bistriţa	h	0-0	
21/8	Poli Iaşi	a	0-2	
29/8	Rapid	h	3-1	Ganea, Alexe 2
13/9	Timişoara	a	0-0	
18/9	Unirea Alba Iulia	h	4-2	Ganea 2, Đokić 2
25/9	Unirea Urziceni	a	1-4	Đokić
3/10	Vaslui	a	1-3	Paulinho
18/10	Univ Craiova	h	3-1	og (Mitchell), Ganea, Miranda
25/10	Internaţional	a	1-2	Miranda
31/10	Ceahlăul	h	1-1	Ganea
8/11	CFR Cluj	a	0-1	
23/11	Steaua	h	2-1	Păun 2
1/12	Oţelul	a	2-3	Ganea, Seto
8/12	Dinamo	h	1-1	og (Moţi)
13/12	Gaz Metan	a	0-0	

2010

21/2	Pandurii	a	2-0	Silva, Paulinho
28/2	Braşov	h	2-1	Ganea 2
6/3	Gloria Bistriţa	a	1-3	Silva
12/3	Poli Iaşi	h	1-1	Ganea
18/3	Rapid	a	1-0	Ganea
22/3	Timişoara	h	1-3	Ganea
27/3	Unirea Alba Iulia	a	1-2	Seto
2/4	Unirea Urziceni	h	0-2	
7/4	Vaslui	h	0-0	
10/4	Univ Craiova	a	0-1	
15/4	Internaţional	h	1-1	Carando
23/4	Ceahlăul	a	0-0	
30/4	CFR Cluj	h	1-0	Stan
5/5	Steaua	a	0-2	
9/5	Oţelul	h	0-3	
16/5	Dinamo	a	3-3	Vădrariu 2, Seto
22/5	Gaz Metan	h	0-0	

No	Name	Nat	DoB	Pos	Aps	(s)	Gls
11	Marius Silviu ALEXE		22/2/90	M	3		2
18	Álvaro Maximiliano ARIAS Invernizzi	URU	3/10/80	D	1	(1)	
	BRUNO Martins SIMÃO	POR	5/5/85	A		(4)	
21	Danilo Ezequiel CARANDO	ARG	5/8/88	A		(6)	1
7	Hristu CHIACU		6/9/86	A	2	(1)	
9	Ştefan CIOBANU		2/5/79	A	1	(2)	
6	Lucian CONDREA		13/1/93	D		(1)	
21	Cornel Flaviu CORNEA		28/7/81	M	2	(2)	
25	Eugen Florin CRĂCIUN		22/3/86	D	15		
9	Dušan ĐOKIĆ	SRB	20/2/80	A	8	(2)	3
15	Cristinel Dimitrie GAFIŢA		10/5/84	A		(6)	
19	Liviu Adrian GANEA		23/2/88	A	26		11
20	Vasile GHEORGHE		5/9/85	M	32	(1)	
11	Vitali GUSSEV	EST	16/3/83	A	4	(8)	
6	Kevin HATCHI	FRA	6/8/81	D	1	(5)	
6	Silviu IZVORANU		3/12/82	D	1	(1)	
2	Alejandro Matías KRUCHOWSKY	ARG	20/1/83	D	4		
23	Marcelo Fabián MÉNDEZ	URU	10/1/83	D	8		
4	Marius Ovidiu MIHALACHE		14/12/84	D	33		
11	Osvaldo Noé MIRANDA	ARG	24/6/84	A	8	(1)	2
82	Bogdan Ionuţ MIRON		2/1/82	G	23		
12	Cristian MUNTEANU		10/11/74	G	10		
19	Nicolae MUŞAT		4/12/86	D		(1)	
3	Radek OPRŠAL	CZE	9/5/78	D	30		

7	Paulo Dinarte Gouveia Pestana "PAULINHO"	BRA	30/1/85	M	19	(9)	2
14	Georgian PĂUN		24/10/85	A	7	(7)	2
13	Daniel Gabriel POPA		27/8/85	G	1		
21	Cornel PREDESCU		21/12/87	M	2		
5	Gheorghe ROHAT		23/1/75	D	27	(2)	
17	Valentin SANDU		28/2/83	D	12	(7)	
6	Dorin Constantin SEMEGHIN		29/3/79	D		(3)	
8	Takayuki SETO	JPN	5/2/86	M	34		3
10	Diego Emilio SILVA	URU	15/4/87	A	8		2
20	Alexandru Constantin STAN		7/2/89	D	12	(9)	1
27	Sorin Daniel STRĂTILĂ		20/10/86	M	28		
17	Marius TIGOIANU		22/9/89	M		(1)	
10	Claudiu TUDOR		29/4/85	A	6	(2)	
26	Abel VALDEZ	ARG	28/4/88	D		(1)	
14	Daniel Petru VĂDRARIU		25/6/90	A	5	(5)	2
27	Cătălin Petruţ VLAICU		4/3/85	D	1	(4)	

FC BRAŞOV

Coach – Dinu Viorel Moldovan
Founded – 1937
Stadium – Silviu Ploeşteanu (12,670)

2009

1/8	Unirea Alba Iulia	a	1-0	Hadnagy
8/8	Astra	h	0-0	
16/8	Vaslui	a	2-2	Ezequias, Roman
21/8	Univ Craiova	h	2-0	Nuno Diogo, Zaharia
28/8	Internaţional	a	3-0	Ilyeş (p), Hadnagy, Munteanu
11/9	Ceahlăul	h	1-0	Ilyeş (p)
20/9	CFR Cluj	a	1-2	og (Hugo Alcântara)
27/9	Steaua	h	0-0	
2/10	Oţelul	a	1-1	Voicu
18/10	Dinamo	h	0-1	
23/10	Gaz Metan	a	1-1	Cristescu
2/11	Pandurii	h	2-0	Măldărăşanu, Ilyeş
7/11	Unirea Urziceni	h	0-0	
22/11	Gloria Bistriţa	a	1-2	Ilyeş
30/11	Poli Iaşi	h	2-0	Zaharia, Sburlea
5/12	Rapid	a	1-2	Voicu
13/12	Timişoara	h	1-0	Nuno Diogo

2010

20/2	Unirea Alba Iulia	h	2-1	Zaharia, Sburlea
28/2	Astra	a	1-2	Ilyeş (p)
8/3	Vaslui	h	1-1	Abrudan
13/3	Univ Craiova	a	0-3	
16/3	Internaţional	h	1-2	Zaharia
20/3	Ceahlăul	a	1-2	Savic
29/3	CFR Cluj	h	0-1	
2/4	Steaua	a	0-1	
6/4	Oţelul	h	3-0	Abrudan, Sburlea, Roman
11/4	Dinamo	a	0-0	
17/4	Gaz Metan	h	3-2	Grigore (p), Sburlea, Hadnagy
24/4	Pandurii	a	0-1	
2/5	Unirea Urziceni	a	0-1	
6/5	Gloria Bistriţa	h	6-0	Abrudan, Munteanu, Sburlea, og (Năstase), Chipciu, Hadnagy
11/5	Poli Iaşi	a	0-0	
16/5	Rapid	h	1-1	Roman
22/5	Timişoara	a	2-1	Savic, Cristescu

No	Name	Nat	DoB	Pos	Aps	(s)	Gls
4	Octavian ABRUDAN		16/3/84	D	25		3
5	Alexandru CHIPCIU		18/9/89	M		(2)	1
1	Dănuţ Dumitru COMAN		28/3/79	G	22		
23	Nicolae CONSTANTIN		3/12/73	D	6		
18	Marian CRISTESCU		17/3/85	M	7	(14)	2
17	Cătălin DEDU		16/5/88	A		(3)	
3	EZEQUIAS Roosevelt Tavares de Melo	BRA	28/1/81	D	28		1

8	Nicolae GRIGORE		19/7/83	M	29	(1)	1
9	Attila HADNAGY		6/3/80	A	16	(6)	4
10	Robert ILYEŞ		4/2/74	M	19	(8)	5
12	Cristian Mihai IONESCU		1/3/78	D	7	(3)	
13	Gabriel KAJCSA		7/7/74	G		(2)	
24	Julio LANDAURI	PER	17/3/86	A	2	(4)	
26	Alexandru MATEIU		10/12/89	M	2	(2)	
27	Marius Constantin MĂLDĂRĂŞANU		19/4/75	M	14	(4)	1
32	Mihai Adrian MINCĂ		8/10/84	G	12		
7	Cătălin Constantin MUNTEANU		26/1/79	M	28	(3)	2
6	Adriano Barbosa Miranda da Luz "NÉNÉ"	CPV	24/8/79	M	2	(7)	
55	NUNO Miguel Pereira DIOGO	POR	13/6/81	D	23	(1)	2
15	Daniel OROS		15/8/84	D	14	(1)	
28	Alexandru Vitorio PIŢURCĂ		28/10/83	A	2	(3)	
14	Mihai ROMAN		16/11/84	M	23	(2)	3
2	RUI Sandro de Carvalho DUARTE	POR	11/10/80	D	21		
19	Dusan SAVIC	MKD	1/10/85	A	5	(5)	2
21	Sabrin SBURLEA		12/5/89	A	18	(13)	5
25	Adrian SENIN		27/8/79	M		(1)	
25	Stelian STANCU		22/9/88	D	7	(2)	
20	Ionuţ Cosmin VOICU		2/8/84	D	18	(6)	2
11	Dorel ZAHARIA		21/2/78	A	24	(4)	4

FC CEAHLĂUL PIATRA NEAMŢ
Coach – Florin Marin; (30/9/09) Gheorghe Mulţescu;
(2/3/10) Zoran Filipović (MNE)
Founded – 1919
Stadium – Ceahlăul (12,500)

2009

2/8	Steaua	h	0-2	
9/8	Oţelul	a	0-0	
15/8	Dinamo	h	0-4	
22/8	Gaz Metan	a	2-0	Fabbron, Gafiţa
29/8	Pandurii	h	1-2	Doicaru
11/9	Braşov	a	0-1	
19/9	Gloria Bistriţa	h	2-1	Forminte, Bădescu (p)
26/9	Poli Iaşi	a	0-2	
2/10	Rapid	h	0-4	
17/10	Timişoara	a	0-6	
24/10	Unirea Alba Iulia	h	1-1	Doicaru
31/10	Astra	a	1-1	Şofroni
7/11	Vaslui	h	0-1	
23/11	Univ Craiova	a	2-3	Bădescu, Cebotari
28/11	Internaţional	h	2-2	Ferariu, Cebotari
4/12	Unirea Urziceni	h	2-3	Ibrahim, Fabbron
12/12	CFR Cluj	a	0-2	

2010

20/2	Steaua	a	3-1	Onciu, Vasilache, Bădescu
26/2	Oţelul	h	0-1	
6/3	Dinamo	a	1-1	Mulisa
12/3	Gaz Metan	h	0-0	
17/3	Pandurii	a	0-0	
20/3	Braşov	h	2-1	Mulisa, Cebotari
28/3	Gloria Bistriţa	a	0-1	
2/4	Poli Iaşi	h	1-0	Vasilache
8/4	Rapid	a	1-1	Cebotari
11/4	Timişoara	h	1-1	Viţelaru
15/4	Unirea Alba Iulia	a	2-3	Bădescu, Cebotari
23/4	Astra	h	0-0	
1/5	Vaslui	a	0-1	
5/5	Univ Craiova	h	2-1	Ibrahim, Cebotari
9/5	Internaţional	a	0-2	
17/5	Unirea Urziceni	a	0-4	
22/5	CFR Cluj	h	2-4	Vasilache, Onciu

No	Name	Nat	DoB	Pos	Aps	(s)	Gls
6	Alexandru Vlad ACHIM		7/4/89	M	18	(6)	
20	George AMBOUROUET	GAB	1/5/86	D	8		
18	Habib-Jean BALDÉ	GUI	8/2/85	A	13	(1)	

8	Daniel Ionuţ BARNA		22/9/86	D	17		
15	Ionuţ BĂDESCU		25/1/79	M	31		4
13	Cosmin BÂRCĂUAN		5/8/78	D	10	(2)	
2	Marius Mihai BURLACU		29/10/85	D	15	(2)	
7	Evgheny CEBOTARI	MDA	16/10/84	M	28	(4)	6
3	Rodrigue DIKABA	COD	28/10/85	D	7		
9	Radu DOICARU		26/2/79	A	11	(2)	2
4	Alexandru DRAGOMIR		18/2/85	A	5	(2)	
33	Ioan Andrei DUMITRAŞ		23/1/88	D	8	(2)	
20	EDSON Rolando Silva Sousa	CPV	3/9/83	A	2	(5)	
23	ERSIN Veli	TUR	2/4/82	D	2		
19	Vinícius de Oliveira FABBRON	BRA	26/3/89	A	8	(5)	2
21	Constantin FERARIU		23/9/86	D	8	(4)	1
20	Liviu Marius FLORICEL		30/6/87	D	2	(1)	
24	Alexandru Gheorghe FORMINTE		19/9/82	D	31		1
14	Cristinel GAFIŢA		14/6/87	A	5	(5)	1
25	Abdoulaye IBRAHIM	TOG	25/10/86	A	10	(6)	2
5	Alexandru ICHIM		21/8/89	D	4		
16	Slaviša JEREMIĆ	SRB	15/2/83	M	4	(6)	
1	Valentin Cosmin LIPITOR		24/2/82	G	5		
18	Vasile Florin MACOVEI		21/1/87	D		(2)	
28	Andrei MARC		29/4/93	M		(2)	
9	Alexandru MARGINĂ		8/3/83	A		(1)	
19	Jimmy MULISA	RWA	3/4/84	A	12	(3)	2
13	Marius Gheorghe ONCIU		23/4/87	M	15	(1)	2
26	Tănăsel Dănuţ PRODAN		13/1/85	M	4	(7)	
12	Andrei ROHEŢKI		18/11/85	G	9	(1)	
4	Valentin ROTARU		10/5/87	A	1	(1)	
20	RUDISON Nogueira Ferreira	BRA	15/2/83	D	2	(5)	
22	George Daniel SAVU		20/3/83	G	3	(1)	
16	Mădălin STAICU		16/7/90	M		(1)	
5	Saša STEVIĆ	BIH	31/5/81	D	15		
10	George Daniel ŞOFRONI		10/6/91	M	2	(6)	1
11	Gabriel TUDOSĂ		17/2/88	A	2	(7)	
10	Ciprian VASILACHE		14/9/83	M	12	(1)	3
21	Krste VELKOSKI	MKD	20/2/88	A	5	(3)	
22	Thomas VILLADSEN	DEN	4/9/84	G	17		
17	Andrei VIŢELARU		3/2/85	D	23		1

CFR 1907 CLUJ
Coach –António Conceição "Toni" (POR);
(14/11/09) Andrea Mandorlini (ITA)
Founded – 1907
Stadium – Dr Constantin Rădulescu (23,200)
MAJOR HONOURS:
Romanian League - (2) 2008, 2010;
Romanian Cup (3) 2008, 2009, 2010.

2009

1/8	Unirea Urziceni	h	2-0	Peralta, Dubarbier
9/8	Steaua	a	2-2	Koné, Flores
15/8	Oţelul	h	1-0	Traoré
23/8	Dinamo	a	0-1	
30/8	Gaz Metan	h	2-0	Traoré, Mara
11/9	Pandurii	a	0-1	
20/9	Braşov	h	2-1	Dubarbier, Cadú
27/9	Gloria Bistriţa	a	2-0	Traoré, Hugo Alcântara
4/10	Poli Iaşi	h	1-1	Cadú (p)
17/10	Rapid	a	4-1	Nei 2, Mureşan, Peralta
25/10	Timişoara	h	0-0	
1/11	Unirea Alba Iulia	a	1-1	Traoré
8/11	Astra	h	1-0	Dubarbier
23/11	Vaslui	a	0-2	
28/11	Univ Craiova	h	2-0	Cadú, Koné
7/12	Internaţional	a	1-0	Hugo Alcântara
12/12	Ceahlăul	h	2-0	Koné 2

2010

22/2	Unirea Urziceni	a	1-0	Traoré
28/2	Steaua	h	1-1	Cadú
7/3	Oţelul	a	0-1	
13/3	Dinamo	h	2-2	Bud, Culio
17/3	Gaz Metan	a	0-0	
20/3	Pandurii	h	1-0	Hugo Alcântara

29/3	Brașov	a	1-0	Bud
3/4	Gloria Bistrița	h	1-0	Koné
8/4	Poli Iași	a	2-0	Nei 2
11/4	Rapid	h	1-0	Mureșan
18/4	Timișoara	a	1-1	Deac
24/4	Unirea Alba Iulia	h	3-2	Bud 3
30/4	Astra	a	0-1	
6/5	FC Vaslui	h	0-0	
10/5	Univ Craiova	a	3-2	Traoré, Bud, Cadú
15/5	Internațional	h	2-1	Bud, Deac
22/5	Ceahlăul	a	4-2	Dică E., Koné, Peralta, Nei

No	Name	Nat	DoB	Pos	Aps	(s)	Gls
28	Andrei Ionuț BOROȘTEAN		25/2/87	M	1		
16	Davide BOTTONE	ITA	11/4/86	M	4	(3)	
85	Cristian BUD		25/6/85	A	11	(4)	7
22	Sergiu Florin BUȘ		2/11/92	A		(1)	
3	Nelson David CABRERA Báez	PAR	22/4/83	D	5		
20	Ricardo Manuel Ferreira de Sousa "CADÚ"	POR	21/12/81	D	28		5
19	Emmanuel Juan CULIO	ARG	30/8/84	M	28		1
31	DANIel Ricardo da Silva Soares	POR	30/1/82	M	17	(4)	
11	Roberto DE ZERBI	ITA	6/6/79	M	1	(3)	
77	Ciprian Ioan DEAC		16/2/86	A	16	(8)	2
30	Emil Cosmin DICĂ		17/7/82	M	6	(8)	1
10	Nicolae Constantin DICĂ		9/5/80	M	10	(3)	
29	Cleidimar Magalhães Silva "DIDY"	BRA	10/9/82	A		(7)	
7	Sebastián DUBARBIER	ARG	19/2/86	M	12	(4)	3
66	EDIMAR Curitiba Fraga	BRA	21/5/86	D	15	(1)	
16	Darío Antonio FLORES	URU	6/2/84	M	3	(2)	1
15	HUGO da Silva ALCÁNTARA	BRA	28/7/79	D	20	(2)	3
17	Yssouf KONÉ	BFA	19/2/82	A	18	(3)	6
25	André Felipe Ribeiro "LEÃO"	POR	20/5/85	M	3	(2)	
23	LEONARDO Henrique Veloso	BRA	29/5/87	D	8	(2)	
23	Bogdan Ion MARA		29/9/77	A	9	(7)	1
6	Gabriel MUREȘAN		13/2/82	D	28		2
99	Claudinei Alexandre Aparecido "NEI"	BRA	2/5/80	A	8	(12)	5
1	NUNO CLARO Simões Coimbra	POR	7/1/77	G	27		
4	Cristian Călin PANIN		9/6/78	D	27	(2)	
8	Sixto Raimundo PERALTA Salso	ARG	16/4/69	M	16	(10)	3
1	Boris PEŠKOVIĆ	SVK	30/6/76	G	5		
13	Felice PICCOLO	ITA	27/8/83	D	9	(1)	
	Diego Alejandro RUIZ	ARG	19/12/80	A		(1)	
44	Eduard Cornel STĂNCIOIU		3/3/81	G	2	(2)	
2	Anthony da Silva "TONY"	POR	20/12/80	D	19	(1)	
9	Lacine TRAORÉ	CIV	20/5/85	A	18	(7)	6
10	Eugen TRICĂ		5/8/76	M		(1)	

FC DINAMO BUCUREȘTI

Coach – Dario Bonetti (ITA); (2/10/09) (Marin Ion);
(24/10/09) Cornel Țălnar
Founded – 1948
Stadium – Dinamo (15,300)
MAJOR HONOURS:
Romanian League - (18) 1955, 1962, 1963, 1964, 1965, 1971, 1973, 1975,
1977, 1982, 1983, 1984, 1990, 1992, 2000, 2002, 2004, 2007;
Romanian Cup - (12) 1959, 1964, 1968, 1982, 1984, 1986, 1990, 2000,
2001, 2003, 2004, 2005.

2009

1/8	Univ Craiova	a	0-0	
7/8	Internațional	h	0-1	
15/8	Ceahlăul	a	4-0	Dănciulescu 2, Cristea Ad,, Torje
23/8	CFR Cluj	h	1-0	Niculae
30/8	Steaua	a	1-0	Tamaș
12/9	Oțelul	h	0-1	
20/9	Unirea Urziceni	h	2-1	Cristea An., Torje
26/9	Gaz Metan	a	0-1	
4/10	Pandurii	h	1-1	Tamaș (p)

18/10	Brașov	a	1-0	Cristea An.
25/10	Gloria Bistrița	h	1-1	Cristea An.
1/11	Poli Iași	a	3-1	Cristea An. 2, Cristea Ad.
8/11	Rapid	h	1-1	Niculescu
23/11	Timișoara	a	0-2	
28/11	Unirea Alba Iulia	h	2-0	Niculescu, Niculae
8/12	Astra	a	1-1	Niculescu
13/12	Vaslui	h	1-1	N'Doye (p)
2010				
21/2	Univ Craiova	h	2-1	Boștină, Niculae
27/2	Internațional	a	3-1	Cristea An. 2, Alexe
6/3	Ceahlăul	h	1-1	og (Vițelaru)
13/3	CFR Cluj	a	2-2	Cristea An., Boștină
17/3	Steaua	h	2-0	Alexe, Cristea An.
21/3	Oțelul	a	3-2	Moți, Alexe, Cristea An.
28/3	Unirea Urziceni	a	4-4	og (Bruno Fernandes), Cristea An. 2 (1p), Torje
2/4	Gaz Metan	h	1-0	Alexe
8/4	Pandurii	a	0-0	
11/4	Brașov	h	0-0	
17/4	Gloria Bistrița	a	2-3	Niculescu, Cristea An. (p)
23/4	Poli Iași	h	1-1	N'Doye
2/5	Rapid	a	2-2	Cristea An., Alexe
6/5	Timișoara	h	1-2	Niculae
10/5	Unirea Alba Iulia	a	2-1	Cristea An. 2 (1p)
16/5	Astra	h	3-3	Scarlatache, Bratu (p), Cristea Ad.
22/5	Vaslui	a	0-2	

No	Name	Nat	DoB	Pos	Aps	(s)	Gls
10	Marius Silviu ALEXE		22/2/90	A	18	(7)	5
8	Gabriel BOȘTINĂ		22/5/77	M	22	(5)	2
15	Florin Daniel BRATU		2/1/80	A	1	(5)	1
20	Adrian CRISTEA		30/11/83	M	18	(10)	3
17	Andrei CRISTEA		15/5/84	M	28	(1)	16
34	George CURCĂ		8/5/81	G	7	(1)	
19	Cristian DAMINUȚA		15/2/80	A		(2)	
10	Ionel Daniel DĂNCIULESCU		6/12/76	A	3	(1)	2
2	Zie DIABATÉ	CIV	2/3/89	D	4	(4)	
12	Emilian Ioan DOLHA		3/11/79	G	22		
18	Lucian GOIAN		10/2/83	D	12	(1)	
21	Dragoș GRIGORE		7/9/86	D	10	(2)	
5	Djakaridja KONÉ	CIV	22/6/86	D	15	(6)	
26	Andrei Silviu MĂRGĂRITESCU		1/1/80	M	4	(2)	
14	Francisco José MOLINERO Calderón	ESP	26/7/85	D	16		
4	Cosmin Iosif MOȚI		3/12/84	D	22	(2)	1
1	Cristian MUNTEANU		10/11/74	G	5		
29	Ousmane N'DOYE	SEN	21/3/78	M	26	(1)	2
9	Marius Constantin NICULAE		16/5/81	A	18	(2)	4
99	Claudiu Iulian NICULESCU		23/6/76	A	11	(13)	4
3	Cristian Corneliu PULHAC		17/8/84	D	29		
6	Laurențiu RUS		7/5/85	M	11	(9)	
25	Manuel Adrian SCARLATACHE		5/12/86	D	26	(1)	1
24	Raphael STĂNESCU		27/6/93	M		(1)	
19	Viorel Ionuț ȘTEFAN		7/1/92	M		(1)	
30	Gabriel Sebastian TAMAȘ		5/11/83	D	12		2
22	Andrei Gabriel TORJE		22/11/89	M	28	(1)	3
24	Voijislav VRANJKOVIĆ	SRB	1/1/83	M		(1)	
27	Paulo Batista Nsimba "ZÉ KALANGA"	ANG	12/10/83	M		(2)	
7	Ianis Alin ZICU		23/10/83	M	5	(13)	
30	Martin ŽIVNÝ	CZE	20/3/81	D	1		

CS GAZ METAN MEDIAȘ

Coach – Cristian Pustai
Founded – 1945
Stadium – Municipal (5,000)

2009

7/8	Univ Craiova	h	2-1	Eric, Kubala
12/8	Vaslui	a	1-2	Bud
16/8	Internațional	a	4-2	Silvășan, Dudiță, Marković, Kubala
22/8	Ceahlăul	h	0-2	

ROMANIA

30/8	CFR Cluj	a	0-2	
13/9	Steaua	h	2-4	Pârvulescu, Bud
19/9	Oţelul	a	1-0	Bud
26/9	Dinamo	h	1-0	Eric
3/10	Unirea Urziceni	h	0-0	
17/10	Pandurii	a	0-0	
23/10	Braşov	h	1-1	Hoban
2/11	Gloria Bistriţa	a	1-1	Silvăşan
7/11	Poli Iaşi	h	2-1	Silvăşan, Hoban
20/11	Rapid	a	1-4	Pârvulescu
29/11	Timişoara	h	2-6	Todea, Eric (p)
6/12	Unirea Alba Iulia	a	0-0	
13/12	Astra	h	0-0	
2010				
21/2	Vaslui	h	0-0	
27/2	Univ Craiova	a	2-1	Liţu, Lazăr
7/3	Internaţional	h	0-0	
12/3	Ceahlăul	a	0-0	
17/3	CFR Cluj	h	0-0	
21/3	Steaua	a	0-2	
26/3	Oţelul	h	0-1	
2/4	Dinamo	a	0-1	
7/4	Unirea Urziceni	a	1-1	Dudiţă
11/4	Pandurii	h	1-0	Kubala
17/4	Braşov	a	2-3	Muntean, Liţu
25/4	Gloria Bistriţa	h	1-1	Liţu
2/5	Poli Iaşi	a	1-1	Eric
5/5	Rapid	h	0-0	
10/5	Timişoara	a	2-0	Eric 2
15/5	Unirea Alba Iulia	h	5-0	Eric 2, Hoban, Khubutia, Dudiţă
22/5	Astra	a	0-0	

No	Name	Nat	DoB	Pos	Aps	(s)	Gls
6	Andrei Dan BOZEŞAN		12/2/88	M	2	(4)	
30	Miloš BUCHTA	CZE	19/7/80	G	27		
99	Cristian BUD		3/4/82	A	12	(4)	3
8	Ionuţ Arghir BUZEAN		18/9/82	D	14	(8)	
9	Cristian Lucian CIGAN		15/7/87	A	2	(14)	
17	Doru DUDIŢĂ		7/9/77	M	12	(13)	3
27	ERIC de Oliveira Pereira	BRA	5/12/85	M	24	(6)	8
29	Vasilios GALANIS	GRE	13/8/87	A	3	(5)	
15	Ovidiu Ştefan HOBAN		27/12/82	D	32		3
30	Akaki KHUBUTIA	GEO	17/3/86	D	19	(3)	1
44	Karel KRATOCHVÍL	CZE	8/6/82	D	11	(2)	
7	Michal KUBALA	SVK	12/6/80	M	26		3
19	Florin Daniel LAZĂR		15/1/80	D	25	(2)	1
9	Alin LIŢU		22/10/86	A	10		3
25	Zarko MARKOVIĆ	SRB	28/1/87	D	11		1
23	Marko MAROVIĆ	SRB	30/1/83	D	9	(3)	
5	Alexandru MUNTEAN		1/1/88	M	23	(8)	1
20	Gheorghe Florin NOHAI		13/4/81	D	12	(4)	
22	Paul PÂRVULESCU		11/8/88	M	27	(2)	2
3	Marius RADU		1/6/77	D	1	(1)	
14	Florin Cosmin SABOU		16/1/80	M	1	(4)	
77	Cristian Radu SILVĂŞAN		25/2/82	A	19	(5)	3
21	Cristian TODEA		18/10/78	M	27	(2)	1
3	Jasmin TRTOVAC	SRB	27/12/86	D	6	(3)	
82	Cosmin Andrei VÂTCĂ		7/3/81	G	7	(1)	
24	Mircea VOICU		17/4/80	M		(1)	
16	Radu Neculai ZAHARIA		25/1/89	D	12	(5)	

ACF GLORIA 1922 BISTRIŢA
Coach – Sandu Tăbîrcă; (5/10/09) Marian Pană;
(5/1/10) Marius Şumudică
Founded – 1922
Stadium – Gloria (12,000)
MAJOR HONOURS:
Romanian Cup - (1) 1994.

2009				
1/8	Timişoara	a	0-1	
8/8	Unirea Alba Iulia	h	1-1	Anca
15/8	Astra	a	0-0	

23/8	Vaslui	h	1-3	Săceanu
29/8	Univ Craiova	a	1-5	Hora
12/9	Internaţional	h	0-1	
19/9	Ceahlăul	a	1-2	Sânmărtean L.
27/9	CFR Cluj	h	0-2	
4/10	Steaua	a	1-1	og (Toja)
18/10	Oţelul	h	2-1	Borbely 2
25/10	Dinamo	a	1-1	Keita
2/11	Gaz Metan	h	1-1	Keita
6/11	Pandurii	a	1-1	Keita
22/11	Braşov	h	2-1	Coroian, Hora (p)
30/11	Unirea Urziceni	a	0-2	
5/12	Poli Iaşi	a	0-0	
11/12	Rapid	h	1-1	Keita
2010				
20/2	Timişoara	h	0-0	
26/2	Unirea Alba Iulia	a	2-1	Júnior Moraes, Coroian
6/3	Astra	h	3-1	Júnior Moraes 2, og (Mihalache)
14/3	Vaslui	a	1-0	Hora
17/3	Univ Craiova	h	2-1	Júnior Moraes (p), Hora
21/3	Internaţional	a	1-2	Júnior Moraes
28/3	Ceahlăul	h	1-0	Petre
3/4	CFR Cluj	a	0-1	
7/4	Steaua	h	1-2	Júnior Moraes
10/4	Oţelul	a	0-3	
17/4	Dinamo	h	3-2	Júnior Moraes 2, Năstase
24/4	Gaz Metan	a	1-1	Frăsinescu
30/4	Pandurii	h	1-0	Coroian
6/5	Braşov	a	0-6	
11/5	Unirea Urziceni	h	0-0	
16/5	Poli Iaşi	h	5-0	Júnior Moraes, Mureşan 2, Coroian, Băjenaru (p)
22/5	Rapid	a	1-2	Júnior Moraes

No	Name	Nat	DoB	Pos	Aps	(s)	Gls
14	Sebastian Zoltan ACHIM		2/6/86	M	10	(5)	
22	Septimiu Călin ALBUŢ		23/5/81	G	32		
20	Adrian Gheorghe ANCA		27/3/76	A	3		1
15	Paul Viorel ANTON		10/5/91	M	1		
30	Liviu BĂJENARU		6/5/83	M	26	(4)	1
29	László Csaba BORBELY		5/7/80	A	9	(3)	2
3	Mădălin Marius CIUCĂ		4/11/82	D	22	(1)	
7	Cristian Ambrozie COROIAN		14/3/73	A	20	(8)	4
8	DIOGO Emanuel Alves RAMOS	POR	8/11/86	A		(1)	
26	Ştefan Andrei ENESCU		12/10/87	M	5	(5)	
18	Cosmin Vali FRĂSINESCU		10/2/85	D	21		1
20	Sergiu HOMEI		6/7/87	D	27	(1)	
24	Ioan Adrian HORA		21/8/88	M	28	(2)	4
9	Sorin Adrian IODI		12/6/76	D	7	(3)	
10	Aluísio Chaves Ribeiro JÚNIOR MORAES	BRA	4/4/87	A	17		10
9	Souleymane KEITA	SEN	4/11/87	M	5	(17)	4
15	Iasmin LATOVLEVICI		11/5/86	D	12		
23	Alexandru MANDEA		27/3/89	M		(4)	
28	Dan MATEI		25/6/81	D	7	(6)	
16	Radu Leon MĂRGINEAN		3/1/83	M		(1)	
11	Tibor Florian MOLDOVAN		3/5/82	A		(5)	
4	Andrei Iosif MUREŞAN		1/8/85	M	18	(1)	2
4	Valentin Vasile NĂSTASE		4/10/74	D	15	(3)	1
29	Răzvan NEAGU		25/5/87	A	2	(3)	
21	Ştefan ODOROABĂ		14/2/81	D	1	(1)	
2	Ciprian Cătălin PETRE		10/12/80	M	18	(5)	1
6	Alin Valer RUS		30/9/75	D	9		
17	Robert Elian SĂCEANU		22/6/83	M	5	(9)	1
27	Dinu SÂNMĂRTEAN		28/7/81	D	12		
10	Lucian Iulian SÂNMĂRTEAN		13/3/80	M	14	(1)	1
1	Petru ŢURCAŞ		16/5/76	G	2		
23	Alexandru Ion VAGNER		19/8/89	M	5		
5	Gabriel Cristian VELCOVICI		2/10/84	M	12	(4)	
16	José Rui Tavares da Veiga "ZÉ RUI"	CPV	16/9/82	M	9	(8)	

FC INTERNAŢIONAL CURTEA DE ARGEŞ

Coach –Ştefan Stoica; (24/12/09) Ionuţ Badea
Founded – 2000
Stadium – Dacia, Mioveni (7,000); Nicolae Dobrin, Piteşti (16,400)

2009

31/7	Oţelul	h	0-1	
7/8	Dinamo	a	1-0	Popa F.
16/8	Gaz Metan	h	2-4	Gado, Neagu
23/8	Pandurii	a	3-2	Răduţ 2 (1p), Vezan
28/8	Braşov	h	0-3	
12/9	Gloria Bistriţa	a	1-0	Răduţ
18/9	Poli Iaşi	h	0-2	
27/9	Rapid	a	0-4	
5/10	Timişoara	h	0-3	
16/10	Unirea Alba Iulia	a	2-1	Stoianof, Koné
25/10	Astra	h	2-1	Itu, Vezan
1/11	Vaslui	a	0-1	
6/11	Univ Craiova	h	0-1	
21/11	Unirea Urziceni	h	1-2	Voiculeţ
28/11	Ceahlăul	a	2-2	Lazăr, Voiculeţ
7/12	CFR Cluj	h	0-1	
13/12	Steaua	a	2-3	Băcilă, Zăgrean
2010				
19/2	Oţelul	a	0-1	
27/2	Dinamo	h	1-3	Apostu
7/3	Gaz Metan	a	0-0	
13/3	Pandurii	h	0-0	
16/3	Braşov	a	2-1	Koné, Băcilă
21/3	Gloria Bistriţa	h	2-1	Koné, Băcilă
27/3	Poli Iaşi	a	0-0	
3/4	Rapid	h	1-2	Băcilă
7/4	Timişoara	a	0-0	
10/4	Unirea Alba Iulia	h	2-1	Voiculeţ, Stan
15/4	Astra	a	1-1	Apostu
26/4	Vaslui	h	1-2	Băcilă
1/5	Univ Craiova	a	3-1	Răduţ, Koné, Stan
6/5	Unirea Urziceni	a	0-1	
9/5	Ceahlăul	h	2-0	Apostu 2 (1p)
15/5	CFR Cluj	a	1-2	Apostu
22/5	Steaua	h	0-2	

No	Name	Nat	DoB	Pos	Aps	(s)	Gls
26	Abiodun AGUNBIADE	NGA	2/1/83	M	6	(4)	
26	Miodrag ANĐELKOVIĆ	SRB	7/7/77	A		(1)	
18	Andrei ANTOHI		16/12/88	A	1	(4)	
9	Bogdan Radu APOSTU		20/4/82	A	14	(4)	5
22	Tomislav ARČABA	AUS	12/12/86	G	4		
2	Cosmin Nicolae BĂCILĂ		10/9/83	D	24	(5)	5
6	Tiberiu BIER		15/7/87	D		(1)	
6	George BLAY	GHA	7/8/80	D	3		
21	Vlad Iulian CHIRICHEŞ		14/11/89	D	14	(1)	
20	Teofil Alexandru CIUCUR		1/3/90	M	2	(2)	
27	Alexandru FILIP		22/7/87	D	2		
24	Dănuţ Cornel FRĂSINEANU		20/8/76	M	22	(2)	
17	Ramses GADO		9/5/82	M	3		1
18	Claudiu Mihai IONESCU		18/8/84	A	1	(3)	
9	Lucian ITU		8/9/78	A	2	(7)	1
4	Silviu IZVORANU		3/12/82	D	10		
26	Marius Dumitru JIANU		29/1/89	A	1	(2)	
5	Emmanuel KONÉ	CIV	31/12/86	M	28	(2)	4
10	Cătălin LAZĂR		16/11/85	M	11	(7)	1
6	Dan MATEI		25/6/81	D	8		
15	Gabriel Eugen MATEI		26/2/90	M	14	(1)	
28	Nasser MENASSEL	FRA	6/1/83	M	17	(7)	
25	Alexandru George NEAGU		24/4/85	D	17	(4)	1
1	Florin Clement PAMPEA		14/7/75	G		(1)	
27	Doru Mihai PINTILII		9/11/84	M	15		
23	Florin POPA		1/6/83	D	4	(1)	1
12	Marius Viorel POPA		31/7/78	G	30		
29	Alin RAŢIU		14/9/82	D	8		
7	Mihai Cosmin RĂDUŢ		18/3/90	M	24	(2)	4
30	Daniel STAN		28/8/78	A	8	(10)	2
11	Ovidiu STOIANOF		28/6/85	A	6	(11)	1
8	Ovidiu VEZAN		20/3/85	M	14	(11)	2
3	Ousmane VIERA Diarrassouba	CIV	21/12/86	D	30		
14	Claudiu Dorian VOICULEŢ		8/8/85	M	24	(3)	3
19	Andrei ZĂGREAN		16/10/86	A	7	(3)	1

FC OŢELUL GALAŢI

Coach – Dorinel Munteanu
Founded – 1964
Stadium – Oţelul (13,500)

2009

31/7	Internaţional	a	1-0	Axente
9/8	Ceahlăul	h	0-0	
15/8	CFR Cluj	a	0-1	
23/8	Steaua	h	0-1	
28/8	Unirea Urziceni	h	1-4	Paraschiv
12/9	Dinamo	a	1-0	Axente
19/9	Gaz Metan	h	0-1	
27/9	Pandurii	a	3-2	Antal, Paraschiv 2
2/10	Braşov	h	1-1	Giurgiu
18/10	Gloria Bistriţa	a	1-2	Antal
23/10	Poli Iaşi	h	4-0	Giurgiu 2, Ibeh, Pena (p)
1/11	Rapid	a	0-3	
8/11	Timişoara	h	3-3	Axente 2, Ibeh
20/11	Unirea Alba Iulia	a	1-3	Paraschiv
1/12	Astra	h	3-2	Ibeh, Pena, Iorga
6/12	Vaslui	a	1-1	Sârghi
12/12	Univ Craiova	h	1-0	Ilie
2010				
19/2	Internaţional	h	1-0	Ochiroşii
26/2	Ceahlăul	a	1-0	Giurgiu
7/3	CFR Cluj	h	1-0	Neagu
12/3	Steaua	a	0-1	
18/3	Unirea Urziceni	a	0-0	
21/3	Dinamo	h	2-3	Paraschiv, Antal
26/3	Gaz Metan	a	1-0	Costin
2/4	Pandurii	h	1-1	Iorga
6/4	Braşov	a	0-3	
10/4	Gloria Bistriţa	h	3-0	Antal (p), Viglianti, Pena
17/4	Poli Iaşi	a	1-1	Ochiroşii
24/4	Rapid	h	0-0	
1/5	Timişoara	a	1-2	Axente
6/5	Unirea Alba Iulia	h	1-0	Sălăgeanu
9/5	Astra	h	3-0	Giurgiu, Costin, Antal
17/5	Vaslui	h	1-0	og (Papp)
22/5	Univ Craiova	a	0-3	

No	Name	Nat	DoB	Pos	Aps	(s)	Gls
8	Liviu Ion ANTAL		2/6/89	M	19	(6)	5
9	Mircea Ionuţ AXENTE		14/3/87	A	15	(10)	5
1	Zdenko BAOTIĆ	BIH	9/3/85	G	6		
2	Marian CÂRJĂ		22/2/88	D	1	(1)	
20	Samoel COJOC		8/7/89	D	1	(9)	
18	Sergiu Ioan Viorel COSTIN		21/11/78	M	28	(1)	2
29	Gabriel Nicu GIURGIU		3/9/82	M	32		5
5	Njegoš GOLOČEVAC	SRB	21/8/83	M	3		
7	Branko GRAHOVAC	MNE	8/7/83	G	17		
15	Jackie Ike IBEH	NGA	16/4/86	M	13	(10)	3
8	Silviu ILIE		27/6/88	M	15	(6)	1
7	Laurenţiu Cătălin IORGA		17/3/88	M	14	(8)	2
12	Stoyan Petrov KOLEV	BUL	3/2/76	G	11		
11	Marius MATEI		1/2/84	A	4	(2)	
10	Gjorgi MOJSOV	MKD	10/6/85	M	3	(4)	
26	Ionuţ NEAGU		26/10/89	M	24	(1)	1
19	Jean Christian N'KONGUE	CMR	7/3/83	A	1	(2)	
10	Răzvan Iulian OCHIROŞII		13/3/89	M	14	(2)	2
10	Gabriel Ioan PARASCHIV		27/3/78	M	22	(9)	5
6	Artur PĂTRAŞ	MDA	10/1/88	M	6	(3)	
27	Marius George PENA		2/5/85	M	15	(8)	3
21	Milan PERENDIJA	SRB	5/1/86	D	8	(4)	
3	Corneliu Emilian RĂPĂ		16/1/90	D	32		
23	Adrian Ioan SĂLĂGEANU		9/4/83	M	23	(3)	1
16	Cristian SÂRGHI		22/2/87	M	21	(2)	1
4	Gabriel SIMINIC		11/3/86	D	5	(1)	
31	Enes ŠIPOVIĆ	BIH	11/9/90	D	1		
37	Gabriel Alejandro VIGLIANTI	ARG	12/6/79	M	10	(6)	1
31	Zhivko ZELEV	BUL	23/7/79	D	10	(1)	

ROMANIA

CS PANDURII LIGNITUL TÂRGU JIU
Coach –Sorin Cârțu; (28/10/09) Liviu Ciobotariu;
(18/3/10) Sorin Cârțu; (11/5/10) Florin Bejinariu
Founded – 1974
Stadium – Tudor Vladimirescu (10,000)

2009

2/8	Astra	a 1-0	Păcurar
8/8	Vaslui	h 1-0	Stângă
16/8	Univ Craiova	a 0-2	
23/8	Internațional	h 2-3	Rašković, Hidișan (p)
29/8	Ceahlăul	a 2-1	Martinović, Nalați
11/9	CFR Cluj	h 1-0	Păcurar (p)
20/9	Steaua	a 0-1	
27/9	Oțelul	h 2-3	Păcurar 2
4/10	Dinamo	a 1-1	Cardoso
17/10	Gaz Metan	h 0-0	
24/10	Unirea Urziceni	h 0-0	
2/11	Brașov	a 0-0	
6/11	Gloria Bistrița	h 1-1	Tilincă
24/11	Poli Iași	a 0-1	
29/11	Rapid	h 1-1	Rusu
6/12	Timișoara	a 0-1	
11/12	Unirea Alba Iulia	h 2-0	Păcurar (p), Štromajer

2010

21/2	Astra	h 0-2	
27/2	Vaslui	a 1-2	Štromajer
8/3	Univ Craiova	h 0-0	
13/3	Internațional	a 0-0	
17/3	Ceahlăul	h 0-0	
20/3	CFR Cluj	a 0-1	
26/3	Steaua	h 0-0	
2/4	Oțelul	a 1-1	Vranješ
8/4	Dinamo	h 0-0	
11/4	Gaz Metan	a 0-1	
15/4	Unirea Urziceni	a 0-3	
24/4	Brașov	h 1-0	Hidișan (p)
30/4	Gloria Bistrița	a 0-1	
5/5	Poli Iași	h 1-1	Štromajer
10/5	Rapid	a 0-1	
17/5	Timișoara	h 0-0	
22/5	Unirea Alba Iulia	a 1-0	Cardoso

No	Name	Nat	DoB	Pos	Aps	(s)	Gls
28	Marko BAŠARA	SRB	27/7/84	M	1		
6	Carlos Alexandre CARDOSO	BRA	11/9/84	D	28		2
11	Enache CĂJU		9/3/83	A		(2)	
4	Alin Nicu CHIBULCUTEAN		20/11/78	D	33		
30	Alexandru Mugurel DEDU		1/3/85	M	6	(3)	
15	Robert Daniel GHINDEANU		23/9/80	D	5	(4)	
29	Constantin GRECU		8/6/88	D	18	(5)	
37	Florin HIDIȘAN		24/6/82	M	10	(11)	2
7	IBÓN PÉREZ Arrieta	ESP	9/6/77	A	1	(9)	
21	Youssouf KAMARA	CIV	10/8/81	A	6	(3)	
11	Predrag LAZIĆ	SRB	15/1/82	M	11	(6)	
18	Novak MARTINOVIĆ	SRB	31/1/85	D	27		1
80	João Pedro MINGOTE Ribeiro	POR	6/8/80	G	14	(1)	
24	Mădălin MURGAN		16/5/83	M	18	(5)	
17	Adrian NALAȚI		21/5/83	M	13	(5)	1
8	Daniel ORAC		6/4/85	M	14	(1)	
5	Alexandru PĂCURAR		20/1/82	M	19	(5)	5
	Marian PLEAȘCĂ		6/2/90	M		(2)	
14	Laurențiu Florin POPETE		27/12/77	M	23	(1)	
23	Milanko RAŠKOVIĆ	SRB	13/3/81	A	18	(7)	1
16	Adrian RUSU		28/7/84	D	21	(2)	1
1	Răzvan Marian STANCA		18/1/80	G	20		
2	Ionuț Sorinel STANCIU		24/2/85	M		(1)	
8	Ionuț Cristian STANCU		17/1/83	D	3	(1)	
21	Florin Cornel STÂNGĂ		22/6/78	A	16		1
20	Jaka ŠTROMAJER	SVN	27/7/83	A	24	(7)	3
25	THIAGO Tremonti	BRA	8/6/85	M	10	(4)	
1	Cosmin TILINCĂ		1/8/80	A	4	(13)	1
32	Alexandru VLĂDUȚI		26/5/89	A		(2)	
27	Stojan VRANJEŠ	BIH	22/6/88	A	11	(1)	1

FC POLITEHNICA IAȘI
Coach – Petre Grigoraș; (11/4/10) (Marian Dinu);
(15/4/10) Dumitru Dumitriu
Founded – 1945
Stadium – Emil Alexandrescu (12,500)

2009

31/7	Rapid	a 1-4	Bujor
9/8	Timișoara	h 1-1	Munteanu
14/8	Unirea Alba Iulia	a 1-2	Bujor
21/8	Astra	h 2-0	Bujor, Constantin
30/8	Vaslui	a 1-2	Miclea
14/9	Univ Craiova	h 1-0	Baldé
18/9	Internațional	a 2-0	Milea, Miclea (p)
26/9	Ceahlăul	h 2-0	Miclea, Beršnjak
4/10	CFR Cluj	a 1-1	Bâlbă (p)
18/10	Steaua	h 0-2	
23/10	Oțelul	a 0-4	
1/11	Dinamo	h 1-3	Ignatov
7/11	Gaz Metan	a 1-2	Miclea
24/11	Pandurii	h 1-0	Bujor
30/11	Brașov	a 0-2	
5/12	Gloria Bistrița	h 0-0	
14/12	Unirea Urziceni	a 0-2	

2010

20/2	Rapid	h 2-1	Negru, Păun
26/2	Timișoara	a 1-2	Păun
7/3	Unirea Alba Iulia	h 1-0	Negru
12/3	Astra	a 1-1	Negru
18/3	Vaslui	h 1-3	Păun
21/3	Univ Craiova	a 1-2	Straton
27/3	Internațional	a 0-0	
2/4	Ceahlăul	a 0-1	
8/4	CFR Cluj	h 0-2	
12/4	Steaua	a 1-2	Păun
17/4	Oțelul	h 1-1	Badea (p)
23/4	Dinamo	a 1-1	Munteanu
2/5	Gaz Metan	a 1-1	Munteanu (p)
5/5	Pandurii	a 1-1	Nuno Viveiros
11/5	Brașov	h 0-0	
16/5	Gloria Bistrița	a 0-5	
22/5	Unirea Urziceni	h 1-2	Diarrassouba

No	Name	Nat	DoB	Pos	Aps	(s)	Gls
99	Valentin BADEA		23/10/82	A	10	(2)	1
21	Ibraima BALDÉ	GNB	15/1/86	A	5	(5)	1
9	Mihai Ionuț BÂLBĂ		1/11/81	A	5	(13)	1
19	George Daniel BÂRLĂDEANU		19/2/88	M	10	(6)	
7	Domen BERŠNJAK	SVN	15/7/81	M	5	(6)	1
13	Cristian Nicolae BRATU		24/12/77	A	10	(5)	
1	Cristian Gigi BRĂNEȚ		14/7/77	G	28		
22	Alexandru BUHUȘI		31/5/90	D	1	(7)	
11	Vlad Alin BUJOR		3/2/89	A	28	(5)	4
77	Cornel BUTA		1/11/77	D	16	(1)	
10	Cristian CONSTANTIN		2/1/77	M	22	(2)	1
3	Ionuț Alexandru COSTACHE		15/3/83	D	19	(2)	
80	Marius CROITORU		2/10/80	M		(1)	
29	Adrian CUCIULA		9/5/86	D	1	(1)	
27	Lamine DIARRASSOUBA	CIV	1/1/86	A	3	(3)	1
8	Stojan IGNATOV	MKD	22/12/79	M	18	(9)	1
23	Adrian ILIE		26/11/81	D	21	(2)	
77	Andrei IONESCU		29/3/88	M	7	(1)	
33	Alexandru Traian MARC		16/1/83	G	2		
18	Romulus Daniel MICLEA		5/4/80	M	13	(11)	4
15	Miloš MIHAJLOV	SRB	15/12/82	D	22		
25	Ciprian MILEA		12/7/84	M	8		1
28	Cristian Lucian MUNTEANU		17/10/80	M	25		3
26	Valentin NEGRU		4/9/82	M	20	(1)	3
27	Salif NOGO	BFA	31/12/86	D	6		
16	NUNO Filipe VIVEIROS	POR	22/6/83	A	5	(8)	1
5	Mihai Marian ONICAȘ		27/1/90	M	10		
14	Georgian PĂUN		24/10/85	M	12		4
5	Andrej PEČNIK	SVN	27/9/81	D	5	(2)	
12	Răzvan PLEȘCA		25/11/82	G	4		

24	Bogdan STRATON	23/8/83	M	15	(5)	1
30	Bogdan Adrian STRĂUŢ	28/4/86	D	18		
25	Paul Cătălin TINCU	26/2/86	M		(1)	

FC RAPID BUCUREŞTI

**Coach –Viorel Hizo; (2/11/09) Nicolae Manea;
(26/3/10) (Ciprian Panait); (31/3/10) Ioan Andone**
Founded – 1923
Stadium – Valentin Stănescu (19,100)
MAJOR HONOURS:
Romanian League - (3) 1967, 1999, 2003;
Romanian Cup - (13) 1935, 1937, 1938, 1939, 1940, 1941, 1942, 1972,
1975, 1998, 2002, 2006, 2007.

2009
31/7	Poli Iaşi	h	4-1	*Juliano Spadacio, João Paulo,*
				Herea, Césinha
8/8	Unirea Urziceni	a	0-1	
14/8	Timişoara	a	0-1	
21/8	Unirea Alba Iulia	h	2-0	*Răduţă 2*
29/8	Astra Ploiesti	a	1-3	*Božović*
13/9	Vaslui	h	3-2	*Herea 2, Buga*
19/9	Univ Craiova	a	4-3	*Iordache A., Buga, Lazăr, Hélder*
27/9	Internaţional	h	4-0	*Herea, Buga 2, Ioniţă*
2/10	Ceahlăul	a	4-0	*Lazăr, Buga 2, Juliano Spadacio*
17/10	CFR Cluj	h	1-4	*Herea*
25/10	Steaua	a	1-1	*Herea*
1/11	Oţelul	h	3-0	*Ioniţă, Grigorie, Herea (p)*
8/11	Dinamo	a	1-1	*Ioniţă*
20/11	Gaz Metan	h	4-1	*Iencsi (p), Juliano Spadacio,*
				Ioniţă, Răduţă
29/11	Pandurii	a	1-1	*Ioniţă*
5/12	Braşov	h	2-1	*Ioniţă, Grigorie*
11/12	Gloria Bistriţa	a	1-1	*Herea (p)*
2010				
20/2	Poli Iaşi	a	1-2	*Răduţă*
28/2	Unirea Urziceni	h	1-1	*Iencsi*
5/3	Timişoara	h	0-3	*(w/o; original result 1-0 Matič)*
14/3	Unirea Alba Iulia	a	1-0	*Ioniţă*
18/3	Astra Ploiesti	h	0-1	
22/3	Vaslui	a	0-1	
27/3	Univ Craiova	h	0-1	
3/4	Internaţional	a	2-1	*Grigorie, Săpunaru*
8/4	Ceahlăul	h	1-1	*Răduţă*
11/4	CFR Cluj	a	0-1	
17/4	Steaua	h	5-1	*Ioniţă 2, Césinha, Constantin,*
				Hélder
24/4	Oţelul	a	0-0	
2/5	Dinamo	h	2-2	*og (Koné), Ioniţă*
5/5	Gaz Metan	a	0-0	
10/5	Pandurii	h	1-0	*Săpunaru*
16/5	Braşov	a	1-1	*Săpunaru (p)*
22/5	Gloria Bistriţa	h	2-1	*Ricardo Fernandes, Božović*

No	Name	Nat	DoB	Pos	Aps	(s)	Gls
29	Tiberiu Gabriel BĂLAN		17/2/81	M	1		
33	Mircea Alexandru BORNESCU		3/5/80	G	24		
19	Vladimir BOŽOVIĆ	MNE	13/11/81	D	23	(1)	2
29	Mugurel Mihai BUGA		16/12/77	A	10	(4)	6
7	Carlos César dos Santos "CÉSINHA"	BRA	12/3/80	M	14	(6)	2
8	Alexandru Cătălin COMAN		16/10/91	M		(2)	
23	Marius Marcel CONSTANTIN		25/10/84	D	19	(3)	1
21	Radomir ĐALOVIĆ	MNE	29/10/82	A		(2)	
16	DIEGO Nicolas CIZ Vaz Torres	URU	31/5/81	A	8	(2)	
27	Alexandru Ionuţ DOBROIU		24/2/88	A		(4)	
27	Edgars GAURAČS	LVA	10/3/88	M	1	(5)	
20	Ştefan Costel GRIGORIE		31/1/82	M	21	(6)	4
2	HÉLDER Maurico da Silva Ferreira	BRA	13/4/88	D	21	(7)	2
10	Nicolae Ovidiu HEREA		26/3/85	M	23	(6)	8
32	Mihai Adrian IENCSI		14/3/75	D	21	(1)	2
11	Alexandru IONIŢĂ		5/8/89	A	23	(4)	10

28	Adrian Gheorghe IORDACHE		12/9/80	D	11	(3)	1
17	Ilie IORDACHE		23/3/85	M	5	(5)	
16	Đorđe IVELJA	SRB	30/6/84	M		(1)	
17	JOÃO PAULO Pinto Ribeiro	POR	8/4/80	A	5	(3)	1
30	JULIANO Gonçalves SPADACIO	POR	16/11/80	M	33		3
15	Costin LAZĂR		24/4/81	M	31		2
5	Ştefan Adrian MARDARE		3/12/87	D	6	(5)	
1	Andrei Daniel MARINESCU		11/2/85	G	7	(1)	
6	Darijan MATIČ	SVN	28/5/83	M	25	(5)	1
13	Cătălin Valentin PĂUN		3/1/88	D	6	(3)	
9	Lucian Dorin RĂDUŢĂ		16/8/88	A	6	(16)	5
3	RICARDO Manuel da Silva FERNANDES	POR	14/1/78	D	16	(1)	1
21	Ionuţ Cristian SĂPUNARU		5/4/84	D	10		3
89	Cătălin George STRATON		9/10/89	G	3		
21	Alin George TENE		13/1/89	A		(2)	
18	Dacian Şerban VARGA		15/10/84	M	1		

FC STEAUA BUCUREŞTI

Coach – Cristiano Bergodi (ITA); (18/9/09) Mihai Stoichiţă
Founded – 1947
Stadium – Steaua (27,000)
MAJOR HONOURS:
European Champion Clubs' Cup – (1) 1986;
UEFA Super Cup – (1) 1986;
Romanian League - (23) 1951, 1952, 1953, 1956, 1960, 1961, 1968,
1976, 1978, 1985, 1986, 1987, 1988, 1989, 1993, 1994, 1995, 1996, 1997,
1998, 2001, 2005, 2006;
Romanian Cup – (21), 1949, 1950, 1951, 1952, 1955, 1962, 1966, 1967, 1969,
1970, 1971, 1976, 1979, 1985, 1987, 1988, 1989, 1992, 1996, 1997, 1999.

2009
2/8	Ceahlăul	a	2-0	*Kapetanos, Toja*
9/8	CFR Cluj	a	2-2	*Surdu, Kapetanos*
16/8	Unirea Urziceni	h	0-1	
23/8	Oţelul	a	1-0	*Surdu*
30/8	Dinamo	h	0-1	
13/9	Gaz Metan	a	4-2	*Stancu, Székely 2 (1p), Nicoliţă*
20/9	Pandurii	h	1-0	*Kapetanos*
27/9	Braşov	a	0-0	
4/10	Gloria Bistriţa	h	1-1	*Marin (p)*
18/10	Poli Iaşi	a	2-0	*Dayro Moreno, Székely*
25/10	Rapid	h	1-1	*Dayro Moreno*
1/11	Timişoara	a	1-0	*Surdu*
9/11	Unirea Alba Iulia	h	2-0	*Kapetanos 2*
23/11	Astra	a	1-2	*Kapetanos*
29/11	Vaslui	h	2-1	*Kapetanos, Székely*
7/12	Univ Craiova	a	2-1	*Kapetanos, Székely*
13/12	Internaţional	h	3-2	*Nicoliţă, Kapetanos (p), Tănase*
2010				
20/2	Ceahlăul	h	1-3	*Kapetanos*
28/2	CFR Cluj	a	1-1	*Stancu*
7/3	Unirea Urziceni	a	2-2	*Petre, Kapetanos*
12/3	Oţelul	h	1-0	*Stancu*
17/3	Dinamo	a	0-2	
21/3	Gaz Metan	h	2-0	*Stancu, Kapetanos (p)*
26/3	Pandurii	a	0-0	
2/4	Braşov	h	1-0	*Pleşan*
7/4	Gloria Bistriţa	a	2-1	*Karamyan Arm., Stancu*
12/4	Poli Iaşi	h	2-1	*Surdu, Kapetanos*
17/4	Rapid	a	1-5	*Kapetanos (p)*
25/4	Timişoara	h	3-3	*Golański, Kapetanos, Zelev*
1/5	Unirea Alba Iulia	a	1-2	*Karamyan Arm.*
5/5	Astra	h	2-0	*Stancu, Karamyan Arm.*
10/5	Vaslui	a	1-2	*Stancu*
16/5	Univ Craiova	h	2-0	*Karamyan Arm. 2*
22/5	Internaţional	a	2-0	*Stancu, Surdu*

No	Name	Nat	DoB	Pos	Aps	(s)	Gls
17	Eugen Cătălin BACIU		25/5/80	D	13	(4)	
99	Krum Georgiev BIBISHKOV	BUL	2/9/82	A		(1)	
26	Eric Cosmin BICFALVI		5/2/88	M	4	(3)	

ROMANIA

23	DAYRO Mauricio MORENO Galindo	COL	16/9/85	M	3	(2)	2
30	Ifeanyi EMEGHARA	NGA	24/3/84	D	9	(2)	
32	Lucian Ionuţ FILIP		25/9/90	D	1	(1)	
24	Sorin GHIONEA		11/5/79	D	12		
3	Dorin Nicolae GOIAN		12/12/80	D	1		
4	Paweł GOLAŃSKI	POL	12/10/82	D	20	(1)	1
10	Rafał GRZELAK	POL	24/6/82	M	2	(4)	
27	Alexandru IACOB		14/4/89	D	1	(1)	
19	Andrei IONESCU		29/3/88	M	6	(2)	
9	Pantelis KAPETANOS	GRE	8/6/83	A	24	(6)	15
11	Arman KARAMYAN	ARM	14/11/79	A	8	(5)	5
77	Artavazd KARAMYAN	ARM	14/11/79	M	4	(4)	
18	Petre MARIN		8/9/73	D	28	(1)	1
21	Florentin MATEI		15/4/93	M		(2)	
16	Bănel NICOLIŢĂ		7/1/85	M	28		2
31	Emil Ducu NINU		23/8/86	D	5	(1)	
21	Răzvan Iulian OCHIROŞII		13/3/89	M		(5)	
25	Mihai Marian ONICAŞ		27/1/90	M	5	(3)	
2	Stelios PARPAS	CYP	25/7/85	D	12	(1)	
22	José Alcides "PEPE" MORENO Mora	COL	10/9/81	A		(6)	
8	Ovidiu PETRE		22/3/82	M	17	(1)	1
22	Mihăiţă PLEŞAN		19/2/83	M	12	(6)	1
5	Ionuţ Alin RADA		6/7/82	D	11		
28	Bogdan Sorin STANCU		28/6/87	A	24	(1)	8
21	Romeo Constantin SURDU		12/1/84	A	17	(15)	5
7	János Joszef SZÉKELY		13/5/83	M	19	(2)	5
6	Cristian TĂNASE		18/2/87	M	13	(8)	1
12	Ciprian Anton TĂTĂRUŞANU		9/2/86	G	15		
14	Juan Carlos TOJA	COL	24/5/85	M	20	(8)	1
15	Alexandru TUDOSE		3/4/87	D	5	(3)	
1	Róbinson ZAPATA Montaño	COL	30/9/78	G	19		
5	Zhivko ZELEV	BUL	23/7/79	D	16		1

FC TIMIŞOARA

Coach – Ioan Ovidiu Sabău
Founded – 2002
Stadium – Dan Păltinişanu (32,019)

2009

1/8	Gloria Bistriţa	h	1-0 Magera
9/8	Poli Iaşi	a	1-1 Parks
14/8	Rapid	h	1-0 Karamyan Arm.
22/8	Unirea Urziceni	a	0-0
30/8	Unirea Alba Iulia	a	3-3 Bucur, Ionescu, Goga
13/9	Astra	h	0-0
20/9	Vaslui	a	1-0 Goga
26/9	Univ Craiova	h	1-1 Mera
5/10	Internaţional	a	3-0 Goga, Bucur, Karamyan Arm.
17/10	Ceahlăul	h	6-0 Magera 2, Chiacu 2, Goga 2
25/10	CFR Cluj-Napca	a	0-0
1/11	Steaua	h	0-1
8/11	Oţelul	a	3-3 Chiacu, Magera, Luchin
23/11	Dinamo	h	2-0 Bucur 2
29/11	Gaz Metan	a	6-2 Bourceanu, Bucur 3 (1p), Alexa, Goga
6/12	Pandurii	h	1-0 Bucur
13/12	Braşov	a	0-1

2010

20/2	Gloria Bistriţa	a	0-0
26/2	Poli Iaşi	h	2-1 Contra, Goga
5/3	Rapid	a	3-0 (w/o; original result 0-1)
14/3	Unirea Urziceni	a	0-0
18/3	Unirea Alba Iulia	h	6-0 Kozák, Magera 2, Mera, Goga, Mansour
22/3	Astra	a	3-1 Magera, Goga 2
29/3	Vaslui	h	0-1
3/4	Univ Craiova	a	2-1 Goga, Magera
7/4	Internaţional	h	0-0
11/4	Ceahlăul	a	1-1 Mansour
18/4	CFR Cluj-Napca	h	1-1 Alexa

25/4	Steaua	a	3-3 Cociş, Contra 2
1/5	Oţelul	h	2-1 Magera, Cociş
6/5	Dinamo	a	2-1 Goga, Cociş
10/5	Gaz Metan	h	0-2
17/5	Pandurii	a	0-0
22/5	Braşov	h	1-2 Chiacu

No	Name	Nat	DoB	Pos	Aps	(s)	Gls
5	Dan ALEXA		28/10/79	D	26	(3)	2
30	Valentin Emanoil BĂDOI		16/12/75	M	2		
17	Balázs BORBÉLY	SVK	2/10/79	D	1	(2)	
55	Alexandru BOURCEANU		24/4/85	M	28	(1)	1
4	Miloš BREZINSKÝ	SVK	2/4/84	D	1		
18	Gheorghe BUCUR		8/4/80	A	14	(2)	8
26	Hristu CHIACU		6/9/86	M	11	(4)	4
18	Marian Adrian CHIŢU		19/8/86	D	4	(1)	
28	Marián ČÍŠOVSKÝ	SVK	2/11/79	D	9		
9	Răzvan COCIŞ		19/2/83	M	8	(1)	3
34	Cosmin Marius CONTRA		15/12/75	D	6	(7)	3
77	Alexandru Paul CURTEAN		27/3/87	M	13	(3)	
77	Adérito Waldemar Alves de Carvalho "DÉDÉ"	ANG	4/7/81	M	1	(2)	
2	ÉDER José Oliveira BONFIM	BRA	3/4/81	D	26	(2)	
31	Marian FUCHS		6/3/92	M		(1)	
21	Dorin Ioan GOGA		2/7/84	A	24	(6)	12
23	Claudiu Mircea IONESCU		20/3/83	M	5	(6)	1
11	Arman KARAMYAN	ARM	14/11/79	A	10	(3)	2
10	Artavazd KARAMYAN	ARM	14/11/79	M	11	(5)	
25	Ján KOZÁK	SVK	22/4/80	D	5	(5)	1
3	Iasmin LATOVLEVICI		11/5/86	D	1	(1)	
16	Srgjan LUCHIN		4/3/86	D	19		1
27	Lukáš MAGERA	CZE	17/1/83	A	17	(9)	9
11	Gueye MANSOUR	SEN	30/12/85	A	2	(4)	2
20	Florin Sandu MAXIM		23/3/81	D	8	(2)	
33	Christian de Jesús MEJÍA Martínez	COL	11/10/90	A	2	(4)	
16	Ioan MERA		5/1/87	D	16		2
6	Daré NIBOMBÉ	TOG	16/6/80	D	25		
29	Costel Fane PANTILIMON		1/2/87	G	21		
9	Winston PARKS	CRC	12/10/81	A	12	(12)	1
13	Cristian Dorel SCUTARU		13/4/87	M	6	(2)	
8	László SEPSI		7/6/86	D	17		
7	Stelian STANCU		22/9/81	D	6	(5)	
37	Nemanja SUPIĆ	BIH	12/1/82	G	1		
99	Pedro Manuel TABORDA Moreira	POR	22/6/78	G	12		
8	Dare VRŠIČ	SVN	26/9/84	A	4	(1)	

FC UNIREA ALBA IULIA

Coach –Adrian Falub; (12/3/10) Blaž Slišković (BIH)
Founded – 1924
Stadium – Cetate (18,000)

2009

1/8	Braşov	h	0-1
8/8	Gloria Bistriţa	a	1-1 Veljović
14/8	Poli Iaşi	h	2-1 Verdeş, Dan (p)
21/8	Rapid	a	0-2
30/8	Timişoara	h	3-3 Dan (p), Bălan, Cristea
12/9	Unirea Urziceni	a	0-1
18/9	Astra	a	2-4 Dan, Grozav
26/9	Vaslui	h	2-0 Cristea, Dâlbea
3/10	Univ Craiova	a	1-3 Verdeş
16/10	Internaţional	h	1-2 og (Chiricheş)
24/10	Ceahlăul	a	1-1 Veljović
1/11	CFR Cluj	h	1-1 Dâlbea
9/11	Steaua	a	0-2
20/11	Oţelul	h	3-1 Dan, Olah, Grozav
28/11	Dinamo	a	0-2
6/12	Gaz Metan	h	0-0
11/12	Pandurii	a	0-2

2010

20/2	Braşov	a	1-2	Cristea
26/2	Gloria Bistriţa	h	1-2	Veljović
7/3	Poli Iaşi	a	0-1	
14/3	Rapid	h	0-1	
18/3	Timişoara	a	0-6	
22/3	Unirea Urziceni	h	1-2	Bucurică
27/3	Astra	h	2-1	Dâlbea, André Galiassi
3/4	Vaslui	a	0-3	
7/4	Univ Craiova	h	2-0	Selagea 2 (1p)
10/4	Internaţional	a	1-2	Cristea
15/4	Ceahlăul	h	3-2	Jovanović 2, Dan
24/4	CFR Cluj	a	2-3	Veljović, og (Mureşan)
1/5	Steaua	h	2-1	Veljović, Dan
6/5	Oţelul	a	0-1	
10/5	Dinamo	h	1-2	Dan
15/5	Gaz Metan	a	0-5	
22/5	Pandurii	h	0-1	

No	Name	Nat	DoB	Pos	Aps	(s)	Gls
3	ANDRÉ Felipe GALIASSI de Sousa	BRA	22/8/80	D	11	(2)	1
17	Ionuţ BĂLAN		2/3/78	M	22	(7)	1
18	Alexandru BĂLŢOI		21/6/82	A	4	(5)	
16	Josip BONACIN	CRO	10/2/84	D	7		
11	Enzo Alejandro BRUNO	ARG	19/3/87	M	10	(6)	
23	Bogdan Nicolae BUCURICĂ		11/2/86	D	27	(2)	1
33	Constantin BUMBAC		29/4/84	D	4	(1)	
12	Cornel CERNEA		22/4/76	G	16		
15	Sergiu Vasile COSTEA		10/1/83	A	1	(11)	
14	Călin Virgil CRISTEA		6/5/88	M	27	(2)	4
19	Florin Cristian DAN		1/4/79	M	30		7
5	Răzvan Dâlbea DÂLBEA		8/10/81	M	30	(2)	3
21	Johnes ELIAS PINTO dos Santos	BRA	28/9/79	M	1	(2)	
7	Gheorghe GROZAV		29/9/90	M	7	(9)	2
21	Fabian Adrian HIMCINSCHI		15/4/94	A		(1)	
33	Nemanja JOVANOVIĆ	SRB	14/8/84	A	14	(2)	2
4	Patrick KANYUKA	COD	19/7/87	D	2	(1)	
88	Mihai LASC		18/2/88	G	1		
7	Silviu MUREŞAN		11/8/91	M		(1)	
20	Adrian OLAH		20/4/81	D	23	(7)	1
3	Marius PISTOL		29/6/87	D	1		
2	Andrei POVERLOVICI		17/10/85	D	22	(2)	
6	Sorin Nicuşor RĂDOI		30/6/85	D	18	(2)	
38	Gabriel ROTARU		8/1/71	G	17		
10	Ciprian SELAGEA		21/1/90	M	5	(7)	2
7	Nicolae Claudiu STANCIU		7/5/93	M	3	(2)	
22	Romeo Constantin STANCU		11/5/78	M		(3)	
8	Norbert VARGA		26/3/80	M	14	(3)	
18	Rade VELJOVIĆ	SRB	9/8/86	A	25	(4)	5
9	Bobi Gheorghiţă VERDEŞ		24/11/80	A	3	(9)	2
22	Vítor Tiago de Freitas "VITINHA"	POR	11/2/86	D	7	(7)	
13	Nikola VUJADINOVIĆ	MNE	31/7/86	D	22		

FC UNIREA URZICENI
Coach – Dan Petrescu; (1/1/10) Roni Levi (ISR)
Founded – 1954
Stadium – Tineretului (8,000)
MAJOR HONOURS:
Romanian League – (1) 2009.

2009

1/8	CFR Cluj	a	0-2	
8/8	Rapid	h	1-0	Pădureţu
16/8	Steaua	a	1-0	Apostol
22/8	Timişoara	h	0-0	
28/8	Oţelul	a	4-1	Bilaşco 2 (1p), Maftei, Onofraş
12/9	Unirea Alba Iulia	h	1-0	Marinescu
20/9	Dinamo	a	1-2	Apostol
25/9	Astra	h	4-1	Rusescu, Varga, Galamaz, Dănălache
3/10	Gaz Metan	a	0-0	

16/10	Vaslui	h	1-2	Onofraş
24/10	Pandurii	a	0-0	
31/10	Univ Craiova	h	3-2	Frunză 2, Bilaşco
7/11	Braşov	a	0-0	
21/11	Internaţional	a	2-1	Bilaşco, Onofraş
30/11	Gloria Bistriţa	h	2-0	Semedo, Bilaşco
4/12	Ceahlăul	a	3-2	Semedo, Onofraş, Brandán (p)
14/12	Poli Iaşi	h	2-0	Brandán, Semedo

2010

22/2	CFR Cluj	h	0-1	
28/2	Rapid	a	1-1	Bilaşco
7/3	Steaua	h	2-2	Frunză, Onofraş
14/3	Timişoara	a	0-0	
18/3	Oţelul	h	0-0	
22/3	Unirea Alba Iulia	a	2-1	Brandán, Onofraş
28/3	Dinamo	h	4-4	Onofraş, Semedo, Bilaşco 2
2/4	Astra	a	2-0	Galamaz, Rusescu
7/4	Gaz Metan	h	1-1	Bilaşco
10/4	Vaslui	a	1-1	Rusescu
15/4	Pandurii	h	3-0	Apostol, Marinescu, og (Rusu)
25/4	Univ Craiova	a	4-1	Bilaşco, Rusescu, Pădureţu, Semedo
2/5	Braşov	h	1-0	Rusescu
6/5	Internaţional	h	1-0	Bilaşco
11/5	Gloria Bistriţa	a	0-0	
17/5	Ceahlăul	h	4-0	Bilaşco, Frunză, Rusescu 2
22/5	Poli Iaşi	a	2-1	Onofraş, Rusescu

No	Name	Nat	DoB	Pos	Aps	(s)	Gls
32	Iulian Cătălin APOSTOL		3/12/80	M	17	(2)	3
1	Giedrius ARLAUSKIS	LTU	1/12/87	G	18		
21	Tiberiu BĂLAN		17/2/81	M	5	(3)	
7	Marius Ioan BILAŞCO		13/7/81	A	28	(2)	12
23	Valeriu Ionuţ BORDEANU		2/2/77	D	14	(5)	
19	Pablo Daniel BRANDÁN	ARG	5/3/83	D	23	(5)	3
22	BRUNO João Nandinga Borges FERNANDES	GNB	6/11/78	D	22		
15	Cristian Costin DĂNĂLACHE		15/7/82	A	4	(5)	1
30	Sorin FRUNZĂ		29/3/78	M	29	(3)	4
6	George Daniel GALAMAZ		5/4/81	D	27	(1)	2
77	Cătălin GRIGORE		6/10/77	G	5		
24	Vasile MAFTEI		1/1/81	D	30		1
20	Laurenţiu Nicolae MARINESCU		25/8/84	M	9	(6)	2
4	Ersin MEHMEDOVIĆ	SRB	10/5/81	D	8	(2)	
29	George Daniel MUNTEANU		6/6/78	D	1		
16	Epaminonda NICU		17/12/79	D	13	(5)	
11	Marius Daniel ONOFRAŞ		17/8/80	A	15	(12)	8
8	Sorin Ion PARASCHIV		17/6/81	M	22	(4)	
10	Răzvan PĂDUREŢU		19/6/81	M	21	(7)	2
18	RICARDO Gomes VILANA	BRA	18/7/81	M	12	(5)	
14	Raul Andrei RUSESCU		9/7/88	A	14	(12)	8
17	António Paulo Sanches SEMEDO	POR	1/6/79	A	17	(9)	5
5	Dinu Marius TODORAN		8/9/78	M	3	(10)	
74	Daniel Ovidiu TUDOR		1/6/74	G	11		
9	Dacian Şerban VARGA		15/10/84	M	6	(2)	1

FC UNIVERSITATEA CRAIOVA
Coach – Daniel Mogoşanu; (21/9/09) Eugen Neagoe;
(7/1/10) Mark Wotte (NED); (3/5/10) Eugen Trică;
(10/5/10) Gheorghe Biţă
Founded – 1948
Stadium – Ion Oblemenco (25,250)
MAJOR HONOURS:
Romanian League – (4) 1974, 1980, 1981, 1991;
Romanian Cup – (6) 1977, 1978, 1981, 1983, 1991, 1993.

2009

1/8	Dinamo	h	0-0	
7/8	Gaz Metan	a	1-2	Costea F.
16/8	Pandurii	h	2-0	Dina, Stoica
21/8	Braşov	a	0-2	
29/8	Gloria Bistriţa	h	5-1	Baird 2, Badea, Costea F., Woobay

ROMANIA

14/9	Poli Iaşi	a	0-1
19/9	Rapid	h	3-4 Costea M., Stoica, Badea
26/9	Timişoara	a	1-1 Costea M.
3/10	Unirea Alba Iulia	h	3-1 Costea F. 3 (1p)
18/10	Astra	a	1-3 Costea F.
24/10	Vaslui	h	1-2 Costea F.
31/10	Unirea Urziceni	a	2-3 Costea M., Woobay
6/11	Internaţional	a	1-0 Dina
23/11	Ceahlăul	h	3-2 Costea M., Costea F., Badea
28/11	CFR Cluj	a	0-2
7/12	Steaua	h	1-2 Prepeliţă
12/12	Oţelul	a	0-1
2010			
21/2	Dinamo	a	1-2 Dina
27/2	Gaz Metan	h	1-2 Trică
8/3	Pandurii	a	0-0
13/3	Braşov	h	3-0 Găman, Barbu, Costea M.
17/3	Gloria Bistriţa	a	1-2 Costea F.
21/3	Poli Iaşi	h	2-1 Iliev, Prepeliţă
27/3	Rapid	a	1-0 Gângioveanu
3/4	Timişoara	h	1-2 Iliev
7/4	Unirea Alba Iulia	a	0-2
10/4	Astra	h	1-0 Dina
18/4	Vaslui	a	1-0 Piţurcă
25/4	Unirea Urziceni	h	1-4 Gângioveanu
1/5	Internaţional	h	1-3 Dina
5/5	Ceahlăul	a	1-2 Costea M.
10/5	CFR Cluj	h	2-3 Piţurcă, Costea M.
16/5	Steaua	a	0-2
22/5	Oţelul	h	3-0 Iliev, Prepeliţă, Bărboianu

No	Name	Nat	DoB	Pos	Aps	(s)	Gls
11	Valentin Vasile BADEA		23/10/82	A	3	(10)	3
17	Michael BAIRD	AUS	1/8/83	A	4	(1)	2
3	Marius Radu BARBU		29/8/89	D	11	(8)	1
32	Emanoil Valentin BĂDOI		16/12/75	D	13	(3)	
27	Silviu BĂLACE		13/11/78	D	15		
2	Ştefan Nicolae BĂRBOIANU		24/1/88	M	24	(5)	1
99	Alin Florian BULEICĂ		12/9/91	D	3	(1)	
5	Marian Sorin BUŞU		8/7/89	D	2		
10	Florin Constantin COSTEA		16/5/85	A	20	(1)	9
9	Mihai Alexandru COSTEA		29/5/88	A	26	(4)	7
86	Cătălin Ştefăniţă CRĂCIUN		26/8/91	A		(8)	
18	Ovidiu Liviu DĂNĂNAE		26/8/85	M	6		
13	Spase DILEVSKI	AUS	13/5/85	M	25		
20	Mihai DINA		15/3/85	M	22	(9)	5
25	Dragoş Petruţ FIRŢULESCU		15/5/89	D	9	(13)	
7	Marius Valerică GĂMAN		25/2/89	D	29		1
28	Constantin GÂNGIOVEANU		4/9/89	M	9	(6)	2
69	Valentin ILIEV	BUL	11/8/80	D	15		3
21	Silviu LUNG jr.		4/6/89	G	29		
22	Pieter MERLIER	BEL	29/3/79	G	5		
4	Josh MITCHELL	AUS	8/6/84	D	9		
88	Jackie NICOLAE		5/1/91	M		(4)	
16	Marius Alexandru OLOGU		16/7/89	M	3		
8	Ivan PAUNOVIĆ	SRB	17/6/86	M	2		
11	Alexandru PIŢURCĂ		28/10/83	A	6	(5)	2
26	Ionuţ Cătălin POPESCU		31/3/90	M		(1)	
30	Andrei PREPELIŢĂ		8/12/85	M	28	(1)	3
26	Mihai ROMAN		31/5/92	A		(2)	
27	Joshua Liam ROSE	AUS	16/12/81	M	13	(2)	
6	Dorel STOICA		15/12/78	D	14		2
8	Florin Costin ŞOAVĂ		24/7/78	M	15	(1)	
33	Eugen TRICĂ		5/8/76	M	7	(9)	1
77	Julius Gibrilla WOOBAY	SLE	19/5/84	A	7	(7)	2

FC VASLUI

**Coach – Cristian Dulca; (21/9/09) (Dorel Zotincă);
(28/9/09) Marius Lăcătuş**
Founded – 2001
Stadium – Municipal (15,000)

2009			
8/8	Pandurii	a	0-1
12/8	Gaz Metan	h	2-1 Genchev, Hugo Luz
16/8	Braşov	h	2-2 Wesley, Zubar
23/8	Gloria Bistriţa	a	3-1 Wesley, Temwanjera, Jovanović
30/8	Poli Iaşi	h	2-1 Costin, Wesley
13/9	Rapid	a	2-3 Jovanović 2
20/9	Timişoara	h	0-1
26/9	Unirea Alba Iulia	a	0-2
3/10	Astra	h	3-1 Gerlem, Temwanjera, Pavlović
16/10	Unirea Urziceni	a	2-1 Gerlem, Wesley
24/10	Univ Craiova	a	2-1 Temwanjera, Genchev
1/11	Internaţional	h	1-0 Akakpo
7/11	Ceahlăul	a	1-0 Temwanjera
23/11	CFR Cluj	h	2-0 Temwanjera, Wesley
29/11	Steaua	a	1-2 Gerlem
6/12	Oţelul	h	1-1 Burdujan
13/12	Dinamo	a	1-1 Wesley
2010			
21/2	Gaz Metan	a	0-0
27/2	Pandurii	h	2-1 Gerlem, Delgado
8/3	Braşov	a	1-1 Delgado
14/3	Gloria Bistriţa	h	0-1
18/3	Poli Iaşi	a	3-1 Wesley 2, Costly
22/3	Rapid	h	1-0 Papp
29/3	Timişoara	a	1-0 Costly
3/4	Unirea Alba Iulia	h	3-0 Wesley 3
7/4	Astra	a	0-0
10/4	Unirea Urziceni	h	1-1 Akakpo
18/4	Univ Craiova	h	0-1
26/4	Internaţional	a	2-1 Costly, Milisavljević
1/5	Ceahlăul	h	1-0 Costly
6/5	CFR Cluj	a	0-0
10/5	Steaua	h	2-1 Burdujan (p), Papp
17/5	Oţelul	a	0-1
22/5	Dinamo	h	2-0 Wesley (p), Costin

No	Name	Nat	DoB	Pos	Aps	(s)	Gls
14	Serge Ognadon AKAKPO	TOG	15/10/87	D	11	(3)	2
17	Silviu Constantin BĂLACE		13/11/78	D	5		
7	Vasile BUHĂESCU		2/2/88	A		(4)	
15	Bogdan Constantin BUHUŞ		30/10/79	D	15	(1)	
9	Lucian BURDUJAN		18/2/84	A	15	(3)	1
30	Raul Răzvan COSTIN		29/1/85	D	16	(8)	2
13	Carlos Yaír COSTLY	HON	18/7/82	A	12	(1)	4
25	Roberto Alfonso DELGADO	ESP	7/5/86	A	8	(14)	2
26	Pavol FARKAŠ	SVK	27/3/85	D	14		
18	Constantin Mihai GÂNGIOVEANU		4/9/89	M	1	(1)	
4	Stanislav GENCHEV	BUL	20/3/81	M	16	(5)	2
10	Willian GERLEM de Jesus Almeida	BRA	7/8/84	A	23	(1)	4
31	Adrian Ion GHEORGHIU		30/11/81	M	6	(2)	
6	GLADSTONE Pereira della Valentina	BRA	29/1/85	D	10	(1)	
81	Cristian HĂISAN		3/3/81	G	11	(1)	
27	HUGO Duarte de Sousa "LUZ"	POR	24/2/82	D	21		1
21	Nemanja JOVANOVIĆ	SRB	3/3/84	A	3	(10)	3
1	Dušan KUCIAK	SVK	21/5/85	G	23		
20	Marko LJUBINKOVIĆ	SRB	7/12/81	M	7	(1)	
6	Neven MARKOVIĆ	SRB	20/2/87	D	2		
20	Zhivko MILANOV	BUL	15/7/84	D	17		
11	Nemanja MILISAVLJEVIĆ	SRB	1/11/84	M	6	(14)	1
25	Răzvan NEAGU		25/5/87	A	2	(6)	
3	Paul PAPP		11/11/89	D	16		2
23	Miloš PAVLOVIĆ	SRB	27/11/83	M	24	(3)	1
17	Dinu SÂNMĂRTEAN		28/7/81	A	3	(1)	
18	Lucian Iulian SÂNMĂRTEAN		13/3/80	M	11	(5)	
19	Mike TEMWANJERA	ZIM	21/5/82	A	16	(2)	5
80	WESLEY Lopes da Silva	BRA	10/11/80	A	31		12
8	Denis ZMEU	MDA	8/5/85	M	4	(9)	
16	Stéphane ZUBAR	FRA	9/10/86	D	25	(1)	1

PROMOTED CLUBS

FC VICTORIA BRĂNEŞTI
Coach – Ilie Stan
Founded – 1968; Stadium – Cătălin Hâldan (2,500)

FC SPORTUL STUDENŢESC BUCUREŞTI
Coach – Tibor Selymes
Founded – 1916; Stadium – Sportul Studenţesc (9,000)

FCM TÂRGU MUREŞ
Coach – Cosmin Bodea; (4/5/10) Adrian Falub
Founded – 2008; Stadium – Trans-Sil (2,500)

FC UNIVERSITATEA CLUJ
Coach – Carmelo Palilla (ITA); (29/8/09) (Marius Popescu); (31/8/09) Cornel Ţălnar; (4/10/09) Cristian Dulca; (9/1/10) Viorel Hizo; (5/4/10) Cristian Dulca
Founded – 1919; Stadium – Clujana (2,000)
MAJOR HONOURS: Romanian Cup – (1) 1965.

SECOND LEVEL FINAL TABLES 2009/10

Seria I

		Pld	W	D	L	F	A	Pts
1	FC Victoria Brăneşti	34	21	8	5	62	28	71
2	FC Sportul Studenţesc Bucureşti	34	20	8	6	65	26	68
3	FC Petrolul Ploieşti	34	18	13	3	58	20	67
4	FC Snagov	34	18	6	10	62	41	60
5	FC Delta Tulcea	34	17	8	9	41	23	59
6	ACS Săgeata Stejaru	34	17	7	10	46	29	58
7	CS Concordia Chiajna	34	16	6	12	36	36	54
8	FC Farul Constanţa	34	16	5	13	52	48	53
9	FCM Dunărea Giurgiu	34	14	7	13	43	41	49
10	FC Botoşani	34	13	10	11	45	36	49
11	FCM Dunărea Galaţi	34	13	6	15	37	39	45
12	FCM Bacău	34	12	7	15	47	57	43
13	FC Steaua II Bucureşti	34	10	11	13	36	36	41
14	FC Gloria Buzău	34	12	7	15	39	43	35
15	FC Dinamo II Bucureşti	34	8	5	21	36	65	29
16	CS Tricolorul Breaza	34	8	4	22	31	66	28
17	CSM Râmnicu Sărat	34	4	7	23	14	68	19
18	FC Cetatea Suceava	34	2	9	23	14	76	15

NB FC Cetatea Suceava withdrew after round 17 – their remaining matches were awarded as 0-3 defeats; FC Gloria Buzău – 8 pts deducted.

Seria II

		Pld	W	D	L	F	A	Pts
1	FCM Târgu Mureş	32	20	9	3	52	20	69
2	FC Universitatea Cluj	32	20	7	5	60	24	67
3	CS Dacia Mioveni	32	19	9	4	46	20	66
4	FCM UTA Arad	32	16	10	6	50	26	58
5	FC Argeş Piteşti	32	16	6	10	48	30	54
6	CS Otopeni	32	15	8	9	59	40	50
7	CS Gaz Metan CFR Craiova	32	12	9	11	39	36	45
8	FC Baia Mare	32	11	11	10	34	35	44
9	FC Bihor Oradea	32	10	12	10	49	40	42
10	FC Arieşul Turda	32	13	3	16	40	43	42
11	FC Silvania Şimleu Silvaniei	32	10	7	15	31	46	37
12	CS Minerul Lupeni	32	8	12	12	33	41	36
13	CSM Râmnicu Vâlcea	32	9	9	14	51	51	36
14	CS Mureşul Deva	32	9	4	19	28	50	31
15	ACS Fortuna Covaci	32	7	5	20	37	59	26
16	CS Jiul Petroşani	31	7	5	19	21	59	26
17	CS Drobeta Turnu Severin	31	5	2	24	12	70	17

NB CFR Timişoara withdrew after round 12 – all their matches annulled; CS Jiul Petroşani & FC Drobeta Turnu Severin withdrew after round 17 – their remaining matches were awarded as 0-3 defeats; CS Otopeni – 3 pts deducted.

DOMESTIC CUP 2009/10

CUPA ROMÂNIEI

FIRST ROUND

(22/9/09)
Gaz Metan Mediaş 1, CSM Râmnicu Vâlcea 1 *(aet; 5-4 on pens)*
Gloria Bistriţa 3, Dunărea Giurgiu 0
Poli Iaşi 3, Pandurii 1
Univ Craiova 4, Gloria II Bistriţa 0

(23/9/09)
Astra 2, Farul 1 *(aet)*
Bacău 0, Steaua 2
Braşov 4, Otopeni 0 *(aet)*
Ceahlăul 1, Gaz Metan CFR Craiova 1 *(aet; 2-3 on pens)*
Chimia Brazi 0, Vaslui 1
Minerul Mehedinţi 1, Internaţional Curtea 1 *(aet; 3-5 on pens)*
Oţelul 1, Unirea Alba Iulia 1 *(aet; 4-3 on pens)*
Timişoara 7, Sănătatea Cluj 0
Unirea Urziceni 3, Sportul Studenţesc 0

(24/9/09)
Bihor 0, Rapid Bucureşti 2
CFR Cluj 2, Dunărea Galaţi 0
Dinamo Bucureşti 5, Zlatna 0

SECOND ROUND

(27/10/09)
Gaz Metan Mediaş 0, Vaslui 1
Unirea Urziceni 0, Braşov 1

(28/10/09)
Astra 2, Timişoara 2 *(aet; 6-5 on pens)*
Gaz Metan CFR Craiova 0, CFR Cluj 1
Gloria Bistriţa 0, Steaua 0 *(aet; 5-4 on pens)*
Poli Iaşi 0, Univ Craiova 3

(29/10/09)
Dinamo Bucureşti 1, Oţelul 0
Internaţional Curtea 2, Rapid Bucureşti 1

QUARTER-FINALS

(17/11/09)
Braşov 3 *(Hadnagy 4, Zaharia 30, Ilyeş 60p)*, Gloria Bistriţa 0

(18/11/09)
Univ Craiova 0, CFR Cluj 1 *(Dubarbier 25)*
Vaslui 1 *(Burdujan 87)*, Internaţional Curtea 0

(19/11/09)
Astra 1 *(Păun 17p)*, Dinamo Bucureşti 2 *(Cristea An. 9, 55)*

SEMI-FINALS

(24/3/10 & 14/4/10)
Dinamo Bucureşti 1 *(Goian 10)*, CFR Cluj 1 *(Koné 25)*
CFR Cluj 2 *(Dică N. 51, Traoré 78)*, Dinamo Bucureşti 1 *(Cristea An. 74)*
(CFR Cluj 3-2)

(25/3/10 & 15/4/10)
Braşov 1 *(Ilyeş 5)*, Vaslui 0
Vaslui 4 *(Costin 28, Wesley 29, Sânmărtean L. 53, Costly 74)*, Braşov 0
(Vaslui 4-1)

FINAL

(26/5/10)
Emil Alexandrescu stadium, Iasi
CFR 1907 CLUJ 0
FC VASLUI 0
(aet; 5-4 on pens)
Referee – Deaconu
CFR CLUJ – Nuno Claro, Panin, Cadú, Piccolo, Edimar, Peralta (Bottone 84), Mureşan, Culio, Deac, De Zerbi (Bud 92), Koné (Dică N. 116).
VASLUI – Häisan, Milanov (Zmeu 88), Papp, Gladstone, Hugo Luz, Gheorghiu, Pavlović, Costin, Sânmărtean L. (Milisavljević 46), Wesley, Burdujan.

RUSSIA

Foreign coaches come unstuck

The resurgence of Russian football suffered a major setback with the national team's non-qualification for the 2010 FIFA World Cup finals in South Africa. Failure to overcome Slovenia in the qualifying play-off was a savage blow not only to the country but also to the reputation of the team's coach, Guus Hiddink.

The revered Dutchman, who had steered Russia so splendidly to the semi-finals of UEFA EURO 2008, was not the only foreign coach to suffer a sudden reversal of fortune while in charge of a Russian team in 2009. In fact, a common theme developed throughout the year - that the country's leading clubs were better off being led by one of their own than by an expensively acquired import.

FC Spartak Moskva set the tone early in the Premier-Liga campaign by ditching Danish legend Michael Laudrup and replacing him with their sporting director Valeriy Karpin. PFC CSKA Moskva also improved after bringing in a Russian, Leonid Slutskiy, after misadventures with Brazilian Zico and – for a very brief period – Spaniard Juande Ramos. There were major benefits, too, at FC Saturn Moskovskaya Oblast and FC Zenit St Petersburg after they both appointed indigenous coaches in place of foreigners.

Dick Advocaat succeeded fellow Dutchman Guus Hiddink as Russia's new national team coach

Advocaat appointed

The Russian Football Association (RFS) appeared to be aloof to this growing trend, however, when they announced in May 2010 that, with Hiddink having already declared that he would be leaving to become the head coach of Turkey, his replacement would be another vastly experienced Dutchman, Dick Advocaat.

Dismissed nine months earlier by Zenit, the club he had led to the Russian league title in 2007 and a European double of UEFA Cup and UEFA Super Cup in 2008, Advocaat's credentials, which included two stints as the head coach of the Netherlands, made him an obvious candidate for the job, but there were understandable reservations about his appointment from within Russia, not least from the overlooked fraternity of Russian coaches.

Advocaat's four-year contract requires him to take the country to the finals of both UEFA EURO 2012 and the 2014 World Cup as a bare minimum. The first of those two tasks should not be over-burdensome as Russia head a relatively straightforward qualifying group including Andorra, Armenia, FYR Macedonia, the Republic of Ireland and Slovakia. But the painful experience of the 2010 World Cup qualifying campaign – in which Hiddink's team lost twice to Germany then squandered a two-goal lead in the play-offs against Slovenia – should caution against complacency. With talented individuals such as Igor Akinfeev, Andrei Arshavin, Yuriy Zhirkov, Diniyar Bilyaletdinov and Alan Dzagoev to call upon, Advocaat knows he has firm foundations on which to construct a winning team.

Credibility restored

Although there could be no consolation for the dismay at missing out on South Africa, the performances of CSKA Moskva and FC Rubin Kazan in European club football during 2009/10 helped to restore some of Russian football's morale and credibility.

CSKA, having jettisoned Zico on the eve of their UEFA Champions League campaign and Juande Ramos halfway through the group stage, made valiant progress under new boss Slutskiy. His first game in charge brought a 3-3 draw away to Manchester United FC at Old Trafford – it would have been a win but for a couple of late United goals – and he followed it up with back-to-back victories against VfL Wolfsburg and Beşiktaş JK that put the Moscow side through to the first knockout round. Furthermore, in the spring, Slutskiy's side sent Sevilla FC packing before bowing out in the quarter-finals to eventual winners FC Internazionale Milano. Although gone, CSKA were certainly not forgotten, players such as Akinfeev, Dzagoev, teenaged full-back Georgiy Schennikov and, especially, imported stars Miloš Krasić, Tomáš Necid and winter arrival Keisuke Honda having all left their imprint on the world's most illustrious club competition.

Aleksandr Bukharov – a key man in Rubin's successful defence of the Russian Premier-Liga title

CSKA's 2-1 win in Seville was their standout result, but it was arguably eclipsed by another victory in Spain by the same scoreline earlier in the competition – Rubin's remarkable defeat of holders FC Barcelona at Camp Nou. Unfortunately, that epic win would be Rubin's only one in their six group games, and they would not join CSKA in the last 16, but on the whole the club from Tatarstan made a decent fist of their UEFA Champions League debut, adding three home draws to that one unforgettable three-pointer. Third place in the group – ahead of competition regulars FC Dynamo Kyiv – put them into the UEFA Europa League, where they easily accounted for Hapoel Tel-Aviv FC before losing out to a late extra-time strike in Wolfsburg in the round of 16.

The pain of Rubin's UEFA Europa League exit was softened by the knowledge that they were already assured a return to the following season's UEFA Champions League – their reward for a second successive Russian Premier-Liga title triumph.

Rubin rule again

Unheralded champions in 2008, Rubin proved in 2009 that their victory was no flash in the pan. If anything, their defence of the title was even more impressive. In contention right from the start, they moved into first place at the end of May and never relinquished their position – despite the double pressure of being defending champions and taking on an extra workload in Europe. The club's long-serving coach Kurban Berdyev, in situ since 2001, reaffirmed his ability to get the best out of the resources at his disposal. He skilfully blended youth and experience and found the perfect

balance between Russian and foreign players, not least up front where local lad Aleksandr Bukharov formed a highly productive partnership with Argentine No10 Alejandro Domínguez, back at the club after two years with Zenit.

In 2008, no Rubin player had managed more than six goals; in 2009, Bukharov and Domínguez bagged 16 apiece to finish joint-second in the Premier-Liga standings. Veteran midfielder Sergei Semak proved himself once again to be an influential and inspirational captain, while there were fine contributions also from goalkeeper Sergei Ryzhikov, diminutive Turkish winger Gökdeniz Karadeniz – scorer of the winning goal in Barcelona – and defensive stalwarts Cristian Ansaldi and César Navas.

Especially effective away from home, Rubin ended the season with 63 points – three more than the previous season's winning tally – but they had to wait a little bit longer for their coronation, securing the title with one game to spare rather than the three of 2008. Their final victory margin was doubled from four points to eight, with closest pursuers Spartak only just hanging on to second place – and, with it, guaranteed group-stage

participation in the 2010/11 UEFA Champions League – after they lost their last three matches.

Brazilian blend

Nevertheless, with Karpin having replaced the hapless Laudrup at the helm, Spartak enjoyed a positive campaign. Their fourth runners-up placing in five years – after a disastrous eighth place in 2008 – was largely down to the season-long excellence of their two Brazilian stars, Welliton and Alex. The former made a sensational return from long-term injury, topping the league's scoring charts with 21 goals, many of which were created for him by his skilful compatriot – a pre-season signing from SC Internacional of Porto Alegre and the best newcomer in the Premier-Liga by a distance.

Zenit beat Spartak 2-1 on the final day to take third place and a UEFA Champions League qualifying berth. The 2008

Rossiyskiy Futbolny Soyuz (RFS)

7 Narodnaya Street
RU-115172 Moskva
tel – +7 495 9261300
fax – +7 495 9261305
website – rfs.ru
email – info@rfs.ru

Year of Formation – 1912
President – Sergei Fursenko
General Secretary – Aleksei Sorokin
Media Officer – Andrei Malosolov
National Stadium – Luzhniki, Moscow (84,000)

INTERNATIONAL HONOURS*
UEFA European Football Championship - (1) 1960.
INTERNATIONAL TOURNAMENT APPEARANCES*
FIFA World Cup - (9) 1958 (qtr-finals), 1962 (qtr-finals), 1966 (4th), 1970 (qtr-finals), 1982 (2nd phase), 1986 (2nd round), 1990, 1994, 2002.
UEFA European Championship - (9) 1960 (Winners), 1964 (runners-up), 1968 (4th), 1972 (runners-up), 1988 (runners-up), 1992, 1996, 2004, 2008 (semi-finals).
TOP FIVE ALL-TIME CAPS
(including USSR/CIS)
Viktor Onopko (113); Oleh Blokhin (112); Rinat Dasaev (91); Albert Shesternyov (90); Anatoliy Demyanenko (80)
TOP FIVE ALL-TIME GOALS
(including USSR/CIS)
Oleh Blokhin (42); Oleh Protasov (29); Vladimir Beschastnykh & Valentin Ivanov (26); Eduard Streltsov (25)

(* before 1992 as USSR; 1992 as CIS)

UEFA Cup winners would have to go a year without European football as their presence in the 2009/10 UEFA Europa League lasted just one round, a shock 5-4 aggregate defeat to Madeira club CD Nacional consigning them to the scrapheap in the play-off round alongside fellow Premier-Liga participants FC Amkar Perm - beaten by Fulham FC – and FC Dinamo Moskva – defeated by PFC CSKA Sofia after an earlier elimination from the UEFA Champions League qualifiers by Celtic FC. With PFC Krylya Sovetov Samara having also suffered a shock UEFA Europa League exit a round earlier – on away goals against Irish minnows Saint Patrick's Athletic FC – there would be no Russian participation whatsoever in the new European competition during the autumn months.

Zenit's defeat by Nacional was an early setback for newly installed coach Anatoliy Davydov, who had replaced Advocaat after a run of four winless league games. European elimination appeared to have a positive effect on the club's domestic form, however, because in 13 Premier-Liga matches under Davydov they accumulated 30 points. This was especially impressive at a time when Zenit were having to overcome the departure to Germany of key players Anatoliy Tymoshchuk and Pavel Pogrebnyak. The return, from Spartak, of tricky Russian international winger Vladimir Bystrov, who scored six goals in ten games, proved timely in the extreme, though, as Zenit soared up the table and pipped FC Lokomotiv Moskva to that coveted third spot.

Reinvigorated by the return of their former long-serving coach Yuriy Syomin, Lokomotiv had to deal with a major mid-season loss of their own when playmaker Bilyaletdinov left for Everton FC, but the goals of Nigerian international Peter Odemwingie and a reborn Dmitriy Sychev helped them to finish the season strongly and end up two points ahead of local rivals CSKA. Although the Army Men won the 2009 Russian Cup and performed well in Europe, fifth place in the Premier-Liga was unacceptable. It was for that reason that neither Zico nor Juande Ramos saw out the season. Like Zenit and Lokomotiv, CSKA had to cope with the mid-season sale of high-profile players as Zhirkov moved to Chelsea FC and Vágner Love, the 2008 Premier-Liga's top scorer, returned to Brazil.

Siberia in Europe

Having both hoped for better, Lokomotiv and CSKA had to be content with places in the 2010/11 UEFA Europa League. More than delighted to join them in that competition were FC Sibir Novosibirsk. The unsung Siberian club booked their ticket to Europe by reaching

the 2010 Russian Cup final, which they narrowly lost, 1-0 in Rostov to Zenit, giving the St Petersburg club's new (foreign) coach, ex-AS Roma boss Luciano Spalletti, an early trophy success.

Sibir reached the final thanks to a memorable hat-trick from their veteran skipper Aleksei Medvedev in the semi-final against FC Alania Vladikavkaz. Both clubs had begun the competition as First Division (second tier) clubs but ended it in the Premier-Liga. Sibir achieved promotion conventionally, as runners-up to First Division champions FC Anzhi Makhachkala – replacing relegated FC Khimki and FC Kuban Krasnodar - whereas 1995 Russian champions Alania, who finished three points below them in third place, owed their top-flight return to the shock demise of FC Moskva, who were forced out of business in early 2010 when their main sponsors suddenly decided to withdraw their financial support.

NATIONAL TEAM RESULTS 2009/10

12/8/09	Argentina	H	Moscow	2-3	Semshov (17), Pavlyuchenko (78)
5/9/09	Liechtenstein (WCQ)	H	St Petersburg	3-0	Berezutskiy V. (17), Pavlyuchenko (39p, 45p)
9/9/09	Wales (WCQ)	A	Cardiff	3-1	Semshov (36), Ignashevich (71), Pavlyuchenko (90+1)
10/10/09	Germany (WCQ)	H	Moscow	0-1	
14/10/09	Azerbaijan (WCQ)	A	Baku	1-1	Arshavin (13)
14/11/09	Slovenia (WCQ)	H	Moscow	2-1	Bilyaletdinov (40, 52)
18/11/09	Slovenia (WCQ)	A	Maribor	0-1	
3/3/10	Hungary	A	Gyor	1-1	Bilyaletdinov (59)

NATIONAL TEAM APPEARANCES 2009/10

Coach – Guus HIDDINK (NED)	8/1/46		Arg	LIE	WAL	GER	AZE	SVN	SVN	Hun	Caps	Goals
Igor AKINFEEV	8/4/86	CSKA Moskva	G	G	G	G	G	G	G	G46	40	-
Aleksandr ANYUKOV	28/9/82	Zenit	D	D	D	D		D	D	D	49	1
Denis KOLODIN	11/1/82	Dinamo Moskva	D76							D83	22	-
Sergei IGNASHEVICH	14/7/79	CSKA Moskva	D	D	D	D	D	D	D	D	56	4
Renat YANBAYEV	7/4/84	Lokomotiv Moskva	D		D		D		D46	D	9	-
Igor DENISOV	17/5/84	Zenit	M	M69		M46	s64	M	M	M89*	12	-
Igor SEMSHOV	6/4/78	Zenit /Dinamo Moskva	M82	s46	M70	M77				M46	43	2
Sergei SEMAK	27/2/76	Rubin	M58	M	M		M	M61	s46	M	65	4
Konstantin ZYRYANOV	5/10/77	Zenit	M	M46	M	M		M	M	M	31	7
Andrei ARSHAVIN	29/5/81	Arsenal (ENG)	A		A	A	A	A	A	s46	51	16
Aleksandr KERZHAKOV	27/11/82	Dinamo Moskva	A46	A	A84	A55			s46 66*		50	15
Roman PAVLYUCHENKO	15/12/81	Tottenham (ENG)	s46	A	s70	s55		A80	A46	s46	34	15
Alan DZAGOEV	17/6/90	CSKA Moskva	s58				M				5	-
Vasiliy BEREZUTSKIY	20/6/82	CSKA Moskva	s76	D58	D		D	D	D	s83	43	2
Pavel POGREBNYAK	8/11/83	Stuttgart (GER)	s82			s77			s77	A46	18	5
Diniyar BILYALETDINOV	27/2/85	Everton (ENG)		M			M	M	M77	M84	33	5
Vladimir BYSTROV	31/1/84	Zenit			M	M	M	M64	s61	s84	31	4
Aleksei BEREZUTSKIY	20/6/82	CSKA Moskva		s58			D				34	-
Aleksei REBKO	23/4/86	FC Moskva		s69	s84		M64				3	-
Yuriy ZHIRKOV	20/8/83	Chelsea (ENG)				D		D	M 92*		34	-
Dmitriy TORBINSKIY	28/4/84	Lokomotiv Moskva					s46	M			19	2
Aleksandr BUKHAROV	12/3/85	Rubin						s64			1	-
Dmitriy SYCHEV	26/10/83	Lokomotiv Moskva							s80		46	15
Vladimir GABULOV	19/10/83	Dinamo Moskva								s46	6	-

 **RUSSIA**

DOMESTIC LEAGUE 2009

PREMIER-LIGA FINAL TABLE

		Pld	Home					Away					Total					Pts
			W	D	L	F	A	W	D	L	F	A	W	D	L	F	A	
1	FC Rubin Kazan	30	9	2	4	31	11	10	4	1	31	10	19	6	5	62	21	63
2	FC Spartak Moskva	30	10	2	3	37	13	7	2	6	24	20	17	4	9	61	33	55
3	FC Zenit St Petersburg	30	10	4	1	24	10	5	5	5	24	17	15	9	6	48	27	54
4	FC Lokomotiv Moskva	30	10	5	0	26	10	5	4	6	17	20	15	9	6	43	30	54
5	PFC CSKA Moskva	30	9	1	5	26	13	7	3	5	22	17	16	4	10	48	30	52
6	FC Moskva	30	9	2	4	24	14	4	7	4	15	14	13	9	8	39	28	48
7	FC Saturn Moskovskaya Oblast	30	9	3	3	22	14	4	3	8	16	27	13	6	11	38	41	45
8	FC Dinamo Moskva	30	6	3	6	12	15	6	3	6	19	22	12	6	12	31	37	42
9	FC Tom Tomsk	30	6	3	6	20	19	5	5	5	11	20	11	8	11	31	39	41
10	PFC Krylya Sovetov Samara	30	6	3	6	19	19	4	3	8	13	23	10	6	14	32	42	36
11	PFC Spartak Nalchik	30	5	6	4	24	17	3	5	7	12	16	8	11	11	36	33	35
12	FC Terek Grozny	30	7	3	5	25	20	2	3	10	8	28	9	6	15	33	48	33
13	FC Amkar Perm	30	5	5	5	16	15	3	4	8	11	22	8	9	13	27	37	33
14	FC Rostov	30	3	8	4	16	16	4	3	8	12	23	7	11	12	28	39	32
15	FC Kuban Krasnodar	30	5	7	3	13	15	1	3	11	10	36	6	10	14	23	51	28
16	FC Khimki	30	2	2	11	12	32	0	2	13	8	32	2	4	24	20	64	10

NB FC Moskva withdrew from 2010 Premier-Liga.

TOP GOALSCORERS

21 WELLITON (Spartak Moskva)
16 Aleksandr BUKHAROV (Rubin)
   Alejandro Damián DOMÍNGUEZ (Rubin)
13 Dmitriy SYCHEV (Lokomotiv)
12 Aleksandr KERZHAKOV (Dinamo)
   ALEX (Spartak Moskva)
11 Shamil LAHIYALOV (Terek)
10 Vladimir BYSTROV (Spartak Moskva/Zenit)
9 Miloš KRASIĆ (CSKA)
   Tomáš NECID (CSKA)
   Jan KOLLER (Krylya Sovetov)

CLUB-BY-CLUB

FC AMKAR PERM

Coach – Dimitar Dimitrov (BUL); (2/9/09) Rashid Rakhimov
Founded – 1993
Stadium – Zvezda (20,000)

2009

14/3	Rostov	h	0-0	
21/3	Krylya Sovetov	a	0-1	
5/4	CSKA	h	0-0	
12/4	Zenit	a	0-0	
19/4	Kuban	h	1-0	Cherenchikov
26/4	Spartak Nalchik	a	1-4	Sikimić
2/5	FC Moskva	h	0-1	
10/5	Terek	a	2-2	Kushev 2
16/5	Rubin	h	2-2	Jean Carlos, Kushev (p)
23/5	Spartak Moskva	a	1-5	Starkov
29/5	Saturn	h	0-2	
14/6	Tom	a	2-1	Peev, Sikimić
11/7	Dinamo	h	3-1	Zhilyaev, Belorukov, Grishin
19/7	Lokomotiv	a	1-1	Sikimić
24/7	Khimki	a	0-2	
2/8	Krylya Sovetov	h	2-0	Kushev (p), Jean Carlos
9/8	CSKA	a	0-1	
16/8	Zenit	h	2-4	Kushev 2
23/8	Kuban	a	0-1	
30/8	Spartak Nalchik	h	1-2	Sikimić
12/9	FC Moskva	a	2-0	Belorukov, Afanasiev
20/9	Terek	h	1-0	Kushev
25/9	Rubin	a	2-1	Sikimić, Peev
4/10	Spartak Moskva	h	1-2	Kushev
17/10	Saturn	a	0-2	
25/10	Tom	h	0-0	
31/10	Dinamo	a	0-0	
8/11	Lokomotiv	a	0-1	
21/11	Khimki	h	2-0	Belorukov, Volkov
29/11	Rostov	a	1-1	Volkov

No	Name	Nat	DoB	Pos	Aps	(s)	Gls
10	Mikhail AFANASIEV	BLR	4/11/86	M	1	(6)	1
21	Dmitriy BELORUKOV		24/3/83	D	28		3
23	Ivan CHERENCHIKOV		25/8/84	D	26		1
18	Nikola DRINČIĆ	MNE	7/9/84	M	28		
30	David DZASOKHOV		6/10/88	M		(1)	
4	Vitaliy FEDORIV	UKR	21/10/87	D	3	(3)	
15	Miklós GAÁL	HUN	13/5/81	D	5	(2)	
32	Vadim GAGLOEV		18/1/89	M		(1)	
5	Vitaliy GRISHIN		9/9/80	M	27		1
17	JEAN CARLOS Sales Bemvindo	BRA	17/3/84	A	18	(4)	2
20	Edin JUNUZOVIĆ	CRO	28/4/86	A		(4)	
28	Vyacheslav KALASHNIKOV		12/5/85	D	14	(2)	
29	Martin KUSHEV	BUL	25/8/73	A	24	(3)	8
27	Mikhail MAKAGONOV		6/2/89	D	1		
42	Sergei NARUBIN		5/12/81	G	21		
13	Mitar NOVAKOVIĆ	MNE	27/9/81	M	27	(1)	
7	Georgi Ivanov PEEV	BUL	11/3/79	M	27	(1)	2
11	Aleksei POMERKO		3/5/90	M	5	(5)	
99	Predrag SIKIMIĆ	SRB	29/8/82	A	8	(13)	5

14	Zahari SIRAKOV	BUL	8/10/77	D	24	
77	Dmitriy SOKOLOV		1/3/88	M	4	(4)
3	Ivan STARKOV		10/1/86	M	5	(6)	1
6	Dimitar TELKIYSKI	BUL	5/5/77	M	1	(3)
1	Igor USMINSKIY		23/4/77	G	9	(1)
8	Sergei VOLKOV		27/9/80	A	8	(6)	2
22	WILLIAM Artur de Oliveira	BRA	20/10/82	M	3	(6)
19	Nikolai ZHILYAEV		5/3/87	A	13	(10)	1

PFC CSKA MOSKVA

Coach – Zico (BRA); (10/9/09) Juande Ramos (ESP);
(26/10/09) Leonid Slutskiy
Founded – 1911
Stadium – Luzhniki (84,000); Arena Khimki (18,000)
MAJOR HONOURS:
UEFA Cup – (1) 2005;
USSR League – (7) 1946, 1947, 1948, 1950, 1951, 1970, 1991;
Russian League – (3) 2003, 2005, 2006;
USSR Cup – (5) 1945, 1948, 1951, 1955, 1991;
Russian Cup – (5) 2002, 2005, 2006, 2008, 2009.

2009

15/3	Saturn	a	3-0	Dzagoev, Ignashevich 2
23/3	Tom	h	0-1	
5/4	Amkar	a	0-0	
12/4	Lokomotiv	h	4-1	Dzagoev 2, Zhirkov, Maazou
19/4	Khimki	a	3-0	Krasić 3
26/4	Rostov	h	1-2	og (Rozhkov)
3/5	Krylya Sovetov	a	3-1	Berezutskiy V., Vágner Love, Maazou
10/5	Dinamo	a	2-1	Necid, Berezutskiy V.
17/5	Zenit	h	2-1	Maazou, Vágner Love (p)
24/5	Kuban	a	0-1	
14/6	FC Moskva	a	0-2	
11/7	Terek	a	1-1	Necid
18/7	Rubin	a	2-1	Ignashevich, Vágner Love
22/7	Spartak Nalchik	h	0-0	
26/7	Spartak Moskva	h	1-2	Šembras
1/8	Tom	a	3-2	Krasić, Dzagoev, Ricardo Jesus
9/8	Amkar	h	1-0	Necid
16/8	Lokomotiv	a	1-2	Dzagoev
22/8	Khimki	h	2-1	Necid, Krasić
30/8	Rostov	a	0-1	
12/9	Krylya Sovetov	h	3-0	Necid, Guilherme 2
20/9	Dinamo	h	3-0	Mamayev, Krasić, Guilherme
26/9	Zenit	a	0-2	
4/10	Kuban	h	4-0	Mark González 2, Krasić, Oliseh
17/10	Spartak Nalchik	a	1-1	Krasić
25/10	FC Moskva	h	1-3	Necid
30/10	Terek	h	1-0	Necid
8/11	Rubin	h	0-2	
21/11	Spartak Moskva	a	3-2	Dzagoev, Necid 2
29/11	Saturn	h	3-0	Dzagoev, Krasić, Mamayev

No	Name	Nat	DoB	Pos	Aps	(s)	Gls
35	Igor AKINFEEV		8/4/86	G	30		
22	Yevgeniy ALDONIN		22/1/80	M	24	(4)	
6	Aleksei BEREZUTSKIY		20/6/82	D	15	(1)	
24	Vasiliy BEREZUTSKIY		20/6/82	D	28		2
88	CANER Erkin	TUR	4/10/88	M	5	(2)	
7	DANIEL da Silva CARVALHO	BRA	1/3/83	A	11	(2)	
10	Alan DZAGOEV		17/6/90	M	26	(1)	7
50	Anton GRIGORYEV		13/12/85	D	4		
20	GUILHERME Milhomem Gusmão	BRA	22/10/88	A	2	(3)	3
4	Sergei IGNASHEVICH		14/7/79	D	29		

21	Luboš KALOUDA	CZE	20/5/87	M	1	(3)	
17	Miloš KRASIĆ	SRB	1/11/84	M	22	(4)	9
12	Ouwo Moussa MAAZOU	NIG	25/8/88	A	6	(9)	3
11	Pavel MAMAYEV		17/9/88	M	26	(2)	2
13	MARK Dennis GONZÁLEZ	CHI	10/7/84	M	4	(1)	2
89	Tomáš NECID	CZE	13/8/89	A	14	(13)	9
15	Chidi ODIAH	NGA	17/12/83	D	11	(2)	
26	Sekou OLISEH	NGA	5/6/90	A		(5)	1
23	Nika PILIEV		21/3/91	M	2	(2)	
25	Elvir RAHIMIĆ	BIH	4/4/76	M	2	(8)	
14	RICARDO JESUS da Silva	BRA	16/5/85	A	1	(5)	1
8	Dmitriy RYZHOV		26/8/89	A		(2)	
42	Georgiy SCHENNIKOV		27/4/91	D	20	(5)	
2	Deividas ŠEMBERAS	LTU	2/8/78	D	25	(1)	1
9	VÁGNER "LOVE" Silva de Sousa	BRA	11/6/84	A	12	(1)	3
18	Yuriy ZHIRKOV		20/8/83	M	10		1

FC DINAMO MOSKVA

Coach – Andrei Kobelev
Founded – 1923
Stadium – Arena Khimki (18,000)
MAJOR HONOURS:
*USSR League – (11) 1936 (spring), 1937, 1940, 1945, 1949, 1954, 1955,
1957, 1959, 1963, 1976 (spring);*
USSR Cup – (6) 1937, 1953, 1967, 1970, 1977, 1984;
Russian Cup – (1) 1995.

2009

14/3	FC Moskva	h	1-0	Kerzhakov
21/3	Khimki	h	3-2	Kokorin, Kerzhakov (p), Dimidko
4/4	Terek	a	0-1	
11/4	Rostov	h	1-0	Kerzhakov (p)
19/4	Rubin	a	0-3	
25/4	Krylya Sovetov	h	0-1	
2/5	Spartak Moskva	a	2-0	Fernández, Kokorin
10/5	CSKA	h	1-2	Kombarov D.
17/5	Saturn	a	0-0	
24/5	Zenit	h	1-0	Khokhlov
30/5	Tom	a	3-2	Kerzhakov 2, Kombarov D.
13/6	Kuban	h	1-1	Kerzhakov (p)
11/7	Amkar	a	1-3	Kolodin
18/7	Spartak Nalchik	h	2-1	Khokhlov, Kerzhakov
25/7	Lokomotiv	a	1-1	Kerzhakov
2/8	Khimki	a	2-0	Aguiar, Kerzhakov
9/8	Terek	h	0-1	
16/8	Rostov	a	1-0	Kerzhakov
23/8	Rubin	h	0-3	
30/8	Krylya Sovetov	a	1-3	Dimidko
13/9	Spartak Moskva	h	1-1	Ropotan
20/9	CSKA	a	0-3	
26/9	Saturn	h	1-0	Aguiar
4/10	Zenit	a	1-2	Fernández
17/10	Tom	h	0-1	
25/10	Kuban	a	1-1	Kombarov D.
31/10	Amkar	h	0-0	
8/11	Spartak Nalchik	a	4-2	Ropotan, Kerzhakov 2, Kombarov D.
21/11	Lokomotiv	h	0-2	
29/11	FC Moskva	a	2-1	Kolodin, Fernández

No	Name	Nat	DoB	Pos	Aps	(s)	Gls
22	Luis Bernardo AGUIAR	URU	17/11/85	M	11	(3)	4
71	Aleksandr DENISOV		23/2/89	M	3	(3)	
15	Aleksandr DIMIDKO		20/1/86	D	9	(5)	2
6	Leandro Sebastián FERNÁNDEZ	ARG	30/1/83	D	27		3
30	Vladimir GABULOV		19/10/83	G	23		

RUSSIA

16	Tsvetan GENKOV	BUL	8/2/84	A	1	(4)	
13	Vladimir GRANAT		22/5/87	D	26	(2)	
10	Aleksandr KERZHAKOV		27/11/82	A	24		12
8	Dmitriy KHOKHLOV		22/12/75	M	29		2
99	Aleksandr KOKORIN		19/3/91	A	15	(9)	2
25	Denis KOLODIN		11/1/82	D	23		2
9	Dmitriy KOMBAROV		22/1/87	M	29		4
7	Kirill KOMBAROV		22/1/87	M	26		
4	Marcin KOWALCZYK	POL	9/4/85	D	15	(3)	
20	Adrian ROPOTAN	ROU	8/5/86	M	12	(6)	2
1	Anton SHUNIN		27/1/87	G	7	(1)	
41	Denis SKEPSKIY	UKR	5/7/87	M		(1)	
11	Fyodor SMOLOV		9/2/90	A	7	(11)	
91	Viktor SVEZHOV		17/5/91	M	5	(3)	
5	Jovan TANASIJEVIĆ	MNE	20/1/78	D	8	(4)	
27	Sergei TEREKHOV		27/6/90	M	2	(1)	
23	Luke WILKSHIRE	AUS	2/10/81	D	27		
14	Artur YUSUPOV		1/9/89	M	1		

FC KHIMKI

Coach – Konstantin Sarsania; (19/9/09) Igor Chugainov
Founded – 1997
Stadium – Arena Khimki (18,000)

2009

14/3	Lokomotiv	a	1-1	Jovanović
21/3	Dinamo	a	2-3	Nizamutdinov, Jovanović
29/3	Rostov	h	0-1	
10/4	Krylya Sovetov	a	0-3	
19/4	CSKA	h	0-3	
25/4	Zenit	a	2-4	Maksimov, Antipenko
3/5	Kuban	h	2-2	Antipenko, Pilipchuk
11/5	Spartak Nalchik	a	0-0	
16/5	FC Moskva	h	1-1	Kirillov
23/5	Terek	a	0-2	
13/6	Spartak Moskva	a	0-1	
6/7	Rubin	h	2-3	Zinoviev, Cvetković
10/7	Saturn	h	1-0	Kirillov
19/7	Tom	a	0-4	
24/7	Amkar	h	2-0	Cvetković, Streltsov
2/8	Dinamo	h	0-2	
9/8	Rostov	a	0-2	
16/8	Krylya Sovetov	h	1-3	Kozhanov
22/8	CSKA	a	1-2	Antipenko
30/8	Zenit	h	0-4	
12/9	Kuban	a	1-2	Blatnjak (p)
18/9	Spartak Nalchik	h	0-2	
26/9	FC Moskva	a	0-3	
3/10	Terek	h	1-2	Kirillov
17/10	Rubin	a	1-2	Antipenko
24/10	Spartak Moskva	h	0-3	
30/10	Saturn	a	0-1	
7/11	Tom	h	1-3	Antipenko
21/11	Amkar	a	0-2	
29/11	Lokomotiv	h	1-3	Antipenko

No	Name	Nat	DoB	Pos	Aps	(s)	Gls
38	Kamalutdin AHMEDOV		14/4/86	D	2	(2)	
20	Aleksandr ANTIPENKO		27/5/82	A	11	(8)	6
1	Roman BEREZOVSKIY	ARM	5/8/74	G	18		
19	Dragan BLATNJAK	BIH	1/8/81	A	22	(2)	1
12	Dmitriy BORODIN		8/10/77	G	2		
21	Viktor BUDYANSKIY		12/1/84	M	7	(2)	
13	Ivan CVETKOVIĆ	SRB	12/2/81	D	16	(5)	2
17	Yevgeniy GAPON		20/4/91	D	11	(2)	
4	Victor GOLOVATENCO	MDA	28/4/84	D	21	(1)	

40	Adil IBRAGIMOV		23/4/89	D	9	(1)	
18	Miodrag JOVANOVIĆ	SRB	24/3/77	D	9	(1)	2
2	Barsegh KIRAKOSYAN	ARM	23/9/82	D	3	(4)	
42	Yuriy KIRILLOV		19/1/90	M	17	(2)	3
16	Mikhail KOMAROV		3/4/84	G	10		
7	Oleg KOZHANOV		5/7/87	A	16	(6)	1
43	Arseniy LOGASHOV		20/8/91	D	5	(1)	
10	Ilia MAKSIMOV		2/2/87	M	12	(3)	1
48	Anton MAMONOV		19/9/89	A	3	(4)	
23	Nenad NASTIĆ	SRB	8/5/81	D	10	(1)	
9	Vladislav NIKIFOROV		21/3/89	A	4	(4)	
31	Eldar NIZAMUTDINOV		31/5/81	A	13	(4)	1
11	Sergei PILIPCHUK		26/11/84	M	10	(3)	1
79	Denis POPOV		4/2/79	A	1	(1)	
22	Maxim ROMASHCHENKO	BLR	31/7/76	M	8		
5	Boris ROTENBERG		18/5/86	D	12	(1)	
8	Oleg SAMSONOV		7/9/87	M	8	(2)	
78	Sébastien SANSONI	FRA	30/1/78	D	8		
15	Dmytro SEMOCHKO	UKR	25/1/79	D	9	(1)	
25	Aleksandr SHVETSOV		17/12/80	M		(1)	
32	Marko ŠIMIĆ	CRO	23/1/88	A		(3)	
33	Ivan STARKOV		10/1/86	M	7	(1)	
99	Errol STEVENS	JAM	9/5/86	A	2	(1)	
3	Andrei STRELTSOV		18/3/84	D	10		1
6	Vule TRIVUNOVIĆ	BIH	13/4/83	D	13	(1)	
28	Jani VIRTANEN	FIN	6/5/84	A		(3)	
27	Maksim ZINOVIEV		15/7/80	M	21	(1)	1

PFC KRYLYA SOVETOV SAMARA

Coach – Leonid Slutskiy; (9/10/09) Yuriy Gazzayev
Founded – 1942
Stadium – Metallurg (32,990)

2009

15/3	Tom	a	1-0	Savin
21/3	Amkar	h	1-0	Koller
5/4	Lokomotiv	a	1-2	Kalachev
10/4	Khimki	h	3-0	Koller, Adjindjal (p), Kalachev
18/4	Rostov	a	0-0	
25/4	Dinamo	a	1-0	Koller
3/5	CSKA	h	1-3	Savin
10/5	Zenit	a	0-2	
17/5	Kuban	h	1-0	Ivanov O.
24/5	Spartak Nalchik	a	1-0	Jarošík
30/5	FC Moskva	h	1-1	Koller
13/6	Terek	a	2-3	Savin 2
11/7	Rubin	h	1-2	Koller
19/7	Spartak Moskva	a	1-1	Kalachev
25/7	Saturn	h	0-2	
2/8	Amkar	a	0-2	
9/8	Lokomotiv	h	1-3	Adamov (p)
16/8	Khimki	a	3-1	Koller, Kalachev 2 (1p)
22/8	Rostov	h	2-2	Koller, Ivanov O.
30/8	Dinamo	h	3-1	Adamov 2, Jarošík
12/9	CSKA	a	0-3	
20/9	Zenit	h	0-1	
27/9	Kuban	a	0-0	
3/10	Spartak Nalchik	h	0-0	
18/10	FC Moskva	a	1-2	Koller
24/10	Terek	h	2-0	Ignatyev, Adamov
30/10	Rubin	a	1-4	Koller
7/11	Spartak Moskva	h	2-1	Bober, og (Stranzl)
21/11	Saturn	a	1-3	Adamov
29/11	Tom	h	1-3	Savin

No	Name	Nat	DoB	Pos	Aps	(s)	Gls
22	Roman ADAMOV		21/6/82	A	9	(5)	5
21	Ruslan ADJINDJAL		22/6/74	M	23		1
63	Alexandr BELOZYOROV		27/10/81	D	27		
7	Anton BOBER		28/9/82	M	24	(2)	1
29	Sergei BUDYLIN		31/10/79	D	12	(1)	
19	Juan Carlos ESCOBAR	COL	30/10/82	M		(8)	
23	Vladislav IGNATYEV		20/1/87	M	11	(15)	1
99	Oleg IVANOV		4/8/86	M	16	(11)	2
33	Stanislav IVANOV		7/10/80	M	9	(1)	
20	Jiří JAROŠÍK	CZE	27/10/77	M	25		2
2	Timofei KALACHEV	BLR	1/5/81	M	25	(1)	5
89	Jan KOLLER	CZE	30/3/73	A	27	(1)	9
9	Denis KOVBA	BLR	6/9/79	M		(1)	
5	Vladislav KULIK		27/2/85	M	17	(3)	
3	LEÍLTON Silva dos Santos	BRA	7/3/82	D	21	(1)	
31	Eduardo Eugenio LOBOS Landaeta	CHI	30/7/81	G	30		
14	OH Beom-seok	KOR	29/7/84	D	1		
18	Yevgeniy PESEGOV		21/2/89	M		(3)	
5	RAMÓN Osni Moreira Lage	BRA	24/5/88	A		(1)	
10	Yevgeniy SAVIN		19/4/84	A	14	(12)	5
4	Roman SHISHKIN		27/1/87	D	25		
8	Ivan TARANOV		22/6/86	D	14	(11)	
71	Sergei TKACHYOV		19/5/89	M		(3)	

FC KUBAN KRASNODAR
Coach – Sergei Ovchinnikov; (10/8/09) Pogos Galstyan (ARM)
Founded – 1928
Stadium – Kuban (35,200)

2009

14/3	Rubin	a	0-3	
21/3	Spartak Moskva	h	1-0	Traoré
4/4	Saturn	a	1-2	Traoré
11/4	Tom	h	0-0	
19/4	Amkar	a	0-1	
26/4	Lokomotiv	h	1-0	Dramani
3/5	Khimki	a	2-2	Zhavnerchik, Kasaev
11/5	Rostov	h	0-0	
17/5	Krylya Sovetov	a	0-1	
24/5	CSKA	h	1-0	Topchu
30/5	Zenit	a	0-2	
13/6	Dinamo	a	1-1	Dramani
12/7	Spartak Nalchik	h	2-2	Tlisov, Traoré
19/7	FC Moskva	a	1-4	Traoré
26/7	Terek	h	1-1	Kasaev
1/8	Spartak Moskva	a	0-4	
8/8	Saturn	h	0-2	
16/8	Tom	a	0-1	
23/8	Amkar	h	1-0	Traoré
29/8	Lokomotiv	a	1-4	Tlisov
12/9	Khimki	h	2-1	Traoré, Djioev
19/9	Rostov	a	3-3	Tlisov 2, Babangida (p)
26/9	Krylya Sovetov	h	0-0	
4/10	CSKA	a	0-4	
17/10	Zenit	h	0-2	
24/10	Dinamo	h	1-1	Traoré
1/11	Spartak Nalchik	a	0-4	
7/11	FC Moskva	h	3-3	Djioev, Dramani, Traoré
21/11	Terek	a	1-0	Shevchenko (p)
29/11	Rubin	h	0-3	

No	Name	Nat	DoB	Pos	Aps	(s)	Gls
30	Haruna BABANGIDA	NGA	1/10/82	A	11	(3)	1
18	Azat BAIRYEV		17/2/89	M	6	(14)	

1	Aleksei BOTVINYEV		25/6/81	G	14		
23	Georgiy DJIOEV		13/6/86	D	25	(2)	2
3	Viktor DMITRIENKO		4/4/91	D		(1)	
7	Ilia DOLMATOV		23/6/85	A		(2)	
12	Haminu DRAMANI	GHA	1/4/86	M	25	(2)	3
20	Dmitriy GORBUSHIN		31/5/86	M		(2)	
14	Anri HAGUSH		23/9/86	D	23		
80	Sani Haruna KAITA	NGA	2/5/86	M	17		
85	Bogdan KARYUKIN		20/8/85	G	8	(3)	
11	Alan KASAEV		8/4/86	M	16		2
34	Aleksandr KHOKHLOV		30/9/88	D	4	(2)	
99	Aleksei KUCHUK	BLR	9/9/86	A		(3)	
4	Krzysztof ŁAGIEWKA	POL	23/1/83	D	2	(1)	
5	Andrei Iosif MUREŞAN	ROU	1/8/85	M	7		
32	Emmanuel Osei OKODUWA	NGA	21/11/83	A	3	(4)	
28	Igor SHEVCHENKO		2/2/85	A	3	(7)	1
19	Aleksei SKVERNYUK	BLR	13/10/85	A	2	(4)	
13	Sreten SRETENOVIĆ	SRB	12/1/85	D	2	(1)	
36	Aleksei STEPANOV		5/12/77	G	8		
21	Aleksandr TIKHONOVETSKIY		11/4/79	A		(5)	
8	Artur TLISOV		10/6/82	M	21	(5)	4
10	Andrei TOPCHU		17/4/80	M	21	(2)	1
17	Dramane TRAORÉ	MLI	17/6/82	A	25	(2)	8
25	Andrei USHENIN		1/12/83	M	14	(5)	
88	WILLIAM Cleite Boaventura	BRA	14/2/80	D	25		
22	Aslan ZASEEV		7/3/82	D	27	(1)	
15	Maxim ZHAVNERCHIK	BLR	9/2/85	M	12	(8)	1
2	José Luís ZUELA dos Santos	ANG	3/8/83	D	9	(1)	

FC LOKOMOTIV MOSKVA
Coach – Rashid Rakhimov; (28/4/09) (Vladimir Maminov);
(1/6/09) Yuriy Syomin
Founded – 1923
Stadium – Lokomotiv (28,800)
MAJOR HONOURS:
Russian League – (2) 2002, 2004;
USSR Cup – (2) 1936, 1957;
Russian Cup – (5) 1996, 1997, 2000, 2001, 2007.

2009

16/3	Khimki	h	1-1	Glushakov
22/3	Rostov	a	1-1	Glushakov
5/4	Krylya Sovetov	h	2-1	Kuzmin, Dujmović
12/4	CSKA	a	1-4	Baša
19/4	Zenit	h	1-1	Rodolfo
26/4	Kuban	a	0-1	
3/5	Spartak Nalchik	h	1-0	Dujmović
10/5	FC Moskva	a	0-0	
16/5	Terek	h	4-0	Odemwingie 2, Glushakov, Mujiri
23/5	Rubin	a	0-2	
30/5	Spartak Moskva	a	2-1	Rodolfo, Minchenkov
14/6	Saturn	a	0-2	
12/7	Tom	h	0-0	
19/7	Amkar	a	1-1	Sychev
25/7	Dinamo	h	1-1	Bilyaletdinov
2/8	Rostov	h	2-0	Bilyaletdinov, Sychev
9/8	Krylya Sovetov	a	3-1	og (Shishkin), Sychev, Gatagov
16/8	CSKA	h	2-1	Bilyaletdinov, Sychev
23/8	Zenit	a	1-1	Wágner
29/8	Kuban	h	4-1	Sychev, Odemwingie, Cociş, Wágner
13/9	Spartak Nalchik	a	1-0	Sychev
19/9	FC Moskva	h	1-0	Sychev
27/10	Terek	a	1-2	Rodolfo
4/10	Rubin	h	2-1	Odemwingie 2
18/10	Spartak Moskva	a	0-3	

24/10	Saturn	h	2-2	Dujmović, Sychev
1/11	Tom	a	3-1	Sychev 2, Odemwingie
8/11	Amkar	h	1-0	Sychev
21/11	Dinamo	a	2-0	Torbinskiy, Wágner
29/11	Khimki	a	3-1	Odemwingie, Sychev 2

No	Name	Nat	DoB	Pos	Aps	(s)	Gls
30	Malkhaz ASATIANI	GEO	4/8/81	D	14		
23	Marko BAŠA	MNE	29/12/82	D	12		1
51	Maxim BELYAEV		30/9/91	D		(1)	
63	Diniyar BILYALETDINOV		27/2/85	M	12	(1)	3
32	Marek ČECH	CZE	8/4/76	G	13		
16	CHARLES Fernando Basílio da Silva	BRA	14/2/85	M	15		
25	Răzvan COCIŞ	ROU	19/2/83	A	11	(4)	1
5	Tomislav DUJMOVIĆ	CRO	26/2/81	M	26		3
20	Ján ĎURICA	SVK	10/12/81	D	6	(4)	
19	Baye Djiby FALL	SEN	20/4/85	A	2	(9)	
15	Vinícius Aparecido Pereira de Santana Campos "FININHO"	BRA	3/11/83	M	2	(5)	
81	Alan GATAGOV		21/1/91	M	13	(8)	1
8	Denis GLUSHAKOV		28/1/87	M	24	(3)	3
85	GUILHERME Alvim Marinato	BRA	12/12/85	G	17		
77	Stanislav IVANOV	MDA	7/10/80	M	4	(3)	
18	Sani Haruna KAITA	NGA	2/5/86	M	1	(2)	
44	Ruslan KAMBOLOV		1/1/90	D	1	(3)	
3	Oleg KUZMIN		9/5/83	D	21	(2)	1
45	Alexand MINCHENKOV		13/1/89	A	4	(8)	1
10	David MUJIRI	GEO	2/1/78	M	3	(6)	1
9	Peter ODEMWINGIE	NGA	15/7/81	A	24	(1)	7
39	Kirill PAVLOV		30/1/90	M	1		
97	Nika PILIEV		21/3/91	M		(1)	
4	RODOLFO Dantas Bispo	BRA	23/10/82	D	23	(1)	3
17	Dmitriy SENNIKOV		24/6/76	D	7	(2)	
11	Dmitriy SYCHEV		26/10/83	A	27		13
7	Dmitriy TORBINSKIY		28/4/84	M	14	(3)	1
13	WÁGNER Ferreira dos Santos	BRA	29/1/85	M	5	(2)	3
55	Renat YANBAYEV		7/4/84	M	28	(2)	

FC MOSKVA

Coach – Miodrag Božović (MNE)
Founded – 1997
Stadium – Eduard Streltsov (13,400)

2009

14/3	Dinamo	a	0-1	
21/3	Terek	h	0-0	
4/4	Rubin	a	0-0	
11/4	Spartak Moskva	h	3-1	Česnauskis, Epureanu, Tarasov
18/4	Saturn	a	1-0	Bracamonte
26/4	Tom	h	2-1	Bracamonte, Jakubko
2/5	Amkar	a	1-0	Jakubko
10/5	Lokomotiv	h	0-0	
16/5	Khimki	a	1-1	Jakubko
24/5	Rostov	h	2-0	Samedov, Jakubko
30/5	Krylya Sovetov	a	1-1	Samedov
14/6	CSKA	h	2-0	Samedov, Krunić
12/7	Zenit	a	0-1	
19/7	Kuban	h	4-1	Česnauskis 2, Samedov, Krunić
26/7	Spartak Nalchik	a	0-0	
1/8	Terek	a	2-1	Vukić, Česnauskis
8/8	Rubin	h	1-3	Marenich
16/8	Spartak Moskva	a	1-2	Vukić
22/8	Saturn	h	3-1	Jakubko, Strelkov, Samedov
29/8	Tom	a	0-0	
12/9	Amkar	h	0-2	

19/9	Lokomotiv	a	0-1	
26/9	Khimki	h	3-0	Jakubko, Golyshev, Vukić
3/10	Rostov	a	2-2	Rebko, Jakubko
18/10	Krylya Sovetov	h	2-1	Golyshev, Rebko
25/10	CSKA	a	3-1	Tarasov, Rebko, Epureanu
31/10	Zenit	h	1-0	Sheshukov
7/11	Kuban	a	3-3	Rebko 2, Jakubko
21/11	Spartak Nalchik	h	0-2	
29/11	Dinamo	h	1-2	og (Kolodin)

No	Name	Nat	DoB	Pos	Aps	(s)	Gls
16	Anton AMELCHENKO	BLR	27/3/85	G	1		
69	Héctor Andrés BRACAMONTE	ARG	16/2/78	A	13		2
88	Edgaras ČESNAUSKIS	LTU	5/2/84	M	24	(1)	4
15	Alexandru EPUREANU	MDA	27/9/86	D	25		2
17	Pavel GOLYSHEV		7/7/87	M	4	(6)	2
33	Akès da Costa GOORE	CIV	31/12/84	D	17		
5	Gia GRIGALAVA		5/8/89	D	13	(1)	
6	Branko ILIĆ	SVN	6/2/83	D	4	(2)	
20	Martin JAKUBKO	SVK	26/2/80	A	18	(5)	8
25	Mariusz JOP	POL	3/8/78	D	1	(2)	
28	Branislav KRUNIĆ	BIH	28/1/79	A	9	(7)	2
7	Aleksandr MARENICH		29/4/89	A	3	(6)	1
14	Kirill NABABKIN		8/9/86	D	28		
23	Isaac OKORONKWO	NGA	1/5/78	D	20		
13	Aleksei REBKO		23/4/86	M	24	(3)	5
21	Artur RYLOV		12/4/89	M		(2)	
19	Aleksandr SAMEDOV		19/7/84	M	27		5
3	Aleksandr SHESHUKOV		15/4/83	D	23	(2)	1
11	Aleksandr STAVPETS		4/7/89	A	8	(11)	
29	Igor STRELKOV		21/3/82	A	3	(18)	1
8	Dmitriy TARASOV		18/3/87	M	22	(3)	2
31	Andrei VASYANOVICH		13/6/88	D	2	(3)	
10	Zvonimir VUKIĆ	SRB	19/7/79	M	12	(12)	3
30	Yuriy ZHEVNOV	BLR	17/4/81	G	29		

FC ROSTOV

Coach – Oleg Dolmatov
Founded – 1930
Stadium – Olimp 2 (15,840)

2009

14/3	Amkar	a	0-0	
22/3	Lokomotiv	h	1-1	Petrović
3/4	Khimki	a	1-0	Lebedenko
11/4	Dinamo	a	0-1	
18/4	Krylya Sovetov	h	0-0	
26/4	CSKA	a	2-1	og (Schennikov), Hong
3/5	Zenit	h	2-1	Gatcan, Akimov
11/5	Kuban	a	0-0	
16/5	Spartak Nalchik	h	1-1	Petrović
24/5	FC Moskva	a	0-2	
30/5	Terek	h	1-1	Astafyev
13/6	Rubin	a	2-0	Akimov 2
11/7	Spartak Moskva	h	0-1	
18/7	Saturn	a	0-4	
25/7	Tom	h	0-0	
2/8	Amkar	a	0-2	
9/8	Khimki	h	2-0	Akimov, Ahmetović
16/8	Dinamo	h	0-1	
22/8	Krylya Sovetov	a	2-2	Akimov, Ahmetović
30/8	CSKA	h	1-0	Osinov
13/9	Zenit	a	0-2	
19/9	Kuban	h	3-3	Pavlenko, Gatcan, Ahmetović
27/9	Spartak Nalchik	a	0-1	
3/10	FC Moskva	h	2-2	Akimov, Lebedenko

18/10	Terek	a	3-1	*Gatcan, Pavlenko, Ahmetović*
25/10	Rubin	h	1-2	*Ahmetović*
1/11	Spartak Moskva	a	1-5	*Gatcan*
7/11	Saturn	h	1-2	*Lebedenko*
21/11	Tom	a	1-2	*Ahmetović*
29/11	Amkar	h	1-1	*Pavlenko*

No	Name	Nat	DoB	Pos	Aps	(s)	Gls
19	Mersudin AHMETOVIĆ	BIH	19/2/85	A	14	(14)	6
9	Dmitriy AKIMOV		14/9/80	A	19	(4)	6
3	Dušan ANĐELKOVIĆ	SRB	15/6/82	D	25		
8	Maksim ASTAFYEV		8/12/82	M	21	(2)	1
5	Aleksandr CHERKES		2/9/76	D	20	(1)	
84	Alexandru GATCAN	MDA	27/3/84	M	23	(3)	4
1	Roman GERUS		14/9/80	G	15		
12	Pyotr GITSELOV		18/7/83	M	2	(5)	
21	HONG Yong-jo	PRK	22/5/82	A	10	(4)	1
27	Stanislav KHOTEEV		7/3/81	G	5	(1)	
7	Aleksandr KULCHIY	BLR	1/11/73	M	27	(1)	
24	Sergei KUZNETSOV		7/5/86	M	1	(4)	
54	Ivan LAPIN		8/5/88	D		(3)	
4	Igor LEBEDENKO		27/5/83	A	25	(4)	3
6	Roman LENGYEL	CZE	3/11/78	D	27		
87	Yevgeniy LUTSENKO		25/2/87	A	3	(3)	
16	Veniamin MANDRYKIN		30/8/81	G	10		
10	Mikhail OSINOV		8/10/75	M	16	(2)	1
25	Aleksandr PAVLENKO		20/1/85	M	9		3
18	Branimir PETROVIĆ	SRB	26/6/82	M	14	(9)	2
14	Aleksandr PONOMARYEV		25/1/86	D		(1)	
83	Mikhail ROZHKOV	KAZ	27/12/83	D	17	(2)	
88	Aleksandr SALUGIN		23/10/88	M	1	(5)	
57	Astemir SHIREEV		23/2/90	D	8	(1)	
51	Andrei SKLYAROV		30/9/89	M	1		
85	Nenad SLIVIĆ	SRB	8/6/85	M	8	(5)	
20	Artur VALIKAEV		8/1/88	D	2	(4)	
26	Ivan ŽIVANOVIĆ	SRB	10/12/81	D	7	(1)	

FC RUBIN KAZAN

Coach – Kurban Berdyev (TKM)
Founded – 1936
Stadium – Central (30,133)
MAJOR HONOURS:
Russian League – (2) 2008, 2009.

2009				
14/3	Kuban	h	3-0	*Bukharov 2, Semak*
22/3	Spartak Nalchik	a	0-0	
4/4	FC Moskva	h	0-0	
11/4	Terek	a	2-1	*Semak, Domínguez*
19/4	Dinamo	h	3-0	*Sharonov, Domínguez (p),*
				og (Kombarov K.)
25/4	Spartak Moskva	h	0-2	
2/5	Saturn	a	5-0	*Domínguez 3, Sibaya, Noboa*
11/5	Tom	h	4-0	*Sharonov, Gökdeniz, Adamov,*
				Hasan
16/5	Amkar	a	2-2	*Adamov, Semak*
23/5	Lokomotiv	h	2-0	*Semak, Gökdeniz*
30/5	Khimki	a	3-2	*Bukharov 3*
13/6	Rostov	h	0-2	
11/7	Krylya Sovetov	a	2-1	*Semak, Bukharov*
18/7	CSKA	h	1-2	*Domínguez (p)*
25/7	Zenit	a	0-0	
31/7	Spartak Nalchik	h	2-0	*Gökdeniz, Domínguez (p)*
8/8	FC Moskva	a	3-1	*Gökdeniz, Bukharov,*
				Domínguez (p)
16/8	Terek	h	4-0	*Bukharov 3, Domínguez*

23/8	Dinamo	a	3-0	*Domínguez 2 (2p), Ryazantsev*
30/8	Spartak Moskva	a	3-0	*Semak, Domínguez, Bukharov*
12/9	Saturn	h	5-1	*Bukharov 2, Domínguez (p),*
				Ryazantsev 2
20/9	Tom	a	0-0	
25/9	Amkar	h	1-2	*Domínguez*
4/10	Lokomotiv	a	1-2	*Salukvadze*
17/10	Khimki	h	2-1	*Gökdeniz, Kasaev*
25/10	Rostov	a	2-1	*Domínguez, Ansaldi*
30/10	Krylya Sovetov	h	4-1	*Noboa, Bukharov 2, Gökdeniz*
8/11	CSKA	a	2-0	*Domínguez, Bukharov*
21/11	Zenit	h	0-0	
29/11	Kuban	a	3-0	*Hasan, Murawski, Portnyagin*

No	Name	Nat	DoB	Pos	Aps	(s)	Gls
21	Roman ADAMOV		21/6/82	A	9	(4)	2
3	Cristian Daniel ANSALDI	ARG	20/9/86	D	25		1
23	Yevgeniy BALYAIKIN		19/5/88	M	5	(12)	
11	Aleksandr BUKHAROV		12/3/85	A	21	(2)	16
5	Pyotr BYSTROV		15/7/79	M	5	(6)	
4	CÉSAR González NAVAS	ESP	14/2/80	D	28		
10	Alejandro Damián DOMÍNGUEZ	ARG	10/6/81	A	19	(4)	16
8	Mahach GADJIEV		18/10/87	M		(1)	
61	GÖKDENİZ Karadeniz	TUR	11/1/80	M	23	(2)	6
32	Andrei GORBANETS		24/8/85	M	5	(6)	
99	HASAN Kabze	TUR	26/5/82	A	2	(12)	2
19	Vitaliy KALESHIN		3/10/80	D	17	(1)	
88	Alan KASAEV		8/4/86	M	6	(4)	1
43	Aleksei KOTLYAROV		11/5/89	M		(1)	
27	Dato KVIRKVELIA	GEO	27/6/80	D	6	(1)	
67	Davron MIRZAYEV	UZB	8/2/89	A		(1)	
42	Rafał MURAWSKI	POL	9/10/81	M	4	(3)	1
16	Christian Fernando NOBOA	ECU	9/4/85	M	20	(2)	2
22	Aleksandr OREKHOV		29/11/83	D	2		
24	Aleksei POPOV		7/7/78	D	7	(3)	
97	Igor PORTNYAGIN		7/1/89	A		(1)	1
14	Serhiy REBROV	UKR	3/6/74	A	3	(4)	
29	Nukri REVISHVILI	GEO	2/3/87	G	1		
15	Aleksandr RYAZANTSEV		5/9/86	M	13	(5)	3
77	Sergei RYZHIKOV		19/9/80	G	29		
9	Lasha SALUKVADZE	GEO	21/12/81	D	8	(2)	1
7	Sergei SEMAK		27/2/76	M	26		6
76	Roman SHARONOV		29/1/76	D	24	(1)	2
6	MacBeth SIBAYA	RSA	25/11/77	M	21	(2)	1
2	Stjepan TOMAS	CRO	6/3/76	D	1		

FC SATURN MOSKOVSKAYA OBLAST

Coach – Jürgen Röber (GER); (15/5/09) Andrei Gordeev
Founded – 1946
Stadium – Saturn (16,726)

2009				
15/3	CSKA	h	0-3	
22/3	Zenit	a	1-2	*Topić*
4/4	Kuban	h	2-1	*Kirichenko 2*
12/4	Spartak Nalchik	a	1-1	*Igonin*
18/4	FC Moskva	h	0-1	
25/4	Terek	a	1-1	*Yevseyev*
2/5	Rubin	h	0-5	
11/5	Spartak Moskva	a	0-4	
17/5	Dinamo	h	0-0	
23/5	Tom	h	0-0	
29/5	Amkar	a	2-0	*Kuzmichov, Kirichenko*
14/6	Lokomotiv	a	2-0	*Zelão, Loskov*
10/7	Khimki	a	0-1	
18/7	Rostov	h	4-0	*Loskov, Nemov, Kirichenko 2*

25/7	Krylya Sovetov	a	2-0	Kirichenko, Vasiev
2/8	Zenit	h	2-2	Kirichenko (p), Nakhushev
8/8	Kuban	a	2-0	Halilovič, Loskov (p)
16/8	Spartak Nalchik	h	1-0	Kuzmichov
22/8	FC Moskva	a	1-3	Angbwa
29/8	Terek	h	3-0	Kuzmichov, Ivanov, Kirichenko
12/9	Rubin	a	1-5	Topić
19/9	Spartak Moskva	h	2-1	Loskov, Topić
26/9	Dinamo	a	0-1	
3/10	Tom	a	1-3	Kuzmichov
17/10	Amkar	h	2-0	Angbwa, Loskov
24/10	Lokomotiv	a	2-2	Karyaka (p), Kuzmichov
30/10	Khimki	h	1-0	Halilovič
7/11	Rostov	a	2-1	Topić, Karyaka
21/11	Krylya Sovetov	h	3-1	Angbwa, Karyaka, og (Jarošík),
29/11	CSKA	a	0-3	

No	Name	Nat	DoB	Pos	Aps	(s)	Gls
24	Benoît Christian ANGBWA	CMR	1/1/82	D	23		3
11	Alexei EREMENKO	FIN	24/3/83	A	2	(5)	
8	Mahach GADJIEV		18/10/87	M		(1)	
6	Dmitriy GRACHYOV		6/10/83	D	8	(1)	
19	Denis HALILOVIČ	SVN	2/3/86	D	6	(1)	2
5	Aleksei IGONIN		18/3/76	D	17	(1)	1
88	Aleksei IVANOV		1/9/81	M	22		1
21	Andrei KARYAKA		1/4/78	M	28		3
1	Antonín KINSKÝ	CZE	31/5/75	G	29		
14	Dmitriy KIRICHENKO		17/1/77	A	22	(5)	8
29	Leonid KOVEL	BLR	29/7/86	A	8	(12)	
28	Vladimir KUZMICHOV		28/7/79	M	24	(4)	5
31	Yevhen LEVCHENKO	UKR	2/1/78	M	2	(5)	
10	Dmitriy LOSKOV		12/2/74	M	17		5
63	Yevgeniy MALKOV		12/7/88	D	3		
15	Ruslan NAKHUSHEV		5/9/84	M	23	(1)	1
7	Pyotr NEMOV		18/10/83	M	29		1
99	Solomon OKORONKWO	NGA	2/8/87	A		(5)	
2	Dmytro PARFENOV	UKR	11/9/74	D	2	(2)	
77	Artyom REBROV		4/3/84	G	1		
41	Aleksandr SAPETA		28/6/89	M	3	(11)	
35	Ivan TEMNIKOV		28/1/89	M		(3)	
8	Marko TOPIĆ	BIH	1/1/76	M	13	(11)	4
61	Farkhod VASIEV	TJK	14/4/90	D	1		1
37	Roman VOROBIYOV		24/3/84	M	9	(9)	
2	Vadim YEVSEYEV		8/1/76	D	12		1
17	Vladimir YURCHENKO	BLR	26/1/89	A		(2)	
3	Luiz Ricardo da Silva "ZELÃO"	BRA	12/11/84	D	26		1

FC SPARTAK MOSKVA
Coach – Michael Laudrup (DEN); (16/4/09) Valeriy Karpin
Founded – 1922
Stadium – Luzhniki (84,000)
MAJOR HONOURS:
USSR League – (12) 1936 (autumn), 1938, 1939, 1952, 1953, 1956, 1958,
1962, 1969, 1979, 1987, 1989;
Russian League – (9) 1992, 1993, 1994, 1996, 1997, 1998, 1999, 2000, 2001;
USSR Cup – (10) 1938, 1939, 1946, 1947, 1950, 1958, 1963, 1965, 1971, 1992;
Russian Cup – (3) 1994, 1998, 2003.

2009

15/3	Zenit	h	1-1	Saenko
22/3	Kuban	a	0-1	
5/4	Spartak Nalchik	h	2-0	Alex, Welliton
11/4	FC Moskva	a	1-3	Alex
18/4	Terek	h	2-0	Bystrov, Welliton
25/4	Rubin	a	2-0	Stranzl, Welliton
2/5	Dinamo	h	0-2	

11/5	Saturn	h	4-0	Makeev, Dzyuba, Welliton 2
17/5	Tom	a	1-1	Dzyuba
23/5	Amkar	h	5-1	Welliton 2, Alex 2, Bazhenov
30/5	Lokomotiv	a	1-2	Alex
13/6	Khimki	h	1-0	Fathi
11/7	Rostov	a	1-0	Welliton
19/7	Krylya Sovetov	h	1-1	Bystrov
26/7	CSKA	a	2-1	Alex 2 (1p)
1/8	Kuban	h	4-0	og (Tlisov), Welliton 2, Bystrov
8/8	Spartak Nalchik	a	4-2	Welliton 3 (1p), Bystrov
16/8	FC Moskva	h	2-1	Yakovlev, Makeev
23/8	Terek	a	3-2	Yakovlev, Welliton 2
30/8	Rubin	h	0-3	
13/9	Dinamo	a	1-1	Bazhenov
19/9	Saturn	a	1-2	Alex (p)
27/9	Tom	h	5-0	Jiránek, Yakovlev, Filipenko, Nizamutdinov, Owusu-Abeyie
4/10	Amkar	a	2-1	Welliton, Fathi
18/10	Lokomotiv	h	3-0	Ananidze, Welliton, Owusu-Abeyie
24/10	Khimki	a	3-0	Welliton 2, Parshivlyuk
1/11	Rostov	h	5-1	Alex 2, Yakovlev, Ananidze, Welliton
7/11	Krylya Sovetov	a	1-2	Alex
21/11	CSKA	h	2-3	Alex (p), Welliton
29/11	Zenit	a	1-2	Fathi

No	Name	Nat	DoB	Pos	Aps	(s)	Gls
12	ALExandre Raphael Meschini	BRA	25/3/82	M	29		12
49	Zhano ANANIDZE	GEO	10/10/92	A	5	(3)	2
21	Nikita BAZHENOV		1/2/85	A	10	(12)	2
7	Denis BOYARINTSEV		6/2/78	M	11	(7)	
23	Vladimir BYSTROV		31/1/84	M	16	(2)	4
17	Serghey COVALCIUC	MDA	20/1/82	M	12	(4)	
20	Ignas DEDURA	LTU	1/6/78	D	2	(2)	
1	Soslan DZHANAEV		13/3/87	G	26		
9	Artyom DZYUBA		22/8/88	A	6	(2)	2
4	Malik FATHI	GER	29/10/83	D	13	(3)	3
58	Yegor FILIPENKO	BLR	10/4/88	D	4	(1)	1
39	Igor GORBATENKO		13/2/89	M		(2)	
30	Maksim GRIGORYEV		6/7/90	M	1	(2)	
18	IBSON Barreto Gonçalves da Silva	BRA	7/11/83	M	4	(2)	
25	Martin JIRÁNEK	CZE	25/5/79	D	29		1
13	Fyodor KUDRYASHOV		5/4/87	D	7		
16	Yevgeniy MAKEEV		24/7/89	M	17	(3)	2
19	Artur MALOYAN		4/2/89	M	1	(2)	
81	Eldar NIZAMUTDINOV		31/5/81	A	2	(3)	1
55	Quincy OWUSU-ABEYIE	GHA	15/4/86	A	1	(7)	2
15	Sergei PARSHIVLYUK		18/3/89	M	21		1
8	Aleksandr PAVLENKO		20/1/85	M	1	(9)	
22	Stipe PLETIKOSA	CRO	8/1/79	G	4		
5	RAFAEL "CARIOCA" de Souza Pereira	BRA	18/6/89	M	22	(1)	
14	Clemente Juan RODRÍGUEZ	ARG	31/7/81	D	3	(4)	
24	Vladislav RYZHKOV		28/2/90	M	2	(2)	
6	Renat SABITOV		13/6/85	D	12	(5)	
10	Ivan SAENKO		17/10/83	A	12	(1)	1
3	Martin STRANZL	AUT	16/6/80	D	19		1
11	WELLITON Soares de Morais	BRA	22/10/86	A	28		21
44	Pavel YAKOVLEV		7/4/91	A	10	(4)	4

PFC SPARTAK NALCHIK

Coach – Yuriy Krasnozhan
Founded – 1935
Stadium – Spartak (14,200)

2009

Date	Opponent	H/A	Score	Scorers
15/3	Terek	a	0-1	
22/3	Rubin	h	0-0	
5/4	Spartak Moskva	a	0-2	
12/4	Saturn	h	1-1	Amisulashvili
18/4	Tom	a	0-1	
26/4	Amkar	h	4-1	Kontsevoi, Kisenkov, Gogua, Goshokov
3/5	Lokomotiv	a	0-1	
11/5	Khimki	h	0-0	
16/5	Rostov	a	1-1	Leandro
24/5	Krylya Sovetov	h	0-1	
14/6	Zenit	h	2-2	Geteriyev 2
12/7	Kuban	a	2-2	Leandro (p), Kontsevoi
18/7	Dinamo	a	1-2	Leandro (p)
22/7	CSKA	a	0-0	
26/7	FC Moskva	h	0-0	
31/7	Rubin	a	0-2	
8/8	Spartak Moskva	h	2-4	Kisenkov, Asildarov
16/8	Saturn	a	0-1	
22/8	Tom	h	3-0	Kisenkov, Asildarov 2 (1p)
31/8	Amkar	a	2-1	Asildarov 2
13/9	Lokomotiv	h	0-1	
18/9	Khimki	a	2-0	Leandro 2
27/9	Rostov	h	1-0	Asildarov
3/10	Krylya Sovetov	a	0-0	
17/10	CSKA	h	1-1	Amisulashvili
25/10	Zenit	a	2-2	Siradze, Leandro
1/11	Kuban	h	4-0	Asildarov (p), Amisulashvili, Kisenkov, Leandro
8/11	Dinamo	h	2-4	Kalimullin, Ricardo Baiano
21/11	FC Moskva	a	2-0	Siradze, Asildarov
29/11	Terek	h	4-2	Leandro, og (Omelyanchuk), Kisenkov, Siradze

No	Name	Nat	DoB	Pos	Aps	(s)	Gls
5	Aleksandre AMISULASHVILI	GEO	20/8/82	D	30		3
55	Shamil ASILDAROV		18/5/83	A	14		8
88	Kantemir BERKHAMOV		7/8/88	M	4	(6)	
9	Marat BIKMOEV	UZB	1/1/86	A	11	(12)	
19	Marat DZAHMISHEV		25/1/80	A	6	(5)	
20	Miodrag DŽUDOVIĆ	MNE	6/9/79	D	29		
99	FELIPE Almeida Félix	BRA	20/4/85	A	1	(2)	
2	António FERREIRA de Oliveira Júnior	BRA	24/8/84	D	10	(3)	
17	Valentin FILATOV		19/3/82	D	7	(3)	
33	Kazbek GETERIYEV		30/6/85	M	25	(3)	2
7	Gogita GOGUA	GEO	4/10/83	M	9	(5)	1
44	Arsen GOSHOKOV		5/6/91	A	3		1
84	Rustem KALIMULLIN		24/6/84	A	16	(5)	1
13	Dmitriy KHOMICH		4/10/84	G	11		
18	Vladimir KISENKOV		8/10/81	D	22		5
14	Roman KONTSEDALOV		11/5/86	M	19	(3)	
11	Artem KONTSEVOI	BLR	20/5/83	A	8	(10)	2
31	LEANDRO da Silva	BRA	26/7/85	D	27	(3)	8
21	David LORIA	KAZ	31/10/81	G	2		
15	Aslan MASHUKOV		4/11/84	M	21	(3)	
26	Sergei OVCHINNIKOV		7/12/84	A		(1)	
16	Franco Martín PARODI	ARG	29/11/89	A	2	(4)	
29	Sergei PILIPCHUK		26/11/84	M	1	(4)	
22	Dejan RADIĆ	SRB	8/7/80	G	17	(1)	
90	RICARDO Lago Santos "BAIANO"	BIH	10/9/80	M	1	(8)	1

No	Name	Nat	DoB	Pos	Aps	(s)	Gls
28	Oleg SAMSONOV		7/7/87	M	7	(3)	
8	David SIRADZE	GEO	21/10/81	A	4	(2)	3
3	Dmitriy YATCHENKO		25/8/86	A	23	(1)	

FC TEREK GROZNY

**Coach – Vyacheslav Hrozniy (UKR);
(20/10/09) Şahin Diniyev (AZE)**
Founded – 1946
Stadium – Sultan Bilimhanov (10,300)
MAJOR HONOURS:
Russian Cup – (1) 2004.

2009

Date	Opponent	H/A	Score	Scorers
15/3	Spartak Nalchik	h	1-0	Cléber
21/3	FC Moskva	a	0-0	
4/4	Dinamo	h	1-0	Djabrailov
11/4	Rubin	h	1-2	Lahiyalov
18/4	Spartak Moskva	a	0-2	
25/4	Saturn	h	1-1	Gvazava
2/5	Tom	a	1-2	Pancu
10/5	Amkar	h	2-2	Pancu 2 (1p)
16/5	Lokomotiv	a	0-4	
23/5	Khimki	h	2-0	Kobenko, Lahiyalov
30/5	Rostov	a	1-1	Lahiyalov
13/6	Krylya Sovetov	h	3-2	Pancu 2, Bendz
11/7	CSKA	h	1-1	Pancu (p)
19/7	Zenit	h	3-2	Georgiev, Lahiyalov, Iliev
26/7	Kuban	a	1-1	Iliev
1/8	FC Moskva	h	1-2	Lahiyalov
9/8	Dinamo	a	1-0	Petre
16/8	Rubin	a	0-4	
23/8	Spartak Moskva	h	2-3	Kutarba, Lahiyalov
29/8	Saturn	a	0-3	
13/9	Tom	h	4-0	Lahiyalov 3 (1p), Petre
20/9	Amkar	a	0-1	
27/9	Lokomotiv	h	2-1	Sadaev, Pancu
3/10	Khimki	a	2-1	Lahiyalov, Djabrailov
18/10	Rostov	h	1-3	Sadaev
24/10	Krylya Sovetov	a	0-2	
30/10	CSKA	a	0-1	
8/11	Zenit	a	0-2	
21/11	Kuban	h	0-1	
29/11	Spartak Nalchik	a	2-4	Djabrailov, Lahiyalov

No	Name	Nat	DoB	Pos	Aps	(s)	Gls
23	Sergei BENDZ		3/4/83	D	3	(7)	1
15	Jean Blaise BOULI	CMR	4/9/80	M	2		
69	Héctor Andrés BRACAMONTE	ARG	16/2/78	A	1	(1)	
5	CLÉBER Guedes de Lima	BRA	29/4/74	D	16	(2)	1
18	Timur DJABRAILOV		5/8/73	D	19	(2)	3
31	Andriy DYKAN	UKR	16/7/77	G	28	(1)	
33	Ismail EDIEV		16/2/88	D	1		
30	Rivadi EDILOV		26/6/88	G	2		
25	Guy Stéphane ESSAME	CMR	25/11/84	M	3	(3)	
7	Blagoy GEORGIEV	BUL	21/12/81	M	25	(2)	1
26	Gogita GOGUA	GEO	4/10/83	M	3	(2)	
22	Levan GVAZAVA	GEO	8/7/80	M	13	(6)	1
4	Zeev HAIMOVICH	ISR	4/4/83	D	11	(1)	
14	Valentin ILIEV	BUL	11/7/80	D	21	(1)	2
17	Adlan KATSAEV		20/2/88	M	7	(4)	
20	Andrei KOBENKO		25/7/82	M	12	(4)	1
57	German KUTARBA		10/9/78	M	1	(1)	1
10	Shamil LAHIYALOV		28/10/79	M	21	(3)	11
6	Silviu Andrei MĂRGĂRITESCU	ROU	11/8/80	M	15	(1)	
3	Mikhail MISCHENKO		27/7/89	D	7	(1)	
28	Sergei OMELYANCHUK	BLR	8/8/80	D	28		
8	Daniel Gabriel PANCU	ROU	18/8/78	A	15	(7)	7
11	Florentin PETRE	ROU	15/1/76	M	15	(4)	2

RUSSIA

29	Aleksandr PRUDNIKOV		26/3/89	A	4	(3)	
13	Zayr SADAEV		6/11/89	A	10	(7)	2
16	Igor SHEVCHENKO		2/2/85	A	2	(6)	
24	Dmitriy SMIRNOV		13/8/80	M	9	(1)	
38	Murad TAGILOV		27/1/90	D		(1)	
39	Anzor TEMBULATOV		8/6/89	M	1		
41	Islam TSUROEV		23/4/89	A		(1)	
40	Rizvan UTSIEV		7/2/88	M	9		
21	Oleg VLASOV		10/12/84	M	5	(11)	
2	Radoslav ZABAVNÍK	SVK	16/9/80	D	21	(5)	

12	Aleksei POLYAKOV		28/2/74	G	4	(1)	
23	Aleksander RADOSAVLJEVIČ	SVN	25/4/79	M	18	(9)	3
5	Sergei SKOBLYAKOV		2/1/77	M	21	(5)	
32	Dmitriy A. SMIRNOV		13/8/80	M	7	(1)	
24	Dmitriy N. SMIRNOV		9/11/80	D	28		
26	Viktor STROYEV		16/1/87	D	8	(2)	
7	Vitaliy VOLKOV		22/3/81	M	7	(10)	
4	Vasiliy YANOTOVSKIY		2/1/76	M	6	(11)	
19	Denis YEVSIKOV		19/2/81	D	4		

FC TOM TOMSK

Coach – Valeriy Nepomniachi
Founded – 1957
Stadium – Trud (15,000)

2009

15/3	Krylya Sovetov	h	0-1	
23/3	CSKA	a	1-0	Maznov
5/4	Zenit	h	0-3	
11/4	Kuban	a	0-0	
18/4	Spartak Nalchik	h	1-0	Kornilenko
26/4	FC Moskva	a	1-2	Kornilenko
2/5	Terek	h	2-1	Jokić, Kornilenko
11/5	Rubin	a	0-4	
17/5	Spartak Moskva	h	1-1	Kharitonov
23/5	Saturn	a	0-0	
30/5	Dinamo	h	2-3	Kornilenko 2
14/6	Amkar	h	1-2	Kornilenko
12/7	Lokomotiv	a	0-0	
19/7	Khimki	h	4-0	Radosavljevič, Klimov 2, Kharitonov
25/7	Rostov	a	0-0	
1/8	CSKA	h	2-3	Michkov, Maznov
9/8	Zenit	a	2-0	Kharitonov, Jokić
16/8	Kuban	h	1-0	Jokić
22/8	Spartak Nalchik	a	0-3	
29/8	FC Moskva	h	0-0	
13/9	Terek	a	0-4	
20/9	Rubin	h	0-0	
27/9	Spartak Moskva	a	0-5	
3/10	Saturn	h	3-1	Kharitonov, Dzyuba 2
17/10	Dinamo	a	1-0	Radosavljevič
25/10	Amkar	a	0-0	
1/11	Lokomotiv	h	1-3	Maznov
7/11	Khimki	a	3-1	Maznov, Radosavljevič, Klimov
21/11	Rostov	h	2-1	Maznov, Klimov
29/11	Krylya Sovetov	a	3-1	Klimov, Dzyuba, Kovalchuk

No	Name	Nat	DoB	Pos	Aps	(s)	Gls
10	Anton ARKHIPOV		4/11/85	A	1	(4)	
21	Valeriu CATINSUS	MDA	27/4/78	D	18	(3)	
22	Vladimir DYADYUN		12/7/88	A	4	(16)	
14	Artyom DZYUBA		22/8/88	A	9	(1)	3
20	Yegor FILIPENKO	BLR	10/4/88	D		(2)	
15	Sergei GOLYATKIN		4/5/88	A		(1)	
13	Ilya GULTYAEV		5/9/88	D	3		
17	Andrei IVANOV		8/10/88	D	19		
37	Đorđe JOKIĆ	SRB	20/1/81	D	27		3
83	Aleksandr KHARITONOV		4/4/83	M	28		4
8	Denis KISILYOV		2/7/77	A		(5)	
3	Valeriy KLIMOV		31/1/74	M	22	(2)	5
9	Sergei KORNILENKO	BLR	14/6/83	A	8	(2)	6
11	Kyrylo KOVALCHUK	UKR	11/6/86	M	4	(4)	1
27	Goran MAZNOV	MKD	22/4/81	A	24	(4)	5
6	Dmitriy MICHKOV		22/2/80	M	29		1
18	Norbert NÉMETH	HUN	5/5/81	M	5	(4)	
25	Sergei PAREIKO	EST	31/1/77	G	26		

FC ZENIT ST PETERSBURG

Coach – Dick Advocaat (NED); (10/8/09) Anatoliy Davydov
Founded – 1925
Stadium – Petrovskiy (22,025)
MAJOR HONOURS:
UEFA Cup – (1) 2008; UEFA Super Cup – (1) 2008;
USSR League – (1) 1984; Russian League – (1) 2007; USSR Cup – (1) 1944;
Russian Cup – (2) 1999, 2010.

2009

15/3	Spartak Moskva	a	1-1	Pogrebnyak
22/3	Saturn	h	2-1	Križanac, Fatih
5/4	Tom	a	3-0	Fernando Meira, Denisov, Fatih
12/4	Amkar	h	0-0	
19/4	Lokomotiv	a	1-1	Kim
25/4	Khimki	h	4-2	og (Trivunović), Semshov, Fatih, Pogrebnyak
3/5	Rostov	a	1-2	Pogrebnyak
10/5	Krylya Sovetov	h	2-0	Zyryanov, Pogrebnyak
17/5	CSKA	a	1-2	Semshov
24/5	Dinamo	a	0-1	
30/5	Kuban	h	2-0	Semshov, Zyryanov
14/6	Spartak Nalchik	a	2-2	Semshov, Anyukov
12/7	FC Moskva	h	1-0	Križanac
19/7	Terek	a	2-3	Huszti, Pogrebnyak
25/7	Rubin	h	0-0	
2/8	Saturn	a	2-2	Kornilenko, Shirokov
9/8	Tom	h	0-2	
15/8	Amkar	a	4-2	Semshov 2, Lombaerts, Huszti
23/8	Lokomotiv	h	1-1	Fatih
30/8	Khimki	a	4-0	Fatih, Bystrov, Rosina, og (Zinoviev)
13/9	Rostov	h	2-0	Zyryanov, Bystrov
20/9	Krylya Sovetov	a	1-0	Bystrov
26/9	CSKA	h	2-0	Kežman, Bystrov
4/10	Dinamo	h	2-1	Fatih, Kežman
18/10	Kuban	a	2-0	Rosina, Bystrov
25/10	Spartak Nalchik	h	2-2	Bystrov, Fatih
31/10	FC Moskva	a	0-1	
8/11	Terek	h	2-0	Fatih, og (Utsiev)
21/11	Rubin	a	0-0	
29/11	Spartak Moskva	h	2-1	Zyryanov, Lombaerts

No	Name	Nat	DoB	Pos	Aps	(s)	Gls
2	Aleksandr ANYUKOV		28/9/82	D	27		1
34	Vladimir BYSTROV		31/1/84	M	10		6
1	Kamil ČONTOFALSKÝ	SVK	3/6/78	G	2		
10	Daniel Miguel Alves Gomes "DANNY"	POR	7/8/83	M	8		
27	Igor DENISOV		17/5/84	M	28		1
9	FATIH Tekke	TUR	9/9/77	A	14	(6)	8
20	Viktor FAYZULIN		22/4/86	M	10	(6)	
3	FERNANDO José da Silva Freitas MEIRA	POR	5/6/78	D	22		
14	Tomáš HUBOČAN	SVK	17/9/85	D	8	(3)	
23	Szabolcs HUSZTI	HUN	18/4/83	M	12	(7)	2
57	Aleksei IONOV		18/2/89	M	5	(5)	
99	Maksim KANUNNIKOV		14/7/91	A		(1)	

88	Mateja KEŽMAN	SRB	12/4/79	A	5	(5)	2
5	KIM Dong-jin	KOR	29/1/82	D	17		1
19	Sergei KORNILENKO	BLR	14/6/83	A	4	(7)	1
4	Ivica KRIŽANAC	CRO	13/4/79	D	18		2
6	Nicolas LOMBAERTS	BEL	20/3/85	D	14	(1)	2
16	Vyacheslav MALAFEEV		4/3/79	G	28		
8	Pavel POGREBNYAK		8/11/83	A	13	(2)	5
17	Alessandro ROSINA	ITA	31/1/84	M	5	(4)	2
21	Igor SEMSHOV		6/4/78	M	20	(6)	6
15	Roman SHIROKOV		6/7/81	M	9	(11)	1
11	Radek ŠÍRL	CZE	20/3/81	M	13	(4)	
44	Anatoliy TYMOSHCHUK	UKR	30/3/79	M	8	(2)	
18	Konstantin ZYRYANOV		5/10/77	M	30		4

PROMOTED CLUBS

FC ANZHI MAKHACHKALA
Coach – Omari Tetradze
Founded – 1991
Stadium – Dinamo (16,000)

FC SIBIR NOVOSIBIRSK
Coach – Igor Kriushenko (BLR)
Founded – 1936
Stadium – Spartak (12,500)

FC ALANIA VLADIKAVKAZ
Coach – Valeriy Petrakov; (11/8/09) Mircea Rednic (ROU)
Founded – 1921
Stadium – Spartak (37,000)
MAJOR HONOURS:
Russian League - (1) 1995.

SECOND LEVEL FINAL TABLE 2009

		Pld	W	D	L	F	A	Pts
1	FC Anzhi Makhachkala	38	21	12	5	61	31	75
2	FC Sibir Novosibirsk	38	22	7	9	60	21	73
3	FC Alania Vladikavkaz	38	21	7	10	57	30	70
4	FC Volga Nizhniy Novgorod	38	17	14	7	54	32	65
5	FC KamAZ Naberezhnye Chelny	38	18	10	10	50	31	64
6	FC Shinnik Yaroslavl	38	18	7	13	46	35	61
7	FC Salyut-Energia Belgorod	38	17	10	11	54	41	61
8	FC Ural Yekaterinburg	38	15	15	8	40	32	60
9	FC Baltika Kaliningrad	38	14	10	14	41	42	52
10	FC Krasnodar	38	14	10	14	50	47	52
11	FC Vityaz Podolsk	38	13	12	13	46	39	51
12	FC Volgar-GazProm-2 Astrakhan	38	12	15	11	40	41	51
13	FC Nizhniy Novgorod	38	14	8	16	37	47	50
14	FC Luch-Energia Vladivostok	38	13	11	14	42	43	50
15	FC SKA–Energia Khabarovsk	38	12	11	15	43	42	47
16	FC Nosta Novotroitsk	38	9	13	16	47	59	40
17	FC Chita	38	10	5	23	27	65	35
18	FC Chernomorets Novorossiysk	38	8	10	20	31	51	34
19	FC Metallurg Lipetsk	38	8	7	23	30	62	31
20	FC MVD Rossii Moskva	38	3	8	27	10	75	17

*NB FC Alania Vladikavkaz promoted as a result of FC Moskva's
withdrawal from 2010 Premier-Liga.*

DOMESTIC CUP 2009/10

KUBOK ROSSII

1/16 FINALS

(15/7/09)
Alania 1, Tom 0
Avangard Kursk 1, Amkar 2
Avangard Podolsk 4, Rostov 2
Baltika 2, Khimki 1
Chelyabinsk 2, Krylya Sovetov 1
FC Krasnodar 1, Spartak Moskva 2
Luch-Energia 3, Saturn 0
Mordovia Saransk 2, Terek 1
Nizhniy Novgorod 2, Spartak Nalchik 0 *(aet)*
Salyut-Energia Belgorod 0, FC Moskva 2
Sibir 1, Kuban 0
SKA–Energia 2, Lokomotiv Moskva 1
Torpedo Vladimir 0, Zenit 2
Ural Yekaterinburg 1, CSKA Moskva 0
Volga Tver 4, Rubin 3 *(aet)*
Volgar-GazProm-2 Astrakhan 2, Dinamo Moskva 0

1/8 FINALS

(5/8/09)
Alania 2, Volgar-GazProm-2 Astrakhan 1 *(aet)*
Amkar 2, Avangard Podolsk 1
Chelyabinsk 0, Mordovia Saransk 2
Luch-Energia 2, SKA–Energia 1 *(aet)*
Spartak Moskva 1, FC Moskva 2
Ural Yekaterinburg 1, Sibir 2
Volga Tver 2, Baltika 2 *(aet; 4-2 on pens)*
Zenit 2, Nizhniy Novgorod 1 *(aet)*

QUARTER- FINALS

(7/4/10)
FC Moskva 0, Amkar 3 *(w/o)*
Mordovia Saransk 0, Alania 3 *(Bazayev J. 26, Kuznetsov 59, Bazayev G. 88)*
Sibir 3 *(Bliznyuk 51, 54p, Astafyev 69)*, Luch-Energia 0
Zenit 2 *(Huszti 23p, Bystrov 59)*, Volga Tver 0

SEMI- FINALS

(21/4/10)
Amkar 0, Zenit 0 *(aet; 2-4 on pens)*
Sibir 3 *(Medvedev 14, 67, 90+1)*, Alania 0

FINAL

(16/5/10)
Olimp 2, Rostov-na-Donu
FC ZENIT ST PETERSBURG 1 *(Shirokov 60p)*
FC SIBIR NOVOSIBIRSK 0
Referee – Kolobaev
ZENIT – Malafeev, Anyukov, Križanac, Lombaerts, Hubočan, Danny, Shirokov, Zyryanov (Fayzulin 80), Denisov, Bystrov (Rosina 90), Kerzhakov (Kanunnikov 83).
SIBIR – Kowalewski, Molosh, Makarenko, Bukhryakov, Valentić, Filipenko, Klimavičius (Nagibin 75), Čížek (Vasilyev 61), Degtyaryov (Antipenko 71), Aravin, Medvedev.

Déjà vu double for Tre Fiori

SP Tre Fiori recovered from a poor start to the season, in which they were defeated on penalties by Andorra's UE Sant Julià in the first qualifying round of the UEFA Champions League, to not only retain the Campionato Sammarinese title but also win the Coppa Titano and therefore complete the double for the first time in the club's history.

In each case Tre Fiori defeated SP Tre Penne after extra-time in the final, and in both matches the decisive strike was delivered by the Florentino club's evergreen 39-year-old striker Sossio Aruta. The standard of football in the tiny principality may not be of the greatest standard, but Aruta, who once played in Italy for Ascoli Calcio, still merited the highest praise for his contributions to Tre Fiori's historic season. He scored 21 goals in all in domestic competition – seven in the regular league campaign, seven in the play-offs and seven in the Cup. Had he been available to coach Floriano Sperindio for the European clash with Sant Julià, he would probably have found the net in that tie too.

Sossio Aruta – the veteran goalgetter of San Marino double winners Tre Fiori

having unexpectedly reached the championship play-off semi-finals, became the first beneficiary of the extra European place allocated to UEFA's smallest member association from 2010/11.

Tre Penne agony

As Tre Fiori celebrated their sixth win in each domestic competition, Tre Penne were left to reflect ruefully on the two trophies that had got away. They actually finished the regular season with a ten-point advantage over Tre Fiori in Group B, having scored more than twice as many goals as their rivals (55 to 26), and subsequently won both of their play-off ties leading up to the championship final without conceding a goal. They also defeated Tre Fiori home and away in the group phase of the Coppa Titano. But, with a first Cup win for a decade as well as a first ever championship win in their sights, they fell agonisingly short in both finals.

Tre Penne did, however, have the consolation of qualifying for European football for the first time, in the UEFA Europa League, and they were joined in that competition by fellow debutants SC Faetano, who,

Federazione Sammarinese Giuoco Calcio (FSGC)

Strada di Montecchio 17
SM-47890 San Marino
tel – +378 0549 990 515
fax – +378 0549 992 348
website – fsgc.sm
email – fsgc@omniway.sm
Year of Formation – 1931

President – Giorgio Crescentini
General Secretary – Luciano Casadei
Media Officer – Elisa Felici
National Stadium – Stadio Olimpico, Serravalle (5,115)

TOP FIVE ALL-TIME CAPS
Damiano Vannucci (53); Mirco Gennari (48); Andy Selva (47); Simone Bacciocchi (46); Ivan Matteoni (44)
TOP FIVE ALL-TIME GOALS
Andy Selva (8)
NB No other player has scored more than one goal.

NATIONAL TEAM RESULTS 2009/10

12/8/09	Slovenia (WCQ)	A	Maribor	0-5
9/9/09	Czech Republic (WCQ)	A	Uherske Hradiste	0-7
14/10/09	Slovenia (WCQ)	H	Serravalle	0-3

NATIONAL TEAM APPEARANCES 2009/10

Coach – Giampaolo MAZZA (ITA) 26/2/56

				SVN	CZE	SVN	Caps	Goals
Aldo SIMONCINI	30/8/86	Bellaria Igea (ITA)		G	G	G	15	-
Matteo ANDREINI	10/10/81	Tre Fiori		D	D		21	-
Fabio VITAIOLI	5/4/84	Novasecchiano (ITA)		D59	D	D	11	-
Simone BACCIOCCHI	22/1/77	Fontanelle (ITA)		D	D 82*		46	-
Alessandro DELLA VALLE	8/6/82	Tropical Coriano (ITA)		D	D		28	-
Davide SIMONCINI	30/8/86	Santa Giustina (ITA)		D66		D	16	-
Damiano VANNUCCI	30/7/77	Perticara (ITA)		M	M		53	-
Nicola CIACCI	7/7/82	Pennarossa		M	M75		14	1
Matteo BUGLI	10/3/83	Corpolo (ITA)		M	M89	s46	17	-
Maicol BERRETTI	1/5/89	San Marino (ITA)		M	M	M46	10	-
Manuel MARANI	7/6/84	Russi (ITA)		A80		M	20	1
Matteo VITAIOLI	27/10/89	San Marino (ITA)		s59	s75	M	9	-
Nicola ALBANI	15/4/81	Murata		s66		D	37	1
Giovanni BONINI	5/9/86	Cailungo		s80	s65		16	-
Mauro MARANI	9/3/75	Murata			D65	D	22	-
Andy SELVA	23/5/76	Hellas Verona (ITA)			A	A62	47	8
Michele CERVELLINI	14/4/88	Juvenes-Dogana			s89	s77	2	-
Carlo VALENTINI	15/3/82	Fontanelle (ITA)				D77	35	-
Michele MARANI	16/11/82	Comarca de Níjar (ESP)				M	33	-
Danilo Ezequiel RINALDI	18/4/86	Virtus				s62	4	-

DOMESTIC LEAGUE 2009/10

CAMPIONATO SAMMARINESE FINAL TABLES
FIRST PHASE

Group A	Pld	W	D	L	F	A	Pts
1 S.S. Cosmos	21	11	5	5	32	24	38
2 Domagnano FC	21	10	7	4	32	21	37
3 AC Juvenes-Dogana	21	10	6	5	34	20	36
4 S.S. Murata	21	9	6	6	35	21	33
5 SP La Fiorita	21	8	8	5	33	30	32
6 S.S. Virtus	21	7	5	9	27	29	26
7 SP Cailungo	21	2	3	16	12	43	9
8 S.S. San Giovanni	21	1	5	15	18	50	8

Group B	Pld	W	D	L	F	A	Pts
1 SP Tre Penne	20	15	3	2	55	22	48
2 SC Faetano	20	12	4	4	41	20	40
3 SP Tre Fiori	20	11	5	4	26	14	38
4 S.S. Pennarossa	20	9	7	4	30	25	34
5 SP Libertas	20	3	10	7	22	29	19
6 S.S. Fiorentino	20	4	1	15	17	45	13
7 S.S. Folgore/Falciano	20	2	5	13	21	42	11

TOP GOALSCORERS
(excluding Play-offs)

13 Simon PARMA (La Fiorita)

12 Calogero MAGGIORE (Cosmos)
   Marco FANTINI (Juvenes-Dogana)
   Mohammed ZABOUL (Murata)
   Valentin GRIGORE (Pennarossa)

11 Paolo MONTAGNA (Cosmos)
   Maurizio DI GIULI (Tre Penne)
   Mirko PALAZZI (Tre Penne)

10 Mirco RICCI (Faetano)
   Alex OLIVIERI (Juvenes-Dogana)
   Enrico CIBELLI (Tre Penne)
   Elton SHABANI (Virtus)

SAN MARINO

CHAMPIONSHIP PLAY-OFFS

FIRST ROUND
(3/5/10)
Faetano 2 *(Moroni 28, Viroli 90+4)*,
Juvenes-Dogana 0

(4/5/10)
Domagnano 0
Tre Fiori 2 *(Amici 63, Andreini 79)*

SECOND ROUND
(7/5/10)
Faetano 0,
Tre Fiori 0 *(aet; 3-0 on pens)*

(8/5/10)
Juvenes-Dogana 2 *(Fantini 45, Fantani 63p)*, Domagnano 4 *(Baiardi 16, 45+1, 58p, Pagliarani 66)*
(Juvenes-Dogana eliminated)

THIRD ROUND
(11/5/10)
Tre Penne 3 *(Franchini 91, Valli 95, Cibelli 101)*, Cosmos 0 *(aet)*

(13/5/10)
Domagnano 0, Tre Fiori 3 *(Aruta 40, 46, 90p)*
(Domagnano eliminated)

FOURTH ROUND
(17/5/10)
Tre Fiori 1 *(Aruta 79)*,Cosmos 0
(Cosmos eliminated)

(21/5/10)
Tre Penne 1 *(Valli 77)*, Faetano 0

SEMI-FINAL
(25/5/10)
Tre Fiori 2 *(Aruta 19, Menin 73)*,
Faetano 1 *(Gianni 90+3)*
(Faetano eliminated)

FINAL
(31/5/10)
Stadio Olimpico, Serravalle
SP TRE FIORI 2 *(Aruta 18, 103)*
SP TRE PENNE 1 *(Palazzi 81)*
(aet)
Referee – Giusti
TRE FIORI – Micheletti, Nardone, Ballanti *(Vendemini 90+1)*, Canarezza *(Menin 73)*, Macerata, Benedettini, Andreini, Vannoni, Aruta, Tarini, Giunta *(Macina 63)*.
TRE PENNE – Valentini, Zavoli *(Pignieri 79)*, Raschi *(Protti 37)*, Francini *(Mikhaylovshiy 57)*, Franchini, Lisi, Cibelli, Chiaruzzi, Valli, Di Giuli, Palazzi.
Sent off: Valli *(111)*

DOMESTIC CUP 2009/10
COPPA TITANO

FIRST PHASE
(Played in Groups)

GROUP A
(12/9/09)
Murata 0,
Tre Fiori 3

Tre Penne 2,
Cailungo 2

(16/9/09)
Murata 1,
Tre Penne 0

Tre Fiori 1,
Cosmos 0

(30/9/09)
Cosmos 3,
Murata 3

Tre Fiori 2,
Cailungo 0

(21/10/09)
Cailungo 0,
Murata 1

Cosmos 1,
Tre Penne 1

(28/10/09)
Cailungo 0,
Cosmos 1

Tre Penne 3,
Tre Fiori 1

(24/1/10)
Cailungo 0, Tre Penne 6
Tre Fiori 2, Murata 0

(30/1/10)
Tre Penne 1,
Murata 2

(31/1/10)
Cosmos 1,
Tre Fiori 3

(17/3/10)
Murata 0,
Cailungo 0

Tre Penne 0,
Cosmos 0

(31/3/10)
Cosmos 3,
Cailungo 0

Tre Fiori 2,
Tre Penne 3

(7/4/10)
Cailungo 0,
Tre Fiori 1

Murata 4,
Cosmos 0

Final Standings
1 Tre Fiori 18 pts;
2 Murata 14 pts;
3 Tre Penne 12 pts *(qualified)*;
4 Cosmos 9 pts;
5 Cailungo 2 pts *(eliminated)*

GROUP B
(13/9/09)
Folgore/Falciano 1,
Faetano 0

Pennarossa 1,
Juvenes-Dogana 1

(16/9/09)
Faetano 2,
Pennarossa 2

Folgore/Falciano 1,
La Fiorita 1

(30/9/09)
Faetano 1,
La Fiorita 1

Juvenes-Dogana 3,
Folgore/Falciano 1

(21/10/09)
Juvenes-Dogana 3,
Faetano 1

La Fiorita 4,
Pennarossa 3

(28/10/09)
La Fiorita 0,
Juvenes-Dogana 1

Pennarossa 2,
Folgore/Falciano 0

(23/1/10)
Faetano 2,
Folgore/Falciano 1

Juvenes-Dogana 1,
Pennarossa 0

(30/1/10)
Pennarossa 2,
Faetano 1

(31/1/10)
La Fiorita 1,
Folgore/Falciano 2

(17/3/10)
Faetano 0,
Juvenes-Dogana 1

Pennarossa 0,
La Fiorita 3

(31/3/10)
Folgore/Falciano 1,
Pennarossa 1

Juvenes-Dogana 2,
La Fiorita 1

(7/4/10)
Folgore/Falciano 1,
Juvenes-Dogana 0

La Fiorita 5,
Faetano 2

Final Standings
1 Juvenes-Dogana 19 pts;
2 Folgore/ Falciano 11 pts *(qualified)*;
3 La Fiorita 11 pts;
4 Pennarossa 9 pts;
5 Faetano 5 pts *(eliminated)*

GROUP C
(12/9/09)
San Giovanni 0,
Libertas 0

(13/9/09)
Fiorentino 0,
Domagnano 2

(16/9/09)
Domagnano 0,
San Giovanni 0

Fiorentino 2,
Virtus 7

(30/9/09)
Domagnano 0,
Virtus 3

Libertas 3,
Fiorentino 0

(21/10/09)
Libertas 3,
Domagnano 1

Virtus 1, San Giovanni 1

(28/10/09)
San Giovanni 0,
Fiorentino 1

Virtus 2, Libertas 1

(23/1/10)
Domagnano 1,
Fiorentino 0

(24/1/10)
Libertas 2, San Giovanni 0

(30/1/10)
San Giovanni 0,
Domagnano 5

(31/1/10)
Virtus 1,
Fiorentino 2

(17/3/10)
Domagnano 1,
Libertas 0

San Giovanni 0,
Virtus 1

(31/3/10)
Fiorentino 2, San Giovanni 2

Libertas 2, Virtus 0

(7/4/10)
Fiorentino 3,
Libertas 3

Virtus 1,
Domagnano 2

Final Standings
1 Libertas 15 pts;
2 Domagnano 14 pts;
3 Virtus 13 pts *(qualified)*;
4 Fiorentino 8 pts;
5 San Giovanni 4 pts *(eliminated)*

QUARTER-FINALS
(21/4/10)
Folgore/Falciano 0, Murata 3 *(Protti 29, 32, Zaboul 49)*
Juvenes-Dogana 1 *(Rosti 90)*, Virtus 2 *(Hirsch 71, 90)*
Libertas 1 *(Mazzoli 68)*, Tre Penne 3 *(Chiaruzzi 21, Palazzi 81, Valli 86)*
Tre Fiori 2 *(Tarini 18, Vannoni 49)*, Domagnano 0

SEMI-FINALS
(24/4/10)
Murata 0, Tre Fiori 3 *(Aruta 47, 68, 77)*
Tre Penne 1 *(Palazzi 48)*, Virtus 0

FINAL
(29/4/10)
Stadio Olimpico, Serravalle
SP TRE FIORI 2 *(Giunta 61, Aruta 95)*
SP TRE PENNE 1 *(Valli 14)*
(aet)
Referee – Rossi
TRE FIORI – Micheletti, Nardone, Ballanti, Andreini, Macerata, Benedettini, Berardi *(Giunta 46)*, Vannoni, Aruta, Tarini *(Macina 90)*, Amici *(Grana 96)*.
TRE PENNE – Valentini, Zavoli, Mikhaylovshiy, Lisi *(Protti 97)*, Franchini, Valentini, Cibelli, Rossi *(Di Giuli 58)*, Valli *(Pignieri 69)*, Chiaruzzi, Palazzi.

Rangers soldier on through tough times

A period of austerity and underachievement for Scottish football continued in 2009/10. The club sides struggled again in European competition, while the national team failed even to come close to qualification for the 2010 FIFA World Cup. On top of that came the resignation of the Scottish Football Association's progressive chief executive, Gordon Smith, leaving the country seeking new leadership and direction going into the new decade.

The most accurate barometer of the strength and health of the Scottish Premier League is the performance of its clubs against those from other European leagues. If the 2008/09 season plumbed new depths for the SPL collective, the 2009/10 season was scarcely an improvement, the outcome being that Scotland will no longer benefit from two UEFA Champions League participants from 2011/12 onwards, with the champions facing the added burden of having to pre-qualify.

It looked as though it might not come to that when Celtic FC, seeking to join Rangers FC in the group stage of the 2009/10 UEFA Champions League, overcame a rare defeat in Glasgow, against FC Dinamo Moskva, by turning the tie around with an even rarer away win, 2-0 in the Russian capital, to qualify for the play-off round. There they predictably succumbed to the might of Arsenal FC in a 'Battle of Britain' that never reached lift-off, dropping into the UEFA Europa League. Still, to remain in continental competition at all, under the tutelage of their new manager Tony Mowbray, was a feat in itself.

Guaranteed gold

Meanwhile, Rangers, whose European campaign had ended almost before it began the previous season, were delighted to have the guarantee of six UEFA Champions League group games – and the pot of gold that came with it during a time of great financial insecurity for the club. They began positively by drawing 1-1 away to VfB Stuttgart, giving their fans hope that another defensive and counterattacking masterclass of the kind that took

them to the 2008 UEFA Cup final might bring further progress from a relatively weak group. Sadly, though, it was not to be. The Gers picked up just one more point thanks to a draw in Romania, which came off the back of a humiliating 4-1 defeat at home to unfancied FC Unirea Urziceni – the same margin of defeat as in their opening home game against Sevilla FC.

For Celtic, it was a similar tale of woe in the UEFA Europa League. The Hoops opened their series of group games with an avoidable, confidence-sapping defeat away to Hapoel Tel-Aviv FC before securing only a draw at home to SK Rapid Wien. Mowbray's men were soon out for the count, and although they staged a memorable

Kris Boyd (left) and Kenny Miller – Rangers' sharpshooting strike duo

comeback from 3-0 down to draw 3-3 in their final tie, against Rapid in the Ernst-Happel-Stadion, it was classic Celtic – finding their best form only when it was too late.

Scotland's three other European entrants – Heart of Midlothian FC, Aberdeen FC and Falkirk FC – had long since put away their continental atlases and roadmaps, having all fallen at the first hurdle in their respective UEFA Europa League qualifiers, while Motherwell FC, who gained access to the same competition via the Fair Play route, ambled past opposition from Wales and Albania before falling heavily at the hands of FC Steaua Bucureşti in the third qualifying round

With European interest extinguished early, all eyes turned to the SPL and the inevitable Old Firm-only battle for the title. Celtic had begun the season with high hopes under Mowbray, who had replaced Gordon Strachan during the summer, and a fine start maintained

2009/10 was not a happy season for Celtic

that optimism. Yet dreadful away form, which started with a 2-1 defeat to Rangers, was to cost Celtic dearly, their first 11 away games yielding four defeats and a draw. Rangers also relied on their home form as they too struggled on their travels in the early part of the season. Still, they compensated by scoring for fun at Ibrox, notably in December when Motherwell and Dundee United FC shipped six and seven goals respectively. Saint Johnstone FC, Falkirk and even the notoriously obstinate Hamilton Academical FC also left Glasgow nursing three-goal defeats during the winter months.

Boyd record

Much of this was down to the Gers' potent strike pairing of Kris Boyd – who overtook Henrik Larsson as the SPL's all-time record scorer when he raised his cumulative tally to 158 goals with five in the 7-1 rout of Dundee United – and Kenny Miller – who enjoyed a much better second season back at Ibrox than his first. As the season progressed Rangers were also able to repair their early defensive frailties, with the impressive Algerian international Madjid Bougherra, when fit and available, offering excellent support to the Peter Pan figure of David Weir, who, astonishingly, would play every minute of the SPL campaign despite turning 40 the day after it concluded – a worthy Player of the Year if ever there was one.

Scottish Football Association (SFA)

THE·SCOTTISH·FOOTBALL
·ASSOCIATION·

Hampden Park
GB-Glasgow G42 9AY
tel – +44 141 616 6000
fax – +44 141 616 6001
website – scottishfa.co.uk
email – info@scottishfa.co.uk
Year of Formation – 1873

President – George Peat
Chief Executive - Stewart Regan
Media Officer – Darryl Broadfoot
National Stadium – Hampden Park, Glasgow (52,054)

INTERNATIONAL TOURNAMENT APPEARANCES
FIFA World Cup – (8) 1954, 1958, 1974, 1978, 1982, 1986, 1990, 1998.
UEFA European Championship – (2) 1992, 1996.
TOP FIVE ALL-TIME CAPS
Kenny Dalglish (102); Jim Leighton (91); Alex McLeish (77); Paul McStay (76); Tommy Boyd (72)
TOP FIVE ALL-TIME GOALS
Kenny Dalglish & Denis Law (30); Hughie Gallacher (24); Lawrie Reilly (22), Ally McCoist (19)

NATIONAL TEAM RESULTS 2009/10

12/8/09	Norway (WCQ)	A	Oslo	0-4	
5/9/09	FYROM (WCQ)	H	Glasgow	2-0	Brown (56), McFadden (80)
9/9/09	Netherlands (WCQ)	H	Glasgow	0-1	
10/10/09	Japan	A	Yokohama	0-2	
14/11/09	Wales	A	Cardiff	0-3	
3/3/10	Czech Republic	H	Glasgow	1-0	Brown (62)

NATIONAL TEAM APPEARANCES 2009/10

Coach – George BURLEY 3/6/56
/(23/11/09) Craig LEVEIN 22/10/64

Player	DOB	Club	NOR	MKD	NED	Jpn	Wal	Cze	Caps	Goals
David MARSHALL	5/3/85	Cardiff (WAL)	G		G		G		5	-
Alan HUTTON	30/11/84	Tottenham (ENG) /Sunderland (ENG)	D	D	D		D	D	15	-
Callum DAVIDSON	25/6/76	Preston (ENG)	D48	D14					19	-
Steven CALDWELL	12/9/80	Burnley (ENG)	D						10	-
Gary CALDWELL	12/4/82	Celtic /Wigan (ENG)	D34*		D	D		D	37	2
Graham ALEXANDER	10/10/71	Burnley (ENG)	M	M					40	-
Darren FLETCHER	1/2/84	Man. United (ENG)	M	M	M		M	M83	47	4
Scott BROWN	25/6/85	Celtic	M	M73	M			M	20	2
Kris COMMONS	30/8/83	Derby (ENG)	M	s67					6	-
Kenny MILLER	23/12/79	Rangers	A	A	A		A55	A63	47	11
Ross McCORMACK	18/8/86	Cardiff (WAL)	A37				s62		5	1
Christophe BERRA	31/1/85	Wolves (ENG)	s37/78		D			s46	7	-
James McFADDEN	14/4/83	Birmingham (ENG)	s48	M			A62		45	15
Steven WHITTAKER	16/6/84	Rangers	s78	s14	D	D		s83	5	-
Craig GORDON	31/12/82	Sunderland (ENG)		G		G		G	39	-
Stephen McMANUS	10/9/82	Celtic			D	D	D	D	22	1
David WEIR	10/5/70	Rangers			D	D			65	1
Steven FLETCHER	26/3/87	Burnley (ENG)			A68		s46	s55	7	1
Shaun MALONEY	24/1/83	Celtic			s68	M83			17	1
Paul HARTLEY	19/10/76	Bristol City (ENG)			s73	M67		s46	25	1
Steven NAISMITH	14/9/86	Rangers				A		A62	3	-
Gary O'CONNOR	7/5/83	Birmingham (ENG)				s83			16	4
Lee WALLACE	1/8/87	Hearts				D	s55	D	3	-
Charlie ADAM	10/12/85	Blackpool (ENG)				M67		s69	4	-
Craig CONWAY	2/5/85	Dundee United				M74			1	-
Graham DORRANS	5/5/87	West Brom (ENG)				M	M71	M	3	-
Ross WALLACE	23/5/85	Preston (ENG)					M46		1	-
Lee MILLER	18/5/83	Aberdeen					A46		3	-
Don COWIE	15/2/83	Watford (ENG)					s46	M78	2	-
Stephen HUGHES	14/11/82	Norwich (ENG)					s67		1	-
Derek RIORDAN	16/1/83	Hibernian					s74	s78	3	-
Danny FOX	29/5/86	Celtic						D55	1	-
Kevin KYLE	7/6/81	Kilmarnock						s62	10	1
Barry ROBSON	7/11/78	Celtic /Middlesbrough (ENG)					s71	M69	8	-
Andy WEBSTER	23/4/82	Dundee United						D46	23	1
Kevin THOMSON	14/10/84	Rangers						M46	2	-
Kris BOYD	18/8/83	Rangers						s63	16	7

As winter turned to spring, Celtic tumbled into disarray. The Hoops had conspicuously failed to find their rhythm under Mowbray and sat well off the pace by the end of December. In came striker Robbie Keane on loan from Tottenham Hotspur FC, and although the Republic of Ireland's record goalscorer would hit 12 goals, it was not nearly enough to propel Celtic to the title. Another defeat at Ibrox, decided by American midfielder Maurice Edu's stoppage-time strike, at the end of February enabled Rangers to go ten points clear with a game in hand. That was the beginning of the end for Mowbray, who was unceremoniously sacked a few weeks later when Celtic were thrashed 4-0 at Saint Mirren FC – their heaviest league defeat to a team other than Rangers for 30 years. Former player Neil Lennon inherited the job, initially as caretaker, before taking command permanently at the end of the season thanks to a closing run of eight straight league victories, including one against Rangers. On the negative side was another humiliating defeat as Celtic inexplicably lost 2-0 to the unheralded Highlanders of Ross County FC in the semi-final of the Scottish Cup, thus ending the season trophyless for the first time in seven years.

Title number 53

In the end Rangers ran away with the title, taking their foot off the pedal only with victory assured. The club's 53rd Scottish championship triumph was wrapped up with three games to spare thanks to a 1-0 win at Hibernian FC on 25 April. They had lost only two games at that point, and although defeat in the final Old Firm encounter of the campaign would make it three, seldom did a loss to Celtic matter so little. Indeed, Rangers beat Celtic on the season's trophy count 2-0 having already lifted the League Cup in March. To many Rangers fans the 1-0 win over Saint Mirren in the Hampden final was the emotional highpoint of the season, coming as it did with an 84th-minute strike from Miller when Rangers were down to nine men.

Dundee United, in their Centenary year, won the other Hampden final, conquering giantkillers Ross County 3-0 with second-half goals from David Goodwillie – an audacious chip – and man of the match Craig Conway (two). The Tangerines had punctured Rangers' treble dreams with a last-minute winner in their replayed quarter-final. The original game, 3-3 at Ibrox, would have been a contender for match of the season had it not been for the astonishing 6-6 draw between Motherwell and Hibernian, both seeking European qualification, in the penultimate round of the league campaign. The home side, led by ex-Scotland manager Craig Brown,

came back from 6-2 down to equalise with a stunning last-gasp volley from Lukas Jutkiewicz.

In the event, thanks to Dundee United's Scottish Cup win, both Motherwell and Hibernian would qualify – with United – for the UEFA Europa League. Hibs, buoyed by the 21 goals of Irishman Anthony Stokes – second only to Boyd in the SPL score charts – finished six points ahead of city rivals Hearts, whose disappointing campaign was eclipsed by that of Aberdeen, who, led by former star centre-forward Mark McGhee, did not even reach the top six after the 'split' and finished ninth. A three-way relegation battle resulted in the demise of Falkirk, with Kilmarnock FC and Saint Mirren surviving at the Bairns' expense. Inverness Caledonian Thistle FC replaced them, coming back up at the first time of asking under ex-England and Rangers defender Terry Butcher at the expense of big-spending Dundee FC.

New Scotland head coach Craig Levein

Levein takes over

For the Tartan Army, the 2010 World Cup was another stay-at-home occasion. A 2-0 win over the Former Yugoslav Republic of Macedonia (FYROM) was the sole highlight of a poor qualifying campaign, but it hardly registered as such following a calamitous 4-0 defeat in Norway that destroyed hopes of a play-off place. George Burley's team eventually finished third in a very weak section, and after further friendly defeats against Japan (0-2) and Wales (0-3), the manager was shown the door. The job was passed on to Dundee United's Craig Levein, who made a positive start with a 1-0 home win over the Czech Republic – one of Scotland's opponents in a five-team UEFA EURO 2012 qualifying group headed by the mighty Spain. Clearly, a place in the play-offs will be the extent of Levein's ambitions as Scotland attempt to end their longest spell in the international wilderness for 40 years.

DOMESTIC LEAGUE 2009/10

SCOTTISH PREMIER LEAGUE FINAL TABLE

		Home					Away					Total					
	Pld	W	D	L	F	A	W	D	L	F	A	W	D	L	F	A	Pts
1 Rangers FC	38	15	4	0	52	13	11	5	3	30	15	26	9	3	82	28	87
2 Celtic FC	38	14	4	1	42	14	11	2	6	33	25	25	6	7	75	39	81
3 Dundee United FC	38	8	4	7	22	21	9	8	2	33	26	17	12	9	55	47	63
4 Hibernian FC	38	9	4	6	29	21	6	5	8	29	34	15	9	14	58	55	54
5 Motherwell FC	38	8	5	5	29	25	5	9	6	23	29	13	14	11	52	54	53
6 Heart of Midlothian FC	38	9	4	6	19	20	4	5	10	16	26	13	9	16	35	46	48
7 Hamilton Academical FC	38	6	7	6	19	17	7	3	9	20	29	13	10	15	39	46	49
8 Saint Johnstone FC	38	6	6	7	31	28	6	5	8	26	33	12	11	15	57	61	47
9 Aberdeen FC	38	6	4	10	20	31	4	7	7	16	21	10	11	17	36	52	41
10 Saint Mirren FC	38	5	9	5	18	18	2	4	13	18	31	7	13	18	36	49	34
11 Kilmarnock FC	38	5	6	8	23	27	3	3	13	6	24	8	9	21	29	51	33
12 Falkirk FC	38	3	6	10	17	29	3	7	9	14	28	6	13	19	31	57	31

NB League split into top and bottom halves after 33 games, with each club playing five further matches exclusively against clubs from its half of the table.

TOP GOALSCORERS

23 Kris BOYD (Rangers)

21 Anthony STOKES (Hibernian)

18 Kenny MILLER (Rangers)

13 Jon DALY (Dundee United)
Derek RIORDAN (Hibernian)

12 Robbie KEANE (Celtic)
Lukas JUTKIEWICZ (Motherwell)
John SUTTON (Motherwell)

10 Marc-Antoine FORTUNÉ (Celtic)
Scott McDONALD (Celtic)
Georgios SAMARAS (Celtic)

CLUB-BY-CLUB

ABERDEEN FC
Manager – Mark McGhee
Founded – 1903
Stadium – Pittodrie (21,421)
MAJOR HONOURS:
UEFA Cup Winners' Cup - (1) 1983;
UEFA Super Cup - (1) 1983;
Scottish League - (4) 1955, 1980, 1984, 1985;
Scottish Cup - (7) 1947, 1970, 1982, 1983, 1984, 1986, 1990;
Scottish League Cup - (5) 1956, 1977, 1986, 1990, 1996.

2009
15/8	Celtic	h	1-3	Aluko
22/8	Hamilton	a	3-0	Mulgrew, Considine, Maguire
29/8	Motherwell	h	0-0	
14/9	Falkirk	a	0-0	
19/9	St Mirren	h	1-0	Mulgrew
26/9	Rangers	a	0-0	
3/10	Kilmarnock	a	1-1	McDonald
17/10	Hearts	h	1-1	Miller
24/10	Dundee United	h	0-2	
31/10	Hibernian	a	0-2	
7/11	St Johnstone	h	2-1	Aluko, Miller (p)
21/11	Motherwell	a	1-1	McDonald
28/11	Rangers	h	1-0	Miller
5/12	Celtic	a	0-3	
12/12	Hamilton	h	1-2	McDonald
19/12	Hibernian	h	0-2	

2010
2/1	Dundee United	a	1-0	Mulgrew
12/1	St Mirren	a	0-1	
23/1	Kilmarnock	a	1-0	Young
27/1	Hearts	a	3-0	Fyvie, Mackie, Young
30/1	Motherwell	h	0-3	
2/2	Falkirk	h	0-1	

10/2	Hibernian	a	2-2	Paton, MacLean
13/2	Celtic	h	4-4	Paton, Mackie, MacLean 2 (1p)
20/2	Falkirk	a	1-3	Mulgrew
27/2	Hearts	h	0-1	
6/3	Hamilton	a	1-1	Diamond
16/3	St Johnstone	a	0-1	
20/3	Dundee United	h	2-2	Diamond, Paton (p)
27/3	St Mirren	h	2-1	Diamond, Aluko
4/4	Kilmarnock	a	0-2	
7/4	Rangers	a	1-3	Mackie
11/4	St Johnstone	h	1-3	Mackie
17/4	Falkirk	h	1-0	MacLean
24/4	St Johnstone	a	1-1	MacLean
1/5	Hamilton	h	1-3	Young
5/5	Kilmarnock	h	1-2	Kerr
8/5	St Mirren	a	1-0	og (Mair)

No	Name	Nat	DoB	Pos	Aps	(s)	Gls
11	Sone ALUKO	NGA	19/2/89	A	15	(7)	3
6	Andrew CONSIDINE		4/1/87	D	15	(1)	1
25	Jonathan CRAWFORD		12/3/90	D	2		
5	Alexander DIAMOND		3/12/85	D	15	(1)	3
16	Stuart DUFF		23/1/82	M	11	(6)	
3	Richard FOSTER		13/7/85	D	37		
34	Fraser FYVIE		27/3/93	M	17	(9)	1
45	Dominic GIBSON		9/6/92	A	1		
18	Davide GRASSI	ITA	13/1/86	D	16	(7)	
52	Jack GRIMMER		1/2/94	M		(2)	
22	Jerel IFIL	ENG	27/6/82	D	25	(2)	
8	Mark KERR		2/3/82	M	37		1
1	Jamie LANGFIELD		22/12/79	G	35		
35	Nicky LOW		6/1/92	D		(1)	
9	Steve MacLEAN		23/8/82	A	15	(1)	5
10	Darren MACKIE		5/1/82	A	21	(11)	4

SCOTLAND

7	Chris MAGUIRE		16/1/89	A	5	(12)	1
20	Paul MARSHALL	ENG	9/7/89	M	6	(3)	
4	Gary McDONALD		10/4/82	M	24		3
31	Mitchel MEGGINSON		27/7/92	A		(2)	
9	Lee MILLER		18/5/83	A	18		3
2	Charlie MULGREW		6/3/86	D	37		4
21	Stuart NELSON	ENG	17/9/81	G	3		
7	Jim PATERSON		25/9/79	M	7		
24	Michael PATON		25/3/89	A	22	(13)	3
19	Peter PAWLETT	ENG	3/2/91	A	11	(3)	
42	Clark ROBERTSON		5/9/93	D	1	(2)	
17	Maurice ROSS		3/2/81	M	6		
15	Tommy WRIGHT	ENG	28/9/84	A		(3)	
14	Derek YOUNG		27/5/80	A	16	(4)	3

CELTIC FC

Manager – Tony Mowbray (ENG); (25/3/10) (Neil Lennon (NIR))
Founded – 1888
Stadium – Celtic Park (60,355)
MAJOR HONOURS:
European Champion Clubs' Cup – (1) 1967;
Scottish League – (42) 1893, 1894, 1896, 1898, 1905, 1906, 1907, 1908, 1909, 1910, 1914, 1915, 1916, 1917, 1919, 1922, 1926, 1936, 1938, 1954, 1966, 1967, 1968, 1969, 1970, 1971, 1972, 1973, 1974, 1977, 1979, 1981, 1982, 1986, 1988, 1998, 2001, 2002, 2004, 2006, 2007, 2008;
Scottish Cup – (34) 1892, 1899, 1900, 1904, 1907, 1908, 1911, 1912, 1914, 1923, 1925, 1927, 1931, 1933, 1937, 1951, 1954, 1965, 1967, 1969, 1971, 1972, 1974, 1975, 1977, 1980, 1985, 1988, 1989, 1995, 2001, 2004, 2005, 2007;
Scottish League Cup – (14) 1957, 1958, 1966, 1967, 1968, 1969, 1970, 1975, 1983, 1998, 2000, 2001, 2006, 2009.

2009

15/8	Aberdeen	a	3-1	McGeady 2, McDonald
22/8	St Johnstone	h	5-2	Fortuné 2, Maloney 2, McDonald
30/8	Hibernian	a	1-0	Samaras
12/9	Dundee United	h	1-1	McDonald
20/9	Hearts	h	2-1	Killen, Loovens
26/9	St Mirren	a	2-0	McCourt, Maloney
4/10	Rangers	a	1-2	McGeady (p)
17/10	Motherwell	h	0-0	
25/10	Hamilton	a	2-1	Maloney, McDonald
31/10	Kilmarnock	h	3-0	McGeady, Samaras, McGinn
8/11	Falkirk	a	3-3	Caldwell, McDonald 2
22/11	Dundee United	a	1-2	Robson (p)
28/11	St Mirren	h	3-1	McDonald 2, Samaras
5/12	Aberdeen	h	3-0	McDonald, Samaras 2
12/12	Motherwell	a	3-2	Samaras, McGeady, Fortuné
20/12	Hearts	a	1-2	Samaras
26/12	Hamilton	h	2-0	Loovens, McGinn

2010

3/1	Rangers	h	1-1	McDonald
16/1	Falkirk	h	1-1	Samaras
24/1	St Johnstone	a	4-1	Fortuné 2, Samaras, McCourt
27/1	Hibernian	h	1-2	Fortuné
30/1	Hamilton	a	1-0	Rasmussen
2/2	Kilmarnock	a	0-1	
10/2	Hearts	h	2-0	Loovens, Fortuné
13/2	Aberdeen	a	4-4	Kamara, Fortuné, Keane, McGeady
20/2	Dundee United	h	1-0	Keane
28/2	Rangers	a	0-1	
7/3	Falkirk	a	2-0	Keane 2
20/3	St Johnstone	h	3-0	Thompson, Keane (p), Samaras
24/3	St Mirren	a	0-4	
27/3	Kilmarnock	h	3-1	Keane 2, Brown
4/4	Hibernian	a	1-0	Keane (p)
13/4	Motherwell	h	2-1	Thompson 2
17/4	Hibernian	h	3-2	Keane, Fortuné, Rasmussen

25/4	Dundee United	a	2-0	Kamara, Keane (p)
1/5	Motherwell	h	4-0	McGeady, O'Dea, Forrest, Keane
4/5	Rangers	h	2-1	Naylor, Fortuné
9/5	Hearts	a	2-1	Keane, Zheng

No	Name	Nat	DoB	Pos	Aps	(s)	Gls
1	Artur BORUC	POL	20/2/80	G	28		
21	Edson BRAAFHEID	NED	8/4/83	D	9	(1)	
8	Scott BROWN		25/6/85	M	19	(2)	1
52	Paul CADDIS		19/4/88	D	3	(7)	
5	Gary CALDWELL		12/4/82	D	14		1
17	Marc CROSAS Luque	ESP	9/1/88	M	14	(3)	
18	Massimo DONATI	ITA	26/3/81	M	2		
16	Willo FLOOD	IRL	10/4/85	M		(1)	
49	James FORREST		7/7/91	M		(2)	1
10	Marc-Antoine FORTUNÉ	FRA	2/7/81	A	22	(8)	10
11	Danny FOX		29/5/86	D	15		
2	Andreas HINKEL	GER	26/3/82	D	30	(1)	
16	Jos HOOIVELD	NED	22/4/83	D	2		
15	Diomansy KAMARA	SEN	8/11/80	A	8	(1)	2
7	Robbie KEANE	IRL	8/7/80	A	15	(1)	12
18	KI Sung-yong	KOR	24/1/89	M	5	(5)	
33	Chris KILLEN	NZL	8/10/81	A	2	(3)	1
22	Glenn LOOVENS	NED	22/9/83	D	20		3
13	Shaun MALONEY		24/1/83	M	8	(1)	4
20	Patrick McCOURT	IRL	16/12/83	M	3	(6)	2
7	Scott McDONALD	AUS	21/8/83	A	16	(2)	10
46	Aiden McGEADY	IRL	4/4/86	M	35		7
14	Niall McGINN		20/7/87	M	6	(11)	2
55	Paul McGOWAN		7/10/87	A	2	(3)	
4	Stephen McMANUS		10/9/82	D	6	(2)	
29	Koki MIZUNO	JPN	6/9/85	M		(1)	
6	Landry N'GUÉMO	CMR	28/11/85	M	30		
3	Lee NAYLOR	ENG	19/3/80	D	11	(1)	1
48	Darren O'DEA	IRL	4/2/87	D	16	(3)	1
19	Morten "Duncan" RASMUSSEN	DEN	31/1/85	A	2	(8)	2
19	Barry ROBSON		7/11/78	M	9	(1)	1
25	Thomas ROGNE	NOR	29/6/90	D	3	(1)	
9	Georgios SAMARAS	GRE	21/2/85	A	20	(12)	10
38	Josh THOMPSON	ENG	25/2/91	D	16	(2)	3
12	Mark WILSON		5/6/84	D	8	(2)	
24	Łukasz ZAŁUSKA	POL	16/6/82	G	10	(1)	
27	ZHENG Zhi	CHN	20/8/80	M	9	(7)	1

DUNDEE UNITED FC

Manager – Craig Levein; (23/12/09) (Peter Houston)
Founded – 1909
Stadium – Tannadice Park (14,223)
MAJOR HONOURS:
Scottish League - (1) 1983;
Scottish Cup - (2) 1994, 2010;
Scottish League Cup - (2) 1980, 1981.

2009

17/8	Hearts	h	2-0	Cadamarteri 2 (1p)
22/8	St Mirren	a	0-0	
29/8	Falkirk	h	2-1	Cadamarteri, Goodwillie
12/9	Celtic	a	1-1	Goodwillie
19/9	Motherwell	h	0-1	
26/9	St Johnstone	a	3-2	Cadamarteri (p), Webster, Casalinuovo
3/10	Hibernian	a	1-1	Webster
17/10	Hamilton	h	1-1	Kenneth
24/10	Aberdeen	a	2-0	Casalinuovo, Gomis
7/11	Kilmarnock	a	2-0	Casalinuovo 2 (1p)
22/11	Celtic	h	2-1	Daly, Dods
28/11	Motherwell	a	2-2	Webster, Daly
5/12	St Mirren	h	3-2	Casalinuovo, Conway, Myrie-Williams

12/12	Hearts	a	0-0		
15/12	Rangers	h	0-3		
26/12	Kilmarnock	h	0-0		
30/12	Rangers	a	1-7	Casalinuovo	
2010					
2/1	Aberdeen	h	0-1		
13/1	Hamilton	a	1-0	Goodwillie	
16/1	Hibernian	h	1-0	Swanson	
24/1	Falkirk	a	4-1	Goodwillie, Daly 3	
27/1	St Johnstone	h	3-3	Daly, Swanson, Myrie-Williams	
30/1	Kilmarnock	a	4-4	Buaben, Conway 2, Daly (p)	
10/2	Hamilton	h	0-2		
13/2	St Mirren	a	2-1	Swanson, Goodwillie	
20/2	Celtic	a	0-1		
27/2	Falkirk	h	3-0	Goodwillie (p), Gomis 2	
7/3	Hearts	h	1-0	Gomis	
20/3	Aberdeen	a	2-2	Daly 2	
27/3	Motherwell	h	3-0	Goodwillie, Buaben, Swanson	
31/3	Hibernian	a	4-2	Daly, Swanson, Goodwillie, Sandaza	
5/4	St Johnstone	a	1-0	Daly	
14/4	Rangers	h	0-0		
18/4	Motherwell	a	3-2	Daly 2, Conway	
25/4	Celtic	h	0-2		
1/5	Rangers	h	1-2	Casalinuovo	
5/5	Hearts	a	0-0		
9/5	Hibernian	h	0-2		

No	Name	Nat	DoB	Pos	Aps	(s)	Gls
13	Steve BANKS	ENG	9/2/72	G	1		
15	Prince BUABEN	GHA	23/4/88	M	33	(1)	2
10	Danny CADAMARTERI	ENG	12/10/79	A	15	(6)	4
24	Greg CAMERON		10/4/88	M		(1)	
21	Damián CASALINUOVO	ARG	6/6/87	A	16	(9)	7
6	Craig CONWAY		2/5/85	M	29	(4)	4
9	Jon DALY	IRL	8/1/83	A	16	(7)	13
2	Sean DILLON	IRL	30/7/83	D	25	(8)	
23	Paul DIXON		22/11/86	D	25		
5	Darren DODS		7/6/75	D	23	(4)	1
35	Ryan DOW		7/6/91	A		(2)	
17	Mark FOTHERINGHAM		22/10/83	M	2	(1)	
16	Morgaro "Jimmy" GOMIS	SEN	14/7/85	M	31		4
25	David GOODWILLIE		28/3/89	A	23	(10)	8
50	Craig HILL	NIR	1/7/91	D	1		
38	Dale HILSON		23/12/92	A		(2)	
18	Gary KENNETH		21/6/87	D	26	(2)	1
19	Mihael KOVAČEVIĆ	SUI	3/3/88	D	24	(2)	
17	Pāvels MIHADJUKS	LVA	27/5/80	D	3		
7	Jennison MYRIE-WILLIAMS	ENG	17/5/88	A	11	(13)	2
1	Dušan PERNIŠ	SVK	28/11/84	G	19		
12	David ROBERTSON		23/8/86	M	8	(6)	
8	Scott ROBERTSON		7/4/85	M	8	(5)	
11	Francisco José SANDAZA Asensio	ESP	30/11/84	A	1	(6)	1
20	Andis SHALA	GER	15/11/88	A	2	(10)	
34	Ross SMITH		4/11/80	D	2	(2)	
14	Daniel SWANSON		28/12/86	M	22	(9)	5
27	Keith WATSON		14/11/89	D	7	(1)	
1	Nicky WEAVER	ENG	2/3/79	G	18		
3	Andy WEBSTER		23/4/82	D	26		3
4	Lee WILKIE		20/4/80	D	1		

FALKIRK FC

Manager – Eddie May; (11/2/10) Steven Pressley
Founded – 1876
Stadium – Falkirk Stadium (7,190)
MAJOR HONOURS:
Scottish Cup - (2) 1913, 1957.

2009					
15/8	Rangers	a	1-4	Finnigan	
22/8	Hibernian	h	1-3	Flynn	
29/8	Dundee United	a	1-2	Finnbogason	
14/9	Aberdeen	h	0-0		
19/9	Hamilton	a	0-0		
26/9	Kilmarnock	h	0-0		
3/10	Motherwell	a	0-1		
17/10	St Mirren	h	1-3	McLean	
24/10	Hearts	a	0-0		
31/10	St Johnstone	a	1-3	Finnigan	
8/11	Celtic	h	3-3	Arfield (p), Pedro Moutinho, Stewart	
21/11	Hamilton	h	2-0	Mitchell, Bullen	
28/11	Hibernian	a	0-2		
5/12	Rangers	h	1-3	Pedro Moutinho	
12/12	St Mirren	a	1-1	Finnigan	
19/12	Kilmarnock	a	2-1	Finnigan, Flynn	
26/12	Hearts	h	0-1		
2010					
16/1	Celtic	a	1-1	Finnigan	
24/1	Dundee United	h	1-4	Pedro Moutinho	
27/1	Motherwell	h	0-0		
30/1	Rangers	a	0-3		
2/2	Aberdeen	a	1-0	Healy	
10/2	Kilmarnock	h	0-1		
13/2	Hearts	a	2-3	og (Kucharski), Pedro Moutinho	
20/2	Aberdeen	h	3-1	Pedro Moutinho, Barr, Showunmi	
27/2	Dundee United	a	0-3		
7/3	Celtic	h	0-2		
13/3	St Johnstone	h	1-2	Twaddle	
20/3	Hamilton	a	2-2	Arfield, Flynn	
23/3	St Johnstone	a	1-1	Flynn	
27/3	Hibernian	h	1-3	Stewart	
3/4	Motherwell	a	1-0	Flynn	
10/4	St Mirren	h	2-1	Pedro Moutinho, og (Higdon)	
17/4	Aberdeen	a	0-1		
24/4	Hamilton	h	0-1		
1/5	St Mirren	h	1-1	Arfield (p)	
5/5	St Johnstone	h	0-0		
8/5	Kilmarnock	a	0-0		

No	Name	Nat	DoB	Pos	Aps	(s)	Gls
18	Brian ALLISON		23/6/88	D	4		
10	Scott ARFIELD		1/11/88	M	35	(1)	3
2	Darren BARR		17/3/85	D	38		1
25	Lee BULLEN		29/3/71	D		(9)	1
28	Jack COMPTON	ENG	2/9/88	M	3	(10)	
30	Kieran DUFFY		4/3/91	D	5	(1)	
24	Kjartan Henry FINNBOGASON	ISL	9/7/86	A	7		1
9	Carl FINNIGAN	ENG	1/10/86	A	20	(7)	5
11	Ryan FLYNN		4/9/88	M	36		5
24	Colin HEALY	IRL	14/3/80	M	17	(2)	1
19	Sean LYNCH		31/1/87	M	3	(5)	
21	Alex MACDONALD		14/4/90	A	4	(7)	
22	Danijel MARČETA	SVN	4/1/89	A	8	(7)	
6	Brian McLEAN	NIR	28/2/85	D	36		1
5	Jackie McNAMARA		24/10/73	D	13		
14	Chris MITCHELL		21/7/88	D	5	(3)	1
35	Stewart MURDOCH		17/12/90	M		(3)	
8	Burton O'BRIEN		10/6/81	M	23	(4)	
1	Robert OLEJNIK	AUT	26/11/86	G	38		
7	PEDRO da Silva MOUTINHO	POR	9/9/79	A	20	(5)	6
26	Pedro Miguel Cardoso Monteiro "PELÉ"	CPV	2/5/78	D	7	(2)	
16	Dayne ROBERTSON		21/6/88	A		(1)	
3	Thomas SCOBBIE		31/3/88	D	19	(1)	
15	Enoch SHOWUNMI	NGA	21/4/82	A	15	(6)	1

SCOTLAND

12	Mark STEWART		22/6/88	A	7	(12)	2
4	Marc TWADDLE		27/8/86	D	30	(3)	1
23	VÍTOR Manuel LIMA Santos	POR	10/8/81	M	22	(4)	
27	Toufik ZERARA	FRA	3/2/86	M	3		

HAMILTON ACADEMICAL FC
Coach – Billy Reid
Founded – 1874
Stadium – New Douglas Park (6,078)

2009

15/8	Kilmarnock	a	0-3	
22/8	Aberdeen	h	0-3	
29/8	Rangers	a	1-4	McLaughlin
13/9	Hibernian	h	2-0	Mensing (p), Antoine-Curier
19/9	Falkirk	h	0-0	
26/9	Hearts	a	1-2	Flávio Paixão
3/10	St Johnstone	h	0-2	
17/10	Dundee United	a	1-1	Antoine-Curier
25/10	Celtic	h	1-2	Antoine-Curier
31/10	St Mirren	a	2-0	Marco Paixão, Canning
7/11	Motherwell	h	2-2	Mensing, Marco Paixão
21/11	Falkirk	a	0-2	
28/11	St Johnstone	a	1-1	Antoine-Curier
6/12	Hearts	h	2-1	McArthur, Mensing
12/12	Aberdeen	a	2-1	Antoine-Curier, Wesolowski
26/12	Celtic	a	0-2	

2010

13/1	Dundee United	h	0-1	
16/1	Rangers	h	0-1	
23/1	Hibernian	a	1-5	Flávio Paixão
26/1	Kilmarnock	h	0-0	
30/1	Celtic	h	0-1	
6/2	Motherwell	a	0-1	
10/2	Dundee United	a	2-0	Flávio Paixão, Marco Paixão
13/2	Motherwell	h	0-0	
21/2	Hearts	a	0-2	
27/2	St Mirren	a	0-0	
6/3	Aberdeen	h	1-1	Flávio Paixão
13/3	St Mirren	h	1-0	Flávio Paixão
20/3	Falkirk	h	2-2	Antoine-Curier, Mensing (p)
24/3	Kilmarnock	a	2-1	Antoine-Curier, Mensing
27/3	St Johnstone	h	1-0	Wesolowski
3/4	Rangers	a	0-1	
10/4	Hibernian	h	4-1	Mensing 2 (2p), Thomas 2
17/4	Kilmarnock	h	3-0	Imrie, Flávio Paixão, Thomas
24/4	Falkirk	a	1-0	Marco Paixão
1/5	Aberdeen	a	3-1	Flávio Paixão, Wesolowski, Mensing (p)
5/5	St Mirren	h	0-0	
8/5	St Johnstone	a	3-2	McLaughlin, Imrie, Wesolowski

No	Name	Nat	DoB	Pos	Aps	(s)	Gls
15	Marvin ANDREWS	TRI	22/12/75	D	2		
9	Mickaël ANTOINE-CURIER	FRA	3/5/83	A	25	(1)	7
35	Guillaume BEUZELIN	FRA	14/4/79	M	3	(4)	
4	Martin CANNING		3/12/81	D	37		1
1	Tomáš ČERNÝ	CZE	10/4/85	G	34		
36	Ali CRAWFORD		30/7/91	A		(7)	
15	Brian EASTON		5/3/88	D	12		
25	David ELEBERT	IRL	21/3/86	D	15	(10)	
14	Stuart ELLIOTT	NIR	23/7/78	M	2	(3)	
12	Grant EVANS		3/1/90	D	5	(4)	
18	FLÁVIO Emanuel Lopes PAIXÃO	POR	19/9/84	A	19	(7)	7
20	Grant GILLESPIE		2/7/81	D		(1)	
3	Richard HASTINGS	CAN	18/5/77	D	17		
23	Dougie IMRIE		3/8/83	A	16		2
5	Ezomo IRIEKPEN	ENG	14/5/82	D	2		

28	Jordan KIRKPATRICK		6/3/92	M	1	(4)	
24	John Paul KISSOCK	ENG	2/12/89	M	2		
26	Leon KNIGHT	ENG	16/9/82	A		(6)	
14	David LOUHOUNGOU	CGO	28/2/89	M		(6)	
3	LUIS Manuel RUBIALES Béjar	ESP	23/8/77	D	3		
11	Derek LYLE		13/2/81	A	4	(1)	
21	MARCO Filipe Lopes PAIXÃO	POR	19/9/84	A	22	(10)	4
34	Gary MASON		15/10/79	M	5		
8	James McARTHUR		7/10/87	M	35		1
2	Trent McCLENAHAN	AUS	4/2/85	D	23	(4)	
6	Mark McLAUGHLIN		2/12/75	D	32		2
38	Brian McQUEEN		1/1/91	D		(1)	
27	Simon MENSING	ENG	27/6/82	D	37		8
17	Stuart MILLS		7/4/90	A		(2)	
19	Sean MURDOCH		31/7/86	G	4	(2)	
10	Alex NEIL		4/6/81	M	22		
9	Richard OFFIONG	ENG	17/12/83	A	1		
37	John SULLIVAN	IRL	6/1/91	M	1	(1)	
29	Stuart TAYLOR		26/11/74	M		(1)	
26	Joël THOMAS	FRA	30/6/87	A	2	(9)	3
5	David VAN ZANTEN	IRL	8/5/82	D	4	(2)	
23	Kevin WELSH		2/9/84	D	1		
7	James WESOLOWSKI	AUS	25/8/87	M	27	(2)	4
33	Kyle WILKIE		20/2/91	M	3	(9)	

HEART OF MIDLOTHIAN FC
Manager – Csaba László (HUN); (29/1/10) Jim Jefferies
Founded – 1874
Stadium – Tynecastle Stadium (17,590)
MAJOR HONOURS:
Scottish League - (4) 1895, 1897, 1958, 1960;
Scottish Cup - (7) 1891, 1896, 1901, 1906, 1956, 1998, 2006;
Scottish League Cup - (4) 1955, 1959, 1960, 1963.

2009

17/8	Dundee United	a	0-2	
23/8	Rangers	h	1-2	Witteveen
30/8	St Johnstone	a	2-2	Gonçalves, Obua
15/9	Kilmarnock	h	1-0	Driver
20/9	Celtic	a	1-2	Suso Santana
26/9	Hamilton	h	2-1	Stewart M. (p), Suso Santana
3/10	St Mirren	h	1-2	Gonçalves
17/10	Aberdeen	a	1-1	Driver
24/10	Falkirk	h	0-0	
31/10	Motherwell	a	0-1	
7/11	Hibernian	h	0-0	
21/11	St Johnstone	h	1-2	Nadé
28/11	Kilmarnock	a	2-1	Jónsson, Nadé
6/12	Hamilton	a	1-2	Jónsson
12/12	Dundee United	h	0-0	
20/12	Celtic	h	2-1	Stewart M. (p), Bouzid
26/12	Falkirk	a	1-0	Stewart M. (p)
30/12	Motherwell	h	1-0	Stewart M. (p)

2010

3/1	Hibernian	a	1-1	Smith
16/1	St Mirren	h	1-0	Stewart M. (p)
23/1	Rangers	a	1-1	Robinson
27/1	Aberdeen	h	0-3	
30/1	St Johnstone	a	0-1	
10/2	Celtic	a	0-2	
13/2	Falkirk	h	3-2	Wallace, Suso Santana, Black
21/2	Hamilton	h	2-0	Obua, Templeton
27/2	Aberdeen	a	1-0	Jónsson
7/3	Dundee United	a	0-1	
13/3	Motherwell	a	1-3	Templeton
20/3	Hibernian	h	2-1	Driver, Glen
27/3	Rangers	h	1-4	Suso Santana
3/4	St Mirren	a	1-1	Žaliūkas
10/4	Kilmarnock	h	1-0	Suso Santana

18/4	Rangers	a	0-2		
24/4	Motherwell	h	0-2		
1/5	Hibernian	a	2-1	Suso Santana, Obua	
5/5	Dundee United	h	0-0		
9/5	Celtic	h	1-2	Žaliūkas	

No	Name	Nat	DoB	Pos	Aps	(s)	Gls
1	János BALOGH	HUN	29/11/82	G	16		
8	Ian BLACK		14/3/85	M	17	(9)	1
21	Ismaël BOUZID	ALG	21/7/83	D	26		1
12	Marius ČINIKAS	LTU	17/5/86	M	1	(1)	
11	Andrew DRIVER	ENG	12/11/87	M	11	(1)	3
22	Calum ELLIOT		30/3/87	A	6	(7)	
36	Gary GLEN		12/3/90	A	10	(8)	1
5	José GONÇALVES	POR	17/8/85	D	19		2
4	Eggert Gunnthor JÓNSSON	ISL	18/8/88	D	27	(1)	3
25	Marián KELLO	SVK	5/9/82	G	14		
10	Laryea KINGSTON	GHA	7/11/80	M	10	(4)	
2	Dawid KUCHARSKI	POL	19/11/84	D	10	(4)	
30	Jamie MACDONALD		17/4/86	G	8	(1)	
19	Jamie MOLE	ENG	1/6/88	A	5	(2)	
46	Paul MULROONEY		27/1/90	M	3	(3)	
14	Christian NADÉ	FRA	18/8/84	A	15	(8)	2
18	Arvydas NOVIKOVAS	LTU	18/12/90	M	5	(8)	
13	David OBUA	UGA	10/4/84	M	30	(2)	3
72	Scott ROBINSON		11/5/92	A	7	(6)	1
6	RUBÉN PALAZUELOS García	ESP	11/3/83	M	26	(1)	
44	Gordon SMITH		14/2/91	A	2	(6)	1
16	Ryan STEVENSON		24/8/84	M	9	(2)	
48	Jonathan STEWART		12/2/90	D		(1)	
23	Michael STEWART		26/2/81	M	24	(1)	5
7	Jesús Manuel "SUSO" SANTANA Abreu	ESP	2/3/85	M	21	(6)	6
24	David TEMPLETON		7/1/89	A	7	(9)	2
46	Craig THOMSON		17/4/91	D	15	(5)	
20	Jason THOMSON		26/7/89	D	15	(1)	
54	Rocky VISCONTE	AUS	22/4/90	M	1	(1)	
3	Lee WALLACE		1/8/87	M	32		1
15	David WITTEVEEN	AUT	5/5/85	A	5	(5)	1
26	Marius ŽALIŪKAS	LTU	10/11/83	D	21	(1)	2

HIBERNIAN FC
Manager – John Hughes
Founded – 1875
Stadium – Easter Road (17,400)
MAJOR HONOURS:
Scottish League - (4) 1903, 1948, 1951, 1952;
Scottish Cup - (2) 1887, 1902;
Scottish League Cup - (3) 1973, 1992, 2007.

2009

15/8	St Mirren	h	2-1	Wotherspoon, Benjelloun
22/8	Falkirk	a	3-1	Bamba, Riordan 2
30/8	Celtic	h	0-1	
13/9	Hamilton	a	0-2	
19/9	St Johnstone	h	3-0	Stokes 2, Riordan
26/9	Motherwell	a	3-1	Nish, Riordan, Zemmama
3/10	Dundee United	h	1-1	Zemmama
17/10	Kilmarnock	h	1-0	Benjelloun (p)
24/10	Rangers	a	1-1	Stokes
31/10	Aberdeen	h	2-0	Nish, Miller
7/11	Hearts	a	0-0	
21/11	St Mirren	h	1-1	Riordan
28/11	Falkirk	h	2-0	og (McLean), Riordan
5/12	Motherwell	h	2-0	Stokes 2
12/12	Kilmarnock	a	1-1	Stokes
19/12	Aberdeen	a	2-0	Stokes 2
27/12	Rangers	h	1-4	Stokes

2010

3/1	Hearts	h	1-1	Stokes
16/1	Dundee United	a	0-1	
23/1	Hamilton	h	5-1	Nish, Stokes 2, Riordan 2
27/1	Celtic	a	2-1	Stokes, Galbraith
30/1	St Mirren	h	2-1	Miller, og (Ross)
10/2	Aberdeen	h	2-2	Stokes, Benjelloun (p)
14/2	Rangers	a	0-3	
17/2	St Johnstone	a	1-5	Stokes
20/2	Motherwell	a	0-1	
27/2	St Johnstone	h	1-1	Stokes (p)
6/3	Kilmarnock	h	1-0	Riordan
20/3	Hearts	a	1-2	Riordan
27/3	Falkirk	a	3-1	Riordan, og (Twaddle), Bamba
31/3	Dundee United	h	2-4	Cregg, Stokes
4/4	Celtic	h	0-1	
10/4	Hamilton	a	1-4	Nish
17/4	Celtic	a	2-3	Riordan, Stokes (p)
25/4	Rangers	h	0-1	
1/5	Hearts	h	1-2	Stokes (p)
5/5	Motherwell	a	6-6	Nish 3, Riordan, Stokes 2
9/5	Dundee United	a	2-0	Nish 2

No	Name	Nat	DoB	Pos	Aps	(s)	Gls
26	Souleymane BAMBA	CIV	13/1/85	D	30		2
19	Abdessalam BENJELLOUN	MAR	28/1/85	A	8	(20)	3
29	Kurtis BYRNE	IRL	9/4/90	A		(4)	
8	Patrick CREGG	IRL	21/2/86	M	10	(5)	1
22	Daniel GALBRAITH		19/8/90	M		(14)	1
28	Alan GOW		9/10/82	A	3	(4)	
20	Paul HANLON		20/1/90	D	16	(2)	
4	Chris HOGG	ENG	12/3/85	D	33		
50	Yves MAKABU-MAKALAMBAY	COD	31/1/86	G	6	(1)	
17	Kevin McBRIDE		14/6/81	M	21	(5)	
2	Kevin McCANN		11/9/87	D	1		
25	Darren McCORMACK		29/9/88	D	7	(2)	
33	Liam MILLER	IRL	13/2/81	M	32	(1)	2
6	Ian MURRAY		20/3/81	D	34		
9	Colin NISH		17/3/81	A	23	(9)	9
11	John RANKIN		27/6/83	M	30	(3)	
10	Derek RIORDAN		16/1/83	A	35	(2)	13
22	Graeme SMITH		8/6/83	G	12		
1	Graham STACK	IRL	26/9/81	G	20		
16	Lewis STEVENSON		5/1/88	D	7	(3)	
18	Anthony STOKES	IRL	25/7/88	A	36	(1)	21
15	Steven THICOT	FRA	14/2/87	D	8	(2)	
3	David VAN ZANTEN	IRL	8/5/82	D	1		
24	David WOTHERSPOON		16/1/90	D	30	(3)	1
7	Merouane ZEMMAMA	MAR	7/10/83	M	15	(6)	2

KILMARNOCK FC
Manager – Jim Jefferies; (14/1/10) Jimmy Calderwood
Founded – 1869
Stadium – Rugby Park (18,128)
MAJOR HONOURS:
Scottish League - (1) 1965;
Scottish Cup - (3) 1920, 1929, 1997.

2009

15/8	Hamilton	h	3-0	Kyle 2, Hamill
22/8	Motherwell	a	1-3	Hamill
29/8	St Mirren	h	1-2	Sammon
15/9	Hearts	a	0-1	
19/9	Rangers	h	0-0	
26/9	Falkirk	a	0-0	
3/10	Aberdeen	h	1-1	Invincibile
17/10	Hibernian	a	0-1	
24/10	St Johnstone	h	2-1	Kyle 2
31/10	Celtic	a	0-3	

SCOTLAND

7/11	Dundee United	h	0-2	
21/11	Rangers	a	0-3	
28/11	Hearts	h	1-2	Bryson
5/12	St Johnstone	a	1-0	Kyle
12/12	Hibernian	h	1-1	Burchill
19/12	Falkirk	h	1-2	Invincibile
26/12	Dundee United	a	0-0	
2010				
2/1	St Mirren	a	0-1	
16/1	Motherwell	h	0-3	
23/1	Aberdeen	a	0-1	
26/1	Hamilton	a	0-0	
30/1	Dundee United	h	4-4	Ford, Kyle, Pascali, Bryson
2/2	Celtic	h	1-0	Maguire
10/2	Falkirk	a	1-0	Bryson
13/2	St Johnstone	h	3-2	Maguire, Hay, Kyle
20/2	St Mirren	h	1-1	Maguire
27/2	Motherwell	a	0-1	
6/3	Hibernian	a	0-1	
9/3	Rangers	h	0-2	
24/3	Hamilton	h	1-2	Maguire
27/3	Celtic	a	1-3	Bryson
4/4	Aberdeen	h	2-0	og (Grassi), Russell
10/4	Hearts	a	0-1	
17/4	Hamilton	a	0-3	
24/4	St Mirren	a	0-1	
1/5	St Johnstone	h	1-2	Wright
5/5	Aberdeen	a	2-1	Kelly, Kyle
8/5	Falkirk	h	0-0	

No	Name	Nat	DoB	Pos	Aps	(s)	Gls
24	Jamie ADAMS		26/8/87	M		(1)	
13	Cameron BELL		18/9/86	G	21		
26	Mark BROWN		28/2/81	G	14		
7	Craig BRYSON		6/11/86	M	33		4
27	Mark BURCHILL		18/8/80	M	9	(7)	1
2	Timothy CLANCY	IRL	8/6/84	D	19	(1)	
1	Alan COMBE		3/4/74	G	3		
20	DAVID FERNÁNDEZ Miramontes	ESP	20/1/76	A	9	(4)	
19	Iain FLANNIGAN		15/1/88	M	3	(4)	
6	Simon FORD	JAM	7/11/81	D	22	(1)	1
4	James FOWLER		26/10/80	M	19	(9)	
23	Jamie HAMILL		29/8/86	M	31	(4)	2
3	Garry HAY		7/9/77	D	27	(1)	1
11	Danny INVINCIBILE	AUS	31/3/79	A	16	(9)	2
22	Liam KELLY	IRL	10/2/90	M	13	(2)	1
29	Rob KIERNAN	ENG	13/1/91	D	2	(2)	
16	Kevin KYLE		7/6/81	A	29	(3)	8
28	Chris MAGUIRE		16/1/89	A	12	(2)	4
15	Ryan O'LEARY		24/8/87	D	10	(1)	
14	Steven OLD	NZL	17/2/86	D	8	(2)	
17	Graeme OWENS	ENG	1/5/88	M	1	(5)	
8	Manuel PASCALI	ITA	9/9/81	M	20	(2)	1
21	Lee ROBINSON	ENG	2/7/86	G		(1)	
9	Alan RUSSELL		13/12/80	A	6	(8)	1
18	Conor SAMMON	IRL	13/4/87	A	14	(9)	1
25	Scott SEVERIN		15/2/79	M	13	(1)	
12	Gavin SKELTON	ENG	27/3/81	M	16	(4)	
10	Mehdi TAOUIL	MAR	20/5/83	M	21	(6)	
5	Frazer WRIGHT		23/12/79	D	27		1

MOTHERWELL FC

Manager – Jim Gannon (IRL); (28/12/09) Craig Brown
Founded – 1886
Stadium – Fir Park (13,677)
MAJOR HONOURS:
Scottish League - (1) 1932;
Scottish Cup - (2) 1952, 1991;
Scottish League Cup - (1) 1951.

2009				
15/8	St Johnstone	a	2-2	Hutchinson, Forbes
22/8	Kilmarnock	h	3-1	Sutton, Forbes (p), Hutchinson
29/8	Aberdeen	a	0-0	
12/9	Rangers	h	0-0	
19/9	Dundee United	a	1-0	Forbes (p)
26/9	Hibernian	h	1-3	Reynolds
3/10	Falkirk	h	1-0	Jutkiewicz
17/10	Celtic	a	0-0	
24/10	St Mirren	a	3-3	Forbes (p), Jutkiewicz 2
31/10	Hearts	h	1-0	Forbes
7/11	Hamilton	a	2-2	Murphy, Jutkiewicz
21/11	Aberdeen	h	1-1	Jutkiewicz
28/11	Dundee United	h	2-2	Sutton, Jutkiewicz
5/12	Hibernian	a	0-2	
12/12	Celtic	h	2-3	Jutkiewicz, Reynolds
19/12	Rangers	a	1-6	Hutchinson
26/12	St Johnstone	h	1-3	Jennings
30/12	Hearts	a	0-1	
2010				
16/1	Kilmarnock	a	3-0	O'Brien 2, Jutkiewicz
23/1	St Mirren	h	2-0	Murphy, Sutton
27/1	Falkirk	a	0-0	
30/1	Aberdeen	a	3-0	Sutton 2, Jutkiewicz
6/2	Hamilton	h	1-0	Jutkiewicz
10/2	Rangers	h	1-1	Hateley
13/2	Hamilton	a	0-0	
20/2	Hibernian	h	1-0	Murphy
27/2	Kilmarnock	h	1-0	Murphy
6/3	St Johnstone	a	2-1	Murphy, Sutton
9/3	St Mirren	a	0-0	
13/3	Hearts	h	3-1	Reynolds, Sutton, O'Brien
27/3	Dundee United	a	0-3	
3/4	Falkirk	h	0-1	
13/4	Celtic	a	1-2	Reynolds
18/4	Dundee United	h	2-3	Sutton 2
24/4	Hearts	a	2-0	Saunders, Sutton
1/5	Celtic	a	0-4	
5/5	Hibernian	h	6-6	Coke 2, Sutton 2, Hateley, Jutkiewicz
9/5	Rangers	a	3-3	Murphy, Jennings, Jutkiewicz (p)

No	Name	Nat	DoB	Pos	Aps	(s)	Gls
6	Giles COKE	ENG	3/6/86	M	25	(7)	2
5	Stephen CRAIGAN	NIR	29/10/76	D	28		
16	Marc FITZPATRICK		11/5/86	D	1	(2)	
27	Ross FORBES		3/3/89	M	22	(6)	5
1	Michael FRASER		8/10/83	G	4	(1)	
3	Steven HAMMELL		18/2/82	D	33		
24	Tom HATELEY	ENG	12/9/89	M	38		2
7	Chris HUMPHREY	ENG	19/9/87	M	6	(22)	
28	Shaun HUTCHINSON	ENG	23/11/90	D	4	(1)	3
8	Steven JENNINGS	ENG	28/10/84	M	21	(8)	2
9	Lukas JUTKIEWICZ	ENG	20/3/89	A	27	(6)	12
14	Keith LASLEY		21/9/79	M	15	(5)	
18	Steven McGARRY		28/9/79	A		(1)	
18	Michael McGLINCHEY	NZL	7/1/87	A	1	(7)	
35	Robert McHUGH		16/7/91	A	2	(8)	
33	Steven MEECHAN		30/3/91	M	1	(1)	
2	Yassin MOUTAOUAKIL	FRA	18/7/86	D	13		
15	Jamie MURPHY		28/8/89	A	24	(11)	6

17	James O'BRIEN	IRL	28/9/87	M	29	(6)	3
46	Jamie POLLOCK		20/2/92	M		(1)	
4	Mark REYNOLDS		7/5/87	D	37		4
21	John RUDDY	ENG	24/10/86	G	34		
43	Steven SAUNDERS		23/2/91	D	22	(3)	1
45	Paul SLANE		25/11/91	A		(2)	
11	John SUTTON	ENG	26/12/83	A	31	(4)	12

RANGERS FC

Manager - Walter Smith

Founded – 1873

Stadium – Ibrox Stadium (51,076)

MAJOR HONOURS:

UEFA Cup Winners' Cup – (1) 1972;
Scottish League – (53) 1891 (joint), 1899, 1900, 1901, 1902, 1911, 1912,
1913, 1918, 1920, 1921, 1923, 1924, 1925, 1927, 1928, 1929, 1930, 1931,
1933, 1934, 1935, 1937, 1939, 1947, 1949, 1950, 1953, 1956, 1957, 1959,
1961, 1963, 1964, 1975, 1976, 1978, 1987, 1989, 1990, 1991, 1992, 1993,
1994, 1995, 1996, 1997, 1999, 2000, 2003, 2005, 2009, 2010;
Scottish Cup – (33) 1894, 1897, 1898, 1903, 1928, 1930, 1932, 1934, 1935,
1936, 1948, 1949, 1950, 1953, 1960, 1962, 1963, 1964, 1966, 1973, 1976,
1978, 1979, 1981, 1992, 1993, 1996, 1999, 2002, 2003, 2008, 2009;
Scottish League Cup – (26) 1947, 1949, 1961, 1962, 1964, 1965, 1971, 1976,
1978, 1979, 1982, 1984, 1985, 1987, 1988, 1989, 1991, 1993, 1994, 1997,
1999, 2002, 2003, 2005, 2008, 2010.

2009

15/8	Falkirk	h	4-1	McCulloch, Miller 2, Naismith
23/8	Hearts	a	2-1	McCulloch, Boyd (p)
29/8	Hamilton	h	4-1	Whittaker 2, Boyd 2
12/9	Motherwell	a	0-0	
19/9	Kilmarnock	a	0-0	
26/9	Aberdeen	h	0-0	
4/10	Celtic	h	2-1	Miller 2
17/10	St Johnstone	a	2-1	Boyd, Papac
24/10	Hibernian	h	1-1	Boyd
7/11	St Mirren	h	2-1	Boyd 2
21/11	Kilmarnock	h	3-0	Boyd, Miller, Whittaker
28/11	Aberdeen	a	0-1	
5/12	Falkirk	a	3-1	Boyd 2, Miller (p)
12/12	St Johnstone	h	3-0	Boyd 2 (1p), Nacho Novo
15/12	Dundee United	a	3-0	Beasley, Miller 2
19/12	Motherwell	h	6-1	Miller 2, Boyd, Lafferty 2, Beasley
27/12	Hibernian	a	4-1	Miller 2, Boyd, Nacho Novo
30/12	Dundee United	h	7-1	Boyd 5 (1p), Whittaker, Bougherra

2010

3/1	Celtic	a	1-1	McCulloch
16/1	Hamilton	a	1-0	Nacho Novo
23/1	Hearts	a	1-1	Little
27/1	St Mirren	a	2-0	Davis, Nacho Novo
30/1	Falkirk	h	3-0	Davis, Fleck, Whittaker
10/2	Motherwell	a	1-1	Boyd
14/2	Hibernian	h	3-0	Whittaker, Boyd (p), Miller
28/2	Celtic	h	1-0	Edu
6/3	St Mirren	a	3-1	McCulloch 2, Nacho Novo
9/3	Kilmarnock	a	2-0	Whittaker, Miller
27/3	Hearts	a	4-1	Wilson, Miller, Naismith 2
30/3	St Johnstone	a	1-4	Papac
3/4	Hamilton	h	1-0	Edu
7/4	Aberdeen	h	3-1	Davis, Lafferty, Miller
14/4	Dundee United	a	0-0	
18/4	Hearts	h	2-0	Lafferty, Miller (p)
25/4	Hibernian	a	1-0	Lafferty
1/5	Dundee United	a	2-1	Boyd, Nacho Novo
4/5	Celtic	a	1-2	Miller
9/5	Motherwell	h	3-3	Boyd, Lafferty 2

No	Name	Nat	DoB	Pos	Aps	(s)	Gls
25	Neil ALEXANDER		10/3/78	G	4	(1)	
20	DaMarcus BEASLEY	USA	24/5/82	M	6	(3)	2
24	Madjid BOUGHERRA	ALG	7/10/82	D	16	(1)	1
9	Kris BOYD		18/8/83	A	28	(3)	23
21	Kirk BROADFOOT		8/8/84	D	12		
7	Steven DAVIS	NIR	1/1/85	M	36		3
2	Maurice EDU	USA	18/4/86	M	8	(7)	2
29	John FLECK		24/8/91	A	8	(7)	1
27	Kyle LAFFERTY	NIR	16/9/87	A	17	(11)	7
48	Andrew LITTLE	NIR	12/5/89	D	2	(4)	1
6	Lee McCULLOCH		14/5/78	D	32	(2)	5
1	Alan McGREGOR		31/1/82	G	34		
18	Kenny MILLER		23/12/79	A	29	(4)	18
10	Ignacio "NACHO" Javier Gómez NOVO	ESP	26/3/79	A	14	(21)	6
14	Steven NAISMITH		14/9/86	A	20	(8)	3
5	Saša PAPAC	BIH	7/2/80	D	34		2
4	PEDRO Miguel da Silva MENDES	POR	26/2/79	M	4		
11	Jérôme ROTHEN	FRA	31/3/78	M	3	(1)	
26	Steven SMITH		30/8/85	D	7	(5)	
8	Kevin THOMSON		14/10/84	M	20	(5)	
3	David WEIR		10/5/70	D	38		
16	Steven WHITTAKER		16/6/84	D	32	(3)	7
66	Daniel WILSON		27/12/91	D	14		1
69	Greg WYLDE		23/3/91	D		(2)	

SAINT JOHNSTONE FC

Coach – Derek McInnes

Founded – 1894

Stadium – McDiarmid Park (10,673)

2009

15/8	Motherwell	h	2-2	Davidson, Gartland
22/8	Celtic	a	2-5	Samuel, Morris
30/8	Hearts	h	2-2	Davidson, Hardie
12/9	St Mirren	a	1-1	Morris
19/9	Aberdeen	a	0-3	
26/9	Dundee United	h	2-3	og (Dods), Hardie
3/10	Hamilton	a	2-0	Anderson, Grainger
17/10	Rangers	h	1-2	Samuel
24/10	Kilmarnock	a	1-2	og (Wright)
31/10	Falkirk	h	3-1	Samuel, Millar, Davidson
7/11	Aberdeen	a	1-2	Craig
21/11	Hearts	a	2-1	Samuel, Johansson
28/11	Hamilton	h	1-1	Filipe Morais
5/12	Kilmarnock	h	0-1	
12/12	Rangers	a	0-3	
19/12	St Mirren	h	1-0	Millar
26/12	Motherwell	a	3-1	MacDonald 3

2010

24/1	Celtic	h	1-4	Craig (p)
27/1	Dundee United	a	3-3	MacDonald, Craig, Moon
30/1	Hearts	h	1-0	Deuchar
10/2	St Mirren	a	1-1	Mackay
13/2	Kilmarnock	a	2-3	MacDonald, Gartland
17/2	Hibernian	h	5-1	Craig 2 (1p), Sheridan 2, Deuchar
27/2	Hibernian	a	1-1	Craig (p)
6/3	Motherwell	h	1-2	Milne
13/3	Falkirk	a	2-1	Craig (p), Deuchar
16/3	Aberdeen	h	1-0	Sheridan
20/3	Celtic	a	0-3	
23/3	Falkirk	h	1-1	Filipe Morais
27/3	Hamilton	a	0-1	
30/3	Rangers	h	4-1	Sheridan, Millar, Craig, Davidson
5/4	Dundee United	h	0-1	
11/4	Aberdeen	a	3-1	Deuchar, Sheridan 2
17/4	St Mirren	h	2-2	Duberry, Sheerin (p)

SCOTLAND

24/4	Aberdeen	h	1-1	og (Nelson)
1/5	Kilmarnock	a	2-1	Deuchar, Samuel
5/5	Falkirk	a	0-0	
8/5	Hamilton	h	2-3	Davidson, Craig

No	Name	Nat	DoB	Pos	Aps	(s)	Gls
24	Steven ANDERSON		19/12/85	D	14	(3)	1
27	Mark CONNOLLY		16/12/91	D	1		
10	Liam CRAIG		27/12/86	M	22	(9)	9
20	Murray DAVIDSON		7/3/88	M	30	(3)	5
17	Kenny DEUCHAR		6/8/80	A	25	(10)	5
28	Michael DUBERRY	ENG	14/10/75	D	17		1
47	Josh FALKINGHAM	ENG	25/8/90	M		(1)	
22	FILIPE Alexandre MORAIS	POR	21/11/85	M	20	(10)	2
18	Graham GARTLAND	IRL	13/7/83	D	20	(1)	2
3	Danny GRAINGER	ENG	28/7/86	D	35	(1)	1
8	Martin HARDIE		22/4/76	M	4	(6)	2
2	Gary IRVINE		17/3/85	D	13	(4)	
23	Andy JACKSON	IRL	9/1/88	A		(2)	
30	Jonatan JOHANSSON	FIN	16/8/75	A	2	(4)	1
16	Peter MacDONALD		17/11/80	A	5	(2)	5
12	David MACKAY		2/5/81	D	36		1
1	Alan MAIN		5/12/67	G	9		
6	Stuart McCAFFREY		30/5/79	D	9	(1)	
7	Chris MILLAR		30/3/83	M	33	(3)	3
9	Steven MILNE		5/5/80	A	10	(6)	1
14	Kevin MOON		8/6/87	M	10	(4)	1
4	Jody MORRIS	ENG	22/12/78	M	33	(1)	2
32	Stephen REYNOLDS		11/6/92	A		(4)	
5	Kevin RUTKIEWICZ		10/5/80	D	7		
21	Collin SAMUEL	TRI	27/8/81	A	16	(11)	5
11	Paul SHEERIN		28/8/74	M	3	(8)	1
26	Cillian SHERIDAN	IRL	23/2/89	A	12	(4)	6
25	Graeme SMITH		3/10/82	G	29		
19	Gavin SWANKIE		22/11/83	M	3	(7)	

SAINT MIRREN FC
Manager – Gus McPherson
Founded – 1877
Stadium – St Mirren Park (8,029)
MAJOR HONOURS:
Scottish Cup - (3), 1926, 1959, 1987.

2009

15/8	Hibernian	a	1-2	McGinn
22/8	Dundee United	h	0-0	
29/8	Kilmarnock	a	2-1	McGinn 2
12/9	St Johnstone	h	1-1	Mehmet (p)
19/9	Aberdeen	a	0-1	
26/9	Celtic	h	0-2	
3/10	Hearts	h	2-1	Thomson, Dargo
17/10	Falkirk	a	3-1	Dargo, Mehmet, Brighton
24/10	Motherwell	h	3-3	Murray 2, Dorman
31/10	Hamilton	h	0-2	
7/11	Rangers	a	1-2	O'Donnell
21/11	Hibernian	h	1-1	Innes
28/11	Celtic	a	1-3	Higdon
5/12	Dundee United	h	2-3	og (Dods), O'Donnell
12/12	Falkirk	h	1-1	Higdon
19/12	St Johnstone	a	0-1	

2010

2/1	Kilmarnock	h	1-0	Innes
12/1	Aberdeen	h	1-0	Innes
16/1	Hearts	a	0-1	
23/1	Motherwell	a	0-2	
27/1	Rangers	h	0-2	
30/1	Hibernian	a	1-2	og (Bamba)
10/2	St Johnstone	h	1-1	og (Mackay)
13/2	Dundee United	h	1-2	Higdon

20/2	Kilmarnock	a	1-1	Mehmet
27/2	Hamilton	h	0-0	
6/3	Rangers	a	1-3	Carey
9/3	Motherwell	h	0-0	
13/3	Hamilton	a	0-1	
24/3	Celtic	h	4-0	Dorman 2, Thomson 2
27/3	Aberdeen	a	1-2	Robb
3/4	Hearts	h	1-1	Carey
10/4	Falkirk	a	1-2	Dorman
17/4	St Johnstone	a	2-2	Carey, Dorman
24/4	Kilmarnock	h	1-0	Dorman
1/5	Falkirk	a	1-1	O'Donnell
5/5	Hamilton	a	0-0	
8/5	Aberdeen	h	0-1	

No	Name	Nat	DoB	Pos	Aps	(s)	Gls
19	David BARRON		10/9/87	D	34		
14	Gary BRADY		7/9/76	M	19	(3)	
16	Tom BRIGHTON		28/3/84	M	1	(7)	1
3	Graham CAREY	IRL	20/5/89	M	10	(5)	3
18	Craig DARGO		3/1/78	A	13	(16)	2
8	Andy DORMAN	WAL	1/5/82	M	29	(5)	6
1	Paul GALLACHER		16/8/79	G	36		
11	Michael HIGDON	ENG	3/9/83	A	22	(11)	3
20	Mark HOWARD	ENG	21/9/86	G	2		
21	Chris INNES		13/7/76	D	18	(3)	3
41	Allan JOHNSTON		14/12/73	A	1	(9)	
17	Rory LOY		19/3/88	A		(8)	
5	Lee MAIR		9/12/80	D	30	(1)	
4	Stephen McGINN		2/12/88	M	18		3
9	Billy MEHMET		3/1/84	A	35	(2)	3
7	Hugh MURRAY		8/1/79	M	35		2
12	Stephen O'DONNELL		10/7/83	M	10	(12)	3
6	John POTTER		15/12/79	D	35		
38	Conor RAMSAY		9/3/93	A		(5)	
15	Steven ROBB		8/3/82	M	12	(8)	1
2	Jack ROSS		5/6/76	D	28		
10	Steven THOMSON		23/1/78	M	30		3

PROMOTED CLUB

INVERNESS CALEDONIAN THISTLE FC
Coach – Terry Butcher (ENG)
Founded – 1994
Stadium – Tulloch Caledonian Stadium (7,189)

SECOND LEVEL FINAL TABLE 2009/10

		Pld	W	D	L	F	A	Pts
1	Inverness Caledonian Thistle FC	36	21	10	5	72	32	73
2	Dundee FC	36	16	13	7	48	34	61
3	Dunfermline Athletic FC	36	17	7	12	54	44	58
4	Queen of the South FC	36	15	11	10	53	40	56
5	Ross County FC	36	15	11	10	46	44	56
6	Partick Thistle FC	36	14	6	16	43	40	48
7	Raith Rovers FC	36	11	9	16	36	47	42
8	Greenock Morton FC	36	11	4	21	40	65	37
9	Airdrie United FC	36	8	9	19	41	56	33
10	Ayr United FC	36	7	10	19	29	60	31

DOMESTIC CUPS 2009/10

SCOTTISH CUP

FOURTH ROUND

(9/1/10)
Aberdeen 2, Hearts 0
Dunfermline 7, Stenhousemuir 1 *(void)*
Hibernian 3, Irvine Meadow 0
Patrick Thistle 0, Dundee United 2
St Mirren 3, Alloa 1

(10/1/10)
Hamilton 3, Rangers 3

(18/1/10)
Albion Rovers 0, Stirling Albion 0
Ayr 1, Brechin 0
Edinburgh City 1, Montrose 3
Forfar 0, St Johnstone 3
Inverness 2, Motherwell 0
Kilmarnock 1, Falkirk 0
Ross County 4, Inverurie Loco Works 0

(19/1/10)
Greenock Morton 0, Celtic 1

(20/1/10)
Livingston 0, Dundee 1

(25/1/10)
Raith Rovers 1, Airdrie 1

Replays

(19/1/10)
Rangers 2, Hamilton 0 *(aet)*

(20/1/10)
Stirling Albion 3, Albion Rovers 1

(26/1/10)
Stenhousemuir 1, Dunfermline 2 *(aet)*

(27/1/10)
Airdrie 1, Raith Rovers 3

FIFTH ROUND

(6/2/10)
Dundee 2, Ayr 1
Hibernian 5, Montrose 1
Kilmarnock 3, Inverness 0
Raith Rovers 1, Aberdeen 1
Ross County 9, Stirling Albion 0

St Johnstone 0, Dundee United 1
St Mirren 0, Rangers 0

(7/2/10)
Dunfermline 2, Celtic 4

Replays

(16/2/10)
Aberdeen 0, Raith Rovers 1
Rangers 1, St Mirren 0

QUARTER-FINALS

(13/3/10)
Celtic 3 *(Keane 63, 81, 83)*, Kilmarnock 0
Dundee 1 *(Forsyth 73)*, Raith Rovers 2 *(Simmons 3, Ellis 10)*
Hibernian 2 *(Nish 7, Riordan 19)*, Ross County 2 *(Hanlon 16og, Gardyne 72)*

(14/3/10)
Rangers 3 *(Boyd 34p, 43p, Nacho Novo 48)*, Dundee United 3 *(Shala 24, Whittaker 63og, Kovačević 80)*

Replays

(23/3/10)
Dundee United 1 *(Robertson D. 90)*, Rangers 0
Ross County 2 *(Wood 70, Boyd 90)*, Hibernian 1 *(Stokes 46)*

SEMI-FINALS

(10/4/10)
Celtic 0, Ross County 2 *(Craig 55, Scott 88)*

(11/4/10)
Dundee United 2 *(Goodwillie 28, Webster 59)*, Raith Rovers 0

FINAL

(15/5/10)
Hampden Park, Glasgow
DUNDEE UNITED FC 3 *(Goodwillie 61, Conway 75, 86)*
ROSS COUNTY FC 0
Referee – McDonald
DUNDEE UNITED – *Perniš, Dillon, Webster, Kenneth, Kovačević (Watson 83), Conway, Swanson (Robertson S. 74), Buaben, Gomis, Daly, Goodwillie (Robertson D. 78).*
ROSS COUNTY – *McGovern, Miller, Morrison, Scott (Wood 79), Boyd, Keddie, Gardyne (Di Giacomo 77), Craig (Lawson 52), Brittain, Vigurs, Barrowman.*

LEAGUE CUP

QUARTER-FINALS

(27/10/09)
Dundee 1 *(Griffiths 29)*, Rangers 3 *(Whittaker 15, MacKenzie 57og, Fleck 85)*
St Johnstone 2 *(Anderson 72, Dods 76og)*, Dundee United 1 *(Buaben 82)*
St Mirren 3 *(Higdon 23, Ross 61, Craigan 81og)*, Motherwell 0

(28/10/09)
Celtic 0, Hearts 1 *(Stewart M. 58p)*

SEMI-FINALS

(2/2/10)
Hearts 0, St Mirren 1 *(Mehmet 51)*

(3/2/10)
Rangers 2 *(Davis 26, McCulloch 37)*, St Johnstone 0

FINAL

(21/3/10)
Hampden Park, Glasgow
RANGERS FC 1 *(Miller 84)*
SAINT MIRREN FC 0
Referee – Thomson
RANGERS – *Alexander, Whittaker, Weir, Wilson, Papac, Thomson, McCulloch, Davis (Edu 46), Miller, Nacho Novo (Smith 89), Boyd (Naismith 79).*
Sent off: *Thomson (53), Wilson (71)*
ST MIRREN – *Gallacher, Ross, Mair, Potter, Barron, Carey, Brady (O'Donnell 85), Thomson, Murray (Dorman 60), Mehmet (Dargo 70), Higdon.*

Victory over Germany to no avail

aving qualified for the 2010 FIFA World Cup with such panache, a 5-0 rout of Romania in Belgrade securing their ticket to South Africa as group winners ahead of France, Serbia's inability to go beyond the opening round at the finals inevitably brought sadness and disappointment to the country's football followers – especially as Radomir Antić's side recorded a famous win over Germany in their second group game.

Unfortunately, that 1-0 victory in Port Elizabeth was sandwiched by defeats against Ghana and Australia and was therefore of no lasting value – even if at the time it was greeted by widespread jubilation across the country. The Serbian fans were certainly put through the whole gamut of emotions during their team's ten-day stay in South Africa. Every one of their three matches was full of incident and controversy, but if it was exciting at the time, the overriding feeling after the team's early exit was one of deep regret and frustration at what might have been.

Out of luck

Had Serbia scored a late equaliser in their final game against Australia – and they vociferously appealed for a late penalty when the ball inadvertently struck the arm of Socceroo striker Tim Cahill – they would have gone through to the last 16 and might even have fancied their chances, given the way the draw had opened up, of going all the way through to the semi-finals. But the luck that went their way against Germany when Miroslav Klose was red-carded in the first half evaded them in their moment of greatest need in Nelspruit.

Over the whole tournament, however, Serbia did not really live up to expectations. Against Ghana – and

their Serbian coach, Milovan Rajevac – they shot themselves in the foot not once but twice, having defender Aleksandar Luković sent off then conceding a needless penalty, from which the Africans scored their late winning goal. A greater level of composure with the final ball should have seen them add to Milan Jovanović's well-taken winning goal against Germany, who also missed a penalty after another silly handball, from, of all people, Nemanja Vidić, who was otherwise imperious, had threatened to allow their undermanned opponents back into the game. Goalkeeper Vladimir Stojković saved that spot-kick but then had a poor game against Australia. It was all swings and roundabouts for Serbia in South Africa.

Antić was not widely blamed for the team's early elimination. In fact, the Football Association of Serbia (FSS) rewarded him with a new contract to cover the UEFA EURO 2012 qualifiers – despite the fact that he was set to serve a four-game ban imposed by FIFA for his complaints about the match officials after the defeat to Australia. If they can improve the quality and precision of their play in the final third, an area in which Marko Pantelić, Nikola Žigić, Zdravko Kuzmanović and even skipper Dejan Stanković were

Milan Jovanović scores Serbia's winner against Germany in Port Elizabeth

all guilty parties in South Africa, Serbia must have a decent chance of giving a transient Italy side a good run for their money in a UEFA EURO 2012 qualifying group that also contains another World Cup first-round faller, Slovenia, as well as Northern Ireland, Estonia and the Faroe Islands.

Antić and his players bear an enormous responsibility for Serbian football, because the likelihood of one of the country's clubs making a telling impact in the international arena – as FK Crvena zvezda did two decades ago – seems remote, both for now and the foreseeable future. There was very little for the Serbian SuperLiga's European representatives to get excited about in 2009/10, with only one of the quartet, FK Partizan, surviving the qualifying rounds and even then in the 'wrong' competition, having transferred over to the UEFA Europa League after falling in the third qualifying round of the UEFA Champions League to Cypriot champions APOEL FC – the same club that had dumped Crvena zvezda out of the UEFA Cup 12 months earlier.

Senegalese striker Lamine Diarra was a key figure in Partizan's Serbian title triumph

Jokanović jettisoned

Although Partizan would make it into the group stage of the UEFA Europa League, their failure in the senior competition led to the departure, allegedly by mutual consent, of coach Slaviša Jokanović. Having led Partizan to the domestic double in each of his first two seasons – a unique feat – it seemed an illogical move for the club to dispense with his services after just one faux pas, particularly as his replacement and erstwhile assistant, Goran Stevanović, was short of experience. Stevanović's newly appointed counterpart at Crvena zvezda, on the other hand, Vladimir Petrović, boasted an impressive coaching CV that included a memorable two-year stint with Serbia and Montenegro Under-21s and a spell in charge of the Chinese national team.

The hope was that Petrović would re-energise 'Red Star' after a calamitous 2008/09 season in which they finished third, 21 points behind champions Partizan. Despite the early setback of European elimination, the appointment of Petrović appeared to have the desired effect as Crvena zvezda threw down the gauntlet to the defending champions with a strong burst of form in the SuperLiga that had them four points ahead of their arch-rivals going into the first 'Eternal Derby' at the end of November. A win would have made Petrović's team clear title favourites, but instead, despite home advantage, they lost, Partizan taking an early lead through their Senegalese striker Lamine

Diarra then recovering from an own goal and a red card for their defender Srđan Knežević to win the game 2-1 with a goal from Cléo – the Brazilian striker they had acquired from Crvena zvezda during the close season.

Still a point in arrears after that win, Partizan had dropped to three points behind Crvena zvezda by the winter break. All of the other teams in the newly expanded 16-team SuperLiga were way off the pace. Indeed third-placed Vojvodina were as close, in terms of points, to bottom-placed FK Čukarički as they were to second-placed Partizan.

The two-horse race resumed in late February, and after three further games Crvena zvezda had stretched their lead to five points. But then came the bombshell of a 2-1 defeat at FK Metalac. Although Metalac were in form, having won their three previous games, the defeat was totally unacceptable to Crvena zvezda president Vladan Lukić, who promptly sacked Petrović and replaced him with youth team coach Ratko Dostanić. The leaders showed no ill effects from the upheaval initially, winning their next four games, but just as the finishing line – and the prospect of a first title in three years – came into view, the wheels came off Red Star's wagon.

SERBIA

Seven straight wins

At the same time Partizan responded to a 3-1 defeat against Vojvodina in the semi-final of the Serbian Cup by sacking Stevanović and installing national Under-19 boss Aleksandar Stanojević, a graduate of the Partizan coaching school, in his place. All of a sudden, as Crvena zvezda wilted, Partizan blossomed. Stanojević's arrival led to a much fresher, more dynamic approach and Partizan reeled off seven straight victories, including 1-0 at home to their fading rivals with a goal from rising midfield star Radosav Petrović – a result that gave them a four-point lead. Five days later, with a 3-0 win at OFK Beograd, the title was theirs.

It was Partizan's 22nd championship win and their third in a row. Only once previously, from 1961-63, had they completed the hat-trick. Furthermore, they achieved it by going through the entire 30-match campaign undefeated, with only one team, FK Javor, taking points off them both home and away. With two wins over Crvena zvezda and ten more goals scored, there could be little doubt that Partizan deserved to be champions, although naturally there was a feeling of devastation

Fudbalski savez Srbije (FSS)

Terazije 35, CP 263
RS-11000 Beograd
tel – +381 11 323 4253
fax – +381 11 323 3433
website – fss.org.rs
email – office@fss.rs
Year of Formation – 1919

President – Tomislav Karadžić
General Secretary – Zoran Laković
Press Officer – Aleksandar Bošković
National Stadium – FK Crvena zvezda, Belgrade (52,000)

INTERNATIONAL TOURNAMENT APPEARANCES*
FIFA World Cup – (11) 1930 (semi-finals), 1950, 1954 (qtr-finals), 1958 (qtr-finals), 1962 (4th), 1974 (2nd phase), 1982, 1990 (qtr-finals), 1998 (2nd round), 2006, 2010.
UEFA European Championship – (5) 1960 (runners-up), 1968 (runners-up), 1976 (4th), 1984, 2000 (qtr-finals).
TOP FIVE ALL-TIME CAPS (including Yugoslavia and Serbia & Montenegro)
Savo Milošević (102); Dejan Stanković (91); Dragan Džajić (85); Dragan Stojković (84); Predrag Mijatović (73)
TOP FIVE ALL-TIME GOALS (including Yugoslavia and Serbia & Montenegro)
Stjepan Bobek (38); Milan Galić & Savo Milošević (37); Blagoje Marjanović (36); Rajko Mitić (32)

(* before 2006 as Yugoslavia; 2006 as Serbia & Montenegro)

NATIONAL TEAM RESULTS 2009/10

12/8/09	South Africa	A	Atteridgeville	3-1	Tošić (56, 77), Lazović (68)
9/9/09	France (WCQ)	H	Belgrade	1-1	Milijaš (13p)
10/10/09	Romania (WCQ)	H	Belgrade	5-0	Žigić (36), Pantelić (50), Kuzmanović (77), Jovanović (87, 90+3)
14/10/09	Lithuania (WCQ)	A	Marijampole	1-2	Tošić (60)
14/11/09	Northern Ireland	A	Belfast	1-0	Lazović (58)
18/11/09	South Korea	N	London (ENG)	1-0	Žigić (7)
3/3/10	Algeria	A	Algiers	3-0	Pantelić (16), Kuzmanović (55), Tošić (64)
7/4/10	Japan	A	Osaka	3-0	Mrđa (15, 23), Tomić (60)
29/5/10	New Zealand	N	Klagenfurt (AUT)	0-1	
2/6/10	Poland	N	Kufstein (AUT)	0-0	
5/6/10	Cameroon	H	Belgrade	4-3	Krasić (16), Stanković D. (25), Milijaš (44p), Pantelić (45)
13/6/10	Ghana (WCF)	N	Pretoria (RSA)	0-1	
18/6/10	Germany (WCF)	N	Port Elizabeth (RSA)	1-0	Jovanović (38)
23/6/10	Australia (WCF)	N	Nelspruit (RSA)	1-2	Pantelić (84)

NATIONAL TEAM APPEARANCES 2009/10

Coach – Radomir ANTIĆ 22/11/48 /(Radovan ĆURĆIĆ) 10/01/72			Rsa	FRA	ROU	LTU	Nir	Kor	Alg	Jpn	Nzl	Pol	Cmr	GHA	GER	AUS	Caps	Goals
Vladimir STOJKOVIĆ	28/7/83	Sporting (POR) /Wigan (ENG)	G	G	G			G		G82	G46	s46	G	G	G	G	36	-
Branislav IVANOVIĆ	22/4/84	Chelsea (ENG)	D	D	D	D		D	D67		D	D	D	D	D	D	34	4
Aleksandar LUKOVIĆ	23/10/82	Udinese (ITA)	D	D	D46	s61	D	D88	D90		D	D	D 74*		D		22	-
Neven SUBOTIĆ	10/12/88	Dortmund (GER)	D		s73	D	s46	D	D86		D	D	D	s76	D		15	1

NATIONAL TEAM APPEARANCES 2009/10 (contd.)

Name		Club	Rsa	FRA	ROU	LTU	Nir	Kor	Alg	Jpn	Nzl	Pol	Cmr	GHA	GER	AUS	Caps	Goals
Ivan OBRADOVIĆ	25/7/88	Partizan /Zaragoza (ESP)	D88	D	D61						D18	D46			D		13	1
Gojko KAČAR	26/1/87	Hertha (GER)	M46	M46		M	s52	s60	s86		s46	s59			s70		18	-
Miloš NINKOVIĆ	25/12/84	Dynamo Kyiv (UKR)	M82	s46		s73	s46	s68	s76		M46	s57			M70	M	11	-
Radosav PETROVIĆ	8/3/89	Partizan	M74				M	M	s82	s63	M	s46	s46	s46	s75		10	-
Miloš KRASIĆ	1/11/84	CSKA Moskva (RUS)	M46	M	M	M46	s46	M	M67			M69	M62	M	M	M62	34	3
Nikola ŽIGIĆ	25/9/80	Valencia (ESP)	A	A	A	A		A	A76		A	A46	A46	A69	A	A67	48	16
Milan JOVANOVIĆ	18/4/81	Standard (BEL)	A46	A73	M	M	A46	M68	M53			M46	M68	M76	M79	M	29	10
Zoran TOŠIĆ	28/4/87	Man. United (ENG) /Köln (GER)	s46				s46	M	s46	s53		M	s46	s68		s62	22	4
Danko LAZOVIĆ	17/5/83	PSV (NED) /Zenit (RUS)	s46	s73				A76	A46	s90	s66	A59	s46	s69	s79	s77	40	10
Zdravko KUZMANOVIĆ	22/9/87	Fiorentina (ITA) /Stuttgart (GER)	s46			s70	s64		M52	M82	s46	M59	M	s62	M75	M77	30	4
Antonio RUKAVINA	26/1/84	1860 München (GER)	s74				D		s67		D						20	-
Marko MILINKOVIĆ	16/4/88	Košice (SVK)	s82														1	-
Nenad TOMOVIĆ	30/8/87	Genoa (ITA)	s88														2	-
Nemanja VIDIĆ	21/10/81	Man. United (ENG)		D	D73		D46	D72			D			D	D	D	48	2
Nenad MILIJAŠ	30/4/83	Wolves (ENG)		M70	M64		M46	M60	M63		M46			M46	M62		18	4
Dejan STANKOVIĆ	11/9/78	Inter (ITA)		M	M				M46		M46	M	M	M	M		91	14
Aleksandar KOLAROV	10/11/85	Lazio (ITA)			D		D67	s72	D46		s18	D	s46		D	D	15	-
Marko PANTELIĆ	15/9/78	Ajax (NED)			A	A73			A46		A66	s46	A57	A		s67	34	7
Ivica DRAGUTINOVIĆ	13/11/75	Sevilla (ESP)			s46	D			s46								49	-
Vladimir DIŠLJENKOVIĆ	2/7/81	Metalurh Donetsk (UKR)				G											7	-
Bojan ISAILOVIĆ	25/3/80	Čukarički /Zagłębie Lubin (POL)					G					G46					4	-
Jagoš VUKOVIĆ	10/6/88	PSV (NED)						s67	s88								2	-
Dejan LEKIĆ	7/6/85	Crvena zvezda						s76			s46	A78					3	-
Boško JANKOVIĆ	1/3/84	Genoa (ITA)									s67						25	5
Željko BRKIĆ	9/7/86	Vojvodina									s82	G86					2	-
Pavle NINKOV	20/4/85	Crvena zvezda									D64						3	-
Milovan MILOVIĆ	24/10/80	Javor									D						1	-
Marko LOMIĆ	13/9/83	Partizan									D						1	-
Vojislav STANKOVIĆ	22/9/87	Partizan									D						1	-
Ljubomir FEJSA	14/8/88	Partizan									M70						2	-
Dušan TADIĆ	20/11/88	Vojvodina									M52						2	-
Nemanja TOMIĆ	21/1/88	Partizan									M85						1	1
Dragan MRĐA	23/1/84	Vojvodina									A	s59	s69	s62			6	2
Aleksandar DAVIDOV	7/10/83	Partizan									s52						1	-
Miroslav VULIĆEVIĆ	29/5/85	Vojvodina									s64						2	-
Nikola MITROVIĆ	2/1/87	Napredak									s70						1	-
Andrija KALUĐEROVIĆ	5/7/87	Rad									s78						1	-
Nikola BELJIĆ	14/5/83	OFK Beograd									s85						1	-
Milan JOVANIĆ	31/7/85	Spartak Zlatibor voda									s86						1	-
Anđelko ĐURIČIĆ	21/11/80	Leiria (POR)										s46					1	-

SERBIA

among Crvena zvezda followers that their team had let the title slip from their grasp.

Just three wins in their last seven games had gifted the SuperLiga crown to Partizan, but if Dostanić stood accused of throwing away the title, he at least had a trophy to proffer in his defence, Crvena zvezda having beaten Vojvodina 3-0 in the final of the Serbian Cup three days before their visit to Partizan's stadium for the fateful league decider. The Cup final win brought Crvena zvezda their first trophy for three years and was a major kick in the teeth for Vojvodina, who had never won the trophy in their 96-year history.

Mrđa magic

The team from Novi Sad would also be denied a place in Europe, dropping from third place at Christmas to fifth in the final league standings. If it was ultimately a disappointing season for the club, who expected better after a hefty outlay on new signings, it was an excellent one for their 26-year-old captain Dragan Mrđa, who won the SuperLiga Golden Boot with 22

Dragan Mrđa of Vojvodina – the SuperLiga top scorer and Player of the Year

goals – five more than runner-up Andrija Kaluđerović of FK Rad and eight more than Partizan duo Diarra and Cléo – and was also named as the official SuperLiga Player of the Season. Furthermore, to prove that good things as well as bad ones come in threes, he was also named in Serbia's World Cup squad.

The Coach of the Year prize went to Zoran Milinković, who miraculously turned newly promoted no-hopers FK Spartak Zlatibor voda into European qualifiers. Spartak finished fourth, one place behind Dejan Đurđević's OFK Beograd, likewise rewarded for a season of over-achievement with a place in the UEFA Europa League. Another club from the capital, Čukarički, enjoyed a strong spring campaign to save themselves from relegation, sending FK Mladi radnik and FK Napredak down instead. Those two vacant places were filled for 2010/11 by SuperLiga newcomers FK Inđija and FK Sevojno, who, in July, merged with FK Sloboda Užice to become FK Sloboda Sevojno.

DOMESTIC LEAGUE 2009/10

SUPERLIGA FINAL TABLE

	Pld	Home					Away					Total					Pts
		W	D	L	F	A	W	D	L	F	A	W	D	L	F	A	
1 FK Partizan	30	14	1	0	37	5	10	5	0	26	9	24	6	0	63	14	78
2 FK Crvena zvezda	30	12	0	3	31	12	11	2	2	22	5	23	2	5	53	17	71
3 OFK Beograd	30	8	3	4	22	19	7	2	6	15	14	15	5	10	37	33	50
4 FK Spartak Zlatibor voda	30	7	5	3	14	7	7	2	6	20	20	14	7	9	34	27	49
5 FK Vojvodina	30	8	2	5	31	12	5	4	6	20	18	13	6	11	51	30	45
6 FK Jagodina	30	10	3	2	25	11	2	4	9	13	23	12	7	11	38	34	43
7 FK Javor	30	5	8	2	14	11	3	6	6	8	12	8	14	8	22	23	38
8 FK Rad	30	9	2	4	25	18	1	5	9	13	21	10	7	13	38	39	37
9 FK Metalac	30	8	2	5	17	16	2	3	10	7	23	10	5	15	24	39	35
10 FK Smederevo	30	6	5	4	11	10	2	5	8	12	20	8	10	12	23	30	34
11 FK Borac Čačak	30	8	4	3	16	10	1	3	11	5	24	9	7	14	21	34	34
12 BSK Borča	30	5	4	6	14	17	4	2	9	13	20	9	6	15	27	37	33
13 FK Čukarički	30	6	4	5	13	16	3	1	11	12	29	9	5	16	25	45	32
14 FK Hajduk Kula	30	6	4	5	17	17	1	5	9	11	23	7	9	14	28	40	30
15 FK Napredak	30	6	4	5	20	16	1	4	10	10	28	7	8	15	30	44	29
16 FK Mladi radnik	30	4	6	5	12	11	1	4	10	7	30	5	10	15	19	47	25

TOP GOALSCORERS

22 Dragan MRĐA (Vojvodina)

17 Andrija KALUĐEROVIĆ (Rad)

14 CLÉO (Partizan)
   Lamine DIARRA (Partizan)

12 Dejan LEKIĆ (Crvena zvezda)
   Milan BOJOVIĆ (Jagodina)

10 Aleksandar JEVTIĆ (Crvena zvezda)
   Vojo UBIPARIP (Spartak)
   Dušan TADIĆ (Vojvodina)

9 Aleksandar ĐUKIĆ (Borča)
   Yaw ANTWI (Napredak)

CLUB-BY-CLUB

FK BORAC ČAČAK
Coach – Žarko Đurović; (24/10/09) Miodrag Martać
Founded – 1926
Stadium – Kraj Morave (5,200)

2009
15/8	Partizan	a	0-5	
22/8	BSK Borča	h	2-0	Stojanović, Stojčev
29/8	Spartak	a	0-1	
12/9	Jagodina	h	2-1	Đoković, Vukovljak
19/9	Rad	a	0-0	
26/9	Napredak	h	0-1	
3/10	Metalac	a	0-1	
17/10	Smederevo	h	3-1	Mugoša 2, Knežević
24/10	Crvena zvezda	a	0-1	
31/10	OFK Beograd	h	2-0	Dmitrović (p), Mugoša
7/11	Mladi radnik	a	1-2	Milovanović
21/11	Vojvodina	a	0-3	
28/11	Javor	h	1-0	Grkajac
6/12	Hajduk	a	0-2	
12/12	Čukarički	h	2-1	Mugoša, Grkajac

2010
27/2	Partizan	h	0-3	
6/3	BSK Borča	a	0-2	
17/3	Spartak	h	1-2	Dmitrović
20/3	Jagodina	a	1-0	Spirovski
24/3	Rad	h	0-0	
27/3	Napredak	a	0-2	
3/4	Metalac	h	1-0	Dmitrović (p)
10/4	Smederevo	a	0-0	
17/4	Crvena zvezda	h	0-0	
21/4	OFK Beograd	a	2-3	Nikodijević, Stojanović (p)
24/4	Mladi radnik	h	1-0	Nikodijević
1/5	Vojvodina	h	0-0	
8/5	Javor	a	1-1	Kostić
13/5	Hajduk	h	1-1	Kostić
16/5	Čukarički	a	0-1	

No	Name	Nat	DoB	Pos	Aps	(s)	Gls
7	André Ronaldo de Souza Esposito "ANDREZINHO"	BRA	11/8/82	M	4	(2)	
13	Zoran ANTIĆ		7/2/75	D	15	(1)	
22	Milan DAVIDOV		1/6/79	M	14		
6	Boban DMITROVIĆ		2/4/72	D	28		3
7	Ivan ĐOKOVIĆ		20/12/82	M	7	(4)	1
4	Dragan DRAGUTINOVIĆ		17/1/80	D	10	(0)	
2	Dušan DUNJIĆ		29/3/87	D	10	(2)	
12	Branko GRAHOVAC	MNE	25/6/83	G	15		
9	Igor GRKAJAC		26/4/87	A	7	(9)	2
4	Aleksandar IGNJATOVIĆ		11/4/88	D	7		
33	Radiša ILIĆ		20/9/77	G	15		
77	Filip KNEŽEVIĆ		8/11/91	M	6	(17)	1
11	Zoran KOSTIĆ		14/11/82	M	25		2
14	Slavko MARIĆ		7/3/84	D	25		
10	Dušan MARTINOVIĆ		22/12/87	M	8	(3)	
17	Marko MASLAĆ		9/9/90	D	6	(1)	
23	Bogdan MILIČIĆ		6/1/89	D	3	(6)	
19	Dragan MILOVANOVIĆ		3/1/86	A	10	(5)	1
5	Nemanja MILUNOVIĆ		31/5/89	D	1		
10	Marko MUGOŠA	MNE	4/4/84	M	12	(1)	4
24	Slađan NIKODIJEVIĆ		1/5/90	A	6	(1)	2
25	Dragiša PEJOVIĆ		31/7/82	D	6	(3)	
21	Nebojša PRTENJAK		10/5/83	M	14	(5)	
16	Danilo RADULOVIĆ		4/7/90	M		(3)	
3	Ilija SPASOJEVIĆ	MNE	9/11/87	A	3	(4)	
22	Stefan SPIROVSKI	MKD	23/8/90	M	8	(4)	1
3	Boban STOJANOVIĆ		27/2/79	A	10	(6)	2
8	Miloš STOJČEV		19/1/87	M	24	(1)	1

26	Miloš TOMAŠEVIĆ		30/4/90	M	5	(3)	
28	Slobodan VUKOVLJAK		13/3/90	A	1	(3)	1
20	WILLIAM Rocha Alves	BRA	7/5/86	M	25	(1)	

BSK BORČA
Coach – Šefki Arifovski; (24/4/10) Miodrag Radanović
Founded – 1937
Stadium – Borča (3,500)

2009
15/8	Mladi radnik	h	2-3	Kajević, Matić
22/8	Borac	a	0-2	
29/8	Javor	h	1-0	Knežević
13/9	Hajduk	a	0-0	
19/9	Čukarički	h	2-0	Babić, Alivodić
26/9	Partizan	a	1-2	Babić
3/10	Vojvodina	h	0-4	
17/10	Spartak	h	0-2	
24/10	Jagodina	a	0-2	
31/10	Rad	h	0-0	
7/11	Napredak	a	2-1	Živadinović, Đukić (p)
21/11	Metalac	h	0-0	
28/11	Smederevo	a	1-1	Đukić (p)
5/12	Crvena zvezda	h	0-1	
12/12	OFK Beograd	a	2-0	Đukić, Savić

2010
27/2	Mladi radnik	a	0-2	
6/3	Borac	h	2-0	Knežević, Đukić (p)
13/3	Javor	a	0-1	
20/3	Hajduk	h	3-0	Kajević, Đukić, Babić
24/3	Čukarički	a	0-1	
27/3	Partizan	h	1-2	Obrovac
3/4	Vojvodina	a	0-2	
10/4	Spartak	a	1-2	Đukić
17/4	Jagodina	h	1-4	Đukić
21/4	Rad	a	0-2	
24/4	Napredak	h	1-1	Đukić
1/5	Metalac	a	3-1	Obrovac (p), Knežević, Alivodić
8/5	Smederevo	h	0-0	
13/5	Crvena zvezda	a	3-1	Đukić, Krstić, Radunović
16/5	OFK Beograd	h	1-0	Krstić

No	Name	Nat	DoB	Pos	Aps	(s)	Gls
9	Enver ALIVODIĆ		27/12/84	A	28	(1)	2
20	Dejan BABIĆ		20/4/89	M	19	(3)	3
24	Marko BOŠKOVIĆ		15/4/82	D	14	(3)	
25	Nikola ČESAREVIĆ		3/10/83	M	8	(7)	
22	Aleksandar ĐUKIĆ		30/11/80	A	25	(4)	9
1	Nemanja DŽODŽO		12/12/86	G	11		
11	Slobodan JANKOVIĆ		29/8/81	G	19		
14	Asmir KAJEVIĆ	MNE	15/2/90	M	10	(11)	2
5	Zoran KNEŽEVIĆ		15/8/86	M	24	(1)	3
18	Vladimir KRSTIĆ		28/6/87	M	10	(10)	2
10	Vladimir MATIĆ		12/7/83	A	8	(7)	1
29	Amir MEMIŠEVIĆ		29/5/88	A		(9)	
8	Miloš MILIVOJEVIĆ		17/11/86	A		(5)	
13	Branislav MILOŠEVIĆ		13/5/88	D	24	(1)	
8	Ivan OBROVAC		8/12/86	M	13		2
7	Nebojša PEJIĆ	BIH	5/1/88	M	9	(3)	
6	Aleksandar RADUNOVIĆ		9/5/80	D	28		1
15	Stefan SAVIĆ	MNE	8/1/91	D	21		1
12	Stefan STOJANOVIĆ		12/1/88	D	8	(1)	
3	Borislav TOPIĆ	BIH	22/5/84	M	14	(1)	
17	Milan VIGNJEVIĆ		30/3/89	M	4	(4)	
28	Ivan VUKADINOVIĆ		21/8/84	D	15	(3)	
4	Dragan ŽARKOVIĆ		16/4/86	D	15	(1)	
26	Predrag ŽIVADINOVIĆ		7/7/83	A	3	(12)	1

SERBIA

FK CRVENA ZVEZDA
Coach – Vladimir Petrović; (21/3/10) Ratko Dostanić
Founded – 1945
Stadium – FK Crvena zvezda (52,000)
MAJOR HONOURS:
European Champion Clubs' Cup - (1) 1991;
World Club Cup - (1) 1991;
Yugoslav/Serbian League - (25) 1951, 1953, 1956, 1957, 1959, 1960, 1964,
1968, 1969, 1970, 1973, 1977, 1980, 1981, 1984, 1988, 1990, 1991, 1992,
1995, 2000, 2001, 2004, 2006, 2007;
Yugoslav/Serbian Cup - (23) 1948, 1949, 1950, 1958, 1959, 1964, 1968,
1970, 1971, 1982, 1985, 1990, 1993, 1995, 1996, 1997, 1999, 2000, 2002,
2004, 2006, 2007, 2010.

2009
15/8	Jagodina	a	3-0	*Lekić 2, Blažić*
23/8	Rad	h	1-0	*Perović*
30/8	Napredak	a	1-1	*Lekić*
12/9	Metalac	h	3-0	*Lekić 2, Lazetić*
20/9	Smederevo	a	3-0	*Perović, Bogdanović (p), Jevtić*
27/9	Vojvodina	a	1-0	*Perović*
3/10	OFK Beograd	h	2-1	*Perović, Bogdanović*
17/10	Mladi radnik	a	1-0	*Awal Issah*
24/10	Borac	h	1-0	*Bogdanović*
31/10	Javor	a	2-0	*Vilotić, Lekić*
7/11	Hajduk	h	1-0	*Sávio*
21/11	Čukarički	a	3-0	*Lekić 2, Jevtić*
28/11	Partizan	h	1-2	*og (Knežević)*
5/12	BSK Borča	a	1-0	*Jevtić*
12/12	Spartak	h	5-2	*Cadú, Perović 2, Blažić, Jevtić*

2010
27/2	Jagodina	h	1-0	*Ignjatijević*
7/3	Rad	a	2-1	*Vilotić, Ignjatijević*
13/3	Napredak	h	2-1	*Ninkov, Jevtić*
20/3	Metalac	a	1-2	*Bogdanović (p)*
24/3	Smederevo	h	2-1	*Cadú (p), Lazović*
28/3	Vojvodina	h	3-0	*Lekić 2, Trifunović*
3/4	OFK Beograd	a	2-0	*Perović, Lekić*
10/4	Mladi radnik	h	4-1	*Jevtić 2, Cadú (p), Sávio*
17/4	Borac	a	0-0	
21/4	Javor	h	0-1	
25/4	Hajduk	a	1-0	*og (Kasalica)*
1/5	Čukarički	h	4-0	*Jevtić 3, Trifunović*
8/5	Partizan	a	0-1	
13/5	BSK Borča	h	1-3	*Sávio*
16/5	Spartak	a	1-0	*Lekić*

No	Name	Nat	DoB	Pos	Aps	(s)	Gls
26	Mohammed AWAL ISSAH	GHA	4/4/86	M	19	(4)	1
25	Marko BLAŽIĆ		2/8/85	M	13	(5)	2
32	Vladimir BOGDANOVIĆ		5/10/86	M	19	(7)	4
20	Carlos Eduardo de Fiori Mendes "CADÚ"	BRA	31/8/86	M	14	(7)	3
19	Nemanja CVETKOVIĆ		8/2/80	D	2	(2)	
18	Slavoljub ĐORĐEVIĆ		15/2/81	D	26		
6	Nikola IGNJATIJEVIĆ		12/12/83	D	21	(1)	2
21	Aleksandar JEVTIĆ		30/3/85	A	17	(11)	10
17	Nikola LAZETIĆ		9/2/78	M	20		1
8	Darko LAZOVIĆ		15/9/90	M	1	(8)	1
9	Dejan LEKIĆ		7/6/85	A	23	(4)	12
14	Nikola MIKIĆ		13/9/85	D	3	(3)	
10	Marko MUGOŠA	MNE	4/4/84	M		(1)	
30	Nemanja NIKOLIĆ	MNE	1/1/88	M	3	(8)	
24	Pavle NINKOV		20/4/85	D	25		1
33	Bojan PAVLOVIĆ		8/11/86	G	1		
23	Slavko PEROVIĆ		9/6/89	A	23	(4)	7
29	Miloš RELJIĆ		12/6/89	A		(1)	
16	Stevan RELJIĆ		31/3/86	D	4		
28	Vujadin SAVIĆ		1/7/90	D	6	(8)	
2	SÁVIO Oliveira do Valle	BRA	1/11/84	D	23	(4)	3
22	Saša STAMENKOVIĆ		5/1/85	G	29		

11	Miloš TRIFUNOVIĆ	15/10/84	A	5	(6)	2
13	Đorđe TUTORIĆ	5/3/83	D		(2)	
3	Nikola VASILJEVIĆ	19/12/83	D	5	(1)	
15	Milan VILOTIĆ	21/10/86	D	28		2

FK ČUKARIČKI
Coach – Miloljub Ostojić; (23/8/09) Srđan Vasiljević; (27/2/10) Simo Krunić
Founded – 1926
Stadium – FK Čukarički Stankom (3,120)

2009
15/8	Javor	h	0-1	
23/8	Hajduk	a	1-2	*Krčmarević*
29/8	Vojvodina	h	1-3	*Tintor*
13/9	Partizan	h	1-1	*Zavišić*
19/9	BSK Borča	a	0-2	
26/9	Spartak	h	0-3	
3/10	Jagodina	a	0-2	
18/10	Rad	h	2-1	*Ribić, Kiso*
24/10	Napredak	a	2-0	*Kiso, Bunjevčević*
31/10	Metalac	h	0-1	
7/11	Smederevo	h	0-1	
21/11	Crvena zvezda	h	0-3	
28/11	OFK Beograd	a	1-3	*Krčmarević (p)*
5/12	Mladi radnik	h	1-1	*Nedeljković*
12/12	Borac	a	1-2	*Nedeljković*

2010
27/2	Javor	a	2-2	*Trajković, Stojmirović*
7/3	Hajduk	h	2-0	*Zavišić, Petronijević*
14/3	Vojvodina	a	0-4	
20/3	Partizan	a	0-3	
24/3	BSK Borča	h	1-0	*Okuka*
27/3	Spartak	a	0-1	
3/4	Jagodina	h	2-1	*Krčmarević, Džiknić*
11/4	Rad	a	0-2	
17/4	Napredak	h	2-1	*Trajković, Grubješić*
21/4	Metalac	a	1-0	*Grubješić*
25/4	Smederevo	h	0-0	
1/5	Crvena zvezda	a	0-4	
8/5	OFK Beograd	h	0-0	
13/5	Mladi radnik	a	4-1	*Grubješić, Stojmirović, Petronijević, Trajković*
16/5	Borac	h	1-0	*Trajković*

No	Name	Nat	DoB	Pos	Aps	(s)	Gls
14	Miljan ANĐELIĆ		25/6/86	D	4	(1)	
25	Mirko BUNJEVČEVIĆ		5/2/78	D	11		1
10	Mihailo DOBRAŠINOVIĆ		19/6/86	M	4	(6)	
9	Jovan DŽIKNIĆ		26/4/89	A	9	(3)	1
7	Nikola GRUBJEŠIĆ		29/6/84	A	14		3
50	Bojan ISAILOVIĆ		25/3/80	G	8		
1	Budimir JANOŠEVIĆ		21/10/89	G	7		
24	Vladimir JEVĐENIJEVIĆ		19/1/86	D	7		
8	Miloš JOKIĆ		7/6/87	M		(3)	
4	Nebojša JOKSIMOVIĆ		1/4/81	D	12		
6	Ivan KECOJEVIĆ	MNE	10/4/88	D	25		
28	Nenad KISO	BIH	30/4/89	M	21	(5)	2
26	Stefan KOČANOVIĆ		14/11/90	A		(1)	
15	Dušan KOLAREVIĆ		19/4/87	M	2	(1)	
33	Nikola KRČMAREVIĆ		18/12/91	M	19	(5)	3
31	Danijel MORARIJU		21/3/91	M	1	(2)	
35	Igor NEDELJKOVIĆ		24/9/91	A	3	(8)	2
13	Dražen OKUKA		5/3/86	D	27		1
15	Tomislav PAJOVIĆ		15/3/86	D	2		
27	Bojan PAVLOVIĆ		1/2/85	M	11	(1)	
14	Miroslav PETRONIJEVIĆ		6/12/87	M	9	(5)	2
3	Ivan POPOVIĆ		3/11/79	D	21		
1	Saša RADIVOJEVIĆ		10/4/79	G	15		
16	Marko RAJIĆ		30/7/91	A	2	(9)	
17	Vladimir RIBIĆ		28/3/81	A	10		1

23	Nikola RNIĆ		11/1/84	M		(12)	
7	Eugene SEPUYA	UGA	1/4/83	A	3		
12	Sreten STANIĆ		15/2/84	M	10	(1)	
2	Vladimir STANOJEVIĆ		1/5/90	D		(2)	
11	Aleksandar STOJMIROVIĆ		11/12/82	M	9	(1)	2
8	Vladimir TINTOR		1/9/79	M	4	(6)	1
10	Nikola TRAJKOVIĆ		5/1/81	M	13		4
12	Aleksandar TRNINIĆ		27/3/87	D	9		
21	Nenad VIŠNJIĆ		25/3/83	D	2	(5)	
20	Bojan ZAVIŠIĆ		9/8/79	D	21	(6)	2
5	Aleksandar ŽIVANOVIĆ		8/4/87	D	15	(1)	

20	Blažo LALEVIĆ	MNE	11/5/84	M	6	(3)	
22	Novica MAKSIMOVIĆ		4/4/88	M	19	(4)	
1	Angel MANOLOV	BUL	30/12/81	G	15		
15	Ivan MARAŠ	MNE	12/11/91	A	1	(9)	
11	Rodoljub MARJANOVIĆ		27/1/88	A	8		2
6	Đorđe MRĐANIN		26/2/81	D	5	(2)	1
24	Vladimir PANJKOVIĆ		30/12/87	D	8	(6)	2
26	Branko PAULJEVIĆ		1/5/87	A	2	(2)	
4	Siniša RADANOVIĆ		23/11/79	D	14		3
4	Branislav STANIĆ		30/7/88	M	4	(4)	
18	Damir TOPČAGIĆ		8/4/90	D	4	(6)	
5	Branislav TRAJKOVIĆ		29/8/89	D	25	(1)	
10	Miloš ŽIVANOVIĆ		24/7/88	A	27	(3)	6

FK HAJDUK KULA

Coach – Bogdan Korak; (28/11/09) Srđan Kovačević;
(27/2/10) Žarko Soldo
Founded – 1925
Stadium – SPC Hajduk (11,710)

2009
16/8	Vojvodina	h	0-3	
23/8	Čukarički	h	2-1	Fejsa, Kekezović
30/8	Partizan	a	0-1	
13/9	BSK Borča	h	0-0	
19/9	Spartak	a	1-1	Radanović (p)
27/9	Jagodina	h	1-1	Živanović
4/10	Rad	a	1-1	Kiš
18/10	Napredak	h	3-1	Živanović, Davidov, Komazec
24/10	Metalac	a	1-2	Komazec
1/11	Smederevo	h	1-2	og (Komadina)
7/11	Crvena zvezda	a	0-1	
22/11	OFK Beograd	h	0-2	
28/11	Mladi radnik	a	3-1	Radanović, Živanović, Bogić
6/12	Borac	h	2-0	Živanović, Davidov
12/12	Javor	a	1-1	Radanović

2010
27/2	Vojvodina	a	2-3	Marjanović 2
7/3	Čukarički	a	0-2	
14/3	Partizan	h	0-2	
20/3	BSK Borča	a	0-3	
24/3	Spartak	h	2-1	Kekezović 2
27/3	Jagodina	a	0-2	
3/4	Rad	h	2-1	Živanović, Panjković
10/4	Napredak	a	0-2	
17/4	Metalac	h	1-1	Panjković
21/4	Smederevo	a	0-0	
25/4	Crvena zvezda	h	0-1	
1/5	OFK Beograd	a	1-2	Kasalica
9/5	Mladi radnik	h	2-0	Kasalica, Komazec
13/5	Borac	a	1-1	Živanović
16/5	Javor	h	1-1	Mrđanin

No	Name	Nat	DoB	Pos	Aps	(s)	Gls
8	Nikola BOGIĆ		30/6/81	M	27		1
19	Nemanja BOŠKOVIĆ		8/5/90	M	1	(1)	
12	Bojan BRAĆ		28/2/89	G	10		
16	Dušan BRKOVIĆ		20/1/89	D	12	(1)	
11	Aleksandar DAVIDOV		7/10/83	A	13		2
6	Bojan DOJKIĆ		25/10/84	D	2	(2)	
17	Srđan ĐUKANOVIĆ		4/11/80	M	1	(2)	
13	Duško DUKIĆ		21/6/86	D	12	(6)	
3	Darko FEJSA		27/8/87	D	22		1
23	Aleksandar JOVANOVIĆ	BIH	24/3/91	M	13	(1)	
20	Marko JOVANOVIĆ		21/11/78	A	1	(1)	
25	Nemanja JOVŠIĆ		7/10/83	G	5		
9	Filip KASALICA	MNE	17/12/88	A	7	(4)	2
16	Aleksandar KAURIN		25/7/92	D		(1)	
7	Dejan KEKEZOVIĆ		16/6/82	M	20	(1)	3
14	Saša KIŠ		7/4/89	M	19	(2)	1
21	Nikola KOMAZEC		15/11/87	A	12	(14)	3
27	Miloš KOVAČEVIĆ		31/3/91	M	1	(1)	
2	Igor KOZOŠ		4/8/74	M	14	(4)	

FK JAGODINA

Coach – Mladen Dodić
Founded – 1918
Stadium – Pod Đurđevim brdom (15,000)

2009
15/8	Crvena zvezda	h	0-3	
22/8	OFK Beograd	a	0-1	
29/8	Mladi radnik	h	2-0	Vusljanin, Marjanović
12/9	Borac	a	1-2	Đilas
19/9	Javor	h	2-0	Bojović, Đilas
27/9	Hajduk	a	1-1	Cilinšek
3/10	Čukarički	h	2-0	Novković, Beljić
17/10	Partizan	a	0-3	
24/10	BSK Borča	h	2-0	Đilas, Bojović
31/10	Spartak	a	1-1	Vusljanin
7/11	Vojvodina	h	2-2	Cilinšek, Vusljanin (p)
21/11	Rad	h	1-0	Cilinšek
29/11	Napredak	a	1-2	Bojović
5/12	Metalac	h	3-1	Novković 2, Đilas
12/12	Smederevo	a	0-2	

2010
27/2	Crvena zvezda	a	0-1	
6/3	OFK Beograd	h	3-2	Ognjenović, Bojović, Živković B.
14/3	Mladi radnik	a	0-0	
20/3	Borac	h	0-1	
24/3	Javor	a	0-0	
27/3	Hajduk	h	2-0	Mihajlović, Bojović (p)
3/4	Čukarički	a	1-2	Đilas
11/4	Partizan	h	0-0	
17/4	BSK Borča	a	4-1	Ognjenović 2, Novković, Bojović
21/4	Spartak	h	3-1	Beljić, Bojović 2 (1)
24/4	Vojvodina	a	1-4	Bojović
2/5	Rad	a	0-1	
8/5	Napredak	h	1-1	Bojović
13/5	Metalac	a	3-2	Novković, Bojović 2 (1p)
16/5	Smederevo	h	2-0	og (Todorov), Đilas

No	Name	Nat	DoB	Pos	Aps	(s)	Gls
16	Kenneth ASAMOAH	GHA	1/8/88	A		(3)	
21	Marko AVRAMOVIĆ		2/4/87	M	2	(2)	
17	Bojan BELJIĆ		8/5/85	A	12	(12)	2
10	Milan BOJOVIĆ		13/4/87	A	23	(3)	12
3	Luka ČANČAREVIĆ		17/6/84	M	7	(5)	
15	Saša CILINŠEK		28/1/82	D	24	(1)	3
19	Vladimir ĐILAS		3/3/83	A	18	(6)	6
4	Marko ĐORĐEVIĆ		22/5/83	D	23		
32	Dušan IVANOV		17/2/91	M		(1)	
21	Milutin IVANOVIĆ		30/10/90	A	3	(4)	
1	Budimir JANOŠEVIĆ		21/10/89	G	7	(1)	
27	Srđan LUKIĆ		1/2/81	D	15		
6	Saša MARJANOVIĆ		13/11/87	M	16	(7)	1
5	Danijel MIHAJLOVIĆ		2/6/85	D	20	(4)	1
16	Nenad NASTIĆ		8/5/81	D	1	(1)	
24	Boban NIKOLIĆ		8/10/80	D	19	(1)	
23	Miloš NIKOLIĆ		22/2/89	M		(1)	
18	Srđan NOVKOVIĆ		29/3/82	M	29	(1)	5

SERBIA

9	Perica OGNJENOVIĆ	24/2/77	A	22	(3)	3
2	Aleksandar SIMČEVIĆ	15/2/87	D	12	(2)	
7	Nenad ŠLJIVIĆ	8/6/85	M	15		
11	Vladan SPASOJEVIĆ	11/10/80	M	4	(11)	
26	Vukašin TOMIĆ	8/4/87	D	1	(4)	
12	Zoran VASKOVIĆ	14/2/79	G	3		
7	Irfan VUSLJANIN	7/1/86	M	11	(2)	3
25	Zlatko ZEČEVIĆ	10/8/83	G	20		
29	Bojan ŽIVKOVIĆ	10/11/81	M	20	(2)	1
2	Miloš R. ŽIVKOVIĆ	5/2/85	D	2		
8	Miloš V. ŽIVKOVIĆ	24/5/84	M	1	(12)	

FK JAVOR
Coach – Radovan Ćurčić
Founded – 1912
Stadium – Kraj Moravice (5,000)

2009
15/8	Čukarički	a	1-0	Luković
23/8	Partizan	h	1-1	Luković
29/8	BSK Borča	a	0-1	
12/9	Spartak	h	1-0	Trifunović
19/9	Jagodina	a	0-2	
26/9	Rad	h	2-2	Trifunović 2
3/10	Napredak	a	1-1	Trifunović
17/10	Metalac	h	2-0	Stojanović (p), Trifunović
24/10	Smederevo	a	1-1	Pavlović
31/10	Crvena zvezda	h	0-2	
8/11	OFK Beograd	a	0-0	
21/11	Mladi radnik	h	0-0	
28/11	Borac	a	0-1	
5/12	Vojvodina	a	1-0	Egharevba
12/12	Hajduk	h	1-1	Dragović

2010
27/2	Čukarički	h	2-2	Gogić, Cvetković
7/3	Partizan	a	0-0	
13/3	BSK Borča	h	1-0	Račić
20/3	Spartak	a	0-0	
24/3	Jagodina	h	0-0	
28/3	Rad	a	2-3	Stojaković, Račić
3/4	Napredak	h	1-0	Milović
10/4	Metalac	a	0-1	
17/4	Smederevo	h	1-0	Nikitović
21/4	Crvena zvezda	a	1-0	Nikitović (p)
24/4	OFK Beograd	h	0-1	
1/5	Mladi radnik	a	0-1	
8/5	Borac	h	1-1	Račić
13/5	Vojvodina	h	1-1	Eliomar
16/5	Hajduk	a	1-1	Panić

No	Name	Nat	DoB	Pos	Aps	(s)	Gls
1	Igor BONDŽULIĆ		5/10/80	G	3		
22	Bojan ČUKIĆ		5/2/88	M	1	(5)	
7	Ivan CVETKOVIĆ		12/2/81	M	14		1
13	Goran DRAGOVIĆ		20/10/81	D	16	(1)	1
3	Frank EGHAREVBA	NGA	15/12/85	A	6	(7)	1
10	ELIOMAR Correia Silva	BRA	16/3/88	M	8	(6)	1
5	Goran GOGIĆ		24/4/86	M	26	(1)	1
26	Vladimir ILIĆ		23/3/82	D	11	(3)	
6	Đuro JANDRIĆ		22/10/83	D		(1)	
12	Damir KAHRIMAN		19/11/84	G	25		
3	Aleksandar LEPOSAVIĆ		3/11/87	A		(1)	
25	Goran LUKOVIĆ		17/5/78	M	19	(5)	2
6	Boris MILIČIĆ		4/4/79	M	6	(3)	
22	Marko MILINKOVIĆ		4/5/92	D	1		
21	Marko MILOVANOVIĆ		12/8/82	D	29		
20	Milovan MILOVIĆ		24/10/80	D	27		1
17	Marko MOMČILOVIĆ		11/6/87	M	2	(4)	
8	Jovan NIKITOVIĆ		26/10/76	M	24	(5)	2
11	Ifeanyi ONYILO	NGA	31/10/90	A	1	(6)	
29	Nenad PANIĆ		12/11/84	M	10	(14)	1

30	Vladan PAVLOVIĆ		24/2/84	D	30		1
24	Filip PETROV	MKD	23/2/89	A	7	(4)	
9	Stevan RAČIĆ		17/1/84	A	12		3
4	Filip STANISAVLJEVIĆ		20/5/87	M	6	(9)	
15	Igor STOJAKOVIĆ		27/5/80	M	24	(4)	1
19	Nenad STOJANOVIĆ		22/10/79	A	9	(7)	1
9	Miloš TRIFUNOVIĆ		15/10/84	A	11	(3)	5
23	Branko VUJOVIĆ	MNE	24/11/80	G	2	(1)	

FK METALAC
Coach – Nenad Milovanović; (1/5/10) Miodrag Starčević
Founded – 1961
Stadium – Kraj Despotovice (4,000)

2009
15/8	Napredak	a	0-2	
22/8	Vojvodina	a	0-1	
29/8	Smederevo	h	0-2	
12/9	Crvena zvezda	a	0-3	
19/9	OFK Beograd	h	2-1	Betoligar 2
26/9	Mladi radnik	a	0-1	
3/10	Borac	h	1-0	Betoligar
17/10	Javor	a	0-2	
24/10	Hajduk	h	2-1	Krasić (p), Teodorović
31/10	Čukarički	a	1-0	Jeremić
8/11	Partizan	h	0-2	
21/11	BSK Borča	a	0-0	
28/11	Spartak	h	0-0	
5/12	Jagodina	a	1-3	Simović
12/12	Rad	h	1-1	Betoligar

2010
27/2	Napredak	h	1-0	Krasić (p)
6/3	Vojvodina	h	3-1	Perić, Betoligar, Krasić
14/3	Smederevo	a	1-0	Betoligar
20/3	Crvena zvezda	h	2-1	Miljković, Simović
24/3	OFK Beograd	a	2-3	Perić, Rakočević
27/3	Mladi radnik	h	1-0	Jakšić
3/4	Borac	a	0-1	
10/4	Javor	h	1-0	Krasić
17/4	Hajduk	a	1-1	Simović
21/4	Čukarički	h	0-1	
24/4	Partizan	a	1-3	Pavlović B.
1/5	BSK Borča	h	1-3	Krasić
8/5	Spartak	a	0-0	
13/5	Jagodina	h	2-3	Betoligar, Simović
16/5	Rad	a	0-3	

No	Name	Nat	DoB	Pos	Aps	(s)	Gls
20	Ljubomir ARSIĆ		21/10/85	M	2		
14	Misdongard BETOLIGAR	CHA	26/9/85	A	25	(2)	7
24	Dragan DRAGUTINOVIĆ		17/1/80	D	12		
21	Danko FILIPOVIĆ		3/10/78	M	1	(1)	
6	Bojan GOJAK		28/8/79	D	17	(9)	
18	Aleksandar IVANOVIĆ		20/11/88	M	2	(4)	
9	Marko JAKŠIĆ		10/8/83	M	4	(8)	1
15	Slaviša JEREMIĆ		15/2/83	M	11		1
9	Saša JOVANOVIĆ		12/1/88	A	1	(3)	
8	Marko KRASIĆ		1/12/85	D	24	(2)	5
10	Milan MIJAJLOVIĆ		18/9/81	A	1	(5)	
15	Aleksandar MILJKOVIĆ		26/2/90	D	1	(4)	1
3	Ljubo NENADIĆ		29/4/86	M	24		
22	Miloš OBRADOVIĆ		30/3/87	M	6	(6)	
5	Vladimir OTAŠEVIĆ		8/6/86	D	29		
22	Bojan PAVLOVIĆ		1/2/85	M	13		1
2	Petar PAVLOVIĆ		3/3/87	D	21	(4)	
10	Milan PERIĆ		14/4/86	A	9	(2)	2
19	Aleksandar PETROVIĆ		1/2/85	M	5	(5)	
13	Darko RAKOČEVIĆ		13/9/81	D	24		1
23	Vladimir SAVIĆEVIĆ		12/5/86	A	4	(8)	
11	Srđan SIMOVIĆ		17/6/85	M	22	(7)	4
7	Nemanja STOŠKOVIĆ		21/2/90	M	2	(12)	

24	Mirko TEODOROVIĆ		6/8/78	M	10	(1)	1
4	Radojica VASIĆ		25/1/76	M	23		
25	Branko VUJOVIĆ	MNE	24/11/80	G	2		
1	Živko ŽIVKOVIĆ		14/4/89	G	28	(1)	
20	Zoran ZUKIĆ		6/6/81	A		(3)	
19	Dragiša ŽUNIĆ		29/6/78	D	7		

18	Nenad SREĆKOVIĆ		11/4/88	D	10	(2)	
12	Miloš STJEPOVIĆ		12/4/79	A		(2)	
22	Goran STOKIĆ		17/9/80	D	26		1
9	Milan SVOJIĆ		9/10/85	A	12	(4)	
3	Aleksandar VASILJEVIĆ		19/6/82	D	11		

FK MLADI RADNIK
Coach – Nebojša Maksimović
Founded – 1926
Stadium – Vašarište (5,000)

2009
15/8	BSK Borča	a	3-2	Matić, Luka, Janković
22/8	Spartak	h	1-1	Luka
29/8	Jagodina	a	0-2	
12/9	Rad	h	0-0	
19/9	Napredak	a	0-0	
26/9	Metalac	h	1-0	Đorđević (p)
3/10	Smederevo	a	0-0	
17/10	Crvena zvezda	h	0-1	
24/10	OFK Beograd	a	0-3	
31/10	Vojvodina	a	0-3	
7/11	Borac	h	2-1	Luka, Franklin
21/11	Javor	a	0-0	
28/11	Hajduk	h	1-3	Franklin
5/12	Čukarički	a	1-1	Franklin
12/12	Partizan	h	1-1	Lazić

2010
27/2	BSK Borča	h	2-0	Luka, Nedeljković
6/3	Spartak	a	0-2	
14/3	Jagodina	h	0-0	
21/3	Rad	a	2-3	Miletić, Prebiračević
24/3	Napredak	h	1-1	Miletić (p)
27/3	Metalac	a	0-1	
3/4	Smederevo	h	0-0	
10/4	Crvena zvezda	a	1-4	Stokić
17/4	OFK Beograd	h	0-2	
21/4	Vojvodina	h	1-3	Jašić
24/4	Borac	a	0-1	
1/5	Javor	h	1-0	Luka
9/5	Hajduk	a	0-2	
13/5	Čukarički	h	1-4	Cenić
16/5	Partizan	a	0-6	

No	Name	Nat	DoB	Pos	Aps	(s)	Gls
17	Goran ANTELJ		6/4/88	A	2	(2)	
5	Boban CENIĆ		13/11/81	D	27		1
10	Živorad ĐORĐEVIĆ		16/10/73	M	13	(5)	1
24	FRANKLIN Ayodele Amankwa	NGA	24/8/87	A	12	(10)	3
29	Dušan JANKOVIĆ		17/8/83	A	1	(6)	1
13	Vladimir JAŠIĆ		4/1/84	D	24	(1)	1
15	Ivica JOVANOVIĆ		4/12/87	A	1	(5)	
4	Milan LAZIĆ		27/10/82	D	18	(3)	1
7	Predrag LUKA		11/5/88	M	30		5
6	Zoran MATIĆ		12/2/85	M	13	(6)	1
20	Igor MIJOVIĆ		11/7/85	D	1		
8	Zoran MILETIĆ		7/3/77	M	9	(14)	2
29	Bojan MIŠIĆ		29/9/79	G	8		
14	Nenad NEDELJKOVIĆ		10/10/86	A	9	(13)	1
26	Goran OBRADOVIĆ		25/12/86	D	3		
21	Nemanja OBRIĆ		15/4/84	M	4	(2)	
17	Bratislav PEJČIĆ		17/1/83	M	6	(1)	
1	Mitar PEJOVIĆ		1/11/83	G	22		
21	Milan PERIĆ		16/4/86	A	3	(2)	
15	Nemanja PREBIRAČEVIĆ		23/1/87	D	8	(1)	1
26	Dušan RAJDA		11/6/83	M	3		
30	Dejan RISTIĆ		6/3/78	M	25		
11	Miroslav SAVANOVIĆ		10/3/85	M	3	(8)	
23	Eugene SEPUYA	UGA	1/4/83	A	4	(2)	
19	Bojan SIMIĆ		29/6/76	D	22		

FK NAPREDAK
Coach – Nenad Sakić; (29/11/09) Jovica Škoro
Founded – 1946
Stadium – SC Mladost (10,800)

2009
15/8	Metalac	h	2-0	Punoševac 2
22/8	Smederevo	a	0-1	
30/8	Crvena zvezda	h	1-1	Punoševac
12/9	OFK Beograd	a	1-1	Antwi
19/9	Mladi radnik	h	0-0	
26/9	Borac	a	1-0	Punoševac (p)
3/10	Javor	h	1-1	Martinović
18/10	Hajduk	a	1-3	Vujović
24/10	Čukarički	h	0-2	
1/11	Partizan	a	1-3	Antwi
7/11	BSK Borča	h	1-2	Binić (p)
21/11	Spartak	a	0-2	
29/11	Jagodina	h	2-1	Leandro, Antwi
6/12	Rad	a	1-2	Binić
13/12	Vojvodina	h	2-0	Binić, Antwi

2010
27/2	Metalac	a	0-1	
6/3	Smederevo	h	2-2	Antwi, Binić
13/3	Crvena zvezda	a	1-2	Mitrović
20/3	OFK Beograd	h	1-2	Antwi
24/3	Mladi radnik	a	1-1	Pavlović P.
27/3	Borac	h	2-0	Vujović 2
3/4	Javor	a	0-1	
10/4	Hajduk	h	2-0	Antwi 2
17/4	Čukarički	a	1-2	Gašić
21/4	Partizan	h	0-1	
24/4	BSK Borča	a	1-1	Pavlović P.
1/5	Spartak	h	2-3	Gašić, Antwi
8/5	Jagodina	a	1-1	Vujović
13/5	Rad	h	2-1	Vranješ, Mitrović (p)
16/5	Vojvodina	a	0-7	

No	Name	Nat	DoB	Pos	Aps	(s)	Gls
16	Radosav ALEKSIĆ		6/3/86	D	6	(6)	
9	Yaw ANTWI	GHA	15/6/85	A	25	(1)	9
5	Ivan BABIĆ		2/1/81	D	23	(1)	
11	Vladan BINIĆ	CZE	25/1/87	M	18	(2)	4
4	Nenad DAMJANOVIĆ	MNE	8/7/86	D	2		
15	Danijel GAŠIĆ		19/1/87	D	20	(1)	2
18	Ezeh IKECHUKWU	NGA	20/12/87	A	2	(6)	
23	Vladimir KRNJINAC		20/3/83	M	25	(2)	
20	LEANDRO Rodrigues Montebeler Scuccuglia	BRA	31/1/82	M	11	(4)	1
8	Dušan MARTINOVIĆ		22/12/87	M	12	(3)	1
6	Nikola MIKIĆ		13/9/85	D	15		
12	Dalibor MILENKOVIĆ		9/1/87	G	7		
25	Stefan MILOSAVLJEVIĆ		11/9/92	M		(1)	
27	Nikola MILOŠEVIĆ		17/4/92	M	2		
21	Nemanja MILOVANOVIĆ		12/6/91	M		(3)	
2	Nenad MILUNOVIĆ		3/6/83	M	2		
22	Nikola MIRKOVIĆ		26/7/91	G	5		
8	Nikola MITROVIĆ		2/1/87	M	14		2
7	Predrag PAVLOVIĆ		19/6/86	M	13	(2)	2
3	Radmilo PAVLOVIĆ		29/8/81	D	2	(5)	
19	Igor PETROVIĆ		18/3/87	D	28	(2)	
18	Josip PROJIĆ		23/8/87	D	9		
13	Bratislav PUNOŠEVAC		9/7/87	A	15	(8)	4
22	Danilo PUSTINJAKOVIĆ		12/3/77	G	9		
3	Ilija RISTANIĆ	BIH	11/2/86	D	3		

SERBIA

4	Milorad SAVIĆ		27/6/91	D		(1)	
1	Bojan ŠEJIĆ		14/7/83	G	9		
6	Marko SPASOJEVIĆ		3/10/90	M	5	(5)	
17	Dragan STOJKOV	MKD	23/2/88	M	10	(9)	
2	Goran STOJKOVIĆ		6/12/83	D		(2)	
14	Ognjen VRANJEŠ	BIH	24/10/89	D	12		1
10	Predrag VUJOVIĆ		20/8/83	A	23	(4)	4
24	Boban VUKMIROVIĆ		5/4/85	D	3	(7)	
24	YONG Lee-ja	PRK	15/5/91	M		(2)	

OFK BEOGRAD

Coach – Dejan Đurđević
Founded – 1911
Stadium – Omladinski stadion (13,900)
MAJOR HONOURS:
Yugoslav League - (5) 1931, 1933, 1935, 1936, 1939;
Yugoslav Cup - (4) 1953, 1955, 1962, 1966.

2009

15/8	Spartak	a	1-0	Simić
22/8	Jagodina	h	1-0	Sinđić
30/8	Rad	a	2-0	Simić, Šćepović
12/9	Napredak	h	1-1	og (Babić)
19/9	Metalac	a	1-2	Žeravica
26/9	Smederevo	h	1-0	Marković
3/10	Crvena zvezda	a	1-2	Jelić
17/10	Vojvodina	a	0-0	
24/10	Mladi radnik	h	3-0	Milić 2, Jelić (p)
31/10	Borac	a	0-2	
8/11	Javor	h	0-0	
22/11	Hajduk	a	2-0	Simić 2
28/11	Čukarički	h	3-1	Simić, Milić, Trivunović
6/12	Partizan	a	0-3	
12/12	BSK Borča	h	1-1	

2010

28/2	Spartak	h	0-1	
6/3	Jagodina	a	2-3	Simić, Milić
14/3	Rad	h	3-2	Milić, Planić, Oumarou
20/3	Napredak	a	2-1	Marković 2
24/3	Metalac	h	3-2	Milić, og (Rakočević), Injac
27/3	Smederevo	a	1-0	Žeravica
3/4	Crvena zvezda	h	0-2	
10/4	Vojvodina	h	2-2	Oumarou, Sinđić
17/4	Mladi radnik	a	2-0	Krstić 2
21/4	Borac	h	3-2	Krstić, Nikolić, Injac
24/4	Javor	a	1-0	Marković
1/5	Hajduk	h	2-1	Žeravica, og (Fejsa)
8/5	Čukarički	a	0-0	
13/5	Partizan	h	0-3	
16/5	BSK Borča	a	0-1	

No	Name	Nat	DoB	Pos	Aps	(s)	Gls
16	Miloš ADAMOVIĆ		6/7/86	M		(1)	
20	Bojan ALEKSIĆ		12/4/91	A		(4)	
7	Nikola BELJIĆ		14/5/83	D	28	(1)	
26	Roberto Carvalho CAUÊ	BRA	22/4/87	D	7	(2)	
17	Nenad INJAC		4/9/85	A	2	(9)	2
9	Petar JELIĆ	BIH	18/10/86	A	9	(6)	2
6	Nikola JOLOVIĆ		4/5/79	D	5	(1)	
23	Darko JOVANDIĆ		4/2/82	D	7	(4)	
19	Miloš KRSTIĆ		7/3/87	A	10	(8)	3
5	Branko LAZAREVIĆ		14/5/84	D	16		
4	Nenad LAZAREVSKI	MKD	3/7/86	D	4		
20	Emir LOTINAC		25/9/87	D	5		
21	Aleksandar MARKOVIĆ		13/3/91	M	17	(4)	4
3	Aleksandar MIJATOVIĆ		20/9/82	D	10	(1)	
29	Nemanja MILIĆ		25/5/90	A	16	(4)	6
17	Zoran MILOVAC		29/10/88	M		(4)	
40	Andrej MRKELA		9/4/92	M		(1)	
11	Danilo NIKOLIĆ		29/7/83	D	20		1
14	Aboubakar OUMAROU	CMR	4/1/87	A	20	(3)	2

15	Petar PLANIĆ		16/3/89	D	21		1
32	Mladen POPOVIĆ		29/8/88	A		(4)	
18	Milan RODIĆ		2/4/91	D	10	(2)	
1	Bojan ŠARANOV		22/10/87	G	28		
28	Stefan ŠĆEPOVIĆ		10/1/90	A	3	(9)	1
22	Nikola SIMIĆ		30/7/81	M	21	(4)	6
8	Uroš SINĐIĆ		19/1/86	M	19	(6)	2
4	Nebojša SKOPLJAK		12/5/87	D	1		
3	Vojislav STANKOVIĆ		22/9/87	D	15		
27	Đorđe TOPALOVIĆ		11/1/79	G	2		
10	Veseljko TRIVUNOVIĆ		13/1/80	M	21	(1)	1
13	Miloš ŽERAVICA		22/7/88	M	13	(11)	3

FK PARTIZAN

Coach – Slaviša Jokanović; (5/9/09) Goran Stevanović;
(16/4/10) Aleksandar Stanojević
Founded – 1945
Stadium – FK Partizan (30,900)
MAJOR HONOURS:
Yugoslav/Serbian League - (22) 1947, 1949, 1961, 1962, 1963, 1965, 1976,
1978, 1983, 1986, 1987, 1993, 1994, 1996, 1997, 1999, 2002, 2003, 2005,
2008, 2009, 2010;
Yugoslav/Serbian Cup (11) 1947, 1952, 1954, 1957, 1989, 1992, 1994, 1998,
2001, 2008, 2009.

2009

15/8	Borac	h	5-0	Ljajić, Diarra 3, Cléo
23/8	Javor	a	1-1	Obradović
30/8	Hajduk	h	1-0	og (Đukanović)
13/9	Čukarički	a	1-1	Ilić B.
20/9	Vojvodina	h	1-0	Ilić B.
26/9	BSK Borča	h	2-1	Cléo (p), Diarra
4/10	Spartak	a	1-1	Diarra
17/10	Jagodina	h	3-0	Krstajić, Diarra, Ljajić
25/10	Rad	a	3-2	Cléo 2, Fejsa
1/11	Napredak	h	3-1	Krstajić, Ljajić, Petrović
8/11	Metalac	a	2-0	Petrović, Moreira
21/11	Smederevo	h	2-1	Diarra, Petrović
28/11	Crvena zvezda	a	2-1	Diarra, Cléo
6/12	OFK Beograd	h	3-0	Ljajić, Petrović, Diarra
12/12	Mladi radnik	a	1-1	Moreira

2010

27/2	Borac	a	3-0	Cléo, Fejsa, Davidov
7/3	Javor	h	0-0	
14/3	Hajduk	a	2-0	Tomić 2
20/3	Čukarički	h	3-0	Davidov, Cléo, Petrović
24/3	Vojvodina	a	2-1	Cléo 2
27/3	BSK Borča	a	2-1	Cléo, Jovanović M.
3/4	Spartak	h	2-0	Lomić 2
11/4	Jagodina	a	0-0	
18/4	Rad	h	2-1	Moreira, Ilić S.
21/4	Napredak	a	1-0	Diarra
24/4	Metalac	h	3-1	Cléo 2, Diarra
1/5	Smederevo	a	2-0	Cléo (p), Ilić S.
8/5	Crvena zvezda	h	1-0	Petrović
13/5	OFK Beograd	a	3-0	Cléo, Ilić B., Petrović
16/5	Mladi radnik	h	6-0	Diarra 3, Ilić B., Davidov, Lomić

No	Name	Nat	DoB	Pos	Aps	(s)	Gls
17	Miloš BOGUNOVIĆ		10/6/85	A	3	(5)	
27	Mladen BOŽOVIĆ	MNE	1/8/84	G	25		
14	Darko BRAŠANAC		12/2/92	M		(3)	
31	Rajko BREŽANČIĆ		21/8/89	D	2	(1)	
9	Cléverson Gabriel Córdova "CLÉO"	BRA	9/8/85	A	24	(3)	14
23	Aleksandar DAVIDOV		7/10/83	M	9	(6)	3
26	Lamine DIARRA	SEN	20/12/83	A	25	(4)	14
4	Nenad ĐORĐEVIĆ		7/8/79	D	14		
5	Ljubomir FEJSA		14/8/88	M	19	(1)	2
52	Goran GAVRANČIĆ		2/8/78	D	3		
19	Brana ILIĆ		16/2/85	A	7	(5)	4

SERBIA

22	Saša ILIĆ		30/12/77	M	13	(1)	2
21	Branislav JOVANOVIĆ		21/9/85	M	6	(7)	
13	Marko JOVANOVIĆ		26/3/88	D	15	(2)	1
6	Radenko KAMBEROVIĆ		13/2/83	D	1	(2)	
24	Srđan KNEŽEVIĆ		15/4/85	D	21	(2)	
20	Mladen KRSTAJIĆ		4/3/74	D	21	(1)	2
22	Adem LJAJIĆ		29/9/91	M	11	(3)	4
11	Marko LOMIĆ		13/9/83	D	24	(1)	3
17	Predrag MIJIĆ		5/11/84	M	1	(3)	
10	Almami Samori da Silva						
	MOREIRA	POR	16/6/78	A	23	(2)	3
37	Ivan OBRADOVIĆ		25/7/88	D	2		1
8	Radosav PETROVIĆ		8/3/89	M	18	(6)	7
30	Aleksandar RADOSAVLJEVIĆ		21/12/82	G	5		
3	Vojislav STANKOVIĆ		22/9/87	D	7	(3)	
2	Siniša STEVANOVIĆ		12/1/89	D	10	(1)	
7	Nemanja TOMIĆ		21/1/88	M	21	(8)	2
77	Nikola VUJOVIĆ	MNE	23/6/81	M		(3)	
25	WASHINGTON Roberto						
	Mariano da Silva	BRA	19/6/85	A		(7)	

9	Andrija KALUĐEROVIĆ		5/7/87	A	25	(4)	17
27	Nemanja KOJIĆ		3/2/90	A		(7)	1
5	Radomir KOKOVIĆ		6/1/84	M	25		1
14	Aleksandar KOSORIĆ	BIH	30/1/87	D	10		
8	LI Chunyu	CHN	9/10/86	M	1		
2	Bojan MALIŠIĆ		14/1/85	D	7	(1)	
19	Luka MILIVOJEVIĆ		7/4/91	M	3	(6)	
14	Nemanja OBRADOVIĆ		29/5/89	A		(4)	
15	Tomislav PAJOVIĆ		15/3/86	D	20	(3)	2
12	Miroslav PETRONIJEVIĆ		6/12/87	M		(5)	
25	Aleksandar PETROVIĆ		8/2/85	D	14		
11	Milan PRŠO		29/6/90	A	7	(4)	2
36	Jovan RADIVOJEVIĆ		19/10/82	M	19	(6)	1
6	Marko RANĐELOVIĆ		16/8/84	D	18	(1)	
21	Nikola RASPOPOVIĆ		18/10/89	M	13	(2)	
20	Bratislav RISTIĆ		21/1/80	M	20	(4)	
28	Marko STANOJEVIĆ		22/6/88	M	8	(4)	2
7	Nenad STOJAKOVIĆ		4/4/80	M	8	(3)	
17	Nikola STOJILJKOVIĆ		17/8/92	A	1		
4	Aleksandar TODOROVSKI	MKD	26/2/84	D	27	(1)	
8	Saša VIDOVIĆ		15/6/82	M	7		

FK RAD
Coach – Marko Nikolić
Founded – 1958
Stadium – FK Rad (6,000)

2009
16/8	Smederevo	h	3-2	Kaluđerović, Radivojević, Jovančić
23/8	Crvena zvezda	a	0-1	
30/8	OFK Beograd	h	0-2	
12/9	Mladi radnik	a	0-0	
19/9	Borac	h	0-0	
26/9	Javor	a	2-2	Jovančić, Andrić
4/10	Hajduk	h	1-1	Jovančić
18/10	Čukarički	a	1-2	Kaluđerović
25/10	Partizan	h	2-3	Kaluđerović 2
31/10	BSK Borča	a	0-0	
7/11	Spartak	h	1-3	Kaluđerović
21/11	Jagodina	a	0-1	
29/11	Vojvodina	h	1-0	Kaluđerović
6/12	Napredak	h	2-1	Andrić 2
12/12	Metalac	a	1-1	Kaluđerović

2010
27/2	Smederevo	a	1-2	Kaluđerović
7/3	Crvena zvezda	h	1-2	Koković (p)
14/3	OFK Beograd	a	2-3	Kaluđerović, Jovančić
21/3	Mladi radnik	h	3-2	Kaluđerović 2, Pajović
24/3	Borac	a	0-0	
28/3	Javor	h	3-2	Kaluđerović 2 (1p), Dimitrijević
3/4	Hajduk	a	1-2	Andrić
11/4	Čukarički	h	2-0	Jovančić, Kaluđerović
18/4	Partizan	a	1-2	Pršo
21/4	BSK Borča	h	2-0	Pršo, Stanojević
24/4	Spartak	a	0-1	
2/5	Jagodina	h	1-0	Kojić
8/5	Vojvodina	a	3-2	Kaluđerović, og (Tumbasević), Stanojević
13/5	Napredak	a	1-2	Kaluđerović
16/5	Metalac	h	3-0	Dimitrijević, Kaluđerović, Pajović

No	Name	Nat	DoB	Pos	Aps	(s)	Gls
18	Srđan AJKOVIĆ	MNE	15/10/91	A		(5)	
22	Nemanja ANDRIĆ		13/6/87	M	23	(5)	4
26	Milan BORJAN		23/10/87	G	13		
3	Đorđe ČOTRA		13/9/84	D	18	(3)	
1	Branislav DANILOVIĆ		24/6/88	G	17		
10	Uroš DELIĆ		10/8/87	M	9	(5)	
7	Miloš DIMITRIJEVIĆ		16/2/84	M	7	(3)	2
23	Vladimir JOVANČIĆ		31/5/87	A	10	(11)	5
16	Milan JOVANOVIĆ		14/10/83	A		(3)	

FK SMEDEREVO
Coach – Blagoje Paunović
Founded – 1924
Stadium – FK Smederevo (17,200)
MAJOR HONOURS:
Yugoslav Cup - (1) 2003.

2009
16/8	Rad	a	2-3	Ćeran, Jovanović
22/8	Napredak	h	1-0	Ranković S.
29/8	Metalac	a	2-0	Ranković S., Stamenković
13/9	Vojvodina	a	1-1	Zečević
20/9	Crvena zvezda	h	0-3	
26/9	OFK Beograd	a	0-1	
3/10	Mladi radnik	h	0-0	
17/10	Borac	a	1-3	Jovanović
24/10	Javor	h	1-1	Ranković S.
1/11	Hajduk	a	2-1	Jovanović, Ćeran
7/11	Čukarički	h	1-0	Mladenović
21/11	Partizan	a	1-2	Ćeran
28/11	BSK Borča	h	1-1	Komadina
5/12	Spartak	a	0-2	
12/12	Jagodina	h	2-0	Ranković S. 2

2010
27/2	Rad	h	2-1	Ognjanović, Ranković S.
6/3	Napredak	a	2-2	Živković 2
14/3	Metalac	h	0-1	
20/3	Vojvodina	h	1-0	Živković
24/3	Crvena zvezda	a	1-2	Živković
27/3	OFK Beograd	h	0-1	
3/4	Mladi radnik	a	0-0	
10/4	Borac	h	0-0	
17/4	Javor	a	0-1	
21/4	Hajduk	h	0-0	
25/4	Čukarički	a	0-0	
1/5	Partizan	h	0-2	
8/5	BSK Borča	a	0-0	
13/5	Spartak	h	2-0	Stojanović, Milosavljević
16/5	Jagodina	a	0-2	

No	Name	Nat	DoB	Pos	Aps	(s)	Gls
19	Branislav ATANACKOVIĆ		5/8/83	D	23		
11	Vojislav BOJATOVIĆ		26/8/82	A	6	(19)	
7	Dragan ĆERAN		6/10/87	A	15		3
3	Miroslav GEGIĆ		27/8/84	M	5	(6)	
2	Nemanja ILIĆ		15/2/88	D	1		
17	Slobodan JANKOVIĆ		1/2/86	A		(3)	
20	Ivan JOVANOVIĆ		1/12/78	A	27		3
6	Aleksandar KOMADINA		8/11/75	D	24	(1)	

4	Željko KOVAČEVIĆ		30/10/81	D	12		
22	Željko KUZMIĆ	BIH	2/11/84	G	6	(1)	
15	Zoran LJUBINKOVIĆ		24/7/82	D	1		
5	Slavko LUKIĆ		14/3/89	D	13	(3)	
23	Aleksandar MILJKOVIĆ		23/8/82	M	11	(2)	
14	Marko MILOSAVLJEVIĆ		20/12/87	M	7	(15)	1
24	Igor MIOVIĆ		11/7/85	A	12	(1)	
7	Marko MITROVIĆ		8/7/78	M	13		
10	Nenad MLADENOVIĆ		13/12/76	A	22	(3)	1
27	Marko NIKOLIĆ		28/9/89	A		(1)	
4	Dejan OGNJANOVIĆ	MNE	21/6/78	A	9		1
8	Miloš RADOSAVLJEVIĆ		10/5/87	M		(2)	
15	Milan RAKIČ	SVN	2/9/81	M	4	(4)	
12	Dejan RANKOVIĆ		25/7/76	G	23		
21	Saša RANKOVIĆ		21/9/79	A	26	(1)	6
33	RENAN Oliveira do Valle	BRA	11/3/86	M	1	(9)	
1	Borivoje RUMENIĆ		10/5/90	G	1		
2	Predrag STAMENKOVIĆ		7/7/77	D	13		1
26	Nenad STANIĆ		14/8/87	M	1		
23	Marko STANOJEVIĆ		8/7/91	D	1		
18	Slaviša STOJANOVIĆ		27/1/89	M	4	(12)	1
16	Zoran TODOROV		31/10/82	M	16	(1)	
9	Milorad ZEČEVIĆ		26/10/72	A	8	(1)	1
13	Dejan ŽIVKOVIĆ		28/4/82	M	25	(3)	4

19	Aleksandar JOVETIĆ		5/1/89	D		(1)	
17	Predrag MIJIĆ		5/11/84	M	10	(4)	1
5	Nikola MILANKOVIĆ		23/4/86	D	20	(2)	1
21	Marko MIRIĆ		26/3/87	M	19	(8)	4
10	Asmir MISINI		29/9/85	A	8	(6)	
11	Aleksandar NOSKOVIĆ		12/12/88	M	4	(24)	4
15	Emmanuel OLETU	NGA	8/12/83	D	11		
24	Zoran PEŠIĆ		25/9/83	D	6		
20	Igor POPOVIĆ		10/8/83	D	25		1
18	Nenad PUHALAK		5/9/92	A		(5)	
2	Darko PUŠKARIĆ		13/7/85	D	18		1
3	Dragan ŠARAC		27/9/75	D	25		1
4	Slobodan SIMOVIĆ		22/5/89	M	12	(2)	2
17	Siniša STEVANOVIĆ		12/1/89	D	15		
8	Vladimir TORBICA		20/9/80	A	24	(1)	1
14	Vojo UBIPARIP		10/5/88	A	25		10
13	Vladimir VESELINOV		25/5/84	M	21		3
23	Lazar VESELINOVIĆ		4/8/86	A	2	(2)	
9	Srđan VUJAKLIJA		21/3/88	A	1	(9)	

FK SPARTAK ZLATIBOR VODA
Coach – Zoran Milenković
Founded – 1921
Stadium – Gradski (25,000)

2009

15/8	OFK Beograd	h	0-1	
22/8	Mladi radnik	a	1-1	Simović
29/8	Borac	h	1-0	Simović
12/9	Javor	a	0-1	
19/9	Hajduk	h	1-1	Mirić
26/9	Čukarički	a	3-0	Ubiparip 2, Mijić
4/10	Partizan	h	1-1	Mirić
17/10	BSK Borča	a	2-0	Veselinov, Nosković
24/10	Vojvodina	h	0-1	
31/10	Jagodina	h	1-1	Janjuš
7/11	Rad	a	3-1	Bratić, Ubiparip 2
21/11	Napredak	h	2-0	Ubiparip 2
28/11	Metalac	a	0-0	
5/12	Smederevo	h	2-0	Janjuš 2
12/12	Crvena zvezda	a	2-5	Janjuš, Nosković

2010

28/2	OFK Beograd	a	1-0	Ubiparip
6/3	Mladi radnik	h	2-0	Veselinov, Nosković
17/3	Borac	a	2-1	Veselinov, Ubiparip
20/3	Javor	h	0-0	
24/3	Hajduk	a	1-2	Mirić
27/3	Čukarički	h	1-0	Popović
3/4	Partizan	a	0-2	
10/4	BSK Borča	h	2-1	Ubiparip, Šarac
18/4	Vojvodina	a	1-0	Milanković
21/4	Jagodina	a	1-3	Torbica
24/4	Rad	h	1-0	Ubiparip
1/5	Napredak	a	3-2	Mirić, Nosković, Puškarić
8/5	Metalac	h	0-0	
13/5	Smederevo	a	0-2	
16/5	Crvena zvezda	h	0-1	

No	Name	Nat	DoB	Pos	Aps	(s)	Gls
7	Marko ADAMOVIĆ		11/3/91	M	13	(2)	
12	Branimir ALEKSIĆ		24/12/90	G	1		
22	Darko BOŠKOVIĆ	MNE	16/9/87	M	10	(15)	
6	Vidak BRATIĆ		20/10/76	D	24		1
9	Milorad JANJUŠ		15/7/82	A	7	(3)	4
1	Milan JOVANIĆ		31/7/85	G	29		

FK VOJVODINA
Coach – Dragoslav Stepanović; (17/10/09) Branko Babić; (14/3/10) Milan Đuričić
Founded – 1914
Stadium – Karađorđe (15,754)
MAJOR HONOURS:
Yugoslav League - (2) 1966, 1989.

2009

16/8	Hajduk	a	3-0	Tadić 2 (1p), Medojević
22/8	Metalac	h	1-0	Mrđa
29/8	Čukarički	a	3-1	Mrđa, Tadić, Djurovski
13/9	Smederevo	h	1-1	Tadić (p)
20/9	Partizan	a	0-1	
27/9	Crvena zvezda	h	0-1	
3/10	BSK Borča	a	4-0	Mrđa 3, Aleksić
17/10	OFK Beograd	h	0-0	
24/10	Spartak	a	1-0	Mrđa
31/10	Mladi radnik	h	3-0	Aleksić, Tadić 2
7/11	Jagodina	a	2-2	Medojević, Stjepanović
21/11	Borac	h	3-0	Mrđa 3
29/11	Rad	a	0-1	
5/12	Javor	h	0-1	
13/12	Napredak	a	0-2	

2010

27/2	Hajduk	h	3-2	Mrđa, Tumbasević 2
6/3	Metalac	a	1-3	Bilbija
14/3	Čukarički	h	4-0	Mrđa 2, Tadić, Merebashvili (p)
20/3	Smederevo	a	0-1	
24/3	Partizan	h	1-2	Djurovski
28/3	Crvena zvezda	a	0-3	
3/4	BSK Borča	h	2-0	Tadić, Mrđa (p)
10/4	OFK Beograd	a	2-2	Tadić, Mudrinski
18/4	Spartak	h	0-1	
21/4	Mladi radnik	a	3-1	Mrđa 2, Katai
24/4	Jagodina	h	4-1	Pletsch, Mrđa, Djurovski, Tadić
1/5	Borac	a	0-0	
8/5	Rad	h	2-3	Mrđa, Djurovski
13/5	Javor	a	1-1	Mrđa
16/5	Napredak	h	7-0	Mrđa 4 (1p), Katai 2, Mudrinski

No	Name	Nat	DoB	Pos	Aps	(s)	Gls
20	Sadick ADAMS	GHA	1/1/91	A		(3)	
6	Nnaemeka AJURU	NGA	28/9/86	M	20	(1)	
33	Danijel ALEKSIĆ		30/4/91	A	7	(5)	2
21	Nemanja BILBIJA	BIH	2/11/90	A	8	(2)	1
1	Željko BRKIĆ		9/7/86	G	23		
10	Mario DJUROVSKI	MKD	11/12/85	M	17	(4)	4
34	Damir DRINIĆ		20/7/89	G	2		
5	Dušan ĐURIŠIĆ	MNE	20/12/77	D	7		

7	Ivan GVOZDENOVIĆ		19/8/78	D	2	(3)	
24	Dejan KARAN		13/8/88	D	10	(3)	
27	Aleksandar KATAI		6/2/91	A	1	(5)	3
12	Aleksandar KESIĆ		18/8/87	G	5		
9	Mikheil KHUTSISHVILI	GEO	28/1/79	A	1	(4)	
2	Joseph Nestroy KIZITO	UGA	27/7/82	D	9		
26	Vladimir KOVAČEVIĆ		11/11/92	D	1	(1)	
28	Risto LAKIĆ	MNE	3/7/83	D	2	(2)	
26	Darko LOVRIĆ		24/11/80	D	13	(1)	
19	Boban MAKSIMOVIĆ	SUI	10/10/85	M		(5)	
3	Slobodan MEDOJEVIĆ		20/10/90	M	22	(3)	2
17	Giorgi MEREBASHVILI	GEO	15/8/86	M	8	(7)	1
13	Vuk MITOŠEVIĆ		12/2/91	M	6		
81	Dragan MRĐA		23/1/84	A	28	(1)	22
19	Ognjen MUDRINSKI		15/11/91	A	1	(5)	2
23	Dušan NESTOROVIĆ		26/6/86	D	10		
7	Slobodan NOVAKOVIĆ		15/10/86	M	4	(2)	
5	Mitar PEKOVIĆ	MNE	28/9/81	D	7	(6)	
25	Marcelo José PLETSCH	BRA	13/5/76	D	23		1
4	Goran SMILJANIĆ		31/1/90	M		(8)	
11	Slaven STJEPANOVIĆ	MNE	2/11/87	A	13	(12)	1
8	Alin STOICA	ROU	10/12/79	M	4		
18	Đorđe ŠUŠNJAR		18/2/92	A		(1)	
31	Dušan TADIĆ		20/11/88	M	26	(1)	10
14	Janko TUMBASEVIĆ	MNE	14/1/85	M	21	(3)	2
22	Miroslav VULIĆEVIĆ		29/5/85	D	29		

PROMOTED CLUBS

FK INĐIJA
Coach – Milan Đuričić; (27/10/09) Momčilo Raičević
Founded – 1933
Stadium – Stadion FK Inđija (3,500)

FK SEVOJNO
Coach – Ljubiša Stamenković
Founded – 1950
Stadium – 7. juli - kraj Valjaonice (4,350)

SECOND LEVEL FINAL TABLE 2009/10

		Pld	W	D	L	F	A	Pts
1	FK Inđija	34	17	9	8	47	26	60
2	FK Sevojno	34	17	7	10	40	24	58
3	FK Kolubara	34	14	14	6	37	29	56
4	FK Bežanija	34	14	11	9	34	28	53
5	FK Novi Sad	34	14	9	11	34	29	51
6	FK Teleoptik	34	14	8	12	36	31	50
7	FK Proleter	34	13	7	14	41	35	46
8	FK Srem	34	12	10	12	34	37	46
9	FK Novi Pazar	34	13	7	14	33	38	46
10	FK Banat	34	11	12	11	31	28	45
11	FK Radnički Sombor	34	12	9	13	30	32	45
12	FK Zemun	34	11	12	11	39	36	43
13	FK Dinamo	34	12	7	15	32	38	43
14	FK Mladost Lučani	34	9	15	10	33	31	42
15	FK Radnički Niš	34	9	14	11	33	35	41
16	FK Sloga	34	9	12	13	28	32	39
17	FK ČSK Pivara	34	6	14	14	32	48	32
18	FK Mladost Apatin	34	7	7	20	24	61	28

NB FK Zemun – 2 pts deducted.

DOMESTIC CUP 2009/10

KUP SRBIJE

FIRST ROUND

(22/9/09)
OFK Beograd 1, Novi Sad 1 (5-4 on pens)

(23/9/09)
BSK Borča 1, Sevojno 1 (4-5 on pens)
Crvena zvezda 6, Mladost Apatin 1
Čukarički 1, Metalac 1 (2-4 on pens)
Hajduk Kula 1, ČSK Pivara 1 (5-4 on pens)
Novi Pazar 2, Mladi radnik 1
Partizan 3, Inđija 0
Partizan Kosovska Mitrovica 0, Napredak 0 (5-4 on pens)
Proleter 3, Javor 1
Rad 2, Mladost Lučani 3
Radnički Svilajnac 1, Banat 3
Smederevo 4, Kolubara 0
Spartak Zlatibor voda 3, Bežanija 0
Srem 1, Borac 1 (1-4 on pens)
Vojvodina 4, Dinamo Vranje 0
Voždovac 0, Jagodina 1

SECOND ROUND

(28/10/09)
Banat 0, Spartak Zlatibor voda 2
Jagodina 1, Sevojno 0
Metalac 0, Borac 1
Mladost Lučani 1, Vojvodina 3
Novi Pazar 0, Crvena zvezda 1
OFK Beograd 3, Partizan Kosovska Mitrovica 1
Proleter 1, Partizan 2
Smederevo 3, Hajduk Kula 0

QUARTER-FINALS

(25/11/09)
Borac 0, OFK Beograd 2 (Marković 80, Sinđić 81)
Crvena zvezda 3 (Vilotić 14, Perović 50, Lekić 66), Spartak Zlatibor voda 2 (Mijić 40, 86)
Jagodina 1 (Bojović 16), Partizan 2 (Diarra 26, Cléo 49)
Vojvodina 1 (Medojević 4), Smederevo 0

SEMI-FINALS

(14/4/10)
Crvena zvezda 1 (Lekić 87), OFK Beograd 0

(15/4/10)
Partizan 1 (Petrović 44), Vojvodina 3 (Mrđa 35, 48, Đurovski 58)

FINAL

(5/5/10)
Stadion Partizana, Beograd
FK CRVENA ZVEZDA 3 (Jevtić 14, Cadú 62, Trifunović 71)
FK VOJVODINA 0
Referee – Stanković
CRVENA ZVEZDA – Stamenković, Ninkov, Đorđević, Vilotić, Reljić S., Lazetić (Perović 69), Bogdanović, Sávio, Cadú (Trifunović 66), Jevtić (Blažić 80), Lekić.
VOJVODINA – Brkić, Vulićević, Karan, Pletsch, Tumbasević, Ajuru, Medojević (Mudrinski 75), Novaković (Stjepanović 67), Djurovski (Mitošević 58), Tadić, Mrđa.

SLOVAKIA

Weiss's young charges emerge with credit

Slovakia were the only FIFA World Cup finals debutants in South Africa. That they reached the second round was a success in itself, but to do so by eliminating the reigning champions in one of the most exciting games of the tournament constituted an achievement of which every Slovakian football follower will forever be immensely proud.

For most of their stay in South Africa, Slovakia were like many of the other competing teams, preferring caution to adventure and defence to attack. However, for one glorious afternoon in Johannesburg, Vladimír Weiss's inexperienced side rediscovered the form that had enabled them to win a qualifying group containing Poland, Slovenia and the Czech Republic. Needing a win against Italy to counter the disappointment of earlier results against New Zealand (1-1) and Paraguay (0-2), they suddenly emerged from their shell, took the game to their vaunted opponents and beat them. The final seconds might have been nerve-shredding, but the 3-2 win, sealed by two goals from centre-forward Róbert Vittek and one, with his first touch, from substitute Kamil Kopúnek, will unquestionably go down as the greatest in Slovakia's short history.

Happy homecoming

Unfortunately, Weiss's men were unable to offer a repeat in the last 16 against the Netherlands, going out with a 2-1 defeat in Durban. They earned a consolation farewell gift when Vittek drove in his fourth goal of the tournament, from the penalty spot, with the last kick of the game. But there could be no complaints about the outcome; nor were there as Weiss magnanimously accepted defeat, safe in the knowledge that he and his players would receive a warm reception on returning home.

Róbert Vittek found the net four times for Slovakia at the World Cup to become his country's all-time top scorer

While Vittek's goals earned him widespread acclaim, Ján Mucha ran him close as Slovakia's stand-out performer with his excellence in goal. Ján Ďurica proved an adaptable defender, the coach's namesake son offered some exciting cameos on the wing, and the introduction into central midfield of Juraj Kucka against Italy proved a masterstroke as the AC Sparta Praha player added some creativity and control to an area in which the team had previously struggled – largely as a result of record cap-holder Miroslav Karhan's absence from the tournament through injury. As for star skipper Marek Hamšík, he showed only fleeting glimpses of his class, the SSC Napoli playmaker perhaps predictably saving his best for the game against Italy.

Žilina triumph

Only two members of Weiss's World Cup squad spent the 2009/10 season in their homeland – Kopúnek of FC Spartak Trnava and Kornel Sálata of ŠK Slovan Bratislava. There was no representation at all for the team that finished top of the Slovakian 1. Liga table, MŠK Žilina. Led by former Czech international Pavel Hapal, the northerners finished three points ahead of Slovan to win their fifth national title in nine years and draw level with the club from the capital as the country's joint-record champions.

Inspired by their workaholic skipper Róbert Jež, Žilina were worthy victors of a season-long duel with the defending champions that remained undecided until the penultimate round, when Hapal's men crushed DAC 1904 Dunajská Streda 4-0 at home, two goals from Tomáš

Slovenský futbalový zväz (SFZ)

Junácka 6
SK-83280 Bratislava
tel – +421 2 4924 9150
fax – +421 2 4924 9595
website – futbalsfz.sk
email – office@futbalsfz.sk
Year of Formation – 1938

President – František Laurinec
General Secretary – Miloš Tomáš

SLOVAKIA

INTERNATIONAL TOURNAMENT APPEARANCES
FIFA World Cup – (1) 2010 (2nd round).

TOP FIVE ALL-TIME CAPS
Miroslav Karhan (96); Róbert Vittek (74); Szilárd Németh (58); Stanislav Varga (54); Robert Tomaschek (52)
TOP FIVE ALL-TIME GOALS
Róbert Vittek (23); Szilárd Németh (22); Marek Mintál (14); Miroslav Karhan (13); Peter Dubovský (12)

Coaching changes

While Žilina stayed loyal to Hapal, Slovan went through three coaches during the campaign. Dušan Uhrin, who had been brought in to replace 2008/09 1. Liga title-winning boss Ladislav Pecko for his European experience, was dismissed in August after a 5-0 defeat by AFC Ajax in the UEFA Europa League (following home and away defeats by Olympiacos FC in the UEFA Champions League qualifiers) and replaced by Michal Hipp, who in turn passed on the reins in January to the inexperienced former Slovakian international defender Dušan Tittel. There would be no league title for Tittel but he did steer Slovan to a resounding 6-0 win over Spartak Trnava in the Slovakian Cup final, delivering a first win in the competition for 11 years.

There was dejection for the other club from the capital, MFK Petržalka, who, having lost their sponsor, benefactor, coach and several players to Slovan, were relegated from the 1. Liga – less than five years after representing Slovakia, as FC Artmedia Bratislava, in the UEFA Champions League. As Petržalka disappeared from view, the team relegated 12 months earlier, FC ViOn Zlaté Moravce, returned to the top flight, while European football beckoned for both Dukla Banská Bystrica – led to third place in the Super Liga by 72-year-old Jozef Jankech – and Nitra – propelled into fourth spot by the 18 goals of 32-year-old Róbert Rák, who, for the second time in five seasons, scooped the 1. Liga's Golden Boot.

Oravec and another from the man who just edged him as the club's leading marksman, Ivan Lietava, paving the way for a night of celebration in the renovated Pod Dubňom stadium.

Žilina had led Slovan by a point at the winter break but were briefly replaced at the top in late March when they lost for the first time at home – aagainst bête noire FC Nitra – then, four days later, lost the head-to-head clash against Slovan 2-0 in Bratislava. But Žilina's strength of character shone through in the run-in as they reeled off six successive wins while Slovan surprisingly dropped nine points over the same period, including three away to their bogey side, MFK Ružomberok.

NATIONAL TEAM RESULTS 2009/10

Date	Opponent		Venue	Score	Scorers
12/8/09	Iceland	A	Reykjavik	1-1	Vittek (35)
5/9/09	Czech Republic (WCQ)	H	Bratislava	2-2	Šesták (59), Hamšík (73p)
9/9/09	Northern Ireland (WCQ)	A	Belfast	2-0	Šesták (15), Hološo (67)
10/10/09	Slovenia (WCQ)	H	Bratislava	0-2	
14/10/09	Poland (WCQ)	A	Chorzow	1-0	Gancarczyk (3og)
14/11/09	United States	H	Bratislava	1-0	Hamšík (26p)
17/11/09	Chile	H	Zilina	1-2	Šesták (17)
3/3/10	Norway	H	Zilina	0-1	
29/5/10	Cameroon	N	Klagenfurt (AUT)	1-1	Kopúnek (6)
5/6/10	Costa Rica	H	Bratislava	3-0	Sequeira (16og), Vittek (47), Šesták (87p)
15/6/10	New Zealand (WCF)	N	Rustenburg (RSA)	1-1	Vittek (50)
20/6/10	Paraguay (WCF)	N	Bloemfontein (RSA)	0-2	
24/6/10	Italy (WCF)	N	Johannesburg (RSA)	3-2	Vittek (25, 73), Kopúnek (89)
28/6/10	Netherlands (WCF)	N	Durban (RSA)	1-2	Vittek (90+4p)

SLOVAKIA

NATIONAL TEAM APPEARANCES 2009/10

Coach – Vladimír WEISS 22/9/64			Isl	CZE	NIR	SVN	POL	Usa	Chi	Nor	Cmr	Crc	NZL	PAR	ITA	NED	Caps	Goals
Ján MUCHA	5/12/82	Legia (POL)	G46	G	G	G	G	G		G		G	G	G	G	G	19	-
Peter PEKARÍK	30/10/86	Wolfsburg (GER)	D	D	D	D	D	s90	D	D84	D88	s46		D	D	D	24	1
Csaba HORVÁTH	2/5/82	Den Haag (NED)	D54														1	-
Radoslav ZABAVNÍK	16/9/80	Terek (RUS) /Mainz (GER)	D	D	D	D			D	s46	D	s77	D	D	D	D88	47	1
Marek ČECH	26/1/83	West Brom (ENG)	D79	s82			D90				D	D46	D				41	5
Miroslav KARHAN	21/6/76	Mainz (GER)	M			s46	s85	M90		M							96	13
Stanislav ŠESTÁK	16/12/82	Bochum (GER)	M	M82	A65		A74	s61	M69			s46	A	A81	A70	s92	36	11
Ján KOZÁK	22/4/80	Slovan Bratislava /Timişoara (ROU)	M46				M85	s90	M46	s84	M46				M		25	2
Marek HAMŠÍK	27/7/87	Napoli (ITA)	M	M75*		M	M	M90	M85	M84	M	M46	M	M	M	M87	36	8
Miroslav STOCH	19/10/89	Twente (NED)	M46		M80	M			M61	s69	s71	M46	M77	s84	s83	M	16	1
Róbert VITTEK	1/4/82	Lille (FRA) /Ankaragücü (TUR)	A63	A	M	M80			M68	s85	A61		A67	A84	A	A92	74	23
Dušan PERNIŠ	28/11/84	Žilina /Dundee United (SCO)	s46								s85						2	-
Filip HOLOŠKO	17/1/84	Beşiktaş (TUR)	s46	M87	s65					s61		s67	s81	s70			40	5
Erik JENDRIŠEK	26/10/86	Kaiserslautern (GER)	s46	s87	s80	s80	A	A	A	M	A46	s77	M		M94	A71	18	2
Martin PETRÁŠ	2/11/79	Cesena (ITA)	s54				D		D46	s84					s94		39	1
Vladimír WEISS	30/11/89	Man. City (ENG) /Bolton (ENG)	s63	M74	M91	M	M65	M82			M77	s46	M	M91	M	M	12	-
Kamil KOPÚNEK	18/5/84	Spartak Trnava	s79		M		M			s74	M	s46			s87	s71	11	2
Martin ŠKRTEĽ	15/12/84	Liverpool (ENG)		D	D	D		D	D		D	D13	D	D	D	D	43	5
Ján ĎURICA	10/12/81	Lokomotiv Moskva (RUS) /Hannover (GER)		D	D	D		D	D		D	D	D	D	D	D	43	1
Zdeno ŠTRBA	9/6/76	Xanthi (GRE)		M	M	M84	D	s90	M79	D74		M46	M	M	M87		24	-
Marek SAPARA	31/7/82	Rosenborg (NOR) /Ankaragücü (TUR)		s74	s91			s79			M71	s46			s87		26	2
Martin JAKUBKO	26/2/80	FC Moskva (RUS) /Saturn (RUS)				A46		s46			s88				s88		25	4
Ján NOVÁK	6/3/85	Košice					s84	s65									4	-
Kornel SALÁTA	24/1/85	Slovan Bratislava					D					s13	D83				5	-
Dušan ŠVENTO	1/8/85	Salzburg (AUT)					s74	s68	s34	s77	s46						20	1
Juraj KUCKA	26/2/87	Sparta Praha (CZE)					s82	M34		M77		s91			M	M	9	-
Ľuboš KAMENÁR	17/6/87	Nantes (FRA)							G								2	-
Dušan KUCIAK	21/5/85	Vaslui (ROU)									G85						3	-

DOMESTIC LEAGUE 2009/10

1. LIGA FINAL TABLE

		Pld	Home W	D	L	F	A	Away W	D	L	F	A	Total W	D	L	F	A	Pts
1	MŠK Žilina	33	15	1	1	37	7	8	3	5	22	10	23	4	6	59	17	73
2	ŠK Slovan Bratislava	33	10	6	1	30	11	11	1	4	24	13	21	7	5	54	24	70
3	Dukla Banská Bystrica	33	10	5	1	27	11	5	6	6	18	19	15	11	7	45	30	56
4	FC Nitra	33	9	2	5	25	17	5	4	8	17	23	14	6	13	42	40	48
5	MFK Ružomberok	33	11	3	3	21	12	2	5	9	12	23	13	8	12	33	35	47
6	FK Senica	33	5	6	5	20	20	7	1	9	14	24	12	7	14	34	44	43
7	FC Spartak Trnava	33	10	2	5	35	17	2	3	11	17	29	12	5	16	52	46	41
8	1. FC Tatran Prešov	33	7	5	4	17	7	4	0	13	15	31	11	5	17	32	38	38
9	MFK Dubnica	33	6	4	6	16	14	2	8	7	11	28	8	12	13	27	42	36
10	DAC 1904 Dunajská Streda	33	5	7	4	19	18	2	5	10	9	29	7	12	14	28	47	33
11	MFK Košice	33	8	1	8	20	24	0	8	8	12	33	8	9	16	32	57	33
12	MFK Petržalka	33	6	5	6	25	21	1	3	12	8	30	7	8	18	33	51	29

TOP GOALSCORERS

- 18 Róbert RÁK (Nitra)
- 13 Ivan LIETAVA (Žilina)
- 12 Ján NOVÁK (Košice)
- 11 Juraj HALENÁR (Slovan)
  - Tomáš ORAVEC (Žilina)
  - Olexandr PYSCHUR (Ružomberok)
- 10 Pavol MASARYK (Slovan)
- 9 Peter DOLEŽAJ (Trnava)
- 8 Ľuboš BERNÁTH (Trnava)
  - Tomáš MAJTÁN (Petržalka/Žilina)

CLUB-BY-CLUB

DAC 1904 DUNAJSKÁ STREDA
Coach – Kurt Garger (AUT); (10/5/10) (Mikuláš Radványi)
Founded – 1904
Stadium – DAC (6,500)
MAJOR HONOURS:
Czechoslovakian Cup – (1) 1987.

2009
11/7	Košice	a	0-2	
18/7	Ružomberok	h	1-1	Koejoe
25/7	Petržalka	a	0-1	
1/8	Tatran	h	3-0	Majus, Seelaus, og (Josl)
8/8	Dubnica	a	3-1	Koejoe 2, Nkendo
15/8	Senica	a	1-0	og (Homola)
22/8	Banská Bystrica	h	0-2	
29/8	Nitra	a	0-2	
19/9	Žilina	a	0-1	
27/9	Trnava	h	2-1	Nkendo, Adiaba
3/10	Košice	h	1-1	Nkendo
17/10	Ružomberok	a	0-0	
24/10	Petržalka	h	3-2	Bognár 3
28/10	Slovan	h	0-0	
31/10	Tatran	a	0-0	
7/11	Dubnica	h	1-1	Koejoe
21/11	Senica	h	1-2	Koejoe
28/11	Banská Bystrica	a	0-2	
5/12	Nitra	h	2-2	Németh K., Adiaba

2010
27/2	Slovan	a	0-2	
6/3	Žilina	h	0-2	
13/3	Trnava	a	0-7	
20/3	Košice	a	1-2	Marcin
24/3	Ružomberok	h	0-0	
27/3	Petržalka	a	1-1	Nikolić
3/4	Tatran	h	2-1	Marcin, Nkendo
10/4	Dubnica	a	1-1	Kazlauskas
17/4	Senica	a	2-2	Yavarzadeh, Bajevski
25/4	Banská Bystrica	h	1-1	Koejoe
1/5	Nitra	a	0-1	
5/5	Slovan	h	0-1	
8/5	Žilina	a	0-4	
15/5	Trnava	h	2-1	Bajevski (p), Halimi

No	Name	Nat	DoB	Pos	Aps	(s)	Gls
14	Martin Diolong ABENA	CMR	14/6/86	M		(1)	
6	Clovis Guy ADIABA Bondoa	CMR	2/1/87	D	20		2
26	Pierre Hervé ATEME Elanga	CMR	25/9/86	A	2	(2)	
29	Aleksandar BAJEVSKI	MKD	8/12/79	M	11	(2)	2
13	Zoltán BOGNÁR		9/2/88	A	7	(7)	3
24	Lukáš BODEČEK	CZE	25/4/88	D		(2)	
18	Jean Paul BOYA	CMR	23/9/84	M	13	(2)	
28	Krisztian BRUNCZVIK		25/10/89	M		(1)	
12	Jacques Aurélien ELONG ELONG	CMR	20/2/81	M	9	(3)	
2	Samuel FUZIK		2/3/85	M	1	(1)	
20	Ilami HALIMI	MKD	8/11/75	M	18	(3)	1
10	Ismail Ahmed HASSAN	FRA	23/5/87	M	16	(1)	
19	David HELÍSEK	CZE	4/9/82	D	31		
27	Marius KAZLAUSKAS	LTU	1/5/84	D	23	(3)	1
9	Samuel KOEJOE	NED	17/8/74	A	25	(5)	6
16	Tomáš LÉNARTH		7/6/90	M	1	(5)	
5	Egidijus MAJUS	LTU	5/1/84	D	18		1
23	Ján MARCIN		7/9/85	D	11	(1)	2
13	Nikola MICHELLINI	BIH	27/2/82	D	7	(1)	
3	Krisztián NÉMETH		5/4/75	D	4	(3)	1
25	Zsolt NÉMETH		1/2/91	D	2	(11)	
4	Staniša NIKOLIĆ	BIH	28/11/80	D	26		1
11	Guillaume NKENDO	CMR	6/6/86	A	14	(6)	4
23	Jean Michel NLEND	CMR	8/5/86	A	1		
1	Juraj NOVOTA		29/11/83	G	28		
24	Sladjan PAJIĆ	SRB	28/3/92	M	1	(4)	
17	Milan PÁLENÍK	CZE	18/5/77	D	1		
15	Stephan PALLA	AUT	15/5/89	D	14		
20	Yüksel SARIYAR	AUT	1/8/79	M	6	(1)	
21	Markus SEELAUS	AUT	16/2/87	M	21	(5)	1
8	Giovanni SPERANZA	ITA	6/3/82	M	7	(7)	
32	Grzegorz SZAMOTULSKI	POL	13/5/76	G	5		

15	Cemil TOSUN	AUT	6/2/87	M	1		
2	Velimir VARGA	SVN	26/1/80	D	3		
11	Nemanja VIDAKOVIĆ	SRB	29/9/85	A	3	(3)	
7	Nyron WAU	NED	24/11/82	M	5		
7	Richard WEMMER	AUT	18/2/81	M	1	(1)	
5	Behshad YAVARZADEH	IRN	7/1/83	M	7	(2)	1

MFK DUBNICA

Coach – Ľuboš Nosický; (18/8/09) Peter Gergely
Founded – 1926
Stadium – Dubnica (6,500)

2009

11/7	Ružomberok	a	1-1	Zápotoka T.
18/7	Petržalka	h	0-0	
25/7	Tatran	a	0-0	
1/8	Senica	a	1-2	Zápotoka T.
8/8	Dunajská Streda	h	1-3	Šulek
15/8	Banská Bystrica	a	0-3	
22/8	Nitra	h	3-0	Filo, Nosek, Kiška
30/8	Slovan	a	1-1	Zápotoka T.
12/9	Žilina	h	0-1	
19/9	Trnava	a	0-1	
26/9	Košice	h	1-0	Ľupták
3/10	Ružomberok	h	1-2	Kiška
17/10	Petržalka	a	0-7	
24/10	Tatran	h	1-0	Ondráš
31/10	Senica	h	0-1	
7/11	Dunajská Streda	a	1-1	Vavrík
21/11	Banská Bystrica	h	1-2	Filo
29/11	Nitra	a	1-0	Jánošík
5/12	Slovan	h	0-1	

2010

27/2	Žilina	a	0-4	
6/3	Trnava	h	2-1	Vavrík, Ondráš
13/3	Košice	a	1-1	Poliaček
20/3	Ružomberok	a	0-1	
24/3	Petržalka	h	2-0	Šulek 2
27/3	Tatran	a	0-2	
3/4	Senica	a	1-1	Bruško (p)
10/4	Dunajská Streda	h	1-1	Filo
17/4	Banská Bystrica	a	1-1	Ľupták
24/4	Nitra	h	1-0	Bruško (p)
1/5	Slovan	a	2-2	Gorelka, Poliaček
5/5	Žilina	h	1-1	Gorelka
8/5	Trnava	a	1-0	Augustíni
15/5	Košice	h	1-1	Gorelka

No	Name	Nat	DoB	Pos	Aps	(s)	Gls
7	Oliver AUGUSTÍNI		12/6/90	M	2	(10)	1
1	Pavol BAJZA		4/9/91	G	14		
3	Lukáš BEŇO		7/1/89	D	4	(2)	
22	Tomáš BRUŠKO		21/2/83	M	12	(1)	2
18	Juraj CHUPÁČ		17/3/88	D	14		
4	Igor DRŽÍK		10/4/82	M	18		
2	Miroslav DUGA		29/1/89	D	16	(6)	
1	Ján ĎURČO		25/2/88	G	8		
20	Michal FILO		28/2/84	A	20	(5)	3
22	Matej GORELKA		3/4/89	M	6	(6)	3
7	Erik GRENDEL		13/10/88	M	8		
19	Milan HARVILKO		18/7/88	M		(1)	
30	Marek IGAZ		13/9/86	G	6	(1)	
18	Peter JÁNOŠÍK		2/1/88	D	16		1
6	Peter KIŠKA		10/5/81	M	2	(8)	2
14	Erik ĽUPTÁK		7/6/90	M	17	(10)	2
13	Juraj MASARÍK		1/3/90	A	1	(3)	
16	Róbert MATEJOV		5/7/88	M	1	(7)	
3	Martin NOSEK		26/1/87	D	32		1
10	Igor OBERT		14/7/82	D	28		

8	Marcel ONDRÁŠ		21/9/85	D	26	(1)	2
6	Pavol POLIAČEK		2/4/88	M	8	(3)	2
9	Andrej PORÁZIK		27/6/77	A	23	(2)	
24	Radoslav STRAKA		10/9/89	M		(3)	
11	Peter ŠULEK		21/9/88	M	27	(3)	3
3	Michal TRHAN		9/3/89	M		(1)	
13	Hector TUBONEMI	NGA	5/9/88	A	2	(9)	
21	Juraj VAVRÍK		9/2/89	M	17	(6)	2
31	Richard ZAJAC		16/8/76	G	5		
13	Ján ZÁPOTOKA		23/3/88	M		(1)	
25	Lukáš ZÁPOTOKA		23/9/85	M	10	(7)	
15	Tomáš ZÁPOTOKA		4/2/87	A	18		3

DUKLA BANSKÁ BYSTRICA

Coach – Jozef Jankech
Founded – 1965
Stadium – Na Štiavničkách (9,800)
MAJOR HONOURS:
Slovakian Cup – (1) 2005.

2009

12/7	Trnava	a	0-0	
18/7	Košice	h	0-0	
25/7	Ružomberok	a	1-1	Bruško
1/8	Petržalka	h	3-0	Uškovič 2, Pich
8/8	Tatran	a	1-0	Pečovský
15/8	Dubnica	h	3-0	Uškovič 3
22/8	Dunajská Streda	a	2-0	Bruško, Pečovský
29/8	Senica	a	2-2	Bruško, Pich
12/9	Nitra	h	0-3	
19/9	Slovan	a	0-3	
26/9	Žilina	h	1-0	Kuzma
3/10	Trnava	h	1-0	Kuzma
17/10	Košice	a	5-0	Gajdoš 3, Kuzma, Seye
24/10	Ružomberok	h	1-1	Kuzma
31/10	Petržalka	a	1-1	Hučko
7/11	Tatran	h	2-1	Adámik 2 (1p)
21/11	Dubnica	a	2-1	Kuzma, Seye
28/11	Dunajská Streda	h	2-0	Seye, Pančík
6/12	Senica	h	1-0	Pančík

2010

27/2	Nitra	a	0-0	
6/3	Slovan	h	2-1	Ďuriš 2
14/3	Žilina	a	1-3	Poljovka (p)
20/3	Trnava	a	0-2	
24/3	Košice	h	2-2	Gajdoš, Adámik
27/3	Ružomberok	a	0-1	
3/4	Petržalka	h	4-0	Ďuriš, Seye, Pleva, Pich
10/4	Tatran	a	1-0	Ďuriš
17/4	Dubnica	h	1-1	Ďuriš
25/4	Dunajská Streda	a	1-1	Ďuriš
1/5	Senica	a	1-2	Uškovič
5/5	Nitra	h	3-1	Uškovič, Pančík, Chmelík
8/5	Slovan	a	0-2	
15/5	Žilina	h	1-1	Turňa

No	Name	Nat	DoB	Pos	Aps	(s)	Gls
5	Jozef ADÁMIK		10/4/85	D	25		3
13	Peter BOROŠ		17/2/80	G	33		
21	Jakub BRAŠEŇ		2/5/89	M	8	(3)	
22	Tomáš BRUŠKO		21/2/83	M	8	(4)	3
26	Ľuboš CHMELÍK		1/5/89	D	12	(5)	1
16	Michal ĎURIŠ		1/6/88	A	18	(6)	6
17	Vratislav GAJDOŠ		13/1/86	M	16	(9)	4
33	Marek HLINKA		4/10/90	D	3	(1)	
3	Tomáš HUČKO		3/10/85	M	24	(4)	1
20	Marek KUZMA		22/6/88	A	19		5
14	Michal PANČÍK		18/8/82	D	30	(1)	3
12	Viktor PEČOVSKÝ		24/5/83	M	14		2
7	Róbert PICH		12/11/88	A	6	(24)	3

8	Dalibor PLEVA		2/4/84	D	27	(2)	1
4	Martin POLJOVKA		9/1/75	D	18		1
11	Jakub POVAŽANEC		31/1/91	M	2	(5)	
24	Jozef REJDOVJAN		18/3/91	M		(1)	
34	Saša SAVIĆ	SRB	5/2/84	D	25		
10	Mouhamadou SEYE	SEN	10/10/88	A	27	(4)	4
2	Gabriel SNITKA		14/8/85	D	1	(7)	
19	Matúš TURŇA		11/5/86	D	24	(4)	1
9	Dušan UŠKOVIČ		9/4/85	A	15	(13)	7
27	Patrik VAJDA		20/3/89	M	8	(1)	

MFK KOŠICE

Coach – Ján Kozák; (8/12/09) Goran Milojević (SRB)
Founded – 2005
Stadium – Lokomotívy v Čermeli (9,200)
MAJOR HONOURS:
Slovakian Cup – (1) 2009.

2009
11/7	Dunajská Streda	h	2-0	Novák, Škutka
18/7	Banská Bystrica	a	0-0	
25/7	Nitra	h	0-1	
2/8	Slovan	a	0-3	
9/8	Žilina	h	0-2	
16/8	Trnava	a	4-5	Novák 4 (1p)
23/8	Senica	h	0-1	
30/8	Ružomberok	h	3-1	Novák, Hovančík, Milinković
13/9	Petržalka	a	0-3	
20/9	Tatran	h	0-1	
26/9	Dubnica	h	0-1	
3/10	Dunajská Streda	a	1-1	Novák
17/10	Banská Bystrica	h	0-5	
24/10	Nitra	a	0-4	
1/11	Slovan	h	1-2	Škutka
8/11	Žilina	a	1-4	Cicman
21/11	Trnava	h	1-4	Serečin
28/11	Senica	a	2-2	Novák, Kaminský
5/12	Ružomberok	a	0-2	

2010
27/2	Petržalka	h	1-0	Đoković
7/3	Tatran	a	1-1	Škutka
13/3	Dubnica	h	1-0	Novák
20/3	Dunajská Streda	h	2-1	Milinković, Megias
24/3	Banská Bystrica	a	2-2	Novák, Đoković
27/3	Nitra	h	2-0	Škutka 2
3/4	Slovan	a	0-0	
11/4	Žilina	h	0-4	
17/4	Trnava	a	0-4	
24/4	Senica	h	2-0	Stoeten, Milinković
1/5	Ružomberok	h	2-0	Milinković, Novák
5/5	Petržalka	a	0-0	
8/5	Tatran	h	3-1	Škutka, Milinković, Đoković
15/5	Dubnica	a	1-1	Novák (p)

No	Name	Nat	DoB	Pos	Aps	(s)	Gls
23	Peter BAŠISTA		6/4/85	D	11		
13	Róbert CICMAN		3/9/84	D	32		1
19	Matúš ČONKA		15/10/90	D	7	(1)	
12	DIONATAN do Nascimento Teixeira	BRA	24/7/92	D	1		
4	Ivan ĐOKOVIĆ	SRB	20/12/82	D	14		3
8	Timon DOBIAS		28/7/89	M	19		
20	Lukáš DŽOGAN		1/1/87	D	1	(1)	
1	FERNANDO López Fernández	ESP	22/6/83	G	14		
40	Juraj HOVANČÍK		22/11/90	M	12	(3)	1
17	Lukáš JANIČ		30/12/86	M	8	(17)	
11	Martin JUHAR		9/3/88	M	14	(2)	
3	Patrik KAMINSKÝ		27/10/78	D	11	(1)	1
24	Kamil KARAŠ		1/3/91	M		(12)	
2	Stanislav KIŠŠ		16/12/78	D	17	(1)	

9	Jaroslav KOLBAS		10/1/85	D	14		
7	Kamil KUZMA		8/3/88	M	24	(1)	
9	Uroš MATIĆ	SRB	23/5/90	M	1	(3)	
23	Antonio Gaspar MEGIAS	ESP	3/7/84	A	11		1
10	Marko MILINKOVIĆ	SRB	16/4/88	M	26	(1)	5
18	Ján NOVÁK		6/3/85	A	28	(1)	12
12	Aleksandar PAUNOVIĆ	SRB	10/3/87	M	3	(6)	
1	Nikola SCHRENG	CRO	15/7/82	G	11		
22	Filip SEREČIN		4/10/89	A	4	(13)	1
4	Radoslav ŠKOLNÍK		14/11/79	D	4		
26	David ŠKUTKA		25/5/88	A	24	(8)	6
6	Stanislav SMREK		1/12/86	D	6	(1)	
30	Bogdan STEFANOVIĆ	SRB	9/7/77	G	8		
6	Jan Gerrit Pérez "STOETEN"	ESP	10/4/86	M	12	(2)	1
15	Mikuláš TÓTH		15/3/88	D		(1)	
10	Blažej VAŠČÁK		21/11/83	M	12	(8)	
14	Miroslav VIAZANKO		27/10/81	M	14	(11)	

FC NITRA

Coach – Ivan Galád
Founded – 1919
Stadium – Pod Zoborom (8,000)

2009
11/7	Žilina	a	1-1	Šimonek
18/7	Trnava	h	1-0	Rák
25/7	Košice	a	1-0	Šimončič
1/8	Ružomberok	h	2-0	Rák (p), Sloboda
8/8	Petržalka	a	0-0	
15/8	Tatran	h	1-0	Šimončič
22/8	Dubnica	a	0-3	
29/8	Dunajská Streda	h	2-0	Štetina, Rák
12/9	Banská Bystrica	a	3-0	Hodúr, Rák, Kolár
19/9	Senica	a	0-0	
26/9	Slovan	h	0-1	
3/10	Žilina	h	0-1	
17/10	Trnava	a	2-1	Hodúr, Rák
24/10	Košice	h	4-0	Rák 2, Áč, Valenta
31/10	Ružomberok	a	0-1	
7/11	Petržalka	h	1-3	Štetina
21/11	Tatran	a	1-3	Rák
29/11	Dubnica	h	0-1	
5/12	Dunajská Streda	a	2-2	Boszorád, Valenta

2010
27/2	Banská Bystrica	h	0-0	
6/3	Senica	h	2-1	Šimonek 2
13/3	Slovan	a	1-2	Kolmokov
20/3	Žilina	a	1-0	og (Oravec)
24/3	Trnava	h	2-2	Rák 2
27/3	Košice	a	0-2	
4/4	Ružomberok	h	3-1	Rák 3 (1p)
10/4	Petržalka	a	2-3	Rák 2
17/4	Tatran	h	4-2	Rák 3, Glenda
24/4	Dubnica	a	0-1	
1/5	Dunajská Streda	h	1-0	Kóňa
5/5	Banská Bystrica	a	1-3	Kašprák (p)
8/5	Senica	a	2-1	Kóňa, Kotora
15/5	Slovan	h	2-5	Kóňa 2

No	Name	Nat	DoB	Pos	Aps	(s)	Gls
11	Michal ÁČ		17/5/85	D	11		1
8	Slavomír BALIŠ		26/9/86	M	4	(5)	
4	Martin BOSZORÁD		13/11/89	M	11	(1)	1
29	Adam BRATSKÝ		30/3/90	M		(2)	
17	Peter BURÁK		17/9/78	D	10		
1	Martin CHUDÝ		23/4/89	G	7	(1)	
12	Martin GABRIEL		17/8/87	D		(1)	
18	Róbert GLENDA		6/3/86	M	11	(8)	1
10	Ivan HODÚR		7/10/79	M	31	(1)	2
31	Lukáš HROŠŠO		19/4/87	G	26		

SLOVAKIA

16	Petr KASPŘÁK	CZE	17/1/84	D	29		1	
7	Ľuboš KOLÁR		1/9/89	M	10	(13)	1	
2	Marián KOLMOKOV		23/3/91	D	12		1	
6	Tomáš KÓŇA		1/3/84	M	30	(1)	4	
26	Igor KOTORA		13/7/89	D	3	(6)	1	
25	Matej KRÁL		28/12/90	M	1			
5	Branislav LABANT		11/5/76	D	4			
23	Ján LEŠKO		6/7/86	D	17	(6)		
13	Irakli LILUASHVILI	GEO	13/10/84	M	1			
9	Matúš MIKUŠ		8/7/91	A	5	(5)		
77	Róbert RÁK		15/1/78	A	29		18	
5	Patrik SAILER		28/6/89	D	1	(2)		
14	Miloš ŠIMONČIČ		27/5/87	M	24	(3)	2	
19	Arnold ŠIMONEK		19/9/90	M	13	(14)	3	
21	Roman SLOBODA		14/1/87	A	3	(10)	1	
8	Lukáš ŠTETINA		28/7/91	D	21	(4)	2	
3	Martin TÓTH		13/10/86	D	29			
20	Róbert VALENTA		10/1/90	A	20	(8)	2	

MFK PETRŽALKA
Coach – Michal Hipp; (25/8/09) (Emil Stranianek);
(31/8/09) Peter Fieber
Founded – 1898
Stadium – Pasienky (13,300)
MAJOR HONOURS:
Slovakian League - (2) 2005, 2008;
Slovakian Cup - (2) 2004, 2008.

2009
11/7	Tatran	h	0-1	
18/7	Dubnica	a	0-0	
25/7	Dunajská Streda	h	1-0	*Kiss F.*
1/8	Banská Bystrica	a	0-3	
8/8	Nitra	h	0-0	
15/8	Slovan	a	1-1	*Hodek*
23/8	Žilina	h	1-0	*og (Tsimakuridze)*
29/8	Trnava	a	0-2	
13/9	Košice	h	3-0	*Tomčák, og (Bašista), Mikulič*
19/9	Ružomberok	a	0-2	
27/9	Senica	h	1-2	*Hodek*
3/10	Tatran	a	0-2	
17/10	Dubnica	h	7-0	*Tomčák, Hodek 2, Majtán 2, Čikoš 2*
24/10	Dunajská Streda	a	2-3	*Kiss F., Majtán*
31/10	Banská Bystrica	h	1-1	*Majtán*
7/11	Nitra	a	3-1	*Sedlák, Ďurica, Hodek*
22/11	Slovan	h	0-2	
28/11	Žilina	a	0-2	
5/12	Trnava	h	2-1	*Hodek, Fodrek (p)*

2010
27/2	Košice	a	0-1	
6/3	Ružomberok	h	2-2	*Fieber, Šedivý*
13/3	Senica	a	0-2	
20/3	Tatran	h	2-3	*Mikulič, Kiss F.*
24/3	Dubnica	a	0-2	
27/3	Dunajská Streda	h	1-1	*Machovec*
3/4	Banská Bystrica	a	0-4	
10/4	Nitra	h	3-2	*Nachtman, Čikoš, Šedivý*
17/4	Slovan	a	1-1	*Cafú*
24/4	Žilina	h	0-4	
1/5	Trnava	a	1-3	*Kiss F.*
5/5	Košice	h	0-0	
8/5	Ružomberok	a	0-1	
15/5	Senica	h	1-2	*Ďurica*

No	Name	Nat	DoB	Pos	Aps	(s)	Gls
17	Radoslav AUGUSTÍN		5/1/87	A	4	(3)	
24	Peter BURÁK		17/9/78	D	8		
7	Andrej BURZA		2/11/79	D	14		
11	Filipe dos Santos "CAFÚ"	BRA	24/7/87	M	5	(4)	1

22	Erik ČIKOŠ		31/7/88	D	33		3	
4	Pavol ĎURICA		17/5/83	M	20	(4)	2	
8	Peter FIEBER		10/12/89	M	11	(9)	1	
20	Branislav FODREK		5/2/81	M	2	(8)	1	
5	Karim GUÉDÉ	TOG	7/1/85	M	14			
16	Jaroslav HÍLEK		6/6/78	M	29			
25	Andrej HODEK		24/5/81	A	14	(5)	6	
30	Miroslav HÝLL		20/9/73	G	2			
18	Tomáš JENČO		29/9/88	G	22			
21	Patrik JOHANCSIK		9/5/90	A	1	(6)		
1	Daniel KISS		14/4/84	G	9			
6	Filip KISS		13/10/90	M	20	(3)	4	
3	Matej KLENOVSKÝ		16/5/91	D		(2)		
23	Roman KONEČNÝ		25/7/83	D	17			
5	Juraj KURÁŇ		11/8/88	M		(2)		
24	Jaroslav MACHOVEC		5/9/86	A	10	(3)	1	
9	Tomáš MAJTÁN		30/3/87	A	16	(1)	4	
12	Martin MAROŠI		23/3/88	D	3	(6)		
10	Martin MIKULIČ		14/3/85	M	10	(3)	2	
19	Stefan MITROVIĆ	SRB	22/5/90	D	8	(1)		
15	Marek MORAVČÍK		27/1/89	D		(1)		
23	Lukáš NACHTMAN	CZE	11/5/84	D	4	(2)	1	
19	Ján NAJMAN		18/8/83	A		(1)		
9	José Giogo PIRES	BRA	18/12/81	M	5	(4)		
13	Pavol SEDLÁK		21/11/79	M	21	(7)	1	
17	Martin STAŠKO		21/8/83	D	16	(2)		
2	Emil STRANIANEK		11/5/90	D		(1)		
25	Ákos SZARKA		24/11/90	A	7	(6)		
14	Peter ŠEDIVÝ		5/1/83	D	21	(1)	2	
11	Marián TOMČÁK		13/7/80	A	17	(1)	4	

MFK RUŽOMBEROK
Coach – Viliam Hyravý; (1/9/09) František Straka (CZE)
Founded – 1906
Stadium – Mestský štadión (5000)
MAJOR HONOURS:
Slovakian League - (1) 2006;
Slovakian Cup - (1) 2006.

2009
11/7	Dubnica	h	1-1	*Sivčević*
18/7	Dunajská Streda	a	1-1	*Zošák (p)*
25/7	Banská Bystrica	h	1-1	*Lačný*
1/8	Nitra	a	0-2	
9/8	Slovan	h	1-3	*Maslo J.*
15/8	Žilina	a	0-1	
22/8	Trnava	h	2-1	*Ďubek 2*
30/8	Košice	a	1-3	*Sloboda*
12/9	Senica	h	0-1	
19/9	Petržalka	h	2-0	*Lačný, Maslo J.*
26/9	Tatran	a	0-1	
3/10	Dubnica	a	2-1	*Pyschur 2 (1p)*
17/10	Dunajská Streda	h	0-0	
24/10	Banská Bystrica	h	1-1	*Pyschur*
31/10	Nitra	h	1-0	*Řezníček*
7/11	Slovan	a	2-0	*Lačný, Pyschur (p)*
21/11	Žilina	h	0-3	
28/11	Trnava	a	1-3	*Lačný*
5/12	Košice	h	2-0	*Pyschur, Lačný*

2010
27/2	Senica	a	1-2	*Pyschur (p)*
6/3	Petržalka	a	2-2	*Ďubek, Gallo*
13/3	Tatran	h	2-0	*Pyschur (p), Ďubek*
20/3	Dubnica	h	1-0	*Pyschur*
24/3	Dunajská Streda	a	0-0	
27/3	Banská Bystrica	h	1-0	*Maslo J.*
4/4	Nitra	a	1-3	*Zošák*
10/4	Slovan	h	2-0	*Higor, Zošák*
18/4	Žilina	a	0-1	
24/4	Trnava	h	2-1	*Pyschur 2 (1p)*

1/5	Košice	a	0-2	
5/5	Senica	h	2-1	Pyschur, Higor
8/5	Petržalka	h	1-0	Higor
15/5	Tatran	a	0-0	

No	Name	Nat	DoB	Pos	Aps	(s)	Gls
21	Pavel BESTA	CZE	2/9/82	M	13		
5	Lukáš BIELÁK		14/12/86	M	3	(5)	
15	Miroslav BOŽOK		19/10/84	M	15	(1)	
15	Ján CHOVANEC		22/3/84	M	13	(1)	
26	Tomáš ĎUBEK		22/1/87	M	31		4
6	FELIPE Viciano Anselmo	BRA	6/1/86	M	3		
2	Michal GALLO		2/6/88	D	23		1
13	Giovano GODEKEN	NED	17/1/90	M	1	(1)	
21	Ľuboš HAJDÚCH		6/3/80	G	4		
12	HIGOR de Sales Coimbra	BRA	7/8/87	A	8	(5)	3
11	Peter HOFERICA		28/6/83	M	5	(7)	
33	Libor HRDLIČKA		2/1/86	G	13		
5	Daniel JURČ		7/3/83	D	3	(2)	
4	Jaroslav KOSTELNÝ		19/4/85	D	14		
23	Ivan KOTORA		27/6/91	M	2	(8)	
8	Vladimír KOVÁČ		29/4/91	M		(3)	
29	Juraj KUHAJDÍK		20/8/84	M	1	(3)	
7	Vladimír KUKOĽ		8/5/86	M	4	(10)	
16	Miloš LAČNÝ		8/3/88	A	16	(2)	5
13	Mamuka LOMIDZE	GEO	16/6/84	D	3	(1)	
9	Andrej LOVÁS		28/5/91	A		(3)	
4	Peter MAJERNÍK		31/12/78	D	12	(1)	
3	Ján MASLO		5/2/86	D	27		3
17	Peter MASLO		2/2/87	M	24	(3)	
31	František OKOLIČÁNI		26/9/82	G	2		
20	Marek ONDRÍK		30/11/90	D	1	(1)	
19	Štefan PEKÁR		3/12/88	A	1	(6)	
1	Pavol PENKSA		7/11/85	G	9		
20	Pavol PILÁR		27/7/86	A	2	(11)	
9	Olexandr PYSCHUR	UKR	26/1/81	A	22		11
21	Jakub ŘEZNÍČEK	CZE	26/5/88	A	4	(5)	1
22	Matej SIVA		10/10/84	D	14		
14	Milomír SIVČEVIĆ	SRB	1/1/79	D	21		1
10	Anton SLOBODA		10/7/87	M	15	(9)	1
30	Roman SMIEŠKA		18/12/86	G	5	(1)	
18	Štefan ZOŠÁK		3/4/84	M	29	(1)	3

FK SENICA
Coach – Ladislav Hudec; (10/2/10) Radim Nečas (CZE)
Founded – 1921
Stadium – Mestský štadión (3,900)

2009

10/7	Slovan	a	0-3	
18/7	Tatran	h	3-2	Belák, Pavlovič, Velický
26/7	Žilina	a	0-3	
1/8	Dubnica	h	2-1	Velický (p), Faldyna
8/8	Trnava	a	0-3	
15/8	Dunajská Streda	h	0-1	
23/8	Košice	a	1-0	Velický
29/8	Banská Bystrica	h	2-2	Faldyna, Števko
12/9	Ružomberok	a	1-0	Piroška
19/9	Nitra	h	0-0	
27/9	Petržalka	a	2-1	Velický (p), Belák
3/10	Slovan	h	0-2	
17/10	Tatran	a	0-0	
24/10	Žilina	h	0-1	
31/10	Dubnica	a	1-0	Piroška (p)
7/11	Trnava	h	0-0	
21/11	Dunajská Streda	a	2-1	Tesák, og (Adiaba)
28/11	Košice	h	2-2	Pavlovič, Piroška (p)
6/12	Banská Bystrica	a	0-1	

2010

27/2	Ružomberok	h	2-1	Vrťo, Sodje

6/3	Nitra	a	1-2	Gajdošík
13/3	Petržalka	h	2-0	Samb 2
21/3	Slovan	a	0-2	
24/3	Tatran	h	1-2	Kanté
27/3	Žilina	a	1-2	Gajdošík
3/4	Dubnica	h	1-1	Vrťo
10/4	Trnava	a	2-1	Hesek, Piroška
17/4	Dunajská Streda	h	2-2	Piroška (p), Pavlovič
24/4	Košice	a	0-2	
1/5	Banská Bystrica	h	2-1	Hesek, Piroška (p)
5/5	Ružomberok	a	1-2	Hesek
8/5	Nitra	h	1-2	Vrťo
15/5	Petržalka	a	2-1	Pilár, Kučera

No	Name	Nat	DoB	Pos	Aps	(s)	Gls
9	Lukáš BAJAN		22/10/81	M	5	(10)	
8	Ivan BELÁK		23/1/78	M	23		2
26	Petr BOLEK	CZE	13/6/84	G	10		
4	Tomáš ČÁP	CZE	21/11/78	D	19	(4)	
10	Petr FALDYNA	CZE	11/7/76	A	16	(3)	2
1	Andrej FIŠAN		8/1/85	G	5		
3	Ján GAJDOŠÍK		12/10/78	D	23		2
6	Jan HALAMA	CZE	14/7/88	D	5	(1)	
11	Richard HEJČÍK		29/5/78	D		(7)	
11	Andrej HESEK		12/6/81	A	13	(1)	3
15	Jiří HOMOLA	CZE	2/8/80	D	24		
15	Norbert HUBEK		18/6/92	A		(3)	
16	Miloš JUHÁSZ		3/10/84	M	15	(4)	
18	Pavol KAMESCH		9/12/74	G	18		
24	Youssouf KANTÉ	FRA	13/8/84	M	2	(2)	1
23	KIM Tae-hyung	KOR	17/3/89	M		(1)	
12	Adam KITTA		27/12/91	M	1	(2)	
14	Lukáš KOŽIČKA		15/10/87	M	1	(1)	
2	Filip KUČERA		4/8/92	M		(1)	1
13	Martin LAURINC		4/1/78	D	25		
5	Samir MERZIĆ	BIH	29/6/84	D	11		
22	Roman MIHÁLIK		22/1/88	D	5	(1)	
23	Tomáš MRVA		6/4/89	D		(2)	
17	Milan PAVLOVIČ		22/11/80	M	18	(3)	3
29	Andrej PETROVSKÝ		23/1/92	D	1	(1)	
28	Robert PILÁR		27/5/91	D	1		
21	Juraj PIROŠKA		27/2/87	A	25	(2)	6
7	Jakub PODANÝ	CZE	15/6/87	M	8	(1)	
20	Victor Abdou SAMB	SEN	12/11/85	M	8	(5)	2
2	Radek SLÁMA	CZE	30/1/80	D	4	(2)	
10	Onome SODJE	NGA	17/1/88	A	11	(2)	1
19	Roland ŠTEVKO		8/4/83	A	12	(9)	1
5	Roman TAREK		4/4/87	D	2	(3)	
7	Lukáš TESÁK		8/3/85	M	14	(3)	1
24	Stanislav VELICKÝ		16/4/81	M	16		4
21	Ján VLASKO		11/1/90	M	9	(1)	
25	Tomáš VRŤO		6/9/88	M	12	(12)	3
33	Vladimír VUKAJLOVIĆ	SRB	25/8/83	M	1		

ŠK SLOVAN BRATISLAVA
Coach – Dušan Uhrin (CZE); (25/8/09) Michal Hipp;
(5/1/10) Dušan Tittel
Founded – 1919
Stadium – Tehelné pole (30,000); Pasienky (13,500)
MAJOR HONOURS:
UEFA Cup Winners´ Cup – (1) 1969;
Czechoslovakian League – (8) 1949, 1950, 1951, 1955, 1970, 1974, 1975, 1992;
Slovakian League – (9) 1940, 1941, 1942, 1944, 1994, 1995, 1996, 1999, 2009;
Czechoslovakian Cup – (5) 1962, 1963, 1968, 1974, 1982;
Slovakian Cup – (4) 1994, 1997, 1999, 2010.

2009

10/7	Senica	h	3-0	Masaryk, Halenár, Kozák
26/7	Trnava	a	2-0	Gaúcho, Slovák (p)
2/8	Košice	h	3-0	Masaryk 2 (1p), Halenár

9/8	Ružomberok	a	3-1	*Masaryk 2, Dobrotka*
15/8	Petržalka	h	1-1	*Halenár*
23/8	Tatran	a	0-3	
30/8	Dubnica	h	1-1	*Dosoudil*
16/9	Žilina	h	2-1	*Halenár, Slovák*
19/9	Banská Bystrica	h	3-0	*Petráš, Halenár 2*
26/9	Nitra	a	1-0	*Saláta*
3/10	Senica	a	2-0	*Sylvestr, Masaryk*
18/10	Žilina	a	0-2	
25/10	Trnava	h	1-1	*Masaryk*
28/10	Dunajská Streda	a	0-0	
1/11	Košice	a	2-1	*Dobrotka, Gaúcho*
7/11	Ružomberok	h	0-2	
22/11	Petržalka	a	2-0	*Sylvestr, Halenár*
28/11	Tatran	h	3-1	*Masaryk 2 (1p), Halenár*
5/12	Dubnica	a	1-0	*Dobrotka*
2010				
27/2	Dunajská Streda	h	2-0	*Halenár, Masaryk*
6/3	Banská Bystrica	a	1-2	*Saláta*
13/3	Nitra	h	2-1	*Halenár 2 (1p)*
21/3	Senica	h	2-0	*Breznaník, Guédé*
24/3	Žilina	h	2-0	*og (Piaček), Had*
28/3	Trnava	a	3-0	*Saláta, Dobrotka, Grendel*
3/4	Košice	h	0-0	
10/4	Ružomberok	a	0-2	
17/4	Petržalka	h	1-1	*Sylvestr*
24/4	Tatran	a	1-0	*Dobrotka*
1/5	Dubnica	h	2-2	*Breznaník, Saláta*
5/5	Dunajská Streda	a	1-0	*Ivana*
8/5	Banská Bystrica	h	2-0	*Kuzma, Guédé*
15/5	Nitra	a	5-2	*Breznaník 2, Ivana, Štepanovský, Sylvestr*

No	Name	Nat	DoB	Pos	Aps	(s)	Gls
18	Mamadou BAGAYOKO	CIV	31/12/89	D	7	(6)	
26	Tomáš BAGI		9/6/91	M		(1)	
35	David BIČÍK	CZE	6/4/81	G	3		
11	Mario BOŽIĆ	BIH	25/5/83	M	19	(7)	
14	Michal BREZNANÍK		16/12/85	D	25	(1)	4
8	Peter ČERŇÁK		21/1/76	M	2	(1)	
6	Martin DOBROTKA		22/1/85	D	29		5
29	Radek DOSOUDIL	CZE	20/6/83	D	26	(1)	1
25	Rogério Márcio Botelho "GAÚCHO"	BRA	28/9/79	A	2	(8)	2
16	Erik GRENDEL		13/10/88	M	17	(3)	1
19	Karim GUÉDÉ	TOG	7/1/85	M	13		2
28	Marián HAD		16/9/82	D	11	(1)	1
9	Juraj HALENÁR		28/6/83	A	18	(3)	11
13	Milan IVANA		26/11/83	A	14	(8)	2
24	Peter JÁNOŠÍK		2/1/88	D	3		
23	Kristián KOLČÁK		30/1/90	D	2	(4)	
24	Ján KOZÁK		22/4/80	M	16		1
8	Jan KRÁLIK	CZE	7/3/87	M		(1)	
7	Marek KUZMA		22/6/88	A	6	(7)	1
20	Pavol MASARYK		12/2/80	A	22	(10)	10
12	Branislav OBŽERA		29/8/81	M	6	(7)	
19	Peter PETRÁŠ		7/5/79	D	11	(2)	1
30	Matúš PUTNOCKÝ		1/11/84	G	30		
2	Kornel SALÁTA		24/1/85	D	28	(1)	4
5	Julio César SERRANO	ARG	1/3/81	M	1	(1)	
77	Bruno Martins SIMÃO	POR	5/5/85	D	6	(1)	
10	Samuel SLOVÁK		17/10/75	M	13		2
21	Peter ŠTEPANOVSKÝ		12/1/88	M	5	(12)	1
17	Jakub SYLVESTR		2/2/89	A	23	(5)	4
8	Timotej VAJDÍK		16/3/92	A		(1)	
7	Jozef VALACHOVIČ		12/7/75	D	5	(1)	

FC SPARTAK TRNAVA

Coach – Karol Pecze; (29/9/09) Peter Zelenský;
(5/10/09) Ľuboš Nosický; (8/12/09) Milan Malatinský;
(12/5/10) Peter Zelenský
Founded – 1923
Stadium – Antona Malatinského (18,642)
MAJOR HONOURS:
Czechoslovakian League - (5) 1968, 1969, 1971, 1972, 1973;
Czechoslovakian Cup – (4) 1967, 1971, 1975, 1986;
Slovakian Cup – (1) 1998.

2009				
12/7	Banská Bystrica	h	0-0	
18/7	Nitra	a	0-1	
26/7	Slovan	h	0-2	
2/8	Žilina	a	1-2	*Doležaj*
8/8	Senica	h	3-0	*Bernáth, Kožuch, Tiago*
16/8	Košice	h	5-4	*Doležaj 3 (1p), Kožuch, Bernáth*
22/8	Ružomberok	a	1-2	*Kožuch*
29/8	Petržalka	h	2-0	*Bernáth, Neto*
12/9	Tatran	a	2-1	*Neto 2*
19/9	Dubnica	h	1-0	*Doležaj (p)*
27/9	Dunajská Streda	a	1-2	*Gueye*
3/10	Banská Bystrica	a	0-1	
17/10	Nitra	h	1-2	*Kožuch*
25/10	Slovan	a	1-1	*Procházka*
31/10	Žilina	h	1-1	*Procházka*
7/11	Senica	a	0-0	
21/11	Košice	a	4-1	*Koné 2, Hruška, Neto*
28/11	Ružomberok	h	3-1	*Jakubička, Bernáth, Doležaj (p)*
5/12	Petržalka	a	1-2	*Hruška*
2010				
27/2	Tatran	h	2-0	*Bernáth, Tiago*
6/3	Dubnica	a	1-2	*Pítio*
13/3	Dunajská Streda	h	7-0	*Bernáth 2, Procházka, Koné, Doležaj, og (Michellini), Kožuch*
20/3	Banská Bystrica	h	2-0	*Doležaj (p), Koné*
24/3	Nitra	a	2-2	*Juhász 2*
28/3	Slovan	h	0-3	
3/4	Žilina	h	1-5	*Guldan*
10/4	Senica	h	1-2	*Guldan*
17/4	Košice	h	4-0	*Banovič, Doležaj, Guldan, Pítio*
24/4	Ružomberok	a	1-2	*Bernáth*
1/5	Petržalka	h	3-1	*Guldan, Kopúnek, Koné*
5/5	Tatran	a	0-3	
8/5	Dubnica	h	0-1	
15/5	Dunajská Streda	a	1-2	*Hruška*

No	Name	Nat	DoB	Pos	Aps	(s)	Gls
21	Patrik BANOVIČ		13/11/91	D	8		1
15	Ľuboš BERNÁTH		3/9/85	A	23	(6)	8
11	Marek BOHÁČEK		17/2/90	M	1	(1)	
30	Ivan BRÁNSKY		28/9/88	G	2		
27	DANILO Cirino de Oliveira	BRA	11/11/86	A	1	(2)	
16	Pavel DEVÁTÝ	CZE	17/6/78	M	5	(3)	
5	Daniel DOKOVIC	NED	18/4/90	D	1		
3	Peter DOLEŽAJ		5/4/81	D	27		9
8	Peter ĎURIŠ		10/4/81	M	15	(5)	
19	Ľubomír GOGOLÁK		24/2/90	A		(8)	
21	Cheikh Amdy GUEYE	SEN	22/8/80	D	3	(1)	1
24	Martin GULDAN		3/9/90	A	8	(1)	4
18	Ľuboš HANZEL		7/5/87	D	13		
4	Tomáš HANZEL		19/2/89	D	1		
23	Lukáš HLAVATOVIČ		22/4/87	M	3	(1)	
30	Miroslav HRDINA		23/9/76	G	2	(1)	
17	Martin HRUŠKA	CZE	11/5/81	M	15	(7)	3
2	Peter JAKUBIČKA		8/9/85	D	22		1
16	Miloš JUHÁSZ		3/1/84	M	10	(1)	2
25	Koro Issa Ahmed KONÉ	CIV	5/7/89	A	14	(12)	5
14	Kamil KOPÚNEK		18/5/84	M	31		1

5	Jozef KOTULA		20/9/76	D	13	
9	Vladimír KOŽUCH		15/10/75	A	14	(6)	5
1	Ivica KRALJ	SRB	26/3/73	G	4	
31	Tomáš MIKINIČ		22/11/92	A	1	(1)
29	Martin MIKOVIČ		12/9/90	M	6	
28	Michel Cury NETO	BRA	24/7/81	M	19	(2)	4
12	Roberto Nascimento dos Santos "PÍTIO"	BRA	5/9/87	A	6	(6)	2
6	Roman PROCHÁZKA		14/3/89	M	27	(2)	3
22	Ladislav RYBÁNSKY		19/12/84	G	14	
27	Peter SCHMIDT		19/11/83	D	6	(2)
1	Ján SLOVENČIAK		5/11/81	G	11	
7	Peter ŠTYVAR		13/8/80	A	4	(5)
26	Igor SÚKENNÍK		25/10/89	M	8	(10)
20	TIAGO Henrique Bernardini Consoni	BRA	2/12/79	D	23		2
10	Martin ŽELEZNÍK		9/11/89	M	2	(12)

1. FC TATRAN PREŠOV
Coach – Roman Pivarník
Founded – 1898
Stadium – Prešov (7,800)

2009
11/7	Petržalka	a	1-0	Belejík
18/7	Senica	a	2-3	Penksa, Ižvolt
25/7	Dubnica	h	0-0	
1/8	Dunajská Streda	a	0-3	
8/8	Banská Bystrica	h	0-1	
15/8	Nitra	a	0-1	
23/8	Slovan	h	3-0	Katona, Poliaček, Pribula
30/8	Žilina	a	0-1	
12/9	Trnava	h	1-2	Katona
20/9	Košice	a	1-0	Papaj
26/9	Ružomberok	h	1-0	Hanek
3/10	Petržalka	h	2-0	Piter-Bučko, Josl
17/10	Senica	h	0-0	
24/10	Dubnica	a	0-1	
31/10	Dunajská Streda	h	0-0	
7/11	Banská Bystrica	a	1-2	Belejík
21/11	Nitra	h	3-1	Farbák, Mariano, Čep
28/11	Slovan	a	1-3	Jurčo
5/12	Žilina	h	1-0	Ižvolt

2010
27/2	Trnava	a	0-2	
7/3	Košice	h	1-1	Jurčo
13/3	Ružomberok	a	0-2	
20/3	Petržalka	a	3-2	Hanek, Katona, Mariano
24/3	Senica	a	2-1	Papaj, Katona
27/3	Dubnica	a	2-0	Papaj, Hanek
3/4	Dunajská Streda	a	1-2	Poliaček
10/4	Banská Bystrica	h	0-1	
17/4	Nitra	a	2-4	Katona, Mariano
24/4	Slovan	h	0-1	
1/5	Nitra	a	0-3	
5/5	Trnava	h	3-0	Hanek, Piter-Bučko, Vršajević
8/5	Košice	a	1-3	Belejík
15/5	Ružomberok	h	0-0	

No	Name	Nat	DoB	Pos	Aps	(s)	Gls
16	Ľuboš BELEJÍK		23/9/85	A	10	(9)	3
3	David ČEP	CZE	4/10/80	D	19	(1)	1
33	Jozef ČERTÍK		29/4/85	M	1	
23	Jakub DIVIŠ	CZE	27/7/86	G	26	
6	Jozef DOLNÝ		13/5/92	A		(1)	
30	Dejan DRAKUL	BIH	23/5/88	M	2	(12)	
	Samuel ĎURECH		5/10/88	D	1	
18	Marian FARBÁK		10/2/83	D	26	(1)	1
29	Dávid GUBA		29/6/91	A	3	(10)	
4	Michal HANEK		18/9/80	D	29	(1)	4

9	Ján HATOK		11/7/90	M		(1)	
5	Matej IŽVOLT		5/6/86	M	14	(8)	2
28	Tomáš JOSL	CZE	12/11/84	D	21		1
7	JUAN PEDRO Garzon Berga	ESP	6/3/90	A		(1)	
14	Pavol JURČO		12/2/86	A	5	(15)	2
11	Peter KATONA		12/4/88	M	28	(3)	5
10	Petr KOBYLÍK	CZE	8/5/85	M	5	
10	Dávid LEŠKO		4/6/88	M		(1)	
15	Peter LIPTÁK		7/9/89	M	6	(1)	
19	Jonathan Bernardo MARIANO	BRA	7/11/88	A	15	(4)	3
21	Ján MUCHA		20/6/78	G	7	
24	Ján PAPAJ		16/6/79	D	28		3
99	Marek PENKSA		4/8/73	A	7	(2)	1
2	Michal PITER-BUČKO		28/10/83	D	23	(2)	2
8	Miroslav POLIAČEK		13/7/83	M	14	(5)	2
6	Juan Carlos POZO Muñoz	ESP	21/1/81	M	5	
25	Jaroslav PREKOP		8/8/79	M	9	
20	Martin PRIBULA		29/11/85	M	11	(3)	1
27	Michal SČASNÝ		19/8/78	D	27	
9	Erik TAKÁČ		26/2/75	A	4	(4)	
26	Lukáš TESÁK		8/3/85	D	9	(2)	
13	Avdija VRŠAJEVIĆ	BIH	6/3/86	M	8	(9)	1

MŠK ŽILINA
Coach – Pavel Hapal (CZE)
Founded – 1908
Stadium – Pod Dubňom (8,000)
MAJOR HONOURS:
Slovakian League - (5) 2002, 2003, 2004, 2007, 2010.

2009
11/7	Nitra	h	1-1	Šourek
26/7	Senica	h	3-0	Lietava 2, Kobylík
2/8	Trnava	h	2-1	Babatunde, Kobylík (p)
9/8	Košice	a	2-0	Lietava, Babatunde
15/8	Ružomberok	h	1-0	Rilke
23/8	Petržalka	h	0-1	
30/8	Tatran	h	1-0	Rilke
12/9	Dubnica	a	1-0	Lietava
16/9	Slovan	a	1-2	Guldan
19/9	Dunajská Streda	h	1-0	Jež
26/9	Banská Bystrica	a	0-1	
3/10	Nitra	a	1-0	Jež
18/10	Slovan	h	2-0	Oravec 2
24/10	Senica	a	1-0	Oravec
31/10	Trnava	a	1-1	Guldan
8/11	Košice	h	4-1	og (Smrek), Oravec 2, Kobylík (p)
21/11	Ružomberok	a	3-0	Lietava 2, Kobylík
28/11	Petržalka	h	2-0	Šourek, Lietava
5/12	Tatran	a	0-1	

2010
27/2	Dubnica	h	4-0	Lietava, Kobylík, Guldan, Majtán
6/3	Dunajská Streda	a	2-0	Oravec 2
14/3	Banská Bystrica	h	3-1	Oravec 2, Majtán
20/3	Nitra	h	0-1	
24/3	Slovan	a	0-2	
27/3	Senica	h	2-1	Majtán, Jež
3/4	Trnava	h	5-1	Lietava 2, Rilke, Piaček, Majtán
11/4	Košice	a	4-0	Lietava 2, Pečalka, Rilke
18/4	Ružomberok	h	1-0	Jež (p)
24/4	Petržalka	a	4-0	Pečalka, og (Nachtman), Mráz, Zlatković
1/5	Tatran	h	1-0	Rilke
5/5	Dubnica	a	1-1	Angelovič
8/5	Dunajská Streda	h	4-0	Oravec 2, Lietava, Pečalka
15/5	Banská Bystrica	a	1-1	Piaček

No	Name	Nat	DoB	Pos	Aps	(s)	Gls
10	Evandro ADAUTO da Silva	BRA	29/5/80	D	13	(1)	
2	Stanislav ANGELOVIČ		26/3/82	D	21		1

SLOVAKIA

28	Bello BABATUNDE	BEN	6/10/89	A	13	(13)	2
25	Dennis CHRISTU	CZE	27/7/89	A	1	(3)	
24	Juraj CHUPÁČ		17/3/88	D	2	(1)	
30	Martin DÚBRAVKA		15/1/89	G	25	(1)	
19	Dominik FOTYIK		16/9/90	A		(3)	
5	Ľubomír GULDAN		30/1/83	D	17	(8)	3
18	Eldar HASANOVIĆ	BIH	12/1/90	M		(1)	
12	Róbert JEŽ		10/7/81	M	30		4
8	David KOBYLÍK	CZE	27/6/74	M	26	(5)	5
22	Martin KRNÁČ		30/1/85	G	1		
21	Josip KVESIĆ	BIH	21/9/90	D	1	(1)	
7	Vladimír LEITNER		28/6/74	D	18	(2)	
39	Ivan LIETAVA		20/7/83	A	25	(1)	13
10	Tomáš MAJTÁN		30/3/87	A	6	(5)	4
6	Patrik MRÁZ		1/2/87	M	22	(6)	1
26	Prince OFORI	BEN	6/10/88	D		(1)	
14	Tomáš ORAVEC		3/7/80	A	15	(7)	11
3	Mário PEČALKA		28/12/80	D	23	(2)	3
22	Dušan PERNIŠ		28/11/84	G	7		
15	Jozef PIAČEK		20/6/83	D	26	(1)	2
16	Martin POLEŤ		31/8/90	D	3	(1)	
9	Emil RILKE	CZE	19/11/83	A	16	(10)	5
29	Michal ŠKVARKA		19/8/92	A	1	(4)	
23	Ondřej ŠOUREK	CZE	26/4/83	D	24		2
32	Giorgi TSIMAKURIDZE	GEO	10/11/83	D	4	(1)	
25	Jakub VOJTUŠ		22/10/93	A		(1)	
11	Martin VYSKOČIL	CZE	15/9/82	M	14	(4)	
4	Adam ŽILÁK		7/12/91	M	4	(6)	
17	Nemanja ZLATKOVIĆ	SRB	21/8/88	M	5	(9)	1

PROMOTED CLUB

FC VION ZLATÉ MORAVCE

Coach – Juraj Jarábek
Founded – 1995
Stadium – Štadión ViOn (3,500)
MAJOR HONOURS:
Slovakian Cup – (1) 2007.

SECOND LEVEL FINAL TABLE 2009/10

		Pld	W	D	L	F	A	Pts
1	FC ViOn Zlaté Moravce	27	18	5	4	54	21	59
2	AS Trenčín	27	13	11	3	53	21	50
3	FK Púchov	27	15	5	7	38	31	50
4	FK LAFC Lučenec	27	10	8	9	36	28	38
5	MFK Dolný Kubín	27	10	7	10	39	31	37
6	MFK Zemplín Michalovce	27	8	6	13	23	33	30
7	MFK Ružomberok B	27	8	5	14	23	45	29
8	FC Rimavská Sobota	27	7	7	13	21	36	28
9	MFK Tatran Liptovský Mikuláš	27	7	5	15	27	42	26
10	FK Slovan Duslo Šaľa	27	4	11	12	15	41	23

NB ZP ŠPORT Podbrezová withdrew after round 5; FK Mesto Prievidza withdrew after round 17; both clubs' matches annulled.

DOMESTIC CUP 2009/10

SLOVENSKÝ POHÁR

SECOND ROUND

(22/9/09)
Čadca 0, Dukla Banská Bystrica 1
Humenné 1, Moldava nad Bodrou 2

MFK Banská Bystrica 1, Ružomberok 3
MFK Vrbové 0, Slovan Bratislava 7
Moravany 0, Trenčín 3
Myjava 0, Senica 0 *(aet; 7-6 on pens)*
Nitra 5, Prievidza 0
Nové Mesto 1, Petržalka 6
Prešov 5, Lučenec 0
Rimavská Sobota 3, Liptovský Mikuláš 1
Sereď 1, Zlaté Moravce 4
SFM Senec 1, DAC Dunajská Streda 1 *(aet; 3-5 on pens)*
Snina 0, MFK Košice 3
Spišská Nová Ves 1, Dubnica 0
Trnava 5, Rača 0
Žilina w/o ŽP Šport Podbrezová

THIRD ROUND

(20/10/09)
Banská Bystrica 1, Nitra 0
Dunajská Streda 1, Prešov 0
Moldava nad Bodrou 1, Spišská Nová Ves 0
Myjava 2, Ružomberok 1
Petržalka 4, Trenčín 0
Slovan 2, Rimavská Sobota 1
Trnava 5, Zlaté Moravce 0
Žilina 1, Košice 2

QUARTER-FINALS

(4/11/09 & 24/11/09)
Dunajská Streda 3 *(Koejoe 38, 57, Nkendo 83)*, Moldava nad Bodrou 0
Moldava nad Bodrou 1 *(Pelegrin 62)*, Dunajská Streda 3 *(Seelaus 49, Bognár 67, Nkendo 70)*
(Dunajská Streda 6-1)
Košice 0, Banská Bystrica 2 *(Pleva 20, Poljovka 27p)*
Banská Bystrica 1 *(Snitka 29)*, Košice 0
(Banská Bystrica 3-0)
Myjava 0, Slovan 3 *(Halenár 42, Masaryk 60, Dobrotka 63)*
Slovan 0, Myjava 0
(Slovan 3-0)
Petržalka 3 *(Majtan 70, Hodek 77, Ďurica 87)*, Trnava 2 *(Doležaj 20, Kopúnek 37)*
Trnava 3 *(Koné 83, 87, Doležaj 40)*, Petržalka 0
(Trnava 5-3)

SEMI-FINALS

(6/4/10 & 20/4/10)
Banská Bystrica 0, Slovan 1 *(Kuzma 2)*
Slovan 1 *(Ivana 40)*, Banská Bystrica 0
(Slovan 2-0)

Dunajská Streda 0, Trnava 1 *(Hanzel Ľ. 40)*
Trnava 2 *(Bernáth 88, Juhász 90)*, Dunajská Streda 0
(Trnava 3-0)

FINAL

(11/5/10)
Mestský štadión, Michalovce
ŠK SLOVAN BRATISLAVA 6 *(Saláta 11, Božić 17, Sylvestr 33, Breznaník 64, Guédé 67, Dobrotka 87)*
FC SPARTAK TRNAVA 0
Referee – Vlk
SLOVAN – Putnocký, Dobrotka, Saláta, Dosoudil, Had, Obžera, Guédé, Božić *(Grendel 53)*, Breznaník *(Ivana 73)*, Masaryk, Sylvestr *(Kuzma 81)*.
TRNAVA – Slovenčiak, Juhász, Banovič *(Hlavatovič 68)*, Kožuch, Schmidt, Procházka, Kopúnek, Neto *(Súkenník 21)*, Mikovič, Štyvar *(Pitio 46)*, Guldan.

Abrupt end to World Cup rollercoaster ride

With just two million inhabitants, Slovenia were the least populous nation present at the 2010 FIFA World Cup. They made it to South Africa by eliminating Russia, the largest country on the planet, in the qualifying play-offs, and although little was expected of them at the finals, they came within seconds of going through to the last 16.

At the final whistle of their final group game, against England in Port Elizabeth, Slovenia looked to have done enough to have reached the knockout phase. But then came the traumatic news from Pretoria that the United States had scored a stoppage-time winner – a goal that relegated Matjaž Kek's team to third place in the group and knocked them out of the competition.

Astonishing adventure

It was a cruel end to what had been an astonishing World Cup adventure, in which Slovenia, seemingly down and out, had won the last four games of their

Goalkeeper Samir Handanović was one of Slovenia's top performers in South Africa

qualifying group to book a play-off date with Russia, then scored a crucial late goal in Moscow before securing qualification with a 1-0 win in Maribor. In South Africa, the rollercoaster ride continued. Slightly fortunate to beat Algeria 1-0 in their opening game after the Africans had gone down to ten men and then gifted Slovenia skipper Robert Koren a late winning goal with a dreadful goalkeeping gaffe, Kek's men then went 2-0 up against the USA with fine goals from Valter Birsa and Zlatan Ljubijankič before allowing the Americans to come back strongly and draw 2-2. In fact, their opponents had a late winning 'goal' disallowed, so there was perhaps some retrospective justice to the manner of Slovenia's demise when, after losing 1-0 to England, Landon Donovan's last-gasp effort against Algeria sealed their fate.

With a win – their first at a major tournament – followed by a draw and a defeat, Slovenia's four-point haul ultimately proved insufficient, but bitter and agonising though the manner of their elimination undoubtedly was, there was no need for recrimination. Some of the Slovenian players were not at their best in South Africa – notably Milivoje Novakovič and Zlatko Dedič in attack – but in general the team punched above their weight, and in goalkeeper Samir Handanovič, right-back Mišo Brečko and set-piece specialist Birsa, Slovenia possessed players more than capable of holding their own at the highest level. The team's unassuming coach also warranted praise. Kek's mild-mannered, almost emotionless reactions to his team's goals betrayed a calm authority. Unlike most of his counterparts, he had virtually no selection headaches, sending out pretty much the same starting XI that had come through the qualifiers. Most of those players did him, and their tiny country, proud.

Slovenia's World Cup 23 contained representatives from 12 European leagues. Only two squad members, NK Maribor defenders Elvedin Džinić and Suad Filepovič, came from the Slovenian Prva Liga, and neither of them actually played. Džinić and Filepovič both travelled south having helped Maribor to victory in the Slovenian

SLOVENIA

NZS

Cup, but the country's record champions were unable to defend their league title, which went instead, against all pre-season odds, to FC Koper.

Glory for golden oldies

The 2009/10 Slovenian season was characterised by the resurgence of some of the country's golden oldies – former Slovenian internationals enjoying an Indian summer back in their homeland. Thirty-four-year-old striker Milan Osterc would have topped the billing with his Golden Boot-winning tally of 23 goals for ND Gorica had it not been for the extraordinary efforts of his fellow UEFA EURO 2000 and 2002 FIFA World Cup participant Miran Pavlin, who, at the age of 38, was the driving force behind Koper's Prva Liga title triumph.

Newly arrived at the Adriatic seaside resort after helping NK Olimpija Ljubljana – the reformed club from the capital with a famous old name – win promotion, Pavlin took on the role of sporting director, as well as team captain, at a club that had narrowly survived relegation the previous season. The ensuing transformation had to be seen to be believed as Pavlin wielded his magic both on and off the pitch. A lightning start catapulted Koper to the top of the table and there they remained, virtually undisturbed, for the remainder of the season. Coach Nedžad Okčić, the same man who had kept Koper up, conducted the title procession, which reached a triumphant conclusion on 24 April with a 2-0 win at NK Rudar Velenje that left Koper holding an unassailable 15-point lead with four games still to play.

Ably assisted by Mitja Brulc, Dalibor Radujko and, in the second half of the season, Dare Vršić, Pavlin masterminded an entertaining, attack-oriented effort that enabled Koper to become only the fifth team to win the Slovenian title. Pavlin himself scored 11 goals – his highest ever seasonal haul – and was in the starting XI for 30 of the 36 matches, with only Brulc (12 goals and 34 appearances) outdoing him in either category.

Cup final thriller

Maribor, still coached by 2008/09 title-winning boss Darko Milanič (another of Slovenia's 'golden generation' from the turn of the millennium), finished 11 points behind Koper in second place.

Nogometna zveza Slovenije (NZS)

NZS

Cerinova 4
PP 3986
SI-1001 Ljubljana
tel - +386 1 530 0400
fax - +386 1 530 0410
website - nzs.si
email - nzs@nzs.si
Year of Formation – 1920

President – Ivan Simič
General Secretary – Aleš Zavrl
Media Officer – Matjaž Krajnik
National Stadium – Ljudski vrt, Maribor (12,432)

INTERNATIONAL TOURNAMENT APPEARANCES
FIFA World Cup – (2) 2002, 2010.
UEFA European Championship - (1) 2000.
TOP FIVE ALL–TIME CAPS
Zlatko Zahovič (80); Milenko Ačimovič & Aleš Čeh (74); Džoni Novak (71); Marinko Galič (66)
TOP FIVE ALL-TIME GOALS
Zlatko Zahovič (35); Milivoje Novakovič & Sašo Udovič (16); Ermin Šiljak (14); Milenko Ačimovič (13)

Hampered by a poor start, they never looked likely to defend their title and had to make do with a sixth Slovenian Cup win – claimed in thrilling fashion when they came from behind twice in the final against NK Domžale with goals from their Brazilian star Marcos Tavares before grabbing glory in the final seconds of extra time with a dramatic winner from David Bunderla.

Domžale, the 2007 and 2008 champions, had a forgettable season in the league, finishing eighth. They were never, however, seriously threatened by relegation, a fate that befell both of the teams below them – NK Drava and, following a heavy play-off defeat, NK IB Ljubljana. The latter, who won the Cup in 2008 and 2009 and were expected to become Slovenian football's nouveaux riches under wealthy benefactor Jože Pečečnik, suffered a chaotic demise, while Olimpija, whose return to the elite engendered much excitement, also failed to live up to expectations, their star player turning out to be not one of the many celebrated thirtysomethings who had earned them promotion but 17-year-old goalkeeper Jan Oblak. The youngster conceded just 28 goals in 33 league games and was rewarded with a dream summer move to Portuguese champions SL Benfica.

Veteran midfielder Miran Pavlin inspired Koper to their first Slovenian title

NZS

NATIONAL TEAM RESULTS 2009/10

12/8/09	San Marino (WCQ)	H	Maribor	5-0	Koren (19, 74), Radosavljevič (39), Kirm (54), Ljubijankič (90+3)
5/9/09	England	A	London	1-2	Ljubijankič (85)
9/9/09	Poland (WCQ)	H	Maribor	3-0	Dedič (13), Novakovič (44), Birsa (62)
10/10/09	Slovakia (WCQ)	A	Bratislava	2-0	Birsa (56), Pečnik (90+3)
14/10/09	San Marino (WCQ)	A	Serravalle	3-0	Novakovič (24), Stevanovič (68), Šuler (81)
14/11/09	Russia (WCQ)	A	Moscow	1-2	Pečnik (88)
18/11/09	Russia (WCQ)	H	Maribor	1-0	Dedič (44)
3/3/10	Qatar	H	Maribor	4-1	Novakovič (14), Cesar (30), Kirm (34), Jokič (66)
4/6/10	New Zealand	H	Maribor	3-1	Novakovič (7, 30), Kirm (44)
13/6/10	Algeria (WCF)	N	Polokwane (RSA)	1-0	Koren (79)
18/6/10	United States (WCF)	N	Johannesburg (RSA)	2-2	Birsa (13), Ljubijankič (42)
23/6/10	England (WCF)	N	Port Elizabeth (RSA)	0-1	

NATIONAL TEAM APPEARANCES 2009/10

Coach - Matjaž KEK	9/9/61		SMR	Eng	POL	SVK	SMR	RUS	RUS	Qat	Nzl	ALG	USA	ENG	Caps	Goals
Samir HANDANOVIČ	14/7/84	Udinese (ITA)	G	G	G	G	G	G	G	G70	G	G	G	G	42	-
Mišo BREČKO	1/5/84	Köln (GER)	D	D	D	D	D85	D	D	D64	D76	D	D	D	34	-
Boštjan CESAR	9/7/82	Grenoble (FRA)	D	D34		D	D	D	D	D78	D	D	D	D	46	3
Marko ŠULER	9/3/83	Gent (BEL)	D	D	D	D	D	D	D	D	D	D	D	D	20	2
Bojan JOKIČ	17/5/86	Sochaux (FRA)/Chievo (ITA)	D	D	D	D	D	D	D	D	D	D	D	D	37	1
Aleksandar RADOSAVLJEVIČ	25/4/79	Tom (RUS)/Larissa (GRE)	M74	M77	M89	M	M	M	M		M64	M78	M87	M	18	1
Nejc PEČNIK	3/1/86	Nacional (POR)	M46	s71	s89	s78		s82	s78		s61	s84	s74/94		10	2
Robert KOREN	20/9/80	West Brom (ENG)	M	M	M	M		M	M	M	M	M	M	M	49	5
Valter BIRSA	7/8/86	Auxerre (FRA)	M	M65	M71	M94	M	M77	M78	M64	M79	M84	M87	M	37	3
Zlatan LJUBIJANKIČ	15/12/83	Gent (BEL)	A	s55	s58		s51	s67		s56	A12	s53	A74	A62	20	5
Etien VELIKONJA	26/12/88	Gorica	A72												1	-
Andraž KIRM	6/9/84	Wisła (POL)	s46	M77	M	M	M	M82	M	M	M84	M	M	M79	29	3
Milivoje NOVAKOVIČ	18/5/79	Köln (GER)	s72	A55	A	A	A	A	A	A	A61	A	A	A	41	16
Armin BAČINOVIČ	24/10/89	Maribor	s74												1	-
Zlatko DEDIČ	5/10/84	Bochum (GER)		A71	A58	A78	A51	A67	A94	A56	s12	A53	s87	s62	27	3
Matej MAVRIČ	29/1/79	Koblenz (GER)		s34	D										32	1
Andrej KOMAC	4/12/79	M. Tel-Aviv (ISR)	s65	s71							s79	s87	s94		43	-
Rene KRHIN	21/5/90	Inter (ITA)	s77					s85		s64	s78				4	-
Dalibor STEVANOVIČ	27/9/84	Vitesse (NED)	s77				s94	M85	s77	s94					15	1
Branko ILIČ	6/2/83	FC Moskva (RUS)							s85		s64	s76			37	-
Mirnes ŠIŠIČ	8/8/81	Giannina (GRE)								s64					12	2
Aleksander ŠELIGA	1/2/80	Sparta (NED)									s70				1	-
Dejan KELHAR	5/4/84	Cercle Brugge (BEL)									s78				1	-
Tim MATAVŽ	13/1/89	Groningen (NED)									s84			s79	2	-

DOMESTIC LEAGUE 2009/10

PRVA LIGA FINAL TABLE

		Home					Away					Total					
	Pld	W	D	L	F	A	W	D	L	F	A	W	D	L	F	A	Pts
1 FC Koper	36	9	6	3	26	17	12	4	2	33	18	21	10	5	59	35	73
2 NK Maribor	36	7	5	6	26	24	11	3	4	32	20	18	8	10	58	44	62
3 ND Gorica	36	7	4	7	38	31	9	3	6	36	29	16	7	13	74	60	55
4 NK Olimpija Ljubljana	36	8	4	6	29	17	8	3	7	22	16	16	7	13	51	33	53
5 NK Celje	36	9	3	6	28	25	5	6	7	25	31	14	9	13	53	56	51
6 NK Nafta	36	11	2	5	34	21	3	5	10	17	32	14	7	15	51	53	49
7 NK Rudar Velenje	36	7	1	10	24	31	8	3	7	22	21	15	4	17	46	52	49
8 NK Domžale	36	6	4	8	27	32	6	5	7	24	27	12	9	15	51	59	45
9 NK IB Ljubljana	36	6	4	8	17	26	3	2	13	18	38	9	6	21	35	64	33
10 NK Drava	36	4	5	9	15	24	3	4	11	19	32	7	9	20	34	56	30

NB NK Olimpija Ljubljana - 2 pts deducted.

TOP GOALSCORERS

23 Milan OSTERC (Gorica)

15 Dragan JELIČ (Maribor)

12 Mitja BRULC (Koper)
   Dalibor VOLAŠ (Maribor/Nafta)

11 Goran CVIJANOVIČ (Gorica)
   Miran PAVLIN (Koper)
   Dalibor RADUJKO (Koper)

10 Slaviša DVORANČIČ (Celje)
   Ivan BREČEVIČ (Gorica)
   MARCOS TAVARES (Maribor)

CLUB-BY-CLUB

NK CELJE

Coach – Milan Djuričić (CRO)
Founded – 1919
Stadium – Petrol Arena (13,400)
MAJOR HONOURS:
Slovenian Cup – (1) 2005.

2009
18/7	Koper	a	0-1	
25/7	Nafta	a	2-2	Dvorančič, Biščan
1/8	Drava	h	1-0	Biščan
9/8	IB Ljubljana	a	2-1	Dvorančič, Biščan
15/8	Gorica	h	2-0	og (Kršič), Dvorančič
22/8	Rudar	a	0-2	
29/8	Maribor	h	2-1	Dvorančič, Andželkovič
12/9	Olimpija	a	2-4	Lovrečič, Korun (p)
19/9	Domžale	h	2-3	Štraus, Biščan
23/9	Koper	h	0-1	
26/9	Nafta	h	2-2	Lovrečič, Dvorančič
4/10	Drava	a	1-0	Rep
17/10	IB Ljubljana	h	3-1	Bjelkanovič, Bezjak, Korun (p)
24/10	Gorica	a	1-1	Gobec
28/10	Rudar	h	0-4	
31/10	Maribor	a	3-3	Biščan (p), Bezjak, Lovrečič (p)
7/11	Olimpija	h	1-1	Duspara
22/11	Domžale	a	5-1	Andželkovič, Dvorančič, Lovrečič (p), Bezjak, Duspara
2/12	Drava	h	3-0	Rep, Duspara, og (Žilić T.)
5/12	Nafta	a	1-2	Dvorančič
9/12	IB Ljubljana	a	0-0	
12/12	Koper	a	0-4	

2010
27/2	Gorica	h	1-4	Bezjak
6/3	Rudar	a	1-3	Lovrečič
13/3	Olimpija	a	3-1	Andželkovič, Bezjak, Bakarič
20/3	Domžale	h	1-0	Močič
28/3	Koper	h	1-3	Popovič
31/3	Maribor	h	0-2	
3/4	Nafta	h	3-2	Lovrečič, Dvorančič, Štraus
10/4	Drava	a	1-0	Duspara
17/4	IB Ljubljana	h	5-1	Lovrečič 2 (2p), Dvorančič 2, Štraus
24/4	Gorica	a	0-3	
30/4	Rudar	h	0-0	
4/5	Maribor	a	1-1	Lovrečič
11/5	Olimpija	h	1-0	Duspara
16/5	Domžale	a	2-2	Gobec, Bezjak

No	Name	Nat	DoB	Pos	Aps	(s)	Gls
6	Milan ANDŽELKOVIČ		1/9/81	D	29		3
13	Saša BAKARIČ		18/3/87	D	27	(2)	1
9	Roman BEZJAK		21/2/89	A	15	(9)	6
7	Dario BIŠČAN		26/8/85	A	14		5
15	Boris BJELKANOVIČ	CRO	27/9/84	D	12	(2)	1
7	Danijel BREZIČ		15/2/76	M	13		
4	Matej CENTRIH		5/9/88	D		(1)	
24	Domagoj DUSPARA	CRO	21/10/87	A	14	(5)	5
8	Slaviša DVORANČIČ		22/1/79	A	23	(2)	10
25	Sebastjan GOBEC		6/12/79	M	29	(2)	2
18	Aljaž HORVAT		16/7/85	M	6	(4)	
21	Aleš KAČIČNIK		28/9/73	D	23	(3)	
5	Amel KAMBEROVIČ	BIH	6/2/91	D	2	(1)	
88	Uroš KORUN		25/5/87	M	10	(4)	2
20	Dejan KRLJANOVIČ		12/7/89	M	2	(4)	
18	Jernej LESKOVAR		10/8/88	D		(4)	
10	Anej LOVREČIČ		10/5/87	M	22	(6)	9
23	Boris MIJATOVIČ		7/2/88	D	13	(3)	
28	Mario MOČIČ		4/5/89	M	9	(8)	1
22	Iztok MOČIVNIK		22/1/92	M	1	(1)	
1	Amel MUJČINOVIČ		20/11/73	G	36		
26	Amel OMEROVIČ		21/7/90	M		(1)	
3	Levin OPARENOVIČ		14/8/84	D	1	(3)	
33	Denis POPOVIČ		15/10/89	M	6	(9)	1
19	Dejan PURIŠIČ		16/7/83	A	12		
55	Rajko REP		20/6/90	M	23	(6)	2
14	Alen ROMIH		16/6/90	D	3	(1)	
27	Óscar Lisandro SACRIPANTI	ARG	7/1/82	A		(1)	
22	Martin ŠARIČ	ARG	18/8/79	M	1		
17	Peter STOJANOVIČ		8/3/90	M	1	(1)	
99	Rok ŠTRAUS		3/3/87	A	25	(1)	3
11	Dejan URBANČ		13/4/84	M	24	(3)	

NK DOMŽALE

Coach – Vlado Badžim; (9/12/09) Darko Birjukov (BIH)
Founded – 1921
Stadium – Športni park (3,212)
MAJOR HONOURS:
Slovenian League - (2) 2007, 2008.

2009

17/7	Drava	h	2-2	Zatkovič, Pekič
25/7	IB Ljubljana	a	0-0	
31/7	Gorica	h	1-4	Teinović
9/8	Rudar	a	1-4	Perme
14/8	Maribor	h	1-3	Teinović
23/8	Olimpija	a	1-3	Perme
28/8	Nafta	h	2-1	Hanžič, Čavuševič
11/9	Koper	h	1-1	Drevenšek
19/9	Celje	a	3-2	Drevenšek 2, Šturm
23/9	Drava	a	1-2	Zatkovič
27/9	IB Ljubljana	h	1-0	Šturm
3/10	Gorica	a	1-1	Elsner
17/10	Rudar	h	2-0	Krcič, Stojanovič
24/10	Maribor	a	2-1	Šturm, Juninho
28/10	Olimpija	h	1-2	Zatkovič
31/10	Nafta	a	2-2	Drevenšek, og (Caban)
7/11	Koper	a	1-0	Čavuševič (p)
22/11	Celje	h	1-5	Juninho
28/11	Drava	h	2-0	Krcič, Juninho
2/12	Gorica	h	2-3	Stojanovič, Hanžič (p)
5/12	IB Ljubljana	a	1-2	Drevenšek
9/12	Rudar	a	2-0	Pekič, Vidovič

2010

27/2	Maribor	h	2-3	Topič, Vidovič
6/3	Olimpija	a	1-1	Topič
13/3	Koper	h	0-1	
20/3	Celje	a	0-1	
27/3	Drava	a	1-2	Topič
31/3	Nafta	h	3-1	Pekič 2, Brezovački
3/4	IB Ljubljana	h	2-1	Šturm (p), Zatkovič
10/4	Gorica	a	3-2	Perme, Zatkovič, og (Mevlja N.)
17/4	Rudar	h	1-1	Pekič
24/4	Maribor	a	1-1	Drevenšek
30/4	Olimpija	h	1-2	og (Salkič)
5/5	Nafta	a	0-2	
11/5	Koper	a	3-1	Perme 2, Šturm
16/5	Celje	h	2-2	Perme, Hanžič (p)

No	Name	Nat	DoB	Pos	Aps	(s)	Gls
87	Tadej APATIČ		7/7/87	D	20	(5)	
30	Jani BENGEZ		8/9/90	M	5		
1	Franci BIČEK		27/11/90	G		(2)	
8	Blaž BREZOVAČKI		29/4/87	D	12	(3)	1
22	Darko BRLJKA		23/12/84	G	13		
28	Džengis ČAVUŠEVIČ		26/11/87	A	14	(6)	2
6	Nik CIMPRIČ		15/8/91	M	2		
20	Marko DREVENŠEK		10/9/87	M	25	(2)	6
29	Luka ELSNER		2/8/82	D	22		1
27	Željko FILIPOVIČ		3/10/88	D	2	(3)	
5	Rok HANŽIČ		6/4/81	D	26		3
25	Wilson Aparecido Xavier Júnior "JUNINHO"	BRA	15/3/84	M	18	(4)	3
18	Saša KOVJENIČ		12/2/90	M	5	(3)	
14	Amer KRCIČ		23/5/89	M	7	(9)	2
26	Tim LO DUCA		17/12/85	A	2	(1)	
16	Blaž MOHOR		21/4/89	M	2	(3)	
10	Damir PEKIČ		15/1/79	A	17	(6)	5
11	Janez PERME		12/4/82	A	7	(13)	6
26	Matic SEFEROVIČ		22/12/86	M	10	(1)	
28	Mato ŠIMUNOVIČ	AUT	27/9/85	A	4	(4)	
17	Dalibor STOJANOVIČ		4/4/89	D	18	(4)	2
9	Jani ŠTURM		20/3/83	A	18	(10)	5
7	Dalibor TEINOVIČ	BIH	22/3/77	M	32	(1)	2

3	Darko TOPIČ	3/3/85	M	22	(5)	3
41	Nejc VIDMAR	31/3/89	G	23		
4	Jovan VIDOVIČ	6/1/89	M	20	(4)	2
15	Alen VUČKIČ	1/2/90	M	3	(5)	
19	Mitja ZATKOVIČ	7/6/83	M	31	(2)	5
2	Darko ZEC	21/2/89	D	16	(4)	

NK DRAVA

Coach – Adnan Zildžović (BIH); (17/10/09) Franci Fridl;
(27/2/10) Milko Djurovski (MKD)
Founded – 1933
Stadium – Ptuj (4,000)

2009

17/7	Domžale	a	2-2	Drevenšek (p), Zajc
26/7	Koper	h	1-3	Drevenšek
1/8	Celje	a	0-1	
8/8	Nafta	a	1-3	Zajc
16/8	IB Ljubljana	h	1-1	Kronaveter
22/8	Gorica	a	2-1	Zajc, Ekpoki
30/8	Rudar	h	1-0	Kronaveter
12/9	Maribor	a	2-2	Ricardo Sousa, Semler
20/9	Olimpija	h	0-3	
23/9	Domžale	h	2-1	Zajc, Prejac
26/9	Koper	a	0-0	
4/10	Celje	h	0-1	
18/10	Nafta	h	1-2	Semler
24/10	IB Ljubljana	a	1-2	Ekpoki
28/10	Gorica	h	1-1	Kronaveter
31/10	Rudar	a	3-0	Kelenc, Kronaveter, Ogu
8/11	Maribor	h	0-2	
21/11	Olimpija	a	0-3	
28/11	Domžale	a	0-2	
2/12	Celje	a	0-3	
6/12	Koper	h	1-1	Ekpoki
9/12	Nafta	a	0-1	

2010

27/2	IB Ljubljana	h	3-1	Ekpoki, Žilić, Pavlovič (p)
6/3	Gorica	a	1-2	Žilić
13/3	Maribor	a	2-3	Pavlovič (p), Filipovič
20/3	Olimpija	h	0-0	
27/3	Domžale	h	2-1	Rakovič, Pavlovič (p)
31/3	Rudar	h	0-1	
3/4	Koper	a	1-1	Lunder
10/4	Celje	h	0-1	
17/4	Nafta	h	0-0	
24/4	IB Ljubljana	a	2-0	Stepanovič, Kelenc
30/4	Gorica	h	2-4	Ekpoki 2
5/5	Rudar	a	2-4	Zajc, Ogu
11/5	Maribor	h	0-1	
16/5	Olimpija	a	0-2	

No	Name	Nat	DoB	Pos	Aps	(s)	Gls
6	Siniša ANDŽELKOVIČ		13/2/86	D	20	(1)	
24	Marko BALAŽIČ		31/7/84	D	27	(3)	
9	Patrik BORDON		6/4/88	A		(4)	
16	Miha BRATUŠEK		14/4/88	G	10		
8	Aleš ČEH		22/7/80	M	2		
7	Marko DREVENŠEK		10/9/87	M	1	(1)	2
11	Abdulrazak EKPOKI	NGA	27/10/82	A	21	(3)	6
15	Aljoša FEKONJA		9/10/91	A	1		
32	Ivan FILIPOVIČ		9/8/87	D	12	(1)	1
1	Gregor FINK		3/7/84	G	16		
8	Franci FRIDL		22/7/72	M	2	(1)	
14	Suvad GRABUS	BIH	14/12/81	D	7		
11	Marko GRIŽONIČ		1/12/82	M	2		
32	Matej HAUPTMAN		20/3/92	M		(1)	
35	Namanja JOZIČ		28/5/84	G	10		
33	Naser KAJTAZI		19/11/92	A		(1)	
10	Doris KELENC		8/2/86	M	34		2

7	Milko KOVAČ		7/1/87	M	1	(1)
22	Rok KRONAVETER		7/12/86	M	18	(1)	4
31	Leon KUKEC		29/8/91	D	1	
25	Kristjan KULČAR		17/8/86	M	4	(3)
91	Robert KUREŽ		20/7/91	M	5	(17)
28	Matjaž LUNDER		4/3/81	D	6		1
19	Gregor MARC		9/3/90	D		(2)
14	Rok MARINIČ		16/5/87	M	6	(1)
18	Jure MATJAŠIČ		31/5/92	M	2	(5)
88	Klemen MEDVED		10/11/88	M	18	(6)
30	John Ugochukwu OGU	NGA	20/4/88	A	29		2
34	David PAUKO		21/2/92	M		(1)
33	Zoran PAVLOVIČ		27/6/76	M	8		3
23	Marko PEČNIK		22/7/90	A	3	
3	Denis PERGER		10/6/93	D		(3)
13	Andrej PREJAC		22/1/85	D	20		1
5	Ermin RAKOVIČ		7/9/77	A	6		1
28	RICARDO André de Pinho SOUSA	POR	11/1/79	A	5		1
26	Marko ROŠKAR		21/10/92	D	7	(2)
9	Borut SEMLER		25/2/85	A	19	(2)	2
6	Nejc SKUBIC		13/6/89	M	10	(2)
7	Bojan STEPANOVIČ		11/1/83	D	4	(2)	1
27	Marko TROJAK		28/3/88	M	2	
20	Renato TURKUŠ		1/5/89	D	1	(3)
2	Marko VINKOVIČ		19/4/91	M	1	
17	Rene VRABL		22/6/89	M	4	(2)
18	Damir ZAGORŠEK		4/9/88	A	1	
87	Gorazd ZAJC		28/12/87	M	19	(5)	5
4	Aleksandar ZEČEVIČ		29/1/85	D	2	(2)
77	Sead ŽILIĆ	BIH	17/9/82	A	8	(3)	2
21	Tonči ŽILIĆ	CRO	26/2/75	M	21	(2)

20/3	Rudar	h	2-1	Brečević, Galešić
27/3	Maribor	h	3-3	Osterc, Cvijanovič, Demirović
31/3	IB Ljubljana	a	5-0	Osterc 2, Galešić, Cvijanovič, Martinović
3/4	Olimpija	a	0-5	
10/4	Domžale	h	2-3	Osterc, Brečević
17/4	Koper	a	2-3	Cvijanovič, Galešić
24/4	Celje	h	3-0	Osterc 2, Demirović
30/4	Drava	a	4-2	Cvijanovič, Osterc, Brečević, Galešić
5/5	IB Ljubljana	h	6-1	Osterc 2, Brečević, Zarifović, Cvijanovič, Nikolič
11/5	Nafta	h	3-1	Cvijanovič 2, Osterc
16/5	Rudar	a	3-2	Mevlja M., Brečević, Kršič

No	Name	Nat	DoB	Pos	Aps	(s)	Gls
18	Sandi ARČON		6/1/91	D		(7)	
9	Gregor BALAŽIČ		12/2/88	M	29		1
25	Ivan BREČEVIČ		28/7/87	A	22	(3)	10
27	Goran CVIJANOVIČ		9/9/86	D	32	(3)	11
24	Enes DEMIROVIČ	BIH	13/6/72	M	29	(2)	5
29	Bojan ĐUKIČ		6/11/86	D	19	(3)	1
13	Domen FRATINA		10/9/87	D	3	(6)	
20	Goran GALEŠIČ	BIH	11/3/89	M	25	(1)	7
4	Gorazd GORINŠEK		29/3/83	M	16		1
35	Miha GREGORIČ		22/8/89	M	7	(7)	
19	Sebastjan KOMEL		18/2/86	M	6	(1)	
10	Admir KRŠIČ		7/11/82	M	26	(3)	4
26	Dino MARTINOVIČ		20/7/90	A		(9)	2
33	Miha MEVLJA		12/6/90	M	7	(7)	1
34	Nejc MEVLJA		12/6/90	D		(4)	
2	Dragoljub NIKOLIČ		26/10/80	D	14	(4)	1
32	Milan OSTERC		4/7/75	A	34		23
22	Mitja PIRIH		13/9/87	G	1		
31	Danijel RAKUŠČEK		10/6/86	M	31	(3)	
12	Vasja SIMČIČ		1/7/83	G	19		
14	Matija ŠKARABOT		4/2/88	M	29		
11	Etien VELIKONJA		26/12/88	A	13	(3)	5
7	Amadej VETRIH		16/9/90	M	1	(9)	
6	Aris ZARIFOVIČ		2/6/88	D	17	(3)	1
28	Dejan ŽIGON		30/3/89	A		(10)	
30	Dragan ŽILIČ	CRO	14/12/74	G	16		

ND GORICA

Coach – Miran Srebrnič; (19/9/09) David Peršič; (23/9/09) Vladan Mladenovič; (28/10/09) David Peršič
Founded – 1947
Stadium – Športni Park (5,000)
MAJOR HONOURS:
Slovenian League - (4) 1996, 2004, 2005, 2006;
Slovenian Cup - (2) 2001, 2002.

2009

18/7	Maribor	a	1-0	Gorinšek
26/7	Olimpija	h	1-2	Galešić
31/7	Domžale	a	4-1	Velikonja 2, Galešić, Osterc
8/8	Koper	h	1-2	Osterc
15/8	Celje	a	0-2	
22/8	Drava	h	1-2	Osterc
29/8	IB Ljubljana	a	1-3	Velikonja
12/9	Nafta	a	1-2	Kršič
19/9	Rudar	h	1-3	Velikonja
23/9	Maribor	h	2-3	Kršič (p), Brečević
27/9	Olimpija	a	1-1	Velikonja
3/10	Domžale	h	1-1	og (Elsner)
17/10	Koper	a	1-1	Osterc
24/10	Celje	a	1-1	Galešić
28/10	Drava	a	1-1	Osterc
31/10	IB Ljubljana	h	4-3	Osterc, Cvijanovič, Đukič, Brečević
7/11	Nafta	h	3-1	Osterc, Demirović, Cvijanovič
21/11	Rudar	a	3-0	Cvijanovič, Kršič, Osterc
28/11	Maribor	a	1-3	Osterc
2/12	Domžale	a	3-2	Osterc 3
5/12	Olimpija	h	1-1	Balažič
9/12	Koper	h	1-2	Brečević
2010				
27/2	Celje	a	4-1	Demirović (p), Brečević 2, Cvijanovič
6/3	Drava	h	2-1	Osterc, Martinović
14/3	Nafta	a	1-0	Demirović

NK IB LJUBLJANA

Coach – Igor Benedejčič; (24/10/09) Borivoje Lučić (BIH)
Founded – 1975
Stadium – Šiška (6,000)
MAJOR HONOURS:
Slovenian Cup – (2) 2008, 2009.

2009

18/7	Olimpija	a	3-1	Horvat, Rakovič, og (Léo Bonfim)
25/7	Domžale	h	0-0	
1/8	Koper	a	1-2	Rakovič
9/8	Celje	h	1-2	Rakovič
16/8	Drava	a	1-1	Mišura
22/8	Nafta	a	1-0	Milenković
29/8	Gorica	h	3-1	Milenković 2, Zadnikar
12/9	Rudar	a	1-2	Gerič (p)
19/9	Maribor	h	2-1	Milenković 2
23/9	Olimpija	h	0-1	
27/9	Domžale	a	0-1	
3/10	Koper	h	0-1	
17/10	Celje	a	1-3	Milenković
24/10	Drava	h	2-1	Iličič, Majcen
28/10	Nafta	h	1-1	Rapnik
31/10	Gorica	a	3-4	Páez 2, Zadnikar
7/11	Rudar	h	3-1	Fink, Tabot, Páez
28/11	Olimpija	a	0-2	
2/12	Koper	a	0-0	

5/12	Domžale	h	2-1	*Páez 2*
9/12	Celje	h	0-0	
12/12	Maribor	a	0-1	
2010				
27/2	Drava	a	1-3	*Horvat*
6/3	Nafta	a	1-3	*Ćehič*
13/3	Rudar	a	2-1	*Iličič, Berič*
20/3	Maribor	h	0-1	
27/3	Olimpija	h	2-1	*Horvat, Fink*
31/3	Gorica	h	0-5	
3/4	Domžale	a	1-2	*Berič*
10/4	Koper	h	0-5	
17/4	Celje	a	1-5	*Berič*
24/4	Drava	h	0-2	
30/4	Nafta	h	1-1	*Berič (p)*
5/5	Gorica	a	1-6	*Iličič (p)*
11/5	Rudar	h	0-1	
16/5	Maribor	a	0-1	

No	Name	Nat	DoB	Pos	Aps	(s)	Gls
20	Asimou AJEWA	TOG	8/6/91	M		(2)	
2	Nemanja ANDRIJEVIĆ		23/7/89	D		(1)	
9	Robert BERIČ		17/6/91	A	14	(2)	4
32	Blaž BOŽIČ		23/10/90	M	17	(8)	
7	Danijel BREZIČ		15/2/76	M	13		
29	Žan CANKAR		13/11/90	D	13	(1)	
23	Damir ĆEHIČ		26/9/91	A	1	(5)	1
30	Matic FINK		27/2/90	M	14	(5)	2
8	Dejan GERIČ		3/5/88	D	6	(4)	1
21	Ben GILL	ENG	4/10/87	D	15	(4)	
33	Suad GRABUS		14/12/81	D	10		
25	Lucas Mario HORVAT	ARG	13/10/85	M	31		3
27	Josip ILIČIČ		29/1/88	A	26	(2)	3
23	Boštjan JELEČEVIĆ		16/3/85	M	6		
6	Alen JOGAN		24/7/85	D	23		
28	Ažbe JUG		3/3/92	G	10		
18	Amer JUKAN		28/11/78	M	1	(2)	
11	Peter KLANČAR		14/11/85	D	2	(6)	
19	Aleš KOKOT		23/10/79	D	13		
16	Luka MAJCEN		25/7/89	A	12	(8)	1
11	Vladimir MILENKOVIĆ	SRB	22/7/82	A	13		6
12	Tomislav MIŠURA	CRO	13/5/81	M	3	(3)	1
20	Théophile NTAMÉ	CMR	17/5/85	D	11	(1)	
17	Gustavo Andrés PÁEZ	VEN	16/4/90	A	16	(4)	5
8	Balša RADOVIĆ		4/1/91	M	1		
10	Ermin RAKOVIĆ		7/9/77	A	6		3
3	Žan RANT ROOS		17/12/90	M		(1)	
35	Matej RAPNIK		24/2/90	D	21		1
22	Matjaž ROZMAN		3/1/87	G	22		
10	Jamie Lee SHELDON	ENG	14/8/91	M	7	(3)	
2	Nejc SKUBIC		13/6/89	D	7	(2)	
5	Enow Juvette TABOT	CMR	8/6/89	D	25		1
1	Andrej TROHA		24/4/81	G	4	(1)	
14	Filip VALENČIČ		7/1/92	M	4	(2)	
26	Luka VRHUNC		11/3/91	M	1	(9)	
24	Dejan ZADNIKAR		2/11/90	A	7	(8)	2
4	Matic ŽITKO		21/2/90	M	13	(2)	
2	Aleksandar ZUKIĆ		5/1/91	D	8	(2)	
15	Janez ZUPANČIČ		17/2/91	M		(1)	

FC KOPER
Coach – Nedžad Okčič
Founded – 1955
Stadium – Bonifika (10,000)
MAJOR HONOURS:
Slovenian League – (1) 2010;
Slovenian Cup - (2) 2006, 2007.

2009				
18/7	Celje	h	1-0	*Božičič*
26/7	Drava	a	3-1	*Radujko, Guberac, Huskič*
1/8	IB Ljubljana	h	2-1	*Brulc, Radujko*
8/8	Gorica	a	2-1	*Kovačevič, Pavlin M.*
15/8	Rudar	h	2-2	*Brulc 2*
23/8	Maribor	a	2-1	*Brulc, Pavlin M.*
29/8	Olimpija	h	2-1	*Brulc, Pavlin M.*
11/9	Domžale	a	1-1	*Pavlin M.*
19/9	Nafta	h	3-1	*Brulc 2 (1p), Božičič*
23/9	Celje	a	1-0	*Rajčevič*
26/9	Drava	h	0-0	
3/10	IB Ljubljana	a	1-0	*Radujko*
17/10	Gorica	h	1-1	*Radujko*
24/10	Rudar	a	2-2	*Pavlin M., Radujko*
28/10	Maribor	h	1-3	*Kovačevič*
31/10	Olimpija	a	1-0	*Radujko*
7/11	Domžale	h	0-1	
21/11	Nafta	a	1-3	*Božičič*
2/12	IB Ljubljana	h	0-0	
6/12	Drava	a	1-1	*Radujko*
9/12	Gorica	a	2-1	*Pavlin M., Brulc*
12/12	Celje	h	4-0	*Pavlin M., Struna Al., Brulc, Bešič*
2010				
27/2	Rudar	h	2-1	*Vršič, Radujko*
6/3	Maribor	a	2-2	*Božičič, Polovanec*
13/3	Domžale	a	1-0	*Brulc*
21/3	Nafta	h	2-0	*Radujko, Vršič*
28/3	Celje	a	3-1	*Pavlin M. 2, Vršič (p)*
31/3	Olimpija	h	1-0	*Pavlin M.*
3/4	Drava	h	1-1	*Radujko*
10/4	IB Ljubljana	a	5-0	*Vršič 3, Radujko, Pavlin M.*
17/4	Gorica	h	3-2	*Vršič, Kovačevič, og (Fratina)*
24/4	Rudar	a	2-0	*Brulc, Vršič*
30/4	Maribor	h	0-0	
5/5	Olimpija	a	1-3	*Bešič*
11/5	Domžale	h	1-3	*Vršič*
16/5	Nafta	a	2-1	*Struna An., Brulc*

No	Name	Nat	DoB	Pos	Aps	(s)	Gls
18	Danijel BEŠIČ		31/7/90	A	3	(3)	2
15	Darijo BIŠĆAN		26/8/85	A	2	(9)	
33	Saša BOŽIČIČ		8/5/83	M	21	(6)	4
25	Mitja BRULC		7/12/79	A	34		12
32	Davor BUBANJA		26/9/87	A	1	(6)	
29	Dragutin GOLUB	CRO	29/8/87	M		(2)	
7	Ivica GUBERAC		5/7/88	M	17	(2)	1
27	Damir HADŽIČ		1/10/84	D	6	(21)	
6	Enes HANDANAGIČ		15/9/79	D	27	(1)	
12	Ermin HASIČ		19/9/75	G	14		
19	Etien HUSKIČ		11/3/88	D	2	(9)	1
9	Patrik IPAVEC		13/7/77	A	2	(5)	
20	Amir KARIČ		31/12/73	M	30		
8	Nebojša KOVAČEVIČ		8/9/77	M	30		3
22	Igor NENEZIČ		23/3/84	G	12		
14	Luka PAVLIN		16/10/88	M		(3)	
11	Miran PAVLIN		8/10/71	M	30		11
31	Frane PETRIČEVIČ	CRO	21/10/79	M		(1)	
5	Kristijan POLOVANEC	CRO	10/10/79	D	21	(2)	1
23	Dalibor RADUJKO		17/6/85	M	26		11
26	Aleksandar RAJČEVIČ		27/11/86	D	30	(2)	1
21	Ivan SESAR	BIH	29/8/89	M	18	(5)	
17	Aljaž STRUNA		4/8/90	M	12	(2)	1
24	Andraž STRUNA		23/4/89	D	21	(1)	1
14	Miloš SUČEVIČ		8/10/88	M		(2)	
30	Admir SUHONJIČ		23/3/81	G	10		
28	Mitja VILER		1/9/86	M	13	(18)	
10	Dare VRŠIČ		26/9/84	A	14		9

SLOVENIA
NZS

NK MARIBOR
Coach – Darko Milanič
Founded – 1960
Stadium – Ljudski vrt (12,432)
MAJOR HONOURS:
Slovenian League - (8) 1997, 1998, 1999, 2000, 2001, 2002, 2003, 2009;
Slovenian Cup - (6) 1992, 1994, 1997, 1999, 2004, 2010.

2009
18/7	Gorica	h	0-1
26/7	Rudar	a	0-1
1/8	Nafta	h	3-1 *Jelič, Volaš, Školnik*
8/8	Olimpija	h	1-0 *Bačinovič*
14/8	Domžale	a	3-1 *Jelič 2, Mihelič*
23/8	Koper	h	1-2 *Jelič*
29/8	Celje	a	1-2 *Jelič*
12/9	Drava	h	2-2 *Školnik, Jelič (p)*
19/9	IB Ljubljana	a	1-2 *Jelič*
23/9	Gorica	a	3-2 *Školnik, Jelič (p), Marcos Tavares*
27/9	Rudar	h	0-2
3/10	Nafta	a	4-2 *Džinič, Mezga, Mihelič, Plut*
17/10	Olimpija	a	1-0 *Marcos Tavares*
24/10	Domžale	h	1-2 *Jelič*
28/10	Koper	a	3-1 *Marcos Tavares, Bačinovič, Jelič (p)*
31/10	Celje	h	3-3 *Jelič, Dodlek, Mihelič (p)*
8/11	Drava	a	2-0 *Mertelj, Jelič (p)*
28/11	Gorica	h	3-1 *Marcos Tavares 2, Plut*
2/12	Nafta	h	1-2 *Marcos Tavares*
6/12	Rudar	a	2-0 *Plut, Jelič*
9/12	Olimpija	h	2-1 *Plut, Marcos Tavares*
12/12	IB Ljubljana	h	1-0 *Plut*

2010
27/2	Domžale	a	3-2 *Mezga, Džinič, Plut*
6/3	Koper	h	2-2 *Plut, Marcos Tavares*
13/3	Drava	h	3-2 *Mezga 2, Marcos Tavares*
20/3	IB Ljubljana	a	1-0 *Mezga*
27/3	Gorica	a	3-3 *Bačinovič, Andjelkovič, Jelič*
31/3	Celje	a	2-0 *Jelič (p), Džinič*
3/4	Rudar	h	0-1
10/4	Nafta	a	1-3 *Marcos Tavares*
16/4	Olimpija	a	1-1 *Mihelič*
24/4	Domžale	h	1-1 *Bunderla*
30/4	Koper	a	0-0
4/5	Celje	h	1-1 *Mihelič (p)*
11/5	Drava	a	1-0 *Mezga*
16/5	IB Ljubljana	h	1-0 *Andjelkovič*

No	Name	Nat	DoB	Pos	Aps	(s)	Gls
16	Janez ALJANČIČ		29/7/82	D	21	(1)	
66	Siniša ANDJELKOVIČ		13/2/86	D	13		2
21	Armin BAČINOVIČ		24/10/89	M	24	(4)	3
39	David BUNDERLA		31/7/87	A	6	(20)	1
2	Matic ČRNIČ		12/6/92	D		(4)	
29	Timotej DODLEK		23/11/89	M	14	(6)	1
3	Elvedin DŽINIČ		25/8/85	D	34		3
15	Suad FILEKOVIČ		16/9/78	D	12		
77	FLÁVIO Beck Júnior	BRA	14/3/87	A	2	(9)	
11	Dragan JELIČ		27/2/86	A	24	(9)	15
6	Dejan JURKIČ		9/12/83	D	7	(1)	
5	Željko KLJAJEVIČ	SRB	14/9/84	D	2		
18	Matjaž LUNDER		4/3/81	D	4		
36	Aleš MAJER		2/8/89	D	6	(4)	
9	MARCOS Magno Morales TAVARES	BRA	30/3/84	A	32	(2)	10
7	Aleš MEJAČ		18/3/83	D	16	(3)	
70	Aleš MERTELJ		22/3/87	M	18	(8)	1
8	Dejan MEZGA	CRO	16/7/85	M	18	(7)	6
10	Rene MIHELIČ		5/7/88	M	25	(8)	5
33	Zoran PAVLOVIČ		27/6/76	M	8		
14	Vito PLUT		8/7/88	A	17	(12)	7
27	Marko POPOVIČ	SRB	25/8/82	M	14	(2)	

12	Marko PRIDIGAR		18/5/85	G	11		
1	Marko RANILOVIČ		25/11/86	G	25		
23	Mitja REŠEK		15/1/91	M		(1)	
20	Miral SAMARDŽIČ		17/2/87	D	16	(1)	
40	Dejan ŠKOLNIK	CRO	1/1/89	M	26	(2)	3
35	Armend SPREČO		27/5/90	A		(1)	
30	Dalibor VOLAŠ		27/2/87	A	1	(3)	1

NK NAFTA
Coach – Ljubinko Drulović (SRB);
(15/8/09) Nebojša Vučičević (SRB)
Founded – 1903
Stadium – Lendava (5,000)

2009
19/7	Rudar	a	0-2
25/7	Celje	h	2-2 *Koplárovics, Sebők*
1/8	Maribor	a	1-3 *Repina*
8/8	Drava	h	3-1 *Mujakovič, Horvat, Sebők*
16/8	Olimpija	a	0-2
22/8	IB Ljubljana	h	0-1
28/8	Domžale	a	1-2 *Sebők*
12/9	Gorica	h	2-1 *Mujakovič, Čeh*
19/9	Koper	a	1-3 *Čeh*
23/9	Rudar	h	5-2 *Miljković 2, Mujakovič (p), Volaš, Gerenčar B.*
26/9	Celje	a	2-2 *Miljković, Volaš*
3/10	Maribor	h	2-4 *Gerenčar B., Volaš (p)*
18/10	Drava	a	2-1 *Gerenčar P., Volaš (p)*
24/10	Olimpija	h	1-0 *Vassiljev*
28/10	IB Ljubljana	a	1-1 *Volaš*
31/10	Domžale	h	2-2 *Čeh, Vassiljev*
7/11	Gorica	a	1-3 *Volaš*
21/11	Koper	h	3-1 *Volaš, Vassiljev, Čeh*
28/11	Rudar	a	1-0 *Volaš*
2/12	Maribor	a	2-1 *Miljković 2*
5/12	Celje	h	2-1 *Čeh, Ošlaj*
9/12	Drava	h	1-0 *Volaš*

2010
28/2	Olimpija	a	0-0
6/3	IB Ljubljana	h	3-1 *Vassiljev, Volaš, Caban*
14/3	Gorica	h	0-1
21/3	Koper	a	0-2
27/3	Rudar	h	2-0 *Buzeti, Benko (p)*
31/3	Domžale	a	1-3 *og (Topič)*
3/4	Celje	a	2-3 *Caban, Miljković*
10/4	Maribor	h	3-1 *Benko 2, Miljković*
17/4	Drava	a	0-0
25/4	Olimpija	h	0-1
30/4	IB Ljubljana	a	1-1 *Mujakovič*
5/5	Domžale	h	2-0 *Volaš, Buzeti*
11/5	Gorica	a	1-3 *Horvat*
16/5	Koper	h	1-2 *Buzeti*

No	Name	Nat	DoB	Pos	Aps	(s)	Gls
8	Jože BENKO		22/3/80	A	8	(5)	3
4	Mihael BUKOVEC		18/9/78	D	12	(9)	
11	Gregor BUNC		23/9/75	M	22	(4)	
24	Rok BUZETI		10/2/88	M	27	(3)	3
23	Stjepan CABAN	CRO	23/2/80	D	25	(2)	2
30	Aleš ČEH		22/7/80	M	21	(1)	5
9	Mitja FLISAR		29/3/89	M		(2)	
15	Borut GERENČAR		20/7/80	M	27	(3)	2
18	Peter GERENČAR		28/4/85	M		(3)	1
5	Leon HORVAT		29/8/86	M	7	(8)	2
10	Siniša JANKOVIČ	SRB	18/1/78	M	7	(5)	
7	Nejc KOLMAN		26/2/89	M	5	(1)	
17	Saša KOLMAN		1/5/84	D	9	(5)	
8	Béla KOPLÁROVICS	HUN	7/6/81	M	9	(1)	1
99	Aleš LUK		23/5/81	G	3		
3	Bojan MATJAŠEC		16/4/84	D	19	(1)	
6	Emil MILJKOVIČ	BIH	26/5/88	A	24	(9)	7

20	Amel MUJAKOVIČ		4/5/82	A	24	(1)	4
22	Tomaž MURKO		7/2/79	G	33		
29	Damjan OŠLAJ		25/8/76	D	22		1
26	Patrik RADUHA		9/2/90	D		(1)	
19	Jernej REPINA		7/1/83	M	2	(8)	1
9	József SEBŐK	HUN	18/6/75	A	8	(1)	3
25	Arpad VAŠ		31/7/89	M	3		
14	Konstantin VASSILJEV	EST	16/8/84	M	31	(1)	4
33	Vedran VINKO		22/2/90	A	2	(5)	
13	Dalibor VOLAŠ		27/2/87	A	21	(4)	11
27	Patrik VOROS		16/10/90	M		(1)	
2	Boštjan ZEMLJIČ		21/9/74	D	25	(2)	

NK OLIMPIJA LJUBLJANA
Coach – Brane Oblak; (15/8/09) Safet Hadžič;
(12/9/09) Robert Pevnik
Founded – 2005
Stadium – ŽAK (5,000)

2009

18/7	IB Ljubljana	h	1-3	Šporar
26/7	Gorica	a	2-1	Cimerotič, Tiganj
31/7	Rudar	h	0-1	
8/8	Maribor	a	0-1	
16/8	Nafta	h	2-0	Roj, Škerjanc
23/8	Domžale	h	3-1	Cimerotič 2, Škerjanc
29/8	Koper	a	1-2	Ibraimi
12/9	Celje	h	4-2	Tiganj 2, Cimerotič, Škerjanc
20/9	Drava	a	3-0	Cimerotič, Roj, Tiganj
23/9	IB Ljubljana	a	1-0	Cvijanovič
27/9	Gorica	h	1-1	Cimerotič
3/10	Rudar	a	3-0	og (Sulejmanovič), Kašnik, Cimerotič
17/10	Maribor	h	0-1	
24/10	Nafta	a	0-1	
28/10	Domžale	a	2-1	Ibraimi, Cimerotič
31/10	Koper	h	0-1	
7/11	Celje	a	1-1	Rujovič
21/11	Drava	h	3-0	Gabriel 2 (1p), Cimerotič
28/11	IB Ljubljana	h	2-0	Gabriel, Rujovič
2/12	Rudar	h	0-1	
5/12	Gorica	a	1-1	Gabriel
9/12	Maribor	h	1-2	Gabriel

2010

28/2	Nafta	h	0-0	
6/3	Domžale	h	1-1	Léo Bonfim
13/3	Celje	h	1-3	Roj
20/3	Drava	a	0-0	
27/3	IB Ljubljana	a	1-2	Purovič (p)
31/3	Koper	a	0-1	
3/4	Gorica	h	5-0	Šporar, Prašnikar, Škerjanc, Ibraimi, Rujovič
10/4	Rudar	a	3-1	Ibraimi 2, Kašnik
16/4	Maribor	h	1-1	Léo Bonfim
25/4	Nafta	a	1-0	Ibraimi (p)
30/4	Domžale	a	2-1	Škerjanc, Kašnik
5/5	Koper	h	3-1	Ibraimi 2, Omladič
11/5	Celje	a	0-1	
16/5	Drava	h	2-0	Prašnikar, Salkič

No	Name	Nat	DoB	Pos	Aps	(s)	Gls
1	Damir BOTONJIČ		14/9/81	G	3		
7	Davor BUBANJA		26/9/87	A	2	(1)	
14	Sebastjan CIMEROTIČ		14/9/74	A	17		9
21	Miroslav CVIJANOVIČ		14/5/85	D	31	(1)	1
28	Andrej DUGOLIN		19/9/86	M	14	(7)	
6	Željko FILIPOVIČ		3/10/88	M	2	(10)	
8	João GABRIEL da Silva	BRA	4/7/84	M	21	(2)	5
9	Agim IBRAIMI	MKD	29/8/88	A	23	(6)	8
15	Sait IDRIZI		26/4/90	M		(9)	
2	Boban JOVIČ		25/6/91	D	13	(3)	
18	David KAŠNIK		16/1/87	D	31	(1)	3
5	LÉOnardo Augusto Bonifácio "BONFIM"	BRA	14/1/83	D	17	(3)	2
30	Željko MITRAKOVIČ		30/12/72	M	2		
22	Jan OBLAK		7/1/93	G	33		
17	Nik OMLADIČ		21/8/89	M	6	(1)	1
11	Luka PAVLIN		16/10/88	M		(1)	
17	Anto PEJIČ	CRO	21/2/89	A	1	(1)	
15	Jalen POKORN		7/6/79	M	31		
20	Luka PRAŠNIKAR		11/6/87	A	8	(5)	2
77	Milan PUROVIČ	MNE	7/5/85	A	5	(2)	1
24	Almir RAHMANOVIČ		25/3/86	M		(1)	
19	Rok ROJ		8/10/86	M	21	(11)	3
13	Mladen RUDONJA		26/7/71	A	1		
10	Enes RUJOVIČ		29/5/89	M	21	(13)	3
33	Erik SALKIČ		10/4/87	D	30	(3)	1
26	Davor ŠKERJANC		7/1/86	M	30		5
3	Miha ŠPORAR		31/7/72	D	24	(5)	2
7	Petar STOJANOVIČ		8/3/90	M	2	(8)	
32	Senad TIGANJ		28/8/75	A	7	(7)	4

NK RUDAR VELENJE
Coach – Marjan Pušnik; (20/3/10) Franci Oblak;
(7/4/10) Bojan Prašnikar
Founded – 1948
Stadium – Ob Jezeru (7,000)
MAJOR HONOURS:
Slovenian Cup – (1) 1998.

2009

19/7	Nafta	h	2-0	Renato, Omladič
26/7	Maribor	h	1-0	og (Kljajevič)
31/7	Olimpija	a	1-0	Grbič
9/8	Domžale	h	4-1	Lo Duca 2, Mešić, Grbič
15/8	Koper	a	2-2	Prašnikar, Renato
22/8	Celje	h	2-0	Renato, Kolsi
30/8	Drava	a	0-1	
12/9	IB Ljubljana	h	2-1	Cipot (p), Grbič
19/9	Gorica	a	3-1	Mešić 2, Prašnikar
23/9	Nafta	a	2-5	Omladič, Tolimir
27/9	Maribor	a	2-0	Mešić, Prašnikar
3/10	Olimpija	h	0-3	
17/10	Domžale	a	0-2	
24/10	Koper	h	2-2	Mešić, Mujakovič
28/10	Celje	a	4-0	Tomažič Šeruga, Cipot (p), Mujakovič, Lo Duca
31/10	Drava	h	0-3	
7/11	IB Ljubljana	a	1-3	Mujakovič
21/11	Gorica	h	0-3	
28/11	Nafta	h	0-1	
2/12	Olimpija	a	1-0	Mujakovič (p)
6/12	Maribor	h	0-2	
9/12	Domžale	h	0-2	

2010

27/2	Koper	a	1-2	Sulejmanovič
6/3	Celje	h	3-1	Tomažič Šeruga, Selimi, Mujakovič
13/3	IB Ljubljana	h	1-2	Grbič
20/3	Gorica	a	1-2	Kronaveter (p)
27/3	Nafta	a	0-2	
31/3	Drava	a	1-0	Selimi
3/4	Maribor	a	1-0	Selimi
10/4	Olimpija	h	1-3	Kronaveter
17/4	Domžale	a	1-1	Kronaveter
24/4	Koper	h	0-2	
30/4	Celje	a	0-0	
5/5	Drava	h	4-2	Torbič, Selimi, Grbič, Stojnič
11/5	IB Ljubljana	a	1-0	Mahmutovič
16/5	Gorica	h	2-3	Cipot, Grbič

SLOVENIA

NZS

No	Name	Nat	DoB	Pos	Aps	(s)	Gls
31	Sebastjan ČELOFIGA		22/4/83	G	1		
6	Fabijan CIPOT		25/8/76	D	28		3
27	Rusmin DEDIČ		11/9/82	D	22		
7	Darko ĐUKIČ		13/8/80	A	1	(1)	
16	Miha GOLOB		9/12/80	M	24	(2)	
10	Denis GRBIČ		15/3/86	M	14	(16)	6
1	Safet JAHIČ		25/1/87	G	4	(2)	
25	Boštjan JELEČEVIČ		16/3/85	D	13	(1)	
3	Aleš JESENIČNIK		28/6/84	D	21		
4	Marko KOLSI	FIN	20/1/85	M	7	(1)	1
24	Denis KRAMAR		7/11/91	M		(1)	
29	Boštjan KREFT		23/2/81	D	4	(3)	
18	Rok KRONAVETER		7/12/86	M	12		3
14	Tim LO DUCA		17/12/85	A	6	(10)	3
17	Amel MAHMUTOVIČ		27/3/89	M	2	(6)	1
9	Mirza MEŠIĆ	BIH	28/6/80	A	16	(2)	5
29	František METELKA	CZE	8/4/80	D	13		
20	Alem MUJAKOVIČ		6/4/78	M	12	(13)	5
21	Nik OMLADIČ		21/8/89	M	9	(3)	2
19	Marko POKLEKA		15/2/82	M	6	(1)	
18	Luka PRAŠNIKAR		11/6/87	A	3	(6)	3
15	RENATO de Morães	BRA	16/8/80	M	18	(3)	3
26	Boban SAVIĆ	SRB	3/4/79	G	31		
7	Nezbedin SELIMI	SUI	6/10/84	A	11	(2)	4
11	Petar STOJNIČ		29/9/81	D	16	(5)	1
5	Almir SULEJMANOVIČ		26/1/78	D	26		1
22	Nikola TOLIMIR		1/4/89	M	28	(2)	1
2	David TOMAŽIČ ŠERUGA		30/4/86	M	21	(7)	2
13	Marian TOMČAK	SVK	13/7/80	M	7	(6)	
19	Dario TORBIČ	CRO	26/10/90	M	3	(2)	1
8	Damjan TRIFKOVIČ		22/7/87	M	17	(4)	

PROMOTED CLUBS

NK PRIMORJE
Coach – Vjekoslav Lokica (CRO)
Founded – 1924
Stadium – Primorje (4,000)

ND TRIGLAV
Coach – Stane Bevc
Founded – 2000
Stadium – Stanko Mlakar (5,000)

SECOND LEVEL FINAL TABLE 2009/10

		Pld	W	D	L	F	A	Pts
1	NK Primorje	27	15	10	2	51	16	55
2	ND Triglav	27	14	5	8	33	25	47
3	NK Aluminij	27	14	4	9	67	34	46
4	ND Dravinja	27	11	6	10	44	32	39
5	NK Bela Krajina	27	11	6	10	28	36	39
6	ND Mura 05	27	9	7	11	36	51	34
7	NK Šenčur	27	7	11	9	31	35	32
8	NK Krško	27	6	10	11	27	45	28
9	NK Livar	27	7	6	14	27	43	27
10	NK MU Šentjur	27	5	7	15	29	56	22

PROMOTION/RELEGATION PLAY-OFFS
(23/5/10)
IB Ljubljana 0, Triglav 1
(30/5/10)
Triglav 3, IB Ljubljana 0
(Triglav 4-0)

DOMESTIC CUP 2009/10

POKAL NZS

FIRST ROUND
(16/9/09)
Ankaran 3, Primorje 4
Črenšovci 1, Tolmin 1 *(aet; 6-5 on pens)*
Gostilna Lobnik Slivnica 0, Mura 5
Idrija 0, Koper 4
Jadran Dekani 0, Nafta 4
Kalcer 1, Olimpija 5
Koroška Dravograd 0, Domžale 5
Odranci 2, Dravinja 1
Stojnci 1, Bela Krajina 0
Triglav 2, Aluminij 1 *(aet)*
Železničar 0, Drava 3
Zreče 0, Celje 8

Byes – Gorica, IB Ljubljana, Maribor, Rudar Velenje

SECOND ROUND
(20/10/09)
Črenšovci 0, Gorica 5

(21/10/09)
Drava 2, Domžale 3
Koper 2, Rudar Velenje 4
Mura 3, Celje 5
Odranci 0, IB Ljubljana 2
Olimpija 0, Maribor 1
Stojnci 2, Nafta 6
Triglav 4, Primorje 0

QUARTER-FINALS
(17/3/10 & 24/3/10)
Domžale 1 *(Zatkovič 57)*, Gorica 1 *(Demirović 7)*
Gorica 0, Domžale 1 *(Pekič 22)*
(Domžale 2-1)

IB Ljubljana 1 *(Tabot 55)*, Nafta 1 *(Volaš 78)*
Nafta 3 *(Volaš 45, Repina 61, Benko 70)*, IB Ljubljana 0
(Nafta 4-1)

Maribor 5 *(Marcos Tavares 55, 67, Jelič 61, Plut 65, Bunderla 75)*, Triglav 1 *(Burgar 11)*
Triglav 2 *(Burgar 61, 90)*, Maribor 2 *(Flavio 59, Mertelj 64)*
(Maribor 7-3)

Rudar Velenje 0, Celje 1 *(Rep 6)*
Celje 1 *(Rep 86)*, Rudar Velenje 0
(Celje 2-0)

SEMI-FINALS
(13/4/10 & 21/4/10)
Maribor 4 *(Jelič 9, Marcos Tavares 21, Mertelj 66, Mezga 86)*, Celje 1
(Lovrečič 71p)
Celje 3 *(Romih 13, Bezjak 22, Purišič 66)*, Maribor 3 *(Jelič 37, Andjelković 76, Plut 90+2)*
(Maribor 7-4)

(14/4/10 & 21/4/10)
Nafta 1 *(Benko 28)*, Domžale 1 *(Pekič 55)*
Domžale 3 *(Zatkovič 3, Topič 29, Pekič 59)*, Nafta 0
(Domžale 4-1)

FINAL
(8/5/10)
Ljudski vrt, Maribor
NK MARIBOR 3 *(Marcos Tavares 42, 55, Bunderla 120)*
NK DOMŽALE 2 *(Brezovački 31, Pekič 45)*
(aet)
Referee - Skomina
MARIBOR – Ranilović, Mejač (Aljančič 83), Džinič, Andjelković, Filekovič,
Bačinovič, Mezga, Školnik (Flávio 78), Marcos Tavares, Jelič (Plut 115), Bunderla.
DOMŽALE – Vidmar, Brezovački, Hanžič, Vidovič, Seferovič (Filipovič 62),
Apatič, Teinovič (Šimunovič 102), Drevenšek, Topič (Šturm 76), Zatkovič, Pekič.

SPAIN

Europe's finest conquer the world

The best team in Europe became the best team in the world as Spain secured football's greatest treasure in Johannesburg's Soccer City stadium on 11 July 2010. The country's first ever FIFA World Cup triumph was a historic, ground-breaking achievement in many ways, and as much for the team's sustained excellence in the years leading up to the event as in South Africa itself, it was a victory of distinction and merit that nobody could justifiably contest.

The fruits of Spain's labour will be savoured for eternity, the gold star forever proudly displayed on their shirts. Vicente del Bosque's side will go down in history as the first European team to win the World Cup outside Europe. They will also be remembered as the first new winners of the trophy other than the host nation for over half a century and the only victors to succeed despite losing their opening match.

Perfect record

With a perfect record in qualifying of ten wins out of ten, plus a 100 per cent success rate also in friendly internationals (13 out of 13) during the two-year reign of Del Bosque, who succeeded Luis Aragonés after the UEFA EURO 2008 triumph, Spain were hot favourites to succeed in South Africa. That they fulfilled those enormous expectations was a tribute to the quality of the coach and the world-class footballers at his disposal, but it was also a consequence of the winning mentality that had been forged by that long sequence of pre-tournament victories.

Although Spain were worthy World Cup winners, the truth is that they did not play to their best in South Africa. They remained defiantly committed to their aesthetic, purist-friendly passing style, but they did not deliver one great performance. Their most memorable display was against Germany in the semi-final, when they dominated dangerous, in-form opponents with their smooth possession game, but even then they had to rely on a good old-fashioned set-piece to defeat them. They scored just eight goals

in seven matches – the lowest tally from a World Cup-winning team – and none in the first 45 minutes of any of their four knockout fixtures. Indeed, there were lengthy spells during the opening periods of their matches against Chile, Portugal and Paraguay when Spain were distinctly second-best. But with a mixture of stout defending and good fortune, they overcame all threats to their well-being and were routinely the stronger side in the latter stages of every match they played, most notably in the final against the Netherlands, with Andrés Iniesta's late winning goal arriving towards the end of an extra-time period in which they had been overwhelmingly superior.

With Fernando Torres injured and out of sorts and the team's midfielders proving surprisingly shot-shy, the responsibility of scoring Spain's goals fell to David Villa, and the top scorer from UEFA EURO 2008 did not disappoint, finding the net five times in four successive games to transform the team's fortunes after their shock opening defeat to Switzerland and catapult

Spain's victorious coach Vicente del Bosque holds aloft the World Cup

them not only to the top of their group but all the way into the semi-finals. But for his sharpness and composure in front of goal, La Roja might well have joined France and Italy as humiliated first-round fallers.

Brothers in arms

Xavi and Iniesta, the brilliant FC Barcelona brothers in arms, became ever more influential as the tournament progressed. Iniesta's winner in the final guarantees him everlasting fame and glory, while Xavi, virtually invisible against Switzerland, gave arguably the most commanding individual display of the tournament with his authoritative masterclass against Germany. For consistency, however, there was no-one who performed better than Carles Puyol. His headed winning goal against Germany was the obvious highlight, but his tireless, committed defending was just as important. As at UEFA EURO 2008, Spain conceded no goals in their knockout encounters – a remarkable statistic and one made possible by not only the excellence of Puyol, goalkeeper/captain Iker Casillas, Gerard Piqué and the other members of the back four but also by the whole team's ability to deny possession to the opposition in threatening areas. Spain's ability to keep hold of the ball for long periods was not just the foundation for their attacks; it proved just as effective as a defensive measure.

On reflection, the opening defeat by Switzerland could be considered a blessing in disguise. At the time it was an ugly stain on an almost unblemished record, but it forced Spain to redouble their efforts and win every game that followed. Their path to victory was no joyride, but it was the conquering of adversity, not to mention the delicious timing of the winning goal in the final, that made success so sweet for Spain and their supporters in the end.

The eruption of joy that swept the nation as the final whistle sounded in Soccer City may never be matched, but Spain's 'golden generation' – a term that, unlike for other countries, has genuine value – are certainly not finished yet. Defenders Puyol and Joan Capdevila will both be 34 when the finals of UEFA EURO 2012 come around, but otherwise there is no reason why the World Cup-winning side cannot remain virtually intact through to Poland/Ukraine and beyond into 2014 for the World Cup defence in Brazil. Del Bosque can also look forward to introducing more fresh young things like Piqué, Sergio Busquets and Pedro, all three of whom came into the side post-UEFA EURO 2008, and there must surely come a time, sooner rather than

Spain's World Cup heroes Xavi and Andrés Iniesta

later, when the immensely gifted Cesc Fàbregas becomes a mainstay in the first XI rather than an occasional substitute.

With La Roja enveloped in glory, Spain finds itself in the unfamiliar position of having its two leading club sides, Barcelona and Real Madrid CF, upstaged by an all-conquering national team. Not that Barça will have the slightest concerns about that particular state of affairs given that no fewer than seven of their players, including new summer signing David Villa, started the World Cup final.

Liga title retained

Spanish celebration of World Cup victory was nationwide, but Catalan pride was also upheld in 2010 as Barcelona made a successful defence of their Liga title, holding off a hyper-tenacious Real to become champions of Spain for the 20th time. – with a record-breaking tally of 99 points. Although the season brought additional silverware in the Spanish Super Cup, the UEFA Super Cup and the FIFA Club World Cup, there was major disappointment in the failure of Josep Guardiola's team of many talents to become the first club to win the UEFA Champions League two years in a row. Their bid for glory was halted in the semi-final by FC Internazionale Milano, a 3-2 aggregate defeat thus denying the Catalans the ultimate pleasure of

travelling to Madrid for the final and raising the trophy again in the lair of their arch-enemy.

For all the Spanish internationals in Guardiola's side, it was a foreigner – albeit one raised in Catalonia – who monopolised the headlines in 2009/10. Lionel Messi may have gone on to suffer a frustrating World Cup for Argentina, but the little maestro's form for Barcelona in the months leading up to it was sensational, leading many observers to group him among the greatest footballers of all time – alongside legends such as Pelé, Johan Cruyff and, of course, his national team coach, Diego Maradona.

Messi's breathtaking brilliance brought him 34 goals in La Liga – a tally that earned him the Pichichi and European Golden Shoe – plus a further eight in Europe, bringing him the UEFA Champions League top scorer prize for the second season in succession. The last four of those came in one scintillating, never-to-be-forgotten quarter-final display against Arsenal FC at Camp Nou – possibly the finest individual performance by any footballer since Maradona beat Belgium virtually on his own in the semi-final of the 1986 World Cup.

Messi and the rest of the Barcelona team would meet their match, however, against José Mourinho's Inter. Fortunate to overcome Chelsea FC at the same stage of the competition 12 months earlier before triumphing in Rome, they would have claimed another dramatic away-goals success had a last-gasp effort from young Bojan Krkić not been ruled out for an earlier handball. On such little things can fortunes swing and history turn.

Clásico double

There was no near-miss for Barça in La Liga, though. Although Real proved a formidable adversary, pursuing them persistently to the last, the two Gran Clásico encounters were both won by the Catalans. Record signing Zlatan Ibrahimović, acquired from Inter for Samuel Eto'o plus a mountain of cash, scored the only goal in the first heavyweight head-to-head at Camp Nou in November, and it was Messi – who else? – who opened the scoring in the April re-match at the Bernabéu before Pedro doubled Barça's advantage early in the second half to cement a victory that ended a 12-match winning sequence for the home side and gave the defending champions a decisive three-point lead – plus head-to-head superiority – with seven games to go.

Barcelona leaked two of those three points with a 0-0 draw against city rivals RCD Espanyol a week later, but their last five games yielded a maximum return, the only serious alarm coming in the penultimate fixture when they allowed Sevilla FC – the team that had knocked them out of the Copa del Rey – to come from three goals down and almost snatch a draw. Their last-day victory over relegation-threatened Real Valladolid CF, in front of almost 100,000 fans in Camp Nou, was considerably less nerve-racking, an own goal and a Pedro strike putting them 2-0 up at half-time before Messi rounded off the campaign in inevitable and appropriate style with a couple of second-half goals.

With 31 of their 38 matches won and only one lost – against bogey side Club Atlético de Madrid in mid-February, the only match in which they also fell behind – it was a performance that invited the highest praise. Their record points tally may have fallen frustratingly one shy of the century, but it was 12 higher than the total they accumulated in 2008/09 and seven higher than the division's previous best – achieved by Real in 1996/97 when there were four more fixtures. Oddly, though, and despite Messi's extraordinary individual contribution, the number of goals scored by the team dropped from 105 to 98. The young Argentinian apart, Barça's best players were local legends Puyol, Xavi and goalkeeper Víctor Valdés, with excellent support from young guns Busquets, Piqué and Pedro. Ibrahimović got off to a great start, scoring in his first five Liga

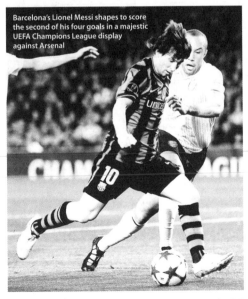

Barcelona's Lionel Messi shapes to score the second of his four goals in a majestic UEFA Champions League display against Arsenal

SPAIN

games, but he generally struggled for consistency, while Iniesta was often injured and the ageing Thierry Henry regularly overlooked.

Barcelona's record-breaking triumph was not just for show; they needed virtually every one of those 99 points to become champions. Real, who entered a new era with the return to the presidency of Galáctico-period supremo Florentino Pérez, a new coach in Manuel Pellegrini, and two expensively acquired global superstars in Cristiano Ronaldo and Kaká, gave everything in their attempt to remove Barça from their perch. Indeed, they too surpassed that record points haul and, unlike their rivals, scored more than 100 goals, but it was those two defeats in the matches that really mattered that consigned them to second place.

Like Barça, Real won all but one of their home games and 13 away. They were especially rampant in the early spring, providing weekly goalfests both at the Bernabéu and on the road. But while lesser teams were vanquished with disdain, the big games found them wanting, those two defeats against Barcelona supplemented by another couple of inopportune off-days against Olympique Lyonnais, which resulted in elimination from the UEFA Champions League at the

Real Federación Española de Fútbol (RFEF)

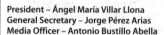

Ramón y Cajal s/n
Apartado de Correos 385
ES-28230 Las Rozas (Madrid)
tel – +34 91 495 9800
fax – +34 91 495 9801
website – rfef.es
email – secretaria@rfef.es
Year of Formation – 1909

President – Ángel María Villar Llona
General Secretary – Jorge Pérez Arias
Media Officer – Antonio Bustillo Abella

INTERNATIONAL HONOURS
FIFA World Cup – (1) 2010.
UEFA European Championship – (2) 1964, 2008.
INTERNATIONAL TOURNAMENT APPEARANCES
FIFA World Cup – (13) 1934, 1950 (4th), 1962, 1966, 1978, 1982 (2nd phase), 1986 (qtr-finals), 1990 (2nd round), 1994 (qtr-finals), 1998, 2002 (qtr-finals), 2006 (2nd round), 2010 (Winners).
UEFA European Championship – (8) 1964 (Winners), 1980, 1984 (runners-up), 1988, 1996 (qtr-finals), 2000 (qtr-finals), 2004, 2008 (Winners).
TOP FIVE ALL-TIME CAPS
Andoni Zubizarreta (126); Iker Casillas (111); Raúl González (102); Xavi Hernández (94); Carles Puyol (90)
TOP FIVE ALL-TIME GOALS
Raúl González (44); David Villa (43); Fernando Ruiz Hierro (29); Fernando Morientes (27); Emilio Butragueño (26)

NATIONAL TEAM RESULTS 2009/10

12/8/09	FYROM	A	Skopje	3-2	Fernando Torres (52), Piqué (54), Riera (56)
5/9/09	Belgium (WCQ)	H	La Coruna	5-0	David Silva (41, 67), David Villa (49, 85), Piqué (50)
9/9/09	Estonia (WCQ)	H	Merida	3-0	Fàbregas (33), Santi Cazorla (82), Mata (90+2)
10/10/09	Armenia (WCQ)	A	Yerevan	2-1	Fàbregas (33), Mata (64p)
14/10/09	Bosnia-Herzegovina (WCQ)	A	Zenica	5-2	Piqué (13), David Silva (14), Negredo (50, 55), Mata (89)
14/11/09	Argentina	H	Madrid	2-1	Xabi Alonso (15, 85p)
18/11/09	Austria	A	Vienna	5-1	Fàbregas (10), David Villa (20, 45), Güiza (56), Pablo Hernández (57)
3/3/10	France	A	Saint-Denis	2-0	David Villa (21), Sergio Ramos (45+1)
29/5/10	Saudi Arabia	N	Innsbruck (AUT)	3-2	David Villa (31), Xabi Alonso (59), Llorente (90)
3/6/10	South Korea	N	Innsbruck (AUT)	1-0	Jesús Navas (87)
8/6/10	Poland	H	Murcia	6-0	David Villa (12), David Silva (14), Xabi Alonso (51), Fàbregas (58), Fernando Torres (76), Pedro (81)
16/6/10	Switzerland (WCF)	N	Durban (RSA)	0-1	
21/6/10	Honduras (WCF)	N	Johannesburg (RSA)	2-0	David Villa (17, 51)
25/6/10	Chile (WCF)	N	Pretoria (RSA)	2-1	David Villa (24), Iniesta (37)
29/6/10	Portugal (WCF)	N	Cape Town (RSA)	1-0	David Villa (63)
3/7/10	Paraguay (WCF)	N	Johannesburg (RSA)	1-0	David Villa (83)
7/7/10	Germany (WCF)	N	Durban (RSA)	1-0	Puyol (73)
11/7/10	Netherlands (WCF)	N	Johannesburg (RSA)	1-0	Iniesta (116) (aet)

NATIONAL TEAM APPEARANCES 2009/10

Coach – Vicente DEL BOSQUE 23/12/50			Mkd	BEL	EST	ARM	BIH	Arg	Aut	Fra	Ksa	Kor	Pol	SUI	HON	CHI	POR	PAR	GER	NED	Caps	Goals
José Manuel REINA	31/8/82	Liverpool (ENG)	G65			G		s88	s46	G46											20	-
Álvaro ARBELOA	17/1/83	Real Madrid	D	D82				D	D	D			D55	s77							16	-
Carles PUYOL	13/4/78	Barcelona	D	D		D		D46		D46	D61		D72	D	D	D	D	D84	D	D	90	3
Gerard PIQUÉ	2/2/87	Barcelona	D	D	D	s46	D77	D	D	D			D	D	D	D	D	D	D	D	23	4
Joan CAPDEVILA	3/2/78	Villarreal	D71	D	D	D	D			s61	D	D	D	D	D	D	D	D	D	D	52	4
XABI ALONSO	25/11/81	Real Madrid	M46	M				M	M	M64	M	s58	M	M	M	M73	M93	M75	M93	M87	76	9
XAVI Hernández	25/1/80	Barcelona	M71	M70	M	M		M46	M46	s46	M74	s58	M55	M	M66	M	M	M	M	M	94	9
SANTI CAZORLA	13/12/84	Villarreal	M46		s66	M															24	2
DAVID SILVA	8/1/86	Valencia		M	M	M77		M82	M65	M46	M80	M61	s80	M55	M62				s86		38	7
DAVID VILLA	3/12/81	Valencia	A46	A	A66			A82	A46	A46	A71	s58	A66	A	A	A	A88	A	A81	A106	65	43
FERNANDO TORRES	20/3/84	Liverpool (ENG)	A64	A66	A54	A55				s46			s66	s61	A70	A55	A58	A56	s81	s106	80	24
Sergio BUSQUETS	16/7/88	Barcelona	s46	M				M	M	M60	M	M	M	M61	M	M	M	M	M	M	20	-
Cesc FÀBREGAS	4/5/87	Arsenal (ENG)	s46	s70	M	M		s46	M	M46		M58		s55	s66	s55		s56		s87	54	6
Albert RIERA	15/4/82	Liverpool (ENG)	s46		s66		M														16	4
Daniel GÜIZA	17/8/80	Fenerbahçe (TUR)	s64		s54			s46	s80												21	6
DIEGO LÓPEZ	3/11/81	Villarreal	s65																		1	-
Ignacio MONREAL	26/2/86	Osasuna	s71			D															2	-
Carlos MARCHENA	31/7/79	Valencia	s71		D	D46		D		s61	D		s72				s93	s84	s93		62	2
Iker CASILLAS	20/5/81	Real Madrid		G	G			G	G88	G46	G	G	G	G	G	G	G	G	G	G	111	-
Raúl ALBIOL	4/9/85	Real Madrid			s82	D		D	s46	D	s46	D									23	-
Marcos SENNA	17/7/76	Villarreal				M	M	s67		s64											28	1
Juan Manuel MATA	28/4/88	Valencia			s77	M67	s82	s82				M58	s70								9	3
SERGIO RAMOS	30/3/86	Real Madrid				D	s77	D	D	D	D61	D	s55	D	D77	D	D	D	D	D	67	5
Álvaro NEGREDO	20/8/85	Sevilla						s55	A	s65	s46										4	2
Andrés INIESTA	11/5/84	Barcelona					s67	M67	M82	M46	M64	M61	M58	M39	M77	M	M	M	M	M	49	7
Andoni IRAOLA	22/6/82	Athletic						D	s60												4	-
JESÚS NAVAS	21/11/85	Sevilla						s82	s46	s64	s61	M	s55	s62	M					s60	9	1
PABLO HERNÁNDEZ	11/4/85	Valencia							s46												2	1
PEDRO Rodríguez	28/7/87	Barcelona									s61	s58	s39	s77			s88	s75	M86	M60	8	1
Fernando LLORENTE	26/2/85	Athletic									s71	A58					s58				8	3
JAVI MARTÍNEZ	2/9/88	Athletic									s74	M80				s73					3	-
VÍCTOR VALDÉS	14/1/82	Barcelona										s46									1	-

first knockout stage for the sixth successive season – a galling statistic for a club of Real's illustrious international repute. For all the fabulous football that Real served up for most of the campaign, with world record signing Ronaldo very much to the fore, it was the team's inability to win those season-defining matches, and in consequence the failure to win a trophy, that led to Pellegrini's dismissal after just one season – and his replacement by man of the moment Mourinho, who did what the Chilean could not, leading his Inter team to UEFA Champions League victory in the final at the Bernabéu.

To make matters worse for Real fans, city rivals Atlético got their hands on the other European trophy, winning the UEFA Europa League after a 2-1 extra-time victory over Fulham FC in the Hamburg final. It was Atlético's first major international conquest since the World Club Cup in 1974 and their first European victory since 1962, when they claimed the UEFA Cup Winners' Cup. The man who led the club to glory was Quique Sánchez Flores – a little over six months after he had been appointed as coach – but the main plaudits were reserved for the team's star forward Diego Forlán, who scored crucial goals against Galatasaray AŞ, Valencia CF and Liverpool FC before bagging the all-important brace against Fulham in the final.

Atlético began their European season alongside Barça and Real in the UEFA Champions League. Having convincingly overcome Panathinaikos FC in the play-off round, they flopped badly in the group stage, costing coach Abel Resino his job. Three points, however, were enough to earn a transfer to the UEFA

Europa League, where Atlético continued to live on the edge, prevailing against Galatasaray only thanks to a last-gasp Forlán strike before using the away-goals rule to eliminate Sporting Clube de Portugal and Valencia and extra time to see off both Liverpool and Fulham.

Sevilla on song

Atlético were unable to make it a cup double, however, as seven days after their European triumph, they ran up against a superior Sevilla side in the final of the Copa del Rey and were defeated 2-0 in Camp Nou, an early goal from Diego Capel and a stoppage-time second from fellow winger Jesús Navas bringing the Andalusian side the trophy for the second time in four seasons and the fifth in all. Like Atlético, Sevilla changed coach in mid-season, with Manuel Jiménez being replaced in March by the club's long-serving assistant, Antonio Álvarez, following a form trough that included elimination from the UEFA Champions League by PFC CSKA Moskva.

Álvarez not only brought Sevilla the Spanish Cup but also won a return ticket to the UEFA Champions League thanks to a winning goal on the final day of the season at UD Almería that came after the final whistle of fellow contenders RCD Mallorca's 2-0 home win over Espanyol. The poor Mallorca players watched on the big screen as young Sevilla substitute Rodri acrobatically converted from close range to knock the islanders down into fifth place. That meant qualification for the UEFA Europa League, where Mallorca, pending licence approval, would be joined by sixth-placed Getafe CF and holders Atlético, whose victory in Hamburg nudged seventh-placed Villarreal CF – initially at least, depending on Mallorca's situation – out of the European frame. Valencia CF, cash-strapped but consistent, finished third – albeit 25 behind runners-up Real Madrid – thanks to another handsome goalscoring contribution from David Villa in his last season before joining Barcelona.

There was a tight contest to avoid relegation from La Liga. Nothing was resolved before the final day, at the start of which five teams were all under threat. In the end both Real Racing Club and Málaga CF managed to escape – the latter with a 1-1 draw against Real Madrid – while Valladolid's defeat in Barcelona sent them down along with newly promoted CD Tenerife and Xerez CD. Three teams from coastal locations came up to replace them – Real Sociedad de Fútbol from San Sebastian, Hércules CF from Alicante and Levante UD from Valencia – as Seville's Real Betis Balompié narrowly missed out.

Diego Forlán clutches the UEFA Europa League trophy after scoring both goals in Atlético Madrid's 2-1 win over Fulham in Hamburg

DOMESTIC LEAGUE 2009/10

LIGA FINAL TABLE

		Home					Away					Total					
	Pld	W	D	L	F	A	W	D	L	F	A	W	D	L	F	A	Pts
1 FC Barcelona	38	18	1	0	57	11	13	5	1	41	13	31	6	1	98	24	99
2 Real Madrid CF	38	18	0	1	60	18	13	3	3	42	17	31	3	4	102	35	96
3 Valencia CF	38	13	5	1	34	12	8	3	8	25	28	21	8	9	59	40	71
4 Sevilla FC	38	10	6	3	33	18	9	0	10	32	31	19	6	13	65	49	63
5 RCD Mallorca	38	15	1	3	42	15	3	7	9	17	29	18	8	12	59	44	62
6 Getafe CF	38	11	4	4	34	22	6	3	10	24	26	17	7	14	58	48	58
7 Villarreal CF	38	13	3	3	35	18	3	5	11	23	39	16	8	14	58	57	56
8 Athletic Club	38	11	4	4	34	24	4	5	10	16	29	15	9	14	50	53	54
9 Club Atlético de Madrid	38	11	3	5	37	24	2	5	12	20	37	13	8	17	57	61	47
10 RC Deportivo La Coruña	38	9	4	6	22	21	4	4	11	13	28	13	8	17	35	49	47
11 RCD Espanyol	38	9	6	4	20	17	2	5	12	9	29	11	11	16	29	46	44
12 CA Osasuna	38	7	8	4	21	16	4	2	13	16	30	11	10	17	37	46	43
13 UD Almería	38	8	6	5	25	23	2	6	11	18	32	10	12	16	43	55	42
14 Real Zaragoza	38	7	6	6	27	23	3	5	11	19	41	10	11	17	46	64	41
15 Real Sporting de Gijón	38	7	7	5	20	18	2	6	11	16	33	9	13	16	36	51	40
16 Real Racing Club	38	4	5	10	17	32	5	7	7	25	27	9	12	17	42	59	39
17 Málaga CF	38	5	8	6	21	21	2	8	9	21	27	7	16	15	42	48	37
18 Real Valladolid CF	38	4	8	7	23	32	3	7	9	14	30	7	15	16	37	62	36
19 CD Tenerife	38	8	6	5	26	29	1	3	15	14	45	9	9	20	40	74	36
20 Xerez CD	38	6	4	9	20	29	2	6	11	18	37	8	10	20	38	66	34

TOP GOALSCORERS

34 Lionel MESSI (Barcelona)
27 Gonzalo HIGUAÍN (Real Madrid)
26 CRISTIANO RONALDO (Real Madrid)
21 DAVID VILLA (Valencia)
18 Diego FORLÁN (Atlético)
16 Zlatan IBRAHIMOVIĆ (Barcelona)
   Roberto SOLDADO (Getafe)
15 LUÍS FABIANO (Sevilla)
14 Fernando LLORENTE (Athletic)
   NINO (Tenerife)

CLUB-BY-CLUB

UD ALMERÍA

Coach – Hugo Sánchez (MEX); (24/12/09) Juan Manuel Lillo
Founded – 1989
Stadium – Juegos Mediterráneos (22,000)

2009

30/8	Valladolid	h	0-0
13/9	Sporting	a	0-1
20/9	Getafe	h	1-0 Míchel
23/9	Atlético	a	2-2 Piatti 2
27/9	Racing	h	2-2 Crusat, Uche
3/10	Barcelona	a	0-1
18/10	Málaga	a	2-1 Cisma, Soriano
25/10	Valencia	h	0-3
1/11	Zaragoza	a	1-2 Juanma Ortiz
8/11	Osasuna	h	2-0 og (Josetxo), Uche
22/11	Mallorca	a	1-3 David Rodríguez
29/11	Athletic	h	1-4 Uche (p)
5/12	Real Madrid	a	2-4 Soriano, Uche
13/12	Deportivo	h	1-1 Uche
20/12	Espanyol	a	0-2

2010

3/1	Xerez	h	1-0 José Ortiz
9/1	Villarreal	a	1-1 Corona
17/1	Tenerife	h	1-1 Goitom
23/1	Sevilla	a	0-1
31/1	Valladolid	a	1-1 Crusat
7/2	Sporting	h	3-1 Crusat, Cisma, Guilherme
14/2	Getafe	a	2-2 Piatti, Soriano
21/2	Atlético	h	1-0 Piatti
28/2	Racing	a	2-0 Soriano, Crusat
6/3	Barcelona	h	2-2 Cisma, og (Puyol)
14/3	Málaga	h	1-0 Soriano
21/3	Valencia	a	0-2
24/3	Zaragoza	h	1-0 Uche
28/3	Osasuna	a	0-1
4/4	Mallorca	h	1-1 Uche
11/4	Athletic	a	1-4 Piatti
15/4	Real Madrid	h	1-2 Crusat
18/4	Deportivo	a	0-0
25/4	Espanyol	h	0-1
1/5	Xerez	a	1-2 Soriano
4/5	Villarreal	h	4-2 Crusat, Uche 2, Piatti
8/5	Tenerife	a	2-2 Piatti, Crusat
15/5	Sevilla	h	2-3 Soriano, Juanma Ortiz

No	Name	Nat	DoB	Pos	Aps	(s)	Gls
18	Wilmar Santiago ACASIETE Ariadela	PER	22/11/77	D	31		
14	Alejandro Rodríguez Rivas "ÁLEX QUILLO"		7/10/86	M		(1)	
25	Hernán Darío BERNARDELLO	ARG	3/8/86	M	35		
24	Leonardo Luis BORZANI	ARG	7/5/82	M	2	(1)	
4	José Manuel Flores Moreno "CHICO"		6/3/87	D	27		
6	Domingo CISMA González		9/2/82	D	29	(4)	3

No	Name	Nat	DoB	Pos	Aps	(s)	Gls
15	Miguel Ángel García Pérez Roldán "CORONA"		12/2/81	M	13	(9)	1
8	Albert CRUSAT Domene		13/5/82	A	31	(2)	7
21	DAVID RODRÍGUEZ Sánchez		14/2/86	M	2	(7)	1
1	DIEGO ALVES Carreira	BRA	24/6/85	G	37		
13	ESTEBAN Andrés Suárez		27/6/75	G	1	(1)	
20	Henok GOITOM	SWE	16/9/84	A	11	(10)	1
3	GUILHERME Oliveira Santos	BRA	5/2/88	D	11	(4)	1
10	JOSÉ ORTIZ Bernal		4/8/77	M		(17)	1
17	Juan Manuel "JUANMA" ORTIZ Palazón		1/3/82	M	24	(11)	2
19	Modeste M'BAMI	CMR	9/10/82	M	28		
16	MÍCHEL Macedo Rocha Machado	BRA	15/2/90	D	28		1
7	Miguel Ángel NIETO de la Calle		12/1/86	M	3	(11)	
2	Hernán Darío PELLERANO	ARG	4/6/84	D	17	(2)	
11	Pablo Daniel PIATTI	ARG	31/3/89	A	28	(7)	7
9	Esteban Andrés SOLARI Poggio	ARG	20/7/80	M		(2)	
23	Fernando SORIANO Marcos		24/9/79	M	33	(2)	7
5	Kalu UCHE	NGA	15/11/82	A	21	(7)	9
22	Fabián Andrés VARGAS	COL	17/4/80	M	6	(4)	

ATHLETIC CLUB

Coach – Joaquín Caparrós
Founded – 1898
Stadium – San Mamés (40,000)
MAJOR HONOURS:
Spanish League – (8) 1930, 1931, 1934, 1936, 1943, 1956, 1983, 1984;
Spanish Cup – (23) 1903, 1904, 1910, 1911, 1914, 1915, 1916, 1921, 1923, 1930, 1931, 1932, 1933, 1943, 1944, 1945, 1950, 1955, 1956, 1958, 1969, 1973, 1984.

2009

30/8	Espanyol	h	1-0	Toquero
13/9	Xerez	a	1-0	og (Prieto)
20/9	Villarreal	h	3-2	Llorente 2, Javi Martínez
23/9	Tenerife	a	0-1	
26/9	Sevilla	h	0-4	
4/10	Valladolid	a	2-2	Susaeta, Muniain
18/10	Sporting	h	1-2	Toquero
25/10	Getafe	a	0-2	
31/10	Atlético	h	1-0	Javi Martínez
8/11	Racing	a	2-0	Gurpegui, Iraola (p)
21/11	Barcelona	h	1-1	Toquero
29/11	Almería	a	4-1	Javi Martínez, Ustaritz, Llorente, De Marcos
6/12	Valencia	h	1-2	Muniain
12/12	Zaragoza	a	2-1	San José, Susaeta
19/12	Osasuna	h	2-0	Yeste, Llorente
2010				
3/1	Mallorca	a	0-2	
10/1	Málaga	a	1-1	Llorente (p)
16/1	Real Madrid	h	1-0	Llorente
23/1	Deportivo	a	1-3	og (Colotto)
30/1	Espanyol	a	0-1	
7/2	Xerez	h	3-2	Muniain, Llorente 2
13/2	Villarreal	a	1-2	Gabilondo
21/2	Tenerife	h	4-1	Llorente (p), Toquero, Iraola, Gabilondo
28/2	Sevilla	a	0-0	
7/3	Valladolid	h	2-0	Toquero 2
13/3	Sporting	a	0-0	
20/3	Getafe	h	2-2	Orbaiz, Llorente (p)
25/3	Atlético	a	0-2	
29/3	Racing	h	4-3	Llorente 2 (1p), Toquero, Susaeta
3/4	Barcelona	a	1-4	Susaeta
11/4	Almería	h	4-1	Javi Martínez 2, Gabilondo, Llorente
15/4	Valencia	a	0-2	
18/4	Zaragoza	h	0-0	
24/4	Osasuna	a	0-0	
2/5	Mallorca	h	1-3	Llorente
5/5	Málaga	h	1-1	Toquero
8/5	Real Madrid	a	1-5	Yeste
15/5	Deportivo	h	2-0	Muniain, Javi Martínez

No	Name	Nat	DoB	Pos	Aps	(s)	Gls
20	AITOR OCIO Carrión		28/11/76	D	3		
36	Isaac Aqueche Barrutia "AKETXE"		3/6/89	A		(1)	
5	Fernando AMOREBIETA Mardaras		29/3/85	D	34		
13	ARMANDO Ribeiro de Aguiar Malda		16/1/71	G	1		
29	Eneko BÓVEDA Altube		14/12/88	M		(1)	
22	Xabier CASTILLO Aranburu		20/3/86	D	18	(1)	
7	DAVID LÓPEZ Moreno		10/9/82	M	7	(10)	
28	Óscar DE MARCOS Arana		14/4/89	M	9	(10)	1
23	Iñigo DÍAZ DE CERIO Conejero		15/5/84	D		(5)	
17	Joseba ETXEBERRIA Lizardi		5/9/77	M	2	(5)	
6	Xabier Echeita Gorritxategi "ETXEITA"		31/10/87	M	1	(2)	
11	Igor GABILONDO del Campo		10/2/79	M	16	(10)	3
18	Carlos GURPEGUI Nausía		19/8/80	M	30	(4)	1
37	IÑIGO PÉREZ Soto		18/1/88	M		(3)	
21	ION VÉLEZ Martínez		17/2/85	A	1	(1)	
1	Gorka IRAIZOZ Moreno		6/3/81	G	37		
15	Andoni IRAOLA Sagarna		22/6/82	D	37		2
26	Ander ITURRASPE Derteano		8/3/89	M	11	(4)	
24	JAVIer MARTÍNEZ Aginaga		2/9/88	M	34		6
3	KOIKILI Lertxundi del Campo		23/12/80	D	20	(1)	
9	Fernando LLORENTE Torres		26/2/85	A	35	(2)	14
27	Iker MUNIAIN Goñi		19/12/92	M	4	(22)	4
8	Iñaki MUÑOZ Oroz		2/7/78	M		(1)	
16	Pablo ORBAIZ Lesaca		6/2/79	M	17	(3)	1
12	Mikel SAN JOSÉ Domínguez		30/5/89	D	24	(1)	1
14	Markel SUSAETA Lasjurain		14/12/87	M	23	(12)	4
2	Gaizka TOQUERO Pinedo		9/8/84	M	26	(5)	8
4	USTARITZ Aldekoaotalora Astarloa		16/2/83	D	15		1
10	Francisco Javier YESTE Navarro		6/12/79	M	13	(9)	2

CLUB ATLÉTICO DE MADRID

Coach – Abel Resino; (22/10/09) (Santiago Denia); (25/10/09) Enrique "Quique" Sánchez Flores
Founded – 1903
Stadium – Vicente Calderón (54,851)
MAJOR HONOURS:
UEFA Cup Winners' Cup – (1) 1962;
UEFA Europa League – (1) 2010;
World Club Cup – (1) 1974;
Spanish League – (9) 1940, 1941, 1950, 1951, 1966, 1970, 1973, 1977, 1996;
Spanish Cup – (9) 1960, 1961, 1965, 1972, 1976, 1985, 1991, 1992, 1996.

2009

30/8	Málaga	a	0-3	
12/9	Racing	h	1-1	Jurado
19/9	Barcelona	a	2-5	Agüero, Forlán
23/9	Almería	h	2-2	Cléber Santana, Forlán
26/9	Valencia	a	2-2	Agüero, Maxi Rodríguez
3/10	Zaragoza	h	2-1	Jurado, Antonio López
18/10	Osasuna	a	0-3	
24/10	Mallorca	h	1-1	Forlán (p)
31/10	Athletic	a	0-1	
7/11	Real Madrid	h	2-3	Forlán, Agüero
21/11	Deportivo	a	1-2	Agüero
29/11	Espanyol	h	4-0	Forlán, Agüero 2, Maxi Rodríguez
5/12	Xerez	a	2-0	Forlán, Agüero
13/12	Villarreal	h	1-2	Simão
20/12	Tenerife	a	1-1	Jurado
2010				
2/1	Sevilla	h	2-1	og (Dragutinović), Antonio López
9/1	Valladolid	a	4-0	Jurado, Forlán, Reyes, Agüero
17/1	Sporting	h	3-2	Forlán, Paulo Assunção, Ibrahima
24/1	Getafe	a	0-1	
31/1	Málaga	h	0-2	
7/2	Racing	a	1-1	Forlán
14/2	Barcelona	h	2-1	Forlán, Simão
21/2	Almería	a	0-1	
28/2	Valencia	h	4-1	Forlán 2 (1p), Agüero, Jurado
7/3	Zaragoza	a	1-1	Ibrahima
15/3	Osasuna	h	1-0	Jurado
21/3	Mallorca	a	1-4	Forlán

25/3	Athletic	h	2-0	Forlán, Agüero
28/3	Real Madrid	a	2-3	Reyes, Forlán (p)
4/4	Deportivo	h	3-0	Juanito, Forlán, Tiago
11/4	Espanyol	a	0-3	
14/4	Xerez	h	1-2	Forlán
17/4	Villarreal	a	1-2	Agüero
25/4	Tenerife	h	3-1	Salvio 2, Agüero
2/5	Sevilla	a	1-3	Tiago
5/5	Valladolid	h	3-1	Juanito, Jurado, Forlán
8/5	Sporting	a	1-1	Ibrahima
15/5	Getafe	h	0-3	

No	Name	Nat	DoB	Pos	Aps	(s)	Gls
10	Sergio Leonel AGÜERO	ARG	2/6/88	A	24	(7)	12
18	ÁLVARO DOMÍNGUEZ Soto		15/5/89	D	26		
3	ANTONIO LÓPEZ Guerrero		13/9/81	D	29	(2)	2
1	Sergio ASENJO Andrés		28/6/89	G	15		
55	BORJA González Tomás		25/8/92	D		(1)	
6	Ignacio CAMACHO Barnola		4/5/90	M	6	(6)	
23	CLÉBER SANTANA Loureiro	BRA	27/6/81	M	8	(6)	1
43	David DE GEA Quintana		7/11/90	G	19		
7	Diego Martín FORLÁN Corazo	URU	19/5/79	A	30	(3)	18
5	John HEITINGA	NED	15/11/83	D	1		
58	IBRAHIMA Baldé	SEN	1/9/90	A	5	(13)	3
42	JOEL Robles Blázquez		17/6/90	G	1	(1)	
16	Juan Gutiérrez Moreno "JUANITO"		23/7/76	D	15	(2)	2
9	José Manuel JURADO Marín		29/6/86	M	29	(9)	7
49	Sergio Gontán Gallardo "KEKO"		28/12/91	M		(1)	
26	Jorge Resurrección Merodio "KOKE"		8/1/92	M	1	(3)	
24	LEANDRO Daniel CABRERA Sasía	URU	17/6/91	D	4		
11	MAXImiliano Rubén RODRÍGUEZ	ARG	2/1/81	M	9	(5)	2
59	Jorge MOLINO Baena		4/3/88	A		(1)	
22	PABLO Ibáñez Tebar		3/8/81	D	6	(1)	
12	PAULO ASSUNÇAO da Silva	BRA	25/1/80	M	29	(1)	1
21	Luis Amaranto PEREA Mosquera	COL	30/1/79	D	27	(1)	
4	Mariano Andrés PERNÍA		4/5/77	D	1		
8	RAÚL GARCÍA Escudero		11/7/86	M	12	(8)	
19	José Antonio REYES Calderón		1/9/83	M	19	(11)	2
13	ROBERTO Jiménez Gago		10/2/86	G	3		
35	RUBÉN Salvador PÉREZ del Mármol		26/4/89	M		(1)	
14	Eduardo Antonio SALVIO	ARG	13/5/90	M	5	(8)	2
20	SIMÃO Pedro Fonseca Sabrosa	POR	31/10/79	M	30	(4)	2
14	Florent SINAMA-PONGOLLE	FRA	20/10/84	A	3	(7)	
5	TIAGO Cardoso Mendes	POR	2/5/81	M	16	(2)	2
17	Tomáš UJFALUŠI	CZE	24/3/78	D	26	(1)	
2	Juan VALERA Espín		21/12/84	D	19	(4)	

FC BARCELONA
Coach – Josep Guardiola
Founded – 1899
Stadium – Camp Nou (98,772)
MAJOR HONOURS:
European Champion Clubs' Cup/UEFA Champions League – (3) 1992, 2006, 2009;
UEFA Cup Winners' Cup - (4) 1979, 1982, 1989, 1997;
Inter Cities Fairs Cup - (3) 1958, 1960, 1966;
UEFA Super Cup - (3) 1992, 1997, 2009;
FIFA Club World Cup - (1) 2009;
Spanish League – (20) 1929, 1945, 1948, 1949, 1952, 1953, 1959, 1960,
1974, 1985, 1991, 1992, 1993, 1994, 1998, 1999, 2005, 2006, 2009, 2010;
Spanish Cup – (25) 1910, 1912, 1913, 1920, 1922, 1925, 1926, 1928, 1942,
1951, 1952, 1953, 1957, 1959, 1963, 1968, 1971, 1978, 1981, 1983, 1988,
1990, 1997, 1998, 2009.

2009

31/8	Sporting	h	3-0	Bojan, Keita, Ibrahimović
12/9	Getafe	a	2-0	Ibrahimović, Messi
19/9	Atlético	h	5-2	Ibrahimović, Messi 2, Dani Alves, Keita
22/9	Racing	a	4-1	Ibrahimović, Messi 2, Piqué
26/9	Málaga	a	2-0	Ibrahimović, Piqué
3/10	Almería	h	1-0	Pedro
17/10	Valencia	a	0-0	
25/10	Zaragoza	h	6-1	Keita 3, Ibrahimović 2, Messi

31/10	Osasuna	a	1-1	Keita
7/11	Mallorca	h	4-2	Pedro 2, Henry, Messi (p)
21/11	Athletic	a	1-1	Dani Alves
29/11	Real Madrid	h	1-0	Ibrahimović
2/12	Xerez	a	2-0	Henry, Ibrahimović
5/12	Deportivo	a	3-1	Messi 2, Ibrahimović
12/12	Espanyol	h	1-0	Ibrahimović (p)
2010				
2/1	Villarreal	h	1-1	Pedro
10/1	Tenerife	a	5-0	Messi 3, Puyol, og (Ezequiel Luna)
16/1	Sevilla	h	4-0	og (Escudé), Pedro, Messi 2
23/1	Valladolid	a	3-0	Xavi, Dani Alves, Messi
30/1	Sporting	a	1-0	Pedro
6/2	Getafe	h	2-1	Messi, Xavi
14/2	Atlético	a	1-2	Ibrahimović
20/2	Racing	h	4-0	Iniesta, Henry, Márquez, Thiago
27/2	Málaga	h	2-1	Pedro, Messi
6/3	Almería	a	2-2	Messi 2
14/3	Valencia	h	3-0	Messi 3
21/3	Zaragoza	a	4-2	Messi 3, Ibrahimović (p)
24/3	Osasuna	h	2-0	Ibrahimović, Bojan
27/3	Mallorca	a	1-0	Ibrahimović
3/4	Athletic	h	4-1	Jeffrén, Bojan 2, Messi
10/4	Real Madrid	a	2-0	Messi, Pedro
14/4	Deportivo	h	3-0	Bojan, Pedro, Touré
17/4	Espanyol	a	0-0	
24/4	Xerez	h	3-1	Jeffrén, Henry, Ibrahimović
1/5	Villarreal	a	4-1	Messi 2, Xavi, Bojan
4/5	Tenerife	h	4-1	Messi 2, Bojan, Pedro
8/5	Sevilla	a	3-2	Messi, Bojan, Pedro
16/5	Valladolid	h	4-0	og (Prieto), Pedro, Messi 2

No	Name	Nat	DoB	Pos	Aps	(s)	Gls
22	Éric ABIDAL	FRA	11/9/79	D	15	(2)	
40	Marc BARTRA Aregall		15/1/91	D		(1)	
11	BOJAN Krkić Pérez		28/8/90	A	11	(12)	8
16	Sergio BUSQUETS Burgos		16/7/88	M	26	(7)	
21	Dmytro CHYHRYNSKIY	UKR	7/11/86	D	10	(2)	
2	DANIel ALVES da Silva	BRA	6/5/83	D	28	(1)	3
32	Andreu FONTÁS Prat		14/11/89	D		(1)	
14	Thierry HENRY	FRA	17/8/77	A	15	(6)	4
9	Zlatan IBRAHIMOVIĆ	SWE	3/10/81	A	23	(6)	16
8	Andrés INIESTA Luján		11/5/84	M	20	(9)	1
35	JEFFRÉN Suárez Bermúdez		20/1/88	M	6	(6)	2
28	JONATHAN dos Santos Ramírez	MEX	26/4/90	M	1	(2)	
15	Seydou KEITA	MLI	16/1/80	M	23	(6)	6
4	Rafael MÁRQUEZ Álvarez	MEX	13/2/79	D	7	(8)	1
19	MAXWELL Scherer Cabeleiro Andrade	BRA	27/8/81	D	25		
10	Lionel Andrés MESSI	ARG	24/6/87	A	30	(5)	34
18	Gabriel Alejandro MILITO	ARG	7/9/80	D	9	(2)	
17	PEDRO Eliezer Rodríguez Ledesma		28/7/87	A	22	(12)	12
3	Gerard PIQUÉ Bernabeu		2/2/87	D	29	(3)	2
5	Carles PUYOL Saforcada		13/4/78	D	31	(1)	1
34	THIAGO Alcántara do Nascimento		11/4/91	M		(1)	1
24	Yaya TOURÉ Gnégnéri	CIV	13/5/83	M	18	(5)	1
1	VÍCTOR VALDÉS Arribas		14/1/82	G	38		
6	XAVIer Hernández Creus		25/1/80	M	31	(3)	3

RC DEPORTIVO LA CORUÑA
Coach – Miguel Ángel Lotina
Founded – 1906
Stadium – Riazor (34,600)
MAJOR HONOURS:
Spanish League – (1) 2000.
Spanish Cup - (2) 1995, 2002.

2009

29/8	Real Madrid	a	2-3	Riki, Valerón
13/9	Málaga	h	1-0	Filipe Luís
19/9	Espanyol	h	2-3	Adrián López, Lassad

SPAIN

23/9	Xerez	a	3-0	Juca, og (Leandro), Riki
27/9	Villarreal	h	1-0	Juca
3/10	Tenerife	a	1-0	Colotto
17/10	Sevilla	h	1-0	Juan Rodríguez
25/10	Valladolid	a	0-4	
1/11	Sporting	h	1-1	Lassad
7/11	Getafe	a	2-0	Mista, Filipe Luís
21/11	Atlético	h	2-1	Colotto, Guardado (p)
29/11	Racing	a	1-0	Lopo
5/12	Barcelona	h	1-3	Adrián López
13/12	Almería	a	1-1	Pablo Álvarez
20/12	Valencia	h	0-0	
2010				
3/1	Zaragoza	a	0-0	
10/1	Osasuna	h	1-0	Juan Rodríguez
17/1	Mallorca	a	0-2	
23/1	Athletic	h	3-1	Filipe Luís, Juca, Pablo Álvarez
30/1	Real Madrid	h	1-3	Riki (p)
7/2	Málaga	a	0-0	
14/2	Espanyol	a	0-2	
20/2	Xerez	h	2-1	Guardado (p), Riki
28/2	Villarreal	a	0-1	
6/3	Tenerife	h	3-1	Juan Rodríguez, Guardado, Colotto
13/3	Sevilla	a	1-1	Adrián López
20/3	Valladolid	h	0-2	
23/3	Sporting	a	1-2	Adrián López
28/3	Getafe	h	1-3	Riki
4/4	Atlético	a	0-3	
11/4	Racing	h	1-1	Riki
14/4	Barcelona	a	0-3	
18/4	Almería	h	0-0	
24/4	Valencia	a	0-1	
1/5	Zaragoza	h	0-1	
5/5	Osasuna	a	1-3	Riki
8/5	Mallorca	h	1-0	Riki
15/5	Athletic	a	0-2	

No	Name	Nat	DoB	Pos	Aps	(s)	Gls
10	ADRIÁN LÓPEZ Álvarez		8/1/88	M	25	(9)	4
29	David AÑÓN González		3/4/89	M	1	(2)	
16	ANTONIO TOMÁS González		19/1/85	M	28	(2)	
1	Daniel ARANZUBIA Aguado		18/9/79	G	36		
9	Rodolfo BODIPO Díaz	EQG	25/10/77	A	6	(9)	
19	Diego Daniel COLOTTO	ARG	10/3/81	D	30		3
3	FILIPE LUÍS Kasmirski	BRA	9/8/85	D	20	(1)	3
18	José Andrés GUARDADO Hernández	MEX	28/9/86	M	23	(3)	3
23	IVÁN PÉREZ Maceira		16/11/85	M	3	(17)	
28	JUAN DOMÍNGUEZ Lamas		8/1/90	M	8	(5)	
22	JUAN Antonio RODRÍGUEZ Villamuela		1/4/82	M	34	(1)	3
6	Juliano Roberto Antonello "JUCA"	BRA	19/11/79	M	14	(2)	3
17	Ángel LAFITA Castillo		7/8/84	M		(1)	
20	LASSAD Hassen Nouioui	TUN	8/7/85	A	10	(9)	2
15	LAURE Sanabria Ruiz		22/3/85	D	19	(1)	
7	Alberto LOPO García		5/5/80	D	34		1
13	MANUel Fernández Muñiz		9/3/86	M	2	(1)	
2	MANUEL PABLO García Díaz		25/1/76	D	33		
24	Miguel Ángel Ferrer Martínez "MISTA"		12/11/78	A	5	(8)	1
14	PABLO ÁLVAREZ Núñez		14/5/80	M	17	(11)	2
4	Adrián López Rodríguez "PISCU"		25/2/87	D	3		
32	RAÚL García Granero		30/11/89	D	4	(1)	
11	Iván Sánchez Rico Soto "RIKI"		11/8/80	A	18	(8)	8
27	David ROCHELA Calvo		19/2/90	D	3	(1)	
33	Diego SEOANE Pérez		26/4/88	D	1		
8	SERGIO González Soriano		10/11/76	M	21	(3)	
21	Juan Carlos VALERÓN Santana		17/6/75	M	12	(12)	1
5	José Eduardo Rosa Vale Castro "ZÉ CASTRO"	POR	13/1/83	D	8	(2)	

RCD ESPANYOL
Coach – Mauricio Pochettino (ARG)
Founded – 1900
Stadium – Cornellá-El Prat (40,500)
MAJOR HONOURS:
Spanish Cup – (4) 1929, 1940, 2000, 2006.

2009				
30/8	Athletic	a	0-1	
12/9	Real Madrid	h	0-3	
19/9	Deportivo	a	3-2	Callejón, Forlín, Verdú
23/9	Málaga	h	2-1	Sahar, Iván Alonso
27/9	Xerez	h	0-0	
4/10	Villarreal	a	0-0	
18/10	Tenerife	h	2-1	Iván Alonso 2
24/10	Sevilla	a	0-0	
1/11	Valladolid	h	1-1	Luis García
8/11	Sporting	a	0-1	
22/11	Getafe	h	0-2	
29/11	Atlético	a	0-4	
6/12	Racing	h	0-4	
12/12	Barcelona	a	0-1	
20/12	Almería	h	2-0	Márquez, Corominas
2010				
2/1	Valencia	a	0-1	
10/1	Zaragoza	h	2-1	Verdú, Marqués
16/1	Osasuna	a	0-2	
24/1	Mallorca	h	1-1	Osvaldo
30/1	Athletic	h	1-0	Luis García
6/2	Real Madrid	a	0-3	
14/2	Deportivo	h	2-0	Verdú, Callejón
21/2	Málaga	a	1-2	Víctor Ruiz
28/2	Xerez	a	1-1	Osvaldo
7/3	Villarreal	h	0-0	
14/3	Tenerife	a	1-4	Verdú
20/3	Sevilla	h	2-0	Osvaldo 2
24/3	Valladolid	a	0-0	
28/3	Sporting	h	0-0	
4/4	Getafe	a	1-1	Osvaldo
11/4	Atlético	h	3-0	Víctor Ruiz, Osvaldo, Iván Alonso
14/4	Racing	a	1-3	Iván Alonso
17/4	Barcelona	h	0-0	
24/4	Almería	a	1-0	Luis García
1/5	Valencia	h	0-2	
5/5	Zaragoza	a	0-1	
8/5	Osasuna	h	2-1	Forlín, Osvaldo
15/5	Mallorca	a	0-2	

No	Name	Nat	DoB	Pos	Aps	(s)	Gls
41	Mahamat AZRACK Yassine	CHA	2/3/88	M		(2)	
37	José Raúl BAENA Urdiales		2/3/89	M	11	(8)	
8	José María CALLEJÓN Bueno		11/2/87	M	31	(5)	2
2	Francisco Javier CHICA Torres		17/5/85	D	27	(1)	
20	Ferran COROMINAS Telecha		5/1/83	A	11	(12)	1
25	CRISTIAN Darío ÁLVAREZ	ARG	13/11/85	G	7	(1)	
3	DAVID GARCÍA de la Cruz		16/1/81	D	21		
9	Iván DE LA PEÑA López		6/5/76	M		(4)	
35	DÍDAC Vilà Roselló		9/6/89	D	11		
18	Juan Daniel FORLÍN	ARG	10/1/88	D	23	(1)	2
24	IVÁN Daniel ALONSO Vallejo	URU	10/4/79	A	19	(15)	5
36	JAVIer LÓPEZ Rodríguez		21/1/86	M		(1)	
40	JORDI AMAT Mas		21/3/92	D	4	(2)	
1	Idriss Carlos KAMENI	CMR	18/2/84	G	31		
10	LUIS GARCÍA Fernández		6/2/81	M	35	(1)	3
19	José Fernando MARQUÉS Martínez		4/12/84	M	10	(11)	1
4	Javier MÁRQUEZ Moreno		11/5/86	D	12	(3)	1
22	MOISÉS HURTADO Pérez		2/1/82	M	30	(1)	
7	Shunsuke NAKAMURA	JPN	24/6/78	M	6	(7)	
17	Pablo Daniel OSVALDO	ITA	12/1/86	A	17	(3)	7
16	Nicolás Martín PAREJA	ARG	19/1/84	D	30		
29	Marc PEDRAZA Sarto		6/2/87	A		(1)	

5	Iván Alexis PILLUD	ARG	24/4/86	D	6	(3)	
12	Facundo Sebastián RONCAGLIA	ARG	10/2/87	D	15	(6)	
14	Ben SAHAR	ISR	10/8/89	M	5	(17)	1
23	Raúl TAMUDO Montero		19/10/77	A	4	(2)	
11	Joan VERDÚ Fernández		5/5/83	M	31	(3)	4
30	VÍCTOR RUIZ Torre		25/1/89	D	21	(1)	2

GETAFE CF
Coach – José Miguel González "Míchel"
Founded – 1983
Stadium – Coliseum Alfonso Pérez (17,000)

2009

30/8	Racing	a	4-1	Rafa López, Soldado 3
12/9	Barcelona	h	0-2	
20/9	Almería	a	0-1	
23/9	Valencia	h	3-1	Manu del Moral 2, Pedro León
27/9	Zaragoza	a	0-3	
4/10	Osasuna	h	2-1	Cata Díaz, Pedro León
18/10	Mallorca	a	1-3	Albín
25/10	Athletic	h	2-0	Soldado, Parejo (p)
31/10	Real Madrid	a	0-2	
7/11	Deportivo	h	0-2	
22/11	Espanyol	a	2-0	Casquero, Pedro Ríos
29/11	Xerez	h	5-1	Soldado 3 (1p) Parejo, Casquero
6/12	Villarreal	a	2-3	Pedro León, Soldado (p)
13/12	Tenerife	h	2-1	Albín 2
19/12	Sevilla	a	2-1	Soldado 2

2010

3/1	Valladolid	h	1-0	Casquero
10/1	Sporting	a	0-1	
17/1	Málaga	a	0-1	
24/1	Atlético	h	1-0	Manu del Moral
31/1	Racing	h	0-0	
6/2	Barcelona	a	1-2	Soldado (p)
14/2	Almería	h	2-2	Casquero, Soldado
22/2	Valencia	a	1-2	Manu del Moral
27/2	Zaragoza	h	0-2	
7/3	Osasuna	a	0-0	
13/3	Mallorca	h	3-0	Parejo, Miku, Manu del Moral (p)
20/3	Athletic	a	2-2	Manu del Moral, Pedro León
25/3	Real Madrid	h	2-4	Parejo, Pedro León
28/3	Deportivo	a	3-1	Miku 2, og (Zé Castro)
4/4	Espanyol	h	1-1	Manu del Moral
10/4	Xerez	a	1-0	Rafa López
13/4	Villarreal	h	3-0	Miku 2, Mané
18/4	Tenerife	a	2-3	Pedro León, Casquero
25/4	Sevilla	h	4-3	Adrián, Pedro León, Manu del Moral, Parejo (p)
1/5	Valladolid	a	0-0	
4/5	Sporting	h	1-1	Soldado
8/5	Málaga	h	2-1	Soldado, Pedro León
15/5	Atlético	a	3-0	Soldado 2, Parejo

No	Name	Nat	DoB	Pos	Aps	(s)	Gls
23	ADRIÁN González Morales		25/5/88	M	19	(6)	1
10	Juan Ángel ALBÍN Leites	URU	17/7/86	A	12	(11)	3
4	David BELENGUER Reverter		17/12/72	D	7	(6)	
18	Derek Owusu BOATENG	GHA	2/5/83	M	26	(3)	
22	Francisco Javier CASQUERO Paredes		11/3/76	M	23	(9)	5
2	Daniel Alberto "CATA" DÍAZ	ARG	13/3/79	D	30		1
6	Fabio CELESTINI	SUI	31/10/75	M	22	(2)	
13	Jordi CODINA Rodríguez		27/4/82	G	22		
11	Cosmin Marius CONTRA	ROU	15/12/75	D		(3)	
21	David CORTÉS Caballero		29/8/79	D	19	(1)	
26	Alberto ESCASI Olmo		28/2/89	M		(1)	
8	Jaime GAVILÁN Martínez		12/5/85	M	16	(11)	
7	KEPA Blanco González		5/1/84	A		(5)	
3	José Manuel Jiménez Ortiz "MANÉ"		21/12/81	D	35		1
14	MANUEL DEL MORAL Fernández		25/2/84	M	21	(15)	8
5	Pedro MARIO Álvarez Abrante		2/2/82	M	12	(1)	

19	Nicolás Ladislao Fedor Flores "MIKU"	VEN	19/8/85	A	11	(5)	5
17	Daniel PAREJO Muñoz		16/4/89	M	16	(12)	6
20	PEDRO LEÓN Sánchez Gil		24/11/86	M	33	(2)	8
16	PEDRO RÍOS Maestre		12/12/81	M	4	(14)	1
15	RAFAel LÓPEZ Gómez		9/4/85	D	27		2
9	Roberto SOLDADO Rillo		27/5/85	A	25	(1)	16
24	Miguel TORRES Gómez		28/1/86	D	22	(4)	
1	Óscar Alfredo USTARI	ARG	3/7/86	G	16		

MÁLAGA CF
Coach – Juan Ramón López Muñiz
Founded – 1994
Stadium – La Rosaleda (28,963)

2009

30/8	Atlético	h	3-0	Baha, Manu Torres, Xavier Torres
13/9	Deportivo	a	0-1	
19/9	Racing	h	1-2	Duda
23/9	Espanyol	a	1-2	Fernando
26/9	Barcelona	h	0-2	
4/10	Xerez	a	1-1	Obinna
18/10	Almería	h	1-2	Edinho
25/10	Villarreal	h	1-2	Luque
1/11	Valencia	h	0-1	
7/11	Tenerife	a	2-2	Edinho, Javi López
22/11	Zaragoza	a	1-1	Iván González
28/11	Sevilla	a	2-2	Fernando, Duda
6/12	Osasuna	h	1-1	Apoño
13/12	Valladolid	a	1-1	Duda
20/12	Mallorca	h	2-1	Fernando, Forestieri

2010

3/1	Sporting	h	2-2	Duda, Weligton
10/1	Athletic	h	1-1	Weligton
17/1	Getafe	h	1-0	Baha
24/1	Real Madrid	a	0-2	
31/1	Atlético	a	2-0	Duda, Javi López
7/2	Deportivo	h	0-0	
14/2	Barcelona	a	3-0	Weligton, Caicedo, Obinna
21/2	Espanyol	h	2-1	Fernando, Obinna
27/2	Barcelona	a	1-2	Valdo
7/3	Xerez	h	2-4	Duda, Valdo
14/3	Almería	a	0-1	
21/3	Villarreal	h	2-0	Baha 2
24/3	Valencia	a	0-1	
27/3	Tenerife	h	1-1	Apoño
3/4	Zaragoza	a	0-2	
10/4	Sevilla	h	1-2	Caicedo
14/4	Osasuna	a	2-2	Caicedo, Baha
18/4	Valladolid	h	0-0	
25/4	Mallorca	a	1-1	Obinna
1/5	Sporting	a	1-1	Caicedo
5/5	Athletic	a	1-1	Duda
8/5	Getafe	a	1-2	Fernando
16/5	Real Madrid	h	1-1	Duda

No	Name	Nat	DoB	Pos	Aps	(s)	Gls
10	Antonio Galdeano Benítez "APOÑO"		13/2/84	M	17	(7)	2
7	Nabil BAHA	MAR	12/8/81	A	21	(11)	5
12	Selim BENACHOUR	TUN	8/9/81	M	18	(5)	
23	Felipe Salvador CAICEDO Corozo	ECU	5/9/88	A	15	(3)	4
21	Ibán Javier CUADRADO Alonso		21/2/79	D	4		
17	Sergio Paulo Barbosa Valente "DUDA"	POR	27/6/80	M	33	(1)	8
22	Arnaldo Edi Lopes da Silva "EDINHO"	POR	7/7/82	M	2	(8)	2
16	EDuardo RAMOS Gómez		17/2/92	M		(3)	
8	FERNANDO Miguel Fernández Escribano		2/6/79	M	29	(1)	5
9	Fernando Martín FORESTIERI	ITA	15/1/90	A	5	(14)	1
14	HÉLDER Miguel do ROSARIO	POR	9/3/80	D	3		
32	IVÁN GONZÁLEZ López		15/2/88	D	22	(1)	

35	Francisco JAVIer LÓPEZ Díaz	20/4/88	A	9	(2)	2
2	JESÚS GÁMEZ Duarte	10/4/85	D	32		
24	Juan Jesús Gutiérrez Robles "JUANITO"	17/2/80	M	25	(5)	
49	Juan Miguel Jiménez López "JUANMI"	20/5/93	A		(5)	
5	Alberto LUQUE Martos	11/3/78	M	4	(12)	1
20	Manuel Gaspar Haro "MANOLO"	3/2/81	D	13	(2)	
4	MANUel TORRES Caturla	14/8/89	D	15	(2)	1
19	Patrick MTILIGA	DEN 28/1/81	D	24		
13	Gustavo Adolfo MUNÚA Vera	URU 27/1/78	G	38		
18	Victor Nsofor OBINNA	NGA 25/3/87	M	16	(10)	4
50	Daniel OROZCO Álvarez	1/2/87	D	4		
37	Pedro Pareja Duque "PEDRITO"	28/4/89	D		(3)	
29	Francisco PORTILLO Soler	13/6/90	A		(1)	
15	Milan STEPANOV	SRB 2/4/83	D	12		
27	Daniel TORIBIO Gutiérrez	5/10/88	D	17	(4)	
11	Valmiro Lopes Rocha "VALDO"	23/4/81	M	10	(9)	2
3	WELIGTON Robson Pena de Oliveira	BRA 26/8/79	D	20	(1)	3
6	XAVIER TORRES Buigues	21/11/86	M	10	(1)	1

RCD MALLORCA
Coach – Gregorio Manzano
Founded – 1916
Stadium – Ono Estadi (23,142)
MAJOR HONOURS:
Spanish Cup – (1) 2003.

2009

30/8	Xerez	h	2-0	Adúriz, Tuni
13/9	Villarreal	a	1-1	Borja Valero
19/9	Tenerife	h	4-0	Mario Suárez, Adúriz, Julio Álvarez, Webo (p)
22/9	Sevilla	a	0-2	
27/9	Valladolid	h	3-0	Nunes, Adúriz, Borja Valero
4/10	Sporting	a	1-4	Martí (p)
18/10	Getafe	h	3-1	Julio Álvarez, Adúriz 2
24/10	Atlético	a	1-1	Borja Valero
1/11	Racing	h	1-0	Webo
7/11	Barcelona	a	2-4	Nunes, Keita
22/11	Almería	h	3-1	Castro 2, Víctor
28/11	Valencia	a	1-1	Borja Valero (p)
6/12	Zaragoza	h	4-1	Adúriz 2, Mario Suárez, Keita
13/12	Osasuna	a	1-0	Castro
20/12	Málaga	h	1-2	Julio Álvarez
2010				
3/1	Athletic	h	2-0	Julio Álvarez, Adúriz
10/1	Real Madrid	a	0-2	
17/1	Deportivo	h	2-0	Mario Suárez, Castro
24/1	Espanyol	a	1-1	Borja Valero (p)
31/1	Xerez	a	1-2	Webo
7/2	Villarreal	h	1-0	Nunes
15/2	Tenerife	a	0-1	
20/2	Sevilla	h	1-3	Borja Valero
28/2	Valladolid	a	2-1	Rubén González, Julio Álvarez
7/3	Sporting	h	3-0	Julio Álvarez, Víctor, Webo
13/3	Getafe	a	0-3	
21/3	Atlético	h	4-1	Víctor, Adúriz, og (Perea), Felipe Mattioni
24/3	Racing	a	0-0	
27/3	Barcelona	h	0-1	
4/4	Almería	a	1-1	Webo
11/4	Valencia	h	3-2	Castro, Webo, og (Manuel Fernandes)
14/4	Zaragoza	a	1-1	Rubén González
19/4	Osasuna	h	2-0	Rubén González, Keita
25/4	Málaga	h	1-1	Adúriz
2/5	Athletic	a	3-1	Castro, Nunes, Adúriz

5/5	Real Madrid	h	1-4	Adúriz
8/5	Deportivo	a	0-1	
15/5	Espanyol	h	2-0	Víctor, Mario Suárez

No	Name	Nat	DoB	Pos	Aps	(s)	Gls
21	Aritz ADÚRIZ Zubeldia		11/2/81	A	33	(1)	12
13	Dudu AWAT	ISR	17/10/77	G	38		
17	AYOZE Díaz Díaz		25/5/82	D	33		
24	BORJA VALERO Iglesias		12/1/85	M	32	(1)	6
22	BRUNO Manuel Rodrigues Silva "CHINA"	POR	5/8/82	M	2	(7)	
11	Gonzalo CASTRO Irazábal	URU	14/9/84	M	32	(3)	6
23	Enrique CORRALES Martín		1/3/82	M	5	(2)	
2	FELIPE MATTIONI Rohde	BRA	15/10/88	D	14	(6)	1
3	José Miguel González Rey "JOSEMI"		15/11/79	D	26	(2)	
10	JULIO ÁLVAREZ Mosquera	VEN	1/5/81	M	21	(5)	6
14	Alhassane KEITA	GUI	26/6/83	M	2	(21)	3
1	Germán Darío LUX	ARG	7/6/82	G		(1)	
6	MARIO SUÁREZ Mata		24/2/87	M	27	(7)	4
8	José Luis MARTÍ Soler		28/4/75	M	27	(9)	1
16	José Carlos de Araújo NUNES	POR	7/3/77	D	34		4
20	Paulo César PEZZOLANO Suárez	URU	25/4/83	A	1	(11)	
4	Iván Andrés RAMIS Barrios		25/10/84	D	26		
5	RUBÉN GONZÁLEZ Rocha		29/1/82	D	16	(3)	3
27	SERGI Enrich Ametller		26/2/90	D		(1)	
31	TOMÁS PINA Isla		14/10/87	M		(1)	
15	Antonio Luis Adrover Colom "TUNI"		14/6/82	M	7	(2)	1
7	Fernando VARELA Ramos		1/9/79	M	10	(5)	
18	VÍCTOR Casadesús Castaño		28/2/85	A	20	(7)	4
9	Pierre Achille WEBO Kouamo	CMR	20/1/82	A	12	(19)	6

CA OSASUNA
Coach – José Antonio Camacho
Founded – 1920
Stadium – Reyno de Navarra (19,800)

2009

30/8	Villarreal	h	1-1	Pandiani
13/9	Tenerife	a	1-2	Pandiani
19/9	Sevilla	h	0-2	
23/9	Valladolid	a	2-1	Pandiani, Galán
27/9	Sporting	h	1-0	Nekounam (p)
4/10	Getafe	a	1-2	Aranda
18/10	Atlético	h	3-0	Pandiani 2, Aranda
25/10	Racing	a	1-1	Pandiani
31/10	Barcelona	h	1-1	og (Piqué)
8/11	Almería	a	0-2	
22/11	Valencia	h	1-3	Shojaei
29/11	Zaragoza	a	1-0	Nekounam
6/12	Málaga	h	1-1	Shojaei
13/12	Mallorca	h	0-1	
19/12	Athletic	a	0-2	
2010				
3/1	Real Madrid	h	0-0	
10/1	Deportivo	a	0-1	
16/1	Espanyol	h	2-0	Juanfran, Pandiani
24/1	Xerez	a	2-1	Monreal, Camuñas
31/1	Villarreal	a	2-0	Juanfran 2
7/2	Tenerife	h	1-0	Aranda
14/2	Sevilla	a	0-1	
21/2	Valladolid	h	1-1	Camuñas
28/2	Sporting	a	2-3	Nekounam (p), Vadócz
7/3	Getafe	h	0-0	
15/3	Atlético	a	0-1	
21/3	Racing	h	1-3	Miguel Flaño
24/3	Barcelona	a	0-2	
28/3	Almería	h	1-0	Pandiani
4/4	Valencia	a	0-3	
11/4	Zaragoza	h	2-0	Aranda, Vadócz
14/4	Málaga	h	2-2	Pandiani 2

19/4	Mallorca	a	0-2	
26/4	Athletic	h	0-0	
2/5	Real Madrid	a	2-3	Aranda, Vadócz
5/5	Deportivo	h	3-1	Camuñas, Pandiani, Juanfran
8/5	Espanyol	a	1-2	Vadócz
16/5	Xerez	h	1-1	Dady

No	Name	Nat	DoB	Pos	Aps	(s)	Gls
32	ALAN BARÓ Calabuig		22/6/86	M		(1)	
20	Carlos Reina ARANDA		27/7/80	A	28	(1)	5
2	César AZPILICUETA Tanco		28/8/89	D	33		
19	Javier CALLEJA Revilla		12/5/78	M	6	(16)	
17	Javier CAMUÑAS Gallego		17/7/80	M	34	(2)	3
18	Eduardo Fernandes Pereira Gomes "DADY"	CPV	13/8/81	A	4	(6)	1
25	Jon ECHAIDE Sola		5/1/88	D	2		
24	Jokin Arcaya ESPARZA		15/6/88	M		(5)	
16	Jorge GALÁN Anaut		22/1/89	M		(20)	1
14	José Romero Urtasun "JOSETXO"		25/2/77	D	18	(1)	
12	Juan Francisco Torres Belén "JUANFRAN"		9/1/85	M	32	(1)	4
4	MIGUEL FLAÑO Bezunartea		19/8/84	D	31	(1)	1
3	Ignacio MONREAL Eraso		26/2/86	D	31		1
6	Javad NEKOUNAM	IRN	7/9/80	M	31		3
15	OIER Sanjurjo Mata		25/5/86	D	8	(3)	
11	Walter Gerardo PANDIANI Urquiza	URU	27/4/76	A	28	(1)	11
9	Javier García PORTILLO		30/3/82	A		(2)	
10	Francisco PUÑAL Martínez		6/9/75	M	27	(6)	
1	RICARDO López Felipe		30/12/71	G	36		
13	ROBERTO Fernández Alvalleros		25/1/79	G	2		
5	ROVÉRSIO Rodrigues de Barros	BRA	17/1/84	D	3		
22	Roberto López Esquiroz "RÚPER"		4/6/87	M	11	(16)	
23	SERGIO Fernández González		23/5/77	D	24		
8	Masoud Soleimani SHOJAEI	IRN	9/6/84	M	18	(18)	2
21	Krisztián VADÓCZ	HUN	30/5/85	M	11	(9)	4

REAL RACING CLUB

Coach – Juan Carlos Mandía; (9/11/09) (Juan José González); (19/11/09) Miguel Ángel Portugal
Founded – 1913
Stadium – El Sardinero (22,222)

2009

30/8	Getafe	h	1-4	Lacen
12/9	Atlético	a	1-1	Serrano
19/9	Málaga	a	2-1	Arana, Morris
22/9	Barcelona	h	1-4	Serrano
27/9	Almería	a	2-2	Tchité, Lacen
4/10	Valencia	h	0-1	
18/10	Zaragoza	a	2-2	Tchité, Serrano
25/10	Osasuna	h	1-1	Arana
1/11	Mallorca	a	0-1	
8/11	Athletic	h	0-2	
21/11	Real Madrid	a	0-1	
29/11	Deportivo	h	0-1	
6/12	Espanyol	a	4-0	Henrique, Canales 2, Tchité (p)
13/12	Xerez	h	3-2	Lacen, Arana, Xisco
20/12	Villarreal	a	0-2	

2010

3/1	Tenerife	h	2-0	Colsa, Xisco
9/1	Sevilla	a	2-1	Canales 2
17/1	Valladolid	h	1-1	Canales
24/1	Sporting	a	1-0	Geijo
31/1	Getafe	h	0-0	
7/2	Atlético	h	1-1	Colsa
14/2	Málaga	h	0-3	
20/2	Barcelona	a	0-4	
28/2	Almería	h	0-2	
8/3	Valencia	a	0-0	
14/3	Zaragoza	h	0-0	

21/3	Osasuna	a	3-1	Colsa, Christian Fernández, Diop
24/3	Mallorca	h	0-0	
29/3	Athletic	a	3-4	Tchité, Iván Bolado 2
4/4	Real Madrid	h	0-2	
11/4	Deportivo	a	1-1	Toni Moral
14/4	Espanyol	h	3-1	Tchité 2 (2p), Arana
18/4	Xerez	a	2-2	Tchité 2 (1p)
25/4	Villarreal	h	1-2	Canales
1/5	Tenerife	a	1-2	Xisco
5/5	Sevilla	h	1-5	Tchité
8/5	Valladolid	a	1-2	Christian Fernández
16/5	Sporting	h	2-0	Tchité 2

No	Name	Nat	DoB	Pos	Aps	(s)	Gls
17	Manuel Jesús ARANA Rodríguez		3/12/84	M	17	(14)	4
27	Sergio CANALES Madrazo		16/2/91	M	19	(7)	6
5	CHRISTIAN FERNÁNDEZ Salas		15/10/85	D	28	(1)	2
8	Gonzalo COLSA Albendea		2/4/79	M	28	(2)	3
1	Fabio COLTORTI	SUI	3/12/80	G	22	(1)	
6	José Ángel CRESPO Rincón		9/2/87	D	13		
21	Papa Kouli DIOP	SEN	19/3/86	M	21	(2)	1
18	EDUardo BEDIA Peláez		23/3/89	M		(5)	
9	Alexandre GEIJO Pazos	SUI	11/3/82	A	8	(11)	1
2	HENRIQUE Adriano Buss	BRA	14/10/86	D	21	(1)	1
9	IVÁN BOLADO Palacios		3/7/89	A	3	(9)	2
9	Juan José Expósito Ruiz "JUANJO"		28/10/85	A		(1)	
4	Mehdi LACEN	ALG	15/5/84	M	28	(5)	3
24	LUIS Javier GARCÍA Sanz		24/6/78	M	4	(11)	
26	Luis Miguel Villa López "LUISMA"		11/8/89	M		(1)	
30	MARIO ORTIZ Ruiz		24/3/89	D		(2)	
22	José MORATÓN Taeño		14/7/79	D	10	(1)	
12	Nasief MORRIS	RSA	16/4/81	D	12		1
10	Pedro Manuel MUNITIS Álvarez		19/6/75	M	27	(2)	
3	ORIOL Lozano Farrán		23/5/81	D	15	(4)	
28	OSMAR Barba Ibáñez		8/6/88	D	1		
14	Pablo PINILLOS Caro		9/7/74	D	22	(1)	
20	László SEPSI	ROU	7/6/87	D	4	(1)	
11	Óscar SERRANO Rodríguez		30/9/81	M	27	(6)	3
7	Mohamed TCHITÉ	COD	31/1/84	A	28	(1)	11
23	Antonio "TONI" MORAL Segura		29/8/81	M	10	(8)	1
13	Antonio Rodríguez Martínez "TOÑO"		17/12/79	G	16		
19	Marc TORREJÓN Moya		18/2/86	D	27		
15	Francisco Jiménez Tejada "XISCO"		26/6/86	A	7	(16)	3

REAL MADRID CF

Coach – Manuel Pellegrini (CHI)
Founded – 1902
Stadium – Santiago Bernabéu (80,354)
MAJOR HONOURS:
European Champion Clubs' Cup/UEFA Champions League – (9) 1956, 1957, 1958, 1959, 1960, 1966, 1998, 2000, 2002;
UEFA Cup – (2) 1985, 1986;
UEFA Super Cup – (1) 2002;
World Club Cup – (3) 1960, 1998, 2002;
Spanish League – (31) 1932, 1933, 1954, 1955, 1957, 1958, 1961, 1962, 1963, 1964, 1965, 1967, 1968, 1969, 1972, 1975, 1976, 1978, 1979, 1980, 1986, 1987, 1988, 1989, 1990, 1995, 1997, 2001, 2003, 2007, 2008;
Spanish Cup – (17) 1905, 1906, 1907, 1908, 1917, 1934, 1936, 1946, 1947, 1962, 1970, 1974, 1975, 1980, 1982, 1989, 1993.

2009

29/8	Deportivo	h	3-2	Raúl, Cristiano Ronaldo (p), Diarra L.
12/9	Espanyol	a	3-0	Granero, Guti, Cristiano Ronaldo
20/9	Xerez	h	5-0	Cristiano Ronaldo 2, Guti, Benzema, Van Nistelrooy
23/9	Villarreal	a	2-0	Cristiano Ronaldo, Kaká (p)
26/9	Tenerife	h	3-0	Benzema 2, Kaká
4/10	Sevilla	h	1-2	Pepe
17/10	Valladolid	h	4-2	Raúl 2, Marcelo, Higuaín

SPAIN

24/10	Sporting	a	0-0	
31/10	Getafe	h	2-0	*Higuaín 2*
7/11	Atlético	a	3-2	*Kaká, Marcelo, Higuaín*
21/11	Racing	h	1-0	*Higuaín*
29/11	Barcelona	a	0-1	
5/12	Almería	h	4-2	*Sergio Ramos, Higuaín, Benzema, Cristiano Ronaldo*
12/12	Valencia	a	3-2	*Higuaín 2, Garay*
19/12	Zaragoza	h	6-0	*Higuaín 2, Van der Vaart 2, Cristiano Ronaldo, Benzema*

2010

3/1	Osasuna	a	0-0	
10/1	Mallorca	h	2-0	*Higuaín, Granero*
16/1	Athletic	a	0-1	
24/1	Málaga	h	2-0	*Cristiano Ronaldo 2*
30/1	Deportivo	a	3-1	*Granero, Benzema 2*
6/2	Espanyol	h	3-0	*Sergio Ramos, Kaká, Higuaín*
13/2	Xerez	a	3-0	*Arbeloa, Cristiano Ronaldo 2*
21/2	Villarreal	h	6-2	*Cristiano Ronaldo, Kaká 2, Higuaín 2, Xabi Alonso (p)*
27/2	Tenerife	a	5-1	*Higuaín 2, Kaká, Cristiano Ronaldo, Raúl*
6/3	Sevilla	h	3-2	*Cristiano Ronaldo, Sergio Ramos, Van der Vaart*
14/3	Valladolid	a	4-1	*Cristiano Ronaldo, Higuaín 3*
20/3	Sporting	h	3-1	*Van der Vaart, Xabi Alonso, Higuaín*
25/3	Getafe	a	4-2	*Cristiano Ronaldo 2, Higuaín 2*
28/3	Atlético	h	3-2	*Xabi Alonso, Arbeloa, Higuaín*
4/4	Racing	a	2-0	*Cristiano Ronaldo (p), Higuaín*
10/4	Barcelona	h	0-2	
15/4	Almería	a	2-1	*Cristiano Ronaldo, Van der Vaart*
18/4	Valencia	h	2-0	*Higuaín, Cristiano Ronaldo*
24/4	Zaragoza	a	2-1	*Raúl, Kaká*
2/5	Osasuna	h	3-2	*Cristiano Ronaldo 2, Marcelo*
5/5	Mallorca	a	4-1	*Cristiano Ronaldo 3, Higuaín*
8/5	Athletic	h	5-1	*Cristiano Ronaldo (p), Higuaín, Sergio Ramos, Benzema, Marcelo*
16/5	Málaga	a	1-1	*Van der Vaart*

No	Name	Nat	DoB	Pos	Aps	(s)	Gls
18	Raúl ALBIOL Tortajada		4/9/85	D	32	(1)	
2	Álvaro ARBELOA Coca		17/1/83	D	30		2
11	Karim BENZEMA	FRA	19/12/87	A	14	(13)	8
1	Íker CASILLAS Fernández		20/5/81	G	38		
9	CRISTIANO RONALDO dos Santos Aveiro	POR	5/2/85	A	28	(1)	26
10	Lassana DIARRA	FRA	10/3/85	M	19	(4)	1
6	Mahamadou DIARRA	MLI	18/5/81	M	4	(11)	
15	Royston DRENTHE	NED	8/4/87	M	3	(5)	
5	Fernando Rubén GAGO	ARG	10/4/86	M	14	(4)	
19	Ezequiel Marcelo GARAY	ARG	10/10/86	D	19	(1)	1
24	Esteban GRANERO Molina		2/7/87	M	21	(10)	3
14	José María GUTIérrez Hernández		31/10/76	M	10	(16)	2
20	Gonzalo Gerardo HIGUAÍN	ARG	10/12/87	A	28	(4)	27
36	Juan Francisco Fuertes "JUANFRAN"		27/4/87			(1)	
8	Ricardo Izecson dos Santos Leite "KAKÁ"	BRA	22/4/82	M	21	(4)	8
12	MARCELO Vieira da Silva Júnior	BRA	12/5/88	D	34	(1)	4
28	MARCOS ALONSO Mendoza		28/12/90	M		(1)	
21	Christoph METZELDER	GER	5/11/80	D	2		
30	Pedro MOSQUERA Parada		21/4/88	M		(1)	
3	Képler Laveran Lima Ferreira "PEPE"	POR	26/2/83	D	10		1
7	RAÚL González Blanco		27/6/77	A	8	(22)	5
4	SERGIO RAMOS García		30/3/86	D	33		4
23	Rafael VAN DER VAART	NED	11/2/83	M	16	(10)	6
17	Ruud VAN NISTELROOY	NED	1/7/76	A		(1)	1
22	XABIer ALONSO Olano		25/11/81	M	34		

SEVILLA FC

Coach – Manuel Jiménez; (24/3/10) Antonio Álvarez
Founded – 1905
Stadium – Ramón Sánchez Pizjuán (45,500)
MAJOR HONOURS:
UEFA Cup – (2) 2006, 2007;
UEFA Super Cup – (1) 2006;
Spanish League – (1) 1946;
Spanish Cup – (5) 1935, 1939, 1948, 2007, 2010.

2009

30/8	Valencia	a	0-2	
12/9	Zaragoza	h	4-1	*Konko, Luís Fabiano 2, Perotti*
19/9	Osasuna	a	2-0	*Negredo, Kanouté*
22/9	Mallorca	h	2-0	*Squillaci, Perotti*
26/9	Athletic	a	4-0	*Renato, Negredo, Kanouté, Jesús Navas*
4/10	Real Madrid	h	2-1	*Jesús Navas, Renato*
17/10	Deportivo	a	0-1	
24/10	Espanyol	h	0-0	
31/10	Xerez	a	2-0	*Negredo, Luís Fabiano*
8/11	Villarreal	h	3-2	*Luís Fabiano 2, Kanouté*
21/11	Tenerife	a	2-1	*Perotti, Renato*
28/11	Málaga	h	2-2	*Luís Fabiano 2*
5/12	Valladolid	h	1-1	*Luís Fabiano (p)*
13/12	Sporting	a	1-0	*Kanouté*
19/12	Getafe	h	1-2	*Negredo*

2010

2/1	Atlético	h	1-2	*Renato*
9/1	Racing	h	1-2	*Romaric*
16/1	Barcelona	a	0-4	
23/1	Almería	h	1-0	*Negredo*
31/1	Valencia	h	2-1	*Negredo 2*
7/2	Zaragoza	a	1-2	*Kanouté*
14/2	Osasuna	h	1-0	*Luís Fabiano*
20/2	Mallorca	a	3-1	*Jesús Navas, Dragutinović, Perotti*
28/2	Athletic	h	0-0	
6/3	Real Madrid	a	2-3	*og (Xabi Alonso), Dragutinović*
13/3	Deportivo	h	1-1	*Fazio*
20/3	Espanyol	a	0-2	
23/3	Xerez	h	1-1	*Kanouté (p)*
28/3	Villarreal	a	0-3	
3/4	Tenerife	h	3-0	*Kanouté, Luís Fabiano, José Carlos*
10/4	Málaga	a	2-1	*Cala, Lolo*
13/4	Valladolid	a	1-2	*Cala*
17/4	Sporting	h	3-0	*Kanouté, Luís Fabiano, Cala*
24/4	Getafe	a	3-4	*Luís Fabiano 2, Kanouté*
2/5	Atlético	h	3-1	*Luís Fabiano, Negredo 2 (2p)*
5/5	Racing	a	5-1	*Negredo 2, Kanouté (p), Jesús Navas, Diego Capel*
8/5	Barcelona	h	2-3	*Kanouté, Luís Fabiano*
15/5	Almería	a	3-2	*Kanouté, og (Chico), Rodri*

No	Name	Nat	DoB	Pos	Aps	(s)	Gls
21	Lautaro Germán ACOSTA	ARG	14/3/88	M	1	(5)	
6	ADRIANO Correia Claro	BRA	26/10/84	D	23	(4)	
28	Juan Torres Ruiz "CALA"		26/11/89	D	5		3
27	Enrique Javier CARREÑO		27/11/86	A		(1)	
15	Ernesto Javier CHEVANTÓN	URU	12/8/80	A		(1)	
16	DIEGO Ángel CAPEL Trinidad		16/2/88	A	14	(15)	1
3	Ivica DRAGUTINOVIĆ	SRB	13/11/75	D	20		2
5	Aldo Pedro DUSCHER	ARG	22/3/79	M	7	(3)	
14	Julien ESCUDÉ	FRA	17/8/79	D	24		
2	Federico Julián FAZIO	ARG	17/3/87	D	10		1
18	FERNANDO NAVARRO Corbacho		25/6/82	D	26	(3)	
13	JAVIer VARAS Herrera		10/9/82	G	5		
7	JESÚS NAVAS González		21/11/85	M	32	(2)	4
30	JOSÉ CARLOS Fernández Vázquez		17/7/87	M	2	(8)	1
12	Frédéric KANOUTÉ	MLI	2/9/77	A	20	(7)	12
9	Arouna KONÉ	CIV	11/11/83	M	3	(9)	
24	Abdoulay KONKO	FRA	9/3/84	D	17	(1)	
23	Manuel Ortiz Toribio "LOLO"		22/8/84	M	9	(12)	1

10	LUÍS FABIANO Clemente	BRA	8/11/80	A	18	(5)	15
37	Antonio LUNA Rodríguez		17/3/91	D	1		
34	MARC VALIENTE Hernández		29/3/87	D	2	(1)	
19	Álvaro NEGREDO Sánchez		20/8/85	A	25	(10)	11
1	Andrés PALOP Cervera		22/10/73	G	33		
25	Diego PEROTTI	ARG	26/7/88	M	22	(6)	4
11	RENATO Dimei Florencio Santos	BRA	15/5/79	M	30	(3)	4
31	RODRIgo Ríos Lozano		6/6/90	A		(2)	1
22	Christian Koffi Ndri "ROMARIC"	CIV	4/6/83	M	10	(9)	1
17	SERGIO SÁNCHEZ Ortega		3/4/86	D	6	(1)	
4	Sebastien SQUILLACI	FRA	11/8/80	D	14	(2)	1
15	Marius STANKEVIČIUS	LTU	15/7/81	D	14	(2)	
8	Didier ZOKORA	CIV	14/12/80	M	25	(1)	

REAL SPORTING DE GIJÓN
Coach – Manuel Preciado
Founded – 1905
Stadium – El Molinón (24,000)

2009

31/8	Barcelona	a	0-3	
13/9	Almería	h	1-0	Diego Castro
20/9	Valencia	a	2-2	Barral, Arnolin
24/9	Zaragoza	h	1-1	Diego Castro
27/9	Osasuna	a	0-1	
4/10	Mallorca	h	4-1	Luis Morán, De las Cuevas 2, Bilić
18/10	Athletic	a	2-1	De las Cuevas 2
24/10	Real Madrid	h	0-0	
1/11	Deportivo	a	1-1	Diego Castro
8/11	Espanyol	h	1-0	Bilić
22/11	Xerez	a	0-0	
28/11	Villarreal	h	1-0	Bilić
6/12	Tenerife	a	1-2	Diego Castro
13/12	Sevilla	h	0-1	
20/12	Valladolid	a	1-2	Luis Morán

2010

3/1	Málaga	h	2-2	Arnolin, Canella
10/1	Getafe	h	1-0	Diego Castro
17/1	Atlético	a	2-3	Diego Castro (p), Luis Morán
24/1	Racing	h	0-1	
30/1	Barcelona	h	0-1	
7/2	Almería	a	1-3	Diego Castro (p)
13/2	Valencia	h	1-1	Diego Castro
21/2	Zaragoza	a	3-1	Bilić, Luis Morán, Barral
28/2	Osasuna	h	3-2	De las Cuevas, Barral, Diego Castro (p)
7/3	Mallorca	a	0-3	
13/3	Athletic	h	0-0	
20/3	Real Madrid	a	1-3	Barral
23/3	Deportivo	h	2-1	Bilić, Diego Castro (p)
28/3	Espanyol	a	0-0	
4/4	Xerez	h	2-2	Rivera, De las Cuevas
10/4	Villarreal	a	0-1	
13/4	Tenerife	h	0-2	
17/4	Sevilla	a	0-3	
25/4	Valladolid	h	0-2	
1/5	Málaga	a	1-1	og (Apoño)
4/5	Getafe	a	1-1	De las Cuevas
8/5	Atlético	h	1-1	De las Cuevas
16/5	Racing	a	0-2	

No	Name	Nat	DoB	Pos	Aps	(s)	Gls
12	Grégory ARNOLIN	FRA	10/11/80	D	35		2
23	David BARRAL Torres		10/5/83	A	23	(10)	4
9	Mate BILIĆ	CRO	23/10/80	A	17	(14)	5
36	BORJA NAVARRO García		14/5/90	A		(2)	
2	Alberto Tomás BOTIA Rabasco		27/1/89	D	26		
15	Roberto CANELLA Suárez		7/2/88	D	28		1
6	CARMELO González Jiménez		9/7/83	M	11	(16)	
20	Miguel Angel DE LAS CUEVAS Barberá		19/6/86	M	32	(5)	8

19	DIEGO CAMACHO Quesada		3/10/76	M	16	(7)	
17	DIEGO CASTRO Jiménez		2/7/82	A	31	(4)	10
16	GERARD Autet Serrabasa		8/9/78	D	8		
14	IVÁN HERNÁNDEZ Soto		27/2/80	D	7	(3)	
3	JOSÉ ÁNGEL Valdés Díaz		5/9/89	M	10	(3)	
38	JUAN MUÑIZ Gallego		13/3/92	A		(1)	
1	JUAN PABLO Colinas Ferreras		2/9/78	G	38		
21	Enrique "KIKE" MATEO Montoya		30/12/79	M	2	(14)	
28	Marcos LANDEIRA Álvarez		2/5/87	A	1		
11	Alberto LORA Ramos		25/3/87	D	31	(1)	
18	LUIS MORÁN Sánchez		26/7/87	M	21	(7)	4
10	Francisco José MALDONADO Collantes		2/6/81	M	6	(9)	
24	Sergio MATABUENA Delgado		12/2/79	M	5	(9)	
8	MIGUEL Marcos Madera		8/11/85	M	12	(1)	
7	PEDRO Santa Cecilia García		10/3/84	M	4	(1)	
31	Cristian PORTILLA Rodríguez		28/8/88	M	3	(1)	
5	Alberto RIVERA Pizarro		18/2/78	M	34		1
22	Rafael SASTRE Reus		22/10/78	D	11	(3)	
37	SERGIO ÁLVAREZ Díaz		23/1/92	M	1		
8	Milan SMILJANIĆ	SRB	19/11/86	M	5	(1)	

CD TENERIFE
Coach – José Luis Oltra
Founded – 1922
Stadium – Heliodoro Rodríguez López (22,500)

2009

29/8	Zaragoza	a	0-1	
13/9	Osasuna	h	2-1	Nino, Ricardo
19/9	Mallorca	a	0-4	
23/9	Athletic	h	1-0	Mikel Alonso
26/9	Real Madrid	a	0-3	
3/10	Deportivo	h	0-1	
18/10	Espanyol	a	1-2	Alfaro
25/10	Xerez	h	1-0	Alfaro
1/11	Villarreal	a	0-5	
7/11	Málaga	h	2-2	Román Martínez, Alfaro
21/11	Sevilla	h	1-2	Nino
29/11	Valladolid	a	3-3	Nino, Ángel, Ayoze
6/12	Sporting	h	2-1	Ricardo, Nino
13/12	Getafe	a	1-2	Juanlu
20/12	Atlético	h	1-1	Nino

2010

3/1	Racing	a	0-2	
10/1	Barcelona	h	0-5	
17/1	Almería	a	1-1	Juanlu
24/1	Valencia	h	0-0	
31/1	Zaragoza	h	1-3	Juanlu
7/2	Osasuna	a	0-1	
15/2	Mallorca	h	1-0	Nino
21/2	Athletic	a	1-4	Alfaro
27/2	Real Madrid	h	1-5	Ayoze
6/3	Deportivo	a	1-3	Juanlu
14/3	Espanyol	h	4-1	Richi, Nino 2, Alfaro
20/3	Xerez	a	1-2	Nino
24/3	Villarreal	h	2-2	Nino, Culebras
27/3	Málaga	a	1-1	Alfaro (p)
3/4	Sevilla	a	0-3	
10/4	Valladolid	h	0-0	
13/4	Sporting	a	2-0	Román Martínez, Alfaro
18/4	Getafe	h	3-2	Nino 3
25/4	Atlético	a	1-3	Román Martínez
1/5	Racing	h	2-1	Román Martínez, Ayoze (p)
4/5	Barcelona	a	1-4	Román Martínez
8/5	Almería	h	2-2	Bertrán, Nino
16/5	Valencia	a	0-1	

No	Name	Nat	DoB	Pos	Aps	(s)	Gls
26	AITOR NÚÑEZ Martín		2/10/87	D	4	(1)	
21	Alejandro ALFARO Ligero		23/11/86	M	36		7
9	ÁNGEL Luis Rodríguez Díaz		26/4/87	M		(24)	1

SPAIN

10	AYOZE García Pérez		22/11/85	D	17	(8)	3
4	Carlos BELLVÍS Llorens		24/4/85	D	15		
2	Marc BERTRÁN Vilanova		22/5/82	D	21		1
24	José Antonio CULEBRAS Arenas		16/1/79	D	16	(2)	1
22	Telmario de Araújo Sacramento "DINEI"	BRA	11/11/83	M	1	(22)	
19	EZEQUIEL LUNA	ARG	19/11/86	D	22	(1)	
3	HÉCTOR Sánchez Cabrera		31/3/85	D	11		
17	Juan Luis Hens Lorite "JUANLU"		7/2/84	M	31	(1)	4
14	Daniel Armand N'gom KOME	CMR	19/5/80	M	19	(10)	
5	Manuel "MANOLO" MARTÍNEZ Lara		15/6/80	D	26	(4)	
23	MIKEL ALONSO Olano		17/5/80	M	21	(7)	1
7	Juan Francisco Martínez Modesto "NINO"		10/6/80	A	37	(1)	14
27	Julián OMAR Ramos Suárez		26/1/88	M	7	(16)	
6	PABLO SICILIA Roig		10/9/81	M	33	(1)	
8	RICARDO León Brito		8/2/83	M	29		2
20	Ricardo Pérez De Zabala Goytre "RICHI"		14/4/77	A	16	(6)	1
15	ROMÁN Fernando MARTÍNEZ	ARG	27/3/83	M	18	(5)	5
11	Gaizka SAIZAR Lecuona		22/7/80	M		(4)	
13	SERGIO ARAGONESES Almeida		1/2/77	G	38		

VALENCIA CF
Coach – Unai Emery
Founded – 1919
Stadium – Mestalla (52,000)
MAJOR HONOURS:
UEFA Cup Winners' Cup – (1) 1980;
UEFA Cup – (1) 2004;
Inter Cities Fairs Cup – (2) 1962, 1963;
UEFA Super Cup – (2) 1980, 2004;
Spanish League – (6) 1942, 1944, 1947, 1971, 2002, 2004;
Spanish Cup – (7) 1941, 1949, 1954, 1967, 1979, 1999, 2008.

2009
30/8	Sevilla	h	2-0	Mata, Pablo Hernández
13/9	Valladolid	a	4-2	David Silva, David Villa 2, Mata
20/9	Sporting	h	2-2	David Villa 2
23/9	Getafe	a	1-3	David Villa
26/9	Atlético	h	2-2	Pablo Hernández, David Villa
4/10	Racing	a	1-0	Žigić
17/10	Barcelona	h	0-0	
25/10	Almería	a	3-0	David Villa, Pablo Hernández, Mata
1/11	Málaga	a	1-0	David Navarro
8/11	Zaragoza	h	3-1	Mata, David Villa, Pablo Hernández
22/11	Osasuna	a	3-1	David Villa, Albelda, Marchena
28/11	Mallorca	h	1-1	David Villa
6/12	Athletic	a	2-1	David Villa, Mathieu
12/12	Real Madrid	h	2-3	David Villa, Joaquín
20/12	Deportivo	a	0-0	

2010
2/1	Espanyol	h	1-0	Žigić
10/1	Xerez	a	3-1	Mata, David Silva, Marchena
17/1	Villarreal	h	4-1	Éver Banega, David Villa 2 (1p), David Silva
24/1	Tenerife	a	0-0	
31/1	Sevilla	a	1-2	David Navarro
6/2	Valladolid	h	2-0	Éver Banega, David Villa
13/2	Sporting	a	1-1	Mata
22/2	Getafe	h	2-1	David Villa 2
28/2	Atlético	a	1-4	David Silva
8/3	Racing	h	0-0	
14/3	Barcelona	a	0-3	
21/3	Almería	h	2-0	Mata, David Silva
24/3	Málaga	h	1-0	David Villa
27/3	Zaragoza	a	0-3	
4/4	Osasuna	h	3-0	Joaquín, David Villa 2 (1p)
11/4	Mallorca	a	2-3	Jordi Alba, Pablo Hernández
15/4	Athletic	h	2-0	David Silva 2
18/4	Real Madrid	a	0-2	
25/4	Deportivo	h	1-0	David Villa (p)
1/5	Espanyol	a	2-0	Žigić 2
4/5	Xerez	h	3-1	Mata 2, David Silva
8/5	Villarreal	a	0-2	
16/5	Tenerife	h	1-0	Alexis

No	Name	Nat	DoB	Pos	Aps	(s)	Gls
6	David ALBELDA Aliques		1/9/77	M	22	(6)	1
20	ALEXIS Ruano Delgado		4/8/85	D	21	(3)	1
8	Rubén BARAJA Vegas		11/7/75	M	7	(11)	
2	BRUNO Saltor Grau		1/10/80	D	25	(1)	
1	CÉSAR SÁNCHEZ Domínguez		2/9/71	G	30		
4	DAVID NAVARRO Pedrós		25/5/80	D	19		2
21	DAVID Jiménez SILVA		8/1/86	M	28	(2)	8
7	DAVID VILLA Sánchez		3/12/81	A	31	(1)	21
15	Ángel DEALBERT Ibáñez		1/1/83	D	22	(2)	
25	Alejandro Damián DOMÍNGUEZ	ARG	10/6/81	M	4	(9)	
24	ÉVER Maximiliano BANEGA	ARG	29/6/88	M	33	(3)	2
17	JOAQUÍN Sánchez Rodríguez		21/7/81	A	17	(11)	2
56	JOEL Johnson Alajarín		20/9/92	D	1		
28	JORGE ALBA Ramos		21/3/89	A	12	(3)	1
43	Manuel Castellano Castro "LILLO"		27/3/89	D	1		
3	Hedwiges MADURO	NED	13/2/85	M	12	(6)	
18	MANUEL Henrique Tavares FERNANDES	POR	5/2/86	M	8	(7)	
5	Carlos MARCHENA López		31/7/79	D	17	(7)	2
10	Juan Manuel MATA García		28/4/88	M	30	(5)	9
22	Jérémy MATHIEU	FRA	29/10/83	D	14	(3)	1
30	Miguel Ángel Herrero "MICHEL"		29/7/88	M		(3)	
23	Luís MIGUEL Brito García Monteiro	POR	4/1/80	D	20	(5)	
16	Nicolás Ladislao Fedor Flores "MIKU"	VEN	19/8/85	A	1	(1)	
13	Miguel Ángel MOYÁ Rumbo		2/4/84	G	8		
19	PABLO HERNÁNDEZ Domínguez		11/4/85	M	25	(8)	5
14	VICENTE Rodríguez Guillén		16/7/81	M	5	(6)	
9	Nikola ŽIGIĆ	SRB	25/9/80	A	5	(8)	4

REAL VALLADOLID CF
Coach – José Luis Mendilíbar; (1/2/10) Onésimo Sánchez; (6/4/10) Javier Clemente
Founded – 1928
Stadium – José Zorrilla (26,512)

2009
30/8	Almería	a	0-0	
13/9	Valencia	h	2-4	Nauzet Alemán, Manucho
20/9	Zaragoza	a	2-1	Marquitos, Sisi
23/9	Osasuna	h	1-2	Diego Costa
27/9	Mallorca	a	0-3	
4/10	Athletic	h	2-2	Diego Costa, Nivaldo
17/10	Real Madrid	a	2-4	Nauzet Alemán, Marquitos
25/10	Deportivo	h	4-0	Nauzet Alemán 2, Diego Costa, Medunjanin
1/11	Espanyol	a	1-1	Medunjanin
8/11	Xerez	h	0-0	
22/11	Villarreal	a	1-3	Diego Costa
29/11	Tenerife	h	3-3	Diego Costa 2, Canobbio (p)
5/12	Sevilla	a	1-1	Manucho
13/12	Málaga	h	1-1	og (Jesús Gámez)
20/12	Sporting	h	2-1	Nivaldo, Medunjanin

2010
3/1	Getafe	a	0-1	
9/1	Atlético	h	0-4	
17/1	Racing	a	1-1	og (Pinillos)
23/1	Barcelona	h	0-3	
31/1	Almería	h	1-1	Arzo
6/2	Valencia	a	0-2	
14/2	Zaragoza	h	1-1	Diego Costa
21/2	Osasuna	a	1-1	Medunjanin
28/2	Mallorca	h	1-2	Bueno

SPAIN

7/3	Athletic	a	0-2	
14/3	Real Madrid	h	1-4	og (Albiol)
20/3	Deportivo	a	2-0	Nauzet Alemán, Medunjanin
24/3	Espanyol	h	0-0	
28/3	Xerez	a	0-3	
4/4	Villarreal	h	0-2	
10/4	Tenerife	a	0-0	
13/4	Sevilla	h	2-1	Diego Costa, Manucho
18/4	Málaga	a	0-0	
25/4	Sporting	a	2-0	Manucho, Baraja
1/5	Getafe	h	0-0	
5/5	Atlético	a	1-3	Jonathan Sesma
8/5	Racing	h	2-1	Baraja, Nauzet Alemán (p)
16/5	Barcelona	a	0-4	

No	Name	Nat	DoB	Pos	Aps	(s)	Gls
18	ÁLVARO RUBIO Robres		18/4/79	M	16		
24	César ARZO Amposta		21/1/86	D	17	(5)	1
12	ASIER Arranz Martín		28/3/87	M	1		
8	Javier BARAJA Vegas		24/8/80	M	18	(7)	2
2	Antonio BARRAGÁN Fernández		12/6/87	D	14	(3)	
10	BORJA Fernández Fernández		14/1/81	M	30	(1)	
11	Alberto BUENO Calvo		20/3/88	M	7	(13)	1
20	Néstor Fabián CANOBBIO	URU	8/3/80	A	21	(3)	1
27	CARLOS LÁZARO Vallejo		13/11/90	M	6	(2)	
15	Asier DEL HORNO Cosgaya		19/1/81	D	13		
22	DIEGO da Silva COSTA	BRA	7/10/88	A	32	(2)	8
13	FABRICIO Agosto Ramírez		31/12/87	G	1		
14	HÉCTOR FONT Romero		15/6/84	M	3	(7)	
25	JACOBO Sanz Ovejero		10/7/83	G	14	(1)	
19	JONATHAN SESMA Suárez		14/11/78	M	14	(3)	1
33	Sergio Gontán Gallardo "KEKO"		28/12/91	M	4	(9)	
9	Mateus Alberto Contreiras Gonçalves "MANUCHO"	ANG	7/3/83	A	20	(8)	4
3	Alberto MARCOS Rey		15/2/74	D	17	(4)	
23	Marcos García Barreno "MARQUITOS"		21/3/87	M	11	(8)	2
5	Haris MEDUNJANIN	BIH	8/3/85	M	9	(15)	5
7	NAUZET ALEMÁN Vera		25/2/85	M	21	(5)	6
4	NIVALDO Batista Santana	BRA	23/6/80	D	23	(2)	2
16	PEDRO José LÓPEZ Muñoz		1/11/83	D	30	(1)	
6	Vítor Hugo Gomes Passos "PELÉ"	POR	4/9/87	M	17	(6)	
17	Luis PRIETO Zalbidegoitia		19/2/79	D	19	(1)	
32	RAÚL Rodríguez NAVAS		11/5/88	D	1		
12	Henrique SERENO Fonseca	POR	18/5/85	D	12		
29	SERGIO GARCÍA de la Iglesia		8/8/89	A		(1)	
21	SISInio González Martínez		21/8/86	M	3	(2)	1
1	Justo Wilmar VILLAR	PAR	30/6/77	G	23		
26	YURI Berchiche Izeta		10/2/90	M	1		

VILLARREAL CF
Coach – Ernesto Valverde; (1/2/10) Juan Carlos Garrido
Founded – 1923
Stadium – El Madrigal (25,400)

2009

30/8	Osasuna	a	1-1	Santi Cazorla
13/9	Mallorca	h	1-1	Rossi
20/9	Athletic	a	2-3	Cani, Santi Cazorla
23/9	Real Madrid	h	0-2	
27/9	Deportivo	a	0-1	
4/10	Espanyol	h	0-0	
18/10	Xerez	a	1-2	Pires
25/10	Málaga	h	2-1	Nilmar, Capdevila
1/11	Tenerife	h	5-0	Llorente 2, Pires, Rossi, Cani
8/11	Sevilla	a	2-3	Pires, David Fuster
22/11	Valladolid	h	3-1	Nilmar 2, Rossi
28/11	Sporting	a	0-1	
6/12	Getafe	h	3-2	Capdevila 2, Santi Cazorla
13/12	Atlético	a	2-1	David Fuster, Llorente
20/12	Racing	h	2-0	Llorente, Rossi

2010

2/1	Barcelona	a	1-1	David Fuster
9/1	Almería	h	1-1	Nilmar
17/1	Valencia	a	1-4	Nilmar
24/1	Zaragoza	h	4-2	Capdevila, Nilmar, Rossi, Ibagaza
31/1	Osasuna	h	0-2	
7/2	Mallorca	a	0-1	
13/2	Athletic	h	2-1	Capdevila, Nilmar
21/2	Real Madrid	a	2-6	Senna, Nilmar
28/2	Deportivo	h	1-0	Llorente
7/3	Espanyol	a	0-0	
14/3	Xerez	h	2-0	Llorente, Escudero
21/3	Málaga	a	0-2	
24/3	Tenerife	a	2-2	Nilmar, Rossi
28/3	Sevilla	h	3-0	Rossi, Llorente, Pires
4/4	Valladolid	a	2-0	Ángel, Nilmar
10/4	Sporting	h	1-0	Godín
13/4	Getafe	a	0-3	
17/4	Atlético	h	2-1	Godín, Rossi
25/4	Racing	a	2-1	Godín, Nilmar
1/5	Barcelona	h	1-4	Llorente
2/5	Almería	a	2-4	Marcano, Ibagaza
8/5	Valencia	h	2-0	Rossi, Llorente
15/5	Zaragoza	a	3-3	Santi Cazorla 2, Rossi

No	Name	Nat	DoB	Pos	Aps	(s)	Gls
18	ÁNGEL Domingo López Ruano		10/3/81	D	22	(2)	1
21	BRUNO Soriano Llido		12/6/84	M	31	(2)	
10	Rubén Gracia Calmache "CANI"		3/8/81	M	27	(8)	2
5	Joan CAPDEVILA Méndez		3/2/78	D	37		5
14	DAVID FUSTER Torrijos		3/2/82	M	11	(11)	3
13	DIEGO LÓPEZ Rodríguez		3/11/81	G	38		
6	Sebastián EGUREN Ledesma	URU	8/1/81	M	9	(5)	
24	Damián Ariel ESCUDERO	ARG	20/4/87	M	3	(10)	1
4	Diego Roberto GODÍN Leal	URU	16/2/86	D	36		3
2	GONZALO Javier RODRÍGUEZ	ARG	10/4/84	D	19	(2)	
11	Ariel Santiago IBAGAZA	ARG	27/10/76	M	14	(10)	2
17	JAVIer Rodríguez VENTA		13/12/75	D	16	(2)	
23	JONATHAN PEREIRA Rodríguez		12/5/87	A		(6)	
32	Francisco José Olivas Alba "KIKO"		21/8/88	D	2		
9	Joseba LLORENTE Echarri		24/11/79	A	20	(9)	9
20	Iván MARCANO Sierra		23/6/87	D	15	(1)	1
28	MARCO Gastón RUBÉN odríguez	ARG	26/10/86	A	1	(3)	
30	MARCOS GULLÓN Ferrera		20/2/89	M		(1)	
31	Javier Magro MATILLA		16/8/88	M	2		
41	Mateo Pablo MUSACCHIO	ARG	26/8/90	D	5	(2)	
12	NILMAR Honorato da Silva	BRA	14/7/84	A	28	(5)	11
7	Robert PIRES	FRA	29/10/73	M	13	(15)	4
22	Giuseppe ROSSI	ITA	1/2/87	A	27	(7)	10
8	SANTIago CAZORLA González		13/12/84	M	16	(8)	5
19	Marcos Antonio SENNA da Silva		17/7/76	M	26	(4)	1

XEREZ CD
Coach – José Ángel Ziganda; (12/1/10) (Antonio Poyatos);
(19/1/10) Néstor Raúl Gorosito (ARG)
Founded – 1947
Stadium – Chapín (20,486)

2009

30/8	Mallorca	a	0-2	
13/9	Athletic	h	0-1	
20/9	Real Madrid	a	0-5	
23/9	Deportivo	h	0-3	
27/9	Espanyol	a	0-0	
4/10	Málaga	h	1-1	Armenteros
18/10	Villarreal	h	2-1	Mario Bermejo, Antoñito
25/10	Tenerife	a	0-1	
31/10	Sevilla	h	0-2	
8/11	Valladolid	a	0-0	

22/11	Sporting	h	0-0	
29/11	Getafe	a	1-5	Aythami
2/12	Barcelona	h	0-2	
5/12	Atlético	h	0-2	
13/12	Racing	a	2-3	Mario Bermejo, Antoñito
2010				
3/1	Almería	a	0-1	
10/1	Valencia	h	1-3	Carlos Calvo
17/1	Zaragoza	a	0-0	
24/1	Osasuna	h	1-2	Mario Bermejo
31/1	Mallorca	h	2-1	Carlos Calvo 2
7/2	Athletic	a	2-3	Moreno, Mario Bermejo
13/2	Real Madrid	h	0-3	
20/2	Deportivo	a	1-2	Mario Bermejo
28/2	Espanyol	h	1-1	Mario Bermejo
7/3	Málaga	a	4-2	Momo 2 (1p), Leandro, Orellana
14/3	Villarreal	a	0-2	
20/3	Tenerife	h	2-1	Mario Bermejo, Aythami
23/3	Sevilla	a	1-1	Leandro
28/3	Valladolid	h	3-0	Víctor Sánchez, Míchel, Mario Bermejo (p)
4/4	Sporting	a	2-2	Mario Bermejo, Alustiza
10/4	Getafe	h	0-1	
14/4	Atlético	a	2-1	Mario Bermejo, Armenteros
18/4	Racing	h	2-2	Orellana, Víctor Sánchez
24/4	Barcelona	a	1-3	Mario Bermejo
1/5	Almería	h	2-1	og (Juanma Ortiz), Mario Bermejo
4/5	Valencia	a	1-3	Armenteros
8/5	Zaragoza	h	3-2	Francis, Míchel, Carlos Calvo
16/5	Osasuna	a	1-1	Antoñito

No	Name	Nat	DoB	Pos	Aps	(s)	Gls
20	ABEL Gómez Moreno		20/2/82	M	9	(8)	
21	Matías ALUSTIZA	ARG	31/5/84	D	1	(10)	1
8	Antonio Ramiro Pérez "ANTOÑITO"		2/2/78	A	2	(23)	3
16	Emiliano Daniel ARMENTEROS	ARG	18/1/86	A	16	(9)	3
23	AYTHAMI Artiles Oliva		2/4/86	D	29	(1)	2
4	Alejandro BERGANTIÑOS García		7/6/85	M	22	(4)	
19	CARLOS CALVO Sobrado		18/9/85	M	26	(9)	4
22	José Manuel CASADO Bizcocho		9/8/86	D	26	(1)	
1	José María Giménez Pérez "CHEMA"		25/4/80	G	3		
7	FRANCIsco Jesús Pérez Malia		17/12/81	D	25		1
24	Sidi Yaya KEITA	MLI	20/3/85	M	24		
5	LEANDRO Andrés Gioda	ARG	1/10/84	D	28	(1)	2
21	Giancarlo MALDONADO Marrero	VEN	29/6/82	A	6	(3)	
9	MARIO BERMEJO Castanedo		7/10/78	A	33	(1)	12
3	Jesús MENDOZA Aguirre		23/2/77	D	12		
17	Miguel Ángel Carrilero González "MÍCHEL"		3/8/77	D	7	(7)	2
11	Jerónimo Figueroa Cabrera "MOMO"		15/7/82	A	22	(4)	2
6	Vicente MORENO Peris		26/10/74	M	15	(7)	1
15	Fabián Ariel ORELLANA Valenzuela	CHI	27/1/86	M	20	(6)	2
18	David PRIETO Gálvez		2/1/83	D	20	(1)	
2	Juan Luis Fernández REDONDO		11/11/77	D	11	(2)	
13	RENAN Brito Soares	BRA	24/1/85	G	35		
14	VÍCTOR SÁNCHEZ Mata		20/1/87	M	22	(3)	2
10	Emilio José VIQUEIRA Moure		20/9/74	M	4	(13)	

REAL ZARAGOZA
Coach – Marcelino García Toral; (13/12/09) José Aurelio Gay
Founded – 1932
Stadium – La Romareda (34,596)
MAJOR HONOURS:
UEFA Cup Winners' Cup – (1) 1995;
Inter Cities Fairs Cup – (1) 1964;
Spanish Cup – (6) 1964, 1966, 1986, 1994, 2001, 2004.

2009				
29/8	Tenerife	h	1-0	Arizmendi
12/9	Sevilla	a	1-4	Arizmendi
20/9	Valladolid	h	1-2	Jorge López

24/9	Sporting	a	1-1	Abel Aguilar
27/9	Getafe	h	3-0	Pavón, Abel Aguilar 2
3/10	Atlético	a	1-2	Ewerthon
18/10	Racing	h	2-2	Pavón, Arizmendi
25/10	Barcelona	a	1-6	Jorge López
1/11	Almería	h	2-1	Lafita, Pulido
8/11	Valencia	a	1-3	Abel Aguilar
22/11	Málaga	a	1-1	Ewerthon (p)
29/11	Osasuna	h	0-1	
6/12	Mallorca	a	1-4	Ander Herrera
12/12	Athletic	h	1-2	Diogo
19/12	Real Madrid	a	0-6	
2010				
3/1	Deportivo	h	0-0	
10/1	Espanyol	a	1-2	og (Moisés Hurtado)
17/1	Xerez	h	0-0	
24/1	Villarreal	a	2-4	Eliseu, Lafita
31/1	Tenerife	a	3-1	Suazo (p), Adrián Colunga, Lafita
7/2	Sevilla	h	2-1	Contini, og (Negredo)
14/2	Valladolid	a	1-1	Suazo
21/2	Sporting	h	1-3	Arizmendi
27/2	Getafe	a	2-0	Suazo 2
7/3	Atlético	h	1-1	Jarošík
14/3	Racing	a	0-0	
21/3	Barcelona	h	2-4	Adrián Colunga 2
24/3	Almería	a	0-1	
27/3	Valencia	h	3-0	Diogo, Arizmendi, Jarošík
3/4	Málaga	h	2-0	Ponzio, Suazo
11/4	Osasuna	a	0-2	
14/4	Mallorca	h	1-1	Suazo
18/4	Athletic	a	0-0	
24/4	Real Madrid	h	1-2	Adrián Colunga
2/5	Deportivo	a	1-0	Adrián Colunga
5/5	Espanyol	h	1-0	Adrián Colunga (p)
8/5	Xerez	a	2-3	Ander Herrera, Gabi
15/5	Villarreal	h	3-3	Eliseu, Adrián Colunga, Pulido

No	Name	Nat	DoB	Pos	Aps	(s)	Gls
16	ABEL Enrique AGUILAR Tapias	COL	6/1/85	M	20	(7)	4
10	ADRIÁN COLUNGA Pérez		17/11/84	A	7	(9)	7
31	Alejandro "ÁLEX" SÁNCHEZ López		6/6/89	A		(3)	
8	ANDER HERRERA Aguera		14/8/89	M	23	(7)	2
19	Ángel Javier ARIZMENDI de Lucas		3/3/84	A	25	(6)	5
4	Roberto Fabián AYALA	ARG	14/4/73	D	13		
20	Marko BABIĆ	CRO	28/1/81	M	7	(7)	
10	BRAULIO Nóbrega Rodríguez		18/9/85	A		(2)	
13	Juan Pablo CARRIZO	ARG	6/5/84	G	16		
4	Matteo CONTINI	ITA	16/4/80	D	15		1
2	Carlos Andrés DIOGO Enseñat	URU	18/7/83	D	13	(2)	2
12	EDMÍLSON José Gomes Moraes	BRA	10/7/76	M	14	(3)	
18	ELISEU Pereira dos Santos	POR	1/10/83	M	19	(2)	2
21	EWERTHON Henrique de Souza	BRA	10/6/81	A	1	(9)	2
14	Gabriel Fernández ARENAS "GABI"		10/7/83	M	29	(3)	1
6	Raúl GONI Bayo		12/10/88	D	6		
21	Jiří JAROŠÍK	CZE	27/10/77	M	20		2
7	JORGE LÓPEZ Montaña		19/9/78	M	20	(9)	2
27	KEVIN LACRUZ Coscolín		13/2/92	M		(3)	
17	Ángel LAFITA Castillo		7/8/84	M	17	(7)	3
26	Víctor LAGUARDIA Cisneros		5/11/89	D	3		
1	Javier LÓPEZ VALLEJO		22/9/75	G	7		
24	Ivan OBRADOVIĆ	SRB	25/7/88	A	6	(3)	
5	PABLO AMO Aguado		15/1/78	D	7	(2)	
3	Javier PAREDES Arango		5/7/82	M	18	(2)	
15	Francisco PAVÓN Barahona		9/1/80	D	11		2
11	Jermaine PENNANT	ENG	15/1/83	M	13	(12)	
23	Leonardo Daniel PONZIO	ARG	29/1/82	M	34		1
22	Rubén Martín PULIDO		2/2/79	D	20	(2)	2
1	ROBERTO Jiménez Gago		10/2/86	G	15		
12	Franck Steve SONGO'O	CMR	14/5/87	M		(5)	
25	Humberto Andrés SUAZO	CHI	10/5/81	A	17		6
9	Ikechukwu UCHE	NGA	5/1/84	A	2	(1)	

PROMOTED CLUBS

REAL SOCIEDAD DE FÚTBOL
Coach – Martín Lasarte (URU)
Founded – 1909
Stadium – Anoeta (32,000)
MAJOR HONOURS:
Spanish League – (2) 1981, 1982;
Spanish Cup – (2) 1909, 1987

HÉRCULES CF
Coach – Esteban Vigo
Founded – 1922
Stadium – José Rico Pérez (30,000)

LEVANTE UD
Coach – Luis García Plaza
Founded – 1939
Stadium – Ciutat de València (25,354)

SECOND LEVEL FINAL TABLE 2009/10

		Pld	W	D	L	F	A	Pts
1	Real Sociedad de Fútbol	42	20	14	8	53	37	74
2	Hércules CF	42	19	14	9	61	34	71
3	Levante UD	42	19	14	9	63	45	71
4	Real Betis Balompié	42	19	14	9	61	38	71
5	FC Cartagena	42	18	11	13	58	49	65
6	Elche CF	42	18	9	15	67	57	63
7	Villarreal CF B	42	16	13	13	60	56	61
8	CD Numancia	42	16	11	15	55	53	59
9	RC Recreativo de Huelva	42	14	15	13	40	42	57
10	Córdoba CF	42	14	13	15	40	46	55
11	Rayo Vallecano de Madrid	42	13	14	15	67	58	53
12	RC Celta de Vigo	42	13	13	16	38	44	52
13	SD Huesca	42	12	16	14	36	40	52
14	Girona FC	42	13	13	16	45	59	52
15	Albacete Balompié	42	12	16	14	60	62	52
16	UD Salamanca	42	13	13	16	44	54	52
17	UD Las Palmas	42	12	15	15	49	49	51
18	Club Gimnàstic de Tarragona	42	14	9	19	42	55	51
19	Cádiz CF	42	12	14	16	49	64	50
20	Real Murcia CF	42	11	17	14	49	51	50
21	Real Unión Club	42	12	10	20	40	59	46
22	CD Castellón	42	7	12	23	37	62	33

DOMESTIC CUP 2009/10

COPA DEL REY

FOURTH ROUND

(27/10/09 & 10/11/09)
Alcorcón v Real Madrid 4-0; 0-1 (4-1)
Lorquí v Sevilla 2-4; 1-5 (3-9)
Marbella v Atlético 0-2; 0-6 (0-8)
Recreativo v Sporting 1-1; 1-1 (aet) (2-2; 4-2 on pens)

(28/10/09 & 10/11/09)
Alcoyano v Valencia 0-1; 2-2 (2-3)
Celta v Tenerife 2-1; 1-0 (3-1)
Leonesa v Barcelona 0-2; 0-5 (0-7)
Murcia v Deportivo 0-1; 0-0 (0-1)

Xerez v Osasuna 1-2; 0-1 (1-3)
Zaragoza v Málaga 1-1; 0-0 (1-1; Málaga on away goal)

(28/10/09 & 11/11/09)
Getafe v Espanyol 2-0; 1-1 (3-1)
Rayo v Athletic 2-0; 2-2 (4-2)

(28/10/09 & 12/11/09)
Hércules v Almería 2-1; 1-0 (3-1)

(29/10/09 & 10/11/09)
Puertollano v Villarreal 1-1; 0-1 (1-2)

(29/10/09 & 11/11/09)
Valladolid v Mallorca 2-1; 0-1 (2-2; Mallorca on away goal)
Salamanca v Racing 1-0; 1-4 (2-4)

FIFTH ROUND

(5/1/10 & 13/1/10)
Barcelona v Sevilla 1-2; 1-0 (2-2; Sevilla on away goal)

(6/1/10 & 12/1/10)
Celta v Villarreal 1-1; 1-0 (2-1)

(6/1/10 & 13/1/10)
Alcorcón v Racing 2-3; 0-0 (2-3)
Valencia v Deportivo 1-2; 2-2 (3-4)

(6/1/10 & 14/1/10)
Recreativo v Atlético 3-0; 1-5 (4-5)

(7/1/10 & 13/1/10)
Hércules v Osasuna 2-1; 0-1 (2-2; Osasuna on away goal)
Málaga v Getafe 2-1; 1-5 (3-6)

(7/1/10 & 14/1/10)
Rayo v Mallorca 2-1; 1-3 (3-4)

QUARTER-FINALS

(20/1/10 & 27/1/10)
Deportivo 0, Sevilla 3 (Negredo 26, Renato 67, Jesús Navas 69)
Sevilla 0, Deportivo 1 (Bodipo 44)
(Sevilla 3-1)

(20/1/10 & 28/1/10)
Mallorca 1 (Castro 90+2), Getafe 2 (Manu del Moral 50, Miku 68)
Getafe 0, Mallorca 1 (Adúriz 45)
(2-2; Getafe on away goals)

(21/1/10 & 27/1/10)
Racing 2 (Colsa 63, Diop 85), Osasuna 1 (Pandiani 88)
Osasuna 0, Racing 3 (Xisco 6, Henrique 23, Canales 79)
(Racing 5-1)

(21/1/10 & 28/1/10)
Atlético 1 (Tiago 11), Celta 1 (Trashorras 2)
Celta 0, Atlético 1 (Forlán 26)
(Atlético 2-1)

SEMI-FINALS

(3/2/10 & 10/2/10)
Sevilla 2 (Luís Fabiano 45, Mario 78og), Getafe 0
Getafe 1 (Soldado 52), Sevilla 0
(Sevilla 2-1)

(4/2/10 & 11/2/10)
Atlético 4 (Simão 9, Reyes 40, Forlán 62p, 71p), Racing 0
Racing 3 (Valera 2og, Xisco 89, Tchité 90), Atlético 2 (Moratón 7og, Jurado 51)
(Atlético 6-3)

FINAL

(19/5/10)
Camp Nou, Barcelona
SEVILLA FC 2 (Diego Capel 5, Jesús Navas 90+1)
CLUB ATLÉTICO DE MADRID 0
Referee – Mejuto González.
SEVILLA – Palop, Konko, Escudé, Squillaci, Luna, Renato (Lolo 90+2), Zokora, Jesús Navas, Diego Capel (Perotti 87), Negredo (Romaric 67), Kanouté.
ATLÉTICO – De Gea, Ujfaluši, Perea, Domínguez, Antonio López, Paulo Assunção (Raúl García 59), Tiago, Reyes, Simão (Jurado 60), Forlán, Agüero.

Unprecedented Double for AIK

2009 was not a year in which Swedish football distinguished itself internationally, with the national team failing to qualify for the 2010 FIFA World Cup and the country's leading clubs collectively falling short in Europe, but it will certainly be recalled with great fondness by the supporters of AIK Solna, who defied all pre-season predictions by winning both the Allsvenskan and Svenska Cupen to claim the first domestic double in their 118-year history.

Few saw it coming. AIK had finished fifth in 2008, 19 points adrift of champions Kalmar FF, and they responded by appointing 33-year-old rookie Mikael Stahre as their coach, replacing the long-serving Rikard Norling. Stahre had previously worked only in the lower leagues with Väsby United, AIK's feeder club, and although he had done well in that capacity, his appointment was widely considered to be a shot in the dark. As it happened, Stahre would prove to be an inspired choice.

Strong start

AIK started the 2009 campaign strongly, winning four of their opening five games. Despite the odd slip-up they were involved in the title race throughout. By the end of May, when the Allsvenskan took a month off to allow the UEFA European Under-21 Championship to take centre stage, the club from the Stockholm suburbs lay fourth, with IFK Göteborg, IF Elfsborg and Helsingborgs IF just above them.

That quartet would eventually be joined in a thrilling tussle at the top by Kalmar, but as the weeks passed AIK and Göteborg began to break away. Matching each other stride for stride in the run-in, the two clubs headed towards a last-day title showdown in Gothenburg on the first day of November.

With each of the two challengers surprisingly drawing their penultimate fixture – Göteborg at home to Halmstads BK and, a day later, AIK at home to Örebro SK – the final-day dénouement was set up to perfection.

AIK, the visitors, held a one-point advantage, which meant that a draw would be good enough for them to take the championship trophy back to Stockholm. Only victory would do for the hosts.

The Gamla Ullevi stadium was packed to capacity for the occasion. It was the first time in 43 years that the only two contenders for the Swedish title had met on the final day. The long-standing city rivalry of Gothenburg versus Stockholm simply added to the tension and excitement. Furthermore, the two clubs had also qualified to contest the final of the Swedish Cup six days later.

Argentine striker Iván Óbolo was a key member of AIK's double-winning side

AIK had won the earlier league meeting 1-0. That was the team's favoured scoreline, one they had managed on nine occasions. Buoyed by the confidence gained from conceding just 19 goals in their previous 29 league games, they set about stifling Göteborg, but the hosts went into the game with the league's second most efficient attack and were also unbeaten at home. Something had to give, and after 32 minutes Göteborg took the lead with a rather fortuitous goal from midfielder Thomas Olsson. Down at the break, the visitors came roaring back in the second half, with Martin Kayongo-Mutamba setting up Brazilian mid-season signing Antônio Flávio for an equaliser that put AIK back in the driving seat. A riveting second period ensued before AIK scored a late second goal – the only one of the season from their veteran captain Daniel Tjernström – to win the match and seal their 11th national title.

IFK Göteborg's Tobias Hysén jointly topped the Allsvenskan scoring charts with 18 goals

South Americans strike

The following weekend's Cup final, played at AIK's Råsundastadion, gave Stahre and his players the opportunity to make history by completing the club's first double. Göteborg, on the other hand, were seeking not only to gain revenge for their league defeat but also to retain the trophy. Once again it was to be AIK's day, a couple of second-half goals from their South American strike duo, Iván Óbolo and Antônio Flávio, giving the club a first Svenska Cupen triumph for ten years and completing the perfect debut season for coach Stahre.

Óbolo, a 28-year-old from Argentina, was AIK's standout performer and top scorer. He started all 30 Allsvenskan matches, as did goalkeeper Daniel Örlund, who kept clean sheets in over half of them. Örlund's task was facilitated by the excellence of the AIK back four, at the heart of which were 23-year-old Per Karlsson and his Dutch partner Jos Hooiveld. Unfortunately, AIK's annus mirabilis looked likely to be an isolated one when Óbolo and Hooiveld left the club, and there was a further blow the following spring when coach Stahre moved to Greece to join Panionios GSS, thus leaving behind a weakened team to contest the 2010/11 UEFA Champions League – a competition in which AIK competed at the group stage on their previous participation in 1999/2000.

Göteborg are no strangers to top-grade European football either, but their two runners-up placings were only sufficient to put them in the qualifying phase of the 2010/11 UEFA Europa League. The first entry into the new competition for the former double UEFA Cup winners proved unsuccessful as they fell at the first hurdle to Hapoel Tel-Aviv FC following a first-leg 3-1 defeat at the Gamla Ullevi. Their scorer in that match was Tobias Hysén, son of legendary Swedish international defender Glenn Hysén, and the 27-year-old enjoyed a productive year on all fronts. Converted from winger to central striker by Göteborg coach Stefan Rehn, he savoured the switch, finding the net 18 times in the Allsvenskan to tie GAIS Göteborg's Brazilian midfielder Wanderson at the top of the goal charts.

Struggle for goals

Elfsborg, the pre-season title favourites, struggled for goals in the final phase of the season, during which they also endured a couple of crushing defeats away to Göteborg (0-4) and Malmö FF (0-5). Nevertheless, with coach Magnus Haglund and captain Anders Svensson continuing to impress, they held on to third place and secured a return to the UEFA Europa League, in which they had been Sweden's top performers in 2009, eliminating SC Braga before bowing out with distinction to S.S. Lazio.

Defending champions Kalmar, who were disappointingly beaten on away goals by Hungary's Debreceni VSC in the second qualifying round of the UEFA Champions League, finished fourth in the

SWEDEN

Sweden's new head coach – Erik Hamrén

Allsvenskan to book a European return. The departure of top scorer Rasmus Elm to AZ Alkmaar in August upset their title challenge, and although coach Nanne Bergstrand's adventurous style made his team pleasing on the eye, the concession of 39 goals – exceeded only by the five lowest-placed teams in the division – proved to be a costly statistic.

Newly promoted BK Häcken surprised everyone by finishing fifth, but there was no such joy for the team that pipped them to the 2008 Superettan (second level) title, Gothenburg rivals Örgryte IS, who were relegated. They were accompanied out of the Allsvenskan by Stockholm's Hammarby Fotboll, who went into freefall, losing 14 of their last 17 matches, to finish bottom. Capital city rivals Djurgårdens IF FF were perilously close to joining them. Victories in each of their last three matches hoisted them into 14th spot, but it was only thanks to a late extra-time winner in the second leg of their play-off, against Assyriska FF, that they retained their top-flight status. Mjällby AIF and Åtvidabergs FF took the two automatic promotion berths.

Svenska Fotbollförbundet (SvFF)

Råsundastadion
PO Box 1216
SE-171 23 Solna
tel – +46 8 7350900
fax – +46 8 7350901
website – svenskfotboll.se
email – svff@svenskfotboll.se
Year of Formation – 1904

President – Lars-Åke Lagrell
General Secretary – Mikael Santoft
Media Officer – Jonas Nystedt
National Stadium – Råsundastadion, Solna (Stockholm)
(35,972)

INTERNATIONAL TOURNAMENT APPEARANCES
FIFA World Cup – (11) 1934 (2nd round), 1938 (4th), 1950 (3rd), 1958 (runners-up), 1970, 1974 (2nd phase), 1978, 1990, 1994 (3rd), 2002 (2nd round), 2006 (2nd round).
UEFA European Championship – (4) 1992 (semi-finals), 2000, 2004 (qtr-finals), 2008.

TOP FIVE ALL-TIME CAPS
Thomas Ravelli (143); Roland Nilsson (116); Björn Nordqvist (115); Niclas Alexandersson (109); Anders Svensson (107)
TOP FIVE ALL-TIME GOALS
Sven Rydell (49); Gunnar Nordahl (43); Henrik Larsson (37); Gunnar Gren (32); Kennet Andersson (31)

The failure of the Swedish national team to qualify for the World Cup – confirmed by an unfortunate 1-0 defeat in Copenhagen against Scandinavian neighbours Denmark in which the team's failure to take chances again proved critical – ended a run of five successive major tournament appearances. Lars Lagerbäck, who had been involved in all of those successes, ended his decade-long association with the team by resigning. He would later go on to lead Nigeria at the World Cup but in the meantime the Sweden job was handed to Erik Hamrén.

Obvious choice

The obvious choice after his exploits in winning the Danish and Norwegian leagues in successive years, Hamrén accepted the appointment with the rider that he could continue to coach Rosenborg BK until the start of the UEFA EURO 2012 qualifying campaign. By May 2010, however, he had already left Trondheim, and with three successive friendly wins over Wales, Bosnia-Herzegovina and Belarus, the first of which brought defender Olof Mellberg his 100th cap, there was some optimism that the 53-year-old would be able to get the team back on track and lead them to Poland/Ukraine from a qualifying group containing San Marino, Moldova, Hungary, Finland and the Netherlands. Whether Zlatan Ibrahimović would be involved, however, remained open to question as the FC Barcelona striker asked to take temporary leave of absence from national service while he considered his future.

988 - The European Football Yearbook 2010/11

NATIONAL TEAM RESULTS 2009/10

Date	Opponent		Venue	Score	Scorers
12/8/09	Finland	H	Solna	1-0	Elmander (42)
5/9/09	Hungary (WCQ)	A	Budapest	2-1	Mellberg (8), Ibrahimović (90+4)
9/9/09	Malta (WCQ)	A	Ta'Qali	1-0	Azzopardi (82og)
10/10/09	Denmark (WCQ)	A	Copenhagen	0-1	
14/10/09	Albania (WCQ)	H	Solna	4-1	Mellberg (6, 42), Berg (40), Svensson (86)
18/11/09	Italy	A	Cesena	0-1	
20/1/10	Oman	A	Muscat	1-0	Svensson (35)
23/1/10	Syria	A	Damascus	1-1	Ranégie (87)
3/3/10	Wales	A	Swansea	1-0	Elmander (43)
29/5/10	Bosnia-Herzegovina	H	Solna	4-2	Toivonen (44), Olsson M. (68, 83), Berg (90+2)
2/6/10	Belarus	A	Minsk	1-0	Wilhelmsson (47)

NATIONAL TEAM APPEARANCES 2009/10

Coach – Lars LAGERBÄCK 16/7/48 /(4/11/09) Erik HAMRÉN 27/6/57

Player	DOB	Club	Fin	HUN	MLT	DEN	ALB	Ita	Oma	Syr	Wal	Bih	Blr	Caps	Goals
Eddie GUSTAFSSON	31/1/77	Salzburg (AUT)	G								G			10	-
Mikael NILSSON	24/6/78	Brøndby (DEN)	D	D	D	D88	D							64	3
Olof MELLBERG	3/9/77	Olympiacos (GRE)	D	D	D	D	D	D			D	D		101	7
Daniel MAJSTOROVIĆ	5/4/77	AEK (GRE)	D46	D	D	D	D	D			D	D	s85	33	2
Behrang SAFARI	9/2/85	Basel (SUI)	D	D	D	D	D	M58			D62	D	s85	15	-
Sebastian LARSSON	6/6/85	Birmingham (ENG)	M46		s82	s63	M	M			D	D	M	22	-
Kim KÄLLSTRÖM	24/8/82	Lyon (FRA)	M79	M	M	M	M21				M80	M75		73	13
Anders SVENSSON	17/7/76	Elfsborg	M46	M	M70	M	M	M	M64	M	M	M		107	17
Samuel HOLMÉN	28/6/84	Brøndby (DEN)	M46	M85	M57	M63				s44	M81			23	2
Marcus BERG	17/8/86	Hamburg (GER)	A	s75	s70	s80	s37					s75	A63	14	3
Johan ELMANDER	27/5/81	Bolton (ENG)	A60	A75	A82		A37	M78			M			47	13
Petter HANSSON	14/12/76	Rennes (FRA)	s46											43	2
Christian WILHELMSSON	8/12/79	Al Hilal (KSA)	s46								M73	M75	M63	62	5
Pontus WERNBLOOM	25/6/86	AZ (NED)	s46							s72	s58	M	M85	7	-
Viktor ELM	13/11/85	Heerenveen (NED)	s46							M46	s80			9	-
Ola TOIVONEN	3/7/86	PSV (NED)	s60							s72	A58	A	M85	7	1
Tobias HYSÉN	9/3/82	Göteborg	s79	s85	s57			A72			s58			11	-
Andreas ISAKSSON	3/10/81	PSV (NED)	G	G	G	G	G					G	G	76	-
Rasmus ELM	17/3/88	AZ (NED)		M	M	M80	M	s46			M58			12	1
Zlatan IBRAHIMOVIĆ	3/10/81	Barcelona (ESP)	A	A	A		A77							62	22
Henrik LARSSON	20/9/71	Helsingborg						A						106	37
Markus ROSENBERG	27/9/82	Werder (GER)							s88	s77	s78			30	6
Daniel ANDERSSON	28/8/77	Malmö								s21				74	-
Mikael LUSTIG	13/12/86	Rosenborg (NOR)						D72	D76	D46	s73	s75	D	7	-
Mikael DORSIN	6/10/81	Rosenborg (NOR)						D58	D	s24			s46	16	-
Oscar WENDT	24/10/85	København (DEN)						s58			s62	D46		9	-
Dusan DJURIC	16/9/84	Zürich (SUI)						s58				s63		8	-
Daniel ÖRLUND	23/6/80	Rosenborg (NOR)							G					1	-

SWEDEN

NATIONAL TEAM APPEARANCES 2009/10 (contd.)

			Fin	HUN	MLT	DEN	ALB	Ita	Oma	Syr	Wal	Bih	Blr	Caps	Goals
Per KARLSSON	2/1/86	AIK						D						1	-
Tom SÖDERBERG	25/8/87	Häcken						D						1	-
Guillermo MOLINS	26/9/88	Malmö						M	s70					2	-
Sebastian ERIKSSON	31/1/89	Göteborg						M44						1	-
Pontus FARNERUD	4/6/80	Stabæk (NOR)						M		s81				11	-
Emir BAJRAMI	7/3/88	Elfsborg						M64	M69		M66			3	-
Daniel LARSSON	25/1/87	Malmö						A76	s69			s63		3	-
Tobias ERIKSSON	19/3/85	Kalmar							s64	s46				2	-
Alexander FARNERUD	1/5/84	Brøndby (DEN)							s64	M46				8	2
Erik LUND	6/11/88	Göteborg							s76	s46				2	-
Mathias RANÉGIE	14/6/84	Häcken							s76	A				2	1
Johan DAHLIN	8/9/86	Malmö							G					2	-
Joel EKSTRAND	4/2/89	Helsingborg							D					1	-
Michael ALMEBÄCK	4/4/88	Örebro							D					1	-
Emil JOHANSSON	11/8/86	Hammarby							D24					1	-
Stefan ISHIZAKI	15/5/82	Elfsborg							M70					12	-
Martin OLSSON	17/5/88	Blackburn (ENG)										s66		1	2
Jonas OLSSON	10/3/83	West Brom (ENG)											D	1	-
Andreas GRANQVIST	16/4/85	Groningen (NED)											D	6	-
Marcus LANTZ	23/10/75	Helsingborg											M	6	-

DOMESTIC LEAGUE 2009

ALLSVENSKAN FINAL TABLE

		Home					Away					Total					Pts
	Pld	W	D	L	F	A	W	D	L	F	A	W	D	L	F	A	
1 AIK Solna	30	10	3	2	17	7	8	4	3	19	13	18	7	5	36	20	61
2 IFK Göteborg	30	11	3	1	39	11	6	3	6	14	13	17	6	7	53	24	57
3 IF Elfsborg	30	9	5	1	25	10	6	5	4	18	24	15	10	5	43	34	55
4 Kalmar FF	30	10	2	3	33	17	4	6	5	20	22	14	8	8	53	39	50
5 BK Häcken	30	8	5	2	25	11	5	4	6	18	19	13	9	8	43	30	48
6 Örebro SK	30	7	5	3	21	15	5	4	6	12	17	12	9	9	33	32	45
7 Malmö FF	30	4	8	3	19	11	7	2	6	21	14	11	10	9	40	25	43
8 Helsingborgs IF	30	8	2	5	19	16	5	2	8	20	23	13	4	13	39	39	43
9 Trelleborgs FF	30	9	2	4	28	15	2	6	7	13	19	11	8	11	41	34	41
10 Gefle IF	30	7	4	4	17	17	3	5	7	11	21	10	9	11	28	38	39
11 GAIS Göteborg	30	4	7	4	22	17	4	4	7	19	21	8	11	11	41	38	35
12 IF Brommapojkarna	30	5	3	7	18	23	4	4	7	14	23	9	7	14	32	46	34
13 Halmstads BK	30	5	3	7	15	21	3	5	7	14	22	8	8	14	29	43	32
14 Djurgårdens IF FF	30	6	3	6	12	13	2	2	11	12	36	8	5	17	24	49	29
15 Örgryte IS	30	4	5	6	16	19	2	2	11	11	30	6	7	17	27	49	25
16 Hammarby Fotboll	30	4	1	10	14	21	2	3	10	8	23	6	4	20	22	44	22

TOP GOALSCORERS

18 WANDERSON (GAIS)
Tobias HYSÉN (Göteborg)

11 Daniel LARSSON (Malmö)

10 Jonas HENRIKSSON (Häcken)
Edward OFERE (Malmö)
ÁLVARO SANTOS (Örgryte)

9 Iván ÓBOLO (AIK)
Rasmus ELM (Kalmar)

8 James KEENE (Elfsborg)
Emir KUJOVIC (Halmstad)
Rasmus JÖNSSON (Helsingborg)
PAULINHO (Häcken)
DANIEL MENDES (Kalmar)
Fredrik JENSEN (Trelleborg)
Kim OLSEN (Örebro)

CLUB-BY-CLUB

AIK SOLNA
Coach – Mikael Stahre
Founded – 1891
Stadium – Råsundastadion (35,972)
MAJOR HONOURS:
Swedish League – (11) 1900, 1901, 1911, 1914, 1916, 1923, 1932, 1937,
1992, 1998, 2009;
Swedish Cup – (8) 1949, 1950, 1976, 1985, 1996, 1997, 1999, 2009.

2009
5/4	Halmstad	h	1-0	Özkan
13/4	Kalmar	a	1-0	Óbolo
16/4	Malmö	h	0-1	
19/4	Brommapojkarna	a	3-2	Lundberg, Óbolo, Jagne
23/4	Örgryte	a	1-0	Óbolo
29/4	Helsingborg	h	0-3	
5/5	Trelleborg	a	0-1	
9/5	Häcken	h	2-0	Jagne, Pavey
18/5	Djurgården	a	1-0	Óbolo
21/5	Elfsborg	h	0-0	
25/5	Gefle	a	0-1	
28/5	Hammarby	h	1-0	Jagne
5/7	Örebro	a	1-1	Jagne
13/7	Göteborg	h	1-0	Johansson
20/7	GAIS	a	2-2	Kayongo-Mutumba, Óbolo
27/7	GAIS	h	1-0	Johansson
30/7	Malmö	a	0-0	
8/8	Brommapojkarna	h	2-1	Jonsson (p), Óbolo
17/8	Halmstad	a	2-1	Óbolo, Pavey
22/8	Kalmar	h	1-1	Johansson
29/8	Trelleborg	h	1-0	Johnson
14/9	Häcken	a	2-0	Antônio Flávio, Óbolo
21/9	Örgryte	h	3-0	Kayongo-Mutumba, Jonsson (p), Óbolo
24/9	Helsingborg	a	2-3	og (Tamboura), Johnson
28/9	Djurgården	h	2-0	Antônio Flávio 2
4/10	Elfsborg	a	0-0	
17/10	Gefle	h	1-0	Özkan
25/10	Hammarby	a	2-1	Antônio Flávio, Pavey
28/10	Örebro	h	1-1	Kayongo-Mutumba
1/11	Göteborg	a	2-1	Antônio Flávio, Tjernström

No	Name	Nat	DoB	Pos	Aps	(s)	Gls
11	ANTÔNIO FLÁVIO Aires dos Santos	BRA	5/1/87	A	12		5
6	Walid ATTA		28/8/86	D	4	(4)	
16	Pierre BENGTSSON		12/4/88	D	3	(11)	
2	Patrik BOJENT		26/12/80	D	2		
9	Miran BURGIČ	SVN	25/9/84	A	1	(7)	
7	Bojan DJORDJIC		6/2/82	M	16	(3)	
26	Pontus ENGBLOM		11/11/91	A		(2)	
24	Daniel GUSTAFSSON		29/8/90	M		(1)	
20	Jos HOOIVELD	NED	22/4/83	D	28		
17	Saihou JAGNE		10/10/86	A	7	(10)	4
4	Nils-Erik JOHANSSON		13/1/80	D	29		3
30	Dulee JOHNSON	LBR	7/11/84	M	14	(1)	2
18	Markus JONSSON		9/3/81	D	28		2
3	Per KARLSSON		2/1/86	D	26		
19	Martin KAYONGO-MUTUMBA		15/6/85	M	24		3
28	Viktor LUNDBERG		4/3/91	M	2	(4)	1
10	Iván ÓBOLO	ARG	28/9/81	A	30		9
5	Jorge ORTÍZ	ARG	20/6/84	M	27		
14	Kenneth PAVEY	ENG	23/8/77	M	15	(4)	3
25	Yussuf SALEH		22/3/84	M	2	(8)	
21	Mikael THORSTENSSON		24/1/85	A	4	(8)	
8	Daniel TJERNSTRÖM		19/2/74	M	17	(9)	1
27	Daniel ÖRLUND		23/6/80	G	30		
29	Gabriel ÖZKAN		23/5/86	M	9	(5)	2

IF BROMMAPOJKARNA
Coach – Kim Bergstrand
Founded – 1942
Stadium – Grimsta IP (8,000)

2009
5/4	Trelleborg	a	0-0	
10/4	Häcken	h	2-0	Guterstam, Runnemo
15/4	Halmstad	a	1-0	Runnemo
19/4	AIK	h	2-3	Guterstam, Chhadeh
24/4	Djurgården	a	2-0	Runnemo, Haglund
1/5	Elfsborg	h	1-1	Guterstam
6/5	Örgryte	a	1-1	og (Brömsen)
11/5	Helsingborg	h	0-3	
17/5	Gefle	a	2-3	Persson (p), Haglund
20/5	Hammarby	h	0-1	
25/5	Örebro	a	2-2	Haglund, Persson (p)
30/5	Göteborg	a	0-4	
4/7	GAIS	h	1-0	Benyahia
12/7	Malmö	h	1-1	Haglund
18/7	Kalmar	a	1-3	Chhadeh
25/7	Kalmar	h	1-2	Petrovic
2/8	Halmstad	h	2-1	Haglund, Benyahia
8/8	AIK	a	1-2	Haglund
16/8	Trelleborg	h	2-2	Guterstam, Asp
25/8	Häcken	a	1-5	Eriksson
31/8	Örgryte	h	1-2	Benyahia
13/9	Helsingborg	a	1-0	Piñones-Arce
20/9	Djurgården	h	1-4	Runnemo
24/9	Elfsborg	a	0-1	
29/9	Gefle	h	1-0	Bahoui
4/10	Hammarby	a	0-1	
18/10	Örebro	h	3-0	Albornoz Ma., Albornoz Mi., Guterstam
23/10	Göteborg	h	0-3	
26/10	GAIS	a	1-0	Haglund
1/11	Malmö	a	1-1	Bahoui

No	Name	Nat	DoB	Pos	Aps	(s)	Gls
4	Mauricio ALBORNOZ		10/3/88	M	13	(12)	1
18	Miiko ALBORNOZ		30/11/90	M	28	(1)	1
16	Pär ASP		14/8/82	D	24		1
17	Sinan AYRANCI		9/7/90	A	1	(7)	
14	Nabil BAHOUI		5/2/91	A	1	(7)	2
23	Dalil BENYAHIA		21/4/90	M	18	(4)	3
13	Tim BJÖRKSTRÖM		8/1/91	D	3		
19	David CARLSSON		7/3/83	A		(2)	
9	Imad CHHADEH	SYR	12/10/79	M	17	(2)	2
22	Max CLAUSS		31/3/89	D		(1)	
21	Andreas ERIKSSON		31/11/81	M	5	(11)	1
24	Ted FONTÉR		6/6/88	D		(1)	
11	Olof GUTERSTAM		4/1/83	A	28	(2)	5
15	Philip HAGLUND		22/3/87	M	28		7
6	Richard HENRIKSSON		5/10/82	D	23		
26	Mikkel JENSEN	DEN	6/1/77	M	4		
3	Markus KARLSSON		30/8/72	D	16		
1	Benny LEKSTRÖM		19/2/81	G	9		
10	Mikael NILSSON		19/8/85	M	1	(4)	
20	Kristoffer NORDFELDT		23/6/89	G	21		
5	Kim ODELIUS		20/6/85	D	20	(4)	

2	Jon PERSSON	31/5/76	D	12	(3)	2
7	Gabriel PETROVIC	25/5/84	M	28	(1)	1
25	Pablo PIÑONES-ARCE	27/8/81	M	14	(2)	1
8	Joakim RUNNEMO	10/3/88	A	16	(6)	4
27	Gustav SANDBERG-MAGNUSSON	30/11/90	M		(1)	

8	Jan TAUER	GER	26/8/83	D	10	(2)	
15	Pa Dembo TOURAY	GAM	31/3/81	G	25		
30	Oskar WAHLSTRÖM		16/8/76	G	5	(1)	
10	Christer YOUSSEF		1/12/87	M	14	(11)	3

DJURGÅRDENS IF FF
Coach – Andrée Jeglertz & Zoran Lukić; (3/6/09) Andrée Jeglertz
Founded – 1891
Stadium – Stockholms stadion (14,417)
MAJOR HONOURS:
Swedish League – (11) 1912, 1915, 1917, 1920, 1955, 1959, 1964, 1966, 2002, 2003, 2005;
Swedish Cup – (4) 1990, 2002, 2004, 2005.

2009

6/4	Örebro	h	1-0	Sjölund (p)
11/4	Göteborg	a	0-6	
15/4	Gefle	h	0-0	
20/4	Hammarby	a	1-3	Kuivasto
24/4	Brommapojkarna	h	0-2	
29/4	Halmstad	a	0-3	
4/5	GAIS	h	2-1	Rajalakso, Mwila
10/5	Malmö	a	1-2	Rajalakso
18/5	AIK	h	0-1	
21/5	Trelleborg	a	0-3	
26/5	Häcken	h	1-0	Mwila
31/5	Örgryte	a	0-0	
5/7	Helsingborg	h	2-1	Haginge, Rajalakso
11/7	Kalmar	a	1-6	Jonson
19/7	Elfsborg	h	1-2	Ceesay
26/7	Elfsborg	a	1-3	Sjölund (p)
3/8	Gefle	a	0-2	
9/8	Hammarby	h	0-1	
17/8	Örebro	a	0-2	
24/8	Göteborg	h	0-0	
31/8	GAIS	a	1-1	Sjölund
14/9	Malmö	h	1-2	Youssef
20/9	Brommapojkarna	a	4-1	Youssef 2, Milić, Burlin
24/9	Halmstad	h	0-2	
28/9	AIK	a	0-2	
3/10	Trelleborg	h	0-0	
19/10	Häcken	a	1-2	Milić
24/10	Örgryte	h	2-1	Haginge, Milić (p)
28/10	Helsingborg	a	2-0	Ayuba, Ikpe Ekong
1/11	Kalmar	h	2-0	Haginge, Johannesson

No	Name	Nat	DoB	Pos	Aps	(s)	Gls
20	Martin ANDERSSON		9/5/82	M	2	(1)	
3	Yosif AYUBA		30/11/90	D	5	(6)	1
27	Dan BURLIN		13/8/80	M	8	(1)	1
14	Kebba CEESAY		14/11/87	D	22	(4)	1
18	Mikael DAHLBERG		6/3/85	A	26	(1)	
5	Petter GUSTAFSSON		1/1/85	D	30		
4	Patrik HAGINGE		2/4/85	D	11	(4)	3
2	Philip HELLQUIST		21/5/91	D	4	(7)	
7	Prince IKPE EKONG	NGA	5/10/78	M	8	(9)	1
16	Markus JOHANNESSON		26/5/75	D	22		1
12	Mattias JONSON		16/1/74	M	8		1
22	Andrej KOMAC	SVN	4/12/79	M	6	(1)	
6	Toni KUIVASTO	FIN	31/12/75	D	29		1
24	Peter MAGNUSSON		16/7/84	D	11	(2)	
28	Trimi MAKOLLI		7/6/92	A		(1)	
19	Hrvoje MILIĆ	CRO	10/5/89	A	17	(9)	3
17	Boyd MWILA	ZAM	28/6/84	A	12	(7)	2
9	Johan OREMO		24/10/86	A	14		
25	Sebastian RAJALAKSO		23/9/88	A	22	(6)	3
11	Daniel SJÖLUND	FIN	22/4/83	M	19		3

IF ELFSBORG
Coach – Magnus Haglund
Founded – 1904
Stadium – Borås Arena (16,899)
MAJOR HONOURS:
Swedish League – (5) 1936, 1939, 1940, 1961, 2006;
Swedish Cup – (2) 2001, 2003.

2009

4/4	Hammarby	h	1-1	Ishizaki (p)
10/4	Örebro	a	1-0	Johansson
16/4	Kalmar	h	1-1	Bajrami
19/4	Gefle	a	2-1	Florén M., Svensson
22/4	Malmö	h	1-0	Florén M.
1/5	Brommapojkarna	a	1-1	Keene
4/5	Göteborg	h	2-0	Mobaeck, Bajrami
10/5	GAIS	a	1-1	Svensson
16/5	Halmstad	h	4-0	Keene 2, Nordmark, Avdic
21/5	AIK	a	0-0	
25/5	Trelleborg	h	1-0	Nordmark
29/5	Häcken	a	1-1	Ericsson
6/7	Örgryte	h	3-0	Ishizaki, Keene, Bajrami
12/7	Helsingborg	a	2-3	Bajrami 2
19/7	Djurgården	a	2-1	Bajrami, Lucic
26/7	Djurgården	h	3-1	Avdic, Nordmark, og (Gustafsson)
2/8	Kalmar	a	1-3	Daníelsson
9/8	Gefle	h	2-3	Ishizaki 2
15/8	Hammarby	a	3-2	Ishizaki 2, Svensson
23/8	Örebro	h	2-1	Mobaeck, Keene
30/8	Göteborg	a	0-4	
12/9	GAIS	h	2-2	Svensson, Jawo
21/9	Malmö	a	0-5	
24/9	Brommapojkarna	h	1-0	Keene
28/9	Halmstad	a	2-1	Ericsson, Avdic
4/10	AIK	h	0-0	
17/10	Trelleborg	a	1-0	Ericsson
25/10	Häcken	h	1-1	og (Östberg)
28/10	Örgryte	a	1-1	Keene
1/11	Helsingborg	h	1-0	Keene

No	Name	Nat	DoB	Pos	Aps	(s)	Gls
5	Martin ANDERSSON		16/1/81	D	19	(3)	
9	Denni AVDIC		15/9/88	A	11	(18)	3
20	Emir BAJRAMI		7/3/88	M	26	(1)	6
31	Ante COVIC	AUS	13/6/75	G	29		
6	Helgi Valur DANÍELSSON	ISL	13/7/81	D	27	(1)	1
10	Martin ERICSSON		4/9/80	M	10	(5)	3
14	Jesper FLORÉN		11/9/90			(2)	
2	Mathias FLORÉN		11/8/76	D	27		2
23	Niklas HULT		13/2/90	M		(1)	
24	Stefan ISHIZAKI		15/5/82	M	20	(2)	6
12	Amadou JAWO		26/9/84	A	4	(6)	1
19	Joel JOHANSSON		16/1/86	A		(14)	1
4	Johan KARLSSON		6/4/75	D	29		
17	James KEENE	ENG	26/12/85	A	23	(4)	8
25	Elmin KURBEGOVIC		3/6/87	M		(1)	
15	Teddy LUCIC		15/4/73	D	25		1
11	Daniel MOBAECK		22/5/80	D	23		2
16	Daniel NORDMARK		4/1/88	M	12	(15)	3
8	Anders SVENSSON		17/7/76	M	26		4
13	Anders WIKSTRÖM		14/12/81	D	18	(2)	
30	Joakim WULFF		24/1/81	G	1		

GAIS GÖTEBORG
Coach – Alexander Axén
Founded – 1894
Stadium – Gamla Ullevi (19,000)
MAJOR HONOURS:
Swedish League – (4) 1919, 1922, 1931, 1954;
Swedish Cup – (1) 1942.

2009

5/4	Örgryte	a	5-1	Lindström 2, Ericsson, Lycén, Wanderson
13/4	Helsingborg	h	1-4	Lycén
16/4	Trelleborg	a	0-3	
19/4	Häcken	h	3-0	Wanderson 2 (1p), Ericsson
23/4	Gefle	a	0-0	
29/4	Hammarby	h	2-2	Ericsson, Wanderson
4/5	Djurgården	a	1-2	Wanderson
10/5	Elfsborg	h	1-1	Lindström
17/5	Örebro	a	0-2	
21/5	Göteborg	h	0-1	
24/5	Kalmar	h	2-2	Wanderson 2
31/5	Malmö	a	2-2	Wanderson 2
4/7	Brommapojkarna	a	0-1	
12/7	Halmstad	h	1-1	Angus
20/7	AIK	h	2-2	Lycén, Ericsson
27/7	AIK	a	0-1	
3/8	Trelleborg	h	0-1	
6/8	Häcken	a	0-1	
17/8	Örgryte	h	1-0	Ericsson
23/8	Helsingborg	a	1-0	Hédinsson
31/8	Djurgården	h	1-1	Spong
12/9	Elfsborg	a	2-2	Wanderson, Hédinsson
17/9	Gefle	h	4-0	Wanderson 3, Hédinsson
23/9	Hammarby	a	2-1	Lundgren, Wanderson
28/9	Örebro	h	3-0	Wanderson 2, Ericsson
5/10	Göteborg	a	1-2	Hédinsson
17/10	Kalmar	a	2-2	Wanderson, Celik
23/10	Malmö	h	1-1	Lindström
26/10	Brommapojkarna	h	0-1	
1/11	Halmstad	a	3-1	Angus, Wanderson, Jónasson

No	Name	Nat	DoB	Pos	Aps	(s)	Gls
22	Björn ANDERSSON		12/6/82	A		(9)	
13	Calum ANGUS	ENG	15/4/86	D	15	(1)	2
6	Reuben AYARNA	GHA	22/10/85	M	7	(12)	
9	Gudjón BALDVINSSON	ISL	15/2/86	A		(5)	
27	Mervan CELIK		26/5/90	M		(6)	1
16	Mikael DAHLGREN		19/7/84	D	8	(3)	
2	Richard EKUNDE	COD	4/8/82	D	22	(1)	
18	Pär ERICSSON		21/7/88	A	28	(2)	6
5	Gudmundur Reynir GUNNARSSON	ISL	21/1/89	D	2	(2)	
20	Kenneth GUSTAFSSON		15/9/83	D	22		
23	Eyjólfur HÉDINSSON	ISL	1/1/85	M	18	(10)	4
32	Tobias HOLMQVIST		23/1/88	A		(2)	
1	Dime JANKULOVSKI		18/9/77	G	30		
4	Hallgrímur JÓNASSON	ISL	4/5/86	D	3	(2)	1
21	Mattias LINDSTRÖM		18/4/80	M	28		4
7	Jonas LUNDÉN		27/12/80	D	21		
15	Fredrik LUNDGREN		26/10/79	M	24		1
10	Tommy LYCÉN		5/10/81	M	15	(6)	3
11	Daniel MORAIS Reis	BRA	12/5/86	A		(1)	
17	Johan MÅRTENSSON		1/4/89	M	25		
14	Daniel NICKLASSON		23/4/81	M	2	(7)	
24	Johan PETTERSSON		12/6/82	M		(2)	
29	Romário Pereira Sipião "ROMARINHO"	BRA	15/4/86	M	6	(6)	
8	Richard SPONG		22/10/85	M	21	(3)	1
3	Andreas TOBIASSON		15/2/86	D	3	(2)	
25	Francisco WANDERSON do Carmo Carneiro	BRA	26/5/90	M	30		18

GEFLE IF
Coach – Per Olsson & Urban Hammar
Founded – 1882
Stadium – Strömvallen (7,200)

2009

6/4	Kalmar	h	1-1	Berggren
12/4	Hammarby	a	2-1	Berggren, Jawo A.
15/4	Djurgården	a	0-0	
19/4	Elfsborg	h	1-2	Berggren
23/4	GAIS	h	0-0	
29/4	Malmö	a	0-0	
4/5	Örebro	h	2-0	Jawo A., Lantto
7/5	Göteborg	a	0-3	
17/5	Brommapojkarna	h	3-2	Chibsah, Berggren, Jawo A.
20/5	Halmstad	a	2-0	Chibsah 2
25/5	AIK	h	1-0	Berggren
30/5	Trelleborg	a	1-2	Jawo A.
5/7	Häcken	h	1-1	Berg
13/7	Örgryte	a	2-2	Westlin, Jawo A.
19/7	Helsingborg	h	0-2	
26/7	Helsingborg	a	0-2	
3/8	Djurgården	h	2-0	Lantto, Westlin
9/8	Elfsborg	a	3-2	Bapupa 2, Lantto
15/8	Kalmar	a	1-1	Bapupa
24/8	Hammarby	h	1-0	og (Armas)
31/8	Örebro	a	0-2	
13/9	Göteborg	h	0-3	
17/9	GAIS	a	0-4	
24/9	Malmö	h	0-3	
29/9	Brommapojkarna	a	0-1	
4/10	Halmstad	h	1-0	Westlin
17/10	AIK	a	0-1	
25/10	Trelleborg	h	2-1	Gerndt, Dahlén
28/10	Häcken	a	0-0	
1/11	Örgryte	h	2-2	Gerndt 2

No	Name	Nat	DoB	Pos	Aps	(s)	Gls
11	Yannick Ngabu BAPUPA	COD	21/1/82	M	23	(1)	3
23	Jonatan BERG		9/5/85	M	18	(3)	1
13	Hans BERGGREN		18/2/73	A	14		5
12	Daniel BERNHARDSSON		31/1/78	D	30		
7	Linus BOLIN		27/11/84	M		(3)	
24	Yussif CHIBSAH	GHA	30/12/83	M	25		2
18	Andreas DAHLÉN		11/12/82	D	26		1
8	Johannes ERICSSON		11/7/76	M	11	(7)	
21	Tomas FERNANDEZ		8/6/90	M		(1)	
16	Alexander GERNDT		14/7/86	A	14	(12)	3
19	Marcus HANSSON		12/2/90	M	6	(7)	
9	Jonatan HELLSTRÖM		9/8/88	D	2	(4)	
1	Mattias HUGOSSON		24/1/74	G	30		
15	Amadou JAWO		26/9/84	M	14		5
5	Omar JAWO		8/11/81	D	28		
17	Jonas LANTTO		22/5/87	A	29	(1)	3
15	Daniel LEINO		29/8/91	A		(2)	
2	Olof MÅRD		31/1/89	D	5		
14	Bernhard NYSTRÖM		8/5/85	M	6	(10)	
3	Daniel THEORIN		4/8/83	D	29		
20	Daniel WESTLIN		24/1/80	A	13	(6)	3
10	Hjalmar ÖHAGEN		17/5/85	M	7	(7)	

SWEDEN

IFK GÖTEBORG

Coach – Stefan Rehn
Founded – 1904
Stadium – Gamla Ullevi (19,000)
MAJOR HONOURS:
UEFA Cup – (2) 1982, 1987;
Swedish League – (18) 1908, 1910, 1918, 1935, 1942, 1958, 1969, 1982,
1983, 1984, 1987, 1990, 1991, 1993, 1994, 1995, 1996, 2007;
Swedish Cup – (5) 1979, 1982, 1983, 1991, 2008.

2009

6/4	Helsingborg	a	0-1	
11/4	Djurgården	h	6-0	*Hysén 2, Selakovic, Söder,*
				Sigurdsson, Wernbloom
15/4	Häcken	a	1-4	*Hysén*
20/4	Örgryte	h	3-0	*Hysén, Selakovic, Sigurdsson*
23/4	Hammarby	a	1-0	*Söder*
28/4	Örebro	h	1-0	*Hysén*
4/5	Elfsborg	a	0-2	
7/5	Gefle	h	3-0	*Wernbloom 2, Sigurdsson*
17/5	Kalmar	h	2-1	*Hysén 2*
21/5	GAIS	a	1-0	*Hysén*
25/5	Malmö	h	2-0	*Wernbloom, Hysén*
30/5	Brommapojkarna	h	4-0	*Bärkroth 2, Wernbloom,*
				Selakovic
6/7	Halmstad	a	0-0	
13/7	AIK	a	0-1	
19/7	Trelleborg	h	3-1	*Johansson J., Olsson, Sigurdsson*
26/7	Trelleborg	a	1-2	*Svensson G.*
2/8	Häcken	h	2-2	*Stiller, Olsson*
9/8	Örgryte	a	2-1	*Hysén 2*
16/8	Helsingborg	h	2-2	*Eriksson, Lund*
24/8	Djurgården	a	0-0	
30/8	Elfsborg	h	4-0	*Stiller 2, Jónsson, Hysén*
13/9	Gefle	a	3-0	*Stiller 2, Svensson G.*
20/9	Hammarby	h	2-0	*Hysén 2*
23/9	Örebro	a	0-0	
26/9	Kalmar	a	1-2	*Stiller*
5/10	GAIS	h	2-1	*Selakovic 2*
19/10	Malmö	a	1-0	*Olsson*
23/10	Brommapojkarna	a	3-0	*Hysén 2, Alexandersson N.*
27/10	Halmstad	h	2-2	*Hysén 2*
1/11	AIK	h	1-2	*Olsson*

No	Name	Nat	DoB	Pos	Aps	(s)	Gls
17	Daniel ALEXANDERSSON		3/12/78	M	1	(8)	
38	Niclas ALEXANDERSSON		29/12/71	D		(5)	1
28	Theódór BJARNASON	ISL	4/3/87	M	9	(2)	
5	Matias BJÄRSMYR		3/1/86	D	13		
21	Niklas BÄRKROTH		19/1/92	A	5	(17)	2
3	Niklas CARLSSON		13/11/79	D		(6)	
1	Kim CHRISTENSEN	DEN	16/7/79	G	30		
24	Mikael DYRESTAM		10/12/91	D	17		
23	Sebastian ERIKSSON		31/1/89	D	25		1
18	Mathias ETÉUS		7/6/90	A		(1)	
7	Tobias HYSÉN		9/3/82	A	26	(1)	18
6	Adam JOHANSSON		21/2/83	D	13		
15	Jakob JOHANSSON		21/6/90	M	7	(10)	1
14	Hjálmar JÓNSSON	ISL	29/7/80	D	24	(1)	1
16	Erik LUND		6/11/88	D	22	(2)	1
29	Kamal MUSTAFA		22/7/91	M	1	(3)	
8	Thomas OLSSON		15/2/76	M	14	(6)	4
22	Tobias SANA		11/7/89	M	1	(4)	
9	Stefan SELAKOVIC		9/1/77	A	29		5
10	Ragnar SIGURDSSON	ISL	19/6/86	D	29		4
19	Hannes STILLER		3/7/78	A	12	(3)	6
13	Gustav SVENSSON		7/2/87	M	29		2
2	Karl SVENSSON		21/3/84	D		(3)	

11	Robin SÖDER		1/4/91	A	11	(1)	2
5	Tuomo TURUNEN	FIN	30/8/87	D	1	(1)	
55	Pontus WERNBLOOM		25/6/86	A	11		5

HALMSTADS BK

Coach – Jan Andersson
Founded – 1914
Stadium – Örjans Vall (15,500)
MAJOR HONOURS:
Swedish League – (4) 1976, 1979, 1997, 2000;
Swedish Cup – (1) 1995.

2009

5/4	AIK	a	0-1	
10/4	Trelleborg	h	1-1	*Kujovic E.*
15/4	Brommapojkarna	h	0-1	
19/4	Kalmar	a	1-0	*Raskaj*
23/4	Helsingborg	a	3-1	*Anselmo, Sise, Rosén*
29/4	Djurgården	h	3-0	*Kujovic E. 2, Johansson A.*
5/5	Häcken	a	2-2	*Johansson A., Anselmo*
10/5	Örgryte	h	2-1	*Görlitz, Johansson A.*
16/5	Elfsborg	a	0-4	
20/5	Gefle	h	0-2	
23/5	Hammarby	a	0-0	
31/5	Örebro	h	1-1	*Görlitz*
6/7	Göteborg	h	0-0	
12/7	GAIS	a	1-1	*Kujovic E.*
20/7	Malmö	a	0-0	
27/7	Malmö	h	0-3	
2/8	Brommapojkarna	a	1-2	*Kujovic E.*
9/8	Kalmar	h	2-0	*Kujovic E., Olsson*
17/8	AIK	h	1-2	*Rosén*
24/8	Trelleborg	a	0-4	
30/8	Häcken	h	0-4	
15/9	Örgryte	a	1-2	*Olsson*
19/9	Helsingborg	h	2-1	*Görlitz, Anselmo*
24/9	Djurgården	a	2-0	*Olsson 2*
28/9	Elfsborg	h	1-2	*Mahamat*
4/10	Gefle	a	0-1	
19/10	Hammarby	h	1-0	*Sparv*
23/10	Örebro	a	1-2	*Kujovic E. (p)*
27/10	Göteborg	a	2-2	*Kujovic E., Sævarsson*
1/11	GAIS	h	1-3	*Lundberg*

No	Name	Nat	DoB	Pos	Aps	(s)	Gls
14	ANSELMO Tadeu Silva						
	do Nascimento	BRA	24/10/80	A	15	(6)	3
20	Magnus BAHNE	FIN	15/3/79	G	27		
25	Kujtim BALA		24/5/90	M		(1)	
5	Markus GUSTAFSSON		12/8/87	D	1	(1)	
7	Michael GÖRLITZ	GER	8/3/87	M	30		3
13	Andreas JOHANSSON		10/3/82	M	12		3
2	Per JOHANSSON		6/5/78	D	12	(2)	
24	Sebastian JOHANSSON		4/9/80	M	3	(5)	
1	Karl-Johan JOHNSSON		28/1/90	G	3		
17	Christian JÄRDLER		3/6/82	D	17	(4)	
4	Tommy JÖNSSON		4/3/76	D	21	(1)	
8	Ajsel KUJOVIC		1/3/86	A	2	(7)	
9	Emir KUJOVIC		22/6/88	A	15	(14)	8
3	Johnny LUNDBERG		15/4/82	D	13	(1)	1
13	Azrack MAHAMAT	CHA	24/8/88	M	4	(4)	1
18	Marcus OLSSON		17/5/88	M	14	(6)	4
11	Alexander PRENT	NED	25/5/83	M	1	(3)	
10	Anel RASKAJ	SRB	19/8/89	M	27		1
6	Mikael ROSÉN		15/8/74	D	13	(11)	2
24	Jónas Gudni SÆVARSSON	ISL	28/11/83	M	12		1
19	Emil SALOMONSSON		28/4/89	M	28		
15	Joe SISE		12/12/89	A	9	(5)	1

SWEDEN

16	Tim SPARV	FIN	20/2/87	M	22	(4)	1
12	Tomas ŽVIRGŽDAUSKAS	LTU	18/3/75	D	29		

HAMMARBY FOTBOLL
Coach – Tony Gustavsson; (31/8/09) Thom Åhlund
Founded – 1897
Stadium – Söderstadion (16,197)
MAJOR HONOURS:
Swedish League – (1) 2001.

2009

4/4	Elfsborg	a	1-1	*Johansson E.*
12/4	Gefle	h	1-2	*Davies*
16/4	Helsingborg	a	0-1	
20/4	Djurgården	h	3-1	*Johansson E., Davies, Söderström*
23/4	Göteborg	h	0-1	
29/4	GAIS	a	2-2	*Paulse, Castro-Tello*
6/5	Kalmar	h	1-4	*Davies*
11/5	Örebro	a	0-2	
17/5	Malmö	h	1-0	*Davies*
20/5	Brommapojkarna	a	1-0	*Chanko*
23/5	Halmstad	h	0-0	
28/5	AIK	a	0-1	
4/7	Trelleborg	h	2-1	*Söderberg, Gerrbrand*
16/7	Häcken	a	0-2	
20/7	Örgryte	h	0-1	
27/7	Örgryte	a	0-0	
3/8	Helsingborg	h	1-2	*Dahl*
9/8	Djurgården	a	1-0	*og (Johannesson)*
15/8	Elfsborg	h	2-3	*Dahl (p), Rafael*
24/8	Gefle	a	0-1	
30/8	Kalmar	a	0-3	
13/9	Örebro	h	0-1	
20/9	Göteborg	a	0-2	
23/9	GAIS	h	1-2	*Gerrbrand*
27/9	Malmö	a	1-3	*Helg*
4/10	Brommapojkarna	h	1-0	*Helg*
19/10	Halmstad	a	0-1	
25/10	AIK	h	1-2	*Helg*
28/10	Trelleborg	a	2-4	*Gerrbrand, Helg*
1/11	Häcken	h	0-1	

No	Name	Nat	DoB	Pos	Aps	(s)	Gls
13	Igor ARMAS	MDA	14/7/87	D	26	(1)	
35	Kristoffer BJÖRKLUND		19/4/78	G	16	(1)	
9	Sebastian CASTRO-TELLO		14/3/87	M	24	(1)	1
6	Louay CHANKO		29/11/79	M	12		1
22	Luiz CLÁUDIO Carvalho da Silva	BRA	27/3/87	A	4	(1)	
20	Andreas DAHL		6/6/84	M	15	(2)	2
10	Charlie DAVIES	USA	25/6/86	A	9		4
7	Carlos GAETE		4/11/87	M	6	(5)	
6	Patrik GERRBRAND		27/4/81	D	13		3
16	Christer GUSTAFSSON		31/12/87	A		(2)	
17	Linus HALLENIUS		1/4/89	A	4	(4)	
26	Simon HELG		10/4/90	M	16	(7)	4
40	Johannes HOPF		16/6/87	G	1		
21	Monday JAMES	NGA	19/10/86	D	7	(1)	
14	Mikkel JENSEN	DEN	6/1/77	M	11	(3)	
2	David JOHANSSON		28/5/82	D	18	(2)	
5	Emil JOHANSSON		11/8/86	D	28		2
18	Haris LAITINEN		5/12/84	M	6	(8)	
3	José MONTEIRO de Macedo		2/6/82	D	12	(8)	
15	Nathan PAULSE	RSA	7/4/82	A	11	(10)	1
19	RAFAEL Leandro Magalhães	BRA	6/2/86	A	9	(3)	1
23	Maic SEMA		2/12/88	M	7	(5)	
1	Rami SHAABAN		30/6/75	G	13		
11	Freddy SÖDERBERG		8/11/84	A	11	(12)	1

8	Fredrik SÖDERSTRÖM		30/1/73	M	24	(2)	1
4	Christian TRAORÉ	DEN	18/4/82	D	20	(2)	
32	Marcus TÖRNSTRAND		10/1/90	D	1		
27	Vladico ZLOJUTRO		4/1/88	M	6	(2)	

HELSINGBORGS IF
Coach – Bo Nilsson
Founded – 1907
Stadium – Olympia (17,200)
MAJOR HONOURS:
Swedish League – (4) 1933, 1934, 1941, 1999;
Swedish Cup – (3) 1941, 1998, 2006.

2009

6/4	Göteborg	h	1-0	*Lantz (p)*
13/4	GAIS	a	4-1	*Jönsson, Sundin, Makondele, Larsson*
16/4	Hammarby	h	1-0	*Andersson C.*
20/4	Örebro	a	0-2	
23/4	Halmstad	h	1-3	*Makondele*
29/4	AIK	a	3-0	*Jönsson 3*
4/5	Malmö	h	1-0	*Larsson*
11/5	Brommapojkarna	a	3-0	*Holgersson, og (Guterstam), Larsson*
18/5	Trelleborg	h	2-2	*Makondele, Andersson C.*
22/5	Häcken	a	0-3	
25/5	Örgryte	h	3-1	*Lantz, Sundin, Unkuri*
31/5	Kalmar	a	0-2	
5/7	Djurgården	a	1-2	*Jönsson*
12/7	Elfsborg	h	3-2	*Jönsson 2, Andersson C.*
19/7	Gefle	a	2-0	*Andersson C., Sundin*
26/7	Gefle	h	2-0	*Larsson, Lantz (p)*
3/8	Hammarby	a	2-1	*Makondele, Sundin*
9/8	Örebro	h	0-1	
16/8	Göteborg	a	2-2	*Makondele 2*
23/8	GAIS	h	0-1	
31/8	Malmö	a	0-0	
13/9	Brommapojkarna	h	0-0	
19/9	Halmstad	a	1-2	*Lantz*
24/9	AIK	h	3-2	*Larsson 2, Landgren*
27/9	Trelleborg	a	2-4	*Jönsson, Andersson C.*
4/10	Häcken	h	1-0	*Larsson*
18/10	Örgryte	a	0-3	
24/10	Kalmar	h	1-1	*Makondele*
28/10	Djurgården	h	0-2	
1/11	Elfsborg	a	0-1	

No	Name	Nat	DoB	Pos	Aps	(s)	Gls
25	Yakubu ALFA	NGA	31/12/90	M		(2)	
21	Christoffer ANDERSSON		22/10/78	M	28		5
1	Daniel ANDERSSON		18/12/72	G	7	(1)	
33	Samuel AZIZ		5/7/91	M		(1)	
14	Marcus BERGHOLTZ		15/12/89	M	6	(6)	
20	Isaac CHANSA	ZAM	23/3/84	M	8	(8)	
26	Joel EKSTRAND		4/2/89	D	24		
30	Pär HANSSON		22/6/86	G	23		
15	Markus HOLGERSSON		12/4/85	D	18	(5)	1
7	Tobias HOLMQVIST		23/1/88	A		(5)	
19	Rasmus JÖNSSON		27/1/90	A	25	(1)	8
4	Andreas LANDGREN		17/3/89	D	18	(3)	1
10	Marcus LANTZ		23/10/75	M	20	(1)	4
17	Henrik LARSSON		20/9/71	A	19	(1)	7
29	Fredrik LIVERSTAM		4/3/88	D	2	(2)	
6	May MAHLANGU	RSA	1/1/89	M	7	(1)	
16	René MAKONDELE	COD	20/4/82	M	29		7
24	Marcus NILSSON		26/2/88	D	25		
5	Hannu PATRONEN	FIN	23/5/84	D	8	(4)	
11	RAFAEL PORCELLIS de Oliveira	BRA	19/1/87	A	1	(6)	

SWEDEN

13	Ólafur Ingi SKÚLASON	ISL	1/4/83	M	11	(3)	
9	Erik SUNDIN		1/3/79	M	11	(8)	4
8	Fredrik SVANBÄCK	FIN	5/12/79	M	4	(4)	
3	Adama TAMBOURA	MLI	18/5/85	D	21	(1)	
18	Mattias UNKURI		16/1/88	M	1	(6)	1
23	Erik WAHLSTEDT		16/4/76	D	14	(1)	

BK HÄCKEN
Coach – Peter Gerhardsson
Founded – 1940
Stadium – Rambergsvallen (8,480)

2009

4/4	Malmö	h	0-1	
10/4	Brommapojkarna	a	0-2	
15/4	Göteborg	h	4-1	Ranégie 2, Paulinho, Karlsson
19/4	GAIS	a	0-3	
22/4	Trelleborg	h	1-0	Nyström
1/5	Kalmar	a	1-2	Paulinho
5/5	Halmstad	h	2-2	Henriksson, Ranégie
9/5	AIK	a	0-2	
18/5	Örgryte	a	1-0	Paulinho
22/5	Helsingborg	h	3-0	Ranégie 2, Henriksson
26/5	Djurgården	a	0-1	
29/5	Elfsborg	h	1-1	Ranégie
5/7	Gefle	a	1-1	Henriksson
16/7	Hammarby	h	2-0	Friberg, Paulinho
20/7	Örebro	a	3-1	Henriksson 3
27/7	Örebro	h	2-2	Chibuike, Henriksson
2/8	Göteborg	a	2-2	Östberg, Karlsson
6/8	GAIS	h	1-0	Friberg
17/8	Malmö	a	2-1	Söderberg, Paulinho
25/8	Brommapojkarna	h	5-1	Chibuike 2, Paulinho 2, Henriksson
30/8	Halmstad	a	4-0	Henriksson 2, Paulinho, Friberg
14/9	AIK	h	0-2	
20/9	Trelleborg	a	2-2	Chibuike, Vinícius Lopes
23/9	Kalmar	h	0-0	
29/9	Örgryte	h	2-0	Chibuike, Bjurström
4/10	Helsingborg	a	0-1	
19/10	Djurgården	h	2-1	Vinícius Lopes, Chibuike
25/10	Elfsborg	a	1-1	Jarlegren
28/10	Gefle	h	0-0	
1/11	Hammarby	a	1-0	Vinícius Lopes

No	Name	Nat	DoB	Pos	Aps	(s)	Gls
28	Jonas BJURSTRÖM		24/3/79	M		(2)	1
18	Dominic CHATTO	NGA	12/7/85	M	18	(1)	
9	John CHIBUIKE	NGA	10/10/88	M	15	(7)	6
22	Daniel FORSSELL		4/1/82	D	2	(8)	
17	Erik FRIBERG		10/2/86	M	24	(4)	3
6	David FRÖLUND		4/6/79	D	27	(1)	
21	Jonas HENRIKSSON		24/3/79	M	30		10
16	Marcus JARLEGREN		16/9/83	D	11	(5)	1
8	Josef KARLSSON		13/7/82	M	23	(5)	2
4	Muhammed Ali KHAN		21/1/86	D		(2)	
1	Christoffer KÄLLQVIST		26/8/83	G	29		
2	Johan LIND		8/2/74	D	23	(2)	
26	Damir MEHIC		18/4/87	G	1	(1)	
14	Peter NYSTRÖM		27/8/84	M	10	(9)	1
10	Paulo José de Oliveira "PAULINHO"	BRA	9/4/86	A	24	(2)	8
13	Mathias RANÉGIE		14/6/84	A	25	(4)	6
7	Janne SAARINEN	FIN	28/2/77	M	11	(2)	
27	Tom SÖDERBERG		25/8/87	D	29		1
11	VINÍCIUS Silva LOPES Souto	BRA	29/1/88	A	2	(22)	3
5	Emil WAHLSTRÖM		2/3/87	D	2	(2)	
12	Robin WIKMAN	FIN	21/1/86	D		(1)	
3	Mattias ÖSTBERG		24/8/77	D	24		1

KALMAR FF
Coach – Nanne Bergstrand
Founded – 1910
Stadium – Fredriksskans IP (8,973)
MAJOR HONOURS:
Swedish League – (1) 2008;
Swedish Cup – (3) 1981, 1987, 2007.

2009

6/4	Gefle	a	1-1	Elm R. (p)
13/4	AIK	h	0-1	
16/4	Elfsborg	a	1-1	Daniel Mendes
19/4	Halmstad	h	0-1	
23/4	Örebro	a	1-2	Elm D.
1/5	Häcken	h	2-1	Daniel Sobralense, Carlsson
6/5	Hammarby	a	4-1	Carlsson, Elm R., Lindberg, Eriksson
11/5	Trelleborg	h	2-0	Eriksson, Daniel Mendes
17/5	Göteborg	a	1-2	Dauda
21/5	Örgryte	h	1-0	Carlsson
24/5	GAIS	a	2-2	Daniel Mendes 2
31/5	Helsingborg	h	2-0	Daniel Sobralense, Elm R.
6/7	Malmö	a	2-1	Elm R. 2
11/7	Djurgården	h	6-1	Elm R. 2, Eriksson 2, Elm D., Dauda
18/7	Brommapojkarna	h	3-1	Elm R., Daniel Mendes, Ricardo Santos
25/7	Brommapojkarna	a	2-1	Larsson, Daniel Mendes
2/8	Elfsborg	h	3-1	Elm D., Elm R., Dauda
9/8	Halmstad	a	0-2	
15/8	Gefle	h	1-1	Daniel Mendes
22/8	AIK	a	1-1	Eriksson
30/8	Hammarby	h	3-0	Eriksson 2, Daniel Mendes
12/9	Trelleborg	a	2-1	Ricardo Santos, Dauda
20/9	Örebro	h	1-3	Ricardo Santos
23/9	Häcken	a	0-0	
26/9	Göteborg	h	2-1	Dauda, Ricardo Santos
3/10	Örgryte	a	2-4	Augustsson, Daniel Sobralense
17/10	GAIS	h	2-2	Daniel Sobralense, Reinaldo
24/10	Helsingborg	a	1-1	Ricardo Santos
27/10	Malmö	h	5-4	Daniel Sobralense 2, Dauda 2, Ricardo Santos
1/11	Djurgården	a	0-2	

No	Name	Nat	DoB	Pos	Aps	(s)	Gls
35	Lourival Rodrigues ASSIS Filho	BRA	3/2/84	M	4	(3)	
7	Jimmie AUGUSTSSON		13/4/81	M	1	(9)	1
5	Tobias CARLSSON		25/2/75	D	10	(1)	3
17	DANIEL Freire MENDES	BRA	18/1/81	A	18	(7)	8
12	DANIEL Lopes da Silva SOBRALENSE	BRA	10/2/82	M	24	(2)	6
11	Abiola DAUDA	NGA	3/2/88	A	19	(9)	7
6	Mikael EKLUND		14/9/81	D	1		
13	David ELM		10/1/83	M	15	(2)	3
18	Rasmus ELM		17/3/88	M	19		9
25	Tobias ERIKSSON		19/3/85	M	29	(1)	7
20	Erik ISRAELSSON		25/2/89	M		(3)	
21	Lars JOHANSSON		2/4/75	M	3	(12)	
23	Matthias JOHANSSON		16/2/92	D	3	(1)	
3	Joachim LANTZ		10/5/77	D	28		
9	Stefan LARSSON		21/1/83	D	30		1
14	LEANDRO "LOVE" Rodrigues da Silva	BRA	31/1/82	A		(1)	
16	Petter LENNARTSSON		13/3/88	D	2		
4	Marcus LINDBERG		31/8/80	D	15	(1)	1
26	Emin NOURI		22/7/85	D	21	(3)	
37	REINALDO da Silva	BRA	25/5/84	M	5	(7)	1
19	RICARDO SANTOS	BRA	13/2/87	A	10	(4)	6

8	Henrik RYDSTRÖM		16/2/76	M	29		
77	Daryl SMYLIE	ENG	10/9/85	M	1	(2)	
1	Petter WASTÅ		2/2/76	G	30		
14	Stefan ÅLANDER		25/4/83	D	13	(2)	
24	Robin ÖSTLIND		14/3/90	A		(1)	

MALMÖ FF
Coach – Roland Nilsson
Founded – 1910
Stadium – Swedbank Stadion (24,000)
MAJOR HONOURS:
Swedish League – (15) 1944, 1949, 1950, 1951, 1953, 1965, 1967, 1970, 1971, 1974, 1975, 1977, 1986, 1988, 2004;
Swedish Cup – (14) 1944, 1946, 1947, 1951, 1953, 1967, 1973, 1974, 1975, 1977, 1980, 1984, 1986, 1989.

2009
4/4	Häcken	a	1-0	*Mutavdžić*
13/4	Örgryte	h	3-0	*Mehmeti 2, Harbuzi*
16/4	AIK	a	1-0	*Mehmeti*
19/4	Trelleborg	h	1-1	*Larsson*
22/4	Elfsborg	a	0-1	
29/4	Gefle	h	0-0	
4/5	Helsingborg	a	0-1	
10/5	Djurgården	h	2-1	*Harbuzi, Wílton Figueiredo*
17/5	Hammarby	a	0-1	
20/5	Örebro	h	0-0	
25/5	Göteborg	a	0-2	
31/5	GAIS	h	2-2	*Molins, Hamad*
6/7	Kalmar	h	1-2	*Wílton Figueiredo*
12/7	Brommapojkarna	a	1-1	*Molins*
20/7	Halmstad	h	0-0	
27/7	Halmstad	a	3-0	*Mehmeti 2, Hamad*
30/7	AIK	h	0-0	
8/8	Trelleborg	a	2-0	*Wílton Figueiredo, Andersson*
17/8	Häcken	h	1-2	*Ricardinho*
24/8	Örgryte	a	0-1	
31/8	Helsingborg	h	0-0	
14/9	Djurgården	a	2-1	*Ofere 2*
21/9	Elfsborg	h	5-0	*Larsson 2, Ofere 2, Molins*
24/9	Gefle	a	3-0	*Ofere 2, Larsson*
27/9	Hammarby	h	3-1	*Larsson 2, Ofere*
4/10	Örebro	a	3-0	*Larsson 3*
19/10	Göteborg	h	0-1	
23/10	GAIS	a	1-1	*Wílton Figueiredo*
27/10	Kalmar	a	4-5	*Larsson 2, Ofere 2*
1/11	Brommapojkarna	h	1-1	*Ofere*

No	Name	Nat	DoB	Pos	Aps	(s)	Gls
8	Daniel ANDERSSON		28/8/77	M	26		1
36	Muamet ASANOVSKI		14/7/91	M		(1)	
11	Jeffrey AUBYNN		12/5/77	M	3	(6)	
27	Johan DAHLIN		8/9/86	G	12		
4	Jimmy DIXON	LBR	10/10/81	D	11		
15	David DURMAZ		21/12/81	D	1		
21	Jimmy DURMAZ		22/3/89	M		(13)	
5	GABRIEL de Paulo Limeira	BRA	20/8/83	D	26		
6	Markus HALSTI	FIN	19/3/84	D	10		
26	Jiloan HAMAD		6/11/90	M	17	(3)	2
79	Labinot HARBUZI		4/4/86	A	11	(2)	2
15	Pontus JANSSON		13/2/91	A		(2)	
10	Rick KRUYS	NED	5/9/85	M	7	(6)	
7	Daniel LARSSON		25/1/87	A	25	(2)	11
24	Agon MEHMETI		20/11/89	A	7	(15)	5
25	Dušan MELICHÁREK	CZE	29/11/83	G	5		
14	Guillermo MOLINS		26/9/88	M	23	(5)	3
16	Miljan MUTAVDŽIĆ	SRB	3/2/86	D	1		1
23	Robin NILSSON		15/9/88	M		(1)	

18	Edward OFERE	NGA	28/3/86	A	19	(9)	10
20	Ricardo Ferreira da Silva						
	"RICARDINHO"	BRA	9/9/84	D	29		1
1	Jonas SANDQVIST		6/5/81	G	13		
29	Jasmin SUDIC		24/11/90	D	18		
2	Ulrich VINZENTS	DEN	11/4/76	D	26		
9	WÍLTON Aguiar FIGUEIREDO	BRA	17/3/82	A	18	(6)	4
3	Robert ÅHMAN PERSSON		26/3/87	M	22	(4)	

TRELLEBORGS FF
Coach – Tom Prahl
Founded – 1926
Stadium – Vångavallen (10,000)

2009
5/4	Brommapojkarna	h	0-0	
10/4	Halmstad	a	1-1	*Pode*
16/4	GAIS	h	3-0	*Pode, Drugge, Haynes*
19/4	Malmö	a	1-1	*Haynes*
22/4	Häcken	a	0-1	
1/5	Örgryte	h	2-1	*Bengtsson R. (p), Sjöhage*
5/5	AIK	h	1-0	*Drugge*
11/5	Kalmar	a	0-2	
18/5	Helsingborg	a	2-2	*Fuxberg, Shala*
21/5	Djurgården	h	3-0	*Jensen 2, Haynes*
25/5	Elfsborg	a	0-1	
30/5	Gefle	h	2-1	*Abelsson, Tavares*
4/7	Hammarby	a	1-2	*Andersson*
13/7	Örebro	h	0-1	
19/7	Göteborg	a	1-3	*Jensen*
26/7	Göteborg	h	2-1	*Drugge, Wihlborg*
3/8	GAIS	a	1-0	*Abelsson*
8/8	Malmö	h	0-2	
16/8	Brommapojkarna	a	2-2	*Wihlborg, Drugge*
24/8	Halmstad	h	4-0	*Jensen 2, Drugge, Wihlborg*
29/8	AIK	a	0-1	
12/9	Kalmar	h	1-2	*Wihlborg*
20/9	Häcken	h	2-2	*Jensen, og (Söderberg)*
24/9	Örgryte	a	2-0	*Sjöhage, Drugge*
27/9	Helsingborg	h	4-2	*Sjöhage 2, Wihlborg, Jensen*
3/10	Djurgården	a	0-0	
17/10	Elfsborg	h	0-1	
25/10	Gefle	a	1-2	*Sjöhage*
28/10	Hammarby	h	4-2	*Jensen, Haynes, Andersson, Sjöhage*
1/11	Örebro	a	1-1	*Abelsson*

No	Name	Nat	DoB	Pos	Aps	(s)	Gls
4	Peter ABELSSON		14/7/77	D	29		3
21	Magnus ANDERSSON		27/4/81	M	26		2
26	Jonathan ASP		6/5/90	M	1		
5	Mikael BENGTSSON		5/12/81	D	13	(1)	
25	Rasmus BENGTSSON		26/6/86	D	12		1
14	Andreas DRUGGE		20/1/83	A	29		6
20	Yousef FAKHRO		3/5/83	D	18	(5)	
18	Marcus FALK OLANDER		21/5/87	M	1	(2)	
23	Max FUXBERG		23/7/85	D	8	(3)	1
8	Kristian HAYNES		20/12/80	M	27		4
13	Fredrik JENSEN		13/6/85	A	20	(9)	8
6	Zoran JOVANOVIĆ		25/9/86	M	5	(8)	
3	Dennis MELANDER		19/1/83	D	24		
15	Emil MÅRTENSSON		9/1/85	M		(2)	
35	Joakim NILSSON		16/5/83	M	10	(2)	
31	Viktor NORING		3/2/91	G	29		
33	Mattias NYLUND		23/9/80	D	3		
1	Fredrik PERSSON		20/2/83	G	1		
17	Thommie PERSSON		4/8/84	D	9	(6)	
32	Marcus PODE		27/3/86	A	14	(5)	2

SWEDEN

28	Fisnik SHALA		16/1/89	A	3	(6)	1
23	Joakim SJÖHAGE		27/9/86	A	10	(18)	6
30	Jens SLOTH		9/9/82	D	11	(1)	
19	Viktor SVENSSON		6/3/90	M	2		
27	Paulino Lopes TAVARES	POR	10/12/84	M	6	(3)	1
7	Mattias THYLANDER		22/10/74	M	3	(3)	
2	Andreas WIHLBORG		18/1/87	M	16		5

ÖREBRO SK
Coach – Sixten Boström (FIN)
Founded – 1908
Stadium – Behrn Arena (14,500)

2009
6/4	Djurgården	a	0-1	
10/4	Elfsborg	h	0-1	
16/4	Örgryte	a	1-0	Olsen
20/4	Helsingborg	h	2-0	Olsen, Tahirović
23/4	Kalmar	h	2-1	Bassombeng, Nordback
28/4	Göteborg	a	0-1	
4/5	Gefle	a	0-2	
11/5	Hammarby	h	2-0	Porokara, Wowoah
17/5	GAIS	h	2-0	Olsen, Nordback
20/5	Malmö	a	0-0	
25/5	Brommapojkarna	h	2-2	Olsen, Nordback
31/5	Halmstad	a	1-1	Wirtanen
5/7	AIK	h	1-1	Gerzic
13/7	Trelleborg	a	1-0	Porokara
20/7	Häcken	h	1-3	Porokara
27/7	Häcken	a	2-2	Bedoya 2
3/8	Örgryte	h	2-2	og (Leinar), og (Jonsson D.)
9/8	Helsingborg	a	1-0	Olsen
17/8	Djurgården	h	2-0	Nordback, Johansson
23/8	Elfsborg	a	1-2	Astvald
31/8	Gefle	h	2-0	Wikström, Adriano Munoz
13/9	Hammarby	a	1-0	Olsen
20/9	Kalmar	a	3-1	Olsen 2, Astvald
23/9	Göteborg	h	0-0	
28/9	GAIS	a	0-3	
4/10	Malmö	h	0-3	
18/10	Brommapojkarna	a	0-3	
23/10	Halmstad	h	2-1	Porokara 2
28/10	AIK	a	1-1	og (Hooiveld)
1/11	Trelleborg	h	1-1	Astvald

No	Name	Nat	DoB	Pos	Aps	(s)	Gls
23	ADRIANO Afonso Thiel MUNOZ	BRA	23/7/78	A	4	(6)	1
19	Michael ALMEBÄCK		4/4/88	D	28		
82	John ALVBÅGE		10/8/82	G	30		
9	Patrik ANTTONEN		6/3/80	D	17	(1)	
29	Marcus ASTVALD		3/9/90	M	13	(5)	3
15	Eric BASSOMBENG	CMR	2/11/83	M	14	(4)	1
17	Alejandro BEDOYA	USA	29/4/87	M	13	(12)	2
25	Nordin GERZIC		9/11/83	M	26	(1)	1
14	Glenn HOLGERSSON		5/11/79	D	2	(1)	
26	Michael JIDSJÖ		7/4/90	A		(1)	
5	Per JOHANSSON		6/4/89	D	2	(10)	1
7	Magnus KIHLBERG		25/10/73	M	28	(1)	
21	Erik NILSSON		30/7/89	M		(2)	
8	Fredrik NORDBACK	FIN	20/3/79	M	25	(2)	4
27	Kristoffer NÄFVER		28/3/86	M		(2)	
6	Kim OLSEN	DEN	2/11/79	A	26	(1)	8
33	Roni POROKARA	FIN	12/12/83	M	29		5
10	Robin STAAF		26/9/86	A		(8)	
99	Emra TAHIROVIĆ		31/7/87	A	1	(8)	1
13	Robert WALKER		6/3/87	M		(2)	
4	Magnus WIKSTRÖM		7/12/77	D	29		1
11	Tommy WIRTANEN	FIN	19/1/83	M	13	(10)	1

| 20 | Samuel WOWOAH | | 17/6/76 | D | 29 | | 1 |
| 3 | Bertin Samuel ZÉ NDILE | CMR | 17/12/88 | D | 1 | (4) | |

ÖRGRYTE IS
Coach – Jan Carlsson
Founded – 1891
Stadium – Gamla Ullevi (19,000)
MAJOR HONOURS:
Swedish League – (12) 1896, 1897, 1898, 1899, 1902, 1904, 1905, 1906,
1907, 1909, 1913, 1985;
Swedish Cup – (1) 2000.

2009
5/4	GAIS	h	1-5	Álvaro Santos
13/4	Malmö	a	0-3	
16/4	Örebro	h	0-1	
20/4	Göteborg	a	0-3	
23/4	AIK	h	0-1	
1/5	Trelleborg	a	1-2	og (Abelsson)
6/5	Brommapojkarna	h	1-1	Lindström C.
10/5	Halmstad	a	1-2	Leinar
18/5	Häcken	h	0-1	
21/5	Kalmar	a	0-1	
25/5	Helsingborg	a	1-3	Leinar
31/5	Djurgården	h	0-0	
6/7	Elfsborg	a	0-3	
13/7	Gefle	h	2-2	Anklev, Anderberg
20/7	Hammarby	a	1-0	Allbäck
27/7	Hammarby	h	0-0	
3/8	Örebro	a	2-2	Álvaro Santos, Allbäck
9/8	Göteborg	h	1-2	Perreira
17/8	GAIS	a	0-1	
24/8	Malmö	h	1-0	Perreira
31/8	Brommapojkarna	a	2-1	Allbäck, Álvaro Santos
15/9	Halmstad	h	2-1	Álvaro Santos, Mellqvist
21/9	AIK	a	0-3	
24/9	Trelleborg	h	0-2	
29/9	Häcken	a	0-2	
3/10	Kalmar	h	4-2	Álvaro Santos 2, Gustafsson, Johansson
18/10	Helsingborg	h	3-0	Álvaro Santos 3 (1p)
24/10	Djurgården	a	1-2	Mellqvist
28/10	Elfsborg	h	1-1	Zavadil
1/11	Gefle	a	2-2	Álvaro Santos, Gustafsson

No	Name	Nat	DoB	Pos	Aps	(s)	Gls
11	Marcus ALLBÄCK		5/7/73	A	18		3
18	ÁLVARO Márcio SANTOS	BRA	30/1/80	A	15	(4)	10
19	Markus ANDERBERG		4/8/88	A	12	(7)	1
30	Bengt ANDERSSON		11/8/66	G	24		
7	Björn ANKLEV		13/4/79	M	26		1
2	Christoffer BENGTSSON		16/11/80	D	2	(4)	
14	Tommy von BRÖMSEN		21/1/81	D	11	(2)	
95	Nathan COE	AUS	1/6/84	G	5		
8	Martin DOHLSTEN		29/4/86	M	5	(6)	
10	Patrik ELMANDER		26/11/78	A	2	(4)	
15	Niclas ELVING		17/1/86	M		(1)	
23	Adam ERIKSSON		2/2/88	D	2	(5)	
29	Danny ERVIK		24/2/89	D	9	(2)	
5	Markus GUSTAFSSON		6/3/89	M	13	(4)	2
24	Sebastian JOHANSSON		4/9/80	M	14		1
26	Dennis JONSSON		16/2/83	D	20	(3)	
17	Robin JONSSON		13/11/87	D	21	(3)	
21	Seif KADHIM		7/2/91	M		(1)	
40	Magnus KÄLLANDER		6/2/69	M	13	(10)	
44	David LEINAR		12/11/79	D	24	(1)	2
20	Christian LINDSTRÖM		11/2/87	M	6	(6)	1
27	Jonathan LINDSTRÖM		14/7/89	M		(1)	

6	Alexander MELLQVIST	29/1/86	M	25	(4)	2
22	Roy MILLER	CRC 24/11/89	D	13	(1)	
16	Alessandro Silva PERREIRA	BRA 15/5/82	D	16	(1)	2
14	Nicolas SANDBERG	24/2/91	A	5	(8)	
3	Johan SJÖBERG	14/11/80	D	1	(1)	
12	David STENMAN	8/10/88	G	1		
9	Pavel ZAVADIL	CZE 30/4/78	M	27		1

PROMOTED CLUBS

MJÄLLBY AIF
Coach – Peter Swärdh
Founded – 1939
Stadium – Strandvallen (7,500)

ÅTVIDABERGS FF
Coach – Daniel Wiklund
Founded – 1907
Stadium – Kopparvallen (8,000)
MAJOR HONOURS:
Swedish League - (2) 1972, 1973; Swedish Cup - (2) 1970, 1971.

SECOND LEVEL FINAL TABLE 2009

		Pld	W	D	L	F	A	Pts
1	Mjällby AIF	30	19	8	3	60	19	65
2	Åtvidabergs FF	30	17	6	7	53	36	57
3	Assyriska FF	30	15	6	9	46	38	51
4	Syrianska FC	30	15	5	10	50	38	50
5	GIF Sundsvall	30	13	8	9	54	48	47
6	Falkenbergs FF	30	14	3	13	44	41	45
7	Ängelholms FF	30	13	5	12	43	45	44
8	Landskrona BoIS	30	12	4	14	51	46	40
9	Ljungskile SK	30	11	7	12	48	43	40
10	Jönköping Södra IF	30	10	6	14	46	54	36
11	IFK Norrköping	30	8	11	11	45	44	35
12	Väsby United	30	8	9	13	28	41	33
13	FC Trollhättan	30	8	8	14	30	46	32
14	Qviding FIF	30	7	10	13	31	45	31
15	IK Sirius	30	8	7	15	37	53	31
16	Vasalunds IF	30	8	5	17	35	64	29
16	Degerfors IF	30	5	9	16	27	47	24

PROMOTION/RELEGATION PLAY-OFFS
(4/11/09)
Assyriska 2, Djurgården 0
(8/11/09)
Djurgården 3, Assyriska 0 *(aet)*
(Djurgården 3-2)

DOMESTIC CUP 2009

SVENSKA CUPEN

THIRD ROUND

(25/4/09)
Ersboda 1, Göteborg 8
Kristianstad 1, Örebro 4
Ljungskile 1, Elfsborg 2 *(aet)*
Syrianska 5, Trelleborg 1 *(aet)*
Åtvidaberg 2, Hammarby 3 *(aet)*

(26/4/09)
Assyriska 2, Häcken 4
Gunnilse 2, Örgryte 0
Hässleholm 0, Djurgården 2
Landskrona 4, GAIS 2
Mjällby 1, Malmö FF 0
Norrköping 1, AIK 2
Qviding 1, Gefle 3
Sirius 2, Brommapojkarna 0 *(aet)*
Skövde 0, Halmstad 2
Sundsvall 1, Kalmar 0
Väsby United 0, Helsingborg 2

FOURTH ROUND

(13/5/09)
Gefle 1, Djurgården 0
Landskrona 1, Göteborg 4
Mjällby 4, Hammarby 2
Sirius 0, AIK 1
Sundsvall 3, Häcken 5
Syrianska 2, Elfsborg 1
Örebro 3, Halmstad 0

(14/5/09)
Gunnilse 0, Helsingborg 7

QUARTER-FINALS

(28/6/09)
Syrianska 1 *(Zatara 80)*, Helsingborg 3 *(Sundin 61, 120, Makondele 92)* *(aet)*

(8/7/09)
Häcken 1 *(Paulinho 59)*, Örebro 0
Mjällby 1 *(Fejzullahu 8)*, AIK 2 *(Óbolo 39, Kayongo-Mutumba 49)*

(9/7/09)
Göteborg 3 *(Hysén 20, 32, Bärkroth 89)*, Gefle 1 *(Jawo A. 77)*

SEMI-FINALS

(6/9/09)
AIK 3 *(Óbolo 21, Johansson 117, Jonsson 120p)*, Häcken 2 *(Vinícius Lopes 87, 95)* *(aet)*

(16/9/09)
Helsingborg 1 *(Sundin 40)*, Göteborg 3 *(Eriksson 17, Hysén 76, Bjarnason 84)*

FINAL

(7/11/09)
Råsunda, Solna
AIK SOLNA 2 *(Óbolo 71, Antônio Flávio 90+1)*
IFK GÖTEBORG 0
Referee – Eriksson
AIK – Örlund, Jonsson, Karlsson, Hooiveld, Johansson, Pavey (Djordjic 66), Ortíz, Johnson, Kayongo-Mutumba (Tjernström 87), Antônio Flávio, Óbolo.
GÖTEBORG – Christensen, Lund, Sigurdsson, Jónsson, Dyrestam (Alexandersson N. 46), Johansson J. (Stiller 69), Svensson G., Selakovic, Bjarnason, Eriksson, Hysén.

Hitzfeld's team falter after dream start

Switzerland's fourth successive appearance at a major tournament ended like two of the previous three – with first-round elimination – but if little was expected of Ottmar Hitzfeld's side before the 2010 FIFA World Cup, there was evident frustration afterwards, especially after they had created the shock of the finals with their opening smash-and-grab 1-0 victory over Spain.

That Spain went on to win every other game and become the new world champions was an irony not lost on the Swiss players as they watched the latter stages of the tournament back home on television. The record books will always show that Switzerland defeated the eventual champions, but, equally, the team's failure to build on that perfect start will always diminish the achievement.

Benaglio stars

The goal that beat Spain in Durban – a scrappy effort from midfielder Gelson Fernandes – was the only one Switzerland managed to score in three matches. Superbly organised at the back, with Diego Benaglio among the very best goalkeepers on view, Hitzfeld's side were extremely disciplined and difficult to penetrate –

as even the pass-masters of Spain discovered. But they could not marry that appetite for destruction with any flair or finishing prowess, and as an attacking force they were almost wholly ineffectual.

Being reduced to ten men only a third of the way through their second encounter, against Chile, was a heavy burden – and, in truth, Valon Behrami's dismissal was very harsh – but less than ten minutes after Switzerland had broken an all-time World Cup finals record for the longest period without conceding a goal, they let one in. The goal came out of the blue, but it did not flatter the South Americans and it left Hitzfeld's team having to defeat Honduras by at least two goals to guarantee their place in the last 16. Needing now to attack rather than defend, they were found badly wanting, and after a painful 0-0 draw in Bloemfontein, coupled with Spain's 2-1 win against Chile, it was time to go home.

The brilliant Benaglio apart, Switzerland were consistently well served in South Africa only by centre-back Stéphane Grichting. The full-backs and midfielders were strong defensively but carried little threat going forward. As for the strikers, record scorer Alexander Frei was barely fit while Blaise Nkufo, who had scored abundantly in qualifying, was practically invisible and Eren Derdiyok, though livelier, squandered a gilt-edged chance late on against Chile.

The build-up to Switzerland's winning goal against Spain

Switzerland's next challenge is to qualify for UEFA EURO 2012. Standing between them and the Poland/Ukraine finals are England, Bulgaria, Wales and Montenegro in a group that looks much tougher than the one they won en route to South Africa. Even so, with the vastly experienced Hitzfeld, not to mention that watertight defence, still in situ, plus the self-belief gained from the win over Spain, a fifth successive major tournament participation is a realistic target.

Gamble pays off

Switzerland's leading club side of recent times, FC Basel 1893, followed the example set by the national association and appointed a German coach in advance of the 2009/10 season, replacing long-serving Christian Gross with ex-FC Bayern München midfielder Thorsten Fink. Given his lack of coaching experience, and indeed lack of success – he had been sacked after a poor 2008/09 campaign with German second division club FC Ingolstadt 04 – the appointment was seen as a major gamble. By the end of the season, though, the sceptics were silenced as Basel celebrated an improbable Super League/ Schweizer Cup double.

Young Boys striker Seydou Doumbia - the Super League's top scorer with 30 goals

Zürich performing in the group stage of the UEFA Champions League and Basel flying the Swiss flag in the UEFA Europa League.

San Siro shock

Zürich benefited from a kind draw in the qualifying stage, having to defeat only the champions of Slovenia and Latvia to make it through to the elite 32, but that was as far as their luck went because the group stage pitted them against three former European champions in Real Madrid CF, AC Milan and Olympique de Marseille. An opening 5-2 home defeat by Real gave an indication of what to expect for Bernard Challandes' side, but although they duly ended up in bottom place, they left with the satisfaction of having taken four points off Milan, the 1-0 victory in San Siro on Matchday 2 – courtesy of captain Hannu Tihinen's neat backheel – ranking as arguably the biggest upset of the competition.

To many the championship was lost by BSC Young Boys rather than won by Basel. The team from Berne led the table for 31 of the 36 matchdays, but the pressure of chasing a first league title in almost a quarter of a century eventually got to them, and two disastrous defeats in their final two matches, the second of them against Basel at the Stade de Suisse, deprived the perpetual runners-up of a trophy that was theirs for the taking.

Young Boys could take consolation from the fact that, in European terms, their prize was the same as Basel's – a place in the third qualifying round of the UEFA Champions League. Furthermore, they also boasted the Super League's top scorer in young Ivory Coast international Seydou Doumbia, who, having already claimed the Golden Boot the previous season, largely as a substitute, with 20 goals, raised that total to 30, in the process firmly establishing himself as one of the first names on coach Vladimir Petrović's teamsheet – despite signing a pre-contract during the winter break to join Russian club PFC CSKA Moskva in the summer.

Doumbia also made his mark on the European stage when he scored Young Boys' winning goal against Athletic Club in Bilbao in the third qualifying round of the UEFA Europa League. Unfortunately, the Spanish club took the tie on away goals with a 2-1 win in Berne, thus ending European activity in the Swiss capital for another year. There would be plenty of continental combat elsewhere in the country, though, with FC

Basel, who had taken just one point from their UEFA Champions League campaign the previous season under Gross, were to make a better fist of the UEFA Europa League group stage under new boss Fink. Like Zürich, they claimed an illustrious Italian scalp, overcoming AS Roma 2-0 at home in their opening fixture. Two further victories against PFC CSKA Sofia left them poised for a place in the round of 32, but a 2-1 defeat in the Stadio Olimpico left them requiring a point at home to Fulham FC to go through and they were beaten again, going down 3-2 on a freezing night at the St. Jakob-Park.

At that stage of the season, with the European setback aggravated by a disappointing league position, seven points adrift of Young Boys, there was speculation that Fink's position might be under threat. But any doubts about the German's ability to handle the pressure were quickly dispelled in the first game after the winter break when Basel demolished Young Boys 4-0 and followed that up with ten wins in their next 12 matches. With the goals flowing and key players such as long-serving Australian Scott Chipperfield and Swiss internationals Benjamin Huggel and Marco Streller all hitting top form, the battle for the title with Young Boys was well and truly joined.

 **SWITZERLAND**

With no other team remotely in contention – Zürich endured a woeful title defence, eventually sacking title-winning coach Challandes in April, while city rivals Grasshopper-Club's spring surge under Ciriaco Sforza came far too late – the destiny of the Super League crown came down to the last-day head-to-head between Young Boys and Basel in Berne.

Six of the best

Although Young Boys enjoyed home advantage, they were the underdogs. Not only had they been thrashed 5-1 on a miserable wet night at FC Luzern three days earlier, they had also dropped into second place on goal difference and were now obliged to beat Basel to take the title. Their opponents, on the other hand, were on a roll. Victorious in each of their previous three league fixtures, they also took time out to win the Swiss Cup for the fifth time in nine seasons, hammering Challenge League (second level) side FC Lausanne-Sport 6-0 in the final.

Two of those six goals were scored by Basel's 21-year-old starlet Valentin Stocker, and he was to open the scoring against Young Boys – just as he had in another last-day title showdown against the same opponents two years previously – with a deft 39th-minute chip. Basel allowed the home side on to them after that and sealed victory on the counter-attack with a Chipperfield header 15 minutes into the second period.

With the 2-0 win came the title, the 13th in Basel's history, and the double, their fourth – rich pickings for a coach who must have wondered what he had let himself in for when his team trailed Young Boys by 13

Schweizerischer Fussballverband/ Association Suisse de Football (SFV/ASF)

Worbstrasse 48
Postfach
CH-3000 Bern 15
tel – +41 31 950 8111
fax – +41 31 950 8181
website – football.ch
email – sfv.asf@football.ch
Year of Formation – 1895

President – Peter Gilliéron
General Secretary – Alex Miescher
Media Officer – Marco von Ah

INTERNATIONAL TOURNAMENT APPEARANCES
FIFA World Cup – (9) 1934, 1938 (qtr-finals), 1950, 1954 (qtr-finals), 1962, 1966, 1994 (2nd round), 2006 (2nd round), 2010.
UEFA European Championship – (3) 1996, 2004, 2008.
TOP FIVE ALL-TIME CAPS
Heinz Hermann (117); Alain Geiger (112); Stéphane Chapuisat (103); Johann Vogel (94); Hakan Yakin (83)
TOP FIVE ALL-TIME GOALS
Alexander Frei (40); Kubilay Türkyilmaz & Xam Abegglen III (34); André Abegglen II & Jacky Fatton (29)

points at the end of August. Ultimately Fink managed to get the best out of senior pros such as Streller, Chipperfield, Huggel and Frei while also furthering the fledgling careers of youngsters such as Stocker, Ghanaian defender Samuel Inkoom and the exciting, diminutive 18-year-old Xherdan Shaqiri, who, whether operating on the wing or as a full-back, did enough to merit a place in Switzerland's World Cup squad.

NATIONAL TEAM RESULTS 2009/10

12/8/09	Italy	H	Basel	0-0	
5/9/09	Greece (WCQ)	H	Basel	2-0	Grichting (83), Padalino (88)
9/9/09	Latvia (WCQ)	A	Riga	2-2	Frei (43), Derdiyok (80)
10/10/10	Luxembourg (WCQ)	A	Luxembourg	3-0	Senderos (6, 8), Huggel (22)
14/10/09	Israel (WCQ)	H	Basel	0-0	
14/11/09	Norway	H	Geneva	0-1	
3/3/10	Uruguay	H	St Gallen	1-3	Inler (29p)
1/6/10	Costa Rica	H	Sion	0-1	
5/6/10	Italy	H	Geneva	1-1	Inler (10)
16/6/10	Spain (WCF)	N	Durban (RSA)	1-0	Fernandes (52)
21/6/10	Chile (WCF)	N	Port Elizabeth (RSA)	0-1	
25/6/10	Honduras (WCF)	N	Bloemfontein (RSA)	0-0	

With Basel taking the title, Lausanne, despite that heavy Cup final defeat, qualified for the UEFA Europa League alongside Grasshoppers and Luzern, respectively fourth and fifth in the league. The lakeside club, whose Cup run included a memorable 4-1 win at Young Boys in the quarter-final, were never candidates for promotion, the Challenge League title going to former UEFA Champions League participants FC Thun, who, led by ex-Basel and Switzerland defender Murat Yakin, just edged out FC Lugano. The latter lost their promotion/relegation play-off to local rivals AC Bellinzona, leaving perennial survivors FC Aarau as the only team to suffer relegation – and thus end an unbroken 29-year stint in Switzerland's top division.

NATIONAL TEAM APPEARANCES 2009/10

			Ita	GRE	LVA	LUX	ISR	Nor	Uru	Crc	Ita	ESP	CHI	HON	Caps	Goals
Coach – Ottmar HITZFELD (GER)	12/1/49															
Diego BENAGLIO	8/9/83	Wolfsburg (GER)	G	G	G	G		G		G	G46	G	G	G	30	-
Philipp DEGEN	15/2/83	Liverpool (ENG)	D67					s46							32	-
Philippe SENDEROS	14/2/85	Arsenal (ENG) /Everton (ENG)	D		D	D	D46			D	D	D36			41	5
Stéphane GRICHTING	30/3/79	Auxerre (FRA)	D	D	D		D		D	D46	D	D	D	D	38	1
Ludovic MAGNIN	20/4/79	Stuttgart (GER) /Zürich	D85	D							s81				62	3
Gökhan INLER	27/6/84	Udinese (ITA)	M		M	M	M	M	M61	M	M	M	M		39	3
Gelson FERNANDES	2/9/86	St-Étienne (FRA)	M	M68	M79		M		s75	s61	M88	M	M77	M46	27	2
Marco PADALINO	8/12/83	Sampdoria (ITA)	M83	M	M76		M			M64					8	1
Tranquillo BARNETTA	22/5/85	Leverkusen (GER)	M78	M	M76	M82	M	M60	s46	M76	s58	M92	s42	M	55	6
Alexander FREI	15/7/79	Basel	A67	A	A	A65	s70	A46		A	A75		A42	s69	77	40
Blaise NKUFO	25/5/75	Twente (NED)	A67	A81	A	A	A			A64	A68	A	A68	A69	34	7
Pirmin SCHWEGLER	9/3/87	Eintracht (GER)	s67						M	M46	s61				4	-
Marco STRELLER	18/6/81	Basel	s67					s46	A46						32	11
Hakan YAKIN	22/2/77	Luzern	s67	s68	s76	s65					s75	s79		s46	83	20
Johan VONLANTHEN	1/2/86	Zürich	s78	s81	s76	M65									40	7
Eren DERDIYOK	12/6/88	Leverkusen (GER)	s83	s61	s79	s65	A70	A46	A	s64	s68	A79	s68	A	24	2
Reto ZIEGLER	16/1/86	Sampdoria (ITA)	s85			s82			D	D46	D	D81	D	D	15	1
Alain NEF	6/2/82	Triestina (ITA)		D61											3	1
Steve VON BERGEN	10/6/83	Hertha (GER)			D	D	D	s46	s46	s46		s36	D	D	14	-
Benjamin HUGGEL	7/7/77	Basel			M	M	M	M61		M61	M	M	M	M78	41	2
Stephan LICHTSTEINER	16/1/84	Lazio (ITA)			D	D	D	D46	D	D	D	D	D	D	31	-
Christoph SPYCHER	30/3/78	Eintracht (GER)			D	D	D	s46							47	-
Marco WÖLFLI	22/8/82	Young Boys					G		G		s46				5	-
Heinz BARMETTLER	21/7/87	Zürich						D							1	-
Albert BUNJAKU	29/11/83	Nürnberg (GER)						s46	s46	s76		s77			4	-
David DEGEN	15/2/83	Young Boys						s60							10	-
Valon BEHRAMI	19/4/85	West Ham (ENG)						s61		M75		M58	M		28	2
Jonathan ROSSINI	5/4/89	Sassuolo (ITA)						D46							1	-
Xherdan SHAQIRI	10/10/91	Basel								M46	s64	s88		s78	4	-
Davide CHIUMIENTO	22/11/84	Luzern						s46							1	-
Mario EGGIMANN	24/1/81	Hannover (GER)											s92		9	-

 **SWITZERLAND**

DOMESTIC LEAGUE 2009/10

SUPER LEAGUE FINAL TABLE

			Home				Away				Total				
	Pld	W	D	L	F	A	W	D	L	F	A	W	D	L	F	A	Pts
1 FC Basel 1893	36	14	2	2	54	18	11	3	4	36	28	25	5	6	90	46	80
2 BSC Young Boys	36	15	2	1	41	13	10	0	8	37	34	25	2	9	78	47	77
3 Grasshopper-Club	36	14	1	3	42	13	7	1	10	23	30	21	2	13	65	43	65
4 FC Luzern	36	12	1	5	46	23	5	6	7	20	32	17	7	12	66	55	58
5 FC Sion	36	11	5	2	44	22	3	4	11	19	35	14	9	13	63	57	51
6 FC St Gallen	36	7	5	6	24	23	6	2	10	29	33	13	7	16	53	56	46
7 FC Zürich	36	9	4	5	31	20	3	5	10	24	38	12	9	15	55	58	45
8 Neuchâtel Xamax FC	36	8	4	6	35	27	3	4	11	20	30	11	8	17	55	57	41
9 AC Bellinzona	36	5	3	10	24	40	2	1	15	18	52	7	4	25	42	92	25
10 FC Aarau	36	4	2	12	18	41	2	3	13	14	47	6	5	25	32	88	23

TOP GOALSCORERS

30 Seydou DOUMBIA (Young Boys)
21 Marco STRELLER (Basel)
Cristian IANU (Luzern)
Émile MPENZA (Sion)
15 Alexander FREI (Basel)
14 Gonzalo ZÁRATE (Grasshoppers)
Moreno COSTANZO (St Gallen)
13 Scott CHIPPERFIELD (Basel)
12 Valentin STOCKER (Basel)
Ideye BROWN (Xamax)

CLUB-BY-CLUB

FC AARAU

Coach – Jeff Saibene (LUX); (12/10/09) Martin Andermatt;
(12/4/10) (Ranko Jakovljević (SRB)); (3/5/10) Alfred Strasser &
Ranko Jakovljević (SRB)
Founded – 1902
Stadium – Brügglifeld (9,250)
MAJOR HONOURS:
Swiss League - (3) 1912, 1914, 1993;
Swiss Cup - (1) 1985.

2009
11/7	Grasshoppers	h	1-0	*Burki*
19/7	Basel	a	1-2	*Bengondo*
26/7	Young Boys	h	0-3	
1/8	Bellinzona	a	1-4	*Bengondo*
8/8	Sion	a	1-1	*Stoll*
16/8	Xamax	h	0-4	
22/8	St Gallen	a	0-1	
29/8	Zürich	h	1-1	*Stojkov*
13/9	Luzern	h	2-4	*Burki, Stojkov (p)*
23/9	Grasshoppers	a	0-4	
26/9	Basel	h	0-2	
4/10	Young Boys	a	0-4	
24/10	Bellinzona	h	1-2	*Stojkov*
28/10	Sion	h	0-0	
1/11	Xamax	a	3-3	*Stojkov 3 (1p)*
7/11	St Gallen	h	0-2	
29/11	Zürich	a	0-2	
6/12	Luzern	a	0-6	

2010
7/2	Bellinzona	h	6-3	*Aquaro, Stoll, Bengondo, Lang,*
				Bastida, Mustafi
20/2	Basel	a	1-2	*Lang*
28/2	Luzern	h	1-2	*Stojkov*
7/3	St Gallen	a	2-2	*Burki, Mustafi*
10/3	Grasshoppers	a	0-2	
13/3	Zürich	h	1-3	*Stojkov*
21/3	Xamax	a	1-2	*Sinanovic*
24/3	Sion	h	0-3	
28/3	Young Boys	a	1-3	*Rapisarda*
3/4	Young Boys	h	1-5	*Lang*
10/4	Sion	a	0-4	
13/4	Xamax	h	1-0	*Lang*
17/4	Zürich	a	1-0	*Mustafi*
24/4	St Gallen	h	2-0	*Marazzi, Burki*

2/5	Luzern	a	0-4	
5/5	Basel	h	0-3	
13/5	Grasshoppers	h	1-4	*Mustafi*
16/5	Bellinzona	a	2-1	*Lang, Marazzi*

No	Name	Nat	DoB	Pos	Aps	(s)	Gls
20	Serghey ALEXEEV	MDA	31/5/86	A		(6)	
3	Giuseppe AQUARO	ITA	21/5/83	D	23		1
13	Sergio José BASTIDA	ARG	3/9/79	M	26	(3)	1
4	BAYKAL Kulakzisoğlu		12/5/83	M	15	(7)	
9	Patrick Alphonse BENGONDO	CMR	27/9/81	A	15	(6)	3
1	Ivan BENITO		27/8/76	G	34		
32	Loris BENITO	ESP	7/1/92	M	4	(3)	
6	Sandro BURKI		16/9/85	M	33		4
15	Jonas ELMER		28/2/88	D	29		
23	Artur IONIŢĂ	ROU	17/8/90	M	1	(7)	
19	Francis Adissa KIOYO	CMR	18/9/79	A	3	(4)	
20	Veli LAMPI	FIN	18/7/84	D	16		
10	Steven LANG		3/9/87	M	34	(1)	5
8	Toni Pekka LEHTINEN	FIN	5/5/84	A	1	(7)	
18	Joel MALL		5/4/91	G	2		
7	David MARAZZI		6/9/84	M	26	(6)	2
12	Mobulu MFUTI		28/8/81	M	7	(4)	
22	Orhan MUSTAFI		4/4/90	A	9	(10)	4
11	Ivan PEJČIĆ	SRB	11/9/82	M	7	(15)	
27	Michele POLVERINO	LIE	26/9/84	M	20	(7)	
21	Giuseppe RAPISARDA		6/9/85	D	18	(3)	1
5	Frédéric SCHAUB		30/4/87	D	6	(7)	
31	Emir SINANOVIC		24/10/88	M	13	(7)	1
17	Aco STOJKOV	MKD	29/4/83	A	23	(1)	8
16	Martin STOLL	GER	9/2/83	D	31		2
30	Sascha STUDER		3/9/91	G		(1)	
33	Skender ZEQIRI	SRB	25/5/90	A		(1)	

FC BASEL 1893

Coach – Thorsten Fink (GER)
Founded – 1893
Stadium – St Jakob-Park (38,500)
MAJOR HONOURS:
Swiss League - (13) 1953, 1967, 1969, 1970, 1972, 1973, 1977, 1980,
2002, 2004, 2005, 2008, 2010;
Swiss Cup - (10) 1933, 1947, 1963, 1967, 1975, 2002, 2003,
2007, 2008, 2010.

SWITZERLAND

2009

12/7	St Gallen	a	0-2	
19/7	Aarau	h	2-1	Stocker, Streller
26/7	Sion	a	2-1	Stocker, Frei
2/8	Luzern	h	1-1	Streller
9/8	Zürich	h	1-1	Huggel
16/8	Grasshoppers	a	1-3	Chipperfield
23/8	Xamax	a	2-2	Streller, Frei (p)
30/8	Young Boys	h	1-2	Frei
13/9	Bellinzona	a	3-2	Huggel 2 (1p), Stocker
23/9	St Gallen	h	4-0	Stocker, Streller 2, Frei
26/9	Aarau	a	2-0	Frei, Stocker
4/10	Sion	h	5-0	Streller 2, Frei, Chipperfield 2
25/10	Luzern	a	5-4	Huggel, Frei 2, Streller 2
28/10	Zürich	a	2-2	Huggel, Stocker
31/10	Grasshoppers	h	3-1	Huggel 2 (1p), Streller
9/11	Xamax	h	4-1	Chipperfield, Frei (p), Shaqiri, Streller
29/11	Young Boys	a	0-2	
6/12	Bellinzona	h	3-2	Frei 2, Cabral

2010

7/2	Young Boys	h	4-0	Frei (p), Streller, Gelabert, Safari
14/2	Xamax	a	3-1	Frei, Streller 2
20/2	Aarau	h	2-1	Huggel, Çağdaş
28/2	Bellinzona	a	2-0	Chipperfield, Streller (p)
6/3	Grasshoppers	h	1-2	Chipperfield
14/3	Luzern	a	1-0	Huggel
21/3	St Gallen	a	4-2	Antônio da Silva, Stocker, Chipperfield, og (Fernando)
24/3	Zürich	h	4-1	Streller 2 (1p), Chipperfield, Zoua
27/3	Sion	a	2-2	Streller 2
1/4	Sion	h	4-3	Almerares 2, Chipperfield, Shaqiri
11/4	Zürich	a	2-1	Shaqiri, Almerares
14/4	St Gallen	h	3-2	Huggel 2 (1p), Stocker
18/4	Luzern	h	5-0	Antônio da Silva, Shaqiri, Stocker 2, Carlitos
25/4	Grasshoppers	a	0-4	
2/5	Bellinzona	h	4-0	Streller 2, Chipperfield 2
5/5	Aarau	a	3-0	Chipperfield, Stocker, Zoua
13/5	Xamax	h	3-0	Gelabert, Frei 2
16/5	Young Boys	a	2-0	Stocker, Chipperfield

No	Name	Nat	DoB	Pos	Aps	(s)	Gls
19	David Ángel ABRAHAM	ARG	15/7/86	D	21		
15	Federico ALMERARES	ARG	2/5/85	A	8	(18)	3
25	ANTÔNIO DA SILVA	BRA	13/6/78	M	21	(4)	2
24	Adilson Tavares Varela "CABRAL"		22/10/88	D	10	(13)	1
4	ÇAĞDAŞ Atan	TUR	29/2/80	D	34		1
30	Carlos Alberto Alves "CARLITOS"	POR	6/9/82	M	15	(7)	1
11	Scott CHIPPERFIELD	AUS	30/12/75	M	24	(2)	13
23	Massimo COLOMBA		24/8/77	G	15	(1)	
1	Franco COSTANZO	ARG	5/9/80	G	20		
28	Beg FERATI		10/11/86	D	9	(8)	
13	Alexander FREI		15/7/79	A	17	(2)	15
6	Marcos Agustín GELABERT	ARG	16/9/81	M	16	(10)	2
8	Benjamin HUGGEL		7/7/77	M	32		11
22	Samuel INKOOM	GHA	22/8/89	D	26	(1)	
29	Orhan MUSTAFI		4/4/90	A		(1)	
10	Marko PEROVIĆ	SRB	11/1/84	M		(1)	
20	Behrang SAFARI	SWE	9/2/85	D	30	(2)	1
33	Serkan SAHIN		15/2/88	D	10	(1)	
7	Pascal SCHÜRPF		15/7/89	M		(6)	
17	Xherdan SHAQIRI		10/10/91	M	20	(12)	4
14	Valentin STOCKER		12/4/89	M	30	(1)	12
9	Marco STRELLER		18/6/81	A	29		21
26	Daniel UNAL		18/1/90	M		(2)	
18	Stefan WESSELS	GER	28/2/79	G	1		
32	Reto ZANNI		9/2/80	D	2	(6)	
31	Jacques ZOUA	CMR	6/9/91	A	6	(8)	2

AC BELLINZONA

Coach – Marco Schällibaum; (3/11/09) (Davide Belotti (ITA)); (12/11/09) Alberto Cavasin (ITA); (12/4/10) Roberto Morinini
Founded – 1904
Stadium – Stadio Comunale (6,000)
MAJOR HONOURS:
Swiss League – (1) 1948.

2009

12/7	Xamax	h	1-1	Ciarrocchi
19/7	Luzern	h	1-2	Conti
25/7	Zürich	a	1-4	Lustrinelli
1/8	Aarau	h	4-1	Gaspar, Lustrinelli 2, Conti
9/8	Young Boys	a	2-4	og (Wölfli), Ciarrocchi
15/8	St Gallen	a	1-1	Lustrinelli
23/8	Grasshoppers	h	0-0	
30/8	Sion	a	1-3	Lustrinelli
13/9	Basel	h	2-3	Ciarrocchi, Hima
24/9	Xamax	a	1-4	Hima
27/9	Luzern	a	0-2	
4/10	Zürich	h	3-2	Sermeter, Gashi, Lustrinelli (p)
24/10	Aarau	a	2-1	Lustrinelli 2
29/10	Young Boys	h	1-7	Sermeter
1/11	St Gallen	h	0-5	
7/11	Grasshoppers	a	0-7	
29/11	Sion	h	3-1	Hima, Lima, Ciarrocchi
6/12	Basel	a	2-3	Ciarrocchi, Lima

2010

7/2	Aarau	a	3-6	Edusei, Lima, Ciarrocchi
21/2	Luzern	a	1-2	Lima
28/2	Basel	h	0-2	
6/3	Sion	a	1-2	Diarra
10/3	St Gallen	h	0-2	
13/3	Xamax	h	3-2	Sermeter, Feltscher 2
21/3	Zürich	a	0-2	
25/3	Young Boys	h	1-3	Diarra
28/3	Grasshoppers	a	0-2	
1/4	Grasshoppers	h	1-2	Sermeter
10/4	Young Boys	a	1-2	Kasami
14/4	Zürich	h	1-4	Hima
17/4	Xamax	a	0-2	
25/4	Sion	h	2-1	Conti, Kalu
2/5	Basel	a	0-4	
6/5	Luzern	h	0-0	
13/5	St Gallen	a	2-1	Kasami, Feltscher
16/5	Aarau	h	1-2	Diarra

No	Name	Nat	DoB	Pos	Aps	(s)	Gls
27	Paolo CARBONE	ITA	13/7/82	D	3	(1)	
14	Maurizio CIARAMITARO	ITA	16/1/82	M	9	(2)	
32	Alessandro CIARROCCHI		3/1/88	A	23	(7)	6
10	Andrea CONTI	ITA	23/8/77	M	17	(8)	3
2	Aimo DIANA	ITA	2/1/78	D	14	(1)	
24	Drissa DIARRA	MLI	7/7/85	M	13	(2)	3
27	Igor DJURIC		30/8/88	D	3		
23	Mark EDUSEI	GHA	29/9/76	M	11		1
21	Frank FELTSCHER		17/5/88	M	20	(7)	3
11	Shkelzen GASHI		15/7/88	M	9	(4)	1
3	Odirlei de Souza GASPAR	BRA	18/5/81	A	4	(5)	1
1	Matteo GRITTI	ITA	11/6/80	G	18	(1)	
17	Yacine HIMA	ALG	25/3/84	M	23	(3)	4
33	Ikechukwu KALU	NGA	18/4/84	A	2	(4)	1
13	Pajtim KASAMI		2/6/92	M	9	(1)	2
25	Iacopo LA ROCCA	ITA	17/2/84	D	22	(3)	
26	Ildefons LIMA	AND	10/12/79	D	23	(1)	4
16	Mauro LUSTRINELLI		26/2/76	A	12	(6)	8
5	Alessandro MANGIARRATTI		15/9/78	D	25	(3)	
19	Genc MEHMETI		4/11/80	M	13	(9)	
34	Dragan MIHAJLOVIĆ	BIH	22/8/91	M		(4)	
2	Hemza MIHOUBI	ALG	13/1/86	D	6	(1)	
11	Igor MIJATOVIĆ	BIH	21/11/92	A		(2)	

7	Angelo RASO	ITA	20/7/81	D	16	(5)	
22	Manuel Garrido RIVERA	PER	16/3/78	M	9	(3)	
20	Fausto ROSSINI	ITA	2/3/78	A	4	(3)	
20	Andrea RUSSOTTO	ITA	25/5/88	M	6	(2)	
8	Gürkan SERMETER		14/2/74	M	15	(7)	4
4	Henry SIQUEIRA BARRAS		15/1/85	D	16	(5)	
6	Jérôme THIESSON		6/8/87	D	32	(2)	
15	Adewale Dauda WAHAB	NGA	4/10/84	M	1	(3)	
30	Carlo ZOTTI	ITA	3/9/82	G	18		

GRASSHOPPER-CLUB
Coach – Ciriaco Sforza
Founded – 1886
Stadium – Letzigrund (26,000)
MAJOR HONOURS:
Swiss League – (27) 1898, 1900, 1901, 1905, 1921, 1927, 1928, 1931, 1937, 1939, 1942, 1943, 1945, 1952, 1956, 1971, 1978, 1982, 1983, 1984, 1990, 1991, 1995, 1996, 1998, 2001, 2003;
Swiss Cup – (18) 1926, 1927, 1932, 1934, 1937, 1938, 1940, 1941, 1942, 1943, 1946, 1952, 1956, 1983, 1988, 1989, 1990, 1994.

2009
11/7	Aarau	a	0-1	
19/7	Sion	h	3-1	Callà, António, Ben Khalifa
26/7	Luzern	a	1-2	Vallori
2/8	Young Boys	a	0-2	
8/8	St Gallen	h	1-3	Schultz
16/8	Basel	h	3-1	António, Callà, Zárate
23/8	Bellinzona	a	0-0	
31/8	Xamax	h	1-3	Salatic
12/9	Zürich	a	3-4	Zárate 2, Ben Khalifa
23/9	Aarau	h	4-0	Zárate, Lulić, Salatic, Schultz
27/9	Sion	a	3-2	Smiljanic (p), Cabanas, Zárate
3/10	Luzern	h	0-0	
24/10	Young Boys	h	2-1	Callà, Smiljanic (p)
28/10	St Gallen	a	0-1	
31/10	Basel	h	1-3	Smiljanic
7/11	Bellinzona	h	7-0	Lulić 2, Zárate 2, Callà, Smiljanic 2 (2p)
28/11	Xamax	a	1-0	Zárate
5/12	Zürich	h	1-0	Cabanas

2010
7/2	Luzern	a	2-4	Callà, Cabanas
6/3	Basel	a	2-1	Colina, Cabanas
10/3	Aarau	h	2-0	Zárate, Zuber
14/3	St Gallen	h	2-1	Rennella, Smiljanic (p)
17/3	Sion	h	2-0	Ben Khalifa, Toko
20/3	Young Boys	a	0-4	
25/3	Xamax	h	2-1	Cabanas, Ben Khalifa
28/3	Bellinzona	h	2-0	Ben Khalifa, Zuber
1/4	Bellinzona	a	2-1	Ben Khalifa, Zárate
5/4	Zürich	a	2-3	Zuber, Cabanas
10/4	Xamax	a	1-0	Zárate
13/4	Young Boys	h	2-1	Zárate, Salatic
18/4	St Gallen	a	1-0	Cabanas
25/4	Basel	h	4-0	Zuber, Cabanas, Smiljanic (p), Zárate
1/5	Sion	a	0-1	
6/5	Zürich	h	4-0	Ben Khalifa, Cabanas, Steuble, Sabanović
13/5	Aarau	a	4-1	Zuber, Zárate, Ben Khalifa, Adili
16/5	Luzern	h	0-1	

No	Name	Nat	DoB	Pos	Aps	(s)	Gls
25	Endogan ADILI		3/8/94	M		(2)	1
30	Guilherme AFONSO		15/1/83	A	3	(4)	
30	ANTÓNIO Carlos dos Santos	BRA	3/10/79	M	6	(3)	2
19	Vullnet BASHI		11/7/90	M	4	(7)	
13	Nassim BEN KHALIFA		13/1/92	A	15	(10)	8
18	Lorenzo BUCCHI	ITA	21/11/83	G	3	(1)	

15	Ricardo CABANAS		17/1/79	M	23	(5)	9
10	Davide CALLÀ		6/10/84	M	21	(1)	5
5	Josip COLINA		8/11/80	D	16	(7)	1
32	Gianluca D'ANGELO		13/3/91	M	6	(7)	
24	Fabio DAPRELÀ		19/2/91	D		(1)	
29	Rolf FELTSCHER		6/10/90	D	13	(8)	
14	Izet HAJROVIC		4/8/91	M		(1)	
27	Bruce LALOMBONGO		29/4/90	M		(2)	
8	Senad LULIĆ	BIH	18/1/86	M	15		3
3	PAULO MENEZES	BRA	14/7/82	D	25	(1)	
11	Vincenzo RENNELLA	ITA	8/10/88	A	10	(1)	1
16	ROGÉRIO Luiz da Silva	BRA	12/6/80	A		(3)	
17	Enzo Daniel RUIZ	URU	31/8/88	D	6	(5)	
21	Samel SABANOVIĆ	SRB	23/12/83		1	(2)	1
35	Veroljub SALATIC		14/11/85	M	34		3
7	Alain SCHULTZ		17/2/83	M	12	(3)	2
21	Haris SEFEROVIC		22/2/92	A		(2)	
6	Boris SMILJANIC		28/9/76	D	29		7
1	Yann SOMMER		17/12/88	G	33		
23	Jeff STRASSER	LUX	5/10/74	M	3	(6)	
24	Martin STEUBLE		9/6/88	A	2	(6)	1
28	Nzuzi Bundebele TOKO	COD	20/12/90	M	14	(4)	1
4	Guillermo Juan VALLORI	ESP	25/6/82	D	26		1
2	Kay VOSER		4/1/87	D	28	(2)	
9	Gonzalo Eulogio ZÁRATE	ARG	6/8/84	A	35		14
31	Steven ZUBER		17/8/91	M	13	(7)	5

FC LUZERN
Coach – Rolf Fringer
Founded – 1901
Stadium – Gersag, Emmenbrücke (8,100)
MAJOR HONOURS:
Swiss League – (1) 1989;
Swiss Cup – (2) 1960, 1992.

2009
19/7	Bellinzona	a	2-1	Ianu, Renggli (p)
22/7	Sion	a	1-3	Ianu (p)
26/7	Grasshoppers	h	2-1	Yakin, Renggli (p)
2/8	Basel	a	1-1	Ianu
9/8	Xamax	h	2-1	Ferreira, Yakin
16/8	Young Boys	h	1-2	João Paiva
22/8	Zürich	a	0-4	
29/8	St Gallen	h	3-1	Yakin, Ianu, Kukeli
13/9	Aarau	a	4-2	Ferreira 2, João Paiva, Ianu
24/9	Sion	h	1-2	Ianu
27/9	Bellinzona	h	2-0	og (Mangiarratti), Lambert
3/10	Grasshoppers	a	0-0	
25/10	Basel	h	4-5	Chiumiento, Renggli (p), Yakin, Ianu
29/10	Xamax	a	1-1	João Paiva
1/11	Young Boys	a	1-1	Ianu
8/11	Zürich	h	1-0	Asamoah-Frimpong
28/11	St Gallen	a	1-1	Asamoah-Frimpong
6/12	Aarau	h	6-0	Tchouga, Asamoah-Frimpong 2, Chiumiento 2, Ianu

2010
7/2	Grasshoppers	h	4-2	Yakin 2, Chiumiento, Ianu
13/2	Young Boys	a	1-2	João Paiva
21/2	Bellinzona	h	2-1	Chiumiento 2 (1p)
28/2	Aarau	a	2-1	Yakin, Chiumiento
7/3	Zürich	a	0-1	
14/3	Basel	h	0-1	
20/3	Sion	a	2-5	Ianu, Yakin
24/3	St Gallen	h	2-3	Chiumiento (p), João Paiva
28/3	Xamax	a	2-1	Ianu 2
3/4	Xamax	h	2-1	Ianu 2
11/4	St Gallen	a	1-3	Ianu
14/4	Sion	h	1-1	Yakin
18/4	Basel	a	0-5	

24/4	Zürich	h	4-1	Renggli, Ianu, Yakin, Chiumiento
2/5	Aarau	h	4-0	Chiumiento 2 (1p), Ferreira, Ianu
6/5	Bellinzona	a	0-0	
13/5	Young Boys	h	5-1	Ferreira, Ianu 2, Kukeli, Siegrist
16/5	Grasshoppers	a	1-0	Ianu

No	Name	Nat	DoB	Pos	Aps	(s)	Gls
2	Joetex ASAMOAH-FRIMPONG	GHA	17/4/82	A	8	(3)	4
30	Silvan BÜCHLI		23/4/90	D	1	(1)	
8	David CHIUMIENTO		22/11/84	M	23	(1)	11
15	Boubacar DIARRA	MLI	15/7/79	D	7	(1)	
33	Lior ETTER		21/1/90	M	1	(14)	
21	Nélson FERREIRA	POR	26/5/82	M	24	(5)	5
16	Cristian Florin IANU	ROU	16/10/83	A	36		21
34	Sascha IMHOLZ		15/11/88	D		(1)	
14	JOÃO Pedro de Lemos PAIVA	POR	8/2/83	A	14	(17)	5
9	Benedikt KOLLER		5/3/90	M		(1)	
18	Swen KÖNIG		3/9/85	G	4		
22	Burim KUKELI	SRB	16/1/84	M	34		2
13	Christophe LAMBERT		23/2/87	D	1	(5)	1
3	Babatunde Adekunle LUKMON	NGA	10/10/84	D	10	(5)	
7	Claudio LUSTENBERGER		6/1/87	D	28		
28	Janko PACAR		18/8/90	A		(5)	
5	Michel RENGGLI		19/3/80	M	34	(1)	4
4	Roland SCHWEGLER		3/2/82	D	13	(3)	
6	Gerardo SEOANE		30/10/78	D	20		
25	Nico SIEGRIST		9/6/91	A	2	(16)	1
26	Dejan SORGIĆ	SRB	15/9/89	A		(5)	
20	Jean-Michel TCHOUGA	CMR	20/12/78	A	1	(3)	1
35	Marijan URTIĆ	CRO	16/1/91	D	2	(3)	
17	Dušan VEŠKOVAĆ	SRB	16/3/86	D	29	(2)	
24	Alain WISS		21/8/90	M	13	(12)	
10	Hakan YAKIN		22/2/77	M	28	(1)	10
1	David ZIBUNG		10/1/84	G	32		
19	Elsad ZVEROTIĆ	MNE	31/10/86	D	31		

NEUCHÂTEL XAMAX FC
Coach – Pierre-André Schürmann; (15/4/10) Jean-Michel Aeby
Founded – 1970
Stadium – La Maladière (11,977)
MAJOR HONOURS:
Swiss League - (2) 1987, 1988.

2009

12/7	Bellinzona	a	1-1	Gavranović
18/7	Zürich	h	3-0	Nuzzolo, Brown 2 (1p)
25/7	St Gallen	a	1-1	Gavranović
1/8	Sion	h	1-3	Brown
9/8	Luzern	a	1-2	Gavranović
16/8	Aarau	a	4-0	Brown 2, Gavranović, Aganović
23/8	Basel	h	2-2	Varela (p), Gavranović
31/8	Grasshoppers	a	3-1	Brown 2 (1p), Wüthrich (p)
13/9	Young Boys	h	3-0	Gavranović, Brown 2
24/9	Bellinzona	h	4-1	Aganović, Nuzzolo, Gavranović, Niasse
27/9	Zürich	a	2-1	Niasse, Brown
3/10	St Gallen	h	4-2	Nuzzolo, Besle, Binya, Wüthrich
25/10	Sion	a	0-1	
29/10	Luzern	h	1-1	Brown
1/11	Aarau	h	3-3	Varela (p), Besle, Gavranović
9/11	Basel	a	1-4	Brown
28/11	Grasshoppers	h	0-1	
6/12	Young Boys	a	0-1	
2010				
6/2	Zürich	a	0-0	
14/2	Basel	h	1-3	Nuzzolo
21/2	Sion	a	1-1	Dampha
28/2	St Gallen	h	0-3	
7/3	Young Boys	h	1-0	Nuzzolo
13/3	Bellinzona	a	2-3	Dampha, Kuljic

21/3	Aarau	h	2-1	Varela (p), Fatadi
25/3	Grasshoppers	a	1-2	Wüthrich
28/3	Luzern	h	1-2	og (König)
3/4	Luzern	a	1-2	Kuljic
10/4	Grasshoppers	h	0-1	
13/4	Aarau	a	0-1	
17/4	Bellinzona	h	2-0	Nuzzolo, Kuljic
25/4	Young Boys	a	1-4	Geiger
1/5	St Gallen	a	1-2	Nuzzolo
6/5	Sion	h	4-1	Kuljic 2 (1p), Gohou 2
13/5	Basel	a	0-3	
16/5	Zürich	h	3-3	Nuzzolo, Etoundi, Gashi

No	Name	Nat	DoB	Pos	Aps	(s)	Gls
11	Admir AGANOVIĆ	BIH	25/8/86	A	3	(17)	2
17	Thierno BAH		5/10/82	M	27	(5)	
4	Stéphane BESLE	FRA	23/1/84	D	31		2
8	Gilles Augustin BINYA	CMR	29/8/84	M	19		1
25	Ideye Aide BROWN	NGA	10/10/88	A	17		12
6	Abdou Rahman DAMPHA	GAM	27/12/91	M	9	(3)	2
21	William EDJENGUÉLÉ	FRA	7/5/87	D	14	(1)	
32	Franck ETOUNDI	CMR	30/8/90	A		(4)	1
3	Mickaël FACCHINETTI		15/2/91	D	2	(1)	
18	Guillaume FAIVRE		20/2/87	G	5	(1)	
16	Abdulla Baba FATADI	BHR	2/11/85	M	8	(9)	1
30	Luca FERRO	ITA	28/8/78	G	31		
10	Shkelzen GASHI		15/7/88	M	5	(7)	1
19	Mario GAVRANOVIĆ	CRO	24/11/89	A	16	(1)	8
33	Bastien GEIGER		26/2/85	D	7		1
9	Gérard Bi Goua GOHOU	CIV	29/12/88	A	6	(5)	2
23	Mike GOMES		19/9/88	D	1	(3)	
12	Selver HODZIC		12/10/78	D	8	(7)	
15	Abdullah Omar ISMAIL	BHR	1/1/87	D	31	(2)	
27	Sanel KULJIC	AUT	10/10/77	A	14	(3)	5
34	Freddy MVENG	CMR	29/5/92	M	2	(4)	
13	Baye Ibrahima NIASSE	SEN	18/4/88	M	8	(4)	2
14	Raphaël NUZZOLO		5/7/83	M	33	(1)	8
24	Frédéric PAGE		28/12/78	D	34		
29	Julio Hernán ROSSI	ARG	22/2/77	A		(5)	
10	Ifet TALJEVIĆ	GER	12/6/80	M		(5)	
5	Damien TIXIER	FRA	23/6/80	D	17	(2)	
7	Carlos VARELA	ESP	15/9/77	M	26		3
22	Sébastien WÜTHRICH		29/5/90	M	22	(7)	3

FC SION
Coach – Didier Tholot (FRA)
Founded – 1909
Stadium – Tourbillon (16,500)
MAJOR HONOURS:
Swiss League - (2) 1992, 1997;
Swiss Cup - (11) 1965, 1974, 1980, 1982, 1986, 1991, 1995, 1996, 1997, 2006, 2009.

2009

19/7	Grasshoppers	a	1-3	Obradović
22/7	Luzern	h	3-1	Dabo, Mpenza, Sarni
26/7	Basel	h	1-2	Mpenza
1/8	Xamax	a	3-1	Mpenza 2 (1p), Serey Die
8/8	Aarau	h	1-1	Fermino
15/8	Zürich	h	3-3	Marin, Obradović, Domínguez (p)
23/8	Young Boys	a	1-3	Adeshina
30/8	Bellinzona	h	3-1	Marin 2, Mpenza (p)
12/9	St Gallen	a	1-1	og (Koubský)
24/9	Luzern	a	2-1	Marin, Domínguez (p)
27/9	Grasshoppers	h	2-3	Mpenza 2
4/10	Basel	a	0-5	
25/10	Xamax	h	1-0	Sarni
28/10	Aarau	a	0-0	
31/10	Zürich	a	1-1	Chihab

SWITZERLAND

8/11	Young Boys	h	3-1	*Adeshina, Nwaneri, Domínguez*
29/11	Bellinzona	a	1-3	*Domínguez*
5/12	St Gallen	h	2-1	*Obradović, Mpenza*
2010				
6/2	St Gallen	a	0-1	
14/2	Zürich	h	1-1	*Vanczák*
21/2	Xamax	h	1-1	*Mpenza*
6/3	Bellinzona	h	2-1	*Bühler 2*
14/3	Young Boys	a	0-1	
17/3	Grasshoppers	a	0-2	
20/3	Luzern	h	5-2	*Mpenza 3, Domínguez, Chihab*
24/3	Aarau	a	3-0	*Yoda, og (Rapisarda), Mpenza*
27/3	Basel	h	2-2	*Marin, Mpenza*
1/4	Basel	a	3-4	*Bühler, Mpenza, Domínguez*
10/4	Aarau	h	4-0	*Vanczák, Mpenza, Domínguez (p), Bühler*
14/4	Luzern	a	1-1	*Zambrella*
18/4	Young Boys	h	4-1	*Mpenza, Obradović, Alioui, Domínguez*
25/4	Bellinzona	a	1-2	*Vanczák*
1/5	Grasshoppers	h	1-0	*Serey Die*
6/5	Xamax	a	1-4	*Mpenza*
13/5	Zürich	a	0-2	
16/5	St Gallen	h	5-1	*Mpenza 3 (1p), Bühler, Neurohr*

No	Name	Nat	DoB	Pos	Aps	(s)	Gls
33	ADAÍLTON José dos Santos Filho	BRA	16/4/83	D	9		
26	Joaquim ADÃO	ANG	14/7/92	M		(1)	
17	Saidu Alade ADESHINA	NGA	4/4/83	A	4	(12)	2
11	Guilherme AFONSO		15/11/85	A	2	(3)	
8	Jamal ALIOUI	MAR	2/6/82	D	29		1
29	ANTÓNIO Carlos dos Santos	BRA	3/10/79	M	1	(1)	
31	Arnaud BÜHLER		17/1/85	D	16	(3)	5
5	Tariq CHIHAB	MAR	22/11/75	D	15	(5)	2
10	Didier CRETTENAND		24/2/86	M	2	(9)	
27	Moustapha DABO	SEN	27/2/86	A	5	(3)	1
23	Álvaro José DOMÍNGUEZ	COL	10/6/81	M	28	(3)	8
16	Enes FERMINO		29/5/87	M	14	(7)	1
2	Guillermo Luis IMHOFF	ARG	11/1/82	D		(1)	
27	Léo LACROIX		27/2/92	D		(1)	
7	Nicolas MARIN	FRA	29/8/80	M	26	(1)	5
24	Mobulu M'FUTI	COD	28/8/81	A	2	(4)	
26	Aleksandar MITRESKI	MKD	5/8/80	M	17	(1)	
2	Yusuf MOHAMED	NGA	5/11/83	D	4	(2)	
25	Émile Lokonda MPENZA	BEL	4/7/78	A	27	(4)	21
28	Kevin NEUROHR		20/9/91	M	1		1
3	Obinna NWANERI	NGA	18/3/82	D	9	(2)	1
22	Goran OBRADOVIĆ	SRB	1/3/76	M	28		4
12	Mucuana Martinho PAÍTO	MOZ	5/7/82	D	23	(5)	
9	Aleksandar PRIJOVIĆ	SRB	21/4/90	M	1	(9)	
15	Bigambo ROCHAT		29/5/91	D	3	(1)	
4	Stéphane SARNI	ITA	31/8/80	D	8	(4)	2
32	Anthony SAUTHIER		5/2/91	M	9	(7)	
14	Sereso "SEREY" Geoffroy Gonzaroua DIE	CIV	7/11/84	M	28	(2)	2
20	Vilmos VANCZÁK	HUN	20/6/83	D	31		3
1	Andris VANINS	LVA	30/4/80	G	36		
21	Abdoul Karim YODA	FRA	25/10/88	M	10	(10)	1
19	Fabrizio ZAMBRELLA		1/3/86	M	8	(6)	1

FC ST GALLEN
Coach – Uli Forte
Founded – 1879
Stadium – AFG Arena (19,694)
MAJOR HONOURS:
Swiss League - (2) 1904, 2000;
Swiss Cup - (1) 1969.

2009				
12/7	Basel	h	2-0	*Frick, Costanzo*
18/7	Young Boys	a	1-1	*Costanzo*
22/7	Zürich	a	0-1	
25/7	Xamax	h	1-1	*Jagne*
8/8	Grasshoppers	a	3-1	*Merenda, Muntwiler, Costanzo*
15/8	Bellinzona	h	1-1	*Costanzo*
22/8	Aarau	h	1-0	*Jagne*
29/8	Luzern	a	1-3	*Frick*
12/9	Sion	h	1-1	*Hämmerli*
23/9	Basel	a	0-4	
26/9	Young Boys	h	2-3	*Abegglen, Zé Vítor (p)*
3/10	Xamax	a	2-4	*Costanzo 2 (1p)*
25/10	Zürich	h	1-3	*Abegglen*
28/10	Grasshoppers	h	1-0	*Frick*
1/11	Bellinzona	a	5-0	*Costanzo 2, Frei, Abegglen, Merenda*
7/11	Aarau	a	2-0	*Frick, Costanzo*
28/11	Luzern	h	1-1	*Nushi*
5/12	Sion	a	1-2	*Schenkel*
2010				
6/2	Sion	h	1-0	*Frei*
21/2	Young Boys	h	1-2	*Merenda*
28/2	Xamax	a	3-0	*Lang, Frei, Merenda*
7/3	Aarau	h	2-2	*Frei, Nushi*
10/3	Bellinzona	a	2-0	*Costanzo 2 (1p)*
14/3	Grasshoppers	a	1-2	*Costanzo*
21/3	Basel	h	2-4	*Imhof, Costanzo (p)*
24/3	Luzern	a	3-2	*Frei 2, Abegglen*
27/3	Zürich	h	1-0	*Merenda*
1/4	Zürich	a	1-1	*Merenda*
11/4	Luzern	h	3-1	*Abegglen 2, Merenda*
14/4	Basel	a	2-3	*Merenda, Costanzo*
18/4	Grasshoppers	h	0-1	
24/4	Aarau	a	0-2	
1/5	Xamax	a	2-1	*Winter, Jagne*
5/5	Young Boys	a	1-2	*Abegglen*
13/5	Bellinzona	h	1-2	*Merenda*
16/5	Sion	a	1-5	*Winter*

No	Name	Nat	DoB	Pos	Aps	(s)	Gls
26	Nico ABEGGLEN		16/2/90	A	17	(10)	7
18	Reto BOLLI		2/3/79	G	1		
11	Mario Antonio CÁCERES	CHI	17/3/81	A		(9)	
21	Diego CICCONE	ITA	21/7/87	M	2	(4)	
20	Moreno COSTANZO		20/2/88	M	33		14
3	FERNANDO César de Souza	BRA	12/9/80	D	32	(1)	
14	Fabian FREI		8/1/89	M	24	(6)	6
10	Mario FRICK	LIE	7/9/74	A	24	(3)	4
24	Marco HÄMMERLI		7/5/85	D	8	(8)	1
31	Daniel IMHOF	CAN	22/11/77	M	16		1
9	Pa Modou JAGNE	GAM	26/12/89	M	6	(15)	3
16	Thomas KNÖPFEL		9/11/83	M		(2)	
19	Jiří KOUBSKÝ	CZE	5/8/82	D	27	(1)	
6	Michael LANG		8/2/91	D	20	(2)	1
34	Sven LEHMANN		18/12/91	A		(1)	
1	Daniel LOPAR		19/4/85	G	21		
27	Ivan MARTIĆ	CRO	2/10/90	M		(1)	
22	Moreno MERENDA		17/5/78	A	16	(16)	9
15	Philipp MUNTWILER		25/2/87	M	10	(1)	1
7	Kristian NUSHI	SRB	31/7/82	M	32	(2)	2
2	Yves OEHRI	LIE	15/3/87	D		(2)	
13	Brice OWONA	CMR	4/3/89	A	3	(8)	
5	Lukas SCHENKEL		1/4/84	D	31		1
28	Manuel SUTTER	AUT	8/3/91	M		(1)	
30	Germano VAILATI		30/8/80	G	14		
25	Adrian WINTER		8/7/86	M	9	(9)	2
8	José "ZÉ" VÍTOR Jardim Vieira	POR	11/2/82	M	23	(2)	1
17	Marc ZELLWEGER		17/10/73	D	27	(2)	

BSC YOUNG BOYS

Coach – Vladimir Petković (BIH)
Founded – 1898
Stadium – Stade de Suisse (32,000)
MAJOR HONOURS:
Swiss League – (11) 1903, 1909, 1910, 1911, 1920, 1929, 1957,
1958, 1959, 1960, 1986;
Swiss Cup – (6) 1930, 1945, 1953, 1958, 1977, 1987.

2009

14/7	Zürich	a	3-2	*Yapi Yapo, Regazzoni, Doumbia (p)*
18/7	St Gallen	h	1-1	*Doumbia*
26/7	Aarau	a	3-0	*Doumbia 2, Degen*
2/8	Grasshoppers	h	2-0	*Doumbia (p), Yapi Yapo*
9/8	Bellinzona	h	4-2	*Doumbia (p), Schneuwly M. 2, Degen*
16/8	Luzern	a	2-1	*Ghezal, Degen*
23/8	Sion	h	3-1	*Schneuwly M., Schneuwly C., Yapi Yapo (p)*
30/8	Basel	a	2-1	*Doumbia, Schneuwly C.*
13/9	Xamax	a	0-3	
23/9	Zürich	h	3-0	*Schneuwly M., Doumbia, Degen*
26/9	St Gallen	a	3-2	*Regazzoni, Doumbia 2*
4/10	Aarau	h	4-0	*Ghezal, Doumbia 3*
24/10	Grasshoppers	a	1-2	*Degen*
29/10	Bellinzona	a	7-1	*Yapi Yapo (p), Doumbia 3, Degen, Sutter, Schneider*
1/11	Luzern	h	1-1	*Dudar*
8/11	Sion	a	1-3	*Coly*
29/11	Basel	h	2-0	*Doumbia, Schneuwly M.*
6/12	Xamax	h	1-0	*Regazzoni*

2010

7/2	Basel	a	0-4	
13/2	Luzern	h	2-1	*Doumbia 2*
21/2	St Gallen	a	2-1	*Regazzoni 2*
27/2	Zürich	h	2-1	*Regazzoni, Bienvenu*
7/3	Xamax	a	0-1	
14/3	Sion	h	1-0	*Lustrinelli*
20/3	Grasshoppers	h	4-0	*Doumbia 3, Bienvenu*
25/3	Bellinzona	a	3-1	*Doumbia 2, Yapi Yapo*
28/3	Aarau	h	3-1	*Schneuwly C., Doumbia 2*
3/4	Aarau	a	5-1	*Doumbia, Regazzoni (p), Raimondi, Hochstrasser 2*
10/4	Bellinzona	h	2-1	*Bienvenu, Affolter*
13/4	Grasshoppers	a	1-2	*Lustrinelli (p)*
18/4	Sion	h	1-4	*Raimondi*
25/4	Xamax	h	4-1	*Doumbia 2, Regazzoni, Hochstrasser*
2/5	Zürich	a	2-0	*Bienvenu, Hochstrasser*
5/5	St Gallen	h	2-1	*Lustrinelli, Bienvenu*
13/5	Luzern	a	1-5	*Doumbia*
16/5	Basel	h	0-2	

No	Name	Nat	DoB	Pos	Aps	(s)	Gls
20	François AFFOLTER		13/3/91	D	33	(1)	1
31	Joetex ASAMOAH-FRIMPONG	GHA	17/4/82	A		(4)	
15	Henri BIENVENU Ntsama	CMR	15/7/88	A	11	(4)	5
29	Matar COLY	SEN	10/11/84	A	2	(11)	1
13	Adriano DE PIERRO		11/1/91	D	4	(3)	
21	David DEGEN		15/2/83	M	28	(2)	6
11	Thierry DOUBAI	CIV	17/7/88	M	13	(7)	
7	Seydou DOUMBIA	CIV	31/12/87	A	29	(3)	30
5	Emiliano Ariel DUDAR	ARG	12/8/81	D	31		1
2	Saïf GHEZAL	TUN	30/6/81	D	16	(1)	2
9	Kaled GOURMI	FRA	18/4/86	A		(2)	
22	Xavier HOCHSTRASSER		1/7/88	M	34		4
3	Aron LIECHTI		15/2/86	D	2	(6)	
6	Hassan LINGANI	CIV	30/12/87	D	3		
35	Mauro LUSTRINELLI		26/2/76	A	5	(8)	3
34	Issam MERDASSI	TUN	16/3/81	D	16	(4)	

17	Giuseppe MORELLO	ITA	12/10/85	A		(1)	
25	Alexandre PASCHE		31/5/91	M	2	(8)	
16	Mario RAIMONDI		10/7/80	M	15	(4)	2
23	Alberto REGAZZONI		4/5/83	A	31	(2)	8
24	Marc SCHNEIDER		23/7/80	D	5	(11)	1
14	Christian SCHNEUWLY		7/2/88	M	11	(18)	3
26	Marco SCHNEUWLY		27/3/85	A	16		5
8	Scott SUTTER		13/5/86	M	26	(2)	1
27	Youssouf TRAORÉ	CIV	29/1/91	M		(2)	
1	Marco WÖLFLI		22/8/82	G	36		
10	Gilles YAPI YAPO	CIV	30/1/82	M	27	(3)	5

FC ZÜRICH

Coach – Bernard Challandes; (19/4/10) Urs Fischer
Founded – 1896
Stadium – Letzigrund (26,000)
MAJOR HONOURS:
Swiss League – (12) 1902, 1924, 1963, 1966, 1968, 1974, 1975, 1976,
1981, 2006, 2007, 2009;
Swiss Cup – (7) 1966, 1970, 1972, 1973, 1976, 2000, 2005.

2009

14/7	Young Boys	h	2-3	*Hassli, Rochat*
18/7	Xamax	a	0-3	
22/7	St Gallen	h	1-0	*Hassli*
25/7	Bellinzona	h	4-1	*Djuric, Rochat, Margairaz (p), Vasquez*
9/8	Basel	a	1-1	*Vonlanthen*
15/8	Sion	a	3-3	*Margairaz, Tihinen, Vonlanthen (p)*
22/8	Luzern	h	4-0	*Alphonse, Hassli, Vonlanthen, Djuric*
29/8	Aarau	a	1-1	*Stahel*
12/9	Grasshoppers	h	4-3	*Alphonse, Aegerter, Vonlanthen, Margairaz*
23/9	Young Boys	a	0-3	
27/9	Xamax	h	1-2	*Vonlanthen*
4/10	Bellinzona	a	2-3	*Schönbächler, Vonlanthen*
25/10	St Gallen	a	3-1	*Djuric, Margairaz, Vonlanthen*
28/10	Basel	h	2-2	*Tico, Gajić*
31/10	Sion	h	1-1	*Alphonse*
8/11	Luzern	a	0-1	
29/11	Aarau	h	2-0	*Djuric, Alphonse*
5/12	Grasshoppers	a	0-1	

2010

6/2	Xamax	h	0-0	
14/2	Sion	a	1-1	*Gajić (p)*
27/2	Young Boys	a	1-2	*Gajić*
7/3	Luzern	h	1-0	*Djuric*
13/3	Aarau	a	3-1	*og (Benito I.), Alphonse, Vonlanthen*
21/3	Bellinzona	h	2-0	*Alphonse, Djuric*
24/3	Basel	a	1-4	*Alphonse*
27/3	St Gallen	a	0-1	
1/4	St Gallen	h	1-1	*Vonlanthen*
5/4	Grasshoppers	h	3-2	*Margairaz (p), Buff, Mehmedi*
11/4	Basel	h	1-2	*Margairaz*
14/4	Bellinzona	a	4-1	*Aegerter, Djuric, Alphonse, Vonlanthen*
17/4	Aarau	h	0-1	
24/4	Luzern	a	1-4	*Djuric*
2/5	Young Boys	h	0-2	
6/5	Grasshoppers	a	0-4	
13/5	Sion	h	2-0	*Mehmedi, Schönbächler*
16/5	Xamax	a	3-3	*Margairaz, Schönbächler, Mehmedi*

No	Name	Nat	DoB	Pos	Aps	(s)	Gls
23	Almen ABDI		21/10/86	M	5	(3)	
7	Silvan AEGERTER		5/5/80	M	18	(1)	2

SWITZERLAND

12	Alexandre ALPHONSE	FRA	17/6/82	A	21	(6)	8
24	Ivan AUDINO		13/7/91	M		(1)	
21	Heinz BARMETTLER		21/7/87	D	18		
26	Martin BÜCHEL	LIE	19/2/87	M		(2)	
26	Oliver BUFF		3/8/92	M	6		1
17	Yassine CHIKHAOUI	TUN	22/9/86	M	6	(2)	
14	Dusan Predrag DJURIC	SWE	16/9/84	M	28	(2)	8
28	Josip DRMIĆ	CRO	8/8/92	A		(4)	
20	Milan GAJIĆ	SRB	17/11/86	M	19	(12)	3
32	Andrea GUATELLI	ITA	5/5/84	G	5		
29	Éric HASSLI	FRA	3/5/81	A	8	(5)	3
16	Philippe KOCH		8/2/91	D	25		
4	Raphael KOCH		20/1/90	D		(1)	
2	Veli LAMPI	FIN	18/7/84	D	10	(2)	
1	Johnny LEONI		30/6/84	G	31		
23	Ludovic MAGNIN		20/4/79	D	15		
5	Xavier MARGAIRAZ		7/1/84	M	25	(6)	7
25	Admir MEHMEDI		16/3/91	A	9	(13)	3
11	Adrian NIKCI		10/11/89	M	10	(11)	
19	Alain ROCHAT		1/2/83	D	30	(2)	2
3	Ricardo RODRIGUEZ		25/8/92	D	4	(2)	
27	Marco SCHÖNBÄCHLER		11/1/90	A	10	(11)	3
13	Florian STAHEL		10/3/85	D	21	(2)	1
10	Onyekachi Donatus Okonkwo "TICO"	NGA	13/5/82	M	26	(3)	1
30	Hannu TIHINEN	FIN	1/7/76	D	26	(1)	1
9	Andrés Javier VASQUEZ	SWE	16/7/87	M		(3)	1
8	Johan VONLANTHEN		1/2/86	M	20	(7)	10

PROMOTED CLUB

FC THUN
Coach – Murat Yakin
Founded – 1898
Stadium – Lachen (10,350)

SECOND LEVEL FINAL TABLE 2009/10

		Pld	W	D	L	F	A	Pts
1	FC Thun	30	18	6	6	70	36	60
2	FC Lugano	30	17	8	5	65	29	59
3	FC Winterthur	30	16	8	6	69	46	56
4	Servette FC	30	14	10	6	49	37	52
5	SC Kriens	30	12	10	8	50	41	46
6	FC Wil 1900	30	11	12	7	44	37	45
7	FC Biel-Bienne	30	10	12	8	54	39	42
8	FC Vaduz	30	11	8	11	44	43	41
9	Yverdon-Sport FC	30	10	9	11	50	38	39
10	FC Lausanne-Sport	30	9	12	9	40	43	39
11	FC Schaffhausen	30	10	9	11	42	51	39
12	FC Wohlen	30	8	7	15	44	55	31
13	FC Locarno	30	7	10	13	46	65	31
14	FC Stade Nyonnais	30	8	7	15	36	64	31
15	FC Le Mont	30	8	3	19	30	56	27
16	FC Gossau	30	2	7	21	27	80	13

PROMOTION/RELEGATION PLAY-OFFS

(21/5/10)
Bellinzona 2, Lugano 1
(24/5/10)
Lugano 0, Bellinzona 0
(Bellinzona 2-1)

DOMESTIC CUP 2009/10

SCHWEIZER CUP/COUPE DE SUISSE

FIRST ROUND

(17/9/09)
Serrières 2, Le Locle 1 *(aet)*

(18/9/09)
Langenthal 0, Biel/Bienne 3

(19/9/09)
Amicitia Riehen 0, Thun 4
Baden 1, Young Boys 3
Belp 0, Solothurn 7
Buochs 1, Kriens 6
Chênois 0, Servette 4
Chiasso 0, Grasshoppers 3
Colombier 1, Lausanne 5
Echallens 0, Sion 1
Frauenfeld 0, Winterthur 8
La Combe 0, Xamax 8
La Tour/Le Pâquier 1, Carouge 3
Laufen 2, Wohlen 3
Linth 2, Gossau 1
Losone 1, Bellinzona 4
Montlingen 0, Lugano 4
Münsingen 1, Aarau 3 *(aet)*
Muotathal 3, Dottikon 1
Regensdorf 1, Rapperswil 3
Schötz 2, Luzern 3
Thalwil 0, Wil 4 *(aet)*
Töss 3, Chur 0
Tuggen 1, Schaffhausen 1
Wängi 1, Locarno 3
Witikon 0, Zürich 10
Zollikofen 1, Härkingen 2

(20/9/09)
Cham 0, Basel 3
Echichens 0, Le Mont 6
Farvagny/Ogoz 0, Yverdon 3
Giubiasco 1, St Gallen 3 *(aet)*
Vernier 0, Nyon 7

SECOND ROUND

(17/10/09)
Carouge 0, Servette 3
Kriens 5, Bellinzona 4
Le Mont 1, Basel 3
Tuggen 1, Winterthur 3 *(aet)*
Xamax 2, Serrières 1
Zürich 7, Locarno 0

(18/10/09)
Biel/Bienne 3, Aarau 2 *(aet)*
Härkingen 1, Solothurn 3
Linth 1, Luzern 4
Lugano 1, Grasshoppers 0
Nyon 1, Lausanne 2
Rapperswil 4, Wohlen 1
St Gallen 2, Wil 1
Thun 2, Sion 1 *(aet)*
Yverdon 1, Young Boys 3

(24/10/09)
Muotathal 0, Töss 3

THIRD ROUND

(20/11/09)
Basel 4, Zürich 2

(21/11/09)
Rapperswil 3, Biel/Bienne 5 *(aet)*
Servette 1, St Gallen 2 *(aet)*
Töss 1, Luzern 2

(22/11/09)
Lugano 1, Lausanne 2
Solothurn 2, Kriens 4
Winterthur 2, Thun 4 *(aet)*
Xamax 0, Young Boys 1

QUARTER-FINALS

(10/12/09)
Luzern 1 *(Siegrist 49)*,
St Gallen 4 *(Frick 13, Lang 40, Jagne 43, Koubský 74)*

(12/12/09)
Basel 3 *(Frei 45, 60, Streller 69)*,
Biel/Bienne 1 *(Hediger 76)*

(13/12/09)
Kriens 2 *(Nogueira 5, Pacar 51)*,
Thun 1 *(Volina 90+1)*
Young Boys 1 *(Doumbia 22)*,
Lausanne 4 *(Rodrigo 17, 53, Sonnerat 33, Pimenta 90+5p)*

SEMI-FINALS

(5/4/10)
Kriens 0, Basel 1 *(Almerares 17)*

St Gallen 1 *(Zé Vítor 22)*,
Lausanne 2 *(Katz 40, Gaspar 79)*

FINAL

(9/5/10)
St Jakob-Park, Basel
FC BASEL 1893 6 *(Stocker 28, 75, Shaqiri 30, Zoua 46, Chipperfield 52, Huggel 89)*
FC LAUSANNE-SPORT 0
Referee – Kever
BASEL – Costanzo, Inkoom *(Zanni 54)*, Abraham, Ferati, Safari, Huggel, Zoua, Antônio da Silva, Shaqiri *(Almerares 79)*, Chipperfield *(Frei 67)*, Stocker.
LAUSANNE – Favre, Nelson *(Geiser 53)*, Buntschu, Meoli, Sonnerat, Ndzomo, Marazzi, Carrupt, Rodrigo, Pimenta *(Stadelmann 70)*, Gaspar *(Hélin 83)*.

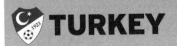

Bursaspor crack the Istanbul cartel

After an extraordinary last-day twist to the Süper Lig season, Bursaspor emerged as the shock champions of Turkey, becoming only the fifth club in history to claim the crown and only the second from outside Istanbul. They also became the fourth different title-winners in as many years.

The unheralded Anatolian outsiders did not go into the 2009/10 campaign with any realistic pretensions of challenging for a title that seemed promised, as ever, to one of the Big Three from the banks of the Bosporus – Fenerbahçe SK, Galatasaray AŞ and defending champions Beşiktaş JK. But with former Beşiktaş boss Ertuğrul Sağlam masterfully pulling the strings, Bursaspor not only held their own against the Istanbul giants but ended the season trumping all three of them.

Although the title race, distorted in part by Ankaraspor's early expulsion, ebbed and flowed for most of the campaign, as it drew to its conclusion only two teams remained in contention – Bursaspor and Fenerbahçe. A brilliant run of eight successive wins took Fener into their final fixture, at home to Trabzonspor, with a one-point lead over their provincial rivals. Everything was set up at a packed Şükrü Saracoğlu stadium for the club to celebrate a record-breaking 18th title. All Christoph Daum's team had to do was stretch their winning run to nine, and anything Bursaspor simultaneously managed at home to Beşiktaş would be inconsequential.

Extraordinary ending

An early goal from Fenerbahçe's Spanish international striker Daniel Güiza seemed to settle early nerves, but not long afterwards, for the first time in 11 league games, Fener conceded a goal – ironically from their old boy Burak Yılmaz. Bursaspor, meanwhile, went 2-0 up against Beşiktaş and were back in the driving seat. There was tension and excitement in both stadiums, especially when Beşiktaş pulled a goal back, but when news filtered through to the Şükrü Saracoğlu that

Beşiktaş had scored a second goal, the Fener players appeared to relax in the closing minutes and settle for the draw rather than push for a title-clinching winner. But the information was incorrect. Bursaspor still led 2-1, and that was how it finished. Fenerbahçe's 1-1 draw was no good. Chaos and disbelief in Istanbul contrasted with unfettered elation in Bursa, where the local team, known as the Crocodiles, had snatched the title from their rivals' grasp in the most extraordinary and unforgettable of circumstances.

The Süper Lig's new history-makers may have required that last-gasp slip-up from their rivals, but they were more than worthy champions. Operating on a budget less than a tenth of the size of Fenerbahçe's, they kept going from first kick to last, defying those – particularly in the Istanbul press - who confidently predicted that their challenge would unravel. Their winning total of 75 points was four more than 2008/09 champions Beşiktaş managed, and they were beaten just five times – only

Bursaspor coach Ertuğrul Sağlam savours his team's shock Süper Lig triumph

TURKEY

once by any of the Big Three, when Fenerbahçe claimed a 1-0 win in Bursa in September.

Bursaspor's 3-2 win over Fener in the reverse fixture five months later was the game in which the underdogs' title aspirations turned serious. Two goals down, they came back to win with two sensational late goals from their exciting young left-winger Ozan İpek. That was the first of six wins on the trot, and although they were halted in their tracks by a 2-1 defeat at İstanbul BB SK in late March, that was their only trip to the big city that yielded no points. Ertuğrul's return to the İnönü stadium, where he had begun the previous (double-winning) season as Beşiktaş's coach before being sacked, yielded three very welcome points in the final league game before Christmas, and although Bursaspor were held 0-0 at Galatasaray in late April, a result that enabled Fenerbahçe to replace them at the top, that precious point could ultimately be considered as the one that brought them the title.

Eclectic band

Although Bursaspor outscored every other team in the division, registering 65 goals, no individual managed more than eight. That was the final tally of both Ozan İpek and Argentine free-kick expert Pablo Batalla. Midfielder Turgay Bahadır struck seven times, and there were half a dozen goals from both Volkan Şen, another gifted winger of high promise, and veteran defender and captain Ömer Erdoğan. Even the goalkeeper chipped in. Not content with his excellent defensive record (28 goals conceded in 30 games), Bulgarian international Dimitar Ivankov also supplied four goals from the penalty spot to match the seasonal hauls of both 20-year-old starlet Sercan Yıldırım and Serbian midfielder Ivan Ergić, a new signing from FC Basel 1893. The post-season task for Ertuğrul was to keep this eclectic band together for

Türkiye Futbol Federasyönü (TFF)

İstinye Mahallesi
Darüssafaka Caddesi No. 45 Kat 2
Sarıyer
TR-34330 İstanbul
tel – +90 212 362 2222
fax – +90 212 323 4968
website – tff.org
email – intdept@tff.org
Year of Formation – 1923

President – Mahmut Özgener
General Secretary – Ahmet Güvener
Media Officer – Türker Tozar

INTERNATIONAL TOURNAMENT APPEARANCES
FIFA World Cup - (2) 1954, 2002 (3rd).
UEFA European Championship - (3) 1996, 2000 (qtr-finals), 2008 (semi-finals).
TOP FIVE ALL-TIME CAPS
Rüştü Reçber (119); Hakan Şükür (112); Bülent Korkmaz (102); Tugay Kerimoğlu (94); Alpay Özalan (90)
TOP FIVE ALL-TIME GOALS
Hakan Şükür (51); Tuncay Şanlı (22); Lefter Küçükandonyadis (21); Cemil Turan & Metin Oktay (19)

the UEFA Champions League, in which Bursaspor, as champions, would be making their debut at the group stage.

Runners-up Fenerbahçe, on the other hand, would be obliged to pre-qualify to join Bursaspor in Europe's blue riband event. What was so nearly a triumphant return to the Şükrü Saracoğlu for coach Daum, who had led Fener to back-to-back Turkish titles in 2004 and 2005, turned out very different. Not only did Trabzonspor deny his club the title on the final day with that 1-1 draw, they also, 11 days previously, prolonged Fener's Turkish Cup misery, defeating them 3-1 in the final of a competition they had not won for 27 years. Since taking the trophy in 1983, Fenerbahçe had now appeared in seven finals and lost the lot. Daum had been in charge for two of those, losing to

NATIONAL TEAM RESULTS 2009/10

12/8/09	Ukraine	A	Kyiv	3-0	*Tuncay (58), Servet (63), Hamit (65)*
5/9/09	Estonia (WCQ)	H	Kayseri	4-2	*Tuncay (28, 72), Sercan (37), Arda (62)*
9/9/09	Bosnia-Herzegovina (WCQ)	A	Zenica	1-1	*Emre Belözoğlu (4)*
10/10/09	Belgium (WCQ)	A	Brussels	0-2	
14/10/09	Armenia (WCQ)	H	Bursa	2-0	*Halil (16), Servet (28)*
3/3/10	Honduras	H	Istanbul	2-0	*Emre Güngör (41), Hamit (55)*
22/5/10	Czech Republic	N	Harrison (USA)	2-1	*Arda (31), Nihat (48)*
26/5/10	Northern Ireland	N	New Britain (USA)	2-0	*Sercan (48), Semih (72)*
29/5/10	United States	A	Philadelphia	1-2	*Arda (27)*

NATIONAL TEAM APPEARANCES 2009/10

			Ukr	EST	BIH	BEL	ARM	Hon	Cze	Nir	Usa	Caps	Goals
Coach: FATIH Terim	14/9/53												
/(15/10/09) (OĞUZ Çetin)	15/2/63												
VOLKAN Demirel	27/10/81	Fenerbahçe	G	G	G	G	G91	G	G		G	43	-
GÖKHAN Gönül	4/1/85	Fenerbahçe	D80	D	D	D	D					17	-
SERVET Çetin	17/3/81	Galatasaray	D	D	D	D	D	D	D	D	D	47	3
GÖKHAN Zan	7/9/81	Galatasaray	D	D36					s9/65		D	33	-
HAKAN Balta	23/3/83	Galatasaray	D	D	D	D						24	1
HAMİT Altıntop	8/12/82	Bayern (GER)	M	M	M46	M	M83	M		M46	M73	56	4
NURİ Şahin	5/9/88	Dortmund (GER)	M82				M		s76	M46		22	1
ARDA Turan	30/1/87	Galatasaray	M86	M	M		M	M61	M82	s66	M	39	7
AYHAN Akman	23/2/77	Galatasaray	M46			M61	M					22	-
NİHAT Kahveci	23/11/79	Beşiktaş	A46				A71		A57		s78	66	18
TUNCAY Şanlı	16/1/82	Middlesbrough (ENG)/Stoke (ENG)	A68	A	A	A	A46	s46		A	A78	75	22
CEYHUN Gülselam	25/12/87	Trabzonspor	s46	s78	M			D33*				6	-
SERCAN Yıldırım	5/4/90	Bursaspor	s46	A	s46					s46	s62	7	2
KAZIM Kazım	26/8/86	Fenerbahçe/Toulouse (FRA)	s68	M61		s61	s83	s84	s46	A62	A62	25	-
SABRİ Sarıoğlu	26/7/84	Galatasaray	s80					D84	D	D	D	32	1
HALİL Altıntop	8/12/82	Schalke (GER)/Eintracht (GER)	s82	s61			A	s46	A46			34	8
İSMAİL Köybaşı	10/7/89	Beşiktaş	s86		s46			D				3	-
EMRE Belözoğlu	7/9/80	Fenerbahçe	M78	M			M	M76	M	s66	M	69	6
ÖNDER Turacı	14/7/81	Fenerbahçe			s36	D46	D					4	-
SEMİH Şentürk	29/4/83	Fenerbahçe				A	s46		s46	s62	s73	22	7
CEYHUN Eriş	15/5/77	Ankaragücü						M46				1	-
YUSUF Şimşek	20/7/75	Beşiktaş						s71				6	-
İBRAHİM Kaş	20/9/86	Beşiktaş							s46			7	-
RÜŞTÜ Reçber	10/5/73	Beşiktaş							s91			119	-
EMRE Güngör	1/8/84	Galatasaray						D	s65			4	1
CANER Erkin	4/10/88	Galatasaray							D		D	8	-
VOLKAN Şen	7/7/87	Bursaspor						M46	s9/46			2	-
MEHMET AURÉLIO	15/12/77	Betis (ESP)						M80				32	2
MEVLÜT Erdinç	25/2/87	PSG (FRA)						A46				12	1
OZAN İpek	10/10/86	Bursaspor						s61		M66		2	-
NECİP Uysal	24/1/91	Beşiktaş						s80				1	-
EMRE Aşık	13/12/73	Galatasaray							D9			34	2
ÇAĞLAR Birinci	2/10/85	Denizlispor							D		D	3	-
OKAN Buruk	19/10/73	İstanbul BB							M9			55	8
SELÇUK Şahin	31/1/81	Fenerbahçe							M77			18	-
TURGAY Bahadır	15/1/84	Bursaspor							s57			1	-
SELÇUK İnan	10/2/85	Trabzonspor							s77	M66	M53	5	-
MEHMET Topal	3/3/86	Galatasaray							s82	s46	s53	16	-
ONUR Kıvrak	1/1/88	Trabzonspor									G	1	-
İBRAHİM Toraman	20/11/81	Beşiktaş									D	29	1

Galatasaray in 2005 and Beşiktaş in 2006, and his unwanted hat-trick was complete as Trabzonspor came from behind to win the trophy for the eighth time.

Trabzonspor's victorious coach was Şenol Güneş, who had also been involved in three of those previous Cup wins – as the team's goalkeeper in 1977, 1978 and 1984 and as coach during the second of his four spells in charge of the Black Sea outfit, in 1995. He was re-installed at his hometown club in December 2009 as a replacement for Belgian coach Hugo Broos, having returned from a three-year stint in South Korea, the country in which he led the Turkish national team to third place at the 2002 FIFA World Cup.

Istanbul eclipsed

While Trabzonspor and Bursaspor carried Turkish football's two main pieces of silverware into the provinces, Istanbul's finest were left to reflect on a season of collective disappointment. It had been over a quarter of a century since the last time both trophies had left the city – when Trabzonspor did the double in 1983/84 – and while Fenerbahçe did at least give their supporters a sniff of victory in both competitions, there was little to savour for the fans of both Galatasaray and Beşiktaş.

Gala went into the season full of ambition and confidence having signed up ex-FC Barcelona boss Frank Rijkaard. Several new players were also brought in at some cost – both in the summer and winter – but after a wonderful start, which produced six straight wins and 20 goals, injuries to key players, such as ex-Liverpool FC duo Milan Baroš and Harry Kewell, began to stall the team's momentum. By February the prospects of a successful debut season for the Dutchman still looked bright, but elimination from the Turkish Cup was followed by a harrowing exit from the UEFA Europa League at the hands of Club Atlético de Madrid, and thereafter the team's form began to slide also in the Süper Lig, a 1-0 home defeat by Fenerbahçe at the end of March effectively extinguishing their last hopes of a trophy.

On an individual level, Fenerbahçe's Emre Belözoğlu and Galatasaray's Arda Turan both enjoyed impressive campaigns, but at Beşiktaş standout performers were few and far between. Resident goalgrabber Bobô managed a dozen goals, but they all came in singles and he received little support from a group of players who had excelled in winning the double the previous season. Coach Mustafa Denizli resigned at the end of a

Emre Belözoğlu enjoyed an excellent season with Fenerbahçe

campaign in which the club's only notable highlight was a 1-0 victory over Manchester United FC at Old Trafford – a complete contrast to their previous UEFA Champions League visit to north-west England, when Liverpool hammered them 8-0. His replacement was Bernd Schuster, out of work since his dismissal from Real Madrid CF in December 2008.

Hiddink takes over

With high-profile foreign coaches the vogue in Istanbul, the Turkish Football Federation (TFF) followed suit by signing up Guus Hiddink to take charge of the national team for the UEFA EURO 2012 qualifying campaign. Hiddink's recent credentials matched those of the man he replaced, Fatih Terim, the two of them having led teams to the semi-finals of UEFA EURO 2008 but not to the 2010 World Cup in South Africa. Whereas Hiddink's Russia stumbled in the play-offs, Terim's Turkey did not even make it that far, finishing third in their qualifying section behind Spain and Bosnia-Herzegovina – an outcome that prompted the coach's resignation. Hiddink will once again be doing battle with Germany – the team that topped Russia's World Cup qualifying group – but if that makes automatic qualification unlikely, a man of his calibre will be fully expected to lead his new charges into the play-offs ahead of Austria, Belgium, Kazakhstan and Azerbaijan.

DOMESTIC LEAGUE 2009/10

SÜPER LİG FINAL TABLE

	Pld	Home W	D	L	F	A	Away W	D	L	F	A	Total W	D	L	F	A	Pts
1 Bursaspor	34	14	1	2	37	9	9	5	3	28	17	23	6	5	65	26	75
2 Fenerbahçe SK	34	13	2	2	33	13	10	3	4	28	15	23	5	6	61	28	74
3 Galatasaray AŞ	34	11	4	2	37	13	8	3	6	24	22	19	7	8	61	35	64
4 Beşiktaş JK	34	10	5	2	28	11	8	5	4	19	14	18	10	6	47	25	64
5 Trabzonspor	34	11	3	3	29	12	5	6	6	24	20	16	9	9	53	32	57
6 İstanbul BB SK	34	9	4	4	24	20	7	4	6	23	24	16	8	10	47	44	56
7 Eskişehirspor	34	11	4	2	24	11	4	6	7	20	23	15	10	9	44	34	55
8 Kayserispor	34	6	7	4	25	14	8	2	7	20	23	14	9	11	45	37	51
9 Antalyaspor	34	9	3	5	29	15	5	4	8	20	23	14	7	13	49	38	49
10 Gençlerbirliği SK	34	6	7	4	18	14	6	4	7	20	21	12	11	11	38	35	47
11 Kasımpaşa SK	34	7	5	5	29	25	3	6	8	21	28	10	11	13	50	53	41
12 MKE Ankaragücü	34	6	8	3	24	16	3	6	8	15	24	9	14	11	39	40	41
13 Gaziantepspor	34	6	6	5	23	20	3	7	7	15	19	9	13	12	38	39	40
14 Manisaspor	34	5	7	5	15	15	3	6	8	12	19	8	13	13	27	34	37
15 Sivasspor	34	6	3	8	23	26	2	7	8	19	33	8	10	16	42	59	34
16 Diyarbakırspor	34	3	4	10	16	31	3	5	9	12	23	6	9	19	28	54	27
17 Denizlispor	34	4	7	6	17	17	2	1	14	13	32	6	8	20	30	49	26
18 Ankaraspor	34	0	0	17	0	51	0	0	17	0	51	0	0	34	0	102	0

NB Ankaraspor expelled after round 4; all of their matches awarded as 0-3 defeats.

TOP GOALSCORERS

21 Ariza MAKUKULA (Kayserispor)
13 JÚLIO CÉSAR (I) (Gaziantepspor)
12 NECATİ Ateş (Antalyaspor)
   BOBÔ (Beşiktaş)
11 ALEX (Fenerbahçe)
   Daniel GÜIZA (Fenerbahçe)
   Milan BAROŠ (Galatasaray)
   MUSTAFA Pektemek (Gençlerbirliği)
   UMUT Bulut (Trabzonspor)
10 İSKENDER Alın (İstanbul BB)

CLUB-BY-CLUB

MKE ANKARAGÜCÜ

Coach - Hikmet Karaman; (17/11/09) Nazmi Erdenerin;
(5/1/10) Roger Lemerre (FRA)
Founded - 1910
Stadium - 19 Mayıs (19,125)
MAJOR HONOURS:
Turkish Cup - (2) 1972, 1981.

2009

8/8	Diyarbakırspor	a	2-2 *Ceyhun 2*
15/8	Manisaspor	h	1-1 *Vassell*
22/8	Bursaspor	a	0-1
29/8	İstanbul BB	h	2-2 *Emre, Vassell*
13/9	Antalyaspor	a	0-1
19/9	Gençlerbirliği	h	1-2 *Barbaros*
26/9	Gaziantepspor	a	3-1 *Metin 2, Emre*
4/10	Galatasaray	h	3-0 *Murat, Emre, Hürriyet*
18/10	Kayserispor	a	0-3
25/10	Ankaraspor	h	3-0 *(w/o)*
31/10	Beşiktaş	a	0-1
8/11	Kasımpaşa	h	2-2 *Koray, Méyé*
22/11	Eskişehirspor	a	0-0
29/11	Denizlispor	h	1-0 *Baki*
6/12	Trabzonspor	a	0-3
12/12	Fenerbahçe	a	2-3 *Vassell, Aydın*
19/12	Sivasspor	h	2-3 *Metin 2*

2010

24/1	Diyarbakırspor	h	0-0
31/1	Manisaspor	a	0-0
7/2	Bursaspor	h	0-0
14/2	İstanbul BB	a	1-1 *Vittek*
21/2	Antalyaspor	h	2-2 *Rajnoch, Muhammet Hanifi*
28/2	Gençlerbirliği	a	1-0 *Vassell*
7/3	Gaziantepspor	h	0-0
14/3	Galatasaray	a	0-3
21/3	Kayserispor	h	3-0 *Geremi (p), Vittek 2*
28/3	Ankaraspor	a	3-0 *(w/o)*
2/4	Beşiktaş	h	0-0
11/4	Kasımpaşa	a	0-2
18/4	Eskişehirspor	h	3-1 *Vittek, Sapara, Geremi (p)*
24/4	Denizlispor	a	0-0
1/5	Trabzonspor	h	1-0 *Vittek*
9/5	Fenerbahçe	h	0-3
15/5	Sivasspor	a	3-3 *İlhan 2, Mehmet*

No	Name	Nat	DoB	Pos	Aps	(s)	Gls
21	ABDULLAH Çetin		18/3/84	M	1		
12	ADEM Koçak		1/9/83	M	9	(6)	
88	AYDIN Karabulut		25/1/88	M	6	(1)	1
15	BAKİ Mercimek		17/9/82	D	5		1
23	BARBAROS Barut		26/1/83	M	9	(2)	1
99	Gustave BEBBE	CMR	22/6/82	A	1	(3)	
26	BİLAL Kısa		22/6/83	M	2	(6)	
35	BORA Körk		9/6/80	G	1		
32	Erich BRABEC	CZE	24/2/77	D	3		
19	Ariel Esteban BROGGI	ARG	15/1/83	D	21		
14	CEYHUN Eriş		15/5/77	M	10		2
46	CIHAN Haspolatlı		4/1/80	M	12	(3)	
29	DIEGO Laiber PADILHA	BRA	9/12/84	D	2		
6	EDİZ Bahtiyaroğlu		2/1/86	D	13	(1)	

TURKEY

No	Name	Nat	DoB	Pos	Aps	(s)	Gls
3	ELYASA Süme		13/8/83	D	21		
30	EMRE Aygün		1/6/85	A	1	(9)	3
75	GEREMI Njitap	CMR	20/12/78	M	12		2
9	Ian HENDERSON	ENG	24/1/85	A	1	(2)	
50	HÜRRİYET Güçer		25/10/81	M	25	(1)	1
7	Leonardo Andrés IGLESIAS	ARG	28/8/79	A	2	(2)	
87	İLHAN Parlak		18/1/87	A	3	(5)	2
39	İLKEM Özkaynak		1/5/82	M	2	(1)	
27	KAAN Kanak		6/10/90	M	1		
40	KAĞAN Söylemezgiller		4/3/88	M	6	(5)	
82	Madiou KONATE	SEN	12/1/82	A	1	(4)	
4	KORAY Çölgeçen		28/5/85	D	14	(1)	1
2	LUIZ HENRIQUE de Souza dos Santos	BRA	23/9/82	D	2		
77	MEHMET Çakır		4/1/84	A	16	(6)	1
10	METİN Akan		28/5/83	A	6	(8)	4
21	Roguy MÉYÉ	GAB	7/10/86	A	7	(1)	1
66	MUHAMMET HANİFİ Yoldaş		20/4/83	D	9		1
11	MURAT Duruer		15/1/88	M	7	(10)	1
60	ÖZGÜR Çek		3/1/91	M	1		
81	Jan RAJNOCH	CZE	30/9/81	D	13		1
33	Fredrik RISP	SWE	15/12/80	D	4		
25	Jérôme ROTHEN	FRA	31/3/78	M	12		
72	Marek SAPARA	SVK	31/7/82	M	13		1
5	SEMAVİ Özgür		6/2/82	M	8	(1)	
34	Štefan SENECKÝ	SVK	6/1/80	G	6		
1	SERKAN Kırıntılı		15/2/85	G	25		
24	Calvin SOSIBO	RSA	15/3/85	D	3		
8	UFUK Bayraktar		1/1/86	M	1	(3)	
28	UMUT Sözen		27/1/90	A		(3)	
13	Darius VASSELL	ENG	13/6/80	A	18	(4)	4
41	Róbert VITTEK	SVK	1/4/82	A	12		5
18	VOLKAN Arslan		29/8/78	M		(4)	
80	Theo Lewis WEEKS	LBR	19/1/90	M	5	(2)	

ANKARASPOR

Coach - Jürgen Röber (GER)
Founded - 1978
Stadium - Yenikent ASAŞ (25,000)

2009

8/8	Antalyaspor	a	0-3	(w/o; original result 1-0 Murat)
16/8	Gençlerbirliği	h	0-3	(w/o; original result 1-1 Méyé)
23/8	Gaziantepspor	a	0-3	(w/o; original result 1-1 Brabec)
31/8	Galatasaray	h	0-3	(w/o; original result 0-2)
12/9	Kayserispor	a	0-3	(w/o)
19/9	Denizlispor	h	0-3	(w/o)
25/9	Beşiktaş	a	0-3	(w/o)
4/10	Kasımpaşa	a	0-3	(w/o)
18/10	Eskişehirspor	h	0-3	(w/o)
25/10	Ankaragücü	h	0-3	(w/o)
1/11	Trabzonspor	h	0-3	(w/o)
8/11	Fenerbahçe	a	0-3	(w/o)
22/11	Sivasspor	h	0-3	(w/o)
29/11	Diyarbakırspor	a	0-3	(w/o)
6/12	Manisaspor	h	0-3	(w/o)
13/12	Bursaspor	a	0-3	(w/o)
19/12	İstanbul BB	h	0-3	(w/o)

2010

24/1	Antalyaspor	h	0-3	(w/o)
31/1	Gençlerbirliği	a	0-3	(w/o)
7/2	Gaziantepspor	h	0-3	(w/o)
14/2	Galatasaray	a	0-3	(w/o)
21/2	Kayserispor	h	0-3	(w/o)
28/2	Denizlispor	a	0-3	(w/o)
7/3	Beşiktaş	h	0-3	(w/o)
14/3	Kasımpaşa	h	0-3	(w/o)
21/3	Eskişehirspor	a	0-3	(w/o)
28/3	Ankaragücü	h	0-3	(w/o)
4/4	Trabzonspor	a	0-3	(w/o)
11/4	Fenerbahçe	h	0-3	(w/o)
18/4	Sivasspor	a	0-3	(w/o)
25/4	Diyarbakırspor	h	0-3	(w/o)
2/5	Manisaspor	a	0-3	(w/o)
9/5	Bursaspor	h	0-3	(w/o)
16/5	İstanbul BB	a	0-3	(w/o)

No	Name	Nat	DoB	Pos	Aps	(s)	Gls
66	ADEM Koçak		1/9/83	M	4		
20	AYDIN Karabulut		25/1/88	M	4		
6	BAKİ Mercimek		17/9/82	D	2		
19	BİLAL Kısa		22/6/83	M	2		
3	Erich BRABEC	CZE	24/2/77	D	4		1
5	EDİZ Bahtiyaroğlu		2/1/86	D	2		
50	HÜRRİYET Güçer		25/10/81	M	4		
17	İLHAN Parlak		18/1/87	A	3	(1)	
9	Madiou KONATE	SEN	12/1/82	A		(3)	
11	MEHMET Çakır		4/1/84	A	2	(1)	
21	Roguy MÉYÉ	GAB	7/10/86	A	1	(3)	1
7	MURAT Tosun		26/2/84	A	2	(1)	1
99	João Alexandre Duarte Ferreira Fernandes "NECA"	POR	31/12/79	M	2	(2)	
41	ÖMER Barış		23/7/82	D	3		
60	ÖZGÜR Çek		3/1/91	M	1		
1	Štefan SENECKÝ	SVK	6/1/80	G	4		
10	Sidney Cristiano dos Santos "TITA"	BRA	20/7/81	A	4		

ANTALYASPOR

Coach - Mehmet Özdilek
Founded - 1966
Stadium - Atatürk (10,000)

2009

8/8	Ankaraspor	h	3-0	(w/o; original result 0-1)
17/8	Beşiktaş	a	0-2	
23/8	Kasımpaşa	h	2-0	Jedinak, Veysel
29/8	Eskişehirspor	a	1-2	Kerim
13/9	Ankaragücü	a	1-0	Necati
18/9	Trabzonspor	a	1-3	Orhan
26/9	Fenerbahçe	h	1-2	Zitouni
4/10	Sivasspor	a	0-2	
18/10	Diyarbakırspor	h	4-1	Jedinak, Necati, Hakan, Ahmet
25/10	Manisaspor	a	2-1	Zitouni, Necati (p)
31/10	Bursaspor	h	1-1	Djiehoua
7/11	İstanbul BB	a	0-1	
22/11	Denizlispor	a	1-1	Yalçın
29/11	Gençlerbirliği	h	2-0	Jedinak 2
6/12	Gaziantepspor	a	1-1	Zitouni
11/12	Galatasaray	h	2-3	Orhan, Jedinak
19/12	Kayserispor	a	2-1	Korhan, og (Makukula)

2010

24/1	Ankaraspor	a	3-0	(w/o)
29/1	Beşiktaş	h	0-1	
7/2	Kasımpaşa	a	2-2	Veysel, Necati (p)
14/2	Eskişehirspor	h	1-2	Veysel
21/2	Ankaragücü	a	2-2	Veysel 2
26/2	Trabzonspor	h	1-1	Necati
7/3	Fenerbahçe	a	0-1	
14/3	Sivasspor	h	3-0	Necati, Veysel, Djiehoua
20/3	Diyarbakırspor	a	0-1	
28/3	Manisaspor	h	0-0	
3/4	Bursaspor	a	1-2	Necati
10/4	İstanbul BB	h	1-3	Yalçın
18/4	Denizlispor	h	2-1	Necati, Djiehoua
24/4	Gençlerbirliği	a	2-0	Necati, Veysel
2/5	Gaziantepspor	h	1-0	Necati
8/5	Galatasaray	a	2-1	Tita, Veysel
15/5	Kayserispor	h	4-0	Tita, Necati 2, Veysel

No	Name	Nat	DoB	Pos	Aps	(s)	Gls
23	AHMET Kuru		23/4/82	A	1	(4)	1
7	Pini BALILI	ISR	18/6/79	A	4	(11)	
77	Radoslav BATAK	MNE	15/8/77	D	12	(2)	
28	Serge DJIEHOUA	CIV	25/9/81	A	12	(7)	3
44	ERHAN Güven		15/5/82	D	14		
58	ERTUĞRUL Arslan		26/1/80	M	22	(6)	
81	FATİH Ceylan		25/11/80	M	4	(6)	
32	GÜRHAN Gürsoy		24/9/87	M		(8)	
8	HAKAN Özmert		3/6/85	M	7	(9)	1
21	Mile JEDINAK	AUS	3/8/84	M	28		5
17	KERİM Zengin		13/4/85	M	17	(2)	1
87	KORHAN Öztürk		28/6/81	M	14	(15)	1
6	MUSA Nizam		8/9/90	D	7	(2)	
10	NECATİ Ateş		3/1/80	A	29		12
5	ORHAN Ak		29/9/79	D	23		2
1	ÖMER Çatkıç		15/10/74	G	31		
18	POLAT Keser		4/12/85	G	2		
15	SEDAT Ağçay		22/9/81	M	24	(6)	
3	ŞENOL Can		3/4/83	D	22	(2)	
86	Sidney Cristiano dos Santos "TITA"	BRA	20/7/81	A	20		2
50	VEYSEL Cihan		4/2/76	A	18	(8)	9
22	VOLKAN Altın		10/8/86	D		(3)	
2	YALÇIN Ayhan		1/5/82	D	29		2
11	Ali ZITOUNI	TUN	11/1/81	A	23	(3)	3

BEŞİKTAŞ JK
Coach - Mustafa Denizli
Founded - 1903
Stadium - İnönü (32,086)
MAJOR HONOURS:
Turkish League- (13) 1957, 1958, 1960, 1966, 1967, 1982, 1986, 1990, 1991, 1992, 1995, 2003, 2009;
Turkish Cup - (8) 1975, 1989, 1990, 1994, 1998, 2006, 2007, 2009.

2009
7/8	İstanbul BB	a	1-1	*Fink*
17/8	Antalyaspor	h	2-0	*Hološko, Tello*
22/8	Gençlerbirliği	a	0-0	
28/8	Gaziantepspor	h	0-0	
12/9	Galatasaray	a	0-3	
19/9	Kayserispor	h	0-1	
25/9	Ankaraspor	a	3-0	*(w/o)*
3/10	Denizlispor	h	1-0	*Rodrigo Tabata*
17/10	Kasımpaşa	h	2-1	*Nihat, Bobô*
24/10	Eskişehirspor	a	1-0	*Ekrem*
31/10	Ankaragücü	h	1-0	*İsmail*
7/11	Trabzonspor	a	2-0	*Ernst, Bobô*
21/11	Fenerbahçe	h	3-0	*Fink, Bobô, Uğur*
29/11	Sivasspor	a	1-0	*Bobô*
4/12	Diyarbakırspor	h	0-0	
13/12	Manisaspor	a	1-1	*Bobô*
18/12	Bursaspor	h	2-3	*Nobre, Bobô (p)*

2010
29/1	Antalyaspor	a	1-0	*Bobô (p)*
5/2	Gençlerbirliği	h	4-1	*Sivok, Bobô, Hološko, Rodrigo Tabata*
13/2	Gaziantepspor	a	0-2	
21/2	Galatasaray	h	1-1	*Sivok*
27/2	Kayserispor	a	2-1	*Tello, Ekrem*
7/3	Ankaraspor	h	3-0	*(w/o)*
10/3	İstanbul BB	h	2-0	*Bobô, Hološko*
15/3	Denizlispor	a	1-0	*Hološko*
19/3	Kasımpaşa	a	2-2	*Tello, Bobô*
27/3	Eskişehirspor	h	3-2	*Nihat, Bobô, Hološko*
2/4	Ankaragücü	a	0-0	
10/4	Trabzonspor	h	0-0	
18/4	Fenerbahçe	a	0-1	
24/4	Sivasspor	h	2-2	*Bobô, Hološko*
2/5	Diyarbakırspor	a	3-1	*İbrahim Toraman, og (Abdullah), Tello*
7/5	Manisaspor	h	2-0	*Nihat, og (Hüseyin)*
16/5	Bursaspor	a	1-2	*Uğur*

No	Name	Nat	DoB	Pos	Aps	(s)	Gls
93	ATINÇ Nukan		20/7/93	D		(1)	
13	Deivson Rogério da Silva "BOBÔ"	BRA	9/1/85	A	22	(7)	12
22	CUMALİ Bişi		15/6/93	A		(1)	
17	EKREM Dağ	AUT	5/12/80	M	21	(3)	2
44	ERHAN Güven		15/5/82	D	3	(1)	
28	Fabian ERNST	GER	30/5/79	M	26	(2)	1
27	Matteo FERRARI	ITA	5/12/79	D	23		
5	Michael FINK	GER	1/2/82	M	28	(2)	2
84	HAKAN Arıkan		17/8/82	G	7	(1)	
23	Filip HOLOŠKO	SVK	17/1/84	A	11	(7)	6
4	İBRAHİM Kaş		20/9/86	D	10	(4)	
20	İBRAHİM Toraman		20/11/81	D	21		
19	İBRAHİM Üzülmez		10/3/74	D	21	(2)	
3	İSMAİL Köybaşı		10/7/89	D	13	(3)	1
87	KORCAN Çelikay		31/12/87	G		(1)	
18	NECİP Uysal		24/1/91	M	7	(4)	
8	NİHAT Kahveci		23/11/79	A	17	(6)	3
11	Marcio "Mert" NOBRE		6/11/80	A	9	(10)	1
7	RIDVAN Şimşek		17/1/91	D	3	(1)	
15	RODRIGO Barbosa TABATA	BRA	19/11/80	M	11	(5)	2
1	RÜŞTÜ Reçber		10/5/73	G	25		
21	SERDAR Özkan		1/1/87	M	5	(7)	
6	Tomáš SIVOK	CZE	15/9/83	D	31		2
14	Rodrigo Alvaro Valenzuela TELLO	CHI	14/10/79	M	23	(3)	4
25	UĞUR İnceman		25/5/81	M	6	(13)	2
29	YUSUF Şimşek		20/7/75	M	9	(7)	

BURSASPOR
Coach - Ertuğrul Sağlam
Founded - 1963
Stadium - Atatürk (19,616)
MAJOR HONOURS:
Turkish League – (1) 2010;
Turkish Cup – (1) 1986.

2009
9/8	Kasımpaşa	h	2-1	*Zápotočný, Sercan*
16/8	Eskişehirspor	a	2-3	*Ömer, Sercan*
22/8	Ankaragücü	h	1-0	*Ömer*
30/8	Trabzonspor	a	1-1	*Turgay*
13/9	Fenerbahçe	h	0-1	
19/9	Sivasspor	a	3-1	*Volkan, Shin 2*
26/9	Diyarbakırspor	h	4-0	*Volkan, Ivankov (p), Ergić, Ozan İpek*
3/10	Manisaspor	a	2-0	*Batalla, Turgay*
17/10	Denizlispor	a	3-2	*Turgay, Batalla, Zápotočný*
24/10	İstanbul BB	h	6-0	*Ömer, Ozan İpek, Batalla, Volkan, Turgay, Ali*
31/10	Antalyaspor	a	1-1	*Ergić*
6/11	Gençlerbirliği	h	1-2	*Ergić*
21/11	Gaziantepspor	a	1-0	*Kırıtă*
27/11	Galatasaray	h	1-0	*Volkan*
6/12	Kayserispor	a	0-3	
13/12	Ankaraspor	h	3-0	*(w/o)*
18/12	Beşiktaş	a	3-2	*Ozan İpek, Ergić, Zápotočný*

2010
31/1	Eskişehirspor	h	3-1	*Ozan İpek, Turgay, Ali*
7/2	Ankaragücü	a	0-0	
15/2	Trabzonspor	h	1-1	*Batalla*
22/2	Fenerbahçe	a	3-2	*Batalla, Ozan İpek 2*

TURKEY

27/2	Sivasspor	h	3-0	Batalla, Turgay, Ozan İpek
6/3	Diyarbakırspor	a	3-0	(w/o; match abandoned after 17 mins at 0-0)
10/3	Kasımpaşa	a	2-0	Batalla, Sercan
14/3	Manisaspor	h	2-0	Ivankov (p), Ömer
22/3	Denizlispor	h	2-1	Ozan İpek, Sercan
26/3	İstanbul BB	a	1-2	Volkan
3/4	Antalyaspor	h	2-1	Ivankov (p), Ömer
11/4	Gençlerbirliği	a	0-0	
16/4	Gaziantepspor	h	2-0	Ömer, Volkan
25/4	Galatasaray	a	0-0	
1/5	Kayserispor	h	2-0	Turgay, Ivankov (p)
9/5	Ankaraspor	a	3-0	(w/o)
16/5	Beşiktaş	h	2-1	Batalla, og (Ibrahim Toraman)

No	Name	Nat	DoB	Pos	Aps	(s)	Gls
21	ALİ Tandoğan		25/12/77	M	31		2
17	Pablo BATALLA	ARG	16/1/84	M	17	(9)	8
11	EREN Albayrak		23/4/91	M		(1)	
25	Ivan ERGİĆ	SRB	21/1/81	M	28	(3)	4
5	HÜSEYİN Çimşir		26/5/79	M	29	(1)	
28	Leonardo Andrés IGLESIAS	ARG	28/8/79	A	1	(8)	
27	Dimitar IVANKOV	BUL	30/10/75	G	30		4
38	İBRAHİM Öztürk		21/6/81	D	16	(2)	
91	İSMAİL HAKTAN Odabaşı		7/8/91	M		(7)	
8	Giani Stelian KIRIŢĂ	ROU	3/3/77	M	2	(6)	1
67	MUHAMMET Demir		10/1/92	A		(1)	
23	MUSTAFA Keçeli		15/9/78	M	26	(1)	
6	OZAN Has		18/2/85	M	8	(14)	
33	OZAN İpek		10/10/86	A	26	(4)	8
4	ÖMER Erdoğan		3/5/77	D	29	(1)	6
55	RAMAZAN Sal		27/6/85	M		(1)	
9	SERCAN Yıldırım		5/4/90	A	22	(3)	4
18	SHIN Young-rok	KOR	27/3/87	A	2	(5)	2
29	José TADEU Mouro Júnior	BRA	1/4/86	M		(6)	
35	TUNA Üzümcü		6/8/82	D	2	(2)	
22	TURGAY Bahadır		15/1/84	A	28	(3)	7
20	VELİ Acar		30/8/81	M	6	(11)	
10	VOLKAN Şen		7/7/87	M	26	(1)	6
1	YAVUZ Özkan		19/5/85	G	2		
32	YENAL Tuncer		28/4/85	D	2		
26	Tomáš ZÁPOTOČNÝ	CZE	13/9/80	D	19	(2)	3

DENİZLİSPOR

Coach - Erhan Altın; (2/9/09) Nurullah Sağlam;
(27/10/09) Hakan Kutlu
Founded - 1966
Stadium - Atatürk (15,000)

2009

9/8	Fenerbahçe	h	0-2	
15/8	Galatasaray	a	1-4	Angelov
29/8	Kayserispor	a	0-3	
12/9	Diyarbakırspor	h	0-0	
16/9	Sivasspor	h	1-1	Ahmet
19/9	Ankaraspor	a	3-0	(w/o)
27/9	Manisaspor	h	1-1	Roberts (p)
3/10	Beşiktaş	a	0-1	
17/10	Bursaspor	h	2-3	Angelov, Roberts
25/10	Kasımpaşa	a	1-3	Bangoura
1/11	İstanbul BB	h	0-1	
8/11	Eskişehirspor	a	0-2	
22/11	Antalyaspor	h	1-1	Roberts
29/11	Ankaragücü	a	0-1	
6/12	Gençlerbirliği	a	0-2	
13/12	Trabzonspor	h	0-1	
19/12	Gaziantepspor	a	1-2	Engin
2010				
22/1	Fenerbahçe	a	1-3	Youla

31/1	Galatasaray	h	1-2	Engin
7/2	Sivasspor	a	0-2	
14/2	Kayserispor	h	1-0	Angelov
21/2	Diyarbakırspor	a	2-0	Chrysostome, Youla
28/2	Ankaraspor	h	3-0	(w/o)
7/3	Manisaspor	a	0-0	
15/3	Beşiktaş	h	0-1	
22/3	Bursaspor	a	1-2	Roberts
28/3	Kasımpaşa	h	3-3	Angelov, Youla, Çağlar
3/4	İstanbul BB	a	1-3	Ahmet
11/4	Eskişehirspor	h	1-0	Angelov
18/4	Antalyaspor	a	1-2	Ahmet
24/4	Ankaragücü	h	0-0	
2/5	Gençlerbirliği	h	2-0	Bajić, Braga
10/5	Trabzonspor	a	1-2	Ahmet
15/5	Gaziantepspor	h	1-1	Ahmet

No	Name	Nat	DoB	Pos	Aps	(s)	Gls
12	ADEM Çalık		26/8/81	A	3	(1)	
60	AHMET Cebe		2/3/83	A	17	(3)	5
26	ALPASLAN Kartal		23/6/77	M		(2)	
71	Emil ANGELOV	BUL	17/7/80	A	25	(3)	5
4	Branimir BAJIĆ	BIH	19/10/79	D	9	(3)	1
15	Ibrahima BANGOURA	GUI	8/12/82	A	9	(4)	1
33	Džemal BERBEROVIĆ	BIH	5/11/81	D	19	(5)	
17	Douglas Daniel BRAGA	BRA	6/7/85	M	27	(2)	1
5	BURAK Akyıldız		3/1/85	D	12	(4)	
6	BURAK Solakel		1/3/82	M	18	(1)	
10	CANER Celep		21/7/84	M	3	(4)	
1	CENK Gönen		21/2/88	G	14		
25	Damien Koffi Anderson CHRYSOSTOME	BEN	24/5/82	D	26		1
61	ÇAĞLAR Birinci		2/10/85	D	24	(1)	1
23	EMİN Aladağ		25/2/83	M	19	(3)	
9	ENGİN Memişler		25/9/87	A	2	(17)	2
88	ERHAN Kartal		1/3/93	M	1		
34	ERKAN Sekman		17/4/84	D	5	(2)	
3	FAHRİ Tatan		30/5/83	M	4	(2)	
45	FATİH Yiğen		1/6/83	M	9	(8)	
22	GÜRAY Vural		11/6/88	M	19	(2)	
14	İBRAHİM Ege		3/2/83	M	10	(2)	
24	İSMAİL Şahmalı		4/1/82	G	1		
13	İZZET Akgül		28/1/82	M		(3)	
21	MEHMET Çoğum		5/2/83	D	10	(1)	
7	MURAT Hacıoğlu		10/6/79	M	7	(2)	
16	MUSTAFA Er		11/1/80	M	1	(2)	
54	OKAN Koç		22/1/82	M	2	(9)	
41	ÖZDEN Öngün		10/9/78	G	17		
11	Darryl ROBERTS	TRI	26/9/83	A	26	(3)	4
8	SÜLEYMAN Olgun		20/4/87	M	1		
19	Norman SYLLA	GUI	27/9/82	A		(1)	
90	UĞUR Aktaş		3/10/90	M		(1)	
77	Souleymane YOULA	GUI	29/11/81	A	12	(2)	3

DİYARBAKIRSPOR

Coach - Ziya Doğan; (5/3/10) Güvenç Kurtar;
(15/4/10) Mehmet Budakın
Founded - 1968
Stadium - Atatürk (12,963)

2009

8/8	Ankaragücü	h	2-2	Adnan, Mendoza
15/8	Trabzonspor	a	2-1	Tazemeta 2
24/8	Fenerbahçe	h	1-3	Tazemeta
30/8	Sivasspor	a	2-0	og (Cihan), Mendoza
12/9	Denizlispor	a	0-0	
19/9	Manisaspor	h	0-0	
26/9	Bursaspor	a	0-4	
3/10	İstanbul BB	h	1-3	Mendoza (p)

18/10	Antalyaspor	a	1-4	*Mendoza (p)*
25/10	Gençlerbirliği	h	1-0	*Tazemeta*
1/11	Gaziantepspor	a	1-2	*Adnan*
8/11	Galatasaray	h	1-2	*Mendoza*
22/11	Kayserispor	a	0-2	
29/11	Ankaraspor	h	3-0	*(w/o)*
4/12	Beşiktaş	a	0-0	
13/12	Kasımpaşa	h	2-2	*Celaleddin, Şener (p)*
19/12	Eskişehirspor	a	0-0	
2010				
24/1	Ankaragücü	a	0-0	
30/1	Trabzonspor	h	1-2	*Tazemeta*
7/2	Fenerbahçe	a	1-1	*Abdelaziz*
13/2	Sivasspor	h	1-1	*Diallo*
21/2	Denizlispor	h	0-2	
28/2	Manisaspor	a	1-2	*Bebbe*
6/3	Bursaspor	h	0-3	*(w/o; match abandoned after 17 mins at 0-0)*
14/3	İstanbul BB	a	0-1	*(match abandoned after 87 mins; result stood)*
20/3	Antalyaspor	h	1-0	*Erhan (p)*
27/3	Gençlerbirliği	a	0-1	
4/4	Gaziantepspor	h	1-3	*Bebbe*
11/4	Galatasaray	a	1-4	*Bebbe*
18/4	Kayserispor	h	0-3	
25/4	Ankaraspor	a	3-0	*(w/o)*
2/5	Beşiktaş	h	1-3	*Tazemeta*
9/5	Kasımpaşa	a	0-1	
15/5	Eskişehirspor	h	0-2	

No	Name	Nat	DoB	Pos	Aps	(s)	Gls
12	Ayman ABDELAZIZ	EGY	20/11/78	M	19		1
6	ABDULLAH Çetin		18/3/84	M	20	(4)	
55	ADNAN Güngör		20/9/80	D	28	(2)	2
3	Bassim Abbas AL OGAILI	IRQ	1/7/82	D	19		
1	Rorys Andrés ARAGÓN	ECU	26/4/78	G	10		
2	Amir AZMY	EGY	14/2/83	D	3	(2)	
13	BAKİ Mercimek		17/9/82	D	5		
21	BARIŞ Ataş		1/2/87	M	30		
60	Gustave BEBBE	CMR	22/6/82	M	13	(1)	3
23	BURAK Karaduman		23/2/85	M	9	(4)	
77	CELALEDDİN Koçak		24/11/77	M	24	(1)	1
36	CEMAL Doğu		26/8/90	D		(1)	
17	Mamadou DIALLO	GUI	2/12/84	D	15	(2)	1
15	Bruce José DJITE	AUS	25/3/87	A	2	(7)	
8	ERDAL Güneş		29/3/82	A	12	(6)	
32	ERDİNÇ Yavuz		4/10/78	D	15	(2)	
7	EREN Şen		28/9/84	A	1	(2)	
10	ERHAN Şentürk		4/5/89	A	8	(16)	1
11	ERSİN Güreler		7/9/78	A		(2)	
48	FEVZİ Tuncay		14/9/77	G	2		
79	GÖKHAN Tokgöz		22/4/79	G	14		
20	HAKAN Güler		3/8/84	A		(1)	
63	İBRAHİM Ülüm		17/9/83	A	3	(5)	
19	Joseph-Désiré JOB	CMR	1/12/77	M	5	(3)	
30	Milan MARTINOVIĆ	SRB	6/8/79	D	6	(2)	
88	MEHMET İstemi		20/4/91	M	1		
18	Andrés MENDOZA	PER	26/4/78	A	11	(4)	5
33	METİN Aktaş		1/8/77	G	4		
34	MUSA Büyük		22/5/80	M	4	(5)	
22	MUSTAFA Özkan		21/2/75	M		(1)	
61	OSMAN Kurtuldu		2/2/81	G	2		
16	Mikkel RASK	DEN	22/6/83	M	2	(3)	
70	Goran STANKOVSKI	MKD	20/11/76	D	2	(5)	
43	ŞENER Aşkaroğlu		24/4/80	M	11	(1)	1
9	Thierry TAZEMETA	CMR	13/10/82	A	18	(2)	6
29	Razundara TJIKUZU	NAM	6/12/79	M	10		
4	TOLGA Doğantez		22/2/75	D	14		
86	UFUK Bayraktar		1/1/86	M		(3)	

14	ÜMİT Bozkurt		20/4/76	D	10	(3)
42	YASİR Elmacı		10/10/81	M		(1)

ESKİŞEHİRSPOR

Coach - Rıza Çalımbay
Founded - 1965
Stadium - Atatürk (18,000)
MAJOR HONOURS:
Turkish Cup – (1) 1971.

2009				
9/8	Manisaspor	a	0-0	
16/8	Bursaspor	h	3-2	*Youla 2 (1p), Mehmet*
22/8	İstanbul BB	a	0-0	
29/8	Antalyaspor	h	2-1	*Mehmet, Youla*
13/9	Gençlerbirliği	a	2-2	*Doğa, og (Kahê)*
19/9	Gaziantepspor	h	3-2	*Ümit (p), Koray, Vučko*
27/9	Galatasaray	a	1-1	*Mehmet*
4/10	Kayserispor	h	0-1	
18/10	Ankaraspor	a	3-0	*(w/o)*
24/10	Beşiktaş	h	0-1	
1/11	Kasımpaşa	a	1-1	*Burak*
8/11	Denizlispor	h	2-0	*Mehmet, Ümit*
22/11	Ankaragücü	h	0-0	
29/11	Trabzonspor	a	1-2	*Adem*
5/12	Fenerbahçe	h	2-1	*Adem 2*
13/12	Sivasspor	a	1-2	*Volkan*
19/12	Diyarbakırspor	h	0-0	
2010				
23/1	Manisaspor	h	1-0	*Adem*
31/1	Bursaspor	a	1-3	*Ümit (p)*
6/2	İstanbul BB	h	2-1	*John, Ümit*
14/2	Antalyaspor	a	2-1	*Erkan, Adem*
20/2	Gençlerbirliği	h	0-0	
28/2	Gaziantepspor	a	1-1	*John*
8/3	Galatasaray	h	2-1	*Koray 2*
14/3	Kayserispor	a	2-1	*Koray, Mehmet*
21/3	Ankaraspor	h	3-0	*(w/o)*
27/3	Beşiktaş	a	2-3	*Ümit 2 (1p)*
4/4	Kasımpaşa	h	2-0	*Sezer, Erkan*
11/4	Denizlispor	a	0-1	
18/4	Ankaragücü	a	1-3	*Adem*
26/4	Trabzonspor	h	1-0	*Ümit*
1/5	Fenerbahçe	a	0-2	
9/5	Sivasspor	h	1-1	*Veysel*
15/5	Diyarbakırspor	a	2-0	*Adem 2*

No	Name	Nat	DoB	Pos	Aps	(s)	Gls
58	ADEM Sarı		9/5/85	A	5	(13)	8
14	ALPER Potuk		8/4/91	M	9	(7)	
29	ATİLLA Koca		16/7/80	G	1		
39	AYDIN Yılmaz		29/1/88	M	4	(5)	
17	BURAK Yılmaz		15/7/85	M	13	(1)	1
55	BÜLENT Ertuğrul		17/9/78	D	20	(3)	
21	BÜLENT Kocabey		8/6/84	M	13	(6)	
28	CANER Celep		21/7/84	M	1	(2)	
20	DOĞA Kaya		30/6/84	M	21		1
5	Abdel Zaher EL SAKA	EGY	30/1/74	D	22	(1)	
77	ERKAN Zengin		5/8/85	M	5	(7)	2
33	FAHRİ Tatan		30/5/83	M	2		
60	FATİH Aydın		1/1/95	A		(1)	
1	Vanja IVEŠA	CRO	21/7/77	G	31		
30	Jaycee JOHN Okwunwanne	BHR	8/10/85	M	8	(4)	2
51	KORAY Arslan		1/10/83	D	26	(3)	4
10	MEHMET Yılmaz		22/5/79	A	23	(1)	5
3	MURAT Önür		15/2/81	D	10	(4)	
13	Safet NADAREVIĆ	BIH	30/8/80	D	21	(2)	
8	RAGIP Başdağ		9/6/78	M	10	(10)	
19	SERDAR Özbayraktar		22/11/81	M		(9)	

TURKEY

45	SEZER Öztürk		3/11/85	A	11	(4)	1
75	SEZGİN Coşkun		23/8/84	D	20	(2)	
99	ÜMİT Karan		1/10/76	A	22	(2)	7
6	VEYSEL Sarı		25/7/88	M	3	(5)	1
7	VOLKAN Yaman		27/8/82	D	19	(1)	1
27	Luka VUČKO	CRO	11/4/84	D	19	(1)	1
11	Souleymane YOULA	GUI	29/11/81	A	13	(1)	3

FENERBAHÇE SK
Coach - Christoph Daum (GER)
Founded - 1907
Stadium - Şükrü Saracoğlu (50,509)
MAJOR HONOURS:
Turkish League – (17) 1959, 1961, 1964, 1965, 1968, 1970, 1974, 1975, 1978, 1983, 1985, 1989, 1996, 2001, 2004, 2005, 2007;
Turkish Cup – (4) 1968, 1974, 1979, 1983.

2009
9/8	Denizlispor	a	2-0	Güiza 2
16/8	Sivasspor	h	3-0	Kazım, Emre, André Santos
24/8	Diyarbakırspor	a	3-1	Gökhan Gönül, Kazım, Semih (p)
30/8	Manisaspor	h	2-1	Güiza, Semih
13/9	Bursaspor	a	1-0	Alex
20/9	İstanbul BB	h	1-0	Wederson
26/9	Antalyaspor	a	2-1	Kazım, Semih
4/10	Gençlerbirliği	h	3-0	Alex 2, Lugano
18/10	Gaziantepspor	a	1-2	Semih
25/10	Galatasaray	h	3-1	Alex 2 (1p), Güiza
1/11	Kayserispor	a	1-1	Cristian
8/11	Ankaraspor	h	3-0	(w/o)
21/11	Beşiktaş	a	0-3	
28/11	Kasımpaşa	h	1-3	Güiza
5/12	Eskişehirspor	a	1-2	Lugano
12/12	Ankaragücü	h	3-2	Alex 2, Güiza
20/12	Trabzonspor	a	1-0	Güiza

2010
22/1	Denizlispor	h	3-1	André Santos, Özer, Güiza
31/1	Sivasspor	a	5-1	Semih 2, Uğur 2, Gökhan Gönül
7/2	Diyarbakırspor	h	1-1	André Santos
14/2	Manisaspor	a	2-2	Cristian, Gökhan Ünal
22/2	Bursaspor	h	2-3	Alex, André Santos
28/2	İstanbul BB	a	1-2	Alex
7/3	Antalyaspor	h	1-0	André Santos
13/3	Gençlerbirliği	a	0-0	
20/3	Gaziantepspor	h	1-0	Güiza
28/3	Galatasaray	a	1-0	Selçuk
4/4	Kayserispor	h	2-0	Gökhan Ünal, Lugano
11/4	Ankaraspor	a	3-0	(w/o)
18/4	Beşiktaş	h	1-0	Alex
25/4	Kasımpaşa	a	1-0	Bekir
1/5	Eskişehirspor	h	2-0	Alex, Özer
9/5	Ankaragücü	a	3-0	Mehmet, Güiza, Cristian
16/5	Trabzonspor	h	1-1	Güiza

No	Name	Nat	DoB	Pos	Aps	(s)	Gls
10	ALEXsandro de Souza	BRA	14/9/77	M	26		11
17	ALİ Bilgin		17/12/81	M		(1)	
27	ANDRÉ Clarindo dos SANTOS	BRA	8/3/83	M	23	(4)	5
15	BEKİR İrtegün		20/4/84	D	4	(3)	1
16	CRISTIAN Nascimento Oliveira Baroni	BRA	25/6/83	M	22	(3)	3
99	DEIVID de Souza	BRA	22/10/79	A	2	(11)	
24	DENİZ Barış		2/7/77	M	5	(9)	
5	EMRE Belözoğlu		7/9/80	M	24	(1)	1
58	FÁBIO Alves da Silva "BILICA"	BRA	14/1/79	D	27	(1)	
77	GÖKHAN Gönül		4/1/85	D	30		2
39	GÖKHAN Ünal		23/7/82	A	1	(9)	2
9	Daniel GÜIZA	ESP	17/8/80	A	24	(3)	11
8	KAZIM Kazım		26/8/86	M	11		3

2	Diego LUGANO	URU	2/11/80	D	25		3
66	MEHMET Topuz		7/9/83	M	25	(3)	1
19	ÖNDER Turacı		14/7/81	D	7	(2)	
20	ÖZER Hurmacı		20/11/86	M	14	(7)	2
3	ROBERTO CARLOS da Silva Rocha	BRA	10/4/73	D	10	(1)	
21	SELÇUK Şahin		31/1/81	M	12	(9)	1
23	SEMİH Şentürk		29/4/83	A	9	(12)	6
25	UĞUR Boral		14/4/82	M	1	(4)	2
1	VOLKAN Demirel		27/10/81	G	32		
6	WEDERSON Luiz da Silva Medeiros	BRA	22/7/81	D	18	(9)	1

GALATASARAY AŞ
Coach - Frank Rijkaard (NED)
Founded - 1905
Stadium - Ali Sami Yen (23,000)
MAJOR HONOURS:
UEFA Cup - (1) 2000; UEFA Super Cup - (1) 2000;
Turkish League – (17) 1962, 1963, 1969, 1971, 1972, 1973, 1987, 1988, 1993, 1994, 1997, 1998, 1999, 2000, 2002, 2006, 2008;
Turkish Cup – (14) 1963, 1964, 1965, 1966, 1973, 1976, 1982, 1985, 1991, 1993, 1996, 1999, 2000, 2005.

2009
9/8	Gaziantepspor	a	3-2	Arda, Mustafa, Nonda
15/8	Denizlispor	h	4-1	Kewell 2 (2p), Arda, og (Burak Akyıldız)
23/8	Kayserispor	h	4-1	Baroš 2, og (Makukula), Elano
31/8	Ankaraspor	a	3-0	(w/o; original result 2-0 Kewell, Nonda)
12/9	Beşiktaş	h	3-0	Mustafa, Baroš 2
21/9	Kasımpaşa	a	3-1	Nonda 3
27/9	Eskişehirspor	h	1-1	Nonda
4/10	Ankaragücü	a	0-3	
18/10	Trabzonspor	h	4-3	Kewell, Servet, Arda, Baroš
25/10	Fenerbahçe	a	1-3	Hakan
1/11	Sivasspor	h	2-0	Nonda, Kewell
8/11	Diyarbakırspor	a	2-1	Sabri, Arda
22/11	Manisaspor	h	1-1	Kewell
27/11	Bursaspor	a	0-1	
6/12	İstanbul BB	h	1-1	Kewell
11/12	Antalyaspor	a	3-2	Keita, Elano, Kewell
19/12	Gençlerbirliği	h	1-0	Nonda

2010
24/1	Gaziantepspor	h	1-0	Mustafa
31/1	Denizlispor	a	2-1	Arda, Jô
6/2	Kayserispor	a	0-0	
14/2	Ankaraspor	h	3-0	(w/o)
21/2	Beşiktaş	a	1-1	Arda
28/2	Kasımpaşa	h	4-1	Arda, Keita 2, Jô (p)
8/3	Eskişehirspor	a	1-2	Elano (p)
14/3	Ankaragücü	h	3-0	Jô, Keita, Baroš
21/3	Trabzonspor	a	0-1	
28/3	Fenerbahçe	h	0-1	
5/4	Sivasspor	a	1-1	Barış
11/4	Diyarbakırspor	h	4-1	Baroš 3, Neill
17/4	Manisaspor	a	2-1	Keita, Baroš
25/4	Bursaspor	h	0-0	
1/5	İstanbul BB	a	1-0	Baroš
8/5	Antalyaspor	h	1-2	og (Yalçın)
16/5	Gençlerbirliği	a	1-2	Emre Çolak

No	Name	Nat	DoB	Pos	Aps	(s)	Gls
10	ARDA Turan		30/1/87	M	27	(2)	7
7	AYDIN Yılmaz		29/1/88	M	3	(8)	
18	AYHAN Akman		23/2/77	M	10	(9)	
1	AYKUT Erçetin		14/9/82	G	7		
8	BARIŞ Özbek		14/9/86	M	14	(4)	1

15	Milan BAROŠ	CZE	28/10/81	A	13	(4)	11
91	BERK Neziroğulları		1/2/91	M		(1)	
88	CANER Erkin		4/10/88	D	18	(1)	
69	CUMHUR Yılmaztürk		5/1/90	M	1		
9	ELANO Ralph Blumer	BRA	14/6/81	M	20	(5)	3
21	EMRE Aşık		13/12/73	D	4	(2)	
37	EMRE Çolak		20/5/91	M	3	(5)	1
2	EMRE Güngör		1/8/84	D	5	(5)	
30	GIOVANI dos Santos	MEX	11/5/89	A	10	(4)	
5	GÖKHAN Zan		7/9/81	D	9		
22	HAKAN Balta		23/3/83	D	23	(2)	1
32	João Alves de Assis Silva "JÔ"	BRA	20/3/87	A	8	(5)	3
11	Abdul Kader KEITA	CIV	6/8/81	M	24	(3)	5
19	Harry KEWELL	AUS	22/9/78	A	12	(5)	9
25	LEOnardo Neoren FRANCO	ARG	20/5/77	G	26		
6	Tobias LINDEROTH	SWE	21/4/79	M		(4)	
14	MEHMET Topal		3/3/86	M	22	(2)	
16	MUSTAFA Sarp		5/11/80	M	23	(7)	3
12	Lucas NEILL	AUS	9/3/78	D	14		1
20	Shabani NONDA	COD	6/3/77	A	6	(7)	7
55	SABRİ Sarıoğlu		26/7/84	M	24		1
39	SERDAR Eylik		1/2/90	M		(1)	
76	SERVET Çetin		17/3/81	D	24		1
3	UĞUR Uçar		5/4/87	D	12	(3)	
74	VOLKAN Yaman		27/8/82	D	1		

GAZİANTEPSPOR
Coach - José Couceiro (POR)
Founded - 1969
Stadium - Kamil Ocak (18,325)

2009

9/8	Galatasaray	h	2-3	*Júlio César I, Rodrigo Tabata (p)*
16/8	Kayserispor	a	1-1	*Beto*
23/8	Ankaraspor	h	3-0	*(w/o; original result 1-1 Júlio César I)*
28/8	Beşiktaş	a	0-0	
13/9	Kasımpaşa	h	1-0	*Beto*
19/9	Eskişehirspor	a	2-3	*Júlio César II, Júlio César I*
26/9	Ankaragücü	h	1-3	*Júlio César I*
2/10	Trabzonspor	a	0-0	
18/10	Fenerbahçe	h	2-1	*Júlio César I 2*
25/10	Sivasspor	a	0-3	
1/11	Diyarbakırspor	h	2-1	*Jorginho, Olcan*
8/11	Manisaspor	a	3-0	*Olcan, Ahmet, Mehmet*
21/11	Bursaspor	h	0-1	
29/11	İstanbul BB	a	1-1	*Júlio César I*
6/12	Antalyaspor	h	1-1	*Júlio César I (p)*
13/12	Gençlerbirliği	a	1-1	*Beto*
19/12	Denizlispor	h	2-1	*Beto, Júlio César I*
2010				
24/1	Galatasaray	a	0-1	
31/1	Kayserispor	h	0-1	
7/2	Ankaraspor	a	3-0	*(w/o)*
13/2	Beşiktaş	h	2-0	*Júlio César I, Deumi*
21/2	Kasımpaşa	a	0-3	
28/2	Eskişehirspor	h	1-1	*Beto*
7/3	Ankaragücü	a	0-0	
12/3	Trabzonspor	h	1-1	*Beto*
20/3	Fenerbahçe	a	0-1	
28/3	Sivasspor	h	2-2	*Júlio César I 2*
4/4	Diyarbakırspor	a	3-1	*Jorginho 2, Erman*
9/4	Manisaspor	h	0-0	
16/4	Bursaspor	a	0-2	
25/4	İstanbul BB	h	2-3	*Beto, Júlio César I*
2/5	Antalyaspor	a	0-1	
8/5	Gençlerbirliği	h	1-1	*og (Murat)*
15/5	Denizlispor	a	1-1	*Soner*

No	Name	Nat	DoB	Pos	Aps	(s)	Gls
72	AHMET Arı		13/1/89	A	12	(10)	1
25	André Roberto Soares da Silva "BETO"	BRA	2/10/81	A	18	(10)	7
77	CENK Güvenç		29/12/91	D	7		
12	Armand DEUMI	CMR	12/3/79	D	25	(1)	1
6	ERKAN Sekman		17/4/84	D	7	(1)	
19	ERMAN Özgür		13/4/77	M	25	(7)	1
20	GÖKHAN Öztürk		22/3/90	M		(1)	
17	HAKAN Bayraktar		11/2/76	M	7	(10)	
37	IVAN Saraiva de Souza	BRA	18/1/82	D	28		
21	İBRAHİM FERDİ Coşkun		20/4/87	M	4	(16)	
11	Jorge Luíz Pereira de Souza "JORGINHO"	BRA	6/5/77	M	19	(6)	3
99	JÚLIO CÉSAR da Silva e Souza (I)	BRA	26/2/80	A	29	(3)	13
55	JÚLIO CÉSAR Santos Correia (II)	BRA	17/11/78	D	18		1
24	Žydrūnas KARČEMARSKAS	LTU	24/5/83	G	3		
39	Roland LINZ	AUT	9/8/81	A		(5)	
22	MAHMUT Bezgin		1/3/86	G	28		
7	MEHMET Yozgatlı		9/1/79	M	2	(5)	1
96	MUHAMMET Şentürk		15/1/88	G	1		
5	MURAT Ceylan		2/3/88	M	27	(4)	
29	OLCAN Adın		30/9/85	M	30		2
23	RECEP Biler		8/5/81	G	1		
10	RODRIGO Barbosa TABATA	BRA	19/11/80	M	3		1
2	SEMİH Kaya		24/2/91	D	1		
16	SERDAR Kurtuluş		23/7/87	D	23		
4	SONER Örnek		28/2/89	D	3		1
28	TOLGA Seyhan		17/1/77	D	15	(2)	
14	Stjepan TOMAS	CRO	6/3/76	D	3	(1)	
61	ÜMİT Tütünci		1/10/84	A	2	(10)	
8	Cristian Rodrigo ZURITA	ARG	24/7/79	M	22	(3)	

GENÇLERBİRLİĞİ SK
Coach - Thomas Doll (GER)
Founded - 1923
Stadium - 19 Mayıs (19,125)
MAJOR HONOURS:
Turkish Cup - (2) 1987, 2001.

2009

9/8	Kayserispor	h	0-0	
16/8	Ankaraspor	a	3-0	*(w/o; original result 1-1 Mustafa)*
22/8	Beşiktaş	h	0-0	
30/8	Kasımpaşa	a	4-0	*Harbuzi, Mustafa, Kahê, Hurşit*
13/9	Eskişehirspor	h	2-2	*Kahê 2*
19/9	Ankaragücü	a	2-1	*Mustafa, Kahê*
25/9	Trabzonspor	h	2-2	*Harbuzi, Bilal*
4/10	Fenerbahçe	a	0-3	
18/10	Sivasspor	h	2-0	*Mustafa, Kahê*
25/10	Diyarbakırspor	a	0-1	
1/11	Manisaspor	h	0-2	
6/11	Bursaspor	a	2-1	*Hurşit, Mustafa*
22/11	İstanbul BB	h	3-1	*Kahê, Hurşit, Cem*
29/11	Antalyaspor	a	0-2	
6/12	Denizlispor	h	2-0	*Mustafa, Bilal*
13/12	Gaziantepspor	h	1-1	*Sandro*
19/12	Galatasaray	a	0-1	
2010				
24/1	Kayserispor	a	1-1	*Burhan*
31/1	Ankaraspor	h	3-0	*(w/o)*
5/2	Beşiktaş	a	1-4	*Hurşit*
14/2	Kasımpaşa	h	0-2	
20/2	Eskişehirspor	a	0-0	
28/2	Ankaragücü	h	0-1	
6/3	Trabzonspor	a	1-3	*Sandro*
13/3	Fenerbahçe	h	0-0	
21/3	Sivasspor	a	2-0	*Mustafa, Kahê*
27/3	Diyarbakırspor	h	1-0	*Mustafa*

4/4	Manisaspor	a	0-0	
11/4	Bursaspor	h	0-0	
17/4	İstanbul BB	a	3-1	Mustafa 2, Harbuzi
24/4	Antalyaspor	h	0-2	
2/5	Denizlispor	a	0-2	
8/5	Gaziantepspor	a	1-1	Mustafa
16/5	Galatasaray	h	2-1	Hurşit, Harbuzi

No	Name	Nat	DoB	Pos	Aps	(s)	Gls
3	ALPARSLAN Erdem		11/12/88	D	1	(1)	
88	AYKUT Demir		22/10/88	D	32		
61	BİLAL Çubukçu		16/5/87	M	3	(14)	2
21	BURHAN Eşer		1/1/85	M	17	(6)	1
40	CEM Can		1/4/81	M	27	(1)	1
19	Bruce José DJITE	AUS	25/3/87	A		(5)	
8	Labinot HARBUZI	SWE	4/4/86	M	19	(3)	4
17	HURŞİT Meriç		31/7/83	M	19	(10)	5
5	İLHAN Eker		1/1/83	D	26		
23	Mile JEDINAK	US	3/8/84	M		(2)	
9	Carlos Eduardo de Souza Floresta "KAHÊ"	BRA	28/8/82	A	24	(6)	7
6	KEREM Şeras		1/1/84	M	17	(6)	
26	MAHMUT Boz		16/4/91	M	5	(2)	
18	Jacques MOMHA	CMR	7/8/82	M	2		
69	MURAT Kalkan		20/5/86	M	9	(3)	
11	MUSTAFA Pektemek		11/8/88	A	23	(7)	11
67	ORHAN Şam		1/6/86	D	32		
58	ÖZKAN Karabulut		16/1/91	G	1		
28	Ivan RADELJIĆ	BIH	14/9/80	D	22		
20	SABAHATTİN Usta		9/6/90	M	1	(1)	
10	SANDRO da Silva Mendonça	BRA	1/10/83	A	14	(8)	2
1	SERDAR Kulbilge		7/7/80	G	31		
7	SERKAN Çalık		15/3/86	M	2	(8)	
52	SEZAİ Zehiroğlu		25/7/88	M		(1)	
16	Patiyo TAMBWE	COD	7/1/84	A	3	(7)	
12	Mariel Everton Cosmo da Silva "TOZO"	BRA	15/8/80	M	19	(5)	
99	ULAŞ Güler		8/4/80	G	1		
30	Jurica VRANJEŠ	CRO	31/1/80	M	13		

İSTANBUL BB SK
Coach - Abdullah Avcı
Founded - 1990
Stadium - Atatürk Olimpiyat (82,576)

2009

7/8	Beşiktaş	h	1-1	İbrahim
16/8	Kasımpaşa	a	3-1	og (Pavlik), İbrahim, Ali
22/8	Eskişehirspor	h	0-0	
29/8	Ankaragücü	a	2-2	İskender, Tum
13/9	Trabzonspor	h	1-6	Gökhan Süzen
20/9	Fenerbahçe	a	0-1	
26/9	Sivasspor	h	1-0	Vinícius
3/10	Diyarbakırspor	a	3-1	Serhat 2, Metin
18/10	Manisaspor	h	1-0	Metin
24/10	Bursaspor	a	0-6	
1/11	Denizlispor	a	1-0	Tum
7/11	Antalyaspor	h	1-0	Tum
22/11	Gençlerbirliği	a	1-3	Tum
29/11	Gaziantepspor	h	1-1	İbrahim
6/12	Galatasaray	a	1-1	Hasan Ali
13/12	Kayserispor	h	1-2	Marquinhos
19/12	Ankaraspor	a	3-0	(w/o)
2010				
30/1	Kasımpaşa	h	4-2	Tum, İskender 2, Tevfik
6/2	Eskişehirspor	a	1-2	Tum
14/2	Ankaragücü	h	1-1	İskender
20/2	Trabzonspor	a	0-0	
28/2	Fenerbahçe	h	2-1	İskender 2

6/3	Sivasspor	a	1-0	Tevfik
10/3	Beşiktaş	a	0-2	
14/3	Diyarbakırspor	h	1-0	Tum (match abandoned after 87 mins; result stood)
20/3	Manisaspor	a	0-1	
26/3	Bursaspor	h	2-1	Kuś, Hasan Ali
3/4	Denizlispor	h	3-1	og (Chrysostome), İbrahim, Tevfik
10/4	Antalyaspor	a	3-1	Tevfik, Ali, İskender
17/4	Gençlerbirliği	h	1-3	İskender
25/4	Gaziantepspor	a	3-2	İskender 2, Tevfik
1/5	Galatasaray	h	0-1	
9/5	Kayserispor	a	1-1	Ali
16/5	Ankaraspor	h	3-0	(w/o)

No	Name	Nat	DoB	Pos	Aps	(s)	Gls
91	ABDÜLKADİR Kayalı		30/1/91	M	5	(1)	
10	ALİ Güzeldal		10/4/86	A	9	(13)	3
23	CAN Arat		21/1/84	D	6	(2)	
6	EFE İnanç		24/3/80	M	23	(3)	
17	EKREM Ekşioğlu		16/1/78	D	25	(3)	
66	ERGÜN Berisha		24/6/88	M		(1)	
9	GÖKHAN Kaba		24/11/83	A	2	(6)	
81	GÖKHAN Süzen		12/7/87	M	18	(6)	1
1	Kenan HASAGIĆ	BIH	1/2/80	G	17		
89	HASAN ALİ Durtuluk		1/1/89	A	3	(10)	2
11	İBRAHİM Akın		4/1/84	A	10	(10)	4
12	İSKENDER Alın		28/2/84	A	24	(3)	10
28	Marcin KUŚ	POL	2/9/81	D	18		1
21	MAHMUT Tekdemir		20/1/88	D	20	(3)	
82	Marcos Roberto da Silva Barbosa "MARQUINHOS"	BRA	21/10/82	D	15		1
3	METİN Depe		10/1/81	D	16	(2)	2
13	Mazuwa N'SUMBU	COD	24/9/82	M	2	(4)	
15	OĞUZ Sabankay		7/8/87	M	1	(8)	
61	OĞUZHAN Bahadır		24/12/79	G	15		
7	OKAN Buruk		19/10/73	M	3	(7)	
53	RIZVAN Şahin		30/10/81	D	16	(2)	
4	SERHAT Gülpınar		1/1/79	M	21	(5)	2
27	Kanfory SYLLA	GUI	7/7/80	D	17	(3)	
41	TANER Gülleri		29/4/76	A		(1)	
88	TEVFİK Köse		12/7/88	A	14	(2)	5
18	Hervé TUM	CMR	15/2/79	A	20		7
5	Marcus Cesário VINÍCIUS	BRA	22/3/85	D	22		1
8	ZEKİ Korkmaz		1/9/88	M	10		

KASIMPAŞA SK
Coach - Besim Durmuş; (7/9/09) Yılmaz Vural
Founded - 1921
Stadium - Recep Tayyip Erdoğan (9,576)

2009

9/8	Bursaspor	a	1-2	Erhan
16/8	İstanbul BB	h	1-3	André Moritz
23/8	Antalyaspor	a	0-2	
30/8	Gençlerbirliği	h	0-4	
13/9	Gaziantepspor	a	0-1	
21/9	Galatasaray	h	1-3	André Moritz
27/9	Kayserispor	a	0-0	
4/10	Ankaraspor	h	3-0	(w/o)
17/10	Beşiktaş	a	1-2	André Moritz (p)
25/10	Denizlispor	h	3-1	Cenk 2, André Moritz
1/11	Eskişehirspor	h	1-1	Karadas
8/11	Ankaragücü	a	2-2	Gökhan, André Moritz
22/11	Trabzonspor	h	3-1	Emre, Murat Erdoğan, André Moritz
28/11	Fenerbahçe	a	3-1	Gökhan, Cenk, Şahin
5/12	Sivasspor	h	2-2	Cenk, Gökhan
13/12	Diyarbakırspor	a	2-2	Cenk, Özgür
19/12	Manisaspor	h	3-1	André Moritz, Gökhan, Sancak

TURKEY

2010

30/1	İstanbul BB	a	2-4	Şahin, Murat Erdoğan
7/2	Antalyaspor	h	2-2	Sancak, Şahin
14/2	Gençlerbirliği	a	2-0	Yekta, André Moritz
21/2	Gaziantepspor	h	3-0	Yekta, Şahin, Murat Erdoğan
28/2	Galatasaray	a	1-4	Yekta
6/3	Kayserispor	h	2-2	Yekta, Merthan
10/3	Bursaspor	h	0-2	
14/3	Ankaraspor	a	3-0	(w/o)
19/3	Beşiktaş	h	2-2	Gökhan, Şahin
28/3	Denizlispor	a	3-3	André Moritz, Gökhan, Özgür
4/4	Eskişehirspor	a	0-2	
11/4	Ankaragücü	h	2-0	Cenk, Şahin
19/4	Trabzonspor	a	0-2	
25/4	Fenerbahçe	h	0-1	
2/5	Sivasspor	a	1-1	Gökhan
9/5	Diyarbakırspor	h	1-0	İsa
16/5	Manisaspor	a	0-0	

No	Name	Nat	DoB	Pos	Aps	(s)	Gls
30	ALİ Güneş		23/11/78	D	10	(6)	
54	ALPASLAN Kartal		23/6/77	M	4		
3	ANDRÉ Felipe GALIASSI de Sousa	BRA	22/8/80	D	3		
10	ANDRÉ Francisco MORITZ	BRA	6/8/86	A	20	(1)	9
44	Martin BARAN	SVK	3/1/88	M	4	(2)	
22	BARIŞ Başdaş		17/1/90	D	18	(3)	
23	Nourdin BOUKHARI	MAR	30/6/80	A	2	(2)	
55	CENK İşler		25/2/74	A	23	(3)	6
34	EMRE Toraman		5/1/79	M	25	(1)	1
13	ERDİ Öner		4/7/86	D	2	(1)	
15	ERGÜN Teber		1/9/85	D	22	(2)	
61	ERHAN Küçük		26/2/81	A	4	(1)	1
24	GÖKHAN Güleç		25/9/85	A	11	(9)	7
9	HÜSEYİN Kartal		1/1/82	A	1		
52	İSA Kaykun		5/6/88	A		(4)	1
99	Azar KARADAS	NOR	9/8/81	A	7		1
80	Christian KELLER	DEN	17/8/80	M	27	(2)	
25	KORAY Avcı		19/5/78	M	24		
28	MERTHAN Açıl		15/2/82	M	17	(5)	1
6	MURAT Akın		22/10/86	M	2	(8)	
33	MURAT Erdoğan		1/8/76	M	26		3
1	MURAT Şahin		4/2/76	G	14		
7	ÖMER Hacısalihoğlu		1/4/77	D		(1)	
2	ÖZGÜR Öçal		5/10/81	D	5	(12)	2
14	Petr PAVLÍK	CZE	22/7/87	D	3		
18	Diego Alejandro RUIZ	ARG	19/12/80	D	3	(1)	
5	SANCAK Kaplan		25/5/82	D	18	(5)	2
20	SEDAT Yeşilkaya		10/6/80	M	1	(10)	
11	SERTAN Eser		18/3/74	M		(2)	
17	ŞAHİN Aygüneş		1/10/90	A	11	(6)	6
68	TOLGA Özgen		28/2/80	G	18		
42	YASİR Elmacı		10/10/81	M	4	(1)	
35	YEKTA Kurtuluş		11/12/85	M	23	(5)	4

KAYSERİSPOR
Coach - Tolunay Kafkas
Founded - 1966
Stadium - Kadir Has (32,876)
MAJOR HONOURS:
Turkish Cup - (1) 2008.

2009

9/8	Gençlerbirliği	a	0-0	
16/8	Gaziantepspor	h	1-1	Aydın
23/8	Galatasaray	a	1-4	Makukula
29/8	Denizlispor	h	3-0	Cángele 2, Makukula
12/9	Ankaraspor	h	3-0	(w/o)
19/9	Beşiktaş	a	1-0	Makukula

27/9	Kasımpaşa	h	0-0	
4/10	Eskişehirspor	a	1-0	Makukula
18/10	Ankaragücü	h	3-0	Cángele, Mehmet Eren, Makukula
23/10	Trabzonspor	a	1-2	Makukula
1/11	Fenerbahçe	h	1-1	Cángele (p)
8/11	Sivasspor	a	4-2	Gökhan Emreciksin 2, Makukula 2
22/11	Diyarbakırspor	h	2-0	Makukula 2
29/11	Manisaspor	a	1-0	Gökhan Emreciksin
6/12	Bursaspor	h	3-0	Ömer, Makukula 2
13/12	İstanbul BB	a	2-1	Makukula, Cángele
19/12	Antalyaspor	h	1-2	Ömer

2010

24/1	Gençlerbirliği	h	1-1	Makukula
31/1	Gaziantepspor	a	1-0	Makukula
6/2	Galatasaray	h	0-0	
14/2	Denizlispor	a	0-1	
21/2	Ankaraspor	a	3-0	(w/o)
27/2	Beşiktaş	h	1-2	Makukula
6/3	Kasımpaşa	a	2-2	Makukula, Abdullah
14/3	Eskişehirspor	h	1-2	Gökhan Emreciksin (p)
21/3	Ankaragücü	a	0-3	
29/3	Trabzonspor	h	1-0	Makukula
4/4	Fenerbahçe	a	0-2	
12/4	Sivasspor	h	2-2	Cángele (p), Makukula
18/4	Diyarbakırspor	a	3-0	Mehmet Eren 2, Saidou
24/4	Manisaspor	h	1-2	Makukula
1/5	Bursaspor	a	0-2	
9/5	İstanbul BB	h	1-1	Makukula
15/5	Antalyaspor	a	0-4	

No	Name	Nat	DoB	Pos	Aps	(s)	Gls
87	ABDULLAH Durak		1/4/87	D	17	(4)	1
5	ALİ Turan		6/9/83	D	16		
25	AYDIN Toscalı		14/8/80	D	30		1
24	BAYRAM Çetin		17/7/85	D	6	(4)	
15	BİLAL AZİZ Özer		1/7/85	M	3	(8)	
10	Franco Darío CÁNGELE	ARG	16/7/84	A	26	(1)	6
2	DURMUŞ Bayram		15/3/86	D	7		
90	FURKAN Özçal		3/9/90	M	12	(6)	
89	GÖKHAN Değirmenci		21/3/89	G	1		
8	GÖKHAN Emreciksin		10/9/84	M	14	(7)	4
38	HAKAN Aslantaş		26/8/85	D	18		
16	Souleymanou HAMIDOU	CMR	22/11/73	G	31		
3	HASAN ALİ Kaldırım		9/12/89	D	4	(2)	
19	Ariza MAKUKULA	POR	4/3/81	A	29		21
67	MEHMET EREN Boyraz		11/10/81	A	31		3
6	MERTER Yüce		18/2/85	M	4		
20	Salomon OLEMBE	CMR	8/12/80	M	3	(2)	
9	ÖMER Şişmanoğlu		1/8/89	A	9	(14)	2
7	Alioum SAIDOU	CMR	19/2/78	M	25		1
61	SAVAŞ Yılmaz		1/1/90	M	4	(8)	
17	SEMİH Aydilek		16/1/89	A	2	(11)	
53	SERDAR Kesimal		24/1/89	D	24	(2)	
45	Mohamed SHAWKY	EGY	5/10/81	M	11		
12	Delio César TOLEDO	PAR	10/2/76	D	15		
21	James TROISI	AUS	3/7/88	A	8	(16)	
11	UMUT Koçin		2/6/88	M	1	(8)	
33	VOLKAN Dikmen		14/10/91	D	1	(1)	

MANİSASPOR
Coach - Mesut Bakkal; (3/2/10) Reha Kapsal
Founded - 1965
Stadium - 19 Mayıs (14,965)

2009

9/8	Eskişehirspor	h	0-0	
15/8	Ankaragücü	a	1-1	Promise
23/8	Trabzonspor	h	1-0	Promise
30/8	Fenerbahçe	a	1-2	Ergin

TURKEY

12/9	Sivasspor	h	3-1	Simpson, Promise, Kemal
19/9	Diyarbakırspor	a	0-0	
27/9	Denizlispor	a	1-1	Simpson
3/10	Bursaspor	h	0-2	
18/10	İstanbul BB	a	0-1	
25/10	Antalyaspor	h	1-2	Promise
1/11	Gençlerbirliği	a	2-0	Ergin, Simpson
8/11	Gaziantepspor	h	0-3	
22/11	Galatasaray	a	1-1	Simpson
29/11	Kayserispor	h	0-1	
6/12	Ankaraspor	a	3-0	(w/o)
13/12	Beşiktaş	h	1-1	Kalabane
19/12	Kasımpaşa	a	1-3	og (Ergün)
2010				
23/1	Eskişehirspor	a	0-1	
31/1	Ankaragücü	h	0-0	
7/2	Trabzonspor	a	0-3	
14/2	Fenerbahçe	h	2-2	Promise 2
20/2	Sivasspor	a	0-1	
28/2	Diyarbakırspor	h	2-1	Yiğit Gökoğlan, Ergin
7/3	Denizlispor	h	0-0	
14/3	Bursaspor	a	0-2	
20/3	İstanbul BB	h	1-0	Mehmet Güven
28/3	Antalyaspor	a	0-0	
4/4	Gençlerbirliği	h	0-0	
9/4	Gaziantepspor	a	0-0	
17/4	Galatasaray	h	1-2	og (Mehmet)
24/4	Kayserispor	a	2-1	Güven, Mehmet Nas
2/5	Ankaraspor	h	3-0	(w/o)
7/5	Beşiktaş	a	0-2	
16/5	Kasımpaşa	h	0-0	

No	Name	Nat	DoB	Pos	Aps	(s)	Gls
23	BULUT Basmaz		6/5/84	G	1	(1)	
3	BURAK Özsaraç		7/6/79	D	29		
55	Jimmy DIXON	LBR	10/10/81	D	10		
50	DİLAVER Güçlü		20/2/86	A		(6)	
34	EREN Aydın		16/1/82	D	27	(1)	
61	ERGİN Keleş		1/1/87	A	11	(11)	3
28	ERSEN Martin		23/5/79	A	1	(4)	
85	FERHAT Çökmüş		14/2/85	M	24	(2)	
6	GABRIEL de Paulo Limeira	BRA	20/8/83	D	2	(3)	
13	GÜVEN Varol		2/6/81	M	26	(2)	1
54	HÜSEYİN Tok		9/9/88	M	10		
1	İLKER Avcıbay		1/10/78	G	27		
15	Oumar KALABANE	GUI	8/4/81	D	13	(1)	1
27	KEMAL Okyay		25/2/85	M	6	(7)	1
8	MEHMET Güven		30/7/87	M	18	(5)	1
7	MEHMET Nas		20/11/79	M	25	(4)	1
29	Jacques MOMHA	CMR	7/8/82	D	2	(3)	
5	NİZAMETTİN Çalışkan		20/3/87	M	19	(6)	
37	ORKUN Usak		5/11/80	G	4		
18	Rahim Assane OUÉDRAOGO	BFA	8/10/80	M	2	(3)	
20	Isaac PROMISE	NGA	2/12/87	A	26	(1)	6
11	REINALDO de Souza	BRA	8/6/80	A		(3)	
10	SEZER Öztürk		3/11/85	M	4	(3)	
9	Joshua SIMPSON	CAN	15/3/83	A	27	(2)	4
43	ŞENER Aşkaroğlu		24/4/80	M	3	(3)	
99	YASER Yıldız		1/6/88	A	3	(7)	
17	YİĞİT Gökoğlu		5/6/89	M	6	(13)	1
4	YİĞİT İncedemir		9/3/85	M	26	(2)	

SİVASSPOR
Coach - Bülent Uygun; (13/10/09) Muhsin Ertuğral; (26/3/10) Mesut Bakkal
Founded - 1967
Stadium - 4 Eylül (18,500)

2009				
8/8	Trabzonspor	h	1-2	Kamanan
16/8	Fenerbahçe	a	0-3	
30/8	Diyarbakırspor	h	0-2	
12/9	Manisaspor	a	1-3	İbrahim Şahin
16/9	Denizlispor	a	1-1	İbrahim Şahin
19/9	Bursaspor	h	1-3	Zita
26/9	İstanbul BB	a	0-1	
4/10	Antalyaspor	h	2-0	Kamanan 2
18/10	Gençlerbirliği	a	0-2	
25/10	Gaziantepspor	h	3-0	Musa, Cihan 2
1/11	Galatasaray	a	0-2	
8/11	Kayserispor	h	2-4	Kamanan, Sedat
22/11	Ankaraspor	a	3-0	(w/o)
29/11	Beşiktaş	h	0-1	
5/12	Kasımpaşa	a	2-2	Erman (p), og(Barış)
13/12	Eskişehirspor	h	2-1	Murat, Sedat
19/12	Ankaragücü	a	3-2	Sedat, İbrahim Şahin, og (Baki)
2010				
24/1	Trabzonspor	a	1-3	Erman
31/1	Fenerbahçe	h	1-5	Mehmet
7/2	Denizlispor	h	2-0	Erman, Musa
13/2	Diyarbakırspor	a	1-1	İbrahim Şahin
20/2	Manisaspor	h	1-0	Cihan
27/2	Bursaspor	a	0-3	
6/3	İstanbul BB	h	0-1	
14/3	Antalyaspor	a	0-3	
21/3	Gençlerbirliği	h	0-2	
28/3	Gaziantepspor	a	2-2	Musa, Cihan
5/4	Galatasaray	h	1-1	Mehmet
12/4	Kayserispor	a	2-2	og (Aydın), Mehmet (p)
18/4	Ankaraspor	h	3-0	(w/o)
24/4	Beşiktaş	a	2-2	Cihan, Kamanan
2/5	Kasımpaşa	h	1-1	Cihan
9/5	Eskişehirspor	a	1-1	Mehmet
15/5	Ankaragücü	h	3-3	Kamanan, Mehmet 2 (1p)

No	Name	Nat	DoB	Pos	Aps	(s)	Gls
61	ABDURRAHMAN Dereli		15/2/81	D	18		
21	Akeem AGBETU	NGA	10/3/88	A	2	(10)	
35	AKIN Vardar		2/4/78	G	17		
78	Lucien AUBEY	COD	24/5/84	D	8	(1)	
18	CİHAN Yılmaz		15/6/83	M	20	(9)	6
11	ERMAN Kılıç		20/9/83	M	20	(8)	3
28	ERSEN Martin		23/5/79	A	8	(3)	
99	FARUK Bayar		11/10/81	M	7	(4)	
3	FERHAT Bıkmaz		6/7/88	D	3	(2)	
58	HAYRETTİN Yerlikaya		13/8/81	D	27		
8	İBRAHİM Dağaşan		15/6/84	M	19	(3)	
21	İBRAHİM Şahin		1/3/84	A	12	(7)	4
20	KADİR Bekmezci		5/7/85	M	15	(4)	
14	Yannick KAMANAN	FRA	5/10/81	A	11	(15)	6
86	Souleymane KEITA	MLI	24/11/86	A	14		
44	Pieter MBEMBA	COD	23/7/88	D		(1)	
9	MEHMET Yıldız		14/9/81	A	13		6
5	MURAT Sözgelmez		21/8/85	D	19	(4)	1
7	MUSA Aydın		1/11/80	M	25	(6)	2
77	ONUR Tuncer		19/2/84	M	3	(1)	
1	Michael PETKOVİĆ	AUS	16/7/76	G	15		
89	RAHMAN Soyudoğru		6/1/89	M		(1)	
4	SEDAT Bayrak		10/4/81	D	23		2
26	SEZER Badur		20/6/84	M	8	(4)	

10	Nabil TAÏDER	TUN	26/5/83	M	6	(2)	
67	UĞUR Kavuk		11/9/79	D	8	(3)	
16	Elrio VAN HEERDEN	RSA	11/7/83	M	6		
23	YASİN Çakmak		6/1/85	D	20	(1)	
6	Bruno Mbanangoyé ZITA	GAB	15/7/80	M	5	(5)	1

TRABZONSPOR

Coach - Hugo Broos (BEL); (4/12/09) Şenol Güneş
Founded - 1967
Stadium - Avni Aker (24,500)
MAJOR HONOURS:
Turkish League (6) 1976, 1977, 1979, 1980, 1981, 1984;
Turkish Cup (8) 1977, 1978, 1984, 1992, 1995, 2003, 2004, 2010.

2009

8/8	Sivasspor	a	2-1	*Selçuk, Ceyhun*
15/8	Diyarbakırspor	h	1-2	*Giray*
23/8	Manisaspor	a	0-1	
30/8	Bursaspor	h	1-1	*Colman*
13/9	İstanbul BB	a	6-1	*Egemen 3, Gökhan, Umut 2*
18/9	Antalyaspor	h	3-1	*Umut, Colman, og (Jedinak)*
25/9	Gençlerbirliği	a	2-2	*Gabrić, Colman*
2/10	Gaziantepspor	h	0-0	
18/10	Galatasaray	a	3-4	*Tayfun, Colman 2*
23/10	Kayserispor	h	2-1	*Gökhan, Ceyhun*
1/11	Ankaraspor	a	3-0	*(w/o)*
7/11	Beşiktaş	h	0-2	
22/11	Kasımpaşa	a	1-3	*Colman (p)*
29/11	Eskişehirspor	h	2-1	*Selçuk, Serkan*
6/12	Ankaragücü	h	3-0	*Umut, Gabrić, Colman*
13/12	Denizlispor	a	1-0	*Gabrić*
20/12	Fenerbahçe	h	0-1	

2010

24/1	Sivasspor	h	3-1	*Umut 2, Colman (p)*
30/1	Diyarbakırspor	a	2-1	*Engin 2*
7/2	Manisaspor	h	3-0	*Umut 2, Ceyhun*
15/2	Bursaspor	a	1-1	*Umut*
20/2	İstanbul BB	h	0-0	
26/2	Antalyaspor	a	1-1	*Burak*
6/3	Gençlerbirliği	h	3-1	*Burak, Gabrić, Umut*
12/3	Gaziantepspor	a	1-1	*Alanzinho*
21/3	Galatasaray	h	1-0	*Colman*
29/3	Kayserispor	a	0-1	
4/4	Ankaraspor	h	3-0	*(w/o)*
10/4	Beşiktaş	a	0-0	
19/4	Kasımpaşa	h	2-0	*Egemen, Umut*
26/4	Eskişehirspor	a	0-1	
1/5	Ankaragücü	a	0-1	
10/5	Denizlispor	h	2-1	*Giray, Murat*
16/5	Fenerbahçe	a	1-1	*Burak*

No	Name	Nat	DoB	Pos	Aps	(s)	Gls
25	Alan Carlos Gomes da Costa "ALANZINHO"	BRA	22/2/83	M	19	(10)	1
11	BARIŞ Memiş		5/1/90	A	1	(5)	
17	BURAK Yılmaz		15/7/85	M	8	(3)	3
3	Hrvoje ČALE	CRO	4/3/85	M	23	(1)	
6	CEYHUN Gülselam		25/12/87	M	12	(16)	3
20	Gustavo COLMAN	ARG	19/4/85	M	29	(1)	9
16	EGEMEN Korkmaz		3/11/82	D	27		4
5	ENGİN Baytar		11/7/83	M	15	(5)	2
15	FERHAT Öztorun		8/5/87	D	8	(6)	
33	Drago GABRİĆ	CRO	27/9/86	M	18	(7)	4
23	GİRAY Kaçar		15/3/85	D	23		2
9	GÖKHAN Ünal		23/7/82	A	8	(5)	2
19	Teófilo GUTIÉRREZ	COL	17/5/85	A	4	(7)	
99	HASAN AHMET Sarı		21/1/92	A		(1)	
21	MURAT Tosun		26/2/84	M		(6)	1

35	ONUR Kıvrak		1/1/88	G	19		
41	ÖMER Barış		23/7/82	D	11		
8	SELÇUK İnan		10/2/85	M	26	(2)	2
30	SERKAN Balcı		22/8/83	M	26	(4)	1
27	SEZER Badur		20/6/84	M	4	(5)	
4	Rigobert SONG	CMR	1/7/76	D	17	(1)	
1	Tony SYLVA	SEN	17/5/75	G	12		
18	TAYFUN Cora		5/12/83	D	7	(2)	1
28	Razundara TJIKUZU	NAM	6/12/79	M	3	(1)	
29	TOLGA Zengin		10/10/83	G	1		
10	UMUT Bulut		15/3/83	A	29	(2)	11
61	Ibrahima YATTARA	GUI	3/6/80	A	2	(3)	

PROMOTED CLUBS

KARDEMİR KARABÜKSPOR

Coach –Yücel İldiz
Founded – 1969
Stadium – Necmettin Şeyhoğlu (7,000)

BUCASPOR

Coach – Kemal Kılıç; (7/10/09) Özcan Kızıltan
Founded – 1928
Stadium – Yeni Buca (10,000)

KONYASPOR

Coach – Hüsnü Özkara; (17/2/10) Fuat Yaman; (26/3/10) Ziya Doğan
Founded – 1981
Stadium – Atatürk (22,459)

SECOND LEVEL FINAL TABLE 2009/10

		Pld	W	D	L	F	A	Pts
1	Kardemir Karabükspor	34	23	8	3	74	28	77
2	Bucaspor	34	19	7	8	69	40	64
3	Adanaspor	34	18	10	6	42	30	64
4	Altay SK	34	17	8	9	48	36	59
5	Karşıyaka SK	34	17	5	12	48	35	56
6	Konyaspor	34	15	10	9	42	37	55
7	Giresunspor	34	15	6	13	51	42	51
8	Orduspor	34	11	11	12	33	32	44
9	Boluspor	34	12	7	15	48	53	43
10	Samsunspor	34	12	6	16	49	47	42
11	Kayseri Erciyesspor	34	10	11	13	42	53	41
12	Gaziantep BBK	34	11	8	15	31	38	41
13	Mersin İdman Yurdu	34	11	8	15	36	44	41
14	Kartal SK	34	11	8	15	32	43	41
15	Çaykur Rizespor	34	10	10	14	37	53	40
16	Hacettepe SK	34	10	8	16	38	50	38
17	Çanakkale Dardanelspor	34	5	19	37	53	35	
18	Kocaelispor	34	2	8	24	23	66	14

PROMOTION PLAY-OFF FINAL TABLE

		Pld	W	D	L	F	A	Pts
1	Konyaspor	3	2	1	0	6	3	7
2	Altay SK	3	1	2	0	4	3	5
3	Karşıyaka SK	3	0	2	1	2	3	2
4	Adanaspor	3	0	1	2	4	7	1

TURKEY

DOMESTIC CUP 2009/10

TÜRKİYE KUPASI

THIRD ROUND

(28/10/09)
Ankaragücü 3, Karşıyaka 2
Denizli Belediye 2, Kastamonu 1 *(aet)*
Denizlispor 4, Gaziantepspor 1 *(aet)*
Diyarbakırspor 0, Tarsus İdman Yurdu 1
Galatasaray 2, Bucaspor 1
Güngören Belediye 0, Bursaspor 1
İstanbul BB 0, Gençlerbirliği 0 *(aet; 4-2 on pens)*
Kasımpaşa 4, Kayseri Erciyes 1
Kayserispor 0, Manisaspor 0 *(aet; 2-4 on pens)*
Konya Şekerspor 3, Adanaspor 2
Mersin İdmanyurdu 2, Antalyaspor 2 *(aet; 6-7 on pens)*
Orduspor 1, Belediye Vanspor 0
Tokatspor 3, Ankaraspor 2
Yalovaspor 1, Eskişehirspor 3 *(aet)*

(29/10/09)
Altay 4, Samsunspor 0

(4/11/09)
Giresunspor 2, Çaykur Rizespor 1 *(aet)*

GROUP STAGE

Group A

(22/12/09)
Antalyaspor 1, Eskişehirspor 0

(23/12/09)
Fenerbahçe 3, Altay 0

(10/1/10)
Eskişehirspor 0, Fenerbahçe 1
Tokatspor 1, Antalyaspor 1

(13/1/10)
Altay 0, Eskişehirspor 5
Fenerbahçe 3, Tokatspor 2

(17/1/10)
Tokatspor 1, Altay 2

(18/1/10)
Antalyaspor 4, Fenerbahçe 3

(26/1/10)
Eskişehirspor 1, Tokatspor 2
Altay 0, Antalyaspor 0

Final Standings
1 Fenerbahçe 9 pts;
2 Antalyaspor 8 pts *(qualified)*

3 Tokatspor 4 pts;
4 Altay 4 pts;
5 Eskişehirspor 3 pts *(eliminated)*

Group B

(23/12/09)
Denizli Belediye 0, Ankaragücü 2
Galatasaray 2, Trabzonspor 1

(9/1/10)
Trabzonspor 6, Denizli Belediye 0

(10/1/10)
Orduspor 0, Galatasaray 3

(13/1/10)
Denizli Belediye 1, Orduspor 2

(14/1/10)
Ankaragücü 0, Trabzonspor 2

(17/1/10)
Galatasaray 5, Denizli Belediye 1
Orduspor 1, Ankaragücü 2

(27/1/10)
Trabzonspor 2, Orduspor 1
Ankaragücü 0, Galatasaray 0

Final Standings
1 Galatasaray 10 pts;
2 Trabzonspor 9 pts *(qualified)*

3 Ankaragücü 7 pts;
4 Orduspor 3 pts;
5 Denizli Belediye 0 pts *(eliminated)*

Group C

(23/12/09)
Giresunspor 1, Bursaspor 2
Sivasspor 1, Tarsus İdman Yurdu 0

(9/1/10)
Denizlispor 0, Sivasspor 0

(10/1/10)
Tarsus İdman Yurdu 1, Giresunspor 2

(13/1/10)
Bursaspor 2, Tarsus İdman Yurdu 1
Giresunspor 0, Denizlispor 1

(17/1/10)
Denizlispor 1, Bursaspor 1
Sivasspor 4, Giresunspor 3

(27/1/10)
Bursaspor 4, Sivasspor 0
Tarsus İdman Yurdu 1, Denizlispor 2

Final Standings
1 Bursaspor 10 pts;
2 Denizlispor 8 pts *(qualified)*

3 Sivasspor 7 pts;
4 Giresunspor 3 pts;
5 Tarsus İdman Yurdu 0 pts *(eliminated)*

Group D

(22/12/09)
Manisaspor 2, Beşiktaş 1

(23/12/09)
Konya Şekerspor 2, Kasımpaşa 1

(9/1/10)
İstanbul BB 1, Konya Şekerspor 0
Kasımpaşa 1, Manisaspor 1

(12/1/10)
Beşiktaş 1, Kasımpaşa 3
Manisaspor 0, İstanbul BB 0

(16/1/10)
İstanbul BB 1, Beşiktaş 0

(17/1/10)
Konya Şekerspor 0, Manisaspor 1

(26/1/10)
Beşiktaş 4, Konya Şekerspor 2
Kasımpaşa 0, İstanbul BB 2

Final Standings
1 İstanbul BB 10 pts;
2 Manisaspor 8 pts *(qualified)*

3 Kasımpaşa 4 pts;
4 Beşiktaş 3 pts;
5 Konya Şekerspor 3 pts *(eliminated)*

QUARTER-FINALS

(3/2/10 & 10/2/10)
Antalyaspor 2 *(Djiehoua 26, Necati 39)*, Galatasaray 1 *(Arda 10)*
Galatasaray 3 *(Elano 26p, Emre Çolak 48, Caner 86)*, Antalyaspor 2 *(Necati 35, 65)*
(4-4; Antalyaspor on away goals)

İstanbul BB 1 *(Tevfik 31)*, Trabzonspor 1 *(Čale 88)*
Trabzonspor 1 *(Giray 40)*, İstanbul BB 0
(Trabzonspor 2-1)

(4/2/10 & 11/2/10)
Fenerbahçe 3 *(André Santos 22, Lugano 25, Semih 40)*, Bursaspor 0
Bursaspor 3 *(Iglesias 18, Ivankov 32p, Turgay 64)*, Fenerbahçe 1 *(Güiza 88)*
(Fenerbahçe 4-3)

Manisaspor 4 *(Hüseyin 16, Güven 30, Simpson 64, 86)*, Denizlispor 1 *(Angelov 20p)*
Denizlispor 0, Manisaspor 1 *(Ergin 33)*
(Manisaspor 5-1)

SEMI-FINALS

(24/3/10 & 13/4/10)
Fenerbahçe 2 *(Güiza 31, Deivid 33)*, Manisaspor 0
Manisaspor 1 *(Güven 16)*, Fenerbahçe 1 *(Alex 65)*
(Fenerbahçe 3-1)

(25/3/10 & 14/4/10)
Trabzonspor 2 *(Alanzinho 65, Umut 86)*, Antalyaspor 0
Antalyaspor 1 *(Djiehoua 43)*, Trabzonspor 0
(Trabzonspor 2-1)

FINAL

(5/5/10)
Şanlıurfa GAP stadium, Sanlıurfa
TRABZONSPOR 3 *(Umut 66, Engin 80, Colman 90+3)*
FENERBAHÇE SK 1 *(Alex 55)*
Referee – Cüneyt Çakır
TRABZONSPOR – Onur, Serkan, Song, Egemen, Čale, Selçuk *(Sezer 83)*, Colman, Engin *(Ceyhun 86)*, Burak, Alanzinho *(Giray 90+1)*, Umut.
FENERBAHÇE – Volkan, Gökhan Gönül *(Gökhan Ünal 87)*, Lugano, Fábio Bilica, Wederson, Mehmet, Selçuk, Emre *(Deivid 67)*, Özer, Alex, Güiza.

Shakhtar reclaim domestic crown

In comparison to the previous season, when FC Shakhtar Donetsk won the UEFA Cup and FC Dynamo Kyiv reached the semi-finals, the 2009/10 campaign was one of intense European disappointment for Ukraine's top two clubs. With the Ukrainian national team also failing to reach the 2010 FIFA World Cup after an unexpected play-off defeat by Greece, it was with a certain reluctance that the country's football followers shifted their attention back towards domestic matters, the main focus of their interest, as ever, being a hard-fought battle for the Premier-Liha championship between Shakhtar and Dynamo.

The title had changed hands repeatedly between the two arch-rivals since Shakhtar's successful defence in 2006, and that trend was maintained as Dynamo, under new Russian coach Valeriy Gazzayev, allowed a healthy autumn lead to be squandered in the spring, enabling Mircea Lucescu's side to surge to victory with 12 wins and a draw in their 13 post-Christmas fixtures. That 37-point haul contrasted sharply with Dynamo's relatively modest second-half-of-the-season return of 29 points, which included an extra fixture – a game in hand away to bottom-of-the-table FC Zakarpattya Uzhhorod that resulted in a humiliating 1-0 defeat.

Solitary defeat

Shakhtar avoided any such pranks and pitfalls against the Premier-Liha's lower order. They were beaten just once, and that, naturally enough, was in the away fixture against Dynamo in late November. At the time that 3-0 defeat looked likely to have serious repercussions for the Orange and Blacks' title hopes, leaving them seven points in arrears – a huge deficit against opponents who had shed only 11 points in the whole of the previous season. To their credit, however, Shakhtar responded by winning each of their last four games before the winter shutdown, and with Dynamo dropping two points in their three fixtures – the game in Uzhhorod having been postponed due to European commitments – the lead that Dynamo took into hibernation was down to just two points.

Nevertheless, with Shakhtar still in Europe and Dynamo out after finishing bottom of their UEFA Champions League group, the advantage appeared to remain with the defending champions. By the time the Premier-Liha resumed at the end of February, however, Shakhtar were also restricted to domestic activity, having unexpectedly crashed out of the UEFA Europa League to English upstarts Fulham FC. Their anger was taken out on their domestic opponents as they overcame all bar one of them – FC Dnipro Dnipropetrovsk – during an irresistible charge to the title that, fittingly, concluded with a 1-0 victory over Dynamo in front of 50,000 joyous supporters in the club's fabulous new Donbass Arena home.

Fernandinho was a central cog in Shakhtar's Ukrainian title-winning team

Shakhtar's fourth Ukrainian title under Lucescu – and fifth in all – was arguably the most rewarding. The season could hardly have started worse for the Romanian, who suffered a heart attack three days before the opening league fixture. He was soon on the mend, though, and able to oversee Shakhtar's involvement in the UEFA Super Cup, where they took FC Barcelona into extra time before losing 1-0. They also ceded key central defender Dmytro Chyhrynskiy to the Catalan giants after that game, but otherwise, thanks to the financial inducements of wealthy club owner Rinat Akhmetov, the UEFA Cup-winning team stayed largely intact.

UKRAINE

Failure to qualify for the UEFA Champions League following a shock away-goals defeat to FC Timişoara in the third qualifying round pitched Shakhtar into the UEFA Europa League, a competition in which, to all intents and purposes, they were defending their trophy. They made light work of the group stage, winning their first four matches and scoring 14 goals in the process, but despite playing Fulham off the park at Craven Cottage for the first 45 minutes of their round of 32 tie, they could not turn their majestic approach play into goals and went out 3-2 on aggregate.

Brazilian influence

The Brazilian influence that had carried Shakhtar to continental glory was just as profound in their recapturing of the Premier-Liha crown. The Fabulous Five of Fernandinho, Ilsinho, Jádson, William and Luiz Adriano were joined in mid-season by the sprightly Douglas Costa, a skilful 19-year-old left-footer bought from Grêmio FBPA, and collectively they lit up Shakhtar's play, scoring 38 of the team's 62 league goals between them. Ironically, it was the least attack-minded of the group, holding midfielder Fernandinho, who gathered the most acclaim. An inspirational figure all season long, he was considered unfortunate by many, Lucescu included, to be overlooked for his country's World Cup squad – a fate that befell every one of Shakhtar's Brazilian contingent.

A couple of Ukrainian newcomers, Vasyl Kobin and Yaroslav Rakytskiy, also enjoyed fine first seasons at Shakhtar. Both were rewarded with regular call-ups to the Ukrainian national team, where they joined club colleagues Olexandr Kucher, Olexiy Hai and goalkeeper Andriy Pyatov as well as the most famous Ukrainian footballer of them all, Andriy Shevchenko,

Federatsiya Futbola Ukrainy (FFU)

Provulok Laboratorniy 7-A
PO Box
UA-01133 Kyiv
tel – +380 44 521 0518
fax – +380 44 521 0550
website – ffu.org.ua
email – info@ffu.org.ua
Year of Formation – 1991

President – Hryhoriy Surkis
General Secretary – Olexandr Bandurko
Press Officer – Serhiy Vasilyev
National Stadium – NSC Olimpiyskiy, Kyiv (65,400)

INTERNATIONAL TOURNAMENT APPEARANCES
FIFA World Cup – (1) 2006 (qtr-finals).
TOP FIVE ALL-TIME CAPS
Andriy Shevchenko (96); Anatoliy Tymoshchuk (95); Olexandr Shovkovskiy (86); Serhiy Rebrov (75); Andriy Gusin (71)
TOP FIVE ALL-TIME GOALS
Andriy Shevchenko (45); Serhiy Rebrov (15); Serhiy Nazarenko (11); Andriy Gusin & Andriy Vorobei (9)

who returned full time to his homeland in August 2009, rejoining Dynamo after a ten-year stint abroad.

Shevchenko was on the verge of turning 33 when he arrived back in Kyiv, and although the AC Milan legend's best years were clearly a long way behind him, his mere presence generated enormous local interest. It was perhaps appropriate that he should celebrate his 100th UEFA Champions League appearance in the colours of the same club with whom he had made his debut. He took his copious haul of European goals to 62 with one against his former rivals FC Internazionale Milano, but he was powerless to extend Dynamo's European involvement beyond Christmas, the four points they took from FC Rubin Kazan being counterbalanced by the Russian

NATIONAL TEAM RESULTS 2009/10

12/8/09	Turkey	H	Kyiv	0-3	
5/9/09	Andorra (WCQ)	H	Kyiv	5-0	Yarmolenko (18), Milevskiy (45+2, 90+2p), Shevchenko (72p), Seleznev (90+4p)
9/9/09	Belarus (WCQ)	A	Minsk	0-0	
10/10/09	England (WCQ)	H	Dnipropetrovsk	1-0	Nazarenko (29)
14/10/09	Andorra (WCQ)	A	Andorra la Vella	6-0	Shevchenko (22), Gusev (61), Lima (69og), Rakytskiy (80), Seleznev (81), Yarmolenko (83)
14/11/09	Greece (WCQ)	A	Athens	0-0	
18/11/09	Greece (WCQ)	H	Donetsk	0-1	
25/5/10	Lithuania	H	Kharkiv	4-0	Aliyev (10, 16), Shevchenko (68p, 78)
29/5/10	Romania	H	Lviv	3-2	Aliyev (15), Konoplyanka (75), Tamaş (78og)
2/6/10	Norway	A	Oslo	1-0	Zozulya (78)

NATIONAL TEAM APPEARANCES 2009/10

Coach – Olexiy MYKHAILYCHENKO 30/3/63
/(2/2/10) Myron MARKEVYCH 1/2/51

Name	DOB	Club	Tur	AND	BLR	ENG	AND	GRE	GRE	Ltu	Rou	Nor	Caps	Goals
Olexandr SHOVKOVSKIY	2/1/75	Dynamo Kyiv	G										86	-
Vitaliy MANDZYUK	24/1/86	Dynamo Kyiv	D	D	D								13	-
Olexandr KUCHER	22/10/82	Shakhtar	D	D	D	D	D	D	D				19	1
Vyacheslav SHEVCHUK	13/5/79	Shakhtar	D46										16	-
Andriy RUSOL	16/1/83	Dnipro	D46							s83		D	49	3
Anatoliy TYMOSHCHUK	30/3/79	Bayern (GER)	M	M	M	M		M	M	M	M	M	95	1
Olexiy HAI	6/11/82	Shakhtar	M46	s71	M	M	s74		s66				22	1
Ruslan ROTAN	29/10/81	Dnipro	M		M	M46				M83	s83	s81	43	6
Maxym KALYNYCHENKO	26/1/79	Dnipro	M46										44	7
Volodymyr HOMENYUK	19/7/85	Dnipro	A46	s81									8	-
Yevhen SELEZNEV	20/7/85	Dnipro	A46	s66		s76				s57	s79	s90	15	4
Dmytro CHYHRYNSKIY	7/11/86	Shakhtar/Barcelona (ESP)	s46	D	D					D	D	D	24	-
Hryhoriy YARMASH	4/1/85	Vorskla	s46										8	-
Serhiy NAZARENKO	16/2/80	Dnipro	s46	s60	M67	M74							41	11
Oleh GUSEV	25/4/83	Dynamo Kyiv	s46	M71	M60	s92	M	M53	s69	M75	M86	M84	57	7
Artem MILEVSKIY	12/1/85	Dynamo Kyiv	s46	A	A	A	A76	A	A	A56	A83		29	4
Andriy SHEVCHENKO	29/9/76	Chelsea (ENG)/Dynamo Kyiv	s46	A81	A89	A92	A74	A	A	A79	A90		96	45
Andriy PYATOV	28/6/84	Shakhtar		G	G	G	G	G	G		G		18	-
Vasyl KOBIN	24/5/85	Shakhtar		D	D	D	D	D	D	D	D58	s56	9	-
Andriy YARMOLENKO	23/10/89	Dynamo Kyiv		M	M	s67	M	s46	M69			M55	7	2
Andriy VORONIN	21/7/79	Liverpool (ENG)	A66	s89									61	6
Yaroslav RAKYTSKIY	3/8/89	Shakhtar			D	D	D	D				D	5	1
Yevhen KHACHERIDI	28/7/87	Dynamo Kyiv			D	D	D	D					4	-
Taras MYKHALYK	28/10/83	Dynamo Kyiv						M	M	M66	D83	M	18	-
Olexandr ALIYEV	3/2/85	Dynamo Kyiv/Lokomotiv Moskva (RUS)						s74	s53	M57	M69	M90	11	3
Olexandr GORYAINOV	29/6/75	Metalist								G			1	-
Yevhen KONOPLYANKA	29/9/89	Dnipro								A	A	A90	3	1
Denys OLIYNYK	16/6/87	Metalist								s56	s58	s84	3	-
Marko DEVIĆ	27/10/83	Metalist								s69		s55	4	-
Volodymyr POLYOVIY	28/7/85	Metalurh Zaporizhya								s75	s62		2	-
Artem FEDETSKIY	26/4/85	Karpaty								s83	s86	s90	3	-
Ihor OSHCHYPKO	25/10/85	Karpaty								D62	D		2	-
Ihor KHUDOBYAK	20/2/85	Karpaty								s90			1	-
Andriy DYKAN	16/7/77	Terek (RUS)										G	1	-
Olexandr YAKOVENKO	23/6/87	Westerlo (BEL)										M56	1	-
Roman ZOZULYA	17/11/89	Dynamo Kyiv										A81	1	1

champions' shock 2-1 win in Barcelona and thus leaving Dynamo bottom of their group after a Matchday 6 2-1 defeat at home to the holders.

Marksman Milevskiy

Ukrainian international striker Artem Milevskiy put Dynamo 1-0 up against Barça in that UEFA Champions League encounter. It was his only European goal of the season but the talented 25-year-old was to strike 17 times in the Premier-Liha – considerably more often than Shevchenko – and win the Golden Boot, edging out FC Metalist Kharkiv's Brazilian forward Jajá by one unit thanks to a last-day double at home to FC Metalurh Zaporizhya.

Milevskiy's individual prize was scant consolation for his club, however, who ended the season trophyless. Although Dynamo were the dominant force domestically in the autumn, with Gazzayev drawing the best from Ukrainian internationals Oleh Gusev, Andriy Yarmolenko and newcomer Yevhen Khacheridi, it was in October that their hopes of a tenth Ukrainian Cup win bit the dust, Shakhtar knocking them out at the quarter-final stage with a 2-0 win in Donetsk. There would be no double for Lucescu's men, though, as they surprisingly fell in the semi-finals to city rivals FC Metalurh Donetsk, who, in turn, lost the final, beaten 3-2 in Kharkiv by SC Tavriya Simferopol.

The Crimean side, winners of the inaugural Ukrainian league title in 1992 but of nothing else since, claimed their first Cup win thanks to an extra-time winner from Nigerian striker Lucky Idahor. Two-nil up at half-time, albeit with the help of a fortunate penalty, Tavriya allowed Metalurh back into the game, but despite being reduced to ten men in extra time, Idahor's header won the day.

Dream debut

Nine days after hosting the Ukrainian Cup final, the newly refurbished OSK Metalist stadium in Kharkiv served as a fitting venue for Myron Markevych's first match in charge of the Ukrainian national team. The long-serving FC Metalist Kharkiv coach had been appointed in February to replace Olexiy Mykhailychenko, whose contract was not renewed after the crushing disappointment of the World Cup play-off defeat by Greece. Markevych saw out the season with Metalist before leading Ukraine out for the first time. It would prove to be a dream debut as a brace of goals apiece from discarded Dynamo Kyiv

playmaker Olexandr Aliyev and the ever-reliable Shevchenko yielded a comprehensive 4-0 win over Lithuania. Two further wins the following week – 3-2 against Romania in Lviv and 1-0 over Norway in Oslo – suggested that Markevych was the right man for the job of preparing Ukraine for the country's biggest ever sporting event, UEFA EURO 2012.

Skipper Shevchenko is already committed to extending his international career so that he can lead out his country on home soil at that tournament, but he could have strong competition by then from 20-year-old Dnipro striker Yevhen Konoplyanka, who, selected up front in each of Markevych's first three games, made a hugely positive impression.

It seemed likely at the end of the season that Markevych would sever his ties with Metalist in order to devote himself full-time to the national team. If so, he bowed out in style, leading the club to a fourth successive third-place finish in the Premier-Liha. Powered by the goals of Jajá, Metalist won six games on the trot in the late autumn before the run was ended with a shock 1-0 defeat by FC Obolon Kyiv on the day the club unveiled their new stadium – and on the 50th birthday of club president Olexandr Yaroslavskiy besides. Obolon subsequently lost the services of their coach Yuriy Maximov, who went on to rescue FC Kryvbas Kryvyi Rih from a seemingly inevitable relegation. Maximov's fire-fighting talent was reflected in the number of points both Obolon and Kryvbas collected with him (21 and 18 respectively) and without him (ten and seven). As those two clubs survived, the relegation places were filled by Zakarpattya and FC Chornomorets Odesa, with PFC Sevastopol and SC Volyn Lutsk moving up to replace them.

Myron Markevych got off to a wonderful start as Ukraine's new head coach

DOMESTIC LEAGUE 2009/10

PREMIER-LIHA FINAL TABLE

		Pld	Home					Away					Total					Pts
			W	D	L	F	A	W	D	L	F	A	W	D	L	F	A	
1	FC Shakhtar Donetsk	30	14	1	0	37	6	10	4	1	25	12	24	5	1	62	18	77
2	FC Dynamo Kyiv	30	14	1	0	40	6	8	4	3	21	10	22	5	3	61	16	71
3	FC Metalist Kharkiv	30	11	2	2	28	10	8	3	4	21	13	19	5	6	49	23	62
4	FC Dnipro Dnipropetrovsk	30	10	4	1	32	13	5	5	5	16	12	15	9	6	48	25	54
5	FC Karpaty Lviv	30	8	5	2	27	16	5	6	4	17	19	13	11	6	44	35	50
6	SC Tavriya Simferopol	30	7	5	3	24	18	5	4	6	14	20	12	9	9	38	38	45
7	FC Arsenal Kyiv	30	7	4	4	23	18	4	5	6	21	23	11	9	10	44	41	42
8	FC Metalurh Donetsk	30	7	4	4	24	9	4	3	8	17	24	11	7	12	41	33	40
9	FC Metalurh Zaporizhya	30	8	2	5	20	16	2	3	10	11	32	10	5	15	31	48	35
10	FC Vorskla Poltava	30	4	7	4	17	16	2	6	7	12	16	6	13	11	29	32	31
11	FC Obolon Kyiv	30	6	3	6	16	17	3	1	11	10	33	9	4	17	26	50	31
12	FC Illychivets Mariupil	30	5	4	6	13	22	2	4	9	18	34	7	8	15	31	56	29
13	FC Zorya Luhansk	30	6	3	6	15	17	1	4	10	8	30	7	7	16	23	47	28
14	FC Kryvbas Kryvyi Rih	30	3	3	9	18	24	4	1	10	13	23	7	4	19	31	47	25
15	FC Chornomorets Odesa	30	3	6	6	12	14	2	3	10	9	30	5	9	16	21	44	24
16	FC Zakarpattya Uzhhorod	30	4	3	8	12	17	1	1	13	6	27	5	4	21	18	44	19

TOP GOALSCORERS

17 Artem MILEVSKIY (Dynamo)
16 JAJÁ (Metalist)
13 Yevhen SELEZNEV (Dnipro)
11 LUIZ ADRIANO (Shakhtar)
10 Andrei VORONKOV (Obolon/Kryvbas)
9 Ionuţ MAZILU (Arsenal)
  Andriy VOROBEI (Arsenal)
  Denys OLIYNYK (Metalist)
  Henrikh MKHITARYAN (Metalurh Donetsk)
  JÁDSON (Shakhtar)

CLUB-BY-CLUB

FC ARSENAL KYIV
Coach – Olexandr Zavarov; (1/2/10) Vyacheslav Hrozniy; (16/4/10) Vasyl Yevseyev; (28/4/10) Yuriy Bakalov
Founded – 2001
Stadium – NTB im. Viktor Bannikov (1,678)

2009

18/7	Zorya	a	0-0	
24/7	Chornomorets	a	3-1	Vorobei, Hrytsai, Khomyn
1/8	Obolon	h	4-1	Mazilu, Josemar 2 (2p), Vorobei
7/8	Dnipro	a	1-1	Mazilu
23/8	Karpaty	h	0-0	
29/8	Zakarpattya	a	1-2	Gusev
20/9	Shakhtar	h	2-4	Vorobei, Yevseyev
26/9	Metalurh Zaporizhya	a	1-2	Mazilu
4/10	Dynamo	h	0-1	
18/10	Tavriya	a	2-2	Yeshchenko, Vorobei
24/10	Kryvbas	h	2-1	Vorobei, Yevseyev
1/11	Illychivets	a	2-1	Khomyn, Zakarlyuka (p)
21/11	Metalurh Donetsk	a	0-3	
29/11	Metalist	h	1-2	Khomyn
5/12	Zorya	h	1-1	Vorobei
12/12	Chornomorets	h	2-0	Mazilu, Vorobei

2010

28/2	Obolon	a	0-0	
7/3	Dnipro	h	1-1	Zakarlyuka (p)
13/3	Karpaty	a	3-3	Shakhov, Şoavă, Shatskikh
19/3	Zakarpattya	h	0-0	
24/3	Vorskla	h	2-0	Mazilu 2
28/3	Shakhtar	a	1-3	Shatskikh
4/4	Metalurh Zaporizhya	h	2-0	Shatskikh, Bogdanov
10/4	Dynamo	a	1-3	Zakarlyuka
15/4	Tavriya	h	1-6	Zakarlyuka (p)
18/4	Kryvbas	a	1-0	Korkishko
23/4	Illychivets	h	3-1	Mazilu 2, Mikoliūnas
30/4	Vorskla	a	5-1	Shatskikh, Şoavă, Mikoliūnas, Vorobei, Mazilu
5/5	Metalurh Donetsk	h	2-0	Mikoliūnas, Vorobei
9/5	Metalist	a	0-1	

No	Name	Nat	DoB	Pos	Aps	(s)	Gls
20	Sendley Sidney BITO	ANT	20/7/83	M	1	(1)	
17	Andriy BOGDANOV		21/1/90	M	11	(1)	1
46	Ruslan CHERNENKO		29/9/92	M		(1)	
18	Aleksandr DANILOV	BLR	10/9/80	M	22	(2)	
27	Ihor DIDYK		2/1/90	D	1		
24	Paul-Hervé ESSOLA	CMR	13/12/81	M		(1)	
8	Rolan GUSEV	RUS	17/9/77	M	4	(13)	1
35	Olexandr HRYTSAI		30/9/77	M	27		1
3	Taras ILNYTSKIY		4/3/83	D	1	(1)	
19	Lasha JAKOBIA	GEO	20/8/84	A		(3)	
11	JOSEMAR dos Santos Silva	BRA	18/10/80	M	8	(10)	2
33	Andriy KHOMYN		2/1/82	D	23	(2)	3
28	Dmytro KORKISHKO		4/5/90	M		(3)	1

UKRAINE

15	Serhiy LYTOVCHENKO		30/1/79	D	2	(1)	
39	Serhiy MATYUKHIN		21/3/80	D	11	(2)	
7	Ionuţ Costinel MAZILU	ROU	9/2/82	A	24	(1)	9
50	Ika MEPORIA		26/1/89	M	1		
13	Saulius MIKOLIŪNAS	LTU	2/5/84	M	5	(15)	3
23	Serhiy POHORILIY		28/7/86	G	2		
1	Vitaliy REVA		19/11/74	G	28		
21	Olexandr ROMANCHUK		21/10/84	D	9	(2)	
30	Yevhen SHAKHOV		30/11/90	M	3		1
15	Maksim SHATSKIKH	UZB	30/8/78	A	13		4
5	Bohdan SHERSHUN		14/5/81	D	21	(2)	
6	Florin Costin ŞOAVĂ	ROU	24/7/78	D	13		2
2	Artem STARHORODSKIY		17/1/82	M	4		
4	Serhiy SYMONENKO		12/6/81	M	12	(4)	
10	Andriy VOROBEI		29/11/78	A	21	(2)	9
29	Andrei YESHCHENKO	RUS	9/2/84	D	25	(1)	1
16	Yevhen YEVSEYEV		16/4/87	D	16	(5)	2
9	Serhiy ZAKARLYUKA		17/8/76	M	16	(2)	4
14	Yaroslav ZAKHAREVYCH		24/9/89	M	6	(1)	
88	Valeriy ZAVAROV		16/8/88	M		(6)	

FC CHORNOMORETS ODESA

Coach – Viktor Hryshko; (12/8/09) (Ihor Nakonechniy);
(1/9/09) Andriy Bal
Founded – 1958
Stadium – Chornomorets (20,836)
MAJOR HONOURS:
Ukrainian Cup – (2) 1992, 1994.

2009

18/7	Dynamo	a	0-5	
24/7	Arsenal	h	1-3	*Vázquez*
31/7	Tavriya	a	1-2	*Rajčević*
8/8	Obolon	h	0-1	
22/8	Kryvbas	a	3-2	*Didenko, Rebenok, Balashov (p)*
29/8	Dnipro	h	0-1	
19/9	Illychivets	a	0-2	
27/9	Karpaty	h	1-1	*Shandruk*
4/10	Vorskla	a	0-0	
17/10	Zakarpattya	h	2-0	*Rebenok, Melnyk V.*
24/10	Metalurh Donetsk	a	0-2	
1/11	Shakhtar	h	0-1	
22/11	Metalurh Zaporizhya	h	0-0	
29/11	Zorya	a	1-0	*Balashov*
5/12	Dynamo	h	0-1	
12/12	Arsenal	a	0-2	

2010

28/2	Tavriya	h	2-0	*Hryshko, Saucedo*
7/3	Obolon	a	0-1	
13/3	Kryvbas	h	3-1	*Vashchuk, Balashov, Saucedo*
20/3	Dnipro	a	1-3	*og (Nazarenko)*
24/3	Metalist	a	1-5	*Shandruk*
28/3	Illychivets	h	1-1	*Balashov*
2/4	Karpaty	a	1-1	*Saucedo*
10/4	Vorskla	h	0-0	
15/4	Zakarpattya	a	1-1	*Vashchuk (p)*
18/4	Metalurh Donetsk	h	1-1	*Zabala*
25/4	Shakhtar	a	0-3	
1/5	Metalist	h	0-2	
5/5	Metalurh Zaporizhya	a	0-1	
9/5	Zorya	h	1-1	*Didenko*

No	Name	Nat	DoB	Pos	Aps	(s)	Gls
55	Olexandr BABYCH		15/2/79	D	2	(1)	
25	Vitaliy BALASHOV		7/2/91	A	14	(10)	4
4	Ruslan BIDNENKO		20/7/81	M	11		
36	Yehor BIDNIY		27/6/88	D	2		
13	Maxym BILETSKIY		7/1/80	D	11		
26	Roman BOCHKUR		27/8/87	D		(1)	
8	Volodymyr BONDARENKO		6/7/81	M	18	(3)	
19	Anatoliy DIDENKO		9/6/82	A	15	(4)	2
2	Volodymyr FEDORIV		29/7/85	D	18		

37	Dmytro HRYSHKO		2/12/85	D	27	(1)	1
20	Oleh HUMENYUK		3/5/83	M	1		
7	Artem KASIYANOV		20/4/83	M	2		
11	Vladimirs KOĻESŅIČENKO	LVA	4/5/80	M	5	(2)	
10	Olexandr KOSYRIN		18/6/77	A	2	(4)	
6	LÉOnardo Cruz de MATOS	BRA	2/4/86	D	13		
9	Ruslan LEVIHA		31/1/83	A	21	(8)	
20	Roman MAXYMYUK		14/6/74	D	1	(1)	
79	Álvaro Alejandro MELLO	URU	13/5/79	M	4	(1)	
43	Serhiy MELNYK		4/9/88	D	2	(1)	
3	Viktor MELNYK		11/8/80	M	10	(6)	1
23	Arrinton NARCISO MINA Villalba	ECU	25/11/82	M	9	(2)	
11	Serhiy NUDNIY		6/10/80	M	2	(1)	
44	Yevhen PAST		16/3/88	G	12		
33	Aleksandr PONOMAREV	RUS	25/1/86	D	3	(2)	
6	Mirko RAJČEVIĆ	MNE	22/3/82	M	2	(4)	1
28	Pavlo REBENOK		23/7/85	M	25	(3)	2
1	Vitaliy RUDENKO		26/1/81	G	11		
18	Mauricio SAUCEDO Guardia	BOL	14/8/85	M	13		3
5	Oleh SHANDRUK		30/1/83	D	26	(1)	2
12	Yevhen SHIRYAYEV		22/2/84	G	7		
15	Vladyslav VASHCHUK		2/1/75	D	22		2
39	Denys VASIN		4/3/89	A	1	(6)	
35	Dmytro VLADOV		12/3/90	M	2	(1)	
16	Olexandr YAKYMENKO		5/9/88	M	5	(4)	
24	Olexandr YATSENKO		24/2/85	D	6		
30	Sebastián VÁZQUEZ	URU	4/11/80	A	9		1
70	Gustavo Pinedo ZABALA	BOL	18/2/88	M	2	(6)	1

FC DNIPRO DNIPROPETROVSK

Coach – Volodymyr Bessonov
Founded – 1918
Stadium – Dnipro-Arena (31,003)
MAJOR HONOURS:
USSR League – (2) 1983, 1988;
USSR Cup – (1) 1989.

2009

19/7	Metalurh Donetsk	a	0-0	
25/7	Metalist	h	2-0	*Kalynychenko, Seleznev*
1/8	Zorya	a	1-0	*Seleznev*
7/8	Arsenal	h	1-1	*Seleznev*
22/8	Obolon	a	0-1	
29/8	Chornomorets	a	1-0	*Homenyuk*
19/9	Karpaty	h	3-0	*Nazarenko 2 (1p), Seleznev*
26/9	Zakarpattya	a	2-0	*Homenyuk 2*
4/10	Shakhtar	a	2-2	*Kalynychenko, Seleznev*
17/10	Metalurh Zaporizhya	a	3-1	*Rotan, Seleznev, Homenyuk*
24/10	Dynamo	h	0-2	
1/11	Tavriya	a	1-2	*Kalynychenko*
22/11	Illychivets	a	3-0	*Seleznev, og (Chuchman), Kalynychenko*
28/11	Vorskla	h	2-2	*Kalynychenko, Seleznev (p)*
6/12	Metalurh Donetsk	h	2-0	*Ferreyra (p), Samodin*
12/12	Metalist	a	2-3	*Seleznev, Kalynychenko*

2010

28/2	Zorya	h	2-2	*Konoplyanka, Homenyuk*
7/3	Arsenal	a	1-1	*Seleznev (p)*
14/3	Obolon	a	2-0	*Samodin, Kalynychenko*
20/3	Chornomorets	h	3-1	*Rusol, Nazarenko, Seleznev*
24/3	Kryvbas	h	3-1	*Nazarenko, Ferreyra, Rusol*
28/3	Karpaty	a	0-1	
3/4	Zakarpattya	h	1-0	*Kalynychenko*
10/4	Shakhtar	a	0-0	
14/4	Metalurh Zaporizhya	h	2-0	*Konoplyanka, Ferreyra*
18/4	Dynamo	a	1-2	*Konoplyanka*
24/4	Tavriya	h	3-1	*Seleznev, Rotan, Ferreyra*
1/5	Kryvbas	a	0-0	
5/5	Illychivets	h	4-1	*Konoplyanka, Rotan, Kravchenko, Seleznev*
9/5	Vorskla	a	1-1	*Nazarenko*

No	Name	Nat	DoB	Pos	Aps	(s)	Gls
21	ALCIDES Eduardo Mendes de Araújo Alves	BRA	13/3/85	D	4	(1)	
7	Olexiy BELIK		15/2/81	A	2	(5)	
12	Yevhen BOROVYK		2/3/85	G	13		
99	Nery Alberto CASTILLO	MEX	13/6/84	A		(3)	
14	Yevhen CHEBERYACHKO		19/6/83	D	27	(1)	
19	Vitaliy DENISOV	UZB	23/2/87	D	28		
15	Paul-Hervé ESSOLA	CMR	13/12/81	M	1	(3)	
18	Osmar Daniel FERREYRA	ARG	9/1/83	M	22	(2)	4
25	Mario HOLEK	CZE	28/10/86	M	12	(8)	
9	Volodymyr HOMENYUK		19/7/85	A	19	(5)	5
26	Maxym KALYNYCHENKO		26/1/79	M	29		8
17	Vitaliy KAVERIN		4/9/90	A	1		
42	Yevhen KONOPLYANKA		29/9/89	A	17	(5)	4
4	Serhiy KRAVCHENKO		24/4/83	M	7	(3)	1
27	Jan LAŠTŮVKA	CZE	7/7/82	G	17		
88	Dmytro LIOPA		23/11/88	M		(2)	
3	Ucha LOBJANIDZE	GEO	23/2/87	D	8	(1)	
44	Vitaliy LYSYTSKIY		16/4/82	D	5	(2)	
5	Vitaliy MANDZYUK		24/1/86	D	7		
28	Serhiy NAZARENKO		16/2/80	M	20	(8)	5
24	Pavlo PASHAYEV		4/1/88	D	16	(6)	
29	Ruslan ROTAN		29/10/81	M	25	(1)	3
16	Andriy RUSOL		16/1/83	D	23		2
10	Sergei SAMODIN	RUS	14/2/85	A	2	(8)	2
11	Yevhen SELEZNEV		20/7/85	A	24	(3)	13
30	Yevhen SHAKHOV		30/11/90	M	1	(4)	

FC DYNAMO KYIV

Coach – Valeriy Gazzayev (RUS)
Founded – 1927
Stadium – Dynamo im. Valeriy Lobanovskiy (16,873)
MAJOR HONOURS:
UEFA Cup Winners' Cup – (2) 1975, 1986;
UEFA Super Cup (1) – 1975;
USSR League – (13) 1961, 1966, 1967, 1968, 1971, 1974, 1975, 1977, 1980, 1981, 1985, 1986, 1990;
Ukrainian League – (13) 1993, 1994, 1995, 1996, 1997, 1998, 1999, 2000, 2001, 2003, 2004, 2007, 2009;
USSR Cup – (9) 1954, 1964, 1966, 1974, 1978, 1982, 1985, 1987, 1990;
Ukrainian Cup – (9) 1993, 1996, 1998, 1999, 2000, 2003, 2005, 2006, 2007.

2009

18/7	Chornomorets	h	5-0	*Kravchenko, Milevskiy (p), Gusev, Yarmolenko, Corrêa*
25/7	Tavriya	h	6-0	*Gusev 2, Milevskiy, Corrêa, Yarmolenko, Guilherme*
1/8	Kryvbas	a	3-1	*Eremenko, Milevskiy, Yarmolenko*
8/8	Illychivets	h	3-1	*Ninković 2, Gusev*
23/8	Vorskla	a	1-1	*Milevskiy (p)*
31/8	Metalurh Donetsk	h	3-1	*Ninković, Yarmolenko, Shevchenko (p)*
20/9	Metalist	a	2-1	*Ghioane, Gusev*
25/9	Zorya	h	2-0	*Milevskiy (p), Ghioane*
4/10	Arsenal	a	1-0	*Shevchenko*
17/10	Obolon	h	2-1	*Milevskiy, Shevchenko*
24/10	Dnipro	a	2-0	*Ghioane, Milevskiy (p)*
31/10	Karpaty	h	1-1	*Ninković*
21/11	Shakhtar	h	3-0	*Milevskiy 2, Yarmolenko*
29/11	Metalurh Zaporizhya	a	0-0	
5/12	Chornomorets	a	1-0	*Yussuf*
13/12	Tavriya	a	3-2	*Milevskiy, Shevchenko, Kravets*

2010

27/2	Kryvbas	h	1-0	*Vukojević*
6/3	Illychivets	a	1-1	*Zozulya*
13/3	Vorskla	h	1-0	*Shevchenko*
19/3	Metalurh Donetsk	a	1-1	*Milevskiy*
24/3	Zakarpattya	a	0-1	
28/3	Metalist	h	3-0	*Mykhalyk, Milevskiy 2*

3/4	Zorya	a	2-0	*Yarmolenko 2*
10/4	Arsenal	h	3-1	*Vukojević, Magrão, Milevskiy*
14/4	Obolon	a	4-0	*Shevchenko 2, Magrão, Zozulya*
18/4	Dnipro	h	2-1	*Magrão, Ghioane*
24/4	Karpaty	a	0-1	
1/5	Zakarpattya	h	2-0	*Milevskiy, Danilo Silva*
5/5	Shakhtar	a	0-1	
9/5	Metalurh Zaporizhya	h	3-0	*Milevskiy 2, og (Krivtsov)*

No	Name	Nat	DoB	Pos	Aps	(s)	Gls
8	Olexandr ALIYEV		3/2/85	M	1	(2)	
3	Ebert William Amâncio "BETÃO"	BRA	11/11/83	D	14	(6)	
31	Stanislav BOHUSH		25/10/83	G	5		
71	Denys BOIKO		29/1/88	G	1		
7	Carlos Rodrigues CORRÊA	BRA	29/12/80	M	2	(1)	2
44	DANILO Aparecido da SILVA	BRA	24/11/86	D	13		1
15	Pape Malickou DIAKHATÉ	SEN	21/6/84	D	1	(1)	
30	Badr EL KADDOURI	MAR	31/1/81	D	4	(4)	
11	Roman EREMENKO	FIN	19/3/87	M	26		1
4	Tiberiu GHIOANE	ROU	18/6/81	M	5	(15)	4
77	GUILHERME Milhomem Gusmão	BRA	22/10/88	A		(4)	1
20	Oleh GUSEV		25/4/83	M	13	(3)	5
35	Denys HARMASH		19/4/90	M	3	(1)	
45	Vladyslav KALITVINTSEV		4/1/93	M	1		
34	Yevhen KHACHERIDI		28/7/87	D	15	(3)	
14	Serhiy KRAVCHENKO		24/4/83	M	1	(2)	1
22	Artem KRAVETS		3/6/89	A	2	(7)	1
44	LEANDRO ALMEIDA da Silva	BRA	14/3/87	D	20	(2)	
21	Gérson Alencor Lima Júnior "MAGRÃO"	BRA	13/6/85	M	20	(1)	3
29	Vitaliy MANDZYUK		24/1/86	D		(2)	
10	Artem MILEVSKIY		12/1/85	A	26	(1)	17
17	Taras MYKHALYK		28/10/83	M	17	(4)	1
26	Andriy NESMACHNIY		28/2/79	D	4	(9)	
36	Miloš NINKOVIĆ	SRB	25/12/84	M	22	(4)	4
8	Kyrylo PETROV		22/6/90	M		(1)	
7	Andriy SHEVCHENKO		29/9/76	A	19	(2)	7
1	Olexandr SHOVKOVSKIY		2/1/75	G	24		
5	Ognjen VUKOJEVIĆ	CRO	20/12/83	M	28		2
61	Andriy YARMOLENKO		23/10/89	A	27	(1)	7
25	Ayila YUSSUF	NGA	4/11/84	M	15	(1)	1
49	Roman ZOZULYA		17/11/89	M	1	(10)	2

FC ILLYCHIVETS MARIUPIL

Coach – Illya Blyznyuk
Founded – 2003
Stadium – Illychivets (12,460)

2009

17/7	Zakarpattya	h	1-0	*Tyshchenko*
25/7	Shakhtar	h	0-2	
2/8	Metalurh Zaporizhya	h	2-1	*Kasiyan, Kashevskiy*
8/8	Dynamo	a	1-3	*Kasiyan*
22/8	Tavriya	h	2-2	*Yaroshenko, Melnyk*
29/8	Kryvbas	a	2-0	*Lima, Tyshchenko*
19/9	Chornomorets	h	2-0	*Tyshchenko, og (Yakymenko)*
27/9	Vorskla	h	0-0	
3/10	Metalurh Donetsk	a	1-4	*Kashevskiy*
18/10	Metalist	h	0-2	
25/10	Zorya	a	2-3	*Kryvosheyenko (p), Melnyk*
1/11	Arsenal	h	1-2	*Melnyk*
22/11	Dnipro	h	0-3	
28/11	Karpaty	a	2-2	*Melnyk, Pukanych*
6/12	Zakarpattya	a	1-0	*Pukanych*
12/12	Shakhtar	a	1-2	*Kirilchik*

2010

27/2	Metalurh Zaporizhya	a	0-2	
6/3	Dynamo	h	1-1	*Tyshchenko*
14/3	Tavriya	a	3-3	*Kasiyan, Yaroshenko, Gabedava*
20/3	Kryvbas	h	0-3	

UKRAINE

<table>
<tr><td>24/3</td><td>Obolon</td><td>a</td><td>1-1</td><td>Yaroshenko</td></tr>
<tr><td>28/3</td><td>Chornomorets</td><td>a</td><td>1-1</td><td>Pukanych</td></tr>
<tr><td>3/4</td><td>Vorskla</td><td>·</td><td>a</td><td>0-3</td></tr>
<tr><td>11/4</td><td>Metalurh Donetsk</td><td>h</td><td>0-4</td><td></td></tr>
<tr><td>15/4</td><td>Metalist</td><td>a</td><td>1-3</td><td>og (Goryainov)</td></tr>
<tr><td>18/4</td><td>Zorya</td><td>h</td><td>1-0</td><td>Yaroshenko (p)</td></tr>
<tr><td>23/4</td><td>Arsenal</td><td>a</td><td>1-3</td><td>Kozoriz</td></tr>
<tr><td>1/5</td><td>Obolon</td><td>h</td><td>1-0</td><td>Yaroshenko (p)</td></tr>
<tr><td>5/5</td><td>Dnipro</td><td>a</td><td>1-4</td><td>Kasiyan</td></tr>
<tr><td>9/5</td><td>Karpaty</td><td>h</td><td>2-2</td><td>Kasiyan, Yaroshenko (p)</td></tr>
</table>

No	Name	Nat	DoB	Pos	Aps	(s)	Gls
6	Darko BOJOVIČ	SVN	1/4/85	M		(1)	
13	Artem CHORNIY		23/10/89	M		(2)	
24	Ihor CHUCHMAN		15/2/85	D	28		
55	Giorgi GABEDAVA	GEO	3/10/89	A	2	(11)	1
20	Anton HAI		25/2/86	M		(1)	
25	Andriy HRYHORYK		31/3/88	M	3	(3)	
66	Stanislav HUDZIKEVYCH		7/3/78	M		(1)	
17	Nikolai KASHEVSKIY	BLR	5/10/80	M	19	(9)	2
27	Olexandr KASIYAN		27/1/89	A	21	(5)	5
23	Yarema KAVATSIV		10/2/86	D		(3)	
33	Pavel KIRILCHIK	BLR	4/1/81	M	3	(12)	1
56	Ivan KOZORIZ		14/9/79	M	3	(4)	1
11	Ivan KRYVOSHEYENKO		11/5/84	A	22	(4)	1
28	Severino LIMA de Maura	BRA	17/5/86	A		(4)	1
84	Vytautas LUKŠA	LTU	14/8/84	M	3	(2)	
4	Vadym MELNYK		16/5/80	D	28	(2)	4
2	Stanislav MYKYTSEI		7/9/89	D	23	(1)	
12	Oleh OSTAPENKO		27/10/77	G	2		
82	Gediminas PAULAUSKAS	LTU	27/10/82	D	7		
5	Adrian PUKANYCH		22/6/83	M	27		3
1	Vsevolod ROMANENKO		24/3/77	G	28		
3	Mantas SAMUSIOVAS	LTU	8/9/78	D	28		
14	Artem SAVIN		20/1/81	D	20	(2)	
40	Yevhen SHMAKOV		7/6/85	M	3		
19	Ihor TYSHCHENKO		11/5/89	M	19	(8)	4
8	Dmytro VOROBEI		10/5/85	M	2		
9	Kostyantyn YAROSHENKO		12/9/86	M	27	(2)	6
51	Olexandr YATSENKO		24/2/85	D	10	(2)	
22	Artur ZAPADNYA		4/6/90	M	2	(3)	

FC KARPATY LVIV
Coach – Oleg Kononov (BLR)
Founded – 1963
Stadium – Ukraina (27,925)
MAJOR HONOURS:
USSR Cup – (1) 1969.

2009

<table>
<tr><td>18/7</td><td>Vorskla</td><td>a</td><td>2-1</td><td>Kuznetsov, Kozhanov</td></tr>
<tr><td>26/7</td><td>Metalurh Donetsk</td><td>h</td><td>2-2</td><td>Fedetskiy, Khudobyak</td></tr>
<tr><td>2/8</td><td>Metalist</td><td>a</td><td>0-1</td><td></td></tr>
<tr><td>8/8</td><td>Zorya</td><td>h</td><td>4-0</td><td>Khudobyak, Kuznetsov, Batista 2 (1p)</td></tr>
<tr><td>23/8</td><td>Arsenal</td><td>a</td><td>0-0</td><td></td></tr>
<tr><td>30/8</td><td>Obolon</td><td>h</td><td>5-0</td><td>Khudobyak 2, Zenjov, Kuznetsov, Batista</td></tr>
<tr><td>19/9</td><td>Dnipro</td><td>a</td><td>0-3</td><td></td></tr>
<tr><td>27/9</td><td>Chornomorets</td><td>a</td><td>1-1</td><td>Fedetskiy</td></tr>
<tr><td>4/10</td><td>Zakarpattya</td><td>h</td><td>1-0</td><td>Kuznetsov</td></tr>
<tr><td>18/10</td><td>Shakhtar</td><td>a</td><td>1-5</td><td>Holodyuk</td></tr>
<tr><td>24/10</td><td>Metalurh Zaporizhya</td><td>h</td><td>3-3</td><td>Kozhanov, Oshchypko, Fedetskiy</td></tr>
<tr><td>31/10</td><td>Dynamo</td><td>a</td><td>1-1</td><td>Zenjov</td></tr>
<tr><td>22/11</td><td>Kryvbas</td><td>a</td><td>2-1</td><td>Holodyuk, Kuznetsov</td></tr>
<tr><td>28/11</td><td>Illychivets</td><td>h</td><td>2-2</td><td>Fedetskiy, Kozhanov</td></tr>
<tr><td>5/12</td><td>Vorskla</td><td>h</td><td>1-0</td><td>Fedetskiy</td></tr>
<tr><td>13/12</td><td>Metalurh Donetsk</td><td>a</td><td>0-1</td><td></td></tr>
</table>

2010

<table>
<tr><td>27/2</td><td>Metalist</td><td>h</td><td>2-1</td><td>Oshchypko (p), Holodyuk</td></tr>
<tr><td>6/3</td><td>Zorya</td><td>a</td><td>2-0</td><td>Oshchypko (p), Fedetskiy</td></tr>
<tr><td>13/3</td><td>Arsenal</td><td>h</td><td>3-3</td><td>Batista, Fedetskiy, Tkachuk</td></tr>
</table>

<table>
<tr><td>20/3</td><td>Obolon</td><td>a</td><td>3-1</td><td>Zenjov, Oshchypko (p), Kozhanov</td></tr>
<tr><td>28/3</td><td>Dnipro</td><td>h</td><td>1-0</td><td>Khudobyak</td></tr>
<tr><td>2/4</td><td>Chornomorets</td><td>h</td><td>1-1</td><td>Batista</td></tr>
<tr><td>7/4</td><td>Tavriya</td><td>h</td><td>1-0</td><td>Oshchypko</td></tr>
<tr><td>11/4</td><td>Zakarpattya</td><td>a</td><td>1-1</td><td>Batista</td></tr>
<tr><td>15/4</td><td>Shakhtar</td><td>h</td><td>0-2</td><td></td></tr>
<tr><td>19/4</td><td>Metalurh Zaporizhya</td><td>a</td><td>1-0</td><td>Oshchypko (p)</td></tr>
<tr><td>24/4</td><td>Dynamo</td><td>h</td><td>1-0</td><td>Batista</td></tr>
<tr><td>1/5</td><td>Tavriya</td><td>a</td><td>1-1</td><td>Tkachuk</td></tr>
<tr><td>5/5</td><td>Kryvbas</td><td>h</td><td>0-2</td><td></td></tr>
<tr><td>9/5</td><td>Illychivets</td><td>a</td><td>2-2</td><td>Tubić, Batista</td></tr>
</table>

No	Name	Nat	DoB	Pos	Aps	(s)	Gls
80	Wiliam Rocha BATISTA	BRA	27/7/80	A	16	(10)	8
28	Volodymyr BIDLOVSKIY		31/5/88	M		(2)	
44	Artem FEDETSKIY		26/4/85	D	28		7
35	Yuriy FURTA		31/5/88	A		(1)	
7	Samson GODWIN	NGA	11/11/83	M	21		
10	Aleksandre GURULI	GEO	9/11/85	A	10	(15)	
24	Yuriy HABOVDA		6/5/89	A		(3)	
17	Oleh HOLODYUK		2/1/88	M	18	(3)	3
36	Volodymyr HUDYMA		20/7/90	A		(1)	
27	Andriy HURSKIY		30/8/88	D		(1)	
13	Mladen KAŠĆELAN	MNE	13/2/83	M	2	(1)	
16	Ihor KHUDOBYAK		20/2/85	M	30		5
18	Mykhailo KOPOLOVETS		29/1/84	M	10	(9)	
9	Denys KOZHANOV		13/6/87	A	29		4
79	Serhiy KUZNETSOV		31/8/82	A	16		5
14	Vlade LAZAREVSKI	MKD	9/6/83	M	2		
30	Yaroslav MARTYNYUK		20/2/89	M	1	(6)	
1	Yuriy MARTYSHCHUK		22/4/86	G	1		
4	Nemanja MILOŠEVIĆ	SRB	3/11/84	D	25	(1)	
8	Ihor OSHCHYPKO		25/10/85	D	24		6
15	Taras PETRIVSKIY		3/2/84	D	11	(3)	
33	Yevhen TARASENKO		3/3/83	D	12	(1)	
25	Andriy TKACHUK		18/11/87	M	15	(13)	2
22	Andriy TLUMAK		7/3/79	G	29		
5	Nemanja TUBIĆ	SRB	8/4/84	A	23		1
11	Sergei ZENJOV	EST	20/4/89	A	7	(18)	3

FC KRYVBAS KRYVYI RIH
Coach – Oleh Taran; (11/1/10) Yuriy Maximov
Founded – 1959
Stadium – Metalurh (29,734)

2009

<table>
<tr><td>18/7</td><td>Shakhtar</td><td>a</td><td>0-3</td><td></td></tr>
<tr><td>26/7</td><td>Metalurh Zaporizhya</td><td>a</td><td>1-2</td><td>Shturko</td></tr>
<tr><td>1/8</td><td>Dynamo</td><td>h</td><td>1-3</td><td>Bylykbashi (p)</td></tr>
<tr><td>8/8</td><td>Tavriya</td><td>a</td><td>1-3</td><td>Motuz</td></tr>
<tr><td>22/8</td><td>Chornomorets</td><td>h</td><td>2-3</td><td>Bartulović (p), Vorobei</td></tr>
<tr><td>29/8</td><td>Illychivets</td><td>h</td><td>0-2</td><td></td></tr>
<tr><td>20/9</td><td>Vorskla</td><td>a</td><td>0-0</td><td></td></tr>
<tr><td>26/9</td><td>Metalurh Donetsk</td><td>h</td><td>0-1</td><td></td></tr>
<tr><td>3/10</td><td>Metalist</td><td>a</td><td>0-1</td><td></td></tr>
<tr><td>17/10</td><td>Zorya</td><td>h</td><td>4-0</td><td>Maximov 2, Bartulović 2 (1p)</td></tr>
<tr><td>24/10</td><td>Arsenal</td><td>a</td><td>1-2</td><td>Karakevych</td></tr>
<tr><td>1/11</td><td>Obolon</td><td>h</td><td>3-2</td><td>Karakevych 2, Bartulović (p)</td></tr>
<tr><td>22/11</td><td>Karpaty</td><td>h</td><td>1-2</td><td>Bartulović (p)</td></tr>
<tr><td>28/11</td><td>Zakarpattya</td><td>a</td><td>0-3</td><td></td></tr>
<tr><td>6/12</td><td>Shakhtar</td><td>h</td><td>0-2</td><td></td></tr>
<tr><td>13/12</td><td>Metalurh Zaporizhya</td><td>h</td><td>1-3</td><td>Bartulović</td></tr>
</table>

2010

<table>
<tr><td>27/2</td><td>Dynamo</td><td>a</td><td>0-1</td><td></td></tr>
<tr><td>7/3</td><td>Tavriya</td><td>h</td><td>0-1</td><td></td></tr>
<tr><td>13/3</td><td>Chornomorets</td><td>a</td><td>1-3</td><td>Voronkov</td></tr>
<tr><td>20/3</td><td>Illychivets</td><td>a</td><td>3-0</td><td>Voronkov 2, Liopa</td></tr>
<tr><td>24/3</td><td>Dnipro</td><td>a</td><td>1-3</td><td>Maximov</td></tr>
<tr><td>28/3</td><td>Vorskla</td><td>h</td><td>1-1</td><td>Liopa (p)</td></tr>
<tr><td>3/4</td><td>Metalurh Donetsk</td><td>h</td><td>1-0</td><td>Voronkov</td></tr>
<tr><td>10/4</td><td>Metalist</td><td>h</td><td>2-2</td><td>Bartulović, Kitsuta</td></tr>
</table>

15/4	Zorya	a	0-1	
18/4	Arsenal	h	0-1	
25/4	Obolon	a	2-1	Morozyuk, Andriyenko
1/5	Dnipro	h	0-0	
5/5	Karpaty	a	2-0	Fedorchuk, Voronkov
9/5	Zakarpattya	h	3-1	Motuz, Morozyuk, Liopa

No	Name	Nat	DoB	Pos	Aps	(s)	Gls
16	Ansi AGOLLI	ALB	11/10/82	M	6	(7)	
2	Denys ANDRIYENKO		12/4/80	D	4	(1)	1
23	Mladen BARTULOVIĆ	CRO	5/10/86	M	23	(4)	7
21	Andriy BOGOMAZOV		15/7/89	M	6	(3)	
18	Ervin BULKU	ALB	3/3/81	M	13	(1)	
17	Dorian BYLYKBASHI	ALB	8/8/80	M	9	(6)	1
4	Serhiy DANYLOVSKIY		20/8/81	M	6	(2)	
6	Oleh DOPILKA		12/3/86	D	7		
37	Valeriy FEDORCHUK		5/10/88	M	9	(1)	1
1	Andriy FEDORENKO		9/1/84	G	3		
4	Olexandr GRANOVSKIY		11/3/76	D	1		
12	Isli HIDI	ALB	15/10/80	G	9		
28	Kęstutis IVAŠKEVIČIUS	LTU	17/4/85	M	9	(4)	
32	Anton KANIBOLOTSKIY		16/5/88	G	13		
11	Roman KARAKEVYCH		13/11/08	A	5	(2)	3
15	Serhiy KARPENKO		19/5/81	D	11		
32	Vyacheslav KERNOZENKO		4/6/76	G	5		
27	Anatoliy KITSUTA		22/12/85	M	13	(1)	1
19	Aleksandre KOBAKHIDZE	GEO	11/2/87	M	12	(11)	
10	Ruslan KOSTYSHYN		8/1/77	M	4	(8)	
5	Vitaliy KOMARNYTSKIY		2/8/81	D	8	(3)	
88	Dmytro LIOPA		23/11/88	M	11	(1)	3
44	Vitaliy LYSYTSKIY		16/4/82	M	14		
30	Olexandr MAXIMOV		13/2/85	M	25		3
8	Olexandr MELASHCHENKO		13/12/78	A		(6)	
18	Pavlo MISKO		12/2/90	A		(1)	
7	Mykola MOROZYUK		17/1/88	M	12		2
20	Serhiy MOTUZ		6/7/82	A	2	(5)	2
7	Andriy OBEREMKO		18/3/84	M	6		
29	Anatoliy OPRYA		25/11/77	M	4		
3	Vyacheslav SERDYUK		28/1/85	D	23	(3)	
22	Yuriy SHTURKO		8/10/84	A	9	(8)	1
2	Artūrs SILAGAILIS	LVA	3/5/87	D	1		
14	Platon SVYRYDOV		20/11/86	M	3	(1)	
9	Dmytro VOROBEI		10/5/85	M	5	(1)	1
8	Andrei VORONKOV	BLR	8/2/89	A	13		5
25	Olexandr ZHDANOV		27/5/84	D	26	(2)	

FC METALIST KHARKIV
Coach – Myron Markevych
Founded – 1925
Stadium – OSK Metalist (41,307)
MAJOR HONOURS:
USSR Cup - (1) 1988.

2009				
19/7	Obolon	a	2-0	Edmar, Oliynyk
25/7	Dnipro	a	0-2	
2/8	Karpaty	h	1-0	Gueye
9/8	Zakarpattya	a	2-0	Lysenko, Zézé
30/8	Metalurh Zaporizhya	a	2-0	Jajá 2
20/9	Dynamo	h	1-2	Dević
23/9	Shakhtar	h	1-1	Oliynyk
27/9	Tavriya	a	0-0	
3/10	Kryvbas	h	1-0	Jajá
18/10	Illychivets	a	2-0	Jajá 2
25/10	Vorskla	h	1-0	Jajá
1/11	Metalurh Donetsk	a	1-0	Dević (p)
21/11	Zorya	h	2-0	Jajá, Oliynyk
29/11	Arsenal	a	2-1	Oliynyk, Obradović (p)
5/12	Obolon	h	0-1	
12/12	Dnipro	h	3-2	Jajá 2 (1p), Rykun

2010				
27/2	Karpaty	a	1-2	Jajá
6/3	Zakarpattya	h	2-1	Dević (p), Jajá
14/3	Shakhtar	a	1-2	Antonov
20/3	Metalurh Zaporizhya	h	4-0	Valyayev, Dević, Edmar, Oliynyk
24/3	Chornomorets	h	5-1	Dević 3, Jajá, og (Ponomarev)
28/3	Dynamo	a	0-3	
3/4	Tavriya	h	1-1	Jajá (p)
10/4	Kryvbas	a	2-2	Oliynyk, Fininho
15/4	Illychivets	h	3-1	Oliynyk, Jajá, Dević
18/4	Vorskla	a	0-0	
24/4	Metalurh Donetsk	h	2-0	Gueye, Jajá
1/5	Chornomorets	a	2-0	Slyusar, Valyayev
5/5	Zorya	a	4-1	Oliynyk 2, Edmar, Jajá
9/5	Arsenal	h	1-0	Fininho

No	Name	Nat	DoB	Pos	Aps	(s)	Gls
69	Olexiy ANTONOV		8/5/86	A	3	(4)	1
19	Serhiy BARYLKO		5/1/87	M		(4)	
23	Ihor BAZHAN		2/12/81	G	4		
4	Andriy BEREZOVCHUK		16/4/81	D	10	(1)	
37	Vitalie BORDIAN	MDA	11/8/84	D	18	(4)	
16	Marcin BURKHARDT	POL	25/9/83	M	1	(6)	
33	Marko DEVIĆ		27/10/83	M	17	(3)	8
8	EDMAR Golovski de Lacerda Aparecida	BRA	16/6/80	M	24	(2)	3
10	Alexei EREMENKO Jr	FIN	24/3/83	A	4	(6)	
15	Vinícius Aparecido Pereira de Santana Campos "FININHO"	BRA	3/11/83	A	7	(1)	2
15	Hernán Daniel FREDES	ARG	27/3/87	M		(4)	
6	Seweryn GANCARCZYK	POL	22/11/81	D	1		
29	Olexandr GORYAINOV		29/6/75	G	26		
30	Papa GUEYE	SEN	7/6/84	D	30		2
50	Jackson Avelino Coelho "JAJÁ"	BRA	28/2/86	A	25		16
14	Volodymyr LYSENKO		20/4/88	A	5	(9)	1
27	Jonathan Ramón MAIDANA	ARG	29/7/85	D	13	(1)	
22	Milan OBRADOVIĆ	SRB	3/8/77	D	25	(1)	1
11	Denys OLIYNYK		16/6/87	M	26	(3)	9
20	Anton POSTUPALENKO		28/8/88	M		(2)	
17	Serhiy PSHENYCHNYKH		19/11/81	D	9	(3)	
77	Artem PUTIVTSEV		29/8/88	M	4	(2)	
25	Olexandr RYKUN		6/5/78	M	16	(2)	1
3	Yevhen SELIN		9/5/88	M	5	(1)	
5	Oleh SHELAYEV		5/11/76	M	20	(6)	
9	Valentyn SLYUSAR		15/9/77	M	5	(14)	1
88	Aleksandar TRIŠOVIĆ	SRB	25/11/83	M	1	(1)	
7	Serhiy VALYAYEV		16/9/78	M	28		2
26	Venance ZÉZÉ	CIV	17/6/81	A	3	(6)	1

FC METALURH DONETSK
Coach – Nikolai Kostov (BUL)
Founded – 1996
Stadium – Metalurh (5,094)

2009				
19/7	Dnipro	h	0-0	
26/7	Karpaty	a	2-2	Godin, Mkhitaryan
2/8	Zakarpattya	h	4-1	Mkhitaryan, Tănasă, Godin, Mguni
9/8	Shakhtar	a	1-4	Kingsley
23/8	Metalurh Zaporizhya	h	3-0	Tănasă 2, Dimitrov (p)
31/8	Dynamo	a	1-3	Tănasă
20/9	Tavriya	h	0-0	
26/9	Kryvbas	a	1-0	Mkhitaryan
3/10	Illychivets	h	4-1	Lazić, Shyshchenko, Kingsley, Tănasă
17/10	Vorskla	a	2-1	Mário Sérgio, Mkhitaryan
24/10	Chornomorets	h	2-0	China, Mkhitaryan
1/11	Metalist	h	0-1	
21/11	Arsenal	h	3-0	Mguni, Dimitrov, Mkhitaryan
29/11	Obolon	a	1-2	Mkhitaryan

UKRAINE

6/12	Dnipro	a	0-2	
13/12	Karpaty	h	1-0	Checher
2010				
27/2	Zakarpattya	a	1-0	Mguni
7/3	Shakhtar	h	0-1	
13/3	Metalurh Zaporizhya	a	2-3	Mguni, Dimitrov
19/3	Dynamo	h	1-1	Mkhitaryan
28/3	Tavriya	a	0-1	
3/4	Kryvbas	h	0-1	
7/4	Zorya	a	1-1	Mguni
11/4	Illychivets	a	4-0	Dimitrov 2 (1p), Tănasă, Mkhitaryan
15/4	Vorskla	h	1-3	Mário Sérgio (p)
18/4	Chornomorets	a	1-1	Mguni
24/4	Metalist	a	0-2	
30/4	Zorya	h	0-0	
5/5	Arsenal	a	0-2	
9/5	Obolon	h	5-0	Soares 2, Dimitrov 2 (1p), Tănasă

No	Name	Nat	DoB	Pos	Aps	(s)	Gls
6	Ararat ARAKELYAN	ARM	1/2/84	M		(3)	
5	Serhiy BILOZOR		15/7/79	D	2	(4)	
4	Vyacheslav CHECHER		15/12/80	D	25		1
27	João Pedro Santos Gonçalves "CHINA"	POR	15/4/82	D	9	(1)	1
33	Serhiy DANYLOVSKIY		20/8/81	M	6	(2)	
3	Artak DASHYAN	ARM	20/11/89	M	1	(3)	
18	Velizar DIMITROV	BUL	13/4/79	M	22	(1)	7
66	Vladimir DIŠLJENKOVIĆ	SRB	2/7/81	G	20		
47	Fábio de Matos Pereira "FABINHO"	BRA	26/2/82	M	2	(5)	
23	Olexiy GODIN		2/2/83	M	15	(6)	2
46	Vitaliy IVANKO		9/4/92	A		(2)	
6	JÚLIO CÉSAR Mendes Moreira	BRA	19/1/83	D		(2)	
39	Sunny Ekeh KINGSLEY	NGA	9/9/81	M	26	(2)	2
3	Ihor KOROTETSKIY		13/9/87	D	11	(3)	
9	Đorđe LAZIĆ	SRB	18/6/83	M	19	(4)	1
20	Constantinos MAKRIDES	CYP	13/1/82	M	4	(1)	
28	MÁRIO SÉRGIO Leal Nogueira	POR	28/7/81	D	29		2
7	Musawengosi MGUNI	ZIM	5/4/83	A	20	(1)	6
22	Henrikh MKHITARYAN	ARM	21/1/89	A	29		9
1	Dmytro NEPOGODOV		17/2/88	G	2		
44	Vasyl PRYIMA		10/6/91	D	21	(3)	
35	Bohdan SHUST		4/3/86	G	5		
88	Serhiy SHYSHCHENKO		13/1/76	A	1	(9)	1
15	Ciprian Ion TĂNASĂ	ROU	2/2/81	A	6	(13)	7
8	Serhiy TKACHENKO		10/2/79	M		(5)	
14	Olexandr VOLOVYK		28/10/85	D	28	(1)	
31	Dmytro VOROBYOV		27/8/77	G	3	(1)	
88	WILLIAM Cleite Boaventura	BRA	14/2/80	D	11	(2)	
10	Chavdar YANKOV	BUL	29/3/84	M	10	(3)	
17	José "ZÉ" SOARES da Silva Filho	BRA	27/7/83	M	3	(11)	2

FC METALURH ZAPORIZHYA

Coach – Oleh Lutkov; (3/9/09) (Volodymyr Khodus);
(22/10/09) Roman Hryhorchuk; (2/11/09) (Volodymyr Khodus);
(8/12/09) Roman Hryhorchuk
Founded – 1935
Stadium – Slavutych-Arena (11,756)

2009				
19/7	Tavriya	a	0-2	
26/7	Kryvbas	h	2-1	og (Zhdanov), Kaskov
2/8	Illychivets	a	1-2	Tigorev
9/8	Vorskla	h	1-1	Arzhanov
23/8	Metalurh Donetsk	a	0-3	
30/8	Metalist	h	0-2	
19/9	Zorya	a	1-3	Rudyka
26/9	Arsenal	h	2-1	Arzhanov, Kaskov

3/10	Obolon	a	1-4	Arzhanov (p)
17/10	Dnipro	h	1-3	Polyoviy
24/10	Karpaty	a	3-3	Teiku, Alozi 2
1/11	Zakarpattya	h	3-0	Vernydub, Alozi, Arzhanov
22/11	Chornomorets	a	0-0	
29/11	Dynamo	h	0-0	
5/12	Tavriya	h	0-1	
9/12	Shakhtar	a	0-2	
13/12	Kryvbas	a	3-1	Arzhanov 2, Modebadze
2010				
27/2	Illychivets	h	2-0	Krivtsov, Alozi
7/3	Vorskla	a	1-1	Krivtsov
13/3	Metalurh Donetsk	h	3-2	Teiku, Pisotskiy, Nevmyvaka
20/3	Metalist	a	0-4	
27/3	Zorya	h	3-1	Arzhanov, Opanasenko 2
4/3	Arsenal	a	0-2	
9/4	Obolon	h	2-1	Nevmyvaka, Alozi
14/4	Dnipro	a	0-2	
19/4	Karpaty	h	0-1	
25/4	Zakarpattya	a	1-0	Nesterov
1/5	Shakhtar	h	0-2	
5/5	Chornomorets	h	1-0	Alozi
9/5	Dynamo	a	0-3	

No	Name	Nat	DoB	Pos	Aps	(s)	Gls
16	Michael Chidi ALOZI	NGA	16/10/86	A	24		6
17	Volodymyr ARZHANOV		29/11/85	M	28		7
24	Dmytro BEZOTOSNIY		15/11/83	G	9		
11	Maxym BILIY		27/4/89	A		(1)	
9	Igor BUGAIOV	MDA	26/6/84	A	2	(1)	
19	Vasile CARAUS	MDA	6/8/88	M	10	(6)	
8	Andriy DEMCHENKO		20/8/76	M		(1)	
22	HWANG Hun-hee	PRK	6/4/87	A		(3)	
10	Mindaugas KALONAS	LTU	28/2/84	A	10	(2)	
30	Artur KASKOV		18/11/91	A	16	(8)	2
15	KIM Pyung-rae	PRK	9/11/87	M	6	(1)	
1	Maxym KOVAL		9/12/92	G	19		
38	Serhiy KRIVTSOV		15/3/91	D	20	(2)	2
18	Darius MICEIKA	LTU	22/2/83	M	14	(2)	
12	Irakli MODEBADZE	GEO	22/4/84	A		(11)	1
21	Andriy NESTEROV		2/7/90	D	3	(5)	1
3	Dmytro NEVMYVAKA		19/3/84	D	22	(3)	2
39	Yevhen OPANASENKO		25/8/90	M	17	(1)	2
31	Yevhen PISOTSKIY		22/4/87	M	6	(15)	1
32	Volodymyr POLYOVIY		28/7/85	M	25	(1)	1
32	Serhiy RUDYKA		14/6/88	M	3	(1)	1
4	Taras STEPANENKO		8/8/89	D	17		
34	Serhiy SYDORCHUK		2/5/91	M		(7)	
44	Serhiy SYLUYK		5/6/85	M		(2)	
5	Adolf Kamgeng TEIKU	CMR	23/6/90	D	25		2
9	Igor TIGIRLAS	MDA	24/2/84	A	10	(3)	
20	Yan TIGOREV	BLR	10/3/84	D	28	(1)	1
7	Vitaliy VERNYDUB		17/10/87	D	14	(1)	1
35	Volodymyr ZHUK		30/5/86	G	2		

FC OBOLON KYIV

Coach – Yuriy Maximov; (14/1/10) Serhiy Kovalets
Founded – 1992
Stadium – Obolon ARENA (5,100)

2009				
19/7	Metalist	h	0-2	
26/7	Zorya	h	3-0	Lozynskiy, Kutsenko, Voronkov
1/8	Arsenal	a	1-4	og (Symonenko)
8/8	Chornomorets	a	1-0	Kutsenko
22/8	Dnipro	h	1-0	Kutsenko
30/8	Karpaty	a	0-5	
19/9	Zakarpattya	h	0-1	
27/9	Shakhtar	a	0-4	
3/10	Metalurh Zaporizhya	h	4-1	Ivashchenko, Rozhok, Voronkov, Kutsenko
17/10	Dynamo	a	1-2	Yavorskiy

24/10	Tavriya	h	1-0	Antonenko	
1/11	Kryvbas	a	2-3	Voronkov, Miroshnychenko	
21/11	Vorskla	a	2-3	Rozhok, Malysh	
29/11	Metalurh Donetsk	h	2-1	Kutsenko, Voronkov	
5/12	Metalist	a	1-0	Voronkov	
12/12	Zorya	a	0-2		
2010					
28/2	Arsenal	h	0-0		
7/3	Chornomorets	h	1-0	Onysko	
14/3	Dnipro	a	0-2		
20/3	Karpaty	h	1-3	Yavorskiy	
24/3	Illychivets	h	1-1	Kotenko	
27/3	Zakarpattya	a	1-0	Rozhok	
3/4	Shakhtar	h	0-1		
9/4	Metalurh Zaporizhya	a	1-2	Konyushenko	
24/4	Dynamo	h	0-4		
19/4	Tavriya	a	0-0		
25/4	Kryvbas	h	1-2	Valeyev	
1/5	Illychivets	a	0-1		
5/5	Vorskla	h	1-1	Konyushenko (p)	
9/5	Metalurh Donetsk	a	0-5		

No	Name	Nat	DoB	Pos	Aps	(s)	Gls
33	Olexandr ANTONENKO		29/12/78	A	3	(3)	1
71	Denys BOIKO		29/1/88	G	15		
17	Olexandr BONDARENKO		28/7/79	A	2	(2)	
23	Victor COMLEONOC	MDA	23/2/79	M	5	(6)	
50	Andriy FARTUSHNYAK		24/3/89	D	2	(5)	
20	Olexandr IVASHCHENKO		19/2/85	A	13	(5)	1
26	Dmytro KARABAYEV		17/8/90	M		(1)	
27	Oleh KARAMUSHKA		30/4/84	D	5		
3	Yevhen KARMALITA		12/4/83	D		(1)	
27	Anatoliy KITSUTA		22/12/85	M	14		
6	Olexandr KLYMENKO		11/2/82	D	4	(2)	
44	Andriy KONYUSHENKO		2/4/77	D	19	(1)	2
49	Ivan KOTENKO		28/4/85	M	10	(1)	1
3	Pavlo KUTAS		3/9/82	D	3		
22	Valeriy KUTSENKO		2/11/86	M	22	(2)	5
5	Ivan LEN		25/7/82	D	11	(2)	
7	Yevhen LOZYNSKIY		7/2/82	D	26		1
14	Ihor MALYSH		15/7/83	M	2	(2)	1
25	Oleh MAZURENKO		8/11/77	M	6	(5)	
2	Artem MIROSHNYCHENKO		9/11/78	M	2	(20)	1
11	Mykola MOROZYUK		17/1/88	M	14		
19	Volodymyr OLEFIR		26/2/80	D	3		
9	Pavlo ONYSKO		12/7/79	A	7	(5)	1
32	Ihor PLASTUN		20/8/90	M	1	(1)	
57	Yuriy PUTRASH		29/1/90	D	2	(1)	
10	Serhiy ROZHOK		25/4/85	M	24		3
4	Ruslan RYABIY		1/3/91	A		(2)	
1	Olexandr RYBKA		10/4/87	G	7		
59	Anton SHEVCHUK		8/2/90	A		(1)	
8	Serhiy SYBIRYAKOV		1/1/82	M	20	(2)	
42	Andriy TOVT		12/3/85	G	8	(1)	
14	Maxym TRUSEVYCH		1/8/85	M	4	(1)	
88	Rinar VALEYEV		22/8/87	M	25	(3)	1
24	Denys VASILIYEV		8/5/87	D	11	(6)	
80	Andrei VORONKOV	BLR	8/2/89	A	12	(2)	5
13	Serhiy YAVORSKIY		5/7/89	D	25		2
28	Yevhen ZARICHNYUK		3/2/89	M	3	(1)	

FC SHAKHTAR DONETSK

Coach – Mircea Lucescu (ROU)
Founded – 1936
Stadium – RSK Olympiyskiy (26,100); Donbass Arena (50,149)
MAJOR HONOURS:
UEFA Cup – (1) 2009;
Ukrainian League – (5) 2002, 2005, 2006, 2008, 2010;
USSR Cup – (4) 1961, 1962, 1980, 1983;
Ukrainian Cup (6) 1995, 1997, 2001, 2002, 2004, 2008.

2009					
18/7	Kryvbas	h	3-0	Jádson 2, Aghahowa	
25/7	Illychivets	a	2-0	Luiz Adriano 2	
1/8	Vorskla	a	1-1	Raţ	
9/8	Metalurh Donetsk	h	4-1	Polyanskiy, Hladkiy 2, Kucher	
31/8	Zorya	h	3-1	Lewandowski, Jádson, Kravchenko	
20/9	Arsenal	a	4-2	Fernandinho (p), Hladkiy, Kravchenko 2	
23/9	Metalist	a	1-1	Kravchenko	
27/9	Obolon	h	4-0	Jádson (p), Ilsinho, Kobin, Willian	
4/10	Dnipro	a	2-2	Luiz Adriano 2	
18/10	Karpaty	h	5-1	Fernandinho 2 (1p), Jádson (p), Luiz Adriano 2 (1p)	
25/10	Zakarpattya	a	1-1	Hai	
1/11	Chornomorets	a	1-0	Jádson	
21/11	Dynamo	a	0-3		
28/11	Tavriya	h	3-0	Luiz Adriano 2, Ilsinho	
6/12	Kryvbas	a	2-0	Fernandinho (p), Hladkiy	
9/12	Metalurh Zaporizhya	h	2-0	Willian, Luiz Adriano (p)	
12/12	Illychivets	h	2-1	Fomin, Kravchenko	
2010					
28/2	Vorskla	h	1-0	Jádson	
7/3	Metalurh Donetsk	a	1-0	Hladkiy	
14/3	Metalist	h	2-1	Lewandowski, Douglas Costa	
20/3	Zorya	a	2-0	Willian, Srna	
28/3	Arsenal	h	3-1	Jádson, Willian, Douglas Costa	
3/4	Obolon	a	1-0	Srna	
10/4	Dnipro	h	0-0		
15/4	Karpaty	a	2-0	Luiz Adriano, Willian	
18/4	Zakarpattya	h	1-0	Hladkiy	
25/4	Chornomorets	h	3-0	Jádson (p), Douglas Costa, Luiz Adriano	
1/5	Metalurh Zaporizhya	a	2-0	Ilsinho, Douglas Costa	
5/5	Dynamo	h	1-0	Ilsinho	
9/5	Tavriya	a	3-2	Kravchenko 2, Douglas Costa	

No	Name	Nat	DoB	Pos	Aps	(s)	Gls
77	Julius AGHAHOWA	NGA	12/2/82	A	4	(5)	1
29	ALEX TEIXEIRA Santos	BRA	6/1/90	M	2	(1)	
36	Olexandr CHIZHOV		10/8/86	D	8	(1)	
27	Dmytro CHYHRYNSKIY		7/11/86	D	4		
20	DOUGLAS COSTA de Souza	BRA	14/9/90	M	4	(9)	5
4	Igor DULJAJ	SRB	29/10/79	D	11	(3)	
7	Fernando Luís Roza "FERNANDINHO"	BRA	4/5/85	M	24		4
24	Ruslan FOMIN		2/3/86	A	4	(8)	1
19	Olexiy HAI		6/11/82	M	5	(8)	1
21	Olexandr HLADKIY		24/8/87	A	15	(7)	6
3	Tomáš HÜBSCHMAN	CZE	4/9/81	M	15	(3)	
11	Ilson Pereira Dias Júnior "ILSINHO"	BRA	12/10/85	M	16	(7)	4
32	Mykola ISHCHENKO		9/3/83	D	12		
8	JÁDSON Rodrigues da Silva	BRA	5/10/83	M	22	(4)	9
12	Rustam KHUDZHAMOV		5/10/82	G	3		
14	Vasyl KOBIN		24/5/85	M	17	(7)	1
23	Kostyantyn KRAVCHENKO		24/9/86	M	5	(6)	7
5	Olexandr KUCHER		22/10/82	D	14		1
18	Mariusz LEWANDOWSKI	POL	18/5/79	D	9	(5)	2
17	LUIZ ADRIANO de Souza da Silva	BRA	12/4/87	A	21	(2)	11
28	Olexiy POLYANSKIY		12/4/86	M	3	(1)	1
30	Andriy PYATOV		28/6/84	G	27		
44	Yaroslav RAKYTSKIY		3/8/89	M	22	(2)	
26	Răzvan Dincă RAŢ	ROU	26/5/81	D	13	(5)	1
13	Vyacheslav SHEVCHUK		13/5/79	D	6		
33	Darijo SRNA	CRO	1/5/82	M	24	(2)	2
90	Vitaliy VITSENETS		3/8/90	M		(2)	
22	WILLIAN Borges da Silva	BRA	9/8/88	M	20	(2)	5

UKRAINE

SC TAVRIYA SIMFEROPOL
Coach – Serhiy Puchkov
Founded – 1958
Stadium – Lokomotyv (19,978)
MAJOR HONOURS:
Ukrainian League – (1) 1992;
Ukrainian Cup – (1) 2010.

2009

19/7	Metalurh Zaporizhya	h	2-0	Kovpak (p), Platon
25/7	Dynamo	a	0-6	
31/7	Chornomorets	h	2-1	Kovpak, Marković
8/8	Kryvbas	h	3-1	Marković, Monakhov, Galyuza
22/8	Illychivets	a	2-2	Gigiadze, Ljubenović
30/8	Vorskla	h	1-0	Platon
20/9	Metalurh Donetsk	a	0-0	
27/9	Metalist	h	0-0	
3/10	Zorya	a	0-0	
18/10	Arsenal	h	2-2	Idahor, Gigiadze (p)
24/10	Obolon	a	0-1	
1/11	Dnipro	h	2-1	Feshchuk, og (Pashayev)
21/11	Zakarpattya	h	3-2	Idahor, Ljubenović, Kovpak (p)
28/11	Shakhtar	a	0-3	
5/12	Metalurh Zaporizhya	a	1-0	Monakhov
13/12	Dynamo	h	2-3	Gigiadze (p), Idahor

2010

28/2	Chornomorets	a	0-2	
7/3	Kryvbas	a	1-0	Kovpak
14/3	Illychivets	h	3-3	Feshchuk, Galyuza, Idahor
19/3	Vorskla	a	1-0	Feshchuk
28/3	Metalurh Donetsk	h	1-0	Holaido
3/4	Metalist	a	1-1	Idahor
7/4	Karpaty	a	0-1	
11/4	Zorya	h	0-1	
15/4	Arsenal	a	6-1	Kovpak 3 (1p), Marković, Ljubenović 2
19/4	Obolon	h	0-0	
24/4	Dnipro	a	1-3	Lutsenko
1/5	Karpaty	h	1-1	Feshchuk
5/5	Zakarpattya	a	1-0	Matyazh
9/5	Shakhtar	h	2-3	Ljubenović, Kovpak

No	Name	Nat	DoB	Pos	Aps	(s)	Gls
29	Matviy BOBAL		27/5/84	A		(1)	
3	Ihor BURYAK		12/1/83	D	1		
25	Vadym DEONAS		25/7/75	G	6		
4	Andriy DONETS		3/1/81	D		(1)	
28	Maxym FESHCHUK		25/11/85	A	12	(7)	4
19	Illya GALYUZA		16/11/79	M	23	(2)	2
20	Vasyl GIGIADZE	GEO	3/6/77	A	19	(9)	3
7	Paweł HAJDUCZEK	POL	17/5/82	M		(3)	
27	Denys HOLAIDO		3/6/84	M	28		1
10	Lucky Isi IDAHOR	NGA	30/8/80	A	12	(13)	5
18	Andrius JOKŠAS	LTU	12/1/79	M		(2)	
6	Saša JURIČIĆ	CRO	14/8/79	D	27	(1)	
33	Oleh KARAMUSHKA		30/4/84	D	3		
8	Andriy KORNEV		1/11/78	M	27		
9	Olexandr KOVPAK		2/2/83	A	25		8
22	Željko LJUBENOVIĆ	SRB	9/7/81	M	29		5
15	Yevhen LUTSENKO		10/11/80	M	19	(8)	1
5	Slobodan MARKOVIĆ	SRB	9/11/78	D	27	3	
18	Ivan MATYAZH		15/2/88	M	6	(3)	1
11	Anton MONAKHOV		31/1/82	D	29		2
24	Ruslan PLATON		12/1/82	A	6	(15)	2
1	Maxym STARTSEV		20/1/80	G	16		
12	Dmytro STOIKO		3/2/75	G	8	(3)	
4	Vyacheslav SVIDERSKIY		1/1/79	D	2		
21	Maxym SYROTA		27/7/87	M	1	(3)	
13	Andriy ZBOROVSKIY		25/2/86	M	2	(8)	
3	Serhiy ZELDI		13/6/86	D	2	(1)	

FC VORSKLA POLTAVA
Coach – Mykola Pavlov
Founded – 1984
Stadium – Vorskla im. Olexiy Butovskiy (24,795)
MAJOR HONOURS:
Ukrainian Cup – (1) 2009.

2009

18/7	Karpaty	h	1-2	og (Milošević)
26/7	Zakarpattya	a	3-1	Markoski 2, Despotovski
3/8	Shakhtar	h	1-1	Yesin
9/8	Metalurh Zaporizhya	a	1-1	Chesnakov
23/8	Dynamo	h	1-1	Sachko
30/8	Tavriya	a	0-1	
20/9	Kryvbas	h	0-0	
27/9	Illychivets	a	0-0	
4/10	Chornomorets	h	0-0	
17/10	Metalurh Donetsk	h	1-2	Markoski
25/10	Metalist	a	0-1	
31/10	Zorya	h	2-0	Bezus, Kulakov
21/11	Obolon	h	3-2	Chesnakov, Bezus, Markoski
28/11	Dnipro	a	2-2	Curri 2 (1p)
5/12	Karpaty	a	0-1	
12/12	Zakarpattya	h	2-0	Curri, Bezus

2010

28/2	Shakhtar	h	0-1	
7/3	Metalurh Zaporizhya	h	1-1	Yanuzi
13/3	Dynamo	a	0-1	
19/3	Tavriya	h	0-1	
24/3	Arsenal	a	0-2	
28/3	Kryvbas	h	1-1	Kulakov
3/4	Illychivets	h	3-0	Yarmash, Markoski 2
10/4	Chornomorets	a	0-0	
15/4	Metalurh Donetsk	a	3-1	Sachko, Yanuzi, Matveyev
18/4	Metalist	h	0-0	
24/4	Zorya	a	1-2	Markoski (p)
30/4	Arsenal	h	1-5	Chichikov
5/5	Obolon	a	1-1	Kulakov
9/5	Dnipro	h	1-1	Matveyev

No	Name	Nat	DoB	Pos	Aps	(s)	Gls
9	Roman BEZUS		26/9/90	M	8	(10)	3
48	Volodymyr CHESNAKOV		12/2/88	D	22	(6)	2
18	Olexiy CHICHIKOV		30/9/87	A	2	(19)	1
20	Debatik CURRI	ALB	28/12/83	D	26		3
4	Armend DALLKU	ALB	16/6/83	D	29		
3	Filip DESPOTOVSKI	MKD	18/11/82	M	11	(3)	1
1	Serhiy DOLHANSKIY		15/9/74	G	21		
11	Denis GLAVINA	CRO	3/3/86	A		(2)	
19	Artem GROMOV		14/1/90	M		(6)	
5	Oleh KRASNOPEROV		25/7/80	M	22	(1)	
8	Serhiy KULAKOV		1/5/86	M	28	(1)	3
7	Jovan MARKOSKI	SRB	23/6/80	M	30		7
2	Olexandr MATVEYEV		11/2/89	D	15	(1)	2
25	Hennadiy MEDVEDEV		7/2/75	D	23		
14	Alexandru ONICA	MDA	29/7/84	M	3	(1)	
17	Vasyl SACHKO		3/5/75	A	20	(3)	2
22	Ihor TYMCHENKO		16/1/86	A		(5)	
12	Serhiy VELYCHKO		9/8/76	G	9		
44	Serhiy VOVKODAV		2/7/88	D		(1)	
27	Ahmed YANUZI	ALB	8/7/88	A	14	(10)	2
37	Hryhoriy YARMASH		4/1/85	D	22	(2)	1
70	Dmytro YESIN		15/4/80	M	25		1

FC ZAKARPATTYA UZHHOROD
Coach – Igor Gamula (RUS)
Founded – 1946
Stadium – Avanhard (10,500)

2009

17/7	Illychivets	a	0-1	
26/7	Vorskla	h	1-3	Shendryk
2/8	Metalurh Donetsk	a	1-4	Braila
9/8	Metalist	h	0-2	
22/8	Zorya	a	0-2	
29/8	Arsenal	h	2-1	Davydov, Gómez (p)
19/9	Obolon	a	1-0	Davydov
26/9	Dnipro	h	0-2	
4/10	Karpaty	a	0-1	
17/10	Chornomorets	a	0-2	
25/10	Shakhtar	h	1-1	Trišović
1/11	Metalurh Zaporizhya	a	0-3	
21/11	Tavriya	a	2-3	Davydov, Tymchenko
28/11	Kryvbas	h	3-0	Tymchenko, Platonov (p), Ksionz
6/12	Illychivets	h	0-1	
12/12	Vorskla	a	0-2	

2010

27/2	Metalurh Donetsk	h	0-1	
6/3	Metalist	a	1-2	Alexeev
14/3	Zorya	h	2-1	Mykulyak, Gómez (p)
19/3	Arsenal	a	0-0	
24/3	Dynamo	h	1-0	Trišović
27/3	Obolon	h	0-1	
3/4	Dnipro	a	0-1	
11/4	Karpaty	h	1-1	Mykulyak
15/4	Chornomorets	h	1-1	Lisytsyn
18/4	Shakhtar	a	0-1	
25/4	Metalurh Zaporizhya	h	0-1	
1/5	Dynamo	a	0-2	
5/5	Tavriya	h	0-1	
9/5	Kryvbas	a	1-3	Mykulyak

No	Name	Nat	DoB	Pos	Aps	(s)	Gls
11	Serghey ALEXEEV	MDA	31/5/86	A	2	(10)	1
2	Igor ANDRONIC	MDA	11/3/88	D	1	(4)	
77	Olexandr ARTEMENKO		19/1/87	M	9	(1)	
33	Dmytro BABENKO		28/6/78	G	23		
14	Sendley Sidney BITO	ANT	20/7/83	A	2	(3)	
13	Andriy BOIKO		27/4/81	D	6	(3)	
27	Vadim BOLOHAN	MDA	15/8/86	D	28		
18	Volodymyr BRAILA		21/8/78	D	14	(3)	1
88	Vladimer BURDULI	GEO	26/10/80	M	1	(3)	
3	Olexandr CHYZHEVSKIY		27/5/71	D	10	(2)	
9	Serhiy DAVYDOV		16/12/84	A	25		3
4	Andriy DONETS		3/1/81	D	12	(1)	
24	Rubén Marcelo GÓMEZ	ARG	26/1/84	M	19	(2)	2
20	Bogdan HAUŞI	ROU	29/9/85	D	9	(2)	
2	Andriy ILCHYSHYN		25/10/81	D		(1)	
22	Olexiy IVANOV		9/1/78	M	8	(5)	
29	Vitaliy KALYNYCHENKO		29/3/83	D	1		
77	Vitaliy KOMARNYTSKIY		2/8/81	D	13		
21	Andriy KOVAL		6/12/83	M		(1)	
22	Ivan KOZORIZ		14/9/79	M	10	(1)	
7	Pavlo KSIONZ		2/1/87	A	4	(3)	1
15	Aurimas KUČYS	LTU	22/2/81	D	5		
29	LEANDRO Messias dos Santos	BRA	29/12/83	D	22		
4	Yevhen LISYTSYN		16/7/81	M	4	(3)	1
5	Aleksandr MALYGIN	RUS	27/11/79	D	10		
14	Ihor MALYSH		15/7/83	M	1	(1)	
13	Volodymyr MAZYAR		28/9/77	A	1	(1)	
23	Vladyslav MYKULYAK		30/8/84	A	20	(6)	3
1	Olexandr NAGY		2/9/85	G	7		
10	Charles NEWUCHE	NGA	14/3/85	A	5	(12)	
6	Valentyn PLATONOV		15/1/77	M	8	(3)	1
25	Anton POSTUPALENKO		28/8/88	M		(1)	

7	Mirko RAJČEVIĆ	MNE	22/3/82	M	12		
30	Serhiy RYZHYKH		12/9/79	M	1	(1)	
6	Dmytro SEMOCHKO		25/1/79	D		(1)	
8	Anton SHENDRYK		26/5/86	D	6	(4)	1
11	Ihor SHOPIN		15/6/78	M		(1)	
1	Olexandr SYTNYK		7/7/84	M		(4)	
30	Aleksandar TRIŠOVIĆ	SRB	25/11/83	M	18		2
21	Ihor TYMCHENKO		16/1/86	A	2	(3)	2
19	Serhiy YESIN		2/4/75	M	3		
5	Olexandr ZOTOV		23/2/75	M	8		

FC ZORYA LUHANSK
Coach – Yuriy Dudnyk; (23/9/09) Yuriy Koval;
(4/1/10) Anatoliy Chantsev
Founded – 1923
Stadium – Avanhard (22,288)
MAJOR HONOURS:
USSR League – (1) 1972.

2009

18/7	Arsenal	h	0-0	
26/7	Obolon	a	0-3	
1/8	Dnipro	h	0-1	
8/8	Karpaty	a	0-4	
22/8	Zakarpattya	h	2-0	Kurilov, Shevchuk
31/8	Shakhtar	a	1-3	Lazarovych
19/9	Metalurh Zaporizhya	h	3-1	Xhihani 2, Melikyan
25/9	Dynamo	a	0-2	
3/10	Tavriya	h	0-0	
17/10	Kryvbas	a	0-4	
25/10	Illychivets	h	3-2	Skoba 2 (2p), Shevchuk
31/10	Vorskla	a	0-2	
21/11	Metalist	a	0-2	
29/11	Chornomorets	h	0-1	
5/12	Arsenal	a	1-1	Lazarovych
12/12	Obolon	h	2-0	Lazarovych, Shevchuk

2010

28/2	Dnipro	a	2-2	Skoba, Lazarovych
6/3	Karpaty	h	0-2	
14/3	Zakarpattya	a	1-2	Shevchuk (p)
20/3	Shakhtar	h	0-2	
27/3	Metalurh Zaporizhya	a	1-3	Lazarovych
3/4	Dynamo	h	0-2	
7/4	Metalurh Donetsk	h	1-1	Lazarovych
11/4	Tavriya	a	1-0	Sylyuk
15/4	Kryvbas	h	1-0	Biliy
18/4	Illychivets	a	0-1	
24/4	Vorskla	h	2-1	Sylyuk, Polyanskiy
30/4	Metalurh Donetsk	a	0-0	
5/5	Metalist	h	1-4	Lazarovych
9/5	Chornomorets	a	1-1	Kamenyuka

No	Name	Nat	DoB	Pos	Aps	(s)	Gls
9	Olexiy ANTONOV		8/5/86	A	13	(2)	
33	Maxym BILIY		27/4/89	A	13		1
10	Ihor CHAIKOVSKIY		7/10/91	M	14		
5	Taras DURAI		31/7/84	D	5	(2)	
2	Andriy GAVRYUSHOV		24/9/77	D	9		
4	Olexiy GORODOV		28/8/78	M	7	(5)	
16	Andriy HRINCHENKO		23/1/86	D	2	(6)	
6	Mykyta KAMENYUKA		3/6/85	M	28		1
9	Yehor KARTUSHOV		5/1/91	A	5	(8)	
40	Dmytro KHOVBOSHA		5/2/89	M		(1)	
38	Oleksiy KHRAMTSOV		8/11/75	D	1		
49	Andriy KOKHMAN		25/5/90	A		(2)	
17	Serhiy KOLESNYCHENKO		23/1/87	M	1	(9)	
33	Andriy KOMARYTSKIY		2/2/82	G	2		
4	Maxym KOVALOV		20/3/89	M	9		
28	Olexiy KURILOV		24/4/88	D	13		1
27	Taras LAZAROVYCH		22/4/82	A	27	(2)	7
52	Serhiy MALIY		5/6/90	D		(2)	

 **UKRAINE**

19	Yegishe MELIKYAN	ARM 13/8/79	D	14		1
22	Vadym MILKO	22/8/86	M	13	(3)	
37	Vladyslav OHYRYA	3/4/90	M		(3)	
44	Harrison OMOKO	NGA 12/12/81	D	16		
3	Olexandr POLOVKOV	4/10/79	D		(1)	
3	Oleksiy POLYANSKIY	12/4/86	M	11	(2)	1
2	Serhiy RUDYKA	14/6/88	M	7	(3)	
7	Artem SEMENENKO	2/9/88	M	3	(3)	
11	Serhiy SHEVCHUK	18/6/85	D	25	(3)	4
99	Ihor SHUKHOVTSEV	13/7/71	G	21		
35	Bohdan SHUST	4/3/86	G	7		
41	Ihor SIKORSKIY	29/7/88	A		(1)	
8	Ihor SKOBA	21/5/82	M	19	(4)	3
44	Serhiy SYLYUK	5/6/85	A	12	(2)	2
10	Giorgi TSIMAKURIDZE	GEO 10/11/83	D	3		
23	Vitaliy VITSENETS	3/8/90	M	5	(2)	
77	Olexandr VOLKOV	7/2/89	A	1	(4)	
14	Parid XHIHANI	ALB 18/7/83	M	13	(9)	2
5	Volodymyr YEZERSKIY	15/11/76	D	11		

PROMOTED CLUBS

PFC SEVASTOPOL
Coach – Oleh Leshchynskiy
Founded – 2002
Stadium – Pivnmorozzavod (3,500)

FC VOLYN LUTSK
Coach – Vitaliy Kvartsyaniy
Founded – 1960
Stadium – Avanhard (10,792)

SECOND LEVEL FINAL TABLE 2009/10

		Pld	W	D	L	F	A	Pts
1	PFC Sevastopol	34	24	4	6	68	27	76
2	FC Volyn Lutsk	34	22	8	4	71	30	74
3	FC Stal Alchevsk	34	19	8	7	55	35	65
4	FC Lviv	34	19	6	9	49	22	63
5	PFC Olexandriya	34	19	6	9	58	34	63
6	FC Krymteplytsia Molodizhne	34	17	8	9	53	28	59
7	FC Naftovyk-Ukrnafta Okhtyrka	34	17	6	11	45	35	57
8	FC Desna Chernihiv	34	12	12	10	38	30	48
9	FC Arsenal Bila Tserkva	34	12	10	12	48	44	46
10	FC Helios Kharkiv	34	12	10	12	42	47	46
11	FC Dnister Ovidiopol	34	12	8	14	44	47	44
12	FC Zirka Kirovohrad	34	11	13	10	38	40	43
13	FC Dynamo-2 Kyiv	34	12	5	17	35	46	41
14	FC Feniks-Illychevets Kalinino	34	10	7	17	39	52	37
15	FC Enerhetyk Burshtyn	34	8	11	15	32	49	35
16	FSC Prykarpattya Ivano-Frankivsk	34	5	7	22	26	68	22
17	FC Kharkiv	34	3	5	26	23	76	14
18	FC Nyva Ternopil	34	3	4	27	18	72	7

NB FC Nyva Ternopil – 6 pts deducted; FC Zirka Kirovohrad – 3 pts deducted.

DOMESTIC CUP 2009/10

KUBOK UKRAÏNY

FIRST ROUND

(15/8/09)
Arsenal Kyiv 1, Dynamo Kyiv 2
CSKA Kyiv 3, Obolon Kyiv 3 *(aet; 2-4 on pens)*
Dnister 1, Shakhtar Donetsk 6
Enerhetyk 0, Metalist Kharkiv 1
FC Kharkiv 1, Karpaty 5
FC Poltava 0, Feniks-Illychivets 2
Kryvbas 5, Zorya 0
Mykolaiv 0, Krymteplytsya 1
Naftovyk-Ukrnafta 2, Metalurh Donetsk 4 *(aet)*
PFC Olexandriya 2, Volyn Lutsk 3
Shakhtar Sverdlovsk 1, Illychivets Mariupil 3
Stal Dniprodzerzhynsk 0, Tavriya
Stal Alchevsk 1, Chornomorets 0
Vorskla 2, Metalurh Zaporizhya 3
Yednist 2, Nyva Ternopil 1
Zakarpattya 2, Dnipro 3

SECOND ROUND

(12/9/09)
Feniks-Illychivets 1, Dnipro 2
Krymteplytsya 1, Metalurh Zaporizhya 2
Metalurh Donetsk 2, Karpaty 1
Metalist Kharkiv 0, Dynamo Kyiv 1
Stal Alchevsk 0, Obolon Kyiv 3
Tavriya 4, Illychivets Mariupil 2
Volyn Lutsk 2, Kryvbas 1
Yednist 1, Shakhtar Donetsk 3

QUARTER-FINALS

(28/10/09)
Dnipro 1 *(Seleznev 24)*, Metalurh Donetsk 2 *(Lazić 72, Ivanko 118)* *(aet)*
Shakhtar Donetsk 2 *(Srna 23, Fernandinho 90+3)*, Dynamo Kyiv 0
Tavriya 4 *(Idahor 13, 43, Platon 19, Monakhov 63)*, Obolon Kyiv 0
Volyn Lutsk 2 *(Kinash 63, Maicon 99p)*, Metalurh Zaporizhya 1 *(Alozi 67)* *(aet)*

SEMI-FINALS

(24/3/10)
Metalurh Donetsk 2 *(Mguni 6, Dimitrov 9)*, Shakhtar Donetsk 1 *(Fernandinho 90+2)*
Volyn Lutsk 1 *(Kurilov 54)*, Tavriya 2 *(Kovpak 6, 44)*

FINAL

(16/5/10)
OSK Metalist, Kharkiv
SC TAVRIYA SIMFEROPOL 3 *(Feshchuk 2, Kovpak 40p, Idahor 97)*
FC METALURH DONETSK 2 *(Mkhitaryan 50, Mário Sérgio 75)*
(aet)
Referee – Derevynskiy
TAVRIYA – Startsev, Marković, Juričić, Monakhov, Kornev, Kovpak, Lutsenko, Galyuza (Matyazh 84), Ljubenović (Gigiadze 70), Holaido, Feshchuk (Idahor 62).
Sent off: Juričić (94), Marković (120+1).
METALURH DONETSK – Dišljenković, Mário Sérgio, Checher, Volovyk, William (Tănasă 106), Pryima (Yankov 67), Dimitrov, Godin, Kingsley (Zé Soares 76), Mkhitaryan, Mguni.

New look for Welsh Premier League

The 2009/10 version of the Welsh Premier League was the last of its kind. The 18-team division was downsized at the end of the season to comprise just a dozen clubs, all of whom were obliged to obtain a licence to participate based on stadium facilities and financial stability. By 2012/13 that number is to be further reduced to ten.

The restructuring meant there was a much larger relegation zone than normal. With neither of the two potential promoted clubs from the feeder leagues meeting the licensing requirements, the bottom five clubs went down, supplemented, astonishingly, by the country's 2008/09 champions Rhyl FC, who failed to provide the necessary financial guarantees.

Rhyl actually finished sixth in the final table, which in itself was a major disappointment. Their title-winning coach Alan Bickerstaff was sacked on the eve of the campaign – after a 12-0 aggregate defeat by FK Partizan in the UEFA Champions League qualifiers – and replaced by ex-Hull City AFC defender Greg Strong. Forced to work with a reduced squad, the new manager got off to a promising start before his team slid out of contention, leaving just two clubs, Llanelli AFC and The New Saints FC, to contest the WPL title. Between them they produced an engaging duel that went right to the wire.

Fixture backlog

A harsh winter forced a larger number of postponements than usual, leading to a fixture backlog that required Llanelli to play their last eight games in 20 days. It was hardly an ideal scenario for the 2007/08 champions, but they braved the ordeal with courage and class, winning six of the matches and drawing the other two. Resident goal machine Rhys Griffiths found the net 11 times during that sequence, thereby hoisting his season's haul to 30 goals and securing the league's Golden Boot for a remarkable fifth season in a row. But it was not enough to bring the title back to South Wales.

TNS, captained by Welsh international defender Steve Evans, back at the club after three years with Wrexham FC, were able to withstand Llanelli's late charge by making one of their own. Having defeated their rivals 1-0 at The Venue in late March – thus completing the double over them after a 2-0 win at Stebonheath Park – Andy Cale's well-drilled outfit won their last six games as well, clinching the title on the final day with a 3-1 win at Aberystwyth Town FC, who, in defeat, surrendered third place – and a UEFA Europa League slot - to the season's surprise package, Port Talbot Town FC.

Cale collects

TNS took the title by two points from Llanelli. It was the club's fourth WPL crown in six years and their fifth in all. Cale had a hand in all five, the first and last as manager and the three in between as head coach, but at the end of the season, after two full campaigns back in charge, he decided to step down. The key to his, and the club's, success in 2009/10 was a settled side. Only 20 players were used, and all but four of those managed to score at least one goal. The team's top scorer was Chris Sharp, son of ex-Everton FC and Scotland striker Graeme Sharp, who arrived in mid-season from Bangor City FC and notched ten goals, half of them in the last two matches. Winger Craig Jones, who joined at the start of the season from Rhyl, also proved a useful new asset, scoring eight goals, including one in each of the wins against Llanelli, to earn the reward of a second successive WPL

TNS's title-winning manager Andy Cale

winner's medal. Another standout performer was goalkeeper Paul Harrison, who conceded the miserly total of 13 goals in 34 matches – a new league record, surpassing the mark set by TNS themselves when they conceded 17 in winning the 2005/06 title.

Bangor joined TNS, Llanelli and Port Talbot in Europe thanks to a thrilling 3-2 victory over the latter in the Welsh Cup final. A 90th-minute header from defender Dave Morley completed a hat-trick of Cup wins for both the club and their manager, Nev Powell, after Port Talbot had threatened to take the game into extra time by coming from 2-0 down to level the scores with five minutes remaining. The other domestic knockout competition, the League Cup, had been lifted a few days earlier by TNS, who defeated Rhyl 3-1 in the final.

Cardiff's Wembley woe

Wales came close to having representation in the English Premier League when Cardiff City FC reached the Championship (second level) play-off final. Fortunate to overcome Leicester City FC on penalties in the semi-final – they would have been eliminated had the standard practice of the away-goals rule applied – they then lost at Wembley to underdogs Blackpool FC, the same club that had narrowly edged another Welsh team, Swansea City FC, out of the last play-off spot.

In contrast to the club scene, 2009/10 was a season of relative tranquillity for the Welsh national team. Manager John Toshack continued to promote young players from Brian Flynn's high-flying Under-21 team, although there was desperately sad news when Aaron Ramsey, the cream of that particular crop, suffered a horrific leg break while playing for Arsenal FC at Stoke City FC at the end of February. The injury, grave but not career-threatening, seemed sure to curtail the gifted 19-year-old's involvement in Wales's UEFA EURO 2012 qualifying campaign, the highlight of which will surely be the Millennium Stadium encounter against England in March 2011.

Cymdeithas Bêl-droed Cymru/ Football Association of Wales (FAW)

11/12 Neptune Court, Vanguard Way
GB-Cardiff CF24 5PJ
tel – +44 29 2043 5830
fax – +44 29 2049 6953
website – faw.org.uk
email – info@faw.org.uk
Year of Formation – 1876

President – Philip Pritchard
Chief Executive – Jonathan Ford
Media Officer – Ceri Stennett
National Stadium – Millennium Stadium, Cardiff (72,500)

INTERNATIONAL TOURNAMENT APPEARANCES
FIFA World Cup – (1) 1958 (qtr-finals).
TOP FIVE ALL-TIME CAPS
Neville Southall (92); Gary Speed (85); Dean Saunders (75); Peter Nicholas & Ian Rush (73)
TOP FIVE ALL-TIME GOALS
Ian Rush (28); Ivor Allchurch & Trevor Ford (23); Dean Saunders (22); Craig Bellamy (17)

Welsh wonderboy Aaron Ramsey suffered a serious leg injury playing for Arsenal

NATIONAL TEAM RESULTS 2009/10

12/8/09	Montenegro	A	Podgorica	1-2	Vokes (47)
9/9/09	Russia (WCQ)	H	Cardiff	1-3	Collins (53)
10/10/09	Finland (WCQ)	A	Helsinki	1-2	Bellamy (17)
14/10/09	Liechtenstein (WCQ)	A	Vaduz	2-0	Vaughan (16), Ramsey (80)
14/11/09	Scotland	H	Cardiff	3-0	Edwards (17), Church (32), Ramsey (35)
3/3/10	Sweden	H	Swansea	0-1	
23/5/10	Croatia	A	Osijek	0-2	

NATIONAL TEAM APPEARANCES 2009/10

Coach – John TOSHACK 22/3/49			Mne	RUS	FIN	LIE	Sco	Swe	Cro	Caps	Goals
Wayne HENNESSEY	24/1/87	Wolves (ENG)	G46	G	G	G		s46	G46	25	-
Chris GUNTER	21/7/89	Nottingham Forest (ENG)	D	D	D	D88		D	D80	22	-
Sam RICKETTS	11/10/81	Bolton (ENG)	D51	D				D	D	38	-
Ashley WILLIAMS	23/8/84	Swansea	D46	D	D	D	D	D	D	20	-
James COLLINS	23/8/83	West Ham (ENG)	D60								
		/Aston Villa (ENG)		D	D	D		D		34	2
Danny GABBIDON	8/8/79	West Ham (ENG)	D	D74				s60		43	-
Jack COLLISON	2/10/88	West Ham (ENG)	M					M71		7	-
Aaron RAMSEY	26/12/90	Arsenal (ENG)	M69	M	M	M	M56			11	2
Joe LEDLEY	23/1/87	Cardiff	M	M				M79		32	2
Simon CHURCH	12/12/88	Reading (ENG)	A46		A62	A	A46	A53	A71	8	1
Robert EARNSHAW	6/4/81	Nottingham Forest (ENG)	A				s46	s46	A74	49	14
Lewin NYATANGA	18/8/88	Bristol City (ENG)	s46		D83	s84	D60	s67	D	33	-
Sam VOKES	21/10/89	Wolves (ENG)	s46	s74	s62			s53	s71	16	2
		/Leeds (ENG)						s46			
Lewis PRICE	19/7/84	Brentford (ENG)	s46							7	-
Neal EARDLEY	6/11/88	Blackpool (ENG)	s51		s83	s88				13	-
Craig MORGAN	18/6/85	Peterborough (ENG)	s60			D	D	D	D	20	-
David COTTERILL	4/12/87	Sheffield United (ENG)	s69					s86			
		/Swansea							s64	16	-
Brian STOCK	24/12/81	Doncaster (ENG)		M					M57	2	-
David EDWARDS	3/2/86	Wolves (ENG)		M	M	M80	M86		M	19	3
Craig BELLAMY	13/7/79	Man. City (ENG)		A	A					58	17
Gareth BALE	16/7/89	Tottenham (ENG)		D	D84	D	D67			24	2
David VAUGHAN	18/2/83	Blackpool (ENG)		M	M			M		17	1
Boaz MYHILL	9/11/82	Hull (ENG)					G	G46	s46	8	-
Jermaine EASTER	15/1/82	MK Dons (ENG)					A			8	-
Andy KING	29/10/88	Leicester (ENG)					s80	s79		3	-
Ched EVANS	28/12/88	Sheffield United (ENG)					A46	A46		12	1
Joe ALLEN	14/3/90	Swansea						s56		2	-
Simon DAVIES	23/10/79	Fulham (ENG)							M64	58	6
Andrew CROFTS	29/5/84	Brighton (ENG)						s71		13	-
Andy DORMAN	1/5/82	St Mirren (SCO)							M62	1	-
Mark BRADLEY	14/1/88	Walsall (ENG)							s57	1	-
Neil TAYLOR	7/2/89	Wrexham							s62	1	-
Hal ROBSON-KANU	21/5/89	Reading (ENG)							s74	1	-
Christian RIBIERO	14/12/89	Bristol City (ENG)							s80	1	-

DOMESTIC LEAGUE 2009/10

PREMIER LEAGUE FINAL TABLE

		Pld	Home					Away					Total					Pts
			W	D	L	F	A	W	D	L	F	A	W	D	L	F	A	
1	The New Saints FC	34	14	3	0	49	6	11	4	2	20	7	25	7	2	69	13	82
2	Llanelli AFC	34	14	2	1	49	14	11	3	3	30	12	25	5	4	79	26	80
3	Port Talbot Town FC	34	12	3	2	35	8	7	5	5	21	15	19	8	7	56	23	65
4	Aberystwyth Town FC	34	8	4	5	27	25	11	3	3	27	16	19	7	8	54	41	64
5	Bangor City FC	34	11	3	3	43	19	8	3	6	32	26	19	6	9	75	45	63
6	Rhyl FC	34	11	3	3	45	17	7	5	5	29	26	18	8	8	74	43	62
7	Airbus UK Broughton FC	34	6	6	5	25	18	6	7	4	24	19	12	13	9	49	37	49
8	Prestatyn Town FC	34	6	7	4	19	20	6	5	6	34	33	12	12	10	53	53	48
9	Neath FC	34	6	6	5	25	21	6	5	6	16	17	12	11	11	41	38	47
10	Carmarthen Town AFC	34	5	4	8	21	21	7	5	5	24	17	12	9	13	45	38	45
11	Bala Town FC	34	5	6	6	18	23	7	3	7	21	24	12	9	13	39	47	45
12	Haverfordwest County AFC	34	6	6	5	22	20	5	5	7	21	27	11	11	12	43	47	44
13	Newtown AFC	34	6	4	7	29	31	4	7	6	25	26	10	11	13	54	57	41
14	Connah's Quay FC	34	7	4	6	20	15	4	4	9	11	27	11	8	15	31	42	41
15	CPD Porthmadog	34	2	4	11	10	28	4	2	11	13	38	6	6	22	23	66	24
16	Welshpool Town FC	34	3	2	12	15	33	3	3	11	15	37	6	5	23	30	70	23
17	Caersws FC	34	3	2	12	13	37	0	2	15	13	57	3	4	27	26	94	13
18	Cefn Druids AFC	34	1	4	12	8	28	0	2	15	8	49	1	6	27	16	77	9

NB Premier League reduced to 12 clubs in 2010/11. Bottom five clubs relegated plus Rhyl FC, who failed to obtain a licence.

TOP GOALSCORERS

30 Rhys GRIFFITHS (Llanelli)

24 Jamie REED (Bangor)

23 Chris SHARP (Bangor/TNS)

20 Matthew WILLIAMS (Rhyl)

17 Luke BOWEN (Aberystwyth)

16 Marc LLOYD-WILLIAMS (Airbus)
Martin ROSE (Port Talbot)

15 Mark CONNOLLY (Rhyl)
Lee HUNT (Rhyl/Bangor)

14 Jack CHRISTOPHER (Haverfordwest)
Craig STEINS (Neath)
Andy MORAN (Prestatyn)

CLUB-BY-CLUB

ABERYSTWYTH TOWN FC

Manager – Brian Coyne (SCO); (28/9/09) Christian Edwards; (4/11/09) Alan Morgan
Founded – 1884
Stadium – Park Avenue (3,000)
MAJOR HONOURS:
Welsh Cup - (1) 1900.

2009

15/8	Caersws	a	4-0	*Waters 2, James S., Kellaway*
21/8	Welshpool	h	1-1	*Evans R.*
29/8	Prestatyn	h	2-3	*Sherbon (p), Bowen L.*
6/9	Carmarthen	a	0-0	
12/9	Airbus	h	0-3	
18/9	Port Talbot	a	2-1	*Bowen L., Kellaway*
26/9	Connah's Quay	h	1-2	*Sherbon*
11/10	Bangor	a	1-0	*Bowen L.*
16/10	Newtown	h	2-1	*James K., Davies*
24/10	Porthmadog	a	1-0	*Bowen L.*
6/11	Bala	h	1-0	*Hughes Gl.*
21/11	Cefn Druids	h	4-1	*Kellaway 2, Hughes Gl. 2*
27/11	Llanelli	a	0-4	
5/12	Rhyl	h	2-2	*og (Doran), Evans G.*
11/12	TNS	a	0-4	
18/12	Caersws	h	3-2	*Bowen L. 2, Thomas*
26/12	Haverfordwest	h	2-1	*Sherbon, Hughes Gl.*

2010

1/1	Haverfordwest	a	1-0	*Sherbon*
16/1	Prestatyn	a	2-0	*Evans G., Bowen L.*
22/1	Carmarthen	h	1-2	*Morgan*
26/1	Neath	h	1-1	*Sherbon*
6/2	Airbus	a	0-2	
12/2	Port Talbot	h	2-1	*Fraughan, Bowen L.*
16/2	Neath	a	3-1	*Morgan, Fraughan, Kellaway*
20/2	Connah's Quay	a	3-0	*Kellaway 2, Sherbon*
6/3	Newtown	a	2-1	*Murtagh, Bowen L.*
12/3	Porthmadog	h	1-0	*Kellaway*
16/3	Bangor	h	2-1	*Fraughan, Murtagh*
19/3	Bala	a	1-1	*Bowen L.*
3/4	Cefn Druids	a	3-0	*Kellaway, Bowen L. 2*
9/4	Llanelli	h	1-1	*Murtagh*
17/4	Rhyl	a	1-1	*Bowen L. (p)*
20/4	Welshpool	a	3-1	*Bowen L. 3*
24/4	TNS	h	1-3	*Bowen L.*

Name	Nat	DoB	Pos	Aps	(s)	Gls
Luke BOWEN		7/3/88	A	34		17
Steve BOWEN		28/6/89	M	22	(2)	
Tom BOWEN		18/4/91	M		(3)	
Liam BUTTON		29/11/92	M		(1)	
Steve CANN		20/1/88	G	29		

Name	Nat	DoB	Pos	Aps	(s)	Gls
Cledan DAVIES		10/3/09	A	10	(14)	1
Christian EDWARDS		25/11/75	D	8	(4)	
Andy EVANS		1/4/78	A		(4)	
Graham EVANS		16/6/80	A	13	(11)	2
Robert EVANS		24/1/89	M	6	(6)	1
Ryan FRAUGHAN	ENG	2/2/91	M	13		3
Anthony HARTNELL		23/9/88	M		(1)	
Gareth HUGHES		8/1/81	D	33		
Glyndwr HUGHES		4/9/77	A	5	(20)	4
Adam JAMES		11/1/84	M	6	(2)	
Kristian JAMES		5/2/82	D	10	(2)	1
Sion JAMES		3/2/80	D	33		1
Geoff KELLAWAY		7/4/86	M	31	(1)	9
Bari MORGAN		13/8/80	M	28	(2)	2
Conall MURTAGH	NIR	29/6/85	M	13		3
Geraint PASSMORE		18/2/86	M	1	(3)	
Joel RICHARDSON	ENG	22/9/90	D	1	(2)	
Dave ROBERTS		10/12/88	G	5		
Luke SHERBON	ENG	6/6/86	M	32	(1)	6
Aneurin THOMAS		27/1/73	D	34		1
Michael WATERS		22/3/85	M	7		2

AIRBUS UK BROUGHTON FC

Manager – Craig Harrison (ENG)
Founded – 1946
Stadium – The Airfield (3,000)

2009

16/8	Llanelli	a	2-2	Lloyd-Williams 2
21/8	Rhyl	h	2-2	Lloyd-Williams, Roberts
29/8	TNS	a	1-2	Lloyd-Williams
6/9	Haverfordwest	h	3-1	Owen, Lloyd-Williams, Cook
12/9	Aberystwyth	a	3-0	Edwards, Owen, Lloyd-Williams
18/9	Welshpool	h	1-2	Lloyd-Williams
25/9	Prestatyn	a	2-2	Feliciello, McManus
10/10	Carmarthen	h	2-2	Edwards (p), Lloyd-Williams
17/10	Caersws	a	4-0	Lloyd-Williams, Desormeaux 2, Owen
24/10	Port Talbot	a	1-2	Lloyd-Williams
6/11	Connah's Quay	h	4-0	Owen, Cook, Roberts, McConnell
21/11	Newtown	h	2-0	Owen, Desormeaux
28/11	Porthmadog	a	1-0	og (Davies)
4/12	Bala	h	0-1	
13/12	Neath	a	0-0	
26/12	Cefn Druids	h	1-1	Lloyd-Williams

2010

23/1	Haverfordwest	a	1-1	Lloyd-Williams
26/1	Rhyl	a	1-2	Edwards (p)
6/2	Aberystwyth	h	2-0	Owen, Lloyd-Williams
9/2	Llanelli	h	0-1	
12/2	Welshpool	a	0-0	
24/2	TNS	h	0-0	
27/2	Carmarthen	a	1-0	Johnson
6/3	Caersws	h	3-0	Smith 2, Allen
10/3	Cefn Druids	a	1-1	Lloyd-Williams
13/3	Port Talbot	h	0-0	
19/3	Connah's Quay	a	1-0	Abraham
24/3	Bangor	h	1-5	Owen
3/4	Newtown	a	3-3	Owen 2, Lloyd-Williams
10/4	Porthmadog	h	1-2	Owen
13/4	Bangor	a	0-3	
16/4	Bala	a	2-1	Owen, Lloyd-Williams
21/4	Prestatyn	h	2-0	Owen, McIntosh
24/4	Neath	h	1-1	McIntosh

	Nat	DoB	Pos	Aps	(s)	Gls
Jack ABRAHAM	ENG	2/10/90	M	23	(3)	1
Mark ALLEN	ENG	2/9/76	D	28	(3)	1
Niall CHALLONER		8/10/92	A		(1)	
Matthew COOK		7/9/85	M	12		2
Danny DESORMEAUX	ENG	15/5/84	M	30		3
Chris DORAN	NIR	12/4/84	G	6		
Ryan EDWARDS		22/6/88	D	32	(1)	3
Giovanni FELICIELLO	ENG	21/11/89	D	29	(1)	1
Josh JOHNSON	TRI	16/4/81	A	4	(9)	1
Marc LLOYD-WILLIAMS		8/2/73	A	28	(6)	16
Gary McCONNELL	ENG	4/1/85	M		(6)	1
James McINTOSH	ENG	6/2/83	A	10	(13)	2
Paul McMANUS	ENG	22/4/90	A	7	(8)	1
Andy MITCHELL	ENG	18/4/90	M		(5)	
Carl OWEN		9/4/80	A	29		12
Rhys ROBERTS		17/7/85	D	23	(1)	2
Kristian ROGERS		2/6/73	G	28		
Jack ROWLANDS	ENG	11/9/89	M	2	(3)	
Tom ROWLANDS		28/10/85	A	7	(5)	
Jamie SMITH	ENG	17/9/74	M	6		2
Gareth SUDLOW		6/10/83	D	9	(7)	
Ashley WILLIAMS	ENG	8/10/87	M	29		
Matty WOODWARD	ENG	14/6/83	M	32	(1)	

BALA TOWN FC

Manager – Colin Caton
Founded – 1880
Stadium – Maes Tegid (2,000)

2009

14/8	Bangor	h	2-1	Evans (p), Jefferies R.
22/8	Newtown	a	1-0	Evans
28/8	Porthmadog	h	0-0	
5/9	Caersws	h	2-0	Toner, Jefferies R.
13/9	Neath	a	1-2	Evans
18/9	Cefn Druids	h	1-0	Evans
27/9	Llanelli	a	0-2	
9/10	Rhyl	h	0-4	
17/10	TNS	a	0-0	
24/10	Haverfordwest	h	1-1	Roberts O.
6/11	Aberystwyth	a	0-1	
20/11	Prestatyn	a	1-2	Jefferies R.
28/11	Carmarthen	h	1-3	Jefferies R.
1/12	Welshpool	h	2-1	Griffiths, Powell (p)
4/12	Airbus	a	1-0	Toner
12/12	Port Talbot	h	1-1	Roberts O.
15/12	Bangor	a	3-6	Toner 2, Evans (p)
26/12	Connah's Quay	a	1-0	Toner

2010

16/1	Porthmadog	a	2-0	Duckett, Evans
23/1	Caersws	a	3-1	Lloyd, Toner, Roberts O.
6/2	Neath	h	1-0	Thompson
12/2	Cefn Druids	a	2-1	Evans, Fisher N.
24/2	Rhyl	a	2-5	Toner 2
5/3	TNS	h	0-1	
9/3	Newtown	h	1-1	Thompson
14/3	Haverfordwest	a	1-1	Evans
19/3	Aberystwyth	h	1-1	Evans
23/3	Carmarthen	a	1-2	Jefferies R.
26/3	Welshpool	a	2-1	Toner, Evans
2/4	Prestatyn	h	2-4	Williams, Evans
5/4	Connah's Quay	h	2-2	Jefferies R., og (Alston B.)
13/4	Llanelli	h	0-1	
16/4	Airbus	h	1-2	Fisher N.
24/4	Port Talbot	a	0-0	

WALES

Name	Nat	DoB	Pos	Aps	(s)	Gls
Jason ASTBURY	ENG	4/6/91	G	1		
Jay BELL	ENG	24/11/89	D	3		
Leon BIMPSON	ENG	16/6/77	G	29		
Mathew BOSWELL	ENG	19/8/77	G	4		
Warren DUCKETT		31/5/84	M	16	(7)	1
Ricky EVANS		29/4/76	M	27		11
Neil FISHER	ENG	8/7/83	A	3	(13)	2
Steven FISHER	ENG	19/6/73	D	20	(2)	
Marc GRIFFITHS	ENG	16/5/84	A	3	(9)	1
Mark HARRIS	ENG	5/12/86	D	9	(4)	
Stuart HAYES		10/11/86	A	5	(3)	
John IRVING	ENG	17/9/88	D	22		
Brett JEFFERIES		5/8/79	D	5	(1)	
Ross JEFFERIES		5/8/79	A	25	(3)	6
Danny JELLICOE		27/9/76	D	32		
Osian JONES		26/2/84	M	20	(3)	
Joe KENNEDY	ENG	24/11/90	D	1	(1)	
Gethin LLOYD		14/11/83	M	24		1
Peter MOORE	ENG	13/9/88	M	16		
Steve MORRISON	ENG	10/9/88	A	3	(2)	
Mark POWELL	ENG	8/5/75	M	34		1
Iwan ROBERTS		2/7/81	D		(2)	
Owain ROBERTS		23/6/79	M	31	(1)	3
Michael THOMPSON	ENG	5/1/84	M	2	(9)	2
John TONER	CAN	9/9/77	A	24	(4)	9
Danny WILLIAMS		12/7/79	M	15		1

BANGOR CITY FC
Manager – Nev Powell (ENG)
Founded – 1876
Stadium – Farrar Road (3,000)
MAJOR HONOURS:
Welsh League - (2) 1994, 1995;
Welsh Cup - (8) 1889, 1896, 1962, 1998, 2000, 2008, 2009, 2010.

2009
14/8	Bala	a	1-2	Stott (p)
22/8	Neath	h	3-1	Reed, Morley, Smyth
28/8	Cefn Druids	a	1-0	Reed
5/9	Llanelli	h	2-3	Sharp 2 (1p)
11/9	Rhyl	a	1-5	Sharp
19/9	TNS	h	0-1	
26/9	Haverfordwest	a	2-2	Reed, Roberts
11/10	Aberystwyth	h	0-1	
17/10	Welshpool	a	2-1	Sharp, Stott
23/10	Prestatyn	h	4-0	Limbert, Reed, Edwards, Sharp
7/11	Carmarthen	a	2-2	Reed, Limbert
21/11	Port Talbot	a	1-2	Swanick
27/11	Connah's Quay	h	0-0	
5/12	Caersws	a	3-1	Swanick, Limbert, Morley
12/12	Newtown	a	5-2	Stott 2, Sharp 2, Reed
15/12	Bala	h	6-3	Sharp 2 (1p), Stott, Morley, Reed 2
27/12	Porthmadog	h	2-0	Reed 2

2010
15/1	Cefn Druids	h	3-1	Sharp 3
23/1	Llanelli	a	2-3	Smyth, Sharp (p)
7/2	Rhyl	h	3-1	Garside, Reed, Edwards
14/2	TNS	a	1-2	Reed
20/2	Haverfordwest	h	3-2	Garside, Reed, Stott
6/3	Welshpool	h	3-2	Brewerton, Reed 2 (1p)
12/3	Prestatyn	a	1-1	Ward
16/3	Aberystwyth	a	1-2	og (Thomas)
20/3	Carmarthen	h	3-2	Hunt, Edwards, Reed
24/3	Airbus	a	5-1	Reed 3, Garside, Jebb
27/3	Neath	a	1-0	Reed

3/4	Port Talbot	h	1-1	Smyth
5/4	Porthmadog	a	2-0	Reed, Hunt
13/4	Airbus	h	3-0	Reed, Jebb, Brewerton
17/4	Caersws	h	7-1	Smyth, Hunt 3, Reed (p), Edwards, Brewerton
20/4	Connah's Quay	a	1-0	Reed
24/4	Newtown	h	0-0	

Name	Nat	DoB	Pos	Aps	(s)	Gls
James BREWERTON		17/11/79	D	32		3
Stephen CONNOR	ENG	21/7/89	A	1	(2)	
Les DAVIES		29/10/84	A	1	(9)	
Sion EDWARDS		1/8/87	M	18	(13)	4
Craig GARSIDE	ENG	11/1/85	M	14	(3)	3
Peter HOY	ENG	16/5/82	D	26	(4)	
Lee HUNT	ENG	5/6/82	A	14		5
Matthew HURDMAN		23/1/91	M		(5)	
Eddie JEBB	ENG	31/12/81	M	15		2
Michael JOHNSTON		16/12/87	D	30		
Kieran KILLACKEY	ENG	12/7/85	M	3	(1)	
Marc LIMBERT		3/10/73	M	13	(12)	3
David MORLEY	ENG	25/9/77	D	27		3
John OWEN		18/8/92	A		(4)	
Jamie REED	NIR	13/8/87	A	34		24
Chris ROBERTS		14/8/85	D	32		1
Matthew SARGENT		5/11/89	M		(1)	
Chris SHARP	SCO	19/6/86	A	17	(1)	13
Paul SMITH		6/12/77	G	34		
Marc SMYTH	ENG	9/1/85	M	20	(4)	4
Ashley STOTT	ENG	14/6/88	A	11	(17)	6
David SWANICK	ENG	16/9/79	D	9	(2)	2
Nicky WARD		30/11/87	M	15		1
Clive WILLIAMS		1/1/91	D	8	(10)	

CAERSWS FC
Manager – Mickey Evans
Founded – 1877
Stadium – Recreation Ground (3,000)

2009
15/8	Aberystwyth	h	0-4	
22/8	Porthmadog	a	1-1	Lewis
29/8	Welshpool	h	3-0	Prosser, Melia, Lewis
5/9	Bala	a	0-2	
12/9	Prestatyn	h	1-5	Lewis
19/9	Neath	a	3-5	Prosser, Melia 2
26/9	Carmarthen	h	0-3	
9/10	Cefn Druids	a	1-1	Smith
17/10	Airbus	h	0-4	
7/11	Port Talbot	h	1-2	Prosser
10/11	Llanelli	a	1-7	Prosser
14/11	Rhyl	a	1-3	Lewis (p)
27/11	TNS	a	0-4	
5/12	Bangor	h	1-3	Smith
12/12	Haverfordwest	h	0-2	
18/12	Aberystwyth	a	2-3	Griffiths 2

2010
23/1	Bala	h	1-3	Prosser
6/2	Prestatyn	a	0-1	
13/2	Neath	h	0-1	
20/2	Carmarthen	a	0-1	
27/2	Cefn Druids	h	1-0	Griffiths
2/3	Connah's Quay	h	1-0	Griffiths
6/3	Airbus	a	0-3	
13/3	Llanelli	h	0-2	
20/3	Port Talbot	a	0-4	

23/3	Welshpool	a	1-3	Griffiths	
27/3	Rhyl	h	2-2	Griffiths, Jenkins C.	
3/4	Connah's Quay	a	0-5		
5/4	Newtown	a	1-4	Jenkins C.	
10/4	TNS	h	0-3		
13/4	Porthmadog	h	1-2	Davies A.	
17/4	Bangor	a	1-7	Prosser	
20/4	Newtown	h	1-1	Holt	
24/4	Haverfordwest	a	1-3	Lewis	

Name	Nat	DoB	Pos	Aps	(s)	Gls
Nick BEDDOES	ENG	27/7/73	D		(1)	
Hugh CLARKE		15/6/71	D	27		
James COLEMAN		5/6/93	A		(2)	
Andy DAVIES		30/10/79	M	23		1
Kevin DAVIES		9/10/85	D	4		
Mark GRIFFITHS	ENG	4/8/87	A	18		6
Matthew HOLT	ENG	27/10/87	D	31		1
David HUGHES		8/4/82	M	3	(1)	
Corey JENKINS		14/2/91	M	9	(10)	2
Lee JENKINS		28/6/79	M	27		
David JONES		29/4/84	G	34		
Graham JONES	ENG	1/12/75	M	26		
Jonathan JONES	ENG	22/2/89	D	1	(1)	
Phil JONES		21/1/80	D	17		
Simon JONES		25/10/84	D	11	(12)	
Tom LAPWORTH		13/3/93	D		(2)	
Geraint LEWIS		20/12/75	M	24		5
Gareth MANSELL		16/2/88	M	5	(2)	
Eddie MAURICE-JONES		20/2/89	A	3		
Chris MELIA	ENG	20/2/81	A	18	(2)	3
Matthew PROSSER		7/4/87	A	30	(3)	6
Matthew ROBERTS		18/1/86	D	13		
Steve ROWLAND		2/11/81	D	15		
Jacob SMITH		2/10/91	A	9	(15)	2
Dave TAYLOR		25/8/65	A		(1)	
James TAYLOR	ENG	10/12/84	M	9	(1)	
Danny WILLIAMS	ENG	7/4/92	M	1		
Kris WILLIAMS	ENG	4/3/92	M		(2)	
Luke WILLIAMS	ENG	20/9/87	M	1		
Scott WILLIAMS		30/10/89	M	15	(9)	

CARMARTHEN TOWN AFC

Manager – Deryn Brace
Founded – 1896
Stadium – Richmond Park (3,000)
MAJOR HONOURS:
Welsh Cup – (1) 2007.

2009

15/8	Rhyl	a	1-2	Williams	
22/8	TNS	a	0-2		
28/8	Haverfordwest	a	1-2	Pritchard	
6/9	Aberystwyth	h	0-0		
12/9	Welshpool	a	3-1	Thomas D. 2, Walters	
19/9	Prestatyn	h	1-2	Fowler	
26/9	Caersws	a	3-0	Smothers, Pierce, Thomas D.	
10/10	Airbus	a	2-2	Hicks, Thomas K.	
17/10	Port Talbot	h	3-1	Hicks, Thomas D., Palmer	
24/10	Connah's Quay	h	1-0	Palmer	
7/11	Bangor	h	2-2	Hicks, Palmer	
21/11	Porthmadog	h	1-3	Hicks	
28/11	Bala	a	3-1	Hicks 2, Thomas D.	
4/12	Neath	h	0-1		
12/12	Cefn Druids	a	1-0	Hicks	
26/12	Llanelli	h	1-2	Hicks (p)	

2010

22/1	Aberystwyth	a	2-1	Hicks, Thomas K.	
30/1	Newtown	a	0-0		
6/2	Welshpool	h	1-1	Thomas D.	
13/2	Prestatyn	a	0-0		
20/2	Caersws	h	1-0	Pritchard	
27/2	Airbus	h	0-1		
6/3	Port Talbot	a	1-0	Smothers	
9/3	TNS	h	1-2	Hicks	
13/3	Connah's Quay	a	0-0		
20/3	Bangor	a	2-3	Walters, Hicks	
23/3	Bala	h	2-1	Thomas D. 2	
27/3	Newtown	h	1-2	Palmer	
3/4	Porthmadog	a	4-1	Hughes C., Thomas D., Walters, Griffiths	
5/4	Llanelli	a	0-1		
13/4	Rhyl	h	0-1		
16/4	Neath	a	1-1	Thomas D.	
20/4	Haverfordwest	h	2-2	Griffiths, Cotterrall	
24/4	Cefn Druids	h	4-0	Thomas K. 2, Griffiths, Thomas D.	

Name	Nat	DoB	Pos	Aps	(s)	Gls
Deryn BRACE		15/3/75	D		(1)	
Nathan COTTERRALL		15/12/76	M	25	(6)	1
Sean CRONIN		17/1/86	D	3		
Mattie DAVIES		8/1/76	A		(1)	
Mark DODDS		29/5/80	D	12		
Paul FOWLER		8/2/85	M	31	(1)	1
Dale GRIFFITHS		2/11/85	D	16	(1)	3
Craig HANFORD		8/7/84	D	24	(1)	
Tim HICKS		5/4/83	A	28	(2)	11
Craig HUGHES		18/12/78	A	21	(4)	1
Richard HUGHES		11/12/86	D	28	(1)	
Steffan JAMES		15/2/92	M		(1)	
Ben MORRIS	ENG	3/5/89	M	1	(8)	
Sam O'SULLIVAN		14/7/86	M	2		
Nicky PALMER		6/11/81	M	19	(9)	4
Dyfan PIERCE		20/12/80	D	14		1
Mark PRITCHARD		23/11/85	A	18	(13)	2
Stuart ROBERTS		22/7/85	A	4	(1)	
Ben SAUL	ENG	24/9/91	M		(2)	
Neil SMOTHERS		8/12/77	D	25		2
Danny THOMAS		13/5/85	A	20	(13)	11
Kris THOMAS		16/1/83	D	30		4
Neil THOMAS		2/6/73	G	34		
Sacha WALTERS		20/6/84	M	16	(7)	3
Steven WILLIAMS		28/4/84	D	3		1

CEFN DRUIDS AFC

Manager – Lee Jones & Wayne Phillips
Founded – 1869
Stadium – Plas Kynaston (3,000)
MAJOR HONOURS:
Welsh Cup – (8) 1880, 1881, 1882, 1885, 1886, 1898, 1899, 1904.

2009

15/8	Port Talbot	h	0-1		
22/8	Connah's Quay	a	1-3	og (Dowridge)	
28/8	Bangor	h	0-1		
5/9	Newtown	a	2-4	Penlington, Bamber	
11/9	Porthmadog	h	1-0	Barnett	
18/9	Bala	a	0-1		
26/9	Neath	h	0-1		
9/10	Caersws	h	1-1	Whitfield	
17/10	Llanelli	a	0-4		
23/10	Rhyl	h	1-1	Whitfield	

WALES

6/11	TNS	a	0-4	
21/11	Aberystwyth	a	1-4	*Rush*
27/11	Welshpool	h	0-1	
4/12	Prestatyn	a	0-2	
12/12	Carmarthen	h	0-1	
26/12	Airbus	a	1-1	*Penlington*
2010				
15/1	Bangor	a	1-3	*Griffiths*
22/1	Newtown	h	0-2	
30/1	Neath	a	1-1	*Whitfield*
6/2	Porthmadog	a	0-1	
12/2	Bala	h	1-2	*Rush*
16/2	Port Talbot	a	0-7	
27/2	Caersws	a	0-1	
6/3	Llanelli	h	2-5	*Rush, Phillips*
10/3	Airbus	h	1-1	*Whitfield*
13/3	Rhyl	a	0-6	
19/3	TNS	h	0-0	
27/3	Haverfordwest	a	0-1	
3/4	Aberystwyth	h	0-3	
5/4	Haverfordwest	h	1-2	*Rush*
9/4	Welshpool	a	1-2	*Caughter*
13/4	Connah's Quay	h	0-1	
16/4	Prestatyn	h	0-5	
24/4	Carmarthen	a	0-4	

Name	Nat	DoB	Pos	Aps	(s)	Gls
Lee BAMBER	ENG	18/1/73	D	8		1
Daniel BARNETT		8/9/88	D	30		1
Chris BUXTON		2/2/91	M	2	(7)	
Gareth CAUGHTER		14/7/80	M	15		1
Jamie CROWTHER		10/2/92	M	9	(7)	
Andrew EDGAR	ENG	4/12/83	M	6		
Aled EVANS		10/4/92	A	5	(6)	
Tony FILSON	ENG	14/2/85	D	2		
Josh GRIFFITHS		19/9/91	M	22	(3)	1
Adam HESP		30/8/91	D	27	(1)	
Adam HUNTER	ENG	25/1/86	D	7	(3)	
James HUSSANEY	ENG	14/12/78	A	1		
Josh JOHNSON	TRI	16/4/81	M	4		
Bobby JONES	ENG	19/7/84	A	1	(1)	
Lee T JONES	ENG	17/10/89	D	12	(1)	
Sean JONES	ENG	16/6/90	D	16		
Gerard MALONEY	ENG	22/5/80	M	1	(2)	
Chris MULLOCK		16/9/88	G	23		
Craig PEJIC	ENG	26/4/85	M	7	(5)	
Gary PENLINGTON		19/8/77	A	7	(8)	2
Waynne PHILLIPS		15/12/70	D	22	(2)	1
Mariusz PROCHENKA	POL	16/8/79	A	3	(2)	
Kieran QUINN	ENG	20/3/86	M	13		
Levi ROBERTS		26/4/91	M		(3)	
Aled ROWLANDS		12/7/71	D	9	(1)	
Tom ROWLANDS		28/10/85	A	5	(3)	
Jonathan RUSH	ENG	13/6/89	A	24	(4)	4
Josh RUSSELL		15/11/90	M	16	(5)	
Adam SKELLON		24/6/93	M		(2)	
Mike TAYLOR		26/5/91	M	9	(7)	
Gary TEBBLE	ENG	29/3/89	A	1	(9)	
Rob THOMAS	ENG	13/11/83	G	11		
Martin WELSH	ENG	10/5/87	M	3		
Craig WHITFIELD	ENG	16/8/89	D	25	(3)	4
Drew WICKENS		2/12/91	D	2		
Ricky WRIGHT		18/3/82	D	26	(2)	

CONNAH'S QUAY FC

Manager – Mark McGregor (ENG); (24/2/10) Ken Price (ENG)
Founded – 1946
Stadium – Deeside Stadium (6,000)

2009				
16/8	Neath	a	1-1	*Herbert*
22/8	Cefn Druids	h	3-1	*Herbert, McNutt, Olsen*
30/8	Llanelli	a	0-5	
5/9	Rhyl	h	0-2	
11/9	TNS	a	0-3	
19/9	Haverfordwest	h	1-1	*McGregor*
26/9	Aberystwyth	a	2-1	*McNutt, Forde*
10/10	Welshpool	h	0-0	
16/10	Prestatyn	a	2-3	*Hayes, Herbert*
24/10	Carmarthen	a	0-1	
6/11	Airbus	a	0-4	
14/11	Port Talbot	h	0-3	
27/11	Bangor	a	0-0	
5/12	Newtown	h	3-1	*Hayes, Herbert, Scheuber*
12/12	Porthmadog	a	1-0	*Hayes*
26/12	Bala	h	0-1	
2010				
23/1	Rhyl	a	1-4	*Burns*
5/2	TNS	h	1-0	*Hayes*
14/2	Haverfordwest	a	0-1	
20/2	Aberystwyth	h	0-3	
2/3	Caersws	a	0-1	
5/3	Prestatyn	h	1-1	*Jones C.*
9/3	Welshpool	a	1-0	*Jones R.*
13/3	Carmarthen	h	0-0	
16/3	Neath	h	2-0	*Herbert 2*
19/3	Airbus	h	0-1	
23/3	Llanelli	h	1-0	*McNutt*
27/3	Port Talbot	a	0-1	
3/4	Caersws	h	5-0	*McNutt, Hayes, McGregor, Pinch D., Burns*
5/4	Bala	a	2-2	*Hayes, McNutt*
13/4	Cefn Druids	a	1-0	*McGregor*
17/4	Newtown	a	0-0	
20/4	Bangor	h	0-1	
24/4	Porthmadog	h	3-0	*Herbert, Burns, Hayes*

Name	Nat	DoB	Pos	Aps	(s)	Gls
Andy ALSTON	ENG	3/11/79	D	29	(1)	
Ben ALSTON	ENG	4/11/86	D	28		
Dominic AUTY		8/1/91	D		(1)	
Tom BAKER	ENG	7/7/78	D	27	(5)	
Aaron BURNS	ENG	8/11/87	A	16		3
Barry CALDER	SCO	23/9/83	M		(1)	
Stuart COOK	ENG	29/3/86	M	5	(3)	
Paul DOWRIDGE		20/11/77	D	3		
Danny FORDE	ENG	8/1/86	M	10	(2)	1
Allan GLOVER	ENG	17/5/80	D	15	(6)	
Mike HAYES	ENG	21/11/87	A	16	(17)	7
Chris HERBERT	ENG	28/2/78	A	15	(9)	7
Alan HOOLEY	ENG	13/7/78	M	20	(3)	
Craig JONES	ENG	7/11/84	A	29		1
Rob JONES	ENG	23/6/89	M	14	(2)	1
Terry McCORMICK	ENG	25/8/83	G	34		
Mark McGREGOR	ENG	16/2/77	D	32	(2)	3
Sam McNUTT	ENG	16/11/79	A	21	(6)	5
Andrew OLSEN	ENG	26/4/82	A	10	(3)	1
Jamie PETRIE	ENG	15/5/86	A	27	(3)	
Danny PINCH		19/8/91	M		(2)	1
Gary PINCH	ENG	3/1/86	D		(1)	
Stuart SCHEUBER		13/4/81	M	23	(5)	1

WALES

HAVERFORDWEST COUNTY AFC
Manager – Derek Brazil (IRL)
Founded – 1899
Stadium – New Bridge Meadow (3,000)

2009

15/8	Welshpool	h	1-0	*Elliott*
22/8	Prestatyn	a	0-3	
28/8	Carmarthen	h	2-1	*Price, Walters*
6/9	Airbus	a	1-3	*Walters*
11/9	Port Talbot	h	1-1	*Williams*
19/9	Connah's Quay	a	1-1	*Bradford*
26/9	Bangor	h	2-2	*Walters 2*
10/10	Newtown	a	1-2	*Walters*
17/10	Porthmadog	h	2-0	*Grimes, Bradford*
24/10	Bala	a	1-1	*Walters*
6/11	Neath	h	1-2	*Bradford*
20/11	Llanelli	h	0-1	
28/11	Rhyl	a	2-1	*Briers, Walters (p)*
5/12	TNS	h	0-0	
12/12	Caersws	a	2-0	*Walters 2*
26/12	Aberystwyth	a	1-2	*Christopher (p)*

2010

1/1	Aberystwyth	h	0-1	
23/1	Airbus	h	1-1	*Christopher*
30/1	Welshpool	a	3-1	*Williams 2, Bradford*
5/2	Port Talbot	a	0-1	
14/2	Connah's Quay	h	1-0	*Dodds*
20/2	Bangor	a	2-3	*Christopher 2*
27/2	Newtown	h	1-2	*Christopher*
6/3	Porthmadog	a	0-0	
10/3	Prestatyn	h	3-3	*Christopher 3 (1p)*
14/3	Bala	h	1-1	*Ramasut*
21/3	Neath	a	2-1	*Christopher 2 (1p)*
27/3	Cefn Druids	h	1-0	*Ramasut*
5/4	Cefn Druids	a	2-1	*Bradford, Christopher*
10/4	Rhyl	h	2-4	*Hudgell, Christopher*
15/4	Llanelli	a	1-1	*Hudgell*
17/4	TNS	a	0-4	
20/4	Carmarthen	a	2-2	*Christopher, Dodds*
24/4	Caersws	h	3-1	*Christopher, Graves, Williams*

Name	Nat	DoB	Pos	Aps	(s)	Gls
Lee BEVAN		10/7/87	D	13	(2)	
Tom BILLING		5/1/82	A	12	(4)	
Dylan BLAIN		11/10/82	D	1	(1)	
Jamie BRADFORD		14/9/83	M	29	(3)	5
Robert BRIERS		29/9/88	M	7	(5)	1
Jack CHRISTOPHER		18/5/87	A	22	(2)	14
Jonathan CLARKE		10/10/86	M	1	(6)	
Mark DODDS		29/5/80	D	14	(2)	2
Gareth ELLIOTT		8/6/83	D	11	(4)	1
Terry EVANS		1/8/76	D	29	(1)	
Kyle GRAVES	ENG	1/4/89	D	34		1
Kristian GRIFFITHS		24/1/87	M	10	(4)	
Jamie GRIMES	ENG	22/11/90	D	27	(3)	1
Josh HARTRICK		20/12/91	M	1	(6)	
Lee HUDGELL		2/11/83	M	12	(4)	2
Lee IDZI		8/2/88	G	34		
Ross JONES		17/2/90	M	5	(2)	
Paul MICHAEL		1/5/86	M	13	(3)	
Kevin MORGAN		7/3/85	M	1	(1)	
Rob MORGANS		5/10/92	M	1	(3)	
Chris O'SULLIVAN		16/2/82	M	12	(2)	
Jarrod PRICE		9/8/83	M	14		1
Tom RAMASUT		30/8/77	M	16	(1)	2
Luke ROBINSON		12/5/91	A	1	(1)	

Damon SEARLE	26/10/71	M	13	(1)	
Robbie WALTERS	17/6/84	A	15	(2)	9
Ricky WATTS	7/11/91	M	2	(6)	
Steffan WILLIAMS	8/6/92	M	20	(7)	4
Nicky WOODROW	25/4/86	A	4	(12)	

LLANELLI AFC
Manager – Andy Legg
Founded – 1892
Stadium – Stebonheath Park (3,000)
MAJOR HONOURS:
Welsh League - (1) 2008.

2009

16/8	Airbus	h	2-2	*Griffiths, Thomas*
21/8	Port Talbot	a	0-0	
30/8	Connah's Quay	h	5-0	*Moses 3, Griffiths, Warlow*
5/9	Bangor	a	3-2	*Griffiths, Legg, Jenkins*
12/9	Newtown	h	3-2	*Griffiths, Moses, Bowen*
20/9	Porthmadog	a	4-0	*Legg, Holloway, Griffiths 2*
27/9	Bala	h	2-0	*Moses 2*
9/10	Neath	a	1-2	*Smitham*
17/10	Cefn Druids	h	4-0	*Bowen, Griffiths, Moses, Corbisiero*
7/11	Rhyl	a	0-0	
10/11	Caersws	h	7-1	*Bowen 2, Moses 2, Griffiths 3*
15/11	TNS	h	0-2	
20/11	Haverfordwest	a	1-0	*Griffiths*
27/11	Aberystwyth	h	4-0	*Mumford, Jarman, Venables, Griffiths*
5/12	Welshpool	a	2-1	*Corbisiero, Griffiths*
13/12	Prestatyn	h	4-1	*Corbisiero, Griffiths 2 (1p), Venables*
26/12	Carmarthen	a	2-1	*Venables, Jarman*

2010

23/1	Bangor	h	3-2	*Venables, Griffiths 2*
6/2	Newtown	a	2-0	*Jones S., Follows*
9/2	Airbus	a	1-0	*Griffiths*
14/2	Porthmadog	h	5-0	*Jones S., Holloway, Venables 2, Evans*
6/3	Cefn Druids	a	5-2	*Thomas 3, Mumford, Moses*
9/3	Port Talbot	h	1-0	*Jarman*
13/3	Caersws	a	2-0	*Griffiths (p), Thomas*
23/3	Connah's Quay	a	0-1	
28/3	TNS	a	0-1	
5/4	Carmarthen	h	1-0	*Griffiths*
9/4	Aberystwyth	a	1-1	*Jones S.*
13/4	Bala	a	1-0	*Griffiths*
15/4	Haverfordwest	h	1-1	*Griffiths*
17/4	Welshpool	h	2-1	*Griffiths, Follows*
20/4	Neath	h	2-1	*Griffiths 2*
22/4	Rhyl	h	3-1	*Follows, Griffiths 2 (1p)*
24/4	Prestatyn	a	5-1	*Griffiths 3, Follows, Phillips*

	Name	Nat	DoB	Pos	Aps	(s)	Gls
26	Ryan BATLEY		17/11/91	D	2	(2)	
7	Jason BOWEN		24/8/72	M	25	(3)	4
8	Antonio CORBISIERO	ENG	17/11/84	M	28		3
25	Stephen EVANS		25/9/80	M	5	(2)	1
20	Jordan FOLLOWS		23/3/90	A	5	(14)	4
28	Craig FRATER		8/12/90	A		(9)	
9	Rhys GRIFFITHS		1/3/80	A	33		30
10	Chris HOLLOWAY		5/2/80	M	17	(5)	2
27	Michael HOWARD	ENG	2/12/78	M	11	(2)	
16	Lee JARMAN		16/12/77	D	18	(3)	3
2	Stephen JENKINS		16/7/72	D	10		1
17	Declan JOHN		14/5/91	M		(1)	

WALES

14	Craig JONES	26/3/87	M	5	(12)	
6	Stuart JONES	14/3/84	D	30		3
21	Andy LEGG	28/7/66	D	21	(6)	2
1	Ashley MORRIS	31/3/84	G	26		
18	Craig MORRIS	27/7/81	G	8		
12	Craig MOSES	12/4/88	A	28	(1)	10
4	Andrew MUMFORD	18/6/81	M	14	(7)	2
22	Lee PHILLIPS	18/3/79	D	10	(4)	1
29	Rory SMITHAM	15/5/87	D	1		1
6	Wyn THOMAS	11/1/79	D	29		5
15	Chris VENABLES	23/7/85	M	30	(1)	6
11	Owain WARLOW	25/10/87	A	18	(5)	1

	Andy HILL	18/10/78	A	6	(7)	
	Ian HILLIER	26/12/79	D	26	(1)	1
	Kieron HOWARD	17/1/91	M	2	(19)	
	Richard INGRAM	15/2/85	M	16	(3)	4
	Kristian JAMES	5/2/82	D	16		
	Chris JONES	14/2/90	A	13	(3)	5
	Chris LLEWELLYN	28/8/79	A	33	(1)	9
	Luke MORGAN	10/10/91	M	4	(3)	
	Stephen POCKETT	11/2/84	M	28	(2)	3
	Carl SHAW	30/5/75	A		(6)	
	Rory SMITHAM	15/5/87	D	3		
	Robert SPENDIFF	24/9/91	A		(3)	
	Craig STEINS	31/7/84	A	25	(6)	14
	Liam THOMAS	6/11/91	M	3	(12)	1
	Wyn WALTERS	28/2/84	G	14		
	Anthony WILLIAMS	20/9/77	G	20		

NEATH FC
Manager – Andy Dyer
Founded – 2005
Stadium – The Gnoll (10,000)

2009

16/8	Connah's Quay	h	1-1	Llewellyn
22/8	Bangor	a	1-3	Llewellyn
28/8	Newtown	h	1-1	Llewellyn
5/9	Porthmadog	a	4-1	Steins 2, Llewellyn, Pockett
13/9	Bala	h	2-1	Steins, Llewellyn
19/9	Caersws	h	5-3	Ingram 3, Castan, Harris
26/9	Cefn Druids	h	1-0	Steins
9/10	Llanelli	h	2-1	Llewellyn 2
17/10	Rhyl	h	2-0	Pockett, Steins
24/10	TNS	a	2-2	Ingram, Steins
6/11	Haverfordwest	a	2-1	Steins 2
21/11	Welshpool	a	0-0	
4/12	Carmarthen	a	1-0	Steins
13/12	Airbus	h	0-0	
27/12	Port Talbot	a	0-2	

2010

23/1	Porthmadog	h	3-2	Jones 3 (1p)
26/1	Aberystwyth	a	1-1	Jones
30/1	Cefn Druids	h	1-1	Hillier
6/2	Bala	a	0-1	
9/2	Newtown	a	0-1	
13/2	Caersws	a	1-0	Llewellyn
16/2	Aberystwyth	h	1-3	Castan
23/2	Prestatyn	h	1-1	Steins
6/3	Rhyl	a	1-0	Llewellyn
13/3	TNS	h	0-1	
16/3	Connah's Quay	a	0-2	
21/3	Haverfordwest	h	1-2	Harris
27/3	Bangor	h	0-1	
4/4	Welshpool	h	4-0	Thomas, Steins 3
7/4	Port Talbot	h	0-2	
13/4	Prestatyn	a	0-0	
16/4	Carmarthen	h	1-1	Jones
20/4	Llanelli	a	1-2	Pockett
24/4	Airbus	a	1-1	Steins

Name	Nat	DoB	Pos	Aps	(s)	Gls
Clayton BLACKMORE		23/9/64	D		(1)	
Carlos CASTAN	ESP	25/2/84	D	34		2
Kevin COOPER	ENG	8/2/75	M	8	(2)	
Sean CRONIN		17/1/86	D	15	(6)	
Steven DAVEY		26/1/91	M		(5)	
Ashley EVANS		18/7/89	M	29	(1)	
Dale EVANS		26/3/87	M	23	(5)	
Rob FOLLAND		3/8/81	D	9	(3)	
Liam HANCOCK		29/7/82	D	30	(1)	
Matthew HARRIS		24/9/88	M	17	(3)	2

NEWTOWN AFC
Manager – Darren Ryan
Founded – 1875
Stadium – GF Grigg Latham Park (6,000)
MAJOR HONOURS:
Welsh Cup – (2) 1879, 1895.

2009

15/8	Porthmadog	a	1-1	Worton
22/8	Bala	h	0-1	
28/8	Neath	a	1-1	Ward
5/9	Cefn Druids	h	4-2	James, Cadwallader, Anoruo, Ward (p)
12/9	Llanelli	a	2-3	Anoruo, Blain
19/9	Rhyl	h	2-4	Ward (p), Anoruo
25/9	TNS	a	2-2	Daniels, James
10/10	Haverfordwest	h	2-1	Breeze, Blain
16/10	Aberystwyth	a	1-2	Stephens
24/10	Welshpool	h	4-1	Mitchell, Anoruo, Stephens 2
6/11	Prestatyn	a	1-1	Cadwallader
21/11	Airbus	a	0-2	
5/12	Connah's Quay	a	1-3	Anoruo
12/12	Bangor	h	2-5	Breeze, Stephens

2010

22/1	Cefn Druids	a	2-0	Stephens (p), Mitchell
30/1	Carmarthen	h	0-0	
6/2	Llanelli	h	0-2	
9/2	Neath	h	1-0	Roberts P.
14/2	Rhyl	a	2-4	Cadwallader, Breeze
20/2	TNS	h	0-2	
27/2	Haverfordwest	a	2-1	Stephens 2
6/3	Aberystwyth	h	1-2	Roberts P.
9/3	Bala	a	1-1	Roberts P.
12/3	Welshpool	a	5-1	Roberts P. 3, Worton, Stephens
16/3	Port Talbot	h	2-2	Stephens 2
20/3	Prestatyn	h	3-2	Cadwallader, Roberts P., og (Hayes)
23/3	Porthmadog	h	1-3	Cadwallader
27/3	Carmarthen	a	2-1	Wright 2
3/4	Airbus	h	3-3	Blain 2, Wright
5/4	Caersws	h	4-1	Stephens, Wright, Blain, Cadwallader
13/4	Port Talbot	a	1-2	Roberts P.
17/4	Connah's Quay	h	0-0	
20/4	Caersws	a	1-1	Worton
24/4	Bangor	a	0-0	

Name	Nat	DoB	Pos	Aps	(s)	Gls
Obi ANORUO	NGA	28/8/91	A	9		5
Dylan BLAIN		10/11/82	M	31	(1)	5
Jamie BREEZE		10/1/92	M	7	(10)	3
Gavin CADWALLADER		18/4/86	D	27	(1)	6
Damien DANIELS	NIR	16/12/81	M	16	(5)	1
Dan DAWSON	ENG	21/10/91	D	5	(7)	
Stuart FRASER		28/3/87	M		(4)	
Richard HARRIS	ENG	14/9/84	M	1		
Jack HUGHES		12/2/90	M	10	(1)	
Craig HUTCHINSON	ENG	28/1/73	M	20	(2)	
Robbie JAMES		20/12/88	D	20	(4)	2
Dave JONES		3/2/90	G	8		
Gareth JONES		18/9/84	D	2	(1)	
Tom JONES		19/6/90	D		(2)	
Matthew LEWIS		1/3/82	M	1	(6)	
David MAGUIRE	NIR	9/10/90	G	13		
Tyrone McFADDEN		7/3/91	M		(1)	
Neil MITCHELL	ENG	1/4/88	M	27	(4)	2
Dave ROBERTS	ENG	10/12/88	G	13		
Paul ROBERTS		29/7/77	A	19		8
Jamie RUSSELL	ENG	15/4/90	M	2	(6)	
Ross STEPHENS		28/5/85	M	33		11
Andrew THOMAS		26/1/75	D	33		
Nicky WARD		30/11/87	A	12		3
Andrew WEBB	ENG	14/9/84	M		(9)	
Craig WILLIAMS		21/12/87	D	31		
Adam WORTON	ENG	10/4/87	M	30	(3)	3
Callum WRIGHT	ENG	31/10/89	M	4	(6)	4

CPD PORTHMADOG

Manager – Tomi Morgan
Founded – 1884
Stadium – Y Traeth (3,000)

2009

15/8	Newtown	h	1-1	Evans M. (p)
22/8	Caersws	h	1-1	Roberts P.
28/8	Bala	a	0-0	
5/9	Neath	h	1-4	Pyrs
11/9	Cefn Druids	a	0-1	
20/9	Llanelli	h	0-4	
26/9	Rhyl	a	0-4	
17/10	Haverfordwest	a	0-2	
24/10	Aberystwyth	h	0-1	
7/11	Welshpool	a	0-2	
14/11	Prestatyn	h	2-0	Parry, Shannon
21/11	Carmarthen	a	3-1	James, Roberts P. 2
28/11	Airbus	h	0-1	
5/12	Port Talbot	a	0-5	
12/12	Connah's Quay	h	0-1	
15/12	TNS	h	1-1	Shannon (p)
27/12	Bangor	a	0-2	

2010

16/1	Bala	h	0-2	
23/1	Neath	a	2-3	Orlik, og (Folland)
6/2	Cefn Druids	h	1-0	Shannon
14/2	Llanelli	a	0-5	
20/2	Rhyl	h	0-2	
6/3	Haverfordwest	h	0-0	
12/3	Aberystwyth	a	0-1	
16/3	TNS	a	0-5	
20/3	Welshpool	h	2-3	Jones Cai, Jones Ch.
23/3	Newtown	a	3-1	Jones Ch. 3 (1p)
27/3	Prestatyn	a	1-1	Rogers (p)
3/4	Carmarthen	h	1-4	Meredith
5/4	Bangor	h	0-2	
10/4	Airbus	a	2-1	Jones Ch. 2
13/4	Caersws	a	2-1	Meredith, Orlik
17/4	Port Talbot	h	0-1	
24/4	Connah's Quay	a	0-3	

Name	Nat	DoB	Pos	Aps	(s)	Gls
Steffano ANTONIAZZI		2/3/88	D	1	(3)	
Ryan DAVIES		31/12/78	D	22		
Andy EVANS		1/4/78	A	2		
Mark EVANS		14/4/90	A	11	(6)	1
Robert EVANS		24/1/89	M	15		
Mike FOSTER		29/11/73	D	25		
Mark GORNALL		7/9/82	D	6	(7)	
Richard HARVEY		25/7/82	G	6		
Ceri JAMES		1/12/83	M	11	(5)	1
Cai JONES		3/10/92	A	11	(2)	1
Carl JONES		30/6/89	M		(1)	
Chris JONES		9/10/85	M	30		6
Eifion JONES		28/9/80	D	3		
Jack JONES		12/10/90	D	15	(6)	
Steve JONES		7/4/89	M	1	(11)	
John KEEGAN	ENG	5/8/81	D	31		
Sion MEREDITH		18/1/78	M	9	(4)	2
Richard MORGAN		28/1/79	G	28		
Tomi MORGAN		4/9/57	A		(1)	
Marcus ORLIK		11/2/85	A	10	(1)	2
Gareth PARRY		4/2/81	M	26	(4)	1
Iddon PRICE		14/4/92	M		(1)	
Dan PYRS		21/10/84	M	28	(3)	1
Euron ROBERTS		18/11/85	D	32		
Paul ROBERTS		29/7/77	A	14	(1)	3
Jamie ROGERS	ENG	14/8/78	A	5	(5)	1
Daniel RYLANCE		25/10/90	M		(1)	
Aden SHANNON		9/4/80	A	16	(5)	3
Aaron STOKOE	ENG	19/6/85	M	6	(4)	
Michael THOMPSON	ENG	5/1/84	M	10	(3)	
Dylan WILLIAMS		23/2/93	M		(10)	

PORT TALBOT TOWN FC

Manager – Mark Jones
Founded – 1901
Stadium – GenQuip Stadium (3,000)

2009

15/8	Cefn Druids	a	1-0	Fahiya
21/8	Llanelli	h	0-0	
29/8	Rhyl	a	0-2	
5/9	TNS	h	2-0	McCreesh 2
11/9	Haverfordwest	a	1-1	John
18/9	Aberystwyth	h	1-2	Rose
26/9	Welshpool	a	2-0	McCreesh 2
10/10	Prestatyn	h	1-1	Surman
17/10	Carmarthen	a	1-3	Rose
24/10	Airbus	h	2-1	Thomas N., McCreesh
7/11	Caersws	a	2-1	McCreesh, Fahiya
14/11	Connah's Quay	a	3-0	Rose, Fahiya, McCreesh
21/11	Bangor	h	2-1	Rose 2 (1p)
5/12	Porthmadog	h	5-0	Thomas N., Rose 2, Barrow, Lewis
12/12	Bala	a	1-1	Thomas N.
27/12	Neath	h	2-0	Barrow, Thomas N.

2010

16/1	Rhyl	h	2-1	McCreesh, Holland
23/1	TNS	a	0-1	
5/2	Haverfordwest	h	1-0	Rose
12/2	Aberystwyth	a	1-2	McCreesh

WALES

16/2	Cefn Druids	h	7-0	Thomas D. 3, John 2, McCreesh 2
20/2	Welshpool	h	3-0	Rose (p), Thomas N., Rees
6/3	Carmarthen	h	0-1	
9/3	Llanelli	a	0-1	
13/3	Airbus	a	0-0	
16/3	Newtown	a	2-2	Rose, Rees
20/3	Caersws	h	4-0	McCreesh, Rees, Rose 2
27/3	Connah's Quay	h	1-0	McCreesh
30/3	Prestatyn	a	3-0	Rose, Thomas D., Fahiya
3/4	Bangor	a	1-1	Grist
7/4	Neath	a	2-0	Thomas D., Rose
13/4	Newtown	h	2-1	Rose, Rees
17/4	Porthmadog	a	1-0	Rose
24/4	Bala	h	0-0	

Name	Nat	DoB	Pos	Aps	(s)	Gls
Gary BANSOR	ENG	25/10/88	D	2	(5)	
Scott BARROW		19/10/88	M	29	(4)	2
Andy BOSLEM		25/7/89	D		(1)	
Leigh DE VULGT		10/3/81	D	34		
Drew FAHIYA		17/4/88	A	19	(12)	4
Lloyd GRIST		13/11/85	M	24	(5)	1
Nicky HOLLAND		24/4/89	M	3	(14)	1
Lee JOHN		4/9/84	M	20	(10)	3
Mark JONES		5/1/89	A		(5)	
Lee KENDALL		8/1/81	G	32		
Karl LEWIS		27/6/81	M	17	(4)	1
Liam McCREESH		9/9/85	M	27	(1)	13
Tony PENNOCK		10/4/71	G	1		
Gareth PHILLIPS		19/8/79	M	20	(5)	
Matthew REES		2/9/82	D	33		4
Duncan ROBERTS	ENG	24/6/79	G	1		
Martin ROSE	ENG	29/2/84	A	32		16
Lee SURMAN		3/4/86	D	31		1
Daniel THOMAS		28/4/84	A	19	(7)	5
Neil THOMAS		22/2/82	M	27	(1)	5
Matthew THOMPSON	ENG	29/5/88	M	3	(10)	

PRESTATYN TOWN FC
Manager – Neil Gibson
Founded – 1946
Stadium – Bastion Road (3,000)

2009

14/8	TNS	a	0-5	
22/8	Haverfordwest	h	3-0	Lewis, Moran, Griffiths
29/8	Aberystwyth	a	3-2	Williams 2, Moran
4/9	Welshpool	h	2-1	Williams, Hayes
12/9	Caersws	a	5-1	Parker 2, Hayes, Moran, Jones
19/9	Carmarthen	a	2-1	Moran, Griffiths
25/9	Airbus	h	2-2	Rogers, O'Neill
10/10	Port Talbot	a	1-1	Griffiths
16/10	Connah's Quay	h	3-2	Moran 2 (1p), Parker
23/10	Bangor	a	0-4	
6/11	Newtown	h	1-1	Parker
14/11	Porthmadog	a	0-2	
20/11	Bala	h	2-1	Hayes, O'Neill
4/12	Cefn Druids	h	2-0	Griffiths, Moran (p)
13/12	Llanelli	a	1-4	O'Neill
18/12	TNS	h	0-1	
26/12	Rhyl	h	0-0	

2010

2/1	Rhyl	a	1-1	Hayes
16/1	Aberystwyth	h	0-2	
22/1	Welshpool	a	5-0	Wilson, Moran 2, Parker 2
6/2	Caersws	h	1-0	Moran

13/2	Carmarthen	h	0-0	
23/2	Neath	a	1-1	Griffiths
5/3	Connah's Quay	a	1-1	Rogers
10/3	Haverfordwest	a	3-3	O'Neill, Fisher-Cooke, Parker (p)
12/3	Bangor	h	1-1	Parker
20/3	Newtown	a	2-3	Rogers, Moran
27/3	Porthmadog	h	1-1	Griffiths
30/3	Port Talbot	h	0-3	
2/4	Bala	a	4-2	Griffiths, Moran (p), Rogers 2
13/4	Neath	h	0-0	
16/4	Cefn Druids	a	5-0	Harris, og (Jones S.), Moran 2, Hayes
21/4	Airbus	a	0-2	
24/4	Llanelli	h	1-5	Evans

Name	Nat	DoB	Pos	Aps	(s)	Gls
Andy DAVIES		12/9/84	D	9	(1)	
Chris DAVIES		21/10/90	M	10	(1)	
Gareth DAVIES		14/3/80	A		3)	
Dan EVANS		1/3/87	M	4	(6)	1
Jon FISHER-COOKE		13/5/82	A	6	(8)	1
Neil GIBSON		11/10/79	M	30	(1)	
Ian GRIFFITHS		2/1/85	A	21	(4)	7
Ross HANNEN		29/4/86	M	8	(3)	
Steve HARRIS	IRL	5/2/86	M	5	(8)	1
David HAYES		15/1/82	D	32		5
Jon HILL-DUNT		13/5/86	G	30		
Steve HOULT		17/1/81	A	14	(8)	
Paul JENKINS		15/4/88	D	1		
Russ JONES		31/5/82	D	27	(1)	1
Jack LEWIS		18/5/88	D	34		1
Adrian MOODY	ENG	29/9/82	D	5	(3)	
Andy MORAN	ENG	7/10/79	A	33		14
Karl MURRAY		24/9/90	M		(2)	
Paul O'NEILL		17/6/82	D	31		4
Michael PARKER		31/10/87	M	25	(2)	8
Steve ROGERS	ENG	16/12/78	A	17	(8)	5
Matt TOWNS	ENG	12/9/82	G	4		
Alec WILLIAMS		19/5/87	M	6	(3)	3
Gareth WILSON	ENG	23/5/78	M	22	(1)	1
Ethan WOODFINE		29/10/90	D		(1)	

RHYL FC
Manager – Greg Strong
Founded – 1874
Stadium – Belle Vue Stadium (3,000)
MAJOR HONOURS:
Welsh League – (2) 2004, 2009;
Welsh Cup – (4) 1952, 1953, 2004, 2006.

2009

15/8	Carmarthen	h	2-1	Strong, Williams M.
21/8	Airbus	a	2-2	Hunt 2
29/8	Port Talbot	h	2-0	Williams M., Hunt
5/9	Connah's Quay	a	2-0	Williams M., Connolly
11/9	Bangor	h	5-1	Hunt 2, Williams M. (p), Williams C., Connolly
19/9	Newtown	a	4-2	Williams M. 2, Strong, Connolly
26/9	Porthmadog	h	4-0	Connolly 3 (1p), Kirk
9/10	Bala	a	4-0	Smith, Doran, Horan, Hunt
17/10	Neath	a	0-2	
23/10	Cefn Druids	a	1-1	Williams M.
7/11	Llanelli	h	0-0	
14/11	Caersws	h	3-1	Connolly, Hunt 2
22/11	TNS	a	0-4	
28/11	Haverfordwest	h	1-2	Strong
5/12	Aberystwyth	a	2-2	Leah, Hunt

12/12	Welshpool	h	4-1	Leah, Williams C., Hunt, Owen
26/12	Prestatyn	a	0-0	
2010				
2/1	Prestatyn	h	1-1	Leah
16/1	Port Talbot	a	1-2	Turner
23/1	Connah's Quay	h	4-1	Connolly, Horan, Williams M. 2
26/1	Airbus	h	2-1	Williams M. (p), Turner
7/2	Bangor	a	1-3	Williams M. (p)
14/2	Newtown	h	4-2	Strong, Williams M., Owens, Kirk
20/2	Porthmadog	a	2-0	Strong, Connolly
24/2	Bala	h	5-2	Pearson, Williams C., Connolly 2, Turner
6/3	Neath	h	0-1	
13/3	Cefn Druids	h	6-0	Williams M. 3 (1p), Connolly, Williams C., Pearson
27/3	Caersws	a	2-2	Owen, Williams M.
2/4	TNS	h	1-2	Williams M.
10/4	Haverfordwest	a	4-2	Connolly 2, Kirk, Williams M.
13/4	Carmarthen	a	1-0	Williams M.
17/4	Aberystwyth	h	1-1	Connolly
22/4	Llanelli	a	1-3	Naylor
24/4	Welshpool	a	2-1	Williams M., Turner

Name	Nat	DoB	Pos	Aps	(s)	Gls
David CAMERON		24/8/75	A		(1)	
James COATES	ENG	22/2/85	G	11		
Mark CONNOLLY	ENG	2/7/84	D	27	(2)	15
Russell COURTNEY	ENG	11/10/88	M	1	(2)	
Jack CUDWORTH	ENG	11/9/90	G	17		
Joseph DIXON	ENG	2/10/85	M		(1)	
Phil DORAN	ENG	30/11/88	D	16	(5)	1
Shaun DOWLING	ENG	9/9/90	D	22		
Sam HEENAN	NZL	21/4/91	M	2	(3)	
Luke HOLDEN	ENG	24/11/88	M	1	(1)	
George HORAN		18/2/82	D	19	(1)	2
Lee HUNT	ENG	5/6/82	A	15		10
Tyrone KIRK	ENG	2/1/86	M	24	(3)	3
John LEAH	ENG	3/8/78	M	33		3
Martyn NAYLOR	ENG	2/8/77	D	16	(4)	1
Phil OJAPAH	ENG	24/7/89	D	7	(2)	
Gareth OWEN		21/10/71	M	27	(2)	2
Andy OWENS	ENG	18/10/89	D	6	(1)	1
Andy PEARSON	ENG	21/12/89	D	12		2
Paul PRITCHARD		26/5/84	G	6	(1)	
Neil ROBERTS		7/4/78	A	2		
Paul SMITH	ENG	17/11/90	M	4	(3)	1
Greg STONES	ENG	4/5/82	D	20	(1)	
Greg STRONG	ENG	5/9/75	D	30	(2)	5
Robert TURNER	ENG	29/9/89	A	7	(1)	4
Chris WILLIAMS		26/2/85	M	22	(5)	4
Matthew WILLIAMS		5/11/82	A	27	(4)	20

THE NEW SAINTS FC

Manager – Andy Cale (ENG)
Founded – 1959
Stadium – The Venue (3,000)
MAJOR HONOURS:
Welsh League - (5) 2000, 2005, 2006, 2007, 2010;
Welsh Cup - (2) 1996, 2005.

2009				
14/8	Prestatyn	h	5-0	Berkeley, Jones 2, Wood, Seargeant
22/8	Carmarthen	h	2-0	Wood, Edwards
29/8	Airbus	h	2-1	Abbott, Wood
5/9	Port Talbot	a	0-2	
11/9	Connah's Quay	h	3-0	Abbott 2, Ruscoe

19/9	Bangor	a	1-0	Murtagh
25/9	Newtown	h	2-2	Marriott R., Ruscoe
17/10	Bala	h	0-0	
24/10	Neath	h	2-2	Berkeley, Wood
6/11	Cefn Druids	h	4-0	Jones (p), Edwards 3
15/11	Llanelli	a	2-0	Jones, Ruscoe
22/11	Rhyl	h	4-0	Abbott, Ruscoe (p), Jones, Berkeley
27/11	Caersws	h	4-0	Wood, Marriott R., Darlington, Seargeant
5/12	Haverfordwest	a	0-0	
11/12	Aberystwyth	h	4-0	Jones 2, Williams 2
15/12	Porthmadog	a	1-1	Wood
18/12	Prestatyn	a	1-0	Evans
2010				
1/1	Welshpool	h	4-0	Williams, Darlington 3
23/1	Port Talbot	h	1-0	Evans
5/2	Connah's Quay	a	0-1	
14/2	Bangor	h	2-1	Ruscoe (p), Darlington
20/2	Newtown	a	2-0	Berkeley, Ruscoe
24/2	Airbus	a	0-0	
5/3	Bala	a	1-0	Abbott
9/3	Carmarthen	a	2-1	Sharp 2
13/3	Neath	a	1-0	McKenna
16/3	Porthmadog	h	5-0	Sharp 2, McKenna, Wood, Holmes T.
19/3	Cefn Druids	a	0-0	
28/3	Llanelli	h	1-0	Jones
2/4	Rhyl	a	2-1	Ruscoe, Sharp
10/4	Caersws	a	3-0	McKenna, Berkeley, Ruscoe
13/4	Welshpool	a	1-0	Berkeley
17/4	Haverfordwest	h	4-0	Sharp 3 (1p), Baker
24/4	Aberystwyth	a	3-1	Sharp 2, Evans

Name	Nat	DoB	Pos	Aps	(s)	Gls
Steve ABBOTT	ENG	31/7/82	A	15	(9)	5
Phil BAKER	ENG	4/11/82	D	31		1
Matthew BERKELEY	ENG	3/8/87	A	21	(6)	6
Alex DARLINGTON		26/12/88	A	7	(11)	5
Aeron EDWARDS		16/2/88	A	16	(3)	4
Steve EVANS		26/2/79	D	31		3
Paul HARRISON	ENG	18/12/84	G	34		
Barry HOGAN	ENG	15/12/83	M	30	(2)	
Danny HOLMES	ENG	6/1/89	D	32		
Tommy HOLMES	ENG	1/9/79	D	18	(1)	1
Craig JONES		20/3/87	M	26	(4)	8
Chris MARRIOTT		24/9/89	D	21	(4)	
Ryan MARRIOTT	ENG	18/11/88	A	3	(4)	2
John McKENNA	ENG	15/5/90	M	9	(8)	3
Conall MURTAGH	NIR	29/6/85	M	4	(2)	1
Scott RUSCOE		15/12/77	M	30	(2)	8
Christian SEARGEANT	ENG	13/11/88	M	11	(8)	2
Chris SHARP	SCO	19/6/86	A	12	(1)	10
Craig WILLIAMS		28/1/83	M	9	(11)	3
Jamie WOOD	CAY	21/9/78	A	14	(10)	7

WELSHPOOL TOWN FC

Manager – Huw Griffiths
Founded – 1878
Stadium – Maes-y-Dre (3,000)

2009				
15/8	Haverfordwest	a	0-1	
21/8	Aberystwyth	a	1-1	Boardman
29/8	Caersws	a	0-3	
4/9	Prestatyn	a	1-2	Lamb
12/9	Carmarthen	h	1-3	Cronshaw

18/9	Airbus	a	2-1	Harris, Lamb
26/9	Port Talbot	h	0-2	
10/10	Connah's Quay	a	0-0	
17/10	Bangor	h	1-2	Stewart
24/10	Newtown	a	1-4	Hughes
7/11	Porthmadog	h	2-0	Doran, Edwards T.
21/11	Neath	h	0-0	
27/11	Cefn Druids	a	1-0	Price (p)
1/12	Bala	a	1-2	Peate
5/12	Llanelli	h	1-2	Jenkins
12/12	Rhyl	a	1-4	Edwards S.
2010				
1/1	TNS	a	0-4	
22/1	Prestatyn	h	0-5	
30/1	Haverfordwest	h	1-3	Hughes
6/2	Carmarthen	a	1-1	Edwards S.
12/2	Airbus	h	0-0	
20/2	Port Talbot	a	0-3	
6/3	Bangor	a	2-3	Cronshaw 2
9/3	Connah's Quay	h	0-1	
12/3	Newtown	h	1-5	Kane
20/3	Porthmadog	a	3-2	Stewart 2, Edwards S.
23/3	Caersws	h	3-1	Williams, Jenkins 2
26/3	Bala	h	1-2	Cronshaw
4/4	Neath	a	0-4	
9/4	Cefn Druids	h	2-1	Williams 2
13/4	TNS	h	0-1	
17/4	Llanelli	a	1-2	Stewart
20/4	Aberystwyth	h	1-3	Boardman
24/4	Rhyl	h	1-2	Griffiths

Name	Nat	DoB	Pos	Aps	(s)	Gls
Martin BEATTIE	ENG	18/1/83	M	30		
Steve BELLERSBY		25/3/81	G	1		
John BOARDMAN	ENG	6/9/80	D	31		2
Phil CLARKE	ENG	20/10/88	D	3		
George CLIFTON	ENG	30/6/90	M		(2)	
Mike CRONSHAW		4/9/90	M	24	(7)	4
Jack CUDWORTH	ENG	11/9/90	G	16		
Calvin DAVIES		14/5/83	A	6	(1)	
Peter DORAN	ENG	30/11/88	M	15		1
Steffan EDWARDS		10/10/89	D	26	(3)	3
Timmy EDWARDS		24/4/72	D	4	(1)	1
Marc GRIFFITHS	ENG	16/5/84	A	14	(2)	1
Richard HARRIS	ENG	14/9/84	M	14		1
George HUGHES		3/10/86	M	34		2
Adam JENKINS	ENG	9/6/93	M	2	(12)	3
Danny JONES		23/4/82	G	2		
Jordan KANE		3/12/91	A	5	(3)	1
Adam KNIGHT	ENG	9/5/86	D	1	(1)	
Carl LAMB	ENG	10/11/84	M	9		2
Dave MAGUIRE	NIR	9/10/90	G	15		
Max PEATE		23/3/89	D	25	(2)	1
Joe PRICE		25/9/90	M	14	(8)	1
Arran PRITCHARD		7/2/91	D	30	(3)	
Eric RAMSEY	ENG	1/8/91	M	10	(4)	
Mark STEWART	ENG	25/7/90	M	8	(10)	4
Gareth WILLIAMS		30/3/82	M	32		3
Geraint WINDSOR		22/6/80	D	3		
Matthew WINDSOR		11/5/93	M		(2)	

SECOND LEVEL FINAL TABLES 2009/10

NORTH		Pld	W	D	L	F	A	Pts
1	Llangefni Town FC	32	25	4	3	95	27	79
2	Flint Town United FC	32	23	6	3	84	29	75
3	Llandudno FC	32	19	8	5	73	31	65
4	Buckley Town FC	32	17	9	6	57	30	60
5	CPD Penrhyncoch	32	16	7	9	51	46	55
6	Guilsfield FC	32	12	9	11	54	54	45
7	Ruthin Town FC	32	13	5	14	48	61	44
8	Holyhead Hotspur FC	32	13	4	15	53	52	40
9	Bethesda Athletic FC	32	10	9	13	70	59	39
10	Denbigh Town FC	32	10	9	13	56	56	39
11	Llangollen Town FC	32	11	3	18	59	78	36
12	Berriew FC	32	10	5	17	50	74	35
13	Mold Alexandra FC	32	11	2	19	53	81	35
14	Lex XI FC	32	9	7	16	45	70	34
15	Llanfairpwll FC	32	9	5	18	38	60	32
16	Caernarfon Town FC	32	8	5	19	50	69	26
17	Gresford Athletic FC	32	5	5	22	28	87	20

NB No promotion; Holyhead Hotspur FC and Caernarfon Town FC - 3pts deducted.

SOUTH		Pld	W	D	L	F	A	Pts
1	Goytre United FC	34	19	12	3	86	47	69
2	Cambrian & Clydach BC	34	19	11	4	73	42	68
3	Afan Lido FC	34	19	6	9	74	37	63
4	Caldicot Town FC	34	16	7	11	78	54	55
5	Bryntirion Athletic AFC	34	15	9	10	67	60	54
6	Taffs Well FC	34	15	5	14	72	60	50
7	Barry Town AFC	34	12	13	9	46	41	49
8	Pontardawe Town FC	34	13	8	13	59	56	47
9	Bridgend Town FC	34	12	9	13	57	55	45
10	ENTO Aberaman Athletic FC	34	12	8	14	56	68	44
11	West End FC	34	12	8	14	62	84	44
12	Cardiff Corinthians AFC	34	12	7	15	63	69	43
13	Garden Village AFC	34	12	6	16	46	52	42
14	Ton Pentre AFC	34	11	8	15	56	65	41
15	Ely Rangers AFC	34	10	6	18	46	67	36
16	Bettws FC	34	9	9	16	38	59	36
17	Dinas Powys AFC	34	9	4	21	50	83	31
18	Caerleon FC	34	8	6	20	37	67	30

NB No promotion.

WALES

DOMESTIC CUP 2009/10

WELSH CUP

SECOND ROUND

(2/10/09)
Aberaman 3, Penrhiwceiber 2
Cambrian & Clydach 3, Troedyrhiw 1
Port Talbot 5, Cwmbran Celtic 0

(3/10/09)
Afan Lido 5, Croesyceiliog 1
Bangor 4, Cefn Druids 1
Borras Park 1, Bala 8
Bridgend 2, Ton Pentre 0
Bryntirion 0, Aberystwyth 3
Caerau Ely 5, Hay 1
Cardiff Bay 3, Aberbargoed 2
Connah's Quay 2, Pwllheli 0
Conwy 0, TNS 2 *(aet)*
Ely Rangers 3, Llwydcoed 2
Flint 7, Barmouth 1
Garden Village 2, Caldicot 6 *(aet)*
Goytre United 0, Pontardawe 3
Gresford 2, Llanrug 3
Holyhead 1, Newtown 1 *(aet; 4-3 on pens)*
Lex XI 1, Airbus 3
Llandudno 3, Berriew 0
Llanfairpwll 1, Rhyl 3
Llangefni 1, Llandudno Junction 2
Llangeinor 2, Pontyclun 1 *(aet)*
Llangollen 1, Glan Conwy 0
Llansantffraid 1, Coedpoeth 2
Neath 2, Llanelli 2 *(aet; 2-3 on pens)*
Penrhyncoch 0, Porthmadog 1
Rhydymwyn 1, Caernarfon 0
Ruthin 1, Caersws 2
Taffs Well 0, Haverfordwest 2
Welshpool 2, Prestatyn 3

(4/10/09)
Carmarthen 4, Pontypridd 1

THIRD ROUND

(31/10/09)
Aberaman 2, Ely Rangers 0
Bala 1, Llanrug 0
Caerau Ely 1, Afan Lido 2
Caersws 4, Coedpoeth 1
Caldicot 0, Port Talbot 3
Cambrian & Clydach 0, TNS 2
Connah's Quay 3, Airbus 2 *(aet)*
Flint 0, Bangor 1
Haverfordwest 1, Aberystwyth 2
Llanelli 3, Carmarthen 1
Llangeinor 1, Holyhead 6
Llangollen 1, Llandudno Junction 3
Pontardawe 2, Llandudno 0
Porthmadog 3, Rhydymwyn 1
Prestatyn 3, Cardiff Bay 0
Rhyl 4, Bridgend 2

FOURTH ROUND

(30/1/10)
Aberystwyth 0, Port Talbot 2
Afan Lido 2, Connah's Quay 1 *(aet)*
Bala 2, Caersws 0
Bangor 3, Aberaman 1
Llandudno Junction 0, TNS 6
Llanelli 4, Holyhead 0
Prestatyn 1, Porthmadog 0
Rhyl 7, Pontardawe 0

QUARTER-FINALS

(27/2/10)
Bala 2 *(Jones 98, Fisher N. 118)*, Afan Lido 0 *(aet)*
Bangor 2 *(Reed 6p, Morley 90)*, Llanelli 0
Prestatyn 4 *(Parker 18, Wilson 44, Gibson 50, Moran 76)*, Rhyl 4
(Connolly 11, 27, Williams M. 30, Turner 90)
(aet; 5-3 on pens)
TNS 2 *(Edwards 14, Darlington 47)*, Port Talbot 2 *(Rose 26, John 35)*
(aet; 3-4 on pens)

SEMI-FINALS

(10/4/10)
Bala Town 0, Port Talbot 1 *(McCreesh 33)*

(11/4/10)
Bangor 2 *(Smyth 11, Garside 43)*, Prestatyn 0

FINAL

(1/5/10)
Parc-y-Scarlets, Llanelli
BANGOR CITY FC 3 *(Hunt 6, Reed 15, Morley 90+1)*
PORT TALBOT TOWN FC 2 *(Fahiya 57, McCreesh 85)*
Referee – John
BANGOR – Smith, Hoy, Roberts, Morley, Brewerton, Garside, Reed *(Davies 90)*, Johnston, Jebb *(Edwards 69)*, Smyth *(Limbert 80)*, Hunt.
PORT TALBOT – Kendall, De Vulgt *(Holland 63)*, Barrow, Phillips, Rees, Surman, Fahiya *(John 66)*, Grist, Rose, McCreesh, Thomas D. *(Lewis 66)*.

Champions

The definitive European football magazine

SAVE 20%

WHEN YOU SUBSCRIBE!

Follow the world's greatest club tournament with the
official magazine of the UEFA Champions League.
Save 20% and pay just £19 for six issues.
Call 08456 760 033 and quote EFY10 or visit

www.themagazineshop.com/CHAM/EFY10

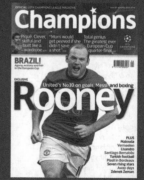

GRAPHIC GUIDE

UEFA COMPETITION PARTICIPANTS 2010/11

This section contains national federation crests, international kits, club badges for the participants of UEFA competitions* and maps for all 53 UEFA member associations.

*subject to UEFA's club licensing regulations.

Key to country pages

○	UEFA Champions League	©	champions
○	UEFA Europa League	*	domestic Cup winners
○	Clubs in top division	[fp]	Fair Play qualifiers
○	Promoted Clubs		
●	Relegated Clubs		

Graphic Guide Index

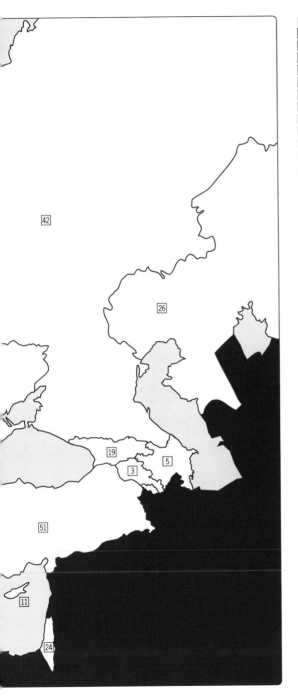

FEDERATION HOME INTERNATIONAL KIT

AWAY INTERNATIONAL KIT

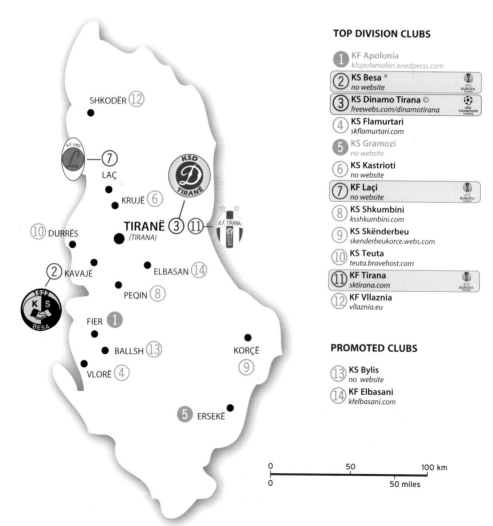

TOP DIVISION CLUBS

1 KF Apolonia
  kfapoloniafier.wordpress.com

2 KS Besa *
  no website

3 KS Dinamo Tirana ©
  freewebs.com/dinamotirana

4 KS Flamurtari
  skflamurtari.com

5 KS Gramozi
  no website

6 KS Kastrioti
  no website

7 KF Laçi
  no website

8 KS Shkumbini
  ksshkumbini.com

9 KS Skënderbeu
  skenderbeukorce.webs.com

10 KS Teuta
  teuta.bravehost.com

11 KF Tirana
  sktirana.com

12 KF Vllaznia
  vllaznia.eu

PROMOTED CLUBS

13 KS Bylis
  no website

14 KF Elbasani
  kfelbasani.com

0   50   100 km

0   50 miles

ANDORRA

FEDERATION   HOME INTERNATIONAL KIT   AWAY INTERNATIONAL KIT

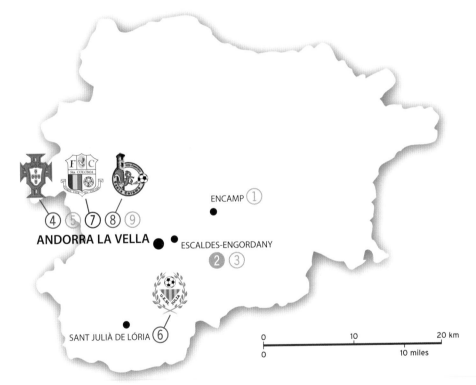

TOP DIVISION CLUBS

1 **FC Encamp**
empresaactiva.net/proves/
futbolclubencamp

2 UE Engordany
no website

3 **Inter Club d'Escaldes**
no website

4 **FC Lusitans**
no website

5 **CE Principat**
ceprincipat.com

6 **UE Sant Julià** *
no website

7 **FC Santa Coloma** ©
no website

8 **UE Santa Coloma**
no website

PROMOTED CLUB

9 **FC Casa del Benfica**
no website

FEDERATION

HOME INTERNATIONAL KIT

AWAY INTERNATIONAL KIT

GYUMRI ⑦

DILIJAN ⑨

YEREVAN
① ② ④ ⑤ ⑥ ⑧

③ KAPAN

0   50   100 km
0   50 miles

TOP DIVISION CLUBS

① FC Ararat Yerevan
fcararat.com

② **FC Banants**
fcbanants.com   EUROPA LEAGUE

③ FC Gandzasar Kapan
no website

④ FC Kilikia
no website

⑤ **FC Mika**
fcmika.am   EUROPA LEAGUE

⑥ **FC Pyunik** © *
fcpyunik.am   CHAMPIONS LEAGUE

⑦ **FC Shirak**
fcshirak.8m.net

⑧ **Ulisses FC**
no website   EUROPA LEAGUE

PROMOTED CLUB

⑨ **FC Impuls**
no website

AUSTRIA

FEDERATION   HOME INTERNATIONAL KIT   AWAY INTERNATIONAL KIT

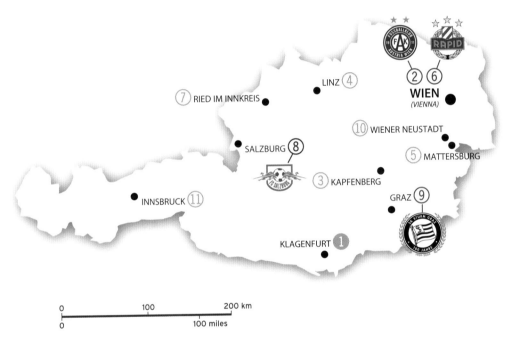

LINZ ④

⑦ RIED IM INNKREIS ●

② ⑥
WIEN
(VIENNA) ●

⑩ WIENER NEUSTADT

SALZBURG ⑧

⑤ MATTERSBURG

③ KAPFENBERG

INNSBRUCK ⑪

GRAZ ⑨

KLAGENFURT ①

0   100   200 km

0   100 miles

TOP DIVISION CLUBS

① **SK Austria Kärnten**
sk-austriakaernten.at

② **FK Austria Wien**
fk-austria.at

③ **Kapfenberger SV**
ksv-fussball.at

④ **LASK Linz**
lask.at

⑤ **SV Mattersburg**
svm.at

⑥ **SK Rapid Wien**
skrapid.at

⑦ **SV Ried**
svried.at

⑧ **FC Salzburg** ©
redbulls.com

⑨ **SK Sturm Graz** *
sksturm.at

⑩ **SC Wiener Neustadt**
fcmagna.at

PROMOTED CLUB

⑪ **FC Wacker Innsbruck**
fc-wacker-innsbruck.at

AZERBAIJAN

AFFA
FEDERATION

HOME INTERNATIONAL KIT

AWAY INTERNATIONAL KIT

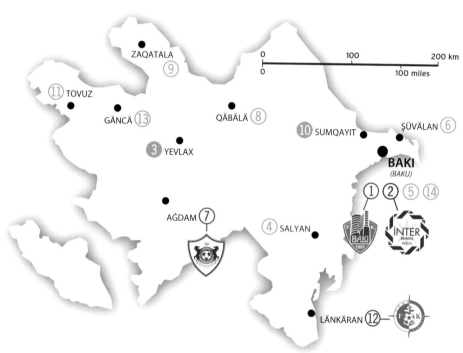

TOP DIVISION CLUBS

① **Bakı FK** *
bakifc.com
EUROPA LEAGUE

② **İnter Bakı PİK** ©
inter.az
CHAMPIONS LEAGUE

③ Karvan İK
karvan.az

④ **Muğan Salyan FK**
no website

⑤ **Neftçi PFK**
neftci.az

⑥ **Olimpik-Şüvälan PFK**
no website

⑦ **Qarabağ FK**
qarabagh.com
EUROPA LEAGUE

⑧ **Qäbälä PFK**
gabalafc.az

⑨ **Simurq PFK**
simurqpfk.com

⑩ Standard FK
standard-fc.az

⑪ **Turan PFK**
no website

⑫ **Xäzär Länkäran FK**
lankaranfc.com
EUROPA LEAGUE

PROMOTED CLUBS

⑬ **Gäncä PFK**
no website

⑭ **MOİK Bakı PFK**
no website

NB Olimpik-Şüvälan PFK changed name to AZAL PFK for 2010/11 season.

BELARUS

FEDERATION   HOME INTERNATIONAL KIT   AWAY INTERNATIONAL KIT

| 0 | 100 | 200 km |
| 0 | 100 miles | |

⑧ NOVOPOLOTSK

VITEBSK ⑭

SMORGON ⑫

BORISOV ①

MOGILEV ④

MINSK ● ZHODINO ⑬

③ ⑦ ⑩

GRODNO ⑨

⑮ BOBRUISK

SOLIGORSK ⑪

BREST ②

⑤ GOMEL

⑥ MIKASHEVICHI

TOP DIVISION CLUBS

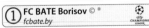

① **FC BATE Borisov** © *
fcbate.by

② **FC Dinamo Brest**
dynamo.brest.by

③ **FC Dinamo Minsk**
dinamo-minsk.com

④ **FC Dnepr Mogilev**
no website

⑤ **FC Gomel**
fcgomel.by

⑥ **FC Granit Mikashevichi**
no website

⑦ **FC Minsk**
no website

⑧ **FC Naftan Novopolotsk**
fcnaftan.com

⑨ **FC Neman Grodno**
fcneman.com

⑩ **FC Partizan Minsk**
mtz-ripo.by

⑪ **FC Shakhtyor Soligorsk**
fcshakhter.by

⑫ **FC Smorgon**
no website

⑬ **FC Torpedo Zhodino**
tarpeda.zhodzina.info

⑭ **FC Vitebsk**
fc.vitebsk.by

PROMOTED CLUB

⑮ **FC Belshina Bobruisk**
no website

NB FC MTZ-RIPO Minsk changed name to FC Partizan Minsk for 2010 season.

FEDERATION

HOME INTERNATIONAL KIT

AWAY INTERNATIONAL KIT

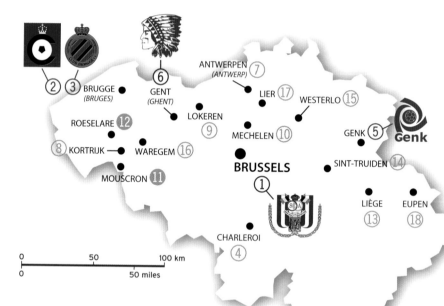

ANTWERPEN (7)
(ANTWERP)

LIER (17) WESTERLO (15)

BRUGGE (2)(3)
(BRUGES)

GENT (6)
(GHENT)

LOKEREN
(9)

MECHELEN (10)

GENK (5)
Genk

ROESELARE (12)

SINT-TRUIDEN (14)

KORTRIJK (8) WAREGEM (16)

BRUSSELS

MOUSCRON (11)

(1)

LIÈGE
(13)

EUPEN
(18)

CHARLEROI
(4)

0   50   100 km

0   50 miles

TOP DIVISION CLUBS

(1) **RSC Anderlecht ©**
rsca.be — CHAMPIONS LEAGUE

(2) **Cercle Brugge KSV**
cerclebrugge.be — EUROPA LEAGUE

(3) **Club Brugge KV**
clubbrugge.be — EUROPA LEAGUE

(4) **R. Charleroi SC**
sporting-charleroi.be

(5) **KRC Genk**
krcgenk.be — EUROPA LEAGUE

(6) **KAA Gent** *
kaagent.be — CHAMPIONS LEAGUE

(7) **KFC Germinal Beerschot Antwerpen**
germinal-beerschot.be

(8) **KV Kortrijk**
kvk.be

(9) **KSC Lokeren OV**
sporting.be

(10) **KV Mechelen**
kvmechelen.be

(11) **R. Excelsior Mouscron**
excelsior.be

(12) **KSV Roeselare**
ksvroeselare.be

(13) **R. Standard de Liège**
standardliege.be

(14) **K. Sint-Truidense VV**
stvv.com

(15) **KVC Westerlo**
kvcwesterlo.be

(16) **SV Zulte Waregem**
svzw.be

PROMOTED CLUBS

(17) **K. Lierse SK**
lierse.com

(18) **K. AS Eupen**
as-eupen.be

BOSNIA-HERZEGOVINA

FEDERATION

HOME INTERNATIONAL KIT

AWAY INTERNATIONAL KIT

TOP DIVISION CLUBS

① **FK Borac Banja Luka** *
borac-sport.com   EUROPA LEAGUE

② **NK Čelik**
nkcelik.ba

③ **FK Laktaši**
no website

④ **FK Leotar**
no website

⑤ **FK Modriča**
fkmodricamaxima.com

⑥ **FK Olimpik Sarajevo**
olimpik.ba

⑦ **FK Rudar Prijedor**
no website

⑧ **FK Sarajevo**
fcsarajevo.ba

⑨ **NK Široki Brijeg**
nk-sirokibrijeg.com   EUROPA LEAGUE

⑩ **FK Slavija Sarajevo**
fkslavija.com

⑪ **FK Sloboda Tuzla**
no website

⑫ **NK Travnik**
nktravnik.ba

⑬ **FK Velež**
fkvelez.ba

⑭ **FK Željezničar** ©
fkzeljeznicar.ba   CHAMPIONS LEAGUE

⑮ **HŠK Zrinjski**
hskzrinjski.ba   EUROPA LEAGUE

⑯ **NK Zvijezda**
zvijezda.info

PROMOTED CLUBS

⑰ **FK Budućnost Banovići**
buducnost.net

⑱ **FK Drina Zvornik**
no website

FEDERATION

HOME INTERNATIONAL KIT

AWAY INTERNATIONAL KIT

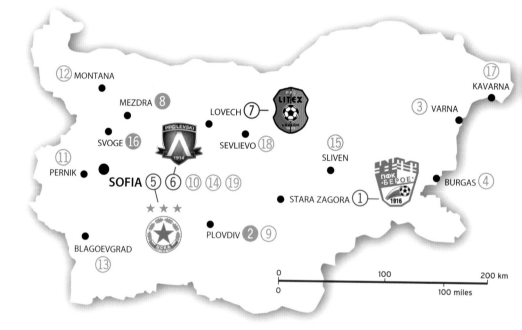

TOP DIVISION CLUBS

(1) **PFC Beroe Stara Zagora** *
    beroe.eu — EUROPA LEAGUE

(2) PFC Botev Plovdiv
    pfcbotev1912.com

(3) PFC Cherno More Varna
    chernomorepfc.bg

(4) PSFC Chernomorets Burgas
    chernomoretz-bs.com

(5) **PFC CSKA Sofia**
    cska.bg — EUROPA LEAGUE

(6) **PFC Levski Sofia**
    levski.bg — EUROPA LEAGUE

(7) **PFC Litex Lovech** ©
    pfclitex.com — CHAMPIONS LEAGUE

(8) PFC Lokomotiv Mezdra
    lokomotivmezdra.host22.com

(9) PFC Lokomotiv Plovdiv 1936
    lokomotivpd.com

(10) **PFC Lokomotiv Sofia**
    lokomotivsofia.bg

(11) **PFC Minyor Pernik**
    minyor-pk.com

(12) **PFC Montana**
    no website

(13) **PFC Pirin Blagoevgrad**
    pirinfc.com

(14) **PFC Slavia Sofia**
    pfcslavia.com

(15) OFC Sliven 2000
    sliven-fc.com

(16) PFC Sportist Svoge
    sportist-svoge.com

PROMOTED CLUBS

(17) PFC Kaliakra Kavarna
    fckaliakra.com

(18) PFC Vidima-Rakovski Sevlievo
    vidimarakovski.bg

(19) **PFC Akademik Sofia**
    akademik-sofia.com

FEDERATION

HOME INTERNATIONAL KIT

AWAY INTERNATIONAL KIT

⑭ VARAŽDIN ● ČAKOVEC ⑨

KOPRIVNICA ⑬

⑤ ZAPREŠIĆ

ZAGREB

⑪ RIJEKA

KARLOVAC

② ③ ⑧ ⑯ ⑱ ⑩ OSIJEK

⑦

VINKOVCI ①

PULA
⑥

ZADAR ⑮

0 ————————— 100 ————————— 200 km
0 ————————————— 100 miles

⑫
ŠIBENIK

SPLIT ④ ⑰

TOP DIVISION CLUBS

FEDERATION

HOME INTERNATIONAL KIT

AWAY INTERNATIONAL KIT

TOP DIVISION CLUBS

① **AEL Limassol FC**
aelfc.com

② **AEP Paphos FC**
pafosfc.com

③ **Anorthosis Famagusta FC**
anorthosisfc.com
EUROPA LEAGUE

④ **APEP Kyperounda FC**
apepfc.com

⑤ **APOEL FC**
apoelfc.com.cy
EUROPA LEAGUE

⑥ **Apollon Limassol FC** *
apollon.com.cy
EUROPA LEAGUE

⑦ **APOP/Kinyras Peyias FC** *
apopkinyrasfc.com

⑧ **Aris Limassol FC**
no website

⑨ **Doxa Katokopia FC**
doxakatokopiasfc.com

⑩ **Enosis Neon Paralimni FC**
no website

⑪ **Ermis Aradippou FC**
ermisaradippoufc.com

⑫ **Ethnikos Achnas FC**
achnafc.com

⑬ **Nea Salamis FC**
neasalamis.com.cy

⑭ **AC Omonia** ©
omonoia.com.cy
CHAMPIONS LEAGUE

PROMOTED CLUBS

⑮ **Alki Larnaca FC**
no website

⑯ **AEK Larnaca FC**
aek.com.cy

⑰ **Olympiakos Nicosia FC**
olympiakos.com.cy

FEDERATION

HOME INTERNATIONAL KIT

AWAY INTERNATIONAL KIT

TOP DIVISION CLUBS

(1) **FC Baník Ostrava**
fcb.cz

(2) **Bohemians 1905**
fc-bohemians.cz

(3) **FC Bohemians Praha**
bohemiansfc.cz

(4) **1. FC Brno**
1fcbrno.cz

(5) **SK Dynamo České Budějovice**
dynamocb.cz

(6) **FK Jablonec**
fkjablonec.cz

(7) **SK Kladno**
skkladno.cz

(8) **FK Mladá Boleslav**
fkmb.cz

(9) **1. FK Příbram**
fkpribram.cz

(10) **SK Sigma Olomouc**
sigmafotbal.cz

(11) **SK Slavia Praha**
slavia.cz

(12) **1. FC Slovácko**
fcslovacko.cz

(13) **FC Slovan Liberec**
fcslovanliberec.cz

(14) **AC Sparta Praha** ©
sparta.cz

(15) **FK Teplice**
fkteplice.cz

(16) **FC Viktoria Plzeň** *
fcviktoria.cz

PROMOTED CLUBS

(17) **FC Hradec Králové**
fchk.cz

(18) **FK Ústí nad Labem**
fkusti.cz

NB 1. FC Brno changed name to FC Zbrojovka Brno for 2010/11 season.

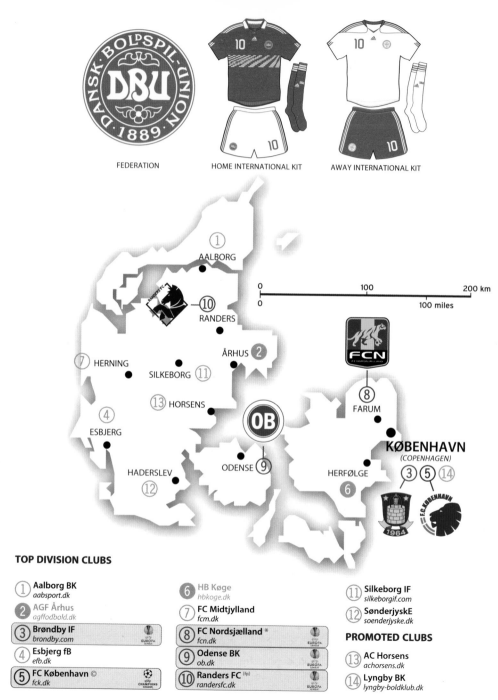

FEDERATION   HOME INTERNATIONAL KIT   AWAY INTERNATIONAL KIT

AALBORG

RANDERS

ÅRHUS

HERNING   SILKEBORG   HORSENS

ESBJERG

HADERSLEV   ODENSE   HERFØLGE

FARUM

KØBENHAVN
(COPENHAGEN)

TOP DIVISION CLUBS

1 **Aalborg BK**
aabsport.dk

2 AGF Århus
agffodbold.dk

3 **Brøndby IF**
brondby.com EUROPA LEAGUE

4 **Esbjerg fB**
efb.dk

5 **FC København** ©
fck.dk CHAMPIONS LEAGUE

6 HB Køge
hbkoge.dk

7 **FC Midtjylland**
fcm.dk

8 **FC Nordsjælland** *
fcn.dk EUROPA LEAGUE

9 **Odense BK**
ob.dk EUROPA LEAGUE

10 Randers FC [fp]
randersfc.dk EUROPA LEAGUE

11 **Silkeborg IF**
silkeborgif.com

12 **SønderjyskE**
soenderjyske.dk

PROMOTED CLUBS

13 **AC Horsens**
achorsens.dk

14 **Lyngby BK**
lyngby-boldklub.dk

ENGLAND

FEDERATION

HOME INTERNATIONAL KIT

AWAY INTERNATIONAL KIT

TOP DIVISION CLUBS

1. **Arsenal FC**
   arsenal.com
2. **Aston Villa FC**
   avfc.co.uk
3. **Birmingham City FC**
   bcfc.com
4. **Blackburn Rovers FC**
   rovers.co.uk
5. **Bolton Wanderers FC**
   bwfc.co.uk
6. **Burnley FC**
   burnleyfootballclub.com
7. **Chelsea FC** © *
   chelseafc.com
8. **Everton FC**
   evertonfc.com
9. **Fulham FC**
   fulhamfc.com
10. **Hull City AFC**
    hullcityafc.net
11. **Liverpool FC**
    liverpoolfc.tv
12. **Manchester City FC**
    mcfc.co.uk
13. **Manchester United FC**
    manutd.com
14. **Portsmouth FC**
    portsmouthfc.co.uk
15. **Stoke City FC**
    stokecityfc.com
16. **Sunderland AFC**
    safc.com
17. **Tottenham Hotspur FC**
    tottenhamhotspur.com
18. **West Ham United FC**
    whufc.com
19. **Wigan Athletic FC**
    wiganlatics.co.uk
20. **Wolverhampton Wanderers FC**
    wolves.co.uk

PROMOTED CLUBS

21. **Newcastle United FC**
    nufc.co.uk
22. **West Bromwich Albion FC**
    wba.co.uk
23. **Blackpool FC**
    blackpoolfc.co.uk

NEWCASTLE 21

16 SUNDERLAND

4 BLACKBURN

BURNLEY 6

BLACKPOOL 23

BOLTON 5

KINGSTON UPON HULL 10

LIVERPOOL

MANCHESTER 12 13

8 11 WIGAN

19

STOKE-ON-TRENT 15

WOLVERHAMPTON 20

WEST BROMWICH 22

BIRMINGHAM

2 3

1 7 9 17 18

LONDON

14 PORTSMOUTH

| 0 | 100 | 200 km |
| 0 | | 100 miles |

FEDERATION

HOME INTERNATIONAL KIT

AWAY INTERNATIONAL KIT

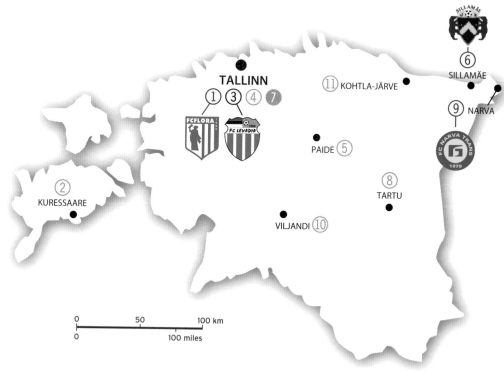

TALLINN

① ③ ④ ⑦

FC FLORA FC LEVADIA

⑪ KOHTLA-JÄRVE

SILLAMÄE

⑥ SILLAMÄE

⑨ NARVA

FC NARVA TRANS 1979

② KURESSAARE

PAIDE ⑤

⑧ TARTU

VILJANDI ⑩

0   50   100 km
0   100 miles

TOP DIVISION CLUBS

① **FC Flora Tallinn**
 fcflora.ee

② **FC Kuressaare**
 fckuressaare.ee

③ **FC Levadia Tallinn** © *
 fclevadia.ee

④ **JK Nõmme Kalju**
 jkkalju.ee

⑤ **Paide Linnameeskond**
 no website

⑥ **JK Sillamäe Kalev**
 fcsillamae.ee

⑦ **JK Tallinna Kalev**
 jkkalev.ee

⑧ **JK Tammeka Tartu**
 jktammeka.ee

⑨ **JK Trans Narva**
 fctrans.ee

⑩ **JK Tulevik Viljandi**
 jktulevik.ee

PROMOTED CLUB

⑪ **FC Lootus Kohtla-Järve**
 fclootus.ee

FAROE ISLANDS

FEDERATION

HOME INTERNATIONAL KIT

AWAY INTERNATIONAL KIT

④ EIDI

⑥ FUGLAFJØRDUR

KLAKSVÍK ⑦

⑩ GØTA

RUNAVÍK ⑧

⑨ SANDAVÁGUR

TOFTIR ③

TÓRSHAVN

② ⑤

ARGÍR ①

⑫ SANDUR

0   20   40 km

0   20 miles

⑪ VÁGUR

TOP DIVISION CLUBS

① **AB Argír**
   ab.fo

② **B36 Tórshavn**
   fcb36.org

③ **B68 Toftir**
   b68.fo

④ **EB/Streymur**
   eb-streymur.fo   EUROPA LEAGUE

⑤ **HB Tórshavn** ©
   hb.fo   CHAMPIONS LEAGUE

⑥ **ÍF Fuglafjørdur**
   if.fo

⑦ KÍ Klaksvík
   ki.fo

⑧ **NSÍ Runavík**
   nsi.fo   EUROPA LEAGUE

⑨ 07 Vestur
   07vestur.fo

⑩ **Víkingur** *
   vikingur.fo   EUROPA LEAGUE

PROMOTED CLUBS

⑪ **VB/Sumba Vágur**
   fcsuduroy.com

⑫ **B71 Sandoy**
   b71-sandoy.com

NB VB/Sumba Vagur changed name to FC Suduroy for 2010 season.

FEDERATION

HOME INTERNATIONAL KIT

AWAY INTERNATIONAL KIT

TOP DIVISION CLUBS

1. **Haka Valkeakoski**
   fchaka.fi
2. **HJK Helsinki ©**
   hjk.fi
3. **FC Honka Espoo**
   fchonka.fi
4. **FC Inter Turku** *
   fcinter.com
5. **FF Jaro**
   ffjaro.fi
6. **JJK Jyväskylä**
   fcjjk.com
7. **KuPS Kuopio**
   kups.fi
8. **FC Lahti**
   fclahti.fi
9. **IFK Mariehamn**
   ifkmariehamn.com
10. **Myllykosken Pallo-47** [lp]
    mypa.fi
11. RoPS Rovaniemi
    rops.fi
12. **Tampere United**
    tampereunited.com
13. **TPS Turku**
    tps.fi
14. **VPS Vaasa**
    vepsu.fi

PROMOTED CLUB

15. **AC Oulu**
    acoulu.fi

FRANCE

FEDERATION

HOME INTERNATIONAL KIT

AWAY INTERNATIONAL KIT

TOP DIVISION CLUBS

1. **AJ Auxerre**
   aja.fr
2. **FC Girondins de Bordeaux**
   girondins.com
3. **US Boulogne CO**
   usbco.asso.fr
4. **Grenoble Foot 38**
   gf38.fr
5. **Le Mans UC 72**
   muc72.fr
6. **RC Lens**
   rclens.fr
7. **LOSC Lille Métropole**
   losc.fr
8. **FC Lorient**
   fclweb.fr
9. **Olympique Lyonnais**
   olweb.fr
10. **Olympique de Marseille ©**
    om.net
11. **AS Monaco FC**
    asm-fc.com
12. **Montpellier Hérault SC**
    mhscfoot.com
13. **AS Nancy-Lorraine**
    asnl.net
14. **OGC Nice**
    ogcnice.com
15. **Paris Saint-Germain FC** *
    psg.fr
16. **Stade Rennais FC**
    staderennais.com
17. **AS Saint-Étienne**
    asse.fr
18. **FC Sochaux-Montbéliard**
    fcsochaux.fr
19. **Toulouse FC**
    tfc.info
20. **Valenciennes FC**
    va-fc.com

PROMOTED CLUBS

21. **SM Caen**
    smcaen.fr
22. **Stade Brestois 29**
    stade-brestois.com
23. **AC Arles-Avignon**
    acarlesavignon.fr

FEDERATION

HOME INTERNATIONAL KIT

AWAY INTERNATIONAL KIT

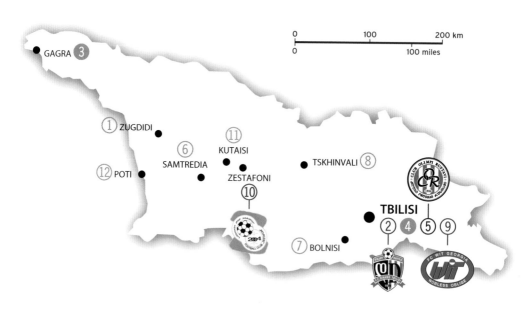

TOP DIVISION CLUBS

① **FC Baia Zugdidi**
no website

② **FC Dinamo Tbilisi** *
fcdinamo.ge

③ **FC Gagra**
fcgagra.ge

④ **FC Lokomotivi Tbilisi**
fcloco.ge

⑤ **FC Olimpi Rustavi** ©
no website

⑥ **FC Samtredia**
no website

⑦ **FC Sioni Bolnisi**
fcsioni.com

⑧ **FC Spartaki Tskhinvali**
no website

⑨ **FC WIT Georgia**
witgeorgia.ge

⑩ **FC Zestafoni**
fczestafoni.ge

PROMOTED CLUBS

⑪ **FC Torpedo-2008 Kutaisi**
no website

⑫ **FC Kolkheti-1913 Poti**
no website

GERMANY

FEDERATION

HOME INTERNATIONAL KIT

AWAY INTERNATIONAL KIT

TOP DIVISION CLUBS

① **Bayer 04 Leverkusen**
bayer04.de

② **FC Bayern München** © *
fcbayern.de

③ VfL Bochum 1848
vfl-bochum.de

④ **BV Borussia Dortmund**
bvb.de

⑤ **VfL Borussia Mönchengladbach**
borussia.de

⑥ **Eintracht Frankfurt**
eintracht.de

⑦ **SC Freiburg**
scfreiburg.com

⑧ **Hamburger SV**
hsv.de

⑨ **Hannover 96**
hannover96.de

⑩ Hertha BSC Berlin
herthabsc.de

⑪ **TSG 1899 Hoffenheim**
tsg-hoffenheim.de

⑫ **1. FC Köln**
fc-koeln.de

⑬ **1. FSV Mainz 05**
mainz05.de

⑭ **1. FC Nürnberg**
fcn.de

⑮ **FC Schalke 04**
schalke04.de

⑯ **VfB Stuttgart**
vfb.de

⑰ **Werder Bremen**
werder.de

⑱ **VfL Wolfsburg**
vfl-wolfsburg.de

PROMOTED CLUBS

⑲ **1. FC Kaiserslautern**
fck.de

⑳ **FC St Pauli**
fcstpauli.com

HAMBURG ⑧⑳

⑰ BREMEN

HANNOVER (HANOVER) ⑨

WOLFSBURG ⑱

⑮ GELSENKIRCHEN

DORTMUND ④

BOCHUM ③

BERLIN ⑩

⑤ MÖNCHENGLADBACH

① LEVERKUSEN

KÖLN (COLOGNE) ⑫

⑬ MAINZ   FRANKFURT ⑥

⑪ SINSHEIM-HOFFENHEIM

KAISERSLAUTERN

NÜRNBERG (NUREMBERG)

⑲   ⑭

STUTTGART

⑯

FREIBURG

⑦

MÜNCHEN (MUNICH)

②

0   100   200 km

0   100 miles

FEDERATION

HOME INTERNATIONAL KIT

AWAY INTERNATIONAL KIT

TOP DIVISION CLUBS

① **AEK Athens FC**
aekfc.gr

② **Aris Thessaloniki FC**
arisfc.gr

③ **Asteras Tripolis FC**
asterastripolis.gr

④ **Atromitos FC**
atromitosfc.gr

⑤ **Ergotelis FC**
ergotelis.gr

⑥ **PAS Giannina FC**
pasgiannina.gr

⑦ **Iraklis FC**
iraklis-fc.gr

⑧ **FC Kavala**
aokavalas.gr

⑨ **Larissa FC**
ael1964.gr

⑩ **Levadiakos FC**
levadiakos.gr

⑪ **Olympiacos FC**
olympiacos.org

⑫ **Panathinaikos FC** © *
pao.gr

⑬ **Panionios GSS**
pgss.gr

⑭ **Panthrakikos FC**
panthrakikos.com

⑮ **PAOK FC**
paokfc.gr

⑯ **Xanthi FC**
skodaxanthifc.gr

PROMOTED CLUBS

⑰ **Olympiacos Volou FC**
no website

⑱ **Kerkyra FC**
aokerkyra.com

⑲ **Panserraikos FC**
panserraikos.eu

HUNGARY

FEDERATION

HOME INTERNATIONAL KIT

AWAY INTERNATIONAL KIT

TOP DIVISION CLUBS

1. **Budapest Honvéd FC**
   honvedfc.hu
2. **Debreceni VSC** © *
   dvsc.hu
3. **Diósgyőri VTK**
   dvtk.eu
4. **Ferencvárosi TC**
   ftc.hu
5. **Győri ETO FC**
   eto.hu
6. **Kaposvári Rákóczi FC**
   rakoczifc.hu
7. **Kecskeméti TE**
   kecskemetite.hu
8. **Lombard-Pápa FC**
   no website
9. **MTK Budapest**
   mtkhungaria.hu
10. **Nyíregyháza Spartacus FC**
    szpari.hu
11. **Paksi SE**
    paksise.hu
12. **Szombathelyi Haladás**
    haladas.hu
13. **Újpest FC**
    ujpestfc.hu
14. **Vasas SC**
    vasasbp.hu
15. **Videoton FC**
    vidi.hu
16. **Zalaegerszegi TE**
    ztefc.hu

PROMOTED CLUBS

17. **Szolnoki MÁV FC**
    szolnokimavfc.hu
18. **BFC Siófok**
    bfc-siofok.hu

ICELAND

FEDERATION

HOME INTERNATIONAL KIT

AWAY INTERNATIONAL KIT

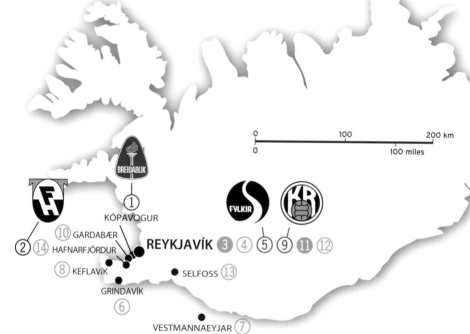

TOP DIVISION CLUBS

(1) **Breidablik** *
breidablik.is — EUROPA LEAGUE

(2) **FH Hafnarfjördur** ©
fh.is — CHAMPIONS LEAGUE

(3) Fjölnir
fjolnir.is

(4) **Fram Reykjavík**
fram.is

(5) **Fylkir**
fylkir.com — EUROPA LEAGUE

(6) **Grindavík**
umfg.is

(7) **ÍBV Vestmannaeyjar**
ibv.is

(8) **Keflavík**
keflavik.is

(9) **KR Reykjavík**
kr.is — EUROPA LEAGUE

(10) **Stjarnan**
stjarnan.is

(11) Thróttur Reykjavík
trottur.is

(12) **Valur Reykjavík**
valur.is

PROMOTED CLUBS

(13) **Selfoss**
no website

(14) **Haukur**
no website

ISRAEL

FEDERATION

HOME INTERNATIONAL KIT

AWAY INTERNATIONAL KIT

KIRYAT SHMONA

AKKO

HAIFA

SAKHNIN

NAZARETH

NETANYA

RAMAT-GAN

RA'ANANA

TEL-AVIV

PETACH-TIKVA

ASHDOD

JERUSALEM

ASHKELON

BEER SHEVA

0   50   100 km

0   50 miles

TOP DIVISION CLUBS

1 **FC Ashdod**
   fcashdod.com

2 **Beitar Jerusalem FC**
   bjerusalem.co.il

3 **Bnei Sakhnin FC**
   abna-sakhnin.com

4 **Bnei Yehuda Tel-Aviv FC**
   fc-bnei-yehuda.co.il

5 **Hapoel Akko FC**
   planetnana.co.il/hapoel_akko

6 **Hapoel Beer Sheva FC**
   no website

7 **Hapoel Haifa FC**
   hhaifa.com

8 **Hapoel Petach-Tikva FC**
   no website

9 **Hapoel Ra'anana FC**
   hapoel-raananafc.ios.st

10 **Hapoel Ramat-Gan FC**
   hapoelrg-fc.co.il

11 **Hapoel Tel-Aviv FC** © *
   hapoelta-fc.co.il

12 **Maccabi Ahi Nazareth FC**
   ahinaza.ios.st

13 **Maccabi Haifa FC**
   maccabi-haifafc.walla.co.il

14 **Maccabi Netanya FC**
   fcmn.co.il

15 **Maccabi Petach-Tikva FC**
   mpt-mib.com

16 **Maccabi Tel-Aviv FC**
   maccabi-tlv.co.il

PROMOTED CLUBS

17 **Hapoel Kiryat Shmona FC**
   no website

18 **Hapoel Ashkelon FC**
   no website

ITALY

FEDERATION

HOME INTERNATIONAL KIT

AWAY INTERNATIONAL KIT

TOP DIVISION CLUBS

1. **Atalanta BC**
   atalanta.it
2. **AS Bari**
   asbari.it
3. **Bologna FC**
   bolognafc.it
4. **Cagliari Calcio**
   cagliaricalcio.it
5. **Calcio Catania**
   calciocatania.it
6. **AC Chievo Verona**
   chievoverona.it
7. **ACF Fiorentina**
   acffiorentina.it
8. **Genoa CFC**
   genoacfc.it
9. **FC Internazionale Milano** © * CHAMPIONS LEAGUE
   inter.it
10. **Juventus** EUROPA LEAGUE
    juventus.com
11. **S.S. Lazio**
    sslazio.it
12. **AS Livorno Calcio**
    livornocalcio.it
13. **AC Milan** CHAMPIONS LEAGUE
    acmilan.com
14. **SSC Napoli** EUROPA LEAGUE
    sscnapoli.it
15. **US Città di Palermo** EUROPA LEAGUE
    ilpalermocalcio.it
16. **Parma FC**
    fcparma.it
17. **AS Roma** CHAMPIONS LEAGUE
    asroma.it
18. **UC Sampdoria** CHAMPIONS LEAGUE
    sampdoria.it
19. **AC Siena**
    acsiena.it
20. **Udinese Calcio**
    udinese.it

PROMOTED CLUBS

21. **US Lecce**
    uslecce.it
22. **AC Cesena**
    cesenacalcio.it
23. **Brescia Calcio**
    bresciaonline.it

TORINO (TURIN) ⑩
MILANO (MILAN) ⑨ ⑬
BERGAMO ①
UDINE ⑳
VERONA ⑥
㉓ BRESCIA
PARMA ⑯
BOLOGNA ③
GENOVA (GENOA)
⑧ ⑱
CESENA ㉒
FIRENZE (FLORENCE) ⑦
LIVORNO
⑫
SIENA ⑲
ROMA (ROME)
⑪ ⑰
NAPOLI (NAPLES) ⑭
BARI ②
LECCE ㉑
CAGLIARI ④
PALERMO ⑮
CATANIA ⑤

0   200   400 km
0   200 miles

KAZAKHSTAN

FEDERATION

HOME INTERNATIONAL KIT

AWAY INTERNATIONAL KIT

URALSK (16)

PETROPAVLOVSK (6)

KOSTANAY
(12)

KOKSHETAU (8)

ATYRAU (2)

AKTOBE
(1)

PAVLODAR (3)

(7) ASTANA

(5) SATPAEV

KARAGANDY (10)

OSKEMEN
(13)

(4)

KYZYLORDA

(14) TALDYKORGAN

ALMATY (15)

TARAZ (11)

(9) SHYMKENT

| 0 | 500 | 1000 km |
| 0 | 500 miles | |

TOP DIVISION CLUBS

(1) **FC Aktobe** ©
fcaktobe.kz

(2) **FC Atyrau** *
fcatyrau.kz

(3) **FC Irtysh Pavlodar**
irtysch.ucoz.ru

(4) FC Kaisar Kyzylorda
fc-kaysar.kz

(5) FC Kazakhmys
fc-kazakhmys.kz

(6) FC Kyzylzhar Petropavlovsk
no website

(7) **FC Lokomotiv Astana**
fc-lokomotiv.kz

(8) **FC Okzhetpes Kokshetau**
okzhetpes.kz

(9) FC Ordabasy Shymkent
fcordabasy.kz

(10) **FC Shakhter Karagandy**
shahter.kz

(11) **FC Taraz**
no website

(12) **FC Tobol Kostanay**
fctobol.kostanay.net

(13) FC Vostok
no website

(14) FC Zhetysu Taldykorgan
fc-zhetisu.kz

NB FC Vostok withdrew from 2010 Superleague.

PROMOTED CLUBS

(15) **FC Kairat Almaty**
fckairat.kz

(16) **FC Akzhaiyk Uralsk**
akzhaik.info

 **LATVIA**

FEDERATION

HOME INTERNATIONAL KIT

AWAY INTERNATIONAL KIT

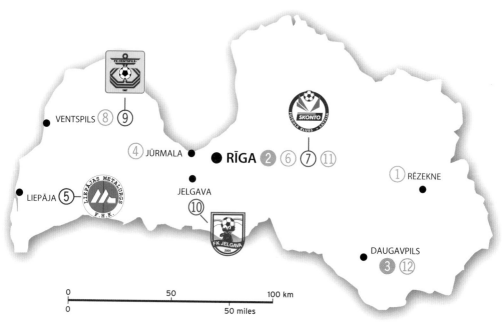

TOP DIVISION CLUBS

① **SK Blāzma Rēzekne**
no website

② **FK Daugava Rīga**
daugava90.lv

③ **FC Dinaburg**
dinaburg.com

④ **FK Jūrmala**
fcjurmala.lv

⑤ **SK Liepājas Metalurgs** ©
sport.metalurgs.lv

⑥ **Olimps/RFS**
no website

⑦ **Skonto FC**
skontofc.lv

⑧ **FK Tranzīts**
no website

⑨ **FK Ventspils**
fkventspils.lv

PROMOTED CLUBS

⑩ **FK Jelgava** *
daugava90.lv

⑪ **FK Jaunība Rīga**
no website

⑫ **FC Daugava Daugavpils**
fcdaugava.lv

LIECHTENSTEIN

FEDERATION

HOME INTERNATIONAL KIT

AWAY INTERNATIONAL KIT

1. **FC Balzers**
   fcbalzers.li
2. **USV Eschen/Mauren**
   usv.li
3. **FC Ruggell**
   fcruggell.li
4. **FC Schaan**
   fcschaan.li
5. **FC Triesen**
   fctriesen.li
6. **FC Triesenberg**
   fctriesenberg.li
7. **FC Vaduz** *
   fcvaduz.li

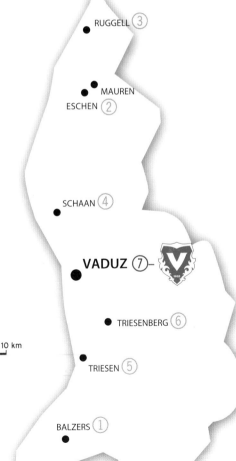

RUGGELL ③

MAUREN
ESCHEN ②

SCHAAN ④

VADUZ ⑦

TRIESENBERG ⑥

TRIESEN ⑤

BALZERS ①

0   5   10 km
0   5 miles

LITHUANIA

FEDERATION

HOME INTERNATIONAL KIT

AWAY INTERNATIONAL KIT

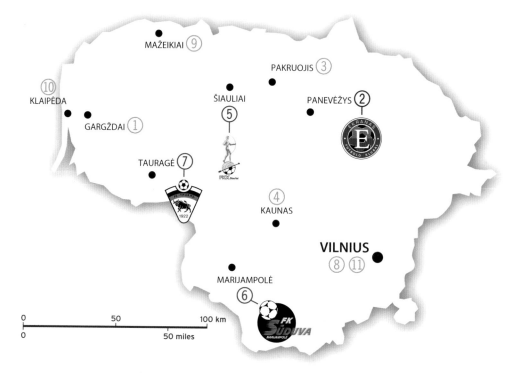

MAŽEIKIAI ⑨

PAKRUOJIS ③

KLAIPĖDA ⑩

ŠIAULIAI ⑤

PANEVĖŽYS ②

GARGŽDAI ①

TAURAGĖ ⑦

KAUNAS ④

VILNIUS ⑧ ⑪

MARIJAMPOLĖ ⑥

0 ——— 50 ——— 100 km
0 ——— 50 miles

TOP DIVISION CLUBS

① **FK Banga**
atlantas.lt

② **FK Ekranas** © *
fkekranas.lt

③ **FK Kruoja**
kruoja.lt

④ **FK LKKA ir Teledema Kaunas**
lkka.teledema.lt

⑤ **FC Šiauliai**
fcsiauliai.lt

⑥ **FK Sūduva**
fksuduva.lt

⑦ **FK Tauras**
fktauras.lt

⑧ **FK Vėtra**
fkvetra.lt

PROMOTED CLUBS

⑨ **FK Mažeikiai**
no website

⑩ **FK Klaipėda**
no website

⑪ **VMFD Žalgiris**
zalgiris-vilnius.lt

FEDERATION   HOME INTERNATIONAL KIT   AWAY INTERNATIONAL KIT

TOP DIVISION CLUBS

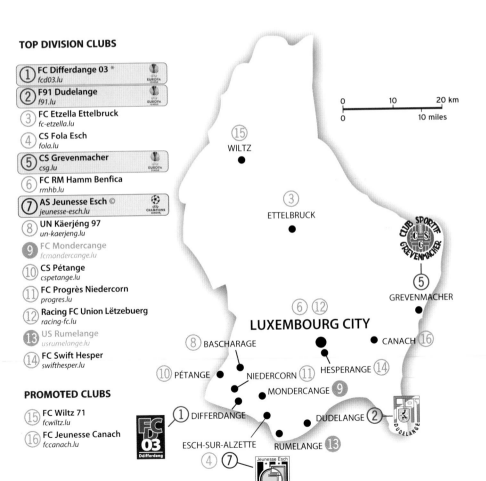

(1) **FC Differdange 03** *
fcd03.lu — EUROPA LEAGUE

(2) **F91 Dudelange**
f91.lu — EUROPA LEAGUE

(3) **FC Etzella Ettelbruck**
fc-etzella.lu

(4) **CS Fola Esch**
fola.lu

(5) **CS Grevenmacher**
csg.lu — EUROPA LEAGUE

(6) **FC RM Hamm Benfica**
rmhb.lu

(7) **AS Jeunesse Esch** ©
jeunesse-esch.lu — CHAMPIONS LEAGUE

(8) **UN Käerjéng 97**
un-kaerjeng.lu

(9) **FC Mondercange**
fcmondercange.lu

(10) **CS Pétange**
cspetange.lu

(11) **FC Progrès Niedercorn**
progres.lu

(12) **Racing FC Union Lëtzebuerg**
racing-fc.lu

(13) **US Rumelange**
usrumelange.lu

(14) **FC Swift Hesper**
swifthesper.lu

PROMOTED CLUBS

(15) **FC Wiltz 71**
fcwiltz.lu

(16) **FC Jeunesse Canach**
fccanach.lu

(15) WILTZ

(3) ETTELBRUCK

(6) (12) **LUXEMBOURG CITY**

(5) GREVENMACHER

(8) BASCHARAGE

CANACH (16)

(10) PÉTANGE   NIEDERCORN (11)   HESPERANGE (14)

MONDERCANGE (9)

(1) DIFFERDANGE   DUDELANGE (2)

ESCH-SUR-ALZETTE   RUMELANGE (13)

(4) (7)

FEDERATION   HOME INTERNATIONAL KIT   AWAY INTERNATIONAL KIT

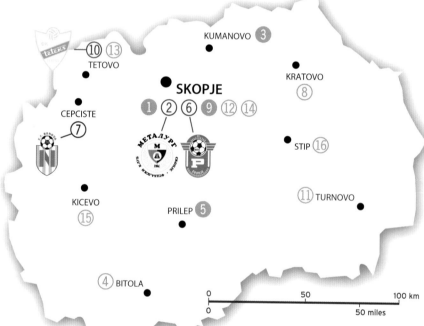

KUMANOVO ③

TETOVO ⑩ ⑬

KRATOVO ⑧

SKOPJE
① ② ⑥ ⑨ ⑫ ⑭

CEPCISTE
⑦

STIP ⑯

KICEVO
⑮

PRILEP ⑤

⑪ TURNOVO

④ BITOLA

0   50   100 km
0   50 miles

TOP DIVISION CLUBS

① **FK Makedonija GP Skopje**
fcmakedonija.com.mk

② **FK Metalurg Skopje**
no website

③ **FK Milano**
fcmilano.com.mk

④ **FK Pelister**
fkpelister.com.mk

⑤ **FK Pobeda**
fkpobeda.com.mk

⑥ **FK Rabotnicki**
fcrabotnicki.com.mk

⑦ **FK Renova** ©
renova.com.mk

⑧ **FK Sileks**
no website

⑨ **FK Sloga Jugomagnat**
no website

⑩ **FK Teteks** *
teteksfans.org

⑪ **FK Turnovo**
no website

⑫ **FK Vardar**
fkvardar.com.mk

PROMOTED CLUBS

⑬ **FK Skendija 79**
kfshkendija79.com.mk

⑭ **FK Skopje**
no website

⑮ **FK Napredok**
no website

⑯ **FK Bregalnica Stip**
bregalnicastip.tk

FEDERATION

HOME INTERNATIONAL KIT

AWAY INTERNATIONAL KIT

TOP DIVISION CLUBS

① **Birkirkara FC** ©
birkirkarafc.com

② **Dingli Swallows FC**
no website

③ **Floriana FC**
florianafc.com

④ **Hamrun Spartans FC**
hamrunspartansfc.com

⑤ **Hibernians FC**
hiberniansfc.org

⑥ **Msida St Joseph FC**
msidastjoseph.com

⑦ **Qormi FC**
qormifc.net

⑧ **Sliema Wanderers FC**
no website

⑨ **Tarxien Rainbows FC**
freewebs.com/tarxienrainbowsfc

⑩ **Valletta FC** *
vallettafcofficial.net

PROMOTED CLUBS

⑪ **Marsaxlokk FC**
mxlokkfc.com

⑫ **Vittoriosa Stars FC**
vittoriosastars.com

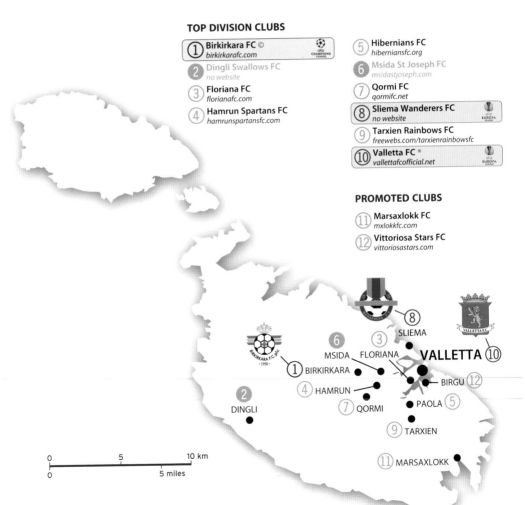

FEDERATION HOME INTERNATIONAL KIT AWAY INTERNATIONAL KIT

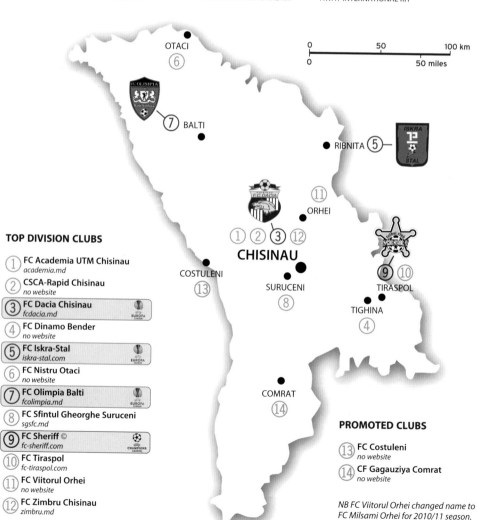

OTACI
⑥

0   50   100 km
0   50 miles

BALTI
⑦

RIBNITA ⑤

ORHEI
⑪

① ② ③ ⑫

CHISINAU

COSTULENI
⑬

SURUCENI
⑧

TIRASPOL
⑨ ⑩

TIGHINA
④

COMRAT
⑭

TOP DIVISION CLUBS

① **FC Academia UTM Chisinau**
   academia.md

② **CSCA-Rapid Chisinau**
   no website

③ **FC Dacia Chisinau**
   fcdacia.md   EUROPA LEAGUE

④ **FC Dinamo Bender**
   no website

⑤ **FC Iskra-Stal**
   iskra-stal.com   EUROPA LEAGUE

⑥ **FC Nistru Otaci**
   no website

⑦ **FC Olimpia Balti**
   fcolimpia.md   EUROPA LEAGUE

⑧ **FC Sfintul Gheorghe Suruceni**
   sgsfc.md

⑨ **FC Sheriff ©**
   fc-sheriff.com   CHAMPIONS LEAGUE

⑩ **FC Tiraspol**
   fc-tiraspol.com

⑪ **FC Viitorul Orhei**
   no website

⑫ **FC Zimbru Chisinau**
   zimbru.md

PROMOTED CLUBS

⑬ **FC Costuleni**
   no website

⑭ **CF Gagauziya Comrat**
   no website

NB FC Viitorul Orhei changed name to
FC Milsami Orhei for 2010/11 season.

FEDERATION HOME INTERNATIONAL KIT AWAY INTERNATIONAL KIT

TOP DIVISION CLUBS

(1) **FK Berane**
no website

(2) **FK Budućnost Podgorica**
fkbuducnost.cg.yu

(3) **FK Dečić**
fkdecictuzi.com

(4) **FK Grbalj**
no website

(5) **FK Kom**
no website

(6) **FK Lovćen**
fklovcen.cg.yu

(7) **FK Mogren**
fkmogren.com

(8) **FK Mornar**
no website

(9) **OFK Petrovac**
ofkpetrovac.com

(10) **FK Rudar Pljevlja** © *
fcrudarpljevlja.com

(11) **FK Sutjeska**
no website

(12) **FK Zeta**
fkzeta.com

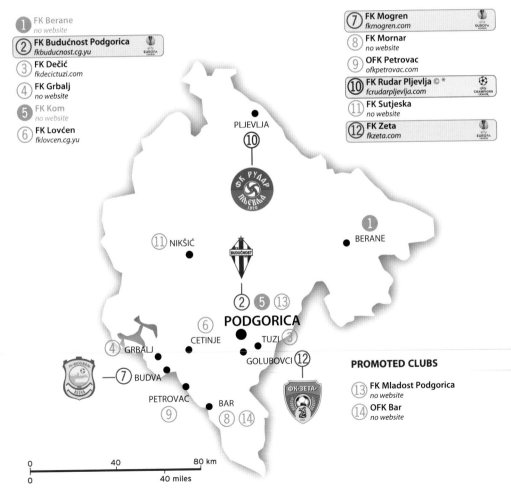

PROMOTED CLUBS

(13) **FK Mladost Podgorica**
no website

(14) **OFK Bar**
no website

PLJEVLJA
(10)

BERANE
(1)

(11) NIKŠIĆ

(2) (5) (13)
PODGORICA

(6)
CETINJE   TUZI (3)

GOLUBOVCI (12)

(4) GRBALJ

(7) BUDVA

PETROVAC
(9)   BAR
(8) (14)

0   40   80 km

0   40 miles

KNVB

FEDERATION

HOME INTERNATIONAL KIT

AWAY INTERNATIONAL KIT

TOP DIVISION CLUBS

1. **ADO Den Haag**
   adodenhaag.nl
2. **AFC Ajax** *
   ajax.nl
3. **AZ Alkmaar**
   az.nl
4. **Feyenoord**
   feyenoord.nl
5. **FC Groningen**
   fcgroningen.nl
6. **sc Heerenveen**
   sc-heerenveen.nl
7. **Heracles Almelo**
   heracles.nl
8. **NAC Breda**
   nac.nl
9. **NEC Nijmegen**
   nec-nijmegen.nl
10. **PSV Eindhoven**
    psv.nl
11. **RKC Waalwijk**
    rkcwaalwijk.nl
12. **Roda JC**
    rodajc.nl
13. **Sparta Rotterdam**
    sparta-rotterdam.nl
14. **FC Twente ©**
    fctwente.nl
15. **FC Utrecht**
    fcutrecht.nl
16. **Vitesse**
    vitesse.nl
17. **VVV-Venlo**
    vvv-venlo.nl
18. **Willem II**
    willem-ii.nl

PROMOTED CLUBS

19. **De Graafschap**
    degraafschap.nl
20. **SBV Excelsior**
    sbvexcelsior.nl

NORTHERN IRELAND

FEDERATION   HOME INTERNATIONAL KIT   AWAY INTERNATIONAL KIT

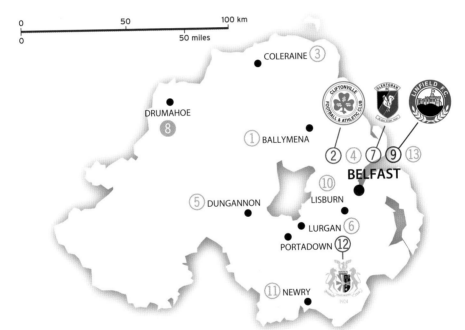

COLERAINE (3)

DRUMAHOE
(8)

(1) BALLYMENA

(2) (4) (7) (9) (13)

BELFAST

(10)

(5) DUNGANNON   LISBURN

LURGAN (6)

PORTADOWN (12)

(11) NEWRY

TOP DIVISION CLUBS

(1) **Ballymena United FC**
ballymenaunitedfc.com

(2) **Cliftonville FC**
cliftonvillefc.net

(3) **Coleraine FC**
colerainefc.com

(4) **Crusaders FC**
crusadersfc.com

(5) **Dungannon Swifts FC**
dungannonswiftsfc.co.uk

(6) **Glenavon FC**
glenavonfc.com

(7) **Glentoran FC**
glentoran.com

(8) Institute FC
stutefc.co.uk

(9) **Linfield FC** © *
linfieldfc.com

(10) **Lisburn Distillery FC**
blue.srv2.com/~lisburn

(11) **Newry City FC**
newrycityfc.com

(12) **Portadown FC**
portadownfc.co.uk

PROMOTED CLUB

(13) **Donegal Celtic FC**
dc-fc.com

FEDERATION

HOME INTERNATIONAL KIT

AWAY INTERNATIONAL KIT

TOP DIVISION CLUBS

1. **Aalesunds FK** *
   aafk.no

2. **FK Bodø/Glimt**
   glimt.no

3. **SK Brann**
   brann.no

4. **Fredrikstad FK**
   fredrikstadfk.no

5. **Lillestrøm SK**
   lsk.no

6. **FC Lyn Oslo**
   lyn.no

7. **Molde FK**
   moldefk.no

8. **Odd Grenland**
   oddgrenland.no

9. **Rosenborg BK** ©
   rbk.no

10. **Sandefjord Fotball**
    sandefjordfotball.no

11. **Stabæk Fotball**
    stabak.no

12. **IK Start**
    ikstart.no

13. **Strømsgodset IF**
    godset.no

14. **Tromsø IL**
    til.no

15. **Viking FK**
    viking-fk.no

16. **Vålerenga Fotball**
    vif-fotball.no

PROMOTED CLUBS

17. **FK Haugesund**
    fkh.no

18. **Hønefoss BK**
    honefossbk.no

19. **Kongsvinger IL**
    kil.no

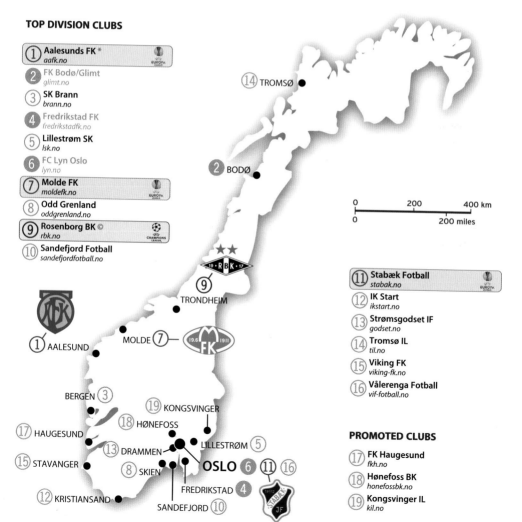

FEDERATION

HOME INTERNATIONAL KIT

AWAY INTERNATIONAL KIT

① GDYNIA   GDAŃSK ⑦

0 _____ 200 _____ 400 km
0 _____ 200 miles

BIAŁYSTOK ④

⑧ ⑫

WARSZAWA
(WARSAW)

⑥ POZNAŃ

⑰ ŁÓDŹ

LUBIN ⑯   BEŁCHATÓW ②

⑱ ZABRZE

⑭ WROCŁAW   BYTOM ⑪   KIELCE ⑤

⑩ GLIWICE   CHORZÓW ⑬

⑨ WODZISŁAW ŚLĄSKI   KRAKÓW ③ ⑮

TOP DIVISION CLUBS

① **Arka Gdynia**
arka.gdynia.pl

② **GKS Bełchatów**
gksbelchatow.com

③ **MKS Cracovia Kraków**
cracovia.pl

④ **Jagiellonia Białystok** *
jagiellonia.pl
EUROPA LEAGUE

⑤ **Korona Kielce**
korona-kielce.pl

⑥ **Lech Poznań** ©
lech.poznan.pl
CHAMPIONS LEAGUE

⑦ **KS Lechia Gdańsk**
lechia.pl

⑧ **Legia Warszawa**
legia.pl

⑨ MKS Odra Wodzisław Śląski
odra.wodzislaw.pl

⑩ **GKS Piast Gliwice**
piast.gliwice.pl

⑪ **KS Polonia Bytom**
poloniabytom.com.pl

⑫ **KSP Polonia Warszawa**
ksppolonia.pl

⑬ **KS Ruch Chorzów**
ruchchorzow.com.pl
EUROPA LEAGUE

⑭ **WKS Śląsk Wrocław**
slaskwroclaw.pl

⑮ **Wisła Kraków**
wisla.krakow.pl
EUROPA LEAGUE

⑯ **Zagłębie Lubin**
zaglebie-lubin.pl

PROMOTED CLUBS

⑰ **RTS Widzew Łódź**
widzew.pl

⑱ **Górnik Zabrze**
gornikzabrze.pl

FEDERATION

HOME INTERNATIONAL KIT

AWAY INTERNATIONAL KIT

TOP DIVISION CLUBS

① **A. Académica de Coimbra**
academica-oaf.pt

② CF Os Belenenses
osbelenenses.com

③ **SL Benfica** ©   CHAMPIONS LEAGUE
slbenfica.pt

④ **SC Braga**   CHAMPIONS LEAGUE
scbraga.pt

⑤ Leixões SC
leixoessc.pt

⑥ **CS Marítimo**   EUROPA LEAGUE
csmaritimo.pt

⑦ **CD Nacional**
cdnacional.pt

⑧ **A. Naval 1° Maio**
naval1demaio.com

⑨ **SC Olhanense**
scolhanense.com

⑩ **FC Paços de Ferreira**
fcpf.pt

⑪ **FC Porto** *   EUROPA LEAGUE
fcporto.pt

⑫ **Rio Ave FC**
rioave-fc.pt

⑬ **Sporting Clube de Portugal**   EUROPA LEAGUE
sporting.pt

⑭ **UD Leiria**
udl.leirianet.pt

⑮ **Vitória FC**
vtfc.pt

⑯ **Vitória SC**
vitoriasc.pt

BRAGA

⑫ VILA DO CONDE   ④

GUIMARÃES ⑯

⑤ MATOSINHOS   PAÇOS DE FERREIRA ⑩

PORTO

⑪

⑰ AVEIRO

⑧ FIGUEIRA DA FOZ

COIMBRA ①

⑭ LEIRIA

② ③ ⑬

LISBOA
(LISBON)

SETÚBAL
⑮

0   100   200 km
0   100 miles

MADEIRA

FUNCHAL ⑥ ⑦

PROMOTED CLUBS

⑰ **SC Beira-Mar**
beiramar.pt

⑱ **Portimonense SC**
portimonensesc.pt

⑱ PORTIMÃO

⑨ OLHÃO

REPUBLIC OF IRELAND

FEDERATION

HOME INTERNATIONAL KIT

AWAY INTERNATIONAL KIT

TOP DIVISION CLUBS

1. **Bohemian FC ©**
   bohemians.ie
2. **Bray Wanderers AFC**
   braywanderers.ie
3. **Cork City FC**
   corkcityfc.ie
4. **Derry City FC**
   derrycityfc.net
5. **Drogheda United FC**
   droghedaunited.ie
6. **Dundalk FC**
   dundalkfc.com
7. **Galway United FC**
   galwayunitedfc.ie
8. **Saint Patrick's Athletic FC**
   stpatsfc.com
9. **Shamrock Rovers FC**
   shamrockrovers.ie
10. **Sligo Rovers FC**
    sligorovers.com

PROMOTED CLUBS

11. **University College Dublin AFC**
    ucdsoccer.com
12. **Sporting Fingal FC ***
    sportingfingal.ie

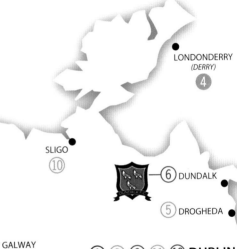

LONDONDERRY
(DERRY)
④

SLIGO
⑩

⑥ DUNDALK

⑤ DROGHEDA

⑦ GALWAY

① ⑧ ⑨ ⑪ ⑫ **DUBLIN**

BRAY
②

③ CORK

0   200   400 km

0   200 miles

FEDERATION

HOME INTERNATIONAL KIT

AWAY INTERNATIONAL KIT

TOP DIVISION CLUBS

① **FC Astra Ploieşti**
no website

② **FC Braşov**
fcbrasov.ro

③ **FC Ceahlăul Piatra Neamţ**
fcceahlaul.ro

④ **CFR 1907 Cluj** © *
cfr1907.ro

⑤ **FC Dinamo Bucureşti**
fcdinamo.ro

⑥ **CS Gaz Metan Mediaş**
gaz-metan-medias.ro

⑦ **ACF Gloria 1922 Bistriţa**
cfgloria.ro

⑧ **FC Internaţional Curtea de Argeş**
fcinternational.ro

⑨ **FC Oţelul Galaţi**
otelul-galati.ro

⑩ **CS Pandurii Lignitul Târgu Jiu**
pandurii-tg-jiu.ro

⑪ **FC Politehnica Iaşi**
politehnicaiasi.ro

⑫ **FC Rapid Bucureşti**
fcrapid.ro

⑬ **FC Steaua Bucureşti**
steauafc.ro

⑭ **FC Timişoara**
politimisoara.ro

⑮ **FC Unirea Alba Iulia**
unireafc.ro

⑯ **FC Unirea Urziceni**
fcunirea.ro

⑰ **FC Universitatea Craiova**
fcuniversitatea.ro

⑱ **FC Vaslui**
fcvaslui.info

PROMOTED CLUBS

⑲ **FC Victoria Brăneşti**
victoriafc.ro

⑳ **FCM Târgu Mureş**
fcm-tirgumures.ro

㉑ **FC Sportul Studenţesc Bucureşti**
fcsportulstudentesc.ro

㉒ **FC Universitatea Cluj**
universitateacluj.ro

RUSSIA

FEDERATION

HOME INTERNATIONAL KIT

AWAY INTERNATIONAL KIT

④ KHIMKI

MOSKVA *(MOSCOW)*

② ③ ⑦ ⑧ ⑫

⑪ RAMENSKOYE

⑯

ST PETERBURG *(ST PETERSBURG)*

⑩ KAZAN

PERM ①

⑨ ROSTOV-NA-DONU

SAMARA ⑤

TOMSK ⑮

KRASNODAR ⑥

NALCHIK

NOVOSIBIRSK ⑱

⑬ GROZNY ⑭

MAKHACHKALA ⑰

VLADIKAVKAZ ⑲

| 0 | 1000 | 2000 km |
| 0 | 1000 miles | |

TOP DIVISION CLUBS

① **FC Amkar Perm**
amkar.ru

② **PFC CSKA Moskva**
pfc-cska.com

③ **FC Dinamo Moskva**
fcdynamo.ru

④ **FC Khimki**
fckhimki.ru

⑤ **PFC Krylya Sovetov Samara**
kc-camapa.ru

⑥ **FC Kuban Krasnodar**
fckuban.ru

⑦ **FC Lokomotiv Moskva**
fclm.ru

⑧ **FC Moskva**
fcmoscow.ru

⑨ **FC Rostov**
fc-rostov.ru

⑩ **FC Rubin Kazan** ©
rubin-kazan.ru

⑪ **FC Saturn Moskovskaya Oblast**
saturn-fc.ru

⑫ **FC Spartak Moskva**
spartak.ru

⑬ **PFC Spartak Nalchik**
spartak-nalchik.ru

⑭ **FC Terek Grozny**
fc-terek.ru

⑮ **FC Tom Tomsk**
football.tomsk.ru

⑯ **FC Zenit St Petersburg** *
fc-zenit.ru

PROMOTED CLUBS

⑰ **FC Anzhi Makhachkala**
fc-anji.ru

⑱ **FC Sibir Novosibirsk**
fc-sibir.ru

⑲ **FC Alania Vladikavkaz**
fc-alania.ru

SAN MARINO

FEDERATION

HOME INTERNATIONAL KIT

AWAY INTERNATIONAL KIT

TOP DIVISION CLUBS

1. **SP Cailungo**
   no website
2. **S.S. Cosmos**
   cosmos.sm
3. **Domagnano FC**
   no website
4. **SC Faetano**
   no website
5. **S.S. Fiorentino**
   no website
6. **S.S. Folgore/Falciano**
   no website
7. **AC Juvenes-Dogana**
   acjuvenesdogana.sm
8. **SP La Fiorita**
   no website
9. **SP Libertas**
   no website
10. **S.S. Murata**
    no website
11. **S.S. Pennarossa**
    pennarossa.com
12. **S.S. San Giovanni**
    no website
13. **SP Tre Fiori** © *
    no website
14. **SP Tre Penne**
    trepenne.sm
15. **S.S. Virtus**
    no website

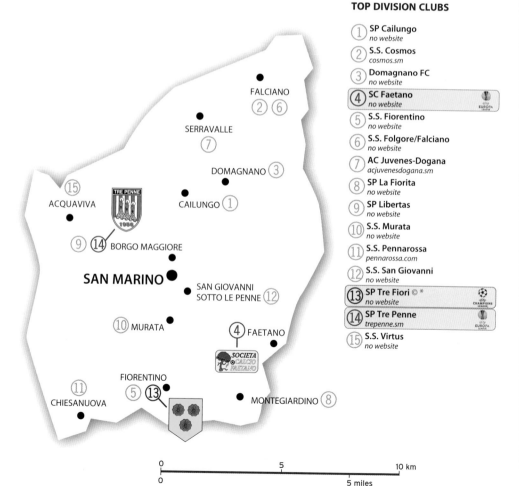

⚔ SCOTLAND

FEDERATION

HOME INTERNATIONAL KIT

AWAY INTERNATIONAL KIT

TOP DIVISION CLUBS

1. **Aberdeen FC**
   afc.co.uk
2. **Celtic FC**
   celticfc.net — CHAMPIONS LEAGUE
3. **Dundee United FC** *
   dundeeunitedfc.co.uk — EUROPA LEAGUE
4. **Falkirk FC**
   falkirkfc.co.uk
5. **Hamilton Academical FC**
   acciesfc.co.uk
6. **Heart of Midlothian FC**
   heartsfc.co.uk
7. **Hibernian FC**
   hibs.co.uk — EUROPA LEAGUE
8. **Kilmarnock FC**
   kilmarnockfc.co.uk
9. **Motherwell FC**
   www.motherwellfc.co.uk — EUROPA LEAGUE
10. **Rangers FC** ©
    rangers.co.uk — CHAMPIONS LEAGUE
11. **Saint Johnstone FC**
    perthstjohnstonefc.co.uk
12. **Saint Mirren FC**
    stmirren.net

PROMOTED CLUB

13. **Inverness Caledonian Thistle FC**
    ictfc.co.uk

INVERNESS ⑬

ABERDEEN ①

⑪ PERTH

DUNDEE ③

⑥ ⑦

FALKIRK ④

EDINBURGH

GLASGOW ② ⑩

MOTHERWELL ⑨

⑫ PAISLEY

HAMILTON ⑤

KILMARNOCK

⑧

0	100	200 km
0		100 miles

SERBIA

FEDERATION

HOME INTERNATIONAL KIT

AWAY INTERNATIONAL KIT

TOP DIVISION CLUBS

1. **FK Borac Čačak**
   boracfk.com

2. **BSK Borča**
   bskborca.org

3. **FK Crvena zvezda** *
   crvenazvezdafk.com — EUROPA LEAGUE

4. **FK Čukarički**
   cukarickistankom.com

5. **FK Hajduk Kula**
   fkhajduk.org.rs

6. **FK Jagodina**
   fkjagodina.org.yu

7. **FK Javor**
   fkjavor.com

8. **FK Metalac**
   no website

9. **FK Mladi radnik**
   mladiradnik.com

10. **FK Napredak**
    fknapredak.com

11. **OFK Beograd**
    ofkbeograd.co.rs — EUROPA LEAGUE

12. **FK Partizan** ©
    partizan.rs — CHAMPIONS LEAGUE

13. **FK Rad**
    fcrad.co.yu

14. **FK Smederevo**
    fksmederevo.com

15. **FK Spartak Zlatibor voda**
    no website — EUROPA LEAGUE

16. **FK Vojvodina**
    fcvojvodina.co.yu

PROMOTED CLUBS

17. **FK Inđija**
    fkindjija.com

18. **FK Sevojno**
    fksevojno.com

NB FK Sevojno merged with FK Sloboda Užice to become FK Sloboda Sevojno for 2010/11 season.

Map

SUBOTICA (15)

KULA (5)

(16) NOVI SAD

INĐIJA (17)

BEOGRAD
(BELGRADE)

SMEDEREVO (14)

POŽAREVAC

(9)

(2) (3) (4) (11) (12) (13)

(8)
GORNJI
MILANOVAC

KRUŠEVAC (10)

(18) SEVOJNO   ČAČAK (1)

JAGODINA

(7) IVANJICA

(6)

0 ——— 50 ——— 100 km
0 ——— 50 miles

FEDERATION   HOME INTERNATIONAL KIT   AWAY INTERNATIONAL KIT

MŠK ŽILINA

⑫
ŽILINA

⑪
PREŠOV

DUBNICA NAD VÁHOM ②

RUŽOMBEROK ⑦

BANSKÁ BYSTRICA ③ FK DUKLA BANSKÁ BYSTRICA

KOŠICE ④

SENICA ⑧

FC NITRA

⑤
NITRA ZLATÉ MORAVCE ⑬

⑩
TRNAVA

BRATISLAVA ⑥ ⑨ SLOVAN BRATISLAVA

DUNAJSKÁ STREDA ①

0   100   200 km
0   100 miles

TOP DIVISION CLUBS

① **DAC 1904 Dunajská Streda**
fcdac1904.com

② **MFK Dubnica**
fkdubnica.sk

③ **Dukla Banská Bystrica**   EUROPA LEAGUE
fkdukla.sk

④ **MFK Košice**
mfkkosice.sk

⑤ **FC Nitra**   EUROPA LEAGUE
fcnitra.sk

⑥ MFK Petržalka
mfkpetrzalka.sk

⑦ **MFK Ružomberok**
futbalruza.sk

⑧ **FK Senica**
no website

⑨ **ŠK Slovan Bratislava** *   EUROPA LEAGUE
slovanfutbal.com

⑩ **FC Spartak Trnava**
spartak.sk

⑪ **1. FC Tatran Prešov**
1fctatran.sk

⑫ **MŠK Žilina** ©   CHAMPIONS LEAGUE
mskzilina.sk

PROMOTED CLUB

⑬ **FC ViOn Zlaté Moravce**
fcvion.sk

FEDERATION   HOME INTERNATIONAL KIT   AWAY INTERNATIONAL KIT

0   50   100 km
0   50 miles

MARIBOR   LENDAVA ⑧
⑦
VELENJE ⑩   PTUJ
⑫ KRANJ   ③
        ②   CELJE ①
    DOMŽALE
            ⑤ ⑨
④   LJUBLJANA
NOVA GORICA
    AJDOVŠČINA ⑪
KOPER ⑥

TOP DIVISION CLUBS

① **NK Celje**
   nk-celje.si

② **NK Domžale**
   nkdomzale.si

③ **NK Drava**
   nkptuj-klub.si

④ **ND Gorica**
   nd-gorica.com   EUROPA LEAGUE

⑤ **NK IB Ljubljana**
   nkinterblock.eu

⑥ **FC Koper** ©
   fckoper.si   CHAMPIONS LEAGUE

⑦ **NK Maribor** *
   nkmaribor.com   EUROPA LEAGUE

⑧ **NK Nafta**
   nknafta.si

⑨ **NK Olimpija Ljubljana**
   nkolimpija.si   EUROPA LEAGUE

⑩ **NK Rudar Velenje**
   nkrudar.com

PROMOTED CLUBS

⑪ **NK Primorje**
   primorje-nklub.si

⑫ **ND Triglav**
   nktriglav.com

SPAIN

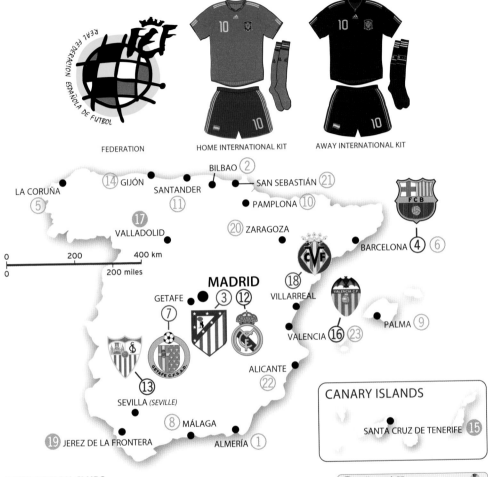

FEDERATION

HOME INTERNATIONAL KIT

AWAY INTERNATIONAL KIT

BILBAO ②

⑭ GIJÓN   SAN SEBASTIÁN ㉑

LA CORUÑA   SANTANDER

⑤   PAMPLONA ⑩

⑰   ⑪   ㉒ ZARAGOZA

VALLADOLID   BARCELONA ④ ⑥

0   200   400 km

0   200 miles

MADRID

GETAFE   ③ ⑫

⑦   VILLARREAL

⑱

VALENCIA ⑯ ㉓

PALMA ⑨

⑬   ALICANTE

SEVILLA (SEVILLE)   ㉒

CANARY ISLANDS

⑧ MÁLAGA

SANTA CRUZ DE TENERIFE ⑮

⑲ JEREZ DE LA FRONTERA   ALMERÍA ①

TOP DIVISION CLUBS

① **UD Almería**
udalmeriasad.com

② **Athletic Club**
athletic-club.net

③ **Club Atlético de Madrid**
clubatleticodemadrid.com

④ **FC Barcelona** ©
fcbarcelona.com

⑤ **RC Deportivo La Coruña**
canaldeportivo.com

⑥ **RCD Espanyol**
rcdespanyol.cat

⑦ **Getafe CF**
getafecf.com

⑧ **Málaga CF**
malagacf.es

⑨ **RCD Mallorca**
rcdmallorca.es

⑩ **CA Osasuna**
osasuna.es

⑪ **Real Racing Club**
realracingclub.es

⑫ **Real Madrid CF**
realmadrid.com

⑬ **Sevilla FC** *
sevillafc.es

⑭ **Real Sporting de Gijón**
realsporting.com

⑮ CD Tenerife
clubdeportivotenerife.es

⑯ **Valencia CF**
valenciacf.es

⑰ Real Valladolid CF
realvalladolid.es

⑱ **Villarreal CF**
villarrealcf.es

⑲ Xerez CD
xerezcd.com

⑳ **Real Zaragoza**
realzaragoza.com

PROMOTED CLUBS

㉑ **Real Sociedad de Fútbol**
realsociedad.com

㉒ **Hércules CF**
herculescf.es

㉓ **Levante UD**
levanteud.com

FEDERATION

HOME INTERNATIONAL KIT

AWAY INTERNATIONAL KIT

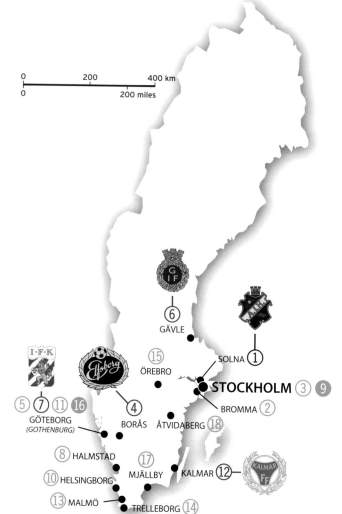

| 0 | 200 | 400 km |
| 0 | 200 miles | |

TOP DIVISION CLUBS

① **AIK Solna** © *
aik.se — CHAMPIONS LEAGUE

② IF Brommapojkarna
brommapojkarna.se

③ Djurgårdens IF FF
dif.se

④ **IF Elfsborg**
elfsborg.se — EUROPA LEAGUE

⑤ GAIS Göteborg
gais.se

⑥ **Gefle IF** [fp]
gefleiffotboll.se — EUROPA LEAGUE

⑦ **IFK Göteborg**
ifkgoteborg.se — EUROPA LEAGUE

⑧ Halmstads BK
hbk.se

⑨ Hammarby Fotboll
hammarbyfotboll.se

⑩ Helsingborgs IF
hif.se

⑪ BK Häcken
bkhacken.se

⑫ **Kalmar FF**
kalmarff.se — EUROPA LEAGUE

⑬ Malmö FF
mff.se

⑭ Trelleborgs FF
trelleborgsff.se

⑮ Örebro SK
orebro-sk.se

⑯ Örgryte IS
ois.se

PROMOTED CLUBS

⑰ Mjällby AIF
maif.se

⑱ Åtvidabergs FF
atvidabergsff.se

GÄVLE ⑥
SOLNA ①
ÖREBRO ⑮
STOCKHOLM ③ ⑨
BROMMA ②
GÖTEBORG (GOTHENBURG) ⑤ ⑦ ⑪ ⑯
BORÅS ④
ÅTVIDABERG ⑱
⑧ HALMSTAD
⑰ MJÄLLBY
KALMAR ⑫
⑩ HELSINGBORG
⑬ MALMÖ
TRELLEBORG ⑭

FEDERATION

HOME INTERNATIONAL KIT

AWAY INTERNATIONAL KIT

BASEL

ZÜRICH (4) (10)

ST GALLEN (8)

(1) AARAU

LUZERN (LUCERNE)

(6) NEUCHÂTEL

BERN
(BERNE) (9)

(11) THUN

LAUSANNE (12)

SION (7)

BELLINZONA (3)

0   100   200 km

0   100 miles

TOP DIVISION CLUBS

(1) FC Aarau
fcaarau.ch

(2) FC Basel 1893 © *
fcb.ch
CHAMPIONS LEAGUE

(3) AC Bellinzona
acbellinzona.ch

(4) Grasshopper-Club
gcz.ch
EUROPA LEAGUE

(5) FC Luzern
fcl.ch
EUROPA LEAGUE

(6) Neuchâtel Xamax FC
xamax.ch

(7) FC Sion
fc-sion-live.ch

(8) FC St Gallen
fcsg.ch

(9) BSC Young Boys
bscyb.ch
CHAMPIONS LEAGUE

(10) FC Zürich
fcz.ch

PROMOTED CLUB

(11) FC Thun
fcthun.ch

ADDITIONAL CLUB

(12) FC Lausanne-Sport
lausanne-sport.ch
EUROPA LEAGUE

FEDERATION

HOME INTERNATIONAL KIT

AWAY INTERNATIONAL KIT

TOP DIVISION CLUBS

① **MKE Ankaragücü**
ankaragucu.org.tr

② **Ankaraspor**
ankaraspor.com.tr

③ **Antalyaspor**
antalyaspor.com.tr

④ **Beşiktaş JK**
bjk.com.tr

⑤ **Bursaspor ©**
bursaspor.org.tr

⑥ **Denizlispor**
denizlispor.org.tr

⑦ **Diyarbakırspor**
diyarbakirspor.org

⑧ **Eskişehirspor**
eskisehirspor.org.tr

⑨ **Fenerbahçe SK**
fenerbahce.org

⑩ **Galatasaray AŞ**
galatasaray.org

⑪ **Gaziantepspor**
gaziantepspor.org.tr

⑫ **Gençlerbirliği SK**
genclerbirligi.org.tr

⑬ **İstanbul BB SK**
ibbspor.com

⑭ **Kasımpaşa SK**
kasimpasaspor.org.tr

⑮ **Kayserispor**
kayserispor.org.tr

⑯ **Manisaspor**
vestelmanisaspor.com

⑰ **Sivasspor**
sivasspor.org.tr

⑱ **Trabzonspor** *
trabzonspor.org.tr

PROMOTED CLUBS

⑲ **Karademir Karabükspor**
kardemirkarabukspor.org.tr

⑳ **Bucaspor**
no website

㉑ **Konyaspor**
konyaspor.org.tr

UKRAINE

FEDERATION

HOME INTERNATIONAL KIT

AWAY INTERNATIONAL KIT

⑱ LUTSK

⑥ LVIV

① ④ ⑪ **KYIV**
(KIEV)

⑮ UZHHOROD

⑭ POLTAVA

③ DNIPROPETROVSK

⑦ KRYVYI RIH

ZAPORIZHYA

⑩

② ODESA

⑧ KHARKIV

⑯ LUHANSK

DONETSK ⑨ ⑫

MARIUPIL

⑤

SIMFEROPOL ⑬

⑰ SEVASTOPOL

| 0 | 200 | 400 km |
| 0 | 200 miles | |

TOP DIVISION CLUBS

① **FC Arsenal Kyiv**
fcarsenal.com.ua

② FC Chornomorets Odesa
chernomorets.odessa.ua

③ **FC Dnipro Dnipropetrovsk**
fcdnipro.dp.ua

④ **FC Dynamo Kyiv**
fcdynamo.kiev.ua

⑤ FC Illychivets Mariupil
fcilyich.com.ua

⑥ **FC Karpaty Lviv**
fckarpaty.lviv.ua

⑦ FC Kryvbas Kryvyi Rih
fckrivbass.dp.ua

⑧ **FC Metalist Kharkiv**
metallist.kharkov.ua

⑨ FC Metalurh Donetsk
metallurg.donetsk.ua

⑩ FC Metalurh Zaporizhya
fcmetalurg.com

⑪ FC Obolon Kyiv
fc.obolon.ua

⑫ **FC Shakhtar Donetsk ©**
shakhtar.com

⑬ **SC Tavriya Simferopol ***
sctavriya.com

⑭ FC Vorskla Poltava
vorskla.com.ua

⑮ FC Zakarpattya Uzhhorod
zakarpatie.com.ua

⑯ FC Zorya Luhansk
zarya-lugansk.com

PROMOTED CLUBS

⑰ PFC Sevastopol
fcsevastopol.com

⑱ FC Volyn Lutsk
fcvolyn.com

FEDERATION

HOME INTERNATIONAL KIT

AWAY INTERNATIONAL KIT

TOP DIVISION CLUBS

1 **Aberystwyth Town FC**
 atfc.org.uk

2 **Airbus UK Broughton FC**
 airbusfc.co.uk

3 **Bala Town FC**
 balatownfc.co.uk

4 **Bangor City FC** *
 bangorcityfc.com

5 Caersws FC
 caerswsfc.co.uk

6 **Carmarthen Town AFC**
 carmarthentownafc.net

7 Cefn Druids AFC
 cefndruidsafc.co.uk

8 Connah's Quay FC
 gapconnahsquay.co.uk

9 **Haverfordwest County AFC**
 haverfordwestcounty.co.uk

10 **Llanelli AFC**
 llanelliafc.org

11 **Neath FC**
 neathathletic.ik.com

12 **Newtown AFC**
 newtownafc.co.uk

13 CPD Porthmadog
 porthmadogfc.com

14 **Port Talbot Town FC**
 porttalbottown.co.uk

15 **Prestatyn Town FC**
 prestatyntownfootballclub.co.uk

16 Rhyl FC
 rhylfc.com

17 **The New Saints FC** ©
 saints-alive.co.uk

18 Welshpool Town FC
 welshpooltownfc.co.uk

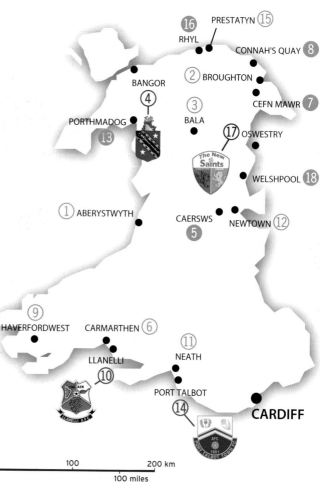

0   100   200 km
0   100 miles

RESPECT
The Opponent

RESPECT
Diversity

RESPECT
The Game

UEFA

Route de Genève 46
Case postale
CH-1260 Nyon 2
Switzerland

Tel: +41 (0) 848 00 2727
Fax: +41 (0) 848 01 2727
Web: UEFA.com
Email: info@uefa.com

Media Desk
Tel: +41 (0) 848 04 2727

Founded: *15 June 1954*

Affiliated national associations: *53*

Number of clubs: *approx. 200,000*

Number of players: *approx. 21,100,000*

Number of female players: *approx. 1,900,000*

Number of referees: *approx. 285,000*

UEFA EXECUTIVE COMMITTEE

President
Michel Platini *(France)*

Vice-Presidents
Senes Erzik *(Turkey)*
Geoffrey Thompson *(England)*
Angel María Villar Llona *(Spain)*
Marios N. Lefkaritis *(Cyprus)*
Joseph Mifsud *(Malta)*

Members
Giancarlo Abete *(Italy)*
Allan Hansen *(Denmark)*
František Laurinec *(Slovakia)*
Avraham Luzon *(Israel)*
Gilberto Madaíl *(Portugal)*
Mircea Sandu *(Romania)*
Hryhoriy Surkis *(Ukraine)*
Michael van Praag *(Netherlands)*
Liutauras Varanavičius *(Lithuania)*
Theo Zwanziger *(Germany)*

Honorary President
Lennart Johansson *(Sweden)*

General Secretary
Gianni Infantino

UEFA Events Calendar 2010/11

NATIONAL TEAM

 UEFA EURO 2012

02/03/07.09.2010	Qualifying round matches
08/09/12.10.2010	Qualifying round matches
Spring 2011	Ticketing sales launch
25/26/29.03.2011	Qualifying round matches
03/04/07.06.2011	Qualifying round matches
08.06.2011	One year to kick-off
02/03/06.09.2011	Qualifying round matches
07/08/11.10.2011	Qualifying round matches
11/12.11.2011	Qualifying play-offs, first leg
15.11.2011	Qualifying play-offs, second leg
December 2011	Final tournament draw (Kyiv, Ukraine)
29.02.2012	100 days to kick-off
08.06-01.07.2012	Final tournament (Poland & Ukraine)
08.06.2012	Opening match (Warsaw, Poland)
01.07.2012	Final (Kyiv, Ukraine)

 2011 UEFA EUROPEAN UNDER-21 CHAMPIONSHIP

03/04.09.2010	Qualifying round matches
07.09.2010	Qualifying round matches
10.09.2010	Play-off draw (Herning, Denmark)
08/09.10.2010	Play-off matches, first leg
11/12.10.2010	Play-off matches, second leg
09.11.2010	Final tournament draw (Aalborg, Denmark)
11-25.06.2011	Final tournament (Denmark)

CLUB

 2010/11 UEFA CHAMPIONS LEAGUE

26.08.2010	Group stage draw (Monaco)
14/15.09.2010	Group stage, Matchday 1
28/29.09.2010	Group stage, Matchday 2
19/20.10.2010	Group stage, Matchday 3
02/03.10.2010	Group stage, Matchday 4
23/24.11.2010	Group stage, Matchday 5
07/08.12.2010	Group stage, Matchday 6
17.12.2010	First knockout round draw (Nyon, Switzerland)
15/16.02.2011	First knockout round, first leg
22/23.02.2011	First knockout round, first leg
08/09.03.2011	First knockout round, second leg
15/16.03.2011	First knockout round, second leg
18.03.2011	Quarter-finals, Semi-finals and Final draw (Nyon, Switzerland)
05/06.04.2011	Quarter-finals, first leg
12/13.04.2011	Quarter-finals, second leg
26/27.04.2011	Semi-finals, first leg
03/04.05.2011	Semi-finals, second leg
28.05.2011	Final (London, England)

 2010/11 UEFA EUROPA LEAGUE

27.08.2010	Group stage draw (Monaco)
16.09.2010	Group stage, Matchday 1
30.09.2010	Group stage, Matchday 2
21.10.2010	Group stage, Matchday 3
04.11.2010	Group stage, Matchday 4
01/02.12.2010	Group stage, Matchday 5
15/16.12.2010	Group stage, Matchday 6
17.12.2010	Round of 32 and Round of 16 draw (Nyon, Switzerland)

UEFA Events Calendar 2010/11

17.02.2011	Round of 32, first leg
24.02.2011	Round of 32, second leg
10.03.2011	Round of 16, first leg
17.03.2011	Round of 16, second leg
18.03.2011	Quarter-finals, Semi-finals and Final draw (Nyon, Switzerland)
07.04.2011	Quarter-finals, first leg
14.04.2011	Quarter-finals, second leg
28.04.2011	Semi-finals, first leg
05.05.2011	Semi-finals, second leg
18.05.2011	Final (Dublin, Republic of Ireland)

2010 UEFA SUPER CUP

27.08.2010	Final (Monaco)

2010 FIFA CLUB WORLD CUP

08-18.12.2010	Final tournament (United Arab Emirates)

YOUTH & AMATEUR

2010/11 UEFA EUROPEAN UNDER-19 CHAMPIONSHIP

01.09-30.11.2010	Qualifying round matches
30.11.2010	Elite round draw (Nyon, Switzerland)
01.03-15.06.2011	Elite round matches
tbd	Final tournament draw (Romania, venue tbd)
20.07-01.08.2011	Final tournament (Romania)

2011/12 UEFA EUROPEAN UNDER-19 CHAMPIONSHIP

30.11.2010	Qualifying round draw (Nyon, Switzerland)

2010/11 UEFA EUROPEAN UNDER-17 CHAMPIONSHIP

01.09-15.11.2010	Qualifying round matches
30.11.2010	Elite round draw (Nyon, Switzerland)
01.03-30.04.2011	Elite round matches
tbd	Final tournament draw (Serbia, venue tbd)
03-15.05.2011	Final tournament (Serbia)

2011/12 UEFA EUROPEAN UNDER-17 CHAMPIONSHIP

30.11.2010	Qualifying round draw (Nyon, Switzerland)

2010/11 UEFA REGIONS' CUP

01.08-30.09.2010	Preliminary round matches
01.08.2010-30.04.2011	Intermediary round matches
15-30.06.2011	Final tournament (venue tbd)

WOMEN'S

2010/11 UEFA WOMEN'S CHAMPIONS LEAGUE

22-23.09.2010	Round of 32, first leg
13-14.10.2010	Round of 32, second leg
03-04.11.2010	Round of 16, first leg
10-11.11.2010	Round of 16, second leg
19.11.2010	Quarter-finals, Semi-finals and Final draw (Nyon, Switzerland)
16-17.03.2011	Quarter-finals, first leg
23-24.03.2011	Quarter-finals, second leg
09-10.04.2011	Semi-finals, first leg
16-17.04.2011	Semi-finals, second leg
26.05.2011	Final (London, England)

UEFA Events Calendar 2010/11

2010/11 UEFA EUROPEAN WOMEN'S UNDER-19 CHAMPIONSHIP

11-16.09.2010	First qualifying round matches
16.11.2010	Second qualifying round draw (Nyon, Switzerland)
31.03-05.04.2011	Second qualifying round matches
April 2011	Final tournament draw (Rimini, Italy)
30.05 - 11.06.2011	Final tournament (Italy)

2011/12 UEFA EUROPEAN WOMEN'S UNDER-19 CHAMPIONSHIP

16.11.2010	First qualifying round draw (Nyon, Switzerland)

2010/11 UEFA EUROPEAN WOMEN'S UNDER-17 CHAMPIONSHIP

01.08-31.10.2010	First qualifying round matches
16.11.2010	Second qualifying round draw (Nyon, Switzerland)
01.03-15.04.2011	Second qualifying round matches
28.07-31.07.2011(tbc)	Final tournament (Nyon, Switzerland)

2011/12 UEFA EUROPEAN WOMEN'S UNDER-17 CHAMPIONSHIP

16.11.2010	First qualifying round draw (Nyon, Switzerland)

2011 FIFA WOMEN'S WORLD CUP

30.08.2010	European play-offs draw (Nyon, Switzerland)
11/12.09.2010	Round 1 Play-off matches (Group winners)
15/16.09.2010	Round 1 Play-off matches (Group winners)
23/24.10.2010	Round 2 Play-off matches (Round 1 winners)
27/28.10.2010	Round 2 Play-off matches (Round 1 winners)
20/27.11.2010	UEFA v CONCACAF Play-off matches
29.11.2010	Final tournament draw (Germany)
26.06-17.07.2011	Final tournament (Germany)

2010 FIFA WOMEN'S UNDER-17 WORLD CUP

05-25.09.2010	Final tournament (Trinidad & Tobago)

FUTSAL

2011/12 UEFA EUROPEAN FUTSAL CHAMPIONSHIP

12.10.2010	Qualifying round draw (Nyon, Switzerland)
20/24.01.2011	Preliminary round matches
24/28.02.2011	Qualifying round matches
tbd	Final tournament draw
February 2012	Final tournament (Croatia)

2010/11 UEFA FUTSAL CUP

25.09-03.10.2010	Main round matches
12.10.2010	Elite round draw (Nyon, Switzerland)
20-28.11.2010	Elite round matches
18.03.2011	Final tournament draw (venue tbd)
28.04-01.05.2011	Final tournament (venue tbd)

tbd = to be decided
tbc = to be confirmed

UEFA™
EURO 2012
POLAND-UKRAINE

QUALIFYING PROCEDURE

The nine group winners qualify directly for the final tournament in Poland and Ukraine. The group runner-up with the best record from matches against the teams placed first, third, fourth and fifth will also qualify directly. The other eight group runners-up will be drawn in four two-legged play-offs, from which the winners will also qualify.

QUALIFYING FIXTURES

GROUP A

Germany, Turkey, Austria, Belgium, Kazakhstan, Azerbaijan

3/9/10	Belgium - Germany
	Kazakhstan – Turkey
7/9/10	Austria – Kazakhstan
	Germany – Azerbaijan
	Turkey – Belgium
8/10/10	Germany – Turkey
	Kazakhstan – Belgium
	Austria – Azerbaijan
12/10/10	Belgium – Austria
	Kazakhstan – Germany
	Azerbaijan – Turkey
25/3/11	Germany – Kazakhstan
	Austria – Belgium
29/3/11	Turkey – Austria
	Belgium – Azerbaijan
3/6/11	Austria – Germany
	Belgium – Turkey
	Kazakhstan – Azerbaijan
7/6/11	Azerbaijan – Germany
2/9/11	Germany – Austria
	Turkey – Kazakhstan
	Azerbaijan – Belgium
6/9/11	Austria – Turkey
	Azerbaijan – Kazakhstan

7/10/11	Turkey – Germany
	Belgium – Kazakhstan
	Azerbaijan – Austria
11/10/11	Germany – Belgium
	Turkey – Azerbaijan
	Kazakhstan – Austria

GROUP B

Russia, Slovakia, Republic of Ireland, FYROM, Armenia, Andorra

3/9/10	Andorra – Russia
	Armenia – Republic of Ireland
	Slovakia – FYROM
7/9/10	Russia – Slovakia
	Republic of Ireland – Andorra
	FYROM – Armenia
8/10/10	Armenia – Slovakia
	Andorra – FYROM
	Republic of Ireland – Russia
12/10/10	Slovakia – Republic of Ireland
	FYROM – Russia
	Armenia – Andorra
26/3/11	Republic of Ireland – FYROM
	Armenia – Russia
	Andorra – Slovakia
4/6/11	Russia – Armenia
	Slovakia – Andorra
	FYROM – Republic of Ireland
2/9/11	Russia – FYROM
	Republic of Ireland – Slovakia
	Andorra – Armenia
6/9/11	Russia – Republic of Ireland
	Slovakia – Armenia
	FYROM – Andorra
7/10/11	Slovakia – Russia
	Armenia – FYROM
	Andorra – Republic of Ireland
11/10/11	Russia – Andorra
	Republic of Ireland – Armenia
	FYROM – Slovakia

GROUP C

Italy, Serbia, Northern Ireland, Slovenia, Estonia, Faroe Islands

11/8/10	Estonia – Faroe Islands
3/9/10	Faroe Islands – Serbia
	Slovenia – Northern Ireland
	Estonia – Italy
7/9/10	Serbia – Slovenia
	Italy – Faroe Islands

8/10/10	Serbia – Estonia
	Northern Ireland – Italy
	Slovenia – Faroe Islands
12/10/10	Italy – Serbia
	Faroe Islands – Northern Ireland
	Estonia – Slovenia
25/3/11	Serbia – Northern Ireland
	Slovenia – Italy
29/3/11	Northern Ireland – Slovenia
	Estonia – Serbia
3/6/11	Italy – Estonia
	Faroe Islands – Slovenia
7/6/11	Faroe Islands – Estonia
10/8/11	Northern Ireland – Faroe Islands
2/9/11	Northern Ireland – Serbia
	Slovenia – Estonia
	Faroe Islands – Italy
6/9/11	Italy – Slovenia
	Serbia – Faroe Islands
	Estonia – Northern Ireland
7/10/11	Serbia – Italy
	Northern Ireland – Estonia
11/10/11	Italy – Northern Ireland
	Slovenia – Serbia

GROUP D

France, Romania, Bosnia-Herzegovina, Belarus, Albania, Luxembourg

3/9/10	Luxembourg – Bosnia-Herzegovina
	France – Belarus
	Romania – Albania
7/9/10	Albania – Luxembourg
	Belarus – Romania
	Bosnia-Herzegovina – France
8/10/10	Albania – Bosnia-Herzegovina
	Luxembourg – Belarus
9/10/10	France – Romania
12/10/10	France – Luxembourg
	Belarus – Albania
25/3/11	Luxembourg – France
26/3/11	Bosnia-Herzegovina – Romania
	Albania – Belarus
29/3/11	Romania – Luxembourg
3/6/11	Romania – Bosnia-Herzegovina
	Belarus – France
7/6/11	Bosnia-Herzegovina – Albania
	Belarus – Luxembourg
2/9/11	Belarus – Bosnia-Herzegovina
	Albania – France
	Luxembourg – Romania

6/9/11	Romania – France
	Bosnia-Herzegovina – Belarus
	Luxembourg – Albania
7/10/11	France – Albania
	Romania – Belarus
	Bosnia-Herzegovina –
	Luxembourg
11/10/11	France – Bosnia-Herzegovina
	Albania – Romania

GROUP E

Netherlands, Sweden, Finland, Hungary, Moldova, San Marino

3/9/10	Moldova – Finland
	Sweden – Hungary
	San Marino – Netherlands
7/9/10	Sweden – San Marino
	Hungary – Moldova
	Netherlands – Finland
0/10	Hungary – San Marino
	Moldova – Netherlands
10/10	Finland – Hungary
	San Marino – Moldova
	Netherlands – Sweden
11/10	Finland – San Marino
11	Hungary – Netherlands
3/11	Netherlands – Hungary
	Sweden – Moldova
1	Moldova – Sweden
	San Marino – Finland
7/6/11	Sweden – Finland
	San Marino – Hungary
2/9/11	Netherlands – San Marino
	Finland – Moldova
	Hungary – Sweden
6/9/11	Finland – Netherlands
	Moldova – Hungary
	San Marino – Sweden
7/10/11	Netherlands – Moldova
	Finland – Sweden
11/10/11	Sweden – Netherlands
	Hungary – Finland
	Moldova – San Marino

GROUP F

Croatia, Greece, Israel, Latvia, Georgia, Malta

2/9/10	Israel – Malta
3/9/10	Greece – Georgia
	Latvia – Croatia

7/9/10	Malta – Latvia
	Croatia – Greece
	Georgia – Israel
8/10/10	Greece – Latvia
	Georgia – Malta
9/10/10	Israel – Croatia
12/10/10	Greece – Israel
	Latvia – Georgia
17/11/10	Croatia – Malta
26/3/11	Israel – Latvia
	Georgia – Croatia
	Malta – Greece
29/3/11	Israel – Georgia
4/6/11	Croatia – Georgia
	Greece – Malta
	Latvia – Israel
2/9/11	Israel – Greece
	Georgia – Latvia
	Malta – Croatia
6/9/11	Croatia – Israel
	Latvia – Greece
	Malta – Georgia
7/10/11	Greece – Croatia
	Latvia – Malta
11/10/11	Croatia – Latvia
	Georgia – Greece
	Malta – Israel

GROUP G

England, Switzerland, Bulgaria, Wales, Montenegro

3/9/10	Montenegro – Wales
	England – Bulgaria
7/9/10	Bulgaria – Montenegro
	Switzerland – England
8/10/10	Wales – Bulgaria
	Montenegro – Switzerland
12/10/10	England – Montenegro
	Switzerland – Wales
26/3/11	Bulgaria – Switzerland
	Wales – England
4/6/11	England – Switzerland
	Montenegro – Bulgaria
2/9/11	Bulgaria – England
	Wales – Montenegro
6/9/11	England – Wales
	Switzerland – Bulgaria
7/10/11	Wales – Switzerland
	Montenegro – England
11/10/11	Switzerland – Montenegro
	Bulgaria – Wales

GROUP H

Portugal, Denmark, Norway, Cyprus, Iceland

3/9/10	Portugal – Cyprus
	Iceland – Norway
7/9/10	Denmark – Iceland
	Norway – Portugal
8/10/10	Portugal – Denmark
	Cyprus – Norway
12/10/10	Iceland – Portugal
	Denmark – Cyprus
26/3/11	Norway – Denmark
	Cyprus – Iceland
4/6/11	Portugal – Norway
	Iceland – Denmark
2/9/11	Norway – Iceland
	Cyprus – Portugal
6/9/11	Iceland – Cyprus
	Denmark – Norway
7/10/11	Portugal – Iceland
	Cyprus – Denmark
11/10/11	Norway – Cyprus
	Denmark – Portugal

GROUP I

Spain, Czech Republic, Scotland, Lithuania, Liechtenstein

3/9/10	Liechtenstein – Spain
	Lithuania – Scotland
7/9/10	Scotland – Liechtenstein
	Czech Republic – Lithuania
8/10/10	Spain – Lithuania
	Czech Republic – Scotland
12/10/10	Liechtenstein – Czech Republic
	Scotland – Spain
25/3/11	Spain – Czech Republic
29/3/11	Czech Republic – Liechtenstein
	Lithuania – Spain
3/6/11	Liechtenstein – Lithuania
2/9/11	Lithuania – Liechtenstein
3/9/11	Scotland – Czech Republic
6/9/11	Spain – Liechtenstein
	Scotland – Lithuania
7/10/11	Czech Republic – Spain
8/10/11	Liechtenstein – Scotland
11/10/11	Spain – Scotland
	Lithuania – Czech Republic

UEFA·com

The official website for European football